Y0-BYV-553

Religion and Society in North America

Clio Bibliography Series No. 12

Gail Schlachter, Editor
Pamela R. Byrne, Executive Editor

Users of the Clio Bibliography Series may refer to current issues of America: History and Life *and* Historical Abstracts *for continuous bibliographic coverage of the subject areas treated by each individual volume in the series.*

1.
The American Political Process
Dwight L. Smith and Lloyd W. Garrison
1972 LC 72-77549 ISBN 0-87436-090-0

2.
Afro-American History
Dwight L. Smith
1974 LC 73-87155 ISBN 0-87436-123-0

3.
Indians of the United States and Canada
Dwight L. Smith
1974 LC 73-87156 ISBN 0-87436-124-9

4.
Era of the American Revolution
Dwight L. Smith
1975 LC 74-14194 ISBN 0-87436-178-8

5.
Women in American History
Cynthia E. Harrison
1979 LC 78-26194 ISBN 0-87436-260-1

6.
The American and Canadian West
Dwight L. Smith
1979 LC 78-24478 ISBN 0-87436-272-5

7.
European Immigration and Ethnicity in the United States and Canada
David L. Brye
1983 LC 82-24306 ISBN 0-87436-258-X

8.
Afro-American History Volume II
Dwight L. Smith
1981 ISBN 0-87436-314-4

9.
Indians of the United States and Canada Volume II
Dwight L. Smith
1982 LC 73-87156 ISBN 0-87436-149-4

10.
The History of Canada
Dwight L. Smith
1983 LC 82-24307 ISBN 0-87436-047-1

11.
Urban America
Neil L. Shumsky and Timothy Crimmins
1983 LC 82-24292 ISBN 0-87436-038-2

12.
Religion and Society in North America
Robert deV. Brunkow
1983 LC 82-24304 ISBN 0-87436-042-0

Religion and Society in North America

An Annotated Bibliography

Robert deV. Brunkow
Editor

Santa Barbara, California
Oxford, England

Library of Congress Cataloging in Publication Data
Main entry under title:

Religion and society in North America: an annotated bibliography.

(Clio bibliography series; no. 12)
Includes index.
1. Religion and sociology—Periodicals—Indexes.
2. North America—Religion—Periodicals—Indexes.
I. Brunkow, Robert deV., 1947- . II. Series.
Z7831.R44 1983 [BL60] 016.2'00973 82-24304
ISBN 0-87436-042-0

American Bibliographical Center—Clio Press, Inc.
2040 Alameda Padre Serra
Santa Barbara, California

European Bibliographical Center—Clio Press
55 St. Thomas Street
Oxford OX1 1JG, England

Printed and bound in the United States of America.

Design and graphics by Lance Klass.
Cover illustration is from the title page of the Geneva Bible of 1599.

TABLE OF CONTENTS

PREFACE vii
INTRODUCTION ix
ABSTRACTS 1
SUBJECT INDEX 323
AUTHOR INDEX 502
LIST OF PERIODICALS 511
LIST OF ABSTRACTERS 514
LIST OF ABBREVIATIONS 515

1. UNITED STATES AND CANADA
   - Multiperiod 1
   - 16th Century-1920 4
   - 1920-1980 7
   - Historians, Historical Archives, Methods, and Societies 12
2. AMERICANIZATION OF INSTITUTIONS 21
3. BUSINESS (INCLUDING PROTESTANT ETHIC) 25
4. COMMUNAL MOVEMENTS AND UTOPIAN THOUGHT 29
5. ECUMENISM AND INTERGROUP RELATIONS 34
   - Ecumenism: Seeking Unity 34
   - Intergroup Relations: Seeking Understanding 38
6. EDUCATION
   - General 40
   - Religion in Public Schools 44
   - Religious Education (including Sunday Schools) 45
7. FAMILY (INCLUDING ABORTION, CHILDBEARING, AND SEX ROLES) 60
8. GOVERNMENT AND POLITICS
   - General 73
   - Church and State 76
   - Civil Religion 88
   - Political Behavior 92
   - Political Theory 102
9. HEALTH 110
10. LABOR 113
11. MISSIONARY IMPULSE
    - Continental Missions 115
    - Foreign Missions 129
12. MODES OF RELIGIOUS EXPRESSION AND REPRESENTATION
    - Architecture 136
    - Arts 141
    - Music 146
    - Radio and Television 149
    - Religious Literature 149
    - Secular Literature 152
13. NEGATIVE IMPULSE
    - General 159
    - Anti-Catholicism 159
    - Anti-Mormonism 162
    - Anti-Semitism 162
    - Racism 162
    - Slavery 164
14. OCCULT 167
15. REVIVALS 170
16. SABBATARIANISM 175
17. SCIENCE 177
18. SOCIAL AND ECONOMIC REFORM
    - General (including Social Gospel) 182
    - Abolition 189
    - Charities 193
    - Civil Rights 195
    - Economic Reform 197
    - Temperance 199
19. SOCIOECONOMIC GROUPS 201
20. WAR AND PACIFISM 204
21. RELIGIOUS GROUPS
    - Christianity, General 210
    - Eastern Orthodox Churches 216
    - Protestant Traditions 216
      - General 216

Protestant Traditions (continued) 216
Adventist Churches (including Millerites) 226
Baptist Churches 227
Christian Church (Disciples of Christ) and Related Churches (including the Churches of Christ) 235
Congregational Churches (including Separatists and United Church of Christ) 236
Dutch Reformed Churches 239
Episcopal Churches (including Church of England) 240
French Reformed Church (Huguenots) . 247
Friends 248
German Reformed Churches 250
Holiness Churches 250
Lutheran Churches 250
Mennonite and Related Churches (including Anabaptist Tradition, Amish, Brethren in Christ, and Hutterites) 254
Methodist Churches 259
Moravian Churches 264
Pentecostal Churches 264
Presbyterian Churches 265
Puritans 270
United Brethren and Related Churches . 275
United Church of Canada 276
Roman Catholic Church and Related Churches 276
General 276
Eastern Rite Catholics 292
Other Christian Traditions 293
Christian Science 293
Doukhobors 293
Jehovah's Witnesses 293
Mormons 293
New Church (Swedenborgians) 304
Shakers 304
Transcendentalists 304
Unitarian-Universalist Churches 305
Judaism 306
General 306
Conservative 312
Orthodox 312
Reform 315
Other Religious Traditions 317
Cults of the Twentieth Century 317
Deism 320
Eastern Religions 320
Spiritualism 321
Theosophy 322
Anti-Religious Movements (including Atheism and Free Thought) 322

PREFACE

Interest in the theological, personal, and societal dimensions of religion has burgeoned in recent years, with a corresponding proliferation of research on the history of religion in North America. As a result, scholars have often been unable to fully utilize all of the materials available to them, and comprehensive bibliographic control of the literature has become essential.

Religion and Society in North America: An Annotated Bibliography, the twelfth volume in the Clio Bibliography Series, provides the scholar, researcher, and student of religion with a convenient guide to the extensive range of periodical literature on the history of religion in the United States and Canada since the seventeenth century. Its 4,304 entries were selected from volumes 11-18 of *America: History and Life*—the largest such database in existence—and have been reedited and reindexed where appropriate to identify the information on religion.

An inclusive selection policy has been followed to make this volume as comprehensive as possible. In addition to articles expressly about religion, the volume cites works that focus on other topics but that contain important information about the religious experience in North America. Only articles on Native American religions unaffected by European contact have been excluded from this work, as their inclusion would duplicate the scholarship covered by *Indians of the United States and Canada, Volume II,* a recent work in this bibliography series. The result is an extensive guide to scholarly studies, published primary sources, bibliographies, and review essays on religion drawn from some 600 periodical titles published mainly during 1973-80. The volume is organized on the premise that religious belief and social behavior are interrelated. Thus the table of contents contains many social headings, and wherever possible entries are classified under social rather than denominational headings. An article on a particular denomination would appear, therefore, under a social heading unless no single social topic dominated or unless the topical subject was not within the scope of any specific social heading.

The classification system, like any other, is arbitrary, and although scholars may disagree on the placement of entries under specific headings, every attempt has been made to organize the broad diversity of articles in a manner that would facilitate the efforts of the researcher to rapidly and effectively locate scholarship on specific subject areas. Additionally, this volume is supported by an extensive index that enables the user to locate virtually every subject of every entry. Religions have been indexed as specifically as possible, but the precise identity of every group could not always be determined. Consequently, a scholar interested in the literature on Southern Baptists, for example, should examine citations under "Baptists" for relevant material in addition to checking entries indexed as "Baptists, Southern."

The indexing system, the American Bibliographical Center's Subject Profile Index (ABC-SPIndex), deserves special attention because it is more sophisticated than a conventional index. In ABC-SPIndex the key terms and historical period of each entry are linked together to form a composite index entry that provides a complete subject profile of the journal article. Each set of index terms is then rotated so that the complete profile appears in the index under each of the subject terms. More detailed information on ABC-SPIndex is available in the headnote at the beginning of the index and in the User's Guide in *America: History and Life,* Part A.

This volume has been made possible through the collaboration of a number of people. Robert S. Michaelsen of the University of California at Santa Barbara provided generous advice on the definition and organization of the bibliography, though he is in no way responsible for its shortcomings. Pamela R. Byrne, Executive Editor of the American Bibliographical Center, proposed the volume and participated in every phase of the project. Managing Editor Suzanne Robitaille Ontiveros and Assistant Editors Lance Klass, David Valiulis, and Shirley Matulich provided editorial and administrative support, while the Data Processing Services Department under the supervision of Kenneth H. Baser, Director, and Deborah Looker, Production Supervisor, expeditiously manipulated the database to fit the editorial specifications of this bibliography. This volume could not have been prepared without the contributions of the worldwide community of scholars who provided the abstracts that make up this work.

Robert deV. Brunkow
Santa Barbara, California

INTRODUCTION

This bibliography reflects the subtle but still drastic shifts in writing about religion in America. The changes are subtle in this sense: no great theorist dominates the field. There has been no sudden breakthrough in the understanding of methods for analysis. It is hard to think of a manifesto that has had much influence on scholars. Yet those changes have still been drastic. Almost without anyone's noticing how the process came about, there have been dramatic alterations in the way the academic community perceives what religion is, where it is, and where it is going.

In the fashionable language of the day, the disciplines of history, sociology, anthropology, and the like have been experiencing a "paradigm-shift." There are new models for coming to terms with the ways Americans are spiritual or how they understand the institutions that mediate the spiritual in their lives. Almost every page of these abstracts will provide some evidence of the changes. They have begun to be taken for granted, yet from the perspective of the past, they are remarkable.

If we could run the bibliographical clock back fifty or perhaps only thirty years, we would find a preoccupation with the routine institutional life of American religion. Most historians wrote "church" history, using denominational models. A Mennonite historian wrote the history of a Mennonite body, a Catholic historian described the career of a bishop or the story of a parish or diocese, a Lutheran historian traced the fates of a Lutheran synod or missionary organization. Meanwhile, "the center held," the center meaning the mainline religious institutions of the nation. Most of the energies went into discussing the bodies that held the allegiance of the largest numbers of members or had the most contacts with the development of secular history.

Today all that has changed. The center did not hold. For the past twenty years the line between insiders and outsiders, mainline and sideline, central and peripheral, and focal and marginal has been blurred or even deliberately scuffed. Denominational histories of the mainline groups are so rare that the American Society of Church History has felt an impulse, perhaps a need, to charter a new set—chiefly to commemorate a century-old sequence of such studies. Denominational history remains important. It tells much, but not enough, about how a hundred million loyalists program their religious life. The denominations are far more efficient organizers of energies, collectors of funds, trainers of ministers, dispatchers of missionaries, or publishers of journals than are interchurch or nondenominational agencies. Yet the public has lost curiosity about what Methodists were doing in the 1890's or Congregationalists in the 1920's.

Some of the new curiosity has shifted to the groups that were once regarded as esoteric or eccentric. Of course, one can always assume that the exotic has its lures. The Presbyterianism or Catholicism down the street is "home," as familiar as faded wallpaper. One prefers some new cuisine to home cooking. Yet not mere faddism inspires the new curiosity. Today articles and books on Theosophy, the Mormons, and the Unification Church are important because they indicate some of the nervousness, the restlessness, of a public that has been looking for new meanings or has found new reasons to be wary of those who offer them. Historians and sociologists can be faulted if they devote more attention to a 50,000-member Asian-based "cult" than to the 50,000,000-member Catholic Church. Yet they do know that the fact that an intense religious group can lure so many gifted young Americans tells something about what America does not now offer or what some Americans think life should.

To be a bit more systematic about the changes, we would do well to notice a basic one. The definition of religion itself has been greatly broadened. Once upon a time the word "religion" connoted what went on in church and synagogue. Anything else passed as philosophy, folklore, or experiment with community. No longer. Without diminishing the importance of church or synagogue, scholars have looked around the world to learn what religion defines and then applied it to America.

Anthropologists and pursuers of the discipline History of Religion have been of most help here. They have shown that primitives, as they used to be called, were religious but did not set aside specific or differentiated institutions. Such institutions developed, some have argued, precisely because the world was becoming disenchanted, demystified, demythified. There had to be a line between sacred and secular. What was everybody's job was nobody's job. So the sacred had to have custodians, and a special caste of priests developed. They nurtured religious rites and institutions. Could it be that today we have much in common with "primitives" and that much of our transaction with the sacred goes unmonitored by religious institutions? It could, and it is a fact that religion is more diffuse and elusive in our time than scholars used to think.

No one can define religion to the satisfaction of all others. But we can see that there are attempts to work with broader definitions when we see how much attention is devoted to a category such as "Civil Religion," "Public Religion," the "Religion of the Republic," and the like. Thanks to the efforts of scholars like Sidney Mead, Will Herberg, and Robert N. Bellah, terms like these have become commonplace. Bellah even argues that the religion to which they refer has become institutionalized. Yet there is no "First Civil Religion Church," no "Seventeenth Synagogue of the Religion of the Republic." Civil religion shows up under what Peter Berger calls the nation's "sacred canopy," in presidential inaugural addresses, American Legion meetings, American Civil Liberties Union debates, and the like.

At the other extreme from this "sacred canopy" of social religion that is broader than the churches is another phenomenon widely noticed by scholars: the "privatization" of religion. Thomas Luckmann has been a leader among those who have said that the fundamental act of coming to terms with being human, with transcending mere biological life—becoming "more" than an animal—is religious. What is more, modern life is so confusing, religion so pluralistic, and society so unsupportive of faith that people have to take their religion *a la carte,* as it were. Their "do-it-yourself" religions are custom-made, held without communal props, and often made up of elements from many faiths and philosophies. So the scholars of religion have to discern what are the "coping mechanisms" or world views of people. What they find enters bibliographies such as these.

Anthropologist Clifford Geertz has led many to this broadening of the definition of religion by his reference to "sets of symbols" that have pervasive influence in the lives of people. He and his associates have created new problems for bibliographers. As the definition of religion grows so broad, the classifier has to ask: "Where does it stop? If everything is religious, is anything religious? Don't definitions bv definition set limits? Where are the limits?" How does one place Oriental Martial Arts beyond the scope of religion and Eastern philosophies within it? Does one?

This bystander has discovered a number of elements used by students of religion today. However they define religion, they tend to call something religious when several of the following factors are present. There must be what Paul Tillich called "ultimate concern." If people are more ready to die for something else than, say, their Christianity, then that something else bids fair to be called their religion. But not all ultimate concern ends up in bibliographies like these. Normally there must be some socialization, some communalizing of the activities. People see a vision together, or hear a prophecy, and they need company in order to check out what they have seen and heard. Most of them will claim that more goes on than everydayishness and ordinariness suggest. They speak of the sacred, the transcendent. This they will support by myth and symbol—religious people prefer mythic-symbolic to ordinary language. They enhance it with rite and ceremony: they celebrate the passages of life and like to observe something the same time each day or week or year. They may make "metaphysical" claims, employing philosophy to show that more is going on behind the backdrop than is seen in daily life. And there are usually behavioral correlates to what they profess. If you are religious, you wear this spot on your forehead, or fast, or go to church, or raise your children this way or that.

Such indicators keep religionists and bibliographers very busy these days. But more has gone on than the mere extension of definition to catch up with the many seepages of religion under American sanctuary doors or the eruptions of effervescences of spirituality in unlikely spots. Three illustrations, out of many possibilities, indicate some of the new directions of scholarship. First, recent trends in the psychological sciences have led scholars of religion to make some daring, and in many cases foolish, ventures into "psychohistory," religious biography which, as it were, stretches dead patients on analysts' couches. Extremes and follies aside, however, it should be said as well that such psychological interest has led to richer and more satisfying attempts to probe motives and to study consequences. Not everything in religion is taken at face value. There are no clerical exemptions when truth claims are taken into consideration.

Of more significance has been the general evolution, perhaps revolution, in understandings of the ways computers and statistics ("Cliometrics") can help in measuring past and present religion. Survey research, interviewing, and polltaking today, for all their limits, tell us much about contemporary faith that would elude those who just reported on formal theology or church politics. So more and more scholars bounce these techniques into the past. They study voting and tax records and learn more about who was baptized, who attended church, and how religion was used in social control than could be known before the new techniques were available.

Add to psychologically-informed and statistically-based inquiries a third broad trend that has been reflected in religious studies. Inspired in part by the "women's revolution," but going beyond it, is a concern for the more intimate details of life. Today historians are writing stories of family life, women's roles, marriage and divorce, sexuality, the stages and passages of life, health care, and much that has always left traces but not inspired curiosity. Today many scholars and their readers care less what a New England Puritan minister said in a sermon than what his parishioners thought they heard and put to work when they arranged their lives in a particular week. Today a historian is less likely to be satisfied with another biography of a nineteenth-century Catholic bishop than with a study of how the "common" Catholic brought pennies to build churches, how these buildings helped them find their identity and social location, and with what activities they filled such edifices.

A summary way of speaking of this change, as I have in *A Nation of Behavers,* is to say that the subtle but still drastic shift has led scholars to correlate belief and behavior in new ways. Too long they took too seriously the cognitive dimensions of faith, as if all the people lived by or even knew the formal creeds or official "high" theologies of their church bodies. The study of religion today reports as much on what the Sunday Church Bulletin says as on what someone's *Systematic Theology, Volume Four* suggests. This is not to say that intellectual history is passé or must disappear. It is also not to say that the study of behavior is the study of mindlessness.

Instead, the behavioral analyses recognize that ideas have consequences just as consequences reveal which ideas were held to. Further, a different set of ideas produces a different set of consequences than many might foresee. Behavior patterns tend to be locked into the deepest ideas humans have, and the most profound creedal notions will issue in actions that go against the grain of the times.

The pages that follow reveal many of these changes. The names of familiar denominations and major theologians will appear frequently. Yet they are accompanied by less familiar religious phenomena and by studies of unknown sets of people. And even the curiosities brought to the familiar will have a different cast than they would have had some time ago.

The last thing I wish to suggest is that the current changes amount to a permanent revolution or a final outcome. Thirty years from now in a new generation, new bibliographies will reveal further development of definitions, curiosities, and techniques. American life has always been kinetic. In the midst of the continuities that religion helps provide for the individual and nation, there is constant change. Scholars have responsibilities to report on what is lasting and what is new. So long as spiritual restlessness persists, and it shows no sign of abating, scholars will be busy chronicling changes. Despite all the prophecies that religion would disappear in a "secular" world, they have discovered that religion is not disappearing. It is constantly being relocated, constantly taking new forms. The odds are that such processes will continue and perhaps even step up. That should keep the typewriters, word-processors, computers, print-out devices, or whatever will have succeeded them thirty years from now very busy at ABC-Clio. And that means that those who track the American spirit will not lack instruments to aid them. For now, there is more than enough in this volume to occupy those who would like to catch up with what has occurred in the recent past. The fare before them is rich, almost stunning, and serves as evidence of the power of spirit and the inventiveness latent in the American public and process.

Martin E. Marty
Fairfax M. Cone Distinguished Service Professor
of the History of Modern Christianity
The University of Chicago

1. UNITED STATES AND CANADA

Multiperiod

1. Ahlstrom, Sydney E. *E PLURIBUS UNUM:* RELIGIOUS PLURALISM AND THE AMERICAN IDEAL. *Soundings 1978 61(3): 328-338.* Examines Puritanism, patriotism, unlimited immigration (1620's-1920's), and slavery as each affected religious pluralism, American idealism, and national characteristics, through World War II.

2. Bainbridge, William Sims and Stark, Rodney. CULT FORMATION: THREE COMPATIBLE MODELS. *Sociol. Analysis 1979 40(4): 283-295.* Draws upon numerous ethnographies to outline three fundamental models of how novel religious ideas are generated and made social. The psychopathology model describes cult innovation as the result of individual psychopathology that finds successful social expression by providing apparent solutions to common intractable human problems. The entrepreneur model states that cult founders consciously develop new systems of religious belief and practice to obtain the rewards that followers may shower upon them. The subculture-evolution model explains that cults are the expression of novel social systems, composed of intimately interacting individuals who achieve radical cultural developments through a series of many small steps. The models are shown to be compatible because each uses two basic concepts: compensators and social exchange. Compensators are somewhat satisfying articles of faith, postulations that strongly desired rewards will be obtained in the distant future or in some other unverifiable context. Magical and religious cults exist through the social exchange of compensators. The models explain how novel packages of compensators are invented and assembled to form new cults. Biblio. J

3. Beit-Hallahmi, Benjamin. PSYCHOLOGY OF RELIGION 1880-1930: THE RISE AND FALL OF A PSYCHOLOGICAL MOVEMENT. *J. of the Hist. of the Behavioral Sci. 1974 10(1): 84-90.* Traces the history of the psychology of religion movement in American psychology. S

4. Bowden, Henry Warner. LANDMARKS IN AMERICAN RELIGIOUS HISTORIOGRAPHY. *J. of the Am. Acad. of Religion 1974 42(1): 128.* Sydney Ahlstrom's *A Religious History of the American People* (New Haven, Conn.: Yale U. Pr., 1972) is "a landmark in modern historiography" which combines a study of organized religious groups with a study of those movements not included in the structured patterns, and which shows how religion has been connected with the social and political life of America. E. R. Lester

5. Bratt, James D.; Brinks, Herbert J.; and Smith, Timothy L. RELIGION AND ETHNICITY IN AMERICA: A CRITIQUE OF TIMOTHY L. SMITH. *Fides et Hist. 1980 12(2): 8-36.* Discussion of Timothy L. Smith's "Religion and Ethnicity in America," including Smith's response. Bratt and Brinks praise Smith for his emphasis on religion in the cultural unity of ethnic groups immigrating to America. However, Bratt criticizes Smith's excessive generalization, and Brink disputes Smith's belief in a future America unified around common religious ideals. In his response, Timothy L. Smith emphasizes that all Judeo-Christian faiths in America have rested on a Biblical understanding of history. Covers 1700-1950. 19 notes. J. A. Kicklighter

6. Bumsted, J. M. RELIGION AND AMERICAN CULTURE. *Can. Rev. of Am. Studies [Canada] 1980 11(1): 49-56.* Review article prompted by publication of: *Sons of the Fathers: The Civil Religion of the American Revolution* (Philadelphia, 1976) by Catherine L. Albanese, *Henry Ward Beecher: Spokesman for a Middle-Class America* (Urbana, 1978) by Clifford E. Clark, Jr., *The Feminization of American Culture* (New York, 1977) by Ann Douglas, *A History of the Churches in the United States and Canada* (New York, 1977) by Robert T. Handy, and *Revivals, Awakenings and Reform: An Essay on Religion and Social Change in America, 1607-1977* (Chicago, 1978) by William G. McLoughlin. These books reflect the recent, inevitable academic ferment that developed when contemporary scholars attempted to reinterpret the history of American religious ideas, practices, and institutions. Note. H. T. Lovin

7. Butler, Jon. THE PEOPLE'S FAITH, IN EUROPE AND AMERICA: FOUR CENTURIES IN REVIEW. *J. of Social Hist. 1978 12(1): 159-167.* Review article prompted by four studies of popular religion: A. N. Galpern's *The Religions of the People in Sixteenth-Century Champagne* (Cambridge: 1976), David E. Harrell, Jr.'s *All Things Are Possible: The Healing and Charismatic Revivals in Modern America* (Bloomington: 1975), Herbert Leventhal's *In the Shadow of the Enlightenment: Occultism and Renaissance Science in Eighteenth-Century America* (New York: 1976), and E. William Monter's *Witchcraft in France and Switzerland: The Borderlands During the Reformation* (Ithaca: 1976). In America the debate over the direction of research on popular religion is nonexistent since what outwardly are called studies of popular religion are in fact variations of church history. European religious historians offer new themes and new methods. Secondary sources; 9 notes. R. S. Sliwoski

8. Cox, Richard J. A BIBLIOGRAPHY OF ARTICLES, BOOKS, AND DISSERTATIONS ON MARYLAND HISTORY, 1978. *Maryland Hist. Mag. 1979 74(4): 358-366.* Lists 192 works on Maryland's history, with cross references, under the following categories: General and Bibliography; Archives and Library; Architecture and Historic Preservation; Art and Decorative Arts; Biography, Autobiography, and Reminiscences; Black History; County and Local; Economic and Business; Education; Ethnic History; Geneaology and Family History; Geography; Legal; Maritime; Military; Politics; Religion; Science and Technology; Social and Cultural; Sports; and Women's History. C. B. Schulz

9. Daniel, W. Harrison. THE SIGNIFICANCE OF THE AMERICAN REVOLUTION IN AMERICAN HISTORY. *Baptist Hist. and Heritage 1976 11(3): 130-148.* The author surveys the historiography of the American Revolution from George Chalmers, William Gordon, Mercy Otis Warren, and David Ramsey to Gordon Wood, Bernard Bailyn, Alan Heimert, and Cecelia Kenyon. The historiography of the American Revolution seems to indicate that each generation has been obliged to write its history of the Revolution for its own time and in the light of its own experiences, value judgments, ideological goals, and current fads. The author then treats the political, economic, social, cultural, and religious significance of the Revolution through the 20th century. Based on secondary sources; 49 notes. H. M. Parker, Jr.

10. Decker, Raymond G. THE SECULARIZATION OF ANGLO-AMERICAN LAW, 1800-1970. *Thought 1974 49(194): 280-298.* Anglo-American constitutional, family, and criminal law have absorbed from the Christian tradition, especially in its Protestant form, metaphysical constructs, moral standards, and linguistic forms. In a pluralistic society a value consensus is lacking. In order to protect individual freedom under these circumstances, the religious elements in the law are being removed. J. C. English

11. Flynt, Wayne. RELIGION IN THE URBAN SOUTH: THE DIVIDED RELIGIOUS MIND OF BIRMINGHAM, 1900-1930. *Alabama Rev. 1977 30(2): 108-134.* Social Gospel activism at the turn of the century brought a number of pastors, priests, and rabbis together in overcoming Birmingham's image of a violent, sin city. Considerable success attended their efforts by World War I. Social work and public welfare were advanced, crime reduced, and prostitution controlled. Latent and powerful anti-Catholic and anti-Semitic elements gained ascendancy in the 1920's. Having turned to secular morality, religious leaders opened the door to the politicization of religion and institutional affairs. Primary and secondary sources; 73 notes. J. F. Vivian

12. Furman, D. E. AMERIKANSKY VARIANT SEKULIARIZATSII [American variant of secularization]. *Voprosy Filosofii [USSR] 1973 (12): 41-53.* The article shows distinctive features of the process of secularization in the United States. The weakness of the Established Church and indigenous religious pluralism resulted in the fact that the ideology of the bourgeois American Revolution did not have an anti-clerical character; it was an ideology of the exclusively socio-political

sphere. A component element of this ideology was recognition of the value of religion and of the equality of different beliefs. This brought into being a system of interaction of two levels of ideology—socio-political and religious—mutually supporting each other. Gradually, more denominations joined this system. An ideological system of this kind prevented the moulding of integral anti-bourgeois outlook and helped channel social progress either into the religious sectarian process, which tends to face away as the sect develops, or into an opportunist process. Secularization in the United States proceeds not in the form of departure from religion, which has become an element of bourgeois American ideology and of spreading non-religious forms of outlook, but in the form of devaluation of the values of religious distinctions and dissolution of religions in amorphous "religion in general." This process is a factor which gradually saps the entire system of bourgeois American ideology and contributes to the disintegration of bourgeois society in the United States. Covers the 17th through 20th centuries. J

13. Griessman, B. Eugene. PHILOSEMITISM AND PROTESTANT FUNDAMENTALISM: THE UNLIKELY ZIONISTS. *Phylon 1976 37(3): 197-211.* "Puritan respect for the Old Testament provided a basis for treating those few Jews who dwelt in the New England colonies in a humane manner." Several of the colonial leaders believed that the American Indians were the Ten Lost Tribes of Israel. This myth stirred missionary activity for converting Indians. A pro-Semitic interpretation of the Abrahamic covenant (Genesis 12) is standard fare in fundamentalist churches. Generally, the conservative and fundamentalist denominations have supported Zionism. The Jewish missions affirm that Jews eventually will accept the Messiah and that it is the duty of Christians to convert Jews to Christianity. Covers 1630-1976. 49 notes. E. P. Stickney

14. Hanrahan, James. A CURRENT BIBLIOGRAPHY OF CANADIAN CHURCH HISTORY. *Study Sessions: Can. Catholic Hist. Assoc. 1973 40: 69-93.* Covers the 17th-20th centuries.

15. Himmelfarb, Milton. PLURAL ESTABLISHMENT. *Commentary 1974 58(6): 69-73.* Discusses the effect of the New Ethnicity on religion, drawing on Matthew Arnold's formulation of the theory of plural establishment in the 19th century. S

16. Hogan, Brian F. A CURRENT BIBLIOGRAPHY OF CANADIAN CHURCH HISTORY. *Study Sessions: Can. Catholic Hist. Assoc. [Canada] 1978 45: 101-141.* Lists recent works on the history of the Catholic, Protestant (including Mennonites and Hutterites), and Eastern Orthodox churches, and smaller groups such as the Jews since the 17th century.

17. Hutchison, William R. AMERICAN RELIGIOUS HISTORY: FROM DIVERSITY TO PLURALISM. *J. of Interdisciplinary Hist. 1974 5(2): 313-318.* Reviews the work of Sydney E. Ahlstrom with special reference to his *A Religious History of the American People* (New Haven, 1972). Focuses on the theme of the failure of pluralism. Suggests several criticisms, but argues that the book "will be lastingly recognized as a *tour de force*." 2 notes. R. Howell

18. Hutchison, William R. OL' ARK'S A-CREAKIN'. *Rev. in Am. Hist. 1974 2(3): 331-336.* The first two installments of the Chicago History of American Religion series, William A. Clebsch's *American Religious Thought: A History* and Edwin Scott Gaustad's *Dissent in American Religion* (both Chicago: U. of Chicago Pr., 1973), break away from the traditional pattern of Puritan-Protestant historiography to include nonorganized religious thought; Clebsch concentrates on Jonathan Edwards, Ralph Waldo Emerson, and William James, while Gaustad focuses on "schismatics, heretics, and misfits" from the 17th to the 20th centuries.

19. Jackson, Charles O. AMERICAN ATTITUDES TO DEATH. *J. of Am. Studies [Great Britain] 1977 11(3): 297-312.* In colonial times, cultural attitudes toward death mirrored the harsh reality of high mortality rates. Never denied, death was treated as the passage to an afterlife, and its impact on bereaved family and community passed rapidly. For the next 100 years following the mid-18th century, attitudes underwent major changes, principally cultural "domestication and sentimentalization" of death. From the mid-19th century to the present, American cultural attitudes sanctioned dissociation of living persons from death and the realm of the deceased because 20th-century secular thought denied the traditional teachings of an afterlife for the dead. Secondary sources; 47 notes. H. T. Lovin

20. Jones, H. G. NORTH CAROLINA BIBLIOGRAPHY, 1975-1976. *North Carolina Hist. Rev. 1977 54(2): 192-216.* This bibliography lists books dealing with North Carolina subjects or by North Carolinians published between 1 July 1975 and 30 June 1976. Only a few serials and government documents are included. Classifications include: bibliography, history, description, and travel, church history, social sciences and institutional history, genealogy, autobiography and biography, and new editions and reprints. T. L. Savitt

21. Jones, Lawrence N. IN GOD WE TRUST: THE BLACK EXPERIENCE BEYOND THE RED SEA. *Crisis 1976 83(4): 132-136.* The black experience in America is similar to the experience of the Children of Israel searching for their vision of the Promised Land. The black understanding of the American creed nurtures hope for the future. While justice and freedom are fraught with many detours, the religious experience of blacks has been the constant guidepost for the realization of the humane community of mankind. Covers the 19th and 20th centuries. A. G. Belles

22. Lankford, John. THE RECOVERY OF AMERICAN RELIGIOUS HISTORY: DEVELOPMENTS SINCE 1964. *Anglican Theological Rev. 1973 55(1): 78-90.* Reviews scholarship, 1964-73, on American religion and its interpretation, 17th-20th centuries.

23. Leighly, John. BIBLICAL PLACE-NAMES IN THE UNITED STATES. *Names 1979 27(1): 46-59.* Surveys 61,742 place-names in the 48 contiguous states as listed in the 1940 US census to discover 803 (1.3% of the total) biblical names, many of which originated in the Northeast (which still has the largest number of such names) in colonial times and spread south and west; generally speaking there are fewer biblical names in the West than in the East, and the northern tier of states differs from the southern tier in the number and type of such names.

24. León, Argeliers. CONSIDERACIONES EN TORNO A LA PRESENCIA DE RASGOS AFRICANOS EN LA CULTURA POPULAR AMERICANA [Thoughts on the presence of African traits in the popular culture of the Americas]. *Santiago [Cuba] 1973-74 (13-14): 49-77.* Examines the economic circumstances which brought Africans to the New World and aspects of the African cultural heritage, transferred via the slave trade, which became deeply ingrained and diffused in the cultures of the slave-importing countries. Such traits are widely discernible in social organization, religious beliefs and practices, superstititions, language, music, dance, art, and folklore. Covers ca 1500-1940's. Secondary sources; biblio. P. J. Taylorson

25. Long, Charles H. A NEW LOOK AT AMERICAN RELIGION. *Anglican Theological Rev. Supplementary Series 1973 (1): 117-125.* The study of American religion has emphasized its European Christian origins but not the contribution of non-Europeans and non-Christians, especially Negroes, since the 17th century. S

26. Marty, Martin E. GOD'S "ALMOST CHOSEN PEOPLE." *Am. Heritage 1977 28(5): 4-7.* Americans cherish the image of piety as evidenced by recent polls. Separation of church and state "removed most occasions for public resentment of formal religion." Resources and needs combined to make religion acceptable and desirable. Consequently, "American religious history is a stunning story of adaptation and diversification of choices." 24 illus. J. F. Paul

27. Maydell, Bodo von. JUEDISCH-KABBALISTISCHE ELEMENTE IN DER RELIGIOESEN GESELLSCHAFT DER FREUNDE (QUAEKER) [Jewish-cabalistic elements in the religious Society of Friends (Quakers)]. *Judaica [Switzerland] 1973 29(3): 97-98.* Cabalistic Jews and Quakers share some basic beliefs, including the concept of the "inner light," the spark of the divine in every human being, and a distrust of hard and fast dogmas. Covers the 17th through 20th centuries.

28. Moore, Marie D., comp. SELECTED BIBLIOGRAPHY OF COMPLETED THESES AND DISSERTATIONS RELATED TO NORTH CAROLINA SUBJECTS, 1974-1978. *North Carolina Hist. Rev. 1979 56(1): 64-107.* Subjects include anthropology, architecture, art, economics, education (the longest section), folklore (the shortest), geography, history (second longest), home economics, journalism, literature, music, political science, psychology, religion, sociology, and speech. Compiled from *Dissertations Abstracts International, Masters Abstracts,* and information from graduate offices and libraries of colleges in North Carolina and other states. T. L. Savitt

29. Owen, John E. RELIGION IN AMERICA. *Contemporary Rev. [Great Britain] 1969 215(1246): 243-246.* A survey of the influence of religious differences in American history and politics from colonial times to the present.

30. Panting, Gerald E. LITERATURBERICHT ÜBER DIE GESCHICHTE KANADAS: VERÖFFENTLICHUNGEN 1945-1969 [Report on writings on the history of Canada: Publications appearing between 1945 and 1969]. *Hist. Zeitschrift [West Germany] 1973 5(special issue): 629-654.* Discusses persons, works, and issues in Canadian historiography, including 131 works in general Canadian history since the 17th century, reference works, source collections, and political, religious, constitutional, economic, social, intellectual, and military history. G. H. Davis

31. Pearson, Samuel C., Jr. A CONTEMPORARY VIEW OF AMERICA'S RELIGIOUS HISTORY: A REVIEW ARTICLE. *Encounter 1974 35(1): 69-72.* Reviews Sydney Ahlstrom's *Religious History of the American People* (New Haven: Yale U. Press, 1972). S

32. Redekop, Calvin. A NEW LOOK AT SECT DEVELOPMENT. *J. for the Sci. Study of Religion 1974 13(3): 345-352.* Discusses the relationship between society and the development of religious sects, such as the Mormons and Mennonites, during the 19th and 20th centuries.

33. Robertson, Roland. RELIGIOUS MOVEMENTS AND MODERN SOCIETIES: TOWARD A PROGRESSIVE PROBLEMSHIFT. *Sociol. Analysis 1979 40(4): 297-314.* Discusses the terms in which study of religious movements has developed, particularly in contemporary US society. The intellectual tradition of interest in religious collectivities is related to Georg Hegel, Max Weber, and Ernst Troeltsch. The shifting of modern societal distinctions between the religious and secular is discussed, as well as the relationships among religion, the modern state, and public and private domains of modern life. 8 notes, ref. J/S

34. Smith, Timothy Lawrence. RELIGION AND ETHNICITY IN AMERICA. *Am. Hist. Rev. 1978 83(5): 1155-1185.* The ethnic mobilization of what became America's immigrant peoples whose origins lay in Europe or the Near East began in most instances in their homelands, amidst a complex rivalry for economic and cultural advantage. Even in the Old World, the developing sense of peoplehood depended heavily upon religious identification, whether they were Protestants, Jews, Catholics, or Eastern Orthodox Christians—in some cases more so than upon language or myths about common descent. Migration to America, both before and after it became a largely urban and industrial society, produced three important alterations in the relationship of faith to ethnic identity: 1) the redefinition, usually in religious terms, of the boundaries of peoplehood, through a broadening of geographic and linguistic expectations and frequently a decisive narrowing of religious ones; 2) an intensification of the psychic basis of theological reflection and ethno-religious commitment, due to the emotional consequences of uprooting and repeated resettlement; and 3) a revitalization of the conviction, deeply rooted in Judaism and Christianity, that the goal of history is the millennialist or messianic one of a common humanity, a brotherhood of faith and faithfulness. The last two developments made the relationship between religion and ethnicity dialectical, faith commitments helping on the one hand to define more sharply the boundaries among subcultures and communities, while the other affirming the hoped-for unity of all humankind. They fostered, therefore, the complex of attitudes toward America which John Higham has recently labeled "pluralistic integration." All three developments demonstrate the dynamic relationship between religion and ethnicity which has recently begun to replace the state model which long prevailed in studies of ethnology. Covers 1800-1975.

35. Sprunk, Larry J. CHARLIE JUMA, SR.—STANLEY. *North Dakota Hist. 1977 44(4): 66-67.* Interviews a second-generation Syrian American, Charlie Juma. During the early 1900's, Syrian immigrants entered North Dakota, primarily to engage in house-to-house peddling. Some Syrians obtained homesteads and farmed near Ross, North Dakota. Religious services for the Syrians were conducted by lay persons in private homes until the erection of a church in 1929. Many Syrians left the area during the Depression and never returned. N. Lederer

36. Stevenson, W. Taylor. HISTORICAL CONSCIOUSNESS AND ECOLOGICAL CRISIS: A THEOLOGICAL PERSPECTIVE. *Anglican Theological Rev. 1976 59(Supplement 7): 99-112.* American attitudes toward wilderness, originating from biblical prescriptions to desacralize and tame the wilderness, are juxtaposed with American historical consciousness, which put nature and civilization in contention with one another; concludes that environmental quality cannot be recovered without recovering historical consciousness. Covers 1700-1975.

37. Stipe, Claude E. RELIGION AND CULTURAL CRISES. *Anglican Theological Rev. 1973 55(3): 289-304.* Subordinate cultures encroached upon by dominant cultures often express anxiety through extremist religious rituals. Covers 1797-1960. S

38. Tharpe, Jac. GOD'S ROLE IN THE NEW WORLD, 1476-1976. *Southern Q. 1976 14(4): 273-285.* Traces American intellectual history, with special focus on religion. The inconsistencies, ironies and paradoxes are accentuated. Reference is made to individualism, self-concept, democracy, and symbolism as they apply to religious thought and activity. The contention is that Americans are paradoxical in their view of God. R. W. Dubay

39. Ward, W. R. WILL HERBERG: AN AMERICAN HYPOTHESIS SEEN FROM EUROPE. *Durham U. J. [Great Britain] 1973 65(3): 260-270.* Discusses religion and religiosity in the United States; prompted by Will Herberg's (b. 1909) *Protestant-Catholic-Jew: An Essay in American Religious Sociology* (Gloucester, Massachusetts: Peter Smith, 1955). Examines Herberg's hypothesis that the relatively high religiosity professed in the United States, coupled with vapidness of the religiousness expressed, is the result of generations of immigrants identifying in religion "the one element in their past which they had not been asked to change." Conflict theory modifications suggested by recent sociologists and historians dealing with US religion are not wholly adequate as explanations of current trends. "Renewed economic growth may make possible the development of a quadripartite Herberg religion of Protestant-Catholic-Jew-Black. Consensus history is after all a correlate of conflict history and it may be that in another decade a fresh wave of religious historians may find the Herberg thesis worth examining." Covers 1790-1970. 23 notes. D. H. Murdoch

40. Wentz, Richard E. THE SAGA OF THE AMERICAN SOUL. *J. of the Am. Acad. of Religion 1974 42(4): 646-657.* Saga is a legitimate theological category, and those who would study the theology of America must become acquainted with the saga. The American Soul is the integrated result of different interpretations of the saga. 15 notes. E. R. Lester

41. Wertz, Richard E. RADICAL CATHOLICITY AND THE AMERICAN EXPERIENCE. *Foundations 1978 21(3): 242-253.* The radical catholicity principle that "the universe is an affair of giving away what is at the same time kept" is a more effective description of America than terms like Protestant, civil religion, etc. Defines "radical catholicity" and "the American experience." Covers the 18th through 20th centuries. 15 notes. E. E. Eminhizer

42. Yoder, Don. INTRODUCTORY BIBLIOGRAPHY ON FOLK RELIGION. *Western Folklore 1974 33(1): 16-34.* A "preliminary bibliography . . .constructed to illustrate the extent of research in the subject areas of folk religion and folk belief." Centers on Europe and North America and includes 271 entries from primary, secondary, and periodical sources. Covers the 16th through 20th centuries. S. L. Myres

43. —. SOUTHERN HISTORY IN PERIODICALS, 1977: A SELECTED BIBLIOGRAPHY. *J. of Southern Hist. 1978 44(2): 233-267.* Includes articles published in 1977 (and some 1976 references which

appeared too late for inclusion in last year's list). The bibliography is divided into the following classifications: general and unclassified, bibliography and historiography, blacks and slavery, economic, military and naval, politics and government, religion, science and medicine, and social, cultural, and intellectual. M. S. Legan

44. —. SOUTHERN HISTORY IN PERIODICALS, 1976: A SELECTED BIBLIOGRAPHY. *J. of Southern Hist 1977 43(2): 237-270.* Lists about 700 articles, most published during 1976, listed under nine categories: "General and unclassified," "Bibliography and historiography," "Blacks and slavery," "Economic," "Military and naval," "Politics and government," "Religion," "Science and medicine," and "Social, cultural, and intellectual." T. D. Schoonover

45. —. SOUTHERN HISTORY IN PERIODICALS 1978: A SELECTED BIBLIOGRAPHY. *J. of Southern Hist. 1979 45(2): 221-254.* About 750 articles published in 1978, except for a few in delayed 1977 publications, are classified under nine headings: General and Unclassified, Bibliography and Historiography, Blacks and Slavery, Economic, Military and Naval, Politics and Government, Religion, Science and Medicine, and Social, Cultural and Intellectual.
T. D. Schoonover

46. —. THESES ON AMERICAN TOPICS IN PROGRESS AND COMPLETED AT BRITISH UNIVERSITIES. *J. of Am. Studies [Great Britain] 1976 10(1): 129-150.* Lists theses at British universities which deal totally or in part with the study of the United States. The titles are classified under the following headings: Arts, Economic History, Economics, Education, Geography, History, International Relations, Drama, Fiction, General Literature, Individual Authors, Poetry, Philosophy, Politics and Government, Religion and Theology, and Sociology.
H. T. Lovin

16th Century-1920

47. Ahlstrom, Sydney E. THE ROMANTIC RELIGIOUS REVOLUTION AND THE DILEMMAS OF RELIGIOUS HISTORY. *Church Hist. 1977 46(2): 149-170.* This presidential address to a 28 December 1975 meeting of the American Society of Church History explores the Romantic movement. Considers subjectivity and idealism, nature and neopantheism, and history and historicism. Religious historians have an obligation to enlarge their concept of religious categories and to accept a historical explanation of reality as an ideal. 34 notes.
M. D. Dibert

48. Ashby, Rickie Zayne. PHILOSOPHICAL AND RELIGIOUS LANGUAGE IN EARLY KENTUCKY WILLS. *Kentucky Folklore Record 1976 22(2): 39-44.* Examines the religious philosophy expounded by Kentuckians in their wills written 1808-53.

49. Barrett, William. THE FAITH TO WILL. *Am. Scholar 1978 47(4): 525-536.* William James spoke about religion from outside of religion itself. He always wrote about religion as an interest, but not as an experience. It is difficult to understand how anyone who has not experienced religion can grasp and understand it. Although the work of James is to be admired, it is incomplete. Covers 1897-1912.
F. F. Harling

50. Barrett, William. OUR CONTEMPORARY, WILLIAM JAMES. *Commentary 1975 60(6): 55-61.* Discusses the current philosophical relevance of the writings of William James, 1870-1910, emphasizing his explorations into psychology, religion, and nihilism.

51. Budick, E. Miller. WHEN THE SOUL SELECTS: EMILY DICKINSON'S ATTACK ON NEW ENGLAND SYMBOLISM. *Am. Literature 1979 51(3): 349-363.* Emily Dickinson's poems on the soul reflect her hostility to the use of symbolic forms, and this hostility was a reaction against the Puritan-Transcendentalist tradition that idealized and symbolized the self. She demonstrates in poems like "The Soul selects her own Society" that a perception of nature dependent upon symbols is a distortion of cosmic reality. Dickinson's poems on the soul are, therefore, specific judgements against American intellectual history. 16 notes. T. P. Linkfield

52. Chesnick, Eugene. WILLIAM JAMES: FICTIONS AND BELIEFS. *South Atlantic Q. 1974 73(2): 236-246.* Discusses William James' two religious treatises: *The Will to Believe* and *The Varieties of Religious Experience*. James found it incredible that God could exist but that His existence could have no effect upon the day-to-day quality of our lives. "For all his yearning to believe, James can hardly be said ever to have undergone any permanent conversion himself." "His appeal for a new credulity for religion was an attempt to restore the balance upset by too long an emphasis on rationalism." Covers 1897-1902. 9 notes.
E. P. Stickney

53. Dargo, George. LAW AND SOCIETY IN TRANSITION. *Rev. in Am. Hist. 1975 3(4): 433-437.* Industrialization and a shift from a religious to a secular orientation resulted in social change and altered legal systems, finds William E. Nelson in *Americanization of the Common Law: The Impact of Legal Change on Massachusetts Society, 1760-1830* (Cambridge, Mass.: Harvard U. Pr., 1975).

54. Ferm, Robert L. JOHN WINTHROP, THE "INFIDEL," AND THE BICENTENNIAL. *Religion in Life 1976 45(2): 146-151.* Discusses the influence of religion, morality and piety in early American history, including the views of Puritan leader John Winthrop in 1630 and of "infidel" Robert Ingersoll in the latter half of the 19th century.

55. Franzoni, Janet Brenner. TROUBLED TIRADER: A PSYCHOBIOGRAPHICAL STUDY OF TOM WATSON. *Georgia Hist. Q. 1973 57(4): 493-510.* Thomas E. Watson (1856-1922), prominent Georgia politician, legislator, congressman, and vice-presidential candidate, was an enigmatic figure. His colorful tirades and efforts ranged in extremes from pro- to anti-black, Catholic, and Jew. Psychological analysis may well hold the key to an understanding of his career. 79 notes.
D. L. Smith

56. French, David. PURITAN CONSERVATISM AND THE FRONTIER: THE ELIZUR WRIGHT FAMILY ON THE CONNECTICUT WESTERN RESERVE. *Old Northwest 1975 1(1): 85-95.* Elizur Wright I and his Yale-educated son, Elizur II, built pioneer farms: the father in wilderness Canaan, Connecticut; the son in the Western Reserve. Both were orthodox Congregationalists, scientists, and mathematicians. In the next generation, Elizur III's study of science led to his questioning Puritan orthodoxy. Elizur II became a conservative religious leader and educator at Tallmadge, Ohio, but his son Elizur III returned to Connecticut to enter Yale University, representing the first generation to return east. Elizur III succeeded at Yale but abandoned the orthodoxy of his heritage. He became a follower of the agnostic Robert Ingersoll (1833-99). Covers 1762-1870. 37 notes. J. N. Dickinson

57. Gerlach, Dominic B. ST. JOSEPH'S INDIAN NORMAL SCHOOL, 1888-1896. *Indiana Mag. of Hist. 1973 69(1): 1-42.* Racial and religious conflicts plagued St. Joseph's, and economic and political problems caused its demise. This Catholic school was supported by public, church, and private funds, but Protestant demands that federal support be withheld from parochial schools deprived the school of essential financing. The Indians resisted the kind of education offered by St. Joseph's; the average annual runaway rate was 50%. By 1895, the anti-Catholic American Protective Association had directed its attention to abolishing the contract schools, and in 1896 the school was closed. Its failure to meet its stated educational objectives was as important a factor as loss of government contracts. N. E. Tutorow

58. Gragg, Larry. A MERE CIVIL FRIENDSHIP: FRANKLIN AND WHITEFIELD. *Hist. Today [Great Britain] 1978 28(9): 574-579.* George Whitefield and Benjamin Franklin had shared business interests, Franklin published Whitefield's works, and they had similar interests in religious liberty and the need for moral improvement, but Whitefield never had the satisfaction of believing that he had converted Franklin.

59. Greenberg, Douglas. THE MIDDLE COLONIES IN RECENT AMERICAN HISTORIOGRAPHY. *William and Mary Q. 1979 36(3): 396-427.* Contends that the mid-Atlantic colonies more represented the varied American character than did the colonies of New England or the South. Attention given particularly to six recent works on colonial New York, New Jersey, and Pennsylvania. Many books and articles, including those dealing with the local level, are cited. Several

generalizations are developed, such as that social conditions changed more rapidly in the three middle colonies than elsewhere; pluralism came at a price, for example in breeding poverty; and the issue of slavery was divisive. Calls for more study in such areas as blacks, Indians, and other ethnic groups. Comments on religious and legal history. Contends that the American Revolution had the most profound effect in providing opportunity to alter insitutions. Based on extensive recent historiography of the middle colonies; 68 notes. H. M. Ward

60. Greenwood, N. H. SOL BARTH: A JEWISH SETTLER ON THE ARIZONA FRONTIER. *J. of Arizona Hist. 1973 14(4): 363-378.* Solomon Barth (ca. 1843-1928) came to the United States from East Prussia in 1856 and crossed the plains that year with a Mormon handcart group. For 20 years he traveled in the Far West, dealing in cattle, farming, trading, and sometimes gambling. He specialized in the opportunity of the moment. In 1873 he won squatters' equities, water rights, thousands of head of sheep, and cash in a card game at a key point on the Little Colorado River, in east central Arizona, at the juncture of two developing trade routes. Consolidating his land titles, he established St. Johns. Barth's fortunes were enhanced when he permitted Mormon colonists to locate there. Mormon-Mexican conflicts, prominence in local politics and graft, and a prison term occupied Barth. His anti-Mormon inclinations were tempered by the years; in the end he requested his funeral to be conducted in the Mormon church. 3 illus., 30 notes. D. L. Smith

61. Gribbin, William. "A GREATER THAN LAFAYETTE IS HERE": DISSENTING VIEWS OF THE LAST AMERICAN VISIT. *South Atlantic Q. 1974 73(3): 348-362.* Reviews the reception accorded the Marquis de Lafayette during his last visit to the United States. On the surface were cheers, gaiety, and joyous celebration, but underneath a certain dissatisfaction was provoked. Lafayette's tour brought forth the questions of slavery, Sabbath-breaking, and Catholicism. The bloom of independence had worn away and the hero's presence served to point up the drabness of everyday problems when compared with the original grand dream. Covers 1824-25. 50 notes. V. L. Human

62. Jackson, Carl T. THE NEW THOUGHT MOVEMENT AND THE NINETEENTH-CENTURY DISCOVERY OF ORIENTAL PHILOSOPHY. *J. of Popular Culture 1975 9(3): 523-548.* Examines the New Thought movement's discovery of ancient Indian philosophy as one example of the late 19th-century Oriental vogue. It developed from Phineas Parkhurst Quimby's discoveries of mental-healing in the 1850's. His disciple Warren Felt Evans then directed attention to the Orient and India; the Vedanta became commonplace in New Thought periodicals. Three of the foremost leaders of the movement, Elizabeth Towne, William Walker Atkinson, and Horatio Dresser reacted to Indian thought in different ways. 91 notes. J. D. Falk

63. Johnson, Jeremiah. RECOLLECTIONS OF INCIDENTS OF THE REVOLUTION OF THE COLONIES OCCURRING IN BROOKLYN: COLLATED FROM THE MANUSCRIPTS AND CONVERSATIONS OF GENERAL JEREMIAH JOHNSON DESCRIPTIVE OF SCENES WHICH HE PERSONALLY WITNESSED: ARRANGED IN CHRONOLOGICAL ORDER AND EDITED BY THOS. W. FIELD. *J. of Long Island Hist. 1976 12(2): 4-21.* Jeremiah Johnson (1766-1852) of Kings County, New York, lived through the British occupation during the American Revolution (1775-83). It caused hardship and dislocation among the local population, affecting their property, religion, and everyday lives. Describes the effects on the army and the treatment of prisoners of war. Includes 19th-century editor Thomas W. Field's biography of Johnson and modern editor Robert T. Murphy's notes on Field. Illus., 2 notes. J. K. Ehrlich

64. Kepner, Diane. FROM SPEARS TO LEAVES: WALT WHITMAN'S THEORY OF NATURE IN "SONG OF MYSELF." *Am. Literature 1979 51(2): 179-204.* Emphasizes the underlying consistency of thought in Whitman's "Song of Myself" in *Leaves of Grass* (1855). Whitman develops a theory of nature, or philosophy of Being, that answers Emerson's demands in "Nature." Whitman's theory is fundamental to his poetry and represents a philosophical reconciliation of materialism to idealism. His theory recognizes a unity in the universe and its qualities of change and changlessness. The fundamental principle of the universe for Whitman is the association between matter and purposely directed energy (God). Each human possesses the intuitive ability to discern the "everlasting interrelatedness of the universe." 2 fig. T. P. Linkfield

65. Kremm, Thomas W. MEASURING RELIGIOUS PREFERENCES IN NINETEENTH-CENTURY URBAN AREAS. *Hist. Methods Newsletter 1975 8(4): 137-141.* Uses the population of Cleveland, Ohio in 1860 to discover mid-19th-century religious preferences in areas that contained a large number of Catholics. 7 notes. D. K. Pickens

66. Lamar, Howard R. PUBLIC VALUES AND PRIVATE DREAMS: SOUTH DAKOTA'S SEARCH FOR IDENTITY, 1850-1900. *South Dakota Hist. 1978 8(2): 117-142.* The history of the last half of the 19th century is first analyzed with regard to the traditional traders, missionaries and settlers. A Missouri mercantile tradition was established, only to be blunted by the Civil War, decline of steamboat transportation, and the railroad companies' choice of routes south of Dakota. Missionary work in southern Dakota brought not only Protestantism but also other elements of cultural New England. The settlers who formed much of the Territory's heritage were also of New England-Yankee origins. Additionally, the established cultures appeared attractive to European religious groups who sought out Dakota, especially during the last three decades of the 19th century. By the time of statehood, South Dakota's public and private values had also included vigorous but sometimes corrupt politics and a proud rural, agrarian economy. Secondary sources; 7 photos, map, 59 notes. A. J. Larson

67. Long, Charles H. "THE OPPRESSIVE ELEMENTS IN RELIGION AND THE RELIGIONS OF THE OPPRESSED." *Harvard Theological Rev. 1976 69(3-4): 397-412.* There was a fundamental difference between William James and Ernst Troeltsch in their philosophies of religion, but Troeltsch nevertheless wrote, in 1912, a very favorable review of James's *The Varieties of Religious Experience.* Discusses how this reception was possible, given their differences. The answer is that in dealing with the religious experience both arrived at the same position, though for different reasons. Contrasts between James's view of religious experience (individual) with that of W. E. B. Du Bois (community). 36 notes. E. E. Eminhizer

68. Lozynsky, Artem. DR. RICHARD MAURICE BUCKE: A RELIGIOUS DISCIPLE OF WHITMAN. *Studies in the Am. Renaissance 1977: 387-403.* The contributions of Richard Maurice Bucke (1837-1902) to the study of the writings of Walt Whitman (1819-92) have been slighted because of the religious significance which Bucke attached to Whitman's work. The poet's apotheosis by Bucke has obscured a proper appreciation of the latter's role, that is, as a religious, and not a literary, disciple. Based on correspondence between Whitman, Bucke, and others; 33 notes. S. Baatz

69. Luckingham, Bradford. RELIGION IN EARLY SAN FRANCISCO. *Pacific Historian 1973 17(4): 56-73.* Traces the development of various religions and their voluntary associations, including charities and schools, in San Francisco during the 1850's. S

70. McDade, Thomas M. MATTHIAS, PROPHET WITHOUT HONOR. *New-York Hist. Soc. Q. 1978 62(4): 311-334.* Among the many religious eccentrics to appear in the 1820's and '30's in New York was Robert Matthews, who had a brief (1828-35) but newsworthy career in New York City. Known as Matthias the Prophet, he was able to dazzle a small group of people, members of the so-called Retrenchment Society, some of whom had money and property. Matthias controlled the group with a mixture of piety, sex, and an ability to win over reasonably sane people, particularly women. Finally, after some wife-swapping and similar activities, one husband died in mysterious circumstances. Murder probably had been done, but not enough evidence existed to indict Matthias. Nevertheless, his hold on the followers began to weaken. By mid-1835, the movement collapsed and Matthias disappeared from sight. The only person to emerge unscathed was a black woman named Isabella Van Wagenen, who later became justly famous as Sojourner Truth. Largely primary sources; 3 illus., 25 notes. C. L. Grant

71. Mead, Sidney E. RELIGIOUS PLURALISM AND THE CHARACTER OF THE REPUBLIC. *Soundings 1978 61(3): 306-327.*

Examines the impact of religious pluralism on national characteristics and the political and social development of American democracy, 1640's-1840's.

72. Miller, J. R. D'ALTON MCCARTHY, EQUAL RIGHTS, AND THE ORIGINS OF THE MANITOBA SCHOOL QUESTION. *Can. Hist. R. 1973 54(4): 369-392.* Examines the historiography of the origins of provincial legislation in Manitoba to eliminate Catholic denominational education in 1890. Offers a revised view of the role of Conservative Member of Parliament D'Alton McCarthy and the Equal Rights Association in this process. There was little connection between McCarthy and the schools legislation. The 1890 Acts were the result of the social transformation of Manitoba, 1870-90. Based on newspaper, pamphlet, and manuscript sources in the Public Archives of Canada, the Public Archives of Manitoba, and the Archiepiscopal Archives of St. Boniface.
A

73. Molson, Francis J. EMILY DICKINSON'S REJECTION OF THE HEAVENLY FATHER. *New England Q. 1974 47(3): 404-426.* Reviews Emily Dickinson's philosophy of religion. Contrary to some opinion, Dickinson did not reject the God of orthodox Protestantism. She strongly believed in a personal God, but insisted that He prove his existence. When her most cherished prayers were not answered, especially her prayers for love, Dickinson turned instead to a God of love, or love itself, within her own heart. She was never content to sacrifice her life for possible future rewards; rather she wished to be rewarded first and then work as payment for the reward. Covers 1840-54. 14 notes.
V. L. Human

74. Moody, Robert. THE LORD SELECTED ME. *Southern Exposure 1979 7(4): 4-10.* In May 1903, in Pine Bluff, Arkansas, young black resident Ellen Burnett had a vision that the city would be destroyed by a storm before five p.m. on 29 May. All who feared the Lord were to leave town before then. Most black residents and some whites left. The town began to feel the economic impact several days before the appointed day, as workers left. Ellen was arrested but later released. Two storms did hit the city on 29 May. Based on newspaper accounts and interviews with residents; 2 photos.
R. V. Ritter

75. Norton, Wesley. "LIKE A THOUSAND PREACHERS FLYING": RELIGIOUS NEWSPAPERS ON THE PACIFIC COAST TO 1865. *California Hist. Q. 1977 56(3): 194-209.* Surveys religious newspapers on the Pacific Coast from the gold rush era through the Civil War. Religious newspapers included secular news as well as religious topics, were generally ambitious, underfinanced, and enjoyed varying runs. They included dailies, weeklies, semimonthlies, monthlies, and other schedules. Most were short-lived, but some lasted to the 20th century. In an era of nativism these papers exercised a moderating influence. For the most part they were antislavery and called for toleration of Chinese. Denominations included Catholic, Jewish, and numerous Protestant sects. With increasing urbanization and the growth of general-readership newspapers, the religious newspapers turned more to coverage of religious affairs and less to worldly matters. Primary and secondary sources; illus., 66 notes, bibliography of West Coast religious newspapers to 1865.
A. Hoffman

76. Piersen, William D. WHITE CANNIBALS, BLACK MARTYRS: FEAR, DEPRESSION, AND RELIGIOUS FAITH AS CAUSES OF SUICIDE AMONG NEW SLAVES. *J. of Negro Hist. 1977 62(2): 147-151.* Suicide, mostly by hanging or drowning, was a part of the largest involuntary intercontinental migration. African slaves, during the three-century span of the Atlantic slave trade, included several hundred thousand suicides. Death was preferable to life for many slaves. Secondary sources; 81 notes.
N. G. Sapper

77. Poelzer, Irene A. THE CATHOLIC NORMAL SCHOOL ISSUE IN THE NORTHWEST TERRITORIES, 1884-1900. *Study Sessions: Can. Catholic Hist. Assoc. 1975 42: 5-28.* The real reason behind the loss of the Catholic Church's right to separate normal schools was not its inability to meet legitimate requirements, but political opportunism and growing intolerance in the North-West during 1884-1900.

78. Quandt, Jean B. RELIGION AND SOCIAL THOUGHT: THE SECULARIZATION OF POSTMILLENNIALISM. *Am. Q. 1973 25(4): 390-409.* The semireligious postmillennialism of the post-Civil War era strongly resembled earlier antebellum evangelical hopes for world redemption. Postmillenialism persisted into the early 20th century but transferred the redemptive power from religious to secular institutions by merging revelation with reason and social Christianity with social science. Primary and secondary sources; 84 notes.
W. D. Piersen

79. Quimby, Rollin W. LLOYD LEWIS MISREADS THE PREACHERS. *Lincoln Herald 1973 75(1): 3-10.* Historian Lloyd Lewis argued in his *Myths After Lincoln* that Union clergymen were Lincoln's chief mythmakers. However, Lewis rearranged quoted sermons on Lincoln's death to fit his thesis. Lincoln's lowly birth, clear thinking, kindness and honesty plus the idea that the Lord took Lincoln away at the right time were basic mythmaking ideas that Lewis's use of rhetorical materials distorted. A chronological examination of the surviving Civil War sermons, church resolutions, and newspaper and magazine articles shows that nothing new was said by either clergy or editors after Lincoln's death. Based on contemporary church papers, reports and sermons, and secondary sources; 31 notes.
A. C. Aimone

80. Rausch, David A. OUR HOPE: PROTOFUNDAMENTALISM'S ATTITUDE TOWARD ZIONISM, 1894-1897. *Jewish Social Studies 1978 40(3-4): 239-250. Our Hope,* founded by Arno C. Gaebelein and edited for its first three years by Dr. Ernst F. Stroeter, was an English-language Christian publication designed to further Fundamentalism in the United States and emphasizing the importance of the Jews and their place in biblical prophecy. Original articles and those taken from Jewish publications were pro-Zionist and stressed the everlasting quality of the nation of Israel. Other pieces discussed Christian missions to the Jews and the Jewish colonization of Palestine. In 1897 the periodical changed from its original purpose to a popular Bible study publication. Attitudes similar to those in the early years of *Our Hope* regarding the restoration of the Jews to Palestine were expressed in the international prophetic conference movement and the Christian missions to the Jews in the 19th century.
N. Lederer

81. Reck, W. Emerson. FOR THE BLESSINGS OF THE YEAR. *Am. Hist. Illus. 1977 12(7): 4-7, 44-46.* The pilgrims were not the first celebrants of Thanksgiving. Martin Frobisher held the first celebration in North America on 27 May 1578 in Newfoundland. English Captain George Popham held the first celebration in the United States on 9 August 1607 near Phippsburg, Maine. Discusses noteworthy Thanksgiving celebrations held by English Captain John Woodlief at the Berkeley Plantation in Charles City County, Virginia, on 4 December 1619, the famous celebration at Plymouth in 1621, the Second Continental Congress's celebration on 18 December 1777, and George Washington's celebrations on 26 November 1789 and 19 February 1795. Abraham Lincoln established the last Thursday in November as Thanksgiving Day in 1863 after a sustained campaign by Sarah J. Hale, editor of *Ladies' Magazine* (later *Godey's Lady's Book);* 1828-63. Primary and secondary sources; 6 illus.
D. Dodd

82. Sancton, Thomas A. LOOKING INWARD: EDWARD BELLAMY'S SPIRITUAL CRISIS. *Am. Q. 1973 25(5): 538-557.* Edward Bellamy (1850-98) suffered a spiritual crisis over his failure to accomplish great deeds as an Emersonian individual. When his alternatives to a failed self—religion, human love, battlefield martyrdom, and a mystical communion with nature—proved either unattainable or unacceptable, he moved into the field of social thought where in the Nationalist Movement he found a glorious cause into which he could submerge his individualism. Primary and secondary sources; 51 notes.
W. D. Piersen

83. Schappes, Morris U. HOW AMERICAN WRITERS SAW THE JEWS: REVIEW ESSAY. *J. of Ethnic Studies 1978 6(2): 75-92.* Surveys and comments on Louis Harap, *The Image of the Jew in American Literature: From Early Republic to Mass Immigration* (1974), "a seminal work opening and defining new areas of perception and evaluation in American life and letters," and "exemplary in conception and execution." Harap examines not only belles lettres, but also popular forms from folklore to journalism and from the dime novel to mass-circulation popular fiction, and concludes that "the history of the Jewish character in American literature is also a chapter in the history of anti-Semitism." Schappes finds Harap even too mild in his criticisms in places, but calls his section on Emma Lazarus "the best single essay in print," and that

on Abraham Cahan excellent. Still Harap is inadequate in his understanding of the Jewish transformation to a primarily ethnic rather than a religious entity. G. J. Bobango

84. Schultz, Joseph P. THE LURIANIC STRAND IN JONATHAN EDWARDS' CONCEPT OF PROGRESS. *Judaica [Switzerland] 1974 30(3): 126-134.* Jonathan Edwards, the great early American theologian, believed that the Millennium would come before the Last Judgment and that it would gradually evolve without miracle or catastrophe; for this concept of progress, Edwards may be indebted to the 16th-century Jewish cabalist Isaac Luria.

85. Smith, Dean. PRINTING: THE TRADE THAT FOUNDED A REPUBLIC. *Am. Hist. Illus. 1979 13(10): 10-21.* Printing played an important role in the development of the American colonies, 1638-1776, providing newspapers, educational, and religious materials, and political tracts and announcements prior to the American Revolution.

86. Smylie, James H. CLERICAL PERSPECTIVES ON DEISM: PAINE'S *THE AGE OF REASON* IN VIRGINIA. *Eighteenth-Cent. Studies 1972-73 6(2): 203-220.* Explores the reasons why Thomas Paine's *The Age of Reason* (1794-95) provoked clerical opposition in Virginia. Analyzes four anti-deistical tracts written and circulated by Old Dominion apologists: 1) Andrew Broaddus' *The Age of Reason and Revelation* (1795), 2) James Muir's *An Examination of the Principles Contained in the Age of Reason* (1795), 3) Moses Hoge's *The Sophist Unmasked* (1797), and 4) an anonymous theologian, "Common Sense," who attacked Paine in nine articles in the *Virginia Gazette and Richmond Chronicle* (March-May 1795). The Virginia clergy attacked Paine for his view of revelation, his exclusive claim to the use of reason, for falsely attributing the ills of the world to Christianity, and for his own basic affirmations in his credo. 67 notes. D. D. Cameron

87. Stannard, David E. CALM DWELLINGS. *Am. Heritage 1979 30(5): 42-55.* Reflecting subtle social changes, rural cemeteries began to appear in the 1830's as an attempt to maintain the symbols, if not the reality, of the viable, traditional family. Tombstones reflect that concern. By the 1840's, there were so many small, fenced-in family cemeteries that complaints began. Economics and changing views on religion led to their eventual decline. 10 illus. J. F. Paul

88. Walker, Charles O. GEORGIA'S RELIGION IN THE COLONIAL ERA, 1733-1790. *Viewpoints: Georgia Baptist Hist. 1976 5: 17-44.* Examines Anglicans, Jews, Lutherans, Presbyterians, Congregationalists, Quakers, and Baptists in Georgia, 1733-90, taking into account the American Revolution and its effect on religious practices in the state.

89. —. THE COCHRAN FANATICISM IN YORK COUNTY. *Maine Hist. Soc. Q. 1980 20(1): 20-39.*

Gaffney, Thomas L. EDITOR'S NOTE, *pp. 20-22.* Summarizes Jacob Cochran's career and gives a bibliography on the subject.

—. THE COCHRAN FANATICISM IN YORK COUNTY, *pp. 23-39.* The unknown author, writing in 1867, gives a morally indignant account of the brief (1817-19) religious career of Jacob Cochran (b. 1785) in York County, Maine. Cochran used his charismatic personality to lead a religious movement known as Cochranism or the Society of Free Brethren and Sisters. He attacked organized Christianity and advocated "spiritual" marriage and free love. After he was convicted of adultery and served time in prison, his movement gradually disappeared. Based on interviews with eyewitnesses. C. A. Watson

1920-1980

90. Albanese, Catherine. REQUIEM FOR MEMORIAL DAY: DISSENT IN THE REDEEMER NATION. *Am. Q. 1974 26(4): 386-398.* If the American symbol system is in crisis and if the cult of the annual commemoration of the dead is declining, "where is the collective expression of death going?" Examines the gradual transformation of the way Americans regard Memorial Day (30 May) and the meaning of death from the viewpoint of the symbol crisis, the history of religions, and social and structural anthropology. Covers 1945-74. 35 notes. C. W. Olson

91. Beckford, James A. EXPLAINING RELIGIOUS MOVEMENTS. *Int. Social Sci. J. [France] 1977 29(2): 235-249.* Trends in religious movements since the 1960's allow for greater sensitivity in religious interpretation: grounding of political movements in social networks and organizational fields, and creation of symbolic articulation of devotees' experiences through social dislocation and reintegration.

92. Bibby, Reginald W. RELIGION AND MODERNITY: THE CANADIAN CASE. *J. for the Sci. Study of Religion 1979 18(1): 1-17.* Surveys religion in Canada in the 1970's, based on a 1975 study, discussing the relationship between organized religion and industrialization.

93. Bibby, Reginald W. THE STATE OF COLLECTIVE RELIGIOSITY IN CANADA: AN EMPIRICAL ANALYSIS. *Can. Rev. of Sociol. and Anthrop. [Canada] 1979 16(1): 105-116.* The institutional specialization which characterizes industrialization knows the concomitant of a decline in the pervasiveness of religion. Maintaining further that collectivities are essential to ideational sustenance, the author explores the state of Judaic-Christianity in an industrializing Canada through an examination of participation in organized religion. Using a basic demographic framework and census and survey data, he begins with an overview of current participation and then examines involvement trends. It is found that organized religion is experiencing a participation decline. Concludes with a discussion of the implications of such findings for traditional religion in Canadian society. Covers 1921-71. 11 tables, biblio. J

94. Boling, T. Edwin. BLACK AND WHITE RELIGION: A COMPARISON IN THE LOWER CLASS. *Sociol. Analysis 1975 36(1): 73-80.* Addresses the problem of the relationship of religion and social class by comparing similarities and differences between blacks and whites within the lower class in a small midwestern city during 1969. Departing from expected patterns, the lower class white religious group members are just as likely to be members of church type organizations as they are to be members of sects. Whites also demonstrated a strong incongruity between organizational membership and religious attitudes. Blacks are largely sect members and do not depart from the expected pattern. By organizational membership and religious attitudes, the blacks are highly congruous. Although the study confirms that lower class blacks and whites share an ideological orientation to sectarianism as measured by religious beliefs, other measures of religiosity (e.g., private prayer and worship attendance) indicate a difference for blacks and whites in the lower class. J

95. Clements, William M. THE JONESBORO TORNADO: A CASE STUDY IN FOLKLORE, POPULAR RELIGION, AND GRASS ROOTS HISTORY. *Red River Valley Hist. R. 1975 2(2): 273-286.* Discusses attitudes in Arkansas concerning a tornado which struck in 1973. S

96. DeJong, Gordon F.; Faulkner, Joseph E.; and Warland, Rex H. DIMENSIONS OF RELIGIOSITY RECONSIDERED: EVIDENCE FROM A CROSS-CULTURAL STUDY. *Social Forces 1976 54(4): 866-889.* This paper supports the multidimensional conceptualization of religiosity by presenting empirical evidence for a strikingly similar dimensional pattern for a group of German and American students. An oblique factor analytic rotation solution identified six dimensions of religiosity: belief, experience, religious practice, religious knowledge, individual moral consequences, and social consequences. Factor intercorrelations show that for both Germans and Americans religious knowledge and social consequences appear to be unique dimensions that are essentially

unrelated to the other dimensions investigated. The remaining dimensions—belief, experience, and religious practice, and to some extent the individual moral consequence dimension—while differentiated in the oblique rotation solution, also form a more generic dimension of religiosity when second-order factor analysis is applied. Our interpretation is that differing numbers of dimensions, and differing content in lower- and higher-order dimensions of religiosity are not logically inconsistent in that they are derived from variant orders of abstraction. Covers 1960-77. J

97. Deloria, Vine, Jr. RELIGION AND THE MODERN AMERICAN INDIAN. *Current Hist. 1974 67(400): 250-253.* From an issue on the American Indian. S

98. Dewing, Rolland. HISTORY OF AMERICAN SPORTS: ACADEMIC FEATHERBEDDING OR NEGLECTED AREA? *Social Sci. J. 1977 14(3): 73-82.* Discusses history in terms of national pastimes, especially sports; discusses sports as a measure of national character, its impact on 20th-century Americans, and its reflection of basic beliefs (political, economic, social, religious, and racial).

99. Dickinson, George E. RELIGIOUS PRACTICES OF ADOLESCENTS IN A SOUTHERN COMMUNITY: 1964-1974. *J. for the Sci. Study of Religion 1976 15(4): 361-364.* Examines differences in church attendance and outward religiosity in Negroes and whites in a Southern community; affiliation with established churches is declining among adolescents.

100. Driedger, Leo. IN SEARCH OF CULTURAL IDENTITY FACTORS: A COMPARISON OF ETHNIC STUDENTS. *Can. Rev. of Sociol. and Anthrop. 1975 12(2): 150-162.* Factor analysis of Likert-type items administered to undergraduate students in 1971 suggests that modes of ethnic identification can be described in terms of six factors: religion, endogamy, language use, ethnic organizations, parochial education, and choice of ingroup friends. A comparison of the factor profiles of seven ethnic groups revealed considerable variations. For example, the Jewish students identified strongly with endogamy and ingroup choice of friends but ranked low on the importance of religion and the use of their ethnic language. The French students' identification with their language and religion was high. Both the French and the Jewish students valued parochial education. Scandinavian and Polish ethnic ingroup identification was the lowest of all seven groups compared. The modes of identification tended to vary with the historically important experiences of ethnic groups. Therefore the measures of the modes exhibited a multifactor structure. J

101. Eckardt, Alice L. THE HOLOCAUST: CHRISTIAN AND JEWISH RESPONSES. *J. of the Am. Acad. of Religion 1974 42(3): 453-469.* Surveys, with some analysis and evaluation, the writings of leading Jewish and Christian scholars who have offered responses to the slaughter of six million Jews by Hitler. While most agree that no solution can be considered adequate, some explanation must be attempted. Stresses the nature of this theological problem for Jews and Christians. 68 notes. E. R. Lester

102. Edwards, Tilden H., Jr. "SPIRITUAL GROWTH," ITS NATURE, SOURCES, AND CONSEQUENCES: ANNOUNCEMENT OF A PRELIMINARY EMPIRICAL INVESTIGATION. *Anglican Theological Rev. Supplementary Series 1973 (2): 132-135.*

103. Elliott, Willis. LEISURE AND THE ESOFUTURE. *Anglican Theological Rev. 1973 55(3): 304-323.* Leisure time can raise individual religious consciousness in the future. S

104. Fennero, Matthew John. SOCIAL GOSPELERS AND SOVIETS, 1921-1926. *J. of Church and State 1977 19(1): 53-73.* Discusses why leading social gospelers Harry F. Ward, Edgar Blake, and Matthew Spinka supported the Bolsheviks' treatment of religion and religious leaders in Russia during 1921-26. Discusses the reaction of conservative American religious leaders. 62 notes.

E. E. Eminhizer

105. Fichter, Joseph H. THE UNCERTAIN FUTURE OF THE CHURCH IN AMERICA. *Thought 1975 50(197): 119-131.* Five trends augur well for the future of organized religion in America: emergence in the larger religious bodies of polities which combine democratic and hierarchical elements, greater cooperation among denominations, tolerance of pluralism within the larger churches, identification with the counter-culture, and commitment to the reform of social institutions.

J. C. English

106. Filsinger, Erik E.; Faulkner, Joseph E.; and Warland, Rex H. EMPIRICAL TAXONOMY OF RELIGIOUS INDIVIDUALS: AN INVESTIGATION AMONG COLLEGE STUDENTS. *Sociol. Analysis 1979 40(2): 136-146.* Factor analytic studies of religion have suggested that several aspects of the religious phenomenon do not necessarily covary with each other. Individuals may manifest their religiosity in different ways through a unique combination of high and/or low values on religious variables. A taxonomy of religious individuals can indicate the different approaches to religiosity, i.e., what types of religious individuals there are. Using hierarchical agglomerative cluster analysis, an empirical taxonomy of religious individuals was developed on questionnaire data from 220 student respondents in 1970. The research instrument was designed to cover the conceptual sphere of traditional religiosity. Seven types were found: the Outsiders, the Conservatives, the Rejectors, the Modern Religious, the Marginally Religious, the Orthodox, and the Culturally Religious. The scientific utility of the typology was supported when differences between the types on additional demographic and religious variables were examined. The contributions made by the study are discussed in terms of the relationship between the present findings and those of past studies. Suggestions are made for subsequent research.

J

107. Fracchia, Charles A. THE WESTERN CONTEXT: ITS IMPACT ON OUR RELIGIOUS CONSCIOUSNESS. *Lutheran Q. 1977 29(1): 13-20.* California has become the center for change, a place where many new religious forms and ideas develop. A strong resurgence of traditional Christianity has taken place; and a strong interest in non-Western religions, such as Hinduism and Buddhism, has occurred. Also from California has come an interest in the new consciousness, which involves a belief in human transformation through contact with a higher reality. Millions of people have become interested in these essentially religious movements. Consequently, contemporary clergy should make themselves familiar with the ideas and practices that have developed from these phenomena. The ministers and priests of California must also direct their attention to two groups: retired, elderly persons and single people. Both groups offer significant challenges to the traditional ideas of the ministry. Covers the 1970's. J. A. Kicklighter

108. Gecas, Viktor; Thomas, Darwin L.; and Weigert, Andrew J. SOCIAL IDENTITIES IN ANGLO AND LATIN ADOLESCENTS. *Social Forces 1973 51(4): 477-484.* Social identities, conceptualized as self-designations and measured by the TST, were examined for samples of high school adolescents in three societies: the United States, Puerto Rico, and Mexico. Four identities were explored in terms of salience, frequency, and valence: gender, religion, family, and peer. For both males and females in Latin and Anglo cultures gender emerged as the most prominent identity. Religious IDs were more frequent for Catholic adolescents. The strongest cultural difference was found with respect to negative religious IDs: these were significantly more frequent for Anglo adolescents. Positive gender and family IDs were more frequent for Latin adolescents, while peer IDs were slightly more common self-designations for Anglos. These tendencies were generally in the expected direction. Social and cultural differences between these Anglo and Latin societies were considered as explanations for variations in adolescent identity structures. J

109. Goldstick, D. FOUR FORMS OF INTELLECTUAL RELIGION. *Queen's Q. [Canada] 1973 80(1): 59-64.* Examines, from an antireligious viewpoint, how modern intellectuals have attempted to come to grips with religious beliefs in the face of attacks on their rationality. Discusses four responses: 1) defense of beliefs from a rational intellectual standpoint, 2) theological liberalism, 3) fideism, and 4) noncognitivism. 5 notes. J. A. Casada

110. Gottlieb, David and Sibbison, Virginia. ETHNICITY AND RELIGIOSITY: SOME SELECTIVE EXPLORATIONS AMONG COLLEGE STUDENTS. *Int. Migration Rev. 1974 8(1): 43-58.* A study of ethnic-religious factors as an integral part of the socialization process in 1972. S

111. Gustafson, Paul M. THE MISSING MEMBER OF TROELTSCH'S TRINITY: THOUGHTS GENERATED BY WEBER'S COMMENTS. *Sociol. Analysis 1975 36(3): 224-226.* Discusses, in a special issue on the concepts of church, sect, and mysticism, American sociologists' neglect in the 20th century of Ernst Troeltsch and Max Weber's conceptions of mysticism.

112. Hadden, Jeffrey K., ed. REVIEW SYMPOSIUM: THE SOCIOLOGY OF RELIGION OF ROBERT N. BELLAH. *J. for the Sci. Study of Religion 1975 14(4): 385-414.* Considers Harvard Professor Robert N. Bellah and his work on the sociology of religion during 1959-75, with emphasis on his theory of civil religion.

113. Hastings, Philip K. and Hoge, Dean R. CHANGES IN RELIGION AMONG COLLEGE STUDENTS, 1948 TO 1974. *J. for the Sci. Study of Religion 1976 15(3): 237-249.* Surveys men at Williams College during 1948-74 and finds an increasing percentage of students rejecting home religious traditions and church participation.

114. Hay, David and Morisy, Ann. REPORTS ON ECSTATIC, PARANORMAL, OR RELIGIOUS EXPERIENCE IN GREAT BRITAIN AND THE UNITED STATES: A COMPARISON OF TRENDS. *J. for the Sci. Study of Religion 1978 17(3): 255-268.* Outlines points of convergence and divergence in the reportage and study of ecstatic, paranormal, and religious experiences in Great Britain, drawing conclusions about the occurrence of such experiences and psychological well-being as it is culturally defined; covers 1975-77.

115. Hertel, Bradley R. and Nelsen, Hart M. ARE WE ENTERING A POST-CHRISTIAN ERA? RELIGIOUS BELIEF AND ATTENDANCE IN AMERICA, 1957-1968. *J. for the Sci. Study of Religion 1974 13(4): 409-419.* Demonstrates that while there has been no appreciable decline in levels of religious belief in recent years, there was a marked decline in the proportion of Americans expressing uncertainty regarding these beliefs and an increase in the proportions openly espousing disbelief.

116. Hoelter, Jon W. and Epley, Rita J. RELIGIOUS CORRELATES OF FEAR OF DEATH. *J. for the Sci. Study of Religion 1979 18(4): 404-411.* Survey results suggest that religiosity can reduce some death related fears while increasing others, 1970's.

117. Klemmack, David L. and Cardwell, Jerry D. INTERFAITH COMPARISON OF MULTIDIMENSIONAL MEASURES OF RELIGIOSITY. *Pacific Sociol. Rev. 1973 16(4): 495-507.*

118. Kluegel, James R. DENOMINATIONAL MOBILITY: CURRENT PATTERNS AND RECENT TRENDS. *J. for the Sci. Study of Religion 1980 19(1): 26-39.* Denominational mobility has been fairly constant in the United States during the 1960's and 1970's, except for the slight increase in the number of people affiliating with sects and the substantial increase of younger people who claim no affiliation.

119. Lankford, John. RELIGION AND POST-INDUSTRIAL SOCIETY IN AMERICA: SOME IMPLICATIONS. *Hist. Mag. of the Protestant Episcopal Church 1978 47(4): 415-425.* Distinguishes between the past Puritan ethic of thrift and the contemporary ethic of consumption. Building on the works of Daniel Bell and Robert Wuthnow, notes the severing of ties with the past in America, the breakup of the Evangelical Synthesis, the value transformation from industrial to post-industrial society, the overriding presence of cultural diversity, and its attendant subjectification of religious belief. People can only "be themselves" when they move from the public to the private world, to family and religion. Thus decentralization in the churches may be expected, together with a greater respect for often successive religious experiences. There is nothing inherent in the nature of post-industrial society that militates against religion. Suggests that this form of society is more open to religion than its predecessors, especially when the role and influence of the electronic media are considered. Secondary sources; 15 notes.

H. M. Parker, Jr.

120. Lankford, John. THE WRITING OF AMERICAN HISTORY IN THE 1960S: A CRITICAL BIBLIOGRAPHY OF MATERIALS OF INTEREST TO SOCIOLOGISTS. *Sociol. Q. 1973 14(1): 99-126.* "This essay is not a contribution to the theoretical literature on the relationships between sociology and history. Rather it is directed at those who have an active commitment to interdisciplinary investigations and who are at work on the common problems and frontiers shared by sociology and history." The series of categories which reflect patterns of sociological concern are as follows: stratification and mobility; politics and power; family; violence; immigration; urbanization; racial, sexual, and cultural minorities; professions; religion; education; economic growth and development; and large scale analysis of American society. 24 notes.

D. D. Cameron

121. Lazerwitz, Bernard. RELIGIOUS IDENTIFICATION AND ITS ETHNIC CORRELATES: A MULTIVARIATE MODEL. *Social Forces 1973 52(2): 204-220.* Separated sets of concepts and procedures have developed from studies on the religious and ethnic identifications of Christians and Jews. This article strives to integrate these research streams through a set of eight identification dimensions. Using prior research by Lenski and Sklare, these eight dimensions are formed into two path analysis models—one for Protestants and one for Jews. These models are then evaluated by data from a probability sample of Chicago area Jews and white Protestants. As would be expected, findings only partially support the hypothesized path models. The data indicate that there is a mainstream of identification that runs from childhood home religious background to religious education to religious behavior to activity in ethnic organizations and to concern over one's children's religious education. Lenski's findings that ethnic community life and religious institutions were somewhat separated is supported for Protestants, but not for Jews. These eight identity dimensions are controlled for two recursive blocks of biosocial and socioeconomic variables and are related to general community organization activities, anomie, and a measure of liberalness. The findings for high-moderate status Jews show weak or negative relations between identification measures and liberalness. Low-status Jews show positive relations between five dimensions and liberalness. Protestants display weak relations between their identity dimensions and liberalness with no evidence of an interaction with social status. Covers the 1960's and 70's. J

122. Leat, Diana. "PUTTING GOD OVER": THE FAITHFUL COUNSELLORS. *Sociol. Rev. [Great Britain] 1973 21(4): 561-572.* Clerical acceptance (1950's-70's) of the principles and means of counselling represents an attempt to adapt traditional pastoral aims to the dominant world view. Based on secondary sources; 15 notes.

M. L. Lifka

123. Machalek, Richard and Martin, Michael. "INVISIBLE" RELIGIONS: SOME PRELIMINARY EVIDENCE. *J. for the Sci. Study of Religion 1976 15(4): 311-322.* Examines the existence of "invisible" religions, religious belief with no actual church affiliation, held by persons in metropolitan areas in the Deep South, which aid them in forming a philosophy of life and coping with day-to-day existence.

124. Mallard, William. SECULARIST AND TRADITIONALIST. *Religion in Life 1973 42(4): 496-507.* Current attitudes toward religion. S

125. McKinney, William J., Jr. H. RICHARD NIEBUHR AND THE QUESTION OF HUMAN SOCIETY. *Religion in Life 1974 43(3): 362-375.* Undertakes "1) to trace the origins and development of the differentiation between social scientific and theological analysis of culture; 2) to specify areas in which this differentiation has left important issues unresolved in contemporary social science; and 3) to examine Niebuhr's contribution . . . " Covers 1930-70. S

126. Millett, David. RELIGIOUS IDENTITY: THE NON-OFFICIAL LANGUAGES AND THE MINORITY CHURCHES. Elliott, Jean Leonard, ed. *Two Nations, Many Cultures: Ethnic Groups in Canada* (Scarborough, Ont.: Prentice-Hall, 1979): 182-194. Discusses the way minority churches, those which provide services in nonofficial languages, help nonwhite immigrants and native peoples in Canada maintain their language and cultural identity in a French- and English-speaking Canada; 1970's.

127. Muelder, Walter George. WHAT SHOULD BE THE CHURCHES' RESPONSE TO THE RELIGIOUS REBIRTH? *Encounter 1978 39(1): 1-18.* Reviews current religio-spiritual trends (civil

rights and the black church, women's liberation, Transcendental Meditation, Jesus People, the Charismatic Movement, Pentecostalism, etc.) from the 1960's to the present and concludes that mainstream churches must be open and tolerant toward these movements, but without syncretistically betraying Christ.

128. Nelsen, Hart M. RELIGIOUS TRANSMISSION VERSUS RELIGIOUS FORMATION: PREADOLESCENT-PARENT INTERACTION. *Sociol. Q. 1980 21(2): 207-218.* Using 1975 data from 2,724 adolescents from intact families in southern Minnesota, measures five factors and concludes that both parental religiousness and support were significant predictors of preadolescent religiousness.

129. Newport, Frank. THE RELIGIOUS SWITCHER IN THE UNITED STATES. *Am. Sociol. Rev. 1979 44(4): 528-552.* Examines trends, patterns and implications of religious mobility in the United States. Previously published data, and analysis of 1975-76 NORC data indicate that about 25% to 32% of American adults have switched religions (including movement out of religion) in their lifetimes. High and low status denominations are gaining members due to switching (more in-mobility than out-mobility), and Baptists, Catholics, and medium status denominations are losing members due to switching. The most common pattern of religious movement is out of religion altogether. Additional analyses show that religious switching patterns are congruent with explanations stressing the switcher's desire to worship with individuals of similar socioeconomic status, that some switching is the result of an individual moving to the religion of a stable spouse, and that movement out of religion is disproportionately composed of young people. J

130. Pargament, Kenneth I.; Steele, Robert E.; and Tyler, Forrest B. RELIGIOUS PARTICIPATION, RELIGIOUS MOTIVATION AND INDIVIDUAL PSYCHOSOCIAL COMPETENCE. *J. for the Sci. Study of Religion 1979 18(4): 412-419.* Results of a survey of church-synagogue members show that religious participation, religious motivation, and psychosocial functioning are related, 1970's.

131. Patrick, John W. PERSONAL FAITH AND THE FEAR OF DEATH AMONG DIVERGENT RELIGIOUS POPULATIONS. *J. for the Sci. Study of Religion 1979 18(3): 298-305.* The relationship of fear of death to Intrinsic and Extrinsic religious commitment was studied in Christian and Buddhist populations to test the hypothesis that these relationships are consistent across widely differing philosophico-religious traditions. Subjects were 91 members of one Buddhist, one Congregationalist and three Southern Baptist churches in Honolulu, Hawaii. Fear of death was negatively related to Intrinsic religion and positively related to Extrinsic religion only for Christian respondents, suggesting the inapplicability of the Intrinsic-Extrinsic dimension for Buddhists. Christian groups reported significantly less fear of death and significantly more positive attitudes about death than did Buddhists, suggesting that religious traditions vary in the effectiveness with which they assist their members in confronting death. J

132. Pfeffer, Leo. ISSUES THAT DIVIDE: THE TRIUMPH OF SECULAR HUMANISM. *J. of Church and State 1977 19(2): 203-216.* Leo Pfeffer's *Creeds in Competition: A Creative Force in American Culture* (New York: Harper & Row, 1958), finds sharp division of ideas between Catholics and Protestants, Jews, and the "unchurched." Examines the sociopolitical issues of the day in light of Vatican II, civil rights, and the Arab-Israeli wars of 1967 and 1973. Finds many former issues mitigated, but others still alive. 11 notes. E. E. Eminhizer

133. Preston, Michael J. CHAIN LETTERS. *Tennessee Folklore Soc. Bull. 1976 42(1): 1-14.* Discusses laws and superstitions regarding pseudo-religious chain letters in the United States from the 1930's-70's.

134. Pruett, Gordon E. HISTORY, TRANSCENDENCE, AND WORLD COMMUNITY IN THE WORK OF WILFRED CANTWELL SMITH. *J. of the Am. Acad. of Religion 1973 41(4): 573-590.* Seeks to clarify Islamist Wilfred Cantwell Smith's position on history and transcendence, the death-of-God theologians, secularism, and the discipline of the history of religions. Smith (b. 1916), in analyzing Islam and Christianity, limits faith and transcendence to a personal awareness of God in history, his objection to the death-of-God movement opposed the arrogant spirit of the theologians as much as their theological concepts. On secularity Smith understands contemporary theologians to mean essentially that the believer's faith should be active in his secular life. Smith's thoughts regarding methodology in a history of religions conclude the article. Covers 1940-73. Based on Smith's published works and other primary and secondary sources; 46 notes. E. R. Lester

135. Rausch, David. AMERICAN EVANGELICALS AND THE JEWS. *Midstream 1977 23(2): 38-41.* Discusses American Jews' fears of anti-Semitism by Protestant Fundamentalists and Evangelicals; considers trends in Fundamentalists' Messianic beliefs, 1970's.

136. Rausch, David A. OUR HOPE: AN AMERICAN FUNDAMENTALIST JOURNAL AND THE HOLOCAUST, 1937-1945. *Fides et Hist. 1980 12(2): 89-103.* Under the leadership of Arno C. Gaebelin, the fundamentalist journal *Our Hope* (1894-1957) was almost unique among American Protestant periodicals, both liberal and conservative, in accurately chronicling the Nazi abuse of European Jewry. Gaebelin began predicting the Jews' problems shortly after Hitler's accession to power. During the late thirties and World War II, his journal described the persecutions and denounced Nazism both in theory and practice, while it advocated a homeland for the Jews in Palestine. 47 notes. J. A. Kicklighter

137. Rice, Dan. REINHOLD NIEBUHR AND JUDAISM. *J. of the Am. Acad. of Religion 1977 45(1): 72.* Identifies and investigates the main themes in the Jewish-Christian dialogue as Reinhold Niebuhr conceived them. Some attention is given to the history of this dialogue. Four major themes are discussed: Zionism and the state of Israel; anti-Semitism; theological issues dividing the two faiths; and the problem of missions. Covers 1930-60. E. R. Lester

138. Richardson, James T. CONVERSION AND COMMITMENT IN CONTEMPORARY RELIGION: AN INTRODUCTION. *Am. Behavioral Scientist 1977 20(6): 799-804.* Discusses conceptualization and methodology concerning conversion and commitment in contemporary religion; introduces a special issue.

139. Richardson, James T. and Fox, Sandie Wightman. RELIGION AND VOTING ON ABORTION REFORM: A FOLLOW-UP STUDY. *J. for the Sci. Study of Religion 1975 14(2): 159-165.* Discusses the effect of religious affiliation on voting behavior of legislators in an unidentified western state on the issue of abortion in 1975. S

140. Robbins, Thomas; Anthony, Dick; and Richardson, James. THEORY AND RESEARCH ON TODAY'S "NEW RELIGIONS." *Sociol. Analysis 1978 39(2): 95-122.* A number of analytical perspectives have been developed to explain the present upsurge of deviant religious movements and heightened spiritual ferment. These include secularization, crisis of community, value crisis, and the increasing need for holistic self-definition in a differentiated society. Viewing the present religious ferment as rooted in a normative breakdown or value crisis affords the basis of a typology of non-traditional movements in which the "types" embody *different responses to increasing moral ambiguity.* An alternative typological strategy has been to assimilate "new religions" to Church-sect theory and to specify the residual concept of "cult." Much of the literature on "new religions" has been social psychological and has focused on processes of conversion and indoctrination. The dominant models appear to be Lofland's interactionist approach and "coercive persuasion" or "brainwashing" theories. The analysis of contemporary religious ferment is vital to an assessment of sociocultural change in advanced societies. Focuses on Christian (including the Jesus People) and other cults. J

141. Robbins, Thomas; Anthony, Dick; and Curtis, Thomas. YOUTH CULTURE RELIGIOUS MOVEMENTS: EVALUATING THE INTEGRATIVE HYPOTHESIS. *Sociol. Q. 1975 16(1): 48-64.* Assesses the "integrative hypothesis" as an aid to understanding the current emergence of new religious movements appealing mainly to young persons. Four ways in which these movements reintegrate young persons into the social system are identified: adjustive socialization, combination, compensation, and redirection. The limitations of each of these as an explanation for the integrative consequences of youth culture religious movements are discussed. A distinction is made between adaptive movements which actually appear to reassimilate social dropouts into conventional instru-

mental routines, and marginal movements which appear to take converts out of conventional roles and routines, but which also perform latent tension management functions for the social system. The correlated properties of adaptive and marginal movements and the tendency for marginal movements to evolve into adaptive movements are discussed. Finally, the problem of reductionism in analyzing religious movements in terms of their latent integrative 'functions' is discussed. Examines Christian and Eastern religion cults. J

142. Rogers, William R. DEPENDENCE AND COUNTER-DEPENDENCY IN PSYCHOANALYSIS AND RELIGIOUS FAITH. *Zygon 1974 9(3): 190-201.*

143. Roof, Wade Clark. ALIENATION AND APOSTASY. *Society 1978 15(4): 41-45.* Examines social indicators of people leaving traditional religions and joining the new Christian and human potential movements in the United States, 1960's-70's.

144. Roof, Wade Clark and Hadaway, Christopher Kirk. DENOMINATIONAL SWITCHING IN THE SEVENTIES: GOING BEYOND STARK AND GLOCK. *J. for the Sci. Study of Religion 1979 18(4): 363-377.* Examines the cultural and symbolic reasons for denominational switching in the 1970's, using Charles Y. Glock's and Rodney Stark's 1960's switching model as a basis for comparison.

145. Roof, Wade Clark and Hadaway, Christopher Kirk. SHIFTS IN RELIGIOUS PREFERENCE: THE MID-SEVENTIES. *J. for the Sci. Study of Religion 1977 16(4): 409-412.* Summarizes, through the use of data tables, shifts in religious preference, indexing American loyalties to institutional religion.

146. Rothfork, John. GROKKING GOD: PHENOMENOLOGY IN NASA AND SCIENCE FICTION. *Res. Studies 1976 44(2): 101-110.* Discusses the phenomenon of religious experience in space exploration, both in actual National Aeronautics and Space Administration personnel and in characters of contemporary science fiction.

147. Schneider, Louis. THE SCOPE OF "THE RELIGIOUS FACTOR" AND THE SOCIOLOGY OF RELIGION: NOTES ON DEFINITION, IDOLATRY AND MAGIC. *Social Res. 1974 41(2): 340-361.* Calls for the development of a better theoretical basis for the limits of the sociology of religion. S

148. Scott, Nathan A., Jr. "NEW HEAV'NS, NEW EARTH"—THE LANDSCAPE OF CONTEMPORARY APOCALYPSE. *J. of Religion 1973 53(1): 1-35.* The liberal estrangement from history, begun in the early 1950's, reached its apex in Theodore Roszak's concept of counter culture of the late 1960's. This disenchantment is characterized by a contemporary apocalypticism defined as "a time of terror and decadence" in which we look forward to a "post-human future." The manifestations of this contemporary mood are documented through the writings of LeRoi Jones, R. D. Laing, Norman O. Brown, Marshall McLuhan, Philip Rieff, and others. The author chides the theological community for failing to mount any significant debate with this new apocalypticism. 70 notes. E. J. O'Brien

149. Shortridge, James R. A NEW REGIONALIZATION OF AMERICAN RELIGION. *J. for the Sci. Study of Religion 1977 16(2): 143-154.* Outlines religious regions; correlations with cultural regionalism yield major inconsistencies in the western Midwest, New England, and the northern Great Plains, 1974.

150. Shortridge, James R. PATTERNS OF RELIGION IN THE UNITED STATES. *Geographical Rev. 1976 66(4): 420-434.* A recently published survey by the National Council of the Churches of Christ in the United States provides data for a detailed examination of current patterns of American religion. Measures are developed and maps prepared for three diagnostic traits: the liberal-conservative division of American Protestantism, religious diversity, and the incidence of church membership. The resultant patterns generally support those found for other culture elements, although the familiar distinction between the New England and the Pennsylvania culture areas is not clear. A religiously distinctive area exists in the northern portions of the Middle West and Great Plains. J

151. Steiber, Steven R. THE INFLUENCE OF THE RELIGIOUS FACTOR ON CIVIL AND SACRED TOLERANCE, 1958-71. *Social Forces 1980 58(3): 811-832.* The 1960's brought with them many changes in both the religious and the non-religious spheres of American society. Detroit area data from 1958 and 1971 reveal that between these years religious tolerance moves closer to preexisting levels of civil tolerance, and black attitudes converge with white attitudes in both spheres. On religious matters, women are less tolerant than men in both the civil and the sacred across religious categories, but the difference is greater in 1958 than in 1971. Church activity exhibits mixed effects across categories of religious preference, and personal piety has a uniformly negative impact on tolerance. Limited support is also found for Wuthnow's "new generations" explanation for the attitude changes analyzed. 4 tables, 4 fig., 9 notes, biblio., appendix. J

152. Toney, Michael B. RELIGIOUS PREFERENCE AND MIGRATION. *Int. Migration Rev. 1973 7(3): 281-288.*

153. Trotter, F. Thomas. VARIATIONS ON THE "DEATH OF GOD" THEME IN RECENT THEOLOGY. *J. of Bible and Religion 1965 33(1): 42-48.* Delineates the theme of the "death of God" by absence, disappearance, silence, withdrawal, or eclipse, focusing on the works of Jean-Paul Sartre, Robert Heidegger, and Martin Buber, and the development of the themes in American theology, 1961-64.

154. Wagenaar, John. B. F. SKINNER ON HUMAN NATURE, CULTURE, AND RELIGION. *Zygon 1975 10(2): 128-143.* Discusses B. F. Skinner's views on human nature, culture, and religion based on his behaviorist philosophy (1948-74). S

155. Washington, Joseph R., Jr. SHAFTS OF LIGHT IN BLACK RELIGIOUS AWAKENING. *Religion in Life 1974 43(2): 150-160.* Covers the 1970's.

156. Wasserman, Ira M. RELIGIOUS AFFILIATIONS AND HOMICIDE: HISTORICAL RESULTS FROM THE RURAL SOUTH. *J. for the Sci. Study of Religion 1978 17(4): 415-418.* Examines the relationship of religious affiliation to murder, comparing whites and blacks; based on information from a 1916 census department study and the 1920 murder rates in the rural South.

157. Watters, William R., Jr. THE LONELINESS OF BEING JEWISH: THE CHRISTIAN'S UNDERSTANDING OF ISRAEL. *Religion in Life 1975 44(2): 212-221.*

158. Westly, Frances. "THE CULT OF MAN": DURKHEIM'S PREDICTIONS AND NEW RELIGIOUS MOVEMENTS. *Sociol. Analysis 1978 39(2): 135-145.* This paper provides a theoretical discussion of Durkheim's predictions concerning religious evolution and their applicability to the new religious movements of the 1970's. Initially, the paper attempts to elicit from Durkheim's work on the past and future of religion a series of precise hypotheses concerning the causes, expressions, and functions of religion in complex societies. Then the paper examines the significance of these hypotheses as alternative explanations for some of the debated features of these movements: the middle class origins of their adherents, their system of ethics and their relationship to scientific and socio-scientific rationalism. Finally, the paper examines the charismatic Renewal Movement and Silva Mind Control to suggest that if Durkheim's predictions concerning the relationship of ritual, belief and social organization hold up in a variety of movements, they may form the basis of comparative work in this area. J

159. Whitt, Hugh P. and Nelsen, Hart M. RESIDENCE, MORAL TRADITIONALISM, AND TOLERANCE OF ATHEISTS. *Social Forces 1975 54(2): 328-340.* A secondary analysis of data from the 1958 Detroit Area Study and the General Household Survey of the Southern Appalachian Studies indicates that the relationship of tolerance of atheists to place of origin and present place of residence cannot be completely explained by the differential distribution of social class variables and religious beliefs across geographical areas. Part of the residence-tolerance relationship stems from residential differences in education and moral traditionalism, but a substantively significant direct effect remains after these and other factors are controlled. These data do not support Glock and Stark's contention that conservative religious doctrines are responsi-

ble for rural-urban differences in tolerance. The relationship of theological variables to tolerant attitudes toward atheists results from their association with education and moral traditionalism. J

160. Wieting, Stephen G. AN EXAMINATION OF INTERGENERATIONAL PATTERNS OF RELIGIOUS BELIEF AND PRACTICE. *Sociol. Analysis 1975 36(2): 137-149.* The paper presents data documenting adolescent-parent intergenerational patterns of belief and practice for a range of religious factors. Results show discontinuity in orientation toward the religious institution; partial continuity over religious beliefs; and similarity in meanings attached to classic religious symbols. The patterns suggest intergenerational differences may be more in the form of expression than in belief; and that symbolic data may be a useful complement to belief and behavioral data for making intergenerational comparisons. Covers 1940-75. J

161. Williams, Preston N. RELIGION AND THE MAKING OF COMMUNITY IN AMERICA. *J. of the Am. Acad. of Religion 1976 44(4): 603-611.* Ethnicity, or group formation based on ties of race, nationality, culture, or religion, is the process by which assimilation has occurred in American life, and the future will see this assimilation producing further consciousness of ethnicity. The role and responsibility of religion in this continuing process is to test and evaluate ethnicity in terms of fundamental human values and to mediate the knowledge of God who unifies across ethnic boundaries. Secondary sources; 9 notes. E. R. Lester

162. Wimberley, Ronald C. DIMENSIONS OF COMMITMENT: GENERALIZING FROM RELIGION TO POLITICS. *J. for the Sci. Study of Religion 1978 17(3): 225-240.* Draws parallels and contrasts in commitment to religion and politics in terms of belief, knowledge, experience, private and public behavior, and social interaction, 1968-78.

163. Winquist, Charles E. and Winzenz, David J. ALTERED STATES OF CONSCIOUSNESS: SACRED AND PROFANE. *Anglican Theological Rev. 1974 56(2): 181-188.* Discusses states of consciousness caused by drugs and by meditation, in the light of psychobiology and religion. S

164. Yoder, Don. TOWARDS A DEFINITION OF FOLK RELIGION. *Western Folklore 1974 33(1): 2-15.* Includes a "brief review of the development of the concept of folk religion," and the problems inherent in defining this area. Based on a five-part analysis, suggests that "Folk religion is the totality of all those views and practices of religion that exist . . . apart from . . . strictly theological and liturgical forms." Covers the 20th century. Based on secondary and primary sources; 31 notes. S. L. Myres

165. —. [CULTURE AND RELIGION].

Singer, Milton. CULTURE AND RELIGION. *Center Mag. 1974 7(6): 47-64.* Discusses social activities developed by organized religion in the past decade.

Varenne, Hervé and Buchdal, David. TWO COMMENTS ON MILTON SINGER'S "CULTURE AND RELIGION." *Center Mag. 1975 8(3): 51-53.* S

166. —. REVIEW SYMPOSIUM: THE SOCIOLOGY OF J. MILTON YINGER. *J. for the Sci. Study of Religion 1978 17(3): 295-325.*

Hadden, Jeffrey K. EDITOR'S INTRODUCTION, *pp. 295-297.* Short preface to reviews includes a selected bibliography of articles and books, 1946-77, by J. Milton Yinger on the sociology of religion.

Bouma, Gary D. EXPLANATION IN YINGER'S SOCIOLOGY OF RELIGION, *pp. 297-301.* Discusses Yinger's definition of religion, his explanation of religion in daily life and his attitudes toward humanistic and social scientific treatment of religion.

Robbins, Thomas. MILTON YINGER AND THE STUDY OF SOCIAL MOVEMENTS, *pp. 302-305.* Examines Yinger's analyses of social movements, especially in religious sect movements of the 1960's-70's and the mode of the surrounding social environment.

Robertson, Roland. THE PROBLEM OF THE TWO KINGDOMS: RELIGION, INDIVIDUAL, AND SOCIETY IN THE WORK OF J. MILTON YINGER, *pp. 306-312.* Exploring Yinger's works, 1946-66, on the interplay between individual religiosity and social secularity.

Means, Richard L. MILTON YINGER'S SOCIOLOGY OF RELIGION: ON SLAYING THE FATHER AND MARRYING THE QUEEN, *pp. 313-318.* Examines the treatment of the philosophy of science, the history of religions, and the problem of symbolic language as they are treated in Yinger's religious sociology.

Yinger, J. Milton. RESPONSE TO PROFESSORS BOUMA, ROBBINS, ROBERTSON, AND MEANS, *pp. 318-325.*

167. —. REVIEW SYMPOSIUM: THE SOCIOLOGY OF RELIGION OF ANDREW M. GREELEY. *J. for the Sci. Study of Religion 1974 13(1): 75-97.*

Hadden, Jeffrey K. EDITOR'S INTRODUCTION, *pp. 75-78.*

McNamara, Patrick H. A THEORETICAL VIEW, *pp. 79-86.*

Marty, Martin E. THE HISTORICAL FOCUS, *pp. 86-90.*

Mueller, Samuel A. THE EMPIRICAL POINT OF VIEW, *pp. 90-97.*

Discusses the thought and writings of theologian Andrew M. Greeley during the 1960's and 70's, emphasizing his sociology of religion concept.

168. —. [SOURCES FOR THE PSYCHOLOGY OF RELIGION].

Capps, Donald; Ransohoff, Paul; and Rambo, Lewis. PUBLICATION TRENDS IN THE PSYCHOLOGY OF RELIGION TO 1974. *J. for the Sci. Study of Religion 1976 15(1): 15-28.* Based on the authors' *Psychology of Religion: An Annotated Bibliography* (Detroit: Gale Res. Publ., 1976), discusses shifting emphasis in research in this discipline and explains a classification schema for publications, 1950-74.

Hunsberger, Bruce. SOURCES OF "PSYCHOLOGY OF RELIGION" JOURNAL ARTICLES: 1950-1974. *J. for the Sci. Study of Religion 1979 18(1): 82-85.* Provides tables taken from Capps, Rambo, and Rashoff's bibliograhy showing the most frequently cited periodicals used as references for articles on the psychology of religion.

Historians, Historical Archives, Methods, and Societies

169. Almaráz, Félix D., Jr. CARLOS EDUARDO CASTAÑEDA, MEXICAN-AMERICAN HISTORIAN: THE FORMATIVE YEARS, 1896-1927. *Pacific Hist. Rev. 1973 42(3): 319-334.* A biography of Carlos Eduardo Castañeda, Texas historiographer best known for *The Mexican Side of the Texas Revolution* and *Our Catholic Heritage in Texas, 1519-1936*. "No Mexican American historian in this century has approximated his solid publishing record of twelve books and seventy-eight articles." Born on 11 November 1896 in a small Mexican border town, Castañeda surmounted the difficulties inherent in his ethnic background, financial position, and geographic setting to establish himself as a scholar of the first rank, teacher, and librarian of the Latin American collection of the University of Texas. 42 notes. B. L. Fenske

170. Anderson, Ann Leger, comp. ARCHIVAL HOLDINGS IN SASKATCHEWAN WOMEN'S HISTORY: PRELIMINARY SURVEY. *Resources for Feminist Res. [Canada] 1979 8(2): 44-56.* Lists materials belonging primarily to the Saskatchewan Archives Board dealing with various topics of Saskatchewan women's history, including women and religion, women's organizations, women in law and politics, and others, 1880's-1970's.

171. Arrington, Leonard J. HISTORIAN AS ENTREPRENEUR: A PERSONAL ESSAY. *Brigham Young U. Studies 1977 17(2): 193-209.* Author traces his own academic development and career. He provides candid insights into the Historical Department of the Mormon Church; the developing historiography of Mormonism, and the Church's attitude toward its vast primary source holdings on western Americana. M. S. Legan

172. Bailyn, Bernard. MORISON: AN APPRECIATION. *Massachusetts Hist. Soc. Pro. 1977 89: 112-123.* A personal memoir of historian Samuel Eliot Morison (1887-1976). A student and professor at Harvard for more than 40 years, Morison was a prolific author of the "old school," known for his narrative flair and his personalized, humanistic books.

Based on the author's relationship with Morison, the recollections of Paul Buck, Oscar Handlin, John H. Parry, and the late Frederick Merk, and other material. G. W. R. Ward

173. Beach, Frank L. THE FIFTY-FOURTH ANNUAL MEETING OF THE AMERICAN CATHOLIC HISTORICAL ASSOCIATION. *Catholic Hist. Rev. 1974 60(1): 65-85.* The meeting was held in San Francisco, California, 28-30 December, 1973.

174. Boileau-DeSerres, Andrée. LES COLLECTIONS RELIGIEUSES DU MUSÉE HISTORIQUE DE VAUDREUIL [The religious collections of the Historical Museum of Vaudreuil]. *Sessions d'Étude: Soc. Can. d'Hist. de l'Église Catholique [Canada] 1978 45: 41-56.* The Musée Historique de Vaudreuil, Quebec, contains a sizable collection of French Canadian popular religious art, 17th-20th centuries.

175. Bowden, Henry Warner. MODERN DEVELOPMENTS IN THE INTERPRETATION OF CHURCH HISTORY. *Hist. Mag. of the Protestant Episcopal Church 1974 43(2): 105-124.* Examines the views of church historians regarding the relation of one's faith commitment to the interpretation of historical events, focusing on Kenneth Scott Latourette (1884-1968) and William Warren Sweet (1881-1959). "Each pursued his craft within the context of modern epistemological and methodological structures, and both of them brought their Christian faith to bear creatively on those standards." They achieved workable hypotheses while reconciling temporal knowledge and transcendental convictions. 44 notes. R. V. Ritter

176. Burrus, Ernest J. A DEDICATION TO THE MEMORY OF ZEPHYRIN ENGELHARDT, O.F.M., 1851-1934. *Arizona and the West 1976 18(3): 212-216.* German-born emigrant Charles Engelhardt (1851-1934) changed his Christian name to Zephyrin when he entered a seminary. After schooling and ordination, he had numerous assignments throughout the country in Indian missions and editorial work. In 1901 he was sent to Mission Santa Barbara in California, where he remained until death. He was a prodigious collector of documents, manuscripts, and rare editions of Southwestern and Western history. He published "an astounding number" of "ponderous tomes" and articles on missionary activity in the Spanish Borderlands of the Southwest. Illus., biblio. D. L. Smith

177. Charlton, Thomas L.; Gaskin, J. M.; and Tonks, A. Ronald. IMPLEMENTING AN ORAL HISTORY PROGRAM. *Baptist Hist. and Heritage 1975 10(3): 138-141.* Comments by three participants in a panel discussion on "Implementing an Oral History Program" indicates that "there are more good subjects to cover through oral history than there are people to cover them." Urges interested people to form a committee—whether on a college campus or in a local church. H. M. Parker, Jr. and S

178. Charlton, Thomas L. ORAL HISTORY: A RESOURCE FOR BAPTIST STUDIES. *Baptist Hist. and Heritage 1975 10(3): 130-137.* Introductory article on the utilization of oral history by Southern Baptists. Oral history should be seen as a research method with the same advantages and disadvantages of other methods of historical inquiry. Historians who use oral history collections have the responsibility of corroborating evidence found in oral memoirs with other primary and secondary sources. Uses four case studies as examples of how oral history can support written documents. Based on oral memoirs; 8 notes. H. M. Parker, Jr.

179. Chiel, Arthur A. GEORGE ALEXANDER KOHUT AND THE JUDAICA COLLECTION IN THE YALE LIBRARY. *Yale U. Lib. Gazette 1979 53(4): 202-210.* George Alexander Kohut's (1874-1933) love for books was inspired by the scholarship of his father, Rabbi Alexander Kohut. The Hebraic bibliophile's interest in Yale was first expressed in an editorial published in the *Jewish Exponent* in November 1901; it culminated in the Alexander Kohut Memorial Collection of Judaica donated to Yale in 1915 by George Alexander Kohut. The original Kohut gift to Yale was supplemented by the establishment of a fellowship in 1919 and a later gift of Heinrich Heine material in 1930. 8 notes. D. A. Yanchisin

180. Claypool, Richard D. and Steelman, Robert F. THE MUSIC COLLECTIONS IN THE MORAVIAN ARCHIVES. *Tr. of the Moravian Hist. Soc. 1979 23(2): 13-49.* Describes the American musical societies of the Moravian Brethren as well as the music collections, and their origins, found in the Moravian Archives, Bethlehem, Pennsylvania. The cataloging of the documents has uncovered many interesting incidents in the development of Moravian music and has suggested areas for further research. Based on the Moravian Archives and presented at the vesper of the Moravian Historical Society, 12 October 1978; 53 notes. C. A. Watson

181. Clebsch, William A. TOWARD A HISTORY OF CHRISTIANITY. *Church Hist. 1974 43(1): 5-16.* None of the numerous books written about the history of Christianity try to explain Christianity in its various cultural contexts. Previous histories have either concerned themselves with the history of doctrine or tried to interpret Christianity through general history categories "mostly borrowed from interpretations of primitive and Oriental religions." A history should be written which tries to understand Christianity in terms of the life styles that have been generated by the Christian faith, particularly in the West. "Christianity has been *relevant*—to times and places, to events and people," and its relationship to major cultural crises in past centuries should be explored. D. C. Richardson

182. Codignola, Luca. L'AMÉRIQUE DU NORD ET LA SACRÉE CONGRÉGATION "DE PROPAGANDA FIDE", 1622-1799: GUIDES ET INVENTAIRES [North America and the Sacred Congregation for the Propagation of the Faith, 1622-1799: guides and inventories]. *Rev. d'Hist. de l'Amérique Française [Canada] 1979 33(2): 197-214.* Lists and critiques available guides and inventories of the archives of the Congregatio de Propaganda Fide relative to North America; all are found inadequate or misleading. The Vatican archives of the Congregation contain many untapped sources of French Canadian history. 61 notes. R. Aldrich

183. Cosette, Joseph. ARCHIVES DE LA COMPAGNIE DE JÉSUS, PROVINCE DU CANADA-FRANÇAIS [Archives of the Jesuits, Province of French Canada]. *Manuscripta 1979 23(1): 26-30.* The archives have been situated at St. Jérôme, Quebec, since 1968. Presents a short history of this institution, which was started by Father Superior Martin in 1842. It became an important source in the history of the Jesuits in Canada since the 17th century. G. E. Pergl

184. Crowell, John C. PERRY MILLER AS HISTORIAN: A BIBLIOGRAPHY OF EVALUATIONS. *Bull. of Biblio. and Mag. Notes 1977 34(2): 77-85.* Includes reviews and evaluations of the historiography of Perry Miller, 1933-77.

185. D'Antoni, Blaise C. THE CHURCH RECORDS OF NORTH LOUISIANA. *Louisiana Hist. 1974 15(1): 59-67.* Outlines preservation efforts, 1930's-74, of colonial period Catholic records.

186. Deweese, Charles W. STATE BAPTIST HISTORICAL JOURNALS. *Baptist Hist. and Heritage 1978 14(4): 34, 36.* Lists periodicals published by Baptist historical societies in Alabama, Georgia, Kentucky, Oklahoma, South Carolina, and Virginia; one since the 1950's, three since the 1960's, and two since the 1970's.

187. Dick, Ernest J. RESOURCES ON MENNONITE HISTORY IN THE PUBLIC ARCHIVES OF CANADA. *Mennonite Life 1975 30(4): 26-28, 1976 31(1): 19-22.* Covers research tools since the 19th century. In two parts.

188. Doherty, Robert W. SOCIOLOGY, RELIGION, AND HISTORIANS. *Hist. Methods Newsletter 1973 6(4): 161-169.* Summarizes recent research on the social reality of religion and its implications for historical analysis. Thomas Luckmann's *Invisible Religion* (1970) provides the bibliographic focus for this piece. Luckmann believes that religion is universal (as a constant search for meaning) and lies at the very center of social and individual existence. Supplies charts dealing with denominational continuum and orientation along with a model of religious change. D. K. Pickens

189. Dove, Kay L. RESOURCES ON CHINA, JAPAN, AND KOREA WITHIN THE PRESBYTERIAN HISTORICAL ARCHIVES IN PHILADELPHIA. *Ch'ing-shih Wen-t'i 1980 4(3): 130-134.* The Presbyterian Historical Society of Philadelphia contains considerable scholarly resources of interest to Asianists. Organized in 1852, the society preserved church history and as such became a repository for missionary reports, letters, journals, and artifacts.
J. R. Pavia, Jr.

190. Drury, Clifford M. REMINISCENCES OF A HISTORIAN. *Western Hist. Q. 1974 5(2): 132-149.* The author studied the Oregon Mission of the American Board of Commissioners for Foreign Missions during his Presbyterian pastorate in Moscow, Idaho. He then served as professor of church history at San Francisco Theological Seminary until his retirement. Of the author's 14 works, 10 deal with the Whitmans, Henry H. Spalding, and other missionaries of the Oregon country. Illus., biblio. D. L. Smith

191. Edwards, Paul M. THE IRONY OF MORMON HISTORY. *Utah Hist. Q. 1973 41(4): 393-409.* Deals with the problems of faith and history as they concern Mormon historiography. The integrity of questions is as important as are questions of integrity. Many Mormon would-be historians waste their energies in "scholastic antiquarianism." There is not, and there never should be, an official Mormon philosophy of history. The historian's first tool is interest in and love of the past with a "willingness to become half lost in the imagination of previous days." Illus., 29 notes. D. L. Smith

192. Esplin, Ronald K. FROM THE RUMORS TO THE RECORDS: HISTORIANS AND THE SOURCES FOR BRIGHAM YOUNG. *Brigham Young U. Studies 1978 18(3): 453-465.* Brigham Young and Mormons have been maligned unjustly in both 19th- and 20th-century sources. Challenges historians to investigate the available primary materials and correct the "systematic distortions." The present arrangement of the extensive Young manuscript collections in the Mormon Church Archives should enable scholars to gain new insights and correct the twisted views of critics. M. S. Legan

193. Esplin, Ronald K. and Evans, Max J. PRESERVING MORMON MANUSCRIPTS: HISTORICAL ACTIVITIES OF THE LDS CHURCH. *Manuscripts 1975 27(3): 166-177.* "Even though Joseph Smith and his associates viewed record keeping as a sacred responsibility" and specifically charged the people to preserve records and keep a history, the problems and turmoils of the 19th century hindered this activity of the Mormon Church. But in the 1890's, when the church's records were in their most perilous state, there appeared the first and most indefatigable record keeper of the church, the Danish emigrant Andrew Jenson, and by 1917 the records and Historian's Office were moved into their first permanent quarters. The article surveys the outstanding collections and activities of the Historian's Office, which has become world famous as a storehouse of information on "the Mormon past, religion in America, the settlement of the West, pioneering, emigration from Europe, migration across the United States, and family history." Illus.
D. A. Yanchisin

194. Evans, Max J. and Watt, Ronald G. SOURCES FOR WESTERN HISTORY AT THE CHURCH OF JESUS CHRIST OF LATTER-DAY SAINTS. *Western Hist. Q. 1977 8(3): 303-312.* One of Joseph Smith's earliest commandments was that "there shall be a record kept among you." A church recorder was then appointed. From that has grown the Library-Archives of the church of Jesus Christ of Latter-Day Saints in Salt Lake City, Utah. It is the custodian of library materials, manuscript collections, archives (church records), and nontextual audiovisual materials, photographs, art, and artifacts which relate to the Mormon experience. It supports facilities for research, writing, interpreting, and publishing. The collections in the library of the Genealogical Society of Utah support the unique Mormon belief of salvation for the dead and eternal family relationships; therefore, this library is not devoted exclusively to Mormonism. The historical holdings of the Mormon church are a vast resource for the study of Western history. 10 notes.
D. L. Smith

195. Findlay, James. THE CONGREGATIONALISTS AND AMERICAN EDUCATION. *Hist. of Educ. Q. 1977 17(4): 449-454.* The Congregational Library in Boston, Massachusetts, contains important documents relating to the history of education in the United States during the 19th and early 20th centuries. Included are records of the American Education Society, founded in 1815, and other organizations supported by the Congregationalists. Their main task was to promote education and Protestantism in the West against Mormons and Catholics. Though the Congregational Library is understaffed, and many manuscripts uncatalogued, the significance of the materials makes them worth an extra effort by historians of culture and of education. 7 notes.
J. C. Billigmeier

196. Flanders, Robert. SOME REFLECTIONS ON THE NEW MORMON HISTORY. *Dialogue 1974 9(1): 34-41.* The New Mormon history shifts away from apologetics and vilification and toward humanism and objectivity. It repudiates the Manichean approach, appreciates the political dimension of early Mormon goals, and is sensitive to the diversity of the Mormon movement including dissenting branches within its scope. Secondary works, 7 notes. D. L. Rowe

197. Frank, Albert H. GEORGE NEISSER: AN EARLY MORAVIAN HISTORIAN. *Tr. of the Moravian Hist. Soc. 1979 23(2): 1-11.* Surveys the known details of the life of George Neisser (1715-84), a Moravian Brethren, from his early lay work in Georgia to his later pastoral work in eastern Pennsylvania and New York. He was sympathetic to the American revolutionary cause, was a student of Moravian hymnology, and compiled biographical, genealogical, and historical information on his church and its members. Based on the Moravian Archives and presented at the vesper of the Moravian Historical Society, 13 October 1977; 65 notes. C. A. Watson

198. Friesen, Steve. THE KAUFFMAN MUSEUM. *Mennonite Life 1977 32(2): 14-20.* In 1907 Charles Kauffman (1882-1961) completed a course in taxidermy and began a museum featuring his mounted specimens, woodcarvings and paintings. In 1940 the collection moved from his home in Freeman, South Dakota, to Bethel College where it merged with the Museum of Natural History and American Relics to become the Kauffman Museum. With Kauffman and his wife as curators, the museum collection expanded over the next 20 years, adding native American artifacts, items from the world-wide Mennonite mission field, and an exhibit on the history of technology. John Schmidt, museum director during 1964-76, stressed professional training for museum workers, better exhibit techniques, and interaction between museums throughout the country. 9 photos. B. Burnett

199. Gardner, Robert G. SPENCER BIDWELL KING, JR. *Viewpoints: Georgia Baptist Hist. 1978 (6): 19-24.* Obituary of Spencer Bidwell King, Jr. (1904-77), discussing his contributions to the Baptist Church in Georgia as a historian of the church and the state, and his work as an educator in state church schools, 1930's-77.

200. Gaustad, Edwin S.; Miller, Darline; and Stokes, G. Allison. RELIGION IN AMERICA. *Am. Q. 1979 31(3): 250-283.* Bibliographical essay on 20th-century studies of religion since the colonial period in relationship to history, psychology, and literature. Recent trends in the study of religion in the United States include the study of pluralism: religions of ethnic groups and religions outside of the Judeo-Christian tradition. 140 notes. S

201. Gerlach, Larry R. and Nicholls, Michael L. THE MORMON GENEALOGICAL SOCIETY AND RESEARCH OPPORTUNITIES IN EARLY AMERICAN HISTORY. *William and Mary Q. 1975 32(4): 625-629.* The Mormon Genealogical Society has the largest genealogical library in the world. The library holds 836,671 rolls of microfilm, including material from eastern as well as western states. There are local records, court records, tax lists, and ecclesiastical records of many churches. The extensive collection of documents from the original 13 states includes 24,044 rolls pertaining to North Carolina. The European collection is substantial. Microfilm can be purchased from the collection. Cites research guides. 8 notes. H. M. Ward

202. Gilreath, James W. THE FORMATION OF THE WESTERN RESERVE HISTORICAL SOCIETY'S SHAKER COLLECTION. *J. of Lib. Hist., Phil. and Comparative Librarianship 1973 8(3-4): 133-142.* Wallace H. Cathcart, as president of the Western Reserve Historical

Society, in 1911-12 founded the finest collection of Shaker books and manuscripts. With the help of Eldress M. Catherine Allen he was able to gain the cooperation of many Shakers in saving the records and books of a rapidly dying sect. Based on documents in the Western Reserve Historical Society Shaker Collection and Archives and on secondary sources; 2 illus., 32 notes. J. R. Willson

203. Goen, C. C. CHURCH HISTORY IS MY VOCATION. *Religion in Life 1975 44(3): 291-301.* Describes the author's fascination for church history and the inherent connection the study of history has with Christianity.

204. Graves, Michael P. A CHECKLIST OF EXTANT QUAKER SERMONS, 1650-1700. *Quaker Hist. 1974 63(1): 53-57.* Lists 79 published and 10 manuscript sermons in the libraries of Friends House (London) and Haverford and Swarthmore Colleges, based on shorthand notes of attenders. Lists principal contributors and number of sermons delivered: Stephen Crisp (32, 1687-92), George Fox (11, 1653, 1671-81), William Penn (10, 1688-94), and George Keith (8, 1694-96, 1700). T. D. S. Bassett

205. Greeley, Andrew M. RELIGION IN A SECULAR SOCIETY. *Social Res. 1974 41(2): 226-241.* Argues that while current writings on American religion are abundant, little is being done to upgrade the quality of these works or to understand the array and impact of trends and fads in religion. S

206. Green, Dee. MORMON ARCHEOLOGY IN THE 1970'S: A NEW DECADE, A NEW APPROACH. *Dialogue 1973 8(2): 49-55.*

207. Handlin, Oscar. A TWENTY YEAR RETROSPECT OF AMERICAN JEWISH HISTORIOGRAPHY. *Am. Jewish Hist. Q. 1976 65(4): 295-309.* Compares his 1948 evaluation of writing of the American Jewish past with the progress made since then. Greater abundance of material and its availability coupled with professionalization of authors and the elimination of an apologetic approach has contributed to greater scholarship. Setting the Jewish experience in America in a comparative, often sociological relationship to the contemporary trends in other immigrant religions and community organizations leads to a better understanding of the story, even though the extent of leakage through intermarriage, conversion, and apathy has not yet been assessed. The history of American anti-Semitism, 1900-40, also still remains to be written. Delivered at the 73rd annual meeting of the American Jewish Historical Society, 4 May 1975. 43 notes. F. Rosenthal

208. Hardy, Robert T. FOR YEARS OF SERVICE: EDWARD C. STARR AS BAPTIST BIBLIOGRAPHER, LIBRARIAN, AND CURATOR. *Foundations 1976 19(1): 5-19.* Mentions Edward Caryl Starr's (b. 1911) background and summarizes his activities as curator of the Samuel Colgate Baptist Historical Library. Discusses his activities as collector, cataloger, bibliographer (the area of his greatest contribution), assistant to scholars, and manager of the library. 2 photos, 38 notes. E. E. Eminhizer

209. Hastings, Robert J. COMMUNICATING HISTORY THROUGH BAPTIST NEWSPAPERS. *Baptist Hist. and Heritage 1977 12(3): 166-169.* No print media in Southern Baptist life equal the Baptist state newspapers in circulation and grass-roots coverage. These papers communicate with Baptist people, share historical articles, and are research sources in Baptist history. Pleads that the papers carry not only the news releases from denominational headquarters, but also stories of the ordinary people. Cites the *Biblical Recorder* of North Carolina as the best state newspaper. Illus. H. M. Parker, Jr.

210. Hastings, Robert J. ORAL HISTORY: BAPTISTS IN THEIR EVERYDAY CLOTHES. *Baptist Hist. and Heritage 1976 11(2): 80-83.* In 1976 the Illinois State Baptist Association published a history of Southern Baptists in the state, *We Were There*. This is the first major Baptist effort to publish a book of such a scope based solely on the methodology of oral history. Nineteen persons were interviewed. In a catechetical manner the author of the book discusses both the advantages and disadvantages of such a procedure. Oral history has its limitations: it excels at personal insights, emotions, and reminiscing, but lacks the details which have a way of escaping human memory. There will always be a place for the step-by-step, detailed, chronological survey of the past. Oral history can put flesh on the skeleton of factual information by helping the historian in his search for the how and why as well as the who, what, when, and where of history. One spin-off of oral history is that it enables the "little person" to make his impact. H. M. Parker, Jr.

211. Hearne, Erwin M., Jr. ILLUSTRATING BAPTIST HISTORY. *Baptist Hist. and Heritage 1977 12(3): 135-141.* Discusses experiences and philosophy in selecting the right psychological moment of an event for portraying that event's historical significance. Focuses especially on the Baptist Heritage Picture Set, a series of line drawings and paintings on Texas Baptist history. Such art media illustrating events in Baptist history can assist Baptists in knowing their heritage. The artists can therefore play a vital role in communicating Baptist history. 2 illus. H. M. Parker, Jr.

212. Hench, John B. HENRY JOEL CADBURY. *Pro. of the Am. Antiquarian Soc. 1975 84(2): 274-277.* Henry Joel Cadbury (1913-74) received his Ph.D. from Harvard University, taught at several preparatory schools and universities, and acquired emeritus rank at Harvard. His research specialties were Quaker and biblical history, and he authored several books on these subjects. Cadbury founded the American Friends Service Committee in 1917, serving two terms as its chairman. He received the Nobel Peace Prize on behalf of the Committee in 1947. V. L. Human

213. Hench, John B. OBITUARY: FREDERICK BARNES TOLLES. *Pro. of the Am. Antiquarian Soc. 1975 85(2): 367-369.* A remembrance of Frederick Barnes Tolles (1915-75). Tolles was born in New Hampshire. He was educated at Harvard University, where he converted from Unitarianism to Quakerism, a decision that was to alter his entire life. He began teaching at Swarthmore College, a Quaker institution, and refused induction in World War II as a conscientious objector, doing alternative work instead. His primary academic interest was in the history of Quakerism in American society, and he published a number of books on the subject. Tolles was elected to membership in the American Antiquarian Society in 1967. He was proud of the honor, but distance and poor health prevented him from taking an active part in the Society's activities. V. L. Human

214. Hershberger, Guy F. IN TRIBUTE TO MELVIN GINGERICH. *Mennonite Hist. Bull. 1975 36(4): 2-4.* Obituary for Melvin Gingerich, a Mennonite educator, historian, and churchman, 1902-75.

215. Hough, Brenda. THE ARCHIVES OF THE SOCIETY FOR THE PROPAGATION OF THE GOSPEL. *Hist. Mag. of the Protestant Episcopal Church 1977 46(3): 309-322.* The Society for the Propagation of the Gospel in Foreign Parts was founded in 1701 to supply the Church of England with missionaries, particularly in the American colonies. The manuscript records of the Society include about 20,000 documents and 2 million letters. Approximately 300 missionaries were sent to America. The Society's records include Annual Reports, the Society's minutes, and the letters and reports from missionaries, which provide insights on the religious, social, economic, and political life of American colonists. Based on primary sources, including numerous references to the missionaries' letters; 64 notes. H. M. Parker, Jr.

216. Hruneni, George A., Jr. BICENTENNIAL POTPOURRI IN THE ARCHIVES OF THE CATHOLIC UNIVERSITY OF AMERICA. *Manuscripts 1976 28(1): 16-26.* Discusses some of the rare items in the Catholic University Archives that tell the American story from colonial times through the Civil War including, 1) a Washington document of payment for 28,430 shingles, 7 September 1785, 2) a letter of Gabriel Richard, a naturalized French emigre, who witnessed the 1832 cholera epidemic in Detroit, 3) a religious comment by Francis P. Kenrick, a prominent frontier clergyman, and 4) a petition to the New York legislature for the relief of widows and orphans, 1803. Also described are loyalist and patriot documents from the American Revolution, notes of missionaries, Indian artifacts, and a number of Civil War documents. 17 notes, 2 illus. D. A. Yanchisin

217. Jones, Clifton H. MANUSCRIPT SOURCES IN RELIGIOUS HISTORY AT THE HISTORICAL RESOURCE CENTER. *South*

Dakota Hist. 1977 7(3): 325-333. Lists 34 processed and three unprocessed manuscript collections at the South Dakota Historical Resource Center. Since Christians settled throughout the state, and as they were usually well educated, their written records constitute a valuable source for historians. Primary sources. A. J. Larson

218. Kingsley, J. Gordon, Jr. COMMUNICATING BAPTIST HISTORY THROUGH CONTEMPORARY MEDIA AND ART FORMS: THEME INTERPRETATION. *Baptist Hist. and Heritage 1977 12(3): 130-134.* Introduces the theme of this issue of *Baptist History and Heritage,* "Communicating Baptist History in Contemporary Media and Art Forms." Baptist history should be communicated in all possible ways. Historically, Baptists have been rather effective in employing contemporary media and art forms to tell their story, beginning with the English tracts of the 17th century. The medium always shapes the message. Note. H. M. Parker, Jr.

219. Klippenstein, Lawrence and Friesen, John. THE MENNONITE HERITAGE CENTRE FOR RESEARCH AND STUDY. *Mennonite Life 1978 33(4): 19-22.* The new Mennonite Heritage Centre at Canadian Mennonite Bible College in Winnipeg, Manitoba, offers the largest public Mennonite archival deposit in the country. The files include several series of German and English newspapers published for Mennonite communities, microfilm records from European points of origin, a 5,000-item photograph collection, and the personal papers of nearly 50 Mennonite leaders (e.g., David Toews, J. J. Thiessen, Benjamin and Heinrich Ewert, H. M. Epp). Works-in-progress include a photo album of Mennonite conscientious objectors in World War II, translations of Russian documents relating to migration, and a detailed catalog of the entire Mennonite studies literary holdings. 7 photos. B. Burnett

220. Kramer, Gerhardt. THE SAXON LUTHERAN MEMORIAL: A CASE HISTORY IN PRESERVATION. *Concordia Hist. Inst. Q. 1978 51(4): 155-167.* Since 1958 leaders of the Concordia Historical Institute had indicated an interest in acquiring the farm of the late Lina Bergt. Bergt was the last direct descendant of Saxon Lutherans who immigrated to Perry County, Missouri, in 1839. Initially the efforts to acquire the property met with failure; however, the farm was purchased in 1960 and restoration was inaugurated. The Saxon Lutheran Memorial was dedicated in 1964. Primary sources; 20 notes. W. T. Walker

221. Kramer, William A. WHY CONCORDIA HISTORICAL INSTITUTE? *Concordia Hist. Inst. Q. 1978 51(2): 70-75.* The Concordia Historical Institute is a depository of Lutheran history in the United States (with a special emphasis on the Missouri Synod) and provides resources in order to encourage and stimulate Christian, especially Lutheran, values and ideas. W. T. Walker

222. Kuhnle, Howard A. THE WORK OF THE CHURCH NECROLOGIST. *Concordia Hist. Inst. Q. 1973 46(4): 158-163.*

223. Leckie, William H. CARL COKE RISTER. *Great Plains J. 1979 18: 120-123.* Carl Coke Rister (1889-1955) was a friendly "Baptist with a Puritan conscience." Describes Rister's teaching techniques and insists that with graduate students he was a particularly fine teacher. Rister taught at Hardin-Simmons (10 years), Oklahoma (22 years), and Texas Tech (3 years). A productive scholar, he wrote 10 books while at Oklahoma and two more were published posthumously. Best known was *Western America,* coauthored with LeRoy Hafen, which was widely used as a textbook. From a special section on "Historians of the Southern Plains." 3 notes. O. H. Zabel

224. Lisenby, Foy. CHARLES HILLMAN BROUGH AS HISTORIAN. *Arkansas Hist. Q. 1976 35(2): 115-126.* Charles Hillman Brough resigned as professor of economics and sociology at the University of Arkansas in 1915 to run for governor of Arkansas. During his academic career he wrote a Ph.D. dissertation on irrigation problems in Utah and the development of Mormonism there, and articles on such subjects as the Clinton, Mississippi race riot of 1875 and the industrial history of Arkansas. He supported the work of the Mississippi state archives and the Arkansas Historical Association. Brough also taught at Mississippi College. Based on the Brough Papers, newspaper accounts, published primary and secondary sources; 41 notes. T. L. Savitt

225. Lowance, Mason I., Jr. KENNETH BALLARD MURDOCK. *Pro. of the Am. Antiquarian Soc. 1976 86(1): 33-38.* A scholar of early American literature, the late Kenneth Murdock pioneered in the revitalization of the Puritan and colonial period. He was a founding editor of several journals, and deeply involved in both teaching and administration. J. Andrew

226. Lyon, T. Edgar. CHURCH HISTORIANS I HAVE KNOWN. *Dialogue 1978 11(4): 14-22.* The author reminisces about the lives and work of four Mormon historians who influenced his own development as a Mormon historian. B. H. Roberts, author of *The History of the Church* and president of the Church of the Latter Day Saints, attempted to break away from writing church history as propaganda. Andrew Jenson represents an earlier type of Mormon historian who collected historical information and documents, a chronicler striving for complete and accurate coverage. Similarly, A. William Lund, assistant historian in the Church Historian's Office, saw his responsibility as preserving documents and books, rather than making them accessible for use. Church historian Howard W. Hunter visited the author in Nauvoo, Illinois, and praised him for the concept of a church history that was people-oriented, not concerned only with abstractions. C. B. Schulz

227. Madaj, M. J. OBITUARIES. *Catholic Hist. Rev. 1978 64(1): 138.* A remembrance of Father Joseph Vincent Swastek (1913-77), who died unexpectedly on 5 September 1977. Swastek was ordained in 1940, and thereupon began graduate work at the University of Notre Dame, Catholic University, Ottawa University, and the University of Michigan. He specialized in Polish American history, in which discipline he was both a pioneer and a leader. He edited the *New Catholic Encyclopedia.* A charter member of the Polish American Historical Association, he was very active in its affairs for a quarter century. He published extensively. V. L. Human

228. Marty, Martin E. RELIGIOUS BEHAVIOR: ITS SOCIAL DIMENSION IN AMERICAN HISTORY. *Social Res. 1974 41(2): 241-264.* Argues that historians of religion have not made available materials which the public needs in order to understand religious issues. S

229. Maser, Frederick E. THE TASK OF THE METHODIST HISTORIAN TODAY. *Methodist Hist. 1974 12(4): 5-26.* The task of the Methodist historian requires integrity in the discovery and use of historical materials, understanding in order to present adequate portraits of Methodist personalities, and the capability to write history that will influence the moral tone of the age. 22 notes. H. L. Calkin

230. May, Lynn E., Jr. BAPTIST INFORMATION RETRIEVAL SYSTEM: A COMPUTERIZED SERVICE. *Baptist Hist. and Heritage 1975 10(2): 79-80.* The Baptist Information Retrieval System is a centralized computer system developed by the Historical Commission of the Southern Baptist Convention with assistance from other Baptist agencies and institutions. Its purpose is to provide reference information on a variety of subjects of interest to Baptists. By the end of 1975 it will contain a minimum of 75,000 subject and author entries from 80 Baptist sources. The availability of massive reference data through the system can save countless hours of research time, eliminate duplication of research, and provide coverage of greater depth and breadth than is now possible. H. M. Parker, Jr.

231. McBeth, Leon and Patterson, W. Morgan. REFLECTIONS ON THE USE OF ORAL HISTORY IN BAPTIST STUDIES. *Baptist Hist. and Heritage 1975 10(3): 149-151.* Comments by two church historians at an oral history workshop in 1973, discussing the advantages and problems of oral history methodology. Suggests that the Church develop oral history as a necessary supplement to more conventional techniques of historical research. H. M. Parker, Jr.

232. McGinty, Park. THREE MODES OF INTERPRETATION: GENEALOGY, TRANSLATION, REARTICULATION. *Hist. of Religions 1975 14(3): 207-227.* Explains the different approaches that scholars have used in interpreting religion: genealogy, translation, and rearticulation. The first is the approach of the unbeliever; the second, of the scholar who sees religion fulfilling certain needs; the third, of the believer. The various conclusions reached by the three systems are examined in their application to five basic controversies: the origin, purpose, human locus, unity, and referent of religion. 8 notes. T. L. Auffenberg

233. Metcalf, Keyes. SAMUEL ELIOT MORISON. *Pro. of the Am. Antiquarian Soc. 1977 87(1): 20-25.* Samuel Eliot Morison (1887-1976) was perhaps the dean of American historians when he died. Traces his career and historical publications including his studies on the Puritans. J. Andrew

234. Moore, John M. THE CENTENNIAL OF THE FRIENDS HISTORICAL ASSOCIATION. *Quaker Hist. 1974 63(1): 34-38.* The Friends Historical Association was founded 4 December 1873 to discuss the Quaker past and encourage the collection of Quaker sources. By spring 1874 they were meeting monthly in the Historical Society of Pennsylvania quarters, reaching a peak of perhaps 20 members by 1882. After James H. Atkinson failed to revive the association in 1910, it gave up its 1875 charter by merging with the 1904 Friends Historical Society of Philadelphia in 1923. Based on its minutes and a 1924 article by Albert Cook Myers. T. D. S. Bassett

235. Moore, Leroy. SIDNEY E. MEAD'S UNDERSTANDING OF AMERICA. *J. of the Am. Acad. of Religion 1976 44(1): 133-153.* Mead is recognized as the dean of the field of American religious history. Sets forth and comments on Mead's approach to history and his understanding of America. E. R. Lester

236. Mulder, William. MORMON SOURCES FOR IMMIGRATION HISTORY. *Immigration Hist. Newsletter 1978 10(2): 1-8.* As an offspring from a basic religious tenet, the library at Brigham Young University (associated with the Mormon Church) contains extensive research and geneological materials with important source material for immigration studies.

237. Noll, Mark A. THE CONFERENCE ON FAITH AND HISTORY AND THE STUDY OF EARLY AMERICAN HISTORY. *Fides et Hist. 1978 11(1): 8-18.* Calls on Christian historians to broaden their audience, their research, and their methodologies while affirming their faith in God's influence on history. Includes an evaluation of the research into early American history (1607-1865) by members of the Conference on Faith and History. Secondary sources; 12 notes. R. E. Butchart

238. Nunis, Doyce B., Jr. A DEDICATION TO THE MEMORY OF MAYNARD J. GEIGER, O.F.M., 1901-1977. *Arizona and the West 1978 20(3): 198-202.* Franciscan Fr. Maynard Joseph Geiger (1901-77) completed his philosophical and theological studies in California and was ordained to the priesthood. His M.A. work at St. Bonaventure College, New York, in English and Spanish were preparatory for his doctorate in Hispanic American history in 1937 at The Catholic University of America, Washington, D. C. His professional career was spent as archivist and historian at Mission Santa Barbara, California. His early writings focused on Spanish Florida. Later his scholarship was concerned with the Franciscan missionaries in California, particularly Junípero Serra. Illus., biblio. D. L. Smith

239. Nunis, Doyce B., Jr. IN MEMORIAM: FATHER MAYNARD J. GEIGER, O.F.M. *California Hist. Q. 1977 56(3): 275-276.* Eulogizes Father Maynard J. Geiger (1901-1977), Franciscan father, archivist of Mission Santa Barbara for almost 40 years, and historian of Franciscan missionary activity in North America, particularly Hispanic California. His published writings included 13 books, among them *The Life and Times of Fray Junípero Serra, Mission Santa Barbara, 1782-1965,* and *Franciscan Missionaries in Hispanic California, 1769-1848.* In addition, he wrote almost 200 articles and for 15 years was editor of *Provincial Annals.* As a speaker he was much in demand by historical groups, and his correspondence with teachers and students was international in scale. Photo. A. Hoffman

240. Nunis, Doyce B., Jr. MEMORIAL TO REV. MAYNARD J. GEIGER, O.F.M. *J. of California Anthrop. 1977 4(2): 155-172.* Maynard J. Geiger (1901-77), a Franciscan priest at Mission Santa Barbara, California, wrote on Mission and Indian life; includes an extensive bibliography of his articles, books, and newspaper articles, 1936-76.

241. O'Farrell, John K. A. THE CANADIAN CATHOLIC HISTORICAL ASSOCIATION'S FORTIETH ANNIVERSARY: A RETROSPECTIVE VIEW. *Study Sessions: Can. Catholic Hist. Assoc. 1973 40: 61-68.* Discusses the Canadian Catholic Historical Association. S

242. O'Toole, James M. CATHOLIC CHURCH RECORDS: A GENEALOGICAL AND HISTORICAL RESOURCE. *New England Hist. and Geneal. Register 1978 132(Oct): 251-263.* In contrast to individual Protestants, Roman Catholics have more frequently relied on the church to keep genealogical records. Describes how church records have been kept at parish and diocesan levels and by interconnecting agencies such as cemeteries, orphanages, schools, welfare agencies, and hospitals. Diaries and papers of priests and bishops often provide additional information on parishioners. Most records which were not lost or destroyed are now preserved in institutional archives. 10 notes. A. E. Huff

243. Oyer, John S. MELVIN GINGERICH, 1902-1975. *Mennonite Q. Rev. 1978 52(2): 91-112.* Melvin Gingerich, a Mennonite scholar, early developed a flair for learning, probably because he came from a long line of churchmen. His books and articles were numerous, the most famous being a history of the Mennonites in Iowa. He also edited several periodicals, acted as research counselor and archivist, and was an active churchman until his death. Never radical or at the forefront of new movements, Gingerich managed to soothe the more ardent spirits at both ends of the political spectrum. 92 notes. V. L. Human

244. Patton, Richard D. COMMUNICATING BAPTIST HISTORY IN A LOCAL CHURCH. *Baptist Hist. and Heritage 1977 12(3): 175-179.* In addition to the minister's role as a teacher of church history, many approaches to communicating history are necessary: study sessions, Sunday School lessons, communicant classes, writing local history, and sermons on great historical and missionary figures. Article is almost bibliographical in its nature, naming numerous works in Baptist history. Urges a good knowledge of Baptist history in anticipation of a richer Baptist future. Note. H. M. Parker, Jr.

245. Pike, Kermit J. SHAKER MANUSCRIPTS AND HOW THEY CAME TO BE PRESERVED. *Manuscripts 1977 29(4): 226-236.* Since their arrival in America, 6 August 1774, the Shakers have amassed records. These records have been deposited in the Western Reserve Historical Society, and are a valuable research tool to social historians. The Society's first president, Wallace H. Cathcart, assisted by Eldress Allen, collected more than 10,000 items and 1,800 volumes in the Society's library. 2 illus., 13 notes. D. A. Yanchisin

246. Powell, Ted F. SAVING THE PAST FOR THE FUTURE: TALES OF INTERNATIONAL SEARCH AND COOPERATION. *Am. Archivist 1976 39(3): 311-318.* Describes the growth of the collections of the Mormon Church's Genealogical Society of Utah, and its facilities and ongoing microfilming programs. Details the difficulties in gathering the documents from all over the world. At present the records form the world's largest genealogical collection and are widely used for historical and medical research. Table. J. A. Benson

247. Price, Brian J. THE ARCHIVES OF THE ARCHDIOCESE OF KINGSTON. *Study Sessions: Can. Catholic Hist. Assoc. 1973 40: 21-26.* Describes material in Kingston archives, including information on bishops of the Archdiocese of Kingston, beginning with Alexander Macdonell (1760?-1840). S

248. Raphael, Marc Lee. NECROLOGY: BERTRAM WALLACE KORN (1918-1979). *Am. Jewish Hist. 1980 69(4): 506-508.* An obituary of Bertram Wallace Korn, historian of American Jews in the antebellum and Civil War periods, and rabbi of Kenesseth Israel Synagogue in Elkins Park, Pennsylvania. Contains a listing and evaluation of his major works. J. D. Sarna

249. Rawls, Andrew B. TEACHING BAPTIST HISTORY WITH AUDIOVISUALS. *Baptist Hist. and Heritage 1977 12(3): 142-151.* Explores the use of audiovisual materials to teach Baptist history and makes some practical suggestions for realizing this potential. Outlines research data which demonstrate the advantages of using both visual and auditory channels in instruction. Rationale provided for using slides as flexible visual medium. Outlines special considerations in slide use and guidelines for producing slides from graphic and photographic materials. 23 notes. H. M. Parker, Jr.

250. Reddig, Ken. THE MENNONITE BRETHREN ARCHIVES IN WINNIPEG. *Mennonite Life 1979 34(4): 11-14.* Dr. Abraham H. Unrhu of Mennonite Brethren Bible College originated the idea of a Mennonite Brethren Archives around 1950. The idea was implemented in the 1960's by Herbert Giesbrecht, then MBBC librarian, now archivist. In 15 years the archives moved from a small faculty office to its present 1,500 square feet in the college library. The collection focuses on material from the Russian immigration and resettlement in Canada and on correspondence relating to the General Conference of Mennonite Brethren. It also includes the John A. Toews Mennonite Historical collection of rare books, the B. B. Jantz Collection, 155,000 pages of church records, and a rich map collection. 8 photos. B. Burnett

251. Reinford, Wilmer. INDEX TO THE JACOB B. MENSCH COLLECTION OF LETTERS, 1861-1912. *Mennonite Q. Rev. 1978 52(1): 77-85.* Lists letters of Jacob B. Mensch (d. 1912), a Mennonite minister from Pennsylvania, who is best remembered for his library of rare books, his many records and diaries, and his Franconia Conference minutes. Lists libraries and archives having microfilm copies of the Mensch Collection and acknowledges the work of Mrs. Mary Mensch Lederach, Mensch's granddaughter, for arranging the letters in alphabetical order. A. W. Howell

252. Reynolds, Arthur. WRITING A LOCAL CHURCH HISTORY. *J. of the Canadian Church Hist. Soc. 1976 18(3): 2-5.* The most important matter in writing local church history is to gather and use the most accurate information. Thus a history must take into account the different impressions events may make on various observers. Also, a history should not be merely a compilation of names and dates, but should tell a story of the interaction of the human and the divine. Finally, the writer of a local church history must always relate it to the universal church and to the larger community of which it is a part. J. A. Kicklighter

253. Rudolph, L. C. WRITING A HISTORY OF YOUR CHURCH. *J. of Presbyterian Hist. 1975 53(4): 363-369.* An elementary introduction to the writing of church history. Directs the writer to possible source materials. H. M. Parker, Jr.

254. Rushing, Stan. A CASE FOR ART IN BAPTIST HISTORIOGRAPHY. *Baptist Hist. and Heritage 1977 12(3): 170-174.* Most Baptists are not enthusiastic about history, but the past can come alive for people when historians give new life to their historiography. A lively style is not a panacea, but it is essential for curing the aversion to the past that afflicts so many people. Urges excitement and fascination in historiography. 13 notes. H. M. Parker, Jr.

255. Sandon, Leo, Jr. H. RICHARD NIEBUHR'S PRINCIPLES OF HISTORIOGRAPHY. *Foundations 1975 18(1): 61-74.* The principles of H. Richard Niebuhr's historiography were Troeltschian, but modified by Henri Bergson. One cannot show the influence of Troeltsch on Niebuhr by explicit statement only. Ernest Troeltsch thought that even though historical investigation was subjective to some degree, it was not a matter of personal judgement. Troeltsch did not think history could be interpreted psychologically only, but that natural cause had to be considered. Niebuhr held in *The Kingdom of God in America* (1937), that historical thought was conceptual thought, and attempted to see American Christianity as an "historic totality" in Troeltschian terms. Henri Bergson held to two kinds of religion and morality: closed morality supported by state religion, and open morality supported by dynamic religion. Niebuhr equates static religion with institutional religion, and sees the true church as a "movement." 55 notes. E. E. Eminhizer

256. Seaburg, Alan. SOME UNITARIAN MANUSCRIPTS AT ANDOVER-HARVARD. *Harvard Lib. Bull. 1978 26(1): 112-120.* Describes the manuscript collections of the Andover-Harvard Theological Library which relate to the history of Unitarianism and Universalism, primarily in the 19th century. W. H. Mulligan, Jr.

257. Searl, Stanford J., Jr. PERRY MILLER AS ARTIST: PIETY AND IMAGINATION IN *THE NEW ENGLAND MIND: THE SEVENTEENTH CENTURY.* *Early Am. Literature 1977-78 12(3): 221-233.* Perry Miller's *The New England Mind: The Seventeenth Century,* searches for the underlying meaning of the Puritan experience. As an artist, Miller uses the creative power of an imaginative vision to offer an insight and understanding into the emotional and spiritual reality of Puritan "piety" and ideas. Though at times it is difficult to distinguish between the narrative voice and the quotations, Miller's attempts to discover and to reveal the religious feelings and the religious ideas of the New England Puritans confirms his status as an intellectual historian. Primary sources; 9 notes. J. N. Friedel

258. Selement, George. PERRY MILLER: A NOTE ON HIS SOURCES IN *THE NEW ENGLAND MIND: THE SEVENTEENTH CENTURY.* *William and Mary Q. 1974 31(3): 453-64.* Considers why Perry Miller's study has had such an influence on colonial historians. Finds that Miller did not meticulously use or even read the great number of sources that he professed to have mastered. Of the 1,506 published New England sources, Miller used only about 15%, and most of these were by a few New England ministers. He neglected Baptist, Plymouth, Quaker, and Antinominian sources; much of his documentation came from European sources. Miller's error was that he did not inform readers that he concentrated only on a select group of ministers. Also comments on recent American historiography of Puritanism. 43 notes. H. M. Ward

259. Skemer, Don C. THE PAPERS OF WILLIAM A. MCDOWELL: A NEW JERSEY PRESBYTERIAN. *South Carolina Hist. Mag. 1978 79(1): 19-22.* William A. McDowell's private papers, a recent accession of the New Jersey Historical Society, hold great research potential for students interested in the history of the Third Presbyterian Church, correspondence with Charleston's parishes and individuals, the Southern religious experience, missionary work, and Charleston civil life in the 1820's-30's.

260. Smylie, James H. THE PRESBYTERIAN HISTORICAL SOCIETY: ONE HUNDRED AND TWENTY-FIVE YEARS. *J. of Presbyterian Hist. 1977 55(1): 1-12.* Describes the programs of the Presbyterian Historical Society headquartered in Philadelphia. It is the oldest denominational historical society in the United States and gradually has developed a broad range of programs. It is the most important archival repository for the records of American Protestant ecumenism. The Society publishes the *Journal of Presbyterian History,* the oldest American denominational historical publication. It supports, subsidizes and promotes scholarly monographs on the Presbyterian and Reformed heritage and has begun to microfilm rare documents held by the Society. In 1973 it inaugurated the Presbyterian and Reformed Sites Registry, and now serves as the archival depository for more than a dozen ecumenical societies including the Student Volunteer Movement and the National Council of Churches of Christ. 5 illus. H. M. Parker, Jr.

261. Speck, William A. KENNETH SCOTT LATOURETTE'S VOCATION AS CHRISTIAN HISTORIAN. *Christian Scholar's R. 1975 4(4): 285-299.* Discusses the efforts of Kenneth Scott Latourette (1884-1968) to reconcile Christian faith and historical scholarship. S

262. Sprunger, Keith L. and Juhnke, James C. MENNONITE ORAL HISTORY. *Mennonite Q. Rev. 1980 54(3): 244-247.* Reproduces the questionnaire used in 1974 by the Department of History in Bethel College to gather oral history on Mennonite conscientious objectors in World War I. Based on authors' association with the project; 4 notes. E. E. Eminhizer

263. Starr, Edward C. THE SAMUEL COLGATE BAPTIST HISTORICAL LIBRARY OF THE AMERICAN BAPTIST HISTORICAL SOCIETY. *Foundations 1976 19(1): 20-23.* Edward Caryl Starr, curator of the American Baptist Historical Society, describes the society's collection, history, and the *Baptist Bibliography* which he is completing. E. E. Eminhizer

264. Stout, Harry S. and Taylor, Robert. SOCIOLOGY, RELIGION, AND HISTORIANS REVISITED: TOWARDS AN HISTORICAL SOCIOLOGY OF RELIGION. *Historical Methods Newsletter 1974 8(1): 29-38.* Discusses Robert W. Doherty's "Sociology, Religion and Historians." Stout and Taylor urge that, unlike Doherty's model, historians use both substantive and functional analysis. This mode of scholarship can be furthered by creating intellectual and social typologies which can be correlated and empirically validated with one another. D. K. Pickens

265. Suelflow, August R. MICROFILM AND PHOTODUPLICATION: A REPORT TO THE LUTHERAN'S LAYMEN'S LEAGUE ON THE MICROFILM ACTIVITIES OF CONCORDIA HISTORICAL INSTITUTE FOR 1972. *Concordia Hist. Inst. Q. 1973 46(4): 183-188.*

266. Suelflow, August R. MICROFILM AND PHOTODUPLICATION: A REPORT TO THE LUTHERAN LAYMEN'S LEAGUE ON THE MICROFILM ACTIVITIES OF THE CONCORDIA HISTORICAL INSTITUTE FOR 1971. *Concordia Hist. Inst. Q. 1973 46(1): 35-39.* Discusses research uses of microfilm and prospects for the future, and lists acquisitions between 1 October 1970 and 30 September 1971. B. W. Henry

267. Thornton, Bob. COMMUNICATING HISTORY THROUGH TELEVISION, VIDEOTAPE, AND FILMS. *Baptist Hist. and Heritage 1977 12(3): 156-165.* The historian can use the film for research, teaching, recreating the past, and capturing the present. Suggests that in the Baptist Church, films should be made on great Baptists of the past; the Southern Baptist Convention should continue being taped; state conventions should be videotaped; interviews should be conducted with noted ministers, teachers, authors, and lay leaders; and noted ministers should videotape their sermons. Urges a central storage, retrieval, and distribution center for video materials in the Southern Baptist Convention. Focuses on technical developments which enhance the potential for communicating religious history through television, videotape, and film; emphasizes the newly emerging disc recorders. H. M. Parker, Jr.

268. Tonks, A. Ronald. ORAL HISTORY AND BAPTIST CHURCHES: HOW TO IMPLEMENT A PROGRAM. *Baptist Hist. and Heritage 1975 10(3): 142-148.* Introductory article on how to implement an oral history program in a local church. Develops the following steps: beginning the program; selecting the interviewers; interview preparation; agreements, legalities and fair play; and interview transcription. Commends oral history as a vehicle to preserve the contributions many individuals have made to the church. 2 notes. H. M. Parker, Jr.

269. Unsigned. THE ARCHIVAL ORGANIZATION OF THE UNITED CHURCH OF CANADA. *Bulletin of the United Church of Can. 1973 (22): 5-15.* Briefly traces the history of the collection and housing of archival material by the Methodist and Presbyterian churches prior to 1925, and by the United Church of Canada since that time. Brief notes on the Central Archives, presently housed at Victoria University in Toronto, and on the regional archives in St. John's, Halifax, Montreal, Hamilton, London, Winnipeg, Saskatoon, Edmonton and Vancouver. Photos. B. D. Tennyson

270. Walker, Charles O. THE COMMITTEE ON BAPTIST HISTORY, 1948-1978. *Viewpoints: Georgia Baptist Hist. 1978 (6): 83-96.* Formed in 1948, the Committee on Baptist History of the Georgia Baptist Convention has sought to identify and establish Baptist landmarks in Georgia, collect historical materials, sponsor a collective history of Georgia Baptists, and maintain a fund for ongoing historical studies.

271. Walker, Charles O. GEORGIA BAPTIST HISTORY INTERESTS. *Viewpoints: Georgia Baptist Hist. 1974 4: 55-66.* Examines interest in Baptist church history among Georgia Baptists. S

272. Wartluft, David J. THE PASTOR AS HISTORIAN. *Concordia Hist. Inst. Q. 1978 51(2): 76-78.* The Lutheran Church pastor can and should be viewed as a historian in three ways. First, the pastor must record and maintain the daily business of his congregation; in this way, he accumulates primary source material. Second, the pastor's own sense of history has an important bearing on how he leads his congregation. Finally, a pastor should preserve materials about himself so that others who follow him will have an opportunity to understand his conception of history. W. T. Walker

273. Wax, Bernard. RHODE ISLAND MATERIALS IN THE AMERICAN JEWISH HISTORICAL SOCIETY COLLECTIONS. *Rhode Island Jewish Hist. Notes 1975 7(1): 171-174.* Covers 1692-1975.

274. Weber, Francis J. SOURCES FOR CATHOLIC HISTORY OF CALIFORNIA: A BIBLIO-ARCHIVAL SURVEY. *Southern California Q. 1975 57(3): 321-335.* Examines source materials relating to the Catholic phase of California history. State government archives were generally neglected and do not provide much material of value; county archives, while better cataloged, also have limited use. The "California Archives," a collection of important documents 1768-1850, were mostly destroyed in the 1906 San Francisco fire, although surviving materials have since been placed in the National Archives. In addition, Hubert H. Bancroft transcribed many of the documents. The Santa Barbara Mission Archives, San Francisco Chancery Archives, and Chancery Archives of the Archdiocese of Los Angeles contain valuable materials dating to the 18th century. Repositories outside California include archival centers in other states, Mexico, Spain, and Rome. There are a number of published guides to these repositories. In the search for documentary evidence on the Catholic contribution to California history, the work has barely begun. Based on descriptions of repositories and secondary studies; 77 notes. A. Hoffman

275. West, Elliot. THOMAS PRINCE AND NEW ENGLAND HISTORY. *J. of Church and State 1974 16(3): 435-452.* Thomas Prince was the pastor of Boston's Old South Church during 1718-58 and the author of *Chronological History of New England,* which expressed a Puritan theology.

276. Whitehill, Walter Muir. IN MEMORIAM: SAMUEL ELIOT MORISON (1887-1976). *New England Q. 1976 49(3): 459-463.* Provides a brief biographical sketch of Samuel Eliot Morison and emphasizes his role in the founding and editorial direction of *The New England Quarterly.* J. C. Bradford

277. Whittaker, David J. [LEONARD J. ARRINGTON: HIS LIFE AND WORK AND A BIBLIOGRAPHY]. *Dialogue 1978 11(4): 23-47.*

LEONARD JAMES ARRINGTON: HIS LIFE AND WORK, *pp. 23-32.* Uses the 20-year anniversary of the 1958 publication of Arrington's *Great Basin Kingdom* as opportunity to celebrate the personal and professional accomplishments of the church historian of the Church of the Latter Day Saints (Mormons). A Mormon by faith, and a historian trained at the University of North Carolina, Arrington personifies the new generation of Mormon historians who have integrated into Mormon studies a larger understanding of institutional, social, and economic developments in western history. Illus., list of six sources.

BIBLIOGRAPHY OF LEONARD JAMES ARRINGTON, *pp. 33-47.* Lists chronologically all work published by Arrington between the beginning of his career in 1935 and the present. For each year, writings are divided into the following categories: articles in professional publications, articles in nonprofessional publications, reviews, books, addresses and duplicated papers, and monographs. C. B. Schulz

278. Wieseltier, Leon. PHILOSOPHY, RELIGION AND HARRY WOLFSON. *Commentary 1976 61(4): 57-64.* Harry Austryn Wolfson (1887-1974) occupied the chair in Hebrew Literature and Philosophy at Harvard for more than 30 years and published prodigiously. His works include *The Philosophy of Spinoza* (1934), *Philo: Foundations of Religious Philosophy in Judaism, Christianity, and Islam* (1947), *The Philosophy of the Church Fathers* (1956), and others. His philosophy of history premised the deepest meaning for philosophy in its encounter with religion. The paganism of the ancients and the skepticism of the moderns pales for Wolfson before the marriage of philosophy and religion exemplified by the medievals. For Wolfson, the Jews held central place in medieval culture. Based on Wolfson's works. S. R. Herstein

279. Zaslow, Morris. DONALD GORDON GRADY KERR 1913-1976. *Can. Hist. Assoc. Hist. Papers [Canada] 1977: 230-231.* A memorial tribute to Donald Gordon Grady Kerr. He made many contributions to the field of Canadian history both through his writings and his teaching in the Protestant school system of Montreal (1938-1943), the University of Western Ontario (1958-1976), and Mount Allison University (1946-1958). R. V. Ritter

280. —. [THE CHARLES J. ROSENBLOOM BEQUEST]. *Yale U. Lib. Gazette 1975 49(4): 309-346.*

Libert, Herman W. THE CHARLES J. ROSENBLOOM BEQUEST, *pp. 309-310.* Charles J. Rosenbloom was a faithful alumni of Yale, a good friend, and an exacting and eclectic collector; his bequest reflected these qualities plus a rare devotion to his God and his country.

Rutter, Suzanna and Gallup, Donald. A CHECK-LIST OF THE BEQUEST, *pp. 311-346.* Lists the 184 items in the Rosenbloom Bequest arranged in 7 categories: 1) English Literature, 53 items; 2) American Literautre, 46 items; 3) Other Literatures, 10 items; 4) Americana, 9 items; 5) Illustrated Books, 34 items; 6) Press Books & Printing, 14 items; 7) The Worship of God, 18 items: Name index, illus. D. A. Yanchisin

281. —. IN MEMORIAM: MAYNARD J. GEIGER, O.F.M. *Pacific Hist. Rev. 1977 46(4): 684-685.* Maynard J. Geiger, archivist at Mission Santa Barbara 1937-77 and historian of Franciscan missionary activities in the Spanish Borderlands, died 13 May 1977. He was born in Lancaster, Pennsylvania, in 1901 and earned his Ph.D. in 1937 from Catholic University. W. K. Hobson

282. —. MIKROFILMADE SVENSKAMERIKANSKA KYRKOARKIV I EMIGRANTINSTITUTET, VÄXJÖ [Microfilmed Swedish-American church archives at the Emigrant Institute, Växjö]. *RA-nytt [Sweden] 1980 (3): 30-35.* Describes the project currently near completion by the Emigrant Institute at Växjö, Sweden, in which the records of Swedish American church congregations and social organizations are being microfilmed. Based on a longer report and inventory issued by the Emigrant Institute.

283. —. T. EDGAR LYON. *Brigham Young U. Studies 1978 19(1): 3-4.* T. Edgar Lyon served on the Editorial Board of the *Brigham Young University Studies* from 1969 until his death on 20 September 1978. Widely published, Lyon was an outstanding scholar in history, Christian studies, and LDS church history. His major area of concentration was the Nauvoo period of Mormon history. M. S. Legan

2. AMERICANIZATION OF INSTITUTIONS

284. Achenbaum, W. Andrew. TOWARD PLURALISM AND ASSIMILATION: THE RELIGIOUS CRISIS OF ANN ARBOR'S WÜRTTEMBERG COMMUNITY. *Michigan Hist. 1974 58(3): 195-218.* The evolution of Ann Arbor's Württemberg community illustrates a point often obscured in the assimilationist-pluralist controversy among historians of American immigration: that in adjusting to American society, most ethnic groups have altered some cultural patterns while preserving others. Ann Arbor Württembergers quickly accommodated themselves politically and economically but maintained their social customs and religious traditions. Following a congregational schism in 1875, one faction endeavored to preserve the pietism and ethnic solidarity of the Württemberg heritage, while the other moved into the mainstream of American Protestantism. Covers 1830-1955. Primary and secondary sources; 2 illus., 8 photos, 54 notes. D. W. Johnson

285. Andresen, Grant W. THE AMERICAN REVOLUTION AND THE SWEDISH CHURCH IN THE DELAWARE VALLEY. *Swedish Pioneer Hist. Q. 1976 27(4): 261-269.* Four congregations of the Swedish Lutheran Church in the Delaware River Valley were the last vestiges of Swedish colonization in America at the beginning of the American Revolution. Ecclesiastically the churches were drawing further away from the mother Church because of the anglicization of the congregations and their dissatisfaction over the policy of transferring ministers without considering the parish sentiment. During the Revolution the congregations were divided in loyalty. The clergymen suffered when they attempted to remain neutral, professing loyalty to the King of Sweden. Recounts the many problems of the congregations and the ministers during the Revolution. By the end of the war the churches had become independent of Swedish control and eventually became Episcopalian. Covers 1655-1831. Primary sources; 18 notes. C. W. Ohrvall

286. Baker, Frank. THE AMERICANIZING OF METHODISM. *Methodist Hist. 1975 13(3): 5-20.* The Americanization of the Methodist Church under Francis Asbury, the true architect of Methodism in America, was completed in broad outline during 1766-1816. Organization, theology, the idea of connectionalism, itineracy and social concerns were largely inherited from the British, but modified to meet the needs of America. 31 notes. H. L. Calkin

287. Bergendoff, Conrad. AUGUSTANA IN AMERICA AND IN SWEDEN. *Swedish Pioneer Hist. Q. 1973 24(4): 238-241.* The Augustana Synod, organized in 1860, is the largest single organization of the Swedish immigrants in the United States. It preserved the immigrants' form of worship and culture but gradually integrated with American society. In 1962 it joined a merger to form the Lutheran Church of America. The Augustana church lives on in the memories of those who still associate themselves with Sweden, and in its influence on the larger church. Paper presented at the conference "The Scandinavian Presence in America," Minneapolis, May 1973. K. J. Puffer

288. Brannan, Emora T. FROM RIGHT TO EXPEDIENCE: LAY REPRESENTATION AND THOMAS EMERSON BOND. *Methodist Hist. 1975 13(3): 123-144.* William S. Stockton and Nicholas Snethen were two principal protagonists of lay representation in the Methodist Episcopal Church after 1820. In 1823 Joshua Soule enlisted Thomas Emerson Bond (1782-1856) in an effort to subvert the reform efforts, a role he continued to fill until his death in 1856. Bond's principal argument was that lay representation was not a right but a matter of expedience. 61 notes. H. L. Calkin

289. Brown, Lawrence L. THE AMERICANIZATION OF THE EPISCOPAL CHURCH. *Hist. Mag. of the Protestant Episcopal Church 1975 44(5): 33-52.* The Episcopal Church suffered so severely from the effects of the American Revolution that it almost became extinct. In order to survive it had to find a new understanding of its meaning in the setting of an independent America, and to establish the institutions necessary for self-government. Traces the Americanizing process from colonial days (when many Puritans converted to Anglicanism) through the poignant post-Revolutionary period (as Anglicans in each state sought to get their respective state conventions structured) through the organization of the General Convention in 1785. Freed of state control, the Episcopal Church was able to restore the true character of the constitution of the church without the loss of distinctive values of Anglican Church being. American Episcopalians organized themselves after the model of Scottish Anglicans. Out of the compromises which made union possible between the state and the General Conventions, the church forged for itself the catholicity and tolerance which characterized the Church of England. Based on secondary sources; illus., 48 notes. H. M. Parker, Jr.

290. Buczek, Daniel S. POLISH AMERICAN PRIESTS AND THE AMERICAN CATHOLIC HIERARCHY: A VIEW FROM THE TWENTIES. *Polish Am. Studies 1976 33(1): 34-43.* Discusses the conflict between Catholic Irish American bishops and the Polish American clergy during the 1920's. Treats only the dioceses of Buffalo, Brooklyn, and Pittsburgh, but states that a revolutionary attitude pervaded the minds of Polish Americans in other dioceses as well. The bishops advocated Americanization in the Polish parishes, but the Poles called this "Irishism." Irish bishops insisted upon English as the language of instruction in all parochial schools, and the Poles fought for bilingualism. The Poles won the battle during the 1920's only to lose the campaign during the 1940's because of the gradual disappearance of the Polish language among the second and third generations. Based on primary and secondary sources; 24 notes. S. R. Pliska

291. Calcote, A. Dean. THE PROPOSED PRAYER BOOK OF 1785. *Hist. Mag. of the Protestant Episcopal Church 1977 46(3): 275-295.* The proposed Book of Common Prayer (American) of 1785 was not an isolated instance of Prayer Book revision in the 18th century, nor was it a radical departure from other proposals. It came after the Revolutionary War, and reflected the desire to omit from the Prayer Book what was not in accordance with Scripture, to avoid repetitions, to extend the comprehensiveness of the Prayer Book, and to bring the Book more into conformity with the politico-religious status of Anglicanism in America in the postwar period. The General Convention of 1785 drew up and accepted the proposed Book, but subsequent state conventions rejected it. The enthusiasm for the Prayer Book revision was well-intended, but misdirected in its attempt to adjust the historic liturgy to the thought forms of its own day. Further thought would be necessary for reaching an agreement on the nature of a book for the whole Church. Primary and secondary sources; 45 notes. H. M. Parker, Jr.

292. Carey, Patrick. THE LAITY'S UNDERSTANDING OF THE TRUSTEE SYSTEM, 1785-1855. *Catholic Hist. Rev. 1978 64(3): 357-376.* American Catholic trusteeism has usually been interpreted as lay insubordination. The author argues that many of the American Catholic laity who were elected trustees for their congregations during the national period tried to adapt the European Catholic Church to American culture by identifying that Church with American republican experiences. Trusteeism, therefore, was not simply a matter of insubordination, but rather a manifestation of the all-pervasive democratic spirit of the times, an implementation of European Catholic practices which were adapted to new republican experiences, and a result of the laity's changing theological perceptions of the Church and their role in it. The trustees were trying to create a republican Catholic Church in America. A

293. Carey, Patrick. TWO EPISCOPAL VIEWS OF LAY-CLERICAL CONFLICTS, 1785-1860. *Records of the Am. Catholic Hist. Soc. of Philadelphia 1976 87(1-4): 85-98.* Episcopal responses to trusteeism in the 19th century show two divergent kinds of opposition. Republican opposition believed that the Catholic Church should appropriate elements of American democracy in its administration while retaining the centrality of episcopal authority. Monarchical opposition was based on attempts of some bishops to establish the Catholic structures of the ancien régime in this country. 42 notes. J. M. McCarthy

294. Chandler, Douglas R. TOWARDS THE AMERICANIZING OF METHODISM. *Methodist Hist. 1974 13(1): 3-16.* The American-

ization of Methodism was a slow and strife-ridden process within its own ranks, as the English transplanted church did not have a natural affinity with the ideas of the new age and the new world. One result was the split of the Methodist Protestant Church from the Methodist Episcopal Church. 26 notes. H. L. Calkin

295. Chinnici, Joseph P. AMERICAN CATHOLICS AND RELIGIOUS PLURALISM, 1775-1820. *J. of Ecumenical Studies 1979 16(4): 727-746.* American Catholics after the American Revolution struggled with issues of pluralism, the separation of Church and state, and religious toleration. While their counterparts in Europe either appropriated Enlightenment thought to bring Catholic theology up-to-date (for example, Muratori, Lami, Demangeot, and Amort) or stuck to strict interpretations of *extra ecclesiam nulla est salus,* English Catholics, influenced by John Locke, moved to new positions and American Catholics, such as John Carroll, were forced to deal directly with these issues and develop a more flexible theology. Sees the new influences as a positive impetus to ecumenism. J. A. Overbeck

296. Curran, Robert Emmett. PRELUDE TO "AMERICANISM": THE NEW YORK ACCADEMIA AND CLERICAL RADICALISM IN THE LATE NINETEENTH CENTURY. *Church Hist. 1978 47(1): 48-65.* Recent discovery of a New York priests' association, The Accademia, started in 1865, shows another facet of the Americanist controversy which attempted to adapt Roman Catholicism to democratic institutions and values. For more than 20 years, the Accademia was regarded as the epitome of unrest fomenting against the established order of American Catholicism. 55 notes. M. D. Dibert

297. Doerries, Reingard R. THE AMERICANIZING OF THE GERMAN IMMIGRANT: A CHAPTER FROM U.S. SOCIAL HISTORY. *Amerikastudien/Am. Studies [West Germany] 1978 23(1): 51-59.* While German historiography has produced a number of studies on the problem of emigration, the question of the absorption of German nationals in foreign societies has largely been neglected. Immigrants from Germany made up one of the largest contingents of the inflow to the United States throughout most of the nineteenth century. As was the case with other nationalities, they formed associations of social, economic, and cultural cooperation in the New World, often designed to maintain an ethnic cohesiveness but in many cases becoming in fact vehicles of Americanization. The social structure of the German-American community is not only of interest as an ethnic microcosm; the study of the ethnic minority and its interaction with the existing American social formations also reveals a number of valuable insights into the makings of American society. The interdisciplinary approach to American social history, drawing on findings in fields such as church history, sociology, applied sociolinguistics, and organizational history shows the multi-faceted Americanization to be a natural social process. J

298. Garland, John M. THE NONECCLESIASTICAL ACTIVITIES OF AN ENGLISH AND A NORTH CAROLINA PARISH: A COMPARATIVE STUDY. *North Carolina Hist. Rev. 1973 50(1): 32-51.* Discusses "to what extent were the activities and the groups of officials of English parishes carried into the New World in the 17th and early 18th centuries, and to what extent were their adoptions modified by circumstances peculiar to colonial functions such as care of the poor, handling of bastardy cases, maintenance of roads, and the supervision of weights and measures. The activities and the official personnel of English parishes were not carried to any large extent into the New World. Circumstances peculiar to colonial America greatly modified both parish organization and parish function. Based on primary sources; 2 tables, 67 notes. R. V. Ritter

299. Gleason, Philip. COMING TO TERMS WITH AMERICAN CATHOLIC HISTORY. *Societas 1973 3(4): 283-312.* Discusses the ambiguity in the use of the crucial terms Americanism and Americanization in the history of American Catholicism. Catholic discussion shows a shift that is "evidence that a profound change has taken place in the way scholars in the historical discipline view the relation of religion to life and the Church to the world." 76 notes. E. P. Stickney

300. Glogower, Rod. THE IMPACT OF THE AMERICAN EXPERIENCE UPON RESPONSA LITERATURE. *Am. Jewish Hist. 1979 69(2): 257-269.* American Jewish issues are reflected in the responsa literature. Questions dealing with ritual slaughtering, divorce laws, attitudes toward the nonobservant, and American social customs all found expression in both questions and answers, particularly in the responsa of Rabbis Moses Aronson, Joseph Fried, Menahem Risikoff, Abraham Yudelovitch, Eliezer Meir Preil, and Moses Feinstein. The responsa literature demonstrates the dynamic between the demands of Jewish law and the realities of Jewish society. Covers ca. 1862-1937. Based on rabbinic responsa. J. D. Sarna

301. Goen, C. C. ECCLESIOCRACY WITHOUT ECCESIOLOGY. *Religion in Life 1979 48(1): 17-31.* Discusses the historical factors that have influenced the erosion of doctrine in American Christianity, including the combination of European traditions with the effects of the American frontier, since the 18th century.

302. Haebler, Peter. HOLYOKE'S FRENCH-CANADIAN COMMUNITY IN TURMOIL: THE ROLE OF THE CHURCH IN ASSIMILATION 1869-1887. *Hist. J. of Western Massachusetts 1979 7(1): 5-21.* Examines the conflict between Father Andre B. Dufresne and his Catholic parishioners in the Holyoke, Massachusetts, French-Canadian parish over his continuation of traditional practices. The extent of the conflict over Dufresne's conduct is an example of the speed with which many French Canadians had changed their outlook on the role of the curé in their lives. 2 illus., 40 notes. W. H. Mulligan, Jr.

303. Hale, Frederick. NORDIC IMMIGRATION: THE NEW PURITANS? *Swedish Pioneer Hist. Q. 1977 28(1): 27-44.* Examines the relations between the established American churches and the Nordic immigrant churches, and the impact of the former on the development and integration of the latter during the second half of the 19th century. Uses the Congregationalist press and the eastern Lutheran press as a basis for examination. The reception of Nordic immigrants was generally favorable, in part due to the similarity of Protestant beliefs. 56 notes. C. W. Ohrvall

304. Hennesey, James. ROMAN CATHOLICISM: THE MARYLAND TRADITION. *Thought 1976 51(202): 282-295.* Distinguishes between two Roman Catholic traditions, a distinctively Anglo-American Catholicism which survives well into the 19th century, and an ultramontane Catholicism which reflects the preoccupations of the European continent. Colonial Maryland played a part in the development of the first tradition's ideas concerning the freedom of conscience and the separation of Church and state. Covers 1634-1786. J. C. English

305. Johnson, Niel M. THE MISSOURI SYNOD LUTHERANS AND THE WAR AGAINST THE GERMAN LANGUAGE. *Nebraska Hist. 1975 56(1): 137-156.* Examines the attack on the Missouri Synod Lutherans for teaching German in church schools. The Nebraska Council of Defense charged them with disloyalty, but in 1923, the US Supreme Court overturned a decision by the Nebraska Supreme Court, and held that laws designed to make English the mother tongue of all children reared in the state were unconstitutional. R. Lowitt

306. Kuzniewski, Anthony. THE POLISH NATIONAL CATHOLIC CHURCH—THE VIEW FROM PEOPLE'S POLAND. *Polish Am. Studies 1974 31(1): 30-34.* Hieronim Kubiak's [*The Polish National Church in the United States of America—1897-1965*] (Krakow: Polish Academy of Science, 1970), "the first good work on the subject," traces the history of the church through three generations of Polish Americans. Marxist in orientation and Polish in viewpoint, the book refers to the origin of the church as a revolutionary plebian movement among the immigrants. During three generations the church passed from a Polish institution to an American institution "only minimally colored by its Polish past." The reviewer sees more ethnicity there than Kubiak does. S. R. Pliska

307. Munch, Peter A. AUTHORITY AND FREEDOM: CONTROVERSY IN NORWEGIAN-AMERICAN CONGREGATIONS. *Norwegian-American Studies 1979 28: 3-34.* Norway-born and trained ministers of the Norwegian Lutheran Church who emigrated to the United States in the 1840's and 1850's to serve the Norwegian settlers discovered congregations transformed by the pervasive American spirit of freedom and egalitarianism. Norwegian Americans rejected Old World notions of pastoral status and authority; they further regarded churches

as voluntary associations. At issue in many congregations was inadequate support of the minister, pastoral attempts to exclude dissenters and otherwise impose authority, or the alleged haughty and overbearing character of the minister. Map, 58 notes. D. K. Lambert Norwegian Lutheran Church.

308. Orban, Edmond. FACTEURS POLITICO-RELIGIEUX ET ANGLICISATION DES FRANCO-AMERICAINS AU VERMONT: INDICATEURS RECENTS [Political and religious factors and the Anglicizing of Franco-Americans in Vermont: recent evidence]. *Can. Ethnic Studies [Canada] 1976 8(2): 34-49.* The decision of the Catholic Church in Vermont in 1960 to end encouragement of the use of the French language has led to the decline of Franco-American institutions in Vermont today. Covers 1917-75.

309. Orban, Edmond. FIN D'UN NATIONALISME: LE CAS RECENT DES FRANCO-AMÉRICAINS DE LA NOUVELLE-ANGLETERRE [End of a nationalism: the recent case of the New England Franco-Americans]. *Can. Rev. of Studies in Nationalism [Canada] 1976 4(1): 91-99.* Studies the nationalism of the Franco-Americans, a group of unassimilated French Canadians in New England, who were distinguished by the use of the French language and the practice of a rural and conservative Catholic faith distinct from the Irish one. After 1940, such nationalism gradually deteriorated and has disappeared today, because of Franco-Americans' exogamous marriages, their mobility due to economic causes, their mixed parishes where priests officiate in English, and a general decrease in their resistance to anglicization. Based on primary and secondary sources; 2 tables, graph, 13 notes.
G. P. Cleyet

310. Orzell, Laurence. A MINORITY WITHIN A MINORITY: THE POLISH NATIONAL CATHOLIC CHURCH. *Polish Am. Studies 1979 36(1): 5-32.* An account of the formative years (1896-1907) of what came to be the largest organized secession from the Catholic Church in the United States. Today, the 280,000 Polish National Catholic, registered in 165 parishes, are proud of their independent status; but interest in local control of parish property rather than full independence seems to have prevailed in the beginning. Describes the Reverend Francis Hodur, the first bishop of the PNCC, and mentions the Reverend Antoni Kozlowski and the Reverend Stephen Kaminski, early bishops of the other Polish Catholic splinter groups in Chicago and Buffalo. Primary and secondary sources in Polish and English; 52 notes.
S. R. Pliska

311. Painter, Borden W. THE VESTRY IN THE MIDDLE COLONIES. *Hist. Mag. of the Protestant Episcopal Church 1978 47(1): 5-36.* Describes the organization, structure, work, and the relationship of the vestry to the clergy of the Anglican Church in colonial New York, New Jersey, Pennsylvania and Delaware during 1690-1775. The Anglican Church was not the established Church in these colonies; discusses how the Church functioned under such conditions. Emphasizes the freedom the vestries had in selecting the clergy because the conditions of church life demanded an increased lay responsibility in all aspects of parochial administration. Generally the vestries acquitted themselves well in assuming their responsibilities, paving the way for the larger role in ecclesiastical life and government which the Episcopal laity were forced to assume after the Revolution. Based largely on records and histories of local churches and dioceses; 142 notes. H. M. Parker, Jr.

312. Painter, Bordon W., Jr. THE VESTRY IN COLONIAL NEW ENGLAND. *Hist. Mag. of the Protestant Episcopal Church 1975 44(4): 381-408.* Because so many of the colonial Anglican clergy and members came out of a Congregational background, and since there was no resident bishop in the colonies, the role of the vestry was an important one in colonial Anglican polity. It reflected the democratic practices of Congregationalism. In New England the vestries acted as the protectors and proponents of Anglicanism where Congregationalism was the established church. The major area of concern was taxation. Discusses the relation of the vestry to the clergy. Foreign-born clergy were not desired. Based on primary sources; 147 notes. H. M. Parker, Jr.

313. Platt, Warren C. THE POLISH NATIONAL CATHOLIC CHURCH: AN INQUIRY INTO ITS ORIGINS. *Church Hist. 1977 46(4): 474-489.* In the United States, the Polish immigrant deprived of old social institutions acquired the capacity to satisfy religious and social particularity. Schisms resulted and parochial life was recognized as an instrument of social cohesion and religious tradition. True to these concerns, the Polish National Catholic Church focused on ethnic nationalism, a force defined by language which would outline the Polish character of the affiliated and the nationalism that accentuated Polish liberation and its coupling with a theology of national religions. The emergence of the Polish National Catholic Church is a testament to the ethnic parish as an effective voluntary association for the preservation of linguistic, cultural, and religious traditions. At the same time, it was a product of the American experience whose traditions of voluntarism and free association allowed its creation and whose religious structure of denominationalism provided the necessary organizational framework. Covers 1880's-1930's. 43 notes. M. D. Dibert

314. Rippinger, Joel. SOME HISTORICAL DETERMINANTS OF AMERICAN BENEDICTINE MONASTICISM, 1846-1900. *Am. Benedictine Rev. 1976 27(1): 63-84.* Investigates significant elements in the development of American Benedictine life. Notes the similarities and the dissimilarities between American and European—specifically German and Swiss—Benedictine life. Stresses the activist character of American life in reshaping the Benedictines' experience in America. Based on primary and secondary sources; 63 notes. J. H. Pragman

315. Rives, Ralph Hardee. NICHOLAS SNETHEN: METHODIST PROTESTANT PIONEER. *Methodist Hist. 1979 17(2): 78-89.* Nicholas Snethen (1769-1845) was an itinerant minister of the Methodist Episcopal Church, author, publisher, orator, educator, advocate of democratic policies in church government, and one of the founders of the Methodist Protestant Church. 55 notes. H. L. Calkin

316. Rowe, Kenneth E. POWER TO THE PEOPLE: GEORGE RICHARD CROOKS, *THE METHODIST*, AND LAY REPRESENTATION IN THE METHODIST EPISCOPAL CHURCH. *Methodist Hist. 1975 13(3): 145-176.* Lay persons sought increased participation in the life of the Methodist Episcopal Church during the 1820's and again in the 1850's-60's. The latter effort began in 1851 and ended with the seating of lay delegates in the General Conference of 1872. George Richard Crooks (1822-97) became the leader for representation and used the pages of *The Methodist*, started in 1860, to counter the arguments of opponents. 84 notes. H. L. Calkin

317. Silvia, Philip T., Jr. THE "FLINT AFFAIR": FRENCH-CANADIAN STRUGGLE FOR *SURVIVANCE*. *Catholic Hist. Rev. 1979 65(3): 414-435.* Examines ethnic tension in Fall River, Massachusetts, 1870's-85, between Irish Americans and French Canadians who, though coreligionists, were divided by cultural and economic differences. Central to this struggle was the militant French-Canadian determination to best preserve their "race," culture and religious heritage by establishing a national parish, Notre Dame de Lourdes, with a French-Canadian serving as pastor. Rome concurred, to the disappointment of Irish-born Thomas F. Hendricken, bishop of Providence, who, despite invoking the spiritual weapon of interdiction, did not prevail in attempting to implement an assimilationist, Americanization approach to church governance. A

318. Simon, Andrea J. ETHNICITY AS A COGNITIVE MODEL: IDENTITY VARIATIONS IN A GREEK IMMIGRANT COMMUNITY. *Ethnic Groups 1979 2(2): 133-154.* Studies Greek Americans in New York City, discerning types of adaptation to the question of ethnic identity versus assimilation. The orientations are organized around two Greek Orthodox churches, St. Demetrios, which has adopted modern architectural styles and dress patterns, and St. Markela, which clings to traditional and Old World ways. Covers the 1970's. 5 notes, ref.
T. W. Smith

319. Thomas, Samuel J. THE AMERICAN PERIODICAL PRESS AND THE APOSTOLIC LETTER *TESTEM BENEVOLENTIAE*. *Catholic Hist. Rev. 1976 62(3): 408-423.* American periodicals reacted sharply to Pope Leo XIII's letter *On Americanism* (1899). Catholic and non-Catholic journals noted the division in the American hierarchy and seemed to intensify it by their impassioned reporting. Protestant writers revealed a self-righteous understanding of liberal Catholicism by their assertion that although certain bishops did adhere to the theological

Americanism condemned by Leo, such Americanism was perfectly Christian (i.e., Protestant). Collectively, non-Catholic periodicals expressed or implied that the letter not only confirmed Leo's ultramontanism and the reintrenchment of the conservative bishops, but also would hinder the process of getting Catholicism accepted into the mainstream of American life. A

320. Warman, John B. OUR METHODIST PROTESTANT HERITAGE. *Methodist Hist. 1979 17(2): 67-77.* Dissension in the Methodist Church was present almost from its beginnings in America. In 1779 and in 1792 there were events which almost split it. Two issues were lay representation and opposition to bishops. In 1830 the reformers left the Methodist Episcopal Church and formed the Methodist Protestant Church which remained a separate entity until Methodist union in 1939. In addition to describing the development of the Methodist Protestant Church, discusses some of the personalities involved: Nicholas Snethen, Asa Shinn, Samuel Clawson, George Brown, and Peter T. Laishley. 8 notes. H. L. Calkin

321. Westerberg, Wesley M. ETHNICITY AND THE FREE CHURCHES. *Swedish Pioneer Hist. Q. 1973 24(4): 231-237.* All the groups in the free church movement in the Scandinavian population of America have undergone the same transitions. Swedish Methodism was never independent of the parent church. The Swedish Baptist Church became an avowedly American denomination in 1945. The Evangelical Free Church of America developed out of two groups which merged in 1950 to become an American denomination. The Salvation Army and the Pentecostal churches are now the only segments of the free church movement carrying on a deliberate ministry to Scandinavians. The Evangelical Covenant Church of America remains reasonably loyal to their ethnic origin and desirous of maintaining it. The newspapers serving the memberships of these churches were one of the great influences in terms of ethnicity. There is nothing comparable for the present generation. Based on personal experience. Covers 1870-1973. K. J. Puffer

322. White, Joyce L. THE AFFILIATION OF SEVEN SWEDISH LUTHERAN CHURCHES WITH THE EPISCOPAL CHURCH. *Hist. Mag. of the Protestant Episcopal Church 1977 46(2): 171-186.* By 1650 the Church of Sweden had established seven mission congregations along the Delaware River. In 1831 the Church left these congregations to go their separate ways. For years they had been largely supplied by Episcopal clergy and the services had long been conducted in English rather than Swedish. The formal steps by which these Swedish Lutheran congregations assimilated into the structure of the Protestant Episcopal Church is presented. Discusses each congregation from its founding through its assimilation into the Episcopal Church. Based on church records and histories. 53 notes. H. M. Parker, Jr.

323. Williams, William Carlos. THE VOYAGE OF THE MAYFLOWER. *Mankind 1977 5(12): 46-47.* The lusty flamboyance of Tudor England became a dessicated smallness of thought and action in the transplantation of the Pilgrims from Old to New England. Their utter isolation in America caused them to turn inward, using their religion as a means of protecting themselves against the American environment. The Pilgrims looked upon the rest of humanity as sinners, while they exalted the emptiness in themselves as a virtue. It was the new continent that shaped their attitudes and contributed to the making of the Puritan legacy that has affected American culture for the worse. Excerpted from *In the American Grain,* published in 1925. N. Lederer

324. Woolverton, John F. PHILADELPHIA'S WILLIAM WHITE: EPISCOPALIAN DISTINCTIVENESS AND ACCOMMODATION IN THE POST-REVOLUTIONARY PERIOD. *Hist. Mag. of the Protestant Episcopal Church 1974 43(4): 275-296.* William White (1748-1836) took the lead in the reorganization of the Episcopal Church after the American Revolution and became the chief architect of the new denomination. Studies White's understanding of the nature of the church, his views on Reformation, his reading of the political thought of his day, and the importance of Philadelphia as the most cosmopolitan town in the land. Through various pressures White moved in a conciliatory, large-minded, and firm manner. He built an institution in which contradictory tendencies could live together side-by-side, and he sought a national identity and unity for his church. 55 notes. R. V. Ritter

3. BUSINESS

(including Protestant Ethic)

325. Adasiak, Allan. MOONRISE IN KODIAK: THE UNIFICATION CHURCH GOES FISHING. *Alaska J. 1980 10(1): 66-72.* Discusses the Unification Church's fishing operation at Kodiak and the local reaction to a cannery opened by the church. Covers 1978-79. Based on local newspapers and interviews; 7 photos. E. E. Eminhizer

326. Agonito, Joseph. ST. INIGOES MANOR: A NINETEENTH CENTURY JESUIT PLANTATION. *Maryland Hist. Mag. 1977 72(1): 83-98.* St. Inigoes in St. Marys County, Maryland, is "the most ancient Jesuit establishment in the United States, and probably the oldest in the world . . . in the possession of the Society." Surveys the history of the plantation and its manor house and church, ravaged by time and twice attacked by the British. Emphasizes the management of Brother Joseph Mobberly during 1806-20 and his handling of the slave population on the estate. Details food, clothing, health care, and the problem of finding capable overseers. The Jesuit regulation of slave marriages was serious and conscientious. Mobberly found managing the Society's 43 slaves frustrating, and he came to believe that free white labor would be as productive and more profitable. By the late 1830's the Jesuits sold off all their slaves. Still in the Society's hands, St. Inigoes has lost ground to the St. Mary's River and a Navy air base. The original manor house burned in 1872. The present church of St. Ignatius was restored in the 1950's and is a reminder of a rich, historic past. Primary sources, including Mobberly's diary; 3 illus., 3 maps, 72 notes. G. J. Bobango

327. Arndt, Karl J. R. DID FREDERICK RAPP CHEAT ROBERT OWEN? *Western Pennsylvania Hist. Mag. 1978 61(4): 358-365.* Questions the accusation that Harmonist Frederick Rapp cheated Robert Owen in the sale of New Harmony to Owen in 1825.

328. Arrington, Chris Rigby. THE FINEST OF FABRICS: MORMON WOMEN AND THE SILK INDUSTRY IN EARLY UTAH. *Utah Hist. Q. 1978 46(4): 376-396.* Mormon church leaders encouraged the Utah silk industry as part of the development of home industries designed to diversify the economy. The work was menial, time-consuming, and not a financial success. Dedicated, ingenious women such as Zina D. H. Young demonstrated resourcefulness and perseverance. They kept the industry alive during 1855-1905. Problems involved were the lack of a steady paying market, the difficulty of getting machinery to manufacture silk thread and cloth, and the lack of skilled workers. Primary and secondary sources; 3 illus., 84 notes. J. L. Hazelton

329. Arrington, Leonard J. and May, Dean. A DIFFERENT MODE OF LIFE: IRRIGATION AND SOCIETY IN NINETEENTH CENTURY UTAH. *Agric. Hist. 1975 49(1): 3-20.* The Mormon system, or irrigated agriculture, in Utah had less impact than usually imagined. Their irrigation projects were influential in inspiring irrigation elsewhere, but were soon considered archaic and unadaptable. The dream that irrigated agriculture would inspire a new and more democratic type of society was not realized—the cooperation of Mormons was more the product of religion than of irrigation. 37 notes. D. E. Bowers

330. Axelrad, Allan M. THE PROTAGONIST OF THE PROTESTANT ETHIC: MAX WEBER'S BEN FRANKLIN. *Rendezvous 1978 13(2): 45-59.* Benjamin Franklin is the leading figure or model for many extremely important ideas developed in Max Weber's *The Protestant Ethic and the Spirit of Capitalism.* The author supports the contention that Weber's portrayal of Franklin is based more on 19th-century stereotypes than on reality. Weber's work portrays only one side of the real Franklin, who was much more complex. However, because Weber was using the Franklin personality as a symbol or ideal type, and because there is much evidence that this particular Franklin persona was widely admired and emulated in 19th-century society, the overall efficacy of the Weber thesis is not impaired or destroyed. Based on German and American published sources; 32 notes. L. K. Blaser

331. Bernhard, Virginia. COTTON MATHER AND THE DOING OF GOOD: A PURITAN GOSPEL OF WEALTH. *New England Q. 1976 49(2): 225-241.* Compares Mather's 1710 *Essays to Do Good* with contemporary British works, which also counseled men to not only *be* good, but to *do* good, and finds Mather's emphasis on individual action, his promise of temporal rewards, and his unitary view of society to be distinctively American. Mather was attempting to counter the rising social and economic dissension of the time by turning self-interest into a force for social betterment, but ended up providing a rationale for the economic individualism and social mobility which were fragmenting the very social order he hoped to buttress. Based on the writings of Mather, Richard Baxter and Robert Nelson and secondary sources; 77 notes. J. C. Bradford

332. Bishop, M. Guy. BUILDING RAILROADS FOR THE KINGDOM: THE CAREER OF JOHN W. YOUNG, 1867-91. *Utah Hist. Q. 1980 48(1): 66-80.* John W. Young (b. 1844), railroad and tourism promoter, and a son of Brigham Young, was a key figure in the development of Utah's transportation facilities and natural resources. He brought together the wealth of eastern financiers and Mormon labor. He helped construct the Utah Central Railroad, the Utah Northern Railroad, the Utah Western, and the Salt Lake and Eastern Railroad. Accused of misuse of his stewardship by the LDS Church, plagued by financial disasters, he ended his business career as an elevator operator in New York City. Based on the John W. Young Papers, LDS Archives; 8 illus., 35 notes. J. L. Hazelton

333. Bosher, J. F. FRENCH PROTESTANT FAMILIES IN CANADIAN TRADE 1740-1760. *Social Hist. [Canada] 1974 7(14): 179-201.* Protestant merchants in Quebec increased in number after the end of the War of Austrian Succession in 1748. By the time Quebec fell in 1759 they may have been preponderant in Franco-Canadian trade. Information on the origins, family ties, and business connections of the 16 identifiable Protestant firms indicates they came from and maintained ties with southwestern France (La Rochelle, Bordeaux, and Montauban) and were willing to trade with anyone, but formed companies and married only with other Protestants. Based on secondary sources and on documents in the Archives nationales, Public Record Office, Bibliothèque de l'Arsenal (Paris), Public Archives of Canada, and departmental and town archives in France; 82 notes. W. K. Hobson

334. Bourg, Carroll J. WORK AND/OR JOB IN ADVANCED INDUSTRIAL SOCIETIES. *Soundings 1974 57(1): 113-125.* Work time, once associated through the Protestant work ethic with moral duty, has been drastically reduced following industrialization, forcing a reevaluation of values and redefinition of leisure. Covers the 19th and 20th centuries.

335. Brandes, Stanley H. FAMILY MISFORTUNE STORIES IN AMERICAN FOLKLORE. *J. of the Folklore Inst. 1975 12(1): 5-17.* Discusses the theme of family misfortune in folktales in the 20th century, including the role of the Protestant Ethic, values, and attitudes toward success and social status.

336. Buettner, George L. CONCORDIA PUBLISHING HOUSE AS I KNEW IT (1888-1955). *Concordia Hist. Inst. Q. 1974 47(2): 62-69.* Discusses his experiences as part of the Concordia Publishing House (1888-1955) in St. Louis, Missouri. S

337. Campeau, Lucien. LE COMMERCE DES CLERCS EN NOUVELLE-FRANCE [Trade by the clergy in New France]. *Rev. de l'U. d'Ottawa [Canada] 1977 47(1-2): 27-35.* In New France, the clergy was forbidden to engage in trade, which was defined as the resale for a profit of merchandise purchased at a smaller price, without any transformation increasing its value beyond the social service rendered. Members of the clergy, who handled a considerable amount of furs which they used only

as currency to pay for imports necessary to church administration activities, were often falsely accused of trading in the manner prohibited by the law. Covers 1627-1760. G. P. Cleyet

338. Clark, Dennis. ETHNIC ENTERPRISE AND URBAN DEVELOPMENT. *Ethnicity 1978 5(2): 108-118.* Examines the role of Irish general contractors in Philadelphia from the time of the potato famine (1846-47) to the 1960's. Construction of churches, parochial schools, and homes for Irish immigrants provided much of the impetus for Irish involvement in general contracting. In the early years, little capital was needed to start as a contractor and aspiring Irish entrepreneurs had access to fellow countrymen who had quickly acquired important construction skills. Irish participation in politics and in construction became closely linked. Discusses the individual careers of leading contractors, and the increasing legal and technological complexity of the business. Based on the Philadelphia *Evening Bulletin,* and secondary sources; 44 notes. L. W. Van Wyk

339. Coleson, Edward. THE REFORMATION AND ECONOMIC DEVELOPMENT TODAY. *Freeman 1973 23(6): 368-376.* Despite its shortcomings there is a great deal to be said in favor of the Weber Thesis. The Reformation did mark a turning point toward a better way of life. American has pursued abundance to excess and there does exist a strong reaction against Western materialism, but the Western world has a better way of life than the often starving, underdeveloped nations. So, well might one ask "what conditions are necessary for prosperity and what, if anything, religion has to contribute toward making progress possible." 22 notes. D. A. Yanchisin

340. Constantin, Charles. THE PURITAN ETHIC AND THE DIGNITY OF LABOR: HIERARCHY VS. EQUALITY. *J. of the Hist. of Ideas 1979 40(4): 543-561.* The Puritan conception of "calling" changed in the 18th century as thinkers in that tradition became familiar with the "Great Chain of Being." Calling, as Puritans had the idea from Martin Luther and John Calvin, was potently equalitarian; all labor, if offered to God as a "living sacrifice," in faith, had high spiritual value. Some Puritans, such as William Perkins, insisted that various labors were more and less honorable, but others, including John Cotton, emphasized the equalitarian implication of calling. In the 18th century Jonathan Edwards and his followers Joseph Bellamy and Samuel Hopkins conceived the "infinite diversity" of the creation, including men, in terms of the hierarchical chain, but continued to insist on the spiritual value of all faithful labor. Their rationalistic contemporaries Charles Chauncey and Jonathan Mayhew derived a less spiritual and equalitarian view from the chain. Based on published primary and secondary sources; 45 notes. D. B. Marti

341. Croft, David James. THE PRIVATE BUSINESS ACTIVITIES OF BRIGHAM YOUNG, 1847-1877. *J. of the West 1977 16(4): 36-51.* The Anti-Bigamy Act (1862) was designed to abolish the Mormons' practice of plural marriage and to limit the economic power of the church. It limited the value of real estate which could be held by the church to $50,000. To get around this provision, the church property was held in trust by the president of the church, Brigham Young. Although his personal accounts and those of the church were kept separately, there was confusion in many minds concerning his personal wealth. When his estate was settled on his death in 1877, it was much smaller than previously thought. R. Alvis

342. Doherty, William T., Jr. THE NINETEENTH CENTURY BUSINESSMAN AND RELIGION. *North Dakota Q. 1978 46(2): 4-18.* Religion in 19th-century America provided an inducement to work and made the business mission sacred; businessmen, including Andrew Carnegie, Commodore Vanderbilt, and John Wanamaker, reciprocated with much philanthropy and time devoted to church activity.

343. Doherty, William T., Jr. THE TWENTIETH CENTURY BUSINESSMAN AND RELIGION. *North Dakota Q. 1979 47(1): 67-79.* Discusses the relationship between religion and business during the 20th century, specifically the transformation of churches into efficiently managed businesses.

344. Doherty, William T., Jr. THE TWENTIETH CENTURY'S SECULAR RELIGION. *North Dakota Q. 1979 47(4): 54-63.* Discusses the reinterpretation of religion by business interests in America from the turn of the century to the Depression, particularly the reinterpretation of the Bible and biblical characters.

345. Ederer, Rupert J. RELIGION AND THE DECLINE OF CAPITALISM IN THE U.S.A. *Rev. Int. d'Hist. de la Banque [Italy] 1975 10: 82-104.* The growing role of the state in the economy and the emergence of a managerial, rather than ownership, class at the head of corporations constitutes a decline of capitalism in the 20th century. This decline parallels the decline of Protestant churches and the rise of a social ethic embodied in the hippie movement and ersatz religions such as Marxism or secularized humanism. The social ethic characterizes Catholicism and Marxism and contrasts with the individualism of Protestantism. Man's true nature, however, is individual and social. The parallel decline of Protestantism and capitalism results as social attitudes and institutions move to an equilibrium which more sharply reflects human nature. Based on the published statements of religious leaders and on secondary sources; 19 notes. D. McGinnis

346. Enders, Donald L. THE STEAMBOAT *MAID OF IOWA:* MORMON MISTRESS OF THE MISSISSIPPI. *Brigham Young U. Studies 1979 19(3): 321-335.* The Mormons at Nauvoo, Illinois, depended on riverboats but felt discriminated against by boat operators, so, in 1843, when Captain Dan Jones, half owner of the *Maid of Iowa,* debarked his Mormon passengers in Nauvoo, Joseph Smith gratefully met the captain and bought the other half interest in the boat. Jones soon converted to Mormonism. The Mormons acquired Jones's half of the *Maid* when he embarked on a career as a missionary, but the boat was sold to non-Mormons in 1845. Based on documents from the Church Archives and published primary and secondary sources; 56 notes. S

347. Esplin, Fred C. THE CHURCH AS BROADCASTER. *Dialogue 1977 10(3): 25-45.* The broadcasting enterprises of the Church of Jesus Christ of Latter-Day Saints (Mormons) include ownership of 16 radio and television stations, and a cable TV system; 1922-77.

348. Falk, Gerhard. OLD CALVIN NEVER DIED: PURITANICAL RHETORIC BY FOUR AMERICAN PRESIDENTS CONCERNING PUBLIC WELFARE. Plesur, Milton, ed. *An American Historian: Essays to Honor Selig Adler* (Buffalo: State U. of N.Y., 1980): 183-190. Discusses the themes of Calvinism and the work ethic from Max Weber's *The Protestant Ethic and the Spirit of Capitalism* (1905) as expressed in the rhetoric of Franklin D. Roosevelt, Herbert C. Hoover, Lyndon B. Johnson, and Richard M. Nixon; 1905-79.

349. Gaventa, John. CASE STUDY: PROPERTY FOR PROPHET. *Southern Exposure 1976 4(3): 101-103.* Nashville, Tennessee, known as the Religious Capital of the South, is the center of several religious publishing houses, Bible distributorships, and hawkers of religious whatnots which comprise a $100 million-a-year business. Covers the 1960's and 70's.

350. Glantz, Oscar. NATIVE SONS AND IMMIGRANTS: SOME BELIEFS AND VALUES OF AMERICAN-BORN AND WEST INDIAN BLACKS AT BROOKLYN COLLEGE. *Ethnicity 1978 5(2): 189-202.* The impressionistic literature on the attitudes of black immigrants from non-Iberian societies of the West Indies, as well as the few empirical studies that have appeared (beginning with Ira Reid's in 1939), suggest that these immigrants are exceptional among blacks in their belief in the efficacy of hard work in the American context, their freedom from anti-white sentiment, and their confidence in the political system. A survey of 657 freshmen and sophomores at Brooklyn College, 200 of them black, confirms these conclusions. This survey's data on white Catholics and Jews are then used to compare their attitudes with those of black immigrants; faith in the work ethic is found to distinguish the latter in this wider context as well. 6 tables, 7 notes, 22 ref. L. W. Van Wyk

351. Hill, Marvin S.; Rooker, C. Keith; and Wimmer, Larry T. THE KIRTLAND ECONOMY REVISITED: A MARKET CRITIQUE OF SECTARIAN ECONOMICS. *Brigham Young U. Studies 1977 17(4): 387-475.* This issue of *BYU Studies* is devoted to an economic analysis of the Mormon experience in Kirtland, Ohio, during the 1830's. Topics include: the viability of the community's economy, whether rising

land prices were due to speculation or to prosperity, Joseph Smith's indebtedness and wealth, and a financial history of the Kirtland Safety Society Bank. Defines Joseph Smith's role in these affairs. Moral judgements concerning Mormons have obscured the fact that valid economic principles were employed, and that individuals participated in these business arrangements because they believed they would profit.
M. S. Legan

352. Kershaw, Gordon E. A QUESTION OF ORTHODOXY: RELIGIOUS CONTROVERSY IN A SPECULATIVE LAND COMPANY: 1759-1775. *New England Q. 1973 46(2): 205-235.* Considers religious controversy in the Kennebec Purchase Company of Massachusetts. The predominantly Congregationalist colonists feared establishment of the Church of England. As in the greater society, the struggle between the two was carried on in the company, proprietors seeking to grant important posts and lucrative contracts to members of their own churches. The harrassed Anglicans finally appealed to the King. The outbreak of the War of Independence wrecked the company as the two groups chose opposing sides. 70 notes. V. L. Human

353. Kolb, Robert. NO CHRISTIAN WOULD DARE PRACTICE USURY. *Concordia Hist. Inst. Q. 1975 48(4): 127-139.* An examination of a letter written by Carl F. W. Walther to Christopher A. Mennicke in 1866 concerning usury. Walther's argument against usury was based on Luther's view of the matter. Walther believed that usury was a moral threat to Lutherans, and that Luther's interpretation of scriptures was a correct condemnation of usury. This 19th-century view was not maintained in later synod meetings in the 20th century. 38 notes.
W. T. Walker

354. Kolbenschlag, M. Claire. THOREAU AND CRUSOE: THE CONSTRUCTION OF AN AMERICAN MYTH AND STYLE. *Amerikastudien/Am. Studies [West Germany] 1977 22(2): 229-246.* The immense popularity of Defoe's *Robinson Crusoe* in early America suggests that it is paradigmatic in style and mythic content for that culture. Thoreau's *Walden,* a later work, is viewed as a counter-genre, representative of a secondary, contrasting mode in American writing. Kenneth Burke's dialectical theory of rhetoric, in which transcendent and mundane terms are transformed in value, illustrates certain structural tendencies in the language which predispose the choice of particular metaphoric contexts. Thus applied to the present study, the social and semantic tensions of both works reveal the polarization of the concepts of 'God' and 'money', and the rhetorical inversions that the capitalist and anti-capitalist imagination invoke respectively in language, myth, and literary genre. If the Crusoe-Franklin myth represents the dominant and prevenient mode of the American consciousness—a downward converison of transcendental aspiration into materialist pragmatism—then, Thoreau's *Walden* parodies, contradicts and disputes this consciousness by inverting the religious-commerical idiom. Both works stand as archetypes of an inherent dialectical tendency that distinguishes American writing to the present. J

355. Kolbenschlag, Madonna Claire. THE PROTESTANT ETHIC AND EVANGELICAL CAPITALISM: THE WEBERIAN THESIS REVISITED. *Southern Q. 1976 14(4): 287-306.* Analyzes the transformation of spiritual motivation into a social, capitalistic impulse. The writings of Max Weber are examined in detail and points of paradox receive focus, along with comparison between historical events and evolution of value systems. Covers 1770-1920. 2 diagrams, 34 notes.
R. W. Dubay

356. Leisy, Bruce R. THE LAST OF THE MENNONITE BREWERS. *Mennonite Life 1976 31(1): 4-9.* Chronicles the beer brewing industry started by the Leisy family in Peoria, Illinois, 1884-1950.

357. Magnusson, Gustav A. THE HOUSE THAT PROCLAIMED THE GOSPEL WITH TYPE AND PRESSES. *Swedish Pioneer Hist. Q. 1979 30(2): 117-128.* The Augustana (Lutheran) Book Concern of Rock Island, Illinois, began as a small print shop in a basement in Galesburg, Illinois, in 1855. It closed in 1967 due to the merger of three national Lutheran church bodies. Based on secondary sources published by the Concern; 6 photos. C. W. Ohrvall

358. Marietta, Jack D. WEALTH, WAR AND RELIGION: THE PERFECTING OF QUAKER ASCETICISM 1740-1783. *Church Hist. 1974 43(2): 230-241.* Quakers have always warned against the perils of wealth, but during the late 18th century an entire generation of American Quakers criticized wealth more than ever before. There are two reasons why the critics linked their grievances over wealth to war: 1) wars illuminated the conflict between wealth and Quaker pacifism, and 2) war lent prophetic dimensions to events that otherwise might have given pause only to the more thoughtful and pious Friends. Two of the strongest critics of wealth, John Woolman and Anthony Benezet, found the ill effects of wealth almost everywhere—in slavery, usury, exorbitant rents, overwork, drunkenness, and cruelty to animals. During war, these ill effects were even more noticable. 41 notes. M. D. Dibert

359. Maros dell'Oro, Angiolo. ECONOMIA QUACCHERA [Quaker economy]. *Econ. e Storia [Italy] 1974 21(4): 462-468.* Examines Quaker religion and ethics as they affect members' attitudes, choices of careers, and probabilities of business success. Lists outstanding Quaker names in the Anglo-Saxon business world in Europe and North America during the 17th and early 18th centuries. Secondary works; 6 notes.
F. Pollaczek

360. May, Dean L. MORMON COOPERATIVES IN PARIS, IDAHO, 1869-1896. *Idaho Yesterdays 1975 19(2): 20-30.* In 1868 the Mormon Church urged its members to establish community cooperatives which would distribute profits and keep business within the church. The settlements around Bear Lake, Idaho, successfully ran community cooperatives for years. Paris had a cooperative store, dairy, tannery, shoe shop, harness shop, shingle mill, tin shop, and tailor shop. Illus., 48 notes.
B. J. Paul

361. May, George S. WILLIAM O. WORTH: ADVENTIST AUTO PIONEER. *Adventist Heritage 1974 1(2): 43-53.* Outlines the career of William O. Worth, Adventist auto manufacturer in Benton Harbor, Michigan, and elsewhere, 1890-1913.

362. McAdams, Donald R. PUBLISHER OF THE GOSPEL: C. H. JONES AND THE PACIFIC PRESS. *Adventist Heritage 1976 3(1): 22-32.* The Pacific Press Publishing Company was founded in Oakland, California, in 1875; Charles Harriman Jones, eventual manager of the house, served the Press during 1879-1923.

363. Miller, Glenn T. BAPTIST BUSINESSMEN IN HISTORICAL PERSPECTIVE. *Baptist Hist. and Heritage 1978 13(1): 55-62.* Baptist attitudes toward business evolved from the theology of English Puritanism. Since the world needs diverse occupations that man might flourish, God called individuals to particular tasks within the social order. No one task is inherently better than any other since each is necessary to the common good. Before the Civil War, Baptists emphasized individual initiative and responsibility in business; since then the emergence of the New South church (represented by Joshua Levering, Isaac Taylor Tichenor and George W. Norton, who brought business techniques into the operation of the Southern Baptist Church), the New Philanthropy (represented by John D. Rockefeller, who endowed the University of Chicago), and the Social Gospel (epitomized by Walter Rauschenbusch and Charles S. Gardner, who stressed the strong sense of responsibility in the traditional ethic over and against the natural tendency to emphasize vocational success as a sign of God's favor) requires adjustments to be made, but the essential, basic theological presuppositions still abide. Covers 1840-1950. 5 notes. H. M. Parker, Jr.

364. Miller, Robert Moats. HARRY EMERSON FOSDICK AND JOHN D. ROCKEFELLER, JR.: THE ORIGINS OF AN ENDURING ASSOCIATION. *Foundations 1978 21(4): 292-304.* Explores the early friendship between America's best known Protestant preacher of the first half of the 20th century, Doctor Harry Emerson Fosdick, and America's wealthiest layman, John D. Rockefeller, Jr. The marriage between religious liberalism and the wealthy layman was fully demonstrated in these two personalities. Religious benevolence served as a form of social control, and liberal as well as conservative laymen sought this control.
H. M. Parker, Jr.

365. Neuchterlein, James A. BRUCE BARTON AND THE BUSINESS ETHOS OF THE 1920'S. *South Atlantic Q. 1977 76(3): 293-308.*

Bruce Barton, a New York City advertising executive, became a household word in the 1920's for his inspirational and theological writings. In his bestseller *The Man Nobody Knows,* Barton equated the business boosterism of the twenties with Christianity. His Christ became a good businessman, building an efficient organization and utilizing catchy advertisements to promote a new personal religion of ethical principles and good fellowship. Monetary gain, personal success, and good works marked both the good Christian and good businessman. Such reformed and naive capitalism provided the foundation for the materialistic New Era and the American Dream of the twenties. Primary and secondary sources; 28 notes. W. L. Olbrich

366. Ogasapian, John. LOWELL AND OLD SAINT ANNE'S: A STUDY IN NINETEENTH-CENTURY INDUSTRIAL-CHURCH RELATIONS. *Hist. Mag. of the Protestant Episcopal Church 1977 46(4): 381-396.* Gives a sociological, economic, and ecclesiastical description of the deteriorating relations of St. Anne's Episcopal parish with the textile industry in Lowell, Massachusetts. The church was at first the only congregation recognized by the mill in a "company" town. However other denominations entered the scene, and relations between the parish and the mill owners dissipated. After years of struggle the congregation finally obtained its corporate independence and control of its property. Much of the struggle between the church and the mill was during the ministry of the Reverend Theodore Edson. Secondary sources, with emphasis on Wilson Waters, *St. Anne's Church, Lowell, Massachusetts;* 20 notes. H. M. Parker, Jr.

367. Rowley, Dennis. NAUVOO: A RIVER TOWN. *Brigham Young U. Studies 1978 18(2): 255-272.* Examines the economic growth of Nauvoo, Illinois, especially the impact of the Mississippi River on its commercial development during 1839-46. While the steamboat era was in progress, the Mormons quickly took advantage of the maritime opportunities to improve their economic position. Whether constructing canals or dams, operating boarding houses for passengers, purchasing steamboats for the river trade, or developing wharves or sawmills, the Mormon leaders sought to improve the commercial position of Nauvoo for the Church's benefit. M. S. Legan

368. Schmandt, Raymond H. SOME FINANCIAL RECORDS OF BISHOP MICHAEL O'CONNOR OF PITTSBURGH. *Western Pennsylvania Hist. Mag. 1979 62(4): 369-376.* Introduces and reprints correspondence, 1843-49, between Mark Anthony Frenaye, financial advisor to Catholic clerics, and Michael O'Connor, first bishop of Pittsburgh.

369. Stortz, Gerald J. ARCHBISHOP LYNCH AND THE TORONTO SAVINGS BANK. *Study Sessions: Can. Catholic Hist. Assoc. [Canada] 1978 45: 5-19.* John Joseph Lynch, the first Roman Catholic archbishop of Toronto, helped set up the Toronto Savings Bank to aid the poor of the city, but was unable to prevent the bank from being used for more secular, profit-oriented aims during the 1870's.

370. Strombeck, Rita. SUCCESS AND THE SWEDISH-AMERICAN IDEOLOGY. *Swedish Pioneer Hist. Q. 1977 28(3): 182-191.* In the America of ca. 1870-1910, the hero was the self-made man who succeeded from humble origins by right moral living and in spite of difficulties. Swedish American journalists and clergymen espoused this doctrine and it became the goal for many Swedish Americans. An example was John A. Johnson, who rose from backwoods cabin to become governor of Minnesota in 1908. Cites articles in Swedish American literature which extol the self-made man doctrine. (Swedish language passages are also translated into English). 12 notes. C. W. Ohrvall

371. Terry, Thomas D. CALIFORNIA GRAPES AND CALIFORNIA MISSIONS. *Agric. Hist. 1975 49(1): 292-293.* The first California wine was made at Franciscan missions in the 18th century. After church lands were secularized, mission vineyards formed the basis for later California wineries. 6 notes. D. E. Bowers

372. Tucker, Barbara M. OUR GOOD METHODISTS: THE CHURCH, THE FACTORY AND THE WORKING CLASS IN ANTE-BELLUM WEBSTER, MASSACHUSETTS. *Maryland Hist. 1977 8(2): 26-37.* Describes the appeal of Methodism to owners and workers in Webster's textile industry. The church provided the "moral foundation of a work effort" which provided owners with a disciplined work force and allowed workers to adjust to industrialism while having their social needs met. Illus., 39 notes. G. O. Gagnon

373. Umetsu, Jun-ichi. PYŪRITAN JISSEN SHISHIN NO KEIZAI-SHI TEKI SEIKAKU [Economic aspects of Puritan life]. *Shakaikeizaishigaku (Socio-Economic Hist.) [Japan] 1977 43(3): 27-46.* Discusses Puritan origins of modern production and exchange, based on Puritan practical tracts from the 17th century.

374. Walker, Jerald C. THE THEOLOGICAL DIMENSION OF ECONOMICS. *Religion in Life 1974 43(1): 22-32.* Questions the purity of objective and scientific economics and describes the theological aspects of economic theory, 1974. S

375. Walker, Ronald W. CRISIS IN ZION: HEBER J. GRANT AND THE PANIC OF 1893. *Arizona and the West 1979 21(3): 257-278.* The Panic of 1893 forced the Utah Mormons to recognize that their longstanding premises of economic independence and isolation were untenable. Their businesses were no more immune from the panic than were non-Mormon businesses. They were forced into the nation's financial mainstream to prevent bankruptcy and ruin and to save the church itself. The panic changed Mormon economics and the church's public image. Influential Mormon businessman Heber J. Grant was prominent in resolving the crisis. 6 illus., 48 notes. D. L. Smith

376. Winter, J. Alan. ELECTIVE AFFINITIES BETWEEN RELIGIOUS BELIEFS AND IDEOLOGIES OF MANAGEMENT IN TWO ERAS. *Am. J. of Sociol. 1974 79(5): 1134-1150.* Weber's concept of 'elective affinity' is used in an examination of the relationships between religious beliefs and ideologies of management in two eras. First, a summary is presented of Weber's thesis that there was an elective affinity between the Protestant ethic and its doctrine of predestination and the ideology of entrepreneurial capitalism with its principles of economic rationality, worldly asceticism, and work as calling. A basis is then shown for an elective affinity between a new Protestant theology stressing a doctrine of the interdependence of men with a loving God and the ideology of managerial capitalism with its principles of human interrelations, worldly humility, and work as satisfaction. Covers the 16th through the 20th centuries. J

377. Zenner, Walter P. and Jarvenpa, Robert. SCOTS IN THE NORTHERN FUR TRADE: A MIDDLEMAN MINORITY PERSPECTIVE. *Ethnic Groups 1980 2(3): 189-210.* Pariah capitalism, as typified by the Jewish and Chinese merchant classes, is often seen in contrast to Weber's Protestant ethic capitalism. Examines a middleman capitalist minority, the Scots, employed by the Hudson's Bay Company of Canada, that shares the ethnic specialization and minority status of pariah capitalism, but the religious, cultural, and business connections of mainstream Protestant capitalism. Table, 7 notes, biblio.

T. W. Smith

4. COMMUNAL MOVEMENTS AND UTOPIAN THOUGHT

378. Arndt, Karl J. R. GEORGE RAPP'S HARMONISTS AND THE BEGINNINGS OF NORWEGIAN MIGRATION TO AMERICA. *Western Pennsylvania Hist. Mag. 1977 60(3): 241-264.* Describes George Rapp's Harmony and New Harmony settlements in Pennsylvania, the immigration of Norwegians, and their letters home to relatives, friends, and interested parties in Norway whom they encouraged to emigrate; 1816-26.

379. Arndt, Karl J. R. LUTHER'S GOLDEN ROSE AT NEW HARMONY, INDIANA. *Concordia Hist. Inst. Q. 1976 49(3): 112-122.* In 1822, in the archway over George Rapp's Harmony Society, a golden rose was carved. Based on one of Luther's early translations of the Book of Micah, the *Güldene Rose* was a symbol of the struggle and strength of the church. Primary sources; 18 notes. W. T. Walker

380. Arndt, Karl J. R. RAPP'S HARMONY SOCIETY AS AN INSTITUTION "CALCULATED TO UNDERMINE AND DESTROY THOSE FUNDAMENTAL PRINCIPLES OF FREE GOVERNMENT, WHICH HAVE CONSPICUOUSLY DISTINGUISHED US FROM ALL THE NATIONS OF THE EARTH." *Western Pennsylvania Hist. Mag. 1980 63(4): 359-366.* Reprints excerpts from George Rapp's Harmony Society's articles of association submitted to the Pennsylvania legislature to request incorporation in 1807; the request was denied.

381. Arndt, Karl J. R. THE STRANGE AND WONDERFUL NEW WORLD OF GEORGE RAPP AND HIS HARMONY SOCIETY. *Western Pennsylvania Hist. Mag. 1974 57(2): 141-166.* Examines the development of religious theory in George Rapp's collective religious settlement, the Harmony Society established in Economy, Pennsylvania. S

382. Bennett, John W. SOCIAL THEORY AND THE SOCIAL ORDER OF THE HUTTERIAN COMMUNITY. *Mennonite Q. Rev. 1977 51(4): 292-307.* An analysis of the social underpinnings of Hutterian society. The cement that holds the society together is belief: the concept that they are living the way Christ meant men to live, whereas the remainder of the world is living in sin. Commitment simply results in controls, not causes. Certainly the Hutterites pay a price for their way: aggression is internalized, later to show up in the forms of stomach trouble and alcoholism. Hutterite society is indeed strict, though change is both possible and continuous, but the internal structure of genuine belief is by far the most significant controlling force. The system has succeeded admirably; Hutterite society is indeed utopian, probably because its members have succeeded in welding together religion and practicality. 3 notes. V. L. Human

383. Bonney, Margaret Atherton. THE SALUBRIA STORY. *Palimpsest 1975 56(2): 34-45.* Salubria, a free thought cooperative community founded in Iowa in 1839 by Abner Kneeland, failed within a few years due to land scarcity, economic adversity, a paucity of free thought advocates, competing townships, and unfavorable topography. Kneeland's controversial religious beliefs, often cited as the major cause of the colony's demise, were of secondary importance; his political activities did bring attention, however, and when combined with religious and economic factors spelled defeat for Salubria. Based on primary and secondary sources; 6 illus., 3 photos. D. W. Johnson

384. Boyer, Paul. A JOYFUL NOYES: REASSESSING AMERICA'S UTOPIAN TRADITION. *Rev. in Am. Hist. 1975 3(1): 25-30.* Review article prompted by Michael Fellman's *The Unbounded Frame: Freedom and Community in Nineteenth Century American Utopianism* (Westport, Conn.: Greenwood Pr., 1973) and Raymond Lee Muncy's *Sex and Marriage in Utopian Communities:19th-Century America* (Bloomington: Indiana U. Pr., 1973).

385. Branson, Branley Allan. THE STRENGTH OF SIMPLICITY. *Américas (Organization of Am. States) 1978 30(8): 38-43.* Discusses the United Society of Believers, or Shakers, and describes the restoration of Pleasant Hill, the largest of the Shaker communities, which was started in Kentucky in 1805.

386. Bromley, David G. and Shupe, Anson D., Jr. THE TNEVNOC CULT. *Sociol. Analysis 1979 40(4): 361-366.* Accompanying the rapid growth of "new religions" in the 1970's has been escalating controversy centering on their methods of socializing new recruits. Examines the Tnevnoc Cult, a communal religious movement that flourished during the 19th century and was embroiled in a similar controversy. Many of the Tnevoc's current socialization practices remain similar to those of the new religions although the Tnevnocs are not now regarded as controversial. By presenting a historical comparison between the Tnevnocs and new religions we demonstrate that the allegedly novel, manipulative socialization practices of the new religions actually are remarkably similar to those employed by the Tnevnocs a century earlier. The reaction of the anti-cult movement to the new religions also has historical parallels which suggest that it is the legitimacy accorded a group rather than its practices which shape public reactions and definitions. Biblio. J

387. Clark, Peter. LEADERSHIP SUCCESSION AMONG THE HUTTERITES. *Can. Rev. of Sociol. and Anthrop. [Canada] 1977 14(3): 294-302.* Forty-two Hutterite colonies were examined in order to determine the degree to which succession to leadership positions departs from a model of complete equality of opportunity. Variation in political mobility patterns within colonies is explained by utilizing a 'demography of opportunity' hypothesis. This hypothesis posits that the degree of inequality of opportunity exhibited by a colony varies directly with the degree to which population growth (growth in the supply of potential position holders) exceeds organizational expansion (expansion in the supply of positions). Covers 1940-76. J

388. Coffey, David M. THE HOPEDALE COMMUNITY. *Hist. J. of Western Massachusetts 1975 4(1): 16-26.* Adin Ballou established Hopedale, a utopian community, (1841) so that moral and religious elements would predominate over family and material considerations. This proved unrealistic. Joint-stock industries were established and by 1846 private investors took control. Antislavery and women's rights were among the causes espoused in the community. E. D. Draper's withdrawal of investment in 1856 ended the community. Based on Heywood's and Ballou's works; 3 illus., 49 notes. S. S. Sprague

389. Cohen, David Steven. THE "ANGEL DANCERS": THE FOLKLORE OF RELIGIOUS COMMUNITARIANISM. *New Jersey Hist. 1977 95(1): 5-20.* Religious sects were associated with American communitarianism. In the 1890's such a sect, known locally as the "Angel Dancers," was established in Woodcliff, New Jersey. Soon after its start, rumors about wild ceremonies, including nude dancing, spread throughout the community. The leaders, Manson T. Huntsman and Jane Howell, and their followers were arrested and tried for keeping a disorderly house, destroying property, and burning Bibles. All but Huntsman and Howell were freed. Deaths and problems over the ownership of their headquarters ended the sect's life. The existence of the "Angel Dancers" demonstrates how rumors affected small religious sects and refutes the supposed compatible relationship between communitarianism and American society. Based on interviews, newspaper articles, and secondary sources; 3 illus., map, 28 notes. E. R. McKinstry

390. Dorfman, Mark H. THE EPHRATA CLOISTER. *Early Am. Life 1979 10(1): 38-41, 64-65.* The Ephrata Cloister in Pennsylvania's Conestoga Valley was a religious commune under the direction of founder Johann Conrad Beissel, Emmanuel Eckerlin, and Beissel once again, ca. 1732-68.

391. Douglas, Paul H. THE MATERIAL CULTURE OF THE HARMONY SOCIETY. *Pennsylvania Folklife 1975 24(3): 2-16.* Uses material culture—specifically, town planning, buildings, and artifacts—to reinterpret social customs and living patterns in Harmony Society, a 19th-century communal society in Harmony and Economy, Pennsylvania and New Harmony, Indiana. S

392. Easton, Carol. A TOUCH OF INNOCENCE. *Westways 1976 68(12): 27-29, 60.* Discusses the life of German American Hutterites in agricultural cooperatives in northwestern states in the 20th century, emphasizing their pacifism and education.

393. Elmen, Paul. BISHOP HILL: UTOPIA ON THE PRAIRIE. *Chicago Hist. 1976 5(1): 45-52.* Chronicles the progress of a group of Swedish immigrants known as Janssonists, who established a religious utopian colony in Bishop Hill, Illinois, 1846-60.

394. Emlen, Robert P. THE HARD CHOICES OF BROTHER JOHN CUMINGS. *Hist. New Hampshire 1979 34(1): 54-65.* John Cumings (1829-1911) had joined the Shaker community at Enfield, New Hampshire, with his family in 1844. His father and brother left the Shakers in the 1860's. Although sorely tempted to join them, John finally decided, in the 1870's, to stay with the Shakers, who came to rely on his mechanical skills. He held the Enfield community together until his death in 1911. In 1923 the surviving Enfield Shakers moved to Canterbury. Based on the Cumings family papers, and other primary and secondary sources. 3 illus., 23 notes. D. F. Chard

395. Ferranti, Frank T. A SHAKER EXPERIENCE. *New England Social Studies Bull. 1974-75 32(2): 17-23.* Describes the Shaker community at Sabbathday Lake, Maine. S

396. Fine, Howard D. THE KORESHAN UNITY: THE CHICAGO YEARS OF A UTOPIAN COMMUNITY. *J. of the Illinois State Hist. Soc. 1975 68(3): 213-227.* Founded in New York State in 1880 and located in Chicago during 1886-1903, the Koreshan Unity still remains in existence in Estero, Florida. It was established as a communistic millennial community by Cyrus Read Teed who experienced a revelation impelling him to create an organization dedicated to the union of religion and science to eliminate suffering and death. Its membership was largely composed of women bound to observe the celibate rules of the group. Teed encountered various obstacles in the early years of the organization, including suits brought against him for alienation of affections by irate husbands of female members. N. Lederer

397. Fish, John O. THE CHRISTIAN COMMONWEALTH COLONY: A GEORGIA EXPERIMENT, 1896-1900. *Georgia Hist. Q. 1973 57(2): 213-226.* Merging two similar out-of-state groups, the Christian Commonwealth Colony was established near Columbus, Georgia, in 1896. It was an experiment by extremist social gospel progressives who asserted that society must be restructured along communistic lines to be truly Christian. The colony collapsed in 1900 because it was not economically viable. 49 notes. D. L. Smith

398. Fogarty, Robert S. ONEIDA: A UTOPIAN SEARCH FOR RELIGIOUS SECURITY. *Labor Hist. 1973 14(2): 202-227.* Examines the origins, conversion factors, and occupations of the original members of the Oneida Community. Most became leaders in the community. The main reasons for joining were related to seeking a religious security; John Humphrey Noyes' writings were an important factor. The community often had to adapt to economic realities, but an essential unity and a puritanical tenacity aided its survival. Covers 1837-86. Based on the *Family Register* of Oneida and on annual inventories; 97 notes. L. L. Athey

399. Francis, Richard. THE IDEOLOGY OF BROOK FARM. *Studies in the Am. Renaissance 1977: 1-48.* Brook Farm was established on the philosophy and principles of Transcendentalism, but, during its brief history, it imbued the main tenets of Fourierism, both through the efforts and beliefs of leading members of the Farm community, and through association with the principal American protégés of François Fourier (1772-1837). Largely through the writings of Albert Brisbane (1809-90), the Transcendentalist ideology obtained an account of individual identity and its relationship to society. William Henry Channing (1810-84), another leading Fourierist, provided the members of Brook Farm with a moral spirit, a sense of free will, and consequently, purposiveness. Based on personal letters, memoirs and notebooks of Farm members and magazine articles; 2 plates, 145 notes. S. Baatz

400. Friedland, Edward I. UTOPIA & THE SCIENCE OF THE POSSIBLE. *Polity 1974 7(1): 105-119.* Reviews two collections of essays on utopian themes: *Utopias: Social Ideals and Communal Experiments,* (Boston: Holbrook Pr., 1971) edited by Peyton Richter; and *Utopia* (New York: Atherton Pr., 1971), edited by George Kateb. Richter "offers a broad sampling of the historical and intellectual spectrum on utopian thought including descriptive material on experimental communities in 19th-century America such as Oneida, Brook Farm, New Harmony, Icaria, and Fruitlands. Includes philosophical and descriptive material and supplies an introductory essay and good bibliographic suggestions. Kateb's focus is upon the present state of utopian thought. Each of the nine essays in his volume is a product of the last two decades." 8 notes. D. D. Cameron

401. Friesen, Gerhard K. AN ADDITIONAL SOURCE ON THE HARMONY SOCIETY OF ECONOMY, PENNSYLVANIA. *Western Pennsylvania Hist. Mag. 1978 61(4): 301-314.* Excerpts from a German book entitled *Scenes of Life in the United States of America and Texas,* collected by Friedrich Wilhelm von Wrede, describing the Harmony Society of Economy, Pennsylvania, based on von Wrede's experiences there on a visit in 1842.

402. Gizycki, Horst von. ALTERNATIVE LEBENSFORMEN (3): DIE CHRISTLICHE KOMMUNITÄT DER KOINONIA-PARTNER IN GEORGIA [Alternative life styles (3): the Christian community of the Koinonia Partners in Georgia]. *Frankfurter Hefte [West Germany] 1976 31(3): 35-42.* Discusses the philosophy and history of Koinonia Farm, a Christian commune founded in Georgia in 1942 by Clarence Jordan; covers 1942-60's.

403. Gizycki, Horst von. ALTERNATIVE LEBENSFORMEN [Alternative life-styles]. *Frankfurter Hefte [West Germany] 1975 30(10): 45-54.* In his search for alternative life-styles, the author visited the Hutterites of Canada and South Dakota, a religious, communalistic group formed in central Europe centuries ago, which fled persecution by Habsburgs and Tsars, coming to the new world during 1874-79.

404. Grant, H. Roger, ed. THE AMANA SOCIETY OF IOWA: TWO VIEWS. *Ann. of Iowa 1975 43(1): 1-23.* Contains two accounts of the Amana Society of Iowa. The first, written by Bertha Horak Shambaugh, appeared in an Iowa state publication in 1901. It offers a view of Amana based on personal observation and research. Topics discussed include the agriculture, manufacturing, housing, education, religion, and government of the Society. The other article, written in 1934 by Barthinius L. Wick, describes the Amana Society's demise in 1932 as a communal religious experiment. Editor's introduction, photos, 26 notes. P. L. Petersen

405. Grant, H. Roger. THE SOCIETY OF BETHEL: A VISITOR'S ACCOUNT. *Missouri Hist. Rev. 1974 68(2): 223-231.* Briefly outlines the background of the Society of Bethel, a German American religious communal experiment in Missouri and Oregon founded by William Keil. Presents a letter of 1852 from Wilhelm Weitling to A. J. McDonald, which gives a visitor's report of the life within the society. Covers 1844-83. Primary and secondary sources; 2 illus., 2 photos, 18 notes. N. J. Street

406. Griffin, Clifford S. MAKING NOYES. *Rev. in Am. Hist. 1977 5(4): 518-523.* Review article prompted by Robert David Thomas's *The Man Who Would Be Perfect: John Humphrey Noyes and the Utopian Impulse* (Philadelphia: U. of Pennsylvania Pr., 1977) a biography of John Humphrey Noyes (1811-86), founder of the Oneida Community.

407. Halliday, E. M. OUR FOREFATHERS IN HOT PURSUIT OF THE GOOD LIFE. *Horizon 1973 15(4): 110-115.* Communal societies in 19th-century America. S

408. Ham, F. Gerald. THE PROPHET AND THE MUMMYJUMS: ISAAC BULLARD AND THE VERMONT PILGRIMS OF 1817.

Wisconsin Mag. of Hist. 1973 56(4): 290-299. The Vermont Pilgrims ("Mummyjums") and their prophet Isaac Bullard imbibed their religious tenets from evangelical revivalism, millennialism, and perfectionism which characterized the religious ferment in New England during the early 19th century. Bullard's faith was distinguished by extreme primitivism and the unquestioned authority of his revelations. Much of the story deals with the hardships experienced by this small band of "Mummyjums" and their leader on their journey from New England through New York, Ohio, and Missouri into the Arkansas Territory in search of the Promised Land. During these wanderings Bullard's experiment disintegrated amidst desertions and deaths. 48 notes. N. C. Burckel

409. Heath, Alden R. APOSTLE IN ZION. *J. of the Illinois State Hist. Soc. 1977 70(2): 98-113.* John Alexander Dowie (1847-1907), Scottish evangelist and founder of the Divine Healing Association, came to the United States from Australia in 1888 and established in 1899 a new communitarian settlement based on strict prohibitions against alcohol, tobacco, labor unions, and doctors. His Christian Catholic Church's experiment at Zion, Illinois, drew thousands of converts, but his own megalomania caused followers to ultimately reject his leadership of that community. 6 illus., map, 52 notes. J/S

410. Jentsch, Theodore W. EDUCATION, OCCUPATION, AND ECONOMICS AMONG OLD ORDER MENNONITES OF THE EAST PENN VALLEY. *Pennsylvania Folklife 1975 24(3): 24-35.* Describes educational, occupational, and economic conditions in an Old Order Mennonite commune (1949-75) in the East Penn Valley of Pennsylvania. S

411. Jones, Arnita Ament. FROM UTOPIA TO REFORM. *Hist. Today [Great Britain] 1976 26(6): 393-401.* Discusses the work of Frances Wright and Robert Dale Owen in reform movements and utopias, includes their philosophy on religion, social order, marriage, politics, and communal living, 1826-32.

412. Kerstan, Reinhold J. THE HUTTERITES: A RADICAL CHRISTIAN ALTERNATIVE. *Fides et Hist. 1973 5(1-2): 62-67.* The Hutterite sect was founded in 1528 in Moravia. They have maintained an agricultural communal form of society and culture. Caught often in the European wars at grave threat to their existence, they migrated to Canada and the United States in the 1870's. They are highly innovative and invariably successful farmers, but cling tenaciously to their original cultural and social patterns. Based on secondary sources; 6 notes. R. Butchart

413. Kirchmann, George. UNSETTLED UTOPIAS: THE NORTH AMERICAN PHALANX AND THE RARITAN BAY UNION. *New Jersey Hist. 1979 97(1): 25-36.* The North American Phalanx, established near Red Bank, New Jersey, in 1843, was one of many communes formed in the United States during the 1840's. By 1848 this community was prosperous financially, operated a successful school, and recorded an absence of personal jealousies and bitterness. Marcus Spring had by that year become the Phalanx's largest stockholder. Through the power that went along with his holdings he tried to influence the community's religious practices. Debates over this and other matters created two factions. In 1852 Spring bought land outside Perth Amboy, New Jersey, persuaded some of the Phalanx's members to leave, and set up the Raritan Bay Union. The North American Phalanx existed until 1854, when a fire destroyed the commune. The Raritan Bay Union was finally turned into the Eagleswood Military Academy in 1859. It closed in 1867. Based on North American Phalanx records and on secondary sources; 5 illus., 29 notes. E. R. McKinstry

414. Klassen, Henry C. THE MENNONITES OF THE NAMAKA FARM. *Mennonite Life 1975 30(4): 8-14.* Describes farming on the Namaka Farm, a 13,000-acre communal Mennonite settlement east of Calgary, 1920's-40's.

415. McCormick, P. L. THE DOUKHOBORS IN 1904. *Saskatchewan Hist. [Canada] 1978 31(1): 12-19.* The year 1904 was pivotal in the early history of the Doukhobors in Canada. The earliest groups came from three different backgrounds and had varying commitments to communal life. They also lacked leadership. The arrival of Peter Verigin in the Yorkton colonies in December 1902 solved the leadership problem and brought a vigorous move to reimpose communalism. A major objective in this, self-sufficiency, was nearly achieved in 1904. The same year, however, saw the arrival of the railway in the area of some of the settlements and the isolation the group had sought was gone forever. Photo, map, 35 notes. C. Held

416. Norton, John E., ed. "FOR IT FLOWS WITH MILK AND HONEY"; TWO IMMIGRANT LETTERS ABOUT BISHOP HILL. *Swedish Pioneer Hist. Q. 1973 24(3): 163-179.* Translates letters by Anders Andersson and Anders Larsson about the colony of Bishop Hill in 1847, which were published in *Aftonbladt.* Andersson, a devoted Janssonist, reported that all arrived in good health. Larsson reported that the Janssonists were laying out their new city, including communal mills, shops, and farms. Erik Jansson was accepted as the Prophet and Bishop Hill as the new spiritual Israel. Illus., notes. K. J. Puffer

417. Olin, Spencer C., Jr. BIBLE COMMUNISM AND THE ORIGINS OF ORANGE COUNTY. *California History 1979 58(3): 220-233.* Describes the establishment of an agricultural colony in what is now Orange County, California, by the Townerites, a dissident group of Oneida colony members, in 1881. Founded in New York in 1848 by John Humphrey Noyes, the Oneida Community achieved notoriety for its espousal of economic communism, the idea of complex marriage, and other radical social practices. The Townerites, led by James W. Towner, purchased property in the Santa Ana area and established an offshoot of the original colony. The Townerites were important in founding Orange County in 1889 and in the region's political, religious, and social life. Argues that the colony merits mention among those middle-class groups who founded Pasadena and Anaheim as expressions of the desire to create economically diversified and culturally and religiously oriented communities. Primary and secondary sources; illus., photos, 31 notes. A. Hoffman

418. Olin, Spencer C., Jr. THE ONEIDA COMMUNITY AND THE INSTABILITY OF CHARISMATIC AUTHORITY. *J. of Am. Hist. 1980 67(2): 285-300.* Provides a new explanation for the breakup of the Oneida Community in central New York in 1881, in terms of the social theory of Max Weber. A dispute over a successor to John Humphrey Noyes in 1875 led to a challenge of the whole concept of charismatic authority, basis for the community's political order. In Weberian terms the contest for power between Noyes and the Townerites became a struggle between charismatic authority and legal-rational authority, and led to the community's demise. Based partly on correspondence, newspaper articles, and other primary sources; 51 notes. T. P. Linkfield

419. Paterwick, Stephen. THE EFFECT OF THE CIVIL WAR ON SHAKER SOCIETIES. *Hist. J. of Western Massachusetts 1973 2(1): 6-26.* The Civil War represented a watershed in Shaker history, separating a period of growth from one of decline. The Kentucky settlements suffered from plunder, arson, and the strenuous efforts to feed, clothe, and nurse soldiers on both sides. All settlements were faced with trade dislocation; and the sale of seeds, fruits, preserves, and livestock languished. The mood of the postwar years was one of crass materialism, and the Shaker population declined. Based on secondary sources; 2 illus., 19 notes. S. S. Sprague

420. Pitzer, Donald E. THE HARMONIST HERITAGE OF THREE TOWNS. *Hist. Preservation 1977 29(4): 4-10.* Discusses the history, architecture, and historic preservation efforts of three communally oriented towns built by the followers of Lutheran dissenter (Johann) George Rapp (1757-1847), who came to the United States from Württemberg. Harmony, Pennsylvania (built 1804), New Harmony, Indiana (1814), and Economy (now Ambridge), Pennsylvania (1825), all face the problem of the restorations and interpretation of an entire town rather than a single building. 6 photos. R. M. Frame, III

421. Pitzer, Donald E. and Elliott, Josephine M. NEW HARMONY'S FIRST UTOPIANS, 1814-1824. *Indiana Mag. of Hist. 1979 75(3): 225-300.* Discusses the communal utopian society of New Harmony, Indiana. Covers the religious mystical basis upon which the community was founded, the leadership qualities of founder George Rapp, other prominent persons, policies and procedures, art, architecture, and artifacts, eminent controversies, schisms, and eventual decline. Notes that the religion engendered at New Harmony continued for another century,

and that the influence of its members extended far beyond the boundaries of the small community. 53 photos, 31 notes. V. L. Human

422. Prieur, Vincent. DE NEW HARMONY À TWIN OAKS: A PROPOS DE QUELQUES RÉCURRENCES DANS L'HISTOIRE DES MOUVEMENTS COMMUNAUTAIRES AMÉRICAINS [From New Harmony to Twin Oaks: the new American communes and their roots in history]. *Mouvement Social [France] 1976 (94): 31-57.* We all know that new American communities emerged from protest movements of the sixties. However, this movement has its roots deep in the 19th century, and has often been neglected. This is unfortunate, since such an approach would lead us to discover the sheer originality of the communitarian utopia of the United States, which can be grossly described as a slow process of Americanization. The purpose of this article is not to discover the depth and to point out the limits of this approach, but to emphasize two main examples in this process as an idea of what is done in a more thoroughgoing research. J

423. Redekop, Calvin. RELIGIOUS INTENTIONAL COMMUNITIES. *Indiana Social Studies Q. 1976 29(1): 52-65.* Discusses sociological and cultural factors in the development of Christian communes and utopias in the United States from 1790-1970.

424. Richling, Barnett. THE AMANA SOCIETY: A HISTORY OF CHANGE. *Palimpsest 1977 58(2): 34-47.* Although the Iowa Amana colonies seem to represent stability in a changing world, they have gradually replaced their communal religious orientation with more secular values. More than 50 years before communalism formally ended in 1932, internal conflicts has begun to weaken the Amana Society. Among factors contributing to its spiritual decline were the deaths of the last Inspirationist prophets, a steady increase in wealth and population, tourism, the automobile, World War I, conversions to Christian Science, and the Great Depression. Primary and secondary sources; 4 illus., 5 photos, note on sources. D. W. Johnson

425. Ritter, Christine C. LIFE IN EARLY AMERICA: FATHER RAPP AND THE HARMONY SOCIETY. *Early Am. Life 1978 9(2): 40-43, 71-72.* Under the leadership of George Rapp (1757-1847), German Protestant immigrants formed the Harmony Society in 1804 in Pennsylvania, and later in Indiana and then Pennsylvania again.

426. Rodgers, James. THE RELIGIOUS ORIGINS OF AMERICAN RADICALISM AND THE IDEOLOGICAL ROOTS OF INTENTIONAL COMMUNITIES. *Rev. Française d'Etudes Américaines [France] 1976 (2): 23-29.* Explores American utopian intentional communities by examining the dissenting and religious character of American radicalism, especially as set forth in the Declaration of Independence, 1730's-1890's.

427. Rollins, Richard M. ADIN BALLOU AND THE PERFECTIONIST'S DILEMMA. *J. of Church and State 1975 17(3): 459-476.* Discusses the religious attitudes of utopian socialist Adin Ballou, 1830-42, including his establishment of the Hopedale Community in Milford, Massachusetts.

428. Schelbert, Leo. DIE STIMME EINES EINSAMEN IN ZION. EIN UNBEKANNTER BRIEF VON BRUDER JAEBEZ AUS EPHRATA, PENNSYLVANIEN, AUS DEM JAHRE 1743 [The voice of one of the solitary of Zion: an unknown letter of Brother Jabez from Ephrata, Pennsylvania, 1743]. *Zeitschrift für Kirchengeschichte [West Germany] 1974 85(1): 77-92.* Brother Jabez (Johan Peter Müller, 1709-96), abbot of the radical pietist (Seventh-Day Baptist) commune at Ephrata, Pennsylvania, wrote to the pietist preacher Jerome Annoni (1697-1770) in Basel, Switzerland describing living conditions in his community.

429. Schwieder, Dorothy A. FRONTIER BRETHREN. *Montana 1978 28(1): 2-15.* Hutterites found in the American West land and isolation, which persecution as European Anabaptists had denied them during the 16th-19th centuries. Communal colonies were first established during 1874-77 near Yankton, South Dakota, spreading during the next century to North Dakota, Montana, Washington, Alberta, Saskatchewan, and Manitoba. Training and education in each colony perpetuated traditions, strengthened communal goals, and reinforced male/female roles in adult life. Colonies are led by an elected minister and a council of 5 to 7 men. When the population reaches 130, a colony seeks to establish a new unit. Intercolonial marriages and religious traditions strengthen group ties. Hutterites were not a product of the American frontier, nor were they shaped by it. Thus Frederick Jackson Turner's frontier thesis and the Great Plains hypothesis of Walter Prescott Webb do not apply to the Hutterite colonies' experiences. Accompanying photographs by Kyrn Taconis are central to the article. Based on secondary sources and author's M.A. thesis; 12 illus., map, biblio. R. C. Myers

430. Sweetland, James H. FEDERAL SOURCES FOR THE STUDY OF COLLECTIVE COMMUNITIES. *Government Publ. Rev. 1980 7A(2): 129-138.* Identifies federal publications primarily from the Labor Department and the Library of Congress on collectivist and communitarian movements in the West, 1830's-1930's.

431. Thomas, Robert David. JOHN HUMPHREY NOYES AND THE ONEIDA COMMUNITY: A 19TH-CENTURY AMERICAN FATHER AND HIS FAMILY. *Psychohistory Rev. 1977-78 6(2-3): 68-87.* Describes the attempts of John Humphrey Noyes, a major utopian reformer, to create a utopian community modeled on the family and Perfectionist religious ideology at the Oneida Community in New York (1848-80). Noyes tried to create a perfect world of inner and outer harmony by regulating the sex, love, marriage, and procreative habits of his community. Order in the community was based on passivity, dependence, and familial submission to Noyes, and through him to God. Based on Noyes's writings and secondary works; 89 notes. J. B. Street

432. Thomas, Samuel W. and Young, Mary Lawrence. THE DEVELOPMENT OF SHAKERTOWN AT PLEASANT HILL, KENTUCKY. *Filson Club Hist. Q. 1975 49(3): 231-255.* Traces the history of the Shaker community at Pleasant Hill, Kentucky. Taking advantage of the favorable climate of opinion created by the Great Revival, three Shaker missionaries settled in Kentucky in 1805 and began to convert some of the native population. Their efforts were successful and by the 1830's the community numbered 500. Describes the buildings constructed at Pleasant Hill and several contemporary accounts of Shaker life. Death, destruction brought by the Civil War, and the materialism of the Gilded Age caused a decline in the community. By 1910 creditors had taken control of the Shaker land and the group was forced to disband. Documentation comes from manuscripts at Case Western Reserve University and Shaker collections in Kentucky; 114 notes. G. B. McKinney

433. Weeks, Robert P. A UTOPIAN KINGDOM IN THE AMERICAN GRAIN. *Wisconsin Mag. of Hist. 1977 61(1): 2-20.* Recounts the bizarre story of James Jesse Strang's establishment of successive utopian communities at Voree, near Burlington, Wisconsin, and then at Beaver Island in northern Lake Michigan in the 1850's. Sees this disciple of Joseph Smith, founder of the Mormon Church, in the context of four elements of the national experience: "the experimental spirit of the Founding Fathers, the utopianism of various nineteenth-century sects and socialist groups, the wild enthusiasm of American revivalism, and certain central features of Mormonism." 7 illus., 29 notes. N. C. Burckel

434. Williams, Richard L. THE SHAKERS, NOW ONLY 12, OBSERVE THEIR 200TH YEAR. *Smithsonian 1974 5(6): 40-49.* The Shakers, "determined in the face of intolerance, sternly hewing to vows of chastity built rich and austere farm communities designed to last." Their principles were to be expressed in celibate life, open confession of sin, non-resistance, community of goods, and universal brotherhood. The two surviving communities, at Canterbury and at Sabbathday Lake, are described; both outposts contain museums. Illus. E. P. Stickney

435. Wilson, J. Donald. "NEVER BELIEVE WHAT YOU HAVE NEVER DOUBTED": MATTI KURIKKA'S DREAM FOR A NEW WORLD UTOPIA. *Turun Hist. Arkisto [Finland] 1980 34: 216-240.* A biography of the Finnish utopian socialist Matti Kurikka (1863-1915), who founded utopian communities in Australia, 1899, and Canada, 1900-04. Kurikka was a Finnish cultural nationalist, a theosophist, and an advocate of free love. These attitudes brought him into conflict with his own followers as well as with orthodox Marxists. Based on Kurikka's letters in a private collection in Finland; 96 notes. R. G. Selleck

436. Winchester, Alice. SHAKERTOWN AT PLEASANT HILL. *Hist. Preservation 1977 29(4): 13-20.* Discusses efforts to preserve Shakertown, Pleasant Hill, Kentucky. The commune was founded in 1805 by missionaries from New Lebanon, New York, and formally dissolved in 1910. Preservation efforts have been active since 1960 and include adaptive use of some of the 27 surviving buildings. 12 photos.

5. ECUMENISM AND INTERGROUP RELATIONS

Ecumenism: Seeking Unity

437. Ames, John T. CUMBERLAND LIBERALS AND THE UNION OF 1906. *J. of Presbyterian Hist. 1974 52(1): 3-18.* In 1906 members of the Cumberland Presbyterian Church (which grew out of an 1800 revival in Logan County, Kentucky) merged with the Presbyterian Church, U.S.A.

438. Armentrout, Don S. LUTHERAN-EPISCOPAL CONVERSATIONS IN THE NINETEENTH CENTURY. *Hist. Mag. of the Protestant Episcopal Church 1975 44(2): 167-187.* While two conversations between Lutherans and Episcopalians are currently taking place, such dialogues are not new. Article delineates the history and results of conversations of the American Protestant Episcopal Church and Lutheran United Synod of the South during 1886-88. The possibilities of any organic union broke down over the matter of the historic episcopacy, in addition to lesser causes. Draws heavily upon contemporary Lutheran journals; 77 notes. H. M. Parker, Jr.

439. Arndt, Karl J. R. MISSOURI AND THE BAD BOLL, 1948. *Concordia Hist. Inst. Q. 1979 52(1): 2-31.* Discussions held between American and German synodic leaders of the Lutheran Church at the Bad Boll Conferences, 1948, were sessions intended to repair torn church affiliations and provide a positive note in the gloom of post-World War II Germany.

440. Bollinger, Heil D. A NEW DIMENSION OF THE STUDENT CHRISTIAN MOVEMENT. *J. of Ecumenical Studies 1979 16(1): 169-174.* The Student Christian Movement has its roots in the 19th century. Inspired by earlier leaders such as John R. Mott, Bishop James K. Matthews, and R. H. Edwin Espy, the movement has pursued its aims of evangelism and social justice. The movement continues to crusade for ecumenism and cultural and social change through nonviolence. 6 notes. S

441. Carmody, John T. THE DEVELOPMENT OF ROBERT MCAFEE BROWN'S ECUMENICAL THOUGHT. *Religion in Life 1974 43(3): 283-293.* Covers 1920-74.

442. Clifford, N. K. THE INTERPRETERS OF THE UNITED CHURCH OF CANADA. *Church Hist. 1977 46(2): 203-214.* Discusses the historiography of the church union movement and the United Church of Canada. Notes the unionists' and dissidents' differences and explains the union movement and its opposition in terms of their responses to religious and social change. Arthur S. Morton laid the foundations for the environmentalist interpretation. C. E. Silcox modified the environmentalists' interpretations, and set the stage for revisionist interpretations. John W. Grant saw the implications of this shift in relation to United Church of Canada history. His concern with consensus and the church's impact on Canadian culture not only marked a transition from environmentalism to consensus but also reflected a shift in emphasis from external to internal factors. Covers 1920-76. 24 notes. M. D. Dibert

443. Clifford, N. K. THE ORIGINS OF THE CHURCH UNION CONTROVERSY. *J. of the Can. Church Hist. Soc. 1976 18(2-3): 34-52.* The key figure of William Patrick in the Presbyterian Church Union controversy has heretofore been neglected. Writers on church union have not emphasized his role, because Patrick was not a Canadian. A Scottish liberal, Patrick rose quickly to a position of leadership in the Presbyterian Church and in 1902 daringly proposed organic union to the Methodist General Conference. This naturally engendered great controversy in the Presbyterian ranks, but Patrick never faltered, believing union was divinely ordained. As the first liberal in a place of authority in the Presbyterian Church and as a newcomer to Canada, Patrick was in a good position to further the cause of union, yet his ignorance of the special conditions of the Canadian situation and his inability to develop many social ties helped to frustrate efforts at union and caused great polarization within the Canadian Presbyterian Church. Based on printed and unprinted primary sources; 45 notes. J. A. Kicklighter

444. DelPino, Julius E. BLACKS IN THE UNITED METHODIST CHURCH FROM ITS BEGINNING TO 1968. *Methodist Hist. 1980 19(1): 3-20.* Traces the experiences of blacks within the Methodist Church from 1769 to 1968. From 1794 to 1870 a number of separate black denominations started; they continue until today. Those who remained within the Methodist Episcopal Church and the Methodist Episcopal Church, South were racially and organizationally divided from the white churches until 1939. At that time a Central Jurisdiction was provided to include all black conferences. This was eliminated by 1968 when the blacks were merged into the white jurisdictions. Map, 38 notes. H. L. Calkin

445. Donald, James M. BISHOP HOPKINS AND THE REUNIFICATION OF THE CHURCH. *Hist. Mag. of the Protestant Episcopal Church 1978 47(1): 73-91.* Bishop John Henry Hopkins of Vermont was the presiding bishop when the General Convention of the Episcopal Church met in Philadelphia in 1865, just a few months after the Civil War. Largely through his personal magnanimity, Hopkins was able to reunite the Episcopal Church in America, which the war had divided, because he recognized that the division had been political and not schismatic. He had supported slavery—one of the few northern Episcopalians to do so—and during the war had carried on what correspondence he could with the southern bishops. Throughout the war as the Presiding Bishop he had continued to call the roll of the dioceses and bishops which included the southern ones. While he opposed the right to secede, he kept political issues out of church affairs. Thus he was the most important figure in maintaining the integrity of the Episcopal Church throughout the war and in bringing about the subsequent reunification in 1865. Based on Hopkin's writings and secondary sources; 90 notes, biblio. H. M. Parker, Jr.

446. Dyck, Cornelius J. and Kreider, Robert. MENNONITE WORLD CONFERENCES IN REVIEW: A PHOTOGRAPHIC ESSAY. *Mennonite Life 1978 33(2): 4-23.* The Mennonite World Conference formed in response to a plea for unity. In 1925 the First World Conference, held in Switzerland under the leadership of Christian Neff (d. 1946), established an office, a treasury, and a registry of churches. The second conference in Danzig, 1930, concentrated on resettlement problems of immigrants. The prime concern of the third conference in Amsterdam, 1936, was Russian Mennonite refugees. Attendance increased at the next six conferences, which had spiritual themes. 48 photos. B. Burnett

447. Frost, Harlan M. THE COUNCIL OF CHURCHES: THE SANDERSON YEARS OF STRUGGLE AND RECOVERY, 1937-1942. *Niagara Frontier 1974 21(3): 59-71.* Chronicles the years 1937-42 in the Council of Churches of Buffalo and Erie County during which time Ross W. Sanderson was the head of the Council.

448. Gilpin, W. Clark. ISSUES RELEVANT TO UNION IN THE HISTORY OF THE CHRISTIAN CHURCH (DISCIPLES OF CHRIST). *Encounter 1980 41(1): 15-23.* Recounts the shifting views of the Disciples of Christ concerning Christian unity and their efforts to unite Christian churches since their founding in 1832; covers 19th-20th centuries.

449. Gunn-Walberg, Kenneth W. THE CHURCH UNION MOVEMENT AND WESTERN CANADA: A STUDY OF THE INFLUENCE OF LIBERALISM AND THE SOCIAL GOSPEL IN THE BIRTH OF THE UNITED CHURCH OF CANADA. *Kyrkohistorisk Årsskrift [Sweden] 1977 77: 156-159.* Discusses the demise of denominationalism in Manitoba, starting in the 1870's, and the formation of the United Church of Canada in 1925. 6 notes.

450. Hargroves, V. Carney. THE PHENOMENON OF THE BAPTIST WORLD ALLIANCE. *Foundations 1974 17(1): 4-7.* Provides an

introduction to a series of articles on the Baptist World Alliance and comments on its international activities and charitable work since 1945.

451. Henderlite, Rachel. PRESBYTERIAN ECUMENICITY: A HERITAGE AND AN OPPORTUNITY. *J. of Presbyterian Hist. 1979 57(2): 87-92, 162-170.* Traces the ecumenical heritage of Presbyterian/Reformed bodies from the days of John Calvin and his efforts to unite the Reformers through contemporary efforts at church union. The historical concept of church unity is very close to the Reformed doctrine that the Church of Jesus Christ is one Catholic Church existing in time and space. As heirs of the Reformation, Presbyterians are under some compulsion to exert their influence to make the unity and catholicity of the church presently visible in those spots where they are engaged in being the church. Discusses contemporary efforts of the Presbyterian Church toward greater unity as well as some of the major current barriers to unity. Secondary sources; 39 notes.
H. M. Parker, Jr.

452. Hinson, E. Glenn. EXPANSIVE CATHOLICISM: ECUMENICAL PERCEPTIONS OF THOMAS MERTON. *Religion in Life 1979 48(1): 63-76.* Discusses Thomas Merton's ecumenism as an outgrowth of his maturing Catholicism and his experiences within the monastic tradition during 1949-68.

453. Hoeveler, J. David, Jr. EVANGELICAL ECUMENISM: JAMES MC COSH AND THE INTELLECTUAL ORIGINS OF THE WORLD ALLIANCE OF REFORMED CHURCHES. *J. of Presbyterian Hist. 1977 55(1): 36-56.* The work of James McCosh (1811-94) for the World Alliance of Reformed Churches (WARC) was a response to the intellectual and cultural challenges that critically confronted western culture in general and the Christian community in particular. The challenge derived from German philosophy. The immense implications of that development, and the solution, lay largely in the counter-cultural thrust of the United States. Out of this conflict, and indeed with much cultural exchange among the nations and the churches, McCosh believed there might emerge a rejuvenated international Protestantism. The WARC would secure its usefulness by linking evangelical religion to philosophical truth. Based largely on McCosh's writings; 2 illus., 55 notes.
H. M. Parker, Jr.

454. Jeter, Joseph R., Jr. THE CHRISTIAN UNITY FOUNDATION. *Hist. Mag. of the Protestant Episcopal Church 1975 44(4): 451-471.* The Christian Unity Foundation was a voluntary and unofficial church organization founded in 1910 by a group of Episcopal bishops, clergy, and laymen, to honor the memory of William Reed Huntington and to promote Christian unity throughout the world through research and conferences. Details the early contributions of Huntington and Rockland Tyng Homans to unity. Efforts to raise sufficient endowment for the Foundation were fruitless. However, several conferences regarding possible union were held with representatives from other churches in the United States. The persistent block to unity was the emphasis placed on the Historic Episcopacy. Lack of funds proved the major stumbling block to its continuance, and the Foundation finally went under in 1942. Based almost wholly on the Homans Papers, Union Theological Seminary, New York; 54 notes.
H. M. Parker, Jr.

455. Jordan, Philip D. COOPERATION WITHOUT INCORPORATION—AMERICA AND THE PRESBYTERIAN ALLIANCE, 1870-1880. *J. of Presbyterian Hist. 1977 55(1): 13-35.* Discusses the Alliance of the Reformed Churches Holding the Presbyterian System which convened its first General Council at Edinburgh in 1877. Although its roots are international, American Churches and leaders contributed to the Alliance. Emphasizes the 1880 Philadelphia meeting and the difficulties raised by the Cumberland Presbyterian Church's efforts to gain admission to the Alliance. Based largely on Alliance proceedings and publications; 2 photos, 45 notes.
H. M. Parker, Jr.

456. Jordan, Philip D. THE EVANGELICAL ALLIANCE AND AMERICAN PRESBYTERIANS, 1867-1873. *J. of Presbyterian Hist. 1973 51(3): 309-326.*

457. Krebs, Sylvia. FUNERAL MEATS AND SECOND MARRIAGES: ALABAMA CHURCHES IN THE PRESIDENTIAL RECONSTRUCTION PERIOD. *Alabama Hist. Q. 1975 37(3): 206-216.* The division in the churches continued following the Civil War, and unification did not occur as some expected, except with the Episcopalians. The problems of the churches were many, but mostly economic, social, and morale-oriented. The factors causing a continuation of division are discussed, as well as the reasons for Episcopal reunion. 35 notes.
E. E. Eminhizer

458. Krummel, John W. THE UNION SPIRIT IN JAPAN IN THE 1880'S. *Methodist Hist. 1978 16(3): 152-168.* The Methodist Protestant Church founded its mission in Yokohama in 1880; it was a blend of denominational pride and inter-denominational cooperation. Frederick C. Klein (1857-1926), the first ordained Methodist Protestant male missionary, changed his attitude toward union with other Methodist denominations in Japan from outright rejection in 1883 to active support in 1887 and continued to work for union until he left Japan in 1893. Based on records in the Archives of the United Methodist Church, Lake Junaluska, North Carolina, and the Wesley Theological Seminary, Washington, D.C. 62 notes.
H. L. Calkin

459. LaFontaine, Charles V. "REPAIRER OF THE BREACH"—MOTHER LURANA WHITE, CO-FOUNDER OF THE SOCIETY OF THE ATONEMENT. *Catholic Hist. Rev. 1976 62(3): 434-454.* Lurana White cofounded the Society of the Atonement with Paul Wattson while both were still members of the Episcopal Church. The Society corporately entered the Roman Church in 1909. From the Episcopal Church the cofounders brought ideals and strategies that enriched the Roman Church, particularly its concept of women's role and function in the church. Wattson contributed the "church unity" aim of the Society, thereby helping Rome raise its ecumenical consciousness. White situated that aim in the Franciscan tradition with a special stress on corporate poverty. The Sisters' apostolate reflected these emphases, especially in missions to the poor and minorities. Covers 1870-1928.
A

460. LaFontaine, Charles V. "LIGHTED FROM THE FIRES OF HELL": THE LAMP MAGAZINE AND THE PRO-ROMAN CONTROVERSY IN THE PROTESTANT EPISCOPAL CHURCH, 1903-1909. *Hist. Mag. of the Protestant Episcopal Church 1976 45(4): 413-433.* Probes the history and function of *The Lamp* magazine as well as the role of the founder, Father Paul Wattson (b. 1863), in the rise and demise of the Anglo-Catholic movement within the Protestant Episcopal Church during the first decade of the 20th century. Through editorials and articles Wattson emphasized the three central concepts of the pro-Roman position of the Episcopal Church: 1) belief in the *de juro divino* primacy of the Pope in the Christian Church and adherence to the doctrine of papal infallibility; 2) belief in the need for corporate reunion of the Churches, particularly the Anglican Church with the Roman; and 3) belief in the validity of Anglican Orders. Wattson joined the Catholic Church in 1909. Among his contributions to Church history was beginning the Church Unity Octave in 1907, which is known today as the Week of Prayer for Christian Unity. Based largely on material from *The Lamp* ; 62 notes.
H. M. Parker, Jr.

461. LaFontaine, Charles V. SISTERS IN PERIL: A CHALLENGE TO PROTESTANT EPISCOPAL-ROMAN CATHOLIC CONCORD, 1909-1918. *New York Hist. 1977 58(4): 440-469.* Discusses the Chapel-of-St. John's-in-the-Wilderness at Graymoor, New York. Paul James Wattson, an Episcopalian priest and founder of the Society of the Atonement, and Lurana Mary White established the Sisters' convent at Graymoor. Father Paul and Mother Lurana sought the reunion of the Anglican and Roman Catholic churches. Disappointed by the latitudinarianism of the Protestant Episcopal Church, they incorporated the Society of the Atonement into the Roman Catholic Church in 1909. Years of litigation over the Sisters' convent property rights in Graymoor ended in 1918 when the New York state legislature resolved the dispute in the Sisters' favor. 5 illus., 60 notes.
R. N. Lokken

462. Levy, I. Judson. CANADIAN BAPTIST ECUMENICAL RELATIONSHIPS. *Foundations 1980 23(1): 84-96.* Traces the contribution of Canadian Baptists to the ecumenical movement through their association with the Canadian Council of Churches, the World Council of Churches, and other interchurch movements. Covers 1907-79. Based on Baptist yearbooks; 16 notes.
E. E. Eminhizer

463. Liggin, Edna. A SHORT CONCISE HISTORY OF THE CONCORD BAPTIST ASSOCIATION. *North Louisiana Hist. Assoc. J. 1976 7(3): 101-103.* On 3 November 1832, 15 representatives from four of the eight Baptist churches then in existence between the Ouachita and Red Rivers in North Louisiana "met at Black Lake Church in what is now Webster Parish to constitute the Concord Missionary Baptist Association." The word "missionary" was later dropped from the association's name. These churches previously had belonged to the Louisiana Baptist Association, which was almost disrupted by the action of the original 15 "Concord Men." The association counted 17 member churches in 1845, the year the Southern Baptist Convention met for the first time. In 1846, the association was large enough to divide its territory, and by 1900, "the original Concord Association had expanded into at least twenty-three smaller associations." In 1972, after 140 years, the association represented 35 churches and had a membership of 14,447. A. N. Garland

464. Lockhart, Wilfred C. ECHOES FROM CANADA. *J. of Ecumenical Studies 1979 16(1): 97-102.* The 1st World Conference of Christian Youth (Amsterdam, 1939) led to an ecumenical conference for US and Canadian churches in Toronto in 1940 as well as to formation of the Canadian Council of Churches. Although the latter's Plan of Union for the United Church of Canada and the Anglican Church in Canada ended in failure in 1975 after 32 years of endeavor, the ecumenical spirit inspired by Amsterdam still persists. S

465. Ludlow, Peter W. THE INTERNATIONAL PROTESTANT COMMUNITY IN THE SECOND WORLD WAR. *J. of Ecclesiastical Hist. [Great Britain] 1978 29(3): 311-362.* During 1900-40 the ecumenical movement found expression in four main types of groups: international, inter-confessional bodies; international youth organizations; international confessional groups; and national committees with international links. Notwithstanding high ambitions on the eve of the war, the movement was divided on the main issues. The war revitalized the ecumenical movement, and was decisive in contributing to the emergence of a vigorous international religious community. Focuses on the history of the Scandinavian Lutherans, with particular attention to the Norwegian Church during the German occupation, and the Reformed Protestant churches of Switzerland, France, and Holland. Also discusses the relation of the above to the resistance movements and ecumenical relief organizations. Reviews the historiography of the various aspects of the subject, and draws attention to major archival collections in Europe and the United States. 301 notes. P. H. Hardacre

466. Macnab, John B. FOSDICK AT FIRST CHURCH. *J. of Presbyterian Hist. 1974 52(1): 59-77.* Following consolidation of three congregations and the establishment of the First Presbyterian Church on Fifth Avenue in New York City, the congregation asked Harry Emerson Fosdick, a liberal theologian who belonged to the Baptist Church, to become its first permanent preacher, an unprecedented position which he filled, 1918-24.

467. Mariner, Kirk. THE NEGRO'S PLACE: VIRGINIA METHODISTS DEBATE UNIFICATION: 1924-1925. *Methodist Hist. 1980 18(3): 155-170.* In 1924 and 1925 a controversy arose in the Methodist Episcopal Church, South, regarding unification with the Methodist Episcopal Church, North. The real issue was race rather than unification since the southern Methodist Episcopal Church membership was almost totally white. In the ensuing debate in Virginia there was a great range of viewpoints on the racial issue. Without agreement on this issue, unification failed to be adopted at that time. Based on periodicals of the period and secondary sources; 78 notes. H. L. Calkin

468. May, Lynn E., Jr. THE ROLE OF ASSOCIATIONS IN BAPTIST HISTORY. *Baptist Hist. and Heritage 1977 12(2): 69-74.* Identifies and examines some of the significant contributions by associations to the growth and development of American Baptists. Baptists are indebted to district associations for many contributions to their life and work. Associations have helped to foster a strong fellowship, develop uniformity of faith and practice, promote missions, support education, promote denominational program, and in other ways assist the churches and the denomination in their world task. After more than three centuries, associations continue to build on the basic plan developed in the 17th century: churches associating together voluntarily to accomplish common objectives they cannot achieve alone. Secondary sources; 8 notes.
H. M. Parker, Jr.

469. McElrath, James L. THE THEME OF CHURCH UNITY IN THE AMERICAN CHURCH CONGRESSES, 1874-1933. *Hist. Mag. of the Protestant Episcopal Church 1973 42(3): 205-222.* Discusses church unity and ecumenism in church congresses held by the American Protestant Episcopal Church between 1874-1933. S

470. Morrow, Hubert W. ADMISSION OF THE CUMBERLAND PRESBYTERIAN CHURCH TO THE WORLD ALLIANCE OF REFORMED CHURCHES. *J. of Presbyterian Hist. 1977 55(1): 58-73.* The constitution of the World Alliance of Reformed Churches (WARC) determined that membership could be open to any church "whose Creed is in harmony with the Consensus of the Reformed Confessions." When the Cumberland Presbyterian Church was organized in the early 19th century, it modified the Westminster Confession of Faith, which was the theological symbol for American Presbyterian Churches, toning down those statements in the Confession that dealt with predestination. When the Church sought admittance to the WARC in 1880, it was denied. Four years later, after considerable discussion and debate in the interim, it was admitted. The initial refusal and the subsequent admission are at the heart of an interesting and controversial chapter in the early history of the WARC. The controversy over the admission of the Cumberland Presbyterian Church, the third largest Presbyterian Church in America, became entangled with the efforts of the WARC to define Consensus and was an important catalyst in the ultimate solution of the problem. Based largely on the Proceedings of the Second and Third General Council of the WARC and publications of the Cumberland Presbyterian Church; 66 notes. H. M. Parker, Jr.

471. Mounger, Dwyn Mecklin. SAMUEL HANSON COX: ANTI-CATHOLIC, ANTI-ANGLICAN, ANTI-CONGREGATIONAL ECUMENIST. *J. of Presbyterian Hist. 1977 55(4): 347-361.* Samuel Hanson Cox (1813-80) was a typical New School Presbyterian in his ecumenical aspirations: he worked energetically to promote interdenominational cooperation through numerous benevolence and mission societies to produce a wholly Protestant America. Thus his ecumenism was more limited than that of similar positions today, for it embraced only denominations which he regarded as "evangelical," which included only those practicing revivalism. He viewed Catholicism, Anglicanism, and the resurgent denominationalism of the 1840's as major threats to a triumphantly Protestant America. To counterbalance such movements, he labored hard for the Evangelical Alliance and the American Alliance and to prevent a North-South schism in the New School Presbyterian Church. Yet all these efforts were doomed to fail because of the slavery issue. As Moderator of the New School in 1846 he was successful in preventing abolitionism from dividing the Church that year; yet division came 11 years later. In his zeal for ecumenism he had been prepared to sacrifice the slave upon the altar of evangelical unity. Based largely on the author's doctoral dissertation on Cox (Union Theological Seminary, New York), writings of Cox, and other biographical data; illus., 58 notes.
H. M. Parker, Jr.

472. Mudge, Lewis S. THE THEOLOGICAL WORK OF THE ALLIANCE: 1957-1962. *J. of Presbyterian Hist. 1977 55(1): 101-106.* Three concerns dominated the period 1957-62, when the World Alliance of Reformed Churches was thinking through its contribution to ecumenical dialogue: 1) establishing theological communication between member churches, 2) finding the appropriate style for Reformed/Presbyterian participation in ecumenical dialogue, and 3) reflecting, as a confessional family, about the meaning of the Reformed faith in the ecumenical movement and in the United States and the rest of the world.
H. M. Parker, Jr.

473. Nall, T. Otto. GREEN LIGHTS AND RED LANTERNS ALONG AUTONOMY ROAD. *Religion in Life 1976 45(1): 53-65.* Examines the concepts of self-determination for Christian churches and ecumenism around the world in the 1960's and 1970's.

474. Norlin, Dennis A. THE RESPONSE IN RELIGIOUS JOURNALS TO SAMUEL SCHMUCKER'S FRATERNAL APPEAL. *Lutheran Q. 1973 25(1): 78-90.* Discusses response to an article by Samuel Simon Schmucker in 1838 on Christian unity. S

475. Paetkau, Peter and Klippenstein, Lawrence. THE CONFERENCE OF MENNONITES IN CANADA: BACKGROUND AND

ORIGINS. *Mennonite Life 1979 34(4): 4-10.* In the 1873-75 migrations from Russia to Manitoba, the largest group, the Bergthal Colony, settled the East Reserve. The second major group settled the West Reserve. A third group, the Rosenorter Mennonite Fellowship, developed under the leadership of Peter Regier in Saskatchewan. In 1902, the groups moved toward unification. Regier, Benjamin Ewert (1870-1958), Johann M. Friesen (b. 1865), Gerhard Epp (1864-1919), and Jocob Hoepner, who became chairman, determined congregational regulations and the extent of mission work appropriate, providing the framework for the Canadian Conference. In 1978, current Conference leaders dedicated a cairn at Hochstadt, Manitoba, to commemorate the work of these pioneers. 6 photos, 2 maps, 19 notes. B. Burnett

476. Painter, Borden W. BISHOP WALTER H. GRAY AND THE ANGLICAN CONGRESS OF 1954. *Hist. Mag. of the Protestant Episcopal Church 1980 49(2): 157-184.* Delineates the efforts of Walter H. Gray, Episcopal Bishop of Connecticut, in his successful effort to convene the Anglican Conference in Minneapolis in August 1954. This congress of representatives of the world's Anglican Churches provides important clues to the nature and character of the worldwide Anglican communion then and now. Based on Gray's correspondence in the Archives of the Church Historical Society (Austin, Texas) and personal papers and secondary sources; 89 notes. H. M. Parker, Jr.

477. Parker, Harold M., Jr. SOUTHERN PRESBYTERIAN ECUMENISM: SIX SUCCESSFUL UNIONS. *J. of Presbyterian Hist. 1978 56(2): 91-106.* In the first 14 years of its history, the Southern Presbyterian Church successfully participated in six organic unions with the Independent Presbyterian Church, the United Synod of the South, the Presbytery of Patapsco, the Kentucky Presbytery of the Associate Reformed Presbyterian Church, and the Old School Synods of Kentucky and Missouri. Discusses the impact of these unions in three categories: numerically, the Church gained members and congregations; geographically, it spread into the Border States and was also strengthened in the states of the old Confederacy; doctrinally, it accommodated its position to several groups. Challenges the premise of Southern Presbyterian purists who have insisted that in every instance the unions took place on the basis of perfect doctrinal affinity. Based on the author's earlier studies of the unions and primary sources; 2 tables, 41 notes. A

478. Pratt, Henry J. ORGANIZATIONAL STRESS AND ADAPTATION TO CHANGING POLITICAL STATUS: THE CASE OF THE NATIONAL COUNCIL OF CHURCHES OF CHRIST IN THE UNITED STATES. *Am. Behavioral Scientist 1974 17(6): 865-883.* Covers 1908-69.

479. Reily, Duncan A. REUNION SHENANIGAN: BISHOP WILLIAM CAPERS' "LETTER" OF 1854. *Methodist Hist. 1977 15(2): 131-139.* In 1875 the New York weekly newspaper *Christian Advocate* published a letter purportedly written by Methodist Bishop William Capers in 1854 on slavery and abolition, and their effect on the uniting of the north and south branches of the Methodist Church. Concludes that the letter was very probably a forgery, intended to influence the Methodist Episcopal Church, South to move toward reunion with the Methodist Episcopal Church. 7 notes. H. L. Calkin

480. Richey, Russell E. "CATHOLIC" PROTESTANTISM AND AMERICAN DENOMINATIONALISM. *J. of Ecumenical Studies 1979 16(2): 213-231.* Catholic Protestantism, an early form of comprehensive, unitive, or ecumenical Christianity, is one ingredient in the religious pluralism known as denominationalism. A succession of theologically irenic "catholic" Protestants from the 16th century is described. Those whose impact on American denominationalism is viewed as most pronounced were British Latitudinarians, Cambridge Platonists, Scottish Moderates, and Dissenters such as Richard Baxter, Daniel Neal, Philip Doddridge, Isaac Watts, and their American counterparts—Cotton Mather, Jonathan Dickinson, and Samuel Davies. Such catholic Christians mediated to 19th-century denominationalism a view of the church as united in fundamentals and charity even if divided by doctrine, practice, and government. J. A. Overbeck

481. Romig, Michael C. GEORGE WARREN RICHARDS: ARCHITECT OF CHURCH UNION. *J. of Presbyterian Hist. 1977 55(1): 74-99.* Discusses the contributions of George Warren Richards (1869-1957) to church union. Examines three areas of Richards's life and thought: the influence of his diverse religious background, his guiding principles of church union and the application of these principles in his church work, and his leadership in the World Alliance of Reformed Churches. Basic to Richards's concept of church union was spiritual unity between the churches seeking organic union. Richards was involved in six efforts toward organic union. The only one consummated formed the Evangelical and Reformed Church in 1934. Covers 1900-55. Based on the writings of Richards; photo, 80 notes. H. M. Parker, Jr.

482. Rudd, Hynda. CONGREGATION KOL AMI: RELIGIOUS MERGER IN SALT LAKE CITY. *Western Staes Jewish Hist. Q. 1978 10(4): 311-326.* Congregation Kol Ami was formed in 1972 by the merger of Congregations B'nai Israel (begun in 1873) and Montefiore (begun ca. 1880). Different opinions about ritual originally had divided Salt Lake City's Jewish community. Eventually grievances dissipated and new religious, social, and economic problems brought the people together. A consolidation committee was formed to discuss the issue, and members of both congregations voted in favor of the merger. The old synagogues were sold and a new synagogue was constructed in 1976. Based on archival, other primary, and secondary sources; 3 photos, 67 notes. B. S. Porter

483. Ruggle, Richard. "BETTER NO BREAD THAN HALF A LOAF," OR "CRUMBS FROM THE HISTORIC EPISCOPATE TABLE": HERBERT SYMONDS AND CHRISTIAN UNITY. *J. of the Can. Church Hist. Soc. 1976 18(2-3): 53-84.* In the first part of this century, an Anglican clergyman, Herbert Symonds, initiated, participated in, and furthered all efforts to involve Anglicans in Canadian church unification. Such efforts led him to suggest that the Church permit non-Anglican clergy to preach in its churches and non-Anglicans to receive communion there as well. Some liberals outside the church derided the proposal in such slogans as "better no bread than half a loaf." But Symonds faced great opposition within the church, even against the ideas of the educational organizations he helped found: the Canadian Society of Church Unity (1898) and the Church Unity League (1913). Symonds and his associates did create some interest in unity, but they were never able to convince the churchmen who were dedicated to the maintenance of the historic episcopate. Nevertheless, by the time of Symonds' death (1921), a General Synod did support the right of bishops to permit Anglican and non-Anglican clergy to preach in each other's churches. Based on primary and secondary sources; 103 notes. J. A. Kicklighter

484. Sandeen, Ernest R. THE DISTINCTIVENESS OF AMERICAN DENOMINATIONALISM: A CASE STUDY FOR THE 1846 EVANGELICAL ALLIANCE. *Church Hist. 1976 45(2): 222-234.* Discusses the Evangelical Alliance in London in 1846 and its participants and questions whether the differences between the religious establishment in Britain and the disestablishment in America are overestimated. 41 notes. M. D. Dibert

485. Schiotz, Fredrik A. OBSERVATIONS ON PARTS OF DR. NELSON'S LUTHERANISM IN NORTH AMERICA, 1914-1970. *Lutheran Q. 1977 29(2): 150-166.* Comments on the parts of E. Clifford Nelson's *Lutheranism in North America, 1914-1970* that deal with efforts toward Lutheran unification in America during 1950-70. Schiotz, who represented the American Lutheran Church (ALC) in its conversations with other Lutheran bodies, believes that Nelson's subjective treatment of the topic has brought about an erroneous, sinister view of his church's work toward unification. Although the work is both useful and important, its failure to credit the ALC with honest purpose, and its obvious prejudices against that body, mean that the story of Lutheran unification in the two decades needs to be considered in greater perspective. 2 notes. J. A. Kicklighter

486. Schmidt, William J. SAMUEL MCCREA CAVERT: AMERICAN BRIDGE TO THE GERMAN CHURCH, 1945-46. *J. of Presbyterian Hist. 1973 51(1): 3-23.* A member of the Provisional Council of the World Council of Churches, the American Presbyterian Samuel McCrea Cavert, was instrumental in the reintegration of postwar German churches into the world church movement, 1945-46.

487. Smith, John Abernathy. ECCLESIASTICAL POLITICS AND THE FOUNDING OF THE FEDERAL COUNCIL OF CHURCHES. *Church Hist. 1974 43(3): 350-365.* Charles Howard Hopkins interpreted the 1908 founding of the Federal Council of the Churches of Christ as a stage in the flowering of the social gospel sect of American Christianity. He and other scholars of the Federal Council of Churches dismissed the efforts of denominational assemblies to achieve unity of Protestant Churches during the 1880's-90's. Near the zenith of their influence, the assemblies were in an unique position to promote Protestant unity. The Federal Council was initially a creation of these assemblies. Unfortunately, the assemblies were a testing ground for the leaders' skill in ecclesiastical politics. After exploring the ecclesiastical politics that occurred in the Presbyterian, Congregationalist, Espicopalian, and the Dutch and German Reformed Churches, the author maintains that this political activity led to the passing of the great age of the assemblies. 64 notes. M. D. Dibert

488. Sweeney, Odile. THE SIGNIFICANCE OF AMSTERDAM FOR THE YWCA: THE CHRISTIAN COMMUNITY IN THE MODERN WORLD. *J. of Ecumenical Studies 1979 16(1): 79-86.* The 1st World Conference of Christian Youth (Amsterdam, 1939) gave the Young Women's Christian Association (YWCA) the inspiration to nurture the perception of itself as a world-wide ecumenical movement of lay Christian women, but with a place for women who were not yet members of any church. Many conferences and publications in support of this perception are noted. S

489. Threinen, Norman J. THE STUERMER UNION MOVEMENT IN CANADA. *Concordia Hist. Inst. Q. 1973 46(4): 148-157.* An early (1922) attempt at unity among Lutheran synods in Western Canada. S

490. Tiller, Carl W. SOME STRANDS IN THE HISTORY OF THE BAPTIST WORLD ALLIANCE. *Foundations 1974 17(1): 20-35.* Traces the history since 1905 of the Baptist World Alliance, a fellowship organization and federation of 95 Baptist conventions located in 75 nations.

491. Vipond, Mary. CANADIAN NATIONAL CONSCIOUSNESS AND THE FORMATION OF THE UNITED CHURCH OF CANADA. *Bull. of the United Church of Can. 1975 24: 4-27.* Examines "the extent to which a feeling of national consciousness and a sense of national responsibility motivated the unionists in the post World War I period." The movement for church union was directly related to the heavy European immigration and the need to evangelize and 'Canadianize' the west." Concludes that the United Church was intended "to accomplish a double mission for a nation whose unity was threatened by ethnic and geographic divisions. . . . The unity of the three Protestant churches was a religious goal, but it was also a national one." Covers 1902-25. Based on United Church archival material, newspapers, and secondary sources; illus., 82 notes. B. D. Tennyson

492. Wright, Malcolm E. EL DORADO COUNTY FEDERATED CHURCH. *Pacific Hist. 1975 19(4): 378-384.* The Presbyterian Church and Methodist Church of Placerville, California, formed a united congregation in the 1920's after separate identities since the 1850's. 3 illus. G. L. Olson

493. Wright, Robert J. ANGLICAN ORDERS IN ECUMENICAL DIALOGUE. *Anglican Theological Rev. Supplementary Issue (2) 1973: 62-68.* Reviews John Jay Hughes' *Stewards of the Lord: A Reappraisal of Anglican Orders* (London and Sydney: Sheed and Ward, 1970). S

494. Zikmund, Barbara Brown. ISSUES RELEVANT TO UNION IN THE HISTORY OF THE UNITED CHURCH OF CHRIST. *Encounter 1980 41(1): 25-36.* Sketches the history of the United Church of Christ, 19th-20th centuries, stressing the "unionist" tradition in the church's heritage.

495. —. AN INTIMATE PORTRAIT OF THE UNION OF AMERICAN HEBREW CONGREGATIONS—A CENTENNIAL DOCUMENTARY. *Am. Jewish Arch. 1973 25(1): 3-116.* Retraces the history of the Union of American Hebrew Congregations for the last 100 years.

Intergroup Relations: Seeking Understanding

496. Agonito, Joseph. ECUMENICAL STIRRINGS: CATHOLIC-PROTESTANT RELATIONS DURING THE EPISCOPACY OF JOHN CARROLL. *Church Hist. 1976 45(3): 358-373.* John Carroll became the first Roman Catholic Bishop of Baltimore in 1790. During his episcopacy, Catholic-Protestant relations were better than they had been during the colonial period and less violent than they would be during the mid-19th century nativist period. During Carroll's episcopacy, Protestants tempered their anti-Catholic sentiments and Catholics found that their separated brethren were not so bad. Carroll and other Catholic leaders hoped that this period was a prediction of future Protestant-Catholic relationships. Such hopes were dashed when the anti-Catholic sentiment was stirred up once more as waves of Catholic immigrants poured into this country. 116 notes. M. D. Dibert

497. Collins, Patrick W. GUSTAVE WEIGEL: AN UNCOMPROMISING ECUMENIST. *J. of Ecumenical Studies 1978 15(4): 684-703.* Gustave Weigel, a Jesuit theologian and educator who died in 1964, was one of the leaders in improving Roman Catholic and Protestant relations since 1950. He defined the Protestant principle as dependence on experience, the intellect, and the Bible. Catholics, on the other hand, depend on magisterial authority more than Protestants. He was an expert on characterizing varieties of Protestantism and became an authority on Protestant theology, particularly that of Paul Tillich. He was active in ecumenical organizations such as Faith and Order, attended the early sessions of Vatican II, and encouraged ecumenical dialogue between students of Woodstock College and Protestant divinity schools. J. A. Overbeck

498. Fader, Larry A. BEYOND THE BIRDS OF APPETITE: THOMAS MERTON'S ENCOUNTER WITH ZEN. *Biography 1979 2(3): 230-254.* An aspect of Father Thomas Merton's career which is not well known is his encounter with Zen and one of its most important interpreters to the West, Diasetz Teitaro Suzuki. The encounter is delineated and its results in terms of Merton's "integrative" approach to inter-religious dialogue critically appraised. 67 notes. J

499. Gephart, Jerry C.; Siegel, Martin A.; and Fletcher, James E. A NOTE ON LIBERALISM AND ALIENATION IN JEWISH LIFE. *Jewish Social Studies 1974 36(3-4): 327-329.* A 1971 survey of the entire Jewish community of Salt Lake City indicated the willingness of the people to submerge their ideological differences in order to have one synagogue to serve the entire community instead of maintaining two separate synagogues, Reform and Conservative. Both groups saw a strengthening of a common Jewish identity but feared that the differences between Reform and Conservative Judaism would be lost through the union of the two synagogues. Primary and secondary sources; 5 notes. P. E. Schoenberg

500. Heim, S. Mark. AMERICAN BAPTIST-ROMAN CATHOLIC DIALOGUE. *Foundations 1978 21(1): 50-70.* Discussion on the church and theology between American Baptists and Roman Catholics started in 1967. Areas discussed include the meaning of the church, theological agreement, freedom versus autonomy, church and state, and the clergy. 37 notes. E. E. Eminhizer

501. Siegman, Henry. JEWS AND CHRISTIANS—BEYOND BROTHERHOOD WEEK. *Worldview 1975 18(12): 31-36.* Discusses the policy established in 1975 by the Vatican in "Guidelines for the Implementation of *Nostra Aetate* No. 4" on how Catholics should improve their relations with Jews, and how the guidelines have been implemented, particularly in the United States and France.

502. Strober, Gerald S. AMERICAN JEWS AND THE PROTESTANT COMMUNITY. *Midstream 1974 20(7): 47-66.* The 1972 Dallas-based General Assembly of the National Council of Churches illustrates the problem of the Jewish community in presenting its agenda and forestalling anti-Jewish or anti-Israeli actions. S

503. Unruh, T. E. THE SEVENTH-DAY ADVENTIST EVANGELICAL CONFERENCES OF 1955-1956. *Adventist Heritage 1977 4(2): 35-46.* The Seventh-Day Adventist and Evangelical Conferences in 1955 and 1956 produced two books defining contemporary Adventist doctrine and belief, and improved relations between Evangelicals and Adventists.

6. EDUCATION

General

504. Adams, William C. AMERICAN PUBLIC OPINION IN THE 1960S ON TWO CHURCH-STATE ISSUES. *J. of Church and State 1975 17(3): 477-494.* Analyzes US attitudes concerning the church and state issues of prayer in public schools and government aid to church schools.

505. Allaire, Georges. INFLUENCE DU MILIEU ÉTUDIANT QUÉBÉCOIS SUR L'ACTION DE L'ÉGLISE CATHOLIQUE [The influence of Quebec student culture on the action of the Catholic Church]. *Action Natl. [Canada] 1978 67(9): 737-744.* In the 1970's, Quebec university students dramatically have abandoned the practice of Catholicism, and many have adopted agnosticism as well. Students generally are indifferent to the Church, and strongly support total freedom of religion, opposing indoctrination in schools. In response, Catholic college chaplains have developed a mission of evangelization, attempting to form Christian campus communities capable of attracting more sophisticated student participation. Biblio. A. W. Novitsky

506. Angrave, James. JOHN STRACHAN AND SCOTTISH INFLUENCE IN THE CHARTER OF KING'S COLLEGE, YORK, 1827. *J. of Can. Studies [Canada] 1976 11(3): 60-68.* The charter of King's College, in Toronto, was modeled on those of Scottish universities known to John Strachan (1776-1867) which gave considerable powers to an academic senate and provided no religious test for students. But, it did provide for an Anglican faculty, president, and visitor. Besides fear of Anglican domination, resistance in the Upper Canadian legislature was motivated by a reluctance to use prime revenue-bearing lands to support the college. So, despite its Scottish liberal character, the charter was not accepted until 1843. Based on official correspondence and secondary works; 35 notes. G. E. Panting

507. Baker, Van R. THE "STERLING HONESTY" OF JOHN ANDREWS. *Hist. Mag. of the Protestant Episcopal Church 1976 45(1): 31-45.* John Andrews (1745-1813), an American Episcopal clergyman, was headmaster of Episcopal Academy in Philadelphia and later vice-provost of the University of Pennsylvania. It is possible that his frankness kept him from advancing higher in the church or faster in academe. He was more interested in education than the parish ministry. Gives numerous instances of Andrews's frankness. For several years he taught moral philosophy at the University of Pennsylvania. In his classes he underscored the very things which he practiced in his dealings with others. Covers 1765-1810. Based largely on primary sources; 58 notes.
H. M. Parker, Jr.

508. Barr, Thomas P. THE POTTAWATOMIE BAPTIST MANUAL LABOR TRAINING SCHOOL. *Kansas Hist. Q. 1977 43(4): 377-431.* Recounts the founding of the Pottawatomie Baptist Manual Labor Training School in Kansas following the signing of the Pottawatomie Indian treaties of 1846. Directed by the Baptist minister and physician Johnston Lykins (1800-76), the school was built in a style unusual for the time. The attic is the most unusual feature of the school and is classified as a flush-gable monitor, thus placing the school apart from nearly all known 19th-century structures. Describes the school's method of operation and cites evidence of its success, in the face of severe health problems and a worsening financial condition. The school ceased operation after the Pottawatomie Indians were moved to the Indian Territory in 1867. In 1873 the school property was sold to a breeder of nationally known trotting horses. 122 notes. W. F. Zornow

509. Burns, S. A. M. CONSIDERING GEORGE GRANT: REVIEW ARTICLE. *Dalhousie Rev. [Canada] 1980 60(1): 146-150.* Review article about *George Grant in Process: Essays and Conversations,* edited by Larry Schmidt (Toronto: Anansi, 1978) which discusses the political and other writings of professor of theology and philosophy George Grant, and their influence on Canadian life since World War II. The divisions in the book are 1) Canadian politics, 2) intellectual background, 3) theology and history, and 4) philosophy. C. H. Held

510. Butchart, Ronald E. SCHOOLING ON THE PLATEAU FRONTIER: COCONINO COUNTY, 1875-1900. *Plateau 1974 47(1): 2-11.* Examines the cultural heritage of Mormon immigrants to Arizona and their impact on the development of frontier schools. S

511. Cleveland, Len G. GEORGIA BAPTISTS AND THE 1954 SUPREME COURT DESEGREGATION DECISION. *Georgia Hist. Q. 1975 59(Supplement): 107-117.* Discusses the reaction of Georgia's Baptist Church to the Supreme Court's *Brown* v. *Board of Education* decision during 1954-61.

512. Cohen, Naomi W. SCHOOLS, RELIGION, AND GOVERNMENT: RECENT AMERICAN JEWISH OPINIONS. *Michael: On the Hist. of the Jews in the Diaspora [Israel] 1975 3: 340-392.* Reproduces 11 documents reflecting American Jewish views on the principle of separation of church and state with regard to state-supported education. On the issue of keeping religion out of public schools, American Jewish organizations energetically supported separation, although Jews in smaller communities may have been inhibited in expressing such an opinion. But on the issue of public aid to church schools the American Jewish consensus broke down. Orthodox and even non-Orthodox circles began to support such aid, long demanded by Catholic groups, as the Jewish day-school movement grew. Primary and secondary sources; 24 notes.
T. Sassoon

513. Crowson, E. T. SAMUEL STANHOPE SMITH: A FOUNDER OF HAMPDEN-SYDNEY COLLEGE. *Virginia Cavalcade 1974 24(2): 52-61.* Hampden-Sydney College was founded by Presbyterian educator Samuel Stanhope Smith six months before the Declaration of Independence was signed, and he went on to make outstanding contributions to early education in America, 1776-1815. S

514. DeVane, F. Arthur. BIRDWOOD JUNIOR COLLEGE: TWO DECADES, 1954-1974. *Viewpoints: Georgia Baptist Hist. 1974 4: 87-98.*

515. Evans, John Whitney. JOHN LA FARGE, *AMERICA,* AND THE NEWMAN MOVEMENT. *Catholic Hist. Rev. 1978 64(4): 614-643.* In 1904 seminarian LaFarge planned to ask the Jesuit authorities in Rome to establish a chaplaincy at Harvard University. In 1926, as editor of *America*, a Jesuit journal, he wrote against such ideas. His position received approval of the Vatican and remained normative for American Catholic officials until after the 1950's. By then, however, LaFarge had relaxed his opposition. This study examines the changing social, educational, and ecclesiastical *milieux* that influenced his thought. It also suggests personal reasons for his contradictory views on Catholic campus ministry. A

516. Fear, Jacqueline. ENGLISH VERSUS THE VERNACULAR: THE SUPPRESSION OF INDIAN LANGUAGES IN RESERVATION SCHOOLS AT THE END OF THE NINETEENTH CENTURY. *Rev. Française d'Études Américaines [France] 1980 5(9): 13-24.* Missionaries, such as the Riggs family working with the Santee Sioux, generally tried to teach Indians to read and write their own tongues, but Bureau of Indian Affairs policy in the late 19th and early 20th centuries was to suppress Indian languages in favor of English.

517. Fletcher, Charlotte. 1784: THE YEAR ST. JOHN'S COLLEGE WAS NAMED. *Maryland Hist. Mag. 1979 74(2): 133-151.* Since 1870, the name of St. John's for the college in Annapolis, Maryland, was believed to have been taken from the college of the same name in Cambridge University, honoring the Evangelist. The Maryland college was named in honor of the Evangelist, but for other reasons. Discussion of the 1784 Charter of the college originated in the Assembly on 27 December, the feast day of St. John the Evangelist. The name of St. John had a special meaning for many of those promoting the college, because of its associations with Freemasonry. The name may also have been chosen to honor George Washington, a Mason. Notes religious controversies surrounding the college's founding. Based on newspapers, official records of the Maryland Assembly, letters, Masonic archival materials; 2 illus., 55 notes.
C. B. Schulz

518. Gerber, David A. SEGREGATION, SEPARATISM, AND SECTARIANISM: OHIO BLACKS AND WILBERFORCE UNIVERSITY'S EFFORT TO OBTAIN FEDERAL FUNDS, 1891. *J. of Negro Educ. 1976 45(1): 1-20.* In 1887 the Ohio legislature established the Combined Normal and Industrial Department at Wilberforce University, a black school owned by the African Methodist Episcopal Church. When federal funds were sought in 1891 for this department, many Ohio blacks opposed it. Instead, Wilberforce agreed to more state funding for the department, leading to further state control of the department which remained almost exclusively black. 44 notes.
B. D. Johnson

519. Godin, Gerald. LA QUESTION DU MANITOBA [The question of Manitoba]. *Action Natl. [Canada] 1980 69(7): 532-548.* Article 22 of the Manitoba Act (Canada, 1870) prohibits discrimination against confessional schools and Article 23 stipulates that both English and French are official languages in that province. Yet, in 1890, the Thomas Greenway government adopted Law 37 abolishing church schools and Law 54 making English the sole official language. Both laws were appealed to the Judicial Committee of the Privy Council in London, and the rights of the minority were recognized by that body. Yet, the laws were effective in reducing the proportion of francophones in Manitoba from 14% in 1890 to 4% in 1979. Such assimilationist policies explain why, of 10 million francophones in North America, 50% reside in Quebec, 45% in the United States, and only 5% in English Canada.
A. W. Novitsky

520. Gordon, Ann D. THE YOUNG LADIES ACADEMY OF PHILADELPHIA. Berkin, Carol Ruth and Norton, Mary Beth, ed. *Women of America: A History* (Boston: Houghton Mifflin Co., 1979): 68-91. Although founded by men in Philadelphia in 1787, the Young Ladies Academy offered girls an education similar to that given to boys. The founders were college-educated and felt that the education of women would raise the tenor of the entire society by cultivating reason and religion. The pupils were daughters of well-to-do families, and, although they did not go on into business or professions, the school did symbolize a recognition of the importance of women's ideas in the late 18th century. Based on published addresses of trustees and students, two of which are included; illus., 11 notes.
K. Talley

521. Greeley, Andrew M. THE "RELIGIOUS FACTOR" AND ACADEMIC CAREERS: ANOTHER COMMUNICATION. *Am. J. of Sociol. 1973 78(5): 1247-1255.* Strong evidence indicates that, despite social, economic, historical, cultural, and perhaps religious obstacles, many more Catholics are electing academic careers. Little is known about either the facts or the dynamics of this change, and there seems to be little interest among sociologists or the funding agencies to inquire about it. While these changes occur, the long-standing assumption that the absence of Catholics in scholarly careers is a proof of Catholic intellectual inferiority remains essentially unchallenged.
J

522. Habibuddin, S. M. SECULARIZATION OF EDUCATION IN THE USA AND INDIA DURING THE 19TH CENTURY. *Indian J. of Pol. [India] 1976 10(1): 27-47.* The United States and India have in common a process of secularization of education that began in the 19th century. In the United States there was a gradual shift of control of schools and colleges from sectarian to secular hands. This was not accomplished without political and constitutional controversy. English education in India was controlled by missionaries in the first half of the century. The government of India early expressed a principle of neutrality and secularism, especially with the 1854 Wood Dispatch. Though this policy was challenged at times, government policy led to a remarkable growth period in Indian education. I D. K. Lambert

523. Heinerman, Joseph. EARLY UTAH PIONEER CULTURAL SOCIETIES. *Utah Hist. Q. 1979 47(1): 70-89.* Mormons always have been concerned with educating lay members. After the colonization of Salt Lake City, church authorities founded or assisted in the founding of intellectual and literary associations to promote cultural interests and strengthen isolationist concepts. Among those formed in the 1850's were the Universal Scientific Society, Polysophical Society, Deseret Theological Institution, Horticultural Society, Deseret Dramatic Association, Deseret Philharmonic Society, and Deseret Typographical Association. Pioneer cultural societies of the 1850's were revived in the 1870's. 7 illus., 75 notes.
J. L. Hazelton

524. Herbst, Jurgen. AMERICAN COLLEGE HISTORY: RE-EXAMINATION UNDERWAY. *Hist. of Educ. Q. 1974 14(2): 259-266.* Reviews Joseph Ellis, *The New England Mind in Transition: Samuel Johnson of Connecticut, 1696-1772* (New Haven: Yale University Press, 1973), Brooks Mather Kelley, *Yale: A History* (New Haven: Yale University Press, 1974), George N. Rainsford, *Congress and Higher Education in the Nineteenth Century* (Knoxville: University of Tennessee Press, 1972), and John S. Whitehead, *The Separation of College and State: Columbia, Dartmouth, Harvard, and Yale, 1776-1876* (New Haven: Yale University Press, 1973). All challenge traditional interpretations of college history.
L. C. Smith

525. Herbst, Jurgen. THE EIGHTEENTH CENTURY ORIGINS OF THE SPLIT BETWEEN PRIVATE AND PUBLIC HIGHER EDUCATION IN THE UNITED STATES. *Hist. of Educ. Q. 1975 15(3): 273-280.* Disintegration of religious homogeneity and strict separation of church and state, which began in the 1730's and continued with American independence, led to the division between private and public institutions of higher education.

526. Hoffmann, John. CONTROLLED SUPERFICIALITY IN THE STUDY OF COLONIAL NEW ENGLAND EDUCATION. *Hist. of Educ. Q. 1976 16(2): 215-228.* Review article prompted by James Axtell *The School Upon the Hill: Education and Society in Colonial New England* (New Haven, Connecticut: Yale U. Pr., 1974).

527. Hornick, Nancy Slocum. ANTHONY BENEZET AND THE AFRICANS' SCHOOL: TOWARD A THEORY OF FULL EQUALITY. *Pennsylvania Mag. of Hist. and Biog. 1975 99(4): 399-421.* Traces the social thought of Anthony Benezet (1713-84), who with the Friends of Philadelphia organized the Africans' School for free Negroes in the 1770's. Benezet was ahead of his time in regarding blacks as the intellectual, moral, and spiritual equal of whites (if not social and economic). His opposition to racial prejudice was a direct result of his pioneering efforts in black education. 52 notes.
C. W. Olson

528. Huel, Raymond. PASTOR VS. POLITICIAN: THE REVEREND MURDOCH MACKINNON AND PREMIER WALTER SCOTT'S AMENDMENT TO THE SCHOOL ACT. *Saskatchewan Hist. [Canada] 1978 32(2): 61-73.* Originally a private exchange of letters between Presbyterian minister Murdoch MacKinnon and Premier Walter Scott, of the Liberal Party, concerning an amendment to the School Act which would force Catholics to support separate schools (thus enhancing the status of those schools) and to which MacKinnon was opposed, the controversy became a vicious public debate from 1913 to 1916. Scott wished to guarantee language and school rights to French Canadians and immigrants, while MacKinnon wished to impose Anglo-Protestant assimilation on them. Details personal vituperations on both sides. Follows MacKinnon's career up to the Church Union and his acceptance of a pastorate in Toronto in 1925. Delineates the preparation of an anti-French, anti-Catholic atmosphere which would lead to the appearance of the Ku Klux Klan in Saskatchewan in 1926. 65 notes.
C. H. Held

529. Humphries, Jack W. THE LAW DEPARTMENT AT OLD AUSTIN COLLEGE. *Southwestern Hist. Q. 1980 83(4): 371-386.* Daniel Baker (1791-1857), a Presbyterian missionary, founded Austin College in Huntsville, Texas, in 1849, and became president in 1854. A law department, the first in Texas, began in 1855. Enrollment was disappointing and the program was soon abandoned, but two of its law graduates became eminent Texas attorneys. Primary sources; 5 illus., 27 notes.
J. H. Broussard

530. Kirk, Russell. LIBERAL LEARNING, MORAL WORTH, AND DEFECATED RATIONALITY. *Modern Age 1975 19(1): 2-9.* In recent decades colleges and universities have offered a limited rationalistic curricula, purged of theology, moral philosophy, and traditional wisdom. This "defecated rationality" exalts private judgment and hedonism at the expense of personal discipline and social order. Covers 1950-73.
M. L. Lifka

531. Lehman, Edward C., Jr. ACADEMIC DISCIPLINE AND FACULTY RELIGIOSITY IN SECULAR AND CHURCH-RELATED COLLEGES. *J. for the Sci. Study of Religion 1974 13(2):*

205-220. Finds different patterns of faculty religiosity in church-related colleges, probably because of the high concentration of faculty pursuing religious vocations. Covers 1965-73. S

532. Liggio, Leonard P. and Peden, Joseph R. SOCIAL SCIENTISTS, SCHOOLING, AND THE ACCULTURATION OF IMMIGRANTS IN 19TH CENTURY AMERICA. *J. of Libertarian Studies 1978 2(1): 69-84.* Fear of ethnic, cultural, and religious diversity expressed in the writings of Benjamin Rush, Benjamin Franklin, and Thomas Jefferson spawned ideas of public education designed to school immigrants in republicanism and citizenship carried out by educational reformers such as Lyman Beecher, Samuel F. B. Morse, William Torrey Harris, and Herbert Spencer 1840's-1910's.

533. Lyons, John. THE (ALMOST) QUIET EVOLUTION: DOUKHOBOR SCHOOLING IN SASKATCHEWAN. *Can. Ethnic Studies [Canada] 1976 8(1): 23-37.* Describes efforts to bring public education to the Saskatchewan Dukhobors since 1905 and the circumstances surrounding their eventual acceptance of public schools.

534. MacDonald, Robert James. HUTTERITE EDUCATION IN ALBERTA; A TEST CASE IN ASSIMILATION, 1920-1970. *Can. Ethnic Studies [Canada] 1976 8(1): 9-22.* Hutterites in Alberta have resisted assimilation through the public schools since 1920, viewing the schools as a threat to their culture.

535. MacPhail, Elizabeth C. SAN DIEGO'S CHINESE MISSION. *J. of San Diego Hist. 1977 23(2): 8-21.* The Chinese Mission School in San Diego, sponsored by the Congregational Church, offered an English education to Chinese members of the community, as well as a place of recreation and religious instruction, 1885-1960.

536. Mathis, Ray. WALTER B. HILL, A NEW CHANCELLOR FOR THE UNIVERSITY OF GEORGIA. *Georgia Hist. Q. 1973 57(1): 76-84.* Describes the conditions that forced one chancellor from office and the election of a new one to head the University of Georgia. Walter B. Hill was a layman, a Georgian, and an alumnus as well as a good leader. The crisis that peaked in 1897 was over in 1901. The Methodists and Baptists were conciliated, agricultural instruction was vitalized, the alumni were organized, enrollment increased, and the state legislature made an appropriation. From the author's doctoral dissertation. 12 notes. D. L. Smith

537. McGlothlin, William J. REV. HORACE HOLLEY: TRANSYLVANIA'S UNITARIAN PRESIDENT, 1818-1827. *Filson Club Hist. Q. 1977 51(3): 234-248.* Analyzes the successful, but controversial, tenure of Horace Holley as president of Transylvania College in Kentucky during 1818-27. Holley, a Yale graduate and successful Unitarian minister in Boston, proved to be an extremely able administrator. He appeared to be creating the large statewide university that he envisioned. Sectarian opposition from the Presbyterians and political opportunism on the part of Kentucky Governor Joseph Desha drove Holley to resign in 1827. The school never recovered and was later absorbed into the University of Kentucky. 66 notes. G. B. McKinney

538. Naylor, Natalie A. THE ANTE-BELLUM COLLEGE MOVEMENT: A REAPPRAISAL OF TEWKSBURY'S FOUNDING OF AMERICAN COLLEGES AND UNIVERSITIES. *Hist. of Educ. Q. 1973 13(3): 261-274.* Discussion of Donald G. Tewksbury's *The Founding of American Colleges and Universities Before the Civil War, With Particular Reference to the Religious Influences Bearing Upon the College Movement* (New York, 1932), 1776-1860.

539. Neusner, Jacob. DEPARTMENTS OF RELIGIOUS STUDIES AND CONTEMPORARY JEWISH STUDIES. *Am. Jewish Hist. Q. 1974 63(4): 356-360.* Although much material of contemporary Jewish studies is not religious in nature, it is often placed in religious studies departments. One of nine related articles in this issue. S

540. Noll, Mark A. CHRISTIAN THINKING AND THE RISE OF THE AMERICAN UNIVERSITY. *Christian Scholar's Rev. 1979 9(1): 3-16.* Analyzes the change in US higher education, 1860-1930, from a broad humanistic approach with a Christian orientation to a technical, empirical orientation following the spread in belief in Social Darwinism and increase in funding from large corporations.

541. Noll, Mark A. THE PRINCETON TRUSTEES OF 1807: NEW MEN AND NEW DIRECTIONS. *Princeton U. Lib. Chronicle 1980 41(3): 208-230.* Lists and provides statistics for the 23 members of the Princeton University Board of Trustees in September 1806, and the new trustees of 1807 (including six new members), who represented ideals and directions new and different from the previous group's revolutionary ideals, and, more importantly, broke the ties between lay and clerical interests.

542. Nortrup, Jack. THE TROUBLES OF AN ITINERANT TEACHER IN THE EARLY NINETEENTH CENTURY. *J. of the Illinois State Hist. Soc. 1978 71(4): 279-287.* Discusses Frances Langdon Willard's (1797-1854) long but frustrating teaching career throughout the eastern, southern, and central states (New York, Vermont, Alabama, and Illinois). During 1835-51, she taught in at least 15 female seminaries and also established one of her own. Her letters to her brother at Alton, Illinois, give proof of her Christian dedication and perseverance: "My girls are to be portions of the mothers of the next generation of *heros, patriots* and *Christians.*" Willard Papers, newspapers, secondary sources; 2 illus., 53 notes. J/S

543. O'Driscoll, Dennis. DIVERGENT IMAGES OF AMERICAN AND BRITISH EDUCATION IN THE ONTARIO CATHOLIC PRESS 1851-1948. *Study Sessions: Can. Catholic Hist. Assoc. [Canada] 1976 43: 5-22.* Examines Canadian attitudes on American and British education through the images presented by the editors of a series of Catholic newspapers published in Ontario 1851-1948.

544. O'Steen, Neal. PIONEER EDUCATION IN THE TENNESSEE COUNTRY. *Tennessee Hist. Q. 1976 35(2): 199-219.* The earliest educators in Tennessee were missionaries. Not until 1780 was the first true school established. The early schools were located in forts, and teaching was loose and unstructured. Religious schools were soon opened, all education was originally permeated with religion, but interest in practical subjects soon started the move to secularization. The first college was established in 1795. The old ideal of education for all was still only a dream when Tennessee became a state; governments paid more lip service to education than to actual financial aid. 72 notes. V. L. Human

545. Perko, F. Michael. THE BUILDING UP OF ZION: RELIGION AND EDUCATION IN NINETEENTH CENTURY CINCINNATI. *Cincinnati Hist. Soc. Bull. 1980 38(2): 96-114.* Discusses why American schooling took the direction of two separate entities, the parochial and the public, using conflict between parochial schools (Catholic, Jewish, and German Lutheran) and public school officials during the 19th century as an example of the concerns over the education of American children.

546. Ralph, John H. and Rubinson, Richard. IMMIGRATION AND THE EXPANSION OF SCHOOLING IN THE UNITED STATES, 1890-1970. *Am. Sociol. Rev. 1980 45(6): 943-954.* Previous studies have shown that the presence of nativist, Protestant-millenial groups was associated with the early expansion of public primary enrollments. Immigrant groups provide an important contrast to such groups, and several interpretive histories of US education stress the relationship between immigration and schooling. Using aggregate, time-series analyses, we find that the effect of immigration on the aggregate rate of growth of schooling has varied as a function of the character of the immigrants themselves. J/S

547. Richardson, Joe M. THE AMERICAN MISSIONARY ASSOCIATION AND BLACK EDUCATION IN CIVIL WAR MISSOURI. *Missouri Hist. Rev. 1975 69(4): 433-488.* The American Missionary Association carried on antislavery work in Missouri before the Civil War, and educational programs during and after the war. In 1862 George Candee, the first educational representative, arrived in St. Louis. Real educational work did not begin until 1863 with the arrival of J. L. Richardson. After concentrating its work in St. Louis, the A.M.A. began to expand into other areas after 1864. After the war it continued modest support in Missouri but transferred most of its activities to the South. Most of the work to educate the 115,000 Negroes in Missouri fell to the blacks themselves, the state, and other benevolent societies, but they were able to build on a foundation already laid by the A.M.A. Based on primary and secondary sources; illus., 40 notes. W. F. Zornow

548. Richardson, Joe M. "WE ARE TRULY DOING MISSIONARY WORK": LETTERS FROM AMERICAN MISSIONARY ASSOCIATION TEACHERS IN FLORIDA, 1864-1874. *Florida Hist. Q. 1975 54(2): 178-195.* The American Missionary Association led the way in aiding Florida's 62,000 freedmen by advocating full citizenship and by establishing schools throughout the state. Although few in number, American Missionary Association teachers instructed hundreds of students and with the aid of other benevolent societies and the Florida legislature, achieved an educational system for black people. Based on the Association's archives at the Amistad Research Center, Dillard University; 11 letters, 22 notes. P. A. Beaber

549. Rogers, George A. and Saunders, R. Frank, Jr. THE AMERICAN MISSIONARY ASSOCIATION IN LIBERTY COUNTY, GEORGIA: AN INVASION OF LIGHT AND LOVE. *Georgia Hist. Q. 1978 62(4): 304-315.* The American Missionary Association provided aid to freedmen in Liberty County, Georgia, after the Civil War. Under the leadership of the Reverend Floyd Snelson and other dedicated teachers, the Congregational "New" Midway Church, Dorchester Academy, and several other facilities were instrumental in the education of blacks. Covers 1870-80's. Primary and secondary sources; 40 notes. G. R. Schroeder

550. Shaffir, William. THE ORGANIZATION OF SECULAR EDUCATION IN A CHASSIDIC JEWISH COMMUNITY. *Can. Ethnic Studies [Canada] 1976 8(1): 38-51.* Examines how the religious community of Lubavitcher chassidim in Montreal, Quebec, attempts to minimize their children's exposure to contradictive materials during their secular learning; covers late 1969 to 1971.

551. Shanabruch, Charles. THE REPEAL OF THE EDWARDS LAW: A STUDY OF RELIGION AND ETHNICITY IN ILLINOIS POLITICS. *Ethnicity 1980 7(3): 310-332.* The Edwards Law (1889) required compulsory education in public schools or public-approved private schools. The requirement that private schools had to be approved by the school board created resentment among Catholic educators and other private school interests. After a four-year struggle between ethnoreligious interest groups and others, the law was modified to end public approval of private schools. 92 notes. T. W. Smith

552. Sklar, Kathryn Kish. THE FOUNDING OF MOUNT HOLYOKE COLLEGE. Berkin, Carol Ruth and Norton, Mary Beth, ed. *Women of America: A History* (Boston: Houghton Mifflin Co., 1979): 177-201. Mount Holyoke Female Seminary was founded in South Hadley, Massachusetts, by Mary Lyon. The college was unique in that it was founded by people of modest means and served their daughters, rather than the children of the privileged. Examines the background of female educators in New England, 1760's-1850's, that influenced Mary Lyon and the liberal Christians who supported the school. Among these was Reverend Joseph Emerson (brother of Ralph Waldo) whose *Discourse on Female Education* (1822) advocated that women should be trained to be teachers rather than "to please the other sex." Based on secondary sources; 15 notes, ref. K. Talley

553. Storey, John W. THE RHETORIC OF PATERNALISM: SOUTHERN BAPTISTS AND NEGRO EDUCATION IN THE LATTER NINETEENTH CENTURY. *Southern Humanities Rev. 1978 12(2): 101-108.* Southern Baptists, 1880's-90's, paternalistically supported black education, but soon even that became little more than rhetoric based on laissez-faire attitudes toward civil rights and economic betterment.

554. Swan, George Steven. THE OUT-CASTE CATHOLICS: REPULSED FROM THE VERGE OF SUCCESS? *J. of Intergroup Relations 1975 4(4): 4-20.* Continued underrepresentation of Catholics in intellectual circles and higher education staffs may be due to their unfashionable ethnic backgrounds, and the solution for this and other discrimination may be the formation of a Catholic-based ethnic rights lobby, 1960's-70's. S

555. Thalheimer, Fred. RELIGIOSITY AND SECULARIZATION IN THE ACADEMIC PROFESSIONS. *Sociol. of Educ. 1973 46(2): 183-202.* Examines the religious and professional orientations of college professors (1973), concluding that religious belief is a better indicator of a professor's concern over the conflict between his convictions and his work than his professional background. S

556. Thornbery, Jerry. NORTHERNS AND THE ATLANTA FREEDMEN, 1865-69. *Prologue 1974 6(4): 236-251.* Immediately following the end of the Civil War there were several federal agencies and northern religious organizations functioning in Atlanta to aid Negroes. The first and most extensive efforts were made by the Union Army. However, the Freedmen's Bureau, the American Missionary Association, and the Methodist Episcopal Church also offered limited assistance. A rudimentary school system was established, but a study of the activities of these organizations reveals considerable limitation because of northern attitudes toward race, work, and welfare. "Northerners as well as Southerners shared a responsibility for Reconstruction's failure." 4 photos, 58 notes. R. V. Ritter

557. Towne, Edgar A. A "SINGLEMINDED" THEOLOGIAN: GEORGE BURMAN FOSTER AT CHICAGO. *Foundations 1977 20(1): 36-59, (2): 163-180.* Part I. George Burman Foster arrived at the University of Chicago Divinity School in 1895. Being a liberal Baptist who tried to express his inner religious experience to a conservative audience, he was controversial throughout his career. Five major controversies centered around him: 1) academic freedom, 2) an attempt to get him excommunicated from the Hyde Park Baptist Church, 3) his transfer from the divinity school to arts, sciences, and letters, 4) ethics and theology, and 5) the issue of Christian theism. Describes how Foster was obtained by the University of Chicago and discusses his controversies. Concludes with the controversy concerning academic freedom. 107 notes. Part II. Foster was accused of holding Unitarian views and did term himself "a frank agnostic." In 1909 Foster's name was deleted from the Northern Baptist conference, but he continued to expound humanism at the university. 82 notes. E. E. Eminhizer/S

558. Vanausdall, Jeanette. RELIGION STUDIES IN THE PUBLIC SCHOOLS. *Social Studies 1979 70(6): 251-253.* Cites historical education foundations in the American colonies to support religion studies in education. Includes plan for implementing religion studies ir the various social sciences. 3 notes. L. R. Raife

559. Vinatieri, Joseph A. THE GROWING YEARS: WESTMINSTER COLLEGE FROM BIRTH TO ADOLESCENCE. *Utah Hist. Q. 1975 43(4): 344-361.* Westminster College, Salt Lake City, Utah, began as Sheldon Jackson College in 1897. In 1910 it merged with Salt Lake Collegiate Institute, organized in 1875 as a foundation for a permanent college and normal school. Both schools were plagued by financial problems and the mutual alienation of Mormons and Protestants. Men involved in the college enterprise were Dr. John M. Coyner, Robert McNiece, Dr. Sheldon Jackson, Dr. Duncan J. McMillan, Dr. Samuel Wishard, Josiah McClain, and William M. Ferry. Covers 1875-1913. Based on primary and secondary sources; 6 illus., 39 notes. J. L. Hazelton

560. Walsh, James P. FATHER PETER YORKE OF SAN FRANCISCO. *Studies [Ireland] 1973 62(245): 19-34.* Discusses the political attitudes of Father Peter Yorke, Catholic clergyman and Irish American, as a Regent of the University of California, 1900-12.

561. Warren, Matthew M. EDUCATION DESCENDS. *Anglican Theological Rev. 1976 59(Supplement 7): 139-149.* Modern education, reflecting American culture, 1945-75, has become utilitarian and has forsaken humanism, religiosity, and basic joy in learning, in favor of technological advance.

562. Wentz, Richard E. A RELIGIOLOGY OF THE MULTICULTURE. *Religion in Life 1973 42(1): 83-92.* Schizoid character of religion in higher education, 1968-73. S

563. Wolters, Raymond. THE PURITAN ETHIC AND BLACK EDUCATION. *Hist. of Educ. Q. 1977 17(1): 63-74.* Review article prompted by James M. McPherson's *The Abolitionist Legacy: from Reconstruction to the NAACP* (Princeton, N.J.: Princeton U. Pr., 1975), which revises conventional views of various American historical problems, argues that the abolitionists studied did not abandon the cause of the freedmen after the Civil War, stresses the importance of missionary

educational activities for blacks, and differs in many ways from the views of C. Vann Woodward, August Mier, Herbert G. Gutman, and others. Covers 1865-1910. 13 notes. L. C. Smith

564. Wood, James E., Jr. RELIGION AND EDUCATION: A CONTINUING DILEMMA. *Ann. of the Am. Acad. of Pol. and Social Sci. 1979 (446): 63-77.* Discusses the role of religion in the public schools and the use of public funds for religious schools. Reviews religion and education in the context of US church-state relations and several decades of judicial interpretations based on the Establishment Clause of the First Amendment. Even with tuition tax-credit legislation, however, the eligibility for such funds may require that church schools maintain an essentially secular character and thereby lose their religious identity and church-relatedness. Covers 1950's-70's. J/S

565. —. [INTELLECTUAL AUTONOMY AMONG PROTESTANTS AND CATHOLICS]. *Am. J. of Sociol. 1974 80 (1): 218-220.*
Humphreys, Claire. THE RELIGIOUS FACTOR: COMMENT ON GREELEY'S CONCLUSION, *pp. 217-219.*
Greeley, Andrew M. GREELEY REPLIES TO HUMPHREYS, *pp. 219-220.*
The authors debate the extent of intellectual autonomy among Protestants and Catholics in the 1960's and 70's—in response to Greely's article on growing Catholic representation in the academy, and reasons for previous underrepresentation, 1960's-70's.

566. —. [SPEAK SCHOOLS]. *Mennonite Hist. Bull. 1975 36(2): 3-6.*
Hollenbach, Raymond E. "SPEAK SCHOOLS" OF THE 19TH CENTURY, pp. 3-4.
Gehman, John B. SPEAK SCHOOL ACCOUNT, HEREFORD, [18]-53, pp. 4-6.
Presents an introduction to John B. Gehman, a Pennsylvania Mennonite, and an excerpt from his diary dealing with Speak Schools. S

Religion in Public Schools

567. Buchanan, Frederick S. UNPACKING THE NEA: THE ROLE OF UTAH'S TEACHERS AT THE 1920 CONVENTION. *Utah Hist. Q. 1973 41(2): 150-161.* In 1920 public school teachers in Utah provoked an attempt to reorganize and "democratize" the National Education Association. Social critic Upton Sinclair in *The Goslings: A Study of the American Schools* (1924) asserted that the Mormon church controlled the NEA in its 1920 convention in Salt Lake City, indicative of a capitalist plot to deprive America's teachers of their democratic rights. By stressing sensationalism, Sinclair glossed over other aspects of the situation. 5 illus., 24 notes. D. L. Smith

568. Carper, James C. A COMMON FAITH FOR THE COMMON SCHOOL? RELIGION AND EDUCATION IN KANSAS, 1861-1900. *Mid-America 1978 60(3): 147-161.* During the latter half of the 19th century religion in education was a major issue in Kansas. Most teachers, and a majority of the population, supported the concept of religious instruction with a Protestant bias in public school systems. Bible reading, mainly from the King James Version, was a normal practice and was used as a basis for moral instruction. Catholics responded with the proposal that tax revenues be divided among the several denominations for the support of their own institutions. This proposal failed after much debate, and public schools still reflected a Protestant bias until the mid-1890's. Eventually, as Kansas society became more secular, religion was divorced from public education. Primary and secondary sources; 64 notes. J. M. Lee

569. Choquette, Robert. ADÉLARD LANGEVIN ET LES QUESTIONS SCOLAIRES DU MANITOBA ET DU NORD-OUEST 1895-1915 [Adélard Langevin and questions concerning the school system in Manitoba and the North-West, 1895-1915]. *Rev. de l'Université d'Ottawa [Canada] 1976 46(3): 324-344.* In 1890, the Liberal government of Manitoba passed a law which abolished church schools; all children were to be educated in the public schools. The Catholic Church, with its own school system, opposed this. The national Conservative Party promised, if victorious in federal elections, to overturn the decision of the provincial government. Instead, the Liberal Party under Wilfrid Laurier won the 1896 elections. Laurier, though French-speaking and Catholic himself, engineered a compromise with Thomas Greenway, the Manitoba premier. All schools would be public, but there would be religious education for those who wished it between 3:30 and 4:00 PM. In addition, the French language would be used where 10 or more pupils were French-speaking (the same rights were given to other non-English-speaking groups), thus partially reversing Greenway's abolition of French as one of the official languages. Most Catholic prelates accepted the compromise, and were suported in this by the Vatican, but Louis Philippe Adélard Langevin, Archbishop of the Diocese of St. Boniface, which included the Prairie Provinces, refused to go along. He accused Laurier of being a traitor to his language and his faith, and continued to demand separate schools for Catholic students throughout his episcopate. 98 notes. J. C. Billigmeier

570. Cummings, Scott; Briggs, Richard; and Mercy, James. PREACHERS VERSUS TEACHERS: LOCAL-COSMOPOLITAN CONFLICT OVER TEXTBOOK CENSORSHIP IN AN APPALACHIAN COMMUNITY. *Rural Sociol. 1977 42(1): 7-21.* Examines a censorship campaign in 1974 by fundamentalists in a small Virginia Appalachian community; focuses on the conflict of cosmopolitan ideas of educators and traditional ideas of religious leaders.

571. Geiger, John O. THE EDGERTON BIBLE CASE: HUMPHREY DESMOND'S POLITICAL EDUCATION OF WISCONSIN CATHOLICS. *J. of Church and State 1979 20(1): 13-28.* Details the case of *State of Wisconsin ex rel. Frederick Weiss, et. al.* v. *District School Board of School District 8* (1890) concerning Bible reading in public schools, and Humphrey Desmond's (1852-1932) support of those who opposed the reading of only the King James version of the Bible by all students including Catholics. The case resulted in the elimination of Bible reading in Wisconsin schools. Covers 1888-90. 47 notes. E. E. Eminhizer

572. Gleason, Philip. BLURRING THE LINE OF SEPARATION: EDUCATION, CIVIL RELIGION, AND TEACHING ABOUT RELIGION. *J. of Church and State 1977 19(3): 517-538.* Following a background discussion of the major cases on church-state relations and education: *Evenson* (1947), *McCollum* (1948), and *Zorach* (1952), discusses American Civil Religion and the teaching about religion. In the latter section he argues that the distinction between "teaching about" and "teaching" is not as clear as some believe. 52 notes. E. E. Eminhizer

573. Gordon, Mary MacDougall. PATRIOTS & CHRISTIANS: A REASSESSMENT OF NINETEENTH-CENTURY SCHOOL REFORMERS. *J. of Social Hist. 1978 11(4): 554-574.* The revisionist preoccupation with social control motivation in the founding of the free public educational system focuses us too much on urban concerns. The fact is that rural schools were as much the goal. Further it ignores the ties between education and nationalism. Concentrates on an educational elite throughout Massachusetts working in the American Institute for Education, founded in 1830 and instrumental before and after Horace Mann emerged through their efforts. They sought a Protestant Christian republic. 57 notes. M. Hough

574. Hatfield, Michael. H. H. PITTS AND RACE AND RELIGION IN NEW BRUNSWICK POLITICS. *Acadiensis [Canada] 1975 4(2): 46-65.* In 1871 New Brunswick adopted a free nonsectarian school system, avoiding an Acadian rebellion only by allowing "a sectarian bias within the non-sectarian system." The dispute resurfaced in 1890 when the Catholic-dominated Bathurst board of trustees began reinstituting strong sectarian policies in their local schools. Herman H. Pitts, a newspaper editor and radical Protestant reformer, cited Bathurst excesses in prodding the province's Protestant majority to institute a "British cultural hegemony." His militant approach failed as the people refused to rekindle the sectarian conflict. Primary and secondary sources; 3 tables, 80 notes. E. A. Churchill

575. Huel, Raymond. THE ANDERSON AMENDMENTS AND THE SECULARIZATION OF SASKATCHEWAN PUBLIC SCHOOLS. *Study Sessions: Can. Catholic Hist. Assoc. [Canada] 1977 44: 61-76.* Dedicated to educational reform, Premier James T. M. Ander-

son advanced two major amendments to Saskatchewan's School Act which prohibited religious garb and symbols in the public schools (1930) and suppressed the French language in grade one (1931). These actions occurred in a climate of anti-Catholicism and spurred nationalism among French-speaking Catholics, including those in Quebec. Covers 1929-34.
G. A. Hewlett

576. Humphreys, James. TEXTBOOK WAR IN WEST VIRGINIA. *Dissent 1976 23(2): 164-170.* The fundamentalist, coal-mining eastern half of Kanawha County, West Virginia, has been protesting the textbooks used in elementary and secondary schools as antireligious, antipatriotic, and obscene, and seeks to eliminate much great modern literature from the curriculum.

577. Kelly, Richard Edward. JOHN GREENLEAF WHITTIER ON BIBLE READING IN THE PUBLIC SCHOOLS: AN UNPUBLISHED LETTER. *Essex Inst. Hist. Collections 1974 110(1): 57-63.* Discusses a letter written by Whittier in 1853 to Giles Merrill Kelley, head of the Amesbury Massachusetts School Committee, requesting toleration for Catholic parents who opposed use of the King James Bible in public schools.
S

578. Michaelsen, Robert S. CONSTITUTIONS, COURTS AND THE STUDY OF RELIGION. *J. of the Am. Acad. of Religion 1977 45(3): 291-308.* The academic study of religion in state universities has not been challenged in the courts by the major separationist groups. In one case a "Bible as Literature" course at the University of Washington was okayed by the Supreme Court. Out of this and other cases involving religion and public schools have come the three cardinal principles of Supreme Court "doctrine" on religion and the state: secular purpose, neutral primary effect, and avoidance of undue entanglement between the state and religious bodies. Table of court cases, biblio.
E. R. Lester

579. Morrison, John L. ALEXANDER CAMPBELL: MORAL EDUCATOR OF THE MIDDLE FRONTIER. *West Virginia Hist. 1975 36(3): 187-201.* Like Horace Mann in New England, Alexander Campbell (1788-1866) urged better education as a means of improving moral behavior on the frontier. He thought people would be reformed not by law, but by schooling, and he criticized traditional education for being sterile and for failing to develop students' minds. Though opposing sectarianism, he wanted the Bible used in schools to teach a "common Christianity" and moral virtue. Campbell's heritage is seen in the many colleges founded by his followers. He admired Thomas Jefferson's educational ideas and was a forerunner of John Dewey's pragmatism. Based on Campbell's writings; 89 notes.
J. H. Broussard

580. Robertson, Ian Ross. THE BIBLE QUESTION IN PRINCE EDWARD ISLAND FROM 1856 TO 1860. *Acadiensis [Canada] 1976 5(2): 3-25.* In 1856 the head of Prince Edward Island's teachers' college suggested daily Bible lessons. The Board of Education rejected the suggestion, but evangelical Protestants launched a campaign for public school Bible-reading. Supported by most Tories, the campaign became the colony's most important political issue until 1860. Sectarian animosity replaced class and ideological divisions as the moving force in Island politics and resulted in an all-Protestant government in a nearly half-Catholic colony. 99 notes.
D. F. Chard

581. Tegborg, Lennart. THE DISAPPEARANCE OF AN AMERICAN DREAM: THE NEW YORK PRAYER CASE IN 1962 IN THE PUBLIC DEBATE. *Kyrkohistorisk Årsskrift [Sweden] 1977 77: 166-171.* Analyzes Protestant and Jewish public opinion about *Engel* v. *Vitale* (US, 1962), which forbade the recitation of a nonsectarian prayer in New York public schools. Opinion was divided, indicating that the ideal of religious unity expressed by the concept of nonsectarianism was obsolete.

582. Tegborg, Lennart. RELIGION OCH ALL MÄN SKOLA I 1940- OCH 1960-TALENS USA [Religion and public school in the USA, 1940-60: A study of an American dilemma]. *Kyrkohistorisk Årsskrift [Sweden] 1975: 96-138.* Analyzes the relationship between church and state in regard to public schools during 1940-60.

583. Thomas, Bettye C. PUBLIC EDUCATION AND BLACK PROTEST IN BALTIMORE, 1865-1900. *Maryland Hist. Mag. 1976 71(3): 381-391.* Reviews the efforts of the Baltimore Association for the Moral and Educational Improvement of the Colored People led by such as Isaac Myers, and Brotherhood of Liberty formed by Harvey Johnson and other Baptist ministers, to acquire public schools, have black teachers hired, secure additional school facilities, and initiate industrial education for black children. Blacks found themselves forced to support Jim Crow legislation and urge all black teachers for the colored schools because the Board of School Commissioners would not allow blacks and whites to teach in the same schools. From 1867 to 1900 black schools grew from 10 to 27 and enrollment from 901 to 9,383. The Mechanical and Industrial Association achieved success only in 1892 with the opening of the Colored Manual Training School. Black leaders were convinced by the Rev. William Alexander and his paper, the *Afro American*, that economic advancement and first-class citizenship depended on equal access to schools, and thus zealously pursued their goals in the face of a white city commission which yielded step-by-step and only very reluctantly. Primary and secondary works; 45 notes.
G. J. Bobango

Religious Education

(including Sunday Schools)

584. Allis, Frederick S., Jr. PHILLIPS ACADEMY: FROM CALVINISM TO COEDUCATION. *Essex Inst. Hist. Collections 1980 116(2): 61-81.* Phillips Academy, in Andover, Massachusetts, was the first incorporated boarding school in the United States and was founded to protect and inculcate the old virtues. Traces the evolution of the academy from basic principles of the first headmaster, Eliphalet Pearson; in the course of 200 years Phillips Academy went from Calvinism to coeducation, 1778-1978. Primary sources; 9 photos, 33 notes.
R. S. Sliwoski

585. Anderson, Harry H., ed. REMEMBRANCES OF NASHOTAH DAYS: TWO LETTERS OF GUSTAF UNONIUS. *Swedish Pioneer Hist. Q. 1976 27(2): 111-115.* Reprints two letters of Gustaf Unonius originally published in the *Nashotah Scholast* in 1884. Unonius was very busy; he feels he should have accomplished more in life. He fondly remembers those he knew at Nashotah House, the Protestant Episcopal seminary. Based on primary sources; 4 notes.
K. J. Puffer

586. Andrew, John. EDUCATING THE HEATHEN: THE FOREIGN MISSION SCHOOL CONTROVERSY AND AMERICAN IDEALS. *J. of Am. Studies [Great Britain] 1978 12(3): 331-342.* The American Board of Commissioners for Foreign Missions established a Foreign Mission School at Cornwall, Connecticut, in 1816. Soon many of the students were American Indians, mostly Cherokee and Choctaws. There students received instruction in agriculture, commerce, mechanics, history, and religious studies. But disagreements plagued the institution and placed it at odds with townsmen until the school closed in 1827 amidst controversies involving some of its Indian students. The conflicts centered on the issue of whether American Indian education and missionary endeavors should focus on preserving the Indians' native culture or be directed toward producing total assimilation of the Indians into white society. Manuscript materials and secondary sources; 43 notes.
H. T. Lovin

587. Arons, Stephen. THE SEPARATION OF SCHOOL AND STATE: *PIERCE* RECONSIDERED. *Harvard Educ. Rev. 1976 46(1): 76-104.* Notes that in *Pierce* v. *Society of Sisters* (US, 1925) the Supreme Court affirmed that the Constitution "protect(s) parents' rights to pass along their values to their children," and argues that a First Amendment reading of that decision may prove present forms of compulsory education to be unconstitutional.

588. Arrington, Leonard J. SEVEN STEPS TO GREATNESS. *Brigham Young U. Studies 1976 16(4): 459-470.* Sketches the historical development of Brigham Young University. Traces the progress of education for Mormon students from the inception of Joseph Smith's interest in the subject, through the establishment of the Dusenberry Grade School, to the founding of Brigham Young Academy in 1875. Includes historical vignettes of significant events and leaders in the evolution of BYU into an institution of higher learning. Focuses on the University's accreditation, graduate program, and expansion. Covers 1831-1975.
M. S. Legan

589. Ashley, Yvonne. "THAT'S THE WAY WE WERE RAISED": AN ORAL INTERVIEW WITH ADA DAMON. *Frontiers 1977 2(2): 59-62.* A Navajo woman recalls her childhood on a reservation near Shiprock, New Mexico, 1900-20; her mother, a medicine woman; and her education at a Christian boarding school and at the Sherman Institute for Indians; part of a special issue on women's oral history.

590. Bailey, Warner M. WILLIAM ROBERTSON SMITH AND AMERICAN BIBLICAL STUDIES. *J. of Presbyterian Hist. 1973 51(3): 285-308.* Smith's theology and its effects on the Biblical Theology Movement in America, 1870-83. S

591. Baird, Frank, Jr., ed. A MISSIONARY EDUCATOR: DR. THOS. MC CULLOCH. *Dalhousie Rev. [Canada] 1972-73 52(4): 611-617.* Discusses Thomas McCulloch's early life, his work as a Presbyterian minister, and efforts in establishing Nova Scotia's Pictou Academy, ending with his acceptance of the presidency of Dalhousie College. Covers 1803-42. 4 notes. R. V. Ritter

592. Baker, Gordon C. CATALOGUE OF SUNDAY SCHOOL BOOKS BELONGING TO THE PLEASANT HILL SUNDAY SCHOOL. *Western Pennsylvania Hist. Mag. 1980 63(2): 185-187.* Lists the entries in a ledger, "Catalogue of Sunday School Books belonging to the Pleasant Hill S.S.," which dates from 1842 to 1857 and includes the *Youth's Friend* book, which covers 1823 to 1830, and is from the New Geneva area of Fayette County, Pennsylvania.

593. Bartel, Deena. UNION COLLEGE: FROM CORN FIELDS TO GOLDEN CORDS. *Adventist Heritage 1976 3(2): 20-29.* Union College in Lincoln, Nebraska, was founded in 1891 by the Seventh-Day Adventists.

594. Baur, John C. FOR CHRIST AND HIS KINGDOM, 1923. *Concordia Hist. Inst. Q. 1977 50(3): 99-105.* Confronted by overcrowded and obsolete facilities at Jefferson Avenue and Miami Street, St. Louis, the leadership of the Concordia Seminary launched a major fund raising project in 1923 to erect a new seminary in Clayton, Missouri. A synodical committee, which consisted of Dr. John H. C. Fritz, Theodore Eckhardt, and Dr. John C. Baur, confronted numerous and complex difficulties in raising the necessary funds during the 1920's. This memoir records the success of the committee in overcoming those problems. Dedication of the new campus occurred in 1926. Based on personal recollections. W. T. Walker

595. Beaman, Robert S. ALEXANDER HALL AT THE PRINCETON THEOLOGICAL SEMINARY. *Princeton Hist. 1977 (2): 45-60.* Alexander Hall, the first building built by the Presbyterian Church to serve as a seminary, heralded the establishment of the Princeton Theological Seminary, 1815.

596. Begnal, Calista. THE SISTERS OF THE CONGREGATION OF NOTRE DAME, NINETEENTH-CENTURY KINGSTON. *Study Sessions: Can. Catholic Hist. Assoc. 1973 40: 27-34.* Examines the efforts of religious women during 1841-48, important years in the history of religious education. S

597. Bender, Norman J. THE ELUSIVE QUEST FOR THE "PRINCETON OF THE WEST." *Colorado Mag. 1975 52(4): 299-316.* Beginning with the efforts of the Rev. Sheldon Jackson in 1874, several abortive attempts were made to found a Presbyterian college in Colorado. A building was built and classes were held at Westminster University from 1907-17. While many factors contributed to the failure of Presbyterian colleges in Colorado, the most important were financial difficulties. Primary sources; 2 illus., 55 notes. O. H. Zabel

598. Bender, Norman J. THE VERY ATMOSPHERE IS CHARGED WITH UNBELIEF: PRESBYTERIANS AND HIGHER EDUCATION IN MONTANA, 1869-1900. *Montana 1978 28(2): 16-25.* To civilize the western frontier and prevent "liberalism," the Presbyterian Church sent missionaries to establish congregations and found a system of Christian schools. Reverend Sheldon Jackson superintended Presbyterian efforts in Montana. Reverend Lyman B. Crittenden and his daughter Mary began the Bozeman Female Seminary in 1873, but experienced difficulties. As a result, Crittenden moved the school, renaming it the Gallatin Valley Female Seminary. In 1878 the school closed altogether. The Presbyterian Board of Aid for Colleges and Academies opened the Bozeman Academy in 1887, but closed it in 1892 when a state supported college opened in Bozeman. In another attempt to found a permanent college, the Presbytery of Montana purchased the five year old Montana Collegiate Institute in Deer Lodge during 1882. Renamed the College of Montana, the school struggled to remain solvent until 1900. It reopened in 1904 but closed finally in 1918. Reverend Duncan M. McMillan served as president for most of the period. While low enrollments and lack of financial support plagued Presbyterian educational efforts, their work did help build a "good" Montana on traditional Christian principals. Based on materials in the Presbyterian Historical Society, Philadelphia, and on secondary works; 10 illus., 23 notes. R. C. Myers

599. Bergendoff, Conrad. AN ANCIENT CULTURE IN A NEW LAND. *Swedish Pioneer Hist. Q. 1976 27(2): 127-134.* Swedish immigrants brought with them the traditions of Swedish Lutheran Church. Augustana College in Rock Island was formed to train clergy. The college and the synod formed a point of contact for cultural transmission and communication within the Swedish community, 1855-1956. Based on secondary sources; 5 notes. K. J. Puffer

600. Bevins, Ann B. SISTERS OF THE VISITATION: 100 YEARS IN SCOTT COUNTY, MT. ADMIRABILIS AND CARDOME. *Register of the Kentucky Hist. Soc. 1976 74(1): 30-39.* Surveys the origins and development of the educational efforts of the Sisters of the Visitation in Scott County, Kentucky. The first academy, Mount Admirabilis, opened in 1875. In 1896, the nuns moved to Cardome, the Georgetown home of former governor James Fisher Robinson. Based on primary and secondary sources; 30 notes. J. F. Paul

601. Bixler, Julius Seelye. ALEXANDER MEIKLEJOHN: THE MAKING OF THE AMHERST MIND. *New England Q. 1974 47(2): 179-195.* During the years 1912-23 when Alexander Meiklejohn was president of Amherst College he profoundly influenced the minds of both students and faculty. In contrast to the earlier Calvinism, he emphasized honest inquiry as the principle to guide the college. His emphasis on a generally intellectual attitude was not caused by indifference to specific moral crusades. Evaluates the possible reasons for his forced resignation in 1923, and speculates on the heights Amherst might have reached if Meikeljohn could have remained another decade. E. P. Stickney

602. Boles, Donald E. CHURCH AND STATE AND THE BURGER COURT: RECENT DEVELOPMENTS AFFECTING PAROCHIAL SCHOOLS. *J. of Church and State 1976 18(1): 21-38.* The Burger Court has been more strict in its interpretations of the first amendment than the Warren Court. Discusses the voting record of the justices on church-state relations and the reasons for their stands on various cases. Points out that the Burger Court has practically ended legislative subterfuge to get around the constitution. Also discusses the fact that higher education cases are approached from a different philosophy. Covers 1950-75. 85 notes. E. E. Eminhizer

603. Boylan, Anne M. THE ROLE OF CONVERSION IN NINETEENTH-CENTURY SUNDAY SCHOOLS. *Am. Studies 1979 20(1): 35-48.* Sunday schools reflected the broader development of new institutions for children to accompany changes in child-rearing methods. Surveys the evangelical Protestant Sunday school and how it expressed ideas about the psychology of children and adolescents. These schools shifted from efforts to enhance literacy to an effort to precipitate early conversion by the 1820's and 1830's. They reflect one more effort to devise institutions to do jobs previously done by the home. Primary and secondary sources; 24 notes. J. A. Andrew

604. Boylan, Anne M. SUNDAY SCHOOLS AND CHANGING EVANGELICAL VIEWS OF CHILDREN IN THE 1820'S. *Church Hist. 1979 48(3): 320-334.* In the urban Northeast, the 1820's were a decade of evangelical fervor and revivalism, and the formative period for Protestant Sunday Schools. The organizational and curricular developments of evangelical Sunday Schools reflect adults' changing theological preconceptions of the children they taught. Although there was little uniformity in schools' development, Sunday School workers at least

evolved an ideal program. This program guided children to conversion, through the Bible class, and back into the school as teachers. 45 notes. M. D. Dibert

605. Buckley, Cathryn. THE EVERETT INSTITUTE. *North Louisiana Hist. Assoc. J. 1977 8(3): 119-124.* Everett Institute was founded in 1893 by the Everett Baptist Association and was located at Spearsville, in Union Parish. Its purpose was to offer the first two years of college courses to prepare its students to enter the state's larger colleges as juniors. George Mason was the Institute's first principal and served during 1894-98. The driving force behind the school's establishment was J. V. B. Waldrop, pastor of the Spearsville Baptist Church. The Institute's name honored John Pickney Everett, one of the founders of the Everett Baptist Association. Although it closed its doors in 1908 the Institute had earned a good reputation in north Louisiana. Primary and secondary sources; 36 notes. A. N. Garland

606. Christensen, Harold T. and Cannon, Kenneth L., II. THE FUNDAMENTALIST EMPHASIS AT BRIGHAM YOUNG UNIVERSITY: 1935-1973. *J. for the Sci. Study of Religion 1978 17(1): 53-57.* Studies of the student body at Brigham Young University show that BYU students are becoming more conservative on religious matters.

607. Cohen, Ronald D. PURITAN EDUCATION IN SEVENTEENTH CENTURY ENGLAND AND NEW ENGLAND. *Hist. of Educ. Q. 1973 13(3): 301-307.* A review essay on Richard L. Greaves's *The Puritan Revolution and Educational Thought: Background for Reform* (Rutgers U. Press, 1970) and Robert Middlekauff's *The Mathers: Three Generations of Puritan Intellectuals, 1596-1728* (Oxford U. Press, 1971). Greaves divides the religious and intellectual life of mid-17th-century Englishmen into three categories: sectary, Puritan, and Anglican. The Puritans stressed organized polity, the sectaries spiritualism and lay piety. Both desired to use the schools and universities for the betterment of society. Middlekauff investigates why education in Puritan New England was so successful in the case of the three generations of Mathers. By "institutionalizing their religious zeal, Richard Mather's generation ignored the most important educational influence upon their own lives, their experiences in the world." In England the sectaries were aware of this fact, divorcing religion from the curriculum. 13 notes. E. P. Stickney

608. Comeault, Gilbert-L. LA QUESTION DES ÉCOLES DU MANITOBA: UN NOUVEL ÉCLAIRAGE [The schools issue in Manitoba: a new light]. *Rev. d'Hist. de l'Amérique Française [Canada] 1979 33(1): 3-23.* Reexamines the schools issue in Manitoba from 1890 to 1916, refuting interpretations still given by most historians. After recalling the policy of Archbishop Msgr. A.-A. Taché, centers on the new line of action of his successor in 1894, Msgr. Adélard Langevin, who opposed the Anglo-Saxon campaign against the principle of bilingual and private schools, and mobilized the Franco-Manitoban political force to protect the other Catholic groups' faith. Based on archival documents and other primary sources; 83 notes. G. P. Cleyet

609. Coogan, M. Jane. THE SISTERS OF CHARITY OF THE BLESSED VIRGIN MARY: THEIR YEARS IN PHILADELPHIA, 1833-1843. *Records of the Am. Catholic Hist. Soc. of Philadelphia 1974 85(3-4): 109-122.* The Sisters of Charity of the Blessed Virgin Mary established themselves in Philadelphia. They conducted a school and supplemented their income by sewing. Unable to win episcopal approval to take final vows, they moved to Dubuque and established a mother house and a boarding academy. 75 notes. J. M. McCarthy

610. Copeland, Robert M. THE REFORMED PRESBYTERIAN THEOLOGICAL SEMINARY IN CINCINNATI, 1845-1849. *Cincinnati Hist. Soc. Bull. 1973 31(3): 151-163.* Discusses the antislavery sentiments of the Reformed Presbyterian Church and how they were reflected in the early integration of the Reformed Presbyterian Theological Seminary.

611. Cottrell, Raymond F. THE BIBLE RESEARCH FELLOWSHIP: A PIONEERING SEVENTH-DAY ADVENTIST ORGANIZATION IN RETROSPECT. *Adventist Heritage 1978 5(1): 39-52.* Details the history and purpose of the Bible Research Fellowship, conducted by the college Bible Teachers of North America during 1943-52.

612. Craven, W. Frank. JOSEPH CLARK AND THE REBUILDING OF NASSAU HALL. *Princeton U. Lib. Chronicle 1979 41(1): 54-68.* Discusses Presbyterian minister Joseph Clark's (1751-1813) manuscript account of his fund raising journey for the rebuilding of Princeton University's Nassau Hall, destroyed by fire in 1802.

613. Cronbach, Abraham. THE SPROUT THAT GREW. *Am. Jewish Arch. 1975 27(1): 51-60.* Points out the contributions of Isaac M. Wise to the Hebrew Union College in Cincinnati, 1870's-1900. S

614. Curry, Thomas J. ETHNIC PAROCHIAL SCHOOLS: DIVERSITY OF ISOLATION? *Rev. in Am. Hist. 1977 5(3): 354-359.* Review article prompted by James W. Sanders's *The Education of an Urban Minority: Catholics in Chicago, 1833-1965* (New York: Oxford U. Pr., 1977).

615. Dallmann, Roger Howard. SPRINGFIELD SEMINARY. *Concordia Hist. Inst. Q. 1977 50(3): 106-130.* During the mid-19th century the spiritual needs of German Lutherans in the Midwest were not being tended. As a result of the efforts of such missionaries as Friedrich Wynecken, Wilhelm Loehe, and Wilhelm Sihler, this situation was remedied by the deployment of additional Lutheran ministers, the opening of Lutheran schools, and the creation in Ft. Wayne of the Concordia Seminary in 1846. The Seminary moved to St. Louis, Missouri, in 1861, and its practical division moved to Springfield, Illinois, in 1874. Through this seminary, during the last half of the 19th century and the first half of the 20th, the Lutheran Church (Missouri Synod) succeeded in serving the spiritual needs of midwestern congregations by establishing additional seminaries, and by developing a viable synodical tradition. Primary sources; 99 notes. W. T. Walker

616. Daniel, W. Harrison. THE GENESIS OF RICHMOND COLLEGE, 1843-1860. *Virginia Mag. of Hist. and Biog. 1975 83(2): 131-149.* When Virginia Baptist Seminary was transformed into Richmond College, the new institution faced many problems. In the early years the trustees developed a curriculum, established rules of behavior for students and faculty, and raised funds to keep the college operating. By the 1850's many problems had been solved. The faculty and student body had increased, and financially the college was flourishing. The Civil War destroyed the gains of the previous decades, however, and rebuilding had to begin after Appomattox. Based largely on the minutes of the Board of Trustees and newspaper accounts; 57 notes. R. F. Oaks

617. Daniel, W. Harrison. MADISON COLLEGE, 1851-1858: A METHODIST PROTESTANT SCHOOL. *Methodist Hist. 1979 17(2): 90-105.* The Methodist Protestant Church, founded in 1830, was unable to establish a college for a number of years. In 1849 the Pittsburgh Conference was offered the buildings of Madison College in Uniontown, Pennsylvania. The General Conference of the church accepted the offer, and the college was opened in 1851. Lack of support, the question of slavery and the admission of blacks, sectional differences, and internal problems led to its closing of 1858. Details on courses, faculty, student costs, and internal problems. 54 notes. H. L. Calkin

618. De Leon, Arnoldo. BLOWOUT 1910 STYLE: A CHICANO SCHOOL BOYCOTT IN WEST TEXAS. *Texana 1974 12(2): 124-140.* In 1910 the San Angelo Board of Education prohibited the integration of Anglos and Mexicans, and the Chicanos organized in an effort to integrate the public schools. They were unsuccessful, but in 1912 the Presbyterian Church established the Mexican Presbyterian Mission School and the Chicanos pulled out of the public schools completely for several years. As time passed, they began to accept the separate school system and drifted back into public schools. Primary and secondary sources; 45 notes. B. D. Ledbetter

619. deValk, Alphonse. CATHOLIC HIGHER EDUCATION AND UNIVERSITY AFFILIATION IN ALBERTA, 1906-1926. *Study Sessions: Can. Catholic Hist. Assoc. [Canada] 1979 (46): 23-47.* Despite protest from some members of the hierarchy, Archbishop Henry Joseph O'Leary continued the work begun by Bishop Emile Legal in 1906 and successfully established St. Joseph's University College, a Catholic adjunct to the University of Alberta, to minister to Catholic students on campus.

620. deValk, Alphonse. INDEPENDENT UNIVERSITY OR FEDERATED COLLEGE?: THE DEBATE AMONG ROMAN CATHOLICS DURING THE YEARS 1918-1921. *Saskatchewan Hist. [Canada] 1977 30(1): 18-32.* Deals with the complicated and often quarrelsome discussions of English-speaking Western Canadian Catholics attempting to establish a location for a college with degree-granting powers in Saskatchewan. The struggle centered on Regina and Saskatoon with the eventual victory going to Saskatoon through the federated college of St. Thomas More and the university there. J. J. Leddy, Father Henry Carr, President Murray (University of Saskatchewan), Archbishop Mathieu, Father Daly, and Father MacMahon played prominent roles in the eventual establishment of the federated college in Saskatoon. 54 notes.
C. Held

621. Dick, Everett. THE FOUNDING OF UNION COLLEGE, 1890-1900. *Nebraska Hist. 1979 60(3): 447-470.* Discusses the founding of Union College in Lincoln, Nebraska, and the first decade of its history. An Adventist college with roots in the reform movement of the 1840's, it also capitalized on an evangelical tradition that appealed to German and Scandinavian immigrants whose children attended the college during the 1890's along with those of native born Americans. Students at the outset were segregated on the basis of sex and ethnic background.
R. Lowitt

622. Dix, William S. THE PRINCETON UNIVERSITY LIBRARY IN THE EIGHTEENTH CENTURY. *Princeton U. Lib. Chronicle 1978 40(1): 1-102.* Gives an account of the Presbyterian origin of Princeton University and the history of its library during the 18th century.

623. Drury, Clifford M. CHURCH-SPONSORED SCHOOLS IN EARLY CALIFORNIA. *Pacific Historian 1976 20(2): 158-166.* Higher education in California began with more than 60 church schools during 1850-74. Based on secondary sources. G. L. Olson

624. Dwyer, Robert J. CATHOLIC EDUCATION IN UTAH: 1875-1975. *Utah Hist. Q. 1975 43(4): 362-378.* The Bishops of Utah Territory, Father Lawrence Scanlan, the Most Reverends Joseph Sarsfield Glass, John J. Mitty, and James E. Kearney, Monsignor Duane G. Hunt, and the Most Reverend Joseph Lennox Federal encouraged the development of Catholic education. Noteworthy schools were Saint Mary's Academy (later Saint Mary-of-the-Wasatch College and Academy for Women), All Hallows College, Judge Memorial High School, and Saint Joseph's High School. A century of educational effort by a religious minority is a tribute to the Catholic Church. Based on primary and secondary sources; 5 illus. J. L. Hazelton

625. Edward, C. ELIZABETH ANN SETON: MOTHER, FOUNDER, SAINT. *Am. Hist. Illus. 1975 10(8): 12-21.* Describes the life of Elizabeth Ann Seton (1774-1821), founder of the White House, the first Catholic parochial school in the United States.

626. Esh, Levi A. THE AMISH PAROCHIAL SCHOOL MOVEMENT. *Mennonite Q. Rev. 1977 51(1): 69-75.* Examines Old Order Amish church schools started after 1937 in Lancaster County, Pennsylvania. E. E. Eminhizer

627. Everman, H. E. EARLY EDUCATIONAL CHANNELS OF BOURBON COUNTY. *Register of the Kentucky Hist. Soc. 1975 73(2): 136-149.* Reports on education in Bourbon County, Kentucky. Education was provided in the home or in religious-oriented private schools until 1846 when public education came into being. Primary and secondary sources; 50 notes. J. F. Paul

628. Ferguson, Anne Williams. CARRY ME NOT, REPEAT NOT, BACK TO OLE VIRGINNY: A BOARDING SCHOOL CHRONICLE OF THE 40'S. *Virginia Q. Rev. 1976 52(2): 243-248.* Presents a humorous description of experiences at Chatham Hall, an Episcopalian boarding school in Virginia in the 1940's. From examining her daughter's experience at another school, the author concludes that the prudery and snobbishness of the 40's has been somewhat reduced, but not entirely eliminated. O. H. Zabel

629. Findlay, James. THE SPCTEW AND WESTERN COLLEGES: RELIGION AND HIGHER EDUCATION IN MID-NINETEENTH CENTURY AMERICA. *Hist. of Educ. Q. 1977 17(1): 31-62.* An extensive study of the Society for the Promotion of Collegiate and Theological Education at the West during 1843-73. Evangelical Protestants were deeply concerned that their distinct worldview be implanted in the then-evolving system of American colleges. The Society also provided key financial support for these colleges in a time of limited state interest in higher education. The work and efforts of Theron Baldwin were particularly important to the Society. The study of the Society sheds light on the "unity, vitality, and aggressiveness" of American evangelical Protestantism itself. Based on extensive archival research and on primary and secondary sources; 84 notes. L. C. Smith

630. Fleming, Sandford. A GREAT ERA IN BAPTIST EDUCATION. *Foundations 1974 17(3): 226-236.* Discusses the administration of Luther Wesley Smith as executive secretary of the Baptist Board of Education and Publication, 1941-56.

631. Franklin, Robert L. GEORGIA BAPTIST STUDENT UNION POWER: DAVID BASCOM NICHOLSON III. *Viewpoints: Georgia Baptist Hist. 1974 4: 67-85.* Examines the activities (1925-52) of David Bascom Nicholson, III, educator, religious leader, and first secretary of the Baptist Student Center in Athens, Georgia. S

632. Galvin, John T. THE DARK AGES OF BOSTON POLITICS. *Massachusetts Hist. Soc. Pro. 1977 89: 88-111.* During the 1880's women emerged as a political force, questions of corruption emerged, the park system developed, the parochial school system was debated, and Irish Americans became a force in local politics. Many of these issues' effects are still felt. Primary and secondary sources; 109 notes.
G. W. R. Ward

633. Gardner, Bettye. ANTE-BELLUM BLACK EDUCATION IN BALTIMORE. *Maryland Hist. Mag. 1976 71(3): 360-366.* "On the eve of the Civil War Baltimore had the largest free black community in the nation." About 15 schools for blacks were operating. From Sabbath schools operated by Methodists, Presbyterians, and Quakers, black education expanded through the efforts of the African Methodist Episcopal Church under Daniel Coker, and the Oblates' Academy "for young girls of color." William Watkins' Academy was perhaps the most prestigious private school for blacks, while the school run by William Lively offered a comprehensive curriculum and "showed the seriousness with which . . . blacks pursued the education of the whole person." All black schools were self-sustaining, receiving no state or local government funds, and whites in Baltimore generally opposed educating the black population, continuing to tax black property holders to maintain schools from which black children were excluded by law. Baltimore's black community, nevertheless, was one of the largest and most cohesive in America due to this experience. Covers 1794-1860. From Baltimore City Records, and secondary materials; 25 notes. G. J. Bobango

634. Gardner, Robert G. WOODLAND FEMALE COLLEGE. *Viewpoints: Georgia Baptist Hist. 1978 (6): 71-82.* History of Woodland Female College in Cedartown, Georgia, associated with the Baptist Church in that state, 1851-87.

635. Gerlach, Don R. and DeMille, George E. [SAMUEL JOHNSON AND KING'S COLLEGE].

SAMUEL JOHNSON AND THE FOUNDING OF KING'S COLLEGE, 1751-1755. *Hist. Mag. of the Protestant Episcopal Church 1975 44(3): 335-352.* King's College was the forerunner of Columbia University, New York. Samuel Johnson was the first president of the college. Underscores the partisan rivalry between the Presbyterians, under the leadership of William Livingston, who opposed the founding of the college for fear of Anglican control, and the Anglicans who, along with the Dutch Reformed, favored establishing the school. At the time the college was conceived, Johnson was rector in Stratford, Connecticut. Because of the low stipend, when he came to King's he also served as assistant rector at Trinity Church. From the beginning the college emphasized not only the classics, but also science, history, and vocational courses. 57 notes.

SAMUEL JOHNSON: PRAESES COLLEGII REGIS, 1755-1763. *Hist. Mag. of the Protestant Episcopal Church 1975 44(4): 417-436.* Chronicles Johnson's accomplishments 1755-63. He laid a good foundation—promulgated the first college statutes, provided the first college hall, collected a library, and modified the curriculum. Based largely on Herbert and Carol Schneider, eds., *Samuel Johnson, President of King's College: His Career and Writings*; 86 notes. H. M. Parker, Jr.

636. Gilborn, Craig. THE REVEREND SAMUEL DAVIES IN GREAT BRITAIN. *Winterthur Portfolio 1973 8: 45-62.* The trustees of the College of New Jersey (now Princeton University) requested that Samuel Davies (1723-61) and Gilbert Tennent (1703-64) undertake a fund-raising trip to Great Britain in November 1753. The ministers were to raise funds for the college, gain clarification of the law regarding the number of meetinghouses allowed dissenters in Virginia, and collect money for the Commissioners for Indian Affairs. Davies' diary of the trip reveals the decline of dissent in England; the extent to which Americans were dependent on foreign money, advice, and personnel; that despite the hazards of travel, communications with England and the continent was remarkably efficient; and that the similarity of conditions in America and Great Britain needs further study. The experience in England indicated that persuasive preaching was the preference of Davies' 18th-century peers. Based on primary and secondary sources; 8 illus., 70 notes. N. A. Kuntz

637. Gina, Terry. KEYSTONE GRADED LESSONS: WATERSHED IN BAPTIST CHURCH SCHOOL EDUCATION. *Foundations 1975 18(3): 261-271.* Traces the development of Sunday school literature among Baptists from 1824 to 1909. Discusses factors which influenced this development, the American Sunday School Union and the *International Uniform Lessons*. Describes and evaluates the first series of the *Keystone Graded Lessons*. 20 notes. E. E. Eminhizer

638. Gladden, Richard K. and Hanson, Grant W. AMERICAN BAPTIST CHURCH SCHOOL CURRICULUM: A ONE HUNDRED AND FIFTY-YEAR STORY. *Foundations 1974 17(3): 214-225.* Discusses Baptists' school curricula 1824-1974, including educational issues of the 1970's.

639. Glauert, Ralph E. AN UNCOMMON COMMITMENT: CLERGYMEN AND THEIR SCHOOLS IN FRONTIER MISSOURI. *Missouri Hist. Soc. Bull. 1977 34(1): 3-16.* Describes schools founded by Protestant clergymen, notably Timothy Flint, Salmon Giddings, and John Mason Peck, in Missouri prior to 1830. The clergy's lot on the Missouri frontier proved difficult. Protestant denominations provided little compensation, thus forcing the clergy to work at other occupations. Many founded secular schools although they deemed teaching secondary to their religious commitments. They were further frustrated because economic poverty compelled them to emphasize secular matters in their schools. The clergy also organized Sunday schools that initially encountered substantial community hostility. Based on reminiscences, unpublished manuscripts, theses, newspapers, and secondary sources; 3 photos, 71 notes. H. T. Lovin

640. Gleason, Philip. THE CURRICULUM OF THE OLD-TIME CATHOLIC COLLEGE: A STUDENT'S VIEW. *Records of the Am. Catholic Hist. Soc. of Philadelphia 1977 88(1-4): 105-122.* Describes and analyzes life at Holy Cross College in Worcester, Massachusetts, through the diary of James A. Healy (later 2nd Bishop of Portland, Maine) during 1849, his last year as a student at the college. 66 notes. J. M. McCarthy

641. Good, Noah G. SUNDAY SCHOOLS: FROM ROBERT RAIKES TO 1980. *Pennsyvania Mennonite Heritage 1980 3(4): 2-11.* Discusses Sunday schools from their beginning in 1780 through the efforts of Robert Raikes, who owned the *Gloucester Journal* and was concerned with the social injustices of the time in England, focusing on Sunday schools associated with the Mennonite Church in America from the first meeting of a Mennonite Sunday school in 1840 in Pennsylvania, until 1980.

642. Greeley, Andrew M. WHO CONTROLS CATHOLIC EDUCATION? *Educ. and Urban Soc. 1977 9(2): 147-166.* Catholic education in primary and secondary schools is administered in a disorganized manner by people who are promoted from within the system. This discourages courage and intelligence. Conservatism is the highest virtue. Discusses the theoretical and real lines of power. Covers 1960's-70's. 5 notes, biblio. C. A. D'Aniello

643. Greer, Allan. THE SUNDAY SCHOOLS OF UPPER CANADA. *Ontario Hist. [Canada] 1975 67(3): 169-184.* The role of Sunday schools in Upper Canada in the early 19th century was to inculcate loyalty to the king, obedience to employers, regular and industrious habits, and fear of God.

644. Grundman, Adolph H. NORTHERN BAPTISTS AND THE FOUNDING OF VIRGINIA UNION UNIVERSITY: THE PERILS OF PATERNALISM. *J. of Negro Hist. 1978 63(1): 26-41.* The American Baptist Home Missionary Society produced a schism among black Baptists in Virginia: separatists who supported the Virginia Seminary and cooperationists who supported Virginia Union University. Afro-American leaders in Virginia used white paternalism to stimulate productive activity among their followers. Covers 1865-1905. Primary materials in the Rochester-Colgate Theological Seminary Archives and secondary materials; 62 notes. N. G. Sapper

645. Hahn, Stephen S. LEXINGTON'S THEOLOGICAL LIBRARY, 1832-1859. *South Carolina Hist. Mag. 1979 80(1): 36-49.* Chronicles the growth of the Lutheran Theological Seminary Library of Lexington, South Carolina, 1832-59.

646. Handy, Robert T. THE INFLUENCE OF CANADIANS ON BAPTIST THEOLOGICAL EDUCATION IN THE UNITED STATES. *Foundations 1980 23(1): 42-56.* Traces the part of Canadians living in the United States in the development of Baptist theological education in the United States. Gives many examples of names and contributions. Covers 1760-1980. 9 notes. E. E. Eminhizer

647. Hart, John W. PRINCETON THEOLOGICAL SEMINARY: THE REORGANIZATION OF 1929. *J. of Presbyterian Hist. 1980 58(2): 124-140.* Traces the dual intricacies through the Board of Trustees of Princeton Theological Seminary and the actions of the General Assembly of the Presbyterian Church in the United States in the 1920's whereby the seminary underwent drastic reorganization. The organizational surgery at Princeton was seen as part of the greater struggle between liberals and conservatives in the Presbyterian Church. The latter sought to preserve Princeton as their headquarters; but with the seminary's reorganization in 1929, a major movement in 19th-century Protestantism, the Princeton Theology, had been reduced to localized agitation. The reorganization showed decisively the intention of the Presbyterian Church to open itself to new expressions of faith. Minutes of the Board of Trustees, Princeton Seminary; Machen Papers, McCormick Library, Westminster Seminary, Philadelphia, contemporary church newspapers, and secondary studies; 81 notes. H. M. Parker, Jr.

648. Helmreich, William B. OLD WINE IN NEW BOTTLES: ADVANCED YESHIVOT IN THE UNITED STATES. *Am. Jewish Hist. 1979 69(2): 234-256.* The Orthodox Rabbi Isaac Elchanan Theological Seminary, founded in 1896 and later merged into Yeshiva University, was the first advanced yeshiva in America. Between the world wars, other yeshivot were founded, spurred by the immigration of important European rabbis. Since World War II, the yeshiva community has grown even more rapidly. It is now an important force in American Jewish life. Based on interviews and secondary sources; 29 notes. J. D. Sarna

649. Hendrix, Scott H. LUTHER AND THE CLIMATE FOR THEOLOGICAL EDUCATION. *Lutheran Q. 1974 26(1): 3-11.* Brings Luther's theology and reforming motivation to bear upon the problem of theological education which was raised in the Lutheran Church-Missouri Synod in July 1973. "The issue is not merely theological disagreement, but the right of a Lutheran theological seminary to pursue the truth according to generally accepted academic criteria. The issue at stake is the same issue which has plagued the church's educational enterprise at crucial points in its history at least since the Middle Ages: the church and academic freedom." Luther's theology "demonstrates how one can be true to one's Christian commitment and at the same time keep the confessional and hierarchical monkey off one's back." 22 notes. D. D. Cameron

650. Herbst, Jurgen. THE FIRST THREE AMERICAN COLLEGES: SCHOOLS OF REFORMATION. *Perspectives in Am. Hist. 1974 8: 7-52.* Harvard University, Yale University, and the College of

William and Mary did not begin as incorporated colleges, but as unincorporated provincial Latin grammer boarding schools tightly controlled by boards of trustees. In their conception and practice they were more similar to the academies and grammar schools of Europe than to medieval universities. The control which external boards exercised over all three institutions reflected the strong Reformation belief in the united authority of church and state. Their avowed primary purpose was to spread the Protestant faith and resist heresy and Roman Catholicism.
W. A. Wiegand

651. Herbst, Jurgen. FROM RELIGION TO POLITICS: DEBATES AND CONFRONTATIONS OVER AMERICAN COLLEGE GOVERNANCE IN THE MID-EIGHTEENTH CENTURY. *Harvard Educ. Rev. 1976 46(3): 397-424.* Discusses political and religious controversies regarding the governance of colleges and universities from the 1740's-60's, emphasizing church and state issues.

652. Hernández Borch, Carmen. LA UNIVERSIDAD CATÓLICA DE PUERTO RICO: SÍNTESIS DE SU HISTORIA [The Catholic University of Puerto Rico: summary of its history]. *Horizontes [Puerto Rico] 1973-74 17(33-34): 5-26.* In commemoration of the 25th anniversary of the Catholic University of Puerto Rico, sets forth the history of the institution from its conception and foundation, discussing its recognition and accreditation, the opening in 1948, academic objectives, the governing body, constituent colleges and faculties, affiliated centers, the law school, library, office of cultural development, intercultural communications institute, community college, publications, orientation center, financing, construction, credit cooperative, and church. Based on secondary sources; 10 illus., 30 notes. P. J. Taylorson

653. Hesten, Richard L. CHURCH SUPPORT FOR HIGHER EDUCATION: ISSUES OF SURVIVAL AND PURPOSE. *J. of Church and State 1978 20(3): 451-468.* The place of the church-related college in American higher education is discussed. Six purposes that can be served by church colleges are: l) to make purpose a central issue in higher education, 2) to prepare for responsible value choices, 3) present a Christian view of human nature, 4) perfect the significance of religion in the American experience, 5) prepare responsible leaders for church and state, and 6) act as proprietor for church and state. Covers 1636-1978. 37 notes.
E. E. Eminhizer

654. Himmelfarb, Harold S. THE INTERACTION EFFECTS OF PARENTS, SPOUSE AND SCHOOLING: COMPARING THE IMPACT OF JEWISH AND CATHOLIC SCHOOLS. *Sociol. Q. 1977 18(4): 468-477.* This paper discusses the literature on the long-range impact of schooling and the types of effects that schools have shown. It compares data on the impact of Jewish schooling on adult religiosity with similar data from a study of Catholic schooling. Like previous studies on other types of schools, the the main effect of Jewish schooling seems to be an accentuation of parental influences. This effect is diminished substantially if not supported by marriage to a religious spouse. However, on some types of religiosity, extensive Jewish schooling produces "conversion" effects which persisted even when pre-school and post-school supports were lacking. Covers 1960's-70's. The implications of these findings are discussed. J

655. Hiner, N. Ray. PREPARING FOR THE HARVEST: THE CONCEPT OF NEW BIRTH AND THE THEORY OF RELIGIOUS EDUCATION ON THE EVE OF THE FIRST AWAKENING. *Fides et Hist. 1976 9(1): 8-25.* The First Great Awakening was, in part, the result of several decades of human endeavor aimed at revitalizing the spiritual life of New England. Jonathan Edwards, Solomon Stoddard, Thomas Foxcroft, Thomas Prince, Cotton Mather, and numerous other Puritan ministers had sought "a strategy to convert the young and reverse the decline in religious fervor." The Awakening was built on a rededication to religious education, a revised concept of salvation that provided a greater role for the seeker, and an insistence upon a regenerate ministry. Based on primary and secondary sources; 72 notes.
R. E. Butchart

656. Holder, Ray. CENTENARY: ROOTS OF A PIONEER COLLEGE (1838-1844). *J. of Mississippi Hist. 1980 42(2): 77-98.* Present-day Centenary College in Shreveport, Louisiana, had its genesis in an antebellum educational renaissance among Mississippi Methodists. The Mississippi Conference, seeking the advantage of an institution of higher learning in closer proximity to its ministerial endeavors, was stimulated by the Wesley Centennial (1838-39) to launch such an enterprise. Discusses the college's Mississippi period before it was removed to Jackson, Louisiana, in 1845. Describes its founders, administrators, faculty, students and student life. Examines controversial issues, particularly the debate over the initial location of the institution in Brandon Springs and its subsequent relocation in the facilities of state-owned Louisiana College which the Methodists acquired. Prominent individuals in the history of Centenary during 1838-44 included: William Winans, David O. Shattuck, Edward McGehee, Thomas C. Thornton, and Charles K. Marshall.
M. S. Legan

657. Holland, Dorothy Garesche. MARYVILLE—THE FIRST HUNDRED YEARS. *Missouri Hist. Soc. Bull. 1973 29(3): 145-162.* Maryville Academy, a convent school founded and operated by the Religious of the Sacred Heart, opened 3 September 1872 and offered elementary, secondary, and collegiate instruction until 1919. The institution became a junior college in 1921 and a "corporate college" of Saint Louis University in 1925. In the 1940's, Maryville abandoned most of its ties to the university, obtained "independent accreditation," and opened its doors to the public. Since 1950, Maryville has broadened its curricula, increased its enrollments, and expanded its facilities, emerging as a "private Catholic co-educational liberal arts college with a marked ecumenical spirit." Based on Maryville College documents, and on interviews and secondary sources; 7 photos, 21 notes. H. T. Lovin

658. Hollow, Elizabeth Patton. DEVELOPMENT OF THE BROWNSVILLE BAPTIST FEMALE COLLEGE: AN EXAMPLE OF FEMALE EDUCATION IN THE SOUTH, 1850-1910. *West Tennessee Hist. Soc. Papers 1978 (32): 48-59.* The West Tennessee Baptist Female College, Brownsville, Tennessee, was chartered in 1850 and was dissolved in 1910. Higher education was available to women in the South before accredited colleges for women were established and before public coeducation was accepted or available. Based largely on the *Proceedings* of the West Tennessee Baptist Convention, publications of the Brownsville Female College, and secondary sources; 4 illus., 61 notes.
H. M. Parker, Jr.

659. Huenemann, Mark W. HUTTERITE EDUCATION AS A THREAT TO SURVIVAL. *South Dakota Hist. 1976 7(1): 15-27.* Currently Hutterite culture is endangered by new legislation in South Dakota which would require secondary education, outside educators using modern audiovisual techniques, the closing of Hutterite attendance centers, and the refusal of school districts to allow new centers for new colonies. Hutterite culture stresses only basic skills, because more education and knowledge are considered dangerous and unnecessary. The basic aim of the Hutterites is to pass on the conservative, thrifty, hard-working doctrines of their ancestors. Covers 1700-1970's. Primary and secondary sources; 5 photos, 26 notes. A. J. Larson

660. Humphrey, David C. ANGLICAN "INFILTRATION" OF EIGHTEENTH CENTURY HARVARD AND YALE. *Hist. Mag. of the Protestant Episcopal Church 1974 43(3): 247-251.* Contrary to the Congregational claims at the time, there never was a grand strategy by Anglicans to infiltrate Harvard and Yale Colleges. The only serious efforts were by local parish clerics, Timothy Cutler in Cambridge and Samuel Johnson in New Haven, but these were fragmented and sporadic, and they were never a serious threat to Congregationalism. 20 notes.
R. V. Ritter

661. Humphrey, David C. THE STRUGGLE FOR SECTARIAN CONTROL OF PRINCETON, 1745-1760. *New Jersey Hist. 1973 91(2): 77-90.* Presbyterians, though claiming that the College of New Jersey (Princeton) was nonsectarian, tried to retain exclusive control over its board of trustees. Discusses resultant problems with the Anglican Church, Quakers, and the Assembly when the charter and financial assistance were requested. Based on primary and secondary sources; 6 illus., 24 notes. E. R. McKinstry

662. Inbar, Efraim. THE HEBREW DAY SCHOOLS: THE ORTHODOX COMMUNAL CHALLENGE. *J. of Ethnic Studies 1979 7(1): 13-29.* Discusses the reasons for the growth of Hebrew Day Schools, which are supported mostly by Orthodox Jews, and discusses the rising

status of Orthodox Jews in the American Jewish community since the 1960's.

663. Jacobson, Robert L. AID TO CHURCH-RELATED SCHOOLS: THE SUPREME COURT SAYS "NO!" *Compact 1973 7(4): 10-13.* Through a series of court rulings, public funding of parochial schools has gradually dwindled to nothing. S

664. Jentsch, Theodore W. CHANGE AND THE SCHOOL IN AN OLD ORDER MENNONITE COMMUNITY. *Mennonite Q. Rev. 1976 50(2): 132-135.* The question of how the Old Order Mennonites have successfully avoided social changes is discussed. The conclusion is that the educational system of this group has preserved them from outside influences. Covers 1653-1975. 6 notes. E. E. Eminhizer

665. Johnsen, Leigh. BROWNSBERGER AND BATTLE CREEK: THE BEGINNING OF SEVENTH-DAY ADVENTIST HIGHER EDUCATION. *Adventist Heritage 1976 3(2): 30-41.* Sidney Brownsberger was chief administrator during 1875-81 of Battle Creek College, the first Seventh-Day Adventist college, founded in 1875 in Battle Creek, Michigan, and later of Healdsburg College in California. Covers 1875-80's.

666. Johnson, Emeroy. SWEDISH ELEMENTARY SCHOOLS IN MINNESOTA LUTHERAN CONGREGATIONS. *Swedish Pioneer Hist. Q. 1979 30(3): 172-182.* After a brief history of the Swedish school program established by the several Lutheran churches in America during the late 19th century, the author describes his experiences as a student and as a teacher. 2 photos, reproduction of a page from *Barnens andra bok* (1890). C. W. Ohrvall

667. Kaiser, Leo M. THE INAUGURAL ADDRESS OF EDWARD WIGGLESWORTH AS FIRST HOLLIS PROFESSOR OF DIVINITY. *Harvard Lib. Bull. 1979 27(3): 319-329.* Provides an introduction to, and reprints the Latin and English versions of, the inaugural address of Edward Wigglesworth on the occasion of his appointment as the first incumbent of the Hollis Professorship of Divinity at Harvard in 1722.

668. Kaiser, Leo M. A LATIN *ORATIUNCULA* OF PRESIDENT JOHN LEVERETT OF HARVARD, OCTOBER 23, 1722. *Manuscripts 1978 22(2): 109-112.* Introduces and reproduces Leverett's oration.

669. Keisker, Walter. THEN . . . NOW. *Concordia Hist. Inst. Q. 1980 53(1): 34-38.* The author remembers the Lutheran St. Paul's College in Concordia, Missouri, where he attended school during 1913-19; compares students and campus then and now.

670. Kennelly, Karen. MARY MOLLOY: WOMEN'S COLLEGE FOUNDER. Stuhler, Barbara and Kreuter, Gretchen, ed. *Women of Minnesota: Selected Biographical Essays* (St. Paul: Minnesota Historical Society Press, 1977): 116-135. Born on 14 June 1880, in Sandusky, Ohio, Mary Aloysia Molloy grew up as the only child of Irish Catholic immigrant parents. In an age when few women attended college, Molloy earned her way through Ohio State University and graduated, in 1903, with more honors than anyone else up to that time. She went on to earn a master's degree and election to Phi Beta Kappa at Ohio State. In 1907 she earned her doctorate at Cornell. That same year, she began her career as a Catholic college educator in Winona, Minnesota, when she accepted a job with the Franciscan Sisters who, under the leadership of Sister Leo Tracy, were creating the liberal arts College of St. Teresa. The two women persevered and successfully established and administered the new collegiate institution for Catholic lay and religious women. Molloy was unique as the lay dean of a Catholic college, but in 1922 she became a nun, Sister Mary Aloysius Molloy, and in 1928 became the college president. As an educator, Molloy worked hard to improve the quality of women's education, wrestled with the unique problems of Catholic colleges, and carefully oversaw the development of her own school. By 1946, when she retired, the college was a firmly established institution producing outstanding graduate women. One of the last among the heroic generation of founders of Minnesota women's colleges, Molloy died on 27 September 1954. Primary and secondary sources; photo, 48 notes. A. E. Wiederrecht

671. Kintrea, Frank. "OLD PEABO" AND THE SCHOOL. *Am. Heritage 1980 31(6): 98-105.* The Reverend Endicott Peabody (1857-1944), an Episcopalian, founded Groton School in Groton, Massachusetts, in 1884 and remained its master until he retired in 1940. During his time, the school achieved fame as a preserve of wealth and privilege. Peabody's acceptance of biblical infallibility and his belief in hard work led to a dogma of "muscular Christianity" at the school. 11 illus. J. F. Paul

672. Kraus, Joe W. THE BOOK COLLECTIONS OF EARLY AMERICAN COLLEGE LIBRARIES. *Lib. Q. 1973 43(2): 142-159.* Previous studies of the libraries of the colleges established in the American colonies have given more attention to the details of institutional history than to the books themselves. As a consequence, the general impression remains that these libraries were little more than antiquated collections of theology. The sources for an evaluation of the resources of these libraries are available in the printed catalogs of the libraries of Harvard (1723-35 and 1790), Yale (1744, 1755, and 1791), Princeton (1760), and Brown (1793). A subject analysis of these catalogs reveals that only about one-half of the titles were theological and that books on history, literature, and science comprised from 32 to 45 percent of the titles. With the exception of the 1793 Brown catalog, the distribution of subjects was remarkably similar despite the differences in size and a time span of seventy years. A bibliographical review of the more important titles indicates that the range of subjects was impressive and that the significant authorities were available in many fields. J

673. Kraybill, Donald B. RELIGIOUS AND ETHNIC SOCIALIZATION IN A MENNONITE HIGH SCHOOL. *Mennonite Q. Rev. 1977 51(4): 329-351.* A study of the effects of ethnic schools on ethnicity in the Mennonite community in Lancaster, Pennsylvania. A comparative study of Mennonites in ethnic and public schools, as well as transfers, with allowance for sex and parental attitudinal changes, suggests that the prime function of the ethnic school, i.e., to solidify members in the precepts of the faith, is hardly fulfilled. The ethnic school does not change student attitudes toward orthodoxy, ethnicity, and ethnic ritual, although the ethnic school students did develop a higher avoidance pattern than their public school counterparts and a greater compatibility with their parents. All results are based on attitudinal changes over a three-year period, with testing both at the beginning and at the end of this period, 1974-76. 8 tables, 4 appendixes. V. L. Human

674. Kreider, Rachel. A MENNONITE COLLEGE THROUGH TOWN EYES. *Mennonite Life 1977 32(2): 4-13.* During the 1860's in the large Mennonite settlement in Median County, Ohio, the Reverend Ephraim Hunsberger (1814-1904) and the General Conference began plans for the first Mennonite college in America. Completed in May 1866, the large brick building cost about $14,000, considerably more than expected. After difficulty in finding a faculty, Wadsworth Institute opened to students in January 1868 with a course of study in English and one in German. A conflict developed between professors Carl Justus van der Smissen and Christian Showalter over educational standards just as Mennonite attention turned from education to immigration problems. The General Conference opened the college to non-Mennonites in 1875, then abruptly closed it in 1879. Based on contemporary newspaper accounts; 8 photos. B. Burnett

675. Kuznicki, Ellen Marie. A HISTORICAL PERSPECTIVE ON THE POLISH AMERICAN PAROCHIAL SCHOOL. *Polish Am. Studies 1978 35(1-2): 5-12.* Covers this school system from its beginning in the 1870's to the phasing-out era in the 1960's. Lists successes and failures of the system and concludes that, above all, "it was an effective Americanizer easing its pupils into English without depriving them of their ethnic heritage." Polish and English sources; 16 notes. S. R. Pliska

676. Lambert, James H. "LE HAUT ENSEIGNEMENT DE LA RELIGION": MGR BOURGET AND THE FOUNDING OF LAVAL UNIVERSITY. *R. de l'U. d'Ottawa [Canada] 1975 45(3): 278-294.* Concentrates "solely on the role of Mgr. Ignace Bourget, second bishop of Montreal," in founding Laval University. "The founding of Laval must be seen in the context of a Catholic ultramontane reaction to a liberal and secularist outburst during and following the French Revolution." Bourget saw the university as the principal instrument for "wresting the elite from

the clutches of liberalism." Covers 1840's-50's. Based on primary and secondary sources; 72 notes. M. L. Frey

677. Lampe, Philip E. THE ACCULTURATION OF MEXICAN AMERICANS IN PUBLIC AND PAROCHIAL SCHOOLS. *Sociol. Analysis 1975 36(1): 57-66.* The influence of the school system on the acculturation of Mexican American students was examined in San Antonio, Texas. During the spring of 1973, 383 eighth-grade minority students from nine public and nine parochial schools were given questionnaires to discover the extent to which their feelings, attitudes and values were similar to those of a group of WASP [White Anglo-Saxon Protestant] respondents. The results revealed that the school system attended made a greater difference than did SES [Socio-economic status] or sex. Parochial school respondents were significantly more acculturated than their public school counterparts, and the difference remained even when other variables such as SES, sex, religiosity, aspirational level and ethnic composition of school were controlled. J

678. Lane, Jack C. LIBERAL ARTS ON THE FLORIDA FRONTIER: THE FOUNDING OF ROLLINS COLLEGE, 1885-1890. *Florida Hist. Q. 1980 59(2): 144-164.* The Congregational Church and the Reverend Edward P. Hooker of the Home Missionary Society promoted the establishment of Rollins College, which followed the Yale Plan and was on solid ground by 1900. Based on church and college records (Winter Park, Fla.); 4 figs., 52 notes. N. A. Kuntz

679. Lannie, Vincent P. CHURCH AND SCHOOL TRIUMPHANT: THE SOURCES OF AMERICAN CATHOLIC EDUCATIONAL HISTORIOGRAPHY. *Hist. of Educ. Q. 1976 16(2): 131-146.* Examines sources from the 19th century.

680. Lauer, Bernarda and Engel, Rose-Anne, ed. RUSSIAN GERMANS AND THE URSULINES OF PRELATE, SASK., 1919-1934. *Study Sessions: Can. Catholic Hist. Assoc. [Canada] 1979 (46): 83-98.* Immigration of Russian Germans (1910's) and relocation of German Ursuline Sisters due to their fears of war and of a renewal of persecution of religion resulted in the establishment of St. Angela's Convent in Prelate, Saskatchewan, in 1919 to educate young and mainly German Catholics from rural areas.

681. Lazerson, Marvin. UNDERSTANDING AMERICAN CATHOLIC EDUCATIONAL HISTORY. *Hist. of Educ. Q. 1977 17(3): 297-317.* The development of the American Catholic parochial school system can be divided into three phases. During the first (1750-1870), parochial schools appeared as ad hoc efforts by parishes, and most Catholic children attended public schools. During the second period (1870-1910), the Catholic hierarchy made a basic commitment to a separate Catholic school system. These parochial schools, like the big-city parishes around them, tended to be ethnically homogeneous; a German child would not be sent to an Irish school, nor vice-versa, nor a Lithuanian pupil to either. Instruction in the language of the old country was common. In the third period (1910-1945), Catholic education was modernized and modelled after the public school systems, and ethnicity was deemphasized in many areas. In cities with large Catholic populations (such as Chicago and Boston) there was a flow of teachers, administrators, and students from one system to the other. 46 notes.
J. C. Billigmeier

682. Leavy, Edward N. and Raps, Eric Alan. THE JUDICIAL DOUBLE STANDARD FOR STATE AID TO CHURCH-AFFILIATED EDUCATIONAL INSTITUTIONS. *J. of Church and State 1979 21(2): 209-222.* The US Supreme Court has ruled that state and federal governments may provide financial support for private colleges and schools for the construction of secular facilities. Based on *Lemon* v. *Kurtzman* (US, 1971), laws providing funding are constitutional if they have a secular purpose, if the primary effect neither advances nor inhibits religion, and if the statute does not foster an excessive government entanglement with religion. In *Roemer* v. *Board of Public Works of Maryland* (US, 1976), a double standard was established: aid to church-related colleges receives less scrutiny than does aid to parochial schools. S

683. Lee, Knute. ESTABLISHING LUTHERAN COLLEGES IN THE UNITED STATES. *Concordia Hist. Inst. Q. 1973 46(1): 18-27.* Reviews the history of church-related institutions in the United States and focuses on the history of Valparaiso University. Covers 1636-1973. Based on manuscript and secondary sources; 3 photos, table, 19 notes.
B. W. Henry

684. Leefe, John. KING'S AND DALHOUSIE: AN EARLY ATTEMPT AT UNIVERSITY CONSOLIDATION IN NOVA SCOTIA. *Nova Scotia Hist. Q. [Canada] 1972 2(1): 41-54.* Discusses the first attempt to unite King's College, an exclusive college founded in 1789 and supported by the Church of England, with Dalhousie College, founded in 1818 by the Presbyterian Church, from 1821 to 1837, which failed.

685. Leslie, W. Bruce. LOCALISM, DENOMINATIONALISM, AND INSTITUTIONAL STRATEGIES IN URBANIZING AMERICA: THREE PENNSYLVANIA COLLEGES, 1870-1915. *Hist. of Educ. Q. 1977 17(3): 235-256.* Examines three private, Protestant, predominantly white, mostly male, Pennsylvania colleges in the period between the Civil War and World War I: Bucknell University (Baptists), Franklin and Marshall College (German Reformed), and Swarthmore College (Hicksite Friends). All three saw a decline in those years of localism and denominational orientation as dependence on the industrial wealth of urban America increased. An example is the effort in the early 20th century of strict Hicksites to stamp out football at Swarthmore; football won. Though members of the founding denomination continued to dominate the respective colleges, they were more secular-minded, ecumenical people than the founders, national and Protestant in outlook rather than local and denominational. 61 notes.
J. C. Billigmeier

686. Lyon, Ralph M. THE EARLY YEARS OF LIVINGSTON FEMALE ACADEMY. *Alabama Hist. Q. 1975 37(3): 192-205.* Lists the four types of schools in the United States in the antebellum period; the academy was a popular form in the South. Details the founding and operation of the Livingston Female Academy, a Presbyterian institution, 1835-1907. 60 notes. E. E. Eminhizer

687. MacPeek, Gertrude A. "TALL OAKS FROM LITTLE ACORNS GROW": THE STORY OF ST. MARY'S EPISCOPAL SCHOOL FOR INDIAN GIRLS. *Daughters of the Am. Revolution Mag. 1973 107(5): 392-398.* Covers 1873-1973.

688. Mayo, Janet. THE AUTHORITY TO GOVERN AND THE RIGHT TO DANCE ON CAMPUS AT CENTENARY COLLEGE. *North Louisiana Hist. Assoc. J. 1978 9(4): 205-218.* Describes the controversy which developed over a dancing resolution passed in 1941 by the Board of Centenary College, a Methodist-controlled college, and the effect it had on the division of power between the Board, the faculty, and the Methodist Church. The major issue that finally emerged was not whether dancing could be permitted on the campus, but rather who possessed the power to govern the college. In the end the Board became the sole authority with the power to govern and operate the college. Through action of the Board, the faculty gained the power to establish curriculum, maintain discipline, and regulate student life. Thus an insignificant controversy over dancing established the policy whereby Centenary College would be governed and operated in the future. Based on minutes of the Board of Trustees of Centenary College, publications and records of the Louisiana Conference of the Methodist Church, South, contemporary newspaper accounts and oral interviews; 67 notes.
H. M. Parker, Jr.

689. Mayse, Edgar C. ERNEST TRICE THOMPSON: PRESBYTERIAN OF THE SOUTH. *J. of Presbyterian Hist. 1978 56(1): 36-46.* Interviews Ernest Trice Thompson, Southern Presbyterian seminary professor and former Moderator of the General Assembly. For more than 40 years at Union Theological Seminary, Richmond, Virginia, he taught in every major field. He has made major contributions in the area of church history, which he taught to men who were becoming pastors. He is interested in the past as it illuminates the present. Illus., 8 notes.
H. M. Parker, Jr.

690. McCall, Duke K. THE SOUTHERN BAPTIST THEOLOGICAL SEMINARY. *Baptist Hist. and Heritage 1977 12(4): 194-197.* Describes the oldest of the six Southern Baptist theological seminaries, which celebrated 100 years of service in Louisville, Kentucky, in 1977. It had been located in Greenville, South Carolina. Mentions leading

personalities, critical events, and that current enrollment is about 3,000.
H. M. Parker, Jr.

691. McCluskey, Neil G. AID TO NONPUBLIC SCHOOLS: HISTORICAL AND SOCIAL PERSPECTIVES. *Current Hist. 1972 62(370): 302-304, 306, 310.* Discusses issues in constitutional law regarding federal aid to education for Catholic elementary schools in the 1960's and 70's.

692. McDonough, Madrienne C. MEMORIES OF A CATHOLIC CONVENT. *Hist. New Hampshire 1978 33(3): 233-245.* In 1902, the author, then six years old, entered the Mount St. Mary Convent school in Manchester for a seven-year stay. Particularly well-remembered was a visit by Bishop Denis M. Bradley, Mass, Benediction, and the Angelus, ghost stories told by an older girl on Sunday evenings, music practice, and morning walks, including walks on special feast days to the old covered bridge over the Merrimack River. Each year of study culminated in Distribution Day, in June, when prizes were awarded with appropriate ceremonies and entertainments. 5 illus., 3 notes. D. F. Chard

693. McFarland, J. Wayne and McFarland, T. A. MEMORIES OF E. A. SUTHERLAND. *Adventist Heritage 1975 2(2): 41-47.* Reminiscences of Edward A. Sutherland, a reform educator in the Seventh-Day Adventist Church, includes highlights of his years as president of Walla Walla College, Walla Walla, Washington; Battle Creek College, Berien Springs, Michigan; and Madison College, Tennessee, 1904-50.

694. McGill, William J. THE BELATED FOUNDING OF ALMA COLLEGE: PRESBYTERIANS AND HIGHER EDUCATION IN MICHIGAN, 1883-1886. *Michigan Hist. 1973 57(2): 93-120.* Presbyterians led in the establishment of sectarian colleges, especially those which eventually survived into the 20th century. In Michigan, however, they did not found a college until well after the boom period. Among other factors, Michigan Presbyterians did not give high priority to the education of their ministry and there were few candidates for the ministry. Alma College was established in 1886, because of efforts of individuals, not of the synod. 5 illus., 82 notes. D. L. Smith

695. McKevitt, Gerald. FROM FRANCISCAN MISSION TO JESUIT COLLEGE: A TROUBLED TRANSITION AT MISSION SANTA CLARA. *Southern California Q. 1976 58(2): 241-254.* Traces the difficulties of establishing a Jesuit college at the site of Mission Santa Clara, a Franciscan mission until its secularization. The first president of the college, Father John Nobili, began the school in 1851 in response to Bishop Joseph Alemany's request for a Catholic college in California. Father Nobili faced many problems, including the poor condition of the mission buildings, lack of equipment and books, a dearth of teachers, and lawsuits over land titles. Father Nobili purchased quitclaim deeds rather than fight land titles in the courts; as a result, the early years of the college found it deeply in debt. Concludes that the college's early difficulties were in large part due to the desire to establish it on the mission grounds in preference to a site with clear title, and to the expenses involved in restoring the mission buildings. Based on University of Santa Clara archival records, other primary sources, and published studies; 36 notes.
A. Hoffman

696. McKevitt, Gerald. THE JESUIT ARRIVAL IN CALIFORNIA AND THE FOUNDING OF SANTA CLARA COLLEGE. *Records of the Am. Catholic Hist. Soc. of Philadelphia 1974 85(3-4): 185-197.* Father Michael Accolti, a Jesuit priest, arrived in San Francisco in 1849. By 1851 he had opened Santa Clara College, the first permanent school in American California, the oldest institution of higher education in the state, and the foundation of the Jesuits' educational apostolate in California. 57 notes. J. M. McCarthy

697. McKevitt, Gerald. PROGRESS AMID POVERTY, SANTA CLARA COLLEGE IN THE 1870'S. *Pacific Hist. 1976 20(4): 407-424.* Founded in 1851 in Santa Clara, California, Santa Clara College had an active building campaign in the 1860's and entered the 1870's with a large debt. Presidents Varsi and Brunengo continued building during the 1870's. The college suffered from competition and economic depression in ensuing decades. Primary and secondary sources; 7 illus., 43 notes.
G. L. Olson

698. McLachlan, James. THE AMERICAN COLLEGE IN THE NINETEENTH CENTURY: TOWARD A REAPPRAISAL. *Teachers Coll. Record 1978 80(2): 288-306.* American historians of higher education have assumed about 19th-century colleges that: they were essentially elitist, their numbers declined after the Civil War, they were narrow and dogmatically Protestant, and they gave way suddenly to universities after 1870. Recent, admittedly fragmentary historical evidence suggests that these schools were far less elitist than formerly believed, that their numbers increased steadily throughout the century, that they were ethnically pluralistic, and they they coexisted with universities. Secondary sources; 48 notes. E. Bailey

699. McLellan, Sara J., ed. CHRONICLES OF SACRED HEART ACADEMY, SALEM 1863-1873. *Oregon Hist. Q. 1979 80(4): 341-364; 1980 81(1): 75-95.* Part I. Extracts from the daily records kept by one of the Sisters of the Holy Names of Jesus and Mary for Sacred Heart Academy (a girls' school after 1863). The account of daily life includes information on the founding of the academy, the curriculum, and visitors to the school. 20 notes. Part II. This portion of the records describes events at the school during 1868-73, including the construction of the new building (1871-73). Primary source; 4 photos, map, 38 notes.
G. R. Schroeder

700. McLoughlin, William G. PARSON BLACKBURN'S WHISKEY AND THE CHEROKEE INDIAN SCHOOLS, 1809-1810. *J. of Presbyterian Hist. 1979 57(4): 427-445.* Relates an incident involving the Reverend Gideon Blackburn's whiskey still and trade with the demise of the first Presbyterian mission among the Cherokee Indians in the Old Southwest. Although the documentary evidence appears to exonerate Blackburn from the charge of trying to sell whiskey to the Indians, nevertheless his being caught in the act of transporting whiskey across Indian lands weakened his credibility and was responsible for closing down Presbyterian schools among the Cherokees. Based largely on Records of the Bureau of Indian Affairs, M-221; illus., 27 notes.
H. M. Parker, Jr.

701. Meyer, Michael A. THE HEBREW UNION COLLEGE—ITS FIRST YEARS. *Cincinnati Hist. Soc. Bull. 1975 33(1): 7-25.* Discusses the activities of Rabbi Isaac Mayer Wise as founder of the Hebrew Union College, America's first rabbinical seminary, in Cincinnati, Ohio, 1817-90's, including students' curricula in Jewish history.

702. Middlekauff, Robert. BEFORE THE PUBLIC SCHOOL: EDUCATION IN COLONIAL AMERICA. *Current Hist. 1972 62(370): 279-281, 307.* Discusses community sponsors for public, private, and religious education from the 1640's to the 1750's, including financing by taxation.

703. Miller, H. Earl. THE OLD SEM AND THE NEW. *Concordia Hist. Inst. Q. 1976 49(2): 52-63.* A comparison of student life-styles in the old and new Lutheran seminaries in St. Louis. The author took six years during 1922-28 to complete a three year course of studies and came to know numerous members of the faculty and a significant number of students. Includes brief biographical sketches of faculty members.
W. T. Walker

704. Miller, Steven I. and Kavanagh, Jack. CATHOLIC SCHOOL INTEGRATION AND SOCIAL POLICY: A CASE STUDY. *J. of Negro Educ. 1975 44(4): 482-492.* A 1972 study of a Catholic high school showed tendencies toward segregation, reflecting views conflicting with Christian dogma.

705. Moorhead, James H. JOSEPH ADDISON ALEXANDER: COMMON SENSE, ROMANTICISM AND BIBLICAL CRITICISM AT PRINCETON. *J. of Presbyterian Hist. 1975 53(1): 51-65.* After receiving his education at the Princeton Theological Seminary, Alexander spent a year studying in Germany and was introduced to the new approach to the Bible. He returned to Princeton in 1834 and began his 25 year teaching career as a biblical scholar who sought to use the results of the new learning to buttress the Princeton orthodoxy. His own life also permits an insight into the strains which the marriage of biblical criticism and orthodoxy produced. Alexander authored some 80 articles for the *Princeton Review* plus five commentaries on biblical books and a sixth volume on biblical studies. Based largely on material from his writings; photo, 62 notes. H. M. Parker, Jr.

706. Morgan, Edmund S. EZRA STILES AND TIMOTHY DWIGHT. *Massachusetts Hist. Soc. Pro. 1957-60 72: 101-117.* Describes the relationship between Ezra Stiles, president of Yale University from 1778 to 1795, and Timothy Dwight, president of Yale from 1795 to 1817, who shared an intense dislike for each other.

707. Mueller, Peter Dietrich. KANSAS VICARAGE. *Concordia Hist. Inst. Q. 1976 49(2): 72-87.* An excerpt from Peter Mueller's *Lebensgeschichte* which was written "after 1930"; this excerpt was translated by the author's grandson, Williard E. Mueller. The article relates the development of Concordia Seminary in Missouri as well as Mueller's student career. Recounts the problems of student life, the memorable teachers and friendships which were developed, and his experiences during his first vicarage at Clay Center, Kansas. Covers 1883-89.
W. T. Walker

708. Mulligan, Robert W. XAVIER: 1831-1861. *Cincinnati Hist. Soc. Bull. 1979 37(1): 7-22.* Xavier University, the first Catholic college in the old Northwest Territory, was founded by Bishop Fenwick in 1831.

709. Naylor, Natalie A. THE THEOLOGICAL SEMINARY IN THE CONFIGURATION OF AMERICAN HIGHER EDUCATION: THE ANTE-BELLUM YEARS. *Hist. of Educ. Q. 1977 17(1): 17-30.* In the early 19th century, theological seminaries developed which were the precursors of later universities and the prototypes of professional graduate schools. Many graduates of these institutions staffed American liberal arts colleges as professors and presidents. Andover, founded in 1808, was the first and the best model for the many institutions which followed. Primary and secondary sources; 33 notes. L. C. Smith

710. Nearing, Peter. REV. JOHN R. MACDONALD, ST. JOSEPH'S COLLEGE AND THE UNIVERSITY OF ALBERTA. *Study Sessions: Can. Catholic Hist. Assoc. 1975 42: 70-90.* John Roderick MacDonald (b. 1891), a Basilian Father, undertook Archbishop O'Leary's 1922-23 project of organizing a Catholic university in Edmonton, thus working toward the evangelization of the large immigrant population of the West, despite his own failing health.

711. Neatby, Hilda. QUEEN'S COLLEGE AND THE SCOTTISH FACT. *Queen's Q. [Canada] 1973 80(1): 1-11.* Discusses the educational and religious controversies behind the founding of Queen's College in 1842. William Morris was the key figure in leading the struggle for Scottish Presbyterians' rights in Canada against the Anglican establishment. His inability to win acceptable concessions for Presbyterian participation on King's College Council led to the decision to found a separate university and thus provided the first chapter in the history of Queen's University. An adaptation of a portion of the author's forthcoming history of Queen's University. J. A. Casada

712. Neely, Sharlotte. THE QUAKER ERA OF CHEROKEE INDIAN EDUCATION, 1880-1892. *Appalachian J. 1975 2(4): 314-322.*

713. Niemeyer, Gerhart. THE NEW NEED FOR THE CATHOLIC UNIVERSITY. *Rev. of Pol. 1975 37(4): 479-489.* In the past, a Catholic university represented a "dogmatically inflexible" Church entwined with secular power. Now the Church is politically weak and dogmatically flexible. Western civilization and culture face destruction "while the technological mastery of nature moves from triumph to triumph." The new role of the Catholic university is "not as an institution where learning is kept on a leash, but, on the contrary, as one with the capacity and equipment to liberate science from the positivist 'taboo on theory,' as it reopens the flow among men, intellectus, and fides." Covers the 20th century. L. E. Ziewacz

714. Noll, Mark A. JACOB GREEN'S PROPOSAL FOR SEMINARIES. *J. of Presbyterian Hist. 1980 58(3): 210-222.* The first Presbyterian seminary in America was not established until 1812. However, the Reverend Jacob Green (1722-90) thought of such a school. Education was of the utmost importance to him, both in the pastorate as well as in his concern for a better-trained ministry. At that time young men studying for the ministry after completing college studied under an "approved divine." On 22 November 1775 he sent a letter to his Congregational friend, the Reverend Joseph Bellamy, in which he laid out his plan for a theological seminary. The letter arose out of his concern about the shortage of ministers and his conviction that the current effort to train them was not succeeding. Reprints the previously unpublished letter. Based on materials by and about Jacob Green, and studies on colonial Presbyterian history; 39 notes. (The letter is in the Bellamy Papers, Hartford Seminary Foundation, Hartford, Connecticut.)
H. M. Parker, Jr.

715. Noonan, Brian. THE CONTRIBUTION OF SEPARATE SCHOOLS TO THE DEVELOPMENT OF SASKATCHEWAN: 1870 TO THE PRESENT. *Study Sessions: Can. Catholic Hist. Assoc. [Canada] 1979 (46): 71-81.* Separate Catholic schools in Saskatchewan have provided a rallying point for minority rights, expressed religious freedom, and allowed for the democratic exercise of the religious education for Catholic youth.

716. Norris, Richard A., Jr. THE EPISCOPAL CHURCH AND THEOLOGICAL EDUCATION: SOME REMARKS. *Anglican Theological Rev. Supplementary Series 1973 (2): 88-95.*

717. Oates, Mary J. ORGANIZED VOLUNTARISM: THE CATHOLIC SISTERS IN MASSACHUSETTS, 1870-1940. *Am. Q. 1978 30(5): 652-680.* Discusses the social and religious forces which caused a much more rapid increase in the number of women in religious work in Boston as opposed to the number of men, and the relative position achieved. A major factor was that of need as emphases in education changed, both overall, and in relation to whether teaching boys or girls. However, they were paid about half what their male counterparts were paid, despite both having taken vows of poverty. It amounted essentially to their subsidizing the schools while having no control over the running of either school or convent. Although the teachers sometimes began with inadequate training, the lifetime commitment resulted in a consistent and steady development. Economic constraints in the women's communities resulted in limited social life, education, and outside contacts, these restrictions tightening in the same period in which men's restrictions were being lifted. 8 tables, 65 notes. R. V. Ritter

718. Ognibene, Richard. THE BAPTIST ACADEMY MOVEMENT IN THE LATE NINETEENTH CENTURY. *Foundations 1979 22(3): 246-260.* Discusses the Baptist and secondary education during 1850-1910, pointing out that although Baptists accepted state-supported elementary education, they reject state-supported secondary education. The reasons for failure of Baptist secondary schools were many and not just competition from developing public high schools. 75 notes.
E. E. Eminhizer

719. Page, F. Hilton. WILLIAM LYALL IN HIS SETTING. *Dalhousie Rev. [Canada] 1980 60(1): 49-66.* Outlines the history of the use of the Scottish School of philosophy in Nova Scotia, especially the curricula at such schools as King's College, Dalhousie, and Pine Hill Divinity Hall (earlier Presbyterian College). Focuses on the life and works of the Reverend William Lyall, doctor of laws and fellow of the Royal Society of Canada. 35 ref. C. H. Held

720. Palmer, Steven C. A THWARTED TRY FOR CHANGE. *Change 1974 6(8): 43-47.* Reports on the attempt of student activists to initiate educational innovation at Southern Methodist University, 1972-present. S

721. Paré, Marius. LE ROLE DES ÉVÊQUES DE CHICOUTIMI DANS L'OEUVRE DU SÉMINAIRE [The role of the bishops of Chicoutimi in the work of the seminary]. *Sessions D'Étude: Soc. Can. d'Hist. de l'Eglise Catholique 1973 40: 113-124.* Gives a history of the bishops of the Séminaire de Chicoutimi in Quebec from its foundation in 1873 to the present. S

722. Parker, Harold M., Jr. A NEW SCHOOL PRESBYTERIAN SEMINARY IN WOODFORD COUNTY. *Register of the Kentucky Hist. Soc. 1976 74(2): 99-111.* Intertwined in the history of Presbyterianism in Kentucky were the themes of division and education. The Old School-New School division in the church in 1837 did not lead to a split in Kentucky until 1840. The slavery issue intruded into the Kentucky situation, and the small New School group had to rely on the North for financial support and for ministers. In 1849, the group accepted the offer of the Macedonia Church to erect a building for a seminary. Two years

later, the effort collapsed because of financial difficulties, lack of leadership, and other problems. Primary and secondary sources; 26 notes.
J. F. Paul

723. Parker, Harold M., Jr. A SCHOOL OF THE PROPHETS AT MARYVILLE. *Tennessee Hist. Q. 1975 34(1): 72-90.* In 1819 Dr. Isaac Anderson began the Southern and Western Theological Seminary in Maryville, Tennessee, with the idea of providing religious training for Presbyterian ministers in an area where there was a shortage. The seminary set a high intellectual standard, grew rapidly, and became a center of abolitionism. Failing financial support, divisions within the church, and agitation over slavery led to the demise of the seminary in the late 1850's. Secondary sources; 55 notes. M. B. Lucas

724. Parzen, Herbert. THE PURGE OF THE DISSIDENTS, HEBREW UNION COLLEGE AND ZIONISM, 1903-1907. *Jewish Social Studies 1975 37(3-4): 291-322.* The assumption of the presidency of this Reform Judaism college in Cincinnati by Dr. Kaufmann Kohler in the fall of 1903 led to the expulsion of its Zionist faculty. Kaufmann, a vehement assimilationist and anti-Zionist, paid only lip service to academic freedom as he moved to curb pro-Zionist utterances and writings by Caspar Levias, Max L. Margolis, and Max Schloessinger. His success in purging the faculty of these individuals met with the general approval of the Reform Judaism constituency. Includes a letter from Max L. Margolis explaining his position to Rabbi Clarke S. Levi. Primary and secondary sources. N. Lederer

725. Patterson, W. Morgan. CHANGING PREPARATION FOR CHANGING MINISTRY. *Baptist Hist. and Heritage 1980 15(1): 14-22, 59.* Surveys the historical development of institutions and their policies and philosophies used in preparing Baptist ministers, from the beginning of the denomination in Great Britain in the early 1600's to contemporary America.

726. Pearson, Daniel M. THE TWO WORLDS OF CARL A. SWENSSON, 1873-1888. *Swedish Pioneer Hist. Q. 1977 28(4): 259-273.* Carl Aaron Swensson was the founder of Bethany College, Lindsborg, Kansas. Several biographical sketches have been written since his death in 1904 but few have analyzed his life and his importance, both in American society and in Midwest Swedish immigrant communities. Swensson's father, Jonas, was a Lutheran minister who despised many aspects of American culture, so he did not allow his children to attend public schools or find American friends. Thus Carl grew up a Swede. He attended Augustana College and Seminary during 1873-79 which further enhanced his Swedish orientation. But he realized that the promise of America was not only that it was Christian, but that it was energetic, strong, and educated. After he graduated, he added Swedish immigrant colonization projects, politics, and railroad promotion to his active concern for religious education. Describes his efforts in these areas. Based on the writings of Swensson; photo, 23 notes. C. W. Ohrvall

727. Peterson, Susan. FROM PARADISE TO PRAIRIE: THE PRESENTATION SISTERS IN DAKOTA, 1880-1896. *South Dakota Hist. 1980 10(3): 210-222.* In 1880, several Sisters of the Presentation of the Blessed Virgin Mary arrived in Dakota Territory from Ireland to serve as missionaries to the Indians. After enduring several years of hardship, confusion, and many moves due to low Indian enrollment, the sisters found themselves teaching children of American and European settlers. By 1896, the sisters had permanent homes in Fargo (North Dakota), and Aberdeen (South Dakota), from which they could continue their work. The experience of the sisters in Dakota had brought them security and a strong sense of value in their educational mission. Based on the Presentation Heights Archives, Aberdeen, South Dakota, and other primary sources; 6 photos, 24 notes. P. L. McLaughlin

728. Peterson, Walfred H. CONFUSION CONFOUNDED: GOVERNMENT AID TO PRIVATE EDUCATION IN THE BURGER COURT. *Christian Scholar's Rev. 1980 9(3): 195-214.* Examines conflicting interpretations of Supreme Court justices on the meaning of the First Amendment when they have considered public aid to private schools with religious affiliations; 1970's.

729. Pfeffer, Leo. UNEASY TRINITY: CHURCH, STATE, AND CONSTITUTION. *Civil Liberties Rev. 1975 2(1): 138-161.* Overview of the debate over the separation of church and state and constitutional issues brought into play, 1930's-70's; discusses tax write-offs for parochial schools, prayer in the classroom, educational requirements for parochial schools, and religious freedom.

730. Pichaske, David R. JUBILEE COLLEGE: BISHOP CHASE'S SCHOOL OF PROPHETS. *Old Northwest 1976 2(3): 281-297.* Episcopal Bishop Philander Chase (1775-1852), who had already founded Kenyon College, founded Jubilee College 15 miles from Peoria, Illinois, in 1840. Convinced that western men must be educated in the west, Chase alienated eastern Episcopal leaders, especially when he sought funds for both Kenyon and Jubilee in England. Chase returned the antipathy of the easterners, but the ill feelings ultimately hurt Jubilee in spite of the energetic bishop's hard work. When Chase died the college began to die as well. Included is an account of life, studies, and costs at Jubilee, which closed in 1862. Based on the Peoria Historical Society's papers, Chicago Diocesean papers, and secondary works; 33 notes. J

731. Poole, David R., Jr. EDUCATIONAL WORK AT WHITEFIELD'S ORPHAN SCHOOL IN GEORGIA. *Methodist Hist. 1977 15(3): 186-195.* George Whitefield established a school near Savannah, Georgia in 1738 to provide an education for orphans and the children of the poor. By 1771 it became a school not only for these but for others who could afford to pay for education. The curriculum was not exceeded even in some exclusive academies in America. It was an outstanding example of American colonial education influenced and shaped by the Great Awakening and its reforming thrust. 58 notes. H. L. Calkin

732. Purdy, J. D. JOHN STRACHAN AND THE DIOCESAN THEOLOGICAL INSTITUTE AT COBOURG, 1842-1852. *Ontario Hist. [Canada] 1973 65(2): 113-123.* John Strachan had pondered the problems of his church before internal disputes (tractarians v. evangelicals) and external attacks (political reform and rival denominations) brought a crisis in the 1840's. Strachan was concerned with obtaining clergy trained to handle frontier conditions. Discusses the resolution of that problem in light of the disputes in the Church of England. Primary and secondary sources; 51 notes. W. B. Whitham

733. Quillian, William F., Jr. CHANGES IN THE CHURCH-RELATED COLLEGE. *J. of Ecumenical Studies 1979 16(1): 133-138.* Reviews the changes that have occurred in church-affiliated colleges in the United States since 1939. While in many cases the church-related college is less distinguishable from the private secular college today than in the past—there may be no compulsory chapel, required courses in religion, or strict rules governing the social behavior of students—there are numerous fundamentalist church-related colleges that are attracting many students in the current conservative mood of the country. Financial strain and government regulations, on the other hand, have caused a shift away from control by the sponsoring church bodies in many cases.
S

734. Quinn, D. Michael. THE BRIEF CAREER OF YOUNG UNIVERSITY AT SALT LAKE CITY. *Utah Hist. Q. 1973 41(1): 69-89.* Young University at Salt Lake City grew out of the earlier Brigham Young Academy. The University "was an early effort to end the migration of Mormon youth to universities and colleges outside Utah . . . Because of its aims and because of its effect upon both the state and Mormon higher education, Young University is an important part of Utah's educational history." Despite only one year of life it contributed directly to the development of the University of Utah, the LDS (Latter Day Saints) Business College, and Brigham Young University (Provo) by way of Brigham Young Academy. 3 photos, 69 notes. R. V. Ritter

735. Quinn, D. Michael. UTAH'S EDUCATIONAL INNOVATION: LDS RELIGION CLASSES, 1890-1929. *Utah Hist. Q. 1975 43(4): 379-389.* The Religion Class Movement was the first effort of the Mormons to supplement secular education. Started in Utah in 1890, it was America's first experiment in providing separate weekday religious training for public-school children. Instruction was given to children for the first nine grades. More than 60,000 elementary-school children annually attended classes prior to their discontinuation in 1929. Since then, Mormons have concentrated on providing instruction to secondary and college students. Based on primary and secondary sources; 2 illus., 34 notes. J. L. Hazelton

736. Rakeffet-Rothkoff, Aaron. THE ATTEMPT TO MERGE THE JEWISH THEOLOGICAL SEMINARY AND YESHIVA COLLEGE, 1926-1927. *Michael: On the Hist. of the Jews in the Diaspora [Israel] 1975 3: 254-280.* The merger attempt of the two leading American traditional rabbinical seminaries was prompted by the fund-raising campaigns launched by both institutions for new campuses in New York City. Some American Jewish lay leaders could not discern the differences between Jewish Theological Seminary and Yeshiva College, for many in the JTS administration and faculty were Orthodox in their theology and practice. Presents 26 documents relating to the attempted merger and serving as the basis for the description in the author's book, *Bernard Revel: Builder of American Jewish Orthodoxy* (Philadelphia, 1972), pp. 94-114. Primary and secondary sources; 40 notes.

737. Rayman, Ronald. THE WINNEBAGO INDIAN SCHOOL EXPERIMENT IN IOWA TERRITORY, 1834-1848. *Ann. of Iowa 1978 44(5): 359-387.* A movement emphasizing assimilation as the solution to the Indian "problem" began in earnest during the administration of Andrew Jackson. The history of the Winnebago school at two locations in Iowa demonstrates that assimilation was a nearly impossible task. Not only did the Winnebago Indians resist the imposition of white culture, but also the school was hampered by personal, political, economic, and Protestant-Catholic disagreements (inspired by Bureau of Indian Affairs appointment of a Presbyterian minister as first principal and refusal to allow Catholic priests to teach the Indians). The most debilitating factor was the "ambivalence and ignorance" of government officials responsible for Indian policy. Based on records of the Bureau of Indian Affairs, National Archives; 3 photos, 67 notes. P. L. Petersen

738. Reynolds, Keld J. LA SIERRA COLLEGE IN ADOLESCENCE. *Adventist Heritage 1979 6(2): 25-37.* History of La Sierra College from its founding in 1922 near Arlington, California, until 1967, when it became the College of Arts and Sciences of Loma Linda University; La Sierra grew out of the closure of the Adventist-run San Fernando Academy.

739. Richardson, Fredrick. AMERICAN BAPTISTS' SOUTHERN MISSION. *Foundations 1975 18(2): 136-145.* American (Northern) Baptists began missions in the South among blacks as soon as possible following the war. The first were supported by the Freedmen's Fund. Discusses the foundation of Northern Baptist educational institutions in the South for blacks. These include Shaw University, started by Henry Tupper in 1865; Wayland Seminary, 1865; Richmond Institute, started by Nathaniel Colver, 1865; Nashville Institute, started by D. W. Phillips in 1866; Augusta Institute by William Jefferson White, 1867; Leland University by Holbrook Chamberlain, 1870; Benedict Institute, 1871; Natchez Seminary, 1877; Spelman Seminary, 1881; and Bishop College, 1881. 49 notes. E. E. Eminhizer

740. Ringenberg, William C. A BRIEF HISTORY OF FORT WAYNE BIBLE COLLEGE. *Mennonite Q. Rev. 1980 54(2): 135-155.* Chronicles the history of the Fort Wayne Bible College, Fort Wayne, Indiana, 1904-77. It was founded by Evangelical Mennonites, the group that followed Henry Egly in the period of the 1860's to the 1880's in Ohio, Indiana, and Illinois. Based on archives and publications of the Fort Wayne Bible College; 68 notes. H. M. Parker, Jr.

741. Ringenberg, William C. THE OBERLIN COLLEGE INFLUENCE IN EARLY MICHIGAN. *Old Northwest 1977 3(2): 111-131.* Three Michigan schools owed their founding and character to men originally associated with Oberlin College, Ohio: Olivet, Adrian, and Hillsdale Colleges. John H. Shipherd, an Oberlin founder, established Olivet College in 1844. Asa Mahan, an early Oberlin president, took over the management of a Wesleyan school which he moved to Adrian in 1859 and named Adrian College. Freewill Baptist Elder David Marks, an Oberlin graduate, urged the hiring of another graduate, Daniel M. Graham, who became Hillsdale's president in 1844. These men carried with them Oberlin's beliefs in abolition, coeducation, Christian perfection, reform, and temperance. Based on college histories and catalogues and on secondary works; 49 notes. J

742. Riser, Ellen Lucille. ST. MICHAEL'S HIGH SCHOOL: A BEACON OF LIGHT. *New Mexico Hist. Rev. 1980 55(2): 139-150.* Reviews the history of St. Michael's High School in Santa Fe, New Mexico, from its founding by the Brothers of Christian Schools in 1859 through its first 100 years. St. Michael's was instrumental in the development of many of the early educational leaders in New Mexico. The school has played an important part in the history of New Mexico as an example for other schools and as the educator of many prominent figures. Newspapers and secondary sources; illus., 30 notes. P. L. McLaughlin

743. Rittenhouse, Floyd O. EDWARD A. SUTHERLAND: INDEPENDENT REFORMER. *Adventist Heritage 1977 4(2): 20-34.* Edward A. Sutherland (1865-1955), Seventh-Day Adventist educator, became president of Battle Creek College in Michigan in 1897 and helped found Madison College in 1904 in Tennessee.

744. Robertson, Ian Ross. PARTY POLITICS AND RELIGIOUS CONTROVERSIALISM IN PRINCE EDWARD ISLAND FROM 1860 TO 1863. *Acadiensis [Canada] 1978 7(2): 29-59.* Sectarian bitterness erupted in Prince Edward Island with a debate over Board of Education membership and the Prince of Wales College Act (1860), seen as a Protestant effort to gain state funds for their college. Feuding escalated from 1861, with attempts to incorporate the Grand Orange Lodge, and because of measures threatening Acadian schools. In 1863 bickering declined. Although verbal, not physical, the battles further divided Islanders and diverted attention from land reform. 132 notes. D. F. Chard

745. Robison, James I. THE FOUNDING OF THE SOUTHERN CALIFORNIA JUNIOR COLLEGE. *Adventist Heritage 1977 4(2): 48-59.* La Sierra Academy, founded in 1922 in Arlington, California, became the Southern California Junior College in 1927 and eventually La Sierra Campus of Loma Linda University.

746. Rosenshine, Jay. HISTORY OF THE SHOLOM ALEICHEM INSTITUTE OF DETROIT, 1926-1971. *Michigan Jewish Hist. 1974 14(2): 9-20.*

747. Ross, Brian. JAMES EUSTACE PURDIE: THE STORY OF PENTECOSTAL THEOLOGICAL EDUCATION. *J. of the Can. Church Hist. Soc. 1975 17(4): 94-103.* Describes the foundations of theological education in the Pentecostal Assemblies of Canada (PAOC). Evangelical, fundamentalist, charismatic, and sectarian, PAOC rather feared theology with its connotations of incessant, cold argument. Yet Pentecostals wanted individuals knowledgeable in biblical subjects to preach and teach. Such a task fell to an evangelical ex-Anglican, James Eustace Purdie, selected to head the Pentecostal Bible School, established in Winnipeg in 1925. Although beginning with a faculty of three and student body of 33, the school under Purdie's direction was very successful. In 1930 the school was moved to Toronto near the church's headquarters, but financial exigencies forced its return to Winnipeg in 1932. There Purdie maintained his leadership of the school for the next 18 years, training individuals of all backgrounds in a biblical, fundamentalist, premillennial, practical atmosphere. Based on primary and secondary sources; 19 notes. J. A. Kicklighter

748. Roth, Gary G. WAKE FOREST COLLEGE AND THE RISE OF SOUTHEASTERN BAPTIST THEOLOGICAL SEMINARY, 1945-1951. *Baptist Hist. and Heritage 1976 11(2): 69-79.* During 1925-50 Southern Baptist membership had increased 67%. For the Southern Baptist Convention, the establishment of a seminary in the southeast would help to meet the increasing demand for trained ministers. For Wake Forest College, the seminary's establishment could serve to meet other, more immediate needs, because the College would be leaving Wake Forest, North Carolina, to go to Winston-Salem. The sale of the college campus to the Southern Baptist Convention for the site of Southeastern Baptist Theological Seminary quieted those critics who objected to moving the college to Winston-Salem. With the seminary utilizing the college's former campus, such usage would be in keeping with the founders' intentions. The availability of the campus was a factor in the establishment of a much-needed seminary. Chronicles the establishment of the seminary at Wake Forest. Based largely on annual reports of the Southern Baptist Convention and the North Carolina Southern Baptist Convention; 31 notes. H. M. Parker, Jr.

749. Royce, Marion V. EDUCATION FOR GIRLS IN QUAKER SCHOOLS IN ONTARIO. *Atlantis [Canada] 1977 3(1): 181-192.* Provides a brief background to the Society of Friends, interest in education

since 17th-century England, and discusses the interest of Quakers in Canada in organizing schools, particularly the educational opportunities for girls, in Ontario, Canada, 1790-1820.

750. Rubenstein, Richard L. STUDYING AT HEBREW UNION COLLEGE: 1942-45. *Midstream 1974 20(6): 68-73.* From the author's *Power Struggle* (New York: Scribner's, 1974). S

751. Ruybalid, M. Keith. MISSION SCHOOL IN THE HOMELAND. *Adventist Heritage 1979 6(1): 41-49.* Discusses the founding of the Spanish-American Seminary near Sandoval, New Mexico, which opened in 1942, from 1928 when the Adventist General Conference Committee agreed to address the needs of Spanish-American children's education in the Southwest, until 1953.

752. Rybolt, John E. KENRICK'S FIRST SEMINARY. *Missouri Hist. Rev. 1977 71(2): 139-155.* St. Mary's of the Barrens was a school for secular and diocesan clergy students until Bishop Joseph Rosati decided to use land obtained from the Antoine Soulard family to build a seminary, Trinity Church, and some rental property. Peter Richard Kenrick, his successor in 1841, later moved the project. Between 1844 and 1848 the seminarians moved from St. Mary's to the city, thereby fulfilling Rosati's and Kenrick's dream to have the school in the city. For some unknown reason the school relocated at Carondelet in 1848 and did not return to St. Louis until 1893. Primary and secondary sources; illus., 56 notes. W. F. Zornow

753. Schwermann, Albert H. MY DEBT OF GRATITUDE TO THE U.S.A. *Concordia Hist. Inst. Q. 1977 50(1): 23-31.* The author was born in Jefferson City, Missouri, in 1891. He became a Lutheran minister in 1913 and served in Mellowdale, Alberta, before becoming the president and a faculty member of Concordia College in Edmonton. His career at Concordia spanned 42 years. Expresses gratitude for the upbringing and educational experiences he enjoyed in the United States. 6 notes. W. T. Walker

754. Selavan, Ida Cohen. THE EDUCATION OF JEWISH IMMIGRANTS IN PITTSBURGH, 1862-1932. *Yivo Ann. of Jewish Social Sci. 1974 (15): 126-144.* Looks at the education of the Jewish immigrants in public school, night school, and adult education. Jews flocked to the public education system and did well. Hebrew, religious, and Yiddish education are also briefly covered. 85 notes. R. J. Wechman

755. Sharp, John E. SOLOMON ZOOK SHARP: EDUCATOR AND OPTIMIST. *Pennsylvania Mennonite Heritage 1979 2(1): 8-11.* Solomon Zook Sharp worked in Mennonite education in Pennsylvania, Tennessee, Kansas, Missouri, California, and Colorado; covers 1860-1931.

756. Simard, Jean Paul and Riverin, Bérard. ORIGINE GÉOGRAPHIQUE ET SOCIAL DES ETUDIANTS DU PETIT-SÉMINAIRE DE CHICOUTIMI ET LEUR ORIENTATION SOCIO-PROFESSIONNELLE: 1873-1930 [Geographic and social origins of the students of the Petit-Séminaire de Chicoutimi and their socioprofessional orientation: 1873-1930]. *Sessions D'Étude: Soc. Can. d'Hist. de l'Eglise Catholique 1973 40: 33-54.*

757. Simard, Ovide-D. SÉMINAIRE DE CHICOUTIMI, 1873-1973: COUP D'OEIL SUR LE SIÈCLE ECOULÉ [Séminaire de Chicoutimi, 1873-1973: a glance at the past century]. *Sessions D'Étude: Soc. Can. de l'Eglise Catholique 1973: 40: 125-130.* The oldest living Superior of the Chicoutimi seminary reflects on its hundred-year existence. S

758. Slavens, Thomas P. THE LIBRARIANSHIP OF HENRY B. SMITH, 1851-77. *Lib. Hist. Rev. [India] 1974 1(4): 1-41.* Summarizes the life of Henry B. Smith (1815-77), American Presbyterian theologian, focusing on his work as the librarian of the Union Theological Seminary in New York City. Covers 1851-77.

759. Slavens, Thomas P. WILLIAM WALKER ROCKWELL AND THE DEVELOPMENT OF THE UNION THEOLOGICAL SEMINARY LIBRARY. *J. of Lib. Hist. 1976 11(1): 26-43.* Describes the major acquisitions and events in the development of the Union Theological Seminary Library in New York City while William Walker Rockwell was librarian. Describes the cataloging scheme for theological materials devised and implemented by Julia Pettee during this time. Covers 1908-58. Based on primary and secondary sources; 83 notes. A. C. Dewees

760. Smith, Wilson. NEW DENOMINATIONAL HISTORY. *Rev. in Am. Hist. 1977 5(3): 314-320.* Review article prompted by Howard Miller's *The Revolutionary College: American Presbyterian Higher Education 1707-1837* (New York: New York U. Pr., 1976).

761. Soper, Marley. "UNSER SEMINAR": THE STORY OF CLINTON GERMAN SEMINARY. *Adventist Heritage 1977 4(1): 44-55.* The Clinton German Seminary (later the Clinton Theological Seminary) in Clinton, Missouri, was for German-speaking Seventh-Day Adventists, 1910-25.

762. Stephens, Bruce M. LIBERALS IN THE WILDERNESS: THE MEADVILLE THEOLOGICAL SCHOOL, 1844-1856. *Pennsylvania Hist. 1975 42(4): 291-302.* The Meadville Theological School was established in 1844 in order to train Unitarian ministers to work in the West. The most prominent founder was Harm Jan Huidekoper, a Meadville businessman and land agent, who believed that the West was ripe for conversion to religious liberalism. His son Frederic, a graduate of Harvard Divinity School, taught at the new institution at no cost during 1844-77. Rufus Phineas Stebbins, president from the school's establishment to 1856, initiated a program of studies modelled on Harvard's. Stebbins devoted much energy to developing ties with the Christian Connection, a nearby church which was a major source of theology students. The entente with the Christian Connection began to deteriorate in 1848, but Stebbins continued to seek an accommodation with that body, and became a member of its Western Reserve Conference. However, the alliance was short-lived, and the Unitarians did not have great success in winning western adherents. Illus., 32 notes. D. C. Swift

763. Stephens, Bruce M. MAIL ORDER SEMINARY: BISHOP JOHN HEYL VINCENT AND THE CHAUTAUQUA SCHOOL OF THEOLOGY. *Methodist Hist. 1976 14(4): 252-295.* John Heyl Vincent (1832-1920), Methodist preacher and bishop, was very conscious of his own lack of education. To assist fellow ministers who also lacked education, he established the degree-granting Chautauqua School of Theology in New York in 1881 to provide correspondence courses and summer sessions. By 1898 the school dropped the granting of degrees and Vincent's dream of theological education for hundreds of untrained Protestant clergymen was short-lived. 16 notes. H. L. Calkin

764. Stephens, Bruce M. WATCHMAN OF THE WALLS OF ZION: SAMUEL MILLER AND THE CHRISTIAN MINISTRY. *J. of Presbyterian Hist. 1978 56(4): 296-309.* Samuel Miller (1769-1850) was appointed professor of ecclesiastical government at the newly-founded Princeton Theological Seminary in 1813. This was the first seminary of the Presbyterian Church. Theretofore Presbyterian clergy were prepared for the ministry by studying under some "approved divine." The seminary provided a more rounded and consistently-trained clergy who were sound biblical critics, defenders of the faith, skilled casuists, useful preachers, faithful pastors, qualified disciplinarians, and examples to their flocks. The educative role of the clergy in society was foremost in Miller's mind. His commitment to theological education, profound piety, devotion to the church, suspicious nature regarding revivalism, critical evaluation of voluntary societies, uncertainty about the democratic ethos, disdain for sectarian disputes, and sense of the millenium all contributed to Miller's understanding of the character and work of the Christian minister. To these ends he trained his students. Covers 1813-50. Based on Miller's writings and biographical studies; illus., 31 notes. H. M. Parker, Jr.

765. Stern, Norton B. and Kramer, William M. THE SAN BERNARDINO HEBREW AND ENGLISH ACADEMY 1868-1872. *Western States Jewish Hist. Q. 1976 8(2): 102-117.* The first Jewish day school in southern California was opened on 27 May 1868 by the Jewish community in San Bernardino. Siegmund Bergel served as the teacher for the San Bernardino Hebrew and English Academy during 1868-72. The subjects included English, Latin, Greek, Hebrew, and other branches of education. Theatrical productions were given each year for different Jewish holidays. Bergel was active in civic affairs. He helped establish the San

Bernardino Literary Society and served as its first president. In 1872, he left for his homeland in Germany. He became internationally known for his work as a Jewish community leader. He died in 1912. Photo, 52 notes.
R. A. Garfinkle

766. Szasz, Margaret Connell. "POOR RICHARD" MEETS THE NATIVE AMERICAN: SCHOOLING FOR YOUNG INDIAN WOMEN IN EIGHTEENTH-CENTURY CONNECTICUT. *Pacific Hist. Rev. 1980 49(2): 215-235.* The Reverend Eleazar Wheelock's experiment in educating Indian girls failed, because his goals were not compatible with the girls' expectations. The girls' education was limited to housekeeping skills and elementary reading and writing. Wheelock expected the girls to assist future Indian husbands who would preach and teach among the Indians, but only one met that goal. Discontented with Indian culture but untrained in the whites' cultural values, the girls did not fit into white society. They confronted the dilemma that future generations of Indians educated in missionary, federal, or public schools were to experience. Covers 1761-69. Based on Dartmouth College archives and manuscripts, diaries and memoirs, Eleazar Wheelock's published work and other contemporary imprints, and other primary sources; 77 notes.
R. N. Lokken

767. Thompson, Dean J. ROBERT MC AFEE BROWN REMEMBERS HENRY PITNEY VAN DUSEN. *J. of Presbyterian Hist. 1978 56(1): 62-78.* Interviews Robert McAfee Brown, who attended Union Theological Seminary, New York City, and then joined the faculty during the presidency (1945-63) of Dr. Henry Pitney Van Dusen (1897-1975). One of the last of the liberals, Van Dusen ran a tight ship as president, yet was open to new concepts and seldom thwarted proposals of faculty members that might run counter to his own ideas. Van Dusen's forte lay in his ability to make both faculty and students think in terms of a worldwide Christian community. Brown gives Van Dusen's administration high marks: "he probably got more things done in the course of his tenure as President of Union Seminary than could have been done under any three other people in three times the time." Illus., 10 notes.
H. M. Parker, Jr.

768. Tobler, Douglas F. KARL G. MAESER'S GERMAN BACKGROUND, 1828-1856: THE MAKING OF ZION'S TEACHER. *Brigham Young U. Studies 1977 17(2): 155-175.* In 1876, at Brigham Young's request, Karl G. Maeser, a convert to Mormonism in 1855, left Germany to come to Provo, Utah, to provide academic and religious direction to Brigham Young Academy. For a man who later exercised such a profound impact on Mormon education, little has been known concerning the European influences in the development of Maeser's character, world view, and educational philosophy. Illuminates the European background and preparation of this Mormon pedagogical reformer.
M. S. Legan

769. Townley, Carrie M. BISHOP WHITAKER'S SCHOOL FOR GIRLS. *Nevada Hist. Soc. Q. 1976 19(3): 171-184.* Analyzes the success and then reasons for the decline and closure in 1894 of a girls' school at Reno which Episcopalian Bishop Ozi William Whitaker founded in 1876. The school prospered while under the supervision of Whitaker, only to lose students and encounter other obstacles between 1888 and 1894. Based on newspaper and primary source materials; 3 photos, 75 notes.
H. T. Lovin

770. Unsicker, Joan I. ARCHEOLOGICAL EXPLORATIONS AT JUBILEE COLLEGE HISTORIC SITE. *Western Illinois Regional Studies 1980 3(1): 36-45.* Describes the findings in 1979 of the excavation site at Jubilee College in central Peoria County, Illinois, which, coupled with historical documents, presents a fairly complete picture of this Episcopal college which was founded in 1839, only to experience several closings until the final one in 1885.

771. —. ACADEMIC FREEDOM AND TENURE: CONCORDIA SEMINARY. *AAUP Bull. 1975 61(1): 49-59.*

772. Vernon, Walter N. EARLY ECHOES FROM BLOOMFIELD ACADEMY. *Chronicles of Oklahoma 1974 52(2): 237-243.* Provides an early history of Bloomfield Academy, a Methodist-supported school for Chickasaw Indian girls, founded in 1853 in Indian Territory. Briefly outlines its management by the Reverend John H. Carr and presents an account of life at the school by Ellen J. Downs, a teacher there during 1856-66. Based on Methodist Church reports and primary source material; photo, 7 notes.
N. J. Street

773. Walch, Timothy. CATHOLIC EDUCATION IN CHICAGO: THE FORMATIVE YEARS, 1840-1890. *Chicago Hist. 1978 7(2): 87-97.* Unable to secure state tax funds for parochial education, Chicago's Catholic community sustained itself on donations and fund raising, an enterprise led by Father Arnold Damen, 1840-90.

774. Warch, Richard. THE SHEPHERD'S TENT: EDUCATION AND ENTHUSIASM IN THE GREAT AWAKENING. *Am. Q. 1978 30(2): 177-198.* The college called the Shepherd's Tent represented an effort on the part of radical advocates of the revivalistic aspects of the Great Awakening to propagate a purified version of religious doctrine through education. Their founding of the short-lived institution reflected their view that Harvard and Yale were not fulfilling their religious mission, owing to the contamination of the spiritual by secular influences in those colleges. The main agents in the formation of the college were James Davenport and Timothy Allen, with moral support provided by such clergymen as Eleazar Wheelock. The school was formed in New London, Connecticut in 1742 to start the process of training New Light exhorters and teachers. Opposition to the venture generated by unsympathetic clergymen was considerable from the beginning and reached a peak during the unfavorable publicity received by the college in the public burning of books incident in 1743. The school was disbanded shortly afterwards. Its existence marks an early effort on the part of those considering themselves to be apart from the majority to form their own educational institutions.
N. Lederer

775. Ward, Leo R. CRASHING THE PHILOSOPHERS' GATE. *Modern Age 1979 23(2): 154-157.* Catholic philosophers and secular philosophers have established an unobstrusive dialogue in the American Philosophical Association. Until mid-century most Catholics earned humanities higher degrees at Catholic institutions which, though often academically rigorous, deadened creativity by disavowing pluralism, synthesis, and inquiry. Covers 1933-79.
C. D'Aniello

776. Ward, Richard Hiram. UNION UNIVERSITY AND ITS PREDECESSORS: HISTORICAL HIGHLIGHTS. *West Tennessee Hist. Soc. Papers 1975 29: 55-63.* Describes the Centennial/Sesquicentennial Celebration of Union University, Jackson, Tennessee, and presents the school's involvement in the history and development of West Tennessee. Beginning as Jackson Male Academy, the school was incorporated 4 February 1826. In 1844 the legislature chartered West Tennessee College in Jackson. In 1848 Union College was established in Murphreesboro. In 1874 the Tennessee Baptist Association accepted an offer to relocate Union in Jackson, and the school was then called Southwestern Baptist University. After meeting certain conditions, the trustees of West Tennessee College conveyed their campus and buildings to the trustees of Southwestern Baptist University. In 1907 the name of the institution was changed to Union University. One of two articles in this issue about Union University. Based on primary sources; 17 photos, 12 notes.
H. M. Parker, Jr.

777. Warford, Malcolm L. THE MAKING AND UNMAKING OF A RADICAL TRADITION: BEREA COLLEGE, 1855-1904. *Encounter 1977 38(2): 149-161.* Berea College was a religious college founded by John Gregg Fee, a Presbyterian missionary, in Kentucky, 1855-1904; emphasizes the abolitionist stance of its founders.

778. Weeks, Louis B., III. LEWIS SHERRILL: THE CHRISTIAN EDUCATOR AND CHRISTIAN EXPERIENCE. *J. of Presbyterian Hist. 1973 51(2): 235-248.* The contributions of Lewis Sherrill (1882-1957), a Presbyterian pastor and educator.
S

779. White, Clinton O. LANGUAGE, RELIGION, SCHOOLS AND POLITICS AMONG GERMAN-AMERICAN CATHOLIC SETTLERS IN ST. PETER'S COLONY, SASKATCHEWAN, 1903-1916. *Study Sessions: Can. Catholic Hist. Assoc. [Canada] 1978 45: 81-99.* Details efforts of German Catholics in St. Peter's Colony to maintain their language and religion in a largely Protestant and English-speaking environment, using their own school system.

780. Williamson, Norman J. LANSDOWNE COLLEGE: A PRODUCT OF THE DEPRESSION OF 1885. *Manitoba Pageant [Canada] 1976 21(4): 15-17.* In 1882 the Collegiate Institute began as a part of the Portage la Prairie school. As an economy measure on 12 June 1885 all first class teachers were fired. Two days later the Collegiate Institute closed. In 1887 the Reverend B. Franklin planned and organized his private college named after Marquis of Lansdowne, the Governor General of Canada. Unable to compete successfully with older, established colleges, Lansdowne College ceased operations in 1893. B. J. LoBue

781. Wulff, O. H. AUTOBIOGRAPHY. *Concordia Hist. Inst. Q. 1975 48(3): 87-98.* An account of O. H. Wulff's career as a professional Lutheran educator. The chronicle starts in Glenview, Illinois, where Wulff was born, moves on to Concordia-River Forest College, and then on to Bristol, Connecticut, where Wulff became an instructor, and later principal of the Immanuel Lutheran School. W. T. Walker

782. Wynne, Edward J., Jr.; Rowe, Kenneth E., ed. BISHOP ASBURY AND THE SUNDAY SCHOOL. *Methodist Hist. 1980 18(4): 272-276.* Reprints, with commentary, a letter and postscript by Francis Asbury, Methodist bishop, in support of Christian education. This letter, dated 16 September 1791, is taken from *Minutes Taken at the Several Conferences of the Methodist-Episcopal Church in America for the Year 1792* (Philadelphia, 1792). 3 notes. H. L. Calkin

783. —. BUDS ON THE TREE OF KNOWLEDGE: EARLY VIEWS OF BRIGHAM YOUNG UNIVERSITY. *Utah Hist. Q. 1975 43(4): 390-395.* This photographic portfolio of Brigham Young University celebrates its centennial with pictures of various scenes, 1897-1924. 13 illus. J. L. Hazelton

784. —. THE FIRST FUND-RAISERS FOR THE HEBREW UNION COLLEGE IN THE FAR EAST. *Western States Jewish Hist. Q. 1975 8(1): 55-58.* Founded in July 1873 by Rabbi Isaac Mayer Wise, the Union of American Hebrew Congregations set as one of its goals the establishment of a Hebrew college. Rabbi Wise used his Anglo-Hebrew weekly paper, *The Israelite*, to solicit funds for the school. Lists of principal Jews in many western communities were published in the paper. These men collected donations from their communities. Provides the lists for California, Nevada, New Mexico, Utah, and Washington Territory. On 4 October 1875 the first classes of the Hebrew Union College were held. 4 notes. R. A. Garfinkle

785. —. GROWING IN THE LORD: 75 YEARS OF LUTHERAN SECONDARY EDUCATION IN MILWAUKEE. *Concordia Hist. Inst. Q. 1978 51(1): 3-8.* From its founding in 1903, the Immanuel Lutheran School had the support of Lutherans in Milwaukee. Established through the efforts of Pastors J. F. G. Harders and Otto Hagedorn who were assisted by Emil Sampe, the Immanuel Lutheran School was the first Lutheran high school in Milwaukee. During the 75 years since its founding the school has grown from 18 to more than 1,000 students. This article is a committee report. W. T. Walker

786. —. HEBREW UNION COLLEGE-JEWISH INSTITUTE OF RELIGION—A CENTENNIAL DOCUMENTARY. *Am. Jewish Arch. 1974 26(2): 103-244.* Founded in Cincinnati in 1875 the Hebrew Union College was conjoined in later years with New York's Jewish Institute of Religion and subsequently added campuses in Los Angeles and Jerusalem. It is not only the Reform movement's leading seminary for the training of rabbis but also a major center of Jewish intellectual endeavor. J

787. —. A HISTORY OF BENEDICTINE HIGH SCHOOL. *Jednota Ann. Furdek 1978 17: 165-176.* Benedictine High School has educated boys in Cleveland, Ohio, since 1928.

788. —. A SAN BERNARDINO CONFIRMAND'S REPORT: 1891. *Western States Jewish Hist. Q. 1979 11(2): 111-113.* The Henrietta Hebrew Benevolent Society sponsored the first Sunday School in San Bernardino, California, in 1891. Fourteen of the students were confirmed in their faith in a ceremony on 14 June 1891. Reform Rabbi Dr. Blum of Los Angeles officiated. Reprint of a letter from *The Sabbath Visitor,* Cincinatti, 31 July 1891; 6 notes. B. S. Porter

7. FAMILY

(including Abortion, Childbearing, and Sex Roles)

789. Abernathy, Mollie C. SOUTHERN WOMEN, SOCIAL RECONSTRUCTION, AND THE CHURCH IN THE 1920'S. *Louisiana Studies 1974 13(4): 289-312.* Southern radical social feminists comprised a special group of Southern women who combined extreme or hard-core feminism and a social reconstructionist program. Despite significant changes in the decades before World War I, the evolution of women's organizations in the South was a decade behind that of their Northern sisters, though many Southern women served in the Y.W.C.A. "Without the radical social feminists spurring on ordinary Southern club and church-women to action little progress pertaining to women would have been accomplished during the reactionary decade of the 1920's." 60 notes. E. P. Stickney

790. Alston, Jon P.; McIntosh, William A.; and Wright, Louise M. EXTENT OF INTERFAITH MARRIAGES AMONG WHITE AMERICANS. *Sociol. Analysis 1976 37(3): 261-264.* The General Social Survey Program makes available data dealing with the religious preferences of respondents and their spouses from national samples of the American population. Seventeen percent of the white population have spouses with different religious preferences. Interfaith marriage is associated with lower church participation and with lower levels of perceived family satisfaction. Covers 1973-75. J

791. Bacon, Margaret H. QUAKER WOMEN AND THE CHARGE OF SEPARATISM. *Quaker Hist. 1980 69(1): 23-26.* The issue of whether women should meet separately began among the Society of Friends three centuries ago with George Fox, who felt that women would be intimidated and silenced in joint meetings. Lucretia Coffin Mott founded the Philadelphia Female Anti-Slavery Society 170 years later. She answered with Fox's reasons Lynn Quaker Abigail Kelley Foster's 1839 argument that to act separately was to violate the principle of equality for which they worked. The admission of women to the American Anti-Slavery Society that year ended the immediate issue. Covers 1837-66. 4 notes. T. D. S. Bassett

792. Bandel, Betty. "WHAT THE GOOD LAWS OF MAN HATH PUT ASUNDER". *Vermont Hist. 1978 46(4): 221-233.* Because the Puritan tradition treated marriage as a civil contract and not a sacrament, and because women were economically important in the age of homespun and knew it, Vermont divorce law, set during 1777-97, allowed several grounds, whereas New York permitted divorce for adultery only. Newspaper advertisements of both spouses, 1795-1815, show that practice was as liberal as the law. Residential requirements were added, early in the 19th century, and later a cooling-off period. 13 notes. T. D. S. Bassett

793. Barrish, Gerald and Welch, Michael R. STUDENT RELIGIOSITY AND DISCRIMINATORY ATTITUDES TOWARD WOMEN. *Sociol. Analysis 1980 41(1): 66-73.* Data on 326 students from three universities were collected to investigate the general relationship between religiosity and sex role stereotyping (i.e., "macho"). The findings call into question the belief that religiosity is presently strongly linked to, and may actually foster, the acceptance of traditionalistic sex role stereotypes among a highly educated segment of the population. Covers 1970's. Table, biblio. J/S

794. Bean, Lee L.; May, Dean L.; and Skolnick, Mark. THE MORMON HISTORICAL DEMOGRAPHY PROJECT. *Hist. Methods Newsletter 1978 11(1): 45-53.* In this research project involving a wide range of specialists, the authors draw on a common data base: Mormon family records who experienced a single demographic event on the Mormon pioneer trail or in Utah. The final plan is to achieve 12 analytical goals: demographic structure and change, nuptiality, polygamy, fertility, natural fertility, mortality, migration, community studies, inheritance, familial correlations, genetic demography, and sex ratios. They briefly cite some results of the project. 2 tables, graph, 2 fig., 16 notes. D. K. Pickens

795. Bednarowski, Mary Farrell. OUTSIDE THE MAINSTREAM: WOMAN'S RELIGION AND WOMEN RELIGIOUS LEADERS IN NINETEENTH CENTURY AMERICA. *J. of the Am. Acad. of Religion 1980 48(2): 207-231.* The character of the divine, human nature, the function of the clergy, and the nature of marriage constitute four religious areas where women's leadership was conspicuous. Analyzes Shakerism, Spiritualism, Christian Science, and Theosophy to point out these characteristics in each and to compare such ideas with the views of modern feminist theologians. E. R. Lester

796. Beecher, Maureen Ursenbach. UNDER THE SUNBONNETS: MORMON WOMEN WITH FACES. *Brigham Young U. Studies 1976 16(4): 471-484.* Mormon women of the 19th century have a stereotyped image compounded of romanticized generalizations and overt sentimentality. Historians should include the impact of women in their writings on the history of the Mormon Church and Mormon culture. Mentions successful Mormon women in education, telegraphy, business, law, and medicine. M. S. Legan

797. Beeton, Beverly. THE HAYES ADMINISTRATION AND THE WOMAN QUESTION. *Hayes Hist. J. 1978 2(1): 52-56.* Rutherford B. Hayes was not an advocate of women's rights; opposing the enfranchisement of women, he viewed women as an elevating influence on men. Despite the efforts of the National Woman Suffrage Association and the American Woman Suffrage Association, Hayes maintained a traditional view of women which was incompatible with political participation. The movement to outlaw the Mormon practice of polygamy, and Congress's move to take away the vote from women in Utah, resulted in Mormon women visiting President and Mrs. Hayes, and sending numerous petitions to Congress. Hayes supported Congress on the Mormon question. Secondary sources; 4 illus., 7 notes. J. N. Friedel

798. Beeton, Beverly. WOMAN SUFFRAGE IN TERRITORIAL UTAH. *Utah Hist. Q. 1978 46(2): 100-120.* During 1867-96, eastern suffragists promoted woman suffrage in Utah as an experiment, and as a way to eliminate polygamy. Compelling Utah motives for enfranchisement were the need to counter the image of downtrodden Mormon women and the desire to promote statehood. Advocates within Utah were William S. Godbe, Annie Thompson Godbe, Charlotte Ives Cobb Godbe, Emmeline B. Wells, Franklin D. Richards, and Emily S. Turner Richards. Utah enfranchisement moved the national suffragists closer to the Victorian Compromise and preoccupation with the franchise. Primary and secondary sources; 4 illus., 45 notes. J. L. Hazelton

799. Bennett, John C. and Bennett, Anne M. THE CHURCH AND THE STRUGGLES FOR LIBERATION. *Foundations 1975 18(1): 53-60.* Covers liberation in a theological context. Women's liberation was the focus of the discussion, but minorities and races were included as they related to women. E. E. Eminhizer

800. Bitton, Davis and Bunker, Gary L. DOUBLE JEOPARDY: VISUAL IMAGES OF MORMON WOMEN TO 1914. *Utah Hist. Q. 1978 46(2): 184-202.* Intolerance of women and Mormons presented special problems for those sharing this double identity in the 19th and early 20th centuries. Pictorial images dealt with the systemic effect of Mormonism upon women, and exploited general stereotypes applied especially to Mormons. Distinct images were created of Mormon women as commodities, embattled, impoverished, subjugated, worldly, uncultured, unsightly, fickle, acquisitive, and domineering. Mormons tried to counteract this negative current because it created a climate in which punitive legislation could be enacted. Primary and secondary sources; 14 illus., 68 notes. J. L. Hazelton

801. Bolin, Winifred D. Wandersee. HARRIET E. BISHOP: MORALIST AND REFORMER. Stuhler, Barbara and Kreuter, Gretchen, ed. *Women of Minnesota: Selected Biographical Essays* (St. Paul: Minne-

sota Historical Society Press, 1977): 7-19. In 1847, Harriet E. Bishop arrived in the frontier community of St. Paul, Minnesota. Trained by Catharine Beecher, Bishop brought with her the missionary zeal of the social reformer and a belief in the moral superiority of women. A Baptist, she established the first public school and the first Sunday School in St. Paul. Discusses her activities as a temperance advocate, largely negative attitudes toward the local Indians, efforts to help the destitute, prose and poetry, and two matrimonial opportunities. Bishop died in 1883. By then she was largely unknown in the growing metropolis, but her life "personified a whole generation of women" who tried to fulfill their destinies within the boundaries of convention and who labored to meet the responsibilities imposed by their presumed innate superiority. Primary and secondary sources; illus., 34 notes. A. E. Wiederrecht

802. Bomberger, Herbert L. THE PARSONAGE: A WAY OF CHRISTIAN FAMILY LIVING. *Lutheran Q. 1974 26(1): 58-63.* Examines the myths, opportunities for growth, and avenues for strengthening marriage and family life within the parsonage. S

803. Bouvier, Leon F. THE FERTILITY OF RHODE ISLAND CATHOLICS: 1968-1969. *Sociol. Analysis 1973 34(2): 124-139.* Analysis of fertility differentials between Catholics and non-Catholics in Rhode Island. Representative samples of the population were derived and interviews conducted in 1968 and 1969. Although Catholics exhibit higher fertility expectation than do non-Catholics, differences are smaller than those observed in earlier national surveys. Furthermore, Catholics indicate an increasing tendency to practice birth control, though not to the extent of non-Catholics. It is suggested that the recent emergence of American Catholics into the 'power structure' has resulted in a loss of minority-status feeling. This may partially explain the developing convergence noted between the two groups. However, a strong religious ideology, limiting birth control to the rhythm method, continues to influence many Catholics and this is preventing a complete convergence in fertility behavior. J

804. Boyd, Lois A. and Brackenridge, R. Douglas. RACHEL HENDERLITE: WOMEN AND CHURCH UNION. *J. of Presbyterian Hist. 1978 56(1): 10-18.* Interviews Rachel Henderlite, the first woman to be ordained in the Southern Presbyterian Church (1965) and also the first female President of the Consultation on Church Union (1976). Because of her years of frustration in religious education before ordination, she recommends that any professional church woman who wants to be active and accepted in the church should seek ordination, and not settle for a lower position such as director of religious education. Illus., 2 notes. H. M. Parker, Jr.

805. Boyd, Lois A. SHALL WOMEN SPEAK? CONFRONTATION IN THE CHURCH, 1876. *J. of Presbyterian Hist. 1978 56(4): 271-296.* The problem of women speaking in Presbyterian pulpits in the 19th century was normally solved on the scriptural injunction which denied the right. In 1876, however, the Reverend Isaac M. See permitted two women to speak from his pulpit in Newark, New Jersey. He was charged before presbytery with disobedience by a colleague. See was found guilty; subsequent appeals before the synod and general assembly sustained the action of presbytery. The "woman question" was too firmly entrenched in the political, social, and religious arenas of the 19th century for Presbyterians to have acted otherwise. Officially the cause of women suffered a setback; however, women maintained separate structures whereby mission work was supported, leadership was developed in education, and very substantial financial support was given to the Presbyterian Church. The base was laid for the 20th century when women would be ordained as officers and ministers. Based on minutes of church courts and church and secular newspapers; 47 notes. H. M. Parker, Jr.

806. Boyer, Paul. MINISTER'S WIFE, WIDOW, RELUCTANT FEMINIST: CATHERINE MARSHALL IN THE 1950S. *Am. Q. 1978 30(5): 703-721.* A study of the role changes forced upon Catherine Marshall by the early death of her husband, Peter Marshall, pastor of New York Avenue Presbyterian Church in Washington, D.C. The early acceptance of the traditional husband-support role fitted her for the position she had held. However, his death thrust her into a literary career in which she was eminently successful. She came to realize that it was in this that she was finding herself, yet her expression of this was always guarded. After her remarriage ten years later, there was again the life of domesticity, yet her writing and speaking career continued unabated. 57 notes. R. V. Ritter

807. Boylan, Anne M. EVANGELICAL WOMANHOOD IN THE NINETEENTH CENTURY: THE ROLE OF WOMEN IN SUNDAY SCHOOLS. *Feminist Studies 1978 4(3): 62-80.* The activities of women in the Sunday School Movement illustrate some of the ways women shaped their roles in 19th-century American society. The model of "evangelical womanhood," as one of several possible roles, was developed by these women during 1800-20. The women of the Sunday School Movement not only shaped their role but designed ways of putting it into practice and transmitting it to succeeding generations by encouraging and training other young women to follow them and by enlarging the scope of Sunday School work to include organized benevolence. A few even went from this beginning to political work for temperance, abolition, and women's rights. 34 notes. L. M. Maloney

808. Brackbill, Yvonne and Howell, Embry M. RELIGIOUS DIFFERENCES IN FAMILY SIZE PREFERENCE AMONG AMERICAN TEENAGERS. *Sociol. Analysis 1974 35(1): 35-44.* Analyzes differences between Catholic and non-Catholic young people in attitudes toward family formation. A sample of 941 students in junior high schools, high schools, and colleges in the Washington, D.C., area responded to a self-administered questionnaire in 1971. Data were obtained on students' background, attitudes toward family formation, girls' career aspirations, and population awareness. In general, results emphasize and reemphasize the continuing importance of a religious differential in family size preference. Religious affiliation was more predictive of preferred family size than was race, sex, age, socio-economic status, number of siblings, type of school, maternal work history, or girls' career aspirations. These results differ from those obtained in recent studies based on short term trends in religious conformity but are consistent with longer term trends. J

809. Brackenridge, R. Douglas. EQUALITY FOR WOMEN? A CASE STUDY IN PRESBYTERIAN POLITY, 1926-1930. *J. of Presbyterian Hist. 1980 58(2): 142-165.* In 1930 women for the first time were eligible for ordination as Ruling Elders in the Presbyterian Church in the United States. Before then, they had raised and contributed substantial amounts of money for the church's benevolent programs, and had served in many unordained capacities. Discusses the appointment of the Committee of Four in 1926 by the General Assembly to look into the matter of ordaining women as Elders. The committee consisted of Robert E. Speer, Lewis S. Mudge, Katherine Bennett, and Margaret Hodge. All were conservative, evangelical, and ecumenical. Details the work of the committee and the General Assemblies of 1926-29 that finally approved the ordination of women as Elders. Emphasizes the difficult context in which the Committee of Four functioned. Based on the Minutes of the General Assembly, numerous personal collections, such as the Mudge Papers, Presbyterian Historical Society, Philadelphia, and the Speer Papers, Princeton Theological Seminary, and contemporary church newspapers; 77 notes. H. M. Parker, Jr.

810. Brady, David W. and Tedin, Kent L. LADIES IN PINK: RELIGION AND POLITICAL IDEOLOGY IN THE ANTI- ERA MOVEMENT. *Social Sci. Q. 1976 56(4): 564-575.* The authors seek to identify the sources of the anti-feminist orientation, 1933-75. J

811. Brooks, Juanita, ed., and Butler, Janet G., ed. UTAH'S PEACE ADVOCATE, THE "MORMONA": ELISE FURER MUSSER. *Utah Hist. Q. 1978 46(2): 151-166.* Excerpts the writings, diaries, and letters of Elise Furer Musser (1877-1967), who was born in Switzerland, migrated to Utah in 1897, and married Burton Musser in 1911. Her social service and political career began with work in Neighborhood House. She became influential in Utah's Democratic Women's Club, serving as state senator (1933-34), and was the only woman delegate to the Buenos Aires Peace Conference in 1936. Her life puts the current women's liberation movement into perspective as a continuum rather than a new, spontaneous phenomenon. Primary sources; 5 illus., 18 notes. J. L. Hazelton

812. Brown, Earl Kent. ARCHETYPES AND STEREOTYPES: CHURCH WOMEN IN THE NINETEENTH CENTURY. *Religion in Life 1974 43(3): 325-337.* The contributions of Barbara Heck, Lois Stiles Parker, Sarah Dickey, Frances Willard, and Anna Howard Shaw

as leaders in the Methodist Church disprove stereotypes about church women in the 19th century. S

813. Brown, Lawrence L. TEXAS BISHOP VETOES WOMEN COUNCIL DELEGATES IN 1921. *Hist. Mag. of the Protestant Episcopal Church 1979 48(1): 93-102.* At the Annual Council of the Episcopal Diocese of Texas in 1921 an amendment to the constitution which would have allowed women as delegates to the Council was adopted by lay and clerical votes, but was vetoed by Bishop George Herbert Kinsolving. Traces the drive for women's rights in the diocese, the origin of the power of the bishop to veto, and why the bishop vetoed the measure: he felt that the church was moving with secular trends, and not in harmony with apostolic precept. It was not until 1969 that the council authorized women as delegates, and the provision was made operative the next year. Based on the Journal of the Annual Council of the Diocese of Texas; 41 notes. H. M. Parker, Jr.

814. Brown, Richard D. RELIGION, NURTURE, AND PERSONALITY-FORMATION IN EARLY AMERICA. *J. of Family Hist. 1979 4(1): 95-100.* Review article prompted by Philip Greven's *The Protestant Temperament: Patterns of Child-Rearing, Religious Experience, and the Self in Early America* (New York: Knopf, 1977) which searches for that perhaps most elusive of all attributes, personality. He identifies three major types that are closely linked to religious perspectives: evangelical, moderate, and genteel. Solid evidence is often lacking to conclusively prove the author's arguments, but this represents a bold attempt to understand the psychological dimensions of colonial America. Note. T. W. Smith

815. Browning, Don S. HOMOSEXUALITY, THEOLOGY, THE SOCIAL SCIENCES AND THE CHURCH. *Encounter 1979 40(3): 223-243.* Evaluates three Protestant studies which examine the issue of homosexuality in theological thinking, 1970's.

816. Bryant, Keith L., Jr. THE ROLE AND STATUS OF THE FEMALE YEOMANRY IN THE ANTEBELLUM SOUTH: THE LITERARY VIEW. *Southern Q. 1980 18(2): 73-88.* In the past historians have given little attention to middle-class white women in the antebellum South. Using literary sources, the author finds that these women occupied significant positions in the antebellum South. For example, they worked, made money for the family, raised the children, established the moral tone in the home, and became important in religious institutions. Their early role in Southern history should not be underestimated. Primary sources; 60 notes. B. D. Ledbetter

817. Bunkle, Phillida. SENTIMENTAL WOMANHOOD AND DOMESTIC EDUCATION, 1830-1870. *Hist. of Educ. Q. 1974 14(1): 13-31.* Attacks the thesis that industrialization and its displacement of the household and family farm as productive centers alone caused the antifeminist ideal of sentimental womanhood to develop. Argues instead that the new domestic education of the 1830's-70's had strong religious influences coming from the second Great Awakening that helped to foster the ideas of morality, motherhood, and domesticity. Based on primary and secondary sources; 43 notes. L. C. Smith

818. Bush, Lester E., Jr. BIRTH CONTROL AMONG THE MORMONS: INTRODUCTION TO AN INSISTENT QUESTION. *Dialogue 1976 10(2): 12-44.* Discusses Mormon doctrine and Church members' values regarding contraception and abortion from the mid-1800's to the present.

819. Bush, Lester E., Jr. MORMOM ELDERS' WAFERS: IMAGES OF MORMON VIRILITY IN PATENT MEDICINE ADS. *Dialogue 1976 10(2): 89-93.* Provides examples of patent medicine ads which portray the stereotype of the virile Mormon male, 1884-1931, in the American patent medicine industry.

820. Calvo, Janis. QUAKER WOMEN MINISTERS IN NINETEENTH CENTURY AMERICA. *Quaker Hist. 1974 63(2): 75-93.* The Quietist-prophetic view that God speaks through pure, obedient, empty vessels enabled the traveling woman Friend to fulfill the conventional image of pure, submissive female, reluctantly accepting God's will to preach. She also accepted her conventional domestic role in everything else. We know little about child care during the mother-minister's absence. 58 notes. T. D. S. Bassett

821. Campbell, D'Ann. WOMEN'S LIFE IN UTOPIA: THE SHAKER EXPERIMENT IN SEXUAL EQUALITY REAPPRAISED: 1810 TO 1860. *New England Q. 1978 51(1): 23-38.* Outlines Shaker attitudes concerning sexual relations and roles and says that Shaker communities had a high female-to-male ratio. Most women joined "to satisfy the basic needs unfulfilled by their own families and communities, especially stability, security, and a promise of eternal salvation." Based on secondary sources and the Shaker MSS Collection, Western Reserve Historical Society, Cleveland, Ohio; 28 notes. J. C. Bradford

822. Campbell, Eugene E. and Campbell, Bruce L. DIVORCE AMONG MORMON POLYGAMISTS: EXTENT AND EXPLANATIONS. *Utah Hist. Q. 1978 46(1): 4-23.* Mormon concepts of millennialism, the feelings of romantic love, and the lack of proven standards of conduct and behavior contributed to the high divorce rate among Mormon polygamists. Church leaders, claiming no special inspiration on the system, and having little experience with polygamy, proposed only individualistic solutions to problems. Ambivalence among leaders pressured by federal laws left members without clear guidance. In these anomic or normless circumstances, muted and ambivalent regulations resulted in a fluid marriage system. Covers 1844-90. Primary and secondary sources; 3 illus., 51 notes. J. L. Hazelton

823. Cannon, Charles A. THE AWESOME POWER OF SEX: THE POLEMICAL CAMPAIGN AGAINST MORMON POLYGAMY. *Pacific Hist. Rev. 1974 43(1): 61-82.* A study of the content and methods of the polemics against Mormon polygamy, concentrating on morality. Polygamy was viewed by its critics as unrestrained sexuality legitimized by religion. Closer examination suggests considerable ambience in regard to sex on the part of the authors and their readers. "The campaign allowed Americans to express vicariously their repressed desires at the same time that they reinforced the rigid sexual values of the existing order." Covers 1860-1900. 60 notes. R. V. Ritter

824. Cannon, Kenneth L., II. BEYOND THE MANIFESTO: POLYGAMOUS COHABITATION AMONG LDS GENERAL AUTHORITIES AFTER 1890. *Utah Hist. Q. 1978 46(1): 24-36.* After 1890, the Mormon church's official position on polygamy coincided with Federal antipolygamy laws, but the actual practice of church leaders did not. Many LDS General Authorities continued living with, and fathering children by their plural wives. As representatives of Mormons they entered into amnesty agreements, but as individuals felt they had the right to obey what they deemed a higher law. Federal investigations, increased social pressures, and stricter church discipline forced factual as well as official compliance. Primary and secondary sources; 2 illus., 30 notes. J. L. Hazelton

825. Christensen, Harold T. MORMON SEXUALITY IN CROSS-CULTURAL PERSPECTIVE. *Dialogue 1976 10(2): 62-75.* Examines several studies of Mormon and non-Mormon college students' attitudes toward premarital sex from the late 1930's to 1968.

826. Cohen, Steven Martin. AMERICAN JEWISH FEMINISM: A STUDY IN CONFLICTS AND COMPROMISES. *Am. Behavioral Scientist 1980 23(4): 519-558.* Investigates the differences between feminism and Judaism and possible individual and structural accommodations to those differences. Covers 1967-79.

827. Cott, Nancy F. PASSIONLESSNESS: AN INTERPRETATION OF VICTORIAN SEXUAL IDEOLOGY, 1790-1850. *Signs 1978 4(2): 219-236.* Reassessing Havelock Ellis's thesis that Victorian "anaesthesia" was a result of social repression, the author coins the terms "passionlessness" to characterize a Victorian woman's lack of sexual aggression. From their sexual and carnal natures in 17th- and 18th-century Anglo-Saxon tradition, women evolved into conservers of morality and purity because of 19th century religious evangelism. The new view appealed to women because it downplayed the sexual characterizations they had sought to escape, and "passionlessness" could be used pragmatically to achieve "voluntary motherhood." Sexual self-control preached by men also promoted passionlessness. Sources deal specifically with New England, literate, Protestant middle-class women. Primary and secondary sources; 61 notes. S. P. Conner

828. Cunningham, Barbara. AN EIGHTEENTH-CENTURY VIEW OF FEMININITY AS SEEN THROUGH THE JOURNALS OF HENRY MELCHIOR MUHLENBERG. *Pennsylvania Hist. 1976 43(3): 197-212.* In some respects, the journals of Henry Melchior Muhlenberg, an 18th-century Pennsylvania Lutheran clergyman, reflect attitudes toward women that historian Barbara Weltner has associated with the 19th-century "Cult of True Womanhood." For Muhlenberg, the ideal woman was religious, pure, submissive, and devoted to household duties. He thought that women were particularly vulnerable to a variety of physical, mental, and spiritual disorders. His views on sexuality prefigure Victorian prudery in some ways, but Muhlenberg did not think that one sex was more or less sensual than the other. "Muhlenberg placed the *female* center of mind, body, and soul very specifically in the uterus." 2 illus., 48 notes. D. C. Swift

829. Dayton, Lucille Sider and Dayton, Donald W. "YOUR DAUGHTERS SHALL PROPHESY": FEMINISM IN THE HOLINESS MOVEMENT. *Methodist Hist. 1976 14(2): 67-92.* The feminist theme permeates the literature of the Holiness Movement in America. It varied in intensity over two centuries from reserved openness, to acceptance of religious activity by women, to favoring the ordination of women. The role of women in holiness traditions was foreshadowed by Susanna Wesley's activities in the 1730's. The Holiness Movement intensified in America as early as 1827, with Phoebe Palmer later having a great impact both evangelically and as a feminist. By 1973 there was considerably less emphasis on feminism in the movement. 116 notes. H. L. Calkin

830. Derr, Jill Mulvay. WOMAN'S PLACE IN BRIGHAM YOUNG'S WORLD. *Brigham Young U. Studies 1978 18(3): 377-395.* A freedom-submission paradox prevaded Brigham Young's attitudes toward Mormon womanhood. Women were to submit to the well-ordered kingdom, which included an all-male priestly hierarchy, but they did gain increasing liberty, particularly during the last decade of Young's administration. Young contributed to their emancipation by giving them spiritual and economic influence within the church organization and by promoting women's education and involvement in trades and professions. Illustrates both sides of Young's paradoxical attitudes. Concludes that Young's efforts in maximizing female integration into the Mormon system of interdependence deserve more recognition. M. S. Legan

831. Deweese, Charles W. DEACONESSES IN BAPTIST HISTORY: A PRELIMINARY STUDY. *Baptist Hist. and Heritage 1977 12(1): 52-57.* Although deaconesses have existed throughout Baptist history, they have never been and are still not widespread. This condition may be due to the brevity of biblical information on the office, varying views of the biblical data which does exist, and a strong proclivity to keep the participation of women in Southern Baptist management positions at a minimal level. Deaconesses flourish best in times when the diaconate has been interpreted more in terms of a wide range of supporting and caring ministries rather than more narrowly in terms of church management and business administration. Covers 1600-1976. Secondary sources; 47 notes. H. M. Parker, Jr.

832. Driggs, Nevada W. HOW COME NEVADA? *Nevada Hist. Soc. Q. 1973 16(3): 180-185.* A memoir of the author's family. Emily Crane and Lorenzo Dow Watson, the author's parents, were parties to a polygamous marriage in Utah when polygamy enjoyed legal and social sanction. When polygamy was outlawed in Utah, polygamists were harassed. Emily Watson and her children fled to Panaca, Nevada, where the author and a younger sister were born. For two years, Lorenzo Watson maintained one family at Panaca and another in Utah, but the problems of keeping two houses so far apart forced him to relocate Emily and their children in Utah. 2 photos. H. T. Lovin

833. Dumont-Johnson, Micheline. LES COMMUNAUTÉS RELIGIEUSES ET LA CONDITION FÉMININE [Religious communities and the feminine condition]. *Recherches Sociographiques [Canada] 1978 19(1): 79-102.* As far back as the French Regime, women's religious communities played an important role in the social and cultural development of Quebec. In the second half of the 19th century one discerns the first manifestations of feminism in Quebec within the structures of these religious communities. With the present one sees their influence and importance disappear since the "Quebecoise" more and more lives within a society that offers avenues for self-development and expression unknown in the past. Based on an analysis of recent monographs; 5 tables, 4 graphs, 76 notes. A. E. LeBlanc

834. Dunn, Mary Maples. SAINTS AND SISTERS: CONGREGATIONAL AND QUAKER WOMEN IN THE EARLY COLONIAL PERIOD. *Am. Q. 1978 30(5): 582-601.* Investigates and contrasts the American Puritan Congregationalists and Quakers as means of getting at the forces which create a dichotomy between the place of men and women in religion, and, ultimately, in society at large. The development in the history of these two communities was very different. For the Quakers, women's position of equality with man in religious functions was largely established when they came to the new world, and women continued to play a much more forceful role than in the Congregational Church. Puritan women were "disciplined to silence." However, the Puritans, being the mainstream of American religious life, had an enduring effect on American culture to a degree far beyond that of the Quakers. 29 notes. R. V. Ritter

835. Dunn, Mary Maples. WOMEN OF LIGHT. Berkin, Carol Ruth and Norton, Mary Beth, ed. *Women of America: A History* (Boston: Houghton Mifflin Co., 1979): 114-136. Presents the general Protestant view of women as an afterthought to man and contrasts it with the Quaker view of women. Sex bias had no place in the recognition of the sense of Christ dwelling within each soul. George Fox championed female ministries as the spiritual regeneration of the converted transcended the curse of original sin. Nearly half of the Quaker missionaries who came to America during 1656-63 were women. Discusses Quaker women such as Margaret Fell, Jane Hoskings, Mary Dyer, Susannah Morris, and Abigale Pike. Based on contemporary documents, 6 of which are included, and secondary sources; illus., 10 notes. K. Talley

836. Ellis, Joseph. THE NEW AMERICAN TRINITY. *Rev. in Am. Hist. 1979 7(1): 58-63.* Review article prompted by Philip Greven's *The Protestant Temperament: Patterns of Child-Rearing, Religious Experience, and the Self in Early America* (New York: Alfred A. Knopf, 1977).

837. Fischer, Christiane. A PROFILE OF WOMEN IN ARIZONA IN FRONTIER DAYS. *J. of the West 1977 16(3): 42-53.* In the 1860's-70's about one-fifth of Arizona's inhabitants were women. Some had difficulty adjusting to primitive living conditions and the isolation of rural ranches, but all worked hard. By 1890 women were more than half the population and were affecting their communities' religious and cultural foundations. Denied reputable and gainful employment in competition with men, they turned to reform work—particularly temperance and woman suffrage. Primary and secondary sources; 7 photos, 57 notes. B. S. Porter

838. Foster, A. Durwood. GOD AND WOMAN: SOME THESES ON THEOLOGY, ETHICS, AND WOMEN'S LIB. *Religion in Life 1973 42(1): 42-55.*

839. Foster, Lawrence. A LITTLE-KNOWN DEFENSE OF POLYGAMY FROM THE MORMON PRESS IN 1842. *Dialogue: J. of Mormon Thought 1974 9(4): 21-34.* An 1842 Mormon pamphlet (apparently authorized by church leaders) which justified polygamy reveals the social and theological rationalization for the practice. Ostensibly, social ills reflected female assumption of male authority; the only solution was restoration of male dominance in the family on the basis of marriage as practiced by the ancient Patriarchs. Since only women alienated from husbands could seek divorce, husbands alienated from wives could reestablish family harmony only by taking another wife. Based on Mormon published sources and manuscripts; illus., 24 notes. D. L. Rowe

840. Fox, Margery. PROTEST IN PIETY: CHRISTIAN SCIENCE REVISITED. *Int. J. of Women's Studies [Canada] 1978 1(4): 401-416.* In the 19th century, Christian Science, through its founder, Mary Baker Eddy, established a religious movement but also a women's protest movement to gain some political power.

841. Frary, Joseph P. REPORT: A CONFERENCE ON "THE QUESTION OF WOMEN PRIESTS." *Anglican Theological Rev. 1973 55(3): 352-353.*

842. Fryer, Judith. AMERICAN EVES IN AMERICAN EDENS. *Am. Scholar 1974-75 44(1): 78-99.* Between the 1840's and the 1880's communitarians were searching for alternative modes of living that would break down the sex roles of traditional American society and create a new role for the American woman. There were two strands in the utopian experimentation, the religious and the secular. Examines the three foremost religious communities: the Shakers, the Mormons, and the Oneida Perfectionists. Most secular communities were implementations of the philosophies of Robert Owen or Charles Fourier. As illustrations, examines the community at New Harmony, Indiana, and the Brook Farm experiment. R. V. Ritter

843. Gambone, Joseph G., ed. THE FORGOTTEN FEMINIST OF KANSAS: THE PAPERS OF CLARINA I. H. NICHOLS, 1854-1885. *Kansas Hist. Q. 1973 39(3): 392-444, 39(4): 515-563, 1974 40(1): 72-135, (2): 241-292, (3): 410-459, (4): 503-562.* Part III. After returning to Kansas from the East in 1857, Mrs. Nichols became associate editor of the *Quindaro Chindowan*, a weekly Free-State journal. Her editorials are reprinted here. Giving up this position, Mrs. Nichols resumed her voluminous correspondence with prominent persons about the territorial strife in Kansas. In numerous letters to Susan B. Anthony she continued her discussion of antifeminism both in Kansas and in the nation as a whole. 142 notes. Part IV. Covers letters written during the late 1860's to the editors of the *Vermont Phoenix*, Wyandotte *Commerical Gazette*, and *Western Home Journal*, in which Mrs. Nichols discusses the status of women in Kansas and what might be done to improve their lot. She wrote at great length against the views of Rev. Eben Blachly, mustering an array of scriptural proof against his assertion that God had intended women to be inferior beings. 6 illus., 110 notes. Part V. In letters written from Wyandotte to the editors of the Topeka *Weekly Leader*, the *Kansas Daily Commonwealth*, and the *Vermont Phoenix*, Mrs. Nichols offers evidence to show that the women of Kansas did not enjoy their constitutional rights, contrary to a misconception apparently widely held in Kansas and other states at the time. She reviews scriptural evidence of the inferiority of women and again concludes that the Bible has been misinterpreted by men. She also elaborates on the ways in which homestead legislation worked to married women's disadvantage. Based on primary and secondary sources; illus., 77 notes. Part VI. Reproduces 1870-72 letters by Mrs. Nichols; from Potter Valley, California, in 1872 she described the daily life of immigrants around San Francisco. 71 notes. Part VII. Reprints more letters, 1873-80. Part VIII. Reprints letters from Mrs. Nichols' correspondence, 1881-85. W. F. Zornow and S

844. Genné, Elizabeth. THE CHANGING WORLDS OF WOMEN. *J. of Ecumenical Studies 1979 16(1): 160-165.* Reviews the vast changes that have occurred in the opportunities, responsibilities, and risks confronting women since the 1st World Conference of Christian Youth (Amsterdam, 1939), both within and outside of religion in the United States. S

845. Gollub, Sylvia L. A CRITICAL LOOK AT RELIGIOUS REQUIREMENTS IN ADOPTION. *Public Welfare 1974 32(2): 23-28.* Evaluates religious matching requirements in administrative adoption policies and practices from 1954 to 1971. S

846. Golomb, Deborah Grand. THE 1893 CONGRESS OF JEWISH WOMEN: EVOLUTION OR REVOLUTION IN AMERICAN JEWISH WOMEN'S HISTORY? *Am. Jewish Hist. 1980 70(1): 52-67.* The social and philanthropic activities of 19th-century Jewish women, particularly clubwomen, coupled with a degree of anti-Semitism in the women's suffrage movement, form the background for the Congress of Jewish Women held in conjunction with the World Parliament of Religions at the World's Columbian Exposition (Chicago, 1893). Hannah G. Solomon (1858-1942) shouldered much of the responsibility for organizing the Congress. She drew inspiration from both American and Jewish sources, particularly from leading clubwoman Mrs. Charles Henrotin and from Rabbi Emil Hirsch. Though the congress did not embrace all Jewish groups—the women were predominantly Reform Jews—and though it did not resolve the tension between loyalty to Judaism or to womankind, as the address by Sadie American demonstrates, it did set the tone for a new kind of participation for Jewish women within Jewish communal life. From the gathering came the idea for a permanent organization, the National Congress of Jewish Women. 30 notes. J. D. Sarna

847. Gorrell, Donald K. ORDINATION OF WOMEN BY THE UNITED BRETHREN IN CHRIST, 1889. *Methodist Hist. 1980 18(2): 136-143.* In 1889, the Church of the United Brethren in Christ revised its constitution. One controversial provision was the ordination of women clergy. Includes the debate regarding the provision finally adopted. Within four months, the Central Illinois Conference of the Church ordained its first woman preacher. Based on church publications, 1889; 13 notes. H. L. Calkin

848. Greeley, Andrew M. RELIGIOUS MUSICAL CHAIRS. *Society 1978 15(4): 53-59.* Analyzes religious exogamy in the United States: marriage outside of one's religion, the tendency to convert or disidentify, and the breakdown in sex and strength of belief, 1960's-70's. Focuses on Protestant churches and the Catholic Church.

849. Gripe, Elizabeth Howell. WOMEN, RESTRUCTURING AND UNREST IN THE 1920'S. *J. of Presbyterian Hist. 1974 52(2): 188-189.* Women gradually increased their participation and position within the structure of the Presbyterian Church throughout the 19th century. Restructuring in 1923, however, removed their principal power base. The church lost some of its support, but "set the stage for the next . . . struggle . . . to achieve ecclesiastical equality in . . . ordination as elders and ministers." 29 notes. D. L. Smith

850. Guggisberg, Hans R. PROTESTANT IDEALS OF EDUCATION IN HISTORICAL PERSPECTIVE: TWO APPROACHES. *J. of the Hist. of Ideas 1980 41(4): 693-698.* Review essay of Gerald Strauss's *Luther's House of Learning: Indoctrination of the Young in the German Reformation* (Baltimore: Johns Hopkins U. Pr., 1978) and Philip Greven's *The Protestant Temperament: Patterns of Child-Rearing, Religious Experience, and the Self in Early America* (New York: Knopf, 1977). Unsuited for direct comparison, the books are mainly considered separately. Greven's work evinces a "latent danger of one-sidedness" which "Strauss, in his more straightforward and at the same time more cautious account, has wisely avoided." D. B. Marti

851. Hales, Jean Gould. CO-LABORERS IN THE CAUSE: WOMEN IN THE ANTE-BELLUM NATIVIST MOVEMENT. *Civil War Hist. 1979 25(2): 119-138.* Denies traditional historiographical claims that nativists refused women an active part in their movement. Argues instead that nativists sympathized with working women, urged women of all classes to join them, and, by virtue of their traditionalist belief in the moral superiority of women, regarded women as natural and valuable allies in their crusade against Catholics and foreigners. Describes the nativist careers of Pennsylvanian Harriet Probasco (1844-45) and Marylander Anna Ella Carroll (1856-61), the activities and ideology of nativists, the roles of women activists, and the resultant acceptance of the expansion of women's social and political roles. The conservative, prostability cult of true womanhood projected by nativism offered women a reassuringly safe outlet from domesticity and thus helped to engender social change. 69 notes. S

852. Hallett, Mary E. NELLIE MCCLUNG AND THE FIGHT FOR THE ORDINATION OF WOMEN IN THE UNITED CHURCH OF CANADA. *Atlantis [Canada] 1979 4(2): 2-16.* Describes Nellie McClung's struggle with the Methodist Church beginning in 1915 and, beginning in 1925, with the United Church of Canada, made up of the Presbyterian, Methodist, and Congregational churches, for the ordination of women in Canada. McClung carried on until December 1928, and others continued until 1946 when the first married woman was ordained in the United Church.

853. Hansen, Klaus J. MORMON SEXUALITY AND AMERICAN CULTURE. *Dialogue 1976 10(2): 45-56.* Describes the formation of Mormons' attitudes toward sex and morality in the context of changing American cultural patterns from Mormonism's beginnings in the 1820's through 19th-century individualism.

854. Headon, Christopher. WOMEN AND ORGANIZED RELIGION IN MID AND LATE NINETEENTH CENTURY CANADA. *J. of the Can. Church Hist. Soc. [Canada] 1978 20(1-2): 3-18.* Within the Christian denominations of Canada, women in the mid- and late-19th century had an alternative to their traditional role. Some served as preaching evangelists, while others joined religious orders to help the

poor. The most important of all activities in which Canadian churchwomen were involved was missionary work, both foreign and domestic, in which they acted to alleviate poverty, teach the young, and eliminate as much as possible the most crude and overt forms of female subordination. Yet, there were many limitations in this advance. Women's organizations in the church were usually considered subordinate and dependent on those dominated by men; and most churchwomen conducted themselves and their activities in accordance with traditional notions of female subservience. Primary and secondary sources; 51 notes.
J. A. Kicklighter

855. Heimer, David D. ABORTION ATTITUDES AMONG CATHOLIC UNIVERSITY STUDENTS. *Sociol. Analysis 1976 37(3): 255-260.* Previous research on abortion attitudes has shown that education is positively associated with acceptance of abortion. There is evidence, however, that this relationship does not apply among Catholics in the 1970's, due apparently to the conservative impact of Catholic colleges. A comparison of abortion attitudes of students at a northwestern Catholic college with attitudes of the general population supports the conclusions of previous research. The level of support for abortion is much lower within the Catholic student sample. Results also stress the importance of religiosity. J

856. Hiner, N. Ray. ADOLESCENCE IN EIGHTEENTH-CENTURY AMERICA. *Hist. of Childhood Q. 1975 3(2): 253-280.* John Demos, Joseph Kett, and others have argued that modern adolescence, as a distinct phase of life marked by marginality and extended dependence, is a relatively recent phenomenon first noticeable in 19th-century America. However, evidence from sermons and religious tracts of the early 18th century suggests that many of the psychological and cultural attributes of adolescence were imputed to youth of that era. Based on primary and secondary sources; 86 notes. R. E. Butchart

857. Hogeland, Ronald W. CHARLES HODGE, THE ASSOCIATION OF GENTLEMEN AND ORNAMENTAL WOMANHOOD: 1825-1855. *J. of Presbyterian Hist. 1975 53(3): 239-255.* Depicts Princeton University scholar Dr. Charles Hodge's attitude toward women. At a time of considerable fervor for improving the status of the American women, Hodge, as Professor of Theology and editor of *The Biblical Repertory and Princeton Review*, emphasized "ornamental womanhood." Princeton gentlemen of Hodge's time did not take seriously social reforms such as the feminists, particularly Charles G. Finney, offered. For the Association of Gentlemen male relationships were of utmost importance, while women were at best an appendage to the central drama of life. Based on the writings of Hodge; 50 notes.
H. M. Parker, Jr.

858. Huefner, Dixie Snow. CHURCH AND POLITICS AT THE IWY CONFERENCE. *Dialogue 1978 11(1): 58-75.* Provides insight about the 24-25 June 1977 Utah Women's Conference authorized by the National Commission on the Observance of International Women's Year (IWY). Mobilized by the Mormon Church Relief Society leadership call for participation of 10 women per ward, 9,000 participants revolted against the state Coordinating Committee, rejected all nationally formulated resolutions, voted against workshop-sponsored resolutions on affirmative action, ERA (Equal Rights Amendment), abortion, sex education, or federal interference in local or family interests, and elected to the 1st National Women's Conference an overwhelmingly Mormon, conservative, antifeminist slate of delegates. The Mormom church, without urging this result, did not prevent use of its machinery by right-wing groups and was not disappointed by conference actions. Based on author's attendance at the conference, and on the conference's official reports; Utah newspapers; 26 notes, appendix. C. B. Schulz

859. Iglitzin, Lynne B. THE PATRIARCHAL HERITAGE. Iglitzin, Lynne B. and Ross, Ruth, eds. *Women in the World* (Santa Barbara, Ca.: Clio Books, 1976): pp. 7-24. Although some advances have been made since the recent revival of feminism, Western and non-Western nations are still characterized as patriarchal. Four sources of patriarchialism—biological, anthropological, religious, and economic ideas and events—contributed to the pervasively male-dominated societies that are the norm today. A model of five attitudes toward women, applied to the contemporary United States, demonstrates that patriarchal attitudes are still prevalent. Primary and secondary sources; 29 notes.
J. Holzinger

860. James, Janet Wilson. WOMEN AND RELIGION: AN INTRODUCTION. *Am. Q. 1978 30(5): 579-581.* The series of essays in this issue explores various facets and expressions of the place of women in religion as seen in Protestantism, Catholicism, and Judaism. The whole is set against two constants: women usually outnumber men, and men exercise the authority. The paradox revealed is one of a religious heritage imparting hopes of freedom, but at the same time blocking women's way. Covers the 17th through 20th centuries. R. V. Ritter

861. Jessee, Dean C. BRIGHAM YOUNG'S FAMILY: PART I, 1824-1845. *Brigham Young U. Studies 1978 18(3): 311-327.* Discusses Young as the head of his domestic household, one of the largest families in Mormondom. Many details of Young's private life are sketchy. Assesses Young's personality on the basis of how well he performed his domestic role. The years of instability, 1824-45, cover the period from his first marriage to the family's exodus from Nauvoo. These years were characterized by numerous and extended absences from his family as he served the Mormon Church in America and England. Article to be continued. M. S. Legan

862. Keller, Rosemary Skinner. CREATING A SPHERE FOR WOMEN IN THE CHURCH: HOW CONSEQUENTIAL AN ACCOMMODATION? *Methodist Hist. 1980 18(2): 83-94.* The "woman issue" was the most controversial question at General Conferences of the Methodist Episcopal Church during 1869-1900. The church denied ordination for women but recognized them as helpers of men in positions of authority. In 1869, the women organized the Women's Foreign Missionary Society and began to send and support women in foreign countries. Concludes that, in developing this autonomous organization, the women began a movement which would eliminate separate spheres for men and women in the church. 26 notes. H. L. Calkin

863. Kern, Louis J. IDEOLOGY AND REALITY: SEXUALITY AND WOMEN'S STATUS IN THE ONEIDA COMMUNITY. *Radical Hist. Rev. 1979 (20): 180-204.* Seemingly liberating factors in the ideology of John Humphrey Noyes's Oneida Community in New York (control over childbearing and sexuality, freedom from marriage, limited occupational flexibility, division of household labor, and laborsaving devices) actually led to the further subjugation of females within the community, because power and status still were allotted only to male members; 1848-79.

864. Keyes, Jane. MARRIAGE PATTERNS AMONG EARLY QUAKERS. *Nova Scotia Hist. Q. [Canada] 1978 8(4): 299-307.* Economic factors persuaded Quakers from Nantucket, Massachusetts, to settle in Dartmouth, Nova Scotia, in 1786; Friends meetings continued until 1789 when most of the settlers returned to Nantucket. Examination of the Minutes of the Dartmouth Friends Meetings for Business revealed that only four marriages of the 10 recorded were between members of the Society of Friends following prescribed procedures. Two were between two members of the Meeting but were not sanctioned, and four were between a member and a non-member. Based on Minutes of the Dartmouth Friends Meetings for Business; table. H. M. Evans

865. King, Anne. ANNE HUTCHINSON AND ANNE BRADSTREET: LITERATURE AND EXPERIENCE, FAITH AND WORKS IN MASSACHUSETTS BAY COLONY. *Int. J. of Women's Studies [Canada] 1978 1(5): 445-467.* Examines the lives and political, religious, and social attitudes of Anne Hutchinson (1591-1643) and Anne Bradstreet (1612-72) who, through polarizing the question of faith versus works and through questioning the position of women, introduced tensions in American life and ideology which led to eventual social change.

866. Klingelsmith, Sharon. WOMEN IN THE MENNONITE CHURCH, 1900-1930. *Mennonite Q. Rev. 1980 54(3): 163-207.* Addresses the role of women in the Mennonite Church as seen in the activities of the Mennonite Women's Missionary Society. Based on the Clara Steiner Collection and other sources; table, 268 notes.
E. E. Eminhizer

867. Koehler, Lyle. THE CASE OF THE AMERICAN JEZEBELS: ANNE HUTCHINSON AND FEMALE AGITATION DURING THE YEARS OF ANTINOMIAN TURMOIL, 1636-1640. *William and Mary Q. 1974 31(1): 55-78.* Places the Antinomian controversy into

the context of female rebellion, defines the role of women in colonial Massachusetts, and describes some of Anne Hutchinson's followers. Female resistance reached its height when many women sympathized with her. The theological charges stemmed from fear of assertion of women's rights. In the aftermath of the trial, other women became assertive and were involved in cases of legal intimidation. Based on court and church records, and on Puritan writings; 70 notes. H. M. Ward

868. Kolmer, Elizabeth. CATHOLIC WOMEN RELIGIOUS AND WOMEN'S HISTORY: A SURVEY OF THE LITERATURE. *Am. Q. 1978 30(5): 639-651.* A bibliographic essay evaluating the existing literature on the history of the Catholic nuns, the bibliographic aids, archival, and other sources available for the investigation of the history of women in religion. Surveys American religious history in general, histories of individual congregations, and unpublished dissertations on related topics. Includes materials available for the study of the relation of Catholic sisters to the contemporary women's movement; also topics needing further study. 24 notes. R. V. Ritter

869. LaSorte, Michael A. NINETEENTH CENTURY FAMILY PLANNING PRACTICES. *J. of Psychohist. 1976 4(2): 163-183.* The decline in the birthrate which began in the early 1800's in the United States is attributable to an increased knowledge and use of contraceptive devices and techniques. Contraception was used more frequently by native-born Protestants than by other groups. Discusses abortion, condoms, coitus interruptus, and coitus reservatus, vaginal extraction and barriers, and the rhythm method. Based on medical publications, marriage manuals, and other primary sources; 102 notes. R. E. Butchart

870. Lavigne, Marie et al. LA FÉDÉRATION NATIONALE SAINT-JEAN-BAPTISTE ET LES REVENDICATIONS FÉMINISTES AU DÉBUT DU XXe SIÈCLE [The Saint John the Baptist National Federation and feminist demands at the start of the 20th century]. *Rev. d'hist. de l'Amérique française [Canada] 1975 29(3): 353-373.* Surveys the history of the Fédération Nationale Saint-Jean-Baptiste from 1907-33, and discusses the role of its founder, Marie Gérin-Lajoie (1867-1945). In order to develop in French-Canadian society, the Fédération, a feminist group, had to make alliances with the Catholic clergy and compromises with the prevailing ideology. While calling for increased political rights for women, it supported the integrity of the family and the traditional female familial role. The organization did not succeed in synthesizing these paradoxical interests, and its influence declined after 1933. Based on documents in the Archives de la Fédération Nationale Saint-Jean-Baptiste (Montréal), Archives de la Communauté des Soeurs de Notre-Dame-du-Bon Conseil (Montréal), and secondary sources; 31 notes. L. B. Chan

871. Lee, Danielle Juteau. LES RELIGIEUSES DU QUÉBEC: LEUR INFLUENCE SUR LA VIE PROFESSIONNELLE DES FEMMES, 1908-1954 [The nuns in Québec: their influence on women's professional life, 1908-54]. *Atlantis [Canada] 1980 5(2): 22-33.* Corrects misunderstandings about the influence of Catholic women's religious orders in Quebec on women's intellectual and professional life; the example of women's fight for a secondary education demonstrates the sisters' avant-garde position, and its importance and consequences.

872. Leon, Joseph J. and Steinhoff, Patricia G. CATHOLICS' USE OF ABORTION. *Sociol. Analysis 1975 36(2): 125-136.* This study considers the methodological difficulties involved in studying abortion behavior and religious preference and uses the conception cohort as a way of handling problems of sampling and comparison. It was hypothesized that Catholic women would have fewer abortions than non-Catholic women according to 1) their proportion in the overall population and 2) their proportion in the pregnant population. Using demographic and medical data collected from hospital records on all abortion patients in the state of Hawaii and all maternity patients during the designated two-month period, a conception cohort was constructed. When the hypothesis was tested using the conception cohort, Catholics were found to have chosen abortion less often than non-Catholic women. Catholic women had a higher rate of pregnancies, but terminated a smaller proportion of these pregnancies by abortion. No difference was found between Catholics and non-Catholics with respect to gestation time and length of time from discovery of pregnancy to abortion. Covers 1965-74. J

873. Letsinger, Norman H. THE STATUS OF WOMEN IN THE SOUTHERN BAPTIST CONVENTION IN HISTORICAL PERSPECTIVE. *Baptist Hist. and Heritage 1977 12(1): 37-44.* The status of women in Southern Baptist circles has improved from a time when women were forbidden to speak in church or serve in positions of leadership to the present where a woman has been elected to a top position of leadership in the Southern Baptist Convention. Although women have not achieved a position of leadership in the Convention concomitant with their role in the local churches and in proportion to their numbers, abilities, and experiences, they have become significantly more involved as messengers (delegates) to the Convention and as members of committees, boards and commissions of the Convention. Covers 1860-1975. Based on annual records of the Southern Baptist Convention and records and histories of associations; 62 notes. H. M. Parker, Jr.

874. Levy, Barry. "TENDER PLANTS": QUAKER FARMERS AND CHILDREN IN THE DELAWARE VALLEY, 1681-1735. *J. of Family Hist. 1978 3(2): 116-135.* Examines the place of children in Quaker theology and their position in Quaker families on Pennsylvania farms in the late 17th century. Studies family organization through demographic analysis of the social, economic, and familial structure of society, and through the socializational and interactional analysis of family relationships. 7 tables, 5 notes, biblio. T. W. Smith

875. Lincoln, C. Eric. THE BLACK FAMILY, THE BLACK CHURCH AND THE TRANSFORMATION OF VALUES. *Religion in Life 1978 47(4): 486-496.* In studying the survival of the black family and the black church, examines the implications of the impact of war on social change and the distinctiveness of the black subculture in the context of American society, 1960's-70's.

876. Lockett, Darby Richardson. FEMINIST FOOTHOLDS IN RELIGION. *Foundations 1976 19(1): 33-39.* Reviews the feminist movement in American Judaism, Catholicism, and Protestantism. Mentions their gains but stresses the general antifeminist attitude found in most religious organizations. Makes suggestions for changing attitudes. Covers 1967-76. Biblio. E. E. Eminhizer

877. Loveland, Anne C. DOMESTICITY AND RELIGION IN THE ANTEBELLUM PERIOD. *Historian 1977 39(3): 455-471.* Investigates the contentions of the "cult of true womanhood" that "religious activity did not take woman from her proper sphere nor did it make her less domestic or submissive." Examines the life and activities of Phoebe Palmer (a Methodist who lived in New York City), as shaped by evangelical religion, and argues that a woman can broaden her sphere of activity without rejecting her domestic obligations. Phoebe Palmer was not restricted to the domestic sphere, but never took up the cause of women's rights because it was too radical for her. 55 notes. R. V. Ritter

878. Lumpkin, William L. THE ROLE OF WOMEN IN 18TH CENTURY VIRGINIA BAPTIST LIFE. *Baptist Hist. and Heritage 1973 8(3): 158-167.*

879. Lynch, John E. THE ORDINATION OF WOMEN: PROTESTANT EXPERIENCE IN ECUMENICAL PERSPECTIVE. *J. of Ecumenical Studies 1975 12(2): 173-197.* Presents the issue of the ordination of women to the professional office of ministry in world Protestantism and the World Council of Churches within the past 10 years. Many churches accept women ministers, but some still hesitate. Scandinavia appears to be more progressive in this regard than either the US or England. Theological and sociological arguments favor the ordination of women, and encourage churches to keep up with social change. J. A. Overbeck

880. Malmsheimer, Lonna M. DAUGHTERS OF ZION: NEW ENGLAND ROOTS OF AMERICAN FEMINISM. *New England Q. 1977 50(3): 484-504.* Traces the evolution of New England attitudes toward women from the 17th century, when they were considered morally and intellectually weaker than men, to the end of the 18th century when they were viewed as morally superior to men. Particularly important in this transformation were the sermons of Cotton Mather (1663-1728), who addressed women as individuals and reinterpreted the meaning and effect of Eve's fall. Once women were perceived to be naturally more moral and benevolent than men they were encouraged to

participate in charitable activities. These activities provided women with social and political experience and a sense of self-esteem which in turn provided a basis from which they expanded their activities in the 19th century. Based on sermons and secondary sources; 40 notes.
J. C. Bradford

881. Maniha, John K. and Maniha, Barbara B. A COMPARISON OF PSYCHOHISTORICAL DIFFERENCES AMONG SOME FEMALE RELIGIOUS AND SECULAR LEADERS. *J. of Psychohistory 1978 5(4): 523-549.* Seeks to determine, through an examination of 26 outstanding American female leaders, why some extraordinary women choose religious rather than secular leadership roles. Female religious leaders more often came from childrearing backgrounds in which they were socialized in traditional sex roles and in which authoritarian males conveyed an image of God as an omnipotent tyrant. Female secular leaders, on the other hand, came from atypical homes in which their intellectual aspirations and abilities were supported by fathers or other males. The study examined the childhoods of Anne Hutchinson, Mary Baker Eddy, Aimee Semple McPherson, Nona Brooks, Ann Lee, Sarah Grimke, Lucy Stone, Susan B. Anthony, Jane Addams, Margaret Sanger, and others. Primary and secondary sources; tables, biblio.
R. E. Butchart

882. Markle, G. E. and Pasco, Sharon. FAMILY LIMITATION AMONG THE OLD ORDER AMISH. *Population Studies [Great Britain] 1977 31(2): 267-280.* This paper shows that the 20th-century Indiana Amish, a high-fertility Anabaptist population, regulate their marital fertility according to their family finances. We linked demographic data from the Indiana Amish Directory with personal property tax records at 5, 15 and 25 years after marriage and found fertility differences by occupation and wealth. Correlations between family size and wealth at the beginning, middle and end of childbearing years were positive. Wealthier women exhibited higher marital fertility, had longer first birth intervals, were older at the birth of their last child, and had larger families than poorer women. Over the past 30 years, marital fertility has remained constant among older women; but birth rates among younger women have been rising rapidly.
J

883. Masson, Margaret W. THE TYPOLOGY OF THE FEMALE AS A MODEL FOR THE REGENERATE: PURITAN PREACHING, 1690-1730. *Signs 1976 2(2): 304-315.* Puritan theology used the norms for the women's roles of bride and wife to describe the regenerate Christian's relation to God. Because men were required to adopt these subordinate behaviors as church members, Puritans could not consider such attributes as innately female. Puritan doctrine required a limited egalitarianism, because both sexes were deemed equally capable of conversion and equally in need of it. Although Cotton Mather and others preached that some vices were sex-related, such as gossiping among women and drinking among men, they rejected the idea that women were innately more evil than men. Based on Puritan sermons, secondary works, and dissertations; 49 notes.
J. Gammage

884. Matthews, Jean V. "WOMAN'S PLACE" AND THE SEARCH FOR IDENTITY IN ANTE-BELLUM AMERICA. *Can. Rev. of Am. Studies [Canada] 1979 10(3): 289-304.* Romanticist ideas, equalitarian ideologies, and redemptive Protestant notions inspired a reexamination of the relationships between men and women in antebellum American society. Alert feminist reformers then made headway by riding the crest of feminine "self-awareness and self-assertion" that the modernist social climate made fashionable. These reformers enlarged women's sphere substantially. They avoided attacks on male workplace and political redoubts, however, choosing instead to levy war on the saloon and other masculine institutions judged disruptive to home and family. Based on writings of feminist reformers and secondary sources; 30 notes.
H. T. Lovin

885. Mauss, Armand L. SHALL THE YOUTH OF ZION FALTER? MORMON YOUTH AND SEX: A TWO-CITY COMPARISON. *Dialogue 1976 10(2): 82-84.* Compares statistics from two surveys during 1967-69 in Salt Lake City and a northern California coastal city which question Mormons' attitudes toward morality, sex, and marriage.

886. May, Henry F. PHILIP GREVEN AND THE HISTORY OF TEMPERAMENT. *Am. Q. 1979 31(1): 107-115.* Review essay of Philip Greven's *The Protestant Temperament: Patterns of Child-Rearing, Religious Experience, and the Self in Early America* (1977); summarizes and critiques the book's central themes as they relate to the "history of temperament." 4 notes.
D. G. Nielson

887. McBeth, Harry Leon. THE ROLE OF WOMEN IN SOUTHERN BAPTIST HISTORY. *Baptist Hist. and Heritage 1977 12(1): 3-25.* Reviews the role of women in early American Baptist life, then relates Southern Baptists' reluctant acceptance of women's organized participation in denominational life. Presents especially valuable material on the gradual movement of women into influential roles in the denomination and on the contributions of women to the growth of Southern Baptists. Covers 1700-1974. Based largely on Southern Baptist periodicals and weeklies of the 19th century and on other secondary materials; 98 notes.
H. M. Parker, Jr.

888. McIntosh, William Alex and Alston, Jon P. ACCEPTANCE OF ABORTION AMONG WHITE CATHOLICS AND PROTESTANTS, 1962 AND 1975. *J. for the Sci. Study of Religion 1977 16(3): 295-304.* Two surveys of white American Protestants and Roman Catholics during 1962-75 asked three questions dealing with the legalization of abortion. Indicates that there has been a slight Protestant-Catholic decrease in attitudinal differences. Nearly all Protestant categories became more favorable toward abortion, while the Catholics who became relatively more accepting of abortion were primarily young.

889. McLaughlin, Eleanor. THE CHRISTIAN PAST: DOES IT HOLD A FUTURE FOR WOMEN? *Anglican Theological Rev. 1975 57(1): 36-56.* Plea for a revisionist approach to church history to reflect a feminist heritage in the Christian tradition.
S

890. McLoughlin, William G. BILLY SUNDAY AND THE WORKING GIRL OF 1915. *J. of Presbyterian Hist. 1976 54(3): 376-384.* Introduces and contains a letter which a Philadelphia working girl wrote to her mother about hearing a sermon which Billy Sunday preached to a "women only" service in 1915. Sunday was not a feminist. It is questionable whether he sympathized with the suffrage movement. He viewed the working girl as a target for unscrupulous young men, and his sermon warned and cautioned them about the temptations they faced on the one hand, and encouraged them to maintain their virtue on the other. According to Sunday, woman's place was in the home. Although the sermon was addressed to a metropolitan women's group, he was merely reaffirming the old rural evangelical beliefs and values of American life. 4 notes.
H. M. Parker, Jr.

891. Micks, Marianne H. EXODUS OR EDEN?: A BATTLE OF IMAGES. *Anglican Theological Rev. Supplementary Series 1973 (1): 126-139.* Examines the role of women in history, how the Protestant church has supported it, and its contemporary manifestations.
S

892. Mineau, G. P.; Bean, L. L.; and Skolnick, M. MORMON DEMOGRAPHIC HISTORY II: THE FAMILY LIFE CYCLE AND NATURAL FERTILITY. *Population Studies [Great Britain] 1979 33(3): 429-446.* Examines the relationship between the marriage age of Mormon women born between 1800 and 1869, and their family size, concluding that the younger the woman's age at marriage, the higher the birth rate, although the age at the last birth was high and unrelated to marriage age.

893. Mitchell, Norma Taylor. FROM SOCIAL TO RADICAL FEMINISM. *Methodist Hist. 1975 13(3): 21-44.* A survey of the diversity in Methodist women's organizations from the establishment of women's foreign and home missionary societies following the Civil War to the Caucus and the Commission on the Status and Role of Women in the United Methodist Church of the 1970's. Changes in the nature of feminism during this period, the accomplishments of the movement, and the problems still to be solved are discussed. 47 notes.
H. L. Calkin

894. Mitchinson, Wendy. CANADIAN WOMEN AND CHURCH MISSIONARY SOCIETIES IN THE NINETEENTH CENTURY: A STEP TOWARDS INDEPENDENCE. *Atlantis [Canada] 1977 2(2, pt. 2): 57-75.* Protestant missionary societies, the first women's groups to form on a national level, allowed women (1870's-90's) outside the sphere of their homes for the first time.

895. Mitchinson, Wendy. THE YWCA AND REFORM IN THE NINETEENTH CENTURY. *Social Hist. [Canada] 1979 12(24): 368-384.* The Young Women's Christian Association began operations in Canada in 1870, mainly to provide decent accommodations for young working women, but its charitable and reform objectives conflicted, and the national organization never provided strong and coordinated direction. The YWCA tended to work for women, not with them, but its concern with working women indicates an acceptance of that change in women's status. Based on primary and secondary sources, including records of the Toronto YWCA; 76 notes. D. F. Chard

896. Monahan, Thomas P. SOME DIMENSIONS OF INTERRELIGIOUS MARRIAGES IN INDIANA, 1962-67. *Social Forces 1973 52(2): 195-203.* Data were selected from Indiana computer tapes, 1962-67, for detailed analysis of intrafaith as compared to interfaith marriages for four religious groups—Protestant, Catholic, Jewish, Other. The influence of age, previous marital status, and occupational class was examined, along with other factors such as age difference and type of ceremony. Although the proportion of mixed marriages among non-Protestants was found to be high and increasing somewhat, a comparison of actual with possible random matings disclosed considerable selectivity, with Jewish persons being by far the most endogamous and Catholics the most intermarried of the minority groups. J

897. Moran, Gerald F. RELIGIOUS RENEWAL, PURITAN TRIBALISM, AND THE FAMILY IN SEVENTEENTH-CENTURY MILFORD, CONNECTICUT. *William and Mary Q. 1979 36(2): 236-254.* The First Church of Milford, Connecticut, has complete records going back to the 17th century, and hence provides a model study for answering many questions, such as those raised by Edmund S. Morgan concerning the whole social and religious context of a Puritan community. Structural restrictiveness actually did not restrain admissions to any large degree. Eventually, however, admissions did decline and the church became isolated from the community at large. In attempts to recapture its earlier vitality the church became increasingly exclusive. There appears to have been an inbred membership and a tribal spirit. Based on church records; 3 tables, graph, 53 notes. H. M. Ward

898. Moriarty, Claire. WOMEN'S RIGHTS VS. CATHOLIC DOGMA: WHY THE CHURCH FATHERS OPPOSE ABORTION. *Int. Socialist Rev. 1973 34(3): 8-11, 44-45.*

899. Moynihan, Daniel Patrick. THE STATE, THE CHURCH, AND THE FAMILY. *Urban and Social Change Rev. 1977 10(1): 7-9.* Religious institutions have forsaken their traditional societal role as a moral force in favor of the government in the 1960's and 70's; examines the implications for the family unit and ethnic groups.

900. Mulvay, Jill C. ELIZA R. SNOW AND THE WOMAN QUESTION. *Brigham Young U. Studies 1976 16(2): 250-264.* Examines the role of Eliza Roxey Snow in originating and leading all female Latter-day Saint organizations. As wife of both Joseph Smith and Brigham Young consecutively, Mrs. Snow was in a position to help define the status of women within Mormon society. Comparisons are drawn between the woman's movement among the Mormons and the other feminist crusades stirring in America at the same time. Attention is given to Mrs. Snow's views on women's suffrage, female relief societies, business and medical efforts by Church women, and female attitudes toward polygamy. Covers 1830-90. M. S. Legan

901. Mulvay, Jill C. THE LIBERAL SHALL BE BLESSED: SARAH M. KIMBALL. *Utah Hist. Q. 1976 44(3): 205-221.* Sarah Melissa Granger Kimball (1818-98), Utah's pioneer suffragist, president of the 15th Ward Relief Society for 40 years, is representative of her generation of Mormon women. Her life encompassed a broad spectrum of Mormon women's concerns and activities. She and others found room within the LDS system for a broad scope of activities and expression. She was shaped by, but also shaped, women's rights and responsibilities within the church and the Utah community. Based on primary and secondary sources; 3 illus., 40 notes. J. L. Hazelton

902. Neal, Marie Augusta. WOMEN IN RELIGION: A SOCIOLOGICAL PERSPECTIVE. *Sociol. Inquiry 1975 45(4): 33-40.* Examines the paucity of feminist interpretations in modern religious sociology and suggests specific areas (family, sexuality, human rights, and law) which bear reinterpretation along feminist lines, 1950's-70's.

903. Noll, William T. WOMEN AS CLERGY AND LAITY IN THE 19TH CENTURY METHODIST PROTESTANT CHURCH. *Methodist Hist. 1977 15(2): 107-121.* Women, both lay and clergy, achieved significant advances in role and status in the Methodist Protestant Church before either the Methodist Episcopal Church or Methodist Episcopal Church, South. Even so their advances were never more than partial. The first constitution of the Methodist Protestant Church limited eligibility to office to white males. Women delegates to annual conferences began to appear in the 1870's, although ordination of women was a more difficult problem. 53 notes. H. L. Calkin

904. Norton, Mary Beth. "MY RESTING REAPING TIMES": SARAH OSBORN'S DEFENSE OF HER "UNFEMININE" ACTIVITIES, 1767. *Signs 1976 2(2): 515-529.* Schoolteacher Sarah Osborn was sharply criticized by her close friend, Congregationalist clergyman Josiah Fish, for assuming a leadership role in the 1766-67 Newport revival. More than 525 colonists, black and white, slave and free, male and female, met weekly at Osborn's. Fish advised her to relinquish her role to a more qualified man so that she could devote her time to feminine pursuits, and complained that her work with blacks was potentially dangerous to the social order. In reply, Osborn carefully downplayed her position as a leader of the groups, but refused to abandon it. Based on the Osborn-Fish correspondence, and on secondary works; 27 notes. J. Gammage

905. Palmquist, Bonnie Beatson. WOMEN IN *MINNESOTA HISTORY*, 1915-1976: AN ANNOTATED BIBLIOGRAPHY OF ARTICLES PERTAINING TO WOMEN. *Minnesota Hist. 1977 45(5): 187-191.* The majority of articles pertaining to women in *Minnesota History* have discussed women in familial and/or social settings, with the next most frequent subject covering women in literature and journalism. Religion and education also mention women fairly frequently, in addition to scattered entries for women and the arts, and female involvement in conservation, crime (as victims), medicine and sciences, native American women, and women in social welfare, reform, and feminist activities. Each entry in the bibliography is included under one of the above major categories and includes name and author and title of article, volume and page numbers, and month and year of publication. Annotations are appended where the article title does not fully explain its contents. N. Lederer

906. Peach, Ceri. WHICH TRIPLE MELTING POT? A RE-EXAMINATION OF ETHNIC INTERMARRIAGE IN NEW HAVEN, 1900-1950. *Ethnic and Racial Studies [Great Britain] 1980 3(1): 1-16.* R. J. R. Kennedy's thesis, developed in the 1940's, that New Haven marriage patterns revealed separate Protestant, Catholic, and Jewish melting pots should be replaced by a description of a society made up of black, Jewish, and white Gentile groups.

907. Peek, Charles W. and Brown, Sharon. SEX PREJUDICE AMONG WHITE PROTESTANTS: LIKE OR UNLIKE ETHNIC PREJUDICE? *Social Forces 1980 59(1): 169-185.* Analysis of 1974-75 attitudes about female participation in politics from two recent national polls reveals divergence between white Protestant prejudice toward women and white Protestant prejudice toward race and ethnic groups documented by previous research. Like ethnic prejudice, political sex prejudice is higher among white Protestants than among unaffiliated whites. Unlike ethnic prejudice, 1) persons affiliated with fundamentalist Protestant groups do not display greater sex prejudice than those affiliated with nonfundamentalist groups; 2) among the sample as a whole and among nonfundamentalists, the less religious are not more prejudiced toward women than the more religious; and 3) within fundamentalist groups the more religious exhibit higher levels of sex prejudice, an association that does not appear due to variations in localism. This divergence seems more a result of a biblical bias against women pervasive among Protestant groups (unlike the absence of biblical statements about most current race and ethnic groups) rather than of women's in-group status (unlike the usual out-group status of race and ethnic groups). J

908. Penfield, Janet Harbison. WOMEN IN THE PRESBYTERIAN CHURCH: AN HISTORICAL OVERVIEW. *J. of Presbyterian Hist. 1977 55(2): 107-123.* Briefly sketches four phases of the participation of

women in the life of the Presbyterian Church: 1) the rise of the "Cent" and "Praying" Societies to about 1815, 2) the development of regional and national women's boards of home and foreign missions from the Civil War to 1923, 3) the roles women played as missionaries from about 1830, and 4) the struggle of women to achieve ecclesiastical parity with men in the Presbyterian Church which ended technically in 1956. While the task of accepting women into total participation in the various areas of church life and ecclesiastical structure has not been fully accomplished, many strides have been taken. The presence today of large numbers of women in the theological seminaries is indicative that in the near future women will be more readily and widely admitted to all levels and institutional structures of the church. Based on secondary sources; picture, 57 notes.
H. M. Parker, Jr.

909. Pepe, Faith L. TOWARD A HISTORY OF WOMEN IN VERMONT: AN ESSAY AND BIBLIOGRAPHY. *Vermont Hist. 1977 45(2): 69-101.* Nineteenth-century Vermont women were neither silent nor inarticulate, although histories have ignored them or, in the few biographies, exaggerated their eccentricities. Provides a review essay and over 200 unannotated entries arranged by 25 subject headings. The entries include diaries, letters, autobiographies, verse, etiquette, domestic economy, broadsides, sermons, student papers, and texts. Half of them cite brief references to women in the larger literature or relate to Vermont natives with achievements elsewhere. 11 photos.
T. D. S. Bassett

910. Petersen, Larry R. and Mauss, Armand L. RELIGION AND "RIGHT TO LIFE": CORRELATES OF OPPOSITION TO ABORTION. *Sociol. Analysis 1976 37(3): 243-254.* The small amount of literature on the relationship between religion and attitudes on abortion does not give us a clear indication of the importance of religion in determining attitudes on abortion. But literature on political attitudes indicates that opposition to "easy" abortion is associated with political conservatism. There is another body of literature indicating that religious and political conservatism/liberalism are highly correlated. The hypothesis inferred from this is that the membership of the more conservative Protestant churches (and probably the Catholic Church) would tend to oppose "easy" abortion, while the membership of the more liberal churches would favor "easy" abortion. An aspect of Rosenberg and Abelson's Affective-Cognitive Consistency Theory provides theoretical backing for this hypothesis. Using a 1972 nationwide sample of National Opinion Research Center data, we found that religious conservatism was indeed positively related to opposition to abortion. Education, church attendance, and religious liberalism/conservatism were found to be the most important predictors of abortion attitudes. J

911. Phillips, J. O. C. THE EDUCATION OF JANE ADDAMS. *Hist. of Educ. Q. 1974 14(1): 49-67.* Analyzes the three determining forces in Jane Addams's life: the ideology of domestic piety, the influence of her Quaker father, and the changing mood in women's education during the 1870's. Follows these themes in her adult life, and shows how Addams' work at Hull House resulted from these early forces. Finds that Addams did not challenge "the basic assumptions of the ideology, nor the doctrines of a separate woman's sphere and a distinct female nature." Based on primary and secondary sources; 38 notes. L. C. Smith

912. Pitcher, B. L.; Peterson, E. T.; and Kunz, P. R. RESIDENCY DIFFERENTIALS IN MORMON FERTILITY. *Population Studies [Great Britain] 1974 28(1): 143-152.* Although one of the most consistent findings of recent fertility studies is the convergence of the religious differentials in fertility, few data have been analyzed to discover Mormon fertility trends and differentials. This paper, based on data obtained on 1,001 Mormon couples, is concerned with describing the effects that the dispersion of Mormon families from the Mormon center in Utah to surrounding areas with various social conditions is having on the fertility of the relocated Mormon families. Data presented clearly show that such families do, on the average, have a lower fertility than do their Mormon contemporaries residing in the homogeneous Mormon society in Utah. They probably compromise their religious obligations to have children with the contradicting demands of their new environment. Their loyalty to these religious beliefs, however, is confirmed by data which show that they tend to have larger families in their new environments than do their non-Mormon neighbors. J

913. Polzin, Theresita. THE POLISH AMERICAN FAMILY: PART I, THE SOCIOLOGICAL ASPECTS OF THE FAMILIES OF POLISH IMMIGRANTS TO AMERICA BEFORE WORLD WAR II, AND THEIR DESCENDANTS. *Polish Rev. 1976 21(3): 103-122.* Examines families in terms of structure (type, size, ascribed roles, and division of labor), value orientations (social, religious, and cultural), and social control (from other family members, church, and community) in the 20th century. To be continued.

914. Pototschnig, Franz. ENTWICKLUNGSTENDENZEN IM KANONISCHEN EHE- UND EHEPROZESSRECHT [Tendencies of development in canon law on marriage and divorce]. *Österreichisches Archiv für Kirchenrecht [Austria] 1978 29(1-2): 52-81.* Discusses the attempts of the Catholic Church, especially in the Netherlands and the United States, to find new forms for the dissolution of Catholic marriages in the light of new developments of mechanical and chemical contraceptives since World War II.

915. Potvin, Raymond H. and Lee, Che-Fu. CATHOLIC COLLEGE WOMEN AND FAMILY-SIZE PREFERENCES: A REANALYSIS. *Sociol. Analysis 1974 35(1): 24-34.* Data on family-size preferences of a 1964-67 cohort of Catholic college women are reanalyzed using standardized matrices and analysis of covariance. The earlier Westoff and Potvin conclusion that the higher fertility preferences of these women educated in Catholic colleges was in part a function of selectivity is sustained, but the conclusion that the Catholic college also maintained high levels is to be modified somewhat. Different types of college affected the general decline in family-size preferences over the four years in different ways depending on the type of high school attended. Though the data are somewhat dated, their reanalysis suggests that changes in preferences should be studied with a model that differentiates individual probabilities of change from group effects, especially if selectivity is a factor. J

916. Pratt, Norma Fain. TRANSITIONS IN JUDAISM: THE JEWISH AMERICAN WOMAN THROUGH THE 1930S. *Am. Q. 1978 30(5): 681-702.* A study of the slow, but steady growth in the status of women in American Judaism, particularly during the 1920's-30's. Rapidity of status growth has depended partly on whether the country of origin was Eastern or Western Europe, but economic factors in the adopted country also had some influence. One can see very clear differences between Reform, Conservative, Orthodox, and secular Jews in their reaction to liberalizing tendencies and demands. A number of Jewish women's organizations have developed significant programs where women have found opportunity for making unique contributions. However, the fear of assimilation into Gentile culture patterns has been a strong inhibiting force among the women themselves. 60 notes. R. V. Ritter

917. Renzi, Mario. IDEAL FAMILY SIZE AS AN INTERVENING VARIABLE BETWEEN RELIGION AND ATTITUDES TOWARDS ABORTION. *J. for the Sci. Study of Religion 1975 14(1): 23-27.* Analyzes data defining the relationships between family size preferences, religion, and attitudes on abortion. S

918. Reynolds, David S. THE FEMINIZATION CONTROVERSY: SEXUAL STEREOTYPES AND THE PARADOXES OF PIETY IN NINETEENTH-CENTURY AMERICA. *New England Q. 1980 53(1): 96-106.* The view presented in Ann Douglas's *The Feminization of American Culture* (New York: 1977) that American religion and culture "became feminized, *i.e.,* more yielding, effeminate," overlooks "that during this period a fervent muscular Christianity began to take shape. In its endorsement of reform, perfectibility, and soldierly endeavor religion of the period tended to be 'masculine' or 'feminist.' In its advocacy of benevolence and emotion it tended to be 'feminine.' " As religion abandoned its strict belief in predestination and the total depravity of man, it adopted beliefs in human capability. Based on an analysis of novels; 36 notes. J. C. Bradford

919. Roberts, Barbara. SEX, POLITICS AND RELIGION: CONTROVERSIES IN FEMALE IMMIGRATION REFORM WORK IN MONTREAL, 1881-1919. *Atlantis [Canada] 1980 6(1): 25-38.* Focuses on the closure of the Home of the Women's Protective (later Women's National) Immigration Society, in Montreal, in 1917 due to numerous circumstances but also as a result of the efforts of a group of Protestant clergy and laymen who wanted to close the women-founded, operated, and controlled institution.

920. Robertson, Darrel M. THE FEMINIZATION OF AMERICAN RELIGION: AN EXAMINATION OF RECENT INTERPRETATIONS OF WOMEN AND RELIGION IN VICTORIAN AMERICA. *Christian Scholar's Rev. 1978 8(3): 238-246.* Traces the feminization of American religion during 1820's-30's, identified as a romanticization or sentimentalization of religion by traditional historians, discussed as feminization in Barbara Welter's essay, "The Feminization of American Religion," published in 1973.

921. Ruether, Rosemary Radford. THE SUBORDINATION AND LIBERATION OF WOMEN IN CHRISTIAN THEOLOGY: SAINT PAUL AND SARAH GRIMKÉ. *Soundings 1978 61(2): 168-181.* Relates beliefs about natural order, social organization, and Christian theology held by Saint Paul and compares them to the beliefs of Sarah Grimké; though working from Christian tenets, they reached radically different conclusions about women's role in society.

922. Ryan, Mary P. A WOMEN'S AWAKENING: EVANGELICAL RELIGION AND THE FAMILIES OF UTICA, N.Y., 1800-1840. *Am. Q. 1978 30(5): 602-623.* A demographic and statistical analysis and interpretation of women's place in the Second Evangelical Awakening as seen in Oneida County, New York, and more particularly in Utica and environs. The study reveals that the Utica women, as wives and mothers and as trustees of an extensive missionary organization, were the ones "who orchestrated the domestic revivals," yet also remained true to a narrowly maternal role and image for their sex. Concludes that "women were more than the majority of the converts, more even than the private guardians of America's souls. The combination and consequence of all these roles left the imprint of a women's awakening on American society as well as on American religion." 7 tables, 29 notes.
R. V. Ritter

923. Segal, Sheila F. FEMINISTS FOR JUDAISM. *Midstream 1975 21(7): 59-65.* Discusses the compatibility of Judaism and feminism (1970's). S

924. Skolnick, M. et al. MORMON DEMOGRAPHIC HISTORY: I. NUPTIALITY AND FERTILITY OF ONCE-MARRIED COUPLES. *Population Studies [Great Britain] 1978 32(1): 5-20.* Traces age at marriage, period and cohort fertility rates, and number of children born to once-married Mormon women, 1820-1920.

925. Slater, Peter G. "FROM THE CRADLE TO THE COFFIN": PARENTAL BEREAVEMENT AND THE SHADOW OF INFANT DAMNATION IN PURITAN SOCIETY. *Psychohistory Rev. 1977-78 6(2-3): 4-24.* High mortality rates among infants in Puritan society confronted parents with a complex and stressful process of bereavement. Anxiety was raised by the principles of original sin, natural iniquity of children, and the uncertainty of salvation or damnation of deceased children. Parents went through psychological processes of idealization, rationalization, and gratification through masochism during the cycle of mourning. Though the Puritan system made successful completion of bereavement difficult, it seems that most parents reached a final stage of equilibrium. Based on contemporary diaries, sermons and poems, and secondary works; 71 notes. J. B. Street

926. Smith, J. E. and Kunz, P. R. POLYGYNY AND FERTILITY IN NINETEENTH-CENTURY AMERICA. *Population Studies [Great Britain] 1976 30(3): 465-480.* Statistics indicate a slightly lower completed marital fertility in polygamous than in monogamous unions among 19th-century Mormons.

927. Smith, Wilford E. MORMOM SEX STANDARDS ON COLLEGE CAMPUSES: OR DEAL US OUT OF THE SEXUAL REVOLUTION! *Dialogue 1976 10(2): 76-81.* Discusses the author's 1950, 1961, and 1972 surveys of Mormon and non-Mormon college students from the northwestern United States, indicating that Mormon students who have a lack of sexual experience attend church frequently and follow the Mormons' emphasis on premarital sexual abstinence.

928. Speizman, Milton D. and Kronick, Jane C., eds. A SEVENTEENTH-CENTURY QUAKER WOMEN'S DECLARATION. *Signs: J. of Women in Culture and Soc. 1975 1(1): 231-245.* Among the earliest champions of essential equality in America were the Quakers, who regarded the Britons George Fox (1624-91) and his wife Margaret Fell as cofounders of their denomination. A reflection of Fell's feminism is found in this reprinted epistle written during the 1670's in a Lancashire women's meeting and sent to the women of Philadelphia. It summarizes the Society of Friends' attitudes on sexual equality, charitable responsibility, and the organization of women's meetings. Primary and secondary sources; 11 notes. T. Simmerman

929. Stannard, David E. DEATH AND THE PURITAN CHILD. *Am. Q. 1974 26(5): 456-476.* Children in 17th and early 18th century New England were at the same time both deeply loved and regarded as being in a state of sin. The state of the child's spiritual health was thus a very serious matter, but so was his physical health, since infant mortality was high. Death was awesome, and the prospects of it conjured up by Puritan parents and clergy frightened the children. 65 notes.
C. W. Olson

930. Stevens, Thelma. A PLACE OF THEIR OWN. *Southern Exposure 1976 4(3): 54-58.* Examines the attempts of women in the 1880's to gain standing in the Methodist Church and the creation of the Women's Division of Christian Service in 1939.

931. Stoloff, Carolyn. WHO JOINS WOMEN'S LIBERATION? *Psychiatry 1973 36(3): 325-340.* Responses to questionnaires sent to female graduate students at the University of Michigan in order to determine the differences between members of the women's liberation movement and others who remained out of the movement indicate that there were distinct differences in socioeconomic, religious, intellectual and political background, and the political attitudes of the students' parents. Those who join the movement are most typically from middle or upper-middle-class urban or suburban families, with a Jewish or "nonformalistically religious" Protestant background, and from homes in which religion was not strongly emphasized. Parents of those who joined the movement are most likely college graduates or employed in professional or intellectual occupations, and they are more politically liberal than parents of the nonjoiners. Most of those in each group reported that they had a close relationship with their mothers, but the participants reported that their mothers were considerably more competitive than mothers of nonparticipants, and somewhat more competitive than their husbands. The women's liberationists tend to be more sexually experienced, and they tended to be participants in the earlier Civil Rights movement and the recent Peace Movement. Subjects in each group, however, subscribed to the women's liberation view of women's rights, roles, and responsibilities. 6 notes, biblio. M. Kaufman

932. Taylor, Sandra C. ABBY M. COLBY: THE CHRISTIAN RESPONSE TO SEXIST SOCIETY. *New England Q. 1979 52(1): 68-79.* Women, who comprised two-thirds of the missionaries to Japan in the late 19th century, received lower pay than men and were only allowed to vote on matters of "women's work" within their organization. Abby M. Colby (1848-1917) was a feminist who served as a Congregational missionary in Japan between 1879 and 1914 and opposed these practices as much as she did Japanese practices of male-dominated marriages, concubinage, and prostitution. Based on Colby's letters in the papers of the American Board of Commissioners for Foreign Missions at Houghton Library, Harvard University; 29 notes. J. C. Bradford

933. Tedin, Kent L. RELIGIOUS PREFERENCE AND PRO/ANTI ACTIVISM ON THE EQUAL RIGHTS AMENDMENT ISSUE. *Pacific Sociol. Rev. 1978 21(1): 55-66.* A sampling of Texas pro- and anti-ERA activists in 1977 shows that religious preference (conservative or liberal) corresponds to levels of activism and support or nonsupport.

934. Thornton, Arland. MARITAL INSTABILITY DIFFERENTIALS AND INTERACTIONS: INSIGHTS FROM MULTIVARIATE CONTINGENCY TABLE ANALYSIS. *Sociol. and Social Res. 1978 62(4): 572-595.* In this paper the marital dissolution experience of women interviewed in the 1970 National Fertility Study is explored. The distribution of discord produced disruptions over several different periods are studied using multivariate contingency table analysis. Nonwhite women and those who marry young have higher dissolution rates than others. Religion was found to be moderately related to marital instability. Fundamentalists and Baptists have somewhat higher rates than women

in other groups, while Catholics are like other Protestants. It was found that the relationship between education and dissolution depends upon race. There appears to be no large or consistent education differential for whites while nonwhite women who fail to complete an education they start have higher dissolution rates than others. The hypothesis that some of the effects of the independent variables interact with marital interval was tested and rejected. The relationships observed appear to persist over the life cycle. J

935. Trifiro, Luigi. UNE INTERVENTION À ROME DANS LA LUTTE POUR LE SUFFRAGE FÉMININ AU QUÉBEC (1922) [An appeal to Rome in the struggle for woman suffrage in Quebec (1922)]. *Rev. d'Hist. de l'Amérique Française [Canada] 1978 32(1): 1-18.* By 1922, Quebec was the only Canadian province that still denied women the right to vote. Facing strong opposition from the conservative Catholic hierarchy, a prosuffrage group launched a direct appeal to the Congress of the International Union of Catholic Women's Leagues in Rome. Despite a somewhat sympathetic hearing, the women of Quebec were refused the franchise for another 20 years. 48 notes. M. R. Yerburgh

936. Ulrich, Laurel Thatcher. VIRTUOUS WOMEN FOUND: NEW ENGLAND MINISTERIAL LITERATURE, 1668-1735. *Am. Q. 1976 28(1): 20-40.* Examines 17th and 18th-century New England ministerial elegies, memorials, funeral sermons, and works of practical piety concerning women indicating a tension existing in male minds between a view of the private worth and the public position of women. Ministers' genuine concern for sex equality eventually generated discrete and ultimately confining notions of femininity. The common historiographical view of Puritan women being regarded as inferior by their male counterparts must be reexamined in the light of the evidence presented. N. Lederer

937. VanBeeck, Frans Josef. INVALID OR MERELY IRREGULAR—COMMENTS BY A RELUCTANT WITNESS. *J. of Ecumenical Studies 1974 11(3): 381-399.* Discusses the question of validity and regularity of the Philadelphia ordination of women into the priesthood of the Protestant Episcopal Church (1974). If the four bishops intended to do what the church does in ordaining the 11 women, then the sacrament of ordination is valid though irregular. The key word is "intended." Those who wish to prove the ordination invalid contend that no sacrament was intended. The Episcopal Church should regularize this ordination and encourage women to enter the priesthood. J. A. Overbeck

938. Vann, Richard T. QUAKER FAMILY LIFE. *J. of Interdisciplinary Hist. 1975 5(4): 739-749.* Review article prompted by J. William Frost, *The Quaker Family in Colonial America* (New York, 1973). The work has substantial virtues, but Frost has overlooked the crucial importance of theory precisely in directing attention to what can count as evidence. 11 notes. R. Howell

939. Wallace, Ruth A. BRINGING WOMEN IN: MARGINALITY IN THE CHURCHES. *Sociol. Analysis 1975 36(4): 291-303.* Discusses possible cases of sex discrimination against women clergy in the Catholic Church and Protestant Churches in the 1970's.

940. Warren, Claude N. THE MANY WIVES OF PEDRO YANUNALI. *J. of California Anthrop. 1977 4(2): 242-248.* Analysis of births, deaths, baptisms, and Catholic marriages and native marriages confirmed at Mission Santa Barbara in California yields kinship information and information on the sociopolitical matrices of the local Chumash Indians; discusses marriages of chief Pedro Yanunali, 1787-1806.

941. Weisberg, D. Kelly. "UNDER GREET TEMPTATIONS HEER": WOMEN AND DIVORCE IN PURITAN MASSACHUSETTS. *Feminist Studies 1975 2(2-3): 183-193.* Explores the "social conditions affecting women and divorce law in Puritan Massachusetts," 1639-92. Massachusetts departed significantly from English divorce law, as divorces were granted more frequently to women than to men. This was because: 1) the Puritan family was an agency of social control and most divorce petitions were due to a husband's breach of familial duty; 2) Puritans regarded single people as especially susceptible to temptation, and divorce allowed deserted women to remarry; 3) remarriage prevented a woman and her children from draining public welfare funds; and 4) women were scarce and valuable. Divorce was not easy, but Massachusetts women enjoyed a legal status not obtained in England until 200 years later. Secondary sources; 49 notes. J. D. Falk

942. Welter, Barbara. THE FEMINIZATION OF AMERICAN RELIGION: 1800-1860. In Hartman, Mary and Banner, Lois W., eds. *Clio's Consciousness Raised: New Perspectives on the History of Women* (New York: Harper Torchbooks, 1974), pp. 137-157. After the American Revolution, religion declined as a male activity. Humility, submission, and weakness were incompatible with the "male" activities of politics and economics, and were relegated to women and religion. Religion, like the family and popular culture, "entered a process of change whereby it became more domesticated, more emotional, more soft and accommodating—in a word, more 'feminine.' " Women made up a large percent of congregations and participated in missionary and volunteer church activities. These women gained experience in organizing and a sense of self-worth valuable for women's independence. 65 notes. S

943. Welter, Barbara. SHE HATH DONE WHAT SHE COULD: PROTESTANT WOMEN'S MISSIONARY CAREERS IN NINETEENTH-CENTURY AMERICA. *Am. Q. 1978 30(5): 624-638.* A study of the rationale for women's place in the missionary enterprise seems to divide between support and help for the husband in his home in a foreign land and unique service she can render the women in the heathen cultures of their field of service. The latter led to a special effort to recruit single women for service overseas through separate women's boards in the various denominations which also supplemented the money raising efforts of the older organizations. This created some struggle with the established male dominated church hierarchies when such recruits demanded a voice in policy. Here was a career in which women found fulfillment. 54 notes. R. V. Ritter

944. White, Jean Bickmore. WOMAN'S PLACE IS IN THE CONSTITUTION: THE STRUGGLE FOR EQUAL RIGHTS IN UTAH IN 1895. *Utah Hist. Q. 1974 42(4): 344-369.* Reviews Utah women's struggle to acquire voting rights when the territory became a state in 1895. Initially, both political parties supported universal suffrage, but opposition soon developed. Militancy was wholly absent, and the women won because their leaders were respected members of the Mormon Church. 5 photos, 58 notes. V. L. Human

945. Williams, Priscilla Parish. RIGHT TO LIFE: THE SOUTHERN STRATEGY. *Southern Exposure 1977 4(4): 82-85.* Anti-abortion forces in the 1970's are emphasizing agitation in the South based on the region's conservatism in matters of feminist interest. Although mainly Catholic, Right To Life organizations are acquiring Southern Protestant backing, aided by state and local efforts to thwart the will of the Supreme Court in permitting abortions on demand. The movement is beginning to strike a responsive chord in Southern Protestant churches. Based on oral interviews. N. Lederer

946. Wyatt, Philip R. JOHN HUMPHREY NOYES AND THE STIRPICULTURAL EXPERIMENT. *J. of the Hist. of Medicine & Allied Sci. 1976 31(1): 55-66.* The Oneida Community, established by John Humphrey Noyes (1811-86) emphasized the desire for perfection. Noyes developed four unique concepts to achieve this goal. These were male continence, complex marriage, community child care, and the stirpicultural experiment. The success of male continence freed women from unwanted pregnancies, and permitted the practice of complex marriage. To assure that children were as perfect as possible, Noyes developed the policy of stirpiculture, the culture of a new race, produced by carefully controlled selective breeding. During 1869-79, 58 live births occurred in the Oneida community as a result of the experiments in scientific breeding. There was a low infant mortality rate, indicating that the combination of selective breeding and community child care had good results. Noyes demonstrated that the nature of man could be improved by controlling the environment and man's biological inheritance. The children became exceptionally successful later in life. 26 notes. M. Kaufman

947. Wyatt-Brown, Bertram. CONSCIENCE AND CAREER: YOUNG ABOLITIONISTS AND MISSIONARIES. Bolt, Christine and Drescher, Seymour, ed. *Anti-Slavery, Religion and Reform: Essays in Memory of Roger Anstey* (Folkestone, England: Dawson, 1980): 183-203. By 1800 an enlightened approach to child-rearing had been developed in many evangelical households in the United States. Although

austere, this type of upbringing offered children love and fostered self-reliance and respect for authority. Children brought up in such homes often became either missionaries or abolitionists. The path chosen seemed to depend on whether, at an impressionable stage of development, the child was affected by a religious experience or a political one. Some of the notable missionaries and abolitionists considered are Henry Lyman, William Lloyd Garrison, John Greenleaf Whittier, Clara Barton, Sarah Grimké, and Elijah Lovejoy. 38 notes.

948. —. [EVANGELICAL CHILD-REARING]. *J. of Social Hist. 1975 9(1): 21-43.*

McLoughlin, William G. EVANGELICAL CHILD-REARING IN THE AGE OF JACKSON: FRANCIS WAYLAND'S VIEW OF WHEN AND HOW TO SUBDUE THE WILLFULNESS OF CHILDREN, *pp. 21-34.* Describes Brown University President Francis Wayland's child-rearing triumph which he submitted anonymously in a letter to the *American Baptist Magazine* in October 1831. 22 notes.

Lipsitt, Lewis P. COMMENT ON "A CASE OF CONVICTION," *pp. 35-43.* Explains the personal and social implications of Wayland's struggle with his son. 5 notes. S

949. —. PREMARITAL PREGNANCY IN AMERICA, 1640-1971.

Smith, Daniel Scott and Hindus, Michael S. AN OVERVIEW AND INTERPRETATION. *J. of Interdisciplinary Hist. 1975 5(4): 537-570.* Analyzes sexual behavior and the social mechanisms controlling it, based on the cycles in premarital pregnancy. 28 notes, appendix.

Hair, P. E. H. SOME DOUBTS. *J. of Interdisciplinary Hist. 1977 7(4): 739-744.* Criticizes the conclusions of Hindus and Smith about the inhibiting effects of Puritanism and Victorian morality.

Smith, Daniel Scott and Hindus, Michael S. A REPLY. *J. of Interdisciplinary Hist. 1977 7(4): 744-746.* Urges that doubts are not equivalent to evidence, and that multiple variables must be considered. Printed sources; table, graph, 9 notes.

R. Howell

8. GOVERNMENT AND POLITICS

General

950. Ahlstrom, Sydney E. RELIGION, REVOLUTION AND THE RISE OF MODERN NATIONALISM: REFLECTIONS ON THE AMERICAN EXPERIENCE. *Church Hist. 1975 44(4): 1630-1876.* During the long revolutionary awakening of America's democratic colonies and their successful war for independence, Europe was experiencing the flowering of Romanticism. Frenchmen with an idealized view of freedom, prosperity, and felicity in the New World turned to social criticism. German thinkers also experienced this leavening influence. In America the same period was quite different. Despite many harsh political debates, the start of the 19th century was not a time of *bouleversement* and social trauma, but rather a period of fulfillment. Apparently, there was little evidence of the spiritual and intellectual revolution sweeping Europe. 26 notes. M. D. Dibert

951. Akers, Charles W. THE LOST REPUTATION OF SAMUEL COOPER AS A LEADER OF THE AMERICAN REVOLUTION. *New England Hist. and Geneal. Register 1976 130: 23-34.* Argues the case for the resurrection of the reputation of the Reverend Samuel Cooper (1725-83) as one of the most influential leaders of Revolutionary Boston and, hence, of the American Revolution generally. Cooper's early efforts had to remain hidden, so as not to compromise his integrity as the minister of Brattle Street Meeting-House. His entry into the political arena, both through his increasingly outspoken sermons during 1775-76 and his partisan support for John Hancock against the Adamses once the Revolution was underway, damaged his reputation after the war. In addition, too many historians have adopted the myth that Samuel Adams alone was the Revolution. Based on primary and secondary sources; 34 notes. S. L. Patterson

952. Archdeacon, Thomas J. AMERICAN HISTORIANS AND THE AMERICAN REVOLUTION: A BICENTENNIAL OVERVIEW. *Wisconsin Mag. of Hist. 1980 63(4): 278-298.* Divides the recent historiography of the American Revolution along the traditional lines of neo-Whigs, emphasizing the rational reaction of colonists to perceived infringements on their rights by a repressive British government and king, and neo-Progressives, stressing the divisions within the colonies along socioeconomic and ethnoreligious lines. Cites the work of Edmund S. Morgan, Benjamin W. Labaree, John Shy, Jack P. Greene, and especially Bernard Bailyn and his students as representative of the neo-Whig school. Leading proponents of the neo-Progressive school include Merrill Jensen, Jackson Turner Main, James Kirby Martin, Joseph Ernst, Marc Egnal, Jesse Lemisch, and Staughton Lynd. 20 illus., 77 notes. N. C. Burckel

953. Baum, Gregory. CHRISTIANITY AND SOCIALISM. *Can. Dimension [Canada] 1979 13(5): 30-35.* Examines the existence of a Christian-Left movement in North America and Latin America, 20th century.

954. Bicha, Karel D. PRAIRIE RADICALS: A COMMON PIETISM. *J. of Church and State 1976 18(1): 79-94.* The "Prairie Radicals" were the activists in the plains area of the United States and Canada following the end of the populist movement. There men had no real common ideological ties. Some were leftist, some rightist, some poor, some wealthy. Argues that pietism was the common tie. There was a prominence of ministerial personnel among the radicals. Their values were pietistic. Most were Baptist, Methodist, Disciples of Christ or Pietistic Lutheran. The influence of their religious origins is analyzed in detail, showing the close similarities of each case. Covers 1890-1975. 59 notes. E. E. Eminhizer

955. Blosser, Janet K. POLITICS AND VOTING IN THE MENNONITE CHURCH IN AMERICA, 1860-1940. *Pennsylvania Mennonite Heritage 1980 3(4): 12-15.* Discusses the moral controversy among Mennonites over political involvement with the government by voting or holding office in North America.

956. Brauer, Jerald. THE PURITAN CONNECTION. *Center Mag. 1976 9(6): 75-79.* Examines Puritanism as the root of the American Revolution, 1630-1776.

957. Briceland, Alan V. THE PHILADELPHIA AURORA, THE NEW ENGLAND ILLUMINATI, AND THE ELECTION OF 1800. *Pennsylvania Mag. of Hist. and Biog. 1976 100(1): 3-36.* During the election of 1800, Thomas Jefferson and the Republicans were accused by the high Federalist clergy of being agents of the Order of Illuminati, a European anti-Christian sect which through control of the societies of Freemasonry was blamed for overthrowing church and state in revolutionary France. Writing in the *Aurora*, 1798-1800, Episcopal clergyman John C. Ogden (d. 1800) helped counteract this Federalist propaganda by portraying New England, the birthplace and main support of Jefferson's opponent, John Adams, as dominated by an intolerant clerical-political aristocracy. Turning the tables on the Federalist clergy, Ogden began in 1799 to freely refer to to the Federalist clergy as the New England Illuminati, imputing to their antimasonry a desire to destroy religious liberty in America. Thus, in the minds of the *Aurora* readers Jefferson was associated with freedom of religion while Adams was tarred with the brush of religious bigotry. Based on primary and secondary sources; 117 notes. E. W. Carp

958. Campbell, Colin. "THE PROTESTANT ETHIC," "RATIONALITY" AND CANADA'S POLITICAL ELITE: ETHNIC AND RELIGIOUS INFLUENCE ON SENATORS. *Soc. Sci. J. 1976 12(3): 159-173.* Analyzes the religious and ethnic values held by Canadian senators in a 1971 study.

959. Cohen, Michael. RELIGIOUS REVIVALISM AND THE ADMINISTRATIVE CENTRALIZATION MOVEMENT. *Administration and Soc. 1977 9(2): 219-232.* The late 19th-century administrative centralization movement, which emphasized the centralizing of unified departments in the executive branch of government, began in an era of intense religious revivals and was promoted by such leading figures as Woodrow Wilson, Luther Gulick, and John Fairlie, who were greatly influenced by the social and political reform tradition of Calvinism.

960. Cohen, Sheldon S. and Gerlach, Larry R. PRINCETON IN THE COMING OF THE AMERICAN REVOLUTION. *New Jersey Hist. 1974 92(2): 69-92.* Examines political attitudes and the role of the Presbyterians at Princeton University prior to the American Revolution, 1765-76.

961. Eisenach, Eldon J. CULTURAL POLITICS AND POLITICAL THOUGHT: THE AMERICAN REVOLUTION MADE AND REMEMBERED. *Am. Studies 1979 20(1): 71-97.* Explores differing interpretations of the American Revolution by examining the patterns of political-cultural conflicts inherent in the sources used to write these histories. Focuses on three areas of conflict and concern: religion, the role of law in political structures, and constitutionalism. Whig interpretations seem to have been more convincing than progressive historiography. Primary and secondary sources; 60 notes. J. A. Andrew

962. Fahmy-Eid, Nadia. ULTRAMONTANISME, IDÉOLOGIE ET CLASSES SOCIALES [Ultramontanism, ideology and social classes]. *Rev. d'Hist. de l'Amérique Française 1975 29(1): 49-68.* During the 19th century, the French middle class of Lower Canada united with the ultramontane clergy against the economic power being wielded by the English middle class of Upper Canada. The clergy of Lower Canada aimed at a state governed by the Church and effectively influenced education and government until Lower Canada became a modern capitalist state. Based on primary and secondary sources; 25 notes. C. Collon

963. Feldblum, Esther. ON THE EVE OF A JEWISH STATE: AMERICAN-CATHOLIC RESPONSES. *Am. Jew. Hist. Q. 1974 64(2): 99-119.* In spite of the Holocaust, American Catholics had reservations about the emergence of a Jewish State. Theological, psychological,

and pragmatic political considerations converged to shape Catholic attitudes. Total linkage of the postwar refugee problem with Palestine was unacceptable to Catholics who had a serious refugee problem of their own. Possible Jewish dominion over the Holy Land irritated theological complacency. The fear of Communism spreading to the Middle East, and the alignment of the Arab states with the USSR, was the main theme around which Catholic opposition to Zionism crystallized from 1945-48. Based on US Church publications, contemporary papers, and magazines; 66 notes. F. Rosenthal

964. Flanagan, Thomas. THE MISSION OF LOUIS RIEL. *Alberta Hist. [Canada] 1975 23(1): 1-12.* Examines visionary Louis Riel's conception of the North-West Rebellion as a messianic religious movement. Covers 1869-85. S

965. Flanagan, Thomas. LOUIS "DAVID" RIEL: PROPHET, PRIEST-KING, INFALLIBLE PONTIFF. *J. of Can. Studies 1974 9(3): 15-25.* Louis Riel's letters, written after his entry into a mental hospital, reveal a traditional Christian eschatological faith with the overtones of a Joachimite dispensation. The letters are well organized rather than demented ravings. During the 1885 Rebellion, Riel tried to put his messianic religious convictions into practice. Based on Public Archives of Canada, and of Manitoba, Archives of the Archdiocese of Montreal and the Seminary of Quebec, periodicals, monographs; 54 notes. G. E. Panting

966. Flanagan, Thomas E. LOUIS RIEL'S RELIGIOUS BELIEFS: A LETTER TO BISHOP TACHÉ. *Saskatchewan Hist. [Canada] 1974 27(1): 15-28.* Louis Riel (1844-85) claimed to be a religious prophet in addition to being a separatist leader. Argues that Riel's religious leadership was "an essential part of the attempt to recover the integrity of the Métis way of life," and that his religious theories were not as fantastic or nonsensical as missionaries and his defense attorneys pointed out. Too much information is gathered from hostile sources. His letter to Bishop Alexandre Taché tends to ameliorate this condition despite Bishop Taché's opinion that Riel was hopelessly insane. 2 portraits, 16 notes. C. Held

967. Frost, J. William. QUAKER VERSUS BAPTIST: A RELIGIOUS AND POLITICAL SQUABBLE IN RHODE ISLAND THREE HUNDRED YEARS AGO. *Quaker Hist. 1974 63(1): 39-52.* George Fox visited Rhode Island three weeks after the May 1672 election put Quakers in power for five years. Quakers had won by taking credit for repeal of sedition, confiscation, and other unpopular laws, thus identifying themselves with popular liberties. Fox's farewell sermon at Newport and the Baptist minister Thomas Olney, Jr.'s reply of a year later continued the Fox-Williams debates of 1672. Fox urged keeping weekly markets and vital records, and warned Friends to use their new power righteously. Olney's much longer polemic called government by inspiration oppressive and generally argued from different assumptions. These tracts illustrated rather than changed Rhode Island politics. Manuscripts preserved in the Rhode Island Historical Soceity and here published and edited. T. D. S. Bassett

968. Gaddy, C. Welton. SIGNIFICANT INFLUENCES OF BAPTISTS ON POLITICS IN AMERICA. *Baptist Hist. and Heritage 1976 11(2): 27-38.* Baptists fought long and successfully to obtain religious freedom in America and to get the First Amendment into the Constitution. But their emphasis on individualism in the religious experience and life has hindered most Southern Baptists from contributing any positive influence on the later American political scene. As individuals and churches they will oppose liquor and gambling, but they will not participate in fights for better housing for the poor, fair labor practices, etc. No leader has appeared among Southern Baptists, as Walter Rauschenbusch did in the North, to interpret the meaning of social Christianity and to call forth concerted efforts on major social problems. Thus the prophetic pulpit is largely absent in Southern Baptist churches. Neither a word of help or hope is extended. Some Southern Baptists have contributed much as individuals to the body politic. Urges the development of the political clout of the Southern Baptist Convention, lest that power become more a myth and less a reality. Covers 18th-20th centuries. Based largely on Annual Reports of the Southern Baptist Convention and secondary sources; 23 notes. H. M. Parker, Jr.

969. Gervin, J. Barry. MIDDLE OCTORARA PRESBYTERIAN CHURCH AND THE REVOLUTION. *J. of the Lancaster County Hist. Soc. 1977 81(2): 65-87.* Discusses the members of Middle Octorara Presbyterian Church, 1740-83, their religious beliefs, and their actions during the American Revolution.

970. Greeley, Andrew M. HOW CONSERVATIVE ARE AMERICAN CATHOLICS? *Pol. Sci. Q. 1977 92(2): 199-218.* The conventional wisdom about Catholic ethnics is false. In the 1970's they have not been more racist, less likely to support civil liberties, more antagonistic toward the counter culture, stronger supporters of the Vietnam War, or heavier supporters of George Wallace than other Americans. Catholics are in fact less conservative than the average, and they have not abandoned the Democratic Party as they have become more affluent and moved to the suburbs. Their conservative image may be based not on substantial issues, but rather on political style; Catholics are more likely to call their precinct captains than to join civic organizations. Based on NORC General Social Surveys, Gallup polls, voting records, and secondary sources; 9 tables, 5 figs., 13 notes. W. R. Hively

971. Gribbin, William. A REPLY OF JOHN ADAMS ON EPISCOPACY AND THE AMERICAN REVOLUTION. *Hist. Mag. of the Protestant Episcopal Church 1975 44(3): 277-283.* In 1824 Jedidiah Morse published his *Annals of the American Revolution; or, A record of the causes and events which produced, and terminated in the establishment and independence of the American republic*. Included in this work was a letter written by John Adams, "Episcopacy, a Cause of the Revolution." The Episcopalians immediately replied to Adams' charge. One such respondent was "W," who was Rev. George Weller, rector of St. Stephen's chapel, North Sassafras, Maryland. Reproduces the letter, with minor editorial annotations. It refutes Adams' claim, concluding that at his advanced age, Adams might better utilize his time in preparing for the world to come rather than in reliving events of his younger days. 8 notes. H. M. Parker, Jr.

972. Haskins, George L. ECCLESIASTICAL ANTECEDENTS OF CRIMINAL PUNISHMENT IN EARLY MASSACHUSETTS. *Massachusetts Hist. Soc. Pro. 1957-60 72: 21-35.* Provides the historical background of ecclesiastical law in colonial Massachusetts dating to the early 17th century in England, whose legal statues had roots in Roman law.

973. Holmes, David L. THE EPISCOPAL CHURCH AND THE AMERICAN REVOLUTION. *Hist. Mag. of the Protestant Episcopal Church 1978 47(3): 261-291.* Challenges the long-accepted hypothesis that all Anglican clergy or laity opposed the American Revolution. Anglican clergy were loyalists in direct proportion to the weakness of Anglicanism in their colony, to the degree of their earlier support of a colonial episcopate, to the "highness" of their churchmanship, to the degree of financial support they received from the Society for the Propagation of the Gospel, and to the numbers of converts and recent immigrants from Britain and Scotland. Estimates that 150 Anglican clergy were loyalists, 123 patriots. The greatest lesson which the Church gained from the Revolution was that it could exist without formal connection with the government of a particular nation. Primary and secondary sources; 55 notes, appendixes. H. M. Parker, Jr.

974. Hughes, Arthur J. "AMAZIN' JIMMY AND A MIGHTY FORTRESS WAS OUR TEDDY": THEODORE ROOSEVELT AND JIMMY CARTER, THE RELIGIOUS LINK. *Presidential Studies Q. 1979 9(1): 80-83.* Both Theodore Roosevelt and Jimmy Carter claimed a strong belief in God, referred repeatedly to their faith, professed a sense of mission in their political functions, and had heroes (Oliver Cromwell and Hyman Rickover, respectively) with similar senses of mission.

975. Jeansonne, Glen. PREACHER, POPULIST, PROPAGANDIST: THE EARLY CAREER OF GERALD L. K. SMITH. *Biography 1979 2(4): 303-327.* Gerald L. K. Smith, born and reared in Wisconsin and educated in Indiana, served as a Christian minister before becoming Huey P. Long's Share Our Wealth Society organizer in 1934. Protestant Fundamentalism and political populism and progressivism prepared Smith for political activism. His evolution from radicalism to reaction is examined and the apparent disjunction explained. J

976. Levitt, Joseph. IMAGES OF BOURASSA. *J. of Can. Studies [Canada] 1978 13(1): 100-113.* The attitudes of Canadian historians, both Anglophone and Francophone, toward Henri Bourassa (1868-1952) consistently have been colored by the position of each on the major issues Bourassa addressed during his more than 40 years in public life (1890's-1930's). Goldwin Smith, a fellow anti-imperialist, introduced him into historical literature in 1902. The isolationism of the 30's and the biculturalism of the 60's (Bourassa, while a champion of Francophone rights, always opposed separatism) occasioned favorable treatment of Bourassa among Anglophones, while Lionel Groulx, his onetime foe, described him in 1971 as "l'incomparable Èveilleur." Bourassa's position on social issues —Catholic, moderately reformist, emphasizing the family and agricultural values—likewise has called forth praise and blame. Calls for a view of Bourassa that is truer to the man himself. Primary sources; 120 notes.
L. W. Van Wyk

977. Lydecker, William J. F. GERRIT LYDEKKER: DOMINE AND LOYALIST. *Halve Maen 1976 50(4): 7-8, 16, 51(1): 9-10, 14.* Part I. Gerrit Lydekker (1729-94), ordained in the Dutch Reformed Church in New York in 1765, became friendly with reactionary Anglican clergy and by 1767 adopted their conservative, Loyalist political views; as a result, soon after the Declaration of Independence he was forced to flee behind the British lines in Manhattan. Part II. Describes Lydekker's attempts to prevent independence while he was leader of the Anglo-Dutch Loyalists in New York City, and his compensation by Great Britain for property losses suffered during the war (which he received after emigrating to London).

978. Maghami, Farhat Ghaem. POLITICAL KNOWLEDGE AMONG YOUTH: SOME NOTES ON PUBLIC OPINION FORMATION. *Can. J. of Pol. Sci. 1974 7(2): 334-340.* Devised a political knowledge scale to test a sampling of Canadian college and university students. Relates findings to socioeconomic background, religion, sex, and education. 5 tables, 8 notes, 2 appendices. R. V. Kubicek

979. McLoughlin, William G. PATRIOTISM AND PIETISM THE DISSENTING DILEMMA: MASSACHUSETTS RURAL BAPTISTS AND THE AMERICAN REVOLUTION. *Foundations 1976 19(2): 121-141.* Traces the persecutions of Baptists in Massachusetts to the time of the American Revolution, and discusses the difficulties Baptists faced in trying to decide who to support in the Revolution. Discusses problems Baptists faced in deciding on the new Constitution in 1788. Biblio.
E. E. Eminhizer

980. Mulder, John M. CALVINISM, POLITICS, AND THE IRONIES OF HISTORY. *Religion in Life 1978 47(2): 148-161.* The pervasive influence of Calvinism in European and American social and political life during the 16th-20th centuries was due to accidents of location, elements in Calvinist theology, and the fact that its reforming zeal, unsuccessful in changing the church, was refocused on society.

981. Murphy, Larry George. THE CHURCH AND BLACK CALIFORNIANS: A MID-NINETEENTH-CENTURY STRUGGLE FOR CIVIL JUSTICE. *Foundations 1975 18(2): 165-183.* Discusses the role of religion in the black community in California. The black church provided opportunity for exercise of skills and expression as well as development of personal status. Black influx to California occurred with the gold rush; the first black church, St. Andrews African Methodist Episcopal, was formed in Sacramento in 1850. Expansion of A. M. E. and Baptist churches was rapid in the following decade. There was some cooperation between black churches, but union between them did not develop as some expected. The black churches considered freedom a right man received from God. Because of this, they became involved in political activity to achieve it. 74 notes. E. E. Eminhizer

982. Perry, William Stevens. THE ALLEGED "TORYISM" OF THE CLERGY OF THE UNITED STATES AT THE BREAKING OUT OF THE WAR OF THE REVOLUTION: AN HISTORICAL EXAMINATION. *Hist. Mag. of the Protestant Episcopal Church 1976 45(2): 133-144.* Reprints a small booklet written about 1895-98 by the Bishop of Iowa and Historiographer of the Episcopal Church. The pamphlet was a one-sided attempt to substantiate the essential loyalty of the Anglican clergy during the Revolutionary War. It also embraced many prominent laymen in the church and attempted to display the patriotic character of the majority of colonial Anglicans.
H. M. Parker, Jr.

983. Petryshyn, J. FROM CLERGYMAN TO COMMUNIST: THE RADICALIZATION OF ALBERT EDWARD SMITH. *J. of Can. Studies [Canada] 1978-79 13(4): 61-71.* After 32 years (1893-1924) as a Methodist pastor in western Canada, influenced by the Social Gospel, Smith passed through a Toronto People's Church to the Communist Party. By 1921, he regarded Christ as a communist thinker and teacher. His experience as a member of the Manitoba legislature (1921-23) had convinced him that a Labour Party required discipline and well-defined objectives. These he found among Communist Party members. Based on United Church Archives, Smith Papers, and secondary sources; 78 notes.
G. E. Panting

984. Powell, Jonathan. PRESBYTERIAN LOYALISTS: A CHAIN OF INTEREST IN PHILADELPHIA. *J. of Presbyterian Hist. 1979 57(2): 135-160.* Ideology did not suddenly become a factor in the politics on the eve of the American Revolution. The members of the chain of interest—it is not lateral divisions between classes of society but the vertical divisons between chains of interest which stretch from a representative in government to the humblest servant—not only traded together but also thought the same way. Property was the most important aspect of liberty; thus independence was an attack on the King's rule and as such was an attack on the basis of all property, and so undermined liberty. Discusses how the most important Loyalist members of the chain of interest in the First Presbyterian Church of Philadelphia were in opposition to the patriots of the Third Presbyterian Church. Yet membership was not the only factor. Marriage, business partnerships, club memberships, etc., also helped to forge the chain of interest. This helps one in understanding the motives which underscored the actions of the Loyalists among Philadelphia Presbyterians. Based on numerous primary collections in Presbyterian Historical Society, recent Ph.D. dissertations, and church records; 3 tables, 2 fig., 94 notes. H. M. Parker, Jr.

985. Schelbert, Leo. THE AMERICAN REVOLUTION: A LESSON IN DISSENT: THE CASE OF JOHN JOACHIM ZUBLY. *Swiss Am. Hist. Soc. Newsletter 1976 12(3): 3-11.* The Reverend John Joachim Zubly of Savannah, Georgia, a Presbyterian, denounced British prerevolutionary theories and practices as unconstitutional and advocated armed resistance; however, his conscientious adherence to the concept of a sacred and inviolable union between England and the colonies led to his subsequent incarceration and sociopolitical ostracism.

986. Schweikart, Larry. THE MORMON CONNECTION: LINCOLN, THE SAINTS, AND THE CRISIS OF EQUALITY. *Western Humanities Rev. 1980 34(1): 1-22.* Briefly traces concepts of equality during the Enlightenment, then discusses these ideas in 19th-century America, particularly among the Mormons, led by Joseph Smith, who relocated numerous times to pursue without harrassment their own ideas of equality; focuses on the Mormons' influence on Abraham Lincoln's political career, and his ideas on equality, slavery, and polygamy, and his handling of Utah territorial affairs, from 1840 to the early 1860's.

987. Stevenson, E. M. A LETTER TO MY COUNTRY FRIENDS. *Nova Scotia Hist. Q. [Canada] 1980 10(2): 143-157.* Excerpts from articles written in 1863 by Robert Murray, editor of the newspaper *Presbyterian Witness.* The articles express his opinions and comments on politics, politicians, the clergy, Parliament and local current events.
H. M. Evans

988. Stowe, Walter Herbert. A STUDY IN CONSCIENCE: SOME ASPECTS OF THE RELATIONS OF THE CLERGY TO THE STATE. *Hist. Mag. of the Protestant Episcopal Church 1975 44(5): 53-75.* Discusses problems of Anglican preachers after the Declaration of Independence had been pronounced. When ordained they had taken an oath to pray for the king. Now they were told for whom they could and could not pray. Two cases are presented of parsons who ceased to hold public worship, confining their pastoral labors to baptisms, weddings, funerals, and calling. Without public worship services, Anglicanism suffered greatly during the war, so that by its conclusion the church was almost in its death throes. The people were not edified by closed churches. As independence was necessary for the United States to achieve its destiny as a nation, so the control of the British state over the American Anglican Church had to be broken for the American Episcopal Church to enter its majority. Based on primary and secondary sources; 32 notes, 2 appendixes. H. M. Parker, Jr.

989. Sullivan, John L. POLITICAL CORRELATES OF SOCIAL, ECONOMIC AND RELIGIOUS DIVERSITY IN THE AMERICAN STATES. *J. of Pol. 1973 35(1): 70-84.* "Computes an index of diversity, (Stanley) Lieberson's Aw [subscript] (diversity within a population), for the 50 American states. It represents the proportion of characteristics upon which two randomly selected individuals will differ, on the average, assuming sampling with replacement. This index is correlated with indicators of party competition (positive), discrimination and inequality (negative), and various policy variables (positive). The index is also related to region in an analysis of variance model, and the within-regional variations are too small to control for region when examining other relationships. South versus non-South comparisons are examined, however, and there is a significant difference in the strength of the relationship between diversity and discrimination—a strong relationship in the South a weaker relationship in the non-South." 6 tables, 11 notes.
A. R. Stoesen

990. Wargelin, Raymond W. CONFRONTATION OF MARXIST RADICALISM WITH THE FINNISH LUTHERAN CHURCH IN FINLAND AND ON THE NORTH AMERICAN CONTINENT. *Lutheran Q. 1976 28(4): 361-377.* Both at home in Finland and in North America where they have immigrated, Finns have been divided by their adherence to Lutheranism and Marxist socialism. As early as the late 19th century, the division became overt as Finnish Marxists attacked the Lutheran Church and its hierarchy in Finland. This situation is now critical because many Finnish governmental officials today are either avowed Marxists or sympathetic to the ideology. In North America, Finns found themselves separated by the same issue with each side competing for adherents and using whatever methods possible to gain them. Today, however, both in Finland and North America, Finnish Lutherans are attempting to maintain a realistic dialogue with the Marxists, while appreciating the common concern of both for human well-being. The Church's concern for human economic improvement may serve to end the traditional alienation of working people from religion. Secondary sources; 53 notes. J. A. Kicklighter

991. Wimberley, Ronald C. and Christenson, James A. CIVIL RELIGION AND CHURCH AND STATE. *Sociol. Q. 1980 21(1): 35-40.* No personal conflicts exist between the belief systems of civil religion and the doctrine of separation of church and state; based on a 1975 survey of more than 3,000 North Carolina respondents.

992. Wolfe, James S. THE RELIGIOUS ISSUE REVISITED: PRESBYTERIAN RESPONSES TO KENNEDY'S PRESIDENTIAL CAMPAIGN. *J. of Presbyterian Hist. 1979 57(1): 1-18.* Most Protestants, Presbyterians included, were apprehensive over the ambivalence of the Roman Catholic Church's position on church and state at the time of John F. Kennedy's race for the presidency in 1960. Divides Kennedy's campaign into three waves: Spring 1959, Spring 1960, and Fall 1960. In each of these major waves Presbyterian laymen and clergy were active when religious issues surfaced. Many thought that Kennedy's Catholicism might be a symbolic detriment in the presidency, but they tended not to worry about it. Most Presbyterians accorded legitimacy to the religious issue; some even examined the deeper question of how religion and politics ought to interact. The main battle lines were formed over the questions of whether the Roman Catholic Church had the aims and means to subvert America and whether as president Kennedy would be party to that subversion. Led by their general assemblies, Presbyterians tended to rule out mere religious affiliation as a basis for judgment and focused on the bearing of Kennedy's religion on his character, record, and policy positions alone as legitimate. Based on Presbyterian religious weekly accounts; 30 notes. H. M. Parker, Jr.

993. Worrall, Arthur J. PERSECUTION, POLITICS AND WAR: ROGER WILLIAMS, QUAKERS, AND KING PHILIP'S WAR. *Quaker Hist. 1977 66(2): 73-86.* The 1672 debate between the Society of Friends and Roger Williams occurred during Williams's efforts to recoup his political position, which was weakened by his faction's law against freedom of assembly and by its stands on taxes and land speculation. The Quakers consolidated their control of Rhode Island until defense needs arising out of King Philip's War (1675-76) allowed the Williams faction to return. Williams was able to have his side of the story about the debate published in Massachusetts, at a time when there was an upsurge in persecution of the Quakers. T. D. S. Bassett

994. —. MENNONITES AND THE POLITICAL ELECTIONS OF 1856: JOHANNES RISSER ON POLITICS AND THE SLAVERY ISSUE. *Mennonite Hist. Bull. 1976 37(4): 1-3.* Reprints three letters from Johannes Risser to his sister and brother-in-law in 1857 discussing the slavery issue, the Democratic Party, and the general state of politics at the time.

995. —. [MORMONS AND WATERGATE]. *Dialogue 1974 9(2): 9-24.*

England, Eugene. HANGING BY A THREAD: MORMONS AND WATERGATE, *pp. 9-18.* Mormon theology posits natural laws of political justice and liberty which are described and guaranteed by the Declaration of Independence and the Constitution. Mormons were wrong to have given unquestioning loyalty to Nixon.

Rushforth, Brent N. WATERGATE: A PERSONAL EXPERIENCE, *pp. 19-24.* In contributing to the Committee to Re-elect the President in illegal ways, the business community revealed moral laxity. The author, in helping to prosecute the Northrop case, rediscovered the value of the gospels in shaping ethics. D. L. Rowe

Church and State

996. Allen, James B. "GOOD GUYS" VS. "GOOD GUYS": RUDGER CLAWSON, JOHN SHARP, AND CIVIL DISOBEDIENCE IN NINETEENTH-CENTURY UTAH. *Utah Hist. Q. 1980 48(2): 148-174.* When the federal government outlawed polygamy in 1862, Mormons faced a moral dilemma of obeying a law that violated their religious convictions or disregarding the law of the land, which it was their religious duty to obey. Rudger Clawson went to prison advocating civil disobedience. Bishop John Sharp despised the law but conformed to it, and was ostracized by Mormons. Based on LDS Archives; 9 illus., 65 notes. J. L. Hazelton

997. Anderson, Philip J. LETTERS OF HENRY JESSEY AND JOHN TOMBES TO THE CHURCHES OF NEW ENGLAND, 1645. *Baptist Q. [Great Britain] 1979 28(1): 30-40.* Discusses letters written in 1645 by Henry Jessey, pastor of the Independent Jacob-Lathrop congregation in London, and John Tombes, a noted Anabaptist minister in the 1640's, urging tolerance by the churches of New England of those who dissented from the practice of infant baptism.

998. Ashdown, Paul G. SAMUEL RINGGOLD: AN EPISCOPAL CLERGYMAN IN KENTUCKY AND TENNESSEE DURING THE CIVIL WAR. *Filson Club Hist. Q. 1979 53(3): 231-238.* Samuel Ringgold served as an Episcopal priest in Bowling Green, Kentucky, and Clarksville, Tennessee. He attempted to maintain political neutrality in an area contested by both armies. Most of the conflicts were with Union army officials who attempted to force Ringgold to adopt a partisan stance. Based on privately held letters; 45 notes.

999. Bailey, Raymond C. POPULAR PETITIONS AND RELIGION IN EIGHTEENTH-CENTURY COLONIAL VIRGINIA. *Hist. Mag. of the Protestant Episcopal Church 1977 46(4): 419-428.* While in form the vestry, comprised of the social elite, controlled the parish government of the established church in 18th-century Virginia, in practice the petitions of local parishioners to the House of Burgesses played a major role in creating new parishes or altering their boundaries and in reversing arbitrary or unpopular decisions of the vestry. As a result, despite the theoretically undemocratic features of parish government at that time, the public interest was safeguarded and considerable popular participation was encouraged. In religious matters, as in many others, colonial Virginians used petitions to play a major role in influencing public policy. *House Journals, Executive Journals of the Council of Colonial Virginia,* and the author's doctoral dissertation in addition to other primary and secondary sources; table, 24 notes.
H. M. Parker, Jr.

1000. Bair, Jo Ann W. and Jensen, Richard L. PROSECUTION OF THE MORMONS IN ARIZONA TERRITORY IN THE 1880'S. *Arizona and the West 1977 19(1): 25-46.* The federal Edmunds Act of 1882 prohibited both polygamy and cohabitation with more than one woman. Expansive Mormon colonization in the Southwest, particularly in Arizona, was regarded as a threat to the status quo. Polygamy became the rallying point for anti-Mormon crusades which usually occurred within the legal system. The legal battles were for control of the land and local government. Once objectives were largely achieved, the anti-Mormon antagonism subsided dramatically during the late 1880's. 6 illus.; 46 notes. D. L. Smith

1001. Baker, Robert A. BAPTISTS AND THE AMERICAN REVOLUTION. *Baptist Hist. and Heritage 1976 11(3): 149-159.* Political liberty would be tragically inadequate if it had not included the most important of all liberties: the right to worship according to the dictates of one's own conscience in a religiously pluralistic society. Religious liberty is the ultimate foundation of democratic institutions. All other human rights are endangered when religious liberty is questioned, hampered, or denied by any group. Emphasizes the contribution of Baptists to religious liberty in the United States. Based on secondary sources; 11 notes. H. M. Parker, Jr.

1002. Barnes, Howard A. THE IDEA THAT CAUSED A WAR: HORACE BUSHNELL VERSUS THOMAS JEFFERSON. *J. of Church and State 1974 16(1): 73-83.* Discusses differing conceptions of church and state between Congregationalist Horace Bushnell and Thomas Jefferson in the early to mid-19th century, emphasizing issues in racism, individualism, and morality.

1003. Barnes, Joseph W. OBEDIAH DOGBERRY, ROCHESTER FREETHINKER. *Rochester Hist. 1974 36(3): 1-24.* Obediah Dogberry fought for religious liberty and freedom of thought in Rochester, New York, through the *Liberal Advocate*, a newspaper published during 1832-34.

1004. Bashore, Melvin L. LIFE BEHIND BARS: MORMON COHABS OF THE 1880S. *Utah Hist. Q. 1979 47(1): 22-41.* More than 1,300 Mormon men and a few women were jailed for polygamy or unlawful cohabitation under the Edmunds Act (US, 1882). So many church, community, and business leaders were jailed that a prison sentence became a mark of honor. Prison diaries reveal problems with bedbugs, lice, poor food, oppressive heat, and overcrowded cells. Tedium was relieved by crafts, glee clubs, bands, sports, speeches, and visiting days. The presence of Mormons exerted a powerful restraining influence on criminals. 7 illus., 37 notes. J. L. Hazelton

1005. Beebe, Robert L. TAX PROBLEMS POSED BY PSEUDO-RELIGIOUS MOVEMENTS. *Ann. of the Am. Acad. of Pol. and Social Sci. 1979 (446): 91-105.* Assume for a moment that in 1847 one Brigham Young had presented himself to your local tax assessor and stated that he was the presiding clergyman of the Church of Jesus Christ of the Latter-Day Saints and that he was therefore entitled to the appropriate real property tax exemptions for property owned by him and his church. Chances are that Mr. Young's requests would have been quickly, if not summarily, denied. And yet, in 1979, if a Mormom clergyman requests an exemption on a Mormon church anywhere in the United States, there will undoubtedly be few if any problems prior to speedy granting of that request. What happened during those 132 years to change the assessor's attitude is, of course, a chapter in American history. When that change in attitude occurred or, more precisely, what standards and criteria might have been applied in each situation is the subject of this paper. J

1006. Betke, Carl. THE MOUNTED POLICE AND THE DOUKHOBORS IN SASKATCHEWAN, 1899-1909. *Saskatchewan Hist. [Canada] 1974 27(1): 1-14.* Following the initial need for the Royal Canadian Mounted Police to safeguard the province from the Indians, the force faced the necessity of being drastically reduced or changing its mission. The latter was the case and many new kinds of services were given by the officers to the settlers in the prairie West. Police comments on the suitability of certain ethnic groups for agricultural pursuits were not required but were made by the constables in their reports. These reports shed light upon the social and economic problems of the period. Personal antipathy toward certain ethnic groups was often overcome if they were successful as farmers. This was true in the case of the Galicians, Mennonites, and Mormons, and particularly the Doukhobors. The Doukhobors' tradition to "submit to no human authority" sorely tried the tolerance of the Mounted Police during their first decade in Canada. The major reason for the problems that did exist is the change in policy toward the Doukhobor settlement, by the federal government. 2 illus., 60 notes. C. Held

1007. Billings, Warren M. A QUAKER IN SEVENTEENTH-CENTURY VIRGINIA: FOUR REMONSTRANCES BY GEORGE WILSON. *William and Mary Q. 1976 33(1): 127-140.* Four documents from the papers of George Wilson, a Quaker missionary in Virginia, reveal his efforts to bring about toleration in 17th-century Virginia. A summary of Wilson's life before he came to Virginia is included. The documents printed here are: memorial to the Virginia authorities (1661), pp. 130-132; letter to deputy-governor Moryson (1662), pp. 132-133; a remonstrance to the Assembly (1662), pp. 134-135; and a memorial to Charles II (1662), pp. 135-140. Wilson was jailed in Virginia. Comments on punitive measures toward the Quakers. Documents from the Wilson Papers, Library of the Religious Society of Friends House, London. 17 notes. H. M. Ward

1008. Bockelman, Wayne L. LOCAL POLITICS IN PRE-REVOLUTIONARY LANCASTER COUNTY. *Pennsylvania Mag. of Hist. and Biog. 1973 97(1): 45-74.* Examines the relationship between local politics and provincial politics in Lancaster County, 1700-76. Locally elected offices, such as sheriff, commissioners, and assessors, were the focus of the political struggles between the Quaker party and the proprietary party. Nonelective local offices such as justices of the peace, clerks of the three courts formed by the judges, and the recorder of deeds, were appointed by the governor to increase the influence of the proprietary party and reward the party faithful. Edward Shippen and James Burd, local leaders of Lancaster County, carried out many governmental and party tasks and were influential in county party politics. Based largely on primary sources; 115 notes. E. W. Carp

1009. Borden, Morton. THE CHRISTIAN AMENDMENT. *Civil War Hist. 1979 25(2): 156-167.* Heeding Protestants' criticism since 1787 of the US Constitution's failure to acknowledge national dependence on God, and specifically on Christ, and accepting the common opinion that the Civil War was a punishment not only for slavery but also for that omission, Protestant fundamentalists in 1863 founded the National Reform Association to support a Christian constitutional amendment. President Abraham Lincoln proclaimed National Fast Day (30 April 1863), acknowledged the truth of the Scriptures, and urged repentance for sin, but he never supported the National Reform Association; nor did Congress. As their goal became less attainable, their supporters fell away and those who remained became fanatical. The National Reform Association persisted until 1945; its members believed that the proclamation and observance of National Fast Day had turned the tide in the Civil War and that a similar constitutional proclamation of dependence on Christ would save the nation. The public never concurred. 37 notes. S

1010. Borden, Morton. FEDERALISTS, ANTIFEDERALISTS, AND RELIGIOUS FREEDOM. *J. of Church and State 1979 21(3): 469-482.* Discusses why no statement on religious liberty appeared in the first-proposed Constitution; Federalists and Antifederalists differed less on philosophy than on implementation. Based on the Federalists' papers, Antifederalists' writings, and secondary sources; 49 notes. E. E. Eminhizer

1011. Botein, Stephen. INCOME AND IDEOLOGY: HARVARD-TRAINED CLERGYMEN IN THE EIGHTEENTH CENTURY. *Eighteenth-Century Studies 1980 13(4): 396-413.* In the inflationary decades preceding 1750, the real income of the New England clergy was cut by more than half. All the arguments mounted by the clergy for increases only worked to reduce their prestige, which was further eroded by the itinerant ministers of the Great Awakening. By Revolution eve, only the Boston clergy lived well from the contributions of their affluent congregations, and so even these churchmen supported the movement to disestablish state religion. 54 notes. W. W. Elison

1012. Bourgeault, Guy. LE NATIONALISME QUEBECOIS ET L'EGLISE [Quebecois nationalism and the Church]. *Can. Rev. of Studies in Nationalism [Canada] 1978 5(2): 189-207.* Discusses the difficulties of the Catholic Church in Quebec in dealing with the contemporary nationalism movement there. Traditionally the Church associated itself with French Canadian aspirations, but it has felt uncomfortable with contemporary expressions of those feelings, characterized as they are by secularism and socialism. The Church's problem in this connection is bound fundamentally to the larger question of the role of the Church in Quebec society today. Covers 1608-1978. Secondary sources; 52 notes. J. A. Kicklighter

1013. Bowler, Clara Ann. THE LITIGIOUS CAREER OF WILLIAM COTTON, MINISTER. *Virginia Mag. of Hist. and Biog. 1978 86(3): 281-294.* The problems involved in transferring the institution of the Anglican Church to frontier Virginia enabled William Cotton (d. 1640), minister in Accomack County, to use the courts to enrich himself by insisting on the traditional tithes and fees due to an Anglican minister, 1633-39. Based on legal histories, court records, and published statutes; 82 notes. R. F. Oaks

1014. Brinsfield, John W. DANIEL DEFOE: WRITER, STATESMAN, AND ADVOCATE OF RELIGIOUS LIBERTY IN SOUTH CAROLINA. *South Carolina Hist. Mag. 1975 76(3): 107-111.* While Daniel Defoe's association with South Carolina's colonial history was brief (1704-06), his pamphlets in defense of religious dissent helped block England's last attempt to disfranchise a legislative body through a religious test. Defoe, a forerunner of the populist Whig tradition, wrote that Carolina's charter was being violated by the exclusion law (proposed by John Lord Granville), and that it threatened Church and State relations. Based on primary sources; 11 notes. R. H. Tomlinson

1015. Buckley, Thomas E. CHURCH-STATE SETTLEMENT IN VIRGINIA: THE PRESBYTERIAN CONTRIBUTION. *J. of Presbyterian Hist. 1976 54(1): 105-119.* Discusses revisionist consideration of the attitude of Presbyterians in postcolonial church-state relations. Not all Presbyterians opposed religious establishment. In Europe they were frequently the recipients of such a status. Virginia Presbyterians grappled with the problem, but the one position they unalterably upheld was the need for an equality of all religious groups in the commonwealth. On this basis they ultimately supported Jefferson's bill before the Virginia legislature. Covers 1770-85. Based largely on primary sources; illus., 40 notes. H. M. Parker, Jr.

1016. Burch, Francis F. A LETTER OF EDWARD J. NOLAN TO PAUL SABATIER: A REFLECTION ON THE SEPARATION OF CHURCH AND STATE IN FRANCE. *Records of the Am. Catholic Hist. Soc. of Philadelphia 1974 85(3-4): 205-207.* Nolan's reaction to the Calvinist clergyman's 1906 open letter disagreeing with Cardinal James Gibbons's contention that separation of church and state in France was part of a government attempt to destroy religion. 5 notes. J. M. McCarthy

1017. Burg, B. R. THE CAMBRIDGE PLATFORM: A REASSERTION OF ECCLESIASTICAL AUTHORITY. *Church Hist. 1974 43(4).* Considered to be one of 17th-century New England's most important documents, the Cambridge Platform (1648) remained the recognized standard for Massachusetts Bay religion until the American Revolution. While there was a doctrinally prescribed equality between church and state in the reformed theories brought over by many immigrants, the relationship of equals was never established in the colony. Although they hoped to establish a noncorrupt church organization, without the ecclesiastical hierarchy which had been dominated by civil authority in the old world, church and state found themselves entangled. Opposition to secular control began to solidify in 1646, and the Cambridge Platform was a visible attempt to proscribe and then diminish civil participation in the colony's religious affairs. This document was a major step toward securing church independence from the civil government. 46 notes. M. D. Dibert

1018. Cadbury, Henry J. THE KING'S MISSIVE. *Quaker Hist. 1974 63(2): 117-123.* Reproduces Charles I's 9 September 1661 mandamus to stop corporal punishment and execution of "vagabond Quakers" in Massachusetts Bay Colony. Also reproduces Samuel Shattuck's letter reporting its delivery and reception. Discusses the May 1661 law by which four were hanged and some 30 jailed, evidence of compliance with the King's order, and the master whose ship brought the letter. 6 notes. T. D. S. Bassett

1019. Callam, Daniel. THE SYLLABUS OF ERRORS: CANADIAN REACTION IN THE SECULAR AND IN THE PROTESTANT PRESS. *Study Sessions: Can. Catholic Hist. Assoc. [Canada] 1979 (46): 5-22.* Reportage of Pope Pius IX's 8 December 1864 encyclical *Quanta cura* (a criticism of growing liberalism in European government and the separation of church and state) and the accompanying *Syllabus of Errors* in the Canadian secular and Protestant presses emphasized the political rather than moral nature of the documents and served to reinforce public opinion that the Catholic Church was intolerant and medieval and largely political in nature.

1020. Campeau, Lucien. MGR DE LAVAL ET LE CONSEIL SOUVERAIN 1659-1684 [Monseigneur Laval and the Sovereign Council 1659-84]. *Rev. d'Hist. de l'Amérique Française [Canada] 1973 27(3): 323-360.* Discusses the relationship between the ecclesiastical and commercial authorities in New France in the late 17th century and how the provincial governors exploited both.

1021. Canavan, Francis. THE IMPACT OF RECENT SUPREME COURT DECISIONS ON RELIGION IN THE UNITED STATES. *J. of Church and State 1974 16(2): 217-236.* Gives a brief summary of major Supreme Court decisions on religion since 1963, in order to assess the impact of these decisions on religion in the United States.

1022. Chianese, Mary Lou. THOMAS JEFFERSON: ENLIGHTENED AMERICAN. *Daughters of the Am. Revolution Mag. 1975 109(5): 417-423.* Reexamines the life and ideas of Thomas Jefferson (1743-1826), author of the Declaration of Independence and the Statute of Virginia for Religious Freedom and founder of the University of Virginia. S

1023. Clark, Tom C. THE SUPREME COURT AND RELIGION. *Christian Scholar's Rev. 1974 4(1): 43-46.* Review of Richard E. Morgan's *The Supreme Court and Religion* (New York: Free Press, 1972). S

1024. Clayton, James L. THE SUPREME COURT, POLYGAMY AND THE ENFORCEMENT OF MORALS IN NINETEENTH CENTURY AMERICA: AN ANALYSIS OF *REYNOLDS V. UNITED STATES*. *Dialogue 1979 12(4): 46-61.* The 1879 Supreme Court decision on the case of Mormon George Reynolds upheld the constitutionality of the antipolygamy act passed by Congress in 1862. The Mormons held that polygamy was protected under the First Amendment guarantee of the free exercise of religion. The Court held that religious belief could not be used to justify an overt act made criminal by the law of the land. The significant basis for the Court's decision, however, was that deviant sexual behavior which offended majority sentiment could not be tolerated. In light of changed public attitudes, the Court's decision could soon be modified. Based on Utah District Court and US Supreme Court records and on secondary sources; 66 notes. R. D. Rahmes

1025. Conway, John S. MYRON C. TAYLOR'S MISSION TO THE VATICAN 1940-50. *Church Hist. 1975 44(1): 85-99.* The mission of Myron C. Taylor, personal representative of Roosevelt and Truman to Pope Pius XII remains an anomaly in US foreign relations. Since the United States maintained no formal mission to the Vatican, Taylor was the main link between the papacy and Washington in the trying days preceding World War II. By remaining aloof from the religious controversies concerning his mission, Taylor maintained cordial relations between Roosevelt and Pius XII in their mutual quest for peace. With the entry of the United States into the conflict, Taylor continued to deal with the Vatican on controversial subjects such as the overthrow of Mussolini and the American bombing of Rome. Present US-Vatican relations have been influenced by Taylor's tenure (1940-1950) as personal envoy. His mission is also significant because Congress later refused to establish a permanent mission to the Vatican. 54 notes. M. D. Dibert

1026. Craig, G. M. TWO CONTRASTING UPPER CANADIAN FIGURES: JOHN ROLPH AND JOHN STRACHAN. *Tr. of the Royal Soc. of Can. 1974 12: 237-248.* Compares and contrasts the careers of John Rolph and John Strachan. Rolph left few records whereas Strachan left many. Both men were born in Britain and were better educated than the average Canadian. Although both men were Anglicans, Rolph opposed the idea of an established church and Strachan strongly supported it and the land endowment allowed the church in Canada. Strachan became the bishop of Toronto; Rolph had a career in law and medicine. In politics Strachan was a Tory and Rolph a rebel who had to flee to the United States after the rebellion of 1837. Only Rolph held elective office, but Strachan held more power. Each man was an eloquent speechmaker, had taught, and was influential in the development of the University of Toronto. Although students may prefer Rolph's reform ideas and his opposition to an established church and the family compact to Strachan's fight for the benefit of a minority denomination, encouragement of the family compact, and francophobia, the latter did provide good leadership to his church and, despite his faults, emerges as the bigger man. Covers 1820-70. J. D. Neville

1027. Ditsky, John. HARD HEARTS AND GENTLE PEOPLE: A QUAKER REPLY TO PERSECUTION. *Can. Rev. of Am. Studies 1974 5(1): 47-51.* Analyzes the response of Francis Howgill to Puritan persecution of Quakers in colonial New England. Quakers denied Puritan charges of heresy. Quakers challenged Puritan usage of civil powers to coerce dissenters, accusing the Puritans of invoking false ecclesiastical doctrines to justify their deeds. Covers the 1650's. Based on tracts by Howgill and John Norton (1606-63); 6 notes. H. T. Lovin

1028. Dix, Fae Decker. UNWILLING MARTYR: THE DEATH OF YOUNG ED DALTON. *Utah Hist. Q. 1973 41(2): 162-177.* Edward Meeks Dalton (1852-86) was killed by a federal deputy marshal who was enforcing the Edmunds-Tucker Act (1882) which forbade polygamy. Young Ed became a martyr. 6 illus., 32 notes. D. L. Smith

1029. Driedger, Leo and Zehr, Dan. THE MENNONITE STATE-CHURCH TRAUMA: ITS EFFECTS ON ATTITUDES OF CANADIAN STUDENTS AND LEADERS. *Mennonite Q. R. 1974 48(4): 515-526.* Discusses some of the social causes for the Canadian Mennonites' perception of social issues, and gives a 1970 statistical analysis of the views of differing Mennonite Conference leaders and university students. S

1030. Dubé, Jean-Claude. LES INTENDANTS DE LA NOUVELLE-FRANCE ET LA RELIGION. [The intendants of New France and religion]. *Sessions d'Étude: Soc. Can. d'Hist. de l'Église Catholique [Canada] 1978 45: 5-17.* The 15 royal intendants in Quebec during 1663-1760 were generally sincere believers in the Catholic faith.

1031. Dunleavy, Janet E. and Dunleavy, Gareth W. RECONSTRUCTION, REFORM, AND ROMANISM, 1865-85: AMERICA AS SEEN BY CHARLES O'CONOR AND CHARLES OWEN O'CONOR DON, M.P. *Éire-Ireland 1980 15(3): 15-35.* Compares the views of the US political system held by Charles O'Conor (1804-84), distinguished Irish American attorney, and Charles Owen O'Conor Don (1838-1906), his prominent Irish kinsman and correspondent. A lawyer's lawyer, Charles O'Conor rose to prominence in the New York Bar and in national affairs. He saw Reconstruction as an opportunity for political reform against the special interest groups of political parties and office-holders who had been able to 1) gain undemocratic power by taking advantage of English-modeled aspects of the US Constitution, and 2) discriminate against Irish American Catholics. The Irish Charles Owen O'Conor (whose title "Don" designated him head of the O'Conors of Connacht), a member of parliament and familiar with the role of parties in the English system, favored not reform of the US political system but solutions worked out by realignment of political factions. Based on the writings of both O'Conors; 50 notes. D. J. Engler

1032. Everett, William. ECCLESIOLOGY AND POLITICAL AUTHORITY, A DIALOGUE WITH HANNAH ARENDT. *Encounter 1975 36(1): 26-36.* Discusses the ideology of church-state relations and its origins in the American Revolution. S

1033. Fain, Elaine. GOING PUBLIC: THE ANGIE WILLIAMS COX LIBRARY, THE VILLAGE OF PARDEEVILLE, AND THE WISCONSIN SUPREME COURT, 1927-1929. *J. of Lib. Hist. 1980 15(1): 53-61.* Describes *Koester* v. *Pardeeville* (1929), in which the Wisconsin Supreme Court ruled that a municipality could support (with tax money) a private library that was empowered by its bylaws to use "discretion" over the inclusion of Catholic publications and that forbade the hiring of Catholics as librarians or trustees. Ramifications of the case involved censorship, religious discrimination, constitutional doctrine of the separation of church and state, and private gifts donated to libraries with stipulations. Although the decision appears unusual, the library still is operating under the provisions. Based on Wisconsin legal and legislative records; 29 notes. D. J. Mycue

1034. Fair, Daryl R. THE CHURCH-STATE POLICY PROCESS. *Policy Studies J. 1975 4(2): 117-122.* Discusses recent Supreme Court decisions in the area of church-state relations and concludes the court favors strict separationism, 1963-75.

1035. Flowers, Ronald B. THE 1960S: A DECISIVE DECADE IN AMERICAN CHURCH-STATE RELATIONSHIPS. *Encounter 1979 40(3): 287-304.* Gives the history of church-state relationships in the United States during the 1960's, providing examples of Supreme Court decisions on church-state issues.

1036. Freeze, Gary. LIKE A HOUSE BUILT UPON SAND: THE ANGLICAN CHURCH AND ESTABLISHMENT IN NORTH CAROLINA, 1765-1776. *Hist. Mag. of the Protestant Episcopal Church 1979 48(4): 405-432.* Of all the establishments of the Church of England in colonial America, North Carolina's was the weakest. To offset this, on the eve of the Revolution, Governor William Tryon energetically pushed for greater conformity in the colony. As a result, the Church became a symbol of royal despotism. Tryon's attempts to impose a more structured, hierarchical society gave colonists reason to revolt, because their principles of fair government and a just society had been violated. Examines Presbyterians and Baptists as dissenters in the colony. Based largely on *Colonial Records of North Carolina,* Clark's *State Records of North Carolina,* and secondary sources; 116 notes.
H. M. Parker, Jr.

1037. Garr, Daniel J. POWER AND PRIORITIES: CHURCH-STATE BOUNDARY DISPUTES IN SPANISH CALIFORNIA. *California History 1978-79 57(4): 364-375.* Traces the conflict between Franciscan missionaries and Spanish efforts to establish civil settlements in Alta California in the late 18th century. Father Junípero Serra opposed establishing the San Jose pueblo in 1777, and Father Fermín de Lasuén protested against the location of Villa de Branciforte 20 years later. The missionaries held that such settlements violated laws guaranteeing the integrity of mission Indian settlements, property, and livestock. Spanish viceroys, however, placed greater priority on the need for civil settlements, increased population of Spanish subjects, and control of territory threatened by encroachment from other countries. To the viceroys and governors, the missionary view unrealistically promoted isolation and perpetual stewardship over the Indians, not true colonization of the province. Primary and secondary sources; illus. (reproductions); 58 notes.
A. Hoffman

1038. Garrett, James Leo, Jr. THE "FREE EXERCISE" CLAUSE OF THE FIRST AMENDMENT: RETROSPECT AND PROSPECT. *J. of Church and State 1975 17(3): 393-398.* Discusses legal decisions regarding the religious freedom clauses in the First Amendment of the US Constitution, 1878-1972.

1039. Gee, Elizabeth D. JUSTICE FOR ALL OR FOR THE "ELECT"? THE UTAH COUNTY PROBATE COURT, 1855-72. *Utah Hist. Q. 1980 48(2): 129-147.* When Utah conferred extraordinary jurisdiction on its county probate courts in 1850, critics charged Mormons with maneuvering to control the judicial system and with partiality toward Mormon litigants. An analysis of procedural operations of the probate court for 1855-56, 1860-61, 1865-66, and 1870-71 cannot completely refute nor substantiate the charge of partisanship. An analysis of nonprocedural decisions and final judgments gives evidence of fair administration of law to all. Based on records of the Utah County Probate Court; 4 illus., 9 tables, 34 notes. J. L. Hazelton

1040. Geldbach, Erich. RELIGIOUS LIBERTY. *Zeitschrift für Religions- und Geistesgeschichte [West Germany] 1977 29(3): 245-251.* Reports on themes discussed at the Bicentennial Conference of Religious Liberty, 25-30 April 1976, in Philadelphia. Despite the continuing problem of the separation of church and state, a topic at the conference, the religious liberty of America was extensive and best represented for the author by his visit to an Amish church meeting and by the presence of the Board of Rabbis of Philadelphia at the conference.
M. A. Hoobs

1041. Gelpi Barrios, Juan. PERSONALIDAD JURÍDICA DE LA IGLESIA EN PUERTO RICO [Juridical personality of the Catholic Church in Puerto Rico]. *Rev. Española de Derecho Canónico [Spain] 1977 33(95-96): 395-415.* Until 1863, when the "congregational corporation" was defined in the United States, the difference in Church and State relations between the United States and Europe consisted in the American notion of trusteeship. Under trusteeship the Catholic Church had opposed denial of its legal status and the undermining of its religious mission, gratefully confirming the new status in the Third Plenary Council in Baltimore, 1884. In Puerto Rico, the 1898 Treaty of Paris concluding the Spanish-American War assured the continued application of the 1851 concordat between Spain and the Holy See to the Church in Puerto Rico. This juridical status of the Church in Puerto Rico was approved by the US Supreme Court in 1908. R. D. Rodríguez

1042. Goulding, Stuart D. ROGER WILLIAMS OF RHODE ISLAND. *Hist. Today [Great Britain] 1975 25(11): 741-748.* Roger Williams returned to Great Britain in 1643 during the English civil war and again in 1651 seeking reaffirmations of Rhode Island's charter.

1043. Green, Jesse C., Jr. THE EARLY VIRGINIA ARGUMENT FOR SEPARATION OF CHURCH AND STATE. *Baptist Hist. and Heritage 1976 11(1): 16-26.* The struggle (ca. 1775-1810) of Virginia Baptists for the disestablishment of the state church and the privilege of freedom of religion for all men has had great implications for both the church and state in America. Three doctrines served as the foundation for the Baptist position: the nature of salvation, the nature of the church, and a belief in the necessity for the separation of civil and ecclesiastical authority. Baptists did not achieve separation of church and state alone (for the active aid of Jefferson and Madison was also a considerable factor), but did serve as a constant reminder of the necessity of securing what they believed to be the inalienable rights of men. Covers 1775-1810. Based largely on the writings of John Leland and other primary sources; 62 notes. H. M. Parker, Jr.

1044. Greenleaf, Richard E. THE INQUISITION IN SPANISH LOUISIANA, 1762-1800. *New Mexico Hist. Rev. 1975 50(1): 45-72.* The first Tribunal of the Inquisition was established in Mexico in 1569, with Mexican and Spanish Inquisition records indicating a close surveillance of Catholics and foreigners who flouted religious orthodoxy and the power of the Spanish government. Many people under surveillance never came to trial, and when the Territory of Louisiana was ceded by Spain to France in 1799, the Mexican Tribunal had a large amount of data on heresy in Louisiana. 56 notes. J. H. Krenkel

1045. Gribbin, William. VERMONT'S UNIVERSALIST CONTROVERSY OF 1824. *Vermont Hist. 1973 41(2): 82-94.* Few protested the choice of Robert Bartlett, a Universalist minister, to give the 1825 election sermon. This phenomenon demonstrates that the Puritan ideal of a community agreeing in polity and theology was almost dead. Universalism was first preached in Vermont in 1795; it organized as an association in 1804 and held a state convention in 1833. The legitimacy of Universalist ordination and right to officiate at marriages had been questioned and their success in proselytism had evoked a large polemical literature. A Methodist's 1817 election sermon was anti-British and antislavery; in 1824 attempts to elect a Methodist narrowly failed. Presbyterian and Congregationalist election sermons, 1823-29, called on the state to suppress sin and on citizens to obey the Higher Law. Bartlett, however, called only for religious liberty under tolerant rulers. 50 notes. T. D. S. Bassett

1046. Groberg, Joseph H. THE MORMON DISFRANCHISEMENTS OF 1882 TO 1892. *Brigham Young U. Studies 1976 16(3): 399-408.* For 10 years the federal government, the territorial legislatures of Idaho and Arizona, and the state legislatures of Idaho and Nevada tried to deny the vote to Mormons because of their religious practices and beliefs. Fearing bloc voting by polygamous religionists, many territorial or state agencies sought to disfranchise them between 1882 and 1892. Details laws and court decisions which may have infringed upon the Mormons' religious liberties. M. S. Legan

1047. Guggisberg, Hans R. RELIGIOUS FREEDOM AND THE HISTORY OF THE CHRISTIAN WORLD IN ROGER WILLIAMS' THOUGHT. *Early Am. Literature 1977 12(1): 36-48.* Roger Williams, the founder of Rhode Island, based his defense of religious liberty on the Holy Scriptures and the history of Christianity. His historical documentation used only those available materials which fit into his general concept of a Christian society. His aim was not universal knowledge and general understanding of the past; history simply provided the facts and examples to support his pleas for religious freedom and the separation of church and state. Primary sources; 46 notes. J. N. Friedel

1048. Harakas, Stanley S. ORTHODOX CHURCH-STATE THEORY AND AMERICAN DEMOCRACY. *Greek Orthodox Theological Rev. 1976 21(4): 399-422.* Discusses the Orthodox symphonia theory in light of American democracy and separation of church and state, 17c-20c.

1049. Harrow, Joan Ray. JOSEPH L. RAWLINS, FATHER OF UTAH STATEHOOD. *Utah Hist. Q. 1976 44(1): 59-75.* Joseph L. Rawlins (1850-1926), Utah educator, lawyer, politician, and statesman, was an active Democrat. As Utah's delegate to Congress from 1893-95, he introduced the Enabling Act that provided for Utah's admission into the Union. He later served as US Senator (1897-1901). While many worked for statehood, few labored as diligently and long as Rawlins to reorient Utah politics, ease church-federal tensions, and shepherd the statehood bill through Congress. Based on primary and secondary sources; 3 illus., 29 notes. J. L. Hazelton

1050. Hartley, William. "IN ORDER TO BE IN FASHION I AM CALLED ON A MISSION": WILFORD WOODRUFF'S PARTING LETTER TO EMMA AS HE JOINS THE "UNDERGROUND." *Brigham Young U. Studies 1974 15(1): 110-112.* In the 1880's as the federal government began enforcing a new antipolygamy law, many Mormons, fearing arrest and conviction for "unlawful cohabitation," fled into exile or the Mormon "underground." This article reprints and describes a letter written in 1885 by Wilford Woodruff, at the time President of the Council of Twelve and Church Historian, to one of his wives, Emma Smith Woodruff, while he was in exile. Most of the letter concerns information about the family's economic affairs, his advice on how to deal with federal officers, his pride in his children's activities, and other personal matters. M. S. Legan

1051. Haw, James. THE PATRONAGE FOLLIES: BENNET ALLEN, JOHN MORTON JORDAN, AND THE FALL OF HORATIO SHARPE. *Maryland Hist. Mag. 1976 71(2): 134-150.* Lord Calvert's attempts at revenue reform in Maryland brought special agent and man-on-the-make John Morton Jordan to the colony in 1766, setting off an intense struggle for power and influence between him and Governor Horatio Sharpe and the influential Daniel and Walter Dulany. At the same time the sycophantic and intensely political Reverend Bennet Allen was forcing Sharpe to violate Maryland's laws against ecclesiastical pluralism by giving Allen control of St. James and All-Saints' Parishes. Four years of internal turmoil culminated in Sharpe's ouster by Baltimore in favor of Robert Eden, protracted brawls in the press and streets over Anglican Allen's machinations and Jordan's schemings, and the conviction on the part of many Marylanders that such misuse of patronage was proof of the Commonwealth thinkers' belief in English ministerial tyranny and the corruption of representative institutions. Based on original correspondence, the Archives of Maryland and secondary sources; 46 notes. G. J. Bobango

1052. Hill, A. Shrady. THE PARSON'S CAUSE. *Hist. Mag. of the Protestant Episcopal Church 1977 46(1): 5-35.* Salaries of colonial Virginia Anglican ministers were paid in tobacco. When the demand for tobacco was high, the clergy prospered; when low, they suffered. Prices were not stable, hence there was considerable uncertainty from year to year over what the clergy could expect in purchasing power. Treats not only the economic ramifications of the arrangement but also deals with the political aspects of a state-supported clergy in an area that was becoming increasingly hostile to Anglicanism. Patrick Henry earned some of his early honors by opposing state support to the established church. Even the courts openly defied the English government. At the same time, the indifference of the clergy toward the colonists failed to gain the support or the respect of the latter. Covers 1750-70. Primary and secondary sources; 79 notes, 2 appendixes. H. M. Parker, Jr.

1053. Hinton, Wayne K. MILLARD FILLMORE, UTAH'S FRIEND IN THE WHITE HOUSE. *Utah Hist. Q. 1980 48(2): 112-128.* Millard Fillmore's moderate attitude when he became president after Zachary Taylor's death in July 1850 temporarily settled the slavery question in the territories. Favoring local rule, Fillmore appointed Mormons to four of seven of Utah's teritorial offices, and made Brigham Young governor. Considering controversy over Young's authoritarian rule and over John M. Bernhisel's election as territorial delegate to be attempts to discredit his administration, Fillmore continued his support of the Mormons. In 1874, Utahans renamed the new territorial seat Fillmore in his honor. Based on Journal History, LDS Archives; 8 illus., 53 notes. J. L. Hazelton

1054. Hogue, William M. THE RELIGIOUS CONSPIRACY THEORY OF THE AMERICAN REVOLUTION: ANGLICAN MOTIVE. *Church Hist. 1976 45(3): 277-292.* Non-Anglicans feared that the Church of England was part of an English conspiracy against their liberties. Consequently, many activities of the Anglican Society for the Propagation of the Gospel in Foreign Parts were looked upon with disdain in anti-Anglican New England. Pamphlets published during this controversy show that although the clash of these rival religions was vigorous, the differences were not, by themselves, sufficiently forceful to motivate Revolutionary thoughts. However, they combined with other forms of British imperialism, and many thinkers began to feel that the mother country was interested not only in building a political empire, but in establishing an ecclesiastical one as well. 62 notes. M. D. Dibert

1055. Holmes, Jack D. L. SPANISH RELIGIOUS POLICY IN WEST FLORIDA: ENLIGHTENED OR EXPEDIENT? *J. of Church and State 1973 15(2): 259-270.* Examines the liberal policy of Spain toward American colonists in the 1780's. S

1056. Huber, Donald L. TIMOTHY CUTLER: THE CONVERT AS CONTROVERSIALIST. *Hist. Mag. of the Protestant Episcopal Church 1975 44(4): 489-496.* In the autumn of 1722 Timothy Cutler, Rector at Yale, converted to Anglicanism. From that time until 1730 he became the chief protagonist of the Church of England in Massachusetts, where the established church was the Congregational. He served as rector of Christ Church, Boston. Delineates some of Cutler's gadfly undertakings as he sought relief for the Anglican church from the Congregationalists. In some instances he was successful, in others he failed; but for the most part he was successful in forcing important concessions from the Congregationalists. For reasons unknown he gradually withdrew from the arena, but only after he had made a mark for himself as controversialist. Based largely on primary sources, including Foote, *Annals of King's Chapel* and Perry, *Historical Collections Relating to the American Colonial Church*; 40 notes. H. M. Parker, Jr.

1057. Hudson, Winthrop S. THE ISSUE OF CHURCH AND STATE: A HISTORICAL PERSPECTIVE. *Religion in Life 1977 46(3): 278-288.* Discusses separation of church and state in the federal government; despite the theoretical separation of the two, religious thought and persuasion have always affected politics, 1776-1976.

1058. Isaac, Rhys. RELIGION AND AUTHORITY: PROBLEMS OF THE ANGLICAN ESTABLISHMENT IN THE ERA OF THE GREAT AWAKENING AND THE PARSONS' CAUSE. *William and Mary Q. 1973 30(1): 3-36.* Traces the internal problems of the church during the breaking up of the coordinate relationship between church and state in Virginia, including vestry disputes, the negative image and low status of the clergy, and clerical corporatist ambitions. Anticlericalism was dramatically abetted by the Parsons' Cause, the trial of the Reverend John Brunskill, and the dismissal of the Reverend Thomas Robinson from the College. The dissenters' influence was growing; and as church power waned, so did the authority of the gentry establishment. Covers 1730-60. Based on church and court records and on secondary sources; 2 tables, 134 notes. H. M. Ward

1059. Johansen, Robin B. and Rosen, Sanford Jay. STATE AND LOCAL REGULATION OF RELIGIOUS SOLICITATION OF FUNDS: A CONSTUTITIONAL PERSPECTIVE. *Ann. of the Am. Acad. of Pol. and Social Sci. 1979 (446): 116-135.* State and local governments, to regulate solicitation on behalf of religious groups, are using existing laws and also enacting new laws in a growing effort by government to regulate and monitor the actions of all religious groups. Implicit in this growing trend is the arrogation by state and local officials and lawmakers of the authority to decide what is "religion" and therefore exempt from regulation. The increased regulation of religious solicitation touches a longstanding tension in American life involving the separation of church and state, and invokes three central themes: our money, our privacy, and our faith. Most laws and regulations currently used to regulate religious solicitation are constitutionally infirm. They are either too vague to protect against arbitrary or capricious enforcement by public officials, or they place officials in the position of deciding what is religious and what is secular activity. The use of traditional time, place, and manner regulations—and sparing use of the existing criminal fraud law—are better means of curbing abuse in religious solicitation, and will prevent dangerous blurring of the boundary between church and state. Covers the 1970's. J/S

1060. Jorgensen, Victor W. and Hardy, B. Carmon. THE TAYLOR-COWLEY AFFAIR AND THE WATERSHED OF MORMON HISTORY. *Utah Hist. Q. 1980 48(1): 4-36.* Conflicting interpretations of the 1890 Woodruff Manifesto led to the continued practice of polygamy among Mormon leaders. The 1904-07 hearings to unseat Senator Reed Smoot broadcast the continued practice of polygamy to the American public. John W. Taylor and Matthias F. Cowley were dropped from the Quorum of the Twelve Apostles in 1905 as a maneuver to help Senator Smoot retain his seat. They were casualties of the radical changes forced upon Mormon theology at this time. Based on family papers and church records in the LDS Archives, and other primary sources; 15 illus., 74 notes. J. L. Hazelton

1061. Keller, Allan. THE CATHOLICS IN MARYLAND. *Early Am. Life 1978 9(3): 18-21, 78-79.* Chronicles the establishment of Maryland as a Catholic colony; covers 1634-92. Discusses the efforts of the colony's proprietor, Cecilius Calvert, 2d Lord Baltimore, to retain the Catholic Church as the official church of the colony, while maintaining strict religious tolerance; touches on agricultural and economic conditions.

1062. Kelley, Dean M. DEPROGRAMMING AND RELIGIOUS LIBERTY. *Civil Liberties Rev. 1977 4(2): 23-33.* Religious deprogramming of members of cult-like religious sects has ramifications involving kidnapping, restraint, and first amendment rights.

1063. Kelley, Dean M. WHEN RELIGION IS PAID TO BE SILENT. *Worldview 1973 16(14): 32-37.* Analyzes ramifications of *U.S. vs. Christian Echoes National Ministry, Inc.*, in which the 10th U.S. Circuit Court of Appeals in Denver "took away a religious organization's tax exemption because it had engaged in political activity," 1950's-70's. M. L. Frey

1064. Kerrine, Theodore M. and Neuhaus, Richard John. MEDIATING STRUCTURES: A PARADIGM FOR DEMOCRATIC PLURALISM. *Ann. of the Am. Acad. of Pol. and Social Sci. 1979 (446): 10-18.* The modern welfare state has tended to undermine the "mediating structures" that link the individual in his private life and the vast institutions of the public order. Such institutions as churches and families are important not only because they are the value-generating and sustaining institutions in democratic society, but also because they are the agencies through which people most frequently interact in public life. The steady erosion of these natural communities by government expansion has resulted in public policies which lack the confidence of the people most directly affected by them. At the same time, there is an increasing desire for government services. Churches have been effectively excluded from considerations of public policy by a view which identifies the public realm solely with the state. Where church participation is acknowledged, the forces of secularization and professionalization continue to assault the religious character of that involvement while the expansionist state attempts to bring churches further within the sphere of government control. The mediating structures proposal calls for an imaginative recognition of institutions like churches in public policy in order to bridge the ever-widening division between belief and public purpose. Covers the 1970's. J

1065. Kessell, John L. FRIARS VERSUS BUREAUCRATS: THE MISSION AS A THREATENED INSTITUTION ON THE ARIZO-

NA-SONORA FRONTIER, 1767-1842. *Western Hist. Q. 1974 5(2): 151-162.* During the Franciscans's control of the Indian missions on the Arizona-Sonora frontier (1767-1842), reforming bureaucrats repeatedly threatened to eclipse the mission as a frontier institution. The missions survived the enlightened despotism of Charles III, the flux of the Napoleonic era, and the turmoil of Mexican independence simply because the bureaucrats could not provide a practical alternative. 32 notes.
D. L. Smith

1066. Kirkpatrick, Gabriel W. BUT NOT TO YIELD. *Daughters of the Am. Revolution Mag. 1973 107(5): 412-413, 496.* Persecution of Quakers in the Massachusetts Bay Colony 1639-61. S

1067. Knopff, Rainer. QUEBEC'S "HOLY WAR" AS "REGIME" POLITICS: REFLECTIONS ON THE GUIBORD CASE. *Can. J. of Pol. Sci. [Canada] 1979 12(2): 315-331. Brown* v. *Les Curé et Marguilliers de l'oeuvre et de la Fabrique de la Paroisse de Montréal* (1874), or the Guibord case, in 19th-century Quebec, was a leading episode of the "Holy War," or quarrel between Ultramontanism and Liberalism. The various court decisions (1870-74) differed in their interpretation of the right of the Church to deprive Joseph Guibord of burial in consecrated ground because of his membership in the anticlerical Institut Canadien, which advocated separation of Church and state. Based on court reports and decisions; 37 notes. G. P. Cleyet

1068. Krugler, John D. LORD BALTIMORE, ROMAN CATHOLICS, AND TOLERATION: RELIGIOUS POLICY IN MARYLAND DURING THE EARLY CATHOLIC YEARS, 1634-1649. *Catholic Hist. Rev. 1979 65(1): 49-75.* The religious policy established in Maryland resulted primarily because Baltimore was Catholic. His policy reflected the realities of being a Catholic in 17th-century England. To overcome the penal legislation and the lack of assistance from Rome, Catholics developed a sense of self-reliance and independence from their "outlawed" Church. Baltimore reflected this pragmatic approach in dealing with the Catholic laity and the Jesuits in Maryland. As an English Catholic, Baltimore rejected the concept that the faith of the subjects must conform to the ruler's. He assumed that religion was essentially a private matter. The Act Concerning Religion (1649) indicated that his original policy failed. A

1069. Lemieux, Donald. SOME LEGAL AND PRACTICAL ASPECTS OF THE OFFICE OF *COMMISSAIRE ORDONNATEUR* OF FRENCH LOUISIANA. *Louisiana Studies 1975 14(4): 379-393.* The French developed a system of checks and balances to control the two officials—the governor and the *commissaire ordonnateur*—who were in charge of colonial administration in Louisiana 1712-69. They were invested with twin powers: the governor acted as the military leader and the chief administrator, the *commissaire ordonnateur* as the chief legal and financial officer. Constant bickering between the two officials, which resulted from a stalemate over duties, slow communication, and personal ambition, weakened the government of Louisiana and reflected the general condition of the bureaucracy. The *commissaire ordonnateur* was sent from France for an indefinite period of time with a salary that was not lucrative; the post was considered as a stepping-stone. Instructions for the post embraced five areas: religion, justice, police, military, and Indians. The *commissaire ordonnateur* often found himself in the predicament of defending his position because he manipulated large sums and directed an army of subordinates who often used their position to profit from commercial activities. Even the most able found their efforts subordinated to the demands of the Colonial System. Based on primary and secondary sources; 52 notes. B. A. Glasrud

1070. Lévesque, Delmas. UN QUÉBEC EN REDÉFINITION [Quebec in redefinition]. *Action Natl. [Canada] 1977 67(1): 16-33.* At the turn of the 20th century, English Canadians saw Quebec as a backward, priest-ridden province dominated by the Catholic Church. Quebec was transformed only by industrialization imported from New England and Ontario, which absorbed the excess farm population. In 200 years, the hegemony of the Catholic Church was challenged only during the 1830's. Catholicism thwarted modernization, but also protected Quebec from the American cultural imperialism which conquered English Canada. In an independent Quebec, the state would be expected to assume the role formerly held by the Church. The text is a lecture prepared for students of L'École Internationale de Bordeaux at the École des Hautes Études Commerciales, Montreal, August, 1972. 5 notes.
A. W. Novitsky

1071. Lippy, Charles H. THE 1780 MASSACHUSETTS CONSTITUTION: RELIGIOUS ESTABLISHMENT OR CIVIL RELIGION? *J. of Church and State 1978 20(3): 533-549.* The Massachusetts Constitutional Convention of 1780 was attempting to establish civil religion, not a particular religion, with the improvement of public morals as the goal. 36 notes. E. E. Eminhizer

1072. Lyman, Edward Leo. ISAAC TRUMBO AND THE POLITICS OF UTAH STATEHOOD. *Utah Hist Q. 1973 41(2): 128-149.* Isaac Trumbo (1858-1912) was engaged in 1887 as a non-Mormon agent to promote favorable news items in Utah's sixth bid for statehood. He was also effective in getting favorable modification of federal laws against the Mormons. His greatest effort was as a lobbyist in Congress. When Utah became a state in 1896, Trumbo made an unsuccessful bid to become one of its first U.S. senators. 5 illus., 74 notes. D. L. Smith

1073. Mackinnon, William P. THE GAP IN THE BUCHANAN REVIVAL: THE UTAH EXPEDITION OF 1857-58. *Utah Hist. Q. 1977 45(1): 36-46.* The writings comprising the current revival of interest in James Buchanan rely excessively on Philip S. Klein's eastern-oriented biography, *President James Buchanan.* This leaves a gap in understanding the Utah Expedition (1857-58) and Buchanan's Mormon policy. Norman F. Furniss' study of Buchanan's western policies can be used as a foundation for a much needed, thorough analysis of the decision to intervene in Utah, related cabinet deliberations, and the impact of both on Buchanan's handling of the Southern secession crisis. Primary and secondary sources; 2 illus., 34 notes. J. L. Hazelton

1074. Maddex, Jack P. FROM THEOCRACY TO SPIRITUALITY: THE SOUTHERN PRESBYTERIAN REVERSAL ON CHURCH AND STATE. *J. of Presbyterian Hist. 1976 54(4): 438-457.* Challenges the premise that Southern Presbyterians embraced the doctrine of the spirituality of the Church before 1861. Claims that antebellum Southern Presbyterians did not teach consistently absolute separation of religion from politics, or even church from state. Most were proslavery social activists who worked through the church to defend slavery and reform its practice. Only during Reconstruction, in drastically altered circumstances, did they take up the cause of a non-secular church—borrowing the concept from the conservative Presbyterians in the border states, such as Stuart Robinson of Louisville. Based on official ecclesiastical documents, current church newspapers and secondary sources; 139 notes.
H. M. Parker, Jr.

1075. Małajny, Ryszard M. STOSUNEK PAŃSTWA DO RELIGII W STANACH ZJEDNOCZONYCH AMERYKI [Attitude of the state to religion in the USA]. *Studia Nauk Politycznych [Poland] 1978 3(33): 117-137.* The division of the state and the church in the United States has been implemented in keeping with the letter of law but not in the sphere of political life and religious ideology. Though the state is separated from religious associations, no such distinction occurs between the state and religious ideology. Thus, the author has confined his brief to the ties between the state and the church in the sphere of political life and religious ideology and discusses the socio-political position of churches and religious sects as well as the religiousness of the American society. The attitude of the state to religion is examined through a survey of a number of decisions about religion by the president, Congress, and Supreme Court. In the three cases effective support of Christianity is observed with a simultaneous legal observance of the state-church division. The active backing of religion by the federal government is well justified by the capitalist state's need to use religion as a stabilizing factor. Thus religion acts as a watchdog of the social order. 51 notes. J

1076. Maloney, Wiley S. SHORT CREEK STORY. *Am. West 1974 11(2): 16-23, 60-62.* Hard evidence of previously rumored polygamy in Short Creek on the Arizona-Utah border began to surface when women applying for relief for their children listed the same man as their husband, some of the wives being only 13, 14, or 15 years of age. State officials in Arizona were alarmed at the resurgence of a so-called fundamentalist movement back to pioneer Mormonism, despite the fact that the church itself had long since outlawed polygamy. Other isolated western communities were allegedly guilty of the same offense. In 1953, Arizona arrested nearly every participating adult and made the children wards of the state; all were jailed or put in protective custody. Utah cooperated, and handled its similar but lesser problem in a modified way. 8 illus.
D. L. Smith

1077. Mansfield, John H. NEW ENGLAND DISSENT, 1630-1833: THE BAPTISTS AND THE SEPARATION OF CHURCH AND STATE. *Am. J. of Legal Hist. 1973 17(2): 185-201.* Reviews William G. McLoughlin's *New England Dissent, 1630-1833: The Baptists and the Separation of Church and State* (Cambridge, Massachusetts: Harvard U. Pr., 1971).

1078. Marty, Martin E. LIVING WITH ESTABLISHMENT AND DISESTABLISHMENT IN NINETEENTH-CENTURY ANGLO-AMERICA. *J. of Church and State 1976 18(1): 61-77.* Secularization of religion is a problem in modern religious study. Makes a comparative study of the effects of disestablishment on American religious life to about 1860 and of establishment on English religious life in the same period. Both got what they wanted; America, a group of national churches, and England, to retain the privileges of the establishment while giving toleration to others. Toleration was extended by legislation in the first half of the 19th century. Arguments defending establishment in England are reviewed, as are those for disestablishment in America. 42 notes.
E. E. Eminhizer

1079. Matter, Robert Allen. MISSIONS IN THE DEFENSE OF SPANISH FLORIDA, 1566-1710. *Florida Hist. Q. 1975 54(1): 18-38.* Refutes the belief that missions played an important role in the defense of Spanish Florida from both Indians and the English. Suggests that a "debilitating church-state feud" about such things as jurisdiction over the Indians and the determination of priorities between military security and religious work actually weakened the Spanish hold on Florida. Illustrations are given from both the Jesuit (1566-72) and Franciscan (1573-1710) periods, showing the discord between the religious orders and the various governors who were responsible for the placement of troops. Concludes that the friars were too involved with their religious duties to see the advantages of a militarily strong colony, and so obstructed military development. Based on primary and secondary sources; 68 notes.
J. E. Findling

1080. McCants, David A. THE AUTHENTICITY OF JAMES MAURY'S ACCOUNT OF PATRICK HENRY'S SPEECH IN THE PARSONS' CAUSE. *Southern Speech Communication J. 1976 42(1): 20-34.* Evaluates the historical reliability of the Reverend James Maury's account of lawyer Patrick Henry's Parsons' Cause speech regarding the role of the clergy in society in Virginia in 1763.

1081. McKillop, Lucille. THE TOURO INFLUENCE—WASHINGTON'S SPIRIT PREVAILS. *Rhode Island Jewish Hist. Notes 1974 6(4): 614-628.* An address on religious liberty made at the Touro Synagogue, Newport, Rhode Island to commemorate an exchange of letters in 1790 between Moses Seixas, President of the Newport Congregation, and George Washington. S

1082. McLoughlin, William G. BARRINGTON CONGREGATIONALISTS VS. SWANSEA BAPTISTS, 1711. *Rhode Island Hist. 1973 32(1): 19-21.* Reproduces and analyzes a 1711 petition which led in 1717 to the separation of Barrington from Swansea. In the petition the Congregationalist minority claimed persecution by the Baptist majority. With the creation of Barrington in 1717 the roles were reversed and the Congregationalist majority taxed the Baptist and Anglican minorities to support the town's meeting house and church. When the longstanding boundary dispute with Massachusetts was finally settled in 1746, Barrington along with a number of other towns became part of Rhode Island. Based on the 1711 petition and secondary sources.
P. J. Coleman

1083. McLoughlin, William G. SOME REMARKS ON THE FRAGILITY OF RELIGIOUS FREEDOM. *Rhode Island Jewish Hist. Notes 1978 7(4): 534-540.* Reflects on the notion and practice of separation of church and state in America since the 17th century.

1084. McLoughlin, William G. TIVERTON'S FIGHT FOR RELIGIOUS LIBERTY, 1692-1724. *Rhode Island Hist. 1979 38(2): 35-37.* For three decades the Massachusetts town of Tiverton refused to tax itself for the support of the Congregational Church, as directed by the provincial legislature. Based on archival records in Boston, Dartmouth, and Tiverton and on minutes of the Rhode Island Quaker meetings; map, 4 notes. P. J. Coleman

1085. Mead, Sidney E. THE THEOLOGY OF THE REPUBLIC AND THE ORTHODOX MIND. *J. of the Am. Acad. of Religion 1976 44(1): 105-113.* The new world in America represented a new kind of commonwealth in Christendom where religious pluralism was encouraged and the rights of sectarian groups and divergent forms of religion were protected. Civil authority placed limits on conflict among Christian groups. Discusses the problems this situation has posed for orthodox groups. E. R. Lester

1086. Meredith, Howard. WHIRLWIND: A STUDY OF CHURCH-STATE RELATIONSHIPS. *Hist. Mag. of the Protestant Episcopal Church 1974 43(4): 297-304.* Conflict arose 1904-14 between the government agent for the Cheyenne Indians and Arapaho Indians, George W. H. Stouch, and the Indian community in western Oklahoma at the Whirlwind Day School. The government's demand for attendance at the Agency Boarding School and the closing of Whirlwind School were strongly resisted by the community and by the Episcopal Bishop of Oklahoma and Indian Territories. The church's role could not be tolerated by a bureaucracy intent on its insensitive program of acculturation. 40 notes.
R. V. Ritter

1087. Miller, J. R. HONORÉ MERCIER, LA MINORITÉ PROTESTANTE DU QUÉBEC ET LA LOI RELATIVE AU RÈGLEMENT DE LA QUESTION DES BIENS DES JÉSUITES [Honoré Mercier, the Protestant minority of Quebec, and the law governing the question of the properties belonging to the Jesuits]. *Rev. d'Hist. de l'Amérique Française [Canada] 1974 27(4): 483-508.* Recounts the attempt of Honoré Mercier, First Minister of Quebec, to resolve the problems occasioned by legislation governing the disposition of lands once granted to the Jesuits, following his rise to power in 1886.

1088. Miller, J. R. THE JESUITS' ESTATES ACT CRISIS: "AN INCIDENT IN A CONSPIRACY OF SEVERAL YEARS' STANDING." *J. of Can. Studies 1974 9(3): 36-50.* Rejects Orange bigotry and general Protestant opposition as a satisfactory explanation for the furor over the Jesuits' Estates Act. Slow economic growth brought pre-Confederation conflicts to the surface of politics, and the Jesuit Estates agitation was in the mainstream of English Canadian life. Covers the 1880's. Based on personal papers, House of Commons debates, newspapers, periodicals, theses, secondary works; 71 notes. G. E. Panting

1089. Moody, Eric N. NEVADA'S ANTI-MORMON LEGISLATION OF 1887 AND SOUTHERN IDAHO ANNEXATION. *Nevada Hist. Soc. Q. 1979 22(1): 21-32.* Although hostility toward Mormons long prevailed in Nevada, the anti-Mormon forces abstained from imposing test oaths on the Mormon populace until 1887 when the legislature enacted laws designed to disenfranchise Mormons. Senator William Stewart promoted the legislation in order to further his scheme to annex the southern portion of Idaho to Nevada. But the new test oath legislation was reversed by the Nevada courts in 1888. Archival newspapers, and secondary sources; 50 notes. H. T. Lovin

1090. Moore, John S. THE STRUGGLE FOR FREEDOM IN VIRGINIA. *Baptist Hist. and Heritage 1976 11(3): 160-168.* The United States became the first nation in the world to insure religious freedom for all in its organic laws. The long struggle of Baptists to achieve this required nearly two centuries, involving much sacrifice and persecution. A large amount of credit must go to the tireless and persevering Virginia Baptists. Covers the 17th and 18th centuries. Based largely on secondary sources; 25 notes. H. M. Parker, Jr.

1091. Mulder, John M. WILLIAM LIVINGSTON: PROPAGANDIST AGAINST EPISCOPACY. *J. of Presbyterian Hist. 1976 54(1): 83-104.* William Livingston opposed the establishment of King's College (now Columbia University). He feared that a college under Episcopal influence would create an atmosphere of authoritarianism in all areas of the colony's life. Thus his opposition to an American episcopacy was not a sudden emergence. Livingston (1723-90) opposed bishops on the Reformation principle of equality of clergy, as well as the complete separation of temporal and spiritual power. He portrayed the effort to establish an Anglican bishop in America as the ecclesiastical side of political imperialism. His battle against episcopacy played some role in formulating the ideology of the Revolution and attracting popular support. His anticlericalism also signaled a profound change in American religious life—the

rise of the articulate layman. Based largely on articles from the *Independent Reflector*, the Livingston Papers in the Massachusetts Historical Society and secondary materials; illus., 82 notes.
H. M. Parker, Jr.

1092. Neier, Aryeh. THE FIRST AMENDMENT: FIRST IN IMPORTANCE. *Crisis 1975 82(9): 356-359.* Of all the constitutional rights, First Amendment rights are first in importance. Freedom of speech, press, worship, and assembly allow those who suffer grievances to call attention to their plight, to share their experiences with others, to organize, and to demand correction. There are foes on the right and the left but the civil rights movement of the 1960's demonstrated the effectiveness of the First Amendment. A. G. Belles

1093. Neri, Michael C. NARCISO DURÁN AND THE SECULARIZATION OF THE CALIFORNIA MISSIONS. *Americas (Acad. of Am. Franciscan Hist.) 1977 33(3): 411-429.* Spanish-born Franciscan Narciso Durán (1776-1846) was the church official primarily responsible for California Indian missions during the post-independence process of secularization. He did not refuse to cooperate with the secular authorities but repeatedly urged ways to lessen the disruption caused. He particularly was concerned with the situation of the Indians themselves but was not indifferent to the larger welfare of Mexican California. Primary sources; 75 notes. D. Bushnell

1094. Patton, Frank, Jr. RELIGION BY PERMISSION OF THE GOVERNMENT. *Worldview 1974 17(12): 31-35.* Discusses church and state and freedom of religion issues involved in the exemption of church property from city real estate taxes in the 1960's and 70's.

1095. Pearson, Samuel C., Jr. CHRISTIANITY IN BRITISH NORTH AMERICA. *Encounter 1978 39(1): 85-91.* In Robert T. Handy's *A History of the Churches in the United States and Canada* (New York, 1977), the author ably presents the view that while the United States and Canada have some similar attitudes toward religion (e.g., neither country has been comfortable with an image of itself as a secular nation), differences in their histories (e.g., US guilt feelings about slavery, and loyalist feelings among 18th-century "English" Canadians) have made Canada less concerned than the United States with rigid separation of church and state.

1096. Pearson, Samuel C., Jr. NATURE'S GOD: A REASSESSMENT OF THE RELIGION OF THE FOUNDING FATHERS. *Religion in Life 1977 46(2): 152-165.* Examines the religious beliefs of the founding fathers, discusses their roots in 18th-century English philosophical thought, and shows their impact upon the religious development of the new nation and the separation of church and state. Covers 1695-1830.

1097. Penton, M. James. JEHOVAH'S WITNESSES AND THE SECULAR STATE: A HISTORICAL ANALYSIS OF DOCTRINE. *J. of Church and State 1979 21(1): 55-72.* Jehovah's Witnesses have been persecuted for refusing military service, not participating in the political system, and avoiding patriotic exercises. Their actions have been based on the concept of the secular state developed by Charles Taze Russell, who believed that Christ's return was imminent and that the secular powers would soon be destroyed. His successor as Watch Tower Society president, Joseph Franklin Rutherford, elaborated on Russell's concepts, developing the concept of higher law. The Witnesses were persecuted in the United States and Canada during World War I. Hostility to the state declined as court victories guaranteed their rights. In the 1960's, doctrine reflected this change by distinguishing between relative and absolute obedience to the state. 72 notes. S

1098. Perin, Roberto. TROPPO ARDENTI SACERDOTI: THE CONROY MISSION REVISITED. *Can. Hist. Rev. [Canada] 1980 61(3): 283-304.* Reassesses the mission of George Conroy (1832-78), an Irish bishop and Apostolic Delegate to the province of Quebec in 1877-78. Worried about the French Canadian clergy's involvement in politics, the Holy See chose Cardinal Paul Cullen's protégé to impose a solution elaborated in Rome. Conroy did not study the roots of the crisis within the Quebec Church, but rather sought to appease the ruling Liberal Party in Ottawa. In so doing, he transformed the Catholic Church from a vital institution, relatively free from the partisan manipulation characterizing Canadian life since the advent of responsible government in 1848, into a tool of the politicians. Until 1878, the Church had been a rampart against an aggressive Anglo-Saxon nationalism which sought to mold Canada in its image. After this date, it was much less effective in resisting the "political compromises" which led to the triumph of this nationalism. Based on the Archives of the Propaganda Fide in Rome and other primary sources; 81 notes. A

1099. Peter, Karl A. THE DEATH OF HUTTERITE CULTURE: A REJOINDER. *Phylon 1979 40(2): 189-194.* James S. Frideres (see *Phylon* 1972 33(3): 260-265) took true statements and applied false conclusions. Restrictive legislation by the Western Canadian provincial governments discriminates against the Hutterites but is not aimed at their "cultural genocide." 6 notes. G. R. Schroeder

1100. Pfisterer, K. Dieterich. RELIGION ALS EIN FERMENT DER FREIHEIT IN DER AMERIKANISCHEN REVOLUTION [Religion as a ferment of liberty in the American Revolution]. *Amerikastudien/Am. Studies [West Germany] 1976 21(2): 217-238.* The controversy over religious liberty was comprised of two movements of independence, one of political liberation from the threat of an English state church, the other of social emancipation from the European state church system. The unconditional and resourceful support of the majority of the clergy throughout the colonies was devoted to this movement and provided an indispensable second line of leadership in staving off Imperial interference with the rule of the clergy and magistrates as the natural aristocracy of the parishes. By the time of the Revolution, heirs of the 'Great Awakening' in New England and Virginia had, on the other hand, launched drives for the abolition of the traditional mainstay of social order in Western Christendom by demanding the very separation of religious and civil authority in the parishes. From the perspective of religious liberty, the American Revolution embraced intellectual, political, and social movements which appealed to different publics. The Baptists provide the clearest illustration of religious liberty as a social movement. They rejected deference in favor of conversion, the parish aristocracy and its coercion for congregational democracy and persuasion. In their drawn-out fight against New England ecclesiastical establishments they insisted on the church as a voluntary association and projected the communicative evangelist rather than the condescending cleric as the successful new leader thus stemming the tide of secularization. They quickly grew into a mass movement during the Revolution and did much to promote the voluntary association approach as a major institution in American civilization. In Virginia they provided much of the pressure that made it possible for Thomas Jefferson's *Bill for Establishing Religious Freedom* (1786) to pass the legislature and they urged James Madison to work for a clearly-worded constitutional guarantee of religious liberty in the First Amendment (1791). On the basis of their voluntary associations they built a culture which included the poor whites and the Negroes, and they added conversion to honor and virtue as central values in Southern civilization. Finally Baptist history serves as a reminder that New England and Virginia are not identical with the American experience. The early radical anti-authoritarianism of the Baptists was modified by the example of Pennsylvania which taught them that voluntary association was an adequate institutional expression both locally and regionally for a religious experience that had been an integral part of the settlement process in America and which had not been distorted by the interference of the state. J

1101. Philip, Kenneth. JOHN COLLIER AND THE CRUSADE TO PROTECT INDIAN RELIGIOUS FREEDOM, 1920-1926. *J. of Ethnic Studies 1973 1(1): 22-38.* As part of the general program of Americanizing the Indian population, the Indian Bureau in the 1920's attempted to suppress various aspects of Indian culture, including the ceremonial dances of the Pueblos. These actions were supported by several missionary-oriented groups such as the Indian Rights Association and the YWCA Indian Department, which considered the dances as immoral and pagan. Defending the native practices of the Indians was John Collier, whose interest in subculture norms had originated from his experience as a social worker among immigrants in New York City. He formed the American Indian Defense Association in 1923 to provide legal aid and to lobby for Indian rights. Although unable to secure positive legislation to guarantee Indian religious freedom, Collier and the association forced the Indian Bureau to curb its program of cultural assimilation and to end its religious persecutions. Based on extensive primary sources, including unpublished papers of John Collier; 76 notes. T. W. Smith

1102. Pilling, Arnold R. NATIVE AMERICAN RELIGIOUS RIGHTS: CONSTITUTIONAL CONSIDERATIONS. *Indian Hist. 1979 12(1): 13-19.* General overview of Supreme Court rulings on religious liberty (under the 1st amendment) is applied to the case of the Eight Mile-Blue Creek land of California containing Indians' sacred areas, where the US Forest Service proposed road construction and logging, 1975.

1103. Poll, Richard D. THE AMERICANISM OF UTAH. *Utah Hist. Q. 1976 44(1): 76-93.* An expanded version of a speech given on Bicentennial Statehood Day, 3 January 1976. Events such as the 1876 centennial celebration, the 1896 statehood celebration, the Domínguez-Vélez de Escalante exploration, daily lives of the early settlers, economic development, and the role of the Mormons illustrate elements in Utah history in common with the American mainstream. Any ambivalence Utah's founders felt toward the United States has been transformed into commitment. Based on primary and secondary sources; 2 illus., 38 notes.
J. L. Hazelton

1104. Preus, J. C. K. FROM NORWEGIAN STATE CHURCH TO AMERICAN FREE CHURCH. *Norwegian-American Studies 1972 25: 186-224.* Examines difficulties encountered by Norwegian Americans in establishing free churches in the United States and in determining the authority which ministers were allotted, methods of finance, difficulties with doctrinal divisions, and sectarian ministers. Focuses on the establishment of a synod in Columbia and Dane counties, Wisconsin, under the leadership of Herman A. Preus. In his diary of the Official Proceedings of the Congregation, kept during 1851-60, he discusses various aspects of the free church. 14 notes. G. A. Hewlett

1105. Punch, Terrence M. THE IRISH CATHOLIC, HALIFAX'S FIRST MINORITY GROUP. *Nova Scotia Hist. Q. [Canada] 1980 10(1): 23-39.* Halifax, founded in 1749, was estimated to be about 16% Irish Catholic in 1767 and about 9% by the end of the 18th century. Although the harsh laws enacted against them were generally not enforced, Irish Catholics had no legal rights in the early history of the city. Catholic membership in the legislature was nonexistent until near the end of the century. In 1829 Lawrence O'Connor Doyle, of Irish parentage, became the first of his faith to become a lawyer and helped to overcome opposition to the Irish. 23 notes. H. M. Evans

1106. Quinlivan, Mary E. FROM PRAGMATIC ACCOMMODATION TO PRINCIPLED ACTION: THE REVOLUTION AND RELIGIOUS ESTABLISHMENT IN VIRGINIA. *West Georgia Coll. Studies in the Social Sci. 1976 15: 55-64.* Describes the situation between religion and politics during the American Revolution in Virginia, and shortly after.

1107. Rainbolt, John Corbin. THE STRUGGLE TO DEFINE "RELIGIOUS LIBERTY" IN MARYLAND, 1776-85. *J. of Church and State 1975 17(3): 443-458.* Discusses political debates regarding the definition and meaning of religious liberty in Maryland government, 1776-85.

1108. Rea, J. E. TWO RICHELIEUS IN CANADA. *Ontario Hist. [Canada] 1978 70(3): 189-200.* Discusses the relations between John Strachan, (Anglican) Archdeacon of Toronto, and Alexander Macdonnell, (Catholic) Bishop of Kingston. The traditional picture is of two men who respected each other, were friends, and worked together for similar ends. Respect and an element of friendship were there, but the men were not close friends as tradition has it. Refers to their attitudes and (usually) behind the scenes to colonial politics in the 1820's and 30's. Mainly secondary sources; 38 notes. W. B. Whitham

1109. Ritchie, Robert C. GOD AND MAMMON IN NEW NETHERLAND. *R. in Am. Hist. 1974 2(3): 353-357.* George L. Smith's *Religion and Trade in New Netherland: Dutch Origins and American Development* (Ithaca, N.Y.: Cornell U. Pr., 1973) points out that Dutch Americans in New York increased their religious liberty during the 17th century due to "economic pressure, weak governments, schismatic movements, and secular influences."

1110. Robison, Joseph B.; Steyer, Beatrice; and Stern, Marc D. THE CULTS AND THE LAW. *Patterns of Prejudice [Great Britain] 1980 14(2): 3-14.* Discusses the use of laws and legal action in combating the proseletyzing methods of some religious cults.

1111. Rock, Rosalind Z. A HISTORY OF LIBRARIES IN NEW MEXICO: SPANISH ORIGINS TO STATEHOOD. *J. of Lib. Hist. 1979 14(3): 253-273.* Traces the development of the Archives of New Mexico, the Territorial Library, and the beginning of public libraries, 1598-1912. During the Spanish and Mexican periods the literate population was small. Coupled with the Church-state conflict which existed through much of the period, lack of public interest hindered the development of a library system. The American territorial government fostered the public library system. Archival, primary, and secondary sources; 76 notes. S

1112. Rodrigues, Lêda Boechat. SUPREMA CORTE DOS ESTADOS UNIDOS: LIBERDADE DE RELIGIÃO E SEPARAÇÃO DA IGREJA E DO ESTADO [The United States Supreme Court: Freedom of religion and separation of church and state]. *Rev. Brasileira de Estudos Pol. [Brazil] 1977 (44): 73-102.* Surveys the US Supreme Court's treatment of the question of freedom of religion and separation of church and state, with respect to obligatory prayers in public schools, aid to parochial schools, exemption from mandatory school attendance beyond the 8th grade, religious observances that interfere with the usual work week, and conscientious objection to military service. While many court decisions have provoked strong criticism, they have brought about profound changes, especially in the last 20 years.
B. J. Chandler

1113. Ryan, Walter A. THE SEPARATION OF CHURCH AND STATE IN ACWORTH, NEW HAMPSHIRE. *Hist. New Hampshire 1979 34(2): 143-153.* Until 1819 each New Hampshire town or parish could establish its own church and pay the minister's salary through public taxes. Acworth, settled in 1767, began to build a meetinghouse in 1783, and acquired its first settled minister in 1789. In 1790 some residents objected to the ministerial tax, and soon the Baptists and Universalists protested the Congregationalist monopoly of the meetinghouse. The dispute simmered until the Toleration Act was passed in 1819. By 1821 Acworth had a separate town house and meetinghouse, and after 1822 Congregationalists paid their minister's salary themselves. Illus., 35 notes.
D. F. Chard

1114. Shaffer, Thomas I. FIRST AMENDMENT: HISTORY AND THE COURTS. *Rev. of Pol. 1978 40(2): 271-279.* Review article prompted by Walter Berns's *The First Amendment and the Future of American Democracy* (New York: Basic Books, 1976), argues that the Supreme Court has "drifted intolerably far away from the principles and circumstances which caused the founding generation of free Americans to amend their written Constitution by limiting the government's control of religion, assembly, and speech." He further argues that the Court "misreads law and misunderstands history." The Court can't be blamed for not following history as Berns states. Church and state problems cannot be dictated to society by Supreme Court edicts alone. Covers 18c-20c. 19 notes. L. E. Ziewacz

1115. Shankman, Arnold. CONVERSE, *THE CHRISTIAN OBSERVER* AND CIVIL WAR CENSORSHIP. *J. of Presbyterian Hist. 1974 52(3): 227-244.* Amasa Converse's Presbyterian newspaper, *The Christian Observer,* was the only paper published simultaneously in the United States and the Confederacy, until federal censorship suppressed it as subversive and Converse moved it South. S

1116. Shapiro, Walter. THE LIBERAL PLOT TO KILL GOD. *Washington Monthly 1975 7(8): 21-30.* Recounts the actions of Jeremy Lansman and Lorenzo Milam, who petitioned the Federal Communications Commission in order to have religious references removed from all broadcasting, 1972-75. S

1117. Shepherd, Allen L. GENTILE IN ZION: ALGERNON SIDNEY PADDOCK AND THE UTAH COMMISSION, 1882-1886. *Nebraska Hist. 1976 57(3): 359-377.* Delineates Algernon Sidney Paddock's service on the Utah Commission. For Paddock (1830-97) these five years in Utah provided an opportunity to remain in public life after not gaining reelection to the Senate, as well as a chance to participate in the antipolygamy campaign against the Mormons. For the Church of Jesus Christ of Latter-Day Saints, these years represented the arrival of a carpetbag federal commission, another attempt by Washington to coerce them to change what they believed to be a divinely inspired way of life.
R. Lowitt

1118. Shupe, Anson D., Jr. "DISEMBODIED ACCESS" AND TECHNOLOGICAL CONSTRAINTS ON ORGANIZATIONAL DEVELOPMENT: A STUDY OF MAIL-ORDER RELIGIONS. *J. for the Sci. Study of Religion 1976 15(2): 177-185.* Discusses the policies and role of the US Postal Service in the organizational structure of "mail-order" religious sects in the 1970's, including proselytization procedures.

1119. Sigall, Michael W. and Ottensoser, Milton D. CHURCH-STATE RELATIONS AND CIVIL LIBERTIES: A COLLEGIATE INTERPRETATION. *J. of Church and State 1974 16(3): 493-508.* Examines the political attitudes of college students in two New York universities in 1972 concerning separation of church and state in granting federal aid to religious schools and the relation of this aid to civil liberties.

1120. Smelser, Marshall. ROGER WILLIAMS. *Am. Hist. Illus. 1975 10(5): 30-38.* Discusses the life and beliefs of Roger Williams (ca 1603-1683), who founded the colony of Rhode Island on the idea of religious tolerance.

1121. Stern, Steve J. KNICKERBOCKERS WHO ASSERTED AND INSISTED: THE DUTCH INTEREST IN NEW YORK POLITICS, 1664-1691. *New-York Hist. Soc. Q. 1974 58(2): 112-138.* A study of New York politics indicates possible inaccuracy of the view in histories of early New York that the Dutch settlers accepted English rule after 1664 passively and were assimilated easily into the colonial society. Dutch politicians asserted themselves on many occasions, such as in retaining comparative freedom for the Dutch Reformed Church, and were able to obtain a share of governmental power. Because English policy was designed to make the transition smooth, the Dutch were able to achieve compromises advantageous to them. Based largely on primary sources; 7 illus., 54 notes. C. L. Grant

1122. Taylor, Orville W. BAPTISTS AND THE IDEALS OF THE NEW NATION: A BICENTENNIAL VIEW. *Viewpoints: Georgia Baptist Hist. 1976 5: 5-16.* On the tenets of freedom of speech, freedom of religion, separation of church and state, freedom of the press, equal opportunities, and innovation the American nation was founded, 1619-1776; draws analogies between these tenets and the history of Baptists in the United States.

1123. Tolzmann, Don Heinrich. THE ST. LOUIS FREE CONGREGATION LIBRARY: A STUDY OF GERMAN-AMERICAN READING INTERESTS. *Missouri Hist. Rev. 1976 70(2): 142-161.* The St. Louis Free Congregation was typical of most congregations of free thinkers. It was formed by immigrants who desired a free society without church and state interference. Many such congregations established schools, singing societies, and libraries. The circulation records of the Free Congregation Library are still available at the Missouri Historical Society in St. Louis. These records provide a valuable guide for an understanding of German-American reading interests in the 19th century. They refute any notion that there was a cultural lag between Germans in America and Europe. Based on primary and secondary sources; illus., 40 notes. W. F. Zornow

1124. Trépanier, Pierre. DUPLESSIS PARMI NOUS [Duplessis among us]. *Action Natl. [Canada] 1978 68(2): 127-132.* There has been rising interest in Maurice Duplessis recently. Robert Rumilly's *Maurice Duplessis et son temps* (Montreal, 1973) provides a favorable view of the former Quebec premier, while Conrad Black's *Duplessis* (Toronto and Montreal, 1977) emphasizes the power of the Church and the infantilism of the Quebecois. For Black, the hallmarks of the Duplessis system were autonomy, frugality, fidelity, and paternalism, based on an alliance between the premier and the church to assure the docility of the people. Biblio. A. W. Novitsky

1125. Trudel, Marcel. LE DESTIN DE L'ÉGLISE SOUS LE RÉGIME MILITAIRE [The destiny of the Church under the military regime]. *Rev. d'Hist. de l'Amérique Française [Canada] 1957 11(1): 10-41.* Great Britain's conquest of French Canada during the French and Indian War, 1756-63, ushered in a period of military government in Quebec. The French-speaking Catholic Church felt oppressed by the Protestant English authorities, and the Church passed through its most difficult period.

1126. Valentine, Foy. AN HISTORICAL VIEW OF CHRISTIANS AND CITIZENSHIP. *Baptist Hist. and Heritage 1974 9(3): 168-178.* Examines the dilemma of allegiance to religious beliefs or loyalty to the state, 1st-20th centuries. S

1127. Waite, P. B. ANNIE AND THE BISHOP: JOHN S. D. THOMPSON GOES TO OTTAWA, 1885. *Dalhousie Rev. [Canada] 1977-78 57(4): 605-618.* Presents the background for John S. D. Thompson's move out of the Supreme Court of Nova Scotia and into the larger world of Canadian politics centering in Ottawa, 1867-94. Details his motives, and especially the motives and influence of his wife, Annie Affleck, through excerpts from their correspondence, which was considerable because of their close emotional ties. Examines the role of the Bishop of Antigonish, John Cameron, and the reluctance of Sir Alexander Campbell in giving up the Ministry of Justice. 40 notes. C. H. Held

1128. Wallfisch, M. Charles. WILLIAM O. DOUGLAS AND RELIGIOUS LIBERTY. *J. of Presbyterian Hist. 1980 58(3): 193-209.* Associate Justice William O. Douglas, son of a Presbyterian home missionary, served the longest term in the history of the US Supreme Court. Examines some events in the interval (1915-80) between the deaths of the two men. Douglas was a theistic humanist. He was a private and public man of deep religious conviction and enduring—though occasionally strained—devotion to the church he had observed his father serving. His religion reflected Protestantism's most basic ethic of duty and individual accountability. Based on books, articles, and Supreme Court opinions by Douglas, other sources, and an interview with Edward L. R. Elson; 53 notes. H. M. Parker, Jr.

1129. Weeks, Louis and Hickey, James C. "IMPLIED TRUST" FOR CONNECTIONAL CHURCHES: *WATSON V. JONES* REVISITED. *J. of Presbyterian Hist. 1976 54(4): 459-470.* Unravels and recounts the complicated history of the famous case of *Watson* v. *Jones*, which dealt with the control and ownership of the property of the Walnut Street Presbyterian Church, Louisville, Kentucky, in the post-Civil War period. The thrust of the case for ecclesiastical as well as civil law is that the governing body of a local church (in this case the session) holds the property and the rights to decision-making in behalf of the highest judicatory of the denomination among those churches that are connectional in their polity. In the more recent *Presbyterian Church in the US* v. *Mary Elizabeth Blue Hull Memorial Presbyterian Church* (1969) the Supreme Court ruled that the First Amendment prohibits civil courts from awarding church property on the basis of the court's interpretation of church doctrine. Thus the basic legal doctrines spawned by *Watson* v. *Jones* over a century ago will probably continue to help determine the role of civil courts in church disputes. Covers 1860-1970. Based on the minutes of the Walnut Street Presbyterian Church and secondary materials; 34 notes. H. M. Parker, Jr.

1130. Wendel, Thomas. JACOBITISM CRUSHED: AN EPISODE CONCERNING LOYALTY AND JUSTICE IN COLONIAL PENNSYLVANIA. *Pennsylvania Hist. 1973 40(1): 59-65.* In 1720, Lieutenant Governor William Keith of Pennsylvania, himself a former Jacobite, capitalized upon the execution of a counterfeiter to prove his loyalty to the Crown and accuse his enemies of lingering attachment to Jacobitism. Governor Keith refused to stay the execution of Edward Hunt until the convicted counterfeiter could appeal to the crown. Keith accused the pastor and vestry of Christ Church of Jacobitism because they insisted upon reading the Anglican funeral liturgy for Hunt. Based on a variety of sources; illus., 21 notes. D. C. Swift

1131. Whelan, Charles M. GOVERNMENTAL ATTEMPTS TO DEFINE CHURCH AND RELIGION. *Ann. of the Am. Acad. of Pol. and Social Sci. 1979 (446): 32-51.* Before 1969 there was very little disagreement between the American churches and the federal and state governments about the legal meanings of church and religion. Since 1969, however, Congress and some federal agencies (notably the Internal Revenue Service) have adopted some legal phraseology that is extremely offensive to the churches because it divorces the charitable, educational and social welfare activities of the churches from their religious mission. The resulting discord, tension and threat to the proper legal understanding of religion and church can be resolved only through changes in the terminology that the government has created. To bring about these changes, the churches must engage in greater collaboration with each other, and in more frequent and cordial discussions with government officials. J/S

1132. White, B. R. EARLY BAPTIST LETTERS. *Baptist Q. [Great Britain] 1977 27(4): 142-148.* Reprints two letters, 1655 and 1658, from John Clarke (1609-76), a Rhode Island Baptist, to Robert Bennett, a member of the London Calvinistic Baptists, which discuss Clarke's ties with Bennett, religious persecution, and a modification of republicanism after the death of Oliver Cromwell.

1133. White, William Griffin, Jr. THE FEMINIST CAMPAIGN FOR THE EXCLUSION OF BRIGHAM HENRY ROBERTS FROM THE FIFTY-SIXTH CONGRESS. *J. of the West 1978 17(1): 45-52.* Citing his polygamy as immoral and illegal, feminists began a successful campaign to keep Utah representative Brigham Henry Roberts from being seated in the House of Representatives, 1900.

1134. Witheridge, David E. NO FREEDOM OF RELIGION FOR AMERICAN INDIANS. *J. of Church and State 1976 18(1): 5-19.* Traces the history of Indian religious liberty from the first settlement of whites to the present time. Points out that Indians have been forced toward Christianity and deprived of their right to worship as they wish. The steps taken in recent years to restore Indian religious rights is discussed along with changing attitudes on the part of whites. 49 notes. E. E. Eminhizer

1135. Withington, Anne Fairfax and Schwartz, Jack. THE POLITICAL TRIAL OF ANNE HUTCHINSON. *New England Q. 1978 51(2): 226-240.* Anne Hutchinson's (1591-1643) trial in 1637 was not to determine guilt or innocence, but a power struggle to solve the political problem of maintaining the social order, and must be judged in these terms. During the first part of the trial she outmaneuvered her accusers. Historians have explained her announcement that she had received divine revelation as a mistake which lost her the case, but the authors conclude that it was no error, but a conscious affirmation of the triviality of all men's endeavors, including both her own and the court's. She knew that she was certain to be found guilty from the beginning of her trial, and decided to make the statement as an act of conscience. Based on trial records and secondary works; 26 notes. J. C. Bradford

1136. Wogaman, J. Philip. THE CHURCHES AND LEGISLATIVE ADVOCACY. *Ann. of the Am. Acad. of Pol. and Social Sci. 1979 (446): 52-62.* Throughout American history, church groups have sought to influence public policy. Indirect challenges persist on the popular level and as a by-product of tax exemption regulations and lobby disclosure legislation. In democratic political theory, this right of churches is grounded in the right of all citizens to be respected as sovereign and to exercise their sovereignty either individually or in groups. Religious freedom points in particular to the transcendence of persons as citizens above the state, and it requires opportunity for political expression. The right of church legislative advocacy is limited by respect for the rights of others and by the requirement that all public policy enactments reflect a primary secular purpose. Churches in fact make important public contributions through legislative advocacy and the state should encourage, not discourage, it. The broad mainstream of Judeo-Christian tradition is deeply supportive of this activity, provided it is pursued with wisdom and restraint. J/S

1137. Wood, James E., Jr. RELIGIOUS LIBERTY AND PUBLIC AFFAIRS IN HISTORICAL PERSPECTIVE. *Baptist Hist. and Heritage 1974 9(3): 154-167.* The role of Baptists in the emergence of religious liberty. S

1138. Wood, James E., Jr. THEOLOGICAL AND HISTORICAL FOUNDATIONS OF RELIGIOUS LIBERTY. *J. of Church and State 1973 15(1): 241-258.*

1139. Worthing, Sharon L. THE STATE TAKES OVER A CHURCH. *Ann. of the Am. Acad. of Pol. and Social Sci. 1979 (446): 136-148.* As political pressure for "public accountability" of charitable organizations and churches increases, lines which delineate the borders of appropriate government surveillance and enforcement activity towards charitable organizations and churches, now somewhat unclear, will be sharpened by contest. Illustrating what can occur when the state loses its sense of restraint is the receivership imposed on the Worldwide Church of God in a proceeding brought by the California Attorney General's office. Instead of constitutionally required separation of church and state, there followed a period in which a state-appointed official took charge of all the administrative affairs of a church and its affiliated charitable organizations. Arguments which have served as a basis for the Attorney General's extreme action are that charitable funds, including church funds, are "public funds," and that the financial affairs of churches are entitled to no First Amendment protection. Proposes that the line which marks the constitutionally protected rights of churches be drawn at a point rather close to that which marks protections for individuals. Also, the financial and religious affairs of churches should be recognized as inextricably linked. Thus, legitimate law enforcement against churches could be conducted without abridging the unique protections of churches under the First Amendment, 1970's. J

1140. Yackel, Peter G. BENEFIT OF CLERGY IN COLONIAL MARYLAND. *Maryland Hist. Mag. 1974 69(4): 383-397.* "Evidence of the influence of the common law on the development of criminal procedure in colonial Maryland" is provided by "the inclusion of benefit of clergy among the procedures" whereby the superior judiciary conducted its criminal business. It was a device in the common law which convicts could employ to avoid execution of the death sentence. Each man was entitled to a single grant only, and only if the crime and the convict's status were "clergyable," and generally only if the candidate was literate. Traces the development of this benefit through medieval English practice, and details a 1710 Maryland case in which the plaintiff invoked the right, it was granted, and he was burned on the thumb to indicate exemption. By this time the literacy test in England had been annulled, but Maryland remained somewhat behind English procedure. Still, "benefit of clergy" and its usage indicated that both judicial and executive officers recognized the severity and many inequities of the criminal code in Maryland, and the need for legal reform, and were thus amenable to the use of this humane device. Based largely on the Archives of Maryland and Parliamentary documents; 3 illus., 43 notes. G. J. Bobango

1141. Zimmer, Anne Y. THE "PAPER WAR" IN MARYLAND, 1772-73: THE PACA-CHASE POLITICAL PHILOSOPHY TESTED. *Maryland Hist. Mag. 1976 71(2): 177-193.* During December 1792-April 1793, "an acrimonious battle of words enlivened the pages of the *Maryland Gazette*" when the Whiggish country-party lawyers William Paca and Samuel Chase—Maryland's equivalent of two Sam Adamses—exchanged a series of letters with rector Jonathan Boucher over the issues of the 40-pound tobacco poll tax for support of the clergy, and the movement for an American bishop symbolized by Boucher. Paca and Chase's position that the 1702 Act of Establishment creating the poll tax was invalid led Boucher to challenge their right as vestrymen of St. Anne's parish to levy taxation for church repairs, since vestrymen also were created by that very law. Instead the lawyers insisted that common law was their justification for representing their parishioners, and turned the argument into a scathing attack on churchmen, bishops, and the proprietary establishment in general. The entire embroglio weakened the position of Maryland clerics as tensions with Britain increased after 1773, and enhanced the political prestige of Paca and Chase in the new politics of confrontation. Primary sources; 23 notes. G. J. Bobango

1142. —. THE LEGACY OF JOSEPH MARTIN DAWSON (1879-1973). *J. of Church and State 1973 15(3): 363-375.* Biography of Joseph Martin Dawson, a Baptist minister and author of numerous articles on the separation of church and state. S

1143. —. [MISSION COLONIZATION AND POLITICAL CONTROL IN SPANISH CALIFORNIA]. *J. of San Diego Hist. 1978 24(1): 97-120.*

Guest, Francis. MISSION COLONIZATION AND POLITICAL CONTROL IN SPANISH CALIFORNIA, *pp. 97-116.* Explores the effects of civil authorities' violations of the Laws of the Indies (secular and religious law concerning Indian rights during Spanish colonization) forbidding proximity of towns to missions. Analyzes the mission system in terms of its predecessors in Mexico, treatment of the Indians 1769-1803 (primarily civil rights and protective segregation), especially at San José (and Mission Santa Clara) and Villa de Branciforte (and Mission Santa Cruz), and tension between religious and civil goals and objectives.

Ramírez, David Piñera. COMMENTARY ON FRANCIS GUEST'S PAPER, "MISSION COLONIZATION AND POLITICAL CONTROL IN SPANISH CALIFORNIA," *pp. 117-120.* Reiterates conclusions of Father Guest and emphasizes the differences between Church and presidio dealings with Indians.

1144. —. TOCQUEVILLE'S RELIGION: AN EXCHANGE. *Pol. Theory 1980 8(1): 9-38.*

Strout, Cushing. TOCQUEVILLE AND REPUBLICAN RELIGION: REVISITING THE VISITOR, *pp. 9-26.* In *Democracy in America,* Alexis de Tocqueville stressed that religion was a unifying force in the United States that supported rather than conflicted with civil authority. He hoped that France could follow the American example.

Bathory, Peter Dennis. TOCQUEVILLE ON CITIZENSHIP AND FAITH: A RESPONSE TO CUSHING STROUT, *pp. 27-38.* Defines Tocqueville's concept of liberalism and contends that Strout did not fully appreciate Tocqueville's fear that religion could lead to authoritarianism.

Civil Religion

1145. Ahlstrom, Sydney E. THE RELIGIOUS DIMENSIONS OF AMERICAN ASPIRATIONS. *Rev. of Pol. 1976 38(3): 332-342.* A general review of man's recorded history brings one to the conclusion that it was in "America that the idea of religiopolitical nationalism was first fully institutionalized and culturally accepted." The Puritans, with their idea of the elect nationhood, transmitted to succeeding generations that the "religious dimension of the nation" was clearly identified with the "nation's essential being" and "sense of mission." The turmoil of the 1960's and 1970's has led to a rejection of the traditional civil religions and "the nation seems to be standing between the times with no song to sing." L. Ziewacz

1146. Akers, Charles W. "A PLACE FOR MY PEOPLE ISRAEL": SAMUEL COOPER'S SERMON OF 7 APRIL 1776. *New England Hist. and Geneal. Register 1978 132(Apr): 123-129.* Following the British evacuation, members of various denominations gathered at the least damaged First Church on 7 April 1776 to hear Samuel Cooper preach in Boston for the first time in a year. A leader of the resistance, he successfully mixed politics and religion. By equating America with Canaan, the promised land, he intimated that independence could be gained and, coincidentally, prosperity could be maintained. The manuscript of the unpublished sermon was found recently among Cooper's papers. A. Huff

1147. Albanese, Catherine. NEWNESS TRANSCENDING: CIVIL RELIGION AND THE AMERICAN REVOLUTION. *Southern Q. 1976 14(4): 307-331.* Examines the role of religion and associated philosophies in the civic and governmental affairs of early American nationhood. Manifestations and personifications of related ideas, symbols and ideals are provided. George Washington receives special consideration. 73 notes. R. W. Dubay

1148. Albanese, Catherine. THE TWO-IN-ONE: REVOLUTIONARY RELIGION IN EIGHTEENTH-CENTURY AMERICA. *Eighteenth-Century Life 1976 3(1): 16-22.* Examines the American Revolution as a two-part entity: the inheritance of past revolutionary tradition and the new revolutionary zeal which the participants discovered upon the advent of the revolution; notes changes in theology, especially about the nature of God, and the origin of civil religion; 1760-75.

1149. Baldwin, Leland D. THE AMERICAN QUEST FOR THE CITY OF GOD: ERRAND INTO THE WILDERNESS. *Western Pennsylvania Hist. Mag. 1976 59(2): 183-213.* Discusses the concept of the City of God, a nondetermined religious, social, and political perfection which Americans (and their European ancestors) have sought since the Puritans first landed in the New World; advocates change which needs to be made in the American psyche in order for these ends to be achieved in the 20th century.

1150. Balitzer, Alfred. SOME THOUGHTS ABOUT CIVIL RELIGION. *J. of Church and State 1974 16(1): 31-50.* Discusses the relationship between civil religion, political institutions and democracy in the United States from the 17th to 20th centuries, including the influence of ideology and the Puritan tradition.

1151. Beam, Christopher M. MILLENNIALISM AND AMERICAN NATIONALISM, 1740-1800. *J. of Presbyterian Hist. 1976 54(1): 182-199.* In the period between the Great Awakening and the end of the 18th century, many Americans firmly believed that the history of the world was inexorably leading up to a millennium of peace and prosperity for a world-encompassing Zion. Presbyterians manifested the same optimistic belief that all the signs of the times indicated that the American Revolution marked the beginning of a new epoch during which the republican principles and the forms of Protestantism embodied by the new nation would extend eventually over the world and usher in the dawn of the promised era. Traces the boundless optimism through the American Revolution, the organization of the nation, the French Revolution, and the great advances in every area of cultural life. Based largely on primary sources; 51 notes. H. M. Parker, Jr.

1152. Bellah, Robert N. RELIGION AND LEGITIMATION IN THE AMERICAN REPUBLIC. *Society 1979 15(4): 16-23.* Clarifies author's term "civil religion": a religious feeling toward the American state that arises because the government takes no stance on religion, 1776-1978.

1153. Bennett, W. Lance. IMITATION, AMBIGUITY, AND DRAMA IN POLITICAL LIFE: CIVIL RELIGION AND THE DILEMMAS OF PUBLIC MORALITY. *J. of Pol. 1979 41(1): 106-133.* Careful analysis of civil religion indicates that the displacement of the high symbols of state risks the abandonment of a collective and binding moral order in any form. Perversion of civil religion was a factor in both the escalation of the Vietnam War and the Watergate coverup, yet civil religion was the basis for the correction for these abuses. 50 notes. A. W. Novitsky

1154. Bercovitch, Sacvan. THE TYPOLOGY OF AMERICA'S MISSION. *Am. Q. 1978 30(2): 135-155.* The civil millenarianism in the 18th-century clergy's concept of America's mission was part of an underlying design which also encompassed, through persistence of language and vision, New England Puritanism and the postmillenarianism of Jonathan Edwards and his followers. The Puritans and the Edwardseans were far less concerned with European chiliastical conceptual frameworks than with the factor of process and the design of gradual fulfillment. Both approaches interwove personal salvation and the progress of the work of the redemption with a suffusion of the idea of the uniqueness of the American experiment. The stress on America's mission became more pronounced and exaggerated in sermons and writings throughout the 18th century. N. Lederer

1155. Berens, John F. "FROM PURITAN TO AMERICAN PROVIDENTIAL THOUGHT." *Cithara 1977 16(2): 59-76.* The Great Awakening of the mid-18th century marked a transition from Puritan, New England, Providential thought to an American, 13-colony-wide Providentialism.

1156. Berens, John F. GOOD NEWS FROM A FAR COUNTRY: A NOTE ON DIVINE PROVIDENCE AND THE STAMP ACT CRISIS. *Church Hist. 1976 45(3): 308-315.* For many Americans the revolutionary experience could be conceptualized best within a religious framework. Sermons, orations, poems, newspapers, essays, and other sources of the popular colonial mind reveal that a significant number of Americans continued to perceive God as the prime mover in human history. They gave America's secular development a prominent place in God's moral government of the world. Because of these beliefs, the Stamp Act was viewed as a threat to the fulfillment of America's providential destiny. Americans saw the Act's repeal as a sign of Almighty intervention in support of his favored people. 49 notes. M. D. Dibert

1157. Berens, John F. "LIKE A PROPHETIC SPIRIT": SAMUEL DAVIES, AMERICAN EULOGISTS, AND THE DEIFICATION OF GEORGE WASHINGTON. *Q. J. of Speech 1977 63(3): 290-297.* During the Early National Period (1789-1815), American eulogists drew upon a homegrown "prophecy" by Samuel Davies, Presbyterian mininster, to give George Washington's legend as the providential agent of Heaven validity and vitality, thus satisfying the new nation's "need for national symbols and its psychological and spiritual craving for a common father figure."

1158. Berens, John F. THE SANCTIFICATION OF AMERICAN NATIONALISM, 1789-1812: PRELUDE TO CIVIL RELIGION IN AMERICA. *Can. Rev. of Studies in Nationalism [Canada] 1976 3(2): 172-191.* Examines the importance of providential thought in American nationalism, 1789-1812, and its role in a kind of "civil religion" which evolved along with the nationalistic movement.

1159. Bishirjian, Richard J. CROLY, WILSON, AND THE AMERICAN CIVIL RELIGION. *Modern Age 1979 23(1): 33-38.* If salvation is thought to be intramundane, political life takes on new historical importance as it becomes enveloped in the history of salvation, and politics becomes the field of prophecy. Two who represent extreme eschatological aspirations in the American millenarianism were Herbert Croly and Woodrow Wilson, 1909-19. Based on author's *A Public Philosophy Reader* (1979). M. L. Lifka

1160. Bowden, Henry Warner. A HISTORIAN'S RESPONSE TO THE CONCEPT OF AMERICAN CIVIL RELIGION. *J. of Church and State 1975 17(3): 495-505.* Discusses the role and definition of civil religion in American life in the 1970's, emphasizing the attitudes of historians.

1161. Cole, William A. and Hammond, Phillip E. RELIGIOUS PLURALISM, LEGAL DEVELOPMENT, AND SOCIETAL COMPLEXITY: RUDIMENTARY FORMS OF CIVIL RELIGION. *J. for the Sci. Study of Religion 1974 13(2): 177-190.* Speculates that civil religion originates because: "1) the condition of religious pluralism creates special problems for social interaction; 2) social interaction, in such situations, is facilitated by a universalistic legal system; 3) a universalistic legal system may, therefore, be elevated to the sacred realm." Covers 1953-72.

1162. Endy, Melvin B. ABRAHAM LINCOLN AND AMERICAN CIVIL RELIGION: A REINTERPRETATION. *Church Hist. 1975 44(2): 229-241.* Abraham Lincoln was in many important respects a preeminent prophet of American civil religion. His conception of revelation and providence and his attitudes toward Negroes and Southern slavery caused him to compromise significantly on his stance concerning the distance between church and state. Thus he was a less impressive spokesman for what he called the central idea of the American experiment, democracy. His flaw may be an inevitable product of a civil religion whose vocational consciousness is informed primarily by the biblical myth of the chosen nation. 66 notes. M. D. Dibert

1163. Erickson, Gary Lee. LINCOLN'S CIVIL RELIGION AND THE LUTHERAN HERITAGE. *Lincoln Herald 1973 75(4): 158-171.* In 1862 various social resolutions concerning the nation were adopted by the General Synod Convention of the Evangelical Lutheran Church, held in Lancaster, Pennsylvania. They were presented to President Lincoln on 13 May 1862. Discusses the background of the social resolutions; the resolutions themselves, which advocated support for the union within the framework of civil religion; and Lincoln's response. Lincoln believed it mandatory to have dialogue with theologians; he cordially received church representatives. Based on the Minutes of the General Synod Convention, 6 May 1864, Baser's *Collected Works of Abraham Lincoln,* and secondary sources; 72 notes. A. C. Aimone

1164. Evans, Mary Ellen. THE MISSING FOOTNOTE OR, THE CURÉ WHO WASN'T THERE. *Records of the Am. Catholic Hist. Soc. of Philadelphia 1973 84(4): 196-216.* Utilizes events of Alexis de Tocqueville's 1831 visit to the United States to describe the political theory of Reverend Samuel Charles Mazzuchelli, who with Tocqueville elaborated the American civil religion a century before the sociologists of the 1970's. 17 notes. J. M. McCarthy

1165. Fenn, Richard K. THE RELEVANCE OF BELLAH'S "CIVIL RELIGION" THESIS TO A THEORY OF SECULARIZATION. *Social Sci. Hist. 1977 1(4): 502-517.* Assesses Robert Bellah's theory of civil religion, applying it to the concept of secularization of society, and concluding that though religious symbols may lend credence to political institutions, they also encourage resistance and opposition and through secularization undermine certain traditional bases of social authority.

1166. Greninger, Edwin T. THANKSGIVING: AN AMERICAN HOLIDAY. *Social Sci. 1979 54(1): 3-15.* Discusses the history and significance of the Thanksgiving celebration in the United States since 1620, in particular, its legal nationwide observance since 1863.

1167. Gustafson, Merlin D. PRESIDENT HOOVER AND THE NATIONAL RELIGION. *J. of Church and State 1974 16(1): 85-100.* Discusses the extent to which Christianity, specifically Protestantism, was considered the "national religion" in the religious attitudes of President Herbert C. Hoover, 1928-32, emphasizing church and state issues.

1168. Hammond, Phillip E. THE SOCIOLOGY OF AMERICAN CIVIL RELIGION: A BIBLIOGRAPHIC ESSAY. *Sociol. Analysis 1976 37(2): 169-182.* Discusses the development of sociological theory regarding the concept of civil religion in the 1960's and 70's, and general attitudes toward it from the 17th to 20th centuries. Presents a bibliography of 20th-century works in American civil religion.

1169. Hatch, Nathan O. THE ORIGINS OF CIVIL MILLENNIALISM IN AMERICA: NEW ENGLAND CLERGYMEN, WAR WITH FRANCE, AND THE REVOLUTION. *William and Mary Q. 1974 31(3): 407-30.* Examines civil millennial expressions in the Revolutionary era, especially the view that the revolutionary movement was a fulfillment of God's cause. Jonathan Edwards and other Great Awakening preachers helped to give credence to the notion that the unfolding of American liberty prepared the way for the millennium. In particular, New England's involvement in King George's War contributed to a shift from solely religious and introspective patterns of apocalyptic thought to a collective sense of struggle against Satan; ministers identified religion with liberty. 75 notes. H. M. Ward

1170. Herberg, Will. AMERICA'S CIVIL RELIGION: WHAT IT IS AND WHENCE IT COMES. *Modern Age 1973 17(3): 226-233.*

1171. Higham, John. HANGING TOGETHER: DIVERGENT UNITIES IN AMERICAN HISTORY. *J. of Am. Hist. 1974 61(1): 5-28.* The 1974 annual presidential address before the Organization of American Historians, devotes attention to three "adhesive forces" characteristic of the development of modernizing societies. "Primordial" unity binds kinsmen and neighbors and has been intense among American Indians, immigrant groups, and American whites of the Southeast. Ideological unity stems from a Puritan, and later a generalized Protestant ideology which was fused with ideas of nationalism into an emphasis on collective mission, dispersal of power, and individual responsibility and opportunity. Since the Civil War the primary unifying force has been technology, exemplified in the engineer, inventor, and scientific manager with emphasis on efficiency and power over nature. For a time technology was considered a servant of a democratic, rational collectivity, but recently technology has been considered specialized, undemocratic in its implications, and contrary or irrelevant to idealism. 56 notes. K. B. West

1172. Hudson, Winthrop S. THIS MOST FAVORED NATION: REFLECTIONS ON THE VOCATION OF AMERICA. *J. of Church and State 1977 19(2): 217-230.* Discusses the idea (held since early settlement) of America being "special" and guided by divine providence. Covers 17th-20th centuries. 26 notes. E. E. Eminhizer

1173. Hughes, Richard T. FROM CIVIL DISSENT TO CIVIL RELIGION: AND BEYOND. *Religion in Life 1980 49(3): 268-288.* Drawing on European antecedents in the Reformation, both Protestants and Rationalists in the United States referred to a primordium: the orthodox Christians looked back to the apostolic church for models of behavior, and the rationalists to nature; both groups identified the United States with the ideal past.

1174. Isetti, Ronald E. THE CHARTER MYTH OF AMERICA: A STUDY OF POLITICAL SYMBOLISM IN THE INAUGURAL ADDRESSES OF THE PRESIDENTS. *Cithara 1976 16(1): 3-17.* The

Presidents have looked upon America not merely as a young nation in a new land, but as Israel in the New World, a biblical vision that was born of the experience of the Protestant settlers of the 17th century, who left England (as it were, Egypt) to found their righteous New Jerusalems, under charter from God, in the American wilderness.

1175. Kessler, Sanford. TOCQUEVILLE ON CIVIL RELIGION AND LIBERAL DEMOCRACY. *J. of Pol. 1977 39(1): 119-146.* The moral crisis of Watergate and the rise of secularism have renewed interest in civil religion. A major spokesman for the political utility of religion was Alexis de Tocqueville, who believed that Christianity was the source of the basic principles of liberal democracy, and the only religion capable of maintaining liberty in a democratic era. His concern was aroused by the mutual antagonism between Christians and liberals in 19th-century France, rooted in the Enlightenment and the French Revolution. In France Christianity was allied with the Old Regime and the Restoration. Christianity was not antagonistic to democracy in the United States, where it was a bulwark against dangerous tendencies toward individualism and materialism, which would lead to atheism and tyranny. 95 notes. A. W. Novitsky

1176. LaFontaine, Charles V. GOD AND NATION IN SELECTED U.S. PRESIDENTIAL INAUGURAL ADDRESSES, 1789-1945. *J. of Church and State 1976 18(1): 39-60, (3): 503-521.* Part I. Suggests that the Presidential Inaugural addresses are a religious statement, in that they constitute the nation's statement of faith. Studies the addresses of George Washington, John Adams, Thomas Jefferson, Abraham Lincoln, Woodrow Wilson, and Franklin Roosevelt. Limits of the study are discussed, indicating that a full study would require examination of all writings of presidents and of their times. The addresses all pay attention to the deity in some form. The most popular term is "God," followed by "providence." "Jesus Christ" and "Christian" do not appear often. Stressed is the view that God is considered a part of the ruling group and government. The government reflects the will of God to some extent. There is a summary of the doctrine of deity found in the addresses, with 9 points, and a summary of the views on the nation and the deity with 17 points. The Civil War caused the first major revision of American concepts of the deity. 65 notes. Part II. Presidents to the time of Abraham Lincoln thought of America as a chosen land, divinely favored. With Lincoln and the Civil War, change occurred. God was chastising the people for their faults and Lincoln saw the war as God's way of reestablishing the nation as it had been. James A. Garfield wanted Congress to respect the religious scruples of the citizens, but at the same time, not to allow any church to usurp power. William McKinley saw God's will in America's obtaining an empire from the Spanish War. Woodrow Wilson went back to Lincoln's view of restoration in 1913. Franklin Roosevelt followed a similar theme in 1933. From this we can see a national theology developing. 1) America as a chosen people and 2) America as an example to the world. 129 notes. E. E. Eminhizer

1177. Lindner, Robert D. CIVIL RELIGION IN HISTORICAL PERSPECTIVE: THE REALITY THAT UNDERLIES THE CONCEPT. *J. of Church and State 1975 17(3): 399-421.* Discusses the history and meaning of the concept of civil religion in Europe and the United States from the 18th to the 20th century, emphasizing the thought of Jean-Jacques Rousseau and the Puritans.

1178. Marx, Leo. "NOBLE SHIT": THE UNCIVIL RESPONSE OF AMERICAN WRITERS TO CIVIL RELIGION IN AMERICA. *Massachusetts Rev. 1973 14(4): 709-739.* Discusses the reactions of Ralph Waldo Emerson, Herman Melville, Mark Twain, George Santayana, Ernest Hemingway, and Norman Mailer to civil religion and its place in the American character.

1179. McCarthy, Rockne. CIVIL RELIGION IN EARLY AMERICA. *Fides et Hist. 1975 8(1): 20-40.* In the absence of a unifying national church, America adopted a civil religion. Acquiescence to the civil religion largely defines the limits of freedom. The elements of the civil religion include a civil theology, civil peoplehood, civil institutions, ceremonial expressions and symbols, and modes of enforcement of the civil religion. Covers 1776-1900. Primary and secondary sources; 65 notes. R. E. Butchart

1180. Miller, Glenn T. IMAGES OF THE FUTURE IN EIGHTEENTH CENTURY AMERICAN THEOLOGY. *Amerikastudien-Am. Studies [West Germany] 1975 20(1): 87-100.* Studies the origins of post-millennial American thinking which many scholars believe was one of the foundations of 19th-century American nationalism and optimism. There were two types of eschatology in 18th-century American theology. The mainline-type stressed the traditional symbols of the day of judgment, heaven and hell. This type of eschatology remained dominant throughout the period. The other type of eschatology, the historicist, sought to interpret history as a series of dispensations or periods. Its advocates saw in the unfulfilled prophecies of Daniel and Revelation the master plan of history. Its symbols were prophecy, the Second Coming of Christ and the millennium. This type of eschatology was closely connected to the 18th-century search for evidences of Christianity. It led men to search for the signs of the times (as empirical verification of the Gospel) and, in particular, for the great event that would signal the transition between the present dispensation and the next age which was believed to be the one before the final period of glory: the millennium. The time of future projected by the historicist eschatology was closely connected to the hopes of the enlightenment. It would be the great age of material and spiritual progress in which pure religion and pure science would transform the world into a paradise. Education is understood to be one of the foundations of this transformation of human life. The Revolution provided the great event necessary for the expansion of the millennium dream into the mainstream of American thought. The time of testing had become part of history: the way into the future was assured. While the age of the millennium was still to come, every event—including many seemingly unimportant ones—brought the United States closer to its destiny. J

1181. Osborn, Ronald E. PERIL TO CHRISTIANITY OR OPPORTUNITY FOR ECUMENISM?: A CONSIDERATION OF AMERICAN CIVIL RELIGION. *Encounter 1976 37(3): 245-258.* Discusses the implications of changing attitudes toward faith and civil religion for Christianity, ecumenism, and theology, 1967-70's, questioning the proper role of the church in society.

1182. Phelan, Michael. TRANSCENDENTAL MEDITATION: A REVITALIZATION OF THE AMERICAN CIVIL RELIGION. *Arch. de Sci. Sociales des Religions [France] 1979 48(1): 5-20.* The practice of Transcendental Meditation has become commonplace in American society. Its success is due to TM's reintegration of cultural values within the US belief system, and it has particularly revitalized civil religion. S

1183. Ross, Don S. THE "CIVIL RELIGION" IN AMERICA. *Religion in Life 1975 44(1): 24-35.* Civil Religion "represents the progressive consensus of general religion shared by religious groupings in America." S

1184. Schelbert, Leo. "AMERICA": VON DER MACHT UND DEM WANDEL EINES ARCHETYPS [America: on the power and change of an archetype]. *Saeculum [West Germany] 1977 28(1): 75-86.* The national self-image of the USA can be seen in a mixture of three archetypes: Puritanism, Pietism, and Enlightenment. The visions of a pure state of god, fraternity, and a nation of order, unity, and reason form the main images of the United States since the 17th-18th centuries.

1185. Schlesinger, Arthur M., Jr. AMERICA, EXPERIMENT OR DESTINY? *Am. Heritage 1977 28(4): 12-17.* Two themes run through American history: the one, America as an experiment; and the other, the belief that Americans are a chosen people. As the populace grows less mindful of its history, the second theme, with its messianic implications, becomes more pronounced. Experiment has declined while destiny has become more accepted. Illus. J. F. Paul

1186. Schlesinger, Arthur M., Jr. AMERICA: EXPERIMENT OR DESTINY. *Am. Hist. Rev. 1977 82(3): 505-530.* This paper traces the evolution through American history of two competing propositions: the view of America as an experiment, fraught with risk, problematic in outcome; and the view of America as a chosen nation with a sacred mission and a sanctified destiny. Both views were derived from the Calvinist ethos; both were sustained and developed by a variety of secular ideas and forces; and the interplay between these divergent propositions has been a pervading theme in the American experience. [Includes comments by James A. Field, Jr. and George E. Mowry]. A

1187. Smidt, Corwin. CIVIL RELIGIOUS ORIENTATIONS AMONG ELEMENTARY SCHOOL CHILDREN. *Sociol. Analysis 1980 41(1): 25-40.* This study focuses upon two major questions concerning civil religion in America: 1) When in life are civil religious orientations initially acquired? and 2) Are civil religious orientations associated with the acquisition of other social and political attitudes? Analysis of data based upon a survey of 825 elementary school children in downstate Illinois suggests that civil religious orientations are learned during childhood, that they are held by a large proportion of elementary school children across both parochial and public school systems, and that these civil religious orientations are associated with the manner in which children relate to their political world. Covers the 1970's. 8 tables, biblio. J

1188. Smith, Kalmin D. THE POLITICS OF CIVIL RELIGION. *Am. Benedictine R. 1975 26(1): 89-106.* American civil religion gives religious value to cultural elements expressed in symbols, beliefs, rituals, and expectations of the American people. Analyzes, evaluates, and criticizes the concept of civil religion in American political theory and practice, 1940-74. Reviews the historic roots of civil religion in the thought of ancient Greek philosophers, St. Augustine, Machiavelli, Spinoza, Montesquieu, and Rousseau. Based on original and secondary sources; 31 notes. J. H. Pragman

1189. Smith, Timothy L. RIGHTEOUSNESS AND HOPE: CHRISTIAN HOLINESS AND THE MILLENNIAL VISION OF AMERICA, 1800-1900. *Am. Q. 1979 31(1): 21-45.* Perfectionism and millenarianism, expounded by such reform-minded evangelists as Charles G. Finney and Asa Mahan, shaped American political as well as religious ideology during the 19th century. Combined with the elements of the American dream, millenarianism played a key role in the nation's search for social "holiness," even while it underscored the role the nation was to play in realizing millenarian expectations for all of mankind. Based on church and other theological publications; 80 notes.
D. G. Nielson

1190. Smylie, James H. THE PRESIDENT AS REPUBLICAN PROPHET AND KING: CLERICAL REFLECTIONS ON THE DEATH OF WASHINGTON. *J. of Church and State 1976 18(2): 233-252.* From a study of 50 sermons and 440 eulogies at the death of Washington in 1799, sees the following conclusions: 1) divine providence was good to America by giving it a Republican leader and making him great, 2) the clergy legitimized the presidential office from the Bible. God had spoken through the Scriptures. They compared Washington with Moses, David, and others, and 3) Washington was a pious man, thankfully. The mystique they wrapped Washington and his office in has made it difficult to criticize either Washington or his successors. 45 notes.
E. E. Eminhizer

1191. Szasz, Ferenc M. DANIEL WEBSTER: ARCHITECT OF AMERICA'S CIVIL RELIGION. *Hist. New Hampshire 1979 34(3-4): 223-243.* When Daniel Webster emerged on the national scene in 1813, the Union was still in its formative stage. By the time of his death in 1852, the Union had become "part of the religion of this people." Webster contributed tremendously to this development. Webster's personal faith consisted of a mild, nondenominational Christianity, paralleled by his faith in the American Union. Many of his speeches reflect his belief that God had singled out the United States for a providential purpose. His Senate speech of 7 March 1850, however, struck a responsive chord throughout the nation. Webster's efforts enabled Lincoln to tap a lasting enthusiasm for the Union. 77 notes. D. F. Chard

1192. Tichi, Cecelia. THE AMERICAN REVOLUTION AND THE NEW EARTH. *Early Am. Literature 1976 11(2): 202-210.* The psychological and spiritual legacy of the American Revolution was reflected in the symbolism used in popular literature, 1770's-1800. The images of progress and human improvement used in spiritual references by the Puritans were translated to the American destiny in the form of the "new earth": the prospect for a new civilization. Seen as the beginning of the Age of Liberty, the American Revolution antedated the idea (joined in literature several decades later by Thoreau) of the wedding of environmental change, conquest of the frontier, and the Edenic myth of the wilderness. G. A. Hewlett

1193. Wellborn, Charles. THE BIBLE AND SOUTHERN POLITICS. *Religion in Life 1975 44(4): 418-427.* Discusses civil religion in the South in the 1960's and 1970's; mentions political speeches.

1194. Whitney, John R. THE CYCLES OF MISSION IN AMERICA. *Anglican Theological Rev. Supplementary Series 1973 (1): 38-57.* Discusses the concept of mission in evolutionary terms, as it has affected America's national destiny. S

1195. Whitson, Mont. CAMPBELL'S POST-PROTESTANTISM AND CIVIL RELIGION. *West Virginia Hist. 1976 37(2): 109-21.* Alexander Campbell (1788-1866) was a left-wing rationalistic New Testament primitivist. He endorsed Locke's idea of separation of church and state, and wanted autonomous local congregations. He was also a millenialist who saw democracy and Christianity as interrelated and believed America was God's agent to bring both to the world. He was a "post-Protestant" in the sense of accepting rather than fearing change, and he emphasized the "common Christianity" of American civil religion while he deplored the minor divisions between denominations. Based on Campbell's writings and secondary sources; 44 notes.
J. H. Broussard

1196. Wilson, Charles Reagan. THE RELIGION OF THE LOST CAUSE: RITUAL AND THE ORGANIZATION OF THE SOUTHERN CIVIL RELIGION, 1865-1920. *J. of Southern Hist. 1980 46(2): 219-238.* The importance of religion in the South has long been noted, but the ties between religion and culture are closer than has been suggested. The post-Civil War years witnessed the birth of a pervasive common civil religion heavy with mythology, ritual, and organization. Southerners have tried to defend on a cultural and religious level what defeat in 1865 made impossible on a political level. The Lost Cause—defeat in a holy war—has left southerners to face guilt, doubt, and the triumph of evil: in other words, to form a tragic sense of life. Base on the *Confederate Veteran,* other organizational publications, and other sources; 36 notes.
T. D. Schoonover

1197. Wimberley, Ronald C. CIVIL RELIGION AND THE CHOICE FOR PRESIDENT: NIXON IN '72. *Social Forces 1980 59(1): 44-61.* This study introduces the concept of civil religion to presidential voting research and tests its explanatory power in comparison to traditionally used variables. Civil religion is a view that the nation is subject to a divine will and that its affairs must be evaluated from that perspective. Social scientists and others have described the presidency as having a central role in American civil religion. As anticipated from such literature, civil religious persons in political, religious, and community samples were more likely to favor Nixon. Among correlates with favored candidate, civil religion ranked ahead of most other variables and, in certain samples, ahead of party. Civil religion was typically more predictive than church religious factors, social background characteristics, and most political variables. J

1198. Wimberley, Ronald C. CONTINUITY IN THE MEASUREMENT OF CIVIL RELIGION. *Sociol. Analysis 1979 40(1): 59-62.* Indicators along the lines of three earlier empirical studies of civil religion are analyzed with items based on documents which Bellah suggests to be primary texts of American civil religion. The assumption that both lines of items form a single dimension is tested through factoring techniques. Reliability is also assessed. Results indicate that items from both sources do converge into a single dimension and discriminate from other types of indicators. Reliability is quite high. This suggests that civil religion as measured in the earlier studies is of the same conceptualization as that in the historical texts. Covers 1967-78. J

1199. —. [ROBERT N. BELLAH, THE NEW ORTHODOXY AND CIVIL RELIGION]. *Sociol. Analysis 1976 37(2): 160-168.*
Fenn, Richard. BELLAH AND THE NEW ORTHODOXY, *pp. 160-166.*
Bellah, Robert N. COMMENT ON "BELLAH AND THE NEW ORTHODOXY," *pp. 167-168.*
Examines the impact of Judeo-Christian thought on conceptions of civil religion, church and state, national self-image, and the "New Israel"

concept in the 19th and 20th centuries; discusses and presents the thought of Robert N. Bellah.

1200. —. [A SYMPOSIUM ON CIVIL RELIGION AND COMMENTS]. *Sociol. Analysis 1976 37(2): 141-159.*
Bourg, Carroll J. A SYMPOSIUM ON CIVIL RELIGION, *pp. 141-149.*
Johnson, Benton. COMMENTS, *pp. 150-152.*
Bellah, Robert N. RESPONSE TO THE PANEL ON CIVIL RELIGION, *pp. 153-159.*
Examines the religious roots of civil religion and their relationship to political attitudes, values, and national self-image from 1775 to the 20th century; discusses and presents the thought of Robert N. Bellah.

Political Behavior

1201. Baum, Dale. KNOW-NOTHINGISM AND THE REPUBLICAN MAJORITY IN MASSACHUSETTS: THE POLITICAL REALIGNMENT OF THE 1850'S. *J. of Am. Hist. 1978 64(4): 959-986.* During the 1850's in Massachusetts, nativism and antislavery were distinct as political forces. The success of the Republican Party in Massachusetts after 1855 did not depend significantly upon attracting former Know-Nothing, anti-Catholic voters. Even though the Native American Party enjoyed a brief and phenomenal success in the state, it still represented only a temporary stop for many voters searching for a true antislavery party. The Know-Nothing Party played a minor role in the transition from a Whig to a Republican Party in Massachusetts politics. Uses ecological regression to trace voters' transitions and alignments during the 1850's. 25 tables, 53 notes. T. P. Linkfield

1202. Abler, Thomas S. FRIENDS, FACTIONS, AND THE SENECA NATION REVOLUTION OF 1848. *Niagara Frontier 1974 21(4): 74-79.* Discusses the split of political parties in the tribal government of the Seneca Indians in 1848 into the New Government Party and the Old Chiefs Party; discusses the Senecas' plea to members of the Society of Friends to aid in settling the dispute and the split in the Quakers which resulted, the Hicksite Quakers siding with the New Government Party and the Orthodox Quakers siding with the Old Chiefs Party.

1203. Alvarez, David J. and True, Edmond J. CRITICAL ELECTIONS AND PARTISAN REALIGNMENT: AN URBAN TEST-CASE. *Polity 1973 5(4): 563-576.* Ward-by-ward voting behavior in Hartford, Connecticut, during 1896-1940 indicates that support for the Democrats came from established middle-class, Protestant sectors of society, rather than from realignment of pro-Democratic Party ethnic groups in 1928.

1204. Archdeacon, Thomas J. NEW YORK MIGHT BE AMERICA. *Rev. in Am. Hist. 1975 3(2): 187-191.* Patricia U. Bonomi's *A Factious People: Politics and Society in Colonial New York* (New York: Columbia U. Pr., 1971) and Milton M. Klein's *The Politics of Diversity: Essays in the History of Colonial New York* (Port Washington, N.Y.: Kennikat Pr., 1974) discuss the effect of ethnic and religious diversity on New York's political institutions in the 1690's-1770's, and the importance of this experience for the political development of the nation after the Revolution.

1205. Argersinger, Peter H. RELIGIOUS POLITICS AND THE PARTY SYSTEM. *Rev. in Am. Hist. 1979 7(4): 547-552.* Review essay of Paul Kleppner's *The Third Electoral System, 1853-1892: Parties, Voters, and Political Cultures* (Chapel Hill: U. of North Carolina Pr., 1979).

1206. Arrington, Leonard J. and Esplin, Ronald K. BUILDING A COMMONWEALTH: THE SECULAR LEADERSHIP OF BRIGHAM YOUNG. *Utah Hist. Q. 1977 45(3): 216-232.* Contemporary observers of Brigham Young (1801-77) emphasized his self-confidence, sincerity, and common sense. He saw his own role as the Lord's steward, as a coordinator of men, money, and material for the greatest good of the community. He accomplished his purpose by keeping in personal contact with key people by letter, personal tours, and meetings in his office. He gave detailed instructions and advice, received regular reports, and provided encouragement for projects large and small. Based on primary and secondary sources; 4 illus., 51 notes.
J. L. Hazelton

1207. Baltzell, E. Digby. THE PROTESTANT ESTABLISHMENT REVISITED. *Am. Scholar 1976 45(4): 499-518.* The thesis of the author's *The Protestant Establishment: Aristocracy and Caste in America* (1963) was that WASPs dominated the American political institutions of the 1960's. By 1976 this had changed, and "perhaps it is best to forget about the WASP establishment, and instead cultivate an open but hierarchical society where all men aspire to be like Washington or Jefferson."
F. F. Harling

1208. Barone, Constance. THE DUTCH. *Hist. J. of Western Massachusetts Supplement 1976: 13-17.* Discusses the Dutch in New York and New Jersey. An individual's allegiance in the American Revolution was linked to his religious affiliation. Members of the Dutch Reformed Church were usually Whigs and adherents of the Conferentie group were Loyalists. Notes. W. H. Mulligan, Jr.

1209. Baum, Dale. KNOW-NOTHINGISM AND THE REPUBLICAN MAJORITY IN MASSACHUSETTS: THE POLITICAL REALIGNMENT OF THE 1850'S. *J. of Am. Hist. 1978 64(4): 959-986.* During the 1850's in Massachusetts, nativism and antislavery were distinct as political forces. The success of the Republican Party in Massachusetts after 1855 did not depend significantly upon attracting former Know-Nothing voters. Even though the Native American Party enjoyed a brief and phenomenal success in the state, it still represented only a temporary stop for many voters searching for a true antislavery party. The Know-Nothing Party played a minor role in the transition from a Whig to a Republican Party in Massachusetts politics. Uses ecological regression to trace voters' transitions and alignments during the 1850's. 25 tables, 53 notes. T. P. Linkfield

1210. Bauman, Mark K. PROHIBITION AND POLITICS: WARREN CANDLER AND AL SMITH'S 1928 CAMPAIGN. *Mississippi Q. 1977-78 31(1): 109-118.* Distaste for mixing religion and politics and a desire not to draw attention to anti-Prohibition elements led Methodist Episcopal Church, South, senior bishop Warren Candler to instruct the clergy in his church not to become involved in the presidential election of 1928 between Catholic, anti-Prohibition candidate Alfred E. Smith and Herbert H. Hoover.

1211. Beardslee, John W., III. THE DUTCH REFORMED CHURCH AND THE AMERICAN REVOLUTION. *J. of Presbyterian Hist. 1976 54(1): 165-181.* Discusses the nature of the divisiveness which plagued the colonial Dutch church, and the relation that it bore to the division between Dutch Whig and Tory during the Revolution. For the Dutch churches, the Revolution was a bitter internal struggle, with lines of division which followed ecclesiastical patterns. A spirit of amnesty made possible the church's survival after the war. The divisiveness was also healed when the church immersed itself in an intensive foreign missions program in the early 18th century. Based on primary and secondary sources; illus., 41 notes. H. M. Parker, Jr.

1212. Belknap, Michal R. JOE MUST GO. *Rev. in Am. Hist. 1979 7(2): 256-261.* Review article prompted by Donald F. Crosby's *God, Church, and Flag: Senator Joseph R. McCarthy and the Catholic Church, 1950-1957* (Chapel Hill: U. of North Carolina Pr., 1978) and David Oshinsky's *Senator Joseph McCarthy and the American Labor Movement* (Columbia: U. of Missouri Pr., 1976).

1213. Bell, Stephen Hugh. PHILLIP PHILLIPS NEELY AND SECESSION. *Alabama Hist. Q. 1976 38(1): 45-50.* The influence of the clergy on secession has been largely overlooked by historians. An examination of Phillip Phillips Neely (1819-68) indicates the impact of this influence. Neely was a Methodist preacher in the black belt of Alabama and influenced the election of secessionists to the Montgomery convention of 1861. Illus., 16 notes. E. E. Eminhizer

1214. Blocker, Jack S., Jr. THE PERILS OF PLURALISM. *Can. R. of Am. Studies 1973 4(2): 201-205.* Review article of: Paul Kleppner's *The Cross of Culture: A Social Analysis of Midwestern Politics, 1850-1900* (New York: Free Press, 1970), and Richard Jensen's *The*

Winning of the Midwest: Social and Political Conflict, 1888-1896 (Chicago: U. of Chicago Press, 1971), analyses of midwestern political behavior in the late 19th century. Unlike earlier histories which emphasized political institutions, debates between political groups, and midwestern power elites, Kleppner and Jensen focus on religion and other cultural forces and conclude these forces were determinative factors in shaping midwestern political activities. Kleppner studied Ohio, Michigan, and Wisconsin. Jensen included Indiana, Iowa, and Illinois in his work.
H. T. Lovin

1215. Bockelman, Wayne L. and Ireland, Owen S. THE INTERNAL REVOLUTION IN PENNSYLVANIA: AN ETHNIC-RELIGIOUS INTERPRETATION. *Pennsylvania Hist. 1974 41(2): 125-159.* Surveys the ethnic and religious composition of the legislative, executive, and judicial branches of Pennsylvania government, 1755-80. During 1756-76, the Quakers remained the largest group in the legislature, but they had lost their overwhelming numerical dominance. Subsequent assemblies saw the emergence of a Presbyterian majority and the decline of Quaker and Anglican strength. Concludes that religious and ethnic conflict was more important than sectional and class conflict. Portrait, 12 charts and graphs, 46 notes.
D. C. Swift

1216. Boudreau, Joseph A. THE MEDIUM AND THE MESSAGE OF WILLIAM ABERHART. *Am. Rev. of Can. Studies 1978 8(1): 18-30.* William Aberhart, evangelist and first Social Credit premier of Alberta, used the radio effectively to promote his program of economic reform among his rural constitutents. He spoke eloquently on political, social, and religious matters, often employing music and drama to heighten effect. Among his major themes were the evils of banks and the domination of the West by Eastern interests. Contrary to the popular view of Aberhart as a political opportunist, his radio broadcasts present him as a sincere, but naive, crusader. Primary and secondary sources, particularly recordings of Aberhart's radio broadcasts; 30 notes.
G.-A. Patzwald

1217. Bradford, Richard H. RELIGION AND POLITICS: ALFRED E. SMITH AND THE ELECTION OF 1928 IN WEST VIRGINIA. *West Virginia Hist. 1975 36(3) 213-221.* In the 1928 Democratic presidential primary, New York Governor Alfred E. Smith faced Missouri Senator James A. Reed in West Virginia. Although Smith never set foot in the state while Reed campaigned vigorously, and although Smith was a Catholic running in a 95% Protestant state, he won the primary, 82,000 to 76,000. In November, Hoover won; but West Virginia had been a Republican state for some time, and Smith did better than previous Democratic candidates. Based on newspapers and secondary sources; 50 notes.
J. H. Broussard.

1218. Brown, Bruce T. GRACE CHURCH, GALESBURG, ILLINOIS, 1864-1866: THE SUPPOSED NEUTRALITY OF THE EPISCOPAL CHURCH DURING THE YEARS OF THE CIVIL WAR. *Hist. Mag. of the Protestant Episcopal Church 1977 46(2): 187-208.* Within the Protestant Episcopal Church of Illinois in the mid-1860's, there was a sharp conflict over both the authority of bishops and the denomination's involvement in political issues. Those who wanted to involve the Church in Civil War politics generally favored the Union; those who wanted to avoid the political arena were probably motivated by Copperhead political persuasions rather than by some ecclesiastical ideal of separation of Church and State. Since the Diocese of Illinois experienced considerable conflict along these lines, as seen in Grace Church, Galesburg, it would not be surprising if that conflict reflected the mood of the national Church. Based on records and history of Grace Church and the Diocese of Illinois, and secondary sources; 55 notes.
H. M. Parker, Jr.

1219. Brownlow, Paul C. THE NORTHERN PROTESTANT PULPIT AND ANDREW JOHNSON. *Southern Speech Communication J. 1974 39(3): 248-259.* The tactics used by Protestant clergy exaggerated Andrew Johnson's characteristics and gave a distorted image of him.
S

1220. Cohen, Steven Martin and Kapsis, Robert E. RELIGION, ETHNICITY, AND PARTY AFFILIATION IN THE U.S.: EVIDENCE FROM POOLED ELECTORAL SURVEYS, 1968-72. *Social Forces 1977 56(2): 637-653.* Analyzes a white Christian subsample of pooled national survey data collected in 1968, 1970, and 1972 to determine whether ethnicity has a direct effect on party identification net of parental party identification. Religion alone (Protestant versus Catholic) is an adequate measure of ethnicity for this analysis, there being little intrareligious variation in party identification by national origin. Second, religion's effect is largely limited to the ethnically identified. Third, its effect holds up when controlling for parental party identification and SES. Fourth, regional variation in the impact of religion is understood as largely flowing from regional variations in the distribution of Catholics.
J

1221. Colburn, Dorothy. NO MORE PASSIVE OBEDIENCE AND NON-RESISTANCE. *Hist. Mag. of the Protestant Episcopal Church 1977 46(4): 455-461.* "No more passive obedience and non-resistance" was a motto painted on the door of the newly completed Anglican church at Appoquiniminck, Delaware, pastored by the Reverend Philip Reading (1720-78), in the summer of 1775. A minister to the colonies under the Society for the Propagation of the Gospel (SPG), and a loyalist Anglican, had he disobeyed the rules of the Church in omitting or changing the words of the prayers, particularly those for the King, he felt he would have subjected the people under his pastoral care to virtual excommunication. What the colonists viewed as "passive obedience and non-resistance" was in reality a very strong stand on his part to protect both his and their lifeline to the Church. He adamantly disobeyed their demands that he sever the tie with the Church by breaking the vows he had made not to change the proscribed forms of worship. Details the struggle of a loyalist clergyman in a rebel land. Based solely on Reading's letters to the London office of the SPG; 19 notes.
H. M. Parker, Jr.

1222. Crosby, Donald F. THE CATHOLIC BISHOPS AND SENATOR JOSEPH MC CARTHY. *Records of the Am. Catholic Hist. Soc. of Philadelphia 1975 86(1-4): 132-148.* One of the prevailing myths of the Joseph R. McCarthy story is that the Catholic bishops were especially enthusiastic in their support of him. Of the 216 prelates who made up the American Catholic hierarchy in 1954 only a handful ever spoke out even obliquely on McCarthy, and of those roughly half were for him and half against. 55 notes.
J. M. McCarthy

1223. Crosby, Donald F. THE JESUITS AND JOE MC CARTHY. *Church Hist. 1977 46(3): 374-388.* Discusses Jesuits during the Communist hunt of Senator Joseph R. McCarthy. There were repeated attempts to link McCarthy with the Jesuits, or paradoxically to link them with the Senator's opponents. The national Jesuit weekly *America* became embroiled in one bitter argument. Illustrates the intense nature of the dispute over McCarthy and the position of the order in the Catholic Church and in the nation's intellectual life. 48 notes.
M. Dibert

1224. Crow, Jeffrey J. TORY PLOTS AND ANGLICAN LOYALTY: THE LLEWELYN CONSPIRACY OF 1777. *North Carolina Hist. Rev. 1978 55(1): 1-17.* Some eastern North Carolina loyalists, many of them men of wealth and social standing, took offense at several laws passed by the 1776 Halifax (North Carolina) congress which adopted the North Carolina state constitution. In addition to being anti-Catholic, these Tories fought the disestablishment of the Anglican Church, the oath of allegiance to the new government, and the military draft. John Llewelyn led a group of dissatisfied loyalists, both militarily and spiritually, against the newly established state government. Several were caught and tried, but most eventually were released. For many Americans the Revolution could be understood only in terms of such local issues as religion, property, and personal relationships. Based on county records, both published and in manuscipt; 4 illus., 62 notes.
T. L. Savitt

1225. Cummings, Scott. A CRITICAL EXAMINATION OF THE PORTRAYAL OF CATHOLIC IMMIGRANTS IN AMERICAN POLITICAL LIFE. *Ethnicity 1979 6(3): 197-214.* The new ethnicity of Catholic minorities, expressed in aggressive political behavior, cannot be equated with conservatism. What is labeled incorrectly as reactionary politics on the part of Catholic ethnics is a part of the traditional antagonism between working-class ethnics and upper-middle-class Protestant reformers in the Democratic Party that has existed since the 1890's. The antielitist and antiprivilege sentiments of the Catholic ethnics were galvanized by the Populist Movement. Biblio.
S

1226. Dalin, David G. JEWISH AND NON-PARTISAN REPUBLICANISM IN SAN FRANCISCO, 1911-1963. *Am. Jewish Hist. 1979 68(4): 492-516.* Until 1963, San Francisco Jews active in politics were, almost invariably, nonpartisan Republicans in line with their German family background, their numbers, and their influence. Congressman Julius Kahn, a 24-year veteran of the House, and Supervisor Jssie Colman, a 27-year veteran, are but two of nine elective office holders, while appointed Jewish board/commission members averaged 27% during 1935-65. This significant participation in local politics is unique to San Francisco. 70 notes, 5 photos. F. Rosenthal

1227. DeVries, George, Jr. THE DUTCH IN THE AMERICAN REVOLUTION: REFLECTIONS AND OBSERVATIONS. *Fides et Hist. 1977 10(1): 43-57.* The response of Dutch Americans and the Reformed Dutch Church to the American Revolution was varied, embracing Tory, Whig, and neutralist positions. The range of responses was dependent upon ecclesiastical, political, or economic considerations, never upon theological or scriptural considerations. Revolution is opposed to Scripture. Based on Biblical, secondary, and primary sources; 75 notes. R.E. Butchart

1228. Donahue, Bernard F. THE POLITICAL USE OF RELIGIOUS SYMBOLS: A CASE STUDY OF THE 1972 PRESIDENTIAL CAMPAIGN. *R. of Pol. 1975 37(1): 48-65.* The electorate expects a presidential candidate to provide a moral as well as a political program. The use of religious terminology in political rhetoric, although not decisive, can have an impact upon voters. In 1972, Richard M. Nixon relied upon the "symbols of American civil religion," while George S. McGovern relied "heavily upon the Judaeo-Christian, biblical religion." Nixon's speeches, reflecting a combination of the work and Puritan ethic, more successfully appealed to the new majority. Secondary sources; 43 notes. L. E. Ziewacz

1229. Erickson, Keith V. JIMMY CARTER: THE RHETORIC OF PRIVATE AND CIVIC PIETY. *Western J. of Speech Communication 1980 44(3): 221-235.* Presidential candidate Jimmy Carter's professed spiritual beliefs made him trustworthy, served to identify him with evangelicals, generated media attention, and reaffirmed American civic piety and faith for voters; 1976.

1230. Fee, Joan L. PARTY IDENTIFICATION AMONG AMERICAN CATHOLICS, 1972, 1973. *Ethnicity 1976 3(1): 53-69.* Examines the relationship between the Catholic Church and the Democratic Party, comparing social and vital statistics to determine culturally what type of Catholic is a Democrat and what the personal perceptions of Catholic Democrats are.

1231. Flynt, Wayne, ed. WILLIAM V. KNOTT AND THE GUBERNATORIAL CAMPAIGN OF 1916. *Florida Hist. Q. 1973 51(4): 423-430.* William V. Knott was a candidate for governor of Florida in 1916 against Sidney J. Catts, preacher and alleged member of the Guardians of Liberty, a secret anti-Catholic organization. The highlight of the campaign was the "Sturkie Resolution," a Democratic Party resolution designed to prevent secret political club members from participating in primaries. The backlash to this resolution combined with anti-Catholic feeling in the state to bring about Catts' election. Based on 1958 manuscript of W. V. Knott; 14 notes. J. E. Findling

1232. Folsom, Burton W., II. THE POLITICS OF ELITES: PROMINENCE AND PARTY IN DAVIDSON COUNTY, TENNESSEE, 1835-1861. *J. of Southern Hist. 1973 39(3): 359-378.* Examines the prominent men of Davidson County, Tennessee, during 1835-61 in terms of political attitudes, affiliation, education, occupation, interrelations, religion, ethnic background, and Unionist sentiment. No clear socioeconomic differences appear between Whig and Democratic party members. Secondary sources; 45 notes. N. J. Street

1233. Friedmann, F. G. RENAISSANCE DES POPULISMUS IN DEN USA: GEISTIG-RELIGIÖSE HINTERGRÜNDE DER PRÄSIDENTSCHAFTSWAHLEN [Renaissance of Populism in the USA: spiritual-religious background of the presidential election]. *Stimmen der Zeit [West Germany] 1976 194(11): 757-765.* Discusses Jimmy Carter's belief in the spiritual foundations of politics, his interest in the ideas of Reinhold Niebuhr, American religious tradition since the Puritans, and the American Populist tradition. Carter emerges also from the folk culture of the South. His faith is a tribute to the spiritual vitality of the United States. R. Stromberg

1234. George, Joseph, Jr. "A CATHOLIC FAMILY NEWSPAPER" VIEWS THE LINCOLN ADMINISTRATION: JOHN MULLALY'S COPPERHEAD WEEKLY. *Civil War Hist. 1978 24(2): 112-132.* In 1859 New York Archbishop John J. Hughes made John Mullaly's new *Metropolitan Record* his "official" organ, if there were no identification with party. Mullaly distrusted abolitionists but supported Lincoln and the Union until the January 1863 Emancipation Proclamation. Archbishop Hughes severed connections with the *Record* in March 1863. Mullaly joined the Copperhead press; he was bitterly anti-Lincoln and a "peace at any price" Democrat. He was arrested for resisting the 1864 draft. Supporting McClellan, he feared the worst. Racism seems to have been Mullaly's main motivation; added were religious fears of Know-Nothingism and Irish economic self-interest. Newqspaper and secondary sources; 57 notes. R. E. Stack

1235. Goodman, Paul. A GUIDE TO AMERICAN CHURCH MEMBERSHIP DATA BEFORE THE CIVIL WAR. *Hist. Methods Newsletter 1977 10(2): 85-89; 1978 10(4): 183-190.* Part I. Reviews the limitations of census returns for finding relationships between religion and voting, then discusses the advantages of town-level membership data from the archives and historical societies of the various denominations. The main advantage of this material is that it begins earlier and is more systematic; therefore, more judicious generalizations can be made. 3 tables. Part II. Includes the guide to the church data previously omitted. Covers 1776-1860. 3 tables, 2 fig. D. K. Pickens

1236. Gribbin, William. ANTIMASONRY, RELIGIOUS RADICALISM, AND THE PARANOID STYLE OF THE 1820'S. *Hist. Teacher 1974 7(2): 239-254.* The Antimasonic movement was a conspiracy to force acquiesence to the ethical outlook of a regional minority. The movement was not unique, because at the same time religious radicals projected a perception of community dynamics remarkably similar to the views of the Antimasons. The paranoid style was the common property, the shared expression, of all kinds of activists in the 1820's. Primary and secondary sources; 43 notes. P. W. Kennedy

1237. Gross, Leonard, ed. "PREPARING FOR '76": A CANADIAN-MENNONITE PERSPECTIVE. *Mennonite Hist. Bull. 1974 35(2): 2-4.* Though "many Canadian and 'American' Mennonites share a common Pennsylvania heritage," some evidence suggests that from the American Revolution through the War of 1812 many Mennonites left Pennsylvania for Canada because of their allegiance to the British Crown. Prints excerpts from the introduction and text of Ezra E. Eby's *A Biographical History of Waterloo Township. . .* (Berlin, Ontario, 1895). S

1238. Gudelunas, William, Jr. NATIVISM AND THE DEMISE OF SCHUYLKILL COUNTY WHIGGERY: ANTI-SLAVERY OR ANTI-CATHOLICISM. *Pennsylvania Hist. 1978 45(3): 225-236.* The Schuylkill County, Pennsylvania, Whigs disintegrated in 1853-54 because they were not the strong anti-Catholic and prohibitionist force that potential supporters wanted. The Kansas-Nebraska Act was not an important factor in the demise of the party in this farming and mining county. Benjamin Bannan, editor of the *Pottsville Miners' Journal,* played a major role in bringing about a coalition of prohibitionist and anti-Catholic forces. Uses quantitative methods based on newspapers and other primary and secondary sources; photo, 3 tables, 48 notes. D. C. Swift

1239. Hachey, Thomas E. ANGLOPHILE SENTIMENTS IN AMERICAN CATHOLICISM IN 1940: A BRITISH OFFICIAL'S CONFIDENTIAL ASSESSMENT. *Records of the Am. Catholic Hist. Soc. of Philadelphia 1974 85(1-2): 48-58.* Presents the text of a confidential report on the 1940 meeting of the American Catholic hierarchy by Robert Wilberforce of the British Library of Information in New York. 12 notes. J. M. McCarthy

1240. Hachey, Thomas E. BRITISH WAR PROPAGANDA AND AMERICAN CATHOLICS, 1918. *Catholic Hist. Rev. 1975 61(1): 48-66.* Examines the British strategy and deliberations concerning propaganda in the United States in January 1918. With the outcome of World

War I still in doubt, the British wished to combat anti-British propaganda and to influence American Catholic opinion. They were concerned that this important and influential constituency not be offended by crude British counterpropaganda. The highly divisive Irish problem was especially serious. Based on documents made available for the first time under the provisions of The British Public Record Act of 1967. S

1241. Hachey, Thomas E. THE INFLUENCE OF ROMAN CATHOLICS AND THEIR CHURCH IN AMERICAN POLITICS: A BRITISH ANALYSIS IN 1943. *Am. Benedictine Rev. 1974 25(1): 123-136.* John R. A. Nicoll, an English-born academic whose specialty was the English theater, served as a consultant to the British Embassy at Washington during World War II. Nicoll's memorandum "The Political Role of Roman Catholics in the United States" (1943), reproduced and analyzed in this article, suggests that Catholic influence would force the Roosevelt administration to become more isolationistic. 14 notes. J. H. Pragman

1242. Hammond, John L. REVIVALS, CONSENSUS, AND AMERICAN POLITICAL CULTURE. *J. of the Am. Acad. of Religion 1978 46(3): 293-314.* A critical analysis of 19th-century revivalism in the United States and the major interpretations which have been proposed to explain its influence on American culture politics. Past interpretations explained the revivals in terms of pietist political dispositions, as an expression of Jacksonian democracy or in terms of a common national culture. Sees weaknesses in each of these theories and concludes that revivalists primarily were attempting to moralize politics. Secondary sources; 14 notes. E. R. Lester

1243. Hastey, Stan L. BAPTIST LAYMEN IN POLITICS IN HISTORICAL PERSPECTIVE. *Baptist Hist. and Heritage 1978 13(1): 45-54.* Challenges the cliche that Baptists, because of championing the concept of separation of church and state, have not been active in politics. Uses the examples of four representative Baptist laymen who distinguished themselves on a national scale: John Hart (1715-79), who signed the Declaration of Independence; Joseph E. Brown (1821-94), who served in numerous capacities in postwar Georgia as well as 11 years in the US Senate; Charles Evans Hughes (1862-1948), Chief Justice of the US Supreme Court; and Brooks Hays (b. 1898), leading American Congressman and Baptist lay leader. Based on autobiographical and biographical studies; 65 notes. H. M. Parker, Jr.

1244. Hays, Brooks. REFLECTIONS ON THE ROLE OF BAPTISTS IN POLITICS AND THE FUTURE OF AMERICA. *Baptist Hist. and Heritage 1976 11(3): 169-178.* The author, former president of the Southern Baptist Convention, gives his "authentic hopes" for the church on the threshold of America's third century: attitudinal conditioning for leadership in social and political action, working toward a better relationship with other religious bodies, pleading for help for the socially and economically deprived, accentuating concern for a strong public school system, and continuing efforts to strengthen the denomination's own educational structure. H. M. Parker, Jr.

1245. Hitchcock, James. PROPHECY AND POLITICS: ABORTION IN THE ELECTION OF 1976. *Worldview 1977 20(3): 25-26, 35-37.* Discusses the intrusion of politics into religion, as in the 1976 Presidential election, where pressure was put on Catholics to disregard abortion as a key moral issue, in the interests of Democratic Party loyalty.

1246. Holt, Michael F. THE POLITICS OF IMPATIENCE: THE ORIGINS OF KNOW NOTHINGISM. *J. of Am. Hist. 1973 60(2): 309-331.* The Know-Nothing Party was the fastest growing political force in many parts of the United States, 1853-56, probably contributing to the disintegration of the Whig Party as much as did the slavery issue. Know-nothingism fed on a surge of anti-Catholic sentiment among workers and the middle class in several eastern and midwestern states. These supporters were bewildered by rapid economic and social change and opposed political manipulators and the convention system. Voters previously identified with the traditional parties were impatient at their failure to take stands, especially on the issues of temperance and public schools. When the Know-Nothing Party nominated Millard Fillmore, many of its supporters turned to the Republicans who adopted the style and some issues of Know-Nothingism. 76 notes. K. B. West

1247. Hutcheson, John D. and Taylor, George A. RELIGIOUS VARIABLES, POLITICAL SYSTEM CHARACTERISTICS, AND POLICY OUTPUTS IN THE AMERICAN STATES. *Am. J. of Pol. Sci. 1973 17(2): 414-421.* Despite the recent theories which perceive economics as the most important variable influencing governmental policy, it is abundantly clear that other factors also are at work, especially religion and political systems. Analysis of governmental decisionmaking suggests that religious influences operate independently of economics. Concludes that economics should neither be ignored nor placed on a pedestal. 2 tables, 20 notes. V. L. Human

1248. Ireland, Owen S. THE ETHNIC-RELIGIOUS DIMENSION OF PENNSYLVANIA POLITICS, 1778-1779. *William and Mary Q. 1973 30(3): 423-448.* Discusses ethnic-religious antagonisms in Pennsylvania politics. Presbyterians were prominent in the Independence movement, and they captured political power. Much of the religious division erupted over the Test Acts, the state constitution, and the Anglican-dominated College of Philadelphia. Quakers were the most vociferous dissenters. Investigates voting patterns in the legislature and counties. Based on ethnic and county histories and on legislative and local records; 9 tables, 43 notes. H. M. Ward

1249. Irvine, William P. EXPLAINING THE RELIGIOUS BASIS OF THE CANADIAN PARTISAN IDENTITY: SUCCESS ON THE THIRD TRY. *Can. J. of Pol. Sci. 1974 7(3): 560-563.* Uses a political socialization model and data from the 1965 national survey to discount religion as a source of electoral cleavage in Canada. 2 tables, 5 notes. R. V. Kubicek

1250. Isaac, Rael Jean. THE SEDUCTION OF THE QUAKERS: FROM FRIENDLY PERSUASION TO PLO SUPPORT. *Midstream 1979 25(9): 23-29.* Discusses the pro-Palestine Liberation Organization (PLO) anti-Israeli position of the American Friends Service Committee during the 1970's.

1251. Jack, Ronald C. EARLY UTAH AND NEVADA ELECTORAL POLITICS. *Nevada Hist. Soc. Q. 1974 17(3): 131-151, (4): 203-224.* Two parts of a projected study of the political behavior of the Nevada and Utah electorate, 1850-70. Part I, (3): 131-151. Focuses on Mormon religious thought and socio-political views during the formative period 1835-50. Examines practices and teachings of early leaders, notably Joseph Smith (1805-1844) and Brigham Young (1801-1877). Primary and secondary sources; 51 notes. Part II, (4): 203-224. Analyzes four clearly observable patterns of electoral behavior among voters in several elections held in the 1850's in the Territory of Utah (which, at that time, included Nevada). Secondary sources; 5 maps, 57 notes. Article to be continued. H. T. Lovin

1252. Jack, Ronald C. EARLY UTAH AND NEVADA ELECTORAL POLITICS. PART 3, ELECTIONS OF THE 1860'S. *Nevada Hist. Soc. Q. 1975 18(1): 2-25.* Continued from a previous article. Analyzes several elections, mostly in Utah, during the 1860's. Significant numbers of non-Mormons came to Utah and Nevada during the 1860's, and thereupon challenged the absolute dominance of the Mormon Church hierarchy over the political processes. The newcomers were partly successful in resisting the Mormon's control over elections, and ultimately formed the Liberal Party in Utah in 1870. Based on newspaper and secondary sources; 4 maps, 52 notes. H. T. Lovin

1253. Jones, Frederick. BISHOPS IN POLITICS: ROMAN CATHOLIC V. PROTESTANT IN NEWFOUNDLAND 1860-2. *Can. Hist. Rev. 1974 55(4): 408-421.* Adds to what has already been written about the ousting of the Liberal government in Newfoundland in 1861 by detailing the several newspaper interventions of the Anglican Bishop, Edward Feild. Describes how these interventions so upset the Roman Catholic Bishop, John Thomas Mullock, an influential reformer, that he lost his growing misgivings about the Liberals and worked for their victory with such imprudence that he facilitated their downfall. Based mainly on Colonial Office correspondence, Society for the Propagation of the Gospel letters and records, and Newfoundland newspapers. A

1254. Jones, Frederick. JOHN BULL'S OTHER IRELAND—NINETEENTH-CENTURY NEWFOUNDLAND. *Dalhousie Rev. [Canada] 1975 55(2): 227-235.* Compares the role of sectarian religion in the politics of 19th-century Newfoundland with that of Ireland, evaluating the reasons for the dissimilar outcome. From early predictions of disaster for Protestants if responsible government should come, to being considered a model at a later date, the fate of Newfoundland is followed through the careers of three important leaders of the day, Roman Catholic bishop John Thomas Mullock, politician Philip Little, and Anglican bishop Edward Feild. 21 notes. C. Held

1255. Kearnes, John. ETHICAL POLITICS: ADVENTISM & THE CASE OF WILLIAM GAGE. *Adventist Heritage 1978 5(1): 3-15.* The entrance of Seventh-Day Adventists into politics via the acceptance of voting for moral principles led to more active participation in 1882, when William C. Gage, an Adventist minister, was elected mayor of Battle Creek, Michigan.

1256. Keefe, Thomas M. THE MUNDELEIN AFFAIR: A REAPPRAISAL. *Records of the Am. Catholic Hist. Soc. of Philadelphia 1978 89(1-4): 74-84.* On 18 May 1937, George Cardinal Mundelein, Archbishop of Chicago, publicly criticized the Hitler government's mistreatment of Catholics, precipitating a serious international incident. Mundelein failed to get American Catholics to focus on conditions in Nazi Germany and created serious strain on German-Vatican relations without alleviating the pressure on German clergy. 41 notes.
J. M. McCarthy

1257. Kelley, Bruce Gunn. ETHNOCULTURAL VOTING TRENDS IN RURAL IOWA, 1890-1898. *Ann. of Iowa 1978 44(6): 441-461.* Tests the ethnocultural model of midwestern voting patterns in the late 19th century developed by historians Paul Kleppner and Richard Jensen by examining the voting behavior of Irish, German, and Bohemian Catholics; German, Danish, Norwegian, and Swedish Lutherans; and Reform Dutch in rural Iowa during the 1890's. Concludes that the shift of "rural Iowa ethnics" to the Republican Party confirms the ethnocultural model as an explanation of voting patterns. Based on primary sources; 6 tables, 2 maps, 42 notes. P. L. Petersen

1258. Kerber, Stephen. PARK TRAMMELL AND THE FLORIDA DEMOCRATIC SENATORIAL PRIMARY OF 1916. *Florida Hist. Q. 1980 58(3): 255-272.* The Florida senatorial contest within the Democratic Party primary of 1916 between incumbent Nathan P. Bryan and Governor Park M. Trammell was closely tied to that state's gubernatorial fight between William V. Knott and Sidney J. Catts. Anti-Catholicism spilled over from the race for governor to influence the senatorial race. Trammell won because he was more attuned to the "grass-root level workings of Florida politics." Based on newspaper accounts and other primary sources; 6 illus., 61 notes. N. A. Kuntz

1259. Kincheloe, Joe L., Jr. SIMILARITIES IN CROWD CONTROL TECHNIQUES FOR THE CAMP MEETING AND POLITICAL RALLY: THE PIONEER ROLE OF TENNESSEE. *Tennessee Hist. Q. 1978 37(2): 155-169.* Tennessee is the focal point for this study of the unique relationship betwen religious and political meetings. As first used by the Tennessee Jacksonians in 1828, the political rally was remarkably similar to the camp meeting. The Whigs soon adopted the same methods. The key was to bring out large crowds to which emotional appeals were made. The politician did not speak to "issues"; the preacher eschewed "theology." Both used evangelistic jargon. Their opponents were the "devil," whether religious or political. Primary and secondary sources; 42 notes. M. B. Lucas

1260. King, Spencer B., Jr. BAPTIST LEADERS IN EARLY GEORGIA POLITICS. *Viewpoints: Georgia Baptist Hist. 1976 5: 45-50.* Covers 1772-1823.

1261. Knoke, David. RELIGION, STRATIFICATION, AND POLITICS: AMERICA IN THE 1960'S. *Am. J. of Pol. Sci. 1974 18(2): 331-345.* The party identifications of the American electorate in the presidential elections of the 1960s are analyzed in an additive model of effects due to occupation, education, income, and religious preference. Religion is seen to have the largest net effect, although the eight-year trend shows education increasing in importance as religion declines slightly. Great variation in party identification between Protestant denominations is noted, indicating that the traditional Protestant-Catholic-Jew trichotomy does not fully reflect the political cleavages between religious groups. J

1262. Kotter, Richard E. THE TRANSCONTINENTAL RAILROAD AND OGDEN CITY POLITICS. *Utah Hist. Q. 1974 42(3): 278-284.* Until 1869 Ogden city election procedures had no residency requirements and permitted election by acclamation. When a large group of railroad workers were to be in town on election day, the city council "passed a new and entirely different set of election ordinances intentionally designed to offset any railroad vote at the polls," including citizenship and residency clauses. Soon after, the ordinance was amended to require real estate and residency only. The Ogden City Council's purpose was to enable President Young to send his son to hold office. However with the rapid influx of non-Mormons into their city, the mayor and councilmen reinstituted the city residency clause. Illus., 14 notes.
E. P. Stickney

1263. Kousser, J. Morgan. THE "NEW POLITICAL HISTORY": A METHODOLOGICAL CRITIQUE. *Rev. in Am. Hist. 1976 4(1): 1-14.* Review article prompted by Ronald Formisano's *The Birth of Mass Political Parties: Michigan, 1827-1861* (1971), F. Sheldon Hackney's *Populism to Progressivism in Alabama* (1969), and Paul Kleppner's *The Cross of Culture: A Social Analysis of Midwestern Politics, 1850-1900* (1970); discusses the use of mass voting behavior in the writing and interpretation of political history.

1264. Kraut, Alan M. and Field, Phyllis F. POLITICS VERSUS PRINCIPLES: THE PARTISAN RESPONSE TO "BIBLE POLITICS" IN NEW YORK STATE. *Civil War Hist. 1979 25(2): 101-118.* To examine the sources of the strength of the US two-party system, investigates the response of the Democratic and Whig parties to the third-party morality-based political challenge of the abolitionist Liberty Party in New York, 1840-47. By 1845, the Liberty Party had become strong enough to affect the outcome of elections, so the major parties forced a referendum over a proposal to remove or modify a stiff property qualification that limited Negro suffrage. Racism prevailed, the measure was soundly defeated, and the Liberty Party soon lost strength. It underwent a schism in 1847 and folded in 1848. 5 tables, 55 notes. S

1265. Kremm, Thomas W. CLEVELAND AND THE FIRST LINCOLN ELECTION: THE ETHNIC RESPONSE TO NATIVISM. *J. of Interdisciplinary Hist. 1977 8(1): 69-86.* Politics in Cleveland, Ohio, on the eve of the Civil War did not revolve exclusively around the question of slavery extension. Accepted theories on the election do not adequately explain ethnic voting patterns in the city. The major division within the electorate was one of Catholics versus non-Catholics. The Republican Party was as much an anti-Catholic coalition as it was an anti-slavery extension organization and non-Catholic voters, ethnic and native-American, voted accordingly. Newspapers and printed sources; 8 tables, 19 notes. R. Howell

1266. Kutcher, Stan. J. W. BENGOUGH AND THE MILLENNIUM IN HOGTOWN: A STUDY OF MOTIVATION IN URBAN REFORM. *Urban Hist. Rev. [Canada] 1976 76(2): 30-49.* The career of John Wilson Bengough (1851-1923), cartoonist and author, illustrates the idealism of certain aspects of the urban reform movement. Religiously motivated, he believed in worshiping God by serving mankind. Concerned with the social conditions of Toronto, he used his weekly satirical magazine, *Grip,* to promote morality in city government. He became involved in politics by serving as an alderman for three years. Frustrated by the necessity of political compromise, he retired from office in 1909, preferring the freedom of an outside critic. Based on the Bengough Papers, secondary sources, and newspapers; 76 notes. C. A. Watson

1267. Lapomarda, Vincent A. A JESUIT RUNS FOR CONGRESS: THE REV. ROBERT F. DRINAN, S. J. AND HIS 1970 CAMPAIGN. *J. of Church and State 1973 15(2): 205-222.* Discusses the issues and the victory of Robert F. Drinan in his political campaign in Massachusetts.
S

1268. Leyburn, James G. PRESBYTERIAN IMMIGRANTS AND THE AMERICAN REVOLUTION. *J. of Presbyterian Hist. 1976 54(1): 9-32.* Focuses on the Scotch-Irish and the Scots, because few English immigrants to the colonies came over as Presbyterians. Most migrants came because of unfavorable economic circumstances. The value of the immigrants to the revolution consisted in the fact that the Presbyterian Church was national in scope. More than any other denomi-

nation, they were in touch with each other from Maine to Georgia. Moreover, their attachment was a patriotism for the cause of the nation as a whole, not the vindication of the rights of one colony alone. Based on primary and secondary sources; illus., 38 notes.
H. M. Parker, Jr.

1269. Lippy, Charles H. RESTORING A LOST IDEAL: CHARLES CHAUNCY AND THE AMERICAN REVOLUTION. *Religion in Life 1975 44(4): 491-502.* Discusses the involvement of New England Congregationalist clergyman Charles Chauncy (1706-87) in the American Revolution.

1270. Lisenby, William Foy. BROUGH, BAPTIST, AND BOMBAST: THE ELECTION OF 1928. *Arkansas Hist. Q. 1973 32(2): 120-131.* Charles Hillman Brough, a prominent Arkansas educator and political figure, clashed with anti-Smith Baptists on prohibition and the teaching of evolution. S

1271. Loewenberg, Robert J. CREATING A PROVISIONAL GOVERNMENT IN OREGON: A REVISION. *Pacific Northwest Q. 1977 68(1): 13-24.* Questions the traditional thesis that the 1843 creation of a provisional government in Oregon Territory resulted from the work of a mysterious Committee of Twelve. Close scrutiny of the documents indicates that this story was fabricated by William Gray, a leader of the faction for independence, who contended that the French Canadians in Oregon joined missionary Jason Lee in traitorous opposition to a provisional government. Ethnic conflict was not a factor since French Canadians and Americans divided evenly over the issue. Lee's opposition was based on a fear of ultimate independence which would weaken mission claims to land that American territorial status would strengthen. Based on primary and secondary sources; 6 photos, 35 notes.
M. L. Tate

1272. Lucet, Charles. JIMMY CARTER: RELIGION ET POLITIQUE AUX USA [Jimmy Carter: Religion and politics in the USA]. *Nouvelle Rev. des Deux Mondes [France] 1977 (1): 110-117.* Describes the rise of Jimmy Carter, an almost unknown governor of Georgia, to the Presidency of the United States, and his attempt to mix his Baptist religion with politics.

1273. Lyman, E. Leo. A MORMON TRANSITION IN IDAHO POLITICS. *Idaho Yesterdays 1977 20(4): 2-11, 24-29.* Mormons in Idaho generally voted Democratic in the years preceding statehood. However, the conflicts over polygamy and political domination by church leaders led to support of Republicans, because the church received more sympathetic treatment from them. When the immediate issues were resolved, Mormons divided their votes equally between the two parties. Covers the 1880's. Primary and secondary sources; 7 illus., 61 notes.
B. J. Paul

1274. Lythgoe, Dennis L. A SPECIAL RELATIONSHIP: J. BRACKEN LEE AND THE MORMON CHURCH. *Dialogue 1978 11(4): 71-87.* Examines the degree of Mormon influence on the election and governing policies of nonchurch Republican and fiscal conservative J. Bracken Lee. In the elections of 1944, 1948, and 1952 Lee enjoyed informal church support and the confidence of J. Reuben Clark, Jr., councilor in the First Presidency, in his campaign for governor of Utah. Elected to that office in 1948 against Mormon incumbent Herbert B. Maw, Lee cultivated church support, and accepted its advice in making some appointments. His controversial refusal to pay federal income tax in 1955 and his veto of Sunday closing laws and criticism of Dwight D. Eisenhower eroded that support, and cost him the governorship in 1956. Some Mormon leaders did continue to ask Lee for favors after his election as Mayor of Salt Lake City in 1960. Interviews; portrait, 70 notes.
C. B. Schulz

1275. Maddox, William S. CHANGING ELECTORAL COALITIONS FROM 1952 TO 1976. *Social Sci. Q. 1979 60(2): 309-313.* Analyzes coalitional factors which significantly affected presidential elections during 1952-76. Coalitions considered are those based on income, race, religion, union, region, urbanism, and age. All have been factors in one election or more, but few have exercised an important influence in all of the elections. Race, union membership, and religion are clearly the dominant indicators of party membership at present; the remaining factors all are pretty much up for grabs in any given election. Table, 4 notes, ref.
V. L. Human

1276. Maller, Allen S. CLASS FACTORS IN THE JEWISH VOTE. *Jewish Social Studies 1977 39(1-2): 159-162.* A study of the mayoral campaign in Los Angeles, California, in 1969 between liberal black candidate Tom Bradley and conservative Sam Yorty indicates the extent to which class factors amid the Jewish voting population are beginning to divide Jews into ascertainable subgroups. Reform rabbis and spokesmen supported Bradley in public meetings as part of their liberal commitment while Orthodox rabbis threw their allegiance to the far more conservative Yorty. Although a majority of Los Angeles Jewish voters supported Bradley, the percentage of Bradley supporters in the most highly affluent Jewish neighborhoods was significantly higher than that in less prosperous Jewish areas. The influence of changing neighborhoods and the school desegregation issue suggests that although Jewish voting patterns are still unique, various issues affecting the well-being and personal status of Jews are having their effect on voting behavior. N. Lederer

1277. Marcus, Jacob Rader. JEWS AND THE AMERICAN REVOLUTION: A BICENTENNIAL DOCUMENTARY. *Am. Jewish Arch. 1975 27(2): 103-276.* When the civil war which we call the American Revolution entered its military phase in 1775, it proved impossible for British North America's tiny Jewish community of perhaps 2,500 souls to remain aloof from the conflict. Most of them, for political or socio-economic reasons or a combination of the two, abandoned their loyalty to the British crown and attached themselves to the Revolutionary cause. When the United States won its independence in 1783, it seemed to the Jews that the world had begun again. J

1278. Maurer, Marvin. QUAKERS IN POLITICS: ISRAEL, P.L.O. AND SOCIAL REVOLUTION. *Midstream 1977 23(9): 36-44.* The American Friends Service Committee sponsored a conference in Chevy Chase, Maryland, in February 1977 on "New Imperatives for Israeli-Palestinian Peace" at which the Religious Society of Friends showed a definite bias toward the Palestinians, comparing today's Palestinians to holocaust victims and criticizing Israel for alleged behavior of a kind which the Society has apparently ignored among groups and nations whom it considers its "clients."

1279. McCarthy, G. Michael. THE BROWN DERBY CAMPAIGN IN WEST TENNESSEE: SMITH, HOOVER, AND THE POLITICS OF RACE. *West Tennessee Hist. Soc. Papers 1973 (27): 81-98.* The hard-fought political campaign between Alfred E. Smith and Herbert C. Hoover in Tennessee dredged up racial, religious, ethical, and political mud and ultimately resulted in Hoover's breaking the solid South for the first time since Reconstruction.

1280. McCarthy, G. Michael. SMITH VS. HOOVER: THE POLITICS OF RACE IN WEST TENNESSEE. *Phylon 1978 39(2): 154-168.* When the Democrats in 1928 nominated for President of the United States Al Smith of New York, a big-city, Catholic, anti-prohibition, pro-immigration, professional politician, there were wide defections in parts of the South, which was overwhelmingly rural and small-town, Protestant, prohibitionist, and anti-immigration. Herbert Hoover won over many southern Democrats because he was from a rural background, was a Protestant, a prohibitionist, and an old stock American. West Tennessee resisted this anti-Smith trend for racial reasons. Blacks were one-third the population in West Tennessee, and the whites feared that they might become politically powerful. The Republican Party had always been the party of the blacks, and in 1928 it reinforced this image by including in its platform a strong anti-lynching plank. The result was white, Democratic solidarity behind Al Smith. Of the 19 counties west of the Tennessee River, only 4 went for Hoover. 71 notes.
J. C. Billigmeier

1281. McLear, Patrick E. THE AGRARIAN REVOLT IN THE SOUTH: A HISTORIOGRAPHICAL ESSAY. *Louisiana Studies 1973 12(2): 443-463.* Surveys and analyzes the literature on the Agrarian Revolt in the South and notes the shortcomings of the theses. Examines economic, political, religious, and social forces to understand the Populist movement. 52 notes. G. W. McGinty

1282. Mekeel, Arthur J. THE RELATION OF THE QUAKERS TO THE AMERICAN REVOLUTION. *Quaker Hist. 1976 65(1): 3-18.* The dilemma of American Friends, especially those Philadelphia merchants with strongest British contacts, was how to maintain loyalty to king and empire while resisting taxation without representation with fellow Quakers and Whigs in England. As the movement to defend the rights of British subjects in America shifted toward treason (i.e., independence), violence, boycott, and smuggling, Friends mainly withdrew from popular front politics and disowned members who continued with the revolutionaries. They suffered exile, sequestration of property, and distraint for resisting conscription or refusing to pay war taxes. They also sent relief to blockaded Boston, to burned Norfolk, and to Philadelphia. 18 notes. T. D. S. Bassett

1283. Metcalf, Michael F. DR. CARL MAGNUS WRANGEL AND PREREVOLUTIONARY PENNSYLVANIA POLITICS. *Swedish Pioneer Hist. Q. 1976 27(4): 247-260.* Carl Magnus Wrangel was provost of the Swedish Lutheran Churches in America from 1757 until his recall to Sweden in 1768. Sheds new light on his controversial ministry and political activities. He arrived from Sweden with broad powers which, combined with his youthfulness, his lack of experience, and his noble origins, contributed to dissension within the ministerial ranks. Wrangel and Henry Melchior Muhlenberg, the renowned German Lutheran minister, strived to reinvigorate Lutheranism. In 1763, Pontiac's Rebellion started a struggle which culminated in an attempt to change Pennsylvania from a proprietary to a royal colony. Both sides worked to persuade the Swedish Lutherans to accept their point of view. Wrangel ultimately supported the proprietary cause. His actions in church and state matters reflect the central problem of the descendants of the original Swedish settlers, their assimilation into the emerging American population and the disintegration of their religious and cultural ties with Sweden. Based in part on original manuscripts; 65 notes. C. W. Ohrvall

1284. Mikkelsen, D. Craig. THE POLITICS OF B. H. ROBERTS. *Dialogue 1974 9(2): 25-43.* Roberts, a turn-of-the-century Utah Democrat, supported the Mormon Church but opposed the church leaders' (particularly President Joseph F. Smith's) use of their religious authority to promote the Republican Party. On the other hand, Roberts used his own position as a church official to promote the League of Nations. Other political issues discussed are women suffrage, prohibition, and the Mormon Church's "Political Manifesto" of 1896. Primary sources; 78 notes. D. L. Rowe

1285. Miller, Howard. THE GRAMMAR OF LIBERTY: PRESBYTERIANS AND THE FIRST AMERICAN CONSTITUTIONS. *J. of Presbyterian Hist. 1976 54(1): 142-164.* When they framed the Articles of Confederation and later the Federal Constitution, Americans worked from years of experience in constitution-making at the state level. Examines the contributions of Presbyterians to constitution-making before 1787 in the crucial states of New Jersey, North Carolina, and Pennsylvania and in the proposed state of Franklin. In each of these situations Presbyterians in 1776 constituted a viable and articulate political force led by able laymen and clergy. Presbyterian influence in constitution-writing is seen in the insistence upon a written constitution and that constitutional government must derive its ultimate authority from the consent of the governed. Presbyterians were active in the efforts to create the first frame of government for all the American states. Based on primary and secondary sources; 36 notes. H. M. Parker, Jr.

1286. Miller, James R. "THIS SAVING REMNANT": MACDONALD AND THE CATHOLIC VOTE IN THE 1891 ELECTION. *Study Sessions [Canada] 1974 41: 33-52.* Discusses the issues involved in the 1891 election in Canada and shows how conservative John Macdonald retained the Catholic vote. A paper read at the 1974 annual meeting of the Canadian Catholic Historical Association. S

1287. Miller, Robert Moats. ONE BIBLE BELT STATE'S ENCOUNTER WITH POPULISM AND "PROGRESSIVE" CAPITALISM. *Rev. in Am. Hist. 1976 4(4): 571-576.* Review article prompted by Frederick A. Bode's *Protestantism and the New South: North Carolina Baptists and Methodists in Political Crisis, 1894-1903* (Charlottesville: U. Pr. of Virginia, 1975); discusses the interaction of religion and politics in North Carolina.

1288. Miscamble, Wilson D. CATHOLICS AND AMERICAN FOREIGN POLICY FROM MCKINLEY TO MCCARTHY: A HISTORIOGRAPHICAL SURVEY. *Diplomatic Hist. 1980 4(3): 223-240.* Catholics exerted no identifiable significant influence on the formulation and conduct of US foreign policy from the Spanish-American War to the Cold War. Even on those rare occasions when the Church made the attempt, the establishment was unable to unify all believers in bringing pressure on the government. Only in its opposition to the lifting of the embargo on the Loyalist government during Spain's Civil War (1936-39) did the Church succeed in influencing policy, and even then other factors contributed heavily to President Franklin D. Roosevelt's decision. The Church "itself was influenced more by the course of American foreign relations than American foreign policy was influenced by Catholics." Mostly secondary sources; 60 notes. T. L. Powers

1289. Montesano, Philip M. SAN FRANCISCO BLACK CHURCHES IN THE EARLY 1860'S: POLITICAL PRESSURE GROUP. *California Hist. Q. 1973 52(2): 145-152.* In the late 1850's and early 1860's the three black churches in San Francisco (the African Methodist Episcopal Zion Church, the Bethel African Methodist Episcopal Church, and the Third Baptist Church) represented the interests of the city's black community, providing spiritual leadership, economic assistance, and aid to Freedmen. They also resisted attempts to deny California blacks their civil rights. Aided by a fledgling black press, the churches successfully campaigned for the repeal of laws forbidding blacks from testifying in court cases involving whites. The Emancipation Proclamation and the increasing preoccupation of nativists with the Chinese community helped the churches' campaign. The issue of voting rights was settled by the 15th Amendment, while other issues, such as school segregation, remained to be solved. Based on primary and secondary sources; illus., photos, 31 notes. A. Hoffman

1290. Morgan, David R. and Meier, Kenneth J. POLITICS AND MORALITY: THE EFFECT OF RELIGION ON REFERENDA VOTING. *Social Sci. Q. 1980 61(1): 144-148.* Analyzes the influence of religious affiliation on referenda concerning public morality issues in Oklahoma. Counties with high socioeconomic status, a larger percentage of Catholics, and smaller percentages of Fundamentalists and other Protestants support referenda on liberalizing liquor and gambling laws. Neither religious affiliation nor socioeconomic status affects Sunday closing referenda. Covers 1959-76. Based on 5 referenda votes, 1970 US Census data, Oklahoma Tax Commission records, and secondary works; table, 13 notes, biblio. L. F. Velicer

1291. Neely, Mark E. RICHARD W. THOMPSON: THE PERSISTENT KNOW NOTHING. *Indiana Mag. of Hist. 1976 72(2): 95-122.* Discusses the anti-Catholic Know-Nothing Party, popular in the 1850's in American politics, and gives an in-depth view of the Party's leader and major speaker, Richard W. Thompson.

1292. Nelsen, Hart M.; Madron, Thomas W.; and Yokley, Raytha L. BLACK RELIGION'S PROMETHEAN MOTIF: ORTHODOXY AND MILITANCY. *Am. J. of Sociol. 1975 81(1): 139-146.* Black religion as inspiration of and opiate for militancy is explored on the basis of data collected in an urban community in the upper South. Orthodoxy is shown to be positively related to militancy, while sectarianism is inversely related. Orthodoxy, viewed as churchlike ideology, is shown to be significantly related to church participation. Sectarianism, interpreted as part of the general culture of less educated blacks, is tangenital to the religious system per se. Sectarianism is unrelated to participation in a religious organization. The results of a secondary analysis of the Gary Marx data are also reported. Covers 1964-75. J

1293. Oaks, Robert F. PHILADELPHIA MERCHANTS AND THE FIRST CONTINENTAL CONGRESS. *Pennsylvania Hist. 1973 40(2): 149-168.* By 1774, merchants still were the largest single group among the Philadelphia radical leadership, yet their influence had declined progressively. Compares the 1769 radical leadership with that in 1774 and notes that fewer Quakers were active in the patriot movement as time passed. Based on the papers of Henry Drinker, a conservative Quaker merchant, and of Thomas Wharton, a conservative-to-moderate merchant; illus., 49 notes. D. C. Swift

1294. Olson, James S. THE NEW YORK ASSEMBLY, THE POLITICS OF RELIGION, AND THE ORIGINS OF THE AMERICAN REVOLUTION, 1768-1771. *Hist. Mag. of the Protestant Episcopal Church 1974 43(1): 21-28.* Reviews the role of religion in the New York Assembly in advancing the ideas which led to the American Revolution. The Assemblymen fell into two groups: the Episcopalians and their allies, and a coalition of religious dissenters. The former exercised a majority on all issues except those of a religious nature, in which instances its unity collapsed. The dissenters feared an established Episcopal Church, and in this group political debate followed consistent patterns. The outbreak of revolt saw the Episcopalians side with England and the dissenters with the rebels. 22 notes. V. L. Human

1295. Patterson, Michael S. THE FALL OF A BISHOP: JAMES CANNON, JR., *VERSUS* CARTER GLASS, 1909-1934. *J. of Southern Hist. 1973 39(4): 493-518.* Examines the fall of Methodist Bishop James Cannon, Jr., from power and political influence. The factors of his decline involved political struggles in Virginia and in the nation at large. Senator Carter Glass, his constant antagonist, sought to discredit Cannon in order to destroy his political influence. Glass, with the help of powerful friends, publicized Cannon's misuse of public, church, and political funds, and questionable stock transactions. Cannon was investigated by Congress, the Methodist Church, and the courts, and was removed from the political arena. Based on contemporary newspaper reports, US government documents, and primary and secondary sources; 92 notes.
N. J. Street

1296. Payne, Ernest A. BRITISH BAPTISTS AND THE AMERICAN REVOLUTION. *Baptist Hist. and Heritage 1976 11(1): 3-15.* During the American Revolutionary War Baptists were not numerous or influential on either side of the Atlantic. In Great Britain, as in the colonies, they considered themselves unfairly treated by the Anglican establishment. In the colonies they resented being taxed to support Congregationalism in New England and Anglicanism in the South. Between the American and British Baptists there was considerable personal contact and correspondence in the 17th and 18th centuries. Only two London Baptist clergymen failed to come out in support of the colonies. Primary and secondary sources; 45 notes. H. M. Parker, Jr.

1297. Peterson, Walfred H. RELIGIOUS LOBBYING: SOME PROBLEMS AND PRACTICES. *Foundations 1976 19(4): 361-373.* Discusses the problems of church lobbying during 1950-73. The reason given for lobbying by churches is to allow Christian organizations some part in American democracy. The major problems are separation of church and state, and of representation. Illustrates the operation of Baptist lobbying groups by examining their work on two issues. 23 notes.
E. E. Eminhizer

1298. Peterson, Walfred H. REPRESENTATION AND A RELIGIOUS PRESSURE GROUP: AN EXAMINATION OF THE BAPTIST JOINT COMMITTEE ON PUBLIC AFFAIRS. *J. of Church and State 1973 15(2): 271-292.*

1299. Pienkos, Donald. POLITICS, RELIGION, AND CHANGE IN POLISH MILWAUKEE, 1900-1930. *Wisconsin Mag. of Hist. 1978 61(3): 178-209.* Analyzes the political behavior of Milwaukee Poles during the Progressive Era, particularly their response to Progressivism and socialism. Describes the role of key leaders, including *Kuryer Polski* editor and publisher Michael Kruszka, socialist alderman Leo Krzyski, state senator Walter Polakowski, and Catholic priest and polemicist Wenceslaus Kruszka. Concludes that Poles did not always support the Democratic Party, that they often supported socialism and LaFollette Progressivism, that they did not always defer to the Catholic Church hierarchy, and that they were more involved with trade unionism than has previously been recognized. 23 illus., 5 tables, 74 notes.
N. C. Burckel

1300. Reynolds, John F. PIETY AND POLITICS: EVANGELISM IN THE MICHIGAN LEGISLATURE, 1837-1861. *Michigan Hist. 1977 61(4): 322-351.* Statistical analysis of roll-call votes in the Michigan House of Representatives during 1837-60 confirms the complexity of political motive during the Jacksonian Era. Neither the class conflict theory nor the ethnocultural, or "evangelical," approach fully explains voting on such issues as slavery, temperance, adultery, and public prayer. Although non-Democrats supported evangelical legislation in greater number, the major political parties were generally similar in their stands regarding such measures. Bills and resolutions regarding slavery were the most divisive partisan issues. Although there was a degree of evangelical cleavage, neither the Democrats nor the Whigs capitalized on it. Primary sources; 30 notes, 8 illus., 2 photos, 4 tables. D. W. Johnson

1301. Robertson, Heard. THE REVEREND JAMES SEYMOUR, FRONTIER PARSON, 1771-1783. *Hist. Mag. of the Protestant Episcopal Church 1976 45(2): 145-153.* During 1771-81 James Seymour was rector of St. Paul's Parish, Augusta, Georgia. He was an avowed loyalist. Delineates the difficulties this obstinate man faced during the American Revolution and the terrible cost in deprivation of property and position and separation from family which he paid. Based largely on the *Journal* of the Society for the Propagation of the Gospel in Foreign Parts and on records of colonial Georgia; illus., 45 notes.
H. M. Parker, Jr.

1302. Rojek, Dean G. THE PROTESTANT ETHIC AND POLITICAL PREFERENCE. *Social Forces 1973 52(2): 168-177.* In a series of articles, Benton Johnson has investigated the effects of ascetic Protestantism on political party preference. His findings indicate that among laymen exposed to fundamentalist teachings, religious involvement would vary directly with Republican party preference. However, among laymen exposed to liberal teachings, religious involvement would vary inversely with Republican identification. This present study shows that church involvement and political party identification are not significantly related. A refinement of Johnson's liberal-fundamentalist dichotomy and his church interaction index again resulted in non-significant findings. Finally, a weighted least-squares procedure was employed yielding a set of linear estimation equations that again showed no significant effect. Results such as these should make the social scientist wary of the dangers associated with the measurement of religion and the contemporary relevance of Weber's Protestant ethic. Covers the 1960's and 70's. J

1303. Schapsmeier, Edward L. and Schapsmeier, Frederick H. RELIGION AND REFORM: A CASE STUDY OF HENRY A. WALLACE AND EZRA TAFT BENSON. *J. of Church and State 1979 21(3): 525-535.* Presbyterian Henry A. Wallace and Mormon Ezra Taft Benson typify moralists of both left and right who functioned fairly well when controlled by moderates, but on their own, adopted extreme moral views, consequently losing what influence they had. Considers their careers, independent of the moderating influences of presidents Roosevelt and Eisenhower. Covers 1933-60. Based on the writeups and papers of Henry A. Wallace and Ezra Taft Benson; 28 notes.
E. E. Eminhizer

1304. Scheidt, David L. THE LUTHERANS IN REVOLUTIONARY PHILADELPHIA. *Concordia Hist. Inst. Q. 1976 49(4): 148-159.* Lutherans settled in the Delaware Valley prior to William Penn's arrival, but not until the 18th century did Lutherans come to Philadelphia in any great numbers. They adapted well and were absorbed by the expanding economic structure of the city; however, they maintained their ethnic identity by residing in the same areas and by speaking in their native German. When the American Revolution came, the Lutherans, as a group, did not demonstrate any enthusiasm for the patriot cause. Based on printed sources; 51 notes. W. T. Walker

1305. Schelin, Robert C. A WHIG'S FINAL QUEST: FILLMORE AND THE KNOW-NOTHINGS. *Niagara Frontier 1979 26(1): 1-11.* History of the American, or Know-Nothing, Party in the United States, which originated in European anti-Catholicism and American nativism, becoming a political force in the 1850's; focuses on the Party's nomination of ex-President Millard Fillmore as presidential candidate at the 1856 nominating convention, and his vain attempts, as a pro-Union candidate, to resurrect the Whig Party.

1306. Sengstock, Mary C. TRADITIONAL AND NATIONALIST IDENTITY IN A CHRISTIAN ARAB COMMUNITY. *Sociol. Analysis 1974 35(3): 201-210.* Christians from Middle Eastern European nations have been less inclined than Muslims to identify with Arab nationalist causes, but a growth of Arab identity has been observed among Middle Eastern Christian immigrants in recent years. Recent immigrants are more likely to identify with Arab nationalism than immigrants who have been in the United States for some time. This paper analyzes religious and nationalist identity in a Chaldean Iraqi community in Detroit, Michigan. It rejects the notion that the earlier immigrants' nationalist sentiments have been "lost" through assimilation, and suggests that the increased nationalist identity of recent immigrants is due in part to an increase in urbanism and bureaucratic participation in the modern Middle East. J

1307. Senkewicz, Robert M. RELIGION AND NON-PARTISAN POLITICS IN GOLD RUSH SAN FRANCISCO. *Southern California Q. 1979 61(4): 351-378.* Examines the makeup and strategies of the 1856 San Francisco Vigilance Committee. The vigilante movement was the effort of importers and merchants who had earlier made several nonpartisan campaigns in local elections. Their effort lacked success until they linked their interests with the Know-Nothing Party in 1854. There followed a series of issues which made religious questions significant in local politics: public aid to Catholic schools, Catholic influence in government operations such as the county hospital, and similar charges. Use of the Catholic issue broadened the base of the merchants, made local government nonpartisan, and through the mechanism of the Vigilance Committee rid San Francisco not only of accused criminals but also of political opponents, including Irish Catholics. The People's Party, as the merchants called themselves, continued as an important political faction until they merged with the Republicans in 1864. 83 notes. A. Hoffman

1308. Shover, John L. ETHNICITY AND RELIGION IN PHILADELPHIA POLITICS, 1924-40. *Am. Q. 1973 25(5): 499-515.* When Philadelphia's ethnic and religious groups confronted vital political choices in 1928, they responded as blacks, Jews, Germans, or Catholics, not as assimilated Americans grouped cross-culturally by occupation, class, or neighborhood. Ethno-religious political consciousness continued to flourish in the 1930's leaving sparse evidence to sustain interpretations of voting behavior predicated on social classes. Based on primary and secondary sources; 6 tables, 40 notes. W. D. Piersen

1309. Smith, James. ANDREW MC KIM, REFORMER. *Nova Scotia Hist. Q. [Canada] 1978 8(3): 225-242.* Andrew McKim (1779-1840), farmer, shoemaker, and Baptist lay preacher, began his political career as a campaigner for Thomas Roach, county member of the provincial parliament. At the age of 56 he ran for a seat in the House of Assembly; the final vote was disputed for two years. He entered a final plea and was awarded a seat in the legislature in February 1838. He served until 1840 when the legislature was dissolved. He entered again but died before the voting was completed. 26 notes. H. M. Evans

1310. Steiner, Bruce E. ANGLICAN OFFICEHOLDING IN PRE-REVOLUTIONARY CONNECTICUT: THE PARAMETERS OF NEW ENGLAND COMMUNITY. *William and Mary Q. 1974 31(3): 369-406.* Discusses Anglican-Congregational relationships in pre-Revolutionary Connecticut; notes the increasing number of Anglicans chosen by Connecticut towns to serve in the Assembly. Anglicans also held various civil, judicial, and military offices, due primarily to their economic success. Other contributing factors were Congregational factionalism, rivalries between outlying societies and original settlements, and effects of the Great Awakening. Anglican congregations consisted mostly of Congregational defectors. Based on primary sources; map, table, 77 notes. H. M. Ward

1311. Tanis, James. THE DUTCH REFORMED CHURCH AND THE AMERICAN REVOLUTION. *Halve Maen 1977 52(2): 1-2, 15, (3): 1-2, 12.* Part I. Discusses the factional war between the "coetus" and the "conferentie" segments of the Dutch Reformed Church during the American Revolution; also offers a background to the conflict, 1750-72. Part II. Concludes the discussion of the Dutch Reformed Church in New York City and in Hackensack during the American Revolution, 1775-83.

1312. Tarr, Dennis L. THE PRESBYTERIAN CHURCH AND THE FOUNDING OF THE UNITED NATIONS. *J. of Presbyterian Hist. 1975 53(1): 3-32.* Examines the major activities and attitudes of the Presbyterian Church during 1941-45 which led it to take an active role in supporting the establishment of the UN. Discusses the close relationships of the church with the Commission on a Just and Durable Peace of the Federal Council of Churches, and pays tribute to Presbyterian John Foster Dulles for his leadership at the San Francisco Conference which brought the UN into being. The influence of the churches on the UN is seen in getting a consideration for human rights into the Charter. Major source materials come from minutes of various Presbyterian judicatories plus the various publications of the church during the period; photo, 121 notes. H. M. Parker, Jr.

1313. Thomson, Randall and Knoke, David. VOLUNTARY ASSOCIATIONS AND VOTING TURNOUT OF AMERICAN ETHNORELIGIOUS GROUPS. *Ethnicity 1980 7(1): 56-69.* Three hypotheses about the effects of voluntary association membership on the voting behavior of American ethnoreligious groups are tested with national survey data spanning 1967-75. Membership in associations is not more likely to mobilize minority group members (blacks and white Catholics) to vote for president, nor does identification with other ethnoreligious group members raise the voting rates of either minority group relative to white Protestants. These results contradict the findings from several community studies and suggest that the ethnoreligious group is no longer the focus of social and political organization it perhaps once was. Primary sources; 5 tables, 3 notes, ref. R. V. Ritter

1314. Tully, Alan. [COLONIAL PENNSYLVANIA].

PROPRIETARY AFFAIRS IN COLONIAL PENNSYLVANIA, 1726-1739. *J. of the Lancaster County Hist. Soc. 1978 82(2): 94-122.* Control of Pennsylvania's proprietary government lapsed following the death of William Penn, when his will was retained in probate. This caused uncertainty in land allotment and collection of quitrents, and border conflicts with Maryland. Thomas Penn, the inheritor of the proprietary government, was able to establish solid policy and cooperation of colonists and government employees. 110 notes.

KING GEORGE'S WAR AND THE QUAKERS: THE DEFENSE CRISIS OF 1732-1742 IN PENNSYLVANIA POLITICS. *J. of the Lancaster County Hist. Soc. 1978 82(4): 174-198.* Discusses Pennsylvania Quakers' pacifism during King George's War and political repercussions (in Pennsylvania) of the Quakers' attitudes and actions. Expanded from the author's book, *William Penn's Legacy: Politics and Social Structure in Provincial Pennsylvania, 1726-1755* (Johns Hopkins U. Pr.).
G. A. Hewlett/G. L. Smith

1315. Vedlitz, Arnold; Alston, Jon P.; and Pinkele, Carl. POLITICS AND THE BLACK CHURCH IN A SOUTHERN COMMUNITY. *J. of Black Studies 1980 10(3): 367-375.* In the late 1940's the black church became the focus for black political activities as black clergymen mediated between black voters and white politicans. Then, "secular social and political institutions began to supplant the Black clergy." In the 1960's civil rights groups declined, more blacks were elected, and black voters became more sophisticated. In Beaumont, Texas, black churches and clergy are still as important politically as any other black organization. Black church members and nonmembers "are equally as likely to be potential political activists." Based on interviews of 100 randomly selected black adults in Beaumont, Texas in 1972; 2 tables, note.
R. G. Sherer

1316. Voss, Carl Hermann. THE AMERICAN CHRISTIAN PALESTINE COMMITTEE: THE MID-1940S IN RETROSPECT. *Midstream 1979 25(6): 49-53.* Reviews the efforts of American Christian groups to influence world opinion, and in particular the British government, to establish a homeland for the Jews in what is now Israel.

1317. Wade, Mason. ODYSSEY OF A LOYALIST RECTOR. *Vermont Hist. 1980 48(2): 96-113.* Ranna Cossitt, missionary of the Society for the Propagation of the Gospel, served in Claremont, New Hampshire, and adjacent Vermont and New Hampshire settlements, and was confined to the limits of Claremont, December 1775-January 1779, when he appeared in New York. Intrigue aiming to win the Connecticut and Champlain Valleys for the Empire, or settle Tories in Canada across the Vermont border, had failed by 1785. He served as rector in Sydney on Cape Breton Island, 1786-1805, and died at Yarmouth, Nova Scotia, in 1815. 58 notes. T. D. S. Bassett

1318. Walker, Randolph Meade. THE ROLE OF THE BLACK CLERGY IN MEMPHIS DURING THE CRUMP ERA. *West Tennessee Hist. Soc. Papers 1979 33: 29-47.* Scrutinizes the black community of Memphis, Tennessee, to understand how "Boss" Edward Hull Crump maintained his power from 1927 to 1948 with the aid of black voters. Most blacks supported him because they wanted to, because he was good to them. However, the limited black political participation was greatly influenced by the clergy, which has always been the dominant agent for public opinion within the Southern black community. Five ministers from that period were interviewed and gave their perspective. A paternalistic dependency did exist among the black clergy of Memphis and Crump. This subservient position helped to form an atmosphere of complacency among the black preachers in Memphis when it came to matters affecting Crump. Crump knew how to handle the black masses with a few hand-picked ministers. While not condoning their actions of the time, the author says that the clergy, largely uneducated, did provide a quality of leadership in a climate that was both oppressive and exploitative. Based largely on oral interviews with clergy, contemporary newspaper accounts, and secondary sources; 84 notes. H. M. Parker, Jr.

1319. Wallot, Jean Pierre. THE LOWER CANADIAN CLERGY AND THE REIGN OF TERROR (1810). *Study Sessions: Can. Catholic Hist. Assoc. 1973 40: 53-60.* Studies the Catholic clergy's reactions and conduct during the crisis of 1810, in which Governor Sir James Craig implemented repressive measures to fend off the threat of democracy and French Canadian nationalism. S

1320. Ward, Michael and Freeman, Mark. DEFENDING GAY RIGHTS: THE CAMPAIGN AGAINST THE BRIGGS AMENDMENT IN CALIFORNIA. *Radical Am. 1979 13(4): 11-26.* The successful 1978 campaign in California to reject Proposition 6 mandating the banning of avowed homosexuals from public schools employment signified an argument in favor of a grass roots approach to organizing. The coalition against the amendment brought together male and female homosexuals, segments of the labor movement, public school employees, high school students, women's groups, and civil libertarians. Some black and Hispanic groups and individuals also favored rejection. The Proposition was opposed in both conservative and liberal areas of the State. Many conservative spokespersons opposed it, along with the Catholic Church. Sectarian left-wing political groups failed to take an avowed stand in favor of rejection. Based on participant observation. N. Lederer

1321. Weber, Francis J. CALIFORNIA PARTICIPATION IN THE SPIRIT OF 1776. *Southern California Q. 1976 58(2): 137-142.* Describes how the California missions and Indians supported the American Revolution. After Spain, in alliance with France, went to war with England in June 1779, King Charles III directed that public prayers be offered for victory. Father Junipero Serra circulated the directive among the Franciscan missions in Alta California. In August 1781 the settlers and mission Indians were requested to pay a "voluntary" tax to support the war effort. 2,683 *pesos* were collected and augmented by another 1,533 *pesos* from Governor Felipe de Neve. Thus, financially as well as spiritually, California played a small part in the War of American Independence. Based on primary and secondary sources; 13 notes. A. Hoffman

1322. Weems, Lovett Hayes, Jr. THE CHURCHES' MINISTRY ON CAPITOL HILL. *Religion in Life 1975 44(3): 318-330.* Describes the lobbying groups in Washington which represent America's established churches and the work they have done in civil rights since 1964. S

1323. Wennersten, John R. THE TRAVAIL OF A TORY PARSON: REVEREND PHILIP HUGHES AND MARYLAND COLONIAL POLITICS 1767-1777. *Hist. Mag. of the Protestant Episcopal Church 1975 44(4): 409-416.* A man of great ambition and tenacity with an unusual stubborn nature, the Reverend Philip Hughes attempted to pursue a rich career for himself as a religious leader in the colonies. That dream floundered on the storm of political revolution in Maryland. His case demonstrates the plight in which many colonial Anglican parsons found themselves during the war. Conscious of status and income, they held on to their offices as loyal subjects of the king until the revolutionists deprived them of their parishes. Based largely on Archives of Maryland; 49 notes. H. M. Parker, Jr.

1324. White, Jean Bickmore. THE RIGHT TO BE DIFFERENT: OGDEN AND WEBER COUNTY POLITICS, 1850-1924. *Utah Hist. Q. 1979 47(3): 254-272.* Weber County, Utah, led the struggle between Mormons and non-Mormons for political domination during the territorial period. Disfranchised by the Edmunds Act of 1882 and the Edmunds-Tucker Act of 1887, Mormons lost power in 1889 to the Liberal Party. After the 1890 Manifesto, Mormons and non-Mormons worked together to eliminate party affiliations along religious lines in order to achieve statehood. Leaders such as Frank J. Cannon and William Glassmann demonstrated that Weber County could challenge Utah's political conservatism. 8 illus., 38 notes. J. L. Hazelton

1325. White, William G. LIEUTENANT GOVERNOR GEORGE A. WILLIAMS: AN ADVENTIST IN POLITICS. *Adventist Heritage 1978 5(1): 24-38.* George A. Williams was Lieutenant Governor of Nebraska during 1925-31.

1326. Whyte, John H. THE CATHOLIC FACTOR IN THE POLITICS OF DEMOCRATIC STATES. *Am. Behavioral Scientist 1974 17(6): 798-812.* The Roman Catholic Church is an important political factor in many democratic states in North America and Western Europe (1870-1974). S

1327. Will, Herman. A DIFFERENT WORLD OF NATIONS: THE CHURCHES, THE UNITED STATES, AND WAR. *J. of Ecumenical Studies 1979 16(1): 138-142.* Since 1945 there has been an enormous increase in the destructive capabilities of the arsenals of the major nations, especially the United States and the USSR. Nevertheless, there has been no World War III (although there have been other serious conflicts), and the world's Christian churches have, for the most part, struggled consistently through the UN and other agencies for the freedom and self-determination of the people of all nations. S

1328. Williamson, Rene De Visme. THE INSTITUTIONAL CHURCH AND POLITICAL ACTIVITY. *Modern Age 1974 18(2): 163-174.*

1329. Wilson, James Q. REAGAN AND THE REPUBLICAN REVIVAL. *Commentary 1980 70(4): 25-32.* Compares the rise of Ronald Reagan and the New Republicans to the 1896 election and William Jennings Bryan's similar appeal to the Democratic Party, an election that resulted in a major realignment of the political parties; events of the 1960's and 1970's may signal the Fourth Great Awakening, because the First Great Awakening (1730-60), the Second Great Awakening (1800-30), and the Third Great Awakening (1890-1920) were all preceded by religious and cultural upheavals similar to those of the 1960's and 1970's.

1330. Wingo, Barbara C. THE 1928 PRESIDENTIAL ELECTION IN LOUISIANA. *Louisiana Hist. 1977 18(4): 405-415.* Although Alfred E. Smith's majority in Louisiana in 1928 (76.3%) was very similar to Democratic majorities in that state in the 1920 and 1924 elections, the composition of his support was markedly different. Reviews and analyzes the election, showing that his strength was in the "wet," Catholic, southern part of the state rather than in the "dry," Protestant north. Black participation remained a factor in the state's Republican Party. Notes some similarities in the support for Smith and Huey P. Long. Primary sources; 3 tables, 66 notes. R. L. Woodward, Jr.

1331. Yellowitz, Irwin. MORRIS HILLQUIT: AMERICAN SOCIALISM AND JEWISH CONCERNS. *Am. Jewish Hist. 1978 68(2): 163-188.* Morris Hillquit (1869-1933), an agnostic and an American socialist leader, posed antireligious appeals and worked to neutralize this issue because it tended to drive away potential supporters. Throughout his career Hillquit, often following the advice of his friend Abraham Cahan, had to accept the reality of his ethnic political base in the New York City Jewish ghetto. Evidence from his political campaigns illustrates this thesis. Ethnic identity and concerns were a stronger influence among socialists in the Jewish community in 1930 than in 1900, and Hillquit recognized this. 42 notes. F. Rosenthal

Political Theory

1332. Admiraal, C. A. ABRAHAM KUYPER EN DE AMERIKAANSE REVOLUTIE [Abraham Kuyper and the American Revolution]. *Spiegel Hist. [Netherlands] 1976 11(7-8): 426-433.* The well-known Dutch statesman Abraham Kuyper (1837-1920) admired American political institutions. He contended that American as well as Dutch political traditions were based upon Calvinism, and not French revolutionary principles. Illus., biblio. G. D. Homan

1333. Akers, Charles W. RELIGION AND THE AMERICAN REVOLUTION: SAMUEL COOPER AND THE BRATTLE STREET CHURCH. *William and Mary Q. 1978 35(3): 477-498.* Reconstructs the part played in the coming of the American Revolution by the Rev. Samuel Cooper and the Brattle Street Congregationalist Church in Boston, during 1754-83. The church members were affluent, and Cooper consistently preached pragmatic sermons, yet he reaffirmed Calvinism. Cooper appealed to the social conscience of the rich. The archenemy in his sermons was France during the French and Indian War; later England was substituted. Although Cooper avoided direct references to politics, his interpretations on the covenant theology aided the revolutionary ideology. Above all, Cooper appealed to the dominance of the elites in Boston society. Uses church records, the Massachusetts archives, and Boston tax records. 76 notes. H. M. Ward

1334. Alderfer, Owen H. BRITISH EVANGELICAL RESPONSE TO THE AMERICAN REVOLUTION: THE WESLEYANS. *Fides et Hist. 1976 8(2): 7-34.* Focuses on the response to the American Revolution of two British Wesleyans, John Wesley (1703-91) and Francis Asbury (1745-1816). Wesley's devotion to the Church of England led him to a Tory position, while Asbury's ministry in America led him toward moderate support for the Revolution. Primary and secondary sources; 83 notes. R. E. Butchart

1335. Anderson, Philip J. WILLIAM LINN, 1752-1808: AMERICAN REVOLUTIONARY AND ANTI-JEFFERSONIAN. *J. of Presbyterian Hist. 1977 55(4): 381-394.* The American Calvinist William Linn (1752-1808) was a typical American Revolutionary clergyman in identifying with the British all that was evil, with the Americans all that was righteous. Recognized as an excellent preacher as well as academician, after the Revolutionary War he held numerous influential pulpits and was associated with several schools. He wrote many books, including a life of George Washington. At first he hailed the French Revolution as an event that would extend God's activity in bringing liberty to the world, but the emerging irreligion turned him from it. Thomas Jefferson he accused of totally removing religion from politics, a course that could only lead to atheism. He thus stands as a poignant reminder of the perplexing dilemma which confronted so many of his clerical generation: the separation of church and state, and yet the perceived responsibility of the Church to keep government "Christian." Based on the writings of Presbyterian Linn and secondary materials; 55 notes. H. M. Parker, Jr.

1336. Andrews, Stuart. JOHN WESLEY AND THE AMERICANS. *Hist. Today [Great Britain] 1976 26(6): 353-359.* Outlines John Wesley's feelings on the American Revolution, as well as his belief that England might also be ripe for revolution.

1337. Andrews, William D. WILLIAM SMITH AND THE RISING GLORY OF AMERICA. *Early Am. Literature 1973 8(1): 33-43.* The theme of the rising glory of America—a regular feature of late 18th-century American literature—is commonly regarded as a creation of the Revolution. However, this theme was well worked out some 20 years before the Revolution in a long poem by Anglican priest William Smith (1727-1803) entitled "Copy of Verses, Addressed to the Gentlemen of the House of Representatives," published in Smith's book, *Some Thoughts on Education* (New York, 1752). Based on primary and secondary sources; 11 notes. D. P. Wharton

1338. Appleby, Joyce. LIBERALISM AND THE AMERICAN REVOLUTION. *New England Q. 1976 49(1): 3-26.* Explains Americans' acceptance of revolution in the mid-18th century by tracing the transformation of colonial society during the previous 50 years, when a society marked by the subordination of the individual to the group and by deference to local leaders was atomized by the forces of population growth and economic change, the Great Awakening, and the pressures of war, and was transformed into a society in which the individual had far greater freedom but much less security. Old institutions lost their meaning and a new, liberal vision of society in which the individual was paramount began to develop. British moves to reorganize the empire were resisted because they threatened the expectations of a new order of freedom and personal advancement. Based on secondary sources; 50 notes. J. C. Bradford

1339. Baker, Donald S. CHARLES WESLEY AND THE AMERICAN WAR OF INDEPENDENCE. *Pro. of the Wesley Hist. Soc. [Great Britain] 1976 40(5): 125-134; (6): 165-182.* Discusses the political poetry of Charles Wesley (1707-88) on the American Revolution derived from manuscripts and a long published narrative poem, "The American War under the Conduct of Sir William Howe." Much of Wesley's information came from his brother John's reproduction of the work of Joseph Galloway (1730-1803), the American conservative and later a Loyalist and critic of the British military leadership. Charles Wesley's interest in the war appears to date from 1779 and reveals his condemnation of American republican attitudes which he associated with the excesses of the Cromwellian era. Wesley's verse denounced the conduct of the war by the British military and naval commanders, the attitude and behavior of successive governments in Britain, and the terms of the peace in 1783, particularly the treatment of the Loyalists. His judgments on the causes and course of the war are "all coloured by his predominant high-church Toryism and his almost fanatical adherence to the person of the King," but he correctly stresses the British desertion of the Loyalists. 82 notes. L. Brown

1340. Baker, Frank. THE SHAPING OF WESLEY'S "CALM ADDRESS." *Methodist Hist. 1975 14(1): 3-12.* Outlines the development and numerous editions of John Wesley's political pamphlet, *A Calm Address to our American Colonies* (1775), which supported the position of the British government. 47 notes. H. L. Calkin

1341. Baker, W. M. TURNING THE SPIT: TIMOTHY ANGLIN AND THE ROASTING OF D'ARCY MC GEE. *Can. Hist. Assoc. Hist. Papers 1974: 135-155.* Discusses debates between Irish Catholic leaders Timothy Warren Anglin and Thomas D'Arcy McGee in Canada, 1863-68, on the character of Irish Canadians, and on McGee's proposed British North American Union, support for Confederation, and attacks on the Fenians.

1342. Barr, William R. THE STRUGGLE FOR FREEDOM IN AMERICA: A THEOLOGICAL CRITIQUE. *Encounter 1976 37(3): 229-244.* Discusses theological aspects of conceptions of freedom in liberation movements from the American Revolution to the 20th century, emphasizing the relationship with attitudes toward government and society.

1343. Becker, William H. REINHOLD NIEBUHR: FROM MARX TO ROOSEVELT. *Historian 1973 35(4): 539-550.* In the early 1930's, theologian Reinhold Niebuhr considered himself to be a Christian Marxist, although 15 years later he believed a decent life could be attained within the framework of capitalism. Students of Niebuhr's thought explain this conversion in a variety of ways. Uses Niebuhr's editorials in *Radical Religion*, 1939-41, as the major source for the contention that increasing appreciation of the policies and programs of the Franklin D. Roosevelt administration was a major factor in the change in viewpoint. 44 notes. N. M. Moen

1344. Bercovitch, Sacvan. HOW THE PURITANS WON THE AMERICAN REVOLUTION. *Massachusetts Rev. 1976 17(4): 597-630.* The American Revolution plays a curious role in American classic literature. Uprisings in other countries meant the unleashing of several discordant national social class elements rather than progress through the uprising of the people at large. The Puritans brought their particular ideology to America, and this became their legacy to their chosen country. Eventually, this ideology became united with others into a single ideal. People who shared this ideal as it evolved included Bancroft, Thoreau, Emerson, Melville, and Hawthorne. Indeed the preface to *The Scarlet Letter* outlines the process by which the Puritans won the Ameri-

can Revolution although it is not identified as such. Secondary sources.
E. R. Campbell

1345. Bercovitch, Sacvan. THE RITUAL OF AMERICAN CONSENSUS. *Can. Rev. of Am. Studies [Canada] 1979 10(3): 271-288.* Americans have long subscribed to theories emphasizing the importance of ideological consensus, which has evolved since the Puritans arrived in 1630, and which explains the historical development of their nation. Offers "an outsider's common-sense guide" through that visionary historical terrain, from the Puritans through the Civil War. 16 notes.
H. T. Lovin

1346. Berens, John F. "A GOD OF ORDER AND NOT OF CONFUSION": THE AMERICAN LOYALISTS AND DIVINE PROVIDENCE, 1774-1783. *Hist. Mag. of the Protestant Episcopal Church 1978 47(2): 211-219.* The basic theological doctrine of the Loyalist American Anglican clergy during the period of the American Revolution was that their cause was supported by a God of order—that God ruled the destiny of nations and He was opposed to the Revolution. Thus the Loyalists, no less than the Patriots, manifested a providential interpretation of the Revolution. To the Loyalists, such a Divine Providence was unmistakably supportive of continued Anglo-American union. It was the misfortune of the Loyalists that during 1774-83 America's protecting Providence proved to be the "God of Liberty" rather than the "God of Order." Based on contemporary materials; 17 notes.
H. M. Parker, Jr.

1347. Berens, John F. RELIGION AND REVOLUTION RECONSIDERED: RECENT LITERATURE ON RELIGION AND NATIONALISM IN EIGHTEENTH-CENTURY AMERICA. *Can. Rev. of Studies in Nationalism [Canada] 1979 6(2): 233-245.* Surveys the historiography of religion and the American Revolution, then reviews recent monographs by Carl Bridenbaugh, Catherine L. Albanese, Henry F. May, James West Davidson, Nathan O. Hatch, and Mark A. Noll. These books lay to rest the notion that providential rhetoric in the Revolutionary era was only rhetoric; refute the contention that millenarianism was always a stimulus to patriotism; and argue that religion and politics were not competing for control of the American mind, but were both central. 7 notes.
R. Aldrich

1348. Berkin, Carol R. JONATHAN BOUCHER: THE LOYALIST AS REBEL. *West Georgia Coll. Studies in the Social Sci. 1976 15: 65-78.* Discusses the attitudes and feelings of Loyalist Jonathan Boucher (1738-89) toward a variety of issues and situations in 18th-century Virginia and Maryland.

1349. Bremer, Francis J. IN DEFENSE OF REGICIDE: JOHN COTTON ON THE EXECUTION OF CHARLES I. *William and Mary Q. 1980 37(1): 103-124.* John Cotton's sermon in September 1650 at the First Church of Boston supported the decision to execute Charles I. Cotton based his arguments on biblical injunctions to resist tyranny. He hoped to encourage New England Puritans to back their coreligionists in England. The sermon reveals Puritan political and eschatalogical views. Cotton justified all the actions of the English Revolution, thinking these were ushering in the millennium. He defended using the army in preserving English liberties. The sermon, previously unpublished, is located in manuscript in the Massachusetts Historical Society, and is reproduced on pp. 110-124. Cites other Puritan writings; 55 notes.
H. M. Ward

1350. Brown, Katherine B. THE CONTROVERSY OVER THE FRANCHISE IN PURITAN MASSACHUSETTS, 1954 TO 1974. *William and Mary Q. 1976 33(2): 212-241.* Surveys the controversy among historians during 1954-74 over the extent of the local and provincial franchise in Massachusetts before 1691. Historical interpretations had not previously veered from the view of Massachusetts as oligarchic. Notes challenges of Richard C. Simmons, Larzer Ziff, Richard S. Dunn, and others to the author's 1954 thesis that the true pattern was closer to that of representative democracy. Comments on historians of individual towns. At the root of the disagreement are varying interpretations of the significance of the franchise laws of 1620-91. Examines the problems of assessment. Further evidence confirms that a liberal franchise existed during the period. Based on Samuel Sewall's diary and on town, county, and colony records. Table, 94 notes.
H. M. Ward

1351. Brydon, G. MacLaren, ed. "PASSIVE OBEDIENCE CONSIDERED": A SERMON BY THE REV. DAVID GRIFFITH BEFORE THE VIRGINIA CONVENTION, DECEMBER, 1775. *Hist. Mag. of the Protestant Episcopal Church 1975 44(5): 77-93.* The sermon, "Passive Obedience Considered," based on Romans 13:1,2, was delivered to the Virginia Convention in December 1775. The Convention had become the *de facto* government of the colony after the governor had prorogued the General Assembly and abolished the county courts. It is thus an excellent document which reflects the attitude of a Virginia Anglican preacher in respect to that colony's relationship to England. Griffith argued that God's intention in appointing temporal rulers was for the advancement of general happiness, and that when such a condition does not exist the people have a right to seek redress, rather than to sit back passively. David Griffith could not believe that God would be angry with His creatures for disregarding the injunctions of those who depart from the rule of rectitude laid down by Him. 2 illus.
H. M. Parker, Jr.

1352. Buchanan, John G. THE JUSTICE OF AMERICA'S CAUSE: REVOLUTIONARY RHETORIC IN THE SERMONS OF SAMUEL COOPER. *New England Q. 1977 50(1): 101-124.* Traces the evolution of Samuel Cooper's (1725-83) political sermons from 1768, when he believed that British and colonial interests were the same and that imperial discord was the product of British and American sin, until the American Revolution, when he compared America to Israel. The Congregationalist explained that America's cause was just, and that Britain had caused the war by attempting to take away America's rights. Both reason and divine revelation required Americans to resist British oppression. Britain's conduct of the war was also immoral, e.g., in its use of mercenaries, incitement of slave rebellions, and use of Indians. Cooper joined theology and Enlightenment ideas to show the justness of America's cause. 49 notes.
J. C. Bradford

1353. Bushman, Richard L. THE BOOK OF MORMON AND THE AMERICAN REVOLUTION. *Brigham Young U. Studies 1976 17(1): 3-20.* Challenges critics of the Mormons who charge that Joseph Smith's *Book of Mormon* merely reflected American political culture in the 19th century. Compares contemporary ideas on government and the American Revolution with political ideas and practices set forth in the *Book of Mormon.* Examines three political concepts that were accepted during the period that Smith was writing: 1) the depiction of the Revolution as heroic resistance against tyranny, 2) the belief that people overthrow their kings under the stimulus of enlightened ideas of human rights, and 3) the conviction that certain constitutional protections were necessary to control power. Smith's work was not exclusively American, but contained political attitudes that had Old World origins, particularly in the history of the Israelite nation.
M. S. Legan

1354. Chapman, Phillip C. JOHN WISE AND THE DEMOCRATIC IMPULSE IN AMERICAN THOUGHT. Chaudhuri, Joyotpaul, ed. *Non-Lockean Roots of American Democratic Thought* (Tucson: U. of Arizona Pr., 1977): 1-16. Among others, John Wise influenced pre-Revolutionary political thought before John Locke and demonstrated America's acceptance of democratic theory in his religious writings.

1355. Chernov, S. A. REINKHOL'D NIBUR: IDEOLOG AMERIKANSKOGO LIBERALIZMA [Reinhold Niebuhr: the ideologue of American liberalism]. *Novaia i Noveishaia Istoriia [USSR] 1972 (3): 143-153.* Niebuhr was raised in an Evangelical background, but soon realized that Evangelicalism alone could not solve the world's problems. The darker sides of American life revealed by the 1929 economic crisis shook his belief in liberalism, and he toyed with Marxism. He condemned Roosevelt's New Deal, and became a member of the American Union for Peace and Democracy. But with the rout of the socialists in the 1936 elections Niebuhr came to support Roosevelt's policy. Eventually he proclaimed it better than socialism. After World War II he became an adherent of the consensus school of political thought. Convinced of his own objectivity, he believed himself an independent thinker. He failed to see that he was a tool of the ruling elite. Based on the works of Niebuhr, J. Dewey, A. Schlesinger, and others; 49 notes.
A. J. Evans

1356. Cherry, Conrad. NATURE AND THE REPUBLIC: THE NEW HAVEN THEOLOGY. *New England Q. 1978 51(4): 509-526.*

Yale President Timothy Dwight (1752-1817) and his students, Nathaniel William Taylor (1786-1858) and Lyman Beecher (1775-1863), were clearly men of their age. They believed that religion must be utilitarian, that men were free to choose salvation or not (they used sentiment and psychology to sway individuals' choices), and that the nation must be a voluntary association. Unlike most Deists and Lockeans, though, they believed that America was a crucial stage in a millenialist unfolding of history and rejected the social contract theory of government. In their view, God ordained republicanism and America had to be a Protestant nation since only Protestantism could make people truly moral and only moral men could preserve free institutions. Based on their writings and secondary sources; 61 notes. J. C. Bradford

1357. Church, F. Forrester. THE FIRST AMERICAN AMNESTY DEBATE: RELIGION AND POLITICS IN MASSACHUSETTS, 1783-1784. *J. of Church and State 1979 21(1): 39-54.* The Preliminary Treaty of Peace of 1783 recommended that the states allow Loyalists to return to negotiate for the restitution of their property. Massachusetts, like most other states, ignored the recommendation. Religious opponents contended that God demanded a purge of the unrighteous; proponents, including John Lathrop, appealed to Christian mercy. Primary sources; 52 notes. S

1358. Clark, Michael D. JONATHAN BOUCHER: HOW HIGH A TORY? *Rev. in Am. Hist. 1979 7(3): 338-343.* Review article prompted by Anne Y. Zimmer's *Jonathan Boucher: Loyalist in Exile* (Detroit: Wayne State U. Pr., 1978); offers an overview of Church of England clergyman Boucher's life in England and Maryland, his Loyalism, and his opposition to the American Revolution; 1770's-90's.

1359. Coffey, John W. NIEBUHR REEXAMINED: CHRISTIAN REALISM AND THE LIBERAL TRADITION. *Modern Age 1974 18(1): 71-82.* Discusses several books and articles written by and about Reinhold Niebuhr in order to examine his rejection of liberal philosophy in favor of Christian realism during the 1920's.

1360. Cooke, J. W. ALBERT TAYLOR BLEDSOE: AN AMERICAN PHILOSOPHER AND THEOLOGIAN OF LIBERTY. *Southern Humanities Rev. 1974 8(2): 215-227.* Analyzes the political philosophy of Albert Taylor Bledsoe (1809-77), whose studies on human liberty were refutations of the ideas of John Locke and Jonathan Edwards. S

1361. Dennis, William Cullen. PURITANISM AS THE BASIS FOR AMERICAN CONSERVATISM. *Modern Age 1974 18(4): 404-413.* Moralistic lectures of church, family, and school taught man to remake the earth, suggesting that whatever he accomplished would be less than God demanded. Americans faced the future with confidence because they believed that a virtuous past could be regained. The typical American has been a backward-looking progressive and a forward-looking conservative. Secondary sources; 20 notes. M. L. Lifka

1362. East, John P. THE CONSERVATISM OF FRANK STRAUS MEYER. *Modern Age 1974 18(3): 226-245.* Frank Straus Meyer as political theorist is not a "traditionalist" nor a "libertarian" nor a "fusionist," but a Christian for whom the Incarnation gives the individual *qua* individual a claim which transcends personal dignity and worth. He dared to confront a world overwhelmingly secular, relativistic, and collectivist. Hence his conservatism is a principled one of the highest order. Covers 1909-72. Based on Meyer's writings and on secondary sources; 108 notes. M. L. Lifka

1363. East, John P. RICHARD M. WEAVER: THE CONSERVATISM OF AFFIRMATION. *Modern Age 1975 19(4): 338-354.* Richard M. Weaver thought that American conservatism, although sharing libertarianism's concern for human freedom, develops a more mature philosophy which seeks meaning, purpose, and truth in human experience. In search of a philosophy sustaining a "recommendation of life," Weaver turned to the Platonic-Christian heritage and its manifestation in the American South. Covers 1930-63. Primary and secondary sources; 131 notes. M. L. Lifka

1364. Ekirch, Arthur A., Jr. CHARLES A. BEARD AND REINHOLD NIEBUHR: CONTRASTING CONCEPTIONS OF NATIONAL INTEREST IN AMERICAN FOREIGN POLICY. *Mid-America 1977 59(2): 103-116.* Two thinkers on American foreign policy were Charles A. Beard and Reinhold Niebuhr. Sharing some common ideas, they came to different conclusions. Beard believed the United States should confine itself to the defense of the Western Hemisphere to preserve national interest. Niebuhr concluded that realism demanded American intervention in world affairs. In recent years Beard's ideas seem to have been most influential, especially in regard to criticism of the Vietnam War. Secondary and archival sources; 45 notes. J. M. Lee

1365. Elliott, David R. ANTITHETICAL ELEMENTS IN WILLIAM ABERHART'S THEOLOGY AND POLITICAL IDEOLOGY. *Can. Hist. Rev. [Canada] 1978 59(1): 38-58.* Close examination of the Social Credit ideology of William Aberhart, Alberta's premier from 1935-1943, indicates that it was clearly antithetical to his previous theology, which was highly sectarian, separatist, apolitical, other-worldly, and eschatologically oriented. Special attention has been paid to document collections which have not been used in previous studies: the Minutes of the Calgary School Board, the Minutes of Westbourne Baptist Church, the Minutes of the Bible Institute Baptist Church, the financial records of the Calgary Prophetic Bible Institute, the W. Norman Smith Papers, and the private collections of Mrs. Iris Miller and Mrs. Irene Barrett. Also used were the Premiers' Papers, Professor J. A. Irving's Papers, the Aberhart Papers, and the Calgary Prophetic Bible Institute Papers, which have been used very slightly by other scholars. This study challenges the statements of Mann (1955) and Irving (1959) that there was a definite connection between Aberhart's theology and political program. Further, Aberhart's political support did not come from the sectarian groups as Mann and Irving suggest, but rather it came from the members of established churches and those with marginal religious commitment. A

1366. Engel, J. Ronald. SIDNEY E. MEAD'S TRAGIC THEOLOGY OF THE REPUBLIC. *J. of the Am. Acad. of Religion 1976 44(1): 155-165.* Explains Mead's theology of the Republic as tragic, and evaluates its adequacy. Notes Mead's views on the Enlightenment and the concepts of democracy and equality. E. R. Lester

1367. Fox, Richard W. REINHOLD NIEBUHR AND THE EMERGENCE OF THE LIBERAL REALIST FAITH, 1930-1945. *R. of Pol. 1976 38(2): 244-265.* Reinhold Niebuhr attracted postwar liberals "not only because of his political analysis and theological achievement but because of his commitment to the realistic use of power." He symbolized for liberals, the intellectual dedicated not only to the pursuit of truth and knowledge, but also an advocate and practioner of democracy. Such activism and faith by Niebuhr almost succeeded in transforming "his own liberal realist faith into the kind of 'political religion' against which he had inveighed since 1930." 35 notes. L. E. Ziewacz

1368. Frank, Douglas. WILLIAM ERNEST HOCKING AND THE DIPLOMACY OF FAITH. Plesur, Milton, ed. *An American Historian: Essays to Honor Selig Adler* (Buffalo: State U. of N.Y., 1980): 214-223. Discusses the political attitudes of idealist philosopher William Ernest Hocking; focuses on his ethical approach to problems of diplomacy and politics, premised on religious faith; 1918-66.

1369. Good, L. Douglas. THE CHRISTIAN NATION IN THE MIND OF TIMOTHY DWIGHT. *Fides et Hist. 1974 7(1): 1-18.* Timothy Dwight (1752-1817) was a leading New England clergyman and educator in the Revolutionary and post-Revolutionary period. His Puritanism and Federalism shaped his political attitudes and his vision of America. He emphasized a righteous electorate, mutual support between church and state, the rectitude of the social elite, and nativism. Dwight had broad impact as President of Yale College for two decades. Based on published writings of Timothy Dwight and secondary sources; 69 notes. R. E. Butchart

1370. Gunter, Mary F. and Taylor, James S. LOYALIST PROPAGANDA IN THE SERMONS OF CHARLES INGLIS, 1770-1780. *Western Speech 1973 37(1): 47-55.*

1371. Hammett, Theodore M. REVOLUTIONARY IDEOLOGY IN MASSACHUSETTS: THOMAS ALLEN'S "VINDICATION" OF THE BERKSHIRE CONSTITUTIONALISTS, 1778. *William and*

Mary Q. 1976 33(3): 514-527. Thomas Allen, a Congregationalist pastor at Pittsfield in Berkshire County, Massachusetts, was a leader of the Constitutional movement which got the state constitution of 1778 rejected. His pamphlet, "Vindication," was a defense of the conduct of the Berkshiremen. Allen made use of Whig and Latitudinarian thought. The document, reprinted here, sets forward objections to the proposed constitution, arguing that a constitution should proceed from a state of nature. 26 notes. H. M. Ward

1372. Harris, Waldo P., III. DANIEL MARSHALL: LONE GEORGIA BAPTIST REVOLUTIONARY PASTOR. *Viewpoints: Georgia Baptist Hist. 1976 5: 51-64.* Daniel Marshall, a convert to the Baptist Church, became a minister in that religion; examines his political stand during and following the American Revolution, and covers the period 1747-1823.

1373. Hoge, Dean R. THEOLOGICAL VIEWS OF AMERICA AMONG PROTESTANTS. *Sociol. Analysis 1976 37(2): 127-139.* A 1973 nationwide survey of United Presbyterian ministers and laypersons asked about the mission of America as a nation in years ahead, the moral stature of America in the world, Communism, internationalism, and related topics. We found more emphasis on America as an example to the nations than on America's active mission in the world. The principle that Christians must judge their nation in universal terms is strongly upheld, but among ministers the present moral stature of America is seen as rather low. Ministers are more universalistic and internationalistic than laypersons. Two discernible "parties" in theological views of America emerged, best defined in terms of internationalism and anti-Communism. J

1374. Jessee, Dean C., ed. JOSEPH SMITH'S 19 JULY 1840 DISCOURSE. *Brigham Young U. Studies 1979 19(3): 390-394.* Introduces and reproduces Joseph Smith's comments on the US Constitution.

1375. Keim, Albert N. JOHN FOSTER DULLES AND THE PROTESTANT WORLD ORDER MOVEMENT ON THE EVE OF WORLD WAR II. *J. of Church and State 1979 21(1): 73-89.* Presbyterian John Foster Dulles's belief that religion could solve the world's problems developed from his participation in the Protestant ecumenical movement and the Oxford Conference (1937). The churches had the duty to enunciate the moral principles on which political activity should be based. Following World War II, Dulles no longer believed that religion could create a universal brotherhood and ethical system; instead, it should support the West in the fight against Communism. Based on the Dulles Papers at Princeton University and published primary sources; 51 notes. S

1376. King, Irving H. DR. JONATHAN SHIPLEY, DEFENDER OF THE COLONIES, 1773-1775. *Hist. Mag. of the Protestant Episcopal Church 1976 45(1): 25-30.* Jonathan Shipley (1714-78) was Anglican Bishop of St. Asaph. He was acquainted with the American colonies through his connection with the Society for the Propagation of the Gospel in Foreign Parts. In 1773 he preached a sermon in London before the Society in which he urged Great Britain to rule the colonies justly. In 1774 he published a speech which was supposed to have been given before the House of Lords. In it he strongly opposed the Stamp Act, the Townshend Duties, and the Tea Act. He also urged Parliament not to alter the charter of Massachusetts Bay that year, but to permit the colonists to continue to enjoy the liberty which the English fathers had given them. He was ignored in every instance. Throughout the war Shipley opposed the English effort. H. M. Parker, Jr.

1377. Kirkham, Donald Henry. JOHN WESLEY'S "CALM ADDRESS": THE RESPONSE OF THE CRITICS. *Methodist Hist. 1975 14(1): 13-23.* The publication of John Wesley's *A Calm Address to Our American Colonies* (1775) led immediately to criticism and controversy. No less than 19 antagonistic tracts appeared after 1775 criticizing Wesley for plagiarism of an earlier tract by Samuel Johnson, having inconsistent political principles, intending to stir up the English public against the colonies, and dabbling in politics. Based on an analysis of contemporary pamphlets; 73 notes. H. L. Calkin

1378. Launitz-Shurer, Leopold, Jr. A LOYALIST CLERGYMAN'S RESPONSE TO THE IMPERIAL CRISIS IN THE AMERICAN COLONIES: A NOTE ON SAMUEL SEABURY'S *LETTERS OF A WESTCHESTER FARMER*. *Hist Mag. of the Protestant Episcopal Church 1975 44(2): 107-119.* The Reverend Samuel Seabury wrote four pamphlets pseudonymously as "A. W. Farmer" during 1774-75. He was an avid American Anglican clergyman who opposed the actions of the First Continental Congress. His pamphlets are recognized as a major source for the study of American loyalist ideology. Attempts to place Seabury's attitudes in the context of New York's political and religious history, and in the broader context of loyalist history and adjustment to independence. Seabury subscribed to the thesis that the American Revolution was the result of a conspiracy organized by a disaffected minority. After the war he was consecrated the first Episcopal bishop in the United States, demonstrating that once the issue of independence was settled, there was room in America for a diversity of opinion. Primary and secondary sources; 34 notes. H. M. Parker, Jr.

1379. Leliaert, Richard M. THE RELIGIOUS SIGNIFICANCE OF DEMOCRACY IN THE THOUGHT OF ORESTES A. BROWNSON. *R. of Pol. 1976 38(1): 3-26.* "Brownson's essays on 'The Origin and Ground of Government' and his *American Republic* epitomize his pre- and post-conversion political thought, respectively." Brownson shifted his thinking in regard to democracy, moving from pure democracy to "constitutional republicanism to a theocratic-democratic Christian commonwealth to the providential mission of the American republic to a virtual belief in the Gotterdammerung of American democracy." Although Brownson maintained faith in democracy, he continually sought to redefine it in terms of theocratic principles. 69 notes. L. E. Ziewacz

1380. Leming, Michael R. THE NATURE OF THE RELATIONSHIP BETWEEN RELIGIOUS ORTHODOXY AND POLITICAL CONSERVATISM. *New Scholar 1974 4(2): 211-221.* Utilizing the ideas and techniques of D. N. Anderson and Benton Johnson, Leming finds that a "significant relationship exists between religious orthodoxy and political conservatism. Furthermore, when socioeconomic status is controlled, the relationship is maintained at the .0001 level of significance." Tables. D. K. Pickens

1381. Martin, Jean-Pierre. JONATHAN MAYHEW: UN THÉOLOGIEN DE LA RÉBELLION [Jonathan Mayhew: a theologian of the Rebellion]. *Rev. Française d'Etudes Américaines [France] 1976 (2): 119-127.* Analyzes a sermon by Jonathan Mayhew given in Boston in 1750 entitled "Discourse concerning Unlimited Submission and Non-Resistance to the Higher Powers: with Some Reflections on the Resistance made to King Charles I," illustrating Mayhew's unorthodox position on the right of rebellion.

1382. McAllister, James L., Jr. FRANCIS ALISON AND JOHN WITHERSPOON: POLITICAL PHILOSOPHERS AND REVOLUTIONARIES. *J. of Presbyterian Hist. 1976 54(1): 33-60.* Compares the contributions of Old Side teacher Francis Alison to those of New Side John Witherspoon. Both taught many students who became prominent American leaders in politics, the professions, and the church during the last third of the 18th century and the early 19th century. As to whether the Old Side or the New Side alignments are reflected in the political philosophy which each taught at his educational institution, what the students learned was fundamentally the same political philosophy, and they saw in their professors men who supplemented their teaching by appropriate political action. Covers 1750-87. Based primarily on the works of Alison and Witherspoon; illus., 135 notes. H. M. Parker, Jr.

1383. McGoldrick, James E. 1776: A CHRISTIAN LOYALIST VIEW. *Fides et Hist. 1977 10(1): 26-42.* Christian participation in the American Revolution was antibiblical. To defend the Revolution required the introduction of Lockean ideas into Protestant theology. Anglican Jonathan Boucher was one of the few ministers who consistently opposed the Revolution on scriptural grounds. His views on civil government were more consistent with biblical doctrine than the views of Christian Whigs. 46 notes. R. E. Butchart

1384. McGreal, Mary Nona. SAMUEL MAZZUCHELLI, PARTICIPANT IN FRONTIER DEMOCRACY. *Records of the Am. Catholic Hist. Soc. of Philadelphia 1976 87(1-4): 99-116.* In his *Memoirs,* Father Samuel Mazzuchelli, a Dominican missionary to the Old Northwest, formulated his views on American democracy, concluding that church and state in the United States are mutually supportive of their respective independence and freedom, that Catholicism is not incompatible with the republican government, that liberty of worship is expedient, and that legal recognition of religious institutions is beneficial. 28 notes. J. M. McCarthy

1385. McLoughlin, William G. 'ENTHUSIASM FOR LIBERTY': THE GREAT AWAKENING AS THE KEY TO THE REVOLUTION. *Pro. of the Am. Antiquarian Soc. 1977 87(1): 69-95.* The American Revolution was a natural outgrowth of the Great Awakening in the 1730's which sought to codify and enforce a particular code of behavior on the nation. Americans believed that republicanism was God's will. This belief preceded the war for independence. Pietistic religion, with its emphasis on individualism and God's power, provided the impetus for revolt. Primary and secondary sources; 31 notes. J. Andrew

1386. Miller, Glenn. THE AMERICAN REVOLUTION AS A RELIGIOUS EVENT: AN ESSAY ON POLITICAL THEOLOGY. *Foundations 1976 19(2): 111-120.* The American Revolution as a religious event is a question of the relationship between the revolutionary myth and its history. The religious contribution comes out of the diversity which weakened crown control, the stress on the importance of the individual in the Great Awakening, and education. The churches faced two issues in the period: independence and war, and the people's need for moral advice. The clergy argued in favor of the just war doctrine. "Liberty: civil and religious" was applied only to the patriots. 4 notes. E. E. Eminhizer

1387. Miller, Glenn T. FEAR GOD AND HONOR THE KING: THE FAILURE OF LOYALIST CIVIL THEOLOGY IN THE REVOLUTIONARY CRISIS. *Hist. Mag. of the Protestant Episcopal Church 1978 47(2): 221-242.* A civil theology is a perspective on government rooted in the religious past of a nation, which may include beliefs about a nation's destiny, the divine origin of its government or its providential role in world affairs. Loyalist civil theologians in the American Revolutionary period attempted to be Whigs and Royalists at the same time; the result was more of an open question than a clear answer. Their only unifying factor was the Book of Common Prayer. The Loyalist clergy were unable to unify the religious minorities—such as Baptists and Quakers—because they failed to understand them, religiously or politically. The failure of the Anglican clergy to provide a theological basis for the Tory faction acceptable to others could well have been one of the factors in the eventual English defeat. Too late, with reason too subtle, they were too disorganized and misunderstood too many of their neighbors to accomplish their task. Primary and secondary sources; 64 notes. H. M. Parker, Jr.

1388. Miller, Rodney K. THE POLITICAL IDEOLOGY OF THE ANGLICAN CLERGY. *Hist. Mag. of the Protestant Episcopal Church 1976 45(3): 227-236.* Discusses the political philosophy of the Anglican clergy in colonial Maryland during the American Revolution. The political ideology of almost all the articulate Anglican clergy was based upon something other than the writings of secular political theorists. Usually a clergyman's political ideas, whether loyalist or patriot, were articulated in terms of Scripture or a legalistic position. Most of the political statements did not qualify as political ideology as they were fragmentary and directed toward one particular object, such as the county committee. Any generalizations concerning these men at this time must be derived primarily from their actions rather than from the speeches or writings of the individual clergymen. Based largely on the writings of Jonathan Boucher and secondary sources; 30 notes. H. M. Parker, Jr.

1389. Moffitt, Robert Emmet. ORESTES BROWNSON AND THE POLITICAL CULTURE OF AMERICAN DEMOCRACY. *Modern Age 1978 22(3): 265-277.* Orestes A. Brownson (1803-76), a steadfast proponent of the doctrine of popular sovereignty in a distinctly republican sense, viewed the people of the state, as vested by God through the natural law, as the repository of political authority. Brownson's disillusionment with the methods and results of the 1840 election occasioned a reconsideration of his political thought. He forged a comprehensive theory featuring continuity and balance and perhaps the most systematic elaboration of political theory by a 19th-century American, in *The American Republican,* 1865. Primary and secondary sources; 28 notes. M. L. Lifka

1390. Montero, Darrel. SUPPORT FOR CIVIL LIBERTIES AMONG A COHORT OF HIGH SCHOOL GRADUATES AND COLLEGE STUDENTS. *J. of Social Issues 1975 31(2): 123-136.* This study examines one facet of political attitudes, support for those civil liberties guaranteed in the Bill of Rights, employing a modified version of the Selvin-Hagstrom Libertarian Index, administered by mail questionnaire to an entire high school senior class four years after graduation in 1968. The varied educational backgrounds, combined with the original relative homogeneity of the sample, allow for a refined analysis of the impact of selected demographic variables (e.g., sex, marital status, religious affiliation, political party identification, and education). The results replicate the well established finding that education is positively and highly related to support of civil liberties. In addition, sex and religion are found to exert an impact upon support for civil liberties. Findings are discussed in reference to the role of higher education in democratic societies. J

1391. Morgan, David T. "THE DUPES OF DESIGNING MEN:" JOHN WESLEY AND THE AMERICAN REVOLUTION. *Hist. Mag. of the Protestant Episcopal Church 1975 44(2): 121-131.* Very much opposed to the events leading up to the American Revolution, John Wesley concluded that the unruly Americans were nothing but dupes of determined enemies of the crown in England, the Radical Whigs. He viewed this handful of "evil men" as having brought Englishmen to the "pitch of madness" which had inflamed America. He was kindly disposed toward the colonies, and believed that peace could be restored if they would accept once more their obligation to fear God and honor the King. After the war began, however, he came to the conclusion that it had been smouldering since 1737. Yet he still remained a strong defender of the status quo, the staunchest kind of political conservative. Based largely on Wesley's writings and other 18th-century materials; 30 notes. H. M. Parker, Jr.

1392. Moses, H. Vincent. NATIONALISM AND THE KINGDOM OF GOD ACCORDING TO HANS KOHN AND CARLTON J. H. HAYES. *J. of Church and State 1975 17(2): 259-274.* Discusses the nationalism and religious attitudes of historians Hans Kohn and Carlton J. H. Hayes in the 1950's and 60's.

1393. Newman, Stephen. A NOTE ON *COMMON SENSE* AND CHRISTIAN ESCHATOLOGY. *Pol. Theory: An Int. J. of Pol. Phil. 1978 6(1): 101-108.* Thomas Paine's *Common Sense* appeared in 1776 and seems at least partly to have relied on the eschatological framework central to American Calvinism to make a case for independence.

1394. Noble, David W. CONSERVATISM IN THE USA. *J. of Contemporary Hist. [Great Britain] 1978 13(4): 635-652.* A historiographical study of conservatism in the United States includes Charles A. Beard, Reinhold Niebuhr, Eric Voegelin, Peter Viereck, Russell Kirk, the *National Review,* and others. New conservatism saw the development of totalitarianism in the West as the result of the increasing rootlessness of the common man. Conservative liberals, however, denied the existence of that kind of alienation in America, where, consequently, respect for constitutional restraint prevented autocracy. Revolutionary conservatives currently seek a respect for the principles of ecology, mandated, if necessary, by legal means. M. P. Trauth

1395. Noll, Mark A. CHRISTIAN AND HUMANISTIC VALUES IN EIGHTEENTH CENTURY AMERICA: A BICENTENNIAL REVIEW. *Christian Scholar's Rev. 1976 6(2-3): 114-126.* Discusses the tradition of Christian humanism throughout the 18th century and the effects of the American Revolution on the seeming rift between secular and humanist beliefs in the political arena; notes the contributions of the Puritans and the Whig political tradition.

1396. Noll, Mark A. THE CHURCH AND THE AMERICAN REVOLUTION: HISTORIOGRAPHICAL PITFALLS, PROBLEMS, AND PROGRESS. *Fides et Hist. 1975 8(1): 2-19.* Historiographical examination of the relationships between the various Protestant Churches and the American Revolution. Calls for fuller investigation of the easy merger of Protestantism and support for the revolution; of the religious sources of Loyalist thought; and of the more complex thought of those patriots who, while supporting the revolution, continued to also press a distinctly Christian ethic. Based on primary and secondary sources; 58 notes. R. E. Butchart

1397. Noll, Mark A. EBENEZER DEVOTION: RELIGION AND SOCIETY IN REVOLUTIONARY CONNECTICUT. *Church Hist. 1976 45(3): 293-307.* Uses the career of Ebenezer Devotion as an example to explore the relationship between church and state in 18th-century New England. Because Devotion not only performed the normal range of ministerial functions but was involved in pre-Revolutionary politics, a study of his life reveals much about such interaction. Throughout his career, Devotion remained ultraconservative in ecclesiastical matters. He was among the opponents of the Great Awakening. In this controversy, he developed two opinions that would be important in his later political thinking. First, he came to view "covenant as an external, legal device through which external legal relationships were established." Second, Devotion defended his right as a minister to attend ecclesiastical councils not on the basis of scripture but because it was "a Liberty . . . that is given by the great Law of Nature." Both positions again manifested themselves in Devotion's opposition to the Stamp Act. His political life was part of and depended upon his religious ideology and ecclesiastical viewpoint. 62 notes. M. D. Dibert

1398. Noll, Mark A. OBSERVATIONS ON THE RECONCILIATION OF POLITICS AND RELIGION IN REVOLUTIONARY NEW JERSEY: THE CASE OF JACOB GREEN. *J. of Presbyterian Hist. 1976 54(2): 217-237.* Jacob Green's perception of the distinction between the church and the world is the key to understanding the nature of his participation in Revolutionary events. The thinking which distinguished church and world in his ecclesiology enabled him to upbraid colonial society for religious and moral shortcomings. He took the Whig view of the Revolutionary crisis seriously; at the same time he was able to transcend libertarian categories and to call American society to account by a higher law to which he owed first allegience. Green's case militates against Bernard Bailyn's conclusion concerning the source of moral reform in Revolutionary America. Green's criticism of society proceeded not primarily from a libertarian perspective but from a religious orientation derived from Edwardsean theology. Based on primary and secondary sources; 80 notes. H. M. Parker, Jr.

1399. Osofsky, Gilbert. WENDELL PHILLIPS AND THE QUEST FOR A NEW AMERICAN NATIONAL IDENTITY. *Can. Rev. of Studies in Nationalism [Canada] 1973 1(1): 15-46.* Buttressed by British and American experience, Wendell Phillips's nationalism was shaped by religion. Its ideology was derived from the European Enlightenment, as expressed by Thomas Paine, Thomas Jefferson, James Madison, and Alexander Hamilton. The Puritan ideal of a Godly Commonwealth, through a pursuit of Christian morality and justice, however, was the main influence on Phillips's nationalism. He would have fragmented the American republic to destroy slavery, and he sought to amalgamate all the American races. Thus, it was the moral end which mattered most in Phillips's nationalism. Based on newspapers, magazines, letters, and secondary sources; 85 notes. T. Spira

1400. Pauley, William E., Jr. TRAGIC HERO: LOYALIST JOHN J. ZUBLY. *J. of Presbyterian Hist. 1976 54(1): 61-81.* The Swiss-born Reverend John J. Zubly (1724-81), pastor of the Independent Presbyterian Church, Savannah, Georgia, heroically articulated the principles upon which the colonies sought redress of grievances from the crown government. He could not or would not, however, alter his principles to include the possibility of political separation from the mother country. He was an independent thinker who analyzed the Anglo-American relationship in ways that closely paralleled the major voices of patriotic thinking in other colonies, but he arrived at different conclusions concerning the wisdom and justice of seeking political separation. Consistent in his thinking to the end, he died a broken man. Based largely on Zubly's writings and sermons; illus., 59 notes. H. M. Parker, Jr.

1401. Payne, Ernest A. NONCONFORMISTS AND THE AMERICAN REVOLUTION: THE SOCIETY'S ANNUAL LECTURE, 1976. *J. of the United Reformed Church Hist. Soc. 1976 1(8): 210-227.* Traces events from 1765 including a vigorous transatlantic correspondence involving Englishmen such as Thomas Hollis, Richard Price, and John Wilkes as well as Americans such as Benjamin Franklin, Isaac Backus, and Charles Chauncy in explaining the drift of Nonconformists into support for the American Revolutionary cause. They came to perceive, as is indicated in Price's *Observations on the Nature of Civil Liberty* (1776), that civil and religious liberty are closely linked. Published sources; 50 notes. S. C. Pearson, Jr.

1402. Pendell, Thomas Roy. IN THE AFTERMATH OF AMSTERDAM: ONE PREACHER'S ODYSSEY. *J. of Ecumenical Studies 1979 16(1): 56-59.* The author, a Methodist minister, credits the spirit of the 1st World Conference of Christian Youth (Amsterdam, 1939) with providing the impetus for his continued involvement in fostering international understanding, especially with the USSR, many of whose representatives have visited his home. S

1403. Raines, John C. THEODICY AND POLITICS. *Worldview 1973 16(14): 44-48.* Analyzes the "religious and social thought of Reinhold Niebuhr as the most sophisticated and complex of the Christian realist presentations." Discusses deepening religious impoverishment in world today. "Both at the level of political interpretation and at the level of theodicy so closely linked to it, the worldview of Christian realism has begun to experience fundamental problems in organizing and consolidating man's interpretation of, and confidence for, life." M. L. Frey

1404. Raymond, Allan. "I FEAR GOD AND HONOUR THE KING": JOHN WESLEY AND THE AMERICAN REVOLUTION. *Church Hist. 1976 45(3): 316-328.* John Wesley, leader of the Methodist movement in England, was a significant figure to the unenfranchised English lower class. Although Wesley could not condone revolution against the King and Parliament, he originally felt that the Americans were constitutionally right and that the ministry had acted unwisely toward them. His fears, roused by the Wilkesite controversy, hinted that there was a deep-seated plot to overthrow the British government and that the American Revolution was part of such a plan. These fears and his desire to maintain royal support for Methodism prompted Wesley to begin his government pamphleteering. Wartime events convinced Wesley that he was right and led him to develop an increasingly bitter attitude toward the Americans. With the French intervention, he turned away from the American phase of the war and pursued a popular anti-Catholic campaign against France. 80 notes. M. D. Dibert

1405. Reynolds, Noel B. THE DOCTRINE OF AN INSPIRED CONSTITUTION. *Brigham Young U. Studies 1976 16(3): 315-340.* Examines the views of the founding fathers and the general political theories of government in the 18th century to determine to what degree the American Constitution was inspired by God. Discusses the attitudes of modern-day historians on the question and criticizes secular revisionist historians for breaking the traditional inspirational view held by the Latter-Day Saints. The ultimate constitutional document may have come as a result of the evolution of God's inspirations rather than by direct revelations to the founding fathers. M. S. Legan

1406. Roselle, Daniel. SERMONS ON THE AMERICAN REVOLUTION: A BICENTENNIAL FEATURE. *Social Educ. 1975 39(5): 286-292.* A collection of five sermons on the American Revolution, by Jonathan Mayhew, Samuel Cooke, Samuel Langdon, John Witherspoon, and Samuel West, stimulated student discussion on religion and the American Revolution. S

1407. Russell, C. Allyn. WILLIAM JENNINGS BRYAN: STATESMAN—FUNDAMENTALIST. *J. of Presbyterian Hist. 1975 53(2): 93-119.* Emphasizes the religious Fundamentalism of Presbyterian William Jennings Bryan (1860-1925) more than his radical statesmanship. His Fundamentalism was not an appendage to his later years. The ingredients of that theological tendency and lifestyle were literally born with him. Suggests the difficulties in applying religious principles to national and international problems. Based largely on Bryan's writings; 103 notes. H. M. Parker, Jr.

1408. Scaff, Lawrence A. CITIZENSHIP IN AMERICA: THEORIES OF THE FOUNDING. Chaudhuri, Joyotpaul, ed. *The Non-Lockean Roots of American Democratic Thought* (Tucson: U. of Arizona Pr., 1977): 44-62. The philosophical foundations of American citizenship are derived partly from John Locke and partly from distinctly American influences such as Puritanism and Thomas Jefferson's democratic philosophy. Covers the 17th and 18th centuries.

1409. Senese, P. M. CATHOLIQUE D'ABORD!: CATHOLICISM AND NATIONALISM IN THE THOUGHT OF LIONEL GROULX. *Can. Hist. Rev. [Canada] 1979 60(2): 154-177.* Examines the thought of Lionel Groulx, sometimes called the father of modern Quebec separatism.

It was his Catholicism, however, that undergirded his French nationalism during 1897-1928. He feared the growing secularization of society he observed as industrialism occurred. Believing that Quebec, with its French Catholic majority, was the only place on the continent where Catholicism might be strengthened to resist the dangers of secularism, he advocated separatism. Nationalism for him was an instrument for the regeneration of Catholicism. Based on Groulx's published and manuscript writings.

1410. Shanklin, Thomas L. and Rowe, Kenneth E., eds. DAVID CREAMER AND THE BALTIMORE MOB RIOT, APRIL 19, 1861. *Methodist Hist. 1975 13(4): 61-64.* Two letters of David Creamer (1812-87), first Methodist hymnologist, written in 1861 and 1863 to George Richard Crooks, editor of *The Methodist*, . . . discuss the Baltimore Riot of 1861 and Creamer's support of the Union cause. 6 notes.
H. L. Calkin

1411. Silver, A. I. SOME QUEBEC ATTITUDES IN AN AGE OF IMPERIALISM AND IDEOLOGICAL CONFLICT. *Can. Hist. Rev. [Canada] 1976 57(4): 440-460.* Uses French-Quebec newspapers, pamphlets, and other printed material to examine late 19th- and early 20th-century attitudes toward world affairs. Finds considerable sympathy for the "civilising mission" in colonial imperialism and for the Catholic, conservative camp in a perceived division of the world on ideological grounds. These sympathies and perceptions seem to have influenced attitudes toward French Canada's place in Canada and in the British Empire.
A

1412. Spalding, James C. LOYALIST AS ROYALIST, PATRIOT AS PURITAN: THE AMERICAN REVOLUTION AS A REPETITION OF THE ENGLISH CIVIL WARS. *Church Hist. 1976 45(3): 329-340.* The struggle of the American Revolution was seen by many as an extension of the English Civil Wars. Thomas Jefferson often compared the two, and Reverend Jonathan Boucher believed that the two events were so similar that they would reach identical conclusions. Because of Boucher's stubborn insistence on the matter, he often delivered his sermons armed with a pair of pistols. 47 notes. M. D. Dibert

1413. Stange, Douglas C. ABOLITION AS TREASON: THE UNITARIAN ELITE DEFENDS LAW, ORDER, AND THE UNION. *Harvard Lib. Bull. 1980 28(2): 152-170.* Describes pre-Civil War opposition of Unitarian conservative clergymen in Boston and St. Louis to the abolitionist movement. By championing law and order, respect for the US Constitution and state law, and separation of politics from moral influence, the ministers upheld the view of businessmen, who were mainly responsible for the fiscal well-being of the churches. The clergy, however, did accept in principle proposals to colonize slaves in foreign lands, realizing the impracticality of the idea because slaveholders would lose too much to agree. Any strong attempt at colonization would generate national disunion, a much worse evil, in the clergy's view, than slavery. Based on the James Freeman Clarke Papers, Houghton Library, Harvard University; William G. Elliot Collection, University Archives, Olin Library, Washington University, St. Louis; and files of the Missouri Historical Society, St. Louis; 81 notes. D. J. Mycue

1414. Stein, Stephen J. AN APOCALYPTIC RATIONALE FOR THE AMERICAN REVOLUTION. *Early Am. Literature 1975 9(3): 211-225.* Samuel Sherwood's sermon "The Church's Flight into the Wilderness" at Norfield, Connecticut, 17 January 1776, developed exegetical arguments in support of the colonies' resistance to the Crown. Those who listened to Sherwood were familiar with the tradition of the jeremiad, and the speaker's apocalyptic justification of the Revolution possessed a special persuasiveness for a Protestant audience conditioned to biblical arguments and interpretations of the *Book of Revelation*. Based on primary and secondary sources; 46 notes. D. P. Wharton

1415. Stevens, Meribah L. ROLE OF THE CLERGY IN ESTABLISHING AMERICAN INDEPENDENCE. *Daughters of the Am. Revolution Mag. 1978 112(9): 860-862.* Though preaching "peace at any cost" during the 1740's, the clergy throughout the colonies became radicalized and began urging independence from the pulpit in the late 1750's; offers specific examples and excerpts from sermons.

1416. Stuart, Reginald C. THE ORIGINS OF AMERICAN NATIONALISM TO 1783: AN HISTORIOGRAPHICAL SURVEY. *Can. Rev. of Studies in Nationalism [Canada] 1979 6(2): 139-151.* Discusses the debate on the existence of nationalism in the American colonies before the American Revolution. Nineteenth-century scholars argued that strong nationalist sentiments underlay the Revolution. Twentieth-century historians have linked nationalism to the American environment, studied changes in politics, economics, and religion, and explored the multiple loyalties present during 1735-76. There is a consensus that the building blocks of nationalism and an embryonic self-consciousness did exist before the Revolution. 36 notes. R. Aldrich

1417. Thompson, Dennis L. THE BASIC DOCTRINES AND CONCEPTS OF REINHOLD NIEBUHR'S POLITICAL THOUGHT. *J. of Church and State 1975 17(2): 275-299.* Discusses the political thought, theology, and views of society of social critic Reinhold Niebuhr, 1927-59.

1418. Trivers, Howard. UNIVERSALISM IN THE THOUGHT OF THE FOUNDING FATHERS. *Virginia Q. Rev. 1976 52(3): 448-462.* The American Republic is unique because it is founded upon universal ideas, particularly those of the Enlightenment and the English and Christian traditions. Our best hope is to put our ideals into practice at home and develop and emphasize common interests with our adversaries, based upon the universal ideas of the Republic. O. H. Zabel

1419. Wald, Alan M. FROM ANTINOMIANISM TO REVOLUTIONARY MARXISM: JOHN WHEELWRIGHT & THE NEW ENGLAND REBEL TRADITION. *Marxist Perspectives 1980 3(2): 44-68.* Describes John Wheelwright (1897-1940), Boston brahmin, modernist poet, and revolutionary socialist, as heir to the New England radical tradition of Hutchinson, Thoreau, and Emerson.

1420. Werly, John M. PREMILLENNIALISM AND THE PARANOID STYLE. *Am. Studies [Lawrence, KS] 1977 18(1): 39-55.* Premillennialists reject reform, have no faith in social progress, and believe that all religious and secular institutions are "infested with satanic influences." The Twenties, a time of great change, produced many such groups. Among the most significant was the Ku Klux Klan. Many critics of the New Deal in the Thirties also fit this mold, such as Huey Long, Gerald L. K. Smith, and Father Charles Coughlin. After World War II Billy James Hargis and other new personalities emerged. All had a paranoid view of American society, and saw conspiracies everywhere. Primary and secondary sources; 35 notes. J. Andrew

1421. Whitaker, Reginald. POLITICAL THOUGHT AND POLITICAL ACTION IN MACKENZIE KING. *J. of Can. Studies [Canada] 1978-79 13(4): 40-60.* The consistency in his political behavior reveals that William Lyon Mackenzie King (1874-1950) had an ideology. As a Protestant, he believed in a God of love and consequently believed in progress. The unfolding of history presented each generation of liberals with new tasks. King was also a technocrat who regarded managerial mediation as essential to an industrial society. The liberal corporatism of his classless Liberal Party was intended to create social harmony; but the class situation in society determined his political actions. Based on W. L. M. King Diary and secondary sources; 47 notes. G. E. Panting

1422. Wu, Nai-te. NI-PU-ÊRH TI CHÊNG CHIH CHIH HSUEH CHIEN CHIEH [The political philosophy of Reinhold Niebuhr]. *Thought and Word [Taiwan] 1974 12(3): 123-133.* A Christian realist, Reinhold Niebuhr's political philosophy is contradictory because he believes in the immorality and irrationality of politics and has faith in human virtue. Aware of his limitations, modern man is torn between liberalism and materialism, or between democracy and Marxism. Politically and historically, this struggle centers on the distribution of wealth. Niebuhr points out the fallacies and dangers of Marxism and communism. Although he is critical of liberalism, Niebuhr believes it is man's hope for the future because of its capacity for change. Based on Niebuhr's works and other secondary works; 32 notes, biblio. C. B. Brown

1423. Yodelis, M. A. BOSTON'S FIRST MAJOR NEWSPAPER WAR: A "GREAT AWAKENING" OF FREEDOM. *Journalism Q. 1974 51(2): 207-212.* During Boston's newspaper war in the 1740's between pro and anti-revivalists, Thomas Fleet in the *Boston Evening Post* wrote and reprinted libertarian statements on freedom of the press.
S

1424. Ziff, Larzer. REVOLUTIONARY RHETORIC AND PURITANISM. *Early Am. Literature 1978 13(1): 45-49.* Puritan history is examined through the Revolutionary rhetoric of John Adams and Thomas Paine. Adams represented the American situation as the organic product of centuries-old attitudes, nurtured in England before their flowering in New England. The importance of Adams's secular version of Puritan history resides in its justification of established institutions. Having been a powerful political movement in England, Puritanism evolved into a culture in America. Nonetheless, the political inclinations were there to be evoked. The persuasiveness of Paine's *Common Sense* was due to its meeting the feelings of a large number of avowed Calvinists. Primary sources; 9 notes, J. N. Friedel

9. HEALTH

1425. Atteberry, Maxine. IT ALL BEGAN IN BATTLE CREEK. *Adventist Heritage 1979 6(2): 38-43.* History of Seventh-Day Adventist nurses' training at California's College of Medical Evangelists (later Loma Linda University), since ca. 1905; such training by the Adventists started at the Battle Creek Sanitarium in Michigan in 1884.

1426. Bardell, Eunice Bonow. PRIMITIVE PHYSICK: JOHN WESLEY'S RECEIPTS. *Pharmacy in Hist. 1979 21(3): 111-121.* Compares the home remedies of the 1747 first edition of *Primitive Physick: or, an Easy and Natural Method of Curing Most Diseases* by John Wesley with the prescribed remedies of 18th-century British medical practitioners. The sources of Wesley's 1745 pamphlet, *A Collection of Receits For the Use of the Poor,* and 1747 book, *Primitive Physick,* and his simply prescribed natural therapeutics were Wesley's observations of the health care of the American Indians of Georgia and the medical treatises of Wesley's predecessors and contemporaries: Dr. George Cheyne (1673-1743); Nicholas Culpeper (1616-1654); Robert Doyle; William Salomon; George Berkeley, Bishop of Cloyne, Ireland; and Dr. Thomas Dover. In the preparation of Wesley's simple remedies, 225 different drugs were used, of which more than 80 percent were of plant origin; 71 of the 225 drugs appeared in the London Pharmacopoeia (1746) and 137 were in the Edinburgh Pharmacopoeia (1744). "John Wesley, as a theologian and itinerant preacher, exerted a tremendous influence on the spiritual well-being of his audience; as a writer of a domestic remedy book he exerted just as tremendous an influence on the medical care provided in the home, in England and America." 3 illus., 61 notes. S. C. Morrison

1427. Berk, Daniel W. ADVENTISM ON THE PICTURE POST CARD. *Adventist Heritage 1978 5(2): 48-53.* Postcards of Adventists' sanitariums, 1900-10's.

1428. Brunel, Gilles and Morissette, Luc. GUÉRISON ET ETHNO-ÉTIOLOGIE POPULAIRE [Healing and popular ethno-etiology]. *Anthropologica [Canada] 1979 21(1): 43-72.* The principles behind Quebec folk healers' classification of diseases agreed with those in folk biology, and there is increased significance of religious syncretism in folk healing.

1429. Bullock, Alice. FRANCIS SCHLATTER: A FOOL FOR GOD. *Palacio 1975 83(1): 38-45.* Francis Schlatter gained notoriety in Peralta, New Mexico, as a mystic and faith healer, 1895-96.

1430. Bush, Lester E., Jr. A PECULIAR PEOPLE: THE PHYSIOLOGICAL ASPECTS OF MORMONISM 1850-1875. *Dialogue 1979 12(3): 61-83.* Variations on the theme of a peculiarly Mormon physiology circulated in medical journals, popular magazines, and government reports during 1860-75. Inferences about the detrimental effect of polygamy on health and physical features, with obvious implications for morality, attracted public attention when Dr. Roberts Bartholow's observations were published as the Surgeon General's Statistical Report. The last known medical report of racial degeneration among Mormons in Utah was Surgeon E. P. Vollum's, also published by the government. Certainly the Mormons' religious resistance to the medical profession did some physical harm. In the 20th century, however, their death rate is below the national average. Primary sources; 2 photos, 59 notes. S

1431. Cassedy, James H. AN AMERICAN CLERICAL CRISIS: MINISTERS' SORE THROAT, 1830-1860. *Bull of the Hist. of Medicine 1979 53(1): 23-38.* For 20 or 30 years, minister's sore throat was a significant occupational disease; and it had broad medical, professional, and social ramifications in the years before the Civil War. It was not identified simply with ministers, but also afflicted lawyers and teachers as well as others. Before 1831, the common sore throat was a mild affliction which did not bother people to any great extent. In 1831, however, a virulent variety came to notice in New England, and it soon spread through the country. Among clergymen, it was more severe, as the Second Great Awakening had stirred up religious zeal that translated into revivals and camp meetings, and to regular prayer meetings. Moreover, Protestant clergymen tried to counter the spread of Catholicism, Unitarianism, and Mormonism, and they anxiously awaited the approach of the millenium. 40 notes. M. Kaufman

1432. Cherry, Charles L. FRIENDS ASYLUM, MORGAN HINCHMAN, AND MORAL INSANITY. *Quaker Hist. 1978 67(1): 20-34.* A member of Philadelphia's North Meeting, Morgan Hinchman, was committed by his family and friends on 7 January 1847 for violent and paranoid behavior. He was discharged on 6 July 1847. He sued for conspiracy to defraud him of his property, and collected $10,000 in damages in a widely publicized, five-week, Philadelphia jury trial. He won because the idea of "moral," or partial, emotional instability lacked popular or consistent judicial acceptance on a religious or rationalist basis. Hinchman was sick, and those who committed him intended to act in his best interests, but they conducted a weak defense. 15 notes. T. D. S. Bassett

1433. Clements, William M. FAITH HEALING NARRATIVES FROM NORTHEAST ARKANSAS. *Indiana Folklore 1976 9(1): 15-40.* Describes the belief systems of one religious sect, the Pentecostals, and relates narratives of faith healing emanating from white Pentecostals in northeast Arkansas, 1937-73.

1434. Cunningham, Raymond J. FROM HOLINESS TO HEALING: THE FAITH CURE IN AMERICA. *Church Hist. 1974 43(4): 499-513.* During the 1870's and 1880's, "faith cure" was a force to contend with in all the major evangelical denominations. The subsidence of the faith cure movement and the controversy surrounding it by the mid-1890's was an important indication of the transition of perfectionism from denominational to sectarian status. The intimate connection between perfectionism and faith cure is clearly revealed in the interwoven ministries of three leading practitioners of faith healing: Charles Cullis, William E. Boardman, and Albert B. Simpson. 130 notes. M. D. Dibert

1435. Daly, Lydia, ed. THE WIT OF LOMA LINDA'S IRISHMAN. *Adventist Heritage 1979 6(2): 49-52.* Excerpts from letters (1918-34) of Dr. Percy Tilson Magan, minister, teacher, medical doctor, and president of the College of Medical Evangelists (now Loma Linda University) in California during 1928-42.

1436. Damsteegt, P. Gerard. HEALTH REFORM AND THE BIBLE IN EARLY SABBATARIAN ADVENTISM. *Adventist Heritage 1978 5(2): 13-21.* Discusses the health reform movement in early-to-mid-19th century America and the use of religious arguments in stressing the importance of healthful living.

1437. Divett, Robert T. HIS CHASTENING ROD: CHOLERA EPIDEMICS AND THE MORMONS. *Dialogue 1979 12(3): 6-15.* Studies the cholera epidemics transmitted from Asia and Europe to Canada and the United States in 1832, 1848, 1853-54, 1863, and 1873. The early Mormons proclaimed them the visitation of God's wrath and urged resignation and faith. The Mormons had a lower mortality rate than others; the plague turned people to righteousness. In 1883 the bacillus which causes cholera was discovered. 29 notes. R. V. Ritter

1438. Divett, Robert T. MEDICINE AND THE MORMONS: A HISTORICAL PERSPECTIVE. *Dialogue 1979 12(3): 16-25.* Studies early medical practice in the United States, including the period of heroic medicine, heavily dependent on massive doses of calomel as a panacea. Samuel Thomson (1769-1843) and his botanic medicine followed, in reaction. Several early Mormons practiced Thomsonian medicine. The two methods were practiced extensively through the Civil War. Heroic use of calomel ceased ca. 1880. 41 notes. R. V. Ritter

1439. Flowers, Ronald B. FREEDOM OF RELIGION VERSUS CIVIL AUTHORITY IN MATTERS OF HEALTH. *Ann. of the Am. Acad. of Pol. and Social Sci. 1979 (446): 149-161.* Decisions of the United States Supreme Court in 1963 and 1972 expanded the scope of the free exercise clause of the First Amendment beyond any previous interpretation of that clause in American judicial history. Although it is still understood that government may prohibit religiously motivated behavior which represents harm to individuals or to the public welfare, civil authorities now may intervene only when the religious activity threatens a compelling state interest. The possibilities of religious activity are abundant, and government intervention is limited to only the gravest offenses of the public order. This article examines some of the areas of health, broadly defined, in which religious attitudes have conflicted with state interests: the handling of poisonous snakes and drinking of poison in religious worship, the use of prohibited drugs in worship, compulsory blood transfusions for those who have theological objections to them, and the application of public health laws to those whose theology rejects medicine altogether. In the light of these cases, as much as the American constitutional system exalts religious liberty, it can never be unfettered. But, even in this area, it is imperative that our governmental units make religious liberty the rule and its curtailment the exception. J

1440. Fowler, Franklin T. THE HISTORY OF SOUTHERN BAPTIST MEDICAL MISSIONS. *Baptist Hist. and Heritage 1975 10(4): 194-203.* Historical chronology of Southern Baptist Medical Missions during 1846-1975, divided into three periods: 1846-1900, 1900-40's, and 1950-1975. In more recent years voluntary short-term service by doctors, dentists and nurses and increasing co-operation with developing nations have characterized the program. Based on ecclesiastical records; 30 notes. H. M. Parker, Jr.

1441. Hayden, Jess, Jr. NIELS BJORN JORGENSEN: PAINLESS DENTIST. *Adventist Heritage 1979 6(2): 44-48.* Denmark-born dentist Niels Bjorn Jorgensen (1894-1974) became acquainted with the Adventists' College of Medical Evangelists (later Loma Linda University) in California in 1923 when he met Dr. Riethmuller, and began teaching at Loma Linda in 1942; Jorgensen was responsible for innovative techniques in teaching dentistry and in sedation and anesthesia in dentistry.

1442. Hirsch, Lester M. PHINEAS PARKHURST QUIMBY. *New-England Galaxy 1978 19(3): 27-31.* Phineas Parkhurst Quimby (1802-66) helped upgrade medical procedures for treating the effects of the mind on the body. Notes his use of hypnotism and psychiatry in the healing of the mentally ill, his concern for his patients, his "clairvoyance," and his influence on Mary Baker Eddy, founder of Christian Science. Covers 1820's-66. P. C. Marshall

1443. Johnson, Greg. A CLASSIFICATION OF FAITH HEALING PRACTICES. *New York Folklore Q. 1975 1(1-2): 91-96.* Defines and describes various 20th-century techniques of faith healing based on charismatic, spiritual, and psychic approaches.

1444. Kay, Margarita Artschwager. THE *FLORILEGIO MEDICINAL:* SOURCE OF SOUTHWEST ETHNOMEDICINE. *Ethnohistory 1977 24(3): 251-259.* In 1711, Jesuit lay brother Juan de Esteyneffer, who had been sent to the Order's College at Chihuahua to care for the old or ailing missionaries, wrote the *Florilegio Medicinal.* This book compiled the herbal lore of various Indians missionized by the Jesuits, combined it with the *materia medica* of Europe and attached these cures to disease conditions that were scientifically recognized in the 18th century. It is suggested that this book has served to standardize herbal therapy throughout the Greater Southwest. J

1445. Koss, Joan D. THERAPEUTIC ASPECTS OF PUERTO RICAN CULT PRACTICES. *Psychiatry 1975 38(2): 160-171.* Studies the social process in Puerto Rican spiritualist cult practices and examines the relationship between patterns of cult social organization and the cult execution of culturally patterned psychotherapeutic processes for committed adherents. S

1446. LaPalm, Loretta. THE HÔTEL-DIEU OF QUEBEC: THE FIRST HOSPITAL NORTH OF THE RIO GRANDE UNDER ITS FIRST TWO SUPERIORS. *Study Sessions [Canada] 1974 41: 53-64.* Gives a history of the Hôtel-Dieu, a hospital founded in 1639 by nuns to provide medical care for the Indians. A paper read at the 1974 annual meeting of the Canadian Catholic Historical Association. S

1447. Lockwood, Rose A. BIRTH, ILLNESS AND DEATH IN 18TH-CENTURY NEW ENGLAND. *J. of Social Hist. 1978 12(1): 111-128.* The diary of Ebenezer Parkman (1703-82), Congregationalist minister of Westborough, Massachusetts, provides the opportunity to reconstruct the social history of medicine in a New England village. The qualitative impressions of Parkman on illness and death, his discussion of the treatment of disease, and the details of the birth of the Parkman children, illustrate the impact of diseases and death on 18th-century New Englanders. What emerged was a pattern of social interdependence. Residents confronted childbirth, illness, and death as a social group. Includes an appendix of the reproductive history of the Parkman family. Based on *The Diary of Ebenezer Parkman, 1703-1782,* ed., Francis G. Walett (Worcester, Ma., 1974), 3 vols., and secondary sources; 70 notes. R. S. Sliwoski

1448. Lyon, Joseph L. and Nelson, Steven. MORMON HEALTH. *Dialogue 1979 12(3): 84-96.* A statistical study of health among Mormons. Studies of the incidence and consequences of the three top killers in the United States—cancer, heart disease, and stroke—indicate that Mormons are below US averages (i.e., have fewer deaths from these causes) in all three cases. Evidence indicates a causal relationship between Mormon life styles and health, but more research is needed. Covers 1930-79. Primary sources; 5 tables, 12 notes. R. V. Ritter

1449. Motto, Sytha. THE SISTERS OF CHARITY AND ST. VINCENT'S HOSPITAL: AN AMPLIFICATION OF SISTER MALLON'S JOURNAL. *New Mexico Hist. Rev. 1977 52(3): 228-236.* Discusses the history of St. Vincent's Hospital, established by the Sisters of Charity in Santa Fe, New Mexico, in 1865. 3 photos, 18 notes. J. H. Krenkel

1450. Norwood, W. Frederick. THE CME SCHOOL OF MEDICINE: ITS STRUGGLE FOR RECOGNITION AND STATUS, 1905-1915. *Adventist Heritage 1979 6(2): 15-24.* History of the College of Medical Evangelists, later Loma Linda University, the Seventh-Day Adventist school of medicine in California, from its founding in 1905 until 1915.

1451. Numbers, Ronald L. DR. JACKSON'S WATER CURE AND ITS INFLUENCE ON ADVENTIST HEALTH REFORM. *Adventist Heritage 1974 1(1): 11-16, 58-59.* Describes changes in Adventist health care by Ellen G. White, a leader of the sabbatarian wing of Adventists, after stays at the hydrotherapy establishment of Dr. James Caleb Jackson in Dansville, New York, in 1864 and 1865.

1452. Numbers, Ronald L. HEALTH REFORM ON THE DELAWARE. *New Jersey Hist. 1974 92(1): 5-12.* Russell Thacher Trall began his medical practice in 1844 when he established the Hygienic Institute in New York City, where he, as a Seventh-Day Adventist, emphasized nonuse of drugs; includes the diary of one of his patients, Merritt Kellogg, during his stay at another of Trall's establishments, the New York Hygeio-Therapeutic College in Florence Heights, New Jersey.

1453. Park, Roberta J. THE ATTITUDES OF LEADING NEW ENGLAND TRANSCENDENTALISTS TOWARD HEALTHFUL EXERCISE, ACTIVE RECREATIONS AND PROPER CARE OF THE BODY, 1830-1860. *J. of Sport Hist. 1977 4(1): 34-50.* Examines attitudes of leading New England transcendentalists, generally finding that Ralph Waldo Emerson (1803-82), William Ellery Channing (1780-1842), Henry David Thoreau (1817-62), Amos Bronson Alcott (1799-1888), and Margaret Fuller (1810-50) agreed on the need for a healthy body. Their writings introduced a wide reading audience to ideas regarding the body as a means to attaining "higher consciousness," and to their attitudes toward health, exercise, play, and recreations. 53 notes. M. Kaufman

1454. Richter, Thomas, ed. SISTER CATHERINE MALLON'S JOURNAL. *New Mexico Hist. Rev. 1977 52(2): 135-155, (3): 237-250.* Part I. Bishop Jean Baptiste Lamy wished to provide social services for the people of New Mexico and asked the Sisters of Charity of Cincinnati, Ohio, to staff the proposed hospital in Santa Fe. Sister Catherine Mallon, one of the original four sisters to come, kept a journal of her experiences. Illus., 38 notes. Part II. Sister Catherine Mallon was one of four nurses who came to New Mexico in 1865 to organize a hospital in Santa Fe. Later she also served in Colorado. Reprints her journal, the original of which is now in Archives of the Sisters of Charity, Mt. St. Joseph, Cincinnati, Ohio. J. H. Krenkel

1455. Roberts, George B. CHRIST CHURCH HOSPITAL. *Hist. Mag. of the Protestant Episcopal Church 1976 45(1): 89-102.* Chronicles the origin and subsequent development of Christ Church Hospital of Philadelphia, which was organized 27 April 1778 as the result of a large bequest from the estate of Dr. John Kearsley (1684-1772). The hospital is a women's residential eleemosynary institution which can accommodate about 85 residents. Emphasizes additions and improvements to the physical plant, and bequests and supervisory personnel. As it prepares to enter its third century of service it will be known as Kearsley Home. H. M. Parker, Jr.

1456. Sayad, Elizabeth Gentry. ALEXIAN BROTHERS' HOSPITAL: UNIQUE HERITAGE. *Missouri Hist. Soc. Bull. 1980 36(4): 264-267.* The Alexian Brothers, an order committed to saving souls through nursing, established their first St. Louis hospital in 1869 under the direction of Brothers Paulus Tollig and Alexius Bernard. The order sought better treatment of mental disease and alcoholism. In the 19th century, Alexian hospital patients were preponderantly German Americans. Until 1920 much of this German order's cultural heritage was retained in the hospital's practices. Based on Alexian Brothers publications; photo, 21 notes. H. T. Lovin

1457. Shapiro, Henry D. GETTING BACK-AND DOWN-TO BASICS. *Rev. in Am. Hist. 1977 5(2): 242-248.* Review article prompted by Ronald L. Numbers's *Prophetess of Health: A Study of Ellen G. White* (New York: Harper & Row, 1976), which discusses White (1827-1915), a leader of the Seventh-Day Adventists.

1458. Shryock, Harold. PORTRAITS FROM THE LOMA LINDA ALBUM. *Adventist Heritage 1979 6(2): 3-14.* Photographs accompanied by the history of the Loma Linda Sanitarium, hospital, and medical school run by the Seventh-Day Adventists in California; covers 1905-19.

1459. Smith, N. Lee. HERBAL REMEDIES: GOD'S MEDICINE? *Dialogue 1979 12(3): 37-60.* As an act of faith, Mormons rely on herbal cures rather than physicians. In the early 19th century Mormons implicitly mistrusted or explicitly opposed all medical practice except that of herbalists, but as medical science advanced, preconceptions changed. The church sanctioned orthodox medicine in 1882. Public acceptance has come more slowly. Official emphasis is still on proven methods, whether medical or herbal; the latter also need careful testing for safety. Primary sources; photo, 77 notes. R. V. Ritter

1460. Teaham, John F. WARREN FELT EVANS AND MENTAL HEALING: ROMANTIC IDEALISM AND PRACTICAL MYSTICISM IN NINETEENTH CENTURY AMERICA. *Church Hist. 1979 48(1): 63-80.* Warren Felt Evans wrote six books that influenced the growth of New Thought, a loosely organized religious movement concerned with health and spiritual integration. His thought and therapy united idealistic philosophy and practical mysticism. As a philosophical idealist with a deeply mystical understanding of experience, Evans developed a general religious and cultural critique. The nature of Evans's mysticism influenced the practical healing techniques he employed to assist others in achieving harmonial consciousness. While influenced by romantic idealism and mysticism, Evans encountered difficulties that intense soul-searching could not alleviate. By advocating scientific and medical knowledge to supplement the cure and insisting that the patient realize that healing is not mysterious or miraculous, Evans linked his therapy with pragmatic character of later mind cure forms. Covers 1864-89. M. Dibert

1461. White, Ellen G. ITS NAME IS "BEAUTIFUL HILL." *Adventist Heritage 1979 6(2): 53-62.* Excerpts from a letter from Ellen G. White (1827-1915), cofounder of the Seventh-Day Adventist Church and one of the founders of the College of Medical Evangelists (later Loma Linda University), to two of her nieces in 1905, urging them to come to California, to help at the Adventists' new Loma Linda Sanitarium.

1462. Whorton, James C. "CHRISTIAN PHYSIOLOGY": WILLIAM ALCOTT'S PRESCRIPTION FOR THE MILLENNIUM. *Bull. of the Hist. of Medicine 1975 49(4): 466-481.* William A. Alcott, M.D. (1798-1859) was a leading health reformer of the Jacksonian age, and a study of his ideas provides a detailed exposition of the ideology of the health reform movement. He was an advocate of "Christian Physiology" or the "directing of biological science toward the social goals of contemporary revivalism." He envisioned a Christian civilization "combining the moral and physical vigor of the Biblical days with the scientific knowledge of the modern era." 64 notes. M. Kaufman

1463. Wilcox, Linda P. THE IMPERFECT SCIENCE: BRIGHAM YOUNG ON MEDICAL DOCTORS. *Dialogue 1979 12(3): 26-36.* Considers Brigham Young's opinions of doctors and the practice of medicine. He had little patience with orthodox medicine dependent on harsh drugs dangerous to the patient. Thomsonianism seemed preferable, though Young generally enjoined prevention. Mormons were to adhere "to the Word of Wisdom and follow . . . common sense rules of health." He often expressed his distrust of the medical profession. As medical knowledge advanced, however, he became more accepting. Covers 1840-75. Primary sources; 54 notes. R. V. Ritter

1464. Zelt, Roger P. SMALLPOX INOCULATIONS IN BOSTON, 1721-1722. *Synthesis 1977 4(1): 3-14.* There was a smallpox epidemic in Boston in 1721. Cotton Mather, having heard of smallpox inoculation in Turkey and Africa, made the controversial suggestion that physicians apply this procedure in Boston. Among the 259 persons inoculated, "the overwhelming majority [were from] . . . the highly educated, politically conservative, and religiously orthodox upper segment of the colonial socio-economic strata." Primary and secondary sources; 16 notes. M. M. Vance

10. LABOR

1465. Askol'dova, S. M. RELIGIIA I AMERIKANSKII TRED-IUNIONIZM V KONTSE XIX-NACHALE XX VEKA [Religion and American trade unionism at the turn of the 20th century]. *Voprosy Istorii [USSR] 1973 (9): 89-104.* The article is devoted to the ideological rapprochement between the church seeking to "modernize" its program and American trade unionism which renounced socialist demands and became an instrument for exerting bourgeois influence on the American proletariat. This rapprochement was aimed at achieving coordinated action in the struggle against the socialist movement in the United States. The collaboration of the AFL with the Catholic Church and the various Protestant trends was adroitly used by the bourgeoisie when it resorted to the ill-famed New Deal for the sake of salvaging capitalism. J

1466. Bouchard, Gérard. SUR L'ÉGLISE CATHOLIQUE ET L'INDUSTRIALISATION AU QUÉBEC: LA RÉLIGION DES EUDISTES ET LES OUVRIERS DU BASSIN DE CHICOUTIMI, 1903-1930 [The Catholic Church and the industrialization of Quebec: religion as practiced by the Eudists and the workers of the Chicoutimi Basin, 1903-30]. *Protée [Canada] 1976 5(2): 31-43.* A tacit alliance between the Church and the working class helped shape religious practices in a working-class parish.

1467. Davies, J. Kenneth. THE SECULARIZATION OF THE UTAH LABOR MOVEMENT. *Utah Hist. Q. 1977 45(2): 108-134.* In the 1850's, the Mormon Church encouraged a religiously oriented worker movement. The 1860's brought nonreligious influences: war induced inflation, large numbers of non-Mormon workers, and association with national unions. Church cooperatives, United Orders, and the Board of Trade movement reduced Mormon influence on the budding unions. Nonintercourse with Gentiles, union violence, and closed shops induced some to leave unions. Political and business secularization of the 1890's ended the church's economic program. By 1896 labor secularization was accomplished. Primary and secondary sources; 5 illus., 51 notes. J. L. Hazelton

1468. Friedmann, F. G. DOROTHY DAY UND DER *CATHOLIC WORKER* [Dorothy Day and the *Catholic Worker*]. *Stimmen der Zeit [West Germany] 1980 198(3): 195-200.* In 1933 Dorothy Day (1897-1980) and Peter Maurin (1877-1949) founded the journal, *Catholic Worker,* that propagated the Catholic social doctrines of Pope Leo XIII and Pius XI in the United States and was met with great support by the mass of American Catholics.

1469. Frigon, F. J. CATHOLICISM AND CRISIS: L'ECOLE SOCIALE POPULAIRE AND THE DEPRESSION IN QUEBEC, 1930-1940. *Rev. de l'U. d'Ottawa 1975 45(1): 54-70.* Analyzes the Roman Catholic Church's reaction to the depression and stresses the importance of the École Sociale Populaire "in promoting a profound reexamination of the church's relationship to the other institutions of French Canada and in encouraging the growth of new ones such as labor unions." Based on primary and secondary sources; 62 notes. M. L. Frey

1470. Lapointe, Michelle. LE SYNDICAT CATHOLIQUE DES ALLUMETTIÈRES DE HULL, 1919-1924 [The Catholic matchmakers' union in Hull, 1919-24]. *Rev. d'Hist. de l'Amerique Française [Canada] 1979 32(4): 603-628.* Analysis of the matchmakers' union in Hull, Quebec, enables the researcher to develop much-needed perspective on the female Catholic workers' movement. It was a vigorous union; membership was impressive. Two strike actions were conducted in a very conservative milieu. The union played an important role in raising the consciousness of its membership and in ensuring, on a modest scale, that the needs of female workers in Canada would receive additional attention in years to come. 40 notes. M. R. Yerburgh

1471. Lavigne, Marie and Stoddart, Jennifer. LES TRAVAILLEUSES MONTRÉALAISES ENTRE LES DEUX GUERRES [Women in the workforce of Montreal between the wars]. *Labour [Canada] 1977 2: 170-183.* Examines the participation of women in the Montreal workforce where they constituted at least 25% of the total throughout the period. Includes an analysis of their distribution in various occupations and the problem of wage discrimination. Comparisons are made with men workers in Montreal and with men and women in Toronto. The unique influence of large numbers of religious women, especially in teaching, is also examined. Most employed women were young (15 to 24), single, and most worked in jobs which did not damage their role and traditional function in the family. Census reports, primary and secondary sources; 3 tables, 34 notes. W. A. Kearns

1472. Menard, Johanne. L'INSTITUT DES ARTISANS DU COMTÉ DE DRUMMOND, 1856-1890 [The Drummond County Mechanics Institute, 1856-1890]. *Recherches Sociographiques [Canada] 1975 16(2): 207-218.* Established in 1856, the Drummond County Mechanics Institute was largely composed of farmers and by 1861, French-Canadian Roman Catholics were in the majority. Until 1880 the institute was a vital part of the community; however, the changing composition of its membership brought an end to this dynamism. A. E. LeBlanc

1473. St. Amant, Jean-Claude. LA PROPAGANDE DE L'ÉCOLE SOCIALE POPULAIRE EN FAVEUR DU SYNDICALISME CATHOLIQUE 1911-1949 [The propaganda of the École Sociale Populaire in favor of Catholic Syndicalism]. *Rev. d'Hist. de l'Amérique Française [Canada] 1978 32(2): 203-228.* Founded by Jesuits in Montreal, the École Sociale Populaire was an educational agency whose primary purpose was to promote improved conditions for workers. It published numerous pamphlets, tracts, and journals on a wide variety of related topics, e.g., the dangers of communism, the perils of alcohol, and the restoration of social order. The School encouraged a brand of unionism that was grounded in the Catholic faith, one that would alleviate the traditional tensions that existed between the working and proprietary classes. 76 notes. M. R. Yerburgh

1474. Schwantes, Carlos A. LABOR UNIONS AND SEVENTH-DAY ADVENTISTS; THE FORMATIVE YEARS, 1877-1903. *Adventist Heritage 1977 4(2): 11-19.* The opposition of the Seventh-Day Adventists to organized labor was a reaction to strikes and violence and to the presence of Catholics and Socialists in labor unions and organizations.

1475. Sutherland, Daniel E. THE SERVANT PROBLEM: AN INDEX OF ANTEBELLUM AMERICANISM. *Southern Studies 1979 18(4): 488-503.* Antebellum Southerners were more like than unlike their Northern neighbors in ordinary attitudes and lives. Both agreed that domestic servants, white or black, were inefficient, unreliable, deceitful, and indolent, and that servant work in itself was degrading. These attitudes applied equally to free white laborers in the North and black slaves in the South. Employers in both areas held paternalistic attitudes tinged with religious obligations. 46 notes. J. J. Buschen

1476. Sylvain, Philippe. LES CHEVALIERS DU TRAVAIL ET LE CARDINAL TASCHEREAU [The Knights of Labor and Cardinal Taschereau]. *Industrial Relations [Canada] 1973 28(3): 550-564.* The Noble and Holy Order of the Knights of Labor, formed in 1869, was one of many secret societies born of militant, discouraged workers. Elzéar Alexandre Taschereau (1820-98), Archbishop of Quebec, was among those who feared an association with Freemasonry in the rapid spread of the secret Knights of Labor. He was instrumental in having the Knights condemned by the Catholic Church in 1884. James Gibbons (1834-1918), Archbishop of Baltimore, however, as a warm supporter of the Knights journeyed to Rome and succeeded in having the ruling overturned. His efforts helped prepare the way for the encyclical *Rerum Novarum* (1891), the charter of Catholic social thought. Based on published Church documents and secondary works; 46 notes. L. R. Atkins

1477. Toy, Eckard V., Jr. THE OXFORD GROUP AND THE STRIKE OF THE SEATTLE LONGSHOREMEN IN 1934. *Pacific Northwest Q. 1978 69(4): 174-184.* Traces the development of the Oxford Group from its founding in 1921 as a Christian mediation group devoted to settling labor and international problems. During the 1934 longshoremen's strike in Seattle, Oxford Group leaders George Light, James Clise, and Walter Horne worked themselves into a mediating role which helped end the deadlock by June. Throughout the negotiations, they unabashedly supported management over labor which was consistent with the entire Oxford Group movement. Primary and secondary sources; 2 photos, 41 notes. M. L. Tate

1478. Troy, Bill and Williams, Claude. THE PEOPLE'S INSTITUTE OF APPLIED RELIGION. *Southern Exposure 1976 4(3): 46-53.* The People's Institute of Applied Religion was established by Claude Williams and his wife Joyce Williams to train religious leaders of the cotton belt in labor unionism, 1940-75.

1479. Wolkinson, Benjamin W. LABOR AND THE JEWISH TRADITION—A REAPPRAISAL. *Jewish Social Studies 1978 40(3-4): 231-238.* Responds to Michael S. Kogan's "Liberty and Labor in the Jewish Tradition," *(Ideas, A Journal of Contemporary Jewish Thought,* Spring, 1975). Argues that union efforts to compel workers to join a union or to pay dues as a condition of employment do not conflict with biblical and talmudic principles concerning the rights of workers. Kogan, supported by Rabbi Jakob J. Petuchkowski, also stated that such union demands were opposed by leading Jewish figures in the trade union movement, including Samuel Gompers. Gompers supported voluntarism in the formulation of AFL policies, but he was very concerned about union security. Even Louis D. Brandeis, an opponent of the closed shop, favored preferential employment of union members. The thesis that union security is antagonistic to Jewish law and tradition regarding freedom of choice ignores the fact that throughout Jewish history freedom of choice has been subordinated to the well-being of the group.

N. Lederer

11. MISSIONARY IMPULSE

Continental Missions

1480. Adams, Eleanor B. FRAY FRANCISCO ATANASIO DOMINGUEZ AND FRAY SILVESTRE VELEZ DE ESCALANTE. *Utah Hist. Q. 1976 44(1): 40-58.* Fray Francisco Atanasio Dominguez (1740-ca 1805), was a commissary visitor and Fray Silvestre Velez de Escalante (ca 1750-80), was a mission friar in New Mexico before their expedition to discover a route from New Mexico to Monterey, California in 1776. Letters and reports on spiritual and economic conditions in New Mexico and the feasibility of the Monterey route reveal both as keen observers, similar in outlook, temperament, and unswerving moral rectitude. Internal and external evidence indicates both were responsible for the expedition diary. Based on primary and secondary sources; 3 illus., 30 notes. J. L. Hazelton

1481. Almeida, Deidre. THE STOCKBRIDGE INDIANS IN THE AMERICAN REVOLUTION. *Hist. J. of Western Massachusetts 1975 4(2): 34-39.* Gives the background of Indian-white relations in Stockbridge, 1680-1737, and explores the Stockbridge Indians' participation in the American Revolution, 1774-76.

1482. Ames, Michael. MISSIONARIES' TOIL FOR SOULS AND SURVIVAL: INTRODUCING CHRISTIANITY TO THE PACIFIC NORTHWEST. *Am. West 1973 10(1): 28-33, 63.* When four Flathead and Nez Perce Indians appeared in St. Louis in 1831 to appeal for religious teachers, American missionary activities were inspired into action. In 1833, the Methodists established themselves in the Oregon country under Jason and Daniel Lee. The Presbyterians followed in 1835 under Samuel Parker and Dr. Marcus Whitman and others. Their activities became the vanguard of American settlement in the Pacific Northwest. Catholic missionaries came to the area in response to invitations from French-Canadian trappers and traders and their close association with the Hudson's Bay Company officials brought friction with the Americans. This lessened when the HBC withdrew from the region and the Oregon question was settled between England and the United States. Based on material from a forthcoming book; map, 12 illus. D. L. Smith

1483. Anderson, Gary Clayton. THE AMERICAN MISSIONARY IN THE TRANS-MISSISSIPPI WEST: SOURCES FOR FUTURE RESEARCH IN INDIAN HISTORY. *Government Publ. Rev. 1980 7A(2): 117-128.* Assesses primary sources available on missionary activities in the Trans-Mississippi West, 1812-1923.

1484. Anderson, Grant K. SAMUEL D. HINMAN AND THE OPENING OF THE BLACK HILLS. *Nebraska Hist. 1979 60(4): 520-542.* Episcopal missionary Samuel D. Hinman acted also as an explorer, treaty maker, and interpreter during negotiations for the Black Hills. As a missionary he devoted three decades to converting the Sioux Indians to Christianity and revising their way of life. During the critical years, 1874-76, he took part in all governmental dealings with the Sioux. R. Lowitt

1485. Archibald, Robert. INDIAN LABOR AT THE CALIFORNIA MISSIONS: SLAVERY OR SALVATION? *J. of San Diego Hist. 1978 24(2): 172-182.* The mission system in California set out to institute social change and transformation of cultural values, often with force which unintentionally resulted in virtual slavery for the Indians; covers 1775-1805.

1486. Arès, Richard. L'INFLUENCE DE L'ESPACE SUR L'ÉVANGÉLISATION DU PAYS [The influence of space on the evangelization of the country]. *Tr. of the Royal Soc. of Can. [Canada] 1976 14: 163-172.* Defines space and evangelization. Notes negative influences such as the great distance required to cross the Atlantic. Once in Canada, one found an immense territory and nomadic indigenous tribes. Great spaces allowed expansion. Priests were among the early explorers, and there was regional development of the Catholic Church. In 1820 British authorities allowed the development of four dioceses: in the Maritimes, at Montreal, at Kingston, and at the Red River. Earlier there had been one diocese of Quebec. Other dioceses were created later. Covers 1615-1851. 11 notes. J. D. Neville

1487. Baker, Frank. JOHN WESLEY'S LAST VISIT TO CHARLESTON. *South Carolina Hist. Mag. 1977 78(4): 265-271.* Chronicles Methodist minister John Wesley's final mission to Charleston, 1737.

1488. Baker, Wesley C. MISSION FUNDING POLICIES: AN HISTORICAL OVERVIEW. *J. of Presbyterian Hist. 1979 57(3): 404-423.* The judicatory system of the American Presbyterian Church came into existence principally as a mission expediter. Many of the basic policies regarding mission funding are thus more implicit than explicit. Yet much can be constructed about mission funding policies from the minutes of almost every General Assembly. Discusses current policies in implementation of mission, designation for mission causes, and roles in mission funding. Covers 1763-1978. Based on minutes of the Presbyterian Church; illus., 16 notes. H. M. Parker, Jr.

1489. Bannon, John Francis. THE MISSION AS A FRONTIER INSTITUTION: SIXTY YEARS OF INTEREST AND RESEARCH. *Western Hist. Q. 1979 10(3): 303-322.* Herbert Eugene Bolton's 1917 faculty research lecture at the University of California at Berkeley, subsequently printed and reprinted several times, became "a veritable seed piece." Entitled "The Mission as a Frontier Institution in the Spanish American Colonies," it continues to affect the study of the Spanish Borderlands history. Reviews a selection of the historiography of the subject under several headings: geographic areas, missions, missions and protection, missions and civilization/Hispanicization, and scholars other than historians who study missions. Selected biblio. D. L. Smith

1490. Barton, J. Hamby. A DOUBLE LETTER: JOHN WESLEY AND THOMAS COKE TO FREEBORN GARRETTSON. *Methodist Hist. 1978 17(1): 59-63.* Printing of letter by John Wesley in 1786 to Freeborn Garrettson together with letter from Thomas Coke to Garrettson, written on the back of Wesley's letter. The letters from Drew University archives pertain to sending preachers to Nova Scotia. Illus. H. L. Calkin

1491. Bass, Dorothy C. GIDEON BLACKBURN'S MISSION TO THE CHEROKEES: CHRISTIANIZATION AND CIVILIZATION. *J. of Presbyterian Hist. 1974 52(3): 203-226.* Gideon Blackburn, a Presbyterian church minister in Tennessee established two mission schools for the Cherokee Indians in 1804 to further the federal policy of acculturation. S

1492. Becker, A. THE LAKE GENEVA MISSION: WAKAW, SASKATCHEWAN. *Saskatchewan Hist. [Canada] 1976 29(2): 51-64.* In 1903 when the Presbyterian Church of Canada decided to establish a medical mission to serve the Dukhobors and Galicians of Western Canada they selected the Reverend George Arthur, originally from Hazel Grove, Prince Edward Island. He served in that position at the Lake Geneva Mission on Crooked Lake until 1908 when he was replaced by Reverend Robert George Scott, M.D., who served until the hospital and mission closed in 1942. A description of hospital problems during World War I and the Depression in Western Canada provides the bulk of the article. 6 photos, 34 notes. C. Held

1493. Bell, Susan N. "OWHYHEE'S PRODIGAL." *Hawaiian J. of Hist. 1976 10: 25-32.* Refers to William Tennooe Kanui, one of five Hawaiian youths who were sent to Connecticut to be trained as missionaries. Kanui spent the years 1809-20 in America. Three months after his return to Hawaii he was excluded from the church for excessive drinking. In later years he became a teacher, restauranteur in California, and a gold miner. He returned to the Congregational Church shortly before his death. R. Alvis

1494. Bewley, Fred W., ed. CAPISTRANO—THE JEWEL OF THE MISSIONS. *California Historian 1976 22(3): 34-36.* Retraces the history of the building (1776) and development by the Franciscans of Mission San Juan Capistrano, whose architecture is famous in California.

1495. Bideaux, Michel. CULTURE ET DÉCOUVERTE DANS LES *RÉLATIONS DES JESUITES* [Culture and discovery in the *Relations of the Jesuits*]. *Dix-Septième Siècle [France] 1976 (112): 3-30.* Examines the view of French missionaries toward American Indians, from the perspectives of a Christian, a humanist, and a 17th-century Frenchman. Based on the 41 little volumes of the *Rélations des Jésuites de la Nouvelle-France* published annually from 1632 to 1672, and other printed primary and secondary works; 108 notes. W. J. Roosen

1496. Bigglestone, William E. OBERLIN COLLEGE AND THE BEGINNING OF THE RED LAKE MISSION. *Minnesota Hist. 1976 45(1): 21-31.* Contrary to earlier accounts, Frederick Ayer instigated the Red Lake Mission and a majority of those who served were Oberlin College people. The mission failed when the number of conversions of Chippewa Indians dropped to near zero. Covers the period 1842-59. The American Board of Commissioners for Foreign Missions played a role in the Mission's formation. Based on manuscript and printed sources; 3 illus., map, 35 notes. S. S. Sprague

1497. Bolton, Herbert Eugene. THE MISSION AS A FRONTIER INSTITUTION IN THE SPANISH AMERICAN COLONIES. Weber, David J., ed. *New Spain's Far Northern Frontier: Essays on Spain in the American West, 1540-1821* (Albuquerque: U. of New Mexico Pr., 1979): 49-65. The missionaries of the American Southwest had the responsibilities of converting and acculturating the Indians, and of exploring, colonizing, and defending the frontier during the 16th-18th centuries. Reprinted from the *American Historical Review* 1917 22(1): 42-61.

1498. Borden, Morton. "TO EDUCATE THE NATIVES." *Am. Hist. Illus. 1975 9(9): 20-27.* Reviews the efforts made to educate American Indians. Educational plans were drawn up at an early date. Missionaries wanted to convert the heathen, and social reformers were convinced that education would civilize him. The early schools were unsuccessful, and the few Indians that did graduate tended to regress. Reforms in teaching methods proved equally ineffective, because the Indian simply did not wish to adopt white culture, even while his own was disintegrating beneath him. Covers 1609-1900. 9 photos.
V. L. Human

1499. Bowden, Henry Warner. SPANISH MISSIONS, CULTURAL CONFLICT AND THE PUEBLO REVOLT OF 1680. *Church Hist. 1975 44(2): 217-228.* In 1598 the upper Rio Grande valley was viewed as an outpost of Spanish civilization, providing an opportunity for colonization, mining, and missionary exploits. From the outset, missionary work seemed to do well, but the repressive measures adopted by the missionaries caused a general native uprising. Methodically, the Indians rid themselves of Spanish intrusion by destroying property, especially churches. The author maintains that the revolt occurred because of religious and cultural differences. 34 notes. M. D. Dibert

1500. Brasser, Ted J. THE CREATIVE VISIONS OF A BLACKFOOT SHAMAN. *Alberta Hist. [Canada] 1975 23(2): 14-16.* Wolf Collar, an Alberta Blackfoot warrior, had several significant dreams in the 1870's, featuring a large bird, Thunder Woman, and her son, Blue Thunder Lodge. Dreams and voices over the years gave Wolf Collar his medicine-man powers. He also became a noted warrior and competent artist. When warfare was declared illegal, Wolf Collar assisted missionary H. W. G. Stocken with a syllabic system in translating the Bible. He died in 1928. D. Chaput

1501. Byrkit, James W. THE WORD ON THE FRONTIER: ANGLO PROTESTANT CHURCHES IN ARIZONA 1859-1899. *J. of Arizona Hist. 1980 21(1): 63-86.* Recounts the ineffective efforts of Protestant churches (Methodist, Presbyterian, Baptist, Episcopal) to achieve influence and bring salvation to Arizonans. Although Methodism had more relative success, Arizonans remained obdurately secular, Catholic, or Mormon. Based on church records and secondary sources; 6 illus., 45 notes. G. O. Gagnon

1502. Carrière, Gaston. THE EARLY EFFORTS OF THE OBLATE MISSIONARIES IN WESTERN CANADA. *Prairie Forum [Canada] 1979 4(1): 1-25.* Discusses the work of Catholic missionaries among Indians in western Canada from 1818 until 1845, when the Oblates of Mary Immaculate arrived to contribute more extensively to the welfare of the Indians; and then until 1870.

1503. Carrière, Gaston, transl. LETTER FROM BISHOP ALEXANDRE TACHÉ TO HIS MOTHER, CONCERNING HIS LIFE WITH THE CHIPEWYAN NATION. *Prairie Forum [Canada] 1978 3(2): 131-156.* Reprints a letter by Bishop Alexandre Antonin Taché to his mother in 1851 describing his experiences with the Chipewyan Indians at the Mission St. Jean-Baptiste on Île-à-la-Crosse in Saskatchewan, and gives a very brief background of Bishop Taché from his birth in 1823 until 1854.

1504. Carriker, Robert C. FATHER JOSEPH BERNARD AMONG "LES ESQUIMAUX." *Alaska J. 1976 6(3): 161-166.* The Roman Catholic missionary effort in Alaska began in 1884. Joseph Bernard, S.J., arrived in 1910 to begin his life as a missionary in the northern part of the state. Describes his experiences with emphasis on the early years. Illus., 10 photos. E. E. Eminhizer

1505. Champion, Walter T., Jr. CHRISTIAN FREDERICK POST AND THE WINNING OF THE WEST. *Pennsylvania Mag. of Hist. and Biog. 1980 104(3): 275-307.* Though much myth has accumulated around Moravian missionary Christian Frederick Post's efforts at Fort Duquesne, myth legitimized by Francis Parkman and debunked by Francis Jennings, Post's services were not without merit. His motivation was religious (converting Indians), not political. Based on American Indian Collection, American Philosophical Society, and printed sources; 86 notes. T. H. Wendell

1506. Champlin, Brad. THE MISSION AT SONOMA. *Pacific Hist. 1978 22(4): 357-360.* Mission San Francisco Solano, northernmost and the last established (1823), is the only one built under Mexican rule. It was founded by a young priest from Mission San Francisco de Asís, Father Jose Altimira, with the cooperation of Governor Luis Arguello. The young padre was succeeded by Padre Buenaventura Fortuni, who brought exceptional organizing ability to its development and growth. Traces its development under successive padres until its secularization in 1834 by order of Mexico City authorities. Illus., 3 notes.
R. V. Ritter

1507. Chaput, Donald. CHARLOTTE DE ROCHEBLAVE: METISSE TEACHER OF THE TEACHERS. *Beaver [Canada] 1977 308(2): 55-58.* Daughter of prominent fur trader Noel de Rocheblave, Charlotte moved from Manitoulin Island to Oka (Lake of Two Mountains), Quebec, in 1813. In the following decades, because of her fluency in French, English, and the various Algonquian dialects, she became the most important instructor of the many priests who studied at Oka in preparation for work in the Red River country, Labrador, and among the Nipissings. Based on ecclesiastical and linguistic sources; 5 illus. A

1508. Christopher, Louise. HENRY WHITEFIELD, CIRCUIT RIDER. *Chicago Hist. 1976 5(1): 2-11.* Discusses the evangelism work done for the Methodist Church by Henry Whitefield; presents an image of Chicago daily life, 1833-71.

1509. Coleman, Michael C. CHRISTIANIZING AND AMERICANIZING THE NEZ PERCE: SUE L. MC BETH AND HER ATTITUDES TO THE INDIANS. *J. of Presbyterian Hist. 1975 53(4): 339-361.* Discusses the personal attitudes of Sue L. McBeth, a Scotland-born American Presbyterian missionary to the Nez Percé Indians, as well as those of the Mission Board of the Presbyterian Church in the last quarter of the 19th century. Her attitude to the Indian culture was one of sustained and relentless hostility. Christianity was equated with Americanism. The only "good" Indian was the converted one. Conversion embraced the totality of life—religion, eating habits, dress, family living, agriculture. The Indian was urged to forsake his old customs and enter the mainstream of American life. Miss McBeth gave a score of years to the training of Nez Percé Christians so that they would become leaders in their church. Based on documents in the Presbyterian Historical Society (American Indian Correspondence Collection) and secondary works; illus., 85 notes. H. M. Parker, Jr.

1510. Coleman, Michael C. NOT RACE, BUT GRACE: PRESBYTERIAN MISSIONARIES AND AMERICAN INDIANS, 1837-1893. *J. of Am. Hist. 1980 67(1): 41-60.* During its first six decades of missionary activity with American Indians, the Board of Foreign Missions of the Presbyterian Church judged Indians as members of inferior, heathen cultures, but not as members of an inferior race. Presbyterian missionaries, convinced of the absolute superiority of the American republic, attempted both a secular and a spiritual transformation of their Indian charges. Missionaries blamed Indian failings upon cultural differences, not upon racial ones. Covers 1837-93. Based on personal records, accounts, and correspondence of missionaries; 78 notes. T. P. Linkfield

1511. Conard, A. Mark. THE CHEROKEE MISSION OF VIRGINIA PRESBYTERIANS. *J. of Presbyterian Hist. 1980 58(1): 35-58.* In the latter 1750's Virginia Presbyterians launched the first Christian mission among the Overhill Cherokee Indians in what is now Tennessee. Discusses the founding, operation, and decline of the labors of John Martin and William Richardson. Based on Richardson's diary (Wilberforce Eames Collection, Manuscript Division, New York Public Library), Eleazar Wheelock MSS (Dartmouth College), Letter Book of the Society for the Propagation of the Gospel in New England (Alderman Library, University of Virginia), ecclesiastical court records and secondary studies; 93 notes. H. M. Parker, Jr.

1512. Conkling, Robert. LEGITIMACY AND CONVERSION IN SOCIAL CHANGE: THE CASE OF FRENCH MISSIONARIES AND THE NORTHEASTERN ALGONKIAN. *Ethnohist. 1974 21(1): 1-24.* Between 1610 and 1750 the Northeastern Algonkian in Maine and the Maritime provinces experienced charismatic political and religious innovations, which were initiated and directed by the French missionaries in the vacuum left by the disintegration of some native social forms. In line with their recognized charismatic authority, the missionaries were able to persuade the Indians to accept new forms of organization and belief and to generate a considerable number of conversions. The legitimacy of the missionaries' domination in Indian affairs, not just their domination per se, played an important role in these changes. The Indians voluntarily accepted the missionaries' introduction of more intensive, external regulation and, through a kind of empiricism analogous to that of science, judged some of their own ideas to be less useful, and therefore inferior, to the new Christian ideas. J

1513. Cumming, John, ed. A MISSIONARY AMONG THE SENECAS: THE JOURNAL OF ABEL BINGHAM, 1822-1828. *New York Hist. 1979 60(2): 157-193.* The journal of a Baptist missionary among the Indians at the Seneca Indian Reservation at Tonawanda in the northwest corner of Genesee County and portions of adjoining counties to the west in New York. It reveals the efforts of a man of little education who could communicate with the Indians only through an interpreter to operate a mission and school for the Christian Senecas. Red Jacket, leader of the pagan Senecas, forced Bingham to move his mission and school off the reservation. The confrontations between Abel Bingham and Red Jacket are recorded in the journal. 5 illus., 51 notes. R. N. Lokken

1514. Davies, Phillips G. DAVID JONES AND GWEN DAVIES, MISSIONARIES IN NEBRASKA TERRITORY, 1853-1860. *Nebraska Hist. 1979 60(1): 77-91.* Documents the life and work of a missionary couple, David Jones Davies (1814-91) and his wife Gwen (1823-1910) whose missionary work among the Omaha Indians in eastern Nebraska spanned the years 1853-60. Both were born in Wales and furthered the work of the Calvinist Methodists in their missionary work. R. Lowitt

1515. De Armond, R. N. ZIEGLER IN BLACK AND WHITE. *Alaska J. 1978 8(2): 162-169.* The Alaskan artist, Eustace Paul Ziegler painted thousands of Alaskan subjects and is exhibited widely. However, his early works in black and white are scattered or lost. Concentrates on these early works as printed in *The Alaskan Churchman.* After art training in the states he went to Cordova, Alaska, as an Episcopal missionary, but continued his drawings in black and white in addition to parish duties. His work reflects the life, culture, and people of the north country. In 1925 he moved to Seattle and began work for the Alaska Steamship Company where he also maintained a studio in a downtown office building. He did approximately 100 works a year from the beginning of the century. 13 photos. R. V. Ritter

1516. Delaney, E. Theo. EPHPHATHA CONFERENCE: A HISTORICAL OVERVIEW. *Concordia Hist. Inst. Q. 1977 50(2): 71-83.* Traces the history of the Ephphatha Conference, a vehicle of Lutheran missionary activity directed toward the deaf during the 1890's-1976. Examines the roles of prominent contributors such as H. A. Bentrup, Augustus H. Reinke, and Enno A. Duemling as well as the relationships that developed between the Conference and other Lutheran institutions. Primary sources; 23 notes. W. T. Walker

1517. Derrick, W. Edwin. COWETA MISSION: STRUGGLE FOR THE MIND AND SOUL OF THE CREEK INDIANS. *Red River Valley Hist. Rev. 1979 4(1): 4-13.* Discusses the efforts of Methodist, Baptist, and Presbyterian missionaries during 1835-60's to Christianize the Creek Indians in Indian Territory and the Creek's opposition to the missionaries' work.

1518. Dobbins, Gaines S. WILLIAM OWEN CARVER, MISSIONARY PATHFINDER. *Baptist Hist. and Heritage 1978 14(4): 2-6, 15.* William Owen Carver (1868-1954), a professor at the Southern Baptist Theological Seminary, taught a "Comparative Religion and Missions" course, which emphasized the Bible's missionary message, and that every Christian should be committed to being a missionary. Carver's ideas represented the turning point in Baptist thought after 50 years of the "great split" between the pro-missionaries and the anti-missionaries.

1519. Doig, Ivan. THE TRIBE THAT LEARNED THE GOSPEL OF CAPITALISM. *Am. West 1974 11(2): 42-47.* William Duncan (b. 1832) served from 1857 until his death in 1918 as Anglican missionary to the Tsimshian Indians. He established the village of Metlakahtla, in northern British Columbia, as a self-sustaining community of Christian Indians, isolated from the moral taints of the white frontier. Later he moved the settlement to the southern tip of Alaska. Schooled in the reform atmosphere of Victorian England and apprenticed in its industrial revolution, Duncan emphasized education, Christian living, organization, and mechanization in his missionary efforts. He was very influential with his converts and earned enormous respect, giving them both Christianity and capitalism. Metlakahtla also became Duncan's fiefdom and trouble came as he aged and became too dictatorial. His town still practices Duncan's faith and thrives as a fishing port. 4 illus. D. L. Smith

1520. Drury, Clifford M. THE SPOKANE INDIAN MISSION AT TSHIMAKAIN, 1838-1848. *Pacific Northwest Q. 1976 67(1): 1-9.* At the urging of Old Chief of the Spokane Indians, the American Board of Commissioners for Foreign Missions launched mission activities at Tshimakain in September 1838. Despite protestations from William Gray that he be given the appointment due to his earlier contact with the tribe, the assignment went to Elkanah Walker and Cushing Eells. The Indians provided labor in constructing the mission, but due to the isolation of the post, life remained hard for the two men and their families. Attempts to convert Old Chief's band to an agricultural lifestyle produced only limited success because unpredictable weather played havoc with crops. Monotony and day-to-day survival instincts characterized the small settlement's history. Yet Walker prepared a small pamphlet of the Spokane language and cultivated good will, which paved the way for later missionaries. The mission was closed in 1848, but the lengthy diaries of Mary and Elkanah Walker remain today as works of historical significance. Primary and secondary sources; 4 photos, 15 notes. M. L. Tate

1521. Drury, Clifford M. WILDERNESS DIARIES: A MISSIONARY COUPLE IN THE PACIFIC NORTHWEST, 1839-48. *Am. West 1976 13(6): 4-9, 62-63.* Reverend Elkanah and Mrs. Mary Walker (c.1810-97) served as missionaries to the Spokane Indians, 1839-48, for the American Board of Commissioners for Foreign Missions. Their service at this eastern Washington mission station is well documented through the parallel diaries of Elkanah, who focused on events outside the home, and of Mary, who wrote particularly of activities at home. Based on the author's earlier publication of Mary's diary and his recent publication of Elkanah's diary. 4 illus., bibliographic note. D. L. Smith

1522. Duncan, Janice K. *RUTH ROVER*: VINDICTIVE FALSEHOOD OR HISTORICAL TRUTH? *J. of the West 1973 12(2): 240-253.* The suppressed *The Grains, or Passages in the Life of Ruth Rover,* written by Margaret Jewett Bailey, clearly documents that Methodist missionaries were more interested in exploiting agricultural and manufacturing opportunities than in spreading Christianity in mid-19th-century Oregon. 48 notes. E. P. Stickney

1523. Eidem, R. J. NORTH DAKOTA PREACHING POINTS: A SYNOPSIS OF SETTLEMENT. *North Dakota Hist. 1978 45(1): 10-13.* North Dakota's settlement pattern can be traced through following the establishment of missionary "preaching points" along the fringe of population residence. These missionary stations, founded primarily by the Methodists, located personnel in areas preliminary to the construction of physical churches. The establishment of "preaching points" paralleled in frequency the peak of frontier settlement attained during North Dakota's Settlement Boom of 1880-85 and again during the Second Settlement Boom of 1898-1914. By 1924 the state was basically fully settled and was also permeated by Methodist "preaching point" stations. Illustrated with maps. Based on secondary sources. N. Lederer

1524. Eisen, George. VOYAGEURS, BLACK-ROBES, SAINTS, AND INDIANS. *Ethnohistory 1977 24(3): 191-205.* Seeks to rediscover the earliest historical sources of Indian games and sport activities as well as the attitudes of the chroniclers toward these diversions. The scope of this study, therefore, is limited to a selection of early works, memoirs and journals of voyageurs, colonial officials and missionaries dating back to the 16th and 17th centuries. Many of these writings remained in manuscript form for centuries and were not previously presented in sport-historical studies. J

1525. Embry, Jessie L. MISSIONARIES FOR THE DEAD: THE STORY OF THE GENEALOGICAL MISSIONARIES OF THE NINETEENTH CENTURY. *Brigham Young U. Studies 1977 17(3): 355-360.* Since Mormons believe in salvation after death, a significant part of their missionary outreach during the late 19th century included genealogical missions. Immigrating saints were encouraged to bring genealogies of persons, living and dead, who might not ever come to Utah or accept the gospel while alive. Records unavailable in Utah were sought by genealogical missionaries returning to their ancestral homelands. Some 178 saints engaged in such missions between 1885 and 1900. Their efforts led to the organization of the Genealogical Society of Utah in 1894. The Church's genealogical library subsequently became the largest in the world with more than 100 branches. M. S. Legan

1526. Ezell, Paul. THE EXCAVATION PROGRAM AT THE SAN DIEGO PRESIDIO. *J. of San Diego Hist. 1976 22(4): 1-20.* Discusses the archaeological excavations of the San Diego Presidio sponsored by the Serra Museum in San Diego, California, 1964-70's, explaining the founding and early history of the mission during 1769-75.

1527. Falls, Helen Emery. BAPTIST WOMEN IN MISSION SUPPORT IN THE NINETEENTH CENTURY. *Baptist Hist. and Heritage 1977 12(1): 26-36.* Summarizes the history of female mite societies from Mary Webb's Boston Society in 1800 until missionary societies replaced most of them following the Civil War. Reviews events leading up to the formal organization of Woman's Missionary Union, Auxiliary to the Southern Baptist Convention, in 1888. Based on secondary sources; 72 notes. H. M. Parker, Jr.

1528. Faries, Richard. AUTOBIOGRAPHY OF ARCHDEACON RICHARD FARIES (DOCUMENTS OF THE CANADIAN CHURCH-5). *J. of the Can. Church Hist. Soc. 1973 15(1): 14-23.* Born and reared in Canada, Faries (1870-1964) devoted his entire career to missionary work with the Indians. He completed this autobiography in 1961 at the request of a church official. He was ordained deacon in 1896 and immediately thereafter began to teach Indian children and to preach to the Indians of the Albany River district, travelling by canoe, dog-team, or foot. He was shortly named missionary to the Swampy Cree Indians and established headquarters at York Factory. His accomplishments included building a new church, converting many Indians to Christianity, and, later, compiling a dictionary of the Cree language. He was named archdeacon of York in 1917 and was ordained priest so that he could perform sacraments. In later years, poor health forced Faries to spend the winter in Toronto, but during the summers he returned to York Factory. 15 notes. J. A. Kicklighter

1529. Farrell, Richard. PROMOTING AGRICULTURE AMONG THE INDIAN TRIBES OF THE OLD NORTHWEST, 1789-1820. *J. of NAL Assoc. 1978 3(1-2): 13-18.* The federal program outlined by Secretary of War Henry Knox in 1789, to civilize American Indians, is considered a failure; it included promoting agriculture to traditional hunters-gatherers and was carried out by Catholic, Quaker, and Moravian groups in the Old Northwest.

1530. Fast, Vera. A RESEARCH NOTE ON THE JOURNALS OF JOHN WEST. *J. of the Can. Church Hist. Soc. [Canada] 1979 21: 30-38.* Describes some of the alterations made by John West, first Anglican priest in western Canada, in his journal of his missionary work there (1820-23), when it was published in its first edition (1824) and in its second (1827). West added some descriptions of animal life he saw and of the peoples he encountered; he provided other accounts to enhance his spiritual role and to describe dangerous or unpleasant situations in which he was involved. On occasion, West omitted material that emphasized his failures with the settlers to whom he ministered or that might have embarrassed the Church Missionary Society in its difficult relationship with the Hudson's Bay Company. Other variations resulted from West's desire to be dramatic, cautious, or exciting. Based on printed and unprinted primary and secondary sources; 8 notes. J. A. Kicklighter

1531. Forbes, Bruce David. THOMAS FULLERTON'S SKETCH OF CHIPPEWA MISSIONS, 1841-44. *Methodist Hist. 1979 17(2): 106-114.* Publication of a document by Thomas Fullerton (1817-89), Methodist Episcopal preacher, about Methodist missions among the Chippewa or Ojibwa Indians along the Minnesota-Wisconsin border, 1841-44. The manuscript is in the Minnesota Historical Society, St. Paul, Minnesota. 3 notes. H. L. Calkin

1532. Forell, George Wolfgang. THE MORAVIAN MISSIONS AMONG THE DELAWARES IN OHIO DURING THE REVOLUTIONARY WAR. *Tr. of the Moravian Hist. Soc. 1977 23(1): 41-60.* The Moravian missions had a profound influence among the Delaware Indians in western Pennsylvania and Ohio during the American Revolution. The effort of the missionaries to secure peace and prosperity for their Indian wards resulted in their bringing pressure on the Delawares to unify in the face of adversity and remain neutral in the war between the Americans and the British. Moravian diaries reveal the fact that the missionaries were in constant contact with Delaware chiefs during the war and had a considerable influence over the thinking of such Indian leaders as Netawatwe and Koquethagachton or White Eyes. Primary and secondary sources. N. Lederer

1533. Franks, Henry A. MISSIONARIES IN THE WEST: AN EXPEDITION OF THE PROTESTANT EPISCOPAL CHURCH IN 1844. *Hist. Mag. of the Protestant Episcopal Church 1975 44(3): 318-333.* In 1844 the Domestic Committee of the Board of Missions of the Protestant Episcopal Church instructed its Secretary, N. Sayre Harris, to make an exploring tour in Indian Territory for the purpose of possible missionary work among the Indians. He was accompanied on the tour by Bishop James Hervey Otey of Tennessee. Reprints a portion (22 March-4 April) of the journal of that trip. The two missionaries visited numerous missionary stations of other churches amonq the Choctaw and Chickasaw Indians. Their journey continued northward after 4 April to Fort Leavenworth, which they reached on 26 April. Because of their efforts, the Protestant Episcopal Church began to play a more active role in the effort to missionize Indians. Map, 41 notes. H. M. Parker, Jr.

1534. Friesen, John W. JOHN MC DOUGALL: THE SPIRIT OF A PIONEER. *Alberta Hist. Rev. 1974 22(2): 9-17.* Reverend John McDougall (ca. 1842-1917) was a pioneer Wesleyan Methodist missionary teacher to the Indians in the Prairie Provinces of Canada. He established several schools, was prominent in church and mission affairs, and was a prolific writer. 5 illus., 25 notes. D. L. Smith

1535. Garrett, Samuel M. GEORGE MUIRSON AND THE MISSION INTO CONNECTICUT. *Hist. Mag. of the Protestant Episcopal Church 1974 43(2): 125-168.* Studies the contributions of George Muirson to Anglicanism in New York and the northern colonies. In 1704 he was appointed schoolmaster in Albany and then in New York City. After his ordination in 1704 as missionary at Rye parish, he later served as missionary to Congregationalist Connecticut. It was in his role in the transplanting of Anglicanism into Connecticut that he made his most significant contribution to American history. Includes in an Appendix a copy from the Society for the Propagation of the Gospel Archives of an extensive letter addressed to John Chamberlayn, in which Muirson describes his work and its problems and successes. R. V. Ritter

1536. Goodheart, Lawrence B. IMPRESSIONS OF WESTERN PENNSYLVANIA: THE MISSION OF ELIZUR WRIGHT, JR., 1828-1829. *Western Pennsylvania Hist. Mag. 1980 63(4): 313-320.* Describes Elizur Wright, Jr. (b. 1804) and his mission to spread evangelical Protestantism in western Pennsylvania in 1828-29 for the American Tract Society, one of a number of societies formed by Presbyterians, Congregationalists, Baptists, and Methodists between 1815 and 1830 to spread evangelical Protestantism into the West.

1537. Grant, John Webster. RENDEZVOUS AT MANITOWANING. *Bull. of the Com. on Arch. of the United Church of Can. [Canada] 1979 28: 22-34.* Competition and suspicion ca. 1820-40 among the Methodist, Catholic, and Anglican churches and the government, in their vying for the Indians of Upper Canada, was reflected in their stands on the Manitoulin project, a government-conceived plan to use the island as an Indian center.

1538. Green, Michael D. WHAT HAPPENED TO THE INDIANS IN THE WAR BETWEEN THE CATHOLICS AND THE PROTESTANTS? *Rev. in Am. Hist. 1980 8(3): 372-376.* Review essay of Francis Paul Prucha's *The Churches and the Indian Schools, 1888-1912* (Lincoln: U. of Nebraska Pr., 1979).

1539. Grulich, Rudolf. SUDETENDEUTSCHE IN DER AMERIKANISCHEN INDIANERMISSION [Sudeten Germans in missionary work among the American Indians]. *Sudetenland [West Germany] 1976 18(2): 97-100.* Describes the activity of missionaries from Sudeten German lands in missionary activities among the Indians of the Americas from Cortez's conquest of Mexico to the early 19th century.

1540. Gruneir, Robert. THE HEBREW MISSION IN TORONTO. *Can. Ethnic Studies [Canada] 1977 9(1): 18-28.* Focuses primarily on the Presbyterian Church and the Protestant-supported Jewish mission founded in 1912. Examines efforts to convert immigrant Jews to Protestantism. Though presented as an aid to social assimilation, conversion (even the hybrid Hebrew-Protestant variety which allowed maintenance of ethnic identity), failed to attract large numbers of Jews. The movement faded after World War I. K. S. McDorman

1541. Guest, Francis F. AN EXAMINATION OF THE THESIS OF S. F. COOK ON THE FORCED CONVERSION OF INDIANS IN THE CALIFORNIA MISSIONS. *Southern California Q. 1979 61(1): 1-77.* Argues against the view of scholar Sherburne Friend Cook that Franciscan missionaries during the last half of the mission period forced Indians into the California missions and then forcibly converted them. Cook mistranslated, misread, misunderstood, and omitted important documentation bearing on the problem. In 1943 he formulated a thesis and proceeded to find evidence to support it, resulting in an influential addition to the Black Legend. Cook's thesis is refuted: missionaries did not administer baptism indiscriminately; expeditions which brought back Indians were military rather than religious in nature; often such expeditions visited Christian and non-Christian villages without seizing Indians; Indians captured for horse-stealing were considered prisoners, not candidates for conversion; only a fraction of the California Indians were ever baptized; many Indians working in Hispanic society during and after the mission period never became Christians; and other important points. Primary and secondary sources; 224 notes, 2 appendixes. A. Hoffman

1542. Habig, M. A. and Diekemper, B., ed.; and Leutenegger, Benedict, transl. BENITO FERNANDEZ: MEMORIAL OF FATHER BENITO FERNANDEZ CONCERNING THE CANARY ISLANDERS, 1741. *Southwestern Hist. Q. 1979 82(3): 265-296.* The Canary Islanders, who dominated the *cabildo* of the Villa San Fernando on the San Antonio River in Texas, sent attorneys to Mexico City to petition the Viceroy Archbishop Juan Antonio de Vizarrón y Equirreta to permit the settlers on the farms to hire the mission Indians to work on the farms, which was opposed by the missionaries. By misrepresenting the situation and the attitude of the Franciscan fathers, they succeeded in 1739 in obtaining the desired order from the viceroy. The major, and newly discovered, testimony which was instrumental in vindicating the missionaries and obtaining revocation of the viceregal order was composed in 1741 by Father Benito Fernandez de Santa Ana of the Mission Purísima Concepción. This memorial is the subject of the present translation. Based on archival and secondary sources; 8 illus., 56 notes. J. L. B. Atkinson

1543. Haury, Samuel S.; Rediger, Beatrice, and Juhnke, James, transl. LETTERS ABOUT THE SPREAD OF THE GOSPEL IN THE HEATHEN WORLD. *Mennonite Life 1979 34(2): 4-7.* Samuel S. Haury, the first conference-sponsored Mennonite missionary in North America, began work among Arapaho Indians in Indian Territory in 1880. Trained in Ohio and Germany, Haury explained in *Briefe ueber die Ausbreitung des Evangeliums in der Heidenwelt* (Halstead, Kansas: Western Publications Company, 1876) that mission, or the spread of the gospel among the heathen, is a work of inner necessity based on the theology that Jesus is the owner of all lost souls. It is the obligation of evangelical Christians to reclaim them. Photo. B. Burnett

1544. Havlik, John F. EVANGELISM: THE CUTTING EDGE. *Baptist Hist. and Heritage 1974 9(1): 30-39, 52.* The role of the Home Mission Board of the Southern Baptist Convention in evangelism and in the interdenominational evangelistic effort, "Key '73." Covers 1845-1973. S

1545. Henderson, John R. MISSIONARY INFLUENCES ON THE HAIDA SETTLEMENT AND SUBSISTENCE PATTERNS, 1876-1920. *Ethnohistory 1974 21(4): 303-316.* In the last quarter of the 19th century Anglican and Methodist missionary societies sent ministers to serve among the Haida of the Queen Charlotte Islands, British Columbia. Each missionary society had its own future goals and appraisals of the Haida's condition. Both approaches lead to the reorganization of the Haida's settlement and subsistence patterns. J

1546. Higginbotham, Mary Alves. THE CREEK PATH MISSION. *J. of Cherokee Studies 1976 1(2): 72-86.* During 1820-37 a school and mission were operated at Creek Path, Alabama, under the auspices of the American Board of Commissioners for Foreign Missions. Its purposes were the education of Cherokee Indians and conversion to Christianity. The major impetus for the mission came from John Brown and his children David and Catherine, all mixed-blood Cherokees. Although the work of the mission was successful, Cherokee removal to the West forced its abandonment in 1837. Primary and secondary sources; map, 3 figs., 83 notes. J. M. Lee

1547. Hill, W. B. "IN WEARINESS AND PAINFULNESS, WAS THE CAUSE BUILT UP." *Adventist Heritage 1977 4(1): 56-59.* Excerpts the autobiography of W. B. Hill for 1877 and 1881, relating his experiences in Minnesota and Iowa as a Seventh-Day Adventist evangelist.

1548. Hinckley, Ted C. "WE ARE MORE TRULY HEATHEN THAN THE NATIVES": JOHN G. BRADY AND THE ASSIMILATION OF ALASKA'S TLINGIT INDIANS. *Western Hist. Q. 1980 11(1): 37-55.* John Green Brady's Alaska career, 1878-1906, gradually shifted from missionary to secular leader. His relations with the Tlingit Indians variously included his roles as missionary-teacher, farmer-settler, businessman, judge, and governor. Brady and other like-minded allies labored to protect and civilize Alaska's natives. As a consequence of their efforts, those Indians "may well enjoy the strongest socioeconomic power base of any Amerindian group." 46 notes. D. L. Smith

1549. Hochbaum, H. Albert. ARCTIC STEEPLES. *Beaver [Canada] 1977 308(3): 28-35.* Descriptive detail, artistic renderings, and brief historical sketches of churches in the central and western Arctic. Fur trading and missionary work did not begin in this section until the 20th century. Catholic and Anglican missions are scattered about the land, serving the few merchants and the Eskimo-Indian communities. 11 illus. D. Chaput

1550. Hoover, Robert Linville. ETHNOHISTORIC SALINAN ACCULTURATION. *Ethnohistory 1977 24(3): 261-268.* No other group of California Indians experienced so intensive or lengthy a period of acculturation as those living within the area of Spanish missions in the south and central coastal areas. And yet, it is possible to trace strands of continuity between the present and the prehistoric past. Recent archival and archaeological studies of the Salinan and other groups of "Mission Indians" have proven a profitable means of filling in details in the historical record and providing an integrated and continuous view of the processes of cultural change. Covers 1770's-1830's. J

1551. Horstman, Otto K. THE SHELBYVILLE TENT MISSION, AUGUST 19-31, 1934. *Concordia Hist. Inst. Q. 1980 53(3): 117-120.* Account of the tent meetings led by the author, an Evangelical Lutheran Synod minister, in Shelbyville, Indiana, 19-31 August 1934, to generate interest in the possible establishment of a mission there.

1552. Humpherys, A. Glen. MISSIONARIES TO THE SAINTS. *Brigham Young U. Studies 1976 17(1): 74-100.* Home missionaries in the Mormons' experience after 1855 established the pattern of church meetings, set speaking styles, and created a tradition of circuit ministries. Church-wide home missionaries were recruited by the General Authorities to travel to and work in various districts. Others were called to represent a particular church agency such as the Relief Society or the Young Men's Mutual Improvement Association. Finally, home missionaries were called by stake presidents and high councils to labor within their assigned stake. In the 20th century the home missionary program has been largely abandoned because of the increased avenues for effective communication between the church and its members.
M. S. Legan

1553. Husband, Michael B. WILLIAM I. MARSHALL AND THE LEGEND OF MARCUS WHITMAN. *Pacific Northwest Q. 1973 64(2): 57-69.* A detailed study of the "Whitman saved Oregon" thesis, Marshall's 20-year crusade to prove it a myth, and the responses of various historians to Marshall's research and methods. Although Marshall's evidence convinced many who had hitherto accepted the story, his proclivity for sarcasm and vituperation marred his work. In 1930, Herbert D. Winters offered further evidence to support Marshall's contentions of the events of 1842-43. 70 notes. R. V. Ritter

1554. Jacob, J. R. THE NEW ENGLAND COMPANY, THE ROYAL SOCIETY AND THE INDIANS. *Social Studies of Sci. 1975 5(4): 450-455.* Notes the contribution of the New England Company and the Royal Society to the evangelization of American Indians, 1660's-70's.

1555. Jessett, Thomas E. ANGLICAN INDIANS IN THE PACIFIC NORTHWEST BEFORE THE COMING OF WHITE MISSIONARIES. *Hist. Mag. of the Protestant Episcopal Church 1976 45(4): 387-412.* Whereas other denominations sent missionaries to the Pacific Northwest to convert the Indians, the Episcopalians did not because the Indians had already been reached for the Episcopal Church through the earlier efforts of Hudson's Bay Company employees. Anglican success among the Indians was quite significant, for in 1825 Hudson's Bay employees sent two boys, Spokan Garry and Kottenay Pelly, to the mission school at Fort Garry. They returned to their tribes and taught agriculture and catechism to their people. Since the response to the Anglican faith was favorable, five more boys were sent back for similar training. As Americans pushed into the Oregon Country, other denominational missionaries came with them. These missionaries were surprised to find Christianized Indians among the Spokanes, Cayuses and Nez Perces. Squabbles among the missionaries, disagreement with Anglican theology, and general confusion on the part of the Indians over the missionaries' strategy gradually reduced the Anglican numbers. When Spokan Garry died, he had long been forgotten by the Church in which he was raised and was buried by a Presbyterian. Based on primary and secondary sources; 37 notes. H. M. Parker, Jr.

1556. Johnston, Patricia Condon. PORTRAYALS OF HENNEPIN, "DISCOVERER" OF THE FALLS OF ST. ANTHONY, 1680. *Minnesota Hist. 1980 47(2): 57-62.* A search for the limited artwork depicting the accomplishment of missionary Father Louis Hennepin, the discoverer of the Falls of St. Anthony on the Mississippi River at modern Minneapolis, in 1680. Despite the notoriety Hennepin gained in his native France for subsequent enlargement of his role as an explorer, there are some notable canvases and a major statue in Minnesota. 8 illus., 9 notes.
C. M. Hough

1557. Juhnke, James C. GENERAL CONFERENCE MENNONITE MISSIONS TO THE AMERICAN INDIANS IN THE LATE NINETEENTH CENTURY. *Mennonite Q. Rev. 1980 54(2): 117-134.* In 1880 General Conference Mennonites began missionary work among the Arapaho Indians and Cheyenne Indians in Indian Territory. Although born of prayer and self-sacrifice, the tragedy of the effort was that the best the Mennonites had to offer—education, medical aid, agricultural development, and the gospel of God's love—was inextricably bound with a massive political and cultural confrontation which turned the good news, for the most part, into bad news. Since it was their first attempt at missionary work among the Indians, the Mennonites could hardly be faulted for their numerous errors, the basic one being their insistent efforts to make whites out of red men. Based largely on Mennonite publications of the period; 55 notes. H. M. Parker, Jr.

1558. Kersey, Harry A. and Pullease, Donald E. BISHOP WILLIAM CRANE GRAY'S MISSION TO THE SEMINOLE INDIANS IN FLORIDA, 1893-1914. *Hist. Mag. of the Protestant Episcopal Church 1973 42(3): 257-274.* Discusses the missionary work of Episcopalian Bishop William Crane Gray to the Seminole Indians during 1893-1914.
S

1559. Kessell, John L. FRIARS, BUREAUCRATS, AND THE SERIS OF SONORA. *New Mexico Hist. R. 1975 50(1): 73-95.* Examines the attempts of the Spanish government and a Christian friar, Father Mariano Buena, to pacify the Seri Indians. Due to bureaucratic problems, funds for building a mission near present-day Nogales, Arizona, were delayed for over four years. Father Juan Gil, Buena's replacement, was murdered by the Indians. S

1560. Kimball, Stanley B. THE UTAH GOSPEL MISSION, 1900-1950. *Utah Hist. Q. 1976 44(2): 149-155.* The Utah Gospel Mission was organized in 1900 by Congregational minister John Danforth Nutting (1854-1949) to convert Mormons. Missionaries traveled in large canvas-covered wagons and later motorized vans, living three to a vehicle and covering Utah, Idaho, Wyoming, and Montana. They left a precious visual heritage—more than 100 glass negatives, mostly from the 1910's-30's, depicting towns, streets, churches, and the missionaries. Included are rare photographs of interiors and hard-to-find non-Mormon churches. Primary and secondary sources; 16 illus., 4 notes.
J. L. Hazelton

1561. Klemp, Alberta H. EARLY METHODISM IN THE NEW MADRID CIRCUIT. *Missouri Hist. Rev. 1974 69(1): 23-47.* Beginning with John Clark, the first Methodist to deliver a sermon in Missouri in 1796 or 1798 and John Travis, the first Methodist circuit rider assigned to Missouri in 1806, traces the frequent restructurings of the Methodist church organization in the West and provides biographical sketches and information on the accomplishments of the circuit riders working in Missouri until 1851. Based on books, articles, and xeroxed records from the Commission of Archives and History, The United Methodist Church, Lake Junaluska, North Carolina; 9 illus., 108 notes.
W. F. Zornow

1562. LaFontaine, Charles V. APOSTLES TO MEATPACKERS: THE ASSOCIATE MISSION OF OMAHA, NEBRASKA, 1891-1902. *Hist. Mag. of the Protestant Episcopal Church 1978 47(3): 333-353.* An associate mission was composed of a small group of unmarried Episcopal priests who, for a given time, pledged to live a community life and devote themselves to missionary work under the guidance and direction of a bishop. Describes such an associate mission in Omaha, 1891-1902. During its brief existence it ministered to 15 congregations, baptized 981, confirmed almost 700, constructed 8 churches and 2 guild halls and founded one parish and four missions. Its work was in three basic areas: working with the poor, operating a parochial school, and preaching. Mission activity died out largely because of an inability to acquire a satisfactory sense of identification. Based largely on an article by John Albert Williams and issues of *The Pulpit and the Cross;* 68 notes.
H. M. Parker, Jr.

1563. Lamirande, Émilien. TRADITIONS ORALES DU XIXe SIÈCLE SUR LA PRÉSENCE DE PRÊTRES ESPAGNOLS EN COLOMBIE-BRITANNIQUE [19th century oral traditions on the presence of Spanish priests in British Columbia]. *Rev. de l'U. d'Ottawa [Canada]*

1977 47(4): 393-412. Identifies and analyzes three main oral traditions and their variants concerning Spanish missionary priests in British Columbia, and specifically at Nootka Sound, Vancouver Island, during 1789-95. The oral traditions were substantially corroborated by the written sources of the period. Primary and secondary sources; 56 notes. Article to be continued. G. J. Rossi

1564. Landon, Fred. BY CANOE TO LAKE SUPERIOR IN 1838. *Inland Seas 1973 29(1): 33-36, 45-46.* Methodist missionary James Evans (1801-46) traveled from Port Sarnia, Ontario, to his new post at Michipicoten River, Ontario. Mentions his comments on his station. K. J. Bauer

1565. Lavender, David. EUSEBIO FRANCISCO KINO: MISSIONARY-EXPLORER OF THE SOUTHWEST. *Am. West 1978 15(3): 4-11.* Eusebio Francisco Kino (d. 1711) was a Jesuit missionary prominent in Spanish expansionism from Sonora, Mexico, into Arizona. As a particular mission enterprise succeeded, the establishment was turned over to secular clergy and the mission properties were divided among the local Indians. The missionaries moved on to begin anew. Kino believed that the inordinately harsh land could be tamed for fruitful uses and that the taming could be accomplished without annihilating the Indians. Adapted from a forthcoming book. 3 illus., map. D. L. Smith

1566. Leutenegger, Benedict and Habig, Marion A., ed. REPORT ON THE SAN ANTONIO MISSIONS IN 1792. *Southwestern Hist. Q. 1974 77(4): 487-498.* The five Indian missions established by the Spanish in the San Antonio area were the most successful in Texas. About the 1770's they began to decline because of the decreasing number of Coahuiltecan Indians that remained to be converted and civilized. Reproduces the 1792 report of José Francisco López, father president of the Texas missions, advocating secularization to recognize the Indians' change from pagan and neophyte to Christian status and to free the missionaries for service elsewhere. 16 notes. D. L. Smith

1567. Lewis, Reid H. THREE HUNDRED YEARS LATER. *Historic Preservation 1974 26(3): 4-9.* Account of the reenactment of the 1673 exploratory voyage up the Mississippi River by Father Jacques Marquette and Louis Jolliet.

1568. Little, J. I. MISSIONARY PRIESTS IN QUEBEC'S EASTERN TOWNSHIPS: THE YEARS OF HARDSHIP AND DISCONTENT, 1825-1853. *Study Sessions: Can. Catholic Hist. Assoc. [Canada] 1978 45: 21-35.* During 1825-53, missionary priests in southeastern Quebec around Sherbrooke close to the American border ministered to a population which, though white, lived much as did the Indians; they were poor, dispersed, backward, and the priests among them had a hard and unglamorous life.

1569. Loewenberg, Robert J. NEW EVIDENCE, OLD CATEGORIES: JASON LEE AS ZEALOT. *Pacific Hist. Rev. 1978 47(3): 343-368.* Traditional interpretation of Jason Lee as a devoted yet worldly missionary, a colonizer who cared little about Indians and a great deal about Americanizing Oregon, requires revision. Hitherto unused letters from Lee and letters and diaries of other Oregon Methodists reveal Lee was primarily an Indian missionary who believed in Christianizing before civilizing. The misinterpretation stems from historians' adherence to a naturalistic philosophy which assumes religious life is a shadow play of more "basic" economic and social realities. Covers 1838-43. Primary and secondary sources; 60 notes. W. K. Hobson

1570. Loewenberg, Robert J. "NOT... BY FEEBLE MEANS": DANIEL LEE'S PLAN TO SAVE OREGON. *Oregon Hist. Q. 1973 74(1): 71-78.* In 1834 Daniel Lee, nephew of Jason Lee (superintendent of the Methodist mission to the Indians of Oregon), arrived in the Willamette Valley and established missionary headquarters north of Salem. He later set up an extension at The Dalles in 1838. Reassesses Daniel's career and presents a letter of his suggesting an elaborate commercial program which would precipitate a more adequately staffed missionary program for the Indians of Oregon. 20 notes. R. V. Ritter

1571. Lotz, Denton. BAPTIST IDENTITY IN MISSION AND EVANGELISM. *Foundations 1978 21(1): 32-49.* The Baptists and their relation to missions is reviewed, showing the historic emphasis Baptists have placed on them. Speculates about the future emphasis Baptists will make on missions. Statistics indicate the impact Baptist missions have had throughout the world. Compares Baptist operation in terms of personnel and monies spent to the 10 largest mission agencies. 5 charts, 34 notes. E. E. Eminhizer

1572. Lynch, Claire. WILLIAM THURSTON BOUTWELL AND THE CHIPPEWAS. *J. of Presbyterian Hist. 1980 58(3): 239-253.* The American Board of Commissioners for Foreign Missions set out to evangelize the Chippewa Indians in Minnesota. In 1831, William Thurston Boutwell (1803-90) went out as a missionary. He spent 16 years with the Indians in northern Minnesota and 43 years preaching to whites and Indians in the lower St. Croix Valley. Among the Indians his ministry was largely a failure, because he sought to make whites out of them. Contains some information on his family. Based on the Boutwell Archives, Minnesota Historical Society; ABCFM Correspondence, Houghton Library, Harvard University; 39 notes. H. M. Parker, Jr.

1573. Maltby, Charles and Weber, Francis J., ed. RUMBLINGS AT PALA. *J. of San Diego Hist. 1975 21(4): 38-42.* Reprint of an 1866 report by Charles Maltby, Superintendent of Indian Affairs for California, concerning the condition of the mission Indians residing in and around the Mission San Antonio de Pala, near Temecula, California. S

1574. Martin, Calvin. THE EUROPEAN IMPACT ON THE CULTURE OF A NORTHEASTERN ALGONQUIAN TRIBE: AN ECOLOGICAL INTERPRETATION. *William and Mary Q. 1974 31(1): 3-26.* Seeks to explain the wildlife extermination through the methodology of cultural ecology. The ecosystem and local human population are the basic units of analysis. The Micmacs of eastern Canada engaged extensively in trade with European fishermen. Taboos and ceremonies governed the preparation of animals as food; other hunting and eating habits affected the environment. The Indians were apostatized by disease, European trade, and Christianity. One important change wrought by the European contact was the unrestrained slaughter of certain wildlife. Based on early French and English records; 94 notes. H. M. Ward

1575. Mathes, W. Michael. SOME REFLECTIONS ON CALIFORNIA, 1776. *J. of San Diego Hist. 1976 22(4): 48-53.* Discusses the establishing of Dominican and Franciscan missions in California following the expulsion of the Jesuits from Spain, 1768-76, emphasizing the works of Fray Junípero Serra.

1576. Mathias, Elizabeth and Varesano, Angelamaria. THE DYNAMICS OF RELIGIOUS REACTIVATION: A STUDY OF A CHARISMATIC MISSIONARY TO SOUTHERN ITALIANS IN THE UNITED STATES. *Ethnicity 1978 5(4): 301-311.* Father Jesu began making an impact among Italian migrant workers in "Migrantville," Pennsylvania in the late 1920's and early 1930's. His approach to Catholicism struck a favorable chord in many Italian Americans not attracted by the dominant Irish and German forms of the faith. Father Jesu, a Spanish-born priest, espoused the traditional Italian manner of religious worship and behavior and stressed the figure of Christ as presented in the Gospels and described during the liturgical year. The priest wore humble clothing and eschewed appeals for money. Miracles were ascribed to him. The followers of Father Jesu eventually attained a foothold among the Italian community in Philadelphia and in other parts of Pennsylvania, New Jersey and New York. Based on field interviews July 1972-December 1973. N. Lederer

1577. McGuckin, Michael. THE LINCOLN CITY MISSION: A. J. CUDNEY AND SEVENTH-DAY ADVENTIST BEGINNINGS IN LINCOLN, NEBRASKA. *Adventist Heritage 1975 2(1): 24-34.* The dedicated evangelism of A. J. Cudney, led to the establishment of Seventh-Day Adventism in Lincoln, Nebraska, and the construction of two missions, 1885-87.

1578. McLoughlin, William G. CHEROKEE ANTI-MISSION SENTIMENT, 1824-1828. *Ethnohistory 1974 21(4): 361-370.* Recently discovered letters written by some Cherokee chiefs in 1824 throw new light on White Path's Rebellion of 1827 in Georgia. They indicate that what appears on the surface to be anti-mission factionalism may, in the case of large, advanced tribes scattered over wide regions, be better understood as conflict over the speed and degree of acculturation, particularly when a prominent group of well-to-do or nominally Christian mixed blood asserts undue influence over political centralization. J

1579. McLoughlin, William G. CIVIL DISOBEDIENCE AND EVANGELISM AMONG THE MISSIONARIES TO THE CHEROKEES, 1829-1839. *J. of Presbyterian Hist. 1973 51(2): 116-140.*

1580. McNairn, Norman A. MISSION TO CANADA. *Methodist Hist. 1975 13(4): 46-60.* An account of the efforts of the Methodist Episcopal Church to expand Methodism into the Provinces of Upper and Lower Canada during 1788-1812. 30 notes. H. L. Calkin

1581. McNairn, Norman A. MISSION TO NOVA SCOTIA. *Methodist Hist. 1974 12(2): 3-18.* Freeborn Garrettson and James Cromwell became the first foreign missionaries of the Methodist Episcopal Church when they went to Nova Scotia in 1785. From 1785 to 1800, 13 American missionaries went there. In 1799, however, William Black decided there was no hope of further help from the United States and turned to England. 36 notes. H. L. Calkin

1582. Miessler, Ernst Gustav Herman and Miessler, H. C., transl. PIONEER LUTHERAN MISSIONARY TO THE CHIPPEWAS: AUTOBIOGRAPHY OF E. G. H. MIESSLER (1826-1916). *Concordia Hist. Inst. Q. 1979 52(4): 146-174.* Silesia-born Ernst Gustav Herman Miessler emigrated to Michigan in 1851 and evangelized among the Chippewa Indians until 1871.

1583. Miles, Edwin A. AFTER JOHN MARSHALL'S DECISION: *WORCESTER* V. *GEORGIA* AND THE NULLIFICATION CRISIS. *J. of Southern Hist. 1973 39(4): 519-544.* Gives the history of the *Worcester* v. *Georgia* case in which the Supreme Court ruled that missionaries Samuel A. Worcester and Dr. Elizur Butler had the right to reside in Cherokee lands, and that Georgia had no right to extend her laws over these lands within her borders. Georgia disregarded the decision and did not release the missionaries, but Worcester and Butler refused to abandon efforts to have the decision enforced. The situation was aggravated in 1833 during the nullification crisis with South Carolina, and associates of Vice President Martin Van Buren acted to solve the dispute. The federal government was thus enabled to use force to put down nullification in South Carolina without added controversy in Georgia, and aided in the preservation of the Union in 1833. Based on contemporary newspaper reports, Georgia and US government documents, and primary and secondary sources; 56 notes. N. J. Street

1584. Miles, William. "AN INVALUABLE LABOR OF LOVE": THE HOLY CHILDHOOD INDIAN SCHOOL PRINTERY. *Am. Book Collector 1973 23(4): 24-28.* Best known for his studies of the California missions, Father Zephyrin Engelhardt (Charles Anthony Engelhardt, 1851-1934) spent most of his life before 1900 in the Midwest. From 1894 to 1900 he was at the Holy Childhood Indian School of Harbor Springs, Michigan, where he established a print shop. Its two most outstanding works were Engelhardt's *The Franciscans in California* and the periodical *Anishinabe Enamiad,* which was issued in the Chippewa language with an English supplement, *The Messenger of the Holy Childhood.* This supplement became a separate paper and was replaced in 1913 by the order's official organ. Illus. D. A. Yanchisin

1585. Miller, Char. THE MAKING OF A MISSIONARY: HIRAM BINGHAM'S ODYSSEY. *Hawaiian J. of Hist. 1979 13: 36-45.* Examines Hiram Bingham's early life in Vermont before he sailed for Hawaii in 1819. Age 21 was a turning point for Bingham (1789-1869), because at that time he was to become his parents' caretaker. Instead, he publicly took the vows of the Lord. His conversion to Congregationalism gave him an excuse to break his commitment to his parents. This decision was due largely but not solely to his ambition. Bingham was raised in a religion that demanded intense commitment that went beyond family ties. The demands of his forceful and uncompromising personality fit the requirements of his missionary vocation. Notes. M. J. Wentworth

1586. Miller, Robert Ryal, ed. and transl. NEW MEXICO IN MID-EIGHTEENTH CENTURY: A REPORT BASED ON GOVERNOR VÉLEZ CACHUPÍN'S INSPECTION. *Southwestern Hist. Q. 1975 79(2): 166-181.* Thomas Vélez Cachupín was Spain's governor of New Mexico for two five-year terms (1749-54 and 1762-67). This translated and edited report was written by him or one of his aides ca. 1754. The report outlines provincial problems, recommends cultivation of friendship and trade with the Comanche Indians to offset French influence, suggests defense improvements in this outpost of empire, provides information on the economy, and suggests ways to improve the effectiveness of the Franciscans' missionary activities. Based on the original 16-page MS in the Real Academia de la Historia in Madrid; 3 tables, 28 notes. C. W. Olson

1587. Millman, T. R. THE DOMESTIC AND FOREIGN MISSIONARY SOCIETY OF THE CHURCH OF ENGLAND IN CANADA, 1883-1902. *J. of the Can. Church Hist. Soc. [Canada] 1977 19(3-4): 166-176.* Describes the major events in the history of the short-lived Domestic and Foreign Missionary Society of the Canadian Anglican Church. First established in 1883, the Society was replaced in 1902 by the Missionary Society of the Church of England in Canada. During its existence it assisted both domestic and foreign missionary efforts. In Canada itself it supported the missionary diocese of Algoma as well as the diocese of the West and Northwest, thus continuing the efforts of earlier groups. The Society was also responsible for the initiation of the Canadian Church's first foreign mission. Although there had been Canadian Anglican missionaries in Japan in earlier years, it was only with the support of the Society that the Church undertook its first major mission there. Based on secondary, printed and unprinted primary sources; 19 notes. J. A. Kicklighter

1588. Moir, John S. ROBERT MC DOWALL AND THE DUTCH REFORMED CHURCH MISSION TO CANADA, 1790-1819. *Halve Maen 1978 53(2): 3-4, 14-15.* Robert James McDowall, a minister in the Reformed Dutch Church from New York, during 1790-1819, was a missionary to Loyalists exiled in present-day Ontario during the American Revolution.

1589. Moldenhauer, Roger and Kramer, William A.. THE DOEDERLEIN DIARY. *Concordia Hist. Inst. Q. 1978 51(3): 99-136.* Gives an introduction with notes by Roger Moldenhauer, a translation of the diary text by William A. Kramer, and notes to the diary by Moldenhauer. The diary begins with the arrival of Paul Ferdinand Doederlein in New York on 17 May 1859. Doederlein, a Lutheran missionary from Bavaria, was charged to spread the gospel to the Crow Indians in western Nebraska. Doederlein set out from Iowa in July, 1859 and his journey took him through Nebraska along the Platte River Road and to Twiss's Upper Platte Agency on the North Platte northwest of Fort Laramie, Wyoming. While the mission to the Crows ended in failure when Doederlein and his colleague Jacob Schmidt withdrew from the region in October, 1857, the diary's value lies in the reflections of the faith of these missionaries and of the hardships which they endured in this service. Primary sources; 38 notes. W. T. Walker

1590. Mondello, Salvatore. [ISABEL CRAWFORD AND THE KIOWAS].

ISABEL CRAWFORD: THE MAKING OF A MISSIONARY. *Foundations 1978 21(4): 322-339.* Presents the early life and education of Isabel Crawford (1865-?), a missionary of the Women's American Baptist Home Missionary Society. Born in Canada, through various family moves while a child she became interested in the plight of the Indians. She received her training in Chicago, during which time she did considerable work in the slums. In June, 1893, she received word that she had been appointed to work as a missionary among the Kiowas of Elk Creek, Indian Territory. Based on the Isabel Crawford Collection, American Baptist Historical Society; 33 notes.

ISABEL CRAWFORD AND THE KIOWA INDIANS. *Foundations 1979 22(1): 28-42.* Describes the labors of Isabel Crawford among the Kiowa Indians in and near the Wichita Mountains of Oklahoma, 1893 to 1906. Her very successful work was abruptly terminated and she was forced to leave the Indians because of her questionable participation in a communion service. Based on the Isabel Crawford Collection, American Baptist Historical Society; 54 notes.

ISABEL CRAWFORD, CHAMPION OF THE AMERICAN INDIANS. *Foundations 1979 22(2): 99-115.* Discusses Isabel Crawford's life from 1907 to her death in 1961. 49 notes.

H. M. Parker, Jr./E. E. Eminhizer

1591. Morrill, Allen C. and Morrill, Eleanor D. THE MCBETH NEZ PERCÉ MISSION CENTENNIAL, UTAH, 1874-1974. *J. of Presbyterian Hist. 1974 52(2): 123-136.* Recounts the background and establishment of a Presbyterian mission among the Nez Percé in Idaho in 1874 by Sue McBeth. Illus., 29 notes. D. L. Smith

1592. Morrison, Kenneth M. "THAT ART OF COYNING CHRISTIANS": JOHN ELIOT AND THE PRAYING INDIANS OF MASSACHUSETTS. *Ethnohist. 1974 21(1): 77-92.* Tribal and cultural fragmentation of the Massachusetts Indians produced the praying towns. The Indians tried to join the English communities after their traditional social, political and economic structures were destroyed by the early seventeenth century plagues and the dominance of English material culture. The praying towns failed because the survivors could not see English institutional structures as a whole and because John Eliot did not realize that the Indians' socially oriented ethics were inoperative within the impersonal English world. Covers 1646-74. J

1593. Morrison, Lorrin L. INTRODUCTION—RED AND WHITE INTERCOURSE IN THE WEST—RELIGION, MIGRATION, EXPLORATION, CONFLICT AND CONQUEST. *J. of the West 1974 13(1): 5-8.* A bibliographical survey of the publishing efforts of *Journal of the West* on Indian-White relations in the history of the West. Covers three previous complete numbers: "Indian Battles and Campaigns" (January, 1970), "Indian Non-Military Intratribal and International Relations" (July 1971) and "The Civil War Era in Indian Territory" (July 1973). This issue and the following one will be the fourth and fifth in the series. R. V. Ritter

1594. Neatby, Leslie H. "THE OLD MAN FROM MAKKOVIK": HERMANN THEODOR JANNASCH. *Beaver [Canada] 1978 309(3): 19-27.* Hermann Theodor Jannasch was born in South Africa to missionary parents, lived there in his youth, then was sent to Germany to prepare for the African missions. His attention shifted to Eskimos, and in 1879 accepted a call from the Moravian Order to go to Labrador. He went first to Nain, on the northern peninsula, working as a storekeeper and religious assistant. In the following decades his responsibilities increased. He also gathered funds in Europe, married, and returned with his family to Labrador. In the 1890's he began the successful mission at Makkovik, Labrador, even constructing the schooner "Agnes." In 1903 Jannasch was recalled to Germany by the Order, and spent much time until his death in 1931 on behalf of the Labrador missions, lecturing and raising funds. Map, 8 illus. D. Chaput

1595. Nettles, Tom J. PATTERNS OF FINANCIAL GIVING FOR MISSION SUPPORT AMONG BAPTISTS. *Baptist Hist. and Heritage 1979 14(1): 27-36.* Investigates the extent of financial support for missionary organizations in the Southern Baptist Convention, examines tendencies toward increasing or decreasing support, and seeks to determine elements in the movement to which Baptists have responded either positively or negatively. Concludes that Southern Baptists will be slow to give if not thoroughly persuaded of the theological or biblical validity of an enterprise. Upon the conviction that those they are supporting are betraying them or are unbiblical, support will be withdrawn. Emphasis on the lostness of man, the reality of the judgment, the sufficiency of Christ, the necessity of hearing the word of truth, and the missionary imperative do much to support a strong mission thrust. Covers 1792-1976. Secondary sources; 2 tables, 30 notes. H. M. Parker, Jr.

1596. Nock, David. E. F. WILSON: EARLY YEARS AS A MISSIONARY IN HURON AND ALGOMA. *J. of the Can. Church Hist. Soc. 1973 15(4): 78-97.* Anglican missionary and educator Edward F. Wilson was sent to the Indians of the diocese of Huron in 1868. He was enthusiastic about converting Indians, intolerant of others' ideas, and thoroughly imbued with Victorian moral precepts. Most of the Indians were already Christians, and his work caused friction with the Methodists. Then he turned to education; but his Industrial School for Ojibway boys was only partly successful, because results did not come fast enough for his patrons and because he did not understand the significance of cultural barriers. By 1885 he had begun to feel that whites should advise Indians only when asked. This change (a result of the Riel Rebellion) revitalized his career. He retired in 1893. 71 notes. J. A. Kicklighter

1597. Norwood, Frederick A. CONFLICT OF CULTURES: METHODIST EFFORTS WITH THE OJIBWAY, 1830-1880. *Religion and Life 1979 48(3): 360-376.* Describes Methodists' unsuccessful attempts to convert the Chippewa Indians of Michigan.

1598. Norwood, Frederick A. STRANGERS IN A STRANGE LAND: REMOVAL OF THE WYANDOT INDIANS. *Methodist Hist. 1975 13(3): 45-60.* A case study in the relation of Methodism to the issue of Indian removal, with particular reference to the Wyandot Indians of Ohio from 1816 to 1843. The efforts to bring about their removal to Kansas, their problems of adjustment, and their relationship with the Methodists are discussed. 37 notes. H. L. Calkin

1599. Ohlmann, Erich H. AN ULTERIOR MOTIVE FOR BAPTIST HOME MISSIONS. *Foundations 1979 22(2): 125-139.* Suggests that evangelism was not the full motivation of American Baptist Home Mission Society's work among non-English-speaking Americans. Argues that Americanization was the ulterior motive. Covers 1832-99. 75 notes. E. E. Eminhizer

1600. Olsson, Nils William. PETER ARVEDSON: EARLY SWEDISH IMMIGRANT EPISCOPALIAN MISSIONARY IN ILLINOIS. *Swedish Pioneer Hist. Q. 1976 27(2): 116-126.* Peter Arvedson or Pehr Arvidsson (1822-80), a Swedish immigrant to Algonquin, Illinois, devoted years of labor to the Protestant Episcopal Church. First as a lay reader and finally as an ordained priest, he held services in a variety of places, including his own farm home. Occasionally he preached in Swedish. Based on primary sources. K. J. Puffer

1601. O'Neill, Ynez Violé. FATHER SERRA PLANS THE FOUNDING OF MISSION SAN JUAN CAPISTRANO. *California Hist. Q. 1977 56(1): 46-51.* Reproduces a memorandum, written by Father Junípero Serra on 21 August 1775, ordering the establishment of the sixth California mission, Mission San Juan Capistrano. Plans included its staffing with two friars, six soldiers, and six Indians; provisions for food, livestock, necessary equipment and tools; and items for the church and sacristy. Fathers Fermín Lasuén and Gregorio Amurrío began work on the mission in October 1775, but news of an Indian massacre at San Diego caused a year's delay. The mission was officially founded on 1 November 1776. Father Serra conducted the first Mass. A translation of the original document appears in the article. Primary and secondary sources; illus., 31 notes. A. Hoffman

1602. Otis, Virginia Ladd. JOHN ELIOT, MISSIONARY TO THE INDIANS. *New-England Galaxy 1975 17(2): 25-31.* Notes the role played by John Eliot in bringing Christianity to the Indians of eastern Massachusetts during 1646-74. Describes his translation of the Bible, his establishment of the village of Natick for Christian Indians, and his ministry to imprisoned Indians during King Philip's War (1675-76). Illus. P. C. Marshall

1603. Peake, F. A. THE ACHIEVEMENTS AND FRUSTRATIONS OF JAMES HUNTER. *J. of the Can. Church Hist. Soc. [Canada] 1977 19(3-4): 138-165.* Describes the missionary work of the Anglican priest James Hunter, an Englishman, in what is now western Canada, during 1844-64. Hunter maintained good relations with the Hudson's Bay Company which had power in the area and made significant contributions to the missionary effort. First, he translated the *Book of Common Prayer* and other religious works into the Cree Indian language. Second, he worked hard to expand Anglican missionary efforts throughout the area known as Rupert's Land, despite some opposition from the Company. His attempts in this area were rewarded by success, but in 1864 Hunter decided to return to England permanently. Ostensibly he did so for the education of his children, but he also may have been frustrated in his desire to occupy a position of leadership within the Church. Upon his return to England, his opportunities in this area were greatly improved. Based on printed and unprinted primary sources; 59 notes, 2 appendixes. J. A. Kicklighter

1604. Peake, Frank A. ROBERT MC DONALD (1829-1913): THE GREAT UNKNOWN MISSIONARY OF THE NORTHWEST. *J. of the Can. Church Hist. Soc. 1975 17(3): 54-72.* Summarizes the career of this Anglican missionary in the Yukon and Mackenzie River valley. Robert McDonald differed from his fellow missionaries in several respects. First, he was of mixed blood; and though he was reared to identify himself with the Protestant, English-speaking society, they never considered him a part of their group. This helps explain why McDonald never became a bishop and why in later life he married a young Indian. Most importantly, his background was a factor in his efforts to understand the culture of the Indians he served. Learning the Tukudh language, McDonald translated the Apostle's Creed, the decalogue, and some hymns. He also learned to preach to the Indians in their own language. Showing appreciation for Indian culture, McDonald selected and trained certain of his converts to direct the others when he was absent. Primary and secondary sources; 23 notes; appendix. J. A. Kicklighter

1605. Perdue, Theda. LETTERS FROM BRAINERD. *J. of Cherokee Studies 1979 4(1): 6-9.* The Brainerd Mission, established in 1817, continued until Cherokee removal in 1838. A major learning exercise for the Cherokee students was the composition of letters to the American Board of Commissioners for Foreign Missions, the founders and administrators of the school. These letters reflect the ideas, thoughts, and values of Cherokee life in their relation to their white neighbors. Based on original letters and secondary sources; 12 notes. J. M. Lee

1606. Phillips, George Harwood. INDIANS AND THE BREAKDOWN OF THE SPANISH MISSION SYSTEM IN CALIFORNIA. *Ethnohistory 1974 21(4): 291-302.* Historians have attributed the collapse of the Spanish mission system in California solely to the activities of land-hungry Mexican officials and aristocrats who cheated the Indian neophytes out of their promised lands when the missions were secularized in the 1830's. As inmates of the mission, a plural institution, the neophytes formed a cultural section that constituted a population majority with distinct burdens and disabilities. Since social identity was ascriptive, there was no way in which they could change their sectional status. The resulting neophyte discontent was largely manifested in a process of continual withdrawal from the missions. Before secularization, however, withdrawal was usually a matter of individual initiative. Afterwards, the neophytes fled from the mission practically en masse, since they had little to fear from their politically emasculated rulers. Their action was a near-unanimous rejection of an oppressive social system, and it clearly exhibits the active role they played in its collapse. J

1607. Phinney, William R. THE NEW YORK CONFERENCE AND CANADIAN METHODISM. *J. of the Can. Church Hist. Soc. [Canada] 1977 19(1-2): 27-41.* Summarizes the Canadian missionary activities of five Methodist missionaries who were affiliated with the New York Conference of the United Methodist Church: Darius Dunham, James Coleman, Nathan Bangs, Peter Vannest, and Samuel Coate. They all went to Canada as volunteers because of their strong personal convictions and, perhaps, their senses of adventure. They enjoyed considerable success in their efforts to bring about the growth of Methodism in Canada, showing how important the New York Conference was to that development. Covers 1766-1862. Primary and secondary sources, 30 notes. This issue is *J. of the Can. Church Hist. Soc.* 1977 19(1-2) and *Bull. of the United Church of Can.* 1977 26.
J. A. Kicklighter

1608. Poethig, Richard P. URBAN/METROPOLITAN MISSION POLICIES: AN HISTORICAL OVERVIEW. *J. of Presbyterian Hist. 1979 57(3): 313-352.* The mission policy of the Presbyterian Church touching the urban area did not begin until 1869. The reason was the church's preoccupation with the frontier. The United Presbsyterian Church of North America did not initiate an urban mission policy until 1905. When the two churches united in 1958 the new united church was thus able to build upon existing foundations, and moved into new urban programs—inner city parishes, industrial evangelism, racial problems, ethnic groups, etc. In more recent years, largely as the result of ecclesiastical reorganization, the urban work on a national level has declined, but the responsibility has been picked up by the lesser church judicatories. Based on minutes of the General Assembly and reports of the Board of National Missions; illus., 27 notes. H. M. Parker, Jr.

1609. Potash, Paul Jeffrey. WELFARE OF THE REGIONS BEYOND. *Vermont Hist. 1978 46(2): 109-128.* New Divinity leaders persuaded the General Association of Connecticut to send missionaries to the new settlements without organized churches or ministers. They concentrated on northwestern Vermont, where the frontier spawned "an irreligious moral code," and the Congregationalists ran "a conspicuously poor third" to Methodists and Baptists. At first pastors volunteered after arranging for the supply of their congregations. After the Missionary Society of Connecticut was organized in 1798 it hired specialized evangelists, who brought revivalism to Vermont and developed "a strong Congregational establishment." Covers 1781-1803. Based on the archives of the Missionary Society of Connecticut; 2 maps, 77 notes.
T. D. S. Bassett

1610. Pritchard, James S. FOR THE GLORY OF GOD: THE QUINTE MISSION, 1668-1680. *Ontario History [Canada] 1973 65(3): 133-148.* Describes the first major Sulpician mission to the Iroquois Indians. Argues that the mission failed due to a complex of reasons including the fitness of the missionaries, dissent within the order, changing conditions among the Indians, and the erection of Fort Frontenac. This last is viewed as less important than it has been seen in the past. 70 notes. W. B. Whitham

1611. Purdy, John R., Jr. ISAAC OWEN—OVERLAND TO CALIFORNIA. *Methodist Hist. 1973 11(4): 46-54.* Isaac Owen (1809-66), Methodist Episcopal missionary in California 1849-66, left his position at Indiana Asbury University (now De Pauw University) and traveled overland to his new appointment. This is the account of his trip, which took 149 days, from January to October 1849. 27 notes. H. L. Calkin

1612. Ramsey, Jarold. THE BIBLE IN WESTERN INDIAN MYTHOLOGY. *J. of Am. Folklore 1977 90(358): 442-454.* Examines the impact of Catholic and Protestant evangelism 1830-50, on the mythologies of the Klamath, Clackamas, Chinook, and Northern Paiutes in Oregon, the Dieguña in California, the Klickitats and Cowlitz in Washington, and the Thompson, Okanagan, Lillooet, and Flathead tribes in British Columbia. Bible stories were incorporated, adapted, or sometimes reworked into new tales within the mythologies of the Pacific Northwest Indians. Primary and secondary sources; 28 notes.
W. D. Piersen

1613. Rausch, David A. ARNO C. GAEBELEIN (1861-1945): FUNDAMENTALIST PROTESTANT ZIONIST. *Am. Jewish Hist. 1978 68(1): 43-56.* Arno C. Gaebelein (1861-1945), originally of the Methodist Episcopal Church, was a central figure in the formulation of Fundamentalism in America. He became a student of Hebrew and Yiddish and a missionary to Jews of New York. In 1893 he began publishing, in Yiddish, *Tiqweth Israel,* or *The Hope of Israel Monthly,* on the pages of which he actively encouraged Jewish settlement of Palestine. This strong Zionist concern was to characterize his work as an evangelist and a teacher at the Dallas Theological Seminary. 28 notes. F. Rosenthal

1614. Rehmer, R. F., ed. SHEEP WITHOUT SHEPHERDS: LETTERS OF TWO LUTHERAN TRAVELING MISSIONARIES, 1835-1837. *Indiana Mag. of Hist. 1975 71(1): 21-84.* As missionaries for two Pennsylvania-based Lutheran bodies, John Christian Frederick Heyer and Ezra Keller each conducted six-month tours of the states of Illinois, Indiana, and Missouri during the 1830's. These 12 letters, together with the editor's introductory essay, reveal a church suffering from cultural, social, and geographical isolation, a serious shortage of trained ministers, synodical differences between "confessional" and "American" Lutheran bodies, and the suspicions of nativists who viewed "foreign" churches with distrust. Despite these and other hardships, Heyer and Keller succeeded in laying the groundwork for the future growth of Lutheranism in these states. Primary and secondary sources; 94 notes.
K. F. Svengalis

1615. Renner, Louis L. FARMING AT HOLY CROSS MISSION. *Alaska J. 1979 9(1): 32-37.* Mixed subsistence farming had been flourishing at Holy Cross Mission (lower Yukon River) a decade before the first official agricultural experiment station was established in 1898. Discusses the history of this farming by the Sisters of St. Ann, the Jesuits, and the Indians in subarctic soil, the hopes, the successes, the setbacks—until October 1956. 8 illus., 30 notes. G. E. Pergl

1616. Rettig, Andrew. A NATIVIST MOVEMENT AT METLAKATLA MISSION. *BC Studies [Canada] 1980 (46): 28-39.* Anglican Church Missionary Society member William Duncan, a layman, established firm and puritanical control over the mission to the Tsimshian

Indians at Metlakatla, British Columbia. When newly ordained clergyman A. J. Hall took over the leadership of the mission in 1877, his emotional and highly charged revivalism produced a spontaneous religious movement, a convergence of precolonial Tsimshian culture and Christianity. The excitement led the Indians to several extraordinary declarations about hearing the voice of God, seeing angels, and discovering the cross of Christ. 61 notes. D. L. Smith

1617. Richardson, Joe M. THE FAILURE OF THE AMERICAN MISSIONARY ASSOCIATION TO EXPAND CONGREGATIONALISM AMONG SOUTHERN BLACKS. *Southern Studies 1979 18(1): 51-73.* Thousands of blacks belonged to white Christian churches before the Civil War, but by 1865 almost all belonged to solely black congregations. The American Missionary Association was founded in 1846 as an evangelical, abolitionist society, which in its first years promoted education, black suffrage, and full citizenship. Association schools held nondenominational prayer meetings and taught religion. The Association ultimately failed to attract permanent black members because of its ties to Congregationalism (which was alien to emotional black religious expression), because of its insistence on white ministers, and because of its paternalistic attitudes. Based on American Missionary Association Archives at Dillard U., New Orleans, and on primary and secondary sources; 71 notes. J. J. Buschen

1618. Rodack, Madeline. THE "LOST" MANUSCRIPT OF ADOLPH BANDELIER. *New Mexico Hist. Rev. 1979 54(3): 183-207.* Of the many works of Adolph Francis Bandelier (1840-1914), one of the most outstanding is his "lost" manuscript, *Histoire de la civilisation et des missions de Sonora, Chihuahua, Nouveau-Mexique et Arizona, jusqu'à l'année 1700,* which is a complete history of the Borderlands up to 1700. Written in 1886-87 for the Golden Jubilee of Pope Leo XIII, it was not found until 1964, in the Vatican Library. A photostatic copy of the text obtained in 1975 by the University of Arizona has been translated and edited, but a lack of funds has delayed publication. Primary sources; 3 illus., 37 notes. P. L. McLaughlin

1619. Rogers, George Truett. AMERICAN BAPTIST MISSIONARIES TO INDIANS OF THE NORTHEAST IN COLONIAL TIMES. *Foundations 1975 18(2): 153-164.* The Baptist Triennial Convention, 1814, began organized mission work on a denominational basis. Before this time mission work was done by individual churches or persons. Describes missionary activities to the Indians by Roger Williams in Massachusetts and his work with Indian languages, Peter Folger in Rhode Island and his attempts at establishing churches among them, and David Jones in the Ohio River Valley. 46 notes.
E. E. Eminhizer

1620. Romo, Oscar I. LANGUAGE MISSIONS IN THE NORTHEAST. *Baptist Hist. and Heritage 1975 10(1): 57-62.* One phase of the work of the Home Missions Board of the Southern Baptist Convention is language missions. Discusses their development in the northeast United States, and provides historical background for the 1975 Home Mission Graded Study of the Southern Baptist Convention. Sixty-eight languages and over 100 dialects are spoken in this region. In several urban areas the language mission of a particular group forms the largest, and frequently the only, Southern Baptist congregation. Southern Baptists have one missionary for every 500,000 language persons. Covers 1950-75.
H. M. Parker, Jr.

1621. Ronda, James P. "WE ARE WELL AS WE ARE": AN INDIAN CRITIQUE OF SEVENTEENTH-CENTURY CHRISTIAN MISSIONS. *William and Mary Q. 1977 24(1): 66-82.* Neither traditional nor revisionist historians have fairly presented the Indians' response to Christianity in 17th-century New England and New France. Discusses Indian concepts of heaven and hell, their criticism of what they regarded as the demonic activity of the missionaries, and their resistance to the campaign against Indian healing rites. Similarities among Catholic, Protestant, and Indian religious ideas are noted. Indian revitalization movements often appeared, and they frustrated Christian proselytization. 62 notes. H. M. Ward

1622. Rouse, Parke, Jr. CONQUISTADORS ON THE CHESAPEAKE. *Américas (Organization of Am. States) 1980 32(8): 28-33.* Spanish Jesuits were settled in Virginia along Chesapeake Bay in 1570 by Pedro Menéndez de Avilés, but the renegade Powhatan Chief Opechancanough killed these missionaries after Menéndez had returned to St. Augustine, Florida.

1623. Rutledge, Arthur B. LAYMEN IN SOUTHERN BAPTIST HOME MISSIONS HISTORY. *Baptist Hist. and Heritage 1978 13(1): 17-25.* Roots of Southern Baptist home missions appeared long before there was any national ecclesiastical organization in America. The Baptist laity opened their homes for worship services, witnessed to their neighbors, preached to ethnic minorities, served as lay preachers, contributed time and money, and were greatly instrumental in organizing new congregations and erecting new churches. Traces trends through the 19th and 20th centuries, underscoring the continuing role of the layman as the denomination has moved out of the South into almost every state. Secondary sources; 51 notes. H. M. Parker, Jr.

1624. Salisbury, Neal. RED PURITANS: THE "PRAYING INDIANS" OF MASSACHUSETTS BAY AND JOHN ELIOT. *William and Mary Q. 1974 31(1): 27-54.* Missionary work among the Indians of New England was viewed as a means of assimilating them into English culture. The values of the two cultures clashed. An overall objective of the missionaries was to manage Indian life so that it fit English policy. The education program sought to purge the Indians of their primitive culture, give them the benefits of civilized society, and instill discipline. John Eliot, who worked through converted sachems, failed from the religious and political points of view because he tried to erase the Indians' identity. Based on published records, contemporary literature, and monographs; 110 notes. H. M. Ward

1625. Santos Hernández, Angel. PRESENCIA MISIONERA EN LA ANTIGUA LUISIANA [Missionary presence in old Louisiana]. *Missionalia Hispanica [Spain] 1975 32(94): 77-101.* Sketches the history of old Louisiana, dealing with its earliest exploration and evangelization connected with the Canadian Indian missions of the Jesuits. The Franciscan Recollects from Paris and the Capuchins were later entrusted with some areas. There were problems of ecclesiastical jurisdiction during the successive French, Spanish, and American periods. In the 20th century the evangelization of several Indian tribes has been the work chiefly of the Jesuits. Based on secondary sources; 29 notes.
J. Correia-Afonso

1626. Sauer, Walter. UNPUBLISHED VIENNESE LETTERS OF BENEDICTINE MISSIONARIES: BONIFACE WIMMER AND JOHN BEDE POLDING. *Am. Benedictine Rev. 1975 26(4): 369-380.* Analyzes and publishes four letters relating to the work of Boniface Wimmer in establishing Benedictine monasticism in North America and one letter relating to the work of John Bede Polding, O.S.B., as the first archbishop of Sydney, Australia. The originals (1847-55) are in the archives of the Benedictine Abbey of Our Blessed Mother of Schotten in Vienna. Original and secondary sources; 40 notes.
J. H. Pragman

1627. Saunders, Charles Frances and Chase, J. Smeaton. MISSION SAN JUAN CAPISTRANO: "LOVELIEST OF THE FRANCISCAN RUINS." *Am. West 1974 11(4): 22-29.* Sketches the history of the California Franciscan Mission San Juan Capistrano from its uncertain beginnings in 1775. The commentary is excerpted from the authors' book, published in 1915. The seven photographs are from a forthcoming book by their photographer, Marvin Wax. D. L. Smith

1628. Schlabach, Theron F. THE HUMBLE BECOME "AGGRESSIVE WORKERS": MENNONITES ORGANIZE FOR MISSION, 1880-1910. *Mennonite Q. Rev. 1978 52(2): 113-126.* For a time the traditionally humble Mennonites became much more aggressive in the United States and Canada, having missions, Sunday Schools, revivalism, etc. Conflicts arose at once; it was not easy to reconcile the old doctrine of defenselessness with the new aggressiveness. The extent of aggressiveness may be questioned: perhaps it was more apparent than real. Many of the institutional changes seem to have been intended to support the much older and traditional Mennonite value system. 47 notes.
V. L. Human

1629. Schlicke, Carl P. NUN IN STATUARY HALL. *Pacific Northwesterner 1980 24(3): 41-45.* Mother Mary Joseph of the Sacred

Heart (1823-1902), born Esther Pariseau near Montreal, founded 29 institutions and conducted extensive missionary activities in the Pacific Northwest after 1856 with the Canadian Sisters of Charity of Providence, for which, in 1977, she was designated one of 91 Americans enshrined in the National Statuary Hall in Washington, D.C.

1630. Schreiber, Clara Seuel. MISSION FESTIVAL IN FREISTADT. *Concordia Hist. Inst. Q. 1977 50(4): 148-151.* At the turn of the 20th century, Mission Festival Sunday was the occasion of a major celebration in Freistadt, Wisconsin. The entire town became involved in the necessary preparations which centered on the arrival of Lutheran missionaries. Based on personal recollections. W. T. Walker

1631. Sessions, Gene A. THE HOLDING FORTH OF JEDDY GRANT. *Dialogue 1979 12(4): 62-70.* Describes the career of Jedediah Morgan Grant, early Mormon missionary. Grant spent most of his preaching career in the eastern and southeastern United States, rather than in the Zion established by the Mormons in Utah. Covers 1833-57. Based on Grant's journal and on secondary sources; 24 notes.
R. D. Rahmes

1632. Shalkop, Antoinette. THE TRAVEL JOURNAL OF VASILII ORLOV. *Pacific Northwest Q. 1977 68(3): 131-140.* Discusses the Alaska Church Collection of Russian Orthodox ecclesiastical documents in the Library of Congress. Presents excerpts from the diary of missionary Vasilii Orlov during his 1886 stay in Alaska. He berated the lack of successful conversions among native peoples and the disrespect shown to missionaries by settlers. A final note discusses the fate of the priest Juvenal who allegedly was murdered by Indians. Photo, map, 22 notes.
M. L. Tate

1633. Shankman, Arnold. THE PECULIAR PEOPLE AND THE JEWS. *Am. Jewish Hist. Q. 1975 64(3): 224-235.* During the last decades of the 19th century, when thousands of European Jews fled to the United States to escape religious persecution, Christian evangelical groups intensified their missionary efforts to convert Jews to Christianity. Among the religious periodicals founded to show the Jew "his need of repentance and of a saviour" was *The Peculiar People*, founded in New York City by the Reverend Herman Friedlaender as a weekly newspaper in 1888. On his sudden death four months later the magazine was taken over by the Reverend William C. Daland, backed by a group of Seventh Day Baptists. Daland served as editor until the paper's demise in 1898. Since Daland's efforts were primarily directed toward conversion of Jews, his interests in Palestinian colonization and his arguments against anti-Semitism were not effective in a wider sense. F. Rosenthal

1634. Sherwood, Roland Harold. PICTOU'S PIONEER MINISTER. *Nova Scotia Hist. Q. 1975 5(4): 337-352.* Describes the primitive way of life and the hardships patiently accepted for the sake of his calling by the Reverend James MacGregor, sent to the "Township of Pictou" in 1786 as a missionary by the Presbyterian Church of Scotland. Records the main events in his 44-year ministry in this parish, until his death on 3 March 1830. R. V. Ritter

1635. Simmons, William S. CONVERSION FROM INDIAN TO PURITAN. *New England Q. 1979 52(2): 197-218.* Thomas Mayhew, Jr. (1621?-1657) of Martha's Vineyard was one of, if not the most, successful missionaries in terms of numbers converted and the permanence and thoroughness of the conversions. His success was based on his thorough knowledge of Indian culture, his ability to picture their old ways in terms of sin, and his use of healing powers to convince them that his god was more powerful than their sachems or gods. The Martha's Vineyard conversions indicate that the transference of cultural dominance is greatest where the traditional culture was most intact, the contending groups roughly equal in power, and the process of conversion gradual. Based on Mayhew's writings; 59 notes. J. C. Bradford

1636. Sizelove, Linda. INDIAN ADAPTATION TO THE SPANISH MISSIONS. *Pacific Hist. 1978 22(4): 393-402.* A study of the interaction between the padres of California's Spanish missions and the stone-age Indian population. The shaman with his hold over the people became the center of the attack on the native culture. The missions used the Indians' fondness for pageantry in music and dance in the worship of the Church. Likewise, Indian decorative motifs were painted in the churches. The Indians were trained in trades, crafts, husbandry, and the Spanish language. However, there was a fundamental conflict of cultures, and the Indians did not adjust well to moral codes, the work regimen, mission life with limitations on movement, and a state-administered governmental system. Decimation as a result of white men's diseases increased. The Indians were not able to change life-styles rapidly enough for a genuine cultural assimilation to take place. 28 notes, biblio.
R. V. Ritter

1637. Smith, Donald B. THE TRANSATLANTIC COURTSHIP OF THE REVEREND PETER JONES. *Beaver [Canada] 1977 308(1): 4-13.* Peter Jones, part Ojibwa, became a Methodist preacher in the 1820's and was successful in converting many of the Indians around Lake Ontario. In 1831 he was sent to England to solicit funds for the missions. He made more than 150 appearances, was successful, and met Eliza Field, daughter of a wealthy factory owner near London. She became interested in mission work, and in him. Jones proposed marriage, which she accepted, though her father resisted for some time. After consent was given, her father found out that Jones' father was still alive, and had two wives. Yet, in 1833, in New York, the couple was married. Based on Jones's accounts and recently discovered diaries kept by Eliza Field; 12 illus.
D. Chaput

1638. Snyder, Marsha. THOMAS VINCENT, THE ARCHDEACON OF MOOSONEE. *Ontario Hist. [Canada] 1976 68(2): 119-135.* Presents a biography of Archdeacon Thomas Vincent and attempts to assess his work for the Anglican Church and the Church Missionary Society in northern Canada. Vincent was born in the North and returned there after his education in the South. He was involved in missionary work before his ordination and thereafter made it his career. Discusses the relationship between the Church Missionary Society and the Hudson's Bay Company, and comments on the impact of Vincent's efforts during his 50 years of service. Remarks on his relationships with colleagues and others, and shows that some of the problems he faced derived, in part, from his intense evangelicism. 98 notes. W. B. Whitham

1639. Steckley, John. BRÉBEUF'S PRESENTATION OF CATHOLICISM IN THE HURON LANGUAGE: A DESCRIPTIVE OVERVIEW. *Rev. de l'U. d'Ottawa [Canada] 1978 48(1-2): 93-115.* Analyzes linguistically Jean de Brébeuf's (1593-1649) Huron translation of R. P. Ledesme's *Doctrine Chrestienne* to investigate the extent to which translated Christian religious tracts were documents of acculturation, and could provide insights into "the cognitive setting in which acculturation was taking place." No other published research on this subject has appeared to the knowledge of the author. Primary sources; 79 notes, biblio., appendix. G. J. Rossi

1640. Stevens, Michael E. CATHOLIC AND PROTESTANT MISSIONARIES AMONG WISCONSIN INDIANS: THE TERRITORIAL PERIOD. *Wisconsin Mag. of Hist. 1974-75 58(2): 140-148.* Compares Catholic and Protestant missionary attitudes toward the Indians in the Wisconsin territory, revealing that both denominations wished to encourage a stable agricultural life among the Indians in order to promote Christianity and to acculturate the Indians, who would otherwise face extinction with the advancing frontier. Protestants "included more of the values of white civilization in their definition of Christianity than did Catholics." While Protestants thought of conversion and civilization as inseparable, Catholics tended to teach in the Indian's native language and praised certain aspects of Indian life. Perhaps because Catholic missionaries were not American-born, as were their Protestant counterparts, and because they were themselves considered foreigners, they found it easier to accept a greater degree of cultural diversity than Protestants. Covers 1830-48. 12 illus., 42 notes. N. C. Burckel

1641. Stineback, David C. THE STATUS OF PURITAN-INDIAN SCHOLARSHIP. *New England Q. 1978 51(1): 80-90.* Analyzes recent Puritan-Indian scholarship. Alden Vaughan has overemphasized Puritan missionary work. Both he and Francis Jennings have underestimated the importance of Puritan theology in determining the Puritans' Indian policy. Believing themselves to be God's chosen people, the Puritans expected Indians to readily accept the superiority of an English way of life and to adopt it. When Indians failed to convert to Christianity and to adopt English ways, the Puritans believed that they must be allied with Satan and they were being used by God to chastise his people for their sins. Indian-Puritan conflict "is best described as a religious confrontation with economic, political, and military ramifications." Primary and secondary sources; 33 notes. J. C. Bradford

1642. Stokes, Durward T. JEREMIAH NORMAN, PIONEER METHODIST MINISTER IN AUGUSTA, AND HIS DIARY. *Richmond County Hist. 1978 10(1): 20-35.* Excerpts from the diary of Jeremiah Norman, an itinerant preacher for the Methodist Episcopal Church on the Augusta Circuit, describes his experiences in the ministry traveling from town to town to deliver his soap box evangelism, 1798-1801.

1643. Tero, Richard D. ALASKA: 1779—FATHER RIOBÓ'S NARRATIVE. *Alaska J. 1973 3(2): 81-88.* Presents the 1779 diary of Spanish priest and missionary Father Juan Antonio García Riobó during his sea voyage to Alaska.

1644. Thomas, C. E. THE WORK OF THE S.P.G. IN NOVA SCOTIA, SECOND HALF-CENTURY. *Nova Scotia Hist Soc. Collections [Canada] 1973 38: 63-90.* The Loyalists' arrival opened a new chapter in the history of the Society for the Propagation of the Gospel in Foreign Parts as 18 of the 31 Church of England clergymen who came as Loyalists remained in the Maritime Provinces. In 1787, Charles Inglis became the first Anglican bishop of Nova Scotia; in 1788, King's College, Windsor was founded; and thereafter new missionary stations were established. All increased the S.P.G.'s work so that hardships were ever present, notably after 1833 when the British government drastically reduced its support to overseas missionaries. A new missionary society from England, The Colonial Church Society, arose; then in 1864, the Nova Scotian Diocesan Synod. E. A. Chard

1645. Thomas, Charles P. MISSIONARY TO THE WILDS OF MAINE. *New-England Galaxy 1977 18(4): 43-53.* Discusses Congregationalist minister Jotham Sewall's role in bringing Protestantism to the settlers in the wilds of northern Maine. Includes extracts from his journal, 1778-1848. 3 illus. P. C. Marshall

1646. Thomas, E. E. REV. WILLIAM TUTTY, M.A.: FIRST MISSIONARY TO THE ENGLISH IN NOVA SCOTIA. *Nova Scotia Hist. Soc. Collections [Canada] 1977 39: 169-186.* Born in Hertfordshire, England (ca. 1715), William Tutty was one of two missionaries appointed by the Society for the Propagation of the Gospel in Foreign Parts (S.P.G.) to sail with Edward Cornwallis in 1749 to what would soon become Halifax. By September 1750, he succeeded in having St. Paul's Church constructed and preached the first service. Tutty then established records of vital statistics for the infant colony. He obtained the appointment of the Reverend Jean Baptiste Moreau as his assistant with the title of "Missionary to the French in Nova Scotia" and ministered to the colony for a little over three years. His letters and reports to the S.P.G. during this interval provided invaluable data with respect to the beginnings of the colony at Halifax. E. A. Chard

1647. Thompson, Paul E. WHO WAS HUDSON STUCK? *Alaska J. 1980 10(1): 62-65.* Describes the life of Hudson Stuck, Episcopal missionary to Alaska during 1904-20, educator, and explorer. 3 photos. E. E. Eminhizer

1648. Tonks, A. Ronald. THE HOME MISSION BOARD: THE EXPECTANT BUT ANXIOUS YEARS, 1845-1860. *Baptist Hist. and Heritage 1973 8(3): 168-187.* Activities of the Domestic Mission Board (Home Mission Board) of the Southern Baptist Convention. S

1649. Upton, L. F. S. COLONISTS AND MICMACS. *J. of Can. Studies 1975 10(3): 44-56.* Discusses colonization and the Christianization of Micmac Indians in Nova Scotia and New Brunswick during 1803-60.

1650. Vernon, Walter N. BEGINNINGS OF INDIAN METHODISM IN OKLAHOMA. *Methodist Hist. 1979 17(3): 127-154.* Methodist preaching to Indians in the Oklahoma-Arkansas area started by 1820 and expanded with the arrival of Creeks, Cherokees, Choctaws, and Chickasaws who were removed from the southeast in the 1830's. Methodists along the route showed compassion and helpfulness toward the Indians as they moved through or settled in a given state. More than 40 schools in Indian territory were started by 1845. Although generally successful, the Methodist itinerant system did not fit a ministry to Indians where longer tenures were needed to understand Indian culture and language. 3 illus., 69 notes. H. L. Calkin

1651. Vittands, Alexander T. THE TRIALS OF PASTOR CLOETER: INDIAN MISSION TO MINNESOTA TERRITORY, 1856-1868. *Old Northwest 1976 2(3): 253-280.* Presents the letters of Lutheran pastor Ottomar Cloeter who attempted to establish a mission in Minnesota Territory in 1856. In spite of Cloeter's great sacrifice and heroic labor the mission effort failed in 1868. Cloeter could not overcome the effects of other whites on Indians who cheated and debauched them. As a result the Indians became distrustful of all whites and suspicious of a religion that some whites preached and others ignored. Further disillusioning the Indians were the attacks of the various Christian denominations upon each other's doctrines. Based on the Minnesota Historical Society's Cloeter Papers, newspapers, and secondary works; 43 notes. J

1652. Voth, M. Agnes. MOTHER M. BEATRICE RENGGLI, O.S.B., FOUNDRESS OF THE AMERICAN OLIVETAN BENEDICTINE SISTERS, JONESBORO, ARKANSAS. *Am. Benedictine Rev. 1974 25(3): 389-409.* Presents a brief biography of Rose Renggli, foundress of the American Olivetan Benedictine Sisters, and a history of Roman Catholic missionary work in Arkansas during the late 19th and early 20th centuries. 15 notes. J. H. Pragman

1653. Wadley, W. THE DIOCESE OF ALGOMA—1873-1973. *J. of the Can. Church Hist. Soc. 1973 15(3): 68-70.* The diocese of Algoma is observing its 100th anniversary as a missionary diocese separated from the diocese of Toronto. Unlike similar dioceses, Algoma was not self-sustaining. It depended for financial support on missionary organizations such as the English Church's Society for the Propagation of the Gospel in Foreign Parts, and on the collective dioceses of the Ecclesiastical Province of Canada. The diocese, covering 70,000 square miles but with only 100,000 communicants, posed a tremendous challenge for the eight original clergy. Summarizes the careers of Algoma's six bishops: Frederick Dawson Fauquier (1873-1881), Edward Sullivan (1882-1896). George Thorneloe (1897-1926), Rocksborough Remington Smith (1927-1939), George Frederick Kingston (1940-1943) and William Lockridge Wright (1944-). In 1955 the diocese became self-supporting. J. A. Kicklighter

1654. Wakely, Francis E. MISSION ACTIVITY AMONG THE IROQUOIS, 1642-1719. *Rochester Hist. 1976 38(4): 1-24.* Examines the efforts of French Jesuits to convert Iroquois Indians in the New World (primarily New York) to Catholicism, and the response from Dutch and British colonizers, 1642-1719.

1655. Waltmann, Henry G. JOHN C. LOWRIE AND PRESBYTERIAN INDIAN ADMINISTRATION, 1870-1882. *J. of Presbyterian Hist. 1976 54(2): 259-276.* John C. Lowrie (1808-1900) supervised the selection and counseling of church-nominated directors for as many as 11 western Indian agencies under the government's Indian "Peace Policy" during 1870-82. He leaned more toward Indian assimilation into American culture than toward cultural pluralism. As one who disparaged the Indians' heritage, leadership, and value systems, he was among those who contributed to their loss of identity and continuing social problems. Likewise, despite his advocacy of justice for the Indians, he did not think in terms of comprehensive equality for their race. Based largely on Lowrie's correspondence in the American Indian Correspondence, Presbyterian Historical Society, Philadelphia; Annual Reports of Board of Foreign Missions of the Presbyterian Church USA; Annual Reports, Board of Indian Commissioners; map, chart, 64 notes. H. M. Parker, Jr.

1656. Ward, Albert E. and Brugge, David M. CHANGING CONTEMPORARY NAVAJO BURIAL PRACTICE AND VALUES. *Plateau 1975 48(1-2): 31-42.* Navajo mortuary beliefs, customs and practices are surveyed from the ethnographic past to the present. It is evident that during the past three decades or so, traditional modes of Navajo funerary behavior have been greatly affected by acculturation. Christian missionary efforts have been an especially important factor. Many contemporary Navajo burial practices are therefore no longer deeply rooted in the past. It is hypothesized that this trend will continue; that the emerging pattern will fuse basic Navajo religious experiences and certain moldable portions of Christianity. The Christian influences will probably continue to be most marked in the superficial burial traits. The most durable meanings in Navajo terms will persist, but they too may eventually give way to complete the acculturation process presently so evident in all Navajo culture. Covers 1949-75. J

1657. Weber, Francis J. THE DEATH OF FRAY LUÍS JAYME: TWO HUNDREDTH ANNIVERSARY. *J. of San Diego Hist. 1976 22(1): 41-43.* Discusses the death of Franciscan missionary Luís Jayme, who was killed by Yuman Indians at Mission San Diego de Alcalá in San Diego, California, 1775.

1658. Weber, Francis J. A JOURNALIST VIEWS MISSION SAN GABRIEL IN 1867. *Records of the Am. Catholic Hist. Soc. of Philadelphia 1974 85(1-2): 68-69.* Describes a 34-page scrapbook of a collection of newspaper articles written in 1867 about Mission San Gabriel. J. M. McCarthy

1659. Weber, Francis J. THE MISSION GRAPE. *Pacific Hist. 1979 23(3): 1-3.* Describes the introduction of viticulture and wine making at the missions of California, introduced first by Jesuit missionary, Padre Juan Ugarte, about 1697 at Mission San Francisco Xavier in Baja California, and from there carried to other California missions. R. V. Ritter

1660. White, Gavin. MISSIONARIES AND TRADERS IN BAFFIN ISLAND 1894-1913. *J. of the Can. Church Hist. Soc. 1975 17(1): 2-10.* Describes the problems of the Anglican Church Missionary Society in their work with the Eskimos of Baffin Island. Because whalers and traders constituted the only government there, E. J. Peck and the other missionaries had to use the traders' ships for transportation and huts for living. Relations between missionaries and traders deteriorated, as the former accused the latter of exploitation and immorality vis-a-vis the Eskimos. The Hudson's Bay Company ultimately took over all trade on the island, and the missionaries seemed to fare better. Based mainly on archival materials of the Church Missionary Society; 26 notes. J. A. Kicklighter

1661. Whyman, Henry C. PETER BERGNER, PIONEER MISSIONARY TO SWEDISH SEAMEN AND IMMIGRANTS. *Swedish Pioneer Hist. Q. 1979 30(2): 103-116.* Peter Bergner (1797-1866) and his family arrived in New York City in 1832 to settle there after Peter had led the sailor's life. He was converted to active Christianity in 1844 and began to preach to immigrant Swedes and Swedish sailors in their own language. These services were held on ships, or floating Bethels, under the auspices of the Methodist Church. This article is the story of Peter Bergner and also of these Bethel Ships. Peter Bergner died in 1866, having worked for the Lord for 17 years. Based on records of the *New York City Tract Society* and several autobiographs and articles in Methodist journals; 3 photos, 25 notes. C. W. Ohrvall

1662. Willauer, G. J., Jr. FIRST PUBLISHERS OF TRUTH IN NEW ENGLAND: A COMPOSITE LIST, 1656-1775. *Quaker Hist. 1976 65(1): 35-44.* The author used 11 MS. lists, in the New England Yearly Meeting Archives at the Rhode Island Historical Society, of Quaker ministers visiting New England, 1656-1775. He found 166 British Friends listed more than twice. Fifty-three of them were women; 30 of them came only to New England; 22 made at least two visits. A third came during the early missionary effort, 1656-72, but with three exceptions during 1677-1712, ministers came every three years or more often. 6 notes. T. D. S. Bassett

1663. Williams, William H. A MEANS TO AN END: OREGON'S PROTESTANT MISSIONARIES VIEW THE INDIANS. *Pacific Historian 1976 20(2): 147-157.* The Pacific Northwest's 19th-century Protestant missionaries, such as Marcus Whitman and Jason Lee, regarded Indians as earthly objects who were a means to an end. They were heathen savages who provided missionaries with an opportunity to do the Lord's work and earn their own salvation. Emphasizes the missionaries of the Methodist Church and the American Board of Commissioners for Foreign Missions. Based on primary sources; 29 notes. G. L. Olson

1664. Wood, Alice S. A CATALOGUE OF JESUIT AND ORNAMENTAL RINGS FROM WESTERN NEW YORK STATE: COLLECTIONS OF CHARLES F. WRAY AND THE ROCHESTER MUSEUM AND SCIENCE CENTER. *Hist. Archaeol. 1974 8: 83-104.* Catalogs "Jesuit" and ornamental rings fron Seneca and Iroquois sites in New York State, the former in particular, associated with the French Jesuit Indian missions of ca. 1630-87, and suggests a chronological and typological sequence for the rings.

1665. Zink, Ella. CHURCH AND IMMIGRATION: THE SISTERS OF SERVICE, ENGLISH CANADA'S FIRST MISSIONARY CONGREGATION OF SISTERS, 1920-1930. *Study Sessions: Can. Catholic Hist. Assoc. [Canada] 1976 43: 23-38.* Sketches the broad background against which the Sisters of Service were founded and developed, beginning in Toronto, and working especially among the largely Protestant populations of new settlers in Western Canada.

1666. —. ERNST LUDWIG HERMANN KUEHN: FRANCONIAN PIONEER. *Concordia Hist. Inst. Q. 1974 47(3): 123-130.* Describes the missionary work of German-born Kuehn and his immigration in 1850 to the United States where he settled in Michigan and became a minister of the Lutheran Church. S

1667. —. GEORGIA'S ATTACK ON THE MISSIONARIES. *J. of Cherokee Studies 1979 4(2): 82-92.* The American Board of Commissioners for Foreign Missions founded and maintained missions for the Cherokee Indians in order to improve Cherokee standards of living and education. To coerce the Cherokees the state of Georgia often harrassed the missionaries, even to the point of jailing Samuel A. Worcester and others. This aroused a great deal of unfavorable publicity for Georgia in other parts of the country. Reproduced from *The New York Spectator,* 23 August 1831. J. M. Lee

1668. —. [IMPACT OF SPANISH COLONIZATION ON CALIFORNIA NATIVES]. *J. of San Diego Hist. 1978 24(1): 121-144.*

Heizer, Robert. IMPACT OF COLONIZATION ON THE NATIVE CALIFORNIA SOCIETIES, *pp. 121-139.* The Spanish mission system (1769-1834), basically inflexible and bent on self-perpetuation, resulted in the enslavement and decimation of the Indians (through disease).

Killea, Lucy L. COMMENTARY ON ROBERT HEIZER'S PAPER "IMPACT OF COLONIZATION ON THE NATIVE CALIFORNIA SOCIETIES," *pp. 140-144.* Relates Heizer's conclusions to the native population under the control of the mission at San Diego, 1769-75.

1669. —. [MORMONS ON VANCOUVER ISLAND].

McCue, Robert J. THE CHURCH OF JESUS CHRIST OF LATTER-DAY SAINTS AND VANCOUVER ISLAND: THE ESTABLISHMENT AND GROWTH OF THE MORMON COMMUNITY. *BC Studies [Canada] 1979 (42): 51-64.* Brigham Young considered Vancouver Island, British Columbia, as a possible haven for the Mormons when they were leaving Illinois. They settled in Utah instead. In 1875, a trickle of Mormon families arrived on Vancouver Island. In tracing the history of the Mormon community of the island, reasons for the scarcity of converts in the early years are suggested, the origins and dates of arrival of Mormon immigrants and missionaries are determined, and the reasons for their choice of the island are examined. 2 tables, 40 notes.

Warburton, Rennie. A COMMENT. *BC Studies 1979 (43): 94-97.* Robert J. McCue's article does not make use of the social sciences in its analysis. It does not consider the psychological values and social conditions that help to explain Mormon growth. It does not, therefore, concern itself with the explanation of why people became Mormons. 13 notes.

McCue, Robert J. A REPLY. *BC Studies 1979 (43): 98.* The "why do people join" question does need further investigation. This matter, however, was beyond the scope of the author's intention. D. L. Smith/S

Foreign Missions

1670. Abu-Ghazaleh, Adnan. AMERICAN MISSIONS AND ARAB NATIONALISM IN 19TH CENTURY SYRIA. *Search: J. for Arab and Islamic Studies 1980 1(2): 135-148.* Surveys the development of a national consciousness among Syrian Arabs between the 1840's and 1918, emphasizing the influence of American religious missionaries on this process.

1671. Akpan, M. B. ALEXANDER CRUMMELL AND HIS AFRICAN "RACE-WORK": AN ASSESSMENT OF HIS CONTRIBUTIONS IN LIBERIA TO AFRICA'S "REDEMPTION," 1853-1873. *Hist. Mag. of the Protestant Episcopal Church 1976 45(2): 177-199.* Highlights the Liberian career of Alexander Crummell, an Episcopalian American Negro educator, as an example of attempts by numerous US Negroes to demonstrate practically their commitments to Africa. His failure to accomplish much stemmed from mulatto attitudes toward the native blacks. The mulattos viewed the natives as intellectually and racially inferior. The author gives insights into the philosophy behind the American Colonization Society, the hopes for the Christianization of the African Negro, and Crummell's fruitless struggle to accomplish lasting goals through his educational philosophy and labors. Based on Crummell's writings; 123 notes. H. M. Parker, Jr.

1672. Allen, James B. and Thorp, Malcolm R. THE MISSION OF THE TWELVE TO ENGLAND, 1840-41: MORMON APOSTLES AND THE WORKING CLASSES. *Brigham Young U. Studies 1975 15(4): 499-526.* Discusses the mission of 12 Mormons from Nauvoo, Illinois, to Great Britain to work among the working classes, 1840-41.

1673. Alter, James P. AMERICAN PRESBYTERIANS IN NORTH INDIA: MISSIONARY MOTIVES AND SOCIAL ATTITUDES UNDER BRITISH COLONIALISM. *J. of Presbyterian Hist. 1975 53(4): 291-312.* Examines Presbyterian missionary motives, objectives, and social attitudes as they developed in the 19th century, first in America and then in British India. In 1834 the first American Presbyterian mission station outside the United States was established at Ludhiana, in the Punjab. From the beginning great emphasis was placed on education. Emphasizes the problem of equality in mission administration until India received her political independence in 1947. With independence, the Presbyterian Board of Foreign Missions relinquished its control, turning over the mission administration to the indigenous Christians. Also stresses the problems of US missionaries in a British colony. Primary and secondary works; 30 notes. H. M. Parker, Jr.

1674. Anchak, G. Ronald. THE DECISION TO GO TO TANGANYIKA. *Mennonite Q. Rev. 1978 52(3): 248-264.* Details the background for the Lancaster Conference Mennonite Church's decision to go into foreign mission work. Cultural differences between the Mennonites and the natives indicate most of the problems the mission faced. Covers 1934-71. 63 notes. E. E. Eminhizer

1675. Arnon, Ruth Soulé. THE CHRISTIAN COLLEGE. *Hist. of Educ. Q. 1974 14(2): 235-249.* Review article prompted by Ira Jerry Burnstein's *The American Movement to Develop Protestant Colleges for Men in Japan, 1868-1912* (Ann Arbor, Michigan: U. of Michigan School of Education, 1967), Richard P. N. Dickinson's *The Christian College in Developing India: a Sociological Inquiry* (London: Oxford U. Pr., 1971), Rao H. Lindsay's *Nineteenth Century American Schools in the Levant: A Study of Purposes* (Ann Arbor, Michigan: U. of Michigan School of Education, 1965), Jessie Gregory Lutz's *China and The Christian Colleges, 1850-1950* (Ithaca: Cornell U. Pr., 1971), and D. C. Masters' *Protestant Church Colleges in Canada: A History* (Toronto: U. of Toronto Pr., 1966). Most find that conflict between secular education and the colleges declined in the face of nationalism. L. C. Smith

1676. Barrere, Dorothy and Sahlins, Marshall. TAHITIANS IN THE EARLY HISTORY OF HAWAIIAN CHRISTIANITY: THE JOURNAL OF TOKETA. *Hawaiian J. of Hist. 1979 13: 19-35.* Toketa of Bora Bora and Kahikona of the Russian American area were Tahitian Congregationalist converts and teachers of reading, writing, and Christian doctrine in the schools of the Hawaiian chiefs in the 1820's and 1830's. Toketa's journal, written in 1822, is probably the first manuscript written in the Hawaiian language by any Polynesian. The influence of the Tahitian teachers, though it left little written trace, was effective. Behind that effectiveness lay the particular cultural values these Tahitians represented to the Hawaiian chiefs. In acting as priests whose ceremonial functions and counsel were necessary to chiefly rule, the Tahitians helped fill the sacerdotal void created by the abolition of the taboos in 1819. Reprints Toketa's journal in English translation. M. J. Wentworth

1677. Beecher, Dale F. REY L. PRATT AND THE MEXICAN MISSION. *Brigham Young U. Studies 1975 15(3): 293-307.* Account of the Mexico City mission at which Rey I. Pratt worked for the Mormon Church, 1906-24; gives accounts of other missions operating concurrently within Mexico, and the events of the Mexican Revolution and resultant civil wars.

1678. Bingham, Afred M. SYBIL'S BONES, A CHRONICLE OF THE THREE HIRAM BINGHAMS. *Hawaiian J. of Hist. 1975 9: 3-36.* Traces the lives of generations of Binghams. The first Hiram Bingham and his wife Sybil were the models for James Michener's missionary sequence in his novel *Hawaii*. He made free use of the first Hiram Bingham's *A Residence of Twenty-one Years in the Sandwich Islands.* In later years the Congregationalist Binghams returned to New England, and were dismissed by the American Board of Commissioners for Foreign Missions. The second Hiram Bingham spent his missionary years in the Gilbert Islands until ill health forced his return to Hawaii. The third Hiram Bingham, the author's father, was responsible for moving the bones of Sybil, the first Hiram's first wife, into a grave next to her husband. Covers 1820-1975. R. Alvis

1679. Booth, Karen Marshall. THE DOMESTIC AND FOREIGN MISSIONARY PAPERS: THE PUERTO RICO PAPERS, 1870-1952. *Hist. Mag. of the Protestant Episcopal Church 1973 42(3): 341-344.* A brief account of Episcopalian missionary activity in Puerto Rico and a mention of the documents from the missionary work which are housed in the archives of the Church Historical Society in Austin, Texas.

1680. Bose, Anima. AMERICAN MISSIONARIES AND HIGHER EDUCATION. *Indica [India] 1974 11(2): 101-122.* In its 1883 report, the Education Commission encouraged private higher education in India. American Protestant missionary societies responded by founding a considerable number of colleges. This activity, partly inspired by the Social Gospel, corresponded to a new emphasis upon the regeneration of society rather than the conversion of individuals. J. C. English

1681. Britsch, R. Lanier. THE CLOSING OF THE EARLY JAPAN MISSION. *Brigham Young U. Studies 1975 15(2): 171-190.* On 7 August 1924, after 23 years of effort and sacrifice by missionaries and church members, the Mormon Church ended its first mission in Japan. The missionary effort of the Mormons, begun in 1901, was not notably successful. Analyzes the conditions in Japan that caused the leaders of the Church to abandon missionary activity there. 2 tables, 49 notes. M. S. Legan

1682. Britsch, R. Lanier. THE EXPANSION OF MORMONISM IN THE SOUTH PACIFIC. *Dialogue 1980 13(1): 53-62.* Describes contemporary Mormon missionary activity in the South Pacific, focusing on the issues of missionary theory and the church as an agent of culture change. Particularly since 1955, more sophisticated methodology has fostered mission autonomy while maintaining strong ties to the mother church. While preserving concern for the ways of local peoples, the Mormons have influenced the island peoples toward a healthy accommodation to the church and to modernization. 7 notes. R. D. Rahmes

1683. Britsch, R. Lanier. THE FOUNDING OF THE SAMOAN MISSION. *Brigham Young U. Studies 1977 18(1): 12-26.* Considers the two separate phases of the Mormons' mission to the Samoan Islands. The first period has as its central figure Walter Murray Gibson, who arrived in Hawaii as a Mormon missionary in 1861. By 1862, Gibson had persuaded two native Hawaiian converts to go to Samoa as missionaries. Recounts their successes and misadventures. The second period details the reopening of the Samoan effort by Joseph Harry Dean in 1888. Examines the religious and political environment within which the reopened Mormon mission functioned in its first year. M. S. Legan

1684. Britsch, R. Lanier. THE LANAI COLONY: A HAWAIIAN EXTENSION OF THE MORMON COLONIAL IDEA. *Hawaiian J. of Hist. 1978 12: 68-83.* In 1854, Elder Ephraim Green (1807-74), a Latter-day Saint missionary to Hawaii, moved to Lanai to establish a new settlement. He was a veteran of the Mormon exodus from the States. When the Hawaiian membership grew to 3,008, and there was antagonism of the government and of Protestant and Catholic missionaries, the decision was made to find a temporary gathering place, and the little island of Lanai was chosen. The planting and settling is described in detail. In 1857 another group of elders were called from Utah to Hawaii. Comments on President Brigham Young's faith in the value of the Hawaiian translation of the Book of Mormon. The water problem in Lanai was so serious, as were also destructive worms and insects, that the numbers in the Hawaii mission fell off rapidly, and the mission was closed. The non-Hawaiian missionaries were called home to Utah. 26 notes. E. P. Stickney

1685. Browning, Mary. THE NAME OF PEASE IS INFAMOUS. *Guam Recorder 1978 8: 3-11.* Describes the efforts of US missionaries and sea captains and British traders to gather evidence against Captain Benjamin Pease, American pirate, slaver, and notorious troublemaker on several Pacific islands, 1867-70.

1686. Campbell, Penelope. PRESBYTERIAN WEST AFRICAN MISSIONS: WOMEN AS CONVERTS AND AGENTS OF SOCIAL CHANGE. *J. of Presbyterian Hist. 1978 56(2): 121-132.* In spite of the secular (colonial administration) and religious (Catholic) forces working against them, Presbyterian women missionaries were able to accomplish a considerable work among female African converts who became the backbone of the indigenous mission churches during 1850-1915. Less vulnerable to societal ways, women were able to grow in the Christian faith. Their groups served both religious needs and social and economic hopes. Also chronicles missionary educational work in late 19th-century West Africa. Based largely on Board of Foreign Missions Correspondence and Report Files, African Letters, in the Presbyterian Historical Society, Philadelphia; 38 notes. H. M. Parker, Jr.

1687. Char, Tin-Yuke. S. P. AHEONG, HAWAII'S FIRST CHINESE EVANGELIST. *Hawaiian J. of Hist. 1977 11: 69-76.* Describes the life, work and family of the Chinese colporteur and missionary, S. P. Aheong (i.e., Siu Pheong) (ca. 1838-76), Congregationalist member of the Hawaiian Evangelical Association. 18 notes. A. E. Standley

1688. Clymer, Kenton J. METHODIST MISSIONARIES AND ROMAN CATHOLICISM IN THE PHILIPPINES, 1899-1916. *Methodist Hist. 1980 18(3): 171-178.* Following the Spanish-American War (1898), representatives of various American Protestant groups began to plan for their religious conquest of the Philippine Islands. It was somewhat embarrassing to the Protestants that the people they were to convert were already Christian (largely of Roman Catholic persuasion). Analyzes the attitude of Methodists, their justifications for the work, and their reception in the Philippines. 32 notes. H. L. Calkin

1689. Clymer, Kenton J. RELIGION AND AMERICAN IMPERIALISM: METHODIST MISSIONARIES IN THE PHILIPPINE ISLANDS, 1899-1913. *Pacific Hist. Rev. 1980 49(1): 29-50.* Most Methodist missionaries supported United States annexation of the Philippines and the violent suppression of Filipino resistance which they blamed on unscrupulous and ambitious Filipino rebel leaders. As unofficial agents of American imperialism, they attempted by means of education and moral suasion to assist the government's efforts to remake Philippine society. Through a limited cooperation between church and state, they promoted the conversion of Filipinos to Protestant Christianity and an American-style democracy. When they suspected Roman Catholic influence on government policy, they applied pressure to insure the conformity of government actions to Protestant norms. Based on accounts by participants in early missionary activity in the Philippines, Methodist Episcopal Church documents and archives, William Howard Taft papers, US Senate documents, and secondary sources; 80 notes. R. N. Lokken

1690. Cole, Garold L. THE BIRTH OF MODERN MEXICO, 1867-1911: AMERICAN TRAVELERS' PERCEPTIONS. *North Dakota Q. 1977 45(2): 54-72.* Most attitudes of American tourists and Protestant missionaries on their visits to Mexico, 1867-1911, were tempered by the then-predominant Social Darwinism; examines thought on the Catholic Church, structured social differences, the hacienda system, railroads, and modernization attempts.

1691. Coleman, Michael C. PRESBYTERIAN MISSIONARY ATTITUDES TOWARD CHINA AND THE CHINESE, 1837-1900. *J. of Presbyterian Hist. 1978 56(3): 185-200.* Focuses on Presbyterian missionary attitudes toward the Chinese from 1837 to the eve of the Boxer Rebellion in 1900. Over six decades the missionaries made little attempt to understand Chinese sociology—family relationships, sex roles, class structure—or Chinese economics, arts, and literature. One positive note is drawn: if the missionaries were predisposed to view Chinese civilization as heathen, and thus inferior, they also saw the people as redeemable, as human beings full of potential. Based largely on periodicals and pamphlets found in the Presbyterian Historical Society, Philadelphia, Annual Reports of the Board of Foreign Missions of the Presbyterian Church and secondary materials; 46 notes. H. M. Parker, Jr.

1692. Cousins, Leone B. WOMAN OF THE YEAR: 1842. *Nova Scotia Hist. Q. [Canada] 1976 6(4): 349-374.* Eliza Ruggles Raymond of Nova Scotia married a minister who was a missionary to escaped slaves and who eventually had a mission on Sierra Leone's Sherbro Island; she aided slaves on slaving vessels, accompanied her husband to Africa, and defended wrongly accused slaves against imprisonment, 1839-50.

1693. Crahan, Margaret E. RELIGIOUS PENETRATION AND NATIONALISM IN CUBA: U.S. METHODIST ACTIVITIES, 1898-1958. *Rev. Interamericana [Puerto Rico] 1978 8(2): 204-224.* Protestant missionary work began immediately after the Spanish-American War. American missionaries, viewing themselves as representatives of a superior culture and religion, were most effective among the island's middle class. In particular, Protestant schools attracted large number of students. Since 1958, however, these churches have been ambivalent in their attitude toward Castro's government. Primary and secondary sources; 49 notes. J. Lewis

1694. Culpepper, Hugo H. BOLD MISSIONS PERSONIFIED: MISSIONARIES WHO HAVE LED THE WAY. *Baptist Hist. and Heritage 1979 14(1): 50-57.* Gives succinct vignettes of three deceased 20th-century Southern Baptist missionaries who personified bold missions: Arthur B. Rutledge (executive in various positions in Home Missions); Agnes Nora Graham (missionary to Chile); and William Maxfield Garrott (missionary to Japan). Based on oral interviews and family correspondence; 12 notes. H. M. Parker, Jr.

1695. Dinnerstein, Myra. THE AMERICAN ZULU MISSION IN THE NINETEENTH CENTURY: CLASH OVER CUSTOMS. *Church Hist. 1976 45(2): 235-246.* By the 1860's the widespread revival of African social customs (particularly bridewealth and concubinage) created controversy which nearly destroyed the American Board Mission among the Zulus. As the mission's early converts assumed a greater role in their own religious lives, missionaries found themselves defending the very customs that they once branded as "heathen." Four factors militated against the further complete domination of the missionaries: 1) the policies of the home office in Boston; 2) the Africans' growing independence fostered by their own initiatives; 3) the missionaries' own unwitting policies; and 4) the Africans' protected status on the reserves. 65 notes. M. D. Dibert

1696. Dunstan, John. GEORGE A. SIMONS AND THE *KHRISTIANSKI POBORNIK:* A NEGLECTED SOURCE ON ST. PETERSBURG METHODISM. *Methodist Hist. 1980 19(1): 21-40.* Methodism got its start in Russia in 1881 or 1882 when the Methodist Episcopal Church started a mission in St. Petersburg. The mission had a struggle until 1906 when the situation began to improve with the naming of George Albert Simons (1874-1952) as leader. One of his first steps was to publish a Russian-language evangelical magazine, the *Khristianski Pobornik.* This publication provides an excellent source on St. Petersburg Methodism from 1909 to 1917. Table, 101 notes. H. L. Calkin

1697. Farah, Caesar E. PROTESTANTISM AND BRITISH DIPLOMACY IN SYRIA. *Int. J. of Middle East Studies [Great Britain] 1976 7(3): 321-344.* American Protestant missionaries arriving in Syria in 1824 met hostility from other Christian sects, and resistance from the

Ottoman Empire because they were not a recognized sect. Therefore, they sought the support of Great Britain who they hoped could obtain recognition from the Ottoman government for their movement. But by 1842 the possibilities of creating a Protestant base in Syria with the support of British diplomacy had only succeeded in stirring up hostility. Primary sources; 98 notes. R. B. Orr

1698. Farah, Caesar E. A TALE OF TWO MISSIONS. *Islamic Q. [Great Britain] 1975 19(1-2): 75-85.* Describes the rivalry between Jesuit and American Protestant missions to assert themselves at a time of intense political and diplomatic activity in Syria following its return to Ottoman administration, 1840-41. The Jesuits were able to elicit a measure of cooperation but American initiatives were unsuccessful due to the prevailing adverse political climate and the lack of a base of support. The educational efforts of both missions suffered setbacks during the 1840's. Based on archives in Harvard, Rome and Vienna, and the Public Records Office, London; 38 notes. P. J. Taylorson

1699. Fletcher, Jesse C. FOREIGN MISSION BOARD STRATEGY. *Baptist Hist. and Heritage 1974 9(4): 210-222.* Discusses the 1974 missionary strategy of the Southern Baptists. S

1700. Fletcher, Jesse C. A HISTORY OF THE FOREIGN MISSION BOARD OF THE SOUTHERN BAPTIST CONVENTION DURING THE CIVIL WAR. *Baptist Hist. and Heritage 1975 10(4): 204-219.* Describes the difficulties that the Southern Baptist Convention encountered during the Civil War in supporting missionaries in such diverse places as China and Africa. Provides insight into a denomination's operations under adverse conditions. The Foreign Mission Board survived the war primarily because of its convictions regarding the worthiness of its efforts, the innovative procedures used by those supporting foreign missions, and the dedication and resiliency of the missionaries. Based on correspondence of the Board; 97 notes.
H. M. Parker, Jr.

1701. Foley, Ruth Howard. I HAD BETTER CALL YOU JOE. *New-England Galaxy 1978 19(4): 43-48.* Neesima Shimeta (1843-90) left Japan to become a Christian. Describes his escape from Hakodate on the American ship *Berlin,* his transfer at Hong Kong to the American vessel *Wild River,* his final arrival in Boston, his befriending by Alpheus Hardy, his enrollment at Phillips Andover, Amherst College, and Andover Theological Seminary, his ordination as a Congregational minister, and his return to Japan. Covers 1860's-90. P. C. Marshall

1702. Franklin, D. Bruce. THE WHITE METHODIST IMAGE OF THE AMERICAN NEGRO EMIGRANT TO LIBERIA, WEST AFRICA, 1833-1848. *Methodist Hist. 1977 15(3): 147-166.* The first missionaries to Sierra Leone and Liberia in 1833 and supporters of colonization believed that the social, political, and economic systems of white Christian civilization were superior to the customs and habits of African black society. Negro American preachers in West Africa were expected to subordinate their activities to the Methodist Episcopal Church in America. In 1848 the whites withdrew their leadership because of inability to survive in Liberia and a desire to maintain a pious image of permitting civilized America-Liberians to carry on the evangelical work in Africa. 46 notes. H. L. Calkin

1703. Goodpasture, H. McKennie. DAVID TRUMBULL: MISSIONARY JOURNALIST AND LIBERTY IN CHILE, 1845-1889. *J. of Presbyterian Hist. 1978 56(2): 149-165.* Sketches the ministry and contributions of the founder of the Presbyterian Church in Chile, the Rev. David Trumbull (1819-89), whose work as a dignified religious and political dissenter was substantial. Religious liberty, the Protestant Church and the quality of public discussion were all on firmer ground because of his labors. Emphasizes his contribution to legislation for religious liberty. Based on Trumbull's correspondence located at Yale, the Presbyterian Historical Society (Philadelphia), and secondary sources; 78 notes.
H. M. Parker, Jr.

1704. Harder, Fred M. *PITCAIRN:* SHIP & SYMBOL. *Adventist Heritage 1979 6(1): 3-15.* The mission ship *Pitcairn* had an impact on Seventh-Day Adventist interest in and support for foreign missions, beginning in 1890 when the *Pitcairn* sailed on her first voyage to the South Seas. Discusses Seventh-Day Adventist missionary work beginning in 1848 when Ellen White had a vision that the Adventist message should be carried worldwide.

1705. Hartwell, Mrs. Charles K. MOBILE TO CHINA: A VALIANT WOMAN'S MISSION. *Alabama Rev. 1978 31(4): 243-255.* Describes Mary Horton Stuart's (1842-1926) early life in Mobile, Alabama, and the 39 years she spent as a Presbyterian missionary in Hangchow, Nanking, and Peking. Of her four sons, John L. Stuart became president of Yenching University and US ambassador to China, and Warren Stuart became president of Hangchow College. Primary and secondary sources; 48 notes. J. F. Vivian

1706. Hassing, Arne. METHODISM FROM AMERICA TO NORWAY. *Norwegian-American Studies 1979 28: 192-216.* Norwegians' fascination with America led not only to Norwegian emigration, but also to the Americanization of Norwegian popular religion. Norway's Dissenter Law of 1845 introduced toleration of non-Lutheran groups and paved the way for American religious influence. Ole Peter Petersen (1822-1901), the key figure in the development of Norwegian Methodism, learned his faith in America from Olof Hedstrom (1803-77), a Norwegian immigrant. Petersen returned to Norway and preached Methodism to a small group of followers at Frederikstad. In 1853, Petersen was formally commissioned to establish the Methodist Episcopal Church in Norway. 59 notes. D. K. Lambert

1707. Hawkins, John N. FRANCIS LISTER HAWKS POTT (1864-1947), CHINA MISSIONARY AND EDUCATOR. *Paedagogica Hist. [Belgium] 1973 13(2): 329-347.* Francis L. H. Pott, an Episcopalian missionary, was president during 1888-1941 of one of the most influential mission colleges in China, St. John's University in Shanghai. 45 notes, biblio. J. M. McCarthy

1708. Hill, Thomas W. A BRIEF HISTORY OF PUBLICATION WORK ON SOUTHERN BAPTIST FOREIGN MISSION FIELDS. *Baptist Hist. and Heritage 1977 12(4): 219-230.* Contains brief historical surveys of publication efforts on Southern Baptist foreign mission fields under the aegis of publication societies since 1899. In 1976 the eight mission areas operated 22 publication centers for 32 foreign countries. The history of the publications programs is presented in terms of the eight geographical areas in which the Foreign Missions Board functions. In 1975-76 approximately nine million periodical pieces, two million books and seven million tracts were published. In the remaining years of the 20th century Foreign Missions Board-related publications will experience a "dramatic growth." Chart. H. M. Parker, Jr.

1709. Hood, Fred J. THE AMERICAN REFORMED TRADITION IN AFRICAN COLONIZATION AND MISSIONS. *J. of Church and State 1977 19(3): 539-555.* The interest in African missions came about in the reformed churches (Congregational, Presbyterian, and Dutch and German Reformed) through their concern over a growing free black population in America. Reviews the sources for this concern and then discusses the influence of the "millennial vision" on this concern. Discusses how they approached the practical implementation of this concern through the form of mission societies, the sending of missionaries, and their relation to the colonization society. Covers the 19th and 20th centuries. 55 notes. E. E. Eminhizer

1710. Hoyt, Frederick B. PROTECTION IMPLIES INTERVENTION: THE U.S. CATHOLIC MISSION AT KANCHOW. *Historian 1976 38(4): 709-727.* The American Catholic mission at Kanchow, China directly influenced American foreign policy from 1929-32. During the Kuomintang era the mission, protected by the American flag, identified itself with the Chinese elite. In 1928 the Communists advanced on Kanchow. The missionaries remained in Kanchow seeking American diplomatic help which forced the Nationalists to protect them. The State Department had two options: 1) persuade the missioners to evacuate or 2) protect the mission. Notes. M. J. Wentworth

1711. Hurford, Grace Gibberd. MISSIONARY SERVICE IN CHINA. *J. of the Can. Church Hist. Soc. [Canada] 1977 19(3-4): 177-181.* A personal recollection by a Canadian missionary-educator in China. During her years of service she was a nurse, English instructor, and Christian teacher. Her work offered many rewarding experiences, but from 1937 on she and her fellow workers had to contend with the problems caused by the Japanese invasion. She was injured only once by Japanese bombs, but the danger was omnipresent. Consequently, her work in China was disrupted by the necessity to move on several occasions and by the orders of the Chinese government to close all schools. Her service in China ended with the conclusion of World War II. J. A. Kicklighter

1712. Israel, Jerry. THE MISSIONARY CATALYST: BISHOP JAMES W. BASHFORD AND THE SOCIAL GOSPEL IN CHINA. *Methodist Hist. 1975 14(1): 24-43.* James W. Bashford, bishop of the Methodist Episcopal Church and missionary to China, saw the Pacific Ocean as the final stage in the development of civilization. He thought the United States had the ability to export its domestic success, particularly in social areas, including educational reform and women's rights. 85 notes. H. L. Calkin

1713. Jackson, Hermione Dannelly. WIFE NUMBER TWO: ELIZA G. SEXTON SHUCK, THE FIRST BAPTIST FOREIGN MISSIONARY FROM ALABAMA. *Baptist Hist. and Heritage 1973 8(2): 69-78.* Church history of a Baptist missionary to China, 1844-51. S

1714. Jimerson, Randall C. THE PAPERS OF THREE HIRAM BINGHAMS. *Yale U. Lib. Gazette 1979 54(2): 85-90.* The contributions of Yale University to American intellectual life are well illustrated in the Bingham Family Papers and the Yale Peruvian Expedition Papers spanning the years 1815 to 1967. The papers of Hiram Bingham I (1789-1869), Hiram Bingham II (1831-1908), Hiram Bingham III (1875-1956), and their wives, reflect developments in American missionary activities, social and family relations, the cultures of Hawaii, Micronesia, and Peru, academic life at Yale and Harvard, Latin American history and archaeology, US politics and foreign policy, and aviation history. D. A. Yanchisin

1715. Jones, Garth N. EXPANDING LDS CHURCH ABROAD: OLD REALITIES COMPOUNDED. *Dialogue 1980 13(1): 8-22.* Discusses the expansion of Mormon missionary effort into countries outside the United States since 1949. This expansion is now focused on areas with rising social expectations and declining resources. This dictates that Mormons reevaluate their basic body of ethics and behavior objectives, returning to voluntary simplicity of lifestyle. 28 notes. R. D. Rahmes

1716. Juhnke, James. MENNONITE MISSION IN CHINA: A PHOTOGRAPHIC ESSAY. *Mennonite Life 1979 34(2): 8-14.* H. C. and Nellie Schmidt Bartel founded the first Mennonite mission in China in 1901 at Caoxian (Tsaohsien). Between 1910 and 1914, Ernest and Maria Dyck Kuhlman and H. J. and Maria Miller Brown also founded China missions. The General Conference Mennonite Church took over the Brown mission at Kai Chow in southern Hubei (Hopeh) province in 1914. 19 photos. B. Burnett

1717. Kastens, Dennis A. NINETEENTH CENTURY CHINESE CHRISTIAN MISSIONS IN HAWAII. *Hawaiian J. of Hist. 1978 12: 61-67.* Asians, beginning in 1872, came to the Sandwich Islands with Judaeo-Christian morals and a biblical faith. After the Opium War in the early 1840's, the mainland of China was opened to western missionaries. The aim of the German and Swiss missionaries was not to found churches and congregations, but to preach the Gospel. Many of the children of converts were trained as teachers and emigrated to Hawaii. With the coming of Protestant missionaries, a number of Christian holidays were added to the social calendar and were observed more reverently than in many parts of the Western world. The first lighted Christmas tree in a church in Hawaii was in the Fort Street Chinese Christian Church in 1881. Much special cooking was done in contemplation of Christmas services; recipes using yeast were from the missionary wives, but today are thought of as part of the Chinese heritage. 15 notes. E. P. Stickney

1718. Kit-Ching, Chau Lau. JOHN KING FAIRBANK, ED., *THE MISSIONARY ENTERPRISE IN CHINA AND AMERICA. J. of Oriental Studies [Hong Kong] 1976 14(2): 190-193.* Fairbank's *The Missionary Enterprise in China and America* (1974), the sixth work in the Harvard studies in American East Asian relations series, is the most comprehensive study ever published on the role of American missions in China. Part I examines the factors which helped mold the pattern of American missionary work. Part II studies the impact of US missionaries in China. Part III is concerned with the image of Chinese missions in American culture. Through this book and other publications, Harvard U. has played a leading role in the postwar advancement in this field. Covers 1860-1949. 12 notes. J. Sokolow

1719. Lancaster, Paul. CHAMPION AMONG THE HEATHEN: AN AMERICAN MISSIONARY CAUGHT IN SOUTH AFRICAN CONFLICT 140 YEARS AGO. *Am. Heritage 1978 29(2): 64-69, 72-77.* George Champion, along with his wife and several others, began a mission in Ginani in Zululand in 1836. Caught between the northward advance of the Boers, and the resistance of black tribes to anything white, Champion was soon forced to flee. Leaving Africa in 1838, he returned to the United States where he died of tuberculosis in 1841, at the age of 31. 15 illus. J. F. Paul

1720. Lebhar, Neil and Minns, Martyn. WHY DID THE YANKEES GO HOME? A STUDY OF EPISCOPAL MISSIONS: 1953-1977. *Hist. Mag. of the Protestant Episcopal Church 1979 48(1): 27-43.* Analyzes the decline of appointed missionaries sent overseas by the Episcopal Church and the amount of funds received for world missions during 1953-77. Some of the reasons for the decline in missionary support were 1) support of missionaries by the national Convention, rather than by dioceses; 2) change in missionary strategy whereby autonomy for missionary churches is encouraged; 3) newer theological presuppositions whereby the Christian faith is viewed as only one of many ways to God; and 4) recent cultural issues at home and abroad which reflect a discernible neo-isolationism in the Church as well as in the nation's foreign relations. Concludes that the major obstacle to Episcopal mission is not poor strategy, but the apathy of the church toward mission in general. Reports on the agencies of the Episcopal Church; 7 tables, 2 graphs, 34 notes. H. M. Parker, Jr.

1721. Lindsey, David. MINISTERING ANGELS IN ALIEN LANDS. *Am. Hist. Illus. 1975 9(10): 19-27.* Discusses the involvement of women in the American overseas missionary movement in the 19th century. Various women's missionary societies, over 700 by mid-century, were formed to promote and support missionary efforts, financing a great portion of the overseas mission crusade. Many women went overseas as missionaries' wives and evangelists. Missionary women were most notably involved in education and medicine, and worked to emancipate non-Christian women from oppression. 10 illus., 2 photos. N. J. Street

1722. Marty, Martin E. THE MISSIONARY MOVEMENT: "HERE AM I; SEND ME, SEND ME!" *Am. Heritage 1978 29(2): 70-71.* The missionary movement began for Protestants about 1792. US missionary enterprises began in 1806 and by 1900, more than 4,000 American missionaries were abroad. Today, many sects are having second thoughts, and some areas are closed to missionaries. Illus. J. F. Paul

1723. McCook, James. SIR GEORGE SIMPSON IN THE HAWAIIAN ISLANDS. *Beaver [Canada] 1976 307(3): 46-53.* George Simpson visited Hawaii for six weeks in early 1842 and became involved in the Hawaiian independence movement. He favored the American Protestant missionaries against the French Catholics and became friends with King Kamahameha III and his leading advisor, William Richards. The Hudson's Bay Co. had been well established on the islands since the 1820's, and Simpson had considerable influence. In 1843 Richards and a Hawaiian delegation visited Simpson in England before going to the continent. Simpson played a key role in having several European powers recognize Hawaii. 11 illus. D. Chaput

1724. Metallo, Michael V. AMERICAN MISSIONARIES, SUN YAT-SEN, AND THE CHINESE REVOLUTION. *Pacific Hist. Rev. 1978 47(2): 261-282.* American missionaries greeted the 1911 Chinese Revolution optimistically, expecting it would improve prospects for the expansion of Christianity. Missionaries also expected the new China to model its political, social, and economic institutions after those of the United States. Sun Yat-sen was especially esteemed. The American business and diplomatic communities in China viewed the revolution far less positively, influencing the William Howard Taft administration's nonrecognition policy. Woodrow Wilson was more sympathetic to the mission-

ary viewpoint, extending diplomatic recognition to China in May 1913. From 1913 on, American missionaries withdrew support from Sun Yat-sen and extended support to elements in China which stood for stability and order rather than for extending the revolution. Based on private papers of missionary societies, documents in the National Archives and Library of Congress, and missionary newspapers; 81 notes.
W. K. Hobson

1725. Millett, Richard. JOHN WESLEY BUTLER AND THE MEXICAN REVOLUTION, 1910-1911. *West Georgia Coll. Studies in the Social Sci. 1978 17: 73-88.* Describes missionary John Wesley Butler's account of the Mexican Revolution, 1910-11; based on excerpts from letters to friends and Methodist Church offices in New York.

1726. Mount, Graeme S. THE CANADIAN PRESBYTERIAN MISSION TO TRINIDAD, 1868-1912. *Rev. Interamericana [Puerto Rico] 1977 7(1): 30-45.* Presbyterian missionaries from Nova Scotia began to work with the East Indian population of Trinidad in 1868. Their most effective tool of conversion was their parochial school system, which was the first to educate East Indians on the island. 4 photos, 2 tables, 78 notes.
J. A. Lewis

1727. Mount, Graeme S. THE PRESBYTERIAN CHURCH IN THE USA AND AMERICAN RULE IN PUERTO RICO, 1898-1917. *J. of Presbyterian Hist. 1979 57(1): 51-64.* Presbyterians were enthusiastic, if unwitting, agents of American empire in Puerto Rico following the Spanish-American War. Proud to be Americans, they sincerely believed that they were doing God's will and providing a valuable service to the former members of Spain's corrupt empire. Their major contribution was in education: they founded many primary and secondary schools. Unlike others, Presbyterian missionaries endeavored to encourage the people to retain their cultural heritage, with the exception of Catholicism, by simply eliminating the worst features of Spanish heritage and promoting the best in the American. All missionaries, for instance, spoke Spanish. Article restates much material in the author's earlier article. Based on Presbyterian publications of the period; photo, 50 notes.
H. M. Parker, Jr.

1728. Mount, Graeme S. PRESBYTERIANISM IN PUERTO RICO: FORMATIVE YEARS, 1899-1914. *J. of Presbyterian Hist. 1977 55(3): 241-254.* The fruits of the Presbyterian Puerto Rico mission appear to be the most numerous of any of that church's undertaking. Article offers suggestions to account for this. For one thing, when the Presbyterians came to Puerto Rico following the Spanish-American War they came with the prestige of being representatives of a liberating power. The fact that they limited their endeavors to the western third of the island in their missionary undertaking meant the conservation of resources and efforts. Further, the Catholic Church in Puerto Rico at that time was in a very weakened condition. Presbyterians capitalized on the poor educational opportunities and developed outstanding schools to correct these deficiencies. It was in education that they made their greatest contributions. Finally, Presbyterian success resulted because natives were trained for the ministry, thus creating an indigenous church leadership. Primary and secondary sources; illus., 3 tables, 63 notes.
H. M. Parker, Jr.

1729. Mufuka, N. Nyamayaro. AMERICAN PRESBYTERIAN MISSIONARIES IN SOUTH-WEST KASAI (CONGO) 1905-1962. *J. of the Can. Church Hist. Soc. [Canada] 1977 19(3-4): 190-207.* Traces the growing involvement and changing attitude of American Presbyterians in the Belgian Congo before it gained independence. Americans first went there in 1871 when the Belgian government employed the American journalist Henry M. Stanley. The missionaries of the American Presbyterian Church acted not in the interests of the government but in those of the Congolese people. They spoke out against the Belgian government's use of forced labor and compared to European missionaries, were less aloof and bigoted in their relations with the African people. But like most Americans, they feared the loss of order when the Belgians unexpectedly proclaimed Congolese independence in 1960. Despite the initial chaos and turmoil, the American missionaries adjusted well to the new conditions and were determined to continue their work in the very different environment that resulted. Primary and secondary sources; 53 notes.
J. A. Kicklighter

1730. Newberry, Daniel Clever. TAQARUB THROUGH EDUCATION. *Middle East J. 1976 30(3): 311-321.* American involvement in Middle Eastern education began with John Jay, who was instrumental in sending American teachers to the Middle East. By 1885 there were more than eight American sponsored colleges in the Ottoman Empire, 75 secondary schools, hundreds of elementary schools, and a college in Egypt. Muslims gradually entered these institutions. Missionary schools were important contributors to the later establishment of public schools and to the education of women. Notes the growth of Area Studies of the Middle East in American educational institutions, with the US Office of Education playing a major role. Arabic language training has just been instituted in the cadet training at Annapolis, Colorado Springs, and West Point.
E. P. Stickney

1731. Newell, Robert C., ed. THE FIRST ROBINS. *Foundations 1978 21(2): 139-149.* Discusses the writings of Baptists Adoniram Judson and Samuel Newell on the beginning of the American foreign mission movement. Adds connecting commentary. Covers 1810-21. 20 notes.
E. E. Eminhizer

1732. Notehelfer, F. G. L. L. JANES IN JAPAN: CARRIER OF AMERICAN CULTURE AND CHRISTIANITY. *J. of Presbyterian Hist. 1975 53(4): 313-338.* Describes the assignment of Presbyterian Leroy Lansing Janes, former soldier and teacher, as a private educator in Kumamoto in the 1870's. Janes' personal integrity and self-discipline appealed greatly to the former samurai youth whom he taught in the Meiji Reformation. Permission was denied him to teach the Christian faith formally, but he was able to inculcate in his students great principles of Americanization and the Christian faith, which he identified as one and the same. At first his teaching embraced agriculture, science, technology, and literature, but later he was able to bring in the Bible and Christian teachings. Thirty-five of his students took the Hanaoka Oath which left an indelible mark on the Protestant movement of the Meiji period. Ultimately every student who took the oath went on to an important public career in the Church, publishing, education, business, or government. Primary and secondary sources; 95 notes.
H. M. Parker, Jr.

1733. Nyhagen, Johan and Cleven, Harry T., transl. JEREMIAH PHILLIPS: PIONEER MISSIONARY AMONG THE SANTALS. *Foundations 1978 21(2): 150-166.* Norwegian Baptists controlled the mission to the Santal tribe in 19th-century India, but the first missionary was an American, Jeremiah Phillips (b. 1812), a Freewill Baptist. The author describes Phillips's work among the Santals. This article originally was published in Norwegian in *Norst Tidsskrift for Mision,* 1970. 128 notes.
E. E. Eminhizer

1734. Pantojas García, Emilio. LA IGLESIA PROTESTANTE Y LA AMERICANIZACIÓN DE PUERTO RICO: 1898-1917 [The Protestant church and the Americanization of Puerto Rico: 1898-1917]. *Rev. de Ciencias Sociales [Puerto Rico] 1974 18(1-2): 97-122.* After US entry to Puerto Rico in 1898, US Protestant missionaries tried deliberately to justify US economic, political, and military exploitation; they called the process "regeneration" and spread their ideas through their control of church, education, and press.

1735. Patterson, James A. MOTIVES IN THE DEVELOPMENT OF FOREIGN MISSIONS AMONG AMERICAN BAPTISTS, 1810-1826. *Foundations 1976 19(4): 298-319.* Assesses the motives behind the American Baptist mission interest. The zeal for venture grew out of the Second Awakening which nearly doubled the Baptist population. The motivation was theological and emphasized the Great Commission in millennial context. Baptists hoped that the Kingdom of God and the Christian ethical system soon would be established, and missions were important to this event. 74 notes.
E. E. Eminhizer

1736. Phillips, Dennis H. THE AMERICAN MISSIONARY IN MOROCCO. *Muslim World 1975 65(1): 1-20.* Narrates the little-known work of American missionaries in Morocco. A. J. Nathan and Henry A. Hammer of the Gospel Missionary Union of Kansas were first to arrive in Tangiers in 1895. They were supplemented by several more missionaries who were sent into the interior. The Muslim population either ignored these missionaries or reacted to them with open hostility, while the British missionaries, who had preceded them, were critical of their American colleagues. The work of the Americans in and around

Tangiers was fruitless and frustrating, though in 1899 they did win their first convert. Despite such difficulties and a lack of tangible results, they persisted in their work, partly because of help received from the American consulate in Morocco and partly because of their strong belief in spreading the gospel throughout the land of "darkness, despair and death." Based on the writings of the missionaries, and secondary works; 56 notes. P. J. Mattar

1737. Pilkington, Luann Foster. THE SHANGHAI PUBLISHING HOUSE. *Methodist Hist. 1979 17(3): 155-177.* The Methodist Episcopal Church, South, at the suggestion of missionaries of the church's China Mission, approved a publishing house in 1898. Almost immediately different viewpoints arose between the Southern Book Committee and the Mission board. By 1901 a site had been selected in China and a manager elected. After continuing conflict and many problems, the property of the publishing house was transferred to the Mission board in 1919. The next year the manufacturing division of the House was discontinued because the Asiatic printers could do the printing more cheaply. 2 illus., 36 notes. H. L. Calkin

1738. Reilly, Michael C. CHARLES HENRY BRENT: PHILIPPINE MISSIONARY AND ECUMENIST. *Philippine Studies 1976 24(3): 303-325.* Provides a biographical article on Charles Henry Brent, first Protestant Episcopal Bishop of the Philippines, 1901-18. Examines Brent's mission and Christian philosophy through his speeches and later writings. He was an advocate of American paternalism, though with liberal positions on most controversial subjects. Based mostly on Brent's publications. 70 notes. D. Chaput

1739. Roy, Andrew T. OVERSEAS MISSION POLICIES: AN HISTORICAL OVERVIEW. *J. of Presbyterian Hist. 1979 57(3): 186-228.* Traces the development and alterations of the foreign mission policies of the United Presbyterian Church in the United States in outline form through 14 periods, each characterized by certain policy characteristics. Covers 1706-1977. Internal documentation, illus. H. M. Parker, Jr.

1740. Saliba, Issa A. THE BIBLE IN ARABIC: THE 19TH-CENTURY PROTESTANT TRANSLATION. *Muslim World 1975 65(4): 254-263.* A brief narrative concerning the Protestant translation of the Bible to Arabic in mid-19th century. Eli Smith (1801-57), a missionary of the American Board of Commissioners for Foreign Missions, commenced translation in 1848 with the help of two Arab scholars, Butrus al-Bustānī and Nāsīf al-Yāziji. When Smith died, he was succeeded by Cornelius VanDyck (1818-95), who chose a Muslim sheik, Yūsuf al-Asīr, to assist him. VanDyck followed the same principles in translating the Bible as his predecessor: conformity to the original text, uniformity in words and phrases, intelligibility, avoiding local dialects, and adherence to ancient grammar and classical usage. The primary concern was to convey the meaning of the Bible. This was reflected in the Arabic New Testament, which was completed in 1860. Based on the archives of the American Board of Commissioners for Foreign Missions and secondary works; 26 notes. P. J. Mattar

1741. Sanderson, Lilian. THE SUDAN INTERIOR MISSION AND THE CONDOMINIUM SUDAN, 1937-1955. *J. of Religion in Africa [Netherlands] 1976 8(1): 13-40.* The Sudan Interior Mission (SIM), headquartered in Canada, had worked in Nigeria and Ethiopia before entering the Sudan in 1937. Provides a year-by-year account of the SIM's activities, including its difficulties with the British government. Of particular importance to the SIM was the development of schools and the role of the British government in the education of Africans. The areas where the SIM went were peopled by Africans who had little interest in missionaries or their schools. 116 notes. H. G. Soff

1742. Saunders, Davis L. CHANGING CONCEPTS OF VOCATION IN SOUTHERN BAPTIST FOREIGN MISSIONS, 1845-1973. *Baptist Hist. and Heritage 1974 8(4): 213-219.* The development of the concept of foreign mission service among Southern Baptists. S

1743. Schloss, Ruth. ELIZA MCCOOK ROOTS: AN AMERICAN IN CHINA, 1900-1934. *Connecticut Antiquarian 1980 32(1): 10-25.* At age 30, Eliza McCook (1869-1934) of Hartford, Connecticut, traveled to China; there she and Logan H. Roots (d. 1945), whom she married in 1902, lived as Episcopalian missionaries (she until her death, he until 1937).

1744. Scovil, G. C. Coster. MSCC AND MY CHINA EXPERIENCE. *J. of the Can. Church Hist. Soc. [Canada] 1977 19(3-4): 182-185.* The recollections of a Canadian Anglican missionary to China. Inspired to his task by a Chinese bishop and earlier Canadian missionaries to China, he entered that country after considerable training in its language, history and culture by the Missionary Society of the Canadian Church. He remained there some 15 months during 1946-47 and was very impressed by the ecumenical spirit that characterized the missionaries of other Christian faiths whom he encountered. He was also pleased by the careful supervision provided by the MSCC. With the recommendation of the Chinese church leaders and the MSCC, however, it was determined that he and his fellow missionaries should leave China because of the growing possibility of a Communist takeover in the years after World War II. J. A. Kicklighter

1745. Smylie, Robert F. JOHN LEIGHTON STUART: A MISSIONARY IN THE SINO-JAPANESE CONFLICT 1937-1941. *J. of Presbyterian Hist. 1975 53(3): 256-276.* As President of Yenching University in 1937 when the Japanese occupied Peking and north China, John Leighton Stuart's unique outlook on China thrust him into the role of intermediary among the varying forces striving for dominance in China. He was disdainful of Chiang Kai-shek who obstinately refused to meet with Japanese officials and sympathized with liberal Japanese who saw the Sino conflict without purpose or end. In 1937-41, all parties in China had confidence in him, but because he was not a US diplomat, he received little sympathy from Roosevelt. Stuart urged an embargo on Japan, financial assistance to China, and settlement of anachronistic foreign rights in China, such as extraterritoriality. Based largely on documents in State Department Archives and the Franklin D. Roosevelt Library in Hyde Park; biblio., 64 notes. H. M. Parker, Jr.

1746. Soremekun, Fola. RELIGION AND POLITICS IN ANGOLA: THE AMERICAN BOARD MISSIONS AND THE PORTUGUESE GOVERNMENT, 1880-1922. *Cahiers d'Études Africaines [France] 1971 11(3): 341-377.* In late 1880, the first three American missionaries arrived in Luanda, Angola, with the object of carrying the Gospel to the Ovimbundu people of the southern highlands of Angola. In the next 42 years they and other Americans worked among the Ovimbundu despite tribal warfare and the official hostility of the Portuguese government, which regarded the Protestant, English-speaking missionaries as a "denationalizing" influence. Eventually, both English and the vernaculars were banned; God's Word could be heard only in Portuguese. 117 notes. J. C. Billigmeier

1747. Sorrill, Bobbie. THE HISTORY OF THE WEEK OF PRAYER FOR FOREIGN MISSIONS. *Baptist Hist. and Heritage 1980 15(4): 28-35.* Traces the history of the Week of Prayer for Foreign Missions to the organization of the Woman's Missionary Union (WMU) in 1888, leader in efforts for the Week of Prayer, and the work of China missionary Lottie Moon in organizing both these events.

1748. Stookey, Robert W. THE HOLY LAND: THE AMERICAN EXPERIENCE. THE CHRISTIAN AMERICAN CONCERN. *Middle East J. 1976 30(3): 351-368.* Traces the American concern for peace in the Holy Land and the growth of ecumenism in the 19th and 20th centuries. Only in the 1820's did Americans begin to visit Palestine. The American Board of Commissioners for Foreign Missions was incorporated in 1812. The ethnocentrism the missionaries took with them "tended to retard the development of a sympathetic and tolerant understanding of the peoples among whom they were to work." Americans became full partners with European scholars in the development of scientific archaeology in biblical studies and related linguistic disciplines. "The Protestantism which Americans took to the Bible land included a general humanitarianism transcending the immediate concern with proselytizing." 21 notes. E. P. Stickney

1749. Thode, Frieda Oehlschlaeger. THE REV. E. L. ARNDT. *Concordia Hist. Inst. Q. 1974 47(2): 90-95.* Chronicles the work of Reverend E. L. Arndt, father of the China mission of the Lutheran Church, 1913-29. S

1750. Thompson, Arthur N. THE WIFE OF THE MISSIONARY. *J. of the Can. Church Hist. Soc. 1973 15(2): 35-44.* A study of the wives of early Anglican missionaries in the Canadian Red River settlement from 1820 to 1840. Born and reared in England, some complained bitterly about their new deprivations. Yet the wives vigorously supported their husbands' work. They bore many children, managed households, taught Sunday school classes, and taught in the missionary boarding schools and cared for the students who lived with them. Although some of the women were hostile to the Indians, most missionary wives treated Indians with warmth and visited them in their homes. In short, the missionaries' wives deserve much credit for their part in maintaining the influence of education and religion in the Red River area. Based on primary and secondary sources; 50 notes. J. A. Kicklighter

1751. Tucker, Kathryn and Tucker, Theodore L. WHAT AMSTERDAM DID TO US. *J. of Ecumenical Studies 1979 16(1): 60-64.* The 1st World Conference of Christian Youth and the presence of African delegates there in Amsterdam in 1939 led to a mission in Africa and an appreciation for the growth of both Christianity and the independence movements there. S

1752. Tucker, Nancy Bernkopf. AN UNLIKELY PEACE: AMERICAN MISSIONARIES AND THE CHINESE COMMUNISTS, 1948-1950. *Pacific Hist. Rev. 1976 45(1): 97-116.* During 1948-50 the Chinese Communists pursued a policy of toleration of religion, including foreign missionaries. The outbreak of the Korean War ended the policy. The toleration policy was more fully observed in urban than in rural areas. Protestants were better treated than Catholics. American missionaries were divided in their response to Chinese Communists: Catholics and fundamentalist Protestants were hostile, but modernist Protestants were more likely to believe cooperation was possible. Other missionaries who decided to cooperate were motivated by the desires of Chinese Christians and by a concern to protect their churches' property holdings in China. Some missionaries also attempted to influence American policy. Many lobbied in 1949 for an end to American aid to the Kuomintang and for recognition of the Communists. Based on manuscripts in church archives, published primary sources, and published and unpublished secondary works; 66 notes. W. K. Hobson

1753. Tullis, LaMond. THE CHURCH MOVES OUTSIDE THE UNITED STATES: SOME OBSERVATIONS FROM LATIN AMERICA. *Dialogue 1980 13(1): 63-73.* The rapid increase in converts in Latin America, particularly since 1975, have posed problems for Mormons. In particular, overtones of American nationalism offend local peoples, and the traditional leadership culture of Latin America conflicts with the Mormon exercise of priesthood authority. Graph.
R. D. Rahmes

1754. Walker, Ronald W. THE WILLARD RICHARDS AND BRIGHAM YOUNG 5 SEPTEMBER 1840 LETTER FROM ENGLAND TO NAUVOO. *Brigham Young U. Studies 1978 18(3): 466-475.* Written by Richards and Young, this 1840 letter was sent to Joseph Smith with the first emigrant group they had officially organized in England. It provides a contemporary Mormon-American view of early Victorian England. Richards and Young examined English life with the objective of identifying English labor's receptivity to the Mormon message. In particular they pointed to the enclosure movement, industrialization, and religion, including the Anglicans and Methodists.
M. S. Legan

1755. Watts, John D. W. HIGHER EDUCATION IN SOUTHERN BAPTIST FOREIGN MISSIONS. *Baptist Hist. and Heritage 1976 11(4): 218-229.* William Carey established the first Baptist institution of higher learning on the foreign mission field at Serampore, India, in 1826. He thus initiated a history of establishing colleges and seminaries on foreign fields which Southern Baptists have continued. Traces the development of institutions of higher learning among Southern Baptist foreign missions, with most emphasis placed upon theological seminaries. The greatest institutional growth has developed since World War II. Based on primary and secondary sources; 28 notes. H. M. Parker, Jr.

1756. —. MENNONITE WOMEN IN MISSION: ROSE LAMBERT, PIONEER. *Mennonite Hist. Bull. 1978 39(4): 1-3.* Reprints two letters by Rose Lambert, a Mennonite missionary in Armenia during 1898-1911; the first letter (1910) refers to her work and the massacre of Armenians in Turkey and the second (1969) offers her opinion on Turkish-Armenian relations.

12. MODES OF RELIGIOUS EXPRESSION AND REPRESENTATION

Architecture

1757. Anderson, Paul L. WILLIAM HARRISON FOLSOM: PIONEER ARCHITECT. *Utah Hist. Q. 1975 43(3): 240-259.* Pioneer architect William Harrison Folsom (1815-1901) was the son of a New Hampshire carpenter. His most important contributions to Mormonism were his accomplishments as architect and builder. As assistant church architect (and later church architect) he planned the Salt Lake Theatre, Manti Temple, and Provo Tabernacle. His name has been almost forgotten, but not his buildings, many of which are listed on the State Register or the National Register of Historic Places. Based on primary and secondary sources; 9 illus., 36 notes. J. L. Hazelton

1758. Arrington, J. Earl. WILLIAM WEEKS, ARCHITECT OF THE NAUVOO TEMPLE. *Brigham Young U. Studies 1979 19(3): 337-359.* Member of a family of New England builders, William Weeks moved to Nauvoo, Illinois, where Joseph Smith approved Weeks's plans for a temple. After Smith's death, the Twelve Apostles took over supervision. In 1847, Weeks was ordered to settle in Utah, but he soon moved to the Midwest and was excommunicated. Later, he returned to Utah because he thought he would be needed for construction of the tabernacle. He was readmitted to the church, but was passed over as architect. In 1857, he moved to California, dying there in 1900. Based on Church Archives, oral interviews, and published primary and secondary sources; photos, diagrams, 110 notes. S

1759. Arrington, Leonard J. and Larkin, Melvin A. THE LOGAN TABERNACLE AND TEMPLE. *Utah Hist. Q. 1973 41(3): 301-314.* Each Mormon community historically underwent three stages, concluding in the construction of a mammoth temple. The temple took years to build and symbolized the unity of the Mormon community. Logan, however, underwent this process in less than three decades. Founded in 1859, Logan began the construction of its tabernacle early in 1865. The edifice was dedicated in 1891. The towers of this five-story structure soar to 165 and 170 feet, and can be seen throughout the Cache Valley, a "reminder of the omnipresence of eternity." Based on primary and secondary sources; plan, 4 photos, 17 notes. H. S. Marks

1760. Batt, Ronald E. JOSEPH BATT AND THE CHAPEL: A BIOGRAPHICAL SKETCH OF AN ALSATIAN IMMIGRANT. *Niagara Frontier 1976 23(2): 49-55.* Discusses the role of Alsatian immigrant, Joseph Batt, in the building of the Chapel of Our Lady Help of Christians in Cheektowaga, in the Buffalo area, 1789-1872.

1761. Benes, Peter. TWIN-PORCH VERSUS SINGLE-PORCH STAIRWELLS: TWO EXAMPLES OF CLUSTER DIFFUSION IN RURAL MEETINGHOUSE ARCHITECTURE. *Old-Time New England 1979 69(3-4): 44-68.* Describes the most common methods of enlarging meetinghouses in New England during the 18th century; discusses, in particular, the merits of the twin-porch versus the single-porch stairwell, which were added to increase pew space.

1762. Bergera, Gary James. "I'M HERE FOR THE CASH": MAX FLORENCE AND THE GREAT MORMON TEMPLE. *Utah Hist. Q. 1979 47(1): 54-63.* Max Florence (1865-1932), a Russian emigrant and former theater owner in Utah, offered in September 1911 to sell to Joseph F. Smith, president of the LDS church, 68 photos secretly taken of the interior of the great Mormon Temple in Salt Lake City. The pictures were taken by Gisbert Bossard, a German convert dissatisfied with church authorities. Smith countered by making public plans to publish an illustrated book with full, accurate descriptions of the temple. Florence's attempts to sell the photos in New York failed. Primary and secondary sources; 3 illus., 41 notes. J. L. Hazelton

1763. Betts, E. Arthur. PLACES OF WORSHIP ON THE HALIFAX SCOTIA SQUARE SITE. *Nova Scotia Hist. Q. [Canada] 1979 9(3): 215-223.* Traces the history of nine churches in Halifax (1784-1825). The places of worship were: Lady Huntingdon's Society Meeting Place, Marchinton's Hall, Zoar Chapel, Burton's Church, Poplar Grove Presbyterian, Salem Chapel, Chalmers, Trinity Free Church, and a building which was used by Baptist, Universalist, and Jewish congregations. None of the buildings are standing today. Primary sources from Public Archives of Nova Scotia and Maritime Conference Archives; map. H. M. Evans

1764. Breibart, Solomon. THE SYNAGOGUES OF KAHAL KADOSH BETH ELOHIM, CHARLESTON. *South Carolina Hist. Mag. 1979 80(3): 215-235.* Provides a brief history of Jews in South Carolina dating to 1695, and describes the synagogues of Kahal Kadosh Beth Elohim (Holy Congregation House of God), from 1749 until 1978, in Charleston; includes photographs and floor plans.

1765. Brosseau, Mathilde. GOTHIC REVIVAL IN CANADIAN ARCHITECTURE. *Can. Hist. Sites [Canada] 1980 (25): 6-204.* This study deals with the evolution of Gothic Revival in Canadian architecture. It goes back to the origins of the style, marks its arrival in the country and traces its four mutations ranging over the greater part of the 19th century and even into the first decades of the 20th century. The first so-called romantic mutation is expressed by buildings that add certain Neo-Gothic traits to a traditional scheme of composition. . . . Toward the middle of the 19th century, this conception gave way to another approach: the ecclesiological and rationalistic style. . . . As early as the 1860's, a desire for inventive freedom created a trend toward picturesque visual effects in Gothic Revival buildings. . . . At the turn of the century, a radical change affects the evolution of Gothic Revival. . . . Religious and institutional architecture, with its inherent ties to the Middle Ages, is almost the only medium for this fourth mutation in Gothic Revival: the *Beaux-Arts* style. During the 1930's, this final expression of Gothic Revival gradually gave way to the imperatives of modern technology in the architectural world. J

1766. Brown, Lisle G. THE SACRED DEPARTMENTS FOR TEMPLE WORK IN NAUVOO: THE ASSEMBLY ROOM AND THE COUNCIL CHAMBER. *Brigham Young U. Studies 1979 19(3): 361-374.* Before completion of the Nauvoo, Illinois, temple, Joseph Smith converted the second story of his store into an assembly room for conducting religious obervances, including initiation into the Mormon Church. After Smith's death, the attic of the unfinished temple was used for the same purpose. Based on Church Archive documents and published primary and secondary sources; 76 notes. S

1767. Brunvand, Jan Harold. THE ARCHITECTURE OF ZION. *Am. West 1976 13(2): 28-35.* Joseph Smith's 1833 master plan for a "City of Zion" specified wide streets following the cardinal points of the compass, with church and civic buildings at the center, and unpainted granaries and barns within the community perimeter, surrounded by open fields. It called for houses of substantial stone or brick masonry construction. These features were adopted to the terrain and environment—elaborate irrigation ditch networks, hay derricks, Lombardy poplar windows, and the thrifty "Mormon fence"—and characterize traditional Mormon small town communities throughout the West in the 19th century. 13 illus. D. L. Smith

1768. Cooper, Patricia Irvin. POSTSCRIPT TO "A QUAKER-PLAN HOUSE IN GEORGIA." *Pioneer Am. 1979 11(3): 142-150.* Discusses the architecture of the Gilmer House, a Quaker-plan house built in 1800 in Oglethorpe County, Georgia, recently moved to Washington, Wilkes County, Georgia.

1769. Cotter, John L. and Orr, David. HISTORICAL ARCHAEOLOGY OF PHILADELPHIA. *Hist. Archaeology 1975 9: 1-10.* Archaeological investigations in quest of evidence of 18th-century site data related to colonial Philadelphia and its part in the American Revolution point to subsequent development. Early excavation of Franklin Court led to others which are summarized. Describes the front step and sidewalk area of Independence Hall; the remnants of the waster deposit of the Bonnin and Morris Pottery factory; the Kensington Methodist Episcopal Church; Walnut Street Prison; the Philadelphia Gaswork Point Breeze Station, where a large archive of historical materials was discovered. The latter is an example of what might be accomplished throughout the nation."Preservation proposals have been advanced which have facilitated the saving of key industrial buildings and machines in Philadelphis." 8 photos, map. E. P. Stickney

1770. Darragh, Ian. THE MAJESTIC ABBEY OF ST. BENOÎT-DU-LAC. *Can. Geographic [Canada] 1979 99(3): 28-35.* Briefly traces the history of the Abbey of St. Benoît-du-Lac, constructed between 1955 and 1962 and located on 300 acres 85 miles east of Montreal, in Brome County, Quebec; describes the work and life of the Benedictines.

1771. Detwiller, Frederic C. THOMAS DAWES'S CHURCH IN BRATTLE SQUARE. *Old-Time New England 1979 69(3-4): 1-17.* The Congregationalist Brattle Square Church in Boston, Massachusetts, built during 1772-73, and designed by Thomas Dawes (who won the informal competition against John Singleton Copley), influenced the design of other 18th-century churches.

1772. Dexter, Lorraine Le H. STEPS FROM THE TRINITY CHURCH TO THE POINT: ZABRISKIE MEMORIAL CHURCH OF ST. JOHN. *Newport Hist. 1975 48(4): 329-347.* History of the construction of the (Catholic) Church of St. John the Evangelist, 1883-1934. 7 photos, reproduction, biblio.

1773. Downs, Arthur Channing, Jr. AMERICA'S FIRST "MEDIEVAL" CHURCHES. *Hist. Mag. of the Protestant Episcopal Church 1976 45(2): 166-176.* In the 1840's the Cambridge Camden Society sent to America plans of the small parish church of St. Michael's, Long Stanton, Cambridgeshire, which had been erected about 1230. Three parish churches in America were built on these plans: one in Philadelphia, one along the Hudson in New York, and one in Baltimore. The last one no longer exists. Details the structure and appointments and alterations of the other two edifices. 5 illus., 2 notes. H. M. Parker, Jr.

1774. Downs, Arthur Channing, Jr. SPECIFICATIONS FOR THE ROOFS OF TRINITY CHURCH, NEW YORK CITY, 1842. *APT Bull. [Canada] 1980 12(2): 112-116.* Details the roof specifications for Trinity Church (Episcopal) on Broadway in New York City, designed by Richard Upjohn (1802-78) in 1839 and completed in 1842.

1775. Elliott, R. Sherman. THE SEVENTH DAY BAPTIST MEETING HOUSE. *Newport Hist. 1975 48(2): 265-279.* Chronicles the history of the presence of Seventh-Day Baptists in Newport and their meeting house, 1664-1929.

1776. Ellis, Bruce T. THE "LOST" CHAPEL OF THE THIRD ORDER OF ST. FRANCIS IN SANTA FE. *New Mexico Hist. Rev. 1978 53(1): 59-74.* The Santa Fe chapel of the Third Order of Saint Francis was not lost. Discusses the dating, location, construction, and other features of the chapel. Covers ca. 1805-32. Illus., 25 notes. J. H. Krenkel

1777. Emlen, Robert P. RAISED, RAZED, AND RAISED AGAIN: THE SHAKER MEETINGHOUSE AT ENFIELD, NEW HAMPSHIRE, 1793-1902. *Hist. New Hampshire 1975 30(3): 133-146.* The Shaker meetinghouse at Enfield, New Hampshire, was "the eighth of ten remarkable meetinghouses." Designed and framed by Brother Moses Johnson, master builder, it was altered in 1815 to provide more space. When membership in the community declined after the 1850's the old church became less important, and from 1889 ceased to be used on a regular basis. In 1902 Annetta and Louis Saint-Gaudens purchased the structure, dismantled it, and had it erected, with modifications, at Cornish, New Hampshire, where it still stands, as the Saint-Gaudens' National Historic Site. 6 illus., 31 notes. D. F. Chard

1778. Fischer, Emil C. A STUDY IN TYPES: RURAL CHURCHES OF THE PLAINS. *Kansas Q. 1974 6(2): 39-53.* Includes 18 plates of 19th-century sketches by Kansas architect Emil C. Fischer. S

1779. Fisher, Brad. ECCLESIOLOGY AND THE DEEP CHANCEL: FROM CAMBRIDGE TO NEW YORK. *Hist. Mag. of the Protestant Episcopal Church 1978 47(3): 313-331.* Describes the emergence of the Ecclesiology Society in Cambridge in 1839 and its impact on using ecclesiastical architecture to revive the lethargy of the Anglican Communion in the first half of the 19th century. Architecture became a means of recognizing the inner spiritual significance of outward, visible forms of church art and architecture. The restoration of the deep chancel was of primary importance in the movement, which also spread to the United States. Based largely on *Ecclesiologist* (1841-59); 93 notes, biblio. H. M. Parker, Jr.

1780. Garvin, James L. ST. JOHN'S CHURCH IN PORTSMOUTH: AN ARCHITECTURAL STUDY. *Hist. New Hampshire 1973 28(3): 153-175.* Built in 1807 after plans by Alexander Parris of Portland, Maine, St. John's Episcopal church was erected on the site of the 1732 "Queen's Chapel" burned in 1806. Documents roles of joiners, suppliers, subscribers, and building committee and agent, from church archives and local histories. Subsequent modifications record "changing religious and aesthetic attitudes" since 1807. 11 illus., 40 notes. T. D. S. Bassett

1781. Goss, Peter L. THE ARCHITECTURAL HISTORY OF UTAH. *Utah Hist. Q. 1975 43(3): 208-239.* Examines two major categories of Utah's architecture: the vernacular (primarily early pioneer structures), and the "high style" (late 19th and early 20th centuries). The vernacular demonstrates the resourcefulness and industry of the pioneers. True skill is displayed in the adaptations of national styles to fit regional needs and conditions. Mormon influence upon religious architecture and town planning is unique. The variety of buildings and styles constitutes a rich heritage that should be preserved. Based on primary and secondary sources; 28 illus., 36 notes. J. L. Hazelton

1782. Goss, Robert C. THE CHURCHES OF SAN XAVIER, ARIZONA AND CABORCA, SONORA: A COMPARATIVE ANALYSIS. *Kiva 1975 40(3): 165-180.* Located less than 200 miles apart on opposite sides of the international border separating Arizona and Sonora, Mexico, are two mission churches, strikingly similar in appearance, but of undetermined relationship. The churches of San Xavier del Bac (erected ca. 1781-97), located near Tucson, Arizona, and Nuestra Señora de la Purísima Concepción del Caborca (erected 1797-1809) in the town of Caborca, Mexico have been referred to as sister or twin churches. Visually the resemblance between the structure is sufficiently strong to suggest kinship. However, of the many Latin cross plan churches built with crossing domes and twin towers in New Spain, a considerable number probably appeared quite similar without necessarily sharing the same plan, architect, or inspiration. Since little evidence concerning the facts of construction of either the San Xavier or Caborca church has been uncovered, the existing structures themselves must be examined for clues that help explain their similarity. This paper investigates the relationship between the two mission churches by analyzing their historical backgrounds, architectural and sculptural styles, structural dimensions, and the materials and probable techniques used in their construction. A comparison of these elements permits judgments to be made concerning the degree and nature of kinship between the churches. J

1783. Griffith, James S. THE FOLK-CATHOLIC CHAPELS OF THE PAPAGUERIA. *Pioneer Am. 1975 7(2): 21-36.* Investigates a small number of Papago Indian chapels and folk-Catholic religious observances on the Papago reservation west of Tucson in southern Arizona. The chapels are primarily repositories for sacred images but are also used for celebrations of public religious feasts. Architecturally, they are simple rectangular buildings, the interiors of which contain altars loaded with sacred images. This study illustrates the usefulness of having folk traditional data readily available for comparative purposes. Based on field work, documents in the archives of Mission Santa Barbara, California, and secondary sources; 11 photos, fig., 19 notes. C. R. Gunter, Jr.

1784. Hartman, Susan B. and Johnson, Richard G. THE RESTORATION OF OLD BETHEL: AN EXAMPLE FOR THE FUTURE. *Pennsylvania Heritage 1980 6(4): 24-28.* Discusses efforts to restore Reading's Bethel African Methodist Episcopal Church (founded in 1834, and designated in the National Register of Historic Places in 1979, thanks to the Bethel A.M.E. Church Restoration Committee).

1785. Heinerman, Joseph. AMELIA'S PALACE: BRIGHAM YOUNG'S GRANDEST RESIDENCE. *Montana 1979 29(1): 54-63.* Brigham Young, president of the Mormon Church, married Amelia Folsom 24 January 1863. She was his twenty-fifth wife, but appeared constantly at his side and assumed all the social duties of his "first wife." In 1875, Young commissioned Joseph Ridges, architect and builder of the Mormon Tabernacle organ, to design and construct an official residence for himself and Amelia. The four-story, Italian villa-style structure was the most magnificient in Salt Lake City. After Young's death in 1877, his successor, John Taylor, had the mansion finished in 1882. Subsequently known as the Gardo House, it served officials of the Mormon church as a residence and office building until 1894. In 1899, Edwin T. Holmes purchased the structure and his wife Susanna had it beautifully redecorated. The Holmeses sold the property to the Mormon Church in 1924 and two years later the federal government purchased it, razed the house, and built a federal bank building. Secondary sources and manuscripts in the collections of the Utah State Historical Society, the University of Utah Library, and the L. D. S. Church Archives, Salt Lake City, as well as the Brigham Young University Library, Provo; 10 illus., 21 notes.
R. C. Myers

1786. Hoffecker, Carol E. CHURCH GOTHIC: A CASE STUDY OF REVIVAL ARCHITECTURE IN WILMINGTON, DELAWARE. *Winterthur Portfolio 1973 (8): 215-231.* Analyzes the reasoning and circumstances that led to the erection of two Gothic revival churches in Wilmington: St. John's Episcopal (1858) and Grace Methodist (1867). The construction of St. John's reflected the congregation's desire, expressed through church leaders, to adhere to the theological statement of the Camden Society of Cambridge University. Gothic revival style was not chosen for social reasons or trends, but reflected developments of the entire Anglican Communion. Grace Methodist, on the other hand, was dressed up with Gothic trappings but lacked the symbols of sacramentalism that had provoked the Anglican Gothic revival. Grace Methodist indicates that the revival had come to symbolize "good taste." Based on primary and secondary sources; 18 illus., 34 notes.
N. A. Kuntz

1787. Horton, Loren N. THE ARCHITECTURAL BACKGROUND OF TRINITY EPISCOPAL CHURCH. *Ann. of Iowa 1977 43(7): 539-548.* Built in 1871-72, Trinity Episcopal Church in Iowa City, Iowa, "is significant as an example of a common design and building technique of the mid-19th century Midwest." The frame church, built with the vertical board and batten construction technique, is of Gothic Revival style. The design was based on plans taken from the 1852 book, *Upjohn's Rural Architecture,* written by the well-known church architect, Richard Upjohn. Primary and secondary sources; 5 illus., 12 notes.
P. L. Petersen

1788. Jacob, Paul. CROIX DE CHEMIN ET DÉVOTIONS POPULAIRES DANS LA BEAUCE [Roadside crosses and popular devotions in La Beauce]. *Sessions d'Étude: Soc. Can. d'Hist. de l'Église Catholique [Canada] 1976 43: 15-34.* Studies 17 roadside shrines in La Beauce County as a key to popular devotion, religious practice, and social customs of the area in the 1970's.

1789. Jacobsen, Florence S. RESTORATIONS BELONG TO EVERYONE. *Brigham Young U. Studies 1978 18(3): 275-285.* Discusses the historical restoration of Mormon homes, particularly Brigham Young's Winter Home in St. George, Utah. Outlines the restoration and potential difficulties of such an undertaking. Cites the necessity of thorough research on the restoration site and discusses Young's life in St. George. The inventories of the furnishings in the St. George home compiled by the executors of Young's estate were equally helpful. These lists later significantly guided in the restoration, which was completed in May 1976.
M. S. Legan

1790. Johannesen, Eric. THE ARCHITECTURAL LEGACY OF GUY TILDEN OF CANTON. *Ohio Hist. 1973 82(3-4): 124-141.* Canton grew sevenfold during the architect's career (1880's-1920's). Tilden worked in styles from Romanesque to Prairie house, and his monuments ranged from cemetery vaults and churches to public and business buildings. Based on Tilden scrapbooks, interviews with descendants, and local histories; 20 illus., 39 notes.
S. S. Sprague

1791. Jordan, Albert F. SOME EARLY MORAVIAN BUILDERS IN AMERICA. *Pennsylvania Folklife 1974 24(1): 2-18.* Discusses the early architecture of Moravian builders (1740-68) in Bethlehem and Nazareth, Pennsylvania.
S

1792. Kirker, Harold. THE BULFINCH DRAWINGS IN THE AMERICAN ANTIQUARIAN SOCIETY. *Pro. of the Am. Antiquarian Soc. 1976 86(1): 125-128.* Reproduces and comments on drawings made for the enlarging of the First Parish meetinghouse in Charlestown, Massachusetts, between 1803 and 1804. Charles Bulfinch's first drawings for this project were revolutionary, suggesting a circular alteration. He later repeated the neoclassical oval in other designs of country houses for friends and relatives. Primary and secondary sources; 6 illus., 7 notes.
J. Andrew

1793. Kowsky, Francis R. THE ARCHITECTURE OF FREDERICK C. WITHERS (1828-1901). *J. of the Soc. of Architectural Historians 1976 35(2): 83-107.* Frederick C. Withers (1828-1901), English-born disciple of Andrew Jackson Downing (1815-52), was a staunch advocate of Gothic Revival architecture in both churches and commercial buildings. His work was High Victorian in secular architecture and traditionalist in church architecture. Discusses numerous church commissions, the influences on his ecclesiastical architecture, and his most well-known building, the brilliantly conceived Jefferson Market Courthouse (1874). Based on Withers' biography, writings, and secondary sources; 34 illus., 84 notes, and a chronologically arranged list of his works.
M. Zolota

1794. Land, Gary. FROM MEETINGHOUSE TO MODERN: ADVENTIST CHURCH ARCHITECTURE IN MICHIGAN. *Adventist Heritage 1977 4(1): 24-31.* Describes and pictures 16 Seventh-Day Adventist churches in Michigan, 1863-1976.

1795. Lathrop, Alan K. A FRENCH ARCHITECT IN MINNESOTA: EMMANUEL L. MASQUERAY, 1861-1917. *Minnesota Hist. 1980 47(2): 42-56.* While working as one of the architects for the Louisiana Purchase Exposition in 1904, Emmanuel L. Masqueray (1861-1917), a French immigrant, École des Beaux-Arts-trained and New York-based, but only moderately notable, met Archbishop John Ireland of Minnesota. Shortly, in 1905, Ireland selected him over 10 nationally known firms or individuals to design a major work—a new Catholic cathedral for St. Paul. For the closing 12 years of his life, Masqueray was in St. Paul, working on similar and smaller ecclesiastical commissions about the Midwest. 18 illus., 45 notes.
C. M. Hough

1796. Lewis, Wilber H. ARTISTS OF SAINT ANNE'S ROCK CHAPEL. *North Louisiana Hist. Assoc. J. 1976 7(2): 64-67.* Saint Anne's Chapel was built in 1891 by Carmelite monks on the grounds of Saint Joseph's Monastery in northern DeSoto Parish. It was "a tiny, one-room chapel of stone—the last of several religious buildings to be erected" at the Monastery. Since 1891, "artists have sketched Saint Anne's Chapel in charcoal or pen and ink, and have painted it with oils, watercolors, and pastels." The Chapel "was forsaken about 1910," and it was not until 1959 that an effort was made to restore it. Restoration was completed in 1961 under the leadership of Father William Kwaaitaal, but when the latter was transferred soon after, again the Chapel deteriorated. In 1975, Father Leger Tremblay began to restore the Chapel and "has definite plans for Saint Anne's rock chapel." 3 photos, line drawing, 10 notes.
A. N. Garland

1797. Marsh, John L. THE COUNTRY CHURCH: A STUDY IN THE NINETEENTH CENTURY TASTE AND TWENTIETH CENTURY COMMITMENT. *J. of Presbyterian Hist. 1980 58(1): 3-16.* Pictorial essay by the author and by photographer Karl E. Nordberg of exterior and interior views of 12 open country or village Presbyterian structures in northwest Pennsylvania. Without, they document a pervasive classicism that gave way in the decade following the Civil War to adaptations of the Gothic Manner; within, both styles, the essential features of the hall church persist. The furnishings, a medley of Victoriana, invariably reflect the country congregations' compulsion to retain the faith by preserving artifacts long associated with it. 30 photos, 8 notes.
H. M. Parker, Jr.

1798. McAllister, James L., Jr. ARCHITECTURE AND CHANGE IN THE DIOCESE OF VIRGINIA. *Hist. Mag. of the Protestant Episcopal Church 1976 45(3): 297-323.* Ecclesiastical architectural form follows function. Traces the architectural changes which occurred in the structures of early Virginia Episcopal edifices as the function of preaching under the earlier evangelical bishops was replaced by emphasis on the sacraments. Instead of the pulpit occupying the center of the front of the church, it was replaced by the altar and chancel, which had not existed in the original structures. Most contemporary Virginia Episcopalians have no idea that many of the buildings in which they now worship were originally erected to emphasize and enhance the importance of preaching in public worship. Based on secondary sources; 5 illus., 83 notes. H. M. Parker, Jr.

1799. McCants, Sister Dorothea Olga. OLD ST. VINCENT ACADEMY. *North Louisiana Hist. Assoc. J. 1973 5(1): 25-27.* The "old St. Vincent Academy structure located at Southern and St. Vincent Avenues, landmark in Shreveport for over half a century, is.... being torn down by workmen engaged by the owners, The Daughters of the Cross." Many people in Shreveport will remember the old building because "salvaged materials of the old building are being put to other use in various areas in and around Shreveport," and because "the two side-altars of handcarved carara marble that once served in the chapel now grace the sanctuary of Shreveport's ... Holy Trinity Church on Marshall Street." Discusses the role of Louis G. Sicard, Jr., and his wife in preserving the memory of the building through the creation of many mementos and souvenirs. 4 photos. A. N. Garland

1800. Morgan, William. THE ARCHITECTURE OF HENRY VAUGHAN AND THE EPISCOPAL CHURCH. *Hist. Mag. of the Protestant Episcopal Church 1973 42(2): 125-136.* An account of the Episcopalian churches designed by the architect Henry Vaughan (1845-1917), most of which are in New England. S

1801. Morrow, Sara Sprott. THE CHURCH OF THE HOLY TRINITY; ENGLISH COUNTRYSIDE TRANQUILITY IN DOWNTOWN NASHVILLE. *Tennessee Hist. Q. 1975 34(4): 333-349.* Describes the origins and development of the Holy Trinity Episcopal Church which began as a mission church in South Nashville during the 1840's. The church, an excellent example of Gothic Revival architecture, was completed in 1853, survived use as a powder magazine during the Civil War, and is being restored under direction of the Tennessee Historical Commission. Secondary sources; 2 illus., 18 notes. M. B. Lucas

1802. Morrow, Sara Sprott. ST. PAUL'S CHURCH, FRANKLIN. *Tennessee Hist. Q. 1975 34(1): 3-18.* In 1827 the Episcopal church had its beginning in Tennessee when James Hervey Otey organized St. Paul's Church in Franklin. The 40 by 80 foot structure with its 18 to 24 inch walls was completed in 1834, a year before Otey was elected the first bishop of Tennessee. During the Civil War the church suffered much damage, but in later years, with the addition of its famed Tiffany stained-glass windows, its appearance improved. Based on primary and secondary sources; illus., 25 notes. M. B. Lucas

1803. Neuerburg, Norman. OLD STONE CHURCH REBORN. *Masterkey 1979 53(4): 131-136.* Discusses the history and restoration of the old stone church at Mission San Juan Capistrano in California from its origins in 1797 to its stabilization in 1916, and the current plans to construct a larger replica on the mission grounds.

1804. Niebling, Howard V. MONASTIC CHURCHES ERECTED BY AMERICAN BENEDICTINES SINCE WORLD WAR II: PART I: CHURCHES BUILT BETWEEN WORLD WAR II AND VATICAN II. *Am. Benedictine Rev. 1975 26(2): 180-226.* The Liturgical Movement inspired new church architectural developments in American Benedictine communities. Reviews and analyzes the churches and chapels built at Mount Saviour Monastery, Elmira, New York; St. Benedict's Monastery, Atchison, Kansas; the Abbey of St. Gregory the Great, Portsmouth, Rhode Island; St. John's Abbey, Collegeville, Minnesota; and St. Louis Priory, Creve Coeur, Missouri. 23 figs., 7 notes. Article to be continued. J. H. Pragman

1805. Niebling, Howard V. MONASTIC CHURCHES ERECTED BY AMERICAN BENEDICTINES SINCE WORLD WAR II: PART II: CHURCHES BUILT DURING AND AFTER VATICAN COUNCIL II. *Am. Benedictine Rev. 1975 26(3): 298-340.* Continued from a previous article. Places Vatican Council II's *Constitution on the Sacred Liturgy* and the *Dogmatic Constitution on the Church* in relation to the building of recent monastic churches. Analyzes these monastic churches: St. Mary's, Morristown, N.J.; St. Anselm's, Manchester, N.H.; Weston Priory, Weston, Vt.; Christ in the Desert, Abiquiu, N.M.; St. Procopius, Lisle, Ill.; St. Martin's, Olympia, Wash.; St. Benedict's, Benet Lake, Wis.; and St. Bede's, Peru, Ill. Flexibility characterizes each of these buildings. 23 illus., 8 notes. J. H. Pragman

1806. Nieuwenhuis, Nelson. ZWEMER HALL: A LANDMARK AT NORTHWESTERN COLLEGE. *Ann. of Iowa 1975 43(2): 103-112.* Erected in 1894, Zwemer Hall was the first building on the campus of Northwestern College in Orange City, Iowa. Today it houses the school's administrative offices and serves as the regional headquarters for the Dutch Reformed Church in America. Recounts the circumstances which led to the construction of the building, the selection of George Pass as architect, the cost of construction, and the dedication of the structure. In 1924, the Northwestern Board of Trustees voted to name the building "Zwemer Hall" in honor of the school's long-time principal, James F. Zwemer. Based largely on a local Dutch-language newspaper; photos, 9 notes. P. L. Petersen

1807. Noppen, Luc. L'ÉVOLUTION DE L'ARCHITECTURE RELIGIEUSE EN NOUVELLE-FRANCE [The evolution of religious architecture in New France]. *Sessions d'Étude: Soc. Can. d'Hist. de l'Église Catholique [Canada] 1976 43: 69-78.* Discusses the principal architectural types characteristic of the period, 1600-1760.

1808. Patrick, James. THE ARCHITECTURE OF ADOLPHUS HEIMAN.

PART I: CS *Tennessee Hist. Q. 1979 38(2): 167-187.* Adolphus Heiman (1809-62) was a successful architect in Nashville, Tennessee. Working as an architect, stonemason, and delineator, he designed the First Baptist Church in 1837, helped plan the ill-fated suspension bridge over the Cumberland, then designed the Adelphi Theater, the Tennessee Hospital for the Insane, the Davidson County Jail, several buildings for the University of Nashville, Hume High School, and three other buildings. Primary sources; 2 illus., photo, 116 notes.

PART II. ROMANTIC CLASSICISM, 1854-1862. *Tennessee Hist. Q. 1979 38(3): 277-295.* Heiman celebrated the flowering southern culture with elegant Grecian, castellated, and Italianate design. Mentions buildings possibly designed by Heiman, who was best known for his design of the Belle Monte in Nashville. 4 illus., 72 notes. W. D. Piersen

1809. Patrick, James. ECCLESIOLOGICAL GOTHIC IN THE ANTEBELLUM SOUTH. *Winterthur Portfolio 1980 15(2): 117-138.* An analysis of Ecclesiological Gothic architecture and its acceptance by the Protestant Episcopal Church. Architects Richard Upjohn and Frank Wills were the most prominent designers in the field. Ecclesiological Gothic became controversial when it challenged the Puritan concept that religious architecture led to idolatry. Covers 1835-60. Based on autobiographies, society reports, religious newspapers and other sources; 3 illus., 15 photos, 2 building plans, 76 notes. N. A. Kuntz

1810. Patton, Helen. LUCAS BRADLEY: CARPENTER, BUILDER, ARCHITECT. *Wisconsin Mag. of Hist. 1974-75 58(2): 107-125.* Lucas Bradley, who learned his building and architectural training from his father, constructed the Second Presbyterian Church in St. Louis. Most of his work, however, is found in Wisconsin in the First Presbyterian Church, the Fourth Ward Schoolhouse, and Racine College, all in Racine, and several buildings on the Beloit College campus. Discusses in detail the composition, plans, and construction of these buildings. Covers 1840-90. 15 illus., 45 notes. N. C. Burckel

1811. Porter, John D. THE CALVARY AT OKA. *Beaver [Canada] 1975 305(4): 18-21.* The village of Oka, a few miles from Montreal, was founded in the early 1700's to accommodate various Iroquois and Algonkin groups. The Sulpician missionaries had a definite assignment: to introduce Christianity to the Indians and convert as many as possible. During 1740-42 the Calvary was constructed, consisting of three chapels, three crosses, and four small oratories. Christian paintings, based on prominent European works, were placed in each of the buildings and were used as instructional devices. The Calvary remains in good condition, a remarkable historic site. 5 illus., map. D. Chaput

1812. Poulsen, Richard C. STONE BUILDINGS OF BEAVER CITY. *Utah Hist. Q. 1975 43(3): 278-285.* Beaver City, Utah, has almost as many stone buildings as all southern Utah combined. Most of the oldest stone dwellings are of black pumice. Tufa, the pink stone, was a later innovation. Beaver City is a unique blend of European folk architecture, eastern US building traditions, and Mormon utilitarianism. Its stone buildings are part of folk tradition. Study of these traditions could lead us to an understanding of the builders as well as of ourselves. Covers 1855-1975. Based on primary and secondary sources; 12 illus., 9 notes. J. L. Hazelton

1813. Priddy, Benjamin, Jr. OLD CHURCHES OF MEMPHIS. *West Tennessee Hist. Soc. Papers 1975 29: 130-161.* Discusses three antebellum and seven postbellum churches in Memphis which reflect 19th-century church architecture. No church structures erected before 1840 survive. In 1844 the first permanent church was erected of brick—a representation of the earliest effort of Memphis congregations to create permanent religious housing. Based on primary and secondary sources; 9 photos, 92 notes. H. M. Parker, Jr.

1814. Puig, Francis J. THE PORCHES OF QUAKER MEETING HOUSES IN CHESTER AND DELAWARE COUNTIES. *Pennsylvania Folklife 1974/75 24(2): 21-30.* Traces the architectural development of Quaker meeting houses, proving that the larger porches or verandas were built, almost without exception, in the second half of the 19th century. S

1815. Ramsey, Ron. EARLY EPISCOPAL CHURCHES. *Red River Valley Hist. 1980 (Fall): 7-11.* Traces the beginnings of Episcopal churches in North Dakota from the construction of Christ Church at Fargo in 1874 until the turn of the century, focusing on architectural style, particularly the influence of New York City architect Richard Upjohn and Gothic Revival and Victorian Gothic styles.

1816. Rice, Cindy. SPRING CITY: A LOOK AT A NINETEENTH-CENTURY MORMON VILLAGE. *Utah Hist. Q. 1975 43(3): 260-277.* Spring City, Utah, is a prototype of the Mormon village, with large lots, broad streets in a typical grid system oriented to the compass points, and its use of local building materials. It is unique in having so many original structures unchanged, its Scandinavian building traditions, and the absence of large commercial establishments. It has all the ingredients needed for an insight into rural life in a 19th-century Mormon village. It merits preservation. Based on primary and secondary sources; 10 illus., 40 notes. J. L. Hazelton

1817. Roberts, Allen D. RELIGIOUS ARCHITECTURE OF THE LDS CHURCH: INFLUENCES AND CHANGES SINCE 1847. *Utah Hist. Q. 1975 43(3): 301-327.* The development of Mormon architecture is as much a story of change in church philosophy and the expansion of church organization as it is the adoption of technological or stylistic improvements. Some influences leading to the variety of styles were: skilled craftsmen were sought as converts and were assigned in Utah according to their skills, the church insisted on community permanence and self-sufficiency, and growth patterns in the church led to different types of buildings to fill new functions. Based on primary and secondary sources; 21 illus., 27 notes. J. L. Hazelton

1818. Robinson, William J. MISSION GUEVAVI: EXCAVATIONS IN THE CONVENTO. *Kiva 1976 42(2): 135-175.* Investigation at an 18th century Jesuit mission near Nogales, Arizona were undertaken in 1964-65 and 1965-66 by the Arizona Archaeological and Historical Society. Nine rooms in the living quarters were fully or partially excavated as well as some outlying structures. Material culture was sparse as the mission had evidently been intentionally stripped upon abandonment about 1773. Architectural remains were not sufficiently diagnostic to determine functions for individual rooms. After abandonment, the mission was re-occupied for local mining activities. Little information was obtained on the location or nature of the Indian village for which the mission was presumably built. J

1819. Schless, Nancy Halverson. PETER HARRISON, THE TOURO SYNAGOGUE, AND THE WREN CITY CHURCH. *Winterthur Portfolio 1973 (8): 187-200.* The Touro Synagogue, Newport, Rhode Island, 1759-63, demonstrates the reliance of Peter Harrison (1716-75) on English architectural books. In spite of brief mention by other authors, the existence of a specific architectural model for the Newport synagogue has been overlooked. The prototype was the Bevis Marks Synagogue in London. The London building was derived from two sources. First, the design recalls the first London synagogue of the Resettlement, the Creechurch Lane synagogue. Secondly, Bevis Marks is related to the most common type of Wren city church of the late 17th century. The Bevis Marks Synagogue marks a halfway point and a catalyst in the "amalgamation of aisled, galleried basilica into religious architecture on both sides of the Atlantic." Based on primary and secondary sources; 19 illus., 16 notes. N. A. Kuntz

1820. Sinclair, James M. ST. ANDREWS CHURCH, LAKE BENNETT. *Alaska J. 1974 4(4): 242-250.* Discusses the construction of St. Andrews Church, a Presbyterian Church in Bennett, British Columbia, built in 1898 during the Klondike gold rush.

1821. Sinclair, John L. WORKING MIRACLES. *Westways 1975 67(12): 41-43, 69.* Story of a chapel of the Spanish Catholic Church in Santa Fe, New Mexico, in the 1850's-70's. S

1822. Skjelver, Mabel C. RANDALL'S CONGREGATIONAL CHURCH AT IOWA CITY. *Ann. of Iowa 1974 42(5): 361-370.* Describes the building of the Congregational United Church of Christ in Iowa City, 1868-69. The church was designed in the Gothic style of architecture by Gurdon Paine Randall of Chicago. 2 illus., photo, 18 notes. C. W. Olson

1823. Spalding, Phinizy. THE RELEVANCE OF LOCAL HISTORY: AUGUSTA AND SACRED HEART. *Richmond County Hist. 1979 11(1): 5-10.* The author discusses his interest in local history, particularly in Georgia, and urges the preservation of Sacred Heart Church in Augusta.

1824. Thomas, James C. SHAKER ARCHITECTURE IN KENTUCKY. *Filson Club Hist. Q. 1979 53(1): 26-36.* Shaker colonies at Pleasant Hill and South Union, Kentucky, provide an excellent example of that sect's early 19th-century interior and exterior architecture. The buildings were constructed in a style called "Shaker Georgian" that emphasized simplicity and practicality. Based on records at Pleasant Hill and on printed memoirs; 4 photos, 25 notes. G. B. McKinney

1825. Turman, Nora Miller. TROMPE L'OEIL IN ACCOMAC: ST. JAMES EPISCOPAL CHURCH. *Virginia Cavalcade 1974 24(4): 5-9.* Discusses the architecture of St. James Episcopal Church, erected 1838 in the village of Accomac, Virginia. S

1826. Van Meter, Mary. ASHER BENJAMIN AND AMERICAN ARCHITECTURE: A NEW ASHER BENJAMIN CHURCH IN BOSTON. *J. of the Soc. of Architectural Hist. 1979 38(3): 262-266.* This is the only standing Greek Revival church of Asher Benjamin in Boston. The church was raised 12 feet above street level to permit the construction of two stores below. The building is now known as the Charles Playhouse. Covers 1833-40. 5 fig., 8 notes. R. J. Jirran

1827. Voye, Nancy S. ASHER BENJAMIN'S WEST CHURCH: A MODEL FOR CHANGE. *Old-Time New England 1976 67(1-2): 7-15.* Sketches of Asher Benjamin's architectural design for Boston's West Church appeared in his *The American Builder's Companion* (1806) as a model for other such buildings, and they represent an early stage in his career as architect. Benjamin later changed his original truss design to strengthen roof structure. 9 illus., 16 notes. R. N. Lokken

1828. Walton, Elisabeth. A NOTE ON WILLIAM W. PIPER AND THE ACADEMY ARCHITECTURE IN OREGON IN THE NINETEENTH CENTURY. *J. of the Soc. of Architectural Historians 1973 32(3): 231-239.* A chronological account of Oregon's academy and university architectural building program. William W. Piper, in collaboration with Elwood M. Burton, designed many Classical schools in Portland, Salem, and Eugene. One of Piper's better known works is the Sacred Heart Academy in Salem. 11 notes. T. H. Bauhs

1829. Warren, William Lamson. PETER BANNER, ARCHITECT OF THE BURLINGTON CHURCH. *Old-Time New England 1978 69(1-2): 48-70.* Concentrates on Peter Banner's design of the First Congregational Society Church (now Unitarian) built in 1815 in Burlington, Vermont, and briefly provides some notes on Banner's background as an architect dating to his arrival in New York from London in 1794.

1830. Webb, Bernard L. LITTLE CHURCHES OF LONG AGO. *Georgia Life 1978 5(3): 21-31.* Discusses Georgia's churches built from 1751 to the 1900's; provides photographs.

1831. Weber, Francis J. GOD'S HOUSE AT SAN BUENAVENTURA. *Pacific Hist. 1978 22(4): 353-356.* The original mission structure having been destroyed by fire, a new masonry church was begun in 1794 or 1795 in Ventura, California. It was completed in 1809; the first services were held that fall. There have been many additions in decoration and arrangement as well as additions to its furnishings through the many years since. Many of the furnishings represent the finest in native art with wood carvings of superb design and artistry. Changes are described down to 1976. R. V. Ritter

1832. Weinberg, Helene Barbara. JOHN LAFARGE AND THE DECORATION OF TRINITY CHURCH, BOSTON. *J. of the Soc. of Architectural Historians 1974 33(4): 323-353.* Details John LaFarge's decoration (1876) of Trinity Church, a Gothic work of Henry Hobson Richardson.

1833. Weinberg, Helene Barbara. THE WORK OF JOHN LA FARGE IN THE CHURCH OF ST. PAUL THE APOSTLE. *Am. Art J. 1974 6(1): 18-34.* Traces the involvement of John La Farge (1835-1910) with the Church of St. Paul the Apostle, New York City, particularly his work on church architecture and decoration between 1876 and 1899. Discusses also his relationship with Isaac Thomas Hecker, Paulist Fathers founder. Letters provide possible evidence of La Farge's early architectural training. Based on documents in Paulist Fathers' Archives, La Farge Family Papers, and other primary and secondary sources; 18 figs., 80 notes, addendum. R. M. Frame III

1834. Whitwell, W. L. SAINT ANDREW'S ROMAN CATHOLIC CHURCH: ROANOKE'S HIGH VICTORIAN GOTHIC LANDMARK. *Virginia Cavalcade 1975 24(3): 124-133.* History and architectural description of Saint Andrew's Church in Roanoke, Virginia. Covers 1882-1975. S

1835. Wilson, Samuel, Jr. RELIGIOUS ARCHITECTURE IN FRENCH COLONIAL LOUISIANA. *Winterthur Portfolio 1973 (8): 63-106.* The original intent of French colonization in Louisiana was religious. That intention, however, was subordinated to France's military and political objectives. The building of religious structures was relegated to state officials and carried out by military engineers. Church construction was therefore subordinated to more worldly needs. Early missionaries were left to their own devices as the first churches were constructed inside forts. Early designs for New Orleans were attempts to translate the concepts of Sebastien Le Prestre, Marechal de Vauban (1633-1707), to New World conditions. Concepts of French architecture influenced Spanish design long after Spain took control of the territory. Covers 1685-1830. Based on primary and secondary sources; 39 illus., 122 notes. N. A. Kuntz

1836. Winter, Robert. ARCHITECTURE ON THE FRONTIER: THE MORMON EXPERIMENT. *Pacific Hist. Rev. 1974 43(1): 50-60.* A study of Mormon architecture suggests that the varieties of frontier building (and not only among the Mormons) reflect a significant continuity with eastern culture. "The influence of the environment, except for materials and landscaping, is well-nigh imperceptible." Covers 1850-56. 8 photos, 20 notes. R. V. Ritter

1837. Wolniewicz, Richard. IN WHOSE IMAGE? CHURCH SYMBOLS AND WORLD VIEWS. *J. of Popular Culture 1978 11(4): 877-894.* Draws juxtapositions between iconography, architecture, decoration, and spatial arrangement in churches, and the extent to which they reflect differences in world view and values of their parishoners, 1970's.

1838. Wright, C. M. NEWPORT QUAKERS AND THEIR GREAT MEETING HOUSE: OR HOW WE CAME TO RESTORE THE GREAT MEETING HOUSE. *Newport Hist. 1974 47(4): 197-217.* Offers a short history of Quakers in Newport, 1657-1974, the history of the construction of one of their meeting houses, 1702-1922, and the preservation of the final building, 1974. 8 reproductions, 4 photos.

Arts

1839. Allard, Joseph. THE PAINTED SERMON: THE SELF-PORTRAIT OF THOMAS SMITH. *J. of Am. Studies [Great Britain] 1976 10(3): 341-348.* Discusses paintings and poetry by Thomas Smith, one of the few Puritan artists of America's colonial period whose paintings still survive. Smith lacked formal artistic training; therefore considerable technical crudity flawed his works. However, his paintings and verse demonstrated artistic power of expression and proved that his modes of expression, too, were used in colonial America for effectively expressing Puritan views and biases. Based on Smith's works and secondary sources; photo, 23 notes. H. T. Lovin

1840. Anderson, Walter. ECSTASY AND REALITY: NEW POSSIBILITIES FOR THE RELIGIOUS COMMUNITIES AND THE ARTS. *J. of Current Social Issues 1974 11(5): 18-21.* "The past two decades have made clear and undeniable that our pluralistic society strains for expression." Cites a minister who said the church's goal should be the provision of bread for the artist. Emphasizes the "tremendous sharing of experiences and the outpouring of affection . . . which would come as direct results of a new home missions venture in which the great lessons of religion and art could be learned concurrently." E. P. Stickney

1841. Benes, Peter. JOHN WIGHT: THE HIEROGLYPH CARVER OF LONDONDERRY. *Old-Time New England 1973 64(2): 31-41.* Tells of an 18th-century Scotch-Irish immigrant gravestone maker in Londonderry, New Hampshire. In more than 44 years he made about 250 burial markers, distributed in the lower Merrimack River Valley of New Hampshire. The author explains John Wight's unique designs on the gravestones he carved, and their religious significance. 18 illus., map, 8 notes. R. N. Lokken

1842. Benes, Peter. THE ROCKINGHAM CARVINGS: FOLK ECCLESIOLOGY IN THE UPPER CONNECTICUT RIVER VALLEY 1786-1812. *New England Hist. and Geneal. Register 1978 132(Apr): 97-114.* The religious inclinations of the settlers undoubtedly had an influence on the Rockingham gravestone carvings. Baptists and Universalists produced an "enthusiastic" town in contrast to "formal" towns based on established Church tradition. The "sun faces" carved by stonecutters workng in Rockingham, Vermont, during 1788-1806 exhibit a unique style. "The Rockingham stonecutters are representative of the best tradition in early American folk art." 53 notes. A. Huff

1843. Bird, Michael. ONTARIO FRAKTUR ART: A DECORATIVE TRADITION IN THREE GERMANIC SETTLEMENTS. *Ontario Hist. [Canada] 1976 68(4): 247-272.* Fraktur art is "the embellishment of a written or printed text . . . to produce a pleasing and often personalised work of art within a religio-ethnic tradition." This tradition is associated with Pennsylvania Germans. Points out minor variations and analyzes the background in Europe and Pennsylvania. Details the arrival and development of this art form in Ontario. Discusses specific artists and analyzes characteristic applications. 36 illus., notes. W. B. Whitham

1844. Briggs, Charles L. WHAT IS A MODERN SANTO? *Palacio 1973 49(4): 40-49.* An adjunct to New Mexico's folk art, santos, polychromed wooden figurines depicting saints and holy persons, were created by José Dolores Lopez (1894-1937) and his son George Lopez (1925-73), in Córdova, New Mexico.

1845. Bronner, Simon J. "WE LIVE WHAT I PAINT AND I PAINT WHAT I SEE": A MENNONITE ARTIST IN NORTHERN INDIANA. *Indiana Folklore 1979 12(1): 5-17.* Discusses Mennonites in the United States from the 1830's and the life and work of ceramic, wood, and canvas painter, Anna Bock (b. 1924) of Elkhart County, Indiana, in the context of the cultural and religious practices of the Old Order Mennonite groups of which she is a member.

1846. Buell, James. THE RELIGIOUS COMMUNITIES, THE ARTS, AND THE SECOND AMERICAN REVOLUTION. *J. of Current Social Issues 1974 11(5): 22-24.* In St. Paul, Minnesota, in October 1973, 75 national consultants gathered for a three-day consultation on the Religious Communities, the Arts and the Second American Revolution. They convened to see how art and religion in their common concerns can relate to the American Bicentennial celebration. As a result some committees have been formed to establish ongoing, self-sustaining, and state-level councils to nurture the relationship between religion and the arts. Illus. E. P. Stickney

1847. Clark, Willene B. AMERICA'S FIRST STAINED GLASS: WILLIAM JAY BOLTON'S WINDOWS AT THE CHURCH OF THE HOLY TRINITY, BROOKLYN, NEW YORK. *Am. Art J. 1979 11(4): 32-53.* William J. Bolton (1816-84), originally of Bath, England, created 60 large fully-leaded, stained glass windows for the Church of the Holy Trinity (now St. Ann and the Holy Trinity Episcopal Church) in Brooklyn during 1845-47. This was the first major complex of Gothic Revival windows in the United States and Bolton should be recognized as one of the founders of the movement. The subjects are of the Old and New Testaments, done in Renaissance style after Raphael. Bolton worked essentially alone to rediscover medieval techniques of glassmaking and then designed windows suitable for the Gothic Revival architecture. 24 illus., 55 notes. J. J. Buschen

1848. Crossin, Alan L. A MANITOBA MEMORIAL. *Manitoba Pageant 1973 18(2): 2-4.* Canadian Memorial Chapel in Vancouver was dedicated 9 November 1928. The first minister, Reverend George Fallis, helped raise funds for 10 stained-glass windows in memory of Canadians killed in World War I. Manitoba is represented by a panel depicting the founding of upper Fort Garry. D. M. Dean

1849. Dawe, Louise Belote. CHRIST CHURCH, LANCASTER COUNTY: BUILT AND ENDOWED BY ROBERT "KING" CARTER. A PICTORIAL ESSAY. *Virginia Cavalcade 1973 23(2): 20-33.* An 18th-century Anglican Church.

1850. Dawson, Joyce Taylor. A NOTE ON RESEARCH IN PROGRESS: THE NEEDLEWORK OF THE URSULINES OF EARLY QUEBEC. *Material Hist. Bull. [Canada] 1978 (5): 73-80.* Describes the needlework in the collection of the Ursuline Sisters of Quebec City consisting of both ecclesiastical and secular needlework in the Ursuline Sisters Convent school, ca. 1655-1890's.

1851. Derfner, Phyllis. EDWARD HICKS: PRACTICAL PRIMITIVISM AND THE "INNER LIGHT." *Art in Am. 1975 63(5): 76-79.* Discusses the 60 variations on Quaker Edward Hicks' painting, *The Peaceable Kingdom,* an example of folk art, produced during 1825-49; analyzes the painting's symbolism of theological, social, and psychological reconciliation between man, God, and nature.

1852. Dow, James R. and Roemig, Madeline. AMANA FOLK ART AND CRAFTSMANSHIP. *Palimpsest 1977 58(2): 54-63.* Colored photographs illustrate a commentary on Amana folk art and craftsmanship. Although the Amana Society valued tradition and utility, the articles illustrated show that Amanites also valued beauty, color, innovation, and creativity. Covers 1843-1932. 15 photos, note on sources. D. W. Johnson

1853. Fedder, Norman J. BEYOND ABSURDITY AND SOCIOPOLITICS: THE RELIGIOUS THEATRE MOVEMENT IN THE SEVENTIES. *Kansas Q. 1980 12(4): 123-131.* Discusses the emergence of an "explicit religious theatre movement" in France, Great Britain, and the United States in the 20th century, focusing on the contributions in America of Fred Eastman, Albert Johnson and Harold Ehrensberger, the culmination of the religious theater movement, especially Jewish and Christian Theatre/Drama, in the late 1950's and early 1960's, the revival of the Religion and Theatre Program of the American Theatre Association in 1974, and other developments until 1978.

1854. Fennimore, Donald L. RELIGION IN AMERICA: METAL OBJECTS IN SERVICE OF THE RITUAL. *Am. Art J. 1978 10(2): 20-42.* The move to America from England was a conservative gesture to preserve values and ideals which appeared to be threatened. This, not being a cultural break, resulted, in the area of religion, in the importation of many items such as communion sets from England, or at least the copying of familiar forms. The metal items which have been preserved illustrate this. A description (with plates) of those in churches and museums reveals patterns of not only religiosity but also taste and fashion, geographical influence, individual craftsmanship, patronage, and the presence or absence of wealth. Covers Protestant, Catholic, and Jewish items 1650-1888. 25 illus., 24 notes. R. V. Ritter

1855. Frueh, Erne R. and Frueh, Florence. STAINED GLASS WINDOWS AT THE SECOND PRESBYTERIAN CHURCH. *Chicago Hist. 1977-78 6(4): 210-217.* The stained glass windows in Chicago's Second Presbyterian Church were designed or executed by Louis C. Tiffany, John La Farge, Louis J. Millet, McCully and Niles, and Sir Edward Burne-Jones between 1872 and 1874.

1856. Gerdts, William H. DANIEL HUNTINGTON'S *MERCY'S DREAM:* A PILGRIMAGE THROUGH BUNYANESQUE IMAGERY. *Winterthur Portfolio 1979 14(2): 171-194.* Critics have failed to realize the influence of John Bunyan's *The Pilgrim's Progress* (1678) on American art, specifically that of the painting *Mercy's Dream* (1841) by Daniel Huntington. Huntington (1816-1906) deliberately selected Bunyan's work to dramatize Protestantism. *Mercy's Dream* combines "moral and redemptive imagery" with the American experience and reflects mythical values of 19th-century American culture. Covers 1841-70. Based on Huntington's correspondence and contemporary art critics and other primary sources; 24 illus., 34 notes. N. A. Kuntz

1857. Guttenberg, John P., Jr. EDWARD HICKS: A JOURNEY TO THE PEACEABLE KINGDOM. *Am. Art and Antiques 1979 2(3): 76-83.* Traces the life and works of 19th century Quaker American folk artist Edward Hicks (1780-1849) of Bucks County, Pennsylvania, whose favorite painting subject was "the Peaceable Kingdom," of which he painted 60 versions.

1858. Hall, E. Boyd. PORTFOLIO OF SPANISH COLONIAL DESIGN. *Palacio 1975 81(2): 1-10.* Discusses folk arts in New Mexico (primarily *santos bultos* and *ex-votos* associated with Catholic iconography), decorative arts, and manuscript production, 16th-17th centuries.

1859. Jacobs, Phoebe Lloyd. JOHN JAMES BARRALET AND THE APOTHEOSIS OF GEORGE WASHINGTON. *Winterthur Portfolio 1977 12: 115-137. Apotheosis of George Washington* was a commemorative engraving by the Irish immigrant John James Barralet (ca. 1747-1815). Americans were familiar with the traditions of European humanism and knew how to interpret allegorical imagery. Barralet's engraving (1802) gave the nation new symbols; classical forms of the apotheosis to serve the needs of the American polity. In so doing, Barralet established a precedent by combining classical, Christian, and American art forms, thereby ensuring that apotheosis would remain popular in America for a long time. Primary and secondary sources; 22 illus., 53 notes. N. A. Kuntz

1860. Jaffe, Irma B. JOHN SINGLETON COPLEY'S *WATSON AND THE SHARK. Am. Art J. 1977 9(1): 15-25.* Discusses religious and political interpretations of Copley's 1778 oil painting, *Watson and the Shark.* It can be seen as Copley's portrayal of a real-life sea drama in terms of Christian resurrection and salvation and at the same time "an allegory of the struggle between the Old World and the New." Neither interpretation excludes the other and they merge on the "religio-cultural level." Based on paintings by Copley, Rubens, Raphael, and others, and on secondary sources; 14 illus., 24 notes. R. M. Frame, III

1861. Johnson, Dale T. DEACON ROBERT PECKHAM: "DELINEATOR OF THE 'HUMAN FACE DIVINE.'" *Am. Art J. 1979 11(1): 27-36.* Congregationalist Robert Peckham (1785-1877) of Massachusetts was a primitive portrait painter, radical abolitionist, and temperance advocate. Attributes to Peckham four major folk paintings, formerly unattributed or misattributed: "The Raymond Children" (ca. 1838), "The Hobby Horse" (ca. 1840), "Rosa Heywood" (ca. 1840), and

"Charles L. Eaton and His Sister" (ca. 1844). These attributions are based on strongly delineated upper skull formations, strong visual confrontation of subjects to viewer, unflattering physical peculiarities, and genealogical and geographical evidence. Primary and secondary sources; 7 illus., 15 notes. J. J. Buschen

1862. Johnson, Kathleen Eagen. 19TH CENTURY MORAVIAN SCHOOLGIRL ART. *Art & Antiques 1980 3(6): 78-83.* Describes the ribbon work, worsted work, watercoloring, velvet painting, and ebony work of Moravian girls who attended Moravian female seminaries in Bethlehem and Lititz (Pennsylvania) and Salem (North Carolina) in the 19th century.

1863. Kamerling, Bruce. THEOSOPHY AND SYMBOLIST ART: THE POINT LOMA ART SCHOOL. *J. of San Diego Hist. 1980 26(4): 230-255.* Theosophy, claiming to be not a religion but rather a movement to "draw out certain basic and universal truths," was founded by Helena Petrovna Blavatsky in 1875; its community on San Diego's Point Loma began in 1897; discusses the attraction of Theosophy to Symbolist artists of the late 19th and early 20th centuries.

1864. Kanellos, Nicolás. FIFTY YEARS OF THEATRE IN THE LATINO COMMUNITIES OF NORTHWEST INDIANA. *Aztlán 1976 7(2): 255-265.* Discusses the development of Latino theater in Gary and East Chicago. By the 1920's, five Latino theater groups were operating in this area, the most prominent being the Cuadro Dramatico del Circulo de Obreros Catholicos "San José," founded to raise funds for construction of a Catholic church and to provide "wholesome recreation" for the community. The Great Depression and its attendant repatriations caused a hiatus in local Latino theater, but beginning in the 1950's, Puerto Rican Baptists made important contributions. The 1960's saw the formation of the Club Aristico Guadalupano, militantly Catholic and anti-Communist, which provided not only drama, but also a broad range of cultural presentations. The Teatro Desengaño del Pueblo, founded by the author in 1972, continues the tradition of these earlier groups, but with a stronger political emphasis. Based largely on contemporary accounts and announcements in the local Latino press; 26 notes. L. W. Van Wyk

1865. Kasson, Joy S. THE VOYAGE OF LIFE: THOMAS COLE AND ROMANTIC DISILLUSIONMENT. *Am. Q. 1975 27(1): 42-56.* The traditional interpretation of Thomas Cole's allegorical painting *The Voyage of Life* (1839) as an exercise in Christian didacticism represents only a portion of its meaning. The painting does express an orthodox Christian idea and is based on long-established iconographic traditions, but in Cole's peculiar combination of images his work forms part of the American and English romantic literary tradition. The painting expresses romantic doubt and disillusionment while providing an ambiguous solution to the problems presented. N. Lederer

1866. Kenney, Alice P. RELIGIOUS ARTIFACTS OF THE DUTCH COLONIAL PERIOD. *Halve Maen 1977 52(4): 1-2, 14, 16, 19.* An analysis of religious objects used since the 17th century shows that the colonial Reformed Dutch Church experienced no significant upheavals during the American Revolution.

1867. Kerr, Joseph R. MEMORIAL WINDOWS: CAMP LEJEUNE'S STAINED GLASS MASTERPIECES. *Marine Corps Gazette 1980 64(12): 45-48.* Stained glass windows designed and installed by the J. and R. Lamb Studios of Tenafly, New Jersey, in the Main Protestant Chapel at Camp Lejeune, North Carolina, when the chapel was built in 1942-43, portray Marine Corps history from 1775 to World War II.

1868. Lange, Yvonne. LITHOGRAPHY, AN AGENT OF TECHNOLOGICAL CHANGE IN RELIGIOUS FOLK ART: A THESIS. *Western Folklore 1974 33(1): 51-64.* Traces the development of relief, intaglio, and surface prints and elaborates on the influences of lithography on the religious folk art of Mexico and the US Southwest, contrasting this with the influence of the same techniques in Puerto Rico. Studies santeros, retablos, and religious prints 1300-1974. 16 illus., 28 notes. S. L. Myres

1869. LeCheminant, Wilford Hill. "ENTITLED TO BE CALLED AN ARTIST": LANDSCAPE AND PORTRAIT PAINTER FREDERICK PIERCY. *Utah Hist. Q. 1980 48(1): 49-65.* In 1855, Frederick Piercy (1830-91), an English convert to Mormonism, wrote and illustrated *Route from Liverpool to Great Salt Lake Valley, Illustrated (Illustrated Route).* Published as a travel guide for Mormon immigrants from Great Britain, today this work is a valuable pictorial record of the western American pioneer. Many histories of the American West have used his illustrations, often without credit. Location of some of his missing English portraits and engravings for the *Illustrated Route* would help restore his art legacy. Piercy was expelled from the LDS Church in 1857, having refused to comply with Brigham Young's order that he return to Utah from Great Britain. Based on letters and diaries in the LDS Archives and other primary sources; 7 illus., 48 notes. J. L. Hazelton

1870. Mather, Eleanore Price. THE INWARD KINGDOM OF EDWARD HICKS: A STUDY IN QUAKER ICONOGRAPHY. *Quaker Hist. 1973 62(1): 3-13.* Edward Hicks (1780-1849), Quaker minister and painter of Newtown, Pennsylvania, produced some 50 pictures of the peaceable kingdom, an allegorical composition developed from an engraving of a painting by British artist Richard Westall, illustrating Isaiah xi, 6-7. Most of Hicks' "Kingdoms" contain a vignette of William Penn signing his treaty with the Indians, as well as portraits of other Quaker leaders. Originally designed to illustrate the Quaker peace testimony, the paintings also state Hicks' esteem of Scripture, and reflect the tensions of the Quaker schism of 1827-28. By 1834 Hicks had settled upon the symbol of the lion eating straw like the ox to express the operation of divine love upon the violent. This symbol replaced the prophetic metaphor of the Messiah as a branch sprung from the family of David (Isaiah xi, 1-2) and the evangelical symbol of the grapevine in the early canvasses, proclaiming redemption by Christ's blood shed on the cross. 2 illus., 33 notes. T. D. S. Bassett

1871. Moffatt, Frederick C. THE EDUCATION OF THE NEW ENGLAND ARTIST: THE EARLY YEARS OF ARTHUR WESLEY DOW. *Essex Inst. Hist. Collections 1976 112(4): 275-289.* Studies the early years of the New England artist, Arthur Wesley Dow (1857-1922) and demonstrates how the rigid Calvinistic climate of New England was modified. Dow, who later taught at the Pratt Institute and the Teachers College, Columbia University, did not receive any formal art instruction until he was 23 years old. Prior to that time he drew old buildings in Ipswich, Massachusetts, which he had been studying as part of his interest in the past. He was influenced by his Congregationalist grammar school teacher, Rev. John P. Cowles, writer and artist Everett Stanley Hubbard, and Rev. Augustine Caldwell, a Methodist minister and printer who encouraged him to reproduce his art work through printing and to seek formal art training. Dow's major contribution to art was the principle that picture-making involved the ordered selection and arrangement of flat shapes on the picture planes. Based on primary and secondary sources; 4 illus., 41 notes. H. M. Parker, Jr.

1872. Morsberger, Robert E. and Morsberger, Katharine M. "CHRIST AND A HORSE-RACE": *BEN-HUR* ON STAGE. *J. of Popular Culture 1974 8(3): 489-502.* Discusses the dramatization of Lew Wallace's novel, *Ben-Hur*, 1880-1900.

1873. Nelson, David et al. ARTS AND RELIGION I HAVE KNOWN. *Arts in Society 1976 13(1): 47-55.* Discussion of the role of art as a revitalizer of the human spirit, as political commentary, and as propaganda for religions and governments.

1874. Nelson, Marion John. A PIONEER AND HIS MASTERPIECE. *Norwegian-American Studies 1965 22: 3-17.* While folk art lasted well into the 20th century in Norway because of delayed modernization, folk art among Norwegian Americans was close to nonexistent. Though some rosepainting was done, most immigrants gave up any former arts in exchange for labor on the family farm. Lars Christenson, a wood-carver living in Benson, Minnesota during 1866-1910, was an exception. From 1897 to 1904, Christenson carved a wood altarpiece, which is presently in the Norwegian-American Historical Museum in Decorah, Iowa. Much of his inspiration for the piece came from native Norwegian Baroque altarpieces he had known as a boy and illustrations from the Doré Bible, combined with his highly individual style. He was a great distance from his Norwegian model, had had little experience in reproducing the human figure, and his primary contacts with art had been Norwegian and Viking folk design. Assesses the Lutheran altarpiece in

terms of influences, iconography, composition, style, size relationships, realistic and decorative carving, and wood used. 18 notes.
G. A. Hewlett

1875. Nelson, Richard Alan. FROM ANTAGONISM TO ACCEPTANCE: MORMONS AND THE SILVER SCREEN. *Dialogue 1977 10(3): 59-69.* Discusses the involvement of Mormons in films since 1911, when the Danish production *A Victim of the Mormons* set an anti-Mormon tone, through the 1970's and serious views of Mormons.

1876. Neuerburg, Norman. THE ANGEL ON THE CLOUD, OR "ANGLO-AMERICAN MYOPIA" REVISITED: A DISCUSSION OF THE WRITINGS OF JAMES L. NOLAN. *Southern California Q. 1980 62(1): 1-48.* Assesses the work of James L. Nolan in analyzing California mission art, especially his criticisms of Anglo-American misperceptions of Catholic religious figures and decorations in mission churches. Nolan's view of this art as part of a total artistic environment is generally accepted, but his research suffers from numerous minor errors, a narrow focus, and omissions, particularly in his failure to consult Mexican and Spanish scholarship. Moreover, Nolan's interpretations of the implications of mission art would probably have been lost on the Indian neophytes despite the best efforts of the missionaries. Nolan should expand the scope of his own research to include comparative analysis with the church art of Hispanic and European countries, not just contrasting California mission art with Anglo-American views. Photos, 123 notes.
A. Hoffman

1877. Newport, John et al. ARTS FROM A CONSERVATIVE PERSPECTIVE. *Arts in Society 1976 13(1): 56-65.* Explains the reticent attitude of Southern Baptists and other conservative religious denominations toward art forms other than music; also discusses folk art.

1878. Nolan, James L. ANGLO-AMERICAN MYOPIA AND CALIFORNIA MISSION ART. *Southern California Q. 1976 58(1): 1-44, (2): 143-204, (3): 261-331.* Part I. California's mission art and liturgical plays have long been misunderstood and misinterpreted by Anglo-American observers. *Los Pastores*, a favorite liturgical play performed in the missions for mission Indian audiences, and mission iconography have been incorrectly identified as to design, characters, and interpretation. Even defenders of mission art, such as Rev. Zephyrin Engelhardt, misinterpreted the religious art of the missionaries. A key misunderstanding concerns the presence of St. Michael in the nativity scene. Anglos have often identified him as St. Gabriel, a reflection of Northern European post-Reformation religious thought rather than a Catholic view. Thus mission art observers view it while lacking a proper frame of reference. Based on primary and secondary sources; photos, 94 notes. Part II. The San Antonio Mission's altar pieces and paintings during the mission's restoration were misinterpreted as to location and meaning. The mission's art is based on the structure of medieval scholasticism which envisioned a geocentric universe and an Apocalyptic world view. This view was taught by Father Junipero Serra in Spain in the early 1740's at the Convent of San Francisco. Books in the Mission San Carlos library also reflect Scotist thought. Thus the Franciscan padres, as typified in the art of Mission San Antonio, attempted to bring their Indian neophytes into a world view based on scholasticism and through that system to Europeanize them. Based on primary and secondary sources, and on art objects and artifacts; illus., photos, 36 notes. Part III. Anglo-American historians of the Spanish missions of California have misunderstood the importance of the visual impact of the iconography of the missions, resulting in reconstruction and restoration of the missions that misidentified saints and moved them about indiscriminately. Mission Santa Barbara is a major example of this cultural myopia. The iconographic system reflects the system found in medieval society from Constantinople to London in an era of general illiteracy when worshipers found the story of genesis and apogenesis imparted visually. The rise of literacy in the wake of the Reformation saw this tradition ended in Protestant societies. The California missions therefore represent the reawakening of a great medieval tradition, the use of a visual language to impart the Catholic faith. Based on primary and secondary sources, photo, 81 notes.
A. Hoffman

1879. Palmer, Arlene M. RELIGION IN CLAY AND GLASS. *Am. Art & Antiques 1979 2(4): 80-87.* Describes the vessels and artifacts made of glass and ceramics for religious activities in the 18th and 19th centuries in America in churches, Moravian communities, and private homes.

1880. Patterson, Nancy Lou. THE IRON CROSS AND THE TREE OF LIFE: GERMAN-ALSATIAN GRAVEMARKERS IN THE WATERLOO REGION AND BRUCE COUNTY ROMAN CATHOLIC CEMETERIES. *Ontario Hist. [Canada] 1976 68(1): 1-16.* Gravemarkers throw light on social values and beliefs. In the Roman Catholic districts of Ontario settled by German Alsatians iron working was an art and iron gravemarkers are characteristic examples of this skill. Discusses the distribution and location of iron gravemarkers in these areas and analyzes the basic characteristics and variations in the design of markers and associated appendages. Covers 1850-1910. 8 illus., 55 notes.
W. B. Whitham

1881. Peavy, Charles D. THE SECULARIZED CHRIST IN CONTEMPORARY CINEMA. *J. of Popular Film 1974 3(2): 139-155.* Covers 1950-74.

1882. Pelzel, Thomas O. THE SAN GABRIEL STATIONS OF THE CROSS FROM AN ART-HISTORICAL PERSPECTIVE. *J. of California Anthrop. 1976 3(1): 115-119.* Examines the paintings of the Stations of the Cross (1800) apparently done by an Indian neophyte, Juan Antonio, at Mission San Gabriel Arcangel and speculates on the influence of Spanish realist tradition as it blended with the artist's native imagination and the tradition of Indian symbolic art. Note.

1883. Phillips, George Harwood. INDIAN PAINTINGS FROM MISSION SAN FERNANDO: AN HISTORICAL INTERPRETATION. *J. of California Anthrop. 1976 3(1): 96-114.* Offers a brief history (1800-1976) of the Stations of the Cross series of paintings done originally for the Mission San Gabriel Arcangel, 1800. Speculates on the background of the apparent artist, Juan Antonio, an Indian convert, and examines his perceptions of the Spanish culture as they are reflected in the paintings. 14 reproductions, 5 notes, biblio.

1884. Regis, Mary. THE HISTORY OF OUR LADY OF LEVOČA. *Jednota Ann. Furdek 1975 14: 25-33.* Traces Slovak devotion to Our Lady of Levoča from the 13th century in the town of Levoča in Spiš county, Slovakia; a replica of the Levoča statue was carved in Slovakia and shipped in 1930 to Bedford, Ohio.

1885. Schorsch, Anita. A KEY TO THE KINGDOM: THE ICONOGRAPHY OF A MOURNING PICTURE. *Winterthur Portfolio 1979 14(1): 41-71.* Analyzes Samuel Folwell's mourning painting, *Sacred to the Illustrious Washington* (ca. 1800). This painting on silk was widely imitated because of its elegance and feeling. Folwell helped to establish allegorical work in America. He connected his painting with the tenets of Reformed Protestantism: a mourning figure; motifs from scripture; a scene offered to all. Based on a comparison of Folwell's work with renowned European artists, and on other primary sources; 35 illus., 49 notes.
N. A. Kuntz

1886. Slater, James A. and Caulfield, Ernest. THE COLONIAL GRAVESTONE CARVINGS OF OBADIAH WHEELER. *Pro. of the Am. Antiquarian Soc. 1974 84(1): 73-104.* Scholarly interest in colonial gravestones of New England has increased in recent years, as "these stones provide rich source material for studies of religious symbolism, cultural interrelationships, artistic styles, mortality data, family composition, and other aspects of early New England culture." Describes in detail gravestones produced by colonial craftsman Obadiah Wheeler during 1702-49, and maps their location throughout eastern Connecticut. 25 plates, 2 tables, 2 fig., 15 notes.
B. L. Fenske

1887. Smylie, James H. PRESBYTERIAN HISTORY IN STAINED GLASS. *J. of Presbyterian Hist. 1979 57(2): 93-116.* For three generations the Willet family of the Willet Stained Glass Studios have produced stained glass windows for the churches of America. Emphasizes some of the major themes and personalities to be found in windows which the Willets have made for some American Presbyterian churches. In their art they have helped to shape a Presbyterian and Reformed iconography. Their contribution to historical Presbyterian faith and life is illustrated in the pictures of some of their stained glass windows. Highlights include such fields as education, domestic and foreign missions, music, theology

and ecumenism. Representations are taken from 16 churches and one college. Eighteen of the pictures are in black and white outline, ten are in color. A commentary accompanies each picture.
H. M. Parker, Jr.

1888. Soria, Regina. ELIHU VEDDER: AN AMERICAN VISIONARY ARTIST. *Am. Art & Antiques 1979 2(4): 38-45.* Biography of American visionary painter Elihu Vedder (1836-1923), who lived and worked in Rome for 60 years, and whose often religious work, from which the word "Vedderesque" was derived, meaning strange or symbolic, was influenced by traumatic childhood experiences and his interest in the symbolic meanings of his dreams.

1889. Stauffer, J. Paul. URIAH SMITH: WOOD ENGRAVER. *Adventist Heritage 1976 3(1): 17-21.* The work of Uriah Smith, wood engraver, appeared in the Seventh-Day Adventist publications *Review and Herald* and *Youth's Instructor* in Battle Creek, Michigan, 1850's-70's.

1890. Steele, Thomas J. THE SPANISH PASSION PLAY IN NEW MEXICO AND COLORADO. *New Mexico Hist. Rev. 1978 53(3): 239-259.* Spanish passion plays have been performed regularly in New Mexico and Colorado, since the 1830's. Interest in them grew or dwindled depending on the priests' interest. 28 notes. J. H. Krenkel

1891. Stewart, Susan. SOCIOLOGICAL ASPECTS OF QUILTING IN THREE BRETHREN CHURCHES IN SOUTHEASTERN PENNSYLVANIA. *Pennsylvania Folklife 1974 23(3): 15-29.* Covers 1700-1974.

1892. Swisher, Bob. GERMAN FOLK ART IN HARMONY CEMETERY. *Appalachian J. 1978 5(3): 313-317.* Photos of 11 tombstones found in Jane Lew, West Virginia, at the Harmony Methodist Church Cemetery show decorative folk symbols representative of local German settlers, 1827-55.

1893. Tanenhaus, Ruth Amdur. PENNSYLVANIA GERMAN QUILTS: AMISH AND MENNONITE FANCYWORK IN A PLAIN TRADITION. *Am. Art & Antiques 1979 2(4): 54-63.* Discusses Anabaptist persecution in 16th-century Europe, the Anabaptist split into the Amish and the Mennonites, and their immigration to Pennsylvania in the 1720's, followed by an account of Amish and Mennonite quiltmaking beginning in 1860 when women began socializing with American women and learned traditional quiltmaking; describes patterns, designs, colors, and materials of quilts made during 1870-1935.

1894. Tatum, W. Barnes and Ingram, Henry Black. WHENCE AND WHITHER THE CINEMATIC JESUS? *Religion in Life 1975 44(4): 470-478.* Analyzes the many films dealing with the life of Christ during the 1920's-70's.

1895. Watt, Ronald G. CALLIGRAPHY IN BRIGHAM YOUNG'S OFFICE. *Utah Hist. Q. 1977 45(3): 265-269.* William Appleby (1811-?) and Joseph M. Simmons, two of Brigham Young's clerks, are responsible for some beautiful handwritten title pages in some little-known financial volumes in the Mormon church archives. Between 7 January 1851 and 4 November 1853, they illuminated nine volumes, one trustee-in-trust ledger, five trustee-in-trust day books, and one tithing record book. With fine lettering and fancy flourishes, this calligraphy is reminiscent of the manuscript illumination of medieval scribes. 4 illus.
J. L. Hazelton

1896. Watters, David. THE PARK AND WHITING FAMILY STONES REVISITED: THE ICONOGRAPHY OF THE CHURCH COVENANT. *Can. Rev. of Am. Studies [Canada] 1978 9(1): 1-15.* Covenant theology dominated Puritan teachings in colonial times, and New England Congregationalist teachings changed little until early in the 19th century. This study of the iconography of tombstones at Grafton and Rockingham, Vermont, reveals the prominence of covenant theology and, moreover, reflects clearly Congregationalists's controversies about baptism of children and teachings about God's promises for those who kept their part of the covenant by remaining faithful to the church. Covers 1770-1803. 5 photos, 20 notes. H. T. Lovin

1897. Weinberg, Helene Barbara. THE DECORATION OF THE UNITED CONGREGATIONAL CHURCH. *Newport Hist. 1974 47(1): 109-120.* Discusses repairs and redecorating done to the United Congregational Church of Newport, Rhode Island, 1879-80. 6 photos, 26 notes.

1898. Weinberg, Helene Barbara. LA FARGE'S ECLECTIC IDEALISM IN THREE NEW YORK CITY CHURCHES. *Winterthur Portfolio 1975 (10): 199-228.* Analyzes John La Farge's (1835-1910) design and painting in three New York City churches; St. Thomas, Church of the Incarnation, and Church of the Ascension. His work suggests the fusion of the ideal and the real, two streams visible in earlier American art. Covers 1877-88. Based on primary and secondary sources; 26 illus., 67 notes. N. A. Kuntz

1899. Weiser, Frederick S. PIETY AND PROTOCOL IN FOLK ART: PENNSYLVANIA GERMAN *FRAKTUR* BIRTH AND BAPTISMAL CERTIFICATES. *Winterthur Portfolio 1973 (8): 19-43.* *Fraktur* describes a typeface dating back to 16th century Germany, but is now used to describe all Pennsylvania German primitive drawings. One of the more common forms of *Fraktur* is the baptismal certificate (*Taufschein*). One basic fact must be remembered in studying the work of Pennsylvania German artists—"the illumination was auxiliary to the text." Analyzes birth and baptismal certificates issued to Pennsylvania German children. The wide variety of design on the certificates indicates that the certificate was an object of design for its own sake. Such designs were employed for their inherent beauty and popular appeal while the text contained religious meaning. Covers 1750-1850. Based on primary and secondary sources; 19 illus., 28 notes. N. A. Kuntz

1900. Welch, Richard F. FOLK ART IN STONE ON LONG ISLAND. *Early Am. Life 1979 10(3): 38-40, 67-69.* Describes early American gravestone art which first appeared in New England circa 1660, lasting as a popular form of religious art until the end of the 18th century.

1901. Wilks, Flo. MAX ROYBAL, SANTERO. *Southwestern Art 1978 7(1): 35-39.* Max Roybal of Albuquerque, New Mexico, is a Penitente and santero—a woodcarver who creates santos, statues of Christ, Mary, and saints.

1902. Wolfe, Ruth. HANNAH COHOON: SHAKER SPIRIT PAINTER. *Art and Antiques 1980 3(3): 88-95.* Describes and discusses the content of the 100 or so Shaker paintings that have been rediscovered since the 1930's which date to the 1840's and 1850's from the Shaker communities of Watervliet and New Lebanon, New York, and Hancock, Massachusetts, and focuses on the four surviving works of Hannah Harrison Cohoon (1788-1864) who joined the Shakers in 1817.

1903. Wroth, William. THE FLOWERING AND DECLINE OF THE NEW MEXICAN *SANTERO:* 1780-1900. Weber, David J., ed. *New Spain's Far Northern Frontier: Essays on Spain in the American West, 1540-1821* (Albuquerque: U. of New Mexico Pr., 1979): 273-282. As the Spanish Franciscans began to leave New Mexico, local artisans began to carve and paint images of saints (*santos*) to fill the void; the folk art flourished until the American occupation when efforts were made to suppress it in order to Americanize and modernize the Catholic Church. Reprinted from Fine Arts Gallery of San Diego, *The Cross and the Sword* (San Diego, 1976).

1904. —. [MENNONITE FRAKTUR]. *Mennonite Q. R. 1974 48(3): 305-342.*

Yoder, Don. FRAKTUR IN MENNONITE CULTURE, *pp. 305-311.* Fraktur is the generic name for the manuscript art of the Pennsylvania Germans, a religious word-oriented folk art which flourished during the 1740's-1860's.

—. COMMENTARY ON THE ILLUSTRATION, *pp. 311-342.* Explanation of 16 photographs of Mennonite frakturs.
S

1905. —. [MYER MYERS, SILVERSMITH]. *Am. Art and Antiques 1979 2(3): 50-59.*

Werner, Alfred. MYER MYERS: SILVERSMITH OF DISTINCTION, *pp. 50-57.* Gives the biography of American silversmith

Myer Myers (1723-1795), one of a few Jews among 3,000,000 American colonists in the 18th century, a prominent member of the New York Jewish community and a colleague of Paul Revere whose fine work was largely unappreciated until the beginning of the 20th century.

Feigenbaum, Rita. CRAFTSMAN OF MANY STYLES, *pp. 58-59.* Describes the varied styles of silversmith Myer Myers who designed pieces for households and churches, and most notably for Jewish rituals in the 18th century.

Music

1906. Albritton, Sherodd. WHAT'S GOING ON WITH THE HYMNAL? *Hist. Mag. of the Protestant Episcopal Church 1979 48(2): 133-145.* Analyzes recent events since 1970 on the possibility of admitting more folk music into the revised, upcoming *Hymnal* of the Protestant Episcopal Church. Author pleads for openness to changes in old texts, admission of new words and tunes, and putting familiar words to new tunes. In a "rapidly changing church and world" there is ample reason for a fresh hymnal. 4 notes. H. M. Parker, Jr.

1907. Anderson, Gillian B. EIGHTEENTH-CENTURY EVALUATIONS OF WILLIAM BILLINGS: A REAPPRAISAL. *Q. J. of the Lib. of Congress 1978 35(1): 48-58.* Contemporary criticisms of William Billings (1746-1800), a native American composer, church singing master, and choir director, who lacked a formal education, reflect the class bias and antipathy to music prevalent during the 18th century. The cultivated upper class felt that the performing of music (even singing) was best left to the lower classes and viewed music as an insignificant, nonessential frill. Although Billings's music was not formally appreciated during his lifetime, it was very popular and is still performed today due to its lively style, appealing text, and suitability for amateur choirs. Based on documents in the Manuscript Division of the Library of Congress and in the Cobb Collection, Massachusetts Historical Society, Boston, and secondary works; 3 illus., 35 notes. A. R. Souby

1908. Bender, Elizabeth, transl. and Kadelbach, Ada. HYMNS WRITTEN BY AMERICAN MENNONITES. *Mennonite Q. Rev. 1974 48(3): 343-370.* Discusses the 50 hymns composed by Mennonites in America before 1860, and includes biographical data on the composers. S

1909. Bennett, James D. A TRIBUTE TO LOUIS H. HAST, LOUISVILLE MUSICIAN. *Filson Club Hist. Q. 1978 52(4): 323-329.* Louis H. Hast, an immigrant from Germany, was a dominant figure in establishing a strong musical tradition in Louisville, Kentucky. In 1878 Hast became organist and choir director for Christ Church Cathedral and introduced classical music to Episcopal Church functions. He also started the Philharmonic and *La Reunion* Musicale and contributed to the Public Library. Newspapers and secondary works; 24 notes. G. B. McKinney

1910. Bensusan, Guy. SOME CURRENT DIRECTIONS IN MEXICAN AMERICAN RELIGIOUS MUSIC. *Latin Am. Res. Rev. 1975 10(2): 186-190.* With Vatican Council II (1962-65), which decreed vernacular Masses, a religious revival began among Mexican Americans, affecting Protestants as well as Catholics and leading many churches to adapt their messages to Mexican American culture and to translate their hymns and literature into Spanish.

1911. Bensusan, Guy. SOME CURRENT DIRECTIONS IN MEXICAN AMERICAN RELIGIOUS MUSIC. *Latin Am. Res. Rev. 1975 10(2): 186-190.* Examines developments in religious music among Catholic and Protestant, including evangelical Mexican Americans, 1963-75.

1912. Beveridge, Lowell P. MUSIC IN NEW ENGLAND FROM JOHN COTTON TO COTTON MATHER (1640-1726). *Hist. Mag. of the Protestant Episcopal Church 1979 48(2): 145-165.* Discusses the Pythagorean and the biblical influences on church music in New England, 1640-1726. Together, the two streams created the characteristic ecclesiastical music of the New England Puritans. Pythagoreanism saved hymnody from pietistic sentimentality, the biblical tradition saved it from the dangers of idolatry. Based on materials of the period; 58 notes. H. M. Parker, Jr.

1913. Butler, Jon. LES "HYMNES OU CANTIQUES SACREZ" D'ELIE NEAU: UN NOUVEAU MANUSCRIT DU "GRAND MYSTIQUE DES GALÈRES" [The "Hymns or Sacred Songs" of Elias Neau: a new manuscript from the "Great Mystic of the Galleys"]. *Bull. de la Soc. de l'Hist. du Protestantisme Français [France] 1978 124(3): 416-423.* Elias Neau, a French Protestant, fled France and established in New York in 1689 the first school in the colonies for black slaves. This work was interrupted for several years when the French captured him and sent him to the galleys, where he wrote a number of religious letters and hymns. Contains a copy of the introduction to a previously unknown additional collection of hymns he later sent to the Anglican missionary society in London. Based on the manuscript possessed by the United Society for the Propagation of the Gospel and secondary works; 6 notes. O. T. Driggs

1914. Card, Edith B. "SAINTS BOUND FOR HEAVEN": THE SINGING SCHOOL LIVES ON. *Southern Q. 1976 15(1): 75-87.* Concerns 19th century song writer William Walker, whose influence on church music in the American South is significant. Examples of his music, explanations relating to its meaning, and justifications for its existence are provided. Covers 1830-50. 23 notes. R. W. Dubay

1915. Cartford, Gerhard M. MUSIC FOR YOUTH IN AN EMERGING CHURCH. *Norwegian-American Studies 1965 22: 162-177.* The singing of hymns was a concern of 19th-century Lutherans. From 1878 to 1914, a proliferation of unofficial, privately edited hymnals and songbooks were published. A new breed of hymnology appeared which sported an upbeat tempo designed to interest young people in the church. A number of these became very popular and went through a number of revisions and reprintings. During 1901-12, a committee was set up among three major church bodies, the Norwegian Lutheran Church in America, the Norwegian Synod, and Hauge's Synod to collaborate on the production of an English-language Standard Hymnal. This was accomplished in 1913 with the publication of *The Lutheran Hymnery* and followed in 1916 by the *Lutheran Hymnery, Junior,* allowing all Norwegian Americans some vestige of similarity in their church ceremonies. G. A. Hewlett

1916. Cavalli, Ennio. GESÚ CRISTO NELLA MUSICA E NELLA CULTURA ROCK [Jesus Christ in rock culture and music]. *Problemi di Ulisse [Italy] 1976 13(81): 176-184.* Jesus has become a counterculture symbol and a favorite theme for rock musicians on both sides of the Atlantic since the 1950's.

1917. Clar, Reva. CANTOR "YOSELE" ROSENBLATT IN LOS ANGELES, 1925. *Western States Jewish Hist. Q. 1980 13(1): 34-36.* Josef "Yosele" Rosenblatt (1880-1933) was widely known in Europe for his recordings of liturgical music and his concert performances. In 1925 he undertook a national tour in the United States on Loew's vaudeville circuit. He sang at Loew's State Theatre in Los Angeles in June 1925, receiving an enthusiastic reception. Based on newspaper accounts; 11 notes. B. S. Porter

1918. Cobb, Buell E., Jr. FASOLA FOLK: SACRED HARP SINGING IN THE SOUTH. *Southern Exposure 1977 5(2-3): 48-53.* Sacred Harp singing began in the 1840's as a nondenominational form of religious music. Today it persists in Southern rural areas and among the Primitive Baptists. The music is based on the use of shaped notes found in collections of hymns. The singing is almost exclusively ensemble, characterized by the generation of large volumes of sound. Singing meetings or conventions are regularly held throughout the year in rural areas of Alabama, Mississippi, Georgia, Florida, Texas, and Tennessee. Teachers train people to sing in the Sacred Harp tradition, but most learning is acquired on the spot. Singing meets usually last all day, with periodic breaks and ample lunches. Several thousand people still participate in Sacred Harp singing on a regular basis. Primary research and interviews. N. Lederer

1919. Crawford, David. GOSPEL SONGS IN COURT: FROM RURAL MUSIC TO URBAN INDUSTRY IN THE 1950's. *J. of Popular Culture 1977 11(3): 551-567.* Analyzes the extended (1957-59) litigation in federal court involving the licensing of performance rights of gospel music. The case, which was finally dismissed without awarding damages to either of the major performance licensing agencies involved, centered largely upon the definition of gospel music. Primary and secondary sources; 25 notes. D. G. Nielson

1920. Crawford, Richard. WATTS FOR SINGING: METRICAL POETRY IN AMERICAN SACRED TUNEBOOKS, 1761-1783. *Early Am. Literature 1976 11(2): 139-146.* Metrical poetry for the purposes of hymnology was printed in two forms, 1761-85: wordbooks and tunebooks. The former were comprised of poems intended to be set to music and are best represented by the works of Isaac Watts. The latter included composed music and though a number of British books are known, two American composers, William Billings and Daniel Read, are notable. G. A. Hewlett

1921. Dix, Fae Decker. NEVER CHANGE A SONG. *Utah Hist. Q. 1976 44(3): 261-266.* In 1919, Professor George H. Durham, the choir leader in Parowan, Utah, attempted to change the wording of an old Mormon hymn in keeping with the move to drop those of a "quarrelsome nature." Mahonri M. Decker was set on keeping alive the spirit of the embattled Mormon pioneer. He refused to cooperate. On Sunday as the choir sang the new words, he loudly and clearly sang the old. Humiliated, his daughter Blanche vowed revenge. Based on primary and secondary sources; 2 illus., 3 notes. J. L. Hazelton

1922. Downey, James. MISSISSIPPI MUSIC: THAT GOSPEL SOUND. *Southern Q. 1979 17(3-4): 216-223.* In studying Mississippi's sense of place, gospel sounds, the sounds of the Bible Belt must be considered. The impact of gospel music is significant throughout the state as it reflects the values of Mississippians. Based on a paper presented at a symposium entitled "The Sense of Place: Mississippi" at the University of Mississippi, October 1978. 9 notes. B. D. Ledbetter

1923. Ellis, Bill. "I WONDER, WONDER, MOTHER": DEATH AND THE ANGELS IN NATIVE AMERICAN BALLADRY. *Western Folklore 1979 38(3): 170-185.* Disagrees with the recent scholarship that suggests that American folk ballads tended to drop supernatural elements from British ballads. The author analyzes a number of American ballads which express two distinct attitudes toward death—"Thy Death" and "One's Own Death— and which "show a society caught between contradictory responses to death." Covers ca. 1830-1930. Based on the texts of American ballads and secondary sources; 37 notes. S. L. Myres

1924. Geiger, Maynard. HARMONIOUS NOTES IN SPANISH CALIFORNIA. *Southern California Q. 1975 57(3): 243-250.* Describes the work of Franciscans, especially Fray Narciso Durán, in teaching Indian neophytes to sing and play musical instruments. Durán worked at the San Jose and Santa Barbara missions 1806-46. He devised rules for Indians to follow in playing from musical notation; some of his compositions, which combined singing and playing of instruments, are still performed. Includes a letter from Durán to the College of San Fernando in 1819 requesting that an organ be provided for Mission San Jose. Based on primary and secondary sources; 24 notes. A. Hoffman

1925. Gilbert, Dan Paul. HOW THE MISSOURI SYNOD ACCEPTED *THE LUTHERAN HYMNAL* OF 1941. *Concordia Hist. Inst. Q. 1978 51(1): 23-27.* During the 1920's a movement within the Missouri Synod developed which led to the 1929 decision that a new hymnal should be produced to replace the Standard Hymnal of 1912. During the 1930's several reports were constructed by committees and their recommendations were considered and, for the most part, approved by the Synod in 1938. The new hymnal appeared in 1941. Primary sources; 18 notes. W. T. Walker

1926. Graybill, Ron. THE LIFE AND LOVE OF ANNIE SMITH. *Adventist Heritage 1975 2(1): 14-23.* Discusses the poetry of Annie Rebekah Smith (1828-55) which became the basis for Seventh Day Adventists' hymns, 1850's.

1927. Halan, Y. C. THE FOLKLORE OF THE APPALACHIANS. *Indian J. of Am. Studies [India] 1977 7(1): 28-40.* The Appalachian region is one of America's most richly folkloristic places. Their folklore reflects the Scotch Irish background of the early settlers, as well as the socioeconomic conditions of the region. Their folk music, ballads, tales, riddles, beliefs, and hymns retained an old, often British, flavor because the region's isolation permitted the preservation and development of a strong folk culture. Today the old ways of entertainment have been almost forgotten. Covers the 18th-20th centuries. 61 notes. L. V. Eid

1928. Harmon, Nolan B. CREATING OFFICIAL METHODIST HYMNALS. *Methodist Hist. 1978 16(4) 230-244.* The Methodist Church appointed Hymnal Commissions in 1930-34 and 1960-64 to produce official hymnals for the church. The members, who included ministers, experts in hymnody, liturgists, and musicians, rejected some old hymns and selected new ones. Each proposed hymn was carefully considered until the contents of the hymn books were agreed and submitted to the General Conferences of the church for final approval. H. L. Calkin

1929. Hart, Columba. THE RELIGIOUS BENT OF WILLIAM HENRY FRY, 1813-64. *Am. Benedictine Rev. 1976 27(4): 400-426.* Studies William Henry Fry, a music critic and composer. Analyzes Fry's life and work, particularly his musical compositions, to determine the extent to which religion influenced the shape of his work. Based on original and secondary sources; 82 notes. J. H. Pragman

1930. Hawley, Richard A. SOME THOUGHTS ON THE POP JESUS. *Anglican Theological Rev. 1973 55(3): 334-346.* Discussion of the emergence of a "modern personality" of Christ through songs and rock operas. Covers the 1960's and 70's. S

1931. Heintze, James R. ALEXANDER MALCOLM: MUSICIAN, CLERGYMAN, AND SCHOOLMASTER. *Maryland Hist. Mag. 1978 73(3): 226-235.* Alexander Malcolm (1685?-1763) was known not only in his native Scotland but throughout Europe and the American colonies as a scholar and teacher of mathematics and music, his fame resting on his 1721 *A Treatise of Musick: Speculative, Practical and Historical.* Malcolm was a schoolmaster in New York, missionary in the Society for the Propagation of the Gospel, rector of St. Anne's Church in Annapolis, and member of the famed Tuesday Club. This last was the source of the musicians for the first opera performance in America, at Upper Marlborough in 1752, along with the members of the Eastern Shore Triumvirate, a musical society based in Talbot County. Primary and secondary sources; 55 notes. G. J. Bobango

1932. Highes, Charles W. THE CHENEYS: A VERMONT SINGING FAMILY. *Vermont Hist. 1977 45(3): 155-168.* The Cheney Family Singers consisted of Moses, four of his sons and a daughter. Moses was a Sanbornton, New Hampshire, farmer, Free Will Baptist preacher, versifier, and singer. Moses Ela taught at singing schools and common schools, directed church choirs, and pioneered musical conventions. Peripatetic as a young man, he settled in Barnard, Vermont. Simeon lived in Dorset, Vermont, was a spiritualist, and published *The American Singing Book* (Boston: White, Smith & Co., 1879). Covers 1839-91. 55 notes. T. D. S. Bassett

1933. Irwin, Joyce. THE THEOLOGY OF "REGULAR SINGING." *New England Q. 1978 51(2): 176-192.* Traces the evolution of Puritan attitudes toward church music and singing styles during the 17th and 18th centuries. Focuses on the "Regular Singing" movement of the 1720's and its attempt to establish common styles of singing through the use of hymnals. Proponents of the movement defended it on the ground that God was to be pleased by the execution as well as the content of singing, while opponents believed that regular singing was destructive of the principles of scripturalism and simplicity which characterized Puritan worship. Based on 18th century pamphlets; 43 notes. J. C. Bradford

1934. Jackson, Irene V. MUSIC AMONG BLACKS IN THE EPISCOPAL CHURCH: SOME PRELIMINARY CONSIDERATIONS. *Hist. Mag. of the Protestant Episcopal Church 1980 49(1): 21-35.* Discusses music among black Episcopalians from the antebellum period to 1975. In the first period blacks contributed to the growing body of Afro-American religious folksong, later to be known as spirituals. "Let us Break Bread Together on our Knees" originated at this time, and even organs appeared in black Episcopal churches. After the Civil War a black "cultivated" tradition appeared in contrast to "folk" or "vernacular" tradition. Now one group is making an effort to move from a hymnbook

tradition to a strictly oral one, with music and text being so familiar to the people that they may enter into the worship service without being bound to the printed page. Seconary sources; 45 notes.
H. M. Parker, Jr.

1935. Kirby, Rich. AND WE'LL SING TOGETHER. *Southern Exposure 1976 4(3): 4-9.* Discusses Southern mountain religious music, including beginnings in the 18th century, its use in revivalistic situations, and contemporary songbooks.

1936. Kroeger, Karl. ISAIAH THOMAS AS A MUSIC PREACHER. *Pro. of the Am. Antiquarian Soc. 1976 86(2): 321-341.* Isaiah Thomas (1750-1831) entered the music publishing field in 1784, and quickly dominated it. His motives were financial. He made a profit and at the same time encouraged New England composers. He produced a number of hymnals. Appends a checklist of music publications by Thomas. Primary and secondary sources; 27 notes. J. Andrew

1937. Marshall, Howard Wight. "KEEP ON THE SUNNY SIDE OF LIFE": PATTERNS AND RELIGIOUS EXPRESSION IN BLUEGRASS GOSPEL MUSIC. *New York Folklore Q. 1974 30(1): 3-43.* Covers 1770-1970.

1938. McKay, David P. COTTON MATHER'S UNPUBLISHED SINGING SERMON. *New England Q. 1975 48(3): 410-422.* Early 18th-century Congregationalists in Boston precipitated a controversy over reading music (singing by note) versus singing by rote (by ear) in their practice of psalmody. Cotton Mather, minister of Boston's Old North Church, entered the "note" or "rote" controversy on 18 April 1721 with a sermon, heretofore unpublished. Mather's sermon is more agreeable and conciliatory than the singing sermons of his contemporaries, and serves to reflect the sensitive side of a man too often regarded as pedantic, narrow-minded, and self-serving. Based on primary sources; 14 notes, text of sermon including 9 notes. B. C. Tharaud

1939. McKay, David P. WILLIAM BILLINGS AND THE COLONIAL MUSIC *PATENT*. *Old-Time New England 1973 63(4): 100-107.* Tells of William Billings's unsuccessful efforts from 1770 to 1778 to obtain from the Massachusetts legislature copyright protection for his *The New England Psalm Singer* (1770) and *The Singing Master's Assistant* (1778). The author suggests that Billings's efforts generally, although not specifically, influenced the passage of the Massachusetts copyright law of 1783 and the federal copyright act of 1790. 20 notes.
R. N. Lokken

1940. Miller, Terry E. VOICES FROM THE PAST: THE SINGING AND PREACHING AT OTTER CREEK CHURCH. *J. of Am. Folklore 1975 88(349): 266-282.* The Otter Creek Predestinarian Church of Putnam County, Indiana, eschews musical notation and relies instead on oral tradition for the melodies of their hymn singing. Isolated from the Northern Baptist movement, the church rejects missions and accepts Daniel Parker's (ca 1782-1884) "two seed" doctrine. The Otter Creek church maintains a traditional song repertory and verbal style of preaching. Covers 1820-1975. Field work and secondary sources; table, 12 notes.
W. D. Piersen

1941. Mumaw, George Shaum. A COUNTRY SINGING SCHOOL TEACHER OF THE 19TH CENTURY: AN AUTOBIOGRAPHY. *Mennonite Hist. Bull. 1975 36(2): 1-3.* An account of George Mumaw's activities as a Mennonite Singing School conductor in Indiana and Ohio, 1900-53. S

1942. Olsen, Deborah M. and Clark, M. Will. MUSICAL HERITAGE OF THE AURORA COLONY. *Oregon Hist. Q. 1978 79(3): 233-268.* Established in 1844 by William Kiel, the Bethel Colony moved to Aurora, Oregon, in 1855 wheré it was known as the Aurora Colony. Well-known throughout Oregon for its members' musical talents, the Colony supported a brass band, known as the Aurora or Pioneer Band, an orchestra, and at least three choirs. The band's repertoire included both German and American tunes, many composed by the band members. The Pioneer Band continued into the 1920's long after the 1877 dissolution of the Colony. Many Aurora instruments have been restored; they were used in an October 1977 performance of Aurora Colony compositions by a recreated Pioneer Band. Based on documents in the Oregon Historial Society, Multnomah County Library, newspaper reports, and published secondary sources; 17 photos, illus., 61 notes.
D. R. McDonald

1943. Phillips, Romeo Eldridge. WHITE RACISM IN BLACK CHURCH MUSIC. *Negro Hist. Bull. 1973 36(1): 17-20.* Covers the 17th-20th centuries.

1944. Ressler, Martin E. A SONG OF PRAISE. *Pennsylvania Mennonite Heritage 1978 1(4): 10-13.* Traces the history since 1590 of the "Lob Lied," Song of Praise, the most widely sung hymn of Mennonite authorship, citing its appearances and variations in 19th and 20th-century hymnals and giving tune and verses.

1945. Reynolds, William J. OUR HERITAGE OF BAPTIST HYMNODY IN AMERICA. *Baptist Hist. and Heritage 1976 11(4): 204-217.* Traces the concept of congregation singing and hymnals among Baptists from England to America up to 1850. Singing was not encouraged in all Baptist churches in the 17th century. Not until the Great Awakening did American Baptists universally employ congregational singing in their worship. This in turn required a hymnbook. At first most of the published hymns were really Psalms after the manner of Isaac Watts. Later "spiritual songs"—which were sung to popular folk tunes—were written. Many of the entries in the early hymnals were centered around the sacraments, particularly baptism. The first American Baptist hymnal was published in 1762. At first the hymnals contained words only; after 1804 they also included the musical scores. Later influences on the songs in the hymnbooks came from camp meetings and the extension of the southern frontier. Secondary sources; 46 notes. H. M. Parker, Jr.

1946. Schreiber, William I. HANS BETZ: POET OF THE *AUSBUND*. *Mennonite Q. Rev. 1979 53(2): 128-136.* Hans Betz's (d. 1537) work was prominent in the first American Mennonite book in German, the *Ausbund* [Anthology] of hymns composed in the Passau, Bavaria, prison. They were printed by Christopher Sauer of Germantown, Pennsylvania, in 1742, and Betz's songs are still staples of Old Order Amish Sunday services and ceremonies. Although little is known about Betz, he may have come from the Meistersinger tradition, adding his own Swiss Anabaptist faith to the German-language hymns. 28 notes.
E. E. Eminhizer/S

1947. Sears, Donald A. MUSIC IN EARLY PORTLAND. *Maine Hist. Soc. Q. 1977 16(3): 131-160.* Traces church influence upon Portland's post-Revolutionary music. Describes the contributions of Supply Belcher (1751-1836), John Merrick (1766-1862) and Dr. Benjamin Vaughan (1751-1838). Notes the development of musical societies, the musical contributions of the Ostinellis, the organization of the Portland Band in 1820, and the opening of a singing school by Francis L. Ilsley in 1833. P. C. Marshall

1948. Southern, Eileen. MUSICAL PRACTICES IN BLACK CHURCHES OF NEW YORK AND PHILADELPHIA, CA. 1800-1844. *Afro-Americans in New York Life and Hist. 1980 4(1): 61-77.* Briefly discusses the importance of Protestant churches for blacks since colonial times, and focuses on black church music in New York City and Philadelphia, Pennsylvania.

1949. Stewart, Thomas H. PSALMS, HYMNS, AND SPIRITUAL SONGS: GENESES OF GOSPEL SONG POEMS. *Tennessee Folklore Soc. Bull. 1980 46(3): 68-72.* The usual roots of the words and themes of gospel songs are the Bible, Protestant theology, and the traditions of Revivalism, 18th-20th centuries.

1950. Stone, Michael. HEAV'N RESCUED LAND: AMERICAN HYMNS AND AMERICAN DESTINY. *J. of Popular Culture 1976 10(1): 133-141.* Examines American hymns of the 19th and early 20th centuries as probable transmitters of the myth of America's destiny, which was usually expressed in religious terms to the general public. Secondary sources; 29 notes. D. G. Nielson

1951. Urkowitz, Steven and Bennett, Lawrence. EARLY AMERICAN VOCAL MUSIC. *J. of Popular Culture 1978 12(1): 5-10.* Early popular vocal music in America, much of it written by itinerant singing school masters, provided the nation with its first instruction in reading musical notation. These singing schools came into existence largely to preserve familiar hymn tunes which, because of oral transmission, were undergoing changes that grated upon the ears of clergymen. Covers 1775-1820. Secondary sources; 5 notes. D. G. Nielson

1952. Walters, Stanley D. STRANGE FIRES: A BIBLICAL ALLUSION IN JOHN WESLEY'S HYMNS. *Methodist Hist. 1978 17(1): 44-58.* John Wesley translated a hymn by Paul Gerhardt in the 1760's, entitled "Jesu, Thy boundless love to me." Several of the 16 verses translated by Wesley under the title "Living by Christ" have appeared in English-language hymnals of various denominations. The metaphor of the sacred fire is based on the book of Leviticus of the Old Testament. Many hymnals of the 1930's have changed the wording and lost the concept of the "sacred fire." 24 notes. H. L. Calkin

1953. Weight, Newell B. THE BIRTH OF MORMON HYMNODY. *Dialogue 1975-76 10(1): 40-43.* Emma Smith, wife of Joseph Smith, made the first collection of Mormon hymns. Some were taken from Protestant hymnals, and some were written by early Mormons including many by William Wines Phelps and Eliza R. Snow. Hymns first appeared in the Mormon journals but were collected and published in a hymnal in 1835. Subjects of these hymns included persecution, missions, revelations, the apocalypse, baptism, and communion. E. L. Rowe

1954. Wolfe, Charles. PRESLEY AND THE GOSPEL TRADITION. *Southern Q. 1979 18(1): 135-150.* Examines the effect of white gospel music on rock and roll singer Elvis Presley (1935-77). He auditioned for and rehearsed with white gospel groups and considered joining a major quartet after his success in the mid-1950's. During his career he used a number of white gospel groups in his back-up music: the Jordannaires (1956-67), the Imperials (1969-71), and T. D. Sumner and the Stamps Quartet (1972-77). The effect of white gospel music on Presley was significant. B. D. Ledbetter

1955. Wolfe, Edward C. AMERICA'S FIRST LUTHERAN CHORALE BOOK. *Concordia Hist. Inst. Q. 1973 46(1): 5-17.* Lutheran German immigrants were troubled by the absence of a standard hymnal with four-part harmonies for each hymn text. Pastor Justus Henry Christian Helmuth (1745-1825) of Philadelphia strongly supported the publication in 1786 of *Erbauliche Lieder-Sammlung,* a standardized book of hymn texts. Helmuth, with the aid and support of his congregation, produced in 1813 the complementary *Choral-Bach fuer die Erbauliche Lieder-Sammlung der deutschen Evangelisch-Lutherischen Gemeinden in Nord Amerika,* containing 266 different tunes and an index relating each hymn text of the *Erbauliche Lieder-Sammlung* to an appropriate tune. Based on primary and secondary sources; 12 notes. B. W. Henry

1956. Wolfe, Edward C. LUTHERAN HYMNODY AND MUSIC PUBLISHED IN AMERICA 1700-1850: A BIBLIOGRAPHY. *Concordia Hist. Inst. Q. 1977 50(4): 164-185.* The significance of music in the history of the American Lutheran Church has been largely overlooked because of the apparent lack of adequate sources. This bibliography attempts to point the way to the sources. It is divided into two parts: hymnals and hymn collections without music, which lists 40 sources with descriptive comments, and chorale books, tunebooks, and other music which contains an annotated list of 21 titles. W. T. Walker

1957. Woolverton, John F. EDITORIAL. *Hist. Mag. of the Protestant Episcopal Church 1979 48(2): 129-132.* Introductory commentary to this issue which deals with the proposed revision of the *Hymnal* (1940) of the Episcopal Church. Underscores the thrust of each article to the field of hymnody in the church. H. M. Parker, Jr.

Radio and Television

1958. Clark, David L. "MIRACLES FOR A DIME": FROM CHAUTAUQUA TENT TO RADIO STATION WITH SISTER AIMEE. *California History 1978-79 57(4): 354-363.* Assesses the activities and accomplishments of Los Angeles evangelist Aimee Semple McPherson. Sister Aimee provided a transition from traditional evangelism to modern use of the media. She was the first woman to hold an FCC broadcaster's license; her station KFSG was the first religious radio station in the United States. Her services employed theatrical devices, including props and stage sets. More traditional Protestant ministers resented her style, but her Angelus Temple proved an irresistible attraction to the lonely, the newly arrived, and the poor in health who seemed to comprise most of the Los Angeles population during 1920's-40's. Her work in Depression relief has been underrated. The success of her church was somewhat flawed by her personal foibles, but the appeal of her evangelical style deserves acknowledgement for its pioneering use of "modern methods of communication for religious purposes." 13 photos. A. Hoffman

1959. Clements, William M. THE RHETORIC OF THE RADIO MINISTRY. *J. of Am. Folklore 1974 87(346): 318-327.* Pentecostal radio preachers in northeastern Arkansas adopt a strategy of folk performance directed at believers familiar with traditional worship services. They transfer their old sermon style and content to the new medium, continuing to manipulate spiritual emotionalism through singing, testimony, and other direct pleas for congregational response. Based on fieldwork and secondary sources; 21 notes. W. D. Piersen

1960. Hollstein, Milton. THE CHURCH AS MEDIA PROPRIETOR. *Dialogue 1977 10(3): 21-24.* Discusses the ability of Mormons to give huge audiences information about their church through the mass media in the 1970's.

1961. Tweedie, Stephen W. VIEWING THE BIBLE BELT. *J. of Popular Culture 1978 11(4): 865-876.* Listener concentration based on audience response to evangelical television programs, 1978, indicates that the highest concentration of listeners is in the Midwest, South, and central Atlantic states.

Religious Literature

1962. Albanese, Catherine. THE KINETIC REVOLUTION: TRANSFORMATION IN THE LANGUAGE OF THE TRANSCENDENTALISTS. *New England Q. 1975 48(3): 319-340.* New England Transcendentalists held a theory of correspondence similar to ancient philosophies of India, China, the Near East, and medieval western Europe. This theory holds that the natural realm mirrors or corresponds to the supernatural realm: even as words are signs of natural facts, natural facts are symbols of corresponding spiritual facts. Hence, since nature changes, words also must change to reflect contemporary forms of the world. To test this theory, the writings of Ralph Waldo Emerson, James Freeman Clarke, Frederic Henry Hedge, George Ripley, Bronson Alcott, and Francis Convers—members of the Transcendental Club which first met in 1836 and later published the *Dial* periodical during 1840-44—are examined. The writings of these men are characterized by an energy which corresponds to the radical ferment and social change of their time, and contrasts with the established language of "Cambridge-educated, Unitarian, Whiggish Boston." Based on primary and secondary sources; 76 notes. B. C. Tharaud

1963. Arner, Robert D. PROVERBS IN EDWARD TAYLOR'S *GODS DETERMINATIONS.* *Southern Folklore Q. 1973 37(1): 1-13.* 1685.

1964. Benton, Robert M. AN ANNOTATED CHECK LIST OF PURITAN SERMONS PUBLISHED IN AMERICA BEFORE 1700. *Bull. of the New York Public Lib. 1970 74(5): 286-337.* Chronological and annotated list of American Puritans' sermons published in New England during 1652-1700, from Charles Evans's *American Bibliography* (1903, New York: Peter Smith, 1941).

1965. Bercovitch, Sacvan. COLONIAL PURITAN RHETORIC AND THE DISCOVERY OF AN AMERICAN IDENTITY. *Can. Rev. of Am. Studies 1975 6(2): 131-150.* Analyzes writings and rhetoric by 17th-century Puritan leaders, most notably Cotton Mather (1663-1728), John Winthrop (1558-1649), and Thomas Hooker (1586?-1647). Through their rhetoric, Puritan leaders attempted to project symbols and images of the coming glory they considered achievable in the Puritan settlements in Massachusetts and Connecticut. Based on primary sources; 25 notes. H. T. Lovin

1966. Bercovitch, Sacvan. "NEHEMIAS AMERICANUS": COTTON MATHER AND THE CONCEPT OF THE REPRESENTATIVE AMERICAN. *Early Am. Literature 1974 8(3): 220-238.* In his life of John Winthrop (1587/88-1649) in *Magnalia Christi Americana* Cotton Mather employed a rhetorical strategy which made it possible for him to internalize his history as spiritual biography, turning it to spiritual autobiography as well. In this manner Mather attempted to define the Representative American—first as Winthrop, then as himself. Based on primary and secondary sources; 35 notes. D. P. Wharton

1967. Bogardus, Ralph F. and Szasz, Ferenc M. REVEREND G. D. FORSSELL AND HIS MAGIC LANTERN SHOWS: A CLUE TO AMERICA'S POPULAR IMAGINATION IN THE 1890'S. *Palimpsest 1977 58(4): 111-119.* In the early 1890's, itinerant minister G. D. Forssell toured Iowa and Minnesota delivering slide lectures on religious subjects. Forssell's presentations were simplistic in outlook and included such themes as the life of Christ, the evils of city life, and temperance. They perhaps provided a foundation for the heightened social consciousness which contributed to the rise of Progressivism. Forssell's Sears Magic Lantern and 70 slides are preserved today at Gibb Farm Museum, St. Paul, Minnesota. 11 illus., note on sources. D. W. Johnson

1968. Bormann, Ernest G. FETCHING GOOD OUT OF EVIL: A RHETORICAL USE OF CALAMITY. *Q. J. of Speech 1977 63(2): 130-139.* The Puritan preachers developed a recurring rhetorical form in which calamity was seen as God's punishment for sins, a retribution which carried with it the implicit promise of a better future once the sin had been propitiated. This pattern appeared during subsequent times of national trial, particularly wars, and was extensively used by Abraham Lincoln in his efforts to hold the Union together during the Civil War. Based on primary and secondary sources; 22 notes. E. C. Bailey

1969. Bray, James. JOHN FISKE: PURITAN PRECURSOR OF EDWARD TAYLOR. *Early Am. Literature 1974 9(1): 27-38.* The Puritan poet John Fiske anticipates Edward Taylor in his use of the Tree of Life metaphor and by his adaptation of the metaphor to a poetic manner best described as Baroque. Fiske's method, like Taylor's, is to use a variety of literary tactics, including puns and anagrams, in an attempt to identify his subject with everything else, a method for which the Tree of Life metaphor is ideally suited. Covers 1650-1721. Based on primary and secondary sources; 26 notes. D. P. Wharton

1970. Bruce, Dickson D., Jr. DEATH AS TESTIMONY IN THE OLD SOUTH. *Southern Humanities Rev. 1978 12(2): 123-131.* Mentions glorification of death scenes in Southern literature and strong support for evangelism, 1800-65.

1971. Burdick, Norman R. THE "COATESVILLE ADDRESS": CROSSROAD OF RHETORIC AND POETRY. *Western J. of Speech Communication 1978 42(2): 73-82.* Analyzes the rhetorical and poetic elements of a speech in 1912 by John Jay Chapman in a prayer meeting observing the first anniversary of the burning alive of a black man in Coatesville, Pennsylvania. The speech revealed Christian fervor.

1972. Clark, Thomas D. AN EXPLORATION OF GENERIC ASPECTS OF CONTEMPORARY AMERICAN CHRISTIAN SERMONS. *Q. J. of Speech 1977 63(4): 384-394.* Contemporary American sermons differ rhetorically from campaign speeches and speeches of social concern in several ways, apparently reflecting the minister's position as interpreter of divine truth. Sermons show more certainty, subordinate the speaker to God, and are more abstract and logically organized, and less future-oriented. Covers 1952-74. Primary and secondary sources; table, 26 notes. E. Bailey

1973. Daly, Robert. PURITAN POETICS: THE WORLD, THE FLESH, AND GOD. *Early Am. Literature 1977 12(2): 136-162.* The American Puritans failed to leave us an "ars poetica," and a pattern of explicit poetics is difficult to discern from their scattered comments. To understand the ideas and attitudes conveyed in Puritan poetry, examines aspects of Puritan thought that, though not explicitly literary, have literary implications: their fear of graven images; their Ramism; and their traditional belief that the sensible world was a book written by God and that man could read something of God in it. Primary and secondary sources; 35 notes. J. N. Friedel

1974. Douglas, Crerar. THE HERMENEUTICS OF AUGUSTUS HOPKINS STRONG. *Foundations 1978 21(1): 71-76.* The Baptist minister Augustus Hopkins Strong's (1836-1921) two books on poetry, *The Great Poets and Their Theology* (Philadelphia: Griffith and Rowland Pr., 1897) and *The American Poets and Their Theology* (Freeport, New York, 1916), need to be studied to understand Strong's theology fully. 10 notes. E. E. Eminhizer

1975. Egan, James. "THIS IS A LAMENTATION AND SHALL BE FOR A LAMENTATION": NATHANIEL WARD AND HIS RHETORIC OF THE JEREMIAD. *Pro. of the Am. Phil. Soc. 1978 122(6): 400-410.* The political condition of England in the 1640's produced pamphlets which may be described as jeremiads, a stylized lamentation over England's Civil War. The author establishes Nathaniel Ward's kinship with the jeremiad by examining the recurring themes, imagery and symbolism, and prophetical cast of his tracts, five of which can be reasonably attributed to Ward, who lives in Massachusetts. Decay in England testified to God's anger with His convenant people. The ultimate establishment of the Protectorate represented the fatal rupture of England's political system. England's failure to respond to a divinely ordained period of probation brought on national ruination and estrangement from God. Such were Ward's views, and thus he saw in New England a symbolic place for true Reformation. Based on Ward's pamphlets, particularly *The Simple Cobbler of Aggawam in America;* 38 notes. H. M. Parker, Jr.

1976. Hahn, T. G. URIAN OAKES'S ELEGIE ON THOMAS SHEPARD. *Am. Literature 1973 45(2): 163-181.* Analyzes the tradition of classical figures and allusions in Urian Oakes' (1631-81) *Elegie Upon the Death of the Reverend Thomas Shepard,* a work of New England poetry. H. M. Burns

1977. Haims, Lynn. THE FACE OF GOD: PURITAN ICONOGRAPHY IN EARLY AMERICAN POETRY, SERMONS, AND TOMBSTONE CARVING. *Early Am. Literature 1979 14(1): 15-47.* Despite cultural injunctions against religious images, New England Puritans revealed in their poetry, sermons, and tombstone carving a need to visualize the face of God. This Puritan desire to anatomize God was related to their cultural isolation, physical danger on the frontier, and fear of failing at their mission in the New World. They sometimes constructed elaborate rationalizations to justify their longing to see God's face. Diagram, 120 notes. T. P. Linkfield

1978. Hensley, Carl Wayne. RHETORICAL VISION AND THE PERSUASION OF A HISTORICAL MOVEMENT: THE DISCIPLES OF CHRIST IN NINETEENTH CENTURY AMERICAN CULTURE. *Q. J. of Speech 1975 61(3): 250-264.* The rhetorical vision of the Disciples of Christ and their use of the dramatic features of the Bible to promote an earthly utopia in the West were part of the 19th-century American dream.

1979. Holmgren, Laton E. A "PIOUS AND LAUDABLE UNDERTAKING": THE BIBLE OF THE REVOLUTION. *Am. Hist. Illus. 1975 10(6): 12-17.* Robert Aitken published the first English Bible printed in America in Philadelphia (1782) and earned official commendation from the Continental Congress.

1980. Jones, Phyllis. BIBLICAL RHETORIC AND THE PULPIT LITERATURE OF NEW ENGLAND. *Early Am. Literature 1976-77 11(3): 245-258.* The use of British Puritan methods of preaching (division of sermons into texts, doctrines, reasons, uses, and applications) as well topical influence from the Bible was typical of New England preaching, 1620's-50's, until presence in the New World had offered adequate metaphors to initiate change.

1981. Jones, Phyllis M. PURITAN'S PROGRESS: THE STORY OF THE SOUL'S SALVATION IN THE EARLY NEW ENGLAND SERMONS. *Early Am. Literature 1980 15(1): 14-28.* Analyzes Puritan sermons in New England from 1625 to 1660 by comparing them in general terms to folk narratives. While similar to folklore in performance, form, and function, these sermons narrated the individual soul's search for salvation. Although the search for faith was never complete, the sermons served the specific needs of both performer and audience. 19 notes. T. P. Linkfield

1982. Marszalek, John F., ed. A CIVIL WAR SERMON AS RECOUNTED IN THE EMMA E. HOLMES DIARY. *Hist. Mag. of the Protestant Episcopal Church 1977 46(1): 57-62.* Discusses a sermon by the Reverend John H. Elliott, rector of Grace Episcopal Church, Camden, South Carolina, on 7 December 1862. The sermon is a rare example of Civil War theological eloquence, and is taken from volume 3 of Emma E. Holmes' Diary, now in possession of the South Carolina Library, University of South Carolina. H. M. Parker, Jr.

1983. Maser, Frederick E. THE DAY AMERICA NEEDED BIBLES. *Religion in Life 1976 45(2): 138-145.* Discusses publisher Robert Aitken's attempt to meet the demand for Bibles in the United States from 1777-82, including the role of the Continental Congress.

1984. McKibbens, Thomas R., Jr. THE ROLE OF PREACHING IN SOUTHERN BAPTIST HISTORY. *Baptist Hist. and Heritage 1980 15(1): 30-36, 64.* Surveys the evolution, distinguishing characteristics, and the dominant role of preaching in the Southern Baptist Church, from 1707 to 1980.

1985. Mühlenfels, Astrid Schmitt-v. JOHN FISKE'S FUNERAL ELEGY ON JOHN COTTON. *Early Am. Literature 1977 12(1): 49-62.* Examines the singularity of John Fiske's elegy on John Cotton against the background of the 17th-century elegiac tradition in New England. Outlines the structure and defines the scope and limitations of the verse. Fiske makes better use of this genre than any writer up to that time, by building the funeral biography around an anagram and by using artistic control rather than a collection of random details and images. Fiske's use of poetic devices humanizes the religious merits of Calvinist doctrine. Primary sources; 41 notes. J. N. Friedel

1986. Nash, Ray. TYPES FOR THE STANDARD PRAYER BOOK OF 1928. *Library [Great Britain] 1974 29(1): 61-79.* Describes the printing problems involved in the production of the 1928 standard Book of Common Prayer for the Protestant Episcopal Church of America. Merrymount Press, which ultimately secured the commission, decided on the use of Janson typeface, the late 17th-century typeface of uncertain provenance. Based on the Merrymount Press Papers in the Huntington Library, San Marino, California; 72 notes. D. H. Murdoch

1987. Neff, LaVonne. LORA E. CLEMENT. *Adventist Heritage 1975 2(2): 48-54.* Lora E. Clement (1890-1958) was editor-in-chief of the Seventh-Day Adventist newspaper, *Youth's Instructor,* 1923-52.

1988. Osborn, Ronald E. THE EFFECT OF PREACHING ON AMERICAN LIFE—AND VICE VERSA: A REVIEW OF SOME RECENT HISTORICAL STUDIES. *Encounter 1975 36(3): 254-269.* Discusses the role of preaching in American life and theology and reviews a number of books on the topic (18c-20c).

1989. Riley, Jobie E. THE RHETORIC OF THE GERMAN-SPEAKING PULPIT IN EIGHTEENTH-CENTURY PENNSYLVANIA. *J. of the Lancaster County Hist. Soc. 1977 81(3): 138-159.* Discusses preaching in German-language churches in Pennsylvania during the 18th century, focusing on German Sectarians, Mennonites, the Church of the Brethren, Quakers, Schwenkfelders, and Separatists, and on some prominent church members.

1990. Schleifer, James T. HOW DEMOCRACY INFLUENCES PREACHING: A PREVIOUSLY UNPUBLISHED FRAGMENT FROM TOCQUEVILLE'S *DEMOCRACY IN AMERICA.* *Yale U. Lib. Gazette 1977 52(2): 75-79.* Tocqueville wrote a number of essays for *Democracy,* which were not included in the final text. Many of these unpublished sketches are contained in the Tocqueville manuscripts at Yale, including "On Religious Eloquence or Preaching" about 19th-century Roman Catholic oratory in America. 23 notes. D. A. Yanchisin

1991. Selement, George. PUBLICATION AND THE PURITAN MINISTER. *William and Mary Q. 1980 37(2): 219-241.* By comparing ministerial publication and ministerial behavior, over five generations, the intellectuality of Puritanism is further clarified. The great majority of the ministers either did not publish or did not consider publication essential to their ministry. Twenty-seven of 531 pastors wrote 70% of the publications. Holding an eminent pulpit helped to bring in subsidization for publication. Comments on the aspects of preparation and the techniques of sermon and tract publishing. Consults a cross-section of Puritan literature and also registers and monographs on printing; 3 tables: number of publications; type, length; 36 notes. H. M. Ward

1992. Stern, Madeleine B. THE FIRST FEMINIST BIBLE: THE "ALDERNEY" EDITION, 1876. *Q. J. of the Lib. of Congress 1977 34(1): 23-31.* Julia Evelina Smith of Connecticut turned to the Bible in search of verification of the Millerite forecast of the Second Coming of Christ. Eventually she completed a word-for-word translation of the Bible, published in 1876. She and her sisters paid $4000 for 1000 copies of it on a subscription basis. Illus., 35 notes. E. P. Stickney

1993. Stout, Harry S. RELIGION, COMMUNICATIONS, AND THE IDEOLOGICAL ORIGINS OF THE AMERICAN REVOLUTION. *William and Mary Q. 1977 34(4): 519-541.* A new style of communication, evidenced in the religious revivals from the Great Awakening to the American Revolution, was the rhetoric of persuasion. This method brought about dialogue, without reference to social or local setting. The popular style in revivals challenged traditional authority and contributed to a more egalitarian and democratic system. Argues that the evangelical experience and not the Commonwealth tradition shaped the language of republican ideology. Elitist culture dwindled and was replaced by mass culture. Secondary sources; sermons, and pamphlets; 80 notes. H. M. Ward

1994. Stuart, Robert Lee. JONATHAN EDWARDS AT ENFIELD: "AND OH THE CHEERFULNESS AND PLEASANTNESS. . . ." *Am. Literature 1976 48(1): 46-59.* A study of the sermon "Sinners in the Hands of an Angry God" delivered by Jonathan Edwards at Enfield, Connecticut, 8 July 1741. Reviews its historical reputation and context, and studies the text with particular attention to the elements of hope contained in it. The frightening rhetoric of the sermon was critically reviewed by Tracy in 1842, Parrington in 1927, and Parkes in 1930. Edwards chose his words to create an emotional response. Though he believed in the sovereignty of God, the responsibility of man to acquire His grace remained. The effectiveness of sermon rhetoric lies in the preacher's achievement of the tension between fear and hope, wherein lies the genius of this sermon. Based on primary and secondary sources; 56 notes. C. J. Nirmal

1995. Taulman, James E. THE LIFE AND WRITINGS OF AMOS COOPER DAYTON (1813-1865). *Baptist Hist. and Heritage 1975 10(1): 36-43.* One of the "Great Triumvirate" of the Landmark movement, Dayton was the first Baptist in the South to write a religious novel. Seeking to disseminate Baptist doctrine through the medium of fiction, he defined the church in one of his novels as a "local" group, organized independently of Christian people—a definition of the church which became a major cornerstone of Landmarkism. Beginning as a Presbyterian, he became a Baptist in 1852, and launched his literary career the following year. He authored 13 volumes of fiction and theology and contributed nearly 1,000 articles to 20 different religious periodicals. Primary and secondary sources; 44 notes. H. M. Parker, Jr.

1996. Van Cromphout, Gustaaf. COTTON MATHER: THE PURITAN HISTORIAN AS RENAISSANCE HUMANIST. *Am. Literature 1977 49(3): 327-337.* Discusses the rhetorical tradition of Renaissance humanism in the *Magnalia Christi Americana* (1702) by Puritan historian and author Cotton Mather.

1997. Waller, John O. URIAH SMITH'S SMALL EPIC: THE WARNING VOICE OF TIME AND PROPHECY. *Adventist Heri-*

tage 1978 5(1): 53-61. "The Warning Voice of Time and Prophecy," a blank verse poem by Uriah Smith about the rise of the Advent movement and the interpretations of prophecy it is based on, appeared in eight installments of the *Advent Review and Sabbath Herald* in 1853.

Secular Literature

1998. Andrews, William D. FRENEAU'S "A POLITICAL LITANY": A NOTE ON INTERPRETATION. *Early Am. Literature 1977 12(2): 193-196.* Describes "A Political Litany" as an early statement of American revolutionary consciousness, and as an early indication of a sense of commitment and mission in Philip Morin Freneau's political and literary development. Examines the poem and its significance in Freneau's intellectual development and poetic vocation in the context of religion. Having spent two years in unfulfilled religious study, this poem's parody and vigorous ironic wit pronounces his contempt for the Church of England, and reflects his self-confidence and assertiveness over intellectual errors and false goals of the past. Secondary sources; 16 notes.
J. N. Friedel

1999. Arrington, Leonard J. and Haupt, Jon. THE MORMON HERITAGE OF VARDIS FISHER. *Brigham Young U. Studies 1977 18(1): 27-47.* Vardis Fisher, one of the leading 20th-century literary recorders of the Mormon experience, never rejected Mormonism entirely. He was not an apostate, but instead possessed a profound religious outlook on life and history. Fisher may be called a literary innovator, for in his efforts to unravel the Mormon mystique he employed modern psychological techniques. Discusses his writings, especially his best-known *Children of God* (1939), in an effort to compile what may be called a psychohistory of Vardis Fisher. M. S. Legan

2000. Bell, James B. ANGLICAN QUILL-DRIVERS IN EIGHTEENTH CENTURY AMERICA. *Hist. Mag. of the Protestant Episcopal Church 1975 44(1): 23-45.* Anglican clergy were never as prolific a group of writers in any of the provinces as were the New England Congregational preachers. They were normally bland and unimaginative in their handling of biblical expositions of great themes of the Christian faith. They seldom commented on current theological and philosophical ideas, yet their histories, prose, and poetry gave a distinctiveness to the intellectual life of the colonial church and were a valuable contribution to colonial culture. Unlike the writings of the Puritan divines, these works were secular rather than sacred in outlook. All their works reveal greater loyalty to England than to America until the Revolution. Based largely on materials of the 18th century; 71 notes. H. M. Parker, Jr.

2001. Bitton, Davis and Bunker, Gary L. MISCHIEVOUS *PUCK* AND THE MORMONS, 1904-1907. *Brigham Young U. Studies 1978 18(4): 504-519.* Analyzes cartoons about Mormons which appeared in *Puck,* an illustrated weekly humor magazine, between 1904 and 1907. Public interest was especially aroused in the aftermath of the controversy over the seating of Mormons in Congress (B. H. Roberts in the House, 1898; Reed Smoot in the Senate, 1904). The cartoons continued to be generally negative, but were more apt to picture Mormons as buffoons rather than as sinister characters. They now included mild spoofing of the sect rather than the earlier virulent anti-Mormonism. Cites a tongue-in-cheek analysis of human relations in Mormon polygamy. *Puck*'s view of Mormonism was a mixture of accommodation to the group as well as a continuation of the Mormon stereotypes. M. S. Legan

2002. Bluestein, Gene. THE BROTHERHOOD OF SINNERS: LITERARY CALVINISM. *New England Q. 1977 50(2): 195-211.* Defines "literary Calvinism" as "the idea that, as a consequence of original sin and predestination, human beings are equal in depravity and thus joined in a brotherhood of sinners within a democratic society whose central mission is to prevent inherent evil from flourishing by circumscribing the individual and institutional energies which always threaten to make themselves felt." Literary Calvinism is a consistent and characteristic strand of all American literary thought and cuts across literary movements including the optimistic and the pessimistic. Traces its appearance in American literature from the 17th to the 19th century. Primary and secondary sources; 13 notes. J. C. Bradford

2003. Borrego, John E. "IF THERE BE SAINTS": FAITH IN THE NOVELS OF SINCLAIR LEWIS. *Hist. Mag. of the Protestant Episcopal Church 1978 47(4): 463-472.* Traces the religious pilgrimage of Sinclair Lewis from his conversion at the academy of Oberlin College to his departure from the faith as a student at Yale. His new faith, based on rationalism and science, made Voltaire and Eugene Debs saints of a secular humanism. Perhaps because of his own experience, Lewis made use of religious and secular faith as themes in such novels as *Elmer Gantry, The God-Seeker,* and *Arrowsmith.* The faith of Christianity, for Lewis, is hollow and meaningless. It cannot offer a worthwhile dream to which an intelligent person would willingly give his life. Secular faith, not empty pietism, should commend man's loyalty. Based on the writings of Lewis, and Mark Shorer's *Sinclair Lewis: An American Life;* 26 notes.
H. M. Parker, Jr.

2004. Bunker, Gary L. and Bitton, Davis. ILLUSTRATED PERIODICAL IMAGES OF MORMONS, 1850-1860. *Dialogue 1977 10(3): 82-94.* Provides a history and examples of the visual images of Mormons in novels and by humorists during the anti-Mormon crusade.

2005. Bushman, Richard L. CARICATURE AND SATIRE IN OLD AND NEW ENGLAND BEFORE THE AMERICAN REVOLUTION. *Massachusetts Hist. Soc. Pro. 1976 88: 19-34.* Before 1760, little visual caricature or literary satire was produced in colonial America, in contrast to the vastness or such material in England. This reticence on the part of Americans, particularly New Englanders, where such material was practically nonexistent, may lie in the incompatability of caricature and satire with Puritanism. Satirists maintain a dismal, hopeless world view, and generally victimize one class or group of society. There was no such group in the homogenous New England culture until the Revolutionary era, and satire did flourish in the 1760's and 1770's. Moreover, it continued to flourish in the post-Revolutionary era, suggesting that the Revolution may not have unified society, but rather divided it into separate ideological groups. Based on the literature of the period and some secondary sources; 32 notes, index. G. W. R. Ward

2006. Cate, Herma R. SHAKERS IN AMERICAN FICTION. *Tennessee Folklore Soc. Bull. 1975 41(1): 19-24.* Discusses the origin of the Shakers, their move to the United States, and their portrayal in American fiction, ca. 1780-1900. S

2007. Cawelti, John. GOD'S COUNTRY, LAS VEGAS AND THE GUNFIGHTER: DIFFERING VISIONS OF THE WEST. *Western Am. Literature 1975 9(4): 273-283.* Two general themes best describe the ways in which American writers have expressed their feelings about the West in the 19th and 20th centuries. The first is the concept of the West as a place to construct a new and better society which will avoid all past mistakes, i.e. God's country. The second theme is of a variant nature since it portrays the West as a means of escape. M. Genung

2008. Clark, James W., Jr. WASHINGTON IRVING AND NEW ENGLAND WITCHLORE. *New York Folklore Q. 1973 29(4): 304-313.*

2009. Crowley, Sue Mitchell. JOHN UPDIKE: "THE RUBBLE OF FOOTNOTES BOUND INTO KIERKEGAARD." *J. of the Am. Acad. of Religion 1977 45(3): 359.* John Updike was greatly influenced in his own religious thinking and in his fictional works by the method and thought of Kierkegaard. This is evident in the concept of self as a synthesis of finitude and infinitude. Three of Updike's early stories are used to establish this thesis. Covers 1932-77. Abstract only.
E. R. Lester

2010. Dahl, Curtis. NEW ENGLAND UNITARIANISM IN FICTIONAL ANTIQUITY: THE ROMANCES OF WILLIAM WARE. *New England Q. 1975 48(1): 104-115.* William Ware, in his three novels, *Zenobia, Aurelian,* and *Julian* was very successful in blending accurate historical description of the ancient world, classical and biblical, with clear expression of the new social and religious ideas of the Boston Unitarians. His novels are as much "drama of thought as drama of action," and the Christianity which competes with other religious views is the liberal Unitarianism of his contemporary Boston, decidedly anachronistic. He was a master of colorful and instructively accurate reconstructions of his ancient settings as background for contemporary commentary. Covers 1837-52. 10 notes. R. V. Ritter

2011. Dobkowski, Michael N. AMERICAN ANTISEMITISM: A REINTERPRETATION. *Am. Q. 1977 29(2): 166-181.* Popular American literature and drama of the 19th and early 20th centuries presented unfavorable stereotypes of the Jews which contributed to a generation of anti-Semitism. Religious novels depicted Jews as bigots. Plays and popular novels included Jewish representations who were greedy and mercenary in business, amoral in social behavior, and generally unscrupulous. By the early 20th century, Jews were associated with radicalism and politically revolutionary movements in popular literature. Primary sources; 59 notes. N. Lederer

2012. Doyle, James. MENNONITES AND MOHAWKS: THE UNIVERSALIST FICTION OF J. L. E. W. SHECUT. *Mennonite Q. Rev. 1977 51(1): 22-30.* John Linnaeus Edward Whitredge Shecut (1770-1836) wrote a novel, *The Eagle of the Mohawks,* which states that the Mennonites were universalists who made up the majority of the Dutch in New Amsterdam. Investigates how Shecut acquired these ideas and why he put them in his work. 15 notes. E. E. Eminhizer

2013. Dumais, Monique. LES FEMMES ET LA RELIGION DAN LES ECRITS DE LANGUE FRANÇAISE AU QUÉBEC [Women and religion in the French-language writings in Quebec]. *Atlantis [Canada] 1979 4(2): 152-162.* Assesses the impact of feminism on the status of women in the Catholic Church in Quebec and in the society as a whole, based on French Canadian literature of the 1960's and 1970's on women and religion.

2014. Ehrlich, James. ASCENSION ROBES AND OTHER MILLERITE FABLES: THE MILLERITES IN AMERICAN LITERATURE. *Adventist Heritage 1975 2(1): 8-13.* Discusses various satirical, humorous, and false accounts of the preaching of William Miller, 1830's-40's, which appeared in the popular press and in fiction.

2015. Elzey, Wayne. THE MOST UNFORGETTABLE MAGAZINE I'VE EVER READ: RELIGION AND SOCIAL HYGIENE IN *THE READER'S DIGEST.* *J. of Popular Culture 1976 10(1): 181-190.* The *Reader's Digest* interprets middle America to middle America through its editorial selection. Articles concerning religious experiences, social order ("hygiene") and reform, and how to attain them, present distilled and "clean" pictures of the symbols and logic of American life that are "unforgettable" and optimistic, and which remind readers that with constant vigilance man is perfectable. Secondary sources; 12 notes. D. G. Nielson

2016. Erisman, Fred. PROLEGOMENA TO A THEORY OF AMERICAN LIFE. *Southern Q. 1976 14(4): 261-272.* Two themes, Puritan and Romantic, are traced through American literature from the founding of the Plymouth colony to the present. Uses the writings of Alexander Hamilton, Nathaniel Hawthorne, Bronson Alcott, James Fenimore Cooper, and Robert Penn Warren. Concludes that Puritan and Romantic philosophies form the elements of continued conflict in American society. 26 notes. R. W. Dubay

2017. Farley, Benjamin W. ERSKINE CALDWELL: PREACHER'S SON AND SOUTHERN PROPHET. *J. of Presbyterian Hist. 1978 56(3): 202-217.* The Reverend Ira Sylvester Caldwell, father of the American novelist Erskine Caldwell, spent his entire ministry as pastor of the Associate Reformed Presbyterian Church, Wrens, Georgia. He placed greater emphasis on the ethical aspects of religion than the theological, a ministry which made a great impression on his son, Erskine. An examination of Erskine Caldwell's novels evidences a much more positive view on religion than is normally assumed. In a prophetic stance he has denounced the deep, engrained religion which is basically pietistic escapism, and the economic-agrarian system. His protest against Anglo-Saxon Protestantism in the South and southern indifference to the victims of sharecropping has been both noble and warranted. Covers 1900-78. Based largely on Caldwell's novels and his correspondence with the author; photo, 53 notes. H. M. Parker, Jr.

2018. Fletcher, Mary Dell. WILLIAM FAULKNER AND RESIDUAL CALVINISM. *Southern Studies 1979 18(2): 199-216.* The character Quentin Compson in *The Sound and the Fury* (1929) reveals the latent Calvinistic heritage in its author, William Faulkner (1897-1962). Not formally a religious man, Faulkner reveals the Southern Scottish Calvinist theology of his heritage and makes use of those aspects serviceable to him, especially the distinctive awareness of good and evil. His views are more a set of attitudes than a theology. Quentin must come to terms with the significance of evil before committing suicide. Quentin's awareness of evil in women, others, and himself leads to his death. 25 notes. J. J. Buschen

2019. Fogle, Richard Harter. HAWTHORNE, HISTORY AND THE HUMAN HEART. *Clio 1976 5(2): 175-180.* To Nathaniel Hawthorne the past was an almost physically oppressive, heavy burden. He stressed the Puritan attitudes of God's providentially chosen people and the idea of God's will as a mysterious force ever separating natural from supernatural and human from divine. Although viewing broad social reforms as futile except as they affected individual hearts and souls, the novelist at times described in his writings a secular and optimistic historical movement of progress and development. In endeavoring to convey the essence of historical truth, Hawthorne made primary use of artistic, particularly visual, symbolism. N. Lederer

2020. Forrey, Robert. DREISER AND THE PROPHETIC TRADITION. *Am. Studies 1974 15(2): 21-35.* Explores the religious element in Theodore Dreiser's (1871-1945) fiction through an examination of his background and writings. Dreiser was concerned with social justice rather than salvation, and with the spirit, not the letter, of religious law. Therefore, he was in the prophetic tradition rather than a tradition of literary naturalism. Based on primary and secondary sources; 38 notes. J. Andrew

2021. Fratto, Toni Flores. "REMEMBER ME": THE SOURCES OF AMERICAN SAMPLER VERSES. *New York Folklore 1976 2(3-4): 205-222.* The traditional, popular, literary, and religious sources of verses on samplers reveal the preoccupations and pastimes of 19th-century America.

2022. Freimarck, Vincent. TIMOTHY DWIGHT'S BRIEF LIVES IN *TRAVELS IN NEW ENGLAND AND NEW YORK.* *Early Am. Literature 1973 8(1): 44-58.* Brief biographical sketches occur regularly throughout Dwight's *Travels in New England and New York.* The subjects of these brief lives were selected according to their capacity to offer moral instruction. Presented as moral portraits, the lives themselves tend to unify the *Travels* as history. Covers 1796-1815. Based on primary and secondary sources; 9 notes. D. P. Wharton

2023. Furtwangler, Albert. FRANKLIN'S APPRENTICESHIP AND THE *SPECTATOR.* *New England Q. 1979 52(3): 377-396.* While an apprentice printer, Benjamin Franklin (1706-90) obtained a volume of the *Spectator* and studied the author's style. When the smallpox epidemic of 1721 opened the door to criticism of Boston's clergy, Franklin imitated the style in the "Silence Dogood" essays he composed for his brother James's (1696-1735) *New England Courant.* Based on Franklin's autobiography and other writings; 14 notes. J. C. Bradford

2024. Garner, Stanton. *ELSIE VENNER:* HOLMES'S DEADLY "BOOK OF LIFE." *Huntington Lib. Q. 1974 37(3): 283-298.* Oliver Wendell Holmes' novel *Elsie Venner* (1861) was an attack on the doctrine of original sin and, more particularly, on the romantic symbolism used by Nathaniel Hawthorne and Herman Melville to portray human corruption. Analyzes this novel in terms of Holmes' contrasts between the world perceived by the novel's narrator and the pessimistic world of Hawthorne and Melville, though reality also proved the fragility and coldness of the New England personality. Based on primary and secondary sources; 19 notes. S. R. Smith

2025. Geary, Edward A. MORMONDOM'S LOST GENERATION: THE NOVELISTS OF THE 1940'S. *Brigham Young U. Studies 1977 18(1): 89-98.* Analyzes a regional literary movement concerning Mormonism during the 1940's. Discusses the roots of a group of regional writers who were born in a transitional period in Mormon country small towns when still vivid remnants of the past existed. Their novels belong to either the pioneer settings, which deal with settlement in Utah, or to the provisional period, when Mormon communities had become settled and often restrictive. Discusses novels belonging to each time frame, including common themes and central plots. Concludes that the most significant theme of this generation of Mormon writers is their sense of expatriation. M. S. Legan

2026. Geary, Edward A. THE POETICS OF PROVINCIALISM: MORMON REGIONAL FICTION. *Dialogue 1978 11(2): 15-24.* Analyzes the literary quality of the second major movement in Mormon fiction, 1930-50, the Mormon regionalists who attempted to capture the distinctive life of their region and their faith. Focuses primarily on the historical fiction of Vardis Fisher, Virginia Sorensen, George Snell, and Maurine Whipple, treating briefly several other authors who also deal with historic themes. All these authors identify themselves with the third generation of Mormonism, as enlightened and liberated Mormons for whom the Mormon utopian experiment was essentially concluded. Whether in epic novels about real Mormon heroes, or introspective novels treating sympathetic fictional characters during the period of Mormon exploration and settlement, the novelists tend to patronize their subjects even as they admire them. Paper read at the second annual meeting of the Association for Mormon Letters, 8 October 1977. 23 notes. C. B. Schulz

2027. Gildner, Judith. IOWANS IN THE ARTS: JOSEPH LANGLAND. *Ann. of Iowa 1977 43(7): 515-533.* Poet Joseph Langland (b. 1917) often uses as a background for his writings the Midwest, especially the farmlands of northeastern Iowa where he spent his youth. In answer to a series of questions submitted to him by Judith Gildner, editor of the *Annals of Iowa,* Langland reflects upon his origins and the "shaping form" of his boyhood during the 1920's and 30's. He describes the impact upon his poetry of his Norwegian ancestry, Lutheran upbringing, early reading, and the sense of being "rooted" which accompanied rural life. Reprints four Langland poems. 2 illus. P. L. Petersen

2028. Godshalk, W. L. WALKER PERCY'S CHRISTIAN VISION. *Louisiana Studies 1974 13(2): 130-141.* A revaluation of Walker Percy's *Love in the Ruins* (New York, 1971) which sets aside the usual existential critical approach in favor of the suggestion that it is "a relatively old vision of the human condition." Percy created a modern Faustus with overweening pride. "Percy is at bottom saying that Western civilization will not be saved by technology . . . Percy is much more the Christian thinker than the existentialist philosopher." R. V. Ritter

2029. Granger, Bruce. JOHN TRUMBULL, ESSAYIST. *Early Am. Literature 1975 10(3): 273-288.* As a young man John Trumbull served a literary apprenticeship as a prose writer, creating two essay serials, *The Meddler* and *The Correspondent*. Trumbull eschewed political controversy in his essays, but unhesitatingly joined in theological and philosophical debate. These early prose efforts contribute to the serial essay tradition in American literature and provide increased understanding of Trumbull's mature poetry. Covers 1769-73. Based on primary and secondary sources; 59 notes. D. P. Wharton

2030. Groos, Seymour and Murphy, Rosalie. FROM STEPHEN CRANE TO WILLIAM FAULKNER: SOME REMARKS ON THE RELIGIOUS SENSE IN AMERICAN LITERATURE. *Cithara 1977 16(2): 90-108.* Traces the important role of the religious sense in American literature even in a secular age, from Stephen Crane to William Faulkner.

2031. Isani, Mukhtar Ali. EARLY VERSIONS OF SOME WORKS BY PHILLIS WHEATLEY. *Early Am. Literature 1979 14(2): 149-155.* Analyzes the revisions in different versions of two of Phillis Wheatley's poems. Both poems appeared in *Poems on Various Subjects, Religious and Moral* (1773). In "To the Right Honourable William, Earl of Dartmouth" the revisions concern change within verses. In revising "On the Death of J.C.," Wheatley added several lines for greater refinement. 7 notes. T. P. Linkfield

2032. Jaenen, Cornelius J. IMAGES OF NEW FRANCE IN THE HISTORY OF LESCARBOT. *Pro. of the Ann. Meeting of the Western Soc. for French Hist. 1978 6: 209-219.* Discusses the historical writings, notably the *Histoire de la Nouvelle-France* (1609), of Canada's first historian and playwright, Marc Lescarbot (1570-1642), in the framework of the conceptual and intellectual constructs used by French writers of the Old Regime to depict the New World and its "new men." Lescarbot, like other writers of the time, resorted to the use of traditional literary, philosophical, and theological constructs. Consequently, there seem to be contradictions in his writings and he fails to develop any single unifying theme in his history of the colony. The concepts identified are: the truly New World, the millennial kingdom, the monstrous world of the damned, the chain of being, the black legend, the utopian vision of New France, the westward march of genius, the noble savage, the *mission civilisatrice* of France, the four stages theory, and aboriginal rights. 8 notes. A/J

2033. Jervey, Edward D. HENRY L. MENCKEN AND AMERICAN METHODISM. *J. of Popular Culture 1978 12(1): 75-87.* Believing that organized religion was a threat to individual freedom, Methodists in particular became a favorite target for the acid pen of H. L. Mencken (1880-1956) from about 1910 through the end of prohibition. At times, the noted editor of *The American Mercury* (1924-33) included all Fundamentalist denominations in his attacks, but he focused largely on the Methodist Episcopal Church (South), which he saw as responsible for the coming of prohibition and even the revival of the Ku Klux Klan. Primary and secondary sources; illus., 70 notes. D. G. Nielson

2034. Johnson, David W. FREESOILERS FOR GOD: KANSAS NEWSPAPER EDITORS AND THE ANTISLAVERY CRUSADE. *Kansas Hist. 1979 2(2): 74-85.* Six Kansas editors publicized the freesoil cause during territorial days. They did not entirely agree on the best means of organizing a state free from slavery, but they did agree that Providence would help this cause. Their religious allusions and imagery reassured many settlers of the inevitable outcome of territorial strife. Often, those who could not accept the idea of direct intervention by Providence found convincing these incessant reminders that God helps those who help themselves. Based on local newspapers; illus., 29 notes. W. F. Zornow

2035. Johnson, Robert L. WILLIAM FAULKNER, CALVINISM AND THE PRESBYTERIANS. *J. of Presbyterian Hist. 1979 57(1): 66-81.* Pursues William Faulkner's connections with Presbyterianism in three dimensions: his personal exposure to Presbyterian influence, the critical studies of Faulkner as a literary Calvinist, and *Light in August,* which is treated as Faulkner's most detailed treatment of Calvinism. Admits that Faulkner was far from being a consistent, thorough-going Calvinist, but does give interesting vignettes which reflect Faulkner's propensity for a Calvinistic view, and demonstrates his philosophy through overarching themes in Faulkner's writings and thoughts. Based on Faulkner's writings and works of literary critics; 39 notes. H. M. Parker, Jr.

2036. Kantrow, Alan M. ANGLICAN CUSTOM, AMERICAN CONSCIOUSNESS. *New England Q. 1979 52(3): 307-325.* Studies of mid-19th century American literature have identified the Puritan "habits of mind" which formed a part of the American imagination, but generally have overlooked equally important New England "habits of mind." Compares Anglican and Puritan attitudes toward worship and prayer and then analyzes Henry James's (1811-82) *The American* (1877) to show how "Catholic Europe provided the broad imaginative analogy by which the American mind covertly reclaimed its Anglican heritage." Based on 18th-century writings and recent literary studies; 33 notes. J. C. Bradford

2037. Kazin, Alfred. THE DRAMA OF GOOD AND EVIL IN AMERICAN WRITING. *Rev. of Pol. 1976 38(3): 343-358.* The Calvinistic background of America, combined with the nationalistic pride resulting from victory in the Revolutionary War and the War of 1812, provided the background for American literature prior to the Civil War that was based on the belief of the "natural and national virtuousness of Americans." American writers after the Civil War to the present day, perceiving a society affected by the corruptive influence of the triumph of capitalism, doubt America's commitment to "public optimism, public egalitarianism, public sanctity." For American writers today, evil is not the absence of good as perceived by Emerson but "the nullity, the positive insignificance of man in a universe definitely not constructed to his personal satisfaction." What must be understood is that nature is neutral concerning good and evil and it is the role of our literature and our writers to raise the questions of morality. L. Ziewacz

2038. Kimball, Gayle. HARRIET BEECHER STOWE'S REVISION OF NEW ENGLAND THEOLOGY. *J. of Presbyterian Hist. 1980 58(1): 64-81.* Basic to the thinking of Harriet Beecher Stowe (1811-96) is the role of women as the central agents of salvation. Her novels depict women as the most effective leaders of souls to Christ, the male clergy as ineffectual shepherds. Her mistrust of masculine reason and "dry theology" and her praise of woman's self-sacrificing Christlike love was the major theme of her more than 30 novels and her articles and letters. She accounted for sin not on the grounds of Adam's fall, but because of the failure in the family, education, and society. Gradually forsaking even the moderate New England theology, she turned to the Episcopal Church, which received as members those who were pious and faithful to the teachings of the church. Based on the writings of Harriet Beecher Stowe and the Schlesinger Archives (Radcliffe College); one photo, 66 notes. H. M. Parker, Jr.

2039. Konvitz, Milton R. HERMAN MELVILLE IN THE HOLY LAND. *Midstream 1979 25(10): 50-57.* Discusses Herman Melville's trip to the Holy Land in 1857, quoting extensively from his journal and his fiction to emphasize his Biblical orientation.

2040. Lambert, Neal. THE REPRESENTATION OF REALITY IN NINETEENTH CENTURY MORMON AUTOBIOGRAPHY. *Dialogue 1978 11(2): 63-74.* Examines 19th-century Mormon diaries and autobiographical writings to illustrate attempts by common people in a utopian community to understand and shape their experiences as well as to preserve them. Long quotations from the *Autobiography of Parley J. Pratt* and the unpublished diaries of Thales Haskel illustrate a humorous approach to that task, while the journal of Hosea Stout shows a sentimental Victorian literary approach to capturing past emotional experience. Lengthy passages from autobiographical accounts by Patience Loader and Mary Goble Pay demonstrate the moving simplicity of stark accounts of pioneering hardships written by uneducated women. In all accounts, details of daily life casually intermingle with a sense of the transcendent purpose of their struggles. Primary sources; 13 notes.
C. B. Schulz

2041. Lauricella, Francis, Jr. THE DEVIL IN DRINK: SWEDENBORGIANISM IN T. S. ARTHUR'S *TEN NIGHTS IN A BARROOM* (1854). *Perspectives in Am. Hist. 1979 12: 353-385.* The theological doctrines articulated by Emanuel Swedenborg (1688-1772), a Swedish theologian, scientist, and mystic, influenced his followers in different ways and for different purposes. For Timothy Shay Arthur, Swedenborgianism and its tenets became a reason for joining the temperance movement. In fact, Arthur found in Swedenborgianism a foundation for taking a conservative stance that, in order to realize a stronger social bond, institutions should restrain a human's tendencies toward doing evil.
W. A. Wiegand

2042. Loving, Jerome M. MELVILLE'S PARDONABLE SIN. *New England Q. 1974 47(2): 262-278.* Though Nathaniel Hawthorne and Herman Melville were close friends, Hawthorne clearly did not share Melville's pessimism as shown in *Moby Dick*. "Melville misinterpreted Hawthorne because he saw in Hawthorne's fiction reflections of his own pessimistic philosophy." Melville considered Ahab's sin a pardonable one. "Ahab is one of his nay-sayers who refuse to accept evil as a part of God's so-called benevolent plan." Melville regarded Ahab's death as a noble one. 30 notes. E. P. Stickney

2043. Masilamoni, E. H. Leelavathi. THE FICTION OF JEWISH AMERICANS: AN INTERVIEW WITH LESLIE FIEDLER. *Southwest Rev. 1979 64(1): 44-59.* Literary critic and novelist Leslie Fiedler discusses forces in American society—anti-Semitism, ethnic identification, and religious differences—as they affect Jews, especially Jewish writers, 1970's.

2044. Mawer, Randall R. "FAREWELL DEAR BABE": BRADSTREET'S ELEGY FOR ELIZABETH. *Early Am. Literature 1980 15(1): 29-41.* Reinterprets Anne Bradstreet's elegy for her young granddaughter Elizabeth, who died in August 1665. Although not as bitter as Bradstreet's other elegies, "Farewell Dear Babe" implicitly rebels against the nature of God's plan. The elegy is not a simple tract, as many scholars have interpreted it. 24 notes. T. P. Linkfield

2045. Mayo, Louise Abbie. HERMAN MELVILLE, THE JEW AND JUDAISM. *Am. Jewish Arch. 1976 28(2): 172-179.* "Melville is the only major American writer in the nineteenth century to include a serious consideration of Jews and Judaism in one of his works—*Clarel*."
J

2046. McCarthy, Kevin M. WITCHCRAFT AND SUPERSTITION IN THE WINTER OF OUR DISCONTENT. *New York Folklore Q. 1974 30(3): 197-211.* Reviews folklore influences in John Steinbeck's *Winter of Our Discontent*. S

2047. McGill, William J. WILLIAM STYRON'S NAT TURNER AND RELIGION. *South Atlantic Q. 1980 79(1): 75-81.* In the late 1960's William Styron wrote *The Confessions of Nat Turner,* a novel in which he stressed the religious dimensions of Virginia slave rebel Turner's life. The author discusses this aspect of Styron's Turner, particularly "the one major attempt at a sermon." Styron attempted to transform Turner's "Confessions," previously transcribed and published by Thomas Gray, into a meditation on history. In the process he transformed an essentially one-dimensional religious fanatic into a more complex, and ultimately more human, figure. His Nat Turner is not Gray's God-mad slave. He is much more than that—a genuine human being, keenly sensitive and profoundly faithful. 14 notes. H. M. Parker, Jr.

2048. McLoughlin, William G., ed. EBENEZER SMITH'S BALLAD OF THE ASHFIELD BAPTISTS, 1772. *New England Q. 1974 47(1): 97-108.* Reprints a poem by Ebenezer Smith protesting the persecution of Baptists in Ashfield, Massachusetts during 1761-71. The reasons for the present publication are that few poems were written by any American on liberty of conscience, and that it is "an excellent example of primitive protest poetry which must have been common in its days but which has since disappeared from historical view." 16 notes.
E. P. Stickney

2049. McNamara, Robert F. WHO WAS WILLIAM JOSEPH WALTER? *Moreana [France] 1976 13(51): 128-131.* William Joseph Walter (1793-1846), was a Catholic and a devotee and biographer of Saint Thomas More, and secretary of the British consul at Philadelphia, where he died.

2050. McWilliams, John P., Jr. FICTIONS OF MERRY MOUNT. *Am. Q. 1977 29(1): 3-30.* The controversy between Thomas Morton and the Pilgrims at Merry Mount has supplied the context in which historical writers have recreated the situation emphasizing their own biases, class values, regional preferences, and generational outlook. The meager and highly tainted historical evidence in existence has led writers such as Charles Francis Adams, Jr. and Lydia Child to accept Governor William Bradford's version of events and moralize upon it. Nathaniel Hawthorne was concerned about the psychological meaning of the conflict and was more evenhanded in his analysis, as was historian John Lothrop Motley. William Carlos Williams used the Merry Mount incident as a vehicle to attack America's Puritan heritage. More recently poet Robert Lowell compared the episode to contemporary events. N. Lederer

2051. Molson, Francis J. FRANCIS J. FINN., S.J.: PIONEERING AUTHOR OF JUVENILES FOR CATHOLIC AMERICANS. *J. of Popular Culture 1977 11(1): 28-41.* Father Francis J. Finn (1859-1928) was a prolific and the first popular author of novels and short stories for American Catholic youths. Examination of Finn's works reveals three primary goals in his stories: to show the compatibility of Americanism and Catholicism, to display the good Catholic boy and girl, and to provide moral and religious instruction. To attain these he employed the conventions of juvenile fiction, changing it as need be to meet changes on the American scene. Primary and secondary sources; 13 notes.
D. G. Nielson

2052. Monteiro, George. RELIGIOUS AND SCRIPTURAL PARODIES. *New York Folklore 1976 2(3-4): 150-166.* Gives examples of the contemporary uses of religious parody as comedy in television, political commentary, advertisements, and oral tradition.

2053. Moseley, James G. RELIGIOUS ETHICS AND THE SOCIAL ASPECTS OF IMAGINATIVE LITERATURE: WILLIAM STYRON AND THE NAT TURNER CONTROVERSY. *J. of the Am. Acad. of Religion 1977 45(3): 360.* Suggests the need for an aesthetics of pluralism based on the reaction to the publication of William Styron's *The Confessions of Nat Turner.* The interpretation of imaginative literature involves a concern for religious ethics. Analysis of the religious scene in American society is, therefore, the proper beginning point for fulfilling this need. Covers the 1970's. Abstract only.
E. R. Lester

2054. Moss, Robert F. SUFFERING, SINFUL CATHOLICS. *Antioch Rev. 1978 36(2): 170-181.* Discusses current popular novels emanating from Catholic writers in America and assesses their meaning for popular cultural conceptions of religious subcultures, 1970's.

2055. Nelson, Rudolph L. "RIPRAP ON THE SLICK ROCK OF METAPHYSICS": RELIGIOUS DIMENSIONS IN THE POETRY OF GARY SNYDER. *Soundings 1974 58(2): 206-221.* The religious impulse in the work of the contemporary American poet Gary Snyder primarily reveals itself in Snyder's interest in Zen.

2056. O'Donnell, Thomas F. THE RETURN OF THE WIDOW BEDOTT: MRS. F. M. WHITCHER OF WHITESBORO AND ELMIRA. *New York Hist. 1974 55(1): 5-34. The Widow Bedott Papers* (first published in book form in 1855) is today unread and forgotten, but it was an American best-seller as late as the mid-1890's, and exemplifies the dialect literature so popular in 19th-century America. *The Widow Bedott Papers* was a forerunner of literary realism, and "one of the most incisive pieces of social criticism to surface in antebellum America." Written by Frances Miriam Berry Whitcher (1811-52), the work portrayed hypocrisy and viciousness in Yankee small-town life in upstate New York. The sketches were drawn from Mrs. Whitcher's personal experience and observation. After marrying the Reverend Benjamin W. Whitcher in 1847, she began writing the papers, which appeared in *Godey's Lady's Book* and other journals, in order to supplement her husband's meager salary. The sketches so outraged the Reverend Whitcher's Presbyterian congregation in Elmira that he was forced to resign his pulpit in June 1849 and move back to his wife's home town of Whitesboro. Primary and secondary sources; 10 illus., 42 notes. G. Kurland

2057. Pinsker, Sanford. THE MENNONITE AS ETHNIC WRITER: A CONVERSATION WITH MERLE GOOD. *J. of Ethnic Studies 1975 3(2): 57-64.* Interview with Merle Good, author of *Happy as the Grass Was Green* (1971) and folk writer of the Pennsylvania Dutch. Discusses the problem of ethnic survival, the Mennonites, and ethnic writing as exploitation. T. W. Smith

2058. Reynolds, David Spencer. SHIFTING INTERPRETATION OF PROTESTANTISM. *J. of Popular Culture 1975 9(3): 593-603.* The Reverend Edward Payson Roe's *Barriers Burned Away* (1873) and the Reverend Charles M. Sheldon's *In His Steps* (1897) illustrate the changes in Protestantism in the latter half of the 19th century. Roe's book reflects the New Theology or liberal Protestantism of Henry Ward Beecher; Sheldon's, the Social Gospel. Both shared the tenets of liberal Protestantism but Sheldon's book shows the increased social consciousness, the interpretation of the immanence of God as the accessibility of the Kingdom of God to all mankind, and the emphasis on human brotherhood. 26 notes. J. D. Falk

2059. Ridgeway, Jacqueline. THE NECESSITY OF FORM TO THE POETRY OF LOUISE BOGAN. *Women's Studies 1977 5(2): 137-149.* Louise Bogan's poetry is formal and objective and reflects such formal aspects of her upbringing as her Irishness, Catholicism, family, and classical education 1920's-70.

2060. Rothfork, John. SCIENCE FICTION AS A RELIGIOUS GUIDE TO THE NEW AGE. *Kansas Q. 1978 10(4): 57-70.* Modern popular religious-psychology-sensitivity movements are reflected and recorded in modern science fiction, which is a new mythology for the coming age 1960's-70's.

2061. Rowland, Beryl. GRACE CHURCH AND MELVILLE'S STORY OF "THE TWO TEMPLES." *Nineteenth-Century Fiction 1973 28(3): 339-346.* The action in Herman Melville's short story "The Two Temples," although eventually placed in London, actually took place in New York City; his use of Grace Church and Trinity Church afforded him the opportunity to assail the ostentation and superficial Christianity of two new and fashionable churches, 1845-50.

2062. Sarna, Jonathan D. HEBREW POETRY IN EARLY AMERICA. *Am. Jewish Hist. 1980 69(3): 364-377.* Historians of American Hebrew literature have long neglected the antebellum period. The author prints seven Hebrew poems—six with English translations—composed in the United States before 1860. They deal with the marriage of Gershom Seixas to Hannah Manuel in 1786, events in the history of Congregation Kahal Kadosh Shearith Israel in New York City, and memorial services for President William Henry Harrison in 1841. Three of the poems are known to have been written by Dob Pique; one by Jacques Judah Lyons and one by Jacob J. M. Falkenau. They signify less as poetic creations than as symbols of ethnic identity. Based on poems found in the American Jewish Historical Society and other primary and secondary sources; 15 notes. A

2063. Schmandt, Raymond H. A FORGOTTEN PHILADELPHIA WRITER: WILLIAM JOSEPH WALTER (1789-1846). *Pennsylvania Mag. of Hist. and Biog. 1978 102(1): 27-39.* Publisher of seven books, 60 essays, and poetry, Walter, an English Catholic and a professor at St. Edmund's College, came to Philadelphia as an established man of letters in 1839. His *Thomas More* was the first volume of his Catholic Family Library, a financial failure. Scholar, editor, anthologizer, Walter was a denominational writer before his denomination was intellectually and financially able to sustain him. Based on archives of the Baltimore Archdiocese, printed sources, and secondary works; 18 notes. T. H. Wendel

2064. Schneider, Gilbert D. DANIEL EMMETT'S NEGRO SERMONS AND HYMNS: AN INVENTORY. *Ohio Hist. 1976 85(1): 67-83.* This study is an inventory of minstrel Daniel Emmett's papers at the Ohio Historical Society and a description of their usefulness to musicologists and students of Negro minstrelsy and black dialect. Based on MS. sources; 2 illus. T. H. Hartig

2065. Scott, Robert Ian. POET'S GODS: STEVENS' WORDS, JEFFERS' WORLD-AS-GOD. *Can. Rev. of Am. Studies [Canada] 1974 5(2): 198-201.* Reviews *Wallace Stevens, Imagination and Faith* (Princeton: Princeton U. Pr., 1974) by Adelaide Kirby Morris and *Robinson Jeffers, Myth, Ritual and Symbol in His Narrative Poems* (Cleveland: Case Western Reserve U. Pr., 1973) by Robert J. Brophy. Stevens regarded the Christian God as unbelievable. Jeffers celebrated "the natural world of God." H. T. Lovin

2066. Sears, John F. TIMOTHY DWIGHT AND THE AMERICAN LANDSCAPE: THE COMPOSING EYE IN DWIGHT'S *TRAVELS IN NEW ENGLAND AND NEW YORK. Early Am. Literature 1976-77 11(3): 311-321.* Written over a number of trips through New England and New York during the 1790's, Timothy Dwight's *Travels in New England and New York* viewed the American wilderness as an area of land waiting to be carved and refined by human hands which might preserve the values of colonial New England.

2067. Sharman, V. THOMAS MCCULLOCH'S STEPSURE: THE RELENTLESS PRESBYTERIAN. *Dalhousie Rev. [Canada] 1972/73 52(4): 618-625.* A critical study of the *Letters of Mephibosheth Stepsure*, a series of 16 letters written by Thomas McCulloch, Secessionist Presbyterian minister, educator, and first principal of Pictou Academy, Nova Scotia. The letters were originally sent to the *Acadian Recorder* in 1821-22, and later published in book form (Halifax, 1862). Half are satiric sketches of those who fail to live productive lives, yet Stepsure, the ideal Presbyterian settler, emerges as an "unsocial, self-centered, and priggish materialist . . . The *Letters* deserve a place in Canadian literature because of the image of the relentless puritan that is so important in our writing." 6 notes. R. V. Ritter

2068. Silver, Charles. PEARL BUCK, EVANGELISM AND WORKS OF LOVE: IMAGES OF THE MISSIONARY IN FICTION. *J. of Presbyterian Hist. 1973 51(2): 216-234.* Covers 1931-69.

2069. Sinclair, D. M. REV. DUNCAN BLACK BLAIR, D.D. (1815-1893): PIONEER PREACHER IN PICTOU COUNTY, GAELIC SCHOLAR AND POET. *Nova Scotia Hist. Soc. Collections [Canada] 1977 39: 155-168.* Duncan B. Blair, a Gaelic poet and Presbyterian preacher, resided in Barney's River, Nova Scotia, 1848-93.

2070. Sinclair, D. M. REV. DUNCAN BLACK BLAIR, D.D. (1815-1893): PIONEER PREACHER IN PICTOU COUNTY, GAELIC SCHOLAR AND POET. *Nova Scotia Hist. Soc. Collections [Canada] 1977 39: 155-168.* Duncan Black Blair's poem "Eas Niagara" is regarded as one of the "two most celebrated Gaelic poems composed on Canadian soil." His Gaelic *Diary* provides not only interesting information on society but also on the youthful author's education, including 1834-38, when he was enrolled at the University of Edinburgh. In 1846 he came to Nova Scotia as a Free Church [Presbyterian] missionary, remained slightly more than one year, only to return in 1848 to accept the call of the congregation at Barney's River-Blue Mountain where he remained until his death in 1893. Regarded as "the best Gaelic scholar in America, in his time" Blair wrote *Rudiments of Gaelic Grammar,* "a most complete Gaelic dictionary," as well as some poetry, examples of which are provided in this article. E. A. Chard

2071. Stathis, Stephen W. and Lythgoe, Dennis L. MORMONISM IN THE NINETEEN-SEVENTIES: THE POPULAR PERCEPTION. *Dialogue 1977 10(3): 95-113.* The public image of Mormonism in newspapers and periodicals in the 1970's often is favorable.

2072. Stott, Graham St. John. ZANE GREY AND JAMES SIMPSON EMMETT. *Brigham Young U. Studies 1978 18(4): 491-503.* In 1907, Zane Grey (1875-1939) spent several months along the Utah-Arizona border with a Mormon, James Simpson Emmett. Grey later acknowledgd that Emmett was the principal influence on his views of Mormons, and the principal inspiration for all his novels about life in Utah. Emmett taught the western writer about bravery, love for the desert, kindness to animals, and endurance. Describes Grey's use of Emmett as a role model for Mormon heroes and villains. This friendship led Grey to moderate or apologize for any Mormon villainy, balance Mormon evil with good, justify Mormons in their conflict with "gentiles," and create a breed of heroes much like his friend. M. S. Legan

2073. Suderman, Elmer F. THE MENNONITE COMMUNITY AND THE PACIFIST CHARACTER IN AMERICAN LITERATURE. *Mennonite Life 1979 34(1): 8-15.* A comparison of four 20th-century novels—*Erloesung* by Peter Epp, *Peace Shall Destroy Many* by Rudy Wiebe, *Mennonite Soldier* by Kenneth Reed, and *The Long Tomorrow* by Lee Brackett—and two plays—*The Blowing and the Bending* by James Juhnke and Harold Moyer, and *The Berserkers* by Warren Kliewer—shows the reactions of Mennonite pacifist communities and characters to a violent world. These worlds lack the radical pacifism that demands a commitment to love and forgiveness and do not present an admirable hero who refuses to fight nor a serious alternative to war. In most, a sense of community strength and church leadership are lacking. 2 photos, 9 notes. B. Burnett

2074. Suderman, Elmer F. RELIGION IN THE POPULAR AMERICAN NOVEL 1870-1900. *J. of Popular Culture 1976 9(4): 1003-1009.* Popular religious fiction written during 1870-1900 was both optimistic and sentimental. Most writers felt that a Christian living in the United States could not help but succeed, for providence had molded the continent to fit man's needs. Human nature was seen as good, and men were continually improving. Life was always good, women were nourished by love, men were strong and upright, and good deeds were almost always rewarded. Most writers were didactic, and few investigated areas of religious doubt or skepticism. They were designed to reinforce, not challenge, conventional religious feelings, and they did not attempt to portray any situation as ambiguous or difficult for a person with God on his side. Primary and secondary sources; 13 notes. J. W. Leedom

2075. Tate, George A. HALLDÓR LAXNESS, THE MORMONS AND THE PROMISED LAND. *Dialogue 1978 11(2): 25-37.* Halldór Laxness, the Icelandic novelist who won the Nobel Prize in 1955 for fiction based on his native literary heritage, completed *Paradise Reclaimed* in 1960, a novel based on the experiences of Eiríkur á Brúnum (1832-1900). Brúnum, an Icelander, converted to Mormonism and spent eight years in Utah before he rejected it and returned to Iceland. Laxness chooses to ignore the renunciation of the church, focusing instead on his fictional hero's ideological odyssey in search of utopia. The mood of the novel is a mixture of melancholy over lost innocence and ironic humor. A paper read at the second annual meeting of the Association for Mormon Letters, 8 October 1977. Based on the novel, literary criticism, and correspondence with Laxness; 51 notes. C. B. Schulz

2076. Topping, Gary. ZANE GREY IN ZION: AN EXAMINATION OF HIS SUPPOSED ANTI-MORMONISM. *Brigham Young U. Studies 1978 18(4): 483-490.* Leonard J. Arrington and Jon Haupt, both Mormon scholars, have seen in Zane Grey's *Riders of the Purple Sage* (1912) a basic hostility toward Mormons. A careful analysis of this work and other evidence of Grey's attitudes toward Mormons does not support the charge. Evidence from Grey's personal correspondence demonstrates his sincere admiration for the group. Although Grey may have possessed a shallow understanding of Mormons and Mormonism, he was an imaginative writer who saw a potential theme in the Mormon-"gentile" encounter, and utilized such a formula to create pro-Mormon works and heroes as well as anti-Mormon works and villains. Grey should not be categorized as an anti-Mormon polemist. M. S. Legan

2077. Vigil, Ralph H. WILLA CATHER AND HISTORICAL REALITY. *New Mexico Hist. Rev. 1975 50(2): 123-139.* Willa Cather's *Death Comes for the Archbishop* (1927) is representative of fictional history and literature dealing with New Mexico. Author deals with Cather's portrayal of Father Antonio Jose Martinez (1793-1867), the parish priest of Taos who favored annexation of New Mexico by the United States. 45 notes. J. H. Krenkel

2078. Vipond, M. BLESSED ARE THE PEACEMAKERS: THE LABOUR QUESTION IN CANADIAN SOCIAL GOSPEL FICTION. *J. of Can. Studies 1975 10(3): 32-43.* Discusses the ideological evolution of social gospel Christianity in Canada in the 1890's as a reaction to increasing industrialization, including the issue of Christian responsibility toward labor.

2079. Warner, Madeleine. THE CHANGING IMAGE OF THE MILLERITES IN THE WESTERN MASSACHUSETTS PRESS. *Adventist Heritage 1975 2(1): 5-7.* The doctrines of William Miller were treated fairly objectively by newspapers in western Massachusetts in the 1830's, but as public opinion changed in the 1840's, so did the press, generally mocking and distorting Millerite philosophy.

2080. Wheeler, Otis B. LOVE AMONG THE RUINS: HAWTHORNE'S SURROGATE RELIGION. *Southern Rev. 1974 10(3): 535-565.* Hawthorne, seeking a sense of God's immanence, found it in the sacramental love tradition. S

2081. White, Paula K. PURITAN THEORIES OF HISTORY IN HAWTHORNE'S FICTION. *Can. Rev. of Am. Studies [Canada] 1978 9(2): 135-153.* Instead of theology as widely believed, Puritan historical theories mostly impressed Nathaniel Hawthorne (1804-64) and so influenced him as to predetermine his subject matter and the "world views" expressed in his fiction. In his writings, Puritan providential and redemptive theories sometimes were applied singly, primarily in short stories; elsewhere both theories were used with varying emphases, especially in longer writings such as *The Scarlet Letter* and *The House of Seven Gables.* Based on Hawthorne's writings and on secondary sources; 13 notes. H. T. Lovin

2082. Williams, John P., Jr. "THOROUGH-GOING DEMOCRAT" AND "MODERN TORY": HAWTHORNE AND THE PURITAN REVOLUTION OF 1776. *Studies in Romanticism 1976 15(4): 549-572.* Discusses Nathaniel Hawthorne's view of American history with special attention paid to his assessment, through his literature, of the American Revolution, his approval of revolutionary motives and distaste for revolutionary events, and finally, the synthesis of his feelings about all of American history from Puritan to Revolutionary times which presented a straightforward account, including the darker side of the national character, proving to be unusual in light of the hyper-patriotism of the Jacksonian Era, 1830-40.

2083. Wright, Rochelle. STUART ENGSTRAND AND BISHOP HILL. *Swedish Pioneer Hist. Q. 1977 28(3): 192-204.* Describes the book, *They Sought for Paradise,* by Stuart Engstrand and compares its plot and characters with historic facts concerning the Bishop Hill Colony. Although a novel, the book does stick close to history. Bishop Hill was a community founded in Illinois in 1846 by Swedish immigrant followers of the religious prophet, Erik Jansson. The novel is a "fascinating fictionalized study of a particular historical figure" and a "commentary on the conflict between individualism and social consciousness." 29 notes. C. W. Ohrvall

2084. Zanger, Jules. "THE PIT AND THE PENDULUM" AND AMERICAN REVIVALISM. *Religion in Life 1980 49(1): 96-105.* Discusses the religious significance of the imagery in Edgar Allan Poe's *The Pit and the Pendulum,* particularly from elements of the Second Great Awakening, ca. 1800-50.

2085. —. [IDEOLOGICAL CURRENTS IN 19TH CENTURY FRENCH-CANADIAN LITERATURE]. *Recherches Sociographiques [Canada] 1964 5(1-2): 101-121.*
Lamontagne, L. LES COURANTS IDÉOLOGIQUES DANS LA LITTÉRATURE CANADIAN-FRANÇAISE DU XIX SIÈCLE [Ideological currents in French-Canadian literature of the 19th century], *pp. 101-119.* Like French romanticism, 19th century French-Canadian literature dealt with similar themes, but it was more objective and focused on religion and patriotism, central to the French-Canadian experience.
Bonenfant, Jean-Charles. COMMENTAIRE [Commentary], *pp. 120-121.* Although Lamontagne offers a detailed historical perspective to understanding 19th-century French-Canadian literature, a more sociological standpoint is needed for further research into the subject.

13. NEGATIVE IMPULSE

General

2086. Canny, Nicholas P. THE IDEOLOGY OF ENGLISH COLONIZATION: FROM IRELAND TO AMERICA. *William and Mary Q. 1973 30(4): 575-598.* Analyzes the English conquest of Ireland in the late 16th century. Examines various colonization schemes during the reign of Elizabeth I. Notes the extreme cruelties of English adventurers such as Essex and Gilbert. The ideology of the English conquest rested on the assumptions that the Irish were pagan, barbarian, and immoral. Relates the ideas of conquest to the need for transplanting malcontents to the New World. Englishmen learned from the experience in Ireland, particularly what not to do; that knowledge aided in American colonization. Discusses ideas of Edmund Spenser and Thomas Smith. Based primarily on rare books and manuscripts in British depositories; 63 notes. H. M. Ward

2087. Crane, Elaine F. UNEASY COEXISTENCE: RELIGIOUS TENSIONS IN EIGHTEENTH CENTURY NEWPORT. *Newport Hist. 1980 53(3): 101-111.* Discusses the occasional religious tensions that surfaced in the unusually tolerant Rhode Island of the 18th century, particularly when it came to Catholics and Sephardic Jews, and the escalation of minor differences among those of different religious persuasions during the revolutionary era.

2088. Curtis, James E. and Lambert, Ronald D. STATUS DISSATISFACTION AND OUT-GROUP REJECTION: CROSS-CULTURAL COMPARISONS WITHIN CANADA. *Can. Rev. of Sociol. and Anthrop. 1975 12(2): 178-192.* An analysis of 1968 data on negative affect towards selected religious, racial, and ethnic out-groups is reported. This is guided by an hypothesis from the literature concerning the effect of status dissatisfaction on attitudes towards minority out-groups. The analysis is for working subsamples of English-speaking Catholics and Protestants and French-speaking Catholics, all native born. The independent variable, status dissatisfaction, is measured by four alternative procedures. Education and occupational status are control variables, employed in analyses within each of the three linguistic-religious groups. There are some slight, but statistically significant, direct relationships between status dissatisfaction and negative affect toward Jews and Blacks in evaluations by French Catholics. However, these findings do not obtain for the other two linguistic-religious subgroups. Interpretations and implications of the findings are discussed. J

2089. Evans, Simon. SPATIAL BIAS IN THE INCIDENCE OF NATIVISM: OPPOSITION TO HUTTERITE EXPANSION IN ALBERTA. *Can. Ethnic Studies [Canada] 1974 6(1-2): 1-16.* Examines the spatial variation in the incidence of overt hostility between the Hutterites and the host population in rural Alberta between 1918 and 1972, as revealed in a study of 50 Hutterite colonies.

2090. Hope, Clifford R., Jr. STRIDENT VOICES IN KANSAS BETWEEN THE WARS. *Kansas Hist. 1979 2(1): 54-64.* Concentrates on Gerald Burton Winrod (1900-57), a pamphleteer and fundamentalist evangelist who, starting in 1933, attacked Jews, Communism, the Catholic Church, Socialism, banking, the New Deal, Freemasonry, and Fascism. Conspiracy theories such as Winrod's are a continuing problem. The 1978 presidential address to the Kansas State Historical Society. Secondary sources; illus., 9 notes. W. F. Zornow

2091. Hurvitz, Nathan. BLACKS AND JEWS IN AMERICAN FOLKLORE. *Western Folklore 1974 33(4): 301-325.* Examines "white Christian American" folklore about Negroes and Jews. Recounts jokes, stories, and folksayings to bear out the thesis that the two minority groups are frequently coupled together in folklore and "are deprecated and rejected individually and jointly by members of the dominant Christian society." S. L. Myres

2092. Perlmutter, Philip. THE AMERICAN STRUGGLE WITH ETHNIC SUPERIORITY. *J. of Intergroup Relations 1977 6(2): 31-56.* Surveys the American tradition of xenophobia and discrimination against different religions and ethnic groups, from the Mayflower Compact to the 1965 immigration law reform.

2093. Roof, Wade Clark. RELIGIOUS ORTHODOXY AND MINORITY PREJUDICE: CAUSAL RELATIONSHIP OR REFLECTION OF LOCALISTIC WORLD VIEW? *Am. J. of Sociol. 1974 80(3): 643-664.* Examines the relationship of religious orthodoxy to prejudice against minorities using a world-view perspective. Instead of regarding the two as causally related, argues that both religious belief and intolerance toward minorities are reflections of a localistic world view formed by individuals with limited social perspectives. Data from a North Carolina survey sample support this explanation, showing that the orthodoxy-prejudice relationship is partially spurious when localism is controlled and that a portion of the influence of education upon prejudice is also expressed indirectly through localism as an intervening orientation. These findings, based upon a causal analysis of anti-Semitic, anti-black, and anti-Catholic attitudes, suggest the need for further attention to "breadth of perspective" as a factor in theories concerning prejudice. Covers 1957-73. J

Anti-Catholicism

2094. Abbey, Sue Wilson. THE KU KLUX KLAN IN ARIZONA, 1921-1925. *J. of Arizona Hist. 1973 14(1): 10-30.* Established in Phoenix and Tucson in 1921, the Ku Klux Klan soon spread to smaller towns and the rural and mining areas. It campaigned for better law enforcement through prohibition and the closing of brothels and gambling halls. The Klan, alarmed at the growth of the Mexican American population and the spread of Catholicism, preached the return to "higher" moral standards and the doctrine of white supremacy. Defeated in the November 1924 elections, the Klan became a victim of its own intolerance when its violence and excesses were widely publicized. 2 illus., 86 notes. D. L. Smith

2095. Bosworth, Timothy W. ANTI-CATHOLICISM AS A POLITICAL TOOL IN MID-EIGHTEENTH-CENTURY MARYLAND. *Catholic Hist. Rev. 1975 61(4): 539-563.* During the 1750's there existed in Maryland a belief that Catholics were on the verge of subverting the colony's Protestant government and delivering it to the French. Investigates anti-Catholic propaganda, relying heavily upon the *Archives of Maryland* and the *Maryland Gazette*. The prospect of a war with Catholic France drew latent anti-Catholicism to the surface and produced a Catholic scare. Politicians then seized upon this fear of Catholics and used it to gain power over the proprietor. Protestants rationalized their actions in terms of the good Protestants defending the British Empire against its enemies, the Catholics.

2096. Calderwood, William. RELIGIOUS REACTIONS TO THE KU KLUX KLAN IN SASKATCHEWAN. *Saskatchewan Hist. 1973 26(3): 103-114.* By 1926 the Ku Klux Klan was organized in most of the Canadian provinces. It fed on long-standing prejudices, but never had spectacular success. Its greatest impact was felt in Saskatchewan in 1927-30 where the prominent political issues of language, sectarianism, immigration, and control of natural resources could all be associated with a "Catholic plot." Evidence is strong that many conservative Protestants embraced and supported the principles of the KKK. 57 notes. D. L. Smith

2097. Camposeo, James M. ANTI-CATHOLIC PREJUDICE IN EARLY NEW ENGLAND: THE DALEY-HALLIGAN MURDER TRIAL. *Hist. J. of Western Massachusetts 1978 6(2): 5-17.* In April 1806 Irish Catholic immigrants Dominic Daley and James Halligan were convicted (with virtually no defense and on a 13-year-old's shaky testimony) in Northampton, Massachusetts, of the murder in 1805 of Marcus Lyon. They were executed in June after hearing Mass and receiving extreme unction from Father (later Cardinal) Jean Louis Lefebvre de

Cheverus, who in a sermon to some of the 15,000 people gathered for the execution tried to diminish the great deal of anti-Irish and anti-Catholic feeling among the people of Massachusetts. 4 illus., 70 notes.
W. H. Mulligan, Jr./S

2098. Casey, Daniel J. HERESY IN THE DIOCESE OF BROOKLYN: AN UNHOLY TRINITY. *New York Affairs 1978 4(4): 73-86.* Discusses three journalist-novelists, Jimmy Breslin, Pete Hamill, and Joe Flaherty, and their criticism of Catholic Irish Americans in Brooklyn, 1960's-70's.

2099. Clark, Andrienne G. WHO MURDERED MARCUS LYON? *New-England Galaxy 1977 19(2): 15-21.* In strongly anti-Catholic, anti-Irish, and anti-immigrant Northampton, Massachusetts, Irish immigrants Dominic Daley and James Halligan were convicted with little defense and on doubtful evidence in April 1806, and hanged in June, for the murder of Marcus Lyon in November 1805. Father (later Cardinal) Jean Louis Lefebvre de Cheverus, in an eloquent sermon to Protestants waiting for the hanging, attempted to diminish their prejudice.
D. J. Engler

2100. Clark, Malcolm, Jr. THE BIGOT DISCLOSED: 90 YEARS OF NATIVISM. *Oregon Hist. Q. 1974 75(2): 108-190.* A history of bigotry in Oregon, illustrated in the nativism of the period on the religious, social, and political scenes. Extreme religious sectarianism was evident at a very early date, exemplified by strong anti-Catholicism. The treatment of Chinese laborers was equally shameful, and became the subject of inflammatory journalism and oratory. Henry Francis Bowers and his American Protective Association brought bigotry into the political arena, followed in turn by the Guardians of Liberty, the I.W.W., and the revived Ku Klux Klan under the leadership of Edward Young Clark. The latter organization had phenomenal growth and influence in the 1920's, with Fred L. Gifford becoming the political boss of Oregon. Despite the Klan's demise, nativism unfortunately is not dead. 17 photos, 179 notes.
R. V. Ritter

2101. Cronon, E. David. FATHER MARQUETTE GOES TO WASHINGTON: THE MARQUETTE STATUE CONTROVERSY. *Wisconsin Mag. of Hist. 1973 56(4): 267-283.* A proposal in 1887 that the state of Wisconsin fund a statue of Jacques Marquette, S.J., for the Statuary Hall in Washington, D.C., touched off such bureaucratic and anti-Catholic controversy that the statue was not placed in the hall until 1896 and not formally accepted by Congress until 1904. 10 illus., 74 notes.
S

2102. Cuddy, Edward. "ARE BOLSHEVIKS ANY WORSE THAN THE IRISH?" ETHNO-RELIGIOUS CONFLICT IN AMERICA DURING THE 1920'S. *Éire-Ireland 1976 11(3): 13-32.* Shattering effects of urbanization and fear of the loss of Anglo-Saxon hegemony in the United States resulted in much anti-Catholicism and anti-Irish sentiment during the 1920's.

2103. Doyle, John E. CHICOPEE'S IRISH (1830-1875). *Hist. J. of Western Massachusetts 1974 3(1): 13-23.* Nineteenth-century Irish settlers came to the Chicopee mills via Canada and other parts of Massachusetts, and by 1848 Chicopee became a predominantly immigrant company town. Irish mores encouraged nativism among Protestants, but the record of Irish participation in the Civil War led to respectability. Primary and secondary sources; 2 illus., 34 notes.
S. S. Sprague

2104. Dyer, Thomas G. AARON'S ROD: THEODORE ROOSEVELT, TOM WATSON, AND ANTI-CATHOLICISM. *Res. Studies 1976 44(1): 60-68.* Discusses Theodore Roosevelt's rebuke of Georgia politician Thomas E. Watson's anti-Catholicism in letters in 1915.

2105. George, Joseph, Jr. THE LINCOLN WRITINGS OF CHARLES P. T. CHINIQUY. *J. of the Illinois State Hist. Soc. 1976 69(1): 17-25.* Examines the claims of the anti-Catholic Charles P. T. Chiniquy (1809-99), a client of Abraham Lincoln in 1856 who later claimed to be a friend of Lincoln and an authority on his religious beliefs, particularly his alleged anti-Catholicism. Chiniquy's claims of a Catholic plot to assassinate Lincoln are false, but several historians have accepted his less sensational but equally unfounded writings about Lincoln's religion. Chiniquy autobiography, Lincoln's *Collected Works,* court records; 2 illus., 45 notes.
J/S

2106. Greeley, Andrew M. ANTI-CATHOLICISM IN THE ACADEMY. *Change 1977 9(6): 40-43.* American academics discriminate against white ethnics, labeling them culturally inferior and socially deficient.
J

2107. Gribbin, William. A MATTER OF FAITH: NORTH AMERICA'S RELIGION AND SOUTH AMERICA'S INDEPENDENCE. *Americas (Acad. of Am. Franciscan Hist.) 1975 31(4): 470-487.* US attitudes toward Latin American independence, at all social levels, were influenced by a strongly Protestant, anti-Catholic bias. Association of Spanish rule with "popery" and the Inquisition intensified US support of the Latin American patriots, but hostility toward Latin Catholic culture hindered understanding of the emerging nations. Contemporary press sources; 81 notes.
D. Bushnell

2108. Gundersen, Joan R. ANTHONY GAVIN'S *A MASTER-KEY TO POPERY*: A VIRGINIA PARSON'S BEST SELLER. *Virginia Mag. of Hist. and Biog. 1974 82(1): 39-46.* Anthony Gavin's *A Master-Key to Popery,* which appeared in Dublin and was reprinted in 1725 in London, was a huge success. In 1773 it was printed in America. It is partly autobiographical for Gavin was a priest in Spain from which he made a spectacular escape. He became an Anglican clergyman and came to Virginia in 1735 where he was unpopular partly because of his anti-slavery views. 31 notes.
E. P. Stickney

2109. Hammett, Theodore M. TWO MOBS OF JACKSONIAN BOSTON: IDEOLOGY AND INTEREST. *J. of Am. Hist. 1976 62(4): 845-868.* Using two dissimilar mob actions occurring in Boston, discusses the interaction of ideas and interests as the main basis for ideological development. Compares the burning of an Ursuline Convent by a mob of poor, Protestant laborers on 11 August 1834 with the Massachusetts Anti-Slavery Society riot of 24 October 1835 (by "wealthier," establishment types). Contemporaries saw one as a danger to society, the latter as righteous action against society's disrupters. These two views represent society's bipartiality in developing ideological responses to events affecting it. Economics and class structure determine "rightness." 5 tables, 70 notes.
V. P. Rilee

2110. Hardy, René. LA RÉBELLION DE 1837-38 ET L'ESSOR DU PROTESTANTISME CANADIEN-FRANÇAIS [The rebellion of 1837-38 and the scope of French-Canadian Protestantism]. *Rev. d'Hist. de l'Amérique Française [Canada] 1975 29(2): 163-189.* English and Swiss Protestant evangelists considered the rebellion of 1837-38 in Lower Canada as a good opportunity to destroy the influence of the Catholic clergy. The English residents of Montreal thought that the conversion of the French-Canadians to Protestantism would guarantee cohesion between the two ethnic groups. Colonial administrators, however, considered the Catholic clergy indispensable to the maintenance of law and order. Based on documents in the Archives de la paroisse Notre-Dame de Québec, Archives de la Chancellerie de l'Archevêché de Montréal, Archives de l'Université du Québec à Trois-Rivières, and secondary works; 106 notes.
L. B. Chan

2111. Houston, Cecil and Smyth, William J. THE ORANGE ORDER AND THE EXPANSION OF THE FRONTIER IN ONTARIO, 1830-1900. *J. of Hist. Geography 1978 4(3): 251-264.* The Orange Order, with its two main tenets, anti-Catholicism and loyalty to Britain, flourished in Ontario. Largely coincident with Protestant Irish settlement, its role pervaded the political, social and community as well as religious lives of its followers. Spatially, Orange lodges were founded as Irish Protestant settlement spread north and west from its original focus on the Lake Ontario plain. Although the number of active members, and thus their influence, may have been overestimated, the Orange influence was considerable and comparable to the Roman Catholic influence in Quebec. Primary and secondary sources; 3 maps, table, graph, 34 notes.
A. J. Larson

2112. Keefe, Thomas M. THE CATHOLIC ISSUE IN THE CHICAGO TRIBUNE BEFORE THE CIVIL WAR. *Mid-America 1975 57(4): 227-245.* Blaming Chicago's troubles on Catholic immigrants, Henry Fowler's editorials began the Chicago *Tribune*'s anti-Catholicism. However, he failed to defeat the Democrats in the 1854 municipal election. Editor Thomas Stewart followed Fowler's example, and with his editorial support the Know-Nothings won the next election. New owners of the *Tribune* Medill, Ray, and Vaughan carried on the Fowler-Stewart policy, which continued after the merger with the *Daily Democratic Press*, linking slavery and Catholicism, expressing sympathy for Italy's struggle for unity, and alleging that Stephen Douglas was a secret Catholic. Based on newspapers and secondary works; 83 notes. T. H. Wendel

2113. Kirwan, Kent A. and Weber, Paul J. DANIEL DE LEON'S ANTI-CATHOLICISM. *Mid-Am. 1976 58(1): 20-30.* Daniel DeLeon's views concerning Catholicism were integral to his vision of the socialist state. The Church was "a political machine ambushed behind religion." Catholicism was the antithesis of socialism and a repudiation of the democratic ideal. Socialism meant individual responsibility; Catholicism, a ruling hierarchy. Education provided the key to the achievement of socialism; here the Church, the leader of capitalism's political force, was a powerful opponent. DeLeon's doctrinaire anti-Catholicism explicates his perception of capitalism. Covers 1891-1914. Based on DeLeon's published works and on secondary sources; 35 notes. T. H. Wendel

2114. Principe, Angelo. IL RISORGIMENTO VISTO DAI PROTESTANTI DELL'ALTO CANADA 1846-1860 [The Risorgimento as seen by Upper Canadian Protestants: 1846-60]. *Rassegna Storica del Risorgimento [Italy] 1979 66(2): 151-163.* Canadian Protestants believed the Catholic Church had kept Italians ignorant, religious fanatics, and morally and politically unable to be independent. The negative attitude changed during 1848-49 when the Italians forced the pope to leave Rome and proclaimed the Roman Republic. They also applauded the House of Savoy for granting religious freedom to the Waldensian Church, for entering the Crimean War on the side of Great Britain, and for Victor Emmanuel's antipapal policy. During the 1859-60 war, which culminated with the Garibaldian success in southern Italy, Canadian Protestants did not see it as the end of the Risorgimento. Before Italy could be considered emancipated it had to be evangelized. Secondary sources; 44 notes. A. Sbacchi

2115. Racine, Philip N. THE KU KLUX KLAN, ANTI-CATHOLICISM, AND ATLANTA'S BOARD OF EDUCATION, 1916-1927. *Georgia Hist. Q. 1973 57(1): 63-75.* The Ku Klux Klan became a power in Atlanta politics during and after World War I. Playing upon strong forces of religious bigotry and fundamentalism, the Klan yet failed to coerce the board of education into adopting anti-Catholic measures. Atlantans viewed the Klan's control of politics as a passing phenomenon, but interference in the education system was intolerable. 55 notes. D. L. Smith

2116. Smith, Norman W. THE KU KLUX KLAN IN RHODE ISLAND. *Rhode Island Hist. 1978 37(2): 35-45.* The Ku Klux Klan flowered briefly in Rhode Island during the 1920's and may have continued in the early 1930's. It attracted more rural than urban supporters, received encouragement from the Protestant clergy, had some links to the Republican Party, and was overwhelmingly anti-Catholic rather than anti-Jew or Negro. Based on interviews, manuscripts in the Rhode Island Historical Society (Providence), newspapers, and secondary accounts; 3 illus., 80 notes. P. J. Coleman

2117. Stegmaier, Mark J. MARYLAND'S FEAR OF INSURRECTION AT THE TIME OF BRADDOCK'S DEFEAT. *Maryland Hist. Mag. 1976 71(4): 467-483.* A significant increase in the number of violent crimes by slaves and servants in Maryland occurred during 1753-55. This combined with normal fears of Catholic subversion and belief in an imminent French and Indian invasion, following General Edward Braddock's defeat on 9 July 1755, to produce a widespread scare of a servile insurrection in the colony. Governor Horatio Sharpe, whom the House of Delegates believed to be an agent of Catholic power in Maryland, used the public rumors and outcry to political and military advantage and frightened the Assembly into arming the western counties against French military incursions. By October 1755 investigations in all but one county had found no signs of slaves or Catholics plotting a revolt; but the relative size of the servile population, the weakness of the militia, and oppression under which slaves and servants struggled, and the general identification of Catholics with disloyalty continued to produce alarm for years to come. Only with the British capture of Fort Duquesne, in 1758, did Maryland's sense of security improve. Based on archival sources; table, 71 notes, appendix of major crimes reported in *Maryland Gazette*, 1745-65. G. J. Bobango

2118. Thomas, Donna. THE *PROVIDENCE VISITOR* AND NATIVIST ISSUES, 1916-1924. *Rhode Island Hist. 1979 38(2): 51-62.* Through its diocesan newspaper, the *Providence Visitor,* the Catholic hierarchy in Providence took a very conservative stand on the social and political issues of the period in an effort to mute nativist suspicion. This pleased the old-stock Protestant forces in the state, but encouraged conservatism within the Church. Based on newspaper files; 6 illus., 36 notes. P. J. Coleman

2119. Thompson, James J., Jr. SOUTHERN BAPTISTS AND ANTI-CATHOLICISM IN THE 1920'S. *Mississippi Q. 1979 32(4): 611-625.* Discusses the reasons for, and the nature of, anti-Catholicism among Southern Baptists who spearheaded the Protestant opposition to Roman Catholicism in the 1920's.

2120. Tweed, Tommy. ON THE TRAIL OF MR. O'B. *Alberta Hist. [Canada] 1975 23(2): 4-13.* An account of the scholarly hitch-hiker Eugene Francis O'Beirne from Ireland, who went to the Red River country in 1863 after wearing out his welcome in Wisconsin and Minnesota. O'Beirne figures prominently in travel narratives of the time as a fraud, interesting conversationalist, and alcoholic. Recent research in archives in Ireland confirms his background as a youth expelled from school and a young adult who gave inflammatory anti-Catholic lectures. After his Red River experiences, O'Beirne went to Queensland, Australia. 5 illus. D. Chaput

2121. Whitmore, Allan R. PORTRAIT OF A MAINE "KNOW-NOTHING": WILLIAM H. CHANEY (1821-1903); HIS EARLY YEARS AND HIS ROLE IN THE ELLSWORTH NATIVIST CONTROVERSY, 1853-1854. *Maine Hist. Soc. Q. 1974 14(1): 1-57.* On 14 October 1854, Jesuit priest John Bapst was tarred, feathered, and ridden on a rail by a nativist mob in Ellsworth, Maine, because of his militant religious activities. Local newspaper editor William Henry Chaney largely created the charged atmosphere producing this riot. A harsh childhood and poverty had made Chaney a combative, defensive individual sensitive to criticism, obsessed with conspiracies, and constantly embroiled in controversies. He strongly denounced Bapst's activities as a Catholic conspiracy and soon inflamed the local citizenry to action. Primary and secondary sources; illus., 164 notes. E. A. Churchill

2122. —. [CALIFORNIOS AND THE IMAGE OF INDOLENCE]. *Western Hist. Q. 1979 10(1): 61-69.*

Weber, David J. HERE RESTS JUAN ESPINOSA: TOWARDS A CLEARER LOOK AT THE IMAGE ON THE "INDOLENT" CALIFORNIOS, *pp. 61-68.* Examines the analysis of indolence of Californios in David J. Langum, "Californios and the Image of Indolence." Finds Langum's religion-nationalism-racism and industrializing explanations leading into "a quagmire on the road to historical explanation." Poses two questions that need answers to put us back "on solid ground." Espinosa is an apocryphal Californio indolent. Covers 1780's-1840's. 23 notes.

Langum, David J. A BRIEF REPLY, *p. 69.* Defends his original position and suggests fallacies in Weber's reasoning. D. L. Smith

2123. —. THOSE MURDEROUS MONKS OF PASCO COUNTY. *Tampa Bay Hist. 1979 1(2): 55-58.* Reprints an anti-Catholic letter to the editor by G. F. D'Equivelley, but signed "French Huguenot," which appeared in Tom Watson's newspaper *The Jeffersonian,* November 1916, and a pamphlet reply by Abbott Charles Mohr, O.S.B., regarding charges and countercharges involving the "Huguenot" and the Benedictines over a disputed land transfer.

Anti-Mormonism

2124. Brown, Lisle G. WEST VIRGINIA AND MORMONISM'S RAREST BOOK. *West Virginia Hist. 1978 39(2-3): 195-199.* The first printing of Joseph Smith's *Book of Commandments* was disrupted by an anti-Mormon mob that wrecked the printing office in Independence, Missouri, in 1833. A few copies of the book were saved, printed on paper furnished by William Lambdin of Wheeling, West Virginia. By 1968 a copy of the book brought $4500. Primary and secondary sources; illus., 16 notes. J. H. Broussard

2125. Brudnoy, David. A DECADE IN ZION: THEODORE SCHROEDER'S INITIAL ASSAULT ON THE MORMONS. *Historian 1975 37(2): 241-256.* Free-thinking Theodore Schroeder (1864-1953) began as a lawyer practicing in Salt Lake City (1889-1900) at a time when national controversies about Mormon polygamy delayed statehood for Utah Territory. Schroeder became a strident critic of Mormonism. His pamphlets and short-lived journal *Lucifer's Lantern* focused on plural marriage, and he campaigned successfully to deny polygamous Brigham Roberts the seat in Congress to which he had been elected. In the years after 1900 when he moved to New York, Schroeder became a prolific contributor to First Amendment studies and a leading advocate of free speech and press causes. The Free Speech League, which he helped form, is one of the forebears of the American Civil Liberties Union. Based on the Schroeder papers at the State Historical Society of Wisconsin, and the library of Southern Illinois University; 31 notes. N. W. Moen

2126. Hindus, Michael Stephen. INEVITABLE ACQUITTAL, TRIAL BY JURY, AND TRIAL BY HISTORY. *Rev. in Am. Hist. 1976 4(3): 397-402.* Review article prompted by Dallin H. Oaks and Marvin S. Hill's *Carthage Conspiracy: The Trial of the Accused Assassins of Joseph Smith* (Urbana: U. of Illinois Pr., 1975) discusses the concepts of frontier justice, Mormon history, and the history of law in the 1844 murder trial.

2127. Sessions, Gene A. MYTH, MORMONISM, AND MURDER IN THE SOUTH. *South Atlantic Q. 1976 75(2): 212-225.* Examines inhumane acts directed against members of the Church of Jesus Christ of Latter-day Saints from the post-Reconstruction period to the early 20th century for the purpose of understanding the broader question of violence in Southern history. Sociological and psychological explanations are analyzed in accounting for such mistreatment. Tennessee, Georgia and Alabama receive primary focus. 29 notes. R. W. Dubay

Anti-Semitism

2128. D'Ancona, David Arnold. AN ANSWER TO ANTI-SEMITISM: SAN FRANCISCO 1883. *Western States Jewish Hist. Q. 1975 8(1): 59-64.* Reprint of a letter to the editor of the *San Francisco Call*, 26 January 1883, in response to anti-Semitic statements published in the San Francisco *Argonaut* by its editor, Frank M. Pixley. Pixley's remarks contained many untruths and misconceptions concerning Jewish religious ceremonies and life-styles. D'Ancona (1827-1908) clearly rebutted Pixley's statements. Pixley recognized his mistakes and ceased his anti-Semitic writings. R. A. Garfinkle

2129. Fried, Lewis. JACOB RIIS AND THE JEWS: THE AMBIVALENT QUEST FOR COMMUNITY. *Am. Studies 1979 20(1): 5-24.* Examines Jacob Riis's treatment of Jews against his general beliefs in civil liberties and social freedom. His thought expressed the tensions between the promise of egalitarianism and the realities of American society, and to him the downtown Jews highlighted this disparity. Their attachment to European cultural traditions confused Riis's impulse for cultural unity and Christian endeavor. Covers 1870-1914. Primary and secondary sources; 2 illus., 59 notes. J. A. Andrew

2130. Littell, Franklin H. UPROOTING ANTISEMITISM: A CALL TO CHRISTIANS. *J. of Church and State 1975 17(1): 15-24.* Christian anti-Semitism, rooted in the theological teaching that Jews are guilty of the crucifixion of Christ, has had social and political implications, exhibited notably in the Holocaust of World War II, as well as in the theology and historiography of such anti-Semitic liberals as Arnold Toynbee.

2131. Simms, Adam. A BATTLE IN THE AIR: DETROIT'S JEWS ANSWER FATHER COUGHLIN. *Michigan Jewish Hist. 1978 18(2): 7-13.* A memorandum written in 1939 by executive director William I. Boxerman outlines the initial stages of the Jewish Community Council's radio campaign against Charles Edward Coughlin's anti-Semitism.

2132. Tuerk, Richard. JACOB RIIS AND THE JEWS. *New-York Hist. Soc. Q. 1979 63(3): 178-201.* The great influx of immigrants during 1875-1920's increased opposition in the United States to immigrants in general and Jews in particular. A result was the post-World War I nativism and the restrictive immigration act of 1924. For some, however, the opposite reaction took place; Jacob Riis, an immigrant himself, was one of these. His most famous work, *How the Other Half Lives,* published in 1890, contained much anti-Semitism, for he believed that Jews from Eastern Europe would never be assimilated. Within a decade he was changing his mind and, after another ten years, much of his prejudice had disappeared. He had begun to accept the idea that people could be different but live in harmony and be "good Americans." Primary sources; illus., 5 photos, 42 notes. C. L. Grant

2133. —. [ANTI-SEMITISM AND CHRISTIAN BELIEFS]. *Am. Sociol. R. 1973 38(1): 33-61.*
Middleton, Russell. DO CHRISTIAN BELIEFS CAUSE ANTI-SEMITISM?, *pp. 33-52.*
Glock, Charles Y. and Stark, Rodney. DO CHRISTIAN BELIEFS CAUSE ANTI-SEMITISM?—A COMMENT, *pp. 53-59.*
Middleton, Russell. RESPONSE, *pp, 59-61.*
Middleton examines Glock and Stark's contention that certain Christian religious beliefs are causally related to anti-Semitism, using data from a 1964 national survey. Religious orthodoxy proves to be uncorrelated with anti-Semitism at the zero-order. A path analysis reveals that the relationships in the causal sequence hypothesized by Glock and Stark are weak. Furthermore, the influence of religious orthodoxy, religious libertarianism, religious particularism, and religious hostility to the historic Jew is not expressed solely through the intervening step of religious hostility to modern Jews; the coefficents for the direct paths to anti-Semitism are in some cases sizable. The five religious belief variables taken together in a simple additive model account for approximately 15% of the variance in anti-Semitism. When socio-economic status, a number of other social attributes, and a number of social psychological traits are held constant, however, the five religious belief variables account uniquely for only 2% of the variance in anti-Semitism. Even here one must be cautious in inferring a causal relationship, particularly since some of the religious measures may simply reflect a more general anti-Semitic ideology. A revised model is presented which includes socioeconomic status and social psychological variables. J

2134. —. A GENTILE REPROVES AN ANTI-SEMITE: FRESNO —1893. *Western States Jewish Hist. Q. 1977 9(4): 299-300.* During a murder trial in Fresno, California, defense lawyer William D. Foote attempted to undermine the testimony of a Jewish prosecution witness by abusing Jews generally. Grove L. Johnson, prosecuting attorney, in offering a rejoinder to Foote's anti-Semitic views, emphasized traditional American religious tolerance and Constitutional rights and privileges. Johnson's speech is quoted at length. 9 notes. B. S. Porter

Racism

2135. Bailey, Kenneth K. THE POST CIVIL WAR RACIAL SEPARATIONS IN SOUTHERN PROTESTANTISM: ANOTHER LOOK. *Church Hist. 1977 46(4): 453-475.* There was a drastic contrast between the remarkably fixed, remarkably unified, harshly separatist racial opinions that developed in the popular white southern churches in the 1880's and 1890's and the more flexible outlooks that earlier seemed ascendant. Racial tendencies in religion were interdenominational, and regionally peculiar. Biracial denominationalism was for a time a viable prospect. Color separations can be attributed to white rather than black initiatives. Based on Conference notes and religious newspaper accounts; 25 notes. M. D. Dibert

2136. Berg, Philip L. RACISM AND THE PURITAN MIND. *Phylon 1975 36(1): 1-7.* A critical inconsistency existed in the early Puritan racial attitude toward Indians. Although the Puritans did not arrive as full-fledged racists, they did arrive with preconceived notions of the Native American. The Indian was not viewed by the settlers as an enemy, but rather as an unfortunate heathen who needed to be saved. However, even when the Indians openly embraced Christianity, the Puritans did not accept them as equals. Gradually, Puritan religious intolerance combined with an increased white desire for more land, and the Puritans began to regard the Indians as racial inferiors whose land could be taken, or whose lives could be ended by war. The Puritans, as with 20th-century whites, refused to look at social explanations of racial difficulties and differences, and instead saw only that the Indians did not willingly adopt Puritan values; hence they were inferior. Based on primary and secondary sources; 27 notes. B. A. Glasrud

2137. Bringhurst, Newell G. AN AMBIGUOUS DECISION: THE IMPLEMENTATION OF MORMON PRIESTHOOD DENIAL FOR THE BLACK MAN—A REEXAMINATION. *Utah Hist. Q. 1978 46(1): 45-64.* Elijah Abel, Walker Lewis, and William McCary were early black members of the Mormon priesthood. Black priesthood denial emerged ambiguously. It was a by-product of Mormon trends after 1844; proslavery tendencies, willingness to enact secular anti-black statutes, a shift in the Mormons' racial values and perceptions, millennialism, and Herrenvolk. Brigham Young declared Negroes ineligible for priesthood in 1849, but this was not publicized until the organization of Utah Territory in 1852 required the resolution of black secular status. Primary and secondary sources; 85 notes. J. L. Hazelton

2138. Bringhurst, Newell G. FORGOTTEN MORMON PERSPECTIVES: SLAVERY, RACE, AND THE BLACK MAN AS ISSUES AMONG NON-UTAH LATTER-DAY SAINTS, 1844-1873. *Michigan Hist. 1977 61(4): 352-370.* James J. Strang and Charles B. Thompson, two Mormon leaders of secondary importance, provided many observations on the subjects of slavery, race, and Negroes. Strang was ambivalent on the antislavery question, accepting a master-servant relationship for his Mormon kingdom yet simultaneously deploring bondage. Thompson was more unequivocal, espousing anti-black concepts forcefully. Thus, Thompson held views which more nearly accorded with those of Brigham Young and the Utah Mormons, while Strang's ambivalence recalled the antislavery side of Mormon thought present under Joseph Smith at Nauvoo in the 1840's. Overall, Mormon thought on slavery and race was complex and often contradictory. Primary sources; 64 notes, illus., 4 photos. D. W. Johnson

2139. Farley, Ena L. METHODISTS AND BAPTISTS ON THE ISSUE OF BLACK EQUALITY IN NEW YORK 1865 TO 1868. *J. of Negro Hist. 1976 61(4): 374-392.* Within three years after Appomattox, the two largest religious denominations in New York—the Baptists and the Methodists—reaffirmed racial segregation in their faith. Based on the records of Baptist and Methodist conferences; 64 notes. N. G. Sapper

2140. Foster, Gaines M. BISHOP CHESHIRE AND BLACK PARTICIPATION IN THE EPISCOPAL CHURCH: THE LIMITATIONS OF RELIGIOUS PATERNALISM. *North Carolina Hist. Rev. 1977 54(1): 49-65.* Joseph Blount Cheshire, Jr. (1850-1932), Episcopal Bishop of North Carolina (1893-1932), held mid-19th-century paternalistic views toward Negroes at the time segregation was rapidly gaining acceptance in the South. As Church leaders attempted entirely to separate and remove black priests from the ruling hierarchy at century's end, Cheshire advocated active black participation. Paradoxically, his religious paternalism did not extend to the social sphere where he maintained a strong attitude of white supremacy and black subservience. Based on contemporary church publications, unpublished autobiographies, Blount manuscript papers, and secondary sources; 9 illus., 33 notes. T. L. Savitt

2141. Gorsuch, Richard L. and Aleshire, Daniel. CHRISTIAN FAITH AND ETHNIC PREJUDICE: A REVIEW AND INTERPRETATION OF RESEARCH. *J. for the Sci. Study of Religion 1974 13(3): 281-307.* Discusses methods for investigating the relationship between religious commitment and racial prejudice during the 1960's and 70's.

2142. Hewitt, John H. THE SACKING OF ST. PHILIP'S CHURCH, NEW YORK. *Hist. Mag. of the Protestant Episcopal Church 1980 49(1): 7-20.* On the night of 11 July 1834 the black Episcopal St. Philip's Church, New York City, was sacked by an antiblack, antiabolition mob. The black rector of the church was Peter Williams, Jr., who would later emerge as a leader in the abolition movement. The mob had been excited by the yellow journalism of the New York newspapers. Reveals the Jim Crow status of New York at this time, with Williams himself not being equal to the white priests in the diocese. His bishop even required him to resign offices he held in abolition societies. Nor was St. Philip's entitled to representation in the Diocesan Convention. Based largely on newspaper accounts of the incident and secondary sources; 78 notes. H. M. Parker, Jr.

2143. Mesar, Joe and Dybdahl, Tom. THE UTOPIA PARK AFFAIR AND THE RISE OF NORTHERN BLACK ADVENTISTS. *Adventist Heritage 1974 1(1): 34-41, 53-54.* A separate Sabbath Day Adventist Church resulted when the First Harlem Church of James K. Humphrey, a leader in the struggle for rights of black Adventists, was expelled from the Seventh-Day Adventists for supporting Humphrey's proposed Utopia Park settlement for blacks 1920's-30's.

2144. Muldoon, James. THE INDIAN AS IRISHMAN. *Essex Inst. Hist. Collections 1975 111(4): 267-289.* Discusses the influence of British and Spanish colonization on Puritans' attitudes toward Indians in Massachusetts in the 17th century, emphasizing the precedent of British stereotypes of Irishmen.

2145. Newman, Harvey K. PIETY AND SEGREGATION: WHITE PROTESTANT ATTITUDES TOWARD BLACKS IN ATLANTA, 1865-1905. *Georgia Hist. Q. 1979 63(2): 238-251.* Following the Civil War, previously integrated Atlanta Protestant churches became segregated. In the interests of maintaining a social order with blacks at the bottom, white church members refused to cooperate with anything that might result in racial equality, even when suggested and exemplified by Bishop Gilbert Haven of the Methodist Episcopal Church. This paternalism and aloofness contributed to racial tensions which led to a tragic massacre in September 1906. Primary and secondary sources; 42 notes. G. R. Schroeder

2146. Petropoulos, Nicholas P. RELIGION AND PREJUDICE AMONG GREEK AMERICANS. *J. for the Sci. Study of Religion 1979 18(1): 68-77.* Discusses the attitudes of Greek Americans towards blacks, based on a study of 152 Greek Americans from Cincinnati, Ohio, linking church attendance and orthodoxy to racial prejudice, 1970's.

2147. Pitcher, W. Alvin. RACISM AND THE CREATIVE RECOVERY OF AMERICAN TRADITIONAL RELIGION. *Anglican Theological Rev. Supplementary Series (1) 1973: 95-116.* Covers 1965-73.

2148. Simms, L. Moody, Jr. THEODORE DU BOSE BRATTON, CHRISTIAN PRINCIPLES, AND THE RACE QUESTION. *J. of Mississippi Hist. 1976 38(1): 47-52.* Describes a 1908 speech by Theodore DuBose Bratton, the Episcopal Bishop of Mississippi, to the Conference for Education in the South. The speech illustrates the attitudes of many white Southern Christian moderates who believed in Negro inferiority and "sought merely to neutralize the harshest aspects of white supremacy." Based on secondary sources; 15 notes. J. W. Hillje

2149. Storey, John W. SOUTHERN BAPTISTS AND THE RACIAL CONTROVERSY IN THE CHURCHES AND SCHOOLS DURING RECONSTRUCTION. *Mississippi Q. 1978 31(2): 211-228.* Separation in Southern Baptist churches and opposition to equal education for blacks stemmed from the fear that equal voice in church and education would force Negroes out of "their place" in Southern society and initiate a new generation of "uppity" blacks.

2150. Thomas, G. E. PURITANS, INDIANS, AND THE CONCEPT OF RACE. *New England Q. 1975 48(1): 3-27.* Reassesses the common view that the Puritans are not to be considered as racist in the modern biological sense of the word in their relations with the Indians. Documents extensively the fact that though Puritan attitudes toward the Indians were complex and the antagonism no doubt involved more than race, "racial characteristics proved to be the one insurmountable barrier." 91 notes. R. V. Ritter

2151. Tuttle, William M., Jr. W. E. B. DU BOIS' CONFRONTATION WITH WHITE LIBERALISM DURING THE PROGRESSIVE ERA: A PHYLON DOCUMENT. *Phylon 1974 35(3): 241-258.* A previously unpublished interview conducted early in 1907 by the Progressive reformer, Ray Stannard Baker, with the black historian and economist from Atlanta University, W. E. B. DuBois, and the southern white Episcopal clergyman, Cary Breckenridge Wilmer. Despite the fact that both Baker and Wilmer were reformers, and both had indicated concern over the plight of Negroes, they appeared unwilling to support or accept DuBois' arguments for political and civil rights for blacks. Portrays the problems blacks faced in the nation when even whites who argued for reform refused to include blacks in the reformist impulse. Based on document located in Manuscript Division of the Library of Congress; 7 notes. B. A. Glasrud

2152. Wunder, John R. LAW AND CHINESE IN FRONTIER MONTANA. *Montana 1980 30(3): 18-31.* In response to social, religious, and economic discrimination in Montana, Chinese settlers turned to the courts for protection and equitable treatment. During 1864-82, Montana's courts listened to Chinese complaints, recognized their seriousness, and judged them equitably. After the first federal statute limiting Chinese immigration in 1882, judicial monitoring broke down, Montana justices reflected public opinion, and the Chinese lost in the courts. Under severe attack were Chinese mining and laundry activities, the major employment opportunities sustaining the Chinese community. Based on all civil and criminal cases involving Chinese before the Montana Supreme Court during 1864-1902, and contemporary newspapers; 6 illus., 54 notes. R. C. Myers

Slavery

2153. Billings, Warren M. THE CASES OF FERNANDO AND ELIZABETH KEY: A NOTE ON THE STATUS OF BLACKS IN SEVENTEENTH-CENTURY VIRGINIA. *William and Mary Q. 1973 30(3): 467-474.* Two court cases in early Virginia shed light on the deteriorating status of Christian blacks. Two blacks sued for their freedom. Elizabeth Key won her freedom; Fernando did not. To avert expensive suits and to insure a permanent labor base, the colony subsequently outlawed baptism as an escape from slavery. Based on court and legislative records; 24 notes. H. M. Ward

2154. Clarke, Erskine. AN EXPERIMENT IN PATERNALISM: PRESBYTERIANS AND SLAVES IN CHARLESTON, SOUTH CAROLINA. *J. of Presbyterian Hist. 1975 53(3): 223-238.* Discusses the attempts of the Presbyterian Church in Charleston in the mid-1840's to establish a separate congregation for Negroes under the administration and pastoral leadership of whites. The intention was good, but the fact that the churches were white-administered and no attempt was made to alleviate the problem of slavery still kept the blacks in a state of paternalism, in spite of the black congregation's numerical success. Covers 1845-60. Based on primary and secondary sources; 38 notes. H. M. Parker, Jr.

2155. Daniel, W. Harrison. THE METHODIST EPISCOPAL CHURCH AND THE NEGRO IN THE EARLY NATIONAL PERIOD. *Methodist Hist. 1973 11(2): 40-53.* The response of the Methodist Episcopal Church to slavery changed from severe condemnation in 1780 to acceptance in 1816. Bishop Francis Asbury (1745-1816) and Bishop Thomas Coke (1747-1814) urged that slavery be eliminated, and the church in 1784 passed resolutions against slave-holding. Later, however, the church was forced to accommodate a practice it condemned by the society of which it was a part. 76 notes. H. L. Calkin

2156. Daniel, W. Harrison. SOUTHERN PRESBYTERIANS AND THE NEGRO IN THE EARLY NATIONAL PERIOD. *J. of Negro Hist. 1973 58(3): 291-312.* Discusses the accommodation of white Presbyterians in the South to the institution of slavery. Although they believed that black people possessed immortal souls, these southerners accepted slavery as the most satisfactory social arrangement. Based on denominational records and on secondary sources; 94 notes. N. G. Sapper

2157. Essig, James David. A VERY WINTRY SEASON: VIRGINIA BAPTISTS AND SLAVERY, 1785-1797. *Virginia Mag. of Hist. and Biog. 1980 88(2): 170-185.* Analyzes Virginia Baptist attitudes toward slavery after the Revolutionary War. Freed from civil abuse by the Revolution, Baptists prospered but were concerned about slave holding as a manifestation of worldliness. Baptists divided on the issue, some for example using liberty as a reason to free slaves, or as a cause to ignore calls for emancipation from their own governing body. Baptists became concerned about other matters as the century turned, but the tendency was to try to reform slavery, a step to the "positive good" stance of the next generation. 67 notes. P. J. Woehrmann

2158. Faust, Drew Gilpin. EVANGELICALISM AND THE MEANING OF THE PROSLAVERY ARGUMENT: THE REVEREND THORNTON STRINGFELLOW OF VIRGINIA. *Virginia Mag. of Hist. and Biog. 1977 85(1): 1-17.* Southern evangelicalism in the antebellum years produced a type of reform movement significantly different from the northern counterpart. The Reverend Thornton Stringfellow had many goals similar to those of northern reformers, especially temperance, improved health, and education. But Stringfellow, a Baptist of the Ketocton Association, was also a passionate defender of the peculiar institution and viewed the defense of slavery as an intimate part of a national reform effort. Based on Stringfellow's published works, newspapers, and secondary sources; 52 notes. R. F. Oaks

2159. Graffagnino, J. Kevin. VERMONT ATTITUDES TOWARD SLAVERY: THE NEED FOR A CLOSER LOOK. *Vermont Hist. 1977 45(1): 31-34.* Although Vermont's 1777 constitution provided against adult slavery and many other public actions establish Vermont's antislavery tradition, abolitionist Samuel J. May was mobbed five times in Vermont; Episcopal Bishop John Henry Hopkins wrote a long defense of slavery; and one-quarter of Vermont's 1860 vote for president was for proslavery candidates. Reprints an 1837 letter written by C. B. Fletcher, a Vermont Congressman's son, that expresses this proslavery minority view. 14 notes. T. D. S. Bassett

2160. Halbrooks, G. Thomas. FRANCIS WAYLAND: INFLUENTIAL MEDIATOR IN THE BAPTIST CONTROVERSY OVER SLAVERY. *Baptist Hist. and Heritage 1978 13(4): 21-35.* Francis Wayland (1796-1865) was President of Brown University, Vice-President of the Triennial Convention, and leading American Baptist spokesman for foreign missions. Describes his mediating efforts to prevent Baptists from dividing over the slavery issue. While he did view slavery as wrong, this Northerner urged that the slaveowner would be innocent if he held the slaves for their own good to prepare them for freedom. For over a decade his mediating position helped to prevent the division which finally occurred in 1845. Concludes by noting the numerous spin-offs in American Baptist history which can be attributed to him, not the least of which was Landmarkism. Based on writings of Wayland and the Manly Collection of Manuscripts at the University of Alabama; 33 notes. H. M. Parker, Jr.

2161. Hertzler, James R. SLAVERY IN THE YEARLY SERMONS BEFORE THE GEORGIA TRUSTEES. *Georgia Hist. Q. 1975 59(Supplement): 118-126.* Discusses the origins of slavery in Georgia, 1731-50, and Biblical justifications for it presented to the Georgia Corporation Trustees.

2162. Ireland, Owen S. GERMANS AGAINST ABOLITION: A MINORITY'S VIEW OF SLAVERY IN REVOLUTIONARY PENNSYLVANIA. *J. of Interdisciplinary Hist. 1973 3(4): 685-706.* Analyzes ethnoreligious alignments over the abolition of slavery in Pennsylvania in 1779-88. Suggests that Germans from Lutheran and Reformed backgrounds were the most consistent opponents of abolition. This cannot be explained satisfactorily on the basis of economic self-interest, commitment to property rights, or worries about Negro poverty. Religious experience, political ideology, and cultural attitudes contributed to the Germans' opposition. A deep fear of social change intensified the impact of these considerations. 4 tables, 46 notes. R. Howell

2163. Jentz, John. A NOTE ON GENOVESE'S ACCOUNT OF THE SLAVES' RELIGION. *Civil War Hist. 1977 23(2): 161-169.* Eugene D. Genovese's *Roll, Jordan, Roll* deserves critical attention, as in its argument that the slaves' religion was unconducive to millenarianism,

hence to a revolutionary political tradition. Millenarianism, as shown in popular black movements, probably did exist; there were not such exaggerated differences between black and white Baptist or Methodist Christianity. Genovese's own account makes the planter regime so pervasively powerful that revolutionary solutions would have been suicidal. His argument "distorts his provocative interpretation of the slaves' religion." Covers 17th century to 1865. Based on secondary sources; 28 notes.
R. E. Stack

2164. Mackinley, Peter W. THE NEW ENGLAND PURITAN ATTITUDE TOWARD BLACK SLAVERY. *Old-Time New England 1973 63(3): 81-88.* Discusses the inconsistency of colonial New England Puritan attitudes toward the slave as an economic unit and as a person "subject to rights established by Hebraic precedent." As the slave population increased, Puritan legislators acted to reduce the civil and personal rights of slaves. Antislavery sentiment nevertheless prevailed and attempts to resolve the inconsistency in the Puritan attitude toward slaves proved futile, as the abolition of slavery in New England began during the American Revolution. Covers 1641-1776. 44 notes.
R. N. Lokken

2165. Maclear, J. F. THOMAS SMYTH, FREDERICK DOUGLASS, AND THE BELFAST ANTISLAVERY CAMPAIGN. *South Carolina Hist. Mag. 1979 80(4): 286-297.* Recounts the controversy in Belfast, Ireland, in 1846 between Frederick Douglass, an ex-slave and an orator of the abolition movement, and Thomas Smyth, a Charleston (South Carolina) Presbyterian minister who supported slave-holding.

2166. Maddex, Jack P., Jr. PROSLAVERY MILLENNIALISM: SOCIAL ESCHATOLOGY IN ANTEBELLUM SOUTHERN CALVINISM. *Am. Q. 1979 31(1): 46-62.* Historians have tended to overlook that American progressive millenarianism contained proslavery as well as antislavery paths to God's society of the future. Although transdenominational, this proslavery millennial view can best be seen in the preachings and writings of Southern Presbyterian theologians. Slavery, however, was not a central issue in the millenarian perspective, North or South, and viewpoints on slavery were not consistent in either region. But, as few in the antebellum South had given credence to the possibility of freedom for the slaves, the destruction of the institution of slavery dealt a severe blow to southern millenarian ideas. Based on church and other theological publications; 100 notes.
D. G. Nielson

2167. Maddex, Jack P., Jr. "THE SOUTHERN APOSTASY" REVISITED: THE SIGNIFICANCE OF PROSLAVERY CHRISTIANITY. *Marxist Perspectives 1979 2(3): 132-141.* Examines studies of religion in the South published between 1844 and 1977 and concludes that the hypothesis that proslavery Christianity was a conscientious religious expression of class ideology appears to accord with the ecclesiastical history of the Old South better than does the longstanding hypothesis that it was a superficial defensive argument devised by thelogians who, at heart, shared the "American" libertarian norms.

2168. Mathews, Donald G. RELIGION AND SLAVERY: THE CASE OF THE AMERICAN SOUTH. Bolt, Christine and Drescher, Seymour, ed. *Anti-Slavery, Religion and Reform: Essays in Memory of Roger Anstey* (Folkestone, England: Dawson, 1980): 207-232. Reviews the conditions of worship and religious activities (especially of the evangelical churches—Methodist, Baptist, and Presbyterian) in the South from 1740 to 1860. Although there were some churches in which Negroes and whites worshipped together and there was considerable expression of antislavery sentiments by black and white Christians, the evangelical churches could not sustain a cohesive abolitionist movement in the South. 28 notes.

2169. Mathews, Donald G. RELIGION IN THE OLD SOUTH: SPECULATION ON METHODOLOGY. *South Atlantic Q 1974 73(1): 34-52.* Historical scholarship has ignored Southerners' views of the Bible. Evangelical Protestantism in the South tried to Christianize the slaves and reform slavery from within, which in turn altered Southern religion. 23 notes.
E. P. Stickney

2170. Miller, Randall M. BLACK CATHOLICS IN THE SLAVE SOUTH: SOME NEEDS AND OPPORTUNITIES FOR STUDY. *Records of the Am. Catholic Hist. Soc. of Philadelphia 1975 86(1-4): 93-106.* Catholic slaveholders as well as Catholic slaves await their historians. The why and how of the Church's function and its failure among blacks and whites of the Old South remain open questions which constitute the main agenda for research for serious students of Catholic Church history in the South. 36 notes.
J. M. McCarthy

2171. Miller, Randall M. "IT IS GOOD TO BE RELIGIOUS": A LOYAL SLAVE ON GOD, MASTERS, AND THE CIVIL WAR. *North Carolina Hist. Rev. 1977 54(1): 66-71.* Halifax County slave Washington Wills acted as body servant first to Methodists George W. Wills (1842-1864) and then to his brother Edward Wills (1846-ca 1900) during the Civil War. Two letters written by Washington Wills about his two soldier-charges demonstrate great respect and a paternalistic attitude towards them. He had strong religious convictions as well. Though opportunities for escape while on the road were available, Washington Wills apparently never took advantage of them. Introduction to letters based on Wills Family Papers, published primary sources, and secondary materials; illus., 20 notes.
T. L. Savitt

2172. Noon, Thomas R. EARLY BLACK LUTHERANS IN THE SOUTH (TO 1865). *Concordia Hist. Inst. Q. 1977 50(2): 50-53.* Prior to the abolition of slavery, Lutherans split on the issue according to regional lines. Southern Lutherans defended slavery because of the economy. In the South, the Lutheran Church involved itself with the blacks; slave owners were urged to provide baptism and religious instruction to their slaves. As a result of this procedure and the nature of slavery, blacks in the South before 1865 became Lutherans because their owners were such and not by choice. 15 notes.
W. T. Walker

2173. Robson, David W. "AN IMPORTANT QUESTION ANSWERED": WILLIAM GRAHAM'S DEFENSE OF SLAVERY IN POST-REVOLUTIONARY VIRGINIA. *William and Mary Q. 1980 37(4): 644-652.* As part of his course on human nature, the Reverend William Graham, rector of Liberty Hall Academy (now Washington and Lee University), gave an annual lecture on slavery to senior students, from the late 1780's to 1796. A brief biography of Graham is included. Contrary to his Pennsylvania upbringing and political principles, Graham avidly defended slavery. The main reason was fear of what would happen if the slaves were freed. To Graham, Christianity and slavery did not conflict. Cites Graham and other literature on slavery; reproduces the "Lecture 30th. An Important Question Answered." 17 notes.
H. M. Ward

2174. Stange, Douglas C. ABOLITIONISM AS MALEFICENCE: SOUTHERN UNITARIANS VERSUS "PURITAN FANATICISM": 1831-1860. *Harvard Lib. Bull. 1978 26(2): 146-171.* Southern Unitarians generally took a much more favorable view on slavery than their Northern coreligionists. By examining the careers of prominent Southern Unitarians, including Samuel Gilman of Charleston, Richard Arnold of Savannah, and Theodore Clapp of New Orleans, presents the full range of Southern Unitarian views on slavery and relations with Northern Unitarians. Notes.
W. H. Mulligan, Jr.

2175. Stein, Stephen J. GEORGE WHITEFIELD ON SLAVERY: SOME NEW EVIDENCE. *Church Hist. 1973 42(2): 243-256.* Attributes authorship of an anonymous 1743 epistle printed in London and entitled *A Letter to the Negroes Lately converted to Christ in America* to George Whitefield (1714-70). The attribution is supported by textual criticism and by the reference in the full title to Jonathan Bryan, a South Carolina plantation owner who knew Whitefield. Whitefield was apparently not the humanitarian many biographers would have one believe, because in his *Letter* he provided a theological defense for slavery. Based on Whitefield's open and private letters, his *Journal,* 19th-century biographies, and other secondary sources; 70 notes.
S. Kerens

2176. Taylor, Orville W. BAPTISTS AND SLAVERY IN ARKANSAS: RELATIONSHIPS AND ATTITUDES. *Arkansas Hist. Q. 1979 38(3): 199-226.* The relationships and attitudes of white Baptists and the slaves are discussed, including church membership, missionary activity, and acceptance and support of slavery. Brief backgrounds on other denominations in Arkansas are provided. Covers 1830-60. Primary and secondary sources; 89 notes.
G. R. Schroeder

2177. Tyner, Wayne C. CHARLES COLCOCK JONES: MISSION TO SLAVES. *J. of Presbyterian Hist. 1977 55(4): 363-380.* A missionary to the slaves, the Reverend Charles Colcock Jones (1804-63) was among those Southern Presbyterian clergymen who accepted slavery as a given in southern society. But while he accepted slavery, he believed that the Christian slave would be a better slave, and taught obedience to masters and contentment with the servile condition. At the same time he must not be classed with those who felt that the promise of heaven was sufficient to pacify slaves. He takes his place with those southern ministers who believed that Christianity should ameliorate the social condition of the slave. Based largely on reports and writings of Jones; illus., 63 notes.
H. M. Parker, Jr.

14. OCCULT

2178. Anderson-Green, Paula Hathaway. "THE LORD'S WORK": SOUTHERN FOLK BELIEF IN SIGNS, WARNINGS, AND DREAM-VISIONS. *Tennessee Folklore Soc. Bull. 1977 43(3): 113-127.* Examines Biblical roots for the belief in premonitions and visions, and the folklore surrounding such occurrences in the South, 20th century.

2179. Beck, Jane C. A TRADITIONAL WITCH OF THE TWENTIETH CENTURY. *New York Folklore Q. 1974 30(2): 101-116.* Study of Dolorez Amelia Gomez of Philadelphia, Pennsylvania, who practices traditional witchcraft. S

2180. Butler, Jon. MAGIC, ASTROLOGY, AND THE EARLY AMERICAN RELIGIOUS HERITAGE, 1600-1760. *Am. Hist. Rev. 1979 84(2): 317-346.* This article criticizes the church-orientation of American religious history and the narrow conceptualizations of religion used by American historians by describing the development and decline of occult religious practices in the colonies before the Revolution. It uses library lists, court records, almanacs, diaries, and other literary evidence to outline a widespread resort to occult practices by colonists from South Carolina to Puritan New England and suggests that these practices supplemented Christianity for some colonists and replaced it for others. The article traces their eighteenth-century decline to a combination of dissension among occult practitioners and supporters, withdrawal of elite support for occult beliefs, continued opposition from mainstream Christian groups, and government use of the law and courts to suppress occult crafts in ways that labeled them socially deviant. A

2181. Cavin, Susan. MISSING WOMEN: ON THE VOODOO TRAIL TO JAZZ. *J. of Jazz Studies 1975 3(1): 4-27.* Discusses the role of voodoo women and black magic cults in the evolution of jazz music in the 19th century, emphasizing the Negro culture of New Orleans.

2182. Cooley, Gilbert E. ROOT DOCTORS AND PSYCHICS IN THE REGION. *Indiana Folklore 1977 10(2): 191-200.* Folklore study of voodoo beliefs among immigrant blacks in Gary, East Chicago, and Hammond, Indiana, indicates that strong retention of beliefs among urban blacks serves as a filter for conflict, antagonism, and frustration encountered in modern city life, 1976.

2183. Costello, John R. CULTURAL VESTIGES AND CULTURAL BLENDS AMONG THE PENNSYLVANIA GERMANS. *New York Folklore 1977 3(1-4): 101-113.* Discusses "the development of three vestiges of German culture which have been maintained among the Pennsylvania Germans since colonial times": the charm, from the pre-Christian-to-*Macbeth* era; the sign of the pentagram, or witch's foot, from the medieval period, or earlier; and the literary character Till Eulenspiegel, from 1515 or earlier.

2184. Davis, Jacaleen. WITCHCRAFT AND SUPERSTITIONS OF TORRANCE COUNTY. *New Mexico Hist. Rev. 1979 54(1): 53-59.* Discusses Spanish legends and beliefs, many of which are present today, concerning witchcraft in Torrance County, New Mexico. The causes and cures of several diseases, including *empacho* or stomach congestion, *suspendido* or suspended colon, and *mal ojo* or the evil eye, are mentioned. The concepts of *curanderos* or healers, *bruja* or witch, and *arbulario* or witch doctor, are also discussed. The people of Torrance County are reluctant to discuss witchcraft, which shows that it still influences them. 26 notes. P. L. McLaughlin

2185. Demos, John. ENTERTAINING SATAN. *Am. Heritage 1978 29(5): 14-23.* Although Salem, Massachusetts, gets most of the attention, incidents of witchcraft occurred throughout colonial New England, particularly between 1630 and 1700. The typical witch was a middle-aged woman, but her victims or accusers are less easily categorized. Interest in witchcraft continues in some communities once afflicted by it. 6 illus. J. F. Paul

2186. Demos, John. JOHN GODFREY AND HIS NEIGHBORS: WITCHCRAFT AND THE SOCIAL WEB IN COLONIAL MASSACHUSETTS. *William and Mary Q. 1976 33(2): 242-265.* John Godfrey, unlike other men accused of witchcraft, was a bachelor. Details Godfrey's life from the time of his arrival in New England, about 1634, until his death in 1675. Godfrey was involved in numerous litigations. He brought suit for slander for being called a witch in 1659, resulting in a trial for witchcraft which ended in acquittal. Tried again in 1666, he was barely acquitted. Afterward he was convicted of various minor crimes. Lists six reasons in the sociocultural context for Godfrey's prosecution as a witch. The problems of Godfrey represent the collective life of the community versus the individual. Based on court and other local records. 64 notes. H. M. Ward

2187. Detweiler, Robert. SHIFTING PERSPECTIVES ON THE SALEM WITCHES. *Hist. Teacher 1975 8(4): 596-610.* Reviews the literature concerning witchcraft in Salem Village. Discusses historical interpretations of this phenomenon, and draws attention to studies in anthropology and psychology concerning witchcraft in other societies. Studies by anthropologists show fear of witchcraft to be a form of behavioral control especially in time of stress. Studies in psychology depict witchcraft as a form of revolt by young people against the restraints imposed by an older generation. Recent historians have built upon studies in both these disciplines. Based on primary and secondary sources; 57 notes. P. W. Kennedy

2188. Grattan-Guinness, I. THE UFO CONTROVERSY IN AMERICA. *Ann. of Sci. [Great Britain] 1976 33(2): 205-210.* Reviews David M. Jacobs' *The UFO Controversy in America* (Bloomington, Indiana and London: Indiana University Press, 1975), adding a psychic and occult perspective to the book's social and political approach.

2189. Hand, Wayland D. LOUIS C. JONES AND THE STUDY OF FOLK BELIEF, WITCHCRAFT, AND POPULAR MEDICINE IN AMERICA. *New York Folklore Q. 1975 1(1-2): 7-13.* Describes contributions to the study of American folklore by Louis C. Jones in articles in numerous folklore journals, notably the *New York Folklore Quarterly* he edited during 1945-49.

2190. Hand, Wayland D. and Tally, Frances M. SUPERSTITION, CUSTOM, AND RITUAL MAGIC: HARRY M. HYATT'S APPROACH TO THE STUDY OF FOLKLORE. *J. of the Folklore Inst. 1979 16(1-2): 28-43.* Harry Midddleton Hyatt (1896-1978) was drawn to folklore by an interest in primitive religion. Hyatt, who directed the Alma Egan Hyatt Foundation (created in 1932), enlisted the aid of his sisters (most importantly of Minnie Hyatt Small), to help him collect beliefs, superstitions, legends, customs, and folk medical practices from his native area. The result, *Folk-Lore from Adams County Illinois* (1935; revised 1965), eventually included more than 10,000 pieces of folklore and was one of the finest and most complete regional collections assembled in the United States. This project acquainted Hyatt with black folk materials and led to the hypothesis that miracle and magic were the crucial traits which separated belief and custom from other forms of folklore. These concerns were reflected in his important collection, *Hoodoo-Conjuration-Witchcraft-Rootwork* (5 vol., 1970-78), which was based on fieldwork throughout the South, 1936-40. The work significantly enlarged the body of American medical pharmacopeia and scatology. 24 notes. C. D. Geist

2191. Hansen, Chadwick. THE METAMORPHOSIS OF TITUBA, OR WHY AMERICAN INTELLECTUALS CAN'T TELL AN INDIAN WITCH FROM A NEGRO. *New England Q. 1974 47(1): 3-12.* Tituba, a Carib Indian woman, was the first confessor in the Salem witchcraft trials. She was a slave brought from the Barbados. The magic she had practiced was English, not Indian as suggested by an historian in 1831. Later historians preferred to consider her half-Indian, or half-Negro to Indian, or Negro to half-Indian and half-Negro. This racial metamorphosis began after the Civil War. The Tituba of Arthur Miller's *The Crucible* (1953) shows racism is still a part of present society. 27 notes. E. P. Stickney

2192. Hartman, Peter and McIntosh, Karyl. EVIL EYE BELIEFS COLLECTED IN UTICA, NEW YORK. *New York Folklore 1978 4(1-4): 60-69.* Discusses evil eye, or malocchio, folklore collected among Italian Americans in Utica, New York, and describes perceptions of the power of the evil eye.

2193. Hurt, Wesley R., Jr. WITCHCRAFT IN NEW MEXICO. *Palacio 1974 80(2): 12-20.* Using data collected from interviews with residents of Bernalillo and Manzana, New Mexico (both relatively remote and undeveloped Spanish and Indian towns), offers examples and explanations of typical *brujo* (witchcraft) stories and beliefs.

2194. Keeney, Steven H. WITCHCRAFT IN COLONIAL CONNECTICUT AND MASSACHUSETTS: AN ANNOTATED BIBLIOGRAPHY. *Bull. of Biblio. and Mag. Notes 1976 33(2): 61-72.*

2195. Layton, Monique. MAGICO-RELIGIOUS ELEMENTS IN THE TRADITIONAL BELIEFS OF MAILLARDVILLE, B. C. *BC Studies [Canada] 1975 (27): 50-61.* The magico-religious elements in the traditional beliefs of the people of Maillardville, British Columbia, are reviewed: remedies, weather, religious symbols, animals, gardening, games. Primary and secondary sources; 19 notes. W. L. Marr

2196. Leininger, Madeleine. WITCHCRAFT PRACTICES AND PSYCHOCULTURAL THERAPY WITH URBAN U.S. FAMILIES. *Human Organization 1973 32(1): 73-83.* The increased interest in witchcraft and the occult is an expression of social-cultural stress. Relates two case-work experiences to support the argument that the treatment of witchcraft victims in traditional mental health clinics may be detrimental. Presents a theoretical model to guide in providing understanding psychocultural therapy in treating witchcraft victims. Abstracts in English, French, and Spanish. Fig., 3 notes, biblio. E. S. Johnson

2197. Leininger, Madeleine. WITCHCRAFT PRACTICES AND PSYCHOCULTURAL THERAPY WITH URBAN U.S. FAMILIES. *Human Organization 1973 32(2): 73-83.* The increased interest in witchcraft and the occult is an expression of social-cultural stress. Two cases support the view that the treatment of witchcraft victims in traditional mental health clinics may be detrimental. Presents a theoretical model to guide psychocultural therapy in treating witchcraft victims. Fig., 3 notes. E. S. Johnson

2198. Lightfoot, William E. WITCHCRAFT MEMORATS FROM EASTERN KENTUCKY. *Indiana Folklore 1978 11(1): 47-62.* Discusses eight categories of folktales pertaining to witchcraft; most literature is intended to serve as a warning against evil.

2199. Long, Eleanor R. APHRODISIACS, CHARMS, AND PHILTRES. *Western Folklore 1973 32(3): 153-163.* Considers the use and history of "love magic." Distinguishes among aphrodisiacs, charms, and philtres, and gives the various ingredients and rituals for their preparation and use. Based on primary and secondary sources; glossary, 37 notes. S. L. Myres

2200. Midelfort, H. C. Erik. THE RENAISSANCE OF WITCHCRAFT RESEARCH. *J. of the Hist. of the Behavioral Sci. 1977 13(3): 294-297.* Reviews five books on witchcraft: Paul Boyer's and Stephen Nissenbaum's *Salem Possessed: The Social Origins of Witchcraft* (Cambridge, Mass.: Harvard U. Pr., 1974); J. J. Cobben's *Jan Wier, Devils, Witches and Magic* (Philadelphia: Wornnace, 1976), translated by Sal A. Prins; Norman Colin's *Europe's Inner Demons: An Enquiry Inspired by the Great Witch-Hunt* (New York: Basic Books, 1975); Richard Kieckhefer's *European Witch Trials: Their Foundations in Popular and Learned Culture, 1300-1500* (Berkeley and Los Angeles: U. of California Pr., 1976); E. William Monter's *Witchcraft In France and Switzerland: The Borderlands during the Reformation* (Ithaca: Cornell U. Pr., 1976). 16 notes. D. K. Pickens

2201. Milspaw, Yvonne J. WITCHCRAFT IN APPALACHIA: PROTECTION FOR THE POOR. *Indiana Folklore 1978 11(1): 71-86.* Folktales collected in West Virginia indicate that persons who claimed to be witches were usually elderly, eccentric women who functioned as manipulators of public fear in order to gain material goods necessary for survival and to command community respect.

2202. Musick, Ruth Ann. WITCHCRAFT AND THE DEVIL IN WEST VIRGINIA. *Appalachian J. 1974 1(4): 271-276.* Tales of the evil eye and the devil told to the author, 1950-67. S

2203. Pearl, Jonathan L. WITCHCRAFT IN NEW FRANCE IN THE SEVENTEENTH CENTURY: THE SOCIAL ASPECT. *Hist. Reflections [Canada] 1977 4(2): 191-205.* Examines the fear of witchcraft in France and New France during the 17th century, particularly how Quebec dealt with witchcraft, providing examples of cases of witchcraft judged in court.

2204. Simmons, Marc. WITCHCRAFT AND BLACK MAGIC: AN INTERPRETIVE VIEW. *Palacio 1974 80(2): 5-11.* Presents historical, psychological, and social views of witchcraft, tracing its presence in Hispanic and Indian cultures, 16th-20th centuries.

2205. Snow, Loudell F. MAIL ORDER MAGIC: THE COMMERCIAL EXPLOITATION OF FOLK BELIEF. *J. of the Folklore Inst. 1979 16(1-2): 44-74.* In the United States, belief in voodoo is most common among ethnic groups whose members perceive themselves as socially, politically, or economically powerless. Though such beliefs may provide individuals with the sense that they control their own destinies, faith in voodoo magic also provides a fertile ground for economic exploitation of folk beliefs. Throughout the United States, but especially among urban blacks, unscrupulous mail order dealers market incense, black cat bones, amulets, herbal teas, exotic roots, and voodoo kits and dolls to individuals who ought to put their limited funds to better use. This fake folklore, often advertised openly as spurious or alleged, is sought by those who hope to protect themselves against evil magic, to alter their economic plight (particularly through mixing gambling and magic), or to influence lovers. Covers 1970-79. Fig., 41 notes, biblio. C. D. Geist

2206. Studer, Gerald C. POWWOWING: FOLK MEDICINE OR WHITE MAGIC? *Pennsylvania Mennonite Heritage 1980 3(3): 17-23.* Examines evidence of modern powwow practice in Pennsylvania, which means "to charm," "to conjure," or "sympathy healing," and was first used by New England Puritans in the mid-17th century from a word of Algonquin Indian origin; and discusses the origin and use of powwowing among the Amish and Mennonites in Pennsylvania.

2207. Tierney, Gail D. BOTANY AND WITCHCRAFT. *Palacio 1974 80(2): 44-50.* Discusses southwestern botanic specimens used to expedite or to cure witchcraft, and plants employed to induce hallucinations and trances, 17th-20th centuries.

2208. Truzzi, Marcello. ASTROLOGY AS POPULAR CULTURE. *J. of Popular Culture 1974 8(4): 906-911.* Covers 1920-75.

2209. Winkler, Louis. PENNSYLVANIA GERMAN ASTRONOMY AND ASTROLOGY III: COMETS AND METEORS. *Pennsylvania Folklife 1972 22(1): 35-41.* Discusses the reaction of Pennsylvania Germans toward the observation of several comets in the 18th century and the early 19th century, specifically their fear that comets precede disaster.

2210. Wrona, Christine. WITCHCRAFT IN EARLY SPRINGFIELD: THE PARSONS CASE. *Hist. J. of Western Massachusetts 1977 6(1): 61-64.* Account of an episode of witchcraft accusation during 1650-55 in Springfield, Massachusetts. Illus., notes. W. H. Mulligan, Jr.

2211. Wrzeszcz, Maciej. "EGZORCYSTA" CZYLI SZATAN W SŁUŻBIE KOMERCJALNEGO KINA [*The Exorcist* or Satan in the service of commercial movies]. *Życie i Myśl [Poland] 1975 25(1): 71-75.* William Friedkin's film *The Exorcist*, about a child possessed by the devil and transformed into a repulsive monster, is in poor taste. Attempting to scare in an atmosphere of sadism and horror, it stands on the borderline of parody. The film was coolly received by the French Catholic press. In an interview with *La vie catholique* Father Constantin Leroy, an exorcist from Nantes, pronounced contemporary cases of the "possessed" as hysteria, hallucination, and collective suggestion calling for spiritual and psychiatric help. The Satan in *The Exorcist* is grotesque but unbelievable because he is too apparent. Yet after Dracula and Frankenstein the film is a sociopsychological masterpiece reflecting the pessimism, skepticism, and disillusionment of the Western world as a result of economic affluence, technological advances, and an ideology lacking in human goals. The irrational tendencies, nostalgia, and attempts to understand the complicated mechanism of the real world lead to an escape in a world of occultism and magic. M. A. J. Swiecicka

2212. Wuthnow, Robert. ASTROLOGY AND MARGINALITY. *J. for the Sci. Study of Religion 1976 15(2): 157-168.* Discusses sociological aspects of interest in astrology and horoscopes as a possible substitute for religion in the San Francisco Bay Area of California in the 1970's, including the influence of the counter culture.

2213. —. THE WITCH OF CLARKSTOWN. *York State Tradition 1974 28(2): 28-30.* Discusses Jane Kanniff, a Rockland County woman suspected of witchcraft in 1816. S

2214. —. WITCHCRAFT ALONG THE RIO GRANDE. *Palacio 1974 80(2): 21-37.* Collection of short pieces from personal accounts, newspaper articles, and private papers, 1880's-1930's, relating encounters with witchcraft in the Southwest among Navajo Indians, Pueblo Indians, and Hispanic Americans; 19c-1930's.

15. REVIVALS

2215. Arnold, Bob. BILLY GRAHAM, SUPERSTAR. *Southern Exposure 1976 4(3): 76-82.* Billy Graham, once a shy, southern boy, became a world-renowned evangelical leader, preaching a gospel of middle class morality and political conservatism, 1940's-70's.

2216. Ashmore, Harry S. THE GREAT RE-AWAKENING. *Virginia Q. Rev. 1975 51(2): 161-185.* Cites the "general agreement that the quality of American life has undergone a profound change" and that confusion besets our secular institutions. See parallels of attitudes with the 18th-century Great Awakening and warns of too easy acceptance of "a new man unencumbered by societal and genetic baggage." Perhaps now is the time for programs of political reform. O. H. Zabel

2217. Baker, James T. THE BATTLE OF ELIZABETH CITY: CHRIST AND ANTICHRIST IN NORTH CAROLINA. *North Carolina Hist. Rev. 1977 54(4): 393-408.* Discusses the battle in 1924 between Elizabeth City newspaper editor William O. Saunders (1886-1940) and Kentucky evangelist Mordecai F. Ham (1877-1961). Ham, well-known for his argumentative style, was derided by Saunders during the opening weeks of a huge revival in Elizabeth City. The controversy changed from Ham's accusations against Chicago Jewish philanthropist Julius Rosenwald to Saunders's modernism vs. Ham's fundamentalism. Based on Saunders' editorials, Ham's published prayers, newspapers, biographies, and reminiscences; 9 illus., 49 notes. T. L. Savitt

2218. Berenbaum, May. "THE GREATEST SHOW THAT EVER CAME TO TOWN": AN ACCOUNT OF THE BILLY SUNDAY CRUSADE IN BUFFALO, NEW YORK, JANUARY 27-MARCH 25, 1917. *Niagara Frontier 1975 22(3): 54-67.*

2219. Berner, Robert L. GRACE AND WORKS IN AMERICA: THE ROLE OF JONATHAN EDWARDS. *Southern Q. 1977 15(2): 125-134.* Examines the Puritan covenants of Grace and Works and their subsequent rejection after the Great Awakening because they were incompatible with American social and political values. Theologian Jonathan Edwards personifies the intellectual struggle. Concludes that contemporary society could benefit from reexamining his attitudes. 7 notes.
R. W. Dubay

2220. Bozeman, Theodore Dwight. NEW (WHIG) LIGHT ON THE AMERICAN GREAT AWAKENINGS. *Rev. in Am. Hist. 1979 7(3): 313-318.* Review article prompted by William G. McLoughlin's *Revivals, Awakenings, and Reform: An Essay on Religion and Social Change in America, 1607-1977* (Chicago: U. of Chicago Pr., 1978); applauds the author's theory of revitalization, but criticizes it for its liberal prejudices and Whig interpretation of history.

2221. Bumsted, J. M. EMOTION IN COLONIAL AMERICA: SOME RELATIONS OF CONVERSION EXPERIENCE IN FREETOWN, MASSACHUSETTS, 1749-1770. *New England Q. 1976 49(1): 97-107.* The Great Awakening's emphasis on spontaneous feeling meant that few conversion relations were recorded for the lower classes and that our understanding of its emotional content has been based on the writings of articulate elites. The Freetown Congregational Church is an exception to this rule, and the nine relations recorded there between 1749 and 1770 are printed here. In common they demonstrate the great guilt felt by their authors before conversion and the emotional release brought by that experience. Based on church records in the Fall River Historical Society; 16 notes. J. C. Bradford

2222. Carroll, Kenneth L. A LOOK AT THE "QUAKER REVIVAL OF 1756." *Quaker Hist. 1976 65(2): 63-80.* Friends decided to withdraw from Pennsylvania government in 1756 rather than compromise their peace views. Their religious revival enabled them to survive the American Revolution and contribute answers to the issues of slavery, Indian rights, religious freedom, and relations with other churches. Quakers must have been influenced by the Great Awakening and the Wesleyan movement. Many meetings in the 20 years before 1756 won new members and sharpened their discipline. Quaker ministers traveling across the Atlantic in both directions brought exhortations, publications and good examples. Based mainly on printed and MS. minutes, epistles sent and received, rules of church order and journals of traveling Friends; biblio.
T. D. S. Bassett

2223. Carwardine, Richard. METHODISM, THE NEW DISSENT AND AMERICAN REVIVALISM. *J. of the United Reformed Church Hist. Soc. [Great Britain] 1978 2(2): 46-54.* The American Second Great Awakening attracted widespread interest among English Calvinist Dissenters from the late 1820's to the 1840's. Explains the rise and fall of that interest in terms of the earlier impact of English Methodism on Calvinist Dissenters. Both Baptists and the "New Dissenters" among the Independents admired elements of Methodism but were hostile to Arminianism and fearful of the enthusiasm and irregularities of Methodist revivals. The American revivalists appeared to offer a theologically and socially acceptable alternative model, and for more than a decade their influence was large. However, by the 1840's the revival had failed among Baptists and Congregationalists, who became increasingly critical of the American system. 48 notes. S. C. Pearson, Jr.

2224. Cherry, Conrad. PROMOTING THE CAUSE AND TESTING THE SPIRITS: JONATHAN EDWARDS ON REVIVALS OF RELIGION—A REVIEW ARTICLE. *J. of Presbyterian Hist. 1973 51(3): 327-337.* Review-essay prompted by C. C. Goen, ed., *The Great Awakening* (New Haven and London: Yale U. Press, 1972; volume four of *The Works of Jonathan Edwards).* S

2225. Clements, William M. THE PHYSICAL LAYOUT OF THE METHODIST CAMP MEETING. *Pioneer Am. 1973 5(1): 9-15.* Indicates that early 19th-century Methodist circuit riders realized that their method of evangelism was reaching few people. In seeking a method whereby they might intensify their religious activities, the camp meeting was originated. It has become identified with Methodism in America. Camp meetings provided an opportunity for people to gather out-of-doors in some "picturesque setting" for a "spiritual vacation." The physical layouts of early camp meeting sites are extensively detailed. Based on field work and secondary sources; illus., 5 photos, 4 notes.
C. R. Gunter, Jr.

2226. Coalter, Milton J., Jr. THE RADICAL PIETISM OF COUNT NICHOLAS ZINZENDORF AS A CONSERVATIVE INFLUENCE ON THE AWAKENER, GILBERT TENNENT. *Church Hist. 1980 49(1): 35-46.* In the middle American colonies, the impact of the related but variant English, Dutch, and German theologies was well represented by Gilbert Tennent, the unquestioned leader of the middle colony Awakening forces. Before 1741 "Tennent sought a rejuvenation of lay spiritual life by emphasizing heartfelt conversion and pious action over theological formulae and ecclesiastical polity." Later, his "fervor for the Awakening cooled and a new concern for reconciliation among his divided Presbyterians took its place. One identifiable catalyst in this remarkable shift was the theological controversy which resulted from a meeting Tennent had with Count Nicholas Zinzendorf [of the Moravian Church] in December 1741." M. D. Dibert

2227. Cole, Nathan and Crawford, Michael J., ed. THE SPIRITUAL TRAVELS OF NATHAN COLE. *William and Mary Q. 1976 33(1): 89-126.* Prints a manuscript, "Spiritual Travels," by Nathan Cole (1711-83), a Connecticut carpenter and farmer. The manuscript covers Cole's spiritual development during 1740-65 and, more broadly, illustrates a side of the Great Awakening. Cole, who became a member of a "Separatist" congregation in 1747, and was fascinated with the preaching of George Whitefield, describes his conversion and subsequent growth as a born-anew Christian. The editor provides descriptive annotation, citing Cole manuscripts at the Connecticut Historical Society, scripture and other sources. 80 notes. H. M. Ward

2228. Cott, Nancy F. YOUNG WOMEN IN THE SECOND GREAT AWAKENING IN NEW ENGLAND. *Feminist Studies 1975 3(1-2): 15-29.* The "second great awakening" in New England Protestant churches occurred between the late 1790's and 1830's. Converts were mainly young unmarried women between the ages of 12 and 20. These young women were textile industry workers, whose industry had been drastically changed by the introduction of spinning and weaving machinery which ended household manufacture and drove young female workers into factories. Employment outside the home led to growing insecurity for young women leaving traditional domestic roles; these women often left the cities of their birth. Conversion helped to provide stability, giving the convert a place in a community and a new family to replace the one left behind. Based on primary and secondary sources; 48 notes. S. R. Herstein

2229. Cox, Richard J. STEPHEN BORDLEY, GEORGE WHITEFIELD, AND THE GREAT AWAKENING IN MARYLAND. *Hist. Mag. of the Protestant Episcopal Church 1977 46(3): 297-307.* Historians have commented little on the Great Awakening in Maryland. Presents a three-page letter by lawyer Stephen Bordley (1710-64) discussing George Whitefield's preaching in Annapolis in December 1739. The letter reveals the responses of upper-class Anglicans in Maryland to the Great Awakening. Bordley faulted Whitefield's theology, but praised his excellent delivery. Based on primary and secondary sources; 33 notes. H. M. Parker, Jr.

2230. Daniels, Bruce E. EMERGING URBANISM AND INCREASING SOCIAL STRATIFICATION IN THE ERA OF THE AMERICAN REVOLUTION. *West Georgia Coll. Studies in the Social Sci. 1976 15: 15-30.* Traces the transition from ruralism to urbanism in British North America, 1740's-70's due to the effects of the Great Awakening and the American Revolution, which challenged the traditional hierarchical view of society.

2231. Dick, Everett N. ADVENT CAMP MEETINGS OF THE 1840'S. *Adventist Heritage 1977 4(2): 3-10.* Describes Adventists' frontier camp meetings of the 1840's in the northeastern states.

2232. Douglas, Walter B. T. GEORGE WHITEFIELD: THE MAN AND HIS MISSION. *Methodist Hist. 1977 16(1): 46-53.* Discusses George Whitefield, 1714-77, an English preacher who had great impact on the evangelical movement in England and America during the 18th century. 22 notes. H. L. Calkin

2233. Durden, Susan. A STUDY OF THE FIRST EVANGELICAL MAGAZINES, 1740-1748. *J. of Ecclesiastical Hist. [Great Britain] 1976 27(3): 255-275.* Considers the purpose and content of three denominational periodicals put out in Great Britain and America during the religious revival of the 1740's. The *Christian History,* published in Massachusetts, reported the activities of George Whitefield. The periodicals reflected the views of Calvinistic Methodists. 110 notes. P. H. Hardacre

2234. Farmerie, Samuel A. and Farmerie, Janice C. THE LETTERS OF DAVID RUSSEL HASWELL. *Western Pennsylvania Hist. Mag. 1977 60(1): 37-54.* A brief biographical sketch of David Russel Haswell, who migrated from Vermont to Pennsylvania in 1808, precedes annotated copies of letters he wrote to his father and brother in Bennington, Vermont, during 1808-31, which tell about his farm and life in Pennsylvania, reveal the evangelical revivals of the period, and relate matters of family interest.

2235. Foster, Mary C. THEOLOGICAL DEBATE IN A REVIVAL SETTING: HAMPSHIRE COUNTY IN THE GREAT AWAKENING. *Fides et Hist. 1974 6(2): 31-47.* Using Hampshire County, Massachusetts, as a case study, discusses the theological debate over justification as it arose in the 1730's and 1740's, the period of the first "awakening." Finds a significant amount of rationalistic Arminianism prior to the first movements of the "awakening." Those espousing Arminianism opposed the revivals, and the basis of their opposition lay in alternative conceptions of the process of justification. They in turn were attacked by Jonathan Edwards. The resulting controversies laid the foundations for the later split in New England society over Unitarianism. Based on manuscript and printed material, as well as secondary sources; 60 notes. R. Butchart

2236. Foster, Mary C. THEOLOGICAL DEBATE IN A REVIVAL SETTING: HAMPSHIRE COUNTY IN THE GREAT AWAKENING. *Fides et Hist. 1974 6(2): 31-47.* Using Hampshire County, Massachusetts, as a case study, discusses the theological debate over justification as it arose in the 1730's and 1740's, the period of the first "awakening." Finds a significant amount of rationalistic Arminianism prior to the first movements of the "awakening." Those espousing Arminianism opposed the revivals, and the basis of their opposition lay in alternative conceptions of the process of justification. They in turn were attacked by Jonathan Edwards. The resulting controversies laid the foundations for the later split in New England society over Unitarianism. Based on manuscript and printed material, as well as secondary sources; 60 notes. R. Butchart

2237. Frantz, John B. THE AWAKENING OF RELIGION AMONG THE GERMAN SETTLERS IN THE MIDDLE COLONIES. *William and Mary Q. 1976 33(2): 266-288.* Discusses German immigration and various German settlements in connection with the German Awakening, which began among German Baptists, particularly the Dunkards. Also evaluates the movement among the Reformed and the Lutheran Churches. Comments on clergymen and evangelists. Moravian missionaries were especially active in the German Awakening, and aided an interdenominationalism. Sectarians, ecumenists, and confessionalists all had pietism in common. German settlers responded enthusiastically to evangelism. As congregations increased, greater structural machinery resulted. The German Awakening was similar to that of other groups. Based on literature of the Great Awakening, church records, and German-language contemporary works. 81 notes. H. M. Ward

2238. Greenberg, Michael. REVIVAL, REFORM, REVOLUTION: SAMUEL DAVIES & THE GREAT AWAKENING IN VIRGINIA. *Marxist Perspectives 1980 3(2): 102-119.* Reviews the role of Samuel Davies, Presbyterian minister, in the Great Awakening in Virginia during the 1740's-50's and the impact of his activities on individual perceptions of religion and Southern abolitionists.

2239. Guelzo, Allen C. GEORGE WHITEFIELD COMES TO NEW ENGLAND. *New-England Galaxy 1978 20(1): 12-21.* Reverend George Whitefield (1714-70), an ordained priest of the Church of England, arrived in Rhode Island from England in 1740 which signified the beginning of the Great Awakening in New England and catapulted the American colonies into the revivalist spirit.

2240. Gura, Philip F. SOWING FOR THE HARVEST: WILLIAM WILLIAMS AND THE GREAT AWAKENING. *J. of Presbyterian Hist. 1978 56(4): 326-341.* William Williams (1655-1741), uncle of Jonathan Edwards and neighbor of Solomon Stoddard, pastored the church in Hatfield, Massachusetts, from 1686 until his death. While historians of the Great Awakening and of developing Presbyterianism in the Connecticut River Valley know less about Williams than about Edwards or Stoddard, urges that there is enough concerning Williams's career to mark him as significant. Williams's conception of the ministry and his emphasis on the doctrine of the Great Salvation complemented Stoddard's treatises on the nature and necessity of the conversion experience. Williams was not a mere imitation of the more famous Stoddard, but a man of considerable accomplishment and influence in his own right. He believed that the millenium would come in the Valley and that he would have had a part in its consummation. Based on Williams's writings; 32 notes. H. M. Parker, Jr.

2241. Hatch, Nathan O. NEW LIGHTS AND THE REVOLUTION IN RURAL NEW ENGLAND. *Rev. in Am. Hist. 1980 8(3): 323-328.* Review essay of Christopher M. Jedrey's *The World of John Cleaveland: Family and Community in Eighteenth-Century New England* (New York: W. W. Norton, 1979), discussing daily life in Chebacco, Massachusetts, and John Cleaveland's activities as a minister of a New Light congregation. Discusses the role of the Great Awakening in the creation of the ideology of the Revolutionary War.

2242. Jeffries, John W. THE SEPARATION IN THE CANTERBURY CONGREGATIONAL CHURCH: RELIGION, FAMILY, AND POLITICS IN A CONNECTICUT TOWN. *New England Q. 1979 52(4): 522-549.* Discusses the Great Awakening and resulting church schisms. In 1743, conflict over the choice of a new minister caused an irreparable division in Canterbury. The split involved more than religious beliefs, but was not along economic, age, sex, or geographical lines. It was between a group of old, important families who dominated local politics and another group of families with as much wealth but with less power in government. Thus "the religious phenomena of revivalism and separatism had important social, political, and institutional contents." Families tied to the political and religious establishment and, thus, with a stake in its continued dominance, came to oppose separation. Based on local records; 78 notes. J. C. Bradford

2243. Johnson, James E. CHARLES G. FINNEY AND THE GREAT "WESTERN" REVIVALS. *Fides et Hist. 1974 6(2): 13-30.* Narrative of the early life (1820-40) and revival preaching of Charles Grandison Finney prior to his emergence as a revivalist of national fame. Finney began his ministry in upstate New York, the "burned-over district," capitalizing on a colloquial style and a pragmatic, individualist theology that marked a break with traditional Calvinism. Based on primary and secondary sources; 82 notes. R. Butchart

2244. Loveland, Anne C. PRESBYTERIANS AND REVIVALISM IN THE OLD SOUTH. *J. of Presbyterian Hist. 1979 57(1): 36-49.* Throughout the antebellum decades Southern Presbyterians utilized the revival as an important source for ministerial candidates and as a way of encouraging support of benevolent programs. The revival was also considered a necessary safeguard of republicanism. Revivals were credited with improving the morality of the communities in which they were conducted. But above all, they were viewed as the chief means of adding members to the Presbyterian Church. Thus revivalism was an important and integral part of Presbyterian life in the Old South. Based on religious newspapers and publications and secondary sources; illus., 50 notes. H. M. Parker, Jr.

2245. Morrison, Howard Alexander. THE FINNEY TAKEOVER OF THE SECOND GREAT AWAKENING DURING THE ONEIDA REVIVALS OF 1825-1827. *New York Hist. 1978 59(1): 27-53.* Analyzes the men and events involved in Charles Grandison Finney's rise to leadership of the Presbyterian-Congregational revival campaign and the second Great Awakening. Finney was not the radical invader from the wild frontier depicted in a number of studies. He was the product of the Presbyterian-Congregational establishment traditions in Connecticut and Oneida County, New York, and his revival style, although it appeared extravagant, was consistent with the revival methodology of the respectable, liberalized orthodoxy. What concerned his rival revivalists was his success in attracting a loyal following among evangelists, clergy, and leadership of New York churches. 5 illus., 63 notes. R. N. Lokken

2246. Muller, H. N., III and Duffy, John J. JEDIDIAH BURCHARD AND VERMONT'S 'NEW MEASURE' REVIVALS: SOCIAL ADJUSTMENT AND THE QUEST FOR UNITY. *Vermont Hist. 1978 46(1): 5-20.* Jedediah Burchard, a traveling actor and circus performer, brought the anxious seat and protracted meetings, techniques used by C. G. Finney in New York and Ohio, to a dozen Vermont villages during 1835-36. His sensationalism and vernacular speech polarized Protestants. A symptom of social unrest, the short-lived Burchard revival was replaced by other excitements, beginning with sympathy for the Canadian Rebellion of 1837-38. 7 illus., 43 notes. T. D. S. Bassett

2247. Nobles, Gregory H. IN THE WAKE OF THE AWAKENING: THE POLITICS OF PURITY IN GRANVILLE, 1754-1776. *Hist. J. of Western Massachusetts 1980 3(1): 48-62.* Examines the tension between the goals of unity and purity in the Congregational Church of Granville, Massachusetts. The congregation shifted from Edwardsean to Stoddardean and back to Edwardsean practices of church admission. The concern for purity led to schisms. Rather than looking with confidence to the future during the prerevolutionary decades, the congregation tried to restore elements of the past. Based on church records, local histories, and secondary sources; 30 notes. S

2248. Noll, Mark A. MOSES MATHER (OLD CALVINIST) AND THE EVOLUTION OF EDWARDSEANISM. *Church Hist. 1980 49(3): 273-285.* Moses Mather, an Old Light Calvinist, played an important role in the evolution of 19th-century Calvinism. Although Mather opposed the 18th-century Great Awakening, his thinking had much in common with ideas advanced during the Second Great Awakening. The author traces the line of descent from New England Puritanism to American Protestantism through the writings of Mather, especially during the first Awakening. M. D. Dibert

2249. Nordbeck, Elizabeth C. ALMOST AWAKENED: THE GREAT REVIVAL IN NEW HAMPSHIRE AND MAINE, 1727-1748. *Hist. New Hampshire 1980 35(1): 23-58.* New England's first revival occurred in 1727, a result of the region's second recorded earthquake. An outbreak of throat distemper in 1735 precipitated another religious awakening. These and other factors helped make northern New Englanders psychologically receptive to the revival of the 1740's, triggered by the preaching of George Whitefield, who arrived in New Hampshire in 1740. The experience of Maine and New Hampshire, however, suggests that lasting ecclesiastical innovations were not automatic. In northern New England the main effect was not a dramatic religious event, but a subtle mood which affected later events. 2 tables, 87 notes. D. F. Chard

2250. Onuf, Peter S. NEW LIGHTS IN NEW LONDON: A GROUP PORTRAIT OF THE SEPARATISTS. *William and Mary Q. 1980 37(4): 627-643.* The New Lights of the Congregational Church were addicted to conflict. The revival in Connecticut occurred among widespread separation within the churches; the semicommercial towns were most susceptible. Two revivals in New London, 1741 and 1742, attracted primarily the young. Ninety-nine separatists formed the Shepherd's Tent. Many of the members of the separatist church had not previously joined an established church. Family ties were the cohesive factors among the separatists. The separatists came from all sections of New London and represented a variety of occupations. The status and wealth of the separatists are examined. Based on church and court records; 3 tables, 30 notes. H. M. Ward

2251. Opie, John. FINNEY'S FAILURE OF NERVE: THE UNTIMELY DEMISE OF EVANGELICAL THEOLOGY. *J. of Presbyterian Hist. 1973 51(2): 155-173.* Charles Grandison Finney's (1792-1875) effect on evangelical theology. S

2252. Parker, Charles A. THE CAMP MEETING ON THE FRONTIER AND THE METHODIST RELIGIOUS RESORT IN THE EAST: BEFORE 1900. *Methodist Hist. 1980 18(3): 179-192.* The first camp meeting with revival services was probably in Kentucky in 1800. At the insistence of Bishop Francis Asbury, the Methodists developed camp meetings as devices for revival and church expansion. By the 1830's and continuing through the 19th century, camp grounds with permanent facilities began to replace the rough frontier revival with a more conservative form of camp meeting and Methodist revival resort. 46 notes. H. L. Calkin

2253. Parker, Russell D. THE PHILOSOPHY OF CHARLES G. FINNEY: HIGHER LAW AND REVIVALISM. *Ohio Hist. 1973 82(3-4): 142-153.* Finney's (1792-1875) contributions to the "higher law" doctrine have been overshadowed by his evangelical endeavors. He favored revivalism over agitation, but would become active politically, as his 1839 resolutions to the Ohio Antislavery Society show. Based on secondary material; illus., 59 notes. S. S. Sprague

2254. Schlabach, Theron F. MENNONITES, REVIVALISM, MODERNITY: 1683-1850. *Church Hist. 1979 48(4): 398-415.* Although the Second Great Awakening of 1780 to 1830 produced the organizing process that fostered ingredients central to theories of modernization, Mennonites did not accept revivalism until about 1880-1920. From early in their history, Mennonite beliefs had implied modernity in the larger social order and accommodated modernizing systems, particularly of an economic and political nature. Their traditionalism was strongest in religion and the group's inner life, but eventually revivalism was able to penetrate even there. Revivalism was for American Mennonites a potent agent of modernization. 51 notes. M. D. Dibert

2255. Schlabach, Theron F. REVEILLE FON *DIE STILLEN IM LANDE!* A STIR AMONG MENNONITES IN THE LATE NINETEENTH CENTURY. *Mennonite Q. Rev. 1977 51(3): 213-226.* In the period between 1860-90, the North American Mennonites and Amish underwent a notable religious revival. This movement has been stereotyped as an "awakening" in Mennonite history. Examines this stereotype by offering alternative explanations and descriptions. It was more a quickening than an awakening; an acculturation than a revival (many shifted to English as their language); and a move from Anabaptist avoidance of personal pride to an individual being allowed to be somebody within the church and society in general. 48 notes. E. E. Eminhizer

2256. Schmitt, Dale J. PREPARATION FOR THE GREAT AWAKENING IN CONNECTICUT. *Religion in Life 1978 47(4): 430-440.* Studies the religious environment in the 18th century before the Great Awakening of the 1740's.

2257. Schmotter, James W. THE IRONY OF CLERICAL PROFESSIONALISM: NEW ENGLAND'S CONGREGATIONAL MINISTERS AND THE GREAT AWAKENING. *Am. Q. 1979 31(2): 148-168.* In the face of lessening prestige and status, a consensus was reached among New England clergy between 1690 and 1740 concerning the need to professionalize the ministry. This was based on an insistence on formal educational training and expertise. During the Great Awakening, however, the consensus unravelled as theological differences, which had been downplayed earlier, were afforded renewed public attention. Based on the writings of New England clergy; fig., 69 notes. D. G. Nielson

2258. Schwartz, Hillel. ADOLESCENCE AND REVIVALS IN ANTE-BELLUM BOSTON. *J. of Religious Hist. [Australia] 1974 8(2): 144-158.* Psychologists and psychiatrists have linked religious revivals to adolescence. In the early 19th century Boston witnessed the impact of four revivalists on its adolescent society: Methodist John Newland Maffett, "Presbygationalist" Charles Grandison Finney, Baptist Jacob Knapp, and Congregationalist Edward Norris Kirk. These men were fully aware that their revivals were part of youthful phenomenon. Based on printed sources; 63 notes. W. T. Walker

2259. Shipps, Howard Fenimore. THE REVIVAL OF 1858 IN MID-AMERICA. *Methodist Hist. 1978 16(3): 128-151.* The Revival of 1858 was brought about by worldliness, a materialistic attitude which threatened to engulf the church. The revival, originating with the laity, seemed to have little if any limitation. It extended to all racial, social, national, and ethnic groups, and to many denominations and cultural divisions. It emphasized the leadership of the Holy Spirit, the prominence of prayer and its ecumenical nature, and the important role of laymen. The revival resulted in an extensive renewal of the church. 43 notes. H. L. Calkin

2260. Shute, Michael N. A LITTLE GREAT AWAKENING: AN EPISODE IN THE AMERICAN ENLIGHTENMENT. *J. of the Hist. of Ideas 1976 37(4): 589-602.* The sermons inspired by the diphtheria epidemic which afflicted New England 1735-40 were "a small chapter in the response of American Calvinism to the growth of Enlightenment ideas." Ministers countered rationalist claims for human autonomy by interpreting the epidemic as a sign that God remained sovereign. The epidemic sermons employed the Lockean psychology, as did Jonathan Edwards' more famous productions, neglecting the older Puritan logic in order to reassert the fundamentals of Puritan belief. Based on published primary and secondary sources; 61 notes. D. B. Marti

2261. Sizer, Sandra. POLITICS AND APOLITICAL RELIGION: THE GREAT URBAN REVIVALS OF THE LATE NINETEENTH CENTURY. *Church Hist. 1979 48(1): 81-98.* The Northern urban revivals of 1857-58 and 1875-77 may be suggestive of the place of the revivalist tradition in American culture. Techniques and ideologies formed there were to be appropriated again by such men as Billy Sunday and Billy Graham. Mass urban revivals were designed to create a community of feeling. Under this strategy of purification from sin for the community, individuals, purified by conversion, would detach themselves from the national tendency to aggressivenss and lust for money. This strategy shows the relation to politics and social conditions of the revivalist tradition, the apolitical political religion of America. M. Dibert

2262. Stansfield, Charles. PITMAN GROVE: A CAMP MEETING AS URBAN NUCLEUS. *Pioneer Am. 1975 7(1): 36-44.* Analyzes Pitman Grove, New Jersey, a community which traces its origin to a combination of social and religious motives. Unlike most mid-19th-century settlements it evolved into a sizeable town, but currently does not appear to be making the necessary urban adjustments. Primary and secondary sources and extensive field work; 3 photos, table, fig., 20 notes. C. R. Gunter, Jr.

2263. Stenerson, Douglas C. AN ANGLICAN CRITIQUE OF THE EARLY PHASE OF THE GREAT AWAKENING IN NEW ENGLAND: A LETTER BY TIMOTHY CUTLER. *William and Mary Q. 1973 30(3): 475-488.* Reprints a letter of 28 May 1739 from Cutler (1684-1765), minister of Christ Church, Boston, to Edmund Gibson (1669-1748), Bishop of London, giving an account of the Great Awakening. He was not wholly unfavorable, but, as a conservative Anglican, he criticized the excesses of emotionalism and was apprehensive of its effects. Cutler examined the roles of Solomon Stoddard (1643-1729) and Jonathan Edwards (1703-58). The preface describes Cutler as a staunch opponent of the Congregational establishment in New England. New England sermon literature cited in annotation; 29 notes. H. M. Ward

2264. Stewart, Gordon. CHARISMA AND INTEGRATION: AN 18TH CENTURY NORTH AMERICAN CASE. *Comparative Studies in Soc. and Hist. 1974 16(2): 138-149.* Considers "the case of Henry Alline, a popular religious revivalist in Nova Scotia during the years of the American Revolutionary War." S

2265. Strout, Cushing. FATHERS AND SONS: NOTES ON "NEW LIGHT" AND "NEW LEFT" YOUNG PEOPLE AS A HISTORICAL COMPARISON. *Psychohistory Rev. 1977-78 6(2-3): 25-31.* Compares the colonial religious revivals of the 1740's and campus radicalism of the 1960's. The "New Light" Calvinist revivals appealed especially to youths in the 15-25 age group, were reactions to the laxity of "family government," and represented a challenge to authority rechanneled by the emotional conversion process. Resemblances are found in the generational conflict and the goal of remaking the university in the 1960's student movement. Both movements rejected compromise and liberal toleration. Analysis of generational conflict supplements, but does not substitute for, other modes of historical investigation. Secondary works; 22 notes. J. B. Street

2266. Sutter, Sem C. MENNONITES AND THE PENNSYLVANIA GERMAN REVIVAL. *Mennonite Q. Rev. 1976 50(1): 37-57.* The view of most church historians is that Mennonites were nearly unaffected by the revivals of the 18th and 19th centuries. Discusses active Mennonite revivalists and their influence on the movement. Those discussed include Martin Boehm (1725-1812) and Christian Newcomer (1750-1830). Groups other than Mennonite, but important to them, are the Baptists in Virginia, the United Brethren in Christ, and the Evangelical Association. Also discusses Mennonite opposition to revivalism. 116 notes. E. E. Eminhizer

2267. Sweet, Douglas H. CHURCH VITALITY AND THE AMERICAN REVOLUTION: HISTORIOGRAPHICAL CONSENSUS AND THOUGHTS TOWARDS A NEW PERSPECTIVE. *Church Hist. 1976 45(3): 341-357.* Although the period from 1770-1800 did not display a consistent pattern of religious dynamism throughout America, there is sufficient evidence to suggest that forces mobilized in the Great Awakening were still alive and led to the Second Great Awakening. Further examination of lay sources may reveal that the evangelism and revivalistic elements of 19th century Protestantism was the resurgence of a continuing process begun in the Great Awakening, rather than a reaction to some supposed ebb tide of religious vitality during the American Revolution. 65 notes. M. D. Dibert

2268. Sweet, Leonard I. THE VIEW OF MAN INHERENT IN NEW MEASURE REVIVALISM. *Church Hist. 1976 45(2): 206-221.* Charles G. Finney often is credited as being the religious spokesman of Jacksonian democracy. Many see the optimistic view of man supposedly inherent in Finney's revivalism as the equivalent of the Jacksonian faith in the worth and dignity of the common man. But historians' reexamination of Finney's thought and activity shows it to be conservative, status conscious and pessimistic about human nature. Finney's new measure revivalism reflected his own image, which was derived from an equality of sin and not from any inherent social equality or democratic ideology. 100 notes. M. D. Dibert

2269. Titon, Jeff Todd. SOME RECENT PENTECOSTAL REVIVALS: A REPORT IN WORDS AND PHOTOGRAPHS. *Georgia Rev. 1978 32(3): 579-605.* Lists some of the most prominent Pentecostal beliefs and describes a typical revival service in the rapidly growing Pentecostal movement. The services described are amply supplemented by verbatim transcriptions of tapes of sermons, prophecy in tongues, and interpretations of that prophecy. 19 illus. M. B. Lucas

2270. Turner, Ronny E. and Edgley, Charles K. "THE DEVIL MADE ME DO IT!" POPULAR CULTURE AND RELIGIOUS VOCABULARIES OF MOTIVE. *J. of Popular Culture 1974 8(1): 28-34.* Members of the religious group A. A. Allen Revival Incorporated of Miracle Valley, Arizona, frequently use the expressions "God did it through me" and "The Devil made me do it" in rationalizing their conduct to others. They attribute their financial, physical, and spiritual activities to the directives of God or Satan. Individuals are thus relieved of much of the guilt when they suffer misfortunes or engage in unrighteous acts since they are not directly responsible. Covers the 1970's. Primary and secondary sources; 16 notes. E. S. Shapiro

2271. Weddle, David L. THE LAW AND THE REVIVAL: A "NEW DIVINITY" FOR THE SETTLEMENTS. *Church Hist. 1978 47(2): 196-214.* Both the revival and the institution of legal order grew from the desire for a just social order. Convinced that man's happiness and the glory of God could be served by a renewed national community formed by respect for law, revivalists joined forces with the legal profession. Since lawyers were dependent on the people's submission to regulations, whether religious or civil, the partnership provided dual benefits and promoted civilization of frontier regions. Charles Grandison Finney, both a lawyer and revivalist, personified this movement and worked out a theology of legal order that sanctified human initiative. In time, the legal profession found their interests for an ordered society could best be served by political means and the partnership dissolved. 62 notes. M. D. Dibert

2272. Williams, John R. THE STRANGE CASE OF DR. FRANKLIN AND MR. WHITEFIELD. *Pennsylvania Mag. of Hist. and Biog. 1978 102(4): 399-421.* Benjamin Franklin, who was not an archetypical deist, and George Whitefield, who was no mere ranter, were sincere friends. Covers 1739-64. Based on published sources and secondary works; 93 notes. T. H. Wendel

2273. Willingham, William F. THE CONVERSION EXPERIENCE DURING THE GREAT AWAKENING IN WINDHAM, CONNECTICUT. *Connecticut Hist. 1980 (21): 34-61.* A demographic analysis of religious conversions in Windham, Connecticut, during the Great Awakening, focusing on Congregational Church membership and religious activity and feeling in 1721, 1735-37, and 1741-43, in the context of social change at the community level.

2274. Willingham, William F. RELIGIOUS CONVERSION IN THE SECOND SOCIETY OF WINDHAM, CONNECTICUT, 1723-43: A CASE STUDY. *Societas 1976 6(2): 109-119.* Finds in the pattern of conversion during the Great Awakening in the Second Society of Windham, Connecticut, confirmation of Philip Greven's thesis that there is a connection in the early to middle 18th century "between the changing character of the family, brought about by geographic mobility, and religious experience." Based upon records and genealogical materials in the Connecticut State Library, other primary and secondary materials; 5 tables, 32 notes. J. D. Hunley

2275. Wimberley, Ronald C.; Hood, Thomas C.; Lipsey, C. M.; Clelland, Donald; and Hay, Marguerite. CONVERSION IN A BILLY GRAHAM CRUSADE: SPONTANEOUS EVENT OR RITUAL PERFORMANCE? *Sociol. Q. 1975 16(2): 162-170.* Literature on religious conversion contains turnabout and ritualistic explanations. This paper examines the nature of the contemporary religious revival or crusade and finds evidence that revival conversions are ritualistic, integrative events. Crusaders are overwhelmingly church members and frequent church attenders. The Graham organization carefully structures the conversion process through local community organization, counselors, screening questions, literature, and church referrals. The crusade also emphasizes the integration of dependent-aged youth. Covers 1968-75. J

16. SABBATARIANISM

2276. Davis, Thomas M. EDWARD TAYLOR TO SAMUEL SEWALL NOVEMBER 17, 1704. *Early Am. Literature 1978 13(1): 107-109.* Though the friendship between Edward Taylor of Westfield and Samuel Sewall of Boston extended for about 60 years, and an extensive correspondence must have existed, only two of Taylor's letters have been located. Reprints the second letter (17 November 1704), a response to an earlier Sewall letter in which Taylor expressed his concern over Jeremiah Drummer's publication of *De Jure Judaeorum Sabbati* (1703). Both Sewall and Taylor objected to Drummer's assertion that the fourth Commandment was exclusively ceremonial and not perpetually binding, and that the observance of the Sabbath rested on positive law rather than on moral or natural law. Primary sources; 5 notes. J. N. Friedel

2277. Hunnicutt, Benjamin Kline. THE JEWISH SABBATH MOVEMENT IN THE EARLY TWENTIETH CENTURY. *Am. Jewish Hist. 1979 69(2): 196-225.* American Jewish leaders long sought means to uphold the Jewish Sabbath in spite of the six-day work week and the national observance of Sunday as a day of rest. Some Reform rabbis advocated a shift of the Jewish Sabbath to Sunday. In the 20th century, however, the Central Conference of American Rabbis, and to a far greater extent the Orthodox Jewish Sabbath Alliance led by Rabbi Bernard Drachman (1861-1945), worked to strengthen the Saturday Sabbath. First they advocated a staggered work week and an end to Sunday blue laws. Later, and more successfully, they joined forces with the American labor movement and advocated a five-day work week—an idea which involved Jewish leaders in broader debates concerning the nature of progress, work, and leisure in the modern world. Drachman's "The Jewish Sabbath Question" (1915) is printed as an appendix. Based on contemporary newspaper accounts, magazine and yearbook articles, court cases, and other primary sources; 34 notes. J. D. Sarna

2278. Jable, J. Thomas. PENNSYLVANIA'S EARLY BLUE LAWS: A QUAKER EXPERIMENT IN THE SUPPRESSION OF SPORTS AND AMUSEMENTS, 1682-1740. *J. of Sport Hist. 1974 1(2): 107-122.* When the Pennsylvania assembly in 1682 adopted William Penn's code, The Body of Laws, they accepted the Quaker principles and especially the strict Sabbath. The Friends expected all citizens to observe their moral standards, although they did not expect to impose their religion on others. When a large number of Anglicans and Presbyterians settled in the colony, however, problems arose from the more liberal view of the Sabbath held by the newcomers. Describes attempts to enforce the Blue Laws. Between 1715-40, the control by the Quakers diminished, as Pennsylvania changed due to increased immigration and a shifting population. As that occurred, amusements and sports developed on a relatively large basis. 4 illus., 63 notes. M. Kaufman

2279. Javersak, David T. "WHEELING'S SUNDAY SENSATION: THE 1889 WHEELING NAILERS." *Upper Ohio Valley Hist. Rev. 1979 8(2): 2-6.* Controversy surrounded the Sunday baseball games of the Wheeling (West Virginia) Nailers in 1889, because a city ordinance forbade all but absolutely necessary work on Sundays.

2280. McArthur, Ben. THE 1893 CHICAGO WORLD'S FAIR: AN EARLY TEST FOR ADVENTIST RELIGIOUS LIBERTY. *Adventist Heritage 1975 2(2): 11-22.* Spearheaded by Alonzo Trevier Jones, Seventh-Day Adventists protested the closing of the Chicago World's Fair on Sundays and succeeded in repealing a practice which they viewed as threatening the separation of church and state and the first step in the establishment of a national (Protestant) religion.

2281. Meen, Sharon P. HOLY DAY OR HOLIDAY? THE GIDDY TROLLEY AND THE CANADIAN SUNDAY, 1890-1914. *Urban Hist. Rev. [Canada] 1980 9(1): 49-63.* The arrival of the electric street car in Canadian cities coincided with changing attitudes toward Sunday. The question of whether or not street cars might run on Sunday prompted a public debate concerning the proper use of the Sabbath—should it be a Holy Day or a holiday? This article examines the nature of the controversy over the Sunday street car and the struggle between the Sunday car and its sabbatarian opponents. Sabbatarians challenged the Sunday car in a variety of ways but found it a most vexing and elusive target. By 1914, the Sunday car had triumphed, running merrily in cities from coast to coast. Its success was due to support it received from the public, governments and the courts. J

2282. Riess, Steven. PROFESSIONAL SUNDAY BASEBALL: A STUDY IN SOCIAL REFORM 1892-1934. *Maryland Historian 1973 4(2): 95-108.* Examines the pattern of social changes in Chicago, New York, and Atlanta which converted Sunday to a recreation day. As America became more urban, bureaucratized, and industrialized, religious conservatism yielded. Baseball became a working-class entertainment and an inculcator of American middle class values. Periodical and secondary sources; 55 notes. G. O. Gagnon

2283. Roth, Arnold. SUNDAY "BLUE LAWS" AND THE CALIFORNIA STATE SUPREME COURT. *Southern California Q. 1973 55(1): 43-47.* Examines the history of Sunday closing laws in California. The first law, passed in 1855, reflected a desire for respectability in the gold rush era and prohibited noisy amusements on the Christian Sabbath. In 1858 a more important law closed stores and stopped sales, but when the case was appealed to the State Supreme Court, a two to one vote declared the law unconstitutional. Another law was enacted in 1861; this time the court upheld it. In most cases the law was ignored, but in 1882 a serious drive to enforce it created a political issue, and it was repealed in 1883. Primary and secondary sources; 24 notes. A. Hoffman

2284. Schrodt, Barbara. SABBATARIANISM AND SPORT IN CANADIAN SOCIETY. *J. of Sport Hist. 1977 4(1): 22-33.* Parliament passed the Lord's Day Act (1906), but stated that a provincial act could allow specific activities prohibited by the federal law. In areas where Sunday professional sports were well established, the activities continued. The Lord's Day Alliance tried to force a strict enforcement of the act, repressing amateur and recreational as well as professional athletics. After World War I, attitudes began to change, Sunday became a day of leisure as well as church worship, and pressures grew for sport on Sunday. The automobile made society more mobile, and Sunday became the ideal time for family leisure activities away from home. Also, increased affluence encouraged the growth of popular Sunday sports such as golf. As time passed, the religious restraints were weakened, and sports gained in influence. Now, the Lord's Day Act no longer prevents Canadians from enjoying sports on Sundays, and Canadian sport is healthier and stronger than ever. 38 notes. M. Kaufman

2285. Vincent, Charles. LOUISIANA'S BLACK LEGISLATORS AND THEIR EFFORTS TO PASS A BLUE LAW DURING RECONSTRUCTION. *J. of Black Studies 1976 7(1): 47-56.* Black legislators in Louisiana during Reconstruction repeatedly tried to have the state's legislature enact a "blue law," but almost yearly resolutions during 1867-75 that would have prohibited (variously) boxing, gambling, horse racing, liquor sales, amusements, and even business transactions on Sunday did not succeed in winning approval. These efforts, which were most vigorous in 1874, drew strong support among the minority of black legislators but little among their white counterparts. Based on primary and secondary sources; notes, biblio. D. C. Neal

2286. Yoder, Paton. TAVERN REGULATION IN VIRGINIA: RATIONALE AND REALITY. *Virginia Mag. of Hist. and Biog. 1979 87(3): 259-278.* Discusses colonial legislation and law enforcement regarding the tavern, an important social institution. Initially rate regulation and licensing were the only concern of government, but during the 18th century laws defined tippling houses, restricted gambling, and regulated credit and Sabbath observance. Liquor by the drink sellers were required with some consistency to accommodate travellers. Makes some comparison with like practices in England, New England, and Virginia of the 19th century. 82 notes. P. J. Woehrmann

2287. Young, David M. WHEN ADVENTISTS BECAME SABBATH-KEEPERS. *Adventist Heritage 1975 2(2): 5-10.* Chronicles Seventh-Day Adventism's tradition of keeping the Sabbath on Saturday, 1841-44, and the influence of Rachel Oakes, Frederick Wheeler, and T. M. Preble of Washington, New Hampshire, in establishing the custom.

17. SCIENCE

2288. Altschuler, Glenn C. FROM RELIGION TO ETHICS: ANDREW D. WHITE AND THE DILEMMA OF A CHRISTIAN RATIONALIST. *Church Hist. 1978 47(3): 308-324.* In 1896 Andrew Dickson White published *A History of the Warfare of Science with Theology in Christendom.* White told his readers that a belief not based on evidence was not only illogical but immoral. Nineteenth-century demands for reason caused religion to give way to the sort of humanitarian ethics advocated by White and others. 54 notes. M. D. Dibert

2289. Andrews, William D. THE LITERATURE OF THE 1727 NEW ENGLAND EARTHQUAKE. *Early Am. Literature 1973 7(3): 281-294.* On 29 October 1727 around 10:40 p.m., New England was shaken by the most severe earthquake it had ever experienced. For the Puritan both common sense and theology demanded that it be analyzed and explained, and within a few months the Boston press produced 26 publications. Both natural philosophy and theology were employed to explain the earthquake in a manner consistent with current naturalistic and religious definitions of reality. The earthquake literature is an exposition of the dynamics of early 18th-century culture. American ministers were forced to repair and adjust their views to make sense of the physical event without seriously decreasing the explanatory capacity of their beliefs about God and nature. Based on primary and secondary sources; 34 notes, biblio. D. P. Wharton

2290. Anthony, Dick; Robbins, Thomas; Doucas, Madeline; and Curtis, Thomas E. PATIENTS AND PILGRIMS: CHANGING ATTITUDES TOWARD PSYCHOTHERAPY OF CONVERTS TO EASTERN MYSTICISM. *Am. Behavioral Scientist 1977 20(6): 861-886.* Examines changing attitudes toward psychotherapy among converts to Eastern religions, following the evolution through preconversion, conversion, and postconversion (often marked by a subscription to participation in psychotherapy).

2291. Baker, Alonzo L. THE SAN FRANCISCO EVOLUTION DEBATES: JUNE 13-14, 1925. *Adventist Heritage 1975 2(2): 23-32.* Debate between Seventh-Day Adventists Alonzo L. Baker and Francis D. Nichol and Science League of America president Maynard Shipley held in San Francisco, California, during 1925 resulted in a judge's decision criticizing evolutionary theory but supported its instruction in the public schools.

2292. Barbour, Ian G. SCIENCE, RELIGION, AND THE COUNTERCULTURE. *Zygon: J. of Religion and Sci. 1975 10(4): 380-397.* The 1960's-70's counter culture's values call for a more humanistic direction to technology.

2293. Bauman, Mark K. JOHN T. SCOPES, LEOPOLD AND LOEB, AND BISHOP WARREN A. CANDLER. *Methodist Hist. 1978 16(2): 92-100.* Warren A. Candler (1857-1941), bishop of the Methodist Episcopal Church, South, offered a conservative analysis of the Scopes trial. Candler opposed liberals and rallied conservatives. He was opposed to the idea of evolution and believed the Leopold-Loeb trial brought the evils of the liberal modernist persuasion into bold relief. Covers 1921-41. Based on Candler's writings; 21 notes. H. L. Calkin

2294. Bedau, Hugo Adam. COMPLEMENTARITY AND THE RELATION BETWEEN SCIENCE AND RELIGION. *Zygon 1974 9(3): 202-224.*

2295. Benton, Robert M. THE JOHN WINTHROPS AND DEVELOPING SCIENTIFIC THOUGHT IN NEW ENGLAND. *Early Am. Literature 1973 7(3): 272-280.* The first-hand observations and second-hand reports in the papers of John Winthrop, Sr. (1588-1649), show him to have had scientific interests. He was not fully a part of the growing scientific movement of the 17th century, for he did not seem interested in testing or experimentation. John Winthrop, Jr. (1606-96), however, made more significant scientific contributions than any 17th-century New England colonist. In him one sees the beginning of the evolution of scientific thought in New England. Without rejecting the religion of his father, he moved away from the restrictions of Puritanism into the light of free scientific inquiry. A later John Winthrop, the great-grandnephew of John Winthrop, Jr., achieved scientific distinction surpassing that of any in his illustrious family. Second Hollis professor of mathematics and natural philosophy at Harvard in 1738 when he was only 24, Professor John Winthrop (1714-79) represented a culmination of that development in scientific thinking which had begun with John Winthrop, Jr. Based on primary and secondary sources; 9 notes. D. P. Wharton

2296. Bideaux, Michel. LE DISCOURS DE L'ORDRE ET LE SÉISME DE 1663 [The order report and earthquake of 1663]. *Rev. de l'U. d'Ottawa [Canada] 1978 48(1-2): 62-83.* Analyzes the *Relation de 1663,* a Jesuit report in which there is a description of the theological and psychological implications of an earthquake which struck Quebec on 5 February 1663. Text of a paper presented at the conference Travel Writings Related to New France, at York University, Toronto, 20-22 February 1979. Primary sources; 99 notes. G. J. Rossi

2297. Birchler, Allen. THE ANTI-EVOLUTIONARY BELIEFS OF WILLIAM JENNINGS BRYAN. *Nebraska Hist. 1973 54(4): 545-559.* Presbyterian Bryan was the foremost spokesman of anti-Darwin forces during the last four years of his life (1921-25). While Bryan's basic beliefs remained unchanged, he was not primarily interested in theological or scientific arguments. His purpose was to prevent the teaching of evolution and to preserve the moral force of Christianity. R. Lowitt

2298. Bitton, Davis and Bunker, Gary L. PHRENOLOGY AMONG THE MORMONS. *Dialogue 1974 9(1): 43-61.* Individual Mormons showed much personal interest in phrenology as late as 1940. The two movements shared a belief in human perfectibility, concern for proper health, certain racial assumptions, and general public condemnation. Because Mormonism had its own theological and religious appeal, however, phrenology never became more than a curiosity to Mormons. The church remained ambivalent but finally outlawed it in 1940. Based on letters, newspapers, and published histories; 5 illus., 64 notes. D. L. Rowe

2299. Blight, James G. SOLOMON STODDARD'S *SAFETY OF APPEARING* AND THE DISSOLUTION OF THE PURITAN FACULTY PSYCHOLOGY. *J. of the Hist. of the Behavioral Sci. 1974 10(2): 238-250.* Discusses the writings of Solomon Stoddard in the context of the dissolution of the faculty psychology of the New England Puritans. S

2300. Bodemer, Charles W. NATURAL RELIGION AND GENERATION THEORY IN COLONIAL AMERICA. *Clio Medica [Netherlands] 1976 11(4): 233-244.* Cotton Mather (1663-1728), a theologian, popularized the scientific discoveries of New England. In *Christian Philosopher* (1721) he expressed the view that nature is the product of divine wisdom. James Logan (1674-1751), an Irish Quaker from Philadelphia, shared Mather's view and made significant contributions in botany. 32 notes. A. J. Papalas

2301. Bozeman, Theodore Dwight. JOSEPH LECONTE: ORGANIC SCIENCE AND "SOCIOLOGY FOR THE SOUTH." *J. of Southern Hist. 1973 39(4): 565-582.* Summarizes the career of Georgia-born Joseph LeConte (1823-1901), and his involvement with organic science. Working within a theological framework, LeConte involved himself in the study of geology, biology, and chemistry as factors proving "the unbreachable dignity of human life," developing a science of sociology which connected with all other sciences and gave a scientific explanation for the turmoil of American society and politics. LeConte felt that proper education in sociology could help to solve the national problems and preserve the Union by proving the potency of "the organic ties that bind." Based on LeConte's autobiography and works, and on secondary sources; 62 notes. N. J. Street

2302. Brodwin, Stanley. EMERSON'S VERSION OF PLOTINUS: THE FLIGHT TO BEAUTY. *J. of the Hist. of Ideas 1974 35(3): 465-483.* Examines Ralph Waldo Emerson's understanding of Plotinus, and the "philosophical despair" resulting from his conclusion that the "One or Divine Beauty" might be weakly grasped by imagination but eluded human understanding. Emerson endeavored to recall science from the "narrow and dead classification" which he thought it had embraced by the 1850's, to a "new enthusiasm in the study of beauty." By 1860, he had worked through "essentially Plotinian ideas of Beauty" in "his own eclectic but original manner," effecting a "harmony of Nature, Science, and Beauty." Based on published primary and secondary sources; 28 notes. D. B. Marti

2303. Bunker, Gary L. and Bitton, Davis. MESMERISM AND MORMONISM. *Brigham Young U. Studies 1975 15(2): 146-170.* Investigates the literature which tried to explain Mormonism in terms of animal magnetism, mesmerism, and their more respectable counterpart, hypnotism. Animal magnetism, which taught that the human body possessed magnetic properties which could be transferred from one person to another, had become an important quasiscientific cult in the early 19th century. Because the unique activities of the Mormons were revealed at about the same time, inevitably writers sought to connect them in order to explain the widespread popular interest in Mormonism.
M. S. Legan

2304. Callahan, Nancy. THE BARTRAMS: PLANTMEN EXTRAORDINAIRE. *Daughters of the Am. Revolution Mag. 1980 114(5): 638-643.* Discusses John Bartram (1699-1777), a Pennsylvania farmer, his son William Bartram (1739-1823), a Philadelphia Quaker, and their interest in botany and natural history; John is known as the father of American botany, and William, the first naturalist-artist in the colonies, wrote extensively about his travels and discoveries.

2305. Campbell, Roy. GERALD B. WINROD VS. THE "EDUCATED DEVILS." *Midwest Q. 1975 16(2): 187-198.* Gerald B. Winrod's 1925 book *Christ Within* (Wichita: Winrod Publication Center, 1925) was the essence of his thought that no man could be a teacher of God and a teacher of evolution. He sought to remove evolution from the schools and blamed evolutionary thought as the cause of almost every evil existing in the world. His ideas were further expressed in *The Red Horse* and *The Defender*, a regular publication he controlled. Based on primary and secondary sources. H. S. Marks

2306. Carter, Paul A. SCIENCE AND THE DEATH OF GOD. *Am. Scholar 1973 42(3): 406-421.* Recalls and describes historical precedents during the past three centuries for the "God is dead" controversy of the 1960's. Throughout modern history the conflict between science and religion has centered on the question of the existence of a personal God. Much of the debate of the 1960's has precedents, especially in the late 19th century and in the 1920's. The vagaries of the history of the "God is dead" debate should indicate that the debate of the 1960's is unlikely to be the last word on the subject. J. B. Street

2307. Cooper, William. JOSEPH MOORE: QUAKER EVOLUTIONIST. *Indiana Mag. of Hist. 1976 72(2): 123-137.* Provides insights into various interpretations of the theory of evolution, in particular, that of Joseph Moore, a Quaker who first introduced the subject for study at Earlham College, Richmond in 1861.

2308. Creelan, Paul G. WATSONIAN BEHAVIORISM AND THE CALVINIST CONSCIENCE. *J. of the Hist. of the Behavioral Sci. 1974 10(1): 95-118.* Examines the relationship between John Broadus Watson's elaboration of a behavioristic science of psychology and his personal conflicts with a fundamentalist Calvinist religious training. Covers 1890-1919. S

2309. Derr, Thomas Sieger. RELIGION'S RESPONSIBILITY FOR THE ECOLOGICAL CRISIS: AN ARGUMENT RUN AMOK. *Worldview 1975 18(1): 39-45.* Examines the implications of medieval historian Lynn White, Jr.'s essay, "The Historical Roots of Our Ecologic Crisis," *Science* (March 1967), which postulates that "the Western Christian tradition is indirectly responsible for the rise of science and technology."

2310. Ellis, William E. THE FUNDAMENTALIST-MODERATE SCHISM OVER EVOLUTION IN THE 1920'S. *Register of the Kentucky Hist. Soc. 1976 74(2): 112-123.* The evolution issue divided moderates and fundamentalists in the four major Protestant denominations in Kentucky during the 1920's. Southern Baptists, Disciples of Christ, Methodists, and Presbyterians all faced internal divisions over this issue. The religious schisms helped block the campaign for antievolution legislation in the state. Primary and secondary sources; 47 notes.
J. F. Paul

2311. Erdt, Terrence. THE CALVINIST PSYCHOLOGY OF THE HEART AND THE "SENSE" OF JONATHAN EDWARDS. *Early Am. Literature 1978 13(2): 165-180.* Many studies of Jonathan Edwards assume that the notion of the sense of heart is derived solely from Locke; these attributes are more rightly due to Augustine and Calvin. In both the Augustinian and Calvinist tradition, the sense of heart is roughly equated with the faculty of the will. Calvinist psychology emphasizes the will in order to preserve the biblical heart concept as the basis of faith. The subsequent Puritan view of the heart was examined in the writings of Edwards and other Puritan writers. Primary and secondary sources; 40 notes. J. N. Friedel

2312. Frank, Robert G., Jr. THE JOHN WARD DIARIES: MIRROR OF SEVENTEENTH-CENTURY SCIENCE AND MEDICINE. *J. of the Hist. of Medicine and Allied Sci. 1974 29(2): 147-179.* The diaries of John Ward, physician and theologian, which are now in the Folger Shakespeare Library, Washington, D.C., describe the life and practice of the cleric-physician of 17th-century England and America. Ward was unique, because he participated in the "Oxford coterie of the 1650s and 1660s whose members founded the Royal Society and remade chemistry, anatomy, and physiology." Using the entries in the diaries, traces Ward's career, from Oxford don to his work as minister and physician. 78 notes.
M. Kaufman

2313. Fulcher, J. Rodney. PURITANS AND THE PASSIONS: THE FACULTY PSYCHOLOGY IN AMERICAN PURITANISM. *J. of the Hist. of the Behavioral Sciences 1973 9(2): 123-139.* Discusses the theme of faculty psychology in American Puritanism in the 17th century, emphasizing the role of the "passions" (emotions) and the intellect.

2314. Gibbons, Russell W. CHIROPRACTIC IN AMERICA: THE HISTORICAL CONFLICTS OF CULTISM AND SCIENCE. *J. of Popular Culture 1977 10(4): 720-731.* Discusses the difficulty which chiropractic medicine has had in gaining recognition as a valid science and medical pursuit, focusing on popular attitudes which have considered it quackery, religious fanaticism, and scientific cultism, 1850's-1970's.

2315. Graham, Louis. THE SCIENTIFIC PIETY OF JOHN WINTHROP OF HARVARD. *New England Q. 1973 46(1): 112-118.* The view that John Winthrop (1714-79) made a radical departure from the Puritan concept of the study of science is a distorted one. In stressing his belief in the continuing providence of God, Winthrop "is far closer to traditional Puritanism than to deism." Edward Wigglesworth, Professor of Divinity at Harvard, wrote in 1777 of Winthrop's admirable scientific piety. This view, it is evident from Winthrop's writings, is a fair one. He was also compared to Boyle and Newton on scientific grounds. 18 notes.
E. P. Stickney

2316. Gray, Ina Turner. MONKEY TRIAL—KANSAS STYLE. *Methodist Hist. 1976 14(4): 235-251.* William Goldsmith (1888-1955) was a professor of biology at Southwestern College, Winfield, Kansas, from 1920-30. While there he published a book on "evolution or Christianity." Soon he and Robert W. Hawkins, professor of religion, were accused by a committee from a local Methodist Episcopal church of teaching evolution and destroying the religious beliefs of the students. After a debate before a Methodist layman's conference, the question was resolved in favor of the college in 1925. 96 notes. H. L. Calkin

2317. Halliburton, R., Jr. THE ANTI-EVOLUTION MOVEMENT IN THE PUBLIC SCHOOLS OF THE UNITED STATES. *Malaysian J. of Educ. [Malaysia] 1975 12(1/2): 31-37.* Fundamentalism is the backbone of the antievolution movement. William Jennings Bryan played a significant role in attempts to enact and enforce "monkey laws." Describes various attempts to proscribe the teaching of Darwinism during 1920-73. Secondary sources; 38 notes. S. A. Farmerie

2318. Hogan, Edward R. ORSON PRATT AS MATHEMATICIAN. *Utah Hist. Q. 1973 41(1): 59-68.* Orson Pratt, one of the original 12 Apostles of the Church of Jesus Christ of Latter-day Saints, demonstrated the same zeal in his study of mathematics and science as in the establishment of his religion in Utah. Evaluates Pratt's achievement in mathematics in the light of his training and circumstances. Concludes that Pratt does not reveal the high level of originality that has sometimes been attributed to him. Covers 1836-70. 3 photos, 20 notes. R. V. Ritter

2319. Hollinger, David A. WHAT IS DARWINISM? IT IS CALVINISM! *Rev. in Am. Hist. 1980 8(1): 80-85.* Review essay of James R. Moore's *The Post-Darwinian Controversies: A study of the Protestant struggle to come to terms with Darwin in Great Britain and America, 1870-1900* (Cambridge: Cambridge U. Pr., 1979).

2320. Houston, Jourdan. SCIENCE IN A SEMINARY: THAT OLD TIME RELIGION. *New-England Galaxy 1975 17(1): 35-42.* Describes changes in the science curriculum at Mount Holyoke Seminary, South Hadley, Massachusetts, 1839-88. The link between religion and science was gradually dissolved and science was taught in its modern form. 4 illus. P. C. Marshall

2321. Lampe, Philip E. VALUES, MORALS AND RELIGION IN THE SOCIAL STUDIES. *Social Studies 1977 68(5): 193-196.* Difficulties in teaching in a value-laden atmosphere are complicated by instructors' attempts to ignore science's debt and responsibility to religion and the morality attached to scientific endeavors.

2322. Ledbetter, Cal, Jr. THE ANTIEVOLUTION LAW: CHURCH AND STATE IN ARKANSAS. *Arkansas Hist. Q. 1979 38(4): 299-327.* Discusses the history of the Arkansas Antievolution Law (1928) from preliminary legislative attempts to pass such an act, through the 1927 popular campaign which initiated the act and voted it into effect. The court cases involving Mrs. Susan Epperson, a Little Rock biology teacher, which resulted in the Supreme Court declaring the Arkansas law unconstitutional in 1968, are also described. 148 notes. G. R. Schroeder

2323. Lee, Sang Hyun. MENTAL ACTIVITY AND THE PERCEPTION OF BEAUTY IN JONATHAN EDWARDS. *Harvard Theological Rev. 1976 69(3-4): 369-396.* Examination of Jonathan Edwards's mental activity theory will lead to a better understanding of his place in the history of aesthetics and epistemology, and will answer some questions raised by current studies of Edwards. Edwards tried to bring together Locke's stress on sensation as the source of knowledge, Shaftesbury's view of the mind as dynamic, and his own view of ultimate reality being beautiful. 76 notes. E. E. Eminhizer

2324. Levinson, H. S. RELIGIOUS TESTIMONY AND EMPIRICAL RESTRAINT: BACONIANISM IN ANTEBELLUM AMERICA. *Rev. in Am. Hist. 1978 6(4): 518-523.* Review article prompted by Theodore Dwight Bozeman's *Protestants in an Age of Science: The Baconian Ideal and Antebellum American Religious Thought* (Chapel Hill: U. of North Carolina Pr., 1977).

2325. Lockwood, Rose. THE SCIENTIFIC REVOLUTION IN SEVENTEENTH-CENTURY NEW ENGLAND. *New England Q. 1980 53(1): 76-95.* A covert war was waged in New England almanacs between science and religion. Almanacs became "a source of popular information about Copernicanism, heliocentricity and theories about the structure of the universe." After 1659 no almanac openly defended Ptolemaic astronomy. The study of astronomical events, e.g., the behavior of comets, led almanac compilers to study the new physics which led to theories of an infinite and eternal universe which could not be reconciled with Puritan theology which was millenialist and predicated on a finite view of a universe created by God at a set time and one which would end. Based on essays in almanacs; 39 notes. J. C. Bradford

2326. Lutz, Cora E. EZRA STILES AND THE DARK DAY. *Yale U. Lib. Gazette 1980 54(4): 163-167.* Ezra Stiles witnessed the Dark Day that occurred in New England on 19 May 1780. He attempted to provide a rational explanation for the seemingly unnatural phenomenon. Based on *The Literary Diary of Ezra Stiles, D. D., LL. D.;* 3 notes. D. A. Yanchisin

2327. Martin, Jean-Pierre. EDWARDS' EPISTEMOLOGY AND THE NEW SCIENCE. *Early Am. Lit. 1973 7(3): 247-255.* Jonathan Edwards (1703-58) was aware of the Newtonian revolution, but his writings remained naively anthropocentric, and as in theological matters, Edwards was embarrassingly conservative. The most striking development of the 18th century was the invention of sciences, grounded on the principle of relativism, that deal with human societies, but for Edwards all men were still but superficial variations on man. Both Descartes and Spinoza insisted that to act and know are complementary and that any appraisal of human freedom entails an evaluation of the boundaries of human knowledge. While Edwards was fully aware of the problem, his own epistemology proceeded from the tradition of the School. To Edwards, knowledge was metaphysical, and proceeded from a concrete intuition. Intuitive knowledge of God, tradition, common sense, and language were the best instruments in the search for truth; the material observations and experimentation of the *natural* philosopher were the way of the lost. Based on primary and secondary sources; illus., 26 notes. D. P. Wharton

2328. Miles, John A., Jr. UNDERSTANDING ALBRIGHT: A REVOLUTIONARY ETUDE. *Harvard Theological Rev. 1976 69(1-2): 151-175.* Defines the philosophical foundations of William Foxwell Albright's (1891-1971) biblical and historical studies in considering in what sense Albright was a radical and in what sense a conservative, and especially his concern about the conflict between religion and science. In his early years, he was concerned with comparative mythology, but abandoned this in favor of archaeology. In selecting historical problems, he chose those problems which new archaeological evidence could enrich. Discusses the influence and importance of Albright's work along with the interplay of his changing philosophy. 49 notes. E. E. Eminhizer

2329. Mills, Eric L. H.M.S. *CHALLENGER*, HALIFAX, AND THE REVEREND DR. HONEYMAN. *Dalhousie Rev. [Canada] 1973 53(3): 529-545.* Describes the discoveries made on the expedition of HMS *Challenger*, a floating oceanographic laboratory which docked in Halifax and was visited by the geologist David Honeyman (1817-89). Covers 1872-76. S

2330. Moore, James R. EVOLUTIONARY THEORY AND CHRISTIAN FAITH: A BIBLIOGRAPHICAL GUIDE TO THE POST-DARWIN CONTROVERSIES. *Christian Scholar's Rev. 1975 4(3): 211-230.*

2331. Moore, John A. CREATIONISM IN CALIFORNIA. *Daedalus 1974 103(3): 173-189.* Since 1963, a trend toward teaching "special creation" as a theory alternative and equal to evolution has gathered momentum in the California school system. Encouraged by the conservative State Board of Education and Max Rafferty, Superintendent until 1970, the creationists seriously influenced the science curriculum. The scientific community, finally aroused in 1972, slowed but did not stop the creationists. The struggle points out the need for scientists to demonstrate rather than assume the reasons for accepting evolution. Based on secondary sources; 29 notes. E. McCarthy

2332. Moses, L. G. "IF THERE BE SERMONS IN STONES, I HAVE NOT HEARD THEM": A BIOGRAPHY OF ROSS RANDALL CALVIN (1889-1970). *Hist. Mag. of the Protestant Episcopal Church 1977 46(3): 333-347.* Sketches the life of Episcopal priest, Ross Randall Calvin (1889-1970), who wrote several valuable books. *Sky Determines: An Interpretation of the Southwest* (U. of New Mexico Pr., 1965) was a popular essay on nature in New Mexico. He contributed to the lore of the Southwest by conveying scientific knowledge in a pleasing and articulate manner. He never equated the beauty of nature with the revelation of God. He served in Silver City and Clovis, New Mexico. Based largely on the Calvin Papers, University of New Mexico, Albuquerque, New Mexico; 66 notes. H. M. Parker, Jr.

2333. Numbers, Ronald L. ARNOLD GUYOT AND THE HARMONY OF SCIENCE AND THE BIBLE. *XIVth International Congress of the History of Science, Proceedings No. 3 (Tokyo and Kyoto: Science Council of Japan, 1975): 239-242.* Arnold Guyot's (1807-84) theory on creation and the Bible combined Genesis with scientific epochs (so that "days" were interpreted as hundreds of thousands of years long) and was popularized in America in the 1850's by James Dwight Dana, editor of the *American Journal of Science.*

2334. Powell, Robert Charles. THE "SUBLIMINAL" VERSUS THE "SUBCONSCIOUS" IN THE AMERICAN ACCEPTANCE OF PSYCHOANALYSIS, 1906-10. *J. of the Hist. of the Behavioral Sci. 1979 15(2): 155-165.* Insofar as Frederic W. H. Myers' conceptions of the "subliminal" were spread by the Boston-based "Emmanuel movement," for medically supervised religious psychotherapy (fl. 1906-1910), the movement probably did more to help than to hinder American acceptance of Freudian ideas. Certainly, many academic psychologists' conceptions of the "unconscious" and "subconscious" were a hindrance. J

2335. Price, John A. THE BOOK OF MORMON VS ANTHROPOLOGICAL PREHISTORY. *Indian Historian 1974 7(3): 35-40.* Discusses the Mormon Church belief, expressed in *The Book of Mormon* (1830), that the American Indians were the lost tribes of Israel, and explores Joseph Smith's knowledge of archaeology and anthropology. S

2336. Ragsdale, W. B. THREE WEEKS IN DAYTON. *Am. Heritage 1975 26(4): 38-41, 99-103.* On hand in Dayton, Tennessee for the Scopes Trial, the author recounts the pre-trial activities in Dayton and discusses some of the main participants, retelling the story of the trial itself. William Jennings Bryan's questioning by Clarence Darrow is covered extensively. 8 illus. J. F. Paul

2337. Raphael, Marc Lee. RABBI JACOB VOORSANGER OF SAN FRANCISCO ON JEWS AND JUDAISM: THE IMPLICATIONS OF THE PITTSBURGH PLATFORM. *Am. Jewish Hist. Q. 1973 63(2): 185-203.* Rabbi Voorsanger (1852-1908) utilized 19th-century Biblical criticism and current philosophies to support his interpretation of the Pittsburgh Platform, the 1885 statement of principles of American Reform Judaism. Strongly influenced by Darwin's studies, he rejected any notions of supernatural revelation and adjusted Jewish theology to the accepted scientific theories of the day. 41 notes. F. Rosenthal

2338. Schultz, Joseph P. THE RELIGIOUS PSYCHOLOGY OF JONATHAN EDWARDS AND THE HASSIDIC MASTERS OF HABAD. *J. of Ecumenical Studies 1973 10(4): 716-727.* Both Jonathan Edwards and the Habad branch of Hassidism sought to overcome the religious polarizations between intellect and emotion. Outlines several similarities between Edwards' theology and Habad thought, especially the unity of the mind, similarity of saints to ordinary men, and methods of discerning authentic religious experience. J. A. Overbeck

2339. Shea, Daniel B., Jr. B. F. SKINNER: THE PURITAN WITHIN. *Virginia Q. Rev. 1974 50(3): 416-437.* Perceives Skinner as portraying views similar to Benjamin Franklin's and Jonathan Edwards's. Using Skinner's *Beyond Freedom and Dignity,* points to personal antecedents and philosophical similarities such as determinism, behaviorism, Puritanism, a certain morality, and imagination of a "utopia while suspecting the worst of human nature . . . " O. H. Zabel

2340. Shils, Edward. FAITH, UTILITY, AND THE LEGITIMACY OF SCIENCE. *Daedalus 1974 103(3): 1-15.* Religious and romanticist opposition to science has gradually subsided, but during the 1960's new criticisms emerged. While science is supported by belief in the intrinsic value of truth and cognitive activity, antipathies center on a loss of morale among scientists themselves, disbelief in the utilitarian value of science, and criticism by nonscientific experts. E. McCarthy

2341. Simpson, Marcus B., Jr. and Simpson, Sallie W. THE REVEREND JOHN CLAYTON'S LETTERS TO THE ROYAL SOCIETY OF LONDON, 1693-1694: AN IMPORTANT SOURCE FOR DR. JOHN BRICKELL'S *NATURAL HISTORY OF NORTH-CAROLINA,* 1737. *North Carolina Hist. Rev. 1977 54(1): 1-16.* Historians have long recognized that Dr. John Brickell plagiarized much of his *Natural History of North-Carolina* (Dublin, 1737) from John Lawson's *A New Voyage to Carolina.* Now a second major source of Brickell's work has been discovered. It is Anglican cleric John Clayton's series of five letters on natural conditions in southeastern Virginia published in the *Philosophical Transactions* (1693-94). At least 35 sections of Brickell's book were lifted from these letters without mention of source. Based on comparisons of the texts named and secondary sources; 6 illus., 73 notes. T. L. Savitt

2342. Sluder, Lawrence Lan. GOD IN THE BACKGROUND: EDWARD TAYLOR AS NATURALIST. *Early Am. Literature 1973 7(3): 266-271.* Taylor's poem, "The Great Bones of Claverack," indicates an area of Taylor's interest in natural science and an aspect of his world view that a strictly theological interpretation of his poetry would miss. It was intended to be an epic poem, in style and subject if not in length. The poetry is closer to Pope than to Donne, Herbert, or other common influences on Taylor. The language is witty, and the tone off-hand, even flippant. "The Great Bones of Claverack" is a temporary aberration from Taylor's religious devotionals in its unusual emphasis on nature and nature's reason with God in the distant background. In this piece Taylor demonstrated that he was capable of approaching his art with the eye of a naturalist, with the humor and rationalism of the arriving 18th century. Based on primary and secondary sources; 12 notes. D. P. Wharton

2343. Stein, Stephen J. JONATHAN EDWARDS AND THE RAINBOW: BIBLICAL EXEGESIS AND POETIC IMAGINATION. *New England Q. 1974 47(3): 440-456.* American theologian Jonathan Edwards became enamored of the rainbow as a student and offered a rather accurate scientific interpretation of it. Later in life, while jotting down Biblical notations, Edwards attempted a theological interpretation of the rainbow. Using as much science as theology, he constructed a virtual religious dogma based on its nature and function. Since Edwards made these notes for personal use, they may represent no more than fanciful recreation for a mind burdened with weightier concerns. 43 notes. V. L. Human

2344. Szasz, Ferenc M. WILLIAM JENNINGS BRYAN, EVOLUTION, AND THE FUNDAMENTALIST-MODERNIST CONTROVERSY. *Nebraska Hist. 1975 56(2): 259-278.* Discusses the fundamentalist-modernist conflict in American religion during the late 19th and early 20th century, examining how Presbyterian William Jennings Bryan influenced the theological issue by casting it in a secular framework revolving around the issue of evolution. While retaining his liberal views, Bryan was far from agreeing with the leading clerical exponents of the evolutionist position. R. Lowitt

2345. Thompson, James J., Jr. SOUTHERN BAPTISTS AND THE ANTIEVOLUTION CONTROVERSY OF THE 1920'S. *Mississippi Q. 1975-76 29(1): 65-81.*

2346. Waldinger, Robert J. SLEEP OF REASON: JOHN P. GRAY AND THE CHALLENGE OF MORAL INSANITY. *J. of the Hist. of Medicine and Allied Sci. 1979 34(2): 163-179.* John P. Gray, psychiatrist and superintendent of the New York State Lunatic Asylum at Utica from 1854 to 1886, was spokesman for the conservatives who were opposed to the doctrine of moral insanity. He delivered expert testimony for the prosecution at the trials of Lewis Payne, who conspired to kill Lincoln, and Charles J. Guiteau, who shot President Garfield. Religion was the keystone of his philosophical attack on the doctrine of moral insanity. The theoretical underpinning of Gray's psychology included a peculiar blend of idealism and materialism that did not fall within any one philosophical system. He forced others to confront the theological, psychological, and political implications of the new theory of emotional breakdown. 53 notes. M. Kaufman

2347. Weaver, Bill L. KENTUCKY BAPTISTS' REACTION TO THE NATIONAL EVOLUTION CONTROVERSY, 1922-1926. *Filson Club Hist. Q. 1975 49(3): 266-275.* The reaction of Kentucky Baptists to the theory of evolution was predictable, attacking the teaching of Darwinian biology in Kentucky schools and colleges. Cumberland College, for example, lost an appropriation from the state Mission Board in 1925 because President E. E. Wood was accused of teaching "theistic evolution." There was a split among Kentucky Baptists over the question of whether to push for a state law prohibiting the teaching of evolution, resulting in the defeat of anti-evolution laws in 1922, 1926, and 1928. Documentation from Baptist state records; 58 notes.

G. B. McKinney

2348. Weitz, Martin M. RELIGION AND PSYCHIATRY. *Colorado Q. 1973 22(1): 59-68.* Defending religion as a useful and reasonable feature of American life, the author suggests that psychiatry and religion may together provide a more complete solution to the problem of depression than is now available. Depression, a major American illness, is being successfully attacked by science, but religion may also be useful in dealing with it.

B. A. Storey

2349. Winkler, Louis. PENNSYLVANIA GERMAN ASTRONOMY AND ASTROLOGY X: CHRISTOPHER WITT'S DEVICE. *Pennsylvania Folklife 1974-75 24(2): 36-39.* Speculates that a unique astronomical-astrological device, the *Horologium Achaz*, was primarily a religious relic of the Pietist sect.

S

2350. Wrobel, Arthur. ORTHODOXY AND RESPECTABILITY IN NINETEENTH-CENTURY PHRENOLOGY. *J. of Popular Culture 1975 9(1): 38-50.* Phrenology synthesized three important intellectual currents: Baconian inductive scientific procedures, Scottish common-sense philosophy, and natural religion based on faith from design in nature. It appealed to a wide spectrum of supporters, conservative to liberal, frivolous and outlandish to respectable and distinguished. In the hands of Orson Squire Fowler and Lorenzo Niles Fowler it contributed to the progress philosophy of perfectionism and millennialism. They transformed the science of phrenology into a practical philosophy of headreadings, personal counseling, and a variety of social issues, which was responsible for its spectacular success during the 1840's-50's, but also for its demise in the 1860's. 49 notes.

J. D. Falk

18. SOCIAL AND ECONOMIC REFORM

General

(including Social Gospel)

2351. Altschuler, Glenn C. WALTER RAUSCHENBUSCH. *Foundations 1979 22(2): 140-151.* Baptist Walter Rauschenbusch has generally been considered a social and theological liberal. Discusses Winthrop Hudson's conflicting view. Rauschenbusch attempted to develop a theological position that would fit his social theory, but it was not liberalism. 33 notes. E. E. Eminhizer

2352. Banner, Lois W. RELIGIOUS BENEVOLENCE AS SOCIAL CONTROL: A CRITIQUE OF AN INTERPRETATION. *J. of Am. Hist. 1973 60(1): 23-41.* Religion in the post-revolutionary period has too often been viewed as a conservative force seeking "social control" not "social improvement" as the major end of benevolent schemes. This view results from a narrow preoccupation with New England Congregationalism and Lyman Beecher, and an erroneous opinion that the clergy was declining. A broader perspective shows genuine humanitarian concern among clergy of many denominations involved in education, antislavery work, and other philanthropic concerns. This benevolence was stimulated by millennarianism and a concern for a "Christian republican" nationalism. These clergymen diagnosed contemporary evils as stemming from a selfish, demagogic materialism which should be combatted through education, self-reliant religion, and voluntary associations. Covers 1790-1815. 53 notes. K. B. West

2353. Barbour, Hugh. WILLIAM PENN, MODEL OF PROTESTANT LIBERALISM. *Church Hist. 1979 48(2): 156-173.* William Penn's practical social reform combined the Quakers' radical hope for the total transforming of men, ethics, and society by God's spirit with a humanist's trust in reason and conscience already at work in all men. This was a new stance for Quakers. Best known in his own time for his practical career, Penn's ideas developed gradually in his laws and tracts. Penn's approaches to history, to toleration, and to theology and ethics cannot be claimed as unique. Yet Penn drew a unique intensity in both his universalism and his radicalism from his Quaker community, from its wrestling with "the Light within," and from his own experience of the unity of world truth and the radical depth of evil. 60 notes. M. D. Dibert

2354. Beck, Jeanne M. HENRY SOMERVILLE AND SOCIAL REFORM: HIS CONTRIBUTION TO CANADIAN CATHOLIC SOCIAL THOUGHT. *Study Sessions: Can. Catholic Hist. Assoc. 1975 42: 91-108.* Henry Somerville, editor of the *Catholic Register* 1933-53, provided an impetus for his generation through his contributions to the development of Catholic social thought and action in Canada by combining the influences of Edwardian England and his own Canadian immigrant experiences after his arrival in 1915.

2355. Behiels, Michael. L'ASSOCIATION CATHOLIQUE DE LA JEUNESSE CANADIENNE-FRANÇAISE AND THE QUEST FOR A MORAL REGENERATION, 1903-1914. *J. of Can. Studies [Canada] 1978 13(2): 27-41.* The Association catholique de la jeunesse canadienne-française was founded (1903) when many developments (e.g., increased immigration, urbanization, and foreign control) gave rise to fears that the French Canadian nation faced imminent demoralization and assimilation. The ACJC's founders promised Archbishop Bruchési of Montreal to remain aloof from politics, and in general the organization's emphasis was moral rather than political. But it did become involved in the drive for increased bilingualism at the national level, and in promoting the interest of French-speaking minorities outside Quebec. The ACJC spokesmen opposed Jewish immigration, and the drive (spearheaded by members of the Masonic lodge Emancipation) to reduce the Church's role in education. They also advocated various industrial reforms, most of them voluntaristic in nature. Based on the ACJC organ *Le Semeur,* other primary, and secondary sources; 88 notes. L. W. Van Wyk

2356. Bélanger, Noël. MGR. COURCHESNE ET L'ACTION CATHOLIQUE [Monsignor Courchesne and Action Catholique]. *Sessions d'Étude: Soc. Can. d'Hist. de l'Église Catholique [Canada] 1976 43: 49-67.* Studies Monsignor Georges Courchesne's work in the Rimouski diocese, 1940-67, with an outline of major dates in the organization of Action Catholique and his rupture with the Church in 1942.

2357. Benedí, Claudio F. THE FORESIGHT OF FÉLIX VARELA. *Américas (DC) 1977 29(4): 9-12.* Félix Varela, a Catholic priest forced to flee from Cuba to New York City in 1823, served in that city as an advocate of human rights and social progress through religion and worked to establish two new Catholic churches; he was appointed pastor to one of them.

2358. Betten, Neil. NATIVISM AND THE KLAN IN TOWN AND CITY: VALPARAISO AND GARY, INDIANA. *Studies in Hist. and Soc. 1973 4(2): 3-16.* A study of the Ku Klux Klan during the 1920's in two urban centers. Indicates that "The Klan grew in Gary and Valparaiso by fashioning its appeal to the concerns of its white Protestant citizens . . ." and focused on such "myriad enemies" as corrupt politicians, bootleggers, prostitutes, imagined radicals, and immigrants who would not or could not instantly assimilate. J. O. Baylen

2359. Bettis, Joseph. THEOLOGY AND POLITICS: KARL BARTH AND REINHOLD NIEBUHR ON SOCIAL ETHICS AFTER LIBERALISM. *Religion in Life 1979 48(1): 53-62.* Discusses the fundamental differences in the viewpoints of Karl Barth and Reinhold Niebuhr, politically influential theologians of the 1920's-30's concerned with social ethics and alternatives to Protestant liberalism, Barth in Europe, and Niebuhr in America, 1920's-60.

2360. Boller, Paul F., Jr. THE PARADOX OF FREEDOM: REINHOLD NIEBUHR'S CHRISTIAN REALISM. *Southwest Rev. 1977 62(1): 31-43.* Discusses Reinhold Niebuhr's belief in social justice, racial equality, pride, and freedom, through a short examination of his works, 1915-63; applies Niebuhr's thought to the freedom movements of the 1960's-70's.

2361. Bower, Robert K. JOSEPH A. DUGDALE: A FRIEND OF TRUTH. *Palimpsest 1975 56(6): 170-183.* Joseph A. Dugdale, an antislavery Hicksite Quaker minister, devoted his life to helping the oppressed. Especially active in the abolitionist movement prior to the Civil War, he turned to such crusades as women's rights, prison reform, temperance, peace, and aid to Indians in later years. He was well known for his children's conventions, which consisted of recreation, recitation, and education, and he knew many famous people of his day. Quiet and relatively anonymous during his lifetime, he has remained obscure since his death in 1896. Illus., 5 photos, note. D. W. Johnson

2362. Brackney, William H. EXPEDIENCE VERSUS CONVICTION: THE BAPTIST RESPONSE TO THE ANTI-MASONIC IMPULSE, 1826-1830. *Foundations 1978 21(2): 167-180.* The disappearance of William Morgan in 1826 caused the rise of the Anti-Masonic movement. The Baptists in western New York, where Morgan lived, were more involved in the controversy than any other denomination. Discusses Baptist involvement. 46 notes. E. E. Eminhizer

2363. Brackney, William H. THE FRUITS OF A CRUSADE: WESLEYAN OPPOSITION TO SECRET SOCIETIES. *Methodist Hist. 1979 17(4): 239-252.* Opposition to secret societies and associations prevailed in the Wesleyan Methodist Connection during the mid-19th century. At the organizational conference in 1843, secret societies were debated. From then until 1860 this became the most controversial issue among the Wesleyans. By 1860 the church had taken a strong position that it could not tolerate ministers or members joining a secret society. The church took this position because of a strong egalitarian-reform tradition which disapproved of any organization which seemed to favor the select. 39 notes. H. L. Calkin

2364. Brown, Wallace. AMERICAN ROMANTIC REFORM. *Hist. Today [Great Britain] 1975 25(8): 552-560.* Covers religious reformers and utopian movements in the decades before the Civil War.

2365. Bryson, Thomas A. WALTER GEORGE SMITH: A CATHOLIC PROGRESSIVE. *Records of the Am. Catholic Hist. Soc. of Philadelphia 1974 85(3-4): 174-184.* Walter George Smith involved himself in municipal reform, fought for a uniform state divorce law and a uniform state commercial law, and helped raise standards of legal education in Pennsylvania. His progressivism sought no sharp change in the social structure but rather the formation of a responsible elite which was to direct the popular impulse toward change into moderate and constructive channels. Covers 1900-22. 38 notes. J. M. McCarthy

2366. Burkett, Randall K. RELIGIOUS DIMENSIONS OF THE UNIVERSAL NEGRO IMPROVEMENT ASSOCIATION AND AFRICAN COMMUNITIES LEAGUE. *Afro-Am. in New York Life and Hist. 1977 1(2): 167-182.* Examines the religious dimension of the Universal Negro Improvement Association, under the leadership of Marcus Garvey, through exploration of meeting structure, format, vocabulary of UNIA members when addressing issues, the role of chaplains, and the religiopolitical symbols of nationhood in the organization, 1920's.

2367. Carlet, Yves. "RESPECTABLES INIQUITÉS": LE TRANSCENDANTALISME ET L'ORDRE SOCIAL" [Respectable Iniquities": Transcendentalism and the social order]. *Rev. Française d'Etudes Américaines [France] 1978 3(5): 19-31.* Questions the interpretation of Transcendentalism as a spiritual or literary quest which leaves its members indifferent to social issues, drawing on the works of Emerson, Thoreau, Ripley, Margaret Fuller, Parker, and Brownson, 1830's-50's.

2368. Carwardine, Richard. AMERICAN EVANGELICAL PROTESTANTISM AND THE REFORM IMPULSE. *J. of the United Reformed Church Hist. Soc. [Great Britain] 1980 2(5): 153-160.* Reviews the following works which address aspects of American evangelical Protestantism in the 19th century: Ronald Walters's *The Antislavery Appeal: American Abolitionism after 1830* (London: Johns Hopkins U. Pr., 1976), Marie Caskey's *Chariot of Fire: Religion and the Beecher Family* (London: Yale U. Pr., 1978), Donald G. Mathews's *Religion in the Old South* (London: U. of Chicago Pr., 1977), and James H. Moorhead's *American Apocalypse: Yankee Protestants and the Civil War* (London: Yale U. Pr., 1978). Each of these volumes develops and refines an understanding of the relationship between evangelicalism and the reform impulse. S. C. Pearson, Jr.

2369. Chapman, James K. HENRY HARVEY STUART (1873-1952): NEW BRUNSWICK REFORMER. *Acadiensis [Canada] 1976 5(2): 79-104.* In his generation Henry Harvey Stuart was the most prominent and widespread voice of dissent in New Brunswick. A single theme dominated his multifarious activities: the regeneration of society through education and social reform. Stuart grew up in poverty. He began teaching in the 1890's, when his Christianity led him to socialism and the social gospel. He organized the province's first socialist party in 1902, promoted unions, edited a union newspaper, and played a role in municipal and provincial politics. 97 notes. D. F. Chard

2370. Christenson, James A. RELIGIOUS INVOLVEMENT, VALUES, AND SOCIAL COMPASSION. *Sociol. Analysis 1976 37(3): 218-227.* People who regularly attend church exhibit no greater social compassion than those who do not attend. However, stronger adherence to religious values has a consistently positive relationship with social compassion issues. Reasons for the dissimilarity between these findings and earlier studies are explored. J

2371. Christian, William A., Sr. INWARDNESS AND OUTWARD CONCERNS: A STUDY OF JOHN WOOLMAN'S THOUGHT. *Quaker Hist. 1978 67(2): 88-104.* John Woolman read devotional literature, believed his dream-visions called for personal testimony on social problems, and was unusually sensitive and self-critical. The answer to his prayers, couched in Biblical, Puritan, Quaker terms, was that God transcends the world and requires its transformation so that human beings will live as equals in one family. Mid-18th century Quaker society was comfortable and, except for a few like Woolman and Benezet, complacently dealt with internal questions of dress, speech, and discipline. "The time was ripe for Woolman to be heard" on oppression of slaves, although not for his pleas for the poor. 16 notes, 55 ref. T. D. S. Bassett

2372. Cloyd, Daniel Lee. PRELUDE TO REFORM: POLITICAL, ECONOMIC, AND SOCIAL THOUGHT OF ALABAMA BAPTISTS, 1877-1890. *Alabama Rev. 1978 31(1): 48-64.* Editorial analysis of *The Alabama Baptist,* 1877-90, supports the contention that Baptists were increasingly interested in socialized religion. Although remaining theologically conservative fundamentalists, Baptists often deplored Gilded Age political corruption, encouraged education and missionary activity among the black community, and championed prohibition. Baptist concern for social issues corresponded more closely to Progressive reform than antebellum religiosity. Primary and secondary sources; 65 notes. J. F. Vivian

2373. Conforti, Joseph A. SAMUEL HOPKINS AND THE NEW DIVINITY: THEOLOGY, ETHICS, AND SOCIAL REFORM IN EIGHTEENTH-CENTURY NEW ENGLAND. *William and Mary Q. 1977 34(4): 572-589.* Examines the controversy among the New Divinity clerics over the nature of true virtue. The Reverend Samuel Hopkins attempted to clarify the ethical theories of Jonathan Edwards, concentrating on defects in Edwards's notions of secondary virtue. Unlike Edwards, who emphasized right affections as the essence of true virtue, Congregationalist Hopkins saw true virtue as right actions which would open the door to social reform. Discusses Hopkins's own position on social issues, including slavery. A unique contribution of the New Divinity was the doctrine of disinterested benevolence. Based on contemporary letters, diaries, and religious writings. 55 notes. H. M. Ward

2374. Corcoran, Theresa. VIDA SCUDDER AND THE LAWRENCE TEXTILE STRIKE. *Essex Inst. Hist. Collections 1979 115(3): 183-195.* During the 1912 Lawrence, Massachusetts, textile strike the Progressive Women's Club of Lawrence invited prominent speakers to address them on 4 March. No outsider stirred the conservatives more than Vida Dutton Scudder, professor at Wellesley College. A founder of the College Settlements Association and Denison House, a distinctively Boston settlement for women, a member of the Socialist Party in 1911, and author of *Socialism and Character* (1912), Scudder had moved into settlements in hopes that they might play their part in radical propaganda. In this she was discouraged, but later became convinced that Christianity offered the one solution to industrialized society, and after 1912 moved into various Christian socialist groups for social reform. Examines Scudder's speech and the reaction to it, the Progressive Women's Club, and the textile strike. Primary and secondary sources; 30 notes. R. S. Sliwoski

2375. Crowley, Weldon S. BENJAMIN RUSH: RELIGION AND SOCIAL ACTIVISM. *Religion in Life 1974 43(2): 227-238.* Covers 1770's-1813.

2376. Davis, Hugh H. THE AMERICAN SEAMEN'S FRIEND SOCIETY AND THE AMERICAN SAILOR, 1828-1838. *Am. Neptune 1979 39(1): 45-57.* Studies the origins and early years of the American Seamen's Friend Society (ASFS), "when its broad strategy was developed and refined and many of its major projects were first undertaken." This benevolent organization's "foremost objectives—to persuade the sailor to avoid the manifold vices which tempted him and to advance the cause of evangelical Christianity—were scarcely accomplished." However, a "vital part of what was done in these years to improve the lot of American seamen resulted from the efforts of the ASFS." Baed on published sources; 54 notes. G. H. Curtis

2377. Dressner, Richard B. WILLIAM DWIGHT PORTER BLISS'S CHRISTIAN SOCIALISM. *Church Hist. 1978 47(1): 66-82.* From the Haymarket Affair until the Red Scare, the Reverend William D. P. Bliss was instrumental in organizing, researching, editing, publishing and lecturing on behalf of the coming of God's kingdom. Along with Walter Rauschenbusch and George Herron, Bliss was certainly one of the most prominent spokesmen for the left wing of the Social Gospel. Apparently, however, there was a divergence between Bliss's radical social philosophy and his political commitments to more moderate causes. Bliss was willing to accommodate his economic and social programs to political exigencies without compromising his vision of Christian redemption. Covers 1876-1926. 61 notes. M. D. Dibert

2378. Driedger, Leo. DOCTRINAL BELIEF: A MAJOR FACTOR IN THE DIFFERENTIAL PERCEPTION OF SOCIAL ISSUES. *Sociol. Q. 1974 15(1): 66-80.* An association between doctrinal beliefs and positions on social issues is posited. This study of the clergy in an industrial city demonstrated that doctrinal orthodoxy had an independent effect on positions taken on issues related to social control, personal morality, use of power by the elite, civil liberties, minority rights, and welfare support. Absolutist clergymen with a doctrinally conservative other-worldly focus were reluctant to change society: they supported social control, personal morality, and considerable use of force by the power elite. Evolutionist, this-worldly clergymen who were more doctrinally liberal were open to change and focused more on issues such as civil liberty, minority rights, and welfare support. J

2379. Durham, Weldon B. "BIG BROTHER" AND THE "SEVEN SISTERS": CAMP LIFE REFORMS IN WORLD WAR I. *Military Affairs 1978 42(2): 57-60.* Volunteer organizations, called the "seven sisters," and special agencies created by the Commission on Training Camp Activities (CTCA) assisted the War Department during World War I to restrict the military trainee's access to liquor and prostitutes and to supply recreation programs. The "seven sisters" represented five religious sects and two nonsectarian groups (including the YMCA, YWCA, Jewish Welfare Board, and Knights of Columbus),and they provided a clean, quiet place for the soldiers to rest, talk, listen, think, play, and write. The CTCA offered millions of lower-class Americans unprecedented access to middle-class leisure activities and helped mold the "ideal young American." Primary and secondary sources; 19 notes. A. M. Osur

2380. Ede, Alfred J. THE SOCIAL THEOLOGIES OF WALTER RAUSCHENBUSCH AND VATICAN II IN DIALOGUE. *Foundations 1975 18(3): 198-208.* The Roman Catholic Church was not friendly to social reform at the end of the 19th century and the early part of the 20th century, when Walter Rauschenbusch (1861-1918) was expressing Protestant concern for social problems. Vatican Council II changed attitudes and an official document, *Pastoral Constitution on the Church in the Modern World (1965)*, set forth a new position on the Roman church and social reform. This article points out the parallels between Baptist Rauschenbusch's thought and the *Pastoral Constitution*. Both recognize the need to overcome social injustice and both are optimistic. 28 notes. E. E. Eminhizer

2381. Emery, George N. THE ORIGINS OF CANADIAN METHODIST INVOLVEMENT IN THE SOCIAL GOSPEL MOVEMENT 1890-1914. *J. of the Can. Church Hist. Soc. [Canada] 1977 19(1-2): 104-119.* The massive, rapid transformation of Canada in the early 20th century through urbanization, immigration, and industrialization brought about the growth of Methodism and other Christian denominations of the social gospel movement. There were a number of reasons. First was the decline of the evangelical tradition with the growing affluence of Methodists and the development of the higher criticism. Moreover, the strong belief in individual perfectionism evolved into concern about society as a whole. In their nationalism, pietism, optimism about the future of man, and desire to avoid theological controversy, many Methodists saw in the social gospel movement an opportunity to express their concern about the growing problems caused by the modern changes. All these factors helped bring Canadian Methodists into the forefront of the social gospel movement in Canada. Primary and secondary sources; table, 38 notes. This issue is *J. of the Can. Church Hist. Soc.* 1977 19(1-2) and *Bull. of the United Church of Can.* 1977 26. J. A. Kicklighter

2382. Ensley, F. Gerald. THE SOCIAL THEOLOGY OF FRANCIS JOHN MC CONNELL. *Religion in Life 1976 45(4): 482-489.* Discusses the social philosophy of Francis John McConnell, a distinguished Methodist intellectual and ecclesiastical leader, during the first half of the 20th century.

2383. Fairbanks, David. RELIGIOUS FORCES AND MORALITY POLICIES IN THE AMERICAN STATES. *Western Pol. Q. 1977 30(3): 411-417.* Shows that religious forces have a greater positive correlation to drafting and enacting laws to regulate alcohol and gambling than does economic development; 1977.

2384. Faramelli, Norman J. NEEDED IN THE SEVENTIES: A MISSIONARY STRATEGY FOR THE WHITE MAJORITY. *Anglican Theological Rev. Supplementary Series 1973 (2): 118-132.*

2385. Frech, Laura P. THE REPUBLICANISM OF HENRY LAURENS. *South Carolina Hist. Mag. 1975 76(2): 69-79.* Despite wealth and social standing, Henry Laurens (1724-92) was an ardent republican and "even something of a leveller." To assist the poor he favored abolition of slavery which he believed would reduce land prices and increase the number of small farmers. While influenced by the Enlightenment, Laurens believed that republicanism required moral regeneration, which would come with Protestant Christianity. Primary sources; 40 notes. R. H. Tomlinson

2386. Fryer, Judith. THE OTHER VICTORIA: "THE WOODHULL" AND HER TIMES. *Old Northwest 1978 4(3): 219-240.* Relates the life and times of two-time presidential candidate Victoria Claflin Woodhull (1838-1927). An advocate of free love, Woodhull, financed by Cornelius Vanderbilt (1794-1877) in New York City, published *Woodhull & Claflin's Weekly,* advocating free love, abortions, divorce, Spiritualism, feminism, Communism, world government, etc. It was also a blackmail sheet. In 1871 Woodhull exposed Henry Ward Beecher's (1813-87) affair with a parishioner when he failed to stop his sisters' attacks on Woodhull. This resulted in Woodhull's arrest and trial on an obscene literature charge, for which she was acquitted. Based on Woodhull's publications and on secondary works; illus., 47 notes. J. N. Dickinson

2387. Garson, Robert A. POLITICAL FUNDAMENTALISM AND POPULAR DEMOCRACY IN THE 1920'S. *South Atlantic Q. 1977 76(2): 219-233.* The 1920's fundamentalist backlash against cosmopolitan modernity was an expression of popular democracy in the Jacksonian tradition. Alienated and frustrated by the crumbling of Victorian mores, the fundamentalists, including pietistic Christian evangelists and the Ku Klux Klan, attempted to preserve traditional ways at the local level. Their vigilantism was intended to keep unpopular new ideas out of local communities and to silence any local adherents. Not sophisticated enough to focus their attack on the mass media, they spent most of their efforts in minimizing the effects of the professional elites in public education on local youth and in carrying punishment to the moral lawbreakers left untouched by civil authorities. In this the fundamentalists evoked the issue of accountability in local education and politics. 24 notes. W. L. Olbrich

2388. Gorrell, Donald K. THE METHODIST FEDERATION FOR SOCIAL SERVICE AND THE SOCIAL CREED. *Methodist Hist. 1975 13(2): 3-32.* The Methodist Federation for Social Service was organized at Washington, D.C., on 3 December 1907. The next year the Methodist Church adopted the Social Creed of Methodism. This was slightly modified and adopted by the Federal Council of Churches of Christ in America. The evolution of the Social Creed occurred because people like Frank M. North and Harry F. Ward in the Methodist Federation labored to arouse the support of Methodism and Protestantism. 88 notes. H. L. Calkin

2389. Gribbin, William. REPUBLICANISM, REFORM, AND THE SENSE OF SIN IN ANTE BELLUM AMERICA. *Cithara 1974 14(1): 25-42.* Discusses social reform movements in antebellum America and their emphasis on sin rather than injustice or inequality. S

2390. Hadden, Jeffrey K.; Longino, Charles F., Jr.; and Reed, Myer S., Jr. FURTHER REFLECTIONS ON THE DEVELOPMENT OF SOCIOLOGY AND THE SOCIAL GOSPEL IN AMERICA. *Sociol. Analysis 1974 35(4): 282-286.* Discusses the question of sociological self-consciousness and the social conditions in which sociology as a discipline emerged during the years 1890-1972. S

2391. Hammerback, John C. and Jensen, Richard J. THE RHETORICAL WORLDS OF CÉSAR CHÁVEZ AND REIES TIJERINA. *Western J. of Speech Communication 1980 44(3): 166-176.* Reies Tijerina, a Chicano political and religious leader, who converted to Protestantism and then returned to Catholicism, in Texas, and Cesar Chavez, a union organizer among California farm laborers, gained political aims for the groups they led through persistent public appearances and development of persuasive rhetorical styles; 1960's-70's.

2392. Harnik, Peter. THE ETHICS OF ENERGY-PRODUCTION AND USE: DEBATE WITHIN THE NATIONAL COUNCIL OF CHURCHES. *Bull. of the Atomic Scientists 1979 35(2): 5-9.* Preparation by the National Council of Churches of a "Policy Statement on the Ethical Implications of Energy Production and Use" emphasized debate on the ethics of the energy problem and resulted in the realization that the energy industry neither encouraged nor welcomed debate on ethics, and that the information gap between so-called experts and the general public remains quite wide, 1976-78.

2393. Hawes, Joseph M. PRISONS IN EARLY NINETEENTH-CENTURY AMERICA: THE PROCESS OF CONVICT REFORMATION. Hawes, Joseph M., ed. *Law and Order in American History* (Port Washington, N.Y.: Kennikat Pr., 1979): 37-52. Compares the ideas of the founders of the Auburn, New York, and Pennsylvania prison systems from 1787 to 1845; Pennsylvania prisons, with Quaker influence, "preferred a noncoercive, practically passive, approach to reform and religion," while the supporters of the Auburn believed that "religion and reform were active human pursuits."

2394. Hoeveler, J. David, Jr. THE UNIVERSITY AND THE SOCIAL GOSPEL: THE INTELLECTUAL ORIGINS OF THE "WISCONSIN IDEA." *Wisconsin Mag. of Hist. 1976 59(4): 282-298.* University of Wisconsin President John Bascom was one of the most important figures in formulating the basis for the Wisconsin Idea because he 1) accepted the outlines of evolutionary science and built the "New Theology" on it, 2) took moral philosophy in new directions through a concern for the problems of government and politics, and 3) used his influence to develop a new philosophy of state which included enhanced powers for government and the state university. Gradually, through the work of Richard T. Ely, Bascom's appointment as director of the newly established School of Economics, Political Science, and History, and John R. Commons, whom Ely brought to Wisconsin, the social gospel ideas of Bascom began to take on a more secular tone. This transition became more obvious in the works of economist Commons and was completed with the ascendancy of geologist Charles R. Van Hise as President of the University and Robert M. La Follette as Governor. Covers 1870-1910. 8 illus., 55 notes. N. C. Burckel

2395. Hutchison, William R. THE AMERICANNESS OF THE SOCIAL GOSPEL: AN INQUIRY IN COMPARATIVE HISTORY. *Church Hist. 1975 44(3): 367-381.* The liberal Social Gospel era of 1885-1925 has been treated as the nadir of the activistic mode. Using comparative analysis, this study explores transatlantic influences and parallel development of European thought during the same period. Basically, such scholarship has been divided into three schools. Many in Europe and America have suggested that the liberal and social movements were international ones, which did not strike national variants. Others have detected an idiosyncratic American contribution and have regretted or deplored it. Lastly, there have been those who considered Protestant liberalism and the Social Gospel as America's special and quite admirable contributions to world religion. 47 notes. M. Dibert

2396. Hynson, Leon O. REFORMATION AND PERFECTION: THE SOCIAL GOSPEL OF BISHOP PECK. *Methodist Hist. 1978 16(2): 82-91.* Jesse T. Peck (1811-83), Bishop of the Methodist Episcopal Church, was a zealous spokesman for a number of social causes within Methodism. His thought became an extension and modification of the Wesleyan union of personal and social sanctification. Peck took the concept of perfection beyond the personal and individual to the social and national. Based on Peck's writings; 18 notes, biblio.
H. L. Calkin

2397. Hynson, Leon O. THE SOCIAL CONCERNS OF WESLEY: THEOLOGICAL FOUNDATIONS. *Christian Scholar's Rev. 1974 4(1): 36-42.* Discusses the social ethics of John Wesley (1703-91), theologian, evangelist, and the founder of Methodism. S

2398. Irvin, Dale T. SOCIAL WITNESS POLICIES: AN HISTORICAL OVERVIEW. *J. of Presbyterian Hist. 1979 57(3): 353-403.* In chronological fashion, embracing eight periods of ecclesiastical history, the many facets of policies regarding the "social gospel" are presented as enacted by the General Assembly of the major American Presbyterian Church. Nothing is said about the role of lesser judicatories—sessions, presbyteries, or synods—or of the numerous contributions of individuals in shaping social witness *extra ecclesiam.* Missing are the contributions of smaller Presbyterian Churches in the American tradition—Cumberland Presbyterian, "Southern" Presbyterian, and the Associate Reformed Presbyterian Church. Traces the policies for social witness from the colonial period to the present day, the latter being well represented, pointing out that General Assembly pronouncements mostly run ahead of the mood of the nation. Covers 1770-1977. Based on minutes and publications of the US Presbyterian Church; illus., 92 notes.
H. M. Parker, Jr.

2399. Jable, J. Thomas. ASPECTS OF REFORM IN EARLY NINETEENTH-CENTURY PENNSYLVANIA. *Pennsylvania Mag. of Hist. and Biog. 1978 102(3): 344-363.* Intense in Pennsylvania, the Second Great Awakening's moral stewards used restrictive legislation and organization to inculcate their regenerative values during 1794-1860. They aimed at, among others, gambling, dancing, pleasure halls, horse racing, and they inculcated Sabbatarianism. Official records, printed sources, and secondary works; 72 notes. T. H. Wendel

2400. Jaehn, Klaus Juergen. THE FORMATION OF WALTER RAUSCHENBUSCH'S SOCIAL CONSCIOUSNESS AS REFLECTED IN HIS EARLY LIFE AND WRITINGS, PART II. *Foundations 1974 17(1): 68-85.* Expounds on Rauschenbusch's theories on Christian Socialism and the social gospel, written by the German American Baptist minister and theologian during 1891-1918. Continued from *Foundations* 1973 16(4).

2401. Jeffries, Vincent and Tygart, Clarence E. THE INFLUENCE OF THEOLOGY, DENOMINATION AND VALUES UPON THE POSITIONS OF CLERGY ON SOCIAL ISSUES. *J. for the Sci. Study of Religion 1974 13(3): 309-324.* Discusses the opinions and behavior of clergymen regarding major social issues during the 1960's and 70's.

2402. Jenkins, William D. THE KU KLUX KLAN IN YOUNGSTOWN, OHIO: MORAL REFORM IN THE TWENTIES. *Historian 1978 41(1): 76-93.* The primary factor in the rapid growth of the Ku Klux Klan in Youngstown, Ohio, was not its white supremacy, anti-Catholicism, anti-Semitism, or nativism, but its desire to improve the morals of the community. An enforcement crusade, begun by the Mahoning County Dry Association, the Federal Council of Churches, and the Federation of Women's Clubs, soon fell under the control of the Klan and its leaders, who also met with surprising political success in local elections. Describes these leaders and Youngtown's attitudes toward other parts of the Klan platform. Speculates on causes of the decline of Klan influence in the area, and concludes that public confidence in the organization as the enforcer of community morals eroded as it proved unable to totally enforce the city's conservative moral code.
M. S. Legan

2403. Jones, Ronald W. CHRISTIAN SOCIAL ACTION AND THE EPISCOPAL CHURCH IN ST. LOUIS, MO.: 1880-1920. *Hist. Mag. of the Protestant Episcopal Church 1976 45(4): 253-274.* Analyzes movements toward social reform emanating from such American Episcopalians as Henry Codman Potter, Goerge C. Hodges, and Philo W. Sprague, and says the Episcopal Diocese of Missouri, much like the Episcopal Church across the nation, was doing little more than "nibbling at the crust of the social reform pie." Only in a few St. Louis ministries was there any activity. The church chose to minister to individuals through institutions rather than to lead actively as an agent for social change. Based on secondary materials; 78 notes, biblio.
H. M. Parker, Jr.

2404. Jordan, Philip D. IMMIGRANTS, METHODISTS AND A "CONSERVATIVE" SOCIAL GOSPEL, 1865-1908. *Methodist Hist. 1978 17(1): 16-43.* While accepting a social creed in the name of Christian liberality in 1908 the Methodist Episcopal Church rejected an open door policy for immigrants. After the Civil War the church saw immigration as a danger to American civilization and to the wages of the laboring classes. At the same time Methodist missionaries saw China as a vast field for evangelism, and therefore the Methodist Episcopal Church opposed American mistreatment of Asians. By 1908, however, restriction of Oriental immigration was supported. Based on Methodist publications. 39 notes. H. L. Calkin

2405. Kalberg, Stephen. THE COMMITMENT TO CAREER REFORM: THE SETTLEMENT MOVEMENT LEADERS. *Social Service Rev. 1975 49(4): 608-628.* Discusses the social, religious, and political attitudes of Settlement Movement reformers during the 1880's and 90's.

2406. Kline, Lawrence O. MONITORING THE NATION'S CONSCIENCE: A PERSPECTIVE ON METHODISM AND AMERICAN SOCIETY. *Methodist Hist. 1974 12(4): 44-62.* Methodism's mission to America has been reformatory from the beginning. The individual with a sense of moral liability was the basic social unit. The growing sense of Methodism's responsibility to America was paralleled with a sense of the nation's responsibility to the world. This was later complicated by the development of an American society of pluralistic values and commitments—not a unified nation measuring up to the expectations of evangelical Protestantism. Covers 1784-1924. 45 notes. H. L. Calkin

2407. Lewis, Ronald L. CULTURAL PLURALISM AND BLACK RECONSTRUCTION: THE PUBLIC CAREER OF RICHARD CAIN. *Crisis 1978 85(2): 57-60, 64-65.* Richard Harvey Cain (1825-87) was a South Carolina State Senator, a US Congressman, a newspaper editor, an African Methodist Episcopal Bishop, and a college president. Born in 1825, he lived through slavery and the Civil War and worked to improve economic, political, and social conditions for blacks during Reconstruction. He died in 1887, having left a legacy of tireles effort and significant progressive change. A. G. Belles

2408. Link, Eugene P. LATTER DAY CHRISTIAN REBEL: HARRY F. WARD. *Mid-America 1974 56(4): 221-230.* Harry F. Ward, the outstanding religious social critic, played a founding role in the formation of the influential Methodist Federation for Social Service. He, rather than Frank M. North, wrote the "Social Creed of the Churches." Ward was later a leader in the American League for Peace and Democracy in the 1930's. Ward was the most significant social Christian since Walter Rauschenbusch. Based on primary and secondary sources; 23 notes. T. D. Schoonover

2409. Lotz, Jim. THE HISTORICAL AND SOCIAL SETTING OF THE ANTIGONISH MOVEMENT. *Nova Scotia Hist. Q. [Canada] 1975 5(2): 99-116.* Studies the Antigonish Movement as a significant Canadian contribution to the theory and practice of social change. It combined educational, economic, and cooperative merchandising elements to solve serious problems developing in rural areas of eastern Nova Scotia. Traces its history from its inception in the 1920's in response to various social trends (urbanization, industrialization, and rural depopulation) as part of the social action movement of the Catholic Church, and as an alternative to the left-wing and right-wing ideologies of the period. "The Movement has acted as a model and a stimulus for grassroots organization elsewhere in Canada and throughout the world." 14 notes. R. V. Ritter

2410. Lucas, Paul R. THE CHURCH AND THE CITY: CONGREGATIONALISM IN MINNEAPOLIS, 1850-1890. *Minnesota Hist. 1974 44(2): 55-69.* Traces the history of three Congregational churches in Minneapolis, Minnesota, and their individual commitments to the social gospel. Based on primary sources; 11 illus., 56 notes. S

2411. Luker, Ralph E. RELIGION AND SOCIAL CONTROL IN THE NINETEENTH-CENTURY AMERICAN CITY. *J. of Urban Hist. 1976 2(3): 363-368.* In earlier years, historians assumed that clergymen and religiously aroused laypeople forged and led reform movements because it was their innate nature to do good and help their fellow man. Current literature, such as in Nathan L. Huggins' *Protestants Against Poverty: Boston's War on Poverty, 1870-1900*, David J. Pivar's *Purity Crusade: Sexual Morality and Social Control, 1868-1900*, and Carroll Smith Rosenberg's *Religion and the Rise of the American City: The New York City Mission Movement, 1812-1870*, shows the religious reformers to be conservatives interested primarily in social control and the preservation of established moral and social values. Examines this social control thesis and the scholarly merits of the works reviewed. Concludes that 19th-century religious reform was not aimed simply at social control or social liberation but at striking a new balance between the two. 8 notes. T. W. Smith

2412. Luker, Ralph E. THE SOCIAL GOSPEL AND THE FAILURE OF RACIAL REFORM, 1877-1898. *Church Hist. 1977 46(1): 80-99.* Preoccupied with the ills of urban-industrial disorder, the prophets of post-Reconstruction social Christianity either ignored or betrayed the Negro and left his fate in the hands of a hostile white South. However, the concepts of the origins and nature of the social gospel make apparent the relation of the social gospel to three surviving traditions of 19th-century racial reform: 1) the home missions movement, 2) the postabolition tradition of civil equity, and 3) the colonization movement. Finally, it sheds light on the response of the social gospel prophets to the lynching problem in the 1890's. 75 notes. M. D. Dibert

2413. Macias, Ysidro Ramón. NUESTROS ANTEPASADOS Y EL MOVIMIENTO [Our ancestors and the movement]. *Aztlán 1974 5(1-2): 143-154.* Examines the spiritual basis for the Mexican American movement. S

2414. MacLeod, David. A LIVE VACCINE: THE YMCA AND MALE ADOLESCENCE IN THE UNITED STATES AND CANADA 1870-1920. *Social Hist. [Canada] 1978 11(21): 5-25.* In the 1850's and 1860's the Young Men's Christian Association (YMCA) engaged in evangelism for all ages, but as job opportunities for teenagers shrank and formal schooling increased, officials devoted more attention to middle-class adolescent boys, who needed protection from corruption, could pay fees, and would be receptive to Christianity. Around 1900, G. Stanley Hall's studies of adolescent psychology further stimulated boy's work. Workers emphasized objective, masculine religious expression, and dealt with sexuality through distraction and sublimation. During 1910-20 Taylor Statten instigated standardized programs. 87 notes. D. F. Chard

2415. MacPhee, Donald A. CARL HENRY'S VOICE STILL SPEAKS. *Fides et Hist. 1973 5(1-2): 113-116.* Reviews Carl F. Henry's *A Plea for Evangelical Demonstration* (Grand Rapids, Michigan: Baker Books, 1971). Henry calls for a greater commitment to social justice from evangelical Christians. He is strongest on evangelical theology, weakest on the relationship of Christians to revolution. R. Butchart

2416. McElroy, James L. SOCIAL CONTROL AND ROMANTIC REFORM IN ANTEBELLUM AMERICA: THE CASE OF ROCHESTER, NEW YORK. *New York Hist. 1977 58(1): 17-46.* Examines reform studies of antebellum Rochester, New York, to test the paradoxical association between radical reform and conservative religious benevolence. Religious revivalism led converts first to religious benevolence and then to radical reform. The divisive anti-slavery issue, secularizaton of social control, and lessened interest in religious revivalism resulted with the decline of conservative religious benevolence. These reform movements were supported mostly by white collar groups. Younger people were attracted to radical reform. 5 illus., table, 69 notes. R. N. Lokken

2417. McInerny, Dennis Q. THOMAS MERTON AND THE AWAKENING OF SOCIAL CONSCIOUSNESS. *Am. Studies (Lawrence, KS) 1974 15(2): 37-53.* Thomas Merton, a notable American Catholic churchman, experienced an awakening of social consciousness in the 1960's and subsequently tried to bring other people to a similar awakening. Merton was concerned with social conditions in the United States, particularly in the cities, and strongly opposed the Vietnam War. He remained an avid social critic to his death in 1968, and he also dedicated himself to nonviolence. Based on primary and secondary sources; 35 notes. J. Andrew

2418. Meyer, Paul R. THE FEAR OF CULTURAL DECLINE: JOSIAH STRONG'S THOUGHT ABOUT REFORM AND EXPANSION. *Church Hist. 1973 42(3): 396-405.* Contends that Josiah Strong's support for domestic reform and overseas expansion resulted from his religious preoccupation with the idea that the Protestant Anglo-Saxon was a major contributor to civilization's progress. Only a thoroughly Anglo-Saxonized population was capable of positive influence when it inevitably became a world ruler. Strong in his early works described Anglo-Saxon cultural superiority as justification for intervention into other nations' internal affairs. As increasing industrialization created social problems, Strong's writing revealed more pessimism, undermining his earlier confidence in an ultimate Anglo-Saxon cultural victory. His early emphasis upon expansion became overshadowed in later years by his fear of Anglo-Saxon cultural decline. Based on Strong's published works; 33 notes. S. Kerens

2419. Michels, Eileen Manning. ALICE O'BRIEN: VOLUNTEER AND PHILANTHROPIST. Stuhler, Barbara and Kreuter, Gretchen, ed. *Women of Minnesota: Selected Biographical Essays* (St. Paul: Minnesota Historical Society Press, 1977): 136-154. Alice O'Brien was born on 1 September 1891 in the affluent Summit Hill area of St. Paul. The daughter of a wealthy lumberman, Alice attended private schools, traveled extensively, and became a prominent philanthropist and art collector. A curious, intelligent, and self-directed individual, Alice O'Brien was part of a large, affectionate, Irish Catholic family. She spent World War I as a volunteer mechanic, nurse, and canteen worker in Europe. She helped make a documentary film of Africa during the 1920's. Thereafter, she returned to St. Paul and participated in many social and political affairs, including the National Prohibition Reform movement and Wendell Willkie's presidential campaign. Her two major interests were the Women's City Club and the Children's Hospital, to which she devoted much time, energy, and money. During her later years, O'Brien continued to financially help many civic organizations. She established the Alice M. O'Brien Foundation to support educational, scientific, religious, and charitable causes; and she became interested in conservation, especially in Florida where she spent many winters. She was on her way to Florida in November 1962 when she died. Primary sources; photo, 48 notes. A. E. Wiederrecht

2420. Middleton, Robert G. VIEWPOINTS: TWO CHEERS FOR THE SIXTIES. *Foundations 1976 19(4): 292-297.* The 1960's were a period in which the Baptist church and individual Christians were involved in social changes. There are now some who feel that these activities repudiated the Christian witness, and are lamenting their part in them. Argues that much of this activity was good, even though there were some misguided programs such as those involving violence. Hope in cases such as race relations was extravagant, but nevertheless the social changes brought about were for the most part beneficial. 4 notes. E. E. Eminhizer

2421. Mohs, Mayo. HEAVENLY VISIONS IN THE INNER CITY. *Horizon 1978 21(2): 22-27.* Discusses attempts of three New York City Protestant churches, Saint Peter's, Riverside, and Saint John the Divine, to combat social problems, 1970's.

2422. Moorhead, James H. SOCIAL REFORM AND THE DIVIDED CONSCIENCE OF ANTEBELLUM PROTESTANTISM. *Church Hist. 1979 48(4): 416-430.* Besides endorsing the antislavery and temperance causes, the great evangelist Charles G. Finney inspired converts to work out their salvation through useful service, including reform. Central to Finney's undertaking of reform was his belief that virtue consisted in disinterested benevolence. Benevolence was a doctrine of fermentation whose utilitarian principles potentially undermined any institutions failing to meet its rigorous test and it encouraged an open-ended search for new ways to realize its imperative. If Finney's career attested to the powerful, even volatile, potential of popular Protestantism for reform, it demonstrated equally the movement's deficiencies in providing a sustained critique of social problems and in offering policies for their improvement. 58 notes. M. D. Dibert

2423. Morrow, Lance. GOSPEL ACCORDING TO JESSE. *Horizon 1978 21(5): 60-63.* Chronicles the efforts of Jesse Jackson, through the Southern Christian Leadership Conference and his present work with People United to Save Humanity, to raise the black lower classes through a program of strong morality and work ethic combined with pride, education, and personal leadership, 1966-78.

2424. Moses, Wilson J. CIVILIZING MISSIONARY: A STUDY OF ALEXANDER CRUMMELL. *J. of Negro Hist. 1975 60(2): 229-251.* The life of Alexander Crummell illustrates the continuity of the black nationalist tradition throughout the 19th century. In addition to influencing W. E. B. Du Bois and William H. Ferris, Crummell, the Episcopalian clergyman, provided both a personal and an ideological link between the African Civilizationism of the 19th century and the separatist, authoritarian, mystical Negro improvement movements among Afro-Americans. Secondary sources; 54 notes. N. G. Sapper

2425. Mulder, John M. THE HEAVENLY CITY AND HUMAN CITIES: WASHINGTON GLADDEN AND URBAN REFORM. *Ohio Hist. 1978 87(2): 151-174.* Examines the relationship between the social gospel and urbanization and the social gospel's influence in urban reform through the preaching and reform efforts of Washington Gladden, one of the earliest influential social gospel leaders. Gladden's activity spanned six decades and ranged from the antislavery movement of the 1850's to the New Freedom of Woodrow Wilson. His constant theme was the need for social reform. In 1882 Gladden moved to Columbus, Ohio, where he held the pulpit of the First Congregational Church for more than 30 years. The capital provided an excellent forum for Gladden's proclamations and spurred the development of ideas on urban, social, and economic reform. He became active in Columbus politics and the progressive movement until his death. Based on primary and secondary sources; 3 illus., 72 notes. N. Summers

2426. Murray, Pauli. BLACK THEOLOGY AND FEMINIST THEOLOGY: A COMPARATIVE VIEW. *Anglican Theological Rev. 1978 60(1): 3-24.* Black and feminist theologies reflect Christian doctrines and are composed of radical political and social reform ideas which could threaten their existence through particularism and exclusivism, 1960's-70's.

2427. North, Gary. THE PURITAN EXPERIMENT WITH SUMPTUARY LEGISLATION. *Freeman 1974 24(6): 341-355.* Covers 1630-90.

2428. Oaks, Bert F. "THINGS FEARFUL TO NAME": SODOMY AND BUGGERY IN SEVENTEENTH-CENTURY NEW ENGLAND. *J. of Social Hist. 1978 12(2): 268-281.* In recent years historians have begun to study human sexuality, but in recent demographic studies of 17th-century New England, there is almost no consideration of variant sexual activities such as homosexuality and bestiality. Corrects this absence with an examination of variant sexual activities documented principally in the court records. Discusses the confusion over terminology, punishments for the various offenses, and the attitudes of the colonials to variant sexual activity. Concludes that nothing is more symbolic of the failure of the city upon a hill than the history of variant sexual activity in 17th-century New England. Primary and secondary sources; 58 notes. R. S. Sliwoski

2429. Orr, J. Edwin. REVIVAL AND SOCIAL CHANGE. *Fides et Hist. 1974 6(2): 1-12.* Periods of religious revival have brought about social reforms. Surveys the five "awakenings" in America and Europe, discussing the various social movements emanating from them. Covers the 15th-19th centuries. Based on secondary sources; 31 notes. R. Butchart

2430. Paz, D. G. MONASTICISM AND SOCIAL REFORM IN LATE NINETEENTH-CENTURY AMERICA: THE CASE OF FATHER HUNTINGTON. *Hist. Mag. of the Protestant Episcopal Church 1979 48(1): 45-66.* Traces the career of one of the most influential and radical social reformers on the national level of the Episcopal Church, the Reverend James Otis Sargent Huntington (1854-1935), founder of the Order of the Holy Cross, the first permanent monastic order for men in the American church. His career illuminates the nature of the Anglican commitment to social justice, the origins of the order itself, and the inevitable tensions within the dual role of religious and reformer. Huntington was a great advocate of Henry George's single tax theory. Based on the Huntington Papers in the Holy Cross Archives, West Park, New York, his publications, religious studies and secular secondary sources; 92 notes. H. M. Parker, Jr.

2431. Quinley, Harold E. THE DILEMMA OF AN ACTIVIST CHURCH: PROTESTANT RELIGION IN THE SIXTIES AND SEVENTIES. *J. for the Sci. Study of Religion 1974 13(1): 1-21.* Discusses sources of political and social activism in the church during the 1960's and 70's; based on a 1968 survey of Protestant clergymen.

2432. Ross, Edyth L. BLACK HERITAGE IN SOCIAL WELFARE: A CASE STUDY OF ATLANTA. *Phylon 1976 37(4): 297-307.* "An examination of the social welfare heritage of black Americans demonstrates their pioneer role in devising many forms of social intervention for promoting the social welfare of the group." The First Congregational Church, the first institutional church of the country, the largest and most progressive Negro church, developed a social welfare program the effectiveness of which is shown by the fact that the death rate in the church was one-third lower than that among the white population. The program played a large part in the restoration of the city's Negro community after the terrible race riot of 1906. Describes the development of the School of Social Service which became affiliated with Atlanta University. 20 notes. E. P. Stickney

2433. Rothchild, Sylvia. A GREAT HAPPENING IN BOSTON: REVOLT OF THE YOUNG. *Present Tense 1976 3(3): 21-26.* Traces the development of the Jewish Student Movement, a renaissance born in 1960 radicalism, from Jewish Boston establishment antipathy to uneasy acceptance by urban and suburban Jewish and Gentile Boston. Describes the establishment and the impact of the student quarterlies *Response* and *Genesis 2*, the Jewish Student Projects, the communal Havurat Shalom, and the *Jewish Catalogue* on the educational and administrative policies of such religious and educational institutions as the Hillel Foundation(s), Boston University, Harvard-Radcliffe, and suburban synagogues. Quotes such movement notables as Alan Mintz, first editor of *Response*; writers Elie Wiesel and Bill Novak; activists Hillel Levine and Rav Kuk; rabbis Arthur Green, Zalman Schachter, Joseph Polak, Ben-Zion Gold, and Lawrence Kushner; professors Bernard Reisman and Leonard Fein. 4 photos. R. B. Mendel

2434. Russell, C. Allyn. MARK ALLISON MATTHEWS: SEATTLE FUNDAMENTALIST AND CIVIC REFORMER. *J. of Presbyterian Hist. 1979 57(4): 446-466.* Concentrates on the social concerns of Mark Allison Matthews (1867-1940), pastor of the First Presbyterian Church, Seattle, Washington. He was a strange mixture of Biblical Fundamentalism and social reform. Under him his congregation became the largest Presbyterian church in the United States. He was an intense critic of religious liberalism at the time of the modernist-fundamentalist controversy, yet participated actively in the civic and political life of Seattle. Describes in detail his pulpit ability, executive acumen, and Fundamentalist theology. Based on the Matthews Papers (Manuscript Division of Suzzallo Library, University of Washington, Seattle); 2 photos, 66 notes. H. M. Parker, Jr.

2435. Scott, James A. RACISM, THE CHURCH, AND EDUCATIONAL STRATEGIES. *Foundations 1974 17(3): 268-280.* Discusses how the church deals with social issues in the 1970's, emphasizing racism, poverty, and education.

2436. Segers, Mary C. EQUALITY AND CHRISTIAN ANARCHISM: THE POLITICAL AND SOCIAL IDEAS OF THE CATHOLIC WORKER MOVEMENT. *Rev. of Pol. 1978 40(2): 196-230.* The Catholic Worker Movement since 1933 has "consistently adopted controversial positions on contemporary social issues and has challenged Americans to think through the implications of public policy." The key to the success of the movement has been on its emphasis on "the fundamental equality and constant humanity of all men and women." The "personalism" of the Catholic Workers serves as a lesson to capitalistic society that all the "civil rights laws and all the affirmative action policies—will have relatively little impact unless there are fundamental changes in capitalist society and unless, on an attitudinal level, equality is believed and accepted as a rule of practical action." 55 notes. L. E. Ziewacz

2437. Sexton, Robert F. THE CRUSADE AGAINST PARI-MUTUEL GAMBLING IN KENTUCKY: A STUDY OF SOUTHERN PROGRESSIVISM IN THE 1920'S. *Filson Club Hist. Q. 1976 50(1): 47-57.* Documents a continued Progressive movement in Kentucky in the 1920's. The anti-gambling crusade sprang from the religious attack on machine politics led by Helm Bruce and the Louisville Churchmen's Federation. The reformers had their greatest support in rural Kentucky, with support from the Ku Klux Klan and fundamentalist clergymen. Alben Barkley became the political spokesman of the anti-gambling group and nearly secured the Democratic gubernatorial nomination in 1923; four years later, former governor J. C. W. Beckham won the party's nomination as the anti-gambling candidate. Urban Democrats deserted Beckham, however, and Republican Slem Sampson was elected. Beckham's defeat marked the end of the Progressive movement in Kentucky. Documented from newspapers and the Barkley Papers at the University of Kentucky; 34 notes. G. B. McKinney

2438. Shapiro, Edward S. ROBERT A. WOODS AND THE SETTLEMENT HOUSE IMPULSE. *Social Service Rev. 1978 52(2): 215-226.* Initially suspected by Catholics as an agency of Protestant proselytization, Boston's South End House, founded by Robert A. Woods, was intended to slow the city's growing religious, ethnic, and social heterogeneity by providing a sense of community; covers 1891-1910.

2439. Shupe, Anson D., Jr. and Wood, James R. SOURCES OF LEADERSHIP IDEOLOGY IN DISSIDENT CLERGY. *Sociol. Analysis 1973 34(3): 185-201.* This study of twelve ministers and their congregations explores several possible sources of ideologies which sustain ministers when their social action stances are out of line with those of their parishioners. Both theology and attitudes toward church polity appear to be important dimensions of such sustaining ideologies. It is suggested that both these dimensions are anchored in socialization and social interaction within the minister's denomination. J

2440. Skoglund, John E., trans. EDWIN DAHLBERG IN CONVERSATION: MEMORIES OF WALTER RAUSCHENBUSCH. *Foundations 1975 18(3): 209-218.* Transcribes an interview with Edwin Dahlberg concerning the life and work of Walter Rauschenbusch as remembered by one student. The interview centers on Baptist Rauschenbusch as teacher and social reformer. 6 notes. E. E. Eminhizer

2441. Smillie, Benjamin G. THE SOCIAL GOSPEL. *Can. Dimension [Canada] 1979 13(5): 35-37.* Discusses the Social Gospel, church aid for the labor movement, and Christian Socialism in 20th-century Canada.

2442. Smith, John S. H. CIGARETTE PROHIBITION IN UTAH, 1921-23. *Utah Hist. Q. 1973 41(4): 358-372.* The tobacco prohibition movement was a lesser known attempt to legislate morality. Utah was one of more than a dozen states to enact such legislation. Traces the movement in the state from 1896 to 1923. In addition to the usual reasons for opposing the use of tobacco, it was a basic tenet of the Mormon Church. It was impossible to keep Mormon-Gentile antagonisms out of the issue. 4 illus., 53 notes. D. L. Smith

2443. Smith, Kenneth and Sweet, Leonard. SHAILER MATHEWS: A CHAPTER IN THE SOCIAL GOSPEL MOVEMENT. *Foundations 1975 18(3): 219-237, (4): 296-320; 1976 19(1): 53-68, (2): 152-170.* Part I. Born in Portland, Maine, 26 May 1863, son of a Baptist businessman, Shailer Mathews was converted in a Moody revival in 1875. Strongly influenced by his grandfather, William Shailer, he attended Waterville College and Colby University. Unsure of a vocation, he attended Newton Seminary where he was introduced to lower criticism. He taught at Colby following graduation from Newton. In 1890 he studied in Germany where he was introduced to Ranke's historical method, as well as new ideas in economics and ethics. As a result he brought the new ideas to Colby and became concerned with social reform. In 1899 he joined men of similar spirit and thinking at the University of Chicago. 54 notes. Part II. Discusses Matthews' approach to dealing with the conflict that developed between religion and science in the last half of the 19th century; also his social views and theology in the context of Christian experience. The later sections are concerned with Mathews' doctrine of God. 96 notes. Part III. Discusses Mathews' view on sin and salvation, and the destiny of man as it reflects evolutionary theories. Mathews saw sin as man's "animal impulses," but man could transcend this. From this idea the article proceeds to discuss the source of sin, its consequences, and the place of Christ in changing man's condition. 88 notes. Part IV. Discusses Mathews' views on the Kingdom of God, ethics, and eschatology, as found in his *The Social Teachings of Jesus* (1897) and *Jesus on Social Institutions* (1928). E. E. Eminhizer

2444. Sokolow, Jayme A. HENRY CLARKE WRIGHT: ANTEBELLUM CRUSADER. *Essex Inst. Hist. Collections 1975 111(2): 122-137.* Examines the origin of Wright's ideas on reform. Evangelical revivalism led to his interest in and advocacy of temperance, immediate abolition of slavery, women's suffrage, pacifism, and humanitarian education. Based on historical essays, newspapers, letters, journals, and Wright's work; 41 notes. R. M. Rollins

2445. Stroupe, Henry S. "CITE THEM BOTH TO ATTEND THE NEXT CHURCH CONFERENCE": SOCIAL CONTROL BY NORTH CAROLINA BAPTIST CHURCHES, 1772-1908. *North Carolina Hist. Rev. 1975 52(2): 156-170.* Baptist church congregations in North Carolina have exercised direct control over the personal conduct of members since the 18th century. Until the early 20th century transgressors were made to fear for their souls and their social standing in the community. Churches excommunicated or suspended white and black congregants for adultery, drunkenness, thievery, lying, swearing, quarreling, etc. Following World War I the church began employing indirect methods for social control, such as the temperance movement and blue laws. Based on manuscript church records, and published primary and secondary sources; 4 illus., table, 37 notes. T. L. Savitt

2446. Strum, Harvey. PROPHET OF RIGHTEOUSNESS. *Alberta Hist. [Canada] 1975 23(4): 21-27.* In 1909 William Jennings Bryan made a speaking tour of western Canada as a fund-raising effort for the Young Men's Christian Association (YMCA). He began at Victoria, B.C., then moved across the prairie provinces. He spoke either on the YMCA movement, or delivered his famous "Prince of Peace" speech. He surprised many Canadians favorably; they were familiar with his role as political leader, but not moral reformer. His political views were especially popular in western Canada as he campaigned against trusts and the plutocracy in general. 3 photos, 34 notes. D. Chaput

2447. Swanson, Merwin. THE "COUNTRY LIFE MOVEMENT" AND THE AMERICAN CHURCHES. *Church Hist. 1977 46(3): 358-373.* During the Progressive Era the country life movement shared many of the urban progressives' analyses and reform plans and applied them to rural America. Progressives in the country life movement believed that even rural neighborhoods had lost their sense of community. Although the country lifers believed that the rural church should serve the rural community because such service was inherently right, they also believed that community service was essential to the survival of rural churches. Programs were instituted to transform rural churches into community centers which would serve the goals of progressive improvement and development. 30 notes. M. D. Dibert

2448. Szasz, Margaret Connell. ALBUQUERQUE CONGREGATIONALISTS AND SOUTHWESTERN SOCIAL REFORM: 1900-1917. *New Mexico Hist. Rev. 1980 55(3): 231-252.* From 1900 to 1917 the Congregationalists of the Albuquerque community participated in the rise of the social gospel and the national movement for social reform. In Albuquerque, the two primary areas of reform were prohibition and education. The Albuquerque Congregationalists, along with other state and local temperance groups, helped to pass the state constitutional amendment for prohibition in 1917. However, it was in the field of education that the Congregationalists made their most enduring contribution to New Mexico. Based on material in the Special Collections Department, University of New Mexico Library, and the First Congregational Church Archives, Albuquerque, New Mexico, and other primary sources; 3 photos, 54 notes. P. L. McLaughlin

2449. Tobin, Eugene M. THE PROGRESSIVE AS HUMANITARIAN: JERSEY CITY'S SEARCH FOR SOCIAL JUSTICE, 1890-1917. *New Jersey Hist. 1975 93(3-4): 77-98.* Social reformers in Jersey City are classified into three groups: private, religious, and public. The Whittier House social settlement tackled problems associated with tenement slums, crime, infant mortality, and juvenile delinquency. Protestants campaigned for broad social welfare reform, while less affluent Catholics opted for assistance on an individual basis for its immigrant communicants. A separate juvenile court was established. World War I changed the priorities of reformers. A typical Jersey City reformer was "a native-stock, middle-class Protestant who resided in the Eighth or Ninth Ward and had some college training." Based on primary and secondary sources; 7 illus., 44 notes. E. R. McKinstry

2450. Wahl, Albert F. LONGWOOD MEETING: PUBLIC FORUM FOR THE AMERICAN DEMOCRATIC FAITH. *Pennsylvania Hist. 1975 42(1): 43-69.* A number of reform-minded Quakers in the mid-19th century became convinced that many of their fellow Quakers were more concerned with the outward forms of their faith than its essence. Groups in Pennsylvania, New York, Ohio, and Michigan severed ties with their respective meetings, and representatives of these Quakers met at the Old Kennett Meeting House in 1853 to form the Pennsylvania Yearly Meeting of Progressive Friends. Two years later they found it necessary to build a new meeting house, and the meeting was hereafter known as the Longwood Meeting. Although a commitment to abolitionism was the most important force in bringing them together, these progressives embraced all the moral reforms of the day and attempted to bring their view of Christian Democracy to others. Until their last meeting in 1940, the Progressive Quakers continued to advocate such reforms as Negro rights, the social gospel, women's liberation, and the rights of labor. Based on proceedings of the Longwood meetings, newspapers, and other sources; 111 notes. D. C. Swift

2451. Whisnant, David E. CONTROVERSY IN GOD'S GREAT DIVISION: THE COUNCIL OF THE MOUNTAINS. *Appalachian J. 1974 2(1): 7-45.* History of the Council of Southern Mountain Workers, a group of social reformers, ministers, doctors, and agriculturalists who seek improvement of living standards in rural southern areas, 1913-72. S

2452. Williams, James H. BACK TO THE BASICS: A NEW CHALLENGE FOR THE BLACK CHURCH. *Explorations in Ethnic Studies 1980 3(1): 13-18.* Discusses some of the black Protestant church's shortcomings and urges it to return to a stronger social role in improving the quality of life for blacks; 1970's.

2453. Wukasch, Peter. BALTIC IMMIGRANTS IN CANADA, 1947-1955. *Concordia Hist. Inst. Q. 1977 50(1): 4-22.* Fleeing Russian expansion, a number of people from Estonia, Latvia, and Lithuania entered Canada during 1947-55. To assist these immigrants the Lutheran Church responded with a multifaceted program led by Rev. Ernest Hahn and Rev. Donald Ortner of St. John's Lutheran Church in Toronto. The church involved itself in social, economic, cultural, and political efforts to safeguard the interests of the displaced Baltic people. Primary sources; 28 notes. W. T. Walker

Abolition

2454. Akers, Charles W. "OUR MODERN EGYPTIANS": PHILLIS WHEATLEY AND THE WHIG CAMPAIGN AGAINST SLAVERY IN REVOLUTIONARY BOSTON. *J. of Negro Hist. 1975 60(3): 397-410.* Unnoticed by previous scholars, one of Phillis Wheatley's most eloquent letters (written in 1774) contains the three elements of her attitude toward slavery: Christian piety, Whiggish patriotism, and racial consciousness. Primary and secondary sources; 42 notes. N. G. Sapper

2455. Allen, Jeffrey Brooke. WERE SOUTHERN WHITE CRITICS OF SLAVERY RACISTS? KENTUCKY AND THE UPPER SOUTH, 1791-1824. *J. of Southern Hist. 1978 44(2): 169-190.* This study, primarily of Kentucky clergymen, challenges the idea that the majority of white antislavery Southerners were racists. Historians have neglected a large group of religious men who defended the equality of blacks. Their antislavery arguments were directed against the abolitionist and the proslavery advocate, both of whom thought in racist terms. Praises the Kentucky clergymen's challenge to racism, but concedes that their eventual conversion to African colonization came, not as a result of their conversion to racism, but because of their having to function in a racist environment. M. S. Legan

2456. Boles, John B. TENSION IN A SLAVE SOCIETY: THE TRIAL OF THE REVEREND JACOB GRUBER. *Southern Studies 1979 18(2): 179-197.* Jacob Gruber (b. 1778), a Methodist preacher from Pennsylvania, in 1818 preached at a camp meeting in Washington County, Maryland, to a mixed audience of blacks and whites. He was subsequently arrested and charged with inciting the slaves present to rebel. Sources indicate that Gruber lacked tact, a sense of proportion, and calm. He was opposed to slavery and often spoke publicly against it. National debate in 1818 to prevent slavery in Missouri made the issue especially sensitive. He was found not guilty for lack of evidence of language actually inciting revolt. The acrimony at the trial reveals the South in the process of discovering itself as a separate minority. Primary sources; 70 notes. J. J. Buschen

2457. Bolt, Christine and Drescher, Seymour. [ANTI-SLAVERY, RELIGION AND REFORM: INTRODUCTION]. Bolt, Christine and Drescher, Seymour, ed. *Anti-Slavery, Religion and Reform: Essays in Memory of Roger Anstey* (Folkestone, England: Dawson, 1980): 1-9. Reviews the various approaches which this collection brings to bear on the study of the antislavery movement. Discusses the social, political, economic, and cultural influences affecting participation—or lack of it—in a reform movement which contained powerful elements of religion, morality, rationalism, optimism, and pragmatism.

2458. Bronner, Edwin B. AN EARLY ANTISLAVERY STATEMENT: 1676. *Quaker Hist. 1973 62(1): 47-50.* Alice Curwen (ca. 1619-79) and her husband Thomas (1610-80) were jailed and whipped in Boston, 1676, traveled in New England, Long Island, East Jersey, and Barbados and returned to England. After a 1675 Barbadian slave insurrection Quakers were not allowed to bring their slaves to meeting or school. Alice Curwen's letter to Martha Tavernor, first printed in 1680, urged the slaveholder to break this law and bring her whole family, including slaves, to worship. 10 notes. T. D. S. Bassett

2459. Brooks, George E., Jr. THE PROVIDENCE AFRICAN SOCIETY'S SIERRA LEONE EMIGRATION SCHEME, 1794-1795: PROLOGUE TO THE AFRICAN COLONIZATION MOVEMENT. *Int. J. of African Hist. Studies 1974 7(2): 183-202.* In November 1794 the African Society of Providence dispatched one of its officers, James Mackenzie, to negotiate arrangements for the settlement of American freedmen in Sierra Leone. Reverend Samuel Hopkins, a prominent Congregationalist clergyman and a well-known advocate of black emigration, was responsible for the fact that no members of the African Society subsequently emigrated, inasmuch as he refused to furnish the prospective colonists with the character references required by the governor of Sierra Leone. Primary and secondary sources; 46 notes.
M. M. McCarthy

2460. Bruns, Roger. BENJAMIN LAY: THE EXPLOITS OF AN ARDENT ABOLITIONIST. *Am. Hist. Illus. 1979 14(2): 16-22.* Discusses the colorful Quaker abolitionist Benjamin Lay, 1690's-1759, who was born in England, moved to Barbados, and on to Philadelphia.

2461. Bruns, Roger A. A QUAKER'S ANTISLAVERY CRUSADE: ANTHONY BENEZET. *Quaker Hist. 1976 65(2): 81-92.* The voices of a few antislavery Friends before 1756 were smothered by the comfortable, respectable weight of American Quakerism. Anthony Benezet believed that Friends were indifferent to the evils of slavery because they did not know them. From the 1759 publication of his first major pamphlet until his death in 1784, he was an "old white-haired busybody of good works scurrying around" to individual Friends and their meetings with letters and tracts, speaking against slave trading and holding. Discrimination continued. Although the Philadelphia Yearly Meeting (comprising Delaware, Pennsylvania, and much of New Jersey) excommmunicated slaveholding members in 1776, it did not abolish the color bar to membership until 1796. 56 notes. T. D. S. Bassett

2462. Burke, Ronald K. THE ANTI-SLAVERY ACTIVITIES OF SAMUEL RINGGOLD WARD IN NEW YORK STATE. *Afro-Americans in New York Life and Hist. 1978 2(1): 17-28.* Samuel Ringgold Ward, a black Northern Congregationalist abolitionist, subscribed to the theory of Christology (becoming Christ-like in thought and action) in preaching reform in New York during 1839-51.

2463. Clar, Bayard S. A SERMON BY PHILLIPS BROOKS ON THE DEATH OF ABRAHAM LINCOLN. *Hist. Mag. of the Protestant Episcopal Church 1980 49(1): 37-50.* Contains the 1893 text of the sermon which Phillips Brooks, 30-year-old rector of Boston's Holy Trinity Church, preached to his Philadelphia congregation on 23 April 1865, following Lincoln's assassination nine days earlier. The sermon vaulted Brooks into national prominence as a preacher. He was a strong antislavery advocate, as the sermon reveals. In it Brooks pointed out that slavery was the curse of the nation. 2 notes.
H. M. Parker, Jr.

2464. Conforti, Joseph. SAMUEL HOPKINS AND THE REVOLUTIONARY ANTISLAVERY MOVEMENT. *Rhode Island Hist. 1979 38(2): 39-49.* A Congregational minister in Newport, Rhode Island, Samuel Hopkins, began speaking out against slavery and the slave trade in the 1770's and went on to become a leading figure in the New England antislavery movement until his death in 1803. Based on manuscripts in New Haven, Newport, New York City, Philadelphia, and Providence, newspapers, pamphlets, and Hopkins's writings; 6 illus., 37 notes.
P. J. Coleman

2465. Cox, Steven. NATHANIEL P. ROGERS AND THE ROGERS COLLECTION. *Hist. New Hampshire 1978 33(1): 52-61.* Nathaniel Peabody Rogers (1794-1846) was New Hampshire's leading abolitionist. Diverted from a legal career by the slavery issue in the early 1830's, he helped found the Portsmouth Anti-Slavery Society in 1833, and became editor of the *Herald of Freedom* in 1838. He espoused nonresistance (pacifism) and attacked churches with Southern connections. His letters are in the Quaker Collection, Haverford College Library, Haverford, Pennsylvania. Consisting of about 800 items, the collection sheds much light on Rogers' life and the abolitionist movement. Primary and secondary sources; 19 notes. D. F. Chard

2466. Essig, James David. THE LORD'S FREE MAN: CHARLES G. FINNEY AND HIS ABOLITIONISM. *Civil War Hist. 1978 24(1): 25-45.* Charles Grandison Finney's theology and antislavery activities reveal a surprisingly committed abolitionism joined to the conviction that indifference to slavery impeded the gospel's spread. Revivalism and abolition could hasten the millennium. His thought closely followed the march of the slavery controversy. During 1833-39, Finney attempted to persuade Southerners to abolish slavery because it was sinful. Through the Civil War, detecting Southern selfishness and malevolence, he turned to violent denunciation and demands for punishment. He succeeded only imperfectly, but did join evangelism to social reform. Unpublished and published papers and secondary works; 94 notes. R. E. Stack

2467. Fellman, Michael. THEODORE PARKER AND THE ABOLITIONIST ROLE IN THE 1850'S. *J. of Am. Hist. 1974 61(3): 666-684.* In the 1850's Theodore Parker, the noted Boston preacher, entered the abolitionist ranks with a message appealing to many people. This Transcendentalist emphasized a higher, natural law of freedom which justified the destruction, by bloodshed if necessary, of "unnatural" statutory law and institutions. Violence was seen as a means of regenerating the revolutionary spirit of Anglo-Saxon New Englanders endangered by materialism and the appearance of the degenerate Irish. Parker called for the preservation of racial purity and ideals from a southern "Spanish" type mixed with an inferior black race possessed of heightened sexuality and a slave mentality. He saw no future for blacks in a racially integrated society, but saw dangers of a future race war if slavery were not ended. 71 notes. K. B. West

2468. Franklin, Benjamin, V. THEODORE DWIGHT'S "AFRICAN DISTRESS": AN EARLY ANTI-SLAVERY POEM. *Yale U. Lib. Gazette 1979 54(1): 26-36.* The first serious antislavery poem to appear in the United States was printed anonymously in the *New-Haven Gazette,* 21 February 1788. Although brief and modest, it was the best poem ever produced by the Connecticut wit, Congregationalist Theodore Dwight. The most authoritative version, reprinted at the conclusion of the article, was produced by the anthologist Samuel Kettrell in *Specimens of American Poetry* (Boston, 1829). 7 notes. D. A. Yanchisin

2469. Friedman, Lawrence J. CONFIDENCE AND PERTINACITY IN EVANGELICAL ABOLITIONISM: LEWIS TAPPAN'S CIRCLE. *Am. Q. 1979 31(1): 81-106.* The "conservative" church-oriented abolitionists who formed Lewis Tappan's circle of reformist friends consisted of such like-minded men as William Jay, Amos Phelps, Theodore Weld, and George Cheever. Each had had positive experiences in his earlier reform activities that, coupled with his common belief in self-help and a God-ordered society, and Lewis Tappan's managerial expertise, provided a group cohesiveness that was unaffected by differences over reform specifics. Covers ca. 1830-61. Based on the journals and papers of the primary participants; 41 notes.
D. G. Nielson

2470. Friedman, Lawrence J. PURIFYING THE WHITE MAN'S COUNTRY: THE AMERICAN COLONIZATION SOCIETY RECONSIDERED 1816-40. *Societas 1976 6(1): 1-24.* Reverend Robert Finley drew together a mixed following of slaveholders, Old School Federalists, Negrophobes, and antislavery philanthropists to found the American Colonization Society in 1816. The stated goal of the organization was to ease American racial difficulties by sending free blacks to Africa, but the motivations and real goals of the society were much more complex and contradictory than this stated purpose would suggest. Because the colonizationists were most ineffective in removing from the nation these allegedly impure elements, the author concludes in part, "For assurances of white purity, Negroes may have been needed as a point of contrast." Based on society's papers on the Library of Congress, and on printed primary and secondary sources; 83 notes.
J. D. Hunley

2471. Frost, J. William. THE ORIGINS OF THE QUAKER CRUSADE AGAINST SLAVERY: A REVIEW OF RECENT LITERATURE. *Quaker Hist. 1978 67(1): 42-58.* Thomas Drake's *Quakers and Slavery,* although limited to published works, remains the starting place for research, even though it is unrevised and unsupplemented for the 19th century. Sydney James, on 18th-century Quaker benevolence, placed abolition in the context of charitable reforms but exaggerated the changes of 1755. After examining 32 other articles and monographs showing the spotty Quaker record of participation in the slave trade, racism, reciprocal transatlantic influences, and Quaker antislavery leadership, concludes that David B. Davis's chapter in *The Problem of Slavery in the Age of Revolution* is the best published account of the Quaker role in starting the abolition process. Suggests that the significance of this role is in the merging of the Woolman- and Benezet-led reform movement. This appealed to rural Friends with few slaves and suspicious of Philadelphia merchants and the disciplinary movement of Philadelphia ministers and elders. The result was "stringent discipline, withdrawal from government, antislavery, and the freedom to prosper. Nineteenth century Quakers were wedded to gentility and social reform." 36 notes.
T. D. S. Bassett

2472. George, Carol V. R. WIDENING THE CIRCLE: THE BLACK CHURCH AND THE ABOLITIONIST CRUSADE, 1830-1860. Perry, Lewis and Fellman, Michael, ed. *Antislavery Reconsidered: New Perspectives on the Abolitionists* (Baton Rouge: Louisiana State U. Pr., 1979): 75-95. Surveys the careers of more than 40 black clergymen from 1830 to 1860 to show the multidimensional quality of their leadership. Working under extremely varied conditions—in slave states and free, as circuit preachers and permanently settled ministers, in exclusively black as well as biracial institutions, and at every level of the hierarchy—black religious leaders contributed to the abolition and civil rights movements and heightened black self-awareness among blacks. 29 notes.
S

2473. Glickstein, Jonathan A. "POVERTY IS NOT SLAVERY": AMERICAN ABOLITIONISTS AND THE COMPETITIVE LABOR MARKET. Perry, Lewis and Fellman, Michael, ed. *Antislavery Reconsidered: New Perspectives on the Abolitionists* (Baton Rouge: Louisiana State U. Pr., 1979): 195-218. Although some abolitionists such as William I. Bowditch believed that the economic system of the industrialized North created a slavery almost as terrible as that of the South, most people in the antislavery movement—especially those who came from evangelical Christianity—believed that, on the positive side, marketplace competition in the United States was so fair that willing workers would not be exploited, and, on the negative side, fear of poverty and poverty itself would act as a spur to industriousness and as proof against indolence. 38 notes.
S

2474. Hovet, Theodore R. CHRISTIAN REVOLUTION: HARRIET BEECHER STOWE'S RESPONSE TO SLAVERY AND THE CIVIL WAR. *New England Q. 1974 47(4): 535-549.* Studies the Christian roots of Mrs. Stowe's antislavery sentiments and the charges forced upon her after the Civil War. Her views of slavery were constructed out of the tenets of Christian perfection. Her antislavery writings indicate also some of the reasons for a change from despair to optimism after the war is won, even though she must admit the ex-slaves have not actually achieved full rights; hence we may speak of the "failure of radical reform in America in the 1850's and 1860's." In her view one could never question the worth of the Civil War by finding fault with the ultimate result. 22 notes.
R. V. Ritter

2475. Howard, Victor B. THE KENTUCKY PRESBYTERIANS IN 1849: SLAVERY AND THE KENTUCKY CONSTITUTION. *Register of the Kentucky Hist. Soc. 1975 73(3): 217-240.* Presbyterians in Kentucky were more opposed to slavery than any other denomination. Led by Robert J. and William Lewis Breckinridge, Presbyterians led the move for emancipation. Although the Emancipation Party of 1849 failed to gain its objectives, remnants of the movement formed the base for the Republican Party in Kentucky. Primary and secondary sources; 63 notes.
J. F. Paul

2476. James, Thomas. THE AUTOBIOGRAPHY OF REV. THOMAS JAMES. *Rochester Hist. 1975 37(4): 1-32.* Reprints an autobiography of Thomas James during 1804-80; he was a minister of the African Methodist Episcopal Church who belonged to the abolitionist movement.

2477. Locke, William R. AN ABOLITIONIST AT GENERAL CONFERENCE. *Methodist Hist. 1979 17(4): 225-238.* William D. Cass was a member of the New Hampshire Conference of the Methodist Episcopal Church. He attended the 1844 General Conference of the Church at which the split over slavery occurred. As an abolitionist Cass took a position against permitting slavery within the church. His personal account of the activities is revealed in the three letters to his wife included here. 39 notes.
H. L. Calkin

2478. Loomis, Sally. EVOLUTION OF PAUL CUFFE'S BLACK NATIONALISM. *Negro Hist. Bull. 1974 37(6): 298-302.* Paul Cuffe (1759-1817), a black Quaker, helped colonize black Americans in Sierra Leone in the 1810's as part of his vision for an international brotherhood that was the "African nation."

2479. Marable, W. Manning. DEATH OF THE QUAKER SLAVE TRADE. *Quaker Hist. 1974 63(1): 17-33.* The first admonitions to Quaker merchants by George Fox in 1656 extended his business ethic to dealing in Indian and African slaves. After Pennsylvania was settled, Friends sanctioned the trade provided all bondsmen were freed after a maximum of 14 years. Difficulties in receiving payment for West Indian slaves sold to Pennsylvania farmers, the rising prices of slaves, and fear of slave insurrection combined with a revival in sensitivity to solidify the Quaker testimony against the slave trade by 1750. 51 notes.
T. D. S. Bassett

2480. Maxwell, John Francis. THE CHARISMATIC ORIGINS OF THE CHRISTIAN ANTI-SLAVERY MOVEMENT IN NORTH AMERICA. *Quaker Hist. 1974 63(2): 108-116.* Quotes George Fox (1671), William Edmundson (1676), Philadelphia Monthly Meeting (1693), William Burling (1718), Benjamin Lay (1738), John Woolman (1762), and Anthony Benezet (1771) on slavery as a moral evil. 12 notes.
T. D. S. Bassett

2481. McKivigan, John R. THE AMERICAN BAPTIST FREE MISSION SOCIETY: ABOLITIONIST REACTION TO THE 1845 BAPTIST SCHISM. *Foundations 1978 21(4): 240-355.* Examines abolitionist relations with Northern Baptists, both before and after the 1845 schism. The American Free Baptist Mission Society was composed of those Baptists who would have no fellowship with Baptists who were in any way connected with the institution of domestic slavery—whether through slave-holding or in accepting contributions from those who held slaves. The group worked outside the normal lines of denominational missionary activity, supporting only missionaries who labored in free states. The persistence of abolitionist criticism of Northern Baptists thus requires a reassessment of the denomination's pre-Civil War antislavery reputation. The number of Northern Baptist associations renouncing fellowship with slaveholders steadily increased during the 1850's and helped sharpen sectional polarization, freeing Northern Baptists to speak more agggressively against slavery. Based on the Annual Reports of the ABFMS and similar benevolent societies; 46 notes.
H. M. Parker, Jr.

2482. Moore, N. Webster. JOHN BERRY MEACHUM (1789-1854): ST. LOUIS PIONEER, BLACK ABOLITIONIST, EDUCATOR,

AND PREACHER. *Missouri Hist. Soc. Bull. 1973 29(2): 96-103.* Meachum, a Virginia slave, purchased his freedom and emigrated to St. Louis in 1815, where he joined in the efforts of a white Baptist missionary, John Mason Peck, "to reclaim the Negroes through religious instruction." In 1825, Meachum was ordained and founded the First African Baptist Church in St. Louis. He initiated educational programs for Negroes in the St. Louis area and purchased and freed about 20 slaves. Secondary sources and manuscript holdings of the Missouri Historical Society; 18 notes. H. T. Lovin

2483. Murray, Andrew E. BRIGHT DELUSION: PRESBYTERIANS AND AFRICAN COLONIZATION. *J. of Presbyterian Hist. 1980 58(3): 224-237.* The basic flaw of the American Colonization Society (ACS) was its effort to ease the troubled consciences of white Americans while ignoring the needs and desires of black people. Points out the paradox in the life of David McDonough, an American slave whose master wanted him trained for leadership in Africa. Details the many frustrations McDonough confronted in his preparation to be a physician, due to prejudice. The ACS did not meet the needs of all blacks. For McDonough and others, colonization attempted to solve the problems of white oppressors by requiring the victims of that oppression to make major sacrifices. Covers ca. 1840-50. Based largely on McDonough's correspondence with the Board of Foreign Missions, Presbyterian Historical Society, Philadelphia, and studies on the American Colonization Society; 30 notes. H. M. Parker, Jr.

2484. Reilly, Timothy F. ROBERT L. STANTON, ABOLITIONIST OF THE OLD SOUTH. *J. of Presbyterian Hist. 1975 53(1): 33-49.* A New Englander by birth and sentiment, Robert Stanton spent nine frustrating years as a pastor in New Orleans and two years as president of Oakland College, Mississippi, prior to the Civil War. The author of a pamphlet, "New Orleans as It Is," Stanton attacked the evils of slavery as he saw it in the Crescent City. While in New Orleans he was overshadowed by B. M. Palmer of the First Presbyterian Church who supported slavery from the pulpit. Stanton held Palmer and other Presbyterian divines morally responsible for the furtherance of slavery and the secession that followed. In 1854 he left the South, settled in Ohio, and became a vociferous opponent of slavery. Based on Stanton's writings and other contemporary publications, photo, 63 notes.
H. M. Parker, Jr.

2485. Rosenthal, Bernard. PURITAN CONSCIENCE AND NEW ENGLAND SLAVERY. *New England Q. 1973 46(1): 62-81.* "The main efforts on behalf of slaves were likely to come from orthodox Puritans." They questioned whether Christians could be slaves—the Bible to the contrary notwithstanding. The actual conversion of Negroes was rare. John Adams in 1795 observed that theological conviction had less to do with emancipation than did the economics of the white working class. A coalition of the clergy and the white working class ended slavery in New England. 56 notes. E. P. Stickney

2486. Schatz, Klaus. EINSATZ FÜR GERECHTIGKEIT UND ABFINDEN MIT DEN VERHÄLTNISSEN [Action for justice and acceptance of the conditions]. *Stimmen der Zeit [West Germany] 1979 197(2): 99-113.* The protest of Dominicans against slavery in South and North America in the 16th century was continued by the Jesuits, who opposed Indian and Negro slavery in Latin America in the 17th and 18th centuries.

2487. Schwarz, Philip J. CLARK T. MOORMAN, QUAKER EMANCIPATOR. *Quaker Hist. 1980 69(1): 27-35.* An 1849 letter from his grandson, Thomas H. Tyrell of Toledo, Ohio, recalls Clark Terrell Moorman's account of how in November 1782 he manumitted his two slaves, Gloster Mingo and Peter Peters, inherited in 1766. He had a dream that a black barred him from heaven. Like other 18th-century abolitionists, Moorman emphasized the bad effects of slavery on whites rather than on blacks. Cedar Creek Monthly Meeting in Caroline County, Virginia, started its campaign to abolish slaveholding among its members in December 1777. Moorman, an average farmer, had to sell land to pay for his free labor. Ultimately, he moved to Ohio. He felt that the manumission brought spiritual blessings in spite of economic losses. County records and Quaker sources; 29 notes. T. D. S. Bassett

2488. Scott, Donald M. ABOLITION AS A SACRED VOCATION. Perry, Lewis and Fellman, Michael, ed. *Antislavery Reconsidered: New Perspectives on the Abolitionists* (Baton Rouge: Louisiana State U. Pr., 1979): 51-74. Many who espoused the immediate abolition of slavery had felt sudden religious revelations that slavery was a sin and had to be extirpated. Gerrit Smith, Theodore Weld, James Birney, and H. B. Stanton were among those who, influenced by the evangelism of the 1820's, called from the pulpit for the swift emancipation of blacks. 32 notes.
S

2489. Stewart, James Brewer. EVANGELICALISM AND THE RADICAL STRAIN IN SOUTHERN ANTISLAVERY THOUGHT DURING THE 1820'S. *J. of Southern Hist. 1973 39(3): 379-396.* Discusses Southern antislavery sentiments during the 1820's among scattered groups of devout Evangelicals, located mostly in the northernmost parts of the South. These few "radicals" believed slavery to be a cause for the decline of religious piety, a contradiction of religious creeds, a crime against humanity, an erosive force on morality and traditional values, and a cause of the diffusion of corruption and civic decay. The Evangelicals attempted to spread their gospel to purify "churchly institutions," and in the process estranged themselves from Southern society. Much of the later abolitionism of the North was similar to or built upon their ideas. Based on contemporary publications and addresses, and secondary sources; 63 notes. N. J. Street

2490. Stirn, James R. URGENT GRADUALISM: THE CASE OF THE AMERICAN UNION FOR THE RELIEF AND IMPROVEMENT OF THE COLORED RACE. *Civil War Hist. 1979 25(4): 309-328.* Briefly during 1835-37, a few mainly Congregationalist Boston religious and business leaders formed, prematurely, the American Union as an alternative to Garrisonianism. Spurning quasicolonizationist views, they pushed urgent, albeit gradual, emancipation through piecemeal reforms such as education and religion, on moderates, North and South. The Union revealed Christian impatience with Southern inaction. Few responded, even when the popular Reverend Leonard Bacon explained how piecemeal cessation of wicked practices would ruin slavery. Terrible disillusionment resulted. The organizers did try significant, tentative steps away from colonization toward pragmatic abolition; respectable Northerners struggled, midway between old ideas, with possibilities of Southern revolt and war. 84 notes. R. E. Stack

2491. Thompson, J. Earl, Jr. ABOLITIONISM AND THEOLOGICAL EDUCATION AT ANDOVER. *New England Q. 1974 47(2): 238-261.* John Greenleaf Whittier, William Lloyd Garrison, and other abolitionists were disillusioned by Andover Seminary's rejection of organized abolitionism. Discusses in detail the development of organized antislavery reform in the Congregationalist seminary's curriculum until it was discontinued in 1835. 69 notes. E. P. Stickney

2492. Thompson, J. Earl, Jr. LYMAN BEECHER'S LONG ROAD TO CONSERVATIVE ABOLITIONISM. *Church Hist. 1973 42(1): 89-109.* Beecher's New School Presbyterian conservative abolitionism underwent three major developmental stages. He was first identified as a New England Colonizationist. The 1834 Lane Seminary rebellion shows Beecher in his second stage as one trying to establish cooperative links between abolitionists and colonizationists notwithstanding their fundamental differences. After the 1837 Presbyterian schism Beecher began to associate with Ohio's New School Presbyterians who by the time of the 1843-44 William Graham heresy trials accepted moderate abolitionism aimed at a gradual end to slavery among church members and, by example, throughout the nation. Based on early 19th-century association journals, newspapers, letters, Beecher's autobiography, and secondary sources; 117 notes. S. Kerens

2493. Thompson, J. Earl, Jr. SLAVERY AND PRESBYTERIANISM IN THE REVOLUTIONARY ERA. *J. of Presbyterian Hist. 1976 54(1): 121-141.* Throughout the Revolutionary epoch Presbyterians attempted to build an antislavery platform upon which the entire church could stand, to unify a young and fragile Christian community avoiding the disruption of schism which had plagued them before the Revolution, and to create a large and strong denomination. Their social goal was to maintain the tranquility, order, and racial homogeneity of white America by protecting the nation against an invasion of degraded freed blacks. They believed that they could reconcile their competing values of hostility

toward slavery, fear of freedom, and loyalty to a united demonination and to a racially homogeneous America by embracing the ideology and program of gradualism. Traces the attitudes of Presbyterian leaders toward slavery—Samuel Davies, Dr. Bejamin Rush, Jacob Green, Samuel Stanhope Smith, Elias Boudinot, Samuel Miller, and David Rice. Based largely on writings of the leaders cited; 91 notes.
H. M. Parker, Jr.

2494. Trendel, Robert. JOHN JAY II: ANTISLAVERY CONSCIENCE OF THE EPISCOPAL CHURCH. *Hist. Mag. of the Protestant Episcopal Church 1976 45(3): 237-252.* The Episcopal Church in New York before and during the Civil War was fearful of schism, of involvement in a divisive and sectional issue, and of offending influential members who were linked economically, socially, or through family ties to slavery interests. John Jay II forced confrontations between the church he loved and human beings he loved, regardless of the costs to his profession, his personal image, his friendships, his status in the community, or the public image of the Episcopal Church in New York. He forced his church, sometimes uncomfortably, to live in the light of truth and justice. Based largely on the John Jay II Papers, in the possession of Mrs. Arthur Iselin (Nelson, New Hampshire), and other primary sources; 49 notes.
H. M. Parker, Jr.

2495. VanDeburg, William L. FREDERICK DOUGLASS: MARYLAND SLAVE TO RELIGIOUS LIBERAL. *Maryland Hist. Mag. 1974 69(1): 27-43.* Young Frederick Douglass was convinced of the omnipotence of God and His role as "Supreme Judge of the Universe." By the 1840's, however, the influence of Reason, Transcendentalism, and Unitarianism convinced him that the abolition movement must be primarily a human enterprise. Despising the passive attitude displayed by many Negro ministers, Douglass even criticized Henry Ward Beecher's reliance on God to end slavery. Increasingly enlightenment terminology crept into Douglass' writings and speeches, and his move to a humanistic theology climaxed with his address in Philadelphia's Horticultural Hall on 26 April 1870 when he lauded Wendell Phillips, Elijah Lovejoy, John Brown, and Abraham Lincoln in celebrating the recently ratified 15th Amendment. Primary and secondary sources; 8 illus., 59 notes.
G. J. Bobango

2496. VanDeburg, William L. FREDERICK DOUGLASS AND THE INSTITUTIONAL CHURCH. *J. of the Am. Acad. of Religion 1977 45(2): 218.* Frederick Douglass was a black abolitionist who remained in the institutional church but was highly critical of the church over the slavery issue. The abolitionist message, for Douglass, must be a vital part of the message of the church. Only those preachers and religious groups giving such an emphasis were considered true Christians. Abstract only.
E. R. Lester

2497. Watner, Carl. THE RADICAL LIBERTARIAN TRADITION IN ANTISLAVERY THOUGHT. *J. of Libertarian Studies 1979 3(3): 299-329.* Radical libertarian antislavery thinking in 18th-century and antebellum America opposed "unjust and criminal property titles in people and in land" and featured such a passion for justice that many thinkers sanctioned violence by slaves or others to secure liberty; focuses on 18th-century Quakers and English radicals and on Lysander Spooner, slave-rescuer John Fairfield, and Henry David Thoreau.

2498. Wolseley, Roland E. SAMUEL E. CORNISH—PIONEER BLACK JOURNALIST AND PASTOR. *Crisis 1976 83(8): 288-289.* Samuel E. Cornish (1796-1859) was born in Delaware in a nonslave home, attended Princeton University, and became a Presbyterian minister in New York City. In 1827 he was editor and copublisher, with John B. Russwurm, of the first black newspaper in the United States, *Freedom's Journal.* Cornish wrote hard-hitting editorials on any issue that he felt retarded black progress. After Russwurm left for Liberia, financial difficulties resulted in the collapse of *Freedom's Journal.* Cornish made several more attempts at journalism, but his real impact was as a strong spokesman for abolition.
A. G. Belles

2499. —. SLAVERY AND THE PROTESTANT ETHIC. *Hist. Reflections [Canada] 1979 6(1): 157-181.*

Anstey, Roger. SLAVERY AND THE PROTESTANT ETHIC, *pp. 157-172.* Analyzes the role of religious forces in the formation and expansion of antislavery movements in the United States and Great Britain and examines its influence in the abolition of the British slave trade, the West Indian emancipation, and US antislavery politics. Theological doctrines—Arminianism, redemptionism, sanctification, and postmillenialism—disposed Protestants to include the slaves among the potentially saved, to hate the institution of slavery, and to strive for earthly reform. Additionally, slavery became a denominational issue, as Anglican Evangelicals, Nonconformists, and Quakers combined to provide the political organization and strategy for abolition and emancipation. 66 notes.

DaCosta, Emilia Viotti. COMMENTARY ONE, *pp. 173-177.* Anstey's reasoning is circular and fails to distinguish causation from concomitance and real motives from the religious rhetoric in which they were dressed. 2 notes.

Davis, David Brion. COMMENTARY TWO, *pp. 177-181.* Explains Anstey's own Christian belief and the way it informed his work on the British abolitionists of the 18th and 19th centuries and their religious conception of politics.
S

Charities

2500. Axe, Ruth Frey. SIGMUND FREY: LOS ANGELES JEWRY'S FIRST PROFESSIONAL SOCIAL WORKER. *Western States Jewish Hist. Q. 1976 8(4): 312-325.* Reform Rabbi Sigmund Frey (1852-1930) came to Los Angeles to be the superintendent for the Jewish Orphan's Home then located at Mission and Macy streets. In 1910 a fire destroyed the home and in November 1912 the new Jewish Orphan's Home was dedicated in Huntington Park, California. Rabbi Frey became a well known author, scholar, journalist, bibliophile, and teacher. In 1921, he resigned as superintendent. Before his death in Los Angeles Rabbi Frey and his wife Hermine traveled several times to Europe. Primary and secondary sources; 4 photos, 5 notes.
R. A. Garfinkle

2501. Barton, Betty L. MORMON POOR RELIEF: A SOCIAL WELFARE INTERLUDE. *Brigham Young U. Studies 1977 18(1): 66-88.* Traces the evolution of Mormon poor relief policies, 1850-1930's. Evaluates the development of relief activities within the church organization and places the Mormons' attitudes toward relief within the context of national relief trends. Distinguishes between the generally accepted view and the Mormon practice of helping others to help themselves and of seeing direct charity as only a last resort. Delineates the church's view on the causes of poverty, the emphasis on the social gospel, and the Mormon practice of "work-relief" as opposed to the dole. Seeks to bridge the gap between early Mormon practices and the rejection of government welfare programs in favor of their own "Security Program" during the Depression.
M. S. Legan

2502. Bibby, Reginald W. and Mauss, Armand L. SKIDDERS AND THEIR SERVANTS: VARIABLE GOALS AND FUNCTIONS OF THE SKID ROAD RESCUE MISSION. *J. for the Sci. Study of Religion 1974 13(4): 421-436.* Studies Seattle's skid road missions and concludes that although the official objectives of the missions are not achieved, the missions live on because they realize the personal goals of their leaders and the men who attend.

2503. Carroll, Kenneth L. IRISH AND BRITISH QUAKERS AND THEIR AMERICAN RELIEF FUNDS, 1778-1797. *Pennsylvania Mag. of Hist. and Biog. 1978 102(4): 437-457.* Philadelphia mainly utilized Irish funds which also relieved New England and southern Quakers. London funds aided Nova Scotian Quaker loyalists and later were utilized by Philadelphia Friends. Based on manuscripts, Friends' House Library, London; Friends' Historical Library, Dublin; Philadelphia Meeting for Sufferings; printed sources and secondary works; 108 notes.
T. H. Wendel

2504. Clement, Priscilla Ferguson. FAMILIES AND FOSTER CARE: PHILADELPHIA IN THE LATE NINETEENTH CENTURY. *Social Service Rev. 1979 53(3): 406-420.* The Home Missionary Society of Philadelphia and the Children's Aid Society of Pennsylvania placed poor, urban, usually white Protestant children in country homes as servants or farm laborers, 1880-1905.

2505. Dumont-Johnson, Micheline. LES GARDERIES AU XIXe SIÈCLE: LES SALLES D'ASILE DES SOEURS GRISES À MONTRÉAL [Child care in the 19th century: Dominican nursery schools in Montreal]. *Rev. d'Hist. de l'Amérique Française [Canada] 1980 34(1): 27-55.* Beginning in the late 1850's, Dominican sisters set up child care centers for infants aged two to seven. In 60 years, they enrolled 60,000 children of working mothers and widows, mostly from the artisan class. Funded by the Church with some assistance from the legislature, they taught the alphabet, counting, religion, and hygiene; time was also provided for meals and play. Much emphasis was placed on proper behavior. Although facilities were crowded and the sisters received no special training, the centers were successful. They disappeared around 1920 after the death of their founder and benefactor and because of changing demography and increased social disapproval of women working outside the home. Based on the journal of the founder and other material in Montreal religious archives; 7 tables, 104 notes. R. Aldrich

2506. Fisher, Albert L. MORMON WELFARE PROGRAMS: PAST AND PRESENT. *Social Sci. J. 1978 15(2): 75-100.* Much of the Mormons' welfare system has depended on contribution of labor, fast offerings, welfare assessments, and tithing to meet the emotional, monetary, and spiritual needs of the church members, who refuse to accept government-sponsored assistance. Covers 1837-1978.

2507. Fisher, Marcelia C. THE ORPHAN'S FRIEND: CHARLES COLLINS TOWNSEND AND THE ORPHANS' HOME OF INDUSTRY. *Palimpsest 1979 60(6): 184-196.* The Reverend Charles Collins Townsend (1808-69) was an Episcopalian missionary and the organizer of The Orphans' Home of Industry in Iowa City, Iowa, 1854-68; it housed 500 children from New York City's streets and slums, until the Johnson County Board of Supervisors asked the city attorney to enjoin the home from bringing any more orphans to town.

2508. Hexter, Maurice B. HISTORICAL REMINISCENCE. *Am. Jewish Hist. 1978 68(2): 122-130.* The author (b. 1871) entered Jewish communal work with the United Jewish Charities in Cincinnati, Ohio, in 1912. His reminiscences of the days before social work went academic and psychological deal with the real problems of illness, desertion, adjustments of immigrants, Hebrew free loans, etc. Then as now the relationship between the social service organizations and the synagogues might be categorized as "mutual distrust tinged with apprehension." F. Rosenthal

2509. Kennedy, Estella. IMMIGRANTS, CHOLERA, AND THE SAINT JOHN SISTERS OF CHARITY, 1854-1864. *Study Sessions: Can. Catholic Hist. Assoc. [Canada] 1977 44: 25-44.* Following a cholera epidemic in 1854, the Sisters of Charity of the Immaculate Conception, was founded in Saint John, New Brunswick, to care for orphaned children, but expanded to include education of youth and care for the elderly during 1854-64.

2510. Kihlstrom, Mary F. THE MORRISTOWN FEMALE CHARITABLE SOCIETY. *J. of Presbyterian Hist. 1980 58(3): 255-272.* Depicts the historical and cultural background of the Morristown Society, known today as the Family Service of Morris County, New Jersey. Focuses on the period from 1813, the year of its founding, to 1870, when active membership was broadened to admit women from churches other than the First Presbyterian Church. The establishment by church women of the Morristown Female Charitable Society and of its sister organizations in New Jersey exemplified the continued modifying influence of the churches upon the harshness of the laws related to the poor. Contains many examples of the types of charitable services rendered by the Society through the years, the kinds of services reflecting the cultural milieu. Based largely on an MA thesis by Edwin W. Be (Rutgers University, 1963), reports of the Society, and local church and community histories; 83 notes. H. M. Parker, Jr.

2511. Knawa, Anne Marie. JANE ADDAMS AND JOSEPHINE DUDZIK: SOCIAL SERVICE PIONEERS. *Polish Am. Studies 1978 35(1-2): 13-22.* Compares the life and work of Sister Mary Theresa (Josephine Dudzik), the founder of the Franciscan Sisters of Chicago, with that of the internationally renowned Jane Addams (1860-1935). Sister Mary Theresa (1860-1918) was an indefatigable worker. Official steps are being taken for her beatification and possible canonization. Polish and English primary and secondary sources; 23 notes. S. R. Pliska

2512. La Fontaine, Charles V. THE ROLE OF FATHER PAUL WATTSON OF GRAYMOOR IN THE FOUNDATION OF THE CATHOLIC NEAR EAST WELFARE ASSOCIATION. *Records of the Am. Catholic Hist. Soc. of Philadelphia 1975 86(1-4): 53-78.* This history of the origins, foundation, and development of the Catholic Near East Welfare Association, 1904-26, reveals the crucial role of Father Paul Wattson (d. 1933). Though not a cofounder of the Association in the strictest sense, he was certainly a primary catalyst and "inspirator" without whom the Association would not have come into being. 94 notes. J. M. McCarthy

2513. Marti, Donald B. LAYMEN, BRING YOUR MONEY: LEE CLAFLIN, METHODIST PHILANTHROPIST, 1791-1871. *Methodist Hist. 1976 14(3): 165-185.* Lee Claflin of Massachusetts was a Methodist layman who made his fortune in the leather trade, western lands, banking, coal liming, and shipping. He gave extensively to Methodist churches, educational institutions, and other programs and organizations of the Methodist Episcopal Church. Based largely on the William and Mary Claflin Collection in the Rutherford B. Hayes Library, Fremont, Ohio; 138 notes. H. L. Calkin

2514. Metz, Judith. 150 YEARS OF CARING: THE SISTERS OF CHARITY IN CINCINNATI. *Cincinnati Hist. Soc. Bull. 1979 37(3): 150-174.* Traces the history of the Sisters of Charity in Cincinnati since 1829, when Fanny Jordan, Victoria Fitzgerald, Beatrice Tyler, and Albina Levy arrived from the Sisters of Charity of St. Joseph in Emmitsburg, Maryland (the first religious community of women in the United States), to devote themselves to the education of children and care for the needy in Cincinnati.

2515. Mohler, Dorothy A. THE ADVOCATE ROLE OF THE ST. VINCENT DE PAUL SOCIETY. *Records of the Am. Catholic Soc. of Philadelphia 1975 86(1-4): 79-92.* The visitation of the poor in their homes was always the principal work of the Saint Vincent de Paul Society, and advocacy activities were special works. Work on behalf of children and Indians were two cases in which, on occasion, members of the Society exercised an advocacy role. These activities were pursued for varying lengths of time—in the case of the Indians, a relatively brief duration. Covers ca. 1900-10. 41 notes. J. M. McCarthy

2516. Moore, Deborah Dash. FROM KEHILLAH TO FEDERATION: THE COMMUNAL FUNCTIONS OF FEDERATED PHILANTHROPY IN NEW YORK CITY, 1917-1933. *Am. Jewish Hist. 1978 68(2): 131-146.* The Federation for the Support of Jewish Philanthropic Societies as an alternative communal structure to that of the Kehillah with its relgious and almost obligatory nuances began in New York City in 1917. A fund raising apparatus that recognized class differences but stressed mass participation and emphasized nonsectarianism remained the framework for a minimal community into the 1930's. Samson Benderly and other Federation leaders recognized early that potentially it could be transformed into a viable, broad, and truly Jewish community. 24 notes. F. Rosenthal

2517. Moore, Julia. THE SISTERS OF ST. JOSEPH: BEGINNINGS IN LONDON DIOCESE 1868-1878. *Study Sessions: Can. Catholic Hist. Assoc. [Canada] 1978 45: 37-55.* An account by the author, a member during the first years (1868-85) of the Sisters of St. Joseph, a Roman Catholic charitable religious organization for women, in London, Ontario, where the sisters were mainly teachers.

2518. Morris, Ann N. THE HISTORY OF THE ST. LOUIS PROTESTANT ORPHAN ASYLUM. *Missouri Hist. Soc. Bull. 1980 36(2, pt. 1): 80-91.* Begun in 1834, the St. Louis Protestant Orphan Asylum later was moved to Webster Groves, where, it was believed, its orphan residents could partake of a more "pure atmosphere" than existed in St. Louis. The institution first accepted largely Protestant children but long ago abandoned such restrictive qualifications. Since 1943, the institution has been called the Edgewood Children's Center. Based on Asylum institutional records, newspapers, and secondary works; 2 illus., 5 tables, 58 notes. H. T. Lovin

2519. Nash, Gary B. POVERTY AND POOR RELIEF IN PREREVOLUTIONARY PHILADELPHIA. *William and Mary Q. 1976 33(1): 3-30.* Discusses the growth of private and public responsibility for the care of the increasing poor in Philadelphia in the 18th century. Emphasizes the role of the Pennsylvania Hospital for the Sick Poor. The relocation of Acadian neutrals in Philadelphia during the French and Indian War and the revival of Irish and German immigration in the 1760's added to the burden of poor relief. Quakers contributed much private philanthrophy. Also notes the new ideology regarding the poor, with some comparison to ideas in England. Based on manuscript records and secondary sources; 3 tables, 79 notes. H. M. Ward

2520. Nieto, Jacob. A 1906 SAN FRANCISCO PROTEST AND APPEAL. *Western States Jewish Hist. Q. 1977 9(3): 246-250.* Rabbi Jacob Nieto criticized the way relief money was distributed to casualties of the San Francisco earthquake of 18 April 1906. After the immediate needs for food, clothing, and shelter had been cared for, financial aid should have been given with a view to reestablishing commercial activities and religious institutions. Many who suffered great losses were too proud to seek aid, and these cases should have been sought out and ministered to in a way that would maintain their privacy and dignity. Reprint of article in *The Jewish Times and Observer,* San Francisco, 9 November 1906, pp. 8-9. B. S. Porter

2521. O'Gallagher, Marianna. CARE OF THE ORPHAN AND THE AGED BY THE IRISH COMMUNITY OF QUEBEC CITY, 1847 AND YEARS FOLLOWING. *Study Sessions: Can. Catholic Hist. Assoc. [Canada] 1976 43: 39-56.* Indicates the history and development of St. Bridget's Home in Quebec, and the work of Father Patrick McMahon, Irish immigrants, and the Catholic Church to provide for the needy, 1847-1972.

2522. Raphael, Marc Lee. FEDERATED PHILANTHROPY IN AN AMERICAN JEWISH COMMUNITY: 1904-1948. *Am. Jewish Hist. 1978 68(2): 147-162.* The story and development of the Federation movement in one American Jewish community, that of Columbus, Ohio, illustrates the paths taken during those decades throughout the country. The shift from local to national and overseas allocations and the increase in contributors and contributions, especially after 1937-38, were accompanied by gradual democratization of the board, even though the bulk of the money continued to be contributed by a tiny minority. Yet the Federation, because of its control of philanthropy, brought secular and religious, traditional and non-traditional, Zionist and non-Zionist Jews together, the only true forum in the community. 28 notes. F. Rosenthal

2523. Rauch, Julia B. QUAKERS AND THE FOUNDING OF THE PHILADELPHIA SOCIETY FOR ORGANIZING CHARITY RELIEF AND REPRESSING MENDICANCY. *Pennsylvania Mag. of Hist. and Bio. 1974 98(4): 438-455.* Blaming poverty on pauperism and insisting on the necessity for character reformation, 19th-century charities failed to meet the needs of the urban poor. The activities of the Philadelphia Society for Organizing Charitable Relief and Repressing Mendicancy (SOC), founded in 1879 by Quakers, reflected the upper-class, moralistic, and repressive nature of charity relief. Since Philadelphia "Quakers did not recognize that an urban, industrialized society required social insurance and other economic security programs," they "ended up supporting a conservative, backward-looking program, one which was repressive toward the poor." Based on primary and secondary sources; 46 notes. E. W. Carp

2524. Rooney, James F. ORGANIZATIONAL SUCCESS THROUGH PROGRAM FAILURE: SKID ROW RESCUE MISSIONS. *Social Forces 1980 58(3): 904-924.* Program failure is essential for many organizations in that effective solution of the problems they address would eliminate the purpose of their existence. Although skid row rescue missions fail on a colossal scale in converting derelicts, they constitute an archetypical example of a general process of providing employment for staff members in a post-industrial society. Institutionalizing survival on perpetual failure occurs through the availability of outside financial support and favorable presentation of the program to a sponsoring group as the best available means of achieving a socially desirable end. A basic question in social policy involves giving continued support to organizations which benefit directly from their failure. Covers the 1960's and 70's. Notes, biblio. J

2525. Sihelvik, LaVerne. DIAMOND JUBILEE OF THE VINCENTIAN SISTERS OF CHARITY. *Jednota Ann. Furdek 1978 17: 197-200.* Established in Pittsburgh, Pennsylvania, in 1902 after coming from what is now Czechoslovakia, the Vincentian Sisters of Charity have provided nursing services for the poor, the incurable, and the aged in the United States and Canada.

2526. Weiner, Lynn. "OUR SISTER'S KEEPERS": THE MINNEAPOLIS WOMAN'S CHRISTIAN ASSOCIATION AND HOUSING FOR WORKING WOMEN. *Minnesota Hist. 1979 46(5): 189-200.* In the late 19th century, many young women made their way to Minneapolis to find work, coming from rural areas and from Europe. The paucity of inexpensive boardinghouses available to these women and the consequent fear that poverty would drive the women into prostitution and other forms of criminal behavior, generated an effort on the part of middle and upper class Minneapolis women to provide suitable, safe and cheap housing for women. Various buildings were donated to the Women's Christian Association (WCA) for this purpose, and both long-term and temporary housing arrangements were made available. The boardinghouses sponsored by the WCA were run along rather puritanical lines but seemed to fill the needs of generations of female sojourners in the city. The WCA also sponsored Travelers' Aid efforts in which young women arriving via train were met by agents and were given advice and assistance. By the end of World War I large-scale migration into Minneapolis had ended and the efforts of the WCA tapered off but did not die out. N. Lederer

2527. —. OAKLAND JEWRY AND THE EARTHQUAKE-FIRE OF 1906. *Western States Jewish Hist. Q. 1977 9(3): 251-252.* When refugees from the fire-stricken, poorer Jewish quarter of San Francisco came to Oakland, Temple Sinai provided immediate aid. Food and clothing were given to the needy and 350 people were given a place to sleep. For about a week the synagogue fed up to 500 people three times a day. A large part of the expenses were paid by the Jewish Ladies' organization of the synagogue. Reprint of article in *Emanu-El,* San Francisco, 4 May 1906. B. S. Porter

Civil Rights

2528. Blackwelder, Julia Kirk. SOUTHERN WHITE FUNDAMENTALISTS AND THE CIVIL RIGHTS MOVEMENT. *Phylon 1979 40(4): 334-341.* Analyzes the response to the civil rights movement of the 1950's and 1960's by the Southern Presbyterian Church, the Church of God, and the Assemblies of God, as seen through articles in their respective denominational publications, *Southern Presbyterian Journal, Church of God Evangel,* and *Pentecostal Evangel.* 21 notes. G. R. Schroeder

2529. Brackenridge, R. Douglas. LAWRENCE W. BOTTOMS: THE CHURCH, BLACK PRESBYTERIANS AND PERSONHOOD. *J. of Presbyterian Hist. 1978 56(1): 47-60.* Interviews Lawrence Bottoms, first Negro Moderator of the Southern Presbyterian Church, and first Negro to head any major white Protestant denomination's Negro work organization. Traces Bottom's life through his educational and pastoral career, giving insights into prejudice which confronted him. Out of such experiences his religious philosophy of personhood emerged. Bottoms strongly urged the Presbyterian Church in the South to reach out to the growing black middle class. Covers 1930-75. Illus., 2 notes. H. M. Parker, Jr.

2530. Carter, George E. MARTIN LUTHER KING: INCIPIENT TRANSCENDENTALIST. *Phylon 1979 40(4): 318-324.* Overemphasis on the influence of Henry David Thoreau's *Civil Disobedience* on Martin Luther King, Jr., has obscured King's resemblance to other Transcendentalists in the areas of: the church leading social change, the concept of God and inner light, and the principle of higher law. Based on King's works and on secondary sources; 44 notes. G. R. Schroeder

2531. Cleveland, Mary L. A BAPTIST PASTOR AND SOCIAL JUSTICE IN CLINTON, TENNESSEE. *Baptist Hist. and Heritage 1979 14(2): 15-19.* Describes the efforts of Baptist pastor Paul Turner in dealing with the violence resulting from forced desegregation in the community of Clinton, Tennessee, in 1956.

2532. Czuchlewski, Paul E. LIBERAL CATHOLICISM AND AMERICAN RACISM, 1924-1960. *Records of the Am. Catholic Hist. Soc. of Philadelphia 1974 85(3-4): 144-162.* During the 1920's-50's, the liberal Catholic intellectual lived in a painful tension between means and ends. An intellectual dedicated to dialogue, a religious man devoted to peace, an antitotalitarian convinced of the virtues of democratic process, and an inheritor of Jeffersonian liberalism and Thomistic organicism committed to limited government, he desired brotherhood but could not seek it through racial militancy or legislative compulsion. 30 notes. J. M. McCarthy

2533. Edmund, T. MARTIN LUTHER KING AND THE BLACK PROTEST MOVEMENT. *Gandhi Marg [India] 1976 20(4): 235-249.* King believed that the Christian doctrine of love operating through Gandhian nonviolence was one of the most potent weapons available to black Americans in their struggle for freedom. Although he mobilized support among Negroes belonging to the middle and upper classes and in the South, he did not attract the support of blacks living in the ghettoes of the northern states, who were interested primarily in economic issues, not civil rights. J. C. English

2534. Fulkerson, Richard P. THE PUBLIC LETTER AS A RHETORICAL FORM: STRUCTURE, LOGIC, AND STYLE IN KING'S "LETTER FROM BIRMINGHAM JAIL." *Q. J. of Speech 1979 65(2): 121-136.* Martin Luther King's famous "Letter from Birmingham Jail" addresses two audiences, the eight clergymen who publicly criticized King for his civil disobedience and a larger national audience of concerned moderates and liberals. King uses the structure of the classical oration coupled with a dual pattern of refutative logic; his style, although informal, is characterized by adaptive, affective, and ethical dimensions. Primary and secondary sources; 25 notes. E. Bailey

2535. Hall, Jacquelyn Dowd. A TRULY SUBVERSIVE AFFAIR: WOMEN AGAINST LYNCHING IN THE TWENTIETH-CENTURY SOUTH. Berkin, Carol Ruth and Norton, Mary Beth, ed. *Women of America: A History* (Boston: Houghton Mifflin Co., 1979): 360-388. Texas suffragist Jessie Daniel Ames founded the Association of Southern Women for the Prevention of Lynching (ASWPL) in 1930 in reaction to the Southern tradition of extralegal racial violence. Earlier organizations had existed, connected with the Methodist Woman's Missionary Council and black YWCA. Jessie Ames also wished to kill the chivalric assumptions inherent in lynchings, which were a potent symbol of white male supremacy and an expression of a "Southern rape complex." Based on ASWPL papers; 2 tables, 15 notes. K. Talley

2536. Harding, Vincent. OUT OF THE CAULDRON OF STRUGGLE: BLACK RELIGION AND THE SEARCH FOR A NEW AMERICA. *Soundings 1978 61(3): 339-354.* Examines the impact of black religion (mainly Christianity) on the black search for equality and freedom, from emancipation to civil rights. Covers the 19th-20th centuries.

2537. Hoehn, Richard A. WHITEWASHING BLACKTHINK. *Lutheran Q. 1975 27(3): 220-229.* The author describes his conversion to "blackthink," a total commitment to multiracial and cultural experiences and to the disadvantaged and his temporary dissociation ("whitewash") from it. Concludes that ministerial students, pastors, and seminary professors should undergo multicultural courses and experiences to develop "blackthink." Covers 1963-75. 2 notes. J. A. Kicklighter

2538. Hunt, Larry L. and Hunt, Janet G. BLACK RELIGION AS BOTH OPIATE AND INSPIRATION OF CIVIL RIGHTS MILITANCY: PUTTING MARX'S DATA TO THE TEST. *Social Forces 1977 56(1): 1-14.* This research evaluates the claim of a general tension between religiosity and civil rights militance among black Americans through a secondary analysis of the 1964 Gary Marx data. It shows that when important secular factors are controlled, Marx's findings of (a) greater militance in largely white denominations (Episcopalian, Presbyterian, Congregationalist, and Roman Catholic), and (b) an inverse correlation between militance and both church attendance and orthodoxy of belief essentially disappear. Additional lines of analysis support the proposal of Nelsen et al. that only a sectlike orientation corrodes militance, while a churchlike orientation actually makes for greater militance. J

2539. Hunt, Larry L. and Hunt, Janet G. RELIGIOUS AFFILIATION AND MILITANCY AMONG URBAN BLACKS: SOME CATHOLIC/PROTESTANT COMPARISONS. *Social Sci. Q. 1977 57(4): 821-833.* Uses Gary Marx's "conventional civil rights militancy" and "black self-image" indices to test whether black Catholics are maintaining their distinctive secular orientation or converging into a common black urban culture. The analysis corroborates the notion that black Catholics attain higher secular status than most black Protestants. However, attitudes toward race relations and social change are complex, and reflect socioeconomic as well as religious backgrounds. Middle class black Catholics tend to display the most distinctive attitudes; they demonstrate racial pride and "structural awareness" but do not favor collective civil rights militancy. Covers the 1960's and 70's. Primary and secondary sources; 3 tables, 5 notes, biblio. W. R. Hively

2540. Kater, John L., Jr. DWELLING TOGETHER IN UNITY: CHURCH, THEOLOGY, AND RACE 1950-1965. *Anglican Theological Rev. 1976 58(4): 444-457.* Examines the response of the Episcopal Church to the Freedom Movement during 1950-65 and links this response to the Church's heritage reaching back to the 1800's.

2541. Kater, John L., Jr. EXPERIMENT IN FREEDOM: THE EPISCOPAL CHURCH AND THE BLACK POWER MOVEMENT. *Hist. Mag. of the Protestant Episcopal Church 1979 48(1): 67-81.* Explores the Episcopal Church's response to the later phase of the movement for black freedom, and describes the course of its history in light of the Church's social theology. The endorsement of the General Convention Special Program of the principle of black self-determination and the commitment of financial support meant that the many older programs at home and abroad had to be curtailed. There is little internal impetus toward a substantive role for the Episcopal Church in the social crises of the present; and it is uncertain whether another period of rapid change would call forth a reassertion of the theological categories of the past for interpreting the Church's place in society. For the present, the challenge lives on in a world where justice and unity and freedom remain unfulfilled dreams for many. Based on Episcopal documents and literature; 41 notes. H. M. Parker, Jr.

2542. Kemper, Donald J. CATHOLIC INTEGRATION IN ST. LOUIS, 1935-1947. *Missouri Hist. Rev. 1978 73(1): 1-22.* In 1947 the Archbishop of St. Louis, Joseph E. Ritter, ordered the admission of black children to local parochial schools, an order that provoked serious resistance from parents. The success of the order came in the wake of a battle going on during the latter years of Archbishop John J. Glennon. Through the Midwest Clergy Conference on Negro Matters, some young priests had set the stage by trying to desegregate Webster College and St. Louis University. It is likely that Rome arranged the liberal Ritter's assignment to speed integration. Primary and secondary sources; illus., 58 notes. W. F. Zornow

2543. Mathews, Donald G. CHARLES COLCOCK JONES AND THE SOUTHERN EVANGELICAL CRUSADE TO FORM A BIRACIAL COMMUNITY. *J. of Southern Hist. 1975 41(3): 299-320.* Charles Colcock Jones, reformist clergyman of the antebellum period, was early disturbed by the slaveholding South in which he resided. He resolved to improve the lot of the Negro, but was sufficiently wise to recognize that any reform must enlist the support of whites. He appealed to the Christian religious conscience, hoping to remake the Negro in the white man's image. He avoided confrontation. Support was reluctantly forthcoming. Jones' personal life was exemplary, but he failed really to change anything. The future biracial utopia he envisioned became a blueprint for postwar religious reformers. 50 notes. V. L. Human

2544. Mays, Benjamin E. PROGRESS AND PROSPECTS IN AMERICAN RACE RELATIONS. *J. of Ecumenical Studies 1979 16(1): 128-132.* There has been enormous progress in race relations in the United States since the 1st World Conference of Christian Youth (Amsterdam, 1939). In education, the necessity to maintain black colleges has assured blacks opportunities that they would not otherwise have had from the 1860's to the 1960's. The existence of black role models in the fields of learning and government is especially meaningful to black youth, and many of those role models exist in or because of black colleges. The churches are moving very slowly toward integration, but the situation is much improved since 1960. In the performing arts and sports there are few barriers to talented blacks in America today. S

2545. McCullum, Hugh and Hatton, Russ. PROJECT NORTH. *Can. Dimension [Canada] 1979 13(5): 43-45.* Describes Project North, begun in 1975, as an attempt by churches to deal with the oppression of Indians, Métis, and Eskimos in Canada.

2546. McQuaid, Kim. WILLIAM APES, PEQUOT: AN INDIAN REFORMER IN THE JACKSON ERA. *New England Q. 1977 50(4): 605-625.* Sketches Methodist William Apes's (b. 1798) troubled youth and shows that his religious approach to Indian-white relations and his belief in racial equality was nonconformist during the era of Indian removal. Focuses on his leadership of the Wampanoag Indians of Mashpee, Massachusetts, in their partially successful struggle for control of their own political, economic and religious affairs. Based on Apes' writings and secondary sources; 29 notes. J. C. Bradford

2547. Mondello, Salvatore. THE INTEGRATION OF JAPANESE BAPTISTS IN AMERICAN SOCIETY. *Foundations 1977 20(3): 254-263.* American Baptists began work among the Japanese immigrants in the 1890's. They opposed discrimination against the Japanese in the National Origins Act of 1924. Deals with Baptist involvement with Japanese Americans during and after World War II. Baptists were very successful in their resettlement efforts at this time. 21 notes. E. E. Eminhizer

2548. Murray, Hugh T., Jr. THE STRUGGLE FOR CIVIL RIGHTS IN NEW ORLEANS IN 1960: REFLECTIONS AND RECOLLECTIONS. *J. of Ethnic Studies 1978 6(1): 25-41.* Narrative of author's student days at Tulane University and involvement with the Tulane Interfaith Council, the Inter-Collegiate Council for Inter-Racial Cooperation, and the NAACP Youth Chapter. His work with voter registration taught him the many devices used to keep blacks away from the polls and his friendship with a black girl exposed him to direct discrimination in public transportation, parks, and restaurants. In the summer of 1960, he attended a CORE workshop in Miami to learn the techniques of nonviolent protest which were then tested in the Shell's City sit-in and white churches. Throughout these events the New Orleans student groups were peripherally in contact with national figures in the civil rights movement. G. J. Bobango

2549. Oliver, John W., Jr. EVANGELICAL CAMPUS AND PRESS MEET BLACK AMERICA'S QUEST FOR CIVIL RIGHTS, 1956-1959: MALONE COLLEGE AND *CHRISTIANITY TODAY*. *Fides et Hist. 1975 8(1): 54-70.* In spite of its call for social progressivism, Protestant evangelicalism, through *Christianity Today* and other organs, took a conservative position on race and other issues. An incident at Malone College in Canton, Ohio, suggests that the evangelical colleges took more liberal positions than evangelical leaders. The integration of Malone's dormitory occurred without incident, and the choir refused to go on a tour of the South when told that a black member would not be allowed to come. Based on interviews, primary and secondary sources; 100 notes. R. E. Butchart

2550. Phillips, Paul D. THE INTERRACIAL IMPACT OF MARSHALL KEEBLE, BLACK EVANGELIST, 1878-1968. *Tennessee Hist. Q. 1977 36(1): 62-74.* Marshall Keeble was a Church of Christ evangelist among Negroes and an ambassador between blacks and whites to improve race relations for 50 years. He followed the accommodationist, nonviolent approach of Booker T. Washington, yet he boasted of his respect for himself and his race and opposed segregation. Primary and secondary sources; 66 notes. M. B. Lucas

2551. Shankman, Arnold. DOROTHY TILLY, CIVIL RIGHTS, AND THE METHODIST CHURCH. *Methodist Hist. 1980 18(2): 95-108.* Dorothy Tilly (1883-1970), an outstanding woman in the Methodist Church in Georgia, was active in civil rights movements during much of her life. Through organizations of the Methodist Church and other organizations, she worked for the abolition of lynchings, the development of better education for black children, the prevention of race riots, and other civil rights movements. 56 notes. H. L. Calkin

2552. Steinkraus, Warren E. MARTIN LUTHER KING'S PERSONALISM AND NON-VIOLENCE. *J. of the Hist. of Ideas 1973 34(1): 97-111.* Martin Luther King, Jr. (1929-68), was a trained philosopher whose commitment to nonviolence was rooted in Personalism. His inherited belief in a personal God was strengthened by his doctoral research on Paul Tillich and Henry Nelson Wieman, who found personality a limiting category, inappropriate for describing God. King viewed personality as absolute and insisted that religious behavior, seeking fellowship with God and reposing trust in His beneficence, requires belief in His personality. King therefore rejected Tillich and Wieman's positions as metaphysically inadequate and "lacking in positive religious value." Philosophic understanding of his personal God enabled King to act with confidence that "man has cosmic companionship" in his ethical endeavors. Belief in the absolute value of personality led him to nonviolence, which only W. G. Muelder among his Personalist teachers espoused. Recognizing no values superior to personality, King condemned violence against any person, under any circumstances. He trusted that the suffering servant, supported by a personal God, could end violence. Based on King's doctoral dissertation, *A Comparison of the Conceptions of God in the Thinking of Paul Tillich and Henry Nelson Wieman* (Boston U., 1955), on his published writings, and on secondary sources; 64 notes. D. B. Marti

2553. Storey, John W. TEXAS BAPTIST LEADERSHIP, THE SOCIAL GOSPEL, AND RACE, 1954-1968. *Southwestern Hist. Q. 1979 83(1): 29-46.* The Southern Baptist Convention's "crisis statement" of June 1968, stressing the church's social involvement, came after 14 years of maneuvering and debate. Since 1954 several Texas Baptist leaders—Ewing S. James, Thomas B. Maston, Acker C. Miller, and Foy Valentine—had pushed the church toward more concern for racial equality. Their course illustrates Walter Rauschenbusch's idea that social action is compatible with conservative theology. Based on interviews and other primary sources; 35 notes. J. H. Broussard

2554. Turner, Ronny E. THE BLACK MINISTER: UNCLE TOM OR ABOLITIONIST? *Phylon 1973 34(1): 86-95.* Discusses the role education played in motivating Negro ministers to become involved in civil rights programs (1969-70) in Buffalo, New York. S

2555. —. JAMES CORDER: "RIGHT HERE ON EARTH." *Southern Exposure 1976 4(3): 39-40.* In this interview Corder, a black minister of four Primitive Baptist Churches in and around Aliceville, Alabama, discusses his religious and civil rights work, 1965-75.

2556. —. JOSEPH ROBERTS: "A FREE PLATFORM." *Southern Exposure 1976 4(3): 40-44.* In this interview Roberts, a minister in Ebenezer Baptist Church in Atlanta, Georgia, discusses his participation in the civil rights movement, 1960-75.

Economic Reform

2557. Andelson, Robert V. MSGR. JOHN A. RYAN'S CRITIQUE OF HENRY GEORGE. *Am. J. of Econ. and Sociol. 1974 33(3): 273-286.* Msgr. John A. Ryan wrote *Distributive Justice* (New York: Macmillan, 1935), a critique of Henry George's single tax doctrine. Ryan's objections are analyzed. Secondary sources; 38 notes. W. L. Marr

2558. Angers, François-Albert. LA PENSÉE ÉCONOMIQUE D'ESDRAS MINVILLE [The economic thought of Esdras Minville]. *Action Natl. [Canada] 1976 65(9-10): 727-761.* Esdras Minville opposed liberal capitalism, but was not an agrarian. He sought a balanced industrialization for Quebec. He saw in *Rerum Novarum* and *Quadragesimo Anno* support for his corporatism and personalism. His nationalism was based on respect for French Canadian culture. 7 notes. A. W. Novitsky

2559. Basen, Neil K. KATE RICHARDS O'HARE: THE "FIRST LADY" OF AMERICAN SOCIALISM, 1901-1917. *Labor Hist. 1980 21(2): 165-199.* Provides a biographical sketch and analysis of Carrie Katherine (Kate) Richards O'Hare. A transitional figure in American socialism, Kate O'Hare represented a paradoxical combination of primitive Christian ideals and American industrial socialism. O'Hare fell short of a Socialist-feminist synthesis, partly because US Socialists were antifeminist. Based on the Wayne State Labor History Archives and the writings of O'Hare; 65 notes. L. L. Athey

2560. Bradley, Preston. HENRY GEORGE, BIBLICAL MORALITY AND ECONOMIC ETHICS: SOME CONCLUSIONS FROM A LIFETIME'S STUDY OF THE RELATION BETWEEN ETHICS AND ECONOMICS. *Am. J. of Econ. and Sociol. 1980 39(3): 209-215.* The basic economic ideas of George cannot be successfully challenged. Religion should never and cannot ever be separated from life. So the application of ethics to economic life is as religious as the statement of Christianity's oldest and most sacred creed. George formulated a reformed system for capitalism based on Biblical morality, the highest ethical standards of the modern age and its most exalted insights. J/S

2561. Crunden, Robert M. GEORGE D. HERRON IN THE 1890S: A NEW FRAME OF REFERENCE FOR THE STUDY OF THE PROGRESSIVE ERA. *Ann. of Iowa 1973 42(2): 81-113.* Examines the career of George David Herron, one of the luminaries of Populism and Progressivism. A member of the National Christian Citizenship League, the Union Reform League, and the National Social Reform Union, Herron's solid Protestant background led him to the Congregational ministry in the 1880's. There he made his name by arguing that "economic competition was always opposed to moral development." In the 1890's Herron was expelled from his church for his radical socialism and from Iowa College for what was regarded as immoral behavior. A study of Herron's career helps "define the limits of progressive reform." Illus., 45 notes. C. W. Olson

2562. Curran, Robert Emmett. THE MCGLYNN AFFAIR AND THE SHAPING OF THE NEW CONSERVATISM IN AMERICAN CATHOLICISM, 1886-1894. *Catholic Hist. Rev. 1980 66(2): 184-204.* Among the issues that divided Catholics into liberal and conservative ranks in the late 1880's, none was as important as the controversy between the New York priest, Edward McGlynn, and his archbishop, Michael Corrigan. The crisis over Father McGlynn's support of Henry George in 1886 fed on the growing fear among certain American bishops and priests of the mounting liberalism within the Church. The persistence of the controversy forced the conservatives to become increasingly dependent on Rome to suppress the liberals. In their very success the conservative bloc largely lost the collegial independence the American hierarchy had struggled to maintain against Roman centralization. A

2563. Foner, Philip S. REVEREND GEORGE WASHINGTON WOODBEY: EARLY TWENTIETH CENTURY BLACK SOCIALIST. *J. of Negro Hist. 1976 61(2): 136-157.* The leading black socialist in the first decade of this century, George Washington Woodbey disappeared from the historical record after 1915. Previously, this Baptist exponent of Christian socialism was in the forefront of left-wing politics in the United States. Secondary sources; 60 notes. N. G. Sapper

2564. Gabbert, Mark. ANGLICANS AND SOCIAL JUSTICE. *Queen's Q. [Canada] 1978 85(2): 191-202.* Discusses the report "For the Elimination of Poverty and Social Injustice," prepared by the National Task Force on the Economy of the General Synod of the Anglican Church of Canada, and accepted by the latter body at its August 1977 meeting. Praises the report's central recommendation of a guaranteed annual income for Canadians, but criticizes its Malthusian approach to world poverty. The report declares that present world production, distributed equally, would simply create universal poverty. This analysis ignores the fact that production is not currently oriented toward satisfying basic human needs, a situation inseparable from capitalism. Calls for a more daring approach on the lines of South American liberation theology. 10 notes. L. W. Van Wyk

2565. Israelsen, L. Dwight. AN ECONOMIC ANALYSIS OF THE UNITED ORDER. *Brigham Young U. Studies 1978 18(4): 536-562.* Discusses economic aspects of the Mormon United Order, which in the last quarter of the 19th century tried to establish a utopian socioeconomic system. Enumerates 15 testable hypotheses which might be applied to the distinct branches (collective, capitalist, commune) of the United Order. Tests statistically two of the hypotheses to account for the eventual failure of the Order. An appendix lists by states all communities known to have been organized under the United Order. M. S. Legan

2566. Jacklin, Thomas M. MISSION TO THE SHARECROPPERS: NEO-ORTHODOX RADICALISM AND THE DELTA FARM VENTURE, 1936-1940. *South Atlantic Q. 1979 78(3): 302-316.* The episode whereby Northern neoorthodox theologians attempted to aid the Southern sharecropper in the late 1930's provides a revealing commentary on the way in which the proponents of the new theology sought in a concrete manner to connect the Word with the world around them. In spite of purchasing two large farms in the Mississippi State delta area which were settled by both white and black tenant farmers, and in spite of the constant infusion of Northern money into the operation to keep it solvent, the attempt of the theologians—who acted like absentee landlords—to provide a model whereby the plight of the sharecropper might be lifted up failed. They forgot that the way of righteousness can be as thorny as the way of sin, a truth which the neoorthodox critics labored long to impress on their liberal colleagues. Based largely on the Reinhold Niebuhr Papers (Manuscript Division), Library of Congress, and contemporary articles in the *Christian Century;* 40 notes. H. M. Parker, Jr.

2567. Kambeitz, Teresita. RELATIONS BETWEEN THE CATHOLIC CHURCH AND CCF IN SASKATCHEWAN, 1930-1950. *Study Sessions: Can. Catholic Hist. Assoc. [Canada] 1979 (46): 49-69.* Relations were spotty at best, due to Church condemnations of socialism, but economic factors and realization of the need for social reform and cooperation within the farming communities led to tolerance and even acceptance of the socialistic Co-operative Commonwealth Federation (CCF) by some Catholics.

2568. Lawson-Peebles, Bob. HENRY GEORGE THE PROPHET. *J. of Am. Studies [Great Britain] 1976 10(1): 37-51.* Reexamines writings, notably *Progress and Poverty* (1879), of Henry George (1839-97) and concludes that George's Single Tax panacea contained strong religious connotations. Widely regarded as an economic panacea, George's Single Tax nevertheless was formulated during his "religious career" and derives from his spiritual preconceptions and aims. Based on George's writings and secondary sources; 37 notes. H. T. Lovin

2569. North, Gary. THE PURITAN EXPERIMENT IN COMMON OWNERSHIP. *Freeman 1974 24(4): 209-220.* When the Plymouth Colony experiments with common ownership of land and produce failed, the Puritans decided to rely on private ownership, 1621-75. S

2570. North, Gary. THE PURITAN EXPERIMENT WITH PRICE CONTROLS. *Freeman 1974 24(5): 270-285.* Covers 1629-76.

2571. Novitsky, Anthony. PETER MAURIN AND THE GREEN REVOLUTION. *Rev. of Pol. 1975 27(1): 83-103.* The ideology of the Catholic Worker Movement is a product of the European Right and not the American Left. The "Easy Essays" of Peter Maurin reflect the ideology of reactionary French Social Catholicism and a repudiation of Enlightenment ideas which underlie American political and social thought. For Maurin, social reconstruction is based on Christian concepts and a rejection of capitalism, a position that is "so old that it looks new." Covers 1920's-33. L. E. Ziewacz

2572. Shapiro, Edward S. CATHOLIC AGRARIAN THOUGHT AND THE NEW DEAL. *Catholic Hist. Rev. 1979 65(4): 583-599.* The American Catholic rural movement welcomed the election of Franklin D. Roosevelt in 1932. It believed the New Deal would embark upon an extensive program of rural rehabilitation, the restoration of the widespread ownership of productive property, and demographic decentralization. While initially favorably disposed toward the Agricultural Adjustment Act, the National Industrial Recovery Act, and other New Deal measures, Catholic ruralists had by the end of the 1930's concluded that the New Deal was a pragmatic response directed at propping up American capitalism rather than embarking upon a fundamental reconstruction of the economy along Catholic and Jeffersonian lines. A

2573. Shapiro, Edward S. THE CATHOLIC RURAL LIFE MOVEMENT AND THE NEW DEAL FARM PROGRAM. *Am. Benedictine Rev. 1977 28(3): 307-332.* Analyzes the Catholic agrarian movement of the 1930's and compares its goals with New Deal farm programs. The New Deal did not alleviate the problems noted by the Catholic agrarian movement. Based on original and secondary sources; 35 notes. J. H. Pragman

2574. —. COOPÉRATION ET DÉVELOPPEMENT AU QUÉBEC [Cooperation and development in Quebec]. *Action Natl. [Canada] 1979 69(4): 304-314.* With a provincial population of 6.25 million, there are nearly .25 million members of cooperatives in Quebec. The cooperative movement, based on Christian social teachings, is a manifestation of a distinctly Quebec culture. The social, economic, cultural, and political transformations of the past few decades have called for new institutions neither capitalist nor Marxist. Cooperatives uniquely recognize people in all dimensions: physical and spiritual; individual and collective, as responsible and participating members of society. Covers 1940-78. Pastoral declaration on the occasion of the Congress of the Fédération de Québec des caisses populaires Desjardins, Quebec 22-24 May 1978.
A. W. Novitsky

Temperance

2575. Birrell, A. J. D.I.K. RINE AND THE GOSPEL TEMPERANCE MOVEMENT IN CANADA. *Can. Hist. Rev. [Canada] 1977 58(1): 23-42.* Examines the rise, message, success, and sudden downfall of D.I.K. Rine and the Gospel Temperance Movement, in Canada during 1877-82. This moral suasionist movement, begun in New England by Francis Murphy, combined religious revivalism with the temperance message in attempting to reclaim alcoholics and hard drinkers. In Canada, led by Rine, a reformed alcoholic and an ex-convict, it met with enormous success, although unlike other contemporary movements it refused to campaign for legislated prohibition. Rine's arrest for indecent assault marked the end of the movement in Canada. A

2576. Bishop, Grace H. CARRY AMELIA NATION. *Daughters of the Am. Revolution Mag. 1977 111(5): 498-503.* Offers a short biography of Carry Amelia Nation (1846-1911), famed temperance worker, highlighting her distrust of all vices and her single-handed campaign against alcohol usage, 1890's-1911.

2577. Blodgett, Geoffrey. THE IMPULSE TO DENY: TWO VIEWS OF THE PROHIBITION MOVEMENT. *Rev. in Am. Hist. 1977 5(3): 373-378.* Review article prompted by Jack S. Blocker, Jr., *Retreat from Reform: The Prohibition Movement in the United States, 1890-1913* (Westport, Conn.: Greenwood Pr., 1976) and Norman H. Clark, *Deliver Us from Evil: An Interpretation of American Prohibition* (New York: W. W. Norton, 1976).

2578. Bordin, Ruth. MARCHING FOR TEMPERANCE: THE WOMAN'S CRUSADE IN ADRIAN. *Chronicle 1980 15(4): 16-23.* The Women's Christian Temperance Union crusade against alcohol in Adrian, Michigan, was part of a larger crusade through the Midwest and parts of the East and West during 1873-74.

2579. Brady, James E. FATHER GEORGE ZURCHER: PROHIBITIONIST PRIEST. *Catholic Hist. Rev. 1976 62(3): 424-433.* In 1884 the Third Plenary Council of the American Catholic Church issued a strong condemnation of the liquor trade. It encouraged Catholics to remove themselves from all aspects of this trade and also forbade the sale of alcoholic beverages at church functions. Father George Zurcher became increasingly unhappy with the widespread disregard with which this proclamation was treated. Zurcher regarded the control of alcohol as a vehicle for both assimilation and social reform. He thus turned to the state to accomplish his goal because the Church would not, he felt, follow its own teaching. A

2580. Brown, Thomas Elton. OKLAHOMA'S BONE DRY LAW AND THE ROMAN CATHOLIC CHURCH. *Chronicles of Oklahoma 1974 52(3): 316-330.* Discusses the controversy between the government of Oklahoma and the Roman Catholic Church during 1907-18 over prohibition laws which did not exempt sacramental wine. The laws were not anti-Catholic in motivation, but were an attempt to make the state "bone dry." Inactivity by the Church in lobbying for exemption is cited as a reason for the problem. The test case challenging the laws was defeated in district court, but the appeal to the state supreme court led to the ruling that religious alcohol was exempt under the law. The Church received public support from the National Prohibition League which recognized the importance of Catholic support for its national campaign. The entire controversy resulted from misunderstandings among those involved. Based on state government documents, contemporary newspaper reports, primary and secondary sources; 4 photos, 68 notes.
N. J. Street

2581. Burnett, Ivan, Jr. METHODIST ORIGINS: JOHN WESLEY AND ALCOHOL. *Methodist Hist. 1975 13(4): 3-17.* John Wesley's (1703-91) position on beverage alcohol must be understood to understand that of American Methodism. Wesley opposed drunkenness but had compassion for the drunkard, and approved of distilled liquors as medicines and favored moderation in their use, but strongly opposed distilleries. 59 notes. H. L. Calkin

2582. Clark, Roger W. CINCINNATI CRUSADERS FOR TEMPERANCE: 1874. *Cincinnati Hist. Soc. Bull. 1974 32(4): 185-199.* Discusses activities and demonstrations of the Women's National Christian Temperance Union in Cincinnati, Ohio, including the role of Wesley Chapel (Methodist Church) and the Ninth Street Baptist Church.

2583. Dannenbaum, Jed. THE CRUSADER: SAMUEL CARY AND CINCINNATI TEMPERANCE. *Cincinnati Hist. Soc. Bull. 1975 33(2): 136-151.* Chronicles Samuel Fenton Cary's fight against alcohol in Cincinnati, Ohio, and his active membership in temperance movements both locally and nationally, 1845-1900.

2584. Dannenbaum, Jed. IMMIGRANTS AND TEMPERANCE: ETHNOCULTURAL CONFLICT IN CINCINNATI, 1845-1860. *Ohio Hist. 1978 87(2): 125-139.* Ethnocultural issues, primarily anti-Catholicism, nativism, and temperance, sparked the breakdown of electoral politics and the realignment of contemporary cultural mores during the 1850's in Cincinnati, Ohio. As German and Irish immigrants grew in political power, native-born Cincinnatians increasingly associated them with rapidly worsening social problems. The issues severely disrupted the local party system and led to the virtual demise of the Whig Party in Cincinnati. Based on newspapers, contemporary comments, and secondary sources; illus., 47 notes. N. Summers

2585. Downey, Fairfax. PREACHER BEECHER AND THE CREATURE. *Smithsonian 1974 5(1): 56-60.* Viewing rum as a danger to Christian society, Lyman Beecher waged a one man war against the demon alcohol from the pulpit of his Presbyterian East Hampton, Long Island church, 1799-1810.

2586. Hougland, James G., Jr.; Wood, James R.; and Mueller, Samuel A. ORGANIZATIONAL "GOAL SUBMERGENCE": THE METHODIST CHURCH AND THE FAILURE OF THE TEMPERANCE MOVEMENT. *Sociol. and Social Res. 1974 58(4): 408-416.* Existing concepts concerning goal change do not describe organizations' adjustments to societal changes which differentially affect organization members, causing some to experience a given goal negatively while others continue to derive positive incentives from it. The authors therefore introduce the concept of 'goal submergence,' which relates goal change to executives' efforts to provide differential incentives to various organizational elements, and illustrate this by the history of the Methodist Church in relation to the temperance movement. Covers 1919-72. J

2587. Kearnes, John. UTAH, SEXTON OF PROHIBITION. *Utah Hist. Q. 1979 47(1): 5-21.* Utah, whose Mormon majority espoused abstinence, was the 36th state to ratify the 21st amendment, which repealed the 18th (Prohibition) amendment. Urban majorities prevailed over rural prohibitionists in spite of concerted efforts of secular and religious leaders. Wets pointed to disrespect for law created by Prohibition. They argued that additional revenue repeal would provide toward recovery from the Depression, and made Prohibition a poltical, not a religious, issue. Drys rejected the economic appeal, pointed out evils rampant before Prohibition, and made prohibition a moral and religious obligation. Covers 1932-33. 8 illus., 59 notes. J. L. Hazelton

2588. Kingsdale, Jon M. THE "POOR MAN'S CLUB": SOCIAL FUNCTIONS OF THE URBAN WORKING-CLASS SALOON. *Am. Q. 1973 25(4): 472-489.* Turn-of-the-century saloons provided an all-male neighborhood social and political center for urban industrial and ethnic groups conserving and reinforcing working-class and ethnic values. Saloons retarded assimilation toward the Anglo-Saxon Protestant ideal and were, therefore, more than symbolic enemies to Prohibitionists concerned with conserving traditional American values and family life. Based on secondary sources; 65 notes. W. D. Piersen

2589. Knight, Virginia C. WOMEN AND THE TEMPERANCE MOVEMENT. *Current Hist. 1976 70(416): 201-203.* Discusses the role of women in temperance movements from the 19th century to 1920, emphasizing the activities of the Women's Christian Temperance Union headed by Frances Willard.

2590. Lender, Mark. DRUNKENNESS AS AN OFFENSE IN EARLY NEW ENGLAND. *Q. J. of Studies on Alcohol 1973 34(2A): 353-366.* One of the dilemmas of 17th-century New England Puritan society was how to deal with the misuse of alcohol, a commodity considered in itself good. Puritans used alcohol frequently and considered it a normal part of their diet and culture, but strongly condemned its misuse. The strength of a few of these condemnations, and the heritage of the modern Temperance Movement, has perpetuated a false image of an intolerant Puritanism irrationally denouncing alcohol and drunkards. The Puritans did not have any consistent method of dealing with drunkenness offenses. New Englanders carefully defined what constituted legal drunkenness, noting that in some persons drunkenness was chronic and closely related to poverty, crime and social disorder. Puritans could only speculate on the causes and remedies of drunkenness. Punishments did not stop the problem and were not the only approaches used to cope with it. Sinning inebriates were forgiven upon repentance; and some local officials even tried to help them without punishment. There was little consistency in dealing with any form of alcohol misuse. Many of the laws against drunkenness were severe but there was never any concerted effort to enforce them. Nothing in these laws was 'Puritan,' as the Anglican colonies and Britain had similar statutes. Thus, images of intolerant Puritan attitudes toward alcohol are distortions. The true picture is one of variety, experimentation and even compassion in the face of a frustrating problem. J

2591. Musselman, Thomas H. A CRUSADE FOR LOCAL OPTION: SHREVEPORT, 1951-1952. *North Louisiana Hist. Assoc. J. 1975 6(2): 59-73.* During the early 1950's, an active political campaign was waged "for the purpose of 'drying up' Shreveport" by members and supporters of the Shreveport Ministerial Association. "Both supporters and opponents of prohibition resorted to unsavory campaign tactics," and the "local option campaign of 1951 and 1952 was bitterly fought and roughly contested." At the end, on election day, 16 July 1952, "voters turned out in near record numbers to defeat prohibition in Shreveport with a total of 28,806 going to the polls." 77 notes.
A. N. Garland

2592. Nelson, Larry E. UTAH GOES DRY. *Utah Hist. Q. 1973 41(4): 340-357.* The prohibition movement in Utah was similar to that in other states. The delay was a product of the particular political situation: although Mormons practiced total abstention themselves as an article of faith, they were reluctant to work for prohibition at the risk of revitalizing old Mormon-Gentile antagonisms. In the end, Utah's law was among the strictest state statutes and more strict than the federal Volstead Act. 7 illus., 71 notes. D. L. Smith

2593. Phillips, Loretta and Phillips, Prentice. HE FOUGHT A HORDE OF DEMONS. *New-England Galaxy 1977 19(1): 45-51.* Describes the personal struggles of John B. Gough against Demon Rum during 1834-43. His preachings against liquor, from 1843 until his death in 1886, persuaded thousands of alcoholics to sign the pledge of total abstinence. 3 illus. P. C. Marshall

2594. Rorabaugh, William J. RISING DEMOCRATIC SPIRITS: IMMIGRANTS, TEMPERANCE, AND TAMMANY HALL, 1854-1860. *Civil War Hist. 1976 22(2): 131-157.* Discusses the emergence of a political coalition among the Irish, Germans, and Anglos in New York City during 1840's-50's. It turned the metropolis into a Democratic stronghold, while the rest of the North was becoming largely Republicanized. Although these groups differed on other matters, hostility to prohibition united immigrant Irish and German Catholics with enough native-born Protestants to control New York City. The corner saloon evolved from an unimportant neighborhood shop to a highly structured nerve center. It became the needed power base from which the coalition could effectively function. E. C. Murdock

2595. Shafer, Elizabeth. ST. FRANCES AND THE CRUSADERS. *Am. Hist. Illus. 1976 11(5): 24-33.* During 1878-98 Frances E. Willard headed the Women's Christian Temperance Union and led a single-handed campaign for prohibition.

2596. Smith, Becky. PROHIBITION IN ALASKA. *Alaska J. 1973 3(3): 170-179.* Discusses eras of alcoholic prohibition in Alaska 1842-1917, emphasizing the activities of the Women's Christian Temperance Union.

2597. Whitaker, F. M. OHIO WCTU AND THE PROHIBITION AMENDMENT CAMPAIGN OF 1883. *Ohio Hist. 1974 83(2): 84-102.* Describes the founding of the Woman's Christian Temperance Union of Ohio in 1874 and its activities through the prohibition amendment campaign of 1883. In its first years the Union struggled with the liquor licensing issue and tried to avoid partisan politics. After a few years of reduced activity, the Union joined the prohibition campaign, which ended in defeat of the amendment. After the campaign of 1883 the Union became more closely associated with the Prohibition Party, and its independent influence declined. Based on minutes of the Ohio WCTU meetings, newspapers, the author's dissertation, and secondary works; 3 photos, 70 notes. J. B. Street

2598. White, Larry. THE RETURN OF THE THIEF: THE REPEAL OF PROHIBITION AND THE ADVENTIST RESPONSE. *Adventist Heritage 1978 5(2): 34-47.* Discusses the response (1932-34) of Seventh-Day Adventists to the campaign for repeal of Prohibition and its aftermath.

2599. Wilson, John and Manton, Kenneth. LOCALISM AND TEMPERANCE. *Sociol. and Social Res. 1975 59(2): 121-135.* "Negative attitudes toward liquor consumption were linked by Gusfield (1969) to localism. A poll before a referendum on liberalizing liquor sales in North Carolina indicated a slight relation between social class and liquor attitudes and stronger relationships between localism and liquor restriction. Interaction effects indicate status preservation concerns expressed in opposing liquor liberalization were concentrated in those of low income, low education, older age, regular church attenders, and the immobile." Covers 1969-70. J

19. SOCIOECONOMIC GROUPS

2600. Blumin, Stuart M. CHURCH AND COMMUNITY: A CASE STUDY OF LAY LEADERSHIP IN NINETEENTH-CENTURY AMERICA. *New York Hist. 1975 56(4): 393-408.* A statistical study of the socioeconomic status, residential tenure, and family background of the leaders of 19th-century Kingston (New York) Protestant and Jewish churches, and their secular leadership in the Kingston community. Although church leaders "comprised a significant minority of the community's secular leadership," the underlying characteristic of community leadership was "membership in a fairly wide and fairly diverse commercial class." Illus., 7 tables, 9 notes. R. N. Lokken

2601. Bouchard, Gérard. LES PRÊTRES, LES CAPITALISTES ET LES OUVRIERS À CHICOUTIMI (1896-1930) [Priests, capitalists and workers in Chicoutimi, 1896-1930]. *Mouvement Social [France] 1980 (112): 5-23.* This paper deals with the working class in a Catholic parish at Chicoutimi (province of Québec) between 1896 and 1930. The creation of this parish had followed the opening of a pulp mill in this mostly commercial town whose population was dominated by traditional elites (priests, professionals, tradesmen). But the mill, along with the skilled and nonskilled workers it attracted in the town and who gathered in a quite isolated ward, was a serious threat to the cultural, social and political order. The elites managed to overcome these disruptive forces through close cooperation with capitalists and powerful control of the working class within the parish life and organization. So this story highlights the social dimension and impact of popular beliefs and worship in a context of industrialization. J

2602. Campbell, Colin. THE SECRET RELIGION OF THE EDUCATED CLASSES. *Sociol. Analysis 1978 39(2): 146-156.* The new religiosity of the sixties is identified as corresponding to Troeltsch's Spiritual and Mystic Religion. Its rise to prominence is thus associated with the gradual displacement of church religion, an interpretation of contemporary events that is consistent with the data on secularization and with the evidence in favor of a new religiosity. An explanation for this transition is sought in Troeltsch's observation that this form of religion possesses greater congruence with the values of students and the educated middle classes than either the church or sect type. As a consequence, the new religiosity is described, following Troeltsch, as the "secret religion of the educated classes." J

2603. Carter, James E. THE SOCIOECONOMIC STATUS OF BAPTIST MINISTERS IN HISTORICAL PERSPECTIVE. *Baptist Hist. and Heritage 1980 15(1): 37-44.* Surveys the upward mobility of Baptist ministers from 1651 to 1980 by analyzing the changes in education, income, public acceptance, and nature of work.

2604. Clelland, Donald A.; Hood, Thomas C.; Lipsey, C. M.; and Wimberley, Ronald. IN THE COMPANY OF THE CONVERTED: CHARACTERISTICS OF A BILLY GRAHAM CRUSADE AUDIENCE. *Sociol. Analysis 1974 35(1): 45-56.* Examination of the social characteristics of a Billy Graham Crusade audience in Knoxville, Tennessee. Basic data sources are 1) a short questionnaire administered to persons in randomly selected seats, 2) a larger follow-up mail questionnaire, and 3) a comparison survey of area residents. Crusade attenders are more educated and of higher income and occupational prestige than area residents. They attend church more frequently and are more conservative on religious beliefs than comparable samples. The thesis of the middle-class respectability of the Graham movement is substantiated by these data. The persistance of revivalism is interpreted as a functional reaffirmation of a threatened life style. J

2605. Ellis, William E. GILBOA TO ICHABOD: SOCIAL AND RELIGIOUS FACTORS IN THE FUNDAMENTALIST-MODERNIST SCHISMS AMONG CANADIAN BAPTISTS, 1895-1934. *Foundations 1977 20(2): 109-126.* Examines the socioeconomic makeup of the Jarvis Street Baptist Church in Toronto, and the change that occurred during the Fundamentalist-Modernist controversy. As the Fundamentalists gained control, the professional and entrepreneur class left to form churches in new upper-class areas. Contrasts the Jarvis Street Church with the Central Baptist Church and compares it to the Conventional churches and Union churches. The Fundamentalist Union churches attracted the working class (91%), while the Conventional churches attracted the professional class. This increased the social stratification of the church. 23 notes. E. E. Eminhizer

2606. Elzey, Wayne. LIMINALITY AND SYMBIOSIS IN POPULAR AMERICAN PROTESTANTISM. *J. of the Am. Acad. of Religion 1975 43(4): 741-756.* While admitting the difficulty of defining and studying popular American Protestantism, the author believes that it is possible to isolate certain descriptive characteristics of it. The article focuses on one form of American Protestantism, that of the urban middle classes, and discusses some of its symbols and thought patterns. Primary and secondary sources; 41 notes. E. R. Lester

2607. Gavelis, Vytautus. A DESCRIPTIVE STUDY OF THE EDUCATIONAL ATTAINMENT, OCCUPATION, AND GEOGRAPHICAL LOCATION OF THE CHILDREN OF LITHUANIAN DISPLACED PERSONS AND OF AMERICAN BORN PARENTS WHO ATTENDED IMMACULATE CONCEPTION PRIMARY SCHOOL IN EAST ST. LOUIS FROM 1948 TO 1968. *Lituanus 1976 22(1): 72-75.* Discusses the summary results of a Ph.D. dissertation comparing the educational and occupational attainment of two groups of children of Lithuanian family background. The parents of one group were American born and English speaking, the other Lithuanian born and non-English speaking. Recommendations for further research based on the results of the study are made. K. N. T. Crowther

2608. Ghent, Joyce Maynard and Jaher, Frederic Cople. THE CHICAGO BUSINESS ELITE, 1830-1930: A COLLECTIVE BIOGRAPHY. *Business Hist. Rev. 1976 50(3): 288-328.* Attempts to determine whether the profile of a business elite, that of Chicago during 1830-1930, conformed to the national pattern found in previous investigations of this subject. Concludes that in education, religion, geography of birth, vintage of wealth, and family background, the commercial elite "had more privileged characteristics than did the national population." It became even less "Algeristic" with each succeeding generation. 32 tables, 19 notes. C. J. Pusateri

2609. Goldberg, Robert A. BENEATH THE HOOD AND ROBE: A SOCIOECONOMIC ANALYSIS OF KU KLUX KLAN MEMBERSHIP IN DENVER, COLORADO, 1921-1925. *Western Hist. Q. 1980 11(2): 181-198.* Except for the young, the elite, and the proletariat, membership in the Denver Ku Klux Klan in the 1920's represented a near occupational cross-section of the local population. White Protestant men from all socioeconomic levels joined to save their communities and homes from so-called disruptive groups: Catholics, Jews, blacks, immigrants, and law violators. 4 tables, 24 notes. D. L. Smith

2610. Goyder, John C. and Pineo, Peter C. MINORITY GROUP STATUS AND SELF-EVALUATED CLASS. *Sociol. Q. 1974 15(2): 199-211.* Self-evaluated class status is shown to vary among white Protestants, Catholics, Jews, and black Protestants. Holding economic status constant, Jews are most likely to select the middle- (or upper-) class label, followed by white Protestants, white Catholics, and black Protestants. Thus, the independent effect of minority status on self-evaluated class status reinforces the ranking directly attributable to the economic levels of each of the four groups. Also, the congruence between self-identified class and objective economic status is closer among Jews and white Protestants than among white Catholics or black Protestants. The hypothesis that affiliation with a minority necessarily reduces class consciousness was, therefore, not supported. J

2611. Groulx, Lionel. UN SEIGNEUR EN SOUTANE [A lord in a cassock]. *Rev. d'Hist. de l'Amérique Française [Canada] 1957 11(2): 201-217.* Discusses the Compagnie de Saint-Sulpice (the Sulpician order), whose members were drawn from the nobility, in New France, 17th-18th centuries.

2612. Horowitz, Irving Louis. RACE, CLASS AND THE NEW ETHNICITY. *Worldview 1975 18(1): 46-53.* Analyzes attitudes of working class ethnic groups toward blacks, religion, Jews, and the class structure, and discusses their increasing conservativism and potential for political power, 1974.

2613. Hunt, Larry L. and Hunt, Janet G. BLACK CATHOLICISM AND OCCUPATIONAL STATUS IN NORTHERN CITIES. *Social Sci. Q. 1978 58(4): 657-670.* The relationship between black Catholicism and occupational status in northern cities is examined using 1968 data for 15 cities. Multiple regression analysis shows that a modest nationwide Catholic advantage in occupational attainment is attributable to opposite trends in eastern and midwestern cities. Suggests that Catholic affiliation implies a status advantage only where it facilitates contact with whites and/or is a minority affiliation that can symbolize a distinctive lifestyle. J

2614. Hurtubise, Pierre. L'ORIGINE SOCIALE DES VOCATIONS CANADIENNES DE NOUVELLE-FRANCE [The social origin of Canadian vocations in New France]. *Sessions d'Étude: Soc. Can. d'Hist. de l'Église Catholique [Canada] 1978 45: 41-56.* Between 1650 and 1762, 841 Canadians became priests, monks, or nuns, of whom 630 were women; they were drawn from all social classes.

2615. Kutolowski, Kathleen Smith. IDENTIFYING THE RELIGIOUS AFFILIATIONS OF 19TH CENTURY LOCAL ELITES. *Hist. Methods Newsletter 1975 9(1): 9-13.* Points out problems and misleading clues awaiting the historian seeking denominational identities for local elites. Despite disadvantages, this material provides insights into the complex relationships of local power elites. D. K. Pickens

2616. Lauer, Robert H. OCCUPATIONAL AND RELIGIOUS MOBILITY IN A SMALL CITY. *Sociol. Q. 1975 16(3): 380-392.* Previous studies have suggested a relationship between occupational and religious mobility, namely, that the latter should follow upon the former in order to provide the mobile individual with a more socially congruent context. The greater the distance of occupational mobility, therefore, the more likely is religious mobility to occur. Analysis of data from a telephone survey of a small Midwestern city reveals that occupational and religious mobility are not related per se; there is, however, a significant relationship between occupational mobility distance and religious mobility. Education is also significantly and positively related to occupational mobility. Highly educated individuals who are occupationally mobile across a great distance are the most religiously mobile group of all. There is also a tendency for the religiously mobile to move into high status Protestant denominations or out of the Christian religion altogether; this pattern is intensified among those who are highly mobile occupationally. The results suggest that religious mobility is a coping mechanism rather than a search for a more socially congruent context. Covers 1955-75. J

2617. Marszalek, John F. THE BLACK LEADER IN 1919—SOUTH CAROLINA AS A CASE STUDY. *Phylon 1975 36(3): 249-259.* Studies comparatively unknown black leaders through use of the South Carolina volume of the *History of the American Negro and His Institutions*, A. B. Caldwell, ed. (Atlanta, 1917-23, seven volumes), with its brief biographical articles. The composite of a black leader emerges as a male in his early forties, a resident of a county with a large black population and large black-to-white population ratio, educated at an all-black religiously oriented South Carolina college, likely to be a Baptist minister, may or may not have owned property, took little part in politics, was a lodge member, and if he read, read religious books. He believed in accommodation, and was convinced that education and self-help would ultimately improve his race's lot. 18 notes. R. V. Ritter

2618. Miller, Rodney K. THE INFLUENCE OF THE SOCIO-ECONOMIC STATUS OF THE ANGLICAN CLERGY OF REVOLUTIONARY MARYLAND ON THEIR POLITICAL ORGANIZATION. *Hist. Mag. of the Protestant Episcopal Church 1978 47(2): 197-210.* A new approach to eight socioeconomic variables demonstrates how members of the Anglican clergy in Maryland were influenced on the eve of the American Revolution. Political orientation among the 44 Maryland Anglicans examined was probably the result of the subtle interaction between the external political and social pressure and the internal pressure of individual conscience and convictions. Biographies and secondary sources; 4 tables, 19 notes, 2 appendixes. H. M. Parker, Jr.

2619. Mueller, Charles W. and Johnson, Weldon T. SOCIOECONOMIC STATUS AND RELIGIOUS PARTICIPATION. *Am. Sociol. Rev. 1975 40(6): 785-800.* The relationship between socioeconomic status and frequency of religious participation is examined for a 1970 U.S. sample of males and females. Although some support is found for the frequently observed positive relationship between these two variables, the data require that such a generalization be qualified. The zero-order relationship generally is stronger for males than females and is positive and weak for Protestants, but is essentially zero for Catholics and negative in sign for Jews and unaffiliated whites. Where the relationship is positive, it is not entirely explainable by the positive relationship of our measure of general social participation with both SES and religious participation. In addition, the examination of interactions with marital status and the presence of children under age 16 indicated that the SES-religious participation relationship is strongest for those who are married and responsible for young children. Even with these significant variations by relevant subpopulations, we conclude that the explanatory power of socioeconomic status in predicting religious participation is small both in absolute terms and in comparison with other possible determinants examined. J

2620. Nelson, Charles H. TOWARD A MORE ACCURATE APPROXIMATION OF CLASS COMPOSITION OF THE ERIK JANSSONISTS. *Swedish Pioneer Hist. Q. 1975 26(1): 3-15.* The occupations of Janssonist emigrants can be identified from ship manifests for the period 1845-47, when the majority emigrated to Illinois. The class distribution of the emigrants was found to be similar to the county they were from, with about two-thirds coming from impoverished classes. Based on a chapter of the author's doctoral dissertation, "Erik Janssonism: A Socio-Cultural Interpretation of the Emergence and Development of a Religious Sect in Sweden in the 1840's." 4 tables, 21 notes. K. J. Puffer

2621. Pierard, Richard V. BILLY GRAHAM—PREACHER OF THE GOSPEL OR MENTOR OF MIDDLE AMERICA? *Fides et Hist. 1973 5(1-2): 127-131.* Lowell D. Streiker and Gerald S. Strober in *Religion and the New Majority: Billy Graham, Middle America, and the Politics of the 70's* (New York: Association Press, 1972) argue that Graham's success lies more in sociological than in spiritual factors, and that he articulates the philosophy, commitment, fears, and hopes of the average American, or "Middle America." The book is fairer than many in its portrayal of Graham's life, but the term "Middle America" is a vague and inadequate sociological construct, the discussion of evangelical Christianity is shallow, and the asserted congruence between Graham-type evangelicalism and mainstream America is doubtful. R. Butchart

2622. Roeber, Anthony Gregg. "HER MERCHANDIZE... SHALL BE HOLINESS TO THE LORD": THE PROGRESS AND DECLINE OF PURITAN GENTILITY AT THE BRATTLE STREET CHURCH, BOSTON, 1715-1745. *New England Hist. and Geneal. Register 1977 131: 175-194.* Examines the life and thought of Benjamin Coleman, pastor of Boston's Brattle Street Church and minister to many of the town's wealthy merchants. The congregation was at the center of a number of controversies which shook Massachusetts during 1715-40, most notably the great credit debates. Coleman's special mission was to bring the "gentility" of 18th-century England to Boston and blend it with Puritan piety. The Puritan gentility had a distinct social dimension. Coleman advocated a social hierarchy with the clergy at the top assisted by a mercantile elite serving as guardians of church and society. However, Coleman never adequately defined his concept of gentility. In the end his ideas were overwhelmed by changes in Puritan thought and in America's attitude toward the mother country. Primary and secondary sources; 56 notes. R. J. Crandall

2623. Roof, Wade Clark. SOCIOECONOMIC DIFFERENTIALS AMONG WHITE SOCIORELIGIOUS GROUPS IN THE UNITED STATES. *Social Forces 1979 58(1): 280-289.* This research addresses the recent claim that Catholics have now replaced traditionally high-status Protestant groups in the national income elite. Evidence from the

NORC [National Opinion Research Center] General Social Surveys fails to support the claim; rather it is found that in income—as in education and occupation—high-status Protestants continue to rank above Catholics. Despite significant gains for Catholics over the past two decades, and thus reduced Protestant-Catholic differentials in status, still the relative rankings of these groups differ very little today from that observed in earlier times. 3 tables, 6 notes, biblio. J

2624. Singleton, Gregory H. POPULAR CULTURE OR THE CULTURE OF THE POPULACE? *J. of Popular Culture 1977 11(1): 254-266.* An examination of how activities within British-origin Protestant church groups influenced the lives of their members in Los Angeles. By the 1920's the British Protestant establishment had split, with the successful members of the new middle class of managers remaining in the established churches, including the Methodist and Episcopal churches, while the less successful joined sects and were more likely to be influenced by Fundamentalism. The former group's identity was economic (class WASP's), while the latter group's was ethnic (ethnic WASP's). Primary and secondary sources; 18 notes. D. G. Nielson/S

2625. Soltow, Lee and May, Dean L. THE DISTRIBUTION OF MORMON WEALTH AND INCOME IN 1857. *Explorations in Econ. Hist. 1979 16(2): 151-162.* A decade after the Mormons migrated to Utah, wealth and income were distributed with a surprisingly even hand. For whatever reason this conformed closely to the Mormon ideology. Based on manuscript records, published documents, and secondary accounts; 4 tables, fig., 16 notes. P. J. Coleman

2626. Stewart, Gordon. SOCIO-ECONOMIC FACTORS IN THE GREAT AWAKENING: THE CASE OF YARMOUTH, NOVA SCOTIA. *Acadiensis [Canada] 1973 3(1): 18-34.* Discusses social and economic tensions of colonial society in Yarmouth, Nova Scotia, during the Great Awakening of the 1760's and 70's.

2627. Stout, Harry S. THE GREAT AWAKENING IN NEW ENGLAND RECONSIDERED: THE NEW ENGLAND CLERGY AS A CASE STUDY. *J. of Social Hist. 1974 8(1): 21-47.* A quantitative analysis of Congregationalist clergymen during the Great Awakening reveals "differences in a social structural context between Old Light and New Light ministers." These differences can be accounted for by variables in the socioeconomic dimension, of which family and militia ties were most significant. The Great Awakening did not create new divisions among ministers but followed previously developed patterns. 8 tables, 59 notes, appendix. L. E. Ziewacz

2628. Tise, Larry Edward. THE INTERREGIONAL APPEAL OF PROSLAVERY THOUGHT: AN IDEOLOGICAL PROFILE OF THE ANTEBELLUM AMERICAN CLERGY. *Plantation Soc. in the Americas 1979 1(1): 58-72.* Clergymen who published defenses of slavery were very successful economically and socially and usually held high church offices. Although the Southern proportion of the group constantly rose, the first generation (born before 1800) was largely born and educated outside the South. Several belonged to non-Southern churches, e.g. Congregational. Since these men shaped the proslavery argument, it was a "logical byproduct of the American mind," not peculiarly Southern. 6 tables, 3 fig., 17 notes. R. G. Sherer

2629. Welch, Michael R. THE UNCHURCHED: BLACK RELIGIOUS NON-AFFILIATES. *J. for the Sci. Study of Religion 1978 17(3): 289-294.* Compares socio-demographic variables (age, marital status, geographical region, residence, sex, occupation, level of education, and income) of nonaffiliated, Protestant, and Catholic Negroes.

20. WAR AND PACIFISM

2630. Alexander, Jon A. T. COLONIAL NEW ENGLAND PREACHING ON WAR AS ILLUSTRATED IN MASSACHUSETTS ARTILLERY ELECTION SERMONS. *J. of Church and State 1975 17(3): 423-442.* Discusses the tradition of religious sermons concerning the legitimacy of war for Christians in Massachusetts and New England, 1640-1740.

2631. Bevil, Gladys Davis Topping. THE FIGHTING CHAPLAIN OF THE REVOLUTION. *Daughters of the Am. Revolution Mag. 1975 109(10): 1108-1112.* Sketches the life of the Reverend John Gano (1727-1804), a Baptist who was chaplain to George Washington during the American Revolution.

2632. Birdwhistell, Jack. EXTRACTS FROM THE DIARY OF B. F. HUNGERFORD, A KENTUCKY BAPTIST PASTOR DURING THE CIVIL WAR. *Baptist Hist. and Heritage 1979 14(2): 24-31.* Provides excerpts from the diary of Kentucky Baptist pastor B. F. Hungerford covering 1863-66, which detail his thoughts on the Civil War.

2633. Bradley, A. Day. JOSHUA BROWN, PRISONER FOR CONSCIENCE SAKE. *J. of the Lancaster County Hist. Soc. 1977 81(1): 25-30.* Joshua Brown, a member of the Society of Friends from Little Britain Township, Pennsylvania, was imprisoned, along with a fellow Friend, in Ninety Six, South Carolina, 1778, primarily because of local distrust of pacifists during the American Revolution.

2634. Brown, Douglas Summers. CHARLES CUMMINGS: THE FIGHTING PARSON OF SOUTHWEST VIRGINIA. *Virginia Cavalcade 1979 28(3): 138-143.* Presbyterian minister Charles Cummings (1733-1812) is "remembered as a late 18th-century pioneer and patriot who defended his region against Indian attacks and the encroachments of the British Empire."

2635. Burnbaugh, Donald F. RELIGION AND REVOLUTION: OPTIONS IN 1776. *Pennsylvania Mennonite Heritage 1978 1(3): 2-9.* The German Dunkards and Mennonites remained neutral due to their basic nonresistant positions, but had pro-British sympathies, as is evidenced in the Pennsylvania and Maryland loyalist movements and an attempt by European Mennonites in 1784 to secure land for settlement.

2636. Campbell, Keith E. and Granberg, Donald. RELIGIOSITY AND ATTITUDE TOWARD THE VIETNAM WAR: A RESEARCH NOTE USING NATIONAL SAMPLES. *Sociol. Analysis 1979 40(3): 254-256.* Two national samples from 1972 and 1968 were used to investigate a possible relationship between religiosity and attitude toward the Vietnam War. Differing from previous findings reported for college students, our analysis indicated neither a negative nor positive relationship between religiosity and criticism of the Vietnam War. Covers 1968-72.

J

2637. Carr, Stephen M. SMEDLEY BUTLER: HERO OR DEMAGOGUE? *Am. Hist. Illus. 1980 15(1): 30-38.* Smedley Butler (1881-1940), raised a Hicksite Quaker in West Chester, Pennsylvania, became a major general in the Marine Corps and was presented with two Congressional Medals of Honor; he was also court-martialed in 1931 for conduct unbecoming an officer after he denounced war and spoke in public against questionable State Department activities in Nicaragua in 1912; Butler continued to speak out until his death.

2638. Childress, James F. REINHOLD NIEBUHR'S CRITIQUE OF PACIFISM. *Rev. of Pol. 1974 36(4): 467-491.*

2639. Chrystal, William G. REINHOLD NIEBUHR AND THE FIRST WORLD WAR. *J. of Presbyterian Hist. 1977 55(3): 285-298.* Reinhold Niebuhr (1892-1970) was recently ordained in the German Evangelical Synod of North America and had just become pastor of a congregation in Detroit when America became involved in World War I. During the war he repeatedly stressed the need to be loyal to the nation of one's birth or adoption. Theologically, however, he went beyond the issue of national loyalty as he endeavored to fashion a realistic ethical perspective of patriotism and pacifism. He endeavored to work out a realistic approach to the moral danger posed by aggressive powers which many idealists and pacifists failed to recognize. During the war he also served his denomination as Executive Secretary of the War Welfare Commission while maintaining his pastorate in Detroit. A pacifist at heart, he saw compromise as a necessity and was willing to support war in order to find peace—"compromising for the sake of righteousness." Based largely on Niebuhr's papers and publications; 41 notes.

H. M. Parker, Jr.

2640. Cook, Blanche Wiesen. AMERICAN JUSTIFICATIONS FOR MILITARY MASSACRES FROM THE PEQUOT WARS TO MYLAI. *Peace and Change 1975 3(2-3): 4-20.* Discusses American justifications for war crimes against Indians, Filipinos, Vietnamese, and others from 1636 to the 1970's.

2641. Curtis, Peter H. A QUAKER AND THE CIVIL WAR: THE LIFE OF JAMES PARNELL JONES. *Quaker Hist. 1978 67(1): 35-41.* Raised as a Quaker in Maine, James Parnell Jones spent two years at Haverford College, and developed a passion for antislavery and temperance reforms in reaction to the "hypocrisy" of conservative, Philadelphia Quakers. He taught school, and graduated from the University of Michigan in 1856, shifting toward the reformist tenets of Progressive or Congregational Friends in the area. When he returned to Maine in 1861 and joined its 7th Regiment, he was disowned, but felt himself still a Friend in all respects except in fighting the war for freedom and union. Based in part on letters to his family in Maine; 33 notes.

T. D. S. Bassett

2642. Davidson, Charles N., Jr. GEORGE ARTHUR BUTTRICK: CHRISTOCENTRIC PREACHER AND PACIFIST. *J. of Presbyterian Hist. 1975 53(2): 143-167.* Although he has changed his mind on other matters, Presbyterian George Arthur Buttrick (b. 1892) has maintained his position on pacifism to the present. Traces Buttrick's pacifism from the early years of his ministry through the two world wars, concluding with a word about the dangers inherent in the idea of an "American Century," borne out by the Vietnam War. Based on an interview with Buttrick and on his writings; illus., 84 notes.

H. M. Parker, Jr.

2643. Davis, Edwin S. THE RELIGION OF GEORGE WASHINGTON: A BICENTENNIAL REPORT. *Air U. Rev. 1976 27(5): 30-34.* Discusses George Washington's religious beliefs and the role that these beliefs played in the development of the Chaplain's corps of the US Army. Several examples of Washington's Anglican derived faith and interest in religious matters are cited by the author. Based on *The Writings of George Washington* and other published works; 20 notes.

J. W. Thacker, Jr.

2644. Dick, Everett N. THE ADVENTIST MEDICAL CADET CORPS AS SEEN BY ITS FOUNDER. *Adventist Heritage 1974 1(2): 18-27.* The Adventist Medical Cadet Corps was founded in 1934 by the author to train Adventist boys to serve in the Army medical department, if conscripted, in order to avoid the moral difficulties encountered with arms bearing and Sabbath observance in the service; covers World War II and Korean War service.

2645. Dick, Everett N. THE MILITARY CHAPLAINCY AND SEVENTH-DAY ADVENTISTS: THE EVOLUTION OF AN ATTITUDE. *Adventist Heritage 1976 3(1): 33-45.* The Seventh-Day Adventist General Conference officers in 1944 attempted to guide Adventist ministers away from military chaplaincy, but by 1955 supplied financial aid and special training for that field.

2646. Durnbaugh, Donald. ENLARGING THE CIRCLE: THE HISTORIC PEACE CHURCHES AND MILITARISM. *Mennonite Life 1978 33(3): 16-18.* The three Historic Peace Churches (Society of Friends, Mennonites, and Church of the Brethren) have worked to promote world peace in the 20th century through four main channels: education, publication, action, and witness to governments. Educational efforts have included seminars and conferences as well as support for such colleges as Haverford and Swarthmore. Propeace publications have ranged from posters to scholarly texts. Action has included devising alternate service for conscientious objectors, nonviolent resistance, and acts of civil disobedience. Peace churches have lobbied for changes in government policy. Currently the three churches are forming the New Call to Peacemaking to revitalize the peace movement. Photo. B. Burnett

2647. Entz, Margaret. WAR BOND DRIVES AND THE KANSAS MENNONITE RESPONSE. *Mennonite Life 1975 30(3): 4-9.* Discusses bonds bought during World War I, 1917-18, by Mennonites living in Kansas.

2648. Fowler, Arlen L. CHAPLAIN D. EGLINTON BARR: A LINCOLN YANKEE. *Hist. Mag. of the Protestant Episcopal Church 1976 45(4): 435-438.* When the Civil War began, Northern-born D. Eglinton Barr was rector of St. John's Episcopal Church, Baton Rouge, Louisiana. Because of his Northern heritage, he was suspect in the eyes of the Confederates. He went to the Federal lines in New Orleans, volunteered as a Chaplain, and was assigned to the 81st Regiment of US Colored Troops. Later he was apprehended and imprisoned by Confederates, but escaped and returned to New Orleans. At the end of the war, with former Confederates returning to power he was not allowed employment. He thus returned to the Army chaplaincy, was again assigned to a black regiment, and conducted school for his troops until he retired in 1872. The Department of Education of Texas presented him with a letter of appreciation for his work in the field of public education. His story provides an insight into the human side of times and events that are often forgotten. Material for the article was found in Selected Appointment, Commission and Personal Branch Records, D. E. Barr file, Record Group 94, National Archives, Washington, D.C. H. M. Parker, Jr.

2649. Frank, Thomas E. CONTENDING VALUES: FRANCIS WAYLAND'S VIEWS ON WAR. *Foundations 1978 21(2): 100-112.* Francis Wayland, president of Brown University during 1827-55, is also known for his *The Elements of Moral Science.* Traces this Baptist's views on war from pacifism to limited war. 70 notes. E. E. Eminhizer

2650. Friesen, Duane K. PEACE STUDIES: MENNONITE COLLEGES IN THE NORTH AMERICAN CONTEXT. *Mennonite Life 1980 35(1): 13-18.* Peace Studies as an academic discipline developed in North American institutions in the mid-60's. COPRED (Consortium of Peace Research, Education and Development), founded in 1970 by 35 peace centers and university departments, coordinates and promotes the study of the nine themes of peace research: theological-philosophical views, nonviolent social change, international war and peace, conflict regulation in society, world order models, knowledge of other cultures, the rich-poor conflict, environmental quality, and peace education. Ethically oriented humanistic disciplines dominate programs at the 14 Mennonite schools; social sciences predominate at nonreligious schools. 4 notes. B. Burnett

2651. Gibson, Harry W. FRONTIER ARMS OF THE MORMONS. *Utah Hist. Q. 1974 42(1): 4-26.* Firearms figured decisively in Mormon history. Firearms assumed significance in the 1830's when the Mormons faced increasingly violent confrontation with Missourians and were expelled from the state. The completion of the transcontinental railroad in 1869 ended the frontier conditions that necessitated the use of firearms for most Mormons. 10 illus., 73 notes. D. L. Smith

2652. Gilbert, Daniel R. BETHLEHEM AND THE AMERICAN REVOLUTION. *Tr. of the Moravian Hist. Soc. 1977 23(1): 17-40.* The Moravians in Bethlehem, Pennsylvania, rendered considerable voluntary and semicoerced support to the American Revolution through the provision of foodstuffs and supplies to the armies, prisoners of war, and the wounded, shelter to troops, and the extension of high quality medical services. Some damage to the town resulted from undisciplined troops, especially in the militia, although the community was never the scene of actual fighting. The prewar isolation of the town was only temporarily affected by the war. Following the shifting of combat to the South, Bethlehem rapidly returned to its prewar state, with the Moravian leaders reestablishing "rigid community control of thought and behavior." Primary and secondary sources. N. Lederer

2653. Griggs, Walter S., Jr. THE SELECTIVE CONSCIENTIOUS OBJECTOR: A VIETNAM LEGACY. *J. of Church and State 1979 21(1): 91-107.* During the Vietnam War, the pacifist-nonpacifist bipolarity that has characterized Christian attitudes on war broke down. Some people claimed to be objectors only to a particular war, but neither legislators nor judges recognized this position as being legitimate. 70 notes. S

2654. Grube, John. LES HÉROS DE LA PAIX [The heroes of peace]. *Action Natl. [Canada] 1980 69(7): 549-561.* François-Albert Angers was a heroic Quebec pacifist whose writings opposed 1) conscription during World War II, 2) European conflicts and the Cold War, and 3) war itself. His opposition to participation in World War II partially derived from the defensive neutrality of the French Canadian minority who saw conscription as a force for their assimilation into English Canada. He argued that Canada, as a small power, was in a position to preserve civilized values during a brutal era. As an ardent Catholic, he constantly recalled the traditional and contemporary teachings of the Church which stressed the ideal of Christian pacifism. 42 notes. A. W. Novitsky

2655. Harrison, Barbara Grizzuti. RED, WHITE AND GRAVEN: WITNESSES AND THE FLAG (BOOK EXCERPT). *Civil Liberties Rev. 1979 5(4): 36-49.* Excerpt from Barbara Grizzuti Harrison's *Visions of Glory: A History and a Memory of Jehovah's Witnesses* (Simon and Schuster, 1978), which traces the Jehovah's Witnesses' fight against the courts for refusing to participate in World War II and for not saluting the US flag, prior to and during World War II.

2656. Hitchcock, Ethan Allen. A CRISIS OF CONSCIENCE. Karsten, Peter, ed. *The Military in America: From the Colonial Era to the Present* (New York: Free Pr., 1980): 111-116. Based on excerpts from his diary written during 1836-54, the author discusses his dilemma as a career military man who, as a Unitarian with a conscience, questions his presence in the military establishment.

2657. Hogan, Brian F. THE GUELPH NOVITIATE RAID: CONSCRIPTION, CENSORSHIP AND BIGOTRY DURING THE GREAT WAR. *Study Sessions: Can. Catholic Hist. Assoc. [Canada] 1978 45: 57-80.* On 7 June 1918, three Jesuit novices were arrested by military police at the Novitiate of St. Stanislaus, near Guelph, Ontario, for evading military service. Protestant militants' refusal to consider novices as clergy entitled to exemption from military service led to the incident and subsequent legal moves and investigation, during which Protestant leaders denounced the raid.

2658. Joseph, Ted. THE UNITED STATES VS. S. H. MILLER: THE STRANGE CASE OF A MENNONITE EDITOR BEING CONVICTED OF VIOLATING THE 1917 ESPIONAGE ACT. *Mennonite Life 1975 30(3): 14-18.* Examines the trial and conviction of Samuel H. Miller, editor of a Mennonite newspaper, for publishing a letter allegedly containing pro-German sentiments, 1917-18.

2659. Juhnke, James C. MOB VIOLENCE AND KANSAS MENNONITES IN 1918. *Kansas Hist. Q. 1977 43(3): 334-350.* Discusses mob violence in central Kansas during 1918 against certain local Mennonites, some of them German-speaking, who refused on account of their pacifist convictions to buy Liberty bonds and to otherwise support the World War I effort. No legal action was ever taken against the vigilantes. Based on archival materials, interviews, contemporary newspaper accounts, and secondary sources; 5 illus., 56 notes. L. W. Van Wyk

2660. Juhnke, James C. THE VICTORIES OF NONRESISTANCE: MENNONITE ORAL TRADITION AND WORLD WAR I. *Fides et Hist. 1974 7(1): 19-25.* The nonresistant Mennonites suffered harsh treatment in America during World War I from civilians and the military. Their oral tradition preserves the memory of that period as personal and group victories over their persecutors. Based on taped interviews in the Schowalter Oral History Collection, Bethel College, and on secondary sources; 19 notes. R. E. Butchart

2661. Keim, Albert N. SERVICE OR RESISTANCE? THE MENNONITE RESPONSE TO CONSCRIPTION IN WORLD WAR II. *Mennonite Q. Rev. 1978 52(2): 141-155.* Mennonites' experiences during World War I caused them to seek an alternative military conscription in the event of another war, an impulse which quickened as World War II approached during the 1930's. Representatives of the Peace Churches approached the federal government with a plan for alternative service in the United States. Neither Congress nor President Roosevelt was enthusiastic about it, but eventually it was adopted. The Mennonites were satisfied with this solution, because they opposed not conscription but war. Some Quakers were more reserved. Ironically, the civilian service units operated under military control, although the individual churches acted as "camp managers." 52 notes. V. L. Human

2662. Klaassen, Walter. MENNONITES AND WAR TAXES. *Pennsylvania Mennonite Heritage 1978 1(2): 17-22.* Traces traditional views of government and taxation held by Anabaptists in Switzerland and Germany during the 16th century; examines Anabaptists' refusal to pay taxes connected with war in the United States from the American Revolution to the Vietnam War.

2663. Kreider, Robert. THE HISTORIC PEACE CHURCHES' MEETING IN 1935. *Mennonite Life 1976 31(2): 21-24.* In the fall of 1935 representatives of the Mennonites, Dunkards (Church of the Brethren), and Quakers met in Newton, Kansas, to discuss the possibilities for peace in a world threatened by war. Mennonite leader H. P. Krehbiel convened the meeting and was instrumental in changing the name of the group from Conference of Pacifist Churches to Historic Peace Churches in response to fundamentalist criticism of "pacifism" as a "secular" word. The conference drafted a message to the Methodist General Conference of 1936 (reprinted) and planned future meetings. 2 photos. R. Burnett

2664. Land, Gary. SEVENTH-DAY ADVENTISTS INTERPRET WORLD WAR ONE: THE PERILS OF PROPHECYING. *Adventist Heritage 1974 1(1): 28-33, 55-56.* Describes the biblical interpretations applied by the leaders and prophets of the Seventh-Day Adventists to the 1912-13 defeat of Turkey by the Balkan League Armies, and to escalating hostilities in Europe leading to World War I.

2665. Lehman, James O. THE MENNONITES OF MARYLAND DURING THE REVOLUTIONARY WAR. *Mennonite Q. Rev. 1976 50(3): 200-229.* Discusses conditions in colonial Maryland, emphasizing problems faced by the Mennonites. The Mennonites centered around Elizabethtown and their relationship with the Committee of Observation which was their point of contact with pro-American revolutionary government. Being conscientious objectors, they generally paid high fines to avoid military service. Details the treatment of Loyalists and neutrals, and the involvement of Mennonites in the American Revolution. 93 notes. E. E. Eminhizer

2666. Lewis, Robert A. A CONTEMPORARY RELIGIOUS ENIGMA: CHURCHES AND WAR. *J. of Pol. and Military Sociol. 1975 3(1): 57-70.* By means of a questionnaire, examines the effects that religious institutions have on youth's attitudes toward war. S

2667. Luce, W. Ray. THE MORMON BATTALION: A HISTORICAL ACCIDENT? *Utah Hist. Q. 1974 42(1): 27-38.* Revises the traditional view of the origins of the Mormon Battalion and its role in the Mexican War. The problem of interpretation arises from an ambiguous letter of instructions written by the secretary of war, William Marcy, and its implementation by Colonel Stephen W. Kearney. 4 illus., 34 notes. D. L. Smith

2668. Luke, Miriam L. THE FIGHTING QUAKERS OF THE AMERICAN REVOLUTION. *Daughters of the Am. Revolution Mag. 1976 110(2): 180-184.* Discusses the Free Quakers who were disowned by the Society of Friends during 1774-83 for fighting in support of the colonies in the American Revolution.

2669. MacCarthy, Esther. CATHOLIC WOMEN AND THE WAR: THE NATIONAL COUNCIL OF CATHOLIC WOMEN, 1919-1946. *Peace and Change 1978 5(1): 23-32.* Examines attitudes toward women and war in the National Catholic Welfare Conference; the National Council of Catholic Women actively participated in the peace movement, 1919-46.

2670. MacMaster, Richard K. NEITHER WHIG NOR TORY: THE PEACE CHURCHES IN THE AMERICAN REVOLUTION. *Fides et Hist. 1977 9(2): 8-24.* The peace churches—Quakers, Mennonites, Dunkards, Schwenkfelders, and Moravians—attempted to take no position during the American Revolution. Claiming a higher sovereign than either Parliament or Congress, they sought to remain aloof from the dispute. Such a position was impossible without persecution, however. Those who refused to bear arms were taxed, and the tax money was used to support the war effort. Thus there was no escape from involvement in the secular issue of Independence. Based on primary and secondary sources; 60 notes. R. E. Butchart

2671. Martens, Hildegard M. ACCOMMODATION AND WITHDRAWAL: THE RESPONSE OF MENNONITES IN CANADA TO WORLD WAR II. *Social Hist. [Canada] 1974 7(14): 306-327.* Canadian Mennonite response to World War II was primarily in the direction of assimilation. There was no united Mennonite policy. Church leaders divided over whether to try and protect baptized members only or to include adherents. They also divided over whether to accept alternative service. The Conference of Historic Peace Churches was formed to negotiate agreements with the Government on matters affecting pacifists. Some individual Mennonites chose jail when unable to satisfy a Mobilization Board of their conscientious objection. Many others, especially recent immigrants, volunteered for active duty. Based on secondary sources and the Conrad Grebel Archives; 79 notes. W. K. Hobson

2672. McNeal, Patricia. CATHOLIC CONSCIENTIOUS OBJECTION DURING WORLD WAR II. *Catholic Hist. 1975 6(2): 222-242.* Focuses on Catholic conscientious objection in World War II. During the war there were 135 Catholics among 11,887 individuals who registered their dissent within the law and were granted conscientious objector (CO) status. These men were placed in Civilian Public Service (CPS) camps. The CPS was created by the Historic Peace Churches as a means of alternative service. The only Catholic group to support CO's was the Catholic Worker. A special group which emerged from the Catholic Worker for this purpose was the Association of Catholic Conscientious Objectors (ACCO). During the war, the ACCO operated two CPS camps for Catholic CO's, published a newspaper, and also worked with 61 Catholics who were imprisoned because they refused to register their dissent within the law. There is no way to show the precise relationship of the Catholic faith to the personal decisions of these men. It is most significant, however, that 73 per cent contended that their faith had a bearing on their decision.

2673. McNeal, Patricia. ORIGINS OF THE CATHOLIC PEACE MOVEMENT. *Rev. of Pol. 1973 35(3): 346-374.* Surveys the Catholic Church's involvement in the peace movement from 1917-68, including such organizations as the Catholic Association for International Peace (CAIP). S

2674. Michel, Jack. THE PHILADELPHIA QUAKERS AND THE AMERICAN REVOLUTION: REFORM IN THE PHILADELPHIA MONTHLY MEETING. *Working Papers from the Regional Econ. Hist. Res. Center 1980 3(4): 53-109.* Covers 1741-90.

2675. Miller, Carman. ENGLISH CANADIAN OPPOSITION TO THE SOUTH AFRICAN WAR AS SEEN THROUGH THE PRESS. *Can. Hist. R. 1974 55(4): 422-438.* Examines the English Canadian opposition to Canadian participation in the Boer War, 1899-1902, attempting to suggest the intellectual and social pattern of dissent. English Canadian opposition, though neither large nor widespread, found its strongest support among farmers, radical labour, Protestant clergy and anglophobic Canadians notably of Irish and German descent who defended their cause with a mélange of arguments from isolationism to Socialism and Christian pacifism. Based primarily on English language Canadian newspaper sources. A

2676. Morgan, David T. THE REVIVALIST AS PATRIOT: BILLY SUNDAY AND WORLD WAR I. *J. of Presbyterian Hist. 1973 51(2): 199-215.*

2677. Pankratz, Herbert L. THE SUPPRESSION OF ALLEGED DISLOYALTY IN KANSAS DURING WORLD WAR I. *Kansas Hist. Q. 1976 42(3): 277-307.* Superpatriots in Kansas during World War I vilified those who did not seem to contribute to the war effort and those suspected of disloyalty. They criticized Germans and other alien minorities, conscientious objectors, religious sects that preached against war, organized labor, socialists, and members of the Non-Partisan League and the Industrial Workers of the World. The Kansas press and public leaders created an atmosphere of intolerance and mass hysteria by mid-1918. Based on primary and secondary sources; illus., 121 notes.
W. F. Zornow

2678. Pearson, Alden B., Jr. A CHRISTIAN MORALIST RESPONDS TO WAR: CHARLES C. MORRISON, *THE CHRISTIAN CENTURY* AND THE MANCHURIAN CRISIS, 1931-33. *World Affairs 1977 139(4): 296-307.* Discusses *The Christian Century,* the most prominent and outspoken Christian periodical on the Japanese threat to peace during the crisis in Manchuria, and its editor, Charles C. Morrison, who had a significant role in determining American foreign policy.

2679. Pfaller, Louis L. FORT KEOGH'S CHAPLAIN IN BUCKSKIN. *Montana 1977 27(1): 14-25.* Eli Washington John Lindesmith served as Catholic Chaplain at Fort Keogh near Miles City, Montana, from 1881 until he retired in 1891. Born in 1827, he became a priest in 1855, serving in Ohio before and after his duty at Fort Keogh. Lindesmith was the only clergyman within a radius of 800 miles for many years and provided religious services for military and non-military residents of the area. Entries in Lindesmith's diary mention ministry to outlaws, prostitutes, soldiers, and prominent settlers like Pierre Wibaux. Lindesmith also built a chapel at Fort Keogh and founded a church in Forsyth. Between his retirement and his death in 1922, he lectured about his experiences, wearing a buckskin suit he acquired in Montana. Based on Lindesmith writings in the Catholic University of America; 9 illus., biblio.
R. C. Myers

2680. Potter, Gail M. PITTSFIELD'S FIGHTING PARSON: THOMAS ALLEN. *New-England Galaxy 1976 18(1): 33-38.* Rev. Thomas Allen was chairman of the Pittsfield, Massachusetts, Committe of Correspondence from 1774 to 1777, and chaplain to three Berkshire regiments. He participated in the battle of Bennington, Vermont. Illus.
P. C. Marshall

2681. Price, Joseph L. ATTITUDES OF KENTUCKY BAPTISTS TOWARD WORLD WAR II. *Foundations 1978 21(2): 123-138.* Southern Baptists' attitudes toward war are examined in George Kelsey's, *Social Ethics Among Southern Baptists 1917-1969* (Metuchen, N.J.: Scarecrow Pr., Inc., 1973). Argues that the book is not accurate, or is to some degree misleading. Examines indepth expressions on World War II in the reports of the Social Service Commission, Kentucky General Association minutes, the Long Run Association, the *Western Recorder,* and First Baptist Church of Paducah. Finds that little attempt was made by these groups to justify the war on biblical grounds, as was suggested by Kelsey. 59 notes.
E. E. Eminhizer

2682. Quinn, D. Michael. THE MORMON CHURCH AND THE SPANISH-AMERICAN WAR: AN END TO SELECTIVE PACIFISM. *Pacific Hist. R. 1974 43(3): 342-366.* The Mormon Church's insistence on the right of discretion in support of a US conflict, dependent on the current prophet, was based on Mormon theocratic philosophy. The erosion of this political and social power was furthered by the elimination of "selective pacifism" in connection with the Spanish-American War. In the face of Mormon suspicion concerning national militarism and a division of opinion within the Church concerning this war, Brigham Young, Jr.'s open opposition to participation is not surprising. He was, however, opposed by other Mormon Church leaders who had come to recognize national authority as supreme. 63 notes.
R. V. Ritter

2683. Radbill, Kenneth A. THE ORDEAL OF ELIZABETH DRINKER. *Pennsylvania Hist. 1980 46(2): 147-172.* During the American Revolution, the Drinkers and other Philadelphia Quakers suffered at the hands of both the patriots and the British. In the summer of 1777, Pennsylvania authorities, suspecting that the Quaker pacifists were really pro-British, arrested Henry Drinker and a number of other Friends and transported them to Winchester, Virginia. This article, based on Elizabeth Drinker's *Journal,* focuses on the British occupation of the city and the eventually successful efforts of Mrs. Drinker and others to obtain the release of the Quaker prisoners in Winchester. The October 1781 assault by Philadelphia mobs on Quaker homes is also discussed. Based on the Elizabeth Drinker *Journal* and other materials; map, 113 notes.
D. C. Swift

2684. Radbill, Kenneth A. QUAKER PATRIOTS: THE LEADERSHIP OF OWEN BIDDLE AND JOHN LACEY, JR. *Pennsylvania Hist. 1978 45(1): 47-60.* Owen Biddle and John Lacey, Jr., Pennsylvania Quakers, left their pacifist tradition to become patriot leaders during the American Revolution. Colonel Biddle served on Pennsylvania's Committee of Safety and its Board of War. The Continental Congress named him assistant commissary general for forage. General Lacey held several field commands and served in the General Assembly. Both were expelled by their meetings; however, Biddle rejoined his meeting after submitting a statement of error. Map, photo, 39 notes.
D. C. Swift

2685. Redkey, Edwin S., ed. ROCKED IN THE CRADLE OF CONSTERNATION. *Am. Heritage 1980 31(6): 70-79.* The Reverend Henry M. Turner, a black chaplain in the Union Army, described the attempts to take Confederate Fort Fisher, North Carolina, during the winter of 1864-65. Several regiments of black soldiers participated with the Union forces under Benjamin F. Butler. Turner's journal contained a daily record and an account of the capture of the fort on 15-16 January 1865. 11 illus.
J. F. Paul

2686. Renner, Richard Wilson. CONSCIENTIOUS OBJECTION AND THE FEDERAL GOVERNMENT, 1787-1792. *Military Affairs 1974 38(4): 142-145.* James Madison recognized conscientious objection to military service in his initial draft of the Second Amendment, but it was removed by the Senate. A similar proposal by him for inclusion in the Federal militia laws lost in the House after extensive debate. While some of the opposition reflected animosity toward the Quakers for their passivity in the patriot cause during the Revolution, most reflected the desire of the states to retain full powers over their militia. Based upon the Congressional debates and contemporary comment; 33 notes.
K. J. Bauer

2687. Richey, Susan. COMMENT ON THE POLITICAL STRATEGY OF CHRISTIAN PACIFISTS: A. J. MUSTE, NORMAN THOMAS, AND REINHOLD NIEBUHR. *Towson State J. of Int. Affairs 1977 11(2): 111-119.* Analyzes the political nature and philosophical perspectives of Christian pacifism as reflected in the writings of A. J. Muste, Norman Thomas, and Reinhold Niebuhr between World War I and World War II.

2688. Rothwell, David R. UNITED CHURCH PACIFISM OCTOBER 1939. *Bull. of the United Church of Can. 1973 (22): 36-55.* Examines the reasons for the issuance of "A Witness Against War," a manifesto signed by 68 United Church of Canada ministers in October 1939 proclaiming opposition to Canadian participation in World War II. The central figure was Reverend R. Edis Fairbairn, who hoped to force the church to recognize the moral dilemma posed by the war and to advertise his conscientious commitment. The manifesto called for no action but sought merely "to bring into fellowship . . . all the Christian pacifists in the United Church." The church moderator suggested that "it is a very serious thing for a minister to split his congregation through controversy," but counselled "tolerance and acceptance of the conscientious rights of others." Concludes that "the pure form of idealism that underlay both the effort to Christianize the social order and to reform international affairs by pacific means was largely a victim of the Second World War." Based on newspapers, interviews and secondary sources; 90 notes.
B. D. Tennyson

2689. Sabine, David B. THE FIFTH WHEEL: THE TROUBLED ORIGINS OF THE CHAPLAINCY. *Civil War Times Illus. 1980 19(2): 14-23.* Although "the 'forgotten man' of a neglected service" at the war's outset, military chaplains in both armies performed well enough to earn respect and to lay the foundation for the modern Chaplain Corps.
D. P. Jordan

2690. Schlabach, Theron, ed.; Reist, Ilse; and Bender, Elizabeth, trans. *AN ACCOUNT* BY JAKOB WALDNER: DIARY OF A CONSCI-

ENTIOUS OBJECTOR IN WORLD WAR I. *Mennonite Q. Rev. 1974 48(1): 73-111.* Young Hutterite Jakob Waldner (b. 1891) describes his life in Camp Funston in Kansas from 1917-18. S

2691. Shankman, Arnold M. SOUTHERN METHODIST NEWSPAPERS AND THE COMING OF THE SPANISH-AMERICAN WAR: A RESEARCH NOTE. *J. of Southern Hist. 1973 39(1): 93-96.* Southern Methodist newspapers did not favor a war to liberate Cuba, supporting instead President William McKinley's efforts to avoid conflict with Spain. "Only when the conflict had already begun did they urge Americans to drive the Spanish forces from Cuba, and some had misgivings even about engaging in war." 23 notes. I. M. Leonard

2692. Sharrow, Walter G. NORTHERN CATHOLIC INTELLECTUALS AND THE COMING OF THE CIVIL WAR. *New-York Hist. Soc. Q. 1974 58(1): 34-56.* The views of Archbishop John Hughes, Orestes Brownson, and James McMaster are representative of northern Catholic intellectuals. They saw the war as a result of divine intervention and a natural consequence of materialism and the weakening effects of Protestantism. They opposed abolitionism and believed the immediate cause of the war to be the intransigence of Southern leaders. Generally conservative, the political outlook of Catholic intellectuals resembled that of conservative Whigs. Unity disappeared as the long war brought about numerous unexpected changes. Based on primary sources; 4 illus., 46 notes. C. L. Grant

2693. Sloan, David. "A TIME OF SIFTING AND WINNOWING:" THE PAXTON RIOTS AND QUAKER NON-VIOLENCE IN PENNSYLVANIA. *Quaker Hist. 1977 66(1): 3-22.* In February 1764 armed "Paxton Boys" marched on Philadelphia demanding justice for the frontier and defense against Indians. Several hundred Quaker youths bore arms to defend the Society of Friends and the city. For three years official committees unsuccessfully tried to persuade members to recant this behavior. Instead of expelling recalcitrants they merely reaffirmed the Quaker peace testimony. 59 notes. T. D. S. Bassett

2694. Starr, Jerold M. RELIGIOUS PREFERENCE, RELIGIOSITY, AND OPPOSITION TO WAR. *Sociol. Analysis 1975 36(4): 323-334.* Discusses the high percentage of Jewish youth involved in the anti-Vietnam War protest movements of the 1960's.

2695. Stover, Earl F. CHAPLAIN HENRY V. PLUMMER, HIS MINISTRY AND HIS COURT MARTIAL. *Nebraska Hist. 1975 56(1): 20-50.* Plummer, the first black Army chaplain, was court-martialed at Fort Robinson, Nebraska, for "conduct unbecoming an officer and gentleman." He was found guilty and dismissed from the service in September 1894. Plummer's army career and the trial which terminated it provide insight into the situation of Negroes in the service during the late 19th century. 8 photos, 84 notes. R. Lowitt

2696. Teichroew, Allan. MENNONITES AND THE CONSCRIPTION TRAP. *Mennonite Life 1975 30(3): 10-13.* Discusses Mennonite feelings surrounding World War I both from the angle of pro-German feelings (many of them having recently immigrated from Germany) and from the vantage point of antidraft sentiment (most being staunch believers in pacifism), 1914-18.

2697. Teichroew, Allan, ed. MILITARY SURVEILLANCE OF MENNONITES IN WORLD WAR I. *Mennonite Q. Rev. 1979 53(2): 95-127.* Reproduces a report on Mennonites by Captain R. J. Malone, which illustrates government surveillance of pacifist groups. The federal government attempted to make the Mennonites appear pro-German. E. E. Eminhizer

2698. Thomas, Ivor B. BAPTIST ANTI-IMPERIALIST VOICE: GEORGE HORR AND *THE WATCHMAN*. *Foundations 1975 18(4): 340-357.* George Horr was an American Baptist who considered the Spanish-American War a mistake. Compares that war with the Vietnam War. Horr's reasons for anti-imperialism are somewhat the same as those for getting out of Vietnam. 50 notes. E. E. Eminhizer

2699. Thompson, James J., Jr. SOUTHERN BAPTISTS AND POST-WAR DISILLUSIONMENT 1918-1920. *Foundations 1978 21(2): 113-122.* Some feel there was disillusionment following World War I. Holds that this idea was not universally true. Examines the Southern Baptists' attitudes on the war and its meaning during 1918-20 as an example of a different view. 35 notes. E. E. Eminhizer

2700. Tygart, Clarence E. SOCIAL MOVEMENT PARTICIPATION: CLERGY AND THE ANTI-VIETNAM WAR MOVEMENT. *Sociol. Analysis 1973 34(3): 202-211.* For a sample of 486 Protestant pastors, the independent variables generally showed a necessary but not sufficient condition for anti-Vietnam war activism. Almost all anti-Vietnam war activists were: 1) non-authoritarian, 2) politically efficacious, 3) self-defined theologically liberal, 4) self-defined politically liberal and 5) civil rights activists. *However,* in multivariate analysis, most of the direct effects of the regression of anti-Vietnam war activism was accounted for by civil rights activism. J

2701. Tyrrell, Alexander. MAKING THE MILLENNIUM: THE MID-NINETEENTH CENTURY PEACE MOVEMENT. *Hist. J. [Great Britain] 1978 21(1): 75-95.* The mid-19th century Anglo-American peace movement culminated in a series of four peace congresses convened in Brussels, Paris, Frankfurt, and London between 1848-51. The author views the peace movement as but one manifestation of a new model of Nonconformist philanthropy. In the 1830's many Nonconformists began to work for the future in explicitly millennial terms. Local groups, such as the London Peace Society, founded in 1816, grew naturally out of the Anglo-American vision of a millennial *respublica christiana.* The specific proposals of the peace movement were a mixture of practicality and idealism. Despite the best intentions of Richard Cobden (1804-65) and others, the American Civil War soon ushered in the demise of the mid-19th-century peace movement. Based on peace congress reports, committee minutes, other primary and secondary sources; 87 notes. L. J. Reith

2702. Ulle, Robert F. PACIFISTS, PAXTON, AND POLITICS: COLONIAL PENNSYLVANIA, 1763-1768. *Pennsylvania Mennonite Heritage 1978 1(4): 18-21.* Discusses the effect on political behavior of the religious convictions of Mennonites and nonresistants versus Presbyterians after the Paxton Massacre, a massacre of peaceful Indians by frontiersmen in 1763.

2703. Weinlick, John R. THE MORAVIANS AND THE AMERICAN REVOLUTION: AN OVERVIEW. *Tr. of the Moravian Hist. Soc. 1977 23(1): 1-16.* The Moravians were pacifists and nonjurors, but there was considerable division on these issues within their ranks during the American Revolution. Although divided, the overwhelming majority of Moravians came to favor American victory. Given the location of the battle, the Moravians rendered more service of a noncombatant nature to the Americans than to the British. Bethlehem, Nazareth, Litiz, Hope, Bethabara, and Salem, Pennsylvania were centers of war production and providers of medical service. In this manner the Moravians aided the Americans far more than if they had merely supplied troops. The war generated the breakdown of the Moravian Indian missionary enterprises and disrupted communication with the Moravian headquarters in Europe. Primary and secondary sources. N. Lederer

2704. Wilbanks, Dana W. AMNESTY: A STUDY IN PUBLIC ETHICS. *Religion in Life 1974 43(4): 401-413.* Probes "the ethical and religious dimensions of the amnesty debate" of the 1970's over the Viet Nam War "in order to expose and analyze underlying issues." S

2705. Wilson, John R. M. THE QUAKER AND THE SWORD: HERBERT HOOVER'S RELATIONS WITH THE MILITARY. *Military Affairs 1974 38(2): 41-47.* Although personally close to his military leaders, Herbert Hoover was a foe of militarism. He believed in preparedness but viewed national defense as the capability to *prevent* an enemy landing in the United States or the Western Hemisphere. Because he opposed large military expenditures during the Depression the Navy suffered greatly, especially in its building programs, while the Army was less affected. Hoover's selection of General Douglas MacArthur as Chief of Staff proved to be outstanding. Based on Hoover's and others' personal papers and official documents; 20 notes. K. J. Bauer

2706. Young, Michael. FACING A TEST OF FAITH: JEWISH PACIFISTS DURING THE SECOND WORLD WAR. *Peace and Change 1975 3(2-3): 34-40.* Pacifist convictions and the necessity to fight the Nazis created a dilemma for the Jews of the Jewish Peace Fellowship in 1943.

2707. Yurtinus, John F. THE MORMON VOLUNTEERS: THE RECRUITMENT AND SERVICE OF A UNIQUE MILITARY COMPANY. *J. of San Diego Hist. 1979 25(3): 242-261.* The Mormon Volunteers were the 81 soldiers who reenlisted in 1847 out of the original 314 soldiers in the Mormon Battalion of the US Army; the Volunteers served in California during 1847-48 in the Mexican War.

2708. Zuber, Richard L. CONSCIENTIOUS OBJECTORS IN THE CONFEDERACY: THE QUAKERS OF NORTH CAROLINA. *Quaker Hist. 1978 67(1): 1-19.* Some 300 pacifist-abolitionist-Unionist North Carolina Quakers, ex-members, and sympathizers were exempt from conscription on payment of $500 ($100 the first year). Seven refused to pay throughout the War. Perhaps 100 labored at the coastal salt works in lieu of commutation the first year. Many "War Quakers," who joined the Society of Friends after the exemption deadline of 11 October 1862, and others who did not meet exemption requirements, were drafted; many Quakers deserted. Draft administration was as varied as Quaker reactions to the War, but generally mild. The Quakers had long made their position clear, had a positive image in the State, and had friends among Unionist Whig politicians such as William A. Graham and Jonathan Worth. 59 notes. T. D. S. Bassett

2709. —. [MENNONITES AND THE CIVIL WAR]. *Mennonite Hist. Bull. 1973 34(4): 1-3.*

Gross, Leonard, ed. JOHN M. BRENNEMAN AND THE CIVIL WAR, pp. 1-3. Two wartime documents by Brenneman—a draft of a petition to President Abraham Lincoln on behalf of the Mennonites, and a covering letter for the petition, sent to Bishop Jacob Nold.

Swope, Wilmer D. DISCOVERY, 1973, p. 3. Relates the discovery of a collection of Mennonites letters in which the above documents were found. S

2710. —. [MENNONITES BEFORE THE REVOLUTION]. *Mennonite Hist. Bull. 1974 35(3): 1-7.*

Gross, Leonard, ed. MENNONITE PETITION TO THE PENNSYLVANIA ASSEMBLY, 1775, p. 1. Prints the German text of "A Short and Sincere Declaration . . . " presented by Mennonites and German Baptists on 7 November 1775 to the Pennsylvania House of Assembly.

Ulle, Robert F., ed. PREPARING FOR REVOLUTION, pp. 2-7. "The following set of [16] documents [now at the Historical Society of Pennsylvania], beginning with the Lancaster 'Association' Resolution of May 1, 1775, footnotes the tension caused when nonresistant Mennonites refused to serve in the military units being established." S

21. RELIGIOUS GROUPS

Christianity, General

2711. Adams, David Wallace and Edmonds, Victor. MAKING YOUR MOVE: THE EDUCATIONAL SIGNIFICANCE OF THE AMERICAN BOARD GAME, 1832 TO 1904. *Hist. of Educ. Q. 1977 17(4): 359-383.* The board game, an American mania, has reflected the changes in values that have occurred in American society. Early board games, such as *Mansion of Happiness* (1832), invented by Anne Abbott, a clergyman's daughter, stressed Christian values as the path to happiness. Later games, the forerunners of Parker Brothers' *Monopoly,* emphasized wealth and economic power as life's goal at a time when the growth of industrial capitalism and increasingly secular outlook made money the *summum bonum* in American society. 48 notes.
J. C. Billigmeier

2712. Albanese, Catherine L. CITIZEN CROCKETT: MYTH, HISTORY, AND NATURE RELIGION. *Soundings [Nashville, TN] 1978 61(1): 87-104.* Examines the mythic religious attitude of the 19th century which supported both dominance of and innocence in nature; examines Davy Crockett as the archetype for man in the wilderness and his evolution as a popular religious and cultural image of the 1830's.

2713. Alston, Jon P. and McIntosh, Wm. Alex. AN ASSESSMENT OF THE DETERMINANTS OF RELIGIOUS PARTICIPATION. *Sociol. Q. 1979 20(1): 49-62.* Assesses patterns of religious participation and church attendance based on a 1974 study of American Protestants and Catholics.

2714. Amero, Richard W. CHRISTMASES IN CALIFORNIA. *J. of San Diego Hist. 1980 26(4): 274-281.* Describes traditional Christmas holiday customs in California from the earliest known description of Christmas in Alta California by Father Juan Crespi in 1769, to celebrations such as *Los Pastores* and *Las Posadas* and parades that are part of San Diego's town celebrations every December.

2715. Amoss, Pamela. SYMBOLIC SUBSTITUTION IN THE INDIAN SHAKER CHURCH. *Ethnohistory 1978 25(3): 225-249.* In the late 1880's a local revitalization movement, the Indian Shaker Church, became an established vehicle for religious expression and social solidarity among Coast Salish Indians. It preserved aboriginal ideas by replacing powerless aboriginal symbols with imported Christian ones and introduced a new concept of solidarity based on ideological community rather than residential community. In the late 1900's the aboriginal religion has been revived with rituals and functions parallel to the Shaker Church. The two systems coexist as alternative or complementary expressions of Indian spirituality. Both persist because they offer individuals opportunity to affiliate with different groups at different times; they embody distinct parts of the Indian historical myth; and they perpetuate comparable but different styles of religious experience.
J

2716. Angus, David L. DETROIT'S GREAT SCHOOL WARS: RELIGION AND POLITICS IN A FRONTIER CITY, 1842-1853. *Michigan Academician 1980 12(3): 261-280.* Latent sectarian differences flared up between Protestants and Catholics during 1842-53 over reading of the King James version of the Bible in public schools and the use of taxes to support parochial schools and encouraged political division along ethnic and religious lines in the city elections of 1853.

2717. Axel, Larry E. THE "CHICAGO SCHOOL" OF THEOLOGY AND HENRY NELSON WIEMAN. *Encounter 1979 40(4): 341-358.* Describes the main characteristics and tendencies of theology at the University of Chicago Divinity School, 1890's-1920's, and the role of Henry Nelson Wieman; 1920's.

2718. Backman, Milton V., Jr. TRUMAN COE'S 1836 DESCRIPTION OF MORMONISM. *Brigham Young U. Studies 1977 17(3): 347-355.* Truman Coe, a Presbyterian minister who had lived among the Mormons in Kirtland, Ohio, for four years, wrote a letter to the *Ohio Observer* on 11 August 1836. It described the early Mormons and analyzed their beliefs, particularly their concept of God. Although the letter contains some alleged distortions, it is reproduced in its entirety because Coe's report is one of the most accurate written by a non-Mormon during the 1830's.
M. S. Legan

2719. Balswick, Jack. THE JESUS PEOPLE MOVEMENT: A GENERATIONAL INTERPRETATION. *J. of Social Issues 1974 30(3): 23-42.* The Jesus People, as members of a distinctive age stratum, exhibit many attributes common to the counterculture: subjectivism, informality, spontaneity, new forms and media of communication. As members of a distinctive religious orientation, they exhibit attributes common to a fundamentalist and Pentecostal Christianity: the inerrancy of scripture, emphasis on the Holy Spirit, and a commitment to "one way" to God. This phenomenological study of the Jesus People suggests that the movement can best be seen as the result of a youthful cohort's "fresh contact" (using Mannheim's concept) with the fundamentalist tradition in Christianity, set within the context to structural conditions in American society in the 1960s and in organized American religion, plus the distinctive life style and orientations of the broader youth counterculture movement. It is suggested that this unique generational movement represents a potential for change in American religious institutions.
J

2720. Barbeau, Art. THY BROTHERS' KEEPER. *J. of the West Virginia Hist. Assoc. 1978 2(1): 25-40.* Among organizations which provided Negroes in the military with recreation, medicine, and social services in World War I, the YMCA practiced racial discrimination, unlike the Salvation Army and the Knights of Columbus.

2721. Barcus, Nancy. EMERSON, CALVINISM, AND AUNT MARY MOODY EMERSON: AN IRREPRESSIBLE DEFENDER OF NEW ENGLAND ORTHODOXY. *Christian Scholar's Rev. 1977 7(2-3): 146-152.* Discusses Mary Moody Emerson's Calvinist orthodoxy and its impact on her nephew, Ralph Waldo Emerson.

2722. Beckford, James A. STRUCTURAL DEPENDENCE IN RELIGIOUS ORGANIZATIONS: FROM "SKID-ROAD" TO WATCH TOWER. *J. for the Sci. Study of Religion 1976 15(2): 169-175.* Discusses the degree of autonomy in the Jehovah's Witness Watch Tower movement and "skid-road" rescue missions in the organizational structure of religious organizations in the 1970's.

2723. Beltman, Brian W. RURAL CHURCH REFORM IN WISCONSIN DURING THE PROGRESSIVE ERA. *Wisconsin Mag. of Hist. 1976 60(1): 2-24.* During 1904-20 many rural Wisconsin churches initiated programs of cooperation and consolidation, as part of and in response to earlier attempts to strengthen rural churches, the rise of the Social Gospel movement, the quest for interchurch unity, and the birth of the Country Life movement. Analysis of four rural counties (Buffalo, LaFayette, Price, and Walworth) indicates a relative rise of Lutheran church membership, a small growth among Catholics, and a decline among non-Lutheran Protestants. Many in this latter group who witnessed the declining membership, overchurching, and unreliable clergymen often saw federation as the panacea. For others, the preacher, as an activist and community leader, was the key to a revitalized church, a church which in turn would become a social center. 7 photos, 2 tables, 62 notes.
N. C. Burckel

2724. Benne, Robert and Hefner, Philip. THE DREAM AND THE WRATH. *Worldview 1974 17(4): 13-15.* The civil religion that propagates the myths of the American dream—liberty, individual initiative, opportunity—fails to account for evil in America and the failure of these myths; Christian theology explains malevolence and misfortune as the wrath of God for the frustration of His will.

2725. Bloy, Myron B., Jr. SECOND EDITION: THE CHRISTIAN NORM. *Center Mag. 1975 8(6): 71-74.* Assesses the respective roles of technology and Christianity in shaping 20th-century values and lifestyles.

2726. Boller, Paul F., Jr. RELIGION AND THE U.S. PRESIDENCY. *J. of Church and State 1979 21(1): 5-21.* Examines the religions of American presidents. Five presidents from James A. Garfield through Jimmy Carter have been born-again Christians. Most have been church members, the largest number (six) being Episcopalians. Calvin Coolidge and Dwight D. Eisenhower became church members after election to the presidency. Some 11 presidents were not affiliated with any religion. Religion was a major issue in only three or four elections. Secondary sources; 50 notes. S

2727. Bouyer, Louis. "SERVICES FOR TRIAL USE": A ROMAN CATHOLIC APPRECIATION. *Anglican Theological Rev. Supplementary Series 1973 (2): 96-100.*

2728. Cashdollar, Charles D. THE SOCIAL IMPLICATIONS OF THE DOCTRINE OF DIVINE PROVIDENCE: A NINETEENTH-CENTURY DEBATE IN AMERICAN THEOLOGY. *Harvard Theological Rev. 1978 71(3-4): 265-284.* This article is in part a response to Langdon Gilkey's "The Concept of Providence in Contemporary Theology," *Journal of Religion* 1963 43: 174 ff. Cashdollar examines the ethical implications of the doctrine of providence in its demise, and traces vigor and substance not emphasized by Gilkey. E. E. Eminhizer

2729. Clark, Michael D. JONATHAN BOUCHER AND THE TOLERATION OF ROMAN CATHOLICS IN MARYLAND. *Maryland Hist. Mag. 1976 71(2): 194-204.* An Anglican minister of Queen Anne's Parish, Jonathan Boucher has been cited "as an exception to the almost universal anti-Catholicism of colonial Protestants, especially for his 1774 sermon 'On the Toleration of Papists.'" Others have noted his hypocrisy in holding out sympathy for Catholics only to enlist them in the Loyalist cause during the Revolution. Actually the more just verdict of him is "opportunism". A devotee of 18th-century paternalistic conservatism, with a "melioristic position," Boucher had an ecumenical disposition which urged the reunion of Catholic, Protestant Englishman, and Presbyterian, with the Anglican confession being the most fit "centre of union." Moreover, the collapse of Jacobitism after 1746 had removed much of the political rationale for Catholic-baiting. Though he urged freedom of religious conviction, Boucher remained fixed in his period's belief that such toleration did not extend to granting equality of political status to dissenters. Primarily extracted from Boucher's own writings and secondary sources; 39 notes. G. J. Bobango

2730. Clements, William M. FIVE BRITISH TRAVELLERS AND RELIGION IN NINETEENTH-CENTURY AMERICA. *Res. Studies 1978 46(1): 44-49.* The treatment of popular religion in British visitors' travel accounts during 1800-30's are subjective and biased, but can provide useful information.

2731. Cole, Phyllis. THE PURITY OF PURITANISM: TRANSCENDENTALIST READINGS OF MILTON. *Studies in Romanticism 1978 17(2): 129-148.* Transcendentalists of the 1820's-30's read the poems of John Milton and found in his glorification of the mind and of contemplation the creative moral force within Puritanism which could overshadow its doctrines of innate depravity.

2732. Davis, Rex and Richardson, James T. THE ORGANIZATION AND FUNCTIONING OF THE CHILDREN OF GOD. *Sociol. Analysis 1976 37(4): 321-339.* Summarizes the early history of the Children of God (COG) in America and elsewhere, and describes and analyzes the current COG international organizational structure and functioning, its feedback and decisionmaking mechanisms, patterns of contact among the various levels of the organization, rules to insure continued growth in the number of colonies, and several major types of COG colonies. Attention is also paid to everyday life in a typical colony, and to the methods of financial support of the organization. The organization has eight major levels, from the *colony* (individual commune) through the King's Counsellorship, which is the apex of the worldwide structure. The author explains why many recent changes in COG have occurred. Covers 1968-76. J/S

2733. Dovre, Paul J. RELIGION: BACKBONE OF THE VALLEY. *Red River Valley Hist. 1980 (Fall): 2-6.* Discusses the importance of Christianity during the frontier and settlement phases of westward development in the United States, particularly in the North Dakota section of the Red River Valley from the 1870's to the 1890's.

2734. Dulles, Avery. HÄRESIEN DER GEGENWART: EIN AUFRUF AMERIKANISCHER THEOLOGEN ZUR SELBSTBESINNUNG DER CHRISTEN [Heresies of the present: A summons of American theologians to a Christian self-evaluation]. *Stimmen der Zeit [West Germany] 1975 193(8): 507-515.* A group of 18 Christian scholars of various denominations met at Hartford, Connecticut, in January 1975 and produced a manifesto which called attention to the dangers of the church losing sight of transcendent and permanent values in its haste to accommodate itself to the customs of the day. It listed 13 errors of this sort, in the hope that this antimodernist stance might replace such recent fads as "honest to God" and "God is dead" theology, and also afford a new basis for ecumenism. R. Stromberg

2735. Everett, William W. LITURGY AND AMERICAN SOCIETY: AN INVOCATION FOR ETHICAL ANALYSIS. *Anglican Theological Rev. 1974 56(1): 16-33.* Liturgy, expressed historically through Christian churches and at present through cultural media, binds the individual to social institutions. S

2736. Feagin, Joe R. THE BLACK CHURCH: INSPIRATION OR OPIATE. *J. of Negro Hist. 1975 60(4): 536-540.* The image of pathology and social disorganization has dominated previous conventional studies of black religious life and organization in the United States. Hart M. Nelsen and Ann Kusener Nelsen in *The Black Church in the Sixties* (Lexington: U. Pr. of Kentucky, 1975) question these traditional views. C. A. McNeill

2737. Fish, Lydia M. JESUS ON THE THRUWAY: THE VANISHING HITCHHIKER STRIKES AGAIN. *Indiana Folklore 1976 9(1): 5-14.* Examines versions of a folktale from the New York Thruway, holding that drivers pick up a 'hippie' hitchhiker, are questioned by him about their belief in the second coming, and turn to find him gone (apparently having disappeared) leaving a still-fastened seatbelt.

2738. Garrett, Clarke. THE SPIRITUAL ODYSSEY OF JACOB DUCHE. *Pro. of the Am. Phil. Sco. 1975 119(2): 143-155.* Jacob Duche, Jr., an Anglican minister, was appointed chaplain to the First and Second Continental Congresses by John Adams. However, his repudiation of the American Revolution in 1777 forced him into exile in Great Britain. His actions actually reflected his apolitical, pietistic turn of mind. A life-long reader of Jacob Boehme and William Law, in exile Duche turned to the writings of Emanuel Swedenborg for solace. Duche was the first American to read him. Based on primary and secondary sources; 73 notes. W. L. Olbrich

2739. Glenn, Norval D. and Gotard, Erin. THE RELIGION OF BLACKS IN THE UNITED STATES: SOME RECENT TRENDS AND CURRENT CHARACTERISTICS. *Am. J. of Sociol. 1977 83(2): 443-451.* Examines the trends in religious practices among blacks, 1960's-70's, finding that though church attendance and faith in the clergy continue undiminished, the number of blacks entering the clergy has declined considerably.

2740. Griffiss, James E. THEOLOGY AND SEXUALITY IN SOME RECENT LITERATURE. *Anglican Theological Rev. 1973 55(2): 225-234.*

2741. Harris, Katherine. FEMINISM AND TEMPERANCE REFORM IN THE BOULDER WCTU. *Frontiers 1979 4(2): 19-24.* Describes the social reform activities of the Boulder, Colorado, chapter of the Women's Christian Temperance Union from its organization in 1881 to 1967; objectives in addition to reform were to raise women's status and increase independence in and out of the home.

2742. Harrison, Michael I. and Maniha, John K. DYNAMICS OF DISSENTING MOVEMENTS WITHIN ESTABLISHED ORGANIZATIONS: TWO CASES AND A THEORETICAL INTERPRETATION. *J. for the Sci. Study of Religion 1978 17(3): 207-224.* Tests the theories of Turner and Killian pertaining to the internalization of dissent within established religious organizations through study of neo-Pentecostal movements in the Protestant Episcopal Church and the Catholic Church, 1950's-70's; concludes that the theory is supported but that other specifications for internalization of dissent may be added.

2743. Hatch, Roger D. INTEGRATING THE ISSUE OF RACE INTO THE HISTORY OF CHRISTIANITY IN AMERICA: AN ESSAY-REVIEW. *J. of the Am. Acad. of Religion 1978 46(4): 545-569.* Sydney E. Ahlstrom, Robert T. Handy, and Martin E. Marty in (respectively) *A Religious History of the American People; Righteous Empire: The Protestant Experience in America;* and *A Christian America: Protestant Hopes and Historical Realities* agree that past attempts to write a history of Christianity in America have not adequately covered the issue of race, but the author contends that each of these historians has failed to make up this lack. Explains the two approaches of these writers: including race as a new topic, thus adding additional chapters; and integrating race into the commonly discussed topics of religious history. Both are insufficient because race is still regarded as somewhat external to the history. Chart, 4 notes, biblio. E. R. Lester

2744. Hill, Samuel S., Jr. A TYPOLOGY OF AMERICAN RESTITUTIONISM: FROM FRONTIER REVIVALISM AND MORMONISM TO THE JESUS MOVEMENT. *J. of the Am. Acad. of Religion 1976 44(1): 65-76.* Restitutionism in America emerged in the early 19th century and is viewed by the author as falling into five types: Institutional Restitutionism, Ideological Restitutionism, Restitution as Spiritual Unification, Restitution as Relational Reconciliation, and Restitution as Inspiration. Discusses each type and illustrates it by a particular denomination. Based on primary and secondary sources; 9 notes. E. R. Lester

2745. Hogan, Brian F. A CURRENT BIBLIOGRAPHY OF CANADIAN CHURCH HISTORY. *Study Sessions: Can. Catholic Hist. Assoc. [Canada] 1979 (46): 99-137.* Books, journal articles, dissertations, and archival sources, 1974-78, arranged alphabetically within subgroupings of guides, sources, general works, church history, communions, regional history, institutions, individual biography, religious practice and pastoral care, missions, and special problems.

2746. Hollinger, David A. CALL IT SLEEP. *Rev. in Am. Hist. 1976 4(1): 38-42.* Review article prompted by David E. Stannard, ed., *Death in America* (Philadelphia: U. of Pennsylvania Pr., 1975). Covers 17th-20th centuries.

2747. Inglis, R. E. LOCHABER: A TYPICAL RURAL COMMUNITY. *Nova Scotia Hist. Soc. Collections [Canada] 1977 39: 89-106.* History of Lochaber, Nova Scotia, 1830-1972, including immigration, the Presbyterian and Catholic churches, schools, and industries.

2748. Janis, Ralph. ETHNIC MIXTURE AND THE PERSISTENCE OF CULTURAL PLURALISM IN THE CHURCH COMMUNITIES OF DETROIT, 1880-1940. *Mid-America 1979 61(2): 99-115.* In 1880 all church officers were male and tended to come from the middle and upper classes. Church membership was homogeneous ethnically (86% to 98%). The economic growth of Detroit changed this considerably by 1940. For example, while Lutheran parishes were uniformly German in 1880, they were less than 70% German in 1940. Other social factors involved in Detroit during this period, though, did not lead to the "melting pot" that might be expected. The cultural and social changes were silent, and other melting pot barriers arose when older ones dropped. 45 notes. J. M. Lee

2749. Johnson, Robert C. KINSEY VS. CHRISTIANITY: A CLASH OF "PARADIGMS" ON HUMAN NATURE. *Q. J. of Speech 1975 61(1): 59-70.* Discusses the Christian reaction to Alfred C. Kinsey's view of human nature presented in his writings about sexual behavior, 1948-54. S

2750. Jordan, Terry G. FOREST FOLK, PRAIRIE FOLK: RURAL RELIGIOUS CULTURE IN NORTH TEXAS. *Southwestern Hist. Q. 1976 80(2): 135-162.* In Cooke and Denton Counties, Texas, fundamentalists from the upper South settled the "Cross Timbers" oak forest and German Catholics settled the prairie land. Rural church architecture shows the cultural differences in the stern, one-room white frame "folk chapel" and the elaborate German "cathedral." Cemetery arrangements and customs also are quite different; German orderliness, attention to family history, and sense of community contrast with the southern protestant simplicity and emphasis on family. Covers 1860-1976. Primary and secondary sources; 18 illus., 2 tables, 28 notes. J. H. Broussard

2751. Jordan, Terry G. "THE ROSES SO RED AND THE LILIES SO FAIR": SOUTHERN FOLK CEMETERIES IN TEXAS. *Southwestern Hist. Q. 1980 83(3): 227-258.* Southern folk cemeteries in Texas are a mixture of cultural origins. From Africa comes the bare "scraped-earth ground and the placing of broken crockery on graves; from pagan Britain come the grave mounds and the cedar or juniper plantings." Shells on the graves, rose bushes and flowers, the use of tombstones, and dove and pomegranate inscriptions derive from pagan Southern Europe. Of Christian British origin are the burial with feet to the east, the wife's position on the left of the husband, and the use of unsanctified ground with fence and lichgate. The use of gravehouses probably originated with the American Indians. Covers 1830-1950. Based on personal observation and other primary sources; 15 illus., 2 maps, table, 35 notes. J. H. Broussard

2752. Kleber, Louis C. RELIGION AMONG THE AMERICAN INDIANS. *Hist. Today [Great Britain] 1978 28(2): 81-87.* Reviews Europeans' impressions of Indian religions and the religious mixing following the introduction of Christianity; covers 16th-20th centuries.

2753. Klein, Janice. ANN LEE AND MARY BAKER EDDY: THE PARENTING OF NEW RELIGIONS. *J. of Psychohistory 1979 6(3): 361-375.* The Christian Science and Shaker religions, founded by Mary Baker Eddy and Ann Lee, respectively, had roots in the personal lives of their founders as well as in their social milieux. Focuses on the former, comparing the life experiences of Eddy and Lee, and suggests ways in which those experiences affected the theologies of the two religions. Covers 1736-1910. Primary and secondary sources; 29 notes. R. E. Butchart

2754. LaFontaine, Charles V. "COBS WITHOUT CORN, WELLS WITHOUT WATER": THE SPIRITUAL ODYSSEY OF JAMES ARTHUR MORROW RICHEY, 1871-1933. *Mid-America 1978 60(2): 107-119.* James Arthur Morrow Richey was a noted convert from the Protestant Episcopal Church to Roman Catholicism. The son of an Episcopal clergyman, Richey was also educated for that ministry. After serving several parishes he became convinced that he could no longer stay in the Episcopal ministry, and in 1910 he was baptised as a Catholic. From then on he was active in the Catholic Church, being employed often as a journalist. Primary and secondary sources; 41 notes. J. M. Lee

2755. Lahey, R. J. THE ROLE OF RELIGION IN LORD BALTIMORE'S COLONIAL ENTERPRISE. *Maryland Hist. Mag. 1977 72(4): 492-511.* Analyzes the facts and the standard versions of Lord Baltimore's involvement in Newfoundland. It is "improbable that Calvert's original interest . . . involved religious considerations of any kind." Assesses how long before 1625 Calvert developed Catholic sympathies. Uses previously unexamined Vatican archives to document the roles of English Carmelite priests who saw in Avalon a potential Catholic mission to offset Puritanism, and a means of reaching the Far East via the supposed Northwest Passage. Calvert's actual attempt to allow Catholics and Protestants to coexist in his colony brought potentially damaging political accusations at home. The inhospitality of land and climate, however, determined Calvert's abandonment of Ferryland in 1629. Primary and secondary sources; 97 notes. G. J. Bobango

2756. Lex, Barbara W. NEUROLOGICAL BASES OF REVITALIZATION MOVEMENTS. *Zygon 1978 13(4): 276-312.* Seeks neurological explanations for the trances experienced at the time of their revelations by prophets such as Handsome Lake among the postrevolutionary Seneca and John Slocum, founder of the Indian Shaker Church among the Indians of the Puget Sound, and for the trance behavior common to the followers of such movements.

2757. Magocsi, Paul R. IMMIGRANTS FROM EASTERN EUROPE: THE CARPATHO-RUSYN COMMUNITY OF PROCTOR, VERMONT. *Vermont Hist. 1974 42(1): 48-52.* 20 families from Bereg, Hungary, attracted by the Vermont Marble Company, came to Proctor about 1914-19. Originally under a Uniate priest, they broke with him in 1917 and, shortly after, with a Greek Orthodox priest. Nine families

organized an independent, Bible-reading, literalist congregation, influenced by the preaching of Charles Lee to nearby Swedes 1920-25. They also published a monthly, *Prorocheskoe Svietlo* (*The Prophetic Light*). It will die with its founders since it does not attract the young.
T. D. S. Bassett

2758. Maloney, Stephen R. THE WORKS AND DAYS OF KARL STERN. *Georgia Rev. 1974 28(2): 245-256.* Karl Stern, a distinguished scientist and musician, is known primarily for his autobiography, *The Pillar of Fire* (1951). An important member of the 20th-century literary phenomenon, the Christian Renaissance and a convert to Catholicism, his greatest contribution has been in fusing a mode of life with a theologically-based philosophy. He viewed Christianity as the core around which to combine the seemingly contradictory insights of philosophy, science, and religion. Covers the 1920's-60's. M. B. Lucas

2759. Marshall, Paul and Welton, Mike. A GUIDE TO CHRISTIAN-MARXIST DIALOGUE. *Can. Dimension [Canada] 1979 13(5): 50-52.* Lists sources on the relationship of theologians and Communists, and their increasing intermingling in the 1970's.

2760. Montgomery, James W. HARRY ORCHARD, SINNER OR SAINT? KIN OF IDAHO KILLER'S LAST VICTIM CONVERTED HIM. *Pacific Northwesterner 1975 19(4): 49-56.* After 20 or more murders, 1899-1906, Idaho killer Harry Orchard was converted to Christianity by the widow and son of his final victim.

2761. Myerson, Joel. FREDERIC HENRY HEDGE AND THE FAILURE OF TRANSCENDENTALISM. *Harvard Lib. Bull. 1975 23(4): 396-410.* Traces Frederic Henry Hedge's alienation from the Transcendentalists during the 1830's-40's. Documents the rift between Hedge and the Emerson-Fuller group as the result of the Bangor minister's dedication to conservative Unitarianism and to purely intellectual questioning of the theological and societal status quo. Based on the Poor and Hedge Family Papers (privately owned), other MSS, and secondary sources; 55 notes. L. D. Smith

2762. Nelsen, Hart M. and Potvin, Raymond H. THE RURAL CHURCH AND RURAL RELIGION: ANALYSIS OF DATA FROM CHILDREN AND YOUTH. *Ann. of the Am. Acad. of Pol. and Social Sci. 1977 (429): 103-114.* The heyday of studies of the rural church was the 1920's-1940's. Even then researchers noted that structural rather than ecological characteristics were especially important in understanding it. A more recent focus has been on rural-urban differences in religiosity. Research done in the 1960's and 1970's indicated differences only on the ideological (belief) dimension. Data from two 1975 studies—one involving children in Minnesota and the other adolescents in a national sample—are reported, showing continuing rural-urban-metropolitan differences in religious belief. There are higher rates of fundamentalism for Protestants in the first two residential categories. For the first sample, the relationship between SES and fundamentalism virtually disappears in the rural area. The importance of residential (and church) propinquity of social classes is suggested as an important intervening variable, and this brings the focus full circle in terms of ecological versus structural and organizational characteristics. Finally, the future of the rural (small) church is discussed. Negative effects of inflation and the overall decline in national church membership and participation and the positive effect of church decentralization as they impinge upon the rural church are discussed. J

2763. Ostrander, Gilman M. NEW ENGLAND RELIGION: UNITARANSCENDENTALISM AND PRESBYGATIONALISM. *Can. Rev. of Am. Studies [Canada] 1980 11(1): 57-63.* Review article prompted by publication of *Transcendental Religion and the New America* (Philadelphia: Temple U. Pr., 1977) by Catherine L. Albanese and *Chariot of Fire: Religion and the Beecher Family* (New Haven: Yale U. Pr., 1978) by Marie Caskey. The books treated more than a half-century of conflicts in the 19th century between conservative Congregationalists and Unitarians and their Transcendentalist allies for control of Calvinist churches and educational institutions in Massachusetts and Connecticut. 6 notes. H. T. Lovin

2764. Peachey, Paul. RADICALIZATION OF THE RELIGIOUS IDIOM AND THE SOCIAL DISLOCATION OF CLERGY. *Anglican Theological Rev. 1973 55(3): 277-289.* Covers 1960-74.

2765. Poulsen, Richard C. BOSOM SERPENTRY AMONG THE PURITANS AND MORMONS. *J. of the Folklore Inst. 1979 16(3): 176-189.* Nathanial Hawthorne's short story, "Egotism: or, the Bosom Serpent," is widely discussed, and some scholars have examined "bosom serpentry" (belief that snakes and other creatures can creep into a human body and live there indefinitely) as folk belief. However, few have attempted to place tales of bosom serpentry within their cultural contexts. Although such tales appear in numerous folk groups, only the New England Puritans, who influenced Hawthorne's story, and the Utah Mormons used them as instruments of spiritual enlightenment. Bosom serpentry appears in Cotton Mather's *Magnalia Christi Americana* and in the writings of Increase Mather to illustrate the divine nature of Puritan beliefs. Mormons used the tales similarly, indicating an adherence to a world view closely tied to that of the 17th century and to Puritanism. Drawn from Puritan writings, limited fieldwork, and secondary sources; 30 notes. C. D. Geist

2766. Quinn, D. Michael, ed. THE FIRST MONTHS OF MORMONISM: A CONTEMPORARY VIEW BY REV. DIEDRICH WILLERS. *New York Hist. 1973 54(3): 317-333.* Translates from the German an unpublished letter by Reverend Diedrich Willers (1798-1883) of the New York Reformed Church, one of the earliest known accounts of the organization of the Mormon Church. Written 18 June 1830, some two months after the Mormon Church was founded, Willer's letter called Joseph Smith the "greatest fraud of our time." Primary and secondary sources; 5 illus., 17 notes. G. Kurland

2767. Raitz, Karl B. THEOLOGY OF THE LANDSCAPE: A COMPARISON OF MORMON AND AMISH-MENNONITE LAND USE. *Utah Hist. Q. 1973 41(1): 23-34.* A comparative study of land use by two closely knit subcultures, using the Mormon village of Escalante, Utah, and the village of Intercourse, Lancaster County, Pennsylvania, as typical examples. Both cases demonstrate that the underlying motivational theological doctrine of a group provides "parameters for behavior which have shaped religious ideals and have also had a pronounced effect on the way each group utilizes its land resources . . . Each subculture has created a distinctive landscape—a landscape born out of theological edict." Two completely different landscape patterns have resulted. 2 photos, 2 maps, 24 notes. R. V. Ritter

2768. Rathbun, John W. GOD IS DEAD: AVANT-GARDE THEOLOGY FOR THE SIXTIES. *Can. Rev. of Am. Studies 1974 5(2): 166-180.* Discusses the writings of notable "God Is Dead" theologians, including Thomas Altizer, William Hamilton, Harvey Cox, and Paul van Buren. Their views closely parallel those of earlier thinkers who established the "long liberal tradition" of the Social Gospel. 6 notes.
H. T. Lovin

2769. Redekop, Calvin and Hostetler, John A. THE PLAIN PEOPLE: AN INTERPRETATION. *Mennonite Q. Rev. 1977 51(4): 266-277.* An analysis of the nature and causes of the Plain People, who include Amish, Hutterites, Mennonites, Molokans, and Dukhobors. The Plain People perceive that religion has failed to integrate larger communities, but have faith that it can integrate small communities. Plain People are not interested in joining the larger majority, a policy which separates them from so-called minority groups. They simply want to be left alone to deal with people on a person-to-person basis. All Plain People groups have a religious bond, almost invariably Protestant. Their major concerns at present are perpetuation of their society in the face of technological change and the acquisition of new lands to support expanding communities. 4 notes. V. L. Human

2770. Richardson, James T. and Stewart, Mary. CONVERSION PROCESS MODELS AND THE JESUS MOVEMENT. *Am. Behavioral Scientist 1977 20(6): 819-838.* Discusses models of conversion as exemplified in the Jesus movement, predisposition for conversion, and the importance of affective interpersonal ties in the conversion process.

2771. Richardson, James T. FROM CULT TO SECT: CREATIVE ECLECTICISM IN NEW RELIGIOUS MOVEMENTS. *Pacific Sociol. Rev. 1979 22(2): 139-166.* Uses the Jesus movement as an example of the evolution of the movement from a cult to a sect in the 1960's and 1970's, providing a model of factors which are present in the evolution from cult to sect.

2772. Robbins, Peggy. A LOOK AT DEATH IN EARLY AMERICA. *Early Am. Life 1979 10(2): 76-80, 82.* Describes variations in social customs associated with death and funerals through the British colonies during the 17th-18th centuries.

2773. Roberts, Wesley A. NEEDED: A HISTORY OF THE BLACK CHURCH IN AMERICA. *Fides et Hist. 1974 6(2): 60-65.* Review essay of Hart M. Nelsen, Raytha L. Yokley and Anne K. Nelsen, eds., *The Black Church in America* (New York: Basic Books 1971); William L. Banks, *The Black Church in the U.S.* (Chicago: Moody Pr., 1972); David L. Lewis, *King: A Critical Biography* (Baltimore: Penguin Books, 1971). Finds that in spite of a decade of important scholarship in Black history, the history of the American Black church is still unavailable. Nor do these latest volumes fill the bill. Nelsen, Yokley and Nelsen's book of readings is outstanding but purely sociological. Banks' book turns out to be a disappointing apologetic for the otherworldliness of Black Christianity. Only in Lewis' biography of Martin Luther King, Jr., is a contribution made to the history of the Black church, especially in its social-protest aspects. Covers the 20th century. R. Butchart

2774. Robinson, David. JONES VERY, THE TRANSCENDENTALIST, AND THE UNITARIAN TRADITION. *Harvard Theological Rev. 1975 68(2): 103-124.* Jones Very, a 19th-century American poet, has been associated with the transcendentalists over the years because of his association with Emerson. It is argued here that he belongs with the unitarians in the Unitarian-Transcendentalists controversy. Reasons suggested include his reverence for scripture as found in his poetry, and in later years his embracement of historical Christian traditions. There is a detailed discussion of the evidence which supports this position. Covers 1833-70. 47 notes. E. E. Eminhizer

2775. Rock, Kenneth W. THE COLORADO GERMANS FROM RUSSIA STUDY PROJECT. *Social Sci. J. 1976 13(2): 119-126.* Reports on previous research and proposes a new study project on the little-known and much misunderstood ethnic community of Russian Germans in Colorado, products of a double migration in the 18th and 19th centuries who made important social and economic contributions to the area. The immigrants included Mennonites, Lutherans, and Catholics.

2776. Sackett, Lee. THE SILETZ INDIAN SHAKER CHURCH. *Pacific Northwest Q. 1973 64(3): 120-126.* Studies the origin and development of the Indian Shaker church in Siletz, Oregon. With the claimed raising from the dead of John Slocum (a Squaxin Indian of southern Puget Sound) in 1881, the new faith spread quickly to the north and south, coming to Siletz about 1891 or 1892. Under the leadership of Jakie Johnson, a permanent building was erected in 1926, and by the early 1930's the new faith included most of the Indians in the area. However, trouble developed over leadership and the use of the Bible, causing a reduction of membership. Analyzes the forces which were favorable and unfavorable to the development of the faith, concluding with brief biographies of four present Shakers. 16 notes. R. V. Ritter

2777. Sanfilippo, M. Helena. PERSONAL RELIGIOUS EXPRESSIONS OF ROMAN CATHOLICISM: A TRANSCENDENTAL CRITIQUE. *Catholic Hist. Rev. 1976 62(3): 366-387.* For the transcendentalists of 19th-century New England, true religion consisted in a joyous pursuit of personal communion with the divine. To this end they found abundant inspiration in the Catholic example, particularly in the Catholic mystics who attained divine union; in Catholic saints, especially the Virgin Mary, who vividly manifested what the transcendentalists believed all men embody—the divine in the human; in the Catholic celebration of sacred times and seasons; and in various other dimensions of Catholic devotion. Aside from warnings about excesses and formalism, the transcendentalist attitude toward Catholic piety was remarkably enthusiastic. A

2778. Saul, Norman E. THE MIGRATION OF THE RUSSIAN-GERMANS TO KANSAS. *Kansas Hist. Q. 1974 40(1): 38-62.* 1974 is the centennial of the arrival in Kansas of Mennonites from the Tauride province of South Russia, as well as Roman Catholic, Lutheran and Baptist Russian-Germans from the Volga River region. The author explains why they left Russia; why they displayed so much interest in coming to Kansas; the distinguishing features of their settlements; the reception given to them by other Kansas residents; and their contributions to the history of Kansas. They may not have introduced hard winter wheat, as most writers have insisted, but they certainly increased the pace of adoption of wheat and helped make possible the rapid expansion of the Kansas wheat industry. Their most lasting contribution was their determination to stay. Unlike other immigrants who merely paused enroute to another frontier, the Russian-Germans stayed through good and bad times to develop the Great Plains. Primary and secondary sources; illus., 74 notes. W. F. Zornow

2779. Saum, Lewis O. PROVIDENCE IN THE POPULAR MIND OF PRE-CIVIL WAR AMERICA. *Indiana Mag. of Hist. 1976 72(4): 315-346.* Examines the dominant historical interpretations of antebellum providentialism and contrasts those interpretations with the sense of Providence revealed in the writings of common people; ca. 1830's-60.

2780. Schleifer, James T. ALEXIS DE TOCQUEVILLE DESCRIBES THE AMERICAN CHARACTER: TWO PREVIOUSLY UNPUBLISHED PORTRAITS. *South Atlantic Q. 1975 74(2): 244-258.* Publication of two heretofore unpublished and unfinished tracts by Alexis de Tocqueville on American religious sects and American political participation. Tocqueville visited Quaker, Methodist, and Shaker religious ceremonies, none of which he could accept with any degree of equanimity. The political activities were equally confusing to him; he questioned why people as happy and as free as Americans ostentatiously claimed to be, spent so much time trying to gain a bit more happiness and freedom. Neither tract is in final form and they fail to show the famed author at his best. Based on documents in the Yale University Tocqueville collection; 63 notes. V. L. Human

2781. Schmandt, Raymond H. A PHILADELPHIA REACTION TO POPE PIUS IX IN 1848. *Records of the Am. Catholic Hist. Soc. of Philadelphia 1977 88(1-4): 63-87.* Reproduces a 24-page pamphlet recording the events of 6 January 1848, a day on which there was a huge, non-denominational public demonstration of enthusiasm for Pope Pius IX's efforts to establish constitutional reforms in the Papal States, a demonstration all the more significant because it came at a time of nativist tensions. J. M. McCarthy

2782. Schneider, Mary L. ARE ALL THINGS REALLY POSSIBLE? *Rev. in Am. Hist. 1977 5(1): 118-123.* Review article prompted by David Edwin Harrell, Jr., *All Things Are Possible: The Healing & Charismatic Revivals in Modern America* (Bloomington: Indiana U. Pr., 1975). Covers 1947-75.

2783. Simmonds, R. B.; Richardson, James T.; and Harder, Mary W. THE JESUS PEOPLE: AN ADJECTIVE CHECK LIST. *J. for the Sci. Study of Religion 1976 15(4): 323-338.* Examines the Jesus movement, 1960's-70's, postulating reasons for its genesis; examines members of the movement in terms of self-identity and compares them to college students of similar age and background; forms a pattern of maladaptivity in self-conceptions related to religiosity.

2784. Simmonds, Robert B. CONVERSION OR ADDICTION: CONSEQUENCE OF JOINING A JESUS MOVEMENT GROUP. *Am. Behavioral Scientist 1977 20(6): 909-924.* Through data collected 1960's-75, on conversion to the Jesus Movement, posits that conversion depends not so much on religious feeling as on psychological addiction (or a shift in addictions, usually from drugs to religion).

2785. Stachiw, Matthew. UKRAINIAN RELIGIOUS, SOCIAL AND POLITICAL ORGANIZATION IN U.S.A. PRIOR TO WORLD WAR II. *Ukrainian Q. 1976 32(4): 385-392.* Until the 1850's emigration from the Ukraine was sporadic and depended on the degree of serfdom imposed and the opportunity to flee to free lands outside of Russian control. After serfdom was abolished in 1861, migration to the Urals and Central Asia was encouraged by the tsarist government. However, US industrial growth in the 1870's produced a demand for labor and enticing offers to immigrants. An estimated 500,000 persons of Ukrainian birth came to the United States prior to 1914. 17 notes. K. N. T. Crowther

2786. Thomas, Samuel J. THE AMERICAN PRESS RESPONSE TO THE DEATH OF POPE PIUS IX AND THE ELECTION OF POPE LEO XIII. *Records of the Am. Catholic Hist. Soc. of Philadel-*

phia 1975 86(1-4): 43-52. When Pope Pius IX died in 1878, the Protestant secular press in the United States expressed respect for Pius the man, but harshly criticized his pontificate and sighed with relief that it had finally ended. This criticism yielded to cautious optimism after the election of Leo XIII, as those journals predicted that his reign would prove more favorable to liberalism, democracy, and the concept of a free church in a free state. The Catholic press response to both events consisted generally of defensive and tactless articles justifying Pius' reign and predicting continuity in Leo's. 29 notes. J. M. McCarthy

2787. Troubetzkoy, Ulrich. HOW VIRGINIA SAVED THE OUTLAWED ENGLISH CAROLS. *Hist. Mag. of the Protestant Episcopal Church 1961 30(3): 198-202.* Puritans banned Maypole festivities and Christmas celebration, including traditional Christmas carols in Great Britain but not Virginia, where tradition was preserved, 1662-70.

2788. Tucker, Glenn. WAS LINCOLN A CONVERTED CHRISTIAN? *Lincoln Herald 1976 78(3): 102-108.* Speculates on the veracity of a claim made by Methodist Church minister James F. Jacquess that in 1847 he was responsible for the conversion to Christianity of Abraham Lincoln in Springfield, Illinois, in 1847.

2789. Viitanen, Wayne. THE WINTER THE MISSISSIPPI RAN BACKWARDS: EARLY KENTUCKIANS REPORT THE NEW MADRID, MISSOURI, EARTHQUAKE OF 1811-1812. *Register of the Kentucky Hist. Soc. 1973 71(1): 51-68.* Three hard earthquakes and some 1,800 lesser tremors shook the lower Mississippi Valley during the winter of 1811-12. Although probably fewer than 100 persons were killed, buildings were destroyed and the Mississippi was wrenched into new paths, reportedly even flowing upstream. Accounts mention strange weather and animal behavior before the quakes and people's reaction to them. Although the quakes continued into May, none were as serious as those of 16 December, 23 January, and 7 February. There were mass conversions to Christianity during the winter. Based on published and unpublished accounts; map, 36 notes. J. F. Paul

2790. Vinyard, Jo Ellen. INLAND URBAN IMMIGRANTS: THE DETROIT IRISH, 1850. *Michigan Hist. 1973 57(2): 121-139.* The Irish were the largest immigrant group in Detroit in 1850. With many opportunities and with negligible religious prejudice, the assets or liabilities of their background determined their economic and social roles in the city. They succeeded, encouraged more Irish to emigrate, and contributed to the growth of Detroit. 5 illus., 3 tables, 41 notes. D. L. Smith

2791. Waddell, Louis M. THE TWELFTH ANNUAL RESEARCH CONFERENCE AT HARRISBURG. *Pennsylvania Hist. 1977 44(4): 348-366.* The 1977 research conference of the Pennsylvania Historical Association and the Pennsylvania Historical and Museum Commission was held in Harrisburg on 1-2 April. Papers were given on religious history, dealing with the Lutheran, Dutch Reformed, Methodist, Roman Catholic, Uniate Catholic, and Orthodox churches. Other sessions dealt with the work of the National Historical Publications and Records Commission and popular culture. D. C. Swift

2792. Wallis, Jim. CONSERVATIVE CHRISTIAN RADICALISM. *Worldview 1974 17(6): 38-40.* Explains major purpose of *The Post-American* as a new publication which "resists the conformity of the church to the values of American power." "The call to follow Jesus Christ," according to the publication, "demands a fundamental break with the dominant values and conformist patterns of the majority culture." M. L. Frey

2793. Wallis, Roy. RECRUITING CHRISTIAN MANPOWER. *Society 1978 15(4): 72-74.* Discusses the use of sexual enticement to recruit converts to the Children of God Christian organization, United States, 1970's, in light of the long Christian tradition of chastity.

2794. Wax, Murray L. and Wax, Rosalie H. RELIGION AMONG AMERICAN INDIANS. *Ann. of the Am. Acad. of Pol. and Social Sci. 1978 436: 27-39.* The traditional worldview of North American Indians is outlined as a basis for explicating the central tribal ceremonials and for comprehending the tribal response to prolonged missionization from Christian denominations. The missionaries operated in a context of authoritarian superiority, and most conceived of themselves as bearing civilization, rather than a plain scriptural message; hence, there was little concern to modify Euro-Christianity to fit with native rituals and values. Today, most Indians are Christians, at least nominally; but, in many cases, the Christianity is integrated with the native worldview, and the individual participates in a variety of both Christian and neotraditional rituals. The destructive impact of the European invasions stimulated millenarian movements, such as the Ghost Dance; the continued vitality of these movements was expressed in the recent occupation of Wounded Knee, which should be comprehended as a religious, rather than a political, action. The Peyote Cult, organized as the Native American Church, constitutes a syncretism of Christian and traditional rites and attitudes, and it is widespread as intertribal and pan-Indian. Further pan-Indian, neotraditional, revivalistic, and millenarian movements may be anticipated. J

2795. Wesson, Kenneth R. TRAVELERS' ACCOUNTS OF THE SOUTHERN CHARACTER: ANTEBELLUM AND EARLY POSTBELLUM PERIOD. *Southern Studies 1978 17(3): 305-318.* Emphasizes how visitors regarded common Southerners rather than wealthy planters or merchants. Most typical was the farmer who was poor, practiced ruinous agricultural techniques, owned a few mangy animals, and lived in a one room cabin. He ate and dressed very simply, did not practice gracious hospitality, but did honor women, had a high honor code and followed some kind of Christianity. He was often lawless, violent, drunk, and lazy, used tobacco freely, loved hunting, and was generally illiterate, using peculiar variants of the English language. Based on travel accounts by visitors to the South, 1850-70; 75 notes. J. Buschen

2796. Whittier, Charles H. and Stathis, Stephen W. THE ENIGMA OF SOLOMON SPALDING. *Dialogue 1977 10(4): 70-73.* Evangelical Congregationalist minister Solomon Spalding (1761-1816) is remembered for his influence on the Book of Mormon.

2797. Wood, Raymund F. EAST AND WEST MEET IN CALIFORNIA IN 1806. *Pacific Historian 1976 20(1): 22-33.* Recounts meeting of Catholicism and Orthodoxy in California, after each set out in opposite directions from Jerusalem several centuries earlier. The first meeting was at San Francisco when Russian Nikolai Rezanov arrived in 1806 seeking to trade for foodstuffs. His betrothal to the daughter of the Spanish Comandante, Maria de la Concepcion Arguello, marked the formal meeting of the two branches of the Church. Based on secondary sources; biblio. G. L. Olson

2798. Wood, Raymund F. JEDEDIAH SMITH, A PROTESTANT IN CATHOLIC CALIFORNIA. *Pacific Hist. 1977 21(3): 268-279.* Jedediah Strong Smith and his men, especially Harrison Rogers, made contact with authorities in California on five occasions during 1826-27. As Protestants, they had many differences of opinion with the Catholics, yet basically they were in agreement, and would have discovered this if they could have set aside their prejudices. 12 notes. G. L. Olson

2799. Woolfolk, George Ruble. THE FREE NEGRO AND TEXAS, 1836-1860. *J. of Mexican Am. Hist. 1973 3(1): 49-75.* Details the intent of Anglo-Protestant and Mexican-Catholic law concerning free blacks in Texas before the Civil War. Based on primary and secondary sources; 57 notes. R. T. Fulton

2800. Wyatt-Brown, Bertram. THE MISSION AND THE MASSES: THE MORAL IMPERATIVES OF THE CITY BOURGEOISIE. *Rev. in Am. Hist. 1979 7(4): 527-534.* Review essay of Paul Boyer's *Urban Masses and Moral Order in America, 1820-1920* (Cambridge, Mass.: Harvard U. Pr., 1978) and Paul E. Johnson's *A Shopkeeper's Millennium: Society and Revivals in Rochester, New York, 1815-1837* (New York: Hill and Wang, 1978).

2801. Yeager, Lyn Allison. THE FLOWERS OF CHRISTMAS. *Tennessee Folklore Soc. Bull. 1973 39(4): 113-118.* Relates contemporary Christmas customs to Roman, Norse, and other pre-Christian customs. L. Russell

2802. —. CECIL CONE: "MIND, BODY, AND SOUL." *Southern Exposure 1976 4(3): 44-45.* In this interview Cone argues that only black Christianity is true to Biblical Christianity and that it will someday convert white Christianity, which is too much imbued with the Greco-Roman worldview.

2803. —. FRITZ MARTI: IMMIGRANT PHILOSOPHER. *Swiss Am. Hist. Soc. Newsletter 1979 15(3): 2-33.*
Schelbert, Leo. CONGRATULATORY MESSAGE, *p. 2.*
—. FRITZ MARTI: THE COURSE OF A BUSY LIFE, *pp. 4-5.*
Marti, Fritz. HAPPENSTANCE OR PROVIDENCE, OR HOW I FOUND ALL MY JOBS, *pp. 6-21.*
—. RELIGION AND PHILOSOPHY: SELECTIONS FROM FRITZ MARTI'S COLLECTED PAPERS, *pp. 22-29.*
Marti, Fritz. THE MARTI SCHOOL, 1947-64. *pp. 30-31.*
—. PHILOSOPHICAL PUBLICATIONS OF FRITZ MARTI, *pp. 32-33.*
Issue dedicated to world-renowned philosopher and educator Dr. Fritz Marti (b. 1894); details his life and career, and lists his philosophical publications, 1922-77.

Eastern Orthodox Churches

2804. Beliajeff, Anton S. THE OLD BELIEVERS IN THE UNITED STATES. *Russian Rev. 1977 36(1): 76-80.* Old Believers are those individuals who cling to the traditional customs of the Russian Orthodox Church as it existed prior to the ecclesiastical reforms of the 17th century. Since the 1890's, small groups of these believers periodically have immigrated to the United States. They became known for their industrious, self-reliant ways. Today, 8,000 Old Believers live primarily in Oregon, Pennsylvania, Michigan, New Jersey, and Alaska. 10 notes.
M. R. Yerburgh

2805. Buryk, Michael. AGAPIUS HONCHARENKO: PORTRAIT OF A UKRAINIAN AMERICAN KOZAK. *Ukrainian Q. 1976 32(1): 16-36.* Outlines the life of Agapius Honcharenko (1832-1916), first Ukrainian Greek Orthodox priest in the United States. Threatened and pursued by Russian authorities for his anti-tsarist writings in radical periodicals published abroad, Honcharenko emigrated to the United States in 1865. The first issue of his newspaper *The Alaska Herald* in 1868 marked the realization of his dream of establishing a Russian publishing house in America. However, Honcharenko's attacks on the monopolistic practices of American companies in Alaska and his criticism of anti-Chinese feeling in the West provoked slander and physical threats which forced his resignation as editor in 1872. Following this Honcharenko hoped to found a cooperative Ukrainian community in California, but this plan also failed. His remaining life was spent on his farm "Ukraina."
K. N. T. Crowther

2806. Croskey, Robert, transl. THE RUSSIAN ORTHODOX CHURCH IN ALASKA: INNOKENTII VENIAMINOV'S SUPPLEMENTARY ACCOUNT (1858). *Pacific Northwest Q. 1975 66(1): 26-29.* Reprints the translation of an 1858 account of the standing of the Russian Orthodox Church in Alaska written by Metropolitan Innokentii Veniaminov, which includes the size and extent of the Church, its relations with the Russian-American Company, sources for its financial support, and its educational activities.

2807. Dunn, Ethel and Dunn, Stephen P. RELIGION AND ETHNICITY: THE CASE OF THE AMERICAN MOLOKANS. *Ethnicity 1977 4(4): 370-379.* An analysis of the nature and activities of the Molokans in California, a small group of religious dissidents who emigrated from Russia around the turn of the century. The San Francisco colony remains, though it has grown but little and has not successfully protected its neighborhood from outside penetration. Certainly the Molokans are no longer peasants, but they can hardly be called an ethnic group. Rather they are simply an offshoot religious sect, whose efforts to develop an ethnicity have largely failed. V. L. Human

2808. Goresky, Isidore, transl. MINUTES OF THE FOUNDING OF ONE OF THE FIRST UKRAINIAN GREEK CATHOLIC CHURCHES IN ALBERTA, MARCH 1900. *Can. Ethnic Studies [Canada] 1974 6(1-2): 67-69.* Translates the minutes of this founding by Ukrainian Canadians in the colony of Rabbit Hill, Alberta.

2809. Grover, Kathryn. THE ORTHODOX RUSSIANS OF CLAREMONT, NEW HAMPSHIRE. *Hist. New Hampshire 1979 34(2): 89-124.* Poles and Russians came to Claremont around 1907 in about the same numbers. By 1918, more than 21 percent of all children in Claremont were born to Russian Orthodox parents. Yet the Russians were always less visible than the Poles. Popular association of Russians with Bolshevism made assimilation difficult, and promoted mobility while war and revolution at home precluded a return to Russia. Internal religious differences may have contributed to residential dispersion and a disintegration of ethnic identity through the 1970's, while some Russians may have sacrificed ethnic solidarity to ease tension. Illus., 60 notes.
D. F. Chard

2810. Orfalea, Greg. HEART OF THE OLD BELIEVERS. *Westways 1976 68(4): 34-37, 68-69.* Leaving their native Russia in order to practice freedom of religion, several members of the Old Believers sect of the Russian Orthodox Church settled in small towns on Alaska's Kenai Peninsula, 1920's.

2811. Papagiannis, Michael D. AMERICA: REFLECTIONS IN RED, WHITE, AND BLUE. *Greek Orthodox Theological Rev. 1976 21(4): 367-384.* Presents reminiscences of first impressions of the United States as an immigrant of Greek descent; discusses the Greek Orthodox Church, politics, education, and social life, 20th century.

2812. Saloutos, Theodore. THE GREEK ORTHODOX CHURCH IN THE UNITED STATES AND ASSIMILATION. *Int. Migration Rev. 1973 7(4): 395-407.* Covers 1918-73.

Protestant Traditions

General

2813. Ainsley, W. Frank and Florin, John W. THE NORTH CAROLINA PIEDMONT: AN ISLAND OF RELIGIOUS DIVERSITY. *West Georgia Coll. Studies in the Social Sci. 1973 12: 30-34.* One of seven articles in this issue on "Geographic Perspectives on Southern Development." S

2814. Arnold, Harvey. REVIEW ARTICLE: CONSERVATIVE THEOLOGY TODAY. *Anglican Theological Rev. 1973 55(3): 354-359.*

2815. Aycock, Martha B., comp. A CHECKLIST OF DOCTORAL DISSERTATIONS ON AMERICAN PRESBYTERIAN AND REFORMED SUBJECTS, 1965-1972. *J. of Presbyterian Hist. 1975 53(2): 168-183.* A nonannotated list of 215 entries divided into five categories: general, Jonathan Edwards, H. Richard Niebuhr, Reinhold Niebuhr, and Paul Tillich. H. M. Parker, Jr.

2816. Bailey, Kenneth K. PROTESTANTISM AND AFRO-AMERICANS IN THE OLD SOUTH: ANOTHER LOOK. *J. of Southern Hist. 1975 41(4): 451-472.* A review of the well-established view that antebellum southern Protestant churches simply served as ecclesiastical arms of secular slavery. It is true that many of the charges are justified, but the other side of the coin has been poorly exposed. Negroes served in all religious capacities from lay offices to full clerical ordination. There were some mixed congregations and white congregations with black pastors. Black clergy were never numerous, but their influence was great. The beginning of the Reconstruction era found many former slaves competent to teach the gospel. 32 notes. V. L. Human

2817. Ballard, Paul H. EVANGELICAL EXPERIENCE: NOTES ON THE HISTORY OF A TRADITION. *J. of Ecumenical Studies 1976 13(1): 51-68.* Evangelicalism is a particular expression of Christianity which emphasizes the centrality of the Bible in personal religious life. Traces the movement from the Reformation through the 20th century in Europe and the United States. J. A. Overbeck

2818. Bédard, Marc-André. LA PRÉSENCE PROTESTANTE EN NOUVELLE-FRANCE [The Protestant presence in New France]. *Rev. d'Hist. de l'Amérique Française [Canada] 1977 31(3): 325-349.* A few Protestants had always dwelt in French Canada, but they led a precarious existence before the permanent arrival of the English in 1759. Totally disorganized, the Protestants were subjected to a series of sectarian excesses designed to force their conversion to Catholicism. During the early years of British hegemony, the Catholic majority was subjected to similar abuses. 69 notes. M. R. Yerburgh

2819. Beeman, Richard R. SOCIAL CHANGE AND CULTURAL CONFLICT IN VIRGINIA: LUNENBURG COUNTY, 1746 TO 1774. *William and Mary Q. 1978 35(3): 455-476.* Traces ideational, demographic, economic, and institutional development in Lunenburg County during 1746-74. Contrasts Lunenburg with other Virginia localities. As population became more dense, the county court and the Anglican Church were able to increase their authority. Discusses the Baptist insurgency in Lunenburg County, but agrees with Rhys Isaac's thesis that social disorder resulted chiefly from the ruling gentry's disregard of public need. Nevertheless, the vitality of the religious opposition made the conflict between "evangelical and gentry styles" a bitter one. Based on local and church records; table, 56 notes. H. M. Ward

2820. Berckman, Edward M. THE CHANGING ATTITUDES OF PROTESTANT CHURCHES TO MOVIES AND TELEVISION. *Encounter 1980 41(3): 293-306.* Examines the attitudes of mainline Protestant Churches toward the visual media since 1921 and finds that, although a tendency to censorship still exists, there is generally increasing tolerance of films and television by Protestants in the United States.

2821. Birchard, Roy. METROPOLITAN COMMUNITY CHURCH: ITS DEVELOPMENT AND SIGNIFICANCE. *Foundations 1977 20(2): 127-132.* The first denomination organized to serve the homosexual community established a church in Los Angeles in 1970. In 1976 there were 90 gay community churches. 8 notes. E. E. Eminhizer

2822. Bosco, Ronald A. LECTURES AT THE PILLORY: THE EARLY AMERICAN EXECUTION SERMON. *Am. Q. 1978 30(2): 156-176.* The 30 execution sermons published in New England between 1674 and 1750 represented an effort by the clergy to utilize to good effect the audiences at public executions. Those sermons emphasized grace and admonished listeners about evil patterns of thought and action. As the genre evolved it contained more social comment than doctrinal discussion, thus taking on the jeremiad format. The sermons, emphasizing that individual failings result from communal shortcomings, were addressed as much if not more to the young than to the age peers of the clergy. N. Lederer

2823. Bowers, Paul C., Jr. and Berquist, Goodwin F., Jr., ed. JAMES KILBOURNE: NEW LIGHT ON HIS STORY. *Ohio Hist. 1978 87(2): 193-206.* Presents, in part, previously unpublished documents and letters of James Kilbourne, founder of Worthington, Ohio. The letters (1844-49) offer an unusually intimate view of an old pioneer reminiscing on the ideals, ambitions, and events that made him a powerful figure in the settlement of the Ohio territory. He reflects on the effect of the Revolutionary War on his family, his father, and himself; his own religious pilgrimage from Congregationalism to Episcopalianism; and his speech in 1849 to the Kilbourne Historical and Genealogical Society of North America. Based on manuscript, contemporary comments, and secondary sources; illus., 22 notes. N. Summers

2824. Bradley, Michael R. THE ROLE OF THE BLACK CHURCH IN THE COLONIAL SLAVE SOCIETY. *Louisiana Studies 1975 14(4): 413-421.* The formation of the black church is the key to the beginning of Afro-American community and culture in colonial America. Because religion was an integral part of West African life, slaves used religion for the creation and recreation of community. The black church developed the concepts of group solidarity, mutual aid and assistance, and concern for everyday matters of life more highly than the white church did. The black church provided opportunities for leadership, a way of coping with slavery, a contact with a black-led group for newly arrived Africans. The church also encouraged survival, and offered a slim hope of improvement, compensation for deprivation, and ways to resist the institution of slavery. From the beginning the role of the black church in the black community has been creation, leadership, reaction to oppression, and support for the people. Based on primary and secondary sources; 28 notes. B. A. Glasrud

2825. Brown, Robert McAfee. REINHOLD NIEBUHR: A STUDY IN HUMANITY AND HUMILITY. *J. of Religion 1974 54(4): 325-332.*

2826. Brunkow, Robert deV. LOVE AND ORDER IN ROGER WILLIAMS' WRITINGS. *Rhode Island Hist. 1976 35(4): 115-126.* Roger Williams believed that existing civil and social relationships in secular things should be preserved. Selfless benevolence should characterize relationships between neighbors, and would preserve order in society. His social theory was grounded in theology. Primary and secondary sources. P. J. Coleman

2827. Burbick, Joan. "ONE UNBROKEN COMPANY": RELIGION AND EMILY DICKINSON. *New England Q. 1980 53(1): 62-75.* Examines religious life at Mount Holyoke College during the time Emily Dickinson studied there, 1848-50, a period marked by the influence of Evangelicalism. Concludes that, contrary to some biographers' views, she did not rebel against religion. Her religion was "fused with the issue of friendship" and for a time she feared that her friends' conversion would separate them from her. For Dickinson "the bonds of friendship determine meaning here as well as in the Christian heaven . . . " and her reaction against religion was "not based on a stance of heroic individualism, but on a continued struggle to avoid isolation and to cement the bonds of friendship." Based on her letters to two friends and on literary biographies; 13 notes. J. C. Bradford

2828. Butler, Jon. A BICENTENNIAL HARVEST: FOUR STUDIES OF THE EARLY AMERICAN COMMUNITY. *J. of Urban Hist. 1978 4(4): 485-497.* Review article on early American communities, prompted by: Thomas J. Archdeacon, *New York, 1664-1710: Conquest and Change,* Edward M. Cook, *The Fathers of the Towns: Leadership and Community in Eighteenth-Century New England,* Estelle F. Feinstein, *Stamford from Puritan to Patriot: The Shaping of a Connecticut Community,* and Stephanie Grauman Wolf, *Urban Village: Population, Community, and Family Structure in Germantown, Pennsylvania, 1683-1800.* Feinstein's and Wolf's works are community studies in the traditional mold, Archdeacon's book is a political history, and Cook's study is a New England-wide analysis of political leadership. Among the common themes are: 1) the failure of religion to harmonize communities, 2) the early rise of modern social thought, and 3) the role of elites in shaping communities. 6 notes. T. W. Smith

2829. Campbell, Bertha J. EARLY HISTORY OF ST. ANDREW'S WESLEY UNITED CHURCH OF CANADA: SPRINGHILL, NOVA SCOTIA. *Nova Scotia Hist. Q. [Canada] 1976 6(2): 173-192.* Discusses St. Andrew's Presbyterian Church and the Wesley Methodist Church in Springhill, Nova Scotia, 1800-1976; originally separate congregations, the two amalgamated in 1964.

2830. Carawan, Guy and Carawan, Candy. THAT HOLDING SPIRIT. *Southern Exposure 1976 4(3): 10-13.* Moving Star Hall, a black church on Johns Island, South Carolina, is the center of a sect of Negroes still similar to 18th-century slave/African-inspired religion.

2831. Carner, Vern. A MILLER LETTER. *Adventist Heritage 1974 1(1): 42-43.* A letter from 1828 by William Miller (1792-1849) in Low Hampton, New York, described the meetings of a group of Baptists.

2832. Carpenter, Joel A. FUNDAMENTALIST INSTITUTIONS AND THE RISE OF EVANGELICAL PROTESTANTISM, 1929-1942. *Church Hist. 1980 49(1): 62-75.* "The revivalistic, millenarian movement that flourished in the urban centers of North America in the late nineteenth and early twentieth centuries continued under the banner of fundamentalism and left no break in the line of succession from Dwight L. Moody to Billy Graham. Fundamentalism bears all the marks of a popular religious movement which drew only part of its identity from opposition to liberal trends in the denominations. The movement had its own ideology and program to pursue." 57 notes. M. D. Dibert

2833. Cashdollar, Charles D. AUGUSTE COMTE AND THE AMERICAN REFORMED THEOLOGIANS. *J. of the Hist. of Ideas 1978 39(1): 61-79.* Examines the reception of Auguste Comte's positivism by American reformed theologians. Received through British intermediaries, positivism was criticized by them for its materialism which denied the validity of all religious experience. Comte put the Reformed theologians on guard against other ideas, notably evolution, which they associated with positivism, and made them dissatisfied with Common Sense philosophy. Common Sense theologians were vitally interested in positivism because of the apparent correspondences between the two philosophies; but ultimately they rebelled against Common Sense because it failed to provide a strong defense against positivism. Comte's emphasis on altruism also forced Reformed theologians to consider the social applications of their religion, and so helped to define the Social Gospel. 48 notes. D. B. Marti

2834. Cawthon, John Ardis. A BRIEF HISTORY OF UNION PARISH BASED UPON A SAMPLING OF INSCRIPTIONS OF TOMBSTONES. *North Louisiana Hist. Assoc. J. 1974 5(2): 68-72.* Established on 13 March 1839, Union Parish was created from the northern part of Ouachita Parish, one of the original parishes in 1812 when Louisiana was made a state, with Farmerville as the parish seat of justice. There were chiefly Baptist and Wesleyan Methodist settlers in the area before Union became a parish. Four state governors—George W. Donaghay, Tom J. Terral, W. W. Heard, and Ruffin G. Pleasant—were born in the parish, although none are buried there. Other prominent names connected with Union Parish are those of Thomas H. Harris, L. M. and Emma Dawson Phillips, Stephen S. and Mary A. Heard, Earl R. Hester, and J. D. and Nancy Baughman. Includes 20th-century material. 2 photos, reproduction, 5 notes. A. N. Garland

2835. Clebsch, William A. SOUTHERN RELIGION RESURRECTED. *Rev. in Am. Hist. 1978 6(3): 337-339.* Review article prompted by Donald G. Mathews's *Religion in the Old South* (Chicago: U. of Chicago Pr., 1977) on the Evangelical churches.

2836. Clements, William. THE AMERICAN FOLK CHURCH IN NORTHEAST ARKANSAS. *J. of the Folklore Inst. 1978 15(2): 161-180.* Discusses folk religion in the United States, as revealed in the teachings, structures, and proceedings of Baptists and Pentecostals in northeastern Arkansas. These churches emphasize an orientation to the past, the literalism of the Scriptures, an awareness of Providence, an emphasis on evangelism, a lack of formalism in their services, the presence of rich emotionalism, moral rigorism, sectarianism, member equality, and plant isolation. Folk churches tend to closely resemble American main-line churches of the turn of the century. Folk churches are distinctive and significant in American life, although they have been little studied. 46 notes, appendix. V. L. Human

2837. Coleman, Richard J. KEY 73: WINNING THE CONTINENT FOR CHRIST, AGAIN. *Worldview 1973 16(1): 27-30.* Discusses this evangelistic movement.

2838. Coles, Robert. *THE NATURE AND DESTINY OF MAN* BY REINHOLD NIEBUHR. *Daedalus 1974 103(1): 97-104.* Niebuhr's *The Nature and Destiny of Man* was a significant attempt by a liberal Protestant theologian to fuse the insights of Marx and Freud with the traditional view of man. To accomplish that, Niebuhr utilized the concept of original sin as the link. Niebuhr saw in messianic Marxism and Freudianism a desperate answer to the confusions of life, and hoped to acknowledge those visionary positions but move beyond them. E. McCarthy

2839. Colmant, Berta. FOUR PREACHER TALES FROM WEST CENTRAL GEORGIA. *Tennessee Folklore Soc. Bull. 1976 42(3): 125-128.* Discusses and presents 19th- and 20th-century humorous folktales involving white and Negro rural preachers from the west central region of Georgia.

2840. Cornwall, Rebecca and Palmer, Richard F. THE RELIGIOUS AND FAMILY BACKGROUND OF BRIGHAM YOUNG. *Brigham Young U. Studies 1978 18(3): 286-310.* Examines the 18th-century religious and family roots of Brigham Young in an effort to determine how that industrious painter and carpenter from western New York came to exercise the leadership of perhaps the "most sensational institutional experiment to come out of the American frontier." The authors search for clues in his heritage, and place Young's New England, Congregational-Methodist forebears within the religious environment of their own age. Young may have been influenced by the mysticism inherent in many of the frontier religions. M. S. Legan

2841. Daniel, W. Harrison. THE EFFECTS OF THE CIVIL WAR ON SOUTHERN PROTESTANTISM. *Maryland Hist. Mag. 1974 69(1): 44-63.* All branches of Protestantism were scarred and afflicted by the Civil War. All denominations carried on extensive activities to care for the wounded, orphans and widows of the Southern armies. Northern troops committed many unjustifiable outrages on Southern churches, while inflation brought serious financial problems to the clergy, many of whom took secular employment. Southern Presbyterians, Lutherans, and Episcopalians all split from their Northern brethren and formed separate organizations, but war brought no revival enthusiasm to the Southern churches as it did in the camps. Federal treatment of Southern clergymen was largely moderate and tolerant, but those who persisted in "political preaching" were punished. All denominations "faced a major rebuilding task in the spring of 1865." Primary and secondary sources; 6 illus., 79 notes. G. J. Bobango

2842. Dawson, Jan C. THE PURITAN AND THE CAVALIER: THE SOUTH'S PERCEPTION OF CONTRASTING TRADITIONS. *J. of Southern Hist. 1978 44(4): 597-614.* William Robert Taylor, in *Cavalier and Yankee,* like other writers on the South, only peripherally recognized the Puritan element in the Southerner's perception of the North. Pre- and post-Civil War Southern writers relied heavily upon English Civil War Puritan-Cavalier imagery and vocabulary to tell the story of disruption and war. The Southerner's inclination to stress the Puritan element in the Yankee has permitted him to emphasize the great moral principals involved in the Civil War, and to continue to assert, as all great conservative forces have, the religious foundation of social and political order. Printed primary and secondary sources; 51 notes. T. D. Schoonover

2843. DeMille, George E. and Gerlach, Don R. SAMUEL JOHNSON AND THE "DARK DAY" AT YALE, 1722. *Connecticut Hist. 1977 (19): 38-63.* At the Yale commencement in 1722 Congregationalist minister Samuel Johnson (1696-1772) and six others questioned the validity of presbyterian orders. Three of them, including Johnson, further stunned Connecticut by going to England, where they were ordained in the Church of England in 1723. Their actions prompted a spread of Anglicanism throughout the colonies, and reaction which resulted in the Great Awakening. S

2844. De Villiers-Westfall, William E. THE DOMINION OF THE LORD: AN INTRODUCTION TO THE CULTURAL HISTORY OF PROTESTANT ONTARIO IN THE VICTORIAN PERIOD. *Queen's Q. [Canada] 1976 83(1): 47-70.* Attempts to delineate the interacting forces of religion and culture in Ontario during the Victorian era. Particular emphasis is placed on the Gothic revival and its relationship "to the general structure of social forces that defined the character of Victorian Canada." Suggests that the leading secular themes of the period's social history were articulated by Lord Durham in his *Report.* Through their religious convictions, Protestants in Ontario (and elsewhere in Canada) became convinced that theirs was a land of boundless possibilities. Covers 1840's-1900. Based on printed sources; 49 notes. J. A. Casada

2845. Dickson, D. Bruce, Jr. RELIGION, SOCIETY AND CULTURE IN THE OLD SOUTH: A COMPARATIVE VIEW. *Am. Q. 1974 26(4): 399-416.* Discusses the religious life and its relationship with the antebellum Southern society of the "plain-folk" small farmers and the Negro slaves. Stresses the impact of evangelicalism upon Methodism and Baptism, and compares and contrasts the differing white and black concepts of religion as an alternative to the oppressions of this world. 48 notes. C. W. Olson

2846. Douglas, Ann. HEAVEN OUR HOME: CONSOLATION LITERATURE IN THE NORTHERN UNITED STATES, 1830-1880. *Am. Q. 1974 26(5): 496-515.* Before and after the Civil War there was a great emphasis on elaborate funerals and conspicuous grief to stress the significance of death and dying. Bookshops were well stocked with death manuals and works on spiritualism and the afterlife. This consolation literature was largely the product of liberal Protestant clergymen and devout women. They "were intent on claiming death as their peculiar property, one conferring on them a special professional mission and prerogative: necessarily they wished to inflate and complicate its importance.... Sentimental as much of their output is in modern eyes, it indisputably served a valid function for those who read it as well as for those who produced it." 62 notes. C. W. Olson

2847. Douglas, Ann. THREE AMERICAN LIVES. *Can. Rev. of Am. Studies 1974 5(2): 190-197.* Reviews Joseph Ellis's *The New England Mind in Transition: Samuel Johnson of Connecticut, 1696-1772* (New Haven: Yale U. Pr., 1973); Louis Harlan's *Booker T. Washington: The Making of a Black Leader, 1856-1901* (New York: Oxford U. Pr., 1972); and Kathryn Sklar's *Catharine Beecher: A Study in American Domesticity* (New Haven: Yale U. Pr., 1973). These biographies of reformers contain little in common, but do provide insights into the task of studying minority cultures. 3 notes. H. T. Lovin

2848. Edwards, Katharine Bush. INSCRIPTIONS FROM THE MT. BETHEL BAPTIST AND EBENEZER METHODIST CHURCH CEMETERIES, ANDERSON COUNTY. *South Carolina Hist. Mag. 1978 79(2): 138-147.* Lists alphabetically the names and attached birth and death dates on gravestones in the Mount Bethel Baptist Church and the Ebenezer Methodist Church cemeteries in Anderson County, South Carolina, from 1856-1978.

2849. Elliott, Emory. THE DOVE AND SERPENT: THE CLERGY IN THE AMERICAN REVOLUTION. *Am. Q. 1979 31(2): 187-203.* The American clergy, using the language and form of the old Puritan clerics, were able to rally the people to the cause of the American Revolution. Instead of finding themselves in a position of respect in the new political system, however, they found their influence and the deference afforded them severely diminished by the end of the war. Only by organizing their messages and service to foster the perceived ordained mission of the new nation did they regain a measure of social status by the turn of the century. Covers 1774-1800. Based on the sermons and writings of Congregational and Presbyterian clergy; 26 notes. D. G. Nielson

2850. Ferm, Deane William. AMERICAN PROTESTANT THEOLOGY, 1900-1970. *Religion in Life 1975 44(1): 59-72.*

2851. Fiering, Norman S. IRRESISTIBLE COMPASSION: AN ASPECT OF EIGHTEENTH-CENTURY SYMPATHY AND HUMANITARIANISM. *J. of the Hist. of Ideas 1976 37(2): 195-218.* "Irresistible compassion" (the idea that people are moved to compassion by some inherent affective principle of their nature) was a "virtual philosophical and psychological dogma" by the mid-18th century. Though not without some ancient sources, this humanitarian dogma was only a century old when it overtook the different view of human nature associated with the Puritans and Thomas Hobbes. The Cambridge Platonists first advanced the idea and were seconded by a roll of familiar thinkers, chiefly British but including some Americans. The author refers to the religious liberalism of the 19th century, exemplified by William Ellery Channing. Published primary and secondary sources; 59 notes. D. B. Marti

2852. Fingard, Judith. HOW THE "FOREIGN" PROTESTANTS CAME TO NOVA SCOTIA, 1749-1752. *Can. Geographical J. [Canada] 1976-77 93(3): 54-59.* Discusses German immigrants who settled in Nova Scotia, 1749-52.

2853. Franch, Michael S. THE CONGREGATIONAL COMMUNITY IN THE CHANGING CITY, 1840-70. *Maryland Hist. Mag. 1976 71(3): 367-380.* The relocation of white, English-language Protestant churches from Baltimore's central city area to newer outlying neighborhoods was due not only to a desire for more select surroundings, but also to urban demographic and economic changes and "the financial imperatives of the American system of voluntary support for religious institutions." Membership in Protestant congregations depended not on geographic residency but on voluntary association: churches regardless of theology were "gathered" organizations. Congregational cohesion depended on whether a church was "pewed" or free-seat, on the social and ethnic homogeneity of the neighborhood, and on members' physical proximity to the church. As economic change allowed members to buy new residences outside the core city area, the "downtown" churches faced bankruptcy and commercial encroachment on their properties. Thus "daughter" churches were founded in the new residential areas, while older core churches came to serve lower-status groups. Primary and secondary sources; 6 maps, 2 tables, 29 notes. G. J. Bobango

2854. Friman, Axel. GUSTAF UNONIUS AND PINE LAKE: JOINING THE EPISCOPAL CHURCH. *Swedish Pioneer Hist. Q. 1978 29(1): 21-33.* Based on the journal of Gustaf Unonius, who with his family and three friends emigrated from Sweden in 1841 to settle in Pine Lake, Wisconsin. Without an evangelical Lutheran church in the area they attempted, through daily household worship, to preserve the teachings of the church. The friendship of the Scandinavians with missionaries of the Protestant Episcopal Church led to a "stabilization" of religion in the area by 1843. Gustaf Unonius was selected to be ordained as the religious leader of the Scandinavian settlers, under the Episcopalian Church. His ordination took place in 1845. He served several congregations in the area until he left in 1848. Discusses Lutheran and Episcopalian churches in the area during 1845-75. Unonius and his family returned to Sweden in 1858 after living for a while in Chicago. 2 photos, 18 notes. C. W. Ohrvall

2855. Gamwell, Franklin I. REINHOLD NIEBUHR'S THEISTIC ETHIC. *J. of Religion 1974 54(4): 387-408.*

2856. Gilkey, Langdon. REINHOLD NIEBUHR'S THEOLOGY OF HISTORY. *J. of Religion 1974 54(4): 360-386.*

2857. Goetsch, Bertha Louise. EARLY CHRISTMAS AT EMMANUEL CHURCH. *Swiss Am. Hist. Soc. Newsletter 1980 16(1): 13-19.* Discusses the arrival of Swiss immigrants in northwestern Ohio from 1848, when they established Mennonite and Reformed churches; the author remembers Christmas festivals at Emmanuel Reformed Church near Bluffton, Ohio, 1890-1900.

2858. Gordon, Ernest. THE PRINCETON GROUP. *Princeton Hist. 1977 (2): 35-44.* Moral Re-Armament was begun at Princeton University by Frank Buchman, an evangelical minister, in 1938.

2859. Greenlaw, William A. A SECOND LOOK AT REINHOLD NIEBUHR'S BIBLICAL-DRAMATIC WORLDVIEW. *Encounter 1976 37(4): 344-355.* Analyzes Reinhold Niebuhr's Christian philosophy of history in the belief that "if World War II (and its attendant horrors), the nuclear balance of terror, and the War in Indochina did not fundamentally faze the American liberal culture Niebuhr sought to critique, it may be that Watergate and the energy, food, and ecological crises will at least open the possibility of his voice being heard again."

2860. Grueningen, John Paul von. BIOGRAPHY OF J. J. VON GRUENINGEN. *Swiss Am. Hist. Soc. Newsletter 1978 14(1): 12-21.* Discusses Johann Jakob von Grueningen's (1845-1911) youth in Switzerland, schooling, immigration to America, and his life career as pastor in a strongly Swiss Reformed Church in Sauk City, Wisconsin, 1876-1911.

2861. Guelzo, Allen C. ETHNOHISTORY AND THE AMERICAN PURSUIT OF THE MILLENIUM. *Fides et Hist. 1980 12(2): 114-124.* A review essay on Anthony F. C. Wallace, *Rockdale: The Growth of an American Village in the Early Industrial Revolution* (New York: Alfred A. Knopf, 1978). An anthropologist, Wallace describes the effects of evangelicalism on the social evolution of Rockdale, a small industrial community south of Philadelphia. Using a paradigm of social change, Wallace shows that religion was a cohesive force among all social classes in the community. Covers 1820-65. 16 notes. J. A. Kicklighter

2862. Gura, Philip F. THE RADICAL IDEOLOGY OF SAMUEL GORTON: NEW LIGHT ON THE RELATION OF ENGLISH TO AMERICAN PURITANISM. *William and Mary Q. 1979 36(1): 78-100.* Discusses Samuel Gorton (1592?-1677) and his confrontations with the Puritan magistrates of Massachusetts Bay Colony and with Roger Williams and Providence Plantations, giving close attention to Gorton's doctrinal views. His antiauthoritarianism and anticlericalism were pronounced. Gorton's radicalism was less eccentric than what many historians have concluded. Links Gorton to English radicalism. Based on Gorton's writings and local records; 53 notes. H. M. Ward

2863. Hale, Frederick. NORWEGIANS, DANES, AND THE ORIGINS OF THE EVANGELICAL FREE TRADITION. *Norwegian-American Studies 1979 28: 82-108.* The revivalist, millenarian environment in America during 1875-95 influenced the development of today's largely Scandinavian Evangelical Free Church of America. Fredrik Franson (1852-1908), a Swedish American, was the major influence on Norwegian and Danish congregations at this time. Franson's views developed from contact with evangelist Dwight L. Moody, and the ideas of the Irish Protestant millenarian, John Nelson Darby (1800-82). Franson introduced his revivalist techniques and eschatological perspectives to congregations in Norway and Denmark during a stay there in 1883-84. 63 notes. D. K. Lambert

2864. Hall, Robert L. TALLAHASSEE'S BLACK CHURCHES, 1865-1885. *Florida Hist. Q. 1979 58(2): 185-196.* Analyzes the establishment of black Protestant churches in Tallahassee, Florida, after the Civil War. Churches aided blacks in airing social and political problems, restrained violent protest, and acted as "agencies of social control for the larger community." The churches performed an accommodating role to the expectations of the white community. Based on local and regional church records and other primary material; 53 notes.
N. A. Kuntz

2865. Hamilton, William B. PREACHERS AND PROFESSIONALISM. *Hist. of Educ. Q. 1979 19(4): 515-522.* Reviews Donald M. Scott's *From Office to Profession: The New England Ministry, 1750-1850.* This book surveys the changes in the status of Congregational-Presbyterian ministers from the late colonial period, when New England pastors served as government officials, until the Civil War, when these clergymen had taken on the same attributes of professionalism as doctors and lawyers. Secondary sources; 13 notes. S. H. Frank

2866. Hammond, John L. REVIVAL RELIGION AND ANTISLAVERY POLITICS. *Am. Sociol. Rev. 1974 39(2): 175-186.* Theories to explain empirical relationships between religion and political behavior (or other secular behavior) have generally asserted either that such relationships are spurious, explained by variations between religious groups in socioeconomic status, or that they are due to group identification with a religious community rather than a theology. The proposition that religious belief directly affects political attitudes and behavior is here tested with respect to revivals and antislavery voting in nineteenth-century Ohio. It has been claimed that revivals preached a new doctrine which demanded active opposition to slavery. The claim that revivalism had a direct, nonspurious effect on antislavery voting is tested in a multiple regression model which incorporates variables representing social structure, ethnicity, denominational membership, and prior political tradition. The effect of revivalism is strong despite all controls; the revivals transformed the religious orientations of those who experienced them, and this transformation affected their voting behavior. J

2867. Harrington, Michael L. EVANGELICISM AND RACISM IN THE DEVELOPMENT OF SOUTHERN RELIGION. *Mississippi Q. 1974 27(2): 201-209.* Review essay on John B. Boles' *The Great Revival, 1785-1805: The Origins of the Southern Evangelical Mind* (Lexington: U. Pr. of Kentucky, 1972) and H. Shelton Smith's *In His Image, But . . . : Racism in Southern Religion* (Durham, N.C.: Duke U. Press, 1972).
S

2868. Hasse, John. THE GARY BLACK RELIGIOUS EXPERIENCE: A PHOTO ESSAY. *Indiana Folklore 1977 10(2): 165-181.* Photo essay and extended description covers evangelical aspects of black churches in Gary, Indiana: gospel music, faith healing, possessing the Holy Spirit, and laying on of hands, 1976.

2869. Hayward, Larry R. F. E. MADDOX: CHAPLAIN OF PROGRESS, 1908. *Arkansas Hist. Q. 1979 38(2): 146-166.* Finis Ewing Maddox (b. 1873) became minister of the First Presbyterian Church of Texarkana, Arkansas, in 1905. He was accused and convicted of heresy in 1908, so he and three-quarters of his congregation withdrew and formed the First Congregational Church. Discusses Maddox's theological modernism and his appeal to churchgoers, as well as the backgrounds of his followers and opponents. Primary and secondary sources; illus., 62 notes. G. R. Schroeder

2870. Heinrich, Thelma C. THE ROLE OF THE CHURCH IN ESTABLISHING AMERICA. *Daughters of the Am. Revolution Mag. 1979 113(9): 980-986.* Discusses how religion, specifically Protestantism, shaped the American consciousness in the 18th century, based on Martin Luther and John Calvin's belief in an individual's responsibility for his own spiritual state.

2871. Hickman, James T. THE POLARITY IN AMERICAN EVANGELICALISM. *Religion in Life 1975 44(1): 47-58.* Conservative Protestantism is polarized into three basic segments; evangelicalism, fundamentalism, and neo-evangelicalism. S

2872. Holifield, E. Brooks. READING THE SIGNS OF THE TIMES. *Rev. in Am. Hist. 1977 5(1): 14-20.* Review article prompted by William R. Hutchison's *The Modernist Impulse in American Protestantism* (Cambridge, Mass.: Harvard U. Pr., 1976). Covers the 19th and 20th centuries.

2873. Humphrey, Richard A. DEVELOPMENT OF RELIGION IN SOUTHERN APPALACHIA: THE PERSONAL QUALITY. *Appalachian J. 1974 1(4): 244-254.* The emphasis on personal religious experience which coincides with the life style of the mountain environment accounts for the predominance of Baptists and Methodists over Presbyterians, 1788-1974. S

2874. Hunt, Richard A. and King, Morton B. MEASURING THE RELIGIOUS VARIABLE: NATIONAL REPLICATION. *J. for the Sci. Study of Religion 1975 14(1): 13-22.* Attempts to determine the key variables defining religion by comparing urban north Texas and national statistics which measure the dimensions of faith and activity of white Protestants. Covers 1965-73. S

2875. Hunter, Lloyd A. MARK TWAIN AND THE SOUTHERN EVANGELICAL MIND. *Missouri Hist. Soc. Bull. 1977 33(4): 246-264.* Analyzes the ways in which the South's particularistic "evangelical faith" influenced the life and thought of Mark Twain. Twain was unable to avoid the religious evangelistic spirit that prevailed on the southern frontier where he resided, though he increasingly disagreed with many aspects of Southern evangelical pietism. He resisted those features that he considered intolerant of individual conscience or repressive to individual humanitarian impulses. Based on Clemens' writings and secondary sources; 5 pictures, 74 notes. H. T. Lovin

2876. James, Sydney V. THE WORLDS OF ROGER WILLIAMS. *Rhode Island Hist. 1978 37(4): 99-109.* Though the evidence is sometimes fragmentary, Roger Williams lived in at least six distinct, sometimes overlapping, worlds of public life. They ranged from the higher ranks of English society, Puritanism, and colonization, to Indian, colonial, and town affairs. In this respect he was not necessarily unique, for many early settlers had to function in a diversity of settings. Published documents and secondary accounts; 4 illus., 33 notes. P. J. Coleman

2877. Janis, Ralph. FLIRTATION AND FLIGHT: ALTERNATIVES TO ETHNIC CONFRONTATION IN WHITE ANGLO-AMERICAN PROTESTANT DETROIT, 1880-1940. *J. of Ethnic Studies 1978 6(2): 1-17.* Examines a large sampling of marriage and baptismal registers, membership rosters, and officer lists of Detroit churches to demonstrate the changing class, cultural, and spatial composition of church-related social organizations over two generations. Solid social interdicts existed against ethnic mixture in 1880. Ethnic uniformity in marriage and membership had declined by 1906, but was resurrected after this by the impact of the auto boom. Ethnocentrism, however, represented a rational 19th-century-rooted search for order by the large majority, who sought viable "acts of adjustment to urban change." Vigilantism, Klanism, and demagoguery were the exception, not the rule, of Detroit Protestants, in their search for "the creative use of social distance, not confrontation," in making the transition to new and modified social boundaries. Primary and secondary research; 2 tables, 26 notes.
G. J. Bobango

2878. Jones, George Fenwick. TWO "SALZBURGER" LETTERS FROM GEORGE WHITEFIELD AND THEOBALD KIEFER II. *Georgia Hist. Q. 1978 62(1): 50-57.* Reprints two letters of request (dating ca. 1738 and 1750) written to Gottfried Francke, director of the Francke Foundation orphanage at Halle, Germany, by George Whitefield, Anglican minister, and Theobald Kiefer, II, boat builder and Lutheran. These concern the settlement of Salzburgers at Ebenezer, Georgia, and their orphanage. The Kiefer letter is in the original German and in English translation. Based on primary sources; 18 notes.
G. R. Schroeder

2879. Jones, Loyal. STUDYING MOUNTAIN RELIGION. *Appalachian J. 1978 5(1): 125-130.* Annotated bibliography of studies of Protestantism in Appalachia, 1905-75; warns researchers against judgmentalism.

2880. Kauffman, Earl H. ANABAPTIST INFLUENCE ON UNITED METHODISM IN CENTRAL PENNSYLVANIA. *Mennonite Hist. Bull. 1977 38(3): 4-5.* Discusses Anabaptist thought and the influence which it had, 1815-1942, on the mainstream of Methodist thought in central Pennsylvania.

2881. Kelley, Mary and Mead, Sidney E. PROTESTANTISM IN THE SHADOW OF ENLIGHTENMENT. *Soundings 1975 58(3): 329-347.* Nothing new in principle has appeared in the history of American Protestantism since the 1920's, and in essential respects little is new since the end of the 18th century. Many of the religious questions surfacing during the 1920's were also inherent in Enlightenment thinking. While the activities of religious leaders and their denominations have greatly increased since the 1920's, their religious thought has been shaped by faddism rather than by intense ideological reasoning. Based on personal memories of the 1920's and on secondary sources.
N. Lederer

2882. Kennedy, E. William. JOHN WARWICK MONTGOMERY AND THE OBJECTIVIST APOLOGETICS MOVEMENT. *Fides et Hist. 1973 5(1/2): 117-121.* Reviews Montgomery's *History and Christianity* (Downers Grove, Illinois: Inter-Varsity, 1972). Montgomery leads an objectivist apologetics movement among American evangelicals which is based on "a stout empirico-historical defense of biblical inerrancy." Designed for campus evangelism, the book attacks all theological positions outside conservative orthodoxy, contends for the historical accuracy of the Bible, and puts an objective event before faith. Sees strengths in Montgomery's critics' arguments. R. Butchart

2883. Kimnach, Wilson H. JONATHAN EDWARDS' EARLY SERMONS: NEW YORK, 1722-1723. *J. of Presbyterian Hist. 1977 55(3): 255-266.* For eight months spanning 1722-23 Jonathan Edwards pastored a Presbyterian congregation in New York. Recent scholarship has identified some 24 sermon manuscripts from this period. These sermons represent a wealth of new material documenting Edwards' mental development. They also permit consideration of the origins of his distinguished preaching career: his handling of visual imagery, his ability as an abstract thinker, his opposition to anything that smacks of "foolish inconsistency" in matters religious and the definition of the Christian life in experiential terms. 11 notes. H. M. Parker, Jr.

2884. Kirkendoll, Chester A. HOW DID THE AMSTERDAM YOUTH CONFERENCE OF 1939 AFFECT THE BLACK CHURCH? *J. of Ecumenical Studies 1979 16(1): 72-78.* Reviews the origins of the black church in America and names some of the delegates (H. Thomas Primm, Carl Downs, Benjamin E. Mays, Clarie Collins Harvey, Dorothy Height et al.) to the 1st World Conference of Christian Youth (Amsterdam, 1939) who later became prominent in the black church and the civil rights movement. Amsterdam "served as a catalytic agent to broaden the horizons of ecumenicity in the Black Church, created the incentive for the Black Church to recapture its prophetic posture, intensified the drive for social equality," and "eliminated concepts that black people had of themselves" as inferior. S

2885. Kirsch, George B. CLERICAL DISMISSALS IN COLONIAL AND REVOLUTIONARY NEW HAMPSHIRE. *Church Hist. 1980 49(2): 160-177.* Ministerial dismissals illustrate the changing roles of the Congregational and Presbyterian clergy in colonial and revolutionary New England. Although New Hampshire may not be representative of the entire region, four broad categories of reasons for ministerial dismissals during 1633-1790 explain patterns of social change in New England. Statistical evidence shows that 77 ministers were dismissed in New Hampshire for personal, religious, financial, and political reasons. 38 notes. M. D. Dibert

2886. Kocher, Helen J. SIDELIGHTS ON THE PURITANS AND PILGRIMS. *Daughters of the Am. Revolution Mag. 1979 113(5): 488-493, 521.* Distinguishes between Puritans and Pilgrims, 1606-1790.

2887. Kraus, Joe W. LIBRARIES OF THE YOUNG MEN'S CHRISTIAN ASSOCIATIONS IN THE NINETEENTH CENTURY. *J. of Lib. Hist. 1975 10(1): 3-21.* A history of the Young Men's Christian Association's libraries, from the association's beginnings in London in 1844 to the present. Surveys the rise and fall of YMCA libraries in the United States with details on some of the larger ones, including the New York YMCA library and its most outstanding librarian, Reuben B. Pool. Based on primary and secondary sources; 55 notes.
A. C. Dewees

2888. Kydd, Ronald. H. C. SWEET: CANADIAN CHURCHMAN. *J. of the Can. Church Hist. Soc. [Canada] 1978 20(1-2): 19-30.* In many ways Dr. H. C. Sweet demonstrated his unique character. First, as missionary, minister, and professor, he served several Christian denominations. Second, he was well-educated and maintained his intellectual curiosity all his life; he obtained the doctorate in theology at the age of 61. Third, he carried out his Christian commitment in a variety of ways. In his early years he was a missionary to Indians in Saskatchewan. Later he served as pastor to a black congregation in Winnipeg. He also devoted a number of years to Christian education through his teaching at two theological institutions. Beloved and respected, H. C. Sweet had such diversity in his career that he merits special attention among Canadian clergy. Covers 1866-1960. Primary and secondary sources; 89 notes.
J. A. Kicklighter

2889. Ledbetter, Patsy. DEFENSE OF THE FAITH: J. FRANK NORRIS AND TEXAS FUNDAMENTALISM, 1920-1929. *Arizona and the West 1973 15(1): 45-62.* Urban growth, loss of individualism, and increased industrialization were regarded as a threat to the traditional values of a predominantly rural nation. This and a backlash from the fervor of the European war years brought a wave of reaction to liberal and scientific thought throughout the country in the 1920's. Religious fundamentalism among the Protestant sects was one of the most important aspects of this reaction. It was basically a response to the attempt of liberal theology to reconcile modern science with Christianity. In Texas, a predominantly rural state with industrialization imminent, fundamentalist sentiment became especially intense in the 1920's. Textbook censorship, agitation in the state legislature, and disturbances in the Protestant churches affected all segments of the population. John Franklyn Norris (1877-1952), a Baptist evangelist known as the "Texas Tornado," led the crusade in the state against alcohol, gambling, Catholicism, Sunday movies, and religious modernism. 5 illus., 32 notes. D. L. Smith

2890. Longino, Charles F., Jr. and Hadden, Jeffrey K. DIMENSIONALITY OF BELIEF AMONG MAINSTREAM PROTESTANT CLERGY. *Social Forces 1976 55(1): 30-42.* In this analysis of 7,443 parish clergy from six mainstream Protestant denominations, we have examined the clustering of religious beliefs. The survey provides a substantially more sophisticated array of theological belief than previous research, and covers sixteen theological content areas. Underlying these belief statements are a small number of factors which are, with minor exceptions, similar across denominations. The key factor which represents the major dimension of belief among Protestant clergy forms a continuum from a relatively literal to a relatively demythologized interpretation of the faith. We have concluded, therefore, that the structure of belief among mainstream Protestant clergy is unidimensional. We would further speculate that the most significant concomitants of belief would stem from this fact. The survey is from 1965. J

2891. Lord, Clyde W. THE MINERAL SPRINGS HOLINESS CAMP MEETINGS. *Louisiana Hist. 1975 16(3): 257-277.* Soon after the Civil War the "National Camp Meeting Association for the Promotion of Holiness" was formed by a prominent group of Methodist clergymen. A rift between the holiness devotees and the Methodist conservative leadership developed and reached a crisis by the mid-1890's when several small holiness sects withdrew and formed the Church of the Nazarene. The camp meetings at Mineral Springs continued from 1903-26. By that time it had become evident that the defenders of Methodist conservatism were fighting a losing battle. Illus., 75 notes. E. P. Stickney

2892. Lucas, Glenn. CANADIAN PROTESTANT CHURCH HISTORY TO 1973. *Bull. of the United Church of Can. [Canada] 1974 (23): 5-50.* Outlines the history of the Methodist, Presbyterian, Anglican, Baptist, Congregational, and Lutheran churches in Canada and the

United Church of Canada since 1825; includes bibliographies and historiography.

2893. Maclear, J. F. THE EVANGELICAL ALLIANCE AND THE ANTISLAVERY CRUSADE. *Huntington Lib. Q. 1979 42(2): 141-164.* In 1846, American and British Protestants attempted to form an international organization to promote missions, reform, and benevolence. British sentiment favored excluding slaveholders, but the question was not settled prior to the organizational meeting in Liverpool, where a heated debate led to the decision to create separate national branches. While the American churchmen were personally opposed to slavery, they resented British attitudes and generally believed that religious unity was more important than abolition. Primary sources; 59 notes.
S. R. Smith

2894. Marsden, George. FUNDAMENTALISM AS AN AMERICAN PHENOMENON, A COMPARISON WITH ENGLISH EVANGELICALISM. *Church Hist. 1977 46(2): 215-232.* Fundamentalism as a Protestant response to modernity was an overwhelmingly American phenomenon. It pervaded the churches and the national culture. Examining fundamentalism reveals significant traits of American culture. Conversely, the American context also provides a key for understanding fundamentalism. Variables in the American environment can be best identified by comparing American fundamentalism with English evangelicalism. Covers the 1920's. 52 notes. M. D. Dibert

2895. Marty, Martin E. THE LOST WORLDS OF REINHOLD NIEBUHR. *Am. Scholar 1976 45(4): 566-572.* Reinhold Niebuhr lived in the realities of two worlds. There was his inner world of Original Sin and the Cross, and an outer world of political activism, pragmatism, empiricism. There was a dynamic relationship between both worlds.
F. F. Harling

2896. Marty, Martin E. REINHOLD NIEBUHR: PUBLIC THEOLOGY AND THE AMERICAN EXPERIENCE. *J. of Religion 1974 54(4): 332-360.*

2897. Mathisen, Robert R. THE SECOND COMING. *Fides et Hist. 1980 12(2): 129-133.* Review essay of Timothy P. Weber's *Living in the Shadow: American Premillennialism, 1875-1925* (New York: Oxford U. Pr., 1979). As historians today recognize the importance of studying religious thought and practice for understanding American cultural development, this work contributes significantly to the social history of the United States in the late 19th and early 20th centuries. Believing that they were witnessing the unfolding of God's plan in history, the premillennialists were devoted to conservative theology and unceasing missionary activity both at home and abroad, in preparation for Christ's return. 9 notes. J. A. Kicklighter

2898. McLoughlin, William G. FREE LOVE, IMMORTALISM, AND PERFECTIONISM IN CUMBERLAND, RHODE ISLAND, 1748-1768. *Rhode Island Hist. 1974 33(3-4): 67-86.* Discusses religious beliefs among a group of perfectionists in Cumberland, Rhode Island; examines a court case generated by the beliefs (among them free love) and examines the movement in terms of the Enlightenment, 1748-68.

2899. Melder, Keith. MASK OF OPPRESSION: THE FEMALE SEMINARY MOVEMENT IN THE UNITED STATES. *New York Hist. 1974 55(3): 261-279.* Challenges the traditional view that the female seminary movement was an instrument of women's liberation in 19th-century American society. The female seminary movement, by fostering the distinction between education for men and education for women, was actually an oppressive institution perpetuating the dependent status of women in society. Its goal of training teachers, housewives, and mothers, and instilling Protestant religious values was a male centered and sexist definition of woman's social role. Based on primary and secondary works; 4 illus., 40 notes. G. Kurland

2900. Millar, W. P. J. THE REMARKABLE REV. THADDEUS OSGOOD: A STUDY IN THE EVANGELICAL SPIRIT IN THE CANADAS. *Social Hist. [Canada] 1977 10(19): 59-76.* Traces career of nondenominational traveling preacher Thaddeus Osgood (1775-1852) in Canada after 1807. He attempted to stimulate a vast spiritual awakening. He believed such an awakening could not be left to faith alone, but must be assisted by such means as day and Sunday schools, education of Indians, temperance movements, sabbatarianism, organization of tract societies, and an attack on urban poverty and vice. By the 1820's he met strong resistance from the sources of denominationalism. By 1835 he had narrowed his activities to the moral improvement of the urban poor, especially children. Based on documents in Public Archives of Canada, Public Record Office, on newspapers, and on other primary sources; 105 notes. W. K. Hobson

2901. Miller, Douglas T. POPULAR RELIGION OF THE 1950'S: NORMAN VINCENT PEALE AND BILLY GRAHAM. *J. of Popular Culture 1975 9(1): 66-76.* Explores the manifestations of the religious boom in billboards, book sales, popular music, films, and the respectability of religion among intellectuals. Popular religion, best illustrated by Norman Vincent Peale's cult of reassurance and Billy Graham's evangelistic crusades, remained superficial and did not challenge or alter American society despite its centrality to popular culture. 30 notes.
J. D. Falk

2902. Moore, Donald S. PRESBYTERIAN NON-CONCURRENCE AND THE UNITED CHURCH OF CANADA. *Bull. of the United Church of Can. 1975 (24): 28-39.* Examines the two major factors "motivating Presbyterian non-concurrence in the Canadian church union of 1925.... One was distaste for the social gospel movement, and the other dislike of the centralized, semi-episcopal structure of the United Church." This paper offers no new interpretations but "is an attempt to detail these attitudes." Based on newspapers; 41 notes.
B. D. Tennyson

2903. Naglack, James J. DEATH IN COLONIAL NEW ENGLAND. *Hist. J. of Western Massachusetts 1975 4(2): 21-33.* Discusses folklore and ritual of death and dying in New England; touches on poems, gravestones, funeral expense, and mourning customs.

2904. Nelsen, Hart M. and Maguire, Mary Ann. THE TWO WORLDS OF CLERGY AND CONGREGATION: DILEMMA FOR MAINLINE DENOMINATIONS. *Sociol. Analysis 1980 41(1): 74-80.* An analysis of a national sample of clergy focuses on the giving of sermons on personal morality, which is part of the religious view of traditionalists. Clergy of mainline, liberal denominations who serve conservative congregations are less likely to give these sermons if they are from a nonfarm rather than a farm background. It is concluded that the study of the dilemma facing the liberal, mainline denominations must include characteristics of their clergy and how they minister to their parishioners. The dilemma facing the mainline denominations includes not only having two quite distinctive audiences (locals and cosmopolitans, or traditionalists and modernists) but also having clergy who, because of changing recruitment patterns, have a proclivity to speak to the world view of the cosmopolitans rather than the locals. Table, biblio. J

2905. Noon, Thomas R. DANIEL PAYNE AND THE LUTHERANS. *Concordia Hist. Inst. Q. 1980 53(2): 51-69.* Discusses the Reverend Doctor Daniel Alexander Payne (1811-93) whose accomplishments include being the first black college president of Wilberforce University (1863-76) and most likely the first black ordained Lutheran pastor in the United States (1839), focusing on his less than seven years involvement with the Lutheran Church due to his redirection to the African Methodist Episcopal Church.

2906. Norton, John E. "...WE HAVE SUCH GREAT NEED OF A TEACHER": OLOF BÄCK, BISHOP HILL, AND THE ANDOVER SETTLEMENT OF LARS PAUL ESBJÖRN. *Swedish Pioneer Hist. Q. 1975 26(4): 215-220.* One of the America-letters of Olof Bäck was written to Pastor Lars Paul Esbjörn of the Swedish State Church. Esbjörn had it published in *Norrlandsposten* in 1849. Bäck had been converted to Methodism. His wife had remained with the Janssonists. The letter tells of Bäck's life in America and expresses the great need for clergymen. Esbjörn, sympathetic to the "Reader" movement, emigrated with many of his congregation. Primary sources; illus., 4 notes.
K. J. Puffer

2907. Norton, Wesley. RELIGIOUS NEWSPAPERS IN ANTEBELLUM TEXAS. *Southwestern Hist. Q. 1975 79(2): 145-165.* Studies the Protestant denominational press in Texas, 1829-61. The Cumberland and Old School Presbyterians, Southern Methodists, and Baptists all published religious newspapers to further denominational interests, promote educational institutions, and provide information on area church activity. Editorials advocated temperance reform and observance of the Sabbath. With one exception they accepted slavery, and they wished to suppress debate on it as a religious issue. None hesitated to endorse secession or back the Confederacy. Perhaps one copy in 10 of all newspapers distributed in Texas by 1860 was denominational, but none survived the Civil War. Based on church newspapers, and on secondary sources; 45 notes. C. W. Olson

2908. Noyes, Richard. A NOTE ON A FOUNDING FATHER'S LIBRARY: THE BOOKS OF BENJAMIN GILES. *Hist. New Hampshire 1979 34(3-4): 244-252.* Benjamin Giles (1717-87), as a central figure in the development of New Hampshire's constitution, can further the understanding of New Hampshire's unique role in this field. Few of Giles's papers have survived, but an inventory of his library, included in his probate records, is revealing. It includes works by Jonathan Edwards and George Whitefield not commonly read by the Founding Fathers. His library had a strongly Calvinistic bias, which, with Giles's known persistence, suggests that the Founding Fathers may have been driven, at least in part, by Puritan energy. 15 notes. D. F. Chard

2909. Nye, Russel B. THE THIRTIES: THE FRAMEWORK OF BELIEF. *Centennial Rev. 1975 19(2): 37-58.* Four major intellectual trends characterize the 1930's: "the discovery of culture; the rediscovery of sin; the acceptance of relativism; the promise of plenty." After publication of Ruth Benedict's *Patterns of Culture* (1934), the concept of culture came to mean "the relationship between each human being, who had his own specific hereditary environment and particular life history, and the culture in which he lived." The relativism advocated by Benedict was reinforced by Carl Becker in the *Heavenly City of the Eighteenth Century Philosophers* (1932), in which he called for recognition of facts and truth as relative, "changing entities, the character and significance of which can be fully grasped only by regarding them in an endless process of differentiation, of unfolding, of waste and repair." Sin came to hold a new meaning in Reinlhold Niebuhr's *Moral Man and Immoral Society* (1932), which directed theology toward the concern of man with God and away from a man-centered faith. A new definition of wealth evolved from John M. Keynes's *The General Theory of Employment, Interest, and Money* (1936), which "shifted the focus of economic theory from prices and costs to income and investment, or from the machinery of the marketplace to the distribution of income and the use people made of it." The long-run effect of these ideas on American intellectual life is as profound as the impact of the New Deal on politics and the function of government. 15 notes. A. R. Stoesen

2910. Parsons, Talcott. RELIGION IN POSTINDUSTRIAL AMERICA: THE PROBLEM OF SECULARIZATION. *Social Res. 1974 41(2): 193-225.* Discusses Protestant secularization, the effects of American civil religion and socialism upon it, and the current relationships between religion and social and cultural movements. Covers 16th-20th centuries. S

2911. Peace, Nancy E. ROGER WILLIAMS: A HISTORIOGRAPHICAL ESSAY. *Rhode Island Hist. 1976 35(4): 103-113.* Analyzes writings about Roger Williams, from accounts by his contemporaries to recent works by theologians. 58 notes. P. J. Coleman

2912. Pearson, Samuel C., Jr. ENLIGHTENMENT INFLUENCE ON PROTESTANT THOUGHT IN EARLY NATIONAL AMERICA. *Encounter 1977 38(3): 193-212.* Examines the continuities in religious thought between Europe and the United States during the Enlightenment, emphasizing anticlericalism and antiecclesiasticalism in the United States and the Second Awakening which took place solely in America; covers 1640's-1830's.

2913. Pearson, Samuel C., Jr. RATIONALIST IN AN AGE OF ENTHUSIASM: THE ANOMALOUS CAREER OF ROBERT CAVE. *Missouri Hist. Soc. Bull. 1979 35(2): 99-108.* A theological liberal, Robert Catlett Cave (1843-1923) became pastor of the Central Christian Church at St. Louis in 1888. From that pulpit he challenged many traditional Christian views, including Biblical literalism, and was, as a consequence, ousted from his pastorate. Case and his followers then formed their own congregation, the Non-Sectarian Church of St. Louis, and, for more than a decade, Cave remained on Protestantism's most "liberal fringe." Eventually he became an advocate of universalist theology based on nature and reason. Archival sources and secondary works; photo, 54 notes. H. T. Lovin

2914. Pickering, Samuel, Jr. THE GRAVE LEADS BUT TO PATHS OF GLORY: DEATHBED SCENES IN AMERICAN CHILDREN'S BOOKS, 1800-1860. *Dalhousie Rev. [Canada] 1979 59(3): 452-464.* Quotes from influential British and American authors, such as James Janeway, Isaiah Thomas, Jason Whitman, J. B. Waterbury, Mary Jane Phillips, William Alcott, and Louis Simpson. Mentions religious periodicals such as the *Arminian, Methodist Magazine,* and *Evangelical Magazine.* 19 notes. C. H. Held

2915. Pierard, Richard V. THE QUEST FOR THE HISTORICAL EVANGELICALISM: A BIBLIOGRAPHICAL EXCURSUS. *Fides et Hist. 1979 11(2): 60-72.* Assesses several recent books on modern American evangelicalism and concludes that the quality of the studies is improving. Notes include several dozen books and articles on the topic beyond those specifically addressed in the text of the article. 56 notes. R. E. Butchart

2916. Reilly, Timothy F. SLAVERY AND THE SOUTHWESTERN EVANGELIST IN NEW ORLEANS (1800-1861). *J. of Mississippi Hist. 1979 41(4): 301-317.* Fundamentalism in New Orleans in the antebellum period produced mixed results. So desperate had Methodist and Baptist organizations become for converts that they were willing to proselytize among blacks and whites alike. Studies these Protestant efforts, and especially some of the clergy's liberal racial philosophies which placed them outside the mainstream in the South's defense of slavery. Key figures in New Orleans Protestantism include William Winans, Benjamin M. Drake, Asa C. Goldsbury, Holland McTyeire, and William Cecil Duncan. New Orleans Catholicism and Protestantism were able to arrange a religious pluralism as the Protestant clergy, with strong roots in the South's agrarian society, sought to create a religious culture that would be responsive to urban needs. M. S. Legan

2917. Richardson, James T.; Stewart, Mary White; and Simmonds, Robert B. CONVERSION TO FUNDAMENTALISM. *Society 1978 15(4): 46-52.* Presents a sociological model of converts to fundamentalist Christian groups and tests it with a survey of members of the Christ Communal Organization in the United States, 1970's.

2918. Ringereide, Mabel. ROMANES: FATHER AND SON. *Bull. of the Com. on Arch. of the United Church of Can. [Canada] 1979 28: 35-46.* A biographical sketch of the Reverend George Romanes, minister of St. Andrew's in Smith Falls, Ontario, 1834-50, and professor and curator at Queen's College, Kingston; and his son George John Romanes (1848-94), British biologist, well-known for his contribution to scientific research and his essay, "Christian Prayer and General Laws."

2919. Robbins, Caroline. FAITH AND FREEDOM (C. 1677-1729). *J. of the Hist. of Ideas 1975 36(1): 47-62.* The last quarter of the 17th and first quarter of the 18th centuries have been neglected by historians of religious ideas and experience. Far from being a period of simple religious decline, it saw developments strongly parallel to those of the present day, with a variety of endeavors to sustain religious affirmations by "interpreting them according to the canons of contemporary scientific and philosophic thought." Reviews European and American religious expressions with interpretive references to leading writers. Primary and secondary sources; 22 notes. D. B. Marti

2920. Rodgers, Daniel T. DEMOCRACY, MEDIOCRITY, AND THE SPIRIT OF MAX WEBER. *Rev. in Am. Hist. 1980 8(4): 465-470.* Review essay of E. Digby Baltzell's *Puritan Boston and Quaker Philadelphia: Two Protestant Ethics and the Spirit of Class Authority and Leadership* (New York: Free Pr., 1979), covering the 17th-20th centuries.

2921. Rowe, David L. ELON GALUSHA AND THE MILLERITE MOVEMENT. *Foundations 1975 18(3): 252-260.* Elon Galusha, a major leader of the Baptists in New York State, was one of a few leading Baptists caught up in the Millerite movement. Describes the attack on

him for his participation in the movement, including his theology and changed view of the church. Since his views were moderate, he used his influence to curb the radicalism of the Millerites. Before his death in 1856, he had returned to the Baptist Church. 19 notes.
E. E. Eminhizer

2922. Runeby, Nils and Barton, H. Arnold, trans. GUSTAV UNONIUS AND PROPAGANDA AGAINST EMIGRATION. *Swedish Pioneer Hist. Q. 1973 24(2): 94-107.* In the struggles between Swedish religious factions in the United States, Gustav Unonius became greatly disillusioned, and a zealous opponent of emigration. He left America in 1858. He was opposed to religious freedom and the American school system. In 1858 he distributed a questionnaire to clergymen concerning Scandinavian settlement. The replies did not agree with his beliefs: the immigrants were generally well off and content. Unonius' efforts to discourage emigration met with positive interest in Sweden. The Riksdag of 1859-60 awarded him a gratification and the Riksdag of 1862-63 discussed emigration. In 1861 Unonius began to bring out his memoirs, perhaps the most cited writing of the earlier emigration. His activity was supported in the Riksdag by individuals of differing political views, but he attained no results. Excerpted from *Den nye världen och den gamla* (Uppsala, 1969). Based on primary and secondary sources; 28 notes.
K. J. Puffer

2923. Scott, Donald M. THE POPULAR LECTURE AND THE CREATION OF A PUBLIC IN MID-NINETEENTH CENTURY AMERICA. *J. of Am. Hist. 1980 66(4): 791-809.* Public lectures as an institution emerged in full form by the mid-1840's. They not only expressed a national culture, but also were one of the institutions by which a white, middle-class, Anglo-Saxon, and Protestant public identified itself. The public lecture was supposed to inspire, entertain, and instruct an audience, but it also had to demonstrate a relationship between its specific topic and a broader, more comprehensive view. The lecture not only provided Americans of the 1840's and 1850's with comprehensive views of culture and knowledge, but also accomplished this task in a democratic form. 78 notes. T. P. Linkfield

2924. Scott, P. G. JAMES BLAIR AND THE SCOTTISH CHURCH: A NEW SOURCE. *William and Mary Q. 1976 33(2): 300-308.* James Blair was a minister in the Church of Scotland before changing to the Church of England and coming to America as a bishop's commissary. In Virginia he became the founder and first president of the College of William and Mary. The minute book of the Presbytery of Dalkeith, Scotland, shows early development of Blair's traits, such as his financial high-handedness and political ability. It also proves his disputed ordination of 1679 in episcopal orders. Points out Blair's views on organization at parish and precinct levels. Compares Blair's Scottish activities with those in Virginia in 1699. In spite of receiving episcopal orders, Blair remained essentially a Scottish churchman. Based on the minutes and on miscellaneous church literature. 34 notes. H. M. Ward

2925. Sernett, Milton C. BEHOLD THE AMERICAN CLERIC: THE PROTESTANT MINISTER AS "PATTERN MAN," 1850-1900. *Winterthur Portfolio 1973 (8): 1-18.* An examination of pastoral theology textbooks reveals a picture of ministers in three areas: the "closet" (private religious life), the study, and the parish. In the "closet" the minister was expected to grow in piety. Thus Victorian America established a model for men who desired ordination. The study was designed to enable ministers to keep pace with the laity and to prepare ministers for their destined roles of leadership. In the parish ministers were to be "everybody's man." Such a requirement established uniformity. Pastoral theology constructed a pattern for ministers on paradoxical propositions. The minister was to be a modern man and an affable gentleman, and still fit into a society that no longer accepted the model or the office. Based on primary and secondary sources; 3 illus., 104 notes. N. A. Kuntz

2926. Sessions, Jim. A MIGHTY FORTRESS: PROTESTANT POWER AND WEALTH. *Southern Exposure 1976 4(3): 83-97.* Explores Protestant growth in the South, 1940-75, including corporate wealth and political power. In pp. 88-92, examines the extensive network of Southern Baptist churches, including wealth, various sects, investments, and political power. In pp. 92-95, discusses assets, educational opportunities, and church organization of the United Methodist Church, 1930's-70's. In pp. 96-98, examines church government, political power, and property of the Presbyterian Church.

2927. Shinn, Roger L. REALISM, RADICALISM, AND ESCHATOLOGY IN REINHOLD NIEBUHR: A REASSESSMENT. *J. of Religion 1974 54(4): 409-423.*

2928. Sides, Sudie Duncan. SLAVE WEDDINGS AND RELIGION. *Hist. Today [Great Britain] 1974 24(2): 77-87.* Describes religious practices and celebrations of Negroes on plantations in the South.

2929. Simonson, Harold P. THE TEMPERED ROMANTICISM OF JOHN MUIR. *Western Am. Literature 1978 13(3): 227-241.* Disagrees with the hypothesis that John Muir had completely traded the Calvinism imbued in him by his father for 19th-century romanticism. Includes examples from Muir's writings and concludes that he really achieved a careful blending of the two philosophies. M. Genung

2930. Singleton, Gregory H. "MERE MIDDLE-CLASS INSTITUTIONS": URBAN PROTESTANTISM IN 19TH-CENTURY AMERICA. *J. of Social Hist. 1973 6(4): 489-504.* Review article prompted by Nathan Irvin Higgins' *Protestants Against Poverty: Boston's Charities, 1870-1900* (Westport, Conn.: Greenwood, 1971), Richard J. Jensen's *The Winning of the Midwest: Social and Political Conflict, 1888-1896* (Chicago: U. of Chicago Pr., 1971), Carroll Smith Rosenberg's *Religion and the Rise of the American City: The New York City Mission Movement, 1812-1870* (Ithaca: Cornell U. Pr., 1971), and Alvin W. Skardon's *Church Leader in the City: Augustus Muhlenberg* (Philadelphia: U. of Pennsylvania Pr., 1971).

2931. Singleton, Gregory H. PROTESTANT VOLUNTARY ORGANIZATIONS AND THE SHAPING OF VICTORIAN AMERICA. *Am. Q. 1975 27(5): 549-560.* In the 19th century the social organization of Protestantism aided in the expansion of American consciousness from localism to nationalism, as exemplified through the changing nature of voluntary associations. This process facilitated the emergence of a corporate society in which all areas of economic, social, and political life were specialized and structured, and had been foreshadowed by the organization of the Protestant establishment before the Civil War. Based on primary and secondary sources. N. Lederer

2932. Smylie, James H. ETHICS IN THE REVIVAL TENT. *Worldview 1973 16(11): 30-35.* Discusses social and political attitudes of Christian Evangelicals toward war and civil authority in the 1970's, including the views of Billy Graham.

2933. Smylie, James H. REINHOLD NEIBUHR: QUADRAGESIMO ANNO. *Religion in Life 1973 42(1): 25-36.* Discusses Niebuhr's *Mortal Man and Immoral Society* (New York: Scribner's, 1932, 1948) on the 40th anniversary of its publication. S

2934. Soland, Martha Jordan. FAITH OF OUR FATHERS. *Daughters of the Am. Revolution Mag. 1975 109(9): 1012-1015, 1075.* Traces American religious history from the beliefs of the Revolutionary leaders to the anti-Catholic sentiments of the Know-Nothing Party during the mid-19th century. S

2935. Spotts, Charles D. BRICKERVILLE OLD ZION REFORMED CHURCH. *J. of the Lancaster County Hist. Soc. 1973 77(2): 61-87.* Covers 1732.

2936. Stearns, Monroe. MOSES IN MASSACHUSETTS. *Midstream 1979 25(2): 13-17.* The Pilgrims and Puritans, first settlers of New England in the 17th century, found analogies between their history and that of the Jews in the Old Testament.

2937. Stein, Stephen J. COTTON MATHER AND JONATHAN EDWARDS ON THE NUMBER OF THE BEAST: EIGHTEENTH-CENTURY SPECULATION ABOUT THE ANTICHRIST. *Pro. of the Am. Antiquarian Soc. 1975 84(2): 293-315.* An analysis of the interpretations of Cotton Mather and Jonathan Edwards on the significance of the biblical number of the Antichrist. Both men based their conclusions primarily on the mathematical determinations of Francis Potter, an English clergyman. Mathematical keys were used by each man, and both decided that Rome, the Pope, and the Catholic Church represented the Antichrist. Americans have frequently equated the Antichrist with unpopular social movements or institutions. 55 notes. V. L. Human

2938. Teunissen, John J. and Hinz, Evelyn J. ROGER WILLIAMS, THOMAS MORE, AND THE NARRAGANSETT UTOPIA. *Early Am. Literature 1976-77 11(3): 281-295.* The Utopian tradition and Renaissance humanism which characterized Thomas More's writing is also found in Roger Williams's *A Key into the Language of America* (London, 1643). Educated in the Renaissance tradition, Williams was able to view Indians as they were rather than in the Puritan sense as representatives of Satan in the howling wilderness.

2939. Teunissen, John J. and Hinz, Evelyn J. ROGER WILLIAMS, ST. PAUL, AND AMERICAN PRIMITIVISM. *Can. Rev. of Am. Studies 1973 4(2): 121-136.* The theological views of Roger Williams (ca. 1603-83), particularly his interpretations of the Epistles of St. Paul, significantly influenced his behavior when he disputed both Puritan orthodoxy and the Quakers. His "kinship with St. Paul" was crucial to the conception of the "true Church of Christ" that Williams attempted to establish in America. In addition, his Pauline predilections conditioned his attitudes toward the Indians. Williams was not a true primitivist but his theology and social attitudes adhere closely to the definitions of primitivism set forth in James Baird's *Ishmael: A Study of the Symbolic Mode in Primitivism* (New York: Harper and Row, 1960). Based on primary and secondary sources; 6 notes. H. T. Lovin

2940. Thompson, Kenneth W. NIEBUHR AS THINKER AND DOER. *J. of Religion 1974 54(4): 424-436.*

2941. Threlfall, John B. THE VERIN FAMILY OF SALEM, MASSACHUSETTS. *New England Hist. and Genealogical Register 1977 131(April): 100-112.* Traces the six sons of Philip Verin (ca. 1580-ca. 1649) who settled in Salem, Massachusetts, in 1635. One son, Robert (b. 1606), probably died on the voyage from England. Joshua (ca. 1611-95) followed Roger Williams to Providence, Rhode Island, but his religious views were too unorthodox for even that unorthodox settlement, and he returned to Salem; he ultimately removed to Barbados. Philip (b. 1619) had Quaker tendencies; he appears no more in the records of Essex County after 1665. Hiliard (1621-83) was a model Salem resident; he held a variety of town offices. Nathaniel (1623-ca. 1665) was a ship captain. John (ca. 1625-89) immigrated to Maine, where he was killed in an Indian ambush. Based on primary and secondary sources.
S. L. Patterson

2942. Tipson, Baird. HOW CAN THE RELIGIOUS EXPERIENCE OF THE PAST BE RECOVERED? THE EXAMPLES OF PURITANISM AND PIETISM. *J. of the Am. Acad. of Religion 1975 43(4): 695-707.* Studies the conversion experience in Anglo-American Puritanism and German Lutheran Pietism by examining a representative theological discussion of conversion from each movement and comparing it with a diary or autobiographical account of an individual's conversion experience. The personal account in each case was influenced largely by the accepted theological discussion which set forth what should happen in the experience. Covers the 17th and 18th centuries. Primary and secondary sources; 46 notes. E. R. Lester

2943. Tucker, Bruce. POLITICS, CULTURE, AND PERSONAL LIFE IN EIGHTEENTH-CENTURY AMERICA: A REVIEW ESSAY. *Eighteenth-Century Studies 1980 13(4): 414-426.* These books on early American history—David H. Fischer's *Growing Old in America* (New York: Oxford U. Pr., 1977), Philip Greven's *The Protestant Temperament* (New York: Knopf, 1977), Kenneth S. Lynn's *A Divided People* (Westport, Conn.: Greenwood, 1977), and David E. Stannard's *A Puritan Way of Death* (New York: Oxford U. Pr., 1977)—investigate how the personal psychology of colonial Americans affected their politics and culture. 15 notes. W. W. Elison

2944. Urofsky, Melvin I. AMERICA AND ISRAEL: TRYING TO FIND THE STRAIGHT PATH. *Reviews in Am. Hist. 1975 3(3): 383-388.* Discusses the evolution, 1945-48, of President Truman's policy on Israel, analyzes the importance of the Zionist cause in the 1948 presidential election, and summarizes the social and theological responses of American Protestantism since the Puritans in this review of Hertzel Fishman's *American Protestantism and a Jewish State* (Detroit, Mich.: Wayne State U. Pr., 1973) and John Snetsinger's *Truman, the Jewish Vote, and the Creation of Israel* (Hoover Institution Studies 39. Stanford, Calif.: Hoover Institution Pr., 1974).

2945. VanDusen, Henry P. A HALF-CENTURY OF LIBERAL THEOLOGY. *Religion in Life 1978 47(3): 343-360.* The introduction of liberalism to theology, 1880's-1930's, entailed devotion to truth, deference to science and scientific method, agnosticism toward the possibility of metaphysical certainty, continuity, and a liberal spirit.

2946. Voskuil, Dennis N. AMERICA ENCOUNTERS KARL BARTH, 1919-1939. *Fides et Hist. 1980 12(2): 61-74.* Despite the success of Karl Barth's crisis theology in his native Germany, and although commentaries on his ideas were published in America as early as 1926, American Protestant theologians were slow to respond. His major work was not translated into English until 1933. Liberals found his neoorthodoxy too traditional; conservatives considered it another modernist expression. Despite growing interest in Barth's ideas, it appears unlikely that his theology will ever have a direct, profound influence on American Protestantism. 36 notes. J. A. Kicklighter

2947. Warman, John B. FRANCIS ASBURY AND JACOB ALBRIGHT. *Methodist Hist. 1978 16(2): 75-81.* Compares Francis Asbury (1745-1816), Bishop of the Methodist Episcopal Church, and Jacob Albright (1759-1808), founder of the Evangelical Association, and their work in the early years of their respective churches in America. 8 notes.
H. L. Calkin

2948. Wentz, Richard E. THE AMERICAN CHARACTER AND THE AMERICAN REVOLUTION: A PENNSYLVANIA GERMAN SAMPLER. *J. of the Am. Acad. of Religion 1976 44(1): 115-131.* Explains the influence of esoteric wisdom and folk religious, cultural, and intellectual history of the American people. These two elements, referred to as the complementary tradition, should be considered along with the more prominent elements of Enlightenment, Calvinism, and Puritanism. Pennsylvania Germans are used as an example of the complementary tradition and its influence. Covers 1775-83. Secondary sources; 71 notes.
E. R. Lester

2949. Wentz, Richard E. RADICAL CATHOLICITY IN AMERICA. *Anglican Theological Rev. 1976 58(1): 3-22.* Discusses the concept of transcendence in Christian and specificially Protestant theology, 1975.

2950. Wentz, Richard E. RADICAL CATHOLICITY: BEYOND PURITANS AND PIETISTS. *Anglican Theological Rev. 1978 60(2): 131-143.* Applies the radical catholicity principle—experiencing the wholeness of existence—to Puritans and Pietists; rather than embrace social wholeness, each sect retreated into dogma and failed to express any truly radical character. Covers the 17th and 18th centuries.

2951. Westerberg, Wesley. SWEDISH-AMERICAN RELIGIOUS AND SECULAR ORGANIZATIONS. Hasselmo, Nils, ed. *Perspectives on Swedish Immigration* (Chicago: Swedish Pioneer Hist. Soc. and Duluth: U. of Minnesota, 1978): 199-204. The Lutheran and Methodist churches provided the first organizations outside the home that Swedish —sometimes together with Norwegian and Danish—immigrants joined. The churches, from which many of the immigrants were already alienated, opposed the secular organizations that arrived later and began to compete for the loyalty of the population. The Masons, Odd Fellows, and the Grange were opposed as secret societies, and many lodges were considered sinful because they tolerated or actually encouraged dancing and drinking. Some old cultural societies such as Society Norden, which also provides social benefits such as medical assistance, still exist, and new ones are still being formed. Competition between the churches and the secular societies has ended. 9 notes. S

2952. Wilson, Major L. PARADOX LOST: ORDER AND PROGRESS IN EVANGELICAL THOUGHT OF MID NINETEENTH CENTURY AMERICA. *Church Hist. 1975 44(3): 352-366.* By focusing on the paradoxical way in which many Americans conceived of themselves within the process of time, this study attempts to elucidate the liberal outlook of 19th-century America. Evangelical thought was a product of the contradictory American belief in progress, which advocated advancement but kept a nostalgic hold on the past. Politically and economically, this concept led Americans to believe in laissez-faire individualism. The evangelical view of man defined something essential in the national consciousness of the era. 40 notes. M. Dibert

2953. Wood, Jerome H., Jr. FOR TRUTH AND REPUTATION: THE NEW ENGLAND FRIENDS' DISPUTE WITH ISAAC BACKUS. *New England Q. 1977 50(3): 458-483.* Analyzes the opposition of Quakers to Backus's (1724-1806) treatment of their early history and views on church and state relations in the first volume of his three-volume *History of New England* (1777). Describes Backus's negotiations with agents of the Quaker New England Meeting for Sufferings and the retraction he included as an appendix to volume two (1784) of his *History,* concluding that the acceptance by both sides of the Bible as the sole source of religious truth and the acceptance of the legitimacy of each other's views "symbolized the voluntarist-biblicist orientation" and the "denominationalist point of view" gaining acceptance at the time. Based primarily on Backus's writings and manuscripts in the Backus Collection of Andover-Newton Theological Library, Newton Center, Massachusetts; 45 notes. J. C. Bradford

2954. Woodrum, Eric. TOWARDS A THEORY OF TENSION IN AMERICAN PROTESTANTISM. *Sociol. Analysis 1978 39(3): 219-227.* A model for tension in American Protestantism is constructed building on Max Weber, modifications of his work, and earlier explanations. It argues that conflicts over "mission" reflect structurally rooted differences in secular accommodation among laity, parish clergy, and supra-congregational staff. Religious professionals' domination of informal power structures and lay independence of church organizations influence outcomes of Protestant disputes. A broad range of primary and secondary information concerning conflict in Protestant bodies is reviewed and found largely consistent with the model. Covers the 19th-20th centuries.

2955. Young, Chester Raymond. THE OBSERVANCE OF OLD CHRISTMAS IN SOUTHERN APPALACHIA. *Appalachian J. 1977 4(4): 147-158.* Social customs and ballads from Appalachian Christmas celebrations are the direct result of resistance to the 1753 adaptation of the Gregorian calendar in England, which created the celebration of "Old Christmas" on 5 January.

2956. Zuckerman, Michael. PILGRIMS IN THE WILDERNESS: COMMUNITY, MODERNITY, AND THE MAYPOLE AT MERRY MOUNT. *New England Q. 1977 50(2): 255-277.* Analyzes relations between Thomas Morton (d. 1647) and his Pilgrim neighbors at Plymouth and Puritan neighbors at Massachusetts Bay. Morton was hated not because he sold guns to the Indians or because he competed for the fur trade, but because his whole outlook on life differed from that of the Puritans. Morton loved the land and the Indians as they were and rejected the Puritan belief that the land was unemployed, if not empty, and open to the English. Morton's adoption of Indian ways was viewed by Puritans as a slip into barbarianism and challenged their commitment to maintain their English identity in what they viewed to be a wilderness. Morton's ultimate offense was to insist on his liberty in a society which demanded the acceptance of authority. Primary and secondary sources; 57 notes. J. C. Bradford

2957. —. AMERICAN PRESBYTERIAN AND REFORMED LIFE—SELECTED 1973 PERIODICAL ARTICLES. *J. of Presbyterian Hist. 1974 52(3): 273-281.* Over 70 annotated entries. S

2958. —. [CHRISTIANITY, CAPITALISM, AND SUCCESS IN NINETEENTH-CENTURY AMERICA]. *Fides et Hist. 1973 5(1-2): 1-28.*

Carey, Ralph A. THE HORATIO ALGER MYTH, *pp. 1-9.* Contemporary understanding of the Horatio Alger myth is often mistaken. Alger emphasized respectability and morality rather than business success. His heroes were not common city boys, but country-bred sons of reputable families who had fallen on bad times. The role of luck or Providence is important, emphasizing providential recognition of middle-class virtues. Alger's benevolent merchant economy provided a romantic escape from the realities of corporate industrialism. His popularity prior to the 20th century reflected a positive response to this attempt to reassert the virtues of the Protestant ethic; his rapid decline paralleled the shift from an ethic of personal virtue to a Gospel of Wealth. Secondary sources; 17 notes.

Marsden, George. THE GOSPEL OF WEALTH, THE SOCIAL GOSPEL, AND THE SALVATION OF SOULS IN NINETEENTH-CENTURY AMERICA, *pp. 10-21.* Argues that the 20th-century equation linking liberal Christianity with social activism and conservative or Evangelical Christianity with personal salvation is a misinterpretation of nineteenth-century religious views. The later identification of Orthodoxy with a lack of social conscience was primarily a facet of the Fundamentalist reaction to the Social Gospel and modernism. Primary and secondary sources; 26 notes.

MacPhee, Donald A. CHRISTIANITY, CAPITALISM, AND SUCCESS IN NINETEENTH-CENTURY AMERICA: A RESPONSE TO CAREY AND MARSDEN, *pp. 22-28.* Carey identified Alger more closely with evangelical Christianity than evidence warrants. The piety of the Alger hero is a mechanical, status-conscious piety rather than a spiritual commitment. Marsden has difficulty with definitions, referring to a Social Gospel long before the rise of the true Social Gospel in the 1890's. Secondary sources; 17 notes. R. Butchart

2959. Kincheloe, Joe L., Jr. EUROPEAN ROOTS OF EVANGELICAL REVIVALISM: METHODIST TRANSMISSION OF THE PIETISTIC SOCIO-RELIGIOUS TRADITION. *Methodist Hist. 1980 18(4): 262-271.* The Pietism of Germany dating from 1674, the radical evangelism of the Reformed Dutch Church, and Methodism in England converged to form the American evangelical heritage. By the early 1800's, the Methodists were exerting an influence on the social and cultural fabric of America. Secondary sources; 24 notes. H. L. Calkin

Adventist Churches
(including Millerites)

2960. Anderson, Godfrey T. "MAKE US A NAME." *Adventist Heritage 1974 1(2): 28-34.* Discusses the controversy in the church in the 1850's preceding the choice in 1860 of the name, "Seventh-day Adventists."

2961. Arthur, David T. AFTER THE GREAT DISAPPOINTMENT: TO ALBANY AND BEYOND. *Adventist Heritage 1974 1(1): 5-10, 58.* The Albany Conference of 1845 after the Great Disappointment of 22 October 1844 (the Millerites' expected date of Christ's return) redefined the old Adventist faith and planned its future, but made permanent the existing divisions among Adventists.

2962. Butler, Jonathan. THE SEVENTH-DAY ADVENTIST AMERICAN DREAM. *Adventist Heritage 1976 3(1): 3-10.* Seventh-Day Adventists interpreted the biblical "two-horned beast" to refer to Protestantism and republicanism, in the mid-19th century.

2963. Carner, Vern. HORACE GREELEY AND THE MILLERITES. *Adventist Heritage 1975 2(1): 33-34.* In an effort to expose readers to both sides of the Millerite issue, New York *Tribune* editor Horace Greeley published the ideas of William Miller as well as excerpts from a book by one of Miller's detractors, Rev. John Dowling, 1842.

2964. Eichler, Margit. LEADERSHIP IN SOCIAL MOVEMENTS. *Sociol. Inquiry [Canada] 1977 47(2): 99-108.* Two types of leadership styles in social movements are constructed on the basis of closed or open access to the source of legitimacy. Several predictions about structural consequences of the open or closed access are then made. The types are applied to four cases: the Nazis, the Manson Family, the Millerites, and Women's Liberation. The hypothese are confirmed. J

2965. Fattic, Grosvenor. "A FEW STERLING PIECES": NINETEENTH CENTURY ADVENTIST TEMPERANCE SONGS. *Adventist Heritage 1975 2(1): 35-41, 68.* Survey of temperance songs of Seventh-Day Adventists in their anti-alcohol campaigns, 1850's-90's.

2966. Gragg, Larry. THE DAYS OF DELUSION. *Am. Hist. Illus. 1978 13(4): 20-25.* In 1831, after 14 years of research and calculation based mainly on the Book of Daniel, William Miller came to the conclusion that Christ would return to rule the world in 1843. Overcoming his natural shyness, he began to preach this message to audiences that reached 1,000-1,500 persons as the fateful year approached. When 1843 passed, Miller shifted his date to the end of the "Jewish" year, 21 March 1844. This passed too, and Miller gave up hope of pinpointing the exact date of Christ's return. Yet his followers settled on 22 October and at last convinced him they were right. 23 October marked the end of the Millerites, whose numbers in their heyday have been estimated at from 50,000 to one million. Based on contemporary newspaper accounts and on Clara E. Sear's *Days of Delusion;* 9 illus. L. W. Van Wyk

2967. Lindén, Ingemar. PATTERNS OF APOCALYPTIC THOUGHT IN THE NINETEENTH CENTURY. *Kyrkohistorisk Årsskrift [Sweden] 1977 77: 172-176.* Discusses millenarianism in the United States (especially William Miller), Great Britain (John Nelson Darby and Henry Drummond), Germany (The Pietists in Würtemberg), and Sweden.

2968. McAdams, Donald R. EDWIN R. PALMER: PUBLISHING SECRETARY EXTRAORDINARY. *Adventist Heritage 1975 2(1): 51-62.* Edwin R. Palmer (1869-1931) was a missionary in Australia for the Seventh-Day Adventists, 1894-1901, and was instrumental in establishing a church publishing house, 1902-15.

2969. Nix, James R. THE AMERICAN CENTENNIAL: AN ADVENTIST PERSPECTIVE. *Adventist Heritage 1976 3(1): 11-16.* Describes the Centennial Exposition of 1876 in Philadelphia from the point of view of John Harvey Kellogg, editor of the Adventist publication *The Health Reformer,* who operated the Adventist exhibit at the fair.

2970. Patt, Jack Michael. THE MILLERITE AWAKENING AND THE GREAT DISAPPOINTMENT OF 1844. *Indian J. of Am. Studies [India] 1973 3(1): 71-82.* Describes the background of religious enthusiasm during the late 18th century, and gives a step-by-step account of the events surrounding the belief in the second coming of the Lord (Parousia) in the year 1844. Outlines the present day religious groups that evolved from this Millerite belief. 31 notes. L. V. Eid

2971. Reynolds, Keld J. EARLY DAYS OF LOMA LINDA . . . AND EVEN BEFORE. *Adventist Heritage 1975 2(1): 42-50.* Discusses Loma Linda, California, through Mexican ownership (as a rancho), 1810-48, early California statehood, and eventually Seventh-Day Adventist purchase after which it became an education and medical facility for the church, 1905-29.

2972. Roach, Robert A. POSTAGE STAMPS, ENVELOPES & ADVENTIST HISTORY. *Adventist Heritage 1979 6(1): 50-55.* Discusses the United States' adoption of postage stamps in 1847 and Seventh-Day Adventist participation in commemorative postage stamp issuance, 1967-78.

2973. Rowe, David L. COMETS AND ECLIPSES: THE MILLERITES, NATURE, AND THE APOCALYPSE. *Adventist Heritage 1976 3(2): 10-19.* Discusses the Millerites' anticipation of the Second Coming of Christ, expected first in 1843 and then on 22 October 1844.

2974. Rowe, David L. A NEW PERSPECTIVE ON THE BURNED-OVER DISTRICT: THE MILLERITES IN UPSTATE NEW YORK. *Church Hist. 1978 47(4): 408-420.* Investigation of the Millerite movement confirms the existence of a particularly strong area of religious fervor in central and western New York. A principal characteristic of the movement was an evangelical reaction against the formalization, or maturation, of the evangelical sects. Such intensity does not fully confirm Whitney R. Cross's delineation of the burned-over district, but a study of the Millerites does confirm Cross's notion that social maturation sparked religious dissent. Dissenting groups such as the Millerites show that the innovative religion of the 1830's and 1840's was rooted in the cultural and institutional life of a "district," which must be thought of as an idea rather than a region. 36 notes. M. D. Dibert

2975. Strayer, Brian. THE TRIUMPH AND TRAGEDY OF NATHAN FULLER. *Adventist Heritage 1977 4(1): 3-12.* Converted to Seventh-Day Adventism in 1857, Nathan Fuller preached in New York and Pennsylvania during 1858-69 until he was expelled from the church for adultery.

2976. Theobald, Robin. THE ROLE OF CHARISMA IN THE DEVELOPMENT OF SOCIAL MOVEMENTS: ELLEN G. WHITE AND THE EMERGENCE OF SEVENTH-DAY ADVENTISM. *Arch. de Sci. Sociales des Religions [France] 1980 49(1): 83-100.* Ellen G. White played a significant role among the Sabbatarean Adventists (they became the Seventh-day Adventists in 1860) during their 1848 meetings, when her visions and pronouncements embodied the spirit of prophecy. By the late 1880's and early 1890's, some of the church leadership came out in opposition to her, and her influence declined. "It is clear that by 1888 a degree of tension had built up between Mrs. White's charismatic authority and the rational-legal authority on which the movement depended for its day-to-day existence." J/S

2977. Thomas, N. Gordon. THE SECOND COMING: A MAJOR IMPULSE OF AMERICAN PROTESTANTISM. *Adventist Heritage 1976 3(2): 3-9.* Discusses the American Protestant view of the Second Coming of Christ, especially that of the Millerites of the 1830's and 1840's.

2978. Watts, Kit. SEVENTH-DAY ADVENTIST HEADQUARTERS: FROM BATTLE CREEK TO TAKOMA PARK. *Adventist Heritage 1976 3(2): 42-50.* Describes the transfer of the Seventh-Day Adventists' national headquarters from Battle Creek, Michigan, to Takoma Park, Maryland, in 1903.

2979. White, Larry. MARGARET W. ROWEN: PROPHETESS OF REFORM AND DOOM. *Adventist Heritage 1979 6(1): 28-40.* Adventist Margaret W. Rowen, who claimed that she had divinely inspired visions, the first on 22 June 1916, and who attempted to prove her divine inspiration in the face of charges by the General Conference and the Southern California Conference of Seventh-Day Adventists by forging documents to prove that she was the successor to prophetess Ellen White, was eventually charged with and convicted of conspiring to murder Dr. Bert E. Fullmer in 1927, even though Fullmer was not murdered.

Baptist Churches

2980. Armour, Rollin S. SIDELIGHTS ON FLORIDA BAPTIST HISTORY: THE WINTER ASSEMBLY AT UMATILLA AND A CONNECTION WITH THE ASSASSINATION OF PRESIDENT LINCOLN. *Baptist Hist. and Heritage 1973 8(4): 225-231.* Two notes: one about the establishment of Southern Baptist winter assembly grounds in 1865; the other about the son of a Baptist pastor, convicted for his part in the assassination of Lincoln. S

2981. Baker, Nathan Larry. BAPTIST POLITY AND PARACHURCH ORGANIZATIONS. *Baptist Hist. and Heritage 1979 14(3): 62-70, 73.* Discusses the 20th-century trend in the proliferation of parachurch groups, and how the Southern Baptist Church has dealt with this issue, particularly during the 1970's.

2982. Baker, Robert A. THE COOPERATIVE PROGRAM IN HISTORICAL PERSPECTIVE. *Baptist Hist. and Heritage 1975 10(3): 169-176.* Discusses the practical impact of the Cooperative Program of the Southern Baptist Convention by contrasting the financial operation of the SBC before and after its inception in 1925. In the 50 years since its inauguration, total gifts to missions and benevolences have increased ninefold. In addition, long-range budget planning, more systematic gathering of tithes and offerings, better support of Southern Baptist benevolences, and many other benefits stem principally from the adoption of the Cooperative Program. 2 notes. H. M. Parker, Jr.

2983. Baker, Robert A. THE MAGNIFICENT YEARS (1917-1931). *Baptist Hist. and Heritage 1973 8(3): 144-157, 167.* A progressive era for the Southern Baptist Convention. S

2984. Baker, Robert A. REFLECTIONS ON THE SOUTHERN BAPTIST CONVENTION AND ITS PEOPLE, 1607-1972. *Baptist Hist. and Heritage 1974 9(4): 223-229.*

2985. Black, Margie. "OUR OWN LOTTIE MOON": THE STORY OF LOTTIE MOON AND HER RELATIONSHIP WITH CARTERSVILLE BAPTIST CHURCH. *Viewpoints: Georgia Baptist Hist. 1974 4: 5-16.* Covers 1870-1903.

2986. Blair, John L., ed. A BAPTIST MINISTER VISITS KENTUCKY: THE JOURNAL OF ANDREW BROADDUS I. *Register of the Kentucky Hist. Soc. 1973 71(4): 393-425.* Reprints edited journal of Reverend Andrew Broaddus I (1770-1848) of a trip made into Kentucky, 9 October-29 November 1817 from the manuscript in the Virginia Baptist Historical Society, Richmond. J. F. Paul

2987. Boling, T. Edwin. DENOMINATIONAL SECTARIANS: PRESERVING THE MYSTIQUE. *Foundations 1978 21(4): 365-372.* As the Southern Baptists advance beyond their regional base where they are a dominant denomination, they move out as a pioneer mission producing groups appropriately termed *dynamic sects.* The combination of denominational support and a sect-type spontaneity suggests the term *denominational sectarians* as descriptive of Southern Baptist pioneer mission organizations. Focuses on some of the interpretive and explanatory characteristics present in this religious movement. As Southern Baptists move North and West they carry with them the mystique of their regional religious experience. Each new congregation is the attempt to confirm a Southern mystique born of a historical sectionalism. The old-time religion, a link to the past, is at the same time a search for a comfortable, predictable future. Based on sociological studies; 19 notes.
H. M. Parker, Jr.

2988. Boling, T. Edwin. LEADERSHIP FOR EVANGELICAL CHURCH EXTENSION: A CASE STUDY OF SOUTHERN BAPTISTS. *Foundations 1978 21(1): 22-31.* Pioneer Southern Baptist churches in Columbus, Ohio, have been studied in terms of local church leadership and the place of the association superintendent of missions in local leadership. The study indicates the superintendent of missions makes decisions outside of the traditional polity context for Baptists in the pioneer areas. The ministers stay longer in their churches than in other areas, and have to assume leadership traditionally held by laymen in other more developed areas. Preaching emphasis is on individual conversion and there is less interdemoninational cooperation. Covers 1969-76. 10 notes. E. E. Eminhizer

2989. Boling, T. Edwin. SOCIAL FACTORS IN CHURCH EXTENSION: SOUTHERN BAPTISTS IN THE NORTH. *Foundations 1975 18(2): 146-152.* Southern Baptist extension in the North is seen as a continuation of rural Southern religious patterns. Extended into urban areas, this pattern establishes identity for a minority ethnic group. The church, because of denominational organization, allows missionary personnel and programs to move into newly settled areas. 8 notes.
E. E. Eminhizer

2990. Bratton, Mary J. JOHN JASPER OF RICHMOND: FROM SLAVE PREACHER TO COMMUNITY LEADER. *Virginia Cavalcade 1979 29(1): 32-39.* Black minister John Jasper (1812-1901), who was born a slave on a Virginia plantation, joined the First African Baptist Church in 1842, and gained national attention in 1878 when he preached a sermon called, "The Sun Do Move."

2991. Brewer, Paul D. THE STATE CONVENTION: IS IT HEADQUARTERS? *Baptist Hist. and Heritage 1979 14(3): 41-51.* Discusses the issue of centralization in the Southern Baptist Church at the state convention level, tracing the functions of the state convention since its beginnings in the early 19th century.

2992. Broach, Claude U. INTRODUCING SOUTHERN BAPTISTS. *Greek Orthodox Theological Rev. 1977 22(4): 367-375.* Describes the membership, beliefs, and policy procedures of contemporary Southern Baptists, focusing on President Jimmy Carter's church in Plains, Georgia.

2993. Bumsted, J. M., ed. THE AUTOBIOGRAPHY OF JOSEPH CRANDALL. *Acadiensis [Canada] 1973 3(1): 79-96.* Discusses the autobiography and memoirs of Reverend Joseph Crandall, patriarch of the Baptist Church in New Brunswick, 1795-1810.

2994. Campbell, Will. THE CALL. *Southern Exposure 1976 4(3): 25-32.* The author reminisces about a Southern Baptist preacher, Thad Garner, whose unorthodox life and ministerial style might have led some to believe he was a nonbeliever.

2995. Carter, James E. THE FRATERNAL ADDRESS OF SOUTHERN BAPTISTS. *Baptist Hist. and Heritage 1977 12(4): 211-218.* "The Fraternal Address of Southern Baptists," issued in 1919, was never officially adopted by the Southern Baptist Convention, although its major author was the influential Dr. E. Y. Mullins. Containing a succinct though incomplete doctrinal position, the purpose of the address was to open communications and cooperation with Baptist groups scattered throughout the world. It was mostly ignored, yet it stands as a statement of Baptist belief. Secondary sources; 43 notes.
H. M. Parker, Jr.

2996. Carter, James E. A REVIEW OF CONFESSIONS OF FAITH ADOPTED BY MAJOR BAPTIST BODIES IN THE UNITED STATES. *Baptist Hist. and Heritage 1977 12(2): 75-91.* Discusses four major American Baptist Confessions: Philadelphia Confession of Faith, 1742; New Hampshire Declaration of Faith, 1833; Baptist Faith and Message, 1925; and Baptist Faith and Message, 1963. Presents each under background, characteristics, and significance. A Baptist confession of faith does not have binding authority; it is a consensus of the belief of the body which issued the statement. Such confessions have a twofold value. They define the doctrinal consensus of Baptist groups at particular times, and they illustrate Baptist history. Based on primary and secondary sources; 90 notes. H. M. Parker, Jr.

2997. Clemmons, William. VOLUNTEER MISSIONS AMONG TWENTIETH CENTURY SOUTHERN BAPTISTS. *Baptist Hist. and Heritage 1979 14(1): 37-49.* A volunteer is not a career worker, receives no wages or honoraria, and has different responsibilities, preparation, and identification in the community than the career worker. The Southern Baptist Convention presently employs thousands of denominational employees, however all agencies and levels of the Church continue to be staffed by thousands of volunteers who give millions of hours each week to make possible the far-flung ministry of Southern Baptists. Examines voluntarism since the 1940's in five Southern Baptist denominational agencies: Women's Missionary Union, Brotherhood Commission, National Student Ministries, Home Missions, and Foreign Missions. Volunteer involvements help church members become more aware of missions by seeing what is going on first-hand. Based on official records of the Southern Baptist Convention; 84 notes. H. M. Parker, Jr.

2998. Compton, Bob. J. M. PENDLETON: A NINETEENTH-CENTURY BAPTIST STATESMAN (1811-1891). *Baptist Hist. and Heritage 1975 10(1): 28-35.* James Madison Pendleton was one of the "Great Triumvirate" who evolved the Landmark Movement in the Baptist Church. Not as rabidly doctrinaire as James R. Graves and Amos Cooper Dayton, he accepted the concept of the universal church, never adhered to the theory of Baptist successionism, and was able and willing to work within the framework of Baptist conventions and societies in a way that many Landmarkers were unable to do. His basic contribution to the Landmark movement lay in his refusal to accept non-immersionists (non-Baptists) as gospel ministers. Although born in the South, he favored the gradual emancipation of slaves, a position which finally forced him out of his pastorate in Tennessee during the Civil War. He subsequently moved to Ohio and later to Pennsylvania. He wrote numerous works, two of which have significantly influenced American Baptist practice and thought until recent days: *Church Manual* (1867) and *Christian Doctrines: A Compendium of Theology* (1878). Based largely on writings of Pendleton as well as local church records; 44 notes.
H. M. Parker, Jr.

2999. Cooke, J. W. STONEY POINT, 1866-1969. *Filson Club Hist. Q. 1976 50(4): 337-352.* Stoney Point is an unincorporated black community located in Warren County, Kentucky. Black ownership of the area began in 1848 with the death of a white plantation owner named William White. White freed at least six of his 50 slaves and provided them with part of his farm and the equipment to work the land. The Stoney Point Missionary Baptist Church, organized in 1866, became the focal point of the community. The church not only acted as a center of worship, but it regulated the social life of its members as well. In 1880 the church had about 250 members; the number has been declining ever since. Race relations with nearby whites were generally peaceful because many of the blacks were forced to work for white farmers to supplement their incomes. Covers 1848-1969. Based on government reports and personal interviews; 20 notes. G. B. McKinney

3000. Corbett, Beatrice. SUSAN MOULTON FRASER MC MASTER. *Inland Seas 1975 31(3): 192-200.* Born in Rhode Island in 1819, Susan Moulton married James Fraser, a Bay City, Michigan, lumberman and Indian agent, in 1851. After Fraser's death in 1866 she built a Baptist church in his memory in Bay City. She married the Toronto banker Senator William McMaster in 1871 and continued to be an active Baptist. She convinced her husband to establish McMaster Hall as a theological college. Based on family information. K. J. Bauer

3001. Daniel, W. Harrison. VIRGINIA BAPTISTS AND THE MYTH OF THE SOUTHERN MIND, 1865-1900. *South Atlantic Q. 1974 73(1): 85-98.* Virginia Baptists in the late 19th century strongly supported the racist prejudices prevalent in the nation at the time. Their sentiments relative to the expansionist activities of the United States were in close harmony with the opinions of religious groups in other areas. They echoed the arguments of the opponents of women's rights. Their views were a part of the mainstream of American social and intellectual development rather than a mirror of a distinctive Southern mind. The concept of the Southern mind is a myth. 54 notes. E. P. Stickney

3002. Davis, Dennis R. THE IMPACT OF EVOLUTIONARY THOUGHT ON WALTER RAUSCHENBUSCH. *Foundations 1978 21(3): 254-271.* Discusses the weakness in Richard Hofstadter's *Social Darwinism in American Thought,* which is too simplistic in certain areas. The Social Gospel movement does not fit Hofstadter's pattern and Baptist Walter Rauschenbusch, the social gospel leader, was not acquainted with the evolutionary theories of Herbert Spencer or Charles Darwin. With this as background, the influence of evolutionary thought on Rauschenbusch is traced; 64 notes. E. E. Eminhizer

3003. Deweese, Charles W. PROMINENT CHURCH COVENANTS OF MARITIME BAPTISTS, 1778-1878. *Baptist Hist. and Heritage 1980 15(2): 24-32.* Describes and reprints examples of several model covenants used by Baptists of the Maritime Provinces in the first century after the founding of the first Baptist church in Nova Scotia.

3004. Deweese, Charles W. RELIEF FOR THE BAPTIST INFORMATION CENTER. *Baptist Hist. and Heritage 1974 9(2): 79-81.* Discusses Volume III of the *Encyclopedia of Southern Baptists,* 1971, which covers developments in Southern Baptist life since 1956.

3005. Deweese, Charles W. SELECTED BAPTIST HISTORICAL LITERATURE IN AMERICA, 1964-1974. *Baptist Hist. and Heritage 1974 9(3): 179-184.*

3006. Deweese, Charles W. SOUTHERN BAPTISTS AND CHURCH COVENANTS. *Baptist Hist. and Heritage 1974 9(1): 2-15.* In 1853 J. Newton Brown published his personal revision of the 1833 New Hampshire Covenant which is used by most churches of the Southern Baptist Convention today. S

3007. Dodd, Damon C. FREEWILL BAPTISTS IN GEORGIA. *Viewpoints: Georgia Baptist Hist. 1978 (6): 55-62.* Chronicles Freewill Baptists from 1727 in North Carolina to their expansion into South Carolina, Alabama, and Florida, focusing on the growth of the sect in Georgia, 1776-1977.

3008. Elifson, Kirk W. RELIGIOUS BEHAVIOR AMONG URBAN SOUTHERN BAPTISTS: A CAUSAL INQUIRY. *Sociol. Analysis 1976 37(1): 32-44.* Separate male and female causal models of religious behavior were developed in accordance with relevant literature and were tested using a 1968 sample of 1014 urban Southern Baptists. Incorporated in the models were demographic, contextual, attitudinal and behavioral measures. The latter two measures were developed via factor analysis, and path analysis was used to assess the respective models. Women were found to be more 'predictable' than men, intergenerational transmission of religious values was minimal for both, and the factor analysis revealed that the content of the attitudinal and behavioral dimensions of religiosity varies slightly by sex. J

3009. Ellis, William E. EDGAR YOUNG MULLINS AND THE CRISES OF MODERATE SOUTHERN BAPTIST LEADERSHIP. *Foundations 1976 19(2): 171-185.* Describes Edgar Young Mullins' (1860-1928) life down to his election as President of Southern Seminary, and discusses his leadership as a moderate in the Southern Baptist Convention. Mullins continually modified his position toward a more conservative position. He lost his place of leadership near the end of his life because of the evolution controversy which was prominent in the South. 61 notes. E. E. Eminhizer

3010. Evans, Teddy H. THE BIG HATCHIE BAPTIST ASSOCIATION, 1903-1978. *West Tennessee Hist. Soc. Papers 1979 33: 95-102.* Continued from a previous article. Part II. Describes the Big Hatchie Baptist Association, located in Haywood, Lauderdale, and Tipton counties in West Tennessee. At present the association consists of 32 congregations. In the 20th century the churches gradually abandoned their adherence to Landmarkism and became more closely integrated into the missionary, educational, and benevolent ministries of the Tennessee and Southern Baptist Conventions. H. M. Parker, Jr.

3011. Evans, Teddy H. THE BIG HATCHIE BAPTIST ASSOCIATION: 1828-1978: PART I 1828-1903. *West Tennessee Hist. Soc. Papers 1978 (32): 148-157.* Trenchant account of the first 75 years of the Big Hatchie Baptist Association, in connection with the Southern Baptist Convention. Emphasizes the work of missions and evangelism as well as the strong leadership of several early pastors. The Landmark movement began within the association, under the leadership of Dr. J. R. Graves. Traces divisions within the association which led to the establishment of other associations. To be continued. H. M. Parker, Jr.

3012. Gardner, Robert G. BAPTIST GENERAL BODIES IN USA. *Baptist Hist. and Heritage 1977 12(2): 92-94.* Lists alphabetically the 53 Baptist bodies in the United States. Most entries include the name and headquarters of the body, date of its founding, number of churches and members, date of the statistics and a reference to the source(s) of the statistics. The 53 bodies have a combined membership of nearly 29,000,000 in 103,000 churches. H. M. Parker, Jr.

3013. Gardner, Robert G. *LANDMARK BANNER AND CHEROKEE BAPTIST. Viewpoints: Georgia Baptist Hist. 1974 4: 27-38.* Examines a Baptist church newspaper, the *Landmark Banner and Cherokee Baptist*, and its role (1859-64) in a religious controversy concerning the Cherokee Georgia Baptist Convention. S

3014. Garrett, James Leo, Jr. DOCTRINAL AUTHORITY, 1925-1975: A STUDY IN FOUR REPRESENTATIVE BAPTIST JOURNALS. *Foundations 1979 22(1): 3-12.* Among Baptists, it is axiomatic that the Bible, at least the New Testament, should occupy the primary position among the sources of doctrinal authority. Discusses how Baptists have actually expressed their convictions about the source of such authority. Examines Baptist periodicals of 1925-75; *British Quarterly* (London), *Review and Expositor* (Louisville), *The Chronicle* (Chester, PA) and its successor *Foundations* (Rochester) and *Southwestern Journal of Theology* (Ft. Worth). Surveys how each journal addressed through numerous authors such topics as "The Nature of Authority," "Revelation and Authority," "The Canon and the Relation of the Testaments," "The Inspiration of the Bible," "Biblical Hermeneutics," "Baptist Confessions of Faith" and "Christian Experience." Based on citations from the articles in the respective journals; 47 notes. H. M. Parker, Jr.

3015. Garrett, James Leo, Jr. JOSEPH MARTIN DAWSON: PASTOR, AUTHOR, DENOMINATIONAL LEADER, SOCIAL ACTIVIST. *Baptist Hist. and Heritage 1979 14(4): 7-15.* Joseph Martin Dawson (1879-1973) attended Baylor University in Texas, became a Baptist pastor while still a student, authored 12 books, was a denominational leader for Baptist institutions and boards, and was known as a social activist.

3016. Garrett, James Leo, Jr. SOURCES OF AUTHORITY IN BAPTIST THOUGHT. *Baptist Hist. and Heritage 1978 13(3): 41-49.* A trenchant, descriptive survey of the sources of authority recognized by

Baptists, based on confessions of faith, writings of systematic theologians and popular monographs on Baptist beliefs. Baptists have regarded the scriptures as either the sole or the supreme doctrinal authority under the lordship of Christ or the sovereignty of God. However disagreements as to the nature of divine revelation and the inspiration of the Bible have existed. Covers the 17th-20th centuries. Based on secondary materials; 59 notes. H. M. Parker, Jr.

3017. Gaustad, Edwin S. THE FIRST BLACK BAPTIST. *Baptist Hist. and Heritage 1980 15(1): 55-56, 64.* Speculates as to the personal background and historical context of one "Jack, a colored man," who joined a Newport, Rhode Island, congregation in 1652.

3018. Halbrooks, G. Thomas. FRANCIS WAYLAND AND "THE GREAT REVERSAL." *Foundations 1977 20(3): 196-214.* By 1823 the Baptist Triennial Convention assumed responsibility for home missions and education as well as foreign missions, its original purpose. Francis Wayland and others felt that this joining of efforts caused problems in fund raising. Luther Rice, the agent, was unable to handle the money which complicated the financial problem of the convention's college. Discusses behind-the-scenes activity to divest the convention of education and home mission responsibility. Covers 1823-26. 44 notes. E. E. Eminhizer

3019. Handy, Robert T. AMERICAN BAPTIST POLITY: WHAT'S HAPPENING AND WHY. *Baptist Hist. and Heritage 1979 14(3): 12-21, 51.* Traces developments in the polity of American Baptist churches since the 17th century.

3020. Harris, Waldo P., III. LOCATIONS ASSOCIATED WITH DANIEL MARSHALL AND THE KIOKEE CHURCH. *Viewpoints: Georgia Baptist Hist. 1978 (6): 25-46.* Chronicles the settlement of land belonging to Daniel Marshall on Great Kiokee Creek in Richmond County, Georgia, 1784-1819, and discusses his work establishing the Kiokee Church, an all-black Baptist Church.

3021. Harrop, G. Gerald. THE ERA OF THE "GREAT PREACHER" AMONG CANADIAN BAPTISTS. *Foundations 1980 23(1): 57-70.* Compares Canadian Baptist preachers William Andrew Cameron (1881-1956), John J. MacNeill (1874-1937), and Englishman Thomas Todhunter Shields (1873-1955), as preachers and church leaders. Covers 1910-41. Based on published sermons and other materials; 23 notes. E. E. Eminhizer

3022. Hastey, Stan L. MAJOR ISSUES IN BAPTIST PUBLIC AFFAIRS, 1936-1971. *Baptist Hist. and Heritage 1974 9(4): 194-209.*

3023. Hastings, C. B. A BAPTIST BIBLIOGRAPHY. *Greek Orthodox Theological Rev. 1977 22(4): 363-365.* A bibliography of works published since the 1950's on the Baptists, including history, theology, and interfaith relations.

3024. Hayden, Roger. BRISTOL BAPTIST COLLEGE AND AMERICA. *Baptist Hist. and Heritage 1979 14(4): 26-33.* Brief discussion of the religious career of Edward Terrill (1634-86), the founder of Bristol Baptist College in Bristol, England, and traces the college's history and its influence on Baptist education and mission in America.

3025. Hays, Brooks. THE CAMPUS YEARS. *Arkansas Hist. Q. 1976 35(3): 203-230.* The author attended the University of Arkansas (in Fayetteville) from 1915-19. Recounts student life and values of that period, with emphasis on the important roles of religion (Baptist), debating societies, fraternities, and World War I. Much of the material is comprised of personal reminiscences; 2 illus. T. L. Savitt

3026. Hendricks, Sylvia C. ADJOURNED IN PEACE: A HISTORY OF PINER BAPTIST CHURCH. *Indiana Mag. of Hist. 1976 72(4): 291-314.* Discusses this rural community church on the Forks of Little Buck Creek in southeast Indiana, 1833-1906.

3027. Hinson, E. Glenn. HISTORICAL PATTERNS OF LAY LEADERSHIP IN MINISTRY IN LOCAL BAPTIST CHURCHES. *Baptist Hist. and Heritage 1978 13(1): 26-34.* Baptists have vacillated with changing times and pressures since the 17th century, but increasingly they have taken advantage of improved lay capabilities and training. Proliferation of organization at both local and denominational levels has meant an expansion of roles which do not require a "called" and educated clergy, but can be filled as readily by lay persons. The ability to capitalize on lay training has greatly contributed to Baptist effectiveness in missions, evangelism, and other programs. For the future, the challenge will be the coordination of lay efforts by professional leaders without relapsing, as in the past, into either clerical or lay dominance. Secondary sources and lay training manuals; 36 notes. H. M. Parker, Jr.

3028. Hobbs, Herschel H. THE BAPTIST FAITH AND MESSAGE: ANCHORED BUT FREE. *Baptist Hist. and Heritage 1978 13(3): 33-40.* The Baptists are not a confessional people. From time to time conventions have adopted articles of faith but such statements are intended merely to be guidelines. Basic to Baptist belief is the competency of the individual soul in religion, based on the principle of the priesthood of all believers. Thus the document "The Baptist Faith and Message" which was adopted at the Southern Baptist Convention in 1963 serves only as information to the churches and as a guideline to the various agencies of the Southern Baptist Church. It still leaves the individual Southern Baptist "anchored but free" in his interpretation of the scriptures. Covers 1920-75. Based on official records; 25 notes. H. M. Parker, Jr.

3029. Howe, Claude L. THE CHARISMATIC MOVEMENT IN SOUTHERN BAPTIST LIFE. *Baptist Hist. and Heritage 1978 13(3): 20-27.* Focuses on those who regard the baptism of the Holy Spirit as a second blessing conversion and consider glossolalia as the evidence of this blessing. Concludes that the charismatic movement has had little impact on the Southern Baptist Church. Covers 1955-77. Secondary sources; 47 notes. H. M. Parker, Jr.

3030. Huddlestun, J. R. SILAS MERCER: FOUNDER AND FATHER. *Viewpoints: Georgia Baptist Hist. 1976 5: 65-80.* Biography of Silas Mercer, a Baptist theologian, 1770-96, examining his doctrinal beliefs, work toward the foundation of new churches, and politics during the American Revolution.

3031. Hudson, Winthrop S. THE INTERRELATIONSHIPS OF BAPTISTS IN CANADA AND THE UNITED STATES. *Foundations 1980 23(1): 22-41.* Emphasizes institutional ties and covers 1760-1970's. Based on the *Canadian Baptist;* 31 notes. E. E. Eminhizer

3032. Isaac, Rhys. EVANGELICAL REVOLT: THE NATURE OF THE BAPTISTS' CHALLENGE TO THE TRADITIONAL ORDER IN VIRGINIA, 1765 TO 1775. *William and Mary Q. 1974 31(3): 345-368.* Describes the rise of the Baptist Church in Virginia, with emphasis on evangelicalism and social life. Contrasts the austerity of the Baptists with the Anglican establishment. Baptist church discipline, mistaken by the gentry for radicalism, served to ameliorate disorder. Comments on the struggle for religious toleration and poses questions about the relation of religion to popular culture. Based chiefly on church records and contemporary journals; 60 notes. H. M. Ward

3033. Johnston, Edwin D. P. HARRIS ANDERSON, ASSISTANT TO PRESIDENT RUFUS C. HARRIS FOR DENOMINATIONAL RELATIONS (1965-1976). *Viewpoints: Georgia Baptist Hist. 1978 6: 11-18.* Chronicles P. Harris Anderson's service in the Baptist Church in Georgia, 1965-76, when he was an assistant to Rufus C. Harris, Mercer University's president (who was in charge of denominational relations), a professor in the Christianity department, and a liaison between various churches throughout the state.

3034. Jones, Loyal. OLD-TIME BAPTISTS AND MAINLINE CHRISTIANITY. *Appalachian J. 1977 4(4): 120-130.* Similarities and distinctions between the fundamentalism and practices of Appalachia's Baptist sects reflect an earlier age in American religious beliefs, and are combined with criticisms of mountain religion and several extended quotes conveying local attitudes toward religion.

3035. Jones, Walter L. GROWING UP IN THE FLATWOODS: JACK SMITH'S MEMORIES OF THE 1860S. *J. of Mississippi Hist. 1980 42(2): 145-151.* Andrew Jackson Smith was born in 1858 in Pon-

totoc County, Mississippi. Smith's account preserves memories of his father's return from the Civil War in 1864 as well as military skirmishes near his home. He describes the family's home and rural life, educational pursuits, and activities of the Shady Grove Baptist Church. Smith's observations of medical practices, death, and activities around the Southern country store preserve an interesting picture of life in the Mississippi flatwoods. Based on a typewritten account of his life that Andrew Jackson Smith sent his daughter, Lida, on his 77th birthday in 1935.
M. S. Legan

3036. Lee, Jerry J. SEPARATION AND CRYSTALLIZATION OF NORTHWEST GEORGIA PRIMITIVE BAPTISTS. *Viewpoints: Georgia Baptist Hist. 1974 4: 39-53.*

3037. Lentz, Lula Gillespie. ILLINOIS COMMENTARY: THE REMINISCENCES OF LULA GILLESPIE LENTZ. *J. of the Illinois State Hist. Soc. 1975 68(3): 267-288, (4): 353-367.* Part I. The author describes life on an Illinois farm in the late 19th century and mentions the farm homestead and furnishings, work routine and daily chores, food preparation, home manufacture of clothing, and sports and games, especially hunting. Discusses the family's practice of its Baptist faith and provides a first-hand account of rural education. Part II. The author describes her experiences of farm life and later town residency, rural education, marriage, and early married life with Eli G. Lentz, a school superintendent and later professor at Southern Illinois Normal University. Covers 1890 to 1929. N. Lederer

3038. Leonard, Bill J. A HISTORY OF THE BAPTIST LAYMEN'S MOVEMENT. *Baptist Hist. and Heritage 1978 13(1): 35-44.* Discusses the early stages of the laymen's movement of the Southern Baptists. Views later developments as they illustrate continuing emphases or changes in the original goals, while focusing on significant trends, ideologies, and church-wide efforts. What began as a mission-centered body had become, in 40 years, a multipurpose agency of an increasingly centralized denomination. The men's movement identified itself so closely with the Southern Baptist Convention that its leaders could insist that a local church must have a Brotherhood if it was to consider itself a fully cooperating congregation within the denomination. Covers ca. 1906-75. Secondary sources; 49 notes. H. M. Parker, Jr.

3039. Leonard, Bill J. THE SOUTHERN BAPTIST DENOMINATIONAL LEADER AS THEOLOGIAN. *Baptist Hist. and Heritage 1980 15(3): 23-32, 61, 63.* Traces the rise in denominationalism in the Southern Baptist Church, and the place of denominational leaders as theologians, focusing on James Bruton Gambrell (1841-1921), A. J. Barton (1867-1942), and J. B. Lawrence, and discusses the challenges of denominationalism and unity for Southern Baptists in the 1970's and 1980's.

3040. Levesque, George A. INHERENT REFORMERS—INHERITED ORTHODOXY: BLACK BAPTISTS IN BOSTON, 1800-1873. *J. of Negro Hist. 1975 60(4): 491-519.* Describes the early development of the black Baptist movement in Boston in the 1800's, including the foundation of a separate church in 1805 under the leadership of Thomas Paul and Scipio Dalton. Overt discrimination was not the principal motive for starting a new church, inasmuch as the parent churches financed and assisted the African offshoot. The black movement grew from a religious revival and an expansion of the black community, forced increasingly to live and work in one particular area. Considers how the new church was drawn into politics and the movement for social reform. 3 tables, 36 notes. C. A. McNeill

3041. Lindsey, Jonathan A. BASIL MANLY: NINETEENTH CENTURY PROTEAN MAN. *Baptist Hist. and Heritage 1973 8(3): 130-143.* Sketches a Southern Baptist preacher and educator, 1798-1868.
S

3042. Manis, Andrew M. SILENCE OR SHOCKWAVES: SOUTHERN BAPTIST RESPONSES TO THE ASSASSINATION OF MARTIN LUTHER KING, JR. *Baptist Hist. and Heritage 1980 15(4): 19-27, 35.* Describes the immediate response of Baptist agencies, leaders, and laity to the assassination of black civil rights leader Martin Luther King, Jr. (1929-68), and the official response by the Southern Baptist Convention in its 1968 National Crisis Statement, and analyzes the controversy among Southern Baptists over King's work.

3043. McBeth, Leon. BAPTIST FUNDAMENTALISM: A CULTURAL INTERPRETATION. *Baptist Hist. and Heritage 1978 13(3): 12-19.* The organized fundamentalist movement of the 1920's was not able to capture the Southern Baptist Convention. Southern Baptists are conservative, Bible-believing people. While sharing many of the same doctrinal beliefs of Fundamentalism, they generally do not share the movement's spirit and temperment. Examines the extent of Baptist involvement in Fundamentalism, reviews several familiar interpretations of Fundamentalism, and concludes that one way to understand it is through a culture-conflict interpretation. Secondary sources; 19 notes.
H. M. Parker, Jr.

3044. McClellan, Albert. THE SHAPING OF THE SOUTHERN BAPTIST MIND. *Baptist Hist. and Heritage 1978 13(3): 2-11.* Contemporary Baptists are no longer a homogeneous people. The Baptist mind may not be as simple and closed as it once was, and it has doctrinal, organizational, and cultural dimensions. Yet there is still a fairly well-defined core of theological understanding common to most Southern Baptists, plus an organizational mind that is probably sanctioned as much by society as by doctrine. The cultural dimensions of Southern Baptist values are harder to perceive and define. Traces significant historical developments since 1700, controversies, and personalities which have helped to mold the Baptist mind. Secondary sources; 8 notes.
H. M. Parker, Jr.

3045. McGinty, Garnie W. MARY JANE CONLY LESHE: PIONEER WOMAN OF BIENVILLE PARISH (1849-1932). *North Louisiana Hist. Assoc. J. 1976 7(2): 61-63.* Mary Jane Conly was the third child of Cullen Thomas Conly, of Savannah, Georgia. When she was about 20 she married Usir Leshe (1839-1934) and moved with him to Bienville Parish. She bore 14 children; one died in infancy, 13 reached adulthood. "The Leshe family were fervent patriots" and Mary Jane Leshe promoted "education and patriotism, instilling frugality, thrift, and industry in her descendants." She was a "deeply religious woman" and "a loyal and devoted member of the Baptist Church." Photo, 4 notes.
A. N. Garland

3046. McKnight, Roger THE JOURNAL OF F. O. NILSSON: AN EARLY MINNESOTA CIRCUIT RIDER. Hasselmo, Nils, ed. *Perspectives on Swedish Immigration* (Chicago: Swedish Pioneer Hist. Soc. and Duluth: U. of Minnesota, 1978): 291-310. Reviews the contents of the journal kept from 1855 to 1865 by Swedish circuit-riding Baptist minister Frederik Olaus Nilsson, a former sailor who led congregations in Sweden and Denmark before emigrating to the United States and reaching Minnesota in 1855. The journal describes the rigors of rural life and circuit-riding and contains many passages describing the stubborn and conservative Nilsson's differences with his scattered flocks. Parts of the journal are kept in English, but most of it is in Swedish, albeit increasingly infiltrated by English terminology. Two doggerel poems are found in the journal. One complains of the difficulty of conducting a ministry of God in a world of deceit and misery, while the other expresses the familiar ambivalent sentiments of an immigrant toward his adopted and his native land. 26 notes. S

3047. Miller, Terry E. OTTER CREEK CHURCH OF INDIANA: LONELY BASTION OF DANIEL PARKER'S "TWO-SEEDISM." *Foundations 1975 18(4): 358-376.* The "two-seed" antimission Baptist movement was started by Daniel Parker by 1820. The Otter Creek Church is one of a half-dozen left of this persuasion. Details the building, its membership, and worship forms. Reprints the articles of faith of the group. 22 notes. E. E. Eminhizer

3048. Mitchell, J. Marcus. THE PAUL FAMILY. *Old-Time New England 1973 63(3): 73-77.* Tells of Thomas Paul, a black Baptist minister who organized the first black church in Boston, his brothers, Nathaniel and Shadrach, who were also ministers, and other members of the Paul family, 1773-1973. Illus. R. N. Lokken

3049. Moody, Dale. THE SHAPING OF SOUTHERN BAPTIST POLITY. *Baptist Hist. and Heritage 1979 14(3): 2-11.* Discusses how the congregation, association, and convention in the Southern Baptist Church have shaped its political organization through Campbellism, Landmarkism, dispensationalism, fundamentalism, and conservatism since the 16th century.

3050. Moore, John Hammond. THEOPHILUS HARRIS'S THOUGHTS ON EMIGRATING TO AMERICA IN 1793. *William and Mary Q. 1979 36(4): 602-614.* Although economic reasons were chief in the mind of Harris, a 24-year-old Welshman, as he contemplated emigration to the United States, his tract stresses political and social conditions in England. The significance of the tract is that Harris gives expression to "old Whig" ideas and also a synthesis of those principles with the new radicalism of his time. Harris and his wife settled in Alexandria, and later in Philadelphia. He also became a Baptist minister. Harris particularly denounces the condition of civil rights, the justice of the courts, moral depravity, the aristocracy, and the long arm of royal authority in England. Reproduction, 8 notes. H. M. Ward

3051. Moore, LeRoy. CRAZY QUILT: SOUTHERN BAPTIST PATTERNS OF THE CHURCH. *Foundations 1977 20(1): 12-35.* The Baptist view of the church has never been uniform. Traces the development of three historic positions: Connectional, which began with the Philadelphia Association in 1704; Localist, which evolved from the 18th-century awakenings; and Individualist, which came from Isaac Backus and the Separate Baptists of New England. These major themes have been changed by centralization following 1845 and the beginning of the Southern Baptist Convention and Landmarkism in the early part of the 20th century. Points out the conflict between these historic positions and the statement of faith and message. Although Southern Baptists hold that they keep power at the local level, they have one of the most authoritarian religious structures in America. 105 notes. E. E. Eminhizer

3052. Newcomb, Horace. BEING SOUTHERN BAPTIST ON THE NORTHERN FRINGE. *Southern Exposure 1976 4(3): 66-72.* The author reminisces about what his membership in the Southern Baptists meant to his childhood, social development, and education, 1940's-70's.

3053. Newsome, Jerry. "PRIMITIVE BAPTISTS": A STUDY IN NAME FORMATION OR WHAT'S IN A WORD. *Viewpoints 1978 6: 63-70.* Discusses the origin of the Primitive Baptists in Georgia, 1835-87.

3054. Norton, John, transl. and ed. ANDERS WIBERG'S ACCOUNT OF A TRIP TO THE UNITED STATES IN 1852-1853. *Swedish Pioneer Hist. Q. 1978 29(2): 89-116, (3): 162-179.* Part I. When he left for the United States, 16 July 1852, Anders Wiberg had been a Swedish Lutheran pastor of pietist leanings. On the ship Wiberg broke completely with the state church of Sweden. He was baptized in Copenhagen by the banished Swedish seaman-lay preacher F. O. Nilsson, father of the Swedish Baptist movement. From New York Wiberg journeyed to the western frontier as a colporteur in the service of the American Baptist Publication Society. His letters home were serialized in the liberal Stockholm newspaper, *Aftonbladet,* and must have profoundly influenced prospective emigrants. They also helped fuel the debate on religious freedom. He remained in America for two years and then returned in 1863 for three more years. The original of the Wiberg manuscript diary is in the archives of Bethelseminariet in Stockholm. 19 notes. Part II. Wiberg describes the conditions of Swedish immigrants in Illinois and their problems in getting there. His return to New York was via St. Louis and the Ohio River to Columbus, Ohio. He comments about Swedes he had met, the country, and other people. He especially was taken with Niagara Falls. 9 notes. C. W. Ohrvall

3055. O'Brien, John T. FACTORY, CHURCH, AND COMMUNITY: BLACKS IN ANTEBELLUM RICHMOND. *J. of Southern Hist. 1978 44(4): 509-536.* Recent studies have shed much light upon the culture of plantation slaves. Yet neglect of urban slaves has left historians with no way to explain such phenomena as the blacks of Richmond successfully organizing and petitioning President Johnson in mid-1865 to ease the US military's control on their lives. Studying and analyzing the social skills which developed from slave labor in the tobacco factories and the well-organized black Protestant churches (especially Baptist churches) permit us to understand the surfacing of these work habits, and the revelation of firm family and community structures in the months after the Civil War. Manuscripts and printed primary and secondary sources; 99 notes. T. D. Schoonover

3056. Patterson, W. Morgan. BAPTIST GROWTH IN AMERICA: EVALUATION OF TRENDS. *Baptist Hist. and Heritage 1979 14(1): 16-26.* Attributes the growth of Southern Baptists since the 18th century, apart from sociological, demographic, and cultural influences, to religious factors: 1) heritage of the revival emphasis, 2) denominational pride growing out of Landmark exclusiveness, 3) development of efficient and adaptable denominational organizations, 4) sense of denominational loyalty, 5) massive program of tuition-free theological education, 6) dispersion of Southern Baptists across the United States, and 7) a gift for organizing and promoting programs and methods to share the gospel in a more effective way. Statistical materials and secondary sources; 3 tables, 36 notes. H. M. Parker, Jr.

3057. Patterson, W. Morgan. THE INFLUENCE OF LANDMARKISM AMONG BAPTISTS. *Baptist Hist. and Heritage 1975 10(1): 44-55.* Identifies specific historical situations in which the Landmark movement influences the Baptist church. The greatest influence was and is among Baptists of the Old Southwest, largely due to the 50 year editorial ministry of James Robinson Graves in Nashville and Memphis. Seaboard Baptists were more settled, and thus less susceptible to the controversies which raged along the frontier and the newly settled lands. Landmarkism was responsible for the idea that the local church, not boards, should be responsible for the conduct and administration of missionary activity, which spawned the gospel missions concept. The Landmark theory of Baptist succession was challenged at the end of the last century, creating the Whitsitt Controversy. Landmarkism has peaked, but its final effects remain to be seen. Based largely on unpublished dissertations and secondary sources; 27 notes.
H. M. Parker, Jr.

3058. Patterson, W. Morgan. THE SOUTHERN BAPTIST THEOLOGIAN AS CONTROVERSIALIST: A CONTRAST. *Baptist Hist. and Heritage 1980 15(3): 7-14.* Compares and contrasts the attitudes and outlooks of Southern Baptist James Robinson Graves (1820-93), founder of the Landmark movement, and Edgar Young Mullins (1860-1928), who was involved in the Fundamentalist-Modernist controversy of the 1920's; and discusses the contributions of both men to the theology of Southern Baptists.

3059. Patton, Richard D. BAPTISTS AND REGENERATE MEMBERSHIP: HISTORICAL PERSPECTIVE AND PRESENT PRACTICE. *Baptist Hist. and Heritage 1978 13(3): 28-32.* Historically, Baptists have insisted on a regenerate, "believer's" membership. Events in recent years among Southern Baptists indicate a laxity in maintaining such a membership. One development is the large nonresident membership which is emerging. Another is an increasing practice of baptizing preschoolers, which is very close to "baby" baptism—a practice which the author decries. Secondary sources; 17 notes.
H. M. Parker, Jr.

3060. Perkin, James R. C. MANY CONFESSIONS, ONE CREED. *Foundations 1980 23(1): 71-83.* Traces the history of Baptists in the Annapolis Valley of Nova Scotia, a model indicating the conditions responsible for many confessions among Baptists. Covers 1760-1980. Based on printed Baptist histories; 21 notes. E. E. Eminhizer

3061. Pousett, Gordon H. FORMATIVE INFLUENCES ON BAPTISTS IN BRITISH COLUMBIA, 1876-1918. *Baptist Hist. and Heritage 1980 15(2): 14-23.* Describes the early American influence on the British Columbia Baptist heritage, the activities of the B.C. Baptist Church Extension Society in the 1890's, geography, economics, immigration, and the impact of World War I.

3062. Priestley, David T. DOCTRINAL STATEMENTS OF GERMAN BAPTISTS IN NORTH AMERICA. *Foundations 1979 22(1): 51-71.* Traces the development of doctrinal statements of German Baptists in Germany and among German Americans. Comments on creedal statements, emphasizing Walter Rauschenbusch. His work among Germans at Rochester Seminary resulted in a definitely Baptist understanding of scripture, rather than a less denominational, generally pietistic and separatist view which had characterized German Baptists in America, 1800's-50's. German Baptists today are organized in the North American Baptist General Conference, with a seminary at Sioux Falls, South Dakota. Based on texts of confessions cited and other studies on Baptist creedal statements; 63 notes. H. M. Parker, Jr.

3063. Proctor, Emerson. BAPTIST CONFESSIONS OF FAITH AND GEORGIA PRIMITIVE BAPTISTS. *Viewpoints: Georgia Baptist Hist. 1976 5: 81-90.* Examines the history of the Baptist Church through confessions of faith, touching on the beginnings of the religion in Great Britain, 1633-80, and the various sects within the United States, including Regular, Orthodox, Separate, Particular, Missionary, and Primitive Baptists, and a small section on the Georgia Primitive Baptists, 1690-1900.

3064. Renault, James Owen. THE CHANGING PATTERNS OF SEPARATE BAPTIST RELIGIOUS LIFE, 1803-1977. *Baptist Hist. and Heritage 1979 14(4): 16-25, 36.* The Separate Baptists began under Shubal Stearns, Daniel Marshall, and Samuel Harris, 1755-80, in New England; they supported evangelism, revivalism, and lay exhorters. Discusses, in particular, the Separate Baptists associated with the General Association of Separate Baptists in Christ, in Kentucky, 1803-1977.

3065. Riest, Irwin W. WILLIAM NEWTON CLARKE: NINETEENTH-CENTURY EVOLUTIONARY AND ESCHATOLOGICAL IMMANENTISM. *Foundations 1975 18(1): 5-25.* Theologians began to interpret Christian faith for the modern mind during 1865-1915. One of those attempting to do this was William Newton Clarke (1841-1912). His important book, *An Outline of Christian Theology* (1894), systematized evangelical liberal theology, stressed God's immanence, discussed history as God's presence in the creation of an evolutionary pattern, and described revelation as an ongoing process between God and man. Discusses the Baptist minister's concept of God's immanence in connection with the creation of man, revelation, and evil. Includes a bibliography of Clarke's books, essays, articles, pamphlets, book reviews and sermons; 87 notes. E. E. Eminhizer

3066. Routh, Porter. THE ROLE OF THE EXECUTIVE COMMITTEE OF THE SOUTHERN BAPTIST CHURCH. *Baptist Hist. and Heritage 1976 11(4): 194-203.* The Executive Committee of the Southern Baptist Church was formed in 1917 and strengthened in 1927. In 1976 a Committee of Seven, having completed a two-year study of the Executive Committee, returned an "Affirmative Appraisal" of the Committee's work to the Convention. Describes the role of the Executive Committee in the Southern Baptist Convention under the following topics: housekeeping, fiscal (with considerable detail), mediation, program statements, press relations, and general duties. Based on the *Annual* of the Southern Baptist Convention; 29 notes. H. M. Parker, Jr.

3067. Russell, C. Allyn. THOMAS TODHUNTER SHIELDS, CANADIAN FUNDAMENTALIST. *Ontario Hist. [Canada] 1978 70(4): 263-280.* Shields's influence came from his prominence as an evangelical Protestant leader, writer, and speaker. He was born in England in 1873, came to Canada in 1888, and began his ministry in 1891. He was appointed to the Jarvis Street Baptist Church, Toronto, in 1910, and remained there until his death in 1955. The major events of his career, the sources and extent of his influence as a Fundamentalist, and significant controversies are described. Some of the basic points of his theology are also given. Mainly contemporary newspapers, or secondary sources, with some bibliographic notes; 4 photos, 59 notes. W. B. Whitham

3068. Russell, C. Allyn. WILLIAM BELL RILEY, ARCHITECT OF FUNDAMENTALISM. *Foundations 1975 18(1): 26-52.* William Bell Riley (1861-1947), recognized as a significant leader in the development of American religion, was involved in the Fundamentalist-Modernist controversy. Under his leadership the membership of the First Baptist Church, Minneapolis, increased from 585 to 3,500 members, and three church schools were founded to provide orthodox training and leadership. Coming out of the revivalistic tradition of Kentucky, Riley influenced Billy Graham, to whom he turned over his schools in 1957. In the 1920's Riley was involved in the anti-evolution movement and became a leader in the World Christian Fundamental Association which retained William Jennings Bryan in the Scopes Case of 1925. Riley's lasting contribution has been in his influence on Graham, the World Christian Fundamental Association, and the conservative nature of Minnesota Baptists. 62 notes. E. E. Eminhizer

3069. Russell, Francis H. A COBBLER AT HIS BENCH: JOHN RUSSELL OF WOBURN, MASSACHUSETTS. *New England Hist. and Geneal. Register 1979 133(Apr): 125-133.* Discusses the Baptist movement in the Massachusetts Bay Colony. The title merely indicates that many of the leaders were men of modest education in contrast to the specially trained Puritan theologians. Breaking out of the Puritan mold in the 17th century required fortitude and sacrifice. Opposition to infant baptism as a means to strike for freedom of individual belief, laid the groundwork for the eventual separation of church and state. 39 notes. J

3070. Short, Ron. THE OLD REGULAR BAPTIST CHURCH. *Southern Exposure 1976 4(3): 60-65.* The Old Regular Baptist Church exists primarily in Appalachia; discusses Appalachian community life 19th-20th centuries.

3071. Shurden, Walter B. THE ASSOCIATIONAL PRINCIPLE, 1707-1814: ITS RATIONALE. *Foundations 1978 21(3): 211-224.* The justification use by Baptists during 1707-1814 for having association is presented. The principle arguments in this period are discussed under three headings: Biblical rationale, theological rationale, and practical rationale. In each case objection to the use of these as justification for Baptist associations is also discussed; 65 notes. E. E. Eminhizer

3072. Shurden, Walter B. BAPTIST ASSOCIATIONS: THE ANNUAL MEETINGS PRIOR TO 1814. *Baptist Hist. and Heritage 1975 10(4): 233-237.* Illustrates the historic value of the Baptist Association ca. 1775-1814. Discusses the organization, worship, correspondence, and queries which were handled in the annual meetings. Based on citations from Association records; 25 notes. H. M. Parker, Jr.

3073. Shurden, Walter B. CHURCH AND ASSOCIATION: A SEARCH FOR BOUNDARIES. *Baptist Hist. and Heritage 1979 14(3): 32-40, 61.* The clash between local Southern Baptist churches and nationwide Southern Baptist associations over autonomy has become a major issue during the 1970's.

3074. Shurden, Walter B. DOCUMENTS ON THE MINISTRY IN SOUTHERN BAPTIST HISTORY. *Baptist Hist. and Heritage 1980 15(1): 45-54, 64.* Reprints and discusses associational circular letters dating from 1800 to 1850 which describe the "call" to the ministry, ordination, preaching, ministerial support, and ministerial education.

3075. Shurden, Walter B. THE PASTOR AS DENOMINATIONAL THEOLOGIAN IN SOUTHERN BAPTIST HISTORY. *Baptist Hist. and Heritage 1980 15(3): 15-22.* Discusses the changing role of Southern Baptist pastors as denominational theologians in three distinct periods: ca. 1700-1859, when "pastors were the primary denominational theologians"; 1859-1960, characterized by the founding of the Southern Baptist Theological Seminary and the professors' preeminence in denominationalism; and 1960-80, characterized by the pastors' resurgence.

3076. Smith, Harold S. THE LIFE AND WORKS OF J. R. GRAVES (1820-1893). *Baptist Hist. and Heritage 1975 10(1): 19-27.* Whereas James Robinson Graves is best known for siring Baptist Landmarkism, the article emphasizes 50 years in which Graves was associated as editor with the *Tennessee Baptist*, a weekly religious paper. The many articles Graves wrote are evidence of an influential pen. Graves was also insistent on an educated Baptist ministry, and was largely instrumental in founding the Southern Baptist Seminary in Greenville, South Carolina, in 1859. Based largely on the *Tennessee Baptist*, with a few references to Graves' works; 48 notes. H. M. Parker, Jr.

3077. Smith, Julia Floyd. MARCHING TO ZION: THE RELIGION OF BLACK BAPTISTS IN COASTAL GEORGIA PRIOR TO 1865. *Viewpoints: Georgia Baptist Hist. 1978 (6): 47-54.* Discusses black Baptist Churches in Georgia, 1750's-1830's.

3078. Sobel, Mechal. "THEY CAN NEVER BOTH PROSPER TOGETHER": BLACK AND WHITE BAPTISTS IN NASHVILLE, TENNESSEE. *Tennessee Hist. Q. 1979 38(3): 296-307.* The First Baptist Church of Nashville, Tennessee, initially welcomed black membership in the 1820's, although blacks' duties and privileges were circumscribed. By 1834, both whites and blacks began to move for greater black autonomy. This led to a separate black meeting in 1841, a black minister—Nelson Merry (1824-84)—and mission in 1853, and finally a separate church in 1865. Based on the Manuscript Minutes of the Southern Baptist Historical Commission, Nashville; 44 notes. W. D. Piersen

3079. Steely, John E. MINISTERIAL CERTIFICATION IN SOUTHERN BAPTIST HISTORY: ORDINATION. *Baptist Hist. and Heritage 1980 15(1): 23-29, 61.* Discusses the lack of change and absence of any standard interpretation in the practice of ordination, from 1677 through 1980, and suggests that the question of female ordination may cause this situation to change.

3080. Sullivan, James L. BAPTIST LAYMEN AS DENOMINATIONAL LEADERS: A HISTORICAL PERSPECTIVE. *Baptist Hist. and Heritage 1978 13(1): 4-16.* The 20th-century laity have served the Southern Baptists through numerous activities—Sunday School, church music, church training, and executive and administrative positions. There is still the danger of pastors dominating the functional aspects of church life. Urges greater lay participation. Secondary sources; 29 notes. H. M. Parker, Jr.

3081. Sullivan, James L. POLITY DEVELOPMENTS IN THE SOUTHERN BAPTIST CONVENTION (1900-1977). *Baptist Hist. and Heritage 1979 14(3): 22-31.*

3082. Sumners, Bill. SOUTHERN BAPTISTS AND WOMEN'S RIGHT TO VOTE, 1910-1920. *Baptist Hist. and Heritage 1977 12(1): 45-51.* Southern Baptists shared differing attitudes on the debate over woman suffrage. The opponents in the church believed equality at the polls would somehow mar the image of the Southern lady. They further questioned the positive effects women might have on government and politics. Others quietly applauded the addition of women to the electorate, foreseeing women playing an integral role in instituting and maintaining prohibition. The Women's Christian Temperance Union and the Anti-Saloon League, both of which contained many Baptists, endorsed woman suffrage. Based largely on Baptists periodicals of the decade; 40 notes. H. M. Parker, Jr.

3083. Sutton, Brett. IN THE GOOD OLD WAY: PRIMITIVE BAPTIST TRADITIONS. *Southern Exposure 1977 5(2-3): 97-104.* Folk revivalists have neglected the rich folk tradition of the Primitive Baptist Church of Appalachia. Church belief centers on predestination and is characterized by a stern, austere attitude toward the outside world. Primitive Baptists have a simple, honest concern with the trials and tribulations of the world, including a realistic approach to death. They do not believe in converting others to their faith and they reject the concept of church growth and expansion. The church relies on oral testimony and lay preaching. Church music is based on 18th- and early 19th-century hymns collected during the church's founding. Although there have been efforts to incorporate newer music into the church, this move has been resisted by many members. Based on participant observation in southwest Virginia. N. Lederer

3084. Thompson, James J., Jr. A FREE-AND-EASY DEMOCRACY: SOUTHERN BAPTISTS AND DENOMINATIONAL STRUCTURE IN THE 1920'S. *Foundations 1979 22(1): 43-50.* Describes problems when the gospel's message becomes lodged in a hierarchical, bureaucratic denomination. This happened to the Southern Baptists in the 1920's, when the Southern Baptist Convention began establishing boards and other denomination-controlled agencies to carry on the work of the church for greater efficiency. The opposition to the growing ecclesiasticism was led by Reverend J. Frank Norris, pastor of the First Baptist Church, Ft. Worth. He emphasized the congregation's role and Baptist democracy, and even insisted that all church employees be elected by popular vote among local church members, in the Baptist tradition of "free-and-easy democracy." The 1930's saw the issue cooling down, but there are still some Baptists who see the essential issue remaining: What is the proper relationship between the individual believer and the local church to an efficient, centralized, denominational apparatus. Based on the J. Frank Norris and William J. McGlothlin papers in the Dargan-Carver Library, Nashville, and the George W. Truett and Lee R. Scarborough papers at the Southwestern Baptist Seminary, Ft. Worth; 17 notes. H. M. Parker, Jr.

3085. Thompson, James J., Jr. SOUTHERN BAPTIST CITY AND COUNTRY CHURCHES IN THE TWENTIES. *Foundations 1974 17(4): 351-363.* In the 1920's Southern Baptists tried to combat the decline in rural church membership and the evils of urbanization in the South with evangelicalism.

3086. Tiller, Carl W. HOW USEFUL ARE OUR RECENT STATISTICAL DATA? *Foundations 1978 21(1): 16-21.* Discusses the problems of Baptist statistics and reveals the methods used by Baptist groups to generate statistical data indicating the shortcomings. It concludes that although inaccurate, the data is not off enough to render it unusable. 8 notes. E. E. Eminhizer

3087. Tonks, A. Ronald. HIGHLIGHTS OF THE RELATIONSHIPS OF SOUTHERN BAPTISTS WITH CANADIAN BAPTISTS. *Baptist Hist. and Heritage 1980 15(2): 5-13.* Discusses the records of some individual Southern Baptists in Canada since the 19th century and the sometimes strained relations between the Southern Baptist Convention and official Canadian Baptist organizations since the 1950's.

3088. Tonks, A. Ronald. THE ORIGIN AND GROWTH OF SOUTHERN BAPTIST WORK IN THE NORTHWEST. *Baptist Hist. and Heritage 1977 12(1): 58-64.* Traces the development of Baptist churches in the Northwest from 1844 to the present. The Northwest Convention of the Southern Baptist Convention has congregations in four American states and four Canadian provinces—the only international "state" convention in the Southern Baptist Convention. Based largely on annual convention records and secondary sources; 51 notes. H. M. Parker, Jr.

3089. Tull, James E. THE LANDMARK MOVEMENT: AN HISTORICAL AND THEOLOGICAL APPRAISAL. *Baptist Hist. and Heritage 1975 10(1): 3-18.* A balanced presentation of the Landmark movement among American Baptists. The central idea of Landmarkism is the authority of the local congregation in Baptist ecclesiology. Landmarkism is viewed as a doctrinal aberration from the English and early American Baptist theology and polity. Traces the movement from its 1851 beginning in Cotton Grove, Tennessee to its present flickering embers. In its extremity Landmarkism was sectarian in its emphasis on the role of the local church, its denial of the validity of "alien" immersion, an adherence to strict, local church communion, and a hostile response to the ecumenical movement—all of which are quite foreign to the ecclesiological traditions which had been developed by English and American Baptists in the 17th and 18th centuries. Based largely on religious newspapers and works written by James R. Graves; 31 notes. H. M. Parker, Jr.

3090. Valentine, Foy. BAPTIST POLITY AND SOCIAL PRONOUNCEMENTS. *Baptist Hist. and Heritage 1979 14(3): 52-61.* Discusses the organization of the Southern Baptist Church and how polity and social pronouncements have been related since the mid-19th century.

3091. Walaskay, Paul William. THE ENTERTAINMENT OF ANGELS: AMERICAN BAPTISTS AND AMERICANIZATION, 1890-1925. *Foundations 1976 19(4): 346-360.* Describes the efforts made by the American Baptists to assimilate and assist immigrants coming to America, 1890-1925. Describes the approaches used to reach those who did not have a Baptist group speaking their language. 51 notes. E. E. Eminhizer

3092. Walker, Arthur L., Jr. THE MAJOR. *Baptist Hist. and Heritage 1974 9(1): 40-47, 54.* Biographical sketch of Harwell G. Davis, president of Howard College and a prominent Alabama Baptist, 1882-1973. S

3093. Williams, Catherine. "I'LL SING YOU A LITTLE SONG." *Am. West 1975 12(6): 18-19, 57.* Reverend Joab Powell (1800-73) and his little colony of Baptists moved from Missouri in 1852 to the Willamette Valley in Oregon. Despite his absurd physical appearance and illiteracy, the itinerant Powell was a powerful and vivid preacher who had "a magnetism and a sympathetic understanding of human beings which drew them to him in spite of his peculiarities." His converts numbered some 3000. He remained very active until shortly before his death. Illus. D. L. Smith

3094. Williams, Michael Patrick. THE BLACK EVANGELICAL MINISTRY IN THE ANTEBELLUM BORDER STATES: PROFILES OF ELDERS JOHN BERRY MEACHUM AND NOAH DAVIS. *Foundations 1978 21(3): 225-241.* Focuses on the problems faced by the black clergy who were accused of accommodationism. Their vilification by their contemporaries was unjust. Studies two Baptist ministers placed in this class, John Berry Meachum of St. Louis (1789-1854) and Noah Davis of Baltimore (1804-66). 48 notes. E. E. Eminhizer

3095. Wilson, Spencer, ed. MONTANA MEMORIES: A MEMOIR BY REV. JAMES HOVEY SPENCER, D. D. *Montana 1979 29(1): 16-29.* James Hovey Spencer (1860-1940) was a Baptist minister in Montana during 1888-97. He completed his memoirs in 1930 and the edited portion dealing with Montana constitutes this article. During his residence in Montana, Spencer served churches at Livingston, Bozeman, Twin Bridges, Dillon, Glendale, Boulder, Basin, Butte, and Anaconda. In his memoirs, Spencer describes early means of transportation, boisterous life in mining communities, frontier hospitality, and his marriage to Cora Wishon. Covers 1888-97. Based on James Hovey Spencer's memoir in his family's possession; 10 illus., 5 notes. R. C. Meyers

3096. Yeager, Lyn Allison. DAVID BADGLEY, PIONEER MINISTER IN THE ILLINOIS TERRITORY. *Foundations 1977 20(3): 263-278.* Virginia Baptists under David Badgley (5 November 1749-16 December 1824) moved to southwest Illinois. Focuses on Badgley's life in connection with the Baptist Church he pastored in New Design, Illinois. Discusses all the major problems facing a pioneer. 71 notes.
E. E. Eminhizer

3097. Yearwood, Lennox. FIRST SHILOH BAPTIST CHURCH OF BUFFALO, NEW YORK: FROM A STOREFRONT TO MAJOR RELIGIOUS INSTITUTION. *Afro-Americans in New York Life and Hist. 1977 1(1): 81-98.* Traces the Shiloh Baptist Church's growth in political and social power within the black community in Buffalo during the 1920's and 1930's.

3098. Zinsmeister, Robert, Jr. THE PIGEON CREEK BAPTIST CHURCH. *Lincoln Herald 1978 80(4): 161-163.* The Pigeon Creek (Indiana) Baptist Church helped shape Abraham Lincoln's character during his formative years. Thomas Lincoln and his son Abraham helped build the church in 1822. Abraham Lincoln never joined the Pigeon Creek Baptist Church, but there is evidence that he was its janitor. The church, a simple log structure, was razed about 1880. Photo.
T. P. Linkfield

3099. —. BAPTIST BIOGRAPHY AND HISTORY IN PERIODICALS, 1979. *Baptist Hist. and Heritage 1980 15(4): 51-53.* Alphabetical list by author of articles published in 1979 that were not included in the *Southern Baptist Periodical Index.*

3100. —. [BAPTIST VIEWS]. *Foundations 1976 19(3): 257-277.*
Edwards, Herbert O. FROM A BLACK PERSPECTIVE AFTER THE BICENTENNIAL: HOPES FOR A NEW FUTURE, *pp. 257-264.* Reviews the relation between white and black Baptists since the American Revolution, with an emphasis on the American Baptist Convention. Concludes that Baptists reflect the general racial attitudes of the nation. 14 notes.
Ashbrook, James B. A WHITE-ANGLOSAXON-AMERICAN BAPTIST (W-AS-AB) PERSPECTIVE, *pp. 265-274.* Analyzes the radical aspects of Baptist heritage. Four radical areas are discussed: 1) class, represented by John Bunyan, 2) political, by Roger Williams, 3) geographical, by William Carey, and 4) social, by Walter Rauschenbusch. The negative ends that these can lead to are indicated along with ways to counter-balance them. Concludes that a white, Anglo-Saxon, American identity leads to seeing all of humanity as the Family of God. 21 notes.
Pemberton, Prentiss. RESPONSE TO HERBERT O. EDWARDS AND JAMES B. ASHBROOK, *pp. 275-277.* Sees Edwards in a prophetic role and Ashbrook in the role of healer. Critical concerns raised were Edwards' need to be more powerful in his role and a list of things it is felt Ashbrook committed.
E. E. Eminhizer

3101. —. [THE NEW ETHNICITY]. *Foundations 1976 19(3): 223-237.*
Shapiro, Deanne Ruth. THE NEW ETHNICITY: MYTH OR REALITY?, *pp. 223-234.* Divides the treatment of ethnic groups into three areas, 1) the "melting pot," 2) cultural pluralism, and 3) the New Ethnicity. In the present period, the ethnic individual is able to look beyond America for identity. Exponents of the New Ethnicity fail to explore fully the theological influence the new views have on the identities of American ethnics. Suggests several areas where further consideration is necessary by those supporting the new ethnic pluralism. 35 notes.
Handy, Robert T. RESPONSE TO DEANNE RUTH SHAPIRO, *pp. 235-237.* Holds that Baptists support the cultural pluralism suggested. Offenses against ethnic minorities did not come in terms of size or percentages, but rather from considering one's own tradition as being the one to which conformity is expected. Note.
E. E. Eminhizer

3102. —. SOUTHERN BAPTIST CHURCHES 200 YEARS OLD OR OLDER. *Baptist Hist. and Heritage 1976 11(4): 232-234.* A compilation of 108 Baptist churches located in Virginia (59), North Carolina (25), South Carolina (20), Georgia (three), and Maryland (one), which are 200 years old or older. Lists each church according to date of founding, name, county in which it is located, and 1975 membership.
H. M. Parker, Jr.

Christian Church (Disciples of Christ) and Related Churches
(including the Churches of Christ)

3103. Eaton, E. L. THE FORGOTTEN CHRISTIANS OF CORNWALLIS TOWNSHIP. *Nova Scotia Hist. Q. 1977 7(1): 41-53.* Sketches the history of the Christian Church (Disciples of Christ) in Cornwallis Township. In 1812, Thomas Campbell established the denomination in Ontario. In 1901, J. A. L. Romig brought the sect to Cornwallis. In 1910, the last minister was recorded. H. M. Evans

3104. Eller, David B. HOOSIER BRETHREN AND THE ORIGINS OF THE RESTORATION MOVEMENT. *Indiana Mag. of Hist. 1980 76(1): 1-20.* The many revivalist religious sects which dominated the Indiana frontier in the early 19th century included the Disciples movement, known popularly as the "Restoration." One of its local leaders, Joseph Hostetler, led a movement in southern Indiana which resulted in the group's becoming a member of the Disciples of Christ, a major American Protestant denomination. Hostetler led some of the German Baptist Brethren (Dunkards) through many doctrinal struggles among individual churches toward membership in the Disciples of Christ. Covers 1800-27. Based on local and family history and church publications; photo, map, 50 notes. A. Erlebacher

3105. Ethridge, F. Maurice and Feagin, Joe R. VARIETIES OF "FUNDAMENTALISM": A CONCEPTUAL AND EMPIRICAL ANALYSIS OF TWO PROTESTANT DENOMINATIONS. *Sociol. Q. 1979 20(1): 37-48.* Examines the results of a study done in 1972 in Texas, dealing with the types of religious fundamentalism in the Disciples of Christ and the Church of Christ, two related Protestant denominations.

3106. Hughes, Richard T. FROM PRIMITIVE CHURCH TO CIVIL RELIGION: THE MILLENNIAL ODYSSEY OF ALEXANDER CAMPBELL. *J. of the Am. Acad. of Religion 1976 44(1): 87-103.* Traces the hope of an earthly millennium in the thought of Alexander Campbell (1788-1866), showing that Campbell initially expected this hope to be realized by a restoration of the Apostolic church by means of his movement. Campbell, founder of the Disciples of Christ, later moved from such thinking to an identification of the nation as the instrument for bringing the millennium. Being disappointed in the nation, however, Campbell finally returned to the idea of restoring the primitive church. Based on primary and secondary sources; 115 notes.
E. R. Lester

3107. Lee, George R. JAMES SHANNON'S SEARCH FOR HAPPINESS. *Missouri Hist. Rev. 1978 73(1): 71-84.* James Shannon (1799-1859) was president of the University of Missouri during 1850-55. After coming to America in 1821 he was president of Sunbury Academy, the College of Louisiana in Jackson, and Bacon College in Harrodsburg. During his years in Missouri Shannon was drawn into the political, social, and religious controversies of the period. He disliked abolition and regarded slavery as divinely inspired. He was caught up in the strife that wracked the Missouri Democratic Party during the 1850's, and as a Disciple of Christ he was often at odds with older denominations. All this obscures his ability as a teacher, scholar, and administrator. While in Missouri he founded two colleges, Christian Women's College and Christian University, the Disciples' school now known as Culver-Stockton where Shannon was president after 1855. Primary and secondary sources; illus., 65 notes. W. F. Zornow

3108. Morrison, John L. ALEXANDER CAMPBELL: FREEDOM FIGHTER OF THE MIDDLE FRONTIER. *West Virginia Hist. 1976 37(4): 291-309.* Alexander Campbell (1788-1866), the Disciples of Christ leader, upheld "primitive" Biblical Christianity against "impure" man-made church traditions. He thought America was destined to free humanity by spreading this Biblical faith through the world. Campbell abhorred war and politicians, defended the Indians against mistreatment, and disliked slavery, although he was not an abolitionist. He viewed women as queens in the home but gave them no place in political or church affairs. Based on Campbell's writings and secondary sources; 126 notes.
J. H. Broussard

3109. Morrison, John L. THE CENTRALITY OF THE BIBLE IN ALEXANDER CAMPBELL'S THOUGHT AND LIFE. *West Virginia Hist. 1974 35(3): 185-204.* Alexander Campbell, founder of the Disciples of Christ, thought the Bible supreme over all "man-made" church authority and disliked the emphasis which many Protestants put on creeds and canons. He rejected infant baptism and sprinkling as un-Biblical and said the Bible could be easily understood without interpretation by human authorities. Reared a Presbyterian, Campbell began preaching Antinomian ideas in his early 20's (1811 and after) without authority from any presbytery and for several decades delivered lectures, sermons, and debates. He insisted that the Bible must be accepted on faith alone and cannot be verified by reason, and that man discovers God by revelation only and not by the study of nature. Based on Campbell's writings; 87 notes. J. H. Broussard

3110. Morrison, John L. A RATIONAL VOICE CRYING IN AN EMOTIONAL WILDERNESS. *West Virginia Hist. 1973 34(2): 125-140.* Summarizes the religious ideas of Alexander Campbell (1786-1866), frontier preacher, author, and founder of the Disciples of Christ. Campbell felt that any man with sufficient intellect, not merely the clergy, could attain sufficient spiritual understanding from God through the application of reason to the Bible. God spoke to man through the Scriptures rationally approached. Campbell denounced emotionalism and mysticism as paths to religious experience, and denounced vigorous sectarianism, seeking a reform of religion away from camp meeting hysteria and sensationalism. 71 notes. C. A. Newton

3111. Pearson, Samuel C., Jr. THE CAVE AFFAIR: PROTESTANT THOUGHT IN THE GILDED AGE. *Encounter 1980 41(2): 179-203.* Recounts the life and theology of Robert Catlett Cave (1843-1924), whose sermon of 1889 in St. Louis, Missouri, which challenged the literal interpretation of the Bible, created a controversy among the Disciples of Christ.

3112. Woehrmann, Paul, ed. THE AUTOBIOGRAPHY OF ABRAHAM SNETHEN, FRONTIER PREACHER. *Filson Club Hist. Q. 1977 51(4): 315-335.* Reproduces part of a manuscript found in the Milwaukee, Wisconsin, Public Library. Although a revised version of this material has been previously published, the actual text is a significant document. There is a real feeling for frontier life and religion in Abraham Snethen's writing. The author was a minister in the Christian Church. Covers 1790's-1830 in Kentucky, Ohio, and Indiana. 75 notes.
G. B. McKinney

Congregational Churches
(including Separatists and United Church of Christ)

3113. Anderson, Gillian B. THE FUNERAL OF SAMUEL COOPER. *New England Q. 1977 50(4): 644-659.* Reprints accounts of Samuel Cooper's (1725-83) New England funeral and shows that it broke with the Congregational norm of simple civil ceremonies and established the pattern for future funerals during the last decades of the 18th century. Cooper's funeral was more religious. It included a sermon delivered over the body, and music was played. Primary sources; 48 notes.
J. C. Bradford

3114. Barnes, Howard A. HORACE BUSHNELL: GENTRY ELITIST. *Connecticut Hist. 1977 (19): 1-24.* Examines the theology of 19th-century Congregationalist minister Horace Bushnell, using the "mass" (as opposed to "class") theory of history per Tocqueville and Mill.

3115. Broadbent, Charles D. A BRIEF PILGRIMAGE: PLYMOUTH CHURCH OF ROCHESTER. *Rochester Hist. 1978 40(4): 1-22.* The Congregational Plymouth Church of Rochester existed from 1853 to 1954 and significantly influenced Rochester's religious community during 1853-1904.

3116. Buell, Lawrence. JOSEPH STEVENS BUCKMINSTER: THE MAKING OF A NEW ENGLAND SAINT. *Can. Rev. of Am. Studies [Canada] 1979 10(1): 1-29.* An important intellectual during the Federalist period, Joseph Stevens Buckminster (1784-1812) managed to conduct a respected and seemingly conventional Congregational ministry at the Brattle Street Church in Boston. At the same time, he helped to foment major ecclesiastical changes, foreshadowed Unitarianism, contributed significantly to producing a literary renaissance in New England, and persuaded Harvard College to revive classical studies and take cognizance of developments in German scholarship. Based on printed primary sources and archival materials; photo, 88 notes. H. T. Lovin

3117. Conforti, Joseph. THE RISE OF THE NEW DIVINITY IN WESTERN NEW ENGLAND, 1740-1800. *Hist. J. of Western Massachusetts 1980 8(1): 37-47.* New Divinity ministers, who held the conservative, evangelical theology of the first Great Awakening, dominated the churches of Western New England. They saw this area as fertile ground for their doctrine and devoted themselves to spreading their message in this area, which became a base from which they could build. Contemporary pamphlets and sermons and secondary sources; 2 illus., 33 notes.
W. H. Mulligan, Jr.

3118. Crawford, Michael J. INDIANS, YANKEES, AND THE MEETINGHOUSE DISPUTE OF NATICK, MASSACHUSETTS, 1743-1800. *New England Hist. and Geneal. Register 1978 132(Oct): 278-292.* The Natick Congregational meetinghouse dispute refutes the "peaceable kingdoms" thesis of 18th-century Massachusetts towns. The General Court intervened to protect the rights of "praying" Indians who built the original meetinghouse and to effect a compromise between the southern faction who lived near the meetinghouse and those who wanted it relocated in the center of town. An eventual solution came three-quarters of a century later as a result of land annexation and trading, a decline in the Indian population and other population shifts. 25 notes.
A. E. Huff

3119. Davies, Phillips G., ed. EARLY WELSH SETTLEMENTS IN ILLINOIS. *J. of the Illinois State Hist. Soc. 1977 70(4): 292-298.* Edits and translates the Illinois chapters of Robert D. Thomas's 1872 *Hanes Cymry America* (history of the Welsh in America). Thomas (1817-88), a Congregational minister and advocate of Welsh emigration to the United States, emigrated to New York City. He describes Welsh churches in the United States as well as major industries employing Welshmen. 2 illus., 4 notes. J

3120. Davies, Phillips G., transl. REVEREND R. D. THOMAS'S "WELSH IN MISSOURI, 1872." *Missouri Hist. Rev. 1978 72(2): 154-175.* Reverend Thomas had Congregational churches in New York,

Pennsylvania, Ohio, and Tennessee. His religious duties did not keep him from writing poetry and prose. Translates chapter 6 of *Hanes Cymry America* (history of the Welsh in America) describing the life of Welsh communities in St. Louis and eight small towns in Missouri. 8 illus., 2 maps, note. W. F. Zornow

3121. Davies, Phillips G., ed. WELSH SETTLEMENTS IN KANSAS. *Kansas Hist. Q. 1977 43(4): 448-469.* Translates a large portion of the seventh chapter of the second part of the Reverend Robert D. Thomas's (1817-88) *Hanes Cymry America* (History of the Welsh in America), published in Welsh at Utica, New York, in 1872. The chapter is of particular interest because it includes considerable firsthand information that Thomas gathered in 1869 in Kansas. Mentions the Congregational Church in Emporia, the Welsh churches in Arvonia, and in Lyon, Osage, Shawnee, Douglas, Leavenworth, and Atchison counties, and other places where Welsh settlers gathered. Mentions several settlers, including Rowland Davies, who established a general store in Bala in 1870 and whose very high opinion of the Kansas prairie Thomas quoted. 80 notes. A. W. Howell

3122. Dumas, David W., ed. RECORDS OF THE REVEREND THOMAS CHEEVER. *New England Hist. and Geneal. Register 1978 132(Jan): 37-43.* Thomas Cheever (d. 1749), the son of Ezekiel Cheever and Ellen (Lothrop), graduated from Harvard in 1677. He was dismissed as minister in Malden, Massachusetts, in 1686, and became pastor in Romney Marsh (now Revere) in 1715, having taught school there in the interim. During this period he continued to perform marriages, as his notebook records attest. The beginning of the notebook, now owned by Winslow Ames of Saunderstown, Rhode Island, probably contains sermon notes; the second part, receipts. 16 notes. A. Huff

3123. Elder, Harris J. HENRY KAMP AND CULTURAL PLURALISM IN OKLAHOMA CITY. *Chronicles of Oklahoma 1977 55(1): 78-92.* In 1906, young Henry Kamp left Germany for St. Louis, Missouri, where his family had previously settled. Intent on setting up his own business, he found bustling Oklahoma City a promising location, and within a few years had established a lucrative grocery business. Kamp, a strong supporter of immigrants maintaining ties with their cultural heritage, helped found the Germania German Club and the German Evangelical and Reformed Church in Oklahoma City. Anti-German sentiment during both world wars forced many German Americans to leave the area, but the Kamp family remained and helped strengthen the German American community. Based on primary and secondary sources; 4 photos, 49 notes. M. L. Tate

3124. Foster, Stephen. PROPHETS ON A FIXED STIPEND: THE CONGREGATIONAL MINISTRY AND THE SOCIAL HISTORY OF COLONIAL NEW ENGLAND. *Rev. in Am. Hist. 1977 5(3): 299-307.* Review article prompted by B. R. Burg's *Richard Mather of Dorchester* (Lexington: U. Pr. of Kentucky, 1976) and J. William T. Youngs, Jr.'s *God's Messengers: Religious Leadership in Colonial New England, 1700-1750* (Baltimore, Md.: Johns Hopkins U. Pr., 1976).

3125. Gregory, Annadora F. THE REVEREND HARMON BROSS AND NEBRASKA CONGREGATIONALISM, 1873-1928. *Nebraska Hist. 1973 54(3): 445-474.* Harmon Bross was active in Congregational Church affairs in Nebraska, 1873-1928. He was pastor of the First Congregational Church at Crete and after 1884 was director of the Nebraska Home Missionary Society in Norfolk and then at Chadron. In 1906 he became pastor of the Congregational Church at Wahoo. Following retirement, Bross moved to Lincoln where for a decade he was assistant state adjutant of the Nebraska Grand Army of the Republic. R. Lowitt

3126. Hovey, Kenneth Alan. THE THEOLOGY OF HISTORY IN *OF PLYMOUTH PLANTATION* AND ITS PREDECESSORS. *Early Am. Literature 1975 10(1): 47-66.* The historiography of William Bradford's *Of Plymouth Plantation* combines the dominant theological emphasis of each of three previous Plymouth histories—"A Brief Relation of the Discovery and Plantation of New England," "Mourt's Relation," and "Good News from New England"—into a single impression of the complex relationship of God and man. Based on primary and secondary sources; 15 notes. D. P. Wharton

3127. Jones, Charles Edwin. THE IMPOLITIC MR. EDWARDS: THE PERSONAL DIMENSION OF THE ROBERT BRECK AFFAIR. *New England Q. 1978 51(1): 64-79.* Describes the controversy surrounding Robert Breck's call to the pastorate at Scotland, Connecticut, in 1736. Jonathan Edwards's backing of the Stoddard-Williams faction of clergymen against Breck would later lead Breck to vote for Edwards's dismissal from his Northampton pastorate in 1751. Based mainly on church records and pamphlets; 45 notes. J. C. Bradford

3128. Klan, Yvonne Mearns. KANAKA WILLIAM. *Beaver [Canada] 1979 309(4): 38-43.* Several hundred Hawaiians were employed by the Hudson's Bay Company along the Columbia River. In 1845, William R. Kaulehelehe was sent from Hawaii to be the Congregationalist minister to the local Hawaiians. He soon became known widely as Kanaka William. The Oregon Treaty of 1846 led to major economic changes, and by the late 1850's few Hawaiians remained along the Columbia. William's house, inside of Fort Vancouver, was deteriorating and said to be expendable. In spite of protests that led to correspondence between London and Washington, it was decided to remove William's house; it was stripped, then burned in March 1860, and shortly after the Company abandoned Fort Vancouver. There is no word of Kanaka William after 1869. 5 illus. D. Chaput

3129. Lippy, Charles H. TRANS-ATLANTIC DISSENT AND THE REVOLUTION: RICHARD PRICE AND CHARLES CHAUNCY. *Eighteenth-Century Life 1977 4(2): 31-37.* Richard Price, British moral philosopher, economic theorist, and dissenting clergyman, corresponded for 20 years with Charles Chauncy, pastor of Boston's prestigious First Church, 1727-87. Price looked favorably upon the American Revolution in global terms of truly universal liberty, but Chauncy took a more practical, local, and perhaps selfish view in his failure to speak out against the enslavement of blacks in the new republic and in his disinclination to extend political power to non-Dissenters.

3130. Lutz, Cora E. THE "GENTLE PURITAN" AND THE "ANGELIC DOCTOR." *Yale U. Lib. Gazette 1978 52(3): 122-126.* Despite his numerous duties as President of Yale College, Ezra Stiles was a voracious reader. So it was not surprising for him to have read thoroughly a medieval manuscript, which contained the text of the *Speculum humanae salvationis* ("Mirror of Man's Salvation"). He described it as "a romish Treatise on Theology," but it is no surprise that Congregationalist Stiles found some value in the words of a disciple of Thomas Aquinas. Covers 1792-94. 9 notes. D. A. Yanchisin

3131. Lutz, Cora E. THE MYSTERY OF THEOPHILUS WHALE. *Yale U. Lib. Gazette 1979 54(2): 79-84.* When Ezra Stiles became minister of the Second Congregational Church at Newport, Rhode Island, he thoroughly investigated the legend of Theophilus Whale, who was said to have been one of the judges who condemned King Charles I to death and who was said to have lived the rest of his life in Rhode Island. Stiles, the first scholar to investigate the story, refuted the legend. D. A. Yanchisin

3132. McLoughlin, William G. THE CHOCTAW SLAVE BURNING: A CRISIS IN MISSION WORK AMONG THE INDIANS. *J. of the West 1974 13(1): 113-127.* On 28 December 1858 a black slave killed his Choctaw master, Richard Harkins. He claimed he had been instigated by another slave, a woman. After he escaped and killed himself, the woman, despite protestations of innocence, was burned at the stake by the widow of the murdered man. The victim was a member, along with the Harkinses, of the Congregational mission church of the Reverend Cyrus Byington. When the incident was revealed a year later it precipitated a crisis over slavery and the relation of the church to slavery among a slave-holding people like the Choctaw Indians. 34 notes. R. V. Ritter

3133. Morrison, Kenneth M. THE WONDERS OF DIVINE MERCY: A REVIEW OF JOHN WILLIAMS' *THE REDEEMED CAPTIVE.* *Am. Rev. of Can. Studies 1979 9(1): 56-62.* In *The Redeemed Captive,* New England Congregationalist minister John Williams recounted his experiences as a captive among French and Indians, 1704-06. Viewing this period almost exclusively in religious terms, Williams saw his Roman Catholic captors as instruments of the wrath of God which was being visited on Protestant New England. *The Redeemed Captive* influenced the views of New England readers well into the 19th century and reminds 20th-century readers of the origins of the continuing conflicts among English, French, and Indians in the northeastern United States and Canada. 28 notes. G.-A. Patzwald

3134. Muller, Dorothea R. CHURCH BUILDING AND COMMUNITY MAKING ON THE FRONTIER, A CASE STUDY: JOSIAH STRONG, HOME MISSIONARY IN CHEYENNE, 1871-1873. *Western Hist. Q. 1979 10(2): 191-216.* Congregationalist minister Josiah Strong (b. 1847) served his first pastorate as a home missionary in Cheyenne, Wyoming, 1871-73. The two years' experience shaped his religious perspective and influenced the development of society and institutions of Cheyenne—its community-making process. Strong's enthusiastic commitment to evangelize the nation and indirectly the world was developed here. He proclaimed a buoyant nationalism in a widely influential volume in the 1880's, and for three decades he led national organizations that espoused his Social Gospel message and perpetuated his dream of America's world-evangelizing role. 71 notes. D. L. Smith

3135. Parker, William H. JONATHAN EDWARDS: FOUNDER OF THE COUNTER-TRADITION OF TRANSCENDENTAL THOUGHT IN AMERICA. *Georgia Rev. 1973 27(4): 543-549.* Jonathan Edwards (1703-58) attempted to fuse the transcendental and naturalistic realms into a single entity, thus exposing the persistent rationalist-empiricist concept that man and society could be constructed to approximate the orderliness of the Newtonian universe. Edwards thus came to resemble Emerson, James, and Niebuhr, who insisted upon the pressing necessity for change. M. B. Lucas

3136. Parsons, Edward Smith. LYMAN ABBOTT. *Religion in Life 1978 47(3): 313-319.* Reminisces about a summer spent in the employ of Congregationalist minister Lyman Abbott, as a research secretary at Cornwall-on-the-Hudson, New York, in 1885.

3137. Potter, Gail M. YORK'S BENEVOLENT TYRANT: SAMUEL MOODY. *New-England Galaxy 1979 20(3): 52-58.* The fiery Reverend Samuel Moody preached to the inhabitants of York, Maine, in the Congregational Church from his ordination in 1700 until his death in 1747.

3138. Pulsifer, Janice Goldsmith. SAMUEL WIGGLESWORTH OF THE HAMLET. *Essex Inst. Hist. Collections 1976 112(2): 89-119.* Discusses Rev. Samuel Wigglesworth (1688-1768), pastor of the church at the Hamlet, the third parish of Ipswich, Massachusetts, from 1714 until his death. Describes the man and his parish and gives interesting vignettes of his education, Congregational ministry, and family. Primary and secondary works, inventory of Wigglesworth's estate; 78 notes.
H. M. Parker, Jr.

3139. Rankin, Jane. THE PILGRIMS WERE NOT MEEK SALLOW SAINTS. *Daughters of the Am. Revolution Mag. 1975 109(9): 972-977, 991.* Describes the Separatists, their flight to Holland in 1607, and their final settlement at Plymouth in 1620. S

3140. Scheick, William J. THE GRAND DESIGN: JONATHAN EDWARDS' *HISTORY OF THE WORK OF REDEMPTION*. *Eighteenth-Cent. Studies 1975 8(3): 300-314.* Reviews the interpretations of Edwards' 1739 series of discourses on the continuity of divine providence as disclosed by history, published posthumously in 1774. Analyzes the work and addresses the troublesome point of what Edwards meant by his claim to have used a new method. Edwards regarded his study as innovative because he treated "history as an allegory of the conversion experience." According to Edwards, both history and the elect soul advance by degrees; Christ's incarnation affects history as the communication of grace affects the soul, but the "actualization of this influence is progressive. As the soul grows in grace and as history approaches eternity . . . the more luminous they become." 40 notes. J. D. Falk

3141. Schmotter, James W. MINISTERIAL CAREERS IN EIGHTEENTH CENTURY NEW ENGLAND: THE GREAT CONTEXT: 1700-1760. *J. of Social Hist. 1975 9(2): 249-267.* In the 18th century the New England Congregational ministry became less attractive as a career, while law and medicine rose in esteem. Although the number of ministers did not slip dramatically, the numbers of prime individuals did, and they were paid less. 5 figs., 32 notes. M. Hough

3142. Selesky, Harold E. ADDITIONAL MATERIAL RELATING TO EZRA STILES. *Yale U. Lib. Gazette 1975 50(2): 112-122.* Additional archives of Ezra Stiles have come to Yale University with the acquisition in the last two years of some printed materials, manuscripts, and a few artifacts, donated by the widow of Lewis Stiles Gannett, a direct descendant of one of Stiles' daughters. Although only a part of Stiles' original collection, the almanacs in the acquisition reflect Stiles' interest in climatological and astronomical phenomena. The acquisition adds to the ecclesiastical and political materials in the Stiles papers. Three letters from Thomas Jefferson to Stiles reflect their kindred interest in science, as well as Jefferson's views on contemporary politics and his confidence in Stiles' discretion. Illus., 4 notes. D. A. Yanchisin

3143. Shea, Daniel B., Jr. JONATHAN EDWARDS: THE FIRST TWO HUNDRED YEARS. *J. of Am. Studies [Great Britain] 1980 14(2): 181-197.* Before 1903, the thinking and literary achievements of American colonial theologian Jonathan Edwards (1703-58) were subjects for lively controversy among historians, theologians and literary analysts, and for 19th-century American eulogists, his work represented the "rising glory in America." These numerous revisionist writings provided essential insights to 20th-century scholars who subsequently have interpreted Edwards's influence on American literature and thought. 40 notes.
H. T. Lovin

3144. Shuffelton, Frank. INDIAN DEVILS AND PILGRIM FATHERS: SQUANTO, HOBOMOK, AND THE ENGLISH CONCEPTION OF INDIAN RELIGION. *New England Q. 1976 49(1): 108-116.* The motivation of Squanto (d. 1622), a Wampanoag Indian, in his dealings with the Pilgrims can only be understood in terms of the polytheism of the Indians. The settlers' Puritanism led them to a simplistic view of the Indians' religion and to recognize only two gods, which they identified with their own God and Satan. The Indians' shamanism was even more difficult for them to understand and they failed to see that Squanto, one of the few survivors of a once important village, was playing the role of a medicine man and using the whites to regain his once important position in Indian society. Hobomok had a secure position among the Indians and his relations with the whites differed from Squanto's because he had no need to use them. Based on Puritan writings and secondary sources; 15 notes. J. C. Bradford

3145. Smith, John E. JONATHAN EDWARDS: PIETY AND PRACTICE IN THE AMERICAN CHARACTER. *J. of Religion 1974 54(2): 166-180.* Attempts to clarify the meaning of Jonathan Edward's appeal to experience, theological empiricism, and to explain how his fidelity to experience led him to connect piety and practice in a way that has had a permanent influence on all forms of religion in America.
S

3146. Stein, Stephen J. THE BIBLICAL NOTES OF BENJAMIN PIERPONT. *Yale U. Lib. Gazette 1976 50(4): 195-218.* Benjamin Pierpont's ministerial career came to an abrupt end when he was dismissed from a temporary pulpit at Deerfield in 1730 for seemingly unproven judgments. In readying for the ministry Pierpont had prepared for his use a *Bible* with interleaved blank sheets, which came into the possession of his brother-in-law, Jonathan Edwards, who used it for his own biblical reflections. Pierpont's fragmentary comments along with Edwards' numerous biblical notes, "Miscellaneous Observations on the Holy Scripture," were preserved in the "Blank Bible" among the Edwards Papers at Yale. "Pierpont's fragmentary biblical commentary shows how one ministerial candidate in New England went about an important part of his theological preparation in the early 18th century." 32 notes.
D. A. Yanchisin

3147. Stein, Stephen J. "FOR THEIR SPIRITUAL GOOD": THE NORTHAMPTON, MASSACHUSETTS, PRAYER BIDS OF THE 1730S AND 1740S. *William and Mary Q. 1980 37(2): 261-285.* Prayer petitions were presented to the pastor, Jonathan Edwards, who incorporated them into the subsequent service. Edwards saved the prayer petitions, and they are found in his papers at Yale University and Andover Newton Theological School. The prayer requests vary from 15 words to 200. They give insight into the relation between religion and life. Most of the requests originate from distress. The prayer bids usually sought some evidence of spiritual good in their lives and capacity to accept God's will. The bids reveal different levels of society in the church. Most made no reference to the minister. Reproduces petition record and cites sermons of Jonathan Edwards; 132 notes. H. M. Ward

3148. Stein, Stephen J. PROVIDENCE AND THE APOCALYPSE IN THE EARLY WRITINGS OF JONATHAN EDWARDS. *Early Am. Literature 1978-79 13(3): 250-267.* Jonathan Edwards's (1703-58) earliest apocalyptic ideas are examined through three principal resources written before mid-1724: "Theological Miscellanies," the "Notes on Scripture," and the "Notes on the Apocalypse." Each contains a diverse assortment of apocalyptic material from the last years of Edward's youth. Though lacking any apparent conceptual or structural focus, illustrates that Edward's interpretation of the vision of the living creatures in Revelation provides an organizing focus by disclosing theological and literary order in the Apocalypse relating to the theme of providence. Primary sources; 63 notes. J. N. Friedel

3149. Stein, Stephen J. THE QUEST FOR THE SPIRITUAL SENSE; THE BIBLICAL HERMENEUTICS OF JONATHAN EDWARDS. *Harvard Theological Rev. 1977 70(1-2): 99-113.* Jonathan Edwards's (1703-58) use and understanding of the Bible has not been addressed to any extent by scholars. Examines Edwards and the Bible by addressing issues of hermeneutical importance. This principal problem in this area is formed in Edwards's quest for the "spiritual sense." 53 notes. E. E. Eminhizer

3150. Tracy, Patricia. THE PASTORATE OF JONATHAN EDWARDS, *Massachusetts Rev. 1979 20(3): 437-451.* Discusses reciprocal relationships between Jonathan Edwards (1703-58), American theologian, philosopher, and Congregational minister, and the congregation to which he ministered. Describes the 1734-35 Northampton revival, and how he took the town's young people as his special constituency. After dismissal from Northampton in 1750, he achieved great success with his theological and philosophical writings. Based on Edwards's works, letters, and an unpublished doctoral dissertation; 40 notes. E. R. Campbell

3151. Waters, John J. THE TRADITIONAL WORLD OF THE NEW ENGLAND PEASANTS: A VIEW FROM SEVENTEENTH-CENTURY BARNSTABLE. *New England Hist. and Genealogical Register 1976 130(1): 3-21.* Explores the values which governed the 17th-century and early 18th-century life of Barnstable County (Cape Cod), Massachusetts. The importance of land, the idea of patrilineage, the reliance on stem families, and the emphasis on religion suggest the Old World background of these immigrants. Property was the most dominant factor, affecting dowries, independence of either the eldest or youngest son, ability of sons and daughters to marry, care of the elderly, and wills. The world of the Barnstable inhabitant was the world of the English peasant. Based on primary sources, especially probate and land records, and on published works; 67 notes. S. L. Patterson

3152. Weddle, David L. THE IMAGE OF THE SELF IN JONATHAN EDWARDS: A STUDY OF AUTOBIOGRAPHY AND THEOLOGY. *J. of the Am. Acad. of Religion 1975 43(1): 70-83.* Explores the relationship between the autobiographical writings of Edwards and his theological works, emphasizing the image of the self as the key to this relationship. To discover oneself is to grasp the reality of God, a concept which could then be applied to such doctrines as sin, redemption, and ethics. Primary and secondary sources; 41 notes. E. R. Lester

3153. Wenska, Walter P. BRADFORD'S TWO HISTORIES: PATTERN AND PARADIGM IN *OF PLYMOUTH PLANTATION.* *Early Am. Literature 1978 13(2): 151-164.* Each of William Bradford's two histories, *Of Plymouth Plantation,* (1630 and 1646-50), present fundamentally different, paradigmatic responses to the American experience. By attending to chronology and the changes in the manner and patterns of their presentation, the reader examines the different impulses behind, purposes, and concerns of each history. Each volume reflects the changing status of the Pilgrims' culture and the stability of their group. In the second, Bradford laments the shift from group consolidation to separation; from the ideal to reality. Primary and secondary sources; 26 notes. J. N. Friedel

3154. Westbrook, Robert B. SOCIAL CRITICISM AND THE HEAVENLY CITY OF JONATHAN EDWARDS. *Soundings (Nashville, TN) 1976 59(4): 396-412.* Jonathan Edwards' social vision was founded on a philosophy in which the good society was maintained by the true virtue of its citizens. This virtue was based on love of God and of other men. As a postmillenialist, Edwards believed that the kingdom of God on earth would appear through the natural workings of the Holy Spirit and would lead to a society ruled by the insight of true virtue. Edwards lost his pulpit in Northampton, Massachusetts, because of his social vision. He made true virtue the *sine qua non* of church association in an increasingly worldly and avaricious environment. N. Lederer

3155. Whitaker, James W., ed., and Davies, Phillips G., transl. WELSH SETTLEMENTS IN IOWA. *Palimpsest 1978 59(1): 24-32.* Presents an edited segment of *Hanes Cymry America* (history of the Welsh in America), published in 1872 and written by Welsh Congregational minister Robert D. Thomas, who served churches in Wales and the United States. Intended as an immigrants' guide, the book was often inaccurate and exaggerated. It did contain useful demographic and genealogical information, as well as information about individuals and social institutions. Photo, note. D. W. Johnson

3156. Wilson, John F. JONATHAN EDWARDS AS HISTORIAN. *Church Hist. 1977 46(1): 5-18.* Presents the Presidential Address delivered at the annual meeting of the American Society of Church History on 28 December 1976. Discusses Jonathan Edwards' *The Work of Redemption* in the context of the social responsibility of historians to offer discriminating perspectives on both traditionality and modernity. 39 notes. M. D. Dibert

3157. Youngs, J. William T., Jr. CONGREGATIONAL CLERICALISM: NEW ENGLAND ORDINATIONS BEFORE THE GREAT AWAKENING. *William and Mary Q. 1974 31(3): 481-90.* Ordination procedures changed from emphasis on the minister as a member of a brotherhood of Christian believers to one of separation of religious leaders. Efforts were made to make the ministry a profession, though a professional class did not develop. As clerical power flowed from the ministers instead of the congregation, festivity ended and new ministers did not preach at their ordinations. Most ordination sermons stressed the special role of ministers; the idea of their higher sanctity also evolved. The greater gulf between minister and congregation came to a head during the Great Awakening. Ebenezer Parkman's ordination in 1724 is considered a case in point. Covers 1630-1740. Based primarily on sermons; 27 notes. H. M. Ward

3158. DeProspo, R. C. THE "NEW SIMPLE IDEA" OF EDWARDS' PERSONAL NARRATIVE. *Early Am. Literature 1979 14(2): 193-204.* In two works during the 1740's, *Religious Affections, The Nature of True Virtue* and "The Distinguishing Marks of the Works of the Spirit of God," Jonathan Edwards uses John Locke's sensational psychology and Puritan piety to describe his personal conversion and the simple idea of grace. Edwards expands Locke's world of sensations to include spiritual truths like grace. Grace is similar to any idea or sensation received by the mind from nature, but it has an immaterial source and cannot be described in images. 28 notes. T. P. Linkfield

Dutch Reformed Churches

3159. Bogert, Frederick W. THE CONEWAGO SETTLEMENT. *Halve Maen 1978 53(3): 3-4, 14, 11.* The Conewago Colony, near Gettysburg, Pennsylvania, was founded by families of the Reformed Dutch Church in America, 1760's-70's; from a series originally published in 1884.

3160. Bouma, Gary D. KEEPING THE FAITHFUL: PATTERNS OF MEMBERSHIP RETENTION IN THE CHRISTIAN REFORMED CHURCH. *Sociol. Analysis 1980 41(3): 259-264.* Why do persons stay members of a conservative Calvinist denomination? Conservative Calvinism is a very demanding meaning system in North America; one that should find a modern, post-industrial society rather inhospitable. The fact that it does have little appeal to those who were not raised with it suggests that this contention is true. The question becomes, how are members retained in this uncongenial atmosphere full of alternative, perhaps more appealing, less demanding meaning systems. This analysis of a survey of former and present members of the Christian Reformed Church indicates that persons leave the CRC because they find the CRC community too demanding, constricting, and intolerant. Those who stayed members of the CRC cited commitment to its conservative Calvinist theology and worship as their primary reasons for continuing. They also mentioned the positive importance of the CRC community to them. Covers 1964-79. J

3161. DeJong, Gerald. THE COMING OF THE DUTCH TO THE DAKOTAS. *South Dakota Hist. 1974 5(1): 20-51.* Dutch ethnic clustering was important in the Dakotas in certain places. Arriving first in the 1880's, they were never as many as the Scandinavians or Germans, but their culture marked a stamp of "Dutchness" on some landscapes. Leaving Holland for the traditional reasons, most Dutch did not go to the Dakotas. As free land became scarce in other midwestern states, Hollanders, like others, spread westward, often in small colonies. A large Dutch settlement in Northwest Iowa allowed near-by cultural contact. The Dutch in the Dakotas suffered all the hardships that settlers in that time experienced. Some left, but the number of Hollanders maintained itself with new arrivals. Their language, clothing and other personal articles, contact with other Dutch Americans, and especially religion continued their cultural traditions long after arrival. Covers 1880's-1951. Based on primary and secondary sources; 10 illus., 63 notes. A. J. Larson

3162. DeJong, Gerald F. THE FOUNDING OF THE DUTCH REFORMED CHURCH ON LONG ISLAND. *Halve Maen 1979 54(2): 1-3, 12-13, 17.* Surveys the establishment and growth of the Reformed Dutch Church in the Long Island settlements of New Amersfoort, Breukelen, Midwout, New Utrecht, and Boswyck, 1636-1700.

3163. Swierenga, Robert. LOCAL-COSMOPOLITAN THEORY AND IMMIGRANT RELIGION: THE SOCIAL BASES OF THE ANTEBELLUM DUTCH REFORMED SCHISM. *J. of Social Hist. 1980 14(1): 113-136.* This analysis of the 1857 schism among Dutch Calvinists in the United States argues that the immigrants' choices between the established Reformed Dutch Church and the breakaway Christian Reformed Church were most affected by the localistic or cosmopolitan outlook of the particular regions of the Netherlands from which they emigrated. Those from areas more isolated from trade and contact with any of the countries bordering the Netherlands tended to become members of the new schismatics. This split developed from an earlier separatist emergency in the established church in the Netherlands. Many of these Separatists came to this country, merged with the Reformed Church here in 1850, then split again in 1857. Based on machine readable profiles of 2,180 Dutch immigrant family heads and single adults for the years 1834-80 from immigration and church records; 11 tables, fig., 44 notes. C. M. Hough

3164. vanMelle, J. J. Ferdinand. IN SEARCH OF JONAS MICHAELIUS. *Halve Maen 1978 53(3): 1-2, 12-13, 17.* Jonas Michaelius (b. 1584), the first minister of the Reformed Dutch Church in America, arrived there in 1628.

3165. VanWyck, Philip. JOHANNES THEODORUS POLHEMIUS. *Halve Maen 1980 55(2): 9-13, 19-21.* A biographical sketch of German-born Johannes Theodorus Polhemius (1598-1676), linguist, scholar, and Reformed Dutch Church minister in Brazil and New Netherland.

3166. —. [NEW YORK CITY RESIDENTS, 1686 AND 1688]. *Halve Maen 1980 55(1): 10-14.*

Scott, Kenneth. CONTRIBUTORS TO BUILDING OF A NEW DUTCH CHURCH IN NEW YORK CITY, 1688, *pp. 10-12.* Lists the 299 contributors to the second Dutch Church built in New York City between 1688 and 1694 (the first was built in 1647).

Stryker-Rodda, Kenn. NOTES ON NEW YORK RESIDENTS, 1686 AND 1688, *pp. 13-14.* Compares the names on Scott's list to a 1686 list of communicants in the Protestant Reformed Dutch Church in New York.

Episcopal Churches
(including Church of England)

3167. Allison, C. FitzSimons. TOWARD AN HISTORICAL HERMENEUTIC FOR UNDERSTANDING PECUSA. *Hist. Mag. of the Protestant Episcopal Church 1979 48(1): 9-25.* John Colet, Erasmus and Thomas More were symbolic of three distinct traditions in the Episcopal Church, in spite of the fact that all three died as Roman Catholics. The three contribute toward an understanding of the Protestant Episcopal Church in the United States. Colet's contribution lay in his confident acceptance of Scripture over the ultimate wisdom of any particular age, thus anticipating the Reformation in England; Desiderius Erasmus symbolized the liberal tradition which appealed to reason as authority, treasuring the freedom of inquiry and scholarship; and More safeguarded the tradition and continuity of the church and defended its transcendent inviolability from encroachments of state or world. The author relates the positive aspects of each tradition as well as the consequences of their loss to the contemporary American Episcopal scene, pointing out that when any one of these traditions is lost, the other two suffer, and when any one succeeds in eliminating the other two, it dies. Covers the 16th-20th centuries. Secondary sources; 12 notes. H. M. Parker, Jr.

3168. Ashdown, Paul G. SAMUEL RINGGOLD: A MISSIONARY IN THE TENNESSEE VALLEY, 1860-1911. *Tennessee Hist. Q. 1979 38(2): 204-213.* Samuel Ringgold (1825-1911) arrived in Bowling Green, Kentucky, as an Episcopal deacon in 1861, just in time to be caught in the middle of a loyalty controversy between the Confederate Episcopal Church and Union troops. Ringgold kept Christ Church (in Bowling Green) neutral and later kept wartime politics out of his church in Knoxville. There Ringgold later became the foremost churchman in eastern Tennessee. Based on copies of Ringgold correspondence and on other sources; 74 notes. W. D. Piersen

3169. Bennett, Robert A. BLACK EPISCOPALIANS: A HISTORY FROM THE COLONIAL PERIOD TO THE PRESENT. *Hist. Mag. of the Protestant Episcopal Church 1974 43(3): 231-246.* An historical survey of the development of Black Episcopalianism in America, offsetting the standard cliches of the incompatibility of the Black temperament and Episcopalianism. Begins with the Colonial period and the early days of the Republic when the vast majority of Black Christians in America were Anglicans as a result of efforts by the Society for the Propagation of the Gospel, chartered in 1701. The efforts of the Black Episcopalians show that the "story of Black America is one of struggle to express itself in the face of opposition and oppression" realizing that the "Church no less than society as a whole struggles with the dilemma of racism." There is an amazing show of strength in the 1970's, with approximately 100,000 Black Episcopalians. 24 notes. R. V. Ritter

3170. Bowers, Paul C., Jr. and Berquist, Goodwin F., Jr. WORTHINGTON, OHIO: JAMES KILBOURN'S EPISCOPAL HAVEN ON THE WESTERN FRONTIER. *Ohio Hist. 1976 85(3): 247-262.* Discusses the founding of Worthington, Ohio, as the first Episcopal parish west of the Alleghenies. Mentions its founder, James Kilbourne, and discusses the Episcopal Church in Connecticut as a factor in promoting the Ohio settlement. Covers 1744-1816. Based on MS., contemporary comments, and secondary sources; 2 illus., 49 notes. N. Summers

3171. Brown, C. G. FREDERICK DENISON MAURICE IN THE UNITED STATES, 1860-1900. *J. of Religious Hist. [Australia] 1978 10(1): 50-69.* After the death of Anglican Frederick Denison Maurice in 1872, the acceptability of his theological views on such matters as revelation and social reform was a matter of debate. Maurice's views fared better in the United States, especially among Episcopalians, than in his native England. However, even within the American Protestant community, Maurice's views proved controversial. Primary sources; 79 notes. W. T. Walker

3172. Carpenter, Charles, ed. HENRY DANA WARD: EARLY DIARIST OF THE KANAWHA VALLEY. *West Virginia Hist. 1975 37(1): 34-48.* Excerpts from the diary of Henry Dana Ward, Yankee Episcopal minister in Charleston, (West) Virginia, 1845-47, discuss the importance of the salt industry in the Kanawha Valley, the operation of his wife's private school in Charleston, and the river traffic on the Ohio. 2 illus., 18 notes. J. H. Broussard

3173. Clapson, Clive. ALL SAINTS CHURCH, KINGSTON. *J. of the Can. Church Hist. Soc. [Canada] 1979 21: 20-29.* Surveys and analyzes the origins and decline of the Anglican parish of All Saints in Kingston, Ontario, during the second half of the 19th century. With the significant population growth of Kingston in midcentury, the diocesan bishop decided to add another parish to the three that already existed in the city. Catholic in its liturgical practices, the church attracted its membership largely from the growing number of workers in Kingston. During its relatively short existence, the parish had many problems which led ultimately to its collapse. Its Catholic orientation as well as its very existence brought about the hostility of the other Kingston parishes; and All Saints had to compete with other popular religious groups for its working class members. A number of its rectors died after short tenures or were unsuitable for the position. Finally, the city's economic and demographic growth came to an end. Covers ca. 1867-1906. Based on printed and unprinted primary sources; 27 notes.
J. A. Kicklighter

3174. Coke, Fletch. CHRIST CHURCH, EPISCOPAL, NASHVILLE. *Tennessee Hist. Q. 1979 38(2): 141-157.* The Episcopal Church was established in Tennessee during the 1820's by James Hervey Otey (1800-63). Christ Church in Nashville was organized in 1829 and solidified in Gothic-styled stone in 1831. A new Victorian Gothic structure was built for the church in 1894. The leadership of Christ Church is reflected in its eight rectors between 1890 and 1944 who were later made bishops. Based on the Christ Church Vestry Book and other primary sources; 84 notes. W. D. Piersen

3175. Deibert, William E. THOMAS BACON, COLONIAL CLERGYMAN. *Maryland Hist. Mag. 1978 73(1): 79-86.* Surveys the American career of the Anglican priest Thomas Bacon (1700-68), rector of St. Peter's Parish, Talbot County, Maryland, and after 1758 of All Saints Church in Frederick. Though he was fundamentalist and conservative in religious and political beliefs, Bacon's ministry had a progressive social content, and he not only preached that slaves should be taught Christianity but also founded perhaps the first charity working school in Maryland. His project of publishing the laws of Maryland flung him into a four-year political battle (centered on inclusion or omission of the 1661 Tonnage Act) between the proprietary and antiproprietary parties in the General Assembly. Minister, musician, physician, educator, gardener, and student of law, he exemplified the 18th-century Renaissance man and achieved a prominence matched by few Maryland clergymen. Primary and secondary sources; illus., 65 notes. G. J. Bobango

3176. DeMille, George E. THE EPISCOPATE OF BISHOP OLDHAM. *Hist. Mag. of the Protestant Episcopal Church 1977 46(1): 37-56.* Discusses the bishopric of the Reverend George Ashton Oldham of the Episcopal Diocese of Albany, New York, during 1922-47. His tenure embraced the Great Depression and World War II. In spite of these difficult times, he developed a strong administration, enlarged program of the diocese, developed new parishes, and increased contributions to the numerous causes of the church. In addition to his administrative acumen, Oldham was a preacher of the first rank. When he retired, he left the Diocese of Albany in a very strong financial position.
H. M. Parker, Jr.

3177. DeMille, George E. and Gerlach, Don R. SAMUEL JOHNSON AT YALE: THE ROOTS OF CONVERSION, 1710-1722. *Connecticut Hist. 1976 (17): 15-41.* Discusses the religious conversion and theological attitudes of Samuel Johnson as a student and teacher at Yale University, who renounced Congregationalism for Anglicanism.

3178. Dennison, Mary S. HOWARD MACQUEARY: HERESY IN OHIO. *Hist. Mag. of the Protestant Episcopal Church 1980 49(2): 109-131.* Priest of St. Paul's Church (Episcopal), Canton, Ohio, the Reverend Howard MacQueary was representative of those clergy in the last quarter of the 19th century who were influenced by Darwinism and European biblical criticism emanating largely from Germany. After writing his only book, *The Evolution of Man and Christianity* (1890), he failed to heed the counsel of his ecclesiastical superior, Bishop Leonard, regarding his preaching. In 1891 he was charged with denying the virgin birth and Jesus's resurrection. His trial, the first of its kind in the Episcopal Church in America, was one of the numerous examples of the impact of European thought on America's churches. Found guilty, MacQueary left the Episcopal Church and later entered the Universalist Church. Based largely on MacQueary's *The Evolution of Man and Christianity*, the Leonard Papers (Archives of the Diocese of Ohio), and contemporary newspaper accounts; 98 notes. H. M. Parker, Jr.

3179. Elmen, Paul. UNONIUS AND THE SWOPE AFFAIR. *Swedish Pioneer Hist. Q. 1976 27(2): 101-107.* In 1851, the vestry of Trinity Church, Chicago, sought the removal of Cornelius E. Swope as rector. Bishop Philander Chase supported the removal and issued a pamphlet to the diocese on the controversy. Gustaf Unonius felt the removal was unjust and issued a pamphlet supporting Swope. Then an anonymous pamphlet was issued defending the bishop. None of the pamphlets dealt with the real issue, the controversy over ritual. Based on primary sources; 16 notes. K. J. Puffer

3180. Esselmont, Harriet A. E. ALEXANDER JOHN DOULL: AN APPRECIATION. *J. of the Can. Church Hist. Soc. [Canada] 1976 18(4): 98-108.* Traces the life and career of Alexander John Doull, the first bishop of Kootenay in the Okanagan Valley, British Columbia. Born in Nova Scotia of a Church of Scotland family, Doull was an orphaned only child. Reared by relatives, he received his advanced education in the British Isles where he converted to Anglicanism and became a priest. After he returned to Canada, Doull served churches in Montreal and Victoria before he became the youngest bishop of the Church of England in Canada. A man of strong convictions, he took active positions on the issues of the day and worked to increase the strength of Anglicanism in his diocese. When he died in 1937, the *Canadian Churchman* declared, "His character was that beautiful combination of strength and beauty, grace and truth which the Apostles found in the Saviour." 25 notes.
J. A. Kicklighter

3181. Friman, Axel. GUSTAF UNONIUS IN MANITOWOC 1848-1849. *Swedish Pioneer Hist. Q. 1976 27(2): 87-100.* The discovery of a journal and letters sheds light on the work of Gustaf Unonius with St. James Church, a newly organized Episcopal parish in Manitowoc, Wisconsin. He preached in English and occasionally in Norwegian at both Manitowoc and Manitowoc Rapids. He left when invited to go to Chicago by Scandinavians. Based on primary sources; illus., 7 notes.
K. J. Puffer

3182. Garrett, Samuel M. AN ANGLICAN VIEW OF ETHICS: THE INVESTIGATION OF A CONTEXT. *Anglican Theological Rev. 1979 61(1): 8-37.* Attempts to describe an Anglican contribution to the study of human conduct, by defining the Anglican viewpoint in England and the United States, 16th-20th centuries.

3183. Gerardi, Donald F. M. SAMUEL JOHNSON AND THE YALE "APOSTASY" OF 1722: THE CHALLENGE OF ANGLICAN SACRAMENTALISM TO THE NEW ENGLAND WAY. *Hist. Mag. of the Protestant Episcopal Church 1978 47(2): 153-175.* Although raised, educated, and ordained in the Congregational Church, Samuel Johnson (1696-1772) began to have serious doubts about the nature of the church. His questionings arose over the issue of worship in general, extemporaneous prayer in particular. It was his sacramental piety, no less than his developing interest in episcopacy, that makes him something other than a New England mind in transition. Calls Johnson's challenge to the New England Way "sacramental Arminiamism." Delineates Johnson's transition through the books he read while teaching at Yale, 1716-19, followed by his pastorate at West Haven, Conn. Most of his reading was done in sacramental Arminiamism of the Caroline Church, which was Laudian in theology and sensitive to history—a view which had turned many men of that day into Patristic scholars. Thus the polity, faith, and piety of High Church Anglicanism in the age of Johnson's transition were all aspects of the sacramental Arminianism which he adopted and which forced him out of Calvinistic Congregationalism into the Episcopal Church. Based on 17th-century Caroline writings and secondary sources; 65 notes. H. M. Parker, Jr.

3184. Gerrard, Ginny. A HISTORY OF THE PROTESTANT EPISCOPAL CHURCH IN SHREVEPORT, LOUISIANA, 1839-1916. *North Louisiana Hist. Assoc. J. 1978 9(4): 193-203.* The Episcopal Church is the oldest Protestant Church in Louisiana and has the oldest congregation in Shreveport. Following a visit to northwestern Louisiana in 1838 by the young and newly-elected Bishop of Louisiana, Leonidas

Polk, the first services were conducted in 1839. St. Paul's church was formally organized in 1845; its name was changed to St. Mark's in 1850. By 1916 the church had seen the services of 10 rectors and was the largest Episcopal church in Shreveport, thus fulfilling Polk's prophecy: "The place has a promising future." Based on the Polk Papers, Jesse duPont Library archives, University of the South, the Journal of the Diocese of Louisiana, files of St. Mark's church and secondary sources; 74 notes.
H. M. Parker, Jr.

3185. Gundersen, Joan R. THE SEARCH FOR GOOD MEN: RECRUITING MINISTERS IN COLONIAL VIRGINIA. *Hist. Mag. of the Protestant Episcopal Church 1979 48(4): 453-464.* Challenges the thesis that, in colonial Virginia, the Anglican Church failed to find good men to serve its churches, or lacked quality among its candidates. Focuses on how Virginians, including George Washington, did find enough suitable men for a greatly expanding church. By 1776, in contrast to 1726, the number of priests had increased to 109 from 42, and more than half were colonial-born, in contrast to none 50 years earlier. Based on author's doctoral dissertation; the Fulham Palace Manuscripts, Virginia Colonial Records Project microfilm; published collections of letters and secondary sources; 2 fig., 58 notes.
H. M. Parker, Jr.

3186. Gundersen, Joan Rezner. THE MYTH OF THE INDEPENDENT VIRGINIA VESTRY. *Hist. Mag. of the Protestant Episcopal Church 1975 44(2): 133-141.* In the 17th century the Virginia vestry kept close control of the right to hire and dismiss the parish parson. This situation changed drastically after 1700, and by mid-century the vestry had lost any effective control over the parish minister; some vestries were faced with frequent elections. The changed condition, which most historians fail to see, is traceable largely to Commissary James Blair, who worked very closely with the Virginia governors to protect the clergy on the one hand, and to check the high-handed vestry on the other. By 1750 it was all but impossible for the vestry to get rid of incompetent clergy. Based on primary sources; 33 notes.
H. M. Parker, Jr.

3187. Hall, Mark Heathcote. BISHOP MCILVAINE, THE RELUCTANT FRONTIERSMAN. *Hist. Mag. of the Protestant Episcopal Church 1975 44(1): 81-96.* The second Bishop of Ohio, Charles Petit McIlvaine served that post for 40 years. A dedicated evangelical, he opposed the Oxford Movement in America. He was elected bishop of Ohio at the age of 32, but the demands of the office, plus the low cultural level of the frontier, had a psychosomatic effect, resulting in severe "head troubles." He found great relief from this illness by making several journeys to England, where he was always well received. Both Oxford and Cambridge awarded him the honorary Doctor of Canon Law. Covers 1800-75. Based almost solely on Carus, *Memorials of the Rt. Rev. Charles Petit McIlvaine* (1881); 49 notes.
H. M. Parker, Jr.

3188. Hatchett, Marion J. A SUNDAY SERVICE IN 1776 OR THEREABOUTS. *Hist. Mag. of the Protestant Episcopal Church 1976 45(4): 369-385.* Describes the liturgy, vestments and architecture of the 18th-century American Episcopal Church. Based on the author's doctoral dissertation; 6 illus., biblio.
H. M. Parker, Jr.

3189. Headon, Christopher F. DEVELOPMENTS IN CANADIAN ANGLICAN WORSHIP IN EASTERN AND CENTRAL CANADA 1840-1868. *J. of the Can. Church Hist. Soc. 1975 17(2): 26-38.* Many Canadian Anglican clergy with Tractarian backgrounds wanted to increase ritual and introduce a variety of innovations in the Canadian Church. These included the increased use of the surplice, more frequent celebration of the Holy Communion, and development of plainsong for congregational singing. The vast number of low churchmen viewed these changes as very dangerous, seeing an obvious drift toward Roman Catholicism. The attitudes of both high and low churchmen toward the innovations cannot be understood without reference to the great changes affecting 19th-century Canada. Secondary and printed primary sources; 51 notes.
J. A. Kicklighter

3190. Headon, Christopher. AN UNPUBLISHED CORRESPONDENCE BETWEEN JOHN MEDLEY AND E. B. PUSEY. *J. of the Can. Church Hist. Soc. 1974 16(4): 72-74.* Selections from letters written by John Medley (1804-92), an Englishman who became first Anglican bishop of Fredericton, New Brunswick, to Edward Bouverie Pusey (1800-82), one of the most prominent leaders of the Oxford Movement. Written during 1840-44 when Medley was in England, the letters were found among Pusey's correspondence at Pusey House, Oxford.
J. A. Kicklighter

3191. Helmreich, Jonathan E. A PRAYER FOR THE SPIRIT OF ACCEPTANCE: THE JOURNAL OF MARTHA WAYLES ROBERTSON, 1860-1866. *Hist. Mag. of the Protestant Episcopal Church 1977 46(4): 397-408.* Martha Wayles Robertson (1812-67) was a member of the Hollywood Episcopal Church, Chesterfield County, South Carolina. The selected entries from her diary, 1860-66, reflect the general feeling of southerners regarding the Civil War: God's blessings on the Confederacy, the intimate intervention of God's hand in history, the growing tendency to pray for the troops of the Confederacy, the growing disdain for the enemy, the fact that Southern defeats were brought by God to humble the South, and the acknowledgement that in the final defeat "we must have been a sinful nation to suffer such severe chastisement!" Based largely on the MS journal of Mrs. Robertson; 35 notes.
H. M. Parker, Jr.

3192. Hendrickson, Walter B. A CHURCH ON THE PRAIRIE: THE FOUNDING AND EARLY YEARS OF TRINITY IN JACKSONVILLE, ILLINOIS—1832-1838. *Hist. Mag. of the Protestant Episcopal Church 1975 44(1): 5-21.* Trinity Church was the first Episcopal congregation organized in Illinois 11 August 1832. With no minister, laymen elected wardens and vestrymen. Details the first edifice, the formation of the Illinois Diocese in 1835, and the ministry of Rev. John Batchelder, Trinity Church's missionary pastor, who served 1833-38. The Episcopal Church had difficulties on a frontier largely dominated by Presbyterians, Congregationalists, Methodists, and other Protestant groups. Based largely on primary sources, including the Parish Register of Trinity Church and the Convention Journal; 56 notes.
H. M. Parker, Jr.

3193. Hewitt, John H. NEW YORK'S BLACK EPISCOPALIANS: IN THE BEGINNING, 1704-1722. *Afro-Americans in New York Life and Hist. 1979 3(1): 9-22.* Elias Neau, a lay member of the Church of England's Society for the Propagation of the Gospel, taught and preached to Negroes in New York City.

3194. Hogue, William M. THE SWEET SINGER OF HARTFORD. *Hist. Mag. of the Protestant Episcopal Church 1976 45(1): 57-77.* The history of the Episcopal Church can be discovered in the literature of an earlier day. Writings of Lydia Huntley Sigourney of Hartford, Connecticut serve as an example. She authored 57 books, contributed to more than 300 periodicals, wrote more than 2,000 poems, many of which became hymns, and was very much a part of the literary scene of her time—the middle third of the 19th century. In her deemphasis of the sacraments, the liturgy, and the Christian year, she unconsciously declared her affinity for the evangelical party of the Episcopal Church. She was very active in the numerous reform movements of her day, and showed special concern for the plight of the American Indian. None of her voluminous productivity, however, is recognized today in any hymnal or poetic anthology. Her poetry nevertheless is a witness to the force of the evangelical movement in shaping the thoughts, words, and deeds of some Episcopalians in the mid-19th century. Based largely on her autobiography and works; 88 notes.
H. M. Parker, Jr.

3195. Holmes, David L. DEVEREUX JARRATT: A LETTER AND A REEVALUATION. *Hist. Mag. of the Protestant Episcopal Church 1978 47(1): 37-49.* A revisionist interpretation of the Virginia Episcopal priest, Devereux Jarratt (1733-1801), who was largely responsible for reviving the Episcopal Church in Virginia after the Revolution. Suggests that a closer analysis of his *Life* reveals layers of complexity as interesting for what it said as for what it left unsaid. The letter was written a few weeks before his death. It displays some of the characteristics of his career—an abiding fellowship for those with whom he agreed, a brotherly feeling for other evangelical denominations, a love for the Bible, a wide background in secular literature, a devotion to Reformation doctrine, a modified Calvinism, a sense of being out of place in his Church and the world, and a resultant striving to be "entirely abstracted from this world." Since few of Jarratt's writings have surfaced the letter is valuable. Based largely on Jarratt's *Life* and includes the letter which was found in the Archives and Historical Collections of the Episcopal Church; 45 notes.
H. M. Parker, Jr.

3196. Holmgren, Eric J. WILLIAM NEWTON AND THE ANGLICAN CHURCH. *Alberta Hist. [Canada] 1975 23(2): 17-25.* William Newton founded the Church of England in Edmonton in 1875 and remained there until 1900. Born, educated, and married in England, his Edmonton years were neither pleasant nor successful. He seemed to be mostly interested in Indians and Métis, possibly because so many whites were Methodist or Roman Catholic, and he antagonized many with his undiplomatic bearing. His book, *Twenty Years on the Saskatchewan,* appeared in 1897. 3 illus., 30 notes. D. Chaput

3197. Jones, Frederick. THE EARLY OPPOSITION TO BISHOP FEILD OF NEWFOUNDLAND. *J. of the Can. Church Hist. Soc. 1974 16(2): 30-41.* Newfoundland was torn between two rival groups when Edward Feild became Anglican bishop there in 1844. The liberals included most of the fishermen, Roman Catholic in religion and Irish in nationality, while the conservatives were Anglican, of English background and included a majority of the merchants. The Protestant Dissenters, Methodists and Presbyterians, were ambivalent in their attitude towards the two groups. Feild's appointment was unfortunate, since the new bishop was High Church and ritualistic while most Anglicans in Newfoundland were Low Church and evangelical. Thus a new source for dispute arose. Feild fought the evangelicals on many issues, and his relations with Roman Catholics and Methodists were not good, either. The conflict between Feild and his Anglican flock typifies the division in the Church of England as a whole. Primary sources; 74 notes.
J. A. Kicklighter

3198. Jones, Frederick. THE MAKING OF A COLONIAL BISHOP: FIELD OF NEWFOUNDLAND. *J. of the Can. Church Hist. Soc. 1973 15(1): 2-13.* Studies the career of Edward Feild, second bishop of Newfoundland (1844-76), before his accession to the episcopate. Feild was born in Worcester, England, in 1801 and was ordained to the priesthood in 1826. As curate-in-charge of Kidlington and rector of English Bicknor, Gloucestershire, Feild dealt with the many difficult problems of his parishes, demonstrating great concern for miseries resulting from industrialization. Believing that education would help alleviate some of the problems, Feild built day schools for his churches. He became widely known as an authority on education and was an Inspector of Schools for the church. In 1844 he reluctantly accepted appointment as a colonial bishop. Based on primary and secondary sources; 79 notes.
J. A. Kicklighter

3199. Jordan, David W. A SEARCH FOR SALVATION IN THE CORRUPT NEW WORLD. *Hist. Mag. of the Protestant Episcopal Church 1974 43(1): 45-55.* Reviews the early colonial experiences of Joseph Presbury, Anglican clergyman and immigrant to Maryland from England, and publishes three letters he wrote to his former clergyman. Presbury was shocked to discover the state of religion in the New World. Church services were sporadic and of poor quality, the clergy were corrupt, and the people were little more than heathens. 3 notes.
V. L. Human

3200. Kater, John L., Jr. FORGOTTEN PROPHET: A NOTE ON THE THEOLOGY OF FREDERIC HASTINGS SMYTH. *Anglican Theological Rev. 1973 55(1): 73-77.* Frederic Hastings Smyth's *Manhood into God* (New York: Round Table Pr., 1940) illuminates his Catholic version of Anglican Christianity which was the basis for establishing the Society of the Catholic Commonwealth, a group of utopian churchmembers based in Cambridge, Massachusetts.

3201. Kinney, John M. BIBLIOGRAPHY OF DIOCESAN HISTORIES. *Hist. Mag. of the Protestant Episcopal Church 1974 43(1): 69-100.* A bibliography of diocesan and missionary histories of the American Episcopal Church. Diocesan listings are categorized by state and foreign mission histories by nation. V. L. Human

3202. Lambert, James H. THE REVEREND SAMUEL SIMPSON WOOD, BA, MA: A FORGOTTEN NOTABLE AND THE EARLY ANGLICAN CHURCH IN CANADA. *J. of the Can. Church Hist. Soc. 1974 16(1): 2-22.* Describes the career of Samuel Wood (1795-1868), an English-born clergyman in the Anglican diocese of Quebec. Educated at the conservative Richmond Grammar School and Cambridge, Wood began his work in Quebec as a missionary. In 1822 he became the first rector of Drummondsville. In 1829 he went to Three Rivers, and remained some 30 years. His chief efforts were devoted to ending the British government's discrimination against Canadian Anglican clergy and to establishing church-related schools and seminaries. His later years were spent as rural dean of Upper Durham, where he was primarily involved in missionary work. Though neither powerful nor spectacular, Wood's career represented many important trends in the evolution of Canadian Anglicanism. Based largely on primary sources; 132 notes.
J. A. Kicklighter

3203. Maclean, Hugh D. AN IRISH APOSTLE AND ARCHDEACON IN CANADA. *J. of the Can. Church Hist. Soc. 1973 15(3): 50-67.* Irish-born William McMurray (1810-94) was an important Canadian Anglican clergyman. Brought to Toronto when he was one, McMurray became a theology student at age 18. In 1832, he became the missionary to the Ojibway Indians in the Sault Ste. Marie area. He was ordained deacon in 1833 and priest in 1839. His work with the Indians was successful, but he resigned after the provincial governor stopped all projects involved in "civilizing" the Indians. He served as assistant curate and rector of Ancaster and Dundas, and in 1857 became rector of Niagara. He received two honorary doctorates as a result of extensive fund-raising in the United States and of lobbying for the church at the Parliament in Quebec City. He rounded out his career as a fund-raiser in Great Britain as rural dean of Lincoln and Welland, and as archdeacon of the new diocese of Niagara 1876-94. 58 notes. J. A. Kicklighter

3204. Mappen, Marc. ANGLICAN HERESY IN EIGHTEENTH CENTURY CONNECTICUT: THE DISCIPLINING OF JOHN BEACH. *Hist. Mag. of the Protestant Episcopal Church 1979 48(4): 465-472.* The only colonial Connecticut Anglican clergyman ever charged with heresy, John Beach (1700-82), was a convert from Congregationalism. He rejected much of the theology of his former colleagues, and even wrote devastating pamphlets against them. In 1755, he published a book asserting that at the moment of death each individual comes into the presence of Christ and is judged then, rather than on Judgment Day. The Connecticut Congregational clergy, spotting this potential heresy, sent a copy of the work to Beach's ecclesiastical superiors in England. Reprimand followed. Beach backed down and went on to serve the Church, being the last Anglican parson in Connecticut to pray for the King's health. Based on the author's doctoral dissertation, records of the Society for the Propagation of the Gospel, Beach's writings, and secondary sources; 28 notes. H. M. Parker, Jr.

3205. Masters, D. C. THE ANGLICAN EVANGELICALS IN TORONTO 1870-1900. *J. of the Can. Church Hist. Soc. [Canada] 1978 20(3-4): 51-66.* Describes the beliefs and contributions of some 55 Anglican evangelicals in the diocese of Toronto during the late 19th century. Consisting of both clergy and laity, the group struggled successfully with the High Church party for influence within the Canadian Church, and consequently had an important role in shaping its future. Emphasizing the role of the individual in his relationship to God, the Evangelicals were also individualistic in their socioeconomic views. Almost all were comfortably middle-class, and advocated private charity for the poor and distressed, while they opposed government intervention to aid working people and the indigent. Like Protestant groups with whom they were on good terms, the Evangelicals advocated total abstinence from alcoholic beverages and maintained a theology centered around God's sovereignty. At the same time, they held to traditional Anglican beliefs in liturgical worship and an ecclesiastical hierarchy. Based on printed and unprinted primary and secondary sources; 36 notes. J. A. Kicklighter

3206. Millman, T. R. BEGINNINGS OF THE SYNODICAL MOVEMENT IN COLONIAL ANGLICAN CHURCHES WITH SPECIAL REFERENCE TO CANADA. *J. of the Can. Church Hist. Soc. [Canada] 1979 21: 3-19.* Surveys the gradual development of lay participation in the governing of Anglican churches in British colonies, particularly Canada. Synods already had been established in the United States to offer the laity the opportunity to share in the authority of the Protestant Episcopal Church; but the bishops in Canada, Australia, and elsewhere still had full authority over their dioceses in the late 18th century. In the 19th century, however, change came about because of the churches' financial needs and because of the desire of Anglicans in Canada and elsewhere to have a greater degree of self-government. In the 1850's, with the support of the Canadian legislature, the dioceses in Canada, despite opposition, established synods to participate in ecclesiastical government. Although the British government did not interfere, the legal fiction was preserved that the crown had full authority over the Anglican Church. Based on printed and unprinted primary sources; 45 notes. J. A. Kicklighter

3207. Millman, T. R. BEGINNINGS OF THE SYNODICAL MOVEMENT IN COLONIAL ANGLICAN CHURCHES WITH SPECIAL REFERENCE TO CANADA. *J. of the Can. Church Hist. Soc. [Canada] 1979 21(6): 7-11.* The inclusion of laymen in the governance of the Anglican Church in Canada seemed hindered by the doctrine of royal supremacy by which the episcopate held all ecclesiastical authority. When the British Parliament ended its financial grants to the church in Canada in 1832, lay participation through synods in the governance of the church provided a means to prevent fiscal disaster. By the 1850's the Canadian legislature recognized the authority of synods in diocesan government. This is an abbreviated version of an earlier article. Covers 1782-1857. J. A. Kicklighter

3208. Millman, T. R. DOCUMENTS OF THE CANADIAN CHURCH—7. *J. of the Can. Church Hist. Soc. 1973 15(3): 71.* Reprints excerpts from the Letters of Patent of 18 July 1850 which created the diocese of Montreal and appointed its first bishop; and from an act of the Parliament of United Canada, 9 June 1852. Sent in response to the June 1973 publication in the *Journal* of a special legal instrument granting the prelate of Quebec the title of lord bishop, these documents demonstrate that the title of lord bishop was given to the bishops of both Montreal and Quebec. J. A. Kicklighter

3209. Millman, Thomas R. A SKETCH OF THE LIFE OF FRANCIS FULFORD. *J. of the Can. Church Hist. Soc. 1975 17(4): 82-93.* Francis Fulford was bishop of Montreal, 1850-68. A native of England, Fulford was aristocratic, well-educated, and experienced as a minister at home. As a bishop in Canada, Fulford made important contributions, especially in establishing diocesan synods, ecclesiastical provinces, and provincial synods in the Canadian Anglican Church. He was also responsible for ecclesiastical legislation which led to the self-governance of the church in Canada and for the construction of a new cathedral after the old one burned down. A man of great faith, Fulford strove for peace within the church and at all times acted in a spirit of moderation. Based on printed primary sources; 30 notes. J. A. Kicklighter

3210. Mills, Frederick V., Sr. THE INTERNAL ANGLICAN CONTROVERSY OVER AN AMERICAN EPISCOPATE. *Hist. Mag. of the Protestant Episcopal Church 1975 44(3): 257-276.* Although the historic episcopate is a principal feature of Anglicanism, American colonial Anglicans were far from unanimous in their disposition toward a resident bishop. Numerous reasons could be marshalled for having an American bishop, but the leading clergy failed to convince the colonists or the mother Church. The opposition in each of the colonies, when added up, reveals why the Americans did not unanimously press for a resident bishop. In addition, the instability of the British ministries in the 1760's, the emphasis upon imperial problems, and the British government's indifference toward ecclesiastical matters were English factors which militated against such action. Primary and secondary sources; 91 notes. H. M. Parker, Jr.

3211. Mills, Frederick V., Sr. THE PROTESTANT EPISCOPAL CHURCHES IN THE UNITED STATES 1783-1789: SUSPENDED ANIMATION OR REMARKABLE RECOVERY? *Hist. Mag. of the Protestant Episcopal Church 1977 46(2): 151-170.* Church historians have interpreted the post-Revolutionary War period as one of stagnation at best, decline at worst, for the Protestant Episcopal Church. However, the records of the plans, hopes, and accomplishments of the churchmen, despite extensive disorganization and a prolonged series of reserves, show that this period was one of remarkable recovery. The achievements of the Episcopalians raise the distinct possibility that religion was not passé between 1775 and 1800, as it has been described. Based on diocesan histories; 2 tables, 82 notes. H. M. Parker, Jr.

3212. Mounger, Dwyn M. HISTORY AS INTERPRETED BY STEPHEN ELLIOTT. *Hist. Mag. of the Protestant Episcopal Church 1975 44(3): 285-317.* Stephen Elliott (1806-66) was the first Episcopal bishop of Georgia. Through his sermons and voluminous writings he conceived of history from the traditional Christian point of view: the fulfillment of the divine will. He was one of the major apologists for the Southern way of life. He viewed slavery as intricately woven into the fabric of Southern life, decried abolitionism, led the way in evangelizing slaves, and favored the Southern cause during the Civil War. Never wavering in his belief that God was on the side of the Stars and Bars, he anticipated Confederate victory down to the last battle. Even the defeat he accepted as the work of God, not of man. His greatest delusion in historical interpretation lay in his claim to be able to read the approval and condemnation of God in the events of history, despite the fact that on occasion he would admit that discernment was difficult. Only the Confederate defeat changed him from a strict Deuteronomist in history. Based largely on Elliott's writings; 117 notes. H. M. Parker, Jr.

3213. Noon, Rozanne E. THE BISHOP'S CHILDREN. *Hist. Mag. of the Protestant Episcopal Church 1974 43(1): 5-20.* Reviews the life, works, and theological philosophies of Frederick Huntington, Episcopal Bishop of Central New York during 1869-1904, and his children. His daughters, Arria and Ruth, shared the Bishop's zeal and energy for good works, but not his view of woman's place as being in the home. His son James also leaned toward a religious life, but deplored the money-raising, good works aspects of the Church, causing conflict with his father; another son, George, was undecided. The death of the Bishop left James to turn to the quiet life he so much desired. 28 notes. V. L. Human

3214. Osmond, Oliver R. THE CHURCHMANSHIP OF JOHN STRACHAN. *J. of the Can. Church Hist. Soc. 1974 16(3): 46-59.* Describes the ecclesiological views of the first bishop of Toronto, John Strachan. Famed as a founder of educational institutions, Strachan was equally devoted to the defense of the Anglican position in Canada. Though born a Presbyterian, Strachan was never fully committed to its beliefs and first received communion at an Anglican church in Kingston. Greatly influenced by the High Church bishop of New York, J. H. Hobart, Strachan insisted that the Anglican Church was a branch of the universal church. He added to this view the idea that the church was independent of both Pope and king. Accusing the Roman Catholic Church of corruption, he emphasized in his own ministry the ancient practices of the church. Fundamentally a High Churchman, Strachan was broadminded and devoted to unity within his diocese. Covers 1802-67. Based on primary and secondary sources; 56 notes. J. A. Kicklighter

3215. Pannekoek, Frits. THE REV. GRIFFITHS OWEN CORBETT AND THE RED RIVER CIVIL WAR OF 1869-70. *Can. Hist. Rev. [Canada] 1976 57(2): 133-149.* Examines the period 1863-69 in Red River. Notes the observations of such an Anglican clerics as Griffiths Corbett. Argues that Red River was a civil war between the English- and French-speaking half-breeds. Based primarily on unpublished documents in the Hudson's Bay Company Archives and the Church Missionary Society Archives, London. A

3216. Petersen, William H. THE TENSIONS OF ANGLICAN IDENTITY IN PECUSA: AN INTERPRETIVE ESSAY. *Hist. Mag. of the Protestant Episcopal Church 1978 47(4): 427-452.* Presents developments in the polity, doctrine, and liturgy of the Protestant Episcopal Church in the United States (PECUSA) during the colonial (1607-1789), national (1789-1928), and modern (1928-78) periods. Finds the Church not so reformed as reforming. In the modern period emphasis is on the liturgy. Suggests that the Thirty-nine Articles have become interesting historical documents to be read by students of Anglican history, though not necessarily subscribed to by all Episcopalians. Secondary sources; 52 notes. H. M. Parker, Jr.

3217. Prichard, Bob. EARLY DEVELOPMENT OF THE DIOCESAN STANDING COMMITTEE. *Hist. Mag. of the Protestant Episcopal Church 1974 43(3): 201-214.* A study of the development during the first 43 years 1789-1832 of the Standing Committee as an effectively functioning unit within the Episcopal framework. During this period bishops grew in power and number while the Standing Committees shrank. In 1832 an attempt was made to retain the usefulness of the Standing Committee, with details of practice being codified for the first time in an attempt to prevent its extinction. 24 notes. R. V. Ritter

3218. Rehkopf, Charles F. REACTIONS TO EVENTS OF THE '60'S AND '70'S. *Hist. Mag. of the Protestant Episcopal Church 1978 47(4): 453-462.* Uses the Episcopal Diocese of Missouri (the eastern part of the state) during the episcopate of George L. Cadigan as a model to demonstrate the influence of the church on society and vice versa. Most of the activity was in the St. Louis area. Cites instances of parish consolidation, renewal and mission on the urban frontier, and ecumenical undertakings to minister to facets of society, religious and secular, since 1960. Whatever the Missouri Diocese did during those turbulent years took place because the leadership felt that the "Church should be there." While it did not succeed in every instance, it endeavored at least to carry out Christ's command to preach the acceptable year of the Lord. H. M. Parker, Jr.

3219. Reilly, Timothy. GENTEEL REFORM VERSUS SOUTHERN ALLEGIANCE: EPISCOPALIAN DILEMMA IN OLD NEW ORLEANS. *Hist. Mag. of the Protestant Episcopal Church 1975 44(4): 437-450.* The first Episcopal church in New Orleans was founded in 1805; the first Bishop of Louisiana, Leonidas Polk, was consecrated in 1838. His basic thrust among Negro slaves was in education. In response to the increasing sectional hostility between North and South, Polk also sought to establish a regional southern university, which was ultimately the University of the South at Sewanee, Tennessee. He was an advocate of gradual emancipation, and supported the efforts of the American Colonization Society up to the eve of the Civil War. He urged humanitarian treatment of slaves. His proselytizing efforts among them resulted in black communicants outnumbering whites in his diocese. He became a planter with slaves, and with the advent of the Civil War his program of genteel reform and educational development was considerably altered. His ministry terminated when he lost his life as a general in the Confederate Army. His religious career was governed by an emotionalism which was intermittently charged by a strong regional identification and an essential conservatism. Based on primary and secondary sources; 50 notes. H. M. Parker, Jr.

3220. Reynierse, Peter J. A HISTORY OF ST. JOHN'S CHURCH, VERSAILLES, KENTUCKY. *Hist. Mag. of the Protestant Episcopal Church 1976 45(1): 47-55.* Chronicles the history of St. John's Episcopal Church, Versailles, Kentucky, largely through its clergy from the earliest services in 1829 to the present. The parish was organized 29 June 1847, and the church was consecrated 10 May 1854. In the early years the shortage of Episcopal priests in Kentucky was the major problem confronting the church; in later years it was the brevity of their pastorates. Cites several anecdotes in the church's history, and describes the numerous improvements and additions to the church property and edifice. Based largely on primary sources, especially the church register; 25 notes. H. M. Parker, Jr.

3221. Rightmyer, Thomas Nelson. THE HOLY ORDERS OF PETER MUHLENBERG. *Hist. Mag. of the Protestant Episcopal Church 1961 30(3): 183-197.* Presents evidence that John Peter Gabriel Muhlenberg, a newly ordained priest in the Church of England, was priest and rector to the Beckford Parish in Dunmore County, Virginia, 1772-76.

3222. Roof, Wade Clark and Perkins, Richard B. ON CONCEPTUALIZING SALIENCE IN RELIGIOUS COMMITMENT. *J. for the Sci. Study of Religion 1975 14(2): 111-128.* Uses a case study of Episcopalians in North Carolina to explore the relation between salience and commitment. S

3223. Rouse, Parke, Jr. JAMES BLAIR OF VIRGINIA. *Hist. Mag. of the Protestant Episcopal Church 1974 43(2): 189-193.* James Blair (1655-1743) was sent out in 1685 as an Episcopal missionary to colonial Virginia. He was a latitudinarian churchman, Whiggish advocate of colonial prerogatives, political hatchet man, for 56 years commissary in Virginia to the Bishop of London, acting governor of Virginia (1740-41), but most important, president for life of the College of William and Mary which he founded and "which has survived to spread throughout the United States some of the Christian humanism that he soaked up from pulpit to classroom in 17th century Scotland." R. V. Ritter

3224. Ryan, H. R. S. and Light, E. S. ON THE NATURE OF SYNODICAL GOVERNMENT IN EPISCOPAL CHURCHES (ILLUSTRATED BY EXPERIENCE IN THE ANGLICAN CHURCH OF CANADA). *J. of the Can. Church Hist. Soc. [Canada] 1979 21(6): 12-17.* Describes how synodical government has functioned in the Anglican Church of Canada. Developing over two centuries, the synodical form of church government gained considerable authority. Anglican bishops in Canada found it necessary to meet with and debate the synods in their diocese; their power to thwart the synods proved limited. Most episcopal authority today stems from the personal prestige of the bishops and from traditional respect for the episcopate. J. C. Kicklighter

3225. Searcey, Mildred. THE LITTLE BROWN JUG. *Hist. Mag. of the Protestant Episcopal Church 1974 43(1): 57-64.* A brief history of the establishment of the Episcopal Church in Pendleton, Oregon. The town was too small to attract clergymen during the 19th century, but eventually a determined group of women succeeded in having a small church built. Informally named "The Little Brown Jug," the building and operation of the church attracted a colorful congregation. Covers 1864-1971. Note. V. L. Human

3226. Siegenthaler, David. NOVA SCOTIA, 1784: A LETTER OF JACOB BAILEY. *J. of the Can. Church Hist. Soc. [Canada] 1977 19(3-4): 131-137.* A letter of an Anglican clergyman in Nova Scotia to another, his close friend, in Massachusetts. Though the letter does not reveal any important information that could not have been acquired from other sources, it has both value and interest because of its unconscious, intimate approach to contemporary events. The Rev. Jacob Bailey (1731-1808) thus remarks on the American Revolution which had forced his removal from Maine to Canada, the severe financial limitations of his current position in Nova Scotia, and the wide diversity of Christian sects in the area. In the letter one can sense some of the difficulties a North American clergyman faced in the later 18th century. Based on secondary sources and an unprinted primary source; 17 notes. J.A. Kicklighter

3227. Skaggs, David Curtis. THE CHAIN OF BEING IN EIGHTEENTH CENTURY MARYLAND: THE PARADOX OF THOMAS CRADOCK. *Hist. Mag. of the Protestant Episcopal Church 1976 45(2): 155-164.* Recent early American historiography stresses the continuity of ideologies and behavior patterns across the Atlantic basin. In the sermons and poetry of the Reverend Thomas Cradock (1718-70) of St. Thomas' Parish (Anglican), Baltimore County, Maryland, we find some of the strongest expositions of the themes inherent in the great chain of being—gradation, plenitude, and continuity. He accepted this paradigm as part of the cultural milieu of his age. On the one hand he sought to uphold the social synthesis learned in his catechism; on the other his incisive, often satirical commentary on those charged with maintaining that cosmology contributed to its downfall in the Revolutionary era. Based largely on Cradock's papers and sermons in the Maryland Diocesan Archives, Maryland Historical Society, Baltimore; 43 notes. H. M. Parker, Jr.

3228. Skaggs, David Curtis and Hartdagen, Gerald E. SINNERS AND SAINTS: ANGLICAN CLERICAL CONDUCT IN COLONIAL MARYLAND. *Hist. Mag. of the Protestant Episcopal Church 1978 47(2): 177-195.* Although there were all too many "sinners" among the colonial Maryland Anglican clergy whose conduct brought reproach to themselves and their church, there were also a number of "saints" who lived virtuously and served well in numerous ecclesiastical and cultural areas. In the past too much emphasis has been placed on the "saints" by some, on the "sinners" by others. Covers 1700-75. Primary and secondary sources; 69 notes. H. M. Parker, Jr.

3229. Skaggs, David Curtis. THOMAS CRADOCK AND THE CHESAPEAKE GOLDEN AGE. *William and Mary Q. 1973 30(1): 93-116.* Reverend Thomas Cradock (1718-70), rector of St. Thomas's parish, Baltimore County, Maryland, was a leading representative of the cultural paradigm of Chesapeake society. This literary biography contains a summary and critique of recent interpretations on Chesapeake society. Cradock's numerous sermons had little relevance to his own time and frequently upbraided his fellow clergy but did not veer from orthodoxy. His poetry, especially his satirical eclogues, though lacking in depth, usefully depicted social and intellectual life in Maryland. Also considers his two translations of the Psalms, with selections from his writings. Based on primary and secondary sources; illus., map, 37 notes. H. M. Ward

3230. Skemp, Sheila. GEORGE BERKELEY'S NEWPORT EXPERIENCE. *Rhode Island Hist. 1978 37(2): 53-63.* George Berkeley's visit to Newport, Rhode Island, 1729-31, had a profound impact on his thought and outlook. He arrived full of hope for religious and educational reforms in the New World; he left a broken and disappointed man. Sectarian conflict in Newport was primarily responsible for transforming him from a practical reformer to a reclusive churchman. Based on published documents and writings, newspapers, and secondary accounts; 6 illus., 39 notes. P. J. Coleman

3231. Spalding, Phinizy. SOME SERMONS BEFORE THE TRUSTEES OF COLONIAL GEORGIA. *Georgia Hist. Q. 1973 57(3): 332-346.* The Associates of Dr. Bray, formed to encourage establishment of philanthropic societies, and the Trustees of the Colony of Georgia, met annually in London and attended church services in a body. Analyzes the 1733-50 sermons as source material for understanding of colonial Georgia and contemporary England. They constitute accurate status reports on the Georgia project. Biblio. D. L. Smith

3232. Sugeno, Frank E., ed. EPISCOPAL AND ANGLICAN HISTORY: 1972: AN ANNOTATED BIBLIOGRAPHY. *Hist. Mag. of the Protestant Episcopal Church 1973 42(4): 451-468.*

3233. Sugeno, Frank E., ed. EPISCOPAL AND ANGLICAN HISTORY: 1973-1975: AN ANNOTATED BIBLIOGRAPHY. *Hist. Mag. of the Protestant Episcopal Church 1977 46(1): 115-148.* An annotated bibliography of books and articles under five major headings: 1) Protestant Episcopal Church in the United States; 2) Anglican Communion; 3) American Christianity; 4) English Christianity; and 5) Bibliographies. Each of these major headings is broken down into the following categories: general history and character; studies of periods; thematic studies; biographies, works and new editions; and local studies.
H. M. Parker, Jr.

3234. Swanton, Carolyn. DR. ALGERNON S. CRAPSEY: RELIGIOUS REFORMER. *Rochester Hist. 1980 42(1): 1-24.* Episcopal minister Algernon Sidney Crapsey (1847-1927) went to Rochester from New York City in 1879 to minister at St. Andrew's Church; focuses on his humanitarian work and concern for his parishioners, and his trial in an ecclesiastical court in 1906 for heresy; found guilty, he was forced to leave the church, but continued his work until his death.

3235. Sydnor, William. [DOCTOR DAVID GRIFFITH OF VIRGINIA].

DAVID GRIFFITH—CHAPLAIN, SURGEON, PATRIOT. *Hist. Mag. of the Protestant Episcopal Church 1975 44(3): 247-256.* Coming out of an obscure pastorate of northern Virginia, David Griffith served three years as chaplain and surgeon of the 3rd Virginia Regiment during the American Revolution. He was with the Continental Line during some of the bloodiest, darkest, and most pivotal engagements in the early years of the war. Later he was the first bishop-elect of the Episcopal Church in Virginia. Based largely on Griffith's letters; 44 notes.

DOCTOR GRIFFITH OF VIRGINIA: EMERGENCE OF A CHURCH LEADER, MARCH, 1779-JUNE 3, 1786. *Hist. Mag. of the Protestant Episcopal Church 1976 45(1): 5-24.* Discusses Griffith's life from the post-Revolutionary War period until he received his honorary doctorate from the University of Pennsylvania in recognition of his leadership in salvaging and rebuilding the Episcopal Church in America from its nadir after the War, through the organization of the General Convention in 1785. Griffith was elected Bishop of Virginia in this period. Article transcends Griffith, however, and gives considerable insights into the total reconstruction of the church in which Griffith played a most prominent role. Based largely on the White Papers of the Church Historical Society, Austin, Texas, and other primary sources; 68 notes.

DR. GRIFFITH OF VIRGINIA: THE BREAKING OF A CHURCH LEADER, SEPTEMBER 1786-AUGUST 3, 1789. *Hist. Mag. of the Protestant Episcopal Church 1976 45(2): 113-132.* Although elected bishop of Virginia, due to lack of funds Griffith was not able to make the journey to England to be consecrated. Failure to vote the funds can be laid at the feet of Virginia Episcopalians. For one thing, they were not sure that they wanted a bishop. For another, they certainly did not want Griffith for they felt that they could not control him. After the Episcopalians refused for three years to raise the funds to send him to England, he abandoned any hope of being consecrated. He thus resigned his bishopric, a broken man, and died three months later. Based largely on the White Papers, Church Historical Society, Austin, Texas, and other miscellaneous primary sources; table, 54 notes. H. M. Parker, Jr.

3236. Tomlinson, Juliette. CHRIST CHURCH, SPRINGFIELD, MASSACHUSETTS: FROM PARISH CHURCH TO THE CATHEDRAL OF THE DIOCESE. *Hist. Mag. of the Protestant Episcopal Church 1974 43(3): 253-260.* The congregation which ultimately became Christ Church was organized in 1817 by Colonel Roswell Lee, Superintendent of Springfield's Armory, and was incorporated by the legislature in 1839. The same year a building was started, and a new stone building following this one in 1875-76. The church prospered as did the whole diocese, so that by the turn of the century division of the diocese was seriously considered. This in turn led to discussions of Christ Church becoming the Diocesan Cathedral for western Massachusetts, a change which was consummated in 1929. R. V. Ritter

3237. Walker, Henry Pickering. PREACHER IN HELLDORADO. *J. of Arizona Hist. 1974 15(3): 223-248.* A narrative account of the six-month ministry in 1882 of Episcopalian Endicott Peabody (1857-1944) in Tombstone, Arizona Territory. The English-educated young Bostonian seminarian related well with the citizenry of the frontier town. He was so well-liked that he has become a part of the legendary history of the town. 2 illus., 46 notes. D. L. Smith

3238. Walsh, James P. "BLACK COTTED RASKOLLS": ANTI-ANGLICAN CRITICISM IN COLONIAL VIRGINIA. *Virginia Mag. of Hist. and Biog. 1980 88(1): 21-36.* Colonial Virginia saw its Anglican clergy as lazy and irresponsible, or alternately as lustful for power. Having to serve geographically large parishes made the clergy appear neglectful. Traces the laity's discontent to clerical rebukes of their sins, and the problem of the clergy's social status. Clergymen complained too, particularly about tenure and salaries, but had opportunity for material improvement and security. Ministers looked to Great Britain, from whence they came, for support in their struggles with Virginians. Covers 1635-1783. 57 notes. P. J. Woehrmann

3239. Walton, John. TRADITION OF THE MIDDLE WAY: THE ANGLICAN CONTRIBUTION TO THE AMERICAN CHARACTER. *Hist. Mag. of the Protestant Episcopal Church 1975 44(5): 7-32.* Anglicanism has made a positive and continuing contribution to the American way of life. Identifies this contribution as 1) a preference for the "middle way," a *via media* not just between Catholics and Protestants, but a *via media vitae*; and 2) an acceptance of pragmatism as the ultimate law. Begins with the English Anglican Richard Hooker, works through the Anglican posture in the American colonies, and concludes by demonstrating similarities and possible historical connections between the distinctive theological pragmatism of early Anglicanism and what is modern American pragmatism. Colonial Anglicanism should be considered a possible major influence on the American character—like Puritanism, the European Enlightenment, and the Frontier. Based largely on primary sources plus extensive use of secondary political theory works; 98 notes. H. M. Parker, Jr.

3240. Watson, Alan D. THE ANGLICAN PARISH IN ROYAL NORTH CAROLINA, 1729-1775. *Hist. Mag. of the Protestant Episcopal Church 1979 48(3): 303-319.* Through a study of two colonial Anglican parishes, St. Paul's (Chowan County) and St. John's (Carteret County), demonstrates ways the church in east North Carolina preached and met the needs of a substantial segment of the population. The parish remained a viable institution throughout the royal era. The assembly continually relieved the parish of its civil responsibilities, reflecting the inability of parishes to cope with such duties on the one hand as well as the increasing competence of county units of government on the other. Yet the parish did retain a competent taxing power which it used to support and enlarge the church establishment and an extensive system of poor relief. Based largely on the records of the two parishes and the two counties and North Carolina colonial and state records; 85 notes.
H. M. Parker, Jr.

3241. Weathersby, Robert W., II. J. H. INGRAHAM AND TENNESSEE: A RECORD OF SOCIAL AND LITERARY CONTRIBUTIONS. *Tennessee Hist. Q. 1975 34(3): 264-272.* Joseph Holt Ingraham (1809-60), though a resident of Nashville for a short duration (1847-51), made a significant and lasting contribution to Tennessee. A novelist called to the Episcopalian ministry late in life, Ingraham studied theology in Nashville where he was a schoolteacher and a vigorous advocate of penal reform and a public school system. Primary and secondary sources; 31 notes. M. B. Lucas

3242. Williams, George W., ed. LETTERS TO THE BISHOP OF LONDON FROM THE COMMISSARIES IN SOUTH CAROLINA. *South Carolina Hist. Mag. 1977 78(1): 1-31; (2): 120-147.* Part I. Reprints 12 letters from the first two Church of England Commissaries in South Carolina, to the Bishop of London, 1715-28. Part II. Reprints some of Commissary Alexander Garden's letters to the Bishop of London, 1724-32. Article to be continued.

3243. Willis, Joe D. and Wettan, Richard G. RELIGION AND SPORT IN AMERICA: THE CASE FOR THE SPORTS BAY IN THE CATHEDRAL CHURCH OF SAINT JOHN THE DIVINE. *J. of Sport Hist. 1977 4(2): 189-207.* A sports bay was installed in one of the 17 bays of the Cathedral Church of St. John the Divine (Episcopal) in New York City during the 1920's. This illustrated the widespread acceptance of sports and the compatibility of religion and sport. By 1900, sports had become a central part of school and church programs. Bishop William Thomas Manning's proposal to include a sports bay in the Cathedral climaxed the developments of the 19th century. Bishop Manning's position on Sunday sports countered the notion of a Puritan Sabbath. 63 notes. M. Kaufman

3244. Wilson, W. Emerson, ed. PHOEBE GEORGE BRADFORD DIARIES. *Delaware Hist. 1974 16(2): 132-151.* Continued from a previous article. This installment publishes Phoebe Bradford's diaries for the period January 1833 to March 1835. Discusses local social events and town gossip, her visit to her birthplace, Mt. Harmon, in Cecil County, Maryland, Bristol College in Pennsylvania, a circus in Wilmington, and her involvement in various local social groups and reform societies as well as the Episcopal church. Illus., 39 notes. Article to be continued. R. M. Miller

3245. Wilson, W. Emerson, ed. PHOEBE GEORGE BRADFORD DIARIES. *Delaware Hist. 1974 16(1): 1-21.* Part I. Selections (1832-33) from the diary of Phoebe George Bradford, daughter of Sidney George, Jr., of Cecil County and wife of Whig editor Moses Bradford, relating to her Mt. Harmon plantation in Maryland, life in Wilmington, family, Wilmington religious fare and ministers, gardening interests, the Female Colonization Society, and prominent or obscure state and national political figures including Henry Clay and the McLane family. 48 notes. Article to be continued. R. M. Miller

3246. Woolverton, John F. WHITHER EPISCOPALIANISM?: A CENTURY OF APOLOGETIC INTERPRETATIONS OF THE EPISCOPAL CHURCH, 1835-1964. *Anglican Theological Rev. Supplementary Series (1) 1973: 140-162.*

3247. —. [THE ANGLICAN CHURCH IN AMERICAN CULTURE]. *Anglican Theological Rev. Supplementary Series 1974 (4): 69-91.*
Brill, Earl H. THE MISSION OF THE CHURCH IN CONTEMPORARY AMERICAN CULTURE: AN OPPORTUNISTIC ANALYSIS, pp. 69-84.
Stoneburner, Tony. RESPONSE TO "THE MISSION OF THE CHURCH IN CONTEMPORARY AMERICAN CULTURE" BY EARL H. BRILL, pp. 84-91.
Examines the role of the Anglican Church in restoring values necessary to the survival of the United States. S

3248. —. [CHRISTIANITY AND THE CLERICAL VOCATION]. *Anglican Theological Rev. Supplementary Series 1974 (4): 47-68.*
Munn, Daniel M. ON BECOMING CHRISTIANS: PATTERNINGS PRELIMINARY TO A THEORY OF MINISTRY, pp. 47-61.
Edwards, O. C., Jr. IN "BECOMING CHRISTIANS," IS THE BECOMING IN THE AORIST OR THE IMPERFECT?: A RESPONSE TO DANIEL MUNN'S PAPER, pp. 61-64.
Munn, Daniel M. et al. DISCUSSION, pp. 64-68.
Examines the role of the Anglican Church and the need for a clear understanding among ministers of their clerical vocation. S

3249. —. [MISSIONS AND THE ANGLICAN CHURCH]. *Anglican Theological Rev. Supplementary Series 1974 (4): 21-46.*
Cochran, David R. CHURCHES OR MISSIONS?, pp. 21-38.
Holmes, Urban T. A RESPONSE TO: CHURCHES OR MISSIONS?, pp. 38-46.
Argues that the weakness of the Anglican Church in the United States is due to faulty theology that departs from the New Testament. S

French Reformed Church (Huguenots)

3250. Dietrich, Bobbie Morrow. CLAUDE PHILLIPE DE RICHEBOURG: A SENSE OF NOBLESS OBLIGE. *Daughters of the Am. Revolution Mag. 1979 113(9): 1012-1014.* Huguenot minister Claude Phillipe de Richebourg (d. ca. 1719), born of French nobility, exemplifies the spirit of the aristocratic immigrants who came to America for religious liberty in the late 17th and early 18th centuries.

3251. DuPasquier, Thierry. RAPPORTS ENTRE LES PROTESTANTS FRANCAIS ET L'AMÉRIQUE DU NORD [Connections between French Protestants and North America]. *Bull. de la Soc. de l'Hist. Protestantisme Français [France] 1976 122(3): 191-199.* Lists principal Huguenot settlements in North America, American Revolution leaders of French Protestant descent, some Protestant members of the French expeditionary force in America, Americans involved in the whaling industry in France in 1786-91 and 1817-30, and some contemporary French Huguenot societies in the United States and Canada. Summarized in English. Based on monographs; 16 notes. O. T. Driggs

3252. Jaenen, Cornelius J. THE PERSISTENCE OF THE PROTESTANT PRESENCE IN NEW FRANCE, 1541-1760. *Pro. of the Ann. Meeting of the Western Soc. for French Hist. 1974 (2): 29-40.* Outlines the varying fortunes of the Huguenots in New France and examines the small Protestant community of 1759. The Catholic Recollet missionaries and the Jesuits successfully campaigned to exclude Protestants from colonial administration and from further settlement in New France by 1627. Protestants continued to trickle in and during 1669-78 Jean Baptiste Colbert's policy of tolerance outweighed the clergy's demand for exclusion of all Huguenots, but Louis XIV's much harsher policy culminated in the Edict of Fontainbleau. Under the Regency and Louis XV, Huguenots reestablished contacts with Canada. In 1759 there were about 1,000 Protestants of whom 471 are identified by name. Their various national origins, their economic and occupational status, and the number of and reasons for abjurations are cited. Protestantism, although not a major factor, continued to be important in the history of New France. Based on Canadian and French archives and other primary sources; 31 notes. J. D. Falk

3253. Ross, Aileen. THE HUGUENOTS. *Pacific Hist. 1974 18(1): 52-65.* Many French Protestants immigrated to colonial America and contributed much to the society and culture. Discusses famous Americans who had Huguenot ancestors: George Washington, Jedediah Strong Smith, Elias Boudinot, John Jay, Pierre Harache, and Bernard Hubley. Biblio. S

3254. Starr, J. Barton. CAMPBELL TOWN: FRENCH HUGUENOTS IN BRITISH WEST FLORIDA. *Florida Hist. Q. 1976 54(4): 532-547.* Located 20 miles north of Pensacola, Campbell Town was a French Huguenot colony led by Lieutenant Governor Montfort Browne. It was established in 1765 to promote the cultivation of grapes and the raising of silkworms. An example of the British government's eagerness to colonize West Florida, Campbell Town nonetheless was abandoned by 1770 due to internal friction, Indian problems, and unhealthy climate. Based mainly on sources in the Colonial Office. 50 notes. P. A. Beaber

3255. Stover, Margaret Harris. HUGUENOT INFLUENCE IN AMERICA. *Daughters of the Am. Revolution Mag. 1979 113(9): 1030-1033.* History of the French Huguenots since the 16th century, focusing on their presence in America; mentions the 1978 Reunion of the Descendants of the Huguenots at Rouen, France.

Friends

3256. Bacon, Margaret H. FRIENDS AND THE 1876 CENTENNIAL: DILEMMAS, CONTROVERSIES AND OPPORTUNITIES. *Quaker Hist. 1977 66(1): 41-50.* Many Quakers praised the Centennial Exposition (1876) for showing peacetime progress, although they disapproved of exalting a revolutionary war, the sale of alcoholic drinks on the grounds, the emphasis on fashions, the nude art, and the boastful attitude behind the whole show. The Orthodox Quakers supported and the Hicksites opposed Sunday closing. Members of the Society of Friends almost completely ignored the fair's failure to recognize Indians, blacks, and women, and avoided the subject of the Centennial in their business meetings. 24 notes. T. D. S. Bassett

3257. Barns, William D. STATUS AND SECTIONALISM IN WEST VIRGINIA. *West Virginia Hist. 1973 34(3): 247-272, (4): 360-381.* Part I. Discusses exploration and settlement of West Virginia, the social status of land speculators, and sectionalism which developed from status, and the effects of immigration of Quakers on religious and community attitudes, 1720's-80's. Part II. West Virginia underwent two "status revolutions" in the last half of the 19th century. The Civil War crushed the ambitions of many former prominent Confederates and speeded the rise of Unionists who had previously been in lesser positions. After the war, promoters of economic development steadily eroded the economic importance and social status of farmers, who finally responded with an "agrarian revolt" by the 1880's. Secondary sources; 148 notes.
G. A. Hewlett/J. H. Broussard

3258. Bradley, A. Day. DANIEL LAWRENCE, QUAKER PRINTER OF BURLINGTON, PHILADELPHIA, AND STANFORD, N.Y. *Quaker Hist. 1976 65(2): 100-108.* Quaker membership records show Daniel Lawrence's seven moves, 1790-1806. Locates in 9 libraries 45 titles (7 in Charles Evans' *American Bibliography* only) printed by Lawrence in 1790-93, 1802-05, and 1810, and one printed from him (N.Y.: 1795). 10 notes. T. D. S. Bassett

3259. Bradley, A. Day. NEW YORK YEARLY MEETING AT POPLAR RIDGE AND THE PRIMITIVE FRIENDS. *Quaker Hist. 1979 68(2): 75-82.* The 1845 separation over evangelical ("Gurneyite") and quietist ("Wilburite") issues divided several Vermont and western New York meetings. When the Wilburite Yearly Meeting at Poplar Ridge decided in 1858 to publish the journal of Joseph Hoag (1762-1846), a Charlotte, Vermont, minister, it split over the deletion of a passage critical of the Otises of New Bedford, Massachusetts. Traces repercussions of "Otisite" or Primitive vs. "Kingite" Friends from Nantucket to Iowa, to their disappearance by 1949. 27 notes. T. D. S. Bassett

3260. Burke, James L. and Bensch, Donald E. MOUNT PLEASANT AND THE EARLY QUAKERS OF OHIO. *Ohio Hist. 1974 83(4): 220-255.* Reviews the origins of the Quaker movement in England in the 17th century, and the migration of Quakers to America and the Ohio territory in the 18th century. Describes the foundation of the Quaker community at Mount Pleasant, Jefferson County, Ohio, and the building of the Meeting House in 1814-15. Describes Quaker life in Mount Pleasant, including the Boarding School (1837-75), and Quakers in the local economy, as well as general Quaker attitudes toward the Indians, slavery, temperance, and peacemaking. Focuses on 1795-1918. Map, 13 photos, 2 tables, biblio. J. B. Street

3261. Butler, Jon. "GOSPEL ORDER IMPROVED:" THE KEITHIAN SCHISM AND THE EXERCISE OF QUAKER MINISTERIAL AUTHORITY IN PENNSYLVANIA. *William and Mary Q. 1974 31(3): 431-452.* The schism among Pennsylvania Quakers in the 1690's is explained chiefly by Keith's ideas rather than by secular issues. Keith tried to carry through reforms aimed at greater discipline in order to compel purity, but rejected ministerial authority. Analyzes Keith's opponents, the "Public Friends" (travelling Quaker ministers) and powerful politicians. In 1692 the Quakers were split after Keith was condemned by the Philadelphia meeting of ministers; he formed a separate yearly meeting. Based on primary and secondary sources; 75 notes.
H. M. Ward

3262. Butler, Jon. INTO PENNSYLVANIA'S SPIRITUAL ABYSS: THE RISE AND FALL OF THE LATER KEITHIANS, 1693-1703. *Pennsylvania Mag. of Hist. and Biog. 1977 101(2): 151-170.* Analyzes the reasons for the rise and decline of Keithianism, a schismatic Quaker sect. George Keith, angered by the contradictions and favoritism of the Society of Friends, broke away from the church and founded a sect of his own. He then went to England to plead his case, and his successors promptly fell to fighting among themselves. The Keithian revolt was a reflection of general dissatisfaction with Quaker society, as were the lesser revolts which quickly destroyed his movement. The Keithian movement went nowhere, but it is a measure of the religious change at the time. 40 notes.
V. L. Human

3263. Canuteson, Richard L. LARS AND MARTHA LARSON: "WE DO WHAT WE CAN FOR THEM." *Norwegian-American Studies 1972 25: 142-166.* Discusses the early life of Lars Larson. In 1807, as part of a commercial venture on board a ship bound to sell lumber, Larson was seized by the British (with whom Norway-Denmark was at war) and imprisoned for seven years. During this time he converted to Quakerism and upon his 1814 return to Norway began teaching the tenets of that religion for which he was severely punished by the government. In 1825, after continual denial of their religious freedom, a group of Norwegians immigrated to the United States. Most settled in Kendall Colony, New York, but Larson and his family moved to Rochester where they associated with the local Quaker church and, until Lars's death in 1844, operated a way station for Norwegian immigrants, often providing food and lodging for as many as 100 people at one time. 61 notes.
G. A. Hewlett

3264. Carroll, Kenneth L., ed. DEATH COMES TO A QUAKERESS. *Quaker Hist. 1975 64(2): 96-104.* Sarah Taylor (ca. 1798-1823), second of nine children of Mary Alexander (Alvord) (1770-1820) and Thomas Tylor (1752-1829), died in Baltimore, a member of Northwest Fork Monthly Meeting, Caroline County, on the Eastern Shore of Maryland, of an operation to remove a large tumor on her neck and shoulder. Copies of two letters from the patient and two from attending friends describing her trip to Baltimore, her condition and the operation, are in a privately owned family record. Family, friends, and the 13 physicians are identified in 23 notes and the introduction.
T. D. S. Bassett

3265. Carroll, Kenneth L. THE IRISH QUAKER COMMUNITY AT CAMDEN. *South Carolina Hist. Mag. 1976 77(2): 69-83.* In 1751, a group of Irish Quakers led by Robert Milhouse and Samuel Wyly came from Dublin and settled at Wateree (Camden), South Carolina. Indian raids troubled the community as did any military effort of the American colonies. Gradually migration to Bush River, Virginia, and North Carolina destroyed the Quaker's Wateree Monthly Meeting. Contains information on life through 1793. Primary sources; 68 notes.
R. H. Tomlinson

3266. Carroll, Kenneth L. THE MARY & CHARLOTTE FIASCO; A LOOK AT 1778 BRITISH QUAKER RELIEF FOR PHILADELPHIA. *Pennsylvania Mag. of Hist. and Biog. 1978 102(2): 212-223.* British Friends, responding to appeals from their Philadelphia brethren, shipped on the *Mary & Charlotte* a cargo arriving mostly spoiled in June 1778. Following several years of mild legal disputes, the London subscribers were compensated for all but the accumulated interest. Based on Epistles Received and Sent, Friends House Library, London; Minutes, Philadelphia Meeting for Suffering; and published sources; 57 notes.
T. H. Wendel

3267. Carroll, Kenneth L., ed. ROBERT PLEASANTS ON QUAKERISM: "SOME ACCOUNT OF THE FIRST SETTLEMENT OF FRIENDS IN VIRGINIA . . . ." *Virginia Mag. of Hist. and Biog. 1978 86(1): 3-16.* Virginia Quaker Robert Pleasants (1722?-1801) wrote an almost unknown account of his sect's history in the colony for publication in a never-completed history of Quakerism. Particularly valuable are his accounts of Quakers' problems during the French and Indian War and the antislavery movement after the Revolution. Covers the 17th and 18th centuries. Edited from the manuscript in the Quaker Collection, Haverford College Library; 61 notes. R. F. Oaks

3268. Champlin, Richard L. QUAKER CLOCKMAKERS OF NEWPORT. *Newport Hist. 1977 50(4): 77-89.* Discusses Quaker clockmakers residing in Newport, Rhode Island, 1780's-1850's.

3269. Clark, Dennis. INVENTION AND CONTENTION IN THE QUAKER CITY. *J. of Urban Hist. 1979 5(2): 265-271.* Review article prompted by Richard G. Miller, *Philadelphia—The Federalist City: A Study in Urban Politics, 1789-1801,* Bruce Sinclair, *Philadelphia's Philosopher Mechanics: A History of the Franklin Institute, 1824-1865,* Michael Feldberg, *The Philadelphia Riots of 1844: A Study of Ethnic Conflict,* and Philip S. Benjamin, *The Philadelphia Quakers in the Industrial Age, 1865-1920.* These books examine three great city-shaping forces: politics, religion, and technology. Their limitation is that they describe and explain the particular rather than the overall structure and complexity of the city. 9 notes. T. W. Smith

3270. Crauder, Bruce. THE DISAPPEARANCE OF OHIO YEARLY MEETING (HICKSITE). *Quaker Hist. 1976 65(2): 93-99.* With about 4,500 members in 1828, Ohio Yearly Meeting (Hicksite) dissolved in 1919 and transferred the remaining 250 members to other bodies. All Ohio Friends meetings in the early 19th century were reduced by the emigration of young families, especially westward, but the Orthodox replaced their losses by evangelism. Complete records exist for only the Yearly Meeting (including eastern Ohio and western Pennsylvania) and Redstone and West Monthly Meetings (in Pennsylvania). 17 notes. T. D. S. Bassett

3271. Cromwell, Jarvis, ed. JAMES W. CROMWELL'S REMINISCENCES OF A QUAKER BOYHOOD. *New-York Hist. Soc. Q. 1975 59(1): 45-70.* Cromwell, a New York City businessman, had a long, successful life (1842-1935). After his retirement in 1920, he wrote his reminiscences, of which this portion is devoted to his early years. It presents an interesting account of urban life in the years before the Civil War. Based on primary sources; 9 illus., 3 notes. C. L. Grant

3272. Fishbourn, William. ONE QUAKER'S VIEW: WILLIAM FISHBOURN'S REMARKS ON THE SETTLEMENT OF PENNSYLVANIA. *Quaker Hist. 1977 66(1): 51-58.* Reprints remarks made in 1739 by William Fishbourn, an immigrant and Quaker merchant. Fishbourn emphasized that the peace, harmony, and prosperity of the first 60 years of Pennsylvania's settlement were derived from William Penn's benevolent constitutional and Indian policies as well as from the original Quaker majority. He attributed difficulties and drawbacks to such non-Quaker forces as the wilderness, English enemies, unfair land dealings, and other un-Quakerly behavior. Fishbourn's membership in the Society of Friends was restored the same year he wrote this essay. 5 notes. T. D. S. Bassett

3273. Frost, J. William. UNLIKELY CONTROVERSIALISTS: CALEB PUSEY AND GEORGE KEITH. *Quaker Hist. 1975 64(1): 16-36.* "The most brilliant" Quaker 17th-century theologian, Keith devoted 25 years (1664-92) to Friends as polemicist, Surveyor-General of New Jersey, and Philadelphia teacher. He was expelled for his arrogance, his theology of the outward body of Christ, and his "devastating critique of the emerging pattern of Pennsylvania society." He opposed birthright membership, slaveholding, and Quaker participation in government. Pusey criticized Keith in 1696 and more vituperatively in 1701-06. 55 notes. T. D. S. Bassett

3274. Hallowell, Benjamin, et al. QUAKER REPORT ON INDIAN AGENCIES IN NEBRASKA, 1869. *Nebraska Hist. 1973 54(2): 151-219.* Reprint of the report of a four-man joint delegation appointed by the Committees on the Indian Concern of the 1869 meeting of Baltimore, Philadelphia, and New York Friends to visit the Indians under Quaker care in Nebraska. Includes an appendix, "The Indians and the Friends," reprinted from the *Omaha Herald.* R. Lowitt

3275. Hoffecker, Carol E., ed. THE DIARIES OF EDMUND CANBY, A QUAKER MILLER, 1822-1848. *Delaware Hist. 1974 16(2): 79-131.* Selections from the diaries of Edmund Canby (1804-48), of the Canby flour milling family of Brandywine. The diaries relate weather conditions, marketing practices, the Canby's Whig principles, family history, the Hicksite schism among Quakers, and social life of New Castle County, Delaware, in the 1820's and 1830's. The first installment covers 1822-35. 2 illus., 24 notes.
Randall M. Miller

3276. Hollingsworth, Gerelyn. IRISH QUAKERS IN COLONIAL PENNSYLVANIA: A FORGOTTEN SEGMENT OF SOCIETY. *J. of the Lancaster County Hist. Soc. 1975 79(3): 150-162.* Describes the background and lives of Irish Quakers in colonial Pennsylvania who settled in Ireland during the 17th century after migrating there from England, and eventually immigrated to America, Pennsylvania in particular, 1682-1750, due to persecution in Ireland.

3277. Hovinen, Elizabeth. QUAKERS OF YONGE STREET. *Can. Geographical J. 1976 92(1): 52-57.* Discusses the members of the Society of Friends who lived in southern Ontario in the 19th century.

3278. LeVan, Sandra W. THE QUAKER AGENTS AT DARLINGTON. *Chronicles of Oklahoma 1973 51(1): 92-99.* Describes the life of the Quaker Indian agents of the Darlington Agency, established by treaty in Western Oklahoma for the Cheyenne Indians and Apache Indians, 1868-86. S

3279. Marietta, Jack. QUAKER FAMILY EDUCATION IN HISTORICAL PERSPECTIVE. *Quaker Hist. 1974 63(1): 3-16.* As New England became less homogeneous, the Puritan denomination failed to transmit its culture by family training and turned to schools. Pennsylvania Quaker sectarians, living "in the world" rather than isolated like the German sects, suffered similar dilution by accommodation. At the cost of nearly 2000 disownments for marrying non-Quakers during 1740-75, they succeeded in insulating the young through family discipline supplemented by practical schooling under Quaker masters. "The Society emerged from the Revolution (after disowning 420 armsbearing Quakers) smaller, more uniform, more endogamous, and more strictly disciplined." 31 notes. T. D. S. Bassett

3280. Ryan, Pat M., ed. MATHIAS HUTCHINSON'S "NOTES OF A JOURNEY" (1819-20). *Quaker Hist. 1979 68(2): 92-114.* A biographical introduction to the journal of this 24-year-old companion of Edward Hicks. Hutchinson was looking for a site to farm, as indicated by his attention to climate, soils, prices, and trade. He moved to Ledyard, Cayuga County, New York, in 1821, and became a substantial farmer, inventor, and Whig assemblyman. The diary, printed in full, documents travel conditions and the central Pennsylvania, western New York, and Ontario frontier to which northeastern Friends were moving. Some Genesee segments appeared in *Rochester History.* Based on Quaker and local histories, and Edward Hicks's parallel *Memoirs;* 65 notes. Article to be continued. T. D. S. Bassett

3281. Smith, Bruce R. BENJAMIN HALLOWELL OF ALEXANDRIA: SCIENTIST, EDUCATOR, QUAKER IDEALIST. *Virginia Mag. of Hist. and Biog. 1977 85(3): 337-361.* Benjamin Hallowell, who lived in Alexandria during 1824-60, influenced the development of education and other civic projects in that city. His *Autobiography* reveals much about his educational philosophy and his difficulties as a Quaker to grapple with such issues as slavery and the Civil War. Covers 1824-60. Based largely on Hallowell's published *Autobiography;* 2 illus., 42 notes.
R. F. Oaks

3282. Williams, Dorothy M. FEATHERS OF PEACE. *Quaker Hist. 1976 65(1): 32-34.* The story that a band of Burgoyne's foraging Indians during the American Revolution, having killed nearby Pennsylvania settlers, came upon the Easton Friends at worship and left them unharmed, is verified from Quaker sources. 9 notes.
T. D. S. Bassett

3283. Worrall, Arthur J. THE IMPACT OF THE DISCIPLINE: IRELAND, NEW ENGLAND, AND NEW YORK. *Quaker Hist. 1979 68(2): 83-91.* The enforcement of rules against marrying non-Quakers and other unacceptable behavior resulted in a loss of members in the 18th century, especially in older-settled areas. This decline is shown in tables of marriages and of cases under discipline and the ratio of excommunication to reconciliation. 4 tables, 11 notes.
T. D. S. Bassett

German Reformed Churches

3284. Myers, Raymond E. THE STORY OF GERMANNA. *Filson Club Hist. Q. 1974 48(1): 27-42.* Virginia's colonial Governor Alexander Spotswood was the driving force behind the organization of the town of Germanna in 1714. Owning land that was rich in iron ore, Spotswood contracted with German Reformed Protestants to immigrate and work the land. At first the project was successful, but religious differences among the Germans and the desire of the immigrants to own their own land brought an end to the experiment. Secondary works; 84 notes. G. B. McKinney

3285. Parsons, William T. "DER GLARNER": ABRAHAM BLUMER OF ZION REFORMED CHURCH, ALLENTOWN. *Swiss Am. Hist. Soc. Newsletter 1977 13(2): 7-22.* Chronicles the ministerial career of Abraham Blumer (1736-1822), a pastor ordained in Switzerland in the German Reformed Church, highlighting his tenure with Pennsylvania parishes, 1771-1801, especially Zion Reformed Church in Allentown.

3286. Yrigoyen, Charles, Jr. EMANUEL V. GERHART: CHURCHMAN, THEOLOGIAN, AND FIRST PRESIDENT OF FRANKLIN AND MARSHALL COLLEGE. *J. of the Lancaster County Hist. Soc. 1974 78(1): 1-28.* Biography of (German) Reformed Church clergyman Emanuel V. Gerhart (1817-1904), touching on his career as a minister and missionary and his writings on theological and philosophical subjects, and finally, his 36 years as professor and President at Franklin and Marshall College in Lancaster, Pennsylvania. 2 photos, 127 notes.

3287. Yrigoyen, Charles, Jr. EMANUEL V. GERHART AND THE MERCERSBURG THEOLOGY. *J. of the Lancaster County Hist. Soc. 1978 82(4): 199-221.* Discusses the life and theological thought of Emanuel Vogel Gerhart (1817-1904), parish minister, missionary, college administrator, professor, theologian, and influential figure in the German Reformed Church in America.

Holiness Churches

3288. Bassett, Paul M. A STUDY IN THE THEOLOGY OF THE EARLY HOLINESS MOVEMENT. *Methodist Hist. 1975 13(3): 61-84.* Theological analysis of the development of the holiness movement in general and in the Church of the Nazarene in particular, 1908-75. 83 notes. H. L. Calkin

3289. Boggs, Beverly. SOME ASPECTS OF WORSHIP IN A HOLINESS CHURCH. *New York Folklore 1977 3(1-4): 29-44.* Describes beliefs of the mainly black congregation of, and music and services at, the Mt. Nebo Church of God in Christ in Binghamton, New York, a Holiness church, based on the author's visits there between 1971 and 1974.

3290. Dann, Norman K. SPATIAL DIFFUSION OF A RELIGIOUS MOVEMENT. *J. for the Sci. Study of Religion 1976 15(4): 351-360.* Studies the Holiness Movement, 1865-1975.

3291. Dunlap, E. Dale. TUESDAY MEETINGS, CAMP MEETINGS, CABINET MEETINGS. *Methodist Hist. 1975 13(3): 85-106.* Scriptural holiness or the Holiness Movement was related to the Methodist Church in the United States during a large part of the 19th century. As an outgrowth of a revival in New York, it received emphasis from "Tuesday Meetings" started by Sarah Langford and Phoebe Palmer in 1835. Later, camp meetings and an effective popular religious press also served to promote the cause of holiness. By the end of the century pressures against the movement arose, and many left the Methodist Church to form splinter religious organizations. 40 notes. H. L. Calkin

3292. Gage, Patricia Anthony. THE SAWDUST TRAIL LIVES ON AT THE HUDSON CAMP MEETING. *North Louisiana Hist. Assoc. J. 1979 10(1): 23-25.* An account of the 1977 camp meeting, with a brief history of the Hudson Holiness Interdenominational Camp site which was established in 1899 in Winn Parish, Louisiana. 2 illus. J. F. Paul

3293. Nelson, Edward O. RECOLLECTIONS OF THE SALVATION ARMY'S SCANDINAVIAN CORPS. *Swedish Pioneer Hist. Q. 1978 29(4): 257-276.* The author came to America from Sweden in 1928. He served in the Salvation Army from 1929 until he retired as a Lieutenant Colonel in 1975. Based on his own experiences, on the experiences of his friends who were also in the "wheel within a wheel" which was the *Frälsningsarmén* or Scandinavia Corps of the Salvation Army, and on books and articles written on the Corps. The Corps, begun in Brooklyn in 1877, at its height had 80 corps wherever Scandinavians, especially Swedes, were located. 4 photos. C. W. Ohrvall

Lutheran Churches

3294. Smith, John Abernathy. THE SCHMUCKER MYTH AND THE EVANGELICAL ALLIANCE. *Concordia Hist. Inst. Q. 1974 47(1): 7-23.* Argues that Samuel Simon Schmucker, leader of the American party in the Lutheran General Synod, was himself largely responsible for the myth that he instigated the Evangelical Alliance during the latter half of the 19th century. S

3295. Anderson, Avis R., ed. PASTOR ON THE PRAIRIE. *Montana 1974 24(1): 36-54.* Biography of Christian Scriver Thorpe (1883-1968), a pastor of the Norwegian Lutheran Church in eastern Montana. His letters 1906-08 reveal many hardships of life on that frontier. S. R. Davison

3296. Bergendoff, Conrad. THE AUGUSTANA PASTOR: SAGA OF A THOUSAND IMMIGRANTS FROM SWEDEN. *Swedish Pioneer Hist. Q. 1980 31(1): 34-50.* A study of the records of more than 800 Swedish-born pastors of the Augustana Lutheran Synod and the 200 Swedish-born women who were their wives. The author believes that this study provides significant sociological material on an influential profession among the immigrants, between the Civil War and World War I. This article is intended as an introduction to a forthcoming biographical dictionary of the pastors of the church. Based on the *Minutes* of the annual conventions of the Synod, a church annual, *Korsbaneret,* and secondary sources; 3 photos. C. W. Ohrvall

3297. Buenger, Theodore Arthur; Buenger, Richard E., transl. AUTOBIOGRAPHY OF THEODORE ARTHUR BUENGER 1886-1957. *Concordia Hist. Inst. Q. 1980 53(3): 98-116.* Autobiography of Theodore Arthur Buenger, son of a German Lutheran minister in Illinois; he was a student at Concordia Seminary in St. Louis, and later a Lutheran (Missouri Synod) minister himself, preaching in German to his largely German-speaking congregations; covers 1886-1909.

3298. Cody, Mary Alice Bull. THE BRAZEAU, MISSOURI, SCENE, 1852-1856: EXCERPTS FROM THE DIARY OF SARAH M. MC PHERSON. *Concordia Hist. Inst. Q. 1974 47(1): 3-6.*

3299. Ellwanger, Walter H. LUTHERANISM IN ALABAMA AND OTHER PARTS OF THE SOUTH. *Concordia Hist. Inst. Q. 1975 48(2): 35-43.* Reviews the development of Lutheranism in the Deep South with comments on the impact of the religion on the region. The works of several prominent Lutherans, including Niles J. Bakke and Rosa J. Young, have been cited with Alabama emerging as the focal point. Mentions congregational development in Mississippi, Louisiana, and the Carolinas. The civil rights movement of the early 1960's witnessed the adjustment of the Lutheran Church to a more liberal position; the Alabama Lutheran Academy and College opened its doors to black students for ministerial and teacher training. Covers 1839-1965. W. T. Walker

3300. Feucht, Oscar E. ST. PAUL'S LUTHERAN CHURCH, WARTBURG, TENNESSEE. *Concordia Hist. Inst. Q. 1975 48(3): 67-86.* The history of St. Paul's Lutheran Church in Wartburg, Tennessee, dates from 1844 when George F. Gerding founded the town and donated land for the church. The church has steadily developed from the pastorates of John F. Wilkes, John L. Hirschmann, Carl A. Bruegemann,

Otto Carl Praetorius, and others. The mission churches which developed out of St. Paul's were located in Deermont, Deer Lodge, and Oakdale, Tennessee. 27 photos, biblio. W. T. Walker

3301. Frizzell, Robert W. 'KILLED BY REBELS': A CIVIL WAR MASSACRE AND ITS AFTERMATH. *Missouri Hist. Rev. 1977 71(4): 369-395.* Of the several massacres in Missouri during the Civil War, the one on 10 October 1864 near Concordia was to have a deep influence on the Germans who had settled on the borders of Lafayette and Saline counties. Always aware of their different values, culture and religious beliefs, the Germans were driven by the violence inflicted on them to become even more isolated and conscious of their origins. The isolationism, which was reflected by their continued use of German and acceptance of the conservative Missouri Synod Lutheranism, lasted into the 20th century. Primary and secondary sources; illus., 93 notes. W. F. Zornow

3302. Guelzo, Allen C. GLORIA DEI: OLD SWEDES' CHURCH. *Early Am. Life. 1977 8(3): 18, 64-66.* The Gloria Dei Congregation was a group of Swedish immigrants who built Old Swedes' Church in Philadelphia, Pennsylvania, during 1638-98.

3303. Hamre, James S. JOHN O. EVJEN: TEACHER, THEOLOGIAN, BIOGRAPHER. *Concordia Hist. Inst. Q. 1974 47(2): 52-61.* Discusses the achievements of John O. Evjen, Lutheran theologian in Minnesota (1874-1942). S

3304. Hamre, James S. A THANKSGIVING DAY ADDRESS BY GEORG SVERDRUP. *Norwegian-American Studies 1970 24: 137-147.* Georg Sverdrup was the leader of the Lutheran Free Church during 1893-1907. The Free Church was brought about by a split in the United Norwegian Lutheran Church in America and had as its main tenets the support for the Augsburg Seminary and an overwhelming belief in the importance of the congregation within the individual church. Reprints a sermon delivered on Thanksgiving Day, 1896, which emphasizes Sverdrup's love of America and its blessings, including opportunity for oppressed peoples in Europe, the federal constitution, and the doctrine of religious freedom. The sermon stresses his belief in the importance of the congregation and the role of women in the development of the church. 8 notes. G. A. Hewlett

3305. Hansel, William H. 50 YEARS IN THE MINISTRY. *Concordia Hist. Inst. Q. 1975 48(1): 4-9.* A brief survey of the author's ministry in the Lutheran Church. Centered in Colorado, Nebraska, and Oklahoma, the author's ministry was involved with the establishment of churches and schools related to the Lutheran Church (Missouri Synod). The German language was a barrier between the Lutheran Church and other denominations in this area. Covers 1907-62. W. T. Walker

3306. Heiges, George L. THE EVANGELICAL LUTHERAN CHURCH OF THE HOLY TRINITY, LANCASTER, PENNSYLVANIA. *J. of the Lancaster County Hist. Soc. 1979 83(1): 2-71, (2): 74-156.* Part I. 1730-1861. Part II: 1862-1980.

3307. Helgeland, John. BERET'S PROBLEM: AN ESSAY ON IMMIGRANT PIONEER RELIGION. *Lutheran Q. 1976 28(1): 45-53.* In the novel *Giants in the Earth* (1927), O. E. Rolvaag considers the problems of cultural adjustment a Norwegian immigrant family faces in life on the South Dakota prairies. Particularly significant is the question of religion. Norwegians, like many other immigrants, were accustomed to an environment in which their religion was part of their essential culture, bounded by space and time. The emigration to the frontier necessitated a massive transformation of religious thinking and brought great problems for some like the heroine, Beret, who finds the unbounded space of her new home extremely difficult to fit into her old religion (adherent versus conversion style of religion). A sermon on God's love unbounded by time and space results in Beret's acceptance of her new situation, while she gradually develops a view based on the division of people into the saved and the unregenerate. Thus the frontier experience was a major factor in the development of a unique Protestant tradition in America. Based on secondary sources; 28 notes. J. A. Kicklighter

3308. Helmreich, Ernst C., ed. and transl. LETTERS OF PASTOR CHRISTIAN HELMREICH: ESTABLISHING A LUTHERAN CONGREGATION IN WEYERTS, NEBRASKA, 1887-1888. *Nebraska Hist. 1977 58(2): 175-192.* Reprints two letters written by Helmreich during 1887-88. They were to his parents in Bavaria about his ordination, and his journey from Illinois to Nebraska where he was called to establish a congregation. R. Lowitt

3309. Holt, Benjamin M. AND SO THEY GAVE ME A 36-INCH BIRTHDAY CARD: A REMEMBRANCE OF 90 EVENTFUL YEARS. *Concordia Hist. Inst. Q. 1974 47(1): 24-38.* Discusses Benjamin M. Holt's activities, especially in the Lutheran Church in Minnesota, 1882-1974. S

3310. Jackson, Claire. HANNAFORD CHURCH SUPPER. *Red River Valley Hist. 1980 (Fall): 15-18.* Account of a lutefisk annual church supper sponsored by the Ladies Aid Society (Norwegian Lutheran) of Hannaford, North Dakota, in 1941.

3311. Johnson, Arthur L.; Brekke, Milo L.; Strommen, Merton P.; and Underwager, Ralph C. AGE DIFFERENCES AND DIMENSIONS OF RELIGIOUS BEHAVIOR. *J. of Social Issues 1974 30(3): 43-67.* Explores the magnitude, sources, and consequences of differences among age strata in various dimensions of religious orientation and practice. A national sample of 4444 Lutheran church members, ages 15-65, completed a 740-item survey. From these data six age groups were empirically formed; these exhibited significant differences on 43 of 52 major scales. Patterns of age strata differences supported a 'selective gap' theory rather than a 'great gap' interpretation of contrasts among age strata. The youth stratum, 19-23, was found to be most heterogeneous in their beliefs, attitudes, or life styles. Although some within-stratum solidarity was evident, it generally was weak and overshadowed by lineage solidarity. Implications of combined aging and cohort effect conclude the discussion. J

3312. Johnson, Emeroy. PER ANDERSSON'S LETTERS FROM CHISAGO LAKE. *Swedish Pioneer Hist. Q. 1973 24(1): 3-31.* The letter of Joris Per Andersson (1817-81), written at Chisago Lake, Minnesota, and mentioned by Helmer Lång in "Moberg, the Emigrant Saga and Reality" *Swedish Pioneer Historical Quarterly,* 1972 23(1): 3-24, is not lost. It is one of 12 letters of 1851-53 in the Gustavus Adolphus College archives with the papers of Eric Norelius, a good friend. Andersson came to Minnesota in 1851 and left in 1856 or 1857. He believed that Chisago Lake was ideal for Swedish settlement and encouraged others to come. Prices for food were high, but a worker made $20 to $30 per month. He gave news about other Swedish settlers, and expressed concern about religion. Letters are translated in full. Based on primary sources; 3 photos, 36 notes. K. J. Puffer

3313. Knudsen, Johannes. ONE HUNDRED YEARS LATER—THE GRUNDTVIGIAN HERITAGE. *Lutheran Q. 1973 25(1): 71-77.* Nikolai Frederik Severin Grundtvig (1783-1872) revitalized the corporate body of the Lutheran Church and healed the dichotomy between religious and secular life. S

3314. Kramer, William A. LIFE IN PERRY COUNTY, MISSOURI, AT THE TURN OF THE CENTURY. *Concordia Hist. Inst. Q. 1975 48(1): 10-25.* There was a closer relationship between the society of Perry County and the Lutheran Church at the turn of the century than today. The people helped support the pastors and teachers of the church. A diversified agrarian system prevailed. Most children attended Lutheran parochial schools for the first six grades before transferring to the public schools. Weddings and funerals were major social events. Based on personal recollection. W. T. Walker

3315. Kramer, William A. A TEACHER EXAMINATION IN 1858. *Concordia Hist. Inst. Q. 1979 52(3): 125-127.* Introduces and reprints a letter from Paul Theodor Buerger to the *Collegium Fratrum* at the seminary in Fort Wayne, Indiana, regarding his teaching examination in Buffalo, New York.

3316. Kukkonen, Walter J. THE MINISTRY OF ENABLING: THE FINNISH TRADITION IN THE LUTHERAN CHURCH IN AMERICA. *Lutheran Q. 1976 28(4): 331-351.* Describes the importance of the Finnish tradition of spiritual faith to the contemporary Lutheran Church. The tradition has several characteristics: close relationship between the

institutional church and spiritual movements among the people; the Bible as the sole repository of the word of God; the nature of faith as inward knowledge of Jesus Christ; and the existence of small groups containing those who love Christ. This tradition can be extremely valuable to the Lutheran Church in America in reaching those outside the denomination and helping people to understand the importance of repentance and self-discovery. Covers 1688-1975. Based on secondary sources; 11 notes.
J. A. Kicklighter

3317. Lemke, Lloyd H. THE HISTORICAL BACKGROUND OF J. P. KOEHLER'S "GESETZLICH WESEN UNTER UNS." *Concordia Hist. Inst. Q. 1976 49(4): 172-177.* Koehler's "Gesetzlich Wesen Unter Uns" first appeared in the *Wisconsin Lutheran Quarterly* during October 1914 and July 1915. The series was motivated by the doctrinal strife which had characterized the Lutheran synods since the election controversy of the 1880's. Primary sources; 7 notes.
W. T. Walker

3318. Lindberg, D. R. PASTORS AMONG THE PEOPLE. *Red River Valley Hist. 1980 (Fall): 12-15.* Discusses the life and work of six Norwegian Lutheran pastors in the Red River Valley in North Dakota: Bersvend Anderson, Olaf Larsen Skattebol, Bjug Harstad, Ibram Libius Lundeby, Ole H. Aaberg, and Christian T. Saugstad; 1871-99.

3319. Løvoll, Odd Sverre. THE *BYGDELAG* MOVEMENT. *Norwegian-American Studies 1972 25: 3-26.* Examines the organization and growth of the bygdelag movement among Norwegian Americans during 1901-25. Centering in the Midwest, the groups consisted of members who hailed from common areas of Norway. Each group (numbering 31 by 1913) served as a cohesive unit to preserve folkcustoms, beliefs, tales, songs, and religious unity. When Norway achieved independence from Sweden in 1905, nationalism among the groups became a strong cohesive factor, as well as the move within several of the groups to begin publishing material relating directly to immigrants of Norwegian descent. Of interest primarily to first- and second-generations, the organizations began to lose momentom following World War I and by 1930 only a small percentage of membership consisted of youth. The movement soon ended thereafter. 34 notes.
G. A. Hewlett

3320. Main, Elaine. THE FRAULEIN CHOOSES BACKWOODS IOWA. *Palimpsest 1978 59(6): 162-167.* Drawn by the work of Sigmund Fritschel who was soliciting funds among German Russian Lutherans, Auguste von Schwartz left Russia to move to Iowa where she worked at Wartburg College as a house mother, 1861-77.

3321. McIntosh, Hugh E. HOW THE SWEDES CAME TO PAXTON. *Swedish Pioneer Hist. Q. 1979 30(1): 35-52.* The removal of Augustana College and Theological Seminary from Chicago to Paxton, Illinois, in 1863 brought about the formation of a Swedish community in the prairie town. Follows the course of events which drew so many Swedes to Paxton so that it attained significance as a community. By 1860 more than half of the 18,625 Swedes in the United States were living in Illinois and Minnesota. At this time the Scandinavians, who had at first joined with other Lutherans, separated and formed the Augustana Synod and the Augustana Seminary in Chicago. This was to be temporary until the Synod could found a colony. Several Midwestern sites were examined. William H. Osborn of the Illinois Central Railroad convinced the group to found its colony along the route of the railroad. Paxton was chosen because of the attractive offers made by the townspeople. Although the school prospered it never became a permanent part of the Paxton community and it moved to Rock Island in 1873. 4 photos, 95 notes.
C. W. Ohrvall

3322. Meyer, Carl S. A VIEW OF THE LUTHERAN CHURCH—MISSOURI SYNOD: 1866. *Concordia Hist. Inst. Q. 1974 47(3): 99-102.* Reprints a letter-to-the-editor from an 1866 edition of the *Evangelische Kirchen-Zeitung,* a German-based Lutheran Church newsletter, from W. Fister, describing the Missouri Synod.
S

3323. Meyer, Judith W. ETHNICITY, THEOLOGY, AND IMMIGRANT CHURCH EXPANSION. *Geographical Rev. 1975 65(2): 180-197.* The Lutheran Church-Missouri Synod, like other immigrant churches in the United States, emphasized its ethnic character and conservative theology with resultant impact on its spatial distribution. Until after World War I, the Missouri Synod expanded primarily into midwestern communities with German-speaking people. Expansion has since taken place in the growing areas of the United States, but the conservative theological outlook of the denomination has concentrated dissemination in areas to which its members have migrated. Covers 1847-1970.
J

3324. Munch, Peter A. PASTOR MUNCH OF WIOTA, 1827-1908. Lovoll, Odd S., ed. *Makers of an American Immigrant Legacy: Essays in Honor of Kenneth O. Bjork* (Northfield, Minn.: Norwegian-American Hist. Assoc., 1980): 62-91. Johan Storm Munch (1827-1908), ordained in Norway, emigrated to Wiota, Wisconsin, in 1855; unpopular because of his opposition to the Norwegian Synod's affiliation with the German Missouri Synod, he resigned as pastor in 1859 and returned to Norway, where he undertook evangelical projects.

3325. Myhrman, Anders. THE FINLAND-SWEDES IN AMERICA. *Swedish Pioneer Hist. Q. 1980 31(1): 16-33.* Focuses on the Finland-Swedish emigrants as immigrants; mentions settlement, occupations, organizations, and lifestyles in the United States and Canada. This article first appeared as *"Finlandssvenskarna i Amerika,"* in *Svenska flokskolans vänners kalender 1970* (Jakobstad, 1970). New information deals with Finland-Swedish churches and societies. Covers 1893-1979. 4 photos.
C. W. Ohrvall

3326. Nelson, E. Clifford. THE SEARCH FOR IDENTITY IN A PLURALISTIC SOCIETY: A HISTORICAL AND THEOLOGICAL INTERPRETATION OF AN AMERICAN LUTHERAN PROBLEM. *Kyrkohistorisk Årsskrift [Sweden] 1977 77: 160-165.* Lutherans in the United States continue to debate about whether confessional unity requires theological uniformity, and about whether denominational identity denies ecclesiastical catholicity; covers 18th-20th centuries.

3327. Noon, Thomas R. THE ALPHA SYNOD OF LUTHERAN FREEDMEN (1889-1891). *Concordia Hist. Inst. Q. 1977 50(2): 64-70.* In 1889 the Alpha Synod was established in North Carolina by black Lutheran leaders. The purpose of the synod was to serve the needs of Lutheran missionary activity among the blacks of the state. At first, the North Carolina Synod responded sympathetically; but it became apparent that a separate black synod was not practical. The Alpha Synod did not function after 1891; but, through the efforts of Rev. Nils J. Bakke, the objectives of the Alpha Synod were realized. Primary sources; 24 notes.
W. T. Walker

3328. Noon, Thomas R. BLACK LUTHERANS LICENSED AND ORDAINED (1865-1889). *Concordia Hist. Inst. Q. 1977 50(2): 54-63.* During the decades following the Civil War, the Lutheran Church had to adjust to the new status of the blacks. The approaches varied slightly from one synod to another but the general movement was toward the creation of a black Lutheran clergy which would administer to the needs of the black people. The North Carolina Synod produced the most lasting results in this endeavor. Primary sources; 32 notes.
W. T. Walker

3329. Ostergren, Robert. A COMMUNITY TRANSPLANTED: THE FORMATIVE EXPERIENCE OF A SWEDISH IMMIGRANT COMMUNITY IN THE UPPER MIDDLE WEST. *J. of Hist. Geography 1979 5(2): 189-212.* Compares the physical and cultural background of Dalarna Province, Sweden, with Isantic County, Minnesota, to which Swedish migration took place. The answers to the establishment of the migrants' old world in the new are mixed. The group's focal point continued to be the Lutheran Church and many of their social customs and ties continued as before, but the economic conditions of frontier Minnesota caused a switch to crops more characteristic of the American frontier. Covers 1840-1910. 7 maps, 6 tables, graph, 31 notes.
A. J. Larson

3330. Rehmer, Rudolph F. OLD DUTCH CHURCH. *Concordia Hist. Inst. Q. 1976 49(3): 98-111.* Discusses the establishment of the Old Dutch Church (St. John's Evangelical Lutheran Church) on the outskirts of Elletsville, Indiana. Examines the building of this Lutheran church, the earliest church constitution, and the church's early development. The constitution described procedures, doctrinal views, and other church matters. Covers 1830-1956. Primary sources; 16 notes.
W. T. Walker

3331. Reith, Ferdinand. A SWEDISH PASTOR AMONG GERMANS: NIELS ALBERT WIHLBORG, 1848-1928. *Concordia Hist. Inst. Q. 1978 51(4): 168-178.* This account of the career of Niels Albert Wihlborg was originally written by his daughter, Ingrid Schroeder; it has been rewritten by Ferdinand Reith, his grandson. Wihlborg was a successful representative of the Lutheran Church (Missouri Synod); he was assigned to Lutheran churches in Minnesota and Missouri during 1893-1918. Previously Wihlborg held a variety of positions including teacher and shopkeeper. Based on personal recollections. W. T. Walker

3332. Repp, Arthur C. A STUDY OF THE AUTHORSHIP OF SCHWAN'S CATECHISM. *Concordia Hist. Inst. Q. 1973 46(3): 106-111.* Surveys the editorship and contributions of others (1893-1912) to Henry C. Schwan's exposition of Luther's Small Catechism. S

3333. Rimbach, Raymond W. JOHN ADAM RIMBACH AND LIFE IN THE NORTHWEST DISTRICT. *Concordia Hist. Inst. Q. 1980 53(1): 2-12.* John Adam Rimbach (1871-1941), born in Ohio, arrived in 1906 in Portland, Oregon; there he was a member of and a leader in the Oregon and Washington District, and pastor of the Lutheran Trinity Church for 35 years.

3334. Rosholt, Malcolm. TWO MEN OF OLD WAUPACA. *Norwegian-American Studies 1965 22: 75-103.* Describes the lives of two Norwegian-American pioneers, O. F. Duus, a Lutheran minister, and Thomas Knoph, a storekeeper in the town of Scandinavia, Wisconsin. The Lutheran Church in Scandinavia, the first in the Waupaca Township, was chartered by the members of the community and Duus in 1854. For the first two years of his ministry, he served two congregations, one in Winchester and the other in Scandinavia, but left the Winchester congregation in 1856. Knoph's country store, opened in 1853, was typical of most frontier areas in that it stocked or could order nearly any supply needed. Knoph's ledgers serve as a measure of areal growth and locally-produced goods since his store was a retail outlet for the area. Based on Duus's journal, church records, and Knoph's store ledger, as well as other primary and secondary sources; 21 notes. G. A. Hewlett

3335. Scharlemann, E. K. and Scharlemann, M. H. [AN INTERVIEW WITH ERNST SCHARLEMANN].

A "HOSPITANT" TO THE SEMINARY. *Concordia Hist. Inst. Q. 1976 49(1): 23-28.* Transcript of a taped interview of Ernst K. Scharlemann, a retired Lutheran pastor, by his son, Martin H. Scharlemann. E. K. Scharlemann arrived in St. Louis during the first decade of this century and attended Concordia Seminary as a "hospitant," one who attended classes but did not write examinations. He later changed his status and graduated in 1909.

A FOREIGNER GOES NATIVE. *Concordia Hist. Inst. Q. 1976 49(2): 64-71.* E. K. Scharlemann reflects upon his pastorate in Hahlen, Illinois from 1909-18. This period witnessed the development of St. Peter's Lutheran Church under his direction and the further extension of Lutheran influence in the Hahlen-Nashville, Illinois area. W. T. Walker

3336. Schlegel, Ronald J. "DADDY" HERZBERGER'S LEGACY. *Concordia Hist. Inst. Q. 1974 47(3): 139-143.* The work of Pastor F. W. Herzberger, missionary to St. Louis, Missouri, for the Lutheran Church, 1899-1930. S

3337. Scholz, Robert F. WAS MUHLENBERG A PIETIST? *Concordia Hist. Inst. Q. 1979 52(2): 50-65.* Denies that Lutheran minister Henry Melchior Muhlenberg, who preached in colonial Pennsylvania during the mid-18th century, was a pietist.

3338. Schreiber, Clara Seuel. PALM SUNDAY IN FREISTADT, 1898. *Concordia Hist. Inst. Q. 1977 50(1): 32-36.* Reminisces about a Lutheran observation of Palm Sunday in Freistadt, Wisconsin, in 1898. 3 photos. W. T. Walker

3339. Schulze, Eldor P. E. C. L. SCHULZE AND H. C. STEUP. *Concordia Hist. Inst. Q. 1973 46(1): 28-34.* Presents brief biographies of his two grandfathers, Pastors Ernst Carl Ludwig Schulze (1854-1918) and Henry Christian Steup (1852-1931?). Illus., 2 photos. B. W. Henry

3340. Sjöborg, Sofia Charlotta; Westerberg, Wesley M., transl. JOURNEY TO FLORIDA, 1871. *Swedish Pioneer Hist. Q. 1975 26(1): 24-45.* Reprints Lutheran Sofia Charlotta Sjöborg's journey from Sweden to New York, then south to central Florida. The company was friendly and happy during the ocean crossing, the time being spent with sermons, religious texts, and singing. Impressions of cities, people, and the countryside are given. Based on primary sources; 14 notes. K. J. Puffer

3341. Skarsten, Trygve R. DANISH CONTRIBUTIONS TO RELIGION IN AMERICA. *Lutheran Q. 1973 25(1): 42-53.* History of Danish Lutherans in the United States, 1619-1973, emphasizing the ministries of Vilhelm Beck (1829-1901) of the Inner Mission Movement and N. F. S. Grundtvig (d. 1872). S

3342. Snyder, Walter W. H. D. WACKER, BESUCHER, REISEPREDIGER, PASTOR IN FRONTIER TEXAS. *Concordia Hist. Inst. Q. 1980 53(2): 70-83.* Examines the meaning and duties of a *Besucher* or "visitor" and a *Reiseprediger* or "circuit rider" of the Missouri Synod of the Lutheran Church, formed during 1847-65, as part of a program to reach German Lutherans in the Western District. Discusses Hermann Dietrich Wacker (1867-1938) who served as a *Besucher, Reiseprediger,* and pastor for the Lutheran Church in parts of Texas and what is now Oklahoma.

3343. Steege, Martin. CHRONICLE OF A MINISTER. *Concordia Hist. Inst. Q. 1976 49(1): 4-22.* An autobiographical review of a career in the Lutheran ministry from induction in the Concordia Collegiate Institute in 1921 to retirement in 1973. Steege's career included pastorates in Trenton and East Rutherford, New Jersey, and Brooklyn, New York. These pastorates witnessed building programs and expansion of Lutheran educational programs. W. T. Walker

3344. Svengalis, Kendall F. THEOLOGICAL CONTROVERSY AMONG INDIANA LUTHERANS 1835-1870. *Concordia Hist. Inst. Q. 1973 46(2): 70-90.* Analyzes religious and political viewpoints. S

3345. Threinen, Norman J. EARLY LUTHERANISM IN WESTERN CANADA. *Concordia Hist. Inst. Q. 1974 47(3): 110-117.* Discusses the role (ca. 1870) of William Wagner, a German immigrant, in establishing Township Berlin, in Manitoba, and his relation to the Lutheran Church, Missouri Synod. S

3346. Waltmann, Henry G. THE STRUGGLE TO ESTABLISH LUTHERANISM IN TIPPECANOE COUNTY, INDIANA, 1826-1850. *Indiana Mag. of Hist. 1979 75(1): 28-52.* Lutheranism scored striking successes in Tippecanoe County between 1826 and 1850. The initial growth of Lutheranism was inhibited by a small German immigrant population, the existence of previously established denominations, and a shortage of clergymen. The latter development was affected by interdenominational disharmony, because four separate schools of Lutheranism were established in Tippecanoe County. 72 notes. J. Moore

3347. Weisheit, Eldon J. THE BLACK BELT REVISITED. *Concordia Hist. Inst. Q. 1975 48(2): 44-50.* A pictorial examination of the recent history of Lutheranism in the Deep South. Twelve photographs depict the development of Lutheranism with primary interest on Alabama. W. T. Walker

3348. Wyneken, Frederick G. and Wyneken, Chet A., transl. CONCISE HISTORY OF EMANUEL LUTHERAN CONGREGATION, CORONA, QUEENS BOROUGH, NEW YORK, 1887-1907. *Concordia Hist. Inst. Q. 1978 51(2): 62-69.* Translation of a church history written in 1967 by Pastor Frederick G. Wyneken in German; the translator is the author's son. Emanuel Lutheran Church was established in 1887 and within 20 years a new facility was in operation. During that 20-year period the church witnessed both triumph and setbacks. Sees divine intervention and guidance in the developing years of the congregation. W. T. Walker

Mennonite and Related Churches
(including Anabaptist tradition, Amish, Brethren in Christ, and Hutterites)

3349. Baer, Hans A. THE EFFECT OF TECHNOLOGICAL INNOVATION ON HUTTERITE CULTURE. *Plains Anthropologist 1976 21(73, pt. 1): 187-198.* The Hutterites of North America are often envied by their rural neighbors as being efficient and productive agriculturalists who combine 20th-century technology with a lifestyle reminiscent of an earlier age. A closer examination of Hutterite culture reveals that a tension exists between these two elements. J

3350. Belk, Fred R. THE FINAL REFUGE: KANSAS AND NEBRASKA MIGRATION OF MENNONITES FROM CENTRAL ASIA AFTER 1884. *Kansas Hist. Q. 1974 40(3): 379-392.* Discusses a nonmilitant group of Mennonites who migrated to the American Middle West from Asia following an intrasect disunity, 1884-93.

3351. Belk, Fred R. TO MEET THE LORD AND ESCAPE THE DRAFT. *Mennonite Life 1974 29(1-2): 38-41.* Reprints a chapter from Fred R. Belk's *The Great Trek of the Russian Mennonites to Central Asia, 1880-1884* (1973) describing the Mennonites' flight from Russia to avoid the draft and to meet the Lord; chronicles their eventual immigration to the Great Plains of the United States.

3352. Bergey, Lorna L. MENNONITE CHANGE: THE LIFE HISTORY OF THE BLENHEIM MENNONITE CHURCH, 1839-1974. *Mennonite Life 1977 32(4): 23-27.* Pennsylvania Germans settled Waterloo and Oxford Counties in southwest Ontario 1830-50, forming a prosperous agricultural community. In 1839 they organized the Blenheim Mennonite Church. Jacob Hallman was pastor. Membership in the church averaged 50 people for 135 years until it merged with the Biehn congregation to form the Nith Valley Mennonite Church in 1975. Reasons for its lack of growth are its location on the fringe of the Waterloo County settlement, the appeal of the livelier Methodist Church, a schism which led to the formation of the Missionary Church, and population changes in the area. B. Burnett

3353. Brado, Edward B. MENNONITES ENRICH THE LIFE OF MANITOBA. *Can. Geographic [Canada] 1979 99(1): 48-51.* Drawn by the offer of land, exemption from military service, and lack of objection to their use of the German language in the schools, Mennonites settled in two areas of Manitoba, the East Reserve and the West Reserve, 1875.

3354. Charles, Daniel E.; Espenshade, Kevin R.; and Kraybill, Donald B. CHANGES IN MENNONITE YOUTH ATTITUDES, 1974-1978. *Pennsylvania Mennonite Heritage 1979 2(4): 20-25.* A study of Lancaster Mennonite High School students reveals a continuing positive identification with the Mennonite Church, but a decreasing acceptance of rituals and practices.

3355. Crowley, William K. OLD ORDER AMISH SETTLEMENT: DIFFUSION AND GROWTH. *Ann. of the Assoc. of Am. Geographers 1978 68(2): 249-264.* Discusses the spread of Amish communities in the United States, 1717-1977.

3356. Denlinger, A. Martha. KATIE HESS REMINISCES. *Pennsylvania Mennonite Heritage 1978 1(4): 2-9.* Discusses Katie Charles Hess's (b. 1883) reminiscences about her childhood in a Mennonite community near Lancaster, Pennsylvania, including her daily life, involvement with the church, and early married years.

3357. Driedger, Leo. THE ANABAPTIST IDENTIFICATION LADDER: PLAIN-URBANE CONTINUITY IN DIVERSITY. *Mennonite Q. Rev. 1977 51(4): 278-291.* A study of social change in Plain People communities. The geographical propinquity of the larger technological society forces changes in the communities whether they want them or not. Not all respond to these changes, but some members have long since moved to urban centers, and conservatism is not uniform within all rural communities. The Hutterites are the most conservative and rural, followed by the Old Order Amish, Old Colony Mennonites, and Urban Mennonites. This "identification ladder" permits variation in individual belief and behavior. If rural communities become untenable, as now seems likely, the Plain People no doubt will be able to maintain their distinctive image in urban areas, much as the Jews have done. Covers 1930-77. Table, 2 notes. V. L. Human

3358. Driedger, Leo. CANADIAN MENNONITE URBANISM: ETHNIC VILLAGERS OR METROPOLITAN REMNANT? *Mennonite Q. Rev. 1975 49(3): 226-241.* Presents a study of the effect of urbanization on traditional Mennonite beliefs and practices in an attempt to determine the amount of erosion, if any, on urban Mennonites in contrast to those in rural areas. Urban Mennonites are lost to other groups in lesser numbers. Institutions (colleges, etc.) are shifting to urbanized areas successfully. The study shows that Canadian Mennonites have suffered less than their American counterparts in urbanization. Covers 1961-71. 3 charts, 19 notes. E. E. Eminhizer

3359. Driedger, Leo. MENNONITE CHANGE: THE OLD COLONY REVISITED, 1955-1977. *Mennonite Life 1977 32(4): 4-12.* Comparison of studies of the Hague-Osler area of Saskatchewan shows that six of the original 15 villages disappeared between 1955 and 1977, and that six more are in decline. The role of the village committee and *Schultze* has been downgraded and Pentecostal evangelism has altered the old conservative religion. Other changes: consolidation of small schools, smaller families, more frequent use of English, more modern and colorful clothing, and introduction of nontraditional foods. Four processes have caused the changes: migration out of the area by the most conservative Mennonites, improved transportation to Saskatoon, influence of industrialization and capitalism, and a general liberalization in education and religion. 9 photos, map, 2 notes, biblio. B. Burnett

3360. Driedger, Leo. NATIVE REBELLION AND MENNONITE INVASION: AN EXAMINATION OF TWO CANADIAN RIVER VALLEYS. *Mennonite Q. R. 1972 46(3): 290-300.* Discusses how Mennonites have reaped settlement benefits from government eviction of Métis and Indian groups, specifically in the Red River Valley of Manitoba and the Saskatchewan River Valley (1869-95). S

3361. Driedger, Leo; Fretz, J. Winfield; and Smucker, Donovan E. A TALE OF TWO STRATEGIES: MENNONITES IN CHICAGO AND WINNIPEG. *Mennonite Q. Rev. 1978 52(4): 294-311.* Mennonites do not seem to survive in the large urban areas, but do well in rural settings. Studies the mission strategies used in Chicago and Winnipeg with an analysis of the results of each and a comparison of the two in detail. Covers 1866-1977. 20 notes. E. E. Eminhizer

3362. Dyck, Peter J. THE DIARY OF ANNA BAERG. *Mennonite Life 1973 28(4): 121-125.* Anna Baerg and other Russian Mennonites emigrated to Canada after the Russian Revolution; excerpts from her diary, 1917-23, detail Russian life, the Revolution, and the trip to Canada.

3363. Ediger, Marlow. OTHER MINORITIES: OLD ORDER AMISH AND HUTTERITES. *Social Studies 1977 68(4): 172-174.* Presents information on Old Order Amish and Hutterites and calls for extension of study of ethnic groups and minorities beyond those commonly associated with those terms.

3364. Ens, Adolph and Penner, Rita. QUEBEC PASSENGER LISTS OF THE RUSSIAN MENNONITE IMMIGRATION, 1874-1880. *Mennonite Q. Rev. 1974 48(4): 527-531.*

3365. Epp, Frank H. 1923: THE BEGINNINGS OF THE GREAT MIGRATION. *Mennonite Life 1973 28(4): 101-103.* Economic depression and cholera in the Ukraine inspired a group of Russian Mennonites to begin immigration to Canada, a country ripe for settlement.

3366. Eshleman, Wilmer J. OLD WEST LAMPETER TOWNSHIP CEMETERIES. *Pennsylvania Mennonite Heritage 1978 1(3): 10-12.* Lists the names found on graves located in Mennonite cemeteries near Lampeter in Lancaster County, Pennsylvania, dating from the 18th century.

3367. Fretz, J. Winfield. THE OLD ORDER MENNONITES IN ONTARIO. *Pennsylvania Mennonite Heritage 1980 3(1): 2-10.* Traces the history of Mennonites in Canada from 1786, when the first Mennonites arrived from Bucks County, Pennsylvania; a split occurred in 1889, when the Old Order Mennonites were established in Ontario.

3368. Fretz, J. Winfield. THE PLAIN AND NOT-SO-PLAIN MENNONITES IN WATERLOO COUNTY, ONTARIO. *Mennonite Q. Rev. 1977 51(4): 377-385.* The Mennonite community in Waterloo County, Ontario, is unique for its mixture of liberal and conservative elements and diversity of ethnic origin. Describes 12 grades of social action ranging from ultraconservative to ultraliberal. However, all factions work together surprisingly well as a result of a governing committee that is loose and resilient. In fact, the groups are not very different beneath the surface, except in their methods. This fact makes accommodation possible. The various groups cooperate if movement by an individual or a family from one group to another is desired. 4 tables.
V. L. Human

3369. Friesen, Steven. MENNONITE SOCIAL CONSCIOUSNESS, 1899-1905. *Mennonite Life 1975 30(2): 19-25.*

3370. Gingerich, Melvin. MENNONITE FAMILY NAMES IN IOWA. *Ann. of Iowa 1974 42(5): 397-403.* Describes the settlement of Mennonites in Iowa from 1839 by tracing family names. Mennonite genealogy in the United States has its origins in Dutch and ethnic Swiss names, both of which are present in Iowa. 4 notes. C. W. Olson

3371. Gingrich, J. Lloyd and Zimmerman, Noah L. SNYDER COUNTY MENNONITES OF LANCASTER CONFERENCE. *Pennsylvania Mennonite Heritage 1979 2(2): 2-16.* Overview of Mennonites in Snyder County, Pennsylvania, 1780's-1970's, includes local history and a listing of clergy serving the parishes.

3372. Goering, Jacob D. and Williams, Robert. GENERATIONAL DRIFT ON FOUR VARIABLES AMONG THE SWISS-VOLHYNIAN MENNONITES IN KANSAS. *Mennonite Q. Rev. 1976 50(4): 290-297.* Studies cultural changes among a group of Russian Mennonites who settled in McPherson County, Kansas, in 1874. The study is concerned with four variables: 1) location, 2) occupation, 3) religious affiliations, and 4) educational level. The findings, which follow a brief historical sketch of the group and a statement on the procedures followed, suggest the following: 1) the group dispersed in the past 100 years to 30 states, 2) farming dropped to less than 50 percent as the chief occupation, 3) unless there was no Mennonite church in the area of relocation, the group remained Mennonites, and 4) about 30 percent of the third generation received some college training. Covers 1874-1974. 5 notes.
E. E. Eminhizer

3373. Gross, Leonard, ed. and Bender, Elizabeth, trans. THE COMING OF THE RUSSIAN MENNONITES TO AMERICA: ANALYSIS OF JOHANN EPP, MENNONITE MINISTER IN RUSSIA 1875. *Mennonite Q. R. 1974 48(4): 460-475.* Introduces and reprints Johann Epp's letter of 1875 arguing against Mennonites' emigration from Russia to North America.

3374. Gross, Leonard, ed. EARLY NINETEENTH-CENTURY PENNSYLVANIA-ONTARIO LETTERS. *Mennonite Hist. Bull. 1975 36(3): 4-7.* Excerpts letters and diary entries of Jacob Brubacher and his brother Henry; the writings reveal their closeness despite the physical distance of the Mennonites in Pennsylvania and Ontario, and describe daily life and economic and social history, 1817-46.

3375. Gross, Leonard, ed. THE MENNONITE GENERAL CONFERENCE SECRETARY BOOK. *Mennonite Hist. Bull. 1973 34(3): 1-8.* Through excerpts from the 1921 Mennonite General Conference Secretary Book, the editor "traces . . . the development of the general conference or assembly idea within the Mennonite Church. Bishop John F. Funk . . . figured prominently in the story, at first enthusiastically furthering the Conference movement, then taking a more cautious stance, and finally, when Mennonite General Conference did actually emerge in 1898, deciding that the idea was being realized all too rapidly." S

3376. Gross, Leonard, ed. MENNONITES AND THE REVOLUTIONARY ERA. *Mennonite Hist. Bull. 1974 35(1): 3-11.* Original documents by and about Christian Funk of Indian Field, Pennsylvania, who "was excommunicated from the brotherhood, and formed his own short-lived Mennonite branch called the 'Funkites.' " Discord arose between Funk and other Mennonites in 1760, and again in 1774-76 when Funk was called a rebel for urging support for the new revolutionary government in Pennsylvania. The discord continued at least through 1809. S

3377. Habegger, David. A STORY RECORDED IN STONE. *Mennonite Life 1978 33(3): 19-21.* An analysis of the Mennonite community cemetery in Lyon County, Kansas, shows that six women, three men, and 14 children were buried there during 1870-1917. The names include: Stoltfuz, Umble, Miller, Stutzman, Stuckey, Steckley, Riehl, Kaufman, Bender, Sutter, Musselman, Rediger, Rich and Schlegel.
B. Burnett

3378. Harms, Marianne. THE MENNONITE RESPONSE TO THE BICENTENNIAL 1975-76. *Mennonite Life 1977 32(2): 28-31.* Provides a compilation of books, leaflets and periodicals published during 1975-76 relating to the Mennonites and the American Bicentennial. The bibliography is divided into four sections: articles, books and leaflets, letters, and news. Over 500 items are listed. B. Burnett

3379. Haury, David A. BERNHARD WARKENTIN AND THE KANSAS MENNONITE PIONEERS. *Mennonite Life 1974 29(4): 70-75.* Discusses the life of Bernhard Warkentin, 1872-1908, his immigration from the Ukraine to Kansas and the influence he had in a large migration of Russian Mennonites in 1873; also highlights his interests in agriculture and milling in Kansas.

3380. Haury, David A. BERNHARD WARKENTIN: A MENNONITE BENEFACTOR. *Mennonite Q. Rev. 1975 49(3): 179-202.* Describes Bernhard Warkentin's early life in Russia, his relationship to Russian Mennonites' immigration to Kansas, and his involvement with the railroads in the West. Warkentin influenced several thousand people to settle in Kansas, where he served on the Board of Guardians and the Kansas Local Relief Committee. Some problems occurred when he married a Methodist. He became a miller for several years, sold out to his father-in-law in 1885, but returned to milling in 1887, and expanded his business several times. He was instrumental in the founding of Bethel College. By 1896, he was a member of the Presbyterian Church. Covers 1847-1908. 116 notes. E. E. Eminhizer

3381. Hertzler, John R. THE 1879 BRETHREN IN CHRIST MIGRATION FROM SOUTHEASTERN PENNSYLVANIA TO DICKINSON COUNTY, KANSAS. *Pennsylvania Mennonite Heritage 1980 3(1): 11-18.* Discusses the migration of 300 people of the Brethren in Christ from Lancaster and surrounding counties in Pennsylvania to Dickinson County, Kansas, in 1879; briefly traces the development of Abilene in Dickinson County from 1867; and describes the history of the Eisenhower clan, ancestors of President Dwight D. Eisenhower, who were among the group to migrate to Kansas (they had arrived in Philadelphia in 1741).

3382. Hostetler, Beulah S. THE CHARTER AS A BASIS FOR RESISTING THE IMPACT OF AMERICAN PROTESTANT MOVEMENTS. *Mennonite Q. Rev. 1978 52(2): 127-140.* A study of the influence of American Protestant movements on the structure and beliefs of Mennonite society. American Protestantism went through waves of change during the last half of the 19th century, including institutionalization, but the Mennonite Church, not without a few defections, clung to its time-honored beliefs. The records of the Franconia Conference during the period 1840-1940, scattered though they are, reveal that the unwritten charter continued to be adhered to. There were calls for institutionalization, the keeping of written records, and creation of a written charter, but to follow the Protestant churches would dangerously suggest equality and that the outside churches were really not very different. 42 notes.
V. L. Human

3383. Hostetler, Beulah S. AN OLD ORDER RIVER BRETHREN LOVE FEAST. *Pennsylvania Folklife 1974-75 24(2): 8-20.* Details a contemporary (1973) love feast given by the Old Order River Brethren, and presents the sect's historical and theological background. S

3384. Hostetler, John A. OLD ORDER AMISH SURVIVAL. *Mennonite Q. Rev. 1977 51(4): 352-361.* An attempt to explain why the Old Order Amish not only survive, but prosper. Conventional theories about revitalization are not relevant, nor are those relating to social cohesiveness and in-group protectionism. The Amish violate all of these, but still their numbers double every 23 years. Their secret is to keep everything on a human level, including schools, industry, and farms. Forces that can, and inevitably would, become bureaucratic and impersonal if existing for their own sake, are prevented from gaining a foothold. American society is dynamic and changing; the Amish must and do change also, but they change as they wish to change, always keeping the human element in mind. Covers 1650-1976. V. L. Human

3385. Jones, Clifton H. "THE HUTERISCH PEOPLE": A VIEW FROM THE 1920'S. *South Dakota Hist. 1976 7(1): 1-14.* Two manuscripts written in 1921 by Bertha W. Clark, not published then because of anti-German sentiment after World War I, include a brief history of the Hutterites and how they came to be located in South Dakota. The attitudes and social and religious life of the Hutterites in the 1920's showed them to be antiwar but not anti-American. The sect was no threat to its neighbors. The Hutterites were described as having Swiss origin and using English, although German was the religious language. Organized baseball, automobiles, and greater knowledge of the outside world were breaking down their isolation. Primary source; 5 photos.
A. J. Larson

3386. Juhnke, James et al. EAST WEST AND HOME. *Mennonite Life 1975 30(1): 10-14.* Testimonials from Russian Mennonites, some of whom remained in Russia, others of whom immigrated to the United States, and still others who moved into central Asia hoping to find religious and economic freedom, 1870's-1920's.

3387. Juhnke, James C.; Klingelsmith, Sharon; and Klippenstein, Lawrence. RADICAL REFORMATION AND MENNONITE BIBLIOGRAPHY 1977-78. *Mennonite Life 1979 34(1): 21-27.* Comprehensive bibliography of significant articles, books, dissertations, and theses published during 1977-78 on Mennonites and other religious groups arising from the Radical Reformation. B. Burnett

3388. Kauffman, S. Duane. MISCELLANEOUS AMISH MENNONITE DOCUMENTS. *Pennsylvania Mennonite Heritage 1979 11(3): 12-16.* Provides excerpts from notes and letters found among the papers of the late Doctor D. Heber Plank of Morgantown, Pennsylvania, which offer glimpses of American Amish history, 1668-1790's.

3389. Keddie, Phillip D. CHANGES IN RURAL MANITOBA'S "ETHNIC MOSAIC" 1921 TO 1961. *Tr. of the Hist. and Sci. Soc. of Manitoba [Canada] 1974-75 3(31): 5-20.* Discusses the changes in four ethnic groups of rural Manitoba during 1921-61, concluding that differing migration rates account for the changing proportions of British, French, Mennonites, and Ukrainian-Polish.

3390. Klippenstein, Lawrence. AELTESTER DAVID STOESZ AND THE BERGTHAL STORY: SOME DIARY NOTES. *Mennonite Life 1976 31(1): 14-18.* Chronicles the years 1872-76 in the life of David Stoesz, a bishop of the Bergthaler Mennonites, during his immigration from the Ukraine to Manitoba.

3391. Klippenstein, Lawrence. DIARY OF A MENNONITE DELEGATION (1873). *Manitoba Pageant 1973 18(2): 18-23.* A delegation of 12 Russian Mennonites visited Manitoba during the summer of 1873. They travelled by steamboat from Moorhead, Minnesota, to Fort Garry and then visited the East Reserve and the Assiniboine River district from Winnipeg West. Records brief observations of their survey. The favorable findings of the delegation were instrumental in sending thousands of Mennonite families to North America. Illus., 4 notes. D. M. Dean

3392. Klippenstein, Lawrence. MANITOBA METIS AND MENNONITE IMMIGRANTS: FIRST CONTACTS. *Mennonite Q. Rev. 1974 48(4): 476-488.* Discusses the first experiences of Russian Mennonites who immigrated to Manitoba in 1873, especially their relationship to the Chippewa Indians and the Métis, natives of mixed blood. S

3393. Klippenstein, Lawrence. A VISIT TO MANITOBA IN 1873: THE RUSSIAN MENNONITE DELEGATION. *Canada 1975 3(1): 48-61.* Discusses a visit by Russian Mennonites to Manitoba for the purpose of investigating settlement possibilities in 1873, emphasizing the role of Mennonite Reverend John F. Funk.

3394. Knight, James A. THE OLD ORDER AMISH: LESSONS FROM KANSAS ETHNOGRAPHY. *Plains Anthropologist 1980 25(89): 229-233.* Although they are widely known in the United States, the Old Order Amish present a puzzling face to both social science and popular media. This puzzle can be seen to arise from inaccurate notions of Amish life and an inadequate analytical paradigm for Amish ethnicity. Both these features are especially evident in the case of the Amish of central Kansas; research in this area suggests that the fundamental sources of Amish distinctiveness are cultural rather than social and independent of technological backwardness or social isolation. Covers 1956-78. J

3395. Krahn, Cornelius. A CENTENNIAL CHRONOLOGY. *Mennonite Life 1973 28(1): 3-9, (2): 40-45.* Part I. Describes Mennonite immigration from Russia to the American prairies, noting the underlying causes of the migration and the chronology of the key events in the movement. 9 illus., biblio. Part II. Chronology of events among Mennonite immigrants in Manitoba, Canada, 1871-74.
J. A. Casada/G. A. Hewlett

3396. Krahn, Cornelius. RADICAL REFORMATION AND MENNONITE BIBLIOGRAPHY. *Mennonite Life 1976 31(1): 23-26.* Sources, both European and American, 1974-75.

3397. Krahn, Cornelius. RADICAL REFORMATION AND MENNONITE BIBLIOGRAPHY 1975-1976. *Mennonite Life 1977 32(1): 26-30.* Contains all significant books, doctoral dissertations, and masters' theses dealing with Anabaptist-Mennonite related subjects published during 1975-76. Topical headings include: 1) radical reformation and Anabaptism, 2) Muenster and Muentzer, reformation and revolution, war and peace, 3) Mennonites and related movements and denominations, 4) service, outreach, family, education, fine arts, and 5) dissertations and theses. B. Burnett

3398. Kreider, Robert. WINDOWS TO THE MENNONITE EXPERIENCE IN AMERICA: A PHOTOGRAPHIC ESSAY. *Mennonite Life 1978 33(2): 24-47.* Fifty-six photographs covering 1880-1940 emphasize social customs, the Mennonite mission to the Cheyenne, and the beginning of Mennonite institutions on the prairie. From the Mennonite Library and Archives, North Newton, Kansas. B. Burnett

3399. Kreider, Robert. 1923: THE YEAR OF OUR DISCONTENT, THE YEAR OF OUR PROMISE. *Mennonite Life 1973 28(4): 99-101.* Describes the immigration of 408 Russian Mennonites to Rosthern, Saskatchewan, in 1923, focusing on the prevailing social conditions in Canada at that time.

3400. Lehman, Daniel R. BISHOP HANS LEHMAN, IMMIGRANT OF 1727. *Pennsylvania Mennonite Heritage 1980 3(4): 16-23.* Discusses Mennonite Bishop Hans Lehman (1702-76) of Rapho Township, Lancaster County, Pennsylvania, who settled there in 1727 upon his arrival to the United States from Switzerland, and a genealogy of his family until the early 20th century.

3401. Lehman, Thomas L. THE PLAIN PEOPLE: RELUCTANT PARTIES IN LITIGATION TO PRESERVE A LIFE STYLE. *J. of Church and State 1974 16(2): 287-300.* Discusses legal cases involving the Amish people of Pennsylvania and Wisconsin from as early as 1755, showing their reluctance to participate in the military practices and school religion of the dominant society.

3402. Liechty, Joseph C. HUMILITY: THE FOUNDATION OF MENNONITE RELIGIOUS OUTLOOK IN THE 1860S. *Mennonite Q. Rev. 1980 54(1): 5-31.* Mennonites and Amish of Swiss and South German extraction have generally prized humility as the highest of virtues, echoing unself-consciously some Christian groups of other times and places. Following the investigations of earlier Mennonite students, the author examines the expression of humility during the mid-19th century within the American Mennonite Church. He challenges the mildly negative evaluation of this era by his predecessors, namely, that the Mennonites lived in a condition of relative religious decay, relieved finally by the Awakening or Quickening which began about 1880. Based on materials in the Mennonite Church Archives, Mennonite publications of the period, and secondary studies; 146 notes. H. M. Parker, Jr.

3403. Loomis, Charles P. A FARMHAND'S DIARY. *Mennonite Q. Rev. 1979 53(3): 235-256.* The diary is part of Walter M. Kollmorgen's *Culture of a Contemporary Rural Community: The Old Order Amish of Lancaster County, Pennsylvania,* a study for the Agriculture Department done in 1940. Discusses the Amish family of Christian King, for whom the author worked during May 1940. Describes agricultural labor, particularly caring for livestock. Also describes meals and how the women prepared them. Gives examples of the Amish rejection of modern conveniences and of how they ran their farms. The Amish believed in self-help and criticized some New Deal programs. 3 diagrams, 8 notes. D. L. Schermerhorn

3404. Mackie, Marlene. OUTSIDERS' PERCEPTION OF THE HUTTERITES. *Mennonite Q. Rev. 1976 50(1): 58-65.* Asks "How is a sacred community perceived by members of the containing society?" and "Do outsiders withhold acceptance of a people which refuses to be integrated?" The study is based on a sample of 590 persons around Edmonton, Alberta. The conclusions are that most appreciate Hutterite uniqueness. Social distance is not based on stereotyped prejudice. Covers 1966-75. 4 tables, 12 notes. E. E. Eminhizer

3405. Miller, David L. DANIEL E. MAST (1848-1930): A BIOGRAPHICAL SKETCH. *Mennonite Hist. Bull. 1978 39(1): 2-6.* Gives a biography of Daniel E. Mast, 1886-1930, an Amish deacon and minister who wrote for a German-language newspaper, *Herald der Wahrheit* in Reno County, Kansas.

3406. Miller, J. Virgil. AMISH-MENNONITES IN NORTHERN ALSACE AND THE PALATINATE IN THE EIGHTEENTH CENTURY AND THEIR CONNECTION WITH IMMIGRANTS TO PENNSYLVANIA. *Mennonite Q. Rev. 1976 50(4): 272-280.* To date, there has been no attempt to locate the residences of the Amish in Alsace and the Palatinate. These people originally settled in this area as early as 1700. In the early days, there were probably no formally organized congregations. The congregations are identified and the names of the families are given. The history of the churches is traced to about 1800. Provides a list of immigrants from these churches to America, with the years they came. 44 notes. E. E. Eminhizer

3407. Olfert, Sharon. THE HILDEBRANDS OF ROSENTHAL, MANITOBA. *Mennonite Life 1979 34(4): 19-26.* The Hildebrand family was centered in Neuenburg, South Russia, from 1818 until 1878 when Bernhard Hildebrand (1840-1910) and family emigrated to Rosenthal, Manitoba. A farming family, they gradually expanded their holdings until the 10 children all had nearby farms. Patriarch Bernhard Hildebrand supported education and foreign missions. Listing of Bernhard Hildebrand family; Rosenthal Village census 1878-80; farm inventory 1880-81. 7 photos, map of Rosenthal householders, late 1870's, 10 notes, biblio. B. Burnett

3408. Oostenbaam, J. A. THE REFORMATION OF THE REFORMATION: FUNDAMENTALS OF ANABAPTIST THEOLOGY. *Mennonite Q. Rev. 1977 51(3): 171-195.* Reviews the problems of classifying the Anabaptists based on their theological views including past approaches. These include approaches which limit the thought patterns of Anabaptists so as to exclude spiritual, Schwanmen, and the antitrinitarians, and those who would extend the thought patterns to include them. Suggests considering whether the Anabaptists were a wing of the Reformation or a new intellectual movement giving a new form to the Christian faith, the latter being the view the Anabaptists had of themselves. Traces the development of the latter view by reviewing the more recent writing on the Anabaptist view of church, faith, and ethics, ending with a detailed analysis. 64 notes. E. E. Eminhizer

3409. Penner, Peter. BY REASON OF STRENGTH: JOHANN WARKENTIN, 1859-1948. *Mennonite Life 1978 33(4): 1-9.* Johann Warkentin (1859-1948), a little-known leader of the Mennonite Brethren Church in Canada, was born in South Russia and migrated to Manitoba in 1879. In 1881 he married Sara Krahn Loewen (d. 1930). Eventually he became a prosperous farmer and they had 19 children. Converted from Old Colony Mennonite to Mennonite Brethren, Warkentin served in the Sunday School, directed the choir, and studied theology. Ordained in the Gospel ministry in 1895, he became assistant moderator to the Reverend David Dyck in the Winkler congregation, and moderator in 1906. As part of his missionary outreach interest, he helped establish a MB group in Winnipeg. Warkentin continued active church leadership until 1931 and remained influential for 10 more years. Based on unpublished material by Ben Warkentin; 6 photos, 15 notes. B. Burnett

3410. Penner, Peter. MENNONITES IN THE ATLANTIC PROVINCES. *Mennonite Life 1976 31(4): 16-20.* Mennonites did not settle in the Canadian Atlantic Provinces until after World War II. Three motivations brought Mennonites to the area after 1954: a desire to withdraw from crowded metropolitan life, an orientation toward social and evangelical service in underdeveloped areas, and the availability of jobs in teaching, engineering, research, and medicine. 5 photos, map, 7 notes. B. Burnett

3411. Regeher, Ted D. MENNONITE CHANGE: THE RISE AND DECLINE OF MENNONITE COMMUNITY ORGANIZATIONS AT COALDALE, ALBERTA. *Mennonite Life 1977 32(4): 13-22.* Russian German immigrants settled Coaldale, Alberta, 1920-30, but because they came as individuals rather than as a colony, they were subject to Canadian regulations and could not transplant distinctly Mennonite institutions and social structures. Organizations evolving from the settlement included churches, a German library, a language preservation society, and Saturday schools. Settlers founded a cooperative cheese factory, a Savings and Credit Union, and a society to provide medical care. Although prosperous, Mennonites at Coaldale had become assimilated into the larger Canadian society by 1976, largely because of the decline of the German language, economic consolidation, superiority of government welfare services, and internal divisions involving religious splits and inadequate leadership. Primary sources; 13 photos. B. Burnett

3412. Ringenberg, William C. DEVELOPMENT AND DIVISION IN THE MENNONITE COMMUNITY IN ALLEN COUNTY, INDIANA. *Mennonite Q. Rev. 1976 50(2): 114-131.* The Allen County Mennonites' background is traced into Europe, with a discussion of the controversy leading to the division by the Amish. The reasons for the settlement in Allen County by the Amish are listed. Local divisions are discussed indicating their effect on marriage and resultant genetic problems. The general development of the Mennonite-Amish community is detailed. Covers 1850-1950. 52 notes. E. E. Eminhizer

3413. Rushby, William F. THE OLD GERMAN BAPTIST BRETHREN: AN INTIMATE CHRISTIAN COMMUNITY IN URBAN-INDUSTRIAL SOCIETY. *Mennonite Q. Rev. 1977 51(4): 362-376.* A consideration of the culture, life-style, and chances for survival of The Old German Baptist Brethren, an ultra-conservative offshoot of a larger church. The Brethren hardly qualify as Plain People, for they accept many modern gadgets and conveniences. They are not nearly so introversionist as some Plain Peoples, but they still survive and maintain their separate identity, though internal numerical growth has been slow. Strict adherence to Church doctrine, rather than differences in clothes or customs, marks off the Brethren. Although this religious emphasis is seen by some sociologists to spell their doom, others argue that it may be the very thing which saves the Brethren from eventual assimilation, for religion is no longer considered important enough to fight over in the larger society. Table, note. V. L. Human

3414. Ruth, John. MENNONITE IDENTITY AND LITERARY ART. *Mennonite Life 1977 32(1): 4-25.* Story-tellers, those who value and transmit the traditions of any culture, give meaning and a spiritual sense to life. Mennonites have lost much of their sense of tradition in their desire to be acculturated. Sentimental nostalgia and ridicule do not touch the souls of people and are not stories. The scruples that Mennonites traditionally have held and which some consider antithetical to art can spur creativity rather than paralyze it by using one's imagination. The artistic challenge today lies in penetrating and articulating the unique values of the Mennonite ethos rather than in betraying them, in transcending social pressures and finding what is true and lasting. B. Burnett

3415. Sauder, David L. METZLER MENNONITE CONGREGATION, 1728-1978. *Pennsylvania Mennonite Heritage 1978 1(2): 9-16.* Established in 1728 in the town of Groffdale, the Metzler Mennonite congregation got its name from the family of Jacob and Maria Metzler who settled in West Earl Township in 1786. Offers a history of the church and lists its bishops, ministers, and deacons, 1728-1978.

3416. Sawatzky, H. L. MANITOBA MENNONITES PAST AND PRESENT. *Mennonite Life 1974 29(1-2): 42-46.* Covers Mennonites in Manitoba 1870-1900.

3417. Schelbert, Leo and Leubking, Sandra. SWISS MENNONITE FAMILY NAMES: AN ANNOTATED CHECKLIST. *Swiss Am. Hist. Soc. Newsletter 1978 14(2): 2-32.* Lists the major family names of the Swiss Brethren who migrated to North America, 1680-1880; gives variant names, Swiss origins, and names of successive first migrated family members.

3418. Schlabach, Theron F. PARADOXES OF MENNONITE SEPARATISM. *Pennsylvania Mennonite Heritage 1979 2(1): 12-17.* Discusses attitudes toward separatism, political activism, and social reform among Mennonites, 1840's-1930's.

3419. Schmidt, Dennis. J. E. ENTZ (1875-1969): SHEPHERD TO HIS FLOCK. *Mennonite Life 1976 31(3): 14-17.* A minister of the First Mennonite Church in Newton, Kansas, John Edward Entz (1875-1969) was committed to pacificism, nonresistance, and evangelical Christianity. He supported the Deaconness movement, worked for high quality music in the church, and produced the *Church Letter* during World War II to keep up morale of men in Civilian Public Service Camps. Because his preaching was monotonous and his message very conservative, he was unseated as an active minister in 1946 and given the title Elder Emeritus. He continued visitation work and other church work until his death. In 1960 he received a Distinguished Alumnus award from Bethel College. Photo. B. Burnett

3420. Schmidt, John F. "THREE YEARS AFTER DATE . . ." *Mennonite Life 1973 28(2): 35-39.* Chronicles events within the congregation of a Mennonite church in Kansas, 1873-80.

3421. Schrag, Martin H. THE BRETHREN IN CHRIST CONCEPT OF THE CHURCH IN TRANSITION, 1870-1910. *Mennonite Q. Rev. 1978 52(4): 312-327.* During 1870-1910 the Brethren in Christ brought into their organization a change in basic outlook which moved toward individualizing the faith. They were influenced by individualistic, perfectionistic, and conservative American Christianity. These influences and the changes they brought about are discussed under the headings: "The New Birth Individualized," "The Christian Life Individualized," and "The Concept of the Church Individualized." Each of these areas is reflected through the adoption of Sunday schools, revivalism, holiness, a periodical, a church school, and centrally organized mission program. 45 notes. E. E. Eminhizer

3422. Schrag, Martin H. THE BRETHREN IN CHRIST ATTITUDE TOWARD THE "WORLD": A HISTORICAL STUDY OF THE MOVEMENT FROM SEPARATION TO AN INCREASING ACCEPTANCE OF AMERICAN SOCIETY. *Mennonite Q. Rev. 1974 48(1): 112-113.* Originally nonconformists, the Brethren in Christ have moved closer to American Protestantism, and have begun to accept economic individualism, higher education, and politics. Covers 1770-1973. S

3423. Schwieder, Dorothy and Schwieder, Elmer. THE BEACHY AMISH IN IOWA: A CASE STUDY. *Mennonite Q. Rev. 1977 51(1): 41-51.* Briefly discusses the history of the Beachy Amish, with emphasis on two colonies in Iowa which have grown rapidly. Notes differences between them and the Old Order Amish. Lists their characteristics, indicating unique features. 33 notes. E. E. Eminhizer

3424. Scott, Stephen E. THE OLD ORDER RIVER BRETHREN CHURCH. *Pennsylvania Mennonite Heritage 1978 1(3): 13-22.* Describes the Old Order River Brethren communities, their membership and leaders since 1855, their schisms, contrasts between the groups, and the 1977 merger between the Musser and Keller-Strickler groups.

3425. Shantz, Jacob Y. NARRATIVE OF JOURNEY TO MANITOBA. *Manitoba Pageant 1973 18(3): 2-6.* In 1873 Jacob Y. Shantz, at the request of the Canadian government, travelled with Bernard Warkentin of South Russia to see what the Manitoba prairies offered Russian Mennonites who wished to migrate. Shantz described the villages and the burgeoning town of Winnipeg. He visited farms owned by recent immigrants and recorded crop prices. His account was translated into several languages and distributed to prospective settlers. D. M. Dean

3426. Showalter, Grace I. THE VIRGINIA MENNONITE RHODES FAMILIES. *Pennsylvania Mennonite Heritage 1980 3(2): 15-22.* History of the Rhodes family and Rhodes descendants of Virginia since the late 1770's and early 1780's, when the first of the Mennonite Rhodes family migrated to Virginia from eastern Pennsylvania, until 1900.

3427. Sprunger, Milton F. COURTSHIP AND MARRIAGE. *Mennonite Life 1976 31(2): 13-16.* Contains the diary account of Indiana Mennonite farmer and widower David Sprunger (1857-1933) in his search for a second wife and mother for his seven children. He married Caroline Tschantz (d. 1939) of Sonneberg, Ohio, 4 April 1895. 2 photos. B. Burnett

3428. Stoltzfus, Victor. AMISH AGRICULTURE: ADAPTIVE STRATEGIES FOR ECONOMIC SURVIVAL OF COMMUNITY LIFE. *Rural Sociol. 1973 38(2): 196-206.* Examines Amish adaptive responses in Coles, Douglas, and Moultrie counties in Illinois to changes in social organization and economic conditions of the outside community and how these aid in securing community cohesiveness, covering 1960-72.

3429. Stoltzfus, Victor. REWARD AND SANCTION: THE ADAPTIVE CONTINUITY OF AMISH LIFE. *Mennonite Q. Rev. 1977 51(4): 308-318.* Analyzes the forces operating to keep Amish society from flying apart in the presence of the larger society. A system of rewards and punishments is in effect: the rewards, though very different from those of the outside world, are seen as being at least equally attractive. Deviants are faced with a number of punishments, running the gamut from simple neighborly admonishment to excommunication. Seldom is the latter necessary, nor is voluntary defection common, for the difficulties of starting all over again in the outside world are a powerful inducement to put up with whatever shortcomings the individual perceives in the society. Fig. V. L. Human

3430. Unruh, John D. and Unruh, John D., Jr. DANIEL UNRUH AND THE MENNONITE SETTLEMENT IN DAKOTA TERRITORY. *Mennonite Q. Rev. 1975 49(3): 203-216.* By 1870, it was clear that Russian Mennonites were going to lose their place in Russia and immigration began. About 10,000 settled in the western United States. Although South Dakota was not recommended by the investigating committee, over 2,000 settled in the area because of Daniel Unruh. Describes his life in Russia. He brought 100 Mennonites to America in 1873. Details their trip across the country and describes their investigation of available lands and final settlement in Dakota. Unruh was successful and relatively wealthy. He devoted some time to the community needs. A negative report on Oregon land by him in 1882 prevented a move there. 49 notes. E. E. Eminhizer

3431. Wagner, Jonathan F. TRANSFERRED CRISIS: GERMAN VOLKISH THOUGHT AMONG RUSSIAN MENNONITE IMMIGRANTS TO WESTERN CANADA. *Can. Rev. of Studies in Nationalism [Canada] 1974 1(2): 202-220.* In 1917, a group of German Mennonite settlers left Russia to relocate in Saskatchewan, western Canada. In 1924, they established *Der Bote,* a German-language newspaper to inform and thus bind the Mennonite community more closely together. *Der Bote* enthusiastically supported Hitler after his advent to power in 1933. Earlier research has largely ignored this sympathy, and has emphasized instead the Mennonites' religious and ethnic diversity, or their contribution to the Canadian mosaic. This revision clears up the Mennonites' Nazi affinities by explaining their devotion to German völkisch thought, actually a mark of insecurity and a revolt against the chaotic conditions of modern living as well as a result of Mennonite hostility to the USSR, which had persecuted them. 55 notes. T. Spira

3432. Wagoner, Gerald C. WENGERITES: PENTECOSTAL BRETHREN IN CHRIST. *Pennsylvania Mennonite Heritage 1978 1(4): 14-17.* Traces the origin and development of this holiness branch of the Brethren in Christ in Ohio and Indiana during 1836-1924, discussing doctrine and leaders.

3433. Wenger, Edna K. BISHOP BENJAMIN W. WEAVER. *Pennsylvania Mennonite Heritage 1980 3(2): 9-14.* Biography of Lancaster Mennonite minister, bishop, and church administrator Benjamin W. Weaver (1853-1928).

3434. Wiebe, Menno. TO BE OR NOT TO BE MENNONITE PEOPLE? *Mennonite Life 1973 28(3): 67-71.* Discusses 20th-century Mennonites and the solidarity which they must express, in terms of spiritual ends and community relations, in order to retain their religious beliefs.

3435. Wittlinger, Carlton O. THE ADVANCE OF WESLEYAN HOLINESS AMONG THE BRETHREN IN CHRIST SINCE 1910. *Mennonite Q. Rev. 1976 50(1): 21-36.* In 1910 the Brethren in Christ, located mainly in Canada and the North Central States, adopted in their general conference a statement embodying the Wesleyan perfectionism. Charles Baker, Bishop of Nottawa District, Ontario, objected to the view that the sanctified no longer had inner desire to sin. No one challenged his view until 1916. In that year, the perfectionists gained control of the *Visitor* and controversy followed. By 1930 the perfectionists were seeking change in the 1910 statement to say "second work of grace." Following this there developed holiness camp meetings. 75 notes.
E. E. Eminhizer

3436. Wittlinger, Carlton O. THE IMPACT OF WESLEYAN HOLINESS ON THE BRETHREN IN CHRIST TO 1910. *Mennonite Q. Rev. 1975 49(4): 259-283.* The Brethren in Christ, a branch of Mennonites, developed divergent views as they came in contact with other Protestant ideas at the end of the 19th century. The Wesleyan influence was important in this change of direction, as can be seen by the number of Charles Wesley's hymns in their hymnal of 1874. Traces the development of Wesley's influence particularly on the Brethren in Kansas. Contact with the American Holiness Movement also caused changes in the doctrinal values held by the Brethren. E. E. Eminhizer

3437. Wittlinger, Carlton O. THE ORIGIN OF THE BRETHREN IN CHRIST. *Mennonite Q. Rev. 1974 48(1): 55-72.* Discusses the 1775-80 founding of the Brethren in Christ in Lancaster County, Pennsylvania, by Jacob Engel (1753-83), the nature of their belief, and disputes between the United States and Canadian branches over the organization's name. S

3438. Yoder, Paton, ed.; Bender, Elizabeth, transl. BAPTISM AS AN ISSUE IN THE AMISH DIVISION OF THE NINETEENTH CENTURY: "TENNESSEE" JOHN STOLTZFUS. *Mennonite Q. Rev. 1979 53(4): 306-323.* Discusses deacon John Stoltzfus's liberal views on baptism and his contribution to the discussion among the Amish of Lancaster and Mifflin counties in Pennsylvania, and of Tennessee, where he moved in 1872. Includes the text of his 1868 "Meditation on Baptism," translated from the German. Based on Stoltzfus's letters and the *Herald of Truth;* 53 notes. E. E. Eminhizer

3439. Yoder, Paton. "TENNESSEE" JOHN STOLTZFUS AND THE GREAT SCHISM IN THE AMISH CHURCH, 1850-1877. *Pennsylvania Mennonite Heritage 1979 11(3): 17-23.* Discusses John Stoltzfus (1805-87), particularly his role in the Great Schism between the liberals and the conservatives in the Amish Church between the 1870's and the turn of the century, in Lancaster County, Pennsylvania.

3440. Zook, Lois Ann. BISHOP JOHN N. DURR AND HIS TIMES. *Pennsylvania Mennonite Heritage 1978 1(1): 18-21.* John N. Durr (1853-1934) served as a bishop in the Mennonite Church in Pennsylvania and was largely responsible for establishing the Southwestern Pennsylvania Mennonite Conference, 1872-1934.

3441. Zook, Lois Ann. MORITZ ZUG, AMISH MENNONITE IMMIGRANT. *Pennsylvania Mennonite Heritage 1979 2(1): 2-7.* Genealogy of the family of Moritz Zug, Pennsylvania Amish, 1742-1886.

3442. —. MENNONITE BEGINNINGS AT ROSTHERN. *Mennonite Life 1976 31(4): 4-15.* Presents an anonymous personal account, perhaps by Peter Klassen, of the first years of the Russian Mennonite settlement in Rosthern, Saskatchewan. In early spring 1892, 27 families staked out homesteads and began planting crops, building homes, and establishing a community. A split between Old Colony Mennonites and liberal Mennonites prevented the establishment of a church until Elder Peter Regier united factions in 1894. Despite frequent prairie fires, a food shortage during the harsh winter of 1892-93, and an 1895 shoot-out with rebellious Cree chief Almighty Voice, morale remained high. Settlers continued to arrive, crop yield was good, and the area prospered. Based on material in the archives of the Conference of Mennonites in Canada; 5 photos, map. B. Burnett

3443. —. PIONEERS, WHEAT, AND FAITH. *Mennonite Life 1974 29(1-2): 24-29.* Pictorial essay showing scenes from pioneer life on the Great Plains among Mennonites who farmed the land, 1870-1974.

Methodist Churches

3444. Allen, Richard. SALEM BLAND: THE YOUNG PREACHER. *J. of the Can. Church Hist. Soc. [Canada] 1977 19(1-2): 75-93.* After World War I, Salem Bland became recognized as a leader in the social gospel and liberal theology movements. The formative period for Bland was his early years as a Methodist minister in Canada. Though successful as a preacher, he held some suspect views and disliked the numerous theological controversies going on around him. Using his various talents, Bland sought to show that there was no important difference between science and religion and that Christian perfection meant not freedom from mistakes, but the constant desire to do what was right. Seeking at all times to combine the good from his own culture and fundamental Christian ideas, Bland rejected the evangelistic approach of both the Methodists and the Salvation Army because he felt that they could not help combine the old and the new. Covers 1880-86. Primary and secondary sources; 69 notes. This issue is *J. of the Can. Church Hist. Soc.* 1977 19(1-2) and *Bull. of the United Church of Can.* 1977 26.
J. A. Kicklighter

3445. Baker, Frank. THE TRANS-ATLANTIC TRIANGLE: RELATIONS BETWEEN BRITISH, CANADIAN, AND AMERICAN METHODISM DURING WESLEY'S LIFETIME. *Bull. of the Com. on Arch. of the United Church of Can. [Canada] 1979 28: 5-21.* The spread of Methodism in the New World was achieved through pioneering laity and consolidating itinerant preachers such as Francis Asbury, Thomas Coke and Philip Embury, encouraged and spurred on by John Wesley.

3446. Boles, John B. JOHN HERSEY: DISSENTING THEOLOGIAN OF ABOLITIONISM, PERFECTIONISM, AND MILLENNIALISM. *Methodist Hist. 1976 14(4): 215-234.* John Hersey (1786-1862), a devout Methodist, turned from mercantilism to preaching in his 20's. Through his preaching and his writings he was a consistent foe of slavery, urged Christians to strive for perfection in their beliefs, stressed that parenthood presented the Christian with great responsibilities, and the millennium was yet to come. Based on Hersey's books; 97 notes. H. L. Calkin

3447. Bradley, Patricia Hayes. "MARK THE PERFECT . . . BEHOLD THE UPRIGHT": FREEBORN GARRETTSON SPEAKS FOR METHODISM. *Methodist Hist. 1978 16(3): 115-127.* Freeborn Garrettson (1752-1827) should be ranked among the best, the most devoted, and the most successful key ministers in the establishment of Methodism in the United States. As a minister, he was a great success even though not greatly gifted in oratory. He was obsessed with the evils of slavery and worked diligently to save sinners from eternal damnation. 108 notes. H. L. Calkin

3448. Breeze, Lawrence E. THE INSKIPS: UNION IN HOLINESS. *Methodist Hist. 1975 13(4): 25-45.* John S. Inskip (1816-84) and his wife, Martha Jane Inskip (1819-90), were leaders in the Holiness Movement within the Methodist Church. In their joint ministerial career they carried their message of Christian perfection throughout the United States and into other lands through evangelism, revivals, class and camp meetings, publications, and preaching. Based largely on a biography of John Inskip by William McDonald and John E. Searles and an unpublished diary of Mrs. Inskip. 88 notes. H. L. Calkin

3449. Brooks, W. H. THE PRIMITIVE METHODISTS IN THE NORTH-WEST. *Saskatchewan Hist. [Canada] 1976 29(1): 26-37.* The branch of evangelical Methodists known as Primitive Methodists since their origin in early 19th-century England, founded an agricultural colony near Grenfell, Saskatchewan, in 1882. Mentions early leaders such as Hugh Bourne, William Clowes, and Lorenzo Dow, as well as a very active leader of the colony, the Reverend William Bee. Presents excerpts from Reverend Bee's letters. Photos, 65 notes. C. Held

3450. Brooks, William H. THE UNIQUENESS OF WESTERN CANADIAN METHODISM 1840-1925. *J. of the Can. Church Hist. Soc. [Canada] 1977 19(1-2): 57-74.* Methodism in western Canada was never truly established as it had been in eastern Canada and the United States. The Ontario missionaries who hoped to find in the west a frontier in which to gain success were bound to be disappointed, because both metropolitanism and railroads began to take hold there quite early. Moreover, the extreme mobility of the settlers and the harsh physical environment made the establishment of western Methodism even more difficult. All these problems meant that the church was not established with any definite character. Some of its members clung to traditional ideas; others turned to social utility. The result was that the institutionalized western Methodist church was devoid of vitality and fell apart. Primary and secondary sources; 35 notes. This issue is *J. of the Can. Church Hist. Soc.* 1977 19(1-2) and *Bull. of the United Church of Can*. 1977 26. J. A. Kicklighter

3451. Calkin, Homer L. THE METHODISTS AND THE CENTENNIAL OF 1876. *Methodist Hist. 1976 14(2): 93-110.* The 1872 General Conference of the Methodist Episcopal Church adopted plans for the recognition of the Centennial of American Independence in 1876. These plans, as well as similar ones of the Methodist Protestant Church and the Evangelical Association, were carried out at the General Conference, Annual Conference, and local church levels. Sermons, editorials, and other publications by Methodists set forth their views regarding America's past, the conditions in 1876, and what lay ahead for the United States. 78 notes. A

3452. Campbell, George Duncan. FATHER TAYLOR, THE SEAMEN'S APOSTLE. *Methodist Hist. 1977 15(4): 251-260.* Discusses Edward Thompson Taylor (1793-1871), sailor turned Methodist preacher, who preached to thousands of seamen from the pulpit of the Seamen's Bethel in Boston (1833-68). 2 illus., 37 notes. H. L. Calkin

3453. Cannon, William R. METHODISM IN A PHILOSOPHY OF HISTORY. *Methodist Hist. 1974 12(4): 27-43.* The concern for world history emerged with the institutionalization of Christianity and the organization of the church as a permanent institution. What John Wesley proposed as "the scheme of salvation and offered as his outline of Christian theology was his anatomy of history." To him history illustrated the positive accomplishments of God's providence. 37 notes. H. L. Calkin

3454. Cannon, William R. THE PIERCES: FATHER AND SON. *Methodist Hist. 1978 17(1): 3-15.* Lovick Pierce (1785-1879) was a Georgia minister in the Methodist Episcopal and later Methodist Episcopal South churches for nearly 75 years. George Foster Pierce (1811-84), his son, was a minister and later bishop of the Methodist Episcopal Church, South. Recounts biographical information for both and describes their contributions to the work of the church. H. L. Calkin

3455. Chapman, Berlin B. A. M. GRIMES: COUNTRY TEACHER AND ITINERANT MINISTER. *West Virginia Hist. 1979 40(3): 287-292.* Addison McLaughlin Grimes (1863-1964), a Methodist Episcopal preacher of Webster County, West Virginia, kept a record of sermons, marriages, funerals, and other religious activities, 1895-1920. Based on newspapers; 3 illus. J. H. Broussard

3456. Clay, Eugene O. PAPA PREACHED AT BODIE. *Pacific Hist. 1979 23(3): 76-81.* The author reminisces about his father's first journey from Smith Valley, Nevada, to preach in the Methodist Church at Bodie, California, and discusses his first funeral in Bodie. R. V. Ritter

3457. Dahl, Curtis. THREE FATHERS, THREE SONS. *Methodist Hist. 1977 15(4): 234-250.* Enoch Mudge (1776-1850) was a Methodist minister and first chaplain of the Seamen's Bethel of New Bedford, Massachusetts. He was a friend of Edward Thompson Taylor, Methodist chaplain of the Seamen's Bethel in Boston and perhaps the model for Herman Melville's Father Mapple in *Moby Dick.* Mudge was at the Bethel for 12 years and greatly influenced the seamen. 2 illus., 36 notes. H. L. Calkin

3458. Dwyer, James A. DER CHRISTLICHE APOLOGETE: GERMAN PROPHET TO AMERICA: 1914-1918. *Methodist Hist. 1977 15(2): 75-94. Der Christliche Apologete* was the official organ of German Methodists in the United States. At the outbreak of World War I in 1914 it took a stand against militarism and resolution of international disputes by warfare. It called for neutrality on the part of the United States, arguing against American entry into the war. As the war progressed in 1917 and 1918, changes were made both in the editorial content of *Apologete* and the administration at Baldwin-Wallace College, both of which were in disfavor with English-speaking Methodists. 48 notes. H. L. Calkin

3459. Engle, Irvin A. PACIFIC GROVE METHODIST CHURCH AND EL CARMELO CEMETERY. *Pacific Historian 1973 17(1): 82-86.* Relates the history of the Methodist Church in Pacific Grove, California, from 1875. S

3460. George, A. Raymond. THE "SUNDAY SERVICE." *Pro. of the Wesley Hist. Soc. [Great Britain] 1976 40(4): 102-105.* Examines the uncertainty concerning the originality of the 1784 copies of John Wesley's *Sunday Service* sent to America. Some of the copies included the manual acts at the Communion and the signation at the Baptism of Infants, while others did not. Considers the role of Thomas Coke in making changes in the 1784 and 1786 versions, suggesting reasons for the changes in the various versions. Based on the editions of the *Sunday Service*; 3 notes. L. Brown

3461. Gravely, William B., ed. A BLACK METHODIST ON RECONSTRUCTION IN MISSISSIPPI: THREE LETTERS BY JAMES LYNCH IN 1868-1869. *Methodist Hist. 1973 11(4): 2-18.* Reprints three letters of 1868-69 in the Matthew Simpson Papers at the Library of Congress from James Lynch (1839-72), black minister of the Methodist Episcopal Church, to Bishop Matthew Simpson (1811-84). Lynch discussed the need to extend the work of the Methodist Episcopal Church in Mississippi during Reconstruction, the need for educational facilities for blacks, and his own political and preaching career. The editor provides biographical data on Lynch and information on the activities of the Methodist Episcopal churches in the South after the Civil War. Based on Methodist periodicals; 46 notes. H. L. Calkin

3462. Gravely, William B. THE DECISION OF A.M.E. LEADER, JAMES LYNCH, TO JOIN THE METHODIST EPISCOPAL CHURCH: NEW EVIDENCE AT OLD ST. GEORGE'S CHURCH, PHILADELPHIA. *Methodist Hist. 1977 15(4): 263-269.* In 1867 James Lynch wrote three letters to Bishop Matthew Simpson. These letters, from the Matthew Simpson Papers at the Philadelphia Conference Historical Society depository in Philadelphia, relate to the decision of Lynch, a black preacher, educator, missionary, and editor, to leave the African Methodist Episcopal Church and join the Methodist Episcopal Church. 5 notes. H. L. Calkin

3463. Gravely, William B. RIDING A COWCATCHER: GILBERT HAVEN VISITS THE ROCKY MOUNTAINS IN 1875. *Colorado Mag. 1976 53(1): 48-62.* Describes the visit of reformer and Methodist Bishop Gilbert Haven in 1875 to various communities in Colorado and to Salt Lake City. Haven presided at church conferences and wrote articles for chuch papers, which included comments upon mining, Mormonism, his ride on a cowcatcher, and church affairs. Primary and secondary sources; 5 illus., 39 notes. O. H. Zabel

3464. Gravely, William B. THE SOCIAL, POLITICAL AND RELIGIOUS SIGNIFICANCE OF THE COLORED METHODIST EPISCOPAL CHURCH (1870). *Methodist Hist. 1979 18(1): 3-25.* In 1865 the Methodist Episcopal Church, South faced the problem of the status of its black members, no longer slaves. The freedmen's options were: membership in the African Methodist Episcopal or the African Methodist Episcopal Zion churches, the southern church, or in northern Methodist missions. In 1870 the decision was made to form a separate organization for blacks, the Colored Methodist Episcopal Church. Under conditions of religious liberty and voluntary choice in religious matters, racial segregation was established institutionally. Based on denominational publications of the period and secondary works; 83 notes. H. L. Calkin

3465. Gundersen, Joan Rezner. A PETITION OF EARLY NORFOLK COUNTY, VIRGINIA, METHODISTS TO THE BISHOP OF LONDON URGING THE ORDINATION OF JOSEPH PILMOOR. *Virginia Mag. of Hist. and Biog. 1975 83(4): 412-421.* Several Norfolk residents petitioned the Bishop of London in 1774 to ordain Methodist preacher Joseph Pilmoor. An analysis of the signers shows that they were a representative sample of Norfolk's population, with the exception that they tended to be patriots more often than the Norfolk population at large. Based on documents in the Fulham Palace Papers (London), newspapers, and secondary sources; 40 notes. R. F. Oaks

3466. Hall, Bob. CASE STUDY: COCA-COLA AND METHODISM. *Southern Exposure 1976 4(3): 98-101.* Examines the Methodist Church in the South since the 1840's, aid from the shareholders of the Coca-Cola Company in 1898, and religious education in the form of Emory University and Vanderbilt University.

3467. Hasse, John. "THE WHITES RUNNIN' BECAUSE THE BLACKS ARE MOVIN' IN": AN INTERVIEW WITH REV. ROOSEVELT ROBINSON. *Indiana Folklore 1977 10(2): 183-190.* The Reverend Roosevelt Robinson, minister of the Centennial United Methodist Church in Gary, Indiana, discusses white flight in Gary, intradenominational differences in black churches, and the history of his church.

3468. Hayes, Alan L. INTRODUCTION. *J. of the Can. Church Hist. Soc. [Canada] 1977 19(1-2): 2-5.* Summarizes a series of papers presented to meetings of the Canadian Methodist Historical Society during 1975-76. Until its 1925 merger into the United Church of Canada, Methodism constituted the largest single Protestant denomination in Canada. Representing a strongly evangelistic faith, Methodist missionaries from both Great Britain and the United States went into many areas of Canada as early as 1765 and were very successful in their efforts at conversion. Eventually Methodism lost its evangelical character and became thoroughly established and institutionalized. Its original character was so strong, however, that there remained some evangelical elements, and a new social reform movement emerged. Canadian Methodism has made significant contributions both to the beliefs of the United Church of Canada and to the development of the secular culture of English Canada. This issue is *J. of the Can. Church Hist. Soc.* 1977 19(1-2) and *Bull. of the United Church of Can.* 1977 26.
J. A. Kicklighter

3469. Hites, Margaret Ann. PETER DOUB, 1796-1869, HIS CONTRIBUTION TO THE RELIGIOUS AND EDUCATIONAL DEVELOPMENT OF NORTH CAROLINA. *Methodist Hist. 1973 11(4): 19-45.* Doub, a Methodist Episcopal preacher in North Carolina, was active in expanding the work of the church in that area, in developing educational facilities for women, and in the church controversy over slavery. Based on Doub's autobiography, journal, and letters in the Perkins Library, Duke University; 71 notes. H. L. Calkin

3470. Hoggard, J. Clinton. PAUL ROBESON: A REMEMBRANCE. *Crisis 1976 83(3): 81-83.* Reminisces about Paul Robeson (1898-1976). Mentions Robeson's Christian upbringing, excellence at Rutgers University in academics and athletics, discrimination encountered, careers in drama and concert singing, political controversies, civil rights activities, continued worship at Mother A.M.E. Zion Church in Manhattan, and retirement due to ill health. A. G. Belles

3471. Hohner, Robert A., ed. FROM THE METHODIST PARSONAGE IN CHARLOTTESVILLE: BERNARD F. LIPSCOMB'S LETTERS TO JAMES CANNON, JR., 1889-1892. *Virginia Mag. of Hist. and Biog. 1975 83(4): 428-474.* Bernard F. Lipscomb, who became the Methodist minister in Charlottesville in 1889, wrote many letters to friends and associates which provide detailed descriptions of the life and problems of Southern Methodist pastors in the late 19th century. The letters to his friend James Cannon, Jr., Methodist pastor in Newport News, are herein published. Letters from the Cannon Papers, Duke University Library, photo, 138 notes. R. F. Oaks

3472. Holder, Ray. METHODIST BEGINNINGS IN NEW ORLEANS 1813-1814. *Louisiana Hist. 1977 18(2): 171-187.* Under orders from the Methodist General Conferences of 1812, itinerant preacher William Winans endeavored to establish Methodism in New Orleans, Louisiana, in 1813-14 with a school and church. He faced considerable opposition in New Orleans, and he believed he did not accomplish much. Not until 1825 did "the continuous history of Methodism in New Orleans" begin. Based on Winans' unfinished autobiography and secondary sources; 80 notes. R. L. Woodward, Jr.

3473. Hotter, Don W. SOME CHANGES RELATED TO THE ORDAINED MINISTRY IN THE HISTORY OF AMERICAN METHODISM. *Methodist Hist. 1975 13(3): 177-194.* The ordained ministry of the Methodist Church has undergone numerous changes from 1771 to the present. These changes relate to the place of the lay preacher, marriage, education, salaries, length of appointment, ministerial training, pastoral counseling, and administering the sacrament of the Lord's Supper. 41 notes. H. L. Calkin

3474. Hudson, Winthrop S. THE METHODIST AGE IN AMERICA. *Methodist Hist. 1974 12(3): 3-15.* The Methodist age in America covered roughly the period from 1825 to 1914. It had a distinct impact on religion in the nation and was marked by growth in church membership and revival meetings. It was distinct also from earlier Puritan evangelicalism and from the Great Awakening. 24 notes.
H. L. Calkin

3475. Hutchinson, Gerald M. JAMES EVANS' LAST YEAR. *J. of the Can. Church Hist. Soc. [Canada] 1977 19(1-2): 42-56.* James Evans served the Methodist Church in Canada with great distinction both as a minister in the Hudson's Bay territory and as a linguist in the creation of a written language for the Cree Indians. Unfortunately, his later years were clouded with controversy. Involved in conflicts with both the Hudson's Bay Company and Roman Catholic missionaries, Evans was accused of immorality with some young girls and went to England where the matter was considered by the Missionary Society. He died suddenly before a verdict was reached; but the view was that while Evans may have acted improperly, he was not guilty of any immorality. The matter has remained a mystery ever since because, until recently, scholars were not permitted to examine the relevant documents. Now it is possible to consider his great accomplishments and explain the great tragedy of his last year. Covers 1833-46. This issue is *J. of the Can. Church Hist. Soc.* 1977 19(1-2) and *Bull. of the United Church of Can.* 1977 26. Primary and secondary sources; 13 notes. J. A. Kicklighter

3476. Keller, Ralph A. METHODIST NEWSPAPERS AND THE FUGITIVE SLAVE LAW: A NEW PERSPECTIVE FOR THE SLAVERY CRISIS IN THE NORTH. *Church Hist. 1974 43(3): 319-339.* Because the antebellum slavery question overlapped into the churches, it is possible to learn a great deal from religious newspapers. The papers, more clearly than conference records or religious journals, show an extensive revulsion to the Fugitive Slave Law. Although the five editors cited found the law repulsive, they were in disagreement about what should be done. Their arguments were often more heated against each other than against the law. Besides being at odds over methods, religious leaders did not feel free to act or speak without concern for the consequences of the church itself. While institutional commitment often tempered the stand a churchman might take regarding a slavery problem, the crisis over slavery and the Union drew the churches into more involvement with social and political issues. Based on the five official newspapers of the Methodist Church; 89 notes. M. D. Dibert

3477. Kewley, Arthur E. THE FIRST FIFTY YEARS OF METHODISM IN NEWFOUNDLAND 1765-1815: WAS IT AUTHENTIC WESLEYANISM? *J. of the Can. Church Hist. Soc. [Canada] 1977 19(1-2): 6-26.* Examines the origins of Methodism in Newfoundland to discover whether the United Church represents the only continuous tradition of pure Methodism in Canada. Finds Methodism in Newfoundland to be totally unique and unconnected, except in name, to any Wesleyan group. Its founder, an Anglican free-lance missionary named Lawrence Coughlin, had practically no connection with English Wesleyans during his stay in Newfoundland and demonstrated little adherence to Wesley's doctrines or to Methodist discipline. The Methodist movement there seemed to fall apart after he left but gradually revived through solid organization, revived missionary concern and skill, and positive popular response. Primary and secondary sources, 43 notes. This issue is *J. of the Can. Church Hist. Soc.* 1977 19(1-2) and *Bull. of the United Church of Can.* 1977 26. J. A. Kicklighter

3478. Kverndal, Roald. THE BETHEL SHIP "JOHN WESLEY": A NEW YORK SHIP SAGA FROM THE MID-1800'S WITH REVERBERATIONS ON BOTH SIDES OF THE ATLANTIC OCEAN. *Methodist Hist. 1977 15(4): 211-233.* Peter Bergner (1797-1866), native of Sweden, was converted to Methodism and began holding religious meetings for Scandinavian sailors in New York in the 1830's. In 1845 the Methodist Episcopal Church acquired a bethel ship, named *John Wesley,* from the Wesleyan Methodists and established a floating chapel for seamen. Religious services for Scandinavian seamen immigrants were held by Bergner, Olof Gustaf Hedstrom (1803-77), and later Ole Peter Petersen (1822-1901), who was also responsible for establishing the Methodist Episcopal Church in Norway. 3 illus., 58 notes. H. L. Calkin

3479. Laurie, Bruce. "NOTHING ON COMPULSION": LIFE STYLES OF PHILADELPHIA ARTISANS, 1820-1850. *Labor Hist. 1974 15(3): 337-366.* Examines the life styles and changing social customs and ideologies of Philadelphia artisans from 1820-1850. Pre-industrial working-class culture with its equal emphasis upon work, leisure, and spontaneity slowly gave way to an emerging industrial culture emphasizing work, discipline, morality, and success. The depression of 1837-43, the temperance crusade, and the impact of evangelical Methodism conveyed a class identity and a modern work ethic to the increasingly diverse artisans. Assesses pre-industrial cultural activities centered in taverns, volunteer fire companies, circuses, and sports. Based on Philadelphia newspapers, census returns, organizational reports, and secondary sources; 106 notes. L. L. Athey

3480. Loewenberg, Robert J. SAVING OREGON AGAIN: A WESTERN PERENNIAL? *Oregon Hist. Q. 1977 78(4): 332-350.* Denies the contention by Clifford M. Drury that Jason Lee, a Methodist missionary, "saved" Oregon for the United States by sponsoring settlement of Oregon by US citizens. Lee supported the colonization of Oregon, but only because colonization would benefit his missionary efforts. The provision of the Gospel to the Indians of Oregon was Lee's major concern. Theories to the contrary are based on "indirect proofs" and "inferences at third and fourth remove from the evidence." Covers 1834-43. Based on documents in the University of Puget Sound and the Washington State Historical Society, and on secondary sources; 48 notes.
D. R. McDonald

3481. Loveland, Anne C. THE "SOUTHERN WORK" OF THE REVEREND JOSEPH C. HARTZELL, PASTOR OF AMES CHURCH IN NEW ORLEANS, 1870-1873. *Louisiana Hist. 1975 16(4): 391-407.* "Like most other Northern Methodist missionaries to the South, Hartzell saw no conflict in linking religious endeavors and Republican politics." Hartzell supervised three Methodist institutions for Negroes: Union Normal School, Thomson Institute, and the Freedmen's Orphan Home which combined educational and missionary efforts. The response of Southern Whites to the educational and missionary work of the Northern Methodists among the freedmen was generally unsympathetic. Another reason for the loss of support was the Republicans ultimately abandoned the social and political goals of Reconstruction. Based largely on correspondence from the Hartzell and Baldwin Papers. Illus., 42 notes. E. P. Stickney

3482. May, James W. FRANCIS ASBURY AND THOMAS WHITE: A REFUGEE PREACHER AND HIS TORY PATRON. *Methodist Hist. 1976 14(3): 141-164.* An account of conditions in the Eastern Shore of Maryland and in Delaware, 1777-80. During this period Francis Asbury, Methodist preacher, sought refuge with Thomas White, a Tory judge considered sympathetic to the English and to the Methodists. 96 notes. H. L. Calkin

3483. McCutcheon, William J. THEOLOGICAL ETHNICITY. *Methodist Hist. 1974 12(3): 40-56.* Ethnicity denotes a measurable social, religious, and theological identity not necessarily restricted to previous linguistic or geographical pasts. Theological ethnicity is reflective thought about God that comes from a denomination as it acts within its own society. In the Methodist Episcopal Church the period from 1919 to 1939 was the "golden age" in its theology. 51 notes. H. L. Calkin

3484. Miller, Virginia P. THE 1870 GHOST DANCE AND THE METHODISTS: AN UNEXPECTED TURN OF EVENTS IN ROUND VALLEY. *J. of California Anthropology 1976 3(2): 66-74.* Discusses the unorthodox acceptance of the Methodist Church among members of the Round Valley Indian Reservation in northern California over the Ghost Dance religion being taught by native religious men, 1870.

3485. Mills, Frederick V., Sr. MENTORS OF METHODISM, 1784-1844. *Methodist Hist. 1973 12(1): 43-57.* Discusses Methodist Episcopal ministers 1784-1844, mentioning their geographical areas of origin, occupations before the ministry, spiritual qualifications, economic and social backgrounds, personal ideals, personal conduct in the pulpit, education, and conditions under which they labored. 74 notes.
H. L. Calkin

3486. Mitchell, Joseph. THE ELECTION OF BISHOP MC KENDREE RECONSIDERED. *Methodist Hist. 1974 12(2): 19-31.* The election of William McKendree as bishop of the Methodist Episcopal Church has traditionally been considered the result of a sermon he preached in May 1808. Concludes that Francis Asbury made McKendree a bishop by using McKendree's sermon to make a pronouncement about his preference for the position. 40 notes. H. L. Calkin

3487. Mitchell, Joseph. SOUTHERN METHODIST NEWSPAPERS DURING THE CIVIL WAR. *Methodist Hist. 1973 11(2): 20-39.* Analyzes the role of church newspapers in preserving the Methodist Episcopal Church, South, during the war and in reviving it afterwards. Describes the difficulties of publication in wartime. Articles and editorials dealt with general news, support of the South and slavery, the church's role in the war, attacks on the North, and avoidance of sins. Contemporary newspapers; 104 notes. H. L. Calkin

3488. Moss, Arthur Bruce. PHILIP EMBURY'S PREACHING MISSION AT CHESTERFIELD, NEW HAMPSHIRE. *Methodist Hist. 1978 16(2): 101-109.* In the fall of 1772 Philip Embury conducted a Methodist preaching mission at Chesterfield, New Hampshire in answer to an invitation from James Robertson, an early settler there. Provides background information, 1754-1805, on Embury and his work, and on the area of New Hampshire where he preached. 27 notes.
H. L. Calkin

3489. Moss, Arthur Bruce. PHILIP EMBURY'S BIBLE. *Methodist Hist. 1979 17(4): 253-260.* An account of the Bible owned by Philip Embury, Irish Methodist who came to America in 1760 and became founder of New York Methodism. The Bible is now at John Street Methodist Church, New York City, to which it was presented in 1834. 15 notes.
H. L. Calkin

3490. Moss, Arthur Bruce. TWO THOMAS WEBB LETTERS AT DREW UNIVERSITY. *Methodist Hist. 1974 13(1): 52-56.* Two unpublished letters of Capt. Thomas Webb, Methodist preacher, written in 1771 to Daniel Montgomery, one of the original class leaders of the Methodist society at Philadelphia, regarding the work of the Methodists in America. 15 notes. H. L. Calkin

3491. Nanez, Alfredo. THE TRANSITION FROM ANGLO TO MEXICAN-AMERICAN LEADERSHIP IN THE RIO GRANDE CONFERENCE. *Methodist Hist. 1978 16(2): 67-74.* From the appointment of the first missionary to Spanish-speaking people in the Southwest United States in 1874 until 1966 the annual conferences of the Spanish

American churches were controlled by the missionaries and agencies of the Methodist Episcopal Church and the Methodist Episcopal Church, South. After continuous struggle the name was established as the Rio Grande Annual Conference and in 1966 the Conference was instructed to serve as the fundamental body of the church in New Mexico and Texas in the same manner as any other conference in the United Methodist Church. 4 notes. H. L. Calkin

3492. Nelson, Arnold and Nelson, Helen. BRINGING HOME THE GOLD. *Alaska J. 1979 9(3): 52-59.* Bringing gold back from the Klondike was a serious business. Describes a trip to and from the Klondike in 1899 by Thomas S. Lippy, owner of the 16 Eldorado mine, and the Reverend Edwin M. Randall, pastor of the First Methodist Church, Seattle, to bring home 255 pounds of gold mined at the 16 Eldorado. Randall published an account of the trip in the *Epworth Herald* 30 December 1899 and 6, 12, and 20 January 1900. 8 photos, 6 notes. E. E. Eminhizer

3493. Neufer, P. Dale. CREEDAL FREEDOM IN AMERICAN METHODISM. *Religion in Life 1974 43(1): 42-51.* Discusses the way John Wesley influenced the concept of creedal freedom in American Methodism during the 19th century. S

3494. Norwood, Frederick A. and Rowe, Kenneth E., ed. A LITTLE KNOWN SOURCE ON PIONEER ITINERACY. *Methodist Hist. 1980 18(3): 205-210.* Discusses the value of journals and letters of George Phillips as an important source of American Methodism. Phillips's papers in the Huntington Library in San Marino, California, cover 1840-64 and pertain to his activities as a Methodist circuit rider in Ohio in the 1840's and in California in the 1850's, and as a Civil War chaplain. 14 notes. H. L. Calkin

3495. Norwood, Frederick A. TWO CONTRASTING VIEWS OF THE INDIANS: METHODIST INVOLVEMENT IN THE INDIAN TROUBLES IN OREGON AND WASHINGTON. *Church Hist. 1980 49(2): 178-187.* Contrasts the attitudes of David E. Blaine, John Beeson, and their families, toward the Indians in Oregon and Washington during the 1850's. Both were Methodists: Blaine was a minister and Beeson a layman. Whereas the Blaines grew disillusioned about the native inhabitants, Beeson became an advocate of the Indian cause, and wrote *A Plea For The Indians.* 27 notes. M. D. Dibert

3496. Paterson, Morton. THE MIND OF A METHODIST: THE PERSONALIST THEOLOGY OF GEORGE JOHN BLEWETT IN ITS HISTORICAL CONTEXT. *Bulletin of the Com. on Arch. of the United Church of Can. [Canada] 1978 (27): 4-41.* Biography of Canadian Methodist George John Blewett (1873-1912) focusing on his work as minister and professor, and his personalism.

3497. Porter, Earl W. THE BASSETT AFFAIR: SOMETHING TO REMEMBER. *South Atlantic Q. 1973 72(4): 451-460.* In 1902 John Spencer Bassett, professor of history at Trinity College (later Duke University) founded, with others, the *South Atlantic Quarterly*. His editorial in 1903 rebuked the dogmatism that refused to acknowledge progress among Negroes. The Board of Trustees supported Bassett, though all the comments from the College made it clear that nobody at Trinity, a Methodist institution, agreed with what Bassett had written. Trinity fought a battle for academic freedom, though making clear that "if the race question were involved, some realistic parameters have to be drawn." 4 notes. E. P. Stickney

3498. Rensi, Ray C. THE GOSPEL ACCORDING TO SAM JONES. *Georgia Hist. Q. 1976 60(3): 251-263.* The 19th-century Georgia revivalist Sam Jones stressed the importance of self-reliance and opposed amusements such as dancing, card-playing, the theater, baseball, the use of cigarettes, and especially liquor. These views were representative of the rural South for which Jones spoke as a minister in the Methodist Episcopal Church, South. Covers 1872-1906. Primary and secondary sources; 44 notes. G. R. Schroeder

3499. Richey, Russell E. THE SOCIAL SOURCES OF DENOMINATIONALISM: METHODISM. *Methodist Hist. 1977 15(3): 167-185.* The denominational church in America is deeply indebted to Methodism, as the principle of organization in Methodism has been the principle of denominationalism. Methodism was the religious movement that first fully, effectively, and nationally exemplified that principle and was a significant social source of denominationalism. Covers the 18th and 19th centuries. Reprinted from *Denominationalism,* edited by Russell E. Richey (Nashville: Abingdon Press, 1977). 32 notes. H. L. Calkin

3500. Ross, Brian R. RALPH CECIL HORNER: A METHODIST SECTARIAN DEPOSED. *J. of the Can. Church Hist. Soc. [Canada] 1977 19(1-2): 94-103.* Finding salvation through an evangelical experience in 1872, Ralph C. Horner dedicated himself to winning souls through evangelism and was ordained a minister in the Montreal Conference of the Methodist Church of Canada in 1887. Horner was very successful as an evangelist but found considerable problems with the authorities of the church. They found his methods excessive and discovered that he would not follow their orders. Though told to accept an assignment as a regular minister, Horner refused to do so. The conference leaders tried to work out an arrangement with him but to no avail. In 1894 Horner was deposed from the ministry of the Methodist Church. Ultimately, in 1900, he organized his own successful Holiness Movement Church in Canada. His strong belief in freedom and his self-confidence in the rightness of his mission made him unable to accept direction from others. Primary sources; 24 notes. This issue is *J. of the Can. Church Hist. Soc.* 1977 19(1-2) and *Bull. of the United Church of Can.* 1977 26. J. A. Kicklighter

3501. Ross, Brian R. RALPH CECIL HORNER: A METHODIST SECTARIAN DEPOSED, 1887-95. *Methodist Hist. 1977 16(1): 21-32.* Ralph Cecil Horner (1854-1921) was ordained a minister in the Methodist Church in 1887 and was suspended seven years later for evangelistic activities. In 1900 he created a separate denominational group, the Holiness Movement Church, in Canada. 24 notes. H. L. Calkin

3502. Rowe, Kenneth E. BISHOP SIMPSON'S CENTENNIAL PRAYER, 1876. *Methodist Hist. 1976 15(1): 68-72.* Matthew Simpson, Bishop of the Methodist Episcopal Church, gave the prayer at the opening day ceremonies of the Centennial Exposition in Philadelphia on 10 May 1876. The prayer, together with an account of the events of the day, is reprinted here. 7 notes. H. L. Calkin

3503. Rowlett, Martha. WOMEN IN THE MINISTRY: CALIFORNIA-NEVADA CONFERENCE OF THE UNITED METHODIST CHURCH. *Pacific Hist. 1978 22(1): 61-70.* Women have contributed to the California-Nevada Conference of the United Methodist Church from its earliest days, serving as evangelists and ministers, particularly in smaller churches. 2 illus. G. L. Olson

3504. Royce, Marion. METHODISM AND THE EDUCATION OF WOMEN IN NINETEENTH CENTURY ONTARIO. *Atlantis [Canada] 1978 3(2): 130-143.* Examines the higher education opportunities for women in Ontario, Canada, during the 19th century, largely encouraged and sponsored by the Methodist Church.

3505. Shockley, Grant S. METHODISM, SOCIETY AND BLACK EVANGELISM IN AMERICA: RETROSPECT AND PROSPECT. *Methodist Hist. 1974 12(4): 145-182.* John Wesley, Francis Asbury, and other early leaders of Methodism showed concern for the blacks and evangelized extensively among them. However, Wesleyan evangelism, which combined piety and social responsibility, gradually accommodated itself to American slavery. In America, Methodism, narrow pietism, and emotional revivalism supplanted Wesleyan evangelism in reference to Negroes. If practiced by Methodists, Wesleyan evangelism would have a unique offering for America today. 83 notes. H. L. Calkin

3506. Spencer, Ralph W. ANNA HOWARD SHAW. *Methodist Hist. 1975 13(2): 33-51.* Anna Howard Shaw (1847-1919) was the first woman ordained in the Methodist Protestant Church, but she is best known for her work on behalf of the woman suffrage movement. Discusses her efforts to get theological and medical training, her service in the ministry, and as an exponent of the Social Gospel Movement. 41 notes. H. L. Calkin

3507. Steele, David L. THE AUTOBIOGRAPHY OF THE REVEREND JOHN YOUNG, 1747-1837. *Methodist Hist. 1974 13(1): 17-40.*

John Young was a Methodist clergyman ordained in 1819. This autobiography, written in 1818 or 1819, covers his early days in North Carolina and includes a statement of his doctrine. 45 notes. H. L. Calkin

3508. Tyrrell, Charles W. PRIMITIVE METHODISM: THE MIDWESTERN STORY. *Methodist Hist. 1976 15(1): 22-42.* The English brought Primitive Methodism to the eastern seaboard in 1829 and to the Midwest in 1842. In Illinois, Wisconsin, and Iowa the Primitive Methodist Church was considered to be a foreign group and was basically missionary in character. There was a constant struggle for survival, and it never consisted of more than a few small churches, with a total membership, in 1976, of 11,000 persons in 82 churches. 20 notes. H. L. Calkin

3509. Waller, John O. JOHN BYINGTON OF BUCKS BRIDGE: THE PRE-ADVENTIST YEARS. *Adventist Heritage 1974 1(2): 5-13, 65-67.* John Byington of Bucks Bridge, New York, was one of the first three presidents of the Seventh-Day Adventist General Conference; he belonged to the Methodist Episcopal and Wesleyan Methodist churches before his conversion to Adventism in 1852.

3510. Zehrer, Karl and Dwyer, James A., transl. THE RELATIONSHIP BETWEEN PIETISM IN HALLE AND EARLY METHODISM. *Methodist Hist. 1979 17(4): 211-224.* Translation of an article originally published in *Pietismus und Neuzeit: Jahrbuch 1975 zur Geschichte des neueren Protestantismus* (Bielefedl, 1975). An account of reactions of German pietists to John and Charles Wesley and George Whitefield in Georgia and England. The pietists did not take the Methodist movement seriously, and the possibilities of mutual influence between 1736 and 1770 are relatively small. Based on correspondence in the Archiv der Frankeschen Stiftungen in Halle, Germany; 66 notes. H. L. Calkin

Moravian Churches

3511. Bolhouse, G. E. THE MORAVIAN CHURCH IN NEWPORT. *Newport Hist. 1979 52(1): 10-16.* History of the Moravian Church in Newport, Rhode Island, 1767-1835; mentions church artifacts now in the Newport Historical Society.

3512. Goodwin, Grethe. MORAVIANS IN MAINE: 1762-1770. *New England Q. 1979 52(2): 250-258.* Sketches the history of the Moravian mission at Broad Bay (now Waldoboro, Maine) from the arrival of pastor Georg Soelle (1709-1773) until the settlers moved to Wachovia, North Carolina. The harsh climate, hostile attitude of other German settlers, and especially a lack of leadership led to the community's failure. Soelle was a good preacher but unable to help to solve the practical problems of the farmers. Based on Soelle's letters in the Moravian Archives, Bethlehem, Pa.; 14 notes. J. C. Bradford

3513. Kortz, Edwin W. THE MESSAGE OF OLDMAN'S CREEK. *Tr. of the Moravian Hist. Soc. 1979 23(2): 75-80.* Notes the history of the Moravian Church in Oldman's Creek, New Jersey, and the role its congregation played in the religious life of the area, ca. 1743-1800. Based on an address given at the Oldman's Creek church building on 3 June 1979. C. A. Watson

3514. Lineback, Donald J. JOHANN HEINRICH MULLER: PRINTER, MORAVIAN, REVOLUTIONARY. *Tr. of the Moravian Hist. Soc. 1977 23(1): 61-76.* Born in northern Germany in 1702, Johann Heinrich Muller joined the Moravians on their voyage to America and eventually became a member of the denomination. His contacts with the founder of the Moravian Church, Count Ludwig von Zinzendorf, resulted in Muller's keeping the group's travel journal and later returning to Germany under Moravian auspices to establish a printing press. Zinzendorf arranged a marriage between Muller and Johanna Dorothea Blaunder, a wealthy widow. Muller used his wife's money to create a publication outlet in America. The marriage was an unhappy one, with Muller evidently unwilling to abide by the dictates of the Moravian faith. After various travels to and from Europe, Muller, in 1762, began publishing *Heinrich Mullers Pennsylvanischer Staatsbote* in German in Philadelphia. This newspaper became a leading champion of the American cause and printed the first German edition of the Declaration of Independence. Primary sources. N. Lederer

3515. Nelson, Vernon H. LIFE IN EARLY AMERICA: THE MORAVIANS AT BETHLEHEM. *Early Am. Life 1978 9(4): 26-29, 62-63.* Examines the influence of the Moravian religious sect on the establishment, growth, religion, art, and social organization of Bethlehem, Pennsylvania, 1741-1865.

3516. Surratt, Jerry L. THE ROLE OF DISSENT IN COMMUNITY EVOLUTION AMONG MORAVIANS IN SALEM, 1772-1860. *North Carolina Hist. R. 1975 52(3): 235-255.* Alterations in the nature of the Salem Moravian theocracy, from *gemeinschaft* to *gesellschaft*, can be traced through the effects of rising dissent on military involvement, relationships between the sexes, and the rise of economic individualism. Salem Brethren were forced, between 1820 and 1850, to permit residents to join the militia, ease the strict rules regarding courting and marriage, abandon the community landholding system, and allow residents to engage in the slave trade. Based primarily on manuscript and printed records at the Moravian Archives, as well as on secondary materials; 7 illus., 74 notes. T. L. Savitt

3517. Weinlick, John R. THE WHITEFIELD TRACT. *Tr. of the Moravian Hist. Soc. 1979 23(2): 51-74.* Describes the founding and early development (1740-50) of the town of Nazareth, Pennsylvania, founded on a tract of land purchased from George Whitefield (1714-70). The Whitefield House, a substantial building built in 1743, served such purposes as a home for new arrivals, a nursery school, a theological seminary, a home for retired Moravian Brethren ministers and missionaries, and finally the current home of the Moravian Historical Society and its museum. Based on Moravian Historical Society records; photo, map, 2 notes. C. A. Watson

3518. Yates, W. Ross. THE PERIOD OF QUESTIONING, BETHLEHEM, 1850-1876. *Tr. of the Moravian Hist. Soc. 1975 22(3): 193-212.* The Period of Questioning for the Moravian community in Bethlehem ensued for several decades following the ending of the lease system and the incorporation of the borough in 1844-45. The moral crisis within the community was reflected in the newly established weekly newspaper, *The Moravian*. The editorials challenged the materialistic nature of American society, insisted on the need for the United States to live as a Christian nation, and wrestled with the problem of slavery. By the aftermath of the Civil War the community had regained its inner stability. Documentation based largely on *The Moravian*. N. Lederer

Pentecostal Churches

3519. Campbell, Will D. COME. *Southern Voices 1974 1(1): 41-48.* Studies the use of serpents by one Appalachian revivalist folk religion as a method of conquering evil. S

3520. Gillespie, Paul and Head, Keith. GRANNY REED: A TESTIMONY. *Southern Exposure 1976 4(3): 33-37.* Interviews Granny Reed, a member of the Church of God in North Carolina, about practices such as faith healing and speaking in tongues, and about her own religious beliefs and interpretations of the Bible.

3521. Griffith, Ezra E. H.; English, Thelouizs; and Mayfield, Violet. POSSESSION, PRAYER, AND TESTIMONY: THERAPEUTIC ASPECTS OF THE WEDNESDAY NIGHT MEETING IN A BLACK CHURCH. *Psychiatry 1980 43(2): 120-128.* Using a black Pentecostal church in New Haven, Connecticut, as an example, discusses the Wednesday evening prayer meeting as "a therapeutic group experience which functions to help some black underprivileged people adapt to the stresses of urban living"; 1978.

3522. Kane, Steven M. HOLY GHOST PEOPLE: THE SNAKEHANDLERS OF SOUTHERN APPALACHIA. *Appalachian J. 1974 1(4): 255-262.* Discusses the Pentecostal Holiness Church and George Went Hensley, 1909-73. S

3523. Kane, Steven M. RITUAL POSSESSION IN A SOUTHERN APPALACHIAN RELIGIOUS SECT. *J. of Am. Folklore 1974 87(346): 293-302.* The possession trances of southern Appalachian serpent-handling sects are stylized, controlled, and conventional activities adopted by people well-adjusted to their Pentecostal religious environment. The "power" of these trances includes glossolalia, serpent and fire handling, strychnine drinking, miracle working, casting out devils, healing, prophecy, and discerning spirits. Based on fieldwork during 1972-74 and secondary sources; 9 notes. W. D. Piersen

3524. Raskoff, Roger W. RECENT LITERATURE ON THE PENTECOSTAL MOVEMENT. *Anglican Theological Rev. Supplementary Series 1973 (2): 113-118.*

3525. Simpson, George Eaton. BLACK PENTECOSTALISM IN THE UNITED STATES. *Phylon 1974 35(2): 203-211.* Reviews the Pentecostal movement in the United States. The Pentecostal group of churches originated in 1906 in the black community of the Los Angeles area. It has since spread across the nation and over much of the world. The many churches which comprise the movement are fundamentalist, emotional rather than intellectual, generally unworldly, and draw their membership from the lower classes. Recent events may be altering this image; other classes are entering the movement and social concerns are increasingly stressed. 43 notes. V. L. Human

Presbyterian Churches

3526. Baird, Anne. JAMES WOODS: A STOCKTON PIONEER. *Pacific Historian 1975 19(2): 103-113.* Recounts efforts of Rev. James Woods to establish the first Presbyterian Church in Stockton, California, in 1850. Primary sources; 3 photos, 35 notes. G. L. Olson

3527. Bozeman, Theodore Dwight. INDUCTIVE AND DEDUCTIVE POLITICS: SCIENCE AND SOCIETY IN ANTEBELLUM PRESBYTERIAN THOUGHT. *J. of Am. Hist. 1977 64(3): 704-722.* Shaken by the revolutions of 1789 and 1848, revivalism, and democratic politics, conservative Presbyterians in America sought justifications for tradition. Increasingly they relied on the doctrine of providential progress which assured that God had planted the solution of social problems into each creature. Conservative Calvinists turned to science and empirical observations to prove that "whatever is, is right." Even slavery would wither when blacks no longer needed the tutelage of white Christians. "Inductive and Deductive Politics," an article in the 1860 *Princeton Review,* was the culmination of these beliefs, a blast at social and scientific theories and a reaffirmation of providential progress and tradition. Primary and secondary sources; 49 notes. J. W. Leedom

3528. Brackenridge, R. Douglas and Garcia-Treto, Francisco O. PRESBYTERIANS AND MEXICAN AMERICANS: FROM PATERNALISM TO PARTNERSHIP. *J. of Presbyterian Hist. 1977 55(2): 160-178.* Traces Presbyterian efforts to minister to migrant and resident Mexicans in New Mexico, Arizona, California, Colorado, and Texas. Depicts the various efforts in areas of churches, evangelism, education and medical units. The basic weakness of the Presbyterians was their paternalistic approach, manifested in their refusal to relinquish ecclesiastical control over the ethnic churches which were established, or to accept or admit Mexican pastors as equals in their ecclesiastical judicatories. Only in recent years has the concept of partnership emerged, and provisions are being made for Mexican leadership to work with Spanish-speaking people. Covers 1830-1977. Based largely on primary sources and the authors' *Iglesia Presbyteriana: A History of Presbyterians and Mexican Americans in the Southwest* (1974); 46 notes.
H. M. Parker, Jr.

3529. Brass, Maynard F. GERMAN PRESBYTERIANS AND THE SYNOD OF THE WEST. *J. of Presbyterian Hist. 1978 56(3): 237-251.* The Synod of the West was a German-ethnic ecclesiastical judicatory of the Presbyterian Church whose three presbyteries and 50 congregations overlapped seven synods of the Church. Organized in 1912, it shaped three aspects of its constituents' church life: their German usage, emphasis on mission activity, and publication. While the Synod thrived in its 47-year existence, its ethnic presence ran counter to the policy of the denomination's social concerns which focused on racial and cultural minority groups, and insisted on integration. The characteristic activities which had formerly bound the people together were gradually lost after the dissolution of the Synod was accomplished in 1959. The identity of German Presbyterians eroded. Based on ecclesiastical resources in the Archives of the University of Dubuque, oral interviews and secondary sources; map, 46 notes. H. M. Parker, Jr.

3530. Butzin, Peter A. POLITICS, PRESBYTERIANS AND THE PAXTON RIOTS, 1763-64. *J. of Presbyterian Hist. 1973 51(1): 70-84.* The rioting which broke out in Paxton Township, Pennsylvania, 1763-64, though ostensibly the result of anti-Indian sentiment spawned by Pontiac's conspiracy, actually was closely connected with political and religious differences between Presbyterians and Quakers in the colony.

3531. Byars, Patti W. JONESBORO PRESBYTERIANS CELEBRATE CENTENNIAL. *Georgia Life 1979 6(2): 34-35.* The Presbyterian Church in Jonesboro, Georgia, was organized on 28 September 1879.

3532. Campbell, Bertha J. EARLY HISTORY OF PRESBYTERIANS OF SPRINGHILL, NOVA SCOTIA. *Nova Scotia Hist. Q. [Canada] 1977 7(1): 1-30.* Traces the history of the Presbyterian Church and its clergy in Springhill, Nova Scotia, from 1874, when the first elders were elected, until 1925, when the congregation joined the United Church of Canada. Primary sources; 48 notes. H. M. Evans

3533. Campbell, Douglas F. and Bouma, Gary D. SOCIAL CONFLICT AND THE PICTOU NOTABLES. *Ethnicity 1978 5(1): 76-88.* Pictou County's per capita representation in four editions of *Who's Who in Canada* and two editions of *Canadian Men and Women of the Times* during 1898-1966 is preeminent among Nova Scotia counties. Yet Pictou is not unique in size, educational facilities, economic development, ethnic composition, or in the dominant position of Scottish Presbyterians. Seeks the explanation for the county's dynamism in the almost equal distribution of local Presbyterians into Kirk and non-Kirk factions, in the resultant conflict, and in the fact that this conflict was almost entirely verbal, thus fostering the skills which make for notability. Secondary sources; 5 tables, 14 notes, 27 ref. L. W. Van Wyk

3534. Cashdollar, Charles D. THE PURSUIT OF PIETY: CHARLES HODGE'S DIARY, 1819-1820. *J. of Presbyterian Hist. 1977 55(3): 267-283.* At a time when Presbyterians, largely through the influence of Scottish realism which had been carried to America by John Witherspoon, placed the role of piety above the conversion experience in importance, a young recent graduate of Princeton Theological Seminary, Charles Hodge (1797-1878), maintained a diary while he was living in Philadelphia. The diary details his spiritual life and pastoral experiences over a seven-month period in 1819-20. This is the only diary he ever kept. It not only relates Philadelphia Presbyterianism of that day, but also touches on the social confines of the ministry, the limited liturgical consciousness within Presbyterianism, and the inner struggles which confronted the spiritually sensitive future theologian, who then returned to Princeton Seminary to begin his lengthy and productive tenure as one of America's great theologians of the 19th century. Based largely on secondary biographical data; illus., 38 notes. H. M. Parker, Jr.

3535. Crouch, Archie. RACIAL-ETHNIC MINISTRY POLICIES: AN HISTORICAL OVERVIEW. *J. of Presbyterian Hist. 1979 57(3): 272-312.* The history of the Presbyterian Church in America in the field of racial and ethnic policies shows a slow movement from a mission of evangelism and civilization to advocacy and finally to an integrated Church in an integrated society. During each stage of development there were prophetic individuals who committed themselves to a vision of a different future, as they lead the church forward. The record also indicates that the church as a whole never quite managed to manifest totally the policies adopted by its assemblies. A chronological presentation is given from the colonial to the present period. Covers 1562-1977. Based on official reports of the church's boards and minutes of the annual General Assemblies; illus., 109 notes. H. M. Parker, Jr.

3536. Dahl, Curtis. THE CLERGYMAN, THE HUSSY, AND OLD HICKORY: EZRA STILES ELY AND THE PEGGY EATON AFFAIR. *J. of Presbyterian Hist. 1974 52(2): 137-155.* The Peggy Eaton affair had considerable effect on the Democratic Party, the presidency of Andrew Jackson, and the ambitions of prominent politicians. Explains the role of the Presbyterian clergyman the Reverend Dr. Ezra Stiles Ely in the scandal. 64 notes. D. L. Smith

3537. Dosker, Nina Ellis. EDWIN M. ELLIS: MONTANA'S BICYCLING MINISTER. *Montana 1980 30(1): 42-51.* Edwin M. Ellis (1853-1940) was a Prebyterian minister and the Montana Superintendent of Sunday School Missions from 1884 until his retirement in 1927. As a minister, he served the Bitterroot Valley; his superintendent duties covered all Montana from his Helena headquarters. To facilitate his travel throughout rural Montana, Ellis used a Columbia Chainless Bicycle during 1892-1913. He became known as Montana's bicycling minister, and many of the churches and sunday schools he founded are still active today. Based on author's reminiscences; 13 illus, note.
R. C. Myers

3538. Evans, E. Raymond. NOTABLE PERSONS IN CHEROKEE HISTORY: STEPHEN FOREMAN. *J. of Cherokee Studies 1977 2(2): 230-239.* Stephen Foreman was born on 22 October 1807 in north Georgia, the son of Anthony Foreman, a Scottish soldier, and Elizabeth Foreman. He was educated for the ministry at Candy's Creek and New Echota, Georgia, and at Union and Princeton Theological Seminaries. In 1833 he was licensed to preach by the Presbyterian Church. He led one group of Cherokee Indians west during the removal of the 1830's. After settling in Park Hill, Oklahoma, he was active in Cherokee government and established a school system. During this time he also translated parts of the Bible from Greek to Cherokee. He died in Oklahoma on 8 December 1881. Illus., 39 notes. J. M. Lee

3539. Farley, Benjamin W. GEORGE W. CABLE: PRESBYTERIAN ROMANCER, REFORMER, BIBLE TEACHER. *J. of Presbyterian Hist. 1980 58(2): 166-181.* In the last 25 years there have been three biographies of George Washington Cable (1844-1925), Southern Presbyterian, ex-Confederate soldier, and author of Creole stories. All three acknowledge his Presbyterian roots, and examine the influence of his church and home on his life and work. Concentrates attention on Cable as a Presbyterian, and explores his life, stories, and reforming activities in light of his Calvinistic heritage. Emphasizes the influence of his early home and training on his work and habits, the role of New Orleans Presbyterianism in his development, and, as his career advanced and his vision matured, how he drew upon and reacted against his Presbyterian heritage. Based on Cable's writings and studies about him, particularly the biography by Lucy Leffingwell Cable Biklè, *George W. Cable, His Life and Letters* (1928); illus., 65 notes.
H. M. Parker, Jr.

3540. Forbes, Bruce David. PRESBYTERIAN BEGINNINGS IN SOUTH DAKOTA: 1840-1900. *South Dakota Hist. 1977 7(2): 115-153.* Chronicles the founding of the Presbyterian Church in South Dakota. Synods in neighboring Minnesota and Iowa influenced and later wrangled to gain Dakota jurisdiction. While national church policies were followed in large part, conditions on the frontier necessitated adjustments. Early mission work among the Indians was successful despite a split in the order. National financial support generally was needed, and the solvency of individual churches followed fluctuations in economic conditions. Presbyterians ranked fifth among South Dakota denominations in the number of adherents. Because of the sparse frontier population, Presbyterians sometimes joined others, usually Congregationalists, to provide settlers with one strong church. Prominent roles were given to women and higher education. Secondary sources; 5 photos, 88 notes.
A. J. Larson

3541. Forbes, Bruce David. WILLIAM HENRY ROBERTS: RESISTANCE TO CHANGE AND BUREAUCRATIC ADAPTATION. *J. of Presbyterian Hist. 1976 54(4): 405-421.* William Henry Roberts (1844-1920) served as Stated Clerk of the General Assembly of the Presbyterian Church in the United States during 1884-1920. On the one hand he represented conservative resistance to change as he sought to preserve Protestant hegemony and resist theological accommodation with a changing intellectual world. But he also represented adaptation as he shared in the bureaucratic organization of his office and the values that were transforming the nation during his lengthy administration. Bureaucratization left its influence in regularized, consolidated ecclesiastical structures and in quantified values. Roberts's activity as an administrative churchman contributed to the process. Presents the evolution of the office of the Stated Clerk under Roberts. Based largely on the Minutes of the Presbyterian General Assembly and secondary sources; illus., 56 notes.
H. M. Parker, Jr.

3542. Geissler, Suzanne B. AARON BURR, JR.: DARLING OF THE PRESBYTERIANS. *J. of Presbyterian Hist. 1978 56(2): 134-147.* Although both his maternal grandfather (Jonathan Edwards) and his father (Aaron Burr, Sr.) had been presidents of the College of New Jersey (Princeton), and thus much was anticipated and expected of him, Aaron Burr, Jr. (1756-1836) never lived up to the hopes which his family and friends held out for him. His prestigious background made him "that darling of the Presbyterians." He was never able to be himself. His ancestry provided him with fame, connections, and a good many votes in the political arena and he ran for President in 1800; however it also provided him with a reputation impossible to live up to, dooming him to a lifetime of comparisons to his illustrious forebears. Secondary sources; illus., 64 notes. H. M. Parker, Jr.

3543. Gillette, Gerald W. JOHN A MACKAY: INFLUENCES ON MY LIFE *J. of Presbyterian Hist. 1978 56(1): 20-34.* Interviews John A. Mackay (b. 1889), former President of Princeton Theological Seminary, former Moderator of the General Assembly of the Presbyterian Church, U.S.A., former missionary to Latin America, and leading Presbyterian statesman and ecumenist. Born in Scotland, he was educated at Princeton and did graduate work in Spain. In addition to the writings of Jonathan Edwards, which he read while still in Scotland, he was greatly influenced by Robert E. Speer (foreign missions) and Benjamin B. Warfield (theology) while at Princeton. Covers 1910-75. Illus., 12 notes.
H. M. Parker, Jr.

3544. Gilliam, Will D., Jr. ROBERT JEFFERSON BRECKENRIDGE, 1800-1871. PART I. *Register of the Kentucky Hist. Soc. 1974 72(3): 207-223.* Breckenridge's public career as a lawyer, legislator, Presbyterian minister, editor, educator, and college president extended from the 1820's to his resignation as head of the Danville Theological Seminary in 1869. Breckenridge favored gradual emancipation and African colonization of freed slaves, and detested abolitionists. He believed in predestination and the authority of the Bible. He was influential in the establishment of Kentucky's public school system. Based on primary and secondary sources; illus., 27 notes. To be continued. J. F. Paul

3545. Gilliam, Will D., Jr. ROBERT JEFFERSON BRECKINRIDGE, 1800-1871. *Register of the Kentucky Hist. Soc. 1974 72(4): 319-336.* Part II. Continued from a previous article. Covers the period from 1832 and emphasizes Presbyterian Breckinridge's importance to his denomination. His views owed much to the writings of Samuel Miller, second professor elected to Princeton Theological Seminary. He endorsed a supernatural Christianity, and the infallibility of the Scriptures. The writings of his grandson, Benjamin Breckinridge Warfield, who was on the Princeton faculty 1887-1921, continued many of Breckinridge's arguments. Breckinridge had accepted his views on faith, but Warfield had a scholarly basis for his understanding. Includes an account of Breckinridge's debate on slavery with George Thompson in Glasgow in 1836. Primary and secondary sources; 17 notes. J. F. Paul

3546. Goin, Mary Elisabeth. CATHERINE MARSHALL: THREE DECADES OF POPULAR RELIGION. *J. of Presbyterian Hist. 1978 56(3): 219-235.* Catherine Marshall is the widow of the popular Reverand Peter Marshall (1902-49), Presbyterian cleric and chaplain of the US Senate. Her books have sold more than 16 million copies, making them a valuable source of information on the popular religion of America in the last three decades. Catherine Marshall places the Christian challenge in terms of an individual response to Jesus rather than in terms of social action—a position that has emerged from her own spiritual crises. Her success as a writer stems from her ability to offer the popular salvation which Americans need at the moment. Based largely on Marshall's books and secondary sources; photo, 55 notes. H. M. Parker, Jr.

3547. Goodloe, James C., IV. KENNETH J. FOREMAN, SR.: A CANDLE ON THE GLACIER. *J. of Presbyterian Hist. 1979 57(4): 467-484.* Kenneth J. Foreman, Sr. (1891-1967), southern Presbyterian theologian and popular writer and speaker, strongly advocated three particular changes in the theology and life of his church—acceptance of critical and historical methods of biblical study, fresh confessions of faith, and involvement of the church in social action. His influence across the church was considerable—having taught religion at Davidson College for 25 years and then theology at Louisville Presbyterian Theological Seminary 13 years. But his greatest influence came from his weekly column in the *Presbyterian Outlook,* which he wrote for 20 years. Based on Foreman's writings; photo, 75 notes. H. M. Parker, Jr.

3548. Gordon, J. King. THE WORLD OF HELEN GORDON. *Manitoba Pageant [Canada] 1978 24(1): 1-14.* The author reminisces about his mother, Helen Skinner Gordon (1876-1961) of Winnipeg, Manitoba, who was a member of the Presbyterial, the Conference Branch, and the Dominion Board of the Woman's Missionary Society of the Presbyterian and United Churches, and whose home is now the clubhouse for the University Women's Club.

3549. Hinckley, Ted C. A VICTORIAN FAMILY IN ALASKA. *Am. West 1979 16(1): 32-37, 60-63.* The Reverend John Green Brady went to Alaska in 1878 as a Presbyterian missionary. Business and politics beckoned. He established the forerunner of Sheldon Jackson College, became a successful lumberman, was appointed judge, and served the territory for three terms as its fifth governor. John and Elizabeth and their five children were models of "Christian upbringing," plain living, and "high thinking." The Brady family was firmly committed to the "Victorian virtues of perspiration, proficiency, and piety," despite the attractions and temptations of frontier Sitka. Includes information through 1906. 7 illus, biblio, note. D. L. Smith

3550. Hoge, Dean R. and Faue, Jeffrey L. SOURCES OF CONFLICT OVER PRIORITIES OF THE PROTESTANT CHURCH. *Social Forces 1973 52(2): 178-194.* Theoretical approaches to internal conflict over priorities in the Presbyterian church are tested using surveys of laymen, ministers, and seminary seniors. Conflicts are greatest over the type and importance of church mission and outreach; there is little conflict over congregational life, religious education, or spiritual nurture. Path analysis shows that theological factors are intervening variables between all background variables and attitudes about church priorities. Orthodoxy and ethicalism act independently and in opposite directions. It is concluded that the conflict is largely theological, explained partly in terms of church-sect tension and partly by conflicting theological orientations in the denomination. Covers the 1960's and 70's. J

3551. Holifield, E. Brooks. MERCERSBURG, PRINCETON, AND THE SOUTH: THE SACRAMENTAL CONTROVERSY IN THE NINETEENTH CENTURY. *J. of Presbyterian Hist. 1976 54(2): 238-257.* Delineates connections between Presbyterian John W. Nevin's Mercersburg mystical presence position on the Lord's Supper and its reception by John B. Adger of Columbia Seminary in South Carolina, and the reaction of Princeton's scion Charles Hodge and connections to Union Seminary in Richmond, Virginia, as represented by Robert L. Dabney. Based almost wholly on the writings of these four men, plus dissertations on Nevin and Hodge; 2 illus., 54 notes. H. M. Parker, Jr.

3552. Holifield, E. Brooks. THOMAS SMYTH: THE SOCIAL IDEAS OF A SOUTHERN EVANGELIST. *J. of Presbyterian Hist. 1973 51(1): 24-40.* Thomas Smyth, a South Carolina pastor in the Presbyterian Church, 1831-70, was concerned with theological ideologies of social order and developed a theological rationale for social conservatism without entirely abandoning Lockean tradition.

3553. Hoobler, James A. KARNAK ON THE CUMBERLAND. *Tennessee Hist. Q. 1976 35(3): 251-262.* Provides a narrative history of the First Presbyterian Church in Nashville, Tennessee, from its organization in 1814 to 1976. Mentions the church's ministers, architectural history, and more important worshippers; and discusses use of the church as a conference and community center. During the Civil War it was an Army hospital, and in 1907 it was the site of the national meeting of the Women's Christian Temperance Union. Based on primary and secondary sources; 2 illus., 20 notes. A. E. Wiederrecht

3554. Hovet, Theodore R. THE CHURCH DISEASED: HARRIET BEECHER STOWE'S ATTACK ON THE PRESBYTERIAN CHURCH. *J. of Presbyterian Hist. 1974 52(2): 167-187.* Harriet Beecher Stowe conducted a prolonged debate with American churches, particularly with the Presbyterian Church. Her concern was that impersonal, intellectual, and institutional emphases were replacing personal, emotional, and individual ones. This was particularly manifest in the church response to slavery. Covers the 1830's-70's. 47 notes. D. L. Smith

3555. Humphrey, Edna H. HUSBAND TO HARRIET. *New-England Galaxy 1976 17(4): 9-14.* Describes the role of Calvin Ellis Stowe in the career of his wife, Harriet Beecher Stowe. Discusses his early life, his thirst for knowledge, and his teaching careers at Dartmouth and Lane Theological Seminary. Calvin depended on Harriet to handle practical matters, and Harriet depended upon Calvin for needed information for her book. 3 illus. P. C. Marshall

3556. Jackson, Gordon E. ARCHIBALD ALEXANDER'S *THOUGHTS ON RELIGIOUS EXPERIENCE,* A CRITICAL REVISITING. *J. of Presbyterian Hist. 1973 51(2): 141-154.* Reviews Alexander's (1772-1851) 1841 book. S

3557. Kerr, Hugh T. THE 1906 BOOK OF COMMON WORSHIP: AN AMUSING FOOTNOTE. *J. of Presbyterian Hist. 1980 58(2): 182-184.* In 1903, the General Assembly of the Presbyterian Church in the United States, feeling the need for a book of simple forms and services to guide the clergy, appointed a committee, headed by Henry Van Dyke. In 1906 the *Book of Common Worship* appeared "for voluntary use." Reaction was swift. Reprints a humorous poem by a Presbyterian layman, William J. Lampton, a journalist for the Louisville *Courier-Journal,* criticizing "canned prayers," and the equally humorous poetic reply by Van Dyke, both written in 1906. H. M. Parker, Jr.

3558. Klein, Maury. [THE SCOTCH IRISH]. *Am. Hist. Illus. 1979 13(9): 30-38, (10): 32-39; 14(1): 8-12, 15-17.* Part I. A RACE IN UPHEAVAL. Discusses social, religious, and political conditions in Ulster during the 17th century and the economic sanctions which caused a great number of Scotch Irish to come to the United States. Parts II and III. THE NATION-BUILDERS. The Scotch Irish settled in Pennsylvania, New York, and Virginia's Shenandoah Valley, establishing agricultural settlements and proving a grim and resolute match for Indians on the western frontier, 1717-76. A general overview of daily life on the frontier focuses on education, religion, social organization, the duties of women, and leisure activities, 1770-76.

3559. Lane, Belden C. PRESBYTERIAN REPUBLICANISM: MILLER AND THE ELDERSHIP AS AN ANSWER TO LAY-CLERICAL TENSIONS. *J. of Presbyterian Hist. 1978 56(4): 311-324.* Samuel Miller (1769-1850) was the first professor of ecclesiastical government in Princeton Theological Seminary, appointed in 1813. Opposed to the democracy of Congregationalism on the one hand, and the clerical privilege of Episcopalianism on the other, Miller raised the office of ruling elder in Presbyterianism on the basis of representative church government. In 1831 he authored a book on the office of the Ruling Elder, the first such in-depth study ever undertaken in Presbyterian-Reformed circles. Examines the social context of lay-clerical tensions whence Miller's work on the eldership developed. His work was a creative attempt to relate the historical distinctiveness of Reformed church polity, with its republican emphasis, to the peculiarities of the American experience. The ruling elder emerged as the best possible way for granting a measure of authority to the laity without opening the church to mob rule. Based on Miller's writings; illus., 29 notes. H. M. Parker, Jr.

3560. LeBeau, Bryan F. THE SUBSCRIPTION CONTROVERSY AND JONATHAN DICKINSON. *J. of Presbyterian Hist. 1976 54(3): 317-335.* The subscription controversy in the colonial American Presbyterian Church developed as both a reflection of Old World English and Scottish divisions and as the basis for one of the most serious ecclesiastical schisms to occur among New World Presbyterians. The controversy developed over the suggestion of requiring ministers to subscribe to the Westminster Standards as prerequisite to ministerial ordination. This study treats the position and role of the Philadelphia pastor and leader Jonathan Dickinson (1688-1747) in the controversy, giving insights into his motives as well as his actions. Covers 1700-75. Based on the writings of Dickinson, records of the Presbyterian Church, and other primary and secondary sources; illus., 101 notes. H. M. Parker, Jr.

3561. Lee, Elizabeth and Abbott, Kenneth A. CHINESE PILGRIMS AND PRESBYTERIANS IN THE UNITED STATES, 1851-1977. *J. of Presbyterian Hist. 1977 55(2): 125-144.* Details the cultural conflict, change, and adjustment between migrant Chinese and settled Americans. Outlines the effects of imperialism and the use of power in the everyday world. Documents the force and pervasiveness of the Holy Spirit to triumph over cultural misunderstanding and oppression and to shine through the goodness and love of true believers of both races. Dispels the myths that the Chinese came over only as sojourners, that the early immigrants were mostly coolies, that there were hardly any families until the 1930's, and that the Chinese were passive and dependent. Chronicles the Presbyterian Church's hesitant acceptance of the Chinese as equals as well as the perennial concerns of Oriental Americans and their ties with those in Asia. Based on the annual reports of Presbyterian agencies and interviews with Chinese pastors and leaders; 4 photos, 73 notes. H. M. Parker, Jr.

3562. Lynd, Staughton. ROBERT S. LYND: THE ELK BASIN EXPERIENCE. *J. of the Hist. of Sociol. 1979-80 2(1): 14-22.* The author describes his father's experiences as a visiting Presbyterian preacher to the Rockefeller oil town of Elk Basin, Wyoming, in 1921.

3563. Maclear, J. F. LYMAN BEECHER IN BRITAIN. *Ohio Hist. 1976 85(4): 293-305.* Discusses Lyman Beecher's (1775-1863) trip to Great Britain in 1846 as a delegate to the World Temperance Convention and the Evangelical Alliance. Based on manuscript sources and contemporary comments; 2 illus., 22 notes. N. Summers

3564. Macnab, John B. BETHLEHEM CHAPEL: PRESBYTERIANS AND ITALIAN AMERICANS IN NEW YORK CITY. *J. of Presbyterian Hist. 1977 55(2): 145-160.* Presents the attempts of New York City Presbyterians, particularly the University Place Church, to minister to the needs of the mass numbers of Italian immigrants who moved into the Greenwich Village area at the turn of the century. The denomination as a whole was quite tardy in responding to the challenge which immigrants presented. Various kinds of programs, both religiously and secularly oriented, were undertaken to assist in Protestantizing and Americanizing the new immigrant. Though a couple of congregations were organized for the Italians, the formal ecclesiastical control remained in the hands of Anglo officials, in spite of a prediction that a strong ethnic church could result only if the people felt they were masters of their work. The hesitancy to turn complete control over to the Italians, coupled with the "caretaker paternalism" whereby the churches were supported by the Anglos, worked to hinder much Presbyterian growth among the Italians. Covers 1900-30. Based on primary sources, including the archives of the First Presbyterian Church in the City of New York; illus., 47 notes. H. M. Parker, Jr.

3565. Martin, Roger A. JOHN J. ZUBLY COMES TO AMERICA. *Georgia Hist. Q. 1977 61(2): 125-139.* Describes the early career of John Joachim Zubly, a Swiss immigrant who became an influential Presbyterian minister in the Savannah area during the colonial period. Primary and secondary sources; 62 notes. G. R. Schroeder

3566. McKim, Donald K. ARCHIBALD ALEXANDER AND THE DOCTRINE OF SCRIPTURE. *J. of Presbyterian Hist. 1976 54(3): 355-375.* Sets forth the doctrine of Scripture as propounded in the published writings of Presbyterian Archibald Alexander (1772-1851), first professor at Princeton Theological Seminary. The influences and experiences which helped mold his thoughts are examined as well as the philosophical background in which his thought was cast. Traces the influence on later Princeton generations down to the reorganization of the seminary in 1929. Based on Alexander's writings; 112 notes. H. M. Parker, Jr.

3567. McLeod, Finlay J. C. RECOLLECTIONS OF VIRDEN 1882. *Manitoba Pageant [Canada] 1976 22(1): 6-10.* Presbyterian Finlay J. C. McLeod was minister for the construction crews of the Canadian Pacific Railway during the winter of 1881-82 when they were passing through the Virden area. His recollections include mention of the earliest settlers and the religious life in the area. B. J. Lo Bue

3568. McLoughlin, William G. INDIAN SLAVEHOLDERS AND PRESBYTERIAN MISSIONARIES, 1837-1861. *Church Hist. 1973 42(4): 535-551.* Indians were not regarded as US citizens but the antebellum caste system allowed them to own black slaves. Missionaries to southern Indian tribes frequently found that their success hinged on their slavery position. The Presbyterian Board of Foreign Missions (PBFM) warned its missionaries not to display abolitionist tendencies. Many incidents involving missionaries and Indian slaves are recorded in the PBFM archives. Based on PBFM archives; 39 notes. M. D. Dibert

3569. Miller, Glenn T. "FASHIONABLE TO PROPHESY": PRESBYTERIANS, THE MILLENNIUM AND THE REVOLUTION. *Amerikastudien/Am. Studies [West Germany] 1976 21(2): 239-260.* After the Revolution, Presbyterians became interested in the issue of millennialism, particularly as the millennial predictions related to the new nation. The paper seeks to document this interest in the doctrine by examining sermons by Presbyterian clergymen and, in particular, examining the reception of Thomas Newton's *Dissertation on the Prophecies in Two Volumes,* which was published in an American edition in 1787. The subscription list of this basic work on the theology of prophecy shows that there was a broad interest in millennial questions in the area where Presbyterians were most numerous and that this interest was to be found among all classes of men. Attention is also paid to Elias Boudinot, the President of the Continental Congress when independence was attained and a very prominent Presbyterian layman. Boudinot's interest in the millennium was almost unbounded, and he spent much of his long retirement searching for answers to the questions posed by the discussion. Unlike many millennialists in the 18th century, Boudinot was determinedly premillennialist in his theology. The paper then goes on to examine the issue of why Presbyterians became interested in the doctrine. There appear to have been two reasons: 1. the doctrine provided a rational framework for belief in the God of history and 2. it provided a hermeneutics of history that could be applied to the situation of a new nation. It is to be remembered that this millennialism was only preparatory for the great outbreak of millenial and millenarian thought in the 19th century which set many American Christians on a quest for the Kingdom of God on earth. J

3570. Miller, Glenn T. GOD'S LIGHT AND MAN'S ENLIGHTENMENT: EVANGELICAL THEOLOGY OF COLONIAL PRESBYTERIANISM. *J. of Presbyterian Hist. 1973 51(2): 97-115.* Discusses the relationship of the theology of Presbyterian Evangelical Calvinists to the Enlightenment. S

3571. Mills, Thora McIlroy. THE CONTRIBUTION OF THE PRESBYTERIAN CHURCH TO THE YUKON DURING THE GOLD RUSH, 1897-1910. *Bull. of the United Church of Can. [Canada] 1976 (25): 5-94.*

3572. Mulder, John M. JOSEPH RUGGLES WILSON: SOUTHERN PRESBYTERIAN PATRIARCH. *J. of Presbyterian Hist. 1974 52(3): 245-271.* Joseph Ruggles Wilson (1822-1903) was one of the founders of the Southern Presbyterian Church and a powerful church official, preacher, and professor. S

3573. Olbricht, Thomas H. CHARLES HODGE AS AN AMERICAN NEW TESTAMENT INTERPRETER. *J. of Presbyterian Hist. 1979 57(2): 117-133.* Although better known as American Presbyterianism's most influential theologian, Charles Hodge (1797-1878) was the first New Testament exegete at Princeton Theological Seminary, and along with Moses Stuart of Andover Seminary, was the first American to publish New Testament commentaries of significance. In doing his studies in Germany, he selected Halle over Göttingen because the former paid more attention to Biblical literature. His works combat the liberalism (Unitarianism) that embraced so much of German thought in America in his day; at the same time he came out quite in accord with the Confessional standards of his own Presbyterian Church. Discusses Hodge's various interpretative principles. Based largely on Hodge's works; 68 notes. H. M. Parker, Jr.

3574. Parker, Harold M. THE NEW SCHOOL SYNOD OF KENTUCKY. *Filson Club Hist. Q. 1976 50(2): 52-89.* Details the division within the Presbyterian Church in Kentucky during 1837-58. Despite the claims of the author, the New School Synod was not a significant institution although it did produce several outstanding clergymen including Archer C. Dickerson, Joseph C. Stiles, and Thomas Cleland. The conflict was generated by ecclesiastical questions rather than doctrinal differences, and, as a result, the New School group rejoined the parent body in 1858. Documentation comes from contemporary tracts, newspapers, and histories; 121 notes. G. B. McKinney

3575. Perry, Everett L. and Perry, Margaret T. NEW CHURCH DEVELOPMENT POLICIES: AN HISTORICAL OVERVIEW. *J. of Presbyterian Hist. 1979 57(3): 229-271.* The establishment of new churches has always been an important work in the growth of American Presbyterian Churches. The history of new church development policy of the United Presbyterian Church in the United States clearly reflects the struggle to maintain the corporate nature of the Church while at the same time recognizing the idea that the local church is a part of the larger church. A chronological approach to the major developments in church erection action and policy is presented for 1640-1978, divided into two major parts: before 1890 and afterwards. Concludes with the development of policies in recent years. Internally documented; illus.
H. M. Parker, Jr.

3576. Pope, Earl A. ALBERT BARNES, *THE WAY OF SALVATION,* AND THEOLOGICAL CONTROVERSY. *J. of Presbyterian Hist. 1979 57(1): 20-34.* In 1829 the Reverend Albert Barnes, pastor of the First Presbyterian Church, Morristown, New Jersey, preached a controversial sermon, *The Way of Salvation.* It ultimately led to his famous heresy trial before the 1836 General Assembly, in which he was vindicated. But the Assembly divided the next year, and Barnes's party was exscinded from the Church. Barnes's sermon was not a major cause in the schism which developed; rather he simply reiterated what had long been affirmed in New England Calvinistic theology in three areas: imputation of sin, the vicarious nature of the atonement, and man's ability to will his salvation. His theological stance was much more in line with Samuel Hopkins than with that of Nathaniel Taylor. Even the Princeton theologians did not fault him; but it was the ultraconservatives, led by Ashbel Green and William Engles, who opposed Barnes, making his trial necessary, and leading ultimately to the division of the Church. Based on Barnes's writings and contemporary religious paper and journal accounts; illus., 48 notes. H. M. Parker, Jr.

3577. Quirk, Charles E. ORIGINS OF THE AUBURN AFFIRMATION. *J. of Presbyterian Hist. 1975 53(2): 120-142.* Chronicles the antecedents of the Auburn Affirmation, a document which circulated early in 1924 and intensified the serious strife existing in the Presbyterian Church USA. The Auburn Affirmation focused crucial constitutional and theological questions for the church. Based largely on religious and secular newspaper and periodical reports and articles of the period; 79 notes.
H. M. Parker, Jr.

3578. Ramsey, David A. and Koedel, R. Craig. THE COMMUNION SEASON—AN 18TH CENTURY MODEL. *J. of Presbyterian Hist. 1976 54(2): 203-216.* Details an 18th-century Presbyterian three- or four-day communion service based on the practice of the Church of Scotland as observed by the Presbyterian Church of Boothbay, Maine.
H. M. Parker, Jr.

3579. Russell, C. Allyn. CLARENCE E. MACARTNEY: FUNDAMENTALIST PRINCE OF THE PULPIT. *J. of Presbyterian Hist. 1974 52(1): 33-58.* Preacher Clarence E. Macartney was an eloquent spokesperson for fundamentalism and orthodoxy in the Presbyterian Church, as well as a symbol of power, 1901-53.

3580. Russell, C. Allyn. J. GRESHAM MACHEN, SCHOLARLY FUNDAMENTALIST. *J. of Presbyterian Hist. 1973 51(1): 41-69.* Focuses on J. Gresham Machen's rabid, albeit scholarly, Fundamentalism, his life as a representation of Southern mores, and his importance as a critic of liberalism within the Presbyterian Church, 1920's-35.

3581. Shriver, George H. PASSAGES IN FRIENDSHIP: JOHN W. NEVIN AND CHARLES HODGE. *J. of Presbyterian Hist. 1980 58(2): 116-122.* A passage is a crisis. A crisis arose in 1872 in the life of John W. Nevin of Mercersburg theology fame as the result of an unfavorable remark by the Princeton theologian and his friend, Charles Hodge. In Volume II of his *Systematic Theology,* Hodge claimed that Nevin was abundant in asserting the simple humanity of Jesus Christ, with the innuendo that he denied Christ's divinity. This was most upsetting to Nevin, who wrote his former mentor a letter, taking exception to what Hodge had written. Reprints the letter of 24 February 1872 to Hodge. 2 illus., 8 notes. H. M. Parker, Jr.

3582. Smylie, James H. NOTABLE PRESBYTERIAN WOMEN. *J. of Presbyterian Hist. 1974 52(2): 99-121.* Biographic sketches of 25 prominent black and white Presbyterian women from Jane Aitken (1764-1832), a Bible printer and bookbinder, to Lois Harkrider Stair (b. 1923), the first woman moderator of the general assembly of the Presbyterian Church. They include a mother and wives of presidents, missionaries, educators, journalists, philanthropists, authors, businesswomen, humanitarian reformers, social workers, and an industrialist. 9 illus., 6 notes.
D. L. Smith

3583. Smylie, James H. "OF SECRET AND FAMILY WORSHIP": HISTORICAL MEDITATIONS. *J. of Presbyterian Hist. 1980 58(2): 95-115.* In 1788, Presbyterians adopted the *Directory of Worship*; it was used until the 1960's. The last chapter of the *Directory* declares that it is the "indispensable duty of each person, alone, in secret, and of every family, by itself, in private, to pray to and worship God." Considers three crises as they are related to the directions given by the *Directory* to Presbyterians: the crisis of the Sabbath and the secularization of time and space, the crisis of the family and the professionalization of religious services, and the crisis of faith and the trivialization of life. Traces these crises historically into the contemporary scene.
H. M. Parker, Jr.

3584. Stevenson, E. M. THE WITNESS. *Nova Scotia Hist. Q. [Canada] 1980 10(1): 41-57.* The weekly newspaper *The Presbyterian Witness and Evangelical Advocate* appeared in Halifax on the first Saturday of January 1848. Under the editorship of James Barnes the *Witness* won support from the Presbyterian community, and continued under the editorship of Robert Murray from 1855 until his death in 1910. Under Mr. Murray, the paper included a new section and a religious department which spoke out against infidelity, drunkenness, popery, and Sabbath desecration and entered into political, social, and religious controversies. 3 notes. H. M. Evans

3585. Stokes, Durward T. THOMAS REESE IN SOUTH CAROLINA. *South Carolina Hist. Mag. 1973 74(3): 151-163.* Thomas Reese (1742-96) was a Presbyterian minister who also devoted his energies to education, writing, and medicine. His ministry, from ordination in 1773, was spent in South Carolina, except for exile during the American Revolution. He was regarded as the outstanding 18th-century Presbyterian minister in South Carolina. 54 notes. D. L. Smith

3586. Stone, William J., Jr. TEXAS' FIRST CHURCH NEWSPAPER: THE TEXAS PRESBYTERIAN, 1846-1865. *Texana 1973 12(3): 239-247.* In 1846 at Victoria, A. J. McGown began publishing the *Texas Presbyterian*. McGown, an ordained Cumberland Presbyterian Church minister, had his problems from the outset. Problems during the 10 years of publication included poor financing, few subscribers, poor mail service, no adequate place to print the paper (he moved from Victoria to Houston and then to Huntsville and threatened other moves), and few qualified correspondents. He ceased publication in 1856 and returned to an active preaching ministry. Primary and secondary sources; 18 notes.
B. D. Ledbetter

3587. Stubbs, Charles H. LITTLE BRITAIN PRESBYTERIAN CHURCH. *J. of the Lancaster County Hist. Soc. 1978 82(3): 165-168.* Discusses the Little Britain Presbyterian Church in Lancaster County, Pennsylvania, ca. 1740-1860.

3588. Teaford, Jon C. TOWARD A CHRISTIAN NATION: RELIGION, LAW AND JUSTICE STRONG. *J. of Presbyterian Hist. 1976 54(4): 422-437.* William Strong (1808-95) was an Associate Justice of the US Supreme Court from 1870 until his resignation in 1880. A prosperous entrepreneur and expert in business law, he was also a Presbyterian Elder and loyal layman in a country which was beginning to deviate from traditional Christian values and the Christian way of life. He was a member of the National Reform Association which in 1864 unsuccessfully proposed an amendment to the preamble of the US Constitution

which would give formal recognition to God and Jesus Christ so that there would be no doubt that the US was a Christian nation ruled by a Christian government. His efforts to promote personal piety in the midst of great social change characterized his own zeal for the moral and spiritual welfare of his country. At the same time he was woefully aware of the shortcomings of the Christian cause in the US in failing to provide religious and social provisions for the masses. He served on the boards of numerous interdenominational agencies in addition to his Presbyterian responsibilities. Based largely on Strong's writings; illus., 40 notes.
H. M. Parker, Jr.

3589. Thompson, Ernest T. BLACK PRESBYTERIANS: EDUCATION AND EVANGELISM AFTER THE CIVIL WAR. *J. of Presbyterian Hist. 1973 51(2): 174-198.* Presbyterians' evangelization and Christian education of their former slaves after the Civil War. S

3590. Troop, Hiram G. THE 250TH ANNIVERSARY OF THE MIDDLE OCTORARA UNITED PRESBYTERIAN CHURCH. *J. of the Lancaster County Hist. Soc. 1977 81(2): 87-91.* Provides a short synopsis of events (1727-1977) in the United Presbyterian Church in Middle Octorara, Pennsylvania.

3591. Weale, David. THE TIME IS COME! MILLENARIANISM IN COLONIAL PRINCE EDWARD ISLAND. *Acadiensis: J. of the Hist. of the Atlantic Region [Canada] 1977 7(1): 35-48.* Hardships led many early 19th-century settlers in Prince Edward Island to despair of their future. Many turned to the millenarian preaching of the Reverend Donald McDonald for consolation. McDonald experienced a conversion in 1828, and led a revival in 1829. At his death in 1867 he had about 5,000 followers, most of them immigrants from the Highlands of Scotland. Millenarianism may have restored their sense of a meaningful future and provided them with an identity. McDonald was affiliated with the Presbyterians, but he remained independent from them. 46 notes.
D. F. Chard

3592. Weeks, Louis. TERAH TEMPLIN: KENTUCKY'S FIRST PRESBYTERIAN PREACHER. *Filson Club Hist. Q. 1979 53(1): 45-60.* Terah Templin was the first Presbyterian minister in Kentucky in 1780. To 1818 he helped organize many congregations, the Transylvania Presbytery, and the Synod of Kentucky. Based on published church minutes; 53 notes. G. B. McKinney

3593. Wilson, Frank T., ed. LIVING WITNESSES: BLACK PRESBYTERIANS IN MINISTRY. III. *J. of Presbyterian Hist. 1977 55(2): 180-238.* A collection of 15 vignettes of contemporary black ministers and prominent laypeople in the United Presbyterian Church in the United States. Clergy, educators, missionaries, and social activists are portrayed in brief essays. 15 photos. H. M. Parker, Jr.

3594. Wilson, Frank T. LIVING WITNESSES: BLACK PRESBYTERIANS IN MINISTRY. II. *J. of Presbyterian Hist. 1975 53(3): 187-222.* Continued from a previous article. Portrays 11 black ministers of the Presbyterian Church, tracing each individual's work in ecclesiastical, civic and service organizations. Covers 1885-1975. 11 photos.
H. M. Parker, Jr.

3595. Wilson, Frank T. LIVING WITNESSES: BLACK PRESBYTERIANS IN MINISTRY. *J. of Presbyterian Hist. 1973 51(4): 347-391.* Prominent black ministers in the United Presbyterian Church. Covers 1855-1973. S

3596. —. PRESBYTERIANS AND THE AMERICAN REVOLUTION: A DOCUMENTARY ACCOUNT. *J. of Presbyterian Hist. 1974 52(4): 303-488.* Reprints documents by Presbyterians on the American Revolution and the national character, 1729-87.

Puritans

3597. Ahluwalia, Harsharan Singh. SALVATION NEW ENGLAND STYLE: A STUDY OF COVENANT THEOLOGY IN MICHAEL WIGGLESWORTH'S *THE DAY OF DOOM*. *Indian J. of Am. Studies [India] 1974 4(1/2): 1-12.* Michael Wigglesworth's poem *Day of Doom* (1662) embodies the official Puritan covenant theology of early New England. Covenant theology was midway between antinomianism (belief that God's grace alone suffices to be saved), and arminianism (belief that free will is the key to salvation). Wigglesworth brilliantly argues for both predestination and the need for human exertion in the salvation process. 14 notes. L. Eid

3598. Archer, John. PURITAN TOWN PLANNING IN NEW HAVEN. *J. of the Soc. of Architectural Historians 1975 34(2): 140-149.* Covers 1628-39.

3599. Babcock, C. Merton. THE PURITAN MINISTER. *New-England Galaxy 1976 17(4): 3-8.* Describes the arduous life of Puritan ministers in 17th-century New England. Details their crowded weekly schedules of church services, prayer meetings, counseling sessions, marriage ceremonies, and funeral orations. Emphasizes their rigorous efforts to suppress evil, their heavy consumption of liquor, and their compassion. 2 illus. P. C. Marshall

3600. Baughman, Ernest W. EXCOMMUNICATIONS AND BANISHMENTS FROM THE FIRST CHURCH IN SALEM AND THE TOWN OF SALEM, 1629-1680. *Essex Inst. Hist. Collections 1977 113(2): 89-104.* Compares the disciplinary actions in *The Records of the First Church in Salem, Massachusetts, 1629-1736* (Salem, Massachusetts, 1974) with other court records and finds discrepancies. In all, 20 substantiated names (two others in doubt) are added to those found in *The Records of the First Church.* Discusses the causes for the excommunication and/or banishment of the newly discovered individuals and those previously known. Primary and secondary sources; 36 notes.
R. S. Sliwoski

3601. Beales, Ross W., Jr. THE HALF-WAY COVENANT AND RELIGIOUS SCRUPULOSITY: THE FIRST CHURCH OF DORCHESTER, MASSACHUSETTS, AS A TEST CASE. *William and Mary Q. 1974 31(3): 465-480.* Dorchester was not inclined to accept the Half-Way Covenant, but acceptance came between 1675 and 1680. In an earlier study of the Dorchester Church, Edmund S. Morgan and Robert G. Pope concluded that the covenant indicated a rise in religious scrupulosity. The present study finds not a desire for re-dedication, but an attempt by a maturing society to accommodate a rising generation. Accepting the Covenant meant extending the church's influence in the community. Based on primary and secondary sources; 2 tables, 45 notes.
H. M. Ward

3602. Bormann, Pauline C. WERE THE PURITANS "PURITANICAL?" *Daughters of the Am. Revolution Mag. 1978 112(5): 434-438, 567.* Examines attitudes of the Puritans toward freedom of worship, education, sex, gaiety, religion, and government, 1630's-80's; sees common misconceptions concerning Puritan thought.

3603. Bosman, Sarah Williams. ROAD TO CONSTITUTIONAL GOVERNMENT IN CONNECTICUT. *Daughters of the Am. Revolution Mag. 1979 113(5): 502-504, 526, 543.* Connecticut was founded by Reverend Thomas Hooker and some Puritan followers during 1635-39 to secure their religious freedom.

3604. Breen, T. H. PERSISTENT LOCALISM: ENGLISH SOCIAL CHANGE AND THE SHAPING OF NEW ENGLAND INSTITUTIONS. *William and Mary Q. 1975 32(1): 3-28.* Religious ideas of the early settlers do not explain the form of institutions in the Massachusetts Bay Colony. Rather the defense in England of the different kinds of local government against arbitrary Stuart centralization made the colonists determined to preserve local institutions from outside interference. Examines social and political dissension in England with relation to ideas formulated by the migrants to New England. Comments on the democratization of the New England colony and town government, churches, and trainbands. Primary and secondary sources; 68 notes. H. M. Ward

3605. Breen, Timothy H. and Foster, Stephen. MOVING TO THE NEW WORLD: THE CHARACTER OF EARLY MASSACHUSETTS IMMIGRATION. *William and Mary Q. 1973 30(2): 189-222.* Investigates the motivation for immigration of 273 migrants to New

England during the 1630's. Migrants were older than hitherto assumed. Most were persons of sufficient means. Compares occupations of migrants coming chiefly from East Anglia and Kent. Profiles some of the migrants. Reasons for leaving England were largely religious and political, related to Puritan unrest. Traces migrant mobility in America for a generation. The new settlers were highly mobile. Based on records in England and America, registers of persons taking loyalty oaths before leaving England, and secondary sources; 88 notes. H. M. Ward

3606. Breen, Timothy H. and Foster, Stephen. THE PURITAN'S GREATEST ACHIEVEMENT: A STUDY OF SOCIAL COHESION IN SEVENTEENTH-CENTURY MASSACHUSETTS. *J. of Am. Hist. 1973 60(1): 5-22.* In their general preoccupation with the causes of violence and unrest, historians have not concerned themselves sufficiently with the causes of peace and social stability. A case in point is Massachusetts, which resolved its social tensions without major upheavals from the 1630's to the 1680's. Nucleated towns and the patriarchal family have received some attention, but more important to social peace was the accepted ideology of Puritan Congregationalism. Inculcated by a widely respected clerical elite, it stressed love and voluntary obedience to law, broad participation in state and church, widespread courts to hear grievances, and a general economic prosperity. In the 1680's the imposition of British authority, the development of the mob as a counterforce, mass hysteria, and economic problems undermined social responsibility. 69 notes. K. B. West

3607. Bremer, Francis J. and Bremer, Barbara A. THOMAS COBBETT'S *PRACTICAL DISCOURSE OF PRAYER*. *Essex Inst. Hist. Collections 1975 111(2): 138-150.* Cobbett's *Practical Discourse* (1657) was precisely that: an analysis and description of how, when, and with whom the Puritans should pray. God commanded his followers to pray and bound Himself to answer their words. They should advance specific individuals, groups, or causes or ask for destruction of others, especially God's enemies. Cobbett believed that there were three distinct types of prayer: secret, family, and public. Based on Cobbett's work, diaries, sermons, journals, letters, and secondary works; 27 notes. R. M. Rollins

3608. Bridenbaugh, Carl. RIGHT NEW-ENGLAND MEN; OR, THE ADAPTABLE PURITANS. *Massachusetts Hist. Soc. Pro. 1976 88: 3-18.* Surveys influences on the settlers of 17th-century New England which transformed the Englishmen of 1640 into the Yankees of 1690. In the face of pressures from climate, physical surroundings, and the need to cultivate friendship with the Indians, the Puritans of New England proved to be adaptable and flexible, rather than rigid. This was due to the homogeneous nature of the society, to their religious faith and willingness to work, and to the high quality of their leadership. Contact with England through commerce and trade also modified social and religious attitudes. On the whole the colonization of New England was a tremendous success. Primary and secondary sources; 21 notes, index. G. W. R. Ward

3609. Caldwell, Patricia. THE ANTINOMIAN LANGUAGE CONTROVERSY. *Harvard Theological Rev. 1976 69(3-4): 345-367.* Anne Hutchinson was at the center of the antinomianism controversy in Massachusetts, 1636-38. In the trial, she gave what appeared to be contradictory statements. This became known as her "lye." The discussion here centers on this issue; defends the "lye" as being a matter of language. The statements which led to the "lye" were not defined by those making them; thus Hutchinson gave them her interpretation, which seemed to differ from those generally assumed. Her use of inner revelation, and the court's rejection of it, led to acceptance of only objective evidence. 45 notes. E. E. Eminhizer

3610. Capps, Donald. ERIKSON'S THEORY OF RELIGIOUS RITUAL: THE CASE OF THE EXCOMMUNICATION OF ANN HIBBENS. *J. for the Sci. Study of Religion 1979 18(4): 337-349.* Analyzes, as a maladaptive religious ritual, the excommunication of Ann Hibbens, 1640-41, from the Congregationalist First Church of Boston, using Erik H. Erikson's ritual theory.

3611. Cherry, Conrad. NEW ENGLAND AS SYMBOL: AMBIGUITY IN THE PURITAN VISION. *Soundings 1975 58(3): 348-362.* The Puritans believed that their destiny necessitated taking seriously their place of settlement. Their accomplishment in holding together "in dynamic tension the promise and the threat" of New England, "the distinctiveness and the relatedness" of their region, provided them a symbol which served as a check against personal pride and social narrowness." When they abandoned the ambiguity of their symbol, the Puritans contributed a good deal to the "presumption and parochialism" with which America came to regard its destiny. Primary and secondary sources; 36 notes. N. Lederer

3612. Clark, Michael. "THE CRUCIFIED PHRASE": SIGN AND DESIRE IN PURITAN SEMIOLOGY. *Early Am. Literature 1978-79 13(3): 278-293.* To determine the presence of saving grace among church members, Puritan church elders used an elaborate scale of conversion such as that developed by William Perkins. Discusses Shepard's and Cotton's optimism and Hooker's skeptism on the application of the scale of conversion as an indicator of the state of man's soul. Hooker's attitudes toward signs of conversion prevailed. In the Puritan hierarchy, the will and reason are above other facilities. The material world is relegated to an insubstantial place in man's spiritual development; perception is an active process of mediation between the world and the Word inscribed in man's heart. Primary sources; 34 notes. J. N. Friedel

3613. Crandall, Ralph J. and Coffman, Ralph J. FROM EMIGRANTS TO RULERS: THE CHARLESTOWN OLIGARCHY IN THE GREAT MIGRATION. *New England Hist. and Genealogical Register 1977 131: (January): 3-27, (April): 3-7, 121-132, (July): 207-213.* Part I. During 1630-40, 273 householders settled in Charlestown, Massachusetts, but only 43 were influential in determining the direction of the town. Evoking a gentry image, these men (literate, older, militantly Puritan, experienced in government, and connected to the right families) controlled town government by 1634. Restriction of the franchise to church members followed. New immigrants who failed to secure the approval of this leadership class could either stay, relegated to a second-class status, or leave to found new communities. The oligarchy's success in banishing several Antinomians to Rhode Island in 1637 underlined its power to establish the religious and economic standards of citizenship for the first generation of immigrants. Based on primary and secondary sources; map, graph, chart of town inhabitants. 52 notes. Part II. Continues the list of names of these inhabitants and gives—where known—birth, marriage, and death dates, spouse's occupation, literacy, origin in England, town offices held, land owned, and other residences. Part III. Concludes the list. S. L. Patterson

3614. Davis, Thomas and Jeske, Jeff, eds. SOLOMON STODDARD'S "ARGUMENTS" CONCERNING ADMISSION TO THE LORD'S SUPPER. *Pro. of the Am. Antiquarian Soc. 1976 86(1): 75-111.* Reprints Solomon Stoddard's arguments in his debate with Increase Mather over the nature of Puritanism. This paper represents Stoddard's position at the 1679 synod, and reflects his change from "a proponent of unregenerate communion to an advocate of the sacrament's alleged converting property." This marked a major deviation from New England orthodoxy. Primary and secondary sources; 28 notes. J. Andrew

3615. Davis, Thomas M. REVIEW ESSAY. *Early Am. Literature 1979 14(1): 110-117.* Although *Solomon Stoddard* by Ralph J. Coffman (Twayne Publishers, 1978) possesses some strengths as a biography, its flaws overshadow the strengths. The text suffers from careless proofing and editing, and Coffman himself is careless and inaccurate with his attempts to modernize original texts. Coffman's discussion of Stoddard's early years at Northampton not only adds little to earlier discussions of that period in his life, but introduces additional confusion. T. P. Linkfield

3616. Faber, Eli. PURITAN CRIMINALS: THE ECONOMIC, SOCIAL, AND INTELLECTUAL BACKGROUND TO CRIME IN SEVENTEENTH-CENTURY MASSACHUSETTS. *Perspectives in Am. Hist. 1977-78 11: 81-144.* Analysis of 315 convicted criminals in 17th-century Middlesex County, Massachusetts, shows that offenders were equally represented in all classes. The percentage of convictions for sexual offenses was highest among the lower classes. Convictions for religious offenses, alcoholic abuse, and defiance of authority were highest among the upper classes. Further analysis shows that Puritans tended to reaccept offenders as contributing members of society after a reasonable period. W. A. Wiegand

3617. Finlayson, Michael G. PURITANISM AND PURITANS: LABELS OR LIBELS? *Can. J. of Hist. 1973 8(3): 201-223.* Between 1560 and 1660, while "the label 'Puritan' enjoyed common currency in England and hence must be a key concept for the historian, nonetheless there was at any one time a wide variety of religious attitudes, the differences between which may not easily be subsumed under a fundamental distinction." The variant definitions of Puritanism do not help the historian to relate "certain aspects of seventeenth century English religious thought with various movements, maybe capitalism, maybe radicalism, perhaps even American democracy." 66 notes. D. D. Cameron

3618. Forrer, Richard. THE PURITAN RELIGIOUS DILEMMA: THE ETHICAL DIMENSIONS OF GOD'S SOVEREIGNTY. *J. of the Am. Acad. of Religion 1976 44(4): 613-628.* Investigates the relationship of religion and ethics, particularly its expression in American Puritanism. Before 1650 the covenant theology was the means of drawing religion and ethics together by declaring that God will reward a particular kind of behavior and punish another. After 1650 this approach came under question. Divine Sovereignty was stressed in Puritan sermons as a way of explaining the seeming inequities in the human situation. This debate in Puritanism continued beyond their day in a broader cultural context. Primary and secondary sources; 65 notes. E. R. Lester

3619. Gadzhiev, K. S. SOVREMENNAIA AMERIKANSKAIA NEOKONSERVATIVNAIA ISTORIOGRAFIIA I NEKOTORYE PROBLEMY PURITANIZMA [Modern American neoconservative historiography and certain problems of Puritanism]. *Vestnik Moskovskogo U. Seriia 9: Istoriia [USSR] 1973 28(3): 18-31.* Criticizes American studies of the 1930's-60's and their interpretation of sociopolitical developments in 17th-century Puritan society. This so-called neoconservative school maintains that New England Puritans gave rise to a purely American culture, differing radically from European traditions, and distinguished by a dominant democratic and religiously tolerant middle class which precluded ideological conflicts typical for European countries. This theory is disputed: Puritan colonization of America, based on bourgeois social concepts, developed similarly to other bourgeois states harboring antagonistic class and sectarian distinctions. 51 notes.

N. Frenkley

3620. Gildrie, Richard P. CONTENTION IN SALEM: THE HIGGINSON-NICHOLET CONTROVERSY, 1672-1676. *Essex Inst. Hist. Collections 1977 113(2): 117-139.* The "spirit of contention" in Massachusetts towns in the late 17th century was connected to social change. In Salem, the hiring of Charles Nicholet in 1672 as an assistant to Reverend John Higginson (1616-1708) illustrates this point. Higginson advised the town to dismiss Nicholet after his trial year, but the majority of townspeople refused. Subsequently, the question of Nicholet's retention, fired by doctrinal and financial disagreements, developed into a struggle for control over the town's religious institution. The battle spread to the Quarterly Court and the Massachusetts General Court which supported the town's leaders in retaining Nicholet but criticized their behavior. Primary and secondary sources; 49 notes.

R. S. Sliwoski

3621. Greenberg, Douglas. NEW WINE IN OLD BOTTLES. *Rev. in Am. Hist. 1977 5(1): 28-35.* Review article prompted by Paul R. Lucas's *Valley of Discord: Church and Society along the Connecticut River, 1636-1725* (Hanover, N.H.: U. Pr. of New England, 1976) and David E. Van Deventer's *The Emergence of Provincial New Hampshire, 1623-1741* (Baltimore, Md.: Johns Hopkins U. Pr., 1976).

3622. Gura, Philip F. COTTON MATHER'S *LIFE OF PHIPS:* "A VICE WITH THE VIZARD OF VERTUE UPON IT." *New England Q. 1977 50(3): 440-457.* Sketches Sir William Phips's (1651-95) career and shows how Cotton Mather's 1697 biography of the governor of Massachusetts was written to justify the actions of his close associate. Mather's commendation of Phips's ambition, patriotism, and rise in society contrasts with the earlier Puritan stress on piety, service to the Lord, and acceptance of one's place in society. Mather's defense marked a shift from a personal piety to public patriotism as the standard of leadership. Facing a crisis in both personal and community terms, Mather hoped that by justifying Phips's actions and reminding people of his ties to Phips, he could both instill in society some of its lost Puritan fervor and bolster his own position as its leader. Based on Mather's writings and secondary sources; 38 notes. J. C. Bradford

3623. Hall, David D. SYMBOLS AND SOCIETY IN COLONIAL NEW ENGLAND. *Rev. in Am. Hist. 1978 6(4): 465-472.* Review article prompted by Emory Elliott's *Power and the Pulpit in Puritan New England* (Princeton, N.J.: Princeton U. Pr., 1975) and Winton U. Solberg's *Redeem the Time: The Puritan Sabbath in Early America* (Cambridge, Mass.: Harvard U. Pr., 1977) which discuss religion in Puritan America from the early 17th century through the mid-18th century.

3624. Hall, Michael and Joyce, William. THE HALF-WAY COVENANT OF 1662: SOME NEW EVIDENCE. *Pro. of the Am. Antiquarian Soc. 1977 87(1): 97-110.* In 1662, representatives of Massachusetts churches held a series of meetings to discuss baptism of infants and church membership. New documents on the debates during the 1662 synod have been uncovered at the American Antiquarian Society. Written by observers and participants, these shed additional light on New England Puritanism and on the discussions and controversies that occurred at the synod, especially the Half-Way Covenant. They indicate opposition to government use of force on issues where there was no consensus. Primary and secondary sources; 16 notes. J. Andrew

3625. Hall, Michael G. GENIUS IN AMERICA: A NEW BIOGRAPHY OF COTTON MATHER. *Rev. in Am. Hist. 1979 7(4): 494-498.* Review essay of David Levin's *Cotton Mather: The Young Life of the Lord's Remembrancer, 1663-1703* (Cambridge, Mass.: Harvard U. Pr., 1978).

3626. Halttunen, Karen. COTTON MATHER AND THE MEANING OF SUFFERING IN THE *MAGNALIA CHRISTI AMERICANA*. *J. of Am. Studies [Great Britain] 1978 12(3): 311-329.* In the 1690's, Puritan clergymen believed moral laxity and impious behavior was too widespread in New England. To counter such developments, Cotton Mather (1663-1728) published the *Magnalia Christi Americana* in 1702. Mather deemed his work, a history of New England's people and their sufferings to establish a Holy Commonwealth, an act of sacrifice by himself to redeem the people of New England by offering up their travails and producing "on their behalf the vicarious atonement of Jesus Christ." Based on Mather's writings and secondary sources; 25 notes. H. T. Lovin

3627. Hambrick-Stowe, Charles E. REFORMED SPIRITUALITY: DIMENSIONS OF PURITAN DEVOTIONAL PRACTICE. *J. of Presbyterian Hist. 1980 58(1): 17-33.* Throughout the 17th century, New Englanders engaged in the widespread practice of piety that actually made New England distinctively Puritan through an elaborate system of public worship and private devotions by which they were able to define their communal purpose. Investigates the devotional habits of four representative Puritans: Captain Roger Clap, the Reverend Thomas Shepard, Samuel Sewall, and Anne Bradstreet. The tradition of Puritan devotion carried within it certain specific spiritual exercises related to life crises and daily routines, developing a spiritual and psychological impact of great power. Sources include the author's dissertation (Boston University, 1980); 20 notes. H. M. Parker, Jr.

3628. Joyce, William and Hall, Michael. THREE MANUSCRIPTS OF INCREASE MATHER. *Pro. of the Am. Antiquarian Soc. 1976 86(1): 113-123.* Directs attention to three important Increase Mather manuscripts not previously described. These include a book-length essay on the New Jerusalem, a work from 1675 on the redemptive value for mankind of Christ's sacrifice, and Mather's copy of the results of the 1679 synod. Primary and secondary sources; 10 notes. J. Andrew

3629. Joyce, William L. NOTE ON INCREASE MATHER'S OBSERVATIONS RESPECTING THE LORD'S SUPPER. *Pro. of the Am. Antiquarian Soc. 1973 83(2): 343-344.* A note correcting an article by Everett Emerson and Mason I. Lowance. The original copy of this Mather sermon, considered lost or no longer extant, in fact exists in the library of the American Antiquarian Society. It does not markedly differ in content from the later copy by Cotton Mather (used by Emerson and Lowance). V. L. Human

3630. Kawashima, Yasuhide. PURITAN PERSUASION: *MAGNALIA CHRISTI AMERICANA,* FROM MATHER TO EMERSON. *Rev. in Am. Hist. 1976 4(2): 164-170.* Review article prompted by Sacvan Bercovitch's *The Puritan Origins of the American Self* (New Haven: Yale

U. Pr., 1975); discusses the origins of the national character as epitomized by the thought and writings of Cotton Mather.

3631. Kingdon, Robert M. PROTESTANT PARISHES IN THE OLD WORLD AND THE NEW: THE CASE OF GENEVA AND BOSTON. *Church Hist. 1979 48(3): 290-309.* The parish is the most important single unit of the Christian church. However, there were considerable differences between the types of parishes developed on opposite sides of the Atlantic in communities dominated on the intellectual level by Calvinist theology. On the European side, the parish remained a geographic unit, drawing together for worship all the inhabitants of a fixed area in the county, or within a city. In America, the parish became an ideological or social unit, drawing together people of common ideas or social attachments, with little regard to their places of residence. Covers the 16th and 17th centuries. 2 maps, 29 notes.
M. D. Dibert

3632. Lowance, Mason I., Jr., ed. and Watters, David, ed. INCREASE MATHER'S "NEW JERUSALEM": MILLENNIALISM IN LATE SEVENTEENTH-CENTURY NEW ENGLAND. *Pro. of the Am. Antiquarian Soc. 1977 87(2): 343-408.* Reproduces the "New Jerusalem," along with a lengthy introduction to Increase Mather and his writings. This document is critical for intellectual historians seeking to understand millennialism in 17th-century New England. The manuscript "establishes Mather's position on the specific conditions of the millennial paradise and shows clearly his premillennial faith in the future perfection of God's society of saints." This document was recently discovered at the American Antiquarian Society in Worcester, Massachusetts. Primary and secondary sources; 110 notes. J. A. Andrew

3633. Lowry, Charles B. "THE CITY ON A HILL' AND KIBBUTZIM: SEVENTEENTH CENTURY UTOPIAS AS IDEAL TYPES. *Am. Jewish Hist. Q. 1974 64(1): 24-41.* A sociological comparison of 17th-century Puritan New England towns and early 20th-century Kibbutzim in Palestine. The kibbutz is defined as a family, comparable to the Puritan family, and both societies are said to operate in a religious setting. Other similarities would include their agricultural character, position of women, and strong intellectual bent. 47 notes. F. Rosenthal

3634. Lucas, Paul R. "AN APPEAL TO THE LEARNED": THE MIND OF SOLOMON STODDARD. *William and Mary Q. 1973 30(2): 257-292.* Examines the assumption that Stoddard dominated religion in western Massachusetts and much of Connecticut, that his theology caused the destruction of orthodox Puritanism, and that he was instrumental in the coming of the Great Awakening. Stoddard's Instituted Church emphasized discipline and was out of step with the democratizing and evangelical tendencies of the greater population. Stoddard's influence derived from his personality, not from religion. In his last years he developed a greater following among the clergy because he changed his tactics. Examines Stoddard's sermons and writings, including the pamphlet warfare between Stoddard and Increase and Cotton Mather. 87 notes. H. M. Ward

3635. Maclear, J. F. NEW ENGLAND AND THE FIFTH MONARCHY: THE QUEST FOR THE MILLENNIUM IN EARLY AMERICAN PURITANISM. *William and Mary Q. 1975 32(2): 223-260.* Urges historians to give weight to the Puritans' apocalyptic view of history and its impact on American thought and institutions. Compares New England and English Puritan eschatology, emphasizing the role of John Cotton as a prophet of Christ's coming. Examines three religious experiments in New England: Cotton's proposal for a Mosaic code; the Constitution of Portsmouth, drawn up by Antinomian exiles; and John Eliot's missionary work among the Indians. Accounts for the decline in the prophetic vision after 1660 and the increasing concern for corruption, which would culminate in the last Judgment. Based on contemporary tracts and interpretive monographs; 83 notes. H. M. Ward

3636. McGiffert, Michael. THE PROBLEM OF THE COVENANT IN PURITAN THOUGHT: PETER BULKELEY'S *GOSPEL-COVENANT*. *New England Hist. and Geneal. Register 1976 130(April): 107-129.* Uses Peter Bulkeley's *Gospel-Covenant* (1646; rev. ed., 1651) to explore the covenant doctrine in Puritan theology. Bulkeley (1583-1659), founder of Concord, Massachusetts, and its minister until his death, published this series of sermons to explain the history and nature of redemption. The means to redemption and salvation was the covenant, first of works (which failed with Adam), then of grace (through Christ). In analyzing Bulkeley's explication of this concept, the author illustrates one of the Puritans' chief theological problems: how to avoid making covenant into contract and thus formalizing and institutionalizing God's relation with His people beyond what He had intended. Primary and secondary sources; 99 notes. S. L. Patterson

3637. Middlekauff, Robert. PURITAN STUDIES AND INTELLECTUAL HISTORY. *Rev. in Am. Hist. 1975 3(2): 173-178.* E. Brooks Holifield's *The Covenant Sealed: The Development of Puritan Sacramental Theology in Old and New England, 1570-1720* (New Haven, Conn.: Yale U. Pr., 1974) and Ernest Benson Lowrie's *The Shape of the Puritan Mind: The Thought of Samuel Willard* (New Haven, Conn.: Yale U. Pr., 1974) discuss the theology of New England Puritans in the 16th and 17th centuries.

3638. Mignon, Charles W. CHRIST THE GLORY OF ALL TYPES: THE INITIAL SERMON FROM EDWARD TAYLOR'S "UPON THE TYPES OF THE OLD TESTAMENT." *William and Mary Q. 1980 37(2): 286-301.* Edward Taylor, minister at Westfield, Massachusetts, delivered this first in a series of 36 sermons on 28 March 1693, with his text from Colossians 2:17. Taylor's typology as it affects Christian living is spelled out. Taylor emphasizes the "Excellency of Christ," which should "allure us" to Him. Persons can find excellent things "working for our reliefs & this is demonstrative of Gods Grace." Sermon reproduced with annotated explanation of the manuscript; 7 notes.
H. M. Ward

3639. Mignon, Charles W. THE NEBRASKA EDWARD TAYLOR MANUSCRIPT: "UPON THE TYPES OF THE OLD TESTAMENT." *Early Am. Literature 1977-78 12(3): 296-301.* Records the discovery of the Edward Taylor (1642-1729) manuscript "Upon the Types of the Old Testment," in 1977. The description of its 36 sermons (1693-1706) demonstrates its importance beyond Taylor scholarship: organized around the central theme of the Types of the Old Testament, it is important to those studying typology in the works of Taylor and in Colonial literature. Includes a list of the dates and texts of the sermons, with pagination. Transcribing, editing, and annotation is necessary for a more thorough understanding and appreciation of this volume. Primary sources; 11 notes. J. N. Friedel

3640. Murphey, Murray G. THE PSYCHODYNAMICS OF PURITAN CONVERSION. *Am. Q. 1979 31(2): 135-147.* The psychodynamics of the Puritan conversion process may be regarded as at least partly analogous to the resolution of the Oedipus complex as described by Freud. Among the Puritan saints, therefore, certain commonalities in personality structure should be expected, because the transforming conversion experience was remarkably similar among them. 26 notes.
D. G. Nielson

3641. Newcomb, Wellington. ANNE HUTCHINSON VERSUS MASSACHUSETTS. *Am. Heritage 1974 25(4): 12-15, 78-81.* Anne Hutchinson's criminal trial in Puritan Boston for her role in the Antinomian controversy. S

3642. Parker, David L. EDWARD TAYLOR'S PREPARATIONISM: A NEW PERSPECTIVE ON THE TAYLOR-STODDARD CONTROVERSY. *Early Am. Literature 1976-77 11(3): 259-278.* In defining the problem of conversion, Edward Taylor redefined the process of conversion and the actual exercise of faith as efficacious, while Solomon Stoddard completely ignored the importance of the moment of saving faith in the hope that communion would inspire conversion, which had the net result of pushing Taylor toward a greater emphasis on preparationism, 1690-94.

3643. Parker, David L. PETRUS RAMUS AND THE PURITANS: THE "LOGIC" OF PREPARATIONIST CONVERSION DOCTRINE. *Early Am. Lit. 1973 8(2): 140-162.* Comparison of the preparationist conversion theories of Thomas Hooker and Thomas Shepard suggests that the influence of the principles of logic formulated by Petrus Ramus was as significant a factor as any other, including Calvin's. Both Hooker and Shepard used the Ramist theory of opposition or contraries to explain the nature of preparation as well as its necessity for salvation. Based on primary and secondary sources; 40 notes.
D. P. Wharton

3644. Pettit, Norman. HOOKER'S DOCTRINE OF ASSURANCE: A CRITICAL PHASE IN NEW ENGLAND SPIRITUAL THOUGHT. *New England Q. 1974 47(4): 518-534.* Thomas Hooker, eminent Puritan divine, through "his doctrine of assurance shaped the New England mind as no other doctrine had done." Hooker "described the order of salvation as a process thoroughly mixed with hopes and fears," and believed that the spiritual life should be seen in the light of ordinary experience. Although opposed by John Cotton and others, he was a man of strong psychological bent, and far ahead of his time. "Doubts and fears had always to be taken into account—together with hope and joy; and for this reason his doctrine of assurance prevailed—corresponding as it did to the experience of those for whom the order of salvation had never been an easy road to follow, but for whom it was an essential part of New England spiritual life." 29 notes.
R. V. Ritter

3645. Poteet, James M. A HOMECOMING: THE BULKELEY FAMILY IN NEW ENGLAND. *New England Q. 1974 47(1): 30-50.* Peter Bulkeley, a Puritan pastor, came to America in 1635 and settled in Concord. He viewed New England as a holy experiment directed by the hand of God. In 1646 his book of sermons expounding the covenant theology was printed in London, the first book by a New England clergyman. While his son Gershom was disillusioned by Puritanism, the third generation accepted it on its own terms. John Bulkeley "found contentment in the routine of a provincial, country preacher." 60 notes.
E. P. Stickney

3646. Poteet, James M. MORE YANKEE THAN PURITAN: JAMES FITCH OF CONNECTICUT. *New England Hist. and Geneal. Register 1979 133(Apr): 102-117.* Traces the private and political scheming of James Fitch, son of a Puritan clergyman born in Saybrook, Connecticut, in 1649. His influence sprang mainly from the acquisition of large land holdings, much of it through friendships with local Indians begun in childhood. He left a legacy of discontent among the inhabitants of Connecticut, quite the opposite of the prevailing Puritan ethics of his father's day. 103 notes. J

3647. Scheick, William J. THE WIDOWER NARRATOR IN NATHANIEL WARD'S *THE SIMPLE COBLER OF AGGAWAM IN AMERICA*. *New England Q. 1974 47(1): 87-96.* Called the pleasantest book ever written by a New England Puritan, Nathaniel Ward's *The Simple Cobler of Aggawam in America* (1647) is of interest not only for the attack on religious toleration, but for its satire and "sheer exuberance of language." The *Cobler* contains references to marriage, adultery, prostitution, and parturition. "The mate he would have each of us find, is truth." 18 notes. E. P. Stickney

3648. Selement, George, ed. JOHN COTTON'S HIDDEN ANTINOMIANISM: HIS SERMON ON REVELATION 4:1-2. *New England Hist. and Genealogical Register 1975 129(July): 278-294.* The role of John Cotton (1584-1652) in the Antinomian controversy has always aroused suspicion. Leaders of the Massachusetts Bay Colony's orthodoxy were wary of him, for as he was Anne Hutchinson's (1591-1643) minister, it could be inferred that her views must somehow reflect his. The ensuing debate eventually produced a unity that enabled the leaders to banish Hutchinson and her followers to Rhode Island. Thomas Shepard (1604-1649), however, remained dubious of Cotton's repudiation, and he used the notes he took from this sermon as proof that Cotton's Antinomianism was "hid only," not repented of. Cotton probably delivered this sermon in 1639, and Shepard copied it into the same notebook that contains the confessions of some of the members admitted to his church. The notebook is now in the possession of the New England Historic Genealogical Society, Boston. Editorial notes explain obscure passages in the sermon. Primary sources; 89 notes. S. L. Patterson

3649. Slethaug, Gordon E. EDWARD TAYLOR'S COPY OF THOMAS TAYLOR'S *TYPES:* A NEW TAYLOR DOCUMENT. *Early Am. Lit. 1973 8(2): 132-139.* Thomas Taylor's *Christ Revealed: Or the Old Testament A Treatise of the Types . . . of our Saviour* (London, 1635), a work of typology and exegesis, is now known to have been possessed by Edward Taylor. Edward Taylor's annotations in this book reveals his keen interest in typology, and several of his *Preparatory Meditations* suggest the influence of Thomas Taylor's study. Based on primary and secondary sources; 9 notes. D. P. Wharton

3650. Sprunger, Keith L. THE DUTCH CAREER OF THOMAS HOOKER. *New England Q. 1973 46(1): 17-44.* Discusses the life in exile of Thomas Hooker, 1631-33. The brief period was formative for his theological and ministerial development. At Amsterdam he witnessed the question of church liberty as well as the issue of his own candidacy. In Delft he entered the company of the most radical non-Separatists, who completely threw out the Prayer Book. Some of the seeds of his ministry to the Congregational Churches of New England had been sown in the Netherlands. 69 notes. E. P. Stickney

3651. Stannard, David Edward. DEATH AND DYING IN PURITAN NEW ENGLAND. *Am. Hist. R. 1973 78(5): 1305-1330.* Every culture, as every individual, must come to terms with the fact of death. The behavior seen as appropriate in the face of death is, in large measure, determined by the vision of what, if anything, the individual's post-mortem status is to be. Christianity has traditionally envisioned different afterlife states determined principally by the merits of one's earthly behavior, thus prescribing peaceful and easy deaths for those who have reason to believe they are saved. The Puritans, with whom the thought of death was something of an obsession, inherited and accepted this prescription for the proper way of dying, but it was in sharp conflict with their predeterministic vision of salvation. The result was a variety of intense cultural and intellectual strains that could not be—and were not—indefinitely endured. A

3652. Stoever, William R. B. NATURE, GRACE AND JOHN COTTON: THE THEOLOGICAL DIMENSION IN THE NEW ENGLAND ANTINOMIAN CONTROVERSY. *Church Hist. 1975 44(1): 22-33.* In 1636, Puritan Massachusetts was confronted with a sectarian outburst which ruined the religious and civil peace of Boston and temporarily threatened the entire colony. Part of the Boston congregation, led by Anne Hutchinson and abetted by John Cotton, charged that many of the Bay clergy were not true ministers of the gospel but a company of unregenerate "legalists" preaching a convenant of "works" instead of a convenant of grace and hindering the work of redemption. In this re-examination of the so-called Antinomian Controversy, importance is placed on the extent to which the Puritans sought to hold together divine sovereignity and human activity. 48 notes. M. D. Dibert

3653. Stout, Harry S. THE MORPHOLOGY OF REMIGRATION: NEW ENGLAND UNIVERSITY MEN AND THEIR RETURN TO ENGLAND, 1640-1660. *J. of Am. Studies [Great Britain] 1976 10(2): 151-172.* Traces the movement of clergymen and other university-trained persons back to England, 1640-60. Puritan political, religious, and social ideologies and the dearth of professional employment opportunities in New England account for the migration of colonials to Europe. The removal from New England of so many potential sources of dissidence helped to produce social stability in the Puritan colonies of New England. The migrations ceased after 1660 for American intellectuals were unwelcome in Restoration England. Primary and secondary works; 7 tables, 69 notes. H. T. Lovin

3654. Struna, Nancy. PURITANS AND SPORTS: THE IRRETRIEVABLE TIDE OF CHANGE. *J. of Sport Hist. 1977 4(1): 1-21.* Developmental examination of sports within the first century of Puritan society in Massachusetts can provide the necessary societal perspective for an understanding of the role of sports in that era. In the first two decades (1630-50), sport was very real, reflecting the values and the diversity within the society. Occasions for sport often detracted from societal values as conceived by magristrates. During 1650-90, there was an attempt to develop a homogeneous society, but by singling out distinct groups the ministers marked an actual fragmentation of the society. From 1690 to 1730, the fragmentation continued. The aftermath of the Glorious Revolution signalled greater freedom from Puritan religious restraint. During the entire first century both Puritans and non-Puritans participated in sports with increasing frequency. "As a behavioral form, sport mirrored developments within Massachusetts Bay, and in turn, was affected by the transformation and diversification of that society." 88 notes.
M. Kaufman

3655. Tipson, Baird. INVISIBLE SAINTS: THE JUDGMENT OF CHARITY IN THE EARLY NEW ENGLAND CHURCHES. *Church Hist. 1975 44(4): 460-471.* Few early New England practices troubled European observers more than the attempt to restrict church membership to the regenerate. Scholars have not been incorrect in assuming that charitable judgment broadly implied a willingness to decide questionable cases favorably. In a narrower context, the judgment of charity was recommended for cases where a Christian wished to decide the spiritual state of his neighbor, especially in the context of his suitability for church membership. 47 notes. M. D. Dibert

3656. Tipson, Baird. THE ROUTINIZED PIETY OF THOMAS SHEPARD'S DIARY. *Early Am. Literature 1978 13(1): 64-80.* Thomas Shepard's spiritual diary (25 November 1640-30 March 1644) contains a unique record of the personal piety of a first-generation New England minister, and offers much insight into the spiritual life of an early American Puritan. In his search for grace and God's revelation, Shepard meditated upon personal experiences. His entries are monotonous and the tone is serious. As a means of systematic introspection and reflection, the Puritan diary could validate divine communication. By citing additional sources on Puritan religious beliefs, the author documents Shepard's reaffirmation of the traditional Puritan position. Based mainly on primary sources; 47 notes. J. N. Friedel

3657. Vartanian, Pershing. COTTON MATHER AND THE PURITAN TRANSITION INTO THE ENLIGHTENMENT. *Early Am. Literature 1973 7(3): 213-224.* The Puritan clergy performed a positive role in the transition to the Enlightenment, which in its initial phase differed more in degree than in substance from late Puritan thought. Interest in the "New Science" led major Puritan figures, including Cotton Mather (1663-1728), into the Enlightenment. As an experimental scientist, Mather made enduring contributions in genetics and preventive medicine, as well as in ornithology. At the end of the 17th century Mather's declining interest in the jeremiad and federal theology was accompanied by a corresponding rise of interest in the "New Science" and the "New Piety," interests which emerged and matured together. Mather's universe became more rational, its mechanical intricacies less mysterious and its operations more orderly and restrained as his religious life became more private and his faith more personal and spontaneous. As he responded to the experimental science, his thought conformed to the beliefs of the early Enlightenment. While his conception of reason was more theistic than naturalistic, Mather did attribute to reason a positive role in human progress. Armed with his piety and his rationalism, he crossed the threshold into the early Enlightenment between 1702 and 1712. Based on primary and secondary sources; 18 notes. D. P. Wharton

3658. Wagner, Peter. AMERICAN PURITAN LITERATURE: A NEGLECTED FIELD OF RESEARCH IN AMERICAN SPORT HISTORY. *Can. J. of Hist. of Sport and Physical Educ. [Canada] 1977 8(2): 62-75.* Puritan writings, especially the jeremiads, reveal that although sports were not highly regarded by the Puritans, 1620-1720, there still was a positive attitude toward physical activity, sports, and games.

3659. Wagner, Peter. LITERARY EVIDENCE OF SPORT IN COLONIAL NEW ENGLAND: THE AMERICAN PURITAN JEREMIAD. *Stadion [West Germany] 1976 2(2): 233-249.* The Puritan sermons of complaint, the "jeremiads," are important additions to sources concerning the social reality of colonial sports. They demonstrate that Puritan settlers engaged in a variety of sports and even neglected their religious duties in taking advantage of both religious and mundane festivities for sport and amusement. Primary and secondary sources; 50 notes. M. Geyer

3660. Wagner, Peter. PURITAN ATTITUDES TOWARD PHYSICAL RECREATION IN 17TH CENTURY NEW ENGLAND. *J. of Sport Hist. 1976 3(2): 139-151.* An analysis of the writings of several leading Puritan ministers indicates that although some church leaders condemned physical recreation, others accepted it. Moreover, the Jeremiads indicated that the rank and file Puritans entertained themselves very early with physical recreation. There was a spectrum of attitude, rather than opposition to amusements. 45 notes. M. Kaufman

3661. Waterhouse, Richard. RELUCTANT IMMIGRANTS: THE ENGLISH BACKGROUND OF THE FIRST GENERATION OF THE NEW ENGLAND PURITAN CLERGY. *Hist. Mag. of the Protestant Episcopal Church 1975 44(4): 473-488.* Examines the English social, educational, and religious backgrounds of the Puritan clergy who migrated to New England in the 17th century, most of them reluctantly. A large proportion migrated only after they were suspended from their ministries, and many others must have left, knowing that if they stayed, suspension was inevitable. Some felt a concern for their English congregations, and several solved this problem by bringing their parishioners with them to New England. Migrations slowed down after the passing of the Act of Uniformity in 1662 because the provisions of the Act were really not enforced. Those who migrated were far from ordinary ministers. They were very well educated, and they held important, well-paying charges. Because they left reluctantly, 26 out of the surviving 68 returned to England with the outbreak of the Civil War, aware that they could resume their ministerial functions. That so few migrated after 1660 suggests that the English Puritan ministers viewed emigration to New England only in terms of a last resort. Based largely on primary sources, including *Calendar of State Papers Domestic*, 1655-66; 89 notes.

H. M. Parker, Jr.

United Brethren and Related Churches

3662. Beal, William C., Jr. THE PLANTING OF THE EVANGELICAL ASSOCIATION IN WESTERN PENNSYLVANIA, 1800-1833. *Methodist Hist. 1978 16(4): 218-229.* The planting of the Evangelical Association in western Pennsylvania occurred in waves during the first, second, and fourth decades of the 19th century. The Association started with a single class and regular preaching appointments under Jacob Albright and John Walter. Under John Dreisbach the work of the association began to accelerate in 1813 until it had expanded throughout western Pennsylvania in 1833. 2 photos, 13 notes. H. L. Calkin

3663. Gorrell, Donald K. OHIO ORIGINS OF THE UNITED BRETHREN IN CHRIST AND THE EVANGELICAL ASSOCIATION. *Methodist Hist. 1977 15(2): 95-106.* During 1806-39, the United Brethren in Christ and the Evangelical Association evolved in Ohio from simple and informal origins to well developed and expanding denominations. Both became identifiable as German-speaking religious groups. Recruitment of itinerant preachers was a constant problem. Other problems were the need for more financial support to build churches, inability to move into the cities, and competition by both groups in the same areas of Ohio. 31 notes. H. L. Calkin

3664. Heisey, Terry M. IMMIGRATION AS A FACTOR IN THE DIVISION OF THE EVANGELICAL ASSOCIATION. *Methodist Hist. 1980 19(1): 41-57.* The schism which divided the Evangelical Association between 1887 and 1894 cannot be attributed to a single cause. It grew out of rivalry between two groups of church leaders, conflict between those favoring law and order and those who were champions of individual rights, and disputes over the theological issue of Christian perfection. However, most of the minority were the American-born, English-speaking core that opposed the newly immigrated Germans who were soon the majority in the Midwest. By 1894, the church had become divided along lines of language and culture. 60 notes.

H. L. Calkin

3665. Ness, John H., Jr. BISHOP MILTON WRIGHT: A MAN OF CONVICTION. *Methodist Hist. 1974 12(2): 32-45.* Biography of Milton Wright (1828-1917), minister, teacher, editor, and bishop of the United Brethren in Christ. Bishop Wright was the father of Orville and Wilbur Wright. H. L. Calkin

3666. O'Malley, J. Steven. THE OTTERBEINS: MEN OF TWO WORLDS. *Methodist Hist. 1976 15(1): 3-21.* The theology of Philip Wilhelm Otterbein (1726-1813), founder of the United Brethren in Christ, and his brothers was influenced by the teachings of the University of Herborn in Germany, which included the symbols of Protestant orthodoxy, the anti-Aristotelian logic of Peter Ramus, mysticism, and the new ideas which were the hallmark of Pietism and the Enlightenment. Otterbein was also influenced by his contacts with significant religious leaders of the 18th century in Europe and America. He served as pastor in Pennsylvania and Maryland. 68 notes. H. L. Calkin

3667. Scanlon, Harold P. THE ORIGIN OF THE ARTICLES OF FAITH OF THE UNITED EVANGELICAL CHURCH. *Methodist Hist. 1980 18(4): 219-238.* The United Evangelical Church was organized

in 1894 after a split with the Evangelical Association. In the same year, the new denomination prepared a discipline including articles of faith based largely on a pamphlet by Milton S. Terry, entitled *Doctrines of Arminian Methodism* (Evanston, Ill.: U. Pr. Print, 1887). The articles remained the doctrine of the church until the United Evangelical Church and the Evangelical Association reunited in 1921. The author includes in tabular form the articles of faith of the United Evangelical Church, the Evangelical Association, and Terry. Secondary sources; 15 notes.
H. L. Calkin

3668. Stein, K. James. WITH PARALLEL STEPS: THE EVANGELICAL BRETHREN AND THE AMERICAN SCENE. *Methodist Hist. 1974 12(3): 16-39.* The Evangelical United Brethren Church was a definite part of the American scene with which it interacted. This relationship was shaped by theological factors—German pietism, Arminianism and evangelical revivalism—and non-theological factors—the frontier and rural ethos of the denomination, the ethnological character of the church, the lower class stratification from which it drew members, and its small size. Specific areas of interaction were slavery, war and peace, capital and labor, and church-and-state relations. Covers 1800-1968. 68 notes.
H. L. Calkin

United Church of Canada

3669. Hobbs, R. Gerald. THE NATURE AND EXERCISE OF AUTHORITY IN THE UNITED CHURCH OF CANADA. *Bull. of the United Church of Can. 1973 (22): 21-35.* Attempts to determine "the reality of the latitudinarian church" which lies behind the "image of institutionalized ecclesiastical anarchy" projected by the United Church of Canada. Concludes that the church is committed to the authority of the Scriptures and of tradition as enshrined in the Basis of Union, and that the church courts possess the necessary authority to exercise discipline. The results of a survey of 24 ministers, "indicate a tentative shift in the direction of a more effective self-discipline administered in a spirit of grace, whether through forms already in existence or as a result of a move closer to the Anglican communion." Covers 1925-73. Based on a questionnaire and records of church conferences; 63 notes.
B. D. Tennyson

3670. Plato, W. R. THE UNITED CHURCH OF CANADA AND EUCHARISTIC WORSHIP. *Bull. of the United Church of Can. 1973 (22): 16-20.* Initial results of a questionnaire sent to 1,000 United Church ministers in 1972 in an attempt to ascertain trends in United Church of Canada eucharistic worship. This is part of a larger study which will seek also to establish possible differences in practice according to geographical location and denominational background. Concludes that over the past 20 years there has been an obvious trend toward more frequent celebration of the Lord's Supper, and that there has been a renewal of interest and personal concern for worship on the part of many ministers.
B. D. Tennyson

Roman Catholic Church and Related Churches

General

3671. Adamec, Joseph V. REVIEWING THE HISTORY OF THE SLOVAK CATHOLIC FEDERATION. *Jednota Ann. Furdek 1980 19: 107-123.* The congresses, conventions, and activities of the Slovak Catholic Federation of America (SSK) since 1911.

3672. Agonito, Joseph. THE JOHN CARROLL PAPERS. *Catholic Hist. Rev. 1977 63(4): 537-572.* Father Thomas O'Brien Hanley, who edited the John Carroll Papers, has brought together the large and diversified body of Archbishop Carroll's writings, scattered in over thirty North American and European archives. Excellent translations of Carroll's numerous Latin, French, and Italian letters have been provided. Carroll's letters, sermons, and theological writings are fully and accurately presented, with explanatory notes attached to each piece. Hanley provides a brief, though historically rich Introduction to each volume, and a fine Index. The JCP reveal, in rich detail, the portrait of a remarkable prelate who established a Church that was American in spirit and yet, at the same time, faithful in essentials to its Roman heritage.
A

3673. Almaráz, Félix D., Jr. CARLOS E. CASTAÑEDA AND *OUR CATHOLIC HERITAGE*: THE INITIAL VOLUMES (1933-1943). *Social Sci. J. 1976 13(2): 27-37.* Studies the background, commitment, and problems encountered by Carlos E. Castañeda in writing *Our Catholic Heritage* on the history of Spanish colonization in Texas 1693-1731.

3674. Angers, François-Albert. LE SENS D'UNE VIE [The sense of a life]. *Action Natl. [Canada] 1976 65(9-10): 800-803.* Reprints the funeral oration for Esdras Minville presented at the church of Saint-Pascal Baylon, 12 December 1975. Minville was, above all else, a Christian. His life was devoted exclusively to the common good of the French Canadian people and was based on the Christian virtues of faith, hope, and charity.
A. W. Novitsky

3675. Aragón, Janie Louise. THE COFRADÍAS OF NEW MEXICO: A PROPOSAL AND A PERIODIZATION. *Aztlán 1978 9: 101-118.* Proposes a methodology for studying Los Hermanos Penitentes, a unit for the social organization of villages and towns of the upper Rio Grande Valley, referring to a large group of cofradías, or brotherhoods, often mentioned, though inadequately understood, by scholars. Lines of investigation are suggested, along with a possible periodization: 1770-1830, 1830-55, 1855-80, 1880-1912, 1912-35, and 1935-65, together with possible primary sources. 29 notes, biblio.
R. V. Ritter

3676. Aspinwall, Bernard. ORESTES A. BROWNSON AND FATHER WILLIAM CUMMING. *Innes Rev. [Great Britain] 1976 27(1): 35-41.* Publishes a letter from Father Cumming to Orestes A. Brownson in 1857 and describes their lives and the history of Scottish Catholics in America in the 1850's.

3677. Aspinwall, Bernard and Tucker, Janey, transl. ORESTES BROWNSON, CRITIQUE COHERENT [Orestes Brownson: A coherent critique]. *Rev. d'Hist. Ecclésiastique [Belgium] 1976 71(1-2): 5-30.* Reinterprets the themes, attitudes, contributions, and importance of this "laicist" Catholic social philosopher. Prominent in English, French, and American intellectual circles, he reflected Jacksonian New England and Saint-Simonism but in an eclecticly independent way and by a vacilating evolution. Both hailed and condemned in his day, he was not a precursor of Marx. Based on published sources, original manuscripts at Notre Dame University and in New York's Paulist Archives, and extensive secondary works.
R. I. Burns

3678. Baker, T. Lindsay. THE EARLY YEARS OF REV. WINCENTY BARZYNSKI. *Polish Am. Studies 1975 32(1): 29-52.* A colorful account of a dedicated, hardworking pioneer who travelled through the early Polish-American communities from Texas to Chicago. Provides an account of American social history, following the Reverend Barzynski's career as a Polish insurrectionist in 1863, a missionary in Texas in 1866, and after 1874 a builder of St. Stanislaus Kortka Church in Chicago, which was to become the largest Catholic parish in the United States. Adding to his many accomplishments Father Barzynski is also credited with starting a printing house, a newspaper, orphanages, and a college, and was one of the cofounders of the Polish Roman Catholic Union, one of the two largest Polish-American associations in the United States. Covers 1838-99.
S. R. Pliska

3679. Baker, T. Lindsay, ed. and trans. FOUR LETTERS FROM TEXAS TO POLAND IN 1855. *Southwestern Hist. Q. 1974 77(3): 381-389.* Panna Marya, Texas, established 1854, is the oldest Polish colony in America. It was the focal point for the first organized Polish peasant immigrants. Reproduces in translation four 1855 letters of Father Leopold Moczygemba and relatives, prime movers in the venture, lauding their new homes and encouraging others to follow. 33 notes.
D. L. Smith

3680. Baker, William M. AN IRISH-CANADIAN JOURNALIST-POLITICIAN AND CATHOLICISM: TIMOTHY ANGLIN OF THE SAINT JOHN FREEMAN. *Study Sessions: Can. Catholic Hist. Assoc. [Canada] 1977 44: 5-24.* Timothy Warren Anglin during 1849-83 supported Catholicism while acting as editor of the *Freeman,* a newspaper in Saint John, New Brunswick.

3681. Barcus, James E. STRUCTURING THE RAGE WITHIN: THE SPIRITUAL AUTOBIOGRAPHIES OF NEWMAN AND ORESTES BROWNSON. *Cithara 1975 15(1): 45-57.* John Henry Newman and Orestes A. Brownson were noted 19th-century Protestants who converted to Roman Catholicism. Each wrote an autobiography which defended his change of religion. Newman's *Apologia pro Vita Sua* (1864) and Brownson's *The Convert* (1857) show many parallels, including a sense of inner rage.

3682. Bardaglio, Peter W. ITALIAN IMMIGRANTS AND THE CATHOLIC CHURCH IN PROVIDENCE, 1890-1930. *Rhode Island Hist. 1975 34(2): 46-57.* The creation of national parishes was not always a success; animosities developed among Italian Americans in Providence, Rhode Island, 1890-1930, when the insensitivity of the Scalabrini order to the cultural traditions of southern Italians combined with their anticlericalism and propensity for disorder to form a rift between northern and southern Italian immigrants in the community.

3683. Barrett, Joseph. A HISTORY OF SAINT DENIS PARISH. *Records of the Am. Catholic Hist. Soc. of Philadelphia 1975 86(1-4): 33-42.* Dennis Kelly, who immigrated to the United States in 1806 and died a wealthy man in 1864, founded St. Denis Parish, the oldest Catholic church in Delaware County. Presents a sketch based on the author's *Sesquicentennial History of Saint Denis Parish.* 11 notes.
J. M. McCarthy

3684. Barry, Colman J. THE BICENTENNIAL REVISITED. *Catholic Hist. Rev. 1977 63(3): 369-391.* The essay is an evaluation of American Catholic religious phenomena during the United States Bicentennial of 1976. Historical comparisons drawn from the history of the Roman Catholic community and other Christian religious experiences in the New World are made and analyzed. The thesis is advanced and defended that, despite current confusion and dissension in the American Catholic community following Vatican Council II, a vibrant and challenging religious renewal is developing that has both ancient roots and major ecumenical associations among divided Christians. A

3685. Barry, Colman J. THE FIRST HURRAH: BONIFACE WIMMER, O.S.B. *Am. Benedictine Rev. 1977 28(1): 30-40.* Reviews *An American Abbot: Boniface Wimmer, O.S.B., 1809-1887* by Jerome Oetgen (Latrobe, Pa.: The Archabbey Press, 1976). Wimmer was responsible for establishing the Benedictine Order on the American frontier. 3 notes.
J. H. Pragman

3686. Bassett, William W. A NEW CANON LAW AND THE CRISIS OF REFORM. *J. of Ecumenical Studies 1973 10(2): 233-258.* Originally mandated by Pope John XXIII, the Pontifical Commission for the Revision of the Code of Canon Law has the task of revising the 1917 Code. The author describes the commission's progress and the ways it might complete its work: 1) restate the church law of 1917, 2) reformulate Church law to conform to pluralism in Roman Catholicism and in Christianity as a whole, or 3) streamline Canon Law to its bare essentials. The author and the Canon Law Society of America prefer the second approach. J. A. Overbeck

3687. Benoit, Virgil. GENTILLY: A FRENCH-CANADIAN COMMUNITY IN THE MINNESOTA RED RIVER VALLEY. *Minnesota Hist. 1975 44(8): 278-289.* Gentilly and its environs in northwestern Minnesota was heavily settled during the 1870's-80's by French Canadians emigrating from Quebec. The French Catholic community has been held together by its religion, conservative family life, and the rural environment. Extensive ties with Canadian relatives still exist. Gentilly achieved a modicum of prosperity through the efforts to establish a cheese factory by the powerful Catholic priest Elie Theillon. Father Theillon was the spiritual and secular leader of Gentilly's French Canadians during 1888-1935. The Catholic Church has been a major factor in preserving the conservative social and economic world view of Gentilly's residents. Based on French and English language primary sources.
N. Lederer

3688. Bergeron, Réjean and Drolet, Yves. LES QUESTIONS INTERNATIONALES DANS LES INÉDITS DE LIONEL GROULX (1895-1905) [International affairs in the unpublished writings of Lionel Groulx, 1895-1905]. *Rev. d'Hist. de l'Amérique Française [Canada] 1980 34(2):245-255.* Lionel Groulx (1878-1967), the historian of French Canada, discussed international issues in his diary and in memoirs of a European visit. He stressed religious questions, lambasted French anti-clericalism, vaunted the papacy of Pius X, and spoke of the messianic role of Quebec as a center of Catholicism. Based on manuscripts held by the University of Montreal; 38 notes. R. Aldrich

3689. Bernardin, Joseph L. A BICENTENNIAL REFLECTION UPON AMERICAN CATHOLIC HISTORY. *Jednota Ann. Furdek 1977 16: 185-188.* Discusses the problems of Catholics from all ethnic groups in the United States since colonial times.

3690. Bielewicz, Bohdan. TWORZENIE SIĘ I ROZWÓJ LOKALNEJ SPOŁECZNOŚCI POLONIJNEJ W STANACH ZJEDNOCZONYCH NA PRZYKŁADZIE MIASTA MILWAUKEE W STANIE WISCONSIN [Formation and development of the local Polish ethnic group in the United States as exemplified by Milwaukee, Wisconsin]. *Przegląd Zachodni [Poland] 1979 35(5-6): 258-283.* The first permanent Polish settler arrived in Wisconsin in 1846. From 1850, Polish immigrants came in increasing numbers until the post-World War I immigration restrictions limited the influx. Some settled in Milwaukee. They settled in tightly knit communities, centered usually around the Polish Roman Catholic Church with a Polish priest. They also formed a rich cultural and organizational life. In 1888 the first Polish daily in the United States, *Kuryer Polski,* began publishing in Milwaukee. Its editor, Michał Kruszka, was elected to the Wisconsin legislature, where he fought for the teaching of Polish in public schools. Poles preferred to vote Democratic, but some supported Republicans and some Socialists. After World War I, acculturation became visible. Primary sources.
M. Krzyzaniak

3691. Bilodeau, Therese. THE FRENCH IN HOLYOKE (1850-1900). *Hist. J. of Western Massachusetts 1974 3(1): 1-12.* Nicholas Proulx, one of the first French Canadians to migrate to Holyoke, recruited workers in Quebec. Management found them obedient, non-union workers whose life revolved around the Catholic Church. Primary and secondary sources; 3 illus., chart, 58 notes. S. S. Sprague

3692. Blejwas, Stanislaus. A POLISH COMMUNITY IN TRANSITION. *Polish Am. Studies 1977 34(1): 26-69.* This account of two parishes in New Britain, Connecticut, mirrors the development of hundreds of Polish parishes throughout the United States during 1890-1955, especially the acculturation and Americanization of the immigrant. Based on sources in English and Polish; 114 notes. S. R. Pliska

3693. Blejwas, Stanislaus A. A POLISH COMMUNITY IN TRANSITION: THE EVOLUTION OF HOLY CROSS PARISH, NEW BRITAIN, CONNECTICUT. *Polish Am. Studies 1978 35(1-2): 23-53.* Discusses a Polish American parish in relation to assimilation and the pressure to Americanize. Since its beginnings in 1928, this parish has become Polish American and no longer strictly Polish. Polish and English primary and secondary sources; 69 notes. S. R. Pliska

3694. Bouchard, Gérard and La Rose, André. LA RÉGLEMENTATION DU CONTENU DES ACTES DE BAPTÊME, MARIAGE, SÉPULTURE, AU QUÉBEC, DES ORIGINES À NOS JOURS [Regulation of the contents of the acts of baptism, marriage, and burial in Quebec from the beginning to our day]. *Rev. d'Hist. de l'Am. Française [Canada] 1976 30(1): 67-77.* From the 16th century to the present, both the Church and the state have been concerned with registering baptisms, marriages, and burials. Church regulation of these practices has always been more detailed than that of the state. Vicars have been recording performances of these acts, and the state has benefited from such assistance. Based on published Church and state documents and secondary works; 6 tables, 37 notes. L. B. Chan

3695. Boucher, Réal. L'ENDETTEMENT DE L'ÉVÊCHÉ DE SAINT-HYACINTHE AU XIXe SIÈCLE: LE RÔLE DÉCISIF DE CHARLES LAROCQUE DANS L'EXTINCTION DE CETTE DETTE [The debt of the diocese of Saint Hyacinthe in the 19th century:

the decisive role of Charles LaRocque in paying off this debt]. *Rev. d'Hist. de l'Amérique Française [Canada] 1980 33(4): 557-574.* The diocese of Saint-Hyacinthe Quebec, suffered from great financial problems from its creation in 1852. Charles LaRocque, appointed bishop in 1866, amortized this debt by levying a tax on parish income and by cutting episcopal expenses. Based on diocesan records; 2 tables, 60 notes.
R. Aldrich

3696. Bouvier, Leon F. and Weller, Robert H. RESIDENCE AND RELIGIOUS PARTICIPATION IN A CATHOLIC SETTING. *Sociol. Analysis 1974 35(4): 273-281.* Examines the relationship between residence, or ecological distribution, and religious behavior in society in the period 1953-69.
S

3697. Bouvy, Jane Faulkner. FOLK CATHOLICISM IN INDIANA. *Indiana Folklore 1976 9(2): 147-164.* Covers the 1970's.

3698. Broderick, Francis L. DEFINING THE AMERICAN CATHOLIC CHURCH. *Rev. in Am. Hist. 1979 7(1): 37-42.* Review article prompted by Neil Betten's *Catholic Activism and the Industrial Worker* (Gainesville: U. Pr. of Florida, 1976) and Jay P. Dolan's *Catholic Revivalism: The American Experience, 1830-1900* (Notre Dame, Ind.: U. of Notre Dame Pr., 1978).

3699. Buchanan, Susan Huelsebusch. LANGUAGE AND IDENTITY: HAITIANS IN NEW YORK CITY. *Int. Migration Rev. 1979 13(2): 298-313.* Examines the dispute in the 1970's between two Haitian factions—those wishing to retain French as the language for masses in a Brooklyn church and those wishing to replace French with Haitian Creole—perceiving the clash (which ended more or less as a defeat for the Creole-speaking faction, although not necessarily as a total victory for the French-language proponents) as a social dilemma inherited from the colonial slave past of Haiti transported to New York.

3700. Buczek, Daniel S. POLISH AMERICANS AND THE ROMAN CATHOLIC CHURCH. *Polish Rev. 1976 21(3): 39-62.* Examines the role which the Catholic Church played in the Americanization of Polish immigrants and the "benign neglect" of the Poles so the hierarchy could hold onto other more renegade ethnic groups who found themselves in a new country, 1860's-1930's.

3701. Bump, Jerome. HOPKINS, THE HUMANITIES, AND THE ENVIRONMENT. *Georgia Rev. 1974 28(2): 227-244.* In the struggle for "ecology," science's counterpart to art, the determining factor will be the humanities, not science. Giving leadership to the scientists and humanists is Jesuit Gerard Manley Hopkins, who in the 1870's developed a beautiful, unified vision of God, man, and nature. To express his concepts he created new words, rhythms, and metaphors which transmit his vision into an elegant call for reconciliation with nature.
M. B. Lucas

3702. Bumsted, J. M. HIGHLAND EMIGRATION TO THE ISLAND OF ST. JOHN AND THE SCOTTISH CATHOLIC CHURCH, 1769-1774. *Dalhousie Rev. [Canada] 1978 58(3): 511-527.* The Catholic Church in Scotland systematically attempted to resettle persecuted Highlanders in what is now called Prince Edward Island between the Seven Years War and the American Revolution; for that reason there is an unusual amount of contemporary documentation. This is a rare thing in the history of Highland emigration. It began with Colin MacDonald of Boysdale's attempts to Protestantize his tenants on South Uist in 1769. The planning for this Hebridean exodus was done by two Edinburgh bishops, George Hay and John MacDonald. Illustrates the Scottish persecutions and the economic problems of the movement. 58 notes.
C. H. Held

3703. Byrne, Cyril. THE MARITIME VISITS OF JOSEPH-OCTAVE PLESSIS, BISHOP OF QUEBEC. *Nova Scotia Hist. Soc. Collections [Canada] 1977 39: 23-48.* Translated parts of travel journals of Joseph-Octave Plessis, Catholic bishop in Quebec, 1812-15, offer his impressions of the Maritime Provinces, primarily Cape Breton, Nova Scotia, and New Brunswick.

3704. Byrne, Cyril. THE MARITIME VISITS OF JOSEPH-OCTAVE PLESSIS, BISHOP OF QUEBEC. *Nova Scotia Hist. Soc. Collections [Canada] 1977 39: 23-47.* The diary of the Bishop of Quebec, Joseph-Octave Plessis, provided considerable detail of the visits which he undertook in 1812 and 1815 to his diocese in Prince Edward Island, Cape Breton, and mainland Nova Scotia, as well as New Brunswick. Several outstanding characteristics of Plessis's attitude are noted: his implicit and explicit acceptance of the British dominance; his adverse judgment of the Acadians; his observation of the "most perfect harmony" between the Scotch and Acadian Catholics on Prince Edward Island; his consciousness of his episcopal office and the dignity which it deserved together with the respectfulness due the performance of the sacred offices of the Church. Interesting details of daily life of the whites and Indians are delineated, as are frequent references to the geography and topography of the Maritime Provinces.
E. A. Chard

3705. Cadwalader, Mary H. CHARLES CARROLL OF CARROLLTON: A SIGNER'S STORY. *Smithsonian 1975 6(9): 64-71.* Presents a biography of Carroll, 1737-1832, a conservative, Catholic financier and Maryland state senator who signed the Declaration of Independence.

3706. Cameron, J. M. FRANK SHEED AND CATHOLICISM. *R. of Pol. 1975 37(3): 275-285.* Frank Sheed, distinguished lay propagator and defender of Catholic doctrine, is a Catholic intellectual who attempts to reconcile the pre-Pope John XXIII Catholicism with Catholicism since that time. Despite the conflict this presents for Sheed, his life is an example of the "possibility of living within such a situation with simplicity and dignity, fidelity to the past, openness to the present and hope for the future." Based on Sheed's book, *The Church and I* (New York: Doubleday, 1974).
L. Ziewacz

3707. Capps, Walter H. THOMAS MERTON'S LEGACY. *Center Mag. 1979 12(2): 2-5.* Trappist monk Thomas Merton studied in Asia and gave new credibility to contemporary monasticism; Merton died in Bangkok, Thailand in 1968.

3708. Carey, Patrick. VOLUNTARYISM: AN IRISH CATHOLIC TRADITION. *Church Hist. 1979 48(1): 49-62.* Many American Irish Catholics saw voluntarism not as uniquely Protestant or American but as part of their Irish Catholic tradition. Focuses on the transition of the tradition from Ireland to the United States and concentrates on the efforts of Father (later Bishop) John England (1786-1842) to articulate and defend that tradition in Ireland and the United States. Outlines the historical context of the tradition and analyzes Father England's advocacy of the practices and principles involved. Family custom, hatred of the British, and other cultural and sociological factors influenced Irish Catholics' identification with the Catholic Church. The system of free will support, moreover, was voluntary in the sense that it had no legal basis of compulsion; custom, necessity, and community pressure insured that it had real sanction in fact as a sort of cultural Catholicism. Covers 1808-50.
M. Dibert

3709. Cartwright, D. G. ECCLESIASTICAL TERRITORIAL ORGANIZATION AND INSTITUTIONAL CONFLICT IN EASTERN AND NORTHERN ONTARIO, 1840-1910. *Hist. Papers [Canada] 1978: 176-198.* The formal organization of ecclesiastical territory tended to precede rather than to follow Catholic settlement in frontier regions. All counties and districts in the province should be under the jurisdiction of the hierarchy of Ontario so that ecclesiastical boundaries could be adjusted to accommodate population movements. Wealthier and more densely populated parishes had to be linked to mission territory in which parishioners were dispersed and frequently in contact with non-Catholics. Mission work among the Indians and the need to secure the faith took precedence over ethnic differences. 2 tables, 4 fig., 53 notes.
E. P. Stickney

3710. Carvalho, Joseph, III and Everett, Robert. STATISTICAL ANALYSIS OF SPRINGFIELD'S FRENCH CANADIANS (1870). *Hist. J. of Western Massachusetts 1974 3(1): 59-63.* Ninety-six percent of all Canadians in Ward 8, in Springfield, Massachusetts, worked in cotton mills. A majority were under the age of 21 and less than one-eighth of those over 21 were US citizens. They were a church centered group. Primary and secondary sources; 4 tables, 17 notes.
S. S. Sprague

3711. Choquette, Robert. ADÉLARD LANGEVIN ET L'ÉRECTION DE L'ARCHIDIOCÈSE DE WINNIPEG [Adélard Langevin and the establishment of the archdiocese of Winnipeg]. *Rev. d'Hist. de l'Amérique Française [Canada] 1974 28(2): 187-208.* Recounts the conflicts which arose after 1905 in Winnipeg between French Catholics and English-speaking Catholics over the administration of Monsignor Adélard Langevin.

3712. Choquette, Robert. JOHN THOMAS MC NAILLY ET L'ÉRECTION DU DIOCÈSE DE CALGARY [John Thomas McNailly and the establishment of the diocese of Calgary]. *Rev. de l'U. d'Ottawa [Canada] 1975 45(4): 401-416.* John Thomas McNailly (1871-1952), the first bishop of Calgary, was an anglophone who defended the interests of the Catholic anglophiles in Calgary, particularly the Irish. The Pope, in selecting McNailly, believed that western Canada was English in both language and culture. Provides brief sketch of McNailly's life and accomplishments and discusses his problems as bishop, particularly with the French Canadians. Primary and secondary sources; 84 notes. M. L. Frey

3713. Choquette, Robert. L'EGLISE D'OTTAWA SOUS MGR GUIGUES, 1848-1874 [The church of Ottawa under Monseigneur Guigues, 1848-74]. *Sessiona d'Étude: Soc. Can. d'Hist. de l'Église Catholique [Canada] 1977 44: 57-62.* The Ottawa diocese was administered by Joseph-Eugène Guigues during 1848-74, where he actively pursued French Canadian colonization in Ontario, church funding, and spiritual and social programs.

3714. Choquette, Robert. OLIVIER-ELZÉAR MATHIEU ET L'ÉRECTION DU DIOCÈSE DE REGINA, SASKATCHEWAN [Olivier-Elzear Mathieu and the establishment of the diocese of Regina, Saskatchewan]. *Rev. de l'U. d'Ottawa 1975 45(1): 101-116.* Discusses the conflict between Anglophiles and Francophiles in Saskatchewan and Mathieu's attempt to reconcile the two groups, 1905-30. Based on primary and secondary sources; 58 notes. M. L. Frey

3715. Choquette, Robert. PROBLÈMES DES MOEURS ET DE DISCIPLINE ECCLÉSTIASTIQUE: LES CATHOLIQUES DES PRAIRIES CANADIENNES DE 1900 À 1930 [Problem of morality and ecclesiastical discipline: Catholics of the Canadian prairies from 1900 to 1930]. *Social Hist. [Canada] 1975 8(15): 102-119.* During 1900-30 the Catholic minority (20 per cent of the population) in the Canadian prairies was split between francophone and anglophone, with the latter in the majority. Francophone clerics were more intransigent than anglophones in enforcing their authority, interpreting doctrine, and in relations with the Protestant majority on such matters as dancing, clerical dress, public schools, and mixed marriages. Adélard Langevin, archbishop of Saint-Boniface, Manitoba (1895-1915), and Monsignor Legal de Saint-Albert of Edmonton provide examples of especially intransigent francophone clerics. John Thomas McNally (1871-1952), archbishop of Calgary, 1913-1924, provides an example of a more liberal anglophone cleric. Based on Edmonton and Saint Boniface archbishopric archives and Calgary diocese archives; table, 55 notes. W. K. Hobson

3716. Clements, Robert B. MICHAEL WILLIAMS AND THE FOUNDING OF *THE COMMONWEAL*. *Records of the Am. Catholic Hist. Soc. of Philadelphia 1974 85(3-4): 163-173.* During Michael Williams's era at *Commonweal* (1922-38), the magazine featured some of the most intelligent and progressive Catholic comment in the United States and was one of the most versatile journals in the country. It combined literature, the arts, public affairs, science, and theology. 24 notes. J. M. McCarthy

3717. Cliche, Marie-Aimée. LA CONFRÉRIE DE LA SAINTE-FAMILLE À QUÉBEC SOUS LE RÉGIME FRANÇAIS, 1663-1760 [The Brotherhood of the Holy Family in Quebec under the French regime, 1663-1760]. *Sessions d'Étude: Soc. Can. d'Hist. de l'Église Catholique [Canada] 1976 43: 79-93.* Describes the formation, recruitment, and nature of the elitist society, the Brotherhood of the Holy Family, founded through collaboration among Bishop François de Laval, Joseph-Marie-Pierre Chaumonot, and followers in Montreal, and its important influence on religious activities in colonial Canadian society.

3718. Cliche, Marie-Aimée. LES ATTITUDES DEVANT LA MORT D'APRÈS LES CLAUSES TESTAMENTAIRES DANS LE GOUVERNEMENT DE QUÉBEC SOUS LE RÉGIME FRANÇAIS [Attitudes before death as evidenced by wills filed with the government of Quebec during the French regime]. *Rev. d'Hist. de l'Amérique Française [Canada] 1978 32(1): 57-94.* Analysis of 799 wills registered in Quebec during 1663-1760 clearly reveals the deep religious convictions of their authors and a fundamental conformity to the teachings of the Catholic Church. Men and women of all socioeconomic classes were more concerned with salvation than with details of burial. Legacies providing for the celebration of Masses and the propagation of good works were favored. 13 tables, 66 notes. M. R. Yerburgh

3719. Conrad, Glenn R. L'IMMIGRATION ALSACIENNE EN LOUISIANE, 1753-1759 [Alsatian immigration into Louisiana, 1753-1759]. *Revue d'hist. de l'Amérique française [Canada] 1975 28(4): 565-577.* Revocation of the Edict of Nantes in 1685 by Louis XIV forced the exodus of many Protestants from France. When France was having difficulty maintaining its hold over Louisiana, 70 years later the government offered to pay the passage to Louisiana for those Protestants living in Alsace, if the immigrants would become Catholic. Many Alsatians accepted the offer and arrived in Louisiana in 1759. Based on primary and secondary sources; 48 notes. L. B. Chan

3720. Coogan, M. Jane. THE REDOUBTABLE JOHN HENNESSY, FIRST ARCHBISHOP OF DUBUQUE. *Mid-America 1980 62(1): 21-34.* Limerick-born John Hennessy (1825-1900) became archbishop of the archdiocese of Dubuque, Iowa, in 1866. During his 34-year reign he sought to establish a Catholic educational system for his diocese. He made several abortive attempts to carry out his grand plan. Little can be told of his episcopate, for he burned all his records before his death. Notes. M. J. Wentworth

3721. Côté, André. LE MONASTÈRE DE MISTASSINI: SA SUPPRESSION OU SA FORMATION EN PRIEURÉ, 1900-1903 [The monastery of Mistassini: its suppression or formation in the priory, 1900-03]. *Sessions D'Étude: Soc. Can. d'Hist. de l'Eglise Catholique 1973 40: 92-111.* Examines the religious controversy between Cistercian authorities and the Archbishop of Quebec, Monseigneur Bégin (and his successor Msgr. Labrecque) over the establishment of a monastery for Trappists. S

3722. Cox, Dwayne. RICHARD HENRY TIERNEY AND THE MEXICAN REVOLUTION, 1914-1917. *Mid-America 1977 59(2): 93-101.* Editor of *America* from March 1914 to February 1925, the Jesuit Richard Henry Tierney campaigned against the anti-Catholic stance of the Mexican revolution during his first three years at this post. He especially opposed the leadership of Venustiano Carranza, whom he saw as a threat to Catholicism everywhere. His crusade was carried out through editorials and speeches until the spring of 1917 when American entry into World War I became the major issue. Although he toiled actively on behalf of the Catholic Church in denouncing governmental practices in Mexico, he did little to influence American foreign policy in this direction. Based on archival and secondary materials; 27 notes. J. M. Lee

3723. Crews, Clyde F. HALLOWED GROUND: THE CATHEDRAL OF THE ASSUMPTION IN LOUISVILLE HISTORY. *Filson Club. Hist. Q. 1977 51(3): 249-261.* Sketches the role of the Cathedral of the Assumption in the life of the Louisville, Kentucky, Catholic community since 1852. Based on newspapers and church records; 50 notes. G. B. McKinney

3724. Cuba, Stanley L. A POLISH COMMUNITY IN THE URBAN WEST: ST. JOSEPH'S PARISH IN DENVER, COLORADO. *Polish Am. Studies 1979 36(1): 33-74.* This parish, hundreds of miles away from Polish American centers of activity, developed through four generations much like other Polish Roman Catholic parishes in the United States. This one is located in Globeville, Denver's leading mixed ethnic enclave. The laying of the cornerstone of the church in 1902 was followed by the arrival of the first pastor, Father Theodore Jarzynski. Covers the parish's role in World War I, the construction of a parochial school in 1926, the upward mobility of the second and third generations, the transitional character of the parish territory, the temporary boosting of Polish nationalism through the arrival of a group of Polish displaced persons after World War II, and the eventual loss of the Polish way, even though often it was propped up and remembered. Primary and secondary sources in Polish and English; 74 notes. S. R. Pliska

3725. Cunningham, Patrick. IRISH CATHOLICS IN A YANKEE TOWN: A REPORT ABOUT BRATTLEBORO, 1847-1898. *Vermont Hist. 1976 44(4): 189-197.* Provides information from Patrick Cunningham about a Catholic parish in Brattleboro, Vermont, during 1847-98. The report was summarized in Bishop John Stephen Michaud's contribution to *The history of the Catholic Church in the New England States* (1899). Gives names, numbers, and dates for arrivals, pastors, places of worship, large contributors, baptisms, marriages, schools, and cemetery. Communicants worked mostly on the railroad or in the Estey organ factory. Notes "the intolerant spirit of a dominant party. . . . old prejudices now happily dead" which made nearly all Catholics Democrats. Based on the original report in Diocesan Archives.
T. D. S. Bassett

3726. Curcione, Nicholas R. FAMILY INFLUENCE ON COMMITMENT TO THE PRIESTHOOD: A STUDY OF ALTAR BOYS. *Sociol. Analysis 1973 34(4): 265-280.* Examines a cohort of altar boys and attempts to determine structural factors that distinguish between those likely to become priests and those not likely to do so. Rather than pursuing a traditional framework, which analyzes organizational commitment in terms of social experiences encountered within an organizational role, a developmental approach is utilized. This perspective focuses on processes by which individuals are selected and socialized to the priesthood prior to actually entering the organization. The data indicate that uniformity of family support is a key structural factor in distinguishing the committed group from the undecided and uncommitted. J

3727. Curtis, Ralph E., Jr. RELATIONS BETWEEN THE QUAPAW NATIONAL COUNCIL AND THE ROMAN CATHOLIC CHURCH, 1876-1927. *Chronicles of Oklahoma 1977 55(2): 211-221.* Since their first contact with French Jesuits in the 17th century, the Quapaw Indians had been nominal Catholics. In 1890, Catholic dominance was challenged when non-Catholic tribal members blocked the use of tribal funds for Church activities. This dissenting group was composed of other Indians who had been assimilated into the Quapaws. By 1927 non-Catholics became sufficiently powerful to close the last remaining Catholic school on Quapaw land. Based on agency reports and newspapers; 2 photos, map, 35 notes. M. L. Tate

3728. DeRose, Christine A. INSIDE "LITTLE ITALY": ITALIAN IMMIGRANTS IN DENVER. *Colorado Mag. 1977 54(3): 277-293.* Italian immigrant history in Denver is characterized by economic difficulties, discrimination, and a lack of internal cohesiveness. Mentions the establishment of numerous societies, Catholic activities, the Angelo Noce-Columbus Day and the Father Mariano Lepore controversies, crime, poverty, business, labor, neighborhoods, and the entrance of several Italian Americans into influential positions in Denver society. Covers 1870-1930. Primary and secondary sources; 11 illus., 43 notes.
D. A. Hartford

3729. Dixon, Blase. THE CATHOLIC UNIVERSITY OF AMERICA AND THE RACIAL QUESTION, 1914-1918. *Records of the Am. Catholic Hist. Soc. of Philadelphia 1973 84(4): 221-224.* The refusal to matriculate Charles H. Wesley in 1914 was the first known instance of racial discrimination at the Catholic University of America. Exclusion of Negroes became a policy in 1919 and the bar was not completely lifted until 1948. 10 notes. J. M. McCarthy

3730. Drolet, Jean Claude. UNE MOUVEMENT DE SPIRITUALITÉ SACERDOTALE AU QUEBEC AU XXe SIÈCLE (1931-1950): LE LACOUTURISME [A movement of priestly spirituality in Quebec in the 20th century (1931-50): Lacouturism]. *Sessions D'Étude: Soc. Can. d'Hist. de l'Eglise Catholique 1973 40: 55-91.* Researches the spiritual movement provoked by Jesuit priest Onésime Lacouture during 1931-39 as it emerged in Quebec. S

3731. Duchschere, Kevin A. JOHN SHANLEY: NORTH DAKOTA'S FIRST CATHOLIC BISHOP. *North Dakota Hist. 1979 46(2): 4-13.* John Shanley, a New York-born priest of Irish descent, became the first Catholic bishop of North Dakota in January 1890, for Jamestown, North Dakota. His earlier clerical career had been mainly spent in St. Paul, Minnesota, where he championed the cause of his black and Italian parishioners and exhibited a pronounced Irish ethnicity and affinity for other ethnics. Throughout his career, Bishop Shanley was an ardent advocate of temperance. In North Dakota the bishop proved to be an indefatigable worker in uniting his far-flung coreligionists through the erection of a network of churches and schools. He displayed considerable sympathy for Indians. He was instrumental in bringing an end to North Dakota's law allowing a 90-day residency for people seeking divorce.
N. Lederer

3732. Eccles, W. J. THE ROLE OF THE CHURCH IN NEW FRANCE. Morton, R. E. and Browning, J. D., ed. *Religion in the 18th Century* (New York: Garland Publ., 1979): 41-57. Describes the religious and secular functions of the Catholic Church in New France during the 17th and 18th centuries; the religious climate was better there than in the mother country.

3733. Ellis, John Tracy. AUSTRALIAN CATHOLICISM: AN AMERICAN PERSPECTIVE. *J. of Religious Hist. [Australia] 1979 10(3): 313-321.* Review article prompted by Patrick O'Farrell's *The Catholic Church and Community in Australia: A History* (West Melbourne: Thomas Nelson, 1977). The strengths of the work—thorough research, lucid writing, mature interpretations—recommend it to the professional community. The development of Catholicism in Australia is similar in many respects to the development of Catholicism in the United States. In both cases, the Church emerged from direct contact with English Catholicism. Comparisons, such as the rather slow development of a Catholic intellectual community, are developed with frequent reference to the social and economic origins of Catholic immigrants. Covers 17c-1977.
W. T. Walker

3734. Faherty, William Barnaby. IN THE FOOTSTEPS OF BISHOP JOSEPH ROSATI. *Italian Americana 1975 1(2): 281-291.* Reviews several works on the life of Bishop Joseph Rosati (1789-1843), focusing on his work for the Catholic Church in the Midwest and Louisiana during the first half of the 19th century. S

3735. Fay, Leo F. CATHOLICS, PAROCHIAL SCHOOLS, AND SOCIAL STRATIFICATION. *Social Sci. Q. 1974 55(2): 520-527.* The intersection of religious, educational, and stratification variables in the Catholic schools is examined. Finds that parents send their children to Catholic elementary and high schools for either religious or mobility-related reasons. Religious reasons tend to be characteristic of middle and upper-middle class parents, who show strong religiosity and have a high opinion of the public schools, while mobility-related reasons are characteristic of lower-middle and working class parents, who show weak religiosity and have a low opinion of the public schools. J

3736. Feldblum, Esther. ISRAEL IN THE HOLY LAND: CATHOLIC RESPONSES, 1948-1950. *J. of Ecumenical Studies 1975 12(2): 199-219.* Examines the varied reactions to the establishment of the State of Israel by the Roman Catholic Church, showing the evolution from a policy of silence to reaction of US Catholics to the internationalization of Jerusalem and the Arab refugee problem, with which many US Catholics were sympathetically concerned. Only after Vatican II could a positive policy toward Israel develop among Roman Catholics.
J. A. Overbeck

3737. Fernández-Shaw, Carlos Manuel. PUENTES HISPÁNICOS ENTRE EL PARAGUAY Y LOS ESTADOS UNIDOS [Spanish bridges between Paraguay and the United States]. *Cuadernos Hispanoamericanos [Spain] 1975 101(301): 98-112.* Outlines common cultural links between Paraguay and the United States deriving ultimately from Spain. These links were most pronounced from the early 16th century, when the Spanish discovered Paraguay and Florida, to the early 19th century. Considers the geographical extent of Spanish influence in North and South America; Spanish linguistic influences to the present day; Catholicism; the importation of animals from Europe; popular culture, music, and literature; explorers and discoverers; and the role of the New World as an inspiration for fantastic and idyllic utopias. Secondary sources; 19 notes. P. J. Taylorson

3738. Flynn, Louis J. THE HISTORY OF SAINT MARY'S CATHEDRAL OF THE IMMACULATE CONCEPTION, KINGSTON, ONTARIO, 1843-1973. *Study Sessions: Can. Catholic Hist. Assoc. 1973 40: 35-40.*

3739. Fox, Francis J. A CHRONICLE: INDICATING THE ESTABLISHMENT OF ECCLESIASTICAL JURISDICTION IN THE AMERICAN SOUTHWEST, PARTICULARLY ARIZONA AND NEW MEXICO. *Records of the Am. Catholic Hist. Soc. of Philadelphia 1978 89(1-4): 109-117.* Outlines the formation of ecclesiastical jurisdictions under the authority of the Spanish kings (1548-1821) and by the suggestions of the American hierarchy (1821-1969). 39 notes.
J. M. McCarthy

3740. Fox, Richard W. RELIGION, POLITICS, AND ETHNICITY: TWO REVIEW ESSAYS. *J. of Ethnic Studies 1974 2(2): 76-82.* In his first essay the author commends Harold J. Abramson's *Ethnic Diversity in Catholic America* (1973) for tabulating and cross-tabulating a large body of data showing the precise dimensions of ethnic diversity among Catholics. The results show the need to revise the claims of sociologists Will Herberg and Ruby Jo Kennedy on the "triple-melting-pot" theory. Abramson shows that "the structural assimilation of Catholic-American sub-groups has not yet occurred, and shows no signs of doing so in the near future." Also, differences among Catholics in religious involvement are not generational, as assumed to now, but ethnic. In his second essay the author examines the "New Political History" of ethnicity and politics, praising Samuel Hays and his students for uncovering "The *local* basis of political commitment." National leaders, indeed, may run on "issues" which are anything but "real" ones, "real" meaning local, ethnocultural issues. Fox discusses other works relevant to this new approach, which stress that commitment to ethnic institutions may retard political "activity" but not political "identification," and point to the need for more research. 3 notes. G. J. Bobango

3741. Gaffey, James P. THE CHANGING OF THE GUARD: THE RISE OF CARDINAL O'CONNELL OF BOSTON. *Catholic Hist. Rev. 1973 59(2): 225-244.* After generations of upheaval and notable independence the Catholic Church in the United States entered a period of quietude and "Romanità." Critical changes within the episcopal leadership, largely unseen, contributed to this shift. One of the most important changes was the ascendancy of William Henry O'Connell (1859-1944), Boston's first cardinal. O'Connell came to Boston by way of the Eternal City and Portland, Maine, largely because of his special contacts at the Roman Curia during the pontificate of Pius X. His rapid advancement scandalized several of the ecclesiastical "Old Guard." In 1921 he succeeded Cardinal James Gibbons (1834-1921) as head of the American hierarchy. Despite his success, he was without effective authority as a national leader. Under Pius's successor, Benedict XV, Rome had virtually repudiated him, and the American hierarchy continued to distrust him as well. O'Connell thus represented a new spirit in the American Church akin to that of the classical Renaissance prince. He stressed a vigorous profession of loyalty to the Vatican and the creation of a formidable ecclesiastical presence. He was a devotee of the arts, publishing hymns and translations. Nevertheless, O'Connell was a misfit among his episcopal colleagues and in the midst of a Puritan society. A

3742. Gaffey, James P. PATTERNS OF ECCLESIASTICAL AUTHORITY: THE PROBLEMS OF THE CHICAGO SUCCESSION, 1865-1881. *Church Hist. 1973 42(2): 257-270.* Describes conflict between Chicago Bishop James Duggan and John McMullen (1832-85), president of the University of St. Mary by the Lake. McMullen and three associates complained to Cardinal Alessandro Barnabo, Congregation de Propaganda Fide, about Duggan's poor administration. St. Louis Archbishop Peter Kenrick supported Duggan in the ensuing investigations. Duggan suspended and banned the four from the Chicago Diocese, prompting a personal appeal to Rome by McMullen. New investigation by Baltimore Archbishop Martin Spalding failed to clear the accusers; Spalding, a traditionalist, did not wish to encourage challenges to local authority. After Duggan was committed to an asylum, Baltimore Chancellor Thomas Foley lifted the McMullen suspensions. McMullen was vindicated in 1881 when he was raised to the episcopacy. The episode illustrates Rome's administrative dependence upon accurate information, the clergy's confidence in Roman justice, and the irony of American bishops being more intolerant than Rome. Based on documents, letters, and secondary sources; 48 notes. S. Kerens

3743. Gagnon, Alain. L'INFLUENCE DE L'ÉGLISE SUR L'ÉVOLUTION SOCIO-ÉCONOMIQUE DU QUÉBEC, DE 1850 À 1950 [The Church's influence on the socioeconomic development of Quebec, 1850-1950]. *Action Natl. [Canada] 1979 69(4): 252-277.* Since 1760, and especially since the Union of 1840, the Catholic Church has dominated Quebec education, social service, cultural defense and economic life. It taught values clearly opposed to those of Anglo-Protestantism with unfortunate economic consequences. Ideologies of mission and agrarianism confirmed this backward tendency, as did a fatalistic acceptance of social inequality, a distrust of industrialism, and a quasi-obsessive fear of urban life. While the hierarchy did intervene in labor disputes and support the right of labor to organize, corporatism was the distinctive response of Quebec Catholicism to modernization. Table, 44 notes, biblio.
A. W. Novitsky

3744. Gannon, Thomas M. THE IMPACT OF STRUCTURAL DIFFERENCES ON THE CATHOLIC CLERGY. *J. for the Sci. Study of Religion 1979 18(4): 350-362.* Among diocesan priests and priests of religious orders, different career trajectories and lifestyles structure different perceptions of the priesthood, 1970's.

3745. Gavigan, Kathleen. THE RISE AND FALL OF PARISH COHESIVENESS IN PHILADELPHIA. *Records of the Am. Catholic Hist. Soc. of Philadelphia 1975 86(1-4): 107-131.* A special characteristic of the Catholic Church in Philadelphia, Pennsylvania, traditionally has been a strong identification with parish communities. This came about as a response to fear and insecurity, and the separation it provided created both strength and weakness for the Catholic community. Because, for many Catholics, the fears and insecurities have dissipated, the result is more vigorous participation in the community at large. Covers 1759-1975. 62 notes. J. M. McCarthy

3746. George, Joseph, Jr. PHILADELPHIA'S CATHOLIC HERALD: THE CIVIL WAR YEARS. *Pennsylvania Mag. of Hist. and Biog. 1979 103(2): 196-221.* Largely aimed at the Irish, the *Catholic Herald and Visitor* (renamed after 1864, *The Universe: The Catholic Herald and Visitor)* was suspicious of Republicans and unsympathetic to blacks, but always determined to support the war and avoid excessive partisanship. Based on Francis X. Reuss Papers, Ryan Memorial Library, Overbrook, Pennsylvania; "Cincinnati Papers, " University of Notre Dame Archives; other manuscripts, newspapers, printed sources, and secondary works; 58 notes. T. H. Wendel

3747. Gleason, Philip. IN SEARCH OF UNITY: AMERICAN CATHOLIC THOUGHT, 1920-1960. *Catholic Hist. Rev. 1979 65(2): 185-205.* Argues that the stress in integral faith in the period 1920 to 1960 heightened the disintegrative effects of postconciliar changes in American Catholicism. By "integral faith" is meant the Catholic religion understood as a unifying principle (intellectually, spiritually, socially, etc.) and as the inspiration of a Catholic culture. The article sketches symptoms of disintegration, surveys the broad outlines of the search for unity in the earlier period, and shows in greater detail how it affected American Catholic thinking on the role of philosophy and theology in undergraduate education. A

3748. Good, Patricia K. IRISH ADJUSTMENT TO AMERICAN SOCIETY: INTEGRATION OR SEPARATION? *Records of the Am. Catholic Hist. Soc. of Philadelphia 1975 86(1-4): 7-23.* Offers insights concerning Irish adjustment to American society by analyzing a late 19th-century Irish Catholic immigrant community in a borough of Pittsburgh. Their St. Andrew Parish fulfilled two major adaptation functions: it operated as an enclosive society supplying the manifest functions of spiritual instruction, sustenance, and consolation as well as the latent functions of mate and friendship choice, and opportunities to express nationalistic and psychological needs. Because its parishioners were able to express basic value orientations of the dominant society, it also stood as a model and means of successful acculturation and adaptation to the American environment. 25 notes. J. M. McCarthy

3749. Greeley, Andrew M. MARGINAL BUT NOT ALIENATED: CONFESSIONS OF A LOUDMOUTHED IRISH PRIEST. *Social Policy 1974 5(1): 4-11.* The author discusses being a Catholic priest and an intellectual in contemporary society.

3750. Griffiths, Naomi. ACADIANS IN EXILE: THE EXPERIENCES OF THE ACADIANS IN THE BRITISH SEAPORTS. *Acadiensis [Canada] 1974 4(1): 67-84.* Caught between the French and English, the Acadians of Nova Scotia remained neutral, developing their own distinctive character by the time of their dispersion in 1755. Those sent to England maintained their separate identity; French officials, emphasizing similarities in language and religion and ignoring cultural differences, saw these Acadians as dislocated loyal French and got them resettled in France in 1763. The Acadians proved unhappy, uncooperative and troublesome and many later emigrated to New Orleans. Based on materials in the British and French Archives, published primary and secondary sources; 86 notes. E. A. Churchill

3751. Haag, Herbert. THE ORIGINAL SIN DISCUSSION, 1966-1971. *J. of Ecumenical Studies 1973 10(2): 259-289.* A new interpretation of Roman Catholic theology appeared in 1967 with *A New Catechism,* popularly referred to as the Dutch Catechism. It questioned the idea that original sin was transmitted hereditarily, by stating simply that the doctrine describes a common guilt shared by all mankind. Haag describes the debate surrounding new interpretations of the doctrine by reference to the works of many Catholic theologians and claims that the traditional theological formulation of the doctrine should be revised. J. A. Overbeck

3752. Harrison, Michael I. THE MAINTENANCE OF ENTHUSIASM: INVOLVEMENT IN A NEW RELIGIOUS MOVEMENT. *Sociol. Analysis 1975 36(2): 150-160.* Religious revivals and renewal movements develop routinized forms of involvement and workable social structures if they are to sustain their participants' intense experiences of conversion and inspiration. From observational and questionnaire data on Catholic Pentecostalism, a highly successful renewal movement, this paper analyzes how such movements focus and sustain the participants' experiences of inspiration. Most participants in the Catholic Pentecostal Movement attend weekly Pentecostal prayer meetings, which are distinguished by their spontaneity, occurrences of speaking in tongues and prophecy, and a sense of direction by the Holy Spirit. Participants who attend other Pentecostal activities become immersed in Pentecostal friendship networks and lead intense devotional lives. Tolerance within the movement of diverse styles and varying degrees of involvement has facilitated broad recruitment. At the same time a sectarian core has emerged which embodies the movement's ideals, provides leadership and insures effective organization. These patterns of involvement appear to promote commitment to the movement in diverse, complementary ways. These various sources of commitment appear to be present in most successful social movements. Uses data for 1969. J

3753. Harrison, Michael I. SOURCES OF RECRUITMENT TO CATHOLIC PENTECOSTALISM. *J. for the Sci. Study of Religion 1974 13(1): 49-64.* Discusses the current popularity of Pentecostalism within the American Catholic Church and its appeal to college students, middle-class adults, and clergy.

3754. Hemmen, Alcuin. THE POST-VATICAN II THRUST OF AMERICAN BENEDICTINES. *Am. Benedictine Rev. 1976 27(4): 379-399.* Review article prompted by *Mönchtum und kirchlicher Heilsdienst, Entstehung und Entwicklung des nordamerikanischen Benediktinertums in 19. Jahrhundert* (1974) by Basil Doppelfeld, O.S.B., who presents and evaluates the history of the founding of St. Vincent Abbey and other abbeys by Abbot Boniface Wimmer and the founding of St. Meinrad Abbey and other abbeys by Benedictine monks from Switzerland. The reviewer concludes on the basis of Doppelfeld's study that American Benedictines must maintain the cenobitical tradition even as they exercise pastoral roles and missionary work in individual congregations. Primary and secondary sources; table, 41 notes. J. H. Pragman

3755. Hennesey, James. AMERICAN JESUIT IN WARTIME ROME: THE DIARY OF VINCENT A. MC CORMICK, S.J., 1942-1945. *Mid-America 1974 56(1): 32-55.* Brooklyn-born Vincent A. McCormick, a Jesuit since 1903, served in Rome from 1934 until after World War II. Among his few personal papers he left several small notebook diaries reflecting his life in Rome during 1942-45. While much of the material involves internal Jesuit matters, many entries refer to contemporary church and political affairs. Some critical remarks are directed toward the Holy See's stance toward the Fascist countries, and secular matters such as the Church's expressed concern at the damage to the San Lorenzo Basilica being more pronounced than its abhorrence of the loss of life from a bombing attack. His own deep loyalty to the Pope and the Church caused him much anguish, some of which is clearly expressed in the diary. Based on the diary and printed secondary sources; 40 notes. T. D. Schoonover

3756. Hennesey, James. SQUARE PEG IN A ROUND HOLE: ON BEING ROMAN CATHOLIC IN AMERICA. *Records of the Am. Catholic Hist. Soc. of Philadelphia 1973 84(4): 167-195.* Roman Catholicism is the largest single religious group in the United States, claiming over 48 million members in 1972. Against the background of the notion that the United States is a Protestant nation, the article seeks to clarify who Roman Catholics are, where they come from, and whether they do or have ever belonged. Covers 1776-1973. 143 notes. J. M. McCarthy

3757. Hill, Beth. THE SISTERS OF ST. ANN. *Alaska J. 1977 7(1): 40-45.* Describes the founding of the Sisters of St. Ann in 1850 and its development to the present. Includes anecdotes about these Catholic sisters, describes their hospital work, and discusses the removal of four of the nuns from Victoria, B.C., to Juneau in 1886. 8 illus., 2 notes. E. E. Eminhizer

3758. Hitchcock, James. THE EVOLUTION OF THE AMERICAN CATHOLIC LEFT. *Am. Scholar 1973-74 43(1): 66-84.* Compares the Catholic New Left of today with that of the 1950's when John Courtney Murray defended church and state separation. The most noted Catholic liberals of the 1960's and 1970's are the Jesuit Fathers Daniel Berrigan and Philip Berrigan. In contrast with Murray they have made a "reassertion of the central importance of religious values in political life, a denial that religion and politics can be separated in any real sense." The activist Catholic New Left has caused considerable confusion and demoralization in the American Catholic Church and has perhaps hastened the declericalization of the Church. The concern for the Gospels, sexual liberation, association with movements that are decidedly non-violent, and failure to preach to the Catholic masses has disturbed the rank-and-file and caused the Church to become more pluralistic. C. W. Olson

3759. Hitchcock, James. SECULAR CLERGY IN 19TH CENTURY AMERICA: A DIOCESAN PROFILE. *Records of the Am. Catholic Hist. Soc. of Philadelphia 1977 88(1-4): 31-62.* The history of the St. Louis archdiocesan clergy during 1841-99 provides a model by which comparative studies of other dioceses can be made, with a view to achieving a historical-sociological understanding of the American priesthood during the critical decades of immigration and gradual Americanization. 15 tables, 136 notes. J. M. McCarthy

3760. Hogan, Brian F. A CURRENT BIBLIOGRAPHY OF CANADIAN CHURCH HISTORY. *Study Sessions: Can. Catholic Hist. Assoc. [Canada] 1976 43: 91-119.* Groups work on Canadian church history according to the following categories: guides, church history, the communions, general works, regional history, institutions since 1800, individual biography and biographical material, religious practice and pastoral care, missions, and special problems.

3761. Horgan, Paul. HE GREW GARDENS IN THE EARTH AND IN THE HEARTS OF MEN. *Smithsonian 1975 6(5): 36-43.* Describes social customs, religion, and Indian-white relations at Santa Fe, New Mexico Territory, 1849-88, under the first American bishop of the Catholic Church there, Jean Baptiste Lamy.

3762. Horgan, Terence B. CARTA DEL ARZOBISPO DE NUEVA YORK, JOHN HUGHES, AL DE BOGOTA, MANUEL JOSE MOSQUERA [Letter from the Archbishop of New York, John Hughes, to that of Bogotá, Manuel José Mosquera]. *Bol. de Hist. y Antigüedades [Colombia] 1979 66(725): 217-234.* With a brief introduction, reproduces a letter of February 1853 from Archbishop John Hughes of New York City to the exiled prelate of Bogotá, answering the latter's queries about the status of the Catholic Church in the United States. Archives of the Archdiocese of New York; 7 notes. Reproduction in Spanish and English. D. Bushnell

3763. Huber, August Kurt. JOHN N. NEUMANN'S STUDENT YEARS IN PRAGUE, 1833-1835. *Records of the Am. Catholic Hist. Soc. of Philadelphia 1978 89(1-4): 3-32.* Examination of Saint John Nepomucene Neumann's diary and letters as well as of documents of the Prague seminary archives and the archive of the Theological Faculty of Prague modifies the traditional picture of Neumann's theological and spiritual formation and highlights the crises and problems of his development. This article appeared originally in *Archiv für Kirchengeschichte von Bohmen-Mahren-Schlesien* (1971). 87 notes.
J. M. McCarthy

3764. Huel, Raymond. THE FRENCH LANGUAGE PRESS IN WESTERN CANADA: *LE PATRIOTE DE L'OUEST,* 1910-41. *Rev. de l'Universite d'Ottawa [Canada] 1976 46(4): 476-499.* The newspaper *Le Patriote de l'Ouest* was founded in Saskatchewan in 1910 with the encouragement of the Roman Catholic bishop and clergy, who regarded the maintenance of the French language and of the Catholic faith as inseparable. *Le Patriote* was located at first in remote Duck Lake, and after 1913 in Regina. The newspaper faced constant financial difficulties. It had to be subsidized constantly by Catholic clergymen, and had a difficult time capturing the imagination of French-speakers in Saskatchewan. In 1933, the Oblates of Mary Immaculate of the Province of Alberta-Saskatchewan took over the newspaper and its publishing company to save it from the Depression. In 1941, *Le Patriote* was merged with *La Liberté* of Winnipeg in the hope that the new, merged journal would survive and help preserve the French language in the West. 142 notes.
J. C. Billigmeier

3765. Huel, Raymond. THE IRISH-FRENCH CONFLICT IN CATHOLIC EPISCOPAL NOMINATIONS: THE WESTERN SEES AND THE STRUGGLE FOR DOMINATION WITHIN THE CHURCH. *Study Sessions: Can. Catholic Hist. Assoc. 1975 42: 51-69.* Describes the bitter competition and internal rivalry between the French-speaking minority and the aggressive Irish Catholics in western Canada for ascendancy in the hierarchy of the Church, showing how the problem went beyond episcopal nomination to concern the nature of Catholicism in Canadian society today (1900-75).

3766. Hurtubise, Pierre. NI JANSENIST, NI GALLICAN, NI ULTRAMONTAIN: FRANÇOIS DE LAVAL [Neither Jansenist, nor Gallican, nor Ultramontane: François de Laval]. *Rev. d'Hist. de l'Amérique Française [Canada] 1974 28(1): 3-26.* Attempts to place the late-17th-century bishop of Quebec, François de Laval, in relationship to the men and ideas of his time, particularly Jansenism and Ultramontanism.

3767. Jaenen, Cornelius J. FRENCH COLONIAL ATTITUDES AND THE EXPLORATION OF JOLLIET AND MARQUETTE. *Wisconsin Mag. of Hist. 1973 56(4): 300-310.* Discusses the explorations of Jolliet and Marquette in the context of French colonial and imperial administration of Louis XIV and Colbert. Although the two explorers had to finance their own expedition, they were expected to extend the French sphere of influence, act as diplomats and Indian negotiators, serve as consultants to the government, increase French geographical knowledge, and minister to the spiritual needs of Indians and colonists. After briefly discussing the separate careers of Jolliet and Marquette, the author traces their historic voyage and concludes with their activities following the exploration of the Mississippi River. Illus., 25 notes.
N. C. Burckel

3768. Johnson, C. Lincoln and Weigert, Andrew J. AN EMERGING FAITHSTYLE: A RESEARCH NOTE ON THE CATHOLIC CHARISMATIC RENEWAL. *Sociol. Analysis 1978 39(2): 165-172.* A survey of a random sample of persons drawn from a national mailing list of Charismatic Services provides background characteristics and attitudinal orientations of Catholic Charismatics toward CCR, society, and the Catholic Church. CCR is not a potential schismatic movement. Rather it appears to be an emergent faithstyle: an alternative answering to a combination of ethical and psychic deprivation experienced by some members of the Catholic Church. Selected comparisons are made with Fichter's earlier study of Catholic Charismatics.
J

3769. Juárez, José Roberto. LA IGLESIA CATÓLICA Y EL CHICANO EN SUD TEXAS, 1836-1911. [The Catholic Church and the Chicano in southern Texas, 1836-1911]. *Aztlán 1973 4(2): 217-255.*

3770. Juliani, Richard J. CHURCH RECORDS AS SOCIAL DATA: THE ITALIANS IN PHILADELPHIA IN THE NINETEENTH CENTURY. *Records of the Am. Catholic Hist. Soc. of Philadelphia 1974 85(1-2): 3-16.* Despite problems of completeness, coverage, and availability, church records can provide fragmentary information on the size and growth of the immigrant community, its duration in the place, occupations of individuals, and their origins in the home country and intentions in the new. They can also provide clues to infant mortality rates and to relations of immigrants with the larger society, and keys to the study of other materials. 24 notes. J. M. McCarthy

3771. Kantowich, Edward. CHURCH AND NEIGHBORHOOD. *Ethnicity 1980 7(4): 349-366.* Examines the role of the Catholic Church in Chicago as a neighborhood institution, ca. 1900-30. Catholics in Chicago, as in the Old World, built their community (or now neighborhood) around the Church. The Church location and national policies of the Catholic Church aided this development. 5 tables, 3 maps, 23 notes.
T. W. Smith

3772. Karlin, Athanasius. THE COMING OF THE FIRST VOLGA GERMAN CATHOLICS TO AMERICA: REWRITTEN FROM A DIARY STARTED FEBRUARY 8, 1887. *J. of the Am. Hist. Soc. of Germans from Russia 1978 1(3): 61-69.* Excerpts of a diary by Athanasius Karlin describing events leading up to his family's emigration from Russia to the United States in 1875, and their earliest experiences in the United States.

3773. Kessell, John L. A MAN CAUGHT BETWEEN TWO WORLDS: DIEGO ROMERO, THE PLAINS APACHES, AND THE INQUISITION. *Am. West 1978 15(3): 12-16.* The governor of Santa Fe, New Mexico, sent Captain Diego Romero (d. 1678) with a packtrain of trade merchandise to the Plains Apache Indians in Texas. The object of the 1660 expedition was to obtain prime buffalo hides and tanned skins. Romero's father had been an honored trader with the Apache so they made him an honorary "captain" also. The ceremony, a probable "marriage" to an Apache maiden, and his relations with other Apache women became the basis for a multiple indictment by the Mexican Inquisition in 1663. He was charged, among other things, with denying the spiritual authority of the priests and deprecating the position of Franciscan missionaries. sentence included banishment from New Mexico for ten years. Before the exile terminated he married under an assumed name. The Inquisition caught up with the "incorrigible backslider" again and sentenced him to six years in the galleys. He died in a Mexican jail while waiting for his first galley assignment. Bibliographic note, 2 illus.
D. L. Smith

3774. Kindermann, A. BÖHMERWALDSOHN UND BISCHOF VON PHILADELPHIA JOHANN NEP. NEUMANN SELIGGESPROCHEN [John Neumann, born in the Bohemian Forest, Bishop of Philadelphia, beatified]. *Sudetenland [West Germany] 1964 6(1): 49-66.* Presents a biography of John Neumann, a Sudeten German, born 28 March 1811 in Prachatitz (now Prachatice, Czechoslovakia), Bohemian Forest. He emigrated to America, joined the order of Redemptorists in 1840 and died 5 January 1860 in Philadelphia, Pennsylvania. Describes his missionary work in America since 1836, posthumous miraculous healings through his intercession, and beatification in March 1963. English summary; illus., 12 notes. N. Frenkley

3775. Kirley, Kevin. A SEMINARY RECTOR IN ENGLISH CANADA DURING AND AFTER THE SECOND VATICAN COUNCIL. *Study Sessions: Can. Catholic Hist. Assoc. [Canada] 1976 43: 57-74.* Surveys the state of the Catholic Church in Toronto before and after Pope John XXIII convoked Vatican Council II in Rome, records some of the rapid and profound transformation in Canada during the Council, 1962-65, and examines the Council's influence on St. Basil's Seminary 1964-67.

3776. Kirschbaum, J. M. JESUITS FIND A HOME IN CANADA. *Jednota Ann. Furdek 1977 16: 107-109.* Jesuits from Czechoslovakia came to Canada in 1950 following the dissolution of religious communities under Communism.

3777. Koller, Douglas B. BELIEF IN THE RIGHT TO QUESTION CHURCH TEACHINGS, 1958-71. *Social Forces 1979 58(1): 290-304.* Between 1958 and 1971 there was a pronounced increase in belief in the right to question church teachings among Detroit Catholics, but there was no significant change among Protestants in general. Certain events calling into question the infallibility of papal pronouncements in the 1960's are suggested as possible forces behind the increase among Catholics. The magnitude of the change is inversely related to age and directly related to education and church attendance. 2 tables, 5 fig., biblio. J

3778. Kring, Hilda Adam. THE CULT OF ST. WALBURGA IN PENNSYLVANIA. *Pennsylvania Folklife 1974-75 24(2): 2-7.* Discusses the history of eighth-century St. Walburga, patron saint of Eichstätt, Germany and of St. Joseph's Convent (1852) in St. Marys, Elk County, which is principally responsible for the continued veneration of her in 20th-century Pennsylvania. S

3779. Kutz, Jack. THE WHIP AND THE CROSS. *Mankind 1974 4(7): 36-40, 60-61.* Traces can still be found of the extra-legal order of flagellants, Los Hermanos Penitentes del Tercer Order de Franciscanos; covers the 13th-20th centuries. S

3780. LaBrèque, Marie-Paule. LES ÉGLISES DANS LES CANTONS DE L'EST, 1800-1860 [The churches in the Eastern Townships, 1800-1860]. *Sessions d'Étude: Soc. Can. d'Hist. de l'Eglise Catholique 1974 41: 87-103.* A history of the establishment of churches in the Eastern Townships of Quebec, including the great material obstacles and the psychological and moral difficulties faced in French settlement. Analyzes the problem of maintaining French education and religion in the isolated colony after the establishment of other settlers (American, Scotch, Irish). Studies the decline of colonization and validity of French rule on Anglo-Saxon land. Describes the establishment of Catholicism and the propagation of the faith under various bishops. Regional and diocesan archives and secondary sources; 49 notes. S. Sevilla

3781. Lalonde, André N. ARCHBISHOP O. E. MATHIEU AND FRANCOPHONE IMMIGRATION TO THE ARCHDIOCESE OF REGINA. *Study Sessions: Can. Catholic Hist. Assoc. [Canada] 1977 44: 45-60.* Olivier-Elzéar Mathieu, Archbishop of the Regina Archdiocese during 1911-31, promoted the immigration of Catholic French Canadians, French, and Americans to Canada's Prairie Provinces, especially Manitoba and Saskatchewan.

3782. Langlais, Antonio. MESSIEURS DE SAINT-SULPICE DEVANT LE CONSEIL SOUVERAIN EN 1667 (LEUR TITRES DE PROPRÍETÉ) [The gentlemen of Saint-Sulpice before the Sovereign Council in 1667: their titles of property]. *Rev. d'Hist. de l'Amérique Française [Canada] 1957 11(3): 393-399.* In 1667, the Sovereign Council, a judicial body in French Canada, confirmed the members of the Compagnie de Saint-Sulpice (the Sulpician order) in possession of property to which they held titles.

3783. Laperrière, Guy. L'ÉGLISE ET L'ARGENT: LES QUÊTES COMMANDÉES DANS LE DIOCÈSE DE SHERBROOKE, 1893-1926 [The church and money: the collections ordered in the diocese of Sherbrooke, 1893-1926]. *Sessions d'Etude Soc. Can. d'Hist. de l'Eglise Catholique 1974 41: 61-86.* Studies the financial sources of the Church in the Quebec diocese of Sherbrooke, based on the collections ordered during the episcopate of Bishop Paul LaRocque. Seeks an explanation for changes in church income and in financial administration. Draws conclusions on the development of the population and agricultural production during this time, as well as on the mentality and the religiousness of the ministers and congregation. Based on diocesan archives and secondary sources; 4 tables, 11 graphs, 55 notes. S. Sevilla

3784. Lauer, Robert H. SOCIALIZATION INTO INEQUALITY: CHILDREN'S PERCEPTION OF OCCUPATIONAL STATUS. *Sociol. and Social Res. 1974 58(2): 176-183.* Occupational status rankings are quite stable, indicating a socialization process. But little work has been done on developmental aspects of stratification. The present research shows the development of and rationale for status perceptions. By grade two, both Catholic and public school pupils are well socialized to accept inequality, and rank occupations accurately in accord with adult values. By grade four, they legitimate the ranking. Public school children gave an increasing (with grade level) emphasis on ability required for occupations and a greater emphasis on income, while Catholic children gave an increasing emphasis on income and a greater emphasis on functions of work. J

3785. Lavallée, Jean-Guy. L'ÉGLISE DE SHERBROOKE ET LES TRAPPISTES (1880-1948) [The Sherbrooke Church and the Trappists]. *Sessions d'Étude: Société Can. d'Histoire de l'Église Catholique [Canada] 1974 41: 9-24.* A history of relations between the Sherbrooke Church and the Trappist Order. Touches on the great anticlerical and secular crises in France in the 19th and 20th centuries, the internal structure and formation of the Order, and broader problems such as the emigration of French-Canadians to the United States, their repatriation in Quebec, and the colonization of less developed regions of the province. The Trappists failed in their attempt to establish a permanent order in Quebec. Based on Archives of the Sherbrooke Arch-diocese; 41 notes. S. Sevilla

3786. Lee, Ellen K. THE CATHOLIC MODJESKA. *Polish Am. Studies 1974 31(1): 20-27.* Describes the great Shakesperean actress, Helena Modrzejewska [or Modjeska, as she anglicized the name]. She came to San Francisco in 1876, at the age of 36, with her husband, son, and a small group of friends hoping to establish a Polish colony near Los Angeles. Though she was recognized in Russian Poland through her association with the Imperial Theater of Warsaw, the language barrier delayed her rise to fame in the United States. Deals mostly with services rendered for the small Catholic churches which she attended. Includes an account of a confrontation in Santa Ana, California in 1897 between Madame Modjeska and the American Protective Association. 23 notes. S. R. Pliska

3787. LeMoignan, Michel. LA VISION AUDACIEUSE DE MGR. F.-X. ROSS, PREMIER ÉVÊQUE DE GASPÉ [The audacious vision of Monsignor F.-X. Ross, first bishop of Gaspé]. *Sessions d'Étude: Soc. Can. d'Hist. de l'Église Catholique [Canada] 1976 43: 35-47.* A biography of Bishop-founder François Xavier Ross (1869-1945), emphasizing his contributions to the educational system, medical facilities, and socioeconomic organization of Gaspé and its environs, 1923-45, and stressing the importance of his writings to the historian.

3788. Leonard, Henry B. ETHNIC CONFLICT AND EPISCOPAL POWER: THE DIOCESE OF CLEVELAND, 1847-1870. *Catholic Hist. Rev. 1976 62(3): 388-407.* In the Diocese of Cleveland the competing socioreligious desires of immigrant groups were frequently divisive. Louis Amadeus Rappe, Cleveland's first bishop, was a staunch Americanizer and an authoritarian administrator who resisted the demands of German and Irish Catholics for separate parishes and schools served by priests of their own nationality, stirred ethnic antagonisms, and raised a fundamental question concerning the proper limits to episcopal authority. By 1870 the diocese had become so disrupted by the issues of ethnicity and authority that Bishop Rappe was forced to resign his office. A

3789. Lévesque, Delmas. L'EXPÉRIENCE QUÉBÉCOIS [The Quebec experience]. *Action Natl. [Canada] 1978 68(2): 91-115.* I. ESSAI SUR NOTRE CULTURE [Part I. Essay on our culture]. Demography has been a major factor in Quebec history: on an anglicized continent, there are only 6,000,000 Quebecois descended from 10,000 immigrants. The collective psyche has also been dominated by the immensity of the land, rigorous climate, abundant natural resources, and a sense of isolation and dependence. Major events included the British conquest, the rebellion of the 1830's, the great depression of the 1930's, and the quiet revolution of the 1960's. While Quebec has been an urban province since the 1920's, only in the 1950's did the contradictions between traditional institutions and society appear. While the clergy were a major factor in maintaining a French identity, their power was destroyed by the resulting transformation. Primary and secondary sources; 6 notes. Part II. The preservation of French traditions in the face of modernization depends on the provincial government of Quebec, a revitalized Catholicism, and cooperative economic institutions. 7 notes. A. W. Novitsky

3790. Lévesque, Georges-Henri. PRÉLUDE À LA RÉVOLUTION TRANQUILLE AU QUÉBEC: NOTES NOUVELLES SUR D'ANCIENS INSTRUMENTS [Prelude to the quiet revolution in Quebec: New notes on old instruments]. *Social Hist. [Canada] 1977 10(19): 134-146.* Personal comments on the historical background to the "quiet revolution" in Quebec. From its founding in 1903 until the 1930's the A.C.J.C. was the only movement of young French Canadians. Its focus was on both Catholicism and nationalism. The dual emphasis was not compatible with the needs of the 1930's, and purely nationalist and purely Catholic youth

movements were formed. The author adopted the nationalist position, and a major controversy developed over an article he planned to publish outlining these views in the *Revue Dominicaine* in 1935. 10 notes.
W. K. Hobson

3791. Little, J. I. THE PARISH AND FRENCH CANADIAN MIGRANTS TO COMPTON, QUEBEC, 1851-1891. *Social Hist. [Canada] 1978 11(21): 134-143.* The Catholic Church in Quebec clearly wanted a society of small independent landowners because of fear that landless laborers would eventually abandon French and Catholicism. In Compton County rural communities were the most stable and homogeneous, reinforcing this bias, but the parish was still an effective institution in towns and where French Canadian farmers were a minority. Studies of a colonization parish, a mixed rural parish, and an industrial parish confirm this. 30 notes. D. F. Chard

3792. Little, John I. LA PATRIE: QUEBEC'S REPATRIATION COLONY, 1875-1880. *Can. Hist. Assoc. Hist. Papers [Canada] 1977: 66-85.* A study of the reaction of Quebec's lay and clerical leaders to the massive exodus of French-speaking Canadians to the United States in the second half of the 19th century. The antidote promoted was reform of the land-holding system, building of colonization roads, and establishing new settlements. To encourage return from New England, the new ministry in 1874 launched its repatriation colony society proposing use of crown lands. Investigates the nature of the considerations involved, how practical were they, and what religious and agrarian values entered into the structuring and operation of the colonies. The Repatriation Act (1875) became the basis for implementation, with the village of La Patrie as headquarters and Jérôme-Adolphe Chicoyne in charge. The effort was only a partial success, for a variety of reasons. 111 notes.
R. V. Ritter

3793. Luebke, Frederick C. CHURCH HISTORY FROM THE BOTTOM UP. *Rev. in Am. Hist. 1976 4(1): 68-72.* Review article prompted by Jay P. Dolan's *The Immigrant Church: New York's Irish and German Catholics, 1815-1865* (Baltimore, Maryland: Johns Hopkins U. Pr., 1975) which discusses the social aspects of religious establishment among ethnic groups.

3794. MacGregor-Villarreal, Mary. CELEBRATING *LAS POSADAS* IN LOS ANGELES. *Western Folklore 1980 39(2): 71-105.* Describes four public *posadas* (traditional Hispanic Christmas celebrations in which the journey of Joseph and Mary to Bethlehem is dramatized) in the Los Angeles neighborhoods of San Gabriel Mission, Pico Adobe, Plaza de la Raza, and Olvera Street. The author compares public and home *posadas,* then analyzes the reasons for presenting public *posadas,* the kinds of modifications necessary for a public event, the conceptions of the organizers, and the basis for their success. Based on field research and interviews; 16 photos, 41 notes, glossary. S. L. Myres

3795. Mahone, Rene C. BIOGRAPHY OF GUAM'S FIRST KNIGHT OF THE CHURCH: DON PEDRO MARTINEZ. *Guam Recorder 1975 5(1): 16-21.* Life of Pedro Martinez, an important citizen of Guam and Catholic, 1909-67.

3796. Matejko, Joanna and Matejko, Alexander. POLISH PIONEERS IN THE CANADIAN PRAIRIES. *Ethnicity 1978 5(4): 351-369.* In the late 1920's Poles became numerically significant in Canada when they totaled about 2.2% of the population. Their importance was considerable in rural areas of Manitoba, Alberta, and Saskatchewan where they began settling during the 1890's. Not considered desirable immigrants by the majority population, the Poles endured prejudice, discrimination, and extreme economic hardship in their early years of settlement. They clung to the Catholic Church as their major social institution. Early good relations with their Ukrainian immigrant neighbors deteriorated following the rise in nationalism during World War I and after. The Depression had a devastating impact on the Polish Canadians in the Prairie Provinces. Many lost their land and moved to urban areas to find work. Those who remained eventually found economic well-being in the 1940's and later. Primary, secondary and oral interview sources. N. Lederer

3797. Matthies, Katherine. CHARLES CARROLL OF CARROLLTON. *Daughters of the Am. Revolution Mag. 1976 110(3): 300-304, 368.* An account of the life of the Maryland patriot (1737-1832).

3798. Maurault, Olivier. LES DIVERS MOTIFS QUI ONT AMENÉ SAINT-SULPICE A MONTRÉAL [The diverse motives which led Saint-Sulpice to Montreal]. *Rev. d'Hist. de l'Amérique Française [Canada] 1957 11(1): 3-9.* Discusses the motives which led the Compagnie de Saint-Sulpice (the Sulpician order) to establish itself in the new French settlement of Montreal in the 1630's-50's, stressing the role of Jean Jacques Olier.

3799. McDonnell, Kilian. THE CATHOLIC CHARISMATIC RENEWAL: REASSESSMENT AND CRITIQUE. *Religion in Life 1975 44(2): 138-154.* Assesses the pentecostal movement in the Catholic Church since 1967. S

3800. McGinty, Brian. THE GREEN & THE GOLD. *Am. West 1978 15(2): 18-21, 65-69.* In the wake of the potato famine in Ireland and the gold discovery in California, thousands of impoverished farmers and artisans migrated to California. By 1860 Irish Americans constituted more than one-fifth of the foreign-born population. Their religious fervor, their passion for politics, and their involvement in the arts left indelible impressions on the history of the Far West. 9 illus., biblio.
D. L. Smith

3801. McGloin, John Bernard. FATHER FLAVIAN FONTAINE AND A COLLEGE OF SORROWS. *Pacific Historian 1973 17(4): 1-12.* Presents the work of Flavian Fontaine who served the Catholic Church at Mission Dolores in San Francisco, 1850-53. S

3802. McGuire, Meredith B. AN INTERPRETIVE COMPARISON OF ELEMENTS OF THE PENTECOSTAL AND UNDERGROUND CHURCH MOVEMENTS IN AMERICAN CATHOLICISM. *Sociol. Analysis 1974 35(1): 57-65.* The underground church and the Catholic pentecostal movement are very different from each other in the substance of their dissent from the rest of the church and society, yet both group-movements are both middle-class in their appeal—thus defying standard sociological explanations based on social and economic deprivation. This comparative study attempts to find and interpret the differences between the underground church movement and the pentecostal movement in American Catholicism. A longitudinal research of sixteen underground groups in Northern New Jersey was conducted from 1969 to 1973, and five pentecostal groups in the same area were studied from 1971 to 1973. The focus of the comparisons was upon economic factors, social status factors, and attitudinal and social-psychological factors. There were few—if any—economic or social status factors found to differentiate the two movements. Social-psychological aspects (especially differential responses to ambiguity and change) appeared to be far more important explanations for the dissimilarity between the two types of groups. J

3803. McKeown, Elizabeth. APOLOGIA FOR AN AMERICAN CATHOLICISM: THE PETITION AND REPORT OF THE NATIONAL CATHOLIC WELFARE COUNCIL TO PIUS XI, APRIL 1922. *Church Hist. 1974 43(4): 514-528.* The 1922 National Catholic Welfare Council Petition and Report to Pius XI is a protest by American bishops against a decree of suppression issued by the Consistorial Congregation of the Vatican, the effect of which would have been the destruction of the newly organized Welfare Council. The formal protest has two parts: a petition to Pius asking for a re-examination of the decision to suppress the Welfare Council, and a report on the activities of the council, its usefulness to the leadership of the Church, and the impossibility of adequately replacing it should the suppression remain in effect. Both the Petition and the Report are rich sources for an examination of the self-image of American Catholicism as it was projected by a significant element of the American hierarchy in 1922. 7 notes. M. D. Dibert

3804. McQuillan, D. Aidan. FRENCH-CANADIAN COMMUNITIES IN THE AMERICAN UPPER MIDWEST DURING THE NINETEENTH CENTURY. *Cahiers de Géographie du Québec [Canada] 1979 23(58): 53-72.* Discusses French-Canadian settlement during the 19th century in Michigan, Illinois, Kansas, and Minnesota and stresses the variance in keeping the use of French, their cultural heritage, and affiliation with the Catholic Church.

3805. Melville, Annabelle M. JOHN CARROLL AND LOUISIANA, 1803-1815. *Catholic Hist. Rev. 1978 64(3): 398-440.* Investigates the relations between John Carroll, Bishop of Baltimore, and his flock in

Louisiana, which suddenly became an American possession in 1803. Primary sources are few, the issues involved were peripheral, and the various personalities in the new territory were contradictory to the extreme. Essentially, Bishop Carroll was concerned to put religious affairs in Louisiana in order, but the various ethnic and political forces each wanted effective power. Bishop Carroll could do little but issue orders which on the wild frontier were ignored more often than not. Curiously, the eventual settlement of the prime issue of ecclesiastical control did not evolve until the year of Bishop Carroll's death, and history does not reveal whether he lived to know of it. 176 notes. V. L. Human

3806. Mensing, Raymond C., Jr. THE RISE AND FALL OF THE PSEUDO POOR CLARE NUNS OF SKIDAWAY ISLAND. *Georgia Hist. Q. 1977 61(4): 318-328.* Details an unsuccessful attempt by four English and Irish women, supposedly of the Poor Clare order, to establish an orphanage and boarding school for black children on Skidaway Island in 1885 by invitation of the Bishop of Savannah, William H. Gross. The nuns were undisciplined and the financial situation was disastrous, leading Bishop Thomas A. Becker to dismiss them in 1887. Primary and secondary sources; 39 notes. G. R. Schroeder

3807. Moberg, David O. and McEnery, Jean N. CHANGES IN CHURCH-RELATED BEHAVIOR AND ATTITUDES OF CATHOLIC STUDENTS, 1961-1971. *Sociol. Analysis 1976 37(1): 53-62.* The Marquette Study of Student Values analyzes religious practices, moral values, and attitudes among Catholic college students. From 1961 to 1971 decreasing frequency of student attendance at Mass and Confession together with attitudinal changes toward religious practices are evident. Changes in attitudes about dating, decreased scrupulosity in areas of personal honesty and responsibility, looser attitudes toward selected items of personal morality, and increased consideration for others also were revealed. Most changes may be interpreted as reflecting decreased compliance with traditional Church norms, increased conformity to values of American society, and conflicting values related to both cultural pluralism and pluralism within the Catholic Church. J

3808. Moberg, David O. and McEnery, Jean N. PRAYER HABITS AND ATTITUDES OF CATHOLIC STUDENTS. *Social Sci. 1976 51(2): 76-85.* Although prayer is found in all cultures and is a very common practice in America, it has received little attention in the sociology of religion. This paper reports selected aspects of the subject, including data from a survey of Catholic college students in 1961 and 1971. The frequency of prayer diminished sharply over the decade, and the reasons for praying shifted toward increased desire to converse with God, but the rank order of four reasons for praying remained the same. Several possible interpretations and implications of the findings are suggested. J

3809. Morissonneau, Christian. LA COLONISATION ÉQUIVOQUE [An uncertain colonization]. *Recherches Sociographiques [Canada] 1978 19(1): 33-53.* The colonist who opened up the Mattawinie district of Quebec formed part of a nomadic tradition that goes back to the early history of French Canada. This tradition was integrated into the geopolitical strategy, the religious project, and the economic development plan of Father T. S. Provost. Covers 17c-1890. Based on the writings of T. S. Provost and other primary and secondary sources; 27 notes. A. E. LeBlanc

3810. Nelsen, Hart M. and Allen, H. David. ETHNICITY, AMERICANIZATION, AND RELIGIOUS ATTENDANCE. *Am. J. of Sociol. 1974 79(4): 906-922.* Two trends in the pattern of Americanization of immigrant groups are noted, one involving decreased second-generation religious interest due to alienation from the ethnic tradition and the other showing an increase in attendance at worship services from first to second generation due to the prominence of religion in American culture. It is suggested, upon a review of the literature, that the pattern of second-generation attendance depends on the extent of difference between the ethnic culture and the dominant American culture. In a secondary analysis of data on New York City Catholics, the respondents are grouped into western, eastern, and southern European categories based on country of origin. There are no meaningful differences in religious attendance among first-generation Catholics; among second-generation respondents there are substantial differences. Western Europeans show an increase in attendance from first to second generation, while southern Europeans show a decrease. It is concluded that the meltingpot concept of assimilation fails to take into account interethnic variations in patterns of Americanization. J

3811. Neri, Michael C. GONZALEZ RUBIO AND CALIFORNIA CATHOLICISM, 1846-1850. *Southern California Q. 1976 58(4): 441-457.* Assesses the work of Father José González Rubio (1804-75), who as governor of the mitre (diocesan administrator) for Upper and Lower California presided over the shift from Mexican to American law and culture during 1846-50. González Rubio faced such problems as intermarriage of Protestants and Catholics, the need for tithing, and a shortage of qualified priests. He believed the mission lands rightfully belonged to the Indians and that Church possessions would be fairly adjudicated by the United States. At the end of his tenure Californians commissioned a painting of him in appreciation of his efforts on their behalf. It is at Mission Santa Barbara. In a time of uncertainty and transition, González Rubio helped the Catholic Church to survive in California. Primary and secondary sources; 63 notes. A. Hoffman

3812. Noone, Bernard. AMERICAN CATHOLIC PERIODICALS AND THE BIBLICAL QUESTION, 1893-1908. *Records of the Am. Catholic Hist. Soc. of Philadelphia 1978 89(1-4): 85-108.* Identifies some of the factors stimulating interest among turn-of-the-century American Catholics in new critical approaches to the Bible. The body of the article surveys treatments of Pentateuch criticism in American Catholic periodicals and presents some general conclusions. 69 notes. J. M. McCarthy

3813. Obidinski, Eugene. THE LOS ANGELES POLONIA. *Polish Am. Studies 1974 31(2): 43-47.* Reviews Neil C. Sandberg's *Ethnic Identity and Assimilation: The Polish-American Community Case Study of Metropolitan Los Angeles* (New York: Praeger, 1974). Discusses the use of "survey research rather than content analysis of documents and symbols," and the delineation of ethnicity in terms of cultural, religious, and national aspects. However, the detailed analysis of methodology with emphasis on the group cohesiveness scale will interest only the sociologist. Covers 1968-74. S. R. Pliska

3814. O'Brien, Miriam. HOOKWORM AND HIBISCUS: THE PHILADELPHIA CONNECTION. *Records of the Am. Catholic Hist. Soc. of Philadelphia 1974 85(3-4): 208-219.* Summarizes the careers of William A. Jones, George J. Caruana, and Edwin V. Byrne. They were Catholic bishops of the Diocese of San Juan, Puerto Rico. Covers 1866-1963. 28 notes. J. M. McCarthy

3815. Oetgen, Jerome, O.S.B. BONIFACE WIMMER AND THE AMERICAN BENEDICTINES. *Am. Benedictine Rev. 1973 24(1): 1-28, 1974 25(1): 1-32.* Continued from a previous article. Part II. Reviews the work (1866-76) of Abbot Wimmer of St. Vincent's in Latrobe, Pennsylvania, in directing the growth of the Benedictines in the United States during the decade after the Civil War. Reviews Abbot Wimmer's participation in Vatican Council I and his understanding of papal infallibility. Based on original documents and secondary sources; 79 notes. Part III. Discusses the missions-minded Abbot Wimmer's direction and expansion of the mission of the Benedictines in America until his death in 1887. 87 notes. J. H. Pragman

3816. Oetgen, Jerome. OSWALD MOOSMÜLLER: MONK AND MISSIONARY. *Am. Benedictine Rev. 1976 27(1): 1-35.* Oswald Moosmüller exemplified the tension between 19th-century Benedictines' missionary zeal and the standards of traditional monastic observance. Moosmüller spent the first part of his monastic life as a missionary serving German Catholic immigrants. Later, he supported the contemplative ideal more vigorously, but his effort to exemplify that ideal at New Cluny in Southern Illinois was a failure. Based on primary and secondary sources; 71 notes. J. H. Pragman

3817. Ousley, Stanley. THE KENTUCKY IRISH AMERICAN. *Filson Club Hist. Q. 1979 53(2): 178-195.* The *Kentucky Irish American,* a Louisville newspaper, was founded in 1898. Until the end of World War I it centered its attention on ethnic and nationalist themes. After 1900 the paper increasingly was "Catholic in orientation and outlook." After 1930 the *Irish American* strongly supported the programs of the Democratic Party. The paper was forced to shut down in 1968. 69 notes. G. M. McKinney

3818. Packard, Hyland B. FROM KILKENNY: THE BACKGROUND OF AN INTELLECTUAL IMMIGRANT. *Éire-Ireland 1975 10(3): 106-125.* Biography of Francis Hackett, noted immigrant intellectual and literary critic covers his early years in Kilkenny and Clongowes Wood, Ireland, 1880's-1901, emphasizing the role of the Catholic Church and education on his later career in the United States.

3819. Painchaud, Robert. FRENCH-CANADIAN HISTORIOGRAPHY AND FRANCO-CATHOLIC SETTLEMENT IN WESTERN CANADA, 1870-1915. *Can. Hist. Rev. [Canada] 1978 59(4): 447-466.* Critically analyzes the usual explanations for the large number of French Canadians who quit Quebec, to become not homesteaders in the Canadian Prairies but rather factory workers in New England or farmers in the American West. It has been common to attribute this to discriminatory measures and attitudes on the part of English Canadians to discourage settlement in western Canada. However such explanations are far too simple, not recognizing the complexity of the forces at work. Nor can it be attributed only to the lack of support of Catholic coreligionists in Quebec. The disagreements indicate a need to reassess the motivations and conclusions which underlie Quebec historiography on the subject. 60 notes. R. V. Ritter

3820. Passi, Michael M. MYTH AS HISTORY, HISTORY AS MYTH: FAMILY AND CHURCH AMONG ITALO-AMERICANS. *J. of Ethnic Studies 1975 3(2): 97-103.* Reviews Silvano Tomasi's *Piety and Power: The Role of the Italian Parishes in the New York Metropolitan Area, 1880-1930* (1975), Richard Gambino's *Blood of My Blood: The Dilemma of the Italian Americans* (1974), and Carla Bianco's *The Two Rosetos* (1974). All three attempt to explain the nature of Italian-American society. Tomasi finds the core to be the Catholic Church and its ethnic parishes, Gambino sees the family system as the central element, and Bianco tackles the issue by comparing Rosetos, Italy, with its namesake in Pennsylvania. Of these three finds Bianco's to be the most illuminating and promising. 14 notes. T. W. Smith

3821. Paučo, Joseph. JOHN SABOL—"MR. JEDNOTA." *Jednota Ann. Furdek 1977 16: 23-27.* John Sabol was elected supreme secretary of the First Catholic Slovak Union (Jednota) in Pennsylvania in 1926 and made important contributions to Slovak American life.

3822. Paučo, Joseph. THE SISTERS OF SS. CYRIL AND METHODIUS. *Jednota Ann. Furdek 1977 16: 7-15.* In Philadelphia, Pennsylvania, on 10 October 1903 Father Matthew Jankola founded the Sisters of SS. Cyril and Methodius, the first and only community of Sisters in the world founded by a Slovak, which became an effective force for cultivating the Slovak language and preserving and promoting Slovak culture in the United States.

3823. Paučo, Jozef. SLOVAK PIONEERS IN AMERICA. *Slovakia 1974 24(47): 67-79.* Recounts the religious accomplishments of Reverend Gregory Vaniščák, O.S.B., and of Reverend Joseph J. Dulík during the first part of the 20th century. S

3824. Pouliot, Léon. UNE LETTRE DE M. FAILLON À MGR. BOURGET [A letter by M. Faillon to Mgr. Bourget]. *Rev. d'Hist. de l'Amérique Française [Canada] 1957 11(1): 107-110.* Presents a letter written in 1850 by Etienne-Michel Faillon to Monseigneur Ignace Bourget about writing a religious history of Montreal.

3825. Powers, Robert M. PAPAGO PRIEST. *Westways 1977 69(2): 41-43, 70.* Discusses the priesthood of Father Lambert Frembling, who after escaping Nazi Germany in 1939 came to Pisinimo, Arizona, to minister to the Papago Indians.

3826. Prinz, Friedrich. DIE KULTURELLEN UND POLITISCHEN LEISTUNGEN DER SUDETENDEUTSCHEN FÜR DIE VEREINIGTEN STAATEN VON AMERIKA [Cultural and political contributions of the Sudeten Germans to the United States of America]. *Bohemia. Jahrbuch des Collegium Carolinum [West Germany] 1977 18: 144-154.* Emphasizes the contributions to Republican and anti-slavery policies of Hans Kudlich (1823-1917), the journalistic, civic and humanitarian work of Oswald Ottendorfer (1826-1900), the writings of Karl Postl (pseudonym Charles Sealsfield, 1793-1864), and the pastoral and missionary importance of Saint John Nepomucene Neumann, Bishop of Philadelphia (1811-60). These German emigrants from Bohemia and Moravia stood out among many of their countrymen who enriched American life; their fate and achievement foreshadowed aspects of the great Sudeten German migration of the mid-20th century. R. E. Weltsch

3827. Radzialowski, Thaddeus. THE VIEW FROM A POLISH GHETTO. SOME OBSERVATIONS ON THE FIRST ONE HUNDRED YEARS IN DETROIT. *Ethnicity 1974 1(2): 125-150.* In the 1870's Polish immigrants built St. Albertus Church on the east side of Detroit and later St. Casimir to the west. The parishes have each been socially self-contained and much feeling exists for them. The Poles see black advancements as threatening their jobs, homes, communities, and churches, while a symbiotic relationship exists with the Jews. Political competition with blacks has been great, but a new Polish pride and determination to fight discrimination and exclusion has recently arisen. 15 notes. E. Barkan

3828. Radzialowski, Thaddeus C. REFLECTIONS ON THE HISTORY OF THE FELICIANS IN AMERICA. *Polish Am. Studies 1975 32(1): 19-28.* Stresses the importance of this sisterhood in Polish-American history. Though originating in Poland in 1855, the order spread to the United States in 1874 and soon became a predominantly American order, with 82% of its membership residing on this side of the Atlantic. Throughout its history it provided social mobility for immigrant women. Although the congregation was involved in the care of orphans, the aged, and the sick, teaching remained its primary concern. Only after the decline and almost total disappearance of the Polish language from parochial schools did the order accept other responsibilities. As a result of their dedication and hard work, the Felicians were able to draw capital and invest it in schools, orphanages, hospitals, and retirement homes. Based on primary and secondary sources; 21 notes. S. R. Pliska

3829. Rael, Juan B. and Martinez, Reyes. ARROYO HONDO: PENITENTES, WEDDINGS, WAKES. *Palacio 1975 81(1): 3-19.* Delineates folk beliefs, social customs, and ceremonies associated with Hispanic culture in New Mexico, 16th-20th centuries.

3830. Ralph, Raymond M. THE CITY AND THE CHURCH: CATHOLIC BEGINNINGS IN NEWARK, 1840-1870. *New Jersey Hist. 1978 96(3-4): 105-118.* By the mid-19th century, reflecting the presence of Irish and German immigrants, Newark, New Jersey's Catholics constituted one of the city's largest religious groups. The church hierarchy had to contend with tensions between these two groups as parishes were established and churches constructed. Raising sufficient money to operate, confronting hostilities from the Protestant community, and dealing with problems involving the public schools were other concerns. The typical Catholic in Newark during the mid-19th century was a blue-collar worker who consciously retained his national characteristics. Based on the archives of the Archdiocese of Newark, church records, and directories and secondary sources; 9 illus., 32 notes. E. R. McKinstry

3831. Real, Michael R. TRENDS IN STRUCTURE AND POLICY IN THE AMERICAN CATHOLIC PRESS. *Journalism Q. 1975 52(2): 265-271.* Immigrants started the American Catholic press in the 19th century and by World War II several large chains had developed, largely under the control of various dioceses and supported by saturation subscription plans. The Second Vatican Council brought a new atmosphere of freedom, so that certain Catholic papers became prestigious and editorially independent, and discussed controversial issues. However, Pope Paul VI's reiteration of the Church's rejection of birth control in 1968 marked a reversal of the trend. Based on interviews, a monitoring of Catholic publications, and study of historical data. Based on primary sources; table, 21 notes. K. J. Puffer

3832. Renggli, M. Beatrice and Voth, M. Agnes, transl. FROM RICKENBACH TO MARYVILLE: AN ACCOUNT OF THE JOURNEY (1874). *Am. Benedictine Rev. 1976 27(3): 247-269.* Translates Mother M. Beatrice Renggli's record of the trip she and four other Benedictine sisters made from Maria Rickenbach Convent in Switzerland to Conception (outside Maryville), Missouri, in 1874. Later, Mother Renggli was the superior of the group of sisters who founded what became

Holy Angels Convent in Jonesboro, Arkansas. Based on original and secondary sources; 22 notes. J. H. Pragman

3833. Rosales, Francisco Arturo. THE REGIONAL ORIGINS OF MEXICANO IMMIGRANTS TO CHICAGO DURING THE 1920'S. *Aztlán 1976 7(2): 187-201.* Of the Mexicano immigrants to the colonias of South Chicago and East Chicago during the 1920's, 68% came from the bajio region in west central Mexico. Their precursors had followed the railroads, for which many of them worked, to the Midwest, and were followed by thousands of immigrants during the revolution, in 1915. The inhabitants of the bajio were less affected by the injustices and hardships that sparked the revolution than by those it occasioned, and hence were less often moved to join it, more often to flee from it, than other Mexicanos. Many of the immigrants were recruited by US steel manufacturers. Many, too, were Catholic militants in exile. Secondary sources; 2 tables, 41 notes. L. W. Van Wyk

3834. Rosoli, Gianfausto. CHIESA E COMUNITÀ ITALIANE NEGLI STATI UNITI (1880-1940) [Church and community among the Italians in the United States (1880-1940)]. *Studium [Italy] 1979 75(1): 25-47.* The Roman Catholic Church played an important role in consolidating and maintaining the Italian community in the United States.

3835. Rusk, Alfred C. THE SECOND VATICAN COUNCIL, 1962-1965, AND BISHOP NEUMANN. *Records of the Am. Catholic Hist. Soc. of Philadelphia 1974 85(3-4): 123-128.* The *Acta* of Vatican Council II in paragraph 50 of the Constitution on the Church refers to the decree of the Congregation of Rites on the heroicity of Bishop John Nepomucene Neumann (1811-60), a decree which clarified the norms for judging heroic virtue in canonization processes. 17 notes. J. M. McCarthy

3836. Ryan, Thomas R. A MEMOIR OF HENRY FRANCIS BROWNSON. *Records of the Am. Catholic Hist. Soc. of Philadelphia 1976 87(1-4): 51-63.* Relatively little is known of Henry Francis Brownson (1835-1900), one of Orestes A. Brownson's sons, editor of his works, and one of the outstanding Catholic laymen of his day. J. M. McCarthy

3837. Ryan, Thomas R. NEWMAN'S INVITATION TO ORESTES A. BROWNSON TO BE LECTURER EXTRAORDINARY AT THE CATHOLIC UNIVERSITY OF IRELAND. *Records of the Am. Catholic Hist. Soc. of Philadelphia 1974 85(1-2): 29-47.* The project to bring Orestes A. Brownson to the Catholic University of Ireland, a project which intrigued John Henry Newman, apparently was scuttled by the furor over Brownson's 1854 article on "Native Americanism" in his *Review*. 35 notes. J. M. McCarthy

3838. Ryan, Thomas R. ORESTES A. BROWNSON'S LECTURES IN ST. LOUIS, MISSOURI, 1852 AND 1854. *Records of the Am. Catholic Hist. Soc. of Philadelphia 1978 89(1-4): 45-59.* Orestes A. Brownson's course of lectures in St. Louis was on the general theme of Catholicity and civilization, in which his aim was to show that all true civilziation is Catholic in origin, that all the nations of the ancient world in proportion as they departed from the patriarchal religion, and all nations of the Christian era in proportion as they recede from the Catholic Church, necessarily tend more and more to barbarism. 20 notes. J. M. McCarthy

3839. Rybolt, John E. MISSOURI IN 1847: THE PASTORAL VISIT OF ARCHBISHOP KENRICK. *Missouri Hist. Soc. Bull. 1979 35(4): 202-209.* Publishes here for the first time a 3 December 1847 letter written by Peter Richard Kenrick, the Archbishop of St. Louis from 1841 to 1895. Kenrick reviewed his work during 1847, much of which required him to travel extensively in the Missouri diocese that was still predominantly a frontier area. This frontier diocese, Kenrick noted, mainly lacked sufficient priests and financial support for implementing the improvements Kenrick prescribed for the diocese. Photo, 44 notes. H. T. Lovin

3840. Savard, Pierre. DES LIVRES, DES IDÉES ET DES HOMMES D'ICI AU XIXe SIÈCLE [Books, ideas and men from here in the 19th century]. *Rev. de l'U. d'Ottawa [Canada] 1979 49(1-2): 117-123.* Reviews 14 books on 19th-century Quebec, published recently and chosen for their richness in information or reliability. They include studies of texts such as those of Crémazié's works, two literary anthologies, a study of sociopolitical thought, an anthology of political songs, biographies of Gérin-Lajoie and of feminist Gaëtane de Montreuil, a synthesis of ideologies, two analyses of the power of the clergy, one on historiography, a study of myths, and analyses of painters Théophile Hamel and Napoléon Bourassa. G. P. Cleyet

3841. Savard, Pierre. SUR LES NOMS DE PAROISSES AU QUÉBEC, DES ORIGINES À 1925 [On parish names in Quebec, from the beginning until 1925]. *Sessions d'Étude: Soc. Can. d'Hist. de l'Eglise Catholique 1974 41: 105-113.* Studies the religious orientation of town and parish names in Quebec, and evaluates the evolution of religious feeling during 1600-1925. Discusses the question of the origin of church names, stressing chronology as a key to recurring themes particular to Quebec: Irish names accompanying emigration, and Jesuit and Franciscan cycles. Catalogues names by number and subject. Based on departmental archives and secondary sources; 9 notes. S. Sevilla

3842. Schmandt, Raymond H. EPISCOPAL SUPPORT OF CATHOLIC INTELLECTUAL ACTIVITY: A NOTE ON THE FOURTH PROVINCIAL COUNCIL OF BALTIMORE. *Catholic Hist. Rev. 1978 64(1): 51-56.* This article publishes from the Baltimore Cathedral Archives a letter written on 17 May 1843 by the Philadelphia Catholic author William Joseph Walter to Archbishop Samuel Eccleston of Baltimore. It reveals the fact that the bishops during the Fourth Provincial Council of Baltimore in 1840 had discussed Walter's literary efforts and made an oblique reference to them in their pastoral letter. It shows that several members of the hierarchy had advanced funds and in other ways encouraged Walter in his writing career. A

3843. Schmandt, Raymond H. THE FRIENDSHIP BETWEEN BISHOP REGIS CANEVIN OF PITTSBURGH AND DR. LAWRENCE FLICK OF PHILADELPHIA. *Western Pennsylvania Hist. Mag. 1978 61(4): 283-300.* Describes the 40 year relationship between two prominent Pennsylvania Catholics, Bishop Regis Canevin (1853-1927) and Dr. Lawrence Flick (1856-1938).

3844. Schmandt, Raymond H. TWO LETTERS OF BISHOP JAMES F. WOOD TO COLONEL BASIL W. DUKE, C.S.A., AT FORT DELAWARE PRISON. *Records of the Am. Catholic Hist. Soc. of Philadelphia 1978 89(1-4): 118-122.* Bishop James F. Wood, having converted Duke's parents to Catholicism and stood as godfather to him, visited Wood at the Fort Delaware prison camp in 1864 and sought to insure his welfare. 2 notes. J. M. McCarthy

3845. Schmidt, Thomas V. EARLY CATHOLIC AMERICANA: SOME ADDITIONS TO PARSONS. *Records of the Am. Catholic Hist. Soc. of Philadelphia 1975 86(1-4): 24-32.* This checklist of early Catholic titles is made up of copies located at Catholic University which were not reported in Wilfrid Parsons' *Early Catholic Americana.* The list is particularly strong in titles dealing with the Hogan Schism in Philadelphia. Covers 1785-1825. 3 notes, biblio. J. M. McCarthy

3846. Scollard, Robert J. REVEREND WILLIAM RICHARD HARRIS, 1846-1923. *Study Sessions [Canada] 1974 41: 65-80.* Gives a biography of William Richard Harris, priest of the Archdiocese of Toronto. A paper read at the 1974 annual meeting of the Canadian Catholic Historical Association. S

3847. Séguin, Norman. COLONISATION ET IMPLANTATION RÉLIGIEUSE AU LAC SAINT-JEAN, DANS LA SECONDE MOITIÉ DU XIXe SIÈCLE [Settlement and the establishment of religion around Lake Saint John, in the second half of the 19th century]. *Protée [Canada] 1976 5(2): 55-59.* The Catholic Church was eminently successful in establishing its influence in the region of Lake St. John, Quebec, beginning with the settlement of Hébertville in 1840.

3848. Sewrey, Charles L. INFALLIBILITY, THE AMERICAN WAY, AND CATHOLIC APOLOGETICS. *J. of Church and State 1973 15(2): 293-302.* Discusses the effect of the proclamation of papal infallibility of 1870 on US Catholics. S

3849. Shaw, Joseph Coolidge. THE "YANKEE PRIEST" SAYS MASS IN BRATTLEBORO: JOSEPH COOLIDGE SHAW DE-

SCRIBES HIS VISIT IN 1848. *Vermont Hist. 1976 44(4): 198-202.* Selections from Joseph Coolidge Shaw's diary, edited by Walter J. Meagher, describe the newly ordained priest's baptizing, marrying, hearing confessions, saying Mass, and talking religion with other patients at the Wesselhoeft Water Cure. After eight weeks at Brattleboro, Shaw entered St. Joseph's Seminary near New York, but died before completing the Jesuit novitiate in Maryland. T. D. S. Bassett

3850. Shaw, Richard. JAMES GORDON BENNETT: IMPROBABLE HERALD OF THE KINGDOM. *Records of the Am. Catholic Hist. Soc. of Philadelphia 1977 88(1-4): 88-100.* From 1835 until after the Civil War, James Gordon Bennett's *New York Herald* far outstripped its rivals in circulation and influence. A Roman Catholic who bore some ill-will to the Church, Bennett was a valuable asset to the cause of immigrant Catholicism by reason of his independent stance and honest criticism of the Church. He gave Catholicism a strong secular voice and his independence refuted nativist slurs. 49 notes. J. M. McCarthy

3851. Simard, Jean. CULTES LITURGIQUES ET DÉVOTIONS POPULAIRES DANS LES COMTÉS DE PORTNEUF ET DU LAC-SAINT-JEAN [Liturgical cults and popular devotions in the counties of Portneuf and Lac-Saint-Jean]. *Sessions d'Études: Soc. Can. d'Hist. de l'Église Catholique [Canada] 1976 43: 5-14.* Presents the results of research and surveys on the close relation between liturgical cults and popular devotions in Quebec, comparing them to similar developments in France in the 1970's.

3852. Simmons, Marc. SETTLEMENT PATTERNS AND VILLAGE PLANS IN COLONIAL NEW MEXICO. Weber, David J., ed. *New Spain's Far Northern Frontier: Essays on Spain in the American West, 1540-1821* (Albuquerque: U. of New Mexico Pr., 1979): 97-115. New Mexico's settlements were founded in an unorganized manner by people driven by economic motivations, frontier individualism, fatalism about the Indian danger, and the desire to escape the paternal control of church and state; they soon dispersed to live near their fields, 17th century-1810. Reprinted from *Journal of the American West* 1969 8(1): 7-21.

3853. Sinclair, John L. HONORING SAN LORENZO. *Westways 1974 66(8): 49-51, 64.* Narrates the five day celebration in honor of martyred Saint Lawrence (d. ca. 258 AD) held annually in the New Mexico village of Bernalillo. S

3854. Sorrell, Richard S. SENTINELLE AFFAIR (1924-1929)—RELIGION AND MILITANT SURVIVANCE IN WOONSOCKET, RHODE ISLAND. *Rhode Island Hist. 1977 36(3): 67-79.* Discusses French Canadians in Woonsocket; examines problems of assimilation, religion, and nationalism. Based on the author's doctoral dissertation; 8 illus., 14 notes. P. J. Coleman

3855. Spigelman, Martin S. RACE ET RELIGION: LES ACADIENS ET LA HIÉRARCHIE CATHOLIQUE IRLANDAISE DU NOUVEAU-BRUNSWICK [Race and religion: the Acadians and the Irish Catholic hierarchy of New Brunswick]. *Rev. d'Hist. de l'Amérique Française 1975 29(1): 69-85.* In 1900, increasing population and economic power led the French-speaking Acadians of New Brunswick to vie for high clerical positions in the Irish dominated Catholic Church. The conflict centered on ethnic and linguistic issues. The Irish feared the Acadians might reach a compromise with the English Protestant population of New Brunswick and sabotaged attempts to teach the French language and to publish French language newspapers. Covers 1860-1900. Based on primary and secondary sources; 62 notes. C. Collon

3856. Steele, Thomas J. THE DEATH CART: ITS PLACE AMONG THE SANTOS OF NEW MEXICO. *Colorado Mag. 1978 55(1): 1-14.* Discusses the appearance of the death cart around 1860, "a constant feature of the Penitente morada" in northern New Mexico and southern Colorado during the latter part of the 19th century and first part of the 20th century. Its surface meanings were: 1) symbol of involuntary death, 2) warning against a "bad death," and 3) encouragement to live for "a good death in a state of grace. But there were cultural implications, too, related to the mid-19th century conquest of the area by the United States and the sublimation of Spanish cutlural life under the pressure of an alien culture. It also served to emphasize confrontation with personal death, mortification, and the Christian paradox itself. Primary and secondary sources; 6 illus., 20 notes. O. H. Zabel

3857. Stekelenburg, H. A. V. M. van. ROOMS-KATHOLIEKE LANDVERHUIZERS NAAR DE VEREENIGDE STATEN [Roman Catholic immigrants to the United States]. *Spiegel Hist. [Netherlands] 1977 12(12): 681-689.* Dutch immigration to the United States became rather substantial, 1845-75. Most of the immigrants who settled in Michigan, Iowa, and Illinois were secessionists of the Reformed Dutch Church. Less is known about a fairly large number of Catholics, most of whom came from the southern provinces of North Brabant and Limburg. The immigrants came primarily for economic reasons and settled in the Fox River Valley of Wisconsin. Much of the original impulse to immigrate came from T. J. van den Broek (1773-1851), the Dutch Catholic missionary among the Indians in Wisconsin. About 8,000 Catholic immigrants came between 1841 and 1875. Illus., biblio. G. D. Homan

3858. Stevens, Clifford. THE CONTEMPLATIVE WITNESS OF THOMAS MERTON. *Am. Benedictine R. 1975 26(4): 395-405.* Presents a panegyric on Thomas Merton as the man who recovered and reestablished the contemplative ideal of a life of prayer for contemporary monasticism 1940's-68. Merton's devotion to the contemplative life places him on a level with St. Stephen Harding and St. Bernard of Clairvaux, founders of the Cistercian Order. Based on original and secondary sources; 17 notes. J. H. Pragman

3859. Stewart, James H. VALUES, INTERESTS, AND ORGANIZATIONAL CHANGE: THE NATIONAL FEDERATION OF PRIESTS' COUNCILS. *Sociol. Analysis 1973 34(4): 281-295.* Examines two types of affiliates to the National Federation of Priests' Councils and their relationship both to values and interests and social change. The major hypotheses are that the value-oriented association members will be more strongly associated with pastoral change than the interest-oriented senators and that the former will be more committed than the latter in employing a more militant approach. Longitudinal data over a three-year period are employed to support the hypotheses. J

3860. Stritch, Thomas J. THREE CATHOLIC BISHOPS FROM TENNESSEE. *Tennessee Hist. Q. 1978 37(1): 3-35.* The three Irish-American Catholic bishops, John Morris (1866-1946), John P. Farrelly (1856-1921), and Samuel A. Stritch (1887-1958), were all Southerners whose lives were intertwined. They were wise, possibly great men who exhibited a tremendous influence on the South. Based on the author's recollections and primary and secondary sources; 2 illus., 70 notes. M. B. Lucas

3861. Stryckman, Paul. LES DÉFIS OCCUPATIONNELS DU CLERGÉ [The occupational challenges of the clergy]. *Recherches Sociographiques [Canada] 1978 19(2): 223-250.* The reduction in religious vocations has resulted in important organizational adaptations for the Roman Catholic clergy in Quebec. Instead of turning toward structural redefinitions to confront the challenge of reduced manpower, the clergy has opted for a reexamination of its occupational activities. Based on extensive interviews with 814 clergymen during 1968-77; 7 tables, 27 notes, biblio. A. E. LeBlanc

3862. Sunter, Ronald. THE SCOTTISH BACKGROUND TO THE IMMIGRATION OF BISHOP ALEXANDER MACDONNELL AND THE GLENGARRY HIGHLANDERS. *Study Sessions: Can. Catholic Hist. Assoc. 1973 40: 11-20.* The British Navy attempted to impress Catholics emigrating to Canada where Bishop Alexander Macdonnell and the Glengarry Highlanders settled and figured prominently in the history of Ontario. Covers the period 1770's-1814.

3863. Suther, Judith D. THE SPIRITUAL TRIAD OF JACQUES AND RAISSA MARITAIN AND THOMAS MERTON. *Encounter 1976 37(2): 129-151.* Discusses the influence of Jacques and Raissa Maritain and Thomas Merton on the intellectual and religious life of the United States since the 1940's, with special emphasis on Maritain's concept of creative innocence in the art of poetry.

3864. Swidler, Arlene. CATHOLICS AND THE 1876 CENTENNIAL. *Catholic Hist. Rev. 1976 62(3): 349-365.* The Catholic periodical literature of 1876 reflected American centennial preoccupations. It summarized Catholic progress, evaluated the position of the Church in 1876, and predicted a glorious future. The more popular Catholic weeklies reported the activities at the Philadelphia Exhibition, the interchurch bickering on whether the exhibition should remain open on Sunday, and the latest activities of the visiting Catholic Emperor of Brazil. The outstanding Catholic contribution to the exposition was the imposing Catholic Centennial Fountain erected by the Catholic Total Abstinence Union. A

3865. Symmons-Symonolewicz, Konstantin. IMMIGRANT PASTOR: ACHIEVEMENTS AND PROFILE. *Polish Rev. 1974 19(3-4): 204-208.* Reviews Daniel Stephen Buczek's *Immigrant Pastor: The Life of the Right Reverend Monsignor Lucyan Bójnowski of New Britain, Connecticut* (Waterbury, Connecticut: Heminway Corporation, 1974). Covers 1895-1960. S

3866. Szafran, Robert F. THE DISTRIBUTION OF INFLUENCE IN RELIGIOUS ORGANIZATIONS. *J. for the Sci. Study of Religions 1976 15(4): 339-350.* Discusses influence and centralization within the dioceses of the Catholic Church, comparing these to outside organizations (League of Women Voters, labor unions) in the 1970's, and concludes that the Church has the most centralized and least apt to be influenced organization of the groups studied.

3867. Szafran, Robert F.; Peterson, Robert W.; and Schoenherr, Richard A. ETHNICITY AND STATUS ATTAINMENT: THE CASE OF THE ROMAN CATHOLIC CLERGY. *Sociol. Q. 1980 21(1): 41-51.* Ethnicity is not a significant factor in status attainment in the clergy; based on a 1972 survey of 2,775 Catholic diocesan priests and bishops.

3868. Tanzone, Daniel F. BISHOP ANDREW GRUTKA. *Jednota Ann. Furdek 1978 17: 81-86.* Discusses the life of Bishop Andrew G. Grutka (b. 1908), a Catholic parish priest in and eventually Bishop of the Diocese of Gary, Indiana; covers 1933-78.

3869. Tanzone, Daniel F. DIAMOND JUBILEE OF HOLY FAMILY SLOVAK PARISH. *Jednota Ann. Furdek 1980 19: 95-102.* The 75th anniversary of this Brooklyn, New York, Catholic parish composed of Slovak immigrants.

3870. Tanzone, Daniel F. JOHN J. KUBAŠEK, PRIEST AND PATRIOT. *Slovakia 1976 26(49): 69-75.* Discusses the life and career of Slovak American Catholic priest John J. Kubašek in Yonkers, New York, 1902-50; emphasizes his work for Slovakian independence from Hungary.

3871. Theriault, Leon. CHEMINEMENT INVERSE DES ACADIANS ET DES ANGLOPHONES DES MARITIMES [Inverse progress among Acadians and the English-speaking population of the Maritimes]. *Tr. of the Royal Soc. of Can. [Canada] 1977 15: 145-168.* Discusses the change in status of French-speaking people in the Maritime Provinces from the defeat of France in 1763 to the present. For the first century, especially after the influx of American Loyalists, the English-speaking population dominated the area. Gradually, the Acadians developed an identity and began to play a more active role. The Catholic Church expanded until it was able to establish dioceses in the area. Conflict between French parishoners and an Irish hierarchy was a problem. Henry Wadsworth Longfellow's poem "Evangeline" and Napoleon Bourassa's novel *Jacques et Marie* helped create an Acadian identity. Colleges such as Saint Anne's founded in 1890 and Sacred Heart founded in 1899 also helped. By the 1970's the Acadians had become an important force in the area, the economy of which had declined. In New Brunswick they have achieved a bilingual province. 55 notes, biblio.
J. D. Neville

3872. Tierney, John J. ANOTHER VIEW OF THE JOHN CARROLL PAPERS. *Catholic Hist. Rev. 1978 64(4): 660-670.* A correction and extension of the three-volume work edited by Thomas O'Brien Hanley, *The John Carroll Papers* (Notre Dame: U. of Notre Dame, 1976). The work has been hailed as a wonderful addition to literary sources, and indeed it is, but it has omissions and inaccuracies, which fall into the following categories: chronology, indexing, footnotes, identification, identical letters, primary vs. secondary sources, and archival material. The *Papers* as they stand must be used with caution if high standards of academic accuracy are to be maintained. The present listing of errors and inaccuracies does not pretend to be exhaustive, but is sufficient to point out the serious shortcomings of the work. 2 notes. V. L. Human

3873. Trépanier, Pierre and Trépannier, Lise. RÉACTIONS QUÉBÉCOISES AU LIVRE D'ANDRÉ SIEGFRIED [Quebec reactions to the work of Andre Siegfried]. *Action Natl. [Canada] 1979 68(5): 394-405, (6): 517-525, (7): 587-601.* Part I. André Siegfried wrote *Le Canada, les deux races, Problèmes politiques contemporains* (Paris, 1906, 1907) after visiting the country in 1898, 1901, and 1904. He saw French Canadians as conquered by the British and dominated by the Catholic clergy, who sought to maintain French culture to preserve Catholicism. Siegfried's interpretation was received favorably in liberal journals, but negatively in the conservative, ultramontane, and religious press. In the debate in Quebec, Siegfried's penetrating analysis of colonialism was hardly mentioned. 31 notes. Part II. The most perceptive analysis of Siegfried's *Le Canada* was published by Fernand Rinfret in *L'Avenir du Nord.* Recognizing that Canada is composed of two races with conflicting religions, languages, customs, ambitions, sentiments and traditions, Rinfret especially appreciated Siegfried's analysis of English and French clashes on questions of education. Siegfried's books appeared in the midst of disputes among Quebecois concerning the value of classical education, and its reception reflected the views of commentators on that issue. 21 notes. Part III. In Quebec, reaction to *Le Canada* was determined by the reader's position concerning the role of the Catholic Church in society. The debate foreshadowed the conflict between the new knowledge of the social sciences and the ancient doctrinal certitudes of the Church that marked Quebec's quiet revolution in the 1950's. 34 notes.
A. W. Novitsky

3874. Trépanier, Pierre. VICTOR BARBEAU ET ALBINY PAQUETTE [Victor Barbeau and Albiny Paquette]. *Action Natl. [Canada] 1978 68(4): 324-330.* Although best known as a writer, linguist, and critic, Victor Barbeau was a prophet of the Quebec consumer cooperative movement. He urged its extension throughout the world as a model for a new society based on rationality of service rather than profit. Albiny Paquette was a medical doctor, mayor, prefect, deputy, provincial secretary, minister of health under Maurice Duplessis, and legislative councillor. He launched crusades against tuberculosis and infant mortality, and was both a political conservative and a staunch Catholic. Covers ca. 1900-45. Review of "Victor Barbeau, hommages et tributes," *Cahiers de l'Académie canadienne-française,* No. 15 (Montreal, Fides, 1978), and Paquette, *33 années à la législature de Québec, Soldat—médecin—maire—député—ministre, Souvenirs d'une vie de travail et de bonheur* (1977). 11 notes. A. W. Novitsky

3875. Treppa, Allan R. JOHN A. LEMKE: AMERICA'S FIRST NATIVE-BORN POLISH AMERICAN PRIEST? *Polish Am. Studies 1978 35(1-2): 78-83.* This Polish American (1866-90) was ordained to the priesthood in Detroit in 1889. Monographs and newspapers in English; 17 notes. S. R. Pliska

3876. Trudel, Marcel. L'HOMME DE MA GÉNÉRATION, HOMME DE L'ANCIEN RÉGIME [The man of my generation, the man of the old order]. *Rev. de l'U. d'Ottawa [Canada] 1977 47(3): 251-269.* Commentary on the liberalizing changes in 20th-century Quebec during the lifetime of the author, with frequent references to secular and religious life during the 17th century. G. J. Rossi

3877. Turk, Eleanor L. THE GERMANS OF ATCHISON, 1854-1859: DEVELOPMENT OF AN ETHNIC COMMUNITY. *Kansas Hist. 1979 2(3): 146-156.* Frederick Jackson Turner said that the frontier blended foreign- and American-born into a composite nationality. John A. Hawgood insisted that German settlers resisted assimilation, and Milton Gordon said that immigrants accommodated to the cultural pattern of the dominant group but retained much of their own heritage. A study of references to Germans in the *Squatter Sovereign, Kansas Zeitung,* and *Freedom's Champion* shows that Gordon is right; native-born Americans and immigrant Germans joined on the issue of freedom in Kansas, but the Germans kept a strong devotion to Roman Catholicism, German schools, and the Turnverein, a culturally separate social center. Americans in Kansas apparently encouraged this cultural pluralism that endured until World War I. Based on books, articles, newspapers; illus., 20 notes. W. F. Zornow

3878. Tusseau, Jean-Pierre. LA FIN "ÉDIFIANTE" D'ARTHUR BUIES [The "edifying" end of Arthur Buies]. *Études Françaises [Canada] 1973 9(1): 45-54.* Discusses the return of French Canadian pamphleteer Arthur Buies to the Catholic Church, 1880's-1901. Based on works of Buies, newspapers, and works of Gagnon; illus., 31 notes. C. Bates

3879. Tybor, M. Martina. SLOVAK AMERICAN CATHOLICS. *Jednota Ann. Furdek 1977 16: 53-66.* Examines the immigration of Catholic Slovaks to America, their problems upon arrival, and their activities to ensure their cohesiveness and their spiritual, cultural, economic, political, and intellectual development in a new environment, 1860's-1970's.

3880. Vaillancourt, François and Ferron, Jean-Olivier. QUI PERD SA LANGUE, PERD SA FOI? [Does he who loses his language also lose his faith?]. *Rev. d'Hist. de l'Amérique Française [Canada] 1979 33(2): 263-265.* A study of the 1941 census of 27 Canadian cities shows a direct correlation among French Canadians between the use of French and the retention of their Catholic faith. Table. R. Aldrich

3881. Vogeler, Ingolf. THE ROMAN CATHOLIC CULTURE REGION OF CENTRAL MINNESOTA. *Pioneer Am. 1976 8(2): 71-83.* Selects for a geographical study of religion, the Roman Catholic Diocese of St. Cloud, Minnesota, which represents the largest percentage of Catholics, by diocese and archdiocese, in Minnesota and the second largest in the Midwest. Three major themes—the genesis and geographical distribution of religions, the spatial organization of religions, and the landscape expression of religious groups—were utilized in analyzing the subject area. Microanalysis of other Catholic regions in North America could verify or modify the findings of this study. Covers 1860-1973. Based on handbooks preserved in the Immigrant Archives, University of Minnesota, Minneapolis, personal interviews, field work, and secondary sources; 7 maps, 5 photos, 25 notes. C. R. Gunter, Jr.

3882. Voisine, Nive. L'ÉPISCOPAT QUÉBÉCOIS AU MOMENT DE LA FORMATION DU DIOCÈSE DE SHERBROOKE, 1874 [The Quebec episcopate at the time of the formation of the diocese of Sherbrooke, 1874]. *Sessions d'Étude Soc. Can. d'Hist. de l'Eglise Catholique 1974 41: 25-41.* A biographical sketch of six bishops of the Sherbrooke Diocese studying conflicts dividing the episcopate, such as opposition to modern thought, to liberalism, and to changes in education. A reunion (1872) to celebrate the bicentennial of the Quebec seat became a confrontation between the two rival clans of bishops, the "idealists": Taschereau, La Rocque, and Langevin; and the "realists": Bourget, and Laflèche. Based on correspondence and publications in Diocese Archives; 43 notes. S. Sevilla

3883. Voisine, Nive. ROME ET LE CANADA: LA MISSION DE MGR CONROY [Rome and Canada: the mission of Monsignor Conroy]. *Rev. d'Hist. de l'Amérique Française [Canada] 1980 33(4): 499-519.* Problems of internal squabbles, political activities, and education created a crisis among the Catholic hierarchy in Canada. In response, the pope sent George Conroy as special legate in 1877. He was successful in limiting the antiliberal political interferences of bishops, setting up a branch of Laval University in Montreal, and reimposing papal authority. Based on Canadian archival materials; 71 notes. R. Aldrich

3884. Vollmar, Edward R. *LA REVISTA CATOLICA. Mid-America 1976 58(2): 85-96.* The origin of *La Revista Catolica,* the Spanish-language publication of the Jesuits of the New Mexico-Colorado Mission of the Neapolitan Province, involved New Mexico's first Bishop, J. B. Lamy, who brought the dispersed Neapolitans to the Southwest in 1867. Father Gaspari instigated the immediately successful Las Vegas (New Mexico)-based *Revista,* and it inspired short-lived Protestant counter publications. Succeeding editors and managers, the move to El Paso (Texas), the 1919 dissolution of the mission, and declining subscriptions all influenced *Revista.* Primary and secondary sources; 20 notes. T. H. Wendel

3885. Wagner, William. THE SISTERS OF SS. CYRIL AND METHODIUS AND THE PRESERVATION OF SLOVAK CULTURE IN AMERICA. *Slovakia 1974 24(47): 132-155.* Discusses the work of the sisters of St. Cyril Academy (1909-73) to preserve Slovak culture in Danville, Pennsylvania. S

3886. Walch, Timothy. CATHOLIC SOCIAL INSTITUTIONS AND URBAN DEVELOPMENTS: THE VIEW FROM NINETEENTH-CENTURY CHICAGO AND MILWAUKEE. *Catholic Hist. Rev. 1978 64(1): 16-32.* The Catholic Church committed itself to the improvement of American life by establishing a variety of urban social institutions. The impact of the Church's efforts, however, varied from one city to the next. In Eastern cities, Catholic institutions served immigrants almost exclusively. But the newness of Chicago and Milwaukee and their drastic need for social institutions precipitated a different kind of experience for the Catholic church in the Midwest. The Church mobilized quickly and offered these cities needed hospitals, asylums and schools. Non-Catholic leaders in Chicago and Milwaukee accepted these institutions with gratitude because they made their cities more attractive and helped to insure future growth. The story of Catholic social institutions in Chicago and Milwaukee highlights the complexity of relations between Catholics and non-Catholics in urban areas and emphasizes the need to look at the Church in a number of regional settings to gain a balanced picture of the American Catholic experience. A

3887. Walsh, James P. and Foley, Timothy. FATHER PETER C. YORKE: IRISH-AMERICAN LEADER. *Studia Hibernica [Ireland] 1974 14: 90-103.* Galway-born Father Peter Yorke (1864-1925) became champion of the Irish working class in San Francisco, advancing their unionization and education under Catholic auspices. He was ordained in 1887, became chancellor of the archdiocese of San Francisco and editor of the diocesan newspaper, *The Monitor*, where he fought the anti-Catholic American Protective Association. After losing editorship of that newspaper he established the Irish-American paper, *The Leader*, in 1902. During his defense of Father Richard Henebry he attacked the Catholic University of America as the preserve of Anglo-Irish-American Churchmen. During World War I he attacked Garret McEnerney, champion of the Home Rule Party and critic of Irish American supporters of Sinn Fein. After the war Yorke quarrelled bitterly with Mayor James Phelan. Though a bright, energetic defender of Irish Americans, he could only cooperate with subordinates, enjoyed excessively the glory attached to popular advocacy, and never accepted the legitimate differences of opponents. Based on Yorke's published writings and MSS at University of San Francisco, newspapers, and secondary sources; 40 notes. T. F. Moriarty

3888. Walsh, James P. A NON-IRISH CATHOLIC AND THE INTELLECTUAL LIFE: MSGR. CHARLES A. RAMM. *Southern California Q. 1973 55(1): 49-58.* Sketches the biography of Msgr. Charles A. Ramm (1863-1951), who devoted his career to brotherhood and public service. He was born in California to German immigrants and attended the University of California, graduating with honors. He converted from Lutheranism, was ordained in 1892, and served 21 years on the State Board of Charities and 32 years on the Board of Regents. In Catholic intellectual life Ramm served by quiet example rather than active advocacy, a tactic made necessary by the dominance of Irish Americans in the American Catholic hierarchy. Based on unpublished sources and secondary works; photos, 50 notes. A. Hoffman

3889. Walsh, James P. PETER YORKE AND PROGRESSIVISM IN CALIFORNIA, 1908. *Éire-Ireland 1975 10(2): 73-81.* Galway-born Father Peter C. Yorke championed the Catholic Church, Irish working people, and Irish nationalism in San Francisco from the 1880's until his death in 1925. Yorke, in his weekly newspaper *The Leader,* was a spokesman for Irish Americans who believed in political brokerage as a way to logically and democratically reconcile conflicting views. The Irish saw Progressive attempts at municipal charter revision in San Francisco in 1908 as the attempted removal of Irish political representation—by privileged, Protestant, University of California-oriented professional and business interests who thought themselves "disinterested" but did not accept cultural pluralism or political dissent. Based on *The Leader,* secondary sources, and correspondence; 28 notes. D. J. Engler

3890. Walters, Jonathan. A REVOLUTIONARY MONASTERY. *Hist. Preservation 1980 32(4): 42-47.* Discusses the history of Wormeley Manor along the Shenandoah River in Virginia, and its 20th-century role for the Trappists as Holy Cross Abbey.

3891. Wangler, Thomas E. A BIBLIOGRAPHY OF THE WRITINGS OF ARCHBISHOP JOHN J. KEANE. *Records of the Am. Catholic Hist. Soc. of Philadelphia 1978 89(1-4): 60-73.* Lists almost all of the surviving articles, pastorals, sermons, discourses, books, and important administrative documents written or spoken by Keane, to be used in conjunction with Patrick Ahern's *The Life of John J. Keane: Educator and Archbishop, 1838-1918* (Bruce, 1955). J. M. McCarthy

3892. Warren, Nancy. "LA FUNCION": VILLAGE FIESTAS IN NORTHERN NEW MEXICO. *Palacio 1978 84(2): 23-29.* A photographic essay of "La Funcion del Santo," yearly fiestas held to honor New Mexican villages' patron saints, 1970's.

3893. Watkins, T. H. THE BROTHERHOOD OF THE MOUNTAINS. *Am. Heritage 1979 30(3): 58-67.* Los Hermanos Penitentes, the Penitent Brothers, was a secret organization whose status in the Catholic Church was shaky from its conception before 1830 until its reform and acceptance by the Church in 1947. The Brothers, whose territory centered in the Sangre de Cristo Mountains in New Mexico, practiced self-flagellation and capped off Holy Week each year with reenacted crucifixions, until the late 1930's. 7 illus. J. F. Paul

3894. Weber, Francis J. AN APPEAL TO LOS ANGELES. *Pacific Hist. 1977 21(4): 359-367.* Reprints an exhortation by Fray José Gonzalez Rubio to the Diocese of Both Californias in 1848. He reminded Catholics of their obligation of tithing. Translation reveals Rubio to be "an enlightened and highly educated man." 10 notes.
G. L. Olson

3895. Weber, Francis J. CALIFORNIA CATHOLICITY IN 1848. *Pacific Historian 1973 17(3): 48-57.*

3896. Weber, Francis J. A CATHOLIC BISHOP MEETS THE RACIAL PROBLEM. *Records of the Am. Catholic Hist. Soc. of Philadelphia 1973 84(4): 217-220.* Describes the efforts of John J. Cantwell, bishop of Monterey-Los Angeles, to design an apostolate for Negroes in the 1920's. 14 notes. J. M. McCarthy

3897. Weber, Francis J. CATHOLICISM AMONG THE MORMONS, 1875-79. *Utah Hist. Q. 1976 44(2): 141-148.* In 1873, Father Laurence Scanlan (1843-1915) became pastor of Salt Lake parish and the anchor-chain of Catholicism in Utah. He found 800 Catholics in the territory, 100 in the Salt Lake area. His letters to the Societè de la Propagation de la Foi for financial assistance are historically pivotal, revealing both his own personality and the complex status of the nascent Catholic community in Mormon territory. Two letters reproduced here are dated 16 November 1875 and 31 October 1879. Primary and secondary sources; illus., 3 notes. J. L. Hazelton

3898. Weigle, Martha. GHOSTLY FLAGELLANTS AND DOÑA SEBASTIANA: TWO LEGENDS OF THE PENITENTE BROTHERHOOD. *Western Folklore 1977 36(2): 135-147.* Examines two important components of the predominantly Hispanic Penitente religious cult of New Mexico and Colorado. Reports on the folklore associated with reported appearances of ghostly skeletal figures during certain rites and also examines the folk art of the carved "death angels" often called Doña Sebastiana; 19c-20c. Primary and secondary sources; illus., 29 notes.
S. L. Myres

3899. Wolf, William J. THE THEOLOGICAL LANDSCAPE, 1936-1974: AN ADDRESS. *Anglican Theological Rev. 1976 59(Supplement 7): 31-42.* Summarizes trends in American Roman Catholic theology, 1936-74: liberalism, neoorthodoxy, secularism, and pluralism.

3900. Wolff, Gerald W. FATHER SYLVESTER EISENMANN AND MARTY MISSION. *South Dakota Hist. 1975 5(4): 360-389.* During 1918-48 Father Sylvester Eisenmann successfully ministered to Sioux Indians on the Yankton Reservation. He supported the Indians' welfare and was extremely generous in the time, effort, and money he invested in their behalf. A tireless worker, he was especially successful in raising funds and in constructing almost 30 major buildings at Marty. His accomplishments were offset somewhat by his paternalism and condescension. These attitudes grew out of his early years and training in southern Indiana. Thus his deep concern and great record of achievement for the Yankton Sioux were diminished because he treated his Indian charges as perpetual children. By rejecting their heritage and underestimating them as human beings, Father Sylvester did them a disservice. Primary and secondary sources; 7 photos, 67 notes.
A. J. Larson

3901. Wolkovich-Valkavičius, William. THE IMPACT OF A CATHOLIC NEWSPAPER ON AN ETHNIC COMMUNITY: THE LITHUANIAN WEEKLY *RYTAS,* 1896-98, WATERBURY, CONNECTICUT. *Lituanus 1978 24(3): 42-53.* Father Joseph Zebris (d. 1915), editor and publisher of the Lithuanian weekly *Rytas,* used his newspaper to improve the welfare of his fellow countrymen in America. Zebris viewed preservation of the Catholic faith as his primary goal and did not hesitate to attack free thinkers in *Rytas.* He was also concerned with the immigrants' assimilation, commending citizenship, literacy, and voting. Through notices of available employment and encouragement of cooperative stores, Zebris aimed to improve the economic welfare of his readers. Health and social services were also a concern. Despite its brief life *Rytas* helped guide Lithuanian immigrants toward assimilation. 10 notes. K. N. T. Crowther

3902. Zubek, Theodoric. REMINISCENCES AND REFLECTIONS OF A SLOVAK REFUGEE PRIEST IN AMERICA. *Jednota Ann. Furdek 1978 17: 259-267.* The author, a Franciscan, recounts Communist persecution of religion in Czechoslovakia, his escape in 1951, his arrival in the United States in 1952, and his ministry in America. Discusses social and spiritual occurrences affecting religious thought in the United States, 1960's-78.

3903. —. FESTIVALS. *Palacio 1975 81(1): 26-30.* Excerpts from WPA files chronicle Hispanic and Catholic holidays in New Mexico: Las Posadas, La Noche Buena, Los Dias, St. John's Day, and Farmers' Patron Day.

3904. —. MILESTONES IN THE LIFE OF SAINT JOHN NEUMANN. *Jednota Ann. Furdek 1978 17: 133-136.* Lists significant events in the life of Bohemia-born Saint John Nepomucene Neumann (1811-60), a Redemptorist and the fourth Bishop of Philadelphia; he was canonized in 1977.

3905. —. A PARISH BORN IN THE GREAT DEPRESSION. *Jednota Ann. Furdek 1977 16: 101-106.* Catholic Slovak Canadians founded Saints Cyril and Methodius Parish in Toronto, Ontario, in 1934; a church was completed in 1941.

Eastern Rite Catholics

3906. Dushnyck, Walter. METROPOLITAN SENYSHYN—GREAT CHURCHMAN AND LEADER. *Ukrainian Q. 1977 33(1): 57-66.* Describes the life and work of Metropolitan Ambrose Senyshyn (1903-1976) of the Philadelphia Archeparchy. Born in the Ukraine and educated there and in Poland, Metropolitan Senyshyn came to the United States in 1933. Here he distinguished himself as a builder and organizer of churches and as a leader of the Ukrainian Catholic (Uniate) order in the United States. K. N. T. Crowther

3907. Fogarty, Gerald P. THE AMERICAN HIERARCHY AND ORIENTAL RITE CATHOLICS, 1890-1907. *Records of the Am. Catholic Hist. Soc. of Philadelphia 1974 85(1-2): 17-28.* Focuses on the role of the American archbishops, who in almost all of their annual meetings from 1890 to 1907 discussed the problem of Oriental rite Catholics coming to this country. They obtained restrictive Church legislation prohibiting retention by these groups of married clergy. 33 notes.
J. M. McCarthy

3908. Kayal, Philip M. RELIGION AND ASSIMILATION: CATHOLIC "SYRIANS" IN AMERICA. *Int. Migration Rev. 1973 7(4): 409-425.*

3909. Procko, Bohdan P. THE ESTABLISHMENT OF THE RUTHENIAN CHURCH IN THE UNITED STATES, 1884-1907. *Pennsylvania Hist. 1975 42(2): 137-154.* In 1884 the first priest of the Byzantine-Slavonic Rite of the Roman Catholic Church came to the United States to minister to Ruthenian Catholics. He established a church in Shenandoah, Pennsylvania. Efforts to provide for the spiritual needs of these people were impeded by divisions between Ukrainians and Rusins and by jurisdictional disputes with the American bishops, who were unwilling to accept married priests of the Byzantine Rite. The appointment of an administrator and, later, an "Apostolic Visitor," did little to improve the situation. Some Uniates left the Church of Rome and joined the Greek Orthodox Church. In 1907 Pope Pius X named a bishop for Ruthenian Catholics in the United States, and a new phase of development began. Illus., 71 notes. D. C. Swift

3910. Procko, Bohdan P. SOTER ORTYNSKY: FIRST RUTHENIAN BISHOP IN THE UNITED STATES, 1907-1916. *Catholic Hist. Rev. 1973 58(4): 513-533.* "Describes the jurisdictional problems that Bishop Soter Ortynsky (1866-1916) faced in his attempt to build an effective administrative system for the Byzantine-Slavic rite of the Catholic Church in the United States. Pope Pius X's appointment of a bishop for the Eastern Rite Catholics, who were then generally known as Ruthenians (primarily Ukrainian and Rusin immigrants from Austria-Hungary), altered a traditional administrative principle of the Roman Catholic Church in the West. This principle constituted an important element in the persistent conflicts between the Ruthenian priests and the Latin hierarchy." J

3911. —. A SHORT HISTORY OF THE SLOVAK CATHOLICS OF THE BYZANTINE PARISH OF THE ASSUMPTION OF THE B.V.M. *Jednota Ann. Furdek 1977 16: 207-209.* This Uniate parish in Hamilton, Ontario, was founded in 1952, and in 1963 the Shrine of Our Lady of Klocočov was dedicated there; Father Francis J. Fuga has been pastor since 1954.

Other Christian Traditions

Christian Science

3912. Johnsen, Thomas C. HISTORICAL CONSENSUS AND CHRISTIAN SCIENCE: THE CAREER OF A MANUSCRIPT CONTROVERSY. *New England Q. 1980 53(1): 3-22.* Analyzes Walter M. Haushalter's (d. 1963) contacts with the Christian Science Church in his attempt to extort money from it in return for suppressing a document which he later published in *Mrs. Eddy Purloins from Hegel* (1936). The key document was a forgery but Haushalter continued to write pamphlets about it until 1959. The church, confident that the document was a fraud, maintained a dignified silence. Based on documents in the archives of The Mother Church, Boston, and on published articles; 59 notes. J. C. Bradford

3913. Marty, Martin E. IN THE MAINSTREAM. *Rev. in Am. Hist. 1974 2(3): 408-413.* Stephen Gottschalk's *The Emergence of Christian Science in American Religious Life* (Berkeley: U. of California Pr., 1973) examines the tenets of Christian Science as propounded by its founder Mary Baker Eddy, the spiritual climate in which the movement grew and passed from "the charismatic to the bureaucratic stage," and its critics and followers, 1885-1910.

3914. Olds, Mason. MARY BAKER EDDY: A SESQUICENTENNIAL ACKNOWLEDGEMENT. *Contemporary Rev. [Great Britain] 1972 220(1277): 294-300.* Surveys the life, work, ideas, and influence of Mary Baker Eddy (1821-1910) and the early growth of Christian Science up to 1926.

Doukhobors

3915. Legebokoff, Peter P. PORTRAIT OF DOUKHOBORS: INTRODUCTION. *Sound Heritage [Canada] 1977 6(4): 12-21.* Offers a history, 1652-1908, of the Christian Community of Universal Brotherhood, also known as Dukhobors; recounts early oppression in Russia and immigration to Nova Scotia in 1899, Saskatchewan in 1905, and British Columbia in 1908.

3916. Mealing, F. M. PORTRAITS OF DOUKHOBORS: PREFACE AND CHRONOLOGY. *Sound Heritage [Canada] 1977 6(4): 1-11.* Discusses the social structure, economic conditions, values, and religious beliefs of the Christian Community of Universal Brotherhood, or Dukhobors, a communalistic religious sect which migrated from Russia to Saskatchewan and eventually settled in British Columbia; includes a chronology, 1652-1976.

3917. Woodcock, George. THE SPIRIT WRESTLERS: DOUKHOBORS IN RUSSIA AND CANADA. *Hist. Today [Great Britain] 1977 27(3): 152-158; (4): 249-255.* Part I. Outlines the history of the Dukhobor sect in Russia 1654-1890's and their emigration to Canada in 1898-99 because of religious persecution. Part II. Describes the Dukhobors as a militant religious sect led by Peter Nerigin, and their emigration from tsarist Russia to Canada, 1898-1902.

3918. —. THE DOUKHOBORS. *Sound Heritage [Canada] 1977 6(4): 23-77.* Fourteen members of the Christian Community of Universal Brotherhood, also known as Dukhobors, reminisce about immigration, the early days in Russia, and daily life in British Columbia, 1880's-1976.

Jehovah's Witnesses

3919. Abrahams, Edward. THE PAIN OF THE MILLENNIUM: CHARLES TAZE RUSSELL AND THE JEHOVAH'S WITNESSES, 1879-1916. *Am. Studies [Lawrence, KS] 1977 18(1): 57-70.* Examines Russell and the Jehovah's Witnesses in their political and social setting. Russell's millenarianism flowed from his perceptions of the major denominations and from the social crises of an industrializing America. He believed that the many conflicting social forces then rampant would lead to anarchy, a belief that reflects the Witnesses' alienation from American society. Primary and secondary sources; illus., 43 notes. J. Andrew

3920. Alston, Jon P. and Aguirre, B. E. CONGREGATIONAL SIZE AND THE DECLINE OF SECTARIAN COMMITMENT: THE CASE OF THE JEHOVAH'S WITNESSES IN SOUTH AND NORTH AMERICA. *Sociol. Analysis 1979 40(1): 63-70.* The analysis of membership and activity data among Jehovah's Witnesses in South and North America during 1950-76 partially supports a number of hypotheses derived from the traditional Troeltsch-Weber church sect model. The average congregation increased in size and levels of commitment decreased. In addition, the relative proportion of those members who were highly committed decreased over time as congregations became larger. Brazil and Paraguay do not fit these hypothesized patterns, and the Witnesses in the United States seemed to become more committed even as the local congregation developed church-like characteristics. Several suggestions are made concerning possible refinements of the church-sect model. J

3921. Blandre, Bernard. RUSSEL ET LES ETUDIANTS DE LA BIBLE [Russel and the Bible Students]. *Rev. de l'hist. des religions [France] 1975 187(2): 181-199.* Charles Taze Russel (1852-1916) is regarded by four American sects as their founder: Jehovah's Witnesses, Interior Lay Missionary Movement, and two groups known as Friends of Man. This division into various groups took place after his death. Born in Pittsburgh, Pennsylvania, in 1852, his mother died when he was nine. As a young man, he was critical of most Christian doctrines, but attracted to the teachings of William Miller and other adventists who speculated upon the return of the Savior. During the repeated crises of the Adventists, when all dates calculated for the second coming proved erroneous, Russel started his own movement in the 1870's. Predictions concerning the second coming of a spiritual Lord and intensive distribution of tract literature and of *Watchtower* materials characterize the organization of his group. F. Rosenthal

Mormons

3922. Adler, Douglas D. and Edwards, Paul M. COMMON BEGINNINGS, DIVERGENT BELIEFS. *Dialogue 1978 11(1): 18-28.* Compares LDS (Church of the Latter-Day Saints, or Mormons) and RLDS (Reorganized Church of the Latter-Day Saints), the two principal religious bodies that accept the authenticity of the Book of Mormon and the prophecy of Joseph Smith. Points of comparison include church positions on lay and professional leadership, role of central authority and local churches, dissent and criticism, temporal issues, geographic distribution, Protestant theology, evangelism, instructional and social opportunities within the church, fiscal policy and tithing, and the philosophical distinctions that separate the two movements. Divergence began in Nauvoo, Illinois, before Joseph Smith's death, and grew with different historical experiences, 1846-60, and afterward. Based on secondary sources; 20 notes. C. B. Schulz

3923. Alexander, Thomas G. WILFORD WOODRUFF AND THE CHANGING NATURE OF MORMON RELIGIOUS EXPERIENCE. *Church Hist. 1976 45(1): 50-69.* Considers the life of a single individual, Wilford Woodruff, in order to explore the attraction and meaning of the Mormon Church. Since Woodruff was important in the movement, it is possible to use his reactions to events and his religious experiences as a model of Mormon thought. Joining the church three years after its formation, Woodruff was involved in every major development in the Church's history except the settlement of Missouri. Consequently, his opinions as expressed in his diary reflect the changing nature of the Mormon religion. Covers 1830-1906. Based in part on the Journal of Wilford Woodruff; 61 notes. M. D. Dibert

3924. Allen, James B. TO THE SAINTS IN ENGLAND: IMPRESSIONS OF A MORMON IMMIGRANT (THE 10 DECEMBER 1840 WILLIAM CLAYTON LETTER FROM NAUVOO TO MANCHESTER). *Brigham Young U. Studies 1978 18(3): 475-480.* William Clayton, a member of the first Mormon emigrant company of Englishmen to America, wrote (on his arrival in Nauvoo, Illinois) his reflections of the journey. Addressing his friends in Manchester, he describes the new country and the hardships and the faith of his fellow Mormons, and offers sage advice to those planning to emigrate. Most significant are Clayton's observations of Joseph Smith and his immediate attachment to him. He expresses deep feelings for those Saints he had left behind, but vows that he would undertake the same journey again. M. S. Legan

3925. Allen, James B. "WE HAD A VERY HARD VOYAGE FOR THE SEASON": JOHN MOON'S ACCOUNT OF THE FIRST EMIGRANT COMPANY OF BRITISH SAINTS. *Brigham Young U. Studies 1977 17(3): 339-341.* An introduction to, and the text of, a letter that John Moon, the leader of the first self-organized emigrant company of British Mormons, wrote to William Clayton, past president of the British Mission, who was preparing for his own emigration. The letter chronicles the experience, trials, testimony, and excitement of the 41 Saints who left Liverpool for America on 6 June 1840. Clayton later included Moon's descriptions in a letter that he wrote on 19 August 1840 to Brigham Young and Willard Richards who were in England on an important mission. M. S. Legan

3926. Anderson, C. LeRoy and Halford, Larry J. THE MORMONS AND THE MORRISITE WAR. *Montana, the Mag. of Western Hist. 1974 24(4): 42-53.* For a brief period in 1861 and 1862, Joseph Morris led a faction challenging the authority of Brigham Young in the Mormon Church. Theological persuasion failing, Young resorted to civil and finally military force to dislodge the Morrisite defectors from their stronghold on the Weber River. Resistance led to Morris' death and the scattering of his followers. Illus., 24 notes. S. R. Davison

3927. Anderson, C. LeRoy. THE SCATTERED MORRISITES. *Montana 1976 26(4): 52-69.* A fragment of the Morrisite group fled Utah in 1862 and settled in Montana's Deer Lodge Valley. The small membership dwindled as rival leaders struggled for supremacy. By 1954, at the death of aged President George Johnson, the Montana Morrisite community had disappeared. Some descendants live in the area, and the church building still stands. Based on contemporary letters and accounts. Illus. S. R. Davison

3928. Anderson, Richard Lloyd. THE FRAUDULENT ARCHKO VOLUME. *Brigham Young U. Studies 1974 15(1): 43-64.* The Archko collection, first published by Cumberland Presbyterian Reverend William D. Mahan in the late 19th century, has been exposed as a modern religious forgery. The forgery purported to provide documents on the life of Christ. Lew Wallace's *Ben-Hur* (1880) formed the basis of a part of Mahan's writings. Other sections in the *Archko Volume* are also critically examined. M. S. Legan

3929. Arrington, Leonard and Jensen, Richard. PANACA: MORMON OUTPOST AMONG THE MINING CAMPS. *Nevada Hist. Soc. Q. 1975 18(4): 207-216.* Describes the efforts of Panaca's Mormons to preserve their community and their sect's particularistic social practices during the 1860's and 1870's. Panaca Mormons, who had founded the oldest permanent Mormon settlement in Nevada, felt that their social and cultural homogeneity was gravely threatened by newcomers of other faiths who flocked to mines and other industries in the region. Based on Mormon Church archives; 12 notes. H. T. Lovin

3930. Arrington, Leonard J. THE MORMON SETTLEMENT OF CASSIA COUNTY, IDAHO, 1873-1921. *Idaho Yesterdays 1979 23(2): 36-46.* Mormon families from Utah settled in south-central and south-western Idaho in the 1870's and 1880's. The settlers came on their own or with the sponsorship of local church leaders, rather than as part of an organized missionary effort from the central church authorities in Utah. The towns of Elba, Almo, Albion, and Oakley were founded. Early church leaders included Francis Marion Lyman, Heber J. Grant, Horton David Haight, and William T. Jack. Based on newspapers, church records, and manuscripts; 4 illus., 59 notes. B. J. Paul

3931. Avery, Valeen Tippetts and Newell, Linda King. LEWIS C. BIDAMON: STEPCHILD OF MORMONDOM. *Brigham Young U. Studies 1979 19(3): 375-388.* Lewis C. Bidamon, unaffiliated with any church, married Emma Smith, widow of Joseph Smith, in 1847, in Nauvoo, Illinois. In 1849, he joined the gold rush to California; he returned in 1850 to Nauvoo and Emma. Despite his love of liquor, lack of religion, and extramarital affairs, Emma continued to love him. Based on Church and Reorganized Church of Latter Day Saints archives; 55 notes. S

3932. Avery, Valeen Tippetts and Newell, Linda King. THE LION AND THE LADY: BRIGHAM YOUNG AND EMMA SMITH. *Utah Hist. Q. 1980 48(1): 81-97.* After Joseph Smith's death in 1844, Emma Hale Smith (later Bidamon) and Brigham Young conflicted over the succession to the Mormons' presidency, and the settling of Joseph's estate. Young felt that Emma had taken property belonging to the Mormons. Emma's legacy of debt left her feeling that Young had swindled her out of wealth. Neither understood that there had been no wealth. Nauvoo, Illinois, was built on speculative economy. Their conflict led to later institutionalized rancor between two churches (the Latter-day Saints and the Reorganized Latter-day Saints) claiming the same founder. Based on Brigham Young Papers, LDS Archives, Emma Smith Bidamon Papers, RLDS Library-Archives, and other primary sources; 6 illus., 42 notes. J. L. Hazelton

3933. Baer, Hans A. THE AARONIC ORDER: THE DEVELOPMENT OF A MODERN MORMON SECT. *Dialogue 1979 12(1): 57-71.* The Aaronic Order is a 400-member millenarian group founded by Maurice L. Glendenning in the early 1930's as the Mormon Church became increasingly oriented toward the middle classes. Many members believe they are lineal descendants of Aaron or Levi of the Old Testament and that they are to perform special religious functions before the second coming of Jesus Christ, which they claim will occur before the year 2000. The order consists of branches in a suburb of Salt Lake City, a congregation in Springdale, the Eskdale commune in western Millard County, and a cooperative community called Partoun in western Juab county. By 1975, ideological differences between fundamentalist Protestantism and the Aaronic order led to the expulsion of members thought to be leaning excessively toward Protestantism. This in turn led to a schism in which 25 other members left the order. 22 notes. S

3934. Barnett, Steven G. COLLECTING MANUSCRIPTS IN MORMON HISTORY. *Manuscripts 1974 26(3): 159-170.* Writes about the major figures of Mormon history, particularly the presidents whose signatures are reproduced at the head of vignettes introducing them and their manuscripts. Mormon materials are little advertised and those items occasionally noted in dealers' catalogs bring "stellar prices." Of course, the serious collector will dig in private fields, but he will encounter stiff competition from Mormon historical institutions. Covers 1823-1974. Illus., 6 notes. D. A. Yanchisin

3935. Beecher, Maureen Ursenbach. ALL THINGS MOVE IN ORDER IN THE CITY: THE NAUVOO DIARY OF ZINA DIANTHA HUNTINGTON JACOBS. *Brigham Young U. Studies 1979 19(3): 285-320.* Reproduces the diary for 1844-45 of Zina Diantha Huntington Jacobs, at one point a wife of Brigham Young, on the Mormons' life in Nauvoo, Illinois. 52 notes. S

3936. Beecher, Maureen Ursenbach. THE ELIZA ENIGMA. *Dialogue 1978 11(1): 30-43.* Examines the role of Eliza Roxey Snow (1804-87), plural wife of Joseph Smith and later Brigham Young, in the Mormon Church. Her poetry, begun in her Ohio youth, was important as an expression of her faith but undistinguished as poetry. She spoke in tongues, and was recognized as a prophet by her contemporaries, but most revelations were derivative, and predictions half-fulfilled. She practiced priestly functions in ministering to women in the early church in Utah. Her skills as "presidentess" were those of a succesful administrator rather than an originator. Based on published manuscript writings of Eliza Snow and her correspondents; illus., 32 notes. C. B. Schulz

3937. Bennion, Sherilyn Cox. THE *WOMAN'S EXPONENT*: FORTY-TWO YEARS OF SPEAKING FOR WOMEN. *Utah Hist. Q. 1976 44(3): 222-239.* Utah's *Women's Exponent* (1872-1914) was one of the earliest periodicals for women in the United States. It was a forum for subjects of interest to women, including religion, fashion, politics, polygamy, and suffrage. It encouraged women writers and reported Relief Society meetings and activities. Its influence among Mormon women was largely due to the ability and dedication of its two editors. Louisa Lula Greene Richards (1849-1944) served 1872-77. Emmeline Blanche Woodward Harris Whitney Wells (b. 1828) served 1877-1914. Based on primary and secondary sources; 4 illus., 41 notes. J. L. Hazelton

3938. Bergera, Gary James. THE ORSON PRATT-BRIGHAM YOUNG CONTROVERSIES: CONFLICT WITHIN THE QUORUMS, 1853-1868. *Dialogue 1980 13(2): 7-49.* The major issue of the conflict between Orson Pratt and Brigham Young was the conflict between Young's notion of dynamic revelation, which provided for the possibility of superceding past revelation, and Pratt's adherence to the written word of divine canon and past revelation. Pratt's demand for rationality and freedom of thought, in the absence of any specific revelation or declaration, threatened Young's prerogative as president of the Mormons for making authoritative theological pronouncements. Called upon to publicly confess his errors, Pratt confessed not that he espoused faulty beliefs, but only that he erred in expounding doctrines considered contrary to the opinions of the president. A public condemnation of Pratt's writings as false doctrine was issued, and thereafter the popularity of his notions waned markedly. Based on letters, sermons, newspapers, and journals of the period and secondary sources; 87 notes. R. D. Rahmes

3939. Bitton, Davis. GEORGE FRANCIS TRAIN AND BRIGHAM YOUNG. *Brigham Young U. Studies 1978 18(3): 410-427.* Train, an entrepreneur, lecturer, and would-be politician, was one of the few people to defend Mormonism during the second half of the 19th century. His adeptness on the lecture circuit and his statements to the press gained him a wide audience. He became, from the Mormons' point of view, a welcomed ally during the 1860's and 70's. A friendship developed between Train and Brigham Young. As a promoter of the transcontinental railroad, Train asked Young to serve as a director for the line and supply needed Mormon labor. Describes Train's visits to Utah, a speech in behalf of the Mormons, and the correspondence between the two men. Reprints Train's poem, "The Death of Brigham Young," which appeared in the Buffalo *Agitator* on 17 October 1877, less than two months after Young's death. M. S. Legan

3940. Bitton, Davis. PEOPLING THE UPPER SNAKE: THE SECOND WAVE OF MORMON SETTLEMENT IN IDAHO. *Idaho Yesterdays 1979 23(2): 47-52.* Mormons migrated into Idaho in the late 19th century because Utah was fully settled. Church leaders encouraged settlement of the sagebrush lands in Idaho. The coming of the railroads and the improvement of irrigation methods, along with the discovery that sugar beets grew well, made farming profitable for the settlers. Based on newspapers and church records; illus., 25 notes. B. J. Paul

3941. Bitton, Davis and Wilcox, Linda P. PESTIFEROUS IRONCLADS: THE GRASSHOPPER PROBLEM IN PIONEER UTAH. *Utah Hist. Q. 1978 46(4): 336-355.* Peak periods of grasshopper devastation in Utah were 1854-56, 1867-72, and 1876-79, with 1855 being the worst. Mormons regarded the devastations as divine trials of faith. They regarded deliverance by gulls, parasites, and wind as miracles, yet continually exerted themselves to repel the grasshoppers by beating them to death, sweeping them into creeks, or burning them. Crop destruction was countered by repeated sowings, larger plantings (to prevent complete destruction), and storage of food in good years. Primary and secondary sources; illus., table, 57 notes. J. L. Hazelton

3942. Bitton, Davis. THE RITUALIZATION OF MORMON HISTORY. *Utah Hist. Q. 1975 43(1): 67-85.* "Ritual" refers to visual symbols simplifying the past into forms that can be memorialized, celebrated, and emotionally appropriated. Examples of ritual in the Mormon Church are founding day, Pioneer Day, the celebrations of special groups such as the Mormon Battalion, organizations such as Daughters of Utah Pioneers, historic sites, shrines, graphic art, pageants, and hagiographical literature. Ritualization aids group cohesion during ridicule and persecution, and simplifies the mastering of history by converts. As simplified history is not completely satisfactory, historians need to criticize and correct inaccuracies, but should not ridicule all ritualization. Covers 1830-1975. Primary and secondary sources; 5 illus., 36 notes. J. L. Hazelton

3943. Bjork, Kenneth O. A COVENANT FOLK, WITH SCANDINAVIAN COLORINGS. *Norwegian-American Studies 1962 21: 212-251.* Though Mormons insisted on communal living among their adherents, some digression from this was allowed for the Scandinavin members of the group. Scandinavin-language newspapers, notably the *Utah posten* and *Bikuben,* covered news and church events during 1873-90's. Political participation in national politics was urged by editorials. Scandinavian-run businesses in Utah were advertised and supported by Mormons of Scandinavian descent. Some missionary work was done by Scandinavian Mormons in the northern Midwest (Wisconsin and Minnesota, predominantly) and reciprocated though never accepted by the Methodist Church and to an extent, the Lutheran Church. Despite integration, the Mormon Church of Utah found that accommodation to Scandinavian language, politics, and cultural heritage kept those members within the Mormon fold. G. A. Hewlett

3944. Bringhurst, Newell G. ELIJAH ABEL AND THE CHANGING STATUS OF BLACKS WITHIN MORMONISM. *Dialogue 1979 12(2): 22-36.* Discusses Elijah Abel, black member of the Mormon priesthood, in relation to the recent decision to abandon denial of the priesthood to blacks. No evidence of priesthood denial is evident prior to 1843; blacks were few, but enjoyed rights and duties equal to those of white members. The policy vacillated thereafter, with Abel usually at the very center of each controversy. The story remains vague and the evidence conflicting, but available data suggests that Brigham Young, rather than Joseph Smith, was finally responsible for the policy of black exclusion. Covers 1830's-70's. Photo, 89 notes. V. L. Human

3945. Britsch, R. Lanier. ANOTHER VISIT WITH WALTER MURRAY GIBSON. *Utah Hist. Q. 1978 46(1): 65-78.* An evaluation of Gwynn Barrett's "Walter Murray Gibson: The Shepherd Saint of Lanai Revisited" reveals that Barrett failed to produce evidence discrediting the works of Thomas G. Thrum and Andrew Jenson. Historical sources relating to Gibson and the Mormons are too abundant and unified to support a new, more sympathetic appraisal of Gibson. They also prove the "tradition" that Gibson stole the Hawaiian island of Lanai from the Mormon Church immediately after his excommunication in 1864, not years later as Barrett asserts. Primary and secondary sources; illus., 37 notes. J. L. Hazelton

3946. Bush, Lester E., Jr. INTRODUCTION. *Dialogue 1979 12(2): 9-12.* A consideration of the decision of the Church of Jesus Christ of Latter Day Saints to accept blacks into the priesthood. One year after the decision of 1978, not much has changed; the mass exodus to or from the faith has not materialized. What remains is a better understanding of the pertinent biblical passages, the traditional position of the church, and the processes which led President Edward Kimball to seek the advice of the Lord on the question of black priesthood. 11 notes. V. L. Human

3947. Cannon, Donald Q. THE KING FOLLETT DISCOURSE: JOSEPH SMITH'S GREATEST SERMON IN HISTORICAL PERSPECTIVE. *Brigham Young U. Studies 1978 18(2): 179-192.* Discusses the historical milieu in which Joseph Smith delivered his greatest sermon on 7 April 1844 in Nauvoo, Illinois. Although it began as a eulogy for King Follett who had been killed on 9 March 1844, in a well accident, Smith expanded his remarks to include revelations whose time, he believed, had come in the spiritual development of the church. The delivered text was preserved by Thomas Bullock, William Clayton, and Willard Richards, who made official records, and by Wilford Woodruff, who took notes for his personal journal. Some effort is made to reconcile the different versions. Analyzes the reactions of Mormons and non-Mormons to the sermon. Traces the publication history of that discourse to the present. M. S. Legan

3948. Coates, Lawrence G. BRIGHAM YOUNG AND MORMON INDIAN POLICIES: THE FORMATIVE PERIOD, 1836-1851. *Brigham Young U. Studies 1978 18(3): 428-452.* Brigham Young's attitudes toward Indians were to profoundly affect Mormon-Indian affairs during his lifetime, and even for decades after his death. Traces Young's relationships with Indians from his first mission to them in western New York in 1835, to the exodus from Nauvoo and on the Great Plains, and through his formulation of a policy toward Indians in Utah. Documents Young's evolving socio-religious-humanitarian philosophy. Young was not averse to open conflict with the Indians of Utah when peaceful means failed. He eventually concluded, however, that "it was cheaper to feed the Indians than fight them." M. S. Legan

3949. Coe, Michael. MORMONS AND ARCHEOLOGY: AN OUTSIDE VIEW. *Dialogue 1973 8(2): 40-48.*

3950. Cook, Lyndon W. ISAAC GALLAND: MORMON BENEFACTOR. *Brigham Young U. Studies 1979 19(3): 261-284.* Isaac Galland (1791-1858) settled in Iowa and speculated in the Half-Breed Tract in Lee County. He interceded with the territorial government to insure a favorable reception of the Mormons and, in 1839, sold them land and converted to their faith. Joseph Smith instructed him to handle some of the Mormons' land transactions. For unknown reasons, he stopped his land activities for the Mormons and left the faith in the 1840's, but continued to associate with them until his death. Map, 107 notes. S

3951. Cook, Lyndon W. JAMES ARLINGTON BENNET AND THE MORMONS. *Brigham Young U. Studies 1979 19(2): 247-249.* Publishes James Arlington Bennet's letter of 6 May 1860 to Joseph Smith III, who had just assumed the presidency of the Reorganized Church of Latter Day Saints. Bennet was an opportunist who parted from the Mormons in 1845 after having been denied the leadership of the Nauvoo Legion.

3952. Cook, Lyndon W. A MORE VIRTUOUS MAN NEVER EXISTED ON THE FOOTSTOOL OF THE GREAT JEHOVAH: GEORGE MILLER ON JOSEPH SMITH. *Brigham Young U. Studies 1979 19(3): 402-407.* Introduces and reproduces a description of Joseph Smith, in 1842, by George Miller, prominent Mormon leader, in a letter to Governor Thomas Reynolds of Missouri. Miller affirmed the good character of Smith and Smith's innocence of a murder charge in Missouri, and protested prejudice against Mormons. 19 notes. S

3953. Corbett, Pearson Starr. SETTLING THE MUDDY RIVER VALLEY. *Nevada Hist. Soc. Q. 1975 18(3): 141-151.* Chronicles the establishment of settlements in the Muddy River region of southern Nevada by Mormons from Utah. As a result of stimulus provided by Mormon Church leaders, the first settlers left Utah in 1865. They settled in Nevada for a few years, and were ousted, but they returned to the region by 1875. Primary sources; 12 notes. H. T. Lovin

3954. Cowan, Richard O. ADVICE FROM A PROPHET: TAKE TIME OUT. *Brigham Young U. Studies 1976 16(3): 415-418.* Comments on the attitudes of the General Authorities of the Mormon Church toward physical recreation and relaxation. Examines and edits several letters exchanged during the 1930's between President Heber J. Grant and Joseph Fielding Smith, who became president some 30 years later. The letters reveal that Grant emphasized golfing and exercise. Smith enjoyed swimming and handball. In his later years he flew in jet planes to relax. M. S. Legan

3955. Cowan, Richard O. THE PRIESTHOOD-AUXILIARY MOVEMENT, 1928-1938. *Brigham Young U. Studies 1978 19(1): 106-120.* During 1928-38, the Mormon Church extensively revised its activities and meetings. Many of the changes combined priesthood activities, which had been separate formerly, with the Sunday School or the Mutual Improvement Association. Major innovations of the so-called Priesthood-Auxiliary Movement still influence church functions. Evaluates the movement's antecedents, the evolution of new meeting patterns, the revitalization and strengthening of the Melchizedek and Aaronic priesthoods, and the correlation of other church activities. Lists the difficulties and contributions of the Priesthood-Auxiliary Movement. M. S. Legan

3956. Crawley, Peter. JOSEPH SMITH AND *A BOOK OF COMMANDMENTS. Princeton U. Lib. Chronicle 1980 42(1): 18-32.* Describes the Princeton University Library's copy of Joseph Smith's *A Book of Commandments for the Government of the Church of Christ,* containing Smith's revelations, and provides a history of the Mormons from the first of the revelations in 1820, and the founding of the church in 1830 in Fayette, New York, until 1846; traces the ownership of the book until Princeton's acquisition of it in 1975.

3957. Dix, Fae Decker, ed. THE JOSEPHINE DIARIES: GLIMPSES OF THE LIFE OF JOSEPHINE STREEPER CHASE, 1881-94. *Utah Hist. Q. 1978 46(2): 167-183.* Josephine Streeper Chase (1835-94) was the polygamous second wife of George Ogden Chase in Centerville, Utah. She was the mother of 15 children and one foster daughter, Sunday school teacher, successful manager of a large household, and faithful church member. Her diary, covering 1881-94, is a priceless journal of daily life in a busy Mormon home, describing with surprising detail housecleaning, outdoor chores, baking, preserving, churning, and hog killing. She voices the spirit and ordeal of her time. Primary and secondary sources; 3 illus., 16 notes. J. L. Hazelton

3958. Ehat, Andrew F., ed. "THEY MIGHT HAVE KNOWN THAT HE WAS NOT A FALLEN PROPHET": THE NAUVOO JOURNAL OF JOSEPH FIELDING. *Brigham Young U. Studies 1979 19(2): 133-166.* Introduces and reproduces Joseph Fielding's journal of 1844-46. Fielding was a Mormon missionary to England in the 1830's and 1840's. In 1843 he was endowed by Joseph Smith to officiate in church ordinances. His diary describes the development of Nauvoo and Fielding's conviction of the truth of his faith. Illus., 105 notes. S

3959. Enders, Donald L. PLATTING THE CITY BEAUTIFUL: A HISTORICAL AND ARCHAEOLOGICAL GLIMPSE OF NAUVOO STREETS. *Brigham Young U. Studies 1979 19(3): 409-415.* Nauvoo, Illinois, was to be laid out in a grid pattern, according to the Mormons' city planning. Unfortunately, buildings encroached property lines, the roads were disjointed, blocks were subdivided, and streets were often impassable in the 1840's. Plate; 23 notes. S

3960. England, Eugene. BRIGHAM'S GOSPEL KINGDOM. *Brigham Young U. Studies 1978 18(3): 328-376.* Discusses Brigham Young's role in the political, economic, social, and religious development of the State of Deseret. Describes the Mormons' sugar experiments and efforts to establish an iron industry to promote the idea of a self-sufficient commonwealth. Details Young's interest in immigration; focuses on the handcart companies and their untimely fate. Traces the origins of the Mountain Meadow Massacre and Young's dynamic leadership during the Mormon War. Young may best be understood through his attitudes toward stewardship which enabled him to use resources in whatever way his judgment and inspiration convinced him was for the good of the kingdom. Covers the 1840's to 1877. M. S. Legan

3961. England, Eugene, ed. GEORGE LAUB'S NAUVOO JOURNAL. *Brigham Young U. Studies 1978 18(2): 151-178.* George Laub began keeping a journal on 1 January 1845, after being converted to Mormonism in Pennsylvania a few years earlier. His record is significant to church history. It includes Joseph Smith's, Brigham Young's, and other church leaders' sermons and speeches. Laub also preserves a brief account of his own life as well as a review of the harsh treatment of Mormons in Illinois. The journal ends with the entry of 6 June 1846, as the Saints prepared to leave Nauvoo for Utah. M. S. Legan

3962. Esplin, Ronald K. BRIGHAM YOUNG AND PRIESTHOOD DENIAL TO THE BLACKS: AN ALTERNATE VIEW. *Brigham Young U. Studies 1979 19(3): 394-402.* Brigham Young's position that Negroes could not be admitted to the Mormon priesthood was a revelation and not the product of personal whims. He had enunciated the belief by 1847, rather than the commonly held date of 1849. 8 notes.

3963. Esplin, Ronald K. LIFE IN NAUVOO, JUNE 1844: VILATE KIMBALL'S MARTYRDOM LETTERS. *Brigham Young U. Studies 1979 19(2): 231-240.* Vilate Kimball's letters to her missionary husband, Apostle Heber C. Kimball, give witness to the emotion-laden atmosphere in Nauvoo, Illinois, during the period of Joseph Smith's flight and murder.

3964. Evans, Max J. WILLIAM C. STAINES: "ENGLISH GENTLEMAN OF REFINEMENT AND CULTURE." *Utah Hist. Q. 1975 43(4): 410-420.* William C. Staines (1818-81) was born in England, joined the Mormon church in 1841, and migrated to Utah in 1847. He occupied prominent positions as territorial librarian (for 12 years) and church emigration agent (for 20 years). He was a promoter, entrepreneur, and businessman in a variety of enterprises. Churchman, politician, horticulturist, amateur scientist, and socialite, he is an example of the diversity of interest and talents found in 19th-century Utah. Based on primary and secondary sources; 2 illus., 40 notes. J. L. Hazelton

3965. Fetzer, Leland. RUSSIAN WRITERS LOOK AT MORMON MANNERS, 1857-72. *Dialogue 1980 13(1): 74-84.* Government and social reforms under Alexander II of Russia had a counterpart in Russian music, painting, and writing. Russian writers were particularly interested in Mormonism, because it was distinctively American and seemingly without European antecedents. Common themes of interest to Russian writers included Mormonism's similarity to Islam, its theocratic structure, its love of labor, and the relation between polygamy and the emancipation of women. Russian writers were never interested in doctrinal concerns, and by 1872 their interest in Mormon social experimentation had expired. Based on Russian publications during this period, and on secondary sources; 27 notes. R. D. Rahmes

3966. Flake, Chad J. MORMON BIBLIOGRAPHY, 1977. *Brigham Young U. Studies 1978 18(4): 570-584.* Sees a poor quality of printing and unsatisfactory paper stock in many Mormon reference materials, particularly religious works such as the *Book of Mormon.* The bibliography lists more than 220 sources on Mormons in their historical, doctrinal, inspirational, artistic, biographical, and genealogical contexts. M. S. Legan

3967. Flake, Chad J. MORMON BIBLIOGRAPHY: 1974. *Brigham Young U. Studies 1975 15(4): 527-536.* Annotated bibliography of articles written in 1974 dealing with Mormonism.

3968. Flake, Chad J. MORMON BIBLIOGRAPHY, 1975. *Brigham Young U. Studies 1976 16(3): 419-428.* This 193-entry bibliography for 1975 relies heavily on volume 16 of *Mormon Americana.* Church periodicals, except for selected references, have been omitted because they appear in another index. Topics are: historical, doctrinal, inspirational, biographical, and the appearance of new periodicals. M. S. Legan

3969. Flake, Chad J. MORMON BIBLIOGRAPHY, 1976. *Brigham Young U. Studies 1977 17(3): 361-372.* This annual bibliography on Mormonism, compiled from *Mormon Americana,* volume 17 (1976), is divided into historical, doctrinal, inspirational, artistic, biographic and family history, and bibliographic sections. The introduction singles out James B. Allen and Glen M. Leonard's work, *The Story of the Latter-day Saints,* as extremely significant, for it marks the first survey by professional historians of the entire scope of Mormon history. M. S. Legan

3970. Francis, Rell G. VIEWS OF MORMON COUNTRY: THE LIFE AND PHOTOGRAPHS OF GEORGE EDWARD ANDERSON. *Am. West 1978 15(6): 14-29.* At the age of 17, after serving as an apprentice where he mastered the principles and techniques of photography, Mormon George Edward (George Ed) Anderson (1860-1928) set up business for himself. He was quick to adopt new ideas and to devise such things as portable studios. He traveled throughout southern Utah to remote villages, mining camps, or wherever opportunity for people-centered civic activities, rural industry, and community celebrations beckoned. About two-thirds of his some 40,000 photographs were studio portraits. He was also motivated by an insatiable quest to document Mormon Church history and subjects. Anderson's work has been featured in several publications and in recent exhibits. Based on a forthcoming book; 18 illus. D. L. Smith

3971. Gardner, Martin R. MORMONISM AND CAPITAL PUNISHMENT: A DOCTRINAL PERSPECTIVE, PAST AND PRESENT. *Dialogue 1979 12(1): 9-26.* Early Mormon leaders such as Joseph Smith, Brigham Young, Jedediah M. Grant, and Heber C. Kimball taught that, according to scripture, some crimes are so heinous that only the spilling of the perpetrator's blood can achieve atonement for his soul. The option of execution by firing squad—the shedding of blood—is peculiar to Utah in the United States due to the Mormons' influence on state laws. Decapitation was another option in the Territory of Utah during 1852-76, as was hanging, which persists. Although elements of utilitarianism appeared in some early Mormon arguments for capital punishment as a deterrent to crime, retribution and atonement were emphasized. In the 20th century there are few references to the blood atonement doctrine. Recently Elder Bruce R. McConkie wrote that there has never been a doctrine of blood atonement in the Church of Latter-Day Saints. 46 notes, ref. S

3972. Gates, Susa Young. FROM IMPULSIVE GIRL TO PATIENT WIFE: LUCY BIGELOW YOUNG. *Utah Hist. Q. 1977 45(3): 270-288.* Lucy Bigelow Young (1830-1905), daughter of Nahum Bigelow and Mary Foster Gibbs, was a lively and impetuous girl who "never intended to marry a married man." Yet she and her sister, Mary Jane Bigelow, were sealed to Brigham Young 14 March 1846 in Utah. She had three children, Eudora, Susa, and Mabel. Excerpts from a typescript "Lucy Bigelow Young," written by Susa Young Gates, illuminate her life and shed light on Brigham Young's character, from a devoted daughter's perspective. Excerpts from a typescript in the manuscript collection of the Utah State Historical Society; 11 illus., 16 notes. J. L. Hazelton

3973. Gentry, Leland H. WHAT OF THE LECTURES OF FAITH? *Brigham Young U. Studies 1978 19(1): 5-19.* The Lectures of Faith were a series of seven theological presentations to the School of the Elders held in Kirtland, Ohio, during the winter of 1834-35. Until 1921, these Lectures were printed with the revelations of God to Joseph Smith in every English edition to the Doctrine and Covenants. Analyzes the Lectures' historical background, their authorship, and their delivery, and discusses why the Lectures were removed from the Doctrine and Covenants. Research has failed to uncover the specific identity of either the writer or the person who delivered them. M. S. Legan

3974. Godfrey, Kenneth W. SOME THOUGHTS REGARDING AN UNWRITTEN HISTORY OF NAUVOO. *Brigham Young U. Studies 1975 15(4): 417-424.* Presents anecdotes about the Mormons in Nauvoo, Illinois, and thoughts regarding the possibility of writing a social history of the town, 1842-46.

3975. Gowans, Fred R. FORT BRIDGER AND THE MORMONS. *Utah Hist. Q. 1974 42(1): 49-67.* Initial Mormon involvement with Fort Bridger at the eastern entrance to the Salt Lake Valley was friendly (starting in 1847). Relations deteriorated rapidly as church leaders became suspicious that mountain man Jim Bridger was exciting the Indians against the Mormons, as friction developed over control of the Green River ferry, as the territorial legislature levied a tax against mountain men, and as Brigham Young sought to control the Fort Bridger area. Bridger sold out to the Mormons in 1855 and Mormon involvement ended in October 1857 when they destroyed the fort. 6 illus., map, 52 notes. D. L. Smith

3976. Hale, Van. THE DOCTRINAL IMPACT OF THE KING FOLLETT DISCOURSE. *Brigham Young U. Studies 1978 18(2): 209-225.* Joseph Smith's King Follett Discourse, delivered on 7 April 1844, in Nauvoo, Illinois, significantly changed the spiritual direction of the Mormons. Evaluates and synthesizes Smith's main theme of the plurality of gods. Treats individually the doctrines enunciated by Smith that:

1) men can become gods; 2) there exist many gods; 3) the gods exist one above another innumerably; and 4) God was once as man is now. Seeks to assess the long-range impact of these revelations on the Church.
M. S. Legan

3977. Hardy, B. Carmon. THE SCHOOLBOY GOD: A MORMON-AMERICAN MODEL. *J. of Religious Hist. [Australia] 1976 9(2): 173-188.* From the very outset, Mormon leaders emphasized the need for education. When one combines this aspect to the Mormons' conception of the universe as a static entity based on fixed laws and purpose, one can readily compare Mormonism with the prevalent concepts accepted by Americans in the 19th century—both were based on a romantic world view and both failed to fulfill their objectives. Primary and secondary sources; 75 notes. W. T. Walker

3978. Hartley, William G. ORDAINED AND ACTING TEACHERS IN THE LESSER PRIESTHOOD, 1851-1883. *Brigham Young U. Studies 1976 16(3): 375-398.* Analyzes the work of the Mormons' Aaronic Priesthood when Edward Hunter presided over the lesser priesthood as presiding bishop of the church. Describes the priesthood's operations, concepts and ideas, and practices, and focuses on the church's efforts to revitalize the lesser order. Emphasizes the loss of possible Aaronic recruits who favored joining the higher Melchizedek Priesthood.
M. S. Legan

3979. Hesslink, George K. KIMBALL YOUNG: SEMINAL AMERICAN SOCIOLOGIST, SWEDISH DESCENDANT, AND GRANDSON OF MORMON LEADER BRIGHAM YOUNG. *Swedish Pioneer Hist. Q. 1974 25(2): 115-132.* Kimball Young (1893-1972), whose mother was Swedish, was a direct descendant of Brigham Young. Summarizes Kimball Young's career, accomplishments, and ancestry. Scandinavian converts to Mormonism experienced a great cultural break. Unfulfilled expectations of the Mormon settlements and perceptions of the Mormon establishment led to disillusionment. Based on primary and secondary sources; photo, table, 34 notes.
K. J. Puffer

3980. Hill, Marvin S. CULTURAL CRISIS IN THE MORMON KINGDOM: A RECONSIDERATION OF THE CAUSES OF KIRTLAND DISSENT. *Church Hist. 1980 49(3): 286-297.* Serious internal discontent developed among the Mormons while they were at Kirtland, Ohio. The failure of the Kirtland bank was a precipitating factor in the rebellion. However, the bank failure may have been more a symbol for general Mormon discontent than a direct factor in the rebellion. Covers ca. 1837-90. 58 notes. M. D. Dibert

3981. Hill, Marvin S. MORMON RELIGION IN NAUVOO: SOME REFLECTIONS. *Utah Hist. Q. 1976 44(2): 170-180.* In comparison with so much that seems secular and worldly, was there much that was religious at Nauvoo, Illinois? Erwin B. Goodenough defines religion as initially a quest for security. Peace, security, the end of social conflict are religious desires. Many things traditionally thought of as secular were not, but were designed to promote social control and social stability. Everything that occurred at Nauvoo of a social or political nature was to Mormons essentially religious. Covers 1833-46. Primary and secondary sources; 2 illus., 49 notes. J. L. Hazelton

3982. Hill, Marvin S. A NOTE ON JOSEPH SMITH'S FIRST VISION AND ITS IMPORT IN THE SHAPING OF EARLY MORMONISM. *Dialogue 1979 12(1): 90-99.* Reviews the religious background of the young Joseph Smith (1805-44) and his family to determine the degree of influence this might have had on the questions he asked (which of the existing Christian religions was the true faith; whether, indeed, there was a Supreme Being). Methodism, Presbyterianism, Universalism, and the thoughts of Thomas Paine and Thomas Jefferson all played a role in Smith's questions about and attitudes toward religion as well as in the doctrines of the Mormon Church which Smith soon founded. As a reflection of Smith's early religious experiences and questions, there remains an uneasy tension between faith and reason in Mormonism to this day. 52 notes. S

3983. Hill, Marvin S. SECULAR OR SECTARIAN HISTORY? A CRITIQUE OF *NO MAN KNOWS MY HISTORY. Church Hist. 1974 43(1): 78-96.* New discoveries about the life of Joseph Smith (1805-44), the Mormon prophet, demand a reappraisal of Fawn Brodie's 1945 biography of Smith, *No Man Knows My History* (New York: Alfred A. Knopf, 1971, 2d edition). Despite her impressive research, Brodie misunderstood Smith's nature and intentions; she judged him on the basis of a secular-sectarian approach. Brodie's biography of Smith, however, has maintained its status despite much change in the way that American intellectual and religious history is viewed. D. C. Richardson

3984. Holbrook, Leona. DANCING AS AN ASPECT OF EARLY MORMON AND UTAH CULTURE. *Brigham Young U. Studies 1975 16(1): 117-138.* Reviews Mormons' high regard for physical activity as an expression of inner joy as well as a way to build a physical strength on which to base a moral and spiritual strength; juxtaposes Mormon belief in dance with that of other Christian religions, and fits all this into the scene in Utah, 1830-80.

3985. Howard, Barbara and Braby, Junia. THE HODGES HANGING. *Palimpsest 1979 60(2): 48-58.* Members of the Danite sect of the Mormon Church, William and Stephen Hodges were indicted and hanged for the murder of two Iowa farmers during a burglary, 1845.

3986. Howard, G. M. MEN, MOTIVES, AND MISUNDERSTANDINGS: A NEW LOOK AT THE MORRISITE WAR OF 1862. *Utah Hist. Q. 1976 44(2): 112-132.* Ostensibly, the issue was law enforcement in the Morrisite War of 1862, but politics and religion were involved. At stake was the unity and leadership of Utah territory. Joseph Morris' (1824-62) predominantly Danish followers were unfamiliar with American law and disenchanted with Mormon orthodoxy. When Robert T. Burton marched a federal posse on Kingston Fort, Morrisites mistakenly thought Mormons were attacking in a religious war. Needless anguish, bloodshed, and lasting scars resulted. Primary and secondary sources; 7 illus., 32 notes. J. L. Hazelton

3987. Irving, Gordon. ENCOURAGING THE SAINTS: BRIGHAM YOUNG'S ANNUAL TOURS OF THE MORMON SETTLEMENTS. *Utah Hist. Q. 1977 45(3): 233-251.* Brigham Young's annual tours of Utah's pioneer settlements had an overall purpose of encouraging the Saints. They also gave him a chance personally to observe and evaluate conditions in the colonies, to give practical and spiritual guidance and instruction, and to strengthen the commitment of the Saints to the church and building up of the kingdom. The tours lifted the spirits of the colonists above the drudgery of pioneer life by providing outside contacts and social activities. Based on primary and secondary sources; 3 illus., 41 notes. J. L. Hazelton

3988. Jackson, Richard H. THE MORMON VILLAGE: GENESIS AND ANTECEDENTS OF THE CITY OF ZION PLAN. *Brigham Young U. Studies 1977 17(2): 223-240.* In 1833 Joseph Smith sent plans for his proposed City of Zion to a group of Missouri Mormons. Many scholars have mistakenly concluded that subsequent Mormon settlements religiously adhered to Smith's plan. Examines the development of Mormon villages, towns, and cities and concludes that most urban development deviated from the Zion plat and from each other as well. However, there are similarities, such as street widths, block sizes, and lot sizes, which seemed to set the Mormon village apart from non-Mormon settlements in the West. M. S. Legan

3989. Jennings, Warren A., ed. "WHAT CRIME HAVE I BEEN GUILTY OF?" EDWARD PARTRIDGE'S LETTER TO AN ESTRANGED SISTER. *Brigham Young U. Studies 1978 18(4): 520-528.* This 1837 letter by Edward Partridge. the first Mormon bishop, although addressed to a brother, was primarily intended for his sister, Emily Dow. The missive, from Missouri to Massachusetts, describes his sorrow at being ostracized by his family after his conversion to Mormonism. Partridge discussed the tenets of his new faith, and the letter contains a common Mormon proselytizing tactic which involved reasoning from scriptural authority rather than emphasizing the revivalism practiced by other denominations. M. S. Legan

3990. Jessee, Dean. HOWARD CORAY'S RECOLLECTIONS OF JOSEPH SMITH. *Brigham Young U. Studies 1977 17(3): 341-347.* Howard Coray, a talented Mormon writer, was a clerk in Joseph Smith's office during the 1840's. The Mormon leader's trust in Coray is attested to by the many important original documents of the Nauvoo era in

Coray's handwriting. In view of the many contradictory sources on Smith, these recollections are significant because of Coray's close contact with Smith during his last years. These two short manuscripts, the first in its entirety, the second extracted, preserve valuable impressions of Smith's personality and his method of conducting Mormon affairs. M. S. Legan

3991. Jessee, Dean. JOSEPH KNIGHT'S RECOLLECTION OF EARLY MORMON HISTORY. *Brigham Young U. Studies 1976 17(1): 29-39.* Joseph Knight, Sr. (1772-1847), became one of the earliest converts to the Mormon religion. Subsequently, his family dedicated itself to the Mormon movement and helped establish several settlements. Reproduces Knight's holograph, "Manuscript of the Early History of Joseph Smith," written some time between Knight's departure from Jackson County, Missouri, in 1833 and his death at Mt. Pisgah, Iowa, in 1847. The manuscript is an important piece of primary material on the life of Joseph Smith and the early vicissitudes of the Mormons. M. S. Legan

3992. Jessee, Dean C. THE WRITINGS OF BRIGHAM YOUNG. *Western Hist. Q. 1973 4(3): 273-294.* The long-standing distorted image of Young is due in part to the magnitude of the task of digesting the massive amount of primary source material about him. Furthermore, a biographer's view is often blurred by the work of ghost writers and of Young's secretaries. Young had many secretaries, and most of his biographers have derived their inaccurate portrait of him from the secretaries' writings. Young's holograph writings provide "an unequaled vantage point" from which to make an accurate study. They closely parallel descriptions of Young by those who knew him best. Describes documents of 1832-75 according to the geographic periods of Young's life; Ohio, England, Illinois, the Great Plains, Utah. 43 notes. D. L. Smith

3993. Keller, Charles L. PROMOTING RAILROADS AND STATEHOOD: JOHN W. YOUNG. *Utah Hist. Q. 1977 45(3): 289-308.* John W. Young, third son of Brigham Young and Mary Ann Angell, was unable to obtain financing for his Salt Lake and Fort Douglas Railroad in the early 1880's because of the unstable Utah economic situation. He attempted to improve that situation by urging either statehood for Utah or relief from federal prosecution of polygamy stipulated by the 1882 Edmunds Act. Through his efforts, the people of Utah agreed to a constitution prohibiting polygamy, a significant step toward gaining statehood. Based on primary and secondary sources; 7 illus., 41 notes. J. L. Hazelton

3994. Kimball, Edward L. "I SUSTAIN HIM AS A PROPHET, I LOVE HIM AS AN AFFECTIONATE FATHER." *Dialogue 1978 11(4): 48-62.* Transcript of an October 1978 interview between *Dialogue* and Edward L. Kimball, the youngest son of Spencer W. Kimball, President of the Church of Jesus Christ of the Latter Day Saints. Kimball, with his brother Andrew, wrote a biography of their father, published in 1977, based on interviews with their parents, friends of the family and leaders of the church, journal entries, personal letters, and family anecdotes. The process of writing the biography made it possible to check the growth of myths about the leader of the Mormon church. Kimball shares his special pride in his father's revelation allowing blacks to hold the priesthood in the Mormon church. C. B. Schulz

3995. Kimball, James L., Jr. A WALL TO DEFEND ZION: THE NAUVOO CHARTER. *Brigham Young U. Studies 1975 15(4): 491-497.* Discusses the success of the Mormon community in ascertaining a city charter for Nauvoo, Illinois, 1839-41, so that their sect might have a town of its own.

3996. Kimball, Stanley B. BRIGHAM AND HEBER. *Brigham Young U. Studies 1978 18(3): 396-409.* Heber C. Kimball's friendship with Brigham Young began in 1829 when both were 27-year-old artisans in Monroe County, New York. Following similar paths into Mormonism, the two men shared many common experiences in the faith as missionaries, as leaders in Nauvoo and during the exodus westward, and as ecclesiastics in the Utah community. Details their parallel careers as Young assumed the church presidency and Kimball became his first counselor. Near the end of his life, Kimball began to experience self-doubts about his and Young's contributions to Mormonism. Despite outside criticisms and his own fears and suppositions, Kimball remained loyal to Young. Kimball died on 22 June 1868. M. S. Legan

3997. Kimball, Stanley B. HEBER C. KIMBALL AND FAMILY, THE NAUVOO YEARS. *Brigham Young U. Studies 1975 15(4): 447-479.* Discusses the Heber C. Kimball family during their tenure in Nauvoo, Illinois, with the rest of the Mormon community, 1839-46.

3998. Kimball, Stanley B. NAUVOO WEST: THE MORMONS OF THE IOWA SHORE. *Brigham Young U. Studies 1978 18(2): 132-142.* Although much of the literature dealing with the Mormons in Illinois has centered on events in Nauvoo, there were those who lived immediately across the Mississippi River in Lee County, Iowa. Discusses the first Mormons in Iowa, who arrived in 1838, their contributions to the general settlement of the region, and the Church's expansion in the Iowa or Zarahemla Stake. Brigham Young used Lee County in 1846 as a staging area for the Mormon trek. M. S. Legan

3999. King, Robert R. THE ENDURING SIGNIFICANCE OF THE MORMON TREK. *Dialogue 1980 13(2): 102-107.* Discusses the contemporary relevance of the Mormon trek to Utah, 1846-69. Seen as a parallel to Israel's Exodus, the trek was significant for establishing group identity. The trek further developed group cooperation and group cohesion, and stimulated organizational development. Finally, the trek created a regional base for the church, facilitating socialization of its second generation to perpetuate its beliefs, norms and goals. 3 notes. R. D. Rahmes

4000. Layton, Stanford J. FORT RAWLINS, UTAH: A QUESTION OF MISSION AND MEANS. *Utah Hist. Q. 1974 42(1): 68-83.* Drunken soldiers from Fort Rawlins assaulted and insulted citizens in nearby Provo, Utah, in September 1870. The so-called Provo Outrage strained relations between Mormon civilians and the military, and growing differences between the local command and higher army headquarters led to the closing of Fort Rawlins in 1871. 5 illus., 24 notes. D. L. Smith

4001. Leonard, Glen M. TRUMAN LEONARD: PIONEER MORMON FARMER. *Utah Hist. Q. 1976 44(3): 240-260.* Truman Leonard (1820-97) was a typical Utah Mormon. Both his plural wives were taken during the flurry of marrying stirred up by the Mormon Reformation. He participated in the Utah War, performed civic duties, and was a missionary four times. He was a religious exile from Nauvoo who mingled a zeal for salvation with hard work on a small but productive Davis County farm. Based on primary and secondary sources; 7 illus., 39 notes. J. L. Hazelton

4002. Lieber, Constance L. "THE GOOSE HANGS HIGH": EXCERPTS FROM THE LETTERS OF MARTHA HUGHES CANNON. *Utah Hist. Q. 1980 48(1): 37-48.* Martha Hughes Cannon (1857-1932) was the fourth polygamous wife of Angus Munn Cannon, president of the Salt Lake Stake of the Mormon Church. To prevent Angus Cannon's arrest for polygamy, Martha exiled herself to England during 1885-87. Her letters reveal loneliness, constant fear of exposure, fear of Cannon's arrest, and jealousy of other wives. The 1890 Manifesto allowed her to live openly in Salt Lake City and continue her medical career. In 1896 she became the first woman state senator in the United States. Based on letters and diaries in the Angus Munn Cannon collection, LDS Archives; 6 illus., 23 notes. J. L. Hazelton

4003. Linford, Lawrence L. ESTABLISHING AND MAINTAINING LAND OWNERSHIP IN UTAH PRIOR TO 1869. *Utah Hist. Q. 1974 42(2): 126-143.* Discusses the regulation of land ownership by Mormons from 1847 to the integration of the Mormon land system with the federal government's system in 1869.

4004. Lyon, T. Edgar. DOCTRINAL DEVELOPMENT OF THE CHURCH DURING THE NAUVOO SOJOURN, 1839-1846. *Brigham Young U. Studies 1975 15(4): 435-446.* Examines evolution in doctrine while the Mormons resided in Nauvoo, Illinois.

4005. Lyon, T. Edgar. RECOLLECTIONS OF "OLD NAUVOOERS": MEMORIES FROM ORAL HISTORY. *Brigham Young U. Studies 1978 18(2): 143-150.* Oral history has played a significant role in the evolution of the Mormon faith. Gives personal recollections of elderly Mormons who testified in church meetings of their impressions and experiences with Joseph Smith and Hyrum Smith. While acknowledging the

subjective limitations of oral history, concludes that such reminiscences do give a more humanistic view of the early Mormon leaders.
M. S. Legan

4006. Lythgoe, Dennis L. POLITICAL FEUD IN SALT LAKE CITY: J. BRACKEN LEE AND THE FIRING OF W. CLEON SKOUSEN. *Utah Hist. Q. 1974 42(4): 316-343.* Portrays the power and personality struggle between Mayor J. Bracken Lee and Police Chief W. Cleon Skousen in Salt Lake City, Utah. The two men disagreed on budgetary matters, and Skousen was fired in 1960. The root of the conflict, however, was that Skousen, a Mormon, held an orthodox morality, whereas Lee, a Mason, was more liberal in his moral views and practices. Although public opinion was against him, Lee was re-elected twice, demonstrating that an unpopular decision need not destroy a political career. 7 photos, 85 notes. V. L. Human

4007. Matheny, Ray T. AN ANALYSIS OF THE PADILLA GOLD PLATES. *Brigham Young U. Studies 1978 19(1): 21-40.* Examines the Padilla Gold Plates, which reputedly contain significant archaeological evidence of the Book of Mormon. The plates were discovered in a tomb in Guerrero, Mexico, sometime during 1952-56. Discusses the circumstances of their reported discovery, a physical description of the artifacts, the apparent method to produce them, and the content of their engravings. Concludes that the Padilla Gold Plates are not authentic, and that their historical value is nil. M. S. Legan

4008. May, Dean L. THE MAKING OF SAINTS: THE MORMON TOWN AS A SETTING FOR THE STUDY OF CULTURAL CHANGE. *Utah Hist. Q. 1977 45(1): 75-92.* Mormon communities are historical specimens of a central theme of American experience: the tension between preservation of order and libertarian ideologies. Past studies of Mormon towns failed to examine the process of change over time. Techniques used for New England towns by such historians as Philip Greven, John Demos, Kenneth Lockridge, and Michael Zuckerman suggest questions to ask about Mormon communities. These scholars identified forces of disintegration. Mormon studies may show forces of reintegration. Primary and secondary sources; illus., 38 notes.
J. L. Hazelton

4009. May, Dean L. PEOPLE ON THE MORMON FRONTIER: KANAB'S FAMILIES OF 1874. *J. of Family Hist. 1976 1(2): 169-192.* Kanab, Utah, a small agricultural community along the Mormon frontier, had a more normal sex-age distribution than was typical for frontier towns but shared with other frontier towns a high rate of population turnover. Discusses how to handle polygamous families and their complex household organization and the distribution of property among members in the Kanab United Order, a communal experiment initiated by Brigham Young. 6 graphs, 2 tables, 17 notes, appendix with ideographs of all 81 families. T. W. Smith

4010. McCormick, John S. AN ANARCHIST DEFENDS THE MORMONS: THE CASE OF DYER D. LUM. *Utah Hist. Q. 1976 44(2): 156-169.* Dyer D. Lum (1839-92), an important American anarchist in the late 19th century, defended Mormonism as a progressive force, condemned the federal government for its attempted suppression of the Mormons, and sought to penetrate below the issue of polygamy to fundamental causes of the confrontation. Morality was not the issue. Friction was caused by the existence of antagonistic economic, social, and cultural orders, and was inevitable. Lum's analysis puts Mormon history in context. Primary and secondary sources; 2 illus., 21 notes.
J. L. Hazelton

4011. McLeod, Dean L. JAMES ROSS: THE EXPERIENCES OF A SCOTTISH IMMIGRANT TO AMERICA. *Family Heritage 1978 1(6): 178-179, 182-183.* James Ross (1822-1900), who emigrated to America in the mid-19th century, was one of the first 600 Scots to join the Mormon Church in 1842, in Scotland.

4012. Michaelsen, Robert S. THOMAS F. O'DEA ON THE MORMONS: RETROSPECT AND ASSESSMENT. *Dialogue 1978 11(1): 44-57.* Thomas F. O'Dea was the foremost non-Mormon to attempt scholarly analysis of Mormon theology, sociology, history, philosophy, and literature. O'Dea's interest in understanding Mormonism, classifying it as a religious movement, delineating the ambivalent relationship between Mormonism and the American ethos, and analyzing Mormonism's strengths and weaknesses, stemmed from his own Catholic background. O'Dea felt the tension that Mormons did in attempting to bridge the gap between the real and the ideal, and raised the critical problem of relevance in the modern world. Based on published and unpublished writings of O'Dea, secondary sources, list of Thomas F. O'Dea's writings on the Mormons; illus., 52 notes. C. B. Schulz

4013. Moench, Melodie. NINETEENTH-CENTURY MORMONS: THE NEW ISRAEL. *Dialogue 1979 12(1): 42-56.* Mormons are said to be especially fond of Old Testament scriptures, but a study of doctrinal Mormon writings does not support this view, because they more frequently refer to the New Testament. The Mormons did, however, perceive themselves as a chosen people similar to Israel, a family with God at its head. Whether God chose the early Mormons to be his new Israel must remain a matter of faith. Covers 1830-1900. 52 notes. S

4014. Moody, Thurman Dean. NAUVOO'S WHISTLING AND WHITTLING BRIGADE. *Brigham Young U. Studies 1975 15(4): 480-490.* Discusses the adaptation of the Whistling and Whittling Brigade, a form of police consisting of the small boys of the community. Following the loss of city government and subsequently the loss of police protection in Nauvoo, Illinois, the Mormon community found it necessary (1845) to provide themselves with this protection, the young boys seemed the safest, because they were harassing rather than threatening.

4015. Moorman, Donald R. SHADOWS OF BRIGHAM YOUNG AS SEEN BY HIS BIOGRAPHERS. *Utah Hist. Q. 1977 45(3): 252-264.* Important biographies of Brigham Young (1801-77), are: Edward W. Tullidge, *Life of Brigham Young,* Morris Robert Werner, *Brigham Young,* Susa Young Gates, *The Life Story of Brigham Young,* Stanley P. Hirshson, *The Lion of the Lord: A Biography of Brigham Young,* and Ray B. West, *Kingdom of the Saints: The Story of Brigham Young and the Mormons.* These representations of sainted father, false prophet, heavenly leader, divine oracle, and unscrupulous financier, do not adequately examine his temperament, Biblicism, and intellectualism. Based on primary and secondary sources; 4 illus., 12 notes.
J. L. Hazelton

4016. Naylor, Thomas H. COLONIA MORELOS AND THE MEXICAN REVOLUTION: CONSUL DYE INSPECTS AN EVACUATED MORMON COLONY, 1912. *J. of Arizona Hist. 1979 20(1): 101-120.* To escape religious persecution in the United States, many Mormons settled in Sonora, Mexico. US Consul Alexander V. Dye went there to inspect and report on conditions after General José Iñez Salazar's soldiers had routed the citizens and destroyed the community in 1912. The principal Mormon communities, at Morelos and Oaxaca, had grown wheat and raised livestock. By the end of August 1912, the survivors had arrived in Douglas, Arizona. After the devastation, the Haymore and Lillywhite families returned for a while, but never again were there Mormons in large numbers. 8 photos, 32 notes. K. E. Gilmont

4017. Paul, Rodman W. THE MORMONS, FROM POVERTY AND PERSECUTION TO PROSPERITY AND POWER. *Am. Heritage 1977 28(4): 74-83.* The Mormon Church has dominated the religious and social life of its members, and frequently their political life and economic activities. Covers 1820-1977. 5 illus. B. J. Paul

4018. Paul, Rodman W. THE MORMONS OF YESTERDAY AND TODAY. *Idaho Yesterdays 1975 19(3): 2-7.* The Mormon theocratic, communistic, and separatist society which developed in Utah in the 19th century has evolved into something quite different in the late 20th century. The church has recently integrated itself politically and socially with middle-class America. Nevertheless, Mormons can still be a part of a close-knit supportive group if they wish. B. J. Paul

4019. Peabody, Velton. A QUARTERLY BIBLIOGRAPHY OF WORKS ON MORMONISM. *Mormonia 1973 2.*
(2): 23-44. Lists book entries 349-393 and article entries 467-607, alphabetically by author. Mentions frequently cited periodicals, most of them Mormon.
(3-4): 47-63. Lists book entries 394-429 and article entries 608-724.
S

4020. Pedersen, Lyman C., Jr. THE DAILY UNION VEDETTE: A MILITARY VOICE ON THE MORMON FRONTIER. *Utah Hist. Q. 1974 42(1): 39-48.* The *Daily Union Vedette* was published at Fort Douglas 1863-67. It was concerned not only with the details of the life of the military post but also with material about Mormons, mining, emigrants, and freighting. 2 illus., 20 notes. D. L. Smith

4021. Peterson, Susan. THE GREAT AND DREADFUL DAY: MORMON FOLKLORE OF THE APOCALYPSE. *Utah Hist. Q. 1976 44(4): 365-378.* Mormon apocalyptic lore expresses not only tensions shared with other members of the modern community, but also those arising from a partial alienation from it. It expresses tensions arising from the desire to cling to faith and to have that faith substantiated by fulfillment. Mormons use the apocalyptic stories to promote and maintain the validity of their world view. The stories mirror folk response to official religious teaching and provide understanding of the hearts and minds of the people. Primary and secondary sources; illus., 41 notes. J. L. Hazelton

4022. Poulsen, Richard C. FATE AND THE PERSECUTORS OF JOSEPH SMITH: TRANSMUTATIONS OF AN AMERICAN MYTH. *Dialogue 1978 11(4): 63-70.* Examines the stories surrounding the fate of the men who murdered Joseph Smith, the founder of the Church of Jesus Christ of Latter-Day Saints. These tales of grotesque and untimely death, especially that of "rotting" of the flesh, are not unique to Mormonism, but have parallels in folk tales of lumberers in late 19th century Michigan, and of Quakers in 17th century Massachusetts. Such tales of vengeance in folklore of persecuted groups serve the function of reinforcing group solidarity, reminding modern descendents of the group of their cultural roots, and helping them cope with the present. Based on compilations of folk tales, secondary sources analyzing folk myths; 29 notes. C. B. Schulz

4023. Poulsen, Richard C. "THIS IS THE PLACE": MYTH AND MORMONDOM. *Western Folklore 1977 36(3): 246-252.* Explores the Mormon migration myth and the reasons for Brigham Young's selection of the Valley of the Great Salt Lake as the place where the Mormons were to settle. Discusses the decision by Mormon leaders to immigrate to the Great Basin. Analysis of popular literature and interviews reveals that most Mormons believe the selection of the site was by vision and or divine revelation. Covers 1842-1976. Based on 30 interviews, other primary and secondary sources; 12 notes. S. L. Myres

4024. Pratt, Orson. "LET BR. PRATT DO AS HE WILL": ORSON PRATT'S 29 JANUARY 1860 CONFESSIONAL DISCOURSE—UNREVISED. *Dialogue 1980 13(2): 50-58.* Presents the unrevised text of a sermon of repentance and confession by Orson Pratt. The confession was revised by the Mormons' Quorum of Apostles prior to official publication to eliminate some controversial material. Pratt acknowledged his errors and committed himself to refrain from further public speculation. Pratt was reluctant to admit that his beliefs themselves were faulty, however, and confessed only his error in publicly expounding doctrines contrary to the opinions of Brigham Young. Note. R. D. Rahmes

4025. Pratt, Steven. ELEANOR MC LEAN AND THE MURDER OF PARLEY P. PRATT. *Brigham Young U. Studies 1975 15(2): 225-256.* Eleanor Jane McComb, who married Hector McLean in 1841, embraced the Mormon faith in 1851 much against her husband's wishes. Later in San Francisco she met Parley Pratt, presiding over the church's Pacific Mission, who baptized several of her children into the Mormon faith, and subsequently took her as one of his wives. In retaliation, McLean, her legal husband, gained custody of their children, tried to have her declared insane, and on 13 May 1857, near Van Buren, Arkansas, murdered Pratt for his relationship with his wife. After Pratt's death, having been spurned by her family, Eleanor McLean Pratt returned to Salt Lake City and taught school in Utah until her death on 24 October 1874. M. S. Legan

4026. Quinn, D. Michael. LATTER-DAY SAINT PRAYER CIRCLES. *Brigham Young U. Studies 1978 19(1): 79-105.* On 3 May 1978, the First Presidency of the Mormon Church discontinued all prayer circles except those conducted as a part of the endowment ceremony in the temples. Traces the evolution of such organizations in Mormon Church history. After suggesting precedents for the LDS Prayer Circle, examines their development during 1829-46. In 1851, the conduct of these meetings was restructured into Special Prayer Circles which functioned until 1929. The Ecclesiastical Prayer Circles remained separate from the other organizations during 1845-1978. Questions of membership, including women, their purposes, and the governance of each of the different prayer circles are discussed. M. S. Legan

4027. Quinn, D. Michael. THE MORMON SUCCESSION CRISIS OF 1844. *Brigham Young U. Studies 1976 16(2): 187-233.* Since no explicit instructions existed concerning Joseph Smith's successor as head of the Mormon Church, a succession crisis arose with his death on 27 June 1844. During 1834-44, however, Smith had by word or action set forth eight precedents for possible elevation to leadership in the Mormon Church. Traces the merits and history of each possible means of succession. The most successful claim came from the Quorum of the Twelve Apostles. On 8 August 1844 the membership of the Church voted to accept the Twelve Apostles as the First Presidency of the Church, thus confirming Brigham Young's leadership by virtue of his being president and senior member of that body. M. S. Legan

4028. Quinn, D. Michael. THE PRACTICE OF REBAPTISM AT NAUVOO. *Brigham Young U. Studies 1978 18(2): 226-232.* While rebaptism was discontinued as an ordinance of the Mormon Church in the 20th century during the presidency of Joseph F. Smith, it occupied a pivotal position in the 19th-century development of the Church. Examines the Mormons' rationales for the practice of rebaptism, particularly during the Nauvoo years. These included its use for entering a new ecclesiastical relationship, for the reformation and remission of sins, for the renewal of covenants through baptism for the dead, for health purposes, and in connection with plural marriage. M. S. Legan

4029. Reilly, P. T. KANAB UNITED ORDER: THE PRESIDENT'S NEPHEW AND THE BISHOP. *Utah Hist. Q. 1974 42(2): 144-164.* Brigham Young's plan to unify all Mormons in his United Order led to disunity in Kanab, Utah, 1874-84, between the order established by Young's nephew John R. Young and the town's bishop Levi Stewart.

4030. Robertson, R. J., Jr. THE MORMON EXPERIENCE IN MISSOURI, 1830-1839. *Missouri Hist. R. 1974 68(3): 280-298, (4): 393-415.* Part I. Discusses Mormon history in Missouri during the 1830's and the difficulties they experienced. First settling in Jackson County, most Mormons had moved by 1836 to Caldwell County due to violence resulting in differences over the treatment of free Negroes. Conflicts between the Mormons and the state militia finally brought about an order to drive them from the state. The Mormons then migrated to Illinois. 10 illus., 15 notes. Part II. Claims that the most important factor in the Mormon experience in Missouri is that wherever a Mormon community existed near non-Mormon settlements, the differences in social organization and philosophy generated social tension and often violence. Based on documents of the Church of Jesus Christ of Latter-day Saints, contemporary newspaper reports, and secondary sources; 13 illus., 64 notes. N. J. Street and S

4031. Rogers, Kristen Smart. WILLIAM HENRY SMART: UINTA BASIN PIONEER LEADER. *Utah Hist. Q. 1977 45(1): 61-74.* William Henry Smart (1862-1937) was a classic example of the severe, disciplined, dedicated men who built Utah. He organized and lead the settlement of Utah's Uinta Basin. He organized realty companies, financed needed businesses and civic enterprises, promoted schools, banks, and newspapers. He gave so freely of his wealth to establish Mormon rule in the Basin that he left there almost penniless. The Uinta Basin bears unmistakably the stamp of his labors. Primary and secondary sources; 3 illus., 42 notes. J. L. Hazelton

4032. Russell, William D. A PRIESTLY ROLE FOR A PROPHETIC CHURCH: THE RLDS CHURCH AND BLACK AMERICANS. *Dialogue 1979 12(2): 37-49.* Reviews and analyzes the position of the Reorganized Church of Jesus Christ of Latter Day Saints on the ordination of women and blacks. Despite the supposed liberalism of the Reorganized Church, it has simply gone along with whatever popular feelings were present at a given moment. Very much in favor of racial equality during the Reconstruction, the church forgot the great cause in the years to follow, not reviving it until racial issues rose again during the

1960's. The RLDS, as opposed to the LDS, has preferred a priestly or pastoral mode of operation, rather than the prophetic mode chosen by the LDS. 48 notes. V. L. Human

4033. Sadler, Richard W. THE IMPACT OF MINING ON SALT LAKE CITY. *Utah Hist. Q. 1979 47(3): 236-253.* The juxtaposition of mining and a dominant religious culture antithetical to mining camp life created a dynamic tension for Salt Lake City. Opposing forces have interacted since 1863. The Mormon impact is obvious. Mining's impact included wealth, pollution, immigrants, unions, and changes in the social and political fabric. Business and religious buildings and residences are visible evidence of mining wealth that contributed to the development of a great urban and regional center. Covers 1863-1978. 7 illus., 23 notes. J. L. Hazelton

4034. Schomakers, G. MORMONEN TREKKEN WESTWAARTS [Mormons move westward]. *Spiegel Historiael [Netherlands] 1974 9(7-8): 422-429.* Details the migration of the Mormons from Nauvoo, Illinois, to Salt Lake City in 1846, and subsequent migrations. Discusses the conflicts between the Mormons in Utah and the federal government in the 1850's. Biblio. G. D. Homan

4035. Sherlock, Richard. FAITH AND HISTORY: THE SNELL CONTROVERSY. *Dialogue 1979 12(1): 27-41.* Heber C. Snell's *Ancient Israel* (1949) expressed modernist views about the Bible which seemed to traditionalist Mormons to conflict with teachings of the Church of Latter-Day Saints. Snell's views had even earlier involved him in controversy with Elder Joseph Fielding Smith; reconciliation of scholarly research concerning ancient Israel and the authorship of the Bible with Mormon revelatory traditions has not yet been attained. Covers 1937-52. 60 notes. S

4036. Singer, Merrill. NATHANIEL BALDWIN, UTAH INVENTOR AND PATRON OF THE FUNDAMENTALIST MOVEMENT. *Utah Hist. Q. 1979 47(1): 42-53.* Nathaniel Baldwin (1878-1961), inventor, writer, and philanthropist, helped Utah become a leading manufacturer of radio loudspeakers and headsets. His products were marketed worldwide and especially were sought by the US Navy in World War I. A Mormon Fundamentalist, he advocated plural marriage. This led to his disfellowship by the LDS Church. Apparently a poor businessman and poor judge of character, he lost his multimillion dollar business, was sent to prison for fraudulent use of the mails for advertising, and died impoverished. 4 illus., 31 notes. J. L. Hazelton

4037. Smaby, Beverly P. THE MORMONS AND THE INDIANS: CONFLICTING ECOLOGICAL SYSTEMS IN THE GREAT BASIN. *Am. Studies 1975 16(1): 35-48.* Focuses on the conflict during 1847-60 when Indian defeat was inevitable. Indian tribes remained flexible and in harmony with the natural ecological system, while Mormons pursued eastern methods of intensive agriculture in nucleated settlements. The two systems quickly conflicted and Indian culture deteriorated under relentless Mormon pressure and population growth. Primary and secondary sources; 56 notes. J. Andrew

4038. Smith, Melvin T. FORCES THAT SHAPED UTAH'S DIXIE: ANOTHER LOOK. *Utah Hist. Q. 1979 47(2): 110-129.* Non-Mormon forces (Indian, Spanish, US government, military, miners, freighting, and merchandising) affected Utah's Dixie only peripherally. Mormon leaders avoided integration with the Gentile world in their development of Dixie. Their purposes were to convert Indians, provide a passenger and freight line into Zion, and provide economic independence. Non-Mormon economic competition after the Civil War led to the establishment of cooperatives, Zino's Cooperative Mercantile Institution, and United Orders. Church leaders inspired Dixie's settlement, but prosperity came only after Dixie integrated with the nation. 8 illus., 59 notes. J. L. Hazelton

4039. Sorenson, John. MORMON WORLD VIEW AND AMERICAN CULTURE. *Dialogue 1973 8(2): 17-29.* Covers the 19th and 20th centuries.

4040. Stathis, Stephen W., ed. A SURVEY OF CURRENT LITERATURE: A SELECTED BIBLIOGRAPHY OF RECENT WORKS ON MORMONS AND MORMONISM. *Dialogue 1978 11(3): 107-123.* A bibliography of more than 300 books published during 1974-78 on the general subject of Mormonism into the following categories: general; apostates and gentiles; architecture; art and music; bibliography; biography and family history; Book of Mormon; Brigham Young; business, labor and mining; doctrine; education; families and marriage; fiction; folklore; genealogy; health and medicine; inspiration; Joseph Smith; journalism and literature; law, politics, and government; local history; minorities; missionary work; priesthood; Reorganized LDS; scriptures; sociology; stake and ward histories; temples, United Order; women; and Word of Wisdom. In addition, a bibliography of Mormon reprints under the categories of general history, biography, doctrine, periodicals, travelogs, and fiction is appended to the compilation. C. B. Schulz

4041. Stathis, Stephen W. A SURVEY OF CURRENT LITERATURE: DISSERTATIONS AND THESES RELATING TO MORMONS AND MORMONISM. *Dialogue 1978 11(2): 96-100.* This compilation of masters theses and doctoral dissertations on Mormon topics completed in the United States during 1973-77 includes 92 titles, arranged alphabetically by author under the following categories: apostates and gentiles; authority, doctrine and theology; auxiliaries; biography; business, economics and labor; culture, drama, literature and music; education; exploration, migration, and settlement; families; folklore; health and medicine; Joseph Smith; military affairs; missionary work; records; scripture; sociology and psychology; and women. C. B. Schulz

4042. Thatcher, Linda. A SURVEY OF CURRENT LITERATURE: SELECTED NEWSPAPER ARTICLES ON MORMONS AND MORMONISM PUBLISHED DURING 1977. *Dialogue 1978 11(4): 104-111.* Compiles and categorizes news articles on Mormonism utilizing the monthly clippings scrapbook of the Public Communications Department of the Church of the Latter Day Saints (LDS). The bibliography does not include those articles on Mormonism in the weekly *Church News* section of the *Deseret News,* or the weekly historical column "Looking Back" in the Logan, Utah *Herald Journal.* One hundred and seventy-six articles, primarily on present-day Mormon activities, from a broad range of national newspapers, are listed under the following categories: general; art, drama, and music; biography; blacks; Book of Mormon; business; doctrine; education; families and Family Home Evening; genealogy; health and medicine; law and politics; literature; missionary work; Nauvoo; polygamy; settlements beyond Utah; Utah's heritage; welfare program and food storage; and women. C. B. Schulz

4043. Turney, Catherine. JOHN DOYLE LEE: VILLAIN OR SCAPEGOAT? *Mankind 1976 5(8): 60-67.* Although the entire Mormon community was antagonistic toward interlopers on their territory, John Doyle Lee was blamed for the massacre of about 140 emigrants at Mountain Meadows, Utah, in September 1857. Paiute Indians attacked the emigrants; a group of Mormons under John D. Lee offered to cover the emigrants' retreat to Cedar City, but massacred them on the way. Lee's close relationship to Brigham Young preserved his freedom until the 1870's when the federal government assumed jurisdiction over criminal cases in Utah. Lee was eventually apprehended, tried, and executed for what was essentially a community crime. Following his death in 1877, his family fought to clear his name, at least in the eyes of the Mormon church, and Lee was reinstated in the church in 1961. N. Lederer

4044. Ursenbach, Maureen, ed. ELIZA SNOW'S NAUVOO JOURNAL. *Brigham Young U. Studies 1975 15(4): 387-391.* Reprints excerpts from the diary of Eliza R. Snow, a Mormon who recorded her life as it coincided with that of the Mormon community in Nauvoo, Illinois, 1842-44.

4045. Ursenbach, Maureen. THREE WOMEN AND THE LIFE OF THE MIND. *Utah Hist. Q. 1975 43(1): 26-40.* Examines the cultural life available for women of intellect in Utah society in the 1850's through the lives of three women: Hannah Tapfield King, Martha Spence Heywood, and Eliza Roxey Snow. With the barren educational landscape during the early pioneer period, the anti-intellectualism of the church, and the demands of frontier life, there was little more stimulation than private meetings of the mind and occasional gatherings of groups such as the Polysophical Society. A strong intellectual thrust remained alive, however, reinforced by the lives of these women and others like them. Primary and secondary sources; 4 illus., 21 notes.

J. L. Hazelton

4046. Wahlquist, Wayne L. A REVIEW OF MORMON SETTLEMENT LITERATURE. *Utah Hist. Q. 1977 45(1): 4-21.* Reviews studies of early Utah settlement. The General Historical Works section indicates types of studies available, including major contributions. The Studies of Mormon Settlement section serves as a guide to future research. Mormon settlement studies are often repetitive and contribute little that is new to the basic analysis of settlement. Further research needs to be nonelitist, open-minded, and with no deviation to irrelevant material. Primary and secondary sources; illus., 25 notes. J. L. Hazelton

4047. Walker, Ronald W. THE COMMENCEMENT OF THE GODBEITE PROTEST: ANOTHER VIEW. *Utah Hist. Q. 1974 42(3): 216-244.* The so-called Godbeite Protest shook Mormonism with considerable intensity, challenging the authority and policies of Brigham Young. The Godbeites were religious revolutionaries seeking the spiritual transformation of Mormonism. The origins of the New Movement lay in Great Britain. A trial in October 1869 resulted in excommunication of William Samuel Godbe—"more for conspiracy than for heresy"—which led to the resignation of a number of others in the New Movement. Covers 1840's-80's. Illus., 80 notes. E. P. Stickney

4048. Watson, Elden J. THE NAUVOO TABERNACLE. *Brigham Young U. Studies 1979 19(3): 416-421.* Orson Hyde traveled to New York, Pennsylvania, and New England to raise funds and collect canvas for the proposed Mormon tabernacle at Nauvoo, Illinois, 1845-46. 19 notes.

4049. Watt, Ronald G. A DIALOGUE BETWEEN WILFORD WOODRUFF AND LYMAN WIGHT. *Brigham Young U. Studies 1976 17(1): 108-113.* Presents several letters between Wilford Woodruff, an assistant church historian who was writing a history of the Twelve Apostles, and Lyman Wight, a former apostle who had been stripped of his position after emigrating to Texas with 150 Mormons shortly after Joseph Smith's death. Wight complied with Woodruff's request for a history of his life, but in his answer asked why the apostles had cut him off from the Mormon Church. Woodruff's reply of 30 June 1858 urged Wight to repent from his errors and come to Salt Lake City, but Wight died before receiving the letter. M. S. Legan

4050. Watt, Ronald G. SAILING "THE OLD SHIP ZION": THE LIFE OF GEORGE D. WATT. *Brigham Young U. Studies 1977 18(1): 48-65.* George D. Watt (1815-81), the first Mormon convert to be baptized in Great Britain, served as a clerk in Brigham Young's office, as a founding editor of the *Journal of Discourses,* as one of the developers of the Deseret alphabet, and as an early proponent of silkworm culture in Utah. He made significant contributions to the Mormons' cause from the 1840's. His knowledge of stenography particularly aided in the compilation of a written record of the early theological teachings. However, Watt's personality, his questioning of many church doctrines, and his perennial financial straits engendered disputes with many of the Mormon elders and led eventually to his excommunication in 1874.

M. S. Legan

4051. White, O. Kendall, Jr. and White, Daryl. ABANDONING AN UNPOPULAR POLICY: AN ANALYSIS OF THE DECISION GRANTING THE MORMON PRIESTHOOD TO BLACKS. *Sociol. Analysis 1980 41(3): 231-245.* The decision in 1978 admitting blacks into the Mormon priesthood is explained as an adaptation to environmental pressures, the logical outcome of organizational practices, and the resolution of internal contradictions. Adverse publicity from the media, pressures from the black community, and threats of successful litigation reflected environmental hostility; an organizational imperative of growth, the quest for respectability, and the internationalization of Mormonism predisposed the church toward adaptation; and challenges from Mormon intellectuals and activists, pressures from black Mormons, and the leadership of President Spencer Kimball reinforced adaptive strategies. Revelation, as a technique of internal control, ensured the consensus of officials and strengthened Mormon hegemony. Covers 1950-78. J

4052. Wilson, Laura Foster. RICHARD BURTON VISITS THE CITY OF THE SAINTS. *Am. West 1975 12(1): 4-9.* English explorer and author Richard Burton (1821-90) traveled across the United States in 1860. His *City of the Saints and Across the Rocky Mountains to California* (1861) was the most complete and knowledgeable account written on the Mormons and Utah for several decades. The book was unique because of its favorable and sympathetic description of the Mormons and their institutions and its hundreds of pages of erudition. 5 illus., biblio. D. L. Smith

4053. Wilson, William A. FOLKLORE OF UTAH'S LITTLE SCANDINAVIA. *Utah Hist. Q. 1979 47(2): 148-166.* The Sanpete-Sevier region of Utah has produced a distinctive body of folklore, almost all growing out of the Mormon experience. Four main themes (settlement, temple building, polygamy, and Scandinavian immigrant tales) reflect dominant attitudes, values, and concerns. More systematic folklore collection needs to be carried out. Sanpete-Sevier folklore will change as today's residents create new lore in coming to terms with the conditions of their lives. Covers 1849-1979. 8 illus., 50 notes.

J. L. Hazelton

4054. Wilson, William A. THE PARADOX OF MORMON FOLKLORE. *Brigham Young U. Studies 1976 17(1): 40-58.* Analyzes Mormon folklore and its influence on church members. Folklore is the part of culture "passed through time and space by the process of oral transmission rather than by institutionalized means of learning or by the mass media." Illustrates how Mormon folklore reinforces church dogma and practice, how it is used to sanction approved forms of behavior, and how it gives people a sense of stability in an unstable world.

M. S. Legan

4055. Wilson, William A. THE STUDY OF MORMON FOLKLORE. *Utah Hist. Q. 1976 44(4): 317-328.* Wayland D. Hand, Thomas E. Cheney, Austin E. Fife, and Hector Lee promoted the study of Mormon folklore. Their purpose was to understand the past. Contemporary folklorists believe folklore tells as much about the culture of the storyteller as about the past. Folklorists must reinterpret Mormon lore to understand the changes in Mormon culture, and reassess the methodological and theoretical approaches used to study this lore. Covers 1892-1975. Primary and secondary sources; illus., 10 notes. J. L. Hazelton

4056. Wilson, William A. "THE VANISHING HITCHHIKER" AMONG THE MORMONS. *Indiana Folklore 1975 8(1-2): 79-97.* Studies indicate that since 1933 the popular ghost story, "The Vanishing Hitchhiker," has not been attached to a specific time and place, but has been a migratory tale that changes to fit cultural contours and has filled the needs of different people, particularly the Mormons during 1955-65.

4057. —. EXPULSION OF A POOR, DELUDED AND MISERABLE SET OF VILLAINS: A CONTEMPORARY ACCOUNT. *Dialogue 1978 11(4): 112-117.* Excerpts portions of six letters from members of the Bradford family of Carrollton, Missouri, to family members remaining in Virginia, during 13 August 1838-22 April 1839. The focus of the excerpts is the unfavorable account given by the Bradfords of the activities of Mormons in Missouri, in Davis and Carroll Counties, and Caldwell City. The letter writers relate the fall 1838 arrest of Mormon leaders in Far West, Missouri, including Joseph Smith, Lyman Wight, Sydney Rigdon, Robeson, Parley Pratt, Doctor Everard, and Colonel Hinkle. The Bradfords involved in the correspondence are descendants of John Bradford (1690-1750) of Fauquier County, Virginia, some of whom remained in Virginia where they were substantial landholders, others of whom migrated westward and took up significant landholdings in Missouri. The Mormon incidents are a brief account in a correspondence more generally concerned with family real estate, health, and financial matters. C. B. Schulz

4058. —. MORMONISM'S NEGRO DOCTRINE. *Dialogue: A J. of Mormon Thought 1973 8(1): 11-86.*

Bush, Lester E., Jr. MORMONISM'S NEGRO DOCTRINE: AN HISTORICAL OVERVIEW, pp. 11-68.

Thomasson, Gordon C. LESTER BUSH'S HISTORICAL OVERVIEW: OTHER PERSPECTIVES, pp. 69-72.

Nibley, Hugh. THE BEST POSSIBLE TEST, pp. 73-77.

England, Eugene. THE MORMON CROSS, pp. 78-86.
The history of Mormon doctrines and attitudes toward Negro participation in church life. S

4059. —. SAINT WITHOUT PRIESTHOOD: THE COLLECTED TESTIMONIES OF EX-SLAVE SAMUEL D. CHAMBERS. *Dialogue 1979 12(2): 13-21.* Samuel D. Chambers, long-time black member of the Church of Jesus Christ of Latter Day Saints, converted to Mormonism in 1844 while a slave youth, and though illiterate and soon isolated from other members of the faith, remained true to its teachings for 25 years, until circumstances permitted him to emigrate to Salt Lake City. He soon became a Deacon, but being black prohibited advancement to the priesthood. Contains publication of minutes of his testimonies during 1873-76, primarily consisting of thanks to God and the church for the good life he enjoyed. 2 photos, 7 notes. V. L. Human

New Church (Swedenborgians)

4060. Deck, Raymond H., Jr. THE "VASTATION" OF HENRY JAMES, SR.: NEW LIGHT ON JAMES'S THEOLOGICAL CAREER. *Bull. of Res. in the Humanities 1980 83(2): 216-247.* Itemizes and evaluates in the context of Henry James, Sr.'s metaphysical writings, the collection of works by Emanuel Swedenborg, James John Garth Wilkinson, and others, which occupied one trunk with which James traveled (now at the Swedenborg School of Religion in Newton, Massachusetts), and the James-Wilkinson correspondence; 1844-55.

4061. Gunn, Giles. HENRY JAMES, SENIOR: AMERICAN ECCENTRIC OR AMERICAN ORIGINAL? *J. of Religion 1974 54(3): 218-243.* Reevaluation of Henry James, Senior, his relation to the American tradition, his grasp of theology and Swedenborgianism, and his contribution to religious thought, 1840's-81. S

4062. Schrock, Nancy Carlson. JOSEPH ANDREWS, ENGRAVER: A SWEDENBORGIAN JUSTIFICATION. *Winterthur Portfolio 1977 12: 165-182.* Joseph Andrews (1806-73) was influenced greatly by Swedenborgianism. Andrews joined the Boston Society of the New Jerusalem in 1830. As a Swedenborgian, he believed in the doctrine of correspondence, that the spiritual world was reflected in the physical world. His journal of 1835-36 indicates how he applied his religious principles. The full impact of Swedenborgianism has yet to be realized. Andrews is given a prominent place because he was the first artist to represent the conservative stand of the Boston Society with regard to art. Study concludes with 1873. Primary and secondary sources; 9 illus., 56 notes. N. A. Kuntz

4063. Tolzmann, Don Heinrich. DR. AXEL LUNDEBERG, SWEDISH AMERICAN SCHOLAR. *Swedish Pioneer Hist. Q. 1973 24(1): 33-48.* Axel Johan Sigurd Mauritz Lundeberg (1852-1940) was born into an influential Swedish family. He was well educated and traveled through Europe reporting on various social systems for Swedish newspapers. In 1888 he arrived in America. From 1890, when he settled in Minneapolis, until his death he was a leading Swede in the Midwest. In 1910 he established a Swedenborgian church; he was its minister until 1919. He was a pacifist during World War I. He collected over 10,000 books and wrote prolifically. Primarily a theologian strongly influenced by Swedish philosophy, he can be characterized as an ethnic intellectual. Reprints one of his poems. Based on primary and secondary sources; 2 photos, 29 notes, biblio. K. J. Puffer

Shakers

4064. Andrews, Edward Deming and Andrews, Faith. THE SHAKER CHILDREN'S ORDER. *Winterthur Portfolio 1973 (8): 201-214.* The Children's Order of the United Society of Believers (Shakers) has been neglected by scholars; yet the order is an important institution for students of American communitarianism. In their early history the Shakers accepted children under indentures. Despite legal contracts almost every Shaker community found itself confronted with angry parents, often bringing forth charges of the most hideous crimes. Life for the children was regulated, with emphasis on cleanliness, modesty, industriousness, and frugality. Education was not designed to produce scholars but to enable the student to better the community. In the early 19th century the Shaker Children's Order served a useful function. In addition to offering care, food, and shelter, the order was a testing ground for the selection of those who were ready to serve the holy cause. It was essential to the development of the Shakers. Based on primary and secondary sources; 5 illus., 34 notes. N. A. Kuntz

4065. Ferguson, Richard G., Jr. CENTRAL THEMES IN SHAKER THOUGHT. *Register of the Kentucky Hist. Soc. 1976 74(3): 216-229.* Defines and criticizes aspects of Shaker theology. Mother Ann Lee founded the Shakers with her arrival in New York in 1774. This offshoot of the Quaker faith built itself around the theory of celibacy, the equality of men and women before God, and human perfectability. Primary and secondary sources; 53 notes. J. F. Paul

4066. Johnson, Theodore E., ed. THE DIARY OF A MAINE SHAKER BOY: DELMER WILSON—1887. *New England Social Studies Bull. 1974 31(1): 52-70.* Reprint from *The Shaker Quarterly* 1968 8(1). S

4067. Ray, Mary Lyn. A REAPPRAISAL OF SHAKER FURNITURE AND SOCIETY. *Winterthur Portfolio 1973 (8): 107-132.* The Shakers have been celebrated for separating from the world. Their rejection of the world, however, was not so strict as reputed. An analysis of their furniture shows their adherence, or lack thereof, to orthodoxy. Shaker furniture was not a distinct style but a "paring down of familiar forms from which applied or inlaid ornament was stripped." A comparison of Shaker furniture before and after the Civil War shows a movement away from orthodoxy resulting in the disintegration of that religious society. As the followers lost their millennial spirit they came into closer contact with the outside world. The loss of followers and their inability to gain converts forced internal change; such change fostered a dependency on worldly products. The consequence was the breakup of the society. Based on primary and secondary sources; 29 illus., 66 notes. N. A. Kuntz

Transcendentalists

4068. Foley, Marya. MARGARET FULLER'S TRANSCENDENTAL VISION. *Res. Studies 1978 46(3): 183-196.* Examines the personal philosophy and spiritualism of Margaret Fuller which embraced transcendentalism and anticipated the thought of Carl Jung, 1840's.

4069. Harding, Brian R. SWEDENBORGIAN SPIRIT AND THOREAUVIAN SENSE: ANOTHER LOOK AT CORRESPONDENCE. *J. of Am. Studies [Great Britain] 1974 8(1): 65-79.* Examines the impact of the "theory of correspondence" (expounded initially by Emanuel Swedenborg [1688-1772]) upon the writings and thinking of Henry David Thoreau (1817-62). Correspondential theory provided Thoreau with valuable insights, and significantly influenced his literary method and style. Based on Thoreau's writings and secondary sources; 25 notes. H. T. Lovin

4070. Mott, Wesley T. EMERSON AND ANTINOMIANISM: THE LEGACY OF THE SERMONS. *Am. Literature 1978 50(3): 369-397.* Relates Ralph Waldo Emerson's spiritual tradition to his position in the broad transcendentalist impulse. Emerson's sermons reflected a spiritual position indicating the classic Puritan middle way between legalism and Antinomianism. While emphasizing faith and grace, Emerson never abandoned the idea that man must also perform works. In a similar fashion, Emerson approached the romantic social reform movements of his time as mixtures of spiritual enthusiasm and practical self-improvement. Emerson's Puritan legacy of balance shaped both his religion and his social consciousness during his intellectual evolution toward Transcendentalism. 26 notes. T. P. Linkfield

4071. Mueller, Roger C. SAMUEL JOHNSON, AMERICAN TRANSCENDENTALIST: A SHORT BIOGRAPHY. *Essex Inst. Hist. Collections 1979 115(1): 9-67.* Johnson was born in Salem, Massachusetts, in 1822. He graduated from Harvard in 1842 and from Harvard Divinity School in 1846. Before leaving Divinity School he collaborated with a classmate, Samuel Longfellow, on *A Book of Hymns for Public and Private Devotion* (Boston, 1846) in which they tried to make hymns "more acceptable to Unitarians in general." Initially a "conservative Unitarian," Johnson, spurred by Theodore Parker's influence, developed his own ministerial model which would go beyond Parker's Christianity into Universal Religion. After graduation Johnson became involved with abolitionist activities which resulted in a speaking engagement to the Lynn congregation and to the formation in 1853 of the Lynn Free Church and Johnson as its minister. For the next 17 years Johnson used the Lynn ministry to establish the outlines of his ideal religion grounded in Transcendentalism. Johnson became increasingly interested in Asian religions and resigned in 1870 to devote more time to his manuscripts on Oriental religions. Until his death in North Andover in 1882 Johnson wrote his *Oriental Religions and Their Relation to Universal Religion* series on India, China, and Persia. "Neither the facts nor the methods of his Oriental books are of much value today," but Johnson significantly affected the "development of Transcendentalism as a religious, philosophical, literary, and educational movement." Primary and secondary sources; 9 photos, fig., 101 notes, biblio. R. S. Sliwoski

4072. Ray, Roberta K. THE ROLE OF THE ORATOR IN THE PHILOSOPHY OF RALPH WALDO EMERSON. *Speech Monographs 1974 41(3): 215-225.* Ralph Waldo Emerson's theory of public address may be characterized as a rhetoric of provocation. Emerson did not see truth as encompassed by the human mind, set down in a book, or defended by logic. It is a state of mind, an attitude of searching for and listening to the voice within, the voice of God. The preacher orator cannot communicate truth directly to other men; he can only provoke them into searching for it on their own. The philosopher, orator, or preacher was, for Emerson, 'only a more or less awkward translator' of ideas already in the consciousness of his audience. An orator functions as a 'divining-rod' to the deeper nature of men, lifting them above themselves and creating within them an appetite for truth. J

4073. Rogers, Charles A. GOD, NATURE, AND PERSONHOOD: THOREAU'S ALTERNATIVE TO INANITY. *Religion in Life 1979 48(1): 101-113.* Henry David Thoreau's transcendentalist vision of the relationship between God and nature, and nature and human beings is a dualism of the spiritual and the phenomenal; covers 1853-1906.

4074. White, Peter. REASON AND INTUITION IN THE THEOLOGY OF THEODORE PARKER. *J. of Religious Hist. [Australia] 1980 11(1): 111-120.* Since the 1920's, historians such as Vernon Parrington, Henry Steele Commager, Herbert W. Schneider, John E. Dirks, and H. Shelton Smith have investigated the complex nature of Unitarian-turned-Transcendentalist Theodore Parker's theology. The basic problem in their assessment of Parker has been their failure to recognize that Transcendentalism, and its essential issue of reason versus intuition, did not emerge in 1800, but rather had a very extensive historical tradition. When this factor is considered, one can detect Parker's debt to the New England rationalist tradition and his concerns of Antinomian dangers which were evident within Transcendentalism. Primary sources; 33 notes. W. T. Walker III

Unitarian-Universalist Churches

4075. Bischoff, Volker. THE "NEW ENGLAND CONSCIENCE," THOMAS GOLD APPLETON, AND MRS. VIVIAN. *New England Q. 1980 53(2): 222-225.* The term "New England Conscience" was first used by Thomas Gold Appleton (1812-84) in an essay by that name published in 1875. Appleton believed that Unitarianism, by seeing God as a loving father rather than as a stern judge and by making the individual aware of his responsibility to society, had modified the stern Calvinism of New Englanders. Henry James (1843-1916), who has previously been cited as the first writer to employ the phrase, was probably familiar with Appleton's work. Based on contemporary publications; 9 notes. J. C. Bradford

4076. Cappon, Lester J. JARED SPARKS: THE PREPARATION OF AN EDITOR. *Massachusetts Hist. Soc. Pro. 1978 90: 3-21.* A study of the background of Jared Sparks, historian and editor of documents pertaining to colonial and revolutionary America, particularly the papers of George Washington. Sparks, an 1815 graduate of Harvard College and a Unitarian minister, received training as editor of the *North American Review* and *The Unitarian Miscellany.* This literary experience helped him formulate his controversial style as an historical editor when he began to collect, copy, and edit the Washington manuscripts, including those at Mount Vernon. Based on the Jared Sparks Papers at the Houghton Library of Harvard University and other primary sources; 81 notes. G. W. R. Ward

4077. Cashdollar, Charles D. EUROPEAN POSITIVISM AND THE AMERICAN UNITARIANS. *Church Hist. 1976 45(4): 490-506.* The reception of European positivism by 19th-century Unitarians led to its infusion into the denomination's swiftly-moving intellectual currents. Positivism in its English and French versions was received by Unitarians more cordially than previously believed and, for some, it helped undermine the Old Unitarianism and suggested forms for the New. Unitarians never adopted European positivism totally; rather, they selected those segments which fit their needs and often modified their original composition in the process. One from whom they borrowed heavily was Auguste Comte, who with F. C. Baur, James Martineau and Charles Darwin were important in the transformation from Old to New Unitarianism. 73 notes. M. D. Dibert

4078. Draxten, Nina. KRISTOFER JANSON'S BEGINNING MINISTRY. *Norwegian-American Studies 1967 23: 126-174.* Kristofer Janson came to America in October 1881, at the urging of Rasmus B. Anderson, initially in order to make a lecture tour of the Midwest in the hopes of stirring interest in a liberal religious organization for Norwegian Americans. Upon his arrival, he was accepted into the ministry in the Unitarian Church and from there moved to Minneapolis, Minnesota, where he began setting up his ministry and recruiting members for his congregation. Though he first met with solid criticism as a freethinker, he eventually gained popular acceptance and was able to establish himself among the Scandinavians in the community. In March 1882, he returned to his native Norway to fetch his wife and family in order to establish a permanent home in the United States. Based on recorded sermons, diaries, and letters of Janson; 70 notes. G. A. Hewlett

4079. Hitchings, Catherine F. UNIVERSALIST AND UNITARIAN WOMEN MINISTERS. *J. of the Universalist Hist. Soc. 1975 10: 3-165.* The entire issue is a biographical dictionary of 163 deceased Universalist and Unitarian women ministers, limited to those who were ordained into the ministry and who served within the United States. Several sketches indicate discrimination endured by these women. Many of them also pursued careers in writing, lecturing, law, medicine, and particularly social welfare. Covers 1860-1976. Based on primary and secondary sources, especially archival materials in the Universalist Historical Society, the Unitarian Universalist Association, and two unpublished biographical manuscripts of women ministers compiled by Unitarian minister Clara Cook Helvie (1876-1969). 13 photos, notes, 2 appendixes. P. A. Beaber

4080. Howe, Charles A. BRITISH UNIVERSALISM, 1787-1825: ELHANAN WINCHESTER, WILLIAM VIDLER AND THE GOSPEL OF UNIVERSAL RESTORATION. *Tr. of the Unitarian Hist. Soc. [Great Britain] 1979 17(1): 1-14.* In 1770 an Englishman, John Murray (1741-1815), arrived in America to found a Universalist movement. In 1787 an American minister, Elhanan Winchester (1759-97), journeyed to England to spread the faith of universal grace and restoration. In 1788 he established a small chapel in Parliament Court, London, and converted William Vidler (1758-1816), a Baptist minister who was subsequently excommunicated by his church. Vidler became minister of the Parliament Court Chapel upon Winchester's return to America in 1794. The author examines Vidler's efforts to spread Universalism in Great Britain until the creed was absorbed by Unitarianism in the 1820's. Secondary sources; 48 notes. G. M. Alexander

4081. Knaplund, Paul. H. TAMBS LYCHE: PROPAGANDIST FOR AMERICA. *Norwegian-American Studies 1970 24: 102-111.* Hans Tambs Lyche, a Norwegian, proved to be one of the greatest champions for pro-America propaganda among Norwegian religious and secular newspapers. During 1880-92, his many moves (from Chicago to New England, then to Georgia and Washington, D.C.) afforded him a fairly adequate view of Americans. Lyche was forced to give up his Unitarian

ministry in the United States because of poor pay; he took a job as a civil engineer. Upon his return to Norway in 1892, he resumed his life as religious leader and began writing extensively for Norwegian papers about his life in America. His positive reports about the American people, their friendliness and generosity, counteracted many anti-American tracts which had appeared in earlier publications and served as a strong bridge between the American and Norwegian peoples. 17 notes.
G. A. Hewlett

4082. Marti, Donald B. THE REVEREND HENRY COLMAN'S AGRICULTURAL MINISTRY. *Agric. Hist. 1977 51(3): 524-539.* Henry Colman's theological emphasis on the improvement of mankind found its secular expression when he left his Massachusetts Unitarian ministry in 1831 to promote agriculture. Though Colman worked as a practical farmer and newspaper editor in Massachusetts and New York, his main contributions were massive surveys of Massachusetts and European agriculture. His reports covered soils, crops, livestock, machinery, fertilizers, drainage, agricultural education, and rural society. He emphasized the practices of the best farmers. Covers 1820-49. 64 notes.
D. E. Bowers

4083. Meyer, D. H. THE SAINT AS HERO: WILLIAM ELLERY CHANNING AND THE NINETEENTH-CENTURY MIND. *Winterthur Portfolio 1973 (8): 171-185.* Analyzes William Ellery Channing's (1780-1842) appeal in the years of his greatest influence, 1830-80. Channing was not an intellectual innovator. He possessed the ability to adapt to change and to present such change in a spirit of optimism. In so doing, Channing summarized what the people wanted to hear and presented it in high literary fashion. By avoiding the extremes of transcendentalism the Unitarian minister was able to offer a safe middleground for man's spirituality. Because Channing offered security supported by sound reasoning, his words became a safe harbor in an age of anxiety. Based on primary and secondary sources; illus., 69 notes.
N. A. Kuntz

4084. Reilly, Timothy F. PARSON CLAPP OF NEW ORLEANS: ANTEBELLUM SOCIAL CRITIC, RELIGIOUS RADICAL, AND MEMBER OF THE ESTABLISHMENT. *Louisiana Hist. 1975 16(2): 167-191.* "Unitarianism in antebellum New Orleans was among the most distinctive religious forces in the Old South. The Church was founded and shepherded by Parson Theodore Clapp, a New England native and former Presbyterian who continually challenged sacred dictums of Christian orthodoxy." Arriving in New Orleans in 1822 and remaining until 1856, Clapp opposed revivalism and theological concepts involving the Trinity, everlasting punishment, and predestination. He defended slavery "because he recognized the supremacy of the large business class in New Orleans and the rest of the South. Such a compromise . . . entitled him to a position of social respectability. Clapp valued the propagation of his radical theology above everything else." Primary and secondary sources; 3 photos, 68 notes.
R. L. Woodward

4085. Stange, Douglas C. FROM TREASON TO ANTISLAVERY PATRIOTISM: UNITARIAN CONSERVATIVES AND THE FUGITIVE SLAVE LAW. *Harvard Lib. Bull. 1977 25(4): 466-488.* Examines the dilemma faced by conservative Boston Unitarians such as Samuel A. Eliot when faced with mutually exclusive demands arising from their opposition to slavery and their commitment to the Union. Presents the actions and discussions of the group and how several individuals resolved the conflict. Notes.
W. H. Mulligan, Jr.

4086. Stephens, Bruce M. FREDERICK HUIDEKOPER (1817-1892): PHILANTHROPIST, SCHOLAR, AND TEACHER. *Pennsylvania Mag. of Hist. and Biog. 1979 103(1): 53-65.* The Harvard-trained son of urbane Harm Jan Huidekoper, Frederick Huidekoper served the Meadville Theological School during 1844-77. His hope was to train Unitarian ministers for service in the West. His published works, which attempt to ground Unitarianism in Jewish monotheism and Christian patristics, display remarkable learning. He opposed the higher criticism. Based on Huidekoper Papers, Crawford County Historical Society, and on secondary sources; 27 notes.
T. H. Wendel

Judaism

General

4087. Alpert, David B. THE MAN FROM KOVNO. *Am. Jewish Arch. 1977 29(2): 107-115.* Not all history is the history of the famous or well-known. This is especially true for the story of American Jewry—where the poor and unlettered played a vital role in its development. Rabbi Abraham Alpert does not rank among the names that have become legend to most American Jews. But to a segment of Boston Jewry, his many efforts to improve the lot of immigrant life in the 20th century earned him a kind of love and respect that the rich and famous could indeed envy.
J

4088. Ascher, Carol. THE RETURN OF JEWISH MYSTICISM: TRY IT, YOU'LL LIKE IT. *Present Tense 1980 7(3): 36-40.* Since the 1960's there has been a rebirth of traditional Jewish mysticism, fueled by the growing interest in other traditions, that has resulted in an alive and growing religious movement.

4089. Becker, Sandra Hartwell and Pearson, Ralph L. THE JEWISH COMMUNITY OF HARTFORD, CONNECTICUT, 1880-1929. *Am. Jewish Arch. 1979 31(2): 184-214.* Traces the development of Jews in Hartford, noting demography, economic change, religious factionalism, and leaders.

4090. Braude, William G. HARRY WOLFSON AS MENTOR. *Rhode Island Jewish Hist. Notes 1975 7(1): 140-148.* Author relates events of his academic and rabbinical career, 1932-54, which was aided and influenced by a Brown University professor, Harry Wolfson.

4091. Driedger, Leo. JEWISH IDENTITY: THE MAINTENANCE OF URBAN RELIGIOUS AND ETHNIC BOUNDARIES. *Ethnic and Racial Studies [Great Britain] 1980 3(1): 67-88.* Jews in Winnipeg, Manitoba, have maintained ethnic enclaves through residential segregation, institutional completeness, cultural identity, and social distance, 1940's-70's.

4092. Edgar, Irving I. THE EARLY SITES AND BEGINNINGS OF CONGREGATION BETH EL: THE MICHIGAN GRAND AVENUE SYNAGOGUE, 1859-1861. *Michigan Jewish Hist. 1973 13(1): 13-20.* Discusses the beginnings of Congregation Beth El in Detroit.
S

4093. Edgar, Irving I. THE EARLY SITES AND BEGINNINGS OF CONGREGATION BETH EL OF DETROIT, MICHIGAN. *Michigan Jewish Hist. 1980 20(1): 20-25.* Continued from a previous article. Part IV. Congregation Beth El of Detroit, Michigan, occupied four sites during 1859-67; focuses on the fourth site, the Rivard Street Synagogue, 1861-67, and the congregation's turn to Reform Judaism; article to be continued.

4094. Edgar, Irving I. RABBI LEO M. FRANKLIN: THE OMAHA YEARS (1892-1899). *Michigan Jewish Hist. 1976 16(2): 10-21.* Details the organizational abilities of Rabbi Leo M. Franklin in his work in Temple Israel in Omaha, Nebraska. 4 letters, 26 notes.

4095. Endelman, Judith E. JUDAICA AMERICANA. *Am. Jewish Hist. Q. 1974 64(1): 55-68.* Annotated bibliography of monographic and periodical literature published since 1960 and received in the library of the American Jewish Historical Society. Twelve topical headings are employed for this annotation (bibliography, biography, cultural life, etc.).
F. Rosenthal

4096. Endelman, Judith E. JUDAICA AMERICANA. *Am. Jewish Hist. Q. 1975 44(3): 245-257.* An annotated bibliography of monographic and periodical literature published since 1960 and received in the library of the American Jewish Historical Society.
F. Rosenthal

4097. Fireman, Bert M. A BAR MITZVAH MESSAGE FROM PRESCOTT, ARIZONA IN 1879. *Western States Jewish Hist. Q. 1980 12(4): 341-344.* On 8 May 1879 Morris Goldwater (1852-1939) wrote a letter, reprinted here, to his younger brother, Baron Goldwater (1866-1928), who was to become the father of US Senator Barry Goldwater of Arizona. The occasion was Baron's 13th birthday and bar mitzvah. The letter congratulated Baron on reaching his religious majority, and advised him to obey his parents and select good companions in order to continue to bring honor to himself and the family. B. S. Porter

4098. Fogelson, George J., ed. A CONVERSION AT SANTA CRUZ, CALIFORNIA, 1877. *Western States Jewish Hist. Q. 1979 11(2): 138-144.* In December 1877, Miss Emma Schlutius was officially accepted as a convert to Judaism in a ceremony at the St. Charles Hotel in Santa Cruz. Miss Schlutius correctly answered questions regarding her motives and tenets of the faith. On her admission to the covenant, her name was changed to Esther. She was shortly afterwards married to Abe Rothschild. Based on an article published in the *Santa Cruz Sentinel* on 8 December 1877; photo, 6 notes. B. S. Porter

4099. Franklin, Harvey B. MEMORIES OF A CALIFORNIA RABBI: STOCKTON, SAN JOSE AND LONG BEACH. *Western States Jewish Hist. Q. 1977 9(2): 122-128.* Rabbi Harvey B. Franklin (1889-1976) spent his rabbinical career at Stockton, 1916-18; Oakland, 1918-20; San Jose, 1920-28; and Long Beach, 1928-57. Early in his career he faced the necessity of developing a religious service that satisfied a mixed and mutually antagonistic congregation of Reform, Orthodox, and Conservative members. Relates several anecdotes, some humorous, of his experiences at each Jewish community. B. S. Porter

4100. Franklin, Lewis A. and Levey, Samson H., ed. THE FIRST JEWISH SERMON IN THE WEST: YOM KIPPUR, 1850, SAN FRANCISCO. *Western States Jewish Hist. Q. 1977 10(1): 3-15.* Lewis Abraham Franklin (1820-79), an English Jew, arrived in San Francisco early in 1849. He opened a tent store in which religious services were conducted on High Holy Days. In 1851 Franklin moved to San Diego where he and his brother Maurice operated a general merchandise store and a hotel. He returned to England in 1860. The Yom Kippur sermon of 1850 centers on atonement and pleads for stricter observance of the Sabbath and a revival of religious (instead of monetary) goals. America provides a unique opportunity for spiritual freedom and self-identity for Jews. Quotes original text; 45 notes. B. S. Porter

4101. Geffen, M. David. DELAWARE JEWRY: THE FORMATIVE YEARS, 1872-1889. *Delaware Hist. 1975 16(4): 269-297.* Although the climate in Delaware was not hostile to Jews, few settled there until the great Jewish migrations from Russia and Eastern Europe in the late 19th century. The Jewish population remained small, concentrated in Wilmington, mercantile in character. The Wilmington Jews met with a favorable reception. They worked hard, earned the respect of the community, and invested their energies in establishing worship services in the city. The Moses Montefiore Mutual Aid Society took the lead in maintaining community life and in providing social and educational services. It also worked hard to bring Jews together for religious purposes, and by its fundraising efforts helped to underwrite the building of a synagogue staffed by a resident rabbi. The Wilmington Jewish community was largely of German origin and lived in a small area near the business district. By the end of the 1880's the Wilmington Jews were receiving an increasing number of Jewish families from Eastern Europe and feeling the cultural distance separating them. Based on contemporary newspapers; 2 illus., 84 notes. R. M. Miller

4102. Gendler, Carol. THE JEWS OF OMAHA: THE FIRST SIXTY YEARS. *Western States Jewish Hist. Q. 1973 5(3): 205-224, (4): 288-305, 6(1): 58-71, 1974 6(2): 141-154, (3): 222-233, (4): 293-304.* Part I. Discusses the role of Jews in the settlement of Omaha, 1820's-30's. Part II. Chronicles the development of the Orthodox and Reform Jewish congregations, the tenures of rabbis, and the erection of synagogues, 1854-1904. Part III. The Jews in Omaha formed several charity and mutual aid societies in the late 1800's. The main social club, the Metropolitan Club, lasted until 1911. Several Jews became leaders in Omaha. Edward Rosewater (1841-1906) served in the state legislature and founded the Omaha *Bee*. He ran for the US Senate twice, but lost. Jonas L. Brandeis (1837-1903), a successful businessman, gave large sums of money to charities. Photo, 41 notes. Part IV. In the late 1880's, thousands of Jews fled from eastern Europe. Several Jewish organizations were set up to help the refugees find homes and jobs in America. The Jews in Omaha came to the aid of those Jews that came to Omaha and wanted to settle there. By 1880, enough Orthodox Jews had settled in Omaha to make it possible to hold orthodox prayer services. The congregations were organized according to the country of origin of the immigrants. A strong Jewish community developed in Omaha. Based on primary and secondary sources; 46 notes. Part V. Because of a depression that hit Omaha in 1890, many wealthy citizens lost their fortunes and had to move elsewhere. Although several wealthy Jews were hard hit by the bad economic conditions, the Jewish population of Omaha continued to grow. This growth necessitated the formation of new organizations to serve the community. The Jews set up their own charities, fraternal groups, and hospital. The Jewish community was a mixture of Orthodox and Reformed Jews working together to take care of their needs. Based on primary and secondary sources; 41 notes. Part VI. The Jews of Omaha became leaders in the professions and politics. Harry B. Zimman served on the city council and was acting mayor when the regular mayor died in 1906. In 1889, the first of many Jewish political groups was founded. A controversy developed over who controlled the "Hebrew vote." The Omaha Jews were planning on building a community center when in 1913 a tornado destroyed the center of the Jewish residential area. The Jewish Relief Committee was established to aid the victims. By 1915, the Jews in Omaha were well established within the larger community, and were taking an active part in its development. Based on primary and secondary sources; photo, 30 notes. R. A. Garfinkle/S

4103. Glanz, Rudolf. FROM FUR RUSH TO GOLD RUSHES: ALASKAN JEWRY FROM THE LATE NINETEENTH TO THE EARLY TWENTIETH CENTURIES. *Western States Jewish Hist. Q. 1975 7(2): 95-107.* The Jewish-owned Alaska Commercial Company, founded in 1868, obtained the fur trading concession from the federal government, giving the company a monopoly in Alaska. The company established 87 trading posts in the territory. When its concession expired in 1890, the company was able to survive because of its other activities. The gold rushes in Alaska attracted many Jews, many establishing small businesses in the gold areas. The first organized Jewish community was in Nome. The Nome Hebrew Benevolent Society was established in 1901. Rabbi Samuel Koch of Seattle conducted religious instruction by correspondence with Jewish children in Alaska, beginning in 1916. Primary and secondary sources; photo, 50 notes. R. A. Garfinkle

4104. Halberstam, Joshua. EDITOR'S INTRODUCTION. *Am. Behavioral Scientist 1980 23(4): 461-466.* Introduces a special issue on contemporary American Judaism and discusses the future of American Jews as a distinct group.

4105. Henig, Gerald S. CALIFORNIA JEWRY AND THE MENDEL BEILISS AFFAIR, 1911-1913. *Western States Jewish Hist. Q. 1979 11(3): 220-230.* Mendel Beiliss was a Jewish laborer in a Russian brick factory, charged with murdering a Christian boy for religious purposes. The nature of the charges, with their anti-Semitic overtones, aroused worldwide protest. California Jews, and especially the Jewish newspapers, recognized that the prosecution of Beiliss was an attempt to justify pogroms. Public rallies attended by Jews and Christians in San Francisco and Oakland condemned the Russian government's action. Beiliss was acquitted, but the jury ruled that the boy was murdered as a ritual victim, and the Jews, as a group, were blamed for his death. Secondary sources; 55 notes. B. S. Porter

4106. Henry, Henry Abraham. A SAN FRANCISCO RABBI REPORTS ON A VISIT TO SACRAMENTO IN 1858. *Western States Jewish Hist. Q. 1978 11(1): 60-63.* A letter from Rabbi Henry Abraham Henry to Rabbi Samuel Meyer Issacs on 17 August 1858 described Rabbi Henry's recent visit to Sacramento, California. Rabbi Henry was invited to preach in the synagogue, and participated in the ceremonial placement of a monument on the grave of Mr. Julius S. Winehill. The president and trustees of the synagogue offered a gratuity for Rabbi Henry's services. Reprinted from the *Jewish Messenger,* New York, 24 September 1858. 2 notes. B. S. Porter

4107. Henry, Marcus H. HENRY ABRAHAM HENRY: SAN FRANCISCO RABBI, 1857-1869. *Western States Jewish Hist. Q. 1977 10(1): 31-37.* Henry Abraham Henry (1806-79) came to the United States from England in 1849. He served congregations in Ohio and New York before coming to San Francisco in 1857. He was minister of San Francisco's Sherith Israel (Polish) synagogue, from 1857-69. A popular lecturer, he officiated at the consecration of many synagogues and the dedications of secular institutions. Rabbi Henry contributed many articles to American Jewish journals. He published his two-part *Synopsis of Jewish History* in 1859. In 1860 he started and edited the weekly *Pacific Messenger.* In 1864 he issued his volume of *Discourses on the Book of Genesis.* His religious views were conservative. He upheld the dignity of his profession to the admiration of both Jews and Christians. Photo.

B. S. Porter

4108. Herscher, Uri D. THE METROPOLIS OF GHETTOS. *J. of Ethnic Studies 1976 4(2): 33-47.* Portrays the "classic" and stereotypical days of the Jewish ghetto from 1890 to 1920, with its sights, smells, tenements, habitual impoverishment and insecurity, and the all-consuming task of earning a living. Despite the hardship and ugliness of life, the ghetto was a world, complete and self-sustaining, with drama, humor, and romance as well. Fever for secular schooling was high, along with an innate distrust for the public, non-Jewish charities and their agencies. Intellectual life thrived in the cafes of Canal Street, prostitutes in Allen Street, and Jewish theaters in the Bowery. The Judaism of Europe grew progressively weaker, but still coexisted with the culture of the new land. World War I saw the garment manufacturers move to 14th Street, and non-Jews begin to move into the Lower East Side; they were willing to pay the higher rents traditionally levied on non-Jews. With these changes, the good old days of the ghetto were numbered. Based largely on personal conversations by the author in 1972 with individuals of immigrant stock who grew up on New York's Lower East Side; 25 notes.

G. J. Bobango

4109. Hertsberg, Steven. THE JEWISH COMMUNITY OF ATLANTA FROM THE END OF THE CIVIL WAR UNTIL THE END OF THE FRANK CASE. *Am. Jewish Hist. Q. 1973 62(3): 250-287.* Atlanta's Jewish community was by 1913 the largest in a South transformed by urbanization, industrialization, and Negro emancipation. There were more than 1,200 Jewish immigrants from Eastern Europe by 1910. Under the leadership of Rabbi David Marx (1872-1962) the established German Jews were led into classical Reform, while the East European and Levantine settlers maintained various forms of traditional Judaism. Thus two separate communities were created. Only in philanthropic activities did the two cooperate. In Atlanta and throughout the United States during this period, discrimination against even the established community of Western European Jews was increasing, setting the stage for the Leo M. Frank tragedy of 1913. 84 notes.

F. Rosenthal

4110. Himmelfarb, Harold S. AGENTS OF RELIGIOUS SOCIALIZATION AMONG AMERICAN JEWS. *Sociol. Q. 1979 20(4): 477-494.* A study of religious socialization among Chicago area Jews suggests that socialization is an ongoing process that continues into adulthood and is most effected by schools and workplaces.

4111. Himmelfarb, Harold S. PATTERNS OF ASSIMILATION: IDENTIFICATION AMONG AMERICAN JEWS. *Ethnicity 1979 6(3): 249-267.* Religious and ethnic identification among American Jews is declining. Younger Jews in the 1970's have tended to be nondenominational or Reformed and to be less interested in Jewish life than are their parents. Orthodoxy has gained popularity among second-generation Orthodox Jews, but the third generation has lost interest in it. Based on questionnaires; 5 notes, biblio., appendix.

S

4112. Hyman, Paula E. IMMIGRANT WOMEN AND CONSUMER PROTEST: THE NEW YORK CITY KOSHER MEAT BOYCOTT OF 1902. *Am. Jewish Hist. 1980 70(1): 91-105.* Immigrant Jewish women rioted on several occasions in spontaneous protest against sharp rises in food prices. Most notable were the May 1902 kosher meat riots in New York City, "evidence of a modern and sophisticated political mentality." In their violent boycott, women displayed an understanding of consumer power, political rhetoric, and the workings of the economic market. A study of nine boycott activists demonstrates that they were not typical of other women political activists of the period, but rather of the larger immigrant Jewish community. The leaders had a distinctive economic objective in mind and a clear political strategy for achieving their goal. Their actions were a prelude to those of women in the garment workers' strikes at the end of the decade. Newspaper accounts and census records; 58 notes.

J. D. Sarna

4113. Kaganoff, N. M. and Endelman, J. E. JUDAICA AMERICANA. *Am. Jewish Hist Q. 1973 62(4): 401-413.* An annotated bibliography of monographic and periodical literature published since 1960 and received in the library of the American Jewish Historical Society.

F. Rosenthal

4114. Kaganoff, Nathan M. and Katz-Hyman, Martha B. JUDAICA AMERICANA. *Am. Jewish Hist. 1980 69(4): 509-527.* "An annotated bibliography of monographic and periodical literature published since 1960 and received in the Library of the American Jewish Historical Society."

J. D. Sarna

4115. Kaganoff, Nathan M. JUDAICA AMERICANA. *Am. Jewish Hist. Q. 1976 65(4): 353-367.* An annotated bibliography of monographical and periodical literature published since 1960 and received in the Library of the American Jewish Historical Society. The current section contains works published in 1974 and 1975. F. Rosenthal

4116. Kaganoff, Nathan M. and Katz-Hyman, Martha B. JUDAICA AMERICANA. *Am. Jewish Hist. Q. 1977 66(4): 513-537.* An annotated bibliography of monographic and periodical literature published since 1960 and received in the library of the American Jewish Historical Society.

F. Rosenthal

4117. Kaganoff, Nathan M. and Katz-Hyman, Martha B. JUDAICA AMERICANA. *Am. Jewish Hist. Q. 1978 67(4): 363-377.* An annotated bibliography of monographic and periodical literature published since 1960 and received in the library of the American Jewish Historical Society.

F. Rosenthal

4118. Kaganoff, Nathan M. and Katz-Hyman, Martha B. JUDAICA AMERICANA. *Am. Jewish Hist. 1978 68(2): 213-230.* Annotated bibliography of new monographic and periodical literature published since 1960 as received in the Library of the American Jewish Historical Society.

F. Rosenthal

4119. Kaganoff, Nathan M. and Katz-Hyman, Martha B. JUDAICA AMERICANA. *Am. Jewish Hist. 1979 68(4): 534-551.* "An annotated bibliography of monographic and periodical literature published since 1960 and received in the Library of the American Jewish Historical Society." Covers general works and special studies.

S

4120. Kaganoff, Nathan M. and Katz-Hyman, Martha B. JUDAICA AMERICANA. *Am. Jewish Hist. 1980 69(3): 378-400.* An annotated bibliography of monographs and periodicals published since 1960 and received in the Library of the American Jewish Historical Society.

J. D. Sarna

4121. Kardonne, Rick. MONTREAL, QUEBEC. *Present Tense 1975 2(2): 50-55.* Discusses the social and religious life of the Jews of Montreal, Quebec during the 1970's and the problems presented by the emigration of Jews from Morocco in the 1960's.

4122. Katz-Hyman, Martha B. A NOTE ON RABBI MOSES ZISKIND FINESILVER, 1847-1922. *Rhode Island Jewish Hist. Notes 1977 7(3): 430-431.* Note offers documentation of the fact that Moses Ziskind Finesilver was the Congregation Sons of Zion's (Providence, Rhode Island) first hazzan (cantor) and shohet (ritual slaughterer), not Eliasar Lipshitz as previously stated; covers 1880-83.

4123. Kinsey, Stephen D. THE DEVELOPMENT OF THE JEWISH COMMUNITY OF SAN JOSE, CALIFORNIA, 1850-1900. *Western States Jewish Hist. Q. 1974 7(1): 70-87, (2): 163-182, (3): 264-273.* Part I. Jews began to arrive in San Jose, California, in the 1850's. In 1861, they established Congregation Bickur Cholim, with Jacob Levy as the first president. There were 35 members in 1869 and the congregation purchased land to construct a synagogue. On 21 August 1870, the synagogue was dedicated. The first ordained rabbi to serve the congregation was Dr. Myer Sol Levy. By 1916 the congregation was a mixture of Orthodox and Reform Jews. Based on primary sources; 3 photos, 79 notes. Part II. The development of the Jewish community in San Jose depended upon merchants who could give their time and money for Jewish activities. Many of these individuals held offices in Jewish community organizations, Congregation Bickur Cholim, Ariel Lodge, B'nai B'rith, and other community groups. Short biographies are included in the article. Based on primary and secondary sources; 5 photos, 108 notes. Part III. Established in 1857, the Beth Olam Cemetery was the first Jewish communal organization in San Jose. Other Jewish community organizations were the Hebrew Ladies Benevolent Society (established 1869), the Hebrew Young Men's Benevolent Association of San Jose (established 1872), and Ariel Lodge No. 248 of B'nai B'rith (established 1875). Even with these few organizations, Congregation Bickur Cholim remained the center of the Jewish community in early San Jose. Based on primary sources; photo, 32 notes. R. A. Garfinkle

4124. Korn, Bertram W. AN AMERICAN JEWISH RELIGIOUS LEADER IN 1860 VOICES HIS FRUSTRATION. *Michael: On the Hist. of the Jews in the Diaspora [Israel] 1975 3: 42-47.* Though some American rabbis in the 1860's were men of stature who helped reorient Judaism and the Jew toward the conditions and demands of their new environment, most were minor religious functionaries who lacked any other speicalized training. One such figure was Henry Loewenthal of Macon, Georgia, who reached the United States from England in 1854. Prints an 1860 letter he wrote to Rabbi Isaac Leeser of Philadelphia, complaining of ill treatment by members of his congregation, Kahal Kadosh Beth Israel, and the poor Jewish example they present to their children. Primary and secondary sources; 12 notes. T. Sassoon

4125. Kramer, William M. THE EMERGENCE OF OAKLAND JEWRY. *Western States Jewish Hist. Q. 1978 10(2): 99-125, (3): 238-259, (4): 353-373; 11(1): 69-86; 1979 11(2): 173-186, (3): 265-278.* Part I. Jewish families were among the pioneers of Oakland, California, in the 1850's. In the early years, the Oakland Hebrew Benevolent Society, founded in 1862, was the religious, social, and charitable center of the community. Later, the first synagogue, founded in 1875, took over the religious and burial functions. Jews from Poland or Prussian-occupied Poland predominated in the community, and most of them worked in some aspect of the clothing industry. David Solis-Cohen, the noted author, was a leader in the Oakland Jewish community in the 1870's. Primary and secondary sources; 3 photos, 111 notes. Part II. In 1879 Oakland's growing Jewish community organized a second congregation, a strictly orthodox group, Poel Zedek. Women's religious organizations flourished, their charitable services extending to needy gentiles as well as Jews. Jewish participants in civic and political affairs included David S. Hirshberg, who served in several Alameda County offices, and Henry Levy, commander of the Oakland Guard militia organization. Oakland Jewry was part of the greater San Francisco community, yet maintained its own charm and character. Primary and secondary sources; 88 notes. Part III. On 6 July 1881 the First Hebrew Congregation of Oakland, California, elected Myer Solomon Levy as its rabbi. The London-born Levy practiced traditional Judaism. In 1884 the community faced the need of finding a larger, more fashionably located synagogue. The Israel Ladies Relief Society held a fair and raised $4,000 for the new building. On 17 June 1885 the First Hebrew's synagogue burned, increasing the urgency for a new building. Construction of the new synagogue began in May 1886 and was completed by September. Primary and secondary sources; 68 notes. Part IV. Oakland's Jews attended excellent schools, both secular and religious. Fannie Bernstein was the first Jewess to graduate from the University of California at Berkeley, in 1883. First Hebrew Congregation sponsored a Sabbath school which had 75 children in 1887. One of the pupils, Meyer Lissner, was a bright youngster whose letters were published in the Jewish press. The Jewish children of Oakland had an active social life with school events, birthday parties, and Bar Mitzvah. The contract of the popular Rabbi Myer S. Levy was renewed for five years, from 1888 to 1893. Primary and secondary sources; 66 notes. Part V. Oakland Jewry was active in public affairs and charitable projects in the 1880's. Rabbi Myer S. Levy was chaplain to the state legislature in 1885, and was invited several times to speak to the congregation of the Unitarian Hamiltonian Church. The Daughters of Israel Relief Society continued its good works both inside and outside the Jewish community. Beth Jacob, the traditional congregation of Old World Polish Jews, continued its separate religious practices while it maintained friendly relations with the members of the first Hebrew Congregation. Primary and secondary sources; 44 notes. Part VI. Oakland's Jewish community had able social and political leadership in David Samuel Hirshberg. Until 1886 he was an officer in the Grand Lodge of B'nai B'rith. He served as Under Sheriff of Alameda County in 1883 and was active in Democratic Party political affairs. In 1885 he was appointed Chief Clerk of the US Mint in San Francisco. As a politician, he had detractors who accused him of using his position in B'nai B'rith to foster his political career. Primary and secondary sources; 56 notes. Part VII. In 1891 Rabbi Myer S. Levy moved to a new position in San Francisco's Congregation Beth Israel, bringing to a close this era of Oakland's Jewish history. Based on published sources; 21 notes. B. S. Porter

4126. Kramer, William M. and Stern, Norton B. A SEARCH FOR THE FIRST SYNAGOGUE IN THE GOLDEN WEST. *Western States Jewish Hist. Q. 1974 7(1): 3-20.* In 1851, the rivalry between German and Polish Jews in San Francisco led to the founding of two separate synagogues within the city. The German synagogue is Temple Emanu-El and the Polish is Temple Sherith Israel. In 1900, Rabbi Jacob Voorsanger of Emanu-El tried to prove that his temple was the first, but he used a misdated lease as his main proof. Research shows that both congregations were founded on 6 April 1851. Primary and secondary sources; photo, 56 notes. R. A. Garfinkle

4127. Krausz, Ernest. THE RELIGIOUS FACTOR IN JEWISH IDENTIFICATION. *Int. Social Sci. J. [France] 1977 29(2): 250-260.* Examines the interconnections between religious and secular life for Jews, concluding that where religion is upheld, the ethnic factor is strong and that where shift in emphasis favors secularization, these will compensate for loss of religious identity; differentiates between Israeli and American Jews, 1957-77.

4128. Lavender, Abraham D. STUDIES OF JEWISH COLLEGE STUDENTS: A REVIEW AND A REPLICATION. *Jewish Social Studies 1977 39(1-2): 37-52.* A comparison of Jewish college students at the University of Maryland in 1971 with those surveyed at the same school by Irving Greenberg in 1949 indicates Jewish college students rank below their parents in overall observance of the Jewish religion, and in the preservation of their Jewish identity. However, the difference is not as great in 1971 as it had been in 1949. Specific findings show that the families of the 1971 freshmen students were economically better off than those of 1949; that synagogue attendance of the parents in both surveys was similar; that by 1971 observance of *kashruth* had declined; that Conservative Judaism had gained in strength at the expense of Orthodoxy; and that Reform Judaism made only minor percentile gains. Based on survey-questionnaires. N. Lederer

4129. Lazerwitz, Bernard and Harrison, Michael. AMERICAN JEWISH DENOMINATIONS: A SOCIAL AND RELIGIOUS PROFILE. *Am. Sociol. Rev. 1979 44(4): 656-666.* Analyzes Jewish denominational patterns as revealed by data from the National Jewish Population Survey of 1970-71. A clear ranking among the denominational subgroups emerges, ranging from those identifying with Orthodoxy, to those identifying with Conservative Judaism, Reform, and finally those having no denominational preferences. This last group has the lowest levels of religious and ethnic identification. The subgroups closer to the Orthodox pole have higher levels of Jewish identification and observance, and are somewhat lower in socioeconomic status and voluntary association activities. The socioeconomic differences are considerably smaller than they are known to have been historically, but differences in the degree of Americanization, as indicated by the number of generations in the United States, remain strong. The data also show that marital patterns and certain secular attitudes and behavior are associated with denominational identification and synagogue membership. Analogies are suggested between the ideological and behavioral divisions within American Judaism and those found in Protestantism. Judaism is becoming increasingly independent of its classic social and economic sources. J

4130. Leibo, Steven A. OUT THE ROAD: THE SAN BRUNO AVENUE JEWISH COMMUNITY OF SAN FRANCISCO, 1901-1968. *Western States Jewish Hist. Q. 1979 11(2): 99-110.* The first synagogue, Ahabat Achim, was formed in 1901, but the major growth of the San Bruno Avenue Jewish community took place after the 1906 earthquake. In its prime, the area comprised about 1200 Jewish residents, most of them poor, Eastern European immigrants. The Esther Hellman Settlement House, usually referred to as the "Clubhouse," was financed by wealthy "downtown" Jews, and provided for educational and social needs of the community. San Bruno Avenue, the main thoroughfare, had numerous stores and businesses operated by the local Jewish residents. Beginning in the 1930's, as they became more affluent, the younger generations moved out of the old neighborhood. Based on interviews and published sources; 3 photos, 47 notes. B. S. Porter

4131. Loewenberg, Robert. THE THEFT OF LIBERALISM—A JEWISH PROBLEM. *Midstream 1977 28(5): 19-33.* The contradictions of modern Jewish liberalism put Jews at odds with reality and force them to choose between particularism and universalism or, more specifically, between Judaism and liberalism, 19th-20th centuries.

4132. Maller, Allen S. REPORT FROM THE MAGAZINE RACK: WHAT ARE THE RABBIS READING? *Am. Jewish Arch. 1979 31(2): 131-141.* Younger Jewish rabbis read less than older ones, indicating that Jews are assimilating into American society, 1970's.

4133. Neusner, Jacob. THE STUDY OF RELIGION AS THE STUDY OF TRADITION: JUDAISM. *Hist. of Religions 1975 14(3): 191-206.* Defines tradition as "something handed on from the past which is made contemporary and transmitted because of its intense contemporaneity." Stresses the importance of literary and legal sources for proper understanding of Jewish tradition. Draws distinctions between the aims and methods of historians of religion and regular historians. Contribution to a Symposium on Methodology and World Religions at the University of Iowa; 8 notes. T. L. Auffenberg

4134. Newman, William M. and Halvorson, Peter L. AMERICAN JEWS: PATTERNS OF GEOGRAPHIC DISTRIBUTION AND CHANGE, 1952-1971. *J. for the Sci. Study of Religion 1979 18(2): 183-193.* Also discusses the effects of geographic change on patterns of American religious pluralism.

4135. Papermaster, Isadore. A HISTORY OF NORTH DAKOTA JEWRY AND THEIR PIONEER RABBI. *Western States Jewish Hist. Q. 1977 10(1): 74-89; 1978 10(2): 170-184, (3): 266-283.* Part I. Rabbi Benjamin Papermaster was born in Lithuania in 1860. He agreed to come to America in 1890 to serve a party of immigrants as its religious leader and teacher. He settled in Grand Forks, North Dakota, amid a growing congregation of Jews from the Ukraine, Rumania, Poland, and Germany. Most of the Jews at that time were peddlers who mortgaged their houses and wagons to build the first synagogue. Papermaster was enthusiastic about America; his letters to his family in Lithuania brought many relatives to join him. Grand Forks was considered a boom town because of the building of the Great Northern Railway. The influx of eastern capital helped the development of Jewish merchants. Based on personal experience and family records; 2 photos, 6 notes. Part II. Until the turn of the century, Papermaster of Grand Forks was the only rabbi serving Jews in all of North Dakota and western Minnesota. Jewish families who started as peddlers became prosperous enough to move out to towns and villages where they opened small shops and stores. Other families followed the Great Northern Railway along its branch lines toward the Canadian border. In Grand Forks, the Jewish community established a modern Hebrew school, a Ladies' Aid Society, and a burial society. 2 photos, 11 notes. Part III. The city of Grand Forks, at the urging of Papermaster, acquired a sanitary meat slaughtering facility with a special department for kosher beef. Papermaster maintained an active interest in local politics, generally favoring the Republican Party but supporting Democrats when he knew them to be good men. Although a member of a Zionist organization, he worried about the antireligious character of the modern movement. During World War I he urged Jewish youths to their patriotic duty of joining the American armed forces. Papermaster died on 24 September 1934. 3 photos, 14 notes. B. S. Porter

4136. Petrusak, Frank and Steinert, Steven. THE JEWS OF CHARLESTON: SOME OLD WINE IN NEW BOTTLES. *Jewish Social Studies 1976 38(3-4): 337-346.* An analysis of survey data for the 1970's indicates that Jewry in Charleston, South Carolina, constitutes a well-defined, highly structured, nonassimilated ethnic group. The Jewish community retains its distinctiveness as a separate entity from the majority population despite great pressures to assimilate. The community has considerable self-identification, and the synagogue and the state of Israel play important roles as ethnic referents. Politically the Charleston Jews are strongly Democratic and have a social welfare and liberal orientation. Primary sources. N. Lederer

4137. Raphael, Marc Lee. AMERICAN JEWISH STUDIES: A PERIODIC REPORT OF THE STATUS OF THE FIELD: REPORT 2: DECEMBER 1978. *Am. Jewish Hist. 1979 68(3): 367-371.* Lists nine conferences, nine colleges and universities offering Jewish studies programs, 26 completed doctoral dissertations (1976-78), and nine dissertations in progress. F. Rosenthal

4138. Raphael, Marc Lee. AMERICAN JEWISH STUDIES: THE STATUS OF THE FIELD. *Am. Jewish Hist. 1979 69(1): 99-102.* A conference calendar for November-December 1979 is provided, as well as a listing of new courses at colleges and universities. Twenty-two completed dissertations and nine dissertations in progress are enumerated. F. Rosenthal

4139. Robinson, Ira. CYRUS ADLER, BERNARD REVEL AND THE PREHISTORY OF ORGANIZED JEWISH SCHOLARSHIP IN THE UNITED STATES. *Am. Jewish Hist. 1980 69(4): 497-505.* The Society of Jewish Academicians was founded in 1916 largely through the initiative of Bernard Revel, then president of the Rabbinical College of America (later Yeshiva University). The society was to serve as a focal point for an American Orthodox Jewish intelligentsia, and to promote the synthesis of Orthodox Judaism and modern scientific thought. Scholars at the Jewish Theological Seminary and Dropsie College, both headed by Cyrus Adler, generally opposed the society for its pretensions, its Orthodoxy, and its lack of ties with Europe. In 1920, opponents formed what is today known as the American Academy for Jewish Research. Revel's society faded away in the 1920's, never becoming a force in American Jewish intellectual life. The Cyrus Adler papers; 25 notes. J. D. Sarna

4140. Roditi, Edouard. NEO-KABBALISM IN THE AMERICAN JEWISH COUNTER-CULTURE. *Midstream 1979 25(8): 8-13.* In response to middle-class Jewish traditionalism and rationalism, young dissident Jews have turned to the mysticism of the Cabala for inspiration, 1940's-70's.

4141. Rosenthal, Marcus. THE JEWISH IMMIGRATION "PROBLEM." *Western States Jewish Hist. Q. 1974 6(4): 278-289.* On 27 January 1905, Rabbi Jacob Voorsanger, the editor of *Emanu-El*, published his feelings against the immigration of large numbers of East European Jews. The author's rebuttal attacks Rabbi Voorsanger's ideas, stating that if American Jews turn against the new arrivals the Christian community will use that as a sign to start a new round of anti-Semitism. Reprinted letter-to-the-editor from *Emanu-El*, San Francisco, 24 February 1905. R. A. Garfinkle

4142. Rosenwaike, Ira. LEON DYER: BALTIMORE AND SAN FRANCISCO JEWISH LEADER. *Western States Jewish Hist. Q. 1977 9(2): 135-143.* Earlier accounts of the life of Leon Dyer (1807-83) have too often relied on legend instead of valid documentary sources. In fact, Dyer was a Baltimore butcher and real estate dealer who developed a business interest in California when his younger brother, Abraham, joined a group of immigrants to that state. Leon Dyer went to San Francisco in 1850 for business reasons and in the few months he spent there, he was chosen the religious leader of a temporary congregation of Jewish settlers. After his return to Baltimore he made several trips to Europe before settling in Louisville, Kentucky, in 1875. Based on documents in the National Archives, Baltimore Land Records, other primary, and secondary sources; 31 notes. B. S. Porter

4143. Scott, William R. RABBI ARNOLD FORD'S BACK-TO-ETHIOPIA MOVEMENT: A STUDY OF BLACK EMIGRATION, 1930-1935. *Pan-African J. [Kenya] 1975 8(2): 191-202.* An account of the career of Rabbi Arnold Ford (1876-1935), early black Nationalist and leader of the back-to-Ethiopia movement. Accompanied by three other members of his congregation, Ford arrived in Addis Ababa in 1930 in an attempt to obtain concessions for the rest of his group, who, it was hoped, would follow soon after. Records the difficulties encountered by those 60 members who made the journey to Addis Ababa during 1930-34. Twenty-five members returned shortly after their arrival and none remained after Ford's death in 1935 and the outbreak of the Italo-Ethiopian War. Primary and secondary sources; 52 notes. M. Feingold

4144. Singerman, Robert, ed. and Grumet, Elinor, ed. WAYWARD ETCHINGS: I. N. CHOYNSKI VISITS SOUTHERN CALIFORNIA, 1881. *Western States Jewish Hist. Q. 1979 11(2): 119-135.* Isidor Nathan Choynski (1834-99) was the West's foremost Jewish journalist of the 19th century. Choynski set out from his home in San Francisco in 1881 to visit several cities in southern, California. His reports on San Luis Obispo, Santa Barbara, Los Angeles, San Gabriel, San Bernardino, Riverside, and San Diego mention the numbers of Jews in these cities, praise their commercial success, and criticize their religious indifference. Based on articles published in *The American Isralite* on 8, 15, and 29 July 1881; 2 photos, 19 notes. B. S. Porter

4145. Sklare, Marshall. JEWISH RELIGION AND ETHNICITY AT THE BICENTENNIAL. *Midstream 1975 21(9): 19-28.* The survival of the Jewish religion in the United States has been deeply dependent upon the Jews' sense of ethnic unity.

4146. Sochen, June. JEWISH WOMEN AS VOLUNTEER ACTIVISTS. *Am. Jewish Hist. 1980 70(1): 23-34.* The rich organizational life of American Jews is based on the energy and talent of women volunteers. Jewish women, after raising their own children, have been expected to devote their energies to communal needs. Single women have often served their communities throughout their lives. The founding of the National Council of Jewish Women in 1893 improved the status of Jewish women. It was followed in 1912 by Hadassah, organized by Henrietta Szold. Both groups reflected and encouraged a new professionalism in Jewish women's activities. The National Council of Jewish Women tended to attract upper middle class Reform Jews; Hadassah more traditional Jews. By the 1930's, Jewish women volunteers had narrowed their activities to self-education and fund raising; women's divisions of Jewish Federations began to appear. More recently, Jewish women's organizations have changed to meet the needs of professional women pressed for time but eager to maintain ties to Judaism. Published sources; 9 notes. J. D. Sarna

4147. Stern, Norton B. and Kramer, William M. THE FIRST JEWISH ORGANIZATION, THE FIRST JEWISH CEMETERY AND THE FIRST KNOWN JEWISH BURIAL IN THE FAR WEST. *Western States Jewish Hist. Q. 1979 11(4): 318-324.* The first Jewish burial in the West took place in San Francisco in December 1849. The deceased was Henry D. Johnson, religious rites were performed by Lewis A. Franklin, and burial was in the Yerba Buena public cemetery. Following this burial, the Jewish community organized the First Hebrew Benevolent Society and established a Jewish cemetery so that Jewish burials could take place in consecrated ground. The Benevolent Society was founded in January 1850, and the land for the cemetery was acquired in April 1950. Johnson's remains were moved to the new cemetery. The first funeral service in the Hart (Jewish) Cemetery was in the fall of 1850 when two victims of the Sacramento cholera epidemic were buried. Newspaper accounts and other published sources; photo, 22 notes. B. S. Porter

4148. Stern, Norton B. A SAN FRANCISCO SYNAGOGUE SCANDAL IN 1893. *Western States Jewish Hist. Q. 1974 6(3): 196-203.* A scandal developed at Temple Sherith Israel in 1893, when a new rabbi was being installed. The cantor, Max Rubin, did not want a new rabbi who would start receiving fees for weddings and funerals, as he had been filling in as reader for over a year and liked the large sum collected for officiating at various functions. In June, 1893, Rabbi Jacob Nieto was elected Rabbi of the congregation, and the scandal soon died down. Primary and secondary sources; 14 notes. R. A. Garfinkle

4149. Tenenbaum, Marc H. HOLY YEAR 1975 AND THE JEWISH JUBILEE YEAR. *Lutheran Q. 1974 26(3): 258-268.* Describes the concept of the Jewish Jubilee Year as an aid to those Christians celebrating the holy year of 1975 proclaimed by Pope Paul VI. Derived from the God-given law on Mount Sinai, the Jubilee had four objectives: freeing the slaves with their families, restoring all purchased land to the original owner, releasing the land from cultivation, and educating the people in the knowledge of the Torah. For centuries, Jews observed the Jubilee every 50 years. It is estimated 1975 is the 20th year of the current Jubilee cycle. Based largely on the Torah; 4 notes. J. A. Kicklighter

4150. Toll, William. THE CHOSEN PEOPLE IN THE WORLD OF CHOICE. *Rev. in Am. Hist. 1980 8(2): 167-175.* Review essay of Lloyd P. Gartner's *History of the Jews of Cleveland* (Cleveland, Ohio: The Western Reserve Historical Society and the Jewish Theological Seminary of America, 1978), Jeffrey S. Gurock's *When Harlem Was Jewish, 1870-1930* (New York: Columbia U. Pr., 1979), Steven Hertzberg's *Strangers within the Gate City: The Jews of Atlanta, 1845-1915* (Philadelphia: Jewish Publication Society of America, 1978), and Mark Lee Raphael's *Jews and Judaism in a Midwestern Community: Columbus, Ohio, 1840-1975* (Columbus: Ohio Historical Society, 1979).

4151. Toury, Jacob. M.E. LEVY'S PLAN FOR A JEWISH COLONY IN FLORIDA: 1825. *Michael: On the Hist. of the Jews in the Diaspora [Israel] 1975 3: 23-33.* Publishes an 1825 letter addressed to Isaac L. Goldsmid of London by the American Jew, Moses Elias Levy, advocating the foundation of a Jewish colony in Florida, the nucleus of which was apparently to be a theological seminary. Levy was also an outspoken proponent of the abolition of Negro slavery and of Jewish political disabilities in Europe. His religious fervor inspired him to advocate a Bible-based socialism. Opposed to Jewish emancipation in Europe because of its ultimate threat to Jewish existence, Levy was a proud defender of the American "right to be different." Primary and secondary sources; 35 notes. T. Sassoon

4152. Twersky, Rebecca. THE FOUNDING OF A JEWISH COMMUNITY: AHAVATH SHALOM OF WEST WARWICK. *Rhode Island Jewish Hist. Notes 1977 7(3): 420-429.* History of the Congregation Ahavath Shalom of West Warwick, Rhode Island, from its inception in 1912 to around 1938.

4153. Urofsky, Melvin I. STEPHEN S. WISE AND THE "JESUS CONTROVERSY." *Midstream 1980 26(6): 36-40.* In December 1925, Reform Rabbi Stephen S. Wise (1874-1949), in a sermon to his Free Synagogue in Carnegie Hall, New York City, said that Jesus Christ was man, not God, that Jesus was a Jew, not a Christian, that Jews had not repudiated Jesus the Jew, and that, for the most part, Christians had not adopted and followed Jesus the Jew; some Orthodox Jews' subsequent attacks on Wise almost destroyed his position of leadership of American Jewry and Zionism.

4154. Warsen, Allen A. THE SURVEY OF THE DETROIT JEWISH COMMUNITY. *Michigan Jewish Hist. 1979 19(2): 8-12.* This congregational chart covers 1850-1922.

4155. Waxman, Chaim I. and Helmreich, William B. RELIGIOUS AND COMMUNAL ELEMENTS OF ETHNICITY: AMERICAN JEWISH COLLEGE STUDENTS AND ISRAEL. *Ethnicity 1977 4(2): 122-132.* Surveys of attitudes among Jewish students in the Northeast show that attitudes on Zionism, Jewishness, and Israel were part of strong and complex self-images based on combinations of Americanism, religiosity, and belief in communalism. Most expressed positive identification with Israel, but few expressed desire to live there. Extent of support of Zionism was based upon its compatibility with their self-professed Americanism (which seemed to consistently outweigh identification with Jewishness). Covers 1973-76. G. A. Hewlett

4156. Weinfeld, Morton. A NOTE ON COMPARING CANADIAN AND AMERICAN JEWRY. *J. of Ethnic Studies 1977 5(1): 95-103.* Evaluates the two factors usually cited to account for the greater communal identification of Canadian Jews compared with their American brethren: 1) that the Canadian community is one generation younger or closer to Europe and 2) the Canadian mosaic is more accepting and supportive of ethnic diversity than is the conformity of the American melting pot ethos. Sees the major empirical differences between the two groups as somewhat misleading because of variations in statistical criteria between the United States and Canada. Still, Canadian Jews rate of intermarriage is much lower, day school enrollment far exceeds that in the United States, retention of Yiddish is stronger in Canada, and religious affiliation of Canadian synagogues leans more to Orthodoxy than does that of American Jews. Canada's new national preoccupation with fostering national sentiment, its official multiculturalism, and its government expenditures to promote ethnic maintenance, which are four times those of the United States explain the greater sense of Jewish identity in Canada. Covers 1961-74. Primary and secondary sources; 3 tables, 13 notes. G. J. Bobango

4157. Zipperstein, Steve et al. THE REAWAKENING OF JEWISH RELIGIOUS LIFE IN AMERICA. *Present Tense 1980 7(3): 23-31.* Presents several essays that view the contemporary reawakening of Jewish life in America with confidence.

4158. Zwerin, Kenneth C. JEWRY AND JUDAISM IN THE HAWAIIAN ISLANDS IN 1935. *Western States Jewish Hist. Q. 1980 12(3): 206-208.* The author officiated at High Holy Days services in Honolulu in 1935. He found 100 Jewish families and 400 Jewish servicemen at the Army and Navy bases on Oahu. The Jewish civilian population had married across religious and racial lines with the Oriental and Polynesian people of the islands. The local non-Jews were friendly and curious about Jewish life and culture. The children of mixed marriages were raised as Jews despite the lack of regular Jewish schools and synagogues. Reprinted from *Emanu-El and the Jewish Journal,* San Francisco, 3 April 1936. B. S. Porter

4159. —. IMPORTANT HISTORIC DOCUMENTS: REGARDING A STATE MARKER FOR THE LAFAYETTE STREET BETH EL CEMETERY. *Michigan Jewish Hist. 1973 13(1): 21-26.* Publishes letters on securing a historic marker for Beth El cemetery in Detroit, Michigan, the first Jewish cemetery owned and maintained by a Jewish congregation, 1850-1971. S

4160. —. JEWS IN EARLY SANTA MONICA: A CENTENNIAL REVIEW. *Western States Jewish Hist. Q. 1975 7(4): 327-350.* Many Los Angeles Jews spent their summers camping out at Santa Monica Canyon before the town was established in 1875. Many of these Jews were the first to purchase lots when the town was laid out by John P. Jones and R. S. Baker in 1875. The Jewish community consisted mostly of vacationers during the summer. The first Jewish religious services were held in 1912 by Los Angeles Rabbi Sigmund Hecht. In 1939, the first permanent Jewish congregation was formed. 16 photos, 56 notes. R. A. Garfinkle

4161. —. THE OLD JEWISH CEMETERY IN CHAVEZ RAVINE, LOS ANGELES: A PICTURE STORY. *Western States Jewish Hist. Q. 1977 9(2): 167-175.* The Hebrew Benevolent Society of Los Angeles established the Home of Peace Jewish Cemetery in 1855. A new cemetery was established in 1902. The remains and monuments were transferred to the new location during 1902-10. Based on photos collected by cemetery superintendent Oscar Willenberg, interviews, and published material; 8 photos, 3 notes. B. S. Porter

4162. —. PACIFIC NORTHWEST JEWRY IN 1888. *Western States Jewish Hist. Q. 1980 12(4): 370-372.* Portland, Oregon, had a Jewish population of 1,500 in 1888. The Jews were among the leaders of the city's commerce and finance. Jewish organizations included Reform Temple Beth Israel and Orthodox congregation Ahavai Sholom, a Hebrew Benevolent Society, B'nai B'rith, and Judith Montefiore Society. Published in *The Jewish Messenger,* New York, 10 February 1888. B. S. Porter

4163. —. PROBLEMS OF A NEVADA JEWISH COMMUNITY IN 1875. *Western States Jewish Hist. Q. 1976 8(2): 160-162.* Reprints a letter to the editor of the *American Israelite*, 3 September 1875, in which an anonymous resident of Eureka, Nevada complained that his Jewish community could not afford a good rabbi for the High Holy Days. He complained that many of the men previously hired to be rabbis had been frauds. R. A. Garfinkle

4164. —. THE RISE AND FALL OF THE JEWISH COMMUNITY OF AUSTIN, NEVADA. *Western States Jewish Q. 1976 9(1): 87-90.* Reprints letters from Jewish correspondents to Jewish newspapers in San Francisco and New York. In 1864 there were 150 Jews, including three families, who kept the principles of the faith and maintained an active Hebrew Benevolent Association in Austin, Nevada. By 1882, silver mining had declined and so had the town's population. Jews numbered only 11. Religious observance was minimal among both Jews and Christians, although the town was remarkably law-abiding. B. S. Porter

4165. —. TWO VIEWS OF AN INTERNATIONAL JEWISH COMMUNITY: BROWNSVILLE, TEXAS AND MATAMOROS, MEXICO. *Western States Jewish Hist. Q. 1978 10(4): 306-310.* Letters to editors of Jewish newspapers in 1876 and 1882 described the Jews of Brownsville (Texas) and Matamoros, (Tamaulipas, Mexico) as a unified religious community. Matamoros, having the greater number of Jewish families, was the location of religious ceremonies on feast and fast days. Some of the leading merchants in both towns were Jews; they were highly respected citizens who took an interest in civic affairs and contributed to every public and religious institution. Reprints letters to the *American Israelite,* Cincinnati, Ohio, 28 July 1876, and the *Jewish Messenger,* New York, 27 January 1882. 7 notes. B. S. Porter

4166. —. YOM KIPPUR FAILINGS: SAN FRANCISCO AND NEW YORK. *Western States Jewish Hist. Q. 1979 12(1): 63-65.* A traveling Jew, Albert Goldie, wishing to attend Yom Kippur services in a San Francisco Reform Congregation, was rudely turned away. Later, in New York City, he was able to find a seat, although the Orthodox synagogue was crowded. Another Jew, Harris Weinstock, corroborated the account with a comment on the contrasting practices of synagogues, which are unfriendly to the poor and nonmembers, and Christian churches, which welcome all who wish to attend services. Reprinted from *The American Israelite,* August 16 and 30, 1906. B. S. Porter

Conservative

4167. Gilson, Estelle. ARTHUR HERTZBERG: WRITER, SCHOLAR, POLEMICIST, RABBI. *Present Tense 1980 7(4): 33-38.* Discusses the views of outspoken American Jewish leader, Conservative rabbi, and historian Arthur Hertzberg, especially those dealing with the American Jewish community.

4168. Hertzberg, Arthur. GROWING UP JEWISH IN AMERICA. *Midstream 1979 25(2): 51-54.* Conservative Rabbi Arthur Hertzberg, author of *Being Jewish in America,* discusses the evolution of his ideas concerning Judaism since the 1940's.

4169. Kaplan, Lawrence J. THE DILEMMA OF CONSERVATIVE JUDAISM. *Commentary 1976 62(5): 44-47.* During the 20 years after World War II Conservative Judaism became the most popular religious movement among American Jews. There has been a crisis in Conservative Judaism in recent years, giving rise to a split between the right and left wings of the movement. The former tend toward Orthodoxy; the latter approach the Reform movement. The left wing argues for religious change through legislation rather than interpretation; the right wing contends that limits on change and liberalization must be maintained. The conflict reflects the most basic issue facing the modern Jewish community: how can Judaism exist in the modern world, while maintaining its distinct identity? Primary and secondary sources. S. R. Herstein

4170. Rosenblum, Herbert. IDEOLOGY AND COMPROMISE: THE EVOLUTION OF THE UNITED SYNAGOGUE CONSTITUTIONAL PREAMBLE. *Jewish Social Studies 1973 35(1): 18-31.* Traces the ideological and institutional development of the Conservative branch of American Judaism, 1910-13. The preambles of the articles of incorporation of the United Synagogue of America, the association for Conservative rabbis, indicate the ideological compromises among diverse groups to achieve unity. Based on primary and secondary sources, particularly letters and documents in the archives of the Jewish Theological Seminary of America; 45 notes. P. E. Schoenberg

Orthodox

4171. Bernstein, Louis. GENERATIONAL CONFLICT IN AMERICAN ORTHODOXY: THE EARLY YEARS OF THE RABBINICAL COUNCIL OF AMERICA. *Am. Jewish Hist. 1979 69(2): 226-233.* The Union of Orthodox Rabbis of the United States and Canada was founded in 1902 by rabbis born and trained in Europe. Over time, tensions developed between these rabbis and American-born rabbis trained in the Rabbi Isaac Elchanan Theological Seminary. In 1926, Rabbi Leo Jung organized the Rabbinical Council of the Union of Orthodox Jewish Congregations of America, primarily to deal with religious questions. Its functions grew until in 1935 it was reorganized into a national rabbinic body: the Rabbinical Council of America. In 1942, this organization merged with the rabbinic association of Hebrew Theological College in Chicago. It is now one of the most important Orthodox institutions in America. Based on Rabbinical Council of America minutes, interviews, and newspaper articles; 17 notes. J. D. Sarna

4172. Braude, William G. SAMUEL BELKIN AT BROWN. *Rhode Island Jewish Hist. Notes 1974 6(4): 610-613.* Reminiscences about Samuel Belkin, President of Yeshiva University, by Rabbi William G. Braude, his friend during their years at Brown University (1932-35). S

4173. Breibart, Solomon. TWO JEWISH CONGREGATIONS IN CHARLESTON, S.C. BEFORE 1791: A NEW CONCLUSION. *Am. Jewish Hist. 1980 69(3): 360-363.* Contrary to accepted scholarly opinion, evidence shows that two Jewish congregations, Kahal Kadosh Beth Elohim and Kahal Kadosh Beth Elohim Unveh Shallom existed simultaneously in Charleston, South Carolina, in the late 18th century. Apparently, a split developed at Kahal Kadosh Beth Elohim, and Portuguese Jews seceded to found their own congregation. Reconciliation was effected by 1791. The name Beth Elohim Unveh Shallom has only been found in sources dated to 1785 and 1786. 9 notes. J. D. Sarna

4174. Burke, John C. THE BREAK IN. *Rhode Island Jewish Hist. Notes 1974 6(4): 532-541.* An account of the forcible reopening of the Touro Synagogue by the Jewish community of Newport, Rhode Island, as told by Judge John C. Burke, who aided in the 1902 struggle. S

4175. Daniels, Doris Groshen. COLONIAL JEWRY: RELIGION, DOMESTIC AND SOCIAL RELATIONS. *Am. Jewish Hist. Q. 1977 61(3): 375-400.* Describes the activities of New York's colonial Jewry. Discusses social relations with Christian surroundings, the influx of Ashkenazi Jews until they outnumbered the Sephardim after 1720, inevitable intermarriages, the role of the synagogue, the nature of strong family bonds, and the problems of 18th-century schools. Abigail Franks, the best-known Jewish lady of the age, had much in common with Abigail Adams. 61 notes. F. Rosenthal

4176. Ellenson, David. A JEWISH LEGAL DECISION BY RABBI BERNARD ILLOWY OF NEW ORLEANS AND ITS DISCUSSION IN NINETEENTH CENTURY EUROPE. *Am. Jewish Hist. 1979 69(2): 174-195.* Dr. Bernard Illowy (1812-71) immigrated to the United States in 1853 and became one of the first Orthodox rabbis in the country. He engaged in disputes with Reform rabbis and rendered decisions in matters of Jewish canon law. In 1864, he placed a ban on a mohel who circumcised sons born to Jewish fathers and non-Jewish mothers. His decision was upheld by various European Orthodox rabbis, including Esriel Hildesheimer, but was contested by Rabbi Zvi Hirsch Kalischer. The episode demonstrates the lax state of Orthodoxy in mid-19th-century America, and shows that Illowy was respected by his European rabbinical colleagues. Based on Illowy's collected writings and on contemporary newspaper accounts; 36 notes. J. D. Sarna

4177. Fasman, Oscar Z. AFTER FIFTY YEARS, AN OPTIMIST. *Am. Jewish Hist. 1979 69(2): 159-173.* Reminiscences of an Orthodox rabbi now in Chicago who formerly served congregations in Tulsa (Oklahoma) and Ottawa (Ontario), and was later president of the Hebrew Theological College, 1929-79. J. D. Sarna

4178. Goldowsky, Seebert J. NEWPORT AS ARARAT. *Rhode Island Jewish Hist. Notes 1974 6(4): 604-609.* An account of the attempts by Mordecai Manuel Noah to establish a Jewish colony, Ararat, first in New York, then successfully in Newport, Rhode Island (1813-21). S

4179. Gutwirth, Jacques. HASSIDIM ET JUDAÏCITÉ À MONTRÉAL [Hasidism and Judaicity in Montreal]. *Recherches Sociographiques 1973 14(3): 291-325.* The Hasidic groupings that established themselves in Montreal during 1941-52 have, through their sociocultural and religious presence, had a direct and salutary impact on the Jewish community of the city. This has become possible through common reference points of Judaism where institutional collaboration takes place. In turn, Montreal's Jewish faction has permitted the Hasidic groupings to implant themselves. Based on field research and secondary sources; 87 notes. A. E. LeBlanc

4180. Hasson, Aron. THE SEPHARDIC JEWS OF RHODES IN LOS ANGELES. *Western States Jewish Hist. Q. 1974 6(4): 241-254.* During 1910-30, many Jews from Rhodes came to settle in Los Angeles. Rhodesli families have remained together and continue their unique Sephardic customs and life styles. In 1917 they formed their own congregation, the Peace and Progress Society, later changed to the Sephardic Hebrew Center. The immigrants spoke Ladino, and their language barrier forced them to take lower-paying jobs. Several immigrants went into the flower business, which became the most successful occupation of the Rhodeslis. Based on interviews and secondary sources; 4 photos, 21 notes. R. A. Garfinkle

4181. Heilman, Samuel C. CONSTRUCTING ORTHODOXY. *Society 1978 15(4): 32-40.* Orthodox Jews are taking part in the modern world and successfully living in the past and the present with some loss of orthodoxy; covers United States in the 1970's.

4182. Kramer, William M. and Clar, Reva. RABBI SIGMUND HECHT: A MAN WHO BRIDGED THE CENTURIES (PART III). *Western States Jewish Hist. Q. 1976 8(2): 169-186.* Continued from a previous article. Rabbi Sigmund Hecht remained neutral toward Zionism. He was appointed to the board of directors of the Los Angeles public library by Mayor Meredith P. Snyder. He backed Mayor Snyder for reelection, but Snyder lost to Owen McAleer. Mayor McAleer appointed George N. Black, a Jewish friend of Hecht, to replace Hecht. Black refused the appointment so McAleer chose another Jew; patronage was strong in Los Angeles then. In 1914, Congregation B'nai B'rith hired Dr. Edgar Fogel Magnin to serve as an associate Rabbi for Rabbi Hecht. Rabbi Hecht died in 1925 after a long and distinguished career. He left many volumes of writings and had been active in many civic and Jewish community groups. 51 notes. R. A. Garfinkle

4183. Kusinitz, Bernard. THE 1902 SIT-IN AT TOURO SYNAGOGUE. *Rhode Island Jewish Hist. Notes 1975 7(1): 42-72.* Discusses a disagreement between members of the Newport, Rhode Island, Touro Synagogue and Congregation Shearith Israel in New York City (who, for legal reasons were official trustees of the Touro Synagogue) which led to the 1902 take-over of Touro Synagogue by the Newport members.

4184. Lewis, Theodore. THE PLIGHT OF ISAAC TOURO. *Rhode Island Jewish Hist. Notes 1977 7(3): 442-443.* Reprints a 1782 document in which Rabbi Isaac Touro of Rhode Island petitions the British Commander-in-Chief for funds to take his family to Jamaica due to persecution by the British during their invasion of Rhode Island.

4185. Lewis, Theodore. TOURO SYNAGOGUE, NEWPORT, R. I. *Newport Hist. 1975 48(3): 281-320.* Offers a history of the presence of Jews in Newport, Rhode Island, 1658-1963, and the synagogue built by them, eventuating in the construction of the Touro Synagogue, 1759. 3 reproductions, 19 photos, appendix.

4186. Liebman, Charles S. ORTHODOX JUDAISM TODAY. *Midstream 1979 25(7): 19-26.* Discusses Orthodoxy in comparison to Conservative and Reform in terms of Jewish commitment, strength, and status in the Jewish community, distinguishing between the positions of strict and modern Orthodoxy.

4187. Mayer, Egon. GAPS BETWEEN GENERATIONS OF ORTHODOX JEWS IN BORO PARK, BROOKLYN, N.Y. *Jewish Social Studies 1977 39(1-2): 93-104.* The generation gap between Jewish parents and children takes on a unique form in the Orthodox Jewish neighborhood of Boro Park. The generations in Boro Park exhibit definite continuities in economic and cultural success from parents to children. However, while the children of Orthodox parents have continued the successful patterns of their parents and have been dependent in their success on that of their elders, tensions generated by status conflict have evolved. Children claim to be more Orthodox than their parents by asserting more sophisticated and deeper understanding of Orthodox ritual and practice. The economic successes of the parents are countered by their children's claims to academic and professional gains. Although both parents and children surround themselves with material evidences of success, the generations display different tastes in the acquisition of such objects. Largely based on survey research. N. Lederer

4188. Morgan, David T. JUDAISM IN EIGHTEENTH-CENTURY GEORGIA. *Georgia Hist. Q. 1974 58(1): 41-54.* Traces the development of Judaism in Georgia until it achieved a permanent institutional form. The first group of Jewish immigrants met official opposition, but they freely observed their religion and remained until the War of Jenkins' Ear brought their departure. A second group arrived in 1762; they were forced out during the American Revolution. They returned after the peace. The state incorporated a Jewish congregation in 1790, evidence that religious freedom had become a reality. 34 notes. D. L. Smith

4189. Pinsker, Sanford. PIETY AS COMMUNITY: THE HASIDIC VIEW. *Social Res. 1975 42(2): 230-246.* Discusses the life, philosophy, and attitudes of Hasidic Jews in the United States, speculating on whether the traditional Jewish community is currently disintegrating.

4190. Pitterman, Marvin and Schiavo, Bartholomew. HAKHAM RAPHAEL HAIM ISAAC CARIGAL: SHALIAH OF HEBRON AND RABBI OF NEWPORT, 5533 (1773). *Rhode Island Jewish Hist. Notes 1974 6(4): 587-603.* Biographical sketch of Hakham Raphael Haim Isaac Carigal's career as rabbi of Newport, Rhode Island (1773), and his contribution to the community's culture and history. S

4191. Rosenwaike, Ira. THE FOUNDING OF BALTIMORE'S FIRST JEWISH CONGREGATION: FACT VS. FICTION. *Am. Jewish Arch. 1976 28(2): 119-125.* Disputes the claim that Isaac Leeser's uncle Zalma Rehine was a founder of the Baltimore Hebrew Congregation. Writers of local history, he urges, "would do well not to rely on some of the hearsay evidence of their predecessors, who often lacked scholarly training." Covers 1830-31. J

4192. Rubinoff, Michael W. C. E. H. KAUVAR: A SKETCH OF A COLORADO RABBI'S LIFE. *Western States Jewish Hist. Q. 1978 10(4): 291-305.* Charles Eliezer Hillel Kauvar (1879-1971) was elected rabbi of Denver's Orthodox Congregation Beth Ha Medrosh Hagodol in 1902. Kauvar's devotion to Zionism caused friction between him and Rabbi William S. Friedman of Denver's Temple Emmanuel. The schism between the two rabbis affected the community at large when, in 1903, Rabbi Kauvar helped found the Jewish Consumptives' Relief Society (later the American Medical Center), open to Jews and non-Jews alike. In 1899 Temple Emmanuel had helped start the Jewish Hospital for Consumptives, an institution with a restricted admission policy. In 1920 Rabbi Kauvar was invited to the chair of rabbinic literature at the Methodist-sponsored University of Denver; he held this post for 45 years. Rabbi Kauvar became rabbi emeritus of his synagogue in 1952. In his later years he received many civic and religious awards and honors. Based on archival and published sources; 2 photos, 39 notes. B. S. Porter

4193. Rubinoff, Michael W. CRISIS IN CONSERVATIVE JUDAISM, DENVER, 1949-1958. *Western States Jewish Hist. Q. 1980 12(4): 326-340.* Rabbi Charles E. H. Kauvar, spiritual leader of Denver's Orthodox Beth Ha Medrosh Hagodol (BHMH) synagogue, believed that Orthodox Judaism was the only legitimate Jewish religious expression. Rabbi Kauvar retired in 1952 but remained active in BHMH. The rabbi's rigid beliefs caused a rift within the congregation, exacerbated by his first two successors' attempts to modify religious services and schedules. In 1957 Rabbi Samuel Adelman, an Orthodox rabbi, was installed at BHMH, resolving the difficulties that had caused controversy and embarrassment in Denver's Jewish community. Based on interviews; Kauvar Scrapbooks, BHMH Congregation, Denver; and Kauvar Papers, American Jewish Archives, Cincinnati; 43 notes. B. S. Porter

4194. Rubinoff, Michael W. RABBI IN A PROGRESSIVE ERA: C.E.H. KAUVAR OF DENVER. *Colorado Mag. 1977 54(3): 220-239.* Russian-born (1879) and New York-educated, Rabbi Charles Eliezer Hillel Kauvar served Denver's orthodox Beth Ha Medrosh Hagodol synagogue during 1902-71. A leading progressive reformer, Kauvar founded the Jewish Consumptives' Relief Society and an orphanage, worked closely with Judge Banjamin Barr Lindsey in attacking juvenile delinquency, and was a long-time leader of Denver's Community Chest. He was a Zionist, urged ecumenism, and vigorously opposed the Ku Klux Klan in the 1920's. Primary and secondary sources; 10 illus., 51 notes. O. H. Zabel

4195. Rudd, Hynda. SHAREY TZEDICK: SALT LAKE'S THIRD JEWISH CONGREGATION. *Western States Jewish Hist. Q. 1976 8(3): 203-208.* Sometime during 1916-19, Congregation Sharey Tzedick of Salt Lake City was formed. The founding members had belonged to the Montefiore synagogue but had become discouraged with the gradual movement away from Orthodox traditions. Sharey Tzedick was set up as an Orthodox temple and the congregation erected a synagogue. For reasons still unclear the congregation folded during the 1930's, and in 1948 its property was sold to the Veterans of Foreign Wars. Photo, 22 notes. R. A. Garfinkle

4196. Salomon, H. P. JOSEPH JESURUN PINTO (1729-1782): A DUTCH HAZAN IN COLONIAL NEW YORK. *Studia Rosenthaliana [Netherlands] 1979 13(1): 18-29.* Recounts the scholarly, professional, and personal activities of a Sephardic cantor who traveled from Amsterdam to London and New York, where he lived, 1759-66, while serving at the Congregation Shearith Israel, whence he returned to London and to Amsterdam, where he died in 1782.

4197. Singer, David. VOICES OF ORTHODOXY. *Commentary 1974 58(1): 54-60.* In view of the "Orthodox renaissance," describes ideological differences between modernist and sectarian branches of Orthodox Judaism. Evaluates two periodicals: *Tradition* and *Jewish Observer.* Covers 1880-1974. S

4198. Stern, Norton B. and Kramer, William M. THE HISTORICAL RECOVERY OF THE PIONEER SEPHARDIC JEWS OF CALIFORNIA. *Western States Jewish Hist. Q. 1975 8(1): 3-25.* Virtually ignored by historians writing about Jews living in California in the 19th century, the Sephardic Jewish community has been rediscovered by historians. In 1853, the Sephardic Jews in San Francisco organized Congregation Shaar Hashamayim, but this group folded in less than a year. The members joined the two Ashkenazim congregations in the city. Because they were no longer an organized group, little was written about them. Discusses prominent California Sephardic Jews, including Abraham Cohen Labatt (and his sons), Joseph Rodriguez Brandon (1828-1916), Elcan Heydenfeldt, Solomon Heydenfeldt (1816-1890), Isaac Nunez Cardozo, California Governor Washington Bartlett (and his brothers Julian and Columbus), Joseph Simpson, Raphael Schoyer, Manuel Mordicai Noah, Elias De Sola, Seixas Solomons, Abraham H. L. Dias (1814-77), and Benjamin Franklin Davega. 3 photos, 78 notes. R. A. Garfinkle

4199. Stern, Norton B. MISSION TO SAN BERNARDINO IN 1879. *Western States Jewish Hist. Q. 1978 10(3): 227-233.* In the summer of 1879, Orthodox Rabbi Aron J. Messing of San Francisco went to San Bernardino, California, for a "missionary visit." This unusual trip was undertaken to raise funds for construction of a synagogue for Messing's San Francisco Congregation Beth Israel. In San Bernardino Messing organized a Sabbath school and a Hebrew Association to promote the spiritual welfare of the community. Rabbi Messing undertook several fundraising journeys but was careful to avoid slander or suspicion by bringing along a trustee from his congregation to receive the collections. Primary and secondary sources; 25 notes. B. S. Porter

4200. Wax, Bernard. "OUR TOURO SYNAGOGUE." *Rhode Island Jewish Hist. Notes 1977 7(3): 440-441.* Discusses the history and symbolism of the Touro Synagogue in Newport, Rhode Island; discusses Jews in Newport since 1654.

4201. —. THE NEWS FROM WOODLAND AND OROVILLE, CALIFORNIA IN 1879. *Western States Jewish Hist. Q. 1979 11(2): 162-166.* Orthodox Rabbi Aron J. Messing of Congregation Beth Israel in San Francisco traveled to scattered Jewish settlements in California encouraging fellow Jews to organize Hebrew societies and Sabbath schools. Following his visits to Woodland and Oroville, both communities established Hebrew associations and Sabbath schools for their children. Based on reports in *The American Israelite,* Cincinnati, 23 May 1879; photo, 23 notes. B. S. Porter

Reform

4202. Berger, Elmer. MEMOIRS OF AN ANTI-ZIONIST JEW. *J. of Palestine Studies [Lebanon] 1975-76 5(1-2): 3-55.* Publishes the memoirs of Reform Rabbi Elmer Berger, an American anti-Zionist, who for over 30 years has led an active opposition to Zionism, racism toward the Arabs, and US support for such policies.

4203. Berman, Myron. RABBI EDWARD NATHAN CALISH AND THE DEBATE OVER ZIONISM IN RICHMOND, VIRGINIA. *Am. Jewish Hist. Q. 1973 62(3): 295-305.* Rabbi Calish, who served the Richmond Jewish community 1891-1945, was a consistent foe of the Zionist movement, and thus shared the position of many Southern Jews of his time and generation. He was one of the original founders of the American Council for Judaism. F. Rosenthal

4204. Clar, Reva. EARLY STOCKTON JEWRY AND ITS CANTOR-RABBI HERMAN DAVIDSON. *Western States Jewish Hist. Q. 1973 5(2): 63-86, (3): 166-187.* Part I. A biography of Herman Davidson (1846-1911) emphasizes his operatic career in Russia, his family life, and his work with Jews in Stockton, 1876-91. Part II. Chronicles the relationship between Davidson, Stockton Jews, and, Reform Judaism; 1893-1911.

4205. Currick, Max C. A VISITOR'S REPORT ON THE WILSHIRE BOULEVARD TEMPLE, LOS ANGELES, AND ON THE ARCHITECTURE OF TEMPLE EMANU-EL, SAN FRANCISCO, IN 1937. *Western States Jewish Hist. Q. 1980 13(1): 49-52.* The author, a rabbi from Erie, Pennsylvania, visited congregations in Los Angeles and San Francisco in 1937. In both cities, attendance at services was good, and the congregations appeared devout and interested in the sermons. San Francisco's Temple Emanu-El, erected in 1925, in the Spanish style, was reminiscent of older European and Near East synagogues. Reprinted from *The Reform Advocate,* Chicago, 19 March 1937.
B. S. Porter

4206. Eisendrath, Maurice N. THE UNION OF AMERICAN HEBREW CONGREGATIONS: CENTENNIAL REFLECTIONS. *Am. Jewish Hist. Q. 1973 63(2): 138-159.* Evaluates the 100-year existence of the Union of American Hebrew Congregations. From a small nucleus of 28 congregations it grew to become the authoritative spokesman for American Reform Judaism and a vital participant in virtually all cooperative Jewish concerns. Describes some alternative modes for synagogues of the future. F. Rosenthal

4207. Gendler, Carol. THE FIRST SYNAGOGUE IN NEBRASKA: THE EARLY HISTORY OF THE CONGREGATION OF ISRAEL OF OMAHA. *Nebraska Hist. 1977 58(3): 323-341.* Examines the beginnings of a formal Jewish community in Omaha, from 1867 through the construction of Temple Israel, dedicated in 1908. Focuses on prominent members of the community, early rabbis who served the Reform congregation, and the tensions between Reform and traditional groups. R. Lowitt

4208. Greenberg, Gershon. THE DIMENSIONS OF SAMUEL ADLER'S RELIGIOUS VIEW OF THE WORLD. *Hebrew Union Coll. Ann. 1975 46: 377-412.* Samuel Adler (1809-91) was a German-born Reform-rabbi who spent the last 35 years of his life as rabbi of Temple Emanuel of New York. For him Judaism is a significant level in the growth of moral consciousness where morality is amplified into an ontological realm, identical to the idealized world of creation. *Wissenschaft* becomes the God-given methodology for achieving insights into the moral possibilities of all literature and history. 100 notes. F. Rosenthal

4209. Greenberg, Gershon. THE HISTORICAL ORIGINS OF GOD AND MAN: SAMUEL HIRSCH'S LUXEMBOURG WRITINGS. *Leo Baeck Inst. Year Book [Great Britain] 1975 20: 129-148.* Samuel Hirsch (1815-89) is significant in modern Jewish history for transplanting Reform Judaism to America. While his American publications are journalistic and pragmatic, concentrating on man and society, his writings during his stay in Luxembourg, 1843-66, concentrate on the theological problem of man and God in history. The contiguity between time and eternity unfolds in history out of which reason and revelation emerge. This refocusing of Hirsch's attention explains his ability to concentrate on the human aspects of religion in America and sublimate his philosophy into the pragmatic world of Reform Judaism's future. 81 notes. F. Rosenthal

4210. Greenberg, Gershon. SAMUEL HIRSCH'S AMERICAN JUDAISM. *Am. Jewish Hist. Q. 1973 62(4): 362-382.* Samuel Hirsch (1815-89), who served as rabbi in Philadelphia 1866-89, wrote extensively on the meaning of Reform Judaism in America. In the nonideological and essentially nontheological atmosphere of the New World, he emphasized the sociohistorical factors in the evolution of Scripture and religion. His articles appeared in *Der Zeitgeist, Die Deborah,* and *The Jewish Times.* 47 notes. F. Rosenthal

4211. Greenberg, Gershon. THE SIGNIFICANCE OF AMERICA IN DAVID EINHORN'S CONCEPTION OF HISTORY. *Am. Jewish Hist. Q. 1973 63(2): 160-184.* Einhorn (1809-79) served several Reform congregations in America during his last 24 years. He was a prolific writer who described the role of Israel in the inevitable progress of history. His interpretation of America as the land where history would culminate and the messianic redemption would come is unique. Based on primary and secondary sources; 61 notes. F. Rosenthal

4212. Karp, Abraham J. IDEOLOGY AND IDENTITY IN JEWISH GROUP SURVIVAL IN AMERICA. *Am. Jewish Hist. Q. 1976 65(4): 310-334.* As a result of enlightenment and emancipation in the early 19th century, the Jews of Western Europe adopted the thesis "Judaism qua Religion"; their brethren in Eastern Europe countered with the antithesis, "Judaism qua nationalism." The American Jews, comprised of and influenced by both communities and by the realities of America, were working out the synthesis of "Religion plus Nationalism." Only in such a way could the threat of the melting pot, total assimilation, be countered. The insight of Horace M. Kallen and of Mordecai Kaplan substantiated the dual image identity—both religious as well as ethnic community—and provides the most creatively viable response to the challenge of Jewish group survival today. Covers 1800-1975. 41 notes.
F. Rosenthal

4213. Katz, Irving I. RABBI KAUFMANN KOHLER BEGAN HIS DETROIT MINISTRY IN 1869. *Michigan Jewish Hist. 1979 19(1): 11-15.* Kaufmann Kohler (1843-1926) was a rabbi in Detroit; discusses his extensive influence in Reform Judaism in America, 1869-1926.

4214. Kerman, Julius C. ADVENTURES IN AMERICA AND THE HOLY LAND. *Am. Jewish Arch. 1976 28(2): 126-141.* "In my forty-three years in the rabbinate I served several communities, enjoying everywhere happy relationships with young and old. The thought that I have influenced some persons to think and live more Jewishly makes me happy." Byelorussian-born Reform Rabbi Kerman also saw service in the Jewish Legion during World War I. J

4215. Knee, Stuart E. FROM CONTROVERSY TO CONVERSION: LIBERAL JUDAISM IN AMERICA AND THE ZIONIST MOVEMENT, 1917-1941. *Ann. of Jewish Social Sci. 1978 17: 260-289.* Deals with the gradual change within US Reform Judaism from firm anti-Zionism to reluctant acceptance of Zionism and gradually to pro-Zionism. The chief catalyst in this change was the advent to power of Adolf Hitler in Germany and the spread of Nazism.
R. J. Wechman

4216. Kramer, William M. and Clar, Reva. EMANUEL SCHREIBER: LOS ANGELES' FIRST REFORM RABBI, 1885-1889. *Western States Jewish Hist. Q. 1977 9(4): 354-370; 1977 10(1): 38-55.* Part I. Emanuel Schreiber left his native Germany in 1881. After serving synagogues in Mobile (Alabama) and Denver (Colorado) he was invited to Los Angeles's Congregation B'nai B'rith, which became the Wilshire Boulevard Temple, in 1885. Some of the traditionalists were offended by Schreiber's radical-Reform policies but the majority of the congregation supported him. He was active in community affairs; most significant was his role in the formation of the Associated Charities which developed into the present United Crusade. San Francisco journalist Isidore N. Choynski criticized Rabbi Schreiber's accumulation of wealth from astute land speculation. Based on newspapers and other published primary and secondary sources; 68 notes. Part II. Religious and social activities at Congregation B'nai B'rith were enhanced by the participation of the rabbi's wife. Reform-Orthodox tensions decreased as Rabbi Schreiber impressed the Jewish community with his considerable knowledge of religious phenomena. Schreiber's relations with the gentile community were excellent; Christian ministers appreciated his learning and invited him to speak to their congregations. Despite his esteemed position in Los Angeles, Schreiber's ambitions caused him to leave. He served at synagogues in Arkansas, Washington, Ohio, and Illinois, 1889-99. He was minister to Chicago's Congregation Emanu-El from 1899 to 1906 when he moved to the east coast. In 1920 he returned to Los Angeles, where he remained until his death in 1932. Based on newspapers and other published primary and secondary sources; illus., 65 notes. B. S. Porter

4217. Kramer, William M. and Clar, Reva. RABBI ABRAHAM BLUM: FROM ALSACE TO NEW YORK BY WAY OF TEXAS AND CALIFORNIA: PART I. *Western States Jewish Hist. Q. 1979 12(1): 73-88; 1980 12(2): 170-184, (3): 266-281.* Part I. Abraham Blum was born and educated in Alsace under the liberal, tolerant rule of France. After emigrating to America in 1866, he served at Reform synagogues in Dayton (Ohio), Augusta (Georgia), and Galveston (Texas), where he distinguished himself in the field of religious education and earned an M.D. degree from the Medical College of Galveston in 1872. His failing health prompted him to seek a position in the mild climate of Los Angeles, California. Based on newspapers and interviews; 2 photos, 66 notes. Part II. Rabbi Blum became superintendant, and his wife principal, of the religious school of Los Angeles Congregation B'nai B'rith (Wilshire Boulevard Temple). Enrollment grew during 1889-94. His relationship with the congregation declined because he did not seem to be an active fund raiser for a new temple. Photo, 63 notes. Part III. Rabbi Blum resigned as rabbi in 1895, but Leopold Loeb, the synagogue's organist, then accused him of improprieties with Mrs. Loeb. Blum denied the charge, but moved to New York City, where he was appointed chaplain for various city and state institutions, apparently was happy and successful, and was active in religious and civic events until his death in 1921. 50 notes.
B. S. Porter

4218. Kramer, William M. and Clar, Reva. RABBI SIGMUND HECHT: A MAN WHO BRIDGED THE CENTURIES. *Western States Jewish Hist. Q. 1975 7(4): 356-375, 8(1): 72-90.* Part I. Sigmund Hecht (b. 1849) emigrated to New York from Hungary with his parents. He completed his rabbinical studies at Temple Emanu-El's Theological School, New York. He soon became the leader of the temple's Sabbath school. In 1877, he became the Rabbi for Congregation Kahl Montgomery (Montgomery, Alabama). In 1885, he helped to establish and then served as the first treasurer of the Conference of Southern Rabbis. In 1888, he was appointed the Rabbi for Congregation Emanu-El, Milwaukee. He was active in many civic and religious groups. Based on primary and secondary sources; 2 photos, 68 notes. Part II. Rabbi Hecht left Milwaukee for Los Angeles in 1899 to become the rabbi at Temple B'nai B'rith. He found the Reform congregation there very disunited. To reunite the congregation he started several new Jewish charitable organizations. In 1911, these separate groups united to form the Los Angeles Federation of Jewish Charities. He fought against movie censorship and anti-Semitism. Includes excerpts from several sermons. Photo, 65 notes. Article to be continued. R. A. Garfinkle

4219. Levy, J. Leonard. A RABBI SAYS "NO." *Western States Jewish Hist. Q. 1973 5(4): 270-272.* J. Leonard Levy (1865-1917), the rabbi in Sacramento 1889-93, rejected an 1892 offer from San Franciscans to head their Reform congregation.

4220. Meyer, Michael A. LETTERS OF ISAAC MAYER WISE TO JOSEPH STOLZ. *Michael: On the Hist. of the Jews in the Diaspora [Israel] 1975 3: 48-58.* Publishes 10 letters written during 1882-1900 by Rabbi Isaac Mayer Wise to Joseph Stolz, one of the early graduates of the rabbinical seminary Wise founded, Hebrew Union College. The letters reveal aspects of a poorly documented area of Wise's activities: the placement and advancement of HUC graduates in American congregations. The letters reflect Wise's fatherly concern for Stolz, as well as his hard-headed approach to rabbinical salaries and prerogatives, and relations with better-established rabbis. Primary and secondary sources; 28 notes.
T. Sassoon

4221. Petuchowski, Jakob J. ABRAHAM GEIGER AND SAMUEL HOLDHEIM: THEIR DIFFERENCES IN GERMANY AND REPERCUSSIONS IN AMERICA. *Leo Baeck Inst. Year Book [Great Britain] 1977 22: 139-160.* In the emergence of a 19th-century German Reform Jewish ideology Abraham Geiger (1810-74) and Samuel Holdheim (1806-60) were dialectic opposites, with Geiger representing the right, traditionalist and Holdheim the left, modernist wing of the movement: evolutionary change versus a revolutionary break with the past. When translated to the United States by German-Jewish immigrants, this dichotomy was represented by Isaac Mayer Wise (1819-1900) and David Einhorn (1809-97). To this day the basic question remains: whether Reform Judaism is predicted on organic growth, i.e. on evolution, or whether it stands for revolution, a break with tradition. 79 notes.
F. Rosenthal

4222. Rockaway, Robert A. THE PROGRESS OF REFORM JUDAISM IN LATE 19TH AND EARLY 20TH CENTURY DETROIT. *Michigan Jewish Hist. 1974 14(1): 8-17.*

4223. Rubinstein, Aryeh. ISAAC MAYER WISE: A NEW APPRAISAL. *Jewish Social Studies 1977 39(1-2): 53-74.* Traditional interpretations of the role of Isaac Mayer Wise as a leader of 19th-century American Judaism depict him as a proponent of moderate reform in Judaism and as a champion of religious unity in the Jewish community. In fact, he was a radical Reformist whose advocacy of reform led to religious disunity and the generation of enemies in the Jewish community. Wise was an opportunistic advocate of reform who craved popularity and a position at the head of American Jewry, and often tailored his pronouncements to suit the audience he was addressing at the moment. Basically, however, his conservative statements were a cover for his almost Deistic views, stressing the role of rationalist thought in Reform Judaism. Primary sources. N. Lederer

4224. Schwartz, Henry. THE FIRST TEMPLE BETH ISRAEL: SAN DIEGO. *Western States Jewish Hist. Q. 1979 11(2): 153-161.* A surge in population growth following rail connection with the east in 1885 helped the growth of San Diego's Jewish congregation and led to the construction of Temple Beth Israel in 1889. The Reform facilities were expanded for another population increase after World War I, but continued growth demanded a new synagogue, built in 1926. The old building was sold at that time but was repurchased by congregation Beth Israel in 1978. The community now intends to restore the historic building and move it to Heritage Park in Old Town. Primary and secondary sources; photo, 45 notes. B. S. Porter

4225. Shook, Robert W. ABRAHAM LEVI: FATHER OF VICTORIA JEWRY. *Western States Jewish Hist. Q. 1977 9(2): 144-154.* Victoria, Texas, was a trade and cattle center serving Texas and northern Mexico since before the Civil War. Abraham Levi (1822-1902) was among the earliest Jewish settlers in Victoria, arriving in 1848 or 1849. By the 1870's the Jewish community included 15 families and had organized a Reform congregation, Temple B'nai Israel. Levi operated a retail store, and engaged in land transactions and private banking. The Levi Bank and Trust Company (now the Victoria Bank and Trust) was franchised in 1910. Levi's activities in the community included serving as president of the Jewish congregation and as a city alderman. Primary and secondary sources; 3 photos, 26 notes. B. S. Porter

4226. Stern, Malcolm H. REFORMING OF REFORM JUDAISM—PAST, PRESENT, AND FUTURE. *Am. Jewish Hist. Q. 1973 63(2): 111-137.* Summarizes the history of Reform Judaism from its beginnings in France and Germany during the time of the French Revolution to its flowering in America during the past 100 years. Includes an extensive bibliography of its history, institutions, biographies, sociological studies, rituals, periodicals, and congregational histories by states.
F. Rosenthal

4227. Stern, Norton B. and Kramer, William M. AN ISAAC MAYER WISE 1890 PLACEMENT LETTER TO SAN FRANCISCO. *Am. Jewish Hist. Q. 1973 63(2): 204-207.* A recently discovered letter of Rabbi Isaac Mayer Wise, president of Hebrew Union College, to Abraham J. Prager, president of Congregation Sherith Israel of San Francisco, 28 April 1890, shows the role of Wise in rabbinic placement. As the patriarch of American Jewry he felt it his responsibility and moral duty to provide objective information when men of his close acquaintance, whether students or colleagues, applied for rabbinic positions. Reproduces the letter. 9 notes. F. Rosenthal

4228. Sutherland, John F. RABBI JOSEPH KRAUSKOPF OF PHILADELPHIA: THE URBAN REFORMER RETURNS TO THE LAND. *Am. Jewish Hist. Q. 1978 67(4): 342-362.* Joseph Krauskopf (1858-1923) came to the United States as a 14-year-old. He graduated with the first class of four at Hebrew Union College in 1883 and was Philadelphia's foremost Reform rabbi during 1887-1922. He introduced English into both services and the religious school, popularized the Jewish Sundry Services, and drafted the Pittsburgh Platform of 1885. His great concern with social reform led him into close cooperation with Jacob Riis. After a visit with Leo Tolstoy at Yasnaya Polyana, Krauskopf became the driving spirit of the Jewish "back-to-the land" movement and of the National Farm School, today known as the Delaware Valley College of Science and Agriculture, the only private agricultural school in the country. Thoroughly part of America's urban milieu, Krauskopf nevertheless sought to modify it with the agrarian myth, an urban-agrarian ambivalence which still influences American thought and action. F. Rosenthal

4229. Urofsky, Melvin I. STEPHEN WISE: THE LAST OF THE SUPERSTARS. *Present Tense 1979 6(4): 21-26.* Recounts the deeds and achievements—especially those devoted to Zionism, ecumenism, charity, and efforts to persuade President Franklin Delano Roosevelt to assist in saving the European Jews during World War II—of the Hungarian-born American Reform rabbi, Stephen Samuel Wise (1874-1949).

4230. Weinberg, Julius. THE TROUBLE WITH REFORM JUDAISM. *Commentary 1979 68(5): 53-60.* Reform Judaism, which has celebrated the centenaries of various aspects of its founding during the 1970's, suffers from a vitiation of interest in its style of worship and belief as it confronts continuing problems of ambivalence toward the significance of Israel for Diaspora Jews and the Reform movement's image as a Judaism of minimalism and convenience which serves as a way-station on the path of assimilation and even apostasy for third- and fourth-generation American Jews of East European ancestry.

4231. —. CONGREGATIONAL POLITICS IN LOS ANGELES—1897. *Western States Jewish Hist. Q. 1974 6(2): 120-123.* There was much in-fighting in the B'nai B'rith Congregation (which became the Wilshire Boulevard Temple) in the 1890's over the type of rabbi for their temple, but no one was trying to solve the temple's financial problems. The wealthy members wanted to keep out the poor Jews by raising dues, but the increase in dues would not cover the temple's debts. Reprint of an article in *Emanu-El*, San Francisco, 9 July 1897. R. A. Garfinkle

4232. —. FIRST SYNAGOGUE AT ALBUQUERQUE: 1900. *Western States Jewish Hist. Q. 1978 11(1): 46-48.* Temple Albert in Albuquerque, New Mexico, was dedicated on 14 September 1900. In a joint ceremony, Pizer Jacobs was installed as the new Reform rabbi. Music and speeches preceded the solemn installation services which were presented to a large audience. Reprinted from *The American Israelite,* Cincinnati, 27 September 1900. Photo, 5 notes. B. S. Porter

4233. —. AN INTIMATE PORTRAIT OF THE UNION OF AMERICAN HEBREW CONGREGATIONS—A CENTENNIAL DOCUMENTARY. *Am. Jewish Arch. 1973 25(1): 3-115.* The Union of American Hebrew Congregations is the national organization encompassing Reform Jewish congregations. Documents cover the founding in 1873, the famous "trefa" (nonkosher) banquet of 1883, Zionism, Jewish-Christian dialogues, Jewish chaplains for the armed forces, tradition and rituals, the exposure of anti-Semitism in the Soviet Union and racism in the United States, opposition to the Vietnam War and the Jewish Chautauqua Society. Based on the Union's archives; 7 photos, 46 notes. E. S. Shapiro

4234. —. THE NEW JEWISH CEMETERY IN EAST LOS ANGELES, 1902. *Western States Jewish Hist. Q. 1978 11(1): 64-68.* Congregation B'nai B'rith (now the Wilshire Boulevard Temple) established the new Home of Peace Cemetery in East Los Angeles in 1902. Oscar Willenberg, the cemetery superintendent, kept a photograph album of scenes from the cemetery, which are presented here. 6 photos, 3 notes. B. S. Porter

4235. —. NEWS FROM THE PORTLAND JEWISH COMMUNITY. *Western States Jewish Hist. Q. 1977 9(3): 235-237.* In 1885, Portland, Oregon, had 1,000 Jewish residents. Religious organizations included two B'nai B'rith lodges, the First Hebrew Benevolent Society, and the Judith Montefiore Society. Rabbi Jacob Bloch headed the Reform Congregation Beth Israel. The congregation, assisted by a leading merchant, Colonel L. Fleischner, undertook to raise funds for construction of a new temple, large enough for the needs of the active and growing Jewish community. Reprint of a report sent from Portland, Oregon, to *The American Israelite,* Cincinnati, Ohio, 8 January 1886; 4 notes. B. S. Porter

4236. —. TWO LETTERS FROM THE JEWISH PATRIARCH OF LOS ANGELES. *Western States Jewish Hist. Q. 1979 11(3): 231-233.* Joseph Newmark (1799-1881), was one of the principal founders of Los Angeles's Congregation B'nai B'rith (Wilshire Boulevard Temple) in 1862. In 1881, several months before his death, he wrote these letters to his granddaughter, Caroline, who lived in St. Louis, Missouri. The letters contain news of family members' health and activities. They are published through the courtesy of the addressee's granddaughter; 17 notes. B. S. Porter

4237. —. WORD FROM PORTLAND A CENTURY AGO. *Western States Jewish Hist. Q. 1979 11(3): 252-254.* Portland, Oregon's, Jewish community recently had received a lecture series by the Reverend Moses May, whose heavy German accent grated on the ears of his Congregation Beth Israel. Social visits between friends and relatives in San Francisco and Portland were frequent. The approaching state elections (3 June 1878) were of great interest because of the nominations of several excellent candidates, including Edward Hirsch, A. Noltner, and Solomon Hirsch. Reprinted from the *Jewish Progress,* San Francisco; 4 notes. B. S. Porter

Other Religious Traditions

Cults of the Twentieth Century

4238. Baechler, Jean. MOURIR À JONESTOWN [Death in Jonestown]. *European J. of Sociol. [Great Britain] 1979 20(2): 173-210.* The massacre at Jonestown, Guyana, on 18 November 1978 was not an act of collective paranoia or religious ecstasy. The death of Jim Jones, the leader of the People's Temple, was the apocalyptic suicide of a criminally sadistic, hate-filled personality after many failures to overcome personal anguish and achieve godlike power. Jones's motive was power, not religious or political commitment. He recruited followers with fragile personalities particularly susceptible to carrying out his demands. As the community changed from a charismatic to an autocratic group, members became willingly enslaved to him, eventually killing themselves because the suicide of their leader and break-up of the sect would be unbearable. 7 notes. R. Aldrich

4239. Bainbridge, William Sims and Stark, Rodney. CLIENT AND AUDIENCE CULTS IN AMERICA. *Sociol. Analysis 1980 41(3): 199-214.* Several sources of good information about client cults and audience cults are analyzed geographically. Data are taken from six directories, *Fate* magazine, Transcendental Meditation initiation records, classified telephone directories, and the Gallup Poll. The geographic distribution found in an earlier study of cult movements is replicated: the Pacific and Mountain regions have very high rates, while the East South Central region is very low. Rates for client cults show distributions reflecting that of cult movements, while audience cults show a much flatter distribution. The distributions result both from differential receptivity to religious deviance and variation in degree of deviance among the measures. Departures from the main trends are analyzed, and prospects for future quantitative research are judged to be quite good. An empirical outgrowth of the attempt to develop a general theory of religion, the research reported here supports key concepts and certain propositions derived from the theory. Many of the cults were concerned with the occult. J/S

4240. Bak, Felix. THE CHURCH OF SATAN IN THE UNITED STATES. *Antonianum [Italy] 1975 50(1-2): 152-193.* The Church of Satan, founded in 1966, exemplifies the most rampant form of satanism in the United States; gives a biography of its founder, Anton Szandor LaVey, analyzes the latter's teachings, writings, the church's satanic rituals, and discusses the satanic movement.

4241. Balch, Robert W. and Taylor, David. SEEKERS AND SAUCERS: THE ROLE OF THE CULTIC MILIEU IN JOINING A UFO CULT. *Am. Behavioral Scientist 1977 20(6): 839-860.* Conversion to UFO cults is found to be marked by a nonnecessity of affective ties between converts and group members as well as lack of ritual behavior; examines the role of the seeker and its importance in converison. Bo and Peep, the cult leaders, developed an eclectic theology that included elements of Christianity and included beliefs about flying saucers, reincarnation, biblical revelation, and the physical resurrection of Christ.

4242. Beitz, U. DIE "COUNTER-CULTURE": "KULTURREVOLUTION" UND KONTERREVOLUTION DER KLEINBÜRGERLICHEN LINKEN IN DEN USA DER 60ER JAHRE [The "Counter Culture": "Cultural revolution" and counter-revolution of the petit bourgeoisie Left in the USA in the 1960's]. *Wissenschaftliche Zeitschrift der Karl-Marx U. Leipzig [East Germany] 1973 22(3-4): 375-387.* The so-called counter culture of the American youth in the 1960's was counter-revolutionary as it originated anarchist, individualistic, religious, and mystical theories. R. Wagnleitner

4243. Bodemann, Y. Michal. MYSTICAL, SATANIC, AND CHILIASTIC FORCES IN COUNTERCULTURAL MOVEMENTS: CHANGING THE WORLD—OR RECONCILING IT. *Youth & Soc. 1974 5(4): 433-447.* Discusses the impact on social reform of the mystical, satanic and chiliastic trends developing in American counter-culture during the 1960's and 70's. S

4244. Bromley, David G.; Shupe, Anson D., Jr.; and Ventimiglia, J. C. ATROCITY TALES, THE UNIFICATION CHURCH, AND THE SOCIAL CONSTRUCTION OF EVIL. *J. of Communication 1979 29(3): 42-53.* Discusses the tactics of deprogrammers and the Unification Church to legitimize their actions, particularly the atrocity story used to discredit the church in the 1970's.

4245. Bromley, David G. and Shupe, Anson D., Jr. FINANCING THE NEW RELIGIONS: A RESOURCE MOBILIZATION APPROACH. *J. for the Sci. Study of Religion 1980 19(3): 227-239.* Analyzes the public fundraising of so-called new religious movements such as Hare Krishna, the Unification Church, and the Children of God in the 1970's, discussing their ritualization of public solicitation and its potential returns for these social movements.

4246. Carroll, Jackson W. TRANSCENDENCE AND MYSTERY IN THE COUNTER-CULTURE. *Religion in Life 1973 42(3): 361-375.* Covers the 1960's and 70's.

4247. Decter, Midge. THE POLITICS OF JONESTOWN. *Commentary 1979 67(5): 29-34.* Examines Reverend Jim Jones's People's Temple as a political outgrowth of 1960's radicalism and leftist sympathies rather than as a freakish religious cult.

4248. Doress, Irvin and Porter, Jack Nusan. KIDS IN CULTS. *Society 1978 15(4): 69-71.* Discusses US cults, 1960's-70's, what youth are looking for when they join cults, and why they decide to stay or leave.

4249. Erickson, Keith V. BLACK MESSIAH: THE FATHER DIVINE PEACE MISSION MOVEMENT. *Q. J. of Speech 1977 63(4): 428-438.* George Baker (d. 1965), who became known as Father Divine, established the Peace Mission religious movement which reached perhaps half a million people, mostly poor Negroes. His popularity derived partly from his providing food and shelter to thousands, but his speeches, ungrammatical and semantically muddled as they were, produced many converts. He succeeded in persuading his followers of his divinity and to reshape their own negative self-images. Covers 1915-65. Primary and secondary sources; 50 notes. E. Bailey

4250. Gianakos, Perry E. THE BLACK MUSLIMS: AN AMERICAN MILLENNIALISTIC RESPONSE TO RACISM AND CULTURAL DERACINATION. *Centennial Rev. 1979 23(4): 430-451.* Traces the Black Muslims' black nationalist origins to the Marcus Garvey movement of the late 1920's and Timothy Drew's (Noble Drew Ali's) Moorish-American Science Temple, and their Islamic origins to Master Wallace Fard Muhammad in Detroit (1930-33). One faction, the Nation of Islam led by Elijah Muhammad, was called the Black Muslims, but in the 1960's "Malcolm X and other Black Muslims denied any connection with the Moorish movement and asserted Fard's uniqueness." Radical salvationists such as the Jehovah's Witnesses and the Mormons also influenced the movement. The author traces American millenarianism to antiquity and the medieval period; it is part of the Christian and Judaic tradition and as such influenced the Black Muslims. Black Muslim orthodoxy will not prevail; there will be an increasing convergence of aims and values of Muslims and black Christians. 48 notes. S

4251. Gutwirth, Jacques. LE SUICIDE-MASSACRE DE GUYANA ET SON CONTEXTE [The suicide-massacre in Guyana and its context]. *Arch. de Sci. Sociales des Religions [France] 1979 47(2): 167-187.* Charles A. Krause and Larry Stern's *Guyana Massacre* (New York: Berkley Books, 1978) and Marshall Kilduff and Ron Javers's *The Suicide Cult* (New York: Bantam Books, 1978) owe much of their value to their authors' first-hand knowledge of the Jonestown affair. Krause accompanied Representative Leo Ryan to Guyana and was present at the ambush in which Ryan was killed. Kilduff investigated the People's Temple when it was still a California organization; his exposé in *New West* magazine was one reason the group emigrated. Javers, like Krause, accompanied the Ryan party. Discusses the childhood and career of cult leader Jim Jones (1931-79), viewing him as in part the victim of the explosive collection of contradictions embodied in his philosophy, in his methods, and (consequently) in his organization. 51 notes.
L. W. Van Wyk

4252. Hall, John R. APOCALYPSE AT JONESTOWN. *Society 1979 16(6): 52-61.* Argues that the mass murder/suicide at Jonestown, Guyana, in 1978 was a function of Jim Jones's Peoples Temple's apocalyptic orientation which went from "heaven-on-earth" to "revolutionary suicide" in response to outside pressures; covers 1953-78.

4253. Johnson, Doyle Paul. DILEMMAS OF CHARISMATIC LEADERSHIP: THE CASE OF THE PEOPLE'S TEMPLE. *Sociol. Analysis 1979 40(4): 315-323.* Designs a theoretical model of charismatic leadership and applies it in an ex post facto interpretation of the evolution of the People's Temple, under Rev. Jones's influence, and its culmination in the mass suicides in Guyana. The theoretical model in this paper provides an alternative to the popular interpretation of the mass suicides in Guyana, and of sects and cults generally, as reflecting psychopathological problems and deficiencies in the social environment. Biblio. J/S

4254. Lincoln, C. Eric and Mamiya, Lawrence H. DADDY JONES AND FATHER DIVINE: THE CULT AS POLITICAL RELIGION. *Religion in Life 1980 49(1): 6-23.* Briefly discusses American religious cults since the end of World War I, focuses on Jim Jones and the People's Temple group he led to Guyana, includes information on the characteristics of a cult leader, the cult itself, and the members, and compares cults and black religion, and Jones and Father Divine, who founded the Peace Mission; 1920's-70's.

4255. Lofland, John. "BECOMING A WORLD-SAVER" REVISITED. *Am. Behavioral Scientist 1977 20(6): 805-818.* Updates a sociological model of conversion (originally formulated in 1965) based on further studies of conversion methods in the Unification Church, 1965-75.

4256. Long, Theodore E. and Hadden, Jeffrey K., ed. SECTS, CULTS AND RELIGIOUS MOVEMENTS. *Sociol. Analysis 1979 40(4): 280-282.* During the late 1960's, youth counterculture became engrossed in the search for a new consciousness through religion. The result was a whole plethora of new religious sects and cults which clashed with the more established religions, and renewed attention to religion as a "public issue of political, legal, and economic significance." Discusses the importance of these developments to sociologists and provides an overview of the seven studies in this issue devoted to sects, cults, and religious movements. S

4257. Lynch, Frederick R. "OCCULT ESTABLISHMENT" OR "DEVIANT RELIGION"? THE RISE AND FALL OF A MODERN CHURCH OF MAGIC. *J. for the Sci. Study of Religion 1979 18(3): 281-298.* The evolution of the cosmology, social organization, and practices of a modern "Church of Magic," as well as the social and psychological characteristics of its members, were examined to determine whether the organization more closely approximated the white, middle class "Occult Establishment" described by Martin Marty, or whether it resembled a "deviant perspective" which attracted "deviant individuals" as suggested by Lofland and Stark. The findings confirmed Marty's description in that the evolution of the belief system, organization, and magical practices of the Church reflected the maturation of the wider "Occult Establishment" in the United States during the late 1960's. However, the model of conversion to a deviant perspective outlined by Lofland and Stark proved useful, not only in noting the emergence of a "deviant perspective" within the Church of the Sun, but also in examining the psychological and social-situational factors which led to adherence to a relatively conventional perspective and praxis. In theoretical and comparative perspective, the members of the Church of the Sun are like those in several other occult and new religious groups, seeking a deeper, more mystical, and more complex understanding of their individual identities within the context of modern "mass society." They also often gain a powerful sense of community from their participation in collective ritual.
J

4258. Marks, John D. FROM KOREA WITH LOVE. *Washington Monthly 1974 5(12): 55-61.* Examines Korean prophet Sun Myung Moon and his Unification Church, with adherents in over 40 countries. Covers 1970-74.
S

4259. Pearson, Fred Lamar, Jr. and Tomberlin, Joseph Aaron. JOHN DOE, ALIAS GOD: A NOTE ON FATHER DIVINE'S GEORGIA CAREER. *Georgia Hist. Q. 1976 60(1): 43-48.* George Baker (later, "Father Divine") was born in Savannah and grew up in the South. He became involved with Samuel Morris, "Father Jehovia," in Baltimore and assumed the title "The Messenger." The trinity was completed with the addition of St. John the Vine Hickerson. There was soon to be conflict over divinity, and Hickerson and "The Messenger" moved in independent directions. Baker went to Valdosta where he began to develop a following, mainly of black females. Eventually (1914) he was taken to court, and after a series of court battles, he was acquitted and left Valdosta with some of his followers. Primary and secondary sources; 29 notes.
M. R. Gillam

4260. Peterson, Keith. FRANK BRUCE ROBINSON AND PSYCHIANA. *Idaho Yesterdays 1979 23(3): 9-15, 26-29.* Frank Bruce Robinson established the world's largest mail-order religion in the 1930's. Operating out of several buildings in Moscow (Idaho), Psychiana was a blend of ideas from the New Thought movement, the beliefs of the power of positive thinking, and the possibility of material success and happiness. Psychiana had appeal to a great many people; they enrolled in correspondence courses to learn more of Robinson's teachings. Covers 1929-48. Based on materials in the University of Idaho library, and in the Latah County Historical Society; 6 illus., 44 notes.
B. J. Paul

4261. Richardson, Evelyn M. THY KINGDOM COME. *Nova Scotia Hist. Q. [Canada] 1975 5(3): 247-264.* A sailing vessel named the *Kingdom Come, Ark of the Holy Ghost and Us Society* ran aground on Big Mud Island approximately 20 miles from Yarmouth in August 1910. Recounts some of the stories of the strange cult and their leader, the Reverend Frank Sanford, who owned the ship—the self-proclaimed incarnation of the prophet Elijah. The cult had as headquarters a communal community near Bangor, Maine. Various legal actions were brought against the leader, and many stories were spread about. The ship, after repair, was ultimatley wrecked off the west coast of Africa, its crew taken off by the companion yacht *Coronet*, also owned by Sanford. Sanford was ultimately imprisoned for manslaughter. He died in 1948.
R. V. Ritter

4262. Richardson, James T. PEOPLE'S TEMPLE AND JONESTOWN: A CORRECTIVE COMPARISON AND CRITIQUE. *J. for the Sci. Study of Religion 1980 19(3): 239-255.* Denies the notion that Jim Jones's People's Temple was similar to other so-called new religions; discusses the implications of not viewing it apart. Covers 1950-79.

4263. Robbins, Thomas and Anthony, Dick. CULTS, BRAINWASHING, AND COUNTER-SUBVERSION. *Ann. of the Am. Acad. of Pol. and Social Sci. 1979 (446): 78-90.* During periods of spiritual ferment, unconventional and sometimes rather authoritarian sects have developed. Such groups have often elicited extreme hostility and distrust and have, moreover, been perceived as fundamentally subversive of civil order and the ideals of Americanism. Counter-subversive movements have sought to mobilize opinion against heterodox sects and to legitimate religious persecution. The current agitation against cults exemplifies a counter-subversive campaign and bears similarities with nineteenth century anti-Masonic, anti-Mormon and anti-Catholic agitation. Both the growth of deviant sects and the emergence of counter-subversive hysteria should be viewed in the context of disturbances in the American civil religion with consequent cultural confusion and normative ambiguity, 19th-20th centuries.
J/S

4264. Robbins, Thomas; Anthony, Dick; Doucas, Madeline; and Curtis, Thomas. THE LAST CIVIL RELIGION: REVEREND MOON AND THE UNIFICATION CHURCH. *Sociol. Analysis 1976 37(2): 111-125.* The increasing domination of the economy by corporate and governmental bureaucracies with concomitant structural differentiation and pluralism has undermined consensual civil religion. In the resulting "mass society" the nuclear family is increasingly isolated because of a lack of secondary groups linking it to the larger polity. However, religions of the youth culture can function as secondary groups and supply legitimations locating young people within the larger society. Some movements do this through tolerant "partial ideologies." Others, such as the Unification Church, attempt to reconstitute an overarching synthesis of threatened patriotic and theistic values within an authoritarian and totalistic organization—in short within a civil religious sect. The existence of authoritarian civil religious sects provides some evidence for Bellah's thesis that without a revolutionary reconstruction of civil religion, either societal disintegration will increase or the nation will relapse into authoritarianism. Covers 1970-76.
J

4265. * Robbins, Thomas and Anthony, Dick. NEW RELIGIONS, FAMILIES AND BRAINWASHING. *Society 1978 15(4): 77-83.* Discusses the forced deprogramming of religious cult converts, and its effectiveness and morality, 1970's.

4266. Schupe, Anson D., Jr. and Bromley, David G. THE MOONIES AND THE ANTI-CULTISTS: MOVEMENT AND COUNTER-MOVEMENT IN CONFLICT. *Sociol. Analysis 1979 40(4): 325-334.* This paper considers a relatively neglected topic in social movements research: the structural conditions under which counter-movements emerge and expand and the relation of the counter-movement's mobilization strategies and tactics to those of the movement(s) which it opposes. The primary movement analyzed is the Unification Church of Sun Myung Moon (as the most prominent of the "new" religious movements in America), and its characteristics as a "world-transforming movement" (in particular its ideology, organizational style, economic resources, and recruitment/socialization practices) are examined in terms of their potential for generating societal conflict. The counter-movement examined is what has been labelled the American anti-cult movement. Drawing upon a wide variety of published and unpublished sources gathered during the authors' three-year study of both movements, the anti-cult movement's institutional origins in the family and (secondarily) in organized religion, as well as the controversial tactics it adopted (including deprogramming), are considered relative to specific aspects of the "Moonies" and similar groups. 4 notes, biblio.
J

4267. Shupe, Anson D., Jr.; Spielmann, Roger; and Stigall, Sam. CULTS OF ANTI-CULTISM. *Society 1980 17(3): 43-46.* Examines organizations which are fighting the Hare Krishna movement, Sun Myung Moon's Unification Church, and other religious sects that spread throughout the United States and Canada during the 1960's and 1970's, and discusses deprogramming cult members.

4268. Shupe, Anson D., Jr.; Spielmann, Roger; and Stigall, Sam. DEPROGRAMMING: THE NEW EXORCISM. *Am. Behavioral Scientist 1977 20(6): 941-956.* Analyzes deprogramming and exorcism in the 1970's, focusing on thought reform and resocialization; offers rationalizations of deprogrammers for participation in such thought control.

4269. Silverberg, David. "HEAVENLY DECEPTION": REV. MOON'S HARD SELL. *Present Tense 1976 4(1): 49-56.* Describes the growth and decline of Reverend Sun Myung Moon's Unification Church. Discusses the Moonie experience, deprogramming, the Divine Principle, anti-Semitism, Jewish involvement and reaction. Covers 1946-76. Primary and secondary sources; 5 photos. R. B. Mendel

4270. Sisk, John P. SALVATION UNLIMITED. *Commentary 1976 61(4): 52-56.* American culture demands immediate gratification. Only a minority are satisfied with slow progress. In the accelerated tempo of post World War II America, salvation has become more than ever identified with speed. Normalcy in our society can appear to be a trap of uninteresting lack of "experience." What may look like a perverse effort to complicate life (e.g., EST, TM, AT, Scientology, etc.), needs to be seen, at least partly, as an effort to simplify life by reducing it to entertainment. S. R. Herstein

4271. Stark, Rodney; Bainbridge, William Sims; and Doyle, Daniel P. CULTS OF AMERICA: A RECONNAISSANCE IN SPACE AND TIME. *Sociol. Analysis 1979 40(4): 347-359.* This paper examines the geographic distribution of American cults based on 501 20th-century independent groups. A third of the nation's cults are in California. However, when population is taken into account, Nevada and New Mexico exceed California in terms of cults per million residents. Regionally, the Pacific states have the highest cult rate (6.9 per million) and the Southern region has the lowest. The Eastern regions have a much larger proportion of cults founded before 1930 than do the southern and western areas. Considerable regional variation also exists in the kinds of cults that predominate. Examination of the dates when existing cults were founded reveals there has been a massive decline over time in the proportion of cults that adopt Christian-sounding names. Finally, trends in the birth dates in 13 families of cults show significant variations. Implications of these findings are considered. 6 tables, biblio. J

4272. Stone, Donald. NEW RELIGIOUS CONSCIOUSNESS AND PERSONAL RELIGIOUS EXPERIENCE. *Sociol. Analysis 1978 39(2): 123-134.* The purpose of this paper is to generalize about characteristics of contemporary religious movements based on ethnographies and survey research data gathered by the Berkeley New Religious Consciousness Project. It is suggested that participants in these religious and quasi-religious groups are attracted by intense experiences of immanence. This is "new" religious consciousness to the extent to which these experiences take place in a context of pluralism, pragmatism, openness to science and rejection of dualistic theology. Religious experiences are seen as particularly attractive in reaction to continuing secularization in which inner-worldly asceticism has lost its sacred underpinnings. The reaction to this loss is distinguished by an "innerworldly mysticism" compatible with science and modern bureaucratic society. The significance of these new religious groups lies in their fostering intuitive styles of consciousness rather than in their membership or longevity. J

4273. Stupple, David. THE "I AM" SECT TODAY: AN *UN* OBITUARY. *J. of Popular Culture 1974 8(4): 897-905.* Discusses the occultist I AM sect and its founders and "Ascended Masters," Edna and Guy Ballard; traces current ritual and belief in contemporary groups, 1930's-75.

4274. Wallis, Roy. IDEOLOGY, AUTHORITY, AND THE DEVELOPMENT OF CULTIC MOVEMENTS. *Social Res. 1974 41(2): 299-327.* Discusses the present sociological interest in religious cults. S

Deism

4275. Currey, Cecil B. BEN FRANKLIN'S RELIGION. *Mankind 1975 5(2): 22-27.* Benjamin Franklin (1706-90), raised in the Congregational Church, in his adult life espoused no church or sect; his theology classifies him as a deist.

4276. Huntley, William B. JEFFERSON'S PUBLIC AND PRIVATE RELIGION. *South Atlantic Q. 1980 79(3): 286-301.* In a study of Thomas Jefferson's religion, one must distinguish between the public and the private. In his public life, his faith can be found in such writings as the Declaration of Independence, the Virginia Bill Establishing Religious Freedom, and the *Notes on the State of Virginia.* His private religion is found in his letters, where he worked out a religion, including an ethic and a theology which he submitted for discussion to friends, particularly John Adams, Joseph Priestley, and Benjamin Rush. Discusses Jefferson's religion in four themes: personal experience with the holy, creation of community through myth and ritual, daily living that expresses cosmic law, and spiritual freedom through discipline. Based on *The Adams-Jefferson Letters,* ed. Cappon; *Writings of Jefferson,* ed. Bergh; *Letters of Benjamin Rush,* ed. Butterfield, secondary sources; 45 notes. H. M. Parker, Jr.

4277. Jurden, D. A. A HISTORIOGRAPHY OF AMERICAN DEISM. *Am. Benedictine Rev. 1974 25(1): 108-122.* Reviews several seminal studies of the history of American Deism and concludes that most studies obscure the varieties, and thus the nature, of Deism that existed in America in the 18th and 19th centuries. This conclusion is demonstrated by a review of the beliefs espoused by significant Deists such as Benjamin Franklin, Thomas Jefferson, Elihu Palmer, and Ethan Allen. 45 notes. J. H. Pragman

4278. Levitsky, Ihor. THE TOLSTOY GOSPEL IN THE LIGHT OF THE JEFFERSON BIBLE. *Can. Slavonic Papers [Canada] 1979 21(3): 347-355.* Comparison of both the rationale and the content of Leo Tolstoy's *Christ's Christianity* (London, 1855) and Thomas Jefferson's *The Life and Morals of Jesus of Nazareth* reveals a remarkable similarity. Both considered that the essential moral teachings of Jesus had been overlaid by a tradition begun by Paul the Apostle that concealed the essence of Christianity and turned it in a detrimental direction. This unorthodox approach was no problem to Jefferson in view of his ability to adjust to public expediencies. For Tolstoy, with his sense of responsibility to conviction, these views created many tensions. Primary sources; 27 notes. R. V. Ritter

4279. Mabee, Charles. THOMAS JEFFERSON'S ANTI-CLERICAL BIBLE. *Hist. Mag. of the Protestant Episcopal Church 1979 48(4): 473-481.* Thomas Jefferson's unpublished "scissors-and-paste" treatment of the gospels during 1813-20 reveals him as an American, not a Marcionite, and as a declericalizer rather than a demythologizer. In endeavoring to rid the scriptures of what he deemed to be priest-ridden interpretations, Jefferson inadvertently grasped one of the basic themes of the gospels: truth is not as it appears in this world. Demonstrates this by drawing attention to the positioning of the gospel passages in Jefferson's work. Thomas Jefferson thus emerges in the "prophetic and apologetic spirit of a true devotee of Jesus." Based on Jefferson's letters and secondary sources; 21 notes. H. M. Parker, Jr.

4280. Wettstein, A. Arnold. RELIGIONLESS RELIGION IN THE LETTERS AND PAPERS FROM MONTICELLO. *Religion in Life 1976 45(2): 152-160.* Discusses anti-sectarianism and the conception of religion and Christianity in the letters of Thomas Jefferson, 1784-1800.

Eastern Religions

4281. Foss, Daniel A. and Larkin, Ralph W. WORSHIPING THE ABSURD: THE NEGATION OF SOCIAL CAUSALITY AMONG THE FOLLOWERS OF GURU MAHARAJ JI. *Sociol. Analysis 1978 39(2): 157-164.* Analyzes the basis of Guru Maharaj Ji's appeal to ex-movement participants in the early 1970's. The youth movement of the 1960's had generated a reinterpretation of reality that called into question conventional reality. When the movement declined, the movement reinterpretation had no possibility for implementation. Left between a reality they rejected and one that could not be implemented, ex-movement participants experienced life as arbitrary and senseless. Guru Maharaj Ji was deified as the mirror of an incomprehensible, meaningless universe. The Divine Light Mission stripped its followers of all notions of causality while simultaneously subsuming and repudiating both conventional and movement interpretations of reality. J

4282. Kurihara, Akira. AMERICAN YOUTH: FROM POLITICS TO RELIGION. *Japan Interpreter [Japan] 1976 11(2): 216-218.* In America and Japan youth are moving away from political activism toward mysticism, reflective introspection, and religious movements such as Transcendental Meditation, Zen, and Sufism. Institutionalized religion seems to be on the wane, but young people show mounting enthusiasm for popular religious movements, which stress ethical content, including an interest in the "emperor system" and "Japan worship." F. W. Iklé

4283. Leneman, Leah. THE HINDU RENAISSANCE OF THE LATE 19TH CENTURY. *Hist. Today [Great Britain] 1980 30(May): 22-27.* Discusses the Hindu revival of the late 19th century in India and the West; provides brief biographies of the people who contributed to the Hindu renaissance, including Ram Mohun Roy (1772-1833), Keshab Chunder Sen (1838-84), Madame Helena Petrovna Blavatsky who was cofounder of the Theosophical Society in 1875 in New York, Annie Besant, President of the Theosophical Society 1907-33, Sri Ramakrishna, and Narendra Vivekananda, who formed Ramakrishna Vedanta centers in Britain, France, and the United States which operate today.

4284. Pilarzyk, Thomas. CONVERSION AND ALTERNATION PROCESSES IN THE YOUTH CULTURE: A COMPARATIVE ANALYSIS OF RELIGIOUS TRANSFORMATIONS. *Pacific Sociol. Rev. 1978 21(4): 379-406.* Within contemporary youth movements there are two processes of religious conversion—sectarian conversion as associated with the Hare Krishna Movement and the cultic alternation process affiliated with the Divine Light Mission, 1960's-70's.

4285. Price, Maeve. THE DIVINE LIGHT MISSION AS A SOCIAL ORGANIZATION. *Sociol. Rev. [Great Britain] 1979 27(2): 279-296.* Examines the organizational structure of the Divine Light Mission, a religious group founded in India in the 1930's by the father of the current Perfect Master, Guru Maharaj Ji, who is the leader of the group.

4286. Rossman, Michael. SHOW US YOUR LOTUS ASS, RENNIE! BLISS AND FEAR IN BERKELEY. *Social Policy 1974 5(3): 33-37.* Discusses the political implications of Rennie Davis's conversion to the teachings of the guru Maharaj Ji and popular attitudes toward Davis' new beliefs as evidenced in a public meeting in Berkeley, California, in 1973.

4287. Sharpe, Eric J. EASTERN RELIGIONS IN THE WESTERN CLASSROOM. *South Asian Rev. [Great Britain] 1975 8(3): 225-237.* Examines the reasons for the revival of Western academic interest in Eastern religions and offers suggestions for the exposition of this subject. The "essence of consciousness" which is central to Hinduism and Buddhism can be communicated across cultural lines. Western preoccupations with these problems represent a theological rather than an educational view. The author analyzes the theories of Indian intellectuals in presenting the essence of their religion. Based on secondary sources and papers developed at the 1969 Shap Working Party on World Religions in Education, conducted by the University of Newcastle; 17 notes. S. H. Frank

4288. Swearer, Donald K. THREE MODES OF ZEN BUDDHISM IN AMERICA. *J. of Ecumenical Studies 1973 10(2): 290-303.* Zen Buddhism long has been popular in America. Discusses two other modes of the religion: the attempt by some, including Alan Watts, to substitute Zen Buddhism for Christianity, and the dialogue set up by Thomas Merton and others between Christianity and Zen Buddhism. Covers 1930-73. J. A. Overbeck

4289. —. AMERICANS IN ASIA: THE SEARCH FOR MEANING IN LIFE. *Center Mag. 1980 13(5): 11-20.* Presents excerpts from interviews with Americans who have gone to places such as Nepal and Thailand to practice Eastern religions.

Spiritualism

4290. Ayers, Edward. SCIENCE AND THE SEANCE. *Rev. in Am. Hist. 1978 6(3): 306-312.* Review article prompted by R. Laurence Moore's *In Search of White Crows: Spiritualism, Parapsychology, and American Culture* (New York: Oxford U. Pr., 1977), which discusses spiritualism as a solution to the confrontation between religion and science by giving the history of spiritualism and spiritualists in American culture since 1850.

4291. Bednarowski, Mary Farrell. SPIRITUALISM IN WISCONSIN IN THE NINETEENTH CENTURY. *Wisconsin Mag. of Hist. 1975 59(1): 2-19.* Three major groups comprised Wisconsin Spiritualism: 1) followers of Mary Hayes Chynoweth in the Madison-Lake Mills-Whitewater area, 2) the Fox River Valley group, including Warren Chase, Nathaniel P. Tallmadge, and R. T. Mason, and 3) those led by Mrs. Julia Severance and Dr. H. S. Brown in the Milwaukee area. All three groups had "a liberal spirit in regard to politics, religion, and social relationships, and a conviction that Spiritualism, as a radical belief untainted by the fears and superstitions fostered by traditional religions, could provide humanity with certain knowledge not only of the nature of laws of this world, but of the next as well." 7 illus., 48 notes. N. C. Burckel

4292. Frazier, Arthur H. HENRY SEYBERT AND THE CENTENNIAL CLOCK AND BELL AT INDEPENDENCE HALL. *Pennsylvania Mag. of Hist. and Biog. 1978 102(1): 40-58.* Following his admired father's death, Henry Seybert almost gave up mineralogy, to which he had significanly contributed, and turned to spiritualism. He wandered for 20 years. After 1846 he became involved in Philadelphia civic affairs. The clock and bell, first projected as a public project in 1860, were personally consummated in 1876. Believing he could obtain heaven by helping the poor, he broadly bequeathed his beneficence, including the founding of Seybert Institute. Based on manuscript and printed sources, and on secondary works; 49 notes. T. H. Wendel

4293. Keys, Thomas Bland. LINCOLN'S VOICE FROM THE GRAVE: A SPIRITUALISTIC CONVERSATION WITH CARL SCHURZ. *Lincoln Herald 1975 77(2): 121-123.* Carl Schurz, summoned to Washington, D.C. by President Andrew Johnson in 1865, assumed it was to discuss the President's plan for reconstructing North Carolina. The night before the meeting, during a seance, Abraham Lincoln supposedly told him the true nature of the meeting and made several prognostications that eventually came true. Based on primary and secondary sources; illus., 17 notes. B. J. LaBue

4294. Moore, R. Laurence. THE SPIRITUALIST MEDIUM: A STUDY OF FEMALE PROFESSIONALISM IN VICTORIAN AMERICA. *Am. Q. 1975 27(2): 200-221.* Female spiritualists in the 19th century gained upward social mobility, self-esteem, and a feeling of helping others through the practice of their profession. Many times physically weak and sickly before engaging in spiritualism, these women were able to endure extensive travel and arduous road conditions in the practice of their work, and often were able to achieve financial independence, respect from males, and a sense of sexual freedom. N. Lederer

4295. Robbins, Peggy. THE LINCOLNS AND SPRITUALISM. *Civil War Times Illus. 1976 15(5): 4-10, 46-47.* Discusses the involvement of Mary Todd Lincoln in spiritualism and the effect which this had on Abraham Lincoln, 1848-64.

4296. Walker, Ronald W. THE LIBERAL INSTITUTE: A CASE STUDY IN NATIONAL ASSIMILATION. *Dialogue 1977 10(4): 74-85.* The Liberal Institute was founded in Salt Lake City, Utah, in 1871 by a group of liberal, intellectual Mormons who rejected the Mormon Church and sought to diminish its role in Utah. They embraced William S. Godbe's protest in 1869 and 1870 but then quickly became spiritualists. They advocated such social reforms as temperance and feminism.

Theosophy

4297. Berge, Dennis E. REMINISCENCES OF LOMALAND: MADAME TINGLEY AND THE THEOSOPHICAL INSTITUTE IN SAN DIEGO. *J. of San Diego Hist. 1975 20(3): 1-32.* Describes the Theosophical movement and the development and history of the Theosophical Institute at Point Loma, 1897-1940, and its founder, Katherine Augusta Tingley. S

4298. Clark, Thomas D. "BATTLE OF THE FAIR THEOSOPHISTS IS ON": ANNIE BESANT'S LECTURE TOUR OF SAN DIEGO. *J. of San Diego Hist. 1977 23(2): 1-7.* Examines the conflict between two women members of the Theosophist Society in San Diego, Annie Besant and Katharine Tingley (the leader of a group of secessionist theosophists, the United Brotherhood of Theosophists), 1897.

4299. Kagan, Paul and Ziebarth, Marilyn. EASTERN THOUGHT ON A WESTERN SHORE: POINT LOMA COMMUNITY. *California Hist. Q. 1973 52(1): 4-15.* From 1897 to 1942 the Universal Brotherhood and Theosophical Society, at Point Loma, near San Diego, was a prominent utopian society. Its leader was Mrs. Katherine Augusta Westcott Tingley (1847-1929). Her brand of Theosophy combined Eastern religious and literary thought with pageantry and ceremony. The progressive school operated by the society won approval during its lifetime. Loss of financial support, dwindling membership, and the adjacent location of a U.S. naval base compelled the society to relocate. 17 photos. A. Hoffman

Anti-Religious Movements

(including atheism and free thought)

4300. Doepke, Dale K. THE WESTERN EXAMINER: A CHRONICLE OF ATHEISM IN THE WEST. *Missouri Hist. Soc. Bull. 1973 30(1): 29-43.* The *Western Examiner,* published in St. Louis 1834-35, provoked "lively and sometimes acrimonious debate." The Mechanics Benevolent Society may have sponsored this controversial magazine. John Bobb appears to have been the original promoter and editor. He and other contributors indulged their freethinking views on religious and political topics. Conservative citizens and the "Christian establishment" were outraged. Based on the *Western Examiner* and other St. Louis publications; 23 notes. H. T. Lovin

4301. Elias, Mohamed. MARK TWAIN AND THE AGA KHAN: MUTUAL IMPRESSIONS. *Indian J. of Am. Studies [India] 1978 8(1): 46-49.* In 1885 the American novelist Mark Twain met the Aga Khan III (1877-1957) in Bombay, India. Both Twain and the Aga Khan instinctively distorted the other's cultural symbols. Aga Khan in his *Memoirs* and Mark Twain in *Following the Equator* discussed the meeting. The Aga Khan greatly admired and was well versed in Twain's works; he wrote amazingly, of the "gentle and saintly" Twain. Playing on the idea that the Aga Khan is regarded by his followers as a proof of God on earth, Twain subtly used the meeting to express some of his bitterness at God. 9 notes. L. V. Eid

4302. Grant, H. Roger, ed. THE SKANEATELES COMMUNITY: A NEW YORK UTOPIA. *Niagara Frontier 1975 22(3): 68-72.* A Utopian community in New York's Finger Lakes area was founded in 1843 by John Anderson Collins with an antireligion orientation; reprints a letter by John Finch describing the surroundings and financial situation of the community in 1845.

4303. Kendall, Kathleen Edgerton and Fisher, Jeanne Y. FRANCES WRIGHT ON WOMEN'S RIGHTS: ELOQUENCE VERSUS ETHOS. *Q. J. of Speech 1974 60(1): 58-68.* Frances Wright, a Scotswoman and first woman public speaker in America, failed to persuade 1828-1830 audiences of the importance of women's rights because of her low extrinsic ethos. She met all the criteria for 'eloquence' defined by Longinus, and contemporary audiences granted her high intrinsic ethos; however, her radical behavior and ideas such as the invasion of the male lecture platform, association with free love practices, and attacks on organized religion violated societal norms and thereby mitigated her effectiveness. J

4304. Kleber, John E. "PAGAN BOB" ON THE COMSTOCK: ROBERT G. INGERSOLL VISITS VIRGINIA CITY. *Nevada Hist. Soc. Q. 1979 22(4): 243-253.* A Gilded Age orator who regularly denounced ecclesiastical orthodoxy and organized religions, Robert Ingersoll (1833-99) twice lectured at Virginia City in 1877 to appreciative audiences. The orator flattered his listeners, praising them for sufficient educational attainments to appreciate ideas and the desirability of high wages in Comstock Lode mines. Moreover, these Nevadans tolerated Ingersoll's freethinking partly because they valued free speech; and they sensed the orator's basic beliefs in "God and nature" that Ingersoll's critics had not recognized. Based on newspaper and secondary sources; 31 notes. H. T. Lovin

SUBJECT INDEX

Subject Profile Index (ABC-SPIndex) carries both generic and specific index terms. Begin a search at the general term but also look under more specific or related terms. Cross-references are included.

Each string of index descriptors is intended to present a profile of a given article; however, no particular relationship between any two terms in the profile is implied. Terms within the profile are listed alphabetically after the leading term. The variety of punctuation and capitalization reflects production methods and has no intrinsic meaning; e.g., there is no difference in meaning between "History, study of" and "History (study of)."

Cities, towns, and counties are listed following their respective states or provinces; e.g., "Ohio (Columbus)." Terms beginning with an arabic numeral are listed after the letter Z. The chronology of the bibliographic entry follows the subject index descriptors. In the chronology, "c" stands for "century"; e.g., "19c" means "19th century."

Note that "United States" is not used as a leading index term; if no country is mentioned, the index entry refers to the United States alone. When an entry refers to both Canada and the United States, both "Canada" and "USA" appear in the string of index descriptors, but "USA" is not a leading term. When an entry refers to any other country and the United States, only the other country is indexed.

The last number in the index string, in italics, refers to the bibliographic entry number.

A

Aaronic Order. Glendenning, Maurice L. Middle classes. Millenarianism. Mormons. Utah. 1930-79. *3933*

Abbott, Lyman. Clergy. Congregationalism. New York (Cornwall-on-the-Hudson). Parsons, Edward Smith. Personal narratives. 1885. *3136*

Abel, Elijah. Clergy. Mormons. Negroes. ca 1830-79. *3944*

Aberhart, William. Alberta. Economic reform. Politics. Prime ministers. Radio. 1934-37. *1216*

—. Alberta. Ideology. Provincial Government. Social Credit Party. Theology. 1935-43. *1365*

Abolition Movement *See also* Antislavery Sentiments; Emancipation.

—. American Free Baptist Mission Society. Baptists. Missions and Missionaries. Schisms. 1830-69. *2481*

—. American Revolution. Letters. Massachusetts (Boston). Wheatley, Phillis. Whigs. 1767-80. *2454*

—. Anderson, Isaac. Presbyterian Church. Southern and Western Theological Seminary. Tennessee (Maryville). 1819-50's. *723*

—. Andover Seminary. Congregationalism. Massachusetts. Seminaries. Theology. 1825-35. *2491*

—. Assassination. Brooks, Phillips. Episcopal Church, Protestant. Lincoln, Abraham. Pennsylvania (Philadelphia). Sermons. 1865. 1893. *2463*

—. Attitudes. Competition. Economic conditions. Evangelicalism. Poverty. ca 1830-60. *2473*

—. Attitudes. New England. Puritans. Slavery. 1641-1776. *2164*

—. Baptists. Education. First African Baptist Church. Meachum, John Berry. Missouri (St. Louis). Negroes. 1815-54. *2482*

—. Baptists. Landmark Movement. Pendleton, James Madison. 1835-91. *2998*

—. Beecher, Lyman. Colonization. Presbyterian Church (New School). 1820-50. *2492*

—. Berea College. Fee, John Gregg. Kentucky. Presbyterian Church. Religious education. 1855-1904. *777*

—. Birney, James. Clergy. Evangelism. Smith, Gerrit. Stanton, H. B. Weld, Theodore. 1820-50. *2488*

—. Breckinridge, Robert Jefferson. Breckinridge, William Lewis. Constitutions, State. Emancipation Party. Kentucky. Presbyterians. 1849. *2475*

—. Cass, William D. Letters. Methodist Episcopal Church (General Conference). 1844. *2477*

—. Childhood. Evangelicalism. Missions and Missionaries. 1800-60. *947*

—. Christianity. Douglass, Frederick. 1830's-60's. *2496*

—. Christianity. Enlightenment. Morality. Nationalism. Phillips, Wendell. 1830-84. *1399*

—. Christology. Clergy. Congregationalism. Negroes. New York. Ward, Samuel Ringgold. 1839-51. *2462*

—. Civil War (antecedents). Clergy. New England. Parker, Theodore. Transcendentalism. Violence. 1850-60. *2467*

—. Civil War (antecedents). Presbyterian Church. South. Stanton, Robert. 1840-55. *2484*

—. Clergy. Conservatism. Constitutions. Massachusetts (Boston). Missouri (St. Louis). Unitarianism. 1828-57. *1413*

—. Clergy. Negroes. Protestant churches. 1830-60. *2472*

—. Constitutional Amendments (15th). Douglass, Frederick. Negroes. Theology. 1825-86. *2495*

—. Cornish, Samuel E. *Freedom's Journal* (newspaper). Journalism. Negroes. Presbyterian Church. 1820's-59. *2498*

—. Davis, David Brion. Drake, Thomas. Friends, Society of (review article). James, Sydney. 1683-1863. 20c. *2471*

—. Douglass, Frederick. Ireland (Belfast). Presbyterian Church. Smyth, Thomas. 1846. *2165*

—. Dugdale, Joseph A. Friends, Society of. Reform. 1810-96. *2361*

—. Education. Freedmen. McPherson, James M. (review article). Missions and Missionaries. Protestantism. 1865-1910. 1975. *563*

—. Evangelicalism. Friendship. Tappan, Lewis. 1830-61. *2469*

—. Finney, Charles G. Revivals. Social reform. South. 1833-69. *2466*

—. Fox, George. Friends, Society of. Pennsylvania. Slave trade. 1656-1754. *2479*

—. Friends, Society of. Haverford College Library (Quaker Collection). New Hampshire. Portsmouth Anti-Slavery Society. Rogers, Nathaniel Peabody. 1830-46. *2465*

—. Friends, Society of (Longwood Meeting). Pennsylvania. Reform. 1850's-1940. *2450*

—. Great Britain. Historiography. Protestantism. 18c-19c. *2499*

—. Hersey, John. Methodist Church. Millenarianism. Perfectionism. 1786-1862. *3446*

—. James, Thomas. Methodist Episcopal Church, African. Personal narratives. 1804-80. *2476*

Abortion. Attitudes. Catholic Church. Colleges and Universities. Students. 1970's. *855*

—. Attitudes. Catholics. Protestants. Whites. 1962-75. *888*

—. Attitudes. Christianity. 1972. *910*

—. Attitudes. Family size preference. 1972. *917*

—. Birth Control. Protestantism. 19c. *869*

—. Catholic Church. Democratic Party. Elections (presidential). 1976. *1245*

—. Catholic Church. Hawaii. Methodology. Women. 1965-74. *872*

—. Catholic Church. Women's Liberation Movement. -1973. *898*

—. Legislators. Voting behavior. Western States. 1975. *139*

—. Protestant churches. Right To Life organizations. South. 1970's. *945*

Abramson, Harold J. Catholics. Ethnicity (review article). Hays, Samuel. Voting and Voting Behavior. 1973. *3740*

Abyssinia. *See* Ethiopia.

Academic disciplines. College teachers. Religiosity. 1965-73. *531*

Academic Freedom. Baptists. Foster, George Burman. Illinois. Theology. University of Chicago Divinity School. 1895-1918. *557*

—. Bassett, John Spencer. Duke University. Methodist Church. North Carolina (Durham). Racism. *South Atlantic Quarterly* (periodical). 1902-03. *3497*

—. Concordia Seminary. Lutheran Church (Missouri Synod). Missouri (St. Louis). Teachers. Tenure. 1968-74. *771*

—. Hebrew Union College. Judaism, Reform. Kohler, Kaufmann. Ohio (Cincinnati). Zionism. 1903-07. *724*

—. Lutheran Church (Missouri Synod). Theology. 1973. *649*

Acadians *See also* French Canadians.

—. Acculturation. Catholic Church. Exiles. France. Great Britain. Nova Scotia. 18c. *3750*

—. Catholic Church. Discrimination. Irish Canadians. New Brunswick. 1860-1900. *3855*

—. Catholic Church. English Canadians. Maritime Provinces. Social Conditions. 1763-1977. *3871*

Accademia (association). Catholic Church. Clergy. New York. 1865-1907. *296*

Acculturation *See also* Assimilation.

—. Acadians. Catholic Church. Exiles. France. Great Britain. Nova Scotia. 18c. *3750*

—. American Indian Defense Association. Collier, John. Indians. Religious liberty. 1920-26. *1101*

—. Americanism. Catholic Church. Leo XIII, Pope (*Testem Benevolentiae*). Periodicals. Protestantism. 1899. *319*

—. Arapaho Indians. Cheyenne Indians. Indians. Mennonites. Missions and Missionaries. 1880-1900. *1557*

—. Blackburn, Gideon. Cherokee Indians. Missions and missionaries. Presbyterian Church. Schools. Tennessee. 1804-10. *1491*

—. Burials. Christianity. Indians. Missions and Missionaries. Navajo Indians. 1949-75. *1656*

—. California (Monterey, San Luis Obispo counties). Catholic Church. Indians. Missions and Missionaries. Salinan Indians. 1770's-1830's. *1550*

—. Canada. Ethnicity. Jews. USA. 1961-74. *4156*

—. Catholic Church. French Canadians. Nationalism. New England. ca 1610-1975. *309*

—. Catholic Church. Indian-White Relations. Missionaries. Protestantism. Wisconsin. 1830-48. *1640*

—. Catholic Church. Irish Americans. Pennsylvania (Pittsburgh). St. Andrew Parish. 1863-90. *3748*

—. Catholic Church. Italian Americans (review article). Social Organization. 1880-20c. *3820*

—. Catholics. Immigration. Slovak Americans. 1860's-1970's. *3879*

—. Cherokee Indians. Georgia. Missions and Missionaries. White Path's Rebellion. 1824-28. *1578*

—. Christianity. Ethnicity. Europe. Immigration. Judaism. Middle East. 19c-20c. *34*

—. Church Schools. Mexican Americans. Public Schools. Texas (San Antonio). 1973. *677*

—. Educational reform. Immigration. Public Schools. 19c-1910's. *532*

—. Frontier and Pioneer Life. Immigrants. Lutheran Church. Rolvaag, O. E. *(Giants in the Earth)*. South Dakota. 1870. 1927. *3307*

—. Literature. Mennonites. 1970's. *3414*
Action Catholique. Catholic Church. Courchesne, Georges. Quebec (Rimouski). 1940-67. *2356*
Actors and Actresses. California (Los Angeles area). Catholic Church. Modjeska, Helena. Polish Americans. 1876-1909. *3786*
Adams, John. American Revolution. New England. Paine, Thomas. Political theory. Puritans. Rhetoric. 17c-1770's. *1424*
—. American Revolution (antecedents). Church of England. Letters. Weller, George. 1770's. 1824-25. *971*
Addams, Jane. Dudzik, Mary Theresa. Franciscan Sisters of Chicago. Illinois. Polish Americans. Social Work. Women. 1860-1918. *2511*
—. Education. Friends, Society of. Hull House. Ideology. Illinois (Chicago). Women. 1875-1930. *911*
Addiction. Conversion. Jesus Movement. 1960's-75. *2784*
Adelman, Samuel. Colorado (Denver). Congregation Beth Ha Medrosh Hagodol. Judaism (Conservative, Orthodox). Kauvar, Charles E. H. Rabbis. 1949-58. *4193*
Adger, John B. Dabney, Robert L. Hodge, Charles. Mercersburg theology. Nevin, John W. Presbyterian Church. Sacramental controversy. 1845-75. *3551*
Adler, Cyrus. American Academy for Jewish Research. Intellectuals. Judaism (Orthodox, Reform). Revel, Bernard. Society of Jewish Academicians. 1916-22. *4139*
Adler, Samuel. Judaism (Reform). Morality. New York City. Theology. ca 1829-91. *4208*
Adolescence *See also* Youth.
—. Baptists. Congregationalism. Finney, Charles G. Massachusetts (Boston). Methodism. Revivals. 1822-42. *2258*
—. Boys. Canada. Protestantism. USA. Young Men's Christian Association. 1870-1920. *2414*
—. Children. Christianity. Rural-Urban Studies. Social classes. 1920's-70's. *2762*
—. Church attendance. Negroes. Religiosity. South. Whites. 1964-74. *99*
—. Family size preference. Population. 1971-74. *808*
—. Hispanic Americans. Identity. Mexico. Puerto Rico. Religiosity. Whites. 1970's. *108*
—. Sermons. 1700-30. *856*
Adoption policies. Children. Public Welfare. 1954-71. *845*
Adrian College. Baptists, Free Will. Hillsdale College. Methodist Church, Wesleyan. Michigan. Oberlin College. Ohio. Olivet College. Social Reform. 1833-70. *741*
Advent Review and Sabbath Herald (newspaper). Adventists. Poetry. Prophecy. Smith, Uriah. 1853. *1997*
Adventist Medical Cadet Corps. Armies. Dick, Everett N. Korean War. Personal narratives. World War II. 1934-53. *2644*
Adventists. 1850's-60's. *2960*
—. *Advent Review and Sabbath Herald* (newspaper). Poetry. Prophecy. Smith, Uriah. 1853. *1997*
—. Albany Conference. Millerites. New York. 1844-45. *2961*
—. Anesthesia. California. Dentistry. Jorgensen, Niels Bjorn. Loma Linda University. Teaching. 1923-74. *1441*
—. Architecture. Churches. Michigan. 1863-1976. *1794*
—. Australia. Missions and Missionaries. Palmer, Edwin R. Publishers and Publishing. 1894-1915. *2968*
—. Automobile Industry and Trade. North Central States. Worth, William O. 1890-1913. *361*
—. Battle Creek College. Brownsberger, Sidney. California. Colleges and Universities. Healdsburg College. Michigan. 1875-80's. *665*
—. Battle Creek College. Madison College. Michigan. Sutherland, Edward A. Tennessee. 1897-1904. *743*
—. Battle Creek Sanitarium. California. Loma Linda University. Medical Education. Michigan. Nurses and Nursing. 1884-1979. *1425*
—. Bible. Medical reform. 1810's-63. *1436*
—. Bible. Prophecy. World War I (antecedents). 1912-18. *2664*
—. Bible. Protestantism. Republicanism. 1850's-60's. *2962*
—. Bible Research Fellowship. Religious Education. 1943-52. *611*
—. Byington, John. Methodist Church, Wesleyan. Methodist Episcopal Church. New York (Bucks Bridge). 1840's-52. *3509*
—. California. Humor. Irish Americans. Letters. Loma Linda University. Magan, Percy Tilson. 1918-34. *1435*
—. California. Letters. Loma Linda Sanitarium. White, Ellen G. 1905. *1461*
—. California. Loma Linda Sanitarium. Photographs. 1905-19. *1458*
—. California. Loma Linda University. Medical Education. 1905-15. *1450*
—. California (Arlington). Loma Linda University. 1922-67. *738*
—. California (Arlington). Loma Linda University. Personal narratives. Robison, James I. 1922. *745*
—. California (Loma Linda). Education. Medicine. 1810-1929. *2971*
—. California (Mountain View, Oakland). Jones, Charles Harriman. Pacific Press Publishing Company. Publishers and Publishing. 1879-1923. *362*
—. California (San Francisco). Debates. Educational Policy. Evolution. Science League of America. 1925. *2291*
—. Camp meetings. Northeastern or North Atlantic states. 1840's. *2231*
—. Centennial Exposition of 1876. Kellogg, John Harvey. Pennsylvania (Philadelphia). 1876. *2969*
—. Chaplains. Military. 1944-55. *2645*
—. Charisma. Prophecy. White, Ellen G. Women. 1848-1901. *2976*
—. Clement, Lora E. Editors and Editing. Women. *Youth's Instructor* (newspaper). 1927-52. *1987*
—. Clinton Theological Seminary. German Americans. Missouri. 1910-25. *761*
—. Colleges and Universities. Educational Reform. Sutherland, Edward A. 1904-50. *693*
—. Constitutional Amendments (21st). Prohibition (repeal). 1932-34. *2598*
—. Cudney, A. J. Evangelism. Nebraska (Lincoln). 1885-87. *1577*
—. Diaries. Kellogg, Merritt. Medicine, practice of. Trall, Russell Thacher. 1844-77. *1452*
—. Dowling, John. Greeley, Horace. Miller, William. New York *Tribune* (newspaper). 1842. *2963*
—. Education. Missions and Missionaries. New Mexico (Sandoval). Spanish-American Seminary. 1928-53. *751*
—. Elections (mayoral). Gage, William C. Michigan (Battle Creek). Morality. 1882. *1255*
—. Engraving. Michigan (Battle Creek). Smith, Uriah. Wood. 1852-70's. *1889*
—. Evangelicals. Theology. 1948-60. *503*
—. Evangelism. Hill, W. B. Iowa. Minnesota. Personal Narratives. 1877. 1881. *1547*
—. Fiction. Miller, William. Press. 1830's-40's. *2014*
—. First Harlem Church. Humphrey, James K. Negroes. New York City. Schisms. Utopia Park. 1920's-30's. *2143*
—. Friends of Man. Interior Lay Missionary Movement. Jehovah's Witnesses. Russell, Charles Taze. 1852-1916. *3921*
—. Fuller, Nathan. New York. Pennsylvania. 1858-71. *2975*
—. Fullmer, Bert E. Rowen, Margaret W. Visions. Women. 1916-29. *2979*
—. Germany. Great Britain. Millenarianism. Miller, William. Sweden. 19c. *2967*
—. Great Disappointment. Millenarianism. Revivals. 18c-1973. *2970*
—. Health. Numbers, Ronald L. (review article). Reform. White, Ellen G. ca 1840's-1915. 1976. *1457*
—. Hydrotherapy. Jackson, James Caleb. Medical reform. New York (Dansville). White, Ellen G. 1864-65. *1451*
—. Hymns. Poetry. Smith, Annie Rebekah. 1850's. *1926*
—. Illinois. Jones, Alonzo Trevier. Religious liberty. Sabbath. World's Columbian Exposition (Chicago, 1893). 1893. *2280*
—. Labor unions and organizations. 1877-1903. *1474*
—. Massachusetts, western. Miller, William. Newspapers. Public opinion. 1840's. *2079*
—. Missions and Missionaries. *Pitcairn* (vessel). Visions. White, Ellen G. 1848-90. *1704*
—. Music. Temperance Movements. 1850's-90's. *2965*
—. Nebraska. State Politics. Williams, George A. 1925-31. *1325*
—. Nebraska (Lincoln). Union College. 1891-1976. *593*
—. New Hampshire (Washington). Oakes, Rachel. Preble, T. M. Sabbath. Wheeler, Frederick. 1841-44. *2287*
—. Postage stamps. 1847-1978. *2972*
—. Postcards. Sanatoriums. 1900's-10's. *1427*
Adventists (headquarters). Maryland (Takoma Park). Michigan (Battle Creek). 1903. *2978*
Advertising *See also* Mail-Order Business; Propaganda.
—. Barton, Bruce *(The Man Nobody Knows)*. Business. Christianity. 1920-29. *365*
—. Men. Mormons. Patent medicines. Stereotypes. Virility. 1884-1931. *819*
Advocate role. Charities. Children. Indians. Poor. St. Vincent de Paul Society. 1900-10. *2515*
Aesthetics. Emerson, Ralph Waldo. Philosophy. Plotinus. Science. Transcendentalism. 1836-60. *2302*
Africa. American Colonization Society. Colonization. McDonough, David. Medical Education. Presbyterian Church. Slavery. 1840-50. *2483*
—. Christianity. Independence movements. Missions and Missionaries. World Conference of Christian Youth, 1st. 1939-74. *1751*
—. Congregationalism. Missions and Missionaries. Presbyterian Church. Reformed Dutch Church. Reformed German Church. 19c-20c. *1709*
—. Economic Conditions. Negroes. Slave trade. Social Customs. ca 1500-1940's. *24*
Africa, West. Missions and Missionaries. Presbyterian Church. Social change. Women. 1850-1915. *1686*
African Society. Colonization. Congregationalism. Freedmen. Hopkins, Samuel. Rhode Island (Providence). Sierra Leone. 1789-95. *2459*
Africans' School. Benezet, Anthony. Education. Friends, Society of. Negroes. Pennsylvania (Philadelphia). 1770's-80's. *527*
Afro-Americans. *See* Negroes.
Aga Khan III. Agnosticism. India (Bombay). Twain, Mark. 1885. *4301*
Age. Birth rate. Marriage. Mormons. Women. 1800-69. *892*
—. Church membership. Lutheran church. Religiosity. 1974. *3311*
Aged *See also* Death and Dying; Public Welfare.
—. Catholic Church. Charities. Education. Immigration. New Brunswick (Saint John). Orphans. Sisters of Charity of the Immaculate Conception. 1854-64. *2509*
—. Folklore. Poor. West Virginia. Witchcraft. Women. 1975. *2201*
Agnosticism. Aga Khan III. India (Bombay). Twain, Mark. 1885. *4301*
—. Catholic Church. Colleges and Universities. Quebec. Students. 1970-78. *505*
—. Ethnicity. Hillquit, Morris. Jews. New York City. Socialism. 1890's-1933. *1331*
—. Ingersoll, Robert. Puritans. Winthrop, John. ca 1630-1890's. *54*
Agricultural Labor *See also* Peasants.
—. Canary Islanders. Fernandez de Santa Ana, Benito. Indians. Missions and Missionaries. Petitions. Provincial Government. Texas (Villa San Fernando). 1741. *1542*
Agricultural Reform. Catholic Church. New Deal. Roosevelt, Franklin D. (administration). Social Theory. 1933-39. *2572*
Agriculture *See also* Agricultural Labor; Country Life; Farms; Land; Land Tenure; Plantations; Rural Development; Winemaking.
—. Amish. Economic conditions. Illinois. Social organization. 1960-72. *3428*
—. Catholic Church. Federal Programs. Friends, Society of. Indian-White Relations. Missions and Missionaries. Moravian Church. Old Northwest. 1789-1820. *1529*
—. Clergy. Colman, Henry. Massachusetts. Unitarianism. 1820-49. *4082*
—. Communalism. Education. German Americans. Hutterites. Pacific Northwest. Pacifism. 20c. *392*
—. Factionalism. Germans, Russian. Mennonites. Personal narratives. Saskatchewan (Rosthern). Settlement. 1891-1900. *3442*
—. Grasshoppers. Pioneers. Utah. 1854-79. *3941*
—. Hutterites. Lifestyles. North America. Social Customs. Technological innovation. 18c-20c. *3349*
—. Idaho. Mormons. Settlement. Snake River. 1880-1914. *3940*
—. Immigration. Kansas. Mennonites. Ukraine. Warkentin, Bernhard. 1872-1908. *3379*

—. Immigration. Lutheran Church. Minnesota (Isantic County). Social customs. Sweden (Dalarna). 1840-1910. *3329*
—. Indians. Mormons. Nevada. Utah. 1847-60. *4037*
—. Judaism (Reform). Krauskopf, Joseph. Social Reform. 1880's-1923. *4228*
—. Landlords and Tenants. Mississippi. Neoorthodoxy. Protestant Churches. Theologians. 1936-40. *2566*
—. Missions and Missionaries. Politics. Settlement. South Dakota. 1850-1900. *66*
Ahlstrom, Sydney E. Christianity (review article). Handy, Robert T. Historiography. Marty, Martin E. Race (issue). 16c-1978. *2743*
Ahlstrom, Sydney E. (review article). Pluralism. Religious history. 1974. *17*
—. Religious history. 1972. *31*
Ahlstrom, Sydney E. (review essay). Historiography. 17c-1974. *4*
Aitken, Robert. Bible. Continental Congress. English language. Pennsylvania (Philadelphia). Publishers and Publishing. 1782. *1979*
—. Bible. Continental Congress. Publishers and Publishing. 1777-82. *1983*
Alabama. Bakke, Niles J. Lutheran Church. South. Young, Rosa J. 1839-1965. *3299*
—. Baptists. Davis, Harwell G. Howard College. 1882-1973. *3092*
—. Baptists, Southern. Reform. Social issues. 1877-90. *2372*
—. Church schools. Livingston Female Academy. Presbyterian Church. Women. 1835-1910. *686*
—. Clergy. Methodist Episcopal Church (South). Neely, Phillip Phillips. Secession. 1861. *1213*
—. Lutheran Church. Photographs. South. 1971-74. *3347*
—. Protestant Churches. Reconstruction. 1865-67. *457*
Alabama (Aliceville). Baptists, Primitive. Civil rights. Corder, James. Negroes. Personal narratives. 1965-75. *2555*
Alabama (Birmingham). Anti-Catholicism. Anti-Semitism. City Politics. Reform. Social Gospel. 1900-30. *11*
Alabama (Creek Path). American Board of Commissioners for Foreign Missions. Cherokee Indians. Missions and Missionaries. 1820-37. *1546*
Alabama (Mobile). China. Missions and Missionaries. Presbyterian Church. Stuart, Mary Horton. Women. 1840's-1947. *1705*
Alaska *See also* Far Western States.
—. Art. Episcopal Church, Protestant. Missions and Missionaries. Ziegler, Eustace Paul. 1900-69. *1515*
—. Assimilation. Brady, John Green. Economic Conditions. Indian-White Relations. Missions and Missionaries. Tlingit Indians. 1878-1906. *1548*
—. Brady, John Green (and family). Business. Governors. Morality. Presbyterian Church. 1878-1906. *3549*
—. Catholic Church. Holy Cross Mission. Indians. Jesuits. Missions and Missionaries. Sisters of St. Ann. Yukon River, lower. 1887-1956. *1615*
—. Catholic Church. Missionaries. Riobó, Juan Antonio García. Spain. Voyages. 1779. *1643*
—. Church finance. Documents. Education. Orthodox Eastern Church, Russian. Russian-American Company. Veniaminov, Metropolitan Innokentii. 1858. *2806*
—. Diaries. Indian-White Relations. Library of Congress (Alaska Church Collection). Missions and Missionaries. Orlov, Vasilii. Orthodox Eastern Church, Russian. 1886. *1632*
—. Discovery and Exploration. Educators. Episcopal Church, Protestant. Missions and Missionaries. Stuck, Hudson. 1904-20. *1647*
—. Fur trade. Gold rushes. Jews. Nome Hebrew Benevolent Society. 1867-1916. *4103*
—. Prohibition. Women's Christian Temperance Union. 1842-1917. *2596*
Alaska Herald (newspaper). Clergy. Far Western States. Honcharenko, Agapius. Orthodox Eastern Church, Greek. Ukrainian Americans. 1832-1916. *2805*
Alaska (Juneau). Catholic Church. Hospitals. Sisters of St. Ann. 1886-1968. *3757*
Alaska (Kenai Peninsula). Freedom of religion. Orthodox Eastern Church, Russian (Old Believers). Russian Americans. 1920's-76. *2810*
Alaska (Kodiak). Canneries. Fishing. Unification Church. 1978-79. *325*
Alaska (Mary's Igloo). Bernard, Joseph. Catholic Church. Eskimos. Missions and Missionaries. 1884-1962. *1504*
Alaska (Metlakahtla). British Columbia. Capitalism. Duncan, William. Missions and Missionaries. Tsimshian Indians. 1857-1974. *1519*
Albanese, Catherine L. Beecher family. Caskey, Marie. Congregationalism. Connecticut. Massachusetts. Presbyterian Church. Transcendentalism (review article). Unitarianism. 1800-60. *2763*
—. Beecher, Henry Ward. Civil Religion. Clark, Clifford E., Jr. Douglas, Ann. Handy, Robert T. McLoughlin, William G. Reform. Revivals (review article). Women. 1607-1978. *6*
Albany Conference. Adventists. Millerites. New York. 1844-45. *2961*
Albany Diocese. Bishops. Episcopal Church, Protestant. New York. Oldham, George Ashton. 1922-47. *3176*
Alberta *See also* Prairie Provinces.
—. Aberhart, William. Economic reform. Politics. Prime ministers. Radio. 1934-37. *1216*
—. Aberhart, William. Ideology. Provincial Government. Social Credit Party. Theology. 1935-43. *1365*
—. Assimilation. Education. Hutterites. 1920-70. *534*
—. Bible. Blackfoot Indians. Indians. Missions and Missionaries. Stocken, H. W. G. Translating and Interpreting. Wolf Collar (shaman). 1870-1928. *1500*
—. Calgary Diocese. Catholic Church. French Canadians. Irish Canadians. McNailly, John Thomas. 1871-1952. *3712*
—. Communes. Farming. Mennonites. Namaka Farm. 1920's-40's. *414*
—. Hutterites. Nativism. Settlement. 1918-72. *2089*
Alberta (Coaldale). Germans, Russian. Mennonites. Organizations. Social Change. 1920-76. *3411*
Alberta (Edmonton). Catholic Church. Colleges and Universities. MacDonald, John Roderick. St. Joseph's College (Alberta). 1922-23. *710*
—. Church of England. Indians. Métis. Newton, William. 1875-1900. *3196*
—. Hutterites. Public Opinion. Social customs. 1966-75. *3404*
Alberta (Edmonton, Mellowdale). Concordia College. Lutheran Church (Missouri Synod). Personal narratives. Schwermann, Albert H. USA. 1891-1976. *753*
Alberta (Rabbit Hill). Orthodox Eastern Church, Greek. Ukrainian Canadians. 1900. *2808*
Alberta, University of. Catholic Church. Colleges and Universities. Legal, Emile. O'Leary, Henry Joseph. St. Joseph's University College. 1906-26. *619*
Albright, Jacob. Asbury, Francis. Evangelical Association. Methodist Episcopal Church. 1765-1816. *2947*
Albright, William Foxwell. Archaeology. Biblical studies. Philosophy of History. Science. 1918-70. *2328*
Alcohol. Economic development. Gambling. Legislation. 1977. *2383*
Alcott, William A. Christian Physiology. Health. ca 1829-60. *1462*
Alexander, Archibald. Presbyterian Church. Princeton Theological Seminary. Scripture, doctrine of. 1772-1929. *3566*
Alexander, Archibald *(Thoughts on Religious Experience)*. Presbyterian Church. Theology. 1841. *3556*
Alexander Hall (building). New Jersey. Presbyterian Church. Princeton Theological Seminary. 1815. *595*
Alexander, Joseph A. Biblical criticism. Princeton Theological Seminary. Seminaries. Theater. 1830-61. *705*
Alexian Brothers. Bernard, Alexius. Catholic Church. German Americans. Hospitals. Missouri (St. Louis). Tollig, Paulus. 1869-1980. *1456*
Alger, Horatio. Capitalism. Evangelicalism. Literature. Social History. Success (concept of). 1820-1910. *2958*
Algoma Diocese. Episcopal Church, Protestant. Missions and Missionaries. Ontario. Society for the Propagation of the Gospel. 1873-1973. *1653*
Algonkian Indians, northeastern. Indians. Maine. Maritime Provinces. Missionaries. Social change. 1610-1750. *1512*
Algonkin Indians. Architecture. Calvary (chapels). Iroquois Indians. Missionaries. Quebec (Oka). Sulpicians. 1700's-1800's. *1811*
Alienation. Christianity. Converts. Cults. Human potential movement. Social indicators. 1960's-70's. *143*
—. Civil War. Ethnicity. German Americans. Lutheran Church (Missouri Synod). Massacres. Missouri (Concordia). 1864. *3301*
—. Ecumenism. Judaism (Conservative, Reform). Liberalism. Utah (Salt Lake City). 1971. *499*
Alison, Francis. American Revolution. Political philosophy. Presbyterian Church. Witherspoon, John. 1750-87. *1382*
All Saints Church. Church of England. Ontario (Kingston). Theology. Working class. 1867-1906. *3173*
Allegory. Art. Folwell, Samuel *(Sacred to the Illustrious Washington)*. Mourning (theme). Painting. Protestantism. ca 1800. *1885*
Allen, Bennet. Church of England. Colonial Government. Ecclesiastical pluralism. Jordan, John Morton. Maryland. Patronage. Sharpe, Horatio. 1759-70. *1051*
Allen, Ethan. Deism. Franklin, Benjamin. Historiography. Jefferson, Thomas. Palmer, Elihu. 1750-1820. *4277*
A. A. Allen Revival, Incorporated. Arizona (Miracle Valley). Fundamentalism. Language. Popular culture. Revivals. 1970's. *2270*
Allen, Thomas. American Revolution. Chaplains. New England. 1774-77. *2680*
Allen, Thomas ("Vindication"). American Revolution. Clergy. Congregationalism. Constitutions, State. Ideology. Massachusetts (Berkshire County). 1778. *1371*
Alline, Henry. Charisma. Integration. Nova Scotia. Revivals. 1776-83. *2264*
Alma College. Colleges and Universities. Michigan. Presbyterians. 1883-86. *694*
Almanacs. Astronomy. Infinity (concept). New England. Puritanism. 1650-85. *2325*
Alpert, Abraham. Immigration. Judaism. Massachusetts (Boston). Rabbis. 20c. *4087*
Alsace-Lorraine. Batt, Joseph. Catholic Church. Chapel of Our Lady of Help of Christians. Immigration. New York (Buffalo area; Cheektowaga). 1789-1872. *1760*
Alta California. *See* California.
Altar boys. Catholic Church. Clergy. Family. -1974. *3726*
Altarpieces. Christenson, Lars. Folk art. Lutheran Church. Minnesota (Benson). Norwegian Americans. Wood Carving. 1887-1904. *1874*
Amana Society. Communalism. Iowa. 1843-1932. *424*
—. Communalism. Iowa. Shambaugh, Bertha Horak. Wick, Barthinius L. ca 1900-34. *404*
—. Folk art. Iowa. 1843-1932. *1852*
America (periodical). Catholic Church. Colleges and Universities. LaFarge, John. Newman Clubs. 1904-50's. *515*
America (views of). Anti-Communist Movements. Internationalism. Presbyterian Church, United. 1973. *1373*
—. Assimilation. Greek Americans. Papagiannis, Michael D. Personnal narratives. 20c. *2811*
America (weekly). Carranza, Venustiano. Catholic Church. Mexico. Revolution. Tierney, Richard Henry. 1914-17. *3722*
American Academy for Jewish Research. Adler, Cyrus. Intellectuals. Judaism (Orthodox, Reform). Revel, Bernard. Society of Jewish Academicians. 1916-22. *4139*
American Anti-Slavery Society. Female Anti-Slavery Society. Foster, Abigail Kelley. Fox, George. Friends, Society of. Mott, Lucretia Coffin. Segregation. 17c. 1837-66. *791*
American Baptist Historical Society. *Baptist Bibliography*. Samuel Colgate Baptist Historical Library. Starr, Edward Caryl. 1935-76. *263*
—. Baptists. Librarians. Samuel Colgate Baptist Historical Library. Starr, Edward Caryl. 1930's-76. *208*
American Baptist Home Mission Society. Americanization. Baptists. Evangelism. 1832-99. *1599*
—. Baptists. Leadership. Missions and Missionaries. Negroes. Paternalism. Virginia Union University. 1865-1905. *644*
American Baptist Publishing Society. Baptists. Converts. Immigration. Lutheran Church. Sweden. Travel (accounts). Wiberg, Anders. 1852-53. *3054*
American Board of Commissioners for Foreign Missions. Alabama (Creek Path). Cherokee Indians. Missions and Missionaries. 1820-37. *1546*

—. Angola. Church and State. Missions and Missionaries. Portugal. Protestant Churches. Umbundu (tribe). 1880-1922. *1746*
—. Arabic. Bible. Missions and Missionaries. Moslems. Protestantism. Translating and Interpreting. 1843-60. *1740*
—. Assimilation. Connecticut (Cornwall). Foreign Mission School. Indian-White Relations. Students. 1816-27. *586*
—. Ayer, Frederick. Chippewa Indians. Minnesota. Missions and Missionaries. Oberlin College. Red Lake Mission. 1842-59. *1496*
—. Bingham family. Congregationalism. Gilbert Islands. Hawaii. Missions and Missionaries. 1820-1975. *1678*
—. Boutwell, William Thurston. Chippewa Indians. Indian-White Relations. Minnesota. Missions and Missionaries. Protestant Churches. 1831-47. *1572*
—. Brainerd Mission. Cherokee Indians. Education. Indian-White Relations. Letters. Southeastern States. 1817-38. *1605*
—. Cherokee Indians. Georgia. Indian-White Relations. Law Enforcement. Missions and Missionaries. Removals, forced. Worcester, Samuel A. 1831. *1667*
—. Indians. Methodist Church. Missionaries. 1830-50. *1663*
—. Missions and Missionaries. Protestant Churches. Social customs. South Africa. Zulus. 1835-60's. *1695*
American Catholic Historical Association. Catholic Church. History. 1973. *173*
American Christian Palestine Committee. Great Britain. Lobbying. Palestine. Zionism. 1940's. *1316*
American Colonization Society. Africa. Colonization. McDonough, David. Medical Education. Presbyterian Church. Slavery. 1840-50. *2483*
—. Crummell, Alexander. Education. Episcopal Church, Protestant. Liberia. Missions and Missionaries. Negroes. 1853-73. *1671*
—. Finley, Robert. Racism. 1816-40. *2470*
American dream. Christianity. Civil religion. Evil. Myths and Symbols. Theology. 1973. *2724*
American exceptionalism. 1775-1975. *1185*
American experience. Niebuhr, Reinhold. Theology, public. 1974. *2896*
American Free Baptist Mission Society. Abolition Movement. Baptists. Missions and Missionaries. Schisms. 1830-69. *2481*
American Friends Service Committee. Arab-Israeli conflict. Foreign Policy. Friends, Society of. Palestine Liberation Organization. 1970's. *1250*
—. Cadbury, Henry Joel (obituary). Friends, Society of. Historians. 1883-1974. *212*
American Indian Defense Association. Acculturation. Collier, John. Indians. Religious liberty. 1920-26. *1101*
American Institute for Education. Country life. Educational Reform. Elites. Massachusetts. Nationalism. Protestantism. 1830-37. *573*
American Israelite (newspaper). Jews. Letters. Nevada (Eureka). 1875. *4163*
American Jewish Historical Society. Archival catalogs and inventories. Judaism. Rhode Island. 1692-1975. *273*
—. Bibliographies. Jews. 1960-75. *4096*
American League for Peace and Democracy. Methodist Federation for Social Service. Social criticism. Ward, Harry F. 1900-40. *2408*
American Mercury (periodical). Editors and Editing. Ku Klux Klan. Mencken, H. L. Methodist Episcopal Church (South). Temperance Movements. 1910-33. *2033*
American Missionary Association. Civil Rights. Education. Florida. Freedmen. 1864-74. *548*
—. Civil War. Education. Missouri. Negroes. 1862-65. *547*
—. Congregationalism. Education. Freedmen. Georgia (Liberty County). 1870-80's. *549*
—. Congregationalism. Missions and Missionaries. Negroes. South. 1846-80. *1617*
—. Federal agencies. Freedmen. Georgia (Atlanta). Methodist Episcopal Church. Reconstruction. 1865-69. *556*
American Philosophical Association. Catholic Church. Colleges and Universities. Philosophy. Religious Education. 1933-79. *775*
American Protective Association. Anti-Catholicism. Chinese Americans. Guardians of Liberty. Ku Klux Klan. Nativism. Oregon. Racism. ca 1840-1945. *2100*
—. Anti-Catholicism. Church Schools. Indiana. Indians. St. Joseph's Indian Normal School. 1888-96. *57*
American Revolution *See also* Declaration of Independence; Loyalists.
—. Abolition Movement. Letters. Massachusetts (Boston). Wheatley, Phillis. Whigs. 1767-80. *2454*
—. Adams, John. New England. Paine, Thomas. Political theory. Puritans. Rhetoric. 17c-1770's. *1424*
—. Alison, Francis. Political philosophy. Presbyterian Church. Witherspoon, John. 1750-87. *1382*
—. Allen, Thomas. Chaplains. New England. 1774-77. *2680*
—. Allen, Thomas ("Vindication"). Clergy. Congregationalism. Constitutions, State. Ideology. Massachusetts (Berkshire County). 1778. *1371*
—. American Revolution. Cleaveland, John. Congregationalism. Daily life. Great Awakening. Ideology. Jedrey, Christopher M. (review article). Massachusetts (Chebacco). New Lights. 1740-79. *2241*
—. American Revolution. Cleaveland, John. Congregationalism. Daily life. Great Awakening. Ideology. Jedrey, Christopher M. (review article). Massachusetts (Chebacco). New Lights. 1740-79. *2241*
—. Americanization. Church of England. 1775-85. *289*
—. Antislavery Sentiments. Congregationalism. Hopkins, Samuel. Rhode Island (Newport). ca 1770-1803. *2464*
—. Antislavery sentiments. Presbyterian Church. Slavery. 1750-1818. *2493*
—. Arendt, Hannah. Church and state. Ideology. ca 1775-83. *1032*
—. Artifacts. Dutch Americans. Reformed Dutch Church. 17c-18c. *1866*
—. Asbury, Francis. Delaware. Loyalists. Maryland. Methodists. White, Thomas. 1777-80. *3482*
—. Asbury, Francis. Great Britain. Methodism. Wesley, John. 1770-90. *1334*
—. Bailey, Jacob. Church of England. Exiles. Letters. Nova Scotia. 1784. *3226*
—. Baptists. Chaplains. Gano, John. Washington, George. 1727-1804. *2631*
—. Baptists. Church of England. Congregationalism. Friends, Society of. Georgia. Judaism. Lutheran Church. Presbyterian Church. 1733-90. *88*
—. Baptists. Clergy. Georgia. Marshall, Daniel. Political Theory. 1747-1823. *1372*
—. Baptists. Colonies. Great Britain. 1775-83. *1296*
—. Baptists. Constitutions. Massachusetts. 1644-1806. *979*
—. Baptists. Georgia. Mercer, Silas. Politics. Theology. 1770-96. *3030*
—. Baptists. New England. Pennsylvania. Religious liberty. Virginia. 1775-91. *1100*
—. Baptists. Religious liberty. 1775-1800. *1001*
—. Bibliographies. Bicentennial Celebrations. Mennonites. 1776. 1975-76. *3378*
—. Biddle, Owen. Friends, Society of. Lacey, John, Jr. Military Service. Pennsylvania. 1775-83. *2684*
—. Bishops. Chaplains. Church of England. Griffith, David. Virginia Regiment, 3rd. 1774-89. *3235*
—. Boucher, Jonathan. Church of England. Civil War. Great Britain. Jefferson, Thomas. Loyalists. 1640-1797. *1412*
—. Boucher, Jonathan. Church of England. Loyalists. 1763-83. *1383*
—. Brattle Street Church. Calvinism. Congregationalism. Cooper, Samuel. Elites. Massachusetts (Boston). 1754-83. *1333*
—. Brattle Street Church. Clergy. Congregationalism. Cooper, Samuel. Massachusetts (Boston). 1770-80. *951*
—. Brown, Joshua. Friends, Society of. Pacifism. Pennsylvania (Little Britain Township). Prisoners. South Carolina (Ninety Six). 1778. *2633*
—. Burgoyne, John. Friends, Society of. Indians. Pennsylvania (Easton). ca 1776. *3282*
—. California. Indians. Missions. Spain. 1776-83. *1321*
—. Calvinism. Church and state. Clergy. Jefferson, Thomas. Linn, William. Presbyterian Church. 1775-1808. *1335*
—. Calvinism. Eschatology. Paine, Thomas *(Common Sense)*. 1776. *1393*
—. Calvinism. Kuyper, Abraham. Netherlands. Political systems. 1775-83. 19c-1920. *1332*
—. Canada. Church of England. Cossitt, Ranna. Loyalists. Missions and Missionaries. New England. 1773-1815. *1317*
—. Canada. France. Huguenots. Settlement. USA. Whaling industry and Trade. 17c-20c. *3251*
—. Chaplains. Church of England. Washington, George. 1775-83. *2643*
—. Charities. Friends, Society of. Great Britain. Ireland. Pennsylvania (Philadelphia). 1778-97. *2503*
—. Chauncy, Charles. Church and State. Congregationalism. Great Britain. Letters. Price, Richard. Slavery. 1727-87. *3129*
—. Chauncy, Charles. Clergy. Congregationalism. New England. 1770's. *1269*
—. Christian humanism. Political attitudes. Puritans. Values. 18c. *1395*
—. Church and State. Church of England. Clergy. 1775-85. *988*
—. Church and State. Virginia. 1776-86. *1106*
—. Church of England. Clergy. Maryland. Political philosophy. 1770-80. *1388*
—. Church of England. Clergy. Maryland. Politics. Social Status. 1775. *2618*
—. Church of England. Clergy. Patriotism. 1770-85. 1895-98. *982*
—. Church of England. Conspiracies. Llewelyn, John. Loyalists. North Carolina. 1776-77. *1224*
—. Church of England. Continental Congress. Loyalists. Seabury, Samuel (pseud. A. W. Farmer). 1774-84. *1378*
—. Church of England. Delaware (Appoquiniminck). Loyalists. Reading, Philip. Society for the Propagation of the Gospel. 1775-78. *1221*
—. Church of England. Freneau, Philip ("A Political Litany"). Intellectuals. Poetry. 1775. *1998*
—. Church of England. Georgia (Augusta). Loyalists. St. Paul's Parish. Seymour, James. 1775-83. *1301*
—. Church of England. Government, Resistance to. Griffith, David. Sermons. Virginia Convention. 1775. *1351*
—. Church of England. Hughes, Philip. Loyalists. Maryland. 1767-77. *1323*
—. Church of England. Loyalists. 1770-1800. *973*
—. Civil Religion. Theology. 1760-75. *1148*
—. Civilian Service. Moravian Church. Pennsylvania. 1775-1783. *2703*
—. Civilian Service. Moravian Church. Pennsylvania (Bethlehem). 1775-83. *2652*
—. Clergy. Congregationalism. Presbyterian Church. Social status. 1774-1800. *2849*
—. Clergy. Delaware River Valley. Episcopal Church, Protestant. Lutheran Church. Swedish Americans. 1655-1831. *285*
—. Clergy. Loyalists. Lydekker, Gerrit. New York City. Reformed Dutch Church. 1765-94. *977*
—. Congregationalism. Cooper, Samuel. Massachusetts (Boston). Rhetoric. Sermons. 1768-80. *1352*
—. Connecticut (Norfield). Protestantism. Sermons. Sherwood, Samuel. 1776. *1414*
—. Conscientious objectors. Loyalists. Maryland (Elizabethtown). Mennonites. 1774-76. *2665*
—. Constitutionalism. Historiography. Law. Politics. 1775-83. 1790-1950. *961*
—. Cooke, Samuel. History Teaching. Langdon, Samuel. Mayhew, Jonathan. Sermons. West, Samuel. Witherspoon, John. 1750-76. 1975. *1406*
—. Cooper, Samuel. Massachusetts (Boston). Sermons. 1776. *1146*
—. Cummings, Charles. Indians. Presbyterian Church. Virginia, southwest. 1760's-80's. *2634*
—. Daily life. Great Britain. Johnson, Jeremiah. Military Occupation. New York City (Brooklyn). Personal narratives. 1775-83. *63*
—. Delaware Indians. Indians. Missions and Missionaries. Moravian Church. Ohio. Pennsylvania, western. 1775-83. *1532*
—. Diaries. Drinker family. Friends, Society of. Pacifism. Pennsylvania (Philadelphia). Prisoners. Virginia (Winchester). 1777-81. *2683*
—. Documents. Judaism. Letters. 1775-90. *1277*
—. Documents. National character. Presbyterians. 1729-87. *3596*

—. Dunkards. Friends, Society of. Mennonites. Moravian Church. Neutrality. Pacifism. Schwenkfelders. Taxation. 1765-83. *2670*
—. Dunkards. Loyalists. Mennonites. Pacifism. 1776-84. *2635*
—. Dutch Americans. New Jersey. New York. Reformed Dutch Church. 1775-83. *1208*
—. Dutch Americans. Reformed Dutch Church. 1740-90. *1227*
—. Education. Great Awakening. Pluralism. Theology. 1776. *1386*
—. Environment. Literature. Millenarianism. Symbolism in Literature. 1770's-1800. *1192*
—. Episcopal Church, Protestant. New York. Nonconformists. Political Factions. Provincial government. 1768-71. *1294*
—. Evangelism. Great Awakening. Protestantism. 1770-1800. *2267*
—. Excommunication. Funk, Christian. Mennonites (Funkite). Pennsylvania (Indian Field). 1760-1809. *3376*
—. Factionalism. Reformed Dutch Church. 1650-1840. *1211*
—. Folk religion. National Characteristics. Pennsylvania Germans. 1775-83. *2948*
—. Free Quakers. Friends, Society of. 1774-83. *2668*
—. Freedom. Liberation movements. Political Attitudes. Theology. 1765-20c. *1342*
—. Friends, Society of. Loyalists. Pennsylvania (Philadelphia). 1770's. *1282*
—. Friends, Society of. Pennsylvania (Philadelphia). Reform. 1741-90. *2674*
—. Georgia. Historians. Hymns. Moravian Church. Neisser, George. New York. Pennsylvania, eastern. ca 1735-84. *197*
—. Georgia (Savannah). Patriotism. Presbyterian Church. Zubly, John Joachim. 1766-81. *985*
—. German Americans. Lutherans. Pennsylvania (Philadelphia). 1776-81. *1304*
—. Germany. *Heinrich Mullers Pennsylvanischer Staatsbote* (newspaper). Moravian Church. Muller, Johann Heinrich. Pennsylvania (Philadelphia). Printing. 1722-82. *3514*
—. Great Awakening. Social Classes. Social theory. Urbanization. 1740's-70's. *2230*
—. Great Britain. Judaism (Orthodox). Rhode Island. Touro, Isaac. 1782. *4184*
—. Great Britain. Loyalists. Methodism. Poetry. Political Commentary. Wesley, Charles. 1775-83. *1339*
—. Great Britain. Methodism. Plagiarism. Politics. Wesley, John *(A Calm Address to our American Colonies)*. 1775-79. *1377*
—. Great Britain. Methodism. Political Attitudes. Wesley, John. Whigs, Radical. 1775-78. *1391*
—. Great Britain. Methodism. Wesley, John. 1760-89. *1404*
—. Great Britain. Nonconformists. 1765-83. *1401*
—. Great Britain. Wesley, John. 1775. *1336*
—. Great Britain. Wesley, John *(A Calm Address to our American Colonies)*. 1770-76. *1340*
—. Green, Jacob. New Jersey. Politics. 1770-90. *1398*
—. Hawthorne, Nathaniel. Literature. National character. Puritan Tradition. 1775-83. 1830-40. *2082*
—. Historiography. 1760-89. 1970-80. *952*
—. Historiography. 18c-20c. *9*
—. Historiography. Millenarianism. Nationalism. Patriotism. Politics. 1740-89. *1347*
—. Historiography. New Jersey. New York. Pennsylvania. Social conditions. 1680-1790's. 1960's-70's. *59*
—. Historiography. Protestant Churches. 1775-82. *1396*
—. Ideology. Literature. Puritans. 1775-83. 19c. *1344*
—. Immigrants. Presbyterian Church. Scotch-Irish. Scottish Americans. 1700-75. *1268*
—. Indian-white relations. Mahican Indians (Stockbridge). Massachusetts (Stockbridge). 1680-1776. *1481*
—. Mormon, Book of. Mormons. Political attitudes. Smith, Joseph. 1820's. *1353*
—. New Jersey (Hackensack). New York City. Reformed Dutch Church (coetus, conferentie). 1750-83. *1311*
—. Pennsylvania (Middle Octorara). Presbyterian Church. 1740-83. *969*
—. Political attitudes. Presbyterians. Princeton University. 1765-76. *960*
—. Puritanism. 1630-1776. *956*
—. Washington, George. 1761-99. *1147*
American Revolution (antecedents). Adams, John. Church of England. Letters. Weller, George. 1770's. 1824-25. *971*
—. Benefices. Church of England. New England. Religious Liberty. Society for the Propagation of the Gospel. 1689-1775. *1054*
—. Business. Friends, Society of. Leadership. Pennsylvania (Philadelphia). Radicals and radicalism. 1769-74. *1293*
—. Church and state. Connecticut. Devotion, Ebenezer. Politics. Theology. 1714-71. *1397*
—. Church of England. Colonial Government. Great Britain. Political theory. Shipley, Jonathan. 1773-75. *1376*
—. Civil religion. Edwards, Jonathan. Great Awakening. King George's War. Millenarianism. 1740-76. *1169*
—. Clergy. Political theory. Sermons. 1750's-75. *1415*
—. Conscientious Objectors. Dunkards. Mennonites. Pennsylvania. Petitions. 1775. *2710*
—. Great Awakening. Individualism. Pietism. Republicanism. 1735-75. *1385*
—. Great Awakening. Liberalism. Social Change. Social theory. ca 1725-75. *1338*
—. Republicanism. Revivals. Rhetoric. 1730-75. *1993*
American, Sadie. Congress of Jewish Women. Jews. Solomon, Hannah G. Women. World Parliament of Religions. World's Columbian Exposition (Chicago, 1893). 1893. *846*
American Seamen's Friend Society. Evangelicalism. Merchant Marine. Ports. 1828-38. *2376*
American Studies. Archives. Catholic University of America. Documents. Kenrick, Francis P. Missions and Missionaries. 1776-1865. *216*
—. Colleges and Universities. Great Britain. Theses. 1975-76. *46*
American Tract Society. Evangelicalism. Missions and Missionaries. Pennsylvania, western. Wright, Elizur, Jr. 1828-29. *1536*
American Union for the Relief and Improvement of the Colored Race. Congregationalism. Emancipation. Massachusetts (Boston). Reform. 1835-37. *2490*
Americanism. Acculturation. Catholic Church. Leo XIII, Pope (*Testem Benevolentiae*). Periodicals. Protestantism. 1899. *319*
Americanization. American Baptist Home Mission Society. Baptists. Evangelism. 1832-99. *1599*
—. American Revolution. Church of England. 1775-85. *289*
—. Asbury, Francis. Methodism. Social Change. 1766-1816. *286*
—. Attitudes. New England. Pilgrims. 17c. *323*
—. Benedictines. Germany. Monasticism. Switzerland. 1846-1900. *314*
—. Catholic Church. Church and state. Europe. Maryland. Religious liberty. ca 1634-1786. *304*
—. Catholic Church. Clergy. Irish Americans. Polish Americans. 1920-40's. *290*
—. Catholic Church. Connecticut (New Britain). Polish Americans. 1890-1955. *3692*
—. Catholic Church. Ecumenism. Europe. Pluralism. Theology. 1775-1820. *295*
—. Catholic Church. French Canadians. Hendricken, Thomas F. Irish Americans. Massachusetts (Fall River). 1870's-85. *317*
—. Catholic Church. French language. Vermont. 1917-75. *308*
—. Catholic Church. Historiography. 1850-1973. *299*
—. Catholics. Church attendance. Ethnicity. New York City. -1974. *3810*
—. Christianity. Janes, Leroy Lansing. Japan (Kumamoto). Missions and Missionaries. Presbyterian Church. 1838-76. *1732*
—. Church of England. Great Britain. North Carolina. Parishes. 1701-12. *298*
—. Church Schools. German language. Lutheran Church (Missouri Synod). Nebraska Council of Defense. Supreme Court. 1917-23. *305*
—. Ecumenism. Episcopal Church, Protestant. Lutheran Church, Swedish. Swedish Americans. 1630-1850. *322*
—. Episcopal Church, Protestant. Pennsylvania (Philadelphia). White, William. ca 1789-1836. *324*
—. Evangelical Covenant Church. Evangelical Free Church of America. Methodism. Pentecostal movement. Salvation Army. Swedish Baptist Church. 1870-1973. *321*
—. German Americans. 19c. *297*
—. Judaism. Law. Rabbis. Rabbis (responsa). Social customs. 1862-1937. *300*
—. Methodist Episcopal Church. Missions and Missionaries. Norway. Petersen, Ole Peter. 1830-53. *1706*
—. Missions and Missionaries. Protestant Churches. Puerto Rico. 1898-1917. *1734*
Americas (North and South). Antislavery Sentiments. Dominicans. Jesuits. 16c-18c. *2486*
Ames Church. Education. Freedmen. Hartzell, Joseph C. Methodist Episcopal Church. Missionaries. Republican Party. South. 1870-73. *3481*
Ames, Jessie Daniel. Association of Southern Women for the Prevention of Lynching. Lynching. Methodist Woman's Missionary Council. Racism. South. Women. Young Women's Christian Association. 1930's. *2535*
Amherst College. Calvinism. Massachusetts. Meiklejohn, Alexander. 1912-23. *601*
Amish. Agriculture. Economic conditions. Illinois. Social organization. 1960-72. *3428*
—. Baptism. Pennsylvania (Lancaster, Mifflin counties). Stoltzfus, John. Tennessee. 1820-74. *3438*
—. Church History. Documents. Pennsylvania (Morgantown). Plank, D. Heber. 1668-1790's. 20c. *3388*
—. Clergy. *Herald der Wahrheit* (newspaper). Kansas (Reno County). Mast, Daniel E. 1886-1930. *3405*
—. Deviant Behavior. Social Organization. 1977. *3429*
—. Doukhobors. Hutterites. Mennonites. Molokans. North America. ca 1650-1977. *2769*
—. Education. Military. Pennsylvania. Trials. Wisconsin. 1755-1974. *3401*
—. Fertility. Income. Indiana. Women. 20c. *882*
—. Folk Art. Mennonites. Pennsylvania. Persecution. Quiltmaking. 16c-1935. *1893*
—. Folk medicine. Magic. Mennonites. Pennsylvania. Powwowing. ca 1650-1979. *2206*
—. France (Alsace). Germany (Palatinate). Immigrants. Pennsylvania. 1693-1803. *3406*
—. Genealogy. Pennsylvania. Zug family. 1718-1886. *3441*
—. Indiana (Allen County). Mennonites. Social Organization. 1850-1950. *3412*
—. Land use. Mennonites. Mormons. Pennsylvania (Intercourse). Theology. Utah (Escalante). 1973. *2767*
—. Mennonites. Revivals. 1860-90. *2255*
—. Pennsylvania (Lancaster County). Schisms. Stoltzfus, John. Theology. 1850-77. *3439*
Amish, Beachy. Iowa. 1920-77. *3423*
Amish, Old Order. Betz, Hans. German language. Hymnals. 16c-20c. *1946*
—. Church schools. Pennsylvania (Lancaster County). 1937-73. *626*
—. Daily Life. Diaries. Farms. King family. Loomis, Charles P. Pennsylvania (Lancaster County). 1940. *3403*
—. Ethnicity. Kansas, central. 1956-78. *3394*
—. Hutterites. Mennonites. Social change. ca 1930-77. *3357*
—. Hutterites. Minorities. Research. 1977. *3363*
—. Settlement. 1717-1977. *3355*
—. Social Change. Tradition. ca 1650-1976. *3384*
Amnesty *See also* Military Service.
—. Ethics. Vietnam War. 1974. *2704*
—. Loyalists. Massachusetts. Property. Public Opinion. 1783-84. *1357*
Amusements. Georgia. Jones, Sam. Methodist Episcopal Church, South. Morality. Revivals. Self-reliance. 1872-1906. *3498*
Anabaptists. Bibliographies. Dissertations. Mennonites. 1975-76. *3397*
—. Bibliographies. Mennonites. 16c-1975. *3396*
—. Bibliographies. Mennonites. 16c-20c. 1977-78. *3387*
—. Germany. Mennonites. Switzerland. Taxation. War. 16c-1973. *2662*
—. Methodism. Pennsylvania, central. 1815-1942. *2880*
—. Reformation. Theology. 16c. 1945-77. *3408*
Anarchism and Anarchists *See also* Communism.
—. Church and State. Lum, Dyer D. Mormons. 1880's. *4010*
Anderson, George Edward. Mormons. Photography. Utah, southern. 1877-1928. *3970*

Anderson, Isaac. Abolition Movement. Presbyterian Church. Southern and Western Theological Seminary. Tennessee (Maryville). 1819-50's. *723*
Anderson, James T. M. Anti-Catholicism. Public schools. Saskatchewan. School Act (Saskatchewan, 1930; amended). Secularization. 1929-34. *575*
Anderson, P. Harris. Baptists. Georgia. Harris, Rufus C. Mercer University. 1965-76. *3033*
Andersson, Joris Per. Letters. Lutheran Church. Minnesota (Chisago Lake). Swedish Americans. 1851-53. *3312*
Andover Seminary. Abolition Movement. Congregationalism. Massachusetts. Seminaries. Theology. 1825-35. *2491*
Andover-Harvard Theological Library. Manuscripts. Massachusetts. Unitarianism. Universalism. 1800-1925. *256*
Andrews, John. Clergy. Education. Episcopal Academy. Pennsylvania, University of. 1765-1810. *507*
Andrews, Joseph. Art. Massachusetts (Boston). Society of the New Jerusalem. Swedenborgianism. 1830-73. *4062*
Anesthesia. Adventists. California. Dentistry. Jorgensen, Niels Bjorn. Loma Linda University. Teaching. 1923-74. *1441*
"Angel Dancers". Communalism. Folklore. Howell, Jane. Huntsman, Manson T. New Jersey (Woodcliff). Rumors. Sects, Religious. 1890-1920. *389*
Angers, François-Albert. Canada. Catholic Church. French Canadians. Pacifism. Values. 1940-79. *2654*
Anglican Communion *See also* Church of England; Episcopal Church, Protestant.
—. Anticlericalism. Church and State. Parsons' Cause. Virginia. 1730-60. *1058*
—. Architecture. Chancels. Ecclesiology Society. Great Britain (Cambridge). 1839-60. *1779*
—. Autobiography. Cree Indians. Faries, Richard. Missions and Missionaries. Ontario (York Factory). 1896-1961. *1528*
—. Bibliographies. 1972. *3232*
—. Bibliographies. Great Britain. 1973-75. *3233*
—. Canada. Education. Great Britain. Missionaries. Protestantism. Sudan Interior Mission. 1937-55. *1741*
—. Catholic Church. Ecumenism. Hughes, John Jay. Religious Orders. -1973. *493*
—. Ethics. Great Britain. 16c-20c. *3182*
—. Manitoba (Red River). Missions and Missionaries. Women. 1820-37. *1750*
—. Massachusetts (Cambridge). Smyth, Frederick Hastings *(Manhood into God)*. Society of the Catholic Commonwealth. Theology. Utopias. 1940. *3200*
Anglican Congress. Ecumenism. Gray, Walter H. Minnesota (Minneapolis). 1940-54. *476*
Anglin, Timothy Warren. Canada. Catholic Church. Debates. Fenian Brotherhood. Irish Canadians. McGee, D'Arcy. 1863-68. *1341*
—. Catholic Church. Irish Canadians. New Brunswick. Newspapers. St. John *Freeman* (newspaper). 1849-83. *3680*
Anglo-Catholics. Catholic Church. Clergy. Ecumenism. Episcopal Church, Protestant. *Lamp* (periodical). Wattson, Paul James. 1903-09. *460*
Anglophiles. Catholic Church. Francophiles. Mathieu, Olivier-Elzéar. Regina Diocese. Saskatchewan. 1905-30. *3714*
—. Catholic Church. Wilberforce, Robert. World War II (antecedents). 1940. *1239*
Anglophones. Catholics. Church Discipline. Church History. Francophones. Morality. Prairie Provinces. 1900-30. *3715*
—. Catholics. French Canadians. Langevin, Adélard. Manitoba. Winnipeg Archdiocese. 1905. *3711*
Anglo-Saxonism. Interventionism. Protestantism. Reform. Strong, Josiah. 1885-1915. *2418*
Angola. American Board of Commissioners for Foreign Missions. Church and State. Missions and Missionaries. Portugal. Protestant Churches. Umbundu (tribe). 1880-1922. *1746*
Animal magnetism. Hypnotism. Mesmerism. Mormons. 19c. *2303*
Annexation. Catholic Church. Converts. Imperialism. Methodist Episcopal Church. Missions and Missionaries. Philippines. 1899-1913. *1689*
—. Church and state. Idaho, southern. Legislation. Mormons. Nevada. Stewart, William. Suffrage. 1887-88. *1089*
Annulments. Birth Control. Canon law. Catholic Church. Divorce. Netherlands. 1945-77. *914*
Anthropology *See also* Acculturation; Archaeology; Ethnology; Language; Race Relations; Social Change.
—. Archaeology. Indians. Lost Tribes of Israel. Mormons. Smith, Joseph. 1830. *2335*
—. Death and dying. Memorial Day. Social Customs. 1945-74. *90*
—. Historiography. Massachusetts (Salem). Psychology. Puritans. Witchcraft. 1691-92. *2187*
Anti-Bigamy Act (US, 1862). Mormons. Wealth. Young, Brigham. 1847-77. *341*
Anti-Catholicism. Alabama (Birmingham). Anti-Semitism. City Politics. Reform. Social Gospel. 1900-30. *11*
—. American Protective Association. Chinese Americans. Guardians of Liberty. Ku Klux Klan. Nativism. Oregon. Racism. ca 1840-1945. *2100*
—. American Protective Association. Church Schools. Indiana. Indians. St. Joseph's Indian Normal School. 1888-96. *57*
—. Anderson, James T. M. Public schools. Saskatchewan. School Act (Saskatchewan, 1930; amended). Secularization. 1929-34. *575*
—. Antichrist. Edwards, Jonathan. Mather, Cotton. Potter, Francis. Puritans. ca 1700-58. *2937*
—. Anti-Semitism. Attitudes. Ku Klux Klan. Morality. Ohio (Youngstown). Reform. 1920's. *2402*
—. Anti-Semitism. Colorado (Denver). Ku Klux Klan. Protestantism. Social Classes. 1921-25. *2609*
—. Anti-Semitism. Conspiracy theories. Fundamentalism. Kansas. Political Commentary. Winrod, Gerald Burton. 1933-57. *2090*
—. Anti-Semitism. Education. Minorities. North Carolina. Prejudice. Religious beliefs. 1957-73. *2093*
—. Antislavery Sentiments. Bannan, Benjamin. Nativism. Pennsylvania (Schuylkill County). Temperance Movements. Whig Party. 1852-54. *1238*
—. Antislavery sentiments. Ideology. Massachusetts (Boston). Riots. Social Classes. Ursulines. 1834-35. *2109*
—. Antislavery Sentiments. Know-Nothing Party. Massachusetts. Republican Party. Voting and Voting Behavior. 1850's. *1201*
—. Arizona. Ku Klux Klan. Morality. 1921-25. *2094*
—. Attitudes. Independence Movements. Latin America. Protestant churches. 1810-25. *2107*
—. Bapst, John. Chaney, William Henry. Editors and editing. Jesuits. Maine (Ellsworth). Nativism. 1853-54. *2121*
—. Baptists. Fundamentalism. Morality. Norris, J. Frank. Texas. 1920's. *2889*
—. Baptists, Southern. 1920's. *2119*
—. Benedictines. D'Equivelley, G. F. Florida (Pasco County). *Jeffersonian* (newspaper). Land. Letters-to-the-editor. Mohr, Charles. 1915-16. *2123*
—. Breslin, Jimmy. Brooklyn Diocese. Flaherty, Joe. Hamill, Pete. Irish Americans. New York City. Novels. 1960's-70's. *2098*
—. Bryan, Nathan P. Catts, Sidney J. Democratic Party. Florida. Political Campaigns (gubernatorial). Primaries (senatorial). Trammell, Park M. 1915-16. *1258*
—. California (San Francisco). City Politics. Know-Nothing Party. People's Party. Vigilance Committee. 1854-56. *1307*
—. Canada. Italy. Political Attitudes. Protestants. Risorgimento. 1846-60. *2114*
—. Capitalism. DeLeon, Daniel. Socialism. 1891-1914. *2113*
—. Catts, Sidney J. Elections (gubernatorial). Florida. Guardians of Liberty. Knott, William V. Sturkie Resolution. 1916. *1231*
—. Cheverus, Jean Louis Lefebvre de. Daley, Dominic. Halligan, James. Irish Americans. Massachusetts (Northampton). Protestantism. Trials. 1805-06. *2097*
—. Cheverus, Jean Louis Lefebvre de. Irish Americans. Lyon, Marcus. Massachusetts (Northampton). Murder. Protestantism. Trials. 1805-06. *2099*
—. Chicago *Tribune* (newspaper). Editors and Editing. Illinois. Political Parties. 1853-61. *2112*
—. Chicopee Manufacturing Company. Immigration. Irish Americans. Massachusetts (Chicopee). Mills. Nativism. Protestantism. 1830-75. *2103*
—. Chiniquy, Charles P. T. Lincoln, Abraham. 1855-65. *2105*
—. Church and State. Clergy. Education, Finance. MacKinnon, Murdoch. Presbyterian Church. Saskatchewan. School Act (Saskatchewan, 1930; amended). Scott, Walter. 1913-26. *528*
—. Church and state. Cox Library. Discrimination. *Koester* v. *Pardeeville* (1929). Libraries. Taxation. Wisconsin (Pardeeville). 1927-29. *1033*
—. Church and state. Ethnic groups. Evangelism. Protestantism. Quebec (Lower Canada). Rebellion of 1837. 1766-1865. *2110*
—. Church of England. Gavin, Anthony *(A Master-Key to Popery)*. Great Britain. Literature. Virginia. 1724-73. *2108*
—. City Politics. Ethnic groups. Immigrants. Ohio (Cincinnati). Temperance Movements. 1845-60. *2584*
—. Civil Rights. Irish Canadians. Law. Nova Scotia (Halifax). 1749-1829. *1105*
—. Clergy. Ku Klux Klan. Protestantism. Republican Party. Rhode Island. 1915-32. *2116*
—. Colleges and Universities. Discrimination, Educational. Ethnic Groups. 1970's. *2106*
—. Colonization. Great Britain. Ideology. Ireland. North America. Protestantism. ca 1550-1600. *2086*
—. Congregationalism. Cox, Samuel Hanson. Ecumenism. Episcopal Church, Protestant. Evangelicalism. Presbyterian Church, New School. Slavery. 1840's. *471*
—. Conscription, Military. Jesuits. Novitiate of St. Stanislaus. Ontario (Guelph). Protestantism. World War I. 1918-19. *2657*
—. Constitutional Law. Ireland. Irish Americans. O'Conor, Charles. O'Conor, Charles Owen. Political reform. Reconstruction. 1865-85. *1031*
—. District of Columbia. Marquette, Jacques. State Politics. Statuary Hall. Wisconsin. 1887-1904. *2101*
—. Elections (presidential). Ethnic Groups. Nativism. Ohio (Cleveland). Republican Party. 1860. *1265*
—. Fillmore, Millard. Know-Nothing Party. Nativism. Political Campaigns (presidential). Whig Party. 1850-56. *1305*
—. France. Maryland. Politicians. Protestants. 1750's. *2095*
—. Georgia. Letters. Roosevelt, Theodore. Watson, Thomas E. 1915. *2104*
—. Georgia (Atlanta). Ku Klux Klan. School boards. 1916-27. *2115*
—. Great Britain. Irish Canadians. Ontario. Orange Order. Patriotism. 1830-1900. *2111*
—. Irish Americans. Urbanization. 1920's. *2102*
—. Know-Nothing Party. 1853-56. *1246*
—. Know-Nothing Party. Massachusetts. Republican Party. Voting and Voting Behavior. 1850's. *1209*
—. Know-Nothing Party. Political Leadership. Thompson, Richard W. 1850's. *1291*
—. Know-Nothing Party. Religious Liberty. 1770's-1850's. *2934*
—. Ku Klux Klan. Protestants. Saskatchewan. 1927-30. *2096*
—. Manitoba (Red River country). O'Beirne, Eugene Francis. Travel. 1860's. *2120*
—. Maryland. Servants. Slave Revolts. 1745-58. *2117*
—. New Brunswick. Pitts, Herman H. Religion in the Public Schools. 1871-90. *574*
Antichrist. Anti-Catholicism. Edwards, Jonathan. Mather, Cotton. Potter, Francis. Puritans. ca 1700-58. *2937*
Anti-Christian sentiments. Christianity. Cochran, Jacob. Free love. Maine (York County). Society of Free Brethren and Sisters. 1817-19. *89*
Anticlericalism. Anglican Communion. Church and State. Parsons' Cause. Virginia. 1730-60. *1058*
—. Bible. Deism. Jefferson, Thomas. Jesus Christ. Translating and Interpreting. 1813-20. *4279*
—. Church of England. Great Britain. Virginia. ca 1635-1783. *3238*
—. Enlightenment. Europe. Protestantism. Revivals. 1640's-1830's. *2912*
Anti-Communist Movements. America (views of). Internationalism. Presbyterian Church, United. 1973. *1373*

—. Catholic Church. Crosby, Donald F. Labor Unions and Organizations. McCarthy, Joseph R. (review article). Oshinsky, David. 1950-54. 1976-78. *1212*
—. Dulles, John Foster. Ecumenism. Morality. Oxford Conference (1937). Presbyterian Church. Protestantism. World order movement. 1937-48. *1375*
Antievolution Law (1928). Arkansas. Church and state. Courts. Epperson, Susan. Evolution. Initiatives. 1900's-68. *2322*
Antifederalists. Constitutions. Federalists. Religious liberty. 1776-92. *1010*
Antigonish Movement. Catholic Church. Nova Scotia. Rural Development. Social change. ca 1928-73. *2409*
Anti-Imperialism *See also* Imperialism; Nationalism.
—. Baptists, American. Horr, George. Spanish-American War. Vietnam War. *Watchman.* 1876-1974. *2698*
Anti-Masonic movement. Baptists. Freemasonry. Morgan, William. New York, western. 1826-30. *2362*
—. Radicals and radicalism. 1820's. *1236*
Antimodernism. Christianity. Ecumenism. Theology. 1975. *2734*
Antinomian Controversy. Church and state. Hutchinson, Anne. Massachusetts. Puritans. Social Organization. Trials. Women. 1637. *1135*
—. Cotton, John. Hutchinson, Anne. Massachusetts. Sermons. Shepard, Thomas. Theology. 1630's. *3648*
—. Cotton, John. Hutchinson, Anne. Massachusetts (Boston). Puritans. 1636. *3652*
—. Feminism. Hutchinson, Anne. Massachusetts. 1630-43. *867*
—. Hutchinson, Anne. Language. Massachusetts. Puritans. Trials. 1636-38. *3609*
—. Hutchinson, Anne. Massachusetts (Boston). Puritans. Trials. Winthrop, John. 1634-38. *3641*
Antinomianism. Bible. Campbell, Alexander. Disciples of Christ. 1810-60. *3109*
—. Cotton, John. Eliot, John. Government. Millenarianism. Missions and Missionaries. New England. Puritans. Rhode Island (Portsmouth). 1630-90. *3635*
—. Emerson, Ralph Waldo. Puritanism. Sermons. Social reform. Transcendentalism. 1820's-30's. *4070*
Antireligious Movements. Communism. Social gospel. USSR. 1921-26. *104*
Anti-Semitism *See also* Jews.
—. Alabama (Birmingham). Anti-Catholicism. City Politics. Reform. Social Gospel. 1900-30. *11*
—. Anti-Catholicism. Attitudes. Ku Klux Klan. Morality. Ohio (Youngstown). Reform. 1920's. *2402*
—. Anti-Catholicism. Colorado (Denver). Ku Klux Klan. Protestantism. Social Classes. 1921-25. *2609*
—. Anti-Catholicism. Conspiracy theories. Fundamentalism. Kansas. Political Commentary. Winrod, Gerald Burton. 1933-57. *2090*
—. Anti-Catholicism. Education. Minorities. North Carolina. Prejudice. Religious beliefs. 1957-73. *2093*
—. Boxerman, William I. Coughlin, Charles Edward. Documents. Michigan (Detroit). 1939. *2131*
—. California (Fresno). Foote, William D. Johnson, Grove L. Trials. 1893. *2134*
—. California (San Francisco). D'Ancona, David Arnold. Letters. Newspapers. Pixley, Frank M. 1883. *2128*
—. Christianity. 1964. *2133*
—. Christians. Toynbee, Arnold. World War II. ca 1940-1975. *2130*
—. Deprogramming. Moon, Sun Myung. Unification Church. 1946-76. *4269*
—. Drama. Literature. Stereotypes. 1830's-1920's. *2011*
—. Europe, Eastern. Immigration. Riis, Jacob. 1890-1914. *2132*
—. Evangelicals. Fundamentalists. Jews. Messianic beliefs. 1970's. *135*
—. Fiction. Fiedler, Leslie. Judaism. Personal narratives. 1970's. *2043*
Antislavery Sentiments *See also* Abolition Movement; Proslavery Sentiments.
—. American Revolution. Congregationalism. Hopkins, Samuel. Rhode Island (Newport). ca 1770-1803. *2464*
—. American Revolution. Presbyterian Church. Slavery. 1750-1818. *2493*
—. Americas (North and South). Dominicans. Jesuits. 16c-18c. *2486*
—. Anti-Catholicism. Bannan, Benjamin. Nativism. Pennsylvania (Schuylkill County). Temperance Movements. Whig Party. 1852-54. *1238*
—. Anti-Catholicism. Ideology. Massachusetts (Boston). Riots. Social Classes. Ursulines. 1834-35. *2109*
—. Anti-Catholicism. Know-Nothing Party. Massachusetts. Republican Party. Voting and Voting Behavior. 1850's. *1201*
—. Barbados. Curwen, Alice. Friends, Society of. Letters. 1675-76. *2458*
—. Benezet, Anthony. Friends, Society of. 1759-84. *2461*
—. British North America. Friends, Society of. Social problems. Woolman, John. 1720-72. *2371*
—. Campbell, Alexander. Civil religion. Disciples of Christ. Indians. Politics. War. Women. 1823-55. *3108*
—. Catholic Church. Emigration. Germans, Sudeten. Journalism. Missions and Missionaries. Neumann, Saint John Nepomucene. Republican Party. 19c-20c. *3826*
—. Christianity. Civil War. Presbyterian Church. Stowe, Harriet Beecher. Women. ca 1850-80. *2474*
—. Civil War. Episcopal Church, Protestant. Jay, John, II. 1840-65. *2494*
—. Civil War. Friends, Society of (Congregational). Jones, James Parnell. Maine. Military Service. 1850's-64. *2641*
—. Clergy. Kentucky. Racism. 1791-1824. *2455*
—. Congregationalism. Connecticut. Dwight, Theodore. Poetry. 1788-1829. *2468*
—. Davies, Samuel. Great Awakening. Presbyterian Church. Virginia. 1740-59. *2238*
—. Editors and Editing. Kansas. Newspapers. Providence. Rhetoric. 1855-58. *2034*
—. Eliot, Samuel A. Fugitive Slave Act (US, 1850). Massachusetts (Boston). Patriotism. Unitarianism. 1850-60. *4085*
—. Evangelicalism. Great Britain. 1846. *2893*
—. Evangelicalism. South. 1820-30. *2489*
—. Friends, Society of. Great Britain. Libertarianism. Radicals and Radicalism. 18c-1865. *2497*
—. Friends, Society of. Lay, Benjamin. Pennsylvania (Philadelphia). 1690's-1759. *2460*
—. Friends, Society of. North America. 1671-1771. *2480*
—. Great Britain. Reform. 18c-19c. *2457*
—. Integration. Ohio (Cincinnati). Presbyterian Church, Reformed. Reformed Presbyterian Theological Seminary. 1845-49. *610*
—. New England. Puritans. 1652-1795. *2485*
—. Ohio. Political attitudes. Revivals. Voting and Voting Behavior. 1825-70. *2866*
Antiwar Sentiment *See also* Peace Movements.
—. Butler, Smedley. Courts Martial and Courts of Inquiry. Friends, Society of (Hicksite). Marines. 1881-1940. *2637*
—. Catholic Association for International Peace. Peace movements. 1917-68. *2673*
—. Clergy. Protestant churches. Vietnam War. ca 1966-73. *2700*
Apache Indians. Cheyenne Indians. Darlington Agency. Friends, Society of. Indian Territory. Indians (agencies). 1868-86. *3278*
Apes, William. Indian-white relations. Massachusetts (Mashpee). Methodist Church. Reform. Wampanoag Indians. 1830-40. *2546*
Aphrodisiacs. Charms. Folk Medicine. Philtres. Witchcraft. -1973. *2199*
Apocalypse. Bible (Revelation). Edwards, Jonathan. Providence. Theology. 1720-24. *3148*
—. Folklore. Mormons. 19c-20c. *4021*
—. Guyana (Jonestown). Jones, Jim. People's Temple. 1953-78. *4252*
Apocalypticism. Counter culture. Philosophy of History. 1950-73. *148*
Apostolic Delegates. Catholic Church. Conroy, George. Nationalism. Politics. Quebec. Vatican. 1877-78. *1098*
Appalachia. Attitudes. Baptists, Southern. Fundamentalism. 1966-77. *3034*
—. Baptists. Lifestyles. Methodism. Presbyterian Church. 1788-1974. *2873*
—. Baptists, Old Regular. Daily life. 19c-20c. *3070*
—. Baptists, Primitive. Folklore. Theology. 1800's-1977. *3083*
—. Bibliographies. Protestantism. 1905-75. *2879*
—. Folk Religion. Pentecostal Movement. Snakehandlers. 1974. *3519*
—. Folklore. Hymns. 18c-20c. *1927*
Appalachia, southern. Ballads. Calendar, Gregorian. "Christmas, Old". Social customs. 1753-1977. *2955*
—. Hensley, George Went. Pentecostal Holiness Church. Snakehandlers. 1909-73. *3522*
—. Pentecostals. Rites and ceremonies. Snakehandlers. Trances. 1909-74. *3523*
Appleby, William. Calligraphy. Mormons. Simmons, Joseph M. Young, Brigham. 1851-53. *1895*
Appleton, Thomas Gold. Calvinism. James, Henry. New England Conscience (term). Unitarianism. 1875-95. *4075*
Appointments to office. Baptists. Georgia, University of (chancellor). Hill, Walter B. Methodists. 1897-1901. *536*
Arabic. American Board of Commissioners for Foreign Missions. Bible. Missions and Missionaries. Moslems. Protestantism. Translating and Interpreting. 1843-60. *1740*
Arab-Israeli conflict. American Friends Service Committee. Foreign Policy. Friends, Society of. Palestine Liberation Organization. 1970's. *1250*
Arabs. Missions and Missionaries. Nationalism. Syria. 1842-1918. *1670*
Arapaho Indians. Acculturation. Cheyenne Indians. Indians. Mennonites. Missions and Missionaries. 1880-1900. *1557*
—. Haury, Samuel S. Indian Territory. Letters. Mennonites. Missions and Missionaries. 1876-80. *1543*
Ararat (colony). Judaism (Orthodox). New York. Noah, Mordecai Manuel. Rhode Island (Newport). 1813-21. *4178*
Archaeology *See also* Anthropology; Artifacts; Excavations; Indians; Museums.
—. Albright, William Foxwell. Biblical studies. Philosophy of History. Science. 1918-70. *2328*
—. Anthropology. Indians. Lost Tribes of Israel. Mormons. Smith, Joseph. 1830. *2335*
—. Engraving. Fraud. Mexico (Guerrero). Mormons. Padilla Gold Plates. 1952-78. *4007*
—. Kensington Methodist Episcopal Church. Methodist Episcopal Church. Pennsylvania (Philadelphia). Preservation. 18c. 1950's-75. *1769*
—. Migration. Mormons. ca 2000 BC-ca 200. 1973. *3949*
—. Mormons. 1958-73. *206*
Architects. Churches. Folsom, William Harrison. Mormons. Utah (Provo, Salt Lake City). ca 1850's-1901. *1757*
Architecture *See also* Construction.
—. Adventists. Churches. Michigan. 1863-1976. *1794*
—. Algonkin Indians. Calvary (chapels). Iroquois Indians. Missionaries. Quebec (Oka). Sulpicians. 1700's-1800's. *1811*
—. Anglican Communion. Chancels. Ecclesiology Society. Great Britain (Cambridge). 1839-60. *1779*
—. Arizona, southern. Catholic Church. Chapels. Folk religion. Papago Indians. 20c. *1783*
—. Banner, Peter. Congregationalism. First Congregational Society Church. New York. Vermont (Burlington). 1794-1815. *1829*
—. Baptists. First Baptist Church. Heiman, Adolphus. Tennessee (Nashville). 1837-62. *1808*
—. Benedictines. Churches. Liturgy. 1945-62. *1804*
—. Benedictines. Churches. Monasteries. Vatican Council II. 1962-75. *1805*
—. Benjamin, Asher. Churches (Greek Revival). Massachusetts (Boston). 1833-40. *1826*
—. Benjamin, Asher. Massachusetts (Boston). Truss design. West Church. 1805-23. *1827*
—. Brattle Street Church. Congregationalism. Dawes, Thomas. Massachusetts (Boston). 18c. *1771*
—. Bulfinch, Charles. First Parish Church. Massachusetts (Charlestown). Meetinghouses. 1803-04. *1792*
—. California. Franciscans. Mission San Juan Capistrano. 1776-1976. *1494*
—. California (Los Angeles, San Francisco). Judaism (Reform). Temple Emanu-El. Wilshire Boulevard Temple. 1937. *4205*

—. Cathedral Church of St. John the Divine. Episcopal Church, Protestant. Manning, William Thomas. New York City. Sabbatarianism. Sports. 19c-1920's. *3243*
—. Cathedrals. Catholic Church. Ireland, John. Masqueray, Emmanuel L. Minnesota (St. Paul). 1904-17. *1795*
—. Catholic Church. Church of St. Paul the Apostle. Decorative Arts. LaFarge, John. New York City. 1876-99. *1833*
—. Catholic Church. Churches. St. Andrew's Church. Virginia (Roanoke). 1882-1975. *1834*
—. Catholic Church. Fundamentalists. German Americans. Rural Settlements. Social customs. Southerners. Texas (Cooke, Denton counties). 1860-1976. *2750*
—. Catholic Church. New France. 1600-1760. *1807*
—. Church of England. Liturgy. Vestments. 18c. *3188*
—. Churches. Country life. Fischer, Emil C. Kansas. 19c. *1778*
—. Churches. Decorative Arts. Values. 1970's. *1837*
—. Churches. Episcopal Church, Protestant. New England. Vaughan, Henry. 1845-1917. *1800*
—. Churches. Episcopal Church, Protestant. St. James Episcopal Church. Virginia (Accomac). 1838. *1825*
—. Churches. Episcopal Church, Protestant. Virginia. 1800-1920. *1798*
—. Churches. Mormons. Utah. 1847-1929. *1817*
—. Churches. Tennessee (Memphis). 19c. *1813*
—. Churches (Gothic Revival). Country Life. Furniture and Furnishings. Pennsylvania, northwest. Presbyterian Church. 1850-1905. 1979. *1797*
—. Churches (Gothic Revival, Victorian Gothic). Episcopal Church, Protestant. North Dakota. Upjohn, Richard. 1874-1903. *1815*
—. City Planning. Mormons. Smith, Joseph. Western states. 1833-90. *1767*
—. City Planning. Mormons. Utah. 1847-1975. *1781*
—. Episcopal Church, Protestant. New Hampshire (Portsmouth). St. John's Episcopal Church. 1807-09. *1780*
—. Frontier. Mormons. ca 1850-56. *1836*
—. Harmony Society. Indiana (New Harmony). Pennsylvania (Economy, Harmony). Preservation. Rapp, George. Restorations. Utopias. 1804-25. 20c. *420*
—. Illinois (Nauvoo). Mormons. Temples. Utah. Weeks, William. 1840's-1900. *1758*
—. Iowa (Orange City). Northwestern College (Zwemer Hall). Reformed Dutch Church. 1890-1924. *1806*
—. Kentucky. Shakers. 1805-60. *1824*
—. Meetinghouses. New England. Stairwells. 18c. *1761*
—. Moravian Church. Pennsylvania (Bethlehem, Nazareth). 1740-68. *1791*
—. Withers, Frederick C. 1840's-1901. *1793*
Architecture, academy. Catholic Church. Oregon (Salem). Piper, William W. Sacred Heart Academy. 1834-83. *1828*
Architecture, folk. Mormons. Stone buildings. Utah (Beaver City). 1855-1975. *1812*
Architecture, Gothic Revival. Bolton, William J. Church of the Holy Trinity. Episcopal Church, Protestant. New York City (Brooklyn). Stained glass windows. 1845-47. *1847*
—. Canada. 1860-1939. *1765*
—. Churches. Congregationalism. Iowa (Iowa City). Randall, Gurdon Paine. 1868-69. *1822*
—. Churches. Episcopal Church, Protestant. Holy Trinity Episcopal Church. Restorations. Tennessee (Nashville). 1840's-1970's. *1801*
—. Churches. Episcopal Church, Protestant. Iowa (Iowa City). Trinity Episcopal Church. Upjohn, Richard. 1871-72. *1787*
—. Episcopal Church, Protestant. South. Upjohn, Richard. Wills, Frank. 1835-60. *1809*
Architecture (Quaker-plan). Friends, society of. Georgia (Oglethorpe, Wilkes counties). Gilmer House. 1800-1978. *1768*
Architecture (Scandinavian). City Planning. Country Life. Mormons. Utah (Spring City). 1851-1975. *1816*
Archival catalogs and inventories. American Jewish Historical Society. Judaism. Rhode Island. 1692-1975. *273*
—. Church History. 1975. *253*
—. Congregatio de Propaganda Fide. France. North America. Vatican. 1622-1799. 1979. *182*
—. Emmett, Daniel. Hymns. Minstrel Shows. Negroes. Ohio Historical Society. Sermons. 1838-96. 1976. *2064*
—. Jenson, Andrew. Manuscripts. Mormon Church (Historian's Office). 1830-1975. *193*
—. Letters. Mennonites. Mensch, Jacob B. Pennsylvania. 1835-1912. *251*
Archives *See also* names of individual archives, e.g. Georgetown University Archives; Court Records; Documents; Manuscripts.
—. American Studies. Catholic University of America. Documents. Kenrick, Francis P. Missions and Missionaries. 1776-1865. *216*
—. Bibliographies. California. Franciscans. Geiger, Maynard J. (obituary). Historiography. Mission Santa Barbara. 1936-76. *240*
—. Bishops. Catholic Church. Church History. Kingston, Archdiocese of. Ontario. 1800-1966. *247*
—. California. Catholic Church. 1768-1975. *274*
—. California. Franciscans. Geiger, Maynard J. (obituary). Historiography. Mission Santa Barbara. 1901-77. *281*
—. California. Franciscans. Geiger, Maynard J. (obituary). Historiography. Mission Santa Barbara. 1937-77. *238*
—. Canada. Jesuits. 17c-1978. *183*
—. Canada. Mennonites. 19c-1975. *187*
—. Canada. Methodist Church. Presbyterian Church. United Church of Canada. 18c-1973. *269*
—. Canadian Mennonite Bible College (Mennonite Heritage Centre). Mennonites. 1979. *219*
—. Cathcart, Wallace H. Shakers. Western Reserve Historical Society. 1911-12. *202*
—. Catholic Church. Church records. Genealogy. 19c-20c. *242*
—. China. Japan. Korea. Missions and Missionaries. Presbyterian Historical Society. 1852-1911. *189*
—. Church History. Concordia Historical Institute. Lutheran Church (Missouri Synod). Missouri (St. Louis). 1978. *221*
—. Church membership. Historical societies. Methodology. Voting and Voting Behavior. 1776-1860. 1977. *1235*
—. Church of England. Missions and Missionaries. Society for the Propagation of the Gospel. 1700-80. *215*
—. Congregationalism. Manuscripts. Stiles, Ezra. Yale University. 1748-1975. *3142*
—. Ecumenism. Historical Societies. Pennsylvania (Philadelphia). Presbyterian Historical Society. 1852-1977. *260*
—. Emigrant Institute. Lutheran Church. Social organizations. Sweden (Växjö). 1800-1970. *282*
—. Giesbrecht, Herbert. Manitoba (Winnipeg). Mennonite Brethren Bible College. 1950-79. *250*
—. Libraries. Mormons. Utah (Salt Lake City). 1830-1970's. *194*
—. Saskatchewan. Women. 1880's-1970's. *170*
Archko collection. Forgeries. Jesus Christ. Mahan, William D. Mormons. Presbyterian Church (Cumberland). Wallace, Lew *(Ben-Hur)*. 1880's. *3928*
Arctic. Canada. Catholic Church. Church of England. Churches. Fur Trade. Missions and Missionaries. 20c. *1549*
Arendt, Hannah. American Revolution. Church and state. Ideology. ca 1775-83. *1032*
Arguello, Maria de la Concepcion. California. Catholic Church. Orthodox Eastern Church, Russian. Rezanov, Nikolai. 1806. *2797*
Aristocracy *See also* Democracy; Nobility; Upper Classes.
—. Clergy. French Americans. Huguenots. Religious liberty. Richebourg, Claude Phillipe de. 1680-1719. *3250*
Arizona *See also* Far Western States.
—. Anti-Catholicism. Ku Klux Klan. Morality. 1921-25. *2094*
—. Bandelier, Adolph Francis. Manuscripts. Mexico (Chihuahua, Sonora). Missions and Missionaries. New Mexico. Vatican Library. 16c-17c. 1886-1964. 1975-79. *1618*
—. Baptists. Catholic Church. Episcopal Church, Protestant. Methodism. Missions and Missionaries. Mormons. Presbyterian Church. 1859-99. *1501*
—. Bar mitzvahs. Goldwater family. Jews. 1879. *4097*
—. Barth, Solomon. Converts. Frontier. Jews. Mormons. 1856-1928. *60*
—. Catholic Church. Colonial Government. Jurisdictions, ecclesiastical. New Mexico. Spain. 1548-1969. *3739*
—. Christianity. Frontier and Pioneer Life. Reform. Suffrage. Temperance Movements. Women. 1850's-1912. *837*
—. Church and State. Franciscans. Indians. Mexico (Sonora). Missions and Missionaries. 1767-1842. *1065*
—. Edmunds Act (US, 1882). Federal government. Mormons. Polygamy. 1880's. *1000*
—. Indians. Jesuits. Kino, Eusebio Francisco. Missions and Missionaries. Spain. 1680's-1711. *1565*
Arizona (Coconino County). Frontier. Immigrants. Mormons. Schools. 1875-1900. *510*
Arizona (Miracle Valley). A. A. Allen Revival, Incorporated. Fundamentalism. Language. Popular culture. Revivals. 1970's. *2270*
Arizona (Nogales). Buena, Mariano. Catholic Church. Gil, Juan. Indians. Seri Indians. 1768-72. *1559*
—. Excavations. Jesuits. Mission Guevavi. 18c. 1964-66. *1818*
Arizona (Pisinimo). Catholic Church. Clergy. Frembling, Lambert. Papago Indians. Refugees. 1939-77. *3825*
Arizona (Short Creek). Church and state. Mormons. Polygamy. Utah. 1953. *1076*
Arizona, southern. Architecture. Catholic Church. Chapels. Folk religion. Papago Indians. 20c. *1783*
Arizona (Tombstone). Clergy. Episcopal Church, Protestant. Peabody, Endicott. 1882. *3237*
Arizona (Tucson). Churches. Mexico (Caborca, Sonora). Mission Nuestra Señora de la Purísima Concepción del Caborca. Mission San Xavier del Bac. ca 1750-1809. *1782*
Arkansas. Antievolution Law (1928). Church and state. Courts. Epperson, Susan. Evolution. Initiatives. 1900's-68. *2322*
—. Baptists. Brough, Charles Hillman. Elections (presidential). Evolution. Prohibition. 1928-29. *1270*
—. Baptists. Slavery. ca 1830-60. *2176*
—. Brough, Charles Hillman. Historians. Mormons. 1890-1915. *224*
Arkansas (Jonesboro). Attitudes. Folk Religion. Folklore. Tornadoes. 1973. *95*
—. Catholic Church. Missions and missionaries. Olivetan Benedictine Sisters, American. Renggli, Rose (Mother Mary Beatrice). 1847-1942. *1652*
Arkansas, northeast. Baptists. Folk religion. Pentecostals. Theology. Worship. 1972-78. *2836*
—. Clergy. Pentecostals. Radio. Rhetoric. 1972-73. *1959*
—. Faith healing. Pentecostals. Sects, Religious. 1937-73. *1433*
Arkansas (Pine Bluff). Burnett, Ellen. Prophecy. Storms. Women. 1903. *74*
Arkansas (Texarkana). Congregationalism. Maddox, Finis Ewing. Presbyterian Church. Schisms. Theology. 1908. *2869*
Arkansas, University of. Baptists. Hays, Brooks. Personal narratives. Students. Values. ca 1915-20. *3025*
Armed Forces. *See* Military.
Armenia *See also* Ottoman Empire.
—. Lambert, Rose. Letters. Mennonites. Missions and Missionaries. Turkey. 1898-1911. 1969. *1756*
Armies *See also* Confederate Army.
—. Adventist Medical Cadet Corps. Dick, Everett N. Korean War. Personal narratives. World War II. 1934-53. *2644*
—. Butler, Benjamin F. Chaplains. Civil War. Diaries. Fort Fisher (battle). Negroes. North Carolina. Turner, Henry M. 1864-65. *2685*
—. California. Mexican War. Military Recruitment. Mormon Volunteers. 1847-48. *2707*
—. Chaplains. Civil War. 1861-65. *2689*
Arminianism. Church of England. Congregationalism. Converts. Johnson, Samuel (1696-1772). New England. Sacramentalism. 1715-22. *3183*
—. Edwards, Jonathan. Great Awakening. Justification. Massachusetts (Hampshire County). 1726-60. *2236*
Arndt, E. L. China. Lutheran Church. Missions and Missionaries. 1913-29. *1749*
Arnold, Matthew. Ethnicity. Plural establishment, theory of. 19c-20c. *15*

Arrington, Leonard J. Grey, Zane *(Riders of the Purple Sage)*. Haupt, Jon. Mormons. Mormons. 1912. 1970's. *2076*
—. Historiography. Mormons. Personal Narratives. Western states. 20c. *171*
Arrington, Leonard J. (tribute). Bibliographies. Historiography. Mormons. 1917-79. *277*
Art *See also* Architecture; Artists; Arts and Crafts; Collectors and Collecting; Decorative Arts; Folk Art; Landscape Painting; Painting; Portraits.
—. Alaska. Episcopal Church, Protestant. Missions and Missionaries. Ziegler, Eustace Paul. 1900-69. *1515*
—. Allegory. Folwell, Samuel *(Sacred to the Illustrious Washington)*. Mourning (theme). Painting. Protestantism. ca 1800. *1885*
—. Andrews, Joseph. Massachusetts (Boston). Society of the New Jerusalem. Swedenborgianism. 1830-73. *4062*
—. Attitudes. Centennial Exposition of 1876. Friends, Society of. Peace. Pennsylvania (Philadelphia). Sabbatarianism. Temperance Movements. 1876. *3256*
—. Baptist Heritage Picture Set. History. Texas. 17c-20c. 1977. *211*
—. Baptists. History. Mass Media. 17c-1977. *218*
—. Bartram, John. Bartram, William. Botany. Friends, Society of. Pennsylvania. Travel (accounts). 1699-1823. *2304*
—. Bunyan, John *(Pilgrim's Progress)*. Huntington, Daniel. *Mercy's Dream* (painting). National characteristics. Protestantism. 1678. 1841-70. *1856*
—. Calvinism. Congregationalism. Dow, Arthur Wesley. Massachusetts (Ipswich). Methodist Church. 1857-80. *1871*
—. Catholic Church. Discovery and Exploration. Hennepin, Louis. Minnesota (Minneapolis). Missions and Missionaries. Mississippi River (Falls of St. Anthony). 1680-1980. *1556*
—. Catholic Church. Folk religion. French Canadians. Musée Historique de Vaudreuil. Quebec. 17c-20c. *174*
—. Copley, John Singleton *(Watson and the Shark)*. 1778. *1860*
—. Daily life. Moravian Church. Pennsylvania (Bethlehem). Social Organization. 1741-1865. *3515*
—. Fraktur. German Canadians. Ontario. 1976. *1843*
—. Illinois (Chicago). Presbyterian Church. Second Presbyterian Church. Stained glass windows. 1872-74. *1855*
Art criticism. California. Catholic Church. Missions and Missionaries. 1769-1980. *1876*
Art, Symbolist. California (San Diego; Point Loma). Theosophy. ca 1875-1910. *1863*
Arthur, Timothy Shay *(Ten Nights in a Bar-Room)*. Swedenborg, Emanuel. Temperance Movements. 18c. 1854. *2041*
Artifacts *See also* Excavations.
—. American Revolution. Dutch Americans. Reformed Dutch Church. 17c-18c. *1866*
—. Ceramics. Glass. Moravian Church. Worship. 18c-19c. *1879*
—. Moravian Church. Rhode Island (Newport). 1767-1835. *3511*
Artisans. Identity. Methodism. Morality. Pennsylvania (Philadelphia). Social customs. Work ethic. Working Class. 1820-50. *3479*
Artists. Carmelites. Louisiana (DeSoto Parish). Restorations. St. Anne's Chapel. 1891-1975. *1796*
Arts. -1974. *1840*
—. Baptists, Southern. Conservatism. Denominationalism. Folk art. 1975. *1877*
—. Bicentennial Celebrations. Consultation on the Religious Communities, the Arts and the Second American Revolution. 1973. *1846*
—. California. Catholic Church. Historiography (Anglo-American). Missions and Missionaries. Scholasticism. 1740's-1976. *1878*
—. Political commentary. Propaganda. 1975. *1873*
Arts and Crafts *See also* Decorative Arts; Folk Art; Needlework; Wood Carving.
—. Girls. Moravian Church. North Carolina. Pennsylvania. Students. 19c. *1862*
Arvedson, Peter. Episcopal Church, Protestant. Illinois. Swedish Americans. 1822-80. *1600*
Asbury, Francis. Albright, Jacob. Evangelical Association. Methodist Episcopal Church. 1765-1816. *2947*
—. American Revolution. Delaware. Loyalists. Maryland. Methodists. White, Thomas. 1777-80. *3482*
—. American Revolution. Great Britain. Methodism. Wesley, John. 1770-90. *1334*
—. Americanization. Methodism. Social Change. 1766-1816. *286*
—. Canada. Coke, Thomas. Embury, Philip. Great Britain. Methodism. USA. 1760-80. *3445*
—. Clergy. Elections. McKendree, William. Methodist Episcopal Church. 1808. *3486*
—. Coke, Thomas. Methodist Episcopal Church. Slavery. 1780-1816. *2155*
—. Letters. Methodist Episcopal Church. Sunday Schools. 1791. *782*
Asia *See also* Asia, Central.
—. 1973-74. *4289*
—. Canada. Colleges and Universities (review article). Missions and Missionaries. Protestant Churches. 1850-1971. *1675*
—. Catholic Church. Merton, Thomas. Monasteries. Trappists. 1940's-68. *3707*
Asia, central. Immigration. Kansas. Mennonites. Nebraska. Pacifism. 1884-93. *3350*
—. Immigration. Mennonites. Russia. 1870's-1920's. *3386*
Asians *See also* East Indians.
—. Conservatism. Immigration. Methodist Episcopal Church. Social Gospel. 1865-1908. *2404*
Assassination *See also* Murder.
—. Abolition Movement. Brooks, Phillips. Episcopal Church, Protestant. Lincoln, Abraham. Pennsylvania (Philadelphia). Sermons. 1865. 1893. *2463*
—. Baptists. Baptists, Southern (winter assembly grounds). Florida (Umatilla). Lincoln, Abraham. 1865. 1925-29. *2980*
—. Baptists, Southern. Civil rights. King, Martin Luther, Jr. 1961-68. *3042*
—. Gray, John P. Moral insanity. New York State Lunatic Asylum. Psychiatry. Trials. 1854-86. *2346*
—. Hill, Marvin S. Illinois (Carthage). Mormons. Oaks, Dallin H. Smith, Joseph. Trials (review article). 1844. 1977. *2126*
Assemblies of God. Church of God. Civil rights movement. Periodicals. Presbyterian Church, Southern. South. 1950's-60's. *2528*
Assimilation *See also* Acculturation; Americanization; Integration.
—. Alaska. Brady, John Green. Economic Conditions. Indian-White Relations. Missions and Missionaries. Tlingit Indians. 1878-1906. *1548*
—. Alberta. Education. Hutterites. 1920-70. *534*
—. American Board of Commissioners for Foreign Missions. Connecticut (Cornwall). Foreign Mission School. Indian-White Relations. Students. 1816-27. *586*
—. Authority. Bishops. Catholic Church. Cleveland Diocese. German Americans. Irish Americans. Ohio. Rappe, Louis Amadeus. 1847-70. *3788*
—. Baptists (American). Immigrants. 1890-1925. *3091*
—. Brethren in Christ. Protestantism. 1770-1973. *3422*
—. Brethren, Old German Baptist. Conservatism. 1881-1977. *3413*
—. Catholic Church. Clergy. Dufresne, Andre B. French Canadians. Massachusetts (Holyoke). 1869-87. *302*
—. Catholic Church. Connecticut (New Britain). Holy Cross Church. Polish Americans. 1928-76. *3693*
—. Catholic Church. Connecticut (Waterbury). Lithuanian Americans. *Rytas* (newspaper). Zebris, Joseph. 1896-98. *3901*
—. Catholic Church. Eastern Orthodox Church, Syrian. Maronite Catholics. Melkite Catholics. Syrian Americans. Uniates. 1900-73. *3908*
—. Catholic Church. French Canadians. Nationalism. Rhode Island (Woonsocket). 1924-29. *3854*
—. Catholic Church. Immigrants. Polish Americans. 1860's-1930's. *3700*
—. Catholic Church. Parishes. Pennsylvania (Philadelphia). 1759-1975. *3745*
—. Christianity. Indians. Missions and Missionaries. Syncretism. 19c-20c. *2794*
—. Church and state. New York. Politics. Reformed Dutch Church. 1664-91. *1121*
—. Eliot, John. Indians. Massachusetts. Praying towns. Puritans. 1646-74. *1592*
—. Ethnicity. 1976. *161*
—. Ethnicity. Greek Americans. New York City. Orthodox Eastern Church. St. Demetrios Church. St. Markela Church. 1970's. *318*
—. Evangelism. Jews. Ontario (Toronto). Presbyterian Church. 1912-18. *1540*
—. German Americans. Michigan (Ann Arbor). Pluralism. Protestantism. 1830-1955. *284*
—. Greek Americans. Papagiannis, Michael D. Personal narratives. USA (impressions). 20c. *2811*
—. Immigrants. Kubiak, Hieronim (review article). Polish National Catholic Church. 1897-1965. *306*
—. Indians. Navajo Indians. New Mexico (Shiprock). Sherman Institute for Indians. Women. 1900-20. *589*
—. Indians (agencies). Lowrie, John C. Missions and Missionaries. Presbyterian Church. 1870-82. *1655*
—. Jews. 1970's. *4111*
—. Jews. Political Attitudes. South Carolina (Charleston). 1970's. *4136*
—. Jews. Rabbis. Reading. 1970's. *4132*
—. Lutheran Church. Muhlenberg, Henry Melchior. Pennsylvania. Politics. Swedish Americans. Wrangel, Carl Magnus. 1749-69. *1283*
—. New Hampshire (Claremont). Orthodox Eastern Church, Russian. Russian Americans. ca 1907-75. *2809*
—. Orthodox Eastern Church, Greek. 1918-73. *2812*
Associates of Dr. Bray. Church of England. Georgia Trustees. Sermons. 1733-50. *3231*
Association Catholique de la Jeunesse Canadienne-Française. Catholic Church. French Canadians. Morality. Quebec. 1903-14. *2355*
Association of Southern Women for the Prevention of Lynching. Ames, Jessie Daniel. Lynching. Methodist Woman's Missionary Council. Racism. South. Women. Young Women's Christian Association. 1930's. *2535*
Assurance, doctrine of. Hooker, Thomas. New England. Puritans. Theology. 1630-60. *3644*
Astrology *See also* Occult Sciences.
—. ca 1920-75. *2208*
—. Astronomy. Comets. Pennsylvania Germans. 18c-19c. *2209*
—. California (San Francisco Bay Area). Counter culture. Horoscopes. 1970's. *2212*
Astronomy *See also* Astrology.
—. Almanacs. Infinity (concept). New England. Puritanism. 1650-85. *2325*
—. Astrology. Comets. Pennsylvania Germans. 18c-19c. *2209*
—. *Horologium Achaz* (scientific device). Pennsylvania Germans. Pietism. Witt, Christopher. 1578-1895. *2349*
Asylums. Catholic Church. Hospitals. Illinois (Chicago). Schools. Wisconsin (Milwaukee). 19c. *3886*
Atheism *See also* Deism; Rationalism.
—. Bobb, John. Missouri (St. Louis). *Western Examiner* (periodical). 1834-35. *4300*
—. Freedom of Speech. *Lucifer's Lantern* (periodical). Mormons. Polygamy. Schroeder, Theodore. Utah. 1889-1900. *2125*
—. Ingersoll, Robert. Lectures. Nevada (Virginia City). Public Opinion. 1877. *4304*
—. Morality. Residence. Theology. Tolerance. Traditionalism. 1958. *159*
Athletics. *See* Sports.
Atkinson, James H. Friends Historical Association. Pennsylvania (Philadelphia). 1873-1923. *234*
Atlantic Provinces *See also* Labrador; Maritime Provinces; New Brunswick; Newfoundland; Nova Scotia; Prince Edward Island.
—. Bishops. Catholic Church. Diaries. Plessis, Joseph-Octave. Quebec Archdiocese. 1812-15. *3704*
—. Mennonites. Settlement. 1950-70. *3410*
Attitudes *See also* Political Attitudes; Public Opinion; Values.
—. Abolition Movement. Competition. Economic conditions. Evangelicalism. Poverty. ca 1830-60. *2473*
—. Abolition Movement. New England. Puritans. Slavery. 1641-1776. *2164*
—. Abortion. Catholic Church. Colleges and Universities. Students. 1970's. *855*
—. Abortion. Catholics. Protestants. Whites. 1962-75. *888*
—. Abortion. Christianity. 1972. *910*
—. Abortion. Family size preference. 1972. *917*
—. Americanization. New England. Pilgrims. 17c. *323*
—. Anti-Catholicism. Anti-Semitism. Ku Klux Klan. Morality. Ohio (Youngstown). Reform. 1920's. *2402*

—. Anti-Catholicism. Independence Movements. Latin America. Protestant churches. 1810-25. *2107*
—. Appalachia. Baptists, Southern. Fundamentalism. 1966-77. *3034*
—. Arkansas (Jonesboro). Folk Religion. Folklore. Tornadoes. 1973. *95*
—. Art. Centennial Exposition of 1876. Friends, Society of. Peace. Pennsylvania (Philadelphia). Sabbatarianism. Temperance Movements. 1876. *3256*
—. Autobiography. Brownson, Orestes A. *(The Convert).* Catholic Church. Converts. Great Britain. Newman, John Henry *(Apologia pro Vita Sua).* Protestantism. 1857-64. *3681*
—. Ballou, Adin Augustus. Hopedale Community. Massachusetts (Milford). Utopias. 1830-42. *427*
—. Baptists. Brown University. War. Wayland, Francis. 1826-65. *2649*
—. Baptists. Business. 1840-1950. *363*
—. Baptists. Slavery. Virginia. 1785-97. *2157*
—. Baptists, Southern. Buddhism. Congregationalism. Death and Dying. Hawaii (Honolulu). 1977. *131*
—. Baptists, Southern. Kelsey, George (review article). Kentucky. World War II. 1941-45. 1973. *2681*
—. Baptists, Southern. World War I. 1918-20. *2699*
—. Benezet, Anthony. Friends, Society of. Wealth. Woolman, John. 1740-83. *358*
—. Billings, William. Music (choral). Upper Classes. 1750-1800. *1907*
—. Bradford family. Letters. Missouri. Mormons. Virginia. 1838-39. *4057*
—. Brooklyn College. Catholic Church. Immigration. Judaism. Negroes. New York City. Protestant Ethic. West Indian Americans. 1939-78. *350*
—. Brownson, Orestes A. Catholic Church. Civil War. Hughes, John. McMaster, James. 1850-65. *2692*
—. California (Berkeley). Converts. Davis, Rennie. Divine Light Mission. Maharaj Ji. Politics. 1973. *4286*
—. Californios. Europeans. Travel (accounts). 1780's-1840's. *2122*
—. Calvinism. Faulkner, William *(The Sound and the Fury).* South. 1929. *2018*
—. Canada. Catholic Church. Ethnic Groups. Jews. Protestantism. Social Status. 1968. *2088*
—. Carter, Jimmy. Civil religion. Evangelicalism. Political Campaigns (presidential). Political Speeches. Rhetoric. 1976. *1229*
—. Catholic Church. Colonial Government. Discovery and Exploration. Games. Indians. Missions and Missionaries. 16c-17c. *1524*
—. Catholic Church. Death and Dying. Quebec. Wills. 1663-1760. *3718*
—. Catholic Church. Israel. Zionism. 1945-48. *963*
—. Catholic Church. Prayer. Students. 1961-71. *3808*
—. Catholic Church. Religiosity. Students. 1961-71. *3807*
—. Censorship. Films. Protestant Churches. Television. 1921-80. *2820*
—. Children. Civil religion. Illinois. 1970's. *1187*
—. China. Missions and Missionaries. Presbyterian Church. 1837-1900. *1691*
—. Chiropractic. Cultism. Medicine (practice of). Science. 1850's-1970's. *2314*
—. Church and state. Civil Religion. Hoover, Herbert C. Protestantism. 1928-32. *1167*
—. Clergy. 1845-60. *307*
—. Clergy. Lyche, Hans Tambs. Newspapers. Norway. Travel (accounts). Unitarianism. 1880-92. *4081*
—. Clergy. Social issues. Theology. 1974. *2378*
—. Colleges and Universities. Religiosity. Sex roles. Stereotypes. Students. Women. 1970's. *793*
—. Colleges and Universities. Religiosity. Students. Vietnam War. 1968-72. *2636*
—. Congregationalism. Dwight, Timothy. New England. New York. Travel (accounts). Wilderness. 1790's. *2066*
—. Conservatism. Religious beliefs. Social Surveys. 1970-74. *1380*
—. Court records. Law Enforcement. New England. Sodomy. 1630-80. *2428*
—. Daily Life. Friends, Society of. Ohio (Mount Pleasant). 1795-1918. *3260*
—. Daily life. Sociology of religion. Yinger, J. Milton. 1946-77. *166*
—. Death and Dying. Social Customs. 17c-1977. *19*
—. Diaries. Hitchcock, Ethan Allen. Military Service. Unitarianism. 1836-54. *2656*
—. Dickinson, Emily. Evangelicalism. Friendship. Mount Holyoke College. 1848-50. *2827*
—. Domestic servants. Upper Classes. 1800-65. *1475*
—. Episcopal Church, Protestant. Fletcher, C. B. Letters. Slavery. Vermont. 1777-1864. *2159*
—. Ethnic groups. Political power. Working class. 1974. *2612*
—. Ethnicity. Israel. Jews. Northeastern or North Atlantic States. Students. Zionism. 1973-76. *4155*
—. Ethnicity. Mennonites. Pennsylvania (Lancaster). Private Schools. Socialization. 1974-76. *673*
—. Exercise. Health. New England. Recreation. Transcendentalists. 1830-60. *1453*
—. France. Indians. Jesuits. Missions and Missionaries. New France. 1611-72. *1495*
—. Friends, Society of. New York (Auburn). Pennsylvania. Prisons. Reform. 1787-1845. *2393*
—. Fundamentalism. Gaebelein, Arno C. *Our Hope* (periodical). Stroeter, Ernst F. Zionism. 1894-97. *80*
—. Great Awakening. Political reform. Social Change. 18c. 1975. *2216*
—. Hasidism. Judaism. Philosophy. 1970's. *4189*
—. Hayes, Carlton J. H. Historiography. Kohn, Hans. Nationalism. 1950's-60's. *1392*
—. Hymnals. New England. Puritans. Regular Singing movement. 1720's. *1933*
—. Indians. Missions and Missionaries. Presbyterian Church. 1837-93. *1510*
—. Jeremiads. Puritans. Sports. 1620-1720. *3658*
—. Lancaster Mennonite High School. Mennonites. Pennsylvania. Rites and Ceremonies. Students. 1974-78. *3354*
—. Mather, Cotton. New England. Puritans. Sermons. Women. 1650-1800. *880*
—. Mexico. Missions and Missionaries. Protestant churches. Social Darwinism. Travel accounts. 1867-1911. *1690*
—. Mormons. Social Organization. Utah. Women. Young, Brigham. 1840's-77. *830*
—. Poetry. Puritans. 16c-17c. *1973*
—. Puritans. 1630's-80's. *3602*
—. Sin, sense of. Social reform. 1830's-60's. *2389*
—. Tolerance. 1958-71. *151*
—. War. Youth. 1975. *2666*
Auburn Affirmation (document). Church government. Presbyterian Church of the United States of America. Theology. 1920-25. *3577*
Audiences. Graham, Billy. Revivalism. Social classes. -1974. *2604*
Audiovisual materials. Baptists. History Teaching. 1977. *249*
Augustana Book Concern. Illinois (Rock Island). Lutheran Church (Augustana Synod). 1850-1967. *357*
Augustana College and Theological Seminary. Bethany College. Immigration. Lutheran Church. Midwest. Politics. Railroads. Religious education. Swedish Americans. Swensson, Carl Aaron. 1873-1904. *726*
—. Illinois (Paxton). Lutheran Church (Augustana Synod). Osborn, William H. Railroads. Swedish Americans. 1853-73. *3321*
—. Illinois (Rock Island). Immigrants. Lutheran Church. Swedish Americans. 1855-1956. *599*
Augustine, Saint. Calvinism. Edwards, Jonathan. Heart concept. New England. Psychology. 17c. *2311*
Aurora Colony. Communes. Music. Oregon. Pioneer Band. Society of Bethel. 1855-1920's. *1942*
Austin College. Baker, Daniel. Legal education. Presbyterian Church. Texas (Huntsville). 1849-57. *529*
Australia. Adventists. Missions and Missionaries. Palmer, Edwin R. Publishers and Publishing. 1894-1915. *2968*
—. Canada. Finland. Kurikka, Matti. Theosophy. Utopias. 1883-1915. *435*
—. Catholic Church. O'Farrell, Patrick (review article). 17c-1977. *3733*
Authoritarianism. Civil religion. Moon, Sun Myung. Unification Church. 1970-76. *4264*
Authority. Assimilation. Bishops. Catholic Church. Cleveland Diocese. German Americans. Irish Americans. Ohio. Rappe, Louis Amadeus. 1847-70. *3788*
—. Baptists, Southern. Theology. 1600-1978. *3016*
—. Bellah, Robert N. Civil religion. Myths and Symbols. Politics. Secularization. 1977. *1165*
—. Bishops. Canada. Church of England. Councils and Synods. Laity. 1780-1979. *3224*
—. Bishops. Church and State. Civil War. Episcopal Church, Protestant. Grace Church. Illinois (Galesburg). 1864-66. *1218*
—. Canada. Church and state. Church of England. Councils and Synods. Laity. 1782-1857. *3207*
—. Canada. Church of England. Councils and Synods. Laity. 1782-1867. *3206*
—. Canada. United Church of Canada. 1925-73. *3669*
—. Charisma. Noyes, John Humphrey. Oneida Community. 1875-81. *418*
—. Church and state. France. Liberalism. Tocqueville, Alexis de. 1830's. *1144*
—. Constitutional Amendments (1st). Health. Religious liberty. Supreme Court. 1963-79. *1439*
—. Cults. Ideology. 1945-74. *4274*
—. Latin America. Missions and Missionaries. Mormons. Nationalism. 1975-80. *1753*
Authors *See also* names of individual authors; Poets.
—. Catholic Church. More, Thomas. Walter, William Joseph. 1820's-46. *2049*
—. Church of England. Clergy. 1650-1775. *2000*
—. Civil religion. National Characteristics. 1830's-1960's. *1178*
—. Marshall, Catherine. Popular Culture. Presbyterian Church. Theology. Women. 1949-78. *3546*
Autobiography *See also* Personal Narratives.
—. Anglican Communion. Cree Indians. Faries, Richard. Missions and Missionaries. Ontario (York Factory). 1896-1961. *1528*
—. Attitudes. Brownson, Orestes A. *(The Convert).* Catholic Church. Converts. Great Britain. Newman, John Henry *(Apologia pro Vita Sua).* Protestantism. 1857-64. *3681*
—. Baptists. Clergy. Crandall, Joseph. New Brunswick. 1795-1810. *2993*
—. Buenger, Theodore Arthur. Clergy. Concordia Seminary. German Americans. Lutheran Church (Missouri Synod). Seminaries. 1886-1909. *3297*
—. Congregationalism. Edwards, Jonathan. Identity. Theology. 1729-58. *3152*
—. Frontier and Pioneer Life. Mormons. 19c. *2040*
Automobile Industry and Trade. Adventists. North Central States. Worth, William O. 1890-1913. *361*
Autonomy. Church Finance. Episcopal Church, Protestant. Isolationism. Missions and Missionaries. Theology. 1953-77. *1720*
Axtell, James (review article). Education. New England. Puritans. Social Organization. 17c-18c. 1974. *526*
Ayer, Frederick. American Board of Commissioners for Foreign Missions. Chippewa Indians. Minnesota. Missions and Missionaries. Oberlin College. Red Lake Mission. 1842-59. *1496*

B

Bäck, Olof. Clergy. Esbjörn, Lars Paul. Janssonists. Letters. Lutheran Church. Methodism. Sweden. 1846-49. *2906*
Backus, Isaac *(History of New England).* Baptists. Friends, Society of. New England Meeting for Sufferings. Sectarianism. Theology. 17c-1784. *2953*
Bacon, Thomas. Church of England. Clergy. Education. Maryland. Politics. Slavery. Theology. ca 1745-68. *3175*
Baconianism. Bozeman, Theodore Dwight (review article). Protestantism. Science. 1800's-60's. 1977. *2324*
Bad Boll Conferences. Ecumenism. Germany. Lutheran Church. 1948. *439*
Badgley, David. Baptists. Illinois (New Design). Pioneers. 1769-1824. *3096*
Baerg, Anna. Canada. Diaries. Immigration. Mennonites. Russian Revolution. Women. 1917-23. *3362*
Bailey, Jacob. American Revolution. Church of England. Exiles. Letters. Nova Scotia. 1784. *3226*

Bailey, Margaret Jewett *(Ruth Rover)*. Business. Methodist Church. Missionaries. Oregon. 1854. *1522*
Baker, Daniel. Austin College. Legal education. Presbyterian Church. Texas (Huntsville). 1849-57. *529*
Baker, Ray Stannard. Civil rights. DuBois, W. E. B. Episcopal Church, Protestant. Liberalism. Negroes. Personal narratives. Whites. Wilmer, Cary Breckenridge. 1900-10. *2151*
Bakke, Niles J. Alabama. Lutheran Church. South. Young, Rosa J. 1839-1965. *3299*
Baldwin, Nathaniel. Fundamentalism. Inventions. Mormons. Polygamy. Radio. Utah. 1900's-61. *4036*
Baldwin, Theron. Congregationalism. Higher education. Presbyterianism. Society for the Promotion of Collegiate and Theological Education at the West. 1843-73. *629*
Ballads. Appalachia, southern. Calendar, Gregorian. "Christmas, Old". Social customs. 1753-1977. *2955*
Ballads, British. Death and Dying. Folk Songs. Supernatural. 1830-1930. *1923*
Ballard, Edna. Ballard, Guy. I AM sect. Occult Sciences. 1930's-75. *4273*
Ballard, Guy. Ballard, Edna. I AM sect. Occult Sciences. 1930's-75. *4273*
Ballou, Adin Augustus. Attitudes. Hopedale Community. Massachusetts (Milford). Utopias. 1830-42. *427*
—. Draper, E. D. Hopedale Community. Massachusetts (Milford). Utopias. 1824-56. *388*
Baltic Area *See also* USSR.
—. Canada. Immigrants. Lutheran Church. 1947-55. *2453*
Baltimore Hebrew Congregation. Judaism (Orthodox). Maryland (Baltimore). Rehine, Zalma. 1830-31. *4191*
Baltimore Riot of 1861. Civil War. Creamer, David. Crooks, George Richard. Letters. Maryland. Methodist Church. 1861-63. *1410*
Baltzell, E. Digby (review article). Friends, Society of. Massachusetts (Boston). Pennsylvania (Philadelphia). Puritans. Social Classes. 17c-1979. *2920*
Bandelier, Adolph Francis. Arizona. Manuscripts. Mexico (Chihuahua, Sonora). Missions and Missionaries. New Mexico. Vatican Library. 16c-17c. 1886-1964. 1975-79. *1618*
Banking. Dissent. Mormons. Ohio (Kirtland). 1837-90. *3980*
Bannan, Benjamin. Anti-Catholicism. Antislavery Sentiments. Nativism. Pennsylvania (Schuylkill County). Temperance Movements. Whig Party. 1852-54. *1238*
Banner, Peter. Architecture. Congregationalism. First Congregational Society Church. New York. Vermont (Burlington). 1794-1815. *1829*
Bapst, John. Anti-Catholicism. Chaney, William Henry. Editors and editing. Jesuits. Maine (Ellsworth). Nativism. 1853-54. *2121*
Baptism. Amish. Pennsylvania (Lancaster, Mifflin counties). Stoltzfus, John. Tennessee. 1820-74. *3438*
—. Baptists. Great Britain (London). Jessey, Henry. Letters. New England. Puritans. Toleration. Tombes, John. 1645. *997*
—. Illinois (Nauvoo). Mormons. Theology. 1830-43. *4028*
Baptismal certificates. Birth certificates. Folk art. Pennsylvania Germans. 1750-1850. *1899*
Baptist Bibliography. American Baptist Historical Society. Samuel Colgate Baptist Historical Library. Starr, Edward Caryl. 1935-76. *263*
Baptist Board of Education and Publication. Church Schools. Smith, Luther Wesley. 1941-56. *630*
Baptist Faith and Message (confession). Baptists, Southern. Theology. 1920-75. *3028*
Baptist Heritage Picture Set. Art. History. Texas. 17c-20c. 1977. *211*
Baptist Information Retrieval System. Information Storage and Retrieval Systems. 1974-75. *230*
Baptist Joint Committee on Public Affairs. Church and State. Pressure groups. 1973. *1298*
Baptist Student Center. Education. Georgia (Athens). Nicholson, David Bascom, III. 1925-52. *631*
Baptist studies. Church History. Oral history. 1940-75. *178*
—. Methodology. Oral history. 1973. *231*
Baptist Triennial Convention. Church Finance. Education. Missions and missionaries. Rice, Luther. Wayland, Francis. 1823-26. *3018*
Baptist World Alliance. Charities. Ecumenism. 1945-73. *450*
—. Ecumenism. 1905-73. *490*
Baptists. 17c-1979. *3019*
—. 1976. *3012*
—. Abolition Movement. American Free Baptist Mission Society. Missions and Missionaries. Schisms. 1830-69. *2481*
—. Abolition Movement. Education. First African Baptist Church. Meachum, John Berry. Missouri (St. Louis). Negroes. 1815-54. *2482*
—. Abolition Movement. Landmark Movement. Pendleton, James Madison. 1835-91. *2998*
—. Academic Freedom. Foster, George Burman. Illinois. Theology. University of Chicago Divinity School. 1895-1918. *557*
—. Adolescence. Congregationalism. Finney, Charles G. Massachusetts (Boston). Methodism. Revivals. 1822-42. *2258*
—. Alabama. Davis, Harwell G. Howard College. 1882-1973. *3092*
—. American Baptist Historical Society. Librarians. Samuel Colgate Baptist Historical Library. Starr, Edward Caryl. 1930's-76. *208*
—. American Baptist Home Mission Society. Americanization. Evangelism. 1832-99. *1599*
—. American Baptist Home Mission Society. Leadership. Missions and Missionaries. Negroes. Paternalism. Virginia Union University. 1865-1905. *644*
—. American Baptist Publishing Society. Converts. Immigration. Lutheran Church. Sweden. Travel (accounts). Wiberg, Anders. 1852-53. *3054*
—. American Revolution. Chaplains. Gano, John. Washington, George. 1727-1804. *2631*
—. American Revolution. Church of England. Congregationalism. Friends, Society of. Georgia. Judaism. Lutheran Church. Presbyterian Church. 1733-90. *88*
—. American Revolution. Clergy. Georgia. Marshall, Daniel. Political Theory. 1747-1823. *1372*
—. American Revolution. Colonies. Great Britain. 1775-83. *1296*
—. American Revolution. Constitutions. Massachusetts. 1644-1806. *979*
—. American Revolution. Georgia. Mercer, Silas. Politics. Theology. 1770-96. *3030*
—. American Revolution. New England. Pennsylvania. Religious liberty. Virginia. 1775-91. *1100*
—. American Revolution. Religious liberty. 1775-1800. *1001*
—. Anderson, P. Harris. Georgia. Harris, Rufus C. Mercer University. 1965-76. *3033*
—. Anti-Catholicism. Fundamentalism. Morality. Norris, J. Frank. Texas. 1920's. *2889*
—. Anti-Masonic movement. Freemasonry. Morgan, William. New York, western. 1826-30. *2362*
—. Appalachia. Lifestyles. Methodism. Presbyterian Church. 1788-1974. *2873*
—. Appointments to office. Georgia, University of (chancellor). Hill, Walter B. Methodists. 1897-1901. *536*
—. Architecture. First Baptist Church. Heiman, Adolphus. Tennessee (Nashville). 1837-62. *1808*
—. Arizona. Catholic Church. Episcopal Church, Protestant. Methodism. Missions and Missionaries. Mormons. Presbyterian Church. 1859-99. *1501*
—. Arkansas. Brough, Charles Hillman. Elections (presidential). Evolution. Prohibition. 1928-29. *1270*
—. Arkansas. Slavery. ca 1830-60. *2176*
—. Arkansas, northeast. Folk religion. Pentecostals. Theology. Worship. 1972-78. *2836*
—. Arkansas, University of. Hays, Brooks. Personal narratives. Students. Values. ca 1915-20. *3025*
—. Art. History. Mass Media. 17c-1977. *218*
—. Assassination. Baptists, Southern (winter assembly grounds). Florida (Umatilla). Lincoln, Abraham. 1865. 1925-29. *2980*
—. Attitudes. Brown University. War. Wayland, Francis. 1826-65. *2649*
—. Attitudes. Business. 1840-1950. *363*
—. Attitudes. Slavery. Virginia. 1785-97. *2157*
—. Audiovisual materials. History Teaching. 1977. *249*
—. Autobiography. Clergy. Crandall, Joseph. New Brunswick. 1795-1810. *2993*
—. Backus, Isaac *(History of New England)*. Friends, Society of. New England Meeting for Sufferings. Sectarianism. Theology. 17c-1784. *2953*
—. Badgley, David. Illinois (New Design). Pioneers. 1769-1824. *3096*
—. Baptism. Great Britain (London). Jessey, Henry. Letters. New England. Puritans. Toleration. Tombes, John. 1645. *997*
—. Bennett, Robert. Clarke, John. Great Britain (London). Letters. Religious Liberty. Rhode Island. 1655-58. *1132*
—. Bethel African Methodist Episcopal Church. California (San Francisco). Civil rights. Methodist Episcopal Zion Church, African. Negroes. Pressure groups. Third Baptist Church. 1860's. *1289*
—. Bible. Church Government. Theology. 1707-1814. *3071*
—. Bible. Periodicals. Theology. 1925-75. *3014*
—. Bibliographies. 1950's-77. *3023*
—. Bibliographies. Clarke, William Newton. Evolution. Immanentism. Theology. 1894-1912. *3065*
—. Bibliographies. Historiography. 1964-74. *3005*
—. Bibliographies. Periodicals. 1979. *3099*
—. Bingham, Abel. Diaries. Indian-White Relations. Iroquois Indians (Seneca). Missions and Missionaries. New York. Red Jacket (leader). Tonawanda Indian Reservation. 1822-28. *1513*
—. Bishop, Harriet E. Minnesota (St. Paul). Reform. Social reform. Women. 1847-83. *801*
—. Bode, Frederick A. (review article). Capitalism. Methodist Church. North Carolina. Populism. 1894-1903. 1975. *1287*
—. Bristol Baptist College. Great Britain (Bristol). Missions and Missionaries. Religious Education. Terrill, Edward. 1634-1979. *3024*
—. British Columbia Baptist Church Extension Society. USA. 1876-1918. *3061*
—. Broaddus, Andrew, I. Clergy. Diaries. Kentucky. Travel. 1817. *2986*
—. *Brown* v. *Board of Education* (US, 1954). Desegregation. Georgia. Supreme Court. 1954-61. *511*
—. Bucknell University. Franklin and Marshall College. Friends, Society of (Hicksite). Pennsylvania. Reformed German Church. Swarthmore College. Urbanization. 1865-1915. *685*
—. California. Negroes. Political activity. St. Andrew's African Methodist Episcopal Church. 1850-73. *981*
—. Cameron, William Andrew. Canada. Clergy. Sermons. Shields, Thomas Todhunter. 1910-41. *3021*
—. Canada. Disciples of Christ. Great Plains. Lutheran Church. Methodism. Pietism. Prairie Radicals. Radicals and Radicalism. 1890-1975. *954*
—. Canada. Ecumenism. USA. 1760-1979. *3031*
—. Canadian Council of Churches. Ecumenism. World Council of Churches. 1907-79. *462*
—. Carey, William. Racial attitudes. Rauschenbusch, Walter. Williams, Roger. 1776-1976. *3100*
—. Carter, Jimmy. Political Campaigns (presidential). 1976. *1272*
—. Catholic Church. Clergy. Rauschenbusch, Walter. Social reform. Theology. Vatican Council II. 1912-65. *2380*
—. Catholic Church. Ecumenism. 1967-77. *500*
—. Catholic Church. Germans, Russian. Immigration. Kansas. Lutheran Church. Mennonites. Wheat industry. 1874-77. *2778*
—. Catholic Church. Hispanic Americans. Indiana (East Chicago, Gary). Theater. 1920-76. *1864*
—. Chaplains. Courts Martial and Courts of Inquiry. Fort Robinson. Nebraska. Negroes. Plummer, Henry V. 1884-94. *2695*
—. Cherokee Georgia Baptist Convention. Georgia. *Landmark Banner and Cherokee Baptist* (newspaper). 1859-64. *3013*
—. Child-rearing. Evangelicalism. Wayland, Francis. 1831. 1975. *948*
—. China. Missions and Missionaries. Shuck, Eliza G. Sexton. 1844-51. *1713*
—. Christian Socialism. Clergy. Rauschenbusch, Walter. Social consciousness. Theology. 1891-1918. *2400*
—. Church and Social Problems. Clergy. Dawson, Joseph Martin. Scholarship. 1879-1973. *3015*

—. Church and State. Church of England. North Carolina. Presbyterians. Provincial Government. Tryon, William. 1765-76. *1036*
—. Church and state. Clergy. Dawson, Joseph Martin. 1879-1973. *1142*
—. Church and state. Congregationalism. Massachusetts (Swansea). Rhode Island (Barrington). 1711-46. *1082*
—. Church and state. Congregationalism. Meetinghouses. New Hampshire (Acworth). Taxation. Toleration Act (New Hampshire, 1819). Universalists. 1783-1822. *1113*
—. Church and state. Lobbying. 1950-73. *1297*
—. Church and state. McLoughlin, William G. (review article). New England. 1630-1833. *1077*
—. Church and state. Virginia. 1775-1810. *1043*
—. Church Government. ca 1775-1814. *3072*
—. Church Government. Ecumenism. 1650-1975. *468*
—. Church government. Virginia. Women. 1765-1800. *878*
—. Church history. Georgia. 1870-1947. *271*
—. Church of England. Elites. Social Change. Values. Virginia (Lunenburg County). 1746-74. *2819*
—. Church of England. Lifestyles. Toleration. Virginia. 1765-75. *3032*
—. Church schools. Curricula. 1824-1974. *638*
—. Circuit riders. Diaries. Immigrants. Minnesota. Nilsson, Frederik Olaus. Swedish Americans. 1855-65. *3046*
—. City Government. Maryland (Baltimore). Negroes. Political protest. Public schools. 1865-1900. *583*
—. Civil rights. King, Martin Luther, Jr. Negroes. Nonviolence. 1950's-68. *2533*
—. Civil Rights. King, Martin Luther, Jr. Theology. Transcendentalism. 1840's-50's. 1950's-60's. *2530*
—. Civil Rights. King, Martin Luther, Jr. ("Letter from Birmingham Jail"). Negroes. 1963. *2534*
—. Civil rights movement. Ebenezer Baptist Church. Georgia (Atlanta). Personal narratives. Roberts, Joseph L., Jr. 1960-75. *2556*
—. Civil War. Diaries. Hungerford, B. F. Kentucky. 1863-66. *2632*
—. Clergy. Dahlberg, Edwin. Personal narratives. Rauschenbusch, Walter. Social reform. 1914-18. *2440*
—. Clergy. Davis, Noah. Maryland (Baltimore). Meachum, John Berry. Missouri (St. Louis). Negroes. Slavery. 1818-66. *3094*
—. Clergy. Education. Income. Social Status. 1651-1980. *2603*
—. Clergy. Emigration. Great Britain. Harris, Theophilus. Politics. Social conditions. 1793-1810. *3050*
—. Clergy. First Presbyterian Church. Fosdick, Harry Emerson. New York City. Presbyterian Church. Theology. 1918-24. *466*
—. Clergy. Frontier and Pioneer Life. Montana. Personal narratives. Spencer, James Hovey. 1888-97. *3095*
—. Clergy. Great Britain. Religious Education. 1600's-1980. *725*
—. Clergy. Hudson, Winthrop. Liberalism. Rauschenbusch, Walter. Social theory. Theology. 1880-1978. *2351*
—. Clergy. Jay Street Church. Massachusetts (Boston). Negroes. Paul, Thomas (and family). 1773-1973. *3048*
—. Clergy. Laity. Leadership. 1609-1970's. *3027*
—. Clergy. Missouri. Oregon (Willamette Valley). Powell, Joab. Westward movement. 1852-73. *3093*
—. Colleges and Universities. Education. Everett Institute. Louisiana (Spearsville). 1893-1908. *605*
—. Colleges and Universities. Georgia (Cedartown). Woodland Female College. 1851-87. *634*
—. Colleges and Universities. Richmond College. Virginia (Richmond). 1843-60. *616*
—. Colleges and Universities. Tennessee (Jackson). Union University. 1825-1975. *776*
—. Committee on Baptist History. Georgia. 1948-78. *270*
—. Conservatism. Evangelism. Graham, Billy. Morality. 1940's-70's. *2215*
—. Converts. Evangelism. Louisiana (New Orleans). Methodism. Slavery. 1800-61. *2916*
—. Country Life. Farms. Illinois (southern). Lentz, Lula Gillespie. Personal narratives. 1883-1929. *3037*
—. Covenants. Maritime Provinces. 1778-1878. *3003*
—. Creeds. 1742-1963. *2996*
—. Creeds. Nova Scotia (Annapolis Valley). 1760-1980. *3060*
—. Creek Indians. Indian Territory. Methodist Church. Missions and Missionaries. Presbyterian Church. 1835-60's. *1517*
—. Cultural pluralism. Ethnicity. Melting pot theory. 1870-1976. *3101*
—. Darwin, Charles. Evolution. Hofstadter, Richard *(Social Darwinism in American Thought)*. Rauschenbusch, Walter. Social Gospel. Spencer, Herbert. 1879-1918. *3002*
—. Dayton, Amos Cooper. Landmark Movement. Novels. South. 1850-65. *1995*
—. Desegregation. Tennessee (Clinton). Turner, Paul. Violence. 1956. *2531*
—. Discrimination. Japanese Americans. Resettlement. World War II. 1890-1970. *2547*
—. Ebenezer Methodist Church. Inscriptions. Methodist Church. Mount Bethel Baptist Church. South Carolina (Anderson County). Tombstones. 1856-1978. *2848*
—. Education. Indians. Kansas. Lykins, Johnston. Potawatomi Indians. Pottawatomie Baptist Manual Labor Training School. 1846-67. *508*
—. Educational Policy. Evolution. Kentucky. Science. 1922-28. *2347*
—. Elementary education. Religious Education. Secondary education. State Aid to Education. 1850-1910. *718*
—. Factionalism. Fundamentalism. Jarvis Street Baptist Church. Modernism. Ontario (Toronto). Social Classes. 1895-1934. *2605*
—. Films. History Teaching. Television. Videotape. 1977. *267*
—. First African Baptist Church. Jasper, John. Negroes. Sermons. Virginia (Richmond). 1812-1901. *2990*
—. Folger, Peter. Indians. Jones, David. Missionaries. Northeastern or North Atlantic States. Williams, Roger. 1638-1814. *1619*
—. Fox, George. Friends, Society of. Olney, Thomas, Jr. Politics. Rhode Island. 1672-73. *967*
—. Fundamentalism. Graham, Billy. Minnesota (Minneapolis). Riley, William Bell. World Christian Fundamental Association. ca 1900-65. *3068*
—. Fundamentalism. Jarvis Street Baptist Church. Ontario (Toronto). Shields, Thomas Todhunter. 1891-1955. *3067*
—. Galusha, Elon. Millerites. New York. 1825-56. *2921*
—. Georgia. Historians. King, Spencer Bidwell, Jr. (obituary). 1930's-77. *199*
—. Georgia. Negroes. 1750's-1830's. *3077*
—. Georgia. Political Leadership. State Politics. 1772-1823. *1260*
—. Georgia (Cartersville). Moon, Lottie. Secondary Education. Women. 1870-1903. *2985*
—. Georgia (Richmond County). Kiokee Church. Marshall, Daniel. Negroes. Settlement. 1784-1819. *3020*
—. Graves, James Robinson. Landmark movement. Missions and Missionaries. South. Whitsitt Controversy. 1850-1950. *3057*
—. Hermeneutics. Poetry. Strong, Augustus Hopkins. Theology. 1897-1916. 1978. *1974*
—. Higher education. Tennessee (Brownsville). West Tennessee Baptist Female College. Women. 1850-1910. *658*
—. Historical societies. Periodicals. South. 1950's-70's. *186*
—. Historiography. 1977. *254*
—. Historiography. Rister, Carl Coke. Western States. 1920's-55. *223*
—. History Teaching. 1977. *244*
—. Hymnals. Singing. 1650-1850. *1945*
—. Imperialism. National Characteristics. Racism. Virginia. Women. 1865-1900. *3001*
—. Indiana. Lincoln, Abraham. Pigeon Creek Baptist Church. 1822-30. *3098*
—. Indiana. Piner Baptist Church. 1833-1906. *3026*
—. Jack (man). Negroes. Rhode Island (Newport). 1630's-52. *3017*
—. Judson, Adoniram. Missions and Missionaries. Newell, Samuel. 1810-21. *1731*
—. Kentucky (Stoney Point). Negroes. Social Conditions. 1848-1969. *2999*
—. *Keystone Graded Lessons*. Literature. Religious Education. Sunday schools. 1824-1909. *637*
—. King, Martin Luther, Jr. Muelder, W. G. Nonviolence. Personalism. Theology. Tillich, Paul. Wieman, Henry Nelson. 1955-68. *2552*
—. Laity. Politics. 1715-1975. *1243*
—. Landmark movement. Sects, Religious. Theology. 1850-1950. *3089*
—. Leshe, Mary Jane Conly. Louisiana (Bienville Parish). 1849-1932. *3045*
—. Letters. Miller, William. New York (Low Hampton). 1828. *2831*
—. Louisiana (Union Parish). Methodist Church, Wesleyan. Tombstones. 1839-1970's. *2834*
—. Massachusetts. 17c. *3069*
—. Massachusetts (Ashfield). Poetry. Political Protest. Religious Liberty. Smith, Ebenezer. 1772. *2048*
—. Massachusetts (Boston). Negroes. Social Reform. 1800-73. *3040*
—. McKim, Andrew. Nova Scotia. Politics. Provincial Legislatures. 1784-1840. *1309*
—. McMaster Hall. McMaster, Susan Moulton Fraser. Michigan (Bay City). Ontario (Toronto). Women. 1819-1916. *3000*
—. Methodism. Negroes. New York. Segregation. 1865-68. *2139*
—. Methodist Church. Ninth Street Baptist Church. Ohio (Cincinnati). Political protest. Temperance Movements. Wesley Chapel. Women's Christian Temperance Union. 1874. *2582*
—. Methodist Church. Presbyterian Church. Slavery. South. 1740-1860. *2168*
—. Methodist Episcopal Church, South. Newspapers. Presbyterian Church (Cumberland, Old School). Texas. 1829-61. *2907*
—. Missions and Missionaries. 1974. *1571*
—. Missions and Missionaries. Moon, Lottie. Week of Prayer for Foreign Missions. Woman's Missionary Union. 1888-1979. *1747*
—. Negroes. New York (Buffalo). Shiloh Baptist Church. 1920's-30's. *3097*
—. Negroes. Protestantism. Socialism. Woodbey, George Washington. 1902-15. *2563*
—. North Carolina. Social control. 1772-1908. *2445*
—. Oral history program. 1970-75. *177*
—. Oral history program. 1975. *268*
—. Political theory. Religious liberty. 1619-1776. 1973. *1122*
—. Politics. Social Reform. 1976. *1244*
—. Public affairs. 1936-71. *3022*
—. Race relations. Social change. Violence. 1960-69. *2420*
—. Religious liberty. 1612-1974. *1137*
—. Religious Liberty. Virginia. 1600-1800. *1090*
—. Slavery. Virginia (Richmond). 1820-65. *3055*
—. Slavery. Wayland, Francis. 1830-45. *2160*
—. Statistics. 1978. *3086*
Baptists, American. Anti-imperialism. Horr, George. Spanish-American War. Vietnam War. *Watchman*. 1876-1974. *2698*
—. Assimilation. Immigrants. 1890-1925. *3091*
—. Crawford, Isabel. Indians. Kiowa Indians. Missions and Missionaries. Oklahoma (Wichita Mountains). Women's American Baptist Home Missionary Society. 1893-1961. *1590*
—. Education. Missions. Negroes. South. 1862-81. *739*
—. Missions and Missionaries. Theology. 1810-26. *1735*
Baptists, Big Hatchie. Baptists, Southern. Ecumenism. Tennessee (Haywood, Lauderdale, Tipton counties). 1903-78. *3010*
—. Baptists, Southern. Evangelism. Landmark movement. Missions and Missionaries. 1828-1903. *3011*
Baptists, Free Will. Adrian College. Hillsdale College. Methodist Church, Wesleyan. Michigan. Oberlin College. Ohio. Olivet College. Social Reform. 1833-70. *741*
—. Cheney Family Singers. Cheney, Moses. Music. Spiritualism. Vermont. 1839-91. *1932*
—. Georgia. 1727-1977. *3007*
—. India. Missions and Missionaries. Phillips, Jeremiah. Santals (tribe). 19c. *1733*
Baptists (Ketocton Association). Evangelicalism. Reform. Slavery. Stringfellow, Thornton. Virginia. 1800-70. *2158*
Baptists, North American. German Americans. Rauschenbusch, Walter. Theology. 1814-1949. *3062*
Baptists, Old Regular. Appalachia. Daily life. 19c-20c. *3070*
Baptists, Primitive. Alabama (Aliceville). Civil rights. Corder, James. Negroes. Personal narratives. 1965-75. *2555*

—. Appalachia. Folklore. Theology. 1800's-1977. *3083*
—. Georgia. 1835-87. *3053*
—. Georgia. Great Britain. 1633-1900. *3063*
—. Georgia, northwest. Sects, Religious. 1830-41. *3036*
—. Music (Sacred Harp). South. 1840's-1977. *1918*
Baptists, Separate. Evangelism. General Association of Separate Baptists in Christ. Kentucky. New England. 1755-1977. *3064*
Baptists, Seventh-Day. Churches. Rhode Island (Newport). 1664-1929. *1775*
—. Communalism. Letters. Müller, Johan Peter. Pennsylvania (Ephrata). Social Conditions. 1743. *428*
—. Conversion. Daland, William C. Friedlaender, Herman. Jews. New York City. *Peculiar People* (newspaper). 1880's-90's. *1633*
Baptists, Southern. 1607-1972. *2984*
—. 1682-1975. *3102*
—. 18c-20c. *3056*
—. 1900-77. *3081*
—. Alabama. Reform. Social issues. 1877-90. *2372*
—. Anti-Catholicism. 1920's. *2119*
—. Appalachia. Attitudes. Fundamentalism. 1966-77. *3034*
—. Arts. Conservatism. Denominationalism. Folk art. 1975. *1877*
—. Assassination. Civil rights. King, Martin Luther, Jr. 1961-68. *3042*
—. Attitudes. Buddhism. Congregationalism. Death and Dying. Hawaii (Honolulu). 1977. *131*
—. Attitudes. Kelsey, George (review article). Kentucky. World War II. 1941-45. 1973. *2681*
—. Attitudes. World War I. 1918-20. *2699*
—. Authority. Theology. 1600-1978. *3016*
—. Baptist Faith and Message (confession). Theology. 1920-75. *3028*
—. Baptists, Big Hatchie. Ecumenism. Tennessee (Haywood, Lauderdale, Tipton counties). 1903-78. *3010*
—. Baptists, Big Hatchie. Evangelism. Landmark movement. Missions and Missionaries. 1828-1903. *3011*
—. Barton, A. J. Denominationalism. Gambrell, James Bruton. Lawrence, J. B. Theology. 1910-80. *3039*
—. Brown, J. Newton. Covenants. New Hampshire Covenant. 1833-1972. *3006*
—. Bureaucracies. Democracy. Norris, J. Frank. 1920-40. *3084*
—. Campbell, Will. Clergy. Garner, Thad. Personal narratives. South. 20c. *2994*
—. Canada. USA. 19c-20c. *3087*
—. Carey, William. Higher education. Missions and Missionaries. 1826-1976. *1755*
—. Carter, Jimmy. Georgia (Plains). 1977. *2992*
—. Charismatic movement. 1955-77. *3029*
—. Church Finance. Cooperative Program. 1845-1975. *2982*
—. Church Finance. Missions and Missionaries. 1792-1976. *1595*
—. Church Government. 1970's. *3073*
—. Church membership. Country life. Evangelicalism. South. Urbanization. 1920's. *3085*
—. Church organization. 1704-1970. *3051*
—. Church organization. Social Policy. 19c-1970's. *3090*
—. Circular letters. Clergy. 1800-50. *3074*
—. Cities. Men. Religiosity. Women. 1968. *3008*
—. Civil Rights. Leadership. Race Relations. Texas. 1954-68. *2553*
—. Civil War. Foreign Mission Board. Missions and Missionaries. 1861-66. *1700*
—. Clergy. Evangelism. Ohio (Columbus). 1969-76. *2988*
—. Clergy. Manly, Basil. Southeastern States. Teachers. 1798-1868. *3041*
—. Concord Baptist Association. Ecumenism. Louisiana (Webster Parish). 1832-1972. *463*
—. Corporate wealth. Methodism. Political power. Presbyterian Church. South. 1930's-75. *2926*
—. Deaconesses. Women. 1600-1976. *831*
—. Developing nations. Medicine, practice of. Missions and missionaries. 1846-1975. *1440*
—. Disciples of Christ. Evolution. Kentucky. Methodist Church. Presbyterian Church. Schisms. 1920's. *2310*
—. Education. Negroes. Paternalism. 1880's-90's. *553*
—. Education. Negroes. Racism. Reconstruction. 1865-76. *2149*
—. *Encyclopedia of Southern Baptists.* 1956-71. *3004*
—. Evangelism. Home Mission Board. 1845-1973. *1544*
—. Evangelism. Social factors. 1940-75. *2989*
—. Evangelism. Voluntarism. 1940's-78. *2997*
—. Evolution. 1920's. *2345*
—. First Baptist Church. Merry, Nelson. Race Relations. Tennessee (Nashville). 1810-65. *3078*
—. Foreign Mission Board. Missions and Missionaries. 1974. *1699*
—. Foreign Mission Board. Missions and Missionaries. Publications programs. 1899-1976. *1708*
—. Fraternal Address. Mullins, Edgar Young. Theology. 1919-20. *2995*
—. Fundamentalism. 1920-75. *3043*
—. Fundamentalism. Graves, James Robinson. Landmark Movement. Modernism. Mullins, Edgar Young. Theology. 1840-1928. *3058*
—. Garrott, William Maxfield. Graham, Agnes Nora. Missions and Missionaries. Rutledge, Arthur B. 20c. *1694*
—. Graves, James Robinson. Newspapers. Seminaries. *Tennessee Baptist* (newspaper). 1820-93. *3076*
—. History. Newspapers. Research. 1977. *209*
—. Illinois State Baptist Association. Oral history. 1976. *210*
—. Individualism. Politics. Social problems. 18c-1976. *968*
—. Kentucky (Louisville). Seminaries. 1877-1977. *690*
—. Laity. 1906-75. *3038*
—. Laity. 20c. *3080*
—. Laity. Missions and missionaries. 1715-1975. *1623*
—. Language. Missions. Northeastern or North Atlantic States. Southern Baptist Convention Home Missions Board. 1950-75. *1620*
—. Missions and missionaries. 1845-1973. *1742*
—. Missions and Missionaries. 1845-60. *1648*
—. Missions and Missionaries. Woman's Missionary Union. 19c. *1527*
—. Mullins, Edgar Young. Theology. 1860-1928. *3009*
—. Newcomb, Horace. Personal narratives. 1940's-70's. *3052*
—. North Carolina. Southeastern Baptist Theological Seminary. Wake Forest College. 1945-51. *748*
—. Ordination. 1677-1980. *3079*
—. Organizational structure. Theology. 16c-20c. *3049*
—. Parachurch groups. 1970's. *2981*
—. Regenerate Membership (doctrine). Theology. 16c-20c. *3059*
—. Sectarianism. Sectionalism. 1970's. *2987*
—. Sermons. 1707-1980. *1984*
—. Suffrage. Women. 1910-20. *3082*
—. Theology. Values. 1700-1977. *3044*
—. Women. 1700-1974. *887*
—. Women. 1860-1975. *873*
Baptists, Southern (centralization). Church Finance. 1917-31. *2983*
Baptists, Southern (Executive Committee). 1917-76. *3066*
Baptists, Southern (Northwest Convention). Canada. USA. 1844-1975. *3088*
Baptists, Southern (state conventions). Centralization. 19c-1970's. *2991*
Baptists, Southern (winter assembly grounds). Assassination. Baptists. Florida (Umatilla). Lincoln, Abraham. 1865. 1925-29. *2980*
Baptists (Two-Seed-in-the-Spirit). Evangelism. Indiana. Otter Creek Predestinarian Church. Parker, Daniel. 1820-1974. *3047*
—. Evangelism. Indiana (Putnam County). Music. Oral tradition. Otter Creek Predestinarian Church. Sermons. 1820-1975. *1940*
Bar mitzvahs. Arizona. Goldwater family. Jews. 1879. *4097*
Barbados. Antislavery sentiments. Curwen, Alice. Friends, Society of. Letters. 1675-76. *2458*
Barbeau, Victor. Catholic Church. Cooperatives. Medical Reform. Paquette, Albiny. Politics. Quebec. 1900-45. *3874*
Barkley, Alben. Gambling, pari-mutuel. Kentucky. Louisville Churchmen's Federation. Progressivism. 1917-27. *2437*
Barnes, Albert *(Way of Salvation).* New Jersey (Morristown). Presbyterian Church. Schisms. Sermons. Theology. Trials. 1829-37. *3576*
Barnes, James. Editorials. Murray, Robert. Nova Scotia (Halifax). *Presbyterian Witness and Evangelical Advocate* (newspaper). 1848-1910. *3584*
Barr, D. Eglinton. Chaplains. Civil War. Episcopal Church, Protestant. South. 1851-72. *2648*
Barralet, John James *(Apotheosis of George Washington).* Engraving. National Self-image. 1802. *1859*
Barrett, Gwynn. Gibson, Walter Murray. Hawaii (Lanai). Historiography. Mormons. 1859-64. 1972-78. *3945*
Barth, Karl. Ethics. Liberalism. Niebuhr, Reinhold. 1920's-60. *2359*
—. Germany. Protestantism. Theology. 1919-39. *2946*
Barth, Solomon. Arizona. Converts. Frontier. Jews. Mormons. 1856-1928. *60*
Bartholow, Roberts. Medical reports. Mormons. Physiology. Polygamy. Utah. Vollum, E. P. 1850-75. *1430*
Bartlett, Robert. Election sermons. Politics. Religious liberty. Universalist Church of America. Vermont. 1817-30. *1045*
Barton, A. J. Baptists, Southern. Denominationalism. Gambrell, James Bruton. Lawrence, J. B. Theology. 1910-80. *3039*
Barton, Bruce *(The Man Nobody Knows).* Advertising. Business. Christianity. 1920-29. *365*
Bartram, John. Art. Bartram, William. Botany. Friends, Society of. Pennsylvania. Travel (accounts). 1699-1823. *2304*
Bartram, William. Art. Bartram, John. Botany. Friends, Society of. Pennsylvania. Travel (accounts). 1699-1823. *2304*
Barzynski, Wincenty. Catholic Church. Illinois (Chicago). Polish Roman Catholic Union. St. Stanislaus Kortka Church. Texas. 1838-99. *3678*
Bascom, John. Commons, John R. Ely, Richard T. Evolution. Political theory. Social gospel. Wisconsin, University of. 1870-1910. *2394*
Baseball. Blue laws. Church and state. Sabbath. West Virginia. Wheeling Nailers (team). 1889. *2279*
—. Sabbath. Social change. Values. 1892-1934. *2282*
Bashford, James W. China. Methodist Episcopal Church. Missions and Missionaries. Social gospel. 1889-1919. *1712*
Bassett, John Spencer. Academic freedom. Duke University. Methodist Church. North Carolina (Durham). Racism. *South Atlantic Quarterly* (periodical). 1902-03. *3497*
Batchelder, John. Episcopal Church, Protestant. Frontier and Pioneer Life. Illinois (Jacksonville). Trinity Church. 1830-40. *3192*
Batt, Joseph. Alsace-Lorraine. Catholic Church. Chapel of Our Lady of Help of Christians. Immigration. New York (Buffalo area; Cheektowaga). 1789-1872. *1760*
Battle Creek College. Adventists. Brownsberger, Sidney. California. Colleges and Universities. Healdsburg College. Michigan. 1875-80's. *665*
—. Adventists. Madison College. Michigan. Sutherland, Edward A. Tennessee. 1897-1904. *743*
Battle Creek Sanitarium. Adventists. California. Loma Linda University. Medical Education. Michigan. Nurses and Nursing. 1884-1979. *1425*
Baur, John C. Concordia Seminary. Fund raising. Lutheran Church (Missouri Synod). Missouri (Clayton, St. Louis). Personal Narratives. 1923-26. *594*
Beach, John. Church of England. Clergy. Congregationalism. Connecticut. Heresy. 1720-82. *3204*
Beard, Charles A. Foreign policy. Niebuhr, Reinhold. 20c. *1364*
Beauty, perception of. Congregationalism. Edwards, Jonathan. Knowledge. Mental activity theory. New England. 1730-69. *2323*
Beck, Vilhelm. Danish Americans. Grundtvig, Nikolai Frederik Severin. Inner Mission Movement. Lutheran Church. 1619-1973. *3341*
Bee, William. Methodist Church, Primitive. Saskatchewan (Grenfell). Settlement. 1882. *3449*
Beecher, Catharine. Church of England. Congregationalism. Johnson, Samuel (1696-1772). Reform (review article). Washington, Booker T. Women. 1696-1901. *2847*

Beecher family. Albanese, Catherine L. Caskey, Marie. Congregationalism. Connecticut. Massachusetts. Presbyterian Church. Transcendentalism (review article). Unitarianism. 1800-60. *2763*
Beecher, Henry Ward. Albanese, Catherine L. Civil Religion. Clark, Clifford E., Jr. Douglas, Ann. Handy, Robert T. McLoughlin, William G. Reform. Revivals (review article). Women. 1607-1978. *6*
—. Feminism. New York City. Radicals and Radicalism. Sex. Social Reform. Spiritualism. Vanderbilt, Cornelius. Woodhull, Victoria Claflin. 1868-90's. *2386*
Beecher, Lyman. Abolition Movement. Colonization. Presbyterian Church (New School). 1820-50. *2492*
—. Clergy. New York (East Hampton). Presbyterian Church. Temperance Movements. 1799-1810. *2585*
—. Congregationalism. Dwight, Timothy. New England. Presbyterian Church. Republicanism. Taylor, Nathaniel William. 1790-1840. *1356*
—. Evangelical Alliance. Great Britain. Presbyterian Church. Temperance Movements. World Temperance Convention. 1846. *3563*
Beeson, John. Blaine, David E. Indian-White Relations. Methodists. Oregon. Washington. 1850-59. *3495*
Behavior. Boucher, Jonathan. Church of England. Loyalists. Maryland. Virginia. 1738-89. *1348*
—. Church of England. Clergy. Maryland. 1700-75. *3228*
—. Communalism. Hutterites. Social theory. ca 1650-1977. *382*
—. Conversion. Graham, Billy. Revivals. 1968-75. *2275*
—. Judaism, Orthodox. 1970's. *4181*
—. Pregnancy. Puritanism. Sex. Social control. 1640-1971. *949*
Behaviorism. Calvinism. Psychology. Watson, John Broadus. 1890-1919. *2308*
—. Skinner, B. F. Social Psychology. 1948-74. *154*
Beiliss, Mendel. California (Oakland, San Francisco). Christianity. Jews. Newspapers. Russia. Trials. 1911-13. *4105*
Beissel, Johann Conrad. Communalism. Eckerlin, Emmanuel. Ephrata Cloister. Pennsylvania (Conestoga Valley). 1732-68. *390*
Belgian Congo (Kasai). Missions and Missionaries. Presbyterian Church. 1871-1964. *1729*
Belk, Fred R. Immigration. Mennonites. Pacifism. Russia. 1880-84. *3351*
Belkin, Samuel. Brown University. Judaism (Orthodox). Rhode Island (Providence). 1932-35. *4172*
Bellah, Robert N. Authority. Civil religion. Myths and Symbols. Politics. Secularization. 1977. *1165*
—. Church and state. Civil religion. Judeo-Christian thought. National self-image. New Israel concept. 19c-20c. *1199*
—. Civil religion. Methodology. 1967-78. *1198*
—. Civil religion. National self-image. Political attitudes. Values. 1775-20c. *1200*
Bellah, Robert N. (review article). Civil religion. Sociology of Religion. 1959-75. *112*
Bellamy, Edward. Individualism. Nationalist Movement. 1865-98. *82*
Benedictine High School. Boys. Catholic Church. Ohio (Cleveland). Secondary Education. 1928-78. *787*
Benedictine sisters. Immigration. Missouri (Conception). Renggli, Rose (Mother Mary Beatrice). Switzerland. Women. 1874. *3832*
Benedictines. Americanization. Germany. Monasticism. Switzerland. 1846-1900. *314*
—. Anti-Catholicism. D'Equivelley, G. F. Florida (Pasco County). *Jeffersonian* (newspaper). Land. Letters-to-the-editor. Mohr, Charles. 1915-16. *2123*
—. Architecture. Churches. Liturgy. 1945-62. *1804*
—. Architecture. Churches. Monasteries. Vatican Council II. 1962-75. *1805*
—. Catholic Church. Frontier and Pioneer Life. Oetgen, Jerome (review article). Wimmer, Boniface. 1809-87. *3685*
—. Catholic Church. Missions and Missionaries. Vatican Council I. Wimmer, Boniface. 1866-87. *3815*
—. Illinois (New Cluny). Immigrants. Missions and Missionaries. Monastic observance. Moosmüller, Oswald. 1832-1901. *3816*
—. Monasteries. Wimmer, Boniface. 19c. 1960's-70's. *3754*
—. Quebec (Brome County). St. Benoît-du-Lac (abbey). 1955-79. *1770*
Benefices. American Revolution (antecedents). Church of England. New England. Religious Liberty. Society for the Propagation of the Gospel. 1689-1775. *1054*
Benefit of clergy. Colonial Government. Common law. Criminal law. Maryland. 1637-1713. *1140*
Benevolence (doctrine). Finney, Charles G. Protestantism. Social reform. 1815-65. *2422*
Benezet, Anthony. Africans' School. Education. Friends, Society of. Negroes. Pennsylvania (Philadelphia). 1770's-80's. *527*
—. Antislavery Sentiments. Friends, Society of. 1759-84. *2461*
—. Attitudes. Friends, Society of. Wealth. Woolman, John. 1740-83. *358*
Bengough, John Wilson. City government. *Grip* (periodical). Ontario (Toronto). Political Reform. Protestantism. 1873-1910. *1266*
Ben-Hur (play, novel). Christianity. Drama. Wallace, Lew. 1880-1900. *1872*
Benjamin, Asher. Architecture. Churches (Greek Revival). Massachusetts (Boston). 1833-40. *1826*
—. Architecture. Massachusetts (Boston). Truss design. West Church. 1805-23. *1827*
Benjamin, Philip S. Feldberg, Michael. Friends, Society of. Miller, Richard G. Pennsylvania (Philadelphia; review article). Sinclair, Bruce. 1790-1920. 1974-76. *3269*
Bennet, James Arlington. Letters. Mormons (Reorganized). 1840's-60. *3951*
Bennett, Anne M. Bennett, John C. Minorities. Theology. Women's liberation. 1974. *799*
Bennett, James Gordon. Catholic Church. Immigration. *New York Herald* (newspaper). 1835-70. *3850*
Bennett, John C. Bennett, Anne M. Minorities. Theology. Women's liberation. 1974. *799*
Bennett, Robert. Baptists. Clarke, John. Great Britain (London). Letters. Religious Liberty. Rhode Island. 1655-58. *1132*
Benson, Ezra Taft. Morality. Mormons. Political Leadership. Presbyterian Church. Wallace, Henry A. 1933-60. *1303*
Bercovitch, Sacvan (review article). Massachusetts. Mather, Cotton. National Characteristics. Puritans. 17c-18c. 1975. *3630*
Berea College. Abolition Movement. Fee, John Gregg. Kentucky. Presbyterian Church. Religious education. 1855-1904. *777*
Bergel, Siegmund. California (San Bernardino). Jews. Religious education. 1868-1912. *765*
Berger, Elmer. Judaism (Reform). Personal Narratives. Rabbis. Zionism. ca 1945-75. *4202*
Bergner, Peter. Bethel Ships. Evangelism. Merchant Marine. Methodist Church. New York City. Swedish Americans. 1832-66. *1661*
—. Immigrants. *John Wesley* (vessel). Methodist Episcopal Church. New York City. Seamen. 1830-77. *3478*
Bergson, Henri. Historiography. Morality. Niebuhr, H. Richard. Troeltsch, Ernst. 1925-37. *255*
Bergthal Colony. Bishops. Immigration. Manitoba. Mennonites. Stoesz, David. Ukraine. 1872-76. *3390*
Berkeley, George. Church of England. Education. Reform. Rhode Island (Newport). Sectarianism. 1704-34. *3230*
Berkeley New Religious Consciousness Project. California (San Francisco Bay area). Cults. 1970's. *4272*
Bernard, Alexius. Alexian Brothers. Catholic Church. German Americans. Hospitals. Missouri (St. Louis). Tollig, Paulus. 1869-1980. *1456*
Bernard, Joseph. Alaska (Mary's Igloo). Catholic Church. Eskimos. Missions and Missionaries. 1884-1962. *1504*
Berns, Walter (review article). Church and state. Constitutional Amendments (1st). Supreme Court. 18c-20c. *1114*
Berrigan, Daniel. Berrigan, Philip. Catholic Church. Church and state. Leftism. Murray, John Courtney. 1950's-70's. *3758*
Berrigan, Philip. Berrigan, Daniel. Catholic Church. Church and state. Leftism. Murray, John Courtney. 1950's-70's. *3758*
Besant, Annie. Blavatsky, Helena Petrovna. Hindu renaissance. India. Theosophy. Vedanta. 1875-1900. *4283*
—. California (San Diego). Schisms. Theosophy. Tingley, Katharine Augusta Westcott. 1897. *4298*
Beth Olam Cemetery. California (San Jose). Congregation Bickur Cholim. Judaism (Orthodox, Reform). Organizations. 1850-1900. *4123*
Bethany College. Augustana College and Theological Seminary. Immigration. Lutheran Church. Midwest. Politics. Railroads. Religious education. Swedish Americans. Swensson, Carl Aaron. 1873-1904. *726*
Bethel African Methodist Episcopal Church. Baptists. California (San Francisco). Civil rights. Methodist Episcopal Zion Church, African. Negroes. Pressure groups. Third Baptist Church. 1860's. *1289*
—. Methodist Episcopal Church, African. Pennsylvania (Reading). Restorations. 1834-1979. *1784*
Bethel College. Conscientious Objectors. Mennonites. Oral history. World War I. 1917-18. 1974. *262*
—. Kansas (North Newton). Kauffman, Charles. Kauffman Museum. Mennonites. Missions and Missionaries. Museums. 1907-76. *198*
Bethel Ships. Bergner, Peter. Evangelism. Merchant Marine. Methodist Church. New York City. Swedish Americans. 1832-66. *1661*
Betten, Neil. Catholic Church (review article). Dolan, Jay P. Working Class. 1830-1978. *3698*
Betz, Hans. Amish, Old Order. German language. Hymnals. 16c-20c. *1946*
Bible. Adventists. Medical reform. 1810's-63. *1436*
—. Adventists. Prophecy. World War I (antecedents). 1912-18. *2664*
—. Adventists. Protestantism. Republicanism. 1850's-60's. *2962*
—. Aitken, Robert. Continental Congress. English language. Pennsylvania (Philadelphia). Publishers and Publishing. 1782. *1979*
—. Aitken, Robert. Continental Congress. Publishers and Publishing. 1777-82. *1983*
—. Alberta. Blackfoot Indians. Indians. Missions and Missionaries. Stocken, H. W. G. Translating and Interpreting. Wolf Collar (shaman). 1870-1928. *1500*
—. American Board of Commissioners for Foreign Missions. Arabic. Missions and Missionaries. Moslems. Protestantism. Translating and Interpreting. 1843-60. *1740*
—. Anticlericalism. Deism. Jefferson, Thomas. Jesus Christ. Translating and Interpreting. 1813-20. *4279*
—. Antinomianism. Campbell, Alexander. Disciples of Christ. 1810-60. *3109*
—. Baptists. Church Government. Theology. 1707-1814. *3071*
—. Baptists. Periodicals. Theology. 1925-75. *3014*
—. British Columbia. California. Christianity. Indians. Missions and Missionaries. Myths and Symbols. Pacific Northwest. 1830-50. *1612*
—. Business. Secularism. 1900-29. *344*
—. Campbell, Alexander. Disciples of Christ. Theology. ca 1830-60. *3110*
—. Catholic Church. Hermeneutics. Periodicals. 1893-1908. *3812*
—. Cave, Robert Catlett. Disciples of Christ. Missouri (St. Louis). Sermons. Theology. 1840's-90's. *3111*
—. Clergy. Congregationalism. Edwards, Jonathan. Marginalia. Massachusetts (Deerfield). Pierpont, Benjamin. Theology. 1726-30. *3146*
—. Congregationalism. Edwards, Jonathan. Hermeneutics. Massachusetts. 1720-58. *3149*
—. Creation theory. Dana, James Dwight. Guyot, Arnold. Protestantism. Science. 1850's. *2333*
—. Darwinism. Episcopal Church, Protestant. Europe. Excommunication. Hermeneutics. MacQueary, Howard. Ohio (Canton). St. Paul's Church. Universalism. 1890-91. *3178*
—. Diaries. Fiction. Melville, Herman. Palestine. Travel. 1857. *2039*
—. Disciples of Christ. Rhetoric. 19c. *1978*
—. Embury, Philip. Ireland. Methodism. New York City. 1760-1834. *3489*
—. Environment. History. Wilderness. 18c-20c. *36*
—. Evangelicals. Inerrancy (doctrine). Montgomery, John W. (review article). Objectivist apologetics. 1972. *2882*

—. Folklore. Protestantism. South. Visions. 20c. *2178*
—. Georgia Trustees. Rhetoric. Sermons. Slavery. 1731-50. *2161*
—. History. Israel. Mormons. Smith, Joseph Fielding. Snell, Heber C. Theology. 1937-52. *4035*
—. Mormons. Theology. 1830-1900. *4013*
—. Music. New England. Puritans. Pythagoreanism. 1640-1726. *1912*
—. Music (Gospel). Protestantism. 18c-1980. *1949*
—. Smith, Julia Evelina. Translating. Women. 1840-76. *1992*
—. Toponymy. 17c-1940. *23*
Bible (King James Version). Catholic Church. Church Schools. City Politics. Education, Finance. Michigan (Detroit). Protestantism. Religion in the Public Schools. 1842-53. *2716*
Bible (New Testament). Exegesis. Germany. Hodge, Charles. Liberalism. Presbyterian Church. Princeton Theological Seminary. 1820-78. *3573*
Bible (New Testament; Epistles). Paul, Saint. Primitivism. Theology. Williams, Roger. 1630-83. *2939*
Bible (Old Testament). Jews. New England. Pilgrims. Puritans. 1620-1700. *2936*
Bible reading. Catholic Church. Desmond, Humphrey. Protestantism. Religion in the Public Schools. *Wisconsin ex rel. Frederick Weiss et al.* v. *District School Board of School District 8* (1890). 1888-90. *571*
—. Catholic Church. Politics. Prince Edward Island. Protestants. Religion in the Public Schools. 1856-60. *580*
—. Letters. Massachusetts (Amesbury). Public schools. Whittier, John Greenleaf. 1853. *577*
Bible Research Fellowship. Adventists. Religious Education. 1943-52. *611*
Bible (Revelation). Apocalypse. Edwards, Jonathan. Providence. Theology. 1720-24. *3148*
Biblical criticism. Alexander, Joseph A. Princeton Theological Seminary. Seminaries. Theater. 1830-61. *705*
Biblical studies. Albright, William Foxwell. Archaeology. Philosophy of History. Science. 1918-70. *2328*
—. Ecumenism. Missions and Missionaries. Palestine. Protestantism. 1812-1975. *1748*
Biblical Theology Movement. Presbyterian Church. Smith, William Robertson. Theology. 1870-83. *590*
Bibliographies. 17c-20c. *200*
—. American Jewish Historical Society. Jews. 1960-75. *4096*
—. American Revolution. Bicentennial Celebrations. Mennonites. 1776. 1975-76. *3378*
—. Anabaptists. Dissertations. Mennonites. 1975-76. *3397*
—. Anabaptists. Mennonites. 16c-1975. *3396*
—. Anabaptists. Mennonites. 16c-20c. 1977-78. *3387*
—. Anglican Communion. 1972. *3232*
—. Anglican Communion. Great Britain. 1973-75. *3233*
—. Appalachia. Protestantism. 1905-75. *2879*
—. Archives. California. Franciscans. Geiger, Maynard J. (obituary). Historiography. Mission Santa Barbara. 1936-76. *240*
—. Arrington, Leonard J. (tribute). Historiography. Mormons. 1917-79. *277*
—. Baptists. 1950's-77. *3023*
—. Baptists. Clarke, William Newton. Evolution. Immanentism. Theology. 1894-1912. *3065*
—. Baptists. Historiography. 1964-74. *3005*
—. Baptists. Periodicals. 1979. *3099*
—. Bishops. Catholic Church. Education. Keane, John J. 1838-1918. *3891*
—. Canada. Catholic Church. ca 1800-1976. *3760*
—. Canada. Christianity. 1974-78. *2745*
—. Canada. Church history. 17c-1973. *14*
—. Canada. Church history. 17c-20c. *16*
—. Canada. Congregationalism. Historiography. Lutheran Church. Methodist Church. Presbyterian Church. United Church of Canada. 1825-1973. *2892*
—. Catholic Church. Catholic University of America. Hogan Schism. Parsons, Wilfrid. Pennsylvania (Philadelphia). Schisms. 1785-1825. 1975. *3845*
—. Christianity. Communism. 1970's. *2759*
—. Christianity. Evolution. 1970's-75. *2330*
—. Civil religion. Sociology of religion. 17c-20c. 1960's-70's. *1168*
—. Clergy. Friends, Society of. Sermons. 1653-1700. *204*
—. Concordia Historical Institute. Lutheran Church. Microforms. 1971-72. *265*
—. Connecticut. Massachusetts. Witchcraft. 17c. 1976. *2194*
—. Diocesan histories. Episcopal Church, Protestant. Missions and Missionaries. ca 1776-1972. *3201*
—. Discovery and Exploration. Historians. Morison, Samuel Eliot (obituary). Puritans. 1887-1976. *233*
—. Dissertations. Edwards, Jonathan. Niebuhr, H. Richard. Niebuhr, Reinhold. Presbyterian Church. Reformed Churches. Tillich, Paul. 18c-20c. 1965-72. *2815*
—. Dissertations. Mormons. Theses. 19c-1977. *4041*
—. Dissertations. North Carolina. Prehistory-1970's. *28*
—. Europe. Folk religion. North America. 1900-74. 16c-20c. *42*
—. Evangelicalism. 1945-79. *2915*
—. Historiography. Miller, Perry. 1933-77. *184*
—. Historiography. Mormons. Settlement. Utah. 1840-1976. *4046*
—. Historiography. Rhode Island. Williams, Roger. 17c-1972. *2911*
—. History. Sociology. 1960-70. *120*
—. Indian-White relations. *Journal of the West* (periodical). Western states. 1970-74. *1593*
—. Jews. 1654-1980. *4114*
—. Jews. 16c-1978. *4118*
—. Jews. 1960-73. *4113*
—. Jews. 1960-74. *4095*
—. Jews. 1960-76. *4116*
—. Jews. 1960-78. *4117*
—. Jews. 1960-79. *4119*
—. Jews. 1974-75. *4115*
—. Judaism. 1960-80. *4120*
—. Judaism (Reform). 1883-1973. *4226*
—. Lutheran Church. Music. 1700-1850. *1956*
—. Maryland. 1788-1978. *8*
—. *Minnesota History* (periodical). Women. 1915-76. *905*
—. Mormonism. 19c-1974. *3967*
—. Mormons. 1976. *3969*
—. Mormons. 1977. *3966*
—. Mormons. 19c-1973. *4019*
—. Mormons. 19c-1975. *3968*
—. Mormons. 19c-20c. 1974-78. *4040*
—. Mormons. Newspapers. 1977. *4042*
—. New England. Puritans. Sermons. 1652-1700. 1903. *1964*
—. North Carolina. 1975-76. *20*
—. Periodicals. 17c-1970's. *44*
—. Periodicals. 1977. *43*
—. Periodicals. Presbyterian Church. Reformed churches. 1973. *2957*
—. Periodicals. Psychology of religion. Research. 1950-74. *168*
—. Periodicals. South. 18c-20c. 1977-78. *45*
—. Sermons. Vermont. Women. 1800-1915. *909*
Bicentennial Celebrations *See also* Centennial Celebrations.
—. American Revolution. Bibliographies. Mennonites. 1776. 1975-76. *3378*
—. Arts. Consultation on the Religious Communities, the Arts and the Second American Revolution. 1973. *1846*
—. Catholic Church. 1976. *3684*
Bicentennial Conference of Religious Liberty. Pennsylvania (Philadelphia). Religious liberty. 1976. *1040*
Bidamon, Emma Smith. Bidamon, Lewis C. Illinois (Nauvoo). Marriage. Mormons. Women. 1842-80. *3931*
—. Illinois (Nauvoo). Mormons. Property. Schisms. Smith, Joseph. Women. Women. Young, Brigham. 1832-79. *3932*
Bidamon, Lewis C. Bidamon, Emma Smith. Illinois (Nauvoo). Marriage. Mormons. Women. 1842-80. *3931*
Biddle, Owen. American Revolution. Friends, Society of. Lacey, John, Jr. Military Service. Pennsylvania. 1775-83. *2684*
Billings, William. Attitudes. Music (choral). Upper Classes. 1750-1800. *1907*
—. Copyright. Massachusetts. Music. 1770-90. *1939*
—. Hymnals. Music. Poetry. Read, Daniel. Watts, Isaac. 1761-85. *1920*
Bingham, Abel. Baptists. Diaries. Indian-White Relations. Iroquois Indians (Seneca). Missions and Missionaries. New York. Red Jacket (leader). Tonawanda Indian Reservation. 1822-28. *1513*
Bingham family. American Board of Commissioners for Foreign Missions. Congregationalism. Gilbert Islands. Hawaii. Missions and Missionaries. 1820-1975. *1678*
—. Congregationalism. Hawaii. Micronesia. Missions and Missionaries. Yale University Library (Bingham Family Papers). 1815-1967. *1714*
Bingham, Hiram. Congregationalism. Converts. Family. Missions and Missionaries. Vermont. 1789-1819. *1585*
Biographical dictionary. Clergy. Unitarianism. Universalism. Women. 1860-1976. *4079*
Birdwood Junior College. Colleges and universities. Georgia (Birdwood). 1954-74. *514*
Birney, James. Abolition Movement. Clergy. Evangelism. Smith, Gerrit. Stanton, H. B. Weld, Theodore. 1820-50. *2488*
Birth certificates. Baptismal certificates. Folk art. Pennsylvania Germans. 1750-1850. *1899*
Birth Control *See also* Abortion; Birth Rate.
—. Abortion. Protestantism. 19c. *869*
—. Annulments. Canon law. Catholic Church. Divorce. Netherlands. 1945-77. *914*
—. Fertility. Rhode Island. 1968-69. *803*
—. Mormons. Values. 19c-20c. *818*
Birth Rate *See also* Birth Control; Fertility; Population.
—. Age. Marriage. Mormons. Women. 1800-69. *892*
Bishop, Harriet E. Baptists. Minnesota (St. Paul). Reform. Social reform. Women. 1847-83. *801*
Bishop Hill Colony. Engstrand, Stuart (review article). Illinois. Jansson, Erik H. 1846-50. 20c. *2083*
—. Illinois. Immigrants. Janssonists. Swedish Americans. Utopias. 1846-60. *393*
—. Illinois. Janssonists. Letters. Swedish Americans. 1847. *416*
Bishop of London. Church of England. Commissaries. Great Britain. South Carolina. 1715-32. *3242*
—. Clergy. Methodists. Ordination. Petitions. Pilmoor, Joseph. Virginia (Norfolk County). 1774. *3465*
Bishops. Albany Diocese. Episcopal Church, Protestant. New York. Oldham, George Ashton. 1922-47. *3176*
—. American Revolution. Chaplains. Church of England. Griffith, David. Virginia Regiment, 3rd. 1774-89. *3235*
—. Archives. Catholic Church. Church History. Kingston, Archdiocese of. Ontario. 1800-1966. *247*
—. Assimilation. Authority. Catholic Church. Cleveland Diocese. German Americans. Irish Americans. Ohio. Rappe, Louis Amadeus. 1847-70. *3788*
—. Atlantic Provinces. Catholic Church. Diaries. Plessis, Joseph-Octave. Quebec Archdiocese. 1812-15. *3704*
—. Authority. Canada. Church of England. Councils and Synods. Laity. 1780-1979. *3224*
—. Authority. Church and State. Civil War. Episcopal Church, Protestant. Grace Church. Illinois (Galesburg). 1864-66. *1218*
—. Bergthal Colony. Immigration. Manitoba. Mennonites. Stoesz, David. Ukraine. 1872-76. *3390*
—. Bibliographies. Catholic Church. Education. Keane, John J. 1838-1918. *3891*
—. British Columbia (Kootenay). Church of England. Doull, Alexander John. 1870-1937. *3180*
—. Byrne, Edwin V. Caruana, George J. Catholic Church. Jones, William A. Puerto Rico. San Juan Diocese. 1866-1963. *3814*
—. Canada. Church of England. Documents. 1850-52. *3208*
—. Canada, western. Catholic Church. French Canadians. Irish Canadians. Nominations for office. 1900-75. *3765*
—. Canevin, Regis. Catholic Church. Flick, Lawrence. Pennsylvania (Philadelphia, Pittsburgh). 1870's-1927. *3843*
—. Catholic Church. Chicago Diocese. Clergy. Duggan, James. Illinois. McMullen, John. Succession. 1865-81. *3742*
—. Catholic Church. Chicoutimi, Séminaire de. Quebec (Saguenay). 1873-1973. *721*
—. Catholic Church. Church Finance. Frenaye, Mark Anthony. Letters. O'Connor, Michael. Pennsylvania (Pittsburgh). 1843-49. *368*
—. Catholic Church. Church of England. Evangelicalism. Feild, Edward. Liturgy. Methodism. Newfoundland. Presbyterian Church. 1765-1852. *3197*

—. Catholic Church. Church of England. Liberal Party. Newfoundland. Provincial government. 1860-62. *1253*
—. Catholic Church. Clergy. Marriage. Uniates. 1890-1907. *3907*
—. Catholic Church. Colombia (Bogotá). Hughes, John. Letters. Mosquera, Manuel José. New York City. 1853. *3762*
—. Catholic Church. Education. Medicine. Quebec (Gaspé). Ross, François Xavier. Social Conditions. 1923-45. *3787*
—. Catholic Church. Farrelly, John P. Irish Americans. Morris, John. Stritch, Samuel A. Tennessee. 19c-1958. *3860*
—. Catholic Church. Indian-white relations. Lamy, Jean Baptiste. New Mexico (Santa Fe). Social customs. 1849-88. *3761*
—. Catholic Church. Intellectuals. Letters. Provincial Council of Baltimore (4th). Walter, William Joseph. 1840-43. *3842*
—. Catholic Church. Irish Americans. Jamestown Diocese. Minnesota (St. Paul). North Dakota. Shanley, John. 1852-1909. *3731*
—. Catholic Church. Kenrick, Peter Richard. Letters. Missouri. Travel. 1847. *3839*
—. Catholic Church. Lynch, John Joseph. Ontario. Poor. Toronto Savings Bank. 1870's. *369*
—. Catholic Church. McCarthy, Joseph R. 1954. *1222*
—. Catholic Church. Quebec. Sherbrooke Diocese. 1868-72. *3882*
—. Catholic Church. Trusteeism. 1785-1860. *293*
—. Church of England. 1750-75. *3210*
—. Church of England. Councils and Synods. Fulford, Francis. Quebec (Montreal). 1850-68. *3209*
—. Church of England. Education. Feild, Edward. Great Britain. Newfoundland. 1826-44. *3198*
—. Church of England. Letters. Medley, John. New Brunswick (Fredericton). Oxford Movement. Pusey, Edward Bouverie. ca 1840-44. *3190*
—. Church of England. Liturgy. Ontario (Toronto). Strachan, John. Theology. 1802-67. *3214*
—. Civil War. Episcopal Church, Protestant. Hopkins, John Henry. 1861-65. *445*
—. Diocesan Standing Committee. Episcopal Church, Protestant. ca 1789-1832. *3217*
—. Durr, John N. Mennonite Conference, Allegheny. Pennsylvania. 1872-1934. *3440*
—. Episcopal Church, Protestant. Huntington, Frederick (and family). New York. Social reform. Theology. Women. 1869-1904. *3213*
—. Episcopal Church, Protestant. Louisiana (Shreveport). Polk, Leonidas. 1830-1916. *3184*
—. Immigration. Lehman, Hans (and family). Mennonites. Pennsylvania (Lancaster County; Rapho Township). Swiss Americans. ca 1727-1909. *3400*
—. Laity. Methodist Protestant Church. Reform. 1779-1832. *320*
—. Methodist Episcopal Church. Peck, Jesse T. Social gospel. 1850-83. *2396*
Black, Conrad. Catholic Church. Church and state. Duplessis, Maurice (review article). Provincial Government. Quebec. Rumilly, Robert. 1930's-77. *1124*
Black Hills. Episcopal Church, Protestant. Hinman, Samuel D. Indians. Missions and Missionaries. Sioux Indians. 1860-76. *1484*
Black Muslims. Christianity. Millenarianism. 1920-79. *4250*
Black Nationalism. Colonization. Cuffe, Paul. Friends, Society of. Sierra Leone. 1810's. *2478*
—. Crummell, Alexander. DuBois, W. E. B. Episcopal Church, Protestant. Ferris, William H. Ideology. 1819-1898. *2424*
Black power. Church and Social Problems. Economic Aid. Episcopal Church, Protestant. General Convention Special Program. Self-determination. 1963-75. *2541*
Black theology. Christianity. Feminism. Negroes. Reform. Theology. 1960's-70's. *2426*
Blackburn, Gideon. Acculturation. Cherokee Indians. Missions and missionaries. Presbyterian Church. Schools. Tennessee. 1804-10. *1491*
—. Cherokee Indians. Indians. Missions and Missionaries. Old Southwest. Presbyterian Church. Schools. Whiskey. 1809-10. *700*
Blackfoot Indians. Alberta. Bible. Indians. Missions and Missionaries. Stocken, H. W. G. Translating and Interpreting. Wolf Collar (shaman). 1870-1928. *1500*
Blacks. *See* Negroes.
Blackthink. Church and Social Problems. Human Relations. Poor. 1963-75. *2537*
Blaine, David E. Beeson, John. Indian-White Relations. Methodists. Oregon. Washington. 1850-59. *3495*
Blair, Duncan Black. Gaelic language. Nova Scotia (Barney's River). Poets. Presbyterianism. Scholarship. 1848-93. *2069*
—. Gaelic language. Nova Scotia (Pictou County). Poetry. Presbyterianism. Scholars. Scotland. 1846-93. *2070*
Blair, James. Church of England. Church of Scotland. College of William and Mary. Converts. Virginia. 1679-1720. *2924*
—. Church of England. Clergy. Vestries. Virginia. 1700-75. *3186*
—. Church of England. College of William and Mary. Governors. Missions and Missionaries. Virginia. ca 1685-1743. *3223*
Bland, Salem. Canada. Methodism. Social Gospel. Theology. 1880-86. *3444*
Blavatsky, Helena Petrovna. Besant, Annie. Hindu renaissance. India. Theosophy. Vedanta. 1875-1900. *4283*
Bledsoe, Albert Taylor. Liberty. Philosophy. Theology. 19c. *1360*
Blenheim Mennonite Church. Mennonites. Ontario (Oxford, Waterloo counties). 1839-1974. *3352*
Blewett, George John. Canada. Methodist Church. Theology. 1873-1912. *3496*
Bliss, William D. P. Christianity. Leftism. Social Gospel. 1876-1926. *2377*
Blocker, Jack S., Jr. Clark, Norman H. Prohibition (review article). 1890-1913. 1976. *2577*
Bloomfield Academy. Chickasaw Indians. Downs, Ellen J. Girls. Indians. Methodist Church. Oklahoma (Penola County). Personal Narratives. Schools. 1853-66. *772*
Blue laws. Baseball. Church and state. Sabbath. West Virginia. Wheeling Nailers (team). 1889. *2279*
—. Church and state. Church of England. Friends, Society of. Law and Society. Pennsylvania. Presbyterian Church. 1682-1740. *2278*
—. Church and state. Legislators. Louisiana. Negroes. Reconstruction. Sabbath. 1867-75. *2285*
Blum, Abraham. California (Los Angeles). Judaism (Reform). New York City. Rabbis. Texas (Galveston). 1866-1921. *4217*
Blumer, Abraham. Pennsylvania (Allentown). Reformed German Church. Swiss Americans. Zion Reformed Church. 1771-1822. *3285*
Boarding Schools. Chatham Hall. Episcopal Church, Protestant. Ferguson, Anne Williams. Personal narratives. Virginia. Women. 1940's. *628*
Boardinghouses. Labor. Minnesota (Minneapolis). Women. Women's Christian Association. 1880's-1979. *2526*
Bobb, John. Atheism. Missouri (St. Louis). *Western Examiner* (periodical). 1834-35. *4300*
Bock, Anna. Indiana (Elkhart County). Mennonites, Old Order. Painting. 1830's-1970's. *1845*
Bode, Frederick A. (review article). Baptists. Capitalism. Methodist Church. North Carolina. Populism. 1894-1903. 1975. *1287*
Boehm, Martin. Mennonites. Newcomer, Christian. Pennsylvania Germans. Revivalism. 1740-1850. *2266*
Boer War. Canada. Clergy. English Canadians. Protestant churches. 1899-1902. *2675*
Boers. Champion, George. Missions and Missionaries. South Africa (Ginani). Zulus. 1836-41. *1719*
Bogan, Louise. Catholic Church. Poetry. Women. 1920's-70. *2059*
Bohemia *See also* Czechoslovakia.
—. Catholic Church. Neumann, Saint John Nepomucene. Pennsylvania (Philadelphia). 1811-1977. *3904*
Bohemia (Prague). Neumann, Saint John Nepomucene. Religious Education. 1833-35. *3763*
Bójnowski, Lucyan. Buczek, Daniel Stephen (review article). Catholic Church. Clergy. Connecticut (New Britain). Polish Americans. 1895-1960. *3865*
Boles, John B. (review article). Evangelicalism. Racism. Revivals. Smith, H. Shelton (review article). South. 1972. *2867*
Bolton, Herbert Eugene. Catholic Church. Colonization. Historiography. Missions and Missionaries. Southwest. Spain. 1917-79. *1489*
Bolton, William J. Architecture, Gothic Revival. Church of the Holy Trinity. Episcopal Church, Protestant. New York City (Brooklyn). Stained glass windows. 1845-47. *1847*
Bond, Thomas Emerson. Church government. Laity. Methodist Episcopal Church. Snethen, Nicholas. Stockton, William S. 1820-56. *288*
Bonomi, Patricia U. Ethnic Groups. Klein, Milton M. New York (review article). Pluralism. Provincial Government. 1690's-1770's. 1971-74. *1204*
Book Collecting *See also* Rare Books.
—. Judaism. Kohut, George Alexander. Yale University Library (Kohut Collection). 1901-33. *179*
Book of Common Prayer. Episcopal Church, Protestant. Merrymount Press. Printing. Typeface. 1922-30. *1986*
—. Episcopal Church, Protestant. Reform. 1785. *291*
Book of Common Worship. Humor. Lampton, William J. Poetry. Presbyterian Church, Southern. Rites and Ceremonies. VanDyke, Henry. 1906. *3557*
Books *See also* Authors; Copyright; Libraries; Literature; Manuscripts; Press; Printing; Publishers and Publishing; Rare Books; Reading; Textbooks.
—. Children's literature. Death and Dying. Periodicals. Protestantism. 1800-60. *2914*
—. Pennsylvania (New Geneva; Pleasant Hill School District). Protestantism. Sunday schools. 1823-57. *592*
Books (editions). Canada, western. Church of England. Diaries. Missions and Missionaries. West, John. 1820-27. *1530*
Bordley, Stephen. Church of England. Great Awakening. Letters. Maryland. Whitefield, George. 1730-40. *2229*
Bosom serpentry (concept). Folklore. Mormons. New England. Puritans. Snakes. Utah. 17c-19c. *2765*
Bossard, Gisbert. Florence, Max. Mormon Temple. Photography. Smith, Joseph Fielding. Utah (Salt Lake City). 1911. *1762*
Bossism. City Politics. Clergy. Crump, Edward Hull. Negroes. Tennessee (Memphis). 1927-48. *1318*
Boston Evening Post (newspaper). Fleet, Thomas. Freedom of the press. Great Awakening. Massachusetts (Boston). Newspapers. 1740's. *1423*
Botany. Art. Bartram, John. Bartram, William. Friends, Society of. Pennsylvania. Travel (accounts). 1699-1823. *2304*
—. Friends, Society of. Logan, James. Mather, Cotton. Natural History. New England. Puritans. 17c-18c. *2300*
Bote (newspaper). Germans, Russian. Mennonites. Nazism. Saskatchewan. USSR. Völkisch thought. 1917-39. *3431*
Bottoms, Lawrence W. Negroes. Personal narratives. Presbyterian Church, Southern. South. 1930-75. *2529*
Boucher, Jonathan. American Revolution. Church of England. Civil War. Great Britain. Jefferson, Thomas. Loyalists. 1640-1797. *1412*
—. American Revolution. Church of England. Loyalists. 1763-83. *1383*
—. Behavior. Church of England. Loyalists. Maryland. Virginia. 1738-89. *1348*
—. Catholic Church. Church of England. Maryland. Religious Liberty. 1774-97. *2729*
—. Chase, Samuel. Church and State. Maryland. Paca, William. Taxation. 1770-73. *1141*
—. Church of England. Great Britain. Loyalists. Maryland. Zimmer, Anne Y. (review article). 1770's-90's. *1358*
Boudinot, Elias. Millenarianism. Newton, Thomas. Presbyterian Church. Theology. 1787-1821. *3569*
Boundaries *See also* Annexation; Geopolitics.
—. Catholic Church. Missions and Missionaries. Ontario. Settlement. 1840-1910. *3709*
Bourassa, Henri. Catholic Church. Politics. Provincial Government. Quebec. 1902-71. *976*
Bourgeoisie. *See* Middle Classes.

Bourget, Ignace. Catholic Church. Church History. Faillon, Etienne-Michel. Letters. Quebec (Montreal). 1850. *3824*
—. Catholic Church. Colleges and Universities. Laval University. Quebec (Quebec). 1840's-50's. *676*
Boutwell, William Thurston. American Board of Commissioners for Foreign Missions. Chippewa Indians. Indian-White Relations. Minnesota. Missions and Missionaries. Protestant Churches. 1831-47. *1572*
Boxerman, William I. Anti-Semitism. Coughlin, Charles Edward. Documents. Michigan (Detroit). 1939. *2131*
Boycotts. Church Schools. Mexican Americans. Mexican Presbyterian Mission School. Presbyterian Church. Public schools. Segregation. Texas (San Angelo). 1910-15. *618*
—. Consumers. Jews. Meat, kosher. New York City. Prices. Riots. Women. 1902. *4112*
Boyer, Paul. City Life. Johnson, Paul E. Middle Classes. Missions and Missionaries. Morality. New York (Rochester). Revivals. 1815-1920. 1978. *2800*
—. Massachusetts (Salem). Nissenbaum, Stephen. Puritans. Witchcraft (review article). 1550-1690. 1974-76. *2200*
Boys. Adolescence. Canada. Protestantism. USA. Young Men's Christian Association. 1870-1920. *2414*
—. Benedictine High School. Catholic Church. Ohio (Cleveland). Secondary Education. 1928-78. *787*
—. Illinois (Nauvoo). Mormons. Police protection. Whistling and Whittling Brigade. 1845. *4014*
Bozeman, Theodore Dwight (review article). Baconianism. Protestantism. Science. 1800's-60's. 1977. *2324*
Bradford family. Attitudes. Letters. Missouri. Mormons. Virginia. 1838-39. *4057*
Bradford, Phoebe George. Daily life. Delaware. Diaries. Episcopal Church, Protestant. 1832-33. *3245*
—. Daily Life. Delaware (Wilmington). Diaries. Episcopal Church, Protestant. 1833-35. *3244*
Bradford, William *(Of Plymouth Plantation).* Historiography. Pilgrims. Plymouth Colony. Social Organization. 1630-50. *3153*
—. Pilgrims. Plymouth Colony. Theology. 1630. *3126*
Bradley, Lucas. Churches. Missouri (St. Louis). Presbyterian Church. Wisconsin (Racine). 1840-90. *1810*
Bradstreet, Anne. Clap, Roger. Devotions. New England. Puritans. Sewall, Samuel. Shepard, Thomas. Worship. 17c. *3627*
—. Elegies. Massachusetts. Poetry. Puritans. Women. 1665. *2044*
—. Hutchinson, Anne. Literature. Massachusetts. Puritans. Social change. Theology. Women. 1630's-70's. *865*
Brady, John Green. Alaska. Assimilation. Economic Conditions. Indian-White Relations. Missions and Missionaries. Tlingit Indians. 1878-1906. *1548*
Brady, John Green (and family). Alaska. Business. Governors. Morality. Presbyterian Church. 1878-1906. *3549*
Brainerd Mission. American Board of Commissioners for Foreign Missions. Cherokee Indians. Education. Indian-White Relations. Letters. Southeastern States. 1817-38. *1605*
Brandeis, Louis D. Gompers, Samuel. Judaism. Kogan, Michael S. Labor Unions and Organizations. 1880's-1975. *1479*
Brattle Street Church. American Revolution. Calvinism. Congregationalism. Cooper, Samuel. Elites. Massachusetts (Boston). 1754-83. *1333*
—. American Revolution. Clergy. Congregationalism. Cooper, Samuel. Massachusetts (Boston). 1770-80. *951*
—. Architecture. Congregationalism. Dawes, Thomas. Massachusetts (Boston). 18c. *1771*
—. Coleman, Benjamin. Elites. Gentility (concept). Massachusetts (Boston). Puritans. 1715-45. *2622*
Bratton, Theodore DuBose. Conference for Education in the South. Episcopal Church, Protestant. Mississippi. Negroes. Racism. 1908. *2148*
Braude, William G. Judaism. Personal narratives. Wolfson, Harry. 1932-54. *4090*
Brazil. Clergy. New Netherland. Polhemius, Johannes Theodorus. Reformed Dutch Church. 1598-1676. *3165*
Brébeuf, Jean de. Catholic Church. Indian-White Relations. Ledesme, R. P. *(Doctrine Chrestienne).* New France. Translating and Interpreting. Wyandot Indians. 16c-17c. *1639*
Breck, Robert. Congregationalism. Connecticut (Scotland). Edwards, Jonathan. Massachusetts (Northampton). 1734-36. *3127*
Breckinridge, Robert Jefferson. Abolition Movement. Breckinridge, William Lewis. Constitutions, State. Emancipation Party. Kentucky. Presbyterians. 1849. *2475*
—. Clergy. Danville Theological Seminary. Education. Emancipation. Kentucky. Presbyterian Church. 1800-71. *3544*
—. Danville Theological Seminary. Emancipation. Kentucky. Presbyterian Church. Theology. 1832-71. *3545*
Breckinridge, William Lewis. Abolition Movement. Breckinridge, Robert Jefferson. Constitutions, State. Emancipation Party. Kentucky. Presbyterians. 1849. *2475*
Brenneman, John M. Civil War. Letters. Mennonites. 1862. *2709*
Brent, Charles Henry. Episcopal Church, Protestant. Missions and Missionaries. Paternalism. Philippines. 1901-18. *1738*
Breslin, Jimmy. Anti-Catholicism. Brooklyn Diocese. Flaherty, Joe. Hamill, Pete. Irish Americans. New York City. Novels. 1960's-70's. *2098*
Brethren churches. Pennsylvania, southeastern. Quiltmaking. 1700-1974. *1891*
Brethren in Christ. Assimilation. Protestantism. 1770-1973. *3422*
—. Canada. Engel, Jacob. Pennsylvania (Lancaster County). Sects, Religious. 1775-1964. *3437*
—. Canada. Holiness movement. North Central States. 1910-50. *3435*
—. Christianity. Education. Evangelism. Holiness movement. Individualism. 1870-1910. *3421*
—. Holiness Movement. Kansas. Mennonites. Methodism. 1870-1910. *3436*
—. Kansas (Dickinson). Pennsylvania, southeastern. Westward Movement. 1879. *3381*
Brethren in Christ (Wengerites). Indiana. Ohio. Pentecostals. 1836-1924. *3432*
Brethren, Old German Baptist. Assimilation. Conservatism. 1881-1977. *3413*
Brethren, Old Order River. Love feast. Pennsylvania. ca 1773-1973. *3383*
—. Mennonites. 1855-1977. *3424*
Brethren, Swiss. Immigration. Mennonites. North America. Surnames. 1680-1880. *3417*
Breweries. Illinois (Peoria). Leisy family. Mennonites. 1884-1950. *356*
Brickell, John. Clayton, John. Letters. Natural History. North Carolina. Plagiarism. 1693-1737. *2341*
Brigham Young University. Centennial Celebrations. Colleges and Universities. Mormons. Utah. 1876-1976. *783*
—. Education. Mormons. Utah (Provo). 1831-1970's. *588*
—. Educators. Germany. Maeser, Karl G. Mormons. 1828-56. 1876. *768*
—. Fundamentalism. Mormons. Students. Utah (Provo). 1935-73. *606*
Brigham Young University Library. Genealogy. Immigration studies. Mormons. Utah (Provo). 1830-1978. *236*
Brisbane, Albert. Brook Farm. Channing, William Henry. Fourierism. Transcendentalism. 1840-46. *399*
Bristol Baptist College. Baptists. Great Britain (Bristol). Missions and Missionaries. Religious Education. Terrill, Edward. 1634-1979. *3024*
British Americans. California (Los Angeles). Popular culture. Protestant Churches. Social Classes. 1920's. 1977. *2624*
British Canadians. Country life. Ethnic groups. French Canadians. Manitoba. Mennonites. Migration. Polish Canadians. Ukrainian Canadians. 1921-61. *3389*
British Columbia. Alaska (Metlakahtla). Capitalism. Duncan, William. Missions and Missionaries. Tsimshian Indians. 1857-1974. *1519*
—. Bible. California. Christianity. Indians. Missions and Missionaries. Myths and Symbols. Pacific Northwest. 1830-50. *1612*
—. Daily life. Doukhobors. Immigration. Personal narratives. Russia. 1880's-1976. *3918*
—. Doukhobors. Russian Canadians. Saskatchewan. 1652-1976. *3916*
British Columbia Baptist Church Extension Society. Baptists. USA. 1876-1918. *3061*
British Columbia (Bennett). Construction. Presbyterian Church. St. Andrew's Church. 1898. *1820*
British Columbia (Kootenay). Bishops. Church of England. Doull, Alexander John. 1870-1937. *3180*
British Columbia (Maillardville). Folklore. Magic. 1973-74. *2195*
British Columbia (Metlakatla). Church Missionary Society. Church of England. Hall, A. J. Indian-White Relations. Missions and Missionaries. Revivals. Tsimshian Indians. 1877. *1616*
British Columbia (Queen Charlotte Islands). Church of England. Haida Indians. Methodist Church. Missions and Missionaries. Settlement. Social Change. 1876-1920. *1545*
British Columbia (Vancouver). Canadian Memorial Chapel (Manitoba memorial window). Stained glass windows. 1928. *1848*
British Columbia (Vancouver Island). Converts. Immigration. Missions and Missionaries. Mormons. 1875-1979. *1669*
British Columbia (Vancouver Island; Nootka Sound). Catholic Church. Indians. Missions and Missionaries. Oral History. Spain. 1789-95. 19c. *1563*
British Empire *See also* Great Britain.
—. Catholic Church. Ideology. Imperialism. Quebec. 19c-20c. *1411*
British North America *See also* Canada; North America.
—. Antislavery Sentiments. Friends, Society of. Social problems. Woolman, John. 1720-72. *2371*
—. Christianity. Deviant Behavior. Government. Historiography. Occult Sciences. 1600-1760. *2180*
—. Death and Dying. Funerals. Social customs. 17c-18c. *2772*
—. Europe. 1677-1729. *2919*
—. Jews. Myers, Myer. Rites and Ceremonies. Silversmithing. 1723-95. *1905*
Broaddus, Andrew, I. Baptists. Clergy. Diaries. Kentucky. Travel. 1817. *2986*
Brodie, Fawn *(No Man Knows My History).* Historiography. Mormons. Smith, Joseph. 19c. 1945-73. *3983*
Brook Farm. Brisbane, Albert. Channing, William Henry. Fourierism. Transcendentalism. 1840-46. *399*
Brooklyn College. Attitudes. Catholic Church. Immigration. Judaism. Negroes. New York City. Protestant Ethic. West Indian Americans. 1939-78. *350*
Brooklyn Diocese. Anti-Catholicism. Breslin, Jimmy. Flaherty, Joe. Hamill, Pete. Irish Americans. New York City. Novels. 1960's-70's. *2098*
Brooks, Phillips. Abolition Movement. Assassination. Episcopal Church, Protestant. Lincoln, Abraham. Pennsylvania (Philadelphia). Sermons. 1865. 1893. *2463*
Brophy, Robert J. Jeffers, Robinson. Morris, Adelaide Kirby. Poetry. Stevens, Wallace. Theology (review article). 20c. *2065*
Bross, Harmon. Congregationalism. Nebraska. 1873-1928. *3125*
Brotherhood of the Holy Family. Catholic Church. Chaumonot, Joseph-Marie-Pierre. Elites. Laval, François de. Quebec (Montreal). 1663-1760. *3717*
Brough, Charles Hillman. Arkansas. Baptists. Elections (presidential). Evolution. Prohibition. 1928-29. *1270*
—. Arkansas. Historians. Mormons. 1890-1915. *224*
Brown, J. Newton. Baptists, Southern. Covenants. New Hampshire Covenant. 1833-1972. *3006*
Brown, Joshua. American Revolution. Friends, Society of. Pacifism. Pennsylvania (Little Britain Township). Prisoners. South Carolina (Ninety Six). 1778. *2633*
Brown, Robert McAfee. Ecumenism. 1920-74. *441*
—. New York City. Personal Narratives. Presbyterian Church. Union Theological Seminary. VanDusen, Henry Pitney. 1945-75. *767*
Brown University. Attitudes. Baptists. War. Wayland, Francis. 1826-65. *2649*
—. Belkin, Samuel. Judaism (Orthodox). Rhode Island (Providence). 1932-35. *4172*
—. Colleges and Universities. Harvard University. Libraries. Princeton University. Yale University. 18c. *672*

Brown v. *Board of Education* (US, 1954). Baptists. Desegregation. Georgia. Supreme Court. 1954-61. *511*
Brown v. *Les Curé et Marguilliers de l'Oeuvre et de la Fabrique de la Paroisse de Montréal* (1874). Catholic Church. Church and state. Guibord, Joseph. Liberalism. Politics. Quebec. Ultramontanism. 1870-74. *1067*
Brownsberger, Sidney. Adventists. Battle Creek College. California. Colleges and Universities. Healdsburg College. Michigan. 1875-80's. *665*
Brownson, Henry Francis. Catholic Church. Editors and Editing. 1835-1900. *3836*
Brownson, Orestes A. Attitudes. Catholic Church. Civil War. Hughes, John. McMaster, James. 1850-65. *2692*
—. Catholic Church. Civilization. Lectures. Missouri (St. Louis). 1852-54. *3838*
—. Catholic Church. Cumming, William. Letters. 1850's. *3676*
—. Catholic Church. Democracy. 1840's-76. *1389*
—. Catholic Church. Democracy. Theocratic principles. 19c. *1379*
—. Catholic Church. Intellectuals. Social Philosophy. 1803-76. *3677*
—. Catholic University of Ireland. Great Britain. Ireland. Newman, John Henry. 1853-54. *3837*
Brownson, Orestes A. *(The Convert).* Attitudes. Autobiography. Catholic Church. Converts. Great Britain. Newman, John Henry *(Apologia pro Vita Sua).* Protestantism. 1857-64. *3681*
Brubacher, Henry. Brubacher, Jacob. Daily life. Letters. Mennonites. Ontario. Pennsylvania. 1817-46. *3374*
Brubacher, Jacob. Brubacher, Henry. Daily life. Letters. Mennonites. Ontario. Pennsylvania. 1817-46. *3374*
Brúnum, Eiríkur á. Iceland. Laxness, Halldór *(Paradise Reclaimed).* Mormons. Novels. 1870-1900. 1960. *2075*
Bryan, Nathan P. Anti-Catholicism. Catts, Sidney J. Democratic Party. Florida. Political Campaigns (gubernatorial). Primaries (senatorial). Trammell, Park M. 1915-16. *1258*
Bryan, William Jennings. Christianity. Evolution. Presbyterian Church. 1921-25. *2297*
—. Church and state. Darwinism. Evolution. Fundamentalism. Public schools. 1920-73. *2317*
—. Darrow, Clarence. Evolution. Scopes Trial. Tennessee (Dayton). Trials. 1925. *2336*
—. Evolution. Fundamentalism. Presbyterian Church. 1875-1920's. *2344*
—. Fund raising. Lectures. Prairie Provinces. Presbyterian Church. Young Men's Christian Association. 1909. *2446*
—. Fundamentalism. Presbyterian Church. 1860-1925. *1407*
—. Political parties. Reagan, Ronald. Revivals. Social Change. 1730-1980. *1329*
Buber, Martin. God is Dead Theology. Heidegger, Robert. Sartre, Jean-Paul. Theology. 1961-64. *153*
Buchanan, James. Church and state. Federal Policy. Historiography. Military. Mormons. Utah. 1857-58. *1073*
Buchman, Frank. Evangelicalism. Moral Re-Armament movement. New Jersey. Princeton University. 1938. *2858*
Buck, Pearl S. Fiction. Missions and Missionaries. Presbyterian Church. 1931-69. *2068*
Bucke, Richard Maurice. Poetry. Whitman, Walt. 1877-1902. *68*
Buckminster, Joseph Stevens. Congregationalism. Massachusetts (Boston). Unitarianism. 1804-12. *3116*
Bucknell University. Baptists. Franklin and Marshall College. Friends, Society of (Hicksite). Pennsylvania. Reformed German Church. Swarthmore College. Urbanization. 1865-1915. *685*
Buczek, Daniel Stephen (review article). Bójnowski, Lucyan. Catholic Church. Clergy. Connecticut (New Britain). Polish Americans. 1895-1960. *3865*
Buddhism *See also* Eastern Religions.
—. Attitudes. Baptists, Southern. Congregationalism. Death and Dying. Hawaii (Honolulu). 1977. *131*
—. Hinduism. Teaching. Western Nations. 1969-75. *4287*
Buddhism (Zen). Catholic Church. Merton, Thomas. Suzuki, Diasetz Teitaro. 1935-70. *498*
—. Christianity. Merton, Thomas. Watts, Alan. 1930-73. *4288*
—. Poetry. Snyder, Gary. 1960-74. *2055*
Budgets *See also* Public Finance.
—. Missions and Missionaries. Presbyterian Church. 1763-1978. *1488*
Buena, Mariano. Arizona (Nogales). Catholic Church. Gil, Juan. Indians. Seri Indians. 1768-72. *1559*
Buenger, Theodore Arthur. Autobiography. Clergy. Concordia Seminary. German Americans. Lutheran Church (Missouri Synod). Seminaries. 1886-1909. *3297*
Buerger, Paul Theodor. *Collegium Fratrum* (organization). Educational Tests and Measurements. Indiana (Fort Wayne). Letters. Lutheran Church. 1858. *3315*
Buettner, George L. Concordia Publishing House. Lutheran Church (Missouri Synod). Missouri (St. Louis). Personal Narratives. Publishers and publishing. 1888-1955. *336*
Buies, Arthur. Catholic Church. 1880's-1901. *3878*
Bulfinch, Charles. Architecture. First Parish Church. Massachusetts (Charlestown). Meetinghouses. 1803-04. *1792*
Bulkeley, Peter (and family). Covenant theology. Massachusetts (Concord). Puritans. 1635-1731. *3645*
Bulkeley, Peter *(Gospel-Covenant).* Covenant theology. Massachusetts. Puritans. 1640's-50's. *3636*
Bullard, Isaac. Christianity. Vermont Pilgrims ("Mummyjums"). 1817-24. *408*
Bunyan, John *(Pilgrim's Progress).* Art. Huntington, Daniel. *Mercy's Dream* (painting). National characteristics. Protestantism. 1678. 1841-70. *1856*
Burchard, Jedediah. Protestants. Revivals. Social Conditions. Vermont. 1835-36. *2246*
Bureau of Indian Affairs. Catholic Church. Indian-White Relations. Iowa. Presbyterian Church. Schools. Winnebago Indians. 1834-48. *737*
—. Educational Policy. Indians (reservations). Language. Missions and Missionaries. 19c-20c. *516*
Bureaucracies. Baptists, Southern. Democracy. Norris, J. Frank. 1920-40. *3084*
—. Church and state. Colonial Government. *Commissaire ordonnateur.* France. Louisiana. 1712-69. *1069*
—. Conservatism. Presbyterian Church, Southern (administration). Roberts, William Henry. Theology. 1884-1920. *3541*
Burg, B. R. Clergy (review article). Congregationalism. Mather, Richard. New England. Youngs, J. William T., Jr. ca 1700-50. 1976. *3124*
Burger, Warren E. Church and state. Church schools. Constitutional Amendments (1st). Supreme Court. 1950-75. *602*
Burgoyne, John. American Revolution. Friends, Society of. Indians. Pennsylvania (Easton). ca 1776. *3282*
Burials. Acculturation. Christianity. Indians. Missions and Missionaries. Navajo Indians. 1949-75. *1656*
Burned-over district (theory). Cross, Whitney R. Dissent. Millerites. New York. 1830's-40's. 20c. *2974*
Burnett, Ellen. Arkansas (Pine Bluff). Prophecy. Storms. Women. 1903. *74*
Burr, Aaron. Political Leadership. Presbyterian Church. 1772-1805. *3542*
Burton, Richard *(City of the Saints).* Mormons. Travel Accounts. Utah. 1860-61. *4052*
Bushnell, Horace. Church and state. Congregationalism. Jefferson, Thomas. ca 1800-60. *1002*
—. Clergy. Congregationalism. Elites. Theology. 19c. *3114*
Business *See also* Advertising; Banking; Consumers; Corporations; Mail-Order Business; Management.
—. Advertising. Barton, Bruce *(The Man Nobody Knows).* Christianity. 1920-29. *365*
—. Alaska. Brady, John Green (and family). Governors. Morality. Presbyterian Church. 1878-1906. *3549*
—. American Revolution (antecedents). Friends, Society of. Leadership. Pennsylvania (Philadelphia). Radicals and radicalism. 1769-74. *1293*
—. Attitudes. Baptists. 1840-1950. *363*
—. Bailey, Margaret Jewett *(Ruth Rover).* Methodist Church. Missionaries. Oregon. 1854. *1522*
—. Bible. Secularism. 1900-29. *344*
—. California (San Francisco; San Bruno Avenue). Esther Hellman Settlement House. Jews. Neighborhoods. 1901-68. *4130*
—. Church administration. 20c. *343*
—. Depressions. Grant, Heber J. Mormons. Utah. 1893. *375*
—. Elites. Illinois (Chicago). 1830-1930. *2608*
—. Ethics. Friends, Society of. 1600-1750. *359*
—. Ethics. Mormons. Theology. Watergate scandal. 1974. *995*
—. Indians. Lee, Daniel. Letters. Methodist Church. Missions and Missionaries. Oregon (Willamette Valley, The Dalles). 1834-43. *1570*
—. Philanthropy. 19c. *342*
—. Tennessee (Nashville). 1960's-70's. *349*
Butler, Benjamin F. Armies. Chaplains. Civil War. Diaries. Fort Fisher (battle). Negroes. North Carolina. Turner, Henry M. 1864-65. *2685*
Butler, Elizur. Cherokee Indians. Indian-White Relations. Marshall, John. Missions and Missionaries. Nullification crisis. Worcester, Samuel A. *Worcester* v. *Georgia* (US, 1832). 1828-33. *1583*
Butler, John Wesley. Letters. Methodist Church. Mexico. Missions and Missionaries. Revolution. 1910-11. *1725*
Butler, Smedley. Antiwar Sentiment. Courts Martial and Courts of Inquiry. Friends, Society of (Hicksite). Marines. 1881-1940. *2637*
Buttrick, George Arthur. Pacifism. Presbyterian Church. 1915-74. *2642*
Bygdelag movement. Ethnicity. Nationalism. North Central States. Norwegian Americans. 1901-30. *3319*
Byington, John. Adventists. Methodist Church, Wesleyan. Methodist Episcopal Church. New York (Bucks Bridge). 1840's-52. *3509*
Byrne, Edwin V. Bishops. Caruana, George J. Catholic Church. Jones, William A. Puerto Rico. San Juan Diocese. 1866-1963. *3814*

C

Cabala. Counter Culture. Jews. Mysticism. Rationalism. Traditionalism. 1940's-70's. *4140*
Cabalism. Friends, Society of. Jews. 17c-20c. *27*
Cable, George Washington. Fiction. Louisiana (New Orleans). Presbyterian Church, Southern. Reform. ca 1870-1925. *3539*
Cadbury, Henry Joel (obituary). American Friends Service Committee. Friends, Society of. Historians. 1883-1974. *212*
Cain, Richard Harvey. Methodist Episcopal Church, African. Negroes. Politics. Reconstruction. Social conditions. South Carolina. 1850's-87. *2407*
Caldwell, Erskine. Caldwell, Ira Sylvester. Novels. Presbyterian Church, Associate Reformed. South. 1900-78. *2017*
Caldwell, Ira Sylvester. Caldwell, Erskine. Novels. Presbyterian Church, Associate Reformed. South. 1900-78. *2017*
Calendar, Gregorian. Appalachia, southern. Ballads. "Christmas, Old". Social customs. 1753-1977. *2955*
Calgary Diocese. Alberta. Catholic Church. French Canadians. Irish Canadians. McNailly, John Thomas. 1871-1952. *3712*
California *See also* Far Western States.
—. Adventists. Anesthesia. Dentistry. Jorgensen, Niels Bjorn. Loma Linda University. Teaching. 1923-74. *1441*
—. Adventists. Battle Creek College. Brownsberger, Sidney. Colleges and Universities. Healdsburg College. Michigan. 1875-80's. *665*
—. Adventists. Battle Creek Sanitarium. Loma Linda University. Medical Education. Michigan. Nurses and Nursing. 1884-1979. *1425*
—. Adventists. Humor. Irish Americans. Letters. Loma Linda University. Magan, Percy Tilson. 1918-34. *1435*
—. Adventists. Letters. Loma Linda Sanitarium. White, Ellen G. 1905. *1461*
—. Adventists. Loma Linda Sanitarium. Photographs. 1905-19. *1458*
—. Adventists. Loma Linda University. Medical Education. 1905-15. *1450*
—. American Revolution. Indians. Missions. Spain. 1776-83. *1321*
—. Architecture. Franciscans. Mission San Juan Capistrano. 1776-1976. *1494*

—. Archives. Bibliographies. Franciscans. Geiger, Maynard J. (obituary). Historiography. Mission Santa Barbara. 1936-76. *240*
—. Archives. Catholic Church. 1768-1975. *274*
—. Archives. Franciscans. Geiger, Maynard J. (obituary). Historiography. Mission Santa Barbara. 1901-77. *281*
—. Archives. Franciscans. Geiger, Maynard J. (obituary). Historiography. Mission Santa Barbara. 1937-77. *238*
—. Arguello, Maria de la Concepcion. Catholic Church. Orthodox Eastern Church, Russian. Rezanov, Nikolai. 1806. *2797*
—. Armies. Mexican War. Military Recruitment. Mormon Volunteers. 1847-48. *2707*
—. Art criticism. Catholic Church. Missions and Missionaries. 1769-1980. *1876*
—. Arts. Catholic Church. Historiography (Anglo-American). Missions and Missionaries. Scholasticism. 1740's-1976. *1878*
—. Baptists. Negroes. Political activity. St. Andrew's African Methodist Episcopal Church. 1850-73. *981*
—. Bible. British Columbia. Christianity. Indians. Missions and Missionaries. Myths and Symbols. Pacific Northwest. 1830-50. *1612*
—. Cantwell, John J. Catholic Church. Negroes. 1920's. *3896*
—. Catholic Church. 1848. *3895*
—. Catholic Church. Charities. Ethnic groups. Ramm, Charles A. 1863-1951. *3888*
—. Catholic Church. Church administration. González Rubio, José. Missions and Missionaries. 1846-50. *3811*
—. Catholic Church. Engelhardt, Zephyrin. Mission Santa Barbara. Missions and Missionaries. Southwestern history. 1851-1934. *176*
—. Catholic Church. Famines. Gold Rushes. Immigration. Irish Americans. 1849-90's. *3800*
—. Catholic Church. Homosexuality. Proposition 6 (1978). Public schools. Referendum. Teachers. 1978. *1320*
—. Catholic Church. Indians. Labor. Missions and Missionaries. 1775-1805. *1485*
—. Catholic Church. Indians (neophytes). Mexico. Missions and missionaries. 1830's. *1606*
—. Catholic Church. Indian-White Relations. Missions and Missionaries. 1770's-1820's. *1636*
—. Catholic Church. Mexico. Rubio, José Gonzalez. Tithing. 1848. *3894*
—. Catholic Church. Mission San Gabriel Arcangel. Newspapers. 1867. *1658*
—. Catholic Church. Mission San Juan Capistrano. Restorations. 1797-1979. *1803*
—. Catholic Church. Mission San Juan Capistrano. Serra, Junípero. 1775-76. *1601*
—. Catholic Church. Mountain Men. Protestantism. Rogers, Harrison. Smith, Jedediah Strong. 1826-27. *2798*
—. Charities. Disaster relief. Economic aid. Jews. Nieto, Jacob. Rabbis. San Francisco Earthquake and Fire. 1906. *2520*
—. Chavez, Cesar. Christianity. Mexican Americans. Political activism. Rhetoric. Texas. Tijerina, Reies. 1960's-70's. *2391*
—. Christianity. Cults. Eastern religions. 1970's. *107*
—. Chumash Indians. Indians. Marriage. Mission Santa Barbara. Social Organization. Yanunali, Pedro (chief). 1787-1806. *940*
—. Church and state. Church Finance. State Government. Worldwide Church of God. 1970's. *1139*
—. Church and state. Colonial Government. Indians. Laws of the Indies. Missions and Missionaries. Spain. 18c. *1143*
—. Church and state. Creationism. Curricula. Educational Policy. Evolution. Science. 1963-74. *2331*
—. Church and State. Franciscans. Indians. Missions and Missionaries. 1775-1800. *1037*
—. Church and state. Sabbatarianism. Supreme Courts, state. 1855-83. *2283*
—. Church schools. Higher education. 1850-74. *623*
—. Circuit riders. Civil War. Frontier and Pioneer Life. Manuscripts. Methodism. Ohio. Phillips, George. 1840-64. *3494*
—. Conversion thesis. Cook, Sherburne Friend. Franciscans. Indians. Missions and Missionaries. ca 1790-1820's. 1943. *1541*
—. Dominicans. Franciscans. Jesuits. Missions and Missionaries. Serra, Junípero. 1768-76. *1575*
—. Durán, Narciso. Franciscans. Indians. Missions. Secularization. 1826-46. *1093*
—. Durán, Narciso. Franciscans. Indians. Missions and Missionaries. Music. 1806-46. *1924*
—. Franciscans. Geiger, Maynard J. (obituary). Historians. Mission Santa Barbara. 1901-77. *239*
—. Franciscans. Mission San Juan Capistrano. 1775-1974. *1627*
—. Franciscans. Missions. Winemaking. 18c-19c. *371*
—. Franklin, Harvey B. Jews. Personal narratives. Rabbis. 1916-57. *4099*
—. Guyana (Jonestown; review article). Jones, Jim. People's Temple. 1931-78. *4251*
—. Jesuits. Nobili, John. Santa Clara, University of. 1850-55. *695*
—. Jesuits. Santa Clara, University of. 1849-51. *696*
—. Jews, Sephardic. Judaism (Orthodox). 1850-1900. *4198*
—. Methodist Episcopal Church. Missions and missionaries. Overland Journeys to the Pacific. Owen, Isaac. 1849. *1611*
—. Missions and Missionaries. Viticulture. 1697-1858. *1659*
California (Arlington). Adventists. Loma Linda University. 1922-67. *738*
—. Adventists. Loma Linda University. Personal narratives. Robison, James I. 1922. *745*
California (Berkeley). Attitudes. Converts. Davis, Rennie. Divine Light Mission. Maharaj Ji. Politics. 1973. *4286*
California (Blue Creek, Eight Mile). Forest Service. Indians. Religious liberty. Supreme Court. 1975. *1102*
California (Bodie). Clay, Eugene O. Funerals. Methodist Church. Nevada (Smith Valley). Personal narratives. Sermons. 1915. *3456*
California (Fresno). Anti-Semitism. Foote, William D. Johnson, Grove L. Trials. 1893. *2134*
California (Huntington Park, Los Angeles). Frey, Sigmund. Jewish Orphan's Home. Judaism (Reform). Social work. 1870's-1930. *2500*
California (Loma Linda). Adventists. Education. Medicine. 1810-1929. *2971*
California (Los Angeles). Blum, Abraham. Judaism (Reform). New York City. Rabbis. Texas (Galveston). 1866-1921. *4217*
—. British Americans. Popular culture. Protestant Churches. Social Classes. 1920's. 1977. *2624*
—. Cantors. Concerts. Judaism. Loew's State Theatre. Music, liturgical. Rosenblatt, Josef "Yosele". Vaudeville. 1925. *1917*
—. Catholic Church. Christmas. Mexican Americans. Neighborhoods. Posadas (celebrations). Rites and Ceremonies. 1975-80. *3794*
—. Catholic Church. Ethnology. Methodology. Polish Americans. Sandberg, Neil C. (review article). 1968-74. *3813*
—. Church finance. Judaism (Reform). Rabbis. Wilshire Boulevard Temple. 1897. *4231*
—. Evangelism. International Church of the Foursquare Gospel. McPherson, Aimee Semple. Radio. 1920-44. *1958*
—. Hecht, Sigmund. Judaism. 1904-25. *4182*
—. Homosexuality. 1970-76. *2821*
—. Immigration. Jews (Rhodesli). Judaism (Orthodox). Sephardic Hebrew Center. 1900-74. *4180*
—. Judaism. Political Campaigns (mayoral). Social Classes. Voting and Voting Behavior. 1969. *1276*
—. Judaism (Reform). Letters. Newmark, Joseph. Rabbis. Wilshire Boulevard Temple. 1881. *4236*
—. Judaism (Reform). Schreiber, Emanuel. Wilshire Boulevard Temple. 1881-1932. *4216*
California (Los Angeles area). Actors and Actresses. Catholic Church. Modjeska, Helena. Polish Americans. 1876-1909. *3786*
California (Los Angeles; Chavez Ravine). Cemeteries. Hebrew Benevolent Society of Los Angeles. Home of Peace Jewish Cemetery. Judaism. Photographs. 1855-1910. *4161*
California (Los Angeles, San Francisco). Architecture. Judaism (Reform). Temple Emanu-El. Wilshire Boulevard Temple. 1937. *4205*
California (Monterey). Discovery and Exploration. Dominguez, Francisco Atanasio. Escalante, Silvestre Velez de. New Mexico. Overland Journeys to the Pacific. 1765-1805. *1480*
California (Monterey, San Luis Obispo counties). Acculturation. Catholic Church. Indians. Missions and Missionaries. Salinan Indians. 1770's-1830's. *1550*
California (Mountain View, Oakland). Adventists. Jones, Charles Harriman. Pacific Press Publishing Company. Publishers and Publishing. 1879-1923. *362*
California, northern. Converts. Ghost Dance. Indians. Methodist Church. Round Valley Indian Reservation. 1870. *3484*
—. Morality. Mormons. Sex. Utah (Salt Lake City). Youth. 1967-69. *885*
California (Oakland). Disaster relief. Jews. Refugees. San Francisco Earthquake and Fire. Temple Sinai. 1906. *2527*
—. Jews. 1852-91. *4125*
California (Oakland, San Francisco). Beiliss, Mendel. Christianity. Jews. Newspapers. Russia. Trials. 1911-13. *4105*
California (Orange County). Communalism. Middle Classes. Oneida Community. Social Organization. Townerites. 1848-1910. *417*
California (Oroville, San Francisco, Woodland). Congregation Beth Israel. Judaism (Orthodox). Messing, Aron J. Religious education. Sabbath Schools. Travel. 1879. *4201*
California (Pacific Grove). Methodist Church. 1875-1975. *3459*
California (Placerville). Ecumenism. El Dorado County Federated Church. Methodist Church. Presbyterian Church. 1850-1950. *492*
California (Sacramento). Judaism (Reform). Letters. Levy, J. Leonard. Rabbis. 1892. *4219*
California (Sacramento, San Francisco). Henry, Henry Abraham. Issacs, Samuel Meyer. Jews. Letters. Rabbis. Travel (accounts). 1858. *4106*
California (San Bernardino). Bergel, Siegmund. Jews. Religious education. 1868-1912. *765*
—. Confirmation. Henrietta Hebrew Benevolent Society. Judaism (Reform). Religious Education. 1891. *788*
—. Congregation Beth Israel. Fund raising. Judaism (Orthodox). Messing, Aron J. 1879. *4199*
California (San Diego). Besant, Annie. Schisms. Theosophy. Tingley, Katharine Augusta Westcott. 1897. *4298*
—. Catholic Church. Excavations. Military Camps and Forts. Missions and Missionaries. Serra Museum. 1769-75. 1964-70's. *1526*
—. Chinese Mission School. Congregationalism. Education. 1885-1960. *535*
—. Christmas. Drama. Parades. Social Customs. 1769-1980. *2714*
—. Colonization. Indians. Missions and Missionaries. Spain. 1769-1834. *1668*
—. Franciscans. Jayme, Luís (death). Mission San Diego de Alcalá. Yuman Indians. 1775. *1657*
—. Judaism (Reform). Population. Temple Beth Israel. 1889-1978. *4224*
California (San Diego; Point Loma). Art, Symbolist. Theosophy. ca 1875-1910. *1863*
—. Church Schools. Theosophical Institute. Tingley, Katherine Augusta Westcott. 1897-1940. *4297*
—. Communes. Theosophy. Tingley, Katherine Augusta Westcott. Universal Brotherhood and Theosophical Society. 1897-1942. *4299*
California (San Francisco). Adventists. Debates. Educational Policy. Evolution. Science League of America. 1925. *2291*
—. Anti-Catholicism. City Politics. Know-Nothing Party. People's Party. Vigilance Committee. 1854-56. *1307*
—. Anti-Semitism. D'Ancona, David Arnold. Letters. Newspapers. Pixley, Frank M. 1883. *2128*
—. Baptists. Bethel African Methodist Episcopal Church. Civil rights. Methodist Episcopal Zion Church, African. Negroes. Pressure groups. Third Baptist Church. 1860's. *1289*
—. Catholic Church. City Politics. Clergy. Irish Americans. Progressivism. Yorke, Peter C. 1900's. *3889*
—. Catholic Church. Clergy. Editors and Editing. Ethnicity. Irish Americans. Yorke, Peter C. ca 1885-1925. *3887*
—. Catholic Church. Clergy. Fontaine, Flavian. Mission Dolores. 1850-53. *3801*
—. Cemeteries. First Hebrew Benevolent Society. Funerals. Jews. Johnson, Henry D. 1849-50. *4147*

—. Dyer, Leon. Jews. Leadership. Maryland (Baltimore). 1820's-75. *4142*
—. *Emanu-El* (newspaper). Immigration. Jews, East European. Letters-to-the-editor. Rabbis. Rosenthal, Marcus. Voorsanger, Jacob. 1905. *4141*
—. Franklin, Lewis Abraham. Judaism. Rabbis. Sermons. Yom Kippur. 1850. *4100*
—. Goldie, Albert. Judaism (Orthodox, Reform). New York City. Poor. Synagogues. Weinstock, Harris. 1906. *4166*
—. Guyana (Jonestown). Jones, Jim. Leftism. People's Temple. 1960's-78. *4247*
—. Henry, Henry Abraham. Judaism. Rabbis. 1857-69. *4107*
—. Jews. Nieto, Jacob. Rabbis. Rubin, Max. Temple Sherith Israel. 1893. *4148*
—. Jews (German, Polish). Synagogues. Temple Emanu-El. Temple Sherith Israel. 1848-1900. *4126*
—. Judaism. Politics. 1935-65. *1226*
—. Voluntary Associations. 1850's. *69*
California (San Francisco Bay Area). Astrology. Counter culture. Horoscopes. 1970's. *2212*
—. Berkeley New Religious Consciousness Project. Cults. 1970's. *4272*
California (San Francisco; Potrero Hill). Ethnicity. Molokans. Sects, Religious. 1906-76. *2807*
California (San Francisco; San Bruno Avenue). Business. Esther Hellman Settlement House. Jews. Neighborhoods. 1901-68. *4130*
California (San Jose). Beth Olam Cemetery. Congregation Bickur Cholim. Judaism (Orthodox, Reform). Organizations. 1850-1900. *4123*
California (Santa Clara). Catholic Church. Santa Clara, University of. 1851-80. *697*
California (Santa Cruz). Converts. Judaism. Schlutius, Emma. 1877. *4098*
California (Santa Monica). Jews. Resorts. 1875-1939. *4160*
California (Sonoma). Catholic Church. Indians. Mission San Francisco Solano. 1823-34. *1506*
California, southern. Choynski, Isidor Nathan. Cities. Jews. Journalism. Travel (accounts). 1881. *4144*
California (Stockton). Clergy. Pioneers. Presbyterian Church. Woods, James. 1850-54. *3526*
—. Davidson, Herman. Judaism (Reform). Opera. Rabbis. Russia. 1846-1911. *4204*
California (Temecula). Catholic Church. Documents. Indians. Maltby, Charles. Mission San Antonio de Pala. 1866. *1573*
California, University of (Regents). Catholic Church. Clergy. Irish Americans. Political attitudes. Yorke, Peter C. 1900-12. *560*
California (Ventura). Catholic Church. Churches. Mission San Buenaventura. ca 1794-1976. *1831*
California-Nevada Conference. Clergy. Methodist Church. Women. 1873-78. *3503*
Californios. Attitudes. Europeans. Travel (accounts). 1780's-1840's. *2122*
Calish, Edward Nathan. Judaism, Reform. Virginia (Richmond). Zionism. Zionism. 1891-1945. *4203*
Calligraphy. Appleby, William. Mormons. Simmons, Joseph M. Young, Brigham. 1851-53. *1895*
Calling (concept). Equality. Great Chain of Being (theme). Protestant Ethic. Puritans. 17c-18c. *340*
Calomel. Medicine (practice of). Mormons. Thomson, Samuel. 1793-1865. *1438*
Calvary (chapels). Algonkin Indians. Architecture. Iroquois Indians. Missionaries. Quebec (Oka). Sulpicians. 1700's-1800's. *1811*
Calvert, Cecilius (2d Lord Baltimore). Catholic Church. Colonization. Maryland. Religious liberty. 1634-92. *1061*
—. Catholic Church. Great Britain. Maryland. Provincial Government. Religious Liberty. 1634-49. *1068*
Calvert, George (1st Lord Baltimore). Catholic Church. Colonization. Newfoundland (Avalon Peninsula). Protestant churches. Religious Liberty. 1620's. *2755*
Calvin, John. Luther, Martin. National Characteristics. Protestantism. 16c-18c. *2870*
Calvin, Ross Randall. Episcopal Church, Protestant. Literature. Nature. New Mexico. 1889-1970. *2332*
Calvinism *See also* Congregationalism; Puritans.
—. American Revolution. Brattle Street Church. Congregationalism. Cooper, Samuel. Elites. Massachusetts (Boston). 1754-83. *1333*
—. American Revolution. Church and state. Clergy. Jefferson, Thomas. Linn, William. Presbyterian Church. 1775-1808. *1335*
—. American Revolution. Eschatology. Paine, Thomas *(Common Sense)*. 1776. *1393*
—. American Revolution. Kuyper, Abraham. Netherlands. Political systems. 1775-83. 19c-1920. *1332*
—. Amherst College. Massachusetts. Meiklejohn, Alexander. 1912-23. *601*
—. Appleton, Thomas Gold. James, Henry. New England Conscience (term). Unitarianism. 1875-95. *4075*
—. Art. Congregationalism. Dow, Arthur Wesley. Massachusetts (Ipswich). Methodist Church. 1857-80. *1871*
—. Attitudes. Faulkner, William *(The Sound and the Fury)*. South. 1929. *2018*
—. Augustine, Saint. Edwards, Jonathan. Heart concept. New England. Psychology. 17c. *2311*
—. Behaviorism. Psychology. Watson, John Broadus. 1890-1919. *2308*
—. Centralization. Executive branch. Public Administration. Reform. Revivals. ca 1880-1930's. *959*
—. Church Membership. Reformed Christian Church. 1964-79. *3160*
—. Congregationalism. Government, Resistance to. Massachusetts (Boston). Mayhew, Jonathan. Political Theory. Sermons. 1750. *1381*
—. Cotton, John. Elegies. Fiske, John. New England. Poetry. Puritans. 17c. *1985*
—. Diphtheria. Enlightenment. Great Awakening. New England. Sermons. 1735-40. *2260*
—. Education. Massachusetts (Andover). Phillips Academy. 1778-1978. *584*
—. Emerson, Mary Moody. Emerson, Ralph Waldo. New England. 19c. *2721*
—. Faulkner, William. Literature. Presbyterian Church. 1920's-75. *2035*
—. Founding fathers. Giles, Benjamin. Libraries. New Hampshire. 1760's-87. *2908*
—. Great Awakening. New Left. New Lights. Youth. 1740's. 1960's. *2265*
—. Literature. 1650-1900. *2002*
—. Literature. Muir, John. Romanticism. 1838-1914. *2929*
—. Massachusetts (Boston). Parishes. Puritans. Switzerland (Geneva). 16c-17c. *3631*
—. Mather, Moses. Revivals. Theology. 1719-1850. *2248*
—. Millenarianism. Presbyterian Church. Proslavery Sentiments. South. 1800-65. *2166*
—. Politics. Social Change. 16c-20c. *980*
—. Secularism. 18c-20c. *1186*
Cambridge Camden Society. Churches (Gothic Revival). Episcopal Church, Protestant. Great Britain. 1840-1975. *1773*
Cambridge Platform. Church and state. Massachusetts. Puritans. 1630-79. *1017*
Cameron, John. Church of England. Letters. Ontario (Ottawa). Politics. Thompson, Annie Affleck. Thompson, John S. D. 1867-94. *1127*
Cameron, William Andrew. Baptists. Canada. Clergy. Sermons. Shields, Thomas Todhunter. 1910-41. *3021*
Camp Funston. Conscientious objectors. Diaries. Hutterites. Kansas. Waldner, Jakob. World War I. 1917-18. *2690*
Camp Lejeune. Lamb Studios. Marines. New Jersey (Tenafly). North Carolina. Protestantism. Stained glass windows. 1775-1943. *1867*
Camp meeting sites. Evangelism. Methodism. 19c. *2225*
Camp meetings. Adventists. Northeastern or North Atlantic states. 1840's. *2231*
—. Church of the Nazarene. Holiness movement. Louisiana (Mineral Springs). Methodist Church. National Camp Meeting Association for the Promotion of Holiness. 1860's-1926. *2891*
—. Crowd control. Political rallies. Rhetoric. Tennessee. 1828-60. *1259*
—. Holiness Movement. Hudson Holiness Interdenominational Camp. Louisiana (Winn Parish). 1899-1977. *3292*
—. Methodism. Resorts. Revivals. 19c. *2252*
Campaigns, Political. *See* Political Campaigns.
Campbell, Alexander. Antinomianism. Bible. Disciples of Christ. 1810-60. *3109*
—. Antislavery sentiments. Civil religion. Disciples of Christ. Indians. Politics. War. Women. 1823-55. *3108*
—. Bible. Disciples of Christ. Theology. ca 1830-60. *3110*
—. Civil religion. Disciples of Christ. Millenarianism. 1810-60. *1195*
—. Civil religion. Disciples of Christ. Millenarianism. 1813-66. *3106*
—. Disciples of Christ. Educational Reform. Frontier. Morality. 1825-1900. *579*
Campbell, Will. Baptists, Southern. Clergy. Garner, Thad. Personal narratives. South. 20c. *2994*
Canada *See also* individual provinces; Atlantic Provinces; British North America; North America; Northwest Territories; Prairie Provinces; Yukon Territory.
—. Acculturation. Ethnicity. Jews. USA. 1961-74. *4156*
—. Adolescence. Boys. Protestantism. USA. Young Men's Christian Association. 1870-1920. *2414*
—. American Revolution. Church of England. Cossitt, Ranna. Loyalists. Missions and Missionaries. New England. 1773-1815. *1317*
—. American Revolution. France. Huguenots. Settlement. USA. Whaling industry and Trade. 17c-20c. *3251*
—. Angers, François-Albert. Catholic Church. French Canadians. Pacifism. Values. 1940-79. *2654*
—. Anglican Communion. Education. Great Britain. Missionaries. Protestantism. Sudan Interior Mission. 1937-55. *1741*
—. Anglin, Timothy Warren. Catholic Church. Debates. Fenian Brotherhood. Irish Canadians. McGee, D'Arcy. 1863-68. *1341*
—. Anti-Catholicism. Italy. Political Attitudes. Protestants. Risorgimento. 1846-60. *2114*
—. Architecture (Gothic Revival). 1860-1939. *1765*
—. Archives. Jesuits. 17c-1978. *183*
—. Archives. Mennonites. 19c-1975. *187*
—. Archives. Methodist Church. Presbyterian Church. United Church of Canada. 18c-1973. *269*
—. Arctic. Catholic Church. Church of England. Churches. Fur Trade. Missions and Missionaries. 20c. *1549*
—. Asbury, Francis. Coke, Thomas. Embury, Philip. Great Britain. Methodism. USA. 1760-80. *3445*
—. Asia. Colleges and Universities (review article). Missions and Missionaries. Protestant Churches. 1850-1971. *1675*
—. Attitudes. Catholic Church. Ethnic Groups. Jews. Protestantism. Social Status. 1968. *2088*
—. Australia. Finland. Kurikka, Matti. Theosophy. Utopias. 1883-1915. *435*
—. Authority. Bishops. Church of England. Councils and Synods. Laity. 1780-1979. *3224*
—. Authority. Church and state. Church of England. Councils and Synods. Laity. 1782-1857. *3207*
—. Authority. Church of England. Councils and Synods. Laity. 1782-1867. *3206*
—. Authority. United Church of Canada. 1925-73. *3669*
—. Baerg, Anna. Diaries. Immigration. Mennonites. Russian Revolution. Women. 1917-23. *3362*
—. Baltic Area. Immigrants. Lutheran Church. 1947-55. *2453*
—. Baptists. Cameron, William Andrew. Clergy. Sermons. Shields, Thomas Todhunter. 1910-41. *3021*
—. Baptists. Disciples of Christ. Great Plains. Lutheran Church. Methodism. Pietism. Prairie Radicals. Radicals and Radicalism. 1890-1975. *954*
—. Baptists. Ecumenism. USA. 1760-1979. *3031*
—. Baptists, Southern. USA. 19c-20c. *3087*
—. Baptists, Southern (Northwest Convention). USA. 1844-1975. *3088*
—. Bibliographies. Catholic Church. ca 1800-1976. *3760*
—. Bibliographies. Christianity. 1974-78. *2745*
—. Bibliographies. Church history. 17c-1973. *14*
—. Bibliographies. Church history. 17c-20c. *16*
—. Bibliographies. Congregationalism. Historiography. Lutheran Church. Methodist Church. Presbyterian Church. United Church of Canada. 1825-1973. *2892*
—. Bishops. Church of England. Documents. 1850-52. *3208*
—. Bland, Salem. Methodism. Social Gospel. Theology. 1880-86. *3444*

—. Blewett, George John. Methodist Church. Theology. 1873-1912. *3496*
—. Boer War. Clergy. English Canadians. Protestant churches. 1899-1902. *2675*
—. Brethren in Christ. Engel, Jacob. Pennsylvania (Lancaster County). Sects, Religious. 1775-1964. *3437*
—. Brethren in Christ. Holiness movement. North Central States. 1910-50. *3435*
—. Capitalism. Fur trade. Hudson's Bay Company. Protestantism. Scottish Canadians. 18c-1970's. *377*
—. Catholic Church. Census. Cities. French Canadians. French language. 1941. *3880*
—. Catholic Church. Church and state. Encyclicals. Pius IX, Pope *(Syllabus of Errors).* Press. Public opinion. 1864-65. *1019*
—. Catholic Church. Clergy. Craig, James Henry. French Canadians. Nationalism. Political repression. Quebec (Lower Canada). 1810. *1319*
—. Catholic Church. Conroy, George. Papal legates. 1873-77. *3883*
—. Catholic Church. Education. French Canadians. Quebec. Rinfret, Fernand. Siegfried, André *(Le Canada, les deux races: Problèmes politiques contemporains).* Social Sciences. 1906-07. *3873*
—. Catholic Church. Geographic Space. Missions and Missionaries. Regionalism. 1615-1851. *1486*
—. Catholic Church. Industrialization. Judaism. Protestant Churches. Religiosity. 1921-71. *93*
—. Catholic Church. Journalism. Social thought. Somerville, Henry. 1915-53. *2354*
—. Catholic Church. Macdonald, John. Voting and Voting Behavior. 1850's-91. *1286*
—. Charities. Nurses and Nursing. Slovak Americans. Slovak Canadians. USA. Vincentian Sisters of Charity. Women. 1902-78. *2525*
—. China. Church of England. Missionary Society of the Canadian Church. Personal narratives. Scovil, G. C. Coster. 1946-47. *1744*
—. China. Hurford, Grace Gibberd. Missions and Missionaries. Personal narratives. Teaching. World War II. 1928-45. *1711*
—. Cholera. Epidemics. Mormons. USA. 1832-83. *1437*
—. Christianity. Church and state. USA. 18c-20c. *1095*
—. Christianity. Civil rights. Eskimos. Indians. Métis. Project North. 1975-79. *2545*
—. Christianity. Missions and Missionaries. Sex roles. Women. 1815-99. *854*
—. Church and state. Cities. Sabbatarianism. Streetcars. Values. 1890-1914. *2281*
—. Church and State. Jesuits' Estates Act. Political Protest. Protestants. 1880-90. *1088*
—. Church and State. Leadership. Mennonite Conference of 1970. Social issues. Students. 1917-74. *1029*
—. Church and state. Lord's Day Act (Canada, 1906). Sabbatarianism. Sports. 1906-77. *2284*
—. Church History. Ecumenism. United Church of Canada. 1920-76. *442*
—. Church of England. Clergy. McMurray, William. 1810-94. *3203*
—. Church of England. Domestic and Foreign Missionary Society. Japan. Missions and Missionaries. 1883-1902. *1587*
—. Church of England. Ecumenism. Symonds, Herbert. 1897-1921. *483*
—. Church of England. Liturgy. Tractarians. 1840-68. *3189*
—. Church of England National Task Force on the Economy (report). Income. Poverty. Social Classes. Theology. 1977. *2564*
—. Church Schools. East Indians. Missions and Missionaries. Presbyterian Church. Trinidad and Tobago. 1868-1912. *1726*
—. Colleges and Universities. Political knowledge. Public opinion. Students. 1974. *978*
—. Communalism. Hutterites. Lifestyles. South Dakota. 1874-1975. *403*
—. Communes. Hutterites. USA. 1870's-1970. *412*
—. Communion. Protestantism. United Church of Canada. 1952-72. *3670*
—. Communist Party. Labour Party. Methodism. Smith, Albert Edward. Social Gospel. 1893-1924. *983*
—. Conference of Historic Peace Churches. Conscientious objectors. Mennonites. World War II. ca 1914-45. *2671*
—. Cree Indians. Evans, James. Methodist Church. Missions and Missionaries. 1833-46. *3475*
—. Czechoslovakia. Jesuits. Refugees. Refugees. 1950. *3776*
—. Deprogramming. Organizations. Sects, religious. USA. 1960's-70's. *4267*
—. Doukhobors. Immigration. Persecution. Russia. Sects, Religious. 1654-1902. *3917*
—. Doukhobors. Immigration. Russia. 1652-1908. *3915*
—. Eby, Ezra E. Immigration. Loyalists. Mennonites. Pennsylvania. 18c-1835. *1237*
—. Ecumenism. Immigration. Nationalism. Protestant churches. United Church of Canada. 1902-25. *491*
—. Ecumenism. Mennonites (Canadian Conference). Pioneers. 1873-1978. *475*
—. Ecumenism. Methodist Church. Patrick, William. Presbyterian Church. 1900-11. *443*
—. Elites. Ethnicity. Protestant ethic. Senators. Values. 1971. *958*
—. Ethnic Groups. Immigrants. Indians. Language. 1970's. *126*
—. Ethnicity. Students. 1971. *100*
—. Evangelism. Holiness Movement Church. Horner, Ralph Cecil. Methodist Church. 1887-1921. *3500*
—. Evangelism. Holiness Movement Church. Horner, Ralph Cecil. Methodist Church. 1887-1921. *3501*
—. Evangelism. Osgood, Thaddeus. Religious Education. 1807-52. *2900*
—. Fairbairn, R. Edis. Pacifism. United Church of Canada. World War II. 1939. *2688*
—. Fiction. Labor. Social gospel. 1890's. *2078*
—. Fort Frontenac. Indian-White Relations. Iroquois Indians. Missions and Missionaries. Quinte Mission. Sulpician order. 1665-80. *1610*
—. Gospel Temperance Movement. Revivalism. Rine, D. I. K. Temperance Movements. 1877-82. *2575*
—. Grant, George. Philosophy. Politics. Schmidt, Larry (review article). Theology. 1945-78. *509*
—. Great Britain. Ontario (Kingston, Smith Falls). Queen's College. Romanes, George. Romanes, George John. Science. Scientific Experiments and Research. Theology. 1830-90. *2918*
—. Historians. Kerr, Donald Gordon Grady (tribute). 1938-76. *279*
—. Historiography. 17c-1973. 1945-69. *30*
—. Ideology. King, William Lyon Mackenzie. Liberal Party. Politics. Protestantism. Social Classes. 1900-50. *1421*
—. Immigrants. Lifestyles. Lutheran Church. Occupations. Settlement. Social Organizations. Swedish Americans. USA. 1893-1979. *3325*
—. Immigration. Mennonites. Ukraine. 1922-23. *3365*
—. Industrialization. 1970's. *92*
—. Labor. Social Gospel. Socialism. 20c. *2441*
—. Letters. Millenarianism. Northwest Rebellion. Riel, Louis. 1876-78. 1885. *965*
—. McClung, Nellie. Methodist Church. Ordination. United Church of Canada. Women. 1915-46. *852*
—. Mennonites. Missions and Missionaries. USA. 1880-1910. *1628*
—. Mennonites. Social Customs. Urbanization. USA. 1961-71. *3358*
—. Methodism. Missions and Missionaries. New York Conference. 1766-1862. *1607*
—. Methodism. Social gospel movement. 1890-1914. *2381*
—. Methodism. United Church of Canada. 18c-20c. *3468*
—. Pentecostal Assemblies of Canada. Pentecostal Bible School. Purdie, James Eustace. Religious education. Theology. 1925-50. *747*
—. Political socialization. Voting and Voting Behavior. 1965. *1249*
—. Presbyterian Church. United Church of Canada. 1925. *2902*
—. Protestantism. Sweet, H. C. 1866-1960. *2888*
—. Social Reform. Women. Young Women's Christian Association. 1870-1900. *895*
Canada, eastern. Christianity. Europe. Micmac Indians. Trade. 15c-18c. *1574*
Canada, western. Bishops. Catholic Church. French Canadians. Irish Canadians. Nominations for office. 1900-75. *3765*
—. Books (editions). Church of England. Diaries. Missions and Missionaries. West, John. 1820-27. *1530*
—. Catholic Church. French Canadians. Historiography. Migration, Internal. Quebec. 1870-1915. *3819*
—. Catholic Church. Immigration. Missions and Missionaries. Sisters of Service. 1920-30. *1665*
—. Catholic Church. Indians. Missions and Missionaries. Oblates of Mary Immaculate. 1818-70. *1502*
—. Church of England. Hudson's Bay Company. Hunter, James. Missions and Missionaries. 1844-64. *1603*
—. Ecumenism. Lutheran Church. Stuermer, Herbert. 1922. *489*
—. Frontier. Methodist Church. Missionaries. 1840-1925. *3450*
Canadian Catholic Historical Association. Catholic Church. Ontario (Toronto). 1933-73. *241*
Canadian Council of Churches. Baptists. Ecumenism. World Council of Churches. 1907-79. *462*
—. Ecumenism. World Conference of Christian Youth, 1st. Youth. 1939-79. *464*
Canadian Memorial Chapel (Manitoba memorial window). British Columbia (Vancouver). Stained glass windows. 1928. *1848*
Canadian Mennonite Bible College (Mennonite Heritage Centre). Archives. Mennonites. 1979. *219*
Canadian Pacific Railway. Clergy. Construction crews. Manitoba (Virden). McLeod, Finlay J. C. Personal narratives. Presbyterian Church. 1881-82. *3567*
Canadians. Religious Education. Theology. USA. 1760-1980. *646*
Canary Islanders. Agricultural Labor. Fernandez de Santa Ana, Benito. Indians. Missions and Missionaries. Petitions. Provincial Government. Texas (Villa San Fernando). 1741. *1542*
Canby, Edmund. Delaware (New Castle County). Diaries. Friends, Society of. Milling. 1822-35. *3275*
Candler, Warren A. Conservatism. Evolution. Leopold, Nathan. Loeb, Richard. Methodist Episcopal Church, South. Scopes, John Thomas. Trials. 1921-41. *2293*
—. Methodist Episcopal Church, South. Political Campaigns (presidential). Prohibition. Smith, Al. 1928. *1210*
Canevin, Regis. Bishops. Catholic Church. Flick, Lawrence. Pennsylvania (Philadelphia, Pittsburgh). 1870's-1927. *3843*
Canneries. Alaska (Kodiak). Fishing. Unification Church. 1978-79. *325*
Cannon, James, Jr. Glass, Carter. Methodist Church. Political Corruption. Virginia. 1909-34. *1295*
Cannon, Martha Hughes. Great Britain. Letters. Mormons. Polygamy. Utah (Salt Lake City). Women. 1885-96. *4002*
Canon law. Annulments. Birth Control. Catholic Church. Divorce. Netherlands. 1945-77. *914*
—. Circumcision. Europe. Illowy, Bernard. Judaism (Orthodox). Louisiana (New Orleans). Rabbis. 1853-65. *4176*
—. Episcopal Church, Protestant. Ordination. Women. 1966-74. *937*
Canon Law Society of America. Catholicism. Pontifical Commission for the Revision of the Code of Canon Law. 1917-73. *3686*
Canonization processes. Heroic virtue. Neumann, Saint John Nepomucene. Vatican Council II. 19c. 1962-65. *3835*
Cantors. California (Los Angeles). Concerts. Judaism. Loew's State Theatre. Music, liturgical. Rosenblatt, Josef "Yosele". Vaudeville. 1925. *1917*
—. Congregation Shearith Israel. Judaism (Orthodox). Netherlands. New York. Pinto, Joseph Jesurun. Travel. 1759-82. *4196*
Cantwell, John J. California. Catholic Church. Negroes. 1920's. *3896*
Capers, William. *Christian Advocate* (newspaper). Ecumenism. Letters. Methodist Episcopal Church. Methodist Episcopal Church (South). Slavery. 1854. 1875. *479*
Capital Punishment. Clergy. New England. Protestantism. Sermons. 1674-1750. *2822*
—. Mormons. Theology. Utah. 1843-1978. *3971*
Capitalism *See also* Socialism.
—. Alaska (Metlakahtla). British Columbia. Duncan, William. Missions and Missionaries. Tsimshian Indians. 1857-1974. *1519*
—. Alger, Horatio. Evangelicalism. Literature. Social History. Success (concept of). 1820-1910. *2958*

—. Anti-Catholicism. DeLeon, Daniel. Socialism. 1891-1914. *2113*
—. Baptists. Bode, Frederick A. (review article). Methodist Church. North Carolina. Populism. 1894-1903. 1975. *1287*
—. Canada. Fur trade. Hudson's Bay Company. Protestantism. Scottish Canadians. 18c-1970's. *377*
—. Catholic Church. Clergy. Elites. Pulp mills. Quebec (Chicoutimi). Working class. 1896-1930. *2601*
—. Church and State. Social Organization. 1960's-70's. *1075*
—. Defoe, Daniel *(Robinson Crusoe)*. Great Britain. Materialism. Thoreau, Henry David *(Walden)*. Transcendentalism. 18c-19c. *354*
—. Ideology. Management. Political Science. Protestantism. Theology. Weber, Max. 16c-1974. *376*
—. Individualism. Protestantism. Social ethic. 20c. *345*
—. Marxism. Niebuhr, Reinhold. *Radical Religion* (periodical). Roosevelt, Franklin D. (administration). 1930-43. *1343*
—. Protestant ethic. Values. Weber, Max. 1770-1920. *355*
Captivity narratives. Catholic Church. Congregationalism. French Canadians. Indians. New England. Williams, John *(The Redeemed Captive)*. 1704-06. *3133*
Cardome (home). Catholic Church. Education. Kentucky (Scott County; Georgetown). Mount Admirabilis (academy). Sisters of the Visitation. 1875-1975. *600*
Carey, William. Baptists. Racial attitudes. Rauschenbusch, Walter. Williams, Roger. 1776-1976. *3100*
—. Baptists, Southern. Higher education. Missions and Missionaries. 1826-1976. *1755*
Caricatures. *See* Cartoons and Caricatures.
Carigal, Hakham Raphael Haim Isaac. Jews. Rhode Island (Newport). 1771-77. *4190*
Carmelites. Artists. Louisiana (DeSoto Parish). Restorations. St. Anne's Chapel. 1891-1975. *1796*
Carranza, Venustiano. *America* (weekly). Catholic Church. Mexico. Revolution. Tierney, Richard Henry. 1914-17. *3722*
Carroll, Anna Ella. Nativism. Probasco, Harriet. Women. 1840's-61. *851*
Carroll, Charles (of Carrollton). Catholic Church. Declaration of Independence. Maryland. Political Leadership. 1737-1832. *3705*
—. Catholic Church. Maryland. 1737-1832. *3797*
Carroll, John. Catholic Church. Clergy. Documents. Hanley, Thomas O'Brien *(The John Carroll Papers)*. Research. 18c-19c. 1976-78. *3872*
—. Catholic Church. Clergy. Frontier and Pioneer Life. Louisiana Purchase. 1803-15. *3805*
—. Catholic Church. Documents. Hanley, Thomas O'Brien (review article). 18c-19c. 1970's. *3672*
—. Catholic Church. Ecumenism. Immigrants. Nativism. Protestants. 1790-1820. *496*
Carter, Jimmy. Attitudes. Civil religion. Evangelicalism. Political Campaigns (presidential). Political Speeches. Rhetoric. 1976. *1229*
—. Baptists. Political Campaigns (presidential). 1976. *1272*
—. Baptists, Southern. Georgia (Plains). 1977. *2992*
—. Cromwell, Oliver. Great Britain. Political Leadership. Rickover, Hyman. Roosevelt, Theodore. 20c. *974*
—. Niebuhr, Reinhold. South. 1976. *1233*
Carter, Robert. Christ Church. Church of England. Churches. Virginia (Lancaster County). 18c. *1849*
Cartoons and Caricatures. Great Britain. New England. Puritans. Satire. 1770-76. *2005*
—. Mormons. *Puck* (periodical). Stereotypes. 1904-07. *2001*
—. Mormons. Stereotypes. Women. 1830-1914. *800*
Caruana, George J. Bishops. Byrne, Edwin V. Catholic Church. Jones, William A. Puerto Rico. San Juan Diocese. 1866-1963. *3814*
Carver, William Owen. Missions and Missionaries. Southern Baptist Theological Seminary. 1859-1954. *1518*
Cary, Samuel Fenton. Ohio (Cincinnati). Temperance movements. 1845-1900. *2583*
Caskey, Marie. Albanese, Catherine L. Beecher family. Congregationalism. Connecticut. Massachusetts. Presbyterian Church. Transcendentalism (review article). Unitarianism. 1800-60. *2763*
—. Mathews, Donald G. Moorhead, James H. Protestantism (review article). Reform. Walters, Ronald. 1830-80. 1976-78. *2368*
Cass, William D. Abolition Movement. Letters. Methodist Episcopal Church (General Conference). 1844. *2477*
Castañeda, Carlos Eduardo. Catholic church. Historians. Mexican Americans. Texas. 1896-1927. *169*
Castañeda, Carlos Eduardo *(Our Catholic Heritage)*. Catholic Church. Colonization. Texas. 1693-1731. 1933-43. *3673*
Cathcart, Wallace H. Archives. Shakers. Western Reserve Historical Society. 1911-12. *202*
—. Manuscripts. Shakers. Western Reserve Historical Society. 1774-1920. *245*
Cathedral Church of St. John the Divine. Architecture. Episcopal Church, Protestant. Manning, William Thomas. New York City. Sabbatarianism. Sports. 19c-1920's. *3243*
Cathedral of the Assumption. Catholic Church. Kentucky (Louisville). 1852-1976. *3723*
Cathedrals. Architecture. Catholic Church. Ireland, John. Masqueray, Emmanuel L. Minnesota (St. Paul). 1904-17. *1795*
Cather, Willa *(Death Comes for the Archbishop)*. Fiction. Martinez, Antonio Jose. New Mexico (Taos). 1830's. 1927. *2077*
Catholic Association for International Peace. Antiwar Sentiment. Peace movements. 1917-68. *2673*
Catholic Church *See also* religious orders by name, e.g. Franciscans, Jesuits, etc.; Vatican.
—. 1776-1973. *3756*
—. Abortion. Attitudes. Colleges and Universities. Students. 1970's. *855*
—. Abortion. Democratic Party. Elections (presidential). 1976. *1245*
—. Abortion. Hawaii. Methodology. Women. 1965-74. *872*
—. Abortion. Women's Liberation Movement. -1973. *898*
—. Acadians. Acculturation. Exiles. France. Great Britain. Nova Scotia. 18c. *3750*
—. Acadians. Discrimination. Irish Canadians. New Brunswick. 1860-1900. *3855*
—. Acadians. English Canadians. Maritime Provinces. Social Conditions. 1763-1977. *3871*
—. Accademia (association). Clergy. New York. 1865-1907. *296*
—. Acculturation. Americanism. Leo XIII, Pope (*Testem Benevolentiae*). Periodicals. Protestantism. 1899. *319*
—. Acculturation. California (Monterey, San Luis Obispo counties). Indians. Missions and Missionaries. Salinan Indians. 1770's-1830's. *1550*
—. Acculturation. French Canadians. Nationalism. New England. ca 1610-1975. *309*
—. Acculturation. Indian-White Relations. Missionaries. Protestantism. Wisconsin. 1830-48. *1640*
—. Acculturation. Irish Americans. Pennsylvania (Pittsburgh). St. Andrew Parish. 1863-90. *3748*
—. Acculturation. Italian Americans (review article). Social Organization. 1880-20c. *3820*
—. Action Catholique. Courchesne, Georges. Quebec (Rimouski). 1940-67. *2356*
—. Actors and Actresses. California (Los Angeles area). Modjeska, Helena. Polish Americans. 1876-1909. *3786*
—. Aged. Charities. Education. Immigration. New Brunswick (Saint John). Orphans. Sisters of Charity of the Immaculate Conception. 1854-64. *2509*
—. Agnosticism. Colleges and Universities. Quebec. Students. 1970-78. *505*
—. Agricultural Reform. New Deal. Roosevelt, Franklin D. (administration). Social Theory. 1933-39. *2572*
—. Agriculture. Federal Programs. Friends, Society of. Indian-White Relations. Missions and Missionaries. Moravian Church. Old Northwest. 1789-1820. *1529*
—. Alaska. Holy Cross Mission. Indians. Jesuits. Missions and Missionaries. Sisters of St. Ann. Yukon River, lower. 1887-1956. *1615*
—. Alaska. Missionaries. Riobó, Juan Antonio García. Spain. Voyages. 1779. *1643*
—. Alaska (Juneau). Hospitals. Sisters of St. Ann. 1886-1968. *3757*
—. Alaska (Mary's Igloo). Bernard, Joseph. Eskimos. Missions and Missionaries. 1884-1962. *1504*
—. Alberta. Calgary Diocese. French Canadians. Irish Canadians. McNailly, John Thomas. 1871-1952. *3712*
—. Alberta (Edmonton). Colleges and Universities. MacDonald, John Roderick. St. Joseph's College (Alberta). 1922-23. *710*
—. Alberta, University of. Colleges and Universities. Legal, Emile. O'Leary, Henry Joseph. St. Joseph's University College. 1906-26. *619*
—. Alexian Brothers. Bernard, Alexius. German Americans. Hospitals. Missouri (St. Louis). Tollig, Paulus. 1869-1980. *1456*
—. Alsace-Lorraine. Batt, Joseph. Chapel of Our Lady of Help of Christians. Immigration. New York (Buffalo area; Cheektowaga). 1789-1872. *1760*
—. Altar boys. Clergy. Family. -1974. *3726*
—. *America* (periodical). Colleges and Universities. LaFarge, John. Newman Clubs. 1904-50's. *515*
—. *America* (weekly). Carranza, Venustiano. Mexico. Revolution. Tierney, Richard Henry. 1914-17. *3722*
—. American Catholic Historical Association. History. 1973. *173*
—. American Philosophical Association. Colleges and Universities. Philosophy. Religious Education. 1933-79. *775*
—. Americanization. Church and state. Europe. Maryland. Religious liberty. ca 1634-1786. *304*
—. Americanization. Clergy. Irish Americans. Polish Americans. 1920-40's. *290*
—. Americanization. Connecticut (New Britain). Polish Americans. 1890-1955. *3692*
—. Americanization. Ecumenism. Europe. Pluralism. Theology. 1775-1820. *295*
—. Americanization. French Canadians. Hendricken, Thomas F. Irish Americans. Massachusetts (Fall River). 1870's-85. *317*
—. Americanization. French language. Vermont. 1917-75. *308*
—. Americanization. Historiography. 1850-1973. *299*
—. Angers, François-Albert. Canada. French Canadians. Pacifism. Values. 1940-79. *2654*
—. Anglican communion. Ecumenism. Hughes, John Jay. Religious Orders. -1973. *493*
—. Anglin, Timothy Warren. Canada. Debates. Fenian Brotherhood. Irish Canadians. McGee, D'Arcy. 1863-68. *1341*
—. Anglin, Timothy Warren. Irish Canadians. New Brunswick. Newspapers. St. John *Freeman* (newspaper). 1849-83. *3680*
—. Anglo-Catholics. Clergy. Ecumenism. Episcopal Church, Protestant. *Lamp* (periodical). Wattson, Paul James. 1903-09. *460*
—. Anglophiles. Francophiles. Mathieu, Olivier-Elzéar. Regina Diocese. Saskatchewan. 1905-30. *3714*
—. Anglophiles. Wilberforce, Robert. World War II (antecedents). 1940. *1239*
—. Annexation. Converts. Imperialism. Methodist Episcopal Church. Missions and Missionaries. Philippines. 1899-1913. *1689*
—. Annulments. Birth Control. Canon law. Divorce. Netherlands. 1945-77. *914*
—. Anti-Communist Movements. Crosby, Donald F. Labor Unions and Organizations. McCarthy, Joseph R. (review article). Oshinsky, David. 1950-54. 1976-78. *1212*
—. Antigonish Movement. Nova Scotia. Rural Development. Social change. ca 1928-73. *2409*
—. Antislavery Sentiments. Emigration. Germans, Sudeten. Journalism. Missions and Missionaries. Neumann, Saint John Nepomucene. Republican Party. 19c-20c. *3826*
—. Apostolic Delegates. Conroy, George. Nationalism. Politics. Quebec. Vatican. 1877-78. *1098*
—. Architecture. Arizona, southern. Chapels. Folk religion. Papago Indians. 20c. *1783*
—. Architecture. Cathedrals. Ireland, John. Masqueray, Emmanuel L. Minnesota (St. Paul). 1904-17. *1795*
—. Architecture. Church of St. Paul the Apostle. Decorative Arts. LaFarge, John. New York City. 1876-99. *1833*
—. Architecture. Churches. St. Andrew's Church. Virginia (Roanoke). 1882-1975. *1834*

—. Architecture. Fundamentalists. German Americans. Rural Settlements. Social customs. Southerners. Texas (Cooke, Denton counties). 1860-1976. *2750*
—. Architecture. New France. 1600-1760. *1807*
—. Architecture, academy. Oregon (Salem). Piper, William W. Sacred Heart Academy. 1834-83. *1828*
—. Archives. Bishops. Church History. Kingston, Archdiocese of. Ontario. 1800-1966. *247*
—. Archives. California. 1768-1975. *274*
—. Archives. Church records. Genealogy. 19c-20c. *242*
—. Arctic. Canada. Church of England. Churches. Fur Trade. Missions and Missionaries. 20c. *1549*
—. Arguello, Maria de la Concepcion. California. Orthodox Eastern Church, Russian. Rezanov, Nikolai. 1806. *2797*
—. Arizona. Baptists. Episcopal Church, Protestant. Methodism. Missions and Missionaries. Mormons. Presbyterian Church. 1859-99. *1501*
—. Arizona. Colonial Government. Jurisdictions, ecclesiastical. New Mexico. Spain. 1548-1969. *3739*
—. Arizona (Nogales). Buena, Mariano. Gil, Juan. Indians. Seri Indians. 1768-72. *1559*
—. Arizona (Pisinimo). Clergy. Frembling, Lambert. Papago Indians. Refugees. 1939-77. *3825*
—. Arkansas (Jonesboro). Missions and missionaries. Olivetan Benedictine Sisters, American. Renggli, Rose (Mother Mary Beatrice). 1847-1942. *1652*
—. Art. Discovery and Exploration. Hennepin, Louis. Minnesota (Minneapolis). Missions and Missionaries. Mississippi River (Falls of St. Anthony). 1680-1980. *1556*
—. Art. Folk religion. French Canadians. Musée Historique de Vaudreuil. Quebec. 17c-20c. *174*
—. Art criticism. California. Missions and Missionaries. 1769-1980. *1876*
—. Arts. California. Historiography (Anglo-American). Missions and Missionaries. Scholasticism. 1740's-1976. *1878*
—. Asia. Merton, Thomas. Monasteries. Trappists. 1940's-68. *3707*
—. Assimilation. Authority. Bishops. Cleveland Diocese. German Americans. Irish Americans. Ohio. Rappe, Louis Amadeus. 1847-70. *3788*
—. Assimilation. Clergy. Dufresne, Andre B. French Canadians. Massachusetts (Holyoke). 1869-87. *302*
—. Assimilation. Connecticut (New Britain). Holy Cross Church. Polish Americans. 1928-76. *3693*
—. Assimilation. Connecticut (Waterbury). Lithuanian Americans. *Rytas* (newspaper). Zebris, Joseph. 1896-98. *3901*
—. Assimilation. Eastern Orthodox Church, Syrian. Maronite Catholics. Melkite Catholics. Syrian Americans. Uniates. 1900-73. *3908*
—. Assimilation. French Canadians. Nationalism. Rhode Island (Woonsocket). 1924-29. *3854*
—. Assimilation. Immigrants. Polish Americans. 1860's-1930's. *3700*
—. Assimilation. Parishes. Pennsylvania (Philadelphia). 1759-1975. *3745*
—. Association Catholique de la Jeunesse Canadienne-Française. French Canadians. Morality. Quebec. 1903-14. *2355*
—. Asylums. Hospitals. Illinois (Chicago). Schools. Wisconsin (Milwaukee). 19c. *3886*
—. Atlantic Provinces. Bishops. Diaries. Plessis, Joseph-Octave. Quebec Archdiocese. 1812-15. *3704*
—. Attitudes. Autobiography. Brownson, Orestes A. *(The Convert)*. Converts. Great Britain. Newman, John Henry *(Apologia pro Vita Sua)*. Protestantism. 1857-64. *3681*
—. Attitudes. Brooklyn College. Immigration. Judaism. Negroes. New York City. Protestant Ethic. West Indian Americans. 1939-78. *350*
—. Attitudes. Brownson, Orestes A. Civil War. Hughes, John. McMaster, James. 1850-65. *2692*
—. Attitudes. Canada. Ethnic Groups. Jews. Protestantism. Social Status. 1968. *2088*
—. Attitudes. Colonial Government. Discovery and Exploration. Games. Indians. Missions and Missionaries. 16c-17c. *1524*
—. Attitudes. Death and Dying. Quebec. Wills. 1663-1760. *3718*
—. Attitudes. Israel. Zionism. 1945-48. *963*
—. Attitudes. Prayer. Students. 1961-71. *3808*
—. Attitudes. Religiosity. Students. 1961-71. *3807*
—. Australia. O'Farrell, Patrick (review article). 17c-1977. *3733*
—. Authors. More, Thomas. Walter, William Joseph. 1820's-46. *2049*
—. Baptists. Clergy. Rauschenbusch, Walter. Social reform. Theology. Vatican Council II. 1912-65. *2380*
—. Baptists. Ecumenism. 1967-77. *500*
—. Baptists. Germans, Russian. Immigration. Kansas. Lutheran Church. Mennonites. Wheat industry. 1874-77. *2778*
—. Baptists. Hispanic Americans. Indiana (East Chicago, Gary). Theater. 1920-76. *1864*
—. Barbeau, Victor. Cooperatives. Medical Reform. Paquette, Albiny. Politics. Quebec. 1900-45. *3874*
—. Barzynski, Wincenty. Illinois (Chicago). Polish Roman Catholic Union. St. Stanislaus Kortka Church. Texas. 1838-99. *3678*
—. Benedictine High School. Boys. Ohio (Cleveland). Secondary Education. 1928-78. *787*
—. Benedictines. Frontier and Pioneer Life. Oetgen, Jerome (review article). Wimmer, Boniface. 1809-87. *3685*
—. Benedictines. Missions and Missionaries. Vatican Council I. Wimmer, Boniface. 1866-87. *3815*
—. Bennett, James Gordon. Immigration. *New York Herald* (newspaper). 1835-70. *3850*
—. Berrigan, Daniel. Berrigan, Philip. Church and state. Leftism. Murray, John Courtney. 1950's-70's. *3758*
—. Bible. Hermeneutics. Periodicals. 1893-1908. *3812*
—. Bible (King James version). Church Schools. City Politics. Education, Finance. Michigan (Detroit). Protestantism. Religion in the Public Schools. 1842-53. *2716*
—. Bible reading. Desmond, Humphrey. Protestantism. Religion in the Public Schools. *Wisconsin ex rel. Frederick Weiss et al.* v. *District School Board of School District 8* (1890). 1888-90. *571*
—. Bible reading. Politics. Prince Edward Island. Protestants. Religion in the Public Schools. 1856-60. *580*
—. Bibliographies. Bishops. Education. Keane, John J. 1838-1918. *3891*
—. Bibliographies. Canada. ca 1800-1976. *3760*
—. Bibliographies. Catholic University of America. Hogan Schism. Parsons, Wilfrid. Pennsylvania (Philadelphia). Schisms. 1785-1825. 1975. *3845*
—. Bicentennial Celebrations. 1976. *3684*
—. Bishops. Byrne, Edwin V. Caruana, George J. Jones, William A. Puerto Rico. San Juan Diocese. 1866-1963. *3814*
—. Bishops. Canada, western. French Canadians. Irish Canadians. Nominations for office. 1900-75. *3765*
—. Bishops. Canevin, Regis. Flick, Lawrence. Pennsylvania (Philadelphia, Pittsburgh). 1870's-1927. *3843*
—. Bishops. Chicago Diocese. Clergy. Duggan, James. Illinois. McMullen, John. Succession. 1865-81. *3742*
—. Bishops. Chicoutimi, Séminaire de. Quebec (Saguenay). 1873-1973. *721*
—. Bishops. Church Finance. Frenaye, Mark Anthony. Letters. O'Connor, Michael. Pennsylvania (Pittsburgh). 1843-49. *368*
—. Bishops. Church of England. Evangelicalism. Feild, Edward. Liturgy. Methodism. Newfoundland. Presbyterian Church. 1765-1852. *3197*
—. Bishops. Church of England. Liberal Party. Newfoundland. Provincial government. 1860-62. *1253*
—. Bishops. Clergy. Marriage. Uniates. 1890-1907. *3907*
—. Bishops. Colombia (Bogotá). Hughes, John. Letters. Mosquera, Manuel José. New York City. 1853. *3762*
—. Bishops. Education. Medicine. Quebec (Gaspé). Ross, François Xavier. Social Conditions. 1923-45. *3787*
—. Bishops. Farrelly, John P. Irish Americans. Morris, John. Stritch, Samuel A. Tennessee. 19c-1958. *3860*
—. Bishops. Indian-white relations. Lamy, Jean Baptiste. New Mexico (Santa Fe). Social customs. 1849-88. *3761*
—. Bishops. Intellectuals. Letters. Provincial Council of Baltimore (4th). Walter, William Joseph. 1840-43. *3842*
—. Bishops. Irish Americans. Jamestown Diocese. Minnesota (St. Paul). North Dakota. Shanley, John. 1852-1909. *3731*
—. Bishops. Kenrick, Peter Richard. Letters. Missouri. Travel. 1847. *3839*
—. Bishops. Lynch, John Joseph. Ontario. Poor. Toronto Savings Bank. 1870's. *369*
—. Bishops. McCarthy, Joseph R. 1954. *1222*
—. Bishops. Quebec. Sherbrooke Diocese. 1868-72. *3882*
—. Bishops. Trusteeism. 1785-1860. *293*
—. Black, Conrad. Church and state. Duplessis, Maurice (review article). Provincial Government. Quebec. Rumilly, Robert. 1930's-77. *1124*
—. Bogan, Louise. Poetry. Women. 1920's-70. *2059*
—. Bohemia. Neumann, Saint John Nepomucene. Pennsylvania (Philadelphia). 1811-1977. *3904*
—. Bójnowski, Lucyan. Buczek, Daniel Stephen (review article). Clergy. Connecticut (New Britain). Polish Americans. 1895-1960. *3865*
—. Bolton, Herbert Eugene. Colonization. Historiography. Missions and Missionaries. Southwest. Spain. 1917-79. *1489*
—. Boucher, Jonathan. Church of England. Maryland. Religious Liberty. 1774-97. *2729*
—. Boundaries. Missions and Missionaries. Ontario. Settlement. 1840-1910. *3709*
—. Bourassa, Henri. Politics. Provincial Government. Quebec. 1902-71. *976*
—. Bourget, Ignace. Church History. Faillon, Etienne-Michel. Letters. Quebec (Montreal). 1850. *3824*
—. Bourget, Ignace. Colleges and Universities. Laval University. Quebec (Quebec). 1840's-50's. *676*
—. Brébeuf, Jean de. Indian-White Relations. Ledesme, R. P. *(Doctrine Chrestienne)*. New France. Translating and Interpreting. Wyandot Indians. 16c-17c. *1639*
—. British Columbia (Vancouver Island; Nootka Sound). Indians. Missions and Missionaries. Oral History. Spain. 1789-95. 19c. *1563*
—. British Empire. Ideology. Imperialism. Quebec. 19c-20c. *1411*
—. Brotherhood of the Holy Family. Chaumonot, Joseph-Marie-Pierre. Elites. Laval, François de. Quebec (Montreal). 1663-1760. *3717*
—. *Brown* v. *Les Curé et Marguilliers de l'Oeuvre et de la Fabrique de la Paroisse de Montréal* (1874). Church and state. Guibord, Joseph. Liberalism. Politics. Quebec. Ultramontanism. 1870-74. *1067*
—. Brownson, Henry Francis. Editors and Editing. 1835-1900. *3836*
—. Brownson, Orestes A. Civilization. Lectures. Missouri (St. Louis). 1852-54. *3838*
—. Brownson, Orestes A. Cumming, William. Letters. 1850's. *3676*
—. Brownson, Orestes A. Democracy. 1840's-76. *1389*
—. Brownson, Orestes A. Democracy. Theocratic principles. 19c. *1379*
—. Brownson, Orestes A. Intellectuals. Social Philosophy. 1803-76. *3677*
—. Buddhism (Zen). Merton, Thomas. Suzuki, Diasetz Teitaro. 1935-70. *498*
—. Buies, Arthur. 1880's-1901. *3878*
—. Bureau of Indian Affairs. Indian-White Relations. Iowa. Presbyterian Church. Schools. Winnebago Indians. 1834-48. *737*
—. California. 1848. *3895*
—. California. Cantwell, John J. Negroes. 1920's. *3896*
—. California. Charities. Ethnic groups. Ramm, Charles A. 1863-1951. *3888*
—. California. Church administration. González Rubio, José. Missions and Missionaries. 1846-50. *3811*
—. California. Engelhardt, Zephyrin. Mission Santa Barbara. Missions and Missionaries. Southwestern history. 1851-1934. *176*
—. California. Famines. Gold Rushes. Immigration. Irish Americans. 1849-90's. *3800*
—. California. Homosexuality. Proposition 6 (1978). Public schools. Referendum. Teachers. 1978. *1320*
—. California. Indians. Labor. Missions and Missionaries. 1775-1805. *1485*
—. California. Indians (neophytes). Mexico. Missions and missionaries. 1830's. *1606*
—. California. Indian-White Relations. Missions and Missionaries. 1770's-1820's. *1636*
—. California. Mexico. Rubio, José Gonzalez. Tithing. 1848. *3894*

—. California. Mission San Gabriel Arcangel. Newspapers. 1867. *1658*
—. California. Mission San Juan Capistrano. Restorations. 1797-1979. *1803*
—. California. Mission San Juan Capistrano. Serra, Junípero. 1775-76. *1601*
—. California. Missions and Missionaries. Viticulture. 1697-1858. *1659*
—. California. Mountain Men. Protestantism. Rogers, Harrison. Smith, Jedediah Strong. 1826-27. *2798*
—. California (Los Angeles). Christmas. Mexican Americans. Neighborhoods. Posadas (celebrations). Rites and Ceremonies. 1975-80. *3794*
—. California (Los Angeles). Ethnology. Methodology. Polish Americans. Sandberg, Neil C. (review article). 1968-74. *3813*
—. California (San Diego). Excavations. Military Camps and Forts. Missions and Missionaries. Serra Museum. 1769-75. 1964-70's. *1526*
—. California (San Francisco). City Politics. Clergy. Irish Americans. Progressivism. Yorke, Peter C. 1900's. *3889*
—. California (San Francisco). Clergy. Editors and Editing. Ethnicity. Irish Americans. Yorke, Peter C. ca 1885-1925. *3887*
—. California (San Francisco). Clergy. Fontaine, Flavian. Mission Dolores. 1850-53. *3801*
—. California (Santa Clara). Santa Clara, University of. 1851-80. *697*
—. California (Sonoma). Indians. Mission San Francisco Solano. 1823-34. *1506*
—. California (Temecula). Documents. Indians. Maltby, Charles. Mission San Antonio de Pala. 1866. *1573*
—. California, University of (Regents). Clergy. Irish Americans. Political attitudes. Yorke, Peter C. 1900-12. *560*
—. California (Ventura). Churches. Mission San Buenaventura. ca 1794-1976. *1831*
—. Calvert, Cecilius (2d Lord Baltimore). Colonization. Maryland. Religious liberty. 1634-92. *1061*
—. Calvert, Cecilius (2d Lord Baltimore). Great Britain. Maryland. Provincial Government. Religious Liberty. 1634-49. *1068*
—. Calvert, George (1st Lord Baltimore). Colonization. Newfoundland (Avalon Peninsula). Protestant churches. Religious Liberty. 1620's. *2755*
—. Canada. Census. Cities. French Canadians. French language. 1941. *3880*
—. Canada. Church and state. Encyclicals. Pius IX, Pope *(Syllabus of Errors)*. Press. Public opinion. 1864-65. *1019*
—. Canada. Clergy. Craig, James Henry. French Canadians. Nationalism. Political repression. Quebec (Lower Canada). 1810. *1319*
—. Canada. Conroy, George. Papal legates. 1873-77. *3883*
—. Canada. Education. French Canadians. Quebec. Rinfret, Fernand. Siegfried, André *(Le Canada, les deux races: Problèmes politiques contemporains)*. Social Sciences. 1906-07. *3873*
—. Canada. Geographic Space. Missions and Missionaries. Regionalism. 1615-1851. *1486*
—. Canada. Industrialization. Judaism. Protestant Churches. Religiosity. 1921-71. *93*
—. Canada. Journalism. Social thought. Somerville, Henry. 1915-53. *2354*
—. Canada. Macdonald, John. Voting and Voting Behavior. 1850's-91. *1286*
—. Canada, western. French Canadians. Historiography. Migration, Internal. Quebec. 1870-1915. *3819*
—. Canada, Western. Immigration. Missions and Missionaries. Sisters of Service. 1920-30. *1665*
—. Canada, western. Indians. Missions and Missionaries. Oblates of Mary Immaculate. 1818-70. *1502*
—. Canadian Catholic Historical Association. Ontario (Toronto). 1933-73. *241*
—. Capitalism. Clergy. Elites. Pulp mills. Quebec (Chicoutimi). Working class. 1896-1930. *2601*
—. Captivity narratives. Congregationalism. French Canadians. Indians. New England. Williams, John *(The Redeemed Captive)*. 1704-06. *3133*
—. Cardome (home). Education. Kentucky (Scott County; Georgetown). Mount Admirabilis (academy). Sisters of the Visitation. 1875-1975. *600*
—. Carroll, Charles (of Carrollton). Declaration of Independence. Maryland. Political Leadership. 1737-1832. *3705*
—. Carroll, Charles (of Carrollton). Maryland. 1737-1832. *3797*
—. Carroll, John. Clergy. Documents. Hanley, Thomas O'Brien *(The John Carroll Papers)*. Research. 18c-19c. 1976-78. *3872*
—. Carroll, John. Clergy. Frontier and Pioneer Life. Louisiana Purchase. 1803-15. *3805*
—. Carroll, John. Documents. Hanley, Thomas O'Brien (review article). 18c-19c. 1970's. *3672*
—. Carroll, John. Ecumenism. Immigrants. Nativism. Protestants. 1790-1820. *496*
—. Castañeda, Carlos Eduardo. Historians. Mexican Americans. Texas. 1896-1927. *169*
—. Castañeda, Carlos Eduardo *(Our Catholic Heritage)*. Colonization. Texas. 1693-1731. 1933-43. *3673*
—. Cathedral of the Assumption. Kentucky (Louisville). 1852-1976. *3723*
—. Cemeteries. German Alsatians. Gravemarkers. Iron work. Ontario (Bruce County; Waterloo). 1850-1910. *1880*
—. Centennial Exposition of 1876. Pennsylvania (Philadelphia). Periodicals. 1876. *3864*
—. Centralization. Influence, distribution of. Organizational structure. 1970's. *3866*
—. Chapel-of-St. John's-in-the-Wilderness. Ecumenism. Episcopal Church, Protestant. New York (Graymoor). Society of the Atonement. Wattson, Paul James. White, Lurana Mary. 1909-18. *461*
—. Chapels. New Mexico (Santa Fe). 1850's-70's. *1821*
—. Chapels. New Mexico (Santa Fe). Third Order of Saint Francis. ca 1805-32. *1776*
—. Chaplains. Diaries. Fort Keogh. Lindesmith, Eli. Montana. 1855-1922. *2679*
—. Charismatic Movement. 1970's. *3768*
—. Charismatic Movement. Italian Americans. Jesu, Father. Pennsylvania (Philadelphia). Working Class. 1920's-30's. *1576*
—. Charities. Education. Moore, Julia. Ontario (London). Personal narratives. Sisters of St. Joseph. Women. 1868-85. *2517*
—. Charities. Irish Canadians. McMahon, Patrick. Poor. Quebec (Quebec). St. Bridget's Home. 1847-1972. *2521*
—. Chicoutimi, Petit-Séminaire de. Quebec (Saguenay). Religious Education. Students. 1873-1930. *756*
—. Chicoutimi, Séminaire de. Church and State. Personal narratives. Personal narratives. Simard, Ovide-D. 1873-1973. *757*
—. Children. Occupational status. Public schools. Socialization. -1974. *3784*
—. China. Communists. Missionaries. Protestant Churches. 1948-50. *1752*
—. China (Kanchow). Foreign policy. Missions and Missionaries. State Department. 1929-32. *1710*
—. Chipewyan Indians. Indian-White Relations. Letters. Mission St. Jean-Baptiste. Saskatchewan (Île-à-la-Crosse). Taché, Alexandre Antonin. 1823-54. *1503*
—. Christian Renaissance. Converts. Literature. Philosophy. Science. Stern, Karl. 1920's-60's. *2758*
—. Church and Social Problems. German Americans. Irish Americans. New Jersey (Newark). 1840-70. *3830*
—. Church and state. Democracy. Dominicans. Mazzuchelli, Samuel Charles *(Memoirs)*. Old Northwest. 1806-63. *1384*
—. Church and State. Europe, Western. North America. Politics. 1870-1974. *1326*
—. Church and State. French language. Langevin, Adélard. Manitoba. Politics. Private schools. 1890-1916. *608*
—. Church and state. Governors, provincial. Laval, François de. New France (Sovereign Council). Trade. 1659-84. *1020*
—. Church and state. Great Britain. Military government. Protestantism. Quebec. 18c. *1125*
—. Church and state. Inquisition. Louisiana. Surveillance. 1762-1800. *1044*
—. Church and state. Kennedy, John F. Political Campaigns (presidential). Presbyterian Church. 1959-60. *992*
—. Church and State. Law. Puerto Rico. ca 1863-1908. *1041*
—. Church and State. New France. Protestantism. ca 1625-1760's. *2818*
—. Church and State. Quebec. 18c-20c. *1070*
—. Church attendance. Protestant Churches. Religiosity. 1974. *2713*
—. Church attendance. Residence. 1953-69. *3696*
—. Church Finance. Economic Development. LaRocque, Paul. Quebec. Sherbrooke Diocese. 1893-1926. *3783*
—. Church finance. Education. Indian-White Relations. Oklahoma. Quapaw Indians. 1876-1927. *3727*
—. Church membership. Ohio (Cleveland). 1860. *65*
—. Church names. Quebec. Toponymy. 1600-1925. *3841*
—. Church of England. Colonial Government. Macdonnell, Alexander. Ontario. Ontario (Kingston, Toronto). Strachan, John. 1820's-30's. *1108*
—. Church of England. Government. Indian-White Relations. Manitoulin project. Methodist Church. Missions and Missionaries. Ontario (Upper Canada). 1820-40. *1537*
—. Church of St. John the Evangelist. Construction. Rhode Island (Newport). 1883-1934. *1772*
—. Church records. Immigrants. Italian Americans. Methodology. Pennsylvania (Philadelphia). 1789-1900. *3770*
—. Church records. Louisiana, north. Preservation. 1716-1840's. 1930's-74. *185*
—. Church Schools. 1750-1945. *681*
—. Church Schools. Constitutional law. Elementary Education. Federal aid to education. 1960's-72. *691*
—. Church Schools. Damen, Arnold. Fund raising. Illinois (Chicago). 1840-90. *773*
—. Church Schools. Dubuque Diocese. Hennessy, John. Iowa. Irish Americans. 1866-1900. *3720*
—. Church Schools. Ethnic Groups. Illinois (Chicago). Sanders, James W. (review article). 1833-1965. 1977. *614*
—. Church Schools. Felicians. Polish Americans. Social Work. Women. 1855-1975. *3828*
—. Church schools. French language. Langevin, Adélard. Laurier, Wilfrid. Liberal Party. Prairie Provinces. Religion in the Public Schools. 1890-1915. *569*
—. Church Schools. Girls. McDonough, Madrienne C. Mount St. Mary Convent. New Hampshire (Manchester). Personal narratives. 1902-09. *692*
—. Church Schools. Glennon, John J. Missouri (St. Louis). Ritter, Joseph E. School Integration. 1935-47. *2542*
—. Church Schools. Manitoba. McCarthy, D'Alton. Provincial legislation. 1870-90. *72*
—. Church Schools. Philosophy. Theology. 1920-60. *3747*
—. Church Schools. Polish Americans. 1874-1960's. *675*
—. Church Schools. Segregation. 1972. *704*
—. Church Schools. Seton, Elizabeth Ann. White House (school). 1774-1821. *625*
—. Churches. Louisiana. 1685-1830. *1835*
—. Cistercians. Mistassini, monastery of. Quebec. Trappists. 1900-03. *3721*
—. Cities. Civil rights movement. Negroes. Protestant churches. Social Classes. 1960's-70's. *2539*
—. Cities. Merton, Thomas. Nonviolence. Reform. Social criticism. 1960's. *2417*
—. Cities. Negroes. North or Northern States. Occupations. Social Status. 1968. *2613*
—. City Life. Illinois (Chicago). Neighborhoods. 1900-30. *3771*
—. City Politics. Construction. Contractors. Irish Americans. Pennsylvania (Philadelphia). 1846-1960's. *338*
—. Civil War. Copperheads. Editors and Editing. *Metropolitan Record* (newspaper). Mullaly, John. New York City. 1861-64. *1234*
—. Civil War. Irish Americans. *Universe: The Catholic Herald and Visitor* (newspaper). 1860-70. *3746*
—. Clergy. Converts. Episcopal Church, Protestant. Richey, James Arthur Morrow. ca 1900-33. *2754*
—. Clergy. Czechoslovakia. Personal narratives. Refugees. Social Change. Zubek, Theodoric. 1950-78. *3902*
—. Clergy. Diaries. Shaw, Joseph Coolidge. Vermont (Brattleboro). 1848. *3849*
—. Clergy. Editors and Editing. Historiography. *New Catholic Encyclopedia*. Polish Americans. Swastek, Joseph Vincent (obituary). 1913-77. *227*

—. Clergy. Ethnicity. Social Status. 1947-80. *3867*
—. Clergy. Germany. Mundelein, George. Nazism. 1937. *1256*
—. Clergy. Greeley, Andrew M. Intellectuals. 1974. *3749*
—. Clergy. Harris, William Richard. Ontario. Toronto Archdiocese. 1846-1923. 1974. *3846*
—. Clergy. Human rights. New York City. Social progress. Varela, Félix. 1823-53. *2357*
—. Clergy. Lemke, John A. Michigan (Detroit). Polish Americans. 1866-90. *3875*
—. Clergy. Massachusetts (Boston). O'Connell, William Henry. 1915-44. *3741*
—. Clergy. Men. Religious Orders. Social classes. Women. 1650-1762. *2614*
—. Clergy. Middle Classes. Pentecostal movement. Students. 1970's. *3753*
—. Clergy. Missouri (St. Louis). 1841-99. *3759*
—. Clergy. National Federation of Priests' Councils. Organizational change. Values. -1973. *3859*
—. Clergy. New France. Trade. 1627-1760. *337*
—. Clergy. Protestant Churches. Sex discrimination. Women. 1970's. *939*
—. Clergy. Quebec. Working conditions. 1968-77. *3861*
—. Clergy. Quebec (review article). 19c. 1979. *3840*
—. Clergy. Values. 1970's. *3744*
—. Coahuiltecan Indians. Missions and Missionaries. Texas (San Antonio). 1792. *1566*
—. Cofradías (brotherhoods). Mexican Americans. New Mexico. Penitentes. Rio Grande Valley. ca 1770-1970. *3675*
—. Colet, John. Episcopal Church, Protestant. Erasmus, Desiderius. Hermeneutics. More, Thomas. 1500-1975. *3167*
—. College of St. Teresa. Franciscan Sisters. Minnesota (Winona). Molloy, Mary Aloysius. Women. 1903-54. *670*
—. Colleges and Universities. 20c. *713*
—. Colleges and Universities. High Schools. Utah. 1875-1975. *624*
—. Colleges and Universities. Maryville Academy. Missouri (St. Louis). 1872-1972. *657*
—. Colonial Government. Discovery and Exploration. France. Jolliet, Louis. Marquette, Jacques. Missions and Missionaries. Mississippi River. Monuments. 1665-1700. *3767*
—. Colonial Government. Intendants. Quebec. 1633-1760. *1030*
—. Colonization. Economic development. French Canadians. Geopolitics. Provost, T. S. Quebec (Mattawinie district). 17c-1890. *3809*
—. Colorado. Diaries. Hospitals. Mallon, Catherine. New Mexico (Santa Fe). Sisters of Charity. 1865-1901. *1454*
—. Colorado. Folk art. New Mexico. Penitentes. 19c-20c. *3898*
—. Colorado. Germans, Russian. Immigration. Mennonites. 18c-19c. *2775*
—. Colorado. New Mexico. Passion plays. Spain. 1830's-1978. *1890*
—. Colorado (Denver). Italian Americans. 1870's-1920's. *3728*
—. Colorado (Denver; Globeville). Polish Americans. St. Joseph Parish. 1902-78. *3724*
—. Colorado, southern. Death Carts. Hispanic Americans. New Mexico, northern. Penitentes. 1860-90's. *3856*
—. *Commonweal* (periodical). Editors and Editing. Williams, Michael. 1922-38. *3716*
—. Communism. Jesuits. McCarthy, Joseph R. 1950-57. *1223*
—. Compulsory education. Edwards Law (Illinois, 1889). Ethnic Groups. Illinois. Private schools. Public schools. State Politics. 1889-93. *551*
—. Confederate Army. Duke, Basil W. Fort Delaware. Prisoners of War. Wood, James F. 1864. *3844*
—. Conflict and Conflict Resolution. Italian Americans. Rhode Island (Providence). 1890-1930. *3682*
—. Congregation of Notre Dame (Sisters). Ontario (Kingston). Religious education. Women. 1841-48. *596*
—. Connecticut (New Haven). Ethnic Groups. Jews. Marriage. Protestantism. 1900-50. *906*
—. Conservatism. Corrigan, Michael. Economic Theory. George, Henry. McGlynn, Edward. New York. 1886-94. *2562*
—. Conservatism. Nativism. Newspapers. Political Commentary. Protestantism. *Providence Visitor* (newspaper). Rhode Island. 1916-24. *2118*
—. Conservatism. Politics. 1970's. *970*
—. Contemplative ideal. Merton, Thomas. Monasticism. 1940's-68. *3858*
—. Conversion. France (Alsace). Immigration policy. Louisiana. Protestants. 1753-59. *3719*
—. Converts. Marriage. Protestantism. 1960's-70's. *848*
—. Co-operative Commonwealth Federation. Saskatchewan. Social reform. Socialism. 1930-50. *2567*
—. Cotton mills. French Canadians. Immigration. Massachusetts (Springfield). Population. Working Class. 1870. *3710*
—. Country Life. Ethnic Groups. Lutheran Church. Reformed Dutch Church. Voting and Voting Behavior. 1890-98. *1257*
—. Cults. Devotions, popular. Quebec (Lake St. John, Portneuf counties). 1970's. *3851*
—. Culture. Paraguay. Spain. 1513-20c. *3737*
—. Culture region. Minnesota. St.Cloud Diocese. 1860-1973. *3881*
—. Cunningham, Patrick. Documents. Irish Americans. Vermont (Brattleboro). 1847-98. *3725*
—. Daily life. Documents. Girls. Holy Names of Jesus and Mary, Sisters of the. Oregon (Salem). Sacred Heart Academy. 1863-73. *699*
—. Daily Life. Nova Scotia (Lochaber). Presbyterians. Rural Settlements. 1830-1972. *2747*
—. Debt. LaRocque, Charles. Quebec. St. Hyacinthe Diocese. 1866-73. *3695*
—. Democracy. Intellectuals. Liberalism. Racism. 1924-59. *2532*
—. Democracy. Laity. Trusteeism. 1785-1855. *292*
—. Democracy. Manuscripts. Sermons. Tocqueville, Alexis de. Yale University. 1831-40. *1990*
—. Democratic Party. 1972-73. *1230*
—. Democratic Party. Elections (presidential). Louisiana. Protestant Churches. Smith, Al. Temperance Movements. 1928. *1330*
—. Democratic Party. Immigrants. New York City. Prohibition. Protestantism. Tammany Hall. 1840-60. *2594*
—. Democratic Party. Irish Americans. *Kentucky Irish American* (newspaper). 1898-1968. *3817*
—. Design. Folk art. Iconography. Manuscripts. New Mexico. 16c-17c. *1858*
—. Devotions, popular. Quebec (Beauce County). Shrines, roadside. Social customs. 1970's. *1788*
—. Dialects. French Language. Haitian Americans. New York City (Brooklyn). 1970's. *3699*
—. Diaries. Germans, Russian. Immigration. Karlin, Athanasius. 1875-87. *3772*
—. Diaries. Healy, James A. Holy Cross College. Massachusetts (Worcester). Religious Education. 1849. *640*
—. Discovery and Exploration. Jolliet, Louis. Marquette, Jacques. Mississippi River. 1673. 1973. *1567*
—. Discrimination. Economic Conditions. Polish Canadians. Prairie Provinces. 1880's-1970's. *3796*
—. Discrimination. Northwest Territories. Teachers colleges. 1884-1900. *77*
—. Dissent. Episcopal Church, Protestant. Pentecostal movement. 1950's-70's. *2742*
—. Dissent. Michigan (Detroit). Protestant Churches. Religious Education. 1958-71. *3777*
—. District of Columbia. Jews. Judaism. Protestant churches. Psychological well-being. Religiosity. Worship. 1970's. *130*
—. Documents. Identity. National Catholic Welfare Council. Vatican. 1922. *3803*
—. Dolan, Jay P. (review article). German Americans. Irish Americans. New York. Social Conditions. 1815-65. 1975. *3793*
—. Drummond County Mechanics Institute. Farmers. Labor Unions and Organizations. Quebec (Drummond County). 1856-90. *1472*
—. Dutch Americans. Immigration. 1845-75. *3857*
—. École Sociale Populaire. Labor Unions and Organizations. Quebec. Social Change. 1911-75. *1469*
—. École Sociale Populaire. Propaganda. Quebec (Montreal). Syndicalism. Working Class. 1911-49. *1473*
—. Economic development. Quebec. Social Conditions. 1850-1950. *3743*
—. Economic Growth. Immigration. Irish Americans. Michigan (Detroit). Toleration. 1850. *2790*
—. Economic Theory. French Canadians. Minville, Esdras. Quebec. 20c. *2558*
—. Ecumenism. Episcopal Church, Protestant. Society of the Atonement. Wattson, Paul James. White, Lurana. Women. 1870-1928. *459*
—. Ecumenism. Merton, Thomas. 1949-68. *452*
—. Ecumenism. Protestantism. Weigel, Gustave. 1950-64. *497*
—. Education. Georgia (Skidaway Island). Negroes. Orphanages. Poor Clares. Women. 1885-87. *3806*
—. Education. Hackett, Francis. Ireland (Kilkenny, Clongowes Wood). Irish Americans. Literature. 1880's-1901. *3818*
—. Education. Historiography. 19c. *679*
—. Education. Indians. Missions and Missionaries. North Dakota. Pioneers. Presentation of the Blessed Virgin Mary, Sisters of the. South Dakota. Women. 1880-96. *727*
—. Education. Missions and Missionaries. Protestant Churches. Prucha, Francis Paul (review article). 1888-1912. *1538*
—. Education. Newspapers. Ontario. 1851-1948. *543*
—. Educational attainment. Immaculate Conception Primary School. Lithuanian Americans. Missouri (St. Louis). Occupations. 1948-68. *2607*
—. Eisenmann, Sylvester. Sioux Indians. South Dakota. Yankton Reservation (Marty Mission). 1918-49. *3900*
—. Elections. Leo XIII, Pope. Pius IX, Pope. Press. Protestantism. 1878. *2786*
—. Elections (presidential). Protestantism. Smith, Al. West Virginia. 1928. *1217*
—. Elites. Ethnicity. Immigrants. Politics. Protestants. Reform. 1890's-1970's. *1225*
—. England, John. Ireland. Voluntarism. 1808-50. *3708*
—. Episcopal Church, Protestant. Liturgy. 1973. *2727*
—. Ethnic groups. 17c-20c. *3689*
—. Ethnic Groups. Judaism. Pennsylvania (Philadelphia). Social classes. Voting and Voting Behavior. 1924-40. *1308*
—. Ethnicity. Political Parties. Protestantism. 1968-72. *1220*
—. Eudists. Industrialization. Quebec (Chicoutimi Basin). Working class. 1903-30. *1466*
—. Europe. Original sin. Theology. 1966-71. *3751*
—. Evangelism. Massachusetts (Boston). Protestantism. Settlement houses. South End House. Woods, Robert A. 1891-1910. *2438*
—. Family. Immigrants. Polish Americans. Social control. Values. 20c. *913*
—. Family. Judaism. Private Schools. 1960's-70's. *654*
—. Family size preference. Population. Women. Women. 1964-74. *915*
—. Farm programs. New Deal. Rural life movement. 1930's. *2573*
—. Feast days. Lawrence, Saint. New Mexico (Bernalillo). Social Customs. 1974. *3853*
—. Feast days. Mexican Americans. New Mexico. 20c. *3903*
—. Fédération Nationale Saint-Jean-Baptiste. Feminism. Gérin-Lajoie, Marie. Quebec. 1907-33. *870*
—. Feild, Edward. Irish Canadians. Mullock, John Thomas. Newfoundland. Politics. Protestant Churches. 19c. *1254*
—. Feminism. Quebec. Religious Orders. Women. 1640-1975. *833*
—. Fiction, juvenile. Finn, Francis J. Youth. 1889-1928. *2051*
—. Fiestas. New Mexico. Rites and Ceremonies. Saints, patron. Villages. 1970's. *3892*
—. First Catholic Slovak Union (Jednota). Pennsylvania. Sabol, John. Slovak Americans. 1920's-60's. *3821*
—. Flagellants. New Mexico. Penitentes. 13c-20c. *3779*
—. Folk art. Lopez, George. Lopez, José Dolores. New Mexico (Cordova). Santos, statues. 20c. *1844*
—. Folk art. New Mexico. Santos (statues). 1780-1900. *1903*
—. Folk religion. Indiana. 1970's. *3697*
—. Folklore. Hispanic Americans. New Mexico. Penitentes. Rites and Ceremonies. Social customs. 16c-20c. *3829*

—. Foreign policy. Historiography. 1898-1955. *1288*
—. Freedmen. Law. Protestantism. Texas. 1836-60. *2799*
—. French Canadians. Groulx, Lionel. Quebec. Secularism. Separatist Movements. 1897-1928. *1409*
—. French Canadians. Guigues, Joseph-Eugène. Ontario. Ottawa Diocese. 1848-74. *3713*
—. French Canadians. Immigration. Massachusetts (Holyoke). Proulx, Nicholas. Working Class. 1850-1900. *3691*
—. French Canadians. LaPatrie (colony). New England. Quebec. Repatriation Act (Canada, 1875). ca 1875-80. *3792*
—. French Canadians. Migration, Internal. Parishes. Quebec (Compton County). Rural-Urban Studies. 1851-91. *3791*
—. French Canadians. Minnesota (Gentilly). Settlement. Theillon, Elie. 1870's-1974. *3687*
—. French Canadians. Minville, Esdras (eulogy). Quebec. 1975. *3674*
—. French Canadians. North Central States. Settlement. Social Customs. 19c. *3804*
—. French Canadians. Quebec. Self-perception. Social Customs. Values. 17c-1978. *3789*
—. French Canadians. Quebec. Social Organization. Women. 1960's-70's. *2013*
—. French language. *Patriote de l'Ouest* (newspaper). Saskatchewan. 1910-41. *3764*
—. Frontier and Pioneer Life. Missions and Missionaries. Southwest. Spain. 16c-18c. *1497*
—. Frontier and Pioneer Life. New Mexico. Settlement. 17c-1810. *3852*
—. Gary Diocese. Grutka, Andrew G. Indiana. 1933-78. *3868*
—. George, Henry. Ryan, John A. Single tax doctrine. Taxation. 1935. *2557*
—. Georgia. Judaism. Psychohistory. State Politics. Watson, Thomas E. 1856-1922. *55*
—. Georgia (Augusta). Local history. Preservation. Sacred Heart Church. 1976-78. *1823*
—. German Americans. Immigrants. Kansas (Atchison). Newspapers. Pluralism. 1854-59. *3877*
—. German Americans. Language. Politics. Religious education. St. Peter's Colony. Saskatchewan. 1903-16. *779*
—. Germans, Russian. Religious Education. St. Angela's Convent. Saskatchewan (Prelate). Ursulines. Women. 1919-34. *680*
—. Gibbons, James. Knights of Labor. Social thought. Taschereau, Elzéar Alexandre. 1880's. *1476*
—. Government. Parish registers. Quebec. 1539-1973. *3694*
—. Great Britain. Isolationism. Nicoll, John R. A. Roosevelt, Franklin D. (administration). World War II. 1943. *1241*
—. Great Britain. Propaganda. World War I. 1918. *1240*
—. Groulx, Lionel. Quebec. 1895-1905. *3688*
—. Guam. Martinez, Pedro. 1909-67. *3795*
—. Hawaii. Independence Movements. Missions and Missionaries. Protestant Churches. Simpson, George. 1842-43. *1723*
—. History. Literature. Religious Orders. Women. 19c-1978. *868*
—. Holy Family Slovak Parish. New York City (Brooklyn). Slovak Americans. 1905-80. *3869*
—. Hospitals. Hôtel-Dieu. Indian-White Relations. Quebec. 1635-98. *1446*
—. Hudson's Bay Company. Indians. Methodist Church. Missions and Missionaries. Oregon. Presbyterian Church. 1830's - 1840's. *1482*
—. Human Relations. Judaism (Orthodox). Protestant Churches. Rhode Island. 18c. *2087*
—. Illinois (Chicago). Immigration. Mexican Americans. Social Conditions. 1910's-20's. *3833*
—. Immigration. Letters. Moczygemba, Leopold. Polish Americans. Texas (Panna Marya). 1855. *3679*
—. Immigration. Manitoba. Mathieu, Olivier-Elzéar. Regina Archdiocese. Saskatchewan. 1911-31. *3781*
—. Immigration. Persecution. Prince Edward Island. Scotland. 1769-74. *3702*
—. Independence Movements. Kubašek, John J. New York (Yonkers). Slovak Americans. 1902-50. *3870*
—. Indians. Juan Antonio (neophyte). Mission San Gabriel Arcangel. Painting (realist tradition). 1800. 1976. *1882*
—. Indians. Juan Antonio (neophyte). Mission San Gabriel Arcangel. Paintings. 1800-1976. *1883*
—. Indians. Louisiana. Missions and Missionaries. 18c-20c. *1625*
—. Indians. Missions and Missionaries. Pueblo Revolt (1680). Southwest. 1590-1680. *1499*
—. International Union of Catholic Women's Leagues (congress). Italy (Rome). Quebec. Suffrage. Women. 1922. *935*
—. Irish Americans. Kelly, Dennis. Pennsylvania (Havertown). St. Denis Parish. 1825-1975. *3683*
—. Israel. 1948-50. *3736*
—. Italian Americans. Social Organization. 1880-1940. *3834*
—. Jankola, Matthew. Pennsylvania (Philadelphia). Sisters of SS. Cyril and Methodius. Slovak Americans. 1903-70's. *3822*
—. Jesuits. *Revista Catolica* (periodical). Southwest. 1875-1962. *3884*
—. Journalism. Newspapers. 1822-1975. *3831*
—. Judaism. Lutheran Church. Ohio (Cincinnati). Public Schools. Religious Education. 19c. *545*
—. Kansas. Protestantism. Religion in the Public Schools. 1861-1900. *568*
—. Kenrick, Peter Richard. Missouri (Carondelet, St. Louis). St. Mary's of the Barrens. Seminaries. 1840-48. *752*
—. Labor Unions and Organizations. Polish Americans. Political Leadership. Progressivism. Socialism. Wisconsin (Milwaukee). 1900-30. *1299*
—. Language. Métis. Missions and Missionaries. Quebec (Oka). Religious Education. Rocheblave, Charlotte de. 19c. *1507*
—. Laval, François de. Quebec. 17c. *3766*
—. Lawyers. Pennsylvania. Progressivism. Smith, Walter George. 1900-22. *2365*
—. Liberalism. Neoorthodoxy. Pluralism. Secularism. Theology. 1936-74. *3899*
—. Literature. Pennsylvania (Philadelphia). Walter, William Joseph *(Thomas More).* 1839-46. *2063*
—. Louisiana. North Central States. Rosati, Joseph (review article). 1818-43. *3734*
—. Louisiana (Shreveport). St. Vincent Academy. -1973. *1799*
—. Maritime Provinces. Plessis, Joseph-Octave. Travel (accounts). 1812-15. *3703*
—. Mary, Virgin. Ohio (Bedford). Our Lady of Levoča (statue). Slovakia (Spiš; Levoča). ca 13c-1975. *1884*
—. Massachusetts (Boston). Religious Orders. Teaching. Voluntarism. Women. 1870-1940. *717*
—. Methodists. Missions and Missionaries. Philippines. 1899-1916. *1688*
—. Mexican Americans. Music. Protestant Churches. 1963-75. *1911*
—. Mexican Americans. Music. Protestantism. 1962-75. *1910*
—. Mexican Americans. Texas, southern. 1836-1911. *3769*
—. Minnesota (St. Paul). O'Brien, Alice. Philanthropy. Women. 1914-62. *2419*
—. Missions and Missionaries. Quebec (Eastern Townships). Social Conditions. 1825-53. *1568*
—. Morality. Oklahoma. Politics. Protestant Churches. Referendum. Sabbatarianism. Voting and Voting Behavior. 1959-76. *1290*
—. National Catholic Welfare Conference. National Council of Catholic Women. Peace Movements. Women. World War II. 1919-46. *2669*
—. National Prohibition League. Oklahoma. Prohibition. Religious Liberty. State Government. 1907-18. *2580*
—. Nationalism. Quebec. 1608-1978. *1012*
—. Needlework. Quebec (Quebec). Ursulines. ca 1655-1890's. *1850*
—. Neumann, Saint John Nepomucene. Pennsylvania (Philadelphia). 1830's-1963. *3774*
—. New England. Theology. Transcendentalists. 19c. *2777*
—. New France. 17c-18c. *3732*
—. New France. Nobility. Sulpicians. 17c-18c. *2611*
—. New Jersey (Jersey City). Progressivism. Protestantism. Social reform. Whittier House. 1890-1917. *2449*
—. New Mexico. Penitentes. Sangre de Cristo Mountains. 19c-1979. *3893*
—. New Mexico (Albuquerque). Penitentes. Roybal, Max. Santos, statues. Wood Carving. 20c. *1901*
—. New Mexico (Santa Fe). St. Vincent's Hospital. Sisters of Charity. 1865-1948. *1449*
—. Novels. Popular Culture. 1970's. *2054*
—. Ohio (Cincinnati). Xavier University. 1831-61. *708*
—. Olier, Jean Jacques. Quebec (Montreal). Sulpicians. 1630's-50's. *3798*
—. Ontario (Kingston). St. Mary's Cathedral of the Immaculate Conception. 1843-1973. *3738*
—. Ontario (Toronto). St. Basil's Seminary. Seminaries. Vatican Council II. 1962-67. *3775*
—. Ontario (Toronto). Saints Cyril and Methodius Parish. Slovak Canadians. 1934-77. *3905*
—. Papal Infallibility. 1870. *3848*
—. Pennsylvania (Danville). St. Cyril Academy. Sisters of SS. Cyril and Methodius. Slovak Americans. Social customs. 1909-73. *3885*
—. Pennsylvania (Philadelphia). Religious education. Sisters of Charity of the Blessed Virgin Mary. 1833-43. *609*
—. Pennsylvania (St. Marys). St. Joseph's Convent. Walburga, Saint. 1852-1974. *3778*
—. Pentecostal movement. 1967-75. *3799*
—. Pentecostal movement. Revivals. 1969. *3752*
—. Polish Americans. Wisconsin (Milwaukee). 1846-1940. *3690*
—. Professions. Quebec. Religious orders. Secondary education. Women. 1908-54. *871*
—. Prohibition. Social reform. Zurcher, George. 1884-1920's. *2579*
—. Protestant Churches. Social Classes. 1970's. *2623*
—. Quebec. Social Change. 17c. 20c. *3876*
—. Quebec (Hébertville, Lake St. John). Settlement. ca 1840-1900. *3847*
—. Religious Education. 1960's-70's. *642*
—. Religious Education. Saskatchewan. Youth. 1870-1978. *715*
—. Slavery. South. 1619-1860. *2170*
—. Slovak Catholic Federation of America. 1911-79. *3671*
Catholic Church (review article). Betten, Neil. Dolan, Jay P. Working Class. 1830-1978. *3698*
Catholic Near East Welfare Association. Charities. Wattson, Paul James. 1904-26. *2512*
Catholic University of America. American Studies. Archives. Documents. Kenrick, Francis P. Missions and Missionaries. 1776-1865. *216*
—. Bibliographies. Catholic Church. Hogan Schism. Parsons, Wilfrid. Pennsylvania (Philadelphia). Schisms. 1785-1825. 1975. *3845*
—. Colleges and Universities. Discrimination. District of Columbia. Negroes. Wesley, Charles H. 1914-48. *3729*
Catholic University of Ireland. Brownson, Orestes A. Great Britain. Ireland. Newman, John Henry. 1853-54. *3837*
Catholic University of Puerto Rico. Colleges and Universities. Puerto Rico. 1900's-74. *652*
Catholic Worker Movement. Equality. Human Rights. Public policy. 1933-78. *2436*
—. Maurin, Peter ("Easy Essays"). Political Theory. Social Reform. 1920's-33. *2571*
Catholic Worker (newspaper). Day, Dorothy. Maurin, Peter. Social justice. 20c. *1468*
Catholicism. Canon Law Society of America. Pontifical Commission for the Revision of the Code of Canon Law. 1917-73. *3686*
—. Clergy. Scanlan, Laurence. Utah. 1875-79. *3897*
—. Colonization. French Canadians. Quebec (Eastern Townships). Settlement. 1800-60. *3780*
—. French Canadians. Lévesque, Georges-Henri. Nationalism. Personal narratives. Quebec. Youth movements. 1930's. *3790*
—. Intellectuals. Sheed, Frank. 20c. *3706*
—. Pentecostal movement. Underground church. 1969-73. *3802*
Catholics. Abortion. Attitudes. Protestants. Whites. 1962-75. *888*
—. Abramson, Harold J. Ethnicity (review article). Hays, Samuel. Voting and Voting Behavior. 1973. *3740*
—. Acculturation. Immigration. Slovak Americans. 1860's-1970's. *3879*
—. Americanization. Church attendance. Ethnicity. New York City. -1974. *3810*

—. Anglophones. Church Discipline. Church History. Francophones. Morality. Prairie Provinces. 1900-30. *3715*
—. Anglophones. French Canadians. Langevin, Adélard. Manitoba. Winnipeg Archdiocese. 1905. *3711*
—. Church membership. Migration, Internal. Protestants. Rhode Island. 1926-71. *152*
—. Church Schools. Social Classes. 1961-73. *3735*
—. College teachers. 1973. *521*
—. College teachers. Discrimination. Higher education. 1960's-70's. *554*
—. Colleges and Universities. Protestants. 1960's-70's. *565*
—. Colleges and Universities. St. Thomas More College. Saskatchewan (Regina, Saskatoon). 1918-21. *620*
—. Conscientious Objectors. World War II. 1941-45. *2672*
—. Great Britain. Immigration. Macdonnell, Alexander. Ontario. Scottish Canadians. 1770's-1814. *3862*
Catts, Sidney J. Anti-Catholicism. Bryan, Nathan P. Democratic Party. Florida. Political Campaigns (gubernatorial). Primaries (senatorial). Trammell, Park M. 1915-16. *1258*
—. Anti-Catholicism. Elections (gubernatorial). Florida. Guardians of Liberty. Knott, William V. Sturkie Resolution. 1916. *1231*
Cave, Robert Catlett. Bible. Disciples of Christ. Missouri (St. Louis). Sermons. Theology. 1840's-90's. *3111*
—. Disciples of Christ. Liberalism. Missouri (St. Louis). Non-Sectarian Church of St. Louis. Theology. 1867-1923. *2913*
Cavert, Samuel McCrea. Christianity. Ecumenism. Germany, West. World Council of Churches. 1945-46. *486*
Cedar Creek Monthly Meeting. Emancipation. Farms. Friends, Society of. Moorman, Clark Terrell. Ohio. Virginia (Caroline County). 1766-1814. *2487*
Cemeteries *See also* Burials.
—. California (Los Angeles; Chavez Ravine). Hebrew Benevolent Society of Los Angeles. Home of Peace Jewish Cemetery. Judaism. Photographs. 1855-1910. *4161*
—. California (San Francisco). First Hebrew Benevolent Society. Funerals. Jews. Johnson, Henry D. 1849-50. *4147*
—. Catholic Church. German Alsatians. Gravemarkers. Iron work. Ontario (Bruce County; Waterloo). 1850-1910. *1880*
—. Christianity. Folklore. Social Customs. Texas. 1830-1950. *2751*
—. Congregation Beth El. Historic markers. Jews. Letters. Michigan (Detroit). 1850-1971. *4159*
—. Family. Rural Cemetery Movement. Social change. Tombstones. 1830's-40's. *87*
—. Judaism (Reform). Wilshire Boulevard Temple. *4234*
—. Kansas (Lyon County). Mennonites. 1870-1925. *3377*
—. Mennonites. Pennsylvania (Lampeter). 18c-20c. *3366*
Censorship *See also* Freedom of Speech; Freedom of the Press.
—. Attitudes. Films. Protestant Churches. Television. 1921-80. *2820*
—. *Christian Observer* (newspaper). Civil War. Converse, Amasa. Presbyterian Church. 1861-65. *1115*
—. Educators. Fundamentalists. Textbooks. Virginia. 1974. *570*
Census *See also* Statistics.
—. Canada. Catholic Church. Cities. French Canadians. French language. 1941. *3880*
Centenary College. Dance. Educational Policy. Louisiana. Methodist Church. 1941. *688*
—. Methodist Church. Mississippi (Brandon Springs). Mississippi Conference. Religious Education. 1838-44. *656*
Centennial Celebrations *See also* Bicentennial Celebrations.
—. Brigham Young University. Colleges and Universities. Mormons. Utah. 1876-1976. *783*
—. Evangelical Association. Methodist Episcopal Church. Methodist Protestant Church. 1872-76. *3451*
—. Georgia (Jonesboro). Presbyterian Church. 1879-1979. *3531*
Centennial Exposition of 1876. Adventists. Kellogg, John Harvey. Pennsylvania (Philadelphia). 1876. *2969*
—. Art. Attitudes. Friends, Society of. Peace. Pennsylvania (Philadelphia). Sabbatarianism. Temperance Movements. 1876. *3256*
—. Catholic Church. Pennsylvania (Philadelphia). Periodicals. 1876. *3864*
—. Methodist Episcopal Church. Pennsylvania (Philadelphia). Prayer. Simpson, Matthew. 1876. *3502*
Centennial United Methodist Church. Indiana (Gary). Methodist Church, United. Methodist Church, United. Negroes. Personal narratives. Robinson, Roosevelt. White flight. 1976. *3467*
Central Conference of American Rabbis. Drachman, Bernard. Judaism. Judaism (Orthodox). Orthodox Jewish Sabbath Alliance. Sabbath. Saturday. 1903-30. *2277*
Centralization. Baptists, Southern (state conventions). 19c-1970's. *2991*
—. Calvinism. Executive branch. Public Administration. Reform. Revivals. ca 1880-1930's. *959*
—. Catholic Church. Influence, distribution of. Organizational structure. 1970's. *3866*
Ceramics. Artifacts. Glass. Moravian Church. Worship. 18c-19c. *1879*
Chain letters. Law. Superstitions. 1930's-70's. *133*
Chain of being. Church of England. Cradock, Thomas. Maryland (Baltimore County). Poetry. Sermons. Social theory. 1700-80. *3227*
Chain of interest (concept). Loyalists. Pennsylvania (Philadelphia). Presbyterian Church. 1770's. *984*
Chaldean Church. Immigrants. Iraqi Americans. Michigan (Detroit). Middle East. Nationalism. Uniates. ca 1940's-74. *1306*
Challenger (vessel). Honeyman, David. Nova Scotia (Halifax). Oceanography. 1872-76. *2329*
Chambers, Samuel D. (testimonies). Converts. Mormons. Negroes. Slavery. Utah (Salt Lake City). 1844-76. *4059*
Champion, George. Boers. Missions and Missionaries. South Africa (Ginani). Zulus. 1836-41. *1719*
Chancels. Anglican Communion. Architecture. Ecclesiology Society. Great Britain (Cambridge). 1839-60. *1779*
Chaney, William Henry. Anti-Catholicism. Bapst, John. Editors and editing. Jesuits. Maine (Ellsworth). Nativism. 1853-54. *2121*
Channing, William Ellery. Clergy. Spirituality. Unitarianism. 1830-80. *4083*
—. Great Britain. Humanitarianism. Irresistible compassion. Theology. ca 1660-19c. *2851*
Channing, William Henry. Brisbane, Albert. Brook Farm. Fourierism. Transcendentalism. 1840-46. *399*
Chapel of Our Lady of Help of Christians. Alsace-Lorraine. Batt, Joseph. Catholic Church. Immigration. New York (Buffalo area; Cheektowaga). 1789-1872. *1760*
Chapel-of-St. John's-in-the-Wilderness. Catholic Church. Ecumenism. Episcopal Church, Protestant. New York (Graymoor). Society of the Atonement. Wattson, Paul James. White, Lurana Mary. 1909-18. *461*
Chapels. Architecture. Arizona, southern. Catholic Church. Folk religion. Papago Indians. 20c. *1783*
—. Catholic Church. New Mexico (Santa Fe). 1850's-70's. *1821*
—. Catholic Church. New Mexico (Santa Fe). Third Order of Saint Francis. ca 1805-32. *1776*
Chaplains. Adventists. Military. 1944-55. *2645*
—. Allen, Thomas. American Revolution. New England. 1774-77. *2680*
—. American Revolution. Baptists. Gano, John. Washington, George. 1727-1804. *2631*
—. American Revolution. Bishops. Church of England. Griffith, David. Virginia Regiment, 3rd. 1774-89. *3235*
—. American Revolution. Church of England. Washington, George. 1775-83. *2643*
—. Armies. Butler, Benjamin F. Civil War. Diaries. Fort Fisher (battle). Negroes. North Carolina. Turner, Henry M. 1864-65. *2685*
—. Armies. Civil War. 1861-65. *2689*
—. Baptists. Courts Martial and Courts of Inquiry. Fort Robinson. Nebraska. Negroes. Plummer, Henry V. 1884-94. *2695*
—. Barr, D. Eglinton. Civil War. Episcopal Church, Protestant. South. 1851-72. *2648*
—. Catholic Church. Diaries. Fort Keogh. Lindesmith, Eli. Montana. 1855-1922. *2679*
—. Garvey, Marcus. Negroes. Universal Negro Improvement Association. 1920's. *2366*
Chapman, John Jay. Christianity. Lynching. Pennsylvania (Coatesville). Poetry. Race Relations. Rhetoric. Speeches, Addresses, etc. 1912. *1971*
Charisma. Adventists. Prophecy. White, Ellen G. Women. 1848-1901. *2976*
—. Alline, Henry. Integration. Nova Scotia. Revivals. 1776-83. *2264*
—. Authority. Noyes, John Humphrey. Oneida Community. 1875-81. *418*
—. Guyana (Jonestown). Jones, Jim. Leadership. Models. People's Temple. Suicide, mass. 1978. *4253*
Charismatic movement. Baptists, Southern. 1955-77. *3029*
—. Catholic Church. 1970's. *3768*
—. Catholic Church. Italian Americans. Jesu, Father. Pennsylvania (Philadelphia). Working Class. 1920's-30's. *1576*
—. Durkheim, Emile. Silva Mind Control. Social organization. 1970's. *158*
—. Europe. Folk Religion (review article). Health. Occult sciences. Science. 16c-19c. 1975-76. *7*
—. Faith healing. Harrell, David Edwin, Jr. (review article). Revivals. 1947-75. *2782*
—. Jesus People. Pentecostalism. Revivals. Transcendental Meditation. 1960's-78. *127*
Charities *See also* Philanthropy; Public Welfare; Rescue Missions.
—. Advocate role. Children. Indians. Poor. St. Vincent de Paul Society. 1900-10. *2515*
—. Aged. Catholic Church. Education. Immigration. New Brunswick (Saint John). Orphans. Sisters of Charity of the Immaculate Conception. 1854-64. *2509*
—. American Revolution. Friends, Society of. Great Britain. Ireland. Pennsylvania (Philadelphia). 1778-97. *2503*
—. Baptist World Alliance. Ecumenism. 1945-73. *450*
—. California. Catholic Church. Ethnic groups. Ramm, Charles A. 1863-1951. *3888*
—. California. Disaster relief. Economic aid. Jews. Nieto, Jacob. Rabbis. San Francisco Earthquake and Fire. 1906. *2520*
—. Canada. Nurses and Nursing. Slovak Americans. Slovak Canadians. USA. Vincentian Sisters of Charity. Women. 1902-78. *2525*
—. Catholic Church. Education. Moore, Julia. Ontario (London). Personal narratives. Sisters of St. Joseph. Women. 1868-85. *2517*
—. Catholic Church. Irish Canadians. McMahon, Patrick. Poor. Quebec (Quebec). St. Bridget's Home. 1847-1972. *2521*
—. Catholic Near East Welfare Association. Wattson, Paul James. 1904-26. *2512*
—. Church of England. Evangelicals. Ontario (Toronto). Temperance Movements. Theology. 1870-1900. *3205*
—. Cities. Evangelism. Muhlenberg, Augustus. Politics. Protestantism (review article). Social Problems. 1812-1900. *2930*
—. Ecumenism. Hungarian Americans. Judaism (Reform). Rabbis. Wise, Stephen Samuel. World War II. Zionism. 1890's-1949. *4229*
—. Edgewood Children's Center. Missouri (Webster Groves). Orphans. Protestantism. St. Louis Protestant Orphan Asylum. 1834-1979. *2518*
—. Episcopal Church, Protestant. Iowa (Iowa City). New York City. Orphans' Home of Industry. Townsend, Charles Collins. 1854-68. *2507*
—. Equality. Missions and Missionaries. Presbyterian Church. Women. 1800-1975. *908*
—. Federation for the Support of Jewish Philanthropic Societies. Judaism. New York City. 1917-33. *2516*
—. Federation movement. Judaism. Ohio (Columbus). 1904-48. *2522*
—. Fosdick, Harry Emerson. Friendship. Liberalism. Protestantism. Rockefeller, John D., Jr. Social control. Wealth. 1920-36. *364*
—. Friends, Society of. Pennsylvania. Philadelphia Society for Organizing Charitable Relief and Repressing Mendicancy. 1800-1900. *2523*
—. Friends, Society of. Pennsylvania Hospital for the Sick Poor. Pennsylvania (Philadelphia). Poor. 18c. *2519*
—. Judaism (Orthodox, Reform). Nebraska (Omaha). Political Leadership. Refugees. Settlement. 1820-1937. *4102*

—. Judaism, Reform. Oregon (Portland). Organizations. Temple Beth Israel. 1885. *4235*
—. Law. Morristown Female Charitable Society. New Jersey. Presbyterian Church. Women. 1813-1978. *2510*
—. Mormons. 1837-1978. *2506*
—. Mormons. Poor. Utah. 1850-1930's. *2501*
Charles I. Congregationalism. Folklore. Regicide. Rhode Island. Stiles, Ezra. Whale, Theophilus. 17c. 1755-85. *3131*
—. Cotton, John. Great Britain. Massachusetts (Boston). Puritans. Regicide. Sermons. 1650. *1349*
—. Friends, Society of. Massachusetts. Persecution. 1661. *1018*
Charms. Aphrodisiacs. Folk Medicine. Philtres. Witchcraft. -1973. *2199*
Charters. Institutionalization. Mennonites (Franconia Conference). Protestant Churches. 1840-1940. *3382*
Chase, Josephine Streeper. Daily life. Diaries. Mormons. Utah (Centerville). Women. 1881-94. *3957*
Chase, Philander. Episcopal Church, Protestant. Illinois (Peoria). Jubilee College. 1840-62. *730*
Chase, Samuel. Boucher, Jonathan. Church and State. Maryland. Paca, William. Taxation. 1770-73. *1141*
Chatham Hall. Boarding Schools. Episcopal Church, Protestant. Ferguson, Anne Williams. Personal narratives. Virginia. Women. 1940's. *628*
Chaumonot, Joseph-Marie-Pierre. Brotherhood of the Holy Family. Catholic Church. Elites. Laval, François de. Quebec (Montreal). 1663-1760. *3717*
Chauncy, Charles. American Revolution. Church and State. Congregationalism. Great Britain. Letters. Price, Richard. Slavery. 1727-87. *3129*
—. American Revolution. Clergy. Congregationalism. New England. 1770's. *1269*
Chautauqua School of Theology. Methodist Church. New York. Seminaries, correspondence. Vincent, John Heyl. 1881-98. *763*
Chavez, Cesar. California. Christianity. Mexican Americans. Political activism. Rhetoric. Texas. Tijerina, Reies. 1960's-70's. *2391*
Cheever, Thomas. Clergy. Congregationalism. Documents. Massachusetts. 1677-1749. *3122*
Cheney Family Singers. Baptists, Free Will. Cheney, Moses. Music. Spiritualism. Vermont. 1839-91. *1932*
Cheney, Moses. Baptists, Free Will. Cheney Family Singers. Music. Spiritualism. Vermont. 1839-91. *1932*
Cherokee Georgia Baptist Convention. Baptists. Georgia. *Landmark Banner and Cherokee Baptist* (newspaper). 1859-64. *3013*
Cherokee Indians. Acculturation. Blackburn, Gideon. Missions and missionaries. Presbyterian Church. Schools. Tennessee. 1804-10. *1491*
—. Acculturation. Georgia. Missions and Missionaries. White Path's Rebellion. 1824-28. *1578*
—. Alabama (Creek Path). American Board of Commissioners for Foreign Missions. Missions and Missionaries. 1820-37. *1546*
—. American Board of Commissioners for Foreign Missions. Brainerd Mission. Education. Indian-White Relations. Letters. Southeastern States. 1817-38. *1605*
—. American Board of Commissioners for Foreign Missions. Georgia. Indian-White Relations. Law Enforcement. Missions and Missionaries. Removals, forced. Worcester, Samuel A. 1831. *1667*
—. Blackburn, Gideon. Indians. Missions and Missionaries. Old Southwest. Presbyterian Church. Schools. Whiskey. 1809-10. *700*
—. Butler, Elizur. Indian-White Relations. Marshall, John. Missions and Missionaries. Nullification crisis. Worcester, Samuel A. *Worcester* v. *Georgia* (US, 1832). 1828-33. *1583*
—. Civil disobedience. Evangelism. Missionaries. 1829-39. *1579*
—. Education. Friends, Society of. 1880-92. *712*
—. Foreman, Stephen. Georgia. Indians. Oklahoma. Presbyterian Church. 1820's-81. *3538*
—. Indians. Martin, John. Missions and Missionaries. Presbyterian Church. Richardson, William. Tennessee. Virginia. 1755-63. *1511*
Cheshire, Joseph Blount, Jr. Episcopal Church, Protestant. Negroes. North Carolina. Paternalism. Race Relations. 1870-1932. *2140*
Cheverus, Jean Louis Lefebvre de. Anti-Catholicism. Daley, Dominic. Halligan, James. Irish Americans. Massachusetts (Northampton). Protestantism. Trials. 1805-06. *2097*
—. Anti-Catholicism. Irish Americans. Lyon, Marcus. Massachusetts (Northampton). Murder. Protestantism. Trials. 1805-06. *2099*
Cheyenne Indians. Acculturation. Arapaho Indians. Indians. Mennonites. Missions and Missionaries. 1880-1900. *1557*
—. Apache Indians. Darlington Agency. Friends, Society of. Indian Territory. Indians (agencies). 1868-86. *3278*
—. Institutions. Mennonites. Missions and Missionaries. Photographs. Social customs. 1880-1940. *3398*
Chicago Diocese. Bishops. Catholic Church. Clergy. Duggan, James. Illinois. McMullen, John. Succession. 1865-81. *3742*
Chicago *Tribune* (newspaper). Anti-Catholicism. Editors and Editing. Illinois. Political Parties. 1853-61. *2112*
Chicago, University of (Divinity School). Academic Freedom. Baptists. Foster, George Burman. Illinois. Theology. 1895-1918. *557*
—. Christianity. Theology. Wieman, Henry Nelson. 1890's-1920's. *2717*
Chicanos. *See* Mexican Americans.
Chickasaw Indians. Bloomfield Academy. Downs, Ellen J. Girls. Indians. Methodist Church. Oklahoma (Penola County). Personal Narratives. Schools. 1853-66. *772*
Chicopee Manufacturing Company. Anti-Catholicism. Immigration. Irish Americans. Massachusetts (Chicopee). Mills. Nativism. Protestantism. 1830-75. *2103*
Chicoutimi, Petit-Séminaire de. Catholic Church. Quebec (Saguenay). Religious Education. Students. 1873-1930. *756*
Chicoutimi, Séminaire de. Bishops. Catholic Church. Quebec (Saguenay). 1873-1973. *721*
—. Catholic Church. Church and State. Personal narratives. Personal narratives. Simard, Ovide-D. 1873-1973. *757*
Chief Justices. *See* Supreme Court.
Child care. Day Nurseries. Dominicans. Quebec (Montreal). Women. 1858-1920. *2505*
Childbirth. Congregationalism. Death and Dying. Diaries. Diseases. Massachusetts (Westborough). Parkman, Ebenezer. Social Organization. 1724-82. *1447*
Childhood. Abolition Movement. Evangelicalism. Missions and Missionaries. 1800-60. *947*
—. Dreams. Italy (Rome). Painting. Symbolism in Art. Vedder, Elihu. 1856-1923. *1888*
—. Leadership. Secularism. Sex roles. Women. 1636-1930. *881*
Child-rearing. Baptists. Evangelicalism. Wayland, Francis. 1831. 1975. *948*
—. Converts. Protestant Churches. Psychology. Religious Education. Sunday schools. 19c. *603*
—. Death and Dying. Fischer, David H. Greven, Philip. Lynn, Kenneth S. Personality (review article). Politics. Protestantism. Stannard, David E. 18c. 1977. *2943*
—. Greven, Philip (review article). Protestantism. 17c-19c. 1977. *886*
—. Greven, Philip (review article). Protestantism. Self-perception. 1620-18c. *836*
—. Personality. Protestantism. 1640-1800. *814*
Children *See also* Birth Rate; Education; Youth.
—. Adolescents. Christianity. Rural-Urban Studies. Social classes. 1920's-70's. *2762*
—. Adoption policies. Public Welfare. 1954-71. *845*
—. Advocate role. Charities. Indians. Poor. St. Vincent de Paul Society. 1900-10. *2515*
—. Attitudes. Civil religion. Illinois. 1970's. *1187*
—. Catholic Church. Occupational status. Public schools. Socialization. -1974. *3784*
—. Death and Dying. New England. Puritans. 17c-1750. *929*
—. Evangelicalism. Northeastern or North Atlantic States. Protestant Churches. Sunday Schools. Theology. 1820's. *604*
—. Family. Friends, Society of. Pennsylvania (Delaware Valley). Theology. 1681-1735. *874*
—. Judaism (Orthodox). New York City (Brooklyn; Boro Park). Parents. Social Status. 1973. *4187*
—. Minnesota, southern. Parents. Religiosity. Socialization. 1975. *128*
Children of God. Christianity. Converts. Sex. 1970's. *2793*
—. Organizational structure. 1968-76. *2732*
Children's Aid Society. Family. Foster care. Home Missionary Society. Pennsylvania (Philadelphia). Protestantism. 1880-1905. *2504*
Children's literature. Books. Death and Dying. Periodicals. Protestantism. 1800-60. *2914*
Children's Order of the United Society of Believers. Education. Shakers. Utopias. Utopias. 1780-1900. *4064*
Chile. Journalism. Missions and Missionaries. Presbyterian Church. Religious liberty. Trumbull, David. 1845-89. *1703*
China. Alabama (Mobile). Missions and Missionaries. Presbyterian Church. Stuart, Mary Horton. Women. 1840's-1947. *1705*
—. Archives. Japan. Korea. Missions and Missionaries. Presbyterian Historical Society. 1852-1911. *189*
—. Arndt, E. L. Lutheran Church. Missions and Missionaries. 1913-29. *1749*
—. Attitudes. Missions and Missionaries. Presbyterian Church. 1837-1900. *1691*
—. Baptists. Missions and Missionaries. Shuck, Eliza G. Sexton. 1844-51. *1713*
—. Bashford, James W. Methodist Episcopal Church. Missions and Missionaries. Social gospel. 1889-1919. *1712*
—. Canada. Church of England. Missionary Society of the Canadian Church. Personal narratives. Scovil, G. C. Coster. 1946-47. *1744*
—. Canada. Hurford, Grace Gibberd. Missions and Missionaries. Personal narratives. Teaching. World War II. 1928-45. *1711*
—. Catholic Church. Communists. Missionaries. Protestant Churches. 1948-50. *1752*
—. Christianity. Fairbank, John King (review article). Missions and Missionaries. ca 1860-1949. 1974. *1718*
—. Diplomacy. Japan. Missions and Missionaries. Presbyterian Church. Stuart, John Leighton. 1937-41. *1745*
—. Diplomatic recognition. Missions and Missionaries. Revolution. Sun Yat-sen. 1911-13. *1724*
—. Episcopal Church, Protestant. Missions and Missionaries. Roots, Eliza McCook. Roots, Logan H. 1900-34. *1743*
China (Caoxian, Kai Chow). Mennonites. Missions and Missionaries. 1901-31. *1716*
China (Kanchow). Catholic Church. Foreign policy. Missions and Missionaries. State Department. 1929-32. *1710*
China (Shanghai). Colleges and Universities. Episcopal Church, Protestant. Missions and Missionaries. Pott, Francis L. H. St. John's University. 1888-1941. *1707*
—. Methodist Episcopal Church, South. Missions and Missionaries. Publishers and Publishing. 1898-1920. *1737*
Chinese Americans. American Protective Association. Anti-Catholicism. Guardians of Liberty. Ku Klux Klan. Nativism. Oregon. Racism. ca 1840-1945. *2100*
—. Christianity. Judaism. Nativism. Newspapers. Pacific Coast. Slavery. 1848-65. *75*
—. Discrimination. Frontier and Pioneer Life. Montana. Public opinion. Supreme courts (state). 1864-1902. *2152*
—. Hawaii. Missions and Missionaries. Protestant Churches. 1872-98. *1717*
—. Immigrants. Presbyterian Church. Race Relations. 1851-1977. *3561*
Chinese Mission School. California (San Diego). Congregationalism. Education. 1885-1960. *535*
Chiniquy, Charles P. T. Anti-Catholicism. Lincoln, Abraham. 1855-65. *2105*
Chipewyan Indians. Catholic Church. Indian-White Relations. Letters. Mission St. Jean-Baptiste. Saskatchewan (Île-à-la-Crosse). Taché, Alexandre Antonin. 1823-54. *1503*
Chippewa Indians. American Board of Commissioners for Foreign Missions. Ayer, Frederick. Minnesota. Missions and Missionaries. Oberlin College. Red Lake Mission. 1842-59. *1496*

—. American Board of Commissioners for Foreign Missions. Boutwell, William Thurston. Indian-White Relations. Minnesota. Missions and Missionaries. Protestant Churches. 1831-47. *1572*
—. Documents. Fullerton, Thomas. Indians. Methodist Episcopal Church. Minnesota. Missions and Missionaries. Wisconsin. 1841-44. *1531*
—. Germans, Russian. Immigration. Manitoba. Mennonites. Métis. 1872-73. *3392*
—. Indian-White Relations. Lutheran Church. Michigan. Miessler, Ernst G. H. Missions and Missionaries. 1851-71. *1582*
—. Indian-White Relations. Methodist Church. Michigan. Missions and Missionaries. 1830-80. *1597*
Chiropractic. Attitudes. Cultism. Medicine (practice of). Science. 1850's-1970's. *2314*
Choctaw Indians. Congregationalism. Harkins, Richard. Missions and Missionaries. Murder. Slavery. 1858-59. *3132*
Cholera. Canada. Epidemics. Mormons. USA. 1832-83. *1437*
Choynski, Isidor Nathan. California, southern. Cities. Jews. Journalism. Travel (accounts). 1881. *4144*
Christ Church. Carter, Robert. Church of England. Churches. Virginia (Lancaster County). 18c. *1849*
—. Churches. Episcopal Church, Protestant. Tennessee (Nashville). 1829-1979. *3174*
—. Civil War. Episcopal Church, Protestant. Kentucky (Bowling Green). Ringgold, Samuel. Tennessee (Knoxville). 1860-1911. *3168*
Christ Church Cathedral. Episcopal Church, Protestant. Massachusetts (Springfield). 1817-1929. *3236*
Christ Church Hospital. Episcopal Church, Protestant. Hospitals. Kearsley, John. Pennsylvania (Philadelphia). Women. 1778-1976. *1455*
Christ Communal Organization. Converts. Fundamentalism. Models. 1970's. *2917*
Christenson, Lars. Altarpieces. Folk art. Lutheran Church. Minnesota (Benson). Norwegian Americans. Wood Carving. 1887-1904. *1874*
Christian Advocate (newspaper). Capers, William. Ecumenism. Letters. Methodist Episcopal Church. Methodist Episcopal Church (South). Slavery. 1854. 1875. *479*
Christian Catholic Church. Dowie, John Alexander. Evangelism. Illinois (Zion). Utopias. 1888-1907. *409*
Christian Century (periodical). Foreign policy. Japan. Manchurian crisis. Morrison, Charles C. 1931-33. *2678*
Christian Commonwealth Colony. Communes. Georgia (Columbus). Social gospel. 1896-1900. *397*
Christian Connection (church). Huidekoper, Harm Jan. Meadville Theological School. Pennsylvania (Meadville). Unitarianism. 1844-56. *762*
Christian History (periodical). Evangelicalism. Great Britain. Methodist Church, Calvinistic. Periodicals. Whitefield, George. 1740's. *2233*
Christian humanism. American Revolution. Political attitudes. Puritans. Values. 18c. *1395*
Christian Observer (newspaper). Censorship. Civil War. Converse, Amasa. Presbyterian Church. 1861-65. *1115*
Christian Physiology. Alcott, William A. Health. ca 1829-60. *1462*
Christian Realism. Eschatology. Niebuhr, Reinhold. Radicalism. 20c. *2927*
—. Freedom. Niebuhr, Reinhold. 1915-63. 1960's-70's. *2360*
—. Liberalism. Niebuhr, Reinhold. Philosophy. 1920's. *1359*
—. Niebuhr, Reinhold. Politics. Theodicy. ca 1940-73. *1403*
Christian Renaissance. Catholic Church. Converts. Literature. Philosophy. Science. Stern, Karl. 1920's-60's. *2758*
Christian Schools, Brothers of. New Mexico (Santa Fe). St. Michael's High School. Secondary Education. 1859-1959. *742*
Christian Science. Documents. Extortion. Forgeries. Haushalter, Walter M. *(Mrs. Eddy Purloins from Hegel).* 1929-59. *3912*
—. Eddy, Mary Baker. Gottschalk, Stephen (review article). Women. 1885-1910. *3913*
—. Eddy, Mary Baker. Lee, Ann. Personality. Shakers. Theology. Women. 1736-1910. *2753*
—. Eddy, Mary Baker. Political power. Political Protest. Women. 1879-99. *840*
—. Eddy, Mary Baker. Women. 1840's-1926. *3914*
—. Leadership. Shakers. Spiritualism. Theosophy. Women. 19c. *795*
Christian Socialism. Baptists. Clergy. Rauschenbusch, Walter. Social consciousness. Theology. 1891-1918. *2400*
Christian Unity Foundation. Ecumenism. Episcopal Church, Protestant. Homans, Rockland Tyng. Huntington, William Reed. 1886-1942. *454*
Christianity *See also* Catholic Church; Councils and Synods; Deism; Missions and Missionaries; Protestantism; Theology.
—. Abolition Movement. Douglass, Frederick. 1830's-60's. *2496*
—. Abolition Movement. Enlightenment. Morality. Nationalism. Phillips, Wendell. 1830-84. *1399*
—. Abortion. Attitudes. 1972. *910*
—. Acculturation. Burials. Indians. Missions and Missionaries. Navajo Indians. 1949-75. *1656*
—. Acculturation. Ethnicity. Europe. Immigration. Judaism. Middle East. 19c-20c. *34*
—. Adolescents. Children. Rural-Urban Studies. Social classes. 1920's-70's. *2762*
—. Advertising. Barton, Bruce *(The Man Nobody Knows).* Business. 1920-29. *365*
—. Africa. Independence movements. Missions and Missionaries. World Conference of Christian Youth, 1st. 1939-74. *1751*
—. Alienation. Converts. Cults. Human potential movement. Social indicators. 1960's-70's. *143*
—. American dream. Civil religion. Evil. Myths and Symbols. Theology. 1973. *2724*
—. Americanization. Janes, Leroy Lansing. Japan (Kumamoto). Missions and Missionaries. Presbyterian Church. 1838-76. *1732*
—. Anti-Christian sentiments. Cochran, Jacob. Free love. Maine (York County). Society of Free Brethren and Sisters. 1817-19. *89*
—. Antimodernism. Ecumenism. Theology. 1975. *2734*
—. Anti-Semitism. 1964. *2133*
—. Antislavery sentiments. Civil War. Presbyterian Church. Stowe, Harriet Beecher. Women. ca 1850-80. *2474*
—. Arizona. Frontier and Pioneer Life. Reform. Suffrage. Temperance Movements. Women. 1850's-1912. *837*
—. Assimilation. Indians. Missions and Missionaries. Syncretism. 19c-20c. *2794*
—. Beiliss, Mendel. California (Oakland, San Francisco). Jews. Newspapers. Russia. Trials. 1911-13. *4105*
—. *Ben-Hur* (play, novel). Drama. Wallace, Lew. 1880-1900. *1872*
—. Bible. British Columbia. California. Indians. Missions and Missionaries. Myths and Symbols. Pacific Northwest. 1830-50. *1612*
—. Bibliographies. Canada. 1974-78. *2745*
—. Bibliographies. Communism. 1970's. *2759*
—. Bibliographies. Evolution. 1970's-75. *2330*
—. Black Muslims. Millenarianism. 1920-79. *4250*
—. Black theology. Feminism. Negroes. Reform. Theology. 1960's-70's. *2426*
—. Bliss, William D. P. Leftism. Social Gospel. 1876-1926. *2377*
—. Brethren in Christ. Education. Evangelism. Holiness movement. Individualism. 1870-1910. *3421*
—. British North America. Deviant Behavior. Government. Historiography. Occult Sciences. 1600-1760. *2180*
—. Bryan, William Jennings. Evolution. Presbyterian Church. 1921-25. *2297*
—. Buddhism (Zen). Merton, Thomas. Watts, Alan. 1930-73. *4288*
—. Bullard, Isaac. Vermont Pilgrims ("Mummyjums"). 1817-24. *408*
—. California. Chavez, Cesar. Mexican Americans. Political activism. Rhetoric. Texas. Tijerina, Reies. 1960's-70's. *2391*
—. California. Cults. Eastern religions. 1970's. *107*
—. Canada. Church and state. USA. 18c-20c. *1095*
—. Canada. Civil rights. Eskimos. Indians. Métis. Project North. 1975-79. *2545*
—. Canada. Missions and Missionaries. Sex roles. Women. 1815-99. *854*
—. Canada, eastern. Europe. Micmac Indians. Trade. 15c-18c. *1574*
—. Cavert, Samuel McCrea. Ecumenism. Germany, West. World Council of Churches. 1945-46. *486*
—. Cemeteries. Folklore. Social Customs. Texas. 1830-1950. *2751*
—. Chapman, John Jay. Lynching. Pennsylvania (Coatesville). Poetry. Race Relations. Rhetoric. Speeches, Addresses, etc. 1912. *1971*
—. Children of God. Converts. Sex. 1970's. *2793*
—. China. Fairbank, John King (review article). Missions and Missionaries. ca 1860-1949. 1974. *1718*
—. Chinese Americans. Judaism. Nativism. Newspapers. Pacific Coast. Slavery. 1848-65. *75*
—. Church and Social Problems. Civil religion. Ecumenism. Theology. 1967-70's. *1181*
—. Church and Social Problems. Labor Unions and Organizations. Socialism. 1880-1913. *1465*
—. Church and State. Orthodoxy. Religious liberty. 17c-20c. *1085*
—. Church history. 1975. *203*
—. Church history. Women. 1975. *889*
—. Civil religion. Democracy. France. Tocqueville, Alexis de. 1820-50. *1175*
—. Civil religion. Nationalism. Senate. Webster, Daniel. 1813-52. *1191*
—. Civil religion. Political Speeches. South. 1960's-70's. *1193*
—. Civil rights. Equality. Negroes. 19c-20c. *2536*
—. Civil Rights. Fernando (slave). Key, Elizabeth. Law. Negroes. Virginia. 1607-90. *2153*
—. Civil Rights. Jews. Riis, Jacob. Social Organization. 1870-1914. *2129*
—. Civil rights. Militance. Negroes. 1960's-70's. *2538*
—. Clergy. Episcopal Church, Protestant. 1974. *3248*
—. Clergy. Radicals and radicalism. Social status. 1960-74. *2764*
—. Cole, Thomas. Iconography. Painting. Romanticism. 1830's-40's. *1865*
—. Colleges and Universities. Curricula. Graham, William. Liberty Hall Academy. Proslavery Sentiments. Virginia. ca 1786-96. *2173*
—. Communes. Georgia. Jordan, Clarence. Koinonia Farm. 1942-60's. *402*
—. Conference on Faith and History. Historiography. 17c-1865. 1977. *237*
—. Conscientious Objectors. Vietnam War. 1960's-70's. *2653*
—. Conservatism. Meyer, Frank Straus. Theology. 1909-72. *1362*
—. Conservatism. Philosophy. South. Weaver, Richard M. ca 1930-63. *1363*
—. Constitutional Amendments. Presbyterian Church. Strong, William. Supreme Court. 1864-80. *3588*
—. Converts. Earthquakes. Mississippi River. Missouri. New Madrid Earthquake. 1811-12. *2789*
—. Converts. Idaho. Murder. Orchard, Harry. 1899-1906. *2760*
—. Cooperatives. Quebec. 1940-78. *2574*
—. Corporations. Education, Finance. Higher education. Social Darwinism. 1860-1930. *540*
—. Country Life. Ecumenism. Progressivism. Protestant Churches. Reform. Wisconsin. 1904-20. *2723*
—. Cults. Jesus People. Morality. 1960's-70's. *140*
—. Death and Dying. Stannard, David E. (review article). 17c-20c. *2746*
—. Deism. Jefferson, Thomas. Letters. Sectarianism. 1784-1800. *4280*
—. Deism. Jefferson, Thomas *(Life and Morals of Jesus of Nazareth).* Jesus Christ. Morality. Russia. Theology. Tolstoy, Leo *(Christ's Christianity).* 1800-85. *4278*
—. Discrimination. Folklore. Jews. Negroes. Stereotypes. 18c-1974. *2091*
—. Divorce. National Fertility Study. Women. 1970's. *934*
—. Eastern religions. Social Organizations. Youth Movements. 1968-74. *141*
—. Economic growth. Ethnic Groups. Michigan (Detroit). Pluralism. 1880-1940. *2748*
—. Economic Theory. Ethics. George, Henry. 1879. *2560*
—. Ecumenism. Self-determination. 1960's-70's. *473*

—. Ecumenism. Women. World Conference of Christian Youth, 1st. Young Women's Christian Association. 1939-79. *488*
—. Education. Games, board. Mansion of Happiness (game). Social Change. Values. 1832-1904. *2711*
—. Enlightenment. Founding fathers. 1776-1976. *1418*
—. Environmental crisis. White, Lynn, Jr. 1c-20c. *2309*
—. Episcopal Church, Protestant. Fiction. Grace Church. Melville, Herman ("The Two Temples"). New York City. Trinity Church. 1845-50. *2061*
—. Ethics. Providence. Theology. 19c. *2728*
—. Ethics. Rationalism. Science. White, Andrew Dickson. 1888-90's. *2288*
—. Ethnic Groups. Voluntary associations. Voting turnout. 1967-75. *1313*
—. Europe. Frontier and Pioneer Life. Theology. 18c-1979. *301*
—. Europeans. Indians. 16c-20c. *2752*
—. Family. Negroes. Social change. Values. War. 1960's-70's. *875*
—. Farmers. Social Customs. South. Travel accounts. 1850-70. *2795*
—. Feminism. Judaism. 1967-76. *876*
—. France. Great Britain. Judaism. Theater. ca 1957-78. *1853*
—. Frontier and Pioneer Life. Manuscripts. South Dakota Historical Resource Center. 1976. *217*
—. Frontier and Pioneer Life. North Dakota. Red River of the North. ca 1870-97. *2733*
—. Gerhardt, Paul. Hymns. Sacred fire. Symbolism in Literature. Translating and Interpreting. Wesley, John. 1760's-1930's. *1952*
—. God is Dead Theology. Islam. Methodology. Religions, history of. Secularism. Smith, Wilfred Cantwell. Theology. 1940-73. *134*
—. Grimké, Sarah. Nature. Paul, Saint. Social organization. Women. 1c. 1830's. *921*
—. Hawthorne, Nathaniel. Literature. Sacramental love tradition. 1838-60. *2080*
—. Historiography. 1974. *181*
—. History. Latourette, Kenneth Scott. 1884-1968. *261*
—. History. Religious liberty. Rhode Island. Williams, Roger. 17c. *1047*
—. Huidekoper, Frederick. Judaism. Meadville Theological School. Pennsylvania. Seminaries. Unitarianism. 1834-92. *4086*
—. Human nature. Kinsey, Alfred C. Sexual behavior. 1948-54. *2749*
—. Indians. Missions and Missionaries. New England. New France. 17c. *1621*
—. Indians. Missions and Missionaries. New England Company. Royal Society. 1660's-70's. *1554*
—. Indian-White Relations. Micmac Indians. Missions and Missionaries. New Brunswick. Nova Scotia. 1803-60. *1649*
—. Industrial Relations. Massachusetts (Lawrence). Scudder, Vida Dutton. Social reform. Socialism. Women. 1912. *2374*
—. Islam. Judaism. Medieval culture. Philosophy of history. Wolfson, Harry Austryn. 6c-16c. 1910-74. *278*
—. Israel. Jews. 1975. *157*
—. Judaism. Metalwork. Rites and Ceremonies. ca 1650-1888. *1854*
—. Judaism. Minority groups. Social Classes. 1974. *2610*
—. Judaism. Niebuhr, Reinhold. 1930-60. *137*
—. Judaism. Pfeffer, Leo. Politics. Secular Humanism. Social Change. 1958-76. *132*
—. Judaism. Women. 17c-1978. *860*
—. Key 73 (evangelistic coalition). 1973. *2837*
—. King, Martin Luther, Jr. Negroes. 1900-70. *2773*
—. Latin America. North America. Socialism. 20c. *953*
—. Letters. Teaching. Willard, Frances Langdon. 1835-51. *542*
—. Lewis, Sinclair. Novels. Science. Secular humanism. 1900-50. *2003*
—. Lifestyles. Technology. Values. 20c. *2725*
—. Lobbying. War. 1939-79. *1327*
—. Longshoremen. Oxford Movement. Strikes. Washington (Seattle). 1921-34. *1477*
—. Marti, Fritz. Philosophy. Scholarship. Swiss Americans. Theology. 1894-1979. *2803*
—. Methodism. Philosophy of history. Wesley, John. ca 1740's-80's. *3453*
—. Methodology. Racism. 1960's-70's. *2141*
—. Muste, A. J. Niebuhr, Reinhold. Pacifism. Political Theory. Thomas, Norman. 1914-38. *2687*
—. National Characteristics. Radical catholicity principle. 18c-20c. *41*
—. Negroes. -1973. *25*
—. Negroes. Race relations. 1939-79. *2544*
—. Negroes. Whites. 1975. *2802*
—. Niebuhr, Reinhold. Philosophy of history. 20c. *2859*
—. Novels. 1870-1900. *2074*
—. O'Hare, Kate Richards. Socialist Party. Women. 1901-17. *2559*
—. Pentecostal movement. 1972-73. *3524*
—. Percy, Walker *(Love in the Ruins)*. Technology. Western civilization. 1971. *2028*
—. *Post-American* (periodical). Values. 1974. *2792*
—. Presidents. 1788-1979. *2726*
—. Proslavery Sentiments. South. 1844-1977. *2167*
—. Sex roles. Social Change. Women. World Conference of Christian Youth, 1st. 1939-79. *844*
—. Sexuality. Theology. 1970's. *2740*
—. Slave Revolts. Styron, William *(Confessions of Nat Turner)*. Turner, Nat. 1820-31. 1968. *2047*
—. Spiritual growth. 1973. *102*
—. Theology. University of Chicago Divinity School. Wieman, Henry Nelson. 1890's-1920's. *2717*
—. Utopias. 1790-1970. *423*
Christianity (review article). Ahlstrom, Sydney E. Handy, Robert T. Historiography. Marty, Martin E. Race (issue). 16c-1978. *2743*
—. Negroes. Nelsen, Ann Kusener. Nelsen, Hart M. 1960's. 1975. *2736*
Christianity Today, periodical. Civil rights. Evangelicalism. Malone College. Race Relations. 1956-59. *2549*
Christianity (unaffiliated). Negroes. Social Indicators. 1977. *2629*
Christians. Anti-Semitism. Toynbee, Arnold. World War II. ca 1940-1975. *2130*
—. Citizenship. Religious beliefs. 100-1974. *1126*
—. Genocide. Jews. Theology. World War II. 1945-74. *101*
—. Massachusetts. Sermons. War. 1640-1740. *2630*
Christliche Apologete (periodical). German Americans. Methodists. Neutrality. World War I. 1914-18. *3458*
Christmas. California (Los Angeles). Catholic Church. Mexican Americans. Neighborhoods. Posadas (celebrations). Rites and Ceremonies. 1975-80. *3794*
—. California (San Diego). Drama. Parades. Social Customs. 1769-1980. *2714*
—. Customs. -1973. *2801*
—. Emmanuel Church. Immigration. Ohio (Bluffton). Reformed Tradition. Swiss Americans. 1840's-1900. *2857*
Christmas carols. Great Britain. Music. Puritans. Virginia. 1662-70. *2787*
"Christmas, Old". Appalachia, southern. Ballads. Calendar, Gregorian. Social customs. 1753-1977. *2955*
Christology. Abolition Movement. Clergy. Congregationalism. Negroes. New York. Ward, Samuel Ringgold. 1839-51. *2462*
Chumash Indians. California. Indians. Marriage. Mission Santa Barbara. Social Organization. Yanunali, Pedro (chief). 1787-1806. *940*
Church administration. Business. 20c. *343*
—. California. Catholic Church. González Rubio, José. Missions and Missionaries. 1846-50. *3811*
Church and Social Problems. Baptists. Clergy. Dawson, Joseph Martin. Scholarship. 1879-1973. *3015*
—. Black power. Economic Aid. Episcopal Church, Protestant. General Convention Special Program. Self-determination. 1963-75. *2541*
—. Blackthink. Human Relations. Poor. 1963-75. *2537*
—. Catholic Church. German Americans. Irish Americans. New Jersey (Newark). 1840-70. *3830*
—. Christianity. Civil religion. Ecumenism. Theology. 1967-70's. *1181*
—. Christianity. Labor Unions and Organizations. Socialism. 1880-1913. *1465*
—. Church membership. Half-Way Covenant. Massachusetts (Dorchester). Puritans. Religious scrupulosity. 1660-1730. *3601*
—. Clergy. Political Activism. Protestant Churches. 1960's-70's. *2431*
—. Congregationalism. Indian-White Relations. Local Politics. Massachusetts (Natick). Meetinghouses. 1650-18c. *3118*
—. Education. Poverty. Racism. 1970's. *2435*
—. Episcopal Church, Protestant. Missions and Missionaries. Social Reform. ca 1960-73. *2384*
—. Episcopal Church, Protestant. Missouri (St. Louis area). 1960's-70's. *3218*
—. Ethics. Evangelicals. Graham, Billy. Political attitudes. War. 1970's. *2932*
—. Negroes. Protestant Churches. 1970's. *2452*
—. Political activity. 1974. *1328*
Church and State *See also* Religion in the Public Schools; Religious Liberty.
—. 17c-1978. *1083*
—. American Board of Commissioners for Foreign Missions. Angola. Missions and Missionaries. Portugal. Protestant Churches. Umbundu (tribe). 1880-1922. *1746*
—. American Revolution. Arendt, Hannah. Ideology. ca 1775-83. *1032*
—. American Revolution. Calvinism. Clergy. Jefferson, Thomas. Linn, William. Presbyterian Church. 1775-1808. *1335*
—. American Revolution. Chauncy, Charles. Congregationalism. Great Britain. Letters. Price, Richard. Slavery. 1727-87. *3129*
—. American Revolution. Church of England. Clergy. 1775-85. *988*
—. American Revolution. Virginia. 1776-86. *1106*
—. American Revolution (antecedents). Connecticut. Devotion, Ebenezer. Politics. Theology. 1714-71. *1397*
—. Americanization. Catholic Church. Europe. Maryland. Religious liberty. ca 1634-1786. *304*
—. Anarchism and Anarchists. Lum, Dyer D. Mormons. 1880's. *4010*
—. Anglican Communion. Anticlericalism. Parsons' Cause. Virginia. 1730-60. *1058*
—. Annexation. Idaho, southern. Legislation. Mormons. Nevada. Stewart, William. Suffrage. 1887-88. *1089*
—. Anti-Catholicism. Clergy. Education, Finance. MacKinnon, Murdoch. Presbyterian Church. Saskatchewan. School Act (Saskatchewan, 1930; amended). Scott, Walter. 1913-26. *528*
—. Anti-Catholicism. Cox Library. Discrimination. *Koester* v. *Pardeeville* (1929). Libraries. Taxation. Wisconsin (Pardeeville). 1927-29. *1033*
—. Anti-Catholicism. Ethnic groups. Evangelism. Protestantism. Quebec (Lower Canada). Rebellion of 1837. 1766-1865. *2110*
—. Antievolution Law (1928). Arkansas. Courts. Epperson, Susan. Evolution. Initiatives. 1900's-68. *2322*
—. Antinomian Controversy. Hutchinson, Anne. Massachusetts. Puritans. Social Organization. Trials. Women. 1637. *1135*
—. Arizona. Franciscans. Indians. Mexico (Sonora). Missions and Missionaries. 1767-1842. *1065*
—. Arizona (Short Creek). Mormons. Polygamy. Utah. 1953. *1076*
—. Assimilation. New York. Politics. Reformed Dutch Church. 1664-91. *1121*
—. Attitudes. Civil Religion. Hoover, Herbert C. Protestantism. 1928-32. *1167*
—. Authority. Bishops. Civil War. Episcopal Church, Protestant. Grace Church. Illinois (Galesburg). 1864-66. *1218*
—. Authority. Canada. Church of England. Councils and Synods. Laity. 1782-1857. *3207*
—. Authority. France. Liberalism. Tocqueville, Alexis de. 1830's. *1144*
—. Baptist Joint Committee on Public Affairs. Pressure groups. 1973. *1298*
—. Baptists. Church of England. North Carolina. Presbyterians. Provincial Government. Tryon, William. 1765-76. *1036*
—. Baptists. Clergy. Dawson, Joseph Martin. 1879-1973. *1142*
—. Baptists. Congregationalism. Massachusetts (Swansea). Rhode Island (Barrington). 1711-46. *1082*
—. Baptists. Congregationalism. Meetinghouses. New Hampshire (Acworth). Taxation. Toleration Act (New Hampshire, 1819). Universalists. 1783-1822. *1113*
—. Baptists. Lobbying. 1950-73. *1297*
—. Baptists. McLoughlin, William G. (review article). New England. 1630-1833. *1077*
—. Baptists. Virginia. 1775-1810. *1043*

—. Baseball. Blue laws. Sabbath. West Virginia. Wheeling Nailers (team). 1889. *2279*
—. Bellah, Robert N. Civil religion. Judeo-Christian thought. National self-image. New Israel concept. 19c-20c. *1199*
—. Berns, Walter (review article). Constitutional Amendments (1st). Supreme Court. 18c-20c. *1114*
—. Berrigan, Daniel. Berrigan, Philip. Catholic Church. Leftism. Murray, John Courtney. 1950's-70's. *3758*
—. Black, Conrad. Catholic Church. Duplessis, Maurice (review article). Provincial Government. Quebec. Rumilly, Robert. 1930's-77. *1124*
—. Blue Laws. Church of England. Friends, Society of. Law and Society. Pennsylvania. Presbyterian Church. 1682-1740. *2278*
—. Blue laws. Legislators. Louisiana. Negroes. Reconstruction. Sabbath. 1867-75. *2285*
—. Boucher, Jonathan. Chase, Samuel. Maryland. Paca, William. Taxation. 1770-73. *1141*
—. *Brown* v. *Les Curé et Marguilliers de l'Oeuvre et de la Fabrique de la Paroisse de Montréal* (1874). Catholic Church. Guibord, Joseph. Liberalism. Politics. Quebec. Ultramontanism. 1870-74. *1067*
—. Bryan, William Jennings. Darwinism. Evolution. Fundamentalism. Public schools. 1920-73. *2317*
—. Buchanan, James. Federal Policy. Historiography. Military. Mormons. Utah. 1857-58. *1073*
—. Bureaucracies. Colonial Government. *Commissaire ordonnateur*. France. Louisiana. 1712-69. *1069*
—. Burger, Warren E. Church schools. Constitutional Amendments (1st). Supreme Court. 1950-75. *602*
—. Bushnell, Horace. Congregationalism. Jefferson, Thomas. ca 1800-60. *1002*
—. California. Church Finance. State Government. Worldwide Church of God. 1970's. *1139*
—. California. Colonial Government. Indians. Laws of the Indies. Missions and Missionaries. Spain. 18c. *1143*
—. California. Creationism. Curricula. Educational Policy. Evolution. Science. 1963-74. *2331*
—. California. Franciscans. Indians. Missions and Missionaries. 1775-1800. *1037*
—. California. Sabbatarianism. Supreme Courts, state. 1855-83. *2283*
—. Cambridge Platform. Massachusetts. Puritans. 1630-79. *1017*
—. Canada. Catholic Church. Encyclicals. Pius IX, Pope *(Syllabus of Errors)*. Press. Public opinion. 1864-65. *1019*
—. Canada. Christianity. USA. 18c-20c. *1095*
—. Canada. Cities. Sabbatarianism. Streetcars. Values. 1890-1914. *2281*
—. Canada. Jesuits' Estates Act. Political Protest. Protestants. 1880-90. *1088*
—. Canada. Leadership. Mennonite Conference of 1970. Social issues. Students. 1917-74. *1029*
—. Canada. Lord's Day Act (Canada, 1906). Sabbatarianism. Sports. 1906-77. *2284*
—. Capitalism. Social Organization. 1960's-70's. *1075*
—. Catholic Church. Chicoutimi, Séminaire de. Personal narratives. Personal narratives. Simard, Ovide-D. 1873-1973. *757*
—. Catholic Church. Democracy. Dominicans. Mazzuchelli, Samuel Charles *(Memoirs)*. Old Northwest. 1806-63. *1384*
—. Catholic Church. Europe, Western. North America. Politics. 1870-1974. *1326*
—. Catholic Church. French language. Langevin, Adélard. Manitoba. Politics. Private schools. 1890-1916. *608*
—. Catholic Church. Governors, provincial. Laval, François de. New France (Sovereign Council). Trade. 1659-84. *1020*
—. Catholic Church. Great Britain. Military government. Protestantism. Quebec. 18c. *1125*
—. Catholic Church. Inquisition. Louisiana. Surveillance. 1762-1800. *1044*
—. Catholic Church. Kennedy, John F. Political Campaigns (presidential). Presbyterian Church. 1959-60. *992*
—. Catholic Church. Law. Puerto Rico. ca 1863-1908. *1041*
—. Catholic Church. New France. Protestantism. ca 1625-1760's. *2818*
—. Catholic Church. Quebec. 18c-20c. *1070*
—. Christianity. Orthodoxy. Religious liberty. 17c-20c. *1085*
—. Church of England. Clergy. Parson's Cause. Tobacco. Virginia. Wages. 1750-70. *1052*
—. Church of England. Colleges and Universities (administration). Friends, Society of. New Jersey. Presbyterians. Princeton University. 1745-60. *661*
—. Church of England. Congregationalism. Connecticut. Factionalism. Great Awakening. Officeholding. 1730-76. *1310*
—. Church of England. Endowments. Land. Ontario (Upper Canada). Rolph, John. Strachan, John. University of Toronto. 1820-70. *1026*
—. Church of England. King's College (charter). Ontario (Toronto). Scotland. Strachan, John. 1815-43. *506*
—. Church of England. Livingston, William. Presbyterian Church. ca 1750-90. *1091*
—. Church property. Freedom of religion. Tax exemption. 1960's-70's. *1094*
—. Church schools. Conscientious objection. Holidays. Prayer. Public finance. Public Schools. Religious Liberty. Supreme Court. 1950-70's. *1112*
—. Church Schools. Constitutional Law. 1930's-70's. *729*
—. Church schools. Education, Finance. Jews. Public Policy. Religion in the Public Schools. 1961-71. *512*
—. Civil religion. 1776-1978. *1152*
—. Civil religion. 1789-1980. *991*
—. Civil religion. Constitutional conventions, state. Massachusetts. Rebellions. 1780. *1071*
—. Civil religion. Lincoln, Abraham. 1812-65. *1162*
—. Civil religion. Political theory. ca 1940's-74. *1188*
—. Civil Rights. Colleges and Universities. Federal Aid to Education. New York. Political attitudes. Students. 1972. *1119*
—. Civil rights. District of Columbia. Lobbying. 1964-72. *1322*
—. Clergy. Henry, Patrick. Maury, James. Parsons' Cause. Personal narratives. Speeches, Addresses, etc. Virginia. 1758-65. *1080*
—. Clergy. Income. New England. 1700-75. *1011*
—. College of William and Mary. Harvard University. Puritans. Yale University. 1636-1700. *650*
—. Colleges and Universities. Constitutions. Religious studies. Supreme Court. 1970's. *578*
—. Colleges and universities. Politics. 1740's-60's. *651*
—. Colleges and Universities (review article). Columbia University. Dartmouth College. Harvard University. Johnson, Samuel (1696-1772). Yale University. 1696-1970. 1972-74. *524*
—. Colonial Government. Defoe, Daniel. Religious liberty. South Carolina. 1704-06. *1014*
—. Colonial Government. Great Britain. Rhode Island. Williams, Roger. 1629-83. *1042*
—. Colonization. Spain. West Florida. 1780's. *1055*
—. Colorado (Denver). Political activity. Tax exemption. *United States* v. *Christian Echoes National Ministry, Inc.* 1950's-1970's. *1063*
—. Compulsory education. Constitutional Amendments (1st). Parents. *Pierce* v. *Society of Sisters* (US, 1925). 1925. 1976. *587*
—. Constitutional Law. Fund raising. Local Government. State Government. 1970's. *1059*
—. County Government. Judicial Administration. Mormons. Partisanship. Probate courts. Utah. 1855-72. *1039*
—. Cowley, Matthias F. Mormons. Polygamy. Smoot, Reed. Taylor, John W. Theology. Woodruff Manifesto. 1890-1911. *1060*
—. Democracy. Orthodox Eastern Church. Symphonia theory. 17c-20c. *1048*
—. Denominationalism. Ecumenism. Evangelical Alliance. Great Britain. 1846. *484*
—. Diaries. Lutheran Church. Norwegian Americans. Preus, Herman A. Wisconsin (Columbia, Dane counties). 1851-60. *1104*
—. Education. Episcopal Church, Protestant. Indians (agencies). Oklahoma, western. Stouch, George W. H. Whirlwind Day School. ca 1904-14. *1086*
—. Education. Great Britain. India. Secularization. 19c. *522*
—. Federal government. Politics. 1776-1976. *1057*
—. Federal Regulation. Law. Religion (definitions). 1950's-70's. *1131*
—. Feminism. House of Representatives. Polygamy. Roberts, Brigham Henry. Utah. 1898-1900. *1133*
—. Founding fathers. Theology. 1695-1830. *1096*
—. France. Gibbons, James. Letters. Nolan, Edward J. Sabatier, Paul. 1906. *1016*
—. Government, Resistance to. Jehovah's Witnesses. Persecution. Theology. 1870's-1960's. *1097*
—. Great Britain. 1780-1860. *1078*
—. Higher education. 1730's-1800. *525*
—. Libraries. New Mexico. 1598-1912. *1111*
—. Lobbying. Mormons. Statehood. Trumbo, Isaac. Utah. 1887-96. *1072*
—. Pluralism. Public policy. 1970's. *1064*
—. Political Parties. Prince Edward Island. Prince of Wales College Act (1860). School Boards. 1860-63. *744*
—. Presbyterian Church. Slavery. South. 1850-80. *1074*
—. Presbyterian Church. Virginia. 1770-85. *1015*
—. Property tax. Sects, Religious. 1847-1979. *1005*
—. Public schools. 1940-60. *582*
—. Rawlins, Joseph L. Statehood. Utah. 1850-1926. *1049*
—. Religiosity. 17c-20c. *26*
—. Religious liberty. -1973. *1138*
—. Supreme Court. 1960's. *1035*
—. Supreme Court decisions. 1963-75. *1034*
Church attendance. Adolescents. Negroes. Religiosity. South. Whites. 1964-74. *99*
—. Americanization. Catholics. Ethnicity. New York City. -1974. *3810*
—. Catholic Church. Protestant Churches. Religiosity. 1974. *2713*
—. Catholic Church. Residence. 1953-69. *3696*
—. Religiosity. Students. Williams College. 1948-74. *113*
—. Religious beliefs. 1957-68. *115*
—. Social compassion. Values. 1973. *2370*
—. Social Status. 1970. *2619*
Church congresses. Ecumenism. Episcopal Church, Protestant. 1874-1933. *469*
Church Councils. *See* Councils and Synods.
Church Discipline. Anglophones. Catholics. Church History. Francophones. Morality. Prairie Provinces. 1900-30. *3715*
—. Friends, Society of. Ireland. New England. New York. 1690-1789. *3283*
Church Finance *See also* Fund Raising.
—. Alaska. Documents. Education. Orthodox Eastern Church, Russian. Russian-American Company. Veniaminov, Metropolitan Innokentii. 1858. *2806*
—. Autonomy. Episcopal Church, Protestant. Isolationism. Missions and Missionaries. Theology. 1953-77. *1720*
—. Baptist Triennial Convention. Education. Missions and missionaries. Rice, Luther. Wayland, Francis. 1823-26. *3018*
—. Baptists, Southern. Cooperative Program. 1845-1975. *2982*
—. Baptists, Southern. Missions and Missionaries. 1792-1976. *1595*
—. Baptists, Southern (centralization). 1917-31. *2983*
—. Bishops. Catholic Church. Frenaye, Mark Anthony. Letters. O'Connor, Michael. Pennsylvania (Pittsburgh). 1843-49. *368*
—. California. Church and state. State Government. Worldwide Church of God. 1970's. *1139*
—. California (Los Angeles). Judaism (Reform). Rabbis. Wilshire Boulevard Temple. 1897. *4231*
—. Catholic Church. Economic Development. LaRocque, Paul. Quebec. Sherbrooke Diocese. 1893-1926. *3783*
—. Catholic Church. Education. Indian-White Relations. Oklahoma. Quapaw Indians. 1876-1927. *3727*
Church Government *See also* Church administration.
—. Auburn Affirmation (document). Presbyterian Church of the United States of America. Theology. 1920-25. *3577*
—. Baptists. ca 1775-1814. *3072*
—. Baptists. Bible. Theology. 1707-1814. *3071*
—. Baptists. Ecumenism. 1650-1975. *468*
—. Baptists. Virginia. Women. 1765-1800. *878*

—. Baptists, Southern. 1970's. *3073*
—. Bond, Thomas Emerson. Laity. Methodist Episcopal Church. Snethen, Nicholas. Stockton, William S. 1820-56. *288*
—. Church of England. House of Burgesses. Petitions. Public policy. Virginia. 1700-75. *999*
—. Crooks, George Richard. Laity. Methodist Episcopal Church. *Methodist* (periodical). 1851-72. *316*
Church History. 17c-20c. 1964-73. *22*
—. 1976. *252*
—. Amish. Documents. Pennsylvania (Morgantown). Plank, D. Heber. 1668-1790's. 20c. *3388*
—. Anglophones. Catholics. Church Discipline. Francophones. Morality. Prairie Provinces. 1900-30. *3715*
—. Archival catalogs and inventories. 1975. *253*
—. Archives. Bishops. Catholic Church. Kingston, Archdiocese of. Ontario. 1800-1966. *247*
—. Archives. Concordia Historical Institute. Lutheran Church (Missouri Synod). Missouri (St. Louis). 1978. *221*
—. Baptist studies. Oral history. 1940-75. *178*
—. Baptists. Georgia. 1870-1947. *271*
—. Bibliographies. Canada. 17c-1973. *14*
—. Bibliographies. Canada. 17c-20c. *16*
—. Bourget, Ignace. Catholic Church. Faillon, Etienne-Michel. Letters. Quebec (Montreal). 1850. *3824*
—. Canada. Ecumenism. United Church of Canada. 1920-76. *442*
—. Christianity. 1975. *203*
—. Christianity. Women. 1975. *889*
—. Clergy. Lutheran Church. 1978. *272*
—. Court records. Excommunication. Massachusetts (Salem). Puritans. 1629-80. *3600*
—. Historiography. Latourette, Kenneth Scott. Sweet, William Warren. ca 1910-65. *175*
—. Personal narratives. Presbyterian Church. Thompson, Ernest Trice. Union Theological Seminary. Virginia (Richmond). 1920-75. *689*
—. Romanticism. 1760-1840. *47*
Church location. Congregationalism. Economic conditions. Maryland (Baltimore). Protestantism. 1840-70. *2853*
Church membership. Age. Lutheran church. Religiosity. 1974. *3311*
—. Archives. Historical societies. Methodology. Voting and Voting Behavior. 1776-1860. 1977. *1235*
—. Baptists, Southern. Country life. Evangelicalism. South. Urbanization. 1920's. *3085*
—. Calvinism. Reformed Christian Church. 1964-79. *3160*
—. Catholic Church. Ohio (Cleveland). 1860. *65*
—. Catholics. Migration, Internal. Protestants. Rhode Island. 1926-71. *152*
—. Church and Social Problems. Half-Way Covenant. Massachusetts (Dorchester). Puritans. Religious scrupulosity. 1660-1730. *3601*
—. Cities. Education. Midwest. Occupational mobility. 1955-75. *2616*
—. Congregationalism. Conservatism. Massachusetts (Granville). 1754-76. *2247*
—. Elites. Research. 19c. 1975. *2615*
—. Ethnicity. Illinois (Chicago). Jews. Protestants. 1960's-70's. *121*
—. Half-Way Covenant. Massachusetts. Puritans. 1662. *3624*
—. New England. Puritans. 1620-1700. *3655*
Church Missionary Society. British Columbia (Metlakatla). Church of England. Hall, A. J. Indian-White Relations. Missions and Missionaries. Revivals. Tsimshian Indians. 1877. *1616*
—. Church of England. Eskimos. Hudson's Bay Company. Missionaries. Northwest Territories (Baffin Island). Peck, E. J. Trade. 1894-1913. *1660*
—. Church of England. Hudson's Bay Company. Missions and Missionaries. Ontario (Moosonee). Vincent, Thomas. 1835-1910. *1638*
Church names. Catholic Church. Quebec. Toponymy. 1600-1925. *3841*
Church of Christ. Disciples of Christ. Fundamentalism. Texas. 1972. *3105*
—. Evangelism. Keeble, Marshall. Race relations. 1878-1968. *2550*
Church of England *See also* Puritans.
—. Adams, John. American Revolution (antecedents). Letters. Weller, George. 1770's. 1824-25. *971*
—. Alberta (Edmonton). Indians. Métis. Newton, William. 1875-1900. *3196*
—. All Saints Church. Ontario (Kingston). Theology. Working class. 1867-1906. *3173*
—. Allen, Bennet. Colonial Government. Ecclesiastical pluralism. Jordan, John Morton. Maryland. Patronage. Sharpe, Horatio. 1759-70. *1051*
—. American Revolution. Americanization. 1775-85. *289*
—. American Revolution. Bailey, Jacob. Exiles. Letters. Nova Scotia. 1784. *3226*
—. American Revolution. Baptists. Congregationalism. Friends, Society of. Georgia. Judaism. Lutheran Church. Presbyterian Church. 1733-90. *88*
—. American Revolution. Bishops. Chaplains. Griffith, David. Virginia Regiment, 3rd. 1774-89. *3235*
—. American Revolution. Boucher, Jonathan. Civil War. Great Britain. Jefferson, Thomas. Loyalists. 1640-1797. *1412*
—. American Revolution. Boucher, Jonathan. Loyalists. 1763-83. *1383*
—. American Revolution. Canada. Cossitt, Ranna. Loyalists. Missions and Missionaries. New England. 1773-1815. *1317*
—. American Revolution. Chaplains. Washington, George. 1775-83. *2643*
—. American Revolution. Church and State. Clergy. 1775-85. *988*
—. American Revolution. Clergy. Maryland. Political philosophy. 1770-80. *1388*
—. American Revolution. Clergy. Maryland. Politics. Social Status. 1775. *2618*
—. American Revolution. Clergy. Patriotism. 1770-85. 1895-98. *982*
—. American Revolution. Conspiracies. Llewelyn, John. Loyalists. North Carolina. 1776-77. *1224*
—. American Revolution. Continental Congress. Loyalists. Seabury, Samuel (pseud. A. W. Farmer). 1774-84. *1378*
—. American Revolution. Delaware (Appoquiniminck). Loyalists. Reading, Philip. Society for the Propagation of the Gospel. 1775-78. *1221*
—. American Revolution. Freneau, Philip ("A Political Litany"). Intellectuals. Poetry. 1775. *1998*
—. American Revolution. Georgia (Augusta). Loyalists. St. Paul's Parish. Seymour, James. 1775-83. *1301*
—. American Revolution. Government, Resistance to. Griffith, David. Sermons. Virginia Convention. 1775. *1351*
—. American Revolution. Hughes, Philip. Loyalists. Maryland. 1767-77. *1323*
—. American Revolution. Loyalists. 1770-1800. *973*
—. American Revolution (antecedents). Benefices. New England. Religious Liberty. Society for the Propagation of the Gospel. 1689-1775. *1054*
—. American Revolution (antecedents). Colonial Government. Great Britain. Political theory. Shipley, Jonathan. 1773-75. *1376*
—. Americanization. Great Britain. North Carolina. Parishes. 1701-12. *298*
—. Anti-Catholicism. Gavin, Anthony (*A Master-Key to Popery*). Great Britain. Literature. Virginia. 1724-73. *2108*
—. Anticlericalism. Great Britain. Virginia. ca 1635-1783. *3238*
—. Architecture. Liturgy. Vestments. 18c. *3188*
—. Archives. Missions and Missionaries. Society for the Propagation of the Gospel. 1700-80. *215*
—. Arctic. Canada. Catholic Church. Churches. Fur Trade. Missions and Missionaries. 20c. *1549*
—. Arminiamism. Congregationalism. Converts. Johnson, Samuel (1696-1772). New England. Sacramentalism. 1715-22. *3183*
—. Associates of Dr. Bray. Georgia Trustees. Sermons. 1733-50. *3231*
—. Authority. Bishops. Canada. Councils and Synods. Laity. 1780-1979. *3224*
—. Authority. Canada. Church and state. Councils and Synods. Laity. 1782-1857. *3207*
—. Authority. Canada. Councils and Synods. Laity. 1782-1867. *3206*
—. Authors. Clergy. 1650-1775. *2000*
—. Bacon, Thomas. Clergy. Education. Maryland. Politics. Slavery. Theology. ca 1745-68. *3175*
—. Baptists. Church and State. North Carolina. Presbyterians. Provincial Government. Tryon, William. 1765-76. *1036*
—. Baptists. Elites. Social Change. Values. Virginia (Lunenburg County). 1746-74. *2819*
—. Baptists. Lifestyles. Toleration. Virginia. 1765-75. *3032*
—. Beach, John. Clergy. Congregationalism. Connecticut. Heresy. 1720-82. *3204*
—. Beecher, Catharine. Congregationalism. Johnson, Samuel (1696-1772). Reform (review article). Washington, Booker T. Women. 1696-1901. *2847*
—. Behavior. Boucher, Jonathan. Loyalists. Maryland. Virginia. 1738-89. *1348*
—. Behavior. Clergy. Maryland. 1700-75. *3228*
—. Berkeley, George. Education. Reform. Rhode Island (Newport). Sectarianism. 1704-34. *3230*
—. Bishop of London. Commissaries. Great Britain. South Carolina. 1715-32. *3242*
—. Bishops. 1750-75. *3210*
—. Bishops. British Columbia (Kootenay). Doull, Alexander John. 1870-1937. *3180*
—. Bishops. Canada. Documents. 1850-52. *3208*
—. Bishops. Catholic Church. Evangelicalism. Feild, Edward. Liturgy. Methodism. Newfoundland. Presbyterian Church. 1765-1852. *3197*
—. Bishops. Catholic Church. Liberal Party. Newfoundland. Provincial government. 1860-62. *1253*
—. Bishops. Councils and Synods. Fulford, Francis. Quebec (Montreal). 1850-68. *3209*
—. Bishops. Education. Feild, Edward. Great Britain. Newfoundland. 1826-44. *3198*
—. Bishops. Letters. Medley, John. New Brunswick (Fredericton). Oxford Movement. Pusey, Edward Bouverie. ca 1840-44. *3190*
—. Bishops. Liturgy. Ontario (Toronto). Strachan, John. Theology. 1802-67. *3214*
—. Blair, James. Church of Scotland. College of William and Mary. Converts. Virginia. 1679-1720. *2924*
—. Blair, James. Clergy. Vestries. Virginia. 1700-75. *3186*
—. Blair, James. College of William and Mary. Governors. Missions and Missionaries. Virginia. ca 1685-1743. *3223*
—. Blue Laws. Church and state. Friends, Society of. Law and Society. Pennsylvania. Presbyterian Church. 1682-1740. *2278*
—. Books (editions). Canada, western. Diaries. Missions and Missionaries. West, John. 1820-27. *1530*
—. Bordley, Stephen. Great Awakening. Letters. Maryland. Whitefield, George. 1730-40. *2229*
—. Boucher, Jonathan. Catholic Church. Maryland. Religious Liberty. 1774-97. *2729*
—. Boucher, Jonathan. Great Britain. Loyalists. Maryland. Zimmer, Anne Y. (review article). 1770's-90's. *1358*
—. British Columbia (Metlakatla). Church Missionary Society. Hall, A. J. Indian-White Relations. Missions and Missionaries. Revivals. Tsimshian Indians. 1877. *1616*
—. British Columbia (Queen Charlotte Islands). Haida Indians. Methodist Church. Missions and Missionaries. Settlement. Social Change. 1876-1920. *1545*
—. Cameron, John. Letters. Ontario (Ottawa). Politics. Thompson, Annie Affleck. Thompson, John S. D. 1867-94. *1127*
—. Canada. China. Missionary Society of the Canadian Church. Personal narratives. Scovil, G. C. Coster. 1946-47. *1744*
—. Canada. Clergy. McMurray, William. 1810-94. *3203*
—. Canada. Domestic and Foreign Missionary Society. Japan. Missions and Missionaries. 1883-1902. *1587*
—. Canada. Ecumenism. Symonds, Herbert. 1897-1921. *483*
—. Canada. Liturgy. Tractarians. 1840-68. *3189*
—. Canada, western. Hudson's Bay Company. Hunter, James. Missions and Missionaries. 1844-64. *1603*
—. Carter, Robert. Christ Church. Churches. Virginia (Lancaster County). 18c. *1849*

—. Catholic Church. Colonial Government. Macdonnell, Alexander. Ontario. Ontario (Kingston, Toronto). Strachan, John. 1820's-30's. *1108*
—. Catholic Church. Government. Indian-White Relations. Manitoulin project. Methodist Church. Missions and Missionaries. Ontario (Upper Canada). 1820-40. *1537*
—. Chain of being. Cradock, Thomas. Maryland (Baltimore County). Poetry. Sermons. Social theory. 1700-80. *3227*
—. Charities. Evangelicals. Ontario (Toronto). Temperance Movements. Theology. 1870-1900. *3205*
—. Church and state. Clergy. Parson's Cause. Tobacco. Virginia. Wages. 1750-70. *1052*
—. Church and State. Colleges and Universities (administration). Friends, Society of. New Jersey. Presbyterians. Princeton University. 1745-60. *661*
—. Church and State. Congregationalism. Connecticut. Factionalism. Great Awakening. Officeholding. 1730-76. *1310*
—. Church and state. Endowments. Land. Ontario (Upper Canada). Rolph, John. Strachan, John. University of Toronto. 1820-70. *1026*
—. Church and State. King's College (charter). Ontario (Toronto). Scotland. Strachan, John. 1815-43. *506*
—. Church and State. Livingston, William. Presbyterian Church. ca 1750-90. *1091*
—. Church Government. House of Burgesses. Petitions. Public policy. Virginia. 1700-75. *999*
—. Church Missionary Society. Eskimos. Hudson's Bay Company. Missionaries. Northwest Territories (Baffin Island). Peck, E. J. Trade. 1894-1913. *1660*
—. Church Missionary Society. Hudson's Bay Company. Missions and Missionaries. Ontario (Moosonee). Vincent, Thomas. 1835-1910. *1638*
—. Clergy. Congregationalism. New England. Vestries. 1630-1775. *312*
—. Clergy. Corbett, Griffiths Owen. Manitoba. Métis. Red River Rebellion. 1863-70. *3215*
—. Clergy. Cotton, William. Lawsuits. Tithes. Virginia (Accomack County). 1633-39. *1013*
—. Clergy. Cradock, Thomas. Maryland (Baltimore County). Poetry. Sermons. 1700-70. *3229*
—. Clergy. Delaware. Northeastern or North Atlantic States. Vestries. 1690-1775. *311*
—. Clergy. Diocesan Theological Institute. Frontier and Pioneer Life. Ontario (Cobourg). Strachan, John. 1840-55. *732*
—. Clergy. Education. Missions and Missionaries. Quebec (Three Rivers). Wood, Samuel. 1822-68. *3202*
—. Clergy. Episcopal Church, Protestant. Ingraham, Joseph Holt. Novels. Prisons. Public Schools. Reform. Tennessee (Nashville). 1847-51. *3241*
—. Clergy. Government. Loyalists. Political Attitudes. Theology. 1770-83. *1387*
—. Clergy. Loyalists. Theology. 1774-83. *1346*
—. Clergy. Muhlenberg, John Peter Gabriel. Virginia (Dunmore County). 1772-76. *3221*
—. Clergy (recruitment). Virginia. 1726-76. *3185*
—. Colonial Government. Ethnic Groups. Friends, society of. Pennsylvania. Reformed churches. 1755-80. *1215*
—. Columbia University. Johnson, Samuel (1696-1772). Livingston, William. Reformed Dutch Church. 1751-63. *635*
—. Congregationalism. Connecticut. Great Britain. Johnson, Samuel (1696-1772). Ordination. Yale University. 1722-23. *2843*
—. Congregationalism. Connecticut (New Haven). Conversion. Johnson, Samuel (1696-1772). Theology. Yale University. 1710-22. *3177*
—. Congregationalism. Cutler, Timothy. Edwards, Jonathan. Gibson, Edmund. Great Awakening. Letters. New England. Stoddard, Solomon. 1739. *2263*
—. Congregationalism. Cutler, Timothy. Massachusetts. 1720-30. *1056*
—. Congregationalism. Harvard University. Yale University. ca 1722-90. *660*
—. Congregationalism. Kennebec Purchase Company. Land. Massachusetts. 1759-75. *352*
—. Connecticut. Letters. Missions and Missionaries. Muirson, George. New York. ca 1697-1708. *1535*
—. Dalhousie University. King's College, University of. Mergers. Nova Scotia. Presbyterian Church. 1821-37. *684*
—. Duche, Jacob, Jr. Great Britain. Pennsylvania (Philadelphia). Pietism. Swedenborgianism. 1750-1800. *2738*
—. Education. Indians. Methodist Church. Missions and Missionaries. Ontario (Algoma, Huron). Wilson, Edward F. 1868-93. *1596*
—. Ethnic Groups. Friends, Society of. Pennsylvania. Presbyterian Church. Provincial Politics. 1775-80. *1248*
—. Great Awakening. New England. Whitefield, George. 1735-70. *2239*
—. Historiography. 1775-1800. *3211*
—. Hunt, Edward. Jacobitism. Keith, William. Patriotism. Pennsylvania. 1720. *1130*
—. Indians. McDonald, Robert. Missions and Missionaries. Northwest Territories. Yukon Territory. 1850's-1913. *1604*
—. Inglis, Charles. Loyalists. Propaganda. Sermons. 1770-80. *1370*
—. James, Henry *(The American)*. National Characteristics. Puritans. 1700-1880. *2036*
—. Laity. Neau, Elias. Negroes. New York City. Society for the Propagation of the Gospel. 1704-22. *3193*
—. Letters. Maryland. Presburg, Joseph. 1713-32. *3199*
—. Loyalists. Nova Scotia. Society for the Propagation of the Gospel. 1787-1864. *1644*
—. Malcolm, Alexander. Maryland (Annapolis). Music. St. Anne's Church. Society for the Propagation of the Gospel. Teaching. 1721-63. *1931*
—. Missions and Missionaries. Nova Scotia (Halifax). St. Paul's Church. Society for the Propagation of the Gospel. Tutty, William. 1749-52. *1646*
—. Morris, William. Ontario (Kingston). Presbyterians. Queen's College. 1836-42. *711*
—. North Carolina, east. Public Administration. St. John's Church. St. Paul's Church. 1729-75. *3240*
—. Patriotism. Poetry. Rising glory of America (theme). Smith, William. 1752. *1337*
Church of England National Task Force on the Economy (report). Canada. Income. Poverty. Social Classes. Theology. 1977. *2564*
Church of God. Assemblies of God. Civil rights movement. Periodicals. Presbyterian Church, Southern. South. 1950's-60's. *2528*
—. North Carolina. Personal narratives. Reed, Granny. 20c. *3520*
Church of God in Christ. Holiness movement. Music. Negroes. New York (Binghamton). 1971-74. *3289*
Church of St. John the Evangelist. Catholic Church. Construction. Rhode Island (Newport). 1883-1934. *1772*
Church of St. Paul the Apostle. Architecture. Catholic Church. Decorative Arts. LaFarge, John. New York City. 1876-99. *1833*
Church of Satan. LaVey, Anton Szandor. Occult Sciences. Satanism. 1966-75. *4240*
Church of Scotland. Blair, James. Church of England. College of William and Mary. Converts. Virginia. 1679-1720. *2924*
—. Communion. Maine (Boothbay). Presbyterian Church. 1750-75. *3578*
Church of the Holy Trinity. Architecture, Gothic Revival. Bolton, William J. Episcopal Church, Protestant. New York City (Brooklyn). Stained glass windows. 1845-47. *1847*
Church of the Nazarene. Camp meetings. Holiness movement. Louisiana (Mineral Springs). Methodist Church. National Camp Meeting Association for the Promotion of Holiness. 1860's-1926. *2891*
—. Holiness movement. 1908-75. *3288*
Church of the Sun. Middle Classes. Occult Sciences. 1960's. *4257*
Church organization. Baptists, Southern. 1704-1970. *3051*
—. Baptists, Southern. Social Policy. 19c-1970's. *3090*
Church property. Church and state. Freedom of religion. Tax exemption. 1960's-70's. *1094*
—. Constitutional Amendments (1st). Courts. Kentucky (Louisville). Presbyterian Church. Walnut Street Presbyterian Church. *Watson* v. *Jones* (US, 1860). 1860-1970. *1129*
Church records. Archives. Catholic Church. Genealogy. 19c-20c. *242*
—. Catholic Church. Immigrants. Italian Americans. Methodology. Pennsylvania (Philadelphia). 1789-1900. *3770*
—. Catholic Church. Louisiana, north. Preservation. 1716-1840's. 1930's-74. *185*
—. Clergy. Grimes, Addison McLaughlin. Methodist Episcopal Church. West Virginia (Webster County). 1880's-1963. *3455*
Church Schools *See also* Religious Education.
—. Acculturation. Mexican Americans. Public Schools. Texas (San Antonio). 1973. *677*
—. Alabama. Livingston Female Academy. Presbyterian Church. Women. 1835-1910. *686*
—. American Protective Association. Anti-Catholicism. Indiana. Indians. St. Joseph's Indian Normal School. 1888-96. *57*
—. Americanization. German language. Lutheran Church (Missouri Synod). Nebraska Council of Defense. Supreme Court. 1917-23. *305*
—. Amish, Old Order. Pennsylvania (Lancaster County). 1937-73. *626*
—. Baptist Board of Education and Publication. Smith, Luther Wesley. 1941-56. *630*
—. Baptists. Curricula. 1824-1974. *638*
—. Bible (King James version). Catholic Church. City Politics. Education, Finance. Michigan (Detroit). Protestantism. Religion in the Public Schools. 1842-53. *2716*
—. Boycotts. Mexican Americans. Mexican Presbyterian Mission School. Presbyterian Church. Public schools. Segregation. Texas (San Angelo). 1910-15. *618*
—. Burger, Warren E. Church and state. Constitutional Amendments (1st). Supreme Court. 1950-75. *602*
—. California. Higher education. 1850-74. *623*
—. California (San Diego; Point Loma). Theosophical Institute. Tingley, Katherine Augusta Westcott. 1897-1940. *4297*
—. Canada. East Indians. Missions and Missionaries. Presbyterian Church. Trinidad and Tobago. 1868-1912. *1726*
—. Catholic Church. 1750-1945. *681*
—. Catholic Church. Constitutional law. Elementary Education. Federal aid to education. 1960's-72. *691*
—. Catholic Church. Damen, Arnold. Fund raising. Illinois (Chicago). 1840-90. *773*
—. Catholic Church. Dubuque Diocese. Hennessy, John. Iowa. Irish Americans. 1866-1900. *3720*
—. Catholic Church. Ethnic Groups. Illinois (Chicago). Sanders, James W. (review article). 1833-1965. 1977. *614*
—. Catholic Church. Felicians. Polish Americans. Social Work. Women. 1855-1975. *3828*
—. Catholic Church. French language. Langevin, Adélard. Laurier, Wilfrid. Liberal Party. Prairie Provinces. Religion in the Public Schools. 1890-1915. *569*
—. Catholic Church. Girls. McDonough, Madrienne C. Mount St. Mary Convent. New Hampshire (Manchester). Personal narratives. 1902-09. *692*
—. Catholic Church. Glennon, John J. Missouri (St. Louis). Ritter, Joseph E. School Integration. 1935-47. *2542*
—. Catholic Church. Manitoba. McCarthy, D'Alton. Provincial legislation. 1870-90. *72*
—. Catholic Church. Philosophy. Theology. 1920-60. *3747*
—. Catholic Church. Polish Americans. 1874-1960's. *675*
—. Catholic Church. Segregation. 1972. *704*
—. Catholic Church. Seton, Elizabeth Ann. White House (school). 1774-1821. *625*
—. Catholics. Social Classes. 1961-73. *3735*
—. Church and State. Conscientious objection. Holidays. Prayer. Public finance. Public Schools. Religious Liberty. Supreme Court. 1950-70's. *1112*
—. Church and state. Constitutional Law. 1930's-70's. *729*
—. Church and State. Education, Finance. Jews. Public Policy. Religion in the Public Schools. 1961-71. *512*
—. City Politics. Massachusetts (Boston). 1880's. *632*
—. Colleges and Universities. Mormons. Utah (Salt Lake City). Young University. 1876-94. *734*
—. Colleges and Universities. State Aid to Education. Supreme Court. 1971-76. *682*
—. Constitutional Amendments (1st). Education, Finance. Government. Religion in the public schools. 1950's-70's. *564*
—. Constitutional Amendments (1st). State Aid to Education. Supreme Court. 1970's. *728*

—. Education. Hasidism (Lubavitch). Judaism. Quebec (Montreal). 1969-71. *550*
—. Education, Finance. Government. Prayer. Public opinion. Religion in the Public Schools. 1962-68. *504*
—. Education, Finance. Public finance. Supreme Court. 1971-73. *663*
—. Francophones. Greenway, Thomas (administration). Language. Legislation. Manitoba Act (Canada, 1870). 1890-99. *519*
—. Higher education. 1636-1978. *653*
—. Kentucky (Bourbon County). ca 1780-1850. *627*
Church suppers. Ladies Aid Society. Lutheran Church (Norwegian). North Dakota (Hannaford). Norwegian Americans. 1941. *3310*
Churches *See also* Cathedrals.
—. Adventists. Architecture. Michigan. 1863-1976. *1794*
—. Architects. Folsom, William Harrison. Mormons. Utah (Provo, Salt Lake City). ca 1850's-1901. *1757*
—. Architecture. Benedictines. Liturgy. 1945-62. *1804*
—. Architecture. Benedictines. Monasteries. Vatican Council II. 1962-75. *1805*
—. Architecture. Catholic Church. St. Andrew's Church. Virginia (Roanoke). 1882-1975. *1834*
—. Architecture. Country life. Fischer, Emil C. Kansas. 19c. *1778*
—. Architecture. Decorative Arts. Values. 1970's. *1837*
—. Architecture. Episcopal Church, Protestant. New England. Vaughan, Henry. 1845-1917. *1800*
—. Architecture. Episcopal Church, Protestant. St. James Episcopal Church. Virginia (Accomac). 1838. *1825*
—. Architecture. Episcopal Church, Protestant. Virginia. 1800-1920. *1798*
—. Architecture. Mormons. Utah. 1847-1929. *1817*
—. Architecture. Tennessee (Memphis). 19c. *1813*
—. Architecture (Gothic Revival). Congregationalism. Iowa (Iowa City). Randall, Gurdon Paine. 1868-69. *1822*
—. Architecture, Gothic Revival. Episcopal Church, Protestant. Holy Trinity Episcopal Church. Restorations. Tennessee (Nashville). 1840's-1970's. *1801*
—. Architecture (Gothic Revival). Episcopal Church, Protestant. Iowa (Iowa City). Trinity Episcopal Church. Upjohn, Richard. 1871-72. *1787*
—. Arctic. Canada. Catholic Church. Church of England. Fur Trade. Missions and Missionaries. 20c. *1549*
—. Arizona (Tucson). Mexico (Caborca, Sonora). Mission Nuestra Señora de la Purísima Concepción del Caborca. Mission San Xavier del Bac. ca 1750-1809. *1782*
—. Baptists, Seventh-Day. Rhode Island (Newport). 1664-1929. *1775*
—. Bradley, Lucas. Missouri (St. Louis). Presbyterian Church. Wisconsin (Racine). 1840-90. *1810*
—. California (Ventura). Catholic Church. Mission San Buenaventura. ca 1794-1976. *1831*
—. Carter, Robert. Christ Church. Church of England. Virginia (Lancaster County). 18c. *1849*
—. Catholic Church. Louisiana. 1685-1830. *1835*
—. Christ Church. Episcopal Church, Protestant. Tennessee (Nashville). 1829-1979. *3174*
—. Dutch Americans. New York City. Reformed Dutch Church. 1686-88. *3166*
—. Episcopal Church, Protestant. New York City. Roofs. Trinity Church. Upjohn, Richard. 1839-42. *1774*
—. Friends, Society of. Meetinghouses. Pennsylvania (Chester, Delaware counties). ca 1700-1903. *1814*
—. Georgia. Photographs. 1751-1900's. *1830*
—. Harrison, Peter. Rhode Island (Newport). Touro Synagogue. Wren, Christoper. 1670-1775. *1819*
—. Idealism. LaFarge, John. New York City. Painting. 1877-88. *1898*
—. Nova Scotia (Halifax). 1784-1825. *1763*
—. Ohio (Canton). Tilden, Guy. 1880's-1920's. *1790*
Churches (Gothic Revival). Architecture. Country Life. Furniture and Furnishings. Pennsylvania, northwest. Presbyterian Church. 1850-1905. 1979. *1797*
—. Cambridge Camden Society. Episcopal Church, Protestant. Great Britain. 1840-1975. *1773*
—. Decorative Arts. LaFarge, John. Massachusetts (Boston). Richardson, Henry Hobson. Trinity Church. 1876. *1832*
—. Delaware (Wilmington). Episcopal Church, Protestant. Grace Methodist Church. Methodist Church. St. John's Episcopal Church. 1850-90. *1786*
Churches (Gothic Revival, Victorian Gothic). Architecture. Episcopal Church, Protestant. North Dakota. Upjohn, Richard. 1874-1903. *1815*
Churches (Greek Revival). Architecture. Benjamin, Asher. Massachusetts (Boston). 1833-40. *1826*
Church-sect model. Jehovah's Witnesses. Latin America. 1950-76. *3920*
Circuit riders. Baptists. Diaries. Immigrants. Minnesota. Nilsson, Frederik Olaus. Swedish Americans. 1855-65. *3046*
—. California. Civil War. Frontier and Pioneer Life. Manuscripts. Methodism. Ohio. Phillips, George. 1840-64. *3494*
—. Clark, John. Evangelism. Methodism. Missouri. Travis, John. 1796-1851. *1561*
—. Frontier and Pioneer Life. German Americans. Lutheran Church (Missouri Synod). Oklahoma. Texas. Wacker, Hermann Dietrich. 1847-1938. *3342*
Circular letters. Baptists, Southern. Clergy. 1800-50. *3074*
Circumcision. Canon law. Europe. Illowy, Bernard. Judaism (Orthodox). Louisiana (New Orleans). Rabbis. 1853-65. *4176*
Cistercians. Catholic Church. Mistassini, monastery of. Quebec. Trappists. 1900-03. *3721*
Cities *See also* headings beginning with the word city and the word urban; names of cities and towns by state; Metropolitan Areas; Rural-Urban Studies; Skid Rows.
—. Baptists, Southern. Men. Religiosity. Women. 1968. *3008*
—. California, southern. Choynski, Isidor Nathan. Jews. Journalism. Travel (accounts). 1881. *4144*
—. Canada. Catholic Church. Census. French Canadians. French language. 1941. *3880*
—. Canada. Church and state. Sabbatarianism. Streetcars. Values. 1890-1914. *2281*
—. Catholic Church. Civil rights movement. Negroes. Protestant churches. Social Classes. 1960's-70's. *2539*
—. Catholic Church. Merton, Thomas. Nonviolence. Reform. Social criticism. 1960's. *2417*
—. Catholic Church. Negroes. North or Northern States. Occupations. Social Status. 1968. *2613*
—. Charities. Evangelism. Muhlenberg, Augustus. Politics. Protestantism (review article). Social Problems. 1812-1900. *2930*
—. Church membership. Education. Midwest. Occupational mobility. 1955-75. *2616*
—. Congregationalism. Gladden, Washington. Ohio (Columbus). Reform. Social gospel. 1850's-1914. *2425*
—. Gartner, Lloyd P. Gurock, Jeffrey S. Hertzberg, Steven. Jews (review article). Raphael, Mark Lee. 1840-1979. *4150*
—. Historiography. Mormons. Social change. Utah. 1849-1970's. *4008*
—. Politics. Revivals. Social conditions. 1857-77. *2261*
—. Reform movements (review article). Social control. 1812-1900. 1970's. *2411*
Cities (review article). New England. New York. Pennsylvania (Philadelphia; Germantown). Protestantism. 1660's-18c. *2828*
Citizenship *See also* Patriotism; Suffrage.
—. Christians. Religious beliefs. 100-1974. *1126*
—. Democracy. Jefferson, Thomas. Locke, John. Puritanism. 17c-18c. *1408*
City charters. Illinois (Nauvoo). Mormons. 1839-41. *3995*
City Government *See also* Cities; City Politics; Public Administration.
—. Baptists. Maryland (Baltimore). Negroes. Political protest. Public schools. 1865-1900. *583*
—. Bengough, John Wilson. *Grip* (periodical). Ontario (Toronto). Political Reform. Protestantism. 1873-1910. *1266*
—. Congregationalism. Massachusetts (Tiverton). Provincial Legislatures. Religious liberty. Taxation. 1692-1724. *1084*
City Life. Boyer, Paul. Johnson, Paul E. Middle Classes. Missions and Missionaries. Morality. New York (Rochester). Revivals. 1815-1920. 1978. *2800*
—. Catholic Church. Illinois (Chicago). Neighborhoods. 1900-30. *3771*
—. Cromwell, James W. Friends, Society of. New York City. Personal narratives. 1842-60. *3271*
—. Ethnic enclaves. Judaism. Manitoba (Winnipeg). 1940's-70's. *4091*
—. Family. Psychocultural therapy. Witchcraft. 1968. *2197*
—. Folklore. Indiana (East Chicago, Gary, Hammond). Negroes. Voodoo. 1976. *2182*
City of God (concept of). National Characteristics. 16c-20c. *1149*
City Planning. Architecture. Mormons. Smith, Joseph. Western states. 1833-90. *1767*
—. Architecture. Mormons. Utah. 1847-1975. *1781*
—. Architecture (Scandinavian). Country Life. Mormons. Utah (Spring City). 1851-1975. *1816*
—. Communes. Harmony Society. Indiana (New Harmony). Pennsylvania (Harmony, Economy). Social customs. 1820's-1905. *391*
—. Connecticut (New Haven). Puritans. 1628-39. *3598*
—. Illinois (Nauvoo). Mormons. 1840's. *3959*
—. Mormons. Settlement. Smith, Joseph. Western states. 19c. *3988*
City Politics *See also* City Government.
—. Alabama (Birmingham). Anti-Catholicism. Anti-Semitism. Reform. Social Gospel. 1900-30. *11*
—. Anti-Catholicism. California (San Francisco). Know-Nothing Party. People's Party. Vigilance Committee. 1854-56. *1307*
—. Anti-Catholicism. Ethnic groups. Immigrants. Ohio (Cincinnati). Temperance Movements. 1845-60. *2584*
—. Bible (King James version). Catholic Church. Church Schools. Education, Finance. Michigan (Detroit). Protestantism. Religion in the Public Schools. 1842-53. *2716*
—. Bossism. Clergy. Crump, Edward Hull. Negroes. Tennessee (Memphis). 1927-48. *1318*
—. California (San Francisco). Catholic Church. Clergy. Irish Americans. Progressivism. Yorke, Peter C. 1900's. *3889*
—. Catholic church. Construction. Contractors. Irish Americans. Pennsylvania (Philadelphia). 1846-1960's. *338*
—. Church Schools. Massachusetts (Boston). 1880's. *632*
—. Lee, J. Bracken. Morality. Mormons. Skousen, W. Cleon. Utah (Salt Lake City). 1956-60. *4006*
Civil disobedience. Cherokee Indians. Evangelism. Missionaries. 1829-39. *1579*
—. Clawson, Rudger. Federal government. Mormons. Polygamy. Sharp, John. Utah. 1862-91. *996*
Civil Liberty. *See* Civil Rights.
Civil Religion. Albanese, Catherine L. Beecher, Henry Ward. Clark, Clifford E., Jr. Douglas, Ann. Handy, Robert T. McLoughlin, William G. Reform. Revivals (review article). Women. 1607-1978. *6*
—. American dream. Christianity. Evil. Myths and Symbols. Theology. 1973. *2724*
—. American Revolution. Theology. 1760-75. *1148*
—. American Revolution (antecedents). Edwards, Jonathan. Great Awakening. King George's War. Millenarianism. 1740-76. *1169*
—. Antislavery sentiments. Campbell, Alexander. Disciples of Christ. Indians. Politics. War. Women. 1823-55. *3108*
—. Attitudes. Carter, Jimmy. Evangelicalism. Political Campaigns (presidential). Political Speeches. Rhetoric. 1976. *1229*
—. Attitudes. Children. Illinois. 1970's. *1187*
—. Attitudes. Church and state. Hoover, Herbert C. Protestantism. 1928-32. *1167*
—. Authoritarianism. Moon, Sun Myung. Unification Church. 1970-76. *4264*
—. Authority. Bellah, Robert N. Myths and Symbols. Politics. Secularization. 1977. *1165*
—. Authors. National Characteristics. 1830's-1960's. *1178*

—. Bellah, Robert N. Church and state. Judeo-Christian thought. National self-image. New Israel concept. 19c-20c. *1199*
—. Bellah, Robert N. Methodology. 1967-78. *1198*
—. Bellah, Robert N. National self-image. Political attitudes. Values. 1775-20c. *1200*
—. Bellah, Robert N. (review article). Sociology of Religion. 1959-75. *112*
—. Bibliographies. Sociology of religion. 17c-20c. 1960's-70's. *1168*
—. Campbell, Alexander. Disciples of Christ. Millenarianism. 1810-60. *1195*
—. Campbell, Alexander. Disciples of Christ. Millenarianism. 1813-66. *3106*
—. Christianity. Church and Social Problems. Ecumenism. Theology. 1967-70's. *1181*
—. Christianity. Democracy. France. Tocqueville, Alexis de. 1820-50. *1175*
—. Christianity. Nationalism. Senate. Webster, Daniel. 1813-52. *1191*
—. Christianity. Political Speeches. South. 1960's-70's. *1193*
—. Church and State. 1776-1978. *1152*
—. Church and state. 1789-1980. *991*
—. Church and State. Constitutional conventions, state. Massachusetts. Rebellions. 1780. *1071*
—. Church and State. Lincoln, Abraham. 1812-65. *1162*
—. Church and State. Political theory. ca 1940's-74. *1188*
—. Counter Culture. Persecution. Public Opinion. Sects, Religious. 19c-20c. *4263*
—. Courts. Religion in the Public Schools. Teaching. 1947-76. *572*
—. Croly, Herbert. Millenarianism. Politics. Wilson, Woodrow. 1909-19. *1159*
—. Democracy. Ideology. Political institutions. Puritan tradition. 17c-20c. *1150*
—. Elections (presidential). Nixon, Richard M. Voting and Voting Behavior. 1972. *1197*
—. Europe. Puritans. Rousseau, Jean-Jacques. 18c-20c. *1177*
—. Finney, Charles G. Mahan, Asa. Millenarianism. National Self-image. Perfectionism. 19c. *1189*
—. Freedom. Social Conditions. 1776-1900. *1179*
—. Golden Age concept. Protestantism. Rationalism. Reformation. 16c-19c. *1173*
—. Government. Morality. Myths and Symbols. 1960's-78. *1153*
—. Historians. 1970's. *1160*
—. Hymns. Myths and Symbols. National Self-image. 1800-1916. *1950*
—. Law and Society. Pluralism. 1953-72. *1161*
—. Lincoln and Lincolniana. Lutheran Church (Evangelical). 1862-63. *1163*
—. Lost Cause (theme). South. 1865-1920. *1196*
—. Mazzuchelli, Samuel Charles. Political theory. Tocqueville, Alexis de. 1831-63. *1164*
—. Nationalism. 17c-1976. *1145*
—. Nationalism. Protestantism. Social Organization. Technology. ca 1630-1974. *1171*
—. Nationalism. Providence. 1789-1812. *1158*
—. Protestantism. Secularization. Socialism. 16c-20c. *2910*
—. Social Conditions. 1973. *1170*
—. Social Organizations. 1975. *1183*
—. Transcendental Meditation. Values. 20c. *1182*
Civil Rights *See also* Academic Freedom; Freedom of Speech; Freedom of the Press; Human Rights; Religious Liberty.
—. Alabama (Aliceville). Baptists, Primitive. Corder, James. Negroes. Personal narratives. 1965-75. *2555*
—. American Missionary Association. Education. Florida. Freedmen. 1864-74. *548*
—. Anti-Catholicism. Irish Canadians. Law. Nova Scotia (Halifax). 1749-1829. *1105*
—. Assassination. Baptists, Southern. King, Martin Luther, Jr. 1961-68. *3042*
—. Baker, Ray Stannard. DuBois, W. E. B. Episcopal Church, Protestant. Liberalism. Negroes. Personal narratives. Whites. Wilmer, Cary Breckenridge. 1900-10. *2151*
—. Baptists. Bethel African Methodist Episcopal Church. California (San Francisco). Methodist Episcopal Zion Church, African. Negroes. Pressure groups. Third Baptist Church. 1860's. *1289*
—. Baptists. King, Martin Luther, Jr. Negroes. Nonviolence. 1950's-68. *2533*
—. Baptists. King, Martin Luther, Jr. Theology. Transcendentalism. 1840's-50's. 1950's-60's. *2530*
—. Baptists. King, Martin Luther, Jr. ("Letter from Birmingham Jail"). Negroes. 1963. *2534*
—. Baptists, Southern. Leadership. Race Relations. Texas. 1954-68. *2553*
—. Canada. Christianity. Eskimos. Indians. Métis. Project North. 1975-79. *2545*
—. Christianity. Equality. Negroes. 19c-20c. *2536*
—. Christianity. Fernando (slave). Key, Elizabeth. Law. Negroes. Virginia. 1607-90. *2153*
—. Christianity. Jews. Riis, Jacob. Social Organization. 1870-1914. *2129*
—. Christianity. Militance. Negroes. 1960's-70's. *2538*
—. *Christianity Today*, periodical. Evangelicalism. Malone College. Race Relations. 1956-59. *2549*
—. Church and state. Colleges and Universities. Federal Aid to Education. New York. Political attitudes. Students. 1972. *1119*
—. Church and State. District of Columbia. Lobbying. 1964-72. *1322*
—. Colonies. Europe. Florida. Judaism. Levy, Moses Elias. 1825. *4151*
—. Deprogramming. Religious liberty. Sects, religious. 1970's. *1062*
—. Georgia. Methodist Church. Tilly, Dorothy. 1900's-70. *2551*
—. Higher education. Political attitudes. 1968. *1390*
Civil rights movement. Assemblies of God. Church of God. Periodicals. Presbyterian Church, Southern. South. 1950's-60's. *2528*
—. Baptists. Ebenezer Baptist Church. Georgia (Atlanta). Personal narratives. Roberts, Joseph L., Jr. 1960-75. *2556*
—. Catholic Church. Cities. Negroes. Protestant churches. Social Classes. 1960's-70's. *2539*
—. Discrimination. Florida (Miami). Louisiana (New Orleans). Murray, Hugh T., Jr. Personal narratives. Tulane Interfaith Council. 1959-60. *2548*
—. Episcopal Church, Protestant. Race Relations. Theology. 1800-1965. *2540*
Civil rights programs. Clergy. Education. Negroes. New York (Buffalo). 1969-70. *2554*
Civil War *See also* battles and campaigns by name; Confederate Army; Confederate States of America; Reconstruction; Secession; Slavery.
—. Alienation. Ethnicity. German Americans. Lutheran Church (Missouri Synod). Massacres. Missouri (Concordia). 1864. *3301*
—. American Missionary Association. Education. Missouri. Negroes. 1862-65. *547*
—. American Revolution. Boucher, Jonathan. Church of England. Great Britain. Jefferson, Thomas. Loyalists. 1640-1797. *1412*
—. Antislavery sentiments. Christianity. Presbyterian Church. Stowe, Harriet Beecher. Women. ca 1850-80. *2474*
—. Antislavery Sentiments. Episcopal Church, Protestant. Jay, John, II. 1840-65. *2494*
—. Antislavery Sentiments. Friends, Society of (Congregational). Jones, James Parnell. Maine. Military Service. 1850's-64. *2641*
—. Armies. Butler, Benjamin F. Chaplains. Diaries. Fort Fisher (battle). Negroes. North Carolina. Turner, Henry M. 1864-65. *2685*
—. Armies. Chaplains. 1861-65. *2689*
—. Attitudes. Brownson, Orestes A. Catholic Church. Hughes, John. McMaster, James. 1850-65. *2692*
—. Authority. Bishops. Church and State. Episcopal Church, Protestant. Grace Church. Illinois (Galesburg). 1864-66. *1218*
—. Baltimore Riot of 1861. Creamer, David. Crooks, George Richard. Letters. Maryland. Methodist Church. 1861-63. *1410*
—. Baptists. Diaries. Hungerford, B. F. Kentucky. 1863-66. *2632*
—. Baptists, Southern. Foreign Mission Board. Missions and Missionaries. 1861-66. *1700*
—. Barr, D. Eglinton. Chaplains. Episcopal Church, Protestant. South. 1851-72. *2648*
—. Bishops. Episcopal Church, Protestant. Hopkins, John Henry. 1861-65. *445*
—. Brenneman, John M. Letters. Mennonites. 1862. *2709*
—. California. Circuit riders. Frontier and Pioneer Life. Manuscripts. Methodism. Ohio. Phillips, George. 1840-64. *3494*
—. Catholic Church. Copperheads. Editors and Editing. *Metropolitan Record* (newspaper). Mullaly, John. New York City. 1861-64. *1234*
—. Catholic Church. Irish Americans. *Universe: The Catholic Herald and Visitor* (newspaper). 1860-70. *3746*
—. Censorship. *Christian Observer* (newspaper). Converse, Amasa. Presbyterian Church. 1861-65. *1115*
—. Christ Church. Episcopal Church, Protestant. Kentucky (Bowling Green). Ringgold, Samuel. Tennessee (Knoxville). 1860-1911. *3168*
—. Constitutional Amendments. Fundamentalism. Lincoln, Abraham. National Fast Day. National Reform Association. 1787-1945. *1009*
—. Country Life. Mississippi (Pontotoc County). Personal narratives. Shady Grove Baptist Church. Smith, Andrew Jackson. 1864-69. *3035*
—. Diaries. Episcopal Church, Protestant. Providence. Robertson, Martha Wayles. South Carolina (Chesterfield County). Women. 1860-66. *3191*
—. Disasters. Lincoln, Abraham. Puritans. Rhetoric. Sermons. 1650-1870. *1968*
—. Elliott, John H. Episcopal Church, Protestant. Sermons. South Carolina (Camden). 1862. *1982*
—. Kentucky. Shakers. Utopias. 1861-65. *419*
—. Letters. Methodist Church. North Carolina (Halifax County). Slavery. Wills, Washington. 1861-65. *2171*
—. North or Northern States. Puritan tradition. South. 1840's-60's. *2842*
—. Protestantism. South. 1861-65. *2841*
Civil War (antecedents). Abolition Movement. Clergy. New England. Parker, Theodore. Transcendentalism. Violence. 1850-60. *2467*
—. Abolition Movement. Presbyterian Church. South. Stanton, Robert. 1840-55. *2484*
Civilian Service. American Revolution. Moravian Church. Pennsylvania. 1775-1783. *2703*
—. American Revolution. Moravian Church. Pennsylvania (Bethlehem). 1775-83. *2652*
—. Conscription, military. Mennonites. World War II. 1930's-45. *2661*
Civilization. Brownson, Orestes A. Catholic Church. Lectures. Missouri (St. Louis). 1852-54. *3838*
Civil-Military Relations. Episcopal Church, Protestant. Kentucky (Bowling Green). Ringgold, Samuel. Tennessee (Clarksville). 1861-65. *998*
—. Fort Rawlins. Mormons. Provo Outrage. Utah. 1870-71. *4000*
Claflin, Lee. Methodist Episcopal Church. Philanthropy. 19c. *2513*
Clap, Roger. Bradstreet, Anne. Devotions. New England. Puritans. Sewall, Samuel. Shepard, Thomas. Worship. 17c. *3627*
Clapp, Theodore. Louisiana (New Orleans). Slavery. Theology. Unitarianism. 1822-56. *4084*
Clark, Bertha W. Hutterites. Pacifism. Social change. South Dakota. 1921. *3385*
Clark, Clifford E., Jr. Albanese, Catherine L. Beecher, Henry Ward. Civil Religion. Douglas, Ann. Handy, Robert T. McLoughlin, William G. Reform. Revivals (review article). Women. 1607-1978. *6*
Clark, John. Circuit riders. Evangelism. Methodism. Missouri. Travis, John. 1796-1851. *1561*
Clark, Joseph. Education, Finance. Fund raising. Personal narratives. Princeton University (Nassau Hall). Travel. 1802-04. *612*
Clark, Norman H. Blocker, Jack S., Jr. Prohibition (review article). 1890-1913. 1976. *2577*
Clarke, John. Baptists. Bennett, Robert. Great Britain (London). Letters. Religious Liberty. Rhode Island. 1655-58. *1132*
Clarke, William Newton. Baptists. Bibliographies. Evolution. Immanentism. Theology. 1894-1912. *3065*
Clawson, Rudger. Civil disobedience. Federal government. Mormons. Polygamy. Sharp, John. Utah. 1862-91. *996*
Clay, Eugene O. California (Bodie). Funerals. Methodist Church. Nevada (Smith Valley). Personal narratives. Sermons. 1915. *3456*
Clayton, John. Brickell, John. Letters. Natural History. North Carolina. Plagiarism. 1693-1737. *2341*
Clayton, William. Great Britain. Immigration. Letters. Moon, John. Mormons. 1840. *3925*
—. Great Britain (Manchester). Illinois (Nauvoo). Immigration. Letters. Mormons. 1840. *3924*

Cleaveland, John. American Revolution. American Revolution. Congregationalism. Daily life. Great Awakening. Ideology. Jedrey, Christopher M. (review article). Massachusetts (Chebacco). New Lights. 1740-79. *2241*
Clebsch, William A. Dissent. Gaustad, Edwin Scott. Religious thought (review article). 17c-20c. *18*
Clemens, Samuel Langhorne. *See* Twain, Mark.
Clement, Lora E. Adventists. Editors and Editing. Women. *Youth's Instructor* (newspaper). 1927-52. *1987*
Clergy *See also* Chaplains; Circuit Riders; Rabbis; Ordination.
—. Abbott, Lyman. Congregationalism. New York (Cornwall-on-the-Hudson). Parsons, Edward Smith. Personal narratives. 1885. *3136*
—. Abel, Elijah. Mormons. Negroes. ca 1830-79. *3944*
—. Abolition Movement. Birney, James. Evangelism. Smith, Gerrit. Stanton, H. B. Weld, Theodore. 1820-50. *2488*
—. Abolition Movement. Christology. Congregationalism. Negroes. New York. Ward, Samuel Ringgold. 1839-51. *2462*
—. Abolition Movement. Civil War (antecedents). New England. Parker, Theodore. Transcendentalism. Violence. 1850-60. *2467*
—. Abolition movement. Conservatism. Constitutions. Massachusetts (Boston). Missouri (St. Louis). Unitarianism. 1828-57. *1413*
—. Abolition Movement. Negroes. Protestant churches. 1830-60. *2472*
—. Accademia (association). Catholic Church. New York. 1865-1907. *296*
—. Agriculture. Colman, Henry. Massachusetts. Unitarianism. 1820-49. *4082*
—. Alabama. Methodist Episcopal Church (South). Neely, Phillip Phillips. Secession. 1861. *1213*
—. *Alaska Herald* (newspaper). Far Western States. Honcharenko, Agapius. Orthodox Eastern Church, Greek. Ukrainian Americans. 1832-1916. *2805*
—. Allen, Thomas ("Vindication"). American Revolution. Congregationalism. Constitutions, State. Ideology. Massachusetts (Berkshire County). 1778. *1371*
—. Altar boys. Catholic Church. Family. -1974. *3726*
—. American Revolution. Baptists. Georgia. Marshall, Daniel. Political Theory. 1747-1823. *1372*
—. American Revolution. Brattle Street Church. Congregationalism. Cooper, Samuel. Massachusetts (Boston). 1770-80. *951*
—. American Revolution. Calvinism. Church and state. Jefferson, Thomas. Linn, William. Presbyterian Church. 1775-1808. *1335*
—. American Revolution. Chauncy, Charles. Congregationalism. New England. 1770's. *1269*
—. American Revolution. Church and State. Church of England. 1775-85. *988*
—. American Revolution. Church of England. Maryland. Political philosophy. 1770-80. *1388*
—. American Revolution. Church of England. Maryland. Politics. Social Status. 1775. *2618*
—. American Revolution. Church of England. Patriotism. 1770-85. 1895-98. *982*
—. American Revolution. Congregationalism. Presbyterian Church. Social status. 1774-1800. *2849*
—. American Revolution. Delaware River Valley. Episcopal Church, Protestant. Lutheran Church. Swedish Americans. 1655-1831. *285*
—. American Revolution. Loyalists. Lydekker, Gerrit. New York City. Reformed Dutch Church. 1765-94. *977*
—. American Revolution (antecedents). Political theory. Sermons. 1750's-75. *1415*
—. Americanization. Catholic Church. Irish Americans. Polish Americans. 1920-40's. *290*
—. Amish. *Herald der Wahrheit* (newspaper). Kansas (Reno County). Mast, Daniel E. 1886-1930. *3405*
—. Andrews, John. Education. Episcopal Academy. Pennsylvania, University of. 1765-1810. *507*
—. Anglo-Catholics. Catholic Church. Ecumenism. Episcopal Church, Protestant. *Lamp* (periodical). Wattson, Paul James. 1903-09. *460*
—. Anti-Catholicism. Church and State. Education, Finance. MacKinnon, Murdoch. Presbyterian Church. Saskatchewan. School Act (Saskatchewan, 1930; amended). Scott, Walter. 1913-26. *528*
—. Anti-Catholicism. Ku Klux Klan. Protestantism. Republican Party. Rhode Island. 1915-32. *2116*
—. Antislavery Sentiments. Kentucky. Racism. 1791-1824. *2455*
—. Antiwar Sentiments. Protestant churches. Vietnam War. ca 1966-73. *2700*
—. Aristocracy. French Americans. Huguenots. Religious liberty. Richebourg, Claude Phillipe de. 1680-1719. *3250*
—. Arizona (Pisinimo). Catholic Church. Frembling, Lambert. Papago Indians. Refugees. 1939-77. *3825*
—. Arizona (Tombstone). Episcopal Church, Protestant. Peabody, Endicott. 1882. *3237*
—. Arkansas, northeastern. Pentecostals. Radio. Rhetoric. 1972-73. *1959*
—. Asbury, Francis. Elections. McKendree, William. Methodist Episcopal Church. 1808. *3486*
—. Assimilation. Catholic Church. Dufresne, Andre B. French Canadians. Massachusetts (Holyoke). 1869-87. *302*
—. Attitudes. 1845-60. *307*
—. Attitudes. Lyche, Hans Tambs. Newspapers. Norway. Travel (accounts). Unitarianism. 1880-92. *4081*
—. Attitudes. Social issues. Theology. 1974. *2378*
—. Authors. Church of England. 1650-1775. *2000*
—. Autobiography. Baptists. Crandall, Joseph. New Brunswick. 1795-1810. *2993*
—. Autobiography. Buenger, Theodore Arthur. Concordia Seminary. German Americans. Lutheran Church (Missouri Synod). Seminaries. 1886-1909. *3297*
—. Bäck, Olof. Esbjörn, Lars Paul. Janssonists. Letters. Lutheran Church. Methodism. Sweden. 1846-49. *2906*
—. Bacon, Thomas. Church of England. Education. Maryland. Politics. Slavery. Theology. ca 1745-68. *3175*
—. Baptists. Broaddus, Andrew, I. Diaries. Kentucky. Travel. 1817. *2986*
—. Baptists. Cameron, William Andrew. Canada. Sermons. Shields, Thomas Todhunter. 1910-41. *3021*
—. Baptists. Catholic Church. Rauschenbusch, Walter. Social reform. Theology. Vatican Council II. 1912-65. *2380*
—. Baptists. Christian Socialism. Rauschenbusch, Walter. Social consciousness. Theology. 1891-1918. *2400*
—. Baptists. Church and Social Problems. Dawson, Joseph Martin. Scholarship. 1879-1973. *3015*
—. Baptists. Church and state. Dawson, Joseph Martin. 1879-1973. *1142*
—. Baptists. Dahlberg, Edwin. Personal narratives. Rauschenbusch, Walter. Social reform. 1914-18. *2440*
—. Baptists. Davis, Noah. Maryland (Baltimore). Meachum, John Berry. Missouri (St. Louis). Negroes. Slavery. 1818-66. *3094*
—. Baptists. Education. Income. Social Status. 1651-1980. *2603*
—. Baptists. Emigration. Great Britain. Harris, Theophilus. Politics. Social conditions. 1793-1810. *3050*
—. Baptists. First Presbyterian Church. Fosdick, Harry Emerson. New York City. Presbyterian Church. Theology. 1918-24. *466*
—. Baptists. Frontier and Pioneer Life. Montana. Personal narratives. Spencer, James Hovey. 1888-97. *3095*
—. Baptists. Great Britain. Religious Education. 1600's-1980. *725*
—. Baptists. Hudson, Winthrop. Liberalism. Rauschenbusch, Walter. Social theory. Theology. 1880-1978. *2351*
—. Baptists. Jay Street Church. Massachusetts (Boston). Negroes. Paul, Thomas (and family). 1773-1973. *3048*
—. Baptists. Laity. Leadership. 1609-1970's. *3027*
—. Baptists. Missouri. Oregon (Willamette Valley). Powell, Joab. Westward movement. 1852-73. *3093*
—. Baptists, Southern. Campbell, Will. Garner, Thad. Personal narratives. South. 20c. *2994*
—. Baptists, Southern. Circular letters. 1800-50. *3074*
—. Baptists, Southern. Evangelism. Ohio (Columbus). 1969-76. *2988*
—. Baptists, Southern. Manly, Basil. Southeastern States. Teachers. 1798-1868. *3041*
—. Beach, John. Church of England. Congregationalism. Connecticut. Heresy. 1720-82. *3204*
—. Beecher, Lyman. New York (East Hampton). Presbyterian Church. Temperance Movements. 1799-1810. *2585*
—. Behavior. Church of England. Maryland. 1700-75. *3228*
—. Bible. Congregationalism. Edwards, Jonathan. Marginalia. Massachusetts (Deerfield). Pierpont, Benjamin. Theology. 1726-30. *3146*
—. Bibliographies. Friends, Society of. Sermons. 1653-1700. *204*
—. Biographical dictionary. Unitarianism. Universalism. Women. 1860-1976. *4079*
—. Bishop of London. Methodists. Ordination. Petitions. Pilmoor, Joseph. Virginia (Norfolk County). 1774. *3465*
—. Bishops. Catholic Church. Chicago Diocese. Duggan, James. Illinois. McMullen, John. Succession. 1865-81. *3742*
—. Bishops. Catholic Church. Marriage. Uniates. 1890-1907. *3907*
—. Blair, James. Church of England. Vestries. Virginia. 1700-75. *3186*
—. Boer War. Canada. English Canadians. Protestant churches. 1899-1902. *2675*
—. Bójnowski, Lucyan. Buczek, Daniel Stephen (review article). Catholic Church. Connecticut (New Britain). Polish Americans. 1895-1960. *3865*
—. Bossism. City Politics. Crump, Edward Hull. Negroes. Tennessee (Memphis). 1927-48. *1318*
—. Brazil. New Netherland. Polhemius, Johannes Theodorus. Reformed Dutch Church. 1598-1676. *3165*
—. Breckinridge, Robert Jefferson. Danville Theological Seminary. Education. Emancipation. Kentucky. Presbyterian Church. 1800-71. *3544*
—. Bushnell, Horace. Congregationalism. Elites. Theology. 19c. *3114*
—. California (San Francisco). Catholic Church. City Politics. Irish Americans. Progressivism. Yorke, Peter C. 1900's. *3889*
—. California (San Francisco). Catholic Church. Editors and Editing. Ethnicity. Irish Americans. Yorke, Peter C. ca 1885-1925. *3887*
—. California (San Francisco). Catholic Church. Fontaine, Flavian. Mission Dolores. 1850-53. *3801*
—. California (Stockton). Pioneers. Presbyterian Church. Woods, James. 1850-54. *3526*
—. California, University of (Regents). Catholic Church. Irish Americans. Political attitudes. Yorke, Peter C. 1900-12. *560*
—. California-Nevada Conference. Methodist Church. Women. 1873-78. *3503*
—. Canada. Catholic Church. Craig, James Henry. French Canadians. Nationalism. Political repression. Quebec (Lower Canada). 1810. *1319*
—. Canada. Church of England. McMurray, William. 1810-94. *3203*
—. Canadian Pacific Railway. Construction crews. Manitoba (Virden). McLeod, Finlay J. C. Personal narratives. Presbyterian Church. 1881-82. *3567*
—. Capital Punishment. New England. Protestantism. Sermons. 1674-1750. *2822*
—. Capitalism. Catholic Church. Elites. Pulp mills. Quebec (Chicoutimi). Working class. 1896-1930. *2601*
—. Carroll, John. Catholic Church. Documents. Hanley, Thomas O'Brien *(The John Carroll Papers).* Research. 18c-19c. 1976-78. *3872*
—. Carroll, John. Catholic Church. Frontier and Pioneer Life. Louisiana Purchase. 1803-15. *3805*
—. Catholic Church. Converts. Episcopal Church, Protestant. Richey, James Arthur Morrow. ca 1900-33. *2754*
—. Catholic Church. Czechoslovakia. Personal narratives. Refugees. Social Change. Zubek, Theodoric. 1950-78. *3902*
—. Catholic Church. Diaries. Shaw, Joseph Coolidge. Vermont (Brattleboro). 1848. *3849*
—. Catholic Church. Editors and Editing. Historiography. *New Catholic Encyclopedia.* Polish Americans. Swastek, Joseph Vincent (obituary). 1913-77. *227*

—. Catholic Church. Ethnicity. Social Status. 1947-80. *3867*
—. Catholic Church. Germany. Mundelein, George. Nazism. 1937. *1256*
—. Catholic Church. Greeley, Andrew M. Intellectuals. 1974. *3749*
—. Catholic Church. Harris, William Richard. Ontario. Toronto Archdiocese. 1846-1923. 1974. *3846*
—. Catholic Church. Human rights. New York City. Social progress. Varela, Félix. 1823-53. *2357*
—. Catholic Church. Lemke, John A. Michigan (Detroit). Polish Americans. 1866-90. *3875*
—. Catholic Church. Massachusetts (Boston). O'Connell, William Henry. 1915-44. *3741*
—. Catholic Church. Men. Religious Orders. Social classes. Women. 1650-1762. *2614*
—. Catholic Church. Middle Classes. Pentecostal movement. Students. 1970's. *3753*
—. Catholic Church. Missouri (St. Louis). 1841-99. *3759*
—. Catholic Church. National Federation of Priests' Councils. Organizational change. Values. -1973. *3859*
—. Catholic church. New France. Trade. 1627-1760. *337*
—. Catholic Church. Protestant Churches. Sex discrimination. Women. 1970's. *939*
—. Catholic Church. Quebec. Working conditions. 1968-77. *3861*
—. Catholic Church. Quebec (review article). 19c. 1979. *3840*
—. Catholic Church. Values. 1970's. *3744*
—. Catholicism. Scanlan, Laurence. Utah. 1875-79. *3897*
—. Channing, William Ellery. Spirituality. Unitarianism. 1830-80. *4083*
—. Cheever, Thomas. Congregationalism. Documents. Massachusetts. 1677-1749. *3122*
—. Christianity. Episcopal Church, Protestant. 1974. *3248*
—. Christianity. Radicals and radicalism. Social status. 1960-74. *2764*
—. Church and Social Problems. Political Activism. Protestant Churches. 1960's-70's. *2431*
—. Church and state. Church of England. Parson's Cause. Tobacco. Virginia. Wages. 1750-70. *1052*
—. Church and state. Henry, Patrick. Maury, James. Parsons' Cause. Personal narratives. Speeches, Addresses, etc. Virginia. 1758-65. *1080*
—. Church and State. Income. New England. 1700-75. *1011*
—. Church History. Lutheran Church. 1978. *272*
—. Church of England. Congregationalism. New England. Vestries. 1630-1775. *312*
—. Church of England. Corbett, Griffiths Owen. Manitoba. Métis. Red River Rebellion. 1863-70. *3215*
—. Church of England. Cotton, William. Lawsuits. Tithes. Virginia (Accomack County). 1633-39. *1013*
—. Church of England. Cradock, Thomas. Maryland (Baltimore County). Poetry. Sermons. 1700-70. *3229*
—. Church of England. Delaware. Northeastern or North Atlantic States. Vestries. 1690-1775. *311*
—. Church of England. Diocesan Theological Institute. Frontier and Pioneer Life. Ontario (Cobourg). Strachan, John. 1840-55. *732*
—. Church of England. Education. Missions and Missionaries. Quebec (Three Rivers). Wood, Samuel. 1822-68. *3202*
—. Church of England. Episcopal Church, Protestant. Ingraham, Joseph Holt. Novels. Prisons. Public Schools. Reform. Tennessee (Nashville). 1847-51. *3241*
—. Church of England. Government. Loyalists. Political Attitudes. Theology. 1770-83. *1387*
—. Church of England. Loyalists. Theology. 1774-83. *1346*
—. Church of England. Muhlenberg, John Peter Gabriel. Virginia (Dunmore County). 1772-76. *3221*
—. Church records. Grimes, Addison McLaughlin. Methodist Episcopal Church. West Virginia (Webster County). 1880's-1963. *3455*
—. Civil rights programs. Education. Negroes. New York (Buffalo). 1969-70. *2554*
—. Columbia River. Congregationalism. Fort Vancouver. Hawaiians. Hudson's Bay Company. Kaulehelehe, William R. Washington. 1845-69. *3128*
—. Concordia Seminary. Illinois (Hahlen, Nashville). Lutheran Church (Missouri Synod). Personal narratives. St. Peter's Lutheran Church. Scharlemann, Ernst K. Seminaries. 1905-18. *3335*
—. Conflict and Conflict Resolution. Laity. Protestantism. 19c-20c. *2954*
—. Congregationalism. Franklin, Benjamin. Massachusetts (Boston). *New England Courant* (newspaper). Smallpox. *Spectator* (newspaper). 1720-23. *2023*
—. Congregationalism. Great Awakening. New England. New Lights. Old Lights. Social Classes. 1734-85. *2627*
—. Congregationalism. Herron, George David. Iowa College. National Christian Citizen League. Populism. Progressivism. Socialism. 1880's-1900. *2561*
—. Congregationalism. Maine (York). Moody, Samuel. 1700-47. *3137*
—. Congregationalism. Massachusetts (Ipswich). Wigglesworth, Samuel. 1714-68. *3138*
—. Congregationalism. New England. 1700-60. *3141*
—. Congregationalism. New England. Presbyterian Church. Professionalism. Scott, Donald M. (review article). 1750-1850. 1979. *2865*
—. Congregations. Morality. Sermons. 1970's. *2904*
—. Consultation on Church Union. Henderlite, Rachel. Personal narratives. Presbyterian Church, Southern. South. Women. 1945-77. *804*
—. Converts. Episcopal Church, Protestant. Lutheran Church. Sweden. Unonius, Gustaf. Wisconsin (Pine Lake). 1841-58. *2854*
—. Council of Southern Mountain Workers. Rural Development. South. Standard of Living. 1913-72. *2451*
—. Counseling. Great Britain. 1950's-70's. *122*
—. Country stores. Duus, O. F. Knoph, Thomas. Ledgers. Lutheran Church. Norwegian Americans. Wisconsin (Waupaca township; Scandinavia). 1853-56. *3334*
—. Davies, Samuel. Eulogies. National Self-image. Presbyterian Church. Washington, George. 1789-1815. *1157*
—. Deism. Paine, Thomas *(Age of Reason).* Virginia. 1794-97. *86*
—. Democratic Party. Eaton, Margaret (Peggy) O'Neale. Ely, Ezra Stiles. Jackson, Andrew. Presbyterian Church. 1829-30. *3536*
—. Denominationalism. Social issues. Theology. Values. 1960's-70's. *2401*
—. Denominationalism. Southern Baptist Theological Seminary. Theology. 18c-1980. *3075*
—. Diaries. Episcopal Church, Protestant. Private Schools. Salt industry. Trade. Ward, Henry Dana. West Virginia (Kanawha Valley, Charleston). 1845-47. *3172*
—. Diaries. Hodge, Charles. Pennsylvania (Philadelphia). Presbyterian Church. Theology. 1819-20. *3534*
—. Diaries. Lutheran Church. Muhlenberg, Henry Melchior. Pennsylvania. Women. 1742-87. *828*
—. Dickinson, Jonathan. Presbyterian Church. Subscription controversy. Westminster Standards. 1700-50. *3560*
—. Disciples of Christ. Frontier. North Central States. Personal narratives. Snethen, Abraham. 1794-1830. 1977. *3112*
—. Documents. Editors and Editing. Historians. Sparks, Jared. Unitarianism. Washington, George. 1815-30. *4076*
—. Dulík, Joseph J. Pioneers. Slovak Americans. Vaniščák, Gregory. 1909-38. *3823*
—. Ecumenism. Lutheran Church (Missouri Synod, Norwegian). Munch, Johan Storm. Norway. Wisconsin (Wiota). 1827-1908. *3324*
—. Ellis, Edwin M. Montana. Presbyterian Church. Sunday schools. Travel. 1870's-1927. *3537*
—. Emanuel Lutheran Church. Lutheran Church. New York City (Queens). Personal narratives. Wyneken, Frederick G. 1887-1907. *3348*
—. Emigration. Intellectuals. New England. 1640-60. *3653*
—. Entz, John Edward. First Mennonite Church. Kansas (Newton). Mennonites. 1875-1969. *3419*
—. Episcopal Church, Protestant. Jarratt, Devereux. Letters. Virginia. 1770-1800. *3195*
—. Episcopal Church, Protestant. Kentucky (Versailles). St. John's Church. 1829-1976. *3220*
—. Episcopal Church, Protestant. Sex Discrimination. Women. 1973. *841*
—. Equality. Mormons (Reorganized). Negroes. Schisms. Women. 1860-1979. *4032*
—. Eulogies. Presidency (mystique). Sermons. Washington, George. 1799. *1190*
—. Folklore. Georgia, west-central. Humor. Protestantism. 19c-20c. *2839*
—. Franklin and Marshall College. Gerhart, Emanuel Vogel. Pennsylvania (Lancaster). Reformed German Church. Theology. 1840-1904. *3286*
—. Friends, Society of. Keith, George. Pennsylvania. Schisms. Schisms. 1660-1720. *3261*
—. Friends, Society of. Women. 19c. *820*
—. Frontier. Letters. Lutheran Church in America, Norwegian. Montana, eastern. Thorpe, Christian Scriver. 1906-08. *3295*
—. Frontier. Missouri. Protestant Churches. Schools. ca 1800-30. *639*
—. Fundamentalism. Macartney, Clarence E. Presbyterian Church. 1901-53. *3579*
—. Funk, John F. Manitoba. Mennonites. Russia. Settlement. Travel. 1873. *3393*
—. Garrettson, Freeborn. Methodism. 1775-1827. *3447*
—. Georgia. Methodist Episcopal Church, South. Pierce, George Foster. Pierce, Lovick. 1785-1884. *3454*
—. Georgia (Savannah). Presbyterian Church. Swiss Americans. Zubly, John Joachim. 1724-58. *3565*
—. German language. Hansel, William H. Lutheran Church (Missouri Synod). Personal narratives. 1907-62. *3305*
—. Germany. Herborn, University of. Maryland. Otterbein, Philip Wilhelm. Pennsylvania. Theology. United Brethren in Christ. 1726-1813. *3666*
—. Gold Mines and Mining. Klondike Stampede. Lippy, Thomas S. Methodist Church. Randall, Edwin M. Transportation. Yukon Territory. 1896-99. *3492*
—. Great Awakening. New England. Professionalism. Theology. 1740-49. *2257*
—. Great Britain. Immigration. New England. Puritans. 1629-65. *3661*
—. Helmreich, Christian. Letters. Lutheran Church. Nebraska (Weyerts). 1887-88. *3308*
—. Historiography. New England. Puritans. Women. 1668-1735. *936*
—. Immigrants. Lutheran Church (Augustana Synod). Swedish Americans. Wives. 1860-1962. *3296*
—. Immigration. Manitoba. Mennonite Brethren Church. Russia. Warkentin, Johann. 1879-1948. *3409*
—. Integration. Kimball, Spencer W. Mormons. Negroes. Revelation. 1950-78. *4051*
—. Janson, Kristofer. Minnesota (Minneapolis). Norwegian Americans. Unitarianism. 1881-82. *4078*
—. Johnson, Andrew. Protestant Churches. Public Opinion. 1865-68. *1219*
—. Kentucky. Presbyterian Church. Templin, Terah. 1780-1818. *3592*
—. Labor. Lynd, Robert S. Oil Industry and Trade. Presbyterian Church. Wyoming (Elk Basin). 1921. *3562*
—. Letters. Lipscomb, Bernard F. Methodist Church. Virginia (Charlottesville). 1889-92. *3471*
—. Letters. Methodist Church. Montgomery, Daniel. Webb, Thomas. 1771. *3490*
—. Lewis, Lloyd. Lincoln, Abraham. Myths and symbols. 1861-65. *79*
—. Lutheran Church. Muhlenberg, Henry Melchior. Pennsylvania. Pietism. 18c. *3337*
—. Lutheran Church. Schulze, Ernst Carl Ludwig. Steup, Henry Christian. 1852-1931. *3339*
—. Lutheran Church (Missouri Synod). Minnesota. Missouri. Swedish Americans. Wihlborg, Niels Albert. 1893-1918. *3331*
—. Lutheran Church (North Carolina Synod). Negroes. 1865-89. *3328*
—. Lutheran Church, Norwegian. North Dakota. Norwegian Americans. Red River of the North. 1871-99. *3318*
—. McGown, A. J. Presbyterian Church, Cumberland. Publishers and Publishing. *Texas Presbyterian* (newspaper). 1846-73. *3586*
—. Mennonites. Pennsylvania (Lancaster). Weaver, Benjamin W. 1853-1928. *3433*

—. Mennonites. Pennsylvania (Snyder County). 1780's-1970's. *3371*
—. Methodist Church. North Carolina. Personal narratives. Young, John. 1747-1837. *3507*
—. Methodist Church. Ordination. Social Change. 1771-1975. *3473*
—. Methodist Episcopal Church. 1784-1844. *3485*
—. Methodist Protestant Church. Shaw, Anna Howard. Social Gospel Movement. Suffrage. Women. 1880-1919. *3506*
—. Methodist Protestant Church. Snethen, Nicholas. 1769-1845. *315*
—. Michaelius, Jonas. New Netherland. Reformed Dutch Church. 1590's-1633. *3164*
—. Miller, Samuel. Presbyterian Church. Princeton Theological Seminary. Religious Education. 1813-50. *764*
—. National Characteristics. Proslavery Sentiments. Social Status. 1699-1865. *2628*
—. Negroes. 1960's-70's. *2739*
—. Negroes. Political Leadership. Texas (Beaumont). 1972. *1315*
—. Negroes. Presbyterian Church. 1885-1975. *3594*
—. Negroes. Presbyterian Church, United. 1855-1973. *3595*
—. Negroes. Protestant churches. Race Relations. South. ca 1800-65. *2816*
—. New England. Puritans. 17c. *3599*
—. Nova Scotia (Springhill). Presbyterian Church. 1874-1925. *3532*
—. Ordination. United Brethren in Christ. Women. 1889. *847*
—. Pennsylvania (Shenandoah). Uniates. 1884-1907. *3909*
—. Presbyterian Church. Reese, Thomas. South Carolina. 1773-96. *3585*
—. Protestant Churches. Religious beliefs. 1965. *2890*
—. Protestant churches. Textbooks. Theology. 1850-1900. *2925*
—. Protestantism. Sore throats. 1830-60. *1431*
—. Publishers and Publishing. Puritanism. 1630-1763. *1991*
—. United Brethren in Christ. Wright, Milton. 1828-1917. *3665*
Clergy (dismissal). Congregationalism. New Hampshire. Presbyterian Church. Social change. 1633-1790. *2885*
—. Episcopal Church, Protestant. Illinois (Chicago). Pamphlets. Rites and Ceremonies. Swope, Cornelius E. Trinity Church. Unonius, Gustaf. 1850-51. *3179*
Clergy, dissident. Ideology. Leadership. Protestant Churches. -1973. *2439*
Clergy (recruitment). Church of England. Virginia. 1726-76. *3185*
Clergy (review article). Burg, B. R. Congregationalism. Mather, Richard. New England. Youngs, J. William T., Jr. ca 1700-50. 1976. *3124*
Clergy (tenure). Higginson, John. Massachusetts (Salem). Nicholet, Charles. Puritans. Social change. 1672-76. *3620*
Cleveland Diocese. Assimilation. Authority. Bishops. Catholic Church. German Americans. Irish Americans. Ohio. Rappe, Louis Amadeus. 1847-70. *3788*
Clinton Theological Seminary. Adventists. German Americans. Missouri. 1910-25. *761*
Clockmakers. Friends, Society of. Rhode Island (Newport). 1780's-1850's. *3268*
Cloeter, Ottomar. Indians. Letters. Lutheran Church. Minnesota. Missions and Missionaries. 1856-68. *1651*
Clothing. Legislation. New England. Puritans. Social Status. 1630-90. *2427*
Coahuiltecan Indians. Catholic Church. Missions and Missionaries. Texas (San Antonio). 1792. *1566*
Coalitions. Elections, presidential. 1952-76. *1275*
Cobbett, Thomas *(Practical Discourse of Prayer)*. New England. Prayer. Puritans. 1630-85. *3607*
Cobden, Richard. Great Britain. Millenarianism. Peace movements. Protestant churches. 1840-60. *2701*
Coca-Cola Company. Emory University. Methodist Church. Religious education. South. Vanderbilt University. 1840's-1970's. *3466*
Cochran, Jacob. Anti-Christian sentiments. Christianity. Free love. Maine (York County). Society of Free Brethren and Sisters. 1817-19. *89*
Coe, Truman. Letters. Mormons. Ohio (Kirtland). Presbyterians. 1836. *2718*
Coffman, Ralph J. (review article). Puritans. Stoddard, Solomon. 1660's-1729. 1978. *3615*
Cofradías (brotherhoods). Catholic Church. Mexican Americans. New Mexico. Penitentes. Rio Grande Valley. ca 1770-1970. *3675*
Cohoon, Hannah Harrison. Massachusetts (Hancock). New York (New Lebanon, Watervliet). Painting. Shakers. 1817-64. *1902*
Coke, Thomas. Asbury, Francis. Canada. Embury, Philip. Great Britain. Methodism. USA. 1760-80. *3445*
—. Asbury, Francis. Methodist Episcopal Church. Slavery. 1780-1816. *2155*
—. Garrettson, Freeborn. Letters. Methodist Church. Missions and Missionaries. Nova Scotia. Wesley, John. 1786. *1490*
—. Great Britain. Methodism. Rites and Ceremonies. Wesley, John *(Sunday Service)*. 1780's. *3460*
Colby, Abby M. Congregationalism. Feminism. Japan. Missions and Missionaries. 1879-1914. *932*
Cole, Nathan ("Spiritual Travels"). Congregationalism. Great Awakening. Whitefield, George. 1740-65. *2227*
Cole, Thomas. Christianity. Iconography. Painting. Romanticism. 1830's-40's. *1865*
Coleman, Benjamin. Brattle Street Church. Elites. Gentility (concept). Massachusetts (Boston). Puritans. 1715-45. *2622*
Colet, John. Catholic Church. Episcopal Church, Protestant. Erasmus, Desiderius. Hermeneutics. More, Thomas. 1500-1975. *3167*
Collectors and Collecting *See also* Art.
—. Folklore. Hyatt, Harry Midddleton. Illinois (Adams County). Negroes. Small, Minnie Hyatt. South. Witchcraft. 1920-78. *2190*
—. Rosenbloom, Charles J. Yale University. 1918-75. *280*
College of St. Teresa. Catholic Church. Franciscan Sisters. Minnesota (Winona). Molloy, Mary Aloysius. Women. 1903-54. *670*
College of William and Mary. Blair, James. Church of England. Church of Scotland. Converts. Virginia. 1679-1720. *2924*
—. Blair, James. Church of England. Governors. Missions and Missionaries. Virginia. ca 1685-1743. *3223*
—. Church and State. Harvard University. Puritans. Yale University. 1636-1700. *650*
College teachers. Academic disciplines. Religiosity. 1965-73. *531*
—. Catholics. 1973. *521*
—. Catholics. Discrimination. Higher education. 1960's-70's. *554*
Colleges and Universities *See also* names of individual institutions; Dissertations; Higher Education; Students.
—. Abortion. Attitudes. Catholic Church. Students. 1970's. *855*
—. Adventists. Battle Creek College. Brownsberger, Sidney. California. Healdsburg College. Michigan. 1875-80's. *665*
—. Adventists. Educational Reform. Sutherland, Edward A. 1904-50. *693*
—. Agnosticism. Catholic Church. Quebec. Students. 1970-78. *505*
—. Alberta (Edmonton). Catholic Church. MacDonald, John Roderick. St. Joseph's College (Alberta). 1922-23. *710*
—. Alberta, University of. Catholic Church. Legal, Emile. O'Leary, Henry Joseph. St. Joseph's University College. 1906-26. *619*
—. Alma College. Michigan. Presbyterians. 1883-86. *694*
—. *America* (periodical). Catholic Church. LaFarge, John. Newman Clubs. 1904-50's. *515*
—. American Philosophical Association. Catholic Church. Philosophy. Religious Education. 1933-79. *775*
—. American Studies. Great Britain. Theses. 1975-76. *46*
—. Anti-Catholicism. Discrimination, Educational. Ethnic Groups. 1970's. *2106*
—. Attitudes. Religiosity. Sex roles. Stereotypes. Students. Women. 1970's. *793*
—. Attitudes. Religiosity. Students. Vietnam War. 1968-72. *2636*
—. Baptists. Education. Everett Institute. Louisiana (Spearsville). 1893-1908. *605*
—. Baptists. Georgia (Cedartown). Woodland Female College. 1851-87. *634*
—. Baptists. Richmond College. Virginia (Richmond). 1843-60. *616*
—. Baptists. Tennessee (Jackson). Union University. 1825-1975. *776*
—. Birdwood Junior College. Georgia (Birdwood). 1954-74. *514*
—. Bourget, Ignace. Catholic Church. Laval University. Quebec (Quebec). 1840's-50's. *676*
—. Brigham Young University. Centennial Celebrations. Mormons. Utah. 1876-1976. *783*
—. Brown University. Harvard University. Libraries. Princeton University. Yale University. 18c. *672*
—. Canada. Political knowledge. Public opinion. Students. 1974. *978*
—. Catholic Church. 20c. *713*
—. Catholic Church. High Schools. Utah. 1875-1975. *624*
—. Catholic Church. Maryville Academy. Missouri (St. Louis). 1872-1972. *657*
—. Catholic University of America. Discrimination. District of Columbia. Negroes. Wesley, Charles H. 1914-48. *3729*
—. Catholic University of Puerto Rico. Puerto Rico. 1900's-74. *652*
—. Catholics. Protestants. 1960's-70's. *565*
—. Catholics. St. Thomas More College. Saskatchewan (Regina, Saskatoon). 1918-21. *620*
—. China (Shanghai). Episcopal Church, Protestant. Missions and Missionaries. Pott, Francis L. H. St. John's University. 1888-1941. *1707*
—. Christianity. Curricula. Graham, William. Liberty Hall Academy. Proslavery Sentiments. Virginia. ca 1786-96. *2173*
—. Church and state. Civil Rights. Federal Aid to Education. New York. Political attitudes. Students. 1972. *1119*
—. Church and State. Constitutions. Religious studies. Supreme Court. 1970's. *578*
—. Church and state. Politics. 1740's-60's. *651*
—. Church Schools. Mormons. Utah (Salt Lake City). Young University. 1876-94. *734*
—. Church Schools. State Aid to Education. Supreme Court. 1971-76. *682*
—. Collegiate Institute. Depressions. Lansdowne College. Manitoba (Portage la Prairie). 1882-93. *780*
—. Colorado. Jackson, Sheldon. Presbyterian Church. Westminster University. 1874-1917. *597*
—. Common Sense school. Curricula. Dalhousie University. King's College. Lyall, William. Nova Scotia. Philosophy. Pine Hill Divinity Hall. Presbyterian Church. 1850-90. *719*
—. Conferences. Curricula. Dissertations. Jewish studies. 1979. *4138*
—. Conferences. Dissertations. Jewish studies. 1978. *4137*
—. Congregationalism. Dwight, Timothy. Human Relations. Stiles, Ezra. Yale University. 1778-95. *706*
—. Congregationalism. Florida (Winter Park). Hooker, Edward P. Rollins College. 1885-1900. *678*
—. Consortium of Peace Research, Education and Development. Mennonites. North America. Peace Studies. 1965-80. *2650*
—. Culver-Stockton University. Democratic Party. Disciples of Christ. Missouri. Shannon, James. Slavery. 1821-59. *3107*
—. Curricula. Ethics.. 1950-73. *530*
—. Curricula. Massachusetts (South Hadley). Mount Holyoke College. Science. Women. 1839-88. *2320*
—. Dalhousie University. McCulloch, Thomas. Missions and Missionaries. Nova Scotia. Pictou Academy. Presbyterian Church. ca 1803-42. *591*
—. Emerson, Joseph. Lyon, Mary. Mount Holyoke College. Protestantism. Women. 1760's-1850's. *552*
—. Foreman, Kenneth J., Sr. Presbyterian Church (southern). *Presbyterian Outlook* (newspaper). Theology. 1922-67. *3547*
—. Fort Wayne Bible College. Indiana. Mennonites, Evangelical. 1904-77. *740*
—. Hebrew Union College. Judaism (Reform). Judaism, Reform. Ohio (Cincinnati). Wise, Isaac Mayer. 1870's-1900. *613*
—. Immigration. Mennonites. Ohio (Median County). Wadsworth Institute. 1825-80. *674*
—. Lutheran Church. Valparaiso University. 1636-1973. *683*
—. Mormons. Presbyterian Church. Utah (Salt Lake City). Westminster College. 1875-1913. *559*
—. Protestantism. 19c. *698*

—. Religiosity. Teachers. 1973. *555*
—. Religious Education. 1939-79. *733*
—. Tewksbury, Donald G. (review article). 1776-1860. 1932. *538*
Colleges and Universities (administration). Church and State. Church of England. Friends, Society of. New Jersey. Presbyterians. Princeton University. 1745-60. *661*
—. Desha, Joseph. Holley, Horace. Kentucky. Politics. Presbyterians. State government. Transylvania College. Unitarianism. 1818-27. *537*
Colleges and Universities (review article). Asia. Canada. Missions and Missionaries. Protestant Churches. 1850-1971. *1675*
—. Church and State. Columbia University. Dartmouth College. Harvard University. Johnson, Samuel (1696-1772). Yale University. 1696-1970. 1972-74. *524*
Collegiate Institute. Colleges and Universities. Depressions. Lansdowne College. Manitoba (Portage la Prairie). 1882-93. *780*
Collegium Fratrum (organization). Buerger, Paul Theodor. Educational Tests and Measurements. Indiana (Fort Wayne). Letters. Lutheran Church. 1858. *3315*
Collier, John. Acculturation. American Indian Defense Association. Indians. Religious liberty. 1920-26. *1101*
Colman, Henry. Agriculture. Clergy. Massachusetts. Unitarianism. 1820-49. *4082*
Colombia (Bogotá). Bishops. Catholic Church. Hughes, John. Letters. Mosquera, Manuel José. New York City. 1853. *3762*
Colonial Government *See also* Imperialism.
—. Allen, Bennet. Church of England. Ecclesiastical pluralism. Jordan, John Morton. Maryland. Patronage. Sharpe, Horatio. 1759-70. *1051*
—. American Revolution (antecedents). Church of England. Great Britain. Political theory. Shipley, Jonathan. 1773-75. *1376*
—. Arizona. Catholic Church. Jurisdictions, ecclesiastical. New Mexico. Spain. 1548-1969. *3739*
—. Attitudes. Catholic Church. Discovery and Exploration. Games. Indians. Missions and Missionaries. 16c-17c. *1524*
—. Benefit of clergy. Common law. Criminal law. Maryland. 1637-1713. *1140*
—. Bureaucracies. Church and state. *Commissaire ordonnateur.* France. Louisiana. 1712-69. *1069*
—. California. Church and state. Indians. Laws of the Indies. Missions and Missionaries. Spain. 18c. *1143*
—. Catholic Church. Church of England. Macdonnell, Alexander. Ontario. Ontario (Kingston, Toronto). Strachan, John. 1820's-30's. *1108*
—. Catholic Church. Discovery and Exploration. France. Jolliet, Louis. Marquette, Jacques. Missions and Missionaries. Mississippi River. Monuments. 1665-1700. *3767*
—. Catholic Church. Intendants. Quebec. 1633-1760. *1030*
—. Church and State. Defoe, Daniel. Religious liberty. South Carolina. 1704-06. *1014*
—. Church and state. Great Britain. Rhode Island. Williams, Roger. 1629-83. *1042*
—. Church of England. Ethnic Groups. Friends, society of. Pennsylvania. Reformed churches. 1755-80. *1215*
—. Documents. Franciscans. Missions and Missionaries. New Mexico. Spain. Vélez Cachupín, Thomas. ca 1754. *1586*
—. Florida. Indians. Military security. Missions. 1566-1710. *1079*
Colonialism *See also* Imperialism.
—. India, north. Missions and Missionaries. Presbyterian Church. ca 1800-1950. *1673*
Colonization *See also* Settlement.
—. Abolition Movement. Beecher, Lyman. Presbyterian Church (New School). 1820-50. *2492*
—. Africa. American Colonization Society. McDonough, David. Medical Education. Presbyterian Church. Slavery. 1840-50. *2483*
—. African Society. Congregationalism. Freedmen. Hopkins, Samuel. Rhode Island (Providence). Sierra Leone. 1789-95. *2459*
—. Anti-Catholicism. Great Britain. Ideology. Ireland. North America. Protestantism. ca 1550-1600. *2086*
—. Black nationalism. Cuffe, Paul. Friends, Society of. Sierra Leone. 1810's. *2478*
—. Bolton, Herbert Eugene. Catholic Church. Historiography. Missions and Missionaries. Southwest. Spain. 1917-79. *1489*
—. California (San Diego). Indians. Missions and Missionaries. Spain. 1769-1834. *1668*
—. Calvert, Cecilius (2d Lord Baltimore). Catholic Church. Maryland. Religious liberty. 1634-92. *1061*
—. Calvert, George (1st Lord Baltimore). Catholic Church. Newfoundland (Avalon Peninsula). Protestant churches. Religious Liberty. 1620's. *2755*
—. Castañeda, Carlos Eduardo *(Our Catholic Heritage).* Catholic Church. Texas. 1693-1731. 1933-43. *3673*
—. Catholic Church. Economic development. French Canadians. Geopolitics. Provost, T. S. Quebec (Mattawinie district). 17c-1890. *3809*
—. Catholicism. French Canadians. Quebec (Eastern Townships). Settlement. 1800-60. *3780*
—. Church and state. Spain. West Florida. 1780's. *1055*
—. Civil Rights. Europe. Florida. Judaism. Levy, Moses Elias. 1825. *4151*
—. Florida (Campbell Town). Great Britain. Huguenots. West Florida. 1763-70. *3254*
—. Hawaii (Lanai). Missions and Missionaries. Mormons. 1850's. *1684*
—. Indians. Jesuits. Menéndez de Avilés, Pedro. Missions and Missionaries. Opechancanough (chief). Powhatan Indians. Spain. Virginia. 1570-72. *1622*
—. Liberia. Methodist Episcopal Church. Missions and Missionaries. Negroes. Sierra Leone. 1833-48. *1702*
—. New England. Pragmatism. Puritans. Social Change. 1620-90. *3608*
Colorado *See also* Western States.
—. Catholic Church. Diaries. Hospitals. Mallon, Catherine. New Mexico (Santa Fe). Sisters of Charity. 1865-1901. *1454*
—. Catholic Church. Folk art. New Mexico. Penitentes. 19c-20c. *3898*
—. Catholic Church. Germans, Russian. Immigration. Mennonites. 18c-19c. *2775*
—. Catholic Church. New Mexico. Passion plays. Spain. 1830's-1978. *1890*
—. Colleges and Universities. Jackson, Sheldon. Presbyterian Church. Westminster University. 1874-1917. *597*
—. Haven, Gilbert. Methodist Church. Rocky Mountains. Utah (Salt Lake City). 1875. *3463*
Colorado (Boulder). Feminism. Social reform. Temperance Movements. Women's Christian Temperance Union. 1881-1967. *2741*
Colorado (Denver). Adelman, Samuel. Congregation Beth Ha Medrosh Hagodol. Judaism (Conservative, Orthodox). Kauvar, Charles E. H. Rabbis. 1949-58. *4193*
—. Anti-Catholicism. Anti-Semitism. Ku Klux Klan. Protestantism. Social Classes. 1921-25. *2609*
—. Catholic Church. Italian Americans. 1870's-1920's. *3728*
—. Church and state. Political activity. Tax exemption. *United States* v. *Christian Echoes National Ministry, Inc.* 1950's-1970's. *1063*
—. Congregation Beth Ha Medrosh Hagodol. Judaism (Orthodox). Kauvar, Charles E. H. 1902-71. *4192*
—. Congregation Beth Ha Medrosh Hagodol. Judaism (Orthodox). Kauvar, Charles E. H. Progressivism. 1902-71. *4194*
Colorado (Denver; Globeville). Catholic Church. Polish Americans. St. Joseph Parish. 1902-78. *3724*
Colorado, southern. Catholic Church. Death Carts. Hispanic Americans. New Mexico, northern. Penitentes. 1860-90's. *3856*
Columbia River. Clergy. Congregationalism. Fort Vancouver. Hawaiians. Hudson's Bay Company. Kaulehelehe, William R. Washington. 1845-69. *3128*
Columbia University. Church and State. Colleges and Universities (review article). Dartmouth College. Harvard University. Johnson, Samuel (1696-1772). Yale University. 1696-1970. 1972-74. *524*
—. Church of England. Johnson, Samuel (1696-1772). Livingston, William. Reformed Dutch Church. 1751-63. *635*
Comets. Astrology. Astronomy. Pennsylvania Germans. 18c-19c. *2209*
Commerce *See also* Banking; Business; Prices; Trade; Transportation.
—. Judaism (Orthodox, Reform). Oregon (Portland). Organizations. 1888. *4162*
—. Puritans. 17c. *373*
Commissaire ordonnateur. Bureaucracies. Church and state. Colonial Government. France. Louisiana. 1712-69. *1069*
Commissaries. Bishop of London. Church of England. Great Britain. South Carolina. 1715-32. *3242*
Commission on the Status and Role of Women in the United Methodist Church. Feminism. Methodism. Social Organizations. 1869-1974. *893*
Commission on Training Camp Activities. Jewish Welfare Board. Knights of Columbus. Leisure. Morality. Social Reform. War Department. World War I. Young Men's Christian Association. Young Women's Christian Association. 1917-18. *2379*
Committee on Baptist History. Baptists. Georgia. 1948-78. *270*
Common law. Benefit of clergy. Colonial Government. Criminal law. Maryland. 1637-1713. *1140*
Common Sense school. Colleges and Universities. Curricula. Dalhousie University. King's College. Lyall, William. Nova Scotia. Philosophy. Pine Hill Divinity Hall. Presbyterian Church. 1850-90. *719*
—. Comte, Auguste. Philosophy. Positivism. Reformed churches. Social Gospel. Theology. ca 1850's-80's. *2833*
Commons, John R. Bascom, John. Ely, Richard T. Evolution. Political theory. Social gospel. Wisconsin, University of. 1870-1910. *2394*
Commonweal (periodical). Catholic Church. Editors and Editing. Williams, Michael. 1922-38. *3716*
Communalism *See also* Communes.
—. Agriculture. Education. German Americans. Hutterites. Pacific Northwest. Pacifism. 20c. *392*
—. Amana Society. Iowa. 1843-1932. *424*
—. Amana Society. Iowa. Shambaugh, Bertha Horak. Wick, Barthinius L. ca 1900-34. *404*
—. "Angel Dancers". Folklore. Howell, Jane. Huntsman, Manson T. New Jersey (Woodcliff). Rumors. Sects, Religious. 1890-1920. *389*
—. Baptists (Seventh-Day). Letters. Müller, Johan Peter. Pennsylvania (Ephrata). Social Conditions. 1743. *428*
—. Behavior. Hutterites. Social theory. ca 1650-1977. *382*
—. Beissel, Johann Conrad. Eckerlin, Emmanuel. Ephrata Cloister. Pennsylvania (Conestoga Valley). 1732-68. *390*
—. California (Orange County). Middle Classes. Oneida Community. Social Organization. Townerites. 1848-1910. *417*
—. Canada. Hutterites. Lifestyles. South Dakota. 1874-1975. *403*
—. Doukhobors. Saskatchewan. 1904. *415*
—. Equal opportunity. Hutterites. Leadership. Population. Prairie Provinces. Social Organization. Succession. 1940's-70's. *387*
—. Free thinkers. Iowa. Kneeland, Abner. Salubria (religious community). 1827-44. *383*
—. Frontier and Pioneer Life. Hutterites. Western states. 1874-1977. *429*
—. German Americans. Harmony Society. Indiana. Pennsylvania. Protestantism. Rapp, George. 1804-47. *425*
—. Holy Ghost and Us Society. *Kingdom Come, Ark of the Holy Ghost and US Society* (vessel). Nova Scotia. Sanford, Frank. Sects, Religious. Shipwrecks. 1910-48. *4261*
—. Kentucky (Pleasant Hill). Shakers. 1805-1922. *432*
—. Maine (Sabbathday Lake). Shakers. 1974. *395*
Communalism (review article). Fellman, Michael. Marriage. Muncy, Raymond Lee. Sex. Social Organization. 19c. 1973. *384*
Communes *See also* names of individual communes; Counter Culture; Utopias.
—. 1774-1886. *407*
—. Alberta. Farming. Mennonites. Namaka Farm. 1920's-40's. *414*
—. Aurora Colony. Music. Oregon. Pioneer Band. Society of Bethel. 1855-1920's. *1942*
—. California (Point Loma). Theosophy. Tingley, Katherine Augusta Westcott. Universal Brotherhood and Theosophical Society. 1897-1942. *4299*
—. Canada. Hutterites. USA. 1870's-1970. *412*

—. Christian Commonwealth Colony. Georgia (Columbus). Social gospel. 1896-1900. *397*
—. Christianity. Georgia. Jordan, Clarence. Koinonia Farm. 1942-60's. *402*
—. City Planning. Harmony Society. Indiana (New Harmony). Pennsylvania (Harmony, Economy). Social customs. 1820's-1905. *391*
—. Convents. Cults. Socialization. Tnevnoc Cult. 19c. 1970-79. *386*
—. Counter culture. Transcendence. 1960's-70's. *4246*
—. Economic conditions. Education. Mennonites, Old Order. Pennsylvania (East Penn Valley). 1949-75. *410*
—. German Americans. Keil, William. Letters. Missouri. Oregon. Society of Bethel. Weitling, Wilhelm. 1844-83. *405*
—. Labor Department. Library of Congress. Publications. Western states. 1830's-1930's. *430*
—. New Jersey (Perth Amboy, Red Bank). North American Phalanx. Raritan Bay Union. Spring, Marcus. 1843-59. *413*
—. Social Organization. 19c-1976. *422*
Communion. Canada. Protestantism. United Church of Canada. 1952-72. *3670*
—. Church of Scotland. Maine (Boothbay). Presbyterian Church. 1750-75. *3578*
—. Mather, Increase. Puritans. Sermons. ca 1680-1710. *3629*
—. New England. Puritanism. Stoddard, Solomon. 1679. *3614*
Communism *See also* Anarchism and Anarchists; Anti-Communist Movements; Leftism; Marxism; Socialism.
—. Antireligious Movements. Social gospel. USSR. 1921-26. *104*
—. Bibliographies. Christianity. 1970's. *2759*
—. Catholic Church. Jesuits. McCarthy, Joseph R. 1950-57. *1223*
Communist Party. Canada. Labour Party. Methodism. Smith, Albert Edward. Social Gospel. 1893-1924. *983*
Communists. Catholic Church. China. Missionaries. Protestant Churches. 1948-50. *1752*
Community centers. Country life movement. Progressives. Rural Settlements. 1900's-20's. *2447*
Competition. Abolition Movement. Attitudes. Economic conditions. Evangelicalism. Poverty. ca 1830-60. *2473*
—. Economic Growth. Mormons. Utah (southern). 500-1979. *4038*
Composers. Fry, William Henry. 1813-64. *1929*
—. Hymnals. Music. New England. Publishers and publishing. Thomas, Isaiah. 1784-19c. *1936*
—. Hymns. Mennonites. ca 1720-1860. *1908*
Compulsory Education *See also* Schools.
—. Catholic Church. Edwards Law (Illinois, 1889). Ethnic Groups. Illinois. Private schools. Public schools. State Politics. 1889-93. *551*
—. Church and State. Constitutional Amendments (1st). Parents. *Pierce* v. *Society of Sisters* (US, 1925). 1925. 1976. *587*
—. Hutterites. Legislation. South Dakota. Values. 1700-1970's. *659*
Comte, Auguste. Common Sense school. Philosophy. Positivism. Reformed churches. Social Gospel. Theology. ca 1850's-80's. *2833*
Concerts. California (Los Angeles). Cantors. Judaism. Loew's State Theatre. Music, liturgical. Rosenblatt, Josef "Yosele". Vaudeville. 1925. *1917*
Concord Baptist Association. Baptists, Southern. Ecumenism. Louisiana (Webster Parish). 1832-1972. *463*
Concordia College. Alberta (Edmonton, Mellowdale). Lutheran Church (Missouri Synod). Personal narratives. Schwermann, Albert H. USA. 1891-1976. *753*
Concordia Collegiate Institute. Lutheran Church. New Jersey (East Rutherford, Trenton). New York City (Brooklyn). Steege, Martin. 1921-73. *3343*
Concordia Historical Institute. Archives. Church History. Lutheran Church (Missouri Synod). Missouri (St. Louis). 1978. *221*
—. Bibliographies. Lutheran Church. Microforms. 1971-72. *265*
—. Farms. Lutheran Church (Missouri Synod). Missouri (Perry County). Preservation. Saxon Lutheran Memorial. 1958-64. *220*
—. Lutheran Church. Microforms. 1970-71. *266*
Concordia Publishing House. Buettner, George L. Lutheran Church (Missouri Synod). Missouri (St. Louis). Personal Narratives. Publishers and publishing. 1888-1955. *336*
Concordia Seminary. Academic freedom. Lutheran Church (Missouri Synod). Missouri (St. Louis). Teachers. Tenure. 1968-74. *771*
—. Autobiography. Buenger, Theodore Arthur. Clergy. German Americans. Lutheran Church (Missouri Synod). Seminaries. 1886-1909. *3297*
—. Baur, John C. Fund raising. Lutheran Church (Missouri Synod). Missouri (Clayton, St. Louis). Personal Narratives. 1923-26. *594*
—. Clergy. Illinois (Hahlen, Nashville). Lutheran Church (Missouri Synod). Personal narratives. St. Peter's Lutheran Church. Scharlemann, Ernst K. Seminaries. 1905-18. *3335*
—. Daily Life. Kansas (Clay Center). Lutheran Church (Missouri Synod). Mueller, Peter. Seminaries. Students. 1883-89. *707*
—. German Americans. Illinois (Springfield). Lutheran Church (Missouri Synod). Missouri (St. Louis). 1846-1938. *615*
Conewago Colony. Pennsylvania. Reformed Dutch Church. 1760's-70's. *3159*
Confederate Army *See also* Confederate States of America.
—. Catholic Church. Duke, Basil W. Fort Delaware. Prisoners of War. Wood, James F. 1864. *3844*
Confederate States of America *See also* names of individual states; Confederate Army; Reconstruction.
—. Conscientious objectors. Friends, Society of. North Carolina. 1861-65. *2708*
Conference for Education in the South. Bratton, Theodore DuBose. Episcopal Church, Protestant. Mississippi. Negroes. Racism. 1908. *2148*
Conference of Historic Peace Churches. Canada. Conscientious objectors. Mennonites. World War II. ca 1914-45. *2671*
Conference on Faith and History. Christianity. Historiography. 17c-1865. 1977. *237*
Conferences. Colleges and universities. Curricula. Dissertations. Jewish studies. 1979. *4138*
—. Colleges and universities. Dissertations. Jewish studies. 1978. *4137*
Confirmation. California (San Bernardino). Henrietta Hebrew Benevolent Society. Judaism (Reform). Religious Education. 1891. *788*
Conflict and Conflict Resolution. Catholic Church. Italian Americans. Rhode Island (Providence). 1890-1930. *3682*
—. Clergy. Laity. Protestantism. 19c-20c. *2954*
—. Presbyterian Church. Theology. 1960's-70's. *3550*
—. Unification Church. 1970's. *4266*
Congo Republic (Leopoldville). *See* Belgian Congo.
Congregatio de Propaganda Fide. Archival Catalogs and Inventories. France. North America. Vatican. 1622-1799. 1979. *182*
Congregation Ahavath Shalom. Judaism. Rhode Island (West Warwick). 1912-38. *4152*
Congregation Beth El. Cemeteries. Historic markers. Jews. Letters. Michigan (Detroit). 1850-1971. *4159*
—. Judaism. Michigan (Detroit). 1859-61. *4092*
—. Judaism. Michigan (Detroit). 1861-67. *4093*
Congregation Beth Elohim. Congregation Beth Elohim Unveh Shallom. Judaism (Orthodox). Portuguese Americans. South Carolina (Charleston). 1784-91. *4173*
Congregation Beth Elohim Unveh Shallom. Congregation Beth Elohim. Judaism (Orthodox). Portuguese Americans. South Carolina (Charleston). 1784-91. *4173*
Congregation Beth Ha Medrosh Hagodol. Adelman, Samuel. Colorado (Denver). Judaism (Conservative, Orthodox). Kauvar, Charles E. H. Rabbis. 1949-58. *4193*
—. Colorado (Denver). Judaism (Orthodox). Kauvar, Charles E. H. 1902-71. *4192*
—. Colorado (Denver). Judaism (Orthodox). Kauvar, Charles E. H. Progressivism. 1902-71. *4194*
Congregation Beth Israel. California (Oroville, San Francisco, Woodland). Judaism (Orthodox). Messing, Aron J. Religious education. Sabbath Schools. Travel. 1879. *4201*
—. California (San Bernardino). Fund raising. Judaism (Orthodox). Messing, Aron J. 1879. *4199*
Congregation Bickur Cholim. Beth Olam Cemetery. California (San Jose). Judaism (Orthodox, Reform). Organizations. 1850-1900. *4123*
Congregation Kahal Kadosh Beth Israel. Georgia (Macon). Judaism. Leeser, Isaac. Letters. Loewenthal, Henry. Rabbis. 1854-70. *4124*
Congregation Kahal Kadosh Shearith Israel. Ethnicity. Falkenau, Jacob J. M. Hebrew. Jews. Lyons, Jacques Judah. New York City. Pique, Dob. Poetry. 1786-1841. *2062*
Congregation Kol Ami. Ecumenism. Judaism. Utah (Salt Lake City). 1964-76. *482*
Congregation Sharey Tzedick. Judaism (Orthodox). Utah (Salt Lake City). 1916-48. *4195*
Congregation Shearith Israel. Cantors. Judaism (Orthodox). Netherlands. New York. Pinto, Joseph Jesurun. Travel. 1759-82. *4196*
—. Judaism (Orthodox). New York City. Rhode Island (Newport). Touro Synagogue. 1893-1902. *4183*
Congregation Sons of Zion. Finesilver, Moses Ziskind. Judaism. Rabbis. Rhode Island (Providence). 1880-83. *4122*
Congregational Library. Education. Massachusetts (Boston). 19c-20c. *195*
Congregationalism *See also* Calvinism; Puritans; Unitarianism; United Church of Christ.
—. Abbott, Lyman. Clergy. New York (Cornwall-on-the-Hudson). Parsons, Edward Smith. Personal narratives. 1885. *3136*
—. Abolition Movement. Andover Seminary. Massachusetts. Seminaries. Theology. 1825-35. *2491*
—. Abolition Movement. Christology. Clergy. Negroes. New York. Ward, Samuel Ringgold. 1839-51. *2462*
—. Adolescence. Baptists. Finney, Charles G. Massachusetts (Boston). Methodism. Revivals. 1822-42. *2258*
—. Africa. Missions and Missionaries. Presbyterian Church. Reformed Dutch Church. Reformed German Church. 19c-20c. *1709*
—. African Society. Colonization. Freedmen. Hopkins, Samuel. Rhode Island (Providence). Sierra Leone. 1789-95. *2459*
—. Albanese, Catherine L. Beecher family. Caskey, Marie. Connecticut. Massachusetts. Presbyterian Church. Transcendentalism (review article). Unitarianism. 1800-60. *2763*
—. Allen, Thomas ("Vindication"). American Revolution. Clergy. Constitutions, State. Ideology. Massachusetts (Berkshire County). 1778. *1371*
—. American Board of Commissioners for Foreign Missions. Bingham family. Gilbert Islands. Hawaii. Missions and Missionaries. 1820-1975. *1678*
—. American Missionary Association. Education. Freedmen. Georgia (Liberty County). 1870-80's. *549*
—. American Missionary Association. Missions and Missionaries. Negroes. South. 1846-80. *1617*
—. American Revolution. American Revolution. Cleaveland, John. Daily life. Great Awakening. Ideology. Jedrey, Christopher M. (review article). Massachusetts (Chebacco). New Lights. 1740-79. *2241*
—. American Revolution. Antislavery Sentiments. Hopkins, Samuel. Rhode Island (Newport). ca 1770-1803. *2464*
—. American Revolution. Baptists. Church of England. Friends, Society of. Georgia. Judaism. Lutheran Church. Presbyterian Church. 1733-90. *88*
—. American Revolution. Brattle Street Church. Calvinism. Cooper, Samuel. Elites. Massachusetts (Boston). 1754-83. *1333*
—. American Revolution. Brattle Street Church. Clergy. Cooper, Samuel. Massachusetts (Boston). 1770-80. *951*
—. American Revolution. Chauncy, Charles. Church and State. Great Britain. Letters. Price, Richard. Slavery. 1727-87. *3129*
—. American Revolution. Chauncy, Charles. Clergy. New England. 1770's. *1269*
—. American Revolution. Clergy. Presbyterian Church. Social status. 1774-1800. *2849*
—. American Revolution. Cooper, Samuel. Massachusetts (Boston). Rhetoric. Sermons. 1768-80. *1352*
—. American Union for the Relief and Improvement of the Colored Race. Emancipation. Massachusetts (Boston). Reform. 1835-37. *2490*
—. Anti-Catholicism. Cox, Samuel Hanson. Ecumenism. Episcopal Church, Protestant. Evangelicalism. Presbyterian Church, New School. Slavery. 1840's. *471*
—. Antislavery Sentiments. Connecticut. Dwight, Theodore. Poetry. 1788-1829. *2468*

—. Architecture. Banner, Peter. First Congregational Society Church. New York. Vermont (Burlington). 1794-1815. *1829*
—. Architecture. Brattle Street Church. Dawes, Thomas. Massachusetts (Boston). 18c. *1771*
—. Architecture (Gothic Revival). Churches. Iowa (Iowa City). Randall, Gurdon Paine. 1868-69. *1822*
—. Archives. Manuscripts. Stiles, Ezra. Yale University. 1748-1975. *3142*
—. Arkansas (Texarkana). Maddox, Finis Ewing. Presbyterian Church. Schisms. Theology. 1908. *2869*
—. Arminiamism. Church of England. Converts. Johnson, Samuel (1696-1772). New England. Sacramentalism. 1715-22. *3183*
—. Art. Calvinism. Dow, Arthur Wesley. Massachusetts (Ipswich). Methodist Church. 1857-80. *1871*
—. Attitudes. Baptists, Southern. Buddhism. Death and Dying. Hawaii (Honolulu). 1977. *131*
—. Attitudes. Dwight, Timothy. New England. New York. Travel (accounts). Wilderness. 1790's. *2066*
—. Autobiography. Edwards, Jonathan. Identity. Theology. 1729-58. *3152*
—. Baldwin, Theron. Higher education. Presbyterianism. Society for the Promotion of Collegiate and Theological Education at the West. 1843-73. *629*
—. Baptists. Church and state. Massachusetts (Swansea). Rhode Island (Barrington). 1711-46. *1082*
—. Baptists. Church and state. Meetinghouses. New Hampshire (Acworth). Taxation. Toleration Act (New Hampshire, 1819). Universalists. 1783-1822. *1113*
—. Beach, John. Church of England. Clergy. Connecticut. Heresy. 1720-82. *3204*
—. Beauty, perception of. Edwards, Jonathan. Knowledge. Mental activity theory. New England. 1730-69. *2323*
—. Beecher, Catharine. Church of England. Johnson, Samuel (1696-1772). Reform (review article). Washington, Booker T. Women. 1696-1901. *2847*
—. Beecher, Lyman. Dwight, Timothy. New England. Presbyterian Church. Republicanism. Taylor, Nathaniel William. 1790-1840. *1356*
—. Bible. Clergy. Edwards, Jonathan. Marginalia. Massachusetts (Deerfield). Pierpont, Benjamin. Theology. 1726-30. *3146*
—. Bible. Edwards, Jonathan. Hermeneutics. Massachusetts. 1720-58. *3149*
—. Bibliographies. Canada. Historiography. Lutheran Church. Methodist Church. Presbyterian Church. United Church of Canada. 1825-1973. *2892*
—. Bingham Family. Hawaii. Micronesia. Missions and Missionaries. Yale University Library (Bingham Family Papers). 1815-1967. *1714*
—. Bingham, Hiram. Converts. Family. Missions and Missionaries. Vermont. 1789-1819. *1585*
—. Breck, Robert. Connecticut (Scotland). Edwards, Jonathan. Massachusetts (Northampton). 1734-36. *3127*
—. Bross, Harmon. Nebraska. 1873-1928. *3125*
—. Buckminster, Joseph Stevens. Massachusetts (Boston). Unitarianism. 1804-12. *3116*
—. Burg, B. R. Clergy (review article). Mather, Richard. New England. Youngs, J. William T., Jr. ca 1700-50. 1976. *3124*
—. Bushnell, Horace. Church and state. Jefferson, Thomas. ca 1800-60. *1002*
—. Bushnell, Horace. Clergy. Elites. Theology. 19c. *3114*
—. California (San Diego). Chinese Mission School. Education. 1885-1960. *535*
—. Calvinism. Government, Resistance to. Massachusetts (Boston). Mayhew, Jonathan. Political Theory. Sermons. 1750. *1381*
—. Captivity narratives. Catholic Church. French Canadians. Indians. New England. Williams, John *(The Redeemed Captive)*. 1704-06. *3133*
—. Charles I. Folklore. Regicide. Rhode Island. Stiles, Ezra. Whale, Theophilus. 17c. 1755-85. *3131*
—. Cheever, Thomas. Clergy. Documents. Massachusetts. 1677-1749. *3122*
—. Childbirth. Death and Dying. Diaries. Diseases. Massachusetts (Westborough). Parkman, Ebenezer. Social Organization. 1724-82. *1447*
—. Choctaw Indians. Harkins, Richard. Missions and Missionaries. Murder. Slavery. 1858-59. *3132*
—. Church and Social Problems. Indian-White Relations. Local Politics. Massachusetts (Natick). Meetinghouses. 1650-18c. *3118*
—. Church and State. Church of England. Connecticut. Factionalism. Great Awakening. Officeholding. 1730-76. *1310*
—. Church location. Economic conditions. Maryland (Baltimore). Protestantism. 1840-70. *2853*
—. Church Membership. Conservatism. Massachusetts (Granville). 1754-76. *2247*
—. Church of England. Clergy. New England. Vestries. 1630-1775. *312*
—. Church of England. Connecticut. Great Britain. Johnson, Samuel (1696-1772). Ordination. Yale University. 1722-23. *2843*
—. Church of England. Connecticut (New Haven). Conversion. Johnson, Samuel (1696-1772). Theology. Yale University. 1710-22. *3177*
—. Church of England. Cutler, Timothy. Edwards, Jonathan. Gibson, Edmund. Great Awakening. Letters. New England. Stoddard, Solomon. 1739. *2263*
—. Church of England. Cutler, Timothy. Massachusetts. 1720-30. *1056*
—. Church of England. Harvard University. Yale University. ca 1722-90. *660*
—. Church of England. Kennebec Purchase Company. Land. Massachusetts. 1759-75. *352*
—. Cities. Gladden, Washington. Ohio (Columbus). Reform. Social gospel. 1850's-1914. *2425*
—. City Government. Massachusetts (Tiverton). Provincial Legislatures. Religious liberty. Taxation. 1692-1724. *1084*
—. Clergy. Columbia River. Fort Vancouver. Hawaiians. Hudson's Bay Company. Kaulehelehe, William R. Washington. 1845-69. *3128*
—. Clergy. Franklin, Benjamin. Massachusetts (Boston). *New England Courant* (newspaper). Smallpox. *Spectator* (newspaper). 1720-23. *2023*
—. Clergy. Great Awakening. New England. New Lights. Old Lights. Social Classes. 1734-85. *2627*
—. Clergy. Herron, George David. Iowa College. National Christian Citizen League. Populism. Progressivism. Socialism. 1880's-1900. *2561*
—. Clergy. Maine (York). Moody, Samuel. 1700-47. *3137*
—. Clergy. Massachusetts (Ipswich). Wigglesworth, Samuel. 1714-68. *3138*
—. Clergy. New England. 1700-60. *3141*
—. Clergy. New England. Presbyterian Church. Professionalism. Scott, Donald M. (review article). 1750-1850. 1979. *2865*
—. Clergy (dismissal). New Hampshire. Presbyterian Church. Social change. 1633-1790. *2885*
—. Colby, Abby M. Feminism. Japan. Missions and Missionaries. 1879-1914. *932*
—. Cole, Nathan ("Spiritual Travels"). Great Awakening. Whitefield, George. 1740-65. *2227*
—. Colleges and Universities. Dwight, Timothy. Human Relations. Stiles, Ezra. Yale University. 1778-95. *706*
—. Colleges and Universities. Florida (Winter Park). Hooker, Edward P. Rollins College. 1885-1900. *678*
—. Connecticut. Evangelism. Revivals. Vermont. 1781-1803. *1609*
—. Connecticut. Free Thinkers. Frontier and Pioneer Life. Ingersoll, Robert. Ohio (Western Reserve). Wright, Elizur (and family). Yale University. 1762-1870. *56*
—. Connecticut. Girls. Indian-White Relations. Religious Education. Wheelock, Eleazar. 1761-69. *766*
—. Connecticut. Hawaii. Kanui, William Tennooe. Missions and Missionaries. Protestant Churches. 1796-1864. *1493*
—. Connecticut. Stiles, Ezra. Theology. Thomism. 1792-94. *3130*
—. Connecticut (Canterbury). Family. Great Awakening. Local politics. Schisms. 1742-50. *2242*
—. Connecticut (New London). Great Awakening. New Lights. Schisms. Shepherd's Tent (college). 1720-50. *2250*
—. Connecticut (New London). Great Awakening. New Lights. Shepherd's Tent (college). 1742-46. *774*
—. Connecticut (Windham). Conversion. Great Awakening. Social Change. 1723-43. *2274*
—. Connecticut (Windham). Converts. Great Awakening. Social change. 1721-43. *2273*
—. Conversion. Great Awakening. Massachusetts (Freetown). Personal narratives. 1749-70. *2221*
—. Converts. Episcopal Church, Protestant. Kilbourne, James. Letters. Ohio (Worthington). Pioneers. 1844-49. *2823*
—. Converts. Japan. Massachusetts. Shimeta, Neesima. Voyages. 1860's-90. *1701*
—. Cooper, Samuel. Funerals. Music. New England. Sermons. Social Customs. 18c. *3113*
—. Covenant theology. Iconography. Theology. Tombstones. Vermont (Grafton, Rockingham). 1770-1803. *1896*
—. Dark Day. New England. Stiles, Ezra. Weather. 1780. *2326*
—. Decorative Arts. Interior decoration. Rhode Island (Newport). United Congregational Church. 1879-80. *1897*
—. Democracy. Massachusetts. Political thought. Wise, John. 17c-18c. *1354*
—. Diaries. Hawaii. Missions and Missionaries. Tahitians. Toketa (teacher). 1820's-30's. *1676*
—. Drummer, Jeremiah. Letters. Massachusetts. Sabbath. Sewall, Samuel. Taylor, Edward. 1704. *2276*
—. Dwight, Timothy. New England. Political attitudes. 1775-1817. *1369*
—. Dwight, Timothy *(Travels in New England and New York)*. Northeastern or North Atlantic States. 1796-1815. *2022*
—. Education. New Mexico (Albuquerque). Prohibition. Social gospel. 1900-17. *2448*
—. Edwards, Jonathan. Epistemology. Science. 1703-58. *2327*
—. Edwards, Jonathan. Goen, C. C. (review essay). Great Awakening. Revivals. 1734-1751. *2224*
—. Edwards, Jonathan. Great Awakening. Intellectuals. Massachusetts (Northampton, Stockbridge). Theology. Youth. ca 1730-1880. *3150*
—. Edwards, Jonathan. Historiography (revisionist). Literature. 1758-1903. *3143*
—. Edwards, Jonathan. Hopkins, Samuel. New Divinity (doctrines). New England. Social reform. Theology. 1730-1803. *2373*
—. Edwards, Jonathan. Judaism. Luria, Isaac. Millenarianism. Progress, concept of. 16c-18c. *84*
—. Edwards, Jonathan. Massachusetts (Northampton). Prayer petitions. 1730-49. *3147*
—. Edwards, Jonathan. New York. Presbyterian Church. Sermons. 1722-23. *2883*
—. Edwards, Jonathan. Philosophy. Theological empiricism. 1740-46. *3145*
—. Edwards, Jonathan. Rainbows. Science. Theology. 1740-45. *2343*
—. Edwards, Jonathan. Transcendentalism. ca 1725-58. *3135*
—. Edwards, Jonathan *(History of the Work of Redemption)*. Historians. 18c. 1976. *3156*
—. Evangelism. Far Western States. Mormons. Nutting, John Danforth. Photographs. Utah Gospel Mission. 1900-50. *1560*
—. Evangelism. New Divinity movement. New England, western. 1740-1800. *3117*
—. Exiles. Great Britain. Hooker, Thomas. Netherlands. New England. Theology. 1631-33. *3650*
—. Family. Methodism. Mormons. New England. New York, western. Young, Brigham. 18c-1830's. *2840*
—. Finney, Charles G. New York (Oneida County). Presbyterian Church. Revivals. 1825-27. *2245*
—. Fish, Josiah. Osborn, Sarah. Revivals. Rhode Island (Newport). Women. 1766-67. *904*
—. Folk Art. Massachusetts. Peckham, Robert. Portraits. ca 1838-44. *1861*
—. Friends, Society of. Women. ca 1620-1765. *834*
—. Georgia (Atlanta). Negroes. Social Work. 1886-1970. *2432*
—. Great Awakening. New England. Ordination. Parkman, Ebenezer. 1630-1740. *3157*
—. Guidebooks. Illinois. Immigration. Thomas, Robert D. *(Hanes Cymry America)*. Welsh Americans. 19c. *3119*
—. Guidebooks. Immigration. Iowa. Thomas, Robert D. *(Hanes Cymry America)*. Welsh Americans. 1790-1890. *3155*

—. Guidebooks. Immigration. Kansas. Thomas, Robert D. *(Hanes Cymry America).* Welsh Americans. 1838-84. *3121*
—. Guidebooks. Immigration. Missouri. Thomas, Robert D. *(Hanes Cymry America).* Welsh Americans. 1872. *3120*
—. Harvard University. Latin language. Leverett, John. Massachusetts (Cambridge). Speeches, Addresses, etc. 1722. *668*
—. Harvard University (Hollis Professorship of Divinity). Latin language. Rhetoric. Wigglesworth, Edward. 1722. *667*
—. Hawaiian Evangelical Association. Missions and Missionaries. Siu Pheong Aheong. ca 1838-76. *1687*
—. Historians. Massachusetts (Boston). Old South Church. Prince, Thomas. 1718-58. *275*
—. Minnesota (Minneapolis). Social gospel. 1850-90. *2410*
—. Missions and Missionaries. Nationalism. Social Gospel. Strong, Josiah. Wyoming (Cheyenne). 1871-1916. *3134*
—. Mormon, Book of. Spalding, Solomon. 1761-1816. *2796*
—. New York (Rochester). Plymouth Church. 1853-1904. *3115*
Congregations. Clergy. Morality. Sermons. 1970's. *2904*
Congress *See also* House of Representatives; Legislation; Senate.
—. Hayes, Rutherford B. Mormons. Polygamy. Suffrage. Women. 1877-81. *797*
Congress of Jewish Women. American, Sadie. Jews. Solomon, Hannah G. Women. World Parliament of Religions. World's Columbian Exposition (Chicago, 1893). 1893. *846*
Connecticut *See also* New England; Northeastern or North Atlantic States.
—. Albanese, Catherine L. Beecher family. Caskey, Marie. Congregationalism. Massachusetts. Presbyterian Church. Transcendentalism (review article). Unitarianism. 1800-60. *2763*
—. American Revolution (antecedents). Church and state. Devotion, Ebenezer. Politics. Theology. 1714-71. *1397*
—. Antislavery Sentiments. Congregationalism. Dwight, Theodore. Poetry. 1788-1829. *2468*
—. Beach, John. Church of England. Clergy. Congregationalism. Heresy. 1720-82. *3204*
—. Bibliographies. Massachusetts. Witchcraft. 17c. 1976. *2194*
—. Church and State. Church of England. Congregationalism. Factionalism. Great Awakening. Officeholding. 1730-76. *1310*
—. Church of England. Congregationalism. Great Britain. Johnson, Samuel (1696-1772). Ordination. Yale University. 1722-23. *2843*
—. Church of England. Letters. Missions and Missionaries. Muirson, George. New York. ca 1697-1708. *1535*
—. Congregationalism. Evangelism. Revivals. Vermont. 1781-1803. *1609*
—. Congregationalism. Free Thinkers. Frontier and Pioneer Life. Ingersoll, Robert. Ohio (Western Reserve). Wright, Elizur (and family). Yale University. 1762-1870. *56*
—. Congregationalism. Girls. Indian-White Relations. Religious Education. Wheelock, Eleazar. 1761-69. *766*
—. Congregationalism. Hawaii. Kanui, William Tennooe. Missions and Missionaries. Protestant Churches. 1796-1864. *1493*
—. Congregationalism. Stiles, Ezra. Theology. Thomism. 1792-94. *3130*
—. Constitutional Law. Government. Hooker, Thomas. Puritans. 1635-39. *3603*
—. Ethics. Fitch, James. Land. Politics. Puritans. 1679-1727. *3646*
—. Great Awakening (antecedents). Protestantism. 1700's-40's. *2256*
Connecticut (Canterbury). Congregationalism. Family. Great Awakening. Local politics. Schisms. 1742-50. *2242*
—. Maine (Sabbathday Lake). Shakers. Theology. Utopias. 1774-1974. *434*
Connecticut (Cornwall). American Board of Commissioners for Foreign Missions. Assimilation. Foreign Mission School. Indian-White Relations. Students. 1816-27. *586*
Connecticut, eastern. Tombstones. Wheeler, Obadiah. 1702-49. *1886*
Connecticut (Enfield). Edwards, Jonathan ("Sinners in the Hands of an Angry God"). Sermons. Theology. 1741. *1994*
Connecticut (Hartford). Democratic Party. Ethnic groups. Middle Classes. Protestantism. Voting and Voting Behavior. 1896-1940. *1203*
—. Episcopal Church, Protestant. Evangelicalism. Literature. Sigourney, Lydia Huntley. Women. 1800-65. *3194*
—. Judaism. 1880-1929. *4089*
Connecticut (Milford). Family. Puritans. 1639-90's. *897*
Connecticut (New Britain). Americanization. Catholic Church. Polish Americans. 1890-1955. *3692*
—. Assimilation. Catholic Church. Holy Cross Church. Polish Americans. 1928-76. *3693*
—. Bójnowski, Lucyan. Buczek, Daniel Stephen (review article). Catholic Church. Clergy. Polish Americans. 1895-1960. *3865*
Connecticut (New Haven). Catholic Church. Ethnic Groups. Jews. Marriage. Protestantism. 1900-50. *906*
—. Church of England. Congregationalism. Conversion. Johnson, Samuel (1696-1772). Theology. Yale University. 1710-22. *3177*
—. City Planning. Puritans. 1628-39. *3598*
—. Negroes. Pentecostal movement. Prayer meetings. Psychology. Social conditions. 1978. *3521*
Connecticut (New London). Congregationalism. Great Awakening. New Lights. Schisms. Shepherd's Tent (college). 1720-50. *2250*
—. Congregationalism. Great Awakening. New Lights. Shepherd's Tent (college). 1742-46. *774*
Connecticut (Norfield). American Revolution. Protestantism. Sermons. Sherwood, Samuel. 1776. *1414*
Connecticut (Scotland). Breck, Robert. Congregationalism. Edwards, Jonathan. Massachusetts (Northampton). 1734-36. *3127*
Connecticut Valley. Folk art. Sun faces (motif). Tombstones. Vermont (Rockingham). 1786-1812. *1842*
—. Great Awakening. Massachusetts (Hatfield). Presbyterian Church. Williams, William. 1686-1741. *2240*
Connecticut (Waterbury). Assimilation. Catholic Church. Lithuanian Americans. *Rytas* (newspaper). Zebris, Joseph. 1896-98. *3901*
Connecticut (Windham). Congregationalism. Conversion. Great Awakening. Social Change. 1723-43. *2274*
—. Congregationalism. Converts. Great Awakening. Social change. 1721-43. *2273*
Conroy, George. Apostolic Delegates. Catholic Church. Nationalism. Politics. Quebec. Vatican. 1877-78. *1098*
—. Canada. Catholic Church. Papal legates. 1873-77. *3883*
Conscientious Objectors *See also* Conscription, Military.
—. American Revolution. Loyalists. Maryland (Elizabethtown). Mennonites. 1774-76. *2665*
—. American Revolution (antecedents). Dunkards. Mennonites. Pennsylvania. Petitions. 1775. *2710*
—. Bethel College. Mennonites. Oral history. World War I. 1917-18. 1974. *262*
—. Camp Funston. Diaries. Hutterites. Kansas. Waldner, Jakob. World War I. 1917-18. *2690*
—. Canada. Conference of Historic Peace Churches. Mennonites. World War II. ca 1914-45. *2671*
—. Catholics. World War II. 1941-45. *2672*
—. Christianity. Vietnam War. 1960's-70's. *2653*
—. Church and State. Church schools. Holidays. Prayer. Public finance. Public Schools. Religious Liberty. Supreme Court. 1950-70's. *1112*
—. Confederate States of America. Friends, Society of. North Carolina. 1861-65. *2708*
—. Constitutional Amendments (2d). Federal government. Friends, Society of. Madison, James. Military service. States' Rights. 1787-92. *2686*
—. Courts. Flag salute. Jehovah's Witnesses. World War II. 1930's-40's. *2655*
—. Mennonites. Oral History. World War I. 1917-20. *2660*
Conscription, Military *See also* Conscientious Objectors; Military Recruitment.
—. Anti-Catholicism. Jesuits. Novitiate of St. Stanislaus. Ontario (Guelph). Protestantism. World War I. 1918-19. *2657*
—. Civilian service. Mennonites. World War II. 1930's-45. *2661*
—. German Americans. Mennonites. Pacifism. Public Opinion. World War I. 1914-18. *2696*
Consensus. Ideology. National Characteristics. Puritans. 1630-1865. *1345*
Conservatism. Abolition movement. Clergy. Constitutions. Massachusetts (Boston). Missouri (St. Louis). Unitarianism. 1828-57. *1413*
—. Arts. Baptists, Southern. Denominationalism. Folk art. 1975. *1877*
—. Asians. Immigration. Methodist Episcopal Church. Social Gospel. 1865-1908. *2404*
—. Assimilation. Brethren, Old German Baptist. 1881-1977. *3413*
—. Attitudes. Religious beliefs. Social Surveys. 1970-74. *1380*
—. Baptists. Evangelism. Graham, Billy. Morality. 1940's-70's. *2215*
—. Bureaucracies. Presbyterian Church, Southern (administration). Roberts, William Henry. Theology. 1884-1920. *3541*
—. Candler, Warren A. Evolution. Leopold, Nathan. Loeb, Richard. Methodist Episcopal Church, South. Scopes, John Thomas. Trials. 1921-41. *2293*
—. Catholic Church. Corrigan, Michael. Economic Theory. George, Henry. McGlynn, Edward. New York. 1886-94. *2562*
—. Catholic Church. Nativism. Newspapers. Political Commentary. Protestantism. *Providence Visitor* (newspaper). Rhode Island. 1916-24. *2118*
—. Catholic Church. Politics. 1970's. *970*
—. Christianity. Meyer, Frank Straus. Theology. 1909-72. *1362*
—. Christianity. Philosophy. South. Weaver, Richard M. ca 1930-63. *1363*
—. Church Membership. Congregationalism. Massachusetts (Granville). 1754-76. *2247*
—. Ideology. Puritanism. 17c. *1361*
—. Liberalism. Mennonites. Ontario (Waterloo County). 1977. *3368*
—. Niebuhr, Reinhold. 20c. *1394*
—. Presbyterian Church. Smyth, Thomas. Social theory. South Carolina. Theology. 1831-70. *3552*
—. Protestants. Quebec (Montreal). Social Reform. Women's Protective Immigration Society. 1882-1917. *919*
Consortium of Peace Research, Education and Development. Colleges and Universities. Mennonites. North America. Peace Studies. 1965-80. *2650*
Conspiracies. American Revolution. Church of England. Llewelyn, John. Loyalists. North Carolina. 1776-77. *1224*
Conspiracy theories. Anti-Catholicism. Anti-Semitism. Fundamentalism. Kansas. Political Commentary. Winrod, Gerald Burton. 1933-57. *2090*
Constitutional Amendments *See also* specific amendments, e.g. Constitutional Amendment (14th).
—. Christianity. Presbyterian Church. Strong, William. Supreme Court. 1864-80. *3588*
—. Civil War. Fundamentalism. Lincoln, Abraham. National Fast Day. National Reform Association. 1787-1945. *1009*
Constitutional Amendments, State. Ohio. Prohibition. Women's Christian Temperance Union. 1874-85. *2597*
Constitutional Amendments (1st). Authority. Health. Religious liberty. Supreme Court. 1963-79. *1439*
—. Berns, Walter (review article). Church and state. Supreme Court. 18c-20c. *1114*
—. Burger, Warren E. Church and state. Church schools. Supreme Court. 1950-75. *602*
—. Church and State. Compulsory education. Parents. *Pierce* v. *Society of Sisters* (US, 1925). 1925. 1976. *587*
—. Church Property. Courts. Kentucky (Louisville). Presbyterian Church. Walnut Street Presbyterian Church. *Watson* v. *Jones* (US, 1860). 1860-1970. *1129*
—. Church Schools. Education, Finance. Government. Religion in the public schools. 1950's-70's. *564*
—. Church Schools. State Aid to Education. Supreme Court. 1970's. *728*
—. Courts. Religious liberty. 1878-1972. *1038*
—. Religious liberty. 1960's-75. *1092*
Constitutional Amendments (2nd). Conscientious objection. Federal government. Friends, Society of. Madison, James. Military service. States' Rights. 1787-92. *2686*

Constitutional Amendments (15th). Abolition movement. Douglass, Frederick. Negroes. Theology. 1825-86. *2495*
Constitutional Amendments (21st). Adventists. Prohibition (repeal). 1932-34. *2598*
—. Mormons. Prohibition (repeal). Utah. 1932-33. *2587*
Constitutional conventions, state. Church and State. Civil religion. Massachusetts. Rebellions. 1780. *1071*
Constitutional Law *See also* Citizenship; Civil Rights; Democracy; Federal Government; Legislation; Political Science; Referendum; Suffrage.
—. Anti-Catholicism. Ireland. Irish Americans. O'Conor, Charles. O'Conor, Charles Owen. Political reform. Reconstruction. 1865-85. *1031*
—. Catholic Church. Church Schools. Elementary Education. Federal aid to education. 1960's-72. *691*
—. Church and state. Church Schools. 1930's-70's. *729*
—. Church and state. Fund raising. Local Government. State Government. 1970's. *1059*
—. Connecticut. Government. Hooker, Thomas. Puritans. 1635-39. *3603*
—. Morality. Mormons. Polygamy. Religious Liberty. *Reynolds* v. *United States* (US, 1878). Supreme Court. 1862-78. *1024*
Constitutionalism. American Revolution. Historiography. Law. Politics. 1775-83. 1790-1950. *961*
Constitutions. Abolition movement. Clergy. Conservatism. Massachusetts (Boston). Missouri (St. Louis). Unitarianism. 1828-57. *1413*
—. American Revolution. Baptists. Massachusetts. 1644-1806. *979*
—. Antifederalists. Federalists. Religious liberty. 1776-92. *1010*
—. Church and State. Colleges and Universities. Religious studies. Supreme Court. 1970's. *578*
—. Founding fathers. Historiography. Political Theory. Theology. 18c. *1405*
—. Mormons. Smith, Joseph. Speeches, Addresses, etc. 1840. *1374*
Constitutions, State. Abolition Movement. Breckinridge, Robert Jefferson. Breckinridge, William Lewis. Emancipation Party. Kentucky. Presbyterians. 1849. *2475*
—. Allen, Thomas ("Vindication"). American Revolution. Clergy. Congregationalism. Ideology. Massachusetts (Berkshire County). 1778. *1371*
—. New Jersey. North Carolina. Pennsylvania. Presbyterian Church. 1775-87. *1285*
Construction *See also* Architecture.
—. British Columbia (Bennett). Presbyterian Church. St. Andrew's Church. 1898. *1820*
—. Catholic Church. Church of St. John the Evangelist. Rhode Island (Newport). 1883-1934. *1772*
—. Catholic church. City Politics. Contractors. Irish Americans. Pennsylvania (Philadelphia). 1846-1960's. *338*
—. Friends, Society of. Historic Preservation. Meetinghouses. Rhode Island (Newport). 1657-1974. *1838*
Construction crews. Canadian Pacific Railway. Clergy. Manitoba (Virden). McLeod, Finlay J. C. Personal narratives. Presbyterian Church. 1881-82. *3567*
Consultation on Church Union. Clergy. Henderlite, Rachel. Personal narratives. Presbyterian Church, Southern. South. Women. 1945-77. *804*
Consultation on the Religious Communities, the Arts and the Second American Revolution. Arts. Bicentennial Celebrations. 1973. *1846*
Consumers. Boycotts. Jews. Meat, kosher. New York City. Prices. Riots. Women. 1902. *4112*
Contemplative ideal. Catholic Church. Merton, Thomas. Monasticism. 1940's-68. *3858*
Continental Congress. Aitken, Robert. Bible. English language. Pennsylvania (Philadelphia). Publishers and Publishing. 1782. *1979*
—. Aitken, Robert. Bible. Publishers and Publishing. 1777-82. *1983*
—. American Revolution. Church of England. Loyalists. Seabury, Samuel (pseud. A. W. Farmer). 1774-84. *1378*
Contractors. Catholic church. City Politics. Construction. Irish Americans. Pennsylvania (Philadelphia). 1846-1960's. *338*
Convents. Communes. Cults. Socialization. Tnevnoc Cult. 19c. 1970-79. *386*
Converse, Amasa. Censorship. *Christian Observer* (newspaper). Civil War. Presbyterian Church. 1861-65. *1115*
Conversion. Addiction. Jesus Movement. 1960's-75. *2784*
—. Baptists, Seventh-Day. Daland, William C. Friedlaender, Herman. Jews. New York City. *Peculiar People* (newspaper). 1880's-90's. *1633*
—. Behavior. Graham, Billy. Revivals. 1968-75. *2275*
—. Catholic Church. France (Alsace). Immigration policy. Louisiana. Protestants. 1753-59. *3719*
—. Church of England. Congregationalism. Connecticut (New Haven). Johnson, Samuel (1696-1772). Theology. Yale University. 1710-22. *3177*
—. Congregationalism. Connecticut (Windham). Great Awakening. Social Change. 1723-43. *2274*
—. Congregationalism. Great Awakening. Massachusetts (Freetown). Personal narratives. 1749-70. *2221*
—. Cultic milieu. UFO cults. 1970's. *4241*
—. Eastern Religions. Mysticism. Psychotherapy. 1970's. *2290*
—. Edwards, Jonathan *(History of the Work of Redemption).* Philosophy of History. Theology. 1739. *3140*
—. Germany. Great Britain. Lutheran Church. Pietism. Puritanism. 17c-18c. *2942*
—. Hooker, Thomas. Preparationism. Puritans. Ramus, Petrus. Shepard, Thomas. Theology. 1608-49. *3643*
—. Jesus Movement. Models. 1970's. *2770*
—. New England. Puritans. Semiology. Theology. 1600's. *3612*
—. Preparationism. Puritans. Stoddard, Solomon. Taylor, Edward. Theology. 1690-94. *3642*
—. Religiosity. 1970's. *138*
Conversion thesis. California. Cook, Sherburne Friend. Franciscans. Indians. Missions and Missionaries. ca 1790-1820's. 1943. *1541*
Converts. 1960's-70's. *118*
—. 1970's. *145*
—. Alienation. Christianity. Cults. Human potential movement. Social indicators. 1960's-70's. *143*
—. American Baptist Publishing Society. Baptists. Immigration. Lutheran Church. Sweden. Travel (accounts). Wiberg, Anders. 1852-53. *3054*
—. Annexation. Catholic Church. Imperialism. Methodist Episcopal Church. Missions and Missionaries. Philippines. 1899-1913. *1689*
—. Arizona. Barth, Solomon. Frontier. Jews. Mormons. 1856-1928. *60*
—. Arminiamism. Church of England. Congregationalism. Johnson, Samuel (1696-1772). New England. Sacramentalism. 1715-22. *3183*
—. Attitudes. Autobiography. Brownson, Orestes A. *(The Convert).* Catholic Church. Great Britain. Newman, John Henry *(Apologia pro Vita Sua).* Protestantism. 1857-64. *3681*
—. Attitudes. California (Berkeley). Davis, Rennie. Divine Light Mission. Maharaj Ji. Politics. 1973. *4286*
—. Baptists. Evangelism. Louisiana (New Orleans). Methodism. Slavery. 1800-61. *2916*
—. Bingham, Hiram. Congregationalism. Family. Missions and Missionaries. Vermont. 1789-1819. *1585*
—. Blair, James. Church of England. Church of Scotland. College of William and Mary. Virginia. 1679-1720. *2924*
—. British Columbia (Vancouver Island). Immigration. Missions and Missionaries. Mormons. 1875-1979. *1669*
—. California, northern. Ghost Dance. Indians. Methodist Church. Round Valley Indian Reservation. 1870. *3484*
—. California (Santa Cruz). Judaism. Schlutius, Emma. 1877. *4098*
—. Catholic Church. Christian Renaissance. Literature. Philosophy. Science. Stern, Karl. 1920's-60's. *2758*
—. Catholic Church. Clergy. Episcopal Church, Protestant. Richey, James Arthur Morrow. ca 1900-33. *2754*
—. Catholic Church. Marriage. Protestantism. 1960's-70's. *848*
—. Chambers, Samuel D. (testimonies). Mormons. Negroes. Slavery. Utah (Salt Lake City). 1844-76. *4059*
—. Child-rearing. Protestant Churches. Psychology. Religious Education. Sunday schools. 19c. *603*
—. Children of God. Christianity. Sex. 1970's. *2793*
—. Christ Communal Organization. Fundamentalism. Models. 1970's. *2917*
—. Christianity. Earthquakes. Mississippi River. Missouri. New Madrid Earthquake. 1811-12. *2789*
—. Christianity. Idaho. Murder. Orchard, Harry. 1899-1906. *2760*
—. Clergy. Episcopal Church, Protestant. Lutheran Church. Sweden. Unonius, Gustaf. Wisconsin (Pine Lake). 1841-58. *2854*
—. Congregationalism. Connecticut (Windham). Great Awakening. Social change. 1721-43. *2273*
—. Congregationalism. Episcopal Church, Protestant. Kilbourne, James. Letters. Ohio (Worthington). Pioneers. 1844-49. *2823*
—. Congregationalism. Japan. Massachusetts. Shimeta, Neesima. Voyages. 1860's-90. *1701*
—. Deprogramming. Sects, Religious. 1970's. *4265*
—. Divine Light Mission. Hare Krsna Movement. Youth. 1960's-70's. *4284*
—. Glock, Charles Y. Models. Social Change. Stark, Rodney. 1960's-70's. *144*
—. Illinois (Springfield). Jacquess, James F. Lincoln, Abraham. Methodist Church. 1847. *2788*
—. Immigration. Kansas. Mennonites. Milling. Presbyterian Church. Warkentin, Bernhard. 1847-1908. *3380*
—. Immigration. Mormons. Ross, James. Scotland. 1842-1900. *4011*
—. Indians. Massachusetts (Martha's Vineyard). Mayhew, Thomas, Jr. Missions and Missionaries. Puritans. 1645-57. *1635*
—. Letters. Lynch, James. Methodist Episcopal Church. Methodist Episcopal Church, African. Negroes. 1867. *3462*
—. Letters. Missouri. Mormons. Ostracism. Partridge, Edward. 1837. *3989*
—. Mormons. Scandinavian Americans. Young, Kimball. 1893-1972. *3979*
—. Personality. Psychology. Puritans. 1630-1740. *3640*
—. Social Change. 1975-76. *129*
Cook, Sherburne Friend. California. Conversion thesis. Franciscans. Indians. Missions and Missionaries. ca 1790-1820's. 1943. *1541*
Cooke, Samuel. American Revolution. History Teaching. Langdon, Samuel. Mayhew, Jonathan. Sermons. West, Samuel. Witherspoon, John. 1750-76. 1975. *1406*
Cooper, Samuel. American Revolution. Brattle Street Church. Calvinism. Congregationalism. Elites. Massachusetts (Boston). 1754-83. *1333*
—. American Revolution. Brattle Street Church. Clergy. Congregationalism. Massachusetts (Boston). 1770-80. *951*
—. American Revolution. Congregationalism. Massachusetts (Boston). Rhetoric. Sermons. 1768-80. *1352*
—. American Revolution. Massachusetts (Boston). Sermons. 1776. *1146*
—. Congregationalism. Funerals. Music. New England. Sermons. Social Customs. 18c. *3113*
Co-operative Commonwealth Federation. Catholic Church. Saskatchewan. Social reform. Socialism. 1930-50. *2567*
Cooperative Program. Baptists, Southern. Church Finance. 1845-1975. *2982*
Cooperatives. Barbeau, Victor. Catholic Church. Medical Reform. Paquette, Albiny. Politics. Quebec. 1900-45. *3874*
—. Christianity. Quebec. 1940-78. *2574*
—. Idaho (Paris). Mormons. Rural Settlements. 1869-96. *360*
Copley, John Singleton *(Watson and the Shark).* Art. 1778. *1860*
Copperheads. Catholic Church. Civil War. Editors and Editing. *Metropolitan Record* (newspaper). Mullaly, John. New York City. 1861-64. *1234*
Copyright *See also* Books; Publishers and Publishing.
—. Billings, William. Massachusetts. Music. 1770-90. *1939*
Coray, Howard. Leadership. Mormons. Personal narratives. Smith, Joseph. 1840's. *3990*

Corbett, Griffiths Owen. Church of England. Clergy. Manitoba. Métis. Red River Rebellion. 1863-70. *3215*
Corder, James. Alabama (Aliceville). Baptists, Primitive. Civil rights. Negroes. Personal narratives. 1965-75. *2555*
Cornish, Samuel E. Abolition Movement. *Freedom's Journal* (newspaper). Journalism. Negroes. Presbyterian Church. 1820's-59. *2498*
Corporate wealth. Baptists, Southern. Methodism. Political power. Presbyterian Church. South. 1930's-75. *2926*
Corporations. Christianity. Education, Finance. Higher education. Social Darwinism. 1860-1930. *540*
Correspondence courses. Idaho (Moscow). New Thought movement. Psychiana (religion). Robinson, Frank Bruce. 1929-48. *4260*
Correspondence, theory of. New England. Transcendentalists. 1836-44. *1962*
—. Swedenborg, Emanuel. Thoreau, Henry David. Transcendentalism. ca 1850-62. *4069*
Corrigan, Michael. Catholic Church. Conservatism. Economic Theory. George, Henry. McGlynn, Edward. New York. 1886-94. *2562*
Cossitt, Ranna. American Revolution. Canada. Church of England. Loyalists. Missions and Missionaries. New England. 1773-1815. *1317*
Cotton, John. Antinomian Controversy. Hutchinson, Anne. Massachusetts (Boston). Puritans. 1636. *3652*
—. Antinomianism. Eliot, John. Government. Millenarianism. Missions and Missionaries. New England. Puritans. Rhode Island (Portsmouth). 1630-90. *3635*
—. Antinomianism. Hutchinson, Anne. Massachusetts. Sermons. Shepard, Thomas. Theology. 1630's. *3648*
—. Calvinism. Elegies. Fiske, John. New England. Poetry. Puritans. 17c. *1985*
—. Charles I. Great Britain. Massachusetts (Boston). Puritans. Regicide. Sermons. 1650. *1349*
Cotton mills. Catholic Church. French Canadians. Immigration. Massachusetts (Springfield). Population. Working Class. 1870. *3710*
Cotton, William. Church of England. Clergy. Lawsuits. Tithes. Virginia (Accomack County). 1633-39. *1013*
Coughlin, Charles Edward. Anti-Semitism. Boxerman, William I. Documents. Michigan (Detroit). 1939. *2131*
Coughlin, Lawrence. Methodism. Newfoundland. 1765-1815. *3477*
Council of Churches of Buffalo and Erie County. New York (Buffalo). Sanderson, Ross W. 1937-42. *447*
Council of Southern Mountain Workers. Clergy. Rural Development. South. Standard of Living. 1913-72. *2451*
Councils and Synods. Authority. Bishops. Canada. Church of England. Laity. 1780-1979. *3224*
—. Authority. Canada. Church and state. Church of England. Laity. 1782-1857. *3207*
—. Authority. Canada. Church of England. Laity. 1782-1867. *3206*
—. Bishops. Church of England. Fulford, Francis. Quebec (Montreal). 1850-68. *3209*
—. Delegates. Episcopal Church, Protestant (Annual Council). Kinsolving, George Herbert. Texas. Veto. Women. 1921-70. *813*
Counseling *See also* Social Work.
—. Clergy. Great Britain. 1950's-70's. *122*
Counter Culture *See also* Communes.
—. Apocalypticism. Philosophy of History. 1950-73. *148*
—. Astrology. California (San Francisco Bay Area). Horoscopes. 1970's. *2212*
—. Cabala. Jews. Mysticism. Rationalism. Traditionalism. 1940's-70's. *4140*
—. Civil religion. Persecution. Public Opinion. Sects, Religious. 19c-20c. *4263*
—. Communes. Transcendence. 1960's-70's. *4246*
—. Fundamentalism. Jesus People. Youth Movements. 1960's. *2719*
—. Jesus Christ. Music, rock and roll. 1950's-70's. *1916*
—. Millenarianism. Mysticism. Satanism. Social reform. 1960's-70's. *4243*
—. Science. Technology. Values. 1960's-70's. *2292*
—. Youth. 1960's. *4242*
Country Life *See also* Rural Settlements.
—. American Institute for Education. Educational Reform. Elites. Massachusetts. Nationalism. Protestantism. 1830-37. *573*
—. Architecture. Churches. Fischer, Emil C. Kansas. 19c. *1778*
—. Architecture. Churches (Gothic Revival). Furniture and Furnishings. Pennsylvania, northwest. Presbyterian Church. 1850-1905. 1979. *1797*
—. Architecture (Scandinavian). City Planning. Mormons. Utah (Spring City). 1851-1975. *1816*
—. Baptists. Farms. Illinois (southern). Lentz, Lula Gillespie. Personal narratives. 1883-1929. *3037*
—. Baptists, Southern. Church membership. Evangelicalism. South. Urbanization. 1920's. *3085*
—. British Canadians. Ethnic groups. French Canadians. Manitoba. Mennonites. Migration. Polish Canadians. Ukrainian Canadians. 1921-61. *3389*
—. Catholic Church. Ethnic Groups. Lutheran Church. Reformed Dutch Church. Voting and Voting Behavior. 1890-98. *1257*
—. Christianity. Ecumenism. Progressivism. Protestant Churches. Reform. Wisconsin. 1904-20. *2723*
—. Civil War. Mississippi (Pontotoc County). Personal narratives. Shady Grove Baptist Church. Smith, Andrew Jackson. 1864-69. *3035*
—. Ethnic groups. Evangelical United Brethren Church. Social classes. Theology. 1800-1968. *3668*
—. Farms. Haswell, David R. Letters. Pennsylvania. Protestants. Revivals. 1808-31. *2234*
—. Iowa. Langland, Joseph. Lutheran Church. Personal narratives. Poetry. Youth. 1917-30's. 1977. *2027*
—. Murder. Negroes. South. Whites. 1916-20. *156*
Country life movement. Community centers. Progressives. Rural Settlements. 1900's-20's. *2447*
Country stores. Clergy. Duus, O. F. Knoph, Thomas. Ledgers. Lutheran Church. Norwegian Americans. Wisconsin (Waupaca township; Scandinavia). 1853-56. *3334*
County Government *See also* Local Government; State Government.
—. Church and state. Judicial Administration. Mormons. Partisanship. Probate courts. Utah. 1855-72. *1039*
Courchesne, Georges. Action Catholique. Catholic Church. Quebec (Rimouski). 1940-67. *2356*
Court records. Attitudes. Law Enforcement. New England. Sodomy. 1630-80. *2428*
—. Church History. Excommunication. Massachusetts (Salem). Puritans. 1629-80. *3600*
Courts *See also* Courts Martial and Courts of Inquiry; Judicial Administration; Supreme Court.
—. Antievolution Law (1928). Arkansas. Church and state. Epperson, Susan. Evolution. Initiatives. 1900's-68. *2322*
—. Church Property. Constitutional Amendments (1st). Kentucky (Louisville). Presbyterian Church. Walnut Street Presbyterian Church. *Watson* v. *Jones* (US, 1860). 1860-1970. *1129*
—. Civil religion. Religion in the Public Schools. Teaching. 1947-76. *572*
—. Conscientious Objectors. Flag salute. Jehovah's Witnesses. World War II. 1930's-40's. *2655*
—. Constitutional Amendments (1st). Religious liberty. 1878-1972. *1038*
Courts Martial and Courts of Inquiry. Antiwar Sentiment. Butler, Smedley. Friends, Society of (Hicksite). Marines. 1881-1940. *2637*
—. Baptists. Chaplains. Fort Robinson. Nebraska. Negroes. Plummer, Henry V. 1884-94. *2695*
Courtship. Diaries. Indiana. Marriage. Mennonites. Sprunger, David. 1893-95. *3427*
—. Field, Eliza. Great Britain (London). Indians. Jones, Peter. Methodism. New York. 1820's-33. *1637*
Covenant theology. Bulkeley, Peter (and family). Massachusetts (Concord). Puritans. 1635-1731. *3645*
—. Bulkeley, Peter *(Gospel-Covenant)*. Massachusetts. Puritans. 1640's-50's. *3636*
—. Congregationalism. Iconography. Theology. Tombstones. Vermont (Grafton, Rockingham). 1770-1803. *1896*
—. Divine Sovereignty. Ethics. Puritanism. 17c-18c. *3618*
—. Edwards, Jonathan. Great Awakening. Puritans. 18c. *2219*
—. New England. Poetry. Puritans. Wigglesworth, Michael *(Day of Doom)*. 1662. *3597*
Covenants. Baptists. Maritime Provinces. 1778-1878. *3003*
—. Baptists, Southern. Brown, J. Newton. New Hampshire Covenant. 1833-1972. *3006*
Cowley, Matthias F. Church and state. Mormons. Polygamy. Smoot, Reed. Taylor, John W. Theology. Woodruff Manifesto. 1890-1911. *1060*
Cox Library. Anti-Catholicism. Church and state. Discrimination. *Koester* v. *Pardeeville* (1929). Libraries. Taxation. Wisconsin (Pardeeville). 1927-29. *1033*
Cox, Samuel Hanson. Anti-Catholicism. Congregationalism. Ecumenism. Episcopal Church, Protestant. Evangelicalism. Presbyterian Church, New School. Slavery. 1840's. *471*
Cradock, Thomas. Chain of being. Church of England. Maryland (Baltimore County). Poetry. Sermons. Social theory. 1700-80. *3227*
—. Church of England. Clergy. Maryland (Baltimore County). Poetry. Sermons. 1700-70. *3229*
Craig, James Henry. Canada. Catholic Church. Clergy. French Canadians. Nationalism. Political repression. Quebec (Lower Canada). 1810. *1319*
Crandall, Joseph. Autobiography. Baptists. Clergy. New Brunswick. 1795-1810. *2993*
Crane, Stephen. Faulkner, William. Literature. 19c-20c. *2030*
Crapsey, Algernon Sidney. Episcopal Church, Protestant. Heresy. Humanitarian Reform. New York (Rochester). St. Andrew's Church. Trials. 1879-1927. *3234*
Crawford, Isabel. Baptists, American. Indians. Kiowa Indians. Missions and Missionaries. Oklahoma (Wichita Mountains). Women's American Baptist Home Missionary Society. 1893-1961. *1590*
Creamer, David. Baltimore Riot of 1861. Civil War. Crooks, George Richard. Letters. Maryland. Methodist Church. 1861-63. *1410*
Creation theory. Bible. Dana, James Dwight. Guyot, Arnold. Protestantism. Science. 1850's. *2333*
Creationism. California. Church and state. Curricula. Educational Policy. Evolution. Science. 1963-74. *2331*
Creative innocence, concept of. Maritain, Jacques. Maritain, Raissa. Merton, Thomas. Poetry. Theology. 1940's-75. *3863*
Cree Indians. Anglican Communion. Autobiography. Faries, Richard. Missions and Missionaries. Ontario (York Factory). 1896-1961. *1528*
—. Canada. Evans, James. Methodist Church. Missions and Missionaries. 1833-46. *3475*
Creeds. Baptists. 1742-1963. *2996*
—. Baptists. Nova Scotia (Annapolis Valley). 1760-1980. *3060*
—. Evangelical Association. Methodism. Terry, Milton S. Theology. United Evangelical Church. 1894-1921. *3667*
—. Methodism. Wesley, John. 19c-20c. *3493*
Creek Indians. Baptists. Indian Territory. Methodist Church. Missions and Missionaries. Presbyterian Church. 1835-60's. *1517*
Crime and Criminals *See also* names of crimes, e.g. Murder, etc.; Capital Punishment; Criminal Law; Pirates; Prisons; Riots; Trials; Violence.
—. Ecclesiastical law. Great Britain. Massachusetts. Roman Law. 17c. *972*
—. Massachusetts (Middlesex County). Puritans. Social classes. 17c. *3616*
Criminal Law *See also* Capital Punishment; Trials.
—. Benefit of clergy. Colonial Government. Common law. Maryland. 1637-1713. *1140*
Crittenden, Lyman B. Higher Education. Jackson, Sheldon. McMillan, Duncan M. Montana. Presbyterian Church. 1869-1918. *598*
Crockett, Davy. Nature. Pioneers. Popular Culture. 1830's. *2712*
Croly, Herbert. Civil religion. Millenarianism. Politics. Wilson, Woodrow. 1909-19. *1159*
Cromwell, James. Garrettson, Freeborn. Methodist Episcopal Church. Missionaries. Nova Scotia. USA. 1785-1800. *1581*
Cromwell, James W. City Life. Friends, Society of. New York City. Personal narratives. 1842-60. *3271*
Cromwell, Oliver. Carter, Jimmy. Great Britain. Political Leadership. Rickover, Hyman. Roosevelt, Theodore. 20c. *974*

Crooks, George Richard. Baltimore Riot of 1861. Civil War. Creamer, David. Letters. Maryland. Methodist Church. 1861-63. *1410*
—. Church government. Laity. Methodist Episcopal Church. *Methodist* (periodical). 1851-72. *316*
Crosby, Donald F. Anti-Communist Movements. Catholic Church. Labor Unions and Organizations. McCarthy, Joseph R. (review article). Oshinsky, David. 1950-54. 1976-78. *1212*
Cross, Whitney R. Burned-over district (theory). Dissent. Millerites. New York. 1830's-40's. 20c. *2974*
Crow Indians. Diaries. Doederlein, Paul Ferdinand. Indians. Lutheran Church. Missions and Missionaries. Wyoming. 1859-60. *1589*
Crowd control. Camp meetings. Political rallies. Rhetoric. Tennessee. 1828-60. *1259*
Crummell, Alexander. American Colonization Society. Education. Episcopal Church, Protestant. Liberia. Missions and Missionaries. Negroes. 1853-73. *1671*
—. Black nationalism. DuBois, W. E. B. Episcopal Church, Protestant. Ferris, William H. Ideology. 1819-1898. *2424*
Crump, Edward Hull. Bossism. City Politics. Clergy. Negroes. Tennessee (Memphis). 1927-48. *1318*
Cuba. Methodist Church. Missions and Missionaries. Nationalism. 1898-1958. *1693*
Cudney, A. J. Adventists. Evangelism. Nebraska (Lincoln). 1885-87. *1577*
Cuffe, Paul. Black nationalism. Colonization. Friends, Society of. Sierra Leone. 1810's. *2478*
Cult practices. Psychotherapy. Puerto Rico. Social organization. Spiritualism. 1975. *1445*
Cultic milieu. Conversion. UFO cults. 1970's. *4241*
Cultism. Attitudes. Chiropractic. Medicine (practice of). Science. 1850's-1970's. *2314*
Cults. 20c. *4271*
—. Alienation. Christianity. Converts. Human potential movement. Social indicators. 1960's-70's. *143*
—. Authority. Ideology. 1945-74. *4274*
—. Berkeley New Religious Consciousness Project. California (San Francisco Bay area). 1970's. *4272*
—. California. Christianity. Eastern religions. 1970's. *107*
—. Catholic Church. Devotions, popular. Quebec (Lake St. John, Portneuf counties). 1970's. *3851*
—. Christianity. Jesus People. Morality. 1960's-70's. *140*
—. Communes. Convents. Socialization. Tnevnoc Cult. 19c. 1970-79. *386*
—. Deviant Behavior. Occult Sciences. Transcendental Meditation. 1948-79. *4239*
—. Evangelism. Law. 1976-78. *1110*
—. Father Divine. Jones, Jim. Negroes. Peace Mission (movement). People's Temple. 1920-79. *4254*
—. Models. 1840's-1970's. *2*
—. Salvation. Social Customs. 1960-76. *4270*
—. Sects, religious. Sociologists. Youth. 1960's-70's. *4256*
—. Youth. 1960's-70's. *4248*
Cultural history. Ontario. Protestantism. 1840's-1900. *2844*
Cultural pluralism. Baptists. Ethnicity. Melting pot theory. 1870-1976. *3101*
—. Jensen, Richard. Kleppner, Paul. North Central States. Political behavior. 1850-1900. *1214*
Culture *See also* Education; Popular Culture; Scholarship.
—. Catholic Church. Paraguay. Spain. 1513-20c. *3737*
—. Mormons. Organizations. Pioneers. Utah. 1850's-70's. *523*
—. Singer, Milton. Social activities. 1964-74. *165*
Culture-region. Catholic Church. Minnesota. St.Cloud Diocese. 1860-1973. *3881*
Culver-Stockton University. Colleges and Universities. Democratic Party. Disciples of Christ. Missouri. Shannon, James. Slavery. 1821-59. *3107*
Cumings, John. New Hampshire (Enfield). Shakers. Utopias. 1829-1923. *394*
Cumming, William. Brownson, Orestes A. Catholic Church. Letters. 1850's. *3676*
Cummings, Charles. American Revolution. Indians. Presbyterian Church. Virginia, southwest. 1760's-80's. *2634*
Cunningham, Patrick. Catholic Church. Documents. Irish Americans. Vermont (Brattleboro). 1847-98. *3725*
Curricula. Baptists. Church schools. 1824-1974. *638*
—. California. Church and state. Creationism. Educational Policy. Evolution. Science. 1963-74. *2331*
—. Christianity. Colleges and Universities. Graham, William. Liberty Hall Academy. Proslavery Sentiments. Virginia. ca 1786-96. *2173*
—. Colleges and Universities. Common Sense school. Dalhousie University. King's College. Lyall, William. Nova Scotia. Philosophy. Pine Hill Divinity Hall. Presbyterian Church. 1850-90. *719*
—. Colleges and universities. Conferences. Dissertations. Jewish studies. 1979. *4138*
—. Colleges and universities. Ethics.. 1950-73. *530*
—. Colleges and Universities. Massachusetts (South Hadley). Mount Holyoke College. Science. Women. 1839-88. *2320*
Curwen, Alice. Antislavery sentiments. Barbados. Friends, Society of. Letters. 1675-76. *2458*
Customs. Christmas. -1973. *2801*
Cutler, Timothy. Church of England. Congregationalism. Edwards, Jonathan. Gibson, Edmund. Great Awakening. Letters. New England. Stoddard, Solomon. 1739. *2263*
—. Church of England. Congregationalism. Massachusetts. 1720-30. *1056*
Czechoslovakia *See also* Bohemia; Europe, Eastern.
—. Canada. Jesuits. Refugees. Refugees. 1950. *3776*
—. Catholic Church. Clergy. Personal narratives. Refugees. Social Change. Zubek, Theodoric. 1950-78. *3902*

D

Dabney, Robert L. Adger, John B. Hodge, Charles. Mercersburg theology. Nevin, John W. Presbyterian Church. Sacramental controversy. 1845-75. *3551*
Dahlberg, Edwin. Baptists. Clergy. Personal narratives. Rauschenbusch, Walter. Social reform. 1914-18. *2440*
Daily Life *See also* Popular Culture.
—. American Revolution. American Revolution. Cleaveland, John. Congregationalism. Great Awakening. Ideology. Jedrey, Christopher M. (review article). Massachusetts (Chebacco). New Lights. 1740-79. *2241*
—. American Revolution. Great Britain. Johnson, Jeremiah. Military Occupation. New York City (Brooklyn). Personal narratives. 1775-83. *63*
—. Amish (Old Order). Diaries. Farms. King family. Loomis, Charles P. Pennsylvania (Lancaster County). 1940. *3403*
—. Appalachia. Baptists, Old Regular. 19c-20c. *3070*
—. Art. Moravian Church. Pennsylvania (Bethlehem). Social Organization. 1741-1865. *3515*
—. Attitudes. Friends, Society of. Ohio (Mount Pleasant). 1795-1918. *3260*
—. Attitudes. Sociology of religion. Yinger, J. Milton. 1946-77. *166*
—. Bradford, Phoebe George. Delaware. Diaries. Episcopal Church, Protestant. 1832-33. *3245*
—. Bradford, Phoebe George. Delaware (Wilmington). Diaries. Episcopal Church, Protestant. 1833-35. *3244*
—. British Columbia. Doukhobors. Immigration. Personal narratives. Russia. 1880's-1976. *3918*
—. Brubacher, Henry. Brubacher, Jacob. Letters. Mennonites. Ontario. Pennsylvania. 1817-46. *3374*
—. Catholic Church. Documents. Girls. Holy Names of Jesus and Mary, Sisters of the. Oregon (Salem). Sacred Heart Academy. 1863-73. *699*
—. Catholic Church. Nova Scotia (Lochaber). Presbyterians. Rural Settlements. 1830-1972. *2747*
—. Chase, Josephine Streeper. Diaries. Mormons. Utah (Centerville). Women. 1881-94. *3957*
—. Concordia Seminary. Kansas (Clay Center). Lutheran Church (Missouri Synod). Mueller, Peter. Seminaries. Students. 1883-89. *707*
—. Diaries. Illinois (Nauvoo). Jacobs, Zina Diantha Huntington. Mormons. Women. 1844-45. *3935*
—. Elections. Judaism. Oregon (Portland). Temple Beth Israel. 1878. *4237*
—. Evangelism. Illinois (Chicago). Methodist Church. Whitefield, Henry. 1833-71. *1508*
Daily Union Vedette (newspaper). Fort Douglas. Mormons. Utah. 1863-67. *4020*
Dakota Indians. *See* Sioux Indians.
Daland, William C. Baptists, Seventh-Day. Conversion. Friedlaender, Herman. Jews. New York City. *Peculiar People* (newspaper). 1880's-90's. *1633*
Daley, Dominic. Anti-Catholicism. Cheverus, Jean Louis Lefebvre de. Halligan, James. Irish Americans. Massachusetts (Northampton). Protestantism. Trials. 1805-06. *2097*
Dalhousie University. Church of England. King's College, University of. Mergers. Nova Scotia. Presbyterian Church. 1821-37. *684*
—. Colleges and Universities. Common Sense school. Curricula. King's College. Lyall, William. Nova Scotia. Philosophy. Pine Hill Divinity Hall. Presbyterian Church. 1850-90. *719*
—. Colleges and universities. McCulloch, Thomas. Missions and Missionaries. Nova Scotia. Pictou Academy. Presbyterian Church. ca 1803-42. *591*
Dalton, Edward Meeks. Edmunds Act (US, 1882). Mormons. Polygamy. Utah. 1852-86. *1028*
Damen, Arnold. Catholic Church. Church Schools. Fund raising. Illinois (Chicago). 1840-90. *773*
Dana, James Dwight. Bible. Creation theory. Guyot, Arnold. Protestantism. Science. 1850's. *2333*
Dance. Centenary College. Educational Policy. Louisiana. Methodist Church. 1941. *688*
—. Mormons. Utah. 1830-80. *3984*
D'Ancona, David Arnold. Anti-Semitism. California (San Francisco). Letters. Newspapers. Pixley, Frank M. 1883. *2128*
Danish Americans. Beck, Vilhelm. Grundtvig, Nikolai Frederik Severin. Inner Mission Movement. Lutheran Church. 1619-1973. *3341*
Danville Theological Seminary. Breckinridge, Robert Jefferson. Clergy. Education. Emancipation. Kentucky. Presbyterian Church. 1800-71. *3544*
—. Breckinridge, Robert Jefferson. Emancipation. Kentucky. Presbyterian Church. Theology. 1832-71. *3545*
Darby, John Nelson. Evangelical Free Church of America. Franson, Fredrik. Millenarianism. Moody, Dwight L. Revivalism. Scandinavian Americans. 1875-95. *2863*
Dark Day. Congregationalism. New England. Stiles, Ezra. Weather. 1780. *2326*
Darlington Agency. Apache Indians. Cheyenne Indians. Friends, Society of. Indian Territory. Indians (agencies). 1868-86. *3278*
Darrow, Clarence. Bryan, William Jennings. Evolution. Scopes Trial. Tennessee (Dayton). Trials. 1925. *2336*
Dartmouth College. Church and State. Colleges and Universities (review article). Columbia University. Harvard University. Johnson, Samuel (1696-1772). Yale University. 1696-1970. 1972-74. *524*
—. Lane Theological Seminary. New England. Presbyterian Church. Stowe, Calvin Ellis. Stowe, Harriet Beecher. 1824-86. *3555*
Darwin, Charles. Baptists. Evolution. Hofstadter, Richard *(Social Darwinism in American Thought).* Rauschenbusch, Walter. Social Gospel. Spencer, Herbert. 1879-1918. *3002*
Darwinism. Bible. Episcopal Church, Protestant. Europe. Excommunication. Hermeneutics. MacQueary, Howard. Ohio (Canton). St. Paul's Church. Universalism. 1890-91. *3178*
—. Bryan, William Jennings. Church and state. Evolution. Fundamentalism. Public schools. 1920-73. *2317*
—. Great Britain. Moore, James R. (review article). Protestantism. 1870-1900. *2319*
Davidson, Herman. California (Stockton). Judaism (Reform). Opera. Rabbis. Russia. 1846-1911. *4204*
Davies, David Jones. Davies, Gwen. Indians. Methodist Church, Calvinistic. Missions and Missionaries. Nebraska, eastern. Omaha Indians. 1853-60. *1514*

Davies, Gwen. Davies, David Jones. Indians. Methodist Church, Calvinistic. Missions and Missionaries. Nebraska, eastern. Omaha Indians. 1853-60. *1514*
Davies, Samuel. Antislavery Sentiments. Great Awakening. Presbyterian Church. Virginia. 1740-59. *2238*
—. Clergy. Eulogies. National Self-image. Presbyterian Church. Washington, George. 1789-1815. *1157*
—. Diaries. Fund raising. Great Britain. New Jersey. Presbyterian Church. Princeton University. 1753-54. *636*
Davis, David Brion. Abolition Movement. Drake, Thomas. Friends, Society of (review article). James, Sydney. 1683-1863. 20c. *2471*
Davis, Harwell G. Alabama. Baptists. Howard College. 1882-1973. *3092*
Davis, Noah. Baptists. Clergy. Maryland (Baltimore). Meachum, John Berry. Missouri (St. Louis). Negroes. Slavery. 1818-66. *3094*
Davis, Rennie. Attitudes. California (Berkeley). Converts. Divine Light Mission. Maharaj Ji. Politics. 1973. *4286*
Dawes, Thomas. Architecture. Brattle Street Church. Congregationalism. Massachusetts (Boston). 18c. *1771*
Dawson, Joseph Martin. Baptists. Church and Social Problems. Clergy. Scholarship. 1879-1973. *3015*
—. Baptists. Church and state. Clergy. 1879-1973. *1142*
Day, Dorothy. *Catholic Worker* (newspaper). Maurin, Peter. Social justice. 20c. *1468*
Day Nurseries. Child care. Dominicans. Quebec (Montreal). Women. 1858-1920. *2505*
Dayton, Amos Cooper. Baptists. Landmark Movement. Novels. South. 1850-65. *1995*
Deaconesses. Baptists, Southern. Women. 1600-1976. *831*
Deaf. Ephphatha Conference. Lutheran Church. Missions and Missionaries. 1893-1976. *1516*
Dean, Joseph Harry. Gibson, Walter Murray. Hawaii. Missions and Missionaries. Mormons. Samoa. 1860's-90. *1683*
Death and Dying *See also* Aged.
—. Anthropology. Memorial Day. Social Customs. 1945-74. *90*
—. Attitudes. Baptists, Southern. Buddhism. Congregationalism. Hawaii (Honolulu). 1977. *131*
—. Attitudes. Catholic Church. Quebec. Wills. 1663-1760. *3718*
—. Attitudes. Social Customs. 17c-1977. *19*
—. Ballads, British. Folk Songs. Supernatural. 1830-1930. *1923*
—. Books. Children's literature. Periodicals. Protestantism. 1800-60. *2914*
—. British North America. Funerals. Social customs. 17c-18c. *2772*
—. Childbirth. Congregationalism. Diaries. Diseases. Massachusetts (Westborough). Parkman, Ebenezer. Social Organization. 1724-82. *1447*
—. Child-rearing. Fischer, David H. Greven, Philip. Lynn, Kenneth S. Personality (review article). Politics. Protestantism. Stannard, David E. 18c. 1977. *2943*
—. Children. New England. Puritans. 17c-1750. *929*
—. Christianity. Stannard, David E. (review article). 17c-20c. *2746*
—. Evangelism. Literature. South. 1800-65. *1970*
—. Folklore. New England. 1630-1790. *2903*
—. Infants. New England. Parents. Puritans. Theology. 1620-1720. *925*
—. Literature. North or Northern States. Protestantism. Women. 1830-80. *2846*
—. New England. Puritans. 17c-18c. *3651*
—. Religiosity. 1970's. *116*
Death Carts. Catholic Church. Colorado, southern. Hispanic Americans. New Mexico, northern. Penitentes. 1860-90's. *3856*
Death Penalty. *See* Capital Punishment.
Debates. Adventists. California (San Francisco). Educational Policy. Evolution. Science League of America. 1925. *2291*
—. Anglin, Timothy Warren. Canada. Catholic Church. Fenian Brotherhood. Irish Canadians. McGee, D'Arcy. 1863-68. *1341*
—. Ecumenism. Methodist Episcopal Church. Methodist Episcopal Church (South). Race. Virginia. 1924-25. *467*
—. Maryland. Religious liberty. State Government. 1776-85. *1107*
Debt. Catholic Church. LaRocque, Charles. Quebec. St. Hyacinthe Diocese. 1866-73. *3695*
Decker, Mahonri M. Hymns. Mormons. Utah (Parowan). 1919. *1921*
Declaration of Independence. Carroll, Charles (of Carrollton). Catholic Church. Maryland. Political Leadership. 1737-1832. *3705*
—. Ideology. Radicals and Radicalism. Utopias. 1730's-1890's. *426*
—. Jefferson, Thomas. Religious liberty. Virginia. 1743-1826. *1022*
Decorative Arts. Architecture. Catholic Church. Church of St. Paul the Apostle. LaFarge, John. New York City. 1876-99. *1833*
—. Architecture. Churches. Values. 1970's. *1837*
—. Churches (Gothic Revival). LaFarge, John. Massachusetts (Boston). Richardson, Henry Hobson. Trinity Church. 1876. *1832*
—. Congregationalism. Interior decoration. Rhode Island (Newport). United Congregational Church. 1879-80. *1897*
Defender (periodical). Evolution. Kansas (Wichita). *Red Horse* (periodical). Science. Winrod, Gerald Burton. 1925-57. *2305*
Defoe, Daniel. Church and State. Colonial Government. Religious liberty. South Carolina. 1704-06. *1014*
Defoe, Daniel *(Robinson Crusoe)*. Capitalism. Great Britain. Materialism. Thoreau, Henry David *(Walden)*. Transcendentalism. 18c-19c. *354*
Deism *See also* Atheism; Christianity; Rationalism.
—. Allen, Ethan. Franklin, Benjamin. Historiography. Jefferson, Thomas. Palmer, Elihu. 1750-1820. *4277*
—. Anticlericalism. Bible. Jefferson, Thomas. Jesus Christ. Translating and Interpreting. 1813-20. *4279*
—. Christianity. Jefferson, Thomas. Letters. Sectarianism. 1784-1800. *4280*
—. Christianity. Jefferson, Thomas *(Life and Morals of Jesus of Nazareth)*. Jesus Christ. Morality. Russia. Theology. Tolstoy, Leo *(Christ's Christianity)*. 1800-85. *4278*
—. Clergy. Paine, Thomas *(Age of Reason)*. Virginia. 1794-97. *86*
—. Franklin, Benjamin. 1706-90. *4275*
—. Jefferson, Thomas. Theology. 1800-25. *4276*
Deity. Illinois (Nauvoo). Mormons. Sermons. Smith, Joseph (King Follett Discourse). Theology. 1844. *3976*
Delaware *See also* Southeastern States.
—. American Revolution. Asbury, Francis. Loyalists. Maryland. Methodists. White, Thomas. 1777-80. *3482*
—. Bradford, Phoebe George. Daily life. Diaries. Episcopal Church, Protestant. 1832-33. *3245*
—. Church of England. Clergy. Northeastern or North Atlantic States. Vestries. 1690-1775. *311*
Delaware (Appoquiniminck). American Revolution. Church of England. Loyalists. Reading, Philip. Society for the Propagation of the Gospel. 1775-78. *1221*
Delaware Indians. American Revolution. Indians. Missions and Missionaries. Moravian Church. Ohio. Pennsylvania, western. 1775-83. *1532*
Delaware (New Castle County). Canby, Edmund. Diaries. Friends, Society of. Milling. 1822-35. *3275*
Delaware River Valley. American Revolution. Clergy. Episcopal Church, Protestant. Lutheran Church. Swedish Americans. 1655-1831. *285*
Delaware (Wilmington). Bradford, Phoebe George. Daily Life. Diaries. Episcopal Church, Protestant. 1833-35. *3244*
—. Churches (Gothic Revival). Episcopal Church, Protestant. Grace Methodist Church. Methodist Church. St. John's Episcopal Church. 1850-90. *1786*
—. Jews. Moses Montefiore Mutual Aid Society. 1850-90. *4101*
Delegates. Councils and Synods. Episcopal Church, Protestant (Annual Council). Kinsolving, George Herbert. Texas. Veto. Women. 1921-70. *813*
DeLeon, Daniel. Anti-Catholicism. Capitalism. Socialism. 1891-1914. *2113*
Democracy *See also* Aristocracy; Federal Government; Middle Classes; Referendum; Socialism; Suffrage.
—. Baptists, Southern. Bureaucracies. Norris, J. Frank. 1920-40. *3084*
—. Brownson, Orestes A. Catholic Church. 1840's-76. *1389*
—. Brownson, Orestes A. Catholic Church. Theocratic principles. 19c. *1379*
—. Catholic Church. Church and state. Dominicans. Mazzuchelli, Samuel Charles *(Memoirs)*. Old Northwest. 1806-63. *1384*
—. Catholic Church. Intellectuals. Liberalism. Racism. 1924-59. *2532*
—. Catholic Church. Laity. Trusteeism. 1785-1855. *292*
—. Catholic Church. Manuscripts. Sermons. Tocqueville, Alexis de. Yale University. 1831-40. *1990*
—. Christianity. Civil religion. France. Tocqueville, Alexis de. 1820-50. *1175*
—. Church and state. Orthodox Eastern Church. Symphonia theory. 17c-20c. *1048*
—. Citizenship. Jefferson, Thomas. Locke, John. Puritanism. 17c-18c. *1408*
—. Civil religion. Ideology. Political institutions. Puritan tradition. 17c-20c. *1150*
—. Congregationalism. Massachusetts. Political thought. Wise, John. 17c-18c. *1354*
—. Education. Fundamentalism. Local Politics. Morality. Social Change. Vigilantism. 1920's. *2387*
—. Enlightenment. Equality. Mead, Sidney E. Theology of the Republic (concept). 17c-20c. *1366*
—. Finney, Charles G. Human nature. Revivalism. Social Theory. 1820-30. *2268*
—. Liberals. Niebuhr, Reinhold. 1930-45. *1367*
—. National characteristics. Pluralism. 1640's-1840's. *71*
Democratic Party. Abortion. Catholic Church. Elections (presidential). 1976. *1245*
—. Anti-Catholicism. Bryan, Nathan P. Catts, Sidney J. Florida. Political Campaigns (gubernatorial). Primaries (senatorial). Trammell, Park M. 1915-16. *1258*
—. Catholic Church. 1972-73. *1230*
—. Catholic Church. Elections (presidential). Louisiana. Protestant Churches. Smith, Al. Temperance Movements. 1928. *1330*
—. Catholic Church. Immigrants. New York City. Prohibition. Protestantism. Tammany Hall. 1840-60. *2594*
—. Catholic Church. Irish Americans. *Kentucky Irish American* (newspaper). 1898-1968. *3817*
—. Clergy. Eaton, Margaret (Peggy) O'Neale. Ely, Ezra Stiles. Jackson, Andrew. Presbyterian Church. 1829-30. *3536*
—. Colleges and Universities. Culver-Stockton University. Disciples of Christ. Missouri. Shannon, James. Slavery. 1821-59. *3107*
—. Connecticut (Hartford). Ethnic groups. Middle Classes. Protestantism. Voting and Voting Behavior. 1896-1940. *1203*
—. Letters. Mennonites. Politics. Risser, Johannes. Slavery. 1856-57. *994*
—. Liberty Party. Negroes. New York. Referendum. Suffrage. Whig Party. 1840-47. *1264*
Demography *See also* Birth Control; Birth Rate; Geopolitics; Population.
—. Pluralism. Religiosity. 1970's. *150*
Denominationalism. 17c-1969. *29*
—. Arts. Baptists, Southern. Conservatism. Folk art. 1975. *1877*
—. Baptists, Southern. Barton, A. J. Gambrell, James Bruton. Lawrence, J. B. Theology. 1910-80. *3039*
—. Church and State. Ecumenism. Evangelical Alliance. Great Britain. 1846. *484*
—. Clergy. Social issues. Theology. Values. 1960's-70's. *2401*
—. Clergy. Southern Baptist Theological Seminary. Theology. 18c-1980. *3075*
—. Ecumenism. Protestantism. 16c-1979. *480*
—. Methodism. 18c-19c. *3499*
Dentistry. Adventists. Anesthesia. California. Jorgensen, Niels Bjorn. Loma Linda University. Teaching. 1923-74. *1441*
Dependence. Psychoanalysis. Religiosity. 1974. *142*
Depression. Psychiatry. 1973. *2348*
Depressions. Business. Grant, Heber J. Mormons. Utah. 1893. *375*
—. Colleges and Universities. Collegiate Institute. Lansdowne College. Manitoba (Portage la Prairie). 1882-93. *780*
—. Juma, Charlie. North Dakota (Ross). Personal narratives. Syrian Americans. 1900's-30's. *35*
Deprogramming. Anti-Semitism. Moon, Sun Myung. Unification Church. 1946-76. *4269*
—. Canada. Organizations. Sects, religious. USA. 1960's-70's. *4267*

—. Civil Rights. Religious liberty. Sects, religious. 1970's. *1062*
—. Converts. Sects, Religious. 1970's. *4265*
—. Exorcism. 1970's. *4268*
—. Unification Church. 1970's. *4244*
D'Equivelley, G. F. Anti-Catholicism. Benedictines. Florida (Pasco County). *Jeffersonian* (newspaper). Land. Letters-to-the-editor. Mohr, Charles. 1915-16. *2123*
Desegregation *See also* Segregation.
—. Baptists. *Brown* v. *Board of Education* (US, 1954). Georgia. Supreme Court. 1954-61. *511*
—. Baptists. Tennessee (Clinton). Turner, Paul. Violence. 1956. *2531*
Desha, Joseph. Colleges and Universities (administration). Holley, Horace. Kentucky. Politics. Presbyterians. State government. Transylvania College. Unitarianism. 1818-27. *537*
Design. Catholic Church. Folk art. Iconography. Manuscripts. New Mexico. 16c-17c. *1858*
Desmond, Humphrey. Bible reading. Catholic Church. Protestantism. Religion in the Public Schools. *Wisconsin ex rel. Frederick Weiss, et. al.* v. *District School Board of School District 8* (1890). 1888-90. *571*
Developing nations. Baptists, Southern. Medicine, practice of. Missions and missionaries. 1846-1975. *1440*
Deviant Behavior. Amish. Social Organization. 1977. *3429*
—. British North America. Christianity. Government. Historiography. Occult Sciences. 1600-1760. *2180*
—. Cults. Occult Sciences. Transcendental Meditation. 1948-79. *4239*
Devil. Folklore. West Virginia. Witchcraft. 1950-67. *2202*
Devotion, Ebenezer. American Revolution (antecedents). Church and state. Connecticut. Politics. Theology. 1714-71. *1397*
Devotions. Bradstreet, Anne. Clap, Roger. New England. Puritans. Sewall, Samuel. Shepard, Thomas. Worship. 17c. *3627*
Devotions, popular. Catholic Church. Cults. Quebec (Lake St. John, Portneuf counties). 1970's. *3851*
—. Catholic Church. Quebec (Beauce County). Shrines, roadside. Social customs. 1970's. *1788*
Dialects. Catholic Church. French Language. Haitian Americans. New York City (Brooklyn). 1970's. *3699*
Diaries. Adventists. Kellogg, Merritt. Medicine, practice of. Trall, Russell Thacher. 1844-77. *1452*
—. Alaska. Indian-White Relations. Library of Congress (Alaska Church Collection). Missions and Missionaries. Orlov, Vasilii. Orthodox Eastern Church, Russian. 1886. *1632*
—. American Revolution. Drinker family. Friends, Society of. Pacifism. Pennsylvania (Philadelphia). Prisoners. Virginia (Winchester). 1777-81. *2683*
—. Amish (Old Order). Daily Life. Farms. King family. Loomis, Charles P. Pennsylvania (Lancaster County). 1940. *3403*
—. Armies. Butler, Benjamin F. Chaplains. Civil War. Fort Fisher (battle). Negroes. North Carolina. Turner, Henry M. 1864-65. *2685*
—. Atlantic Provinces. Bishops. Catholic Church. Plessis, Joseph-Octave. Quebec Archdiocese. 1812-15. *3704*
—. Attitudes. Hitchcock, Ethan Allen. Military Service. Unitarianism. 1836-54. *2656*
—. Baerg, Anna. Canada. Immigration. Mennonites. Russian Revolution. Women. 1917-23. *3362*
—. Baptists. Bingham, Abel. Indian-White Relations. Iroquois Indians (Seneca). Missions and Missionaries. New York. Red Jacket (leader). Tonawanda Indian Reservation. 1822-28. *1513*
—. Baptists. Broaddus, Andrew, I. Clergy. Kentucky. Travel. 1817. *2986*
—. Baptists. Circuit riders. Immigrants. Minnesota. Nilsson, Frederik Olaus. Swedish Americans. 1855-65. *3046*
—. Baptists. Civil War. Hungerford, B. F. Kentucky. 1863-66. *2632*
—. Bible. Fiction. Melville, Herman. Palestine. Travel. 1857. *2039*
—. Books (editions). Canada, western. Church of England. Missions and Missionaries. West, John. 1820-27. *1530*
—. Bradford, Phoebe George. Daily life. Delaware. Episcopal Church, Protestant. 1832-33. *3245*
—. Bradford, Phoebe George. Daily Life. Delaware (Wilmington). Episcopal Church, Protestant. 1833-35. *3244*
—. Camp Funston. Conscientious objectors. Hutterites. Kansas. Waldner, Jakob. World War I. 1917-18. *2690*
—. Canby, Edmund. Delaware (New Castle County). Friends, Society of. Milling. 1822-35. *3275*
—. Catholic Church. Chaplains. Fort Keogh. Lindesmith, Eli. Montana. 1855-1922. *2679*
—. Catholic Church. Clergy. Shaw, Joseph Coolidge. Vermont (Brattleboro). 1848. *3849*
—. Catholic Church. Colorado. Hospitals. Mallon, Catherine. New Mexico (Santa Fe). Sisters of Charity. 1865-1901. *1454*
—. Catholic Church. Germans, Russian. Immigration. Karlin, Athanasius. 1875-87. *3772*
—. Catholic Church. Healy, James A. Holy Cross College. Massachusetts (Worcester). Religious Education. 1849. *640*
—. Chase, Josephine Streeper. Daily life. Mormons. Utah (Centerville). Women. 1881-94. *3957*
—. Childbirth. Congregationalism. Death and Dying. Diseases. Massachusetts (Westborough). Parkman, Ebenezer. Social Organization. 1724-82. *1447*
—. Church and State. Lutheran Church. Norwegian Americans. Preus, Herman A. Wisconsin (Columbia, Dane counties). 1851-60. *1104*
—. Civil War. Episcopal Church, Protestant. Providence. Robertson, Martha Wayles. South Carolina (Chesterfield County). Women. 1860-66. *3191*
—. Clergy. Episcopal Church, Protestant. Private Schools. Salt industry. Trade. Ward, Henry Dana. West Virginia (Kanawha Valley, Charleston). 1845-47. *3172*
—. Clergy. Hodge, Charles. Pennsylvania (Philadelphia). Presbyterian Church. Theology. 1819-20. *3534*
—. Clergy. Lutheran Church. Muhlenberg, Henry Melchior. Pennsylvania. Women. 1742-87. *828*
—. Congregationalism. Hawaii. Missions and Missionaries. Tahitians. Toketa (teacher). 1820's-30's. *1676*
—. Courtship. Indiana. Marriage. Mennonites. Sprunger, David. 1893-95. *3427*
—. Crow Indians. Doederlein, Paul Ferdinand. Indians. Lutheran Church. Missions and Missionaries. Wyoming. 1859-60. *1589*
—. Daily life. Illinois (Nauvoo). Jacobs, Zina Diantha Huntington. Mormons. Women. 1844-45. *3935*
—. Davies, Samuel. Fund raising. Great Britain. New Jersey. Presbyterian Church. Princeton University. 1753-54. *636*
—. Emigration. Florida. Lutheran Church. Sjöborg, Sofia Charlotta. Sweden. 1871. *3340*
—. Episcopal Church, Protestant. Harris, N. Sayre. Indian Territory. Missions and Missionaries. Otey, James Hervey. 1844. *1533*
—. Evangelism. Georgia (Augusta Circuit). Methodist Episcopal Church. Norman, Jeremiah. 1798-1801. *1642*
—. Federal government. Malone, R. J. Mennonites. Military Intelligence. Surveillance. World War I. 1914-19. *2697*
—. Fielding, Joseph. Illinois (Nauvoo). Mormons. 1844-46. *3958*
—. Gehman, John B. Mennonites. Pennsylvania (Hereford). Speak Schools. 1853. *566*
—. Grant, Jedediah Morgan. Missions and Missionaries. Mormons. 1833-57. *1631*
—. Great Britain. North America. Physicians. Theologians. Ward, John. 17c. *2312*
—. Illinois (Nauvoo). Laub, George. Mormons. Smith, Joseph. Young, Brigham. 1845-46. *3961*
—. Illinois (Nauvoo). Mormons. Snow, Eliza Roxey. Women. 1842-44. *4044*
—. Indians. Missions and Missionaries. Spokan Indians. Walker, Elkanah. Walker, Mary. Washington, eastern. 1839-48. *1521*
—. Jesuits. McCormick, Vincent A. Vatican. World War II. 1942-45. *3755*
—. Lutheran Church. McPherson, Sarah M. Missouri (Brazeau). 1852-56. *3298*
—. Maine. Missions and Missionaries. Protestantism. Sewall, Jotham. 1778-1848. *1645*
—. Maine. Shakers. Wilson, Delmer. 1887. *4066*
—. Massachusetts (Cambridge). Piety. Puritans. Shepard, Thomas. 1640-44. *3656*
—. Mormons. Musser, Elise Furer. Political Leadership. Social Reform. Utah. Women. 1897-1967. *811*
—. Mormons. Woodruff, Wilford. 1830-1906. *3923*
Dick, Everett N. Adventist Medical Cadet Corps. Armies. Korean War. Personal narratives. World War II. 1934-53. *2644*
Dickey, Sarah. Heck, Barbara. Leadership. Methodist Church. Parker, Lois Stiles. Shaw, Anna Howard. Stereotypes. Willard, Frances E. Women. 19c. *812*
Dickinson, Emily. Attitudes. Evangelicalism. Friendship. Mount Holyoke College. 1848-50. *2827*
—. Identity. Intellectual history. Myths and Symbols. Poetry. Puritanism. Transcendentalism. Women. 1860's. *51*
—. Protestantism. Women. 1840-54. *73*
Dickinson, Jonathan. Clergy. Presbyterian Church. Subscription controversy. Westminster Standards. 1700-50. *3560*
Diocesan histories. Bibliographies. Episcopal Church, Protestant. Missions and Missionaries. ca 1776-1972. *3201*
Diocesan Standing Committee. Bishops. Episcopal Church, Protestant. ca 1789-1832. *3217*
Diocesan Theological Institute. Church of England. Clergy. Frontier and Pioneer Life. Ontario (Cobourg). Strachan, John. 1840-55. *732*
Diphtheria. Calvinism. Enlightenment. Great Awakening. New England. Sermons. 1735-40. *2260*
Diplomacy. China. Japan. Missions and Missionaries. Presbyterian Church. Stuart, John Leighton. 1937-41. *1745*
—. Great Britain. Missionaries. Ottoman Empire. Protestantism. 1824-42. *1697*
—. Hocking, William Ernest. Idealism. Philosophy. Political attitudes. 1918-66. *1368*
—. Pius XII, Pope. Taylor, Myron C. Vatican. World War II. 1940-50. *1025*
Diplomatic recognition. China. Missions and Missionaries. Revolution. Sun Yat-sen. 1911-13. *1724*
Directory of Worship. Presbyterian Church. Worship. 1788-1979. *3583*
Disaster relief. California. Charities. Economic aid. Jews. Nieto, Jacob. Rabbis. San Francisco Earthquake and Fire. 1906. *2520*
—. California (Oakland). Jews. Refugees. San Francisco Earthquake and Fire. Temple Sinai. 1906. *2527*
Disasters *See also* names of particular disasters, e.g. San Francisco Earthquake and Fire (1906); Earthquakes; Storms.
—. Civil War. Lincoln, Abraham. Puritans. Rhetoric. Sermons. 1650-1870. *1968*
Disciples of Christ. Antinomianism. Bible. Campbell, Alexander. 1810-60. *3109*
—. Antislavery sentiments. Campbell, Alexander. Civil religion. Indians. Politics. War. Women. 1823-55. *3108*
—. Baptists. Canada. Great Plains. Lutheran Church. Methodism. Pietism. Prairie Radicals. Radicals and Radicalism. 1890-1975. *954*
—. Baptists, Southern. Evolution. Kentucky. Methodist Church. Presbyterian Church. Schisms. 1920's. *2310*
—. Bible. Campbell, Alexander. Theology. ca 1830-60. *3110*
—. Bible. Cave, Robert Catlett. Missouri (St. Louis). Sermons. Theology. 1840's-90's. *3111*
—. Bible. Rhetoric. 19c. *1978*
—. Campbell, Alexander. Civil religion. Millenarianism. 1810-60. *1195*
—. Campbell, Alexander. Civil religion. Millenarianism. 1813-66. *3106*
—. Campbell, Alexander. Educational Reform. Frontier. Morality. 1825-1900. *579*
—. Cave, Robert Catlett. Liberalism. Missouri (St. Louis). Non-Sectarian Church of St. Louis. Theology. 1867-1923. *2913*
—. Church of Christ. Fundamentalism. Texas. 1972. *3105*
—. Clergy. Frontier. North Central States. Personal narratives. Snethen, Abraham. 1794-1830. 1977. *3112*
—. Colleges and Universities. Culver-Stockton University. Democratic Party. Missouri. Shannon, James. Slavery. 1821-59. *3107*

—. Dunkards. Hostetler, Joseph. Indiana. Restoration movement. Revivals. 1800-27. *3104*
—. Ecumenism. 19c-20c. *448*
—. Nova Scotia (Cornwallis Township). 1812-1910. *3103*
Discovery and Exploration *See also* Westward Movement.
—. Alaska. Educators. Episcopal Church, Protestant. Missions and Missionaries. Stuck, Hudson. 1904-20. *1647*
—. Art. Catholic Church. Hennepin, Louis. Minnesota (Minneapolis). Missions and Missionaries. Mississippi River (Falls of St. Anthony). 1680-1980. *1556*
—. Attitudes. Catholic Church. Colonial Government. Games. Indians. Missions and Missionaries. 16c-17c. *1524*
—. Bibliographies. Historians. Morison, Samuel Eliot (obituary). Puritans. 1887-1976. *233*
—. California (Monterey). Dominguez, Francisco Atanasio. Escalante, Silvestre Velez de. New Mexico. Overland Journeys to the Pacific. 1765-1805. *1480*
—. Catholic Church. Colonial Government. France. Jolliet, Louis. Marquette, Jacques. Missions and Missionaries. Mississippi River. Monuments. 1665-1700. *3767*
—. Catholic Church. Jolliet, Louis. Marquette, Jacques. Mississippi River. 1673. 1973. *1567*
Discrimination *See also* Civil Rights; Minorities; Racism; Segregation; Sex Discrimination.
—. Acadians. Catholic Church. Irish Canadians. New Brunswick. 1860-1900. *3855*
—. Anti-Catholicism. Church and state. Cox Library. *Koester* v. *Pardeeville* (1929). Libraries. Taxation. Wisconsin (Pardeeville). 1927-29. *1033*
—. Baptists. Japanese Americans. Resettlement. World War II. 1890-1970. *2547*
—. Catholic Church. Economic Conditions. Polish Canadians. Prairie Provinces. 1880's-1970's. *3796*
—. Catholic Church. Northwest Territories. Teachers colleges. 1884-1900. *77*
—. Catholic University of America. Colleges and Universities. District of Columbia. Negroes. Wesley, Charles H. 1914-48. *3729*
—. Catholics. College teachers. Higher education. 1960's-70's. *554*
—. Chinese Americans. Frontier and Pioneer Life. Montana. Public opinion. Supreme courts (state). 1864-1902. *2152*
—. Christianity. Folklore. Jews. Negroes. Stereotypes. 18c-1974. *2091*
—. Civil Rights movement. Florida (Miami). Louisiana (New Orleans). Murray, Hugh T., Jr. Personal narratives. Tulane Interfaith Council. 1959-60. *2548*
—. Ethnicity. Hutterites. Legislation. Prairie Provinces. Provincial government. 1960's-79. *1099*
—. Ethnocentrism. 1620-1965. *2092*
—. Georgia (Atlanta). Judaism (Orthodox, Reform). 1865-1915. *4109*
Discrimination, Educational. Anti-Catholicism. Colleges and Universities. Ethnic Groups. 1970's. *2106*
—. Protestantism. Women. 1818-91. *2899*
Diseases *See also* names of diseases, e.g. diphtheria, etc.; Epidemics; Medicine (practice of).
—. Childbirth. Congregationalism. Death and Dying. Diaries. Massachusetts (Westborough). Parkman, Ebenezer. Social Organization. 1724-82. *1447*
Diseases (classification). Etiology. Folk Medicine. Quebec. 1976-77. *1428*
Disfranchisement. Federal government. Mormons. State Legislatures. Suffrage. 1882-92. *1046*
Dissent. Banking. Mormons. Ohio (Kirtland). 1837-90. *3980*
—. Burned-over district (theory). Cross, Whitney R. Millerites. New York. 1830's-40's. 20c. *2974*
—. Catholic Church. Episcopal Church, Protestant. Pentecostal movement. 1950's-70's. *2742*
—. Catholic Church. Michigan (Detroit). Protestant Churches. Religious Education. 1958-71. *3777*
—. Clebsch, William A. Gaustad, Edwin Scott. Religious thought (review article). 17c-20c. *18*
—. Economic conditions. Military Service. Moravian Church. North Carolina (Salem). Slavery. Social change. Women. 1772-1860. *3516*
Dissertations *See also* Theses.
—. Anabaptists. Bibliographies. Mennonites. 1975-76. *3397*
—. Bibliographies. Edwards, Jonathan. Niebuhr, H. Richard. Niebuhr, Reinhold. Presbyterian Church. Reformed Churches. Tillich, Paul. 18c-20c. 1965-72. *2815*
—. Bibliographies. Mormons. Theses. 19c-1977. *4041*
—. Bibliographies. North Carolina. Prehistory-1970's. *28*
—. Colleges and universities. Conferences. Curricula. Jewish studies. 1979. *4138*
—. Colleges and universities. Conferences. Jewish studies. 1978. *4137*
District of Columbia *See also* Southeastern States.
—. Anti-Catholicism. Marquette, Jacques. State Politics. Statuary Hall. Wisconsin. 1887-1904. *2101*
—. Catholic Church. Jews. Judaism. Protestant churches. Psychological well-being. Religiosity. Worship. 1970's. *130*
—. Catholic University of America. Colleges and Universities. Discrimination. Negroes. Wesley, Charles H. 1914-48. *3729*
—. Church and State. Civil rights. Lobbying. 1964-72. *1322*
—. Johnson, Andrew. Lincoln, Abraham. Schurz, Carl. Seance. Spiritualism. 1865. *4293*
—. Missions and Missionaries. National Statuary Hall. Pacific Northwest. Pariseau, Mother Mary Joseph. Sisters of Charity of Providence. Women. 1856-1902. 1977. *1629*
Divine Light Mission. Attitudes. California (Berkeley). Converts. Davis, Rennie. Maharaj Ji. Politics. 1973. *4286*
—. Converts. Hare Krsna Movement. Youth. 1960's-70's. *4284*
—. Maharaj Ji. Organizational Theory. 1930's-70's. *4285*
—. Maharaj Ji. Youth movements. 1970's. *4281*
Divine Sovereignty. Covenant Theology. Ethics. Puritanism. 17c-18c. *3618*
Divinity (issue). Hodge, Charles *(Systematic Theology).* Jesus Christ. Nevin, John W. Presbyterian Church. Theology. 1872. *3581*
Divorce *See also* Family; Marriage.
—. Annulments. Birth Control. Canon law. Catholic Church. Netherlands. 1945-77. *914*
—. Christianity. National Fertility Study. Women. 1970's. *934*
—. Law. Massachusetts. Puritans. Social conditions. Women. 1639-92. *941*
—. Law. Vermont. 1777-1815. *792*
—. Mormons. Polygamy. Utah. 1844-90. *822*
Documents *See also* Manuscripts.
—. Alaska. Church finance. Education. Orthodox Eastern Church, Russian. Russian-American Company. Veniaminov, Metropolitan Innokentii. 1858. *2806*
—. American Revolution. Judaism. Letters. 1775-90. *1277*
—. American Revolution. National character. Presbyterians. 1729-87. *3596*
—. American Studies. Archives. Catholic University of America. Kenrick, Francis P. Missions and Missionaries. 1776-1865. *216*
—. Amish. Church History. Pennsylvania (Morgantown). Plank, D. Heber. 1668-1790's. 20c. *3388*
—. Anti-Semitism. Boxerman, William I. Coughlin, Charles Edward. Michigan (Detroit). 1939. *2131*
—. Bishops. Canada. Church of England. 1850-52. *3208*
—. California (Temecula). Catholic Church. Indians. Maltby, Charles. Mission San Antonio de Pala. 1866. *1573*
—. Carroll, John. Catholic Church. Clergy. Hanley, Thomas O'Brien *(The John Carroll Papers).* Research. 18c-19c. 1976-78. *3872*
—. Carroll, John. Catholic Church. Hanley, Thomas O'Brien (review article). 18c-19c. 1970's. *3672*
—. Catholic Church. Cunningham, Patrick. Irish Americans. Vermont (Brattleboro). 1847-98. *3725*
—. Catholic Church. Daily life. Girls. Holy Names of Jesus and Mary, Sisters of the. Oregon (Salem). Sacred Heart Academy. 1863-73. *699*
—. Catholic Church. Identity. National Catholic Welfare Council. Vatican. 1922. *3803*
—. Cheever, Thomas. Clergy. Congregationalism. Massachusetts. 1677-1749. *3122*
—. Chippewa Indians. Fullerton, Thomas. Indians. Methodist Episcopal Church. Minnesota. Missions and Missionaries. Wisconsin. 1841-44. *1531*
—. Christian Science. Extortion. Forgeries. Haushalter, Walter M. *(Mrs. Eddy Purloins from Hegel).* 1929-59. *3912*
—. Clergy. Editors and Editing. Historians. Sparks, Jared. Unitarianism. Washington, George. 1815-30. *4076*
—. Colonial Government. Franciscans. Missions and Missionaries. New Mexico. Spain. Vélez Cachupín, Thomas. ca 1754. *1586*
—. Episcopal Church, Protestant. Excavations. Illinois (Peoria County). Jubilee College. 1839-1979. *770*
—. Episcopal Church, Protestant. Missions and Missionaries. Puerto Rico. 1870-1952. *1679*
—. Free Thinkers. German Americans. Immigrants. Missouri. Reading. Religious liberty. St. Louis Free Congregation Library. 1850-99. *1123*
—. Friends, Society of. Methodism. National Characteristics. Political participation. Shakers. Tocqueville, Alexis de. 1831-40. *2780*
—. Friends, Society of. Missions and Missionaries. Religious Liberty. Virginia. Wilson, George. 1650-62. *1007*
—. Funk, John F. Mennonites (General Conference). 1864-1921. *3375*
—. Indian-White Relations. Missions and Missionaries. Western States. 1812-1923. *1483*
Doederlein, Paul Ferdinand. Crow Indians. Diaries. Indians. Lutheran Church. Missions and Missionaries. Wyoming. 1859-60. *1589*
Dogberry, Obediah. Free thinkers. Freedom of thought. *Liberal Advocate* (newspaper). New York (Rochester). Religious liberty. 1832-34. *1003*
Doherty, Robert W. Historiography. Methodology. Sociology of Religion. 1974. *264*
Dolan, Jay P. Betten, Neil. Catholic Church (review article). Working Class. 1830-1978. *3698*
Dolan, Jay P. (review article). Catholic Church. German Americans. Irish Americans. New York. Social Conditions. 1815-65. 1975. *3793*
Domestic and Foreign Missionary Society. Canada. Church of England. Japan. Missions and Missionaries. 1883-1902. *1587*
Domestic servants. Attitudes. Upper Classes. 1800-65. *1475*
Domesticity. Industrialization. Revivals. Womanhood, sentimental. 1830-70. *817*
—. Methodism. New York City. Palmer, Phoebe. Women. ca 1825-60. *877*
Dominguez, Francisco Atanasio. California (Monterey). Discovery and Exploration. Escalante, Silvestre Velez de. New Mexico. Overland Journeys to the Pacific. 1765-1805. *1480*
Dominicans. Americas (North and South). Antislavery Sentiments. Jesuits. 16c-18c. *2486*
—. California. Franciscans. Jesuits. Missions and Missionaries. Serra, Junípero. 1768-76. *1575*
—. Catholic Church. Church and state. Democracy. Mazzuchelli, Samuel Charles *(Memoirs).* Old Northwest. 1806-63. *1384*
—. Child care. Day Nurseries. Quebec (Montreal). Women. 1858-1920. *2505*
Doub, Peter. Education. Methodist Episcopal Church. North Carolina. Slavery. Women. 1796-1869. *3469*
Douglas, Ann. Albanese, Catherine L. Beecher, Henry Ward. Civil Religion. Clark, Clifford E., Jr. Handy, Robert T. McLoughlin, William G. Reform. Revivals (review article). Women. 1607-1978. *6*
—. Feminization. Protestantism. Reform. Sex roles. Stereotypes. ca 1820-75. 1977-80. *918*
Douglas, William O. Humanism. Presbyterian Church. Religious liberty. Supreme Court. 1915-80. *1128*
Douglass, Frederick. Abolition Movement. Christianity. 1830's-60's. *2496*
—. Abolition movement. Constitutional Amendments (15th). Negroes. Theology. 1825-86. *2495*
—. Abolition movement. Ireland (Belfast). Presbyterian Church. Smyth, Thomas. 1846. *2165*
Doukhobors. Amish. Hutterites. Mennonites. Molokans. North America. ca 1650-1977. *2769*

—. British Columbia. Daily life. Immigration. Personal narratives. Russia. 1880's-1976. *3918*
—. British Columbia. Russian Canadians. Saskatchewan. 1652-1976. *3916*
—. Canada. Immigration. Persecution. Russia. Sects, Religious. 1654-1902. *3917*
—. Canada. Immigration. Russia. 1652-1908. *3915*
—. Communalism. Saskatchewan. 1904. *415*
—. Ethnic groups. Federal government. Royal Canadian Mounted Police. Saskatchewan. Settlement. 1899-1909. *1006*
—. Galicians. Hospitals. Lake Geneva Mission. Missions and Missionaries. Presbyterian Church. Saskatchewan (Wakaw). 1903-42. *1492*
—. Public schools. Saskatchewan. 1905-50. *533*
Doull, Alexander John. Bishops. British Columbia (Kootenay). Church of England. 1870-1937. *3180*
Dow, Arthur Wesley. Art. Calvinism. Congregationalism. Massachusetts (Ipswich). Methodist Church. 1857-80. *1871*
Dowie, John Alexander. Christian Catholic Church. Evangelism. Illinois (Zion). Utopias. 1888-1907. *409*
Dowling, John. Adventists. Greeley, Horace. Miller, William. New York *Tribune* (newspaper). 1842. *2963*
Downs, Ellen J. Bloomfield Academy. Chickasaw Indians. Girls. Indians. Methodist Church. Oklahoma (Penola County). Personal Narratives. Schools. 1853-66. *772*
Drachman, Bernard. Central Conference of American Rabbis. Judaism. Judaism (Orthodox). Orthodox Jewish Sabbath Alliance. Sabbath. Saturday. 1903-30. *2277*
Drake, Thomas. Abolition Movement. Davis, David Brion. Friends, Society of (review article). James, Sydney. 1683-1863. 20c. *2471*
Drama *See also* Films; Theater.
—. Anti-Semitism. Literature. Stereotypes. 1830's-1920's. *2011*
—. *Ben-Hur* (play, novel). Christianity. Wallace, Lew. 1880-1900. *1872*
—. California (San Diego). Christmas. Parades. Social Customs. 1769-1980. *2714*
Draper, E. D. Ballou, Adin Augustus. Hopedale Community. Massachusetts (Milford). Utopias. 1824-56. *388*
Dreams. Childhood. Italy (Rome). Painting. Symbolism in Art. Vedder, Elihu. 1856-1923. *1888*
Dreiser, Theodore. Fiction. Social justice. 1900-45. *2020*
Dress. *See* Clothing.
Driggs, Nevada W. Nevada (Panaca). Personal narratives. Polygamy. Utah. 1890-93. *832*
Drinan, Robert F. Jesuits. Massachusetts. Political campaigns. 1970. *1267*
Drinker family. American Revolution. Diaries. Friends, Society of. Pacifism. Pennsylvania (Philadelphia). Prisoners. Virginia (Winchester). 1777-81. *2683*
Drugs (psychoactive). Meditation. ca 1974. *163*
Drummer, Jeremiah. Congregationalism. Letters. Massachusetts. Sabbath. Sewall, Samuel. Taylor, Edward. 1704. *2276*
Drummond County Mechanics Institute. Catholic Church. Farmers. Labor Unions and Organizations. Quebec (Drummond County). 1856-90. *1472*
Drunkenness. New England. Puritans. 17c. *2590*
Drury, Clifford M. Historians. Missions and Missionaries. Oregon. Presbyterian Church. Washington. 1928-74. *190*
—. Indians. Lee, Jason. Methodism. Missions and Missionaries. Oregon. Settlement. 1834-43. 1970's. *3480*
Dualism. Theology. Thoreau, Henry David. Transcendentalism. 1853-1906. *4073*
DuBois, W. E. B. Baker, Ray Stannard. Civil rights. Episcopal Church, Protestant. Liberalism. Negroes. Personal narratives. Whites. Wilmer, Cary Breckenridge. 1900-10. *2151*
—. Black nationalism. Crummell, Alexander. Episcopal Church, Protestant. Ferris, William H. Ideology. 1819-1898. *2424*
—. James, William *(Varieties of Religious Experience)*. Troeltsch, Ernst (review). 1912. *67*
Dubuque Diocese. Catholic Church. Church Schools. Hennessy, John. Iowa. Irish Americans. 1866-1900. *3720*
Duche, Jacob, Jr. Church of England. Great Britain. Pennsylvania (Philadelphia). Pietism. Swedenborgianism. 1750-1800. *2738*
Dudzik, Mary Theresa. Addams, Jane. Franciscan Sisters of Chicago. Illinois. Polish Americans. Social Work. Women. 1860-1918. *2511*
Dufresne, Andre B. Assimilation. Catholic Church. Clergy. French Canadians. Massachusetts (Holyoke). 1869-87. *302*
Dugdale, Joseph A. Abolition Movement. Friends, Society of. Reform. 1810-96. *2361*
Duggan, James. Bishops. Catholic Church. Chicago Diocese. Clergy. Illinois. McMullen, John. Succession. 1865-81. *3742*
Duke, Basil W. Catholic Church. Confederate Army. Fort Delaware. Prisoners of War. Wood, James F. 1864. *3844*
Duke University. Academic freedom. Bassett, John Spencer. Methodist Church. North Carolina (Durham). Racism. *South Atlantic Quarterly* (periodical). 1902-03. *3497*
Dulík, Joseph J. Clergy. Pioneers. Slovak Americans. Vaniščák, Gregory. 1909-38. *3823*
Dulles, John Foster. Anti-Communist Movements. Ecumenism. Morality. Oxford Conference (1937). Presbyterian Church. Protestantism. World order movement. 1937-48. *1375*
—. Federal Council of the Churches of Christ in America. Presbyterian Church. UN. 1941-45. *1312*
Duncan, William. Alaska (Metlakahtla). British Columbia. Capitalism. Missions and Missionaries. Tsimshian Indians. 1857-1974. *1519*
Dunkards. American Revolution. Friends, Society of. Mennonites. Moravian Church. Neutrality. Pacifism. Schwenkfelders. Taxation. 1765-83. *2670*
—. American Revolution. Loyalists. Mennonites. Pacifism. 1776-84. *2635*
—. American Revolution (antecedents). Conscientious Objectors. Mennonites. Pennsylvania. Petitions. 1775. *2710*
—. Disciples of Christ. Hostetler, Joseph. Indiana. Restoration movement. Revivals. 1800-27. *3104*
—. Evangelism. German Americans. Great Awakening. Immigration. Lutheran Church. Moravian Church. Northeastern or North Atlantic States. Reformed churches. 1720-60. *2237*
—. Friends, Society of. Historic Peace Churches (meeting). Kansas (Newton). Krehbiel, H. P. Mennonites. Pacifism. 1935-36. *2663*
—. Friends, Society of. Mennonites. Militarism. Pacifism. 1900-78. *2646*
Duplessis, Maurice (review article). Black, Conrad. Catholic Church. Church and state. Provincial Government. Quebec. Rumilly, Robert. 1930's-77. *1124*
Durán, Narciso. California. Franciscans. Indians. Missions. Secularization. 1826-46. *1093*
—. California. Franciscans. Indians. Missions and Missionaries. Music. 1806-46. *1924*
Durkheim, Emile. Charismatic Movement. Silva Mind Control. Social organization. 1970's. *158*
Durr, John N. Bishops. Mennonite Conference, Allegheny. Pennsylvania. 1872-1934. *3440*
Dutch Americans. American Revolution. Artifacts. Reformed Dutch Church. 17c-18c. *1866*
—. American Revolution. New Jersey. New York. Reformed Dutch Church. 1775-83. *1208*
—. American Revolution. Reformed Dutch Church. 1740-90. *1227*
—. Catholic Church. Immigration. 1845-75. *3857*
—. Churches. New York City. Reformed Dutch Church. 1686-88. *3166*
—. Genealogy. Iowa. Mennonites. Settlement. Swiss Americans. 1839-1974. *3370*
—. Immigration. North Dakota. Reformed Dutch Church. South Dakota. 1880's-1951. *3161*
—. Mennonites. New Netherland (New Amsterdam). Shecut, John L. E. W. *(The Eagle of the Mohawks)*. Universalists. 17c. 1800-36. *2012*
—. New Netherland. Religious liberty. Smith, George L. (review article). Trade. 17c. *1109*
—. New York (Long Island). Reformed Dutch Church. 1636-1700. *3162*
Duus, O. F. Clergy. Country stores. Knoph, Thomas. Ledgers. Lutheran Church. Norwegian Americans. Wisconsin (Waupaca township; Scandinavia). 1853-56. *3334*
Dwellings. Jacobsen, Florence S. Mormons. Personal narratives. Restorations. Utah (St. George). Young, Brigham. 19c. 1970's. *1789*
—. Mormons. Utah (Salt Lake City). Young, Amelia Folsom. Young, Brigham. 1863-1926. *1785*
Dwight, Theodore. Antislavery Sentiments. Congregationalism. Connecticut. Poetry. 1788-1829. *2468*
Dwight, Timothy. Attitudes. Congregationalism. New England. New York. Travel (accounts). Wilderness. 1790's. *2066*
—. Beecher, Lyman. Congregationalism. New England. Presbyterian Church. Republicanism. Taylor, Nathaniel William. 1790-1840. *1356*
—. Colleges and Universities. Congregationalism. Human Relations. Stiles, Ezra. Yale University. 1778-95. *706*
—. Congregationalism. New England. Political attitudes. 1775-1817. *1369*
Dwight, Timothy *(Travels in New England and New York)*. Congregationalism. Northeastern or North Atlantic States. 1796-1815. *2022*
Dye, Alexander V. Mexico (Sonora). Mormons. Revolution. Settlement. 1912. *4016*
Dyer, Leon. California (San Francisco). Jews. Leadership. Maryland (Baltimore). 1820's-75. *4142*

E

Earlham College. Evolution. Friends, Society of. Moore, Joseph. Virginia (Richmond). 1861. *2307*
Earthquakes. Christianity. Converts. Mississippi River. Missouri. New Madrid Earthquake. 1811-12. *2789*
—. Jesuits. Quebec. *Relation de 1663* (report). 1663. *2296*
—. Literature. New England. Puritans. 1727. *2289*
East Indians *See also* Asians.
—. Canada. Church Schools. Missions and Missionaries. Presbyterian Church. Trinidad and Tobago. 1868-1912. *1726*
Eastern Religions *See also* Buddhism, Hinduism.
—. California. Christianity. Cults. 1970's. *107*
—. Christianity. Social Organizations. Youth Movements. 1968-74. *141*
—. Conversion. Mysticism. Psychotherapy. 1970's. *2290*
Eastern Rite Catholics. *See* Uniates.
Eaton, Margaret (Peggy) O'Neale. Clergy. Democratic Party. Ely, Ezra Stiles. Jackson, Andrew. Presbyterian Church. 1829-30. *3536*
Ebenezer Baptist Church. Baptists. Civil rights movement. Georgia (Atlanta). Personal narratives. Roberts, Joseph L., Jr. 1960-75. *2556*
Ebenezer Methodist Church. Baptists. Inscriptions. Methodist Church. Mount Bethel Baptist Church. South Carolina (Anderson County). Tombstones. 1856-1978. *2848*
Eby, Ezra E. Canada. Immigration. Loyalists. Mennonites. Pennsylvania. 18c-1835. *1237*
Ecclesiastical law. Crime and criminals. Great Britain. Massachusetts. Roman Law. 17c. *972*
Ecclesiastical pluralism. Allen, Bennet. Church of England. Colonial Government. Jordan, John Morton. Maryland. Patronage. Sharpe, Horatio. 1759-70. *1051*
Ecclesiology Society. Anglican Communion. Architecture. Chancels. Great Britain (Cambridge). 1839-60. *1779*
Eckerlin, Emmanuel. Beissel, Johann Conrad. Communalism. Ephrata Cloister. Pennsylvania (Conestoga Valley). 1732-68. *390*
École Sociale Populaire. Catholic Church. Labor Unions and Organizations. Quebec. Social Change. 1911-75. *1469*
—. Catholic Church. Propaganda. Quebec (Montreal). Syndicalism. Working Class. 1911-49. *1473*
Ecology *See also* Environment; Wilderness.
—. Hopkins, Gerard Manley. Humanities. Jesuits. Poetry. Science. ca 1840-70's. *3701*
Economic Aid. Black power. Church and Social Problems. Episcopal Church, Protestant. General Convention Special Program. Self-determination. 1963-75. *2541*
—. California. Charities. Disaster relief. Jews. Nieto, Jacob. Rabbis. San Francisco Earthquake and Fire. 1906. *2520*

Economic Conditions *See also* terms beginning with Economic.
—. Abolition Movement. Attitudes. Competition. Evangelicalism. Poverty. ca 1830-60. *2473*
—. Africa. Negroes. Slave trade. Social Customs. ca 1500-1940's. *24*
—. Agriculture. Amish. Illinois. Social organization. 1960-72. *3428*
—. Alaska. Assimilation. Brady, John Green. Indian-White Relations. Missions and Missionaries. Tlingit Indians. 1878-1906. *1548*
—. Catholic Church. Discrimination. Polish Canadians. Prairie Provinces. 1880's-1970's. *3796*
—. Church location. Congregationalism. Maryland (Baltimore). Protestantism. 1840-70. *2853*
—. Communes. Education. Mennonites, Old Order. Pennsylvania (East Penn Valley). 1949-75. *410*
—. Dissent. Military Service. Moravian Church. North Carolina (Salem). Slavery. Social change. Women. 1772-1860. *3516*
—. Ethnic groups. Folklore. Mail-Order Business. Social Conditions. Voodoo. 1970-79. *2205*
—. Frontier and Pioneer life. Indians. Missions and Missionaries. Presbyterian Church. South Dakota. 1840-1900. *3540*
—. Great Awakening. Nova Scotia (Yarmouth). Social Conditions. 1760's-70's. *2626*
—. Judaism. Social Status. 1970-71. *4129*
—. Mormons. Ohio (Kirtland). Smith, Joseph. 1830's. *351*
—. Mormons. Polygamy. Railroads. Salt Lake and Fort Douglas Railroad. Statehood. Utah. Young, John W. 1883-1924. *3993*
—. Mormons. United Order. ca 1870's-90's. *2565*
Economic development. Alcohol. Gambling. Legislation. 1977. *2383*
—. Catholic Church. Church Finance. LaRocque, Paul. Quebec. Sherbrooke Diocese. 1893-1926. *3783*
—. Catholic Church. Colonization. French Canadians. Geopolitics. Provost, T. S. Quebec (Mattawinie district). 17c-1890. *3809*
—. Catholic Church. Quebec. Social Conditions. 1850-1950. *3743*
—. Government. Quebec (Lower Canada). Social classes. Ultramontanism. 19c. *962*
—. Protestant Ethic. Reformation. -1973. *339*
Economic Growth *See also* Industrialization; Modernization.
—. Catholic Church. Immigration. Irish Americans. Michigan (Detroit). Toleration. 1850. *2790*
—. Christianity. Ethnic Groups. Michigan (Detroit). Pluralism. 1880-1940. *2748*
—. Competition. Mormons. Utah (southern). 500-1979. *4038*
—. Illinois (Nauvoo). Mississippi River. Mormons. Steamboats. 1839-46. *367*
Economic reform. Aberhart, William. Alberta. Politics. Prime ministers. Radio. 1934-37. *1216*
Economic Theory. Catholic Church. Conservatism. Corrigan, Michael. George, Henry. McGlynn, Edward. New York. 1886-94. *2562*
—. Catholic Church. French Canadians. Minville, Esdras. Quebec. 20c. *2558*
—. Christianity. Ethics. George, Henry. 1879. *2560*
—. Theology. 1974. *374*
Economics *See also* Business; Commerce; Depressions; Finance; Income; Labor; Land; Population; Prices; Property; Socialism; Trade.
—. Political systems. Public Policy. ca 1920-72. *1247*
Ecumenism. Alienation. Judaism (Conservative, Reform). Liberalism. Utah (Salt Lake City). 1971. *499*
—. Americanization. Catholic Church. Europe. Pluralism. Theology. 1775-1820. *295*
—. Americanization. Episcopal Church, Protestant. Lutheran Church, Swedish. Swedish Americans. 1630-1850. *322*
—. Anglican communion. Catholic Church. Hughes, John Jay. Religious Orders. -1973. *493*
—. Anglican Congress. Gray, Walter H. Minnesota (Minneapolis). 1940-54. *476*
—. Anglo-Catholics. Catholic Church. Clergy. Episcopal Church, Protestant. *Lamp* (periodical). Wattson, Paul James. 1903-09. *460*
—. Anti-Catholicism. Congregationalism. Cox, Samuel Hanson. Episcopal Church, Protestant. Evangelicalism. Presbyterian Church, New School. Slavery. 1840's. *471*
—. Anti-Communist Movements. Dulles, John Foster. Morality. Oxford Conference (1937). Presbyterian Church. Protestantism. World order movement. 1937-48. *1375*
—. Antimodernism. Christianity. Theology. 1975. *2734*
—. Archives. Historical Societies. Pennsylvania (Philadelphia). Presbyterian Historical Society. 1852-1977. *260*
—. Bad Boll Conferences. Germany. Lutheran Church. 1948. *439*
—. Baptist World Alliance. 1905-73. *490*
—. Baptist World Alliance. Charities. 1945-73. *450*
—. Baptists. Canada. USA. 1760-1979. *3031*
—. Baptists. Canadian Council of Churches. World Council of Churches. 1907-79. *462*
—. Baptists. Catholic Church. 1967-77. *500*
—. Baptists. Church Government. 1650-1975. *468*
—. Baptists, Big Hatchie. Baptists, Southern. Tennessee (Haywood, Lauderdale, Tipton counties). 1903-78. *3010*
—. Baptists, Southern. Concord Baptist Association. Louisiana (Webster Parish). 1832-1972. *463*
—. Biblical studies. Missions and Missionaries. Palestine. Protestantism. 1812-1975. *1748*
—. Brown, Robert McAfee. 1920-74. *441*
—. California (Placerville). El Dorado County Federated Church. Methodist Church. Presbyterian Church. 1850-1950. *492*
—. Canada. Church History. United Church of Canada. 1920-76. *442*
—. Canada. Church of England. Symonds, Herbert. 1897-1921. *483*
—. Canada. Immigration. Nationalism. Protestant churches. United Church of Canada. 1902-25. *491*
—. Canada. Mennonites (Canadian Conference). Pioneers. 1873-1978. *475*
—. Canada. Methodist Church. Patrick, William. Presbyterian Church. 1900-11. *443*
—. Canada, Western. Lutheran Church. Stuermer, Herbert. 1922. *489*
—. Canadian Council of Churches. World Conference of Christian Youth, 1st. Youth. 1939-79. *464*
—. Capers, William. *Christian Advocate* (newspaper). Letters. Methodist Episcopal Church. Methodist Episcopal Church (South). Slavery. 1854. 1875. *479*
—. Carroll, John. Catholic Church. Immigrants. Nativism. Protestants. 1790-1820. *496*
—. Catholic Church. Chapel-of-St. John's-in-the-Wilderness. Episcopal Church, Protestant. New York (Graymoor). Society of the Atonement. Wattson, Paul James. White, Lurana Mary. 1909-18. *461*
—. Catholic Church. Episcopal Church, Protestant. Society of the Atonement. Wattson, Paul James. White, Lurana. Women. 1870-1928. *459*
—. Catholic Church. Merton, Thomas. 1949-68. *452*
—. Catholic Church. Protestantism. Weigel, Gustave. 1950-64. *497*
—. Cavert, Samuel McCrea. Christianity. Germany, West. World Council of Churches. 1945-46. *486*
—. Charities. Hungarian Americans. Judaism (Reform). Rabbis. Wise, Stephen Samuel. World War II. Zionism. 1890's-1949. *4229*
—. Christian Unity Foundation. Episcopal Church, Protestant. Homans, Rockland Tyng. Huntington, William Reed. 1886-1942. *454*
—. Christianity. Church and Social Problems. Civil religion. Theology. 1967-70's. *1181*
—. Christianity. Country Life. Progressivism. Protestant Churches. Reform. Wisconsin. 1904-20. *2723*
—. Christianity. Self-determination. 1960's-70's. *473*
—. Christianity. Women. World Conference of Christian Youth, 1st. Young Women's Christian Association. 1939-79. *488*
—. Church and State. Denominationalism. Evangelical Alliance. Great Britain. 1846. *484*
—. Church congresses. Episcopal Church, Protestant. 1874-1933. *469*
—. Clergy. Lutheran Church (Missouri Synod, Norwegian). Munch, Johan Storm. Norway. Wisconsin (Wiota). 1827-1908. *3324*
—. Congregation Kol Ami. Judaism. Utah (Salt Lake City). 1964-76. *482*
—. Debates. Methodist Episcopal Church. Methodist Episcopal Church (South). Race. Virginia. 1924-25. *467*
—. Denominationalism. Protestantism. 16c-1979. *480*
—. Disciples of Christ. 19c-20c. *448*
—. Education. Mackay, John A. Personal narratives. Presbyterian Church of the United States of America. Princeton Theological Seminary. Theology. 1910-75. *3543*
—. Episcopal Church, Protestant. Lutheran Church (United Synod of the South). 1860-90. *438*
—. Europe. Protestant Churches. World War II. 1900-45. *465*
—. Evangelical Alliance. Evangelicalism. Presbyterian Church. 1867-73. *456*
—. Evangelical and Reformed Church. Presbyterian Church. Richards, George Warren. World Alliance of Reformed Churches. 1900-55. *481*
—. Evangelism. Protestantism. Social change. Social justice. Student Christian Movement. 19c-20c. *440*
—. Federal Council of the Churches of Christ in America. Hopkins, Charles Howard. Politics. Protestant Churches. Social gospel. 1880-1908. *487*
—. France. Jews. Vatican. 1975. *501*
—. Great Awakening. Moravian Church. Presbyterian Church. Tennent, Gilbert. Theology. Zinzendorf, Nikolaus. 1740-41. *2226*
—. Japan (Yokohama). Klein, Frederick C. Methodist Protestant Church. Missions and Missionaries. 1880-93. *458*
—. Jews. National Council of Churches (General Assembly). Protestant churches. 1969-74. *502*
—. Liberalism. Manitoba. Social gospel. United Church of Canada. 1870's-1925. *449*
—. Lutheran Church. Schmucker, Samuel Simon. 1838. *474*
—. Lutheran Church, American. Nelson, E. Clifford. Schiotz, Fredrik A. 1945-69. *485*
—. Methodist Church. Nova Scotia (Springhill). Presbyterian Church. St. Andrew's Wesley United Church of Canada. United Church of Canada. 1800-1976. *2829*
—. National Council of Churches. Organizational stress. 1908-69. *478*
—. Negroes. Protestantism. Reform. World Conference of Christian Youth, 1st. Youth. 1939-79. *2884*
—. Pennsylvania (Philadelphia). Presbyterian Church, Cumberland. World Alliance of Reformed Churches. 1870-80. *455*
—. Pluralism. Social reform. Tolerance. 1975. *105*
—. Presbyterian Church. 1549-1979. *451*
—. Presbyterian Church, Cumberland. Presbyterian Church of the United States of America. 1906. *437*
—. Presbyterian Church, Cumberland. Theology. World Alliance of Reformed Churches. 1880-84. *470*
—. Presbyterian Church, Southern. South. 1861-74. *477*
—. Reformed churches. World Alliance of Reformed Churches. 1957-62. *472*
—. United Church of Christ. 19c-20c. *494*
Eddy, Mary Baker. Christian Science. Gottschalk, Stephen (review article). Women. 1885-1910. *3913*
—. Christian Science. Lee, Ann. Personality. Shakers. Theology. Women. 1736-1910. *2753*
—. Christian Science. Political power. Political Protest. Women. 1879-99. *840*
—. Christian Science. Women. 1840's-1926. *3914*
—. Hypnotism. New England. Psychiatry. Quimby, Phineas Parkhurst. 1820's-66. *1442*
Edgewood Children's Center. Charities. Missouri (Webster Groves). Orphans. Protestantism. St. Louis Protestant Orphan Asylum. 1834-1979. *2518*
Editorials. Barnes, James. Murray, Robert. Nova Scotia (Halifax). *Presbyterian Witness and Evangelical Advocate* (newspaper). 1848-1910. *3584*
Editors and Editing *See also* Press.
—. Adventists. Clement, Lora E. Women. *Youth's Instructor* (newspaper). 1927-52. *1987*

—. *American Mercury* (periodical). Ku Klux Klan. Mencken, H. L. Methodist Episcopal Church (South). Temperance Movements. 1910-33. *2033*
—. Anti-Catholicism. Bapst, John. Chaney, William Henry. Jesuits. Maine (Ellsworth). Nativism. 1853-54. *2121*
—. Anti-Catholicism. Chicago *Tribune* (newspaper). Illinois. Political Parties. 1853-61. *2112*
—. Antislavery Sentiments. Kansas. Newspapers. Providence. Rhetoric. 1855-58. *2034*
—. Brownson, Henry Francis. Catholic Church. 1835-1900. *3836*
—. California (San Francisco). Catholic Church. Clergy. Ethnicity. Irish Americans. Yorke, Peter C. ca 1885-1925. *3887*
—. Catholic Church. Civil War. Copperheads. *Metropolitan Record* (newspaper). Mullaly, John. New York City. 1861-64. *1234*
—. Catholic Church. Clergy. Historiography. *New Catholic Encyclopedia*. Polish Americans. Swastek, Joseph Vincent (obituary). 1913-77. *227*
—. Catholic Church. *Commonweal* (periodical). Williams, Michael. 1922-38. *3716*
—. Clergy. Documents. Historians. Sparks, Jared. Unitarianism. Washington, George. 1815-30. *4076*
—. Germany. Mennonites. Miller, Samuel H. Trials. World War I. 1917-18. *2658*
—. "Letter to My Country Friends" (series). Murray, Robert. Nova Scotia (Halifax). *Presbyterian Witness* (newspaper). 1863. *987*
—. Mormons. Utah. *Woman's Exponent* (periodical). Women. 1872-1914. *3937*
Edmunds Act (US, 1882). Arizona. Federal government. Mormons. Polygamy. 1880's. *1000*
—. Dalton, Edward Meeks. Mormons. Polygamy. Utah. 1852-86. *1028*
—. Mormons. Polygamy. Prisons. Utah. 1880's. *1004*
Edson, Theodore. Episcopal Church, Protestant. Massachusetts (Lowell). St. Anne's Parish. Textile industry. 1800-65. *366*
Education *See also* subjects with the subdivision study and teaching, e.g. Art History (study and teaching); headings beginning with education and educational; Audiovisual Materials; Colleges and Universities; Curricula; Discrimination, Educational; Elementary Education; Federal Aid to Education; Higher Education; Religious Education; Scholarship; Schools; Secondary Education; Teaching; Textbooks.
—. Abolition Movement. Baptists. First African Baptist Church. Meachum, John Berry. Missouri (St. Louis). Negroes. 1815-54. *2482*
—. Abolition Movement. Freedmen. McPherson, James M. (review article). Missions and Missionaries. Protestantism. 1865-1910. 1975. *563*
—. Addams, Jane. Friends, Society of. Hull House. Ideology. Illinois (Chicago). Women. 1875-1930. *911*
—. Adventists. California (Loma Linda). Medicine. 1810-1929. *2971*
—. Adventists. Missions and Missionaries. New Mexico (Sandoval). Spanish-American Seminary. 1928-53. *751*
—. Africans' School. Benezet, Anthony. Friends, Society of. Negroes. Pennsylvania (Philadelphia). 1770's-80's. *527*
—. Aged. Catholic Church. Charities. Immigration. New Brunswick (Saint John). Orphans. Sisters of Charity of the Immaculate Conception. 1854-64. *2509*
—. Agriculture. Communalism. German Americans. Hutterites. Pacific Northwest. Pacifism. 20c. *392*
—. Alaska. Church finance. Documents. Orthodox Eastern Church, Russian. Russian-American Company. Veniaminov, Metropolitan Innokentii. 1858. *2806*
—. Alberta. Assimilation. Hutterites. 1920-70. *534*
—. American Board of Commissioners for Foreign Missions. Brainerd Mission. Cherokee Indians. Indian-White Relations. Letters. Southeastern States. 1817-38. *1605*
—. American Colonization Society. Crummell, Alexander. Episcopal Church, Protestant. Liberia. Missions and Missionaries. Negroes. 1853-73. *1671*
—. American Missionary Association. Civil Rights. Florida. Freedmen. 1864-74. *548*
—. American Missionary Association. Civil War. Missouri. Negroes. 1862-65. *547*
—. American Missionary Association. Congregationalism. Freedmen. Georgia (Liberty County). 1870-80's. *549*
—. American Revolution. Great Awakening. Pluralism. Theology. 1776. *1386*
—. Ames Church. Freedmen. Hartzell, Joseph C. Methodist Episcopal Church. Missionaries. Republican Party. South. 1870-73. *3481*
—. Amish. Military. Pennsylvania. Trials. Wisconsin. 1755-1974. *3401*
—. Andrews, John. Clergy. Episcopal Academy. Pennsylvania, University of. 1765-1810. *507*
—. Anglican Communion. Canada. Great Britain. Missionaries. Protestantism. Sudan Interior Mission. 1937-55. *1741*
—. Anti-Catholicism. Anti-Semitism. Minorities. North Carolina. Prejudice. Religious beliefs. 1957-73. *2093*
—. Axtell, James (review article). New England. Puritans. Social Organization. 17c-18c. 1974. *526*
—. Bacon, Thomas. Church of England. Clergy. Maryland. Politics. Slavery. Theology. ca 1745-68. *3175*
—. Baptist Student Center. Georgia (Athens). Nicholson, David Bascom, III. 1925-52. *631*
—. Baptist Triennial Convention. Church Finance. Missions and missionaries. Rice, Luther. Wayland, Francis. 1823-26. *3018*
—. Baptists. Clergy. Income. Social Status. 1651-1980. *2603*
—. Baptists. Colleges and Universities. Everett Institute. Louisiana (Spearsville). 1893-1908. *605*
—. Baptists. Indians. Kansas. Lykins, Johnston. Potawatomi Indians. Pottawatomie Baptist Manual Labor Training School. 1846-67. *508*
—. Baptists, American. Missions. Negroes. South. 1862-81. *739*
—. Baptists, Southern. Negroes. Paternalism. 1880's-90's. *553*
—. Baptists, Southern. Negroes. Racism. Reconstruction. 1865-76. *2149*
—. Berkeley, George. Church of England. Reform. Rhode Island (Newport). Sectarianism. 1704-34. *3230*
—. Bibliographies. Bishops. Catholic Church. Keane, John J. 1838-1918. *3891*
—. Bishops. Catholic Church. Medicine. Quebec (Gaspé). Ross, François Xavier. Social Conditions. 1923-45. *3787*
—. Bishops. Church of England. Feild, Edward. Great Britain. Newfoundland. 1826-44. *3198*
—. Breckinridge, Robert Jefferson. Clergy. Danville Theological Seminary. Emancipation. Kentucky. Presbyterian Church. 1800-71. *3544*
—. Brethren in Christ. Christianity. Evangelism. Holiness movement. Individualism. 1870-1910. *3421*
—. Brigham Young University. Mormons. Utah (Provo). 1831-1970's. *588*
—. California (San Diego). Chinese Mission School. Congregationalism. 1885-1960. *535*
—. Calvinism. Massachusetts (Andover). Phillips Academy. 1778-1978. *584*
—. Canada. Catholic Church. French Canadians. Quebec. Rinfret, Fernand. Siegfried, André *(Le Canada, les deux races: Problèmes politiques contemporains)*. Social Sciences. 1906-07. *3873*
—. Cardome (home). Catholic Church. Kentucky (Scott County; Georgetown). Mount Admirabilis (academy). Sisters of the Visitation. 1875-1975. *600*
—. Catholic Church. Charities. Moore, Julia. Ontario (London). Personal narratives. Sisters of St. Joseph. Women. 1868-85. *2517*
—. Catholic Church. Church finance. Indian-White Relations. Oklahoma. Quapaw Indians. 1876-1927. *3727*
—. Catholic Church. Georgia (Skidaway Island). Negroes. Orphanages. Poor Clares. Women. 1885-87. *3806*
—. Catholic Church. Hackett, Francis. Ireland (Kilkenny, Clongowes Wood). Irish Americans. Literature. 1880's-1901. *3818*
—. Catholic Church. Historiography. 19c. *679*
—. Catholic Church. Indians. Missions and Missionaries. North Dakota. Pioneers. Presentation of the Blessed Virgin Mary, Sisters of the. South Dakota. Women. 1880-96. *727*
—. Catholic Church. Missions and Missionaries. Protestant Churches. Prucha, Francis Paul (review article). 1888-1912. *1538*
—. Catholic Church. Newspapers. Ontario. 1851-1948. *543*
—. Cherokee Indians. Friends, Society of. 1880-92. *712*
—. Children's Order of the United Society of Believers. Shakers. Utopias. Utopias. 1780-1900. *4064*
—. Christianity. Games, board. Mansion of Happiness (game). Social Change. Values. 1832-1904. *2711*
—. Church and Social Problems. Poverty. Racism. 1970's. *2435*
—. Church and State. Episcopal Church, Protestant. Indians (agencies). Oklahoma, western. Stouch, George W. H. Whirlwind Day School. ca 1904-14. *1086*
—. Church and State. Great Britain. India. Secularization. 19c. *522*
—. Church membership. Cities. Midwest. Occupational mobility. 1955-75. *2616*
—. Church of England. Clergy. Missions and Missionaries. Quebec (Three Rivers). Wood, Samuel. 1822-68. *3202*
—. Church of England. Indians. Methodist Church. Missions and Missionaries. Ontario (Algoma, Huron). Wilson, Edward F. 1868-93. *1596*
—. Church Schools. Hasidism (Lubavitch). Judaism. Quebec (Montreal). 1969-71. *550*
—. Civil rights programs. Clergy. Negroes. New York (Buffalo). 1969-70. *2554*
—. Communes. Economic conditions. Mennonites, Old Order. Pennsylvania (East Penn Valley). 1949-75. *410*
—. Congregational Library. Massachusetts (Boston). 19c-20c. *195*
—. Congregationalism. New Mexico (Albuquerque). Prohibition. Social gospel. 1900-17. *2448*
—. Democracy. Fundamentalism. Local Politics. Morality. Social Change. Vigilantism. 1920's. *2387*
—. Doub, Peter. Methodist Episcopal Church. North Carolina. Slavery. Women. 1796-1869. *3469*
—. Ecumenism. Mackay, John A. Personal narratives. Presbyterian Church of the United States of America. Princeton Theological Seminary. Theology. 1910-75. *3543*
—. Engelhardt, Zephyrin. Franciscans. Holy Childhood Indian School Printery. Indians. Michigan (Harbor Springs). Printing. 1894-1913. *1584*
—. Episcopal Church, Protestant. Girls. Indians. St. Mary's Episcopal School for Indian Girls. South Dakota (Springfield). 1873-1973. *687*
—. Episcopal Church, Protestant. Louisiana (New Orleans). Polk, Leonidas. Slavery. 1805-65. *3219*
—. Evangelism. Freedmen. Presbyterians. 1872-1900. *3589*
—. Family. Friends, Society of. Pennsylvania. Social Customs. Socialization. ca 1740-76. *3279*
—. France. Hymns. Neau, Elias. New York. Protestant Churches. Slaves. ca 1689-1722. *1913*
—. Friends, Society of. Girls. Ontario. 1790-1820. *749*
—. Friends, Society of. Hallowell, Benjamin. Science. Virginia (Alexandria). 1824-60. *3281*
—. Frontier and Pioneer Life. Tennessee. 1758-96. *544*
—. Georgia (Savannah). Great Awakening. Orphans. Whitefield, George. 1738-71. *731*
—. Great Britain. Greaves, Richard L. Mather (family). Middlekauff, Robert. New England. Puritans. 1596-1728. *607*
—. Indian-White Relations. Missionaries. Social reform. ca 1609-1900. *1498*
—. Mennonites. Sharp, Solomon Zook. 1860-1931. *755*
—. Mennonites, old order. Pennsylvania. Social change. 1653-1975. *664*
—. Middle classes. Religiosity. Troeltsch, Ernst. 1960's-70's. *2602*
—. Middle East. Missions and Missionaries. 19c-20c. *1730*
—. Missions and Missionaries. Presbyterian Church. Puerto Rico. Social Customs. 1898-1917. *1727*
—. Mormons. Religious education. Utah. 1890-1929. *735*

—. Mormons. Theology. Universe. 1830-75. *3977*
—. New Brunswick. Socialism. Stuart, Henry Harvey. 1873-1952. *2369*
—. Ohio (Cincinnati). Sisters of Charity of St. Joseph. Social Work. Women. 1809-1979. *2514*
—. Pennsylvania (Philadelphia). Women. Young Ladies Academy. 1780's-90's. *520*
—. Political Parties. 1960's-74. *1261*
—. Religiosity. Social Conditions. Technology. 1945-75. *561*
Education, Finance *See also* Federal Aid to Education; State Aid to Education.
—. 1640's-1750's. *702*
—. Anti-Catholicism. Church and State. Clergy. MacKinnon, Murdoch. Presbyterian Church. Saskatchewan. School Act (Saskatchewan, 1930; amended). Scott, Walter. 1913-26. *528*
—. Bible (King James version). Catholic Church. Church Schools. City Politics. Michigan (Detroit). Protestantism. Religion in the Public Schools. 1842-53. *2716*
—. Christianity. Corporations. Higher education. Social Darwinism. 1860-1930. *540*
—. Church and State. Church schools. Jews. Public Policy. Religion in the Public Schools. 1961-71. *512*
—. Church Schools. Constitutional Amendments (1st). Government. Religion in the public schools. 1950's-70's. *564*
—. Church schools. Government. Prayer. Public opinion. Religion in the Public Schools. 1962-68. *504*
—. Church schools. Public finance. Supreme Court. 1971-73. *663*
—. Clark, Joseph. Fund raising. Personal narratives. Princeton University (Nassau Hall). Travel. 1802-04. *612*
Education (review article). Germany. Greven, Philip. Protestantism. Strauss, Gerald. Youth. 16c-19c. *850*
Educational attainment. Catholic Church. Immaculate Conception Primary School. Lithuanian Americans. Missouri (St. Louis). Occupations. 1948-68. *2607*
Educational innovation. Methodist Church, United. Southern Methodist University. Student activists. Texas (Dallas). 1972-74. *720*
Educational Policy. Adventists. California (San Francisco). Debates. Evolution. Science League of America. 1925. *2291*
—. Baptists. Evolution. Kentucky. Science. 1922-28. *2347*
—. Bureau of Indian Affairs. Indians (reservations). Language. Missions and Missionaries. 19c-20c. *516*
—. California. Church and state. Creationism. Curricula. Evolution. Science. 1963-74. *2331*
—. Centenary College. Dance. Louisiana. Methodist Church. 1941. *688*
—. Fundamentalism. Public schools. Textbooks. West Virginia (Kanawha County). 1975. *576*
—. Presbyterian Church. Princeton University (trustees). 1806-07. *541*
Educational Reform *See also* Compulsory Education; Education; Educators; School Integration.
—. Acculturation. Immigration. Public Schools. 19c-1910's. *532*
—. Adventists. Colleges and Universities. Sutherland, Edward A. 1904-50. *693*
—. American Institute for Education. Country life. Elites. Massachusetts. Nationalism. Protestantism. 1830-37. *573*
—. Campbell, Alexander. Disciples of Christ. Frontier. Morality. 1825-1900. *579*
Educational Tests and Measurements. Buerger, Paul Theodor. *Collegium Fratrum* (organization). Indiana (Fort Wayne). Letters. Lutheran Church. 1858. *3315*
Educators *See also* Teachers.
—. Alaska. Discovery and Exploration. Episcopal Church, Protestant. Missions and Missionaries. Stuck, Hudson. 1904-20. *1647*
—. Brigham Young University. Germany. Maeser, Karl G. Mormons. 1828-56. 1876. *768*
—. Censorship. Fundamentalists. Textbooks. Virginia. 1974. *570*
—. Hampden-Sydney College. Smith, Samuel Stanhope. Virginia (Farmville area). 1776-1815. *513*
Edwards, Jonathan. American Revolution (antecedents). Civil religion. Great Awakening. King George's War. Millenarianism. 1740-76. *1169*
—. Anti-Catholicism. Antichrist. Mather, Cotton. Potter, Francis. Puritans. ca 1700-58. *2937*
—. Apocalypse. Bible (Revelation). Providence. Theology. 1720-24. *3148*
—. Arminianism. Great Awakening. Justification. Massachusetts (Hampshire County). 1726-60. *2236*
—. Augustine, Saint. Calvinism. Heart concept. New England. Psychology. 17c. *2311*
—. Autobiography. Congregationalism. Identity. Theology. 1729-58. *3152*
—. Beauty, perception of. Congregationalism. Knowledge. Mental activity theory. New England. 1730-69. *2323*
—. Bible. Clergy. Congregationalism. Marginalia. Massachusetts (Deerfield). Pierpont, Benjamin. Theology. 1726-30. *3146*
—. Bible. Congregationalism. Hermeneutics. Massachusetts. 1720-58. *3149*
—. Bibliographies. Dissertations. Niebuhr, H. Richard. Niebuhr, Reinhold. Presbyterian Church. Reformed Churches. Tillich, Paul. 18c-20c. 1965-72. *2815*
—. Breck, Robert. Congregationalism. Connecticut (Scotland). Massachusetts (Northampton). 1734-36. *3127*
—. Church of England. Congregationalism. Cutler, Timothy. Gibson, Edmund. Great Awakening. Letters. New England. Stoddard, Solomon. 1739. *2263*
—. Congregationalism. Epistemology. Science. 1703-58. *2327*
—. Congregationalism. Goen, C. C. (review essay). Great Awakening. Revivals. 1734-1751. *2224*
—. Congregationalism. Great Awakening. Intellectuals. Massachusetts (Northampton, Stockbridge). Theology. Youth. ca 1730-1880. *3150*
—. Congregationalism. Historiography (revisionist). Literature. 1758-1903. *3143*
—. Congregationalism. Hopkins, Samuel. New Divinity (doctrines). New England. Social reform. Theology. 1730-1803. *2373*
—. Congregationalism. Judaism. Luria, Isaac. Millenarianism. Progress, concept of. 16c-18c. *84*
—. Congregationalism. Massachusetts (Northampton). Prayer petitions. 1730-49. *3147*
—. Congregationalism. New York. Presbyterian Church. Sermons. 1722-23. *2883*
—. Congregationalism. Philosophy. Theological empiricism. 1740-46. *3145*
—. Congregationalism. Rainbows. Science. Theology. 1740-45. *2343*
—. Congregationalism. Transcendentalism. ca 1725-58. *3135*
—. Covenant theology. Great Awakening. Puritans. 18c. *2219*
—. Grace. Locke, John. Psychology. Theology. 1740's. *3158*
—. Hasidism (Habad). Psychology. Theology (comparative). 18c. *2338*
—. Massachusetts (Northampton). Millenarianism. Social Theory. 1720's-50's. *3154*
—. Millenarianism. Mission, concept of. New England. Puritans. 18c. *1154*
Edwards, Jonathan *(History of the Work of Redemption).* Congregationalism. Historians. 18c. 1976. *3156*
—. Philosophy of History. Theology. 1739. *3140*
Edwards, Jonathan ("Sinners in the Hands of an Angry God"). Connecticut (Enfield). Sermons. Theology. 1741. *1994*
Edwards Law (Illinois, 1889). Catholic Church. Compulsory education. Ethnic Groups. Illinois. Private schools. Public schools. State Politics. 1889-93. *551*
Einhorn, David. History. Judaism, Reform. Millenarianism. 1830-79. *4211*
Eisenmann, Sylvester. Catholic Church. Sioux Indians. South Dakota. Yankton Reservation (Marty Mission). 1918-49. *3900*
El Dorado County Federated Church. California (Placerville). Ecumenism. Methodist Church. Presbyterian Church. 1850-1950. *492*
Elders. Laity. Miller, Samuel. Presbyterian Church. Republicanism. 1813-50. *3559*
Election sermons. Bartlett, Robert. Politics. Religious liberty. Universalist Church of America. Vermont. 1817-30. *1045*
Elections *See also* Political Campaigns; Presidents; Primaries; Referendum; Suffrage; Voting and Voting Behavior.
—. Asbury, Francis. Clergy. McKendree, William. Methodist Episcopal Church. 1808. *3486*
—. Catholic Church. Leo XIII, Pope. Pius IX, Pope. Press. Protestantism. 1878. *2786*
—. Daily Life. Judaism. Oregon (Portland). Temple Beth Israel. 1878. *4237*
—. Labor. Law. Mormons. Railroads. Utah (Ogden). 1869-70. *1262*
—. Lee, J. Bracken. Mormons. State Government. Utah. 1944-56. *1274*
—. Liberal Party. Mormons. Nevada. Utah. 1860-70. *1252*
Elections (gubernatorial). Anti-Catholicism. Catts, Sidney J. Florida. Guardians of Liberty. Knott, William V. Sturkie Resolution. 1916. *1231*
Elections (mayoral). Adventists. Gage, William C. Michigan (Battle Creek). Morality. 1882. *1255*
Elections (presidential). Abortion. Catholic Church. Democratic Party. 1976. *1245*
—. Anti-Catholicism. Ethnic Groups. Nativism. Ohio (Cleveland). Republican Party. 1860. *1265*
—. Arkansas. Baptists. Brough, Charles Hillman. Evolution. Prohibition. 1928-29. *1270*
—. Catholic Church. Democratic Party. Louisiana. Protestant Churches. Smith, Al. Temperance Movements. 1928. *1330*
—. Catholic church. Protestantism. Smith, Al. West Virginia. 1928. *1217*
—. Civil religion. Nixon, Richard M. Voting and Voting Behavior. 1972. *1197*
—. Coalitions. 1952-76. *1275*
—. Episcopal Church, Protestant. Illuminati controversy. Ogden, John C. Philadelphia *Aurora* (newspaper). Religious liberty. 1798-1800. *957*
—. Hoover, Herbert C. Racism. Smith, Al. Tennessee, west. 1928. *1280*
Elegies. Bradstreet, Anne. Massachusetts. Poetry. Puritans. Women. 1665. *2044*
—. Calvinism. Cotton, John. Fiske, John. New England. Poetry. Puritans. 17c. *1985*
Elementary education. Baptists. Religious Education. Secondary education. State Aid to Education. 1850-1910. *718*
—. Catholic Church. Church Schools. Constitutional law. Federal aid to education. 1960's-72. *691*
—. Johnson, Emeroy. Lutheran Church. Minnesota. Personal narratives. Religious education. Swedish Americans. ca 1854-ca 1920. *666*
Eliot, John. Antinomianism. Cotton, John. Government. Millenarianism. Missions and Missionaries. New England. Puritans. Rhode Island (Portsmouth). 1630-90. *3635*
—. Assimilation. Indians. Massachusetts. Praying towns. Puritans. 1646-74. *1592*
—. Indians. Massachusetts. Missions and Missionaries. Puritans. 1620-80. *1624*
—. Indians. Massachusetts (Natick). Missions and Missionaries. Puritans. 1646-74. *1602*
Eliot, Samuel A. Antislavery Sentiments. Fugitive Slave Act (US, 1850). Massachusetts (Boston). Patriotism. Unitarianism. 1850-60. *4085*
Elites *See also* Social Classes; Social Status.
—. American Institute for Education. Country life. Educational Reform. Massachusetts. Nationalism. Protestantism. 1830-37. *573*
—. American Revolution. Brattle Street Church. Calvinism. Congregationalism. Cooper, Samuel. Massachusetts (Boston). 1754-83. *1333*
—. Baptists. Church of England. Social Change. Values. Virginia (Lunenburg County). 1746-74. *2819*
—. Brattle Street Church. Coleman, Benjamin. Gentility (concept). Massachusetts (Boston). Puritans. 1715-45. *2622*
—. Brotherhood of the Holy Family. Catholic Church. Chaumonot, Joseph-Marie-Pierre. Laval, François de. Quebec (Montreal). 1663-1760. *3717*
—. Bushnell, Horace. Clergy. Congregationalism. Theology. 19c. *3114*
—. Business. Illinois (Chicago). 1830-1930. *2608*
—. Canada. Ethnicity. Protestant ethic. Senators. Values. 1971. *958*
—. Capitalism. Catholic Church. Clergy. Pulp mills. Quebec (Chicoutimi). Working class. 1896-1930. *2601*
—. Catholic Church. Ethnicity. Immigrants. Politics. Protestants. Reform. 1890's-1970's. *1225*
—. Church membership. Research. 19c. 1975. *2615*
—. Government. Politics. Protestants. 1960's-70's. *1207*

—. Immigrants. Local government. Massachusetts (Charlestown). Puritans. 1630-40. *3613*
—. Political attitudes. Social Classes. Tennessee (Davidson County). 1835-61. *1232*
Elliott, Emory. New England. Puritans (review article). Sabbath. Sermons. Solberg, Winton U. 17c-18c. 1975-77. *3623*
Elliott, John H. Civil War. Episcopal Church, Protestant. Sermons. South Carolina (Camden). 1862. *1982*
Elliott, Stephen. Episcopal Church, Protestant. Philosophy of History. Providence. South. 1840-66. *3212*
Ellis, Edwin M. Clergy. Montana. Presbyterian Church. Sunday schools. Travel. 1870's-1927. *3537*
Ely, Ezra Stiles. Clergy. Democratic Party. Eaton, Margaret (Peggy) O'Neale. Jackson, Andrew. Presbyterian Church. 1829-30. *3536*
Ely, Richard T. Bascom, John. Commons, John R. Evolution. Political theory. Social gospel. Wisconsin, University of. 1870-1910. *2394*
Emancipation *See also* Freedmen.
—. American Union for the Relief and Improvement of the Colored Race. Congregationalism. Massachusetts (Boston). Reform. 1835-37. *2490*
—. Breckinridge, Robert Jefferson. Clergy. Danville Theological Seminary. Education. Kentucky. Presbyterian Church. 1800-71. *3544*
—. Breckinridge, Robert Jefferson. Danville Theological Seminary. Kentucky. Presbyterian Church. Theology. 1832-71. *3545*
—. Cedar Creek Monthly Meeting. Farms. Friends, Society of. Moorman, Clark Terrell. Ohio. Virginia (Caroline County). 1766-1814. *2487*
Emancipation Party. Abolition Movement. Breckinridge, Robert Jefferson. Breckinridge, William Lewis. Constitutions, State. Kentucky. Presbyterians. 1849. *2475*
Emanuel Lutheran Church. Clergy. Lutheran Church. New York City (Queens). Personal narratives. Wyneken, Frederick G. 1887-1907. *3348*
Emanu-El (newspaper). California (San Francisco). Immigration. Jews, East European. Letters-to-the-editor. Rabbis. Rosenthal, Marcus. Voorsanger, Jacob. 1905. *4141*
Embury, Philip. Asbury, Francis. Canada. Coke, Thomas. Great Britain. Methodism. USA. 1760-80. *3445*
—. Bible. Ireland. Methodism. New York City. 1760-1834. *3489*
—. Methodist Church. New Hampshire (Chesterfield). Sermons. 1754-1805. *3488*
Emerson, Joseph. Colleges and Universities. Lyon, Mary. Mount Holyoke College. Protestantism. Women. 1760's-1850's. *552*
Emerson, Mary Moody. Calvinism. Emerson, Ralph Waldo. New England. 19c. *2721*
Emerson, Ralph Waldo. Aesthetics. Philosophy. Plotinus. Science. Transcendentalism. 1836-60. *2302*
—. Antinomianism. Puritanism. Sermons. Social reform. Transcendentalism. 1820's-30's. *4070*
—. Calvinism. Emerson, Mary Moody. New England. 19c. *2721*
—. Hedge, Frederic Henry. Maine (Bangor). Transcendentalism. Unitarianism. 1833. *2761*
—. Oration. Theology. Transcendentalism. ca 1836-60. *4072*
Emigrant Institute. Archives. Lutheran Church. Social organizations. Sweden (Växjö). 1800-1970. *282*
Emigration *See also* Demography; Immigration; Population; Race Relations; Refugees.
—. Antislavery Sentiments. Catholic Church. Germans, Sudeten. Journalism. Missions and Missionaries. Neumann, Saint John Nepomucene. Republican Party. 19c-20c. *3826*
—. Baptists. Clergy. Great Britain. Harris, Theophilus. Politics. Social conditions. 1793-1810. *3050*
—. Clergy. Intellectuals. New England. 1640-60. *3653*
—. Diaries. Florida. Lutheran Church. Sjöborg, Sofia Charlotta. Sweden. 1871. *3340*
—. Epp, Johann. Letters. Mennonites. North America. Russia. 1875. *3373*
—. Ethiopia (Addis Ababa). Ford, Arnold. Judaism. Negroes. 1930-35. *4143*
—. Evangelism. Friends, Society of (Hicksite). Ohio Yearly Meeting. 1828-1919. *3270*
—. Foreign Relations. France. Quebec (Sherbrooke). Trappists. 1903-14. *3785*
—. Illinois. Janssonists. Sects, Religious. Social Classes. Sweden. 1845-47. *2620*
—. Protestantism. Sweden. Unonius, Gustaf. 1858-63. *2922*
Emmanuel Church. Christmas. Immigration. Ohio (Bluffton). Reformed Tradition. Swiss Americans. 1840's-1900. *2857*
Emmanuel movement. Freud, Sigmund. Myers, Frederic W. H. Psychoanalysis. 1906-10. *2334*
Emmett, Daniel. Archival catalogs and inventories. Hymns. Minstrel Shows. Negroes. Ohio Historical Society. Sermons. 1838-96. 1976. *2064*
Emmett, James Simpson. Friendship. Grey, Zane. Mormons. Novels (western). Utah. 1907. *2072*
Emory University. Coca-Cola Company. Methodist Church. Religious education. South. Vanderbilt University. 1840's-1970's. *3466*
Emotions. Intellect. Psychology, faculty. Puritanism. 17c. *2313*
Employment *See also* Occupations.
—. Program failure. Public Policy. Rescue missions. Skid rows. Social Reform. 1960's-70's. *2524*
Encyclicals. Acculturation. Americanism. Catholic Church. Leo XIII, Pope *(Testem Benevolentiae)*. Periodicals. Protestantism. 1899. *319*
—. Canada. Catholic Church. Church and state. Pius IX, Pope *(Syllabus of Errors)*. Press. Public opinion. 1864-65. *1019*
Encyclopedia of Southern Baptists. Baptists, Southern. 1956-71. *3004*
Endowments *See also* Charities.
—. Church and state. Church of England. Land. Ontario (Upper Canada). Rolph, John. Strachan, John. University of Toronto. 1820-70. *1026*
Energy. Ethics. National Council of Churches. 1976-78. *2392*
Engel, Jacob. Brethren in Christ. Canada. Pennsylvania (Lancaster County). Sects, Religious. 1775-1964. *3437*
Engel v. *Vitale* (US, 1962). New York. Nonsectarianism. Prayer. Public opinion. Public schools. 1962. *581*
Engelhardt, Zephyrin. California. Catholic Church. Mission Santa Barbara. Missions and Missionaries. Southwestern history. 1851-1934. *176*
—. Education. Franciscans. Holy Childhood Indian School Printery. Indians. Michigan (Harbor Springs). Printing. 1894-1913. *1584*
England, John. Catholic Church. Ireland. Voluntarism. 1808-50. *3708*
English Canadians. Acadians. Catholic Church. Maritime Provinces. Social Conditions. 1763-1977. *3871*
—. Boer War. Canada. Clergy. Protestant churches. 1899-1902. *2675*
English language. Aitken, Robert. Bible. Continental Congress. Pennsylvania (Philadelphia). Publishers and Publishing. 1782. *1979*
Engraving. Adventists. Michigan (Battle Creek). Smith, Uriah. Wood. 1852-70's. *1889*
—. Archaeology. Fraud. Mexico (Guerrero). Mormons. Padilla Gold Plates. 1952-78. *4007*
—. Barralet, John James *(Apotheosis of George Washington)*. National Self-image. 1802. *1859*
Engstrand, Stuart (review article). Bishop Hill Colony. Illinois. Jansson, Erik H. 1846-50. 20c. *2083*
Enlightenment *See also* Rationalism.
—. Abolition Movement. Christianity. Morality. Nationalism. Phillips, Wendell. 1830-84. *1399*
—. Anticlericalism. Europe. Protestantism. Revivals. 1640's-1830's. *2912*
—. Calvinism. Diphtheria. Great Awakening. New England. Sermons. 1735-40. *2260*
—. Christianity. Founding fathers. 1776-1976. *1418*
—. Democracy. Equality. Mead, Sidney E. Theology of the Republic (concept). 17c-20c. *1366*
—. Mather, Cotton. Puritans. Theology. 1680-1728. *3657*
—. National self-image. Pietism. Puritanism. 17c-20c. *1184*
—. Presbyterian Evangelical Calvinists. Theology. 17c-19c. *3570*
—. Protestantism. Theology. 1920's-75. *2881*
Entz, John Edward. Clergy. First Mennonite Church. Kansas (Newton). Mennonites. 1875-1969. *3419*
Environment *See also* Ecology.
—. American Revolution. Literature. Millenarianism. Symbolism in Literature. 1770's-1800. *1192*
—. Bible. History. Wilderness. 18c-20c. *36*
Environmental crisis. Christianity. White, Lynn, Jr. 1c-20c. *2309*
Ephphatha Conference. Deaf. Lutheran Church. Missions and Missionaries. 1893-1976. *1516*
Ephrata Cloister. Beissel, Johann Conrad. Communalism. Eckerlin, Emmanuel. Pennsylvania (Conestoga Valley). 1732-68. *390*
Epidemics *See also* names of contagious diseases, e.g. Smallpox, etc.
—. Canada. Cholera. Mormons. USA. 1832-83. *1437*
—. Inoculation. Massachusetts (Boston). Mather, Cotton. Smallpox. 1721-22. *1464*
Episcopal Academy. Andrews, John. Clergy. Education. Pennsylvania, University of. 1765-1810. *507*
Episcopal Church, Protestant. 1835-1964. *3246*
—. Abolition Movement. Assassination. Brooks, Phillips. Lincoln, Abraham. Pennsylvania (Philadelphia). Sermons. 1865. 1893. *2463*
—. Alaska. Art. Missions and Missionaries. Ziegler, Eustace Paul. 1900-69. *1515*
—. Alaska. Discovery and Exploration. Educators. Missions and Missionaries. Stuck, Hudson. 1904-20. *1647*
—. Albany Diocese. Bishops. New York. Oldham, George Ashton. 1922-47. *3176*
—. Algoma Diocese. Missions and Missionaries. Ontario. Society for the Propagation of the Gospel. 1873-1973. *1653*
—. American Colonization Society. Crummell, Alexander. Education. Liberia. Missions and Missionaries. Negroes. 1853-73. *1671*
—. American Revolution. Clergy. Delaware River Valley. Lutheran Church. Swedish Americans. 1655-1831. *285*
—. American Revolution. New York. Nonconformists. Political Factions. Provincial government. 1768-71. *1294*
—. Americanization. Ecumenism. Lutheran Church, Swedish. Swedish Americans. 1630-1850. *322*
—. Americanization. Pennsylvania (Philadelphia). White, William. ca 1789-1836. *324*
—. Anglo-Catholics. Catholic Church. Clergy. Ecumenism. *Lamp* (periodical). Wattson, Paul James. 1903-09. *460*
—. Anti-Catholicism. Congregationalism. Cox, Samuel Hanson. Ecumenism. Evangelicalism. Presbyterian Church, New School. Slavery. 1840's. *471*
—. Antislavery Sentiments. Civil War. Jay, John, II. 1840-65. *2494*
—. Architecture. Cathedral Church of St. John the Divine. Manning, William Thomas. New York City. Sabbatarianism. Sports. 19c-1920's. *3243*
—. Architecture. Churches. New England. Vaughan, Henry. 1845-1917. *1800*
—. Architecture. Churches. St. James Episcopal Church. Virginia (Accomac). 1838. *1825*
—. Architecture. Churches. Virginia. 1800-1920. *1798*
—. Architecture. Churches (Gothic Revival, Victorian Gothic). North Dakota. Upjohn, Richard. 1874-1903. *1815*
—. Architecture. New Hampshire (Portsmouth). St. John's Episcopal Church. 1807-09. *1780*
—. Architecture, Gothic Revival. Bolton, William J. Church of the Holy Trinity. New York City (Brooklyn). Stained glass windows. 1845-47. *1847*
—. Architecture, Gothic Revival. Churches. Holy Trinity Episcopal Church. Restorations. Tennessee (Nashville). 1840's-1970's. *1801*
—. Architecture (Gothic Revival). Churches. Iowa (Iowa City). Trinity Episcopal Church. Upjohn, Richard. 1871-72. *1787*
—. Architecture, Gothic Revival. South. Upjohn, Richard. Wills, Frank. 1835-60. *1809*
—. Arizona. Baptists. Catholic Church. Methodism. Missions and Missionaries. Mormons. Presbyterian Church. 1859-99. *1501*
—. Arizona (Tombstone). Clergy. Peabody, Endicott. 1882. *3237*
—. Arvedson, Peter. Illinois. Swedish Americans. 1822-80. *1600*

—. Attitudes. Fletcher, C. B. Letters. Slavery. Vermont. 1777-1864. *2159*
—. Authority. Bishops. Church and State. Civil War. Grace Church. Illinois (Galesburg). 1864-66. *1218*
—. Autonomy. Church Finance. Isolationism. Missions and Missionaries. Theology. 1953-77. *1720*
—. Baker, Ray Stannard. Civil rights. DuBois, W. E. B. Liberalism. Negroes. Personal narratives. Whites. Wilmer, Cary Breckenridge. 1900-10. *2151*
—. Barr, D. Eglinton. Chaplains. Civil War. South. 1851-72. *2648*
—. Batchelder, John. Frontier and Pioneer Life. Illinois (Jacksonville). Trinity Church. 1830-40. *3192*
—. Bible. Darwinism. Europe. Excommunication. Hermeneutics. MacQueary, Howard. Ohio (Canton). St. Paul's Church. Universalism. 1890-91. *3178*
—. Bibliographies. Diocesan histories. Missions and Missionaries. ca 1776-1972. *3201*
—. Bishops. Civil War. Hopkins, John Henry. 1861-65. *445*
—. Bishops. Diocesan Standing Committee. ca 1789-1832. *3217*
—. Bishops. Huntington, Frederick (and family). New York. Social reform. Theology. Women. 1869-1904. *3213*
—. Bishops. Louisiana (Shreveport). Polk, Leonidas. 1830-1916. *3184*
—. Black Hills. Hinman, Samuel D. Indians. Missions and Missionaries. Sioux Indians. 1860-76. *1484*
—. Black nationalism. Crummell, Alexander. DuBois, W. E. B. Ferris, William H. Ideology. 1819-1898. *2424*
—. Black power. Church and Social Problems. Economic Aid. General Convention Special Program. Self-determination. 1963-75. *2541*
—. Boarding Schools. Chatham Hall. Ferguson, Anne Williams. Personal narratives. Virginia. Women. 1940's. *628*
—. Book of Common Prayer. Merrymount Press. Printing. Typeface. 1922-30. *1986*
—. Book of Common Prayer. Reform. 1785. *291*
—. Bradford, Phoebe George. Daily life. Delaware. Diaries. 1832-33. *3245*
—. Bradford, Phoebe George. Daily Life. Delaware (Wilmington). Diaries. 1833-35. *3244*
—. Bratton, Theodore DuBose. Conference for Education in the South. Mississippi. Negroes. Racism. 1908. *2148*
—. Brent, Charles Henry. Missions and Missionaries. Paternalism. Philippines. 1901-18. *1738*
—. Calvin, Ross Randall. Literature. Nature. New Mexico. 1889-1970. *2332*
—. Cambridge Camden Society. Churches (Gothic Revival). Great Britain. 1840-1975. *1773*
—. Canon Law. Ordination. Women. 1966-74. *937*
—. Catholic Church. Chapel-of-St. John's-in-the-Wilderness. Ecumenism. New York (Graymoor). Society of the Atonement. Wattson, Paul James. White, Lurana Mary. 1909-18. *461*
—. Catholic Church. Clergy. Converts. Richey, James Arthur Morrow. ca 1900-33. *2754*
—. Catholic Church. Colet, John. Erasmus, Desiderius. Hermeneutics. More, Thomas. 1500-1975. *3167*
—. Catholic Church. Dissent. Pentecostal movement. 1950's-70's. *2742*
—. Catholic Church. Ecumenism. Society of the Atonement. Wattson, Paul James. White, Lurana. Women. 1870-1928. *459*
—. Catholic Church. Liturgy. 1973. *2727*
—. Charities. Iowa (Iowa City). New York City. Orphans' Home of Industry. Townsend, Charles Collins. 1854-68. *2507*
—. Chase, Philander. Illinois (Peoria). Jubilee College. 1840-62. *730*
—. Cheshire, Joseph Blount, Jr. Negroes. North Carolina. Paternalism. Race Relations. 1870-1932. *2140*
—. China. Missions and Missionaries. Roots, Eliza McCook. Roots, Logan H. 1900-34. *1743*
—. China (Shanghai). Colleges and Universities. Missions and Missionaries. Pott, Francis L. H. St. John's University. 1888-1941. *1707*
—. Christ Church. Churches. Tennessee (Nashville). 1829-1979. *3174*
—. Christ Church. Civil War. Kentucky (Bowling Green). Ringgold, Samuel. Tennessee (Knoxville). 1860-1911. *3168*
—. Christ Church Cathedral. Massachusetts (Springfield). 1817-1929. *3236*
—. Christ Church Hospital. Hospitals. Kearsley, John. Pennsylvania (Philadelphia). Women. 1778-1976. *1455*
—. Christian Unity Foundation. Ecumenism. Homans, Rockland Tyng. Huntington, William Reed. 1886-1942. *454*
—. Christianity. Clergy. 1974. *3248*
—. Christianity. Fiction. Grace Church. Melville, Herman ("The Two Temples"). New York City. Trinity Church. 1845-50. *2061*
—. Church and Social Problems. Missions and Missionaries. Social Reform. ca 1960-73. *2384*
—. Church and Social Problems. Missouri (St. Louis area). 1960's-70's. *3218*
—. Church and State. Education. Indians (agencies). Oklahoma, western. Stouch, George W. H. Whirlwind Day School. ca 1904-14. *1086*
—. Church congresses. Ecumenism. 1874-1933. *469*
—. Church of England. Clergy. Ingraham, Joseph Holt. Novels. Prisons. Public Schools. Reform. Tennessee (Nashville). 1847-51. *3241*
—. Churches. New York City. Roofs. Trinity Church. Upjohn, Richard. 1839-42. *1774*
—. Churches (Gothic Revival). Delaware (Wilmington). Grace Methodist Church. Methodist Church. St. John's Episcopal Church. 1850-90. *1786*
—. Civil rights movement. Race Relations. Theology. 1800-1965. *2540*
—. Civil War. Diaries. Providence. Robertson, Martha Wayles. South Carolina (Chesterfield County). Women. 1860-66. *3191*
—. Civil War. Elliott, John H. Sermons. South Carolina (Camden). 1862. *1982*
—. Civil-Military Relations. Kentucky (Bowling Green). Ringgold, Samuel. Tennessee (Clarksville). 1861-65. *998*
—. Clergy. Converts. Lutheran Church. Sweden. Unonius, Gustaf. Wisconsin (Pine Lake). 1841-58. *2854*
—. Clergy. Diaries. Private Schools. Salt industry. Trade. Ward, Henry Dana. West Virginia (Kanawha Valley, Charleston). 1845-47. *3172*
—. Clergy. Jarratt, Devereux. Letters. Virginia. 1770-1800. *3195*
—. Clergy. Kentucky (Versailles). St. John's Church. 1829-1976. *3220*
—. Clergy. Sex Discrimination. Women. 1973. *841*
—. Clergy (dismissal). Illinois (Chicago). Pamphlets. Rites and Ceremonies. Swope, Cornelius E. Trinity Church. Unonius, Gustaf. 1850-51. *3179*
—. Congregationalism. Converts. Kilbourne, James. Letters. Ohio (Worthington). Pioneers. 1844-49. *2823*
—. Connecticut (Hartford). Evangelicalism. Literature. Sigourney, Lydia Huntley. Women. 1800-65. *3194*
—. Crapsey, Algernon Sidney. Heresy. Humanitarian Reform. New York (Rochester). St. Andrew's Church. Trials. 1879-1927. *3234*
—. Diaries. Harris, N. Sayre. Indian Territory. Missions and Missionaries. Otey, James Hervey. 1844. *1533*
—. Documents. Excavations. Illinois (Peoria County). Jubilee College. 1839-1979. *770*
—. Documents. Missions and Missionaries. Puerto Rico. 1870-1952. *1679*
—. Ecumenism. Lutheran Church (United Synod of the South). 1860-90. *438*
—. Edson, Theodore. Massachusetts (Lowell). St. Anne's Parish. Textile industry. 1800-65. *366*
—. Education. Girls. Indians. St. Mary's Episcopal School for Indian Girls. South Dakota (Springfield). 1873-1973. *687*
—. Education. Louisiana (New Orleans). Polk, Leonidas. Slavery. 1805-65. *3219*
—. Elections (presidential). Illuminati controversy. Ogden, John C. Philadelphia *Aurora* (newspaper). Religious liberty. 1798-1800. *957*
—. Elliott, Stephen. Philosophy of History. Providence. South. 1840-66. *3212*
—. Evangelism. Frontier and Pioneer Life. McIlvaine, Charles Petit. Ohio. Oxford Movement. 1800-75. *3187*
—. Florida. Gray, William Crane. Indian-White Relations. Missions and missionaries. Seminole Indians. 1893-1914. *1558*
—. Folk Songs. Hymnals. 1970-78. *1906*
—. German Americans. Hast, Louis H. Kentucky (Louisville). Music. 1848-90. *1909*
—. Girls. Nevada (Reno). Schools. Whitaker, Ozi William. 1876-94. *769*
—. Great Britain. Maurice, Frederick Denison. Protestantism. Revelation. Social reform. Theology. 1860-1900. *3171*
—. Groton School. Massachusetts. Peabody, Endicott. Religious education. 1884-1940. *671*
—. Hudson's Bay Company. Indians. Missions and Missionaries. Pacific Northwest. 1825-75. *1555*
—. Huntington, James Otis Sargent. Monasticism. Order of the Holy Cross. Single tax. Social reform. 1878-90. *2430*
—. Hymnody. 1640-1978. *1957*
—. Kilbourne, James. Ohio (Worthington). Settlement. 1744-1816. *3170*
—. Letters. Nashotah House. Seminaries. Unonius, Gustaf. Wisconsin (Nashotah). 1884. *585*
—. Missions. Theology. 1972-73. *3249*
—. Missions and Missionaries (associate). Nebraska (Omaha). 1891-1902. *1562*
—. Missouri (St. Louis). Social reform. 1880-1920. *2403*
—. Music. Negroes. 1790-1975. *1934*
—. National Characteristics. Pragmatism. 1650-1975. *3239*
—. Negroes. Racism. Society for the Propagation of the Gospel. ca 1700-1974. *3169*
—. New York City. Newspapers. Racism. Riots. St. Philip's Church. Williams, Peter, Jr. 1830-50. *2142*
—. North Carolina. Religious commitment. Salience. 1975. *3222*
—. Oregon (Pendleton). 1864-1971. *3225*
—. Otey, James Hervey. St. Paul's Church. Tennessee (Franklin). 1827-34. *1802*
—. Rites and Ceremonies. Theology. 1607-1978. *3216*
—. St. James Church. Unonius, Gustaf. Wisconsin (Manitowoc). 1848-49. *3181*
—. Theology. 1973. *716*
—. Values. 1974. *3247*
Episcopal Church, Protestant (Annual Council). Councils and Synods. Delegates. Kinsolving, George Herbert. Texas. Veto. Women. 1921-70. *813*
Epistemology. Congregationalism. Edwards, Jonathan. Science. 1703-58. *2327*
Epp, Johann. Emigration. Letters. Mennonites. North America. Russia. 1875. *3373*
Epperson, Susan. Antievolution Law (1928). Arkansas. Church and state. Courts. Evolution. Initiatives. 1900's-68. *2322*
Equal opportunity. Communalism. Hutterites. Leadership. Population. Prairie Provinces. Social Organization. Succession. 1940's-70's. *387*
Equal Rights Amendment. Ideology. Women. 1933-75. *810*
—. Political Participation. Texas. Women. 1977. *933*
Equality. Calling (concept). Great Chain of Being (theme). Protestant Ethic. Puritans. 17c-18c. *340*
—. Catholic Worker Movement. Human Rights. Public policy. 1933-78. *2436*
—. Charities. Missions and Missionaries. Presbyterian Church. Women. 1800-1975. *908*
—. Christianity. Civil rights. Negroes. 19c-20c. *2536*
—. Clergy. Mormons (Reorganized). Negroes. Schisms. Women. 1860-1979. *4032*
—. Democracy. Enlightenment. Mead, Sidney E. Theology of the Republic (concept). 17c-20c. *1366*
—. Lincoln, Abraham. Mormons. Polygamy. Slavery. Smith, Joseph. 1840-64. *986*
—. New England. Sex roles. Shakers. Women. 1810-60. *821*
Erasmus, Desiderius. Catholic Church. Colet, John. Episcopal Church, Protestant. Hermeneutics. More, Thomas. 1500-1975. *3167*
Erikson, Erik H. Excommunication. First Church. Hibbens, Ann. Massachusetts (Boston). Puritans. Rites and Ceremonies. 1640-41. 1960's-70's. *3610*
Esbjörn, Lars Paul. Bäck, Olof. Clergy. Janssonists. Letters. Lutheran Church. Methodism. Sweden. 1846-49. *2906*

Escalante, Silvestre Velez de. California (Monterey). Discovery and Exploration. Dominguez, Francisco Atanasio. New Mexico. Overland Journeys to the Pacific. 1765-1805. *1480*
Eschatology. American Revolution. Calvinism. Paine, Thomas *(Common Sense)*. 1776. *1393*
—. Christian Realism. Niebuhr, Reinhold. Radicalism. 20c. *2927*
—. Future. Millenarianism. Theology. 18c. *1180*
Eskimos. Alaska (Mary's Igloo). Bernard, Joseph. Catholic Church. Missions and Missionaries. 1884-1962. *1504*
—. Canada. Christianity. Civil rights. Indians. Métis. Project North. 1975-79. *2545*
—. Church Missionary Society. Church of England. Hudson's Bay Company. Missionaries. Northwest Territories (Baffin Island). Peck, E. J. Trade. 1894-1913. *1660*
—. Jannasch, Hermann Theodor. Labrador. Missions and Missionaries. Moravian Church. 1855-1931. *1594*
Esteyneffer, Juan de *(Florilegio Medicinal)*. Herbs. Indians. Jesuits. Medicine (practice of). Missions and Missionaries. Southwest. 1711. *1444*
Esther Hellman Settlement House. Business. California (San Francisco; San Bruno Avenue). Jews. Neighborhoods. 1901-68. *4130*
Ethics *See also* Morality; Values.
—. Amnesty. Vietnam War. 1974. *2704*
—. Anglican Communion. Great Britain. 16c-20c. *3182*
—. Barth, Karl. Liberalism. Niebuhr, Reinhold. 1920's-60. *2359*
—. Business. Friends, Society of. 1600-1750. *359*
—. Business. Mormons. Theology. Watergate scandal. 1974. *995*
—. Christianity. Economic Theory. George, Henry. 1879. *2560*
—. Christianity. Providence. Theology. 19c. *2728*
—. Christianity. Rationalism. Science. White, Andrew Dickson. 1888-90's. *2288*
—. Church and Social Problems. Evangelicals. Graham, Billy. Political attitudes. War. 1970's. *2932*
—. Colleges and universities. Curricula. 1950-73. *530*
—. Connecticut. Fitch, James. Land. Politics. Puritans. 1679-1727. *3646*
—. Covenant theology. Divine Sovereignty. Puritanism. 17c-18c. *3618*
—. Energy. National Council of Churches. 1976-78. *2392*
—. Literature. Pluralism. Styron, William *(Confessions of Nat Turner)*. 1970's. *2053*
—. Liturgy. Social Organization. 1970's. *2735*
—. Methodist Church. Theology. Wesley, John. 1744-91. 1879-1974. *2397*
—. Theology. Women's Liberation Movement. 1973. *838*
Ethiopia (Addis Ababa). Emigration. Ford, Arnold. Judaism. Negroes. 1930-35. *4143*
Ethnic enclaves. City Life. Judaism. Manitoba (Winnipeg). 1940's-70's. *4091*
Ethnic Groups *See also* Minorities.
—. Anti-Catholicism. Church and state. Evangelism. Protestantism. Quebec (Lower Canada). Rebellion of 1837. 1766-1865. *2110*
—. Anti-Catholicism. City Politics. Immigrants. Ohio (Cincinnati). Temperance Movements. 1845-60. *2584*
—. Anti-Catholicism. Colleges and Universities. Discrimination, Educational. 1970's. *2106*
—. Anti-Catholicism. Elections (presidential). Nativism. Ohio (Cleveland). Republican Party. 1860. *1265*
—. Attitudes. Canada. Catholic Church. Jews. Protestantism. Social Status. 1968. *2088*
—. Attitudes. Political power. Working class. 1974. *2612*
—. Bonomi, Patricia U. Klein, Milton M. New York (review article). Pluralism. Provincial Government. 1690's-1770's. 1971-74. *1204*
—. British Canadians. Country life. French Canadians. Manitoba. Mennonites. Migration. Polish Canadians. Ukrainian Canadians. 1921-61. *3389*
—. California. Catholic Church. Charities. Ramm, Charles A. 1863-1951. *3888*
—. Canada. Immigrants. Indians. Language. 1970's. *126*
—. Catholic Church. 17c-20c. *3689*
—. Catholic Church. Church Schools. Illinois (Chicago). Sanders, James W. (review article). 1833-1965. 1977. *614*
—. Catholic Church. Compulsory education. Edwards Law (Illinois, 1889). Illinois. Private schools. Public schools. State Politics. 1889-93. *551*
—. Catholic Church. Connecticut (New Haven). Jews. Marriage. Protestantism. 1900-50. *906*
—. Catholic Church. Country Life. Lutheran Church. Reformed Dutch Church. Voting and Voting Behavior. 1890-98. *1257*
—. Catholic Church. Judaism. Pennsylvania (Philadelphia). Social classes. Voting and Voting Behavior. 1924-40. *1308*
—. Christianity. Economic growth. Michigan (Detroit). Pluralism. 1880-1940. *2748*
—. Christianity. Voluntary associations. Voting turnout. 1967-75. *1313*
—. Church of England. Colonial Government. Friends, society of. Pennsylvania. Reformed churches. 1755-80. *1215*
—. Church of England. Friends, Society of. Pennsylvania. Presbyterian Church. Provincial Politics. 1775-80. *1248*
—. Connecticut (Hartford). Democratic Party. Middle Classes. Protestantism. Voting and Voting Behavior. 1896-1940. *1203*
—. Country life. Evangelical United Brethren Church. Social classes. Theology. 1800-1968. *3668*
—. Doukhobors. Federal government. Royal Canadian Mounted Police. Saskatchewan. Settlement. 1899-1909. *1006*
—. Economic Conditions. Folklore. Mail-Order Business. Social Conditions. Voodoo. 1970-79. *2205*
—. Evangelical Association. Schisms. 1887-94. *3664*
—. Family. Government. Morality. Religious institutions. 1960's-70's. *899*
—. Michigan (Detroit). Protestant Churches. Social organization. 1880-1940. *2877*
—. Prohibitionists. Saloons. Values. Working Class. 1890-1920. *2588*
—. Rites and ceremonies. 1797-1960. *37*
Ethnicity. 1700-1950. *5*
—. Acculturation. Canada. Jews. USA. 1961-74. *4156*
—. Acculturation. Christianity. Europe. Immigration. Judaism. Middle East. 19c-20c. *34*
—. Agnosticism. Hillquit, Morris. Jews. New York City. Socialism. 1890's-1933. *1331*
—. Alienation. Civil War. German Americans. Lutheran Church (Missouri Synod). Massacres. Missouri (Concordia). 1864. *3301*
—. Americanization. Catholics. Church attendance. New York City. -1974. *3810*
—. Amish, Old Order. Kansas, central. 1956-78. *3394*
—. Arnold, Matthew. Plural establishment, theory of. 19c-20c. *15*
—. Assimilation. 1976. *161*
—. Assimilation. Greek Americans. New York City. Orthodox Eastern Church. St. Demetrios Church. St. Markela Church. 1970's. *318*
—. Attitudes. Israel. Jews. Northeastern or North Atlantic States. Students. Zionism. 1973-76. *4155*
—. Attitudes. Mennonites. Pennsylvania (Lancaster). Private Schools. Socialization. 1974-76. *673*
—. Baptists. Cultural pluralism. Melting pot theory. 1870-1976. *3101*
—. Bygdelag movement. Nationalism. North Central States. Norwegian Americans. 1901-30. *3319*
—. California (San Francisco). Catholic Church. Clergy. Editors and Editing. Irish Americans. Yorke, Peter C. ca 1885-1925. *3887*
—. California (San Francisco; Potrero Hill). Molokans. Sects, Religious. 1906-76. *2807*
—. Canada. Elites. Protestant ethic. Senators. Values. 1971. *958*
—. Canada. Students. 1971. *100*
—. Catholic Church. Clergy. Social Status. 1947-80. *3867*
—. Catholic Church. Elites. Immigrants. Politics. Protestants. Reform. 1890's-1970's. *1225*
—. Catholic Church. Political Parties. Protestantism. 1968-72. *1220*
—. Church membership. Illinois (Chicago). Jews. Protestants. 1960's-70's. *121*
—. Congregation Kahal Kadosh Shearith Israel. Falkenau, Jacob J. M. Hebrew. Jews. Lyons, Jacques Judah. New York City. Pique, Dob. Poetry. 1786-1841. *2062*
—. Discrimination. Hutterites. Legislation. Prairie Provinces. Provincial government. 1960's-79. *1099*
—. Evangelical and Reformed Church. German Americans. Kamp, Henry. Oklahoma (Oklahoma City). 1906-57. *3123*
—. Immigrants. Lutheran Church (Missouri Synod). Migration. Theology. 1847-1970. *3323*
—. Jews. Maryland, University of. Parents. Students. 1949-71. *4128*
—. Judaism. 1975. *4145*
—. Language. Nationalism. Parishes. Polish National Catholic Church. 1880's-1930's. *313*
—. Religiosity. Students. 1972. *110*
Ethnicity (review article). Abramson, Harold J. Catholics. Hays, Samuel. Voting and Voting Behavior. 1973. *3740*
Ethnocentrism. Discrimination. 1620-1965. *2092*
Ethnology *See also* Acculturation; Anthropology; Folklore; Language; Negroes; Race Relations.
—. California (Los Angeles). Catholic Church. Methodology. Polish Americans. Sandberg, Neil C. (review article). 1968-74. *3813*
Etiology. Diseases (classification). Folk Medicine. Quebec. 1976-77. *1428*
Eudists. Catholic Church. Industrialization. Quebec (Chicoutimi Basin). Working class. 1903-30. *1466*
Eulogies. Clergy. Davies, Samuel. National Self-image. Presbyterian Church. Washington, George. 1789-1815. *1157*
—. Clergy. Presidency (mystique). Sermons. Washington, George. 1799. *1190*
Europe *See also* Europe, Eastern; Europe, Western.
—. Acculturation. Christianity. Ethnicity. Immigration. Judaism. Middle East. 19c-20c. *34*
—. Americanization. Catholic Church. Church and state. Maryland. Religious liberty. ca 1634-1786. *304*
—. Americanization. Catholic Church. Ecumenism. Pluralism. Theology. 1775-1820. *295*
—. Anticlericalism. Enlightenment. Protestantism. Revivals. 1640's-1830's. *2912*
—. Bible. Darwinism. Episcopal Church, Protestant. Excommunication. Hermeneutics. MacQueary, Howard. Ohio (Canton). St. Paul's Church. Universalism. 1890-91. *3178*
—. Bibliographies. Folk religion. North America. 1900-74. 16c-20c. *42*
—. British North America. 1677-1729. *2919*
—. Canada, eastern. Christianity. Micmac Indians. Trade. 15c-18c. *1574*
—. Canon law. Circumcision. Illowy, Bernard. Judaism (Orthodox). Louisiana (New Orleans). Rabbis. 1853-65. *4176*
—. Catholic Church. Original sin. Theology. 1966-71. *3751*
—. Charismatic movement. Folk Religion (review article). Health. Occult sciences. Science. 16c-19c. 1975-76. *7*
—. Christianity. Frontier and Pioneer Life. Theology. 18c-1979. *301*
—. Civil religion. Puritans. Rousseau, Jean-Jacques. 18c-20c. *1177*
—. Civil Rights. Colonies. Florida. Judaism. Levy, Moses Elias. 1825. *4151*
—. Ecumenism. Protestant Churches. World War II. 1900-45. *465*
—. History, comparative. Liberalism. Protestant Churches. Social Gospel. 1885-1975. *2395*
—. Nationalism. Revolution. Romanticism. Social criticism. 1630-1876. *950*
—. Revivals. Social reform. 1400-1900. *2429*
Europe, Eastern. Anti-Semitism. Immigration. Riis, Jacob. 1890-1914. *2132*
Europe, Western. Catholic Church. Church and State. North America. Politics. 1870-1974. *1326*
—. Evangelicalism. Methodism. Pietism. Reformed Dutch Church. Revivals. Social Conditions. 1674-19c. *2959*
Europeans. Attitudes. Californios. Travel (accounts). 1780's-1840's. *2122*
—. Christianity. Indians. 16c-20c. *2752*
Evangelical Alliance. Beecher, Lyman. Great Britain. Presbyterian Church. Temperance Movements. World Temperance Convention. 1846. *3563*
—. Church and State. Denominationalism. Ecumenism. Great Britain. 1846. *484*
—. Ecumenism. Evangelicalism. Presbyterian Church. 1867-73. *456*
—. Lutheran Church (General Synod). Schmucker, Samuel Simon. 1843-51. *3294*

Evangelical and Reformed Church. Ecumenism. Presbyterian Church. Richards, George Warren. World Alliance of Reformed Churches. 1900-55. *481*
—. Ethnicity. German Americans. Kamp, Henry. Oklahoma (Oklahoma City). 1906-57. *3123*
Evangelical Association. Albright, Jacob. Asbury, Francis. Methodist Episcopal Church. 1765-1816. *2947*
—. Centennial Celebrations. Methodist Episcopal Church. Methodist Protestant Church. 1872-76. *3451*
—. Creeds. Methodism. Terry, Milton S. Theology. United Evangelical Church. 1894-1921. *3667*
—. Ethnic groups. Schisms. 1887-94. *3664*
—. Ohio. United Brethren in Christ. 1806-39. *3663*
—. Pennsylvania, western. 1800-33. *3662*
Evangelical Covenant Church. Americanization. Evangelical Free Church of America. Methodism. Pentecostal movement. Salvation Army. Swedish Baptist Church. 1870-1973. *321*
Evangelical Free Church of America. Americanization. Evangelical Covenant Church. Methodism. Pentecostal movement. Salvation Army. Swedish Baptist Church. 1870-1973. *321*
—. Darby, John Nelson. Franson, Fredrik. Millenarianism. Moody, Dwight L. Revivalism. Scandinavian Americans. 1875-95. *2863*
Evangelical United Brethren Church. Country life. Ethnic groups. Social classes. Theology. 1800-1968. *3668*
Evangelicalism. 1975. *2871*
—. Abolition Movement. Attitudes. Competition. Economic conditions. Poverty. ca 1830-60. *2473*
—. Abolition Movement. Childhood. Missions and Missionaries. 1800-60. *947*
—. Abolition Movement. Friendship. Tappan, Lewis. 1830-61. *2469*
—. Alger, Horatio. Capitalism. Literature. Social History. Success (concept of). 1820-1910. *2958*
—. American Seamen's Friend Society. Merchant Marine. Ports. 1828-38. *2376*
—. American Tract Society. Missions and Missionaries. Pennsylvania, western. Wright, Elizur, Jr. 1828-29. *1536*
—. Anti-Catholicism. Congregationalism. Cox, Samuel Hanson. Ecumenism. Episcopal Church, Protestant. Presbyterian Church, New School. Slavery. 1840's. *471*
—. Antislavery Sentiments. Great Britain. 1846. *2893*
—. Antislavery sentiments. South. 1820-30. *2489*
—. Attitudes. Carter, Jimmy. Civil religion. Political Campaigns (presidential). Political Speeches. Rhetoric. 1976. *1229*
—. Attitudes. Dickinson, Emily. Friendship. Mount Holyoke College. 1848-50. *2827*
—. Baptists. Child-rearing. Wayland, Francis. 1831. 1975. *948*
—. Baptists (Ketocton Association). Reform. Slavery. Stringfellow, Thornton. Virginia. 1800-70. *2158*
—. Baptists, Southern. Church membership. Country life. South. Urbanization. 1920's. *3085*
—. Bibliographies. 1945-79. *2915*
—. Bishops. Catholic Church. Church of England. Feild, Edward. Liturgy. Methodism. Newfoundland. Presbyterian Church. 1765-1852. *3197*
—. Boles, John B. (review article). Racism. Revivals. Smith, H. Shelton (review article). South. 1972. *2867*
—. Buchman, Frank. Moral Re-Armament movement. New Jersey. Princeton University. 1938. *2858*
—. Children. Northeastern or North Atlantic States. Protestant Churches. Sunday Schools. Theology. 1820's. *604*
—. *Christian History* (periodical). Great Britain. Methodist Church, Calvinistic. Periodicals. Whitefield, George. 1740's. *2233*
—. *Christianity Today*, periodical. Civil rights. Malone College. Race Relations. 1956-59. *2549*
—. Connecticut (Hartford). Episcopal Church, Protestant. Literature. Sigourney, Lydia Huntley. Women. 1800-65. *3194*
—. Ecumenism. Evangelical Alliance. Presbyterian Church. 1867-73. *456*
—. Europe, Western. Methodism. Pietism. Reformed Dutch Church. Revivals. Social Conditions. 1674-19c. *2959*
—. Faith Healing. Indiana (Gary). Music (gospel). Negroes. Theology. 1976. *2868*
—. Farmers. Negroes. South. 1800-60. *2845*
—. Graham, Billy. Middle America. Streiker, Lowell D. (review essay). Strober, Gerald S. (review essay). -1972. *2621*
—. Henry, Carl F. (review essay). Social justice. 1971. *2415*
—. Individualism. Liberalism. 1815-60. *2952*
—. Jones, Charles Colcock. Race Relations. South. Utopias. 1804-63. *2543*
—. Mathews, Donald G. (review article). South. 18c-19c. 1977. *2835*
—. Methodism. Values. 1784-1924. *2406*
—. New York (Utica). Revivals. Women. 1800-40. *922*
—. Pennsylvania (Rockdale). Social change. Wallace, Allen F. C. (review article). 1820-65. *2861*
—. Sex roles. Sunday School Movement. Women. 1790-1880. *807*
—. Television. 1978. *1961*
—. Theology. 1517-20c. *2817*
Evangelicals. Adventists. Theology. 1948-60. *503*
—. Anti-Semitism. Fundamentalists. Jews. Messianic beliefs. 1970's. *135*
—. Bible. Inerrancy (doctrine). Montgomery, John W. (review article). Objectivist apologetics. 1972. *2882*
—. Charities. Church of England. Ontario (Toronto). Temperance Movements. Theology. 1870-1900. *3205*
—. Church and Social Problems. Ethics. Graham, Billy. Political attitudes. War. 1970's. *2932*
—. South. Twain, Mark. 1870-1910. *2875*
Evangelische Kirchen-Zeitung (newspaper). Fister, W. Letters-to-the-editor. Lutheran Church (Missouri Synod). 1866. *3322*
Evangelism. Abolition Movement. Birney, James. Clergy. Smith, Gerrit. Stanton, H. B. Weld, Theodore. 1820-50. *2488*
—. Adventists. Cudney, A. J. Nebraska (Lincoln). 1885-87. *1577*
—. Adventists. Hill, W. B. Iowa. Minnesota. Personal Narratives. 1877. 1881. *1547*
—. American Baptist Home Mission Society. Americanization. Baptists. 1832-99. *1599*
—. American Revolution. Great Awakening. Protestantism. 1770-1800. *2267*
—. Anti-Catholicism. Church and state. Ethnic groups. Protestantism. Quebec (Lower Canada). Rebellion of 1837. 1766-1865. *2110*
—. Assimilation. Jews. Ontario (Toronto). Presbyterian Church. 1912-18. *1540*
—. Baptists. Conservatism. Graham, Billy. Morality. 1940's-70's. *2215*
—. Baptists. Converts. Louisiana (New Orleans). Methodism. Slavery. 1800-61. *2916*
—. Baptists, Big Hatchie. Baptists, Southern. Landmark movement. Missions and Missionaries. 1828-1903. *3011*
—. Baptists, Separate. General Association of Separate Baptists in Christ. Kentucky. New England. 1755-1977. *3064*
—. Baptists, Southern. Clergy. Ohio (Columbus). 1969-76. *2988*
—. Baptists, Southern. Home Mission Board. 1845-1973. *1544*
—. Baptists, Southern. Social factors. 1940-75. *2989*
—. Baptists, Southern. Voluntarism. 1940's-78. *2997*
—. Baptists (Two-Seed-in-the-Spirit). Indiana. Otter Creek Predestinarian Church. Parker, Daniel. 1820-1974. *3047*
—. Baptists (Two-Seed-in-the-Spirit). Indiana (Putnam County). Music. Oral tradition. Otter Creek Predestinarian Church. Sermons. 1820-1975. *1940*
—. Bergner, Peter. Bethel Ships. Merchant Marine. Methodist Church. New York City. Swedish Americans. 1832-66. *1661*
—. Brethren in Christ. Christianity. Education. Holiness movement. Individualism. 1870-1910. *3421*
—. California (Los Angeles). International Church of the Foursquare Gospel. McPherson, Aimee Semple. Radio. 1920-44. *1958*
—. Camp meeting sites. Methodism. 19c. *2225*
—. Canada. Holiness Movement Church. Horner, Ralph Cecil. Methodist Church. 1887-1921. *3500*
—. Canada. Holiness Movement Church. Horner, Ralph Cecil. Methodist Church. 1887-1921. *3501*
—. Canada. Osgood, Thaddeus. Religious Education. 1807-52. *2900*
—. Catholic Church. Massachusetts (Boston). Protestantism. Settlement houses. South End House. Woods, Robert A. 1891-1910. *2438*
—. Charities. Cities. Muhlenberg, Augustus. Politics. Protestantism (review article). Social Problems. 1812-1900. *2930*
—. Cherokee Indians. Civil disobedience. Missionaries. 1829-39. *1579*
—. Christian Catholic Church. Dowie, John Alexander. Illinois (Zion). Utopias. 1888-1907. *409*
—. Church of Christ. Keeble, Marshall. Race relations. 1878-1968. *2550*
—. Circuit riders. Clark, John. Methodism. Missouri. Travis, John. 1796-1851. *1561*
—. Congregationalism. Connecticut. Revivals. Vermont. 1781-1803. *1609*
—. Congregationalism. Far Western States. Mormons. Nutting, John Danforth. Photographs. Utah Gospel Mission. 1900-50. *1560*
—. Congregationalism. New Divinity movement. New England, western. 1740-1800. *3117*
—. Cults. Law. 1976-78. *1110*
—. Daily life. Illinois (Chicago). Methodist Church. Whitefield, Henry. 1833-71. *1508*
—. Death and Dying. Literature. South. 1800-65. *1970*
—. Diaries. Georgia (Augusta Circuit). Methodist Episcopal Church. Norman, Jeremiah. 1798-1801. *1642*
—. Dunkards. German Americans. Great Awakening. Immigration. Lutheran Church. Moravian Church. Northeastern or North Atlantic States. Reformed churches. 1720-60. *2237*
—. Ecumenism. Protestantism. Social change. Social justice. Student Christian Movement. 19c-20c. *440*
—. Education. Freedmen. Presbyterians. 1872-1900. *3589*
—. Emigration. Friends, Society of (Hicksite). Ohio Yearly Meeting. 1828-1919. *3270*
—. Episcopal Church, Protestant. Frontier and Pioneer Life. McIlvaine, Charles Petit. Ohio. Oxford Movement. 1800-75. *3187*
—. Faith healing. Perfectionism. Theology. 1870-90. *1434*
—. Great Awakening. Great Britain. Whitefield, George. 1714-70. *2232*
—. Herzberger, F. W. Lutheran Church. Missouri (St. Louis). 1899-1930. *3336*
—. Horstman, Otto K. Indiana (Shelbyville). Lutheran Church, Evangelical. Missions and Missionaries. Personal narratives. 1934. *1551*
—. Illinois (Chicago). Manitoba (Winnipeg). Mennonites. 1866-1977. *3361*
—. Methodism. Slavery. Wesley, John. 1725-1974. *3505*
—. Michigan. Political parties. State Legislatures. 1837-61. *1300*
—. Models. Unification Church. 1965-75. *4255*
—. New York (Buffalo). Sunday, Billy. 1917. *2218*
—. Postal Service. Sects, Religious. 1970's. *1118*
—. Protestantism. Slavery. South. 18-19c. *2169*
—. Reform. Wright, Henry Clarke. 1820-60. *2444*
Evans, James. Canada. Cree Indians. Methodist Church. Missions and Missionaries. 1833-46. *3475*
—. Methodism. Missions and Missionaries. Ontario (Lake Superior). Voyages. 1837-38. *1564*
Evans, Warren Felt. Idealism. Mental healing. Mysticism. New Thought Movement. Romanticism. 1864-89. *1460*
Everett Institute. Baptists. Colleges and Universities. Education. Louisiana (Spearsville). 1893-1908. *605*
Evil. American dream. Christianity. Civil religion. Myths and Symbols. Theology. 1973. *2724*
Evil eye. Folklore. Italian Americans. New York (Utica). 20c. *2192*
Evjen, John O. Lutheran Church. Minnesota. Theologians. 1874-1942. *3303*
Evolution *See also* Creation Theory.
—. Adventists. California (San Francisco). Debates. Educational Policy. Science League of America. 1925. *2291*
—. Antievolution Law (1928). Arkansas. Church and state. Courts. Epperson, Susan. Initiatives. 1900's-68. *2322*

—. Arkansas. Baptists. Brough, Charles Hillman. Elections (presidential). Prohibition. 1928-29. *1270*
—. Baptists. Bibliographies. Clarke, William Newton. Immanentism. Theology. 1894-1912. *3065*
—. Baptists. Darwin, Charles. Hofstadter, Richard *(Social Darwinism in American Thought)*. Rauschenbusch, Walter. Social Gospel. Spencer, Herbert. 1879-1918. *3002*
—. Baptists. Educational Policy. Kentucky. Science. 1922-28. *2347*
—. Baptists, Southern. 1920's. *2345*
—. Baptists, Southern. Disciples of Christ. Kentucky. Methodist Church. Presbyterian Church. Schisms. 1920's. *2310*
—. Bascom, John. Commons, John R. Ely, Richard T. Political theory. Social gospel. Wisconsin, University of. 1870-1910. *2394*
—. Bibliographies. Christianity. 1970's-75. *2330*
—. Bryan, William Jennings. Christianity. Presbyterian Church. 1921-25. *2297*
—. Bryan, William Jennings. Church and state. Darwinism. Fundamentalism. Public schools. 1920-73. *2317*
—. Bryan, William Jennings. Darrow, Clarence. Scopes Trial. Tennessee (Dayton). Trials. 1925. *2336*
—. Bryan, William Jennings. Fundamentalism. Presbyterian Church. 1875-1920's. *2344*
—. California. Church and state. Creationism. Curricula. Educational Policy. Science. 1963-74. *2331*
—. Candler, Warren A. Conservatism. Leopold, Nathan. Loeb, Richard. Methodist Episcopal Church, South. Scopes, John Thomas. Trials. 1921-41. *2293*
—. *Defender* (periodical). Kansas (Wichita). *Red Horse* (periodical). Science. Winrod, Gerald Burton. 1925-57. *2305*
—. Earlham College. Friends, Society of. Moore, Joseph. Virginia (Richmond). 1861. *2307*
—. Friends, Society of. Pennsylvania. Provincial Government. Revivals. 1735-75. *2222*
—. Goldsmith, William. Hawkins, Robert W. Kansas (Winfield). Methodist Episcopal Church. Southwestern College. 1920-25. *2316*
Excavations *See also* Artifacts.
—. Arizona (Nogales). Jesuits. Mission Guevavi. 18c. 1964-66. *1818*
—. California (San Diego). Catholic Church. Military Camps and Forts. Missions and Missionaries. Serra Museum. 1769-75. 1964-70's. *1526*
—. Documents. Episcopal Church, Protestant. Illinois (Peoria County). Jubilee College. 1839-1979. *770*
Excommunication. American Revolution. Funk, Christian. Mennonites (Funkite). Pennsylvania (Indian Field). 1760-1809. *3376*
—. Bible. Darwinism. Episcopal Church, Protestant. Europe. Hermeneutics. MacQueary, Howard. Ohio (Canton). St. Paul's Church. Universalism. 1890-91. *3178*
—. Church History. Court records. Massachusetts (Salem). Puritans. 1629-80. *3600*
—. Erikson, Erik H. First Church. Hibbens, Ann. Massachusetts (Boston). Puritans. Rites and Ceremonies. 1640-41. 1960's-70's. *3610*
—. Godbe, William Samuel. Mormonism. Schisms. 1840's-80's. *4047*
Executive Branch *See also* Presidency.
—. Calvinism. Centralization. Public Administration. Reform. Revivals. ca 1880-1930's. *959*
Exegesis. Bible (New Testament). Germany. Hodge, Charles. Liberalism. Presbyterian Church. Princeton Theological Seminary. 1820-78. *3573*
—. Luther, Martin *(Small Catechism)*. Schwan, Henry C. 1893-1912. *3332*
Exercise. Attitudes. Health. New England. Recreation. Transcendentalists. 1830-60. *1453*
Exiles. Acadians. Acculturation. Catholic Church. France. Great Britain. Nova Scotia. 18c. *3750*
—. American Revolution. Bailey, Jacob. Church of England. Letters. Nova Scotia. 1784. *3226*
—. Congregationalism. Great Britain. Hooker, Thomas. Netherlands. New England. Theology. 1631-33. *3650*
—. Letters. Mormons. Polygamy. Utah. Woodruff, Emma Smith. Woodruff, Wilford. 1885. *1050*
—. Loyalists. McDowall, Robert James. Missions and Missionaries. Ontario (Upper Canada). Reformed Dutch Church. 1790-1819. *1588*
Exorcism. Deprogramming. 1970's. *4268*
The Exorcist, film (review article). Occult sciences. Social Psychology. 1975. *2211*
Extortion. Christian Science. Documents. Forgeries. Haushalter, Walter M. *(Mrs. Eddy Purloins from Hegel)*. 1929-59. *3912*

F

Factionalism. Agriculture. Germans, Russian. Mennonites. Personal narratives. Saskatchewan (Rosthern). Settlement. 1891-1900. *3442*
—. American Revolution. Reformed Dutch Church. 1650-1840. *1211*
—. Baptists. Fundamentalism. Jarvis Street Baptist Church. Modernism. Ontario (Toronto). Social Classes. 1895-1934. *2605*
—. Church and State. Church of England. Congregationalism. Connecticut. Great Awakening. Officeholding. 1730-76. *1310*
—. Nova Scotia (Pictou County). Presbyterian Church. Scottish Canadians. Social Conditions. 1898-1966. *3533*
Faillon, Etienne-Michel. Bourget, Ignace. Catholic Church. Church History. Letters. Quebec (Montreal). 1850. *3824*
Fairbairn, R. Edis. Canada. Pacifism. United Church of Canada. World War II. 1939. *2688*
Fairbank, John King (review article). China. Christianity. Missions and Missionaries. ca 1860-1949. 1974. *1718*
Faith healing. Arkansas, northeast. Pentecostals. Sects, Religious. 1937-73. *1433*
—. Charismatic movement. Harrell, David Edwin, Jr. (review article). Revivals. 1947-75. *2782*
—. Evangelicalism. Indiana (Gary). Music (gospel). Negroes. Theology. 1976. *2868*
—. Evangelism. Perfectionism. Theology. 1870-90. *1434*
—. Medicine. 20c. *1443*
—. Mysticism. New Mexico (Peralta). Schlatter, Francis. 1895-96. *1429*
Falkenau, Jacob J. M. Congregation Kahal Kadosh Shearith Israel. Ethnicity. Hebrew. Jews. Lyons, Jacques Judah. New York City. Pique, Dob. Poetry. 1786-1841. *2062*
Family *See also* Divorce; Marriage; Women.
—. Altar boys. Catholic Church. Clergy. -1974. *3726*
—. Bingham, Hiram. Congregationalism. Converts. Missions and Missionaries. Vermont. 1789-1819. *1585*
—. Catholic Church. Immigrants. Polish Americans. Social control. Values. 20c. *913*
—. Catholic Church. Judaism. Private Schools. 1960's-70's. *654*
—. Cemeteries. Rural Cemetery Movement. Social change. Tombstones. 1830's-40's. *87*
—. Children. Friends, Society of. Pennsylvania (Delaware Valley). Theology. 1681-1735. *874*
—. Children's Aid Society. Foster care. Home Missionary Society. Pennsylvania (Philadelphia). Protestantism. 1880-1905. *2504*
—. Christianity. Negroes. Social change. Values. War. 1960's-70's. *875*
—. City life. Psychocultural therapy. Witchcraft. 1968. *2197*
—. Congregationalism. Connecticut (Canterbury). Great Awakening. Local politics. Schisms. 1742-50. *2242*
—. Congregationalism. Methodism. Mormons. New England. New York, western. Young, Brigham. 18c-1830's. *2840*
—. Connecticut (Milford). Puritans. 1639-90's. *897*
—. Education. Friends, Society of. Pennsylvania. Social Customs. Socialization. ca 1740-76. *3279*
—. Ethnic groups. Government. Morality. Religious institutions. 1960's-70's. *899*
—. Farms. Literature. Sex roles. Social Status. South. Women. 1800-60. *816*
—. France. Protestantism. Quebec. Trade. 1740-60. *333*
—. Friends, Society of. Frost, J. William (review article). 17c-18c. 1973-75. *938*
—. Generations. Religiosity. 1940-75. *160*
—. Government. Ideology. Massachusetts. Puritans. Social cohesion. 1630-85. *3606*
—. Illinois (Nauvoo). Mormons. New York. Young, Brigham. 1824-45. *861*
—. Land. Mormons. Pioneer life. Utah (Kanab). 1874-80. *4009*
—. Lutheran Church. Parsonages. 1974. *802*
—. New York. Noyes, John Humphrey. Oneida Community. Sex. 1848-80. *431*
Family Histories. *See* Genealogy.
Family misfortune, theme of. Folklore. Protestant Ethic. 20c. *335*
Family size preference. Abortion. Attitudes. 1972. *917*
—. Catholic Church. Population. Women. Women. 1964-74. *915*
—. Population. Teenagers. 1971-74. *808*
Famines. California. Catholic Church. Gold Rushes. Immigration. Irish Americans. 1849-90's. *3800*
Far Western States *See also* individual states (including Alaska and Hawaii).
—. *Alaska Herald* (newspaper). Clergy. Honcharenko, Agapius. Orthodox Eastern Church, Greek. Ukrainian Americans. 1832-1916. *2805*
—. Congregationalism. Evangelism. Mormons. Nutting, John Danforth. Photographs. Utah Gospel Mission. 1900-50. *1560*
Faries, Richard. Anglican Communion. Autobiography. Cree Indians. Missions and Missionaries. Ontario (York Factory). 1896-1961. *1528*
Farm programs. Catholic Church. New Deal. Rural life movement. 1930's. *2573*
Farmers *See also* Peasants.
—. Catholic Church. Drummond County Mechanics Institute. Labor Unions and Organizations. Quebec (Drummond County). 1856-90. *1472*
—. Christianity. Social Customs. South. Travel accounts. 1850-70. *2795*
—. Evangelicalism. Negroes. South. 1800-60. *2845*
Farming. Alberta. Communes. Mennonites. Namaka Farm. 1920's-40's. *414*
Farms. Amish (Old Order). Daily Life. Diaries. King family. Loomis, Charles P. Pennsylvania (Lancaster County). 1940. *3403*
—. Baptists. Country Life. Illinois (southern). Lentz, Lula Gillespie. Personal narratives. 1883-1929. *3037*
—. Cedar Creek Monthly Meeting. Emancipation. Friends, Society of. Moorman, Clark Terrell. Ohio. Virginia (Caroline County). 1766-1814. *2487*
—. Concordia Historical Institute. Lutheran Church (Missouri Synod). Missouri (Perry County). Preservation. Saxon Lutheran Memorial. 1958-64. *220*
—. Country Life. Haswell, David R. Letters. Pennsylvania. Protestants. Revivals. 1808-31. *2234*
—. Family. Literature. Sex roles. Social Status. South. Women. 1800-60. *816*
—. Germans, Russian. Hildebrand, Bernhard (and family). Manitoba (Rosenthal). Mennonites. 1795-1915. *3407*
Farrelly, John P. Bishops. Catholic Church. Irish Americans. Morris, John. Stritch, Samuel A. Tennessee. 19c-1958. *3860*
Fasman, Oscar Z. Hebrew Theological College. Judaism (Orthodox). Oklahoma (Tulsa). Ontario (Ottawa). Personal narratives. Rabbis. 1929-79. *4177*
Father Divine. Cults. Jones, Jim. Negroes. Peace Mission (movement). People's Temple. 1920-79. *4254*
—. Father Jehovia (pseud. of Samuel Morris). Georgia (Valdosta). Negroes. St. John the Vine Hickerson. 1899-1914. *4259*
—. Negroes. Peace Mission (movement). Sermons. 1915-65. *4249*
Father Jehovia (pseud. of Samuel Morris). Father Divine. Georgia (Valdosta). Negroes. St. John the Vine Hickerson. 1899-1914. *4259*
Faulkner, William. Calvinism. Literature. Presbyterian Church. 1920's-75. *2035*
—. Crane, Stephen. Literature. 19c-20c. *2030*
Faulkner, William *(The Sound and the Fury)*. Attitudes. Calvinism. South. 1929. *2018*
Feast days. Catholic Church. Lawrence, Saint. New Mexico (Bernalillo). Social Customs. 1974. *3853*
—. Catholic Church. Mexican Americans. New Mexico. 20c. *3903*
Federal agencies. American Missionary Association. Freedmen. Georgia (Atlanta). Methodist Episcopal Church. Reconstruction. 1865-69. *556*

Federal aid to education. Catholic Church. Church Schools. Constitutional law. Elementary Education. 1960's-72. *691*
—. Church and state. Civil Rights. Colleges and Universities. New York. Political attitudes. Students. 1972. *1119*
—. Methodist Episcopal Church, African. Negroes. Ohio. Wilberforce University (Combined Normal and Industrial Department). 1887-91. *518*
Federal Communications Commission. Lansman, Jeremy. Milam, Lorenzo. Radio. Religious references. Television. 1972-75. *1116*
Federal Council of the Churches of Christ in America. Dulles, John Foster. Presbyterian Church. UN. 1941-45. *1312*
—. Ecumenism. Hopkins, Charles Howard. Politics. Protestant Churches. Social gospel. 1880-1908. *487*
—. Methodist Federation for Social Service. North, Frank M. Social Creed of Methodism. Ward, Harry F. 1907-12. *2388*
Federal Government *See also* names of individual agencies, bureaus, and departments, e.g. Bureau of Indian Affairs, Office of Education, but State Department, Defense Department, etc.; Congress; Constitutions; Executive Branch; Government; Legislation; Supreme Court.
—. Arizona. Edmunds Act (US, 1882). Mormons. Polygamy. 1880's. *1000*
—. Church and state. Politics. 1776-1976. *1057*
—. Civil disobedience. Clawson, Rudger. Mormons. Polygamy. Sharp, John. Utah. 1862-91. *996*
—. Conscientious objection. Constitutional Amendments (2nd). Friends, Society of. Madison, James. Military service. States' Rights. 1787-92. *2686*
—. Diaries. Malone, R. J. Mennonites. Military Intelligence. Surveillance. World War I. 1914-19. *2697*
—. Disfranchisement. Mormons. State Legislatures. Suffrage. 1882-92. *1046*
—. Doukhobors. Ethnic groups. Royal Canadian Mounted Police. Saskatchewan. Settlement. 1899-1909. *1006*
—. Mormons. Utah. Westward Movement. 1846-50's. *4034*
Federal Policy. Buchanan, James. Church and state. Historiography. Military. Mormons. Utah. 1857-58. *1073*
Federal Programs. Agriculture. Catholic Church. Friends, Society of. Indian-White Relations. Missions and Missionaries. Moravian Church. Old Northwest. 1789-1820. *1529*
Federal Regulation. Church and State. Law. Religion (definitions). 1950's-70's. *1131*
Federalists. Antifederalists. Constitutions. Religious liberty. 1776-92. *1010*
Federation for the Support of Jewish Philanthropic Societies. Charities. Judaism. New York City. 1917-33. *2516*
Federation movement. Charities. Judaism. Ohio (Columbus). 1904-48. *2522*
Fédération Nationale Saint-Jean-Baptiste. Catholic Church. Feminism. Gérin-Lajoie, Marie. Quebec. 1907-33. *870*
Fee, John Gregg. Abolition Movement. Berea College. Kentucky. Presbyterian Church. Religious education. 1855-1904. *777*
Feild, Edward. Bishops. Catholic Church. Church of England. Evangelicalism. Liturgy. Methodism. Newfoundland. Presbyterian Church. 1765-1852. *3197*
—. Bishops. Church of England. Education. Great Britain. Newfoundland. 1826-44. *3198*
—. Catholic Church. Irish Canadians. Mullock, John Thomas. Newfoundland. Politics. Protestant Churches. 19c. *1254*
Feldberg, Michael. Benjamin, Philip S. Friends, Society of. Miller, Richard G. Pennsylvania (Philadelphia; review article). Sinclair, Bruce. 1790-1920. 1974-76. *3269*
Felicians. Catholic Church. Church Schools. Polish Americans. Social Work. Women. 1855-1975. *3828*
Fell, Margaret. Feminism. Friends, Society of. Great Britain (Lancashire). Pennsylvania (Philadelphia). Women. 1670's. *928*
Fellman, Michael. Communalism (review article). Marriage. Muncy, Raymond Lee. Sex. Social Organization. 19c. 1973. *384*
Female Anti-Slavery Society. American Anti-Slavery Society. Foster, Abigail Kelley. Fox, George. Friends, Society of. Mott, Lucretia Coffin. Segregation. 17c. 1837-66. *791*
Feminism *See also* Women's Liberation Movement.
—. Antinomian controversy. Hutchinson, Anne. Massachusetts. 1630-43. *867*
—. Beecher, Henry Ward. New York City. Radicals and Radicalism. Sex. Social Reform. Spiritualism. Vanderbilt, Cornelius. Woodhull, Victoria Claflin. 1868-90's. *2386*
—. Black theology. Christianity. Negroes. Reform. Theology. 1960's-70's. *2426*
—. Catholic Church. Fédération Nationale Saint-Jean-Baptiste. Gérin-Lajoie, Marie. Quebec. 1907-33. *870*
—. Catholic Church. Quebec. Religious Orders. Women. 1640-1975. *833*
—. Christianity. Judaism. 1967-76. *876*
—. Church and state. House of Representatives. Polygamy. Roberts, Brigham Henry. Utah. 1898-1900. *1133*
—. Colby, Abby M. Congregationalism. Japan. Missions and Missionaries. 1879-1914. *932*
—. Colorado (Boulder). Social reform. Temperance Movements. Women's Christian Temperance Union. 1881-1967. *2741*
—. Commission on the Status and Role of Women in the United Methodist Church. Methodism. Social Organizations. 1869-1974. *893*
—. Fell, Margaret. Friends, Society of. Great Britain (Lancashire). Pennsylvania (Philadelphia). Women. 1670's. *928*
—. Holiness Movement. Palmer, Phoebe. Wesley, Susanna. 1732-1973. *829*
—. Identity. Social Reform. 1820's-60. *884*
—. Judaism. 1967-79. *826*
—. Judaism. 1970's. *923*
—. Kansas. Letters. Nichols, Clarina I. H. Sex roles. Theology. 1857-69. *843*
—. Mormons. National Women's Conference, 1st. Utah Women's Conference. Women. 1977. *858*
—. Patriarchal attitudes. Prehistory-1970's. *859*
—. Protestant Churches. Radicals and Radicalism. Social reform. South. Women. 1920's. *789*
—. Protestant churches. Women. -1973. *891*
Feminization. Douglas, Ann. Protestantism. Reform. Sex roles. Stereotypes. ca 1820-75. 1977-80. *918*
—. Historiography. Welter, Barbara. Women. 1820's-30's. 1970's. *920*
—. Missions and Missionaries. Voluntary Associations. Women. 1800-60. *942*
Fenian Brotherhood. Anglin, Timothy Warren. Canada. Catholic Church. Debates. Irish Canadians. McGee, D'Arcy. 1863-68. *1341*
Ferguson, Anne Williams. Boarding Schools. Chatham Hall. Episcopal Church, Protestant. Personal narratives. Virginia. Women. 1940's. *628*
Fernandez de Santa Ana, Benito. Agricultural Labor. Canary Islanders. Indians. Missions and Missionaries. Petitions. Provincial Government. Texas (Villa San Fernando). 1741. *1542*
Fernando (slave). Christianity. Civil Rights. Key, Elizabeth. Law. Negroes. Virginia. 1607-90. *2153*
Ferris, William H. Black nationalism. Crummell, Alexander. DuBois, W. E. B. Episcopal Church, Protestant. Ideology. 1819-1898. *2424*
Fertility. Amish. Income. Indiana. Women. 20c. *882*
—. Birth Control. Rhode Island. 1968-69. *803*
—. Marriage. Mormons. 1820-1920. *924*
—. Migration. Mormons. -1974. *912*
—. Mormons. Polygamy. 19c. *926*
Fiction *See also* Novels.
—. Adventists. Miller, William. Press. 1830's-40's. *2014*
—. Anti-Semitism. Fiedler, Leslie. Judaism. Personal narratives. 1970's. *2043*
—. Bible. Diaries. Melville, Herman. Palestine. Travel. 1857. *2039*
—. Buck, Pearl S. Missions and Missionaries. Presbyterian Church. 1931-69. *2068*
—. Cable, George Washington. Louisiana (New Orleans). Presbyterian Church, Southern. Reform. ca 1870-1925. *3539*
—. Canada. Labor. Social gospel. 1890's. *2078*
—. Cather, Willa *(Death Comes for the Archbishop)*. Martinez, Antonio Jose. New Mexico (Taos). 1830's. 1927. *2077*
—. Christianity. Episcopal Church, Protestant. Grace Church. Melville, Herman ("The Two Temples"). New York City. Trinity Church. 1845-50. *2061*
—. Dreiser, Theodore. Social justice. 1900-45. *2020*
—. Hawthorne, Nathaniel. Massachusetts. Philosophy of History. Puritans. 1820's-60's. *2081*
—. Hawthorne, Nathaniel. Melville, Herman *(Moby Dick)*. Pessimism. 1850-51. *2042*
—. Kierkegaard, Sören. Updike, John. 1932-77. *2009*
—. Mormons. Regionalism. 1930-50. *2026*
—. Shakers. ca 1780-1900. *2006*
Fiction, juvenile. Catholic Church. Finn, Francis J. Youth. 1889-1928. *2051*
Fiedler, Leslie. Anti-Semitism. Fiction. Judaism. Personal narratives. 1970's. *2043*
Field, Eliza. Courtship. Great Britain (London). Indians. Jones, Peter. Methodism. New York. 1820's-33. *1637*
Fielding, Joseph. Diaries. Illinois (Nauvoo). Mormons. 1844-46. *3958*
Fiestas. Catholic Church. New Mexico. Rites and Ceremonies. Saints, patron. Villages. 1970's. *3892*
Filipinos. Indians. Vietnamese. War crimes. 1636-1970's. *2640*
Fillmore, Millard. Anti-Catholicism. Know-Nothing Party. Nativism. Political Campaigns (presidential). Whig Party. 1850-56. *1305*
—. Mormons. Territorial government. Utah. 1850-53. *1053*
Films *See also* Actors and Actresses; Audiovisual Materials.
—. Attitudes. Censorship. Protestant Churches. Television. 1921-80. *2820*
—. Baptists. History Teaching. Television. Videotape. 1977. *267*
—. Jesus Christ. 1920's-70's. *1894*
—. Jesus Christ. 1950's-74. *1881*
—. Mormons. 1911-70's. *1875*
Finance *See also* Business; Commerce; Economics; Public Finance.
—. Mormons. Railroads. Tourism. Utah. Young, John W. 1867-91. *332*
Finch, John. Letters. New York (Finger Lakes area). Skaneateles Community. Utopias. 1843-45. *4302*
Finesilver, Moses Ziskind. Congregation Sons of Zion. Judaism. Rabbis. Rhode Island (Providence). 1880-83. *4122*
Finland. Australia. Canada. Kurikka, Matti. Theosophy. Utopias. 1883-1915. *435*
—. Finnish Americans. Lutheranism. Marxism. Reform. 1900-76. *990*
Finley, Robert. American Colonization Society. Racism. 1816-40. *2470*
Finn, Francis J. Catholic Church. Fiction, juvenile. Youth. 1889-1928. *2051*
Finney, Charles G. Abolition Movement. Revivals. Social reform. South. 1833-69. *2466*
—. Adolescence. Baptists. Congregationalism. Massachusetts (Boston). Methodism. Revivals. 1822-42. *2258*
—. Benevolence (doctrine). Protestantism. Social reform. 1815-65. *2422*
—. Civil Religion. Mahan, Asa. Millenarianism. National Self-image. Perfectionism. 19c. *1189*
—. Congregationalism. New York (Oneida County). Presbyterian Church. Revivals. 1825-27. *2245*
—. Democracy. Human nature. Revivalism. Social Theory. 1820-30. *2268*
—. Higher law (doctrine). Ohio Antislavery Society. Political Participation. Revivalism. 1835-60. *2253*
—. Law and Society. Revivals. 1800-50. *2271*
—. New York. Revivals. 1820-40. *2243*
—. Revivals. Theology. 1821-75. *2251*
Finnish Americans. Finland. Lutheranism. Marxism. Reform. 1900-76. *990*
—. Lutheran Church. Theology. 1688-1970's. *3316*
Firearms. Mormons. 1830's-1869. *2651*
First African Baptist Church. Abolition Movement. Baptists. Education. Meachum, John Berry. Missouri (St. Louis). Negroes. 1815-54. *2482*
—. Baptists. Jasper, John. Negroes. Sermons. Virginia (Richmond). 1812-1901. *2990*
First Baptist Church. Architecture. Baptists. Heiman, Adolphus. Tennessee (Nashville). 1837-62. *1808*
—. Baptists, Southern. Merry, Nelson. Race Relations. Tennessee (Nashville). 1810-65. *3078*
First Catholic Slovak Union (Jednota). Catholic Church. Pennsylvania. Sabol, John. Slovak Americans. 1920's-60's. *3821*

First Church. Erikson, Erik H. Excommunication. Hibbens, Ann. Massachusetts (Boston). Puritans. Rites and Ceremonies. 1640-41. 1960's-70's. *3610*

First Congregational Society Church. Architecture. Banner, Peter. Congregationalism. New York. Vermont (Burlington). 1794-1815. *1829*

First Harlem Church. Adventists. Humphrey, James K. Negroes. New York City. Schisms. Utopia Park. 1920's-30's. *2143*

First Hebrew Benevolent Society. California (San Francisco). Cemeteries. Funerals. Jews. Johnson, Henry D. 1849-50. *4147*

First Mennonite Church. Clergy. Entz, John Edward. Kansas (Newton). Mennonites. 1875-1969. *3419*

First Parish Church. Architecture. Bulfinch, Charles. Massachusetts (Charlestown). Meetinghouses. 1803-04. *1792*

First Presbyterian Church. Baptists. Clergy. Fosdick, Harry Emerson. New York City. Presbyterian Church. Theology. 1918-24. *466*

—. Presbyterian Church. Tennessee (Nashville). 1814-1976. *3553*

Fischer, David H. Child-rearing. Death and Dying. Greven, Philip. Lynn, Kenneth S. Personality (review article). Politics. Protestantism. Stannard, David E. 18c. 1977. *2943*

Fischer, Emil C. Architecture. Churches. Country life. Kansas. 19c. *1778*

Fish, Josiah. Congregationalism. Osborn, Sarah. Revivals. Rhode Island (Newport). Women. 1766-67. *904*

Fishbourn, William. Friends, Society of. Pennsylvania. Settlement. 1680-1739. *3272*

Fisher, Vardis. Literature. Mormons. 1915-68. *1999*

Fishing *See also* Whaling Industry and Trade.

—. Alaska (Kodiak). Canneries. Unification Church. 1978-79. *325*

Fiske, John. Calvinism. Cotton, John. Elegies. New England. Poetry. Puritans. 17c. *1985*

—. Poetry. Puritans. Taylor, Edward. Tree of Life metaphor. 1650-1721. *1969*

Fister, W. *Evangelische Kirchen-Zeitung* (newspaper). Letters-to-the-editor. Lutheran Church (Missouri Synod). 1866. *3322*

Fitch, James. Connecticut. Ethics. Land. Politics. Puritans. 1679-1727. *3646*

Flag salute. Conscientious Objectors. Courts. Jehovah's Witnesses. World War II. 1930's-40's. *2655*

Flagellants. Catholic Church. New Mexico. Penitentes. 13c-20c. *3779*

Flaherty, Joe. Anti-Catholicism. Breslin, Jimmy. Brooklyn Diocese. Hamill, Pete. Irish Americans. New York City. Novels. 1960's-70's. *2098*

Fleet, Thomas. *Boston Evening Post* (newspaper). Freedom of the press. Great Awakening. Massachusetts (Boston). Newspapers. 1740's. *1423*

Fletcher, C. B. Attitudes. Episcopal Church, Protestant. Letters. Slavery. Vermont. 1777-1864. *2159*

Flick, Lawrence. Bishops. Canevin, Regis. Catholic Church. Pennsylvania (Philadelphia, Pittsburgh). 1870's-1927. *3843*

Florence, Max. Bossard, Gisbert. Mormon Temple. Photography. Smith, Joseph Fielding. Utah (Salt Lake City). 1911. *1762*

Florida *See also* South; Southeastern States.

—. American Missionary Association. Civil Rights. Education. Freedmen. 1864-74. *548*

—. Anti-Catholicism. Bryan, Nathan P. Catts, Sidney J. Democratic Party. Political Campaigns (gubernatorial). Primaries (senatorial). Trammell, Park M. 1915-16. *1258*

—. Anti-Catholicism. Catts, Sidney J. Elections (gubernatorial). Guardians of Liberty. Knott, William V. Sturkie Resolution. 1916. *1231*

—. Civil Rights. Colonies. Europe. Judaism. Levy, Moses Elias. 1825. *4151*

—. Colonial Government. Indians. Military security. Missions. 1566-1710. *1079*

—. Diaries. Emigration. Lutheran Church. Sjöborg, Sofia Charlotta. Sweden. 1871. *3340*

—. Episcopal Church, Protestant. Gray, William Crane. Indian-White Relations. Missions and missionaries. Seminole Indians. 1893-1914. *1558*

Florida (Campbell Town). Colonization. Great Britain. Huguenots. West Florida. 1763-70. *3254*

Florida (Estero). Illinois (Chicago). Koreshan Unity. Millenarianism. Teed, Cyrus Read. Utopias. 1886-1903. *396*

Florida (Miami). Civil Rights movement. Discrimination. Louisiana (New Orleans). Murray, Hugh T., Jr. Personal narratives. Tulane Interfaith Council. 1959-60. *2548*

Florida (Pasco County). Anti-Catholicism. Benedictines. D'Equivelley, G. F. *Jeffersonian* (newspaper). Land. Letters-to-the-editor. Mohr, Charles. 1915-16. *2123*

Florida (Tallahassee). Negroes. Protestant Churches. Race Relations. Social control. 1865-85. *2864*

Florida (Umatilla). Assassination. Baptists. Baptists, Southern (winter assembly grounds). Lincoln, Abraham. 1865. 1925-29. *2980*

Florida (Winter Park). Colleges and Universities. Congregationalism. Hooker, Edward P. Rollins College. 1885-1900. *678*

Folger, Peter. Baptists. Indians. Jones, David. Missionaries. Northeastern or North Atlantic States. Williams, Roger. 1638-1814. *1619*

Folk Art *See also* Art; Arts and Crafts.

—. Altarpieces. Christenson, Lars. Lutheran Church. Minnesota (Benson). Norwegian Americans. Wood Carving. 1887-1904. *1874*

—. Amana Society. Iowa. 1843-1932. *1852*

—. Amish. Mennonites. Pennsylvania. Persecution. Quiltmaking. 16c-1935. *1893*

—. Arts. Baptists, Southern. Conservatism. Denominationalism. 1975. *1877*

—. Baptismal certificates. Birth certificates. Pennsylvania Germans. 1750-1850. *1899*

—. Catholic Church. Colorado. New Mexico. Penitentes. 19c-20c. *3898*

—. Catholic Church. Design. Iconography. Manuscripts. New Mexico. 16c-17c. *1858*

—. Catholic Church. Lopez, George. Lopez, José Dolores. New Mexico (Cordova). Santos, statues. 20c. *1844*

—. Catholic Church. New Mexico. Santos (statues). 1780-1900. *1903*

—. Congregationalism. Massachusetts. Peckham, Robert. Portraits. ca 1838-44. *1861*

—. Connecticut Valley. Sun faces (motif). Tombstones. Vermont (Rockingham). 1786-1812. *1842*

—. Friends, Society of. Hicks, Edward *(Peaceable Kingdom).* Painting. Pennsylvania (Bucks County). 1780-1849. *1857*

—. Friends, Society of. Hicks, Edward *(Peaceable Kingdom).* Symbolism in Art. 1825-49. *1851*

—. German Americans. Harmony Methodist Church Cemetery. Methodist Church. Tombstones. West Virginia (Jane Lew). 1827-55. *1892*

—. Lithography. Mexico. Puerto Rico. Southwest. 1300-1974. *1868*

—. New England. New York (Long Island). Tombstones. 1660-18c. *1900*

Folk medicine. Amish. Magic. Mennonites. Pennsylvania. Powwowing. ca 1650-1979. *2206*

—. Aphrodisiacs. Charms. Philtres. Witchcraft. -1973. *2199*

—. Diseases (classification). Etiology. Quebec. 1976-77. *1428*

—. Folklore. Jones, Louis C. Witchcraft. 1945-49. *2189*

—. Georgia. Great Britain. Indians. Medicine (practice of). Methodism. Wesley, John. 1740's. *1426*

Folk religion. ca 1900-74. *164*

—. American Revolution. National Characteristics. Pennsylvania Germans. 1775-83. *2948*

—. Appalachia. Pentecostal Movement. Snakehandlers. 1974. *3519*

—. Architecture. Arizona, southern. Catholic Church. Chapels. Papago Indians. 20c. *1783*

—. Arkansas (Jonesboro). Attitudes. Folklore. Tornadoes. 1973. *95*

—. Arkansas, northeast. Baptists. Pentecostals. Theology. Worship. 1972-78. *2836*

—. Art. Catholic Church. French Canadians. Musée Historique de Vaudreuil. Quebec. 17c-20c. *174*

—. Bibliographies. Europe. North America. 1900-74. 16c-20c. *42*

—. Catholic Church. Indiana. 1970's. *3697*

Folk Religion (review article). Charismatic movement. Europe. Health. Occult sciences. Science. 16c-19c. 1975-76. *7*

Folk Songs. Ballads, British. Death and Dying. Supernatural. 1830-1930. *1923*

—. Episcopal Church, Protestant. Hymnals. 1970-78. *1906*

Folklore *See also* Folk Medicine; Folk Songs; Occult Sciences.

—. Aged. Poor. West Virginia. Witchcraft. Women. 1975. *2201*

—. "Angel Dancers". Communalism. Howell, Jane. Huntsman, Manson T. New Jersey (Woodcliff). Rumors. Sects, Religious. 1890-1920. *389*

—. Apocalypse. Mormons. 19c-20c. *4021*

—. Appalachia. Baptists, Primitive. Theology. 1800's-1977. *3083*

—. Appalachia. Hymns. 18c-20c. *1927*

—. Arkansas (Jonesboro). Attitudes. Folk Religion. Tornadoes. 1973. *95*

—. Bible. Protestantism. South. Visions. 20c. *2178*

—. Bosom serpentry (concept). Mormons. New England. Puritans. Snakes. Utah. 17c-19c. *2765*

—. British Columbia (Maillardville). Magic. 1973-74. *2195*

—. Catholic Church. Hispanic Americans. New Mexico. Penitentes. Rites and Ceremonies. Social customs. 16c-20c. *3829*

—. Cemeteries. Christianity. Social Customs. Texas. 1830-1950. *2751*

—. Charles I. Congregationalism. Regicide. Rhode Island. Stiles, Ezra. Whale, Theophilus. 17c. 1755-85. *3131*

—. Christianity. Discrimination. Jews. Negroes. Stereotypes. 18c-1974. *2091*

—. City life. Indiana (East Chicago, Gary, Hammond). Negroes. Voodoo. 1976. *2182*

—. Clergy. Georgia, west-central. Humor. Protestantism. 19c-20c. *2839*

—. Collectors and Collecting. Hyatt, Harry Midddleton. Illinois (Adams County). Negroes. Small, Minnie Hyatt. South. Witchcraft. 1920-78. *2190*

—. Death and dying. New England. 1630-1790. *2903*

—. Devil. West Virginia. Witchcraft. 1950-67. *2202*

—. Economic Conditions. Ethnic groups. Mail-Order Business. Social Conditions. Voodoo. 1970-79. *2205*

—. Evil eye. Italian Americans. New York (Utica). 20c. *2192*

—. Family misfortune, theme of. Protestant Ethic. 20c. *335*

—. Folk medicine. Jones, Louis C. Witchcraft. 1945-49. *2189*

—. Gomez, Dolorez Amelia. Pennsylvania (Philadelphia). Witchcraft. 1974. *2179*

—. Jesus Christ. New York Thruway. Vanishing hitchhiker (theme). 1971. *2737*

—. Kentucky, eastern. Witchcraft. 1977. *2198*

—. Methodology. Mormons. 1892-1970's. *4055*

—. Mormons. Murder. Smith, Joseph. 1659-1900. *4022*

—. Mormons. Oral tradition. 19c-20c. *4054*

—. Mormons. Polygamy. Scandinavian Americans. Temples. Utah (Sanpete-Sevier area). 1849-1979. *4053*

—. Mormons. Settlement. Utah (Great Salt Lake valley). Young, Brigham. 1842-1970's. *4023*

—. Mormons. Vanishing hitchhiker (theme). 1933-74. *4056*

—. Music, bluegrass gospel. Southeastern States. 1770-1970. *1937*

—. New England. Puritans. Sermons. 1625-60. *1981*

—. Novels. Steinbeck, John *(Winter of Our Discontent).* Witchcraft. 1961. *2046*

—. Poetry. Samplers. Social Customs. 19c. *2021*

Folsom, William Harrison. Architects. Churches. Mormons. Utah (Provo, Salt Lake City). ca 1850's-1901. *1757*

Folwell, Samuel *(Sacred to the Illustrious Washington).* Allegory. Art. Mourning (theme). Painting. Protestantism. ca 1800. *1885*

Fontaine, Flavian. California (San Francisco). Catholic Church. Clergy. Mission Dolores. 1850-53. *3801*

Foote, William D. Anti-Semitism. California (Fresno). Johnson, Grove L. Trials. 1893. *2134*

Ford, Arnold. Emigration. Ethiopia (Addis Ababa). Judaism. Negroes. 1930-35. *4143*

Foreign Mission Board. Baptists, Southern. Civil War. Missions and Missionaries. 1861-66. *1700*

—. Baptists, Southern. Missions and Missionaries. 1974. *1699*

—. Baptists, Southern. Missions and Missionaries. Publications programs. 1899-1976. *1708*

Foreign Mission School. American Board of Commissioners for Foreign Missions. Assimilation. Connecticut (Cornwall). Indian-White Relations. Students. 1816-27. *586*
Foreign Policy. American Friends Service Committee. Arab-Israeli conflict. Friends, Society of. Palestine Liberation Organization. 1970's. *1250*
—. Beard, Charles A. Niebuhr, Reinhold. 20c. *1364*
—. Catholic Church. China (Kanchow). Missions and Missionaries. State Department. 1929-32. *1710*
—. Catholic Church. Historiography. 1898-1955. *1288*
—. *Christian Century* (periodical). Japan. Manchurian crisis. Morrison, Charles C. 1931-33. *2678*
—. Israel. Protestantism. Zionism (review article). 1945-48. *2944*
Foreign Relations *See also* Boundaries; Diplomacy; Geopolitics.
—. Emigration. France. Quebec (Sherbrooke). Trappists. 1903-14. *3785*
Foreman, Kenneth J., Sr. Colleges and Universities. Presbyterian Church (southern). *Presbyterian Outlook* (newspaper). Theology. 1922-67. *3547*
Foreman, Stephen. Cherokee Indians. Georgia. Indians. Oklahoma. Presbyterian Church. 1820's-81. *3538*
Forest Service. California (Eight Mile, Blue Creek). Indians. Religious liberty. Supreme Court. 1975. *1102*
Forgeries. Archko collection. Jesus Christ. Mahan, William D. Mormons. Presbyterian Church (Cumberland). Wallace, Lew *(Ben-Hur).* 1880's. *3928*
—. Christian Science. Documents. Extortion. Haushalter, Walter M. *(Mrs. Eddy Purloins from Hegel).* 1929-59. *3912*
Formisano, Ronald P. Hackney, F. Sheldon. Kleppner, Paul. Methodology. Politics (review article). 1827-1900. 1969-71. *1263*
Forssell, G. D. Iowa. Lectures. Minnesota. Progressivism. Social Conditions. 1890-95. *1967*
Fort Bridger. Mormons. Mountain men. Utah. 1847-57. *3975*
Fort Delaware. Catholic Church. Confederate Army. Duke, Basil W. Prisoners of War. Wood, James F. 1864. *3844*
Fort Douglas. *Daily Union Vedette* (newspaper). Mormons. Utah. 1863-67. *4020*
Fort Duquesne. Frontier and Pioneer Life. Indian-White Relations. Moravian Church. Pennsylvania. Post, Christian Frederick. 1758-59. *1505*
Fort Fisher (battle). Armies. Butler, Benjamin F. Chaplains. Civil War. Diaries. Negroes. North Carolina. Turner, Henry M. 1864-65. *2685*
Fort Frontenac. Canada. Indian-White Relations. Iroquois Indians. Missions and Missionaries. Quinte Mission. Sulpician order. 1665-80. *1610*
Fort Keogh. Catholic Church. Chaplains. Diaries. Lindesmith, Eli. Montana. 1855-1922. *2679*
Fort Rawlins. Civil-Military Relations. Mormons. Provo Outrage. Utah. 1870-71. *4000*
Fort Robinson. Baptists. Chaplains. Courts Martial and Courts of Inquiry. Nebraska. Negroes. Plummer, Henry V. 1884-94. *2695*
Fort Vancouver. Clergy. Columbia River. Congregationalism. Hawaiians. Hudson's Bay Company. Kaulehelehe, William R. Washington. 1845-69. *3128*
Fort Wayne Bible College. Colleges and Universities. Indiana. Mennonites, Evangelical. 1904-77. *740*
Forts. *See* Military Camps and Forts.
Fosdick, Harry Emerson. Baptists. Clergy. First Presbyterian Church. New York City. Presbyterian Church. Theology. 1918-24. *466*
—. Charities. Friendship. Liberalism. Protestantism. Rockefeller, John D., Jr. Social control. Wealth. 1920-36. *364*
Foster, Abigail Kelley. American Anti-Slavery Society. Female Anti-Slavery Society. Fox, George. Friends, Society of. Mott, Lucretia Coffin. Segregation. 17c. 1837-66. *791*
Foster care. Children's Aid Society. Family. Home Missionary Society. Pennsylvania (Philadelphia). Protestantism. 1880-1905. *2504*
Foster, George Burman. Academic Freedom. Baptists. Illinois. Theology. University of Chicago Divinity School. 1895-1918. *557*
Founding Fathers. Calvinism. Giles, Benjamin. Libraries. New Hampshire. 1760's-87. *2908*
—. Christianity. Enlightenment. 1776-1976. *1418*
—. Church and state. Theology. 1695-1830. *1096*
—. Constitutions. Historiography. Political Theory. Theology. 18c. *1405*
Fourierism. Brisbane, Albert. Brook Farm. Channing, William Henry. Transcendentalism. 1840-46. *399*
Fowler, Lorenzo Niles. Fowler, Orson Squire. Millenarianism. Philosophy. Phrenology. ca 1820-60's. *2350*
Fowler, Orson Squire. Fowler, Lorenzo Niles. Millenarianism. Philosophy. Phrenology. ca 1820-60's. *2350*
Fox, George. Abolition Movement. Friends, Society of. Pennsylvania. Slave trade. 1656-1754. *2479*
—. American Anti-Slavery Society. Female Anti-Slavery Society. Foster, Abigail Kelley. Friends, Society of. Mott, Lucretia Coffin. Segregation. 17c. 1837-66. *791*
—. Baptists. Friends, Society of. Olney, Thomas, Jr. Politics. Rhode Island. 1672-73. *967*
Fraktur. Art. German Canadians. Ontario. 1976. *1843*
—. Mennonites. Pennsylvania Germans. 1740's-1860's. *1904*
France *See also* Alsace-Lorraine.
—. Acadians. Acculturation. Catholic Church. Exiles. Great Britain. Nova Scotia. 18c. *3750*
—. American Revolution. Canada. Huguenots. Settlement. USA. Whaling industry and Trade. 17c-20c. *3251*
—. Anti-Catholicism. Maryland. Politicians. Protestants. 1750's. *2095*
—. Archival Catalogs and Inventories. Congregatio de Propaganda Fide. North America. Vatican. 1622-1799. 1979. *182*
—. Attitudes. Indians. Jesuits. Missions and Missionaries. New France. 1611-72. *1495*
—. Authority. Church and state. Liberalism. Tocqueville, Alexis de. 1830's. *1144*
—. Bureaucracies. Church and state. Colonial Government. *Commissaire ordonnateur.* Louisiana. 1712-69. *1069*
—. Catholic Church. Colonial Government. Discovery and Exploration. Jolliet, Louis. Marquette, Jacques. Missions and Missionaries. Mississippi River. Monuments. 1665-1700. *3767*
—. Christianity. Civil religion. Democracy. Tocqueville, Alexis de. 1820-50. *1175*
—. Christianity. Great Britain. Judaism. Theater. ca 1957-78. *1853*
—. Church and state. Gibbons, James. Letters. Nolan, Edward J. Sabatier, Paul. 1906. *1016*
—. Ecumenism. Jews. Vatican. 1975. *501*
—. Education. Hymns. Neau, Elias. New York. Protestant Churches. Slaves. ca 1689-1722. *1913*
—. Emigration. Foreign Relations. Quebec (Sherbrooke). Trappists. 1903-14. *3785*
—. Family. Protestantism. Quebec. Trade. 1740-60. *333*
—. Great Britain. Positivism. Unitarianism. 1816-90. *4077*
—. Huguenots. 16c-1978. *3255*
—. Huguenots. New France. 1541-1760. *3252*
—. Indians. Jesuits. Missions and Missionaries. New York, western. Rings. ca 1630-87. *1664*
—. New France. Trials. Witchcraft. 17c. *2203*
France (Alsace). Amish. Germany (Palatinate). Immigrants. Pennsylvania. 1693-1803. *3406*
—. Catholic Church. Conversion. Immigration policy. Louisiana. Protestants. 1753-59. *3719*
Franchise. *See* Citizenship; Suffrage.
Franciscan Sisters. Catholic Church. College of St. Teresa. Minnesota (Winona). Molloy, Mary Aloysius. Women. 1903-54. *670*
Franciscan Sisters of Chicago. Addams, Jane. Dudzik, Mary Theresa. Illinois. Polish Americans. Social Work. Women. 1860-1918. *2511*
Franciscans. Architecture. California. Mission San Juan Capistrano. 1776-1976. *1494*
—. Archives. Bibliographies. California. Geiger, Maynard J. (obituary). Historiography. Mission Santa Barbara. 1936-76. *240*
—. Archives. California. Geiger, Maynard J. (obituary). Historiography. Mission Santa Barbara. 1901-77. *281*
—. Archives. California. Geiger, Maynard J. (obituary). Historiography. Mission Santa Barbara. 1937-77. *238*
—. Arizona. Church and State. Indians. Mexico (Sonora). Missions and Missionaries. 1767-1842. *1065*
—. California. Church and State. Indians. Missions and Missionaries. 1775-1800. *1037*
—. California. Conversion thesis. Cook, Sherburne Friend. Indians. Missions and Missionaries. ca 1790-1820's. 1943. *1541*
—. California. Dominicans. Jesuits. Missions and Missionaries. Serra, Junípero. 1768-76. *1575*
—. California. Durán, Narciso. Indians. Missions. Secularization. 1826-46. *1093*
—. California. Durán, Narciso. Indians. Missions and Missionaries. Music. 1806-46. *1924*
—. California. Geiger, Maynard J. (obituary). Historians. Mission Santa Barbara. 1901-77. *239*
—. California. Mission San Juan Capistrano. 1775-1974. *1627*
—. California. Missions. Winemaking. 18c-19c. *371*
—. California (San Diego). Jayme, Luís (death). Mission San Diego de Alcalá. Yuman Indians. 1775. *1657*
—. Colonial Government. Documents. Missions and Missionaries. New Mexico. Spain. Vélez Cachupín, Thomas. ca 1754. *1586*
—. Education. Engelhardt, Zephyrin. Holy Childhood Indian School Printery. Indians. Michigan (Harbor Springs). Printing. 1894-1913. *1584*
—. Indian-White Relations. Inquisition. Marriage. Missions and Missionaries. New Mexico. Plains Apache Indians. Romero, Diego. 1660-78. *3773*
Francke, Gottfried. Georgia (Ebenezer). Germany. Immigrants. Kiefer, Theobald, II. Letters. Lutheran Church. Orphanages. Pietism. Whitefield, George. 1738. 1750. *2878*
Francophiles. Anglophiles. Catholic Church. Mathieu, Olivier-Elzéar. Regina Diocese. Saskatchewan. 1905-30. *3714*
Francophones. Anglophones. Catholics. Church Discipline. Church History. Morality. Prairie Provinces. 1900-30. *3715*
—. Church schools. Greenway, Thomas (administration). Language. Legislation. Manitoba Act (Canada, 1870). 1890-99. *519*
Franklin and Marshall College. Baptists. Bucknell University. Friends, Society of (Hicksite). Pennsylvania. Reformed German Church. Swarthmore College. Urbanization. 1865-1915. *685*
—. Clergy. Gerhart, Emanuel Vogel. Pennsylvania (Lancaster). Reformed German Church. Theology. 1840-1904. *3286*
Franklin, Benjamin. Allen, Ethan. Deism. Historiography. Jefferson, Thomas. Palmer, Elihu. 1750-1820. *4277*
—. Clergy. Congregationalism. Massachusetts (Boston). *New England Courant* (newspaper). Smallpox. *Spectator* (newspaper). 1720-23. *2023*
—. Deism. 1706-90. *4275*
—. Friendship. Morality. Publishers and Publishing. Religious liberty. Whitefield, George. 1739-70. *58*
—. Great Awakening. Great Britain. Theology. Whitefield, George. 1739-64. *2272*
—. Protestant Ethic. Weber, Max *(The Protestant Ethic and the Spirit of Capitalism).* 18c-1978. *330*
Franklin, Harvey B. California. Jews. Personal narratives. Rabbis. 1916-57. *4099*
Franklin, Leo M. Judaism. Nebraska (Omaha). Rabbis. Temple Israel. 1892-99. *4094*
Franklin, Lewis Abraham. California (San Francisco). Judaism. Rabbis. Sermons. Yom Kippur. 1850. *4100*
Franson, Fredrik. Darby, John Nelson. Evangelical Free Church of America. Millenarianism. Moody, Dwight L. Revivalism. Scandinavian Americans. 1875-95. *2863*
Fraternal Address. Baptists, Southern. Mullins, Edgar Young. Theology. 1919-20. *2995*
Fraud. Archaeology. Engraving. Mexico (Guerrero). Mormons. Padilla Gold Plates. 1952-78. *4007*
—. Owen, Robert. Pennsylvania (New Harmony). Rapp, Frederick. Real Estate. 1825. *327*

Free love. Anti-Christian sentiments. Christianity. Cochran, Jacob. Maine (York County). Society of Free Brethren and Sisters. 1817-19. *89*
—. Perfectionists. Rhode Island (Cumberland). Theology. 1748-68. *2898*
Free Quakers. American Revolution. Friends, Society of. 1774-83. *2668*
Free thinkers. Communalism. Iowa. Kneeland, Abner. Salubria (religious community). 1827-44. *383*
—. Congregationalism. Connecticut. Frontier and Pioneer Life. Ingersoll, Robert. Ohio (Western Reserve). Wright, Elizur (and family). Yale University. 1762-1870. *56*
—. Documents. German Americans. Immigrants. Missouri. Reading. Religious liberty. St. Louis Free Congregation Library. 1850-99. *1123*
—. Dogberry, Obediah. Freedom of thought. *Liberal Advocate* (newspaper). New York (Rochester). Religious liberty. 1832-34. *1003*
Free World. *See* Western Nations.
Freedmen. Abolition Movement. Education. McPherson, James M. (review article). Missions and Missionaries. Protestantism. 1865-1910. 1975. *563*
—. African Society. Colonization. Congregationalism. Hopkins, Samuel. Rhode Island (Providence). Sierra Leone. 1789-95. *2459*
—. American Missionary Association. Civil Rights. Education. Florida. 1864-74. *548*
—. American Missionary Association. Congregationalism. Education. Georgia (Liberty County). 1870-80's. *549*
—. American Missionary Association. Federal agencies. Georgia (Atlanta). Methodist Episcopal Church. Reconstruction. 1865-69. *556*
—. Ames Church. Education. Hartzell, Joseph C. Methodist Episcopal Church. Missionaries. Republican Party. South. 1870-73. *3481*
—. Catholic Church. Law. Protestantism. Texas. 1836-60. *2799*
—. Education. Evangelism. Presbyterians. 1872-1900. *3589*
—. Methodist Episcopal Church, Colored. Methodist Episcopal Church, South. Religious liberty. Segregation. South. 1865-70. *3464*
Freedom. American Revolution. Liberation movements. Political Attitudes. Theology. 1765-20c. *1342*
—. Christian realism. Niebuhr, Reinhold. 1915-63. 1960's-70's. *2360*
—. Civil religion. Social Conditions. 1776-1900. *1179*
Freedom of religion. Alaska (Kenai Peninsula). Orthodox Eastern Church, Russian (Old Believers). Russian Americans. 1920's-76. *2810*
—. Church and state. Church property. Tax exemption. 1960's-70's. *1094*
Freedom of Speech *See also* Freedom of the Press.
—. Atheism. *Lucifer's Lantern* (periodical). Mormons. Polygamy. Schroeder, Theodore. Utah. 1889-1900. *2125*
Freedom of the Press *See also* Censorship.
—. *Boston Evening Post* (newspaper). Fleet, Thomas. Great Awakening. Massachusetts (Boston). Newspapers. 1740's. *1423*
Freedom of thought. Dogberry, Obediah. Free thinkers. *Liberal Advocate* (newspaper). New York (Rochester). Religious liberty. 1832-34. *1003*
Freedom's Journal (newspaper). Abolition Movement. Cornish, Samuel E. Journalism. Negroes. Presbyterian Church. 1820's-59. *2498*
Freemasons. Anti-Masonic movement. Baptists. Morgan, William. New York, western. 1826-30. *2362*
—. Anti-Masonic Movement. Radicals and Radicalism. 1820's. *1236*
—. Maryland (Annapolis). St. John's College. State Legislatures. 1784. *517*
Frembling, Lambert. Arizona (Pisinimo). Catholic Church. Clergy. Papago Indians. Refugees. 1939-77. *3825*
Frenaye, Mark Anthony. Bishops. Catholic Church. Church Finance. Letters. O'Connor, Michael. Pennsylvania (Pittsburgh). 1843-49. *368*
French Americans. Aristocracy. Clergy. Huguenots. Religious liberty. Richebourg, Claude Phillipe de. 1680-1719. *3250*
French Canadians *See also* Acadians.
—. Acculturation. Catholic Church. Nationalism. New England. ca 1610-1975. *309*
—. Alberta. Calgary Diocese. Catholic Church. Irish Canadians. McNailly, John Thomas. 1871-1952. *3712*
—. Americanization. Catholic Church. Hendricken, Thomas F. Irish Americans. Massachusetts (Fall River). 1870's-85. *317*
—. Angers, François-Albert. Canada. Catholic Church. Pacifism. Values. 1940-79. *2654*
—. Anglophones. Catholics. Langevin, Adélard. Manitoba. Winnipeg Archdiocese. 1905. *3711*
—. Art. Catholic Church. Folk religion. Musée Historique de Vaudreuil. Quebec. 17c-20c. *174*
—. Assimilation. Catholic Church. Clergy. Dufresne, Andre B. Massachusetts (Holyoke). 1869-87. *302*
—. Assimilation. Catholic Church. Nationalism. Rhode Island (Woonsocket). 1924-29. *3854*
—. Association Catholique de la Jeunesse Canadienne-Française. Catholic Church. Morality. Quebec. 1903-14. *2355*
—. Bishops. Canada, western. Catholic Church. Irish Canadians. Nominations for office. 1900-75. *3765*
—. British Canadians. Country life. Ethnic groups. Manitoba. Mennonites. Migration. Polish Canadians. Ukrainian Canadians. 1921-61. *3389*
—. Canada. Catholic Church. Census. Cities. French language. 1941. *3880*
—. Canada. Catholic Church. Clergy. Craig, James Henry. Nationalism. Political repression. Quebec (Lower Canada). 1810. *1319*
—. Canada. Catholic Church. Education. Quebec. Rinfret, Fernand. Siegfried, André *(Le Canada, les deux races: Problèmes politiques contemporains)*. Social Sciences. 1906-07. *3873*
—. Canada, western. Catholic Church. Historiography. Migration, Internal. Quebec. 1870-1915. *3819*
—. Captivity narratives. Catholic Church. Congregationalism. Indians. New England. Williams, John *(The Redeemed Captive)*. 1704-06. *3133*
—. Catholic Church. Colonization. Economic development. Geopolitics. Provost, T. S. Quebec (Mattawinie district). 17c-1890. *3809*
—. Catholic Church. Cotton mills. Immigration. Massachusetts (Springfield). Population. Working Class. 1870. *3710*
—. Catholic Church. Economic Theory. Minville, Esdras. Quebec. 20c. *2558*
—. Catholic Church. Groulx, Lionel. Quebec. Secularism. Separatist Movements. 1897-1928. *1409*
—. Catholic Church. Guigues, Joseph-Eugène. Ontario. Ottawa Diocese. 1848-74. *3713*
—. Catholic Church. Immigration. Massachusetts (Holyoke). Proulx, Nicholas. Working Class. 1850-1900. *3691*
—. Catholic Church. LaPatrie (colony). New England. Quebec. Repatriation Act (Canada, 1875). ca 1875-80. *3792*
—. Catholic Church. Migration, Internal. Parishes. Quebec (Compton County). Rural-Urban Studies. 1851-91. *3791*
—. Catholic Church. Minnesota (Gentilly). Settlement. Theillon, Elie. 1870's-1974. *3687*
—. Catholic Church. Minville, Esdras (eulogy). Quebec. 1975. *3674*
—. Catholic Church. North Central States. Settlement. Social Customs. 19c. *3804*
—. Catholic Church. Quebec. Self-perception. Social Customs. Values. 17c-1978. *3789*
—. Catholic Church. Quebec. Social Organization. Women. 1960's-70's. *2013*
—. Catholicism. Colonization. Quebec (Eastern Townships). Settlement. 1800-60. *3780*
—. Catholicism. Lévesque, Georges-Henri. Nationalism. Personal narratives. Quebec. Youth movements. 1930's. *3790*
—. Government, provisional. Gray, William. Lee, Jason. Methodist Church. Missions and Missionaries. Oregon. 1843. *1271*
—. Literature. Patriotism. Quebec. Sociology. 19c. *2085*
French language. Americanization. Catholic Church. Vermont. 1917-75. *308*
—. Canada. Catholic Church. Census. Cities. French Canadians. 1941. *3880*
—. Catholic Church. Church and State. Langevin, Adélard. Manitoba. Politics. Private schools. 1890-1916. *608*
—. Catholic Church. Church schools. Langevin, Adélard. Laurier, Wilfrid. Liberal Party. Prairie Provinces. Religion in the Public Schools. 1890-1915. *569*
—. Catholic Church. Dialects. Haitian Americans. New York City (Brooklyn). 1970's. *3699*
—. Catholic Church. *Patriote de l'Ouest* (newspaper). Saskatchewan. 1910-41. *3764*
Freneau, Philip ("A Political Litany"). American Revolution. Church of England. Intellectuals. Poetry. 1775. *1998*
Freud, Sigmund. Emmanuel movement. Myers, Frederic W. H. Psychoanalysis. 1906-10. *2334*
Freudianism. Marxism. Niebuhr, Reinhold (review article). Original sin. Protestantism. Theology. 1939-70. *2838*
Frey, Sigmund. California (Huntington Park, Los Angeles). Jewish Orphan's Home. Judaism (Reform). Social work. 1870's-1930. *2500*
Friedlaender, Herman. Baptists, Seventh-Day. Conversion. Daland, William C. Jews. New York City. *Peculiar People* (newspaper). 1880's-90's. *1633*
Friends Asylum. Hinchman, Morgan. Mental Illness. Moral insanity. Pennsylvania (Philadelphia). Trials. 1847. *1432*
Friends Historical Association. Atkinson, James H. Pennsylvania (Philadelphia). 1873-1923. *234*
Friends of Man. Adventists. Interior Lay Missionary Movement. Jehovah's Witnesses. Russell, Charles Taze. 1852-1916. *3921*
Friends, Society of. Abolition Movement. Dugdale, Joseph A. Reform. 1810-96. *2361*
—. Abolition Movement. Fox, George. Pennsylvania. Slave trade. 1656-1754. *2479*
—. Abolition Movement. Haverford College Library (Quaker Collection). New Hampshire. Portsmouth Anti-Slavery Society. Rogers, Nathaniel Peabody. 1830-46. *2465*
—. Addams, Jane. Education. Hull House. Ideology. Illinois (Chicago). Women. 1875-1930. *911*
—. Africans' School. Benezet, Anthony. Education. Negroes. Pennsylvania (Philadelphia). 1770's-80's. *527*
—. Agriculture. Catholic Church. Federal Programs. Indian-White Relations. Missions and Missionaries. Moravian Church. Old Northwest. 1789-1820. *1529*
—. American Anti-Slavery Society. Female Anti-Slavery Society. Foster, Abigail Kelley. Fox, George. Mott, Lucretia Coffin. Segregation. 17c. 1837-66. *791*
—. American Friends Service Committee. Arab-Israeli conflict. Foreign Policy. Palestine Liberation Organization. 1970's. *1250*
—. American Friends Service Committee. Cadbury, Henry Joel (obituary). Historians. 1883-1974. *212*
—. American Revolution. Baptists. Church of England. Congregationalism. Georgia. Judaism. Lutheran Church. Presbyterian Church. 1733-90. *88*
—. American Revolution. Biddle, Owen. Lacey, John, Jr. Military Service. Pennsylvania. 1775-83. *2684*
—. American Revolution. Brown, Joshua. Pacifism. Pennsylvania (Little Britain Township). Prisoners. South Carolina (Ninety Six). 1778. *2633*
—. American Revolution. Burgoyne, John. Indians. Pennsylvania (Easton). ca 1776. *3282*
—. American Revolution. Charities. Great Britain. Ireland. Pennsylvania (Philadelphia). 1778-97. *2503*
—. American Revolution. Diaries. Drinker family. Pacifism. Pennsylvania (Philadelphia). Prisoners. Virginia (Winchester). 1777-81. *2683*
—. American Revolution. Dunkards. Mennonites. Moravian Church. Neutrality. Pacifism. Schwenkfelders. Taxation. 1765-83. *2670*
—. American Revolution. Free Quakers. 1774-83. *2668*
—. American Revolution. Loyalists. Pennsylvania (Philadelphia). 1770's. *1282*
—. American Revolution. Pennsylvania (Philadelphia). Reform. 1741-90. *2674*
—. American Revolution (antecedents). Business. Leadership. Pennsylvania (Philadelphia). Radicals and radicalism. 1769-74. *1293*
—. Antislavery sentiments. Barbados. Curwen, Alice. Letters. 1675-76. *2458*
—. Antislavery Sentiments. Benezet, Anthony. 1759-84. *2461*

—. Antislavery Sentiments. British North America. Social problems. Woolman, John. 1720-72. *2371*
—. Antislavery Sentiments. Great Britain. Libertarianism. Radicals and Radicalism. 18c-1865. *2497*
—. Antislavery Sentiments. Lay, Benjamin. Pennsylvania (Philadelphia). 1690's-1759. *2460*
—. Antislavery Sentiments. North America. 1671-1771. *2480*
—. Apache Indians. Cheyenne Indians. Darlington Agency. Indian Territory. Indians (agencies). 1868-86. *3278*
—. Architecture (Quaker-plan). Georgia (Oglethorpe, Wilkes counties). Gilmer House. 1800-1978. *1768*
—. Art. Attitudes. Centennial Exposition of 1876. Peace. Pennsylvania (Philadelphia). Sabbatarianism. Temperance Movements. 1876. *3256*
—. Art. Bartram, John. Bartram, William. Botany. Pennsylvania. Travel (accounts). 1699-1823. *2304*
—. Attitudes. Benezet, Anthony. Wealth. Woolman, John. 1740-83. *358*
—. Attitudes. Daily Life. Ohio (Mount Pleasant). 1795-1918. *3260*
—. Attitudes. New York (Auburn). Pennsylvania. Prisons. Reform. 1787-1845. *2393*
—. Backus, Isaac *(History of New England)*. Baptists. New England Meeting for Sufferings. Sectarianism. Theology. 17c-1784. *2953*
—. Baltzell, E. Digby (review article). Massachusetts (Boston). Pennsylvania (Philadelphia). Puritans. Social Classes. 17c-1979. *2920*
—. Baptists. Fox, George. Olney, Thomas, Jr. Politics. Rhode Island. 1672-73. *967*
—. Benjamin, Philip S. Feldberg, Michael. Miller, Richard G. Pennsylvania (Philadelphia; review article). Sinclair, Bruce. 1790-1920. 1974-76. *3269*
—. Bibliographies. Clergy. Sermons. 1653-1700. *204*
—. Black nationalism. Colonization. Cuffe, Paul. Sierra Leone. 1810's. *2478*
—. Blue Laws. Church and state. Church of England. Law and Society. Pennsylvania. Presbyterian Church. 1682-1740. *2278*
—. Botany. Logan, James. Mather, Cotton. Natural History. New England. Puritans. 17c-18c. *2300*
—. Business. Ethics. 1600-1750. *359*
—. Cabalism. Jews. 17c-20c. *27*
—. Canby, Edmund. Delaware (New Castle County). Diaries. Milling. 1822-35. *3275*
—. Cedar Creek Monthly Meeting. Emancipation. Farms. Moorman, Clark Terrell. Ohio. Virginia (Caroline County). 1766-1814. *2487*
—. Charities. Pennsylvania. Philadelphia Society for Organizing Charitable Relief and Repressing Mendicancy. 1800-1900. *2523*
—. Charities. Pennsylvania Hospital for the Sick Poor. Pennsylvania (Philadelphia). Poor. 18c. *2519*
—. Charles I. Massachusetts. Persecution. 1661. *1018*
—. Cherokee Indians. Education. 1880-92. *712*
—. Children. Family. Pennsylvania (Delaware Valley). Theology. 1681-1735. *874*
—. Church and State. Church of England. Colleges and Universities (administration). New Jersey. Presbyterians. Princeton University. 1745-60. *661*
—. Church discipline. Ireland. New England. New York. 1690-1789. *3283*
—. Church of England. Colonial Government. Ethnic Groups. Pennsylvania. Reformed churches. 1755-80. *1215*
—. Church of England. Ethnic Groups. Pennsylvania. Presbyterian Church. Provincial Politics. 1775-80. *1248*
—. Churches. Meetinghouses. Pennsylvania (Chester, Delaware counties). ca 1700-1903. *1814*
—. City Life. Cromwell, James W. New York City. Personal narratives. 1842-60. *3271*
—. Clergy. Keith, George. Pennsylvania. Schisms. Schisms. 1660-1720. *3261*
—. Clergy. Women. 19c. *820*
—. Clockmakers. Rhode Island (Newport). 1780's-1850's. *3268*
—. Confederate States of America. Conscientious objectors. North Carolina. 1861-65. *2708*
—. Congregationalism. Women. ca 1620-1765. *834*
—. Conscientious objection. Constitutional Amendments (2nd). Federal government. Madison, James. Military service. States' Rights. 1787-92. *2686*
—. Construction. Historic Preservation. Meetinghouses. Rhode Island (Newport). 1657-1974. *1838*
—. Documents. Methodism. National Characteristics. Political participation. Shakers. Tocqueville, Alexis de. 1831-40. *2780*
—. Documents. Missions and Missionaries. Religious Liberty. Virginia. Wilson, George. 1650-62. *1007*
—. Dunkards. Historic Peace Churches (meeting). Kansas (Newton). Krehbiel, H. P. Mennonites. Pacifism. 1935-36. *2663*
—. Dunkards. Mennonites. Militarism. Pacifism. 1900-78. *2646*
—. Earlham College. Evolution. Moore, Joseph. Virginia (Richmond). 1861. *2307*
—. Education. Family. Pennsylvania. Social Customs. Socialization. ca 1740-76. *3279*
—. Education. Girls. Ontario. 1790-1820. *749*
—. Education. Hallowell, Benjamin. Science. Virginia (Alexandria). 1824-60. *3281*
—. Evolution. Pennsylvania. Provincial Government. Revivals. 1735-75. *2222*
—. Family. Frost, J. William (review article). 17c-18c. 1973-75. *938*
—. Fell, Margaret. Feminism. Great Britain (Lancashire). Pennsylvania (Philadelphia). Women. 1670's. *928*
—. Fishbourn, William. Pennsylvania. Settlement. 1680-1739. *3272*
—. Folk art. Hicks, Edward *(Peaceable Kingdom)*. Painting. Pennsylvania (Bucks County). 1780-1849. *1857*
—. Folk art. Hicks, Edward *(Peaceable Kingdom)*. Symbolism in Art. 1825-49. *1851*
—. Frontier and Pioneer Life. Hutchinson, Mathias. New York, western. Ontario. Pennsylvania, central. Travel (accounts). 1819-20. *3280*
—. Great Britain. Law. *Mary and Charlotte* (vessel). Pennsylvania (Philadelphia). War relief. 1778-84. *3266*
—. Great Britain. Missions and Missionaries. New England. 1656-1775. *1662*
—. Hicks, Edward *(Peaceable Kingdom)*. Iconography. ca 1824-44. *1870*
—. Historiography. Tolles, Frederick Barnes (obituary). 1915-75. *213*
—. Hoover, Herbert C. Military. 1929-33. *2705*
—. Howgill, Francis. New England. Persecution. Puritans. ca 1650-60. *1027*
—. Humanism. Intellectuals. Penn, William. Radicals and Radicalism. Social reform. 1650-1700. *2353*
—. Indian Wars. Nonviolence. Paxton Boys. Pennsylvania (Philadelphia). 1764-67. *2693*
—. Indians. Paxton Boys. Pennsylvania. Politics. Presbyterian Church. Riots. 1763-64. *3530*
—. Irish Americans. Milhouse, Robert. South Carolina (Camden). Wyly, Samuel. 1751-93. *3265*
—. Irish Americans. Pennsylvania. Settlement. 1682-1750. *3276*
—. Israel. Palestinians. 1977. *1278*
—. Keith, George. Pennsylvania. Pusey, Caleb. Schisms. Theology. 17c. *3273*
—. Keith, George. Pennsylvania. Schisms. 1693-1703. *3262*
—. King George's War. Pacifism. Penn, Thomas. Pennsylvania. Politics. Provincial Government. 1726-42. *1314*
—. King Philip's War. New England. Politics. Toleration. Williams, Roger *(George Fox)*. 1672-77. *993*
—. Larson, Lars. Larson, Martha. New York (Rochester). Norwegian Americans. Religious Liberty. Women. 1807-44. *3263*
—. Lawrence, Daniel. North or Northern States. Printing. 1788-1812. *3258*
—. Local politics. Pennsylvania (Lancaster County). Provincial politics. 1700-76. *1008*
—. Marriage. Nova Scotia (Dartmouth). 1786-89. *864*
—. Maryland (Baltimore). Medicine (practice of). Surgery. Taylor, Sarah. Women. 1823. *3264*
—. Maryland (Baltimore). Methodist Episcopal Church, African. Negroes. Presbyterian Church. Private Schools. Sunday Schools. 1794-1860. *633*
—. Massachusetts. New York Yearly Meeting. Schisms. Vermont. 1845-1949. *3259*
—. Massachusetts. Persecution. Southwick (family). 1639-61. *1066*
—. New York. Political Factions. Seneca Indians. Tribal government. 1848. *1202*
—. Ontario, southern. 19c. *3277*
—. Pleasants, Robert. Virginia. 17c-18c. *3267*
—. Protestantism. Sex roles. Women. 17c-18c. *835*
—. Sectionalism. Social status. West Virginia. 18c-19c. *3257*
Friends, Society of (Committees on the Indian Concern). Indians (agencies). Nebraska. 1869. *3274*
Friends, Society of (Congregational). Antislavery Sentiments. Civil War. Jones, James Parnell. Maine. Military Service. 1850's-64. *2641*
Friends, Society of (Hicksite). Antiwar Sentiment. Butler, Smedley. Courts Martial and Courts of Inquiry. Marines. 1881-1940. *2637*
—. Baptists. Bucknell University. Franklin and Marshall College. Pennsylvania. Reformed German Church. Swarthmore College. Urbanization. 1865-1915. *685*
—. Emigration. Evangelism. Ohio Yearly Meeting. 1828-1919. *3270*
Friends, Society of (Longwood Meeting). Abolition Movement. Pennsylvania. Reform. 1850's-1940. *2450*
Friends, Society of (review article). Abolition Movement. Davis, David Brion. Drake, Thomas. James, Sydney. 1683-1863. 20c. *2471*
Friendship. Abolition Movement. Evangelicalism. Tappan, Lewis. 1830-61. *2469*
—. Attitudes. Dickinson, Emily. Evangelicalism. Mount Holyoke College. 1848-50. *2827*
—. Charities. Fosdick, Harry Emerson. Liberalism. Protestantism. Rockefeller, John D., Jr. Social control. Wealth. 1920-36. *364*
—. Emmett, James Simpson. Grey, Zane. Mormons. Novels (western). Utah. 1907. *2072*
—. Franklin, Benjamin. Morality. Publishers and Publishing. Religious liberty. Whitefield, George. 1739-70. *58*
—. Kimball, Heber C. Mormons. Utah. Young, Brigham. 1829-68. *3996*
Frontier. Architecture. Mormons. ca 1850-56. *1836*
—. Arizona. Barth, Solomon. Converts. Jews. Mormons. 1856-1928. *60*
—. Arizona (Coconino County). Immigrants. Mormons. Schools. 1875-1900. *510*
—. Campbell, Alexander. Disciples of Christ. Educational Reform. Morality. 1825-1900. *579*
—. Canada, western. Methodist Church. Missionaries. 1840-1925. *3450*
—. Clergy. Disciples of Christ. North Central States. Personal narratives. Snethen, Abraham. 1794-1830. 1977. *3112*
—. Clergy. Letters. Lutheran Church in America, Norwegian. Montana, eastern. Thorpe, Christian Scriver. 1906-08. *3295*
—. Clergy. Missouri. Protestant Churches. Schools. ca 1800-30. *639*
Frontier and Pioneer Life *See also* Indians; Overland Journeys to the Pacific; Pioneers.
—. Acculturation. Immigrants. Lutheran Church. Rolvaag, O. E. *(Giants in the Earth)*. South Dakota. 1870. 1927. *3307*
—. Arizona. Christianity. Reform. Suffrage. Temperance Movements. Women. 1850's-1912. *837*
—. Autobiography. Mormons. 19c. *2040*
—. Baptists. Clergy. Montana. Personal narratives. Spencer, James Hovey. 1888-97. *3095*
—. Batchelder, John. Episcopal Church, Protestant. Illinois (Jacksonville). Trinity Church. 1830-40. *3192*
—. Benedictines. Catholic Church. Oetgen, Jerome (review article). Wimmer, Boniface. 1809-87. *3685*
—. California. Circuit riders. Civil War. Manuscripts. Methodism. Ohio. Phillips, George. 1840-64. *3494*
—. Carroll, John. Catholic Church. Clergy. Louisiana Purchase. 1803-15. *3805*
—. Catholic Church. Missions and Missionaries. Southwest. Spain. 16c-18c. *1497*
—. Catholic Church. New Mexico. Settlement. 17c-1810. *3852*
—. Chinese Americans. Discrimination. Montana. Public opinion. Supreme courts (state). 1864-1902. *2152*
—. Christianity. Europe. Theology. 18c-1979. *301*

—. Christianity. Manuscripts. South Dakota Historical Resource Center. 1976. *217*
—. Christianity. North Dakota. Red River of the North. ca 1870-97. *2733*
—. Church of England. Clergy. Diocesan Theological Institute. Ontario (Cobourg). Strachan, John. 1840-55. *732*
—. Circuit riders. German Americans. Lutheran Church (Missouri Synod). Oklahoma. Texas. Wacker, Hermann Dietrich. 1847-1938. *3342*
—. Communalism. Hutterites. Western states. 1874-1977. *429*
—. Congregationalism. Connecticut. Free Thinkers. Ingersoll, Robert. Ohio (Western Reserve). Wright, Elizur (and family). Yale University. 1762-1870. *56*
—. Economic conditions. Indians. Missions and Missionaries. Presbyterian Church. South Dakota. 1840-1900. *3540*
—. Education. Tennessee. 1758-96. *544*
—. Episcopal Church, Protestant. Evangelism. McIlvaine, Charles Petit. Ohio. Oxford Movement. 1800-75. *3187*
—. Fort Duquesne. Indian-White Relations. Moravian Church. Pennsylvania. Post, Christian Frederick. 1758-59. *1505*
—. Friends, Society of. Hutchinson, Mathias. New York, western. Ontario. Pennsylvania, central. Travel (accounts). 1819-20. *3280*
—. Heywood, Martha Spence. Intellectuals. King, Hannah Tapfield. Mormons. Snow, Eliza Roxey. Utah. Women. 1850-70. *4045*
—. Immigration. Irish Americans. New York. Pennsylvania. Presbyterian Church. Virginia (Shenandoah Valley). 17c-1776. *3558*
Frost, J. William (review article). Family. Friends, Society of. 17c-18c. 1973-75. *938*
Fry, William Henry. Composers. 1813-64. *1929*
Fuga, Francis J. Ontario (Hamilton). Shrine of Our Lady of Klocočov. Slovak Canadians. Uniates. 1952-77. *3911*
Fugitive Slave Act (US, 1850). Antislavery Sentiments. Eliot, Samuel A. Massachusetts (Boston). Patriotism. Unitarianism. 1850-60. *4085*
—. Methodist Church. Newspapers. Slavery. 1850. *3476*
Fulford, Francis. Bishops. Church of England. Councils and Synods. Quebec (Montreal). 1850-68. *3209*
Fuller, Margaret. Philosophy. Spiritualism. Transcendentalism. Women. 1840's. *4068*
Fuller, Nathan. Adventists. New York. Pennsylvania. 1858-71. *2975*
Fullerton, Thomas. Chippewa Indians. Documents. Indians. Methodist Episcopal Church. Minnesota. Missions and Missionaries. Wisconsin. 1841-44. *1531*
Fullmer, Bert E. Adventists. Rowen, Margaret W. Visions. Women. 1916-29. *2979*
Fund raising. Baur, John C. Concordia Seminary. Lutheran Church (Missouri Synod). Missouri (Clayton, St. Louis). Personal Narratives. 1923-26. *594*
—. Bryan, William Jennings. Lectures. Prairie Provinces. Presbyterian Church. Young Men's Christian Association. 1909. *2446*
—. California (San Bernardino). Congregation Beth Israel. Judaism (Orthodox). Messing, Aron J. 1879. *4199*
—. Catholic Church. Church Schools. Damen, Arnold. Illinois (Chicago). 1840-90. *773*
—. Church and state. Constitutional Law. Local Government. State Government. 1970's. *1059*
—. Clark, Joseph. Education, Finance. Personal narratives. Princeton University (Nassau Hall). Travel. 1802-04. *612*
—. Davies, Samuel. Diaries. Great Britain. New Jersey. Presbyterian Church. Princeton University. 1753-54. *636*
—. Hebrew Union College. Judaism (Reform). Union of American Hebrew Congregations. Western States. Wise, Isaac Mayer. 1873-75. *784*
—. Hyde, Orson. Illinois (Nauvoo). Mormons. Northeastern or North Atlantic States. Tabernacle project. 1845-46. *4048*
—. Jewish Theological Seminary. Judaism (Orthodox). Mergers. New York City. Seminaries. Yeshiva College. 1925-28. *736*
—. Sects, Religious. 1945-79. *4245*
Fundamentalism. 1929-42. *2832*
—. A. A. Allen Revival, Incorporated. Arizona (Miracle Valley). Language. Popular culture. Revivals. 1970's. *2270*
—. Anti-Catholicism. Anti-Semitism. Conspiracy theories. Kansas. Political Commentary. Winrod, Gerald Burton. 1933-57. *2090*
—. Anti-Catholicism. Baptists. Morality. Norris, J. Frank. Texas. 1920's. *2889*
—. Appalachia. Attitudes. Baptists, Southern. 1966-77. *3034*
—. Attitudes. Gaebelein, Arno C. *Our Hope* (periodical). Stroeter, Ernst F. Zionism. 1894-97. *80*
—. Baldwin, Nathaniel. Inventions. Mormons. Polygamy. Radio. Utah. 1900's-61. *4036*
—. Baptists. Factionalism. Jarvis Street Baptist Church. Modernism. Ontario (Toronto). Social Classes. 1895-1934. *2605*
—. Baptists. Graham, Billy. Minnesota (Minneapolis). Riley, William Bell. World Christian Fundamental Association. ca 1900-65. *3068*
—. Baptists. Jarvis Street Baptist Church. Ontario (Toronto). Shields, Thomas Todhunter. 1891-1955. *3067*
—. Baptists, Southern. 1920-75. *3043*
—. Baptists, Southern. Graves, James Robinson. Landmark Movement. Modernism. Mullins, Edgar Young. Theology. 1840-1928. *3058*
—. Brigham Young University. Mormons. Students. Utah (Provo). 1935-73. *606*
—. Bryan, William Jennings. Church and state. Darwinism. Evolution. Public schools. 1920-73. *2317*
—. Bryan, William Jennings. Evolution. Presbyterian Church. 1875-1920's. *2344*
—. Bryan, William Jennings. Presbyterian Church. 1860-1925. *1407*
—. Christ Communal Organization. Converts. Models. 1970's. *2917*
—. Church of Christ. Disciples of Christ. Texas. 1972. *3105*
—. Civil War. Constitutional Amendments. Lincoln, Abraham. National Fast Day. National Reform Association. 1787-1945. *1009*
—. Clergy. Macartney, Clarence E. Presbyterian Church. 1901-53. *3579*
—. Counter culture. Jesus People. Youth Movements. 1960's. *2719*
—. Democracy. Education. Local Politics. Morality. Social Change. Vigilantism. 1920's. *2387*
—. Educational Policy. Public schools. Textbooks. West Virginia (Kanawha County). 1975. *576*
—. Gaebelein, Arno C. Genocide. Germany. Jews. *Our Hope* (periodical). 1937-45. *136*
—. Gaebelein, Arno C. Methodist Episcopal Church. Missions and Missionaries. Zionism. 1893-1945. *1613*
—. Great Britain. 1920's. *2894*
—. Ham, Mordecai F. Newspapers. North Carolina (Elizabeth City). Revivals. Saunders, William O. 1924. *2217*
—. Immigrants. Orthodox Eastern Church, Greek. Ruthenians. Uniates. Vermont (Proctor). 1914-73. *2757*
—. Jews. 17c-1976. *13*
—. Long, Huey P. North Central States. Populism. Progressivism. Smith, Gerald L. K. 1934-48. *975*
—. Machen, J. Gresham. Presbyterian Church. South. 1920's-35. *3580*
—. Matthews, Mark Allison. Presbyterian Church. Social reform. Washington (Seattle). 1900-40. *2434*
—. Theology, conservative (review essay). 1920-74. *2814*
Fundamentalists. Anti-Semitism. Evangelicals. Jews. Messianic beliefs. 1970's. *135*
—. Architecture. Catholic Church. German Americans. Rural Settlements. Social customs. Southerners. Texas (Cooke, Denton counties). 1860-1976. *2750*
—. Censorship. Educators. Textbooks. Virginia. 1974. *570*
Funerals. British North America. Death and Dying. Social customs. 17c-18c. *2772*
—. California (Bodie). Clay, Eugene O. Methodist Church. Nevada (Smith Valley). Personal narratives. Sermons. 1915. *3456*
—. California (San Francisco). Cemeteries. First Hebrew Benevolent Society. Jews. Johnson, Henry D. 1849-50. *4147*
—. Congregationalism. Cooper, Samuel. Music. New England. Sermons. Social Customs. 18c. *3113*
Funk, Christian. American Revolution. Excommunication. Mennonites (Funkite). Pennsylvania (Indian Field). 1760-1809. *3376*
Funk, John F. Clergy. Manitoba. Mennonites. Russia. Settlement. Travel. 1873. *3393*
—. Documents. Mennonites (General Conference). 1864-1921. *3375*
Fur trade. Alaska. Gold rushes. Jews. Nome Hebrew Benevolent Society. 1867-1916. *4103*
—. Arctic. Canada. Catholic Church. Church of England. Churches. Missions and Missionaries. 20c. *1549*
—. Canada. Capitalism. Hudson's Bay Company. Protestantism. Scottish Canadians. 18c-1970's. *377*
Furniture and Furnishings *See also* Decorative Arts; Wood Carving.
—. Architecture. Churches (Gothic Revival). Country Life. Pennsylvania, northwest. Presbyterian Church. 1850-1905. 1979. *1797*
—. Orthodoxy. Shakers. Social Change. Theology. 1815-1969. *4067*
Future. Eschatology. Millenarianism. Theology. 18c. *1180*
—. Leisure. Religious consciousness. 1973-. *103*

G

Gaebelein, Arno C. Attitudes. Fundamentalism. *Our Hope* (periodical). Stroeter, Ernst F. Zionism. 1894-97. *80*
—. Fundamentalism. Genocide. Germany. Jews. *Our Hope* (periodical). 1937-45. *136*
—. Fundamentalism. Methodist Episcopal Church. Missions and Missionaries. Zionism. 1893-1945. *1613*
Gaelic language. Blair, Duncan Black. Nova Scotia (Barney's River). Poets. Presbyterianism. Scholarship. 1848-93. *2069*
—. Blair, Duncan Black. Nova Scotia (Pictou County). Poetry. Presbyterianism. Scholars. Scotland. 1846-93. *2070*
Gage, William C. Adventists. Elections (mayoral). Michigan (Battle Creek). Morality. 1882. *1255*
Galicians. Doukhobors. Hospitals. Lake Geneva Mission. Missions and Missionaries. Presbyterian Church. Saskatchewan (Wakaw). 1903-42. *1492*
Galland, Isaac. Iowa (Lee County). Land. Mormons. Smith, Joseph. Speculation. 1830's-58. *3950*
Galusha, Elon. Baptists. Millerites. New York. 1825-56. *2921*
Gambling. Alcohol. Economic development. Legislation. 1977. *2383*
Gambling, pari-mutuel. Barkley, Alben. Kentucky. Louisville Churchmen's Federation. Progressivism. 1917-27. *2437*
Gambrell, James Bruton. Baptists, Southern. Barton, A. J. Denominationalism. Lawrence, J. B. Theology. 1910-80. *3039*
Games *See also* Sports.
—. Attitudes. Catholic Church. Colonial Government. Discovery and Exploration. Indians. Missions and Missionaries. 16c-17c. *1524*
Games, board. Christianity. Education. Mansion of Happiness (game). Social Change. Values. 1832-1904. *2711*
Gano, John. American Revolution. Baptists. Chaplains. Washington, George. 1727-1804. *2631*
Garner, Thad. Baptists, Southern. Campbell, Will. Clergy. Personal narratives. South. 20c. *2994*
Garrettson, Freeborn. Clergy. Methodism. 1775-1827. *3447*
—. Coke, Thomas. Letters. Methodist Church. Missions and Missionaries. Nova Scotia. Wesley, John. 1786. *1490*
—. Cromwell, James. Methodist Episcopal Church. Missionaries. Nova Scotia. USA. 1785-1800. *1581*
Garrott, William Maxfield. Baptists, Southern. Graham, Agnes Nora. Missions and Missionaries. Rutledge, Arthur B. 20c. *1694*
Gartner, Lloyd P. Cities. Gurock, Jeffrey S. Hertzberg, Steven. Jews (review article). Raphael, Mark Lee. 1840-1979. *4150*
Garvey, Marcus. Chaplains. Negroes. Universal Negro Improvement Association. 1920's. *2366*
Gary Diocese. Catholic Church. Grutka, Andrew G. Indiana. 1933-78. *3868*
Gates, Susa Young. Marriage. Mormons. Personal narratives. Utah. Women. Young, Brigham. Young, Lucy Bigelow. 1830-1905. *3972*

Gaustad, Edwin Scott. Clebsch, William A. Dissent. Religious thought (review article). 17c-20c. *18*
Gavin, Anthony *(A Master-Key to Popery)*. Anti-Catholicism. Church of England. Great Britain. Literature. Virginia. 1724-73. *2108*
Gehman, John B. Diaries. Mennonites. Pennsylvania (Hereford). Speak Schools. 1853. *566*
Geiger, Abraham. Holdheim, Samuel. Judaism, Reform. Theology. 19c. *4221*
Geiger, Maynard J. (obituary). Archives. Bibliographies. California. Franciscans. Historiography. Mission Santa Barbara. 1936-76. *240*
—. Archives. California. Franciscans. Historiography. Mission Santa Barbara. 1901-77. *281*
—. Archives. California. Franciscans. Historiography. Mission Santa Barbara. 1937-77. *238*
—. California. Franciscans. Historians. Mission Santa Barbara. 1901-77. *239*
Genealogical Society of Utah. Mormons. Research. Utah. 1894-1976. *246*
Genealogy. Amish. Pennsylvania. Zug family. 1718-1886. *3441*
—. Archives. Catholic Church. Church records. 19c-20c. *242*
—. Brigham Young University Library. Immigration studies. Mormons. Utah (Provo). 1830-1978. *236*
—. Dutch Americans. Iowa. Mennonites. Settlement. Swiss Americans. 1839-1974. *3370*
—. Huguenots. Immigration. 16c-20c. *3253*
—. Libraries. Mormon Genealogical Society. 1607-1850. 1975. *201*
—. Methodology. Rearticulation. Religious studies. Translating and Interpreting. 1975. *232*
—. Missions and Missionaries. Mormons. Utah. 1885-1900. *1525*
General Association of Separate Baptists in Christ. Baptists, Separate. Evangelism. Kentucky. New England. 1755-1977. *3064*
General Convention Special Program. Black power. Church and Social Problems. Economic Aid. Episcopal Church, Protestant. Self-determination. 1963-75. *2541*
Generations. Family. Religiosity. 1940-75. *160*
Genetics. New York. Noyes, John Humphrey. Oneida Community. Stirpicultural experiment. Utopias. 1848-86. *946*
Genocide. Christians. Jews. Theology. World War II. 1945-74. *101*
—. Fundamentalism. Gaebelein, Arno C. Germany. Jews. *Our Hope* (periodical). 1937-45. *136*
Genovese, Eugene D. (review article). Millenarianism. Protestantism. Slavery. South. 17c-1865. *2163*
Gentility (concept). Brattle Street Church. Coleman, Benjamin. Elites. Massachusetts (Boston). Puritans. 1715-45. *2622*
Geographic distribution. Holiness Movement. 1865-1975. *3290*
—. Jews. 1952-71. *4134*
Geographic Space. Canada. Catholic Church. Missions and Missionaries. Regionalism. 1615-1851. *1486*
Geopolitics *See also* Boundaries; Demography.
—. Catholic Church. Colonization. Economic development. French Canadians. Provost, T. S. Quebec (Mattawinie district). 17c-1890. *3809*
George, Henry. Catholic Church. Conservatism. Corrigan, Michael. Economic Theory. McGlynn, Edward. New York. 1886-94. *2562*
—. Catholic Church. Ryan, John A. Single tax doctrine. Taxation. 1935. *2557*
—. Christianity. Economic Theory. Ethics. 1879. *2560*
—. Single Tax. ca 1870's-90's. *2568*
Georgia *See also* South; Southeastern States.
—. Acculturation. Cherokee Indians. Missions and Missionaries. White Path's Rebellion. 1824-28. *1578*
—. American Board of Commissioners for Foreign Missions. Cherokee Indians. Indian-White Relations. Law Enforcement. Missions and Missionaries. Removals, forced. Worcester, Samuel A. 1831. *1667*
—. American Revolution. Baptists. Church of England. Congregationalism. Friends, Society of. Judaism. Lutheran Church. Presbyterian Church. 1733-90. *88*
—. American Revolution. Baptists. Clergy. Marshall, Daniel. Political Theory. 1747-1823. *1372*
—. American Revolution. Baptists. Mercer, Silas. Politics. Theology. 1770-96. *3030*
—. American Revolution. Historians. Hymns. Moravian Church. Neisser, George. New York. Pennsylvania, eastern. ca 1735-84. *197*
—. Amusements. Jones, Sam. Methodist Episcopal Church, South. Morality. Revivals. Self-reliance. 1872-1906. *3498*
—. Anderson, P. Harris. Baptists. Harris, Rufus C. Mercer University. 1965-76. *3033*
—. Anti-Catholicism. Letters. Roosevelt, Theodore. Watson, Thomas E. 1915. *2104*
—. Baptists. *Brown* v. *Board of Education* (US, 1954). Desegregation. Supreme Court. 1954-61. *511*
—. Baptists. Cherokee Georgia Baptist Convention. *Landmark Banner and Cherokee Baptist* (newspaper). 1859-64. *3013*
—. Baptists. Church history. 1870-1947. *271*
—. Baptists. Committee on Baptist History. 1948-78. *270*
—. Baptists. Historians. King, Spencer Bidwell, Jr. (obituary). 1930's-77. *199*
—. Baptists. Negroes. 1750's-1830's. *3077*
—. Baptists. Political Leadership. State Politics. 1772-1823. *1260*
—. Baptists, Freewill. 1727-1977. *3007*
—. Baptists, Primitive. 1835-87. *3053*
—. Baptists, Primitive. Great Britain. 1633-1900. *3063*
—. Catholic Church. Judaism. Psychohistory. State Politics. Watson, Thomas E. 1856-1922. *55*
—. Cherokee Indians. Foreman, Stephen. Indians. Oklahoma. Presbyterian Church. 1820's-81. *3538*
—. Christianity. Communes. Jordan, Clarence. Koinonia Farm. 1942-60's. *402*
—. Churches. Photographs. 1751-1900's. *1830*
—. Civil rights. Methodist Church. Tilly, Dorothy. 1900's-70. *2551*
—. Clergy. Methodist Episcopal Church, South. Pierce, George Foster. Pierce, Lovick. 1785-1884. *3454*
—. Folk Medicine. Great Britain. Indians. Medicine (practice of). Methodism. Wesley, John. 1740's. *1426*
—. Germany (Halle). Methodism. Pietism. 1736-70. *3510*
—. Judaism (Orthodox). Religious liberty. 1733-90. *4188*
Georgia (Athens). Baptist Student Center. Education. Nicholson, David Bascom, III. 1925-52. *631*
Georgia (Atlanta). American Missionary Association. Federal agencies. Freedmen. Methodist Episcopal Church. Reconstruction. 1865-69. *556*
—. Anti-Catholicism. Ku Klux Klan. School boards. 1916-27. *2115*
—. Baptists. Civil rights movement. Ebenezer Baptist Church. Personal narratives. Roberts, Joseph L., Jr. 1960-75. *2556*
—. Congregationalism. Negroes. Social Work. 1886-1970. *2432*
—. Discrimination. Judaism (Orthodox, Reform). 1865-1915. *4109*
—. Haven, Gilbert. Negroes. Protestant Churches. Segregation. 1865-1906. *2145*
Georgia (Augusta). American Revolution. Church of England. Loyalists. St. Paul's Parish. Seymour, James. 1775-83. *1301*
—. Catholic Church. Local history. Preservation. Sacred Heart Church. 1976-78. *1823*
Georgia (Augusta Circuit). Diaries. Evangelism. Methodist Episcopal Church. Norman, Jeremiah. 1798-1801. *1642*
Georgia (Birdwood). Birdwood Junior College. Colleges and universities. 1954-74. *514*
Georgia (Cartersville). Baptists. Moon, Lottie. Secondary Education. Women. 1870-1903. *2985*
Georgia (Cedartown). Baptists. Colleges and Universities. Woodland Female College. 1851-87. *634*
Georgia (Columbus). Christian Commonwealth Colony. Communes. Social gospel. 1896-1900. *397*
Georgia (Ebenezer). Francke, Gottfried. Germany. Immigrants. Kiefer, Theobald, II. Letters. Lutheran Church. Orphanages. Pietism. Whitefield, George. 1738. 1750. *2878*
Georgia (Jonesboro). Centennial Celebrations. Presbyterian Church. 1879-1979. *3531*
Georgia (Liberty County). American Missionary Association. Congregationalism. Education. Freedmen. 1870-80's. *549*
Georgia (Macon). Congregation Kahal Kadosh Beth Israel. Judaism. Leeser, Isaac. Letters. Loewenthal, Henry. Rabbis. 1854-70. *4124*
Georgia, northwest. Baptists, Primitive. Sects, Religious. 1830-41. *3036*
Georgia (Oglethorpe, Wilkes counties). Architecture (Quaker-plan). Friends, society of. Gilmer House. 1800-1978. *1768*
Georgia (Plains). Baptists, Southern. Carter, Jimmy. 1977. *2992*
Georgia (Richmond County). Baptists. Kiokee Church. Marshall, Daniel. Negroes. Settlement. 1784-1819. *3020*
Georgia (Savannah). American Revolution. Patriotism. Presbyterian Church. Zubly, John Joachim. 1766-81. *985*
—. Clergy. Presbyterian Church. Swiss Americans. Zubly, John Joachim. 1724-58. *3565*
—. Education. Great Awakening. Orphans. Whitefield, George. 1738-71. *731*
Georgia (Skidaway Island). Catholic Church. Education. Negroes. Orphanages. Poor Clares. Women. 1885-87. *3806*
Georgia Trustees. Associates of Dr. Bray. Church of England. Sermons. 1733-50. *3231*
—. Bible. Rhetoric. Sermons. Slavery. 1731-50. *2161*
Georgia, University of (chancellor). Appointments to office. Baptists. Hill, Walter B. Methodists. 1897-1901. *536*
Georgia (Valdosta). Father Divine. Father Jehovia (pseud. of Samuel Morris). Negroes. St. John the Vine Hickerson. 1899-1914. *4259*
Georgia, west-central. Clergy. Folklore. Humor. Protestantism. 19c-20c. *2839*
Gerhardt, Paul. Christianity. Hymns. Sacred fire. Symbolism in Literature. Translating and Interpreting. Wesley, John. 1760's-1930's. *1952*
Gerhart, Emanuel Vogel. Clergy. Franklin and Marshall College. Pennsylvania (Lancaster). Reformed German Church. Theology. 1840-1904. *3286*
—. Mercersburg Theological Seminary. Pennsylvania. Reformed German Church. Theology. 1831-1904. *3287*
Gérin-Lajoie, Marie. Catholic Church. Fédération Nationale Saint-Jean-Baptiste. Feminism. Quebec. 1907-33. *870*
German Alsatians. Catholic Church. Cemeteries. Gravemarkers. Iron work. Ontario (Bruce County; Waterloo). 1850-1910. *1880*
German Americans *See also* Pennsylvania Germans.
—. Adventists. Clinton Theological Seminary. Missouri. 1910-25. *761*
—. Agriculture. Communalism. Education. Hutterites. Pacific Northwest. Pacifism. 20c. *392*
—. Alexian Brothers. Bernard, Alexius. Catholic Church. Hospitals. Missouri (St. Louis). Tollig, Paulus. 1869-1980. *1456*
—. Alienation. Civil War. Ethnicity. Lutheran Church (Missouri Synod). Massacres. Missouri (Concordia). 1864. *3301*
—. American Revolution. Lutherans. Pennsylvania (Philadelphia). 1776-81. *1304*
—. Americanization. 19c. *297*
—. Architecture. Catholic Church. Fundamentalists. Rural Settlements. Social customs. Southerners. Texas (Cooke, Denton counties). 1860-1976. *2750*
—. Assimilation. Authority. Bishops. Catholic Church. Cleveland Diocese. Irish Americans. Ohio. Rappe, Louis Amadeus. 1847-70. *3788*
—. Assimilation. Michigan (Ann Arbor). Pluralism. Protestantism. 1830-1955. *284*
—. Autobiography. Buenger, Theodore Arthur. Clergy. Concordia Seminary. Lutheran Church (Missouri Synod). Seminaries. 1886-1909. *3297*
—. Baptists, North American. Rauschenbusch, Walter. Theology. 1814-1949. *3062*
—. Catholic Church. Church and Social Problems. Irish Americans. New Jersey (Newark). 1840-70. *3830*
—. Catholic Church. Dolan, Jay P. (review article). Irish Americans. New York. Social Conditions. 1815-65. 1975. *3793*
—. Catholic Church. Immigrants. Kansas (Atchison). Newspapers. Pluralism. 1854-59. *3877*
—. Catholic Church. Language. Politics. Religious education. St. Peter's Colony. Saskatchewan. 1903-16. *779*

—. *Christliche Apologete* (periodical). Methodists. Neutrality. World War I. 1914-18. *3458*
—. Circuit riders. Frontier and Pioneer Life. Lutheran Church (Missouri Synod). Oklahoma. Texas. Wacker, Hermann Dietrich. 1847-1938. *3342*
—. Communalism. Harmony Society. Indiana. Pennsylvania. Protestantism. Rapp, George. 1804-47. *425*
—. Communes. Keil, William. Letters. Missouri. Oregon. Society of Bethel. Weitling, Wilhelm. 1844-83. *405*
—. Concordia Seminary. Illinois (Springfield). Lutheran Church (Missouri Synod). Missouri (St. Louis). 1846-1938. *615*
—. Documents. Free Thinkers. Immigrants. Missouri. Reading. Religious liberty. St. Louis Free Congregation Library. 1850-99. *1123*
—. Dunkards. Evangelism. Great Awakening. Immigration. Lutheran Church. Moravian Church. Northeastern or North Atlantic States. Reformed churches. 1720-60. *2237*
—. Episcopal Church, Protestant. Hast, Louis H. Kentucky (Louisville). Music. 1848-90. *1909*
—. Ethnicity. Evangelical and Reformed Church. Kamp, Henry. Oklahoma (Oklahoma City). 1906-57. *3123*
—. Folk art. Harmony Methodist Church Cemetery. Methodist Church. Tombstones. West Virginia (Jane Lew). 1827-55. *1892*
—. Good, Merle. Literature. Mennonites. Pennsylvania. Personal narratives. 1975. *2057*
—. Helmuth, Justus Henry Christian. Hymnals. Lutheran Church. 1786-1813. *1955*
—. Immigration. Reformed German Church. Spotswood, Alexander. Virginia (Germanna). 1714-21. *3284*
—. Lutheran Church. Pennsylvania. Reformed Chnrches. Slavery. Social change. 1779-88. *21o2*
—. Mennonites. Military conscription. Pacifism. Public opinion. World War I. 1914-18. *2696*
—. Occult Sciences. Pennsylvania. 17c-20c. *2183*
—. Presbyterian Church (Synod of the West). 1912-59. *3529*
German Canadians. Art. Fraktur. Ontario. 1976. *1843*
—. Immigrants. Nova Scotia. Protestants. 1749-52. *2852*
German Evangelical Synod of North America. Niebuhr, Reinhold. Pacifism. Patriotism. Theology. World War I. 1915-18. *2639*
German language. Americanization. Church Schools. Lutheran Church (Missouri Synod). Nebraska Council of Defense. Supreme Court. 1917-23. *305*
—. Amish, Old Order. Betz, Hans. Hymnals. 16c-20c. *1946*
—. Clergy. Hansel, William H. Lutheran Church (Missouri Synod). Personal narratives. 1907-62. *3305*
—. Pennsylvania. Protestant Churches. Sermons. 18c. *1989*
Germans, Russian. Agriculture. Factionalism. Mennonites. Personal narratives. Saskatchewan (Rosthern). Settlement. 1891-1900. *3442*
—. Alberta (Coaldale). Mennonites. Organizations. Social Change. 1920-76. *3411*
—. Baptists. Catholic Church. Immigration. Kansas. Lutheran Church. Mennonites. Wheat industry. 1874-77. *2778*
—. *Bote* (newspaper). Mennonites. Nazism. Saskatchewan. USSR. Völkisch thought. 1917-39. *3431*
—. Catholic Church. Colorado. Immigration. Mennonites. 18c-19c. *2775*
—. Catholic Church. Diaries. Immigration. Karlin, Athanasius. 1875-87. *3772*
—. Catholic Church. Religious Education. St. Angela's Convent. Saskatchewan (Prelate). Ursulines. Women. 1919-34. *680*
—. Chippewa Indians. Immigration. Manitoba. Mennonites. Métis. 1872-73. *3392*
—. Farms. Hildebrand, Bernhard (and family). Manitoba (Rosenthal). Mennonites. 1795-1915. *3407*
Germans, Sudeten. Antislavery Sentiments. Catholic Church. Emigration. Journalism. Missions and Missionaries. Neumann, Saint John Nepomucene. Republican Party. 19c-20c. *3826*
—. Indians. Missions and Missionaries. 1519-19c. *1539*
Germany *See also* component parts, e.g. Bavaria, Prussia, etc.; Alsace-Lorraine; Germany, West.
—. Adventists. Great Britain. Millenarianism. Miller, William. Sweden. 19c. *2967*
—. American Revolution. *Heinrich Mullers Pennsylvanischer Staatsbote* (newspaper). Moravian Church. Muller, Johann Heinrich. Pennsylvania (Philadelphia). Printing. 1722-82. *3514*
—. Americanization. Benedictines. Monasticism. Switzerland. 1846-1900. *314*
—. Anabaptists. Mennonites. Switzerland. Taxation. War. 16c-1973. *2662*
—. Bad Boll Conferences. Ecumenism. Lutheran Church. 1948. *439*
—. Barth, Karl. Protestantism. Theology. 1919-39. *2946*
—. Bible (New Testament). Exegesis. Hodge, Charles. Liberalism. Presbyterian Church. Princeton Theological Seminary. 1820-78. *3573*
—. Brigham Young University. Educators. Maeser, Karl G. Mormons. 1828-56. 1876. *768*
—. Catholic Church. Clergy. Mundelein, George. Nazism. 1937. *1256*
—. Clergy. Herborn, University of. Maryland. Otterbein, Philip Wilhelm. Pennsylvania. Theology. United Brethren in Christ. 1726-1813. *3666*
—. Conversion. Great Britain. Lutheran Church. Pietism. Puritanism. 17c-18c. *2942*
—. Editors and Editing. Mennonites. Miller, Samuel H. Trials. World War I. 1917-18. *2658*
—. Education (review article). Greven, Philip. Protestantism. Strauss, Gerald. Youth. 16c-19c. *850*
—. Francke, Gottfried. Georgia (Ebenezer). Immigrants. Kiefer, Theobald, II. Letters. Lutheran Church. Orphanages. Pietism. Whitefield, George. 1738. 1750. *2878*
—. Fundamentalism. Gaebelein, Arno C. Genocide. Jews. *Our Hope* (periodical). 1937-45. *136*
—. Religiosity. Students. 1960-77. *96*
Germany (Halle). Georgia. Methodism. Pietism. 1736-70. *3510*
Germany (Palatinate). Amish. France (Alsace). Immigrants. Pennsylvania. 1693-1803. *3406*
Germany, West. Cavert, Samuel McCrea. Christianity. Ecumenism. World Council of Churches. 1945-46. *486*
Ghettos. Jews. New York City (Lower East Side). 1890-1920. *4108*
Ghost Dance. California, northern. Converts. Indians. Methodist Church. Round Valley Indian Reservation. 1870. *3484*
Gibbons, James. Catholic Church. Knights of Labor. Social thought. Taschereau, Elzéar Alexandre. 1880's. *1476*
—. Church and state. France. Letters. Nolan, Edward J. Sabatier, Paul. 1906. *1016*
Gibson, Edmund. Church of England. Congregationalism. Cutler, Timothy. Edwards, Jonathan. Great Awakening. Letters. New England. Stoddard, Solomon. 1739. *2263*
Gibson, Walter Murray. Barrett, Gwynn. Hawaii (Lanai). Historiography. Mormons. 1859-64. 1972-78. *3945*
—. Dean, Joseph Harry. Hawaii. Missions and Missionaries. Mormons. Samoa. 1860's-90. *1683*
Giesbrecht, Herbert. Archives. Manitoba (Winnipeg). Mennonite Brethren Bible College. 1950-79. *250*
Gil, Juan. Arizona (Nogales). Buena, Mariano. Catholic Church. Indians. Seri Indians. 1768-72. *1559*
Gilbert Islands. American Board of Commissioners for Foreign Missions. Bingham family. Congregationalism. Hawaii. Missions and Missionaries. 1820-1975. *1678*
Giles, Benjamin. Calvinism. Founding fathers. Libraries. New Hampshire. 1760's-87. *2908*
Gilmer House. Architecture (Quaker-plan). Friends, society of. Georgia (Oglethorpe, Wilkes counties). 1800-1978. *1768*
Gingerich, Melvin (obituary). Historians. Mennonites. 1902-75. *214*
—. History. Mennonites. 1902-75. *243*
Girls. Arts and Crafts. Moravian Church. North Carolina. Pennsylvania. Students. 19c. *1862*
—. Bloomfield Academy. Chickasaw Indians. Downs, Ellen J. Indians. Methodist Church. Oklahoma (Penola County). Personal Narratives. Schools. 1853-66. *772*
—. Catholic Church. Church Schools. McDonough, Madrienne C. Mount St. Mary Convent. New Hampshire (Manchester). Personal narratives. 1902-09. *692*
—. Catholic Church. Daily life. Documents. Holy Names of Jesus and Mary, Sisters of the. Oregon (Salem). Sacred Heart Academy. 1863-73. *699*
—. Congregationalism. Connecticut. Indian-White Relations. Religious Education. Wheelock, Eleazar. 1761-69. *766*
—. Education. Episcopal Church, Protestant. Indians. St. Mary's Episcopal School for Indian Girls. South Dakota (Springfield). 1873-1973. *687*
—. Education. Friends, Society of. Ontario. 1790-1820. *749*
—. Episcopal Church, Protestant. Nevada (Reno). Schools. Whitaker, Ozi William. 1876-94. *769*
Gladden, Washington. Cities. Congregationalism. Ohio (Columbus). Reform. Social gospel. 1850's-1914. *2425*
Glass. Artifacts. Ceramics. Moravian Church. Worship. 18c-19c. *1879*
Glass, Carter. Cannon, James, Jr. Methodist Church. Political Corruption. Virginia. 1909-34. *1295*
Glendenning, Maurice L. Aaronic Order. Middle classes. Millenarianism. Mormons. Utah. 1930-79. *3933*
Glennon, John J. Catholic Church. Church Schools. Missouri (St. Louis). Ritter, Joseph E. School Integration. 1935-47. *2542*
Glock, Charles Y. Converts. Models. Social Change. Stark, Rodney. 1960's-70's. *144*
Gloria Dei Congregation. Lutheran Church. Old Swedes' Church. Pennsylvania (Philadelphia). Swedish Americans. 1638-98. *3302*
Goal submergence concept. Methodist Church. Social Organizations. Temperance movements. 1919-72. *2586*
God is Dead Theology. Buber, Martin. Heidegger, Robert. Sartre, Jean-Paul. Theology. 1961-64. *153*
—. Christianity. Islam. Methodology. Religions, history of. Secularism. Smith, Wilfred Cantwell. Theology. 1940-73. *134*
—. Science. Theology. 1600-1970. *2306*
—. Social Gospel. Theology, avant-garde. 1960's. *2768*
Godbe, William Samuel. Excommunication. Mormonism. Schisms. 1840's-80's. *4047*
Godfrey, John. Massachusetts. Puritans. Social Conditions. Trials. Witchcraft. 1634-75. *2186*
Goen, C. C. (review essay). Congregationalism. Edwards, Jonathan. Great Awakening. Revivals. 1734-1751. *2224*
Gold Mines and Mining. Clergy. Klondike Stampede. Lippy, Thomas S. Methodist Church. Randall, Edwin M. Transportation. Yukon Territory. 1896-99. *3492*
Gold rushes. Alaska. Fur trade. Jews. Nome Hebrew Benevolent Society. 1867-1916. *4103*
—. California. Catholic Church. Famines. Immigration. Irish Americans. 1849-90's. *3800*
—. Presbyterian Church. Yukon Territory. 1897-1910. *3571*
Golden Age concept. Civil religion. Protestantism. Rationalism. Reformation. 16c-19c. *1173*
Goldie, Albert. California (San Francisco). Judaism (Orthodox, Reform). New York City. Poor. Synagogues. Weinstock, Harris. 1906. *4166*
Goldsmith, William. Evolution. Hawkins, Robert W. Kansas (Winfield). Methodist Episcopal Church. Southwestern College. 1920-25. *2316*
Goldwater family. Arizona. Bar mitzvahs. Jews. 1879. *4097*
Gomez, Dolorez Amelia. Folklore. Pennsylvania (Philadelphia). Witchcraft. 1974. *2179*
Gompers, Samuel. Brandeis, Louis D. Judaism. Kogan, Michael S. Labor Unions and Organizations. 1880's-1975. *1479*
González Rubio, José. California. Catholic Church. Church administration. Missions and Missionaries. 1846-50. *3811*
Good, Merle. German Americans. Literature. Mennonites. Pennsylvania. Personal narratives. 1975. *2057*
Gordon, Helen Skinner. King, Gordon J. Manitoba (Winnipeg). Personal narratives. Presbyterian Church. Woman's Missionary Society of the Presbyterian and United Churches. 1890's-1961. *3548*

Gorton, Samuel. Great Britain. Massachusetts. Puritanism. Radicals and Radicalism. Rhode Island. Rhode Island. Theology. 1636-77. *2862*
Gospel Missionary Union of Kansas. Missions and Missionaries. Morocco (Tangiers). 1895-1905. *1736*
Gospel Temperance Movement. Canada. Revivalism. Rine, D. I. K. Temperance Movements. 1877-82. *2575*
Gottschalk, Stephen (review article). Christian Science. Eddy, Mary Baker. Women. 1885-1910. *3913*
Gough, John B. Temperance Movements. 1828-86. *2593*
Government *See also* City Government; Constitutions; County Government; Federal Government; Local Government; Military Government; Political Science; Politics; Provincial Government; Public Administration; State Government.
—. Antinomianism. Cotton, John. Eliot, John. Millenarianism. Missions and Missionaries. New England. Puritans. Rhode Island (Portsmouth). 1630-90. *3635*
—. British North America. Christianity. Deviant Behavior. Historiography. Occult Sciences. 1600-1760. *2180*
—. Catholic Church. Church of England. Indian-White Relations. Manitoulin project. Methodist Church. Missions and Missionaries. Ontario (Upper Canada). 1820-40. *1537*
—. Catholic Church. Parish registers. Quebec. 1539-1973. *3694*
—. Church of England. Clergy. Loyalists. Political Attitudes. Theology. 1770-83. *1387*
—. Church Schools. Constitutional Amendments (1st). Education, Finance. Religion in the public schools. 1950's-70's. *564*
—. Church schools. Education, Finance. Prayer. Public opinion. Religion in the Public Schools. 1962-68. *504*
—. Civil religion. Morality. Myths and Symbols. 1960's-78. *1153*
—. Connecticut. Constitutional Law. Hooker, Thomas. Puritans. 1635-39. *3603*
—. Economic Development. Quebec (Lower Canada). Social classes. Ultramontanism. 19c. *962*
—. Elites. Politics. Protestants. 1960's-70's. *1207*
—. Ethnic groups. Family. Morality. Religious institutions. 1960's-70's. *899*
—. Family. Ideology. Massachusetts. Puritans. Social cohesion. 1630-85. *3606*
Government Employees. *See* Civil Service.
Government, provisional. French Canadians. Gray, William. Lee, Jason. Methodist Church. Missions and Missionaries. Oregon. 1843. *1271*
Government, Resistance to *See also* Revolution.
—. American Revolution. Church of England. Griffith, David. Sermons. Virginia Convention. 1775. *1351*
—. Calvinism. Congregationalism. Massachusetts (Boston). Mayhew, Jonathan. Political Theory. Sermons. 1750. *1381*
—. Church and State. Jehovah's Witnesses. Persecution. Theology. 1870's-1960's. *1097*
Governors. Alaska. Brady, John Green (and family). Business. Morality. Presbyterian Church. 1878-1906. *3549*
—. Blair, James. Church of England. College of William and Mary. Missions and Missionaries. Virginia. ca 1685-1743. *3223*
Governors, provincial. Catholic Church. Church and state. Laval, François de. New France (Sovereign Council). Trade. 1659-84. *1020*
Grace. Edwards, Jonathan. Locke, John. Psychology. Theology. 1740's. *3158*
Grace Church. Authority. Bishops. Church and State. Civil War. Episcopal Church, Protestant. Illinois (Galesburg). 1864-66. *1218*
—. Christianity. Episcopal Church, Protestant. Fiction. Melville, Herman ("The Two Temples"). New York City. Trinity Church. 1845-50. *2061*
Grace Methodist Church. Churches (Gothic Revival). Delaware (Wilmington). Episcopal Church, Protestant. Methodist Church. St. John's Episcopal Church. 1850-90. *1786*
Graham, Agnes Nora. Baptists, Southern. Garrott, William Maxfield. Missions and Missionaries. Rutledge, Arthur B. 20c. *1694*
Graham, Billy. Audiences. Revivalism. Social classes. -1974. *2604*
—. Baptists. Conservatism. Evangelism. Morality. 1940's-70's. *2215*
—. Baptists. Fundamentalism. Minnesota (Minneapolis). Riley, William Bell. World Christian Fundamental Association. ca 1900-65. *3068*
—. Behavior. Conversion. Revivals. 1968-75. *2275*
—. Church and Social Problems. Ethics. Evangelicals. Political attitudes. War. 1970's. *2932*
—. Evangelicalism. Middle America. Streiker, Lowell D. (review essay). Strober, Gerald S. (review essay). -1972. *2621*
—. Peale, Norman Vincent. Popular culture. Protestantism. 1950's. *2901*
Graham, William. Christianity. Colleges and Universities. Curricula. Liberty Hall Academy. Proslavery Sentiments. Virginia. ca 1786-96. *2173*
Grant, George. Canada. Philosophy. Politics. Schmidt, Larry (review article). Theology. 1945-78. *509*
Grant, Heber J. Business. Depressions. Mormons. Utah. 1893. *375*
—. Letters. Mormons. Recreation. Smith, Joseph Fielding. 1930's. *3954*
Grant, Jedediah Morgan. Diaries. Missions and Missionaries. Mormons. 1833-57. *1631*
Grasshoppers. Agriculture. Pioneers. Utah. 1854-79. *3941*
Gravemarkers. Catholic Church. Cemeteries. German Alsatians. Iron work. Ontario (Bruce County; Waterloo). 1850-1910. *1880*
Graves, James Robinson. Baptists. Landmark movement. Missions and Missionaries. South. Whitsitt Controversy. 1850-1950. *3057*
—. Baptists, Southern. Fundamentalism. Landmark Movement. Modernism. Mullins, Edgar Young. Theology. 1840-1928. *3058*
—. Baptists, Southern. Newspapers. Seminaries. *Tennessee Baptist* (newspaper). 1820-93. *3076*
Gray, John P. Assassination. Moral insanity. New York State Lunatic Asylum. Psychiatry. Trials. 1854-86. *2346*
Gray, Walter H. Anglican Congress. Ecumenism. Minnesota (Minneapolis). 1940-54. *476*
Gray, William. French Canadians. Government, provisional. Lee, Jason. Methodist Church. Missions and Missionaries. Oregon. 1843. *1271*
Gray, William Crane. Episcopal Church, Protestant. Florida. Indian-White Relations. Missions and missionaries. Seminole Indians. 1893-1914. *1558*
Great Awakening. American Revolution. American Revolution. Cleaveland, John. Congregationalism. Daily life. Ideology. Jedrey, Christopher M. (review article). Massachusetts (Chebacco). New Lights. 1740-79. *2241*
—. American Revolution. Education. Pluralism. Theology. 1776. *1386*
—. American Revolution. Evangelism. Protestantism. 1770-1800. *2267*
—. American Revolution. Social Classes. Social theory. Urbanization. 1740's-70's. *2230*
—. American Revolution (antecedents). Civil religion. Edwards, Jonathan. King George's War. Millenarianism. 1740-76. *1169*
—. American Revolution (antecedents). Individualism. Pietism. Republicanism. 1735-75. *1385*
—. American Revolution (antecedents). Liberalism. Social Change. Social theory. ca 1725-75. *1338*
—. Antislavery Sentiments. Davies, Samuel. Presbyterian Church. Virginia. 1740-59. *2238*
—. Arminianism. Edwards, Jonathan. Justification. Massachusetts (Hampshire County). 1726-60. *2236*
—. Attitudes. Political reform. Social Change. 18c. 1975. *2216*
—. Bordley, Stephen. Church of England. Letters. Maryland. Whitefield, George. 1730-40. *2229*
—. *Boston Evening Post* (newspaper). Fleet, Thomas. Freedom of the press. Massachusetts (Boston). Newspapers. 1740's. *1423*
—. Calvinism. Diphtheria. Enlightenment. New England. Sermons. 1735-40. *2260*
—. Calvinism. New Left. New Lights. Youth. 1740's. 1960's. *2265*
—. Church and State. Church of England. Congregationalism. Connecticut. Factionalism. Officeholding. 1730-76. *1310*
—. Church of England. Congregationalism. Cutler, Timothy. Edwards, Jonathan. Gibson, Edmund. Letters. New England. Stoddard, Solomon. 1739. *2263*
—. Church of England. New England. Whitefield, George. 1735-70. *2239*
—. Clergy. Congregationalism. New England. New Lights. Old Lights. Social Classes. 1734-85. *2627*
—. Clergy. New England. Professionalism. Theology. 1740-49. *2257*
—. Cole, Nathan ("Spiritual Travels"). Congregationalism. Whitefield, George. 1740-65. *2227*
—. Congregationalism. Connecticut (Canterbury). Family. Local politics. Schisms. 1742-50. *2242*
—. Congregationalism. Connecticut (New London). New Lights. Schisms. Shepherd's Tent (college). 1720-50. *2250*
—. Congregationalism. Connecticut (New London). New Lights. Shepherd's Tent (college). 1742-46. *774*
—. Congregationalism. Connecticut (Windham). Conversion. Social Change. 1723-43. *2274*
—. Congregationalism. Connecticut (Windham). Converts. Social change. 1721-43. *2273*
—. Congregationalism. Conversion. Massachusetts (Freetown). Personal narratives. 1749-70. *2221*
—. Congregationalism. Edwards, Jonathan. Goen, C. C. (review essay). Revivals. 1734-1751. *2224*
—. Congregationalism. Edwards, Jonathan. Intellectuals. Massachusetts (Northampton, Stockbridge). Theology. Youth. ca 1730-1880. *3150*
—. Congregationalism. New England. Ordination. Parkman, Ebenezer. 1630-1740. *3157*
—. Connecticut Valley. Massachusetts (Hatfield). Presbyterian Church. Williams, William. 1686-1741. *2240*
—. Covenant theology. Edwards, Jonathan. Puritans. 18c. *2219*
—. Dunkards. Evangelism. German Americans. Immigration. Lutheran Church. Moravian Church. Northeastern or North Atlantic States. Reformed churches. 1720-60. *2237*
—. Economic Conditions. Nova Scotia (Yarmouth). Social Conditions. 1760's-70's. *2626*
—. Ecumenism. Moravian Church. Presbyterian Church. Tennent, Gilbert. Theology. Zinzendorf, Nikolaus. 1740-41. *2226*
—. Education. Georgia (Savannah). Orphans. Whitefield, George. 1738-71. *731*
—. Evangelism. Great Britain. Whitefield, George. 1714-70. *2232*
—. Franklin, Benjamin. Great Britain. Theology. Whitefield, George. 1739-64. *2272*
—. Massachusetts (Hampshire County). Theology. 1730's-40's. *2235*
—. New England. Puritans. Religious Education. 1690-1750. *655*
—. Providence. 18c. *1155*
Great Awakening (antecedents). Connecticut. Protestantism. 1700's-40's. *2256*
Great Britain *See also* British Empire; Ireland; Scotland.
—. Abolition Movement. Historiography. Protestantism. 18c-19c. *2499*
—. Acadians. Acculturation. Catholic Church. Exiles. France. Nova Scotia. 18c. *3750*
—. Adventists. Germany. Millenarianism. Miller, William. Sweden. 19c. *2967*
—. American Christian Palestine Committee. Lobbying. Palestine. Zionism. 1940's. *1316*
—. American Revolution. Asbury, Francis. Methodism. Wesley, John. 1770-90. *1334*
—. American Revolution. Baptists. Colonies. 1775-83. *1296*
—. American Revolution. Boucher, Jonathan. Church of England. Civil War. Jefferson, Thomas. Loyalists. 1640-1797. *1412*
—. American Revolution. Charities. Friends, Society of. Ireland. Pennsylvania (Philadelphia). 1778-97. *2503*
—. American Revolution. Chauncy, Charles. Church and State. Congregationalism. Letters. Price, Richard. Slavery. 1727-87. *3129*
—. American Revolution. Daily life. Johnson, Jeremiah. Military Occupation. New York City (Brooklyn). Personal narratives. 1775-83. *63*
—. American Revolution. Judaism (Orthodox). Rhode Island. Touro, Isaac. 1782. *4184*

—. American Revolution. Loyalists. Methodism. Poetry. Political Commentary. Wesley, Charles. 1775-83. *1339*
—. American Revolution. Methodism. Plagiarism. Politics. Wesley, John *(A Calm Address to our American Colonies).* 1775-79. *1377*
—. American Revolution. Methodism. Political Attitudes. Wesley, John. Whigs, Radical. 1775-78. *1391*
—. American Revolution. Methodism. Wesley, John. 1760-89. *1404*
—. American Revolution. Nonconformists. 1765-83. *1401*
—. American Revolution. Wesley, John. 1775. *1336*
—. American Revolution. Wesley, John *(A Calm Address to our American Colonies).* 1770-76. *1340*
—. American Revolution (antecedents). Church of England. Colonial Government. Political theory. Shipley, Jonathan. 1773-75. *1376*
—. American Studies. Colleges and Universities. Theses. 1975-76. *46*
—. Americanization. Church of England. North Carolina. Parishes. 1701-12. *298*
—. Anglican Communion. Bibliographies. 1973-75. *3233*
—. Anglican Communion. Canada. Education. Missionaries. Protestantism. Sudan Interior Mission. 1937-55. *1741*
—. Anglican Communion. Ethics. 16c-20c. *3182*
—. Anti-Catholicism. Church of England. Gavin, Anthony *(A Master-Key to Popery).* Literature. Virginia. 1724-73. *2108*
—. Anti-Catholicism. Colonization. Ideology. Ireland. North America. Protestantism. ca 1550-1600. *2086*
—. Anti-Catholicism. Irish Canadians. Ontario. Orange Order. Patriotism. 1830-1900. *2111*
—. Anticlericalism. Church of England. Virginia. ca 1635-1783. *3238*
—. Antislavery Sentiments. Evangelicalism. 1846. *2893*
—. Antislavery Sentiments. Friends, Society of. Libertarianism. Radicals and Radicalism. 18c-1865. *2497*
—. Antislavery Sentiments. Reform. 18c-19c. *2457*
—. Asbury, Francis. Canada. Coke, Thomas. Embury, Philip. Methodism. USA. 1760-80. *3445*
—. Attitudes. Autobiography. Brownson, Orestes A. *(The Convert).* Catholic Church. Converts. Newman, John Henry *(Apologia pro Vita Sua).* Protestantism. 1857-64. *3681*
—. Baptists. Clergy. Emigration. Harris, Theophilus. Politics. Social conditions. 1793-1810. *3050*
—. Baptists. Clergy. Religious Education. 1600's-1980. *725*
—. Baptists, Primitive. Georgia. 1633-1900. *3063*
—. Beecher, Lyman. Evangelical Alliance. Presbyterian Church. Temperance Movements. World Temperance Convention. 1846. *3563*
—. Bishop of London. Church of England. Commissaries. South Carolina. 1715-32. *3242*
—. Bishops. Church of England. Education. Feild, Edward. Newfoundland. 1826-44. *3198*
—. Boucher, Jonathan. Church of England. Loyalists. Maryland. Zimmer, Anne Y. (review article). 1770's-90's. *1358*
—. Brownson, Orestes A. Catholic University of Ireland. Ireland. Newman, John Henry. 1853-54. *3837*
—. Calvert, Cecilius (2d Lord Baltimore). Catholic Church. Maryland. Provincial Government. Religious Liberty. 1634-49. *1068*
—. Cambridge Camden Society. Churches (Gothic Revival). Episcopal Church, Protestant. 1840-1975. *1773*
—. Canada. Ontario (Kingston, Smith Falls). Queen's College. Romanes, George. Romanes, George John. Science. Scientific Experiments and Research. Theology. 1830-90. *2918*
—. Cannon, Martha Hughes. Letters. Mormons. Polygamy. Utah (Salt Lake City). Women. 1885-96. *4002*
—. Capitalism. Defoe, Daniel *(Robinson Crusoe).* Materialism. Thoreau, Henry David *(Walden).* Transcendentalism. 18c-19c. *354*
—. Carter, Jimmy. Cromwell, Oliver. Political Leadership. Rickover, Hyman. Roosevelt, Theodore. 20c. *974*
—. Cartoons and Caricatures. New England. Puritans. Satire. 1770-76. *2005*
—. Catholic Church. Church and state. Military government. Protestantism. Quebec. 18c. *1125*
—. Catholic Church. Isolationism. Nicoll, John R. A. Roosevelt, Franklin D. (administration). World War II. 1943. *1241*
—. Catholic Church. Propaganda. World War I. 1918. *1240*
—. Catholics. Immigration. Macdonnell, Alexander. Ontario. Scottish Canadians. 1770's-1814. *3862*
—. Channing, William Ellery. Humanitarianism. Irresistible compassion. Theology. ca 1660-19c. *2851*
—. Charles I. Cotton, John. Massachusetts (Boston). Puritans. Regicide. Sermons. 1650. *1349*
—. *Christian History* (periodical). Evangelicalism. Methodist Church, Calvinistic. Periodicals. Whitefield, George. 1740's. *2233*
—. Christianity. France. Judaism. Theater. ca 1957-78. *1853*
—. Christmas carols. Music. Puritans. Virginia. 1662-70. *2787*
—. Church and state. 1780-1860. *1078*
—. Church and state. Colonial Government. Rhode Island. Williams, Roger. 1629-83. *1042*
—. Church and State. Denominationalism. Ecumenism. Evangelical Alliance. 1846. *484*
—. Church and State. Education. India. Secularization. 19c. *522*
—. Church of England. Congregationalism. Connecticut. Johnson, Samuel (1696-1772). Ordination. Yale University. 1722-23. *2843*
—. Church of England. Duche, Jacob, Jr. Pennsylvania (Philadelphia). Pietism. Swedenborgianism. 1750-1800. *2738*
—. Clayton, William. Immigration. Letters. Moon, John. Mormons. 1840. *3925*
—. Clergy. Counseling. 1950's-70's. *122*
—. Clergy. Immigration. New England. Puritans. 1629-65. *3661*
—. Cobden, Richard. Millenarianism. Peace movements. Protestant churches. 1840-60. *2701*
—. Coke, Thomas. Methodism. Rites and Ceremonies. Wesley, John *(Sunday Service).* 1780's. *3460*
—. Colonization. Florida (Campbell Town). Huguenots. West Florida. 1763-70. *3254*
—. Congregationalism. Exiles. Hooker, Thomas. Netherlands. New England. Theology. 1631-33. *3650*
—. Conversion. Germany. Lutheran Church. Pietism. Puritanism. 17c-18c. *2942*
—. Crime and criminals. Ecclesiastical law. Massachusetts. Roman Law. 17c. *972*
—. Darwinism. Moore, James R. (review article). Protestantism. 1870-1900. *2319*
—. Davies, Samuel. Diaries. Fund raising. New Jersey. Presbyterian Church. Princeton University. 1753-54. *636*
—. Diaries. North America. Physicians. Theologians. Ward, John. 17c. *2312*
—. Diplomacy. Missionaries. Ottoman Empire. Protestantism. 1824-42. *1697*
—. Education. Greaves, Richard L. Mather (family). Middlekauff, Robert. New England. Puritans. 1596-1728. *607*
—. Episcopal Church, Protestant. Maurice, Frederick Denison. Protestantism. Revelation. Social reform. Theology. 1860-1900. *3171*
—. Evangelism. Great Awakening. Whitefield, George. 1714-70. *2232*
—. Folk Medicine. Georgia. Indians. Medicine (practice of). Methodism. Wesley, John. 1740's. *1426*
—. France. Positivism. Unitarianism. 1816-90. *4077*
—. Franklin, Benjamin. Great Awakening. Theology. Whitefield, George. 1739-64. *2272*
—. Friends, Society of. Law. *Mary and Charlotte* (vessel). Pennsylvania (Philadelphia). War relief. 1778-84. *3266*
—. Friends, Society of. Missions and Missionaries. New England. 1656-1775. *1662*
—. Fundamentalism. 1920's. *2894*
—. Gorton, Samuel. Massachusetts. Puritanism. Radicals and Radicalism. Rhode Island. Rhode Island. Theology. 1636-77. *2862*
—. Immigrants. Landscape Painting. Mormons. Piercy, Frederick *(Illustrated Route).* Portraits. Travel guides. Western states. 1848-57. *1869*
—. Iroquois Indians. Jesuits. Missions and Missionaries. Netherlands. New York. 1642-1719. *1654*
—. Jeremiads. New England. Pamphlets. Puritans. Ward, Nathaniel. 1645-50. *1975*
—. Law. Protestantism. Secularization. 1800-1970. *10*
—. Letters. Mormons. Richards, Willard. Young, Brigham. 1840. *1754*
—. Local government. Massachusetts. New England. Political theory. Puritans. Social change. 1600-50. *3604*
—. Methodism. Nonconformists. Revivals. 1828-43. *2223*
—. Missions and Missionaries. Mormons. Working class. 1840-41. *1672*
—. Murray, John. Universalism. Vidler, William. Winchester, Elhanan. 1770-1825. *4080*
—. New England. Puritans. Rhetoric. Sermons. 1620's-50's. *1980*
—. New England. Williams, Roger. 1629-82. *2876*
—. Psychology. Religious experience. 1975-77. *114*
—. Puritanism. 1560-1660. *3617*
—. Travel accounts. 1800-30's. *2730*
Great Britain (Bristol). Baptists. Bristol Baptist College. Missions and Missionaries. Religious Education. Terrill, Edward. 1634-1979. *3024*
Great Britain (Cambridge). Anglican Communion. Architecture. Chancels. Ecclesiology Society. 1839-60. *1779*
Great Britain (Lancashire). Fell, Margaret. Feminism. Friends, Society of. Pennsylvania (Philadelphia). Women. 1670's. *928*
Great Britain (London). Baptism. Baptists. Jessey, Henry. Letters. New England. Puritans. Toleration. Tombes, John. 1645. *997*
—. Baptists. Bennett, Robert. Clarke, John. Letters. Religious Liberty. Rhode Island. 1655-58. *1132*
—. Courtship. Field, Eliza. Indians. Jones, Peter. Methodism. New York. 1820's-33. *1637*
—. Libraries. Pool, Reuben B. Young Men's Christian Association. 1844-1974. *2887*
Great Britain (Manchester). Clayton, William. Illinois (Nauvoo). Immigration. Letters. Mormons. 1840. *3924*
Great Chain of Being (concept). Calling (concept). Equality. Protestant Ethic. Puritans. 17c-18c. *340*
Great Disappointment. Adventists. Millenarianism. Revivals. 18c-1973. *2970*
—. Millenarianism. Miller, William. 1831-44. *2966*
—. Millenarianism. Millerites. Nature. 1830's-44. *2973*
Great Plains. Baptists. Canada. Disciples of Christ. Lutheran Church. Methodism. Pietism. Prairie Radicals. Radicals and Radicalism. 1890-1975. *954*
—. Immigration. Manitoba. Mennonites. Russia. 1871-74. *3395*
—. Indian-White Relations. Mormons. New York, western. Utah. Young, Brigham. 1835-51. *3948*
—. Mennonites. Pioneer life. Wheat. 1870-1974. *3443*
Greaves, Richard L. Education. Great Britain. Mather (family). Middlekauff, Robert. New England. Puritans. 1596-1728. *607*
Greek Americans. Assimilation. Ethnicity. New York City. Orthodox Eastern Church. St. Demetrios Church. St. Markela Church. 1970's. *318*
—. Assimilation. Papagiannis, Michael D. Personal narratives. USA (impressions). 20c. *2811*
—. Negroes. Ohio (Cincinnati). Racism. 1970's. *2146*
Greeley, Andrew M. Catholic Church. Clergy. Intellectuals. 1974. *3749*
Greeley, Andrew M. (review essay). Sociology of religion concept. Theology. 1960's-70's. *167*
Greeley, Horace. Adventists. Dowling, John. Miller, William. New York *Tribune* (newspaper). 1842. *2963*
Green, Jacob. American Revolution. New Jersey. Politics. 1770-90. *1398*
—. Presbyterian Church. Seminaries. 1775. *714*
Greenway, Thomas (administration). Church schools. Francophones. Language. Legislation. Manitoba Act (Canada, 1870). 1890-99. *519*

Greven, Philip. Child-rearing. Death and Dying. Fischer, David H. Lynn, Kenneth S. Personality (review article). Politics. Protestantism. Stannard, David E. 18c. 1977. *2943*
—. Education (review article). Germany. Protestantism. Strauss, Gerald. Youth. 16c-19c. *850*
Greven, Philip (review article). Child-rearing. Protestantism. 17c-19c. 1977. *886*
—. Child-rearing. Protestantism. Self-perception. 1620-18c. *836*
Grey, Zane. Emmett, James Simpson. Friendship. Mormons. Novels (western). Utah. 1907. *2072*
Grey, Zane *(Riders of the Purple Sage)*. Arrington, Leonard J. Haupt, Jon. Mormons. Mormons. 1912. 1970's. *2076*
Griffith, David. American Revolution. Bishops. Chaplains. Church of England. Virginia Regiment, 3rd. 1774-89. *3235*
—. American Revolution. Church of England. Government, Resistance to. Sermons. Virginia Convention. 1775. *1351*
Grimes, Addison McLaughlin. Church records. Clergy. Methodist Episcopal Church. West Virginia (Webster County). 1880's-1963. *3455*
Grimké, Sarah. Christianity. Nature. Paul, Saint. Social organization. Women. 1c. 1830's. *921*
Grip (periodical). Bengough, John Wilson. City government. Ontario (Toronto). Political Reform. Protestantism. 1873-1910. *1266*
Groton School. Episcopal Church, Protestant. Massachusetts. Peabody, Endicott. Religious education. 1884-1940. *671*
Groulx, Lionel. Catholic Church. French Canadians. Quebec. Secularism. Separatist Movements. 1897-1928. *1409*
—. Catholic Church. Quebec. 1895-1905. *3688*
Group survival. Identity. Ideology. Judaism (Reform). 1800-1975. *4212*
Gruber, Jacob. Maryland (Washington County). Methodism. Slave Revolts. Trials. 1818-20. *2456*
Grueningen, Johann Jakob von. Reformed Swiss Church. Swiss Americans. Wisconsin (Sauk City). 1876-1911. *2860*
Grundtvig, Nikolai Frederik Severin. Beck, Vilhelm. Danish Americans. Inner Mission Movement. Lutheran Church. 1619-1973. *3341*
—. Lutheran Church. Reform. 19c-1972. *3313*
Grutka, Andrew G. Catholic Church. Gary Diocese. Indiana. 1933-78. *3868*
Guam. Catholic Church. Martinez, Pedro. 1909-67. *3795*
Guardians of Liberty. American Protective Association. Anti-Catholicism. Chinese Americans. Ku Klux Klan. Nativism. Oregon. Racism. ca 1840-1945. *2100*
—. Anti-Catholicism. Catts, Sidney J. Elections (gubernatorial). Florida. Knott, William V. Sturkie Resolution. 1916. *1231*
Guibord, Joseph. *Brown* v. *Les Curé et Marguilliers de l'Oeuvre et de la Fabrique de la Paroisse de Montréal* (1874). Catholic Church. Church and state. Liberalism. Politics. Quebec. Ultramontanism. 1870-74. *1067*
Guidebooks. Congregationalism. Illinois. Immigration. Thomas, Robert D. *(Hanes Cymry America)*. Welsh Americans. 19c. *3119*
—. Congregationalism. Immigration. Iowa. Thomas, Robert D. *(Hanes Cymry America)*. Welsh Americans. 1790-1890. *3155*
—. Congregationalism. Immigration. Kansas. Thomas, Robert D. *(Hanes Cymry America)*. Welsh Americans. 1838-84. *3121*
—. Congregationalism. Immigration. Missouri. Thomas, Robert D. *(Hanes Cymry America)*. Welsh Americans. 1872. *3120*
Guigues, Joseph-Eugène. Catholic Church. French Canadians. Ontario. Ottawa Diocese. 1848-74. *3713*
Gurock, Jeffrey S. Cities. Gartner, Lloyd P. Hertzberg, Steven. Jews (review article). Raphael, Mark Lee. 1840-1979. *4150*
Guyana (Jonestown). Apocalypse (concept). Jones, Jim. People's Temple. 1953-78. *4252*
—. California (San Francisco). Jones, Jim. Leftism. People's Temple. 1960's-78. *4247*
—. Charisma. Jones, Jim. Leadership. Models. People's Temple. Suicide, mass. 1978. *4253*
—. Jones, Jim. People's Temple. Personality. Suicide, mass. 1965-78. *4238*
—. Jones, Jim. People's Temple. Sects, Religious. ca 1950-79. *4262*
Guyana (Jonestown; review article). California. Jones, Jim. People's Temple. 1931-78. *4251*
Guyot, Arnold. Bible. Creation theory. Dana, James Dwight. Protestantism. Science. 1850's. *2333*

H

Hackett, Francis. Catholic Church. Education. Ireland (Kilkenny, Clongowes Wood). Irish Americans. Literature. 1880's-1901. *3818*
Hackney, F. Sheldon. Formisano, Ronald P. Kleppner, Paul. Methodology. Politics (review article). 1827-1900. 1969-71. *1263*
Hadassah. Jews. National Council of Jewish Women. Professionalism. Voluntary Associations. Women. 1890-1980. *4146*
Haida Indians. British Columbia (Queen Charlotte Islands). Church of England. Methodist Church. Missions and Missionaries. Settlement. Social Change. 1876-1920. *1545*
Haitian Americans. Catholic Church. Dialects. French Language. New York City (Brooklyn). 1970's. *3699*
Half-Way Covenant. Church and Social Problems. Church membership. Massachusetts (Dorchester). Puritans. Religious scrupulosity. 1660-1730. *3601*
—. Church membership. Massachusetts. Puritans. 1662. *3624*
Hall, A. J. British Columbia (Metlakatla). Church Missionary Society. Church of England. Indian-White Relations. Missions and Missionaries. Revivals. Tsimshian Indians. 1877. *1616*
Halligan, James. Anti-Catholicism. Cheverus, Jean Louis Lefebvre de. Daley, Dominic. Irish Americans. Massachusetts (Northampton). Protestantism. Trials. 1805-06. *2097*
Hallowell, Benjamin. Education. Friends, Society of. Science. Virginia (Alexandria). 1824-60. *3281*
Hallucinations. Plants. Southwest. Trances. Witchcraft. 17c-20c. *2207*
Ham, Mordecai F. Fundamentalism. Newspapers. North Carolina (Elizabeth City). Revivals. Saunders, William O. 1924. *2217*
Hamill, Pete. Anti-Catholicism. Breslin, Jimmy. Brooklyn Diocese. Flaherty, Joe. Irish Americans. New York City. Novels. 1960's-70's. *2098*
Hampden-Sydney College. Educators. Smith, Samuel Stanhope. Virginia (Farmville area). 1776-1815. *513*
Handsome Lake (Seneca). Indian Shaker Church. Neurology. Revitalization movements. Slocum, John. Trances. 18c-20c. *2756*
Handy, Robert T. Ahlstrom, Sydney E. Christianity (review article). Historiography. Marty, Martin E. Race (issue). 16c-1978. *2743*
—. Albanese, Catherine L. Beecher, Henry Ward. Civil Religion. Clark, Clifford E., Jr. Douglas, Ann. McLoughlin, William G. Reform. Revivals (review article). Women. 1607-1978. *6*
Hangings. Hodges, Stephen. Hodges, William. Iowa. Mormons (Danites). Murder. 1845. *3985*
Hanley, Thomas O'Brien (review article). Carroll, John. Catholic Church. Documents. 18c-19c. 1970's. *3672*
Hanley, Thomas O'Brien *(The John Carroll Papers)*. Carroll, John. Catholic Church. Clergy. Documents. Research. 18c-19c. 1976-78. *3872*
Hansel, William H. Clergy. German language. Lutheran Church (Missouri Synod). Personal narratives. 1907-62. *3305*
Harap, Louis (review article). Jews. Literature. 1775-1914. 1974. *83*
Hare Krishna Movement. Converts. Divine Light Mission. Youth. 1960's-70's. *4284*
Harkins, Richard. Choctaw Indians. Congregationalism. Missions and Missionaries. Murder. Slavery. 1858-59. *3132*
Harmony Methodist Church Cemetery. Folk art. German Americans. Methodist Church. Tombstones. West Virginia (Jane Lew). 1827-55. *1892*
Harmony Society. Architecture. Indiana (New Harmony). Pennsylvania (Economy, Harmony). Preservation. Rapp, George. Restorations. Utopias. 1804-25. 20c. *420*
—. City Planning. Communes. Indiana (New Harmony). Pennsylvania (Harmony, Economy). Social customs. 1820's-1905. *391*
—. Communalism. German Americans. Indiana. Pennsylvania. Protestantism. Rapp, George. 1804-47. *425*
—. Indiana (New Harmony). Rapp, George. Utopias. 1814-47. *421*
—. Indiana (New Harmony). Rapp, George. Utopias. 1822-30. *379*
—. Pennsylvania. Rapp, George. State Legislatures. Utopias. 1805-07. *380*
—. Pennsylvania (Economy). Rapp, George. Utopias. 1785-1847. *381*
—. Pennsylvania (Economy). Wrede, Friedrich Wilhelm von. 1842. *401*
Harrell, David Edwin, Jr. (review article). Charismatic movement. Faith healing. Revivals. 1947-75. *2782*
Harris, N. Sayre. Diaries. Episcopal Church, Protestant. Indian Territory. Missions and Missionaries. Otey, James Hervey. 1844. *1533*
Harris, Rufus C. Anderson, P. Harris. Baptists. Georgia. Mercer University. 1965-76. *3033*
Harris, Theophilus. Baptists. Clergy. Emigration. Great Britain. Politics. Social conditions. 1793-1810. *3050*
Harris, William Richard. Catholic Church. Clergy. Ontario. Toronto Archdiocese. 1846-1923. 1974. *3846*
Harrison, Peter. Churches. Rhode Island (Newport). Touro Synagogue. Wren, Christoper. 1670-1775. *1819*
Hartzell, Joseph C. Ames Church. Education. Freedmen. Methodist Episcopal Church. Missionaries. Republican Party. South. 1870-73. *3481*
Harvard University. Brown University. Colleges and Universities. Libraries. Princeton University. Yale University. 18c. *672*
—. Church and State. College of William and Mary. Puritans. Yale University. 1636-1700. *650*
—. Church and State. Colleges and Universities (review article). Columbia University. Dartmouth College. Johnson, Samuel (1696-1772). Yale University. 1696-1970. 1972-74. *524*
—. Church of England. Congregationalism. Yale University. ca 1722-90. *660*
—. Congregationalism. Latin language. Leverett, John. Massachusetts (Cambridge). Speeches, Addresses, etc. 1722. *668*
Harvard University (Hollis Professorship of Divinity). Congregationalism. Latin language. Rhetoric. Wigglesworth, Edward. 1722. *667*
Hasidism. Attitudes. Judaism. Philosophy. 1970's. *4189*
—. Judaism. Quebec (Montreal). 1942-71. *4179*
Hasidism (Habad). Edwards, Jonathan. Psychology. Theology (comparative). 18c. *2338*
Hasidism (Lubavitch). Church Schools. Education. Judaism. Quebec (Montreal). 1969-71. *550*
Hast, Louis H. Episcopal Church, Protestant. German Americans. Kentucky (Louisville). Music. 1848-90. *1909*
Haswell, David R. Country Life. Farms. Letters. Pennsylvania. Protestants. Revivals. 1808-31. *2234*
Haupt, Jon. Arrington, Leonard J. Grey, Zane *(Riders of the Purple Sage)*. Mormons. Mormons. 1912. 1970's. *2076*
Haury, Samuel S. Arapaho Indians. Indian Territory. Letters. Mennonites. Missions and Missionaries. 1876-80. *1543*
Haushalter, Walter M. *(Mrs. Eddy Purloins from Hegel)*. Christian Science. Documents. Extortion. Forgeries. 1929-59. *3912*
Haven, Gilbert. Colorado. Methodist Church. Rocky Mountains. Utah (Salt Lake City). 1875. *3463*
—. Georgia (Atlanta). Negroes. Protestant Churches. Segregation. 1865-1906. *2145*
Haverford College Library (Quaker Collection). Abolition Movement. Friends, Society of. New Hampshire. Portsmouth Anti-Slavery Society. Rogers, Nathaniel Peabody. 1830-46. *2465*
Hawaii *See also* Far Western States.
—. Abortion. Catholic Church. Methodology. Women. 1965-74. *872*
—. American Board of Commissioners for Foreign Missions. Bingham family. Congregationalism. Gilbert Islands. Missions and Missionaries. 1820-1975. *1678*
—. Bingham Family. Congregationalism. Micronesia. Missions and Missionaries. Yale University Library (Bingham Family Papers). 1815-1967. *1714*

—. Catholic Church. Independence Movements. Missions and Missionaries. Protestant Churches. Simpson, George. 1842-43. *1723*
—. Chinese Americans. Missions and Missionaries. Protestant Churches. 1872-98. *1717*
—. Congregationalism. Connecticut. Kanui, William Tennooe. Missions and Missionaries. Protestant Churches. 1796-1864. *1493*
—. Congregationalism. Diaries. Missions and Missionaries. Tahitians. Toketa (teacher). 1820's-30's. *1676*
—. Dean, Joseph Harry. Gibson, Walter Murray. Missions and Missionaries. Mormons. Samoa. 1860's-90. *1683*
—. Judaism. Personal narratives. Zwerin, Kenneth C. 1935. *4158*
Hawaii (Honolulu). Attitudes. Baptists, Southern. Buddhism. Congregationalism. Death and Dying. 1977. *131*
Hawaii (Lanai). Barrett, Gwynn. Gibson, Walter Murray. Historiography. Mormons. 1859-64. 1972-78. *3945*
—. Colonization. Missions and Missionaries. Mormons. 1850's. *1684*
Hawaiian Evangelical Association. Congregationalism. Missions and Missionaries. Siu Pheong Aheong. ca 1838-76. *1687*
Hawaiians. Clergy. Columbia River. Congregationalism. Fort Vancouver. Hudson's Bay Company. Kaulehelehe, William R. Washington. 1845-69. *3128*
Hawkins, Robert W. Evolution. Goldsmith, William. Kansas (Winfield). Methodist Episcopal Church. Southwestern College. 1920-25. *2316*
Hawthorne, Nathaniel. American Revolution. Literature. National character. Puritan Tradition. 1775-83. 1830-40. *2082*
—. Christianity. Literature. Sacramental love tradition. 1838-60. *2080*
—. Fiction. Massachusetts. Philosophy of History. Puritans. 1820's-60's. *2081*
—. Fiction. Melville, Herman *(Moby Dick)*. Pessimism. 1850-51. *2042*
—. History. Novels. Puritan tradition. Social reform. Symbolism in Literature. 1825-63. *2019*
Hayes, Carlton J. H. Attitudes. Historiography. Kohn, Hans. Nationalism. 1950's-60's. *1392*
Hayes, Rutherford B. Congress. Mormons. Polygamy. Suffrage. Women. 1877-81. *797*
Hays, Brooks. Arkansas, University of. Baptists. Personal narratives. Students. Values. ca 1915-20. *3025*
Hays, Samuel. Abramson, Harold J. Catholics. Ethnicity (review article). Voting and Voting Behavior. 1973. *3740*
Healdsburg College. Adventists. Battle Creek College. Brownsberger, Sidney. California. Colleges and Universities. Michigan. 1875-80's. *665*
Health. Adventists. Numbers, Ronald L. (review article). Reform. White, Ellen G. ca 1840's-1915. 1976. *1457*
—. Alcott, William A. Christian Physiology. ca 1829-60. *1462*
—. Attitudes. Exercise. New England. Recreation. Transcendentalists. 1830-60. *1453*
—. Authority. Constitutional Amendments (1st). Religious liberty. Supreme Court. 1963-79. *1439*
—. Charismatic movement. Europe. Folk Religion (review article). Occult sciences. Science. 16c-19c. 1975-76. *7*
—. Lifestyles. Mormons. ca 1930-79. *1448*
Healy, James A. Catholic Church. Diaries. Holy Cross College. Massachusetts (Worcester). Religious Education. 1849. *640*
Heart concept. Augustine, Saint. Calvinism. Edwards, Jonathan. New England. Psychology. 17c. *2311*
Hebrew. Congregation Kahal Kadosh Shearith Israel. Ethnicity. Falkenau, Jacob J. M. Jews. Lyons, Jacques Judah. New York City. Pique, Dob. Poetry. 1786-1841. *2062*
Hebrew Benevolent Association. Jews. Letters. Nevada (Austin). Silver mining. 1864-82. *4164*
Hebrew Benevolent Society of Los Angeles. California (Los Angeles; Chavez Ravine). Cemeteries. Home of Peace Jewish Cemetery. Judaism. Photographs. 1855-1910. *4161*
Hebrew Day Schools. Judaism (Orthodox). Religious education. 1960's-70's. *662*
Hebrew Theological College. Fasman, Oscar Z. Judaism (Orthodox). Oklahoma (Tulsa). Ontario (Ottawa). Personal narratives. Rabbis. 1929-79. *4177*
Hebrew Union College. Academic Freedom. Judaism, Reform. Kohler, Kaufmann. Ohio (Cincinnati). Zionism. 1903-07. *724*
—. Colleges and Universities. Judaism (Reform). Judaism, Reform. Ohio (Cincinnati). Wise, Isaac Mayer. 1870's-1900. *613*
—. Fund raising. Judaism (Reform). Union of American Hebrew Congregations. Western States. Wise, Isaac Mayer. 1873-75. *784*
—. Jewish Institute of Religion. Seminaries. 1875-1974. *786*
—. Judaism, Reform. Letters. Prager, Abraham J. Rabbis. Wise, Isaac Mayer. 1854-1900. *4227*
—. Judaism (Reform). Letters. Rabbis. Stolz, Joseph. Wise, Isaac Mayer. 1882-1900. *4220*
—. Judaism (Reform). Ohio (Cincinnati). 1942-45. *750*
—. Judaism (Reform). Ohio (Cincinnati). Rabbis. Seminaries. Wise, Isaac Mayer. 1817-90's. *701*
Hecht, Sigmund. California (Los Angeles). Judaism. 1904-25. *4182*
—. Judaism (Reform). 1877-1911. *4218*
Heck, Barbara. Dickey, Sarah. Leadership. Methodist Church. Parker, Lois Stiles. Shaw, Anna Howard. Stereotypes. Willard, Frances E. Women. 19c. *812*
Hedge, Frederic Henry. Emerson, Ralph Waldo. Maine (Bangor). Transcendentalism. Unitarianism. 1833. *2761*
Hegel, Georg. Religious movements. Troeltsch, Ernst. Weber, Max. 19c-20c. *33*
Heidegger, Robert. Buber, Martin. God is Dead Theology. Sartre, Jean-Paul. Theology. 1961-64. *153*
Heiman, Adolphus. Architecture. Baptists. First Baptist Church. Tennessee (Nashville). 1837-62. *1808*
Heinrich Mullers Pennsylvanischer Staatsbote (newspaper). American Revolution. Germany. Moravian Church. Muller, Johann Heinrich. Pennsylvania (Philadelphia). Printing. 1722-82. *3514*
Helmreich, Christian. Clergy. Letters. Lutheran Church. Nebraska (Weyerts). 1887-88. *3308*
Helmuth, Justus Henry Christian. German Americans. Hymnals. Lutheran Church. 1786-1813. *1955*
Henderlite, Rachel. Clergy. Consultation on Church Union. Personal narratives. Presbyterian Church, Southern. South. Women. 1945-77. *804*
Hendricken, Thomas F. Americanization. Catholic Church. French Canadians. Irish Americans. Massachusetts (Fall River). 1870's-85. *317*
Hennepin, Louis. Art. Catholic Church. Discovery and Exploration. Minnesota (Minneapolis). Missions and Missionaries. Mississippi River (Falls of St. Anthony). 1680-1980. *1556*
Hennessy, John. Catholic Church. Church Schools. Dubuque Diocese. Iowa. Irish Americans. 1866-1900. *3720*
Henrietta Hebrew Benevolent Society. California (San Bernardino). Confirmation. Judaism (Reform). Religious Education. 1891. *788*
Henry, Carl F. (review essay). Evangelicalism. Social justice. 1971. *2415*
Henry, Henry Abraham. California (Sacramento, San Francisco). Issacs, Samuel Meyer. Jews. Letters. Rabbis. Travel (accounts). 1858. *4106*
—. California (San Francisco). Judaism. Rabbis. 1857-69. *4107*
Henry, Patrick. Church and state. Clergy. Maury, James. Parsons' Cause. Personal narratives. Speeches, Addresses, etc. Virginia. 1758-65. *1080*
Hensley, George Went. Appalachia, southern. Pentecostal Holiness Church. Snakehandlers. 1909-73. *3522*
Herald der Wahrheit (newspaper). Amish. Clergy. Kansas (Reno County). Mast, Daniel E. 1886-1930. *3405*
Herberg, Will. Historiography. Religiosity. Sociology of Religion. 1790's-1970's. *39*
Herborn, University of. Clergy. Germany. Maryland. Otterbein, Philip Wilhelm. Pennsylvania. Theology. United Brethren in Christ. 1726-1813. *3666*
Herbs. Esteyneffer, Juan de *(Florilegio Medicinal)*. Indians. Jesuits. Medicine (practice of). Missions and Missionaries. Southwest. 1711. *1444*
—. Medicine (practice of). Mormons. Physicians. 1820-1979. *1459*
Heresy. Beach, John. Church of England. Clergy. Congregationalism. Connecticut. 1720-82. *3204*
—. Crapsey, Algernon Sidney. Episcopal Church, Protestant. Humanitarian Reform. New York (Rochester). St. Andrew's Church. Trials. 1879-1927. *3234*
—. Mormons. Pratt, Orson. Revelation. Young, Brigham. 1853-68. *3938*
Hermeneutics. Baptists. Poetry. Strong, Augustus Hopkins. Theology. 1897-1916. 1978. *1974*
—. Bible. Catholic Church. Periodicals. 1893-1908. *3812*
—. Bible. Congregationalism. Edwards, Jonathan. Massachusetts. 1720-58. *3149*
—. Bible. Darwinism. Episcopal Church, Protestant. Europe. Excommunication. MacQueary, Howard. Ohio (Canton). St. Paul's Church. Universalism. 1890-91. *3178*
—. Catholic Church. Colet, John. Episcopal Church, Protestant. Erasmus, Desiderius. More, Thomas. 1500-1975. *3167*
Heroic virtue. Canonization processes. Neumann, Saint John Nepomucene. Vatican Council II. 19c. 1962-65. *3835*
Herron, George David. Clergy. Congregationalism. Iowa College. National Christian Citizen League. Populism. Progressivism. Socialism. 1880's-1900. *2561*
Hersey, John. Abolition Movement. Methodist Church. Millenarianism. Perfectionism. 1786-1862. *3446*
Hertzberg, Arthur. Historians. Judaism (Conservative). Rabbis. 1980. *4167*
—. Judaism (Conservative). Personal narratives. Rabbis. 1940's-79. *4168*
Hertzberg, Steven. Cities. Gartner, Lloyd P. Gurock, Jeffrey S. Jews (review article). Raphael, Mark Lee. 1840-1979. *4150*
Herzberger, F. W. Evangelism. Lutheran Church. Missouri (St. Louis). 1899-1930. *3336*
Hess, Katie Charles. Mennonites. Pennsylvania. Personal narratives. Women. 1883-1978. *3356*
Hexter, Maurice B. Jews. Ohio (Cincinnati). Personal narratives. Social Work. United Jewish Charities. 1910's. *2508*
Heyer, John Christian Frederick. Illinois. Indiana. Keller, Ezra. Letters. Lutheranism. Missions and Missionaries. Missouri. ca 1820-40. *1614*
Heywood, Martha Spence. Frontier and Pioneer Life. Intellectuals. King, Hannah Tapfield. Mormons. Snow, Eliza Roxey. Utah. Women. 1850-70. *4045*
Hibbens, Ann. Erikson, Erik H. Excommunication. First Church. Massachusetts (Boston). Puritans. Rites and Ceremonies. 1640-41. 1960's-70's. *3610*
Hicks, Edward *(Peaceable Kingdom)*. Folk art. Friends, Society of. Painting. Pennsylvania (Bucks County). 1780-1849. *1857*
—. Friends, Society of. Symbolism in Art. 1825-49. *1851*
—. Iconography. ca 1824-44. *1870*
Higginson, John. Clergy (tenure). Massachusetts (Salem). Nicholet, Charles. Puritans. Social change. 1672-76. *3620*
High Schools *See also* Secondary Education.
—. Catholic Church. Colleges and Universities. Utah. 1875-1975. *624*
Higher Education *See also* Colleges and Universities.
—. Baldwin, Theron. Congregationalism. Presbyterianism. Society for the Promotion of Collegiate and Theological Education at the West. 1843-73. *629*
—. Baptists. Tennessee (Brownsville). West Tennessee Baptist Female College. Women. 1850-1910. *658*
—. Baptists, Southern. Carey, William. Missions and Missionaries. 1826-1976. *1755*
—. California. Church schools. 1850-74. *623*
—. Catholics. College teachers. Discrimination. 1960's-70's. *554*
—. Christianity. Corporations. Education, Finance. Social Darwinism. 1860-1930. *540*
—. Church and state. 1730's-1800. *525*
—. Church Schools. 1636-1978. *653*
—. Civil Rights. Political attitudes. 1968. *1390*
—. Crittenden, Lyman B. Jackson, Sheldon. McMillan, Duncan M. Montana. Presbyterian Church. 1869-1918. *598*
—. India. Missionaries. Protestant Churches. Social Gospel. 1883. *1680*
—. Jewish studies. Religious studies departments. 1972-74. *539*

—. Madison College. Methodist Protestant Church. Pennsylvania (Uniontown). 1851-58. *617*
—. Methodist Church. Ontario. Women. 19c. *3504*
—. Miller, Howard (review article). Presbyterian Church. 1707-1837. 1976. *760*
—. Religiosity. 1968-73. *562*
—. Religiosity. Students. 1970. *106*
Higher law (doctrine). Finney, Charles G. Ohio Antislavery Society. Political Participation. Revivalism. 1835-60. *2253*
Hildebrand, Bernhard (and family). Farms. Germans, Russian. Manitoba (Rosenthal). Mennonites. 1795-1915. *3407*
Hill, Marvin S. Assassination. Illinois (Carthage). Mormons. Oaks, Dallin H. Smith, Joseph. Trials (review article). 1844. 1977. *2126*
Hill, W. B. Adventists. Evangelism. Iowa. Minnesota. Personal Narratives. 1877. 1881. *1547*
Hill, Walter B. Appointments to office. Baptists. Georgia, University of (chancellor). Methodists. 1897-1901. *536*
Hillquit, Morris. Agnosticism. Ethnicity. Jews. New York City. Socialism. 1890's-1933. *1331*
Hillsdale College. Adrian College. Baptists, Free Will. Methodist Church, Wesleyan. Michigan. Oberlin College. Ohio. Olivet College. Social Reform. 1833-70. *741*
Hinchman, Morgan. Friends Asylum. Mental Illness. Moral insanity. Pennsylvania (Philadelphia). Trials. 1847. *1432*
Hindu renaissance. Besant, Annie. Blavatsky, Helena Petrovna. India. Theosophy. Vedanta. 1875-1900. *4283*
Hinduism *See also* Eastern Religions.
—. Buddhism. Teaching. Western Nations. 1969-75. *4287*
Hinman, Samuel D. Black Hills. Episcopal Church, Protestant. Indians. Missions and Missionaries. Sioux Indians. 1860-76. *1484*
Hirsch, Samuel. History. Judaism, Reform. Theology. 1815-89. *4209*
—. Judaism (Reform). 1866-89. *4210*
Hispanic Americans. Adolescents. Identity. Mexico. Puerto Rico. Religiosity. Whites. 1970's. *108*
—. Baptists. Catholic Church. Indiana (East Chicago, Gary). Theater. 1920-76. *1864*
—. Catholic Church. Colorado, southern. Death Carts. New Mexico, northern. Penitentes. 1860-90's. *3856*
—. Catholic Church. Folklore. New Mexico. Penitentes. Rites and Ceremonies. Social customs. 16c-20c. *3829*
Historians. American Friends Service Committee. Cadbury, Henry Joel (obituary). Friends, Society of. 1883-1974. *212*
—. American Revolution. Georgia. Hymns. Moravian Church. Neisser, George. New York. Pennsylvania, eastern. ca 1735-84. *197*
—. Arkansas. Brough, Charles Hillman. Mormons. 1890-1915. *224*
—. Baptists. Georgia. King, Spencer Bidwell, Jr. (obituary). 1930's-77. *199*
—. Bibliographies. Discovery and Exploration. Morison, Samuel Eliot (obituary). Puritans. 1887-1976. *233*
—. California. Franciscans. Geiger, Maynard J. (obituary). Mission Santa Barbara. 1901-77. *239*
—. Canada. Kerr, Donald Gordon Grady (tribute). 1938-76. *279*
—. Castañeda, Carlos Eduardo. Catholic church. Mexican Americans. Texas. 1896-1927. *169*
—. Civil religion. 1970's. *1160*
—. Clergy. Documents. Editors and Editing. Sparks, Jared. Unitarianism. Washington, George. 1815-30. *4076*
—. Congregationalism. Edwards, Jonathan *(History of the Work of Redemption).* 18c. 1976. *3156*
—. Congregationalism. Massachusetts (Boston). Old South Church. Prince, Thomas. 1718-58. *275*
—. Drury, Clifford M. Missions and Missionaries. Oregon. Presbyterian Church. Washington. 1928-74. *190*
—. Gingerich, Melvin (obituary). Mennonites. 1902-75. *214*
—. Hertzberg, Arthur. Judaism (Conservative). Rabbis. 1980. *4167*
—. Jews. Kenesseth Israel Synagogue. Korn, Bertram Wallace (obituary). Pennsylvania (Elkins Park). 1918-79. *248*
—. Letters. Mormons. Schisms. Wight, Lyman. Woodruff, Wilford. 1857-58. *4049*
—. Massachusetts (Salem). Racism. Tituba (Indian). Witchcraft. 1648-1953. *2191*
—. Methodism. 1974. *229*
—. Morison, Samuel Eliot (obituary). *New England Quarterly* (periodical). Puritans. 1928-76. *276*
Historic markers. Cemeteries. Congregation Beth El. Jews. Letters. Michigan (Detroit). 1850-1971. *4159*
Historic Peace Churches (meeting). Dunkards. Friends, Society of. Kansas (Newton). Krehbiel, H. P. Mennonites. Pacifism. 1935-36. *2663*
Historic Preservation. Construction. Friends, Society of. Meetinghouses. Rhode Island (Newport). 1657-1974. *1838*
Historical Sites and Parks *See also* Restorations.
—. Meetinghouses. New Hampshire (Cornish, Enfield). Shakers. 1793-1902. *1777*
Historical societies. Archives. Church membership. Methodology. Voting and Voting Behavior. 1776-1860. 1977. *1235*
—. Archives. Ecumenism. Pennsylvania (Philadelphia). Presbyterian Historical Society. 1852-1977. *260*
—. Baptists. Periodicals. South. 1950's-70's. *186*
Historiography *See also* Historians; Philosophy of History.
—. Abolition Movement. Great Britain. Protestantism. 18c-19c. *2499*
—. Ahlstrom, Sydney E. Christianity (review article). Handy, Robert T. Marty, Martin E. Race (issue). 16c-1978. *2743*
—. Ahlstrom, Sydney E. (review essay). 17c-1974. *4*
—. Allen, Ethan. Deism. Franklin, Benjamin. Jefferson, Thomas. Palmer, Elihu. 1750-1820. *4277*
—. American Revolution. 1760-89. 1970-80. *952*
—. American Revolution. 18c-20c. *9*
—. American Revolution. Constitutionalism. Law. Politics. 1775-83. 1790-1950. *961*
—. American Revolution. Millenarianism. Nationalism. Patriotism. Politics. 1740-89. *1347*
—. American Revolution. New Jersey. New York. Pennsylvania. Social conditions. 1680-1790's. 1960's-70's. *59*
—. American Revolution. Protestant Churches. 1775-82. *1396*
—. Americanization. Catholic Church. 1850-1973. *299*
—. Anthropology. Massachusetts (Salem). Psychology. Puritans. Witchcraft. 1691-92. *2187*
—. Archives. Bibliographies. California. Franciscans. Geiger, Maynard J. (obituary). Mission Santa Barbara. 1936-76. *240*
—. Archives. California. Franciscans. Geiger, Maynard J. (obituary). Mission Santa Barbara. 1901-77. *281*
—. Archives. California. Franciscans. Geiger, Maynard J. (obituary). Mission Santa Barbara. 1937-77. *238*
—. Arrington, Leonard J. Mormons. Personal Narratives. Western states. 20c. *171*
—. Arrington, Leonard J. (tribute). Bibliographies. Mormons. 1917-79. *277*
—. Attitudes. Hayes, Carlton J. H. Kohn, Hans. Nationalism. 1950's-60's. *1392*
—. Baptists. 1977. *254*
—. Baptists. Bibliographies. 1964-74. *3005*
—. Baptists. Rister, Carl Coke. Western States. 1920's-55. *223*
—. Barrett, Gwynn. Gibson, Walter Murray. Hawaii (Lanai). Mormons. 1859-64. 1972-78. *3945*
—. Bergson, Henri. Morality. Niebuhr, H. Richard. Troeltsch, Ernst. 1925-37. *255*
—. Bibliographies. Canada. Congregationalism. Lutheran Church. Methodist Church. Presbyterian Church. United Church of Canada. 1825-1973. *2892*
—. Bibliographies. Miller, Perry. 1933-77. *184*
—. Bibliographies. Mormons. Settlement. Utah. 1840-1976. *4046*
—. Bibliographies. Rhode Island. Williams, Roger. 17c-1972. *2911*
—. Bolton, Herbert Eugene. Catholic Church. Colonization. Missions and Missionaries. Southwest. Spain. 1917-79. *1489*
—. Bradford, William *(Of Plymouth Plantation).* Pilgrims. Plymouth Colony. Social Organization. 1630-50. *3153*
—. Bradford, William *(Of Plymouth Plantation).* Pilgrims. Plymouth Colony. Theology. 1630. *3126*
—. British North America. Christianity. Deviant Behavior. Government. Occult Sciences. 1600-1760. *2180*
—. Brodie, Fawn *(No Man Knows My History).* Mormons. Smith, Joseph. 19c. 1945-73. *3983*
—. Buchanan, James. Church and state. Federal Policy. Military. Mormons. Utah. 1857-58. *1073*
—. Canada. 17c-1973. 1945-69. *30*
—. Canada, western. Catholic Church. French Canadians. Migration, Internal. Quebec. 1870-1915. *3819*
—. Catholic Church. Clergy. Editors and Editing. *New Catholic Encyclopedia.* Polish Americans. Swastek, Joseph Vincent (obituary). 1913-77. *227*
—. Catholic Church. Education. 19c. *679*
—. Catholic Church. Foreign policy. 1898-1955. *1288*
—. Christianity. 1974. *181*
—. Christianity. Conference on Faith and History. 17c-1865. 1977. *237*
—. Church History. Latourette, Kenneth Scott. Sweet, William Warren. ca 1910-65. *175*
—. Church of England. 1775-1800. *3211*
—. Cities. Mormons. Social change. Utah. 1849-1970's. *4008*
—. Clergy. New England. Puritans. Women. 1668-1735. *936*
—. Constitutions. Founding fathers. Political Theory. Theology. 18c. *1405*
—. Doherty, Robert W. Methodology. Sociology of Religion. 1974. *264*
—. Feminization. Welter, Barbara. Women. 1820's-30's. 1970's. *920*
—. Friends, Society of. Tolles, Frederick Barnes (obituary). 1915-75. *213*
—. Herberg, Will. Religiosity. Sociology of Religion. 1790's-1970's. *39*
—. Hunter, Howard W. Jenson, Andrew. Lund, A. William. Lyon, T. Edgar. Mormons. Roberts, Brigham Henry. 1913-70. *226*
—. Indians. Lee, Jason. Methodism. Missions and Missionaries. Oregon. 1838-43. *1569*
—. Indian-White Relations. Missions and Missionaries. New England. Puritans. Theology. 17c-20c. *1641*
—. Intuition. New England. Parker, Theodore. Reason. Theology. Transcendentalism. Unitarianism. 18c-1860. 1920-79. *4074*
—. Jews. Scholarship. 1948-76. *207*
—. Lescarbot, Marc *(Histoire de la Nouvelle-France).* New France. 1606-30's. *2032*
—. Manuscripts. Mormons. Research. Young, Brigham. 19c-1978. *192*
—. Marshall, William I. Missions and Missionaries. Oregon. Whitman, Marcus. Winters, Herbert D. ca 1842-43. 1930. *1553*
—. Massachusetts. Merry Mount incident. Morton, Thomas. Pilgrims. 1625-1970's. *2050*
—. Massachusetts. Political Systems. Puritans. Suffrage. 1620-99. 1954-74. *1350*
—. Mather, Cotton *(Magnalia Christi Americana).* Puritans. Winthrop, John. 1702. *1966*
—. Miller, Perry. New England. Puritanism. 1620-1775. 1939-74. *258*
—. Morison, Samuel Eliot (obituary). Puritans. 1887-1976. *172*
—. Mormons. 1973. *191*
—. Mormons. Stereotypes. Women. 19c. 1976. *796*
—. Mormons. Young, Brigham. 1801-77. 1977. *4015*
—. Nationalism. 1735-83. 19c-1960's. *1416*
—. Populism. South. 1865-1900. *1281*
Historiography (Anglo-American). Arts. California. Catholic Church. Missions and Missionaries. Scholasticism. 1740's-1976. *1878*
Historiography, neoconservative. New England. Puritans. Social Organization. 17c. 1930's-60's. *3619*
Historiography (revisionist). Congregationalism. Edwards, Jonathan. Literature. 1758-1903. *3143*
History *See also* particular branches of history, e.g. business history, oral history, psychohistory, science, history of; Philosophy of History.
—. American Catholic Historical Association. Catholic Church. 1973. *173*
—. Art. Baptist Heritage Picture Set. Texas. 17c-20c. 1977. *211*
—. Art. Baptists. Mass Media. 17c-1977. *218*

—. Baptists, Southern. Newspapers. Research. 1977. *209*
—. Bible. Environment. Wilderness. 18c-20c. *36*
—. Bible. Israel. Mormons. Smith, Joseph Fielding. Snell, Heber C. Theology. 1937-52. *4035*
—. Bibliographies. Sociology. 1960-70. *120*
—. Catholic Church. Literature. Religious Orders. Women. 19c-1978. *868*
—. Christianity. Latourette, Kenneth Scott. 1884-1968. *261*
—. Christianity. Religious liberty. Rhode Island. Williams, Roger. 17c. *1047*
—. Einhorn, David. Judaism, Reform. Millenarianism. 1830-79. *4211*
—. Gingerich, Melvin (obituary). Mennonites. 1902-75. *243*
—. Hawthorne, Nathaniel. Novels. Puritan tradition. Social reform. Symbolism in Literature. 1825-63. *2019*
—. Hirsch, Samuel. Judaism, Reform. Theology. 1815-89. *4209*
—. Niebuhr, Reinhold. Theology. 1974. *2856*
—. Protestantism. Theology. 1900-70. *2850*
—. Social Psychology. 17c-20c. *228*
—. Sociology. -1973. *188*
History, comparative. Europe. Liberalism. Protestant Churches. Social Gospel. 1885-1975. *2395*
History Teaching. American Revolution. Cooke, Samuel. Langdon, Samuel. Mayhew, Jonathan. Sermons. West, Samuel. Witherspoon, John. 1750-76. 1975. *1406*
—. Audiovisual materials. Baptists. 1977. *249*
—. Baptists. 1977. *244*
—. Baptists. Films. Television. Videotape. 1977. *267*
Hitchcock, Ethan Allen. Attitudes. Diaries. Military Service. Unitarianism. 1836-54. *2656*
Hobomok (shaman). Indian-White Relations. Pilgrims. Plymouth Colony. Polytheism. Squanto (Wampanoag Indian). Theology. ca 1620-30. *3144*
Hocking, William Ernest. Diplomacy. Idealism. Philosophy. Political attitudes. 1918-66. *1368*
Hodge, Charles. Adger, John B. Dabney, Robert L. Mercersburg theology. Nevin, John W. Presbyterian Church. Sacramental controversy. 1845-75. *3551*
—. Bible (New Testament). Exegesis. Germany. Liberalism. Presbyterian Church. Princeton Theological Seminary. 1820-78. *3573*
—. Clergy. Diaries. Pennsylvania (Philadelphia). Presbyterian Church. Theology. 1819-20. *3534*
—. New Jersey (Princeton). Princeton University. Women. 1825-55. *857*
Hodge, Charles *(Systematic Theology)*. Divinity (issue). Jesus Christ. Nevin, John W. Presbyterian Church. Theology. 1872. *3581*
Hodges, Stephen. Hangings. Hodges, William. Iowa. Mormons (Danites). Murder. 1845. *3985*
Hodges, William. Hangings. Hodges, Stephen. Iowa. Mormons (Danites). Murder. 1845. *3985*
Hodur, Francis. Polish National Catholic Church. 1896-1907. *310*
Hofstadter, Richard *(Social Darwinism in American Thought)*. Baptists. Darwin, Charles. Evolution. Rauschenbusch, Walter. Social Gospel. Spencer, Herbert. 1879-1918. *3002*
Hogan Schism. Bibliographies. Catholic Church. Catholic University of America. Parsons, Wilfrid. Pennsylvania (Philadelphia). Schisms. 1785-1825. 1975. *3845*
Holdheim, Samuel. Geiger, Abraham. Judaism, Reform. Theology. 19c. *4221*
Holidays. Church and State. Church schools. Conscientious objection. Prayer. Public finance. Public Schools. Religious Liberty. Supreme Court. 1950-70's. *1112*
Holifield, E. Brooks. Lowrie, Ernest Benson. New England. Puritans (review article). Sacraments. Theology. Willard, Samuel. 16c-17c. 1974. *3637*
Holiness movement. Brethren in Christ. Canada. North Central States. 1910-50. *3435*
—. Brethren in Christ. Christianity. Education. Evangelism. Individualism. 1870-1910. *3421*
—. Brethren in Christ. Kansas. Mennonites. Methodism. 1870-1910. *3436*
—. Camp meetings. Church of the Nazarene. Louisiana (Mineral Springs). Methodist Church. National Camp Meeting Association for the Promotion of Holiness. 1860's-1926. *2891*
—. Camp meetings. Hudson Holiness Interdenominational Camp. Louisiana (Winn Parish). 1899-1977. *3292*
—. Church of God in Christ. Music. Negroes. New York (Binghamton). 1971-74. *3289*
—. Church of the Nazarene. 1908-75. *3288*
—. Feminism. Palmer, Phoebe. Wesley, Susanna. 1732-1973. *829*
—. Geographic distribution. 1865-1975. *3290*
—. Inskip, John S. Inskip, Martha Jane. Methodist Church. Revivals. Women. 1836-90. *3448*
—. Methodist Church. Revivals. 1835-1920. *3291*
Holiness Movement Church. Canada. Evangelism. Horner, Ralph Cecil. Methodist Church. 1887-1921. *3500*
—. Canada. Evangelism. Horner, Ralph Cecil. Methodist Church. 1887-1921. *3501*
Holley, Horace. Colleges and Universities (administration). Desha, Joseph. Kentucky. Politics. Presbyterians. State government. Transylvania College. Unitarianism. 1818-27. *537*
Holmes, Oliver Wendell *(Elsie Venner)*. Literature. New England. Original Sin. 1861. *2024*
Holt, Benjamin M. Lutheran Church. Minnesota. Personal narratives. 1882-1974. *3309*
Holy Childhood Indian School Printery. Education. Engelhardt, Zephyrin. Franciscans. Indians. Michigan (Harbor Springs). Printing. 1894-1913. *1584*
Holy Cross Abbey. Trappists. Virginia (Shenandoah Valley). Wormeley Manor. 1744-1980. *3890*
Holy Cross Church. Assimilation. Catholic Church. Connecticut (New Britain). Polish Americans. 1928-76. *3693*
Holy Cross College. Catholic Church. Diaries. Healy, James A. Massachusetts (Worcester). Religious Education. 1849. *640*
Holy Cross Mission. Alaska. Catholic Church. Indians. Jesuits. Missions and Missionaries. Sisters of St. Ann. Yukon River, lower. 1887-1956. *1615*
Holy Family Slovak Parish. Catholic Church. New York City (Brooklyn). Slovak Americans. 1905-80. *3869*
Holy Ghost and Us Society. Communalism. *Kingdom Come, Ark of the Holy Ghost and US Society* (vessel). Nova Scotia. Sanford, Frank. Sects, Religious. Shipwrecks. 1910-48. *4261*
Holy Trinity Episcopal Church. Architecture, Gothic Revival. Churches. Episcopal Church, Protestant. Restorations. Tennessee (Nashville). 1840's-1970's. *1801*
Holy Trinity Parish. Lutheran Church (Evangelical). Pennsylvania (Lancaster). 1730-1980. *3306*
Homans, Rockland Tyng. Christian Unity Foundation. Ecumenism. Episcopal Church, Protestant. Huntington, William Reed. 1886-1942. *454*
Home Mission Board. Baptists, Southern. Evangelism. Home Mission Board. 1845-1973. *1544*
Home Missionary Society. Children's Aid Society. Family. Foster care. Pennsylvania (Philadelphia). Protestantism. 1880-1905. *2504*
Home of Peace Jewish Cemetery. California (Los Angeles; Chavez Ravine). Cemeteries. Hebrew Benevolent Society of Los Angeles. Judaism. Photographs. 1855-1910. *4161*
Homicide. *See* Murder.
Homosexuality. California. Catholic Church. Proposition 6 (1978). Public schools. Referendum. Teachers. 1978. *1320*
—. California (Los Angeles). 1970-76. *2821*
—. Protestant Churches. Theology. 1970's. *815*
Honcharenko, Agapius. *Alaska Herald* (newspaper). Clergy. Far Western States. Orthodox Eastern Church, Greek. Ukrainian Americans. 1832-1916. *2805*
Honeyman, David. *Challenger* (vessel). Nova Scotia (Halifax). Oceanography. 1872-76. *2329*
Hooker, Edward P. Colleges and Universities. Congregationalism. Florida (Winter Park). Rollins College. 1885-1900. *678*
Hooker, Thomas. Assurance, doctrine of. New England. Puritans. Theology. 1630-60. *3644*
—. Congregationalism. Exiles. Great Britain. Netherlands. New England. Theology. 1631-33. *3650*
—. Connecticut. Constitutional Law. Government. Puritans. 1635-39. *3603*
—. Conversion. Preparationism. Puritans. Ramus, Petrus. Shepard, Thomas. Theology. 1608-49. *3643*
—. Mather, Cotton. Puritans. Rhetoric. Winthrop, John. 17c. *1965*
Hoover, Herbert C. Attitudes. Church and state. Civil Religion. Protestantism. 1928-32. *1167*
—. Elections (presidential). Racism. Smith, Al. Tennessee, west. 1928. *1280*
—. Friends, Society of. Military. 1929-33. *2705*
—. Johnson, Lyndon B. Nixon, Richard M. Protestant ethic. Public welfare. Rhetoric. Roosevelt, Franklin D. Weber, Max. 1905-79. *348*
—. Political Campaigns (presidential). Smith, Al. Tennessee, west. 1928. *1279*
Hopedale Community. Attitudes. Ballou, Adin Augustus. Massachusetts (Milford). Utopias. 1830-42. *427*
—. Ballou, Adin Augustus. Draper, E. D. Massachusetts (Milford). Utopias. 1824-56. *388*
Hopkins, Charles Howard. Ecumenism. Federal Council of the Churches of Christ in America. Politics. Protestant Churches. Social gospel. 1880-1908. *487*
Hopkins, Gerard Manley. Ecology. Humanities. Jesuits. Poetry. Science. ca 1840-70's. *3701*
Hopkins, John Henry. Bishops. Civil War. Episcopal Church, Protestant. 1861-65. *445*
Hopkins, Samuel. African Society. Colonization. Congregationalism. Freedmen. Rhode Island (Providence). Sierra Leone. 1789-95. *2459*
—. American Revolution. Antislavery Sentiments. Congregationalism. Rhode Island (Newport). ca 1770-1803. *2464*
—. Congregationalism. Edwards, Jonathan. New Divinity (doctrines). New England. Social reform. Theology. 1730-1803. *2373*
Horner, Ralph Cecil. Canada. Evangelism. Holiness Movement Church. Methodist Church. 1887-1921. *3500*
—. Canada. Evangelism. Holiness Movement Church. Methodist Church. 1887-1921. *3501*
Horologium Achaz (scientific device). Astronomy. Pennsylvania Germans. Pietism. Witt, Christopher. 1578-1895. *2349*
Horoscopes. Astrology. California (San Francisco Bay Area). Counter culture. 1970's. *2212*
Horr, George. Anti-imperialism. Baptists, American. Spanish-American War. Vietnam War. *Watchman*. 1876-1974. *2698*
Horstman, Otto K. Evangelism. Indiana (Shelbyville). Lutheran Church, Evangelical. Missions and Missionaries. Personal narratives. 1934. *1551*
Hospitals. Alaska (Juneau). Catholic Church. Sisters of St. Ann. 1886-1968. *3757*
—. Alexian Brothers. Bernard, Alexius. Catholic Church. German Americans. Missouri (St. Louis). Tollig, Paulus. 1869-1980. *1456*
—. Asylums. Catholic Church. Illinois (Chicago). Schools. Wisconsin (Milwaukee). 19c. *3886*
—. Catholic Church. Colorado. Diaries. Mallon, Catherine. New Mexico (Santa Fe). Sisters of Charity. 1865-1901. *1454*
—. Catholic Church. Hôtel-Dieu. Indian-White Relations. Quebec. 1635-98. *1446*
—. Christ Church Hospital. Episcopal Church, Protestant. Kearsley, John. Pennsylvania (Philadelphia). Women. 1778-1976. *1455*
—. Doukhobors. Galicians. Lake Geneva Mission. Missions and Missionaries. Presbyterian Church. Saskatchewan (Wakaw). 1903-42. *1492*
Hostetler, Joseph. Disciples of Christ. Dunkards. Indiana. Restoration movement. Revivals. 1800-27. *3104*
Hôtel-Dieu. Catholic Church. Hospitals. Indian-White Relations. Quebec. 1635-98. *1446*
House of Burgesses. Church Government. Church of England. Petitions. Public policy. Virginia. 1700-75. *999*
House of Representatives *See also* Legislation; Senate.
—. Church and state. Feminism. Polygamy. Roberts, Brigham Henry. Utah. 1898-1900. *1133*
Howard College. Alabama. Baptists. Davis, Harwell G. 1882-1973. *3092*
Howell, Jane. "Angel Dancers". Communalism. Folklore. Huntsman, Manson T. New Jersey (Woodcliff). Rumors. Sects, Religious. 1890-1920. *389*
Howgill, Francis. Friends, Society of. New England. Persecution. Puritans. ca 1650-60. *1027*

Hudson Holiness Interdenominational Camp. Camp meetings. Holiness Movement. Louisiana (Winn Parish). 1899-1977. *3292*
Hudson, Winthrop. Baptists. Clergy. Liberalism. Rauschenbusch, Walter. Social theory. Theology. 1880-1978. *2351*
Hudson's Bay Company. Canada. Capitalism. Fur trade. Protestantism. Scottish Canadians. 18c-1970's. *377*
—. Canada, western. Church of England. Hunter, James. Missions and Missionaries. 1844-64. *1603*
—. Catholic Church. Indians. Methodist Church. Missions and Missionaries. Oregon. Presbyterian Church. 1830's - 1840's. *1482*
—. Church Missionary Society. Church of England. Eskimos. Missionaries. Northwest Territories (Baffin Island). Peck, E. J. Trade. 1894-1913. *1660*
—. Church Missionary Society. Church of England. Missions and Missionaries. Ontario (Moosonee). Vincent, Thomas. 1835-1910. *1638*
—. Clergy. Columbia River. Congregationalism. Fort Vancouver. Hawaiians. Kaulehelehe, William R. Washington. 1845-69. *3128*
—. Episcopal Church, Protestant. Indians. Missions and Missionaries. Pacific Northwest. 1825-75. *1555*
Hughes, John. Attitudes. Brownson, Orestes A. Catholic Church. Civil War. McMaster, James. 1850-65. *2692*
—. Bishops. Catholic Church. Colombia (Bogotá). Letters. Mosquera, Manuel José. New York City. 1853. *3762*
Hughes, John Jay. Anglican communion. Catholic Church. Ecumenism. Religious Orders. -1973. *493*
Hughes, Philip. American Revolution. Church of England. Loyalists. Maryland. 1767-77. *1323*
Huguenots. American Revolution. Canada. France. Settlement. USA. Whaling industry and Trade. 17c-20c. *3251*
—. Aristocracy. Clergy. French Americans. Religious liberty. Richebourg, Claude Phillipe de. 1680-1719. *3250*
—. Colonization. Florida (Campbell Town). Great Britain. West Florida. 1763-70. *3254*
—. France. 16c-1978. *3255*
—. France. New France. 1541-1760. *3252*
—. Genealogy. Immigration. 16c-20c. *3253*
Huidekoper, Frederick. Christianity. Judaism. Meadville Theological School. Pennsylvania. Seminaries. Unitarianism. 1834-92. *4086*
Huidekoper, Harm Jan. Christian Connection (church). Meadville Theological School. Pennsylvania (Meadville). Unitarianism. 1844-56. *762*
Hull House. Addams, Jane. Education. Friends, Society of. Ideology. Illinois (Chicago). Women. 1875-1930. *911*
Human nature. Christianity. Kinsey, Alfred C. Sexual behavior. 1948-54. *2749*
—. Democracy. Finney, Charles G. Revivalism. Social Theory. 1820-30. *2268*
Human potential movement. Alienation. Christianity. Converts. Cults. Social indicators. 1960's-70's. *143*
Human Relations *See also* Discrimination; Family; Labor; Marriage; Race Relations.
—. Blackthink. Church and Social Problems. Poor. 1963-75. *2537*
—. Catholic Church. Judaism (Orthodox). Protestant Churches. Rhode Island. 18c. *2087*
—. Colleges and Universities. Congregationalism. Dwight, Timothy. Stiles, Ezra. Yale University. 1778-95. *706*
—. Rhode Island. Social Theory. Williams, Roger. 1643-76. *2826*
Human rights. Catholic Church. Clergy. New York City. Social progress. Varela, Félix. 1823-53. *2357*
—. Catholic Worker Movement. Equality. Public policy. 1933-78. *2436*
Humanism. Douglas, William O. Presbyterian Church. Religious liberty. Supreme Court. 1915-80. *1128*
—. Friends, Society of. Intellectuals. Penn, William. Radicals and Radicalism. Social reform. 1650-1700. *2353*
—. Indians. More, Thomas *(Utopia)*. Rhode Island (Narragansett). Utopias. Williams, Roger *(A Key into the Language of America)*. 1640's. *2938*
—. Mather, Cotton *(Magnalia Christi Americana)*. Puritans. Renaissance. Rhetoric. 1702. *1996*
Humanitarian Reform. Crapsey, Algernon Sidney. Episcopal Church, Protestant. Heresy. New York (Rochester). St. Andrew's Church. Trials. 1879-1927. *3234*
Humanitarianism. Channing, William Ellery. Great Britain. Irresistible compassion. Theology. ca 1660-19c. *2851*
Humanities *See also* such subjects as Art, Literature, Music, Philosophy, etc.
—. Ecology. Hopkins, Gerard Manley. Jesuits. Poetry. Science. ca 1840-70's. *3701*
Humility. Mennonites. 1840-80. *3402*
Humor *See also* Satire.
—. Adventists. California. Irish Americans. Letters. Loma Linda University. Magan, Percy Tilson. 1918-34. *1435*
—. *Book of Common Worship*. Lampton, William J. Poetry. Presbyterian Church, Southern. Rites and Ceremonies. VanDyke, Henry. 1906. *3557*
—. Clergy. Folklore. Georgia, west-central. Protestantism. 19c-20c. *2839*
—. Illustration. Mormons. Novels. Periodicals. 1850-60. *2004*
—. Parody. Popular Culture. 1976. *2052*
Humphrey, James K. Adventists. First Harlem Church. Negroes. New York City. Schisms. Utopia Park. 1920's-30's. *2143*
Hungarian Americans. Charities. Ecumenism. Judaism (Reform). Rabbis. Wise, Stephen Samuel. World War II. Zionism. 1890's-1949. *4229*
Hungerford, B. F. Baptists. Civil War. Diaries. Kentucky. 1863-66. *2632*
Hunt, Edward. Church of England. Jacobitism. Keith, William. Patriotism. Pennsylvania. 1720. *1130*
Hunter, Howard W. Historiography. Jenson, Andrew. Lund, A. William. Lyon, T. Edgar. Mormons. Roberts, Brigham Henry. 1913-70. *226*
Hunter, James. Canada, western. Church of England. Hudson's Bay Company. Missions and Missionaries. 1844-64. *1603*
Huntington, Daniel. Art. Bunyan, John *(Pilgrim's Progress)*. *Mercy's Dream* (painting). National characteristics. Protestantism. 1678. 1841-70. *1856*
Huntington, Frederick (and family). Bishops. Episcopal Church, Protestant. New York. Social reform. Theology. Women. 1869-1904. *3213*
Huntington, James Otis Sargent. Episcopal Church, Protestant. Monasticism. Order of the Holy Cross. Single tax. Social reform. 1878-90. *2430*
Huntington, William Reed. Christian Unity Foundation. Ecumenism. Episcopal Church, Protestant. Homans, Rockland Tyng. 1886-1942. *454*
Huntsman, Manson T. "Angel Dancers". Communalism. Folklore. Howell, Jane. New Jersey (Woodcliff). Rumors. Sects, Religious. 1890-1920. *389*
Hurford, Grace Gibberd. Canada. China. Missions and Missionaries. Personal narratives. Teaching. World War II. 1928-45. *1711*
Hutchinson, Anne. Antinomian Controversy. Church and state. Massachusetts. Puritans. Social Organization. Trials. Women. 1637. *1135*
—. Antinomian Controversy. Cotton, John. Massachusetts (Boston). Puritans. 1636. *3652*
—. Antinomian controversy. Feminism. Massachusetts. 1630-43. *867*
—. Antinomian controversy. Massachusetts (Boston). Puritans. Trials. Winthrop, John. 1634-38. *3641*
—. Antinomianism. Cotton, John. Massachusetts. Sermons. Shepard, Thomas. Theology. 1630's. *3648*
—. Antinomianism. Language. Massachusetts. Puritans. Trials. 1636-38. *3609*
—. Bradstreet, Anne. Literature. Massachusetts. Puritans. Social change. Theology. Women. 1630's-70's. *865*
Hutchinson, Mathias. Friends, Society of. Frontier and Pioneer Life. New York, western. Ontario. Pennsylvania, central. Travel (accounts). 1819-20. *3280*
Hutchison, William R. (review article). Modernism. Protestantism. 19c-1976. *2872*
Hutterites. Agriculture. Communalism. Education. German Americans. Pacific Northwest. Pacifism. 20c. *392*
—. Agriculture. Lifestyles. North America. Social Customs. Technological innovation. 18c-20c. *3349*
—. Alberta. Assimilation. Education. 1920-70. *534*
—. Alberta. Nativism. Settlement. 1918-72. *2089*
—. Alberta (Edmonton). Public Opinion. Social customs. 1966-75. *3404*
—. Amish. Doukhobors. Mennonites. Molokans. North America. ca 1650-1977. *2769*
—. Amish, Old Order. Mennonites. Social change. ca 1930-77. *3357*
—. Amish, Old Order. Minorities. Research. 1977. *3363*
—. Behavior. Communalism. Social theory. ca 1650-1977. *382*
—. Camp Funston. Conscientious objectors. Diaries. Kansas. Waldner, Jakob. World War I. 1917-18. *2690*
—. Canada. Communalism. Lifestyles. South Dakota. 1874-1975. *403*
—. Canada. Communes. USA. 1870's-1970. *412*
—. Clark, Bertha W. Pacifism. Social change. South Dakota. 1921. *3385*
—. Communalism. Equal opportunity. Leadership. Population. Prairie Provinces. Social Organization. Succession. 1940's-70's. *387*
—. Communalism. Frontier and Pioneer Life. Western states. 1874-1977. *429*
—. Compulsory Education. Legislation. South Dakota. Values. 1700-1970's. *659*
—. Discrimination. Ethnicity. Legislation. Prairie Provinces. Provincial government. 1960's-79. *1099*
Hyatt, Harry Midddleton. Collectors and Collecting. Folklore. Illinois (Adams County). Negroes. Small, Minnie Hyatt. South. Witchcraft. 1920-78. *2190*
Hyde, Orson. Fund raising. Illinois (Nauvoo). Mormons. Northeastern or North Atlantic States. Tabernacle project. 1845-46. *4048*
Hydrotherapy. Adventists. Jackson, James Caleb. Medical reform. New York (Dansville). White, Ellen G. 1864-65. *1451*
Hymnals. Amish, Old Order. Betz, Hans. German language. 16c-20c. *1946*
—. Attitudes. New England. Puritans. Regular Singing movement. 1720's. *1933*
—. Baptists. Singing. 1650-1850. *1945*
—. Billings, William. Music. Poetry. Read, Daniel. Watts, Isaac. 1761-85. *1920*
—. Composers. Music. New England. Publishers and publishing. Thomas, Isaiah. 1784-19c. *1936*
—. Episcopal Church, Protestant. Folk Songs. 1970-78. *1906*
—. German Americans. Helmuth, Justus Henry Christian. Lutheran Church. 1786-1813. *1955*
—. Lutheran Church (Hauge's Synod, Norwegian Synod). Lutheran Church in America, Norwegian. Norwegian Americans. Youth. 1878-1916. *1915*
—. Methodist Church. 1930-34. 1960-64. *1928*
Hymnody. Episcopal Church, Protestant. 1640-1978. *1957*
Hymns. Adventists. Poetry. Smith, Annie Rebekah. 1850's. *1926*
—. American Revolution. Georgia. Historians. Moravian Church. Neisser, George. New York. Pennsylvania, eastern. ca 1735-84. *197*
—. Appalachia. Folklore. 18c-20c. *1927*
—. Archival catalogs and inventories. Emmett, Daniel. Minstrel Shows. Negroes. Ohio Historical Society. Sermons. 1838-96. 1976. *2064*
—. Christianity. Gerhardt, Paul. Sacred fire. Symbolism in Literature. Translating and Interpreting. Wesley, John. 1760's-1930's. *1952*
—. Civil Religion. Myths and Symbols. National Self-image. 1800-1916. *1950*
—. Composers. Mennonites. ca 1720-1860. *1908*
—. Decker, Mahonri M. Mormons. Utah (Parowan). 1919. *1921*
—. Education. France. Neau, Elias. New York. Protestant Churches. Slaves. ca 1689-1722. *1913*
—. Mormons. Smith, Emma. 1835. *1953*
—. Music. Schools. Singing. 1775-1820. *1951*
Hypnotism. Animal magnetism. Mesmerism. Mormons. 19c. *2303*
—. Eddy, Mary Baker. New England. Psychiatry. Quimby, Phineas Parkhurst. 1820's-66. *1442*

I

I AM sect. Ballard, Edna. Ballard, Guy. Occult Sciences. 1930's-75. *4273*
Iceland. Brúnum, Eiríkur á. Laxness, Halldór *(Paradise Reclaimed)*. Mormons. Novels. 1870-1900. 1960. *2075*
Iconography. Catholic Church. Design. Folk art. Manuscripts. New Mexico. 16c-17c. *1858*
—. Christianity. Cole, Thomas. Painting. Romanticism. 1830's-40's. *1865*
—. Congregationalism. Covenant theology. Theology. Tombstones. Vermont (Grafton, Rockingham). 1770-1803. *1896*
—. Friends, Society of. Hicks, Edward *(Peaceable Kingdom)*. ca 1824-44. *1870*
—. New England. Poetry. Puritans. Sermons. Tombstones. 17c. *1977*
Idaho *See also* Far Western States.
—. Agriculture. Mormons. Settlement. Snake River. 1880-1914. *3940*
—. Christianity. Converts. Murder. Orchard, Harry. 1899-1906. *2760*
—. McBeth, Sue L. Missions and Missionaries. Nez Percé Indians. Presbyterian Church. 1874. *1591*
—. Mormons. Political Attitudes. Voting and Voting Behavior. 1880's. *1273*
Idaho (Cassia County). Mormons. Settlement. 1873-1921. *3930*
Idaho (Moscow). Correspondence courses. New Thought movement. Psychiana (religion). Robinson, Frank Bruce. 1929-48. *4260*
Idaho (Paris). Cooperatives. Mormons. Rural Settlements. 1869-96. *360*
Idaho, southern. Annexation. Church and state. Legislation. Mormons. Nevada. Stewart, William. Suffrage. 1887-88. *1089*
Ideal States. *See* Utopias.
Idealism. Churches. LaFarge, John. New York City. Painting. 1877-88. *1898*
—. Diplomacy. Hocking, William Ernest. Philosophy. Political attitudes. 1918-66. *1368*
—. Evans, Warren Felt. Mental healing. Mysticism. New Thought Movement. Romanticism. 1864-89. *1460*
—. National characteristics. Pluralism. Puritan tradition. 1620's-1940's. *1*
Identity. Adolescents. Hispanic Americans. Mexico. Puerto Rico. Religiosity. Whites. 1970's. *108*
—. Artisans. Methodism. Morality. Pennsylvania (Philadelphia). Social customs. Work ethic. Working Class. 1820-50. *3479*
—. Autobiography. Congregationalism. Edwards, Jonathan. Theology. 1729-58. *3152*
—. Catholic Church. Documents. National Catholic Welfare Council. Vatican. 1922. *3803*
—. Dickinson, Emily. Intellectual history. Myths and Symbols. Poetry. Puritanism. Transcendentalism. Women. 1860's. *51*
—. Feminism. Social Reform. 1820's-60. *884*
—. Group survival. Ideology. Judaism (Reform). 1800-1975. *4212*
—. Lutheran Church. Theology. 18c-20c. *3326*
—. Mormons. Utah. Westward Movement. 1846-69. *3999*
Ideology. Aberhart, William. Alberta. Provincial Government. Social Credit Party. Theology. 1935-43. *1365*
—. Addams, Jane. Education. Friends, Society of. Hull House. Illinois (Chicago). Women. 1875-1930. *911*
—. Allen, Thomas ("Vindication"). American Revolution. Clergy. Congregationalism. Constitutions, State. Massachusetts (Berkshire County). 1778. *1371*
—. American Revolution. American Revolution. Cleaveland, John. Congregationalism. Daily life. Great Awakening. Jedrey, Christopher M. (review article). Massachusetts (Chebacco). New Lights. 1740-79. *2241*
—. American Revolution. Arendt, Hannah. Church and state. ca 1775-83. *1032*
—. American Revolution. Literature. Puritans. 1775-83. 19c. *1344*
—. Anti-Catholicism. Antislavery sentiments. Massachusetts (Boston). Riots. Social Classes. Ursulines. 1834-35. *2109*
—. Anti-Catholicism. Colonization. Great Britain. Ireland. North America. Protestantism. ca 1550-1600. *2086*
—. Authority. Cults. 1945-74. *4274*
—. Black nationalism. Crummell, Alexander. DuBois, W. E. B. Episcopal Church, Protestant. Ferris, William H. 1819-1898. *2424*
—. British Empire. Catholic Church. Imperialism. Quebec. 19c-20c. *1411*
—. Canada. King, William Lyon Mackenzie. Liberal Party. Politics. Protestantism. Social Classes. 1900-50. *1421*
—. Capitalism. Management. Political Science. Protestantism. Theology. Weber, Max. 16c-1974. *376*
—. Civil religion. Democracy. Political institutions. Puritan tradition. 17c-20c. *1150*
—. Clergy, dissident. Leadership. Protestant Churches. -1973. *2439*
—. Consensus. National Characteristics. Puritans. 1630-1865. *1345*
—. Conservatism. Puritanism. 17c. *1361*
—. Declaration of Independence. Radicals and Radicalism. Utopias. 1730's-1890's. *426*
—. Equal Rights Amendment. Women. 1933-75. *810*
—. Family. Government. Massachusetts. Puritans. Social cohesion. 1630-85. *3606*
—. Group survival. Identity. Judaism (Reform). 1800-1975. *4212*
—. Middle Classes. Pluralism. Secularization. Social Change. 17c-20c. *12*
Illinois *See also* North Central States.
—. Academic Freedom. Baptists. Foster, George Burman. Theology. University of Chicago Divinity School. 1895-1918. *557*
—. Addams, Jane. Dudzik, Mary Theresa. Franciscan Sisters of Chicago. Polish Americans. Social Work. Women. 1860-1918. *2511*
—. Adventists. Jones, Alonzo Trevier. Religious liberty. Sabbath. World's Columbian Exposition (Chicago, 1893). 1893. *2280*
—. Agriculture. Amish. Economic conditions. Social organization. 1960-72. *3428*
—. Anti-Catholicism. Chicago *Tribune* (newspaper). Editors and Editing. Political Parties. 1853-61. *2112*
—. Arvedson, Peter. Episcopal Church, Protestant. Swedish Americans. 1822-80. *1600*
—. Attitudes. Children. Civil religion. 1970's. *1187*
—. Bishop Hill Colony. Engstrand, Stuart (review article). Jansson, Erik H. 1846-50. 20c. *2083*
—. Bishop Hill Colony. Immigrants. Janssonists. Swedish Americans. Utopias. 1846-60. *393*
—. Bishop Hill Colony. Janssonists. Letters. Swedish Americans. 1847. *416*
—. Bishops. Catholic Church. Chicago Diocese. Clergy. Duggan, James. McMullen, John. Succession. 1865-81. *3742*
—. Catholic Church. Compulsory education. Edwards Law (Illinois, 1889). Ethnic Groups. Private schools. Public schools. State Politics. 1889-93. *551*
—. Congregationalism. Guidebooks. Immigration. Thomas, Robert D. *(Hanes Cymry America)*. Welsh Americans. 19c. *3119*
—. Emigration. Janssonists. Sects, Religious. Social Classes. Sweden. 1845-47. *2620*
—. Heyer, John Christian Frederick. Indiana. Keller, Ezra. Letters. Lutheranism. Missions and Missionaries. Missouri. ca 1820-40. *1614*
Illinois (Adams County). Collectors and Collecting. Folklore. Hyatt, Harry Midddleton. Negroes. Small, Minnie Hyatt. South. Witchcraft. 1920-78. *2190*
Illinois (Carthage). Assassination. Hill, Marvin S. Mormons. Oaks, Dallin H. Smith, Joseph. Trials (review article). 1844. 1977. *2126*
Illinois (Chicago). Addams, Jane. Education. Friends, Society of. Hull House. Ideology. Women. 1875-1930. *911*
—. Art. Presbyterian Church. Second Presbyterian Church. Stained glass windows. 1872-74. *1855*
—. Asylums. Catholic Church. Hospitals. Schools. Wisconsin (Milwaukee). 19c. *3886*
—. Barzynski, Wincenty. Catholic Church. Polish Roman Catholic Union. St. Stanislaus Kortka Church. Texas. 1838-99. *3678*
—. Business. Elites. 1830-1930. *2608*
—. Catholic Church. Church Schools. Damen, Arnold. Fund raising. 1840-90. *773*
—. Catholic Church. Church Schools. Ethnic Groups. Sanders, James W. (review article). 1833-1965. 1977. *614*
—. Catholic Church. City Life. Neighborhoods. 1900-30. *3771*
—. Catholic Church. Immigration. Mexican Americans. Social Conditions. 1910's-20's. *3833*
—. Church membership. Ethnicity. Jews. Protestants. 1960's-70's. *121*
—. Clergy (dismissal). Episcopal Church, Protestant. Pamphlets. Rites and Ceremonies. Swope, Cornelius E. Trinity Church. Unonius, Gustaf. 1850-51. *3179*
—. Daily life. Evangelism. Methodist Church. Whitefield, Henry. 1833-71. *1508*
—. Evangelism. Manitoba (Winnipeg). Mennonites. 1866-1977. *3361*
—. Florida (Estero). Koreshan Unity. Millenarianism. Teed, Cyrus Read. Utopias. 1886-1903. *396*
—. Judaism. Socialization. 1974. *4110*
Illinois (Galesburg). Authority. Bishops. Church and State. Civil War. Episcopal Church, Protestant. Grace Church. 1864-66. *1218*
Illinois (Hahlen, Nashville). Clergy. Concordia Seminary. Lutheran Church (Missouri Synod). Personal narratives. St. Peter's Lutheran Church. Scharlemann, Ernst K. Seminaries. 1905-18. *3335*
Illinois (Jacksonville). Batchelder, John. Episcopal Church, Protestant. Frontier and Pioneer Life. Trinity Church. 1830-40. *3192*
Illinois (Nauvoo). Architecture. Mormons. Temples. Utah. Weeks, William. 1840's-1900. *1758*
—. Baptism. Mormons. Theology. 1830-43. *4028*
—. Bidamon, Emma Smith. Bidamon, Lewis C. Marriage. Mormons. Women. 1842-80. *3931*
—. Bidamon, Emma Smith. Mormons. Property. Schisms. Smith, Joseph. Women. Women. Young, Brigham. 1832-79. *3932*
—. Boys. Mormons. Police protection. Whistling and Whittling Brigade. 1845. *4014*
—. City charters. Mormons. 1839-41. *3995*
—. City planning. Mormons. 1840's. *3959*
—. Clayton, William. Great Britain (Manchester). Immigration. Letters. Mormons. 1840. *3924*
—. Daily life. Diaries. Jacobs, Zina Diantha Huntington. Mormons. Women. 1844-45. *3935*
—. Deity. Mormons. Sermons. Smith, Joseph (King Follett Discourse). Theology. 1844. *3976*
—. Diaries. Fielding, Joseph. Mormons. 1844-46. *3958*
—. Diaries. Laub, George. Mormons. Smith, Joseph. Young, Brigham. 1845-46. *3961*
—. Diaries. Mormons. Snow, Eliza Roxey. Women. 1842-44. *4044*
—. Economic growth. Mississippi River. Mormons. Steamboats. 1839-46. *367*
—. Family. Mormons. New York. Young, Brigham. 1824-45. *861*
—. Fund raising. Hyde, Orson. Mormons. Northeastern or North Atlantic States. Tabernacle project. 1845-46. *4048*
—. Jones, Dan. *Maid of Iowa* (vessel). Mormons. Smith, Joseph. Steamboats. 1843-45. *346*
—. Kimball, Heber C. (and family). Mormons. 1839-46. *3997*
—. Kimball, Vilate. Letters. Mormons. Murder. Smith, Joseph. Women. 1844. *3963*
—. Lyon, T. Edgar. Mormons. Oral history. Smith, Hyrum. Smith, Joseph. 1840's-1978. *4005*
—. Mormons. 1842-46. *3974*
—. Mormons. Religiosity. Social stability. 1833-46. *3981*
—. Mormons. Rites and Ceremonies. Smith, Joseph. Temples. 1841-45. *1766*
—. Mormons. Sermons. Smith, Joseph (King Follett Discourse). Theology. 1844-1978. *3947*
—. Mormons. Theology. 1839-46. *4004*
Illinois (New Cluny). Benedictines. Immigrants. Missions and Missionaries. Monastic observance. Moosmüller, Oswald. 1832-1901. *3816*
Illinois (New Design). Badgley, David. Baptists. Pioneers. 1769-1824. *3096*
Illinois (Paxton). Augustana College and Theological Seminary. Lutheran Church (Augustana Synod). Osborn, William H. Railroads. Swedish Americans. 1853-73. *3321*
Illinois (Peoria). Breweries. Leisy family. Mennonites. 1884-1950. *356*
—. Chase, Philander. Episcopal Church, Protestant. Jubilee College. 1840-62. *730*
Illinois (Peoria County). Documents. Episcopal Church, Protestant. Excavations. Jubilee College. 1839-1979. *770*
Illinois (Rock Island). Augustana Book Concern. Lutheran Church (Augustana Synod). 1850-1967. *357*

—. Augustana College and Theological Seminary. Immigrants. Lutheran Church. Swedish Americans. 1855-1956. *599*
Illinois (southern). Baptists. Country Life. Farms. Lentz, Lula Gillespie. Personal narratives. 1883-1929. *3037*
Illinois (Springfield). Concordia Seminary. German Americans. Lutheran Church (Missouri Synod). Missouri (St. Louis). 1846-1938. *615*
—. Converts. Jacquess, James F. Lincoln, Abraham. Methodist Church. 1847. *2788*
Illinois State Baptist Association. Baptists, Southern. Oral history. 1976. *210*
Illinois (Zion). Christian Catholic Church. Dowie, John Alexander. Evangelism. Utopias. 1888-1907. *409*
Illowy, Bernard. Canon law. Circumcision. Europe. Judaism (Orthodox). Louisiana (New Orleans). Rabbis. 1853-65. *4176*
Illuminati controversy. Elections (presidential). Episcopal Church, Protestant. Ogden, John C. Philadelphia *Aurora* (newspaper). Religious liberty. 1798-1800. *957*
Illustration. Humor. Mormons. Novels. Periodicals. 1850-60. *2004*
Immaculate Conception Primary School. Catholic Church. Educational attainment. Lithuanian Americans. Missouri (St. Louis). Occupations. 1948-68. *2607*
Immanentism. Baptists. Bibliographies. Clarke, William Newton. Evolution. Theology. 1894-1912. *3065*
Immanuel Lutheran School. Lutheran Church. Secondary education. Wisconsin (Milwaukee). 1903-78. *785*
—. Lutheran Church (Missouri Synod). Personal narratives. Religious education. Wulff, O. H. 1908-75. *781*
Immigrants. Acculturation. Frontier and Pioneer Life. Lutheran Church. Rolvaag, O. E. *(Giants in the Earth).* South Dakota. 1870. 1927. *3307*
—. American Revolution. Presbyterian Church. Scotch-Irish. Scottish Americans. 1700-75. *1268*
—. Amish. France (Alsace). Germany (Palatinate). Pennsylvania. 1693-1803. *3406*
—. Anti-Catholicism. City Politics. Ethnic groups. Ohio (Cincinnati). Temperance Movements. 1845-60. *2584*
—. Arizona (Coconino County). Frontier. Mormons. Schools. 1875-1900. *510*
—. Assimilation. Baptists (American). 1890-1925. *3091*
—. Assimilation. Catholic Church. Polish Americans. 1860's-1930's. *3700*
—. Assimilation. Kubiak, Hieronim (review article). Polish National Catholic Church. 1897-1965. *306*
—. Augustana College and Theological Seminary. Illinois (Rock Island). Lutheran Church. Swedish Americans. 1855-1956. *599*
—. Baltic Area. Canada. Lutheran Church. 1947-55. *2453*
—. Baptists. Circuit riders. Diaries. Minnesota. Nilsson, Frederik Olaus. Swedish Americans. 1855-65. *3046*
—. Benedictines. Illinois (New Cluny). Missions and Missionaries. Monastic observance. Moosmüller, Oswald. 1832-1901. *3816*
—. Bergner, Peter. *John Wesley* (vessel). Methodist Episcopal Church. New York City. Seamen. 1830-77. *3478*
—. Bishop Hill Colony. Illinois. Janssonists. Swedish Americans. Utopias. 1846-60. *393*
—. Canada. Ethnic Groups. Indians. Language. 1970's. *126*
—. Canada. Lifestyles. Lutheran Church. Occupations. Settlement. Social Organizations. Swedish Americans. USA. 1893-1979. *3325*
—. Carroll, John. Catholic Church. Ecumenism. Nativism. Protestants. 1790-1820. *496*
—. Catholic Church. Church records. Italian Americans. Methodology. Pennsylvania (Philadelphia). 1789-1900. *3770*
—. Catholic Church. Democratic Party. New York City. Prohibition. Protestantism. Tammany Hall. 1840-60. *2594*
—. Catholic Church. Elites. Ethnicity. Politics. Protestants. Reform. 1890's-1970's. *1225*
—. Catholic Church. Family. Polish Americans. Social control. Values. 20c. *913*
—. Catholic Church. German Americans. Kansas (Atchison). Newspapers. Pluralism. 1854-59. *3877*
—. Chaldean Church. Iraqi Americans. Michigan (Detroit). Middle East. Nationalism. Uniates. ca 1940's-74. *1306*
—. Chinese Americans. Presbyterian Church. Race Relations. 1851-1977. *3561*
—. Clergy. Lutheran Church (Augustana Synod). Swedish Americans. Wives. 1860-1962. *3296*
—. Documents. Free Thinkers. German Americans. Missouri. Reading. Religious liberty. St. Louis Free Congregation Library. 1850-99. *1123*
—. Elites. Local government. Massachusetts (Charlestown). Puritans. 1630-40. *3613*
—. Ethnicity. Lutheran Church (Missouri Synod). Migration. Theology. 1847-1970. *3323*
—. Francke, Gottfried. Georgia (Ebenezer). Germany. Kiefer, Theobald, II. Letters. Lutheran Church. Orphanages. Pietism. Whitefield, George. 1738. 1750. *2878*
—. Fundamentalism. Orthodox Eastern Church, Greek. Ruthenians. Uniates. Vermont (Proctor). 1914-73. *2757*
—. German Canadians. Nova Scotia. Protestants. 1749-52. *2852*
—. Great Britain. Landscape Painting. Mormons. Piercy, Frederick *(Illustrated Route).* Portraits. Travel guides. Western states. 1848-57. *1869*
—. Jews. Pennsylvania (Pittsburgh). Religious Education. 1862-1932. *754*
—. Letters. Norwegian Americans. Pennsylvania (Harmony, New Harmony). Rapp, George. 1816-26. *378*
—. Massachusetts. Puritans. 1590-1660. *3605*
—. McDonald, Donald. Millenarianism. Presbyterianism. Prince Edward Island. Scottish Canadians. ca 1828-67. *3591*
—. Netherlands. Reformed Christian Church. Reformed Dutch Church. Schisms. 1834-80. *3163*
—. Protestantism. Scandinavian Americans. 1849-1900. *303*
Immigration *See also* Assimilation; Demography; Emigration; Population; Race Relations; Refugees; Social Problems.
—. Acculturation. Catholics. Slovak Americans. 1860's-1970's. *3879*
—. Acculturation. Christianity. Ethnicity. Europe. Judaism. Middle East. 19c-20c. *34*
—. Acculturation. Educational reform. Public Schools. 19c-1910's. *532*
—. Aged. Catholic Church. Charities. Education. New Brunswick (Saint John). Orphans. Sisters of Charity of the Immaculate Conception. 1854-64. *2509*
—. Agriculture. Kansas. Mennonites. Ukraine. Warkentin, Bernhard. 1872-1908. *3379*
—. Agriculture. Lutheran Church. Minnesota (Isantic County). Social customs. Sweden (Dalarna). 1840-1910. *3329*
—. Alpert, Abraham. Judaism. Massachusetts (Boston). Rabbis. 20c. *4087*
—. Alsace-Lorraine. Batt, Joseph. Catholic Church. Chapel of Our Lady of Help of Christians. New York (Buffalo area; Cheektowaga). 1789-1872. *1760*
—. American Baptist Publishing Society. Baptists. Converts. Lutheran Church. Sweden. Travel (accounts). Wiberg, Anders. 1852-53. *3054*
—. Anti-Catholicism. Chicopee Manufacturing Company. Irish Americans. Massachusetts (Chicopee). Mills. Nativism. Protestantism. 1830-75. *2103*
—. Anti-Semitism. Europe, Eastern. Riis, Jacob. 1890-1914. *2132*
—. Asia, central. Kansas. Mennonites. Nebraska. Pacifism. 1884-93. *3350*
—. Asia, central. Mennonites. Russia. 1870's-1920's. *3386*
—. Asians. Conservatism. Methodist Episcopal Church. Social Gospel. 1865-1908. *2404*
—. Attitudes. Brooklyn College. Catholic Church. Judaism. Negroes. New York City. Protestant Ethic. West Indian Americans. 1939-78. *350*
—. Augustana College and Theological Seminary. Bethany College. Lutheran Church. Midwest. Politics. Railroads. Religious education. Swedish Americans. Swensson, Carl Aaron. 1873-1904. *726*
—. Baerg, Anna. Canada. Diaries. Mennonites. Russian Revolution. Women. 1917-23. *3362*
—. Baptists. Catholic Church. Germans, Russian. Kansas. Lutheran Church. Mennonites. Wheat industry. 1874-77. *2778*
—. Belk, Fred R. Mennonites. Pacifism. Russia. 1880-84. *3351*
—. Benedictine sisters. Missouri (Conception). Renggli, Rose (Mother Mary Beatrice). Switzerland. Women. 1874. *3832*
—. Bennett, James Gordon. Catholic Church. *New York Herald* (newspaper). 1835-70. *3850*
—. Bergthal Colony. Bishops. Manitoba. Mennonites. Stoesz, David. Ukraine. 1872-76. *3390*
—. Bishops. Lehman, Hans (and family). Mennonites. Pennsylvania (Lancaster County; Rapho Township). Swiss Americans. ca 1727-1909. *3400*
—. Brethren, Swiss. Mennonites. North America. Surnames. 1680-1880. *3417*
—. British Columbia. Daily life. Doukhobors. Personal narratives. Russia. 1880's-1976. *3918*
—. British Columbia (Vancouver Island). Converts. Missions and Missionaries. Mormons. 1875-1979. *1669*
—. California. Catholic Church. Famines. Gold Rushes. Irish Americans. 1849-90's. *3800*
—. California (Los Angeles). Jews (Rhodesli). Judaism (Orthodox). Sephardic Hebrew Center. 1900-74. *4180*
—. California (San Francisco). *Emanu-El* (newspaper). Jews, East European. Letters-to-the-editor. Rabbis. Rosenthal, Marcus. Voorsanger, Jacob. 1905. *4141*
—. Canada. Doukhobors. Persecution. Russia. Sects, Religious. 1654-1902. *3917*
—. Canada. Doukhobors. Russia. 1652-1908. *3915*
—. Canada. Eby, Ezra E. Loyalists. Mennonites. Pennsylvania. 18c-1835. *1237*
—. Canada. Ecumenism. Nationalism. Protestant churches. United Church of Canada. 1902-25. *491*
—. Canada. Mennonites. Ukraine. 1922-23. *3365*
—. Canada, Western. Catholic Church. Missions and Missionaries. Sisters of Service. 1920-30. *1665*
—. Catholic Church. Colorado. Germans, Russian. Mennonites. 18c-19c. *2775*
—. Catholic Church. Cotton mills. French Canadians. Massachusetts (Springfield). Population. Working Class. 1870. *3710*
—. Catholic Church. Diaries. Germans, Russian. Karlin, Athanasius. 1875-87. *3772*
—. Catholic Church. Dutch Americans. 1845-75. *3857*
—. Catholic Church. Economic Growth. Irish Americans. Michigan (Detroit). Toleration. 1850. *2790*
—. Catholic Church. French Canadians. Massachusetts (Holyoke). Proulx, Nicholas. Working Class. 1850-1900. *3691*
—. Catholic Church. Illinois (Chicago). Mexican Americans. Social Conditions. 1910's-20's. *3833*
—. Catholic Church. Letters. Moczygemba, Leopold. Polish Americans. Texas (Panna Marya). 1855. *3679*
—. Catholic Church. Manitoba. Mathieu, Olivier-Elzéar. Regina Archdiocese. Saskatchewan. 1911-31. *3781*
—. Catholic Church. Persecution. Prince Edward Island. Scotland. 1769-74. *3702*
—. Catholics. Great Britain. Macdonnell, Alexander. Ontario. Scottish Canadians. 1770's-1814. *3862*
—. Chippewa Indians. Germans, Russian. Manitoba. Mennonites. Métis. 1872-73. *3392*
—. Christmas. Emmanuel Church. Ohio (Bluffton). Reformed Tradition. Swiss Americans. 1840's-1900. *2857*
—. Clayton, William. Great Britain. Letters. Moon, John. Mormons. 1840. *3925*
—. Clayton, William. Great Britain (Manchester). Illinois (Nauvoo). Letters. Mormons. 1840. *3924*
—. Clergy. Great Britain. New England. Puritans. 1629-65. *3661*
—. Clergy. Manitoba. Mennonite Brethren Church. Russia. Warkentin, Johann. 1879-1948. *3409*
—. Colleges and Universities. Mennonites. Ohio (Median County). Wadsworth Institute. 1825-80. *674*
—. Congregationalism. Guidebooks. Illinois. Thomas, Robert D. *(Hanes Cymry America).* Welsh Americans. 19c. *3119*
—. Congregationalism. Guidebooks. Iowa. Thomas, Robert D. *(Hanes Cymry America).* Welsh Americans. 1790-1890. *3155*
—. Congregationalism. Guidebooks. Kansas. Thomas, Robert D. *(Hanes Cymry America).* Welsh Americans. 1838-84. *3121*

—. Congregationalism. Guidebooks. Missouri. Thomas, Robert D. *(Hanes Cymry America)*. Welsh Americans. 1872. *3120*
—. Converts. Kansas. Mennonites. Milling. Presbyterian Church. Warkentin, Bernhard. 1847-1908. *3380*
—. Converts. Mormons. Ross, James. Scotland. 1842-1900. *4011*
—. Dunkards. Evangelism. German Americans. Great Awakening. Lutheran Church. Moravian Church. Northeastern or North Atlantic States. Reformed churches. 1720-60. *2237*
—. Dutch Americans. North Dakota. Reformed Dutch Church. South Dakota. 1880's-1951. *3161*
—. Frontier and Pioneer Life. Irish Americans. New York. Pennsylvania. Presbyterian Church. Virginia (Shenandoah Valley). 17c-1776. *3558*
—. Genealogy. Huguenots. 16c-20c. *3253*
—. German Americans. Reformed German Church. Spotswood, Alexander. Virginia (Germanna). 1714-21. *3284*
—. Great Plains. Manitoba. Mennonites. Russia. 1871-74. *3395*
—. Iowa. Lutheran Church. Schwartz, Auguste von. Wartburg College. Women. 1861-77. *3320*
—. Italian Americans. New York City (Greenwich Village). Presbyterian Church. University Place Church. 1900-30. *3564*
—. Jews. Morocco. Quebec (Montreal). 1960's-70's. *4121*
—. Manitoba. Mennonites. Russia. Shantz, Jacob Y. Travel accounts. 1873. *3425*
—. Manitoba. Mennonites. Russian Canadians. Travel accounts. 1873. *3391*
—. Mennonites. Passenger lists. Quebec. Russia. 1874-80. *3364*
—. Mennonites. Russia. South Dakota. Unruh, Daniel. 1820-82. *3430*
—. Mennonites. Russian Canadians. Saskatchewan (Rosthern). Social conditions. 1923. *3399*
—. Protestantism. Public Schools. 1890-1970. *546*
—. Russia. Ukrainian Americans. 1850's-1945. *2785*
Immigration policy. Catholic Church. Conversion. France (Alsace). Louisiana. Protestants. 1753-59. *3719*
Immigration studies. Brigham Young University Library. Genealogy. Mormons. Utah (Provo). 1830-1978. *236*
Imperialism *See also* Colonialism; Militarism.
—. Annexation. Catholic Church. Converts. Methodist Episcopal Church. Missions and Missionaries. Philippines. 1899-1913. *1689*
—. Baptists. National Characteristics. Racism. Virginia. Women. 1865-1900. *3001*
—. British Empire. Catholic Church. Ideology. Quebec. 19c-20c. *1411*
Inaugural addresses. Myths and Symbols. National Characteristics. Presidents. Protestantism. 17c-20c. *1174*
—. Presidents. 1789-1941. *1176*
Income. Amish. Fertility. Indiana. Women. 20c. *882*
—. Baptists. Clergy. Education. Social Status. 1651-1980. *2603*
—. Canada. Church of England National Task Force on the Economy (report). Poverty. Social Classes. Theology. 1977. *2564*
—. Church and State. Clergy. New England. 1700-75. *1011*
—. Mormons. Utah. Wealth. 1857. *2625*
Independence Hall. Pennsylvania (Philadelphia). Philanthropy. Seybert, Henry. Spiritualism. 1793-1882. *4292*
Independence Movements *See also* Anti-Imperialism; Nationalism; Self-Determination; Separatist Movements.
—. Africa. Christianity. Missions and Missionaries. World Conference of Christian Youth, 1st. 1939-74. *1751*
—. Anti-Catholicism. Attitudes. Latin America. Protestant churches. 1810-25. *2107*
—. Catholic Church. Hawaii. Missions and Missionaries. Protestant Churches. Simpson, George. 1842-43. *1723*
—. Catholic Church. Kubašek, John J. New York (Yonkers). Slovak Americans. 1902-50. *3870*
India. Baptists (freewill). Missions and Missionaries. Phillips, Jeremiah. Santals (tribe). 19c. *1733*
—. Besant, Annie. Blavatsky, Helena Petrovna. Hindu renaissance. Theosophy. Vedanta. 1875-1900. *4283*
—. Church and State. Education. Great Britain. Secularization. 19c. *522*
—. Higher education. Missionaries. Protestant Churches. Social Gospel. 1883. *1680*
India (Bombay). Aga Khan III. Agnosticism. Twain, Mark. 1885. *4301*
India, north. Colonialism. Missions and Missionaries. Presbyterian Church. ca 1800-1950. *1673*
Indian Shaker Church. Handsome Lake (Seneca). Neurology. Revitalization movements. Slocum, John. Trances. 18c-20c. *2756*
—. Indians. Revitalization movements. Rites and Ceremonies. Salishan Indians. 1840's-1978. *2715*
—. Johnson, Jakie. Missions and Missionaries. Oregon (Siletz). Siletz Indians. ca 1881-1970. *2776*
Indian Territory. Apache Indians. Cheyenne Indians. Darlington Agency. Friends, Society of. Indians (agencies). 1868-86. *3278*
—. Arapaho Indians. Haury, Samuel S. Letters. Mennonites. Missions and Missionaries. 1876-80. *1543*
—. Baptists. Creek Indians. Methodist Church. Missions and Missionaries. Presbyterian Church. 1835-60's. *1517*
—. Diaries. Episcopal Church, Protestant. Harris, N. Sayre. Missions and Missionaries. Otey, James Hervey. 1844. *1533*
Indian Wars. Friends, Society of. Nonviolence. Paxton Boys. Pennsylvania (Philadelphia). 1764-67. *2693*
Indiana *See also* North Central States.
—. American Protective Association. Anti-Catholicism. Church Schools. Indians. St. Joseph's Indian Normal School. 1888-96. *57*
—. Amish. Fertility. Income. Women. 20c. *882*
—. Baptists. Lincoln, Abraham. Pigeon Creek Baptist Church. 1822-30. *3098*
—. Baptists. Piner Baptist Church. 1833-1906. *3026*
—. Baptists (Two-Seed-in-the-Spirit). Evangelism. Otter Creek Predestinarian Church. Parker, Daniel. 1820-1974. *3047*
—. Brethren in Christ (Wengerites). Ohio. Pentecostals. 1836-1924. *3432*
—. Catholic Church. Folk religion. 1970's. *3697*
—. Catholic Church. Gary Diocese. Grutka, Andrew G. 1933-78. *3868*
—. Colleges and Universities. Fort Wayne Bible College. Mennonites, Evangelical. 1904-77. *740*
—. Communalism. German Americans. Harmony Society. Pennsylvania. Protestantism. Rapp, George. 1804-47. *425*
—. Courtship. Diaries. Marriage. Mennonites. Sprunger, David. 1893-95. *3427*
—. Disciples of Christ. Dunkards. Hostetler, Joseph. Restoration movement. Revivals. 1800-27. *3104*
—. Heyer, John Christian Frederick. Illinois. Keller, Ezra. Letters. Lutheranism. Missions and Missionaries. Missouri. ca 1820-40. *1614*
—. Lutherans. Politics. Theology. 1835-70. *3344*
—. Marriage, interfaith. 1962-67. *896*
—. Mennonites. Mumaw, George Shaum. Ohio. Personal narratives. Singing Schools. 1900-57. *1941*
Indiana (Allen County). Amish. Mennonites. Social Organization. 1850-1950. *3412*
Indiana (East Chicago, Gary). Baptists. Catholic Church. Hispanic Americans. Theater. 1920-76. *1864*
Indiana (East Chicago, Gary, Hammond). City life. Folklore. Negroes. Voodoo. 1976. *2182*
Indiana (Elkhart County). Bock, Anna. Mennonites, Old Order. Painting. 1830's-1970's. *1845*
Indiana (Elletsville). Lutheran Church (Evangelical). St. John's Evangelical Lutheran Church (Old Dutch Church). 1830-1956. *3330*
Indiana (Fort Wayne). Buerger, Paul Theodor. *Collegium Fratrum* (organization). Educational Tests and Measurements. Letters. Lutheran Church. 1858. *3315*
Indiana (Gary). Centennial United Methodist Church. Methodist Church, United. Methodist Church, United. Negroes. Personal narratives. Robinson, Roosevelt. White flight. 1976. *3467*
—. Evangelicalism. Faith Healing. Music (gospel). Negroes. Theology. 1976. *2868*
Indiana (Gary, Valparaiso). Ku Klux Klan. Nativism. Protestantism. 1920's. *2358*
Indiana (New Harmony). Architecture. Harmony Society. Pennsylvania (Economy, Harmony). Preservation. Rapp, George. Restorations. Utopias. 1804-25. 20c. *420*
—. City Planning. Communes. Harmony Society. Pennsylvania (Harmony, Economy). Social customs. 1820's-1905. *391*
—. Harmony Society. Rapp, George. Utopias. 1814-47. *421*
—. Harmony Society. Rapp, George. Utopias. 1822-30. *379*
Indiana (Putnam County). Baptists (Two-Seed-in-the-Spirit). Evangelism. Music. Oral tradition. Otter Creek Predestinarian Church. Sermons. 1820-1975. *1940*
Indiana (Shelbyville). Evangelism. Horstman, Otto K. Lutheran Church, Evangelical. Missions and Missionaries. Personal narratives. 1934. *1551*
Indiana (Tippecanoe County). Lutheran Church. 1826-50. *3346*
Indians *See also* terms beginning with the word Indian; names of Indian tribe, e.g. Delaware Indians; Acculturation; Asians; East Indians.
—. 20c. *97*
—. Acculturation. American Indian Defense Association. Collier, John. Religious liberty. 1920-26. *1101*
—. Acculturation. Arapaho Indians. Cheyenne Indians. Mennonites. Missions and Missionaries. 1880-1900. *1557*
—. Acculturation. Burials. Christianity. Missions and Missionaries. Navajo Indians. 1949-75. *1656*
—. Acculturation. California (Monterey, San Luis Obispo counties). Catholic Church. Missions and Missionaries. Salinan Indians. 1770's-1830's. *1550*
—. Advocate role. Charities. Children. Poor. St. Vincent de Paul Society. 1900-10. *2515*
—. Agricultural Labor. Canary Islanders. Fernandez de Santa Ana, Benito. Missions and Missionaries. Petitions. Provincial Government. Texas (Villa San Fernando). 1741. *1542*
—. Agriculture. Mormons. Nevada. Utah. 1847-60. *4037*
—. Alaska. Catholic Church. Holy Cross Mission. Jesuits. Missions and Missionaries. Sisters of St. Ann. Yukon River, lower. 1887-1956. *1615*
—. Alberta. Bible. Blackfoot Indians. Missions and Missionaries. Stocken, H. W. G. Translating and Interpreting. Wolf Collar (shaman). 1870-1928. *1500*
—. Alberta (Edmonton). Church of England. Métis. Newton, William. 1875-1900. *3196*
—. Algonkian Indians, northeastern. Maine. Maritime Provinces. Missionaries. Social change. 1610-1750. *1512*
—. American Board of Commissioners for Foreign Missions. Methodist Church. Missionaries. 1830-50. *1663*
—. American Protective Association. Anti-Catholicism. Church Schools. Indiana. St. Joseph's Indian Normal School. 1888-96. *57*
—. American Revolution. Burgoyne, John. Friends, Society of. Pennsylvania (Easton). ca 1776. *3282*
—. American Revolution. California. Missions. Spain. 1776-83. *1321*
—. American Revolution. Cummings, Charles. Presbyterian Church. Virginia, southwest. 1760's-80's. *2634*
—. American Revolution. Delaware Indians. Missions and Missionaries. Moravian Church. Ohio. Pennsylvania, western. 1775-83. *1532*
—. Anthropology. Archaeology. Lost Tribes of Israel. Mormons. Smith, Joseph. 1830. *2335*
—. Antislavery sentiments. Campbell, Alexander. Civil religion. Disciples of Christ. Politics. War. Women. 1823-55. *3108*
—. Arizona. Church and State. Franciscans. Mexico (Sonora). Missions and Missionaries. 1767-1842. *1065*
—. Arizona. Jesuits. Kino, Eusebio Francisco. Missions and Missionaries. Spain. 1680's-1711. *1565*
—. Arizona (Nogales). Buena, Mariano. Catholic Church. Gil, Juan. Seri Indians. 1768-72. *1559*
—. Assimilation. Christianity. Missions and Missionaries. Syncretism. 19c-20c. *2794*
—. Assimilation. Eliot, John. Massachusetts. Praying towns. Puritans. 1646-74. *1592*
—. Assimilation. Navajo Indians. New Mexico (Shiprock). Sherman Institute for Indians. Women. 1900-20. *589*

—. Attitudes. Catholic Church. Colonial Government. Discovery and Exploration. Games. Missions and Missionaries. 16c-17c. *1524*
—. Attitudes. France. Jesuits. Missions and Missionaries. New France. 1611-72. *1495*
—. Attitudes. Missions and Missionaries. Presbyterian Church. 1837-93. *1510*
—. Baptists. Education. Kansas. Lykins, Johnston. Potawatomi Indians. Pottawatomie Baptist Manual Labor Training School. 1846-67. *508*
—. Baptists. Folger, Peter. Jones, David. Missionaries. Northeastern or North Atlantic States. Williams, Roger. 1638-1814. *1619*
—. Baptists, American. Crawford, Isabel. Kiowa Indians. Missions and Missionaries. Oklahoma (Wichita Mountains). Women's American Baptist Home Missionary Society. 1893-1961. *1590*
—. Bible. British Columbia. California. Christianity. Missions and Missionaries. Myths and Symbols. Pacific Northwest. 1830-50. *1612*
—. Black Hills. Episcopal Church, Protestant. Hinman, Samuel D. Missions and Missionaries. Sioux Indians. 1860-76. *1484*
—. Blackburn, Gideon. Cherokee Indians. Missions and Missionaries. Old Southwest. Presbyterian Church. Schools. Whiskey. 1809-10. *700*
—. Bloomfield Academy. Chickasaw Indians. Downs, Ellen J. Girls. Methodist Church. Oklahoma (Penola County). Personal Narratives. Schools. 1853-66. *772*
—. British Columbia (Vancouver Island; Nootka Sound). Catholic Church. Missions and Missionaries. Oral History. Spain. 1789-95. 19c. *1563*
—. Business. Lee, Daniel. Letters. Methodist Church. Missions and Missionaries. Oregon (Willamette Valley, The Dalles). 1834-43. *1570*
—. California. Catholic Church. Labor. Missions and Missionaries. 1775-1805. *1485*
—. California. Chumash Indians. Marriage. Mission Santa Barbara. Social Organization. Yanunali, Pedro (chief). 1787-1806. *940*
—. California. Church and state. Colonial Government. Laws of the Indies. Missions and Missionaries. Spain. 18c. *1143*
—. California. Church and State. Franciscans. Missions and Missionaries. 1775-1800. *1037*
—. California. Conversion thesis. Cook, Sherburne Friend. Franciscans. Missions and Missionaries. ca 1790-1820's. 1943. *1541*
—. California. Durán, Narciso. Franciscans. Missions. Secularization. 1826-46. *1093*
—. California. Durán, Narciso. Franciscans. Missions and Missionaries. Music. 1806-46. *1924*
—. California (Eight Mile, Blue Creek). Forest Service. Religious liberty. Supreme Court. 1975. *1102*
—. California, northern. Converts. Ghost Dance. Methodist Church. Round Valley Indian Reservation. 1870. *3484*
—. California (San Diego). Colonization. Missions and Missionaries. Spain. 1769-1834. *1668*
—. California (Sonoma). Catholic Church. Mission San Francisco Solano. 1823-34. *1506*
—. California (Temecula). Catholic Church. Documents. Maltby, Charles. Mission San Antonio de Pala. 1866. *1573*
—. Canada. Christianity. Civil rights. Eskimos. Métis. Project North. 1975-79. *2545*
—. Canada. Ethnic Groups. Immigrants. Language. 1970's. *126*
—. Canada, western. Catholic Church. Missions and Missionaries. Oblates of Mary Immaculate. 1818-70. *1502*
—. Captivity narratives. Catholic Church. Congregationalism. French Canadians. New England. Williams, John *(The Redeemed Captive)*. 1704-06. *3133*
—. Catholic Church. Education. Missions and Missionaries. North Dakota. Pioneers. Presentation of the Blessed Virgin Mary, Sisters of the. South Dakota. Women. 1880-96. *727*
—. Catholic Church. Hudson's Bay Company. Methodist Church. Missions and Missionaries. Oregon. Presbyterian Church. 1830's - 1840's. *1482*
—. Catholic Church. Juan Antonio (neophyte). Mission San Gabriel Arcangel. Painting (realist tradition). 1800. 1976. *1882*
—. Catholic Church. Juan Antonio (neophyte). Mission San Gabriel Arcangel. Paintings. 1800-1976. *1883*
—. Catholic Church. Louisiana. Missions and Missionaries. 18c-20c. *1625*
—. Catholic Church. Missions and Missionaries. Pueblo Revolt (1680). Southwest. 1590-1680. *1499*
—. Cherokee Indians. Foreman, Stephen. Georgia. Oklahoma. Presbyterian Church. 1820's-81. *3538*
—. Cherokee Indians. Martin, John. Missions and Missionaries. Presbyterian Church. Richardson, William. Tennessee. Virginia. 1755-63. *1511*
—. Chippewa Indians. Documents. Fullerton, Thomas. Methodist Episcopal Church. Minnesota. Missions and Missionaries. Wisconsin. 1841-44. *1531*
—. Christianity. Europeans. 16c-20c. *2752*
—. Christianity. Missions and Missionaries. New England. New France. 17c. *1621*
—. Christianity. Missions and Missionaries. New England Company. Royal Society. 1660's-70's. *1554*
—. Church of England. Education. Methodist Church. Missions and Missionaries. Ontario (Algoma, Huron). Wilson, Edward F. 1868-93. *1596*
—. Church of England. McDonald, Robert. Missions and Missionaries. Northwest Territories. Yukon Territory. 1850's-1913. *1604*
—. Cloeter, Ottomar. Letters. Lutheran Church. Minnesota. Missions and Missionaries. 1856-68. *1651*
—. Colonial Government. Florida. Military security. Missions. 1566-1710. *1079*
—. Colonization. Jesuits. Menéndez de Avilés, Pedro. Missions and Missionaries. Opechancanough (chief). Powhatan Indians. Spain. Virginia. 1570-72. *1622*
—. Converts. Massachusetts (Martha's Vineyard). Mayhew, Thomas, Jr. Missions and Missionaries. Puritans. 1645-57. *1635*
—. Courtship. Field, Eliza. Great Britain (London). Jones, Peter. Methodism. New York. 1820's-33. *1637*
—. Crow Indians. Diaries. Doederlein, Paul Ferdinand. Lutheran Church. Missions and Missionaries. Wyoming. 1859-60. *1589*
—. Davies, David Jones. Davies, Gwen. Methodist Church, Calvinistic. Missions and Missionaries. Nebraska, eastern. Omaha Indians. 1853-60. *1514*
—. Diaries. Missions and Missionaries. Spokan Indians. Walker, Elkanah. Walker, Mary. Washington, eastern. 1839-48. *1521*
—. Drury, Clifford M. Lee, Jason. Methodism. Missions and Missionaries. Oregon. Settlement. 1834-43. 1970's. *3480*
—. Economic conditions. Frontier and Pioneer life. Missions and Missionaries. Presbyterian Church. South Dakota. 1840-1900. *3540*
—. Education. Engelhardt, Zephyrin. Franciscans. Holy Childhood Indian School Printery. Michigan (Harbor Springs). Printing. 1894-1913. *1584*
—. Education. Episcopal Church, Protestant. Girls. St. Mary's Episcopal School for Indian Girls. South Dakota (Springfield). 1873-1973. *687*
—. Eliot, John. Massachusetts. Missions and Missionaries. Puritans. 1620-80. *1624*
—. Eliot, John. Massachusetts (Natick). Missions and Missionaries. Puritans. 1646-74. *1602*
—. Episcopal Church, Protestant. Hudson's Bay Company. Missions and Missionaries. Pacific Northwest. 1825-75. *1555*
—. Esteyneffer, Juan de *(Florilegio Medicinal)*. Herbs. Jesuits. Medicine (practice of). Missions and Missionaries. Southwest. 1711. *1444*
—. Filipinos. Vietnamese. War crimes. 1636-1970's. *2640*
—. Folk Medicine. Georgia. Great Britain. Medicine (practice of). Methodism. Wesley, John. 1740's. *1426*
—. France. Jesuits. Missions and Missionaries. New York, western. Rings. ca 1630-87. *1664*
—. Friends, Society of. Paxton Boys. Pennsylvania. Politics. Presbyterian Church. Riots. 1763-64. *3530*
—. Germans, Sudeten. Missions and Missionaries. 1519-19c. *1539*
—. Historiography. Lee, Jason. Methodism. Missions and Missionaries. Oregon. 1838-43. *1569*
—. Humanism. More, Thomas *(Utopia)*. Rhode Island (Narragansett). Utopias. Williams, Roger *(A Key into the Language of America)*. 1640's. *2938*
—. Irish. Massachusetts. Puritans. Stereotypes. 17c. *2144*
—. Kansas. Methodism. Ohio. Removal policy. Wyandot Indians. 1816-60. *1598*
—. Massachusetts. Morton, Thomas. Pilgrims. Puritans. Values. 1625-45. *2956*
—. McBeth, Sue L. Missions and Missionaries. Nez Percé Indians. Presbyterian Church. 1873-93. *1509*
—. McDougall, John. Methodist Church, Wesleyan. Missions and Missionaries. Prairie Provinces. 1860-1917. *1534*
—. Mennonites. Métis. Red River of the North. Red River of the North. Removals, forced. Saskatchewan River Valley. Settlement. 1869-95. *3360*
—. Methodism. Missions and Missionaries. Oklahoma. 1820-45. *1650*
—. Mexican Americans. Navajo Indians. Pueblo Indians. Southwest. Witchcraft. 19c-1930's. *2214*
—. Mexican Americans. New Mexico (Bernalillo, Manzana). Witchcraft. 1970-74. *2193*
—. Mexican Americans. Witchcraft. 16c-20c. *2204*
—. Missionaries. Presbyterian Board of Foreign Missions. Slavery. 1837-61. *3568*
—. Religious liberty. 1609-1976. *1134*
Indians (agencies). Apache Indians. Cheyenne Indians. Darlington Agency. Friends, Society of. Indian Territory. 1868-86. *3278*
—. Assimilation. Lowrie, John C. Missions and Missionaries. Presbyterian Church. 1870-82. *1655*
—. Church and State. Education. Episcopal Church, Protestant. Oklahoma, western. Stouch, George W. H. Whirlwind Day School. ca 1904-14. *1086*
—. Friends, Society of (Committees on the Indian Concern). Nebraska. 1869. *3274*
Indians (neophytes). California. Catholic Church. Mexico. Missions and missionaries. 1830's. *1606*
Indians (reservations). Bureau of Indian Affairs. Educational Policy. Language. Missions and Missionaries. 19c-20c. *516*
Indian-White Relations. Acculturation. Catholic Church. Missionaries. Protestantism. Wisconsin. 1830-48. *1640*
—. Agriculture. Catholic Church. Federal Programs. Friends, Society of. Missions and Missionaries. Moravian Church. Old Northwest. 1789-1820. *1529*
—. Alaska. Assimilation. Brady, John Green. Economic Conditions. Missions and Missionaries. Tlingit Indians. 1878-1906. *1548*
—. Alaska. Diaries. Library of Congress (Alaska Church Collection). Missions and Missionaries. Orlov, Vasilii. Orthodox Eastern Church, Russian. 1886. *1632*
—. American Board of Commissioners for Foreign Missions. Assimilation. Connecticut (Cornwall). Foreign Mission School. Students. 1816-27. *586*
—. American Board of Commissioners for Foreign Missions. Boutwell, William Thurston. Chippewa Indians. Minnesota. Missions and Missionaries. Protestant Churches. 1831-47. *1572*
—. American Board of Commissioners for Foreign Missions. Brainerd Mission. Cherokee Indians. Education. Letters. Southeastern States. 1817-38. *1605*
—. American Board of Commissioners for Foreign Missions. Cherokee Indians. Georgia. Law Enforcement. Missions and Missionaries. Removals, forced. Worcester, Samuel A. 1831. *1667*
—. American Revolution. Mahican Indians (Stockbridge). Massachusetts (Stockbridge). 1680-1776. *1481*
—. Apes, William. Massachusetts (Mashpee). Methodist Church. Reform. Wampanoag Indians. 1830-40. *2546*
—. Baptists. Bingham, Abel. Diaries. Iroquois Indians (Seneca). Missions and Missionaries. New York. Red Jacket (leader). Tonawanda Indian Reservation. 1822-28. *1513*
—. Beeson, John. Blaine, David E. Methodists. Oregon. Washington. 1850-59. *3495*
—. Bibliographies. *Journal of the West* (periodical). Western states. 1970-74. *1593*

—. Bishops. Catholic Church. Lamy, Jean Baptiste. New Mexico (Santa Fe). Social customs. 1849-88. *3761*
—. Brébeuf, Jean de. Catholic Church. Ledesme, R. P. *(Doctrine Chrestienne).* New France. Translating and Interpreting. Wyandot Indians. 16c-17c. *1639*
—. British Columbia (Metlakatla). Church Missionary Society. Church of England. Hall, A. J. Missions and Missionaries. Revivals. Tsimshian Indians. 1877. *1616*
—. Bureau of Indian Affairs. Catholic Church. Iowa. Presbyterian Church. Schools. Winnebago Indians. 1834-48. *737*
—. Butler, Elizur. Cherokee Indians. Marshall, John. Missions and Missionaries. Nullification crisis. Worcester, Samuel A. *Worcester* v. *Georgia* (US, 1832). 1828-33. *1583*
—. California. Catholic Church. Missions and Missionaries. 1770's-1820's. *1636*
—. Canada. Fort Frontenac. Iroquois Indians. Missions and Missionaries. Quinte Mission. Sulpician order. 1665-80. *1610*
—. Catholic Church. Chipewyan Indians. Letters. Mission St. Jean-Baptiste. Saskatchewan (Île-à-la-Crosse). Taché, Alexandre Antonin. 1823-54. *1503*
—. Catholic Church. Church finance. Education. Oklahoma. Quapaw Indians. 1876-1927. *3727*
—. Catholic Church. Church of England. Government. Manitoulin project. Methodist Church. Missions and Missionaries. Ontario (Upper Canada). 1820-40. *1537*
—. Catholic Church. Hospitals. Hôtel-Dieu. Quebec. 1635-98. *1446*
—. Chippewa Indians. Lutheran Church. Michigan. Miessler, Ernst G. H. Missions and Missionaries. 1851-71. *1582*
—. Chippewa Indians. Methodist Church. Michigan. Missions and Missionaries. 1830-80. *1597*
—. Christianity. Micmac Indians. Missions and Missionaries. New Brunswick. Nova Scotia. 1803-60. *1649*
—. Church and Social Problems. Congregationalism. Local Politics. Massachusetts (Natick). Meetinghouses. 1650-18c. *3118*
—. Congregationalism. Connecticut. Girls. Religious Education. Wheelock, Eleazar. 1761-69. *766*
—. Documents. Missions and Missionaries. Western States. 1812-1923. *1483*
—. Education. Missionaries. Social reform. ca 1609-1900. *1498*
—. Episcopal Church, Protestant. Florida. Gray, William Crane. Missions and missionaries. Seminole Indians. 1893-1914. *1558*
—. Fort Duquesne. Frontier and Pioneer Life. Moravian Church. Pennsylvania. Post, Christian Frederick. 1758-59. *1505*
—. Franciscans. Inquisition. Marriage. Missions and Missionaries. New Mexico. Plains Apache Indians. Romero, Diego. 1660-78. *3773*
—. Great Plains. Mormons. New York, western. Utah. Young, Brigham. 1835-51. *3948*
—. Historiography. Missions and Missionaries. New England. Puritans. Theology. 17c-20c. *1641*
—. Hobomok (shaman). Pilgrims. Plymouth Colony. Polytheism. Squanto (Wampanoag Indian). Theology. ca 1620-30. *3144*
—. Missions and Missionaries. Protestant Churches. Spokan Indians. Walker, Elkanah. Washington (Tshimakain). 1838-48. *1520*
—. New England. Puritans. Race. 1620-90. *2150*
—. Puritans. Racism. 17c. *2136*
Individualism. American Revolution (antecedents). Great Awakening. Pietism. Republicanism. 1735-75. *1385*
—. Baptists, Southern. Politics. Social problems. 18c-1976. *968*
—. Bellamy, Edward. Nationalist Movement. 1865-98. *82*
—. Brethren in Christ. Christianity. Education. Evangelism. Holiness movement. 1870-1910. *3421*
—. Capitalism. Protestantism. Social ethic. 20c. *345*
—. Evangelicalism. Liberalism. 1815-60. *2952*
Industrial Relations *See also* Labor Unions and Organizations; Strikes.
—. Christianity. Massachusetts (Lawrence). Scudder, Vida Dutton. Social reform. Socialism. Women. 1912. *2374*
Industrialization *See also* Economic Growth; Modernization.
—. Canada. 1970's. *92*
—. Canada. Catholic Church. Judaism. Protestant Churches. Religiosity. 1921-71. *93*
—. Catholic Church. Eudists. Quebec (Chicoutimi Basin). Working class. 1903-30. *1466*
—. Domesticity. Revivals. Womanhood, sentimental. 1830-70. *817*
—. Labor. Leisure. Protestant Ethic. Values. 19c-20c. *334*
—. Law and society. Massachusetts. Nelson, William E. (review article). Secularization. Social change. 1760-1830. *53*
Inerrancy (doctrine). Bible. Evangelicals. Montgomery, John W. (review article). Objectivist apologetics. 1972. *2882*
Infants. Death and Dying. New England. Parents. Puritans. Theology. 1620-1720. *925*
Infinity (concept). Almanacs. Astronomy. New England. Puritanism. 1650-85. *2325*
Influence, distribution of. Catholic Church. Centralization. Organizational structure. 1970's. *3866*
Information Storage and Retrieval Systems. Baptist Information Retrieval System. 1974-75. *230*
Ingersoll, Robert. Agnosticism. Puritans. Winthrop, John. ca 1630-1890's. *54*
—. Atheism. Lectures. Nevada (Virginia City). Public Opinion. 1877. *4304*
—. Congregationalism. Connecticut. Free Thinkers. Frontier and Pioneer Life. Ohio (Western Reserve). Wright, Elizur (and family). Yale University. 1762-1870. *56*
Inglis, Charles. Church of England. Loyalists. Propaganda. Sermons. 1770-80. *1370*
Ingraham, Joseph Holt. Church of England. Clergy. Episcopal Church, Protestant. Novels. Prisons. Public Schools. Reform. Tennessee (Nashville). 1847-51. *3241*
Initiatives. Antievolution Law (1928). Arkansas. Church and state. Courts. Epperson, Susan. Evolution. 1900's-68. *2322*
Inner Mission Movement. Beck, Vilhelm. Danish Americans. Grundtvig, Nikolai Frederik Severin. Lutheran Church. 1619-1973. *3341*
Inoculation. Epidemics. Massachusetts (Boston). Mather, Cotton. Smallpox. 1721-22. *1464*
Inquisition. Catholic Church. Church and state. Louisiana. Surveillance. 1762-1800. *1044*
—. Franciscans. Indian-White Relations. Marriage. Missions and Missionaries. New Mexico. Plains Apache Indians. Romero, Diego. 1660-78. *3773*
Inscriptions. Baptists. Ebenezer Methodist Church. Methodist Church. Mount Bethel Baptist Church. South Carolina (Anderson County). Tombstones. 1856-1978. *2848*
Inskip, John S. Holiness Movement. Inskip, Martha Jane. Methodist Church. Revivals. Women. 1836-90. *3448*
Inskip, Martha Jane. Holiness Movement. Inskip, John S. Methodist Church. Revivals. Women. 1836-90. *3448*
Institutionalization. Charters. Mennonites (Franconia Conference). Protestant Churches. 1840-1940. *3382*
Institutions. Cheyenne Indians. Mennonites. Missions and Missionaries. Photographs. Social customs. 1880-1940. *3398*
Insurrections. *See* Rebellions.
Integration *See also* Assimilation.
—. Alline, Henry. Charisma. Nova Scotia. Revivals. 1776-83. *2264*
—. Antislavery sentiments. Ohio (Cincinnati). Presbyterian Church, Reformed. Reformed Presbyterian Theological Seminary. 1845-49. *610*
—. Clergy. Kimball, Spencer W. Mormons. Negroes. Revelation. 1950-78. *4051*
Intellect. Emotions. Psychology, faculty. Puritanism. 17c. *2313*
Intellectual history. 1476-1976. *38*
—. Dickinson, Emily. Identity. Myths and Symbols. Poetry. Puritanism. Transcendentalism. Women. 1860's. *51*
Intellectuals. -1973. *109*
—. Adler, Cyrus. American Academy for Jewish Research. Judaism (Orthodox, Reform). Revel, Bernard. Society of Jewish Academicians. 1916-22. *4139*
—. American Revolution. Church of England. Freneau, Philip ("A Political Litany"). Poetry. 1775. *1998*
—. Bishops. Catholic Church. Letters. Provincial Council of Baltimore (4th). Walter, William Joseph. 1840-43. *3842*
—. Brownson, Orestes A. Catholic Church. Social Philosophy. 1803-76. *3677*
—. Catholic Church. Clergy. Greeley, Andrew M. 1974. *3749*
—. Catholic Church. Democracy. Liberalism. Racism. 1924-59. *2532*
—. Catholicism. Sheed, Frank. 20c. *3706*
—. Clergy. Emigration. New England. 1640-60. *3653*
—. Congregationalism. Edwards, Jonathan. Great Awakening. Massachusetts (Northampton, Stockbridge). Theology. Youth. ca 1730-1880. *3150*
—. Friends, Society of. Humanism. Penn, William. Radicals and Radicalism. Social reform. 1650-1700. *2353*
—. Frontier and Pioneer Life. Heywood, Martha Spence. King, Hannah Tapfield. Mormons. Snow, Eliza Roxey. Utah. Women. 1850-70. *4045*
—. McConnell, Francis John. Methodist Church. Social Reform. Theology. 1894-1937. *2382*
—. New England. Poetry. Radicals and Radicalism. Socialism. Wheelwright, John (1897-1940). 18c-1940. *1419*
Intendants. Catholic Church. Colonial Government. Quebec. 1633-1760. *1030*
Interior decoration. Congregationalism. Decorative Arts. Rhode Island (Newport). United Congregational Church. 1879-80. *1897*
Interior Lay Missionary Movement. Adventists. Friends of Man. Jehovah's Witnesses. Russell, Charles Taze. 1852-1916. *3921*
Internal Migration. *See* Migration, Internal.
International Church of the Foursquare Gospel. California (Los Angeles). Evangelism. McPherson, Aimee Semple. Radio. 1920-44. *1958*
International cooperation. Methodism. Pendell, Thomas Roy. Personal narratives. USSR. World Conference of Christian Youth, 1st. 1939-79. *1402*
International Union of Catholic Women's Leagues (congress). Catholic Church. Italy (Rome). Quebec. Suffrage. Women. 1922. *935*
Internationalism. America (views of). Anti-Communist Movements. Presbyterian Church, United. 1973. *1373*
Interventionism. Anglo-Saxonism. Protestantism. Reform. Strong, Josiah. 1885-1915. *2418*
Intuition. Historiography. New England. Parker, Theodore. Reason. Theology. Transcendentalism. Unitarianism. 18c-1860. 1920-79. *4074*
Inventions. Baldwin, Nathaniel. Fundamentalism. Mormons. Polygamy. Radio. Utah. 1900's-61. *4036*
Iowa *See also* North Central States.
—. Adventists. Evangelism. Hill, W. B. Minnesota. Personal Narratives. 1877. 1881. *1547*
—. Amana Society. Communalism. 1843-1932. *424*
—. Amana Society. Communalism. Shambaugh, Bertha Horak. Wick, Barthinius L. ca 1900-34. *404*
—. Amana Society. Folk art. 1843-1932. *1852*
—. Amish, Beachy. 1920-77. *3423*
—. Bureau of Indian Affairs. Catholic Church. Indian-White Relations. Presbyterian Church. Schools. Winnebago Indians. 1834-48. *737*
—. Catholic Church. Church Schools. Dubuque Diocese. Hennessy, John. Irish Americans. 1866-1900. *3720*
—. Communalism. Free thinkers. Kneeland, Abner. Salubria (religious community). 1827-44. *383*
—. Congregationalism. Guidebooks. Immigration. Thomas, Robert D. *(Hanes Cymry America).* Welsh Americans. 1790-1890. *3155*
—. Country Life. Langland, Joseph. Lutheran Church. Personal narratives. Poetry. Youth. 1917-30's. 1977. *2027*
—. Dutch Americans. Genealogy. Mennonites. Settlement. Swiss Americans. 1839-1974. *3370*
—. Forssell, G. D. Lectures. Minnesota. Progressivism. Social Conditions. 1890-95. *1967*
—. Hangings. Hodges, Stephen. Hodges, William. Mormons (Danites). Murder. 1845. *3985*
—. Immigration. Lutheran Church. Schwartz, Auguste von. Wartburg College. Women. 1861-77. *3320*
Iowa College. Clergy. Congregationalism. Herron, George David. National Christian Citizen League. Populism. Progressivism. Socialism. 1880's-1900. *2561*

Iowa (Iowa City). Architecture (Gothic Revival). Churches. Congregationalism. Randall, Gurdon Paine. 1868-69. *1822*
—. Architecture (Gothic Revival). Churches. Episcopal Church, Protestant. Trinity Episcopal Church. Upjohn, Richard. 1871-72. *1787*
—. Charities. Episcopal Church, Protestant. New York City. Orphans' Home of Industry. Townsend, Charles Collins. 1854-68. *2507*
Iowa (Lee County). Galland, Isaac. Land. Mormons. Smith, Joseph. Speculation. 1830's-58. *3950*
—. Mormons. Settlement. Young, Brigham. 1838-46. *3998*
Iowa (Orange City). Architecture. Northwestern College (Zwemer Hall). Reformed Dutch Church. 1890-1924. *1806*
Iraqi Americans. Chaldean Church. Immigrants. Michigan (Detroit). Middle East. Nationalism. Uniates. ca 1940's-74. *1306*
Ireland *See also* Great Britain.
—. American Revolution. Charities. Friends, Society of. Great Britain. Pennsylvania (Philadelphia). 1778-97. *2503*
—. Anti-Catholicism. Colonization. Great Britain. Ideology. North America. Protestantism. ca 1550-1600. *2086*
—. Anti-Catholicism. Constitutional Law. Irish Americans. O'Conor, Charles. O'Conor, Charles Owen. Political reform. Reconstruction. 1865-85. *1031*
—. Bible. Embury, Philip. Methodism. New York City. 1760-1834. *3489*
—. Brownson, Orestes A. Catholic University of Ireland. Great Britain. Newman, John Henry. 1853-54. *3837*
—. Catholic Church. England, John. Voluntarism. 1808-50. *3708*
—. Church discipline. Friends, Society of. New England. New York. 1690-1789. *3283*
Ireland (Belfast). Abolition movement. Douglass, Frederick. Presbyterian Church. Smyth, Thomas. 1846. *2165*
Ireland (Clongowes Wood, Kilkenny). Catholic Church. Education. Hackett, Francis. Irish Americans. Literature. 1880's-1901. *3818*
Ireland, John. Architecture. Cathedrals. Catholic Church. Masqueray, Emmanuel L. Minnesota (St. Paul). 1904-17. *1795*
Irish. Indians. Massachusetts. Puritans. Stereotypes. 17c. *2144*
Irish Americans. Acculturation. Catholic Church. Pennsylvania (Pittsburgh). St. Andrew Parish. 1863-90. *3748*
—. Adventists. California. Humor. Letters. Loma Linda University. Magan, Percy Tilson. 1918-34. *1435*
—. Americanization. Catholic Church. Clergy. Polish Americans. 1920-40's. *290*
—. Americanization. Catholic Church. French Canadians. Hendricken, Thomas F. Massachusetts (Fall River). 1870's-85. *317*
—. Anti-Catholicism. Breslin, Jimmy. Brooklyn Diocese. Flaherty, Joe. Hamill, Pete. New York City. Novels. 1960's-70's. *2098*
—. Anti-Catholicism. Cheverus, Jean Louis Lefebvre de. Daley, Dominic. Halligan, James. Massachusetts (Northampton). Protestantism. Trials. 1805-06. *2097*
—. Anti-Catholicism. Cheverus, Jean Louis Lefebvre de. Lyon, Marcus. Massachusetts (Northampton). Murder. Protestantism. Trials. 1805-06. *2099*
—. Anti-Catholicism. Chicopee Manufacturing Company. Immigration. Massachusetts (Chicopee). Mills. Nativism. Protestantism. 1830-75. *2103*
—. Anti-Catholicism. Constitutional Law. Ireland. O'Conor, Charles. O'Conor, Charles Owen. Political reform. Reconstruction. 1865-85. *1031*
—. Anti-Catholicism. Urbanization. 1920's. *2102*
—. Assimilation. Authority. Bishops. Catholic Church. Cleveland Diocese. German Americans. Ohio. Rappe, Louis Amadeus. 1847-70. *3788*
—. Bishops. Catholic Church. Farrelly, John P. Morris, John. Stritch, Samuel A. Tennessee. 19c-1958. *3860*
—. Bishops. Catholic Church. Jamestown Diocese. Minnesota (St. Paul). North Dakota. Shanley, John. 1852-1909. *3731*
—. California. Catholic Church. Famines. Gold Rushes. Immigration. 1849-90's. *3800*
—. California (San Francisco). Catholic Church. City Politics. Clergy. Progressivism. Yorke, Peter C. 1900's. *3889*
—. California (San Francisco). Catholic Church. Clergy. Editors and Editing. Ethnicity. Yorke, Peter C. ca 1885-1925. *3887*
—. California, University of (Regents). Catholic Church. Clergy. Political attitudes. Yorke, Peter C. 1900-12. *560*
—. Catholic Church. Church and Social Problems. German Americans. New Jersey (Newark). 1840-70. *3830*
—. Catholic Church. Church Schools. Dubuque Diocese. Hennessy, John. Iowa. 1866-1900. *3720*
—. Catholic church. City Politics. Construction. Contractors. Pennsylvania (Philadelphia). 1846-1960's. *338*
—. Catholic Church. Civil War. *Universe: The Catholic Herald and Visitor* (newspaper). 1860-70. *3746*
—. Catholic Church. Cunningham, Patrick. Documents. Vermont (Brattleboro). 1847-98. *3725*
—. Catholic Church. Democratic Party. *Kentucky Irish American* (newspaper). 1898-1968. *3817*
—. Catholic Church. Dolan, Jay P. (review article). German Americans. New York. Social Conditions. 1815-65. 1975. *3793*
—. Catholic Church. Economic Growth. Immigration. Michigan (Detroit). Toleration. 1850. *2790*
—. Catholic Church. Education. Hackett, Francis. Ireland (Kilkenny, Clongowes Wood). Literature. 1880's-1901. *3818*
—. Catholic Church. Kelly, Dennis. Pennsylvania (Havertown). St. Denis Parish. 1825-1975. *3683*
—. Friends, Society of. Milhouse, Robert. South Carolina (Camden). Wyly, Samuel. 1751-93. *3265*
—. Friends, Society of. Pennsylvania. Settlement. 1682-1750. *3276*
—. Frontier and Pioneer Life. Immigration. New York. Pennsylvania. Presbyterian Church. Virginia (Shenandoah Valley). 17c-1776. *3558*
Irish Canadians. Acadians. Catholic Church. Discrimination. New Brunswick. 1860-1900. *3855*
—. Alberta. Calgary Diocese. Catholic Church. French Canadians. McNailly, John Thomas. 1871-1952. *3712*
—. Anglin, Timothy Warren. Canada. Catholic Church. Debates. Fenian Brotherhood. McGee, D'Arcy. 1863-68. *1341*
—. Anglin, Timothy Warren. Catholic Church. New Brunswick. Newspapers. St. John *Freeman* (newspaper). 1849-83. *3680*
—. Anti-Catholicism. Civil Rights. Law. Nova Scotia (Halifax). 1749-1829. *1105*
—. Anti-Catholicism. Great Britain. Ontario. Orange Order. Patriotism. 1830-1900. *2111*
—. Bishops. Canada, western. Catholic Church. French Canadians. Nominations for office. 1900-75. *3765*
—. Catholic Church. Charities. McMahon, Patrick. Poor. Quebec (Quebec). St. Bridget's Home. 1847-1972. *2521*
—. Catholic Church. Feild, Edward. Mullock, John Thomas. Newfoundland. Politics. Protestant Churches. 19c. *1254*
Iron work. Catholic Church. Cemeteries. German Alsatians. Gravemarkers. Ontario (Bruce County; Waterloo). 1850-1910. *1880*
Iroquois Indians. Algonkin Indians. Architecture. Calvary (chapels). Missionaries. Quebec (Oka). Sulpicians. 1700's-1800's. *1811*
—. Canada. Fort Frontenac. Indian-White Relations. Missions and Missionaries. Quinte Mission. Sulpician order. 1665-80. *1610*
—. Great Britain. Jesuits. Missions and Missionaries. Netherlands. New York. 1642-1719. *1654*
Iroquois Indians (Seneca). Baptists. Bingham, Abel. Diaries. Indian-White Relations. Missions and Missionaries. New York. Red Jacket (leader). Tonawanda Indian Reservation. 1822-28. *1513*
Irresistible compassion. Channing, William Ellery. Great Britain. Humanitarianism. Theology. ca 1660-19c. *2851*
Irrigation. Mormons. Social Change. Utah. 1840-1900. *329*
Irving, Washington. New England. Witchlore. 1809-24. *2008*
Islam *See also* Moslems.
—. Christianity. God is Dead Theology. Methodology. Religions, history of. Secularism. Smith, Wilfred Cantwell. Theology. 1940-73. *134*
—. Christianity. Judaism. Medieval culture. Philosophy of history. Wolfson, Harry Austryn. 6c-16c. 1910-74. *278*
Isolationism. Autonomy. Church Finance. Episcopal Church, Protestant. Missions and Missionaries. Theology. 1953-77. *1720*
—. Catholic Church. Great Britain. Nicoll, John R. A. Roosevelt, Franklin D. (administration). World War II. 1943. *1241*
Israel *See also* entries under Palestinian; Palestine.
—. Attitudes. Catholic Church. Zionism. 1945-48. *963*
—. Attitudes. Ethnicity. Jews. Northeastern or North Atlantic States. Students. Zionism. 1973-76. *4155*
—. Bible. History. Mormons. Smith, Joseph Fielding. Snell, Heber C. Theology. 1937-52. *4035*
—. Catholic Church. 1948-50. *3736*
—. Christianity. Jews. 1975. *157*
—. Foreign Policy. Protestantism. Zionism (review article). 1945-48. *2944*
—. Friends, Society of. Palestinians. 1977. *1278*
Issacs, Samuel Meyer. California (Sacramento, San Francisco). Henry, Henry Abraham. Jews. Letters. Rabbis. Travel (accounts). 1858. *4106*
Italian Americans. Catholic Church. Charismatic Movement. Jesu, Father. Pennsylvania (Philadelphia). Working Class. 1920's-30's. *1576*
—. Catholic Church. Church records. Immigrants. Methodology. Pennsylvania (Philadelphia). 1789-1900. *3770*
—. Catholic Church. Colorado (Denver). 1870's-1920's. *3728*
—. Catholic Church. Conflict and Conflict Resolution. Rhode Island (Providence). 1890-1930. *3682*
—. Catholic Church. Social Organization. 1880-1940. *3834*
—. Evil eye. Folklore. New York (Utica). 20c. *2192*
—. Immigration. New York City (Greenwich Village). Presbyterian Church. University Place Church. 1900-30. *3564*
Italian Americans (review article). Acculturation. Catholic Church. Social Organization. 1880-20c. *3820*
Italy *See also* Tuscany, Venetian Republic, etc.
—. Anti-Catholicism. Canada. Political Attitudes. Protestants. Risorgimento. 1846-60. *2114*
Italy (Rome). Catholic Church. International Union of Catholic Women's Leagues (congress). Quebec. Suffrage. Women. 1922. *935*
—. Childhood. Dreams. Painting. Symbolism in Art. Vedder, Elihu. 1856-1923. *1888*

J

Jack (man). Baptists. Negroes. Rhode Island (Newport). 1630's-52. *3017*
Jackson, Andrew. Clergy. Democratic Party. Eaton, Margaret (Peggy) O'Neale. Ely, Ezra Stiles. Presbyterian Church. 1829-30. *3536*
Jackson, James Caleb. Adventists. Hydrotherapy. Medical reform. New York (Dansville). White, Ellen G. 1864-65. *1451*
Jackson, Jesse. Negroes. People United to Save Humanity. Social Status. Southern Christian Leadership Conference. 1966-78. *2423*
Jackson, Sheldon. Colleges and Universities. Colorado. Presbyterian Church. Westminster University. 1874-1917. *597*
—. Crittenden, Lyman B. Higher Education. McMillan, Duncan M. Montana. Presbyterian Church. 1869-1918. *598*
Jacobitism. Church of England. Hunt, Edward. Keith, William. Patriotism. Pennsylvania. 1720. *1130*
Jacobs, David M. (review article). Occult sciences. UFO controversy. 1975. *2188*
Jacobs, Pizer. Judaism (Reform). New Mexico (Albuquerque). Temple Albert (dedication). 1900. *4232*
Jacobs, Zina Diantha Huntington. Daily life. Diaries. Illinois (Nauvoo). Mormons. Women. 1844-45. *3935*
Jacobsen, Florence S. Dwellings. Mormons. Personal narratives. Restorations. Utah (St. George). Young, Brigham. 19c. 1970's. *1789*
Jacquess, James F. Converts. Illinois (Springfield). Lincoln, Abraham. Methodist Church. 1847. *2788*

James, Henry. Appleton, Thomas Gold. Calvinism. New England Conscience (term). Unitarianism. 1875-95. *4075*

James, Henry *(The American)*. Church of England. National Characteristics. Puritans. 1700-1880. *2036*

James, Henry (1811-82). Letters. Swedenborg, Emanuel. Theology. Wilkinson, James John Garth. 1844-55. *4060*

—. Literature. Swedenborgianism. Theology. 1840's-81. *4061*

James, Sydney. Abolition Movement. Davis, David Brion. Drake, Thomas. Friends, Society of (review article). 1683-1863. 20c. *2471*

James, Thomas. Abolition Movement. Methodist Episcopal Church, African. Personal narratives. 1804-80. *2476*

James, William. ca 1897-1912. *49*

—. Nihilism. Psychology. 1870-1910. 1975. *50*

James, William *(Varieties of Religious Experience)*. DuBois, W. E. B. Troeltsch, Ernst (review). 1912. *67*

James, William *(Varieties of Religious Experience, Will to Believe)*. Rationalism. 1897-1902. *52*

Jamestown Diocese. Bishops. Catholic Church. Irish Americans. Minnesota (St. Paul). North Dakota. Shanley, John. 1852-1909. *3731*

Janes, Leroy Lansing. Americanization. Christianity. Japan (Kumamoto). Missions and Missionaries. Presbyterian Church. 1838-76. *1732*

Jankola, Matthew. Catholic Church. Pennsylvania (Philadelphia). Sisters of SS. Cyril and Methodius. Slovak Americans. 1903-70's. *3822*

Jannasch, Hermann Theodor. Eskimos. Labrador. Missions and Missionaries. Moravian Church. 1855-1931. *1594*

Janson, Kristofer. Clergy. Minnesota (Minneapolis). Norwegian Americans. Unitarianism. 1881-82. *4078*

Jansson, Erik H. Bishop Hill Colony. Engstrand, Stuart (review article). Illinois. 1846-50. 20c. *2083*

Janssonists. Bäck, Olof. Clergy. Esbjörn, Lars Paul. Letters. Lutheran Church. Methodism. Sweden. 1846-49. *2906*

—. Bishop Hill Colony. Illinois. Immigrants. Swedish Americans. Utopias. 1846-60. *393*

—. Bishop Hill Colony. Illinois. Letters. Swedish Americans. 1847. *416*

—. Emigration. Illinois. Sects, Religious. Social Classes. Sweden. 1845-47. *2620*

Japan. Archives. China. Korea. Missions and Missionaries. Presbyterian Historical Society. 1852-1911. *189*

—. Canada. Church of England. Domestic and Foreign Missionary Society. Missions and Missionaries. 1883-1902. *1587*

—. China. Diplomacy. Missions and Missionaries. Presbyterian Church. Stuart, John Leighton. 1937-41. *1745*

—. *Christian Century* (periodical). Foreign policy. Manchurian crisis. Morrison, Charles C. 1931-33. *2678*

—. Colby, Abby M. Congregationalism. Feminism. Missions and Missionaries. 1879-1914. *932*

—. Congregationalism. Converts. Massachusetts. Shimeta, Neesima. Voyages. 1860's-90. *1701*

—. Missions and Missionaries. Mormons. 1901-24. *1681*

—. Mysticism. Youth. 1976. *4282*

Japan (Kumamoto). Americanization. Christianity. Janes, Leroy Lansing. Missions and Missionaries. Presbyterian Church. 1838-76. *1732*

Japan (Yokohama). Ecumenism. Klein, Frederick C. Methodist Protestant Church. Missions and Missionaries. 1880-93. *458*

Japanese Americans. Baptists. Discrimination. Resettlement. World War II. 1890-1970. *2547*

Jarratt, Devereux. Clergy. Episcopal Church, Protestant. Letters. Virginia. 1770-1800. *3195*

Jarvis Street Baptist Church. Baptists. Factionalism. Fundamentalism. Modernism. Ontario (Toronto). Social Classes. 1895-1934. *2605*

—. Baptists. Fundamentalism. Ontario (Toronto). Shields, Thomas Todhunter. 1891-1955. *3067*

Jasper, John. Baptists. First African Baptist Church. Negroes. Sermons. Virginia (Richmond). 1812-1901. *2990*

Jay, John, II. Antislavery Sentiments. Civil War. Episcopal Church, Protestant. 1840-65. *2494*

Jay Street Church. Baptists. Clergy. Massachusetts (Boston). Negroes. Paul, Thomas (and family). 1773-1973. *3048*

Jayme, Luís (death). California (San Diego). Franciscans. Mission San Diego de Alcalá. Yuman Indians. 1775. *1657*

Jedrey, Christopher M. (review article). American Revolution. American Revolution. Cleaveland, John. Congregationalism. Daily life. Great Awakening. Ideology. Massachusetts (Chebacco). New Lights. 1740-79. *2241*

Jeffers, Robinson. Brophy, Robert J. Morris, Adelaide Kirby. Poetry. Stevens, Wallace. Theology (review article). 20c. *2065*

Jefferson, Thomas. Allen, Ethan. Deism. Franklin, Benjamin. Historiography. Palmer, Elihu. 1750-1820. *4277*

—. American Revolution. Boucher, Jonathan. Church of England. Civil War. Great Britain. Loyalists. 1640-1797. *1412*

—. American Revolution. Calvinism. Church and state. Clergy. Linn, William. Presbyterian Church. 1775-1808. *1335*

—. Anticlericalism. Bible. Deism. Jesus Christ. Translating and Interpreting. 1813-20. *4279*

—. Bushnell, Horace. Church and state. Congregationalism. ca 1800-60. *1002*

—. Christianity. Deism. Letters. Sectarianism. 1784-1800. *4280*

—. Citizenship. Democracy. Locke, John. Puritanism. 17c-18c. *1408*

—. Declaration of Independence. Religious liberty. Virginia. 1743-1826. *1022*

—. Deism. Theology. 1800-25. *4276*

Jefferson, Thomas *(Life and Morals of Jesus of Nazareth)*. Christianity. Deism. Jesus Christ. Morality. Russia. Theology. Tolstoy, Leo *(Christ's Christianity)*. 1800-85. *4278*

Jeffersonian (newspaper). Anti-Catholicism. Benedictines. D'Equivelley, G. F. Florida (Pasco County). Land. Letters-to-the-editor. Mohr, Charles. 1915-16. *2123*

Jehovah's Witnesses. Adventists. Friends of Man. Interior Lay Missionary Movement. Russell, Charles Taze. 1852-1916. *3921*

—. Church and State. Government, Resistance to. Persecution. Theology. 1870's-1960's. *1097*

—. Church-sect model. Latin America. 1950-76. *3920*

—. Conscientious Objectors. Courts. Flag salute. World War II. 1930's-40's. *2655*

—. Millenarianism. Russell, Charles Taze. 1879-1916. *3919*

—. Organizational structure. Rescue missions. Skid Rows. Watch Tower movement. 1970's. *2722*

Jensen, Richard. Cultural Pluralism. Kleppner, Paul. North Central States. Political behavior. 1850-1900. *1214*

Jenson, Andrew. Archival catalogs and inventories. Manuscripts. Mormon Church (Historian's Office). 1830-1975. *193*

—. Historiography. Hunter, Howard W. Lund, A. William. Lyon, T. Edgar. Mormons. Roberts, Brigham Henry. 1913-70. *226*

Jeremiads. Attitudes. Puritans. Sports. 1620-1720. *3658*

—. Great Britain. New England. Pamphlets. Puritans. Ward, Nathaniel. 1645-50. *1975*

—. New England. Puritans. Sermons. Sports. 17c-18c. *3659*

Jessey, Henry. Baptism. Baptists. Great Britain (London). Letters. New England. Puritans. Toleration. Tombes, John. 1645. *997*

Jesu, Father. Catholic Church. Charismatic Movement. Italian Americans. Pennsylvania (Philadelphia). Working Class. 1920's-30's. *1576*

Jesuits. Alaska. Catholic Church. Holy Cross Mission. Indians. Missions and Missionaries. Sisters of St. Ann. Yukon River, lower. 1887-1956. *1615*

—. Americas (North and South). Antislavery Sentiments. Dominicans. 16c-18c. *2486*

—. Anti-Catholicism. Bapst, John. Chaney, William Henry. Editors and editing. Maine (Ellsworth). Nativism. 1853-54. *2121*

—. Anti-Catholicism. Conscription, Military. Novitiate of St. Stanislaus. Ontario (Guelph). Protestantism. World War I. 1918-19. *2657*

—. Archives. Canada. 17c-1978. *183*

—. Arizona. Indians. Kino, Eusebio Francisco. Missions and Missionaries. Spain. 1680's-1711. *1565*

—. Arizona (Nogales). Excavations. Mission Guevavi. 18c. 1964-66. *1818*

—. Attitudes. France. Indians. Missions and Missionaries. New France. 1611-72. *1495*

—. California. Dominicans. Franciscans. Missions and Missionaries. Serra, Junípero. 1768-76. *1575*

—. California. Nobili, John. Santa Clara, University of. 1850-55. *695*

—. California. Santa Clara, University of. 1849-51. *696*

—. Canada. Czechoslovakia. Refugees. Refugees. 1950. *3776*

—. Catholic Church. Communism. McCarthy, Joseph R. 1950-57. *1223*

—. Catholic Church. *Revista Catolica* (periodical). Southwest. 1875-1962. *3884*

—. Colonization. Indians. Menéndez de Avilés, Pedro. Missions and Missionaries. Opechancanough (chief). Powhatan Indians. Spain. Virginia. 1570-72. *1622*

—. Diaries. McCormick, Vincent A. Vatican. World War II. 1942-45. *3755*

—. Drinan, Robert F. Massachusetts. Political campaigns. 1970. *1267*

—. Earthquakes. Quebec. *Relation de 1663* (report). 1663. *2296*

—. Ecology. Hopkins, Gerard Manley. Humanities. Poetry. Science. ca 1840-70's. *3701*

—. Esteyneffer, Juan de *(Florilegio Medicinal)*. Herbs. Indians. Medicine (practice of). Missions and Missionaries. Southwest. 1711. *1444*

—. France. Indians. Missions and Missionaries. New York, western. Rings. ca 1630-87. *1664*

—. Great Britain. Iroquois Indians. Missions and Missionaries. Netherlands. New York. 1642-1719. *1654*

—. Lacouture, Onésime. Quebec. Spiritual movement. 1931-50. *3730*

—. Land Tenure. Legislation. Mercier, Honoré. Protestant Churches. Quebec. 1886. *1087*

—. Maryland (St. Marys County). Plantations. St. Inigoes Church. Slavery. 1806-1950. *326*

—. Missions and Missionaries. Ottoman Empire. Protestant Churches. Syria. 1840's. *1698*

Jesuits' Estates Act. Canada. Church and State. Political Protest. Protestants. 1880-90. *1088*

Jesus Christ. Anticlericalism. Bible. Deism. Jefferson, Thomas. Translating and Interpreting. 1813-20. *4279*

—. Archko collection. Forgeries. Mahan, William D. Mormons. Presbyterian Church (Cumberland). Wallace, Lew *(Ben-Hur)*. 1880's. *3928*

—. Christianity. Deism. Jefferson, Thomas *(Life and Morals of Jesus of Nazareth)*. Morality. Russia. Theology. Tolstoy, Leo *(Christ's Christianity)*. 1800-85. *4278*

—. Counter culture. Music, rock and roll. 1950's-70's. *1916*

—. Divinity (issue). Hodge, Charles *(Systematic Theology)*. Nevin, John W. Presbyterian Church. Theology. 1872. *3581*

—. Films. 1920's-70's. *1894*

—. Films. 1950's-74. *1881*

—. Folklore. New York Thruway. Vanishing hitchhiker (theme). 1971. *2737*

—. Judaism (Orthodox, Reform). New York City. Sermons. Theology. Wise, Stephen Samuel. 1925-26. *4153*

—. Music (pop). 1960's-1970's. *1930*

Jesus Movement. Addiction. Conversion. 1960's-75. *2784*

—. Conversion. Models. 1970's. *2770*

—. Religiosity. Self-conceptions. 1960's-70's. *2783*

—. Sects, Religious. 1960's-70's. *2771*

Jesus People. Charismatic Movement. Pentecostalism. Revivals. Transcendental Meditation. 1960's-78. *127*

—. Christianity. Cults. Morality. 1960's-70's. *140*

—. Counter culture. Fundamentalism. Youth Movements. 1960's. *2719*

—. Mormons. Protestant Churches. Restitutionism. Revivals. 19c-20c. *2744*

Jewish Institute of Religion. Hebrew Union College. Seminaries. 1875-1974. *786*

Jewish Jubilee Year. Social Customs. ca 3000 BC-1975. *4149*

Jewish Observer (periodical). Judaism, Orthodox. *Tradition* (periodical). 1880-1974. *4197*

Jewish Orphan's Home. California (Huntington Park, Los Angeles). Frey, Sigmund. Judaism (Reform). Social work. 1870's-1930. *2500*

Jewish Peace Fellowship. Pacifism. World War II. 1943. *2706*

Jewish Student Movement. Massachusetts (Boston). Radicals and Radicalism. Social Change. Youth Movements. 1960-75. *2433*
Jewish studies. Colleges and universities. Conferences. Curricula. Dissertations. 1979. *4138*
—. Colleges and universities. Conferences. Dissertations. 1978. *4137*
—. Higher Education. Religious studies departments. 1972-74. *539*
Jewish Theological Seminary. Fund raising. Judaism (Orthodox). Mergers. New York City. Seminaries. Yeshiva College. 1925-28. *736*
Jewish Welfare Board. Commission on Training Camp Activities. Knights of Columbus. Leisure. Morality. Social Reform. War Department. World War I. Young Men's Christian Association. Young Women's Christian Association. 1917-18. *2379*
Jews *See also* Anti-Semitism; Judaism; Zionism.
—. Acculturation. Canada. Ethnicity. USA. 1961-74. *4156*
—. Agnosticism. Ethnicity. Hillquit, Morris. New York City. Socialism. 1890's-1933. *1331*
—. Alaska. Fur trade. Gold rushes. Nome Hebrew Benevolent Society. 1867-1916. *4103*
—. *American Israelite* (newspaper). Letters. Nevada (Eureka). 1875. *4163*
—. American Jewish Historical Society. Bibliographies. 1960-75. *4096*
—. American, Sadie. Congress of Jewish Women. Solomon, Hannah G. Women. World Parliament of Religions. World's Columbian Exposition (Chicago, 1893). 1893. *846*
—. Anti-Semitism. Evangelicals. Fundamentalists. Messianic beliefs. 1970's. *135*
—. Arizona. Bar mitzvahs. Goldwater family. 1879. *4097*
—. Arizona. Barth, Solomon. Converts. Frontier. Mormons. 1856-1928. *60*
—. Assimilation. 1970's. *4111*
—. Assimilation. Evangelism. Ontario (Toronto). Presbyterian Church. 1912-18. *1540*
—. Assimilation. Political Attitudes. South Carolina (Charleston). 1970's. *4136*
—. Assimilation. Rabbis. Reading. 1970's. *4132*
—. Attitudes. Canada. Catholic Church. Ethnic Groups. Protestantism. Social Status. 1968. *2088*
—. Attitudes. Ethnicity. Israel. Northeastern or North Atlantic States. Students. Zionism. 1973-76. *4155*
—. Baptists, Seventh-Day. Conversion. Daland, William C. Friedlaender, Herman. New York City. *Peculiar People* (newspaper). 1880's-90's. *1633*
—. Beiliss, Mendel. California (Oakland, San Francisco). Christianity. Newspapers. Russia. Trials. 1911-13. *4105*
—. Bergel, Siegmund. California (San Bernardino). Religious education. 1868-1912. *765*
—. Bibliographies. 1654-1980. *4114*
—. Bibliographies. 16c-1978. *4118*
—. Bibliographies. 1960-73. *4113*
—. Bibliographies. 1960-74. *4095*
—. Bibliographies. 1960-76. *4116*
—. Bibliographies. 1960-78. *4117*
—. Bibliographies. 1960-79. *4119*
—. Bibliographies. 1974-75. *4115*
—. Boycotts. Consumers. Meat, kosher. New York City. Prices. Riots. Women. 1902. *4112*
—. British North America. Myers, Myer. Rites and Ceremonies. Silversmithing. 1723-95. *1905*
—. Business. California (San Francisco; San Bruno Avenue). Esther Hellman Settlement House. Neighborhoods. 1901-68. *4130*
—. Cabala. Counter Culture. Mysticism. Rationalism. Traditionalism. 1940's-70's. *4140*
—. Cabalism. Friends, Society of. 17c-20c. *27*
—. California. Charities. Disaster relief. Economic aid. Nieto, Jacob. Rabbis. San Francisco Earthquake and Fire. 1906. *2520*
—. California. Franklin, Harvey B. Personal narratives. Rabbis. 1916-57. *4099*
—. California (Oakland). 1852-91. *4125*
—. California (Oakland). Disaster relief. Refugees. San Francisco Earthquake and Fire. Temple Sinai. 1906. *2527*
—. California (Sacramento, San Francisco). Henry, Henry Abraham. Issacs, Samuel Meyer. Letters. Rabbis. Travel (accounts). 1858. *4106*
—. California (San Francisco). Cemeteries. First Hebrew Benevolent Society. Funerals. Johnson, Henry D. 1849-50. *4147*
—. California (San Francisco). Dyer, Leon. Leadership. Maryland (Baltimore). 1820's-75. *4142*
—. California (San Francisco). Nieto, Jacob. Rabbis. Rubin, Max. Temple Sherith Israel. 1893. *4148*
—. California (Santa Monica). Resorts. 1875-1939. *4160*
—. California, southern. Choynski, Isidor Nathan. Cities. Journalism. Travel (accounts). 1881. *4144*
—. Carigal, Hakham Raphael Haim Isaac. Rhode Island (Newport). 1771-77. *4190*
—. Catholic Church. Connecticut (New Haven). Ethnic Groups. Marriage. Protestantism. 1900-50. *906*
—. Catholic Church. District of Columbia. Judaism. Protestant churches. Psychological well-being. Religiosity. Worship. 1970's. *130*
—. Cemeteries. Congregation Beth El. Historic markers. Letters. Michigan (Detroit). 1850-1971. *4159*
—. Christianity. Civil Rights. Riis, Jacob. Social Organization. 1870-1914. *2129*
—. Christianity. Discrimination. Folklore. Negroes. Stereotypes. 18c-1974. *2091*
—. Christianity. Israel. 1975. *157*
—. Christians. Genocide. Theology. World War II. 1945-74. *101*
—. Church and State. Church schools. Education, Finance. Public Policy. Religion in the Public Schools. 1961-71. *512*
—. Church membership. Ethnicity. Illinois (Chicago). Protestants. 1960's-70's. *121*
—. Congregation Kahal Kadosh Shearith Israel. Ethnicity. Falkenau, Jacob J. M. Hebrew. Lyons, Jacques Judah. New York City. Pique, Dob. Poetry. 1786-1841. *2062*
—. Delaware (Wilmington). Moses Montefiore Mutual Aid Society. 1850-90. *4101*
—. Ecumenism. France. Vatican. 1975. *501*
—. Ecumenism. National Council of Churches (General Assembly). Protestant churches. 1969-74. *502*
—. Ethnicity. Maryland, University of. Parents. Students. 1949-71. *4128*
—. Fundamentalism. 17c-1976. *13*
—. Fundamentalism. Gaebelein, Arno C. Genocide. Germany. *Our Hope* (periodical). 1937-45. *136*
—. Geographic distribution. 1952-71. *4134*
—. Ghettos. New York City (Lower East Side). 1890-1920. *4108*
—. Hadassah. National Council of Jewish Women. Professionalism. Voluntary Associations. Women. 1890-1980. *4146*
—. Harap, Louis (review article). Literature. 1775-1914. 1974. *83*
—. Hebrew Benevolent Association. Letters. Nevada (Austin). Silver mining. 1864-82. *4164*
—. Hexter, Maurice B. Ohio (Cincinnati). Personal narratives. Social Work. United Jewish Charities. 1910's. *2508*
—. Historians. Kenesseth Israel Synagogue. Korn, Bertram Wallace (obituary). Pennsylvania (Elkins Park). 1918-79. *248*
—. Historiography. Scholarship. 1948-76. *207*
—. Immigrants. Pennsylvania (Pittsburgh). Religious Education. 1862-1932. *754*
—. Immigration. Morocco. Quebec (Montreal). 1960's-70's. *4121*
—. Laity. Leadership. New York (Kingston). Political Leadership. Protestant Churches. Social Status. 1825-60. *2600*
—. Letters-to-the-editor. Mexico (Tamaulipas; Matamoros). Newspapers. Texas (Brownsville). 1876-82. *4165*
—. New England. Old Testament. Pilgrims. Puritans. 1620-1700. *2936*
—. North Dakota (Grand Forks). Papermaster, Benjamin. 1890-1934. *4135*
—. Political Protest. Vietnam War. Youth. 1960's. *2694*
—. Secularization. Self-perception. 1957-77. *4127*
Jews, East European. California (San Francisco). *Emanu-El* (newspaper). Immigration. Letters-to-the-editor. Rabbis. Rosenthal, Marcus. Voorsanger, Jacob. 1905. *4141*
Jews (German, Polish). California (San Francisco). Synagogues. Temple Emanu-El. Temple Sherith Israel. 1848-1900. *4126*
Jews (review article). Cities. Gartner, Lloyd P. Gurock, Jeffrey S. Hertzberg, Steven. Raphael, Mark Lee. 1840-1979. *4150*
Jews (Rhodesli). California (Los Angeles). Immigration. Judaism (Orthodox). Sephardic Hebrew Center. 1900-74. *4180*
Jews, Sephardic. California. Judaism (Orthodox). 1850-1900. *4198*
John Wesley (vessel). Bergner, Peter. Immigrants. Methodist Episcopal Church. New York City. Seamen. 1830-77. *3478*
Johnson, Andrew. Clergy. Protestant Churches. Public Opinion. 1865-68. *1219*
—. District of Columbia. Lincoln, Abraham. Schurz, Carl. Seance. Spiritualism. 1865. *4293*
Johnson, Benton. Political parties. Protestant ethic. 1960's-70's. *1302*
Johnson, Emeroy. Elementary Education. Lutheran Church. Minnesota. Personal narratives. Religious education. Swedish Americans. ca 1854-ca 1920. *666*
Johnson, Grove L. Anti-Semitism. California (Fresno). Foote, William D. Trials. 1893. *2134*
Johnson, Henry D. California (San Francisco). Cemeteries. First Hebrew Benevolent Society. Funerals. Jews. 1849-50. *4147*
Johnson, Jakie. Indian Shaker Church. Missions and Missionaries. Oregon (Siletz). Siletz Indians. ca 1881-1970. *2776*
Johnson, Jeremiah. American Revolution. Daily life. Great Britain. Military Occupation. New York City (Brooklyn). Personal narratives. 1775-83. *63*
Johnson, Lyndon B. Hoover, Herbert C. Nixon, Richard M. Protestant ethic. Public welfare. Rhetoric. Roosevelt, Franklin D. Weber, Max. 1905-79. *348*
Johnson, Paul E. Boyer, Paul. City Life. Middle Classes. Missions and Missionaries. Morality. New York (Rochester). Revivals. 1815-1920. 1978. *2800*
Johnson, Samuel (1822-82). Massachusetts. Orientalism. Theology. Transcendentalism. 1840's-82. *4071*
Johnson, Samuel (1696-1772). Arminiamism. Church of England. Congregationalism. Converts. New England. Sacramentalism. 1715-22. *3183*
—. Beecher, Catharine. Church of England. Congregationalism. Reform (review article). Washington, Booker T. Women. 1696-1901. *2847*
—. Church and State. Colleges and Universities (review article). Columbia University. Dartmouth College. Harvard University. Yale University. 1696-1970. 1972-74. *524*
—. Church of England. Columbia University. Livingston, William. Reformed Dutch Church. 1751-63. *635*
—. Church of England. Congregationalism. Connecticut. Great Britain. Ordination. Yale University. 1722-23. *2843*
—. Church of England. Congregationalism. Connecticut (New Haven). Conversion. Theology. Yale University. 1710-22. *3177*
Jolliet, Louis. Catholic Church. Colonial Government. Discovery and Exploration. France. Marquette, Jacques. Missions and Missionaries. Mississippi River. Monuments. 1665-1700. *3767*
—. Catholic Church. Discovery and Exploration. Marquette, Jacques. Mississippi River. 1673. 1973. *1567*
Jones, Alonzo Trevier. Adventists. Illinois. Religious liberty. Sabbath. World's Columbian Exposition (Chicago, 1893). 1893. *2280*
Jones, Charles Colcock. Evangelicalism. Race Relations. South. Utopias. 1804-63. *2543*
—. Missions and Missionaries. Presbyterian Church. Slavery. South. 1825-63. *2177*
Jones, Charles Harriman. Adventists. California (Mountain View, Oakland). Pacific Press Publishing Company. Publishers and Publishing. 1879-1923. *362*
Jones, Dan. Illinois (Nauvoo). *Maid of Iowa* (vessel). Mormons. Smith, Joseph. Steamboats. 1843-45. *346*
Jones, David. Baptists. Folger, Peter. Indians. Missionaries. Northeastern or North Atlantic States. Williams, Roger. 1638-1814. *1619*
Jones, James Parnell. Antislavery Sentiments. Civil War. Friends, Society of (Congregational). Maine. Military Service. 1850's-64. *2641*
Jones, Jim. Apocalypse (concept). Guyana (Jonestown). People's Temple. 1953-78. *4252*

—. California. Guyana (Jonestown; review article). People's Temple. 1931-78. *4251*
—. California (San Francisco). Guyana (Jonestown). Leftism. People's Temple. 1960's-78. *4247*
—. Charisma. Guyana (Jonestown). Leadership. Models. People's Temple. Suicide, mass. 1978. *4253*
—. Cults. Father Divine. Negroes. Peace Mission (movement). People's Temple. 1920-79. *4254*
—. Guyana (Jonestown). People's Temple. Personality. Suicide, mass. 1965-78. *4238*
—. Guyana (Jonestown). People's Temple. Sects, Religious. ca 1950-79. *4262*
Jones, Louis C. Folk medicine. Folklore. Witchcraft. 1945-49. *2189*
Jones, Peter. Courtship. Field, Eliza. Great Britain (London). Indians. Methodism. New York. 1820's-33. *1637*
Jones, Sam. Amusements. Georgia. Methodist Episcopal Church, South. Morality. Revivals. Self-reliance. 1872-1906. *3498*
Jones, William A. Bishops. Byrne, Edwin V. Caruana, George J. Catholic Church. Puerto Rico. San Juan Diocese. 1866-1963. *3814*
Jordan, Clarence. Christianity. Communes. Georgia. Koinonia Farm. 1942-60's. *402*
Jordan, John Morton. Allen, Bennet. Church of England. Colonial Government. Ecclesiastical pluralism. Maryland. Patronage. Sharpe, Horatio. 1759-70. *1051*
Jorgensen, Niels Bjorn. Adventists. Anesthesia. California. Dentistry. Loma Linda University. Teaching. 1923-74. *1441*
Journal of the West (periodical). Bibliographies. Indian-White relations. Western states. 1970-74. *1593*
Journalism *See also* Editors and Editing; Films; Freedom of the Press; Newspapers; Periodicals; Press.
—. Abolition Movement. Cornish, Samuel E. *Freedom's Journal* (newspaper). Negroes. Presbyterian Church. 1820's-59. *2498*
—. Antislavery Sentiments. Catholic Church. Emigration. Germans, Sudeten. Missions and Missionaries. Neumann, Saint John Nepomucene. Republican Party. 19c-20c. *3826*
—. California, southern. Choynski, Isidor Nathan. Cities. Jews. Travel (accounts). 1881. *4144*
—. Canada. Catholic Church. Social thought. Somerville, Henry. 1915-53. *2354*
—. Catholic Church. Newspapers. 1822-1975. *3831*
—. Chile. Missions and Missionaries. Presbyterian Church. Religious liberty. Trumbull, David. 1845-89. *1703*
Journals. *See* Diaries.
Juan Antonio (neophyte). Catholic Church. Indians. Mission San Gabriel Arcangel. Painting (realist tradition). 1800. 1976. *1882*
—. Catholic Church. Indians. Mission San Gabriel Arcangel. Paintings. 1800-1976. *1883*
Jubilee College. Chase, Philander. Episcopal Church, Protestant. Illinois (Peoria). 1840-62. *730*
—. Documents. Episcopal Church, Protestant. Excavations. Illinois (Peoria County). 1839-1979. *770*
Judaism *See also* Anti-Semitism; Jews; Zionism.
—. 1979. *4104*
—. 1980. *4157*
—. Acculturation. Christianity. Ethnicity. Europe. Immigration. Middle East. 19c-20c. *34*
—. Alpert, Abraham. Immigration. Massachusetts (Boston). Rabbis. 20c. *4087*
—. American Jewish Historical Society. Archival catalogs and inventories. Rhode Island. 1692-1975. *273*
—. American Revolution. Baptists. Church of England. Congregationalism. Friends, Society of. Georgia. Lutheran Church. Presbyterian Church. 1733-90. *88*
—. American Revolution. Documents. Letters. 1775-90. *1277*
—. Americanization. Law. Rabbis. Rabbis (responsa). Social customs. 1862-1937. *300*
—. Anti-Semitism. Fiction. Fiedler, Leslie. Personal narratives. 1970's. *2043*
—. Attitudes. Brooklyn College. Catholic Church. Immigration. Negroes. New York City. Protestant Ethic. West Indian Americans. 1939-78. *350*
—. Attitudes. Hasidism. Philosophy. 1970's. *4189*
—. Bibliographies. 1960-80. *4120*
—. Book Collecting. Kohut, George Alexander. Yale University Library (Kohut Collection). 1901-33. *179*
—. Brandeis, Louis D. Gompers, Samuel. Kogan, Michael S. Labor Unions and Organizations. 1880's-1975. *1479*
—. Braude, William G. Personal narratives. Wolfson, Harry. 1932-54. *4090*
—. California (Los Angeles). Cantors. Concerts. Loew's State Theatre. Music, liturgical. Rosenblatt, Josef "Yosele". Vaudeville. 1925. *1917*
—. California (Los Angeles). Hecht, Sigmund. 1904-25. *4182*
—. California (Los Angeles). Political Campaigns (mayoral). Social Classes. Voting and Voting Behavior. 1969. *1276*
—. California (Los Angeles; Chavez Ravine). Cemeteries. Hebrew Benevolent Society of Los Angeles. Home of Peace Jewish Cemetery. Photographs. 1855-1910. *4161*
—. California (San Francisco). Franklin, Lewis Abraham. Rabbis. Sermons. Yom Kippur. 1850. *4100*
—. California (San Francisco). Henry, Henry Abraham. Rabbis. 1857-69. *4107*
—. California (San Francisco). Politics. 1935-65. *1226*
—. California (Santa Cruz). Converts. Schlutius, Emma. 1877. *4098*
—. Canada. Catholic Church. Industrialization. Protestant Churches. Religiosity. 1921-71. *93*
—. Catholic Church. District of Columbia. Jews. Protestant churches. Psychological well-being. Religiosity. Worship. 1970's. *130*
—. Catholic Church. Ethnic Groups. Pennsylvania (Philadelphia). Social classes. Voting and Voting Behavior. 1924-40. *1308*
—. Catholic Church. Family. Private Schools. 1960's-70's. *654*
—. Catholic Church. Georgia. Psychohistory. State Politics. Watson, Thomas E. 1856-1922. *55*
—. Catholic Church. Lutheran Church. Ohio (Cincinnati). Public Schools. Religious Education. 19c. *545*
—. Central Conference of American Rabbis. Drachman, Bernard. Judaism (Orthodox). Orthodox Jewish Sabbath Alliance. Sabbath. Saturday. 1903-30. *2277*
—. Charities. Federation for the Support of Jewish Philanthropic Societies. New York City. 1917-33. *2516*
—. Charities. Federation movement. Ohio (Columbus). 1904-48. *2522*
—. Chinese Americans. Christianity. Nativism. Newspapers. Pacific Coast. Slavery. 1848-65. *75*
—. Christianity. Feminism. 1967-76. *876*
—. Christianity. France. Great Britain. Theater. ca 1957-78. *1853*
—. Christianity. Huidekoper, Frederick. Meadville Theological School. Pennsylvania. Seminaries. Unitarianism. 1834-92. *4086*
—. Christianity. Islam. Medieval culture. Philosophy of history. Wolfson, Harry Austryn. 6c-16c. 1910-74. *278*
—. Christianity. Metalwork. Rites and Ceremonies. ca 1650-1888. *1854*
—. Christianity. Minority groups. Social Classes. 1974. *2610*
—. Christianity. Niebuhr, Reinhold. 1930-60. *137*
—. Christianity. Pfeffer, Leo. Politics. Secular Humanism. Social Change. 1958-76. *132*
—. Christianity. Women. 17c-1978. *860*
—. Church Schools. Education. Hasidism (Lubavitch). Quebec (Montreal). 1969-71. *550*
—. City Life. Ethnic enclaves. Manitoba (Winnipeg). 1940's-70's. *4091*
—. Civil Rights. Colonies. Europe. Florida. Levy, Moses Elias. 1825. *4151*
—. Congregation Ahavath Shalom. Rhode Island (West Warwick). 1912-38. *4152*
—. Congregation Beth El. Michigan (Detroit). 1859-61. *4092*
—. Congregation Beth El. Michigan (Detroit). 1861-67. *4093*
—. Congregation Kahal Kadosh Beth Israel. Georgia (Macon). Leeser, Isaac. Letters. Loewenthal, Henry. Rabbis. 1854-70. *4124*
—. Congregation Kol Ami. Ecumenism. Utah (Salt Lake City). 1964-76. *482*
—. Congregation Sons of Zion. Finesilver, Moses Ziskind. Rabbis. Rhode Island (Providence). 1880-83. *4122*
—. Congregationalism. Edwards, Jonathan. Luria, Isaac. Millenarianism. Progress, concept of. 16c-18c. *84*
—. Connecticut (Hartford). 1880-1929. *4089*
—. Daily Life. Elections. Oregon (Portland). Temple Beth Israel. 1878. *4237*
—. Economic Conditions. Social Status. 1970-71. *4129*
—. Emigration. Ethiopia (Addis Ababa). Ford, Arnold. Negroes. 1930-35. *4143*
—. Ethnicity. 1975. *4145*
—. Feminism. 1967-79. *826*
—. Feminism. 1970's. *923*
—. Franklin, Leo M. Nebraska (Omaha). Rabbis. Temple Israel. 1892-99. *4094*
—. Hasidism. Quebec (Montreal). 1942-71. *4179*
—. Hawaii. Personal narratives. Zwerin, Kenneth C. 1935. *4158*
—. Illinois (Chicago). Socialization. 1974. *4110*
—. Liberalism. 19c-20c. *4131*
—. Melville, Herman *(Clarel)*. 19c. *2045*
—. Michigan (Detroit). 1850-1922. *4154*
—. Michigan (Detroit). Religious Education. Sholom Aleichem Institute. 1926-71. *746*
—. Mysticism. 1960's-80. *4088*
—. Religious studies. Tradition. 20c. *4133*
—. Women. 1920's-30's. *916*
Judaism (Conservative). Hertzberg, Arthur. Historians. Rabbis. 1980. *4167*
—. Hertzberg, Arthur. Personal narratives. Rabbis. 1940's-79. *4168*
—. Theology. 1945-70's. *4169*
—. United Synagogue of America. 1910-13. *4170*
Judaism (Conservative, Orthodox). Adelman, Samuel. Colorado (Denver). Congregation Beth Ha Medrosh Hagodol. Kauvar, Charles E. H. Rabbis. 1949-58. *4193*
Judaism (Conservative, Reform). Alienation. Ecumenism. Liberalism. Utah (Salt Lake City). 1971. *499*
Judaism (Orthodox). 1970-79. *4186*
—. American Revolution. Great Britain. Rhode Island. Touro, Isaac. 1782. *4184*
—. Ararat (colony). New York. Noah, Mordecai Manuel. Rhode Island (Newport). 1813-21. *4178*
—. Baltimore Hebrew Congregation. Maryland (Baltimore). Rehine, Zalma. 1830-31. *4191*
—. Behavior. 1970's. *4181*
—. Belkin, Samuel. Brown University. Rhode Island (Providence). 1932-35. *4172*
—. California. Jews, Sephardic. 1850-1900. *4198*
—. California (Los Angeles). Immigration. Jews (Rhodesli). Sephardic Hebrew Center. 1900-74. *4180*
—. California (Oroville, San Francisco, Woodland). Congregation Beth Israel. Messing, Aron J. Religious education. Sabbath Schools. Travel. 1879. *4201*
—. California (San Bernardino). Congregation Beth Israel. Fund raising. Messing, Aron J. 1879. *4199*
—. Canon law. Circumcision. Europe. Illowy, Bernard. Louisiana (New Orleans). Rabbis. 1853-65. *4176*
—. Cantors. Congregation Shearith Israel. Netherlands. New York. Pinto, Joseph Jesurun. Travel. 1759-82. *4196*
—. Catholic Church. Human Relations. Protestant Churches. Rhode Island. 18c. *2087*
—. Central Conference of American Rabbis. Drachman, Bernard. Judaism. Orthodox Jewish Sabbath Alliance. Sabbath. Saturday. 1903-30. *2277*
—. Children. New York City (Brooklyn; Boro Park). Parents. Social Status. 1973. *4187*
—. Colorado (Denver). Congregation Beth Ha Medrosh Hagodol. Kauvar, Charles E. H. 1902-71. *4192*
—. Colorado (Denver). Congregation Beth Ha Medrosh Hagodol. Kauvar, Charles E. H. Progressivism. 1902-71. *4194*
—. Congregation Beth Elohim. Congregation Beth Elohim Unveh Shallom. Portuguese Americans. South Carolina (Charleston). 1784-91. *4173*
—. Congregation Sharey Tzedick. Utah (Salt Lake City). 1916-48. *4195*
—. Congregation Shearith Israel. New York City. Rhode Island (Newport). Touro Synagogue. 1893-1902. *4183*
—. Fasman, Oscar Z. Hebrew Theological College. Oklahoma (Tulsa). Ontario (Ottawa). Personal narratives. Rabbis. 1929-79. *4177*
—. Fund raising. Jewish Theological Seminary. Mergers. New York City. Seminaries. Yeshiva College. 1925-28. *736*
—. Georgia. Religious liberty. 1733-90. *4188*

—. Hebrew Day Schools. Religious education. 1960's-70's. *662*
—. *Jewish Observer* (periodical). *Tradition* (periodical). 1880-1974. *4197*
—. Jung, Leo. Rabbinical Council of America. 1926-42. *4171*
—. Letters. Religious Liberty. Rhode Island (Newport). Seixas, Moses. Washington, George. 1790. 1974. *1081*
—. New York. Schools. Social relations. 18c. *4175*
—. Religious Education. Yeshivot (schools). 1896-1979. *648*
—. Rhode Island (Newport). Touro Synagogue. 1654-1977. *4200*
—. Rhode Island (Newport). Touro Synagogue. 1658-1963. *4185*
—. Rhode Island (Newport). Touro Synagogue. 1902. *4174*
Judaism (Orthodox, Reform). Adler, Cyrus. American Academy for Jewish Research. Intellectuals. Revel, Bernard. Society of Jewish Academicians. 1916-22. *4139*
—. Beth Olam Cemetery. California (San Jose). Congregation Bickur Cholim. Organizations. 1850-1900. *4123*
—. California (San Francisco). Goldie, Albert. New York City. Poor. Synagogues. Weinstock, Harris. 1906. *4166*
—. Charities. Nebraska (Omaha). Political Leadership. Refugees. Settlement. 1820-1937. *4102*
—. Commerce. Oregon (Portland). Organizations. 1888. *4162*
—. Discrimination. Georgia (Atlanta). 1865-1915. *4109*
—. Jesus Christ. New York City. Sermons. Theology. Wise, Stephen Samuel. 1925-26. *4153*
Judaism, Reform. 1970's. *4230*
—. Academic Freedom. Hebrew Union College. Kohler, Kaufmann. Ohio (Cincinnati). Zionism. 1903-07. *724*
—. Adler, Samuel. Morality. New York City. Theology. ca 1829-91. *4208*
—. Agriculture. Krauskopf, Joseph. Social Reform. 1880's-1923. *4228*
—. Architecture. California (Los Angeles, San Francisco). Temple Emanu-El. Wilshire Boulevard Temple. 1937. *4205*
—. Berger, Elmer. Personal Narratives. Rabbis. Zionism. ca 1945-75. *4202*
—. Bibliographies. 1883-1973. *4226*
—. Blum, Abraham. California (Los Angeles). New York City. Rabbis. Texas (Galveston). 1866-1921. *4217*
—. California (Huntington Park, Los Angeles). Frey, Sigmund. Jewish Orphan's Home. Social work. 1870's-1930. *2500*
—. California (Los Angeles). Church finance. Rabbis. Wilshire Boulevard Temple. 1897. *4231*
—. California (Los Angeles). Letters. Newmark, Joseph. Rabbis. Wilshire Boulevard Temple. 1881. *4236*
—. California (Los Angeles). Schreiber, Emanuel. Wilshire Boulevard Temple. 1881-1932. *4216*
—. California (Sacramento). Letters. Levy, J. Leonard. Rabbis. 1892. *4219*
—. California (San Bernardino). Confirmation. Henrietta Hebrew Benevolent Society. Religious Education. 1891. *788*
—. California (San Diego). Population. Temple Beth Israel. 1889-1978. *4224*
—. California (Stockton). Davidson, Herman. Opera. Rabbis. Russia. 1846-1911. *4204*
—. Calish, Edward Nathan. Virginia (Richmond). Zionism. Zionism. 1891-1945. *4203*
—. Cemeteries. Wilshire Boulevard Temple. *4234*
—. Charities. Ecumenism. Hungarian Americans. Rabbis. Wise, Stephen Samuel. World War II. Zionism. 1890's-1949. *4229*
—. Charities. Oregon (Portland). Organizations. Temple Beth Israel. 1885. *4235*
—. Colleges and Universities. Hebrew Union College. Judaism, Reform. Ohio (Cincinnati). Wise, Isaac Mayer. 1870's-1900. *613*
—. Colleges and Universities. Hebrew Union College. Judaism (Reform). Ohio (Cincinnati). Wise, Isaac Mayer. 1870's-1900. *613*
—. Einhorn, David. History. Millenarianism. 1830-79. *4211*
—. Fund raising. Hebrew Union College. Union of American Hebrew Congregations. Western States. Wise, Isaac Mayer. 1873-75. *784*
—. Geiger, Abraham. Holdheim, Samuel. Theology. 19c. *4221*
—. Group survival. Identity. Ideology. 1800-1975. *4212*
—. Hebrew Union College. Letters. Prager, Abraham J. Rabbis. Wise, Isaac Mayer. 1854-1900. *4227*
—. Hebrew Union College. Letters. Rabbis. Stolz, Joseph. Wise, Isaac Mayer. 1882-1900. *4220*
—. Hebrew Union College. Ohio (Cincinnati). 1942-45. *750*
—. Hebrew Union College. Ohio (Cincinnati). Rabbis. Seminaries. Wise, Isaac Mayer. 1817-90's. *701*
—. Hecht, Sigmund. 1877-1911. *4218*
—. Hirsch, Samuel. 1866-89. *4210*
—. Hirsch, Samuel. History. Theology. 1815-89. *4209*
—. Jacobs, Pizer. New Mexico (Albuquerque). Temple Albert (dedication). 1900. *4232*
—. Kahal Kadosh Beth Elohim (synagogue). South Carolina (Charleston). 1695-1978. *1764*
—. Kerman, Julius C. Palestine. Personal narratives. Rabbis. World War I. 1913-71. *4214*
—. Kohler, Kaufmann. Michigan (Detroit). 1869-1926. *4213*
—. Leadership. Levi, Abraham. Temple B'nai Israel. Texas (Victoria). 1850-1902. *4225*
—. Michigan (Detroit). 19c-20c. *4222*
—. Nazism. Zionism. 1917-41. *4215*
—. Nebraska (Omaha). Temple Israel. 1867-1908. *4207*
—. Pittsburgh Platform (1885). Science. Theology. Voorsanger, Jacob. 1872-1908. *2337*
—. Theology. Wise, Isaac Mayer. 19c. *4223*
—. Union of American Hebrew Congregations. 1873-1973. *495*
—. Union of American Hebrew Congregations. 1873-1973. *4206*
—. Union of American Hebrew Congregations. 1873-1973. *4233*
Judeo-Christian thought. Bellah, Robert N. Church and state. Civil religion. National self-image. New Israel concept. 19c-20c. *1199*
Judicial Administration. Church and state. County Government. Mormons. Partisanship. Probate courts. Utah. 1855-72. *1039*
Judson, Adoniram. Baptists. Missions and Missionaries. Newell, Samuel. 1810-21. *1731*
Juma, Charlie. Depressions. North Dakota (Ross). Personal narratives. Syrian Americans. 1900's-30's. *35*
Jung, Leo. Judaism (Orthodox). Rabbinical Council of America. 1926-42. *4171*
Jurisdictions, ecclesiastical. Arizona. Catholic Church. Colonial Government. New Mexico. Spain. 1548-1969. *3739*
Justification. Arminianism. Edwards, Jonathan. Great Awakening. Massachusetts (Hampshire County). 1726-60. *2236*

K

Kahal Kadosh Beth Elohim (synagogue). Judaism (Reform). South Carolina (Charleston). 1695-1978. *1764*
Kamp, Henry. Ethnicity. Evangelical and Reformed Church. German Americans. Oklahoma (Oklahoma City). 1906-57. *3123*
Kanniff, Jane. New York (Rockland County; Clarkstown, Clarksville). Witchcraft. 1816. *2213*
Kansas *See also* Western States.
—. Agriculture. Immigration. Mennonites. Ukraine. Warkentin, Bernhard. 1872-1908. *3379*
—. Anti-Catholicism. Anti-Semitism. Conspiracy theories. Fundamentalism. Political Commentary. Winrod, Gerald Burton. 1933-57. *2090*
—. Antislavery Sentiments. Editors and Editing. Newspapers. Providence. Rhetoric. 1855-58. *2034*
—. Architecture. Churches. Country life. Fischer, Emil C. 19c. *1778*
—. Asia, central. Immigration. Mennonites. Nebraska. Pacifism. 1884-93. *3350*
—. Baptists. Catholic Church. Germans, Russian. Immigration. Lutheran Church. Mennonites. Wheat industry. 1874-77. *2778*
—. Baptists. Education. Indians. Lykins, Johnston. Potawatomi Indians. Pottawatomie Baptist Manual Labor Training School. 1846-67. *508*
—. Brethren in Christ. Holiness Movement. Mennonites. Methodism. 1870-1910. *3436*
—. Camp Funston. Conscientious objectors. Diaries. Hutterites. Waldner, Jakob. World War I. 1917-18. *2690*
—. Catholic Church. Protestantism. Religion in the Public Schools. 1861-1900. *568*
—. Congregationalism. Guidebooks. Immigration. Thomas, Robert D. *(Hanes Cymry America)*. Welsh Americans. 1838-84. *3121*
—. Converts. Immigration. Mennonites. Milling. Presbyterian Church. Warkentin, Bernhard. 1847-1908. *3380*
—. Feminism. Letters. Nichols, Clarina I. H. Sex roles. Theology. 1857-69. *843*
—. Indians. Methodism. Ohio. Removal policy. Wyandot Indians. 1816-60. *1598*
—. Liberty bonds. Mennonites. Pacifism. Vigilantism. World War I. 1918. *2659*
—. Mennonites. 1873-80. *3420*
—. Mennonites. War bond drives. World War I. 1917-18. *2647*
—. Pacifism. Patriotism. Sects, Religious. World War I. 1917-18. *2677*
Kansas (Atchison). Catholic Church. German Americans. Immigrants. Newspapers. Pluralism. 1854-59. *3877*
Kansas, central. Amish, Old Order. Ethnicity. 1956-78. *3394*
Kansas (Clay Center). Concordia Seminary. Daily Life. Lutheran Church (Missouri Synod). Mueller, Peter. Seminaries. Students. 1883-89. *707*
Kansas (Dickinson). Brethren in Christ. Pennsylvania, southeastern. Westward Movement. 1879. *3381*
Kansas (Lyon County). Cemeteries. Mennonites. 1870-1925. *3377*
Kansas (McPherson County). Mennonites. Russian Americans. Social Change. 1874-1974. *3372*
Kansas (Newton). Clergy. Entz, John Edward. First Mennonite Church. Mennonites. 1875-1969. *3419*
—. Dunkards. Friends, Society of. Historic Peace Churches (meeting). Krehbiel, H. P. Mennonites. Pacifism. 1935-36. *2663*
Kansas (North Newton). Bethel College. Kauffman, Charles. Kauffman Museum. Mennonites. Missions and Missionaries. Museums. 1907-76. *198*
Kansas (Reno County). Amish. Clergy. *Herald der Wahrheit* (newspaper). Mast, Daniel E. 1886-1930. *3405*
Kansas (Wichita). *Defender* (periodical). Evolution. *Red Horse* (periodical). Science. Winrod, Gerald Burton. 1925-57. *2305*
Kansas (Winfield). Evolution. Goldsmith, William. Hawkins, Robert W. Methodist Episcopal Church. Southwestern College. 1920-25. *2316*
Kanui, William Tennooe. Congregationalism. Connecticut. Hawaii. Missions and Missionaries. Protestant Churches. 1796-1864. *1493*
Karlin, Athanasius. Catholic Church. Diaries. Germans, Russian. Immigration. 1875-87. *3772*
Kateb, George. Richter, Peyton. Utopias (review article). 19c. 1971. *400*
Kauffman, Charles. Bethel College. Kansas (North Newton). Kauffman Museum. Mennonites. Missions and Missionaries. Museums. 1907-76. *198*
Kauffman Museum. Bethel College. Kansas (North Newton). Kauffman, Charles. Mennonites. Missions and Missionaries. Museums. 1907-76. *198*
Kaulehelehe, William R. Clergy. Columbia River. Congregationalism. Fort Vancouver. Hawaiians. Hudson's Bay Company. Washington. 1845-69. *3128*
Kauvar, Charles E. H. Adelman, Samuel. Colorado (Denver). Congregation Beth Ha Medrosh Hagodol. Judaism (Conservative, Orthodox). Rabbis. 1949-58. *4193*
—. Colorado (Denver). Congregation Beth Ha Medrosh Hagodol. Judaism (Orthodox). 1902-71. *4192*
—. Colorado (Denver). Congregation Beth Ha Medrosh Hagodol. Judaism (Orthodox). Progressivism. 1902-71. *4194*
Keane, John J. Bibliographies. Bishops. Catholic Church. Education. 1838-1918. *3891*
Kearsley, John. Christ Church Hospital. Episcopal Church, Protestant. Hospitals. Pennsylvania (Philadelphia). Women. 1778-1976. *1455*
Keeble, Marshall. Church of Christ. Evangelism. Race relations. 1878-1968. *2550*

Keil, William. Communes. German Americans. Letters. Missouri. Oregon. Society of Bethel. Weitling, Wilhelm. 1844-83. *405*
Keisker, Walter. Lutheran Church. Missouri (Concordia). Personal narratives. Religious Education. St. Paul's College. Students. 1913-19. 1980. *669*
Keith, George. Clergy. Friends, Society of. Pennsylvania. Schisms. Schisms. 1660-1720. *3261*
—. Friends, Society of. Pennsylvania. Pusey, Caleb. Schisms. Theology. 17c. *3273*
—. Friends, Society of. Pennsylvania. Schisms. 1693-1703. *3262*
Keith, William. Church of England. Hunt, Edward. Jacobitism. Patriotism. Pennsylvania. 1720. *1130*
Keller, Ezra. Heyer, John Christian Frederick. Illinois. Indiana. Letters. Lutheranism. Missions and Missionaries. Missouri. ca 1820-40. *1614*
Kellogg, John Harvey. Adventists. Centennial Exposition of 1876. Pennsylvania (Philadelphia). 1876. *2969*
Kellogg, Merritt. Adventists. Diaries. Medicine, practice of. Trall, Russell Thacher. 1844-77. *1452*
Kelly, Dennis. Catholic Church. Irish Americans. Pennsylvania (Havertown). St. Denis Parish. 1825-1975. *3683*
Kelsey, George (review article). Attitudes. Baptists, Southern. Kentucky. World War II. 1941-45. 1973. *2681*
Kenesseth Israel Synagogue. Historians. Jews. Korn, Bertram Wallace (obituary). Pennsylvania (Elkins Park). 1918-79. *248*
Kennebec Purchase Company. Church of England. Congregationalism. Land. Massachusetts. 1759-75. *352*
Kennedy, John F. Catholic Church. Church and state. Political Campaigns (presidential). Presbyterian Church. 1959-60. *992*
Kenrick, Francis P. American Studies. Archives. Catholic University of America. Documents. Missions and Missionaries. 1776-1865. *216*
Kenrick, Peter Richard. Bishops. Catholic Church. Letters. Missouri. Travel. 1847. *3839*
—. Catholic Church. Missouri (Carondelet, St. Louis). St. Mary's of the Barrens. Seminaries. 1840-48. *752*
Kensington Methodist Episcopal Church. Archaeology. Methodist Episcopal Church. Pennsylvania (Philadelphia). Preservation. 18c. 1950's-75. *1769*
Kentucky. Abolition Movement. Berea College. Fee, John Gregg. Presbyterian Church. Religious education. 1855-1904. *777*
—. Abolition Movement. Breckinridge, Robert Jefferson. Breckinridge, William Lewis. Constitutions, State. Emancipation Party. Presbyterians. 1849. *2475*
—. Antislavery Sentiments. Clergy. Racism. 1791-1824. *2455*
—. Architecture. Shakers. 1805-60. *1824*
—. Attitudes. Baptists, Southern. Kelsey, George (review article). World War II. 1941-45. 1973. *2681*
—. Baptists. Broaddus, Andrew, I. Clergy. Diaries. Travel. 1817. *2986*
—. Baptists. Civil War. Diaries. Hungerford, B. F. 1863-66. *2632*
—. Baptists. Educational Policy. Evolution. Science. 1922-28. *2347*
—. Baptists, Separate. Evangelism. General Association of Separate Baptists in Christ. New England. 1755-1977. *3064*
—. Baptists, Southern. Disciples of Christ. Evolution. Methodist Church. Presbyterian Church. Schisms. 1920's. *2310*
—. Barkley, Alben. Gambling, pari-mutuel. Louisville Churchmen's Federation. Progressivism. 1917-27. *2437*
—. Breckinridge, Robert Jefferson. Clergy. Danville Theological Seminary. Education. Emancipation. Presbyterian Church. 1800-71. *3544*
—. Breckinridge, Robert Jefferson. Danville Theological Seminary. Emancipation. Presbyterian Church. Theology. 1832-71. *3545*
—. Civil War. Shakers. Utopias. 1861-65. *419*
—. Clergy. Presbyterian Church. Templin, Terah. 1780-1818. *3592*
—. Colleges and Universities (administration). Desha, Joseph. Holley, Horace. Politics. Presbyterians. State government. Transylvania College. Unitarianism. 1818-27. *537*
—. Language. Religious Beliefs. Wills. 1808-53. *48*
—. Pleasant Hill (community). Restorations. Shakers. Utopias. 1805-1970's. *385*
—. Presbyterian Church (New Church Synod). Schisms. 1837-58. *3574*
Kentucky (Bourbon County). Church schools. ca 1780-1850. *627*
Kentucky (Bowling Green). Christ Church. Civil War. Episcopal Church, Protestant. Ringgold, Samuel. Tennessee (Knoxville). 1860-1911. *3168*
—. Civil-Military Relations. Episcopal Church, Protestant. Ringgold, Samuel. Tennessee (Clarksville). 1861-65. *998*
Kentucky, eastern. Folklore. Witchcraft. 1977. *2198*
Kentucky Irish American (newspaper). Catholic Church. Democratic Party. Irish Americans. 1898-1968. *3817*
Kentucky (Louisville). Baptists, Southern. Seminaries. 1877-1977. *690*
—. Cathedral of the Assumption. Catholic Church. 1852-1976. *3723*
—. Church Property. Constitutional Amendments (1st). Courts. Presbyterian Church. Walnut Street Presbyterian Church. *Watson* v. *Jones* (US, 1860). 1860-1970. *1129*
—. Episcopal Church, Protestant. German Americans. Hast, Louis H. Music. 1848-90. *1909*
Kentucky (Pleasant Hill). Communalism. Shakers. 1805-1922. *432*
Kentucky (Pleasant Hill; Shakertown). Preservation. Shakers. Utopias. 1805-1976. *436*
Kentucky (Scott County; Georgetown). Cardome (home). Catholic Church. Education. Mount Admirabilis (academy). Sisters of the Visitation. 1875-1975. *600*
Kentucky (Stoney Point). Baptists. Negroes. Social Conditions. 1848-1969. *2999*
Kentucky (Versailles). Clergy. Episcopal Church, Protestant. St. John's Church. 1829-1976. *3220*
Kentucky (Woodford County). Presbyterian Church (New School). Seminaries. 1837-51. *722*
Kerman, Julius C. Judaism (Reform). Palestine. Personal narratives. Rabbis. World War I. 1913-71. *4214*
Kerr, Donald Gordon Grady (tribute). Canada. Historians. 1938-76. *279*
Key, Elizabeth. Christianity. Civil Rights. Fernando (slave). Law. Negroes. Virginia. 1607-90. *2153*
Key 73 (evangelistic coalition). Christianity. 1973. *2837*
Keystone Graded Lessons. Baptists. Literature. Religious Education. Sunday schools. 1824-1909. *637*
Khristianski Pobornik (periodical). Methodist Episcopal Church. Missions and Missionaries. Russia (St. Petersburg). Simons, George Albert. 1881-1917. *1696*
Kibbutzim. New England. Palestine. Puritans. Social Organization. Towns. 17c. 20c. *3633*
Kiefer, Theobald, II. Francke, Gottfried. Georgia (Ebenezer). Germany. Immigrants. Letters. Lutheran Church. Orphanages. Pietism. Whitefield, George. 1738. 1750. *2878*
Kierkegaard, Sören. Fiction. Updike, John. 1932-77. *2009*
Kilbourne, James. Congregationalism. Converts. Episcopal Church, Protestant. Letters. Ohio (Worthington). Pioneers. 1844-49. *2823*
—. Episcopal Church. Protestant. Ohio (Worthington). Settlement. 1744-1816. *3170*
Kimball, Edward L. Kimball, Spencer W. Mormons. Personal narratives. 1943-78. *3994*
Kimball, Heber C. Friendship. Mormons. Utah. Young, Brigham. 1829-68. *3996*
Kimball, Heber C. (and family). Illinois (Nauvoo). Mormons. 1839-46. *3997*
Kimball, Sarah Melissa Granger. Mormons. Suffrage. Utah. Women. 15th Ward Relief Society. 1818-98. *901*
Kimball, Spencer W. Clergy. Integration. Mormons. Negroes. Revelation. 1950-78. *4051*
—. Kimball, Edward L. Mormons. Personal narratives. 1943-78. *3994*
Kimball, Vilate. Illinois (Nauvoo). Letters. Mormons. Murder. Smith, Joseph. Women. 1844. *3963*
King family. Amish (Old Order). Daily Life. Diaries. Farms. Loomis, Charles P. Pennsylvania (Lancaster County). 1940. *3403*
King George's War. American Revolution (antecedents). Civil religion. Edwards, Jonathan. Great Awakening. Millenarianism. 1740-76. *1169*
—. Friends, Society of. Pacifism. Penn, Thomas. Pennsylvania. Politics. Provincial Government. 1726-42. *1314*
King, Gordon J. Gordon, Helen Skinner. Manitoba (Winnipeg). Personal narratives. Presbyterian Church. Woman's Missionary Society of the Presbyterian and United Churches. 1890's-1961. *3548*
King, Hannah Tapfield. Frontier and Pioneer Life. Heywood, Martha Spence. Intellectuals. Mormons. Snow, Eliza Roxey. Utah. Women. 1850-70. *4045*
King, Martin Luther, Jr. Assassination. Baptists, Southern. Civil rights. 1961-68. *3042*
—. Baptists. Civil rights. Negroes. Nonviolence. 1950's-68. *2533*
—. Baptists. Civil Rights. Theology. Transcendentalism. 1840's-50's. 1950's-60's. *2530*
—. Baptists. Muelder, W. G. Nonviolence. Personalism. Theology. Tillich, Paul. Wieman, Henry Nelson. 1955-68. *2552*
—. Christianity. Negroes. 1900-70. *2773*
King, Martin Luther, Jr. ("Letter from a Birmingham Jail"). Baptists. Civil Rights. Negroes. 1963. *2534*
King Philip's War. Friends, Society of. New England. Politics. Toleration. Williams, Roger *(George Fox)*. 1672-77. *993*
King, Spencer Bidwell, Jr. (obituary). Baptists. Georgia. Historians. 1930's-77. *199*
King, William Lyon Mackenzie. Canada. Ideology. Liberal Party. Politics. Protestantism. Social Classes. 1900-50. *1421*
Kingdom Come, Ark of the Holy Ghost and US Society (vessel). Communalism. Holy Ghost and Us Society. Nova Scotia. Sanford, Frank. Sects, Religious. Shipwrecks. 1910-48. *4261*
King's College (charter). Church and State. Church of England. Ontario (Toronto). Scotland. Strachan, John. 1815-43. *506*
King's College, University of. Church of England. Dalhousie University. Mergers. Nova Scotia. Presbyterian Church. 1821-37. *684*
—. Colleges and Universities. Common Sense school. Curricula. Dalhousie University. Lyall, William. Nova Scotia. Philosophy. Pine Hill Divinity Hall. Presbyterian Church. 1850-90. *719*
Kingston, Archdiocese of. Archives. Bishops. Catholic Church. Church History. Ontario. 1800-1966. *247*
Kino, Eusebio Francisco. Arizona. Indians. Jesuits. Missions and Missionaries. Spain. 1680's-1711. *1565*
Kinsey, Alfred C. Christianity. Human nature. Sexual behavior. 1948-54. *2749*
Kinsolving, George Herbert. Councils and Synods. Delegates. Episcopal Church, Protestant (Annual Council). Texas. Veto. Women. 1921-70. *813*
Kiokee Church. Baptists. Georgia (Richmond County). Marshall, Daniel. Negroes. Settlement. 1784-1819. *3020*
Kiowa Indians. Baptists, American. Crawford, Isabel. Indians. Missions and Missionaries. Oklahoma (Wichita Mountains). Women's American Baptist Home Missionary Society. 1893-1961. *1590*
Klein, Frederick C. Ecumenism. Japan (Yokohama). Methodist Protestant Church. Missions and Missionaries. 1880-93. *458*
Klein, Milton M. Bonomi, Patricia U. Ethnic Groups. New York (review article). Pluralism. Provincial Government. 1690's-1770's. 1971-74. *1204*
Kleppner, Paul. Cultural Pluralism. Jensen, Richard. North Central States. Political behavior. 1850-1900. *1214*
—. Formisano, Ronald P. Hackney, F. Sheldon. Methodology. Politics (review article). 1827-1900. 1969-71. *1263*
Kleppner, Paul (review article). Political Parties. 1853-92. 1979. *1205*
Klondike Stampede. Clergy. Gold Mines and Mining. Lippy, Thomas S. Methodist Church. Randall, Edwin M. Transportation. Yukon Territory. 1896-99. *3492*
Kneeland, Abner. Communalism. Free thinkers. Iowa. Salubria (religious community). 1827-44. *383*
Knight, Joseph, Sr. Manuscripts. Mormons. Smith, Joseph. 1772-1847. *3991*

Knights of Columbus. Commission on Training Camp Activities. Jewish Welfare Board. Leisure. Morality. Social Reform. War Department. World War I. Young Men's Christian Association. Young Women's Christian Association. 1917-18. *2379*
—. Military. Negroes. Salvation Army. World War I. Young Men's Christian Association. 1917-18. *2720*
Knights of Labor. Catholic Church. Gibbons, James. Social thought. Taschereau, Elzéar Alexandre. 1880's. *1476*
Knoph, Thomas. Clergy. Country stores. Duus, O. F. Ledgers. Lutheran Church. Norwegian Americans. Wisconsin (Waupaca township; Scandinavia). 1853-56. *3334*
Knott, William V. Anti-Catholicism. Catts, Sidney J. Elections (gubernatorial). Florida. Guardians of Liberty. Sturkie Resolution. 1916. *1231*
Knowledge. Beauty, perception of. Congregationalism. Edwards, Jonathan. Mental activity theory. New England. 1730-69. *2323*
Know-Nothing Party. Anti-Catholicism. 1853-56. *1246*
—. Anti-Catholicism. Antislavery Sentiments. Massachusetts. Republican Party. Voting and Voting Behavior. 1850's. *1201*
—. Anti-Catholicism. California (San Francisco). City Politics. People's Party. Vigilance Committee. 1854-56. *1307*
—. Anti-Catholicism. Fillmore, Millard. Nativism. Political Campaigns (presidential). Whig Party. 1850-56. *1305*
—. Anti-Catholicism. Massachusetts. Republican Party. Voting and Voting Behavior. 1850's. *1209*
—. Anti-Catholicism. Political Leadership. Thompson, Richard W. 1850's. *1291*
—. Anti-Catholicism. Religious Liberty. 1770's-1850's. *2934*
Koehler, J. P. Lutheran Church. Theology. *Wisconsin Lutheran Quarterly* (periodical). 1880's-1915. *3317*
Koester v. *Pardeeville* (1929). Anti-Catholicism. Church and state. Cox Library. Discrimination. Libraries. Taxation. Wisconsin (Pardeeville). 1927-29. *1033*
Kogan, Michael S. Brandeis, Louis D. Gompers, Samuel. Judaism. Labor Unions and Organizations. 1880's-1975. *1479*
Kohler, Kaufmann. Academic Freedom. Hebrew Union College. Judaism, Reform. Ohio (Cincinnati). Zionism. 1903-07. *724*
—. Judaism, Reform. Michigan (Detroit). 1869-1926. *4213*
Kohn, Hans. Attitudes. Hayes, Carlton J. H. Historiography. Nationalism. 1950's-60's. *1392*
Kohut, George Alexander. Book Collecting. Judaism. Yale University Library (Kohut Collection). 1901-33. *179*
Koinonia Farm. Christianity. Communes. Georgia. Jordan, Clarence. 1942-60's. *402*
Korea. Archives. China. Japan. Missions and Missionaries. Presbyterian Historical Society. 1852-1911. *189*
Korean War. Adventist Medical Cadet Corps. Armies. Dick, Everett N. Personal narratives. World War II. 1934-53. *2644*
Koreshan Unity. Florida (Estero). Illinois (Chicago). Millenarianism. Teed, Cyrus Read. Utopias. 1886-1903. *396*
Korn, Bertram Wallace (obituary). Historians. Jews. Kenesseth Israel Synagogue. Pennsylvania (Elkins Park). 1918-79. *248*
Kramer, William A. Lutheran Church. Missouri (Perry County). Personal narratives. ca 1890-1910. *3314*
Krauskopf, Joseph. Agriculture. Judaism (Reform). Social Reform. 1880's-1923. *4228*
Krehbiel, H. P. Dunkards. Friends, Society of. Historic Peace Churches (meeting). Kansas (Newton). Mennonites. Pacifism. 1935-36. *2663*
Ku Klux Klan. *American Mercury* (periodical). Editors and Editing. Mencken, H. L. Methodist Episcopal Church (South). Temperance Movements. 1910-33. *2033*
—. American Protective Association. Anti-Catholicism. Chinese Americans. Guardians of Liberty. Nativism. Oregon. Racism. ca 1840-1945. *2100*
—. Anti-Catholicism. Anti-Semitism. Attitudes. Morality. Ohio (Youngstown). Reform. 1920's. *2402*
—. Anti-Catholicism. Anti-Semitism. Colorado (Denver). Protestantism. Social Classes. 1921-25. *2609*
—. Anti-Catholicism. Arizona. Morality. 1921-25. *2094*
—. Anti-Catholicism. Clergy. Protestantism. Republican Party. Rhode Island. 1915-32. *2116*
—. Anti-Catholicism. Georgia (Atlanta). School boards. 1916-27. *2115*
—. Anti-Catholicism. Protestants. Saskatchewan. 1927-30. *2096*
—. Indiana (Gary, Valparaiso). Nativism. Protestantism. 1920's. *2358*
Kubašek, John J. Catholic Church. Independence Movements. New York (Yonkers). Slovak Americans. 1902-50. *3870*
Kubiak, Hieronim (review article). Assimilation. Immigrants. Polish National Catholic Church. 1897-1965. *306*
Kuehn, Ernst Ludwig Hermann. Lutheran Church. Michigan. Missions and Missionaries. 1850-98. *1666*
Kuhnle, Howard A. Lutheran Church. Necrology. 1950-73. *222*
Kurikka, Matti. Australia. Canada. Finland. Theosophy. Utopias. 1883-1915. *435*
Kuyper, Abraham. American Revolution. Calvinism. Netherlands. Political systems. 1775-83. 19c-1920. *1332*

L

Labor *See also* Agricultural Labor; Capitalism; Communism; Employment; Industrial Relations; Socialism; Strikes; Wages; Working Class; Working Conditions.
—. Boardinghouses. Minnesota (Minneapolis). Women. Women's Christian Association. 1880's-1979. *2526*
—. California. Catholic Church. Indians. Missions and Missionaries. 1775-1805. *1485*
—. Canada. Fiction. Social gospel. 1890's. *2078*
—. Canada. Social Gospel. Socialism. 20c. *2441*
—. Clergy. Lynd, Robert S. Oil Industry and Trade. Presbyterian Church. Wyoming (Elk Basin). 1921. *3562*
—. Elections. Law. Mormons. Railroads. Utah (Ogden). 1869-70. *1262*
—. Industrialization. Leisure. Protestant Ethic. Values. 19c-20c. *334*
—. Match industry. Quebec (Hull). Syndicat Catholique des Allumettières. Women. 1919-24. *1470*
—. Occupations. Quebec (Montreal). Sex roles. Women. 1911-41. *1471*
Labor Department. Communes. Library of Congress. Publications. Western states. 1830's-1930's. *430*
Labor Unions and Organizations *See also* names of labor unions and organizations, e.g. American Federation of Labor, United Automobile Workers, etc.; Strikes.
—. Adventists. 1877-1903. *1474*
—. Anti-Communist Movements. Catholic Church. Crosby, Donald F. McCarthy, Joseph R. (review article). Oshinsky, David. 1950-54. 1976-78. *1212*
—. Brandeis, Louis D. Gompers, Samuel. Judaism. Kogan, Michael S. 1880's-1975. *1479*
—. Catholic Church. Drummond County Mechanics Institute. Farmers. Quebec (Drummond County). 1856-90. *1472*
—. Catholic Church. École Sociale Populaire. Quebec. Social Change. 1911-75. *1469*
—. Catholic Church. Polish Americans. Political Leadership. Progressivism. Socialism. Wisconsin (Milwaukee). 1900-30. *1299*
—. Christianity. Church and Social Problems. Socialism. 1880-1913. *1465*
—. Mormons. Utah. 1850-96. *1467*
—. People's Institute of Applied Religion. South. Williams, Claude. Williams, Joyce. 1940-75. *1478*
Labour Party. Canada. Communist Party. Methodism. Smith, Albert Edward. Social Gospel. 1893-1924. *983*
Labrador *See also* Atlantic Provinces; Newfoundland.
—. Eskimos. Jannasch, Hermann Theodor. Missions and Missionaries. Moravian Church. 1855-1931. *1594*
Lacey, John, Jr. American Revolution. Biddle, Owen. Friends, Society of. Military Service. Pennsylvania. 1775-83. *2684*
Lacouture, Onésime. Jesuits. Quebec. Spiritual movement. 1931-50. *3730*
Ladies Aid Society. Church suppers. Lutheran Church (Norwegian). North Dakota (Hannaford). Norwegian Americans. 1941. *3310*
LaFarge, John. *America* (periodical). Catholic Church. Colleges and Universities. Newman Clubs. 1904-50's. *515*
—. Architecture. Catholic Church. Church of St. Paul the Apostle. Decorative Arts. New York City. 1876-99. *1833*
—. Churches. Idealism. New York City. Painting. 1877-88. *1898*
—. Churches (Gothic Revival). Decorative Arts. Massachusetts (Boston). Richardson, Henry Hobson. Trinity Church. 1876. *1832*
Lafayette, Marquis de. Public Opinion. Social Problems. Travel. 1824-25. *61*
Laity. Authority. Bishops. Canada. Church of England. Councils and Synods. 1780-1979. *3224*
—. Authority. Canada. Church and state. Church of England. Councils and Synods. 1782-1857. *3207*
—. Authority. Canada. Church of England. Councils and Synods. 1782-1867. *3206*
—. Baptists. Clergy. Leadership. 1609-1970's. *3027*
—. Baptists. Politics. 1715-1975. *1243*
—. Baptists, Southern. 1906-75. *3038*
—. Baptists, Southern. 20c. *3080*
—. Baptists, Southern. Missions and missionaries. 1715-1975. *1623*
—. Bishops. Methodist Protestant Church. Reform. 1779-1832. *320*
—. Bond, Thomas Emerson. Church government. Methodist Episcopal Church. Snethen, Nicholas. Stockton, William S. 1820-56. *288*
—. Catholic Church. Democracy. Trusteeism. 1785-1855. *292*
—. Church government. Crooks, George Richard. Methodist Episcopal Church. *Methodist* (periodical). 1851-72. *316*
—. Church of England. Neau, Elias. Negroes. New York City. Society for the Propagation of the Gospel. 1704-22. *3193*
—. Clergy. Conflict and Conflict Resolution. Protestantism. 19c-20c. *2954*
—. Elders. Miller, Samuel. Presbyterian Church. Republicanism. 1813-50. *3559*
—. Jews. Leadership. New York (Kingston). Political Leadership. Protestant Churches. Social Status. 1825-60. *2600*
—. Revivals. 1858. *2259*
Lake Geneva Mission. Doukhobors. Galicians. Hospitals. Missions and Missionaries. Presbyterian Church. Saskatchewan (Wakaw). 1903-42. *1492*
Lake Michigan. Michigan (Beaver Island). Mormons. Strang, James Jesse. Utopias. Wisconsin (Voree). 1820-56. *433*
Lamb Studios. Camp Lejeune. Marines. New Jersey (Tenafly). North Carolina. Protestantism. Stained glass windows. 1775-1943. *1867*
Lambdin, William. Mormons. Rare Books. Smith, Joseph *(Book of Commandments).* West Virginia (Wheeling). 1830-33. *2124*
Lambert, Rose. Armenia. Letters. Mennonites. Missions and Missionaries. Turkey. 1898-1911. 1969. *1756*
Lamp (periodical). Anglo-Catholics. Catholic Church. Clergy. Ecumenism. Episcopal Church, Protestant. Wattson, Paul James. 1903-09. *460*
Lampton, William J. *Book of Common Worship.* Humor. Poetry. Presbyterian Church, Southern. Rites and Ceremonies. VanDyke, Henry. 1906. *3557*
Lamy, Jean Baptiste. Bishops. Catholic Church. Indian-white relations. New Mexico (Santa Fe). Social customs. 1849-88. *3761*
Lancaster Mennonite High School. Attitudes. Mennonites. Pennsylvania. Rites and Ceremonies. Students. 1974-78. *3354*
Land *See also* Agriculture; Land Tenure; Real Estate.
—. Anti-Catholicism. Benedictines. D'Equivelley, G. F. Florida (Pasco County). *Jeffersonian* (newspaper). Letters-to-the-editor. Mohr, Charles. 1915-16. *2123*
—. Church and state. Church of England. Endowments. Ontario (Upper Canada). Rolph, John. Strachan, John. University of Toronto. 1820-70. *1026*

—. Church of England. Congregationalism. Kennebec Purchase Company. Massachusetts. 1759-75. *352*
—. Connecticut. Ethics. Fitch, James. Politics. Puritans. 1679-1727. *3646*
—. Family. Mormons. Pioneer life. Utah (Kanab). 1874-80. *4009*
—. Galland, Isaac. Iowa (Lee County). Mormons. Smith, Joseph. Speculation. 1830's-58. *3950*
—. Law. New France. Sulpicians. 1667. *3782*
—. Massachusetts (Barnstable County). Peasants. Pilgrims. Values. 1620's-1720's. *3151*
—. Moravian Church. Pennsylvania (Nazareth). Settlement. Whitefield House. 1740-1978. *3517*
Land Tenure *See also* Peasants; Real Estate.
—. Jesuits. Legislation. Mercier, Honoré. Protestant Churches. Quebec. 1886. *1087*
Land use. Amish. Mennonites. Mormons. Pennsylvania (Intercourse). Theology. Utah (Escalante). 1973. *2767*
Landlords and Tenants. Agriculture. Mississippi. Neoorthodoxy. Protestant Churches. Theologians. 1936-40. *2566*
Landmark Banner and Cherokee Baptist (newspaper). Baptists. Cherokee Georgia Baptist Convention. Georgia. 1859-64. *3013*
Landmark Movement. Abolition Movement. Baptists. Pendleton, James Madison. 1835-91. *2998*
—. Baptists. Dayton, Amos Cooper. Novels. South. 1850-65. *1995*
—. Baptists. Graves, James Robinson. Missions and Missionaries. South. Whitsitt Controversy. 1850-1950. *3057*
—. Baptists. Sects, Religious. Theology. 1850-1950. *3089*
—. Baptists, Big Hatchie. Baptists, Southern. Evangelism. Missions and Missionaries. 1828-1903. *3011*
—. Baptists, Southern. Fundamentalism. Graves, James Robinson. Modernism. Mullins, Edgar Young. Theology. 1840-1928. *3058*
Landownership. Mormons. Utah. 1847-69. *4003*
Landscape Painting. Great Britain. Immigrants. Mormons. Piercy, Frederick *(Illustrated Route)*. Portraits. Travel guides. Western states. 1848-57. *1869*
Lane Theological Seminary. Dartmouth College. New England. Presbyterian Church. Stowe, Calvin Ellis. Stowe, Harriet Beecher. 1824-86. *3555*
Langdon, Samuel. American Revolution. Cooke, Samuel. History Teaching. Mayhew, Jonathan. Sermons. West, Samuel. Witherspoon, John. 1750-76. 1975. *1406*
Langevin, Adélard. Anglophones. Catholics. French Canadians. Manitoba. Winnipeg Archdiocese. 1905. *3711*
—. Catholic Church. Church and State. French language. Manitoba. Politics. Private schools. 1890-1916. *608*
—. Catholic Church. Church schools. French language. Laurier, Wilfrid. Liberal Party. Prairie Provinces. Religion in the Public Schools. 1890-1915. *569*
Langland, Joseph. Country Life. Iowa. Lutheran Church. Personal narratives. Poetry. Youth. 1917-30's. 1977. *2027*
Language *See also* Literature; Rhetoric; Translating and Interpreting.
—. A. A. Allen Revival, Incorporated. Arizona (Miracle Valley). Fundamentalism. Popular culture. Revivals. 1970's. *2270*
—. Antinomianism. Hutchinson, Anne. Massachusetts. Puritans. Trials. 1636-38. *3609*
—. Baptists, Southern. Missions. Northeastern or North Atlantic States. Southern Baptist Convention Home Missions Board. 1950-75. *1620*
—. Bureau of Indian Affairs. Educational Policy. Indians (reservations). Missions and Missionaries. 19c-20c. *516*
—. Canada. Ethnic Groups. Immigrants. Indians. 1970's. *126*
—. Catholic Church. German Americans. Politics. Religious education. St. Peter's Colony. Saskatchewan. 1903-16. *779*
—. Catholic Church. Métis. Missions and Missionaries. Quebec (Oka). Religious Education. Rocheblave, Charlotte de. 19c. *1507*
—. Church schools. Francophones. Greenway, Thomas (administration). Legislation. Manitoba Act (Canada, 1870). 1890-99. *519*
—. Ethnicity. Nationalism. Parishes. Polish National Catholic Church. 1880's-1930's. *313*
—. Kentucky. Religious Beliefs. Wills. 1808-53. *48*
Lansdowne College. Colleges and Universities. Collegiate Institute. Depressions. Manitoba (Portage la Prairie). 1882-93. *780*
Lansman, Jeremy. Federal Communications Commission. Milam, Lorenzo. Radio. Religious references. Television. 1972-75. *1116*
LaPatrie (colony). Catholic Church. French Canadians. New England. Quebec. Repatriation Act (Canada, 1875). ca 1875-80. *3792*
LaRocque, Charles. Catholic Church. Debt. Quebec. St. Hyacinthe Diocese. 1866-73. *3695*
LaRocque, Paul. Catholic Church. Church Finance. Economic Development. Quebec. Sherbrooke Diocese. 1893-1926. *3783*
Larson, Lars. Friends, Society of. Larson, Martha. New York (Rochester). Norwegian Americans. Religious Liberty. Women. 1807-44. *3263*
Larson, Martha. Friends, Society of. Larson, Lars. New York (Rochester). Norwegian Americans. Religious Liberty. Women. 1807-44. *3263*
Latin America. Anti-Catholicism. Attitudes. Independence Movements. Protestant churches. 1810-25. *2107*
—. Authority. Missions and Missionaries. Mormons. Nationalism. 1975-80. *1753*
—. Christianity. North America. Socialism. 20c. *953*
—. Church-sect model. Jehovah's Witnesses. 1950-76. *3920*
Latin language. Congregationalism. Harvard University. Leverett, John. Massachusetts (Cambridge). Speeches, Addresses, etc. 1722. *668*
—. Congregationalism. Harvard University (Hollis Professorship of Divinity). Rhetoric. Wigglesworth, Edward. 1722. *667*
Latourette, Kenneth Scott. Christianity. History. 1884-1968. *261*
—. Church History. Historiography. Sweet, William Warren. ca 1910-65. *175*
Laub, George. Diaries. Illinois (Nauvoo). Mormons. Smith, Joseph. Young, Brigham. 1845-46. *3961*
Laurens, Henry. Philosophy. Republicanism. Social Reform. South Carolina. 1764-77. *2385*
Laurier, Wilfrid. Catholic Church. Church schools. French language. Langevin, Adélard. Liberal Party. Prairie Provinces. Religion in the Public Schools. 1890-1915. *569*
Laval, François de. Brotherhood of the Holy Family. Catholic Church. Chaumonot, Joseph-Marie-Pierre. Elites. Quebec (Montreal). 1663-1760. *3717*
—. Catholic Church. Church and state. Governors, provincial. New France (Sovereign Council). Trade. 1659-84. *1020*
—. Catholic Church. Quebec. 17c. *3766*
Laval University. Bourget, Ignace. Catholic Church. Colleges and Universities. Quebec (Quebec). 1840's-50's. *676*
LaVey, Anton Szandor. Church of Satan. Occult Sciences. Satanism. 1966-75. *4240*
Law *See also* Canon Law; Constitutional Law; Courts; Criminal Law; Judicial Administration; Lawyers; Legislation.
—. American Revolution. Constitutionalism. Historiography. Politics. 1775-83. 1790-1950. *961*
—. Americanization. Judaism. Rabbis. Rabbis (responsa). Social customs. 1862-1937. *300*
—. Anti-Catholicism. Civil Rights. Irish Canadians. Nova Scotia (Halifax). 1749-1829. *1105*
—. Catholic Church. Church and State. Puerto Rico. ca 1863-1908. *1041*
—. Catholic Church. Freedmen. Protestantism. Texas. 1836-60. *2799*
—. Chain letters. Superstitions. 1930's-70's. *133*
—. Charities. Morristown Female Charitable Society. New Jersey. Presbyterian Church. Women. 1813-1978. *2510*
—. Christianity. Civil Rights. Fernando (slave). Key, Elizabeth. Negroes. Virginia. 1607-90. *2153*
—. Church and State. Federal Regulation. Religion (definitions). 1950's-70's. *1131*
—. Cults. Evangelism. 1976-78. *1110*
—. Divorce. Massachusetts. Puritans. Social conditions. Women. 1639-92. *941*
—. Divorce. Vermont. 1777-1815. *792*
—. Elections. Labor. Mormons. Railroads. Utah (Ogden). 1869-70. *1262*
—. Friends, Society of. Great Britain. *Mary and Charlotte* (vessel). Pennsylvania (Philadelphia). War relief. 1778-84. *3266*
—. Great Britain. Protestantism. Secularization. 1800-1970. *10*
—. Land. New France. Sulpicians. 1667. *3782*
—. Leadership. Mormons. Polygamy. Utah. 1890-1905. *824*
—. Mormons. Tobacco. Utah. 1896-1923. *2442*
Law and Society. Blue Laws. Church and state. Church of England. Friends, Society of. Pennsylvania. Presbyterian Church. 1682-1740. *2278*
—. Civil religion. Pluralism. 1953-72. *1161*
—. Finney, Charles G. Revivals. 1800-50. *2271*
—. Industrialization. Massachusetts. Nelson, William E. (review article). Secularization. Social change. 1760-1830. *53*
Law Enforcement. American Board of Commissioners for Foreign Missions. Cherokee Indians. Georgia. Indian-White Relations. Missions and Missionaries. Removals, forced. Worcester, Samuel A. 1831. *1667*
—. Attitudes. Court records. New England. Sodomy. 1630-80. *2428*
—. Licenses. Sabbath. Taverns. Virginia. ca 1630-1850. *2286*
Lawrence, Daniel. Friends, Society of. North or Northern States. Printing. 1788-1812. *3258*
Lawrence, J. B. Baptists, Southern. Barton, A. J. Denominationalism. Gambrell, James Bruton. Theology. 1910-80. *3039*
Lawrence, Saint. Catholic Church. Feast days. New Mexico (Bernalillo). Social Customs. 1974. *3853*
Laws of the Indies. California. Church and state. Colonial Government. Indians. Missions and Missionaries. Spain. 18c. *1143*
Lawsuits. Church of England. Clergy. Cotton, William. Tithes. Virginia (Accomack County). 1633-39. *1013*
—. Licenses. Music, gospel. Performance licensing. 1950's. *1919*
Lawyers. Catholic Church. Pennsylvania. Progressivism. Smith, Walter George. 1900-22. *2365*
Laxness, Halldór *(Paradise Reclaimed)*. Brúnum, Eiríkur á. Iceland. Mormons. Novels. 1870-1900. 1960. *2075*
Lay, Benjamin. Antislavery Sentiments. Friends, Society of. Pennsylvania (Philadelphia). 1690's-1759. *2460*
Leadership *See also* Political Leadership.
—. American Baptist Home Mission Society. Baptists. Missions and Missionaries. Negroes. Paternalism. Virginia Union University. 1865-1905. *644*
—. American Revolution (antecedents). Business. Friends, Society of. Pennsylvania (Philadelphia). Radicals and radicalism. 1769-74. *1293*
—. Baptists. Clergy. Laity. 1609-1970's. *3027*
—. Baptists, Southern. Civil Rights. Race Relations. Texas. 1954-68. *2553*
—. California (San Francisco). Dyer, Leon. Jews. Maryland (Baltimore). 1820's-75. *4142*
—. Canada. Church and State. Mennonite Conference of 1970. Social issues. Students. 1917-74. *1029*
—. Charisma. Guyana (Jonestown). Jones, Jim. Models. People's Temple. Suicide, mass. 1978. *4253*
—. Childhood. Secularism. Sex roles. Women. 1636-1930. *881*
—. Christian Science. Shakers. Spiritualism. Theosophy. Women. 19c. *795*
—. Clergy, dissident. Ideology. Protestant Churches. -1973. *2439*
—. Communalism. Equal opportunity. Hutterites. Population. Prairie Provinces. Social Organization. Succession. 1940's-70's. *387*
—. Coray, Howard. Mormons. Personal narratives. Smith, Joseph. 1840's. *3990*
—. Dickey, Sarah. Heck, Barbara. Methodist Church. Parker, Lois Stiles. Shaw, Anna Howard. Stereotypes. Willard, Frances E. Women. 19c. *812*
—. Jews. Laity. New York (Kingston). Political Leadership. Protestant Churches. Social Status. 1825-60. *2600*
—. Judaism (Reform). Levi, Abraham. Temple B'nai Israel. Texas (Victoria). 1850-1902. *4225*

—. Law. Mormons. Polygamy. Utah. 1890-1905. *824*
—. Manson Family. Millerites. Nazism. Social Organization. Women's Liberation Movement. 19c-20c. *2964*
—. Mormons. Poetry. Prophecy. Snow, Eliza Roxey. Utah. Women. 1804-87. *3936*
—. Mormons. Utah. Young, Brigham. 1801-77. *1206*
—. Mormons. Utah. Young, Brigham. 1840's-77. *3960*
—. Negroes. South Carolina. 1919. *2617*
League of Nations. Mormons. Prohibition. Republican Party. Roberts, Brigham Henry. Smith, Joseph Fielding. Suffrage. Utah. Women. ca 1900. *1284*
LeConte, Joseph. Philosophy of Science. Sociology. South. ca 1840-60. *2301*
Lectures *See also* Speeches, Addresses, etc.
—. Atheism. Ingersoll, Robert. Nevada (Virginia City). Public Opinion. 1877. *4304*
—. Brownson, Orestes A. Catholic Church. Civilization. Missouri (St. Louis). 1852-54. *3838*
—. Bryan, William Jennings. Fund raising. Prairie Provinces. Presbyterian Church. Young Men's Christian Association. 1909. *2446*
—. Forssell, G. D. Iowa. Minnesota. Progressivism. Social Conditions. 1890-95. *1967*
—. Protestantism. Public Opinion. 1840's-50's. *2923*
Lectures of Faith. Mormons. Theology. 1834-1921. *3973*
Ledesme, R. P. *(Doctrine Chrestienne).* Brébeuf, Jean de. Catholic Church. Indian-White Relations. New France. Translating and Interpreting. Wyandot Indians. 16c-17c. *1639*
Ledgers. Clergy. Country stores. Duus, O. F. Knoph, Thomas. Lutheran Church. Norwegian Americans. Wisconsin (Waupaca township; Scandinavia). 1853-56. *3334*
Lee, Ann. Christian Science. Eddy, Mary Baker. Personality. Shakers. Theology. Women. 1736-1910. *2753*
—. New York. Shakers. Theology. 1774-20c. *4065*
Lee, Daniel. Business. Indians. Letters. Methodist Church. Missions and Missionaries. Oregon (Willamette Valley, The Dalles). 1834-43. *1570*
Lee, J. Bracken. City Politics. Morality. Mormons. Skousen, W. Cleon. Utah (Salt Lake City). 1956-60. *4006*
—. Elections. Mormons. State Government. Utah. 1944-56. *1274*
Lee, Jason. Drury, Clifford M. Indians. Methodism. Missions and Missionaries. Oregon. Settlement. 1834-43. 1970's. *3480*
—. French Canadians. Government, provisional. Gray, William. Methodist Church. Missions and Missionaries. Oregon. 1843. *1271*
—. Historiography. Indians. Methodism. Missions and Missionaries. Oregon. 1838-43. *1569*
Lee, John Doyle. Mormons. Mountain Meadows Massacre. Utah. 1857-77. *4043*
Leeser, Isaac. Congregation Kahal Kadosh Beth Israel. Georgia (Macon). Judaism. Letters. Loewenthal, Henry. Rabbis. 1854-70. *4124*
Leftism *See also* Communism; New Left; Radicals and Radicalism; Socialism.
—. Berrigan, Daniel. Berrigan, Philip. Catholic Church. Church and state. Murray, John Courtney. 1950's-70's. *3758*
—. Bliss, William D. P. Christianity. Social Gospel. 1876-1926. *2377*
—. California (San Francisco). Guyana (Jonestown). Jones, Jim. People's Temple. 1960's-78. *4247*
—. Methodist Episcopal Zion Church, African. Music. Negroes. Robeson, Paul. 1898-1976. *3470*
Legal education. Austin College. Baker, Daniel. Presbyterian Church. Texas (Huntsville). 1849-57. *529*
Legal, Emile. Alberta, University of. Catholic Church. Colleges and Universities. O'Leary, Henry Joseph. St. Joseph's University College. 1906-26. *619*
Legislation *See also* Congress; Law.
—. Alcohol. Economic development. Gambling. 1977. *2383*
—. Annexation. Church and state. Idaho, southern. Mormons. Nevada. Stewart, William. Suffrage. 1887-88. *1089*
—. Church schools. Francophones. Greenway, Thomas (administration). Language. Manitoba Act (Canada, 1870). 1890-99. *519*
—. Clothing. New England. Puritans. Social Status. 1630-90. *2427*
—. Compulsory Education. Hutterites. South Dakota. Values. 1700-1970's. *659*
—. Discrimination. Ethnicity. Hutterites. Prairie Provinces. Provincial government. 1960's-79. *1099*
—. Jesuits. Land Tenure. Mercier, Honoré. Protestant Churches. Quebec. 1886. *1087*
—. Lobbying. Religious Liberty. 1950's-70's. *1136*
Legislators. Abortion. Voting behavior. Western States. 1975. *139*
—. Blue laws. Church and state. Louisiana. Negroes. Reconstruction. Sabbath. 1867-75. *2285*
Lehman, Hans (and family). Bishops. Immigration. Mennonites. Pennsylvania (Lancaster County; Rapho Township). Swiss Americans. ca 1727-1909. *3400*
Leisure *See also* Recreation.
—. Commission on Training Camp Activities. Jewish Welfare Board. Knights of Columbus. Morality. Social Reform. War Department. World War I. Young Men's Christian Association. Young Women's Christian Association. 1917-18. *2379*
—. Future. Religious consciousness. 1973-. *103*
—. Industrialization. Labor. Protestant Ethic. Values. 19c-20c. *334*
Leisy family. Breweries. Illinois (Peoria). Mennonites. 1884-1950. *356*
Lemke, John A. Catholic Church. Clergy. Michigan (Detroit). Polish Americans. 1866-90. *3875*
Lentz, Lula Gillespie. Baptists. Country Life. Farms. Illinois (southern). Personal narratives. 1883-1929. *3037*
Leo XIII, Pope. Catholic Church. Elections. Pius IX, Pope. Press. Protestantism. 1878. *2786*
Leo XIII, Pope (*Testem Benevolentiae*). Acculturation. Americanism. Catholic Church. Periodicals. Protestantism. 1899. *319*
Leonard, Truman. Mormons. Utah (Davis County). 1820-97. *4001*
Leopold, Nathan. Candler, Warren A. Conservatism. Evolution. Loeb, Richard. Methodist Episcopal Church, South. Scopes, John Thomas. Trials. 1921-41. *2293*
Lescarbot, Marc *(Histoire de la Nouvelle-France).* Historiography. New France. 1606-30's. *2032*
Leshe, Mary Jane Conly. Baptists. Louisiana (Bienville Parish). 1849-1932. *3045*
"Letter to My Country Friends" (series). Editors and Editing. Murray, Robert. Nova Scotia (Halifax). *Presbyterian Witness* (newspaper). 1863. *987*
Letters. Abolition Movement. American Revolution. Massachusetts (Boston). Wheatley, Phillis. Whigs. 1767-80. *2454*
—. Abolition Movement. Cass, William D. Methodist Episcopal Church (General Conference). 1844. *2477*
—. Adams, John. American Revolution (antecedents). Church of England. Weller, George. 1770's. 1824-25. *971*
—. Adventists. California. Humor. Irish Americans. Loma Linda University. Magan, Percy Tilson. 1918-34. *1435*
—. Adventists. California. Loma Linda Sanitarium. White, Ellen G. 1905. *1461*
—. American Board of Commissioners for Foreign Missions. Brainerd Mission. Cherokee Indians. Education. Indian-White Relations. Southeastern States. 1817-38. *1605*
—. *American Israelite* (newspaper). Jews. Nevada (Eureka). 1875. *4163*
—. American Revolution. Bailey, Jacob. Church of England. Exiles. Nova Scotia. 1784. *3226*
—. American Revolution. Chauncy, Charles. Church and State. Congregationalism. Great Britain. Price, Richard. Slavery. 1727-87. *3129*
—. American Revolution. Documents. Judaism. 1775-90. *1277*
—. Andersson, Joris Per. Lutheran Church. Minnesota (Chisago Lake). Swedish Americans. 1851-53. *3312*
—. Anti-Catholicism. Georgia. Roosevelt, Theodore. Watson, Thomas E. 1915. *2104*
—. Anti-Semitism. California (San Francisco). D'Ancona, David Arnold. Newspapers. Pixley, Frank M. 1883. *2128*
—. Antislavery sentiments. Barbados. Curwen, Alice. Friends, Society of. 1675-76. *2458*
—. Arapaho Indians. Haury, Samuel S. Indian Territory. Mennonites. Missions and Missionaries. 1876-80. *1543*
—. Archival catalogs and inventories. Mennonites. Mensch, Jacob B. Pennsylvania. 1835-1912. *251*
—. Armenia. Lambert, Rose. Mennonites. Missions and Missionaries. Turkey. 1898-1911. 1969. *1756*
—. Asbury, Francis. Methodist Episcopal Church. Sunday Schools. 1791. *782*
—. Attitudes. Bradford family. Missouri. Mormons. Virginia. 1838-39. *4057*
—. Attitudes. Episcopal Church, Protestant. Fletcher, C. B. Slavery. Vermont. 1777-1864. *2159*
—. Bäck, Olof. Clergy. Esbjörn, Lars Paul. Janssonists. Lutheran Church. Methodism. Sweden. 1846-49. *2906*
—. Baltimore Riot of 1861. Civil War. Creamer, David. Crooks, George Richard. Maryland. Methodist Church. 1861-63. *1410*
—. Baptism. Baptists. Great Britain (London). Jessey, Henry. New England. Puritans. Toleration. Tombes, John. 1645. *997*
—. Baptists. Bennett, Robert. Clarke, John. Great Britain (London). Religious Liberty. Rhode Island. 1655-58. *1132*
—. Baptists. Miller, William. New York (Low Hampton). 1828. *2831*
—. Baptists (Seventh-Day). Communalism. Müller, Johan Peter. Pennsylvania (Ephrata). Social Conditions. 1743. *428*
—. Bennet, James Arlington. Mormons (Reorganized). 1840's-60. *3951*
—. Bible reading. Massachusetts (Amesbury). Public schools. Whittier, John Greenleaf. 1853. *577*
—. Bishop Hill Colony. Illinois. Janssonists. Swedish Americans. 1847. *416*
—. Bishops. Catholic Church. Church Finance. Frenaye, Mark Anthony. O'Connor, Michael. Pennsylvania (Pittsburgh). 1843-49. *368*
—. Bishops. Catholic Church. Colombia (Bogotá). Hughes, John. Mosquera, Manuel José. New York City. 1853. *3762*
—. Bishops. Catholic Church. Intellectuals. Provincial Council of Baltimore (4th). Walter, William Joseph. 1840-43. *3842*
—. Bishops. Catholic Church. Kenrick, Peter Richard. Missouri. Travel. 1847. *3839*
—. Bishops. Church of England. Medley, John. New Brunswick (Fredericton). Oxford Movement. Pusey, Edward Bouverie. ca 1840-44. *3190*
—. Bordley, Stephen. Church of England. Great Awakening. Maryland. Whitefield, George. 1730-40. *2229*
—. Bourget, Ignace. Catholic Church. Church History. Faillon, Etienne-Michel. Quebec (Montreal). 1850. *3824*
—. Brenneman, John M. Civil War. Mennonites. 1862. *2709*
—. Brickell, John. Clayton, John. Natural History. North Carolina. Plagiarism. 1693-1737. *2341*
—. Brownson, Orestes A. Catholic Church. Cumming, William. 1850's. *3676*
—. Brubacher, Henry. Brubacher, Jacob. Daily life. Mennonites. Ontario. Pennsylvania. 1817-46. *3374*
—. Buerger, Paul Theodor. *Collegium Fratrum* (organization). Educational Tests and Measurements. Indiana (Fort Wayne). Lutheran Church. 1858. *3315*
—. Business. Indians. Lee, Daniel. Methodist Church. Missions and Missionaries. Oregon (Willamette Valley, The Dalles). 1834-43. *1570*
—. Butler, John Wesley. Methodist Church. Mexico. Missions and Missionaries. Revolution. 1910-11. *1725*
—. California (Los Angeles). Judaism (Reform). Newmark, Joseph. Rabbis. Wilshire Boulevard Temple. 1881. *4236*
—. California (Sacramento). Judaism (Reform). Levy, J. Leonard. Rabbis. 1892. *4219*
—. California (Sacramento, San Francisco). Henry, Henry Abraham. Issacs, Samuel Meyer. Jews. Rabbis. Travel (accounts). 1858. *4106*
—. Cameron, John. Church of England. Ontario (Ottawa). Politics. Thompson, Annie Affleck. Thompson, John S. D. 1867-94. *1127*
—. Canada. Millenarianism. Northwest Rebellion. Riel, Louis. 1876-78. 1885. *965*

—. Cannon, Martha Hughes. Great Britain. Mormons. Polygamy. Utah (Salt Lake City). Women. 1885-96. *4002*
—. Capers, William. *Christian Advocate* (newspaper). Ecumenism. Methodist Episcopal Church. Methodist Episcopal Church (South). Slavery. 1854. 1875. *479*
—. Catholic Church. Chipewyan Indians. Indian-White Relations. Mission St. Jean-Baptiste. Saskatchewan (Île-à-la-Crosse). Taché, Alexandre Antonin. 1823-54. *1503*
—. Catholic Church. Immigration. Moczygemba, Leopold. Polish Americans. Texas (Panna Marya). 1855. *3679*
—. Cemeteries. Congregation Beth El. Historic markers. Jews. Michigan (Detroit). 1850-1971. *4159*
—. Christianity. Deism. Jefferson, Thomas. Sectarianism. 1784-1800. *4280*
—. Christianity. Teaching. Willard, Frances Langdon. 1835-51. *542*
—. Church and state. France. Gibbons, James. Nolan, Edward J. Sabatier, Paul. 1906. *1016*
—. Church of England. Congregationalism. Cutler, Timothy. Edwards, Jonathan. Gibson, Edmund. Great Awakening. New England. Stoddard, Solomon. 1739. *2263*
—. Church of England. Connecticut. Missions and Missionaries. Muirson, George. New York. ca 1697-1708. *1535*
—. Church of England. Maryland. Presburg, Joseph. 1713-32. *3199*
—. Civil War. Methodist Church. North Carolina (Halifax County). Slavery. Wills, Washington. 1861-65. *2171*
—. Clayton, William. Great Britain. Immigration. Moon, John. Mormons. 1840. *3925*
—. Clayton, William. Great Britain (Manchester). Illinois (Nauvoo). Immigration. Mormons. 1840. *3924*
—. Clergy. Episcopal Church, Protestant. Jarratt, Devereux. Virginia. 1770-1800. *3195*
—. Clergy. Frontier. Lutheran Church in America, Norwegian. Montana, eastern. Thorpe, Christian Scriver. 1906-08. *3295*
—. Clergy. Helmreich, Christian. Lutheran Church. Nebraska (Weyerts). 1887-88. *3308*
—. Clergy. Lipscomb, Bernard F. Methodist Church. Virginia (Charlottesville). 1889-92. *3471*
—. Clergy. Methodist Church. Montgomery, Daniel. Webb, Thomas. 1771. *3490*
—. Cloeter, Ottomar. Indians. Lutheran Church. Minnesota. Missions and Missionaries. 1856-68. *1651*
—. Coe, Truman. Mormons. Ohio (Kirtland). Presbyterians. 1836. *2718*
—. Coke, Thomas. Garrettson, Freeborn. Methodist Church. Missions and Missionaries. Nova Scotia. Wesley, John. 1786. *1490*
—. Communes. German Americans. Keil, William. Missouri. Oregon. Society of Bethel. Weitling, Wilhelm. 1844-83. *405*
—. Congregation Kahal Kadosh Beth Israel. Georgia (Macon). Judaism. Leeser, Isaac. Loewenthal, Henry. Rabbis. 1854-70. *4124*
—. Congregationalism. Converts. Episcopal Church, Protestant. Kilbourne, James. Ohio (Worthington). Pioneers. 1844-49. *2823*
—. Congregationalism. Drummer, Jeremiah. Massachusetts. Sabbath. Sewall, Samuel. Taylor, Edward. 1704. *2276*
—. Converts. Lynch, James. Methodist Episcopal Church. Methodist Episcopal Church, African. Negroes. 1867. *3462*
—. Converts. Missouri. Mormons. Ostracism. Partridge, Edward. 1837. *3989*
—. Country Life. Farms. Haswell, David R. Pennsylvania. Protestants. Revivals. 1808-31. *2234*
—. Democratic Party. Mennonites. Politics. Risser, Johannes. Slavery. 1856-57. *994*
—. Emigration. Epp, Johann. Mennonites. North America. Russia. 1875. *3373*
—. Episcopal Church, Protestant. Nashotah House. Seminaries. Unonius, Gustaf. Wisconsin (Nashotah). 1884. *585*
—. Exiles. Mormons. Polygamy. Utah. Woodruff, Emma Smith. Woodruff, Wilford. 1885. *1050*
—. Feminism. Kansas. Nichols, Clarina I. H. Sex roles. Theology. 1857-69. *843*
—. Finch, John. New York (Finger Lakes area). Skaneateles Community. Utopias. 1843-45. *4302*
—. Francke, Gottfried. Georgia (Ebenezer). Germany. Immigrants. Kiefer, Theobald, II. Lutheran Church. Orphanages. Pietism. Whitefield, George. 1738. 1750. *2878*
—. Grant, Heber J. Mormons. Recreation. Smith, Joseph Fielding. 1930's. *3954*
—. Great Britain. Mormons. Richards, Willard. Young, Brigham. 1840. *1754*
—. Hebrew Benevolent Association. Jews. Nevada (Austin). Silver mining. 1864-82. *4164*
—. Hebrew Union College. Judaism, Reform. Prager, Abraham J. Rabbis. Wise, Isaac Mayer. 1854-1900. *4227*
—. Hebrew Union College. Judaism (Reform). Rabbis. Stolz, Joseph. Wise, Isaac Mayer. 1882-1900. *4220*
—. Heyer, John Christian Frederick. Illinois. Indiana. Keller, Ezra. Lutheranism. Missions and Missionaries. Missouri. ca 1820-40. *1614*
—. Historians. Mormons. Schisms. Wight, Lyman. Woodruff, Wilford. 1857-58. *4049*
—. Illinois (Nauvoo). Kimball, Vilate. Mormons. Murder. Smith, Joseph. Women. 1844. *3963*
—. Immigrants. Norwegian Americans. Pennsylvania (Harmony, New Harmony). Rapp, George. 1816-26. *378*
—. James, Henry (1811-82). Swedenborg, Emanuel. Theology. Wilkinson, James John Garth. 1844-55. *4060*
—. Judaism (Orthodox). Religious Liberty. Rhode Island (Newport). Seixas, Moses. Washington, George. 1790. 1974. *1081*
—. Lutheran Church. Mennicke, Christopher A. Usury. Walther, Carl F. W. 1866. *353*
—. Lynch, James. Methodist Episcopal Church. Mississippi. Negroes. Reconstruction. 1868-69. *3461*
—. Métis. Prairie Provinces. Religious beliefs. Riel, Louis. Taché, Alexandre Antonin. 1880's. *966*
—. Miller, George. Mormons. Smith, Joseph. 1842. *3952*
—. Missionaries. Wimmer, Boniface. 1847-55. *1626*
—. Mormons. New York. Reformed Dutch Church. Willers, Diedrich. 1830. *2766*
Letters-to-the-editor. Anti-Catholicism. Benedictines. D'Equivelley, G. F. Florida (Pasco County). *Jeffersonian* (newspaper). Land. Mohr, Charles. 1915-16. *2123*
—. California (San Francisco). *Emanu-El* (newspaper). Immigration. Jews, East European. Rabbis. Rosenthal, Marcus. Voorsanger, Jacob. 1905. *4141*
—. *Evangelische Kirchen-Zeitung* (newspaper). Fister, W. Lutheran Church (Missouri Synod). 1866. *3322*
—. Jews. Mexico (Tamaulipas; Matamoros). Newspapers. Texas (Brownsville). 1876-82. *4165*
Leverett, John. Congregationalism. Harvard University. Latin language. Massachusetts (Cambridge). Speeches, Addresses, etc. 1722. *668*
Lévesque, Georges-Henri. Catholicism. French Canadians. Nationalism. Personal narratives. Quebec. Youth movements. 1930's. *3790*
Levi, Abraham. Judaism (Reform). Leadership. Temple B'nai Israel. Texas (Victoria). 1850-1902. *4225*
Levin, David (review article). Mather, Cotton. Puritans. 1663-1703. 1978. *3625*
Levy, J. Leonard. California (Sacramento). Judaism (Reform). Letters. Rabbis. 1892. *4219*
Levy, Moses Elias. Civil Rights. Colonies. Europe. Florida. Judaism. 1825. *4151*
Lewis, Lloyd. Clergy. Lincoln, Abraham. Myths and symbols. 1861-65. *79*
Lewis, Sinclair. Christianity. Novels. Science. Secular humanism. 1900-50. *2003*
Liberal Advocate (newspaper). Dogberry, Obediah. Free thinkers. Freedom of thought. New York (Rochester). Religious liberty. 1832-34. *1003*
Liberal Institute. Mormons. Social Reform. Spiritualism. Utah (Salt Lake City). 1869-84. *4296*
Liberal Party. Bishops. Catholic Church. Church of England. Newfoundland. Provincial government. 1860-62. *1253*
—. Canada. Ideology. King, William Lyon Mackenzie. Politics. Protestantism. Social Classes. 1900-50. *1421*
—. Catholic Church. Church schools. French language. Langevin, Adélard. Laurier, Wilfrid. Prairie Provinces. Religion in the Public Schools. 1890-1915. *569*
—. Elections. Mormons. Nevada. Utah. 1860-70. *1252*
Liberalism. Alienation. Ecumenism. Judaism (Conservative, Reform). Utah (Salt Lake City). 1971. *499*
—. American Revolution (antecedents). Great Awakening. Social Change. Social theory. ca 1725-75. *1338*
—. Authority. Church and state. France. Tocqueville, Alexis de. 1830's. *1144*
—. Baker, Ray Stannard. Civil rights. DuBois, W. E. B. Episcopal Church, Protestant. Negroes. Personal narratives. Whites. Wilmer, Cary Breckenridge. 1900-10. *2151*
—. Baptists. Clergy. Hudson, Winthrop. Rauschenbusch, Walter. Social theory. Theology. 1880-1978. *2351*
—. Barth, Karl. Ethics. Niebuhr, Reinhold. 1920's-60. *2359*
—. Bible (New Testament). Exegesis. Germany. Hodge, Charles. Presbyterian Church. Princeton Theological Seminary. 1820-78. *3573*
—. *Brown* v. *Les Curé et Marguilliers de l'Oeuvre et de la Fabrique de la Paroisse de Montréal* (1874). Catholic Church. Church and state. Guibord, Joseph. Politics. Quebec. Ultramontanism. 1870-74. *1067*
—. Catholic Church. Democracy. Intellectuals. Racism. 1924-59. *2532*
—. Catholic Church. Neoorthodoxy. Pluralism. Secularism. Theology. 1936-74. *3899*
—. Cave, Robert Catlett. Disciples of Christ. Missouri (St. Louis). Non-Sectarian Church of St. Louis. Theology. 1867-1923. *2913*
—. Charities. Fosdick, Harry Emerson. Friendship. Protestantism. Rockefeller, John D., Jr. Social control. Wealth. 1920-36. *364*
—. Christian realism. Niebuhr, Reinhold. Philosophy. 1920's. *1359*
—. Conservatism. Mennonites. Ontario (Waterloo County). 1977. *3368*
—. Ecumenism. Manitoba. Social gospel. United Church of Canada. 1870's-1925. *449*
—. Europe. History, comparative. Protestant Churches. Social Gospel. 1885-1975. *2395*
—. Evangelicalism. Individualism. 1815-60. *2952*
—. Judaism. 19c-20c. *4131*
—. Marxism. Niebuhr, Reinhold. Philosophy. 1927-69. *1422*
—. Niebuhr, Reinhold. Political Theory. ca 1920-72. *1355*
—. Protestantism. Theology. 1880's-1930's. *2945*
Liberals. Democracy. Niebuhr, Reinhold. 1930-45. *1367*
Liberation movements. American Revolution. Freedom. Political Attitudes. Theology. 1765-20c. *1342*
Liberia *See also* Africa, West.
—. American Colonization Society. Crummell, Alexander. Education. Episcopal Church, Protestant. Missions and Missionaries. Negroes. 1853-73. *1671*
—. Colonization. Methodist Episcopal Church. Missions and Missionaries. Negroes. Sierra Leone. 1833-48. *1702*
Libertarianism. Antislavery Sentiments. Friends, Society of. Great Britain. Radicals and Radicalism. 18c-1865. *2497*
Liberty. Bledsoe, Albert Taylor. Philosophy. Theology. 19c. *1360*
Liberty bonds. Kansas. Mennonites. Pacifism. Vigilantism. World War I. 1918. *2659*
Liberty Hall Academy. Christianity. Colleges and Universities. Curricula. Graham, William. Proslavery Sentiments. Virginia. ca 1786-96. *2173*
Liberty Party. Democratic Party. Negroes. New York. Referendum. Suffrage. Whig Party. 1840-47. *1264*
Librarians. American Baptist Historical Society. Baptists. Samuel Colgate Baptist Historical Library. Starr, Edward Caryl. 1930's-76. *208*
—. New York City. Presbyterian Church. Smith, Henry B. Union Theological Seminary. 1851-77. *758*
Libraries *See also* names of individual libraries; Archives; Museums.
—. Anti-Catholicism. Church and state. Cox Library. Discrimination. *Koester* v. *Pardeeville* (1929). Taxation. Wisconsin (Pardeeville). 1927-29. *1033*
—. Archives. Mormons. Utah (Salt Lake City). 1830-1970's. *194*

—. Brown University. Colleges and Universities. Harvard University. Princeton University. Yale University. 18c. *672*
—. Calvinism. Founding fathers. Giles, Benjamin. New Hampshire. 1760's-87. *2908*
—. Church and state. New Mexico. 1598-1912. *1111*
—. Genealogy. Mormon Genealogical Society. 1607-1850. 1975. *201*
—. Great Britain (London). Pool, Reuben B. Young Men's Christian Association. 1844-1974. *2887*
—. Lutheran Church. South Carolina. Theological Seminary Library of Lexington, South Carolina. 1832-59. *645*
—. New York City. Pettee, Julia. Presbyterian Church. Rockwell, William Walker. Union Theological Seminary Library. 1908-58. *759*
Library of Congress. Communes. Labor Department. Publications. Western states. 1830's-1930's. *430*
Library of Congress (Alaska Church Collection). Alaska. Diaries. Indian-White Relations. Missions and Missionaries. Orlov, Vasilii. Orthodox Eastern Church, Russian. 1886. *1632*
Licenses. Law enforcement. Sabbath. Taverns. Virginia. ca 1630-1850. *2286*
—. Lawsuits. Music, gospel. Performance licensing. 1950's. *1919*
Lifestyles. Agriculture. Hutterites. North America. Social Customs. Technological innovation. 18c-20c. *3349*
—. Appalachia. Baptists. Methodism. Presbyterian Church. 1788-1974. *2873*
—. Baptists. Church of England. Toleration. Virginia. 1765-75. *3032*
—. Canada. Communalism. Hutterites. South Dakota. 1874-1975. *403*
—. Canada. Immigrants. Lutheran Church. Occupations. Settlement. Social Organizations. Swedish Americans. USA. 1893-1979. *3325*
—. Christianity. Technology. Values. 20c. *2725*
—. Health. Mormons. ca 1930-79. *1448*
—. Lutheran Church. Missouri (St. Louis). Seminaries. Students. 1922-28. *703*
Lincoln, Abraham. Abolition Movement. Assassination. Brooks, Phillips. Episcopal Church, Protestant. Pennsylvania (Philadelphia). Sermons. 1865. 1893. *2463*
—. Anti-Catholicism. Chiniquy, Charles P. T. 1855-65. *2105*
—. Assassination. Baptists. Baptists, Southern (winter assembly grounds). Florida (Umatilla). 1865. 1925-29. *2980*
—. Baptists. Indiana. Pigeon Creek Baptist Church. 1822-30. *3098*
—. Church and State. Civil religion. 1812-65. *1162*
—. Civil War. Constitutional Amendments. Fundamentalism. National Fast Day. National Reform Association. 1787-1945. *1009*
—. Civil War. Disasters. Puritans. Rhetoric. Sermons. 1650-1870. *1968*
—. Clergy. Lewis, Lloyd. Myths and symbols. 1861-65. *79*
—. Converts. Illinois (Springfield). Jacquess, James F. Methodist Church. 1847. *2788*
—. District of Columbia. Johnson, Andrew. Schurz, Carl. Seance. Spiritualism. 1865. *4293*
—. Equality. Mormons. Polygamy. Slavery. Smith, Joseph. 1840-64. *986*
—. Lincoln, Mary Todd. Spiritualism. 1848-64. *4295*
Lincoln and Lincolniana. Civil Religion. Lutheran Church (Evangelical). 1862-63. *1163*
Lincoln, Mary Todd. Lincoln, Abraham. Spiritualism. 1848-64. *4295*
Lindesmith, Eli. Catholic Church. Chaplains. Diaries. Fort Keogh. Montana. 1855-1922. *2679*
Linn, William. American Revolution. Calvinism. Church and state. Clergy. Jefferson, Thomas. Presbyterian Church. 1775-1808. *1335*
Lippy, Thomas S. Clergy. Gold Mines and Mining. Klondike Stampede. Methodist Church. Randall, Edwin M. Transportation. Yukon Territory. 1896-99. *3492*
Lipscomb, Bernard F. Clergy. Letters. Methodist Church. Virginia (Charlottesville). 1889-92. *3471*
Literary movement, regional. Mormons. Novels. Utah. 1940's. *2025*
Literary Symbolism. *See* Symbolism in Literature.
Literature *See also* Authors; Books; Drama; Fiction; Humor; Journalism; Language; Novels; Poetry; Satire; Symbolism in Literature.
—. Acculturation. Mennonites. 1970's. *3414*
—. Alger, Horatio. Capitalism. Evangelicalism. Social History. Success (concept of). 1820-1910. *2958*
—. American Revolution. Environment. Millenarianism. Symbolism in Literature. 1770's-1800. *1192*
—. American Revolution. Hawthorne, Nathaniel. National character. Puritan Tradition. 1775-83. 1830-40. *2082*
—. American Revolution. Ideology. Puritans. 1775-83. 19c. *1344*
—. Anti-Catholicism. Church of England. Gavin, Anthony *(A Master-Key to Popery).* Great Britain. Virginia. 1724-73. *2108*
—. Anti-Semitism. Drama. Stereotypes. 1830's-1920's. *2011*
—. Baptists. *Keystone Graded Lessons.* Religious Education. Sunday schools. 1824-1909. *637*
—. Bradstreet, Anne. Hutchinson, Anne. Massachusetts. Puritans. Social change. Theology. Women. 1630's-70's. *865*
—. Calvin, Ross Randall. Episcopal Church, Protestant. Nature. New Mexico. 1889-1970. *2332*
—. Calvinism. 1650-1900. *2002*
—. Calvinism. Faulkner, William. Presbyterian Church. 1920's-75. *2035*
—. Calvinism. Muir, John. Romanticism. 1838-1914. *2929*
—. Catholic Church. Christian Renaissance. Converts. Philosophy. Science. Stern, Karl. 1920's-60's. *2758*
—. Catholic Church. Education. Hackett, Francis. Ireland (Kilkenny, Clongowes Wood). Irish Americans. 1880's-1901. *3818*
—. Catholic Church. History. Religious Orders. Women. 19c-1978. *868*
—. Catholic Church. Pennsylvania (Philadelphia). Walter, William Joseph *(Thomas More).* 1839-46. *2063*
—. Christianity. Hawthorne, Nathaniel. Sacramental love tradition. 1838-60. *2080*
—. Congregationalism. Edwards, Jonathan. Historiography (revisionist). 1758-1903. *3143*
—. Connecticut (Hartford). Episcopal Church, Protestant. Evangelicalism. Sigourney, Lydia Huntley. Women. 1800-65. *3194*
—. Crane, Stephen. Faulkner, William. 19c-20c. *2030*
—. Death and Dying. Evangelism. South. 1800-65. *1970*
—. Death and Dying. North or Northern States. Protestantism. Women. 1830-80. *2846*
—. Earthquakes. New England. Puritans. 1727. *2289*
—. Ethics. Pluralism. Styron, William *(Confessions of Nat Turner).* 1970's. *2053*
—. Family. Farms. Sex roles. Social Status. South. Women. 1800-60. *816*
—. Fisher, Vardis. Mormons. 1915-68. *1999*
—. French Canadians. Patriotism. Quebec. Sociology. 19c. *2085*
—. German Americans. Good, Merle. Mennonites. Pennsylvania. Personal narratives. 1975. *2057*
—. Harap, Louis (review article). Jews. 1775-1914. 1974. *83*
—. Holmes, Oliver Wendell *(Elsie Venner).* New England. Original Sin. 1861. *2024*
—. James, Henry (1811-82). Swedenborgianism. Theology. 1840's-81. *4061*
—. Marriage. Marshall, Catherine. Presbyterian Church. Sex roles. Women. 1950's. *806*
—. McCulloch, Thomas *(Letters of Mephibosheth Stepsure).* Nova Scotia. Presbyterian Church. Satire. 1821-22. *2067*
—. Mennonites. Pacifism. 20c. *2073*
—. Morality. Social Conditions. 17c-1976. *2037*
—. Murdock, Kenneth Ballard (obituary). Puritans. 20c. *225*
—. New York. Presbyterian Church. Satire. Social criticism. Whitcher, Frances Miriam Berry *(Widow Bedott Papers).* 1847-55. *2056*
—. Puritanism. Romanticism. 1620-1946. *2016*
—. Theology. Trumbull, John. 1769-73. *2029*
—. Western States. 19c-20c. *2007*
Lithography. Folk art. Mexico. Puerto Rico. Southwest. 1300-1974. *1868*
Lithuanian Americans. Assimilation. Catholic Church. Connecticut (Waterbury). *Rytas* (newspaper). Zebris, Joseph. 1896-98. *3901*
—. Catholic Church. Educational attainment. Immaculate Conception Primary School. Missouri (St. Louis). Occupations. 1948-68. *2607*
Little Britain Presbyterian Church. Pennsylvania (Lancaster County). Presbyterian Church. 1740-1860. *3587*
Liturgy. Architecture. Benedictines. Churches. 1945-62. *1804*
—. Architecture. Church of England. Vestments. 18c. *3188*
—. Bishops. Catholic Church. Church of England. Evangelicalism. Feild, Edward. Methodism. Newfoundland. Presbyterian Church. 1765-1852. *3197*
—. Bishops. Church of England. Ontario (Toronto). Strachan, John. Theology. 1802-67. *3214*
—. Canada. Church of England. Tractarians. 1840-68. *3189*
—. Catholic Church. Episcopal Church, Protestant. 1973. *2727*
—. Ethics. Social Organization. 1970's. *2735*
Livingston Female Academy. Alabama. Church schools. Presbyterian Church. Women. 1835-1910. *686*
Livingston, William. Church and State. Church of England. Presbyterian Church. ca 1750-90. *1091*
—. Church of England. Columbia University. Johnson, Samuel (1696-1772). Reformed Dutch Church. 1751-63. *635*
Llewelyn, John. American Revolution. Church of England. Conspiracies. Loyalists. North Carolina. 1776-77. *1224*
"Lob Lied" (song). Mennonites. 1590-1978. *1944*
Lobbying *See also* Political Factions.
—. American Christian Palestine Committee. Great Britain. Palestine. Zionism. 1940's. *1316*
—. Baptists. Church and state. 1950-73. *1297*
—. Christianity. War. 1939-79. *1327*
—. Church and State. Civil rights. District of Columbia. 1964-72. *1322*
—. Church and state. Mormons. Statehood. Trumbo, Isaac. Utah. 1887-96. *1072*
—. Legislation. Religious Liberty. 1950's-70's. *1136*
Local Government *See also* Local Politics; Public Administration.
—. Church and state. Constitutional Law. Fund raising. State Government. 1970's. *1059*
—. Elites. Immigrants. Massachusetts (Charlestown). Puritans. 1630-40. *3613*
—. Great Britain. Massachusetts. New England. Political theory. Puritans. Social change. 1600-50. *3604*
Local history. Catholic Church. Georgia (Augusta). Preservation. Sacred Heart Church. 1976-78. *1823*
Local option campaign. Louisiana. Prohibition. Shreveport Ministerial Association. 1950-52. *2591*
Local Politics *See also* Local Government.
—. Church and Social Problems. Congregationalism. Indian-White Relations. Massachusetts (Natick). Meetinghouses. 1650-18c. *3118*
—. Congregationalism. Connecticut (Canterbury). Family. Great Awakening. Schisms. 1742-50. *2242*
—. Democracy. Education. Fundamentalism. Morality. Social Change. Vigilantism. 1920's. *2387*
—. Friends, society of. Pennsylvania (Lancaster County). Provincial politics. 1700-76. *1008*
Localism. North Carolina. Social classes. Temperance Movements. 1969-70. *2599*
Locke, John. Citizenship. Democracy. Jefferson, Thomas. Puritanism. 17c-18c. *1408*
—. Edwards, Jonathan. Grace. Psychology. Theology. 1740's. *3158*
Loeb, Richard. Candler, Warren A. Conservatism. Evolution. Leopold, Nathan. Methodist Episcopal Church, South. Scopes, John Thomas. Trials. 1921-41. *2293*
Loewenthal, Henry. Congregation Kahal Kadosh Beth Israel. Georgia (Macon). Judaism. Leeser, Isaac. Letters. Rabbis. 1854-70. *4124*
Loew's State Theatre. California (Los Angeles). Cantors. Concerts. Judaism. Music, liturgical. Rosenblatt, Josef "Yosele". Vaudeville. 1925. *1917*
Logan, James. Botany. Friends, Society of. Mather, Cotton. Natural History. New England. Puritans. 17c-18c. *2300*
Loma Linda Sanitarium. Adventists. California. Letters. White, Ellen G. 1905. *1461*
—. Adventists. California. Photographs. 1905-19. *1458*

Loma Linda University. Adventists. Anesthesia. California. Dentistry. Jorgensen, Niels Bjorn. Teaching. 1923-74. *1441*
—. Adventists. Battle Creek Sanitarium. California. Medical Education. Michigan. Nurses and Nursing. 1884-1979. *1425*
—. Adventists. California. Humor. Irish Americans. Letters. Magan, Percy Tilson. 1918-34. *1435*
—. Adventists. California. Medical Education. 1905-15. *1450*
—. Adventists. California (Arlington). 1922-67. *738*
—. Adventists. California (Arlington). Personal narratives. Robison, James I. 1922. *745*
Long, Huey P. Fundamentalism. North Central States. Populism. Progressivism. Smith, Gerald L. K. 1934-48. *975*
Longshoremen. Christianity. Oxford Movement. Strikes. Washington (Seattle). 1921-34. *1477*
Loomis, Charles P. Amish (Old Order). Daily Life. Diaries. Farms. King family. Pennsylvania (Lancaster County). 1940. *3403*
Lopez, George. Catholic Church. Folk art. Lopez, José Dolores. New Mexico (Cordova). Santos, statues. 20c. *1844*
Lopez, José Dolores. Catholic Church. Folk art. Lopez, George. New Mexico (Cordova). Santos, statues. 20c. *1844*
Lord's Day Act (Canada, 1906). Canada. Church and state. Sabbatarianism. Sports. 1906-77. *2284*
Lost Cause (theme). Civil religion. South. 1865-1920. *1196*
Lost Tribes of Israel. Anthropology. Archaeology. Indians. Mormons. Smith, Joseph. 1830. *2335*
Louisiana. Blue laws. Church and state. Legislators. Negroes. Reconstruction. Sabbath. 1867-75. *2285*
—. Bureaucracies. Church and state. Colonial Government. *Commissaire ordonnateur*. France. 1712-69. *1069*
—. Catholic Church. Church and state. Inquisition. Surveillance. 1762-1800. *1044*
—. Catholic Church. Churches. 1685-1830. *1835*
—. Catholic Church. Conversion. France (Alsace). Immigration policy. Protestants. 1753-59. *3719*
—. Catholic Church. Democratic Party. Elections (presidential). Protestant Churches. Smith, Al. Temperance Movements. 1928. *1330*
—. Catholic Church. Indians. Missions and Missionaries. 18c-20c. *1625*
—. Catholic Church. North Central States. Rosati, Joseph (review article). 1818-43. *3734*
—. Centenary College. Dance. Educational Policy. Methodist Church. 1941. *688*
—. Local option campaign. Prohibition. Shreveport Ministerial Association. 1950-52. *2591*
Louisiana (Bienville Parish). Baptists. Leshe, Mary Jane Conly. 1849-1932. *3045*
Louisiana (DeSoto Parish). Artists. Carmelites. Restorations. St. Anne's Chapel. 1891-1975. *1796*
Louisiana (Mineral Springs). Camp meetings. Church of the Nazarene. Holiness movement. Methodist Church. National Camp Meeting Association for the Promotion of Holiness. 1860's-1926. *2891*
Louisiana (New Orleans). Baptists. Converts. Evangelism. Methodism. Slavery. 1800-61. *2916*
—. Cable, George Washington. Fiction. Presbyterian Church, Southern. Reform. ca 1870-1925. *3539*
—. Canon law. Circumcision. Europe. Illowy, Bernard. Judaism (Orthodox). Rabbis. 1853-65. *4176*
—. Civil Rights movement. Discrimination. Florida (Miami). Murray, Hugh T., Jr. Personal narratives. Tulane Interfaith Council. 1959-60. *2548*
—. Clapp, Theodore. Slavery. Theology. Unitarianism. 1822-56. *4084*
—. Education. Episcopal Church, Protestant. Polk, Leonidas. Slavery. 1805-65. *3219*
—. Methodist Church. Winans, William. 1813-14. *3472*
—. Music (jazz). Negroes. Voodoo. Women. ca 19c. *2181*
Louisiana, north. Catholic Church. Church records. Preservation. 1716-1840's. 1930's-74. *185*
Louisiana Purchase. Carroll, John. Catholic Church. Clergy. Frontier and Pioneer Life. 1803-15. *3805*
Louisiana (Shreveport). Bishops. Episcopal Church, Protestant. Polk, Leonidas. 1830-1916. *3184*
—. Catholic Church. St. Vincent Academy. -1973. *1799*
Louisiana (Spearsville). Baptists. Colleges and Universities. Education. Everett Institute. 1893-1908. *605*
Louisiana (Union Parish). Baptists. Methodist Church, Wesleyan. Tombstones. 1839-1970's. *2834*
Louisiana (Webster Parish). Baptists, Southern. Concord Baptist Association. Ecumenism. 1832-1972. *463*
Louisiana (Winn Parish). Camp meetings. Holiness Movement. Hudson Holiness Interdenominational Camp. 1899-1977. *3292*
Louisville Churchmen's Federation. Barkley, Alben. Gambling, pari-mutuel. Kentucky. Progressivism. 1917-27. *2437*
Love feast. Brethren, Old Order River. Pennsylvania. ca 1773-1973. *3383*
Lowrie, Ernest Benson. Holifield, E. Brooks. New England. Puritans (review article). Sacraments. Theology. Willard, Samuel. 16c-17c. 1974. *3637*
Lowrie, John C. Assimilation. Indians (agencies). Missions and Missionaries. Presbyterian Church. 1870-82. *1655*
Loyalists. American Revolution. Asbury, Francis. Delaware. Maryland. Methodists. White, Thomas. 1777-80. *3482*
—. American Revolution. Boucher, Jonathan. Church of England. 1763-83. *1383*
—. American Revolution. Boucher, Jonathan. Church of England. Civil War. Great Britain. Jefferson, Thomas. 1640-1797. *1412*
—. American Revolution. Canada. Church of England. Cossitt, Ranna. Missions and Missionaries. New England. 1773-1815. *1317*
—. American Revolution. Church of England. 1770-1800. *973*
—. American Revolution. Church of England. Conspiracies. Llewelyn, John. North Carolina. 1776-77. *1224*
—. American Revolution. Church of England. Continental Congress. Seabury, Samuel (pseud. A. W. Farmer). 1774-84. *1378*
—. American Revolution. Church of England. Delaware (Appoquiniminck). Reading, Philip. Society for the Propagation of the Gospel. 1775-78. *1221*
—. American Revolution. Church of England. Georgia (Augusta). St. Paul's Parish. Seymour, James. 1775-83. *1301*
—. American Revolution. Church of England. Hughes, Philip. Maryland. 1767-77. *1323*
—. American Revolution. Clergy. Lydekker, Gerrit. New York City. Reformed Dutch Church. 1765-94. *977*
—. American Revolution. Conscientious objectors. Maryland (Elizabethtown). Mennonites. 1774-76. *2665*
—. American Revolution. Dunkards. Mennonites. Pacifism. 1776-84. *2635*
—. American Revolution. Friends, Society of. Pennsylvania (Philadelphia). 1770's. *1282*
—. American Revolution. Great Britain. Methodism. Poetry. Political Commentary. Wesley, Charles. 1775-83. *1339*
—. Amnesty. Massachusetts. Property. Public Opinion. 1783-84. *1357*
—. Behavior. Boucher, Jonathan. Church of England. Maryland. Virginia. 1738-89. *1348*
—. Boucher, Jonathan. Church of England. Great Britain. Maryland. Zimmer, Anne Y. (review article). 1770's-90's. *1358*
—. Canada. Eby, Ezra E. Immigration. Mennonites. Pennsylvania. 18c-1835. *1237*
—. Chain of interest (concept). Pennsylvania (Philadelphia). Presbyterian Church. 1770's. *984*
—. Church of England. Clergy. Government. Political Attitudes. Theology. 1770-83. *1387*
—. Church of England. Clergy. Theology. 1774-83. *1346*
—. Church of England. Inglis, Charles. Propaganda. Sermons. 1770-80. *1370*
—. Church of England. Nova Scotia. Society for the Propagation of the Gospel. 1787-1864. *1644*
—. Exiles. McDowall, Robert James. Missions and Missionaries. Ontario (Upper Canada). Reformed Dutch Church. 1790-1819. *1588*
—. Presbyterian Church. Zubly, John Joachim. 1770-81. *1400*
Lucas, Paul R. New England (review article). Puritans. Social Organization. VanDeventer, David E. 1623-1741. 1976. *3621*
Lucifer's Lantern (periodical). Atheism. Freedom of Speech. Mormons. Polygamy. Schroeder, Theodore. Utah. 1889-1900. *2125*
Lum, Dyer D. Anarchism and Anarchists. Church and State. Mormons. 1880's. *4010*
Lund, A. William. Historiography. Hunter, Howard W. Jenson, Andrew. Lyon, T. Edgar. Mormons. Roberts, Brigham Henry. 1913-70. *226*
Lundeberg, Axel Johan Sigurd Mauritz. Minnesota. Swedenborgianism. Swedish Americans. 1852-1940. *4063*
Luria, Isaac. Congregationalism. Edwards, Jonathan. Judaism. Millenarianism. Progress, concept of. 16c-18c. *84*
Luther, Martin. Calvin, John. National Characteristics. Protestantism. 16c-18c. *2870*
Luther, Martin *(Small Catechism)*. Exegesis. Schwan, Henry C. 1893-1912. *3332*
Lutheran Church. Acculturation. Frontier and Pioneer Life. Immigrants. Rolvaag, O. E. *(Giants in the Earth)*. South Dakota. 1870. 1927. *3307*
—. Age. Church membership. Religiosity. 1974. *3311*
—. Agriculture. Immigration. Minnesota (Isantic County). Social customs. Sweden (Dalarna). 1840-1910. *3329*
—. Alabama. Bakke, Niles J. South. Young, Rosa J. 1839-1965. *3299*
—. Alabama. Photographs. South. 1971-74. *3347*
—. Altarpieces. Christenson, Lars. Folk art. Minnesota (Benson). Norwegian Americans. Wood Carving. 1887-1904. *1874*
—. American Baptist Publishing Society. Baptists. Converts. Immigration. Sweden. Travel (accounts). Wiberg, Anders. 1852-53. *3054*
—. American Revolution. Baptists. Church of England. Congregationalism. Friends, Society of. Georgia. Judaism. Presbyterian Church. 1733-90. *88*
—. American Revolution. Clergy. Delaware River Valley. Episcopal Church, Protestant. Swedish Americans. 1655-1831. *285*
—. Andersson, Joris Per. Letters. Minnesota (Chisago Lake). Swedish Americans. 1851-53. *3312*
—. Archives. Emigrant Institute. Social organizations. Sweden (Växjö). 1800-1970. *282*
—. Arndt, E. L. China. Missions and Missionaries. 1913-29. *1749*
—. Assimilation. Muhlenberg, Henry Melchior. Pennsylvania. Politics. Swedish Americans. Wrangel, Carl Magnus. 1749-69. *1283*
—. Augustana College and Theological Seminary. Bethany College. Immigration. Midwest. Politics. Railroads. Religious education. Swedish Americans. Swensson, Carl Aaron. 1873-1904. *726*
—. Augustana College and Theological Seminary. Illinois (Rock Island). Immigrants. Swedish Americans. 1855-1956. *599*
—. Bäck, Olof. Clergy. Esbjörn, Lars Paul. Janssonists. Letters. Methodism. Sweden. 1846-49. *2906*
—. Bad Boll Conferences. Ecumenism. Germany. 1948. *439*
—. Baltic Area. Canada. Immigrants. 1947-55. *2453*
—. Baptists. Canada. Disciples of Christ. Great Plains. Methodism. Pietism. Prairie Radicals. Radicals and Radicalism. 1890-1975. *954*
—. Baptists. Catholic Church. Germans, Russian. Immigration. Kansas. Mennonites. Wheat industry. 1874-77. *2778*
—. Beck, Vilhelm. Danish Americans. Grundtvig, Nikolai Frederik Severin. Inner Mission Movement. 1619-1973. *3341*
—. Bibliographies. Canada. Congregationalism. Historiography. Methodist Church. Presbyterian Church. United Church of Canada. 1825-1973. *2892*
—. Bibliographies. Concordia Historical Institute. Microforms. 1971-72. *265*
—. Bibliographies. Music. 1700-1850. *1956*
—. Buerger, Paul Theodor. *Collegium Fratrum* (organization). Educational Tests and Measurements. Indiana (Fort Wayne). Letters. 1858. *3315*
—. Canada. Immigrants. Lifestyles. Occupations. Settlement. Social Organizations. Swedish Americans. USA. 1893-1979. *3325*

—. Canada, Western. Ecumenism. Stuermer, Herbert. 1922. *489*
—. Catholic Church. Country Life. Ethnic Groups. Reformed Dutch Church. Voting and Voting Behavior. 1890-98. *1257*
—. Catholic Church. Judaism. Ohio (Cincinnati). Public Schools. Religious Education. 19c. *545*
—. Chippewa Indians. Indian-White Relations. Michigan. Miessler, Ernst G. H. Missions and Missionaries. 1851-71. *1582*
—. Church and State. Diaries. Norwegian Americans. Preus, Herman A. Wisconsin (Columbia, Dane counties). 1851-60. *1104*
—. Church History. Clergy. 1978. *272*
—. Clergy. Converts. Episcopal Church, Protestant. Sweden. Unonius, Gustaf. Wisconsin (Pine Lake). 1841-58. *2854*
—. Clergy. Country stores. Duus, O. F. Knoph, Thomas. Ledgers. Norwegian Americans. Wisconsin (Waupaca township; Scandinavia). 1853-56. *3334*
—. Clergy. Diaries. Muhlenberg, Henry Melchior. Pennsylvania. Women. 1742-87. *828*
—. Clergy. Emanuel Lutheran Church. New York City (Queens). Personal narratives. Wyneken, Frederick G. 1887-1907. *3348*
—. Clergy. Helmreich, Christian. Letters. Nebraska (Weyerts). 1887-88. *3308*
—. Clergy. Muhlenberg, Henry Melchior. Pennsylvania. Pietism. 18c. *3337*
—. Clergy. Schulze, Ernst Carl Ludwig. Steup, Henry Christian. 1852-1931. *3339*
—. Cloeter, Ottomar. Indians. Letters. Minnesota. Missions and Missionaries. 1856-68. *1651*
—. Colleges and Universities. Valparaiso University. 1636-1973. *683*
—. Concordia Collegiate Institute. New Jersey (East Rutherford, Trenton). New York City (Brooklyn). Steege, Martin. 1921-73. *3343*
—. Concordia Historical Institute. Microforms. 1970-71. *266*
—. Conversion. Germany. Great Britain. Pietism. Puritanism. 17c-18c. *2942*
—. Country Life. Iowa. Langland, Joseph. Personal narratives. Poetry. Youth. 1917-30's. 1977. *2027*
—. Crow Indians. Diaries. Doederlein, Paul Ferdinand. Indians. Missions and Missionaries. Wyoming. 1859-60. *1589*
—. Deaf. Ephphatha Conference. Missions and Missionaries. 1893-1976. *1516*
—. Diaries. Emigration. Florida. Sjöborg, Sofia Charlotta. Sweden. 1871. *3340*
—. Diaries. McPherson, Sarah M. Missouri (Brazeau). 1852-56. *3298*
—. Dunkards. Evangelism. German Americans. Great Awakening. Immigration. Moravian Church. Northeastern or North Atlantic States. Reformed churches. 1720-60. *2237*
—. Ecumenism. Schmucker, Samuel Simon. 1838. *474*
—. Elementary Education. Johnson, Emeroy. Minnesota. Personal narratives. Religious education. Swedish Americans. ca 1854-ca 1920. *666*
—. Evangelism. Herzberger, F. W. Missouri (St. Louis). 1899-1930. *3336*
—. Evjen, John O. Minnesota. Theologians. 1874-1942. *3303*
—. Family. Parsonages. 1974. *802*
—. Finnish Americans. Theology. 1688-1970's. *3316*
—. Francke, Gottfried. Georgia (Ebenezer). Germany. Immigrants. Kiefer, Theobald, II. Letters. Orphanages. Pietism. Whitefield, George. 1738. 1750. *2878*
—. German Americans. Helmuth, Justus Henry Christian. Hymnals. 1786-1813. *1955*
—. German Americans. Pennsylvania. Reformed Churches. Slavery. Social change. 1779-88. *2162*
—. Gloria Dei Congregation. Old Swedes' Church. Pennsylvania (Philadelphia). Swedish Americans. 1638-98. *3302*
—. Grundtvig, Nikolai Frederik Severin. Reform. 19c-1972. *3313*
—. Holt, Benjamin M. Minnesota. Personal narratives. 1882-1974. *3309*
—. Identity. Theology. 18c-20c. *3326*
—. Immanuel Lutheran School. Secondary education. Wisconsin (Milwaukee). 1903-78. *785*
—. Immigration. Iowa. Schwartz, Auguste von. Wartburg College. Women. 1861-77. *3320*
—. Indiana (Tippecanoe County). 1826-50. *3346*
—. Keisker, Walter. Missouri (Concordia). Personal narratives. Religious Education. St. Paul's College. Students. 1913-19. 1980. *669*
—. Koehler, J. P. Theology. *Wisconsin Lutheran Quarterly* (periodical). 1880's-1915. *3317*
—. Kramer, William A. Missouri (Perry County). Personal narratives. ca 1890-1910. *3314*
—. Kuehn, Ernst Ludwig Hermann. Michigan. Missions and Missionaries. 1850-98. *1666*
—. Kuhnle, Howard A. Necrology. 1950-73. *222*
—. Letters. Mennicke, Christopher A. Usury. Walther, Carl F. W. 1866. *353*
—. Libraries. South Carolina. Theological Seminary Library of Lexington, South Carolina. 1832-59. *645*
—. Lifestyles. Missouri (St. Louis). Seminaries. Students. 1922-28. *703*
—. Methodist Church. Orthodox Eastern Church. Pennsylvania Historical and Museum Commission. Pennsylvania Historical Association. Reformed Dutch Church. Research conference. Uniates. 1977. *2791*
—. Methodist Church. Social Organizations. Swedish Americans. 1850-1951. *2951*
—. Methodist Episcopal Church, African. Negroes. Payne, Daniel Alexander. Wilberforce University. 1830-93. *2905*
—. Mission Festival Sunday. Missions and Missionaries. Personal narratives. Schreiber, Clara Seuel. Wisconsin (Freistadt). 1900. *1630*
—. Palm Sunday. Personal narratives. Schreiber, Clara Seuel. Wisconsin (Freistadt). 1898. *3338*
—. St. Paul's Lutheran Church. Tennessee (Wartburg). 1844-1975. *3300*
—. Slavery. South. 1790-1865. *2172*
Lutheran Church (Alpha Synod). Negroes. North Carolina. 1889-91. *3327*
Lutheran Church, American. Ecumenism. Nelson, E. Clifford. Schiotz, Fredrik A. 1945-69. *485*
Lutheran Church (Augustana Synod). Augustana Book Concern. Illinois (Rock Island). 1850-1967. *357*
—. Augustana College and Theological Seminary. Illinois (Paxton). Osborn, William H. Railroads. Swedish Americans. 1853-73. *3321*
—. Clergy. Immigrants. Swedish Americans. Wives. 1860-1962. *3296*
—. Swedish Americans. 1860-1973. *287*
Lutheran Church (Evangelical). Civil Religion. Lincoln and Lincolniana. 1862-63. *1163*
—. Evangelism. Horstman, Otto K. Indiana (Shelbyville). Missions and Missionaries. Personal narratives. 1934. *1551*
—. Holy Trinity Parish. Pennsylvania (Lancaster). 1730-1980. *3306*
—. Indiana (Elletsville). St. John's Evangelical Lutheran Church (Old Dutch Church). 1830-1956. *3330*
Lutheran Church (General Synod). Evangelical Alliance. Schmucker, Samuel Simon. 1843-51. *3294*
Lutheran Church (Hauge's Synod, Norwegian Synod). Hymnals. Lutheran Church in America, Norwegian. Norwegian Americans. Youth. 1878-1916. *1915*
Lutheran Church in America, Norwegian. Clergy. Frontier. Letters. Montana, eastern. Thorpe, Christian Scriver. 1906-08. *3295*
—. Hymnals. Lutheran Church (Hauge's Synod, Norwegian Synod). Norwegian Americans. Youth. 1878-1916. *1915*
Lutheran Church (Missouri Synod). Academic freedom. Concordia Seminary. Missouri (St. Louis). Teachers. Tenure. 1968-74. *771*
—. Academic freedom. Theology. 1973. *649*
—. Alberta (Edmonton, Mellowdale). Concordia College. Personal narratives. Schwermann, Albert H. USA. 1891-1976. *753*
—. Alienation. Civil War. Ethnicity. German Americans. Massacres. Missouri (Concordia). 1864. *3301*
—. Americanization. Church Schools. German language. Nebraska Council of Defense. Supreme Court. 1917-23. *305*
—. Archives. Church History. Concordia Historical Institute. Missouri (St. Louis). 1978. *221*
—. Autobiography. Buenger, Theodore Arthur. Clergy. Concordia Seminary. German Americans. Seminaries. 1886-1909. *3297*
—. Baur, John C. Concordia Seminary. Fund raising. Missouri (Clayton, St. Louis). Personal Narratives. 1923-26. *594*
—. Buettner, George L. Concordia Publishing House. Missouri (St. Louis). Personal Narratives. Publishers and publishing. 1888-1955. *336*
—. Circuit riders. Frontier and Pioneer Life. German Americans. Oklahoma. Texas. Wacker, Hermann Dietrich. 1847-1938. *3342*
—. Clergy. Concordia Seminary. Illinois (Hahlen, Nashville). Personal narratives. St. Peter's Lutheran Church. Scharlemann, Ernst K. Seminaries. 1905-18. *3335*
—. Clergy. German language. Hansel, William H. Personal narratives. 1907-62. *3305*
—. Clergy. Minnesota. Missouri. Swedish Americans. Wihlborg, Niels Albert. 1893-1918. *3331*
—. Concordia Historical Institute. Farms. Missouri (Perry County). Preservation. Saxon Lutheran Memorial. 1958-64. *220*
—. Concordia Seminary. Daily Life. Kansas (Clay Center). Mueller, Peter. Seminaries. Students. 1883-89. *707*
—. Concordia Seminary. German Americans. Illinois (Springfield). Missouri (St. Louis). 1846-1938. *615*
—. Ethnicity. Immigrants. Migration. Theology. 1847-1970. *3323*
—. *Evangelische Kirchen-Zeitung* (newspaper). Fister, W. Letters-to-the-editor. 1866. *3322*
—. Immanuel Lutheran School. Personal narratives. Religious education. Wulff, O. H. 1908-75. *781*
—. *Lutheran Hymnal*. Music. 1923-41. *1925*
—. Manitoba (Township Berlin). Wagner, William. ca 1870. *3345*
—. Oregon (Portland). Rimbach, John Adam. Trinity Church. Washington. 1906-41. *3333*
Lutheran Church (Missouri Synod, Norwegian). Clergy. Ecumenism. Munch, Johan Storm. Norway. Wisconsin (Wiota). 1827-1908. *3324*
Lutheran Church (North Carolina Synod). Clergy. Negroes. 1865-89. *3328*
Lutheran Church (Norwegian). Church suppers. Ladies Aid Society. North Dakota (Hannaford). Norwegian Americans. 1941. *3310*
—. Clergy. North Dakota. Norwegian Americans. Red River of the North. 1871-99. *3318*
Lutheran Church, Swedish. Americanization. Ecumenism. Episcopal Church, Protestant. Swedish Americans. 1630-1850. *322*
Lutheran Church (United Synod of the South). Ecumenism. Episcopal Church, Protestant. 1860-90. *438*
Lutheran Free Church. Norwegian Americans. Religious Liberty. Sermons. Sverdrup, Georg. Thanksgiving. 1896-1907. *3304*
Lutheran Hymnal. Lutheran Church (Missouri Synod). Music. 1923-41. *1925*
Lutheranism. Finland. Finnish Americans. Marxism. Reform. 1900-76. *990*
—. Heyer, John Christian Frederick. Illinois. Indiana. Keller, Ezra. Letters. Missions and Missionaries. Missouri. ca 1820-40. *1614*
Lutherans. American Revolution. German Americans. Pennsylvania (Philadelphia). 1776-81. *1304*
—. Indiana. Politics. Theology. 1835-70. *3344*
Lyall, William. Colleges and Universities. Common Sense school. Curricula. Dalhousie University. King's College. Nova Scotia. Philosophy. Pine Hill Divinity Hall. Presbyterian Church. 1850-90. *719*
Lyche, Hans Tambs. Attitudes. Clergy. Newspapers. Norway. Travel (accounts). Unitarianism. 1880-92. *4081*
Lydekker, Gerrit. American Revolution. Clergy. Loyalists. New York City. Reformed Dutch Church. 1765-94. *977*
Lykins, Johnston. Baptists. Education. Indians. Kansas. Potawatomi Indians. Pottawatomie Baptist Manual Labor Training School. 1846-67. *508*
Lynch, James. Converts. Letters. Methodist Episcopal Church. Methodist Episcopal Church, African. Negroes. 1867. *3462*
—. Letters. Methodist Episcopal Church. Mississippi. Negroes. Reconstruction. 1868-69. *3461*
Lynch, John Joseph. Bishops. Catholic Church. Ontario. Poor. Toronto Savings Bank. 1870's. *369*

Lynching. Ames, Jessie Daniel. Association of Southern Women for the Prevention of Lynching. Methodist Woman's Missionary Council. Racism. South. Women. Young Women's Christian Association. 1930's. *2535*
—. Chapman, John Jay. Christianity. Pennsylvania (Coatesville). Poetry. Race Relations. Rhetoric. Speeches, Addresses, etc. 1912. *1971*
Lynd, Robert S. Clergy. Labor. Oil Industry and Trade. Presbyterian Church. Wyoming (Elk Basin). 1921. *3562*
Lynn, Kenneth S. Child-rearing. Death and Dying. Fischer, David H. Greven, Philip. Personality (review article). Politics. Protestantism. Stannard, David E. 18c. 1977. *2943*
Lyon, Marcus. Anti-Catholicism. Cheverus, Jean Louis Lefebvre de. Irish Americans. Massachusetts (Northampton). Murder. Protestantism. Trials. 1805-06. *2099*
Lyon, Mary. Colleges and Universities. Emerson, Joseph. Mount Holyoke College. Protestantism. Women. 1760's-1850's. *552*
Lyon, T. Edgar. Historiography. Hunter, Howard W. Jenson, Andrew. Lund, A. William. Mormons. Roberts, Brigham Henry. 1913-70. *226*
—. Illinois (Nauvoo). Mormons. Oral history. Smith, Hyrum. Smith, Joseph. 1840's-1978. *4005*
Lyon, T. Edgar (obituary). Mormons. 19c-20c. *283*
Lyons, Jacques Judah. Congregation Kahal Kadosh Shearith Israel. Ethnicity. Falkenau, Jacob J. M. Hebrew. Jews. New York City. Pique, Dob. Poetry. 1786-1841. *2062*

M

Macartney, Clarence E. Clergy. Fundamentalism. Presbyterian Church. 1901-53. *3579*
Macdonald, John. Canada. Catholic Church. Voting and Voting Behavior. 1850's-91. *1286*
MacDonald, John Roderick. Alberta (Edmonton). Catholic Church. Colleges and Universities. St. Joseph's College (Alberta). 1922-23. *710*
Macdonnell, Alexander. Catholic Church. Church of England. Colonial Government. Ontario. Ontario (Kingston, Toronto). Strachan, John. 1820's-30's. *1108*
—. Catholics. Great Britain. Immigration. Ontario. Scottish Canadians. 1770's-1814. *3862*
MacGregor, James. Missions and Missionaries. Nova Scotia (Pictou). Presbyterian Church of Scotland. 1786-1830. *1634*
Machen, J. Gresham. Fundamentalism. Presbyterian Church. South. 1920's-35. *3580*
Mackay, John A. Ecumenism. Education. Personal narratives. Presbyterian Church of the United States of America. Princeton Theological Seminary. Theology. 1910-75. *3543*
MacKinnon, Murdoch. Anti-Catholicism. Church and State. Clergy. Education, Finance. Presbyterian Church. Saskatchewan. School Act (Saskatchewan, 1930; amended). Scott, Walter. 1913-26. *528*
MacQueary, Howard. Bible. Darwinism. Episcopal Church, Protestant. Europe. Excommunication. Hermeneutics. Ohio (Canton). St. Paul's Church. Universalism. 1890-91. *3178*
Maddox, Finis Ewing. Arkansas (Texarkana). Congregationalism. Presbyterian Church. Schisms. Theology. 1908. *2869*
Madison College. Adventists. Battle Creek College. Michigan. Sutherland, Edward A. Tennessee. 1897-1904. *743*
—. Higher Education. Methodist Protestant Church. Pennsylvania (Uniontown). 1851-58. *617*
Madison, James. Conscientious objection. Constitutional Amendments (2nd). Federal government. Friends, Society of. Military service. States' Rights. 1787-92. *2686*
Maeser, Karl G. Brigham Young University. Educators. Germany. Mormons. 1828-56. 1876. *768*
Magan, Percy Tilson. Adventists. California. Humor. Irish Americans. Letters. Loma Linda University. 1918-34. *1435*
Magazines. *See* Periodicals.
Magic. Amish. Folk medicine. Mennonites. Pennsylvania. Powwowing. ca 1650-1979. *2206*
—. British Columbia (Maillardville). Folklore. 1973-74. *2195*
—. Sociology of religion. 1940-73. *147*
Mahan, Asa. Civil Religion. Finney, Charles G. Millenarianism. National Self-image. Perfectionism. 19c. *1189*
Mahan, William D. Archko collection. Forgeries. Jesus Christ. Mormons. Presbyterian Church (Cumberland). Wallace, Lew (*Ben-Hur*). 1880's. *3928*
Maharaj Ji. Attitudes. California (Berkeley). Converts. Davis, Rennie. Divine Light Mission. Politics. 1973. *4286*
—. Divine Light Mission. Organizational Theory. 1930's-70's. *4285*
—. Divine Light Mission. Youth movements. 1970's. *4281*
Mahican Indians (Stockbridge). American Revolution. Indian-white relations. Massachusetts (Stockbridge). 1680-1776. *1481*
Maid of Iowa (vessel). Illinois (Nauvoo). Jones, Dan. Mormons. Smith, Joseph. Steamboats. 1843-45. *346*
Mail-Order Business. Economic Conditions. Ethnic groups. Folklore. Social Conditions. Voodoo. 1970-79. *2205*
Maine *See also* New England; Northeastern or North Atlantic States.
—. Algonkian Indians, northeastern. Indians. Maritime Provinces. Missionaries. Social change. 1610-1750. *1512*
—. Antislavery Sentiments. Civil War. Friends, Society of (Congregational). Jones, James Parnell. Military Service. 1850's-64. *2641*
—. Diaries. Missions and Missionaries. Protestantism. Sewall, Jotham. 1778-1848. *1645*
—. Diaries. Shakers. Wilson, Delmer. 1887. *4066*
—. New Hampshire. Revivals. Whitefield, George. 1727-48. *2249*
Maine (Bangor). Emerson, Ralph Waldo. Hedge, Frederic Henry. Transcendentalism. Unitarianism. 1833. *2761*
Maine (Boothbay). Church of Scotland. Communion. Presbyterian Church. 1750-75. *3578*
Maine (Ellsworth). Anti-Catholicism. Bapst, John. Chaney, William Henry. Editors and editing. Jesuits. Nativism. 1853-54. *2121*
Maine (Portland). Music. 1785-1836. *1947*
Maine (Sabbathday Lake). Communalism. Shakers. 1974. *395*
—. Connecticut (Canterbury). Shakers. Theology. Utopias. 1774-1974. *434*
Maine (Waldoboro). Missions and Missionaries. Moravian Church. Soelle, Georg. 1762-70. *3512*
Maine (York). Clergy. Congregationalism. Moody, Samuel. 1700-47. *3137*
Maine (York County). Anti-Christian sentiments. Christianity. Cochran, Jacob. Free love. Society of Free Brethren and Sisters. 1817-19. *89*
Malcolm, Alexander. Church of England. Maryland (Annapolis). Music. St. Anne's Church. Society for the Propagation of the Gospel. Teaching. 1721-63. *1931*
Mallon, Catherine. Catholic Church. Colorado. Diaries. Hospitals. New Mexico (Santa Fe). Sisters of Charity. 1865-1901. *1454*
Malone College. *Christianity Today*, periodical. Civil rights. Evangelicalism. Race Relations. 1956-59. *2549*
Malone, R. J. Diaries. Federal government. Mennonites. Military Intelligence. Surveillance. World War I. 1914-19. *2697*
Maltby, Charles. California (Temecula). Catholic Church. Documents. Indians. Mission San Antonio de Pala. 1866. *1573*
Management *See also* Industrial Relations.
—. Capitalism. Ideology. Political Science. Protestantism. Theology. Weber, Max. 16c-1974. *376*
Manchurian crisis. *Christian Century* (periodical). Foreign policy. Japan. Morrison, Charles C. 1931-33. *2678*
Manitoba *See also* Prairie Provinces.
—. Anglophones. Catholics. French Canadians. Langevin, Adélard. Winnipeg Archdiocese. 1905. *3711*
—. Bergthal Colony. Bishops. Immigration. Mennonites. Stoesz, David. Ukraine. 1872-76. *3390*
—. British Canadians. Country life. Ethnic groups. French Canadians. Mennonites. Migration. Polish Canadians. Ukrainian Canadians. 1921-61. *3389*
—. Catholic Church. Church and State. French language. Langevin, Adélard. Politics. Private schools. 1890-1916. *608*
—. Catholic Church. Church Schools. McCarthy, D'Alton. Provincial legislation. 1870-90. *72*
—. Catholic Church. Immigration. Mathieu, Olivier-Elzéar. Regina Archdiocese. Saskatchewan. 1911-31. *3781*
—. Chippewa Indians. Germans, Russian. Immigration. Mennonites. Métis. 1872-73. *3392*
—. Church of England. Clergy. Corbett, Griffiths Owen. Métis. Red River Rebellion. 1863-70. *3215*
—. Clergy. Funk, John F. Mennonites. Russia. Settlement. Travel. 1873. *3393*
—. Clergy. Immigration. Mennonite Brethren Church. Russia. Warkentin, Johann. 1879-1948. *3409*
—. Ecumenism. Liberalism. Social gospel. United Church of Canada. 1870's-1925. *449*
—. Great Plains. Immigration. Mennonites. Russia. 1871-74. *3395*
—. Immigration. Mennonites. Russia. Shantz, Jacob Y. Travel accounts. 1873. *3425*
—. Immigration. Mennonites. Russian Canadians. Travel accounts. 1873. *3391*
—. Mennonites. 1870-1900. *3416*
—. Mennonites. Pioneers. 1875. *3353*
Manitoba Act (Canada, 1870). Church schools. Francophones. Greenway, Thomas (administration). Language. Legislation. 1890-99. *519*
Manitoba (Portage la Prairie). Colleges and Universities. Collegiate Institute. Depressions. Lansdowne College. 1882-93. *780*
Manitoba (Red River). Anglican Communion. Missions and Missionaries. Women. 1820-37. *1750*
Manitoba (Red River country). Anti-Catholicism. O'Beirne, Eugene Francis. Travel. 1860's. *2120*
Manitoba (Rosenthal). Farms. Germans, Russian. Hildebrand, Bernhard (and family). Mennonites. 1795-1915. *3407*
Manitoba (Township Berlin). Lutheran Church, Missouri Synod. Wagner, William. ca 1870. *3345*
Manitoba (Virden). Canadian Pacific Railway. Clergy. Construction crews. McLeod, Finlay J. C. Personal narratives. Presbyterian Church. 1881-82. *3567*
Manitoba (Winnipeg). Archives. Giesbrecht, Herbert. Mennonite Brethren Bible College. 1950-79. *250*
—. City Life. Ethnic enclaves. Judaism. 1940's-70's. *4091*
—. Evangelism. Illinois (Chicago). Mennonites. 1866-1977. *3361*
—. Gordon, Helen Skinner. King, Gordon J. Personal narratives. Presbyterian Church. Woman's Missionary Society of the Presbyterian and United Churches. 1890's-1961. *3548*
Manitoulin project. Catholic Church. Church of England. Government. Indian-White Relations. Methodist Church. Missions and Missionaries. Ontario (Upper Canada). 1820-40. *1537*
Manly, Basil. Baptists, Southern. Clergy. Southeastern States. Teachers. 1798-1868. *3041*
Manning, William Thomas. Architecture. Cathedral Church of St. John the Divine. Episcopal Church, Protestant. New York City. Sabbatarianism. Sports. 19c-1920's. *3243*
Mansion of Happiness (game). Christianity. Education. Games, board. Social Change. Values. 1832-1904. *2711*
Manson Family. Leadership. Millerites. Nazism. Social Organization. Women's Liberation Movement. 19c-20c. *2964*
Manuscripts *See also* Documents.
—. Andover-Harvard Theological Library. Massachusetts. Unitarianism. Universalism. 1800-1925. *256*
—. Archival catalogs and inventories. Jenson, Andrew. Mormon Church (Historian's Office). 1830-1975. *193*
—. Archives. Congregationalism. Stiles, Ezra. Yale University. 1748-1975. *3142*
—. Arizona. Bandelier, Adolph Francis. Mexico (Chihuahua, Sonora). Missions and Missionaries. New Mexico. Vatican Library. 16c-17c. 1886-1964. 1975-79. *1618*
—. California. Circuit riders. Civil War. Frontier and Pioneer Life. Methodism. Ohio. Phillips, George. 1840-64. *3494*
—. Cathcart, Wallace H. Shakers. Western Reserve Historical Society. 1774-1920. *245*

—. Catholic Church. Democracy. Sermons. Tocqueville, Alexis de. Yale University. 1831-40. *1990*
—. Catholic Church. Design. Folk art. Iconography. New Mexico. 16c-17c. *1858*
—. Christianity. Frontier and Pioneer Life. South Dakota Historical Resource Center. 1976. *217*
—. Historiography. Mormons. Research. Young, Brigham. 19c-1978. *192*
—. Knight, Joseph, Sr. Mormons. Smith, Joseph. 1772-1847. *3991*
—. Massachusetts. Mather, Increase. Puritans. Theology. 1670's. *3628*
—. McDowell, William A. New Jersey Historical Society. Presbyterian Church. South Carolina (Charleston). Third Presbyterian Church. 1820's-30's. *259*
—. Mormon history. 1823-1974. *3934*
Marginalia. Bible. Clergy. Congregationalism. Edwards, Jonathan. Massachusetts (Deerfield). Pierpont, Benjamin. Theology. 1726-30. *3146*
Marines. Antiwar Sentiment. Butler, Smedley. Courts Martial and Courts of Inquiry. Friends, Society of (Hicksite). 1881-1940. *2637*
—. Camp Lejeune. Lamb Studios. New Jersey (Tenafly). North Carolina. Protestantism. Stained glass windows. 1775-1943. *1867*
Maritain, Jacques. Creative innocence, concept of. Maritain, Raissa. Merton, Thomas. Poetry. Theology. 1940's-75. *3863*
Maritain, Raissa. Creative innocence, concept of. Maritain, Jacques. Merton, Thomas. Poetry. Theology. 1940's-75. *3863*
Maritime Provinces *See also* Atlantic Provinces.
—. Acadians. Catholic Church. English Canadians. Social Conditions. 1763-1977. *3871*
—. Algonkian Indians, northeastern. Indians. Maine. Missionaries. Social change. 1610-1750. *1512*
—. Baptists. Covenants. 1778-1878. *3003*
—. Catholic Church. Plessis, Joseph-Octave. Travel (accounts). 1812-15. *3703*
Maronite Catholics. Assimilation. Catholic Church. Eastern Orthodox Church, Syrian. Melkite Catholics. Syrian Americans. Uniates. 1900-73. *3908*
Marquette, Jacques. Anti-Catholicism. District of Columbia. State Politics. Statuary Hall. Wisconsin. 1887-1904. *2101*
—. Catholic Church. Colonial attitudes. Discovery and Exploration. Discovery and Exploration. France. Jolliet, Louis. Missions and Missionaries. Mississippi River. Monuments. 1665-1700. *3767*
—. Catholic Church. Discovery and Exploration. Jolliet, Louis. Mississippi River. 1673. 1973. *1567*
Marriage *See also* Divorce; Family; Sex; Women.
—. Age. Birth rate. Mormons. Women. 1800-69. *892*
—. Bidamon, Emma Smith. Bidamon, Lewis C. Illinois (Nauvoo). Mormons. Women. 1842-80. *3931*
—. Bishops. Catholic Church. Clergy. Uniates. 1890-1907. *3907*
—. California. Chumash Indians. Indians. Mission Santa Barbara. Social Organization. Yanunali, Pedro (chief). 1787-1806. *940*
—. Catholic Church. Connecticut (New Haven). Ethnic Groups. Jews. Protestantism. 1900-50. *906*
—. Catholic Church. Converts. Protestantism. 1960's-70's. *848*
—. Communalism (review article). Fellman, Michael. Muncy, Raymond Lee. Sex. Social Organization. 19c. 1973. *384*
—. Courtship. Diaries. Indiana. Mennonites. Sprunger, David. 1893-95. *3427*
—. Fertility. Mormons. 1820-1920. *924*
—. Franciscans. Indian-White Relations. Inquisition. Missions and Missionaries. New Mexico. Plains Apache Indians. Romero, Diego. 1660-78. *3773*
—. Friends, Society of. Nova Scotia (Dartmouth). 1786-89. *864*
—. Gates, Susa Young. Mormons. Personal narratives. Utah. Women. Young, Brigham. Young, Lucy Bigelow. 1830-1905. *3972*
—. Literature. Marshall, Catherine. Presbyterian Church. Sex roles. Women. 1950's. *806*
—. Plantations. Protestantism. Slaves. South. ca 1750's-1860. *2928*
Marriage, interfaith. Indiana. 1962-67. *896*
—. Whites. 1973-75. *790*
Marshall, Catherine. Authors. Popular Culture. Presbyterian Church. Theology. Women. 1949-78. *3546*
—. Literature. Marriage. Presbyterian Church. Sex roles. Women. 1950's. *806*
Marshall, Daniel. American Revolution. Baptists. Clergy. Georgia. Political Theory. 1747-1823. *1372*
—. Baptists. Georgia (Richmond County). Kiokee Church. Negroes. Settlement. 1784-1819. *3020*
Marshall, John. Butler, Elizur. Cherokee Indians. Indian-White Relations. Missions and Missionaries. Nullification crisis. Worcester, Samuel A. *Worcester* v. *Georgia* (US, 1832). 1828-33. *1583*
Marshall, William I. Historiography. Missions and Missionaries. Oregon. Whitman, Marcus. Winters, Herbert D. ca 1842-43. 1930. *1553*
Marti, Fritz. Christianity. Philosophy. Scholarship. Swiss Americans. Theology. 1894-1979. *2803*
Martin, John. Cherokee Indians. Indians. Missions and Missionaries. Presbyterian Church. Richardson, William. Tennessee. Virginia. 1755-63. *1511*
Martinez, Antonio Jose. Cather, Willa *(Death Comes for the Archbishop)*. Fiction. New Mexico (Taos). 1830's. 1927. *2077*
Martinez, Pedro. Catholic Church. Guam. 1909-67. *3795*
Marty, Martin E. Ahlstrom, Sydney E. Christianity (review article). Handy, Robert T. Historiography. Race (issue). 16c-1978. *2743*
Marxism *See also* Anarchism and Anarchists; Communism; Socialism.
—. Capitalism. Niebuhr, Reinhold. *Radical Religion* (periodical). Roosevelt, Franklin D. (administration). 1930-43. *1343*
—. Finland. Finnish Americans. Lutheranism. Reform. 1900-76. *990*
—. Freudianism. Niebuhr, Reinhold (review article). Original sin. Protestantism. Theology. 1939-70. *2838*
—. Liberalism. Niebuhr, Reinhold. Philosophy. 1927-69. *1422*
Mary and Charlotte (vessel). Friends, Society of. Great Britain. Law. Pennsylvania (Philadelphia). War relief. 1778-84. *3266*
Mary, Virgin. Catholic Church. Ohio (Bedford). Our Lady of Levoča (statue). Slovakia (Spiš; Levoča). ca 13c-1975. *1884*
Maryland *See also* Southeastern States.
—. Allen, Bennet. Church of England. Colonial Government. Ecclesiastical pluralism. Jordan, John Morton. Patronage. Sharpe, Horatio. 1759-70. *1051*
—. American Revolution. Asbury, Francis. Delaware. Loyalists. Methodists. White, Thomas. 1777-80. *3482*
—. American Revolution. Church of England. Clergy. Political philosophy. 1770-80. *1388*
—. American Revolution. Church of England. Clergy. Politics. Social Status. 1775. *2618*
—. American Revolution. Church of England. Hughes, Philip. Loyalists. 1767-77. *1323*
—. Americanization. Catholic Church. Church and state. Europe. Religious liberty. ca 1634-1786. *304*
—. Anti-Catholicism. France. Politicians. Protestants. 1750's. *2095*
—. Anti-Catholicism. Servants. Slave Revolts. 1745-58. *2117*
—. Bacon, Thomas. Church of England. Clergy. Education. Politics. Slavery. Theology. ca 1745-68. *3175*
—. Baltimore Riot of 1861. Civil War. Creamer, David. Crooks, George Richard. Letters. Methodist Church. 1861-63. *1410*
—. Behavior. Boucher, Jonathan. Church of England. Loyalists. Virginia. 1738-89. *1348*
—. Behavior. Church of England. Clergy. 1700-75. *3228*
—. Benefit of clergy. Colonial Government. Common law. Criminal law. 1637-1713. *1140*
—. Bibliographies. 1788-1978. *8*
—. Bordley, Stephen. Church of England. Great Awakening. Letters. Whitefield, George. 1730-40. *2229*
—. Boucher, Jonathan. Catholic Church. Church of England. Religious Liberty. 1774-97. *2729*
—. Boucher, Jonathan. Chase, Samuel. Church and State. Paca, William. Taxation. 1770-73. *1141*
—. Boucher, Jonathan. Church of England. Great Britain. Loyalists. Zimmer, Anne Y. (review article). 1770's-90's. *1358*
—. Calvert, Cecilius (2d Lord Baltimore). Catholic Church. Colonization. Religious liberty. 1634-92. *1061*
—. Calvert, Cecilius (2d Lord Baltimore). Catholic Church. Great Britain. Provincial Government. Religious Liberty. 1634-49. *1068*
—. Carroll, Charles (of Carrollton). Catholic Church. 1737-1832. *3797*
—. Carroll, Charles (of Carrollton). Catholic Church. Declaration of Independence. Political Leadership. 1737-1832. *3705*
—. Church of England. Letters. Presburg, Joseph. 1713-32. *3199*
—. Clergy. Germany. Herborn, University of. Otterbein, Philip Wilhelm. Pennsylvania. Theology. United Brethren in Christ. 1726-1813. *3666*
—. Debates. Religious liberty. State Government. 1776-85. *1107*
Maryland (Annapolis). Church of England. Malcolm, Alexander. Music. St. Anne's Church. Society for the Propagation of the Gospel. Teaching. 1721-63. *1931*
—. Freemasonry. St. John's College. State Legislatures. 1784. *517*
Maryland (Baltimore). Baltimore Hebrew Congregation. Judaism (Orthodox). Rehine, Zalma. 1830-31. *4191*
—. Baptists. City Government. Negroes. Political protest. Public schools. 1865-1900. *583*
—. Baptists. Clergy. Davis, Noah. Meachum, John Berry. Missouri (St. Louis). Negroes. Slavery. 1818-66. *3094*
—. California (San Francisco). Dyer, Leon. Jews. Leadership. 1820's-75. *4142*
—. Church location. Congregationalism. Economic conditions. Protestantism. 1840-70. *2853*
—. Friends, Society of. Medicine (practice of). Surgery. Taylor, Sarah. Women. 1823. *3264*
—. Friends, Society of. Methodist Episcopal Church, African. Negroes. Presbyterian Church. Private Schools. Sunday Schools. 1794-1860. *633*
Maryland (Baltimore County). Chain of being. Church of England. Cradock, Thomas. Poetry. Sermons. Social theory. 1700-80. *3227*
—. Church of England. Clergy. Cradock, Thomas. Poetry. Sermons. 1700-70. *3229*
Maryland (Elizabethtown). American Revolution. Conscientious objectors. Loyalists. Mennonites. 1774-76. *2665*
Maryland (St. Marys County). Jesuits. Plantations. St. Inigoes Church. Slavery. 1806-1950. *326*
Maryland (Takoma Park). Adventists (headquarters). Michigan (Battle Creek). 1903. *2978*
Maryland, University of. Ethnicity. Jews. Parents. Students. 1949-71. *4128*
Maryland (Washington County). Gruber, Jacob. Methodism. Slave Revolts. Trials. 1818-20. *2456*
Maryville Academy. Catholic Church. Colleges and Universities. Missouri (St. Louis). 1872-1972. *657*
Masons. *See* Freemasons.
Masqueray, Emmanuel L. Architecture. Cathedrals. Catholic Church. Ireland, John. Minnesota (St. Paul). 1904-17. *1795*
Mass Media *See also* Films; Newspapers; Radio; Television.
—. Art. Baptists. History. 17c-1977. *218*
—. Mormons. 1970's. *1960*
Massachusetts *See also* New England; Northeastern or North Atlantic States.
—. Abolition Movement. Andover Seminary. Congregationalism. Seminaries. Theology. 1825-35. *2491*
—. Agriculture. Clergy. Colman, Henry. Unitarianism. 1820-49. *4082*
—. Albanese, Catherine L. Beecher family. Caskey, Marie. Congregationalism. Connecticut. Presbyterian Church. Transcendentalism (review article). Unitarianism. 1800-60. *2763*
—. American Institute for Education. Country life. Educational Reform. Elites. Nationalism. Protestantism. 1830-37. *573*
—. American Revolution. Baptists. Constitutions. 1644-1806. *979*
—. Amherst College. Calvinism. Meiklejohn, Alexander. 1912-23. *601*
—. Amnesty. Loyalists. Property. Public Opinion. 1783-84. *1357*
—. Andover-Harvard Theological Library. Manuscripts. Unitarianism. Universalism. 1800-1925. *256*

—. Anti-Catholicism. Antislavery Sentiments. Know-Nothing Party. Republican Party. Voting and Voting Behavior. 1850's. *1201*
—. Anti-Catholicism. Know-Nothing Party. Republican Party. Voting and Voting Behavior. 1850's. *1209*
—. Antinomian Controversy. Church and state. Hutchinson, Anne. Puritans. Social Organization. Trials. Women. 1637. *1135*
—. Antinomian controversy. Feminism. Hutchinson, Anne. 1630-43. *867*
—. Antinomianism. Cotton, John. Hutchinson, Anne. Sermons. Shepard, Thomas. Theology. 1630's. *3648*
—. Antinomianism. Hutchinson, Anne. Language. Puritans. Trials. 1636-38. *3609*
—. Assimilation. Eliot, John. Indians. Praying towns. Puritans. 1646-74. *1592*
—. Baptists. 17c. *3069*
—. Bercovitch, Sacvan (review article). Mather, Cotton. National Characteristics. Puritans. 17c-18c. 1975. *3630*
—. Bible. Congregationalism. Edwards, Jonathan. Hermeneutics. 1720-58. *3149*
—. Bibliographies. Connecticut. Witchcraft. 17c. 1976. *2194*
—. Billings, William. Copyright. Music. 1770-90. *1939*
—. Bradstreet, Anne. Elegies. Poetry. Puritans. Women. 1665. *2044*
—. Bradstreet, Anne. Hutchinson, Anne. Literature. Puritans. Social change. Theology. Women. 1630's-70's. *865*
—. Bulkeley, Peter *(Gospel-Covenant)*. Covenant theology. Puritans. 1640's-50's. *3636*
—. Cambridge Platform. Church and state. Puritans. 1630-79. *1017*
—. Charles I. Friends, Society of. Persecution. 1661. *1018*
—. Cheever, Thomas. Clergy. Congregationalism. Documents. 1677-1749. *3122*
—. Christians. Sermons. War. 1640-1740. *2630*
—. Church and State. Civil religion. Constitutional conventions, state. Rebellions. 1780. *1071*
—. Church membership. Half-Way Covenant. Puritans. 1662. *3624*
—. Church of England. Congregationalism. Cutler, Timothy. 1720-30. *1056*
—. Church of England. Congregationalism. Kennebec Purchase Company. Land. 1759-75. *352*
—. Congregationalism. Converts. Japan. Shimeta, Neesima. Voyages. 1860's-90. *1701*
—. Congregationalism. Democracy. Political thought. Wise, John. 17c-18c. *1354*
—. Congregationalism. Drummer, Jeremiah. Letters. Sabbath. Sewall, Samuel. Taylor, Edward. 1704. *2276*
—. Congregationalism. Folk Art. Peckham, Robert. Portraits. ca 1838-44. *1861*
—. Crime and criminals. Ecclesiastical law. Great Britain. Roman Law. 17c. *972*
—. Divorce. Law. Puritans. Social conditions. Women. 1639-92. *941*
—. Drinan, Robert F. Jesuits. Political campaigns. 1970. *1267*
—. Eliot, John. Indians. Missions and Missionaries. Puritans. 1620-80. *1624*
—. Episcopal Church, Protestant. Groton School. Peabody, Endicott. Religious education. 1884-1940. *671*
—. Family. Government. Ideology. Puritans. Social cohesion. 1630-85. *3606*
—. Fiction. Hawthorne, Nathaniel. Philosophy of History. Puritans. 1820's-60's. *2081*
—. Friends, Society of. New York Yearly Meeting. Schisms. Vermont. 1845-1949. *3259*
—. Friends, Society of. Persecution. Southwick (family). 1639-61. *1066*
—. Godfrey, John. Puritans. Social Conditions. Trials. Witchcraft. 1634-75. *2186*
—. Gorton, Samuel. Great Britain. Puritanism. Radicals and Radicalism. Rhode Island. Rhode Island. Theology. 1636-77. *2862*
—. Great Britain. Local government. New England. Political theory. Puritans. Social change. 1600-50. *3604*
—. Historiography. Merry Mount incident. Morton, Thomas. Pilgrims. 1625-1970's. *2050*
—. Historiography. Political Systems. Puritans. Suffrage. 1620-99. 1954-74. *1350*
—. Immigrants. Puritans. 1590-1660. *3605*
—. Indians. Irish. Puritans. Stereotypes. 17c. *2144*
—. Indians. Morton, Thomas. Pilgrims. Puritans. Values. 1625-45. *2956*
—. Industrialization. Law and society. Nelson, William E. (review article). Secularization. Social change. 1760-1830. *53*
—. Johnson, Samuel (1822-82). Orientalism. Theology. Transcendentalism. 1840's-82. *4071*
—. Manuscripts. Mather, Increase. Puritans. Theology. 1670's. *3628*
—. Mather, Cotton *(Life of Phips)*. Phips, William. Politics. Puritans. 1690-1705. *3622*
—. Mather, Increase. Millenarianism. "New Jerusalem" (manuscript). Puritans. 1669-1710. *3632*
—. Puritans. Sports. 1630-1730. *3654*
—. Puritans. Taylor, Edward. Taylor, Thomas *(Christ Revealed)*. Typology. 1635-98. *3649*
Massachusetts (Amesbury). Bible reading. Letters. Public schools. Whittier, John Greenleaf. 1853. *577*
Massachusetts (Andover). Calvinism. Education. Phillips Academy. 1778-1978. *584*
Massachusetts (Ashfield). Baptists. Poetry. Political Protest. Religious Liberty. Smith, Ebenezer. 1772. *2048*
Massachusetts (Barnstable County). Land. Peasants. Pilgrims. Values. 1620's-1720's. *3151*
Massachusetts (Berkshire County). Allen, Thomas ("Vindication"). American Revolution. Clergy. Congregationalism. Constitutions, State. Ideology. 1778. *1371*
Massachusetts (Boston). Abolition Movement. American Revolution. Letters. Wheatley, Phillis. Whigs. 1767-80. *2454*
—. Abolition movement. Clergy. Conservatism. Constitutions. Missouri (St. Louis). Unitarianism. 1828-57. *1413*
—. Adolescence. Baptists. Congregationalism. Finney, Charles G. Methodism. Revivals. 1822-42. *2258*
—. Alpert, Abraham. Immigration. Judaism. Rabbis. 20c. *4087*
—. American Revolution. Brattle Street Church. Calvinism. Congregationalism. Cooper, Samuel. Elites. 1754-83. *1333*
—. American Revolution. Brattle Street Church. Clergy. Congregationalism. Cooper, Samuel. 1770-80. *951*
—. American Revolution. Congregationalism. Cooper, Samuel. Rhetoric. Sermons. 1768-80. *1352*
—. American Revolution. Cooper, Samuel. Sermons. 1776. *1146*
—. American Union for the Relief and Improvement of the Colored Race. Congregationalism. Emancipation. Reform. 1835-37. *2490*
—. Andrews, Joseph. Art. Society of the New Jerusalem. Swedenborgianism. 1830-73. *4062*
—. Anti-Catholicism. Antislavery sentiments. Ideology. Riots. Social Classes. Ursulines. 1834-35. *2109*
—. Antinomian Controversy. Cotton, John. Hutchinson, Anne. Puritans. 1636. *3652*
—. Antinomian controversy. Hutchinson, Anne. Puritans. Trials. Winthrop, John. 1634-38. *3641*
—. Antislavery Sentiments. Eliot, Samuel A. Fugitive Slave Act (US, 1850). Patriotism. Unitarianism. 1850-60. *4085*
—. Architecture. Benjamin, Asher. Churches (Greek Revival). 1833-40. *1826*
—. Architecture. Benjamin, Asher. Truss design. West Church. 1805-23. *1827*
—. Architecture. Brattle Street Church. Congregationalism. Dawes, Thomas. 18c. *1771*
—. Baltzell, E. Digby (review article). Friends, Society of. Pennsylvania (Philadelphia). Puritans. Social Classes. 17c-1979. *2920*
—. Baptists. Clergy. Jay Street Church. Negroes. Paul, Thomas (and family). 1773-1973. *3048*
—. Baptists. Negroes. Social Reform. 1800-73. *3040*
—. *Boston Evening Post* (newspaper). Fleet, Thomas. Freedom of the press. Great Awakening. Newspapers. 1740's. *1423*
—. Brattle Street Church. Coleman, Benjamin. Elites. Gentility (concept). Puritans. 1715-45. *2622*
—. Buckminster, Joseph Stevens. Congregationalism. Unitarianism. 1804-12. *3116*
—. Calvinism. Congregationalism. Government, Resistance to. Mayhew, Jonathan. Political Theory. Sermons. 1750. *1381*
—. Calvinism. Parishes. Puritans. Switzerland (Geneva). 16c-17c. *3631*
—. Catholic Church. Clergy. O'Connell, William Henry. 1915-44. *3741*
—. Catholic Church. Evangelism. Protestantism. Settlement houses. South End House. Woods, Robert A. 1891-1910. *2438*
—. Catholic Church. Religious Orders. Teaching. Voluntarism. Women. 1870-1940. *717*
—. Charles I. Cotton, John. Great Britain. Puritans. Regicide. Sermons. 1650. *1349*
—. Church Schools. City Politics. 1880's. *632*
—. Churches (Gothic Revival). Decorative Arts. LaFarge, John. Richardson, Henry Hobson. Trinity Church. 1876. *1832*
—. Clergy. Congregationalism. Franklin, Benjamin. *New England Courant* (newspaper). Smallpox. *Spectator* (newspaper). 1720-23. *2023*
—. Congregational Library. Education. 19c-20c. *195*
—. Congregationalism. Historians. Old South Church. Prince, Thomas. 1718-58. *275*
—. Epidemics. Inoculation. Mather, Cotton. Smallpox. 1721-22. *1464*
—. Erikson, Erik H. Excommunication. First Church. Hibbens, Ann. Puritans. Rites and Ceremonies. 1640-41. 1960's-70's. *3610*
—. Jewish Student Movement. Radicals and Radicalism. Social Change. Youth Movements. 1960-75. *2433*
—. Mather, Cotton. Psalmody. Puritans. Sermons. Singing. 1721. *1938*
—. Methodist Church. Seamen's Bethel. Taylor, Edward Thompson. 1793-1871. *3452*
—. Novels. Unitarianism. Ware, William. 1837-52. *2010*
Massachusetts (Boston, New Bedford). Methodist Church. Mudge, Enoch. Seamen's Bethel. Taylor, Edward Thompson. 1776-1850. *3457*
Massachusetts (Cambridge). Anglican Communion. Smyth, Frederick Hastings *(Manhood into God)*. Society of the Catholic Commonwealth. Theology. Utopias. 1940. *3200*
—. Congregationalism. Harvard University. Latin language. Leverett, John. Speeches, Addresses, etc. 1722. *668*
—. Diaries. Piety. Puritans. Shepard, Thomas. 1640-44. *3656*
Massachusetts (Charlestown). Architecture. Bulfinch, Charles. First Parish Church. Meetinghouses. 1803-04. *1792*
—. Elites. Immigrants. Local government. Puritans. 1630-40. *3613*
Massachusetts (Chebacco). American Revolution. American Revolution. Cleaveland, John. Congregationalism. Daily life. Great Awakening. Ideology. Jedrey, Christopher M. (review article). New Lights. 1740-79. *2241*
Massachusetts (Chicopee). Anti-Catholicism. Chicopee Manufacturing Company. Immigration. Irish Americans. Mills. Nativism. Protestantism. 1830-75. *2103*
Massachusetts (Concord). Bulkeley, Peter (and family). Covenant theology. Puritans. 1635-1731. *3645*
Massachusetts (Deerfield). Bible. Clergy. Congregationalism. Edwards, Jonathan. Marginalia. Pierpont, Benjamin. Theology. 1726-30. *3146*
Massachusetts (Dorchester). Church and Social Problems. Church membership. Half-Way Covenant. Puritans. Religious scrupulosity. 1660-1730. *3601*
Massachusetts (Fall River). Americanization. Catholic Church. French Canadians. Hendricken, Thomas F. Irish Americans. 1870's-85. *317*
Massachusetts (Freetown). Congregationalism. Conversion. Great Awakening. Personal narratives. 1749-70. *2221*
Massachusetts (Granville). Church Membership. Congregationalism. Conservatism. 1754-76. *2247*
Massachusetts (Hampshire County). Arminianism. Edwards, Jonathan. Great Awakening. Justification. 1726-60. *2236*
—. Great Awakening. Theology. 1730's-40's. *2235*
Massachusetts (Hancock). Cohoon, Hannah Harrison. New York (New Lebanon, Watervliet). Painting. Shakers. 1817-64. *1902*
Massachusetts (Hatfield). Connecticut Valley. Great Awakening. Presbyterian Church. Williams, William. 1686-1741. *2240*
Massachusetts (Holyoke). Assimilation. Catholic Church. Clergy. Dufresne, Andre B. French Canadians. 1869-87. *302*

—. Catholic Church. French Canadians. Immigration. Proulx, Nicholas. Working Class. 1850-1900. *3691*
Massachusetts (Ipswich). Art. Calvinism. Congregationalism. Dow, Arthur Wesley. Methodist Church. 1857-80. *1871*
—. Clergy. Congregationalism. Wigglesworth, Samuel. 1714-68. *3138*
Massachusetts (Lawrence). Christianity. Industrial Relations. Scudder, Vida Dutton. Social reform. Socialism. Women. 1912. *2374*
Massachusetts (Lowell). Edson, Theodore. Episcopal Church, Protestant. St. Anne's Parish. Textile industry. 1800-65. *366*
Massachusetts (Martha's Vineyard). Converts. Indians. Mayhew, Thomas, Jr. Missions and Missionaries. Puritans. 1645-57. *1635*
Massachusetts (Mashpee). Apes, William. Indian-white relations. Methodist Church. Reform. Wampanoag Indians. 1830-40. *2546*
Massachusetts (Middlesex County). Crime and Criminals. Puritans. Social classes. 17c. *3616*
Massachusetts (Milford). Attitudes. Ballou, Adin Augustus. Hopedale Community. Utopias. 1830-42. *427*
—. Ballou, Adin Augustus. Draper, E. D. Hopedale Community. Utopias. 1824-56. *388*
Massachusetts (Natick). Church and Social Problems. Congregationalism. Indian-White Relations. Local Politics. Meetinghouses. 1650-18c. *3118*
—. Eliot, John. Indians. Missions and Missionaries. Puritans. 1646-74. *1602*
Massachusetts (Northampton). Anti-Catholicism. Cheverus, Jean Louis Lefebvre de. Daley, Dominic. Halligan, James. Irish Americans. Protestantism. Trials. 1805-06. *2097*
—. Anti-Catholicism. Cheverus, Jean Louis Lefebvre de. Irish Americans. Lyon, Marcus. Murder. Protestantism. Trials. 1805-06. *2099*
—. Breck, Robert. Congregationalism. Connecticut (Scotland). Edwards, Jonathan. 1734-36. *3127*
—. Congregationalism. Edwards, Jonathan. Prayer petitions. 1730-49. *3147*
—. Edwards, Jonathan. Millenarianism. Social Theory. 1720's-50's. *3154*
Massachusetts (Northampton, Stockbridge). Congregationalism. Edwards, Jonathan. Great Awakening. Intellectuals. Theology. Youth. ca 1730-1880. *3150*
Massachusetts (Plymouth). Netherlands. Pilgrims. 1607-20. *3139*
Massachusetts (Salem). Anthropology. Historiography. Psychology. Puritans. Witchcraft. 1691-92. *2187*
—. Boyer, Paul. Nissenbaum, Stephen. Puritans. Witchcraft (review article). 1550-1690. 1974-76. *2200*
—. Church History. Court records. Excommunication. Puritans. 1629-80. *3600*
—. Clergy (tenure). Higginson, John. Nicholet, Charles. Puritans. Social change. 1672-76. *3620*
—. Historians. Racism. Tituba (Indian). Witchcraft. 1648-1953. *2191*
—. Verin, Philip (sons). 1635-90. *2941*
Massachusetts (South Hadley). Colleges and Universities. Curricula. Mount Holyoke College. Science. Women. 1839-88. *2320*
Massachusetts (Springfield). Catholic Church. Cotton mills. French Canadians. Immigration. Population. Working Class. 1870. *3710*
—. Christ Church Cathedral. Episcopal Church, Protestant. 1817-1929. *3236*
—. Parsons case. Puritans. Witchcraft. 1650-55. *2210*
Massachusetts (Stockbridge). American Revolution. Indian-white relations. Mahican Indians (Stockbridge). 1680-1776. *1481*
Massachusetts (Swansea). Baptists. Church and state. Congregationalism. Rhode Island (Barrington). 1711-46. *1082*
Massachusetts (Tiverton). City Government. Congregationalism. Provincial Legislatures. Religious liberty. Taxation. 1692-1724. *1084*
Massachusetts (Webster). Methodism. Protestant Ethic. Textile industry. Working class. 1820's-50's. *372*
Massachusetts (Westborough). Childbirth. Congregationalism. Death and Dying. Diaries. Diseases. Parkman, Ebenezer. Social Organization. 1724-82. *1447*
Massachusetts, western. Adventists. Miller, William. Newspapers. Public opinion. 1840's. *2079*
Massachusetts (Westfield). Puritans. Sermons. Taylor, Edward ("Upon the Types of the Old Testament"). Theology. Typology. 1693. *3638*
Massachusetts (Worcester). Catholic Church. Diaries. Healy, James A. Holy Cross College. Religious Education. 1849. *640*
Massacres. Alienation. Civil War. Ethnicity. German Americans. Lutheran Church (Missouri Synod). Missouri (Concordia). 1864. *3301*
—. Mennonites. Pacifism. Paxton Boys. Pennsylvania. Politics. Presbyterian Church. 1763-68. *2702*
Mast, Daniel E. Amish. Clergy. *Herald der Wahrheit* (newspaper). Kansas (Reno County). 1886-1930. *3405*
Match industry. Labor. Quebec (Hull). Syndicat Catholique des Allumettières. Women. 1919-24. *1470*
Materialism. Capitalism. Defoe, Daniel *(Robinson Crusoe)*. Great Britain. Thoreau, Henry David *(Walden)*. Transcendentalism. 18c-19c. *354*
—. *Moravian* (newspaper). Nationalism. Pennsylvania (Bethlehem). Slavery. 1850-76. *3518*
Mathematics. Mormons. Pratt, Orson. Utah. ca 1836-70. *2318*
Mather, Cotton. Anti-Catholicism. Antichrist. Edwards, Jonathan. Potter, Francis. Puritans. ca 1700-58. *2937*
—. Attitudes. New England. Puritans. Sermons. Women. 1650-1800. *880*
—. Bercovitch, Sacvan (review article). Massachusetts. National Characteristics. Puritans. 17c-18c. 1975. *3630*
—. Botany. Friends, Society of. Logan, James. Natural History. New England. Puritans. 17c-18c. *2300*
—. Enlightenment. Puritans. Theology. 1680-1728. *3657*
—. Epidemics. Inoculation. Massachusetts (Boston). Smallpox. 1721-22. *1464*
—. Hooker, Thomas. Puritans. Rhetoric. Winthrop, John. 17c. *1965*
—. Levin, David (review article). Puritans. 1663-1703. 1978. *3625*
—. Massachusetts (Boston). Psalmody. Puritans. Sermons. Singing. 1721. *1938*
Mather, Cotton *(Essays to Do Good)*. Morality. Puritans. Social Organization. 1700-25. *331*
Mather, Cotton *(Life of Phips)*. Massachusetts. Phips, William. Politics. Puritans. 1690-1705. *3622*
Mather, Cotton *(Magnalia Christi Americana)*. Historiography. Puritans. Winthrop, John. 1702. *1966*
—. Puritans. Renaissance. Rhetoric. 1702. *1996*
—. New England. Puritans. Suffering (meaning). 1690's-1702. *3626*
Mather (family). Education. Great Britain. Greaves, Richard L. Middlekauff, Robert. New England. Puritans. 1596-1728. *607*
Mather, Increase. Communion. Puritans. Sermons. ca 1680-1710. *3629*
—. Manuscripts. Massachusetts. Puritans. Theology. 1670's. *3628*
—. Massachusetts. Millenarianism. "New Jerusalem" (manuscript). Puritans. 1669-1710. *3632*
Mather, Moses. Calvinism. Revivals. Theology. 1719-1850. *2248*
Mather, Richard. Burg, B. R. Clergy (review article). Congregationalism. New England. Youngs, J. William T., Jr. ca 1700-50. 1976. *3124*
Mathews, Donald G. Caskey, Marie. Moorhead, James H. Protestantism (review article). Reform. Walters, Ronald. 1830-80. 1976-78. *2368*
Mathews, Donald G. (review article). Evangelicalism. South. 18c-19c. 1977. *2835*
Mathews, Shailer. Modernism. Science. Social gospel movement. Theology. 1864-1930. *2443*
Mathieu, Olivier-Elzéar. Anglophiles. Catholic Church. Francophiles. Regina Diocese. Saskatchewan. 1905-30. *3714*
—. Catholic Church. Immigration. Manitoba. Regina Archdiocese. Saskatchewan. 1911-31. *3781*
Matthews, Mark Allison. Fundamentalism. Presbyterian Church. Social reform. Washington (Seattle). 1900-40. *2434*
Matthews, Robert ("Matthias the Prophet"). New York City. Retrenchment Society. Sects, Religious. 1828-35. *70*
Maurice, Frederick Denison. Episcopal Church, Protestant. Great Britain. Protestantism. Revelation. Social reform. Theology. 1860-1900. *3171*
Maurin, Peter. *Catholic Worker* (newspaper). Day, Dorothy. Social justice. 20c. *1468*
Maurin, Peter ("Easy Essays"). Catholic Worker Movement. Political Theory. Social Reform. 1920's-33. *2571*
Maury, James. Church and state. Clergy. Henry, Patrick. Parsons' Cause. Personal narratives. Speeches, Addresses, etc. Virginia. 1758-65. *1080*
Mayhew, Jonathan. American Revolution. Cooke, Samuel. History Teaching. Langdon, Samuel. Sermons. West, Samuel. Witherspoon, John. 1750-76. 1975. *1406*
—. Calvinism. Congregationalism. Government, Resistance to. Massachusetts (Boston). Political Theory. Sermons. 1750. *1381*
Mayhew, Thomas, Jr. Converts. Indians. Massachusetts (Martha's Vineyard). Missions and Missionaries. Puritans. 1645-57. *1635*
Mazzuchelli, Samuel Charles. Civil religion. Political theory. Tocqueville, Alexis de. 1831-63. *1164*
Mazzuchelli, Samuel Charles *(Memoirs)*. Catholic Church. Church and state. Democracy. Dominicans. Old Northwest. 1806-63. *1384*
McBeth, Sue L. Idaho. Missions and Missionaries. Nez Percé Indians. Presbyterian Church. 1874. *1591*
—. Indians. Missions and Missionaries. Nez Percé Indians. Presbyterian Church. 1873-93. *1509*
McCarthy, D'Alton. Catholic Church. Church Schools. Manitoba. Provincial legislation. 1870-90. *72*
McCarthy, Joseph R. Bishops. Catholic Church. 1954. *1222*
—. Catholic Church. Communism. Jesuits. 1950-57. *1223*
McCarthy, Joseph R. (review article). Anti-Communist Movements. Catholic Church. Crosby, Donald F. Labor Unions and Organizations. Oshinsky, David. 1950-54. 1976-78. *1212*
McClung, Nellie. Canada. Methodist Church. Ordination. United Church of Canada. Women. 1915-46. *852*
McConnell, Francis John. Intellectuals. Methodist Church. Social Reform. Theology. 1894-1937. *2382*
McCormick, Vincent A. Diaries. Jesuits. Vatican. World War II. 1942-45. *3755*
McCosh, James. Philosophy. Protestantism. World Alliance of Reformed Churches. 1850-75. *453*
McCulloch, Thomas. Colleges and universities. Dalhousie University. Missions and Missionaries. Nova Scotia. Pictou Academy. Presbyterian Church. ca 1803-42. *591*
McCulloch, Thomas *(Letters of Mephibosheth Stepsure)*. Literature. Nova Scotia. Presbyterian Church. Satire. 1821-22. *2067*
McDonald, Donald. Immigrants. Millenarianism. Presbyterianism. Prince Edward Island. Scottish Canadians. ca 1828-67. *3591*
McDonald, Robert. Church of England. Indians. Missions and Missionaries. Northwest Territories. Yukon Territory. 1850's-1913. *1604*
McDonough, David. Africa. American Colonization Society. Colonization. Medical Education. Presbyterian Church. Slavery. 1840-50. *2483*
McDonough, Madrienne C. Catholic Church. Church Schools. Girls. Mount St. Mary Convent. New Hampshire (Manchester). Personal narratives. 1902-09. *692*
McDougall, John. Indians. Methodist Church, Wesleyan. Missions and Missionaries. Prairie Provinces. 1860-1917. *1534*
McDowall, Robert James. Exiles. Loyalists. Missions and Missionaries. Ontario (Upper Canada). Reformed Dutch Church. 1790-1819. *1588*
McDowell, William A. Manuscripts. New Jersey Historical Society. Presbyterian Church. South Carolina (Charleston). Third Presbyterian Church. 1820's-30's. *259*
McGee, D'Arcy. Anglin, Timothy Warren. Canada. Catholic Church. Debates. Fenian Brotherhood. Irish Canadians. 1863-68. *1341*

McGlynn, Edward. Catholic Church. Conservatism. Corrigan, Michael. Economic Theory. George, Henry. New York. 1886-94. *2562*
McGovern, George S. Nixon, Richard M. Political Campaigns (presidential). Rhetoric. Voting and Voting Behavior. 1972. *1228*
McGown, A. J. Clergy. Presbyterian Church, Cumberland. Publishers and Publishing. *Texas Presbyterian* (newspaper). 1846-73. *3586*
McIlvaine, Charles Petit. Episcopal Church, Protestant. Evangelism. Frontier and Pioneer Life. Ohio. Oxford Movement. 1800-75. *3187*
McKendree, William. Asbury, Francis. Clergy. Elections. Methodist Episcopal Church. 1808. *3486*
McKim, Andrew. Baptists. Nova Scotia. Politics. Provincial Legislatures. 1784-1840. *1309*
McLean, Eleanor. McLean, Hector. Mormons. Murder. Pratt, Parley P. Women. 1841-57. *4025*
McLean, Hector. McLean, Eleanor. Mormons. Murder. Pratt, Parley P. Women. 1841-57. *4025*
McLeod, Finlay J. C. Canadian Pacific Railway. Clergy. Construction crews. Manitoba (Virden). Personal narratives. Presbyterian Church. 1881-82. *3567*
McLoughlin, William G. Albanese, Catherine L. Beecher, Henry Ward. Civil Religion. Clark, Clifford E., Jr. Douglas, Ann. Handy, Robert T. Reform. Revivals (review article). Women. 1607-1978. *6*
McLoughlin, William G. (review article). Baptists. Church and state. New England. 1630-1833. *1077*
—. Revivals. Social Change. 1607-1978. *2220*
McMahon, Patrick. Catholic Church. Charities. Irish Canadians. Poor. Quebec (Quebec). St. Bridget's Home. 1847-1972. *2521*
McMaster Hall. Baptists. McMaster, Susan Moulton Fraser. Michigan (Bay City). Ontario (Toronto). Women. 1819-1916. *3000*
McMaster, James. Attitudes. Brownson, Orestes A. Catholic Church. Civil War. Hughes, John. 1850-65. *2692*
McMaster, Susan Moulton Fraser. Baptists. McMaster Hall. Michigan (Bay City). Ontario (Toronto). Women. 1819-1916. *3000*
McMillan, Duncan M. Crittenden, Lyman B. Higher Education. Jackson, Sheldon. Montana. Presbyterian Church. 1869-1918. *598*
McMullen, John. Bishops. Catholic Church. Chicago Diocese. Clergy. Duggan, James. Illinois. Succession. 1865-81. *3742*
McMurray, William. Canada. Church of England. Clergy. 1810-94. *3203*
McNailly, John Thomas. Alberta. Calgary Diocese. Catholic Church. French Canadians. Irish Canadians. 1871-1952. *3712*
McPherson, Aimee Semple. California (Los Angeles). Evangelism. International Church of the Foursquare Gospel. Radio. 1920-44. *1958*
McPherson, James M. (review article). Abolition Movement. Education. Freedmen. Missions and Missionaries. Protestantism. 1865-1910. 1975. *563*
McPherson, Sarah M. Diaries. Lutheran Church. Missouri (Brazeau). 1852-56. *3298*
Meachum, John Berry. Abolition Movement. Baptists. Education. First African Baptist Church. Missouri (St. Louis). Negroes. 1815-54. *2482*
—. Baptists. Clergy. Davis, Noah. Maryland (Baltimore). Missouri (St. Louis). Negroes. Slavery. 1818-66. *3094*
Mead, Sidney E. Democracy. Enlightenment. Equality. Theology of the Republic (concept). 17c-20c. *1366*
—. National Characteristics. Religious history. 20c. *235*
Meadville Theological School. Christian Connection (church). Huidekoper, Harm Jan. Pennsylvania (Meadville). Unitarianism. 1844-56. *762*
—. Christianity. Huidekoper, Frederick. Judaism. Pennsylvania. Seminaries. Unitarianism. 1834-92. *4086*
Meat, kosher. Boycotts. Consumers. Jews. New York City. Prices. Riots. Women. 1902. *4112*
Medical Education. Adventists. Battle Creek Sanitarium. California. Loma Linda University. Michigan. Nurses and Nursing. 1884-1979. *1425*
—. Adventists. California. Loma Linda University. 1905-15. *1450*
—. Africa. American Colonization Society. Colonization. McDonough, David. Presbyterian Church. Slavery. 1840-50. *2483*
Medical reform. Adventists. Bible. 1810's-63. *1436*
—. Adventists. Hydrotherapy. Jackson, James Caleb. New York (Dansville). White, Ellen G. 1864-65. *1451*
—. Barbeau, Victor. Catholic Church. Cooperatives. Paquette, Albiny. Politics. Quebec. 1900-45. *3874*
Medical reports. Bartholow, Roberts. Mormons. Physiology. Polygamy. Utah. Vollum, E. P. 1850-75. *1430*
Medicine *See also* headings beginning with the word medical; Faith Healing; Hospitals; Mental Healing; Nurses and Nursing; Physicians.
—. Adventists. California (Loma Linda). Education. 1810-1929. *2971*
—. Bishops. Catholic Church. Education. Quebec (Gaspé). Ross, François Xavier. Social Conditions. 1923-45. *3787*
—. Faith healing. 20c. *1443*
Medicine (practice of) *See also* Diseases; Nurses and Nursing.
—. Adventists. Diaries. Kellogg, Merritt. Trall, Russell Thacher. 1844-77. *1452*
—. Attitudes. Chiropractic. Cultism. Science. 1850's-1970's. *2314*
—. Baptists, Southern. Developing nations. Missions and missionaries. 1846-1975. *1440*
—. Calomel. Mormons. Thomson, Samuel. 1793-1865. *1438*
—. Esteyneffer, Juan de *(Florilegio Medicinal)*. Herbs. Indians. Jesuits. Missions and Missionaries. Southwest. 1711. *1444*
—. Folk Medicine. Georgia. Great Britain. Indians. Methodism. Wesley, John. 1740's. *1426*
—. Friends, Society of. Maryland (Baltimore). Surgery. Taylor, Sarah. Women. 1823. *3264*
—. Herbs. Mormons. Physicians. 1820-1979. *1459*
—. Mormons. Young, Brigham. ca 1840-75. *1463*
Medieval culture. Christianity. Islam. Judaism. Philosophy of history. Wolfson, Harry Austryn. 6c-16c. 1910-74. *278*
Meditation. Drugs (psychoactive). ca 1974. *163*
Medley, John. Bishops. Church of England. Letters. New Brunswick (Fredericton). Oxford Movement. Pusey, Edward Bouverie. ca 1840-44. *3190*
Meetinghouses. Architecture. Bulfinch, Charles. First Parish Church. Massachusetts (Charlestown). 1803-04. *1792*
—. Architecture. New England. Stairwells. 18c. *1761*
—. Baptists. Church and state. Congregationalism. New Hampshire (Acworth). Taxation. Toleration Act (New Hampshire, 1819). Universalists. 1783-1822. *1113*
—. Church and Social Problems. Congregationalism. Indian-White Relations. Local Politics. Massachusetts (Natick). 1650-18c. *3118*
—. Churches. Friends, Society of. Pennsylvania (Chester, Delaware counties). ca 1700-1903. *1814*
—. Construction. Friends, Society of. Historic Preservation. Rhode Island (Newport). 1657-1974. *1838*
—. Historical Sites and Parks. New Hampshire (Cornish, Enfield). Shakers. 1793-1902. *1777*
Meiklejohn, Alexander. Amherst College. Calvinism. Massachusetts. 1912-23. *601*
Melkite Catholics. Assimilation. Catholic Church. Eastern Orthodox Church, Syrian. Maronite Catholics. Syrian Americans. Uniates. 1900-73. *3908*
Melting pot theory. Baptists. Cultural pluralism. Ethnicity. 1870-1976. *3101*
Melville, Herman. Bible. Diaries. Fiction. Palestine. Travel. 1857. *2039*
Melville, Herman *(Clarel)*. Judaism. 19c. *2045*
Melville, Herman *(Moby Dick)*. Fiction. Hawthorne, Nathaniel. Pessimism. 1850-51. *2042*
Melville, Herman ("The Two Temples"). Christianity. Episcopal Church, Protestant. Fiction. Grace Church. New York City. Trinity Church. 1845-50. *2061*
Memoirs. *See* Autobiography; Personal Narratives.
Memorial Day. Anthropology. Death and dying. Social Customs. 1945-74. *90*
Men. Advertising. Mormons. Patent medicines. Stereotypes. Virility. 1884-1931. *819*
—. Baptists, Southern. Cities. Religiosity. Women. 1968. *3008*
—. Catholic Church. Clergy. Religious Orders. Social classes. Women. 1650-1762. *2614*
Mencken, H. L. *American Mercury* (periodical). Editors and Editing. Ku Klux Klan. Methodist Episcopal Church (South). Temperance Movements. 1910-33. *2033*
Menéndez de Avilés, Pedro. Colonization. Indians. Jesuits. Missions and Missionaries. Opechancanough (chief). Powhatan Indians. Spain. Virginia. 1570-72. *1622*
Mennicke, Christopher A. Letters. Lutheran Church. Usury. Walther, Carl F. W. 1866. *353*
Mennonite Brethren Bible College. Archives. Giesbrecht, Herbert. Manitoba (Winnipeg). 1950-79. *250*
Mennonite Brethren Church. Clergy. Immigration. Manitoba. Russia. Warkentin, Johann. 1879-1948. *3409*
Mennonite Conference of 1970. Canada. Church and State. Leadership. Social issues. Students. 1917-74. *1029*
Mennonite World Conference. Neff, Christian. 1910-78. *446*
Mennonites. Acculturation. Arapaho Indians. Cheyenne Indians. Indians. Missions and Missionaries. 1880-1900. *1557*
—. Acculturation. Literature. 1970's. *3414*
—. Agriculture. Factionalism. Germans, Russian. Personal narratives. Saskatchewan (Rosthern). Settlement. 1891-1900. *3442*
—. Agriculture. Immigration. Kansas. Ukraine. Warkentin, Bernhard. 1872-1908. *3379*
—. Alberta. Communes. Farming. Namaka Farm. 1920's-40's. *414*
—. Alberta (Coaldale). Germans, Russian. Organizations. Social Change. 1920-76. *3411*
—. American Revolution. Bibliographies. Bicentennial Celebrations. 1776. 1975-76. *3378*
—. American Revolution. Conscientious objectors. Loyalists. Maryland (Elizabethtown). 1774-76. *2665*
—. American Revolution. Dunkards. Friends, Society of. Moravian Church. Neutrality. Pacifism. Schwenkfelders. Taxation. 1765-83. *2670*
—. American Revolution. Dunkards. Loyalists. Pacifism. 1776-84. *2635*
—. American Revolution (antecedents). Conscientious Objectors. Dunkards. Pennsylvania. Petitions. 1775. *2710*
—. Amish. Doukhobors. Hutterites. Molokans. North America. ca 1650-1977. *2769*
—. Amish. Folk Art. Pennsylvania. Persecution. Quiltmaking. 16c-1935. *1893*
—. Amish. Folk medicine. Magic. Pennsylvania. Powwowing. ca 1650-1979. *2206*
—. Amish. Indiana (Allen County). Social Organization. 1850-1950. *3412*
—. Amish. Land use. Mormons. Pennsylvania (Intercourse). Theology. Utah (Escalante). 1973. *2767*
—. Amish. Revivals. 1860-90. *2255*
—. Amish, Old Order. Hutterites. Social change. ca 1930-77. *3357*
—. Anabaptists. Bibliographies. 16c-1975. *3396*
—. Anabaptists. Bibliographies. 16c-20c. 1977-78. *3387*
—. Anabaptists. Bibliographies. Dissertations. 1975-76. *3397*
—. Anabaptists. Germany. Switzerland. Taxation. War. 16c-1973. *2662*
—. Arapaho Indians. Haury, Samuel S. Indian Territory. Letters. Missions and Missionaries. 1876-80. *1543*
—. Archival catalogs and inventories. Letters. Mensch, Jacob B. Pennsylvania. 1835-1912. *251*
—. Archives. Canada. 19c-1975. *187*
—. Archives. Canadian Mennonite Bible College (Mennonite Heritage Centre). 1979. *219*
—. Armenia. Lambert, Rose. Letters. Missions and Missionaries. Turkey. 1898-1911. 1969. *1756*
—. Asia, central. Immigration. Kansas. Nebraska. Pacifism. 1884-93. *3350*
—. Asia, central. Immigration. Russia. 1870's-1920's. *3386*
—. Atlantic Provinces. Settlement. 1950-70. *3410*
—. Attitudes. Ethnicity. Pennsylvania (Lancaster). Private Schools. Socialization. 1974-76. *673*
—. Attitudes. Lancaster Mennonite High School. Pennsylvania. Rites and Ceremonies. Students. 1974-78. *3354*

—. Baerg, Anna. Canada. Diaries. Immigration. Russian Revolution. Women. 1917-23. *3362*
—. Baptists. Catholic Church. Germans, Russian. Immigration. Kansas. Lutheran Church. Wheat industry. 1874-77. *2778*
—. Belk, Fred R. Immigration. Pacifism. Russia. 1880-84. *3351*
—. Bergthal Colony. Bishops. Immigration. Manitoba. Stoesz, David. Ukraine. 1872-76. *3390*
—. Bethel College. Conscientious Objectors. Oral history. World War I. 1917-18. 1974. *262*
—. Bethel College. Kansas (North Newton). Kauffman, Charles. Kauffman Museum. Missions and Missionaries. Museums. 1907-76. *198*
—. Bishops. Immigration. Lehman, Hans (and family). Pennsylvania (Lancaster County; Rapho Township). Swiss Americans. ca 1727-1909. *3400*
—. Blenheim Mennonite Church. Ontario (Oxford, Waterloo counties). 1839-1974. *3352*
—. Boehm, Martin. Newcomer, Christian. Pennsylvania Germans. Revivalism. 1740-1850. *2266*
—. *Bote* (newspaper). Germans, Russian. Nazism. Saskatchewan. USSR. Völkisch thought. 1917-39. *3431*
—. Brenneman, John M. Civil War. Letters. 1862. *2709*
—. Brethren in Christ. Holiness Movement. Kansas. Methodism. 1870-1910. *3436*
—. Brethren, Old Order River. 1855-1977. *3424*
—. Brethren, Swiss. Immigration. North America. Surnames. 1680-1880. *3417*
—. Breweries. Illinois (Peoria). Leisy family. 1884-1950. *356*
—. British Canadians. Country life. Ethnic groups. French Canadians. Manitoba. Migration. Polish Canadians. Ukrainian Canadians. 1921-61. *3389*
—. Brubacher, Henry. Brubacher, Jacob. Daily life. Letters. Ontario. Pennsylvania. 1817-46. *3374*
—. Canada. Conference of Historic Peace Churches. Conscientious objectors. World War II. ca 1914-45. *2671*
—. Canada. Eby, Ezra E. Immigration. Loyalists. Pennsylvania. 18c-1835. *1237*
—. Canada. Immigration. Ukraine. 1922-23. *3365*
—. Canada. Missions and Missionaries. USA. 1880-1910. *1628*
—. Canada. Social Customs. Urbanization. USA. 1961-71. *3358*
—. Catholic Church. Colorado. Germans, Russian. Immigration. 18c-19c. *2775*
—. Cemeteries. Kansas (Lyon County). 1870-1925. *3377*
—. Cemeteries. Pennsylvania (Lampeter). 18c-20c. *3366*
—. Cheyenne Indians. Institutions. Missions and Missionaries. Photographs. Social customs. 1880-1940. *3398*
—. China (Caoxian, Kai Chow). Missions and Missionaries. 1901-31. *1716*
—. Chippewa Indians. Germans, Russian. Immigration. Manitoba. Métis. 1872-73. *3392*
—. Civilian service. Conscription, military. World War II. 1930's-45. *2661*
—. Clergy. Entz, John Edward. First Mennonite Church. Kansas (Newton). 1875-1969. *3419*
—. Clergy. Funk, John F. Manitoba. Russia. Settlement. Travel. 1873. *3393*
—. Clergy. Pennsylvania (Lancaster). Weaver, Benjamin W. 1853-1928. *3433*
—. Clergy. Pennsylvania (Snyder County). 1780's-1970's. *3371*
—. Colleges and Universities. Consortium of Peace Research, Education and Development. North America. Peace Studies. 1965-80. *2650*
—. Colleges and Universities. Immigration. Ohio (Median County). Wadsworth Institute. 1825-80. *674*
—. Composers. Hymns. ca 1720-1860. *1908*
—. Conscientious objectors. Oral History. World War I. 1917-20. *2660*
—. Conservatism. Liberalism. Ontario (Waterloo County). 1977. *3368*
—. Converts. Immigration. Kansas. Milling. Presbyterian Church. Warkentin, Bernhard. 1847-1908. *3380*
—. Courtship. Diaries. Indiana. Marriage. Sprunger, David. 1893-95. *3427*
—. Democratic Party. Letters. Politics. Risser, Johannes. Slavery. 1856-57. *994*
—. Diaries. Federal government. Malone, R. J. Military Intelligence. Surveillance. World War I. 1914-19. *2697*
—. Diaries. Gehman, John B. Pennsylvania (Hereford). Speak Schools. 1853. *566*
—. Dunkards. Friends, Society of. Historic Peace Churches (meeting). Kansas (Newton). Krehbiel, H. P. Pacifism. 1935-36. *2663*
—. Dunkards. Friends, Society of. Militarism. Pacifism. 1900-78. *2646*
—. Dutch Americans. Genealogy. Iowa. Settlement. Swiss Americans. 1839-1974. *3370*
—. Dutch Americans. New Netherland (New Amsterdam). Shecut, John L. E. W. *(The Eagle of the Mohawks).* Universalists. 17c. 1800-36. *2012*
—. Editors and Editing. Germany. Miller, Samuel H. Trials. World War I. 1917-18. *2658*
—. Education. Sharp, Solomon Zook. 1860-1931. *755*
—. Emigration. Epp, Johann. Letters. North America. Russia. 1875. *3373*
—. Evangelism. Illinois (Chicago). Manitoba (Winnipeg). 1866-1977. *3361*
—. Farms. Germans, Russian. Hildebrand, Bernhard (and family). Manitoba (Rosenthal). 1795-1915. *3407*
—. Fraktur. Pennsylvania Germans. 1740's-1860's. *1904*
—. German Americans. Good, Merle. Literature. Pennsylvania. Personal narratives. 1975. *2057*
—. German Americans. Military conscription. Pacifism. Public opinion. World War I. 1914-18. *2696*
—. Gingerich, Melvin (obituary). Historians. 1902-75. *214*
—. Gingerich, Melvin (obituary). History. 1902-75. *243*
—. Great Plains. Immigration. Manitoba. Russia. 1871-74. *3395*
—. Great Plains. Pioneer life. Wheat. 1870-1974. *3443*
—. Hess, Katie Charles. Pennsylvania. Personal narratives. Women. 1883-1978. *3356*
—. Humility. 1840-80. *3402*
—. Immigration. Manitoba. Russia. Shantz, Jacob Y. Travel accounts. 1873. *3425*
—. Immigration. Manitoba. Russian Canadians. Travel accounts. 1873. *3391*
—. Immigration. Passenger lists. Quebec. Russia. 1874-80. *3364*
—. Immigration. Russia. South Dakota. Unruh, Daniel. 1820-82. *3430*
—. Immigration. Russian Canadians. Saskatchewan (Rosthern). Social conditions. 1923. *3399*
—. Indiana. Mumaw, George Shaum. Ohio. Personal narratives. Singing Schools. 1900-57. *1941*
—. Indians. Métis. Red River of the North. Red River of the North. Removals, forced. Saskatchewan River Valley. Settlement. 1869-95. *3360*
—. Kansas. 1873-80. *3420*
—. Kansas. Liberty bonds. Pacifism. Vigilantism. World War I. 1918. *2659*
—. Kansas. War bond drives. World War I. 1917-18. *2647*
—. Kansas (McPherson County). Russian Americans. Social Change. 1874-1974. *3372*
—. Literature. Pacifism. 20c. *2073*
—. "Lob Lied" (song). 1590-1978. *1944*
—. Manitoba. 1870-1900. *3416*
—. Manitoba. Pioneers. 1875. *3353*
—. Massacres. Pacifism. Paxton Boys. Pennsylvania. Politics. Presbyterian Church. 1763-68. *2702*
—. Metzler congregation. Pennsylvania (Groffdale). 1728-1978. *3415*
—. Missions and Missionaries. Women's Missionary Society. 1900-30. *866*
—. Modernization. Revivals. 1683-1850. *2254*
—. Morality. North America. Officeholding. Voting and Voting Behavior. 1860-1940. *955*
—. Mormons. Sects, Religious. ca 19c-20c. *32*
—. Pennsylvania. Raikes, Robert. Sunday schools. 1780-1980. *641*
—. Politics. Separatism. Social Reform. 1840's-1930's. *3418*
—. Religious beliefs. Values. 20c. *3434*
—. Rhodes families. Virginia. 1770's-1900. *3426*
—. Saskatchewan (Hague-Osler area). Social Change. 1895-1977. *3359*
—. Social consciousness. 1890-1905. *3369*
Mennonites (Allegheny Conference). Bishops. Durr, John N. Pennsylvania. 1872-1934. *3440*
Mennonites (Canadian Conference). Canada. Ecumenism. Pioneers. 1873-1978. *475*
Mennonites, Evangelical. Colleges and Universities. Fort Wayne Bible College. Indiana. 1904-77. *740*
Mennonites (Franconia Conference). Charters. Institutionalization. Protestant Churches. 1840-1940. *3382*
Mennonites (Funkite). American Revolution. Excommunication. Funk, Christian. Pennsylvania (Indian Field). 1760-1809. *3376*
Mennonites (General Conference). Documents. Funk, John F. 1864-1921. *3375*
Mennonites (Lancaster Conference). Missions and Missionaries. Tanzania. 1934-71. *1674*
Mennonites, Old Order. Bock, Anna. Indiana (Elkhart County). Painting. 1830's-1970's. *1845*
—. Communes. Economic conditions. Education. Pennsylvania (East Penn Valley). 1949-75. *410*
—. Education. Pennsylvania. Social change. 1653-1975. *664*
—. Ontario. 1786-1980. *3367*
Mensch, Jacob B. Archival catalogs and inventories. Letters. Mennonites. Pennsylvania. 1835-1912. *251*
Mental activity theory. Beauty, perception of. Congregationalism. Edwards, Jonathan. Knowledge. New England. 1730-69. *2323*
Mental healing. Evans, Warren Felt. Idealism. Mysticism. New Thought Movement. Romanticism. 1864-89. *1460*
Mental Illness *See also* Psychiatry.
—. Friends Asylum. Hinchman, Morgan. Moral insanity. Pennsylvania (Philadelphia). Trials. 1847. *1432*
Mercer, Silas. American Revolution. Baptists. Georgia. Politics. Theology. 1770-96. *3030*
Mercer University. Anderson, P. Harris. Baptists. Georgia. Harris, Rufus C. 1965-76. *3033*
Mercersburg Theological Seminary. Gerhart, Emanuel Vogel. Pennsylvania. Reformed German Church. Theology. 1831-1904. *3287*
Mercersburg theology. Adger, John B. Dabney, Robert L. Hodge, Charles. Nevin, John W. Presbyterian Church. Sacramental controversy. 1845-75. *3551*
Merchant Marine. American Seamen's Friend Society. Evangelicalism. Ports. 1828-38. *2376*
—. Bergner, Peter. Bethel Ships. Evangelism. Methodist Church. New York City. Swedish Americans. 1832-66. *1661*
Mercier, Honoré. Jesuits. Land Tenure. Legislation. Protestant Churches. Quebec. 1886. *1087*
Mercy's Dream (painting). Art. Bunyan, John *(Pilgrim's Progress).* Huntington, Daniel. National characteristics. Protestantism. 1678. 1841-70. *1856*
Mergers. Church of England. Dalhousie University. King's College, University of. Nova Scotia. Presbyterian Church. 1821-37. *684*
—. Fund raising. Jewish Theological Seminary. Judaism (Orthodox). New York City. Seminaries. Yeshiva College. 1925-28. *736*
Merry Mount incident. Historiography. Massachusetts. Morton, Thomas. Pilgrims. 1625-1970's. *2050*
Merry, Nelson. Baptists, Southern. First Baptist Church. Race Relations. Tennessee (Nashville). 1810-65. *3078*
Merrymount Press. Book of Common Prayer. Episcopal Church, Protestant. Printing. Typeface. 1922-30. *1986*
Merton, Thomas. Asia. Catholic Church. Monasteries. Trappists. 1940's-68. *3707*
—. Buddhism (Zen). Catholic Church. Suzuki, Diasetz Teitaro. 1935-70. *498*
—. Buddhism (Zen). Christianity. Watts, Alan. 1930-73. *4288*
—. Catholic Church. Cities. Nonviolence. Reform. Social criticism. 1960's. *2417*
—. Catholic Church. Contemplative ideal. Monasticism. 1940's-68. *3858*
—. Catholic Church. Ecumenism. 1949-68. *452*
—. Creative innocence, concept of. Maritain, Jacques. Maritain, Raissa. Poetry. Theology. 1940's-75. *3863*
Mesmerism. Animal magnetism. Hypnotism. Mormons. 19c. *2303*
Messianic beliefs. Anti-Semitism. Evangelicals. Fundamentalists. Jews. 1970's. *135*

Messianic Movements. Northwest Rebellion. Prairie Provinces. Riel, Louis. 1869-85. *964*
Messing, Aron J. California (Oroville, San Francisco, Woodland). Congregation Beth Israel. Judaism (Orthodox). Religious education. Sabbath Schools. Travel. 1879. *4201*
—. California (San Bernardino). Congregation Beth Israel. Fund raising. Judaism (Orthodox). 1879. *4199*
Metalwork. Christianity. Judaism. Rites and Ceremonies. ca 1650-1888. *1854*
Methodism. Adolescence. Baptists. Congregationalism. Finney, Charles G. Massachusetts (Boston). Revivals. 1822-42. *2258*
—. American Revolution. Asbury, Francis. Great Britain. Wesley, John. 1770-90. *1334*
—. American Revolution. Great Britain. Loyalists. Poetry. Political Commentary. Wesley, Charles. 1775-83. *1339*
—. American Revolution. Great Britain. Plagiarism. Politics. Wesley, John *(A Calm Address to our American Colonies)*. 1775-79. *1377*
—. American Revolution. Great Britain. Political Attitudes. Wesley, John. Whigs, Radical. 1775-78. *1391*
—. American Revolution. Great Britain. Wesley, John. 1760-89. *1404*
—. Americanization. Asbury, Francis. Social Change. 1766-1816. *286*
—. Americanization. Evangelical Covenant Church. Evangelical Free Church of America. Pentecostal movement. Salvation Army. Swedish Baptist Church. 1870-1973. *321*
—. Anabaptists. Pennsylvania, central. 1815-1942. *2880*
—. Appalachia. Baptists. Lifestyles. Presbyterian Church. 1788-1974. *2873*
—. Arizona. Baptists. Catholic Church. Episcopal Church, Protestant. Missions and Missionaries. Mormons. Presbyterian Church. 1859-99. *1501*
—. Artisans. Identity. Morality. Pennsylvania (Philadelphia). Social customs. Work ethic. Working Class. 1820-50. *3479*
—. Asbury, Francis. Canada. Coke, Thomas. Embury, Philip. Great Britain. USA. 1760-80. *3445*
—. Bäck, Olof. Clergy. Esbjörn, Lars Paul. Janssonists. Letters. Lutheran Church. Sweden. 1846-49. *2906*
—. Baptists. Canada. Disciples of Christ. Great Plains. Lutheran Church. Pietism. Prairie Radicals. Radicals and Radicalism. 1890-1975. *954*
—. Baptists. Converts. Evangelism. Louisiana (New Orleans). Slavery. 1800-61. *2916*
—. Baptists. Negroes. New York. Segregation. 1865-68. *2139*
—. Baptists, Southern. Corporate wealth. Political power. Presbyterian Church. South. 1930's-75. *2926*
—. Bible. Embury, Philip. Ireland. New York City. 1760-1834. *3489*
—. Bishops. Catholic Church. Church of England. Evangelicalism. Feild, Edward. Liturgy. Newfoundland. Presbyterian Church. 1765-1852. *3197*
—. Bland, Salem. Canada. Social Gospel. Theology. 1880-86. *3444*
—. Brethren in Christ. Holiness Movement. Kansas. Mennonites. 1870-1910. *3436*
—. California. Circuit riders. Civil War. Frontier and Pioneer Life. Manuscripts. Ohio. Phillips, George. 1840-64. *3494*
—. Camp meeting sites. Evangelism. 19c. *2225*
—. Camp meetings. Resorts. Revivals. 19c. *2252*
—. Canada. Communist Party. Labour Party. Smith, Albert Edward. Social Gospel. 1893-1924. *983*
—. Canada. Missions and Missionaries. New York Conference. 1766-1862. *1607*
—. Canada. Social gospel movement. 1890-1914. *2381*
—. Canada. United Church of Canada. 18c-20c. *3468*
—. Christianity. Philosophy of history. Wesley, John. ca 1740's-80's. *3453*
—. Circuit riders. Clark, John. Evangelism. Missouri. Travis, John. 1796-1851. *1561*
—. Clergy. Garrettson, Freeborn. 1775-1827. *3447*
—. Coke, Thomas. Great Britain. Rites and Ceremonies. Wesley, John *(Sunday Service)*. 1780's. *3460*
—. Commission on the Status and Role of Women in the United Methodist Church. Feminism. Social Organizations. 1869-1974. *893*
—. Congregationalism. Family. Mormons. New England. New York, western. Young, Brigham. 18c-1830's. *2840*
—. Coughlin, Lawrence. Newfoundland. 1765-1815. *3477*
—. Courtship. Field, Eliza. Great Britain (London). Indians. Jones, Peter. New York. 1820's-33. *1637*
—. Creeds. Evangelical Association. Terry, Milton S. Theology. United Evangelical Church. 1894-1921. *3667*
—. Creeds. Wesley, John. 19c-20c. *3493*
—. Denominationalism. 18c-19c. *3499*
—. Documents. Friends, Society of. National Characteristics. Political participation. Shakers. Tocqueville, Alexis de. 1831-40. *2780*
—. Domesticity. New York City. Palmer, Phoebe. Women. ca 1825-60. *877*
—. Drury, Clifford M. Indians. Lee, Jason. Missions and Missionaries. Oregon. Settlement. 1834-43. 1970's. *3480*
—. Europe, Western. Evangelicalism. Pietism. Reformed Dutch Church. Revivals. Social Conditions. 1674-19c. *2959*
—. Evangelicalism. Values. 1784-1924. *2406*
—. Evangelism. Slavery. Wesley, John. 1725-1974. *3505*
—. Evans, James. Missions and Missionaries. Ontario (Lake Superior). Voyages. 1837-38. *1564*
—. Folk Medicine. Georgia. Great Britain. Indians. Medicine (practice of). Wesley, John. 1740's. *1426*
—. Georgia. Germany (Halle). Pietism. 1736-70. *3510*
—. Great Britain. Nonconformists. Revivals. 1828-43. *2223*
—. Gruber, Jacob. Maryland (Washington County). Slave Revolts. Trials. 1818-20. *2456*
—. Historians. 1974. *229*
—. Historiography. Indians. Lee, Jason. Missions and Missionaries. Oregon. 1838-43. *1569*
—. Indians. Kansas. Ohio. Removal policy. Wyandot Indians. 1816-60. *1598*
—. Indians. Missions and Missionaries. Oklahoma. 1820-45. *1650*
—. International cooperation. Pendell, Thomas Roy. Personal narratives. USSR. World Conference of Christian Youth, 1st. 1939-79. *1402*
—. Massachusetts (Webster). Protestant Ethic. Textile industry. Working class. 1820's-50's. *372*
—. South Carolina (Charleston). Wesley, John. 1737. *1487*
—. Temperance Movements. Wesley, John. 1725-91. *2581*
Methodist Church *See also* United Brethren in Christ.
—. Abolition Movement. Hersey, John. Millenarianism. Perfectionism. 1786-1862. *3446*
—. Academic freedom. Bassett, John Spencer. Duke University. North Carolina (Durham). Racism. *South Atlantic Quarterly* (periodical). 1902-03. *3497*
—. American Board of Commissioners for Foreign Missions. Indians. Missionaries. 1830-50. *1663*
—. Apes, William. Indian-white relations. Massachusetts (Mashpee). Reform. Wampanoag Indians. 1830-40. *2546*
—. Archives. Canada. Presbyterian Church. United Church of Canada. 18c-1973. *269*
—. Art. Calvinism. Congregationalism. Dow, Arthur Wesley. Massachusetts (Ipswich). 1857-80. *1871*
—. Bailey, Margaret Jewett *(Ruth Rover)*. Business. Missionaries. Oregon. 1854. *1522*
—. Baltimore Riot of 1861. Civil War. Creamer, David. Crooks, George Richard. Letters. Maryland. 1861-63. *1410*
—. Baptists. Bode, Frederick A. (review article). Capitalism. North Carolina. Populism. 1894-1903. 1975. *1287*
—. Baptists. Creek Indians. Indian Territory. Missions and Missionaries. Presbyterian Church. 1835-60's. *1517*
—. Baptists. Ebenezer Methodist Church. Inscriptions. Mount Bethel Baptist Church. South Carolina (Anderson County). Tombstones. 1856-1978. *2848*
—. Baptists. Ninth Street Baptist Church. Ohio (Cincinnati). Political protest. Temperance Movements. Wesley Chapel. Women's Christian Temperance Union. 1874. *2582*
—. Baptists. Presbyterian Church. Slavery. South. 1740-1860. *2168*
—. Baptists, Southern. Disciples of Christ. Evolution. Kentucky. Presbyterian Church. Schisms. 1920's. *2310*
—. Bergner, Peter. Bethel Ships. Evangelism. Merchant Marine. New York City. Swedish Americans. 1832-66. *1661*
—. Bibliographies. Canada. Congregationalism. Historiography. Lutheran Church. Presbyterian Church. United Church of Canada. 1825-1973. *2892*
—. Blewett, George John. Canada. Theology. 1873-1912. *3496*
—. Bloomfield Academy. Chickasaw Indians. Downs, Ellen J. Girls. Indians. Oklahoma (Penola County). Personal Narratives. Schools. 1853-66. *772*
—. British Columbia (Queen Charlotte Islands). Church of England. Haida Indians. Missions and Missionaries. Settlement. Social Change. 1876-1920. *1545*
—. Business. Indians. Lee, Daniel. Letters. Missions and Missionaries. Oregon (Willamette Valley, The Dalles). 1834-43. *1570*
—. Butler, John Wesley. Letters. Mexico. Missions and Missionaries. Revolution. 1910-11. *1725*
—. California (Bodie). Clay, Eugene O. Funerals. Nevada (Smith Valley). Personal narratives. Sermons. 1915. *3456*
—. California, northern. Converts. Ghost Dance. Indians. Round Valley Indian Reservation. 1870. *3484*
—. California (Pacific Grove). 1875-1975. *3459*
—. California (Placerville). Ecumenism. El Dorado County Federated Church. Presbyterian Church. 1850-1950. *492*
—. California-Nevada Conference. Clergy. Women. 1873-78. *3503*
—. Camp meetings. Church of the Nazarene. Holiness movement. Louisiana (Mineral Springs). National Camp Meeting Association for the Promotion of Holiness. 1860's-1926. *2891*
—. Canada. Cree Indians. Evans, James. Missions and Missionaries. 1833-46. *3475*
—. Canada. Ecumenism. Patrick, William. Presbyterian Church. 1900-11. *443*
—. Canada. Evangelism. Holiness Movement Church. Horner, Ralph Cecil. 1887-1921. *3500*
—. Canada. Evangelism. Holiness Movement Church. Horner, Ralph Cecil. 1887-1921. *3501*
—. Canada. McClung, Nellie. Ordination. United Church of Canada. Women. 1915-46. *852*
—. Canada, western. Frontier. Missionaries. 1840-1925. *3450*
—. Cannon, James, Jr. Glass, Carter. Political Corruption. Virginia. 1909-34. *1295*
—. Catholic Church. Church of England. Government. Indian-White Relations. Manitoulin project. Missions and Missionaries. Ontario (Upper Canada). 1820-40. *1537*
—. Catholic Church. Hudson's Bay Company. Indians. Missions and Missionaries. Oregon. Presbyterian Church. 1830's - 1840's. *1482*
—. Centenary College. Dance. Educational Policy. Louisiana. 1941. *688*
—. Centenary College. Mississippi (Brandon Springs). Mississippi Conference. Religious Education. 1838-44. *656*
—. Chautauqua School of Theology. New York. Seminaries, correspondence. Vincent, John Heyl. 1881-98. *763*
—. Chippewa Indians. Indian-White Relations. Michigan. Missions and Missionaries. 1830-80. *1597*
—. Church of England. Education. Indians. Missions and Missionaries. Ontario (Algoma, Huron). Wilson, Edward F. 1868-93. *1596*
—. Churches (Gothic Revival). Delaware (Wilmington). Episcopal Church, Protestant. Grace Methodist Church. St. John's Episcopal Church. 1850-90. *1786*
—. Civil rights. Georgia. Tilly, Dorothy. 1900's-70. *2551*
—. Civil War. Letters. North Carolina (Halifax County). Slavery. Wills, Washington. 1861-65. *2171*

—. Clergy. Gold Mines and Mining. Klondike Stampede. Lippy, Thomas S. Randall, Edwin M. Transportation. Yukon Territory. 1896-99. *3492*
—. Clergy. Letters. Lipscomb, Bernard F. Virginia (Charlottesville). 1889-92. *3471*
—. Clergy. Letters. Montgomery, Daniel. Webb, Thomas. 1771. *3490*
—. Clergy. North Carolina. Personal narratives. Young, John. 1747-1837. *3507*
—. Clergy. Ordination. Social Change. 1771-1975. *3473*
—. Coca-Cola Company. Emory University. Religious education. South. Vanderbilt University. 1840's-1970's. *3466*
—. Coke, Thomas. Garrettson, Freeborn. Letters. Missions and Missionaries. Nova Scotia. Wesley, John. 1786. *1490*
—. Colorado. Haven, Gilbert. Rocky Mountains. Utah (Salt Lake City). 1875. *3463*
—. Converts. Illinois (Springfield). Jacquess, James F. Lincoln, Abraham. 1847. *2788*
—. Cuba. Missions and Missionaries. Nationalism. 1898-1958. *1693*
—. Daily life. Evangelism. Illinois (Chicago). Whitefield, Henry. 1833-71. *1508*
—. Dickey, Sarah. Heck, Barbara. Leadership. Parker, Lois Stiles. Shaw, Anna Howard. Stereotypes. Willard, Frances E. Women. 19c. *812*
—. Ecumenism. Nova Scotia (Springhill). Presbyterian Church. St. Andrew's Wesley United Church of Canada. United Church of Canada. 1800-1976. *2829*
—. Embury, Philip. New Hampshire (Chesterfield). Sermons. 1754-1805. *3488*
—. Ethics. Theology. Wesley, John. 1744-91. 1879-1974. *2397*
—. Folk art. German Americans. Harmony Methodist Church Cemetery. Tombstones. West Virginia (Jane Lew). 1827-55. *1892*
—. French Canadians. Government, provisional. Gray, William. Lee, Jason. Missions and Missionaries. Oregon. 1843. *1271*
—. Fugitive Slave Act (US, 1850). Newspapers. Slavery. 1850. *3476*
—. Goal submergence concept. Social Organizations. Temperance movements. 1919-72. *2586*
—. Higher education. Ontario. Women. 19c. *3504*
—. Holiness Movement. Inskip, John S. Inskip, Martha Jane. Revivals. Women. 1836-90. *3448*
—. Holiness Movement. Revivals. 1835-1920. *3291*
—. Hymnals. 1930-34. 1960-64. *1928*
—. Intellectuals. McConnell, Francis John. Social Reform. Theology. 1894-1937. *2382*
—. Louisiana (New Orleans). Winans, William. 1813-14. *3472*
—. Lutheran Church. Orthodox Eastern Church. Pennsylvania Historical and Museum Commission. Pennsylvania Historical Association. Reformed Dutch Church. Research conference. Uniates. 1977. *2791*
—. Lutheran Church. Social Organizations. Swedish Americans. 1850-1951. *2951*
—. Massachusetts (Boston). Seamen's Bethel. Taylor, Edward Thompson. 1793-1871. *3452*
—. Massachusetts (Boston, New Bedford). Mudge, Enoch. Seamen's Bethel. Taylor, Edward Thompson. 1776-1850. *3457*
—. Mexican Americans. Rio Grande Annual Conference. Southwest. 1874-1978. *3491*
—. Missions and Missionaries. North Dakota. Settlement. 1871-1914. *1523*
—. Negroes. 1769-1968. *444*
Methodist Church, Calvinistic. *Christian History* (periodical). Evangelicalism. Great Britain. Periodicals. Whitefield, George. 1740's. *2233*
—. Davies, David Jones. Davies, Gwen. Indians. Missions and Missionaries. Nebraska, eastern. Omaha Indians. 1853-60. *1514*
Methodist Church, Primitive. Bee, William. Saskatchewan (Grenfell). Settlement. 1882. *3449*
—. North Central States. 1842-1976. *3508*
Methodist Church, United. Centennial United Methodist Church. Indiana (Gary). Methodist Church, United. Negroes. Personal narratives. Robinson, Roosevelt. White flight. 1976. *3467*
—. Centennial United Methodist Church. Indiana (Gary). Methodist Church, United. Negroes. Personal narratives. Robinson, Roosevelt. White flight. 1976. *3467*
—. Educational innovation. Southern Methodist University. Student activists. Texas (Dallas). 1972-74. *720*
Methodist Church, Wesleyan. Adrian College. Baptists, Free Will. Hillsdale College. Michigan. Oberlin College. Ohio. Olivet College. Social Reform. 1833-70. *741*
—. Adventists. Byington, John. Methodist Episcopal Church. New York (Bucks Bridge). 1840's-52. *3509*
—. Baptists. Louisiana (Union Parish). Tombstones. 1839-1970's. *2834*
—. Indians. McDougall, John. Missions and Missionaries. Prairie Provinces. 1860-1917. *1534*
Methodist Church (Women's Division of Christian Service). Women. 1880's-1975. *930*
Methodist Connection, Wesleyan. Secret societies. 1843-60. *2363*
Methodist Episcopal Church. Adventists. Byington, John. Methodist Church, Wesleyan. New York (Bucks Bridge). 1840's-52. *3509*
—. Albright, Jacob. Asbury, Francis. Evangelical Association. 1765-1816. *2947*
—. American Missionary Association. Federal agencies. Freedmen. Georgia (Atlanta). Reconstruction. 1865-69. *556*
—. Americanization. Missions and Missionaries. Norway. Petersen, Ole Peter. 1830-53. *1706*
—. Ames Church. Education. Freedmen. Hartzell, Joseph C. Missionaries. Republican Party. South. 1870-73. *3481*
—. Annexation. Catholic Church. Converts. Imperialism. Missions and Missionaries. Philippines. 1899-1913. *1689*
—. Archaeology. Kensington Methodist Episcopal Church. Pennsylvania (Philadelphia). Preservation. 18c. 1950's-75. *1769*
—. Asbury, Francis. Clergy. Elections. McKendree, William. 1808. *3486*
—. Asbury, Francis. Coke, Thomas. Slavery. 1780-1816. *2155*
—. Asbury, Francis. Letters. Sunday Schools. 1791. *782*
—. Asians. Conservatism. Immigration. Social Gospel. 1865-1908. *2404*
—. Bashford, James W. China. Missions and Missionaries. Social gospel. 1889-1919. *1712*
—. Bergner, Peter. Immigrants. *John Wesley* (vessel). New York City. Seamen. 1830-77. *3478*
—. Bishops. Peck, Jesse T. Social gospel. 1850-83. *2396*
—. Bond, Thomas Emerson. Church government. Laity. Snethen, Nicholas. Stockton, William S. 1820-56. *288*
—. California. Missions and missionaries. Overland Journeys to the Pacific. Owen, Isaac. 1849. *1611*
—. Capers, William. *Christian Advocate* (newspaper). Ecumenism. Letters. Methodist Episcopal Church (South). Slavery. 1854. 1875. *479*
—. Centennial Celebrations. Evangelical Association. Methodist Protestant Church. 1872-76. *3451*
—. Centennial Exposition of 1876. Pennsylvania (Philadelphia). Prayer. Simpson, Matthew. 1876. *3502*
—. Chippewa Indians. Documents. Fullerton, Thomas. Indians. Minnesota. Missions and Missionaries. Wisconsin. 1841-44. *1531*
—. Church government. Crooks, George Richard. Laity. *Methodist* (periodical). 1851-72. *316*
—. Church records. Clergy. Grimes, Addison McLaughlin. West Virginia (Webster County). 1880's-1963. *3455*
—. Claflin, Lee. Philanthropy. 19c. *2513*
—. Clergy. 1784-1844. *3485*
—. Colonization. Liberia. Missions and Missionaries. Negroes. Sierra Leone. 1833-48. *1702*
—. Converts. Letters. Lynch, James. Methodist Episcopal Church, African. Negroes. 1867. *3462*
—. Cromwell, James. Garrettson, Freeborn. Missionaries. Nova Scotia. USA. 1785-1800. *1581*
—. Debates. Ecumenism. Methodist Episcopal Church (South). Race. Virginia. 1924-25. *467*
—. Diaries. Evangelism. Georgia (Augusta Circuit). Norman, Jeremiah. 1798-1801. *1642*
—. Doub, Peter. Education. North Carolina. Slavery. Women. 1796-1869. *3469*
—. Evolution. Goldsmith, William. Hawkins, Robert W. Kansas (Winfield). Southwestern College. 1920-25. *2316*
—. Fundamentalism. Gaebelein, Arno C. Missions and Missionaries. Zionism. 1893-1945. *1613*
—. *Khristianski Pobornik* (periodical). Missions and Missionaries. Russia (St. Petersburg). Simons, George Albert. 1881-1917. *1696*
—. Letters. Lynch, James. Mississippi. Negroes. Reconstruction. 1868-69. *3461*
—. Methodist Protestant Church. Schisms. 1775-1820. *294*
—. Missions and Missionaries. Ontario (Upper Canada). Quebec (Lower Canada). 1788-1812. *1580*
—. Missions and Missionaries. Women's Foreign Missionary Society. 1869-1900. *862*
—. Theology. 1919-39. *3483*
Methodist Episcopal Church, African. Abolition Movement. James, Thomas. Personal narratives. 1804-80. *2476*
—. Baptists. California. Negroes. Political Activity. St. Andrew's African Methodist Episcopal Church. 1850-73. *981*
—. Bethel African Methodist Episcopal Church. Pennsylvania (Reading). Restorations. 1834-1979. *1784*
—. Cain, Richard Harvey. Negroes. Politics. Reconstruction. Social conditions. South Carolina. 1850's-87. *2407*
—. Converts. Letters. Lynch, James. Methodist Episcopal Church. Negroes. 1867. *3462*
—. Federal Aid to Education. Negroes. Ohio. Wilberforce University (Combined Normal and Industrial Department). 1887-91. *518*
—. Friends, Society of. Maryland (Baltimore). Negroes. Presbyterian Church. Private Schools. Sunday Schools. 1794-1860. *633*
—. Lutheran Church. Negroes. Payne, Daniel Alexander. Wilberforce University. 1830-93. *2905*
Methodist Episcopal Church, Colored. Freedmen. Methodist Episcopal Church, South. Religious liberty. Segregation. South. 1865-70. *3464*
Methodist Episcopal Church (General Conference). Abolition Movement. Cass, William D. Letters. 1844. *2477*
Methodist Episcopal Church (South). Alabama. Clergy. Neely, Phillip Phillips. Secession. 1861. *1213*
—. *American Mercury* (periodical). Editors and Editing. Ku Klux Klan. Mencken, H. L. Temperance Movements. 1910-33. *2033*
—. Amusements. Georgia. Jones, Sam. Morality. Revivals. Self-reliance. 1872-1906. *3498*
—. Baptists. Newspapers. Presbyterian Church (Cumberland, Old School). Texas. 1829-61. *2907*
—. Candler, Warren A. Conservatism. Evolution. Leopold, Nathan. Loeb, Richard. Scopes, John Thomas. Trials. 1921-41. *2293*
—. Candler, Warren A. Political Campaigns (presidential). Prohibition. Smith, Al. 1928. *1210*
—. Capers, William. *Christian Advocate* (newspaper). Ecumenism. Letters. Methodist Episcopal Church. Slavery. 1854. 1875. *479*
—. China (Shanghai). Missions and Missionaries. Publishers and Publishing. 1898-1920. *1737*
—. Clergy. Georgia. Pierce, George Foster. Pierce, Lovick. 1785-1884. *3454*
—. Debates. Ecumenism. Methodist Episcopal Church. Race. Virginia. 1924-25. *467*
—. Freedmen. Methodist Episcopal Church, Colored. Religious liberty. Segregation. South. 1865-70. *3464*
—. Newspapers. South. 1861-65. *3487*
—. Newspapers. South. Spanish-American War. 1898. *2691*
Methodist Episcopal Zion Church, African. Baptists. Bethel African Methodist Episcopal Church. California (San Francisco). Civil rights. Negroes. Pressure groups. Third Baptist Church. 1860's. *1289*
—. Leftism. Music. Negroes. Robeson, Paul. 1898-1976. *3470*
Methodist Era. Revival meetings. 1825-1914. *3474*
Methodist Federation for Social Service. American League for Peace and Democracy. Social criticism. Ward, Harry F. 1900-40. *2408*
—. Federal Council of the Churches of Christ in America. North, Frank M. Social Creed of Methodism. Ward, Harry F. 1907-12. *2388*
Methodist (periodical). Church government. Crooks, George Richard. Laity. Methodist Episcopal Church. 1851-72. *316*

Methodist Protestant Church. Bishops. Laity. Reform. 1779-1832. *320*
—. Centennial Celebrations. Evangelical Association. Methodist Episcopal Church. 1872-76. *3451*
—. Clergy. Shaw, Anna Howard. Social Gospel Movement. Suffrage. Women. 1880-1919. *3506*
—. Clergy. Snethen, Nicholas. 1769-1845. *315*
—. Ecumenism. Japan (Yokohama). Klein, Frederick C. Missions and Missionaries. 1880-93. *458*
—. Higher Education. Madison College. Pennsylvania (Uniontown). 1851-58. *617*
—. Methodist Episcopal Church. Schisms. 1775-1820. *294*
—. Women. 19c. *903*
Methodist Woman's Missionary Council. Ames, Jessie Daniel. Association of Southern Women for the Prevention of Lynching. Lynching. Racism. South. Women. Young Women's Christian Association. 1930's. *2535*
Methodists. American Revolution. Asbury, Francis. Delaware. Loyalists. Maryland. White, Thomas. 1777-80. *3482*
—. Appointments to office. Baptists. Georgia, University of (chancellor). Hill, Walter B. 1897-1901. *536*
—. Beeson, John. Blaine, David E. Indian-White Relations. Oregon. Washington. 1850-59. *3495*
—. Bishop of London. Clergy. Ordination. Petitions. Pilmoor, Joseph. Virginia (Norfolk County). 1774. *3465*
—. Catholic Church. Missions and Missionaries. Philippines. 1899-1916. *1688*
—. *Christliche Apologete* (periodical). German Americans. Neutrality. World War I. 1914-18. *3458*
Methodology *See also* Models; Research.
—. Abortion. Catholic Church. Hawaii. Women. 1965-74. *872*
—. Archives. Church membership. Historical societies. Voting and Voting Behavior. 1776-1860. 1977. *1235*
—. Baptist studies. Oral history. 1973. *231*
—. Bellah, Robert N. Civil religion. 1967-78. *1198*
—. California (Los Angeles). Catholic Church. Ethnology. Polish Americans. Sandberg, Neil C. (review article). 1968-74. *3813*
—. Catholic Church. Church records. Immigrants. Italian Americans. Pennsylvania (Philadelphia). 1789-1900. *3770*
—. Christianity. God is Dead Theology. Islam. Religions, history of. Secularism. Smith, Wilfred Cantwell. Theology. 1940-73. *134*
—. Christianity. Racism. 1960's-70's. *2141*
—. Doherty, Robert W. Historiography. Sociology of Religion. 1974. *264*
—. Folklore. Mormons. 1892-1970's. *4055*
—. Formisano, Ronald P. Hackney, F. Sheldon. Kleppner, Paul. Politics (review article). 1827-1900. 1969-71. *1263*
—. Genealogy. Rearticulation. Religious studies. Translating and Interpreting. 1975. *232*
Métis. Alberta (Edmonton). Church of England. Indians. Newton, William. 1875-1900. *3196*
—. Canada. Christianity. Civil rights. Eskimos. Indians. Project North. 1975-79. *2545*
—. Catholic Church. Language. Missions and Missionaries. Quebec (Oka). Religious Education. Rocheblave, Charlotte de. 19c. *1507*
—. Chippewa Indians. Germans, Russian. Immigration. Manitoba. Mennonites. 1872-73. *3392*
—. Church of England. Clergy. Corbett, Griffiths Owen. Manitoba. Red River Rebellion. 1863-70. *3215*
—. Indians. Mennonites. Red River of the North. Red River of the North. Removals, forced. Saskatchewan River Valley. Settlement. 1869-95. *3360*
—. Letters. Prairie Provinces. Religious beliefs. Riel, Louis. Taché, Alexandre Antonin. 1880's. *966*
Metropolitan Areas *See also* Cities; Urbanization.
—. Missions and Missionaries. Presbyterian Church. 1869-1977. *1608*
—. Religiosity. South. 1970's. *123*
Metropolitan Record (newspaper). Catholic Church. Civil War. Copperheads. Editors and Editing. Mullaly, John. New York City. 1861-64. *1234*
Metzler congregation. Mennonites. Pennsylvania (Groffdale). 1728-1978. *3415*
Mexican Americans. Acculturation. Church Schools. Public Schools. Texas (San Antonio). 1973. *677*
—. Boycotts. Church Schools. Mexican Presbyterian Mission School. Presbyterian Church. Public schools. Segregation. Texas (San Angelo). 1910-15. *618*
—. California. Chavez, Cesar. Christianity. Political activism. Rhetoric. Texas. Tijerina, Reies. 1960's-70's. *2391*
—. California (Los Angeles). Catholic Church. Christmas. Neighborhoods. Posadas (celebrations). Rites and Ceremonies. 1975-80. *3794*
—. Castañeda, Carlos Eduardo. Catholic church. Historians. Texas. 1896-1927. *169*
—. Catholic Church. Cofradías (brotherhoods). New Mexico. Penitentes. Rio Grande Valley. ca 1770-1970. *3675*
—. Catholic Church. Feast days. New Mexico. 20c. *3903*
—. Catholic Church. Illinois (Chicago). Immigration. Social Conditions. 1910's-20's. *3833*
—. Catholic Church. Music. Protestant Churches. 1963-75. *1911*
—. Catholic Church. Music. Protestantism. 1962-75. *1910*
—. Catholic Church. Texas, southern. 1836-1911. *3769*
—. Indians. Navajo Indians. Pueblo Indians. Southwest. Witchcraft. 19c-1930's. *2214*
—. Indians. New Mexico (Bernalillo, Manzana). Witchcraft. 1970-74. *2193*
—. Indians. Witchcraft. 16c-20c. *2204*
—. Methodist Church. Rio Grande Annual Conference. Southwest. 1874-1978. *3491*
—. New Mexico (Torrance County). Superstitions. Witchcraft. 1970's. *2184*
—. Presbyterian Church. Southwest. 1830-1977. *3528*
—. Social Reform. 1974. *2413*
Mexican Presbyterian Mission School. Boycotts. Church Schools. Mexican Americans. Presbyterian Church. Public schools. Segregation. Texas (San Angelo). 1910-15. *618*
Mexican War. Armies. California. Military Recruitment. Mormon Volunteers. 1847-48. *2707*
—. Mormon Battalion. 1846. *2667*
Mexico. Adolescents. Hispanic Americans. Identity. Puerto Rico. Religiosity. Whites. 1970's. *108*
—. *America* (weekly). Carranza, Venustiano. Catholic Church. Revolution. Tierney, Richard Henry. 1914-17. *3722*
—. Attitudes. Missions and Missionaries. Protestant churches. Social Darwinism. Travel accounts. 1867-1911. *1690*
—. Butler, John Wesley. Letters. Methodist Church. Missions and Missionaries. Revolution. 1910-11. *1725*
—. California. Catholic Church. Indians (neophytes). Missions and missionaries. 1830's. *1606*
—. California. Catholic Church. Rubio, José Gonzalez. Tithing. 1848. *3894*
—. Folk art. Lithography. Puerto Rico. Southwest. 1300-1974. *1868*
Mexico (Caborca, Sonora). Arizona (Tucson). Churches. Mission Nuestra Señora de la Purísima Concepción del Caborca. Mission San Xavier del Bac. ca 1750-1809. *1782*
Mexico (Chihuahua, Sonora). Arizona. Bandelier, Adolph Francis. Manuscripts. Missions and Missionaries. New Mexico. Vatican Library. 16c-17c. 1886-1964. 1975-79. *1618*
Mexico (Guerrero). Archaeology. Engraving. Fraud. Mormons. Padilla Gold Plates. 1952-78. *4007*
Mexico (Mexico City). Missions. Mormons. Pratt, Rey I. 1906-24. *1677*
Mexico (Sonora). Arizona. Church and State. Franciscans. Indians. Missions and Missionaries. 1767-1842. *1065*
—. Dye, Alexander V. Mormons. Revolution. Settlement. 1912. *4016*
Mexico (Tamaulipas; Matamoros). Jews. Letters-to-the-editor. Newspapers. Texas (Brownsville). 1876-82. *4165*
Meyer, Frank Straus. Christianity. Conservatism. Theology. 1909-72. *1362*
Michaelius, Jonas. Clergy. New Netherland. Reformed Dutch Church. 1590's-1633. *3164*
Michigan *See also* North Central States.
—. Adrian College. Baptists, Free Will. Hillsdale College. Methodist Church, Wesleyan. Oberlin College. Ohio. Olivet College. Social Reform. 1833-70. *741*
—. Adventists. Architecture. Churches. 1863-1976. *1794*
—. Adventists. Battle Creek College. Brownsberger, Sidney. California. Colleges and Universities. Healdsburg College. 1875-80's. *665*
—. Adventists. Battle Creek College. Madison College. Sutherland, Edward A. Tennessee. 1897-1904. *743*
—. Adventists. Battle Creek Sanitarium. California. Loma Linda University. Medical Education. Nurses and Nursing. 1884-1979. *1425*
—. Alma College. Colleges and Universities. Presbyterians. 1883-86. *694*
—. Chippewa Indians. Indian-White Relations. Lutheran Church. Miessler, Ernst G. H. Missions and Missionaries. 1851-71. *1582*
—. Chippewa Indians. Indian-White Relations. Methodist Church. Missions and Missionaries. 1830-80. *1597*
—. Evangelism. Political parties. State Legislatures. 1837-61. *1300*
—. Kuehn, Ernst Ludwig Hermann. Lutheran Church. Missions and Missionaries. 1850-98. *1666*
Michigan (Adrian). Temperance Movements. Women's Christian Temperance Union. 1873-74. *2578*
Michigan (Ann Arbor). Assimilation. German Americans. Pluralism. Protestantism. 1830-1955. *284*
Michigan (Battle Creek). Adventists. Elections (mayoral). Gage, William C. Morality. 1882. *1255*
—. Adventists. Engraving. Smith, Uriah. Wood. 1852-70's. *1889*
—. Adventists (headquarters). Maryland (Takoma Park). 1903. *2978*
Michigan (Bay City). Baptists. McMaster Hall. McMaster, Susan Moulton Fraser. Ontario (Toronto). Women. 1819-1916. *3000*
Michigan (Beaver Island). Lake Michigan. Mormons. Strang, James Jesse. Utopias. Wisconsin (Voree). 1820-56. *433*
Michigan (Detroit). Anti-Semitism. Boxerman, William I. Coughlin, Charles Edward. Documents. 1939. *2131*
—. Bible (King James version). Catholic Church. Church Schools. City Politics. Education, Finance. Protestantism. Religion in the Public Schools. 1842-53. *2716*
—. Catholic Church. Clergy. Lemke, John A. Polish Americans. 1866-90. *3875*
—. Catholic Church. Dissent. Protestant Churches. Religious Education. 1958-71. *3777*
—. Catholic Church. Economic Growth. Immigration. Irish Americans. Toleration. 1850. *2790*
—. Cemeteries. Congregation Beth El. Historic markers. Jews. Letters. 1850-1971. *4159*
—. Chaldean Church. Immigrants. Iraqi Americans. Middle East. Nationalism. Uniates. ca 1940's-74. *1306*
—. Christianity. Economic growth. Ethnic Groups. Pluralism. 1880-1940. *2748*
—. Congregation Beth El. Judaism. 1859-61. *4092*
—. Congregation Beth El. Judaism. 1861-67. *4093*
—. Ethnic Groups. Protestant Churches. Social organization. 1880-1940. *2877*
—. Judaism. 1850-1922. *4154*
—. Judaism. Religious Education. Sholom Aleichem Institute. 1926-71. *746*
—. Judaism, reform. 19c-20c. *4222*
—. Judaism, Reform. Kohler, Kaufmann. 1869-1926. *4213*
—. Polish Americans. St. Albertus Church. St. Casimir Church. 1870-1970. *3827*
Michigan (Harbor Springs). Education. Engelhardt, Zephyrin. Franciscans. Holy Childhood Indian School Printery. Indians. Printing. 1894-1913. *1584*
Micmac Indians. Canada, eastern. Christianity. Europe. Trade. 15c-18c. *1574*
—. Christianity. Indian-White Relations. Missions and Missionaries. New Brunswick. Nova Scotia. 1803-60. *1649*
Microforms. Bibliographies. Concordia Historical Institute. Lutheran Church. 1971-72. *265*
—. Concordia Historical Institute. Lutheran Church. 1970-71. *266*

Micronesia. Bingham Family. Congregationalism. Hawaii. Missions and Missionaries. Yale University Library (Bingham Family Papers). 1815-1967. *1714*
Middle America. Evangelicalism. Graham, Billy. Streiker, Lowell D. (review essay). Strober, Gerald S. (review essay). -1972. *2621*
Middle classes. Aaronic Order. Glendenning, Maurice L. Millenarianism. Mormons. Utah. 1930-79. *3933*
—. Boyer, Paul. City Life. Johnson, Paul E. Missions and Missionaries. Morality. New York (Rochester). Revivals. 1815-1920. 1978. *2800*
—. California (Orange County). Communalism. Oneida Community. Social Organization. Townerites. 1848-1910. *417*
—. Catholic Church. Clergy. Pentecostal movement. Students. 1970's. *3753*
—. Church of the Sun. Occult Sciences. 1960's. *4257*
—. Connecticut (Hartford). Democratic Party. Ethnic groups. Protestantism. Voting and Voting Behavior. 1896-1940. *1203*
—. Education. Religiosity. Troeltsch, Ernst. 1960's-70's. *2602*
—. Ideology. Pluralism. Secularization. Social Change. 17c-20c. *12*
—. Myths and Symbols. Protestantism. 1975. *2606*
—. *Reader's Digest* (periodical). Values. 1976. *2015*
Middle East. Acculturation. Christianity. Ethnicity. Europe. Immigration. Judaism. 19c-20c. *34*
—. Chaldean Church. Immigrants. Iraqi Americans. Michigan (Detroit). Nationalism. Uniates. ca 1940's-74. *1306*
—. Education. Missions and Missionaries. 19c-20c. *1730*
Middlekauff, Robert. Education. Great Britain. Greaves, Richard L. Mather (family). New England. Puritans. 1596-1728. *607*
Midwest *See also* North Central States.
—. Augustana College and Theological Seminary. Bethany College. Immigration. Lutheran Church. Politics. Railroads. Religious education. Swedish Americans. Swensson, Carl Aaron. 1873-1904. *726*
—. Church membership. Cities. Education. Occupational mobility. 1955-75. *2616*
Miessler, Ernst G. H. Chippewa Indians. Indian-White Relations. Lutheran Church. Michigan. Missions and Missionaries. 1851-71. *1582*
Migration *See also* Emigration; Immigration; Refugees; Resettlement.
—. Archaeology. Mormons. ca 2000 BC-ca 200. 1973. *3949*
—. British Canadians. Country life. Ethnic groups. French Canadians. Manitoba. Mennonites. Polish Canadians. Ukrainian Canadians. 1921-61. *3389*
—. Ethnicity. Immigrants. Lutheran Church (Missouri Synod). Theology. 1847-1970. *3323*
—. Fertility. Mormons. -1974. *912*
Migration, Internal. Canada, western. Catholic Church. French Canadians. Historiography. Quebec. 1870-1915. *3819*
—. Catholic Church. French Canadians. Parishes. Quebec (Compton County). Rural-Urban Studies. 1851-91. *3791*
—. Catholics. Church membership. Protestants. Rhode Island. 1926-71. *152*
Milam, Lorenzo. Federal Communications Commission. Lansman, Jeremy. Radio. Religious references. Television. 1972-75. *1116*
Milhouse, Robert. Friends, Society of. Irish Americans. South Carolina (Camden). Wyly, Samuel. 1751-93. *3265*
Militancy. Christianity. Civil rights. Negroes. 1960's-70's. *2538*
—. Negroes. Orthodoxy. South. 1964-75. *1292*
Militarism *See also* Civil-Military Relations; Imperialism; Military Government.
—. Dunkards. Friends, Society of. Mennonites. Pacifism. 1900-78. *2646*
Military *See also* headings beginning with the words military and paramilitary; Armies; Civil-Military Relations; Conscription, Military; War.
—. Adventists. Chaplains. 1944-55. *2645*
—. Amish. Education. Pennsylvania. Trials. Wisconsin. 1755-1974. *3401*
—. Buchanan, James. Church and state. Federal Policy. Historiography. Mormons. Utah. 1857-58. *1073*
—. Friends, Society of. Hoover, Herbert C. 1929-33. *2705*
—. Knights of Columbus. Negroes. Salvation Army. World War I. Young Men's Christian Association. 1917-18. *2720*
Military Camps and Forts *See also* names of military camps and forts, e.g. Fort Apache.
—. California (San Diego). Catholic Church. Excavations. Missions and Missionaries. Serra Museum. 1769-75. 1964-70's. *1526*
Military Government *See also* Military Occupation.
—. Catholic Church. Church and state. Great Britain. Protestantism. Quebec. 18c. *1125*
Military Intelligence. Diaries. Federal government. Malone, R. J. Mennonites. Surveillance. World War I. 1914-19. *2697*
Military Occupation *See also* Military Government.
—. American Revolution. Daily life. Great Britain. Johnson, Jeremiah. New York City (Brooklyn). Personal narratives. 1775-83. *63*
Military Recruitment *See also* Conscription, Military.
—. Armies. California. Mexican War. Mormon Volunteers. 1847-48. *2707*
Military security. Colonial Government. Florida. Indians. Missions. 1566-1710. *1079*
Military Service. American Revolution. Biddle, Owen. Friends, Society of. Lacey, John, Jr. Pennsylvania. 1775-83. *2684*
—. Antislavery Sentiments. Civil War. Friends, Society of (Congregational). Jones, James Parnell. Maine. 1850's-64. *2641*
—. Attitudes. Diaries. Hitchcock, Ethan Allen. Unitarianism. 1836-54. *2656*
—. Conscientious objection. Constitutional Amendments (2nd). Federal government. Friends, Society of. Madison, James. States' Rights. 1787-92. *2686*
—. Dissent. Economic conditions. Moravian Church. North Carolina (Salem). Slavery. Social change. Women. 1772-1860. *3516*
Millenarianism *See also* Apocalypse; Eschatology.
—. Aaronic Order. Glendenning, Maurice L. Middle classes. Mormons. Utah. 1930-79. *3933*
—. Abolition Movement. Hersey, John. Methodist Church. Perfectionism. 1786-1862. *3446*
—. Adventists. Germany. Great Britain. Miller, William. Sweden. 19c. *2967*
—. Adventists. Great Disappointment. Revivals. 18c-1973. *2970*
—. American Revolution. Environment. Literature. Symbolism in Literature. 1770's-1800. *1192*
—. American Revolution. Historiography. Nationalism. Patriotism. Politics. 1740-89. *1347*
—. American Revolution (antecedents). Civil religion. Edwards, Jonathan. Great Awakening. King George's War. 1740-76. *1169*
—. Antinomianism. Cotton, John. Eliot, John. Government. Missions and Missionaries. New England. Puritans. Rhode Island (Portsmouth). 1630-90. *3635*
—. Black Muslims. Christianity. 1920-79. *4250*
—. Boudinot, Elias. Newton, Thomas. Presbyterian Church. Theology. 1787-1821. *3569*
—. Calvinism. Presbyterian Church. Proslavery Sentiments. South. 1800-65. *2166*
—. Campbell, Alexander. Civil religion. Disciples of Christ. 1810-60. *1195*
—. Campbell, Alexander. Civil religion. Disciples of Christ. 1813-66. *3106*
—. Canada. Letters. Northwest Rebellion. Riel, Louis. 1876-78. 1885. *965*
—. Civil religion. Croly, Herbert. Politics. Wilson, Woodrow. 1909-19. *1159*
—. Civil Religion. Finney, Charles G. Mahan, Asa. National Self-image. Perfectionism. 19c. *1189*
—. Cobden, Richard. Great Britain. Peace movements. Protestant churches. 1840-60. *2701*
—. Congregationalism. Edwards, Jonathan. Judaism. Luria, Isaac. Progress, concept of. 16c-18c. *84*
—. Counter culture. Mysticism. Satanism. Social reform. 1960's-70's. *4243*
—. Darby, John Nelson. Evangelical Free Church of America. Franson, Fredrik. Moody, Dwight L. Revivalism. Scandinavian Americans. 1875-95. *2863*
—. Edwards, Jonathan. Massachusetts (Northampton). Social Theory. 1720's-50's. *3154*
—. Edwards, Jonathan. Mission, concept of. New England. Puritans. 18c. *1154*
—. Einhorn, David. History. Judaism, Reform. 1830-79. *4211*
—. Eschatology. Future. Theology. 18c. *1180*
—. Florida (Estero). Illinois (Chicago). Koreshan Unity. Teed, Cyrus Read. Utopias. 1886-1903. *396*
—. Fowler, Lorenzo Niles. Fowler, Orson Squire. Philosophy. Phrenology. ca 1820-60's. *2350*
—. Genovese, Eugene D. (review article). Protestantism. Slavery. South. 17c-1865. *2163*
—. Great Disappointment. Miller, William. 1831-44. *2966*
—. Great Disappointment. Millerites. Nature. 1830's-44. *2973*
—. Immigrants. McDonald, Donald. Presbyterianism. Prince Edward Island. Scottish Canadians. ca 1828-67. *3591*
—. Jehovah's Witnesses. Russell, Charles Taze. 1879-1916. *3919*
—. Massachusetts. Mather, Increase. "New Jerusalem" (manuscript). Puritans. 1669-1710. *3632*
—. Millerites. Protestantism. 1830's-40's. *2977*
—. Missions and Missionaries. Theology. Weber, Timothy P. (review article). 1875-1925. *2897*
—. Nationalism. Protestantism. 1740-1800. *1151*
—. Politics. Social Conditions. 1920's-50's. *1420*
—. Secularization. 1850-1914. *78*
Miller, George. Letters. Mormons. Smith, Joseph. 1842. *3952*
Miller, Howard (review article). Higher Education. Presbyterian Church. 1707-1837. 1976. *760*
Miller, Perry. Bibliographies. Historiography. 1933-77. *184*
—. Historiography. New England. Puritanism. 1620-1775. 1939-74. *258*
Miller, Perry *(The New England Mind: The Seventeenth Century)*. New England. Puritans. 17c. 1939. *257*
Miller, Richard G. Benjamin, Philip S. Feldberg, Michael. Friends, Society of. Pennsylvania (Philadelphia; review article). Sinclair, Bruce. 1790-1920. 1974-76. *3269*
Miller, Samuel. Clergy. Presbyterian Church. Princeton Theological Seminary. Religious Education. 1813-50. *764*
—. Elders. Laity. Presbyterian Church. Republicanism. 1813-50. *3559*
Miller, Samuel H. Editors and Editing. Germany. Mennonites. Trials. World War I. 1917-18. *2658*
Miller, William. Adventists. Dowling, John. Greeley, Horace. New York *Tribune* (newspaper). 1842. *2963*
—. Adventists. Fiction. Press. 1830's-40's. *2014*
—. Adventists. Germany. Great Britain. Millenarianism. Sweden. 19c. *2967*
—. Adventists. Massachusetts, western. Newspapers. Public opinion. 1840's. *2079*
—. Baptists. Letters. New York (Low Hampton). 1828. *2831*
—. Great Disappointment. Millenarianism. 1831-44. *2966*
Millerites. Adventists. Albany Conference. New York. 1844-45. *2961*
—. Baptists. Galusha, Elon. New York. 1825-56. *2921*
—. Burned-over district (theory). Cross, Whitney R. Dissent. New York. 1830's-40's. 20c. *2974*
—. Great Disappointment. Millenarianism. Nature. 1830's-44. *2973*
—. Leadership. Manson Family. Nazism. Social Organization. Women's Liberation Movement. 19c-20c. *2964*
—. Millenarianism. Protestantism. 1830's-40's. *2977*
Milling. Canby, Edmund. Delaware (New Castle County). Diaries. Friends, Society of. 1822-35. *3275*
—. Converts. Immigration. Kansas. Mennonites. Presbyterian Church. Warkentin, Bernhard. 1847-1908. *3380*
Mills. Anti-Catholicism. Chicopee Manufacturing Company. Immigration. Irish Americans. Massachusetts (Chicopee). Nativism. Protestantism. 1830-75. *2103*
Milton, John. Puritanism. Transcendentalism. 1820's-30's. *2731*
Mines. Mormons. Utah (Salt Lake City). 1863-1979. *4033*
Mining camps. Mormons. Nevada (Panaca). Social Customs. ca 1860-80. *3929*
Ministers. *See* Clergy.
Minnesota *See also* North Central States.

—. Adventists. Evangelism. Hill, W. B. Iowa. Personal Narratives. 1877. 1881. *1547*
—. American Board of Commissioners for Foreign Missions. Ayer, Frederick. Chippewa Indians. Missions and Missionaries. Oberlin College. Red Lake Mission. 1842-59. *1496*
—. American Board of Commissioners for Foreign Missions. Boutwell, William Thurston. Chippewa Indians. Indian-White Relations. Missions and Missionaries. Protestant Churches. 1831-47. *1572*
—. Baptists. Circuit riders. Diaries. Immigrants. Nilsson, Frederik Olaus. Swedish Americans. 1855-65. *3046*
—. Catholic Church. Culture region. St.Cloud Diocese. 1860-1973. *3881*
—. Chippewa Indians. Documents. Fullerton, Thomas. Indians. Methodist Episcopal Church. Missions and Missionaries. Wisconsin. 1841-44. *1531*
—. Clergy. Lutheran Church (Missouri Synod). Missouri. Swedish Americans. Wihlborg, Niels Albert. 1893-1918. *3331*
—. Cloeter, Ottomar. Indians. Letters. Lutheran Church. Missions and Missionaries. 1856-68. *1651*
—. Elementary Education. Johnson, Emeroy. Lutheran Church. Personal narratives. Religious education. Swedish Americans. ca 1854-ca 1920. *666*
—. Evjen, John O. Lutheran Church. Theologians. 1874-1942. *3303*
—. Forssell, G. D. Iowa. Lectures. Progressivism. Social Conditions. 1890-95. *1967*
—. Holt, Benjamin M. Lutheran Church. Personal narratives. 1882-1974. *3309*
—. Lundeberg, Axel Johan Sigurd Mauritz. Swedenborgianism. Swedish Americans. 1852-1940. *4063*
Minnesota (Benson). Altarpieces. Christenson, Lars. Folk art. Lutheran Church. Norwegian Americans. Wood Carving. 1887-1904. *1874*
Minnesota (Chisago Lake). Andersson, Joris Per. Letters. Lutheran Church. Swedish Americans. 1851-53. *3312*
Minnesota (Gentilly). Catholic Church. French Canadians. Settlement. Theillon, Elie. 1870's-1974. *3687*
Minnesota History (periodical). Bibliographies. Women. 1915-76. *905*
Minnesota (Isantic County). Agriculture. Immigration. Lutheran Church. Social customs. Sweden (Dalarna). 1840-1910. *3329*
Minnesota (Minneapolis). Anglican Congress. Ecumenism. Gray, Walter H. 1940-54. *476*
—. Art. Catholic Church. Discovery and Exploration. Hennepin, Louis. Missions and Missionaries. Mississippi River (Falls of St. Anthony). 1680-1980. *1556*
—. Baptists. Fundamentalism. Graham, Billy. Riley, William Bell. World Christian Fundamental Association. ca 1900-65. *3068*
—. Boardinghouses. Labor. Women. Women's Christian Association. 1880's-1979. *2526*
—. Clergy. Janson, Kristofer. Norwegian Americans. Unitarianism. 1881-82. *4078*
—. Congregationalism. Social gospel. 1850-90. *2410*
Minnesota (St. Paul). Architecture. Cathedrals. Catholic Church. Ireland, John. Masqueray, Emmanuel L. 1904-17. *1795*
—. Baptists. Bishop, Harriet E. Reform. Social reform. Women. 1847-83. *801*
—. Bishops. Catholic Church. Irish Americans. Jamestown Diocese. North Dakota. Shanley, John. 1852-1909. *3731*
—. Catholic Church. O'Brien, Alice. Philanthropy. Women. 1914-62. *2419*
Minnesota, southern. Children. Parents. Religiosity. Socialization. 1975. *128*
Minnesota (Winona). Catholic Church. College of St. Teresa. Franciscan Sisters. Molloy, Mary Aloysius. Women. 1903-54. *670*
Minorities *See also* Discrimination; Ethnic Groups; Nationalism; Population; Racism; Segregation.
—. Amish, Old Order. Hutterites. Research. 1977. *3363*
—. Anti-Catholicism. Anti-Semitism. Education. North Carolina. Prejudice. Religious beliefs. 1957-73. *2093*
—. Bennett, Anne M. Bennett, John C. Theology. Women's liberation. 1974. *799*
—. Christianity. Judaism. Social Classes. 1974. *2610*
Minstrel Shows. Archival catalogs and inventories. Emmett, Daniel. Hymns. Negroes. Ohio Historical Society. Sermons. 1838-96. 1976. *2064*
Minville, Esdras. Catholic Church. Economic Theory. French Canadians. Quebec. 20c. *2558*
Minville, Esdras (eulogy). Catholic Church. French Canadians. Quebec. 1975. *3674*
Mission, concept of. -1973. *1194*
—. Edwards, Jonathan. Millenarianism. New England. Puritans. 18c. *1154*
Mission Dolores. California (San Francisco). Catholic Church. Clergy. Fontaine, Flavian. 1850-53. *3801*
Mission Festival Sunday. Lutheran Church. Missions and Missionaries. Personal narratives. Schreiber, Clara Seuel. Wisconsin (Freistadt). 1900. *1630*
Mission Guevavi. Arizona (Nogales). Excavations. Jesuits. 18c. 1964-66. *1818*
Mission Nuestra Señora de la Purísima Concepción del Caborca. Arizona (Tucson). Churches. Mexico (Caborca, Sonora). Mission San Xavier del Bac. ca 1750-1809. *1782*
Mission St. Jean-Baptiste. Catholic Church. Chipewyan Indians. Indian-White Relations. Letters. Saskatchewan (Île-à-la-Crosse). Taché, Alexandre Antonin. 1823-54. *1503*
Mission San Antonio de Pala. California (Temecula). Catholic Church. Documents. Indians. Maltby, Charles. 1866. *1573*
Mission San Buenaventura. California (Ventura). Catholic Church. Churches. ca 1794-1976. *1831*
Mission San Diego de Alcalá. California (San Diego). Franciscans. Jayme, Luís (death). Yuman Indians. 1775. *1657*
Mission San Francisco Solano. California (Sonoma). Catholic Church. Indians. 1823-34. *1506*
Mission San Gabriel Arcangel. California. Catholic Church. Newspapers. 1867. *1658*
—. Catholic Church. Indians. Juan Antonio (neophyte). Painting (realist tradition). 1800. 1976. *1882*
—. Catholic Church. Indians. Juan Antonio (neophyte). Paintings. 1800-1976. *1883*
Mission San Juan Capistrano. Architecture. California. Franciscans. 1776-1976. *1494*
—. California. Catholic Church. Restorations. 1797-1979. *1803*
—. California. Catholic Church. Serra, Junípero. 1775-76. *1601*
—. California. Franciscans. 1775-1974. *1627*
Mission San Xavier del Bac. Arizona (Tucson). Churches. Mexico (Caborca, Sonora). Mission Nuestra Señora de la Purísima Concepción del Caborca. ca 1750-1809. *1782*
Mission Santa Barbara. Archives. Bibliographies. California. Franciscans. Geiger, Maynard J. (obituary). Historiography. 1936-76. *240*
—. Archives. California. Franciscans. Geiger, Maynard J. (obituary). Historiography. 1901-77. *281*
—. Archives. California. Franciscans. Geiger, Maynard J. (obituary). Historiography. 1937-77. *238*
—. California. Catholic Church. Engelhardt, Zephyrin. Missions and Missionaries. Southwestern history. 1851-1934. *176*
—. California. Chumash Indians. Indians. Marriage. Social Organization. Yanunali, Pedro (chief). 1787-1806. *940*
—. California. Franciscans. Geiger, Maynard J. (obituary). Historians. 1901-77. *239*
Missionaries. Acculturation. Catholic Church. Indian-White Relations. Protestantism. Wisconsin. 1830-48. *1640*
—. Alaska. Catholic Church. Riobó, Juan Antonio García. Spain. Voyages. 1779. *1643*
—. Algonkian Indians, northeastern. Indians. Maine. Maritime Provinces. Social change. 1610-1750. *1512*
—. Algonkin Indians. Architecture. Calvary (chapels). Iroquois Indians. Quebec (Oka). Sulpicians. 1700's-1800's. *1811*
—. American Board of Commissioners for Foreign Missions. Indians. Methodist Church. 1830-50. *1663*
—. Ames Church. Education. Freedmen. Hartzell, Joseph C. Methodist Episcopal Church. Republican Party. South. 1870-73. *3481*
—. Anglican Communion. Canada. Education. Great Britain. Protestantism. Sudan Interior Mission. 1937-55. *1741*
—. Bailey, Margaret Jewett *(Ruth Rover)*. Business. Methodist Church. Oregon. 1854. *1522*
—. Baptists. Folger, Peter. Indians. Jones, David. Northeastern or North Atlantic States. Williams, Roger. 1638-1814. *1619*
—. Canada, western. Frontier. Methodist Church. 1840-1925. *3450*
—. Catholic Church. China. Communists. Protestant Churches. 1948-50. *1752*
—. Cherokee Indians. Civil disobedience. Evangelism. 1829-39. *1579*
—. Church Missionary Society. Church of England. Eskimos. Hudson's Bay Company. Northwest Territories (Baffin Island). Peck, E. J. Trade. 1894-1913. *1660*
—. Cromwell, James. Garrettson, Freeborn. Methodist Episcopal Church. Nova Scotia. USA. 1785-1800. *1581*
—. Diplomacy. Great Britain. Ottoman Empire. Protestantism. 1824-42. *1697*
—. Education. Indian-White Relations. Social reform. ca 1609-1900. *1498*
—. Higher education. India. Protestant Churches. Social Gospel. 1883. *1680*
—. Indians. Presbyterian Board of Foreign Missions. Slavery. 1837-61. *3568*
—. Letters. Wimmer, Boniface. 1847-55. *1626*
—. Nova Scotia. Raymond, Eliza Ruggles. Sierra Leone (Sherbro Island). Slaves. Women. 1839-50. *1692*
Missionary Society of the Canadian Church. Canada. China. Church of England. Personal narratives. Scovil, G. C. Coster. 1946-47. *1744*
Missions. American Revolution. California. Indians. Spain. 1776-83. *1321*
—. Baptists, American. Education. Negroes. South. 1862-81. *739*
—. Baptists, Southern. Language. Northeastern or North Atlantic States. Southern Baptist Convention Home Missions Board. 1950-75. *1620*
—. California. Durán, Narciso. Franciscans. Indians. Secularization. 1826-46. *1093*
—. California. Franciscans. Winemaking. 18c-19c. *371*
—. Colonial Government. Florida. Indians. Military security. 1566-1710. *1079*
—. Episcopal Church, Protestant. Theology. 1972-73. *3249*
—. Mexico (Mexico City). Mormons. Pratt, Rey I. 1906-24. *1677*
Missions and Missionaries. Abolition Movement. American Free Baptist Mission Society. Baptists. Schisms. 1830-69. *2481*
—. Abolition Movement. Childhood. Evangelicalism. 1800-60. *947*
—. Abolition Movement. Education. Freedmen. McPherson, James M. (review article). Protestantism. 1865-1910. 1975. *563*
—. Acculturation. Arapaho Indians. Cheyenne Indians. Indians. Mennonites. 1880-1900. *1557*
—. Acculturation. Blackburn, Gideon. Cherokee Indians. Presbyterian Church. Schools. Tennessee. 1804-10. *1491*
—. Acculturation. Burials. Christianity. Indians. Navajo Indians. 1949-75. *1656*
—. Acculturation. California (Monterey, San Luis Obispo counties). Catholic Church. Indians. Salinan Indians. 1770's-1830's. *1550*
—. Acculturation. Cherokee Indians. Georgia. White Path's Rebellion. 1824-28. *1578*
—. Adventists. Australia. Palmer, Edwin R. Publishers and Publishing. 1894-1915. *2968*
—. Adventists. Education. New Mexico (Sandoval). Spanish-American Seminary. 1928-53. *751*
—. Adventists. *Pitcairn* (vessel). Visions. White, Ellen G. 1848-90. *1704*
—. Africa. Christianity. Independence movements. World Conference of Christian Youth, 1st. 1939-74. *1751*
—. Africa. Congregationalism. Presbyterian Church. Reformed Dutch Church. Reformed German Church. 19c-20c. *1709*
—. Africa, West. Presbyterian Church. Social change. Women. 1850-1915. *1686*
—. Agricultural Labor. Canary Islanders. Fernandez de Santa Ana, Benito. Indians. Petitions. Provincial Government. Texas (Villa San Fernando). 1741. *1542*
—. Agriculture. Catholic Church. Federal Programs. Friends, Society of. Indian-White Relations. Moravian Church. Old Northwest. 1789-1820. *1529*
—. Agriculture. Politics. Settlement. South Dakota. 1850-1900. *66*
—. Alabama (Creek Path). American Board of Commissioners for Foreign Missions. Cherokee Indians. 1820-37. *1546*

—. Alabama (Mobile). China. Presbyterian Church. Stuart, Mary Horton. Women. 1840's-1947. *1705*
—. Alaska. Art. Episcopal Church, Protestant. Ziegler, Eustace Paul. 1900-69. *1515*
—. Alaska. Assimilation. Brady, John Green. Economic Conditions. Indian-White Relations. Tlingit Indians. 1878-1906. *1548*
—. Alaska. Catholic Church. Holy Cross Mission. Indians. Jesuits. Sisters of St. Ann. Yukon River, lower. 1887-1956. *1615*
—. Alaska. Diaries. Indian-White Relations. Library of Congress (Alaska Church Collection). Orlov, Vasilii. Orthodox Eastern Church, Russian. 1886. *1632*
—. Alaska. Discovery and Exploration. Educators. Episcopal Church, Protestant. Stuck, Hudson. 1904-20. *1647*
—. Alaska (Mary's Igloo). Bernard, Joseph. Catholic Church. Eskimos. 1884-1962. *1504*
—. Alaska (Metlakahtla). British Columbia. Capitalism. Duncan, William. Tsimshian Indians. 1857-1974. *1519*
—. Alberta. Bible. Blackfoot Indians. Indians. Stocken, H. W. G. Translating and Interpreting. Wolf Collar (shaman). 1870-1928. *1500*
—. Algoma Diocese. Episcopal Church, Protestant. Ontario. Society for the Propagation of the Gospel. 1873-1973. *1653*
—. American Baptist Home Mission Society. Baptists. Leadership. Negroes. Paternalism. Virginia Union University. 1865-1905. *644*
—. American Board of Commissioners for Foreign Missions. Angola. Church and State. Portugal. Protestant Churches. Umbundu (tribe). 1880-1922. *1746*
—. American Board of Commissioners for Foreign Missions. Arabic. Bible. Moslems. Protestantism. Translating and Interpreting. 1843-60. *1740*
—. American Board of Commissioners for Foreign Missions. Ayer, Frederick. Chippewa Indians. Minnesota. Oberlin College. Red Lake Mission. 1842-59. *1496*
—. American Board of Commissioners for Foreign Missions. Bingham family. Congregationalism. Gilbert Islands. Hawaii. 1820-1975. *1678*
—. American Board of Commissioners for Foreign Missions. Boutwell, William Thurston. Chippewa Indians. Indian-White Relations. Minnesota. Protestant Churches. 1831-47. *1572*
—. American Board of Commissioners for Foreign Missions. Cherokee Indians. Georgia. Indian-White Relations. Law Enforcement. Removals, forced. Worcester, Samuel A. 1831. *1667*
—. American Board of Commissioners for Foreign Missions. Protestant Churches. Social customs. South Africa. Zulus. 1835-60's. *1695*
—. American Board of Commissioners for Missions. Angola. Church and State. Portugal. Protestant Churches. Umbundu (tribe). 1880-1922. *1746*
—. American Colonization Society. Crummell, Alexander. Education. Episcopal Church, Protestant. Liberia. Negroes. 1853-73. *1671*
—. American Missionary Association. Congregationalism. Negroes. South. 1846-80. *1617*
—. American Revolution. Canada. Church of England. Cossitt, Ranna. Loyalists. New England. 1773-1815. *1317*
—. American Revolution. Delaware Indians. Indians. Moravian Church. Ohio. Pennsylvania, western. 1775-83. *1532*
—. American Studies. Archives. Catholic University of America. Documents. Kenrick, Francis P. 1776-1865. *216*
—. American Tract Society. Evangelicalism. Pennsylvania, western. Wright, Elizur, Jr. 1828-29. *1536*
—. Americanization. Christianity. Janes, Leroy Lansing. Japan (Kumamoto). Presbyterian Church. 1838-76. *1732*
—. Americanization. Methodist Episcopal Church. Norway. Petersen, Ole Peter. 1830-53. *1706*
—. Americanization. Protestant Churches. Puerto Rico. 1898-1917. *1734*
—. Anglican Communion. Autobiography. Cree Indians. Faries, Richard. Ontario (York Factory). 1896-1961. *1528*
—. Anglican Communion. Manitoba (Red River). Women. 1820-37. *1750*
—. Annexation. Catholic Church. Converts. Imperialism. Methodist Episcopal Church. Philippines. 1899-1913. *1689*
—. Antinomianism. Cotton, John. Eliot, John. Government. Millenarianism. New England. Puritans. Rhode Island (Portsmouth). 1630-90. *3635*
—. Antislavery Sentiments. Catholic Church. Emigration. Germans, Sudeten. Journalism. Neumann, Saint John Nepomucene. Republican Party. 19c-20c. *3826*
—. Arabs. Nationalism. Syria. 1842-1918. *1670*
—. Arapaho Indians. Haury, Samuel S. Indian Territory. Letters. Mennonites. 1876-80. *1543*
—. Archives. China. Japan. Korea. Presbyterian Historical Society. 1852-1911. *189*
—. Archives. Church of England. Society for the Propagation of the Gospel. 1700-80. *215*
—. Arctic. Canada. Catholic Church. Church of England. Churches. Fur Trade. 20c. *1549*
—. Arizona. Bandelier, Adolph Francis. Manuscripts. Mexico (Chihuahua, Sonora). New Mexico. Vatican Library. 16c-17c. 1886-1964. 1975-79. *1618*
—. Arizona. Baptists. Catholic Church. Episcopal Church, Protestant. Methodism. Mormons. Presbyterian Church. 1859-99. *1501*
—. Arizona. Church and State. Franciscans. Indians. Mexico (Sonora). 1767-1842. *1065*
—. Arizona. Indians. Jesuits. Kino, Eusebio Francisco. Spain. 1680's-1711. *1565*
—. Arkansas (Jonesboro). Catholic Church. Olivetan Benedictine Sisters, American. Renggli, Rose (Mother Mary Beatrice). 1847-1942. *1652*
—. Armenia. Lambert, Rose. Letters. Mennonites. Turkey. 1898-1911. 1969. *1756*
—. Arndt, E. L. China. Lutheran Church. 1913-29. *1749*
—. Art. Catholic Church. Discovery and Exploration. Hennepin, Louis. Minnesota (Minneapolis). Mississippi River (Falls of St. Anthony). 1680-1980. *1556*
—. Art criticism. California. Catholic Church. 1769-1980. *1876*
—. Arts. California. Catholic Church. Historiography (Anglo-American). Scholasticism. 1740's-1976. *1878*
—. Asia. Canada. Colleges and Universities (review article). Protestant Churches. 1850-1971. *1675*
—. Assimilation. Christianity. Indians. Syncretism. 19c-20c. *2794*
—. Assimilation. Indians (agencies). Lowrie, John C. Presbyterian Church. 1870-82. *1655*
—. Attitudes. Catholic Church. Colonial Government. Discovery and Exploration. Games. Indians. 16c-17c. *1524*
—. Attitudes. China. Presbyterian Church. 1837-1900. *1691*
—. Attitudes. France. Indians. Jesuits. New France. 1611-72. *1495*
—. Attitudes. Indians. Presbyterian Church. 1837-93. *1510*
—. Attitudes. Mexico. Protestant churches. Social Darwinism. Travel accounts. 1867-1911. *1690*
—. Authority. Latin America. Mormons. Nationalism. 1975-80. *1753*
—. Autonomy. Church Finance. Episcopal Church, Protestant. Isolationism. Theology. 1953-77. *1720*
—. Baptist Triennial Convention. Church Finance. Education. Rice, Luther. Wayland, Francis. 1823-26. *3018*
—. Baptists. 1974. *1571*
—. Baptists. Bingham, Abel. Diaries. Indian-White Relations. Iroquois Indians (Seneca). New York. Red Jacket (leader). Tonawanda Indian Reservation. 1822-28. *1513*
—. Baptists. Bristol Baptist College. Great Britain (Bristol). Religious Education. Terrill, Edward. 1634-1979. *3024*
—. Baptists. China. Shuck, Eliza G. Sexton. 1844-51. *1713*
—. Baptists. Creek Indians. Indian Territory. Methodist Church. Presbyterian Church. 1835-60's. *1517*
—. Baptists. Graves, James Robinson. Landmark movement. South. Whitsitt Controversy. 1850-1950. *3057*
—. Baptists. Judson, Adoniram. Newell, Samuel. 1810-21. *1731*
—. Baptists. Moon, Lottie. Week of Prayer for Foreign Missions. Woman's Missionary Union. 1888-1979. *1747*
—. Baptists, American. Crawford, Isabel. Indians. Kiowa Indians. Oklahoma (Wichita Mountains). Women's American Baptist Home Missionary Society. 1893-1961. *1590*
—. Baptists (American). Theology. 1810-26. *1735*
—. Baptists, Big Hatchie. Baptists, Southern. Evangelism. Landmark movement. 1828-1903. *3011*
—. Baptists (freewill). India. Phillips, Jeremiah. Santals (tribe). 19c. *1733*
—. Baptists, Southern. 1845-1973. *1742*
—. Baptists, Southern. 1845-60. *1648*
—. Baptists, Southern. Carey, William. Higher education. 1826-1976. *1755*
—. Baptists, Southern. Church Finance. 1792-1976. *1595*
—. Baptists, Southern. Civil War. Foreign Mission Board. 1861-66. *1700*
—. Baptists, Southern. Developing nations. Medicine, practice of. 1846-1975. *1440*
—. Baptists, Southern. Foreign Mission Board. 1974. *1699*
—. Baptists, Southern. Foreign Mission Board. Publications programs. 1899-1976. *1708*
—. Baptists, Southern. Garrott, William Maxfield. Graham, Agnes Nora. Rutledge, Arthur B. 20c. *1694*
—. Baptists, Southern. Laity. 1715-1975. *1623*
—. Baptists, Southern. Woman's Missionary Union. 19c. *1527*
—. Bashford, James W. China. Methodist Episcopal Church. Social gospel. 1889-1919. *1712*
—. Belgian Congo (Kasai). Presbyterian Church. 1871-1964. *1729*
—. Benedictines. Catholic Church. Vatican Council I. Wimmer, Boniface. 1866-87. *3815*
—. Benedictines. Illinois (New Cluny). Immigrants. Monastic observance. Moosmüller, Oswald. 1832-1901. *3816*
—. Bethel College. Kansas (North Newton). Kauffman, Charles. Kauffman Museum. Mennonites. Museums. 1907-76. *198*
—. Bible. British Columbia. California. Christianity. Indians. Myths and Symbols. Pacific Northwest. 1830-50. *1612*
—. Biblical studies. Ecumenism. Palestine. Protestantism. 1812-1975. *1748*
—. Bibliographies. Diocesan histories. Episcopal Church, Protestant. ca 1776-1972. *3201*
—. Bingham Family. Congregationalism. Hawaii. Micronesia. Yale University Library (Bingham Family Papers). 1815-1967. *1714*
—. Bingham, Hiram. Congregationalism. Converts. Family. Vermont. 1789-1819. *1585*
—. Black Hills. Episcopal Church, Protestant. Hinman, Samuel D. Indians. Sioux Indians. 1860-76. *1484*
—. Blackburn, Gideon. Cherokee Indians. Indians. Old Southwest. Presbyterian Church. Schools. Whiskey. 1809-10. *700*
—. Blair, James. Church of England. College of William and Mary. Governors. Virginia. ca 1685-1743. *3223*
—. Boers. Champion, George. South Africa (Ginani). Zulus. 1836-41. *1719*
—. Bolton, Herbert Eugene. Catholic Church. Colonization. Historiography. Southwest. Spain. 1917-79. *1489*
—. Books (editions). Canada, western. Church of England. Diaries. West, John. 1820-27. *1530*
—. Boundaries. Catholic Church. Ontario. Settlement. 1840-1910. *3709*
—. Boyer, Paul. City Life. Johnson, Paul E. Middle Classes. Morality. New York (Rochester). Revivals. 1815-1920. 1978. *2800*
—. Brent, Charles Henry. Episcopal Church, Protestant. Paternalism. Philippines. 1901-18. *1738*
—. British Columbia (Metlakatla). Church Missionary Society. Church of England. Hall, A. J. Indian-White Relations. Revivals. Tsimshian Indians. 1877. *1616*
—. British Columbia (Queen Charlotte Islands). Church of England. Haida Indians. Methodist Church. Settlement. Social Change. 1876-1920. *1545*
—. British Columbia (Vancouver Island). Converts. Immigration. Mormons. 1875-1979. *1669*
—. British Columbia (Vancouver Island; Nootka Sound). Catholic Church. Indians. Oral History. Spain. 1789-95. 19c. *1563*
—. Buck, Pearl S. Fiction. Presbyterian Church. 1931-69. *2068*

—. Budgets. Presbyterian Church. 1763-1978. *1488*
—. Bureau of Indian Affairs. Educational Policy. Indians (reservations). Language. 19c-20c. *516*
—. Business. Indians. Lee, Daniel. Letters. Methodist Church. Oregon (Willamette Valley, The Dalles). 1834-43. *1570*
—. Butler, Elizur. Cherokee Indians. Indian-White Relations. Marshall, John. Nullification crisis. Worcester, Samuel A. *Worcester* v. *Georgia* (US, 1832). 1828-33. *1583*
—. Butler, John Wesley. Letters. Methodist Church. Mexico. Revolution. 1910-11. *1725*
—. California. Catholic Church. Church administration. González Rubio, José. 1846-50. *3811*
—. California. Catholic Church. Engelhardt, Zephyrin. Mission Santa Barbara. Southwestern history. 1851-1934. *176*
—. California. Catholic Church. Indians. Labor. 1775-1805. *1485*
—. California. Catholic Church. Indians (neophytes). Mexico. 1830's. *1606*
—. California. Catholic Church. Indian-White Relations. 1770's-1820's. *1636*
—. California. Church and state. Colonial Government. Indians. Laws of the Indies. Spain. 18c. *1143*
—. California. Church and State. Franciscans. Indians. 1775-1800. *1037*
—. California. Conversion thesis. Cook, Sherburne Friend. Franciscans. Indians. ca 1790-1820's. 1943. *1541*
—. California. Dominicans. Franciscans. Jesuits. Serra, Junípero. 1768-76. *1575*
—. California. Durán, Narciso. Franciscans. Indians. Music. 1806-46. *1924*
—. California. Methodist Episcopal Church. Overland Journeys to the Pacific. Owen, Isaac. 1840. *1611*
—. California. Viticulture. 1697-1858. *1659*
—. California (San Diego). Catholic Church. Excavations. Military Camps and Forts. Serra Museum. 1769-75. 1964-70's. *1526*
—. California (San Diego). Colonization. Indians. Spain. 1769-1834. *1668*
—. Canada. Catholic Church. Geographic Space. Regionalism. 1615-1851. *1486*
—. Canada. China. Hurford, Grace Gibberd. Personal narratives. Teaching. World War II. 1928-45. *1711*
—. Canada. Christianity. Sex roles. Women. 1815-99. *854*
—. Canada. Church of England. Domestic and Foreign Missionary Society. Japan. 1883-1902. *1587*
—. Canada. Church Schools. East Indians. Presbyterian Church. Trinidad and Tobago. 1868-1912. *1726*
—. Canada. Cree Indians. Evans, James. Methodist Church. 1833-46. *3475*
—. Canada. Fort Frontenac. Indian-White Relations. Iroquois Indians. Quinte Mission. Sulpician order. 1665-80. *1610*
—. Canada. Mennonites. USA. 1880-1910. *1628*
—. Canada. Methodism. New York Conference. 1766-1862. *1607*
—. Canada, Western. Catholic Church. Immigration. Sisters of Service. 1920-30. *1665*
—. Canada, western. Catholic Church. Indians. Oblates of Mary Immaculate. 1818-70. *1502*
—. Canada, western. Church of England. Hudson's Bay Company. Hunter, James. 1844-64. *1603*
—. Carver, William Owen. Southern Baptist Theological Seminary. 1859-1954. *1518*
—. Catholic Church. China (Kanchow). Foreign policy. State Department. 1929-32. *1710*
—. Catholic Church. Church of England. Government. Indian-White Relations. Manitoulin project. Methodist Church. Ontario (Upper Canada). 1820-40. *1537*
—. Catholic Church. Coahuiltecan Indians. Texas (San Antonio). 1792. *1566*
—. Catholic Church. Colonial Government. Discovery and Exploration. France. Jolliet, Louis. Marquette, Jacques. Mississippi River. Monuments. 1665-1700. *3767*
—. Catholic Church. Education. Indians. North Dakota. Pioneers. Presentation of the Blessed Virgin Mary, Sisters of the. South Dakota. Women. 1880-96. *727*
—. Catholic Church. Education. Protestant Churches. Prucha, Francis Paul (review article). 1888-1912. *1538*
—. Catholic Church. Frontier and Pioneer Life. Southwest. Spain. 16c-18c. *1497*
—. Catholic Church. Hawaii. Independence Movements. Protestant Churches. Simpson, George. 1842-43. *1723*
—. Catholic Church. Hudson's Bay Company. Indians. Methodist Church. Oregon. Presbyterian Church. 1830's - 1840's. *1482*
—. Catholic Church. Indians. Louisiana. 18c-20c. *1625*
—. Catholic Church. Indians. Pueblo Revolt (1680). Southwest. 1590-1680. *1499*
—. Catholic Church. Language. Métis. Quebec (Oka). Religious Education. Rocheblave, Charlotte de. 19c. *1507*
—. Catholic Church. Methodists. Philippines. 1899-1916. *1688*
—. Catholic Church. Quebec (Eastern Townships). Social Conditions. 1825-53. *1568*
—. Charities. Equality. Presbyterian Church. Women. 1800-1975. *908*
—. Cherokee Indians. Indians. Martin, John. Presbyterian Church. Richardson, William. Tennessee. Virginia. 1755-63. *1511*
—. Cheyenne Indians. Institutions. Mennonites. Photographs. Social customs. 1880-1940. *3398*
—. Chile. Journalism. Presbyterian Church. Religious liberty. Trumbull, David. 1845-89. *1703*
—. China. Christianity. Fairbank, John King (review article). ca 1860-1949. 1974. *1718*
—. China. Diplomacy. Japan. Presbyterian Church. Stuart, John Leighton. 1937-41. *1745*
—. China. Diplomatic recognition. Revolution. Sun Yat-sen. 1911-13. *1724*
—. China. Episcopal Church, Protestant. Roots, Eliza McCook. Roots, Logan H. 1900-34. *1743*
—. China (Caoxian, Kai Chow). Mennonites. 1901-31. *1716*
—. China (Shanghai). Colleges and Universities. Episcopal Church, Protestant. Pott, Francis L. H. St. John's University. 1888-1941. *1707*
—. China (Shanghai). Methodist Episcopal Church, South. Publishers and Publishing. 1898-1920. *1737*
—. Chinese Americans. Hawaii. Protestant Churches. 1872-98. *1717*
—. Chippewa Indians. Documents. Fullerton, Thomas. Indians. Methodist Episcopal Church. Minnesota. Wisconsin. 1841-44. *1531*
—. Chippewa Indians. Indian-White Relations. Lutheran Church. Michigan. Miessler, Ernst G. H. 1851-71. *1582*
—. Chippewa Indians. Indian-White Relations. Methodist Church. Michigan. 1830-80. *1597*
—. Choctaw Indians. Congregationalism. Harkins, Richard. Murder. Slavery. 1858-59. *3132*
—. Christianity. Indians. New England. New France. 17c. *1621*
—. Christianity. Indians. New England Company. Royal Society. 1660's-70's. *1554*
—. Christianity. Indian-White Relations. Micmac Indians. New Brunswick. Nova Scotia. 1803-60. *1649*
—. Church and Social Problems. Episcopal Church, Protestant. Social Reform. ca 1960-73. *2384*
—. Church Missionary Society. Church of England. Hudson's Bay Company. Ontario (Moosonee). Vincent, Thomas. 1835-1910. *1638*
—. Church of England. Clergy. Education. Quebec (Three Rivers). Wood, Samuel. 1822-68. *3202*
—. Church of England. Connecticut. Letters. Muirson, George. New York. ca 1697-1708. *1535*
—. Church of England. Education. Indians. Methodist Church. Ontario (Algoma, Huron). Wilson, Edward F. 1868-93. *1596*
—. Church of England. Indians. McDonald, Robert. Northwest Territories. Yukon Territory. 1850's-1913. *1604*
—. Church of England. Nova Scotia (Halifax). St. Paul's Church. Society for the Propagation of the Gospel. Tutty, William. 1749-52. *1646*
—. Cloeter, Ottomar. Indians. Letters. Lutheran Church. Minnesota. 1856-68. *1651*
—. Coke, Thomas. Garrettson, Freeborn. Letters. Methodist Church. Nova Scotia. Wesley, John. 1786. *1490*
—. Colby, Abby M. Congregationalism. Feminism. Japan. 1879-1914. *932*
—. Colleges and universities. Dalhousie University. McCulloch, Thomas. Nova Scotia. Pictou Academy. Presbyterian Church. ca 1803-42. *591*
—. Colonial Government. Documents. Franciscans. New Mexico. Spain. Vélez Cachupín, Thomas. ca 1754. *1586*
—. Colonialism. India, north. Presbyterian Church. ca 1800-1950. *1673*
—. Colonization. Hawaii (Lanai). Mormons. 1850's. *1684*
—. Colonization. Indians. Jesuits. Menéndez de Avilés, Pedro. Opechancanough (chief). Powhatan Indians. Spain. Virginia. 1570-72. *1622*
—. Colonization. Liberia. Methodist Episcopal Church. Negroes. Sierra Leone. 1833-48. *1702*
—. Congregationalism. Connecticut. Hawaii. Kanui, William Tennooe. Protestant Churches. 1796-1864. *1493*
—. Congregationalism. Diaries. Hawaii. Tahitians. Toketa (teacher). 1820's-30's. *1676*
—. Congregationalism. Hawaiian Evangelical Association. Siu Pheong Aheong. ca 1838-76. *1687*
—. Congregationalism. Nationalism. Social Gospel. Strong, Josiah. Wyoming (Cheyenne). 1871-1916. *3134*
—. Converts. Indians. Massachusetts (Martha's Vineyard). Mayhew, Thomas, Jr. Puritans. 1645-57. *1635*
—. Crow Indians. Diaries. Doederlein, Paul Ferdinand. Indians. Lutheran Church. Wyoming. 1859-60. *1589*
—. Cuba. Methodist Church. Nationalism. 1898-1958. *1693*
—. Davies, David Jones. Davies, Gwen. Indians. Methodist Church, Calvinistic. Nebraska, eastern. Omaha Indians. 1853-60. *1514*
—. Deaf. Ephphatha Conference. Lutheran Church. 1893-1976. *1516*
—. Dean, Joseph Harry. Gibson, Walter Murray. Hawaii. Mormons. Samoa. 1860's-90. *1683*
—. Diaries. Episcopal Church, Protestant. Harris, N. Sayre. Indian Territory. Otey, James Hervey. 1844. *1533*
—. Diaries. Grant, Jedediah Morgan. Mormons. 1833-57. *1631*
—. Diaries. Indians. Spokan Indians. Walker, Elkanah. Walker, Mary. Washington, eastern. 1839-48. *1521*
—. Diaries. Maine. Protestantism. Sewall, Jotham. 1778-1848. *1645*
—. District of Columbia. National Statuary Hall. Pacific Northwest. Pariseau, Mother Mary Joseph. Sisters of Charity of Providence. Women. 1856-1902. 1977. *1629*
—. Documents. Episcopal Church, Protestant. Puerto Rico. 1870-1952. *1679*
—. Documents. Friends, Society of. Religious Liberty. Virginia. Wilson, George. 1650-62. *1007*
—. Documents. Indian-White Relations. Western States. 1812-1923. *1483*
—. Doukhobors. Galicians. Hospitals. Lake Geneva Mission. Presbyterian Church. Saskatchewan (Wakaw). 1903-42. *1492*
—. Drury, Clifford M. Historians. Oregon. Presbyterian Church. Washington. 1928-74. *190*
—. Drury, Clifford M. Indians. Lee, Jason. Methodism. Oregon. Settlement. 1834-43. 1970's. *3480*
—. Economic conditions. Frontier and Pioneer life. Indians. Presbyterian Church. South Dakota. 1840-1900. *3540*
—. Ecumenism. Japan (Yokohama). Klein, Frederick C. Methodist Protestant Church. 1880-93. *458*
—. Education. Middle East. 19c-20c. *1730*
—. Education. Presbyterian Church. Puerto Rico. Social Customs. 1898-1917. *1727*
—. Eliot, John. Indians. Massachusetts. Puritans. 1620-80. *1624*
—. Eliot, John. Indians. Massachusetts (Natick). Puritans. 1646-74. *1602*
—. Episcopal Church, Protestant. Florida. Gray, William Crane. Indian-White Relations. Seminole Indians. 1893-1914. *1558*
—. Episcopal Church, Protestant. Hudson's Bay Company. Indians. Pacific Northwest. 1825-75. *1555*
—. Eskimos. Jannasch, Hermann Theodor. Labrador. Moravian Church. 1855-1931. *1594*

—. Esteyneffer, Juan de *(Florilegio Medicinal)*. Herbs. Indians. Jesuits. Medicine (practice of). Southwest. 1711. *1444*
—. Evangelism. Horstman, Otto K. Indiana (Shelbyville). Lutheran Church, Evangelical. Personal narratives. 1934. *1551*
—. Evans, James. Methodism. Ontario (Lake Superior). Voyages. 1837-38. *1564*
—. Exiles. Loyalists. McDowall, Robert James. Ontario (Upper Canada). Reformed Dutch Church. 1790-1819. *1588*
—. Feminization. Voluntary Associations. Women. 1800-60. *942*
—. France. Indians. Jesuits. New York, western. Rings. ca 1630-87. *1664*
—. Franciscans. Indian-White Relations. Inquisition. Marriage. New Mexico. Plains Apache Indians. Romero, Diego. 1660-78. *3773*
—. French Canadians. Government, provisional. Gray, William. Lee, Jason. Methodist Church. Oregon. 1843. *1271*
—. Friends, Society of. Great Britain. New England. 1656-1775. *1662*
—. Fundamentalism. Gaebelein, Arno C. Methodist Episcopal Church. Zionism. 1893-1945. *1613*
—. Genealogy. Mormons. Utah. 1885-1900. *1525*
—. Germans, Sudeten. Indians. 1519-19c. *1539*
—. Gospel Missionary Union of Kansas. Morocco (Tangiers). 1895-1905. *1736*
—. Great Britain. Iroquois Indians. Jesuits. Netherlands. New York. 1642-1719. *1654*
—. Great Britain. Mormons. Working class. 1840-41. *1672*
—. Heyer, John Christian Frederick. Illinois. Indiana. Keller, Ezra. Letters. Lutheranism. Missouri. ca 1820-40. *1614*
—. Historiography. Indians. Lee, Jason. Methodism. Oregon. 1838-43. *1569*
—. Historiography. Indian-White Relations. New England. Puritans. Theology. 17c-20c. *1641*
—. Historiography. Marshall, William I. Oregon. Whitman, Marcus. Winters, Herbert D. ca 1842-43. 1930. *1553*
—. Idaho. McBeth, Sue L. Nez Percé Indians. Presbyterian Church. 1874. *1591*
—. Indian Shaker Church. Johnson, Jakie. Oregon (Siletz). Siletz Indians. ca 1881-1970. *2776*
—. Indians. McBeth, Sue L. Nez Percé Indians. Presbyterian Church. 1873-93. *1509*
—. Indians. McDougall, John. Methodist Church, Wesleyan. Prairie Provinces. 1860-1917. *1534*
—. Indians. Methodism. Oklahoma. 1820-45. *1650*
—. Indian-White Relations. Protestant Churches. Spokan Indians. Walker, Elkanah. Washington (Tshimakain). 1838-48. *1520*
—. Japan. Mormons. 1901-24. *1681*
—. Jesuits. Ottoman Empire. Protestant Churches. Syria. 1840's. *1698*
—. Jones, Charles Colcock. Presbyterian Church. Slavery. South. 1825-63. *2177*
—. *Khristianski Pobornik* (periodical). Methodist Episcopal Church. Russia (St. Petersburg). Simons, George Albert. 1881-1917. *1696*
—. Kuehn, Ernst Ludwig Hermann. Lutheran Church. Michigan. 1850-98. *1666*
—. Lutheran Church. Mission Festival Sunday. Personal narratives. Schreiber, Clara Seuel. Wisconsin (Freistadt). 1900. *1630*
—. MacGregor, James. Nova Scotia (Pictou). Presbyterian Church of Scotland. 1786-1830. *1634*
—. Maine (Waldoboro). Moravian Church. Soelle, Georg. 1762-70. *3512*
—. Mennonites. Women's Missionary Society. 1900-30. *866*
—. Mennonites (Lancaster Conference). Tanzania. 1934-71. *1674*
—. Methodist Church. North Dakota. Settlement. 1871-1914. *1523*
—. Methodist Episcopal Church. Ontario (Upper Canada). Quebec (Lower Canada). 1788-1812. *1580*
—. Methodist Episcopal Church. Women's Foreign Missionary Society. 1869-1900. *862*
—. Metropolitan Areas. Presbyterian Church. 1869-1977. *1608*
—. Millenarianism. Theology. Weber, Timothy P. (review article). 1875-1925. *2897*
—. Modernization. Mormons. Pacific, South. 1955-80. *1682*
—. Mormons. 1855-20c. *1552*
—. Mormons. 1949-80. *1715*
—. Oceania. Pease, Benjamin. Pirates. 1867-70. *1685*
—. Organizations. Protestant Churches. Women. 1870's-90's. *894*
—. Presbyterian Church. 1706-1977. *1739*
—. Presbyterian Church. Puerto Rico. 1899-1914. *1728*
—. Presbyterian Church. Race Relations. 1562-1977. *3535*
—. Protestant Churches. 1792-1970. *1722*
—. Protestant Churches. Women. 19c. *943*
—. Women. 19c. *1721*
Missions and Missionaries (associate). Episcopal Church, Protestant. Nebraska (Omaha). 1891-1902. *1562*
Mississippi. Agriculture. Landlords and Tenants. Neoorthodoxy. Protestant Churches. Theologians. 1936-40. *2566*
—. Bratton, Theodore DuBose. Conference for Education in the South. Episcopal Church, Protestant. Negroes. Racism. 1908. *2148*
—. Letters. Lynch, James. Methodist Episcopal Church. Negroes. Reconstruction. 1868-69. *3461*
—. Music, gospel. Values. 1890-1978. *1922*
Mississippi (Brandon Springs). Centenary College. Methodist Church. Mississippi Conference. Religious Education. 1838-44. *656*
Mississippi Conference. Centenary College. Methodist Church. Mississippi (Brandon Springs). Religious Education. 1838-44. *656*
Mississippi (Pontotoc County). Civil War. Country Life. Personal narratives. Shady Grove Baptist Church. Smith, Andrew Jackson. 1864-69. *3035*
Mississippi River. Catholic Church. Colonial Government. Discovery and Exploration. France. Jolliet, Louis. Marquette, Jacques. Missions and Missionaries. Monuments. 1665-1700. *3767*
—. Catholic Church. Discovery and Exploration. Jolliet, Louis. Marquette, Jacques. 1673. 1973. *1567*
—. Christianity. Converts. Earthquakes. Missouri. New Madrid Earthquake. 1811-12. *2789*
—. Economic growth. Illinois (Nauvoo). Mormons. Steamboats. 1839-46. *367*
Mississippi River (Falls of St. Anthony). Art. Catholic Church. Discovery and Exploration. Hennepin, Louis. Minnesota (Minneapolis). Missions and Missionaries. 1680-1980. *1556*
Missouri *See also* North Central States.
—. Adventists. Clinton Theological Seminary. German Americans. 1910-25. *761*
—. American Missionary Association. Civil War. Education. Negroes. 1862-65. *547*
—. Attitudes. Bradford family. Letters. Mormons. Virginia. 1838-39. *4057*
—. Baptists. Clergy. Oregon (Willamette Valley). Powell, Joab. Westward movement. 1852-73. *3093*
—. Bishops. Catholic Church. Kenrick, Peter Richard. Letters. Travel. 1847. *3839*
—. Christianity. Converts. Earthquakes. Mississippi River. New Madrid Earthquake. 1811-12. *2789*
—. Circuit riders. Clark, John. Evangelism. Methodism. Travis, John. 1796-1851. *1561*
—. Clergy. Frontier. Protestant Churches. Schools. ca 1800-30. *639*
—. Clergy. Lutheran Church (Missouri Synod). Minnesota. Swedish Americans. Wihlborg, Niels Albert. 1893-1918. *3331*
—. Colleges and Universities. Culver-Stockton University. Democratic Party. Disciples of Christ. Shannon, James. Slavery. 1821-59. *3107*
—. Communes. German Americans. Keil, William. Letters. Oregon. Society of Bethel. Weitling, Wilhelm. 1844-83. *405*
—. Congregationalism. Guidebooks. Immigration. Thomas, Robert D. *(Hanes Cymry America)*. Welsh Americans. 1872. *3120*
—. Converts. Letters. Mormons. Ostracism. Partridge, Edward. 1837. *3989*
—. Documents. Free Thinkers. German Americans. Immigrants. Reading. Religious liberty. St. Louis Free Congregation Library. 1850-99. *1123*
—. Heyer, John Christian Frederick. Illinois. Indiana. Keller, Ezra. Letters. Lutheranism. Missions and Missionaries. ca 1820-40. *1614*
Missouri (Brazeau). Diaries. Lutheran Church. McPherson, Sarah M. 1852-56. *3298*
Missouri (Caldwell, Jackson counties). Mormons. Negroes. Social Problems. 1830-39. *4030*
Missouri (Carondelet, St. Louis). Catholic Church. Kenrick, Peter Richard. St. Mary's of the Barrens. Seminaries. 1840-48. *752*
Missouri (Clayton, St. Louis). Baur, John C. Concordia Seminary. Fund raising. Lutheran Church (Missouri Synod). Personal Narratives. 1923-26. *594*
Missouri (Conception). Benedictine sisters. Immigration. Renggli, Rose (Mother Mary Beatrice). Switzerland. Women. 1874. *3832*
Missouri (Concordia). Alienation. Civil War. Ethnicity. German Americans. Lutheran Church (Missouri Synod). Massacres. 1864. *3301*
—. Keisker, Walter. Lutheran Church. Personal narratives. Religious Education. St. Paul's College. Students. 1913-19. 1980. *669*
Missouri (Perry County). Concordia Historical Institute. Farms. Lutheran Church (Missouri Synod). Preservation. Saxon Lutheran Memorial. 1958-64. *220*
—. Kramer, William A. Lutheran Church. Personal narratives. ca 1890-1910. *3314*
Missouri (St. Louis). Abolition Movement. Baptists. Education. First African Baptist Church. Meachum, John Berry. Negroes. 1815-54. *2482*
—. Abolition movement. Clergy. Conservatism. Constitutions. Massachusetts (Boston). Unitarianism. 1828-57. *1413*
—. Academic freedom. Concordia Seminary. Lutheran Church (Missouri Synod). Teachers. Tenure. 1968-74. *771*
—. Alexian Brothers. Bernard, Alexius. Catholic Church. German Americans. Hospitals. Tollig, Paulus. 1869-1980. *1456*
—. Archives. Church History. Concordia Historical Institute. Lutheran Church (Missouri Synod). 1978. *221*
—. Atheism. Bobb, John. *Western Examiner* (periodical). 1834-35. *4300*
—. Baptists. Clergy. Davis, Noah. Maryland (Baltimore). Meachum, John Berry. Negroes. Slavery. 1818-66. *3094*
—. Bible. Cave, Robert Catlett. Disciples of Christ. Sermons. Theology. 1840's-90's. *3111*
—. Bradley, Lucas. Churches. Presbyterian Church. Wisconsin (Racine). 1840-90. *1810*
—. Brownson, Orestes A. Catholic Church. Civilization. Lectures. 1852-54. *3838*
—. Buettner, George L. Concordia Publishing House. Lutheran Church (Missouri Synod). Personal Narratives. Publishers and publishing. 1888-1955. *336*
—. Catholic Church. Church Schools. Glennon, John J. Ritter, Joseph E. School Integration. 1935-47. *2542*
—. Catholic Church. Clergy. 1841-99. *3759*
—. Catholic Church. Colleges and Universities. Maryville Academy. 1872-1972. *657*
—. Catholic Church. Educational attainment. Immaculate Conception Primary School. Lithuanian Americans. Occupations. 1948-68. *2607*
—. Cave, Robert Catlett. Disciples of Christ. Liberalism. Non-Sectarian Church of St. Louis. Theology. 1867-1923. *2913*
—. Concordia Seminary. German Americans. Illinois (Springfield). Lutheran Church (Missouri Synod). 1846-1938. *615*
—. Episcopal Church, Protestant. Social reform. 1880-1920. *2403*
—. Evangelism. Herzberger, F. W. Lutheran Church. 1899-1930. *3336*
—. Lifestyles. Lutheran Church. Seminaries. Students. 1922-28. *703*
Missouri (St. Louis area). Church and Social Problems. Episcopal Church, Protestant. 1960's-70's. *3218*
Missouri (Webster Groves). Charities. Edgewood Children's Center. Orphans. Protestantism. St. Louis Protestant Orphan Asylum. 1834-1979. *2518*
Mistassini, monastery of. Catholic Church. Cistercians. Quebec. Trappists. 1900-03. *3721*
Mobility. *See* Geographic Mobility; Social Mobility.
Moczygemba, Leopold. Catholic Church. Immigration. Letters. Polish Americans. Texas (Panna Marya). 1855. *3679*
Models *See also* Methodology.
—. Charisma. Guyana (Jonestown). Jones, Jim. Leadership. People's Temple. Suicide, mass. 1978. *4253*
—. Christ Communal Organization. Converts. Fundamentalism. 1970's. *2917*
—. Conversion. Jesus Movement. 1970's. *2770*

—. Converts. Glock, Charles Y. Social Change. Stark, Rodney. 1960's-70's. *144*
—. Cults. 1840's-1970's. *2*
—. Evangelism. Unification Church. 1965-75. *4255*
Modernism. Baptists. Factionalism. Fundamentalism. Jarvis Street Baptist Church. Ontario (Toronto). Social Classes. 1895-1934. *2605*
—. Baptists, Southern. Fundamentalism. Graves, James Robinson. Landmark Movement. Mullins, Edgar Young. Theology. 1840-1928. *3058*
—. Hutchison, William R. (review article). Protestantism. 19c-1976. *2872*
—. Mathews, Shailer. Science. Social gospel movement. Theology. 1864-1930. *2443*
Modernization *See also* Developing Nations; Economic Theory; Industrialization; Social Change.
—. Mennonites. Revivals. 1683-1850. *2254*
—. Missions and Missionaries. Mormons. Pacific, South. 1955-80. *1682*
Modjeska, Helena. Actors and Actresses. California (Los Angeles area). Catholic Church. Polish Americans. 1876-1909. *3786*
Mohr, Charles. Anti-Catholicism. Benedictines. D'Equivelley, G. F. Florida (Pasco County). *Jeffersonian* (newspaper). Land. Letters-to-the-editor. 1915-16. *2123*
Molloy, Mary Aloysius. Catholic Church. College of St. Teresa. Franciscan Sisters. Minnesota (Winona). Women. 1903-54. *670*
Molokans. Amish. Doukhobors. Hutterites. Mennonites. North America. ca 1650-1977. *2769*
—. California (San Francisco; Potrero Hill). Ethnicity. Sects, Religious. 1906-76. *2807*
Monasteries. Architecture. Benedictines. Churches. Vatican Council II. 1962-75. *1805*
—. Asia. Catholic Church. Merton, Thomas. Trappists. 1940's-68. *3707*
—. Benedictines. Wimmer, Boniface. 19c. 1960's-70's. *3754*
Monastic observance. Benedictines. Illinois (New Cluny). Immigrants. Missions and Missionaries. Moosmüller, Oswald. 1832-1901. *3816*
Monasticism. Americanization. Benedictines. Germany. Switzerland. 1846-1900. *314*
—. Catholic Church. Contemplative ideal. Merton, Thomas. 1940's-68. *3858*
—. Episcopal Church, Protestant. Huntington, James Otis Sargent. Order of the Holy Cross. Single tax. Social reform. 1878-90. *2430*
Montana *See also* Western States.
—. Baptists. Clergy. Frontier and Pioneer Life. Personal narratives. Spencer, James Hovey. 1888-97. *3095*
—. Catholic Church. Chaplains. Diaries. Fort Keogh. Lindesmith, Eli. 1855-1922. *2679*
—. Chinese Americans. Discrimination. Frontier and Pioneer Life. Public opinion. Supreme courts (state). 1864-1902. *2152*
—. Clergy. Ellis, Edwin M. Presbyterian Church. Sunday schools. Travel. 1870's-1927. *3537*
—. Crittenden, Lyman B. Higher Education. Jackson, Sheldon. McMillan, Duncan M. Presbyterian Church. 1869-1918. *598*
Montana (Deer Lodge Valley). Mormons (Morrisites). 1862-1954. *3927*
Montana, eastern. Clergy. Frontier. Letters. Lutheran Church in America, Norwegian. Thorpe, Christian Scriver. 1906-08. *3295*
Montgomery, Daniel. Clergy. Letters. Methodist Church. Webb, Thomas. 1771. *3490*
Montgomery, John W. (review article). Bible. Evangelicals. Inerrancy (doctrine). Objectivist apologetics. 1972. *2882*
Monuments. Catholic Church. Colonial Government. Discovery and Exploration. France. Jolliet, Louis. Marquette, Jacques. Missions and Missionaries. Mississippi River. 1665-1700. *3767*
Moody, Dwight L. Darby, John Nelson. Evangelical Free Church of America. Franson, Fredrik. Millenarianism. Revivalism. Scandinavian Americans. 1875-95. *2863*
Moody, Samuel. Clergy. Congregationalism. Maine (York). 1700-47. *3137*
Moon, John. Clayton, William. Great Britain. Immigration. Letters. Mormons. 1840. *3925*
Moon, Lottie. Baptists. Georgia (Cartersville). Secondary Education. Women. 1870-1903. *2985*
—. Baptists. Missions and Missionaries. Week of Prayer for Foreign Missions. Woman's Missionary Union. 1888-1979. *1747*
Moon, Sun Myung. Anti-Semitism. Deprogramming. Unification Church. 1946-76. *4269*
—. Authoritarianism. Civil religion. Unification Church. 1970-76. *4264*
—. Unification Church. 1970's. *4258*
Moore, James R. (review article). Darwinism. Great Britain. Protestantism. 1870-1900. *2319*
Moore, Joseph. Earlham College. Evolution. Friends, Society of. Virginia (Richmond). 1861. *2307*
Moore, Julia. Catholic Church. Charities. Education. Ontario (London). Personal narratives. Sisters of St. Joseph. Women. 1868-85. *2517*
Moore, R. Laurence (review article). Science. Spiritualism. 1850-1977. *4290*
Moorhead, James H. Caskey, Marie. Mathews, Donald G. Protestantism (review article). Reform. Walters, Ronald. 1830-80. 1976-78. *2368*
Moorman, Clark Terrell. Cedar Creek Monthly Meeting. Emancipation. Farms. Friends, Society of. Ohio. Virginia (Caroline County). 1766-1814. *2487*
Moosmüller, Oswald. Benedictines. Illinois (New Cluny). Immigrants. Missions and Missionaries. Monastic observance. 1832-1901. *3816*
Moral insanity. Assassination. Gray, John P. New York State Lunatic Asylum. Psychiatry. Trials. 1854-86. *2346*
—. Friends Asylum. Hinchman, Morgan. Mental Illness. Pennsylvania (Philadelphia). Trials. 1847. *1432*
Moral Re-Armament movement. Buchman, Frank. Evangelicalism. New Jersey. Princeton University. 1938. *2858*
Morality *See also* Ethics; Values.
—. Abolition Movement. Christianity. Enlightenment. Nationalism. Phillips, Wendell. 1830-84. *1399*
—. Adler, Samuel. Judaism (Reform). New York City. Theology. ca 1829-91. *4208*
—. Adventists. Elections (mayoral). Gage, William C. Michigan (Battle Creek). 1882. *1255*
—. Alaska. Brady, John Green (and family). Business. Governors. Presbyterian Church. 1878-1906. *3549*
—. Amusements. Georgia. Jones, Sam. Methodist Episcopal Church, South. Revivals. Self-reliance. 1872-1906. *3498*
—. Anglophones. Catholics. Church Discipline. Church History. Francophones. Prairie Provinces. 1900-30. *3715*
—. Anti-Catholicism. Anti-Semitism. Attitudes. Ku Klux Klan. Ohio (Youngstown). Reform. 1920's. *2402*
—. Anti-Catholicism. Arizona. Ku Klux Klan. 1921-25. *2094*
—. Anti-Catholicism. Baptists. Fundamentalism. Norris, J. Frank. Texas. 1920's. *2889*
—. Anti-Communist Movements. Dulles, John Foster. Ecumenism. Oxford Conference (1937). Presbyterian Church. Protestantism. World order movement. 1937-48. *1375*
—. Artisans. Identity. Methodism. Pennsylvania (Philadelphia). Social customs. Work ethic. Working Class. 1820-50. *3479*
—. Association Catholique de la Jeunesse Canadienne-Française. Catholic Church. French Canadians. Quebec. 1903-14. *2355*
—. Atheism. Residence. Theology. Tolerance. Traditionalism. 1958. *159*
—. Baptists. Conservatism. Evangelism. Graham, Billy. 1940's-70's. *2215*
—. Benson, Ezra Taft. Mormons. Political Leadership. Presbyterian Church. Wallace, Henry A. 1933-60. *1303*
—. Bergson, Henri. Historiography. Niebuhr, H. Richard. Troeltsch, Ernst. 1925-37. *255*
—. Boyer, Paul. City Life. Johnson, Paul E. Middle Classes. Missions and Missionaries. New York (Rochester). Revivals. 1815-1920. 1978. *2800*
—. California, northern. Mormons. Sex. Utah (Salt Lake City). Youth. 1967-69. *885*
—. Campbell, Alexander. Disciples of Christ. Educational Reform. Frontier. 1825-1900. *579*
—. Catholic Church. Oklahoma. Politics. Protestant Churches. Referendum. Sabbatarianism. Voting and Voting Behavior. 1959-76. *1290*
—. Christianity. Cults. Jesus People. 1960's-70's. *140*
—. Christianity. Deism. Jefferson, Thomas *(Life and Morals of Jesus of Nazareth)*. Jesus Christ. Russia. Theology. Tolstoy, Leo *(Christ's Christianity)*. 1800-85. *4278*
—. City Politics. Lee, J. Bracken. Mormons. Skousen, W. Cleon. Utah (Salt Lake City). 1956-60. *4006*
—. Civil religion. Government. Myths and Symbols. 1960's-78. *1153*
—. Clergy. Congregations. Sermons. 1970's. *2904*
—. Commission on Training Camp Activities. Jewish Welfare Board. Knights of Columbus. Leisure. Social Reform. War Department. World War I. Young Men's Christian Association. Young Women's Christian Association. 1917-18. *2379*
—. Constitutional Law. Mormons. Polygamy. Religious Liberty. *Reynolds* v. *United States* (US, 1878). Supreme Court. 1862-78. *1024*
—. Democracy. Education. Fundamentalism. Local Politics. Social Change. Vigilantism. 1920's. *2387*
—. Ethnic groups. Family. Government. Religious institutions. 1960's-70's. *899*
—. Franklin, Benjamin. Friendship. Publishers and Publishing. Religious liberty. Whitefield, George. 1739-70. *58*
—. Literature. Social Conditions. 17c-1976. *2037*
—. Mather, Cotton *(Essays to Do Good)*. Puritans. Social Organization. 1700-25. *331*
—. Mather, Cotton *(Magnalia Christi Americana)*. New England. Puritans. Suffering (meaning). 1690's-1702. *3626*
—. Mennonites. North America. Officeholding. Voting and Voting Behavior. 1860-1940. *955*
—. Mormons. Polemics. Polygamy. ca 1860-1900. *823*
—. Mormons. Sex. Social Change. 1820's-90's. *853*
—. Mormons. Sex. Students. 1930's-68. *825*
—. Mormons. Sex. Students. Western States. 1950-72. *927*
—. Presbyterian Church. Republicanism. Revivals. South. 1825-60. *2244*
—. Protestantism. Sex. Women. 1790-1850. *827*
—. Science. Social studies. Teaching. 1977. *2321*
Moravian Archives. Music. Pennsylvania (Bethlehem). 1740-1978. *180*
Moravian Church. Agriculture. Catholic Church. Federal Programs. Friends, Society of. Indian-White Relations. Missions and Missionaries. Old Northwest. 1789-1820. *1529*
—. American Revolution. Civilian Service. Pennsylvania. 1775-1783. *2703*
—. American Revolution. Civilian Service. Pennsylvania (Bethlehem). 1775-83. *2652*
—. American Revolution. Delaware Indians. Indians. Missions and Missionaries. Ohio. Pennsylvania, western. 1775-83. *1532*
—. American Revolution. Dunkards. Friends, Society of. Mennonites. Neutrality. Pacifism. Schwenkfelders. Taxation. 1765-83. *2670*
—. American Revolution. Georgia. Historians. Hymns. Neisser, George. New York. Pennsylvania, eastern. ca 1735-84. *197*
—. American Revolution. Germany. *Heinrich Mullers Pennsylvanischer Staatsbote* (newspaper). Muller, Johann Heinrich. Pennsylvania (Philadelphia). Printing. 1722-82. *3514*
—. Architecture. Pennsylvania (Bethlehem, Nazareth). 1740-68. *1791*
—. Art. Daily life. Pennsylvania (Bethlehem). Social Organization. 1741-1865. *3515*
—. Artifacts. Ceramics. Glass. Worship. 18c-19c. *1879*
—. Artifacts. Rhode Island (Newport). 1767-1835. *3511*
—. Arts and Crafts. Girls. North Carolina. Pennsylvania. Students. 19c. *1862*
—. Dissent. Economic conditions. Military Service. North Carolina (Salem). Slavery. Social change. Women. 1772-1860. *3516*
—. Dunkards. Evangelism. German Americans. Great Awakening. Immigration. Lutheran Church. Northeastern or North Atlantic States. Reformed churches. 1720-60. *2237*
—. Ecumenism. Great Awakening. Presbyterian Church. Tennent, Gilbert. Theology. Zinzendorf, Nikolaus. 1740-41. *2226*
—. Eskimos. Jannasch, Hermann Theodor. Labrador. Missions and Missionaries. 1855-1931. *1594*

—. Fort Duquesne. Frontier and Pioneer Life. Indian-White Relations. Pennsylvania. Post, Christian Frederick. 1758-59. *1505*
—. Land. Pennsylvania (Nazareth). Settlement. Whitefield House. 1740-1978. *3517*
—. Maine (Waldoboro). Missions and Missionaries. Soelle, Georg. 1762-70. *3512*
—. New Jersey (Oldman's Creek). 1743-1800. *3513*
Moravian (newspaper). Materialism. Nationalism. Pennsylvania (Bethlehem). Slavery. 1850-76. *3518*
More, Thomas. Authors. Catholic Church. Walter, William Joseph. 1820's-46. *2049*
—. Catholic Church. Colet, John. Episcopal Church, Protestant. Erasmus, Desiderius. Hermeneutics. 1500-1975. *3167*
More, Thomas *(Utopia).* Humanism. Indians. Rhode Island (Narragansett). Utopias. Williams, Roger *(A Key into the Language of America).* 1640's. *2938*
Moreton, Andrew. *See* Defoe, Daniel.
Morgan, Richard E. (review article). Supreme Court. 1972-74. *1023*
Morgan, William. Anti-Masonic movement. Baptists. Freemasonry. New York, western. 1826-30. *2362*
Morison, Samuel Eliot (obituary). Bibliographies. Discovery and Exploration. Historians. Puritans. 1887-1976. *233*
—. Historians. *New England Quarterly* (periodical). Puritans. 1928-76. *276*
—. Historiography. Puritans. 1887-1976. *172*
Mormon Battalion. Mexican War. 1846. *2667*
Mormon, Book of. American Revolution. Mormons. Political attitudes. Smith, Joseph. 1820's. *1353*
—. Congregationalism. Spalding, Solomon. 1761-1816. *2796*
Mormon Church (Historian's Office). Archival catalogs and inventories. Jenson, Andrew. Manuscripts. 1830-1975. *193*
Mormon Genealogical Society. Genealogy. Libraries. 1607-1850. 1975. *201*
Mormon history. 1945-74. *196*
—. Manuscripts. 1823-1974. *3934*
—. Ritualization. Utah. 1830-1975. *3942*
Mormon Temple. Bossard, Gisbert. Florence, Max. Photography. Smith, Joseph Fielding. Utah (Salt Lake City). 1911. *1762*
Mormon Volunteers. Armies. California. Mexican War. Military Recruitment. 1847-48. *2707*
Mormonism. Bibliographies. 19c-1974. *3967*
—. Excommunication. Godbe, William Samuel. Schisms. 1840's-80's. *4047*
Mormons. 1820-1977. *4017*
—. Aaronic Order. Glendenning, Maurice L. Middle classes. Millenarianism. Utah. 1930-79. *3933*
—. Abel, Elijah. Clergy. Negroes. ca 1830-79. *3944*
—. Advertising. Men. Patent medicines. Stereotypes. Virility. 1884-1931. *819*
—. Age. Birth rate. Marriage. Women. 1800-69. *892*
—. Agriculture. Idaho. Settlement. Snake River. 1880-1914. *3940*
—. Agriculture. Indians. Nevada. Utah. 1847-60. *4037*
—. American Revolution. Mormon, Book of. Political attitudes. Smith, Joseph. 1820's. *1353*
—. Amish. Land use. Mennonites. Pennsylvania (Intercourse). Theology. Utah (Escalante). 1973. *2767*
—. Anarchism and Anarchists. Church and State. Lum, Dyer D. 1880's. *4010*
—. Anderson, George Edward. Photography. Utah, southern. 1877-1928. *3970*
—. Animal magnetism. Hypnotism. Mesmerism. 19c. *2303*
—. Annexation. Church and state. Idaho, southern. Legislation. Nevada. Stewart, William. Suffrage. 1887-88. *1089*
—. Anthropology. Archaeology. Indians. Lost Tribes of Israel. Smith, Joseph. 1830. *2335*
—. Anti-Bigamy Act (US, 1862). Wealth. Young, Brigham. 1847-77. *341*
—. Apocalypse. Folklore. 19c-20c. *4021*
—. Appleby, William. Calligraphy. Simmons, Joseph M. Young, Brigham. 1851-53. *1895*
—. Archaeology. 1958-73. *206*
—. Archaeology. Engraving. Fraud. Mexico (Guerrero). Padilla Gold Plates. 1952-78. *4007*
—. Archaeology. Migration. ca 2000 BC-ca 200. 1973. *3949*
—. Architects. Churches. Folsom, William Harrison. Utah (Provo, Salt Lake City). ca 1850's-1901. *1757*
—. Architecture. Churches. Utah. 1847-1929. *1817*
—. Architecture. City Planning. Smith, Joseph. Western states. 1833-90. *1767*
—. Architecture. City Planning. Utah. 1847-1975. *1781*
—. Architecture. Frontier. ca 1850-56. *1836*
—. Architecture. Illinois (Nauvoo). Temples. Utah. Weeks, William. 1840's-1900. *1758*
—. Architecture, folk. Stone buildings. Utah (Beaver City). 1855-1975. *1812*
—. Architecture (Scandinavian). City Planning. Country Life. Utah (Spring City). 1851-1975. *1816*
—. Archives. Libraries. Utah (Salt Lake City). 1830-1970's. *194*
—. Archko collection. Forgeries. Jesus Christ. Mahan, William D. Presbyterian Church (Cumberland). Wallace, Lew *(Ben-Hur).* 1880's. *3928*
—. Arizona. Baptists. Catholic Church. Episcopal Church, Protestant. Methodism. Missions and Missionaries. Presbyterian Church. 1859-99. *1501*
—. Arizona. Barth, Solomon. Converts. Frontier. Jews. 1856-1928. *60*
—. Arizona. Edmunds Act (US, 1882). Federal government. Polygamy. 1880's. *1000*
—. Arizona (Coconino County). Frontier. Immigrants. Schools. 1875-1900. *510*
—. Arizona (Short Creek). Church and state. Polygamy. Utah. 1953. *1076*
—. Arkansas. Brough, Charles Hillman. Historians. 1890-1915. *224*
—. Arrington, Leonard J. Grey, Zane *(Riders of the Purple Sage).* Haupt, Jon. Mormons. 1912. 1970's. *2076*
—. Arrington, Leonard J. Grey, Zane *(Riders of the Purple Sage).* Haupt, Jon. Mormons. 1912. 1970's. *2076*
—. Arrington, Leonard J. Historiography. Personal Narratives. Western states. 20c. *171*
—. Arrington, Leonard J. (tribute). Bibliographies. Historiography. 1917-79. *277*
—. Assassination. Hill, Marvin S. Illinois (Carthage). Oaks, Dallin H. Smith, Joseph. Trials (review article). 1844. 1977. *2126*
—. Atheism. Freedom of Speech. *Lucifer's Lantern* (periodical). Polygamy. Schroeder, Theodore. Utah. 1889-1900. *2125*
—. Attitudes. Bradford family. Letters. Missouri. Virginia. 1838-39. *4057*
—. Attitudes. Social Organization. Utah. Women. Young, Brigham. 1840's-77. *830*
—. Authority. Latin America. Missions and Missionaries. Nationalism. 1975-80. *1753*
—. Autobiography. Frontier and Pioneer Life. 19c. *2040*
—. Baldwin, Nathaniel. Fundamentalism. Inventions. Polygamy. Radio. Utah. 1900's-61. *4036*
—. Banking. Dissent. Ohio (Kirtland). 1837-90. *3980*
—. Baptism. Illinois (Nauvoo). Theology. 1830-43. *4028*
—. Barrett, Gwynn. Gibson, Walter Murray. Hawaii (Lanai). Historiography. 1859-64. 1972-78. *3945*
—. Bartholow, Roberts. Medical reports. Physiology. Polygamy. Utah. Vollum, E. P. 1850-75. *1430*
—. Benson, Ezra Taft. Morality. Political Leadership. Presbyterian Church. Wallace, Henry A. 1933-60. *1303*
—. Bible. History. Israel. Smith, Joseph Fielding. Snell, Heber C. Theology. 1937-52. *4035*
—. Bible. Theology. 1830-1900. *4013*
—. Bibliographies. 1976. *3969*
—. Bibliographies. 1977. *3966*
—. Bibliographies. 19c-1973. *4019*
—. Bibliographies. 19c-1975. *3968*
—. Bibliographies. 19c-20c. 1974-78. *4040*
—. Bibliographies. Dissertations. Theses. 19c-1977. *4041*
—. Bibliographies. Historiography. Settlement. Utah. 1840-1976. *4046*
—. Bibliographies. Newspapers. 1977. *4042*
—. Bidamon, Emma Smith. Bidamon, Lewis C. Illinois (Nauvoo). Marriage. Women. 1842-80. *3931*
—. Bidamon, Emma Smith. Illinois (Nauvoo). Property. Schisms. Smith, Joseph. Women. Women. Young, Brigham. 1832-79. *3932*
—. Birth control. Values. 19c-20c. *818*
—. Bosom serpentry (concept). Folklore. New England. Puritans. Snakes. Utah. 17c-19c. *2765*
—. Boys. Illinois (Nauvoo). Police protection. Whistling and Whittling Brigade. 1845. *4014*
—. Brigham Young University. Centennial Celebrations. Colleges and Universities. Utah. 1876-1976. *783*
—. Brigham Young University. Education. Utah (Provo). 1831-1970's. *588*
—. Brigham Young University. Educators. Germany. Maeser, Karl G. 1828-56. 1876. *768*
—. Brigham Young University. Fundamentalism. Students. Utah (Provo). 1935-73. *606*
—. Brigham Young University Library. Genealogy. Immigration studies. Utah (Provo). 1830-1978. *236*
—. British Columbia (Vancouver Island). Converts. Immigration. Missions and Missionaries. 1875-1979. *1669*
—. Brodie, Fawn *(No Man Knows My History).* Historiography. Smith, Joseph. 19c. 1945-73. *3983*
—. Brúnum, Eiríkur á. Iceland. Laxness, Halldór *(Paradise Reclaimed).* Novels. 1870-1900. 1960. *2075*
—. Buchanan, James. Church and state. Federal Policy. Historiography. Military. Utah. 1857-58. *1073*
—. Burton, Richard *(City of the Saints).* Travel Accounts. Utah. 1860-61. *4052*
—. Business. Depressions. Grant, Heber J. Utah. 1893. *375*
—. Business. Ethics. Theology. Watergate scandal. 1974. *995*
—. California, northern. Morality. Sex. Utah (Salt Lake City). Youth. 1967-69. *885*
—. Calomel. Medicine (practice of). Thomson, Samuel. 1793-1865. *1438*
—. Canada. Cholera. Epidemics. USA. 1832-83. *1437*
—. Cannon, Martha Hughes. Great Britain. Letters. Polygamy. Utah (Salt Lake City). Women. 1885-96. *4002*
—. Capital punishment. Theology. Utah. 1843-1978. *3971*
—. Cartoons and Caricatures. *Puck* (periodical). Stereotypes. 1904-07. *2001*
—. Cartoons and Caricatures. Stereotypes. Women. 1830-1914. *800*
—. Chambers, Samuel D. (testimonies). Converts. Negroes. Slavery. Utah (Salt Lake City). 1844-76. *4059*
—. Charities. 1837-1978. *2506*
—. Charities. Poor. Utah. 1850-1930's. *2501*
—. Chase, Josephine Streeper. Daily life. Diaries. Utah (Centerville). Women. 1881-94. *3957*
—. Church and state. County Government. Judicial Administration. Partisanship. Probate courts. Utah. 1855-72. *1039*
—. Church and state. Cowley, Matthias F. Polygamy. Smoot, Reed. Taylor, John W. Theology. Woodruff Manifesto. 1890-1911. *1060*
—. Church and state. Lobbying. Statehood. Trumbo, Isaac. Utah. 1887-96. *1072*
—. Church Schools. Colleges and Universities. Utah (Salt Lake City). Young University. 1876-94. *734*
—. Cities. Historiography. Social change. Utah. 1849-1970's. *4008*
—. City charters. Illinois (Nauvoo). 1839-41. *3995*
—. City planning. Illinois (Nauvoo). 1840's. *3959*
—. City Planning. Settlement. Smith, Joseph. Western states. 19c. *3988*
—. City Politics. Lee, J. Bracken. Morality. Skousen, W. Cleon. Utah (Salt Lake City). 1956-60. *4006*
—. Civil disobedience. Clawson, Rudger. Federal government. Polygamy. Sharp, John. Utah. 1862-91. *996*
—. Civil-Military Relations. Fort Rawlins. Provo Outrage. Utah. 1870-71. *4000*
—. Clayton, William. Great Britain. Immigration. Letters. Moon, John. 1840. *3925*
—. Clayton, William. Great Britain (Manchester). Illinois (Nauvoo). Immigration. Letters. 1840. *3924*
—. Clergy. Integration. Kimball, Spencer W. Negroes. Revelation. 1950-78. *4051*
—. Coe, Truman. Letters. Ohio (Kirtland). Presbyterians. 1836. *2718*
—. Colleges and Universities. Presbyterian Church. Utah (Salt Lake City). Westminster College. 1875-1913. *559*

—. Colonization. Hawaii (Lanai). Missions and Missionaries. 1850's. *1684*
—. Competition. Economic Growth. Utah (southern). 500-1979. *4038*
—. Congregationalism. Evangelism. Far Western States. Nutting, John Danforth. Photographs. Utah Gospel Mission. 1900-50. *1560*
—. Congregationalism. Family. Methodism. New England. New York, western. Young, Brigham. 18c-1830's. *2840*
—. Congress. Hayes, Rutherford B. Polygamy. Suffrage. Women. 1877-81. *797*
—. Constitutional Amendments (21st). Prohibition (repeal). Utah. 1932-33. *2587*
—. Constitutional Law. Morality. Polygamy. Religious Liberty. *Reynolds* v. *United States* (US, 1878). Supreme Court. 1862-78. *1024*
—. Constitutions. Smith, Joseph. Speeches, Addresses, etc. 1840. *1374*
—. Converts. Immigration. Ross, James. Scotland. 1842-1900. *4011*
—. Converts. Letters. Missouri. Ostracism. Partridge, Edward. 1837. *3989*
—. Converts. Scandinavian Americans. Young, Kimball. 1893-1972. *3979*
—. Cooperatives. Idaho (Paris). Rural Settlements. 1869-96. *360*
—. Coray, Howard. Leadership. Personal narratives. Smith, Joseph. 1840's. *3990*
—. Culture. Organizations. Pioneers. Utah. 1850's-70's. *523*
—. Daily life. Diaries. Illinois (Nauvoo). Jacobs, Zina Diantha Huntington. Women. 1844-45. *3935*
—. *Daily Union Vedette* (newspaper). Fort Douglas. Utah. 1863-67. *4020*
—. Dalton, Edward Meeks. Edmunds Act (US, 1882). Polygamy. Utah. 1852-86. *1028*
—. Dance. Utah. 1830-80. *3984*
—. Dean, Joseph Harry. Gibson, Walter Murray. Hawaii. Missions and Missionaries. Samoa. 1860's-90. *1683*
—. Decker, Mahonri M. Hymns. Utah (Parowan). 1919. *1921*
—. Deity. Illinois (Nauvoo). Sermons. Smith, Joseph (King Follett Discourse). Theology. 1844. *3976*
—. Diaries. Fielding, Joseph. Illinois (Nauvoo). 1844-46. *3958*
—. Diaries. Grant, Jedediah Morgan. Missions and Missionaries. 1833-57. *1631*
—. Diaries. Illinois (Nauvoo). Laub, George. Smith, Joseph. Young, Brigham. 1845-46. *3961*
—. Diaries. Illinois (Nauvoo). Snow, Eliza Roxey. Women. 1842-44. *4044*
—. Diaries. Musser, Elise Furer. Political Leadership. Social Reform. Utah. Women. 1897-1967. *811*
—. Diaries. Woodruff, Wilford. 1830-1906. *3923*
—. Disfranchisement. Federal government. State Legislatures. Suffrage. 1882-92. *1046*
—. Divorce. Polygamy. Utah. 1844-90. *822*
—. Dwellings. Jacobsen, Florence S. Personal narratives. Restorations. Utah (St. George). Young, Brigham. 19c. 1970's. *1789*
—. Dwellings. Utah (Salt Lake City). Young, Amelia Folsom. Young, Brigham. 1863-1926. *1785*
—. Dye, Alexander V. Mexico (Sonora). Revolution. Settlement. 1912. *4016*
—. Economic Conditions. Ohio (Kirtland). Smith, Joseph. 1830's. *351*
—. Economic Conditions. Polygamy. Railroads. Salt Lake and Fort Douglas Railroad. Statehood. Utah. Young, John W. 1883-1924. *3993*
—. Economic Conditions. United Order. ca 1870's-90's. *2565*
—. Economic growth. Illinois (Nauvoo). Mississippi River. Steamboats. 1839-46. *367*
—. Editors and Editing. Utah. *Woman's Exponent* (periodical). Women. 1872-1914. *3937*
—. Edmunds Act (US, 1882). Polygamy. Prisons. Utah. 1880's. *1004*
—. Education. Religious education. Utah. 1890-1929. *735*
—. Education. Theology. Universe. 1830-75. *3977*
—. Elections. Labor. Law. Railroads. Utah (Ogden). 1869-70. *1262*
—. Elections. Lee, J. Bracken. State Government. Utah. 1944-56. *1274*
—. Elections. Liberal Party. Nevada. Utah. 1860-70. *1252*
—. Emmett, James Simpson. Friendship. Grey, Zane. Novels (western). Utah. 1907. *2072*
—. Equality. Lincoln, Abraham. Polygamy. Slavery. Smith, Joseph. 1840-64. *986*
—. Exiles. Letters. Polygamy. Utah. Woodruff, Emma Smith. Woodruff, Wilford. 1885. *1050*
—. Family. Illinois (Nauvoo). New York. Young, Brigham. 1824-45. *861*
—. Family. Land. Pioneer life. Utah (Kanab). 1874-80. *4009*
—. Federal government. Utah. Westward Movement. 1846-50's. *4034*
—. Feminism. National Women's Conference, 1st. Utah Women's Conference. Women. 1977. *858*
—. Fertility. Marriage. 1820-1920. *924*
—. Fertility. Migration. -1974. *912*
—. Fertility. Polygamy. 19c. *926*
—. Fiction. Regionalism. 1930-50. *2026*
—. Fillmore, Millard. Territorial government. Utah. 1850-53. *1053*
—. Films. 1911-70's. *1875*
—. Finance. Railroads. Tourism. Utah. Young, John W. 1867-91. *332*
—. Firearms. 1830's-1869. *2651*
—. Fisher, Vardis. Literature. 1915-68. *1999*
—. Folklore. Methodology. 1892-1970's. *4055*
—. Folklore. Murder. Smith, Joseph. 1659-1900. *4022*
—. Folklore. Oral tradition. 19c-20c. *4054*
—. Folklore. Polygamy. Scandinavian Americans. Temples. Utah (Sanpete-Sevier area). 1849-1979. *4053*
—. Folklore. Settlement. Utah (Great Salt Lake valley). Young, Brigham. 1842-1970's. *4023*
—. Folklore. Vanishing hitchhiker (theme). 1933-74. *4056*
—. Fort Bridger. Mountain men. Utah. 1847-57. *3975*
—. Friendship. Kimball, Heber C. Utah. Young, Brigham. 1829-68. *3996*
—. Frontier and Pioneer Life. Heywood, Martha Spence. Intellectuals. King, Hannah Tapfield. Snow, Eliza Roxey. Utah. Women. 1850-70. *4045*
—. Fund raising. Hyde, Orson. Illinois (Nauvoo). Northeastern or North Atlantic States. Tabernacle project. 1845-46. *4048*
—. Galland, Isaac. Iowa (Lee County). Land. Smith, Joseph. Speculation. 1830's-58. *3950*
—. Gates, Susa Young. Marriage. Personal narratives. Utah. Women. Young, Brigham. Young, Lucy Bigelow. 1830-1905. *3972*
—. Genealogical Society of Utah. Research. Utah. 1894-1976. *246*
—. Genealogy. Missions and Missionaries. Utah. 1885-1900. *1525*
—. Grant, Heber J. Letters. Recreation. Smith, Joseph Fielding. 1930's. *3954*
—. Great Britain. Immigrants. Landscape Painting. Piercy, Frederick *(Illustrated Route).* Portraits. Travel guides. Western states. 1848-57. *1869*
—. Great Britain. Letters. Richards, Willard. Young, Brigham. 1840. *1754*
—. Great Britain. Missions and Missionaries. Working class. 1840-41. *1672*
—. Great Plains. Indian-White Relations. New York, western. Utah. Young, Brigham. 1835-51. *3948*
—. Health. Lifestyles. ca 1930-79. *1448*
—. Herbs. Medicine (practice of). Physicians. 1820-1979. *1459*
—. Heresy. Pratt, Orson. Revelation. Young, Brigham. 1853-68. *3938*
—. Historians. Letters. Schisms. Wight, Lyman. Woodruff, Wilford. 1857-58. *4049*
—. Historiography. 1973. *191*
—. Historiography. Hunter, Howard W. Jenson, Andrew. Lund, A. William. Lyon, T. Edgar. Roberts, Brigham Henry. 1913-70. *226*
—. Historiography. Manuscripts. Research. Young, Brigham. 19c-1978. *192*
—. Historiography. Stereotypes. Women. 19c. 1976. *796*
—. Historiography. Young, Brigham. 1801-77. 1977. *4015*
—. Humor. Illustration. Novels. Periodicals. 1850-60. *2004*
—. Hymns. Smith, Emma. 1835. *1953*
—. Idaho. Political Attitudes. Voting and Voting Behavior. 1880's. *1273*
—. Idaho (Cassia County). Settlement. 1873-1921. *3930*
—. Identity. Utah. Westward Movement. 1846-69. *3999*
—. Illinois (Nauvoo). 1842-46. *3974*
—. Illinois (Nauvoo). Jones, Dan. *Maid of Iowa* (vessel). Smith, Joseph. Steamboats. 1843-45. *346*
—. Illinois (Nauvoo). Kimball, Heber C. (and family). 1839-46. *3997*
—. Illinois (Nauvoo). Kimball, Vilate. Letters. Murder. Smith, Joseph. Women. 1844. *3963*
—. Illinois (Nauvoo). Lyon, T. Edgar. Oral history. Smith, Hyrum. Smith, Joseph. 1840's-1978. *4005*
—. Illinois (Nauvoo). Religiosity. Social stability. 1833-46. *3981*
—. Illinois (Nauvoo). Rites and Ceremonies. Smith, Joseph. Temples. 1841-45. *1766*
—. Illinois (Nauvoo). Sermons. Smith, Joseph (King Follett Discourse). Theology. 1844-1978. *3947*
—. Illinois (Nauvoo). Theology. 1839-46. *4004*
—. Income. Utah. Wealth. 1857. *2625*
—. Iowa (Lee County). Settlement. Young, Brigham. 1838-46. *3998*
—. Irrigation. Social Change. Utah. 1840-1900. *329*
—. Japan. Missions and Missionaries. 1901-24. *1681*
—. Jesus People. Protestant Churches. Restitutionism. Revivals. 19c-20c. *2744*
—. Kimball, Edward L. Kimball, Spencer W. Personal narratives. 1943-78. *3994*
—. Kimball, Sarah Melissa Granger. Suffrage. Utah. Women. 15th Ward Relief Society. 1818-98. *901*
—. Knight, Joseph, Sr. Manuscripts. Smith, Joseph. 1772-1847. *3991*
—. Labor Unions and Organizations. Utah. 1850-96. *1467*
—. Lake Michigan. Michigan (Beaver Island). Strang, James Jesse. Utopias. Wisconsin (Voree). 1820-56. *433*
—. Lambdin, William. Rare Books. Smith, Joseph *(Book of Commandments).* West Virginia (Wheeling). 1830-33. *2124*
—. Landownership. Utah. 1847-69. *4003*
—. Law. Leadership. Polygamy. Utah. 1890-1905. *824*
—. Law. Tobacco. Utah. 1896-1923. *2442*
—. Leadership. Poetry. Prophecy. Snow, Eliza Roxey. Utah. Women. 1804-87. *3936*
—. Leadership. Utah. Young, Brigham. 1801-77. *1206*
—. Leadership. Utah. Young, Brigham. 1840's-77. *3960*
—. League of Nations. Prohibition. Republican Party. Roberts, Brigham Henry. Smith, Joseph Fielding. Suffrage. Utah. Women. ca 1900. *1284*
—. Lectures of Faith. Theology. 1834-1921. *3973*
—. Lee, John Doyle. Mountain Meadows Massacre. Utah. 1857-77. *4043*
—. Leonard, Truman. Utah (Davis County). 1820-97. *4001*
—. Letters. Miller, George. Smith, Joseph. 1842. *3952*
—. Letters. New York. Reformed Dutch Church. Willers, Diedrich. 1830. *2766*
—. Liberal Institute. Social Reform. Spiritualism. Utah (Salt Lake City). 1869-84. *4296*
—. Literary movement, regional. Novels. Utah. 1940's. *2025*
—. Lyon, T. Edgar (obituary). 19c-20c. *283*
—. Mass media. 1970's. *1960*
—. Mathematics. Pratt, Orson. Utah. ca 1836-70. *2318*
—. McLean, Eleanor. McLean, Hector. Murder. Pratt, Parley P. Women. 1841-57. *4025*
—. Medicine, practice of. Young, Brigham. ca 1840-75. *1463*
—. Mennonites. Sects, Religious. ca 19c-20c. *32*
—. Mexico (Mexico City). Missions. Pratt, Rey I. 1906-24. *1677*
—. Mines. Utah (Salt Lake City). 1863-1979. *4033*
—. Mining camps. Nevada (Panaca). Social Customs. ca 1860-80. *3929*
—. Missions and Missionaries. 1855-20c. *1552*
—. Missions and Missionaries. 1949-80. *1715*
—. Missions and Missionaries. Modernization. Pacific, South. 1955-80. *1682*
—. Missouri (Caldwell, Jackson counties). Negroes. Social Problems. 1830-39. *4030*
—. Morality. Polemics. Polygamy. ca 1860-1900. *823*
—. Morality. Sex. Social Change. 1820's-90's. *853*
—. Morality. Sex. Students. 1930's-68. *825*

—. Morality. Sex. Students. Western States. 1950-72. *927*
—. Morris, Joseph. Schisms. Utah (Weber River). War. Young, Brigham. 1861-62. *3926*
—. Morrisite War. Utah. 1862. *3986*
—. National Education Association. Public schools. Sinclair, Upton. Teachers. Utah. 1920-24. *567*
—. Negroes. Priesthood. 1978-79. *3946*
—. Negroes. Priesthood. Utah. 1844-52. *2137*
—. Negroes. Priesthood. Young, Brigham. 1843-52. *3955*
—. Negroes. Race Relations. Theology. 1831-1973. *4058*
—. Negroes. Social Theory. Strang, James Jesse. Thompson, Charles B. 1844-73. *2138*
—. Nevada. Smith, Joseph. Utah. Voting and Voting Behavior. Young, Brigham. 1835-50's. *1251*
—. Nevada (Muddy River Valley). Settlement. 1865-75. *3953*
—. Newspapers. Periodicals. Public Opinion. 1970's. *2071*
—. O'Dea, Thomas F. Scholarship. 1957-74. *4012*
—. Oneida Community. Sex roles. Shakers. Utopias. Women. ca 1825-90. *842*
—. Pacifism. Spanish-American War. Young, Brigham, Jr. ca 1840-98. *2682*
—. Paddock, Algernon Sidney. Polygamy. Utah Commission. 1882-86. *1117*
—. Philanthropy. Settlement. Smart, William Henry. Utah (Uinta Basin). 1862-1937. *4031*
—. Phrenology. 1842-1940. *2298*
—. Pioneer life. Travel. Utah. Young, Brigham. 1850-77. *3987*
—. Politics. Utah (Weber County; Ogden). 1850-1924. *1324*
—. Polygamy. 1842. *839*
—. Population. 19c. 1978. *794*
—. Pratt, Orson (confession). Theology. 1860. *4024*
—. Prayer circles. 1829-1978. *4026*
—. Priesthood (Aaronic). 1851-83. *3978*
—. Priesthood-Auxiliary movement. 1928-38. *3955*
—. Princeton University Library. Smith, Joseph (*Book of Commandments*). 1820-1975. *3956*
—. Prohibition. Utah. 1900's-1910's. *2592*
—. Public Opinion. Railroads. Train, George Francis. Utah. Young, Brigham. 1860's-70's. *3939*
—. Radio. Television. 1922-77. *347*
—. Russia. 1857-72. *3965*
—. Scandinavian Americans. Utah. ca 1873-1900. *3943*
—. Schisms. 1840-1978. *3922*
—. Silk industry. Utah. Women. 1855-1905. *328*
—. Smith, Joseph. Succession. Young, Brigham. 1834-44. *4027*
—. Smith, Joseph. Theology. ca 1800-44. *3982*
—. Snow, Eliza Roxey. Women. 1830-90. *900*
—. Social change. Utah. 1830-1974. *4018*
—. South. Violence. 1884-1905. *2127*
—. Speeches, Addresses, etc. Utah. 1776-1976. *1103*
—. Staines, William C. Utah. 1818-81. *3964*
—. Statehood. Suffrage. Utah. Women. 1867-96. *798*
—. Stewart, Levi. United Order. Utah (Kanab). Young, Brigham. Young, John R. 1874-84. *4029*
—. Suffrage. Utah. Women. 1895. *944*
—. Temples. Utah (Logan). 1850-1900. *1759*
—. Theology. 19c-1973. *4039*
—. Utah. Watt, George D. 1840's-81. *4050*
—. Young, Brigham. 1832-75. *3992*
Mormons (Danites). Hangings. Hodges, Stephen. Hodges, William. Iowa. Murder. 1845. *3985*
Mormons (Morrisites). Montana (Deer Lodge Valley). 1862-1954. *3927*
Mormons (Reorganized). Bennet, James Arlington. Letters. 1840's-60. *3951*
—. Clergy. Equality. Negroes. Schisms. Women. 1860-1979. *4032*
Morocco. Immigration. Jews. Quebec (Montreal). 1960's-70's. *4121*
Morocco (Tangiers). Gospel Missionary Union of Kansas. Missions and Missionaries. 1895-1905. *1736*
Morris, Adelaide Kirby. Brophy, Robert J. Jeffers, Robinson. Poetry. Stevens, Wallace. Theology (review article). 20c. *2065*
Morris, John. Bishops. Catholic Church. Farrelly, John P. Irish Americans. Stritch, Samuel A. Tennessee. 19c-1958. *3860*
Morris, Joseph. Mormons. Schisms. Utah (Weber River). War. Young, Brigham. 1861-62. *3926*
Morris, William. Church of England. Ontario (Kingston). Presbyterians. Queen's College. 1836-42. *711*
Morrisite War. Mormons. Utah. 1862. *3986*
Morrison, Charles C. *Christian Century* (periodical). Foreign policy. Japan. Manchurian crisis. 1931-33. *2678*
Morristown Female Charitable Society. Charities. Law. New Jersey. Presbyterian Church. Women. 1813-1978. *2510*
Morton, Thomas. Historiography. Massachusetts. Merry Mount incident. Pilgrims. 1625-1970's. *2050*
—. Indians. Massachusetts. Pilgrims. Puritans. Values. 1625-45. *2956*
Moses Montefiore Mutual Aid Society. Delaware (Wilmington). Jews. 1850-90. *4101*
Moslems *See also* Islam.
—. American Board of Commissioners for Foreign Missions. Arabic. Bible. Missions and Missionaries. Protestantism. Translating and Interpreting. 1843-60. *1740*
Mosquera, Manuel José. Bishops. Catholic Church. Colombia (Bogotá). Hughes, John. Letters. New York City. 1853. *3762*
Mott, Lucretia Coffin. American Anti-Slavery Society. Female Anti-Slavery Society. Foster, Abigail Kelley. Fox, George. Friends, Society of. Segregation. 17c. 1837-66. *791*
Mount Admirabilis (academy). Cardome (home). Catholic Church. Education. Kentucky (Scott County; Georgetown). Sisters of the Visitation. 1875-1975. *600*
Mount Bethel Baptist Church. Baptists. Ebenezer Methodist Church. Inscriptions. Methodist Church. South Carolina (Anderson County). Tombstones. 1856-1978. *2848*
Mount Holyoke College. Attitudes. Dickinson, Emily. Evangelicalism. Friendship. 1848-50. *2827*
—. Colleges and Universities. Curricula. Massachusetts (South Hadley). Science. Women. 1839-88. *2320*
—. Colleges and Universities. Emerson, Joseph. Lyon, Mary. Protestantism. Women. 1760's-1850's. *552*
Mount St. Mary Convent. Catholic Church. Church Schools. Girls. McDonough, Madrienne C. New Hampshire (Manchester). Personal narratives. 1902-09. *692*
Mountain Meadows Massacre. Lee, John Doyle. Mormons. Utah. 1857-77. *4043*
Mountain Men. California. Catholic Church. Protestantism. Rogers, Harrison. Smith, Jedediah Strong. 1826-27. *2798*
—. Fort Bridger. Mormons. Utah. 1847-57. *3975*
Mountaineers. Music. Revivals. South. 1798-1970. *1935*
Mourning (theme). Allegory. Art. Folwell, Samuel (*Sacred to the Illustrious Washington*). Painting. Protestantism. ca 1800. *1885*
Movies. *See* Films.
Moving Star Hall. Negroes. Protestantism. South Carolina (Johns Island). 18c-1970. *2830*
Mudge, Enoch. Massachusetts (Boston, New Bedford). Methodist Church. Seamen's Bethel. Taylor, Edward Thompson. 1776-1850. *3457*
Muelder, W. G. Baptists. King, Martin Luther, Jr. Nonviolence. Personalism. Theology. Tillich, Paul. Wieman, Henry Nelson. 1955-68. *2552*
Mueller, Peter. Concordia Seminary. Daily Life. Kansas (Clay Center). Lutheran Church (Missouri Synod). Seminaries. Students. 1883-89. *707*
Muhlenberg, Augustus. Charities. Cities. Evangelism. Politics. Protestantism (review article). Social Problems. 1812-1900. *2930*
Muhlenberg, Henry Melchior. Assimilation. Lutheran Church. Pennsylvania. Politics. Swedish Americans. Wrangel, Carl Magnus. 1749-69. *1283*
—. Clergy. Diaries. Lutheran Church. Pennsylvania. Women. 1742-87. *828*
—. Clergy. Lutheran Church. Pennsylvania. Pietism. 18c. *3337*
Muhlenberg, John Peter Gabriel. Church of England. Clergy. Virginia (Dunmore County). 1772-76. *3221*
Muir, John. Calvinism. Literature. Romanticism. 1838-1914. *2929*
Muirson, George. Church of England. Connecticut. Letters. Missions and Missionaries. New York. ca 1697-1708. *1535*
Mullaly, John. Catholic Church. Civil War. Copperheads. Editors and Editing. *Metropolitan Record* (newspaper). New York City. 1861-64. *1234*
Müller, Johan Peter. Baptists (Seventh-Day). Communalism. Letters. Pennsylvania (Ephrata). Social Conditions. 1743. *428*
Muller, Johann Heinrich. American Revolution. Germany. *Heinrich Mullers Pennsylvanischer Staatsbote* (newspaper). Moravian Church. Pennsylvania (Philadelphia). Printing. 1722-82. *3514*
Mullins, Edgar Young. Baptists, Southern. Fraternal Address. Theology. 1919-20. *2995*
—. Baptists, Southern. Fundamentalism. Graves, James Robinson. Landmark Movement. Modernism. Theology. 1840-1928. *3058*
—. Baptists, Southern. Theology. 1860-1928. *3009*
Mullock, John Thomas. Catholic Church. Feild, Edward. Irish Canadians. Newfoundland. Politics. Protestant Churches. 19c. *1254*
Mumaw, George Shaum. Indiana. Mennonites. Ohio. Personal narratives. Singing Schools. 1900-57. *1941*
Munch, Johan Storm. Clergy. Ecumenism. Lutheran Church (Missouri Synod, Norwegian). Norway. Wisconsin (Wiota). 1827-1908. *3324*
Muncy, Raymond Lee. Communalism (review article). Fellman, Michael. Marriage. Sex. Social Organization. 19c. 1973. *384*
Mundelein, George. Catholic Church. Clergy. Germany. Nazism. 1937. *1256*
Murder *See also* Assassination; Capital Punishment.
—. Anti-Catholicism. Cheverus, Jean Louis Lefebvre de. Irish Americans. Lyon, Marcus. Massachusetts (Northampton). Protestantism. Trials. 1805-06. *2099*
—. Choctaw Indians. Congregationalism. Harkins, Richard. Missions and Missionaries. Slavery. 1858-59. *3132*
—. Christianity. Converts. Idaho. Orchard, Harry. 1899-1906. *2760*
—. Country Life. Negroes. South. Whites. 1916-20. *156*
—. Folklore. Mormons. Smith, Joseph. 1659-1900. *4022*
—. Hangings. Hodges, Stephen. Hodges, William. Iowa. Mormons (Danites). 1845. *3985*
—. Illinois (Nauvoo). Kimball, Vilate. Letters. Mormons. Smith, Joseph. Women. 1844. *3963*
—. McLean, Eleanor. McLean, Hector. Mormons. Pratt, Parley P. Women. 1841-57. *4025*
Murdock, Kenneth Ballard (obituary). Literature. Puritans. 20c. *225*
Murray, Hugh T., Jr. Civil Rights movement. Discrimination. Florida (Miami). Louisiana (New Orleans). Personal narratives. Tulane Interfaith Council. 1959-60. *2548*
Murray, John. Great Britain. Universalism. Vidler, William. Winchester, Elhanan. 1770-1825. *4080*
Murray, John Courtney. Berrigan, Daniel. Berrigan, Philip. Catholic Church. Church and state. Leftism. 1950's-70's. *3758*
Murray, Robert. Barnes, James. Editorials. Nova Scotia (Halifax). *Presbyterian Witness and Evangelical Advocate* (newspaper). 1848-1910. *3584*
—. Editors and Editing. "Letter to My Country Friends" (series). Nova Scotia (Halifax). *Presbyterian Witness* (newspaper). 1863. *987*
Musée Historique de Vaudreuil. Art. Catholic Church. Folk religion. French Canadians. Quebec. 17c-20c. *174*
Museums *See also* names of museums, e.g. American Museum of Natural History, etc.; Archives; Libraries.
—. Bethel College. Kansas (North Newton). Kauffman, Charles. Kauffman Museum. Mennonites. Missions and Missionaries. 1907-76. *198*
Music *See also* Ballads; Composers; Folk Songs; Hymns; Opera; Singing.
—. Adventists. Temperance Movements. 1850's-90's. *2965*
—. Aurora Colony. Communes. Oregon. Pioneer Band. Society of Bethel. 1855-1920's. *1942*
—. Baptists, Free Will. Cheney Family Singers. Cheney, Moses. Spiritualism. Vermont. 1839-91. *1932*
—. Baptists (Two-Seed-in-the-Spirit). Evangelism. Indiana (Putnam County). Oral tradition. Otter Creek Predestinarian Church. Sermons. 1820-1975. *1940*

—. Bible. New England. Puritans. Pythagoreanism. 1640-1726. *1912*
—. Bibliographies. Lutheran Church. 1700-1850. *1956*
—. Billings, William. Copyright. Massachusetts. 1770-90. *1939*
—. Billings, William. Hymnals. Poetry. Read, Daniel. Watts, Isaac. 1761-85. *1920*
—. California. Durán, Narciso. Franciscans. Indians. Missions and Missionaries. 1806-46. *1924*
—. Catholic Church. Mexican Americans. Protestant Churches. 1963-75. *1911*
—. Catholic Church. Mexican Americans. Protestantism. 1962-75. *1910*
—. Christmas carols. Great Britain. Puritans. Virginia. 1662-70. *2787*
—. Church of England. Malcolm, Alexander. Maryland (Annapolis). St. Anne's Church. Society for the Propagation of the Gospel. Teaching. 1721-63. *1931*
—. Church of God in Christ. Holiness movement. Negroes. New York (Binghamton). 1971-74. *3289*
—. Composers. Hymnals. New England. Publishers and publishing. Thomas, Isaiah. 1784-19c. *1936*
—. Congregationalism. Cooper, Samuel. Funerals. New England. Sermons. Social Customs. 18c. *3113*
—. Episcopal Church, Protestant. German Americans. Hast, Louis H. Kentucky (Louisville). 1848-90. *1909*
—. Episcopal Church, Protestant. Negroes. 1790-1975. *1934*
—. Hymns. Schools. Singing. 1775-1820. *1951*
—. Leftism. Methodist Episcopal Zion Church, African. Negroes. Robeson, Paul. 1898-1976. *3470*
—. Lutheran Church (Missouri Synod). *Lutheran Hymnal.* 1923-41. *1925*
—. Maine (Portland). 1785-1836. *1947*
—. Moravian Archives. Pennsylvania (Bethlehem). 1740-1978. *180*
—. Mountaineers. Revivals. South. 1798-1970. *1935*
—. Negroes. New York City. Pennsylvania (Philadelphia). Protestant churches. ca 1800-44. *1948*
—. Negroes. Racism. 17c-20c. *1943*
—. Protestantism. South. Walker, William. 1830-50. *1914*
Music, bluegrass gospel. Folklore. Southeastern States. 1770-1970. *1937*
Music (choral). Attitudes. Billings, William. Upper Classes. 1750-1800. *1907*
Music (Gospel). Bible. Protestantism. 18c-1980. *1949*
—. Evangelicalism. Faith Healing. Indiana (Gary). Negroes. Theology. 1976. *2868*
—. Lawsuits. Licenses. Performance licensing. 1950's. *1919*
—. Mississippi. Values. 1890-1978. *1922*
Music (jazz). Louisiana (New Orleans). Negroes. Voodoo. Women. ca 19c. *2181*
Music, liturgical. California (Los Angeles). Cantors. Concerts. Judaism. Loew's State Theatre. Rosenblatt, Josef "Yosele". Vaudeville. 1925. *1917*
Music (pop). Jesus Christ. 1960's-1970's. *1930*
Music, rock and roll. Counter culture. Jesus Christ. 1950's-70's. *1916*
Music (rock and roll, white gospel). Presley, Elvis. 1956-77. *1954*
Music (Sacred Harp). Baptists, Primitive. South. 1840's-1977. *1918*
Musser, Elise Furer. Diaries. Mormons. Political Leadership. Social Reform. Utah. Women. 1897-1967. *811*
Muste, A. J. Christianity. Niebuhr, Reinhold. Pacifism. Political Theory. Thomas, Norman. 1914-38. *2687*
Myers, Frederic W. H. Emmanuel movement. Freud, Sigmund. Psychoanalysis. 1906-10. *2334*
Myers, Myer. British North America. Jews. Rites and Ceremonies. Silversmithing. 1723-95. *1905*
Mysticism. Cabala. Counter Culture. Jews. Rationalism. Traditionalism. 1940's-70's. *4140*
—. Conversion. Eastern Religions. Psychotherapy. 1970's. *2290*
—. Counter culture. Millenarianism. Satanism. Social reform. 1960's-70's. *4243*
—. Evans, Warren Felt. Idealism. Mental healing. New Thought Movement. Romanticism. 1864-89. *1460*
—. Faith healing. New Mexico (Peralta). Schlatter, Francis. 1895-96. *1429*
—. Japan. Youth. 1976. *4282*
—. Judaism. 1960's-80. *4088*
—. Sociology. Troeltsch, Ernst. Weber, Max. 20c. *111*
Myths and Symbols. American dream. Christianity. Civil religion. Evil. Theology. 1973. *2724*
—. Authority. Bellah, Robert N. Civil religion. Politics. Secularization. 1977. *1165*
—. Bible. British Columbia. California. Christianity. Indians. Missions and Missionaries. Pacific Northwest. 1830-50. *1612*
—. Civil religion. Government. Morality. 1960's-78. *1153*
—. Civil Religion. Hymns. National Self-image. 1800-1916. *1950*
—. Clergy. Lewis, Lloyd. Lincoln, Abraham. 1861-65. *79*
—. Dickinson, Emily. Identity. Intellectual history. Poetry. Puritanism. Transcendentalism. Women. 1860's. *51*
—. Inaugural addresses. National Characteristics. Presidents. Protestantism. 17c-20c. *1174*
—. Middle classes. Protestantism. 1975. *2606*
—. New England. Puritans. Regionalism. Theology. 17c. *3611*
—. Psychology. Science fiction. Sensitivity movement. 1960's-70's. *2060*

N

Namaka Farm. Alberta. Communes. Farming. Mennonites. 1920's-40's. *414*
Names, Place. *See* Toponymy.
Nashotah House. Episcopal Church, Protestant. Letters. Seminaries. Unonius, Gustaf. Wisconsin (Nashotah). 1884. *585*
Nation, Carry Amelia. Prohibition. Temperance Movements. Women. 1890's-1911. *2576*
National Aeronautics and Space Administration. Religious experience. Science fiction. Space exploration. 1960-76. *146*
National Camp Meeting Association for the Promotion of Holiness. Camp meetings. Church of the Nazarene. Holiness movement. Louisiana (Mineral Springs). Methodist Church. 1860's-1926. *2891*
National Catholic Welfare Conference. Catholic Church. National Council of Catholic Women. Peace Movements. Women. World War II. 1919-46. *2669*
National Catholic Welfare Council. Catholic Church. Documents. Identity. Vatican. 1922. *3803*
National Characteristics *See also* National Self-image; Nationalism.
—. American Revolution. Documents. Presbyterians. 1729-87. *3596*
—. American Revolution. Folk religion. Pennsylvania Germans. 1775-83. *2948*
—. American Revolution. Hawthorne, Nathaniel. Literature. Puritan Tradition. 1775-83. 1830-40. *2082*
—. Art. Bunyan, John *(Pilgrim's Progress).* Huntington, Daniel. *Mercy's Dream* (painting). Protestantism. 1678. 1841-70. *1856*
—. Authors. Civil religion. 1830's-1960's. *1178*
—. Baptists. Imperialism. Racism. Virginia. Women. 1865-1900. *3001*
—. Bercovitch, Sacvan (review article). Massachusetts. Mather, Cotton. Puritans. 17c-18c. 1975. *3630*
—. Calvin, John. Luther, Martin. Protestantism. 16c-18c. *2870*
—. Christianity. Radical catholicity principle. 18c-20c. *41*
—. Church of England. James, Henry *(The American).* Puritans. 1700-1880. *2036*
—. City of God (concept of). 16c-20c. *1149*
—. Clergy. Proslavery Sentiments. Social Status. 1699-1865. *2628*
—. Consensus. Ideology. Puritans. 1630-1865. *1345*
—. Democracy. Pluralism. 1640's-1840's. *71*
—. Documents. Friends, Society of. Methodism. Political participation. Shakers. Tocqueville, Alexis de. 1831-40. *2780*
—. Episcopal Church, Protestant. Pragmatism. 1650-1975. *3239*
—. Idealism. Pluralism. Puritan tradition. 1620's-1940's. *1*
—. Inaugural addresses. Myths and Symbols. Presidents. Protestantism. 17c-20c. *1174*
—. Mead, Sidney E. Religious history. 20c. *235*
—. Providence. 17c-20c. *1172*
—. Sports. 20c. *98*
National Christian Citizen League. Clergy. Congregationalism. Herron, George David. Iowa College. Populism. Progressivism. Socialism. 1880's-1900. *2561*
National Council of Catholic Women. Catholic Church. National Catholic Welfare Conference. Peace Movements. Women. World War II. 1919-46. *2669*
National Council of Churches. Ecumenism. Organizational stress. 1908-69. *478*
—. Energy. Ethics. 1976-78. *2392*
National Council of Churches (General Assembly). Ecumenism. Jews. Protestant churches. 1969-74. *502*
National Council of Jewish Women. Hadassah. Jews. Professionalism. Voluntary Associations. Women. 1890-1980. *4146*
National Education Association. Mormons. Public schools. Sinclair, Upton. Teachers. Utah. 1920-24. *567*
National Fast Day. Civil War. Constitutional Amendments. Fundamentalism. Lincoln, Abraham. National Reform Association. 1787-1945. *1009*
National Federation of Priests' Councils. Catholic Church. Clergy. Organizational change. Values. -1973. *3859*
National Fertility Study. Christianity. Divorce. Women. 1970's. *934*
National Prohibition League. Catholic Church. Oklahoma. Prohibition. Religious Liberty. State Government. 1907-18. *2580*
National Reform Association. Civil War. Constitutional Amendments. Fundamentalism. Lincoln, Abraham. National Fast Day. 1787-1945. *1009*
National Self-image *See also* National Characteristics.
—. Barralet, John James *(Apotheosis of George Washington).* Engraving. 1802. *1859*
—. Bellah, Robert N. Church and state. Civil religion. Judeo-Christian thought. New Israel concept. 19c-20c. *1199*
—. Bellah, Robert N. Civil religion. Political attitudes. Values. 1775-20c. *1200*
—. Civil Religion. Finney, Charles G. Mahan, Asa. Millenarianism. Perfectionism. 19c. *1189*
—. Civil Religion. Hymns. Myths and Symbols. 1800-1916. *1950*
—. Clergy. Davies, Samuel. Eulogies. Presbyterian Church. Washington, George. 1789-1815. *1157*
—. Enlightenment. Pietism. Puritanism. 17c-20c. *1184*
National Statuary Hall. District of Columbia. Missions and Missionaries. Pacific Northwest. Pariseau, Mother Mary Joseph. Sisters of Charity of Providence. Women. 1856-1902. 1977. *1629*
National Women's Conference, 1st. Feminism. Mormons. Utah Women's Conference. Women. 1977. *858*
Nationalism *See also* Anti-Imperialism; Independence Movements; Minorities; Patriotism; Self-Determination; Separatist Movements.
—. Abolition Movement. Christianity. Enlightenment. Morality. Phillips, Wendell. 1830-84. *1399*
—. Acculturation. Catholic Church. French Canadians. New England. ca 1610-1975. *309*
—. American Institute for Education. Country life. Educational Reform. Elites. Massachusetts. Protestantism. 1830-37. *573*
—. American Revolution. Historiography. Millenarianism. Patriotism. Politics. 1740-89. *1347*
—. Apostolic Delegates. Catholic Church. Conroy, George. Politics. Quebec. Vatican. 1877-78. *1098*
—. Arabs. Missions and Missionaries. Syria. 1842-1918. *1670*
—. Assimilation. Catholic Church. French Canadians. Rhode Island (Woonsocket). 1924-29. *3854*
—. Attitudes. Hayes, Carlton J. H. Historiography. Kohn, Hans. 1950's-60's. *1392*
—. Authority. Latin America. Missions and Missionaries. Mormons. 1975-80. *1753*
—. Bygdelag movement. Ethnicity. North Central States. Norwegian Americans. 1901-30. *3319*

—. Canada. Catholic Church. Clergy. Craig, James Henry. French Canadians. Political repression. Quebec (Lower Canada). 1810. *1319*
—. Canada. Ecumenism. Immigration. Protestant churches. United Church of Canada. 1902-25. *491*
—. Catholic Church. Quebec. 1608-1978. *1012*
—. Catholicism. French Canadians. Lévesque, Georges-Henri. Personal narratives. Quebec. Youth movements. 1930's. *3790*
—. Chaldean Church. Immigrants. Iraqi Americans. Michigan (Detroit). Middle East. Uniates. ca 1940's-74. *1306*
—. Christianity. Civil religion. Senate. Webster, Daniel. 1813-52. *1191*
—. Civil religion. 17c-1976. *1145*
—. Civil Religion. Protestantism. Social Organization. Technology. ca 1630-1974. *1171*
—. Civil religion. Providence. 1789-1812. *1158*
—. Congregationalism. Missions and Missionaries. Social Gospel. Strong, Josiah. Wyoming (Cheyenne). 1871-1916. *3134*
—. Cuba. Methodist Church. Missions and Missionaries. 1898-1958. *1693*
—. Ethnicity. Language. Parishes. Polish National Catholic Church. 1880's-1930's. *313*
—. Europe. Revolution. Romanticism. Social criticism. 1630-1876. *950*
—. Historiography. 1735-83. 19c-1960's. *1416*
—. Materialism. *Moravian* (newspaper). Pennsylvania (Bethlehem). Slavery. 1850-76. *3518*
—. Millenarianism. Protestantism. 1740-1800. *1151*
—. Protestantism. Social organization. Voluntary associations. 19c. *2931*
Nationalist Movement. Bellamy, Edward. Individualism. 1865-98. *82*
Nativism. Alberta. Hutterites. Settlement. 1918-72. *2089*
—. American Protective Association. Anti-Catholicism. Chinese Americans. Guardians of Liberty. Ku Klux Klan. Oregon. Racism. ca 1840-1945. *2100*
—. Anti-Catholicism. Antislavery Sentiments. Bannan, Benjamin. Pennsylvania (Schuylkill County). Temperance Movements. Whig Party. 1852-54. *1238*
—. Anti-Catholicism. Bapst, John. Chaney, William Henry. Editors and editing. Jesuits. Maine (Ellsworth). 1853-54. *2121*
—. Anti-Catholicism. Chicopee Manufacturing Company. Immigration. Irish Americans. Massachusetts (Chicopee). Mills. Protestantism. 1830-75. *2103*
—. Anti-Catholicism. Elections (presidential). Ethnic Groups. Ohio (Cleveland). Republican Party. 1860. *1265*
—. Anti-Catholicism. Fillmore, Millard. Know-Nothing Party. Political Campaigns (presidential). Whig Party. 1850-56. *1305*
—. Carroll, Anna Ella. Probasco, Harriet. Women. 1840's-61. *851*
—. Carroll, John. Catholic Church. Ecumenism. Immigrants. Protestants. 1790-1820. *496*
—. Catholic Church. Conservatism. Newspapers. Political Commentary. Protestantism. *Providence Visitor* (newspaper). Rhode Island. 1916-24. *2118*
—. Chinese Americans. Christianity. Judaism. Newspapers. Pacific Coast. Slavery. 1848-65. *75*
—. Indiana (Gary, Valparaiso). Ku Klux Klan. Protestantism. 1920's. *2358*
Natural History *See also* Botany; Museums.
—. Botany. Friends, Society of. Logan, James. Mather, Cotton. New England. Puritans. 17c-18c. *2300*
—. Brickell, John. Clayton, John. Letters. North Carolina. Plagiarism. 1693-1737. *2341*
Nature *See also* Ecology; Wilderness.
—. Calvin, Ross Randall. Episcopal Church, Protestant. Literature. New Mexico. 1889-1970. *2332*
—. Christianity. Grimké, Sarah. Paul, Saint. Social organization. Women. 1c. 1830's. *921*
—. Crockett, Davy. Pioneers. Popular Culture. 1830's. *2712*
—. Great Disappointment. Millenarianism. Millerites. 1830's-44. *2973*
—. Philosophy. Poetry. Whitman, Walt ("Song of Myself"). 1855. *64*
Navajo Indians. Acculturation. Burials. Christianity. Indians. Missions and Missionaries. 1949-75. *1656*
—. Assimilation. Indians. New Mexico (Shiprock). Sherman Institute for Indians. Women. 1900-20. *589*
—. Indians. Mexican Americans. Pueblo Indians. Southwest. Witchcraft. 19c-1930's. *2214*
Naval Recruiting and Enlistment. *See* Military Conscription; Military Recruiting.
Nazism. *Bote* (newspaper). Germans, Russian. Mennonites. Saskatchewan. USSR. Völkisch thought. 1917-39. *3431*
—. Catholic Church. Clergy. Germany. Mundelein, George. 1937. *1256*
—. Judaism, Reform. Zionism. 1917-41. *4215*
—. Leadership. Manson Family. Millerites. Social Organization. Women's Liberation Movement. 19c-20c. *2964*
Near East. *See* Middle East.
Neau, Elias. Church of England. Laity. Negroes. New York City. Society for the Propagation of the Gospel. 1704-22. *3193*
—. Education. France. Hymns. New York. Protestant Churches. Slaves. ca 1689-1722. *1913*
Nebraska *See also* Western States.
—. Adventists. State Politics. Williams, George A. 1925-31. *1325*
—. Asia, central. Immigration. Kansas. Mennonites. Pacifism. 1884-93. *3350*
—. Baptists. Chaplains. Courts Martial and Courts of Inquiry. Fort Robinson. Negroes. Plummer, Henry V. 1884-94. *2695*
—. Bross, Harmon. Congregationalism. 1873-1928. *3125*
—. Friends, Society of (Committees on the Indian Concern). Indians (agencies). 1869. *3274*
Nebraska Council of Defense. Americanization. Church Schools. German language. Lutheran Church (Missouri Synod). Supreme Court. 1917-23. *305*
Nebraska, eastern. Davies, David Jones. Davies, Gwen. Indians. Methodist Church, Calvinistic. Missions and Missionaries. Omaha Indians. 1853-60. *1514*
Nebraska (Lincoln). Adventists. Cudney, A. J. Evangelism. 1885-87. *1577*
—. Adventists. Union College. 1891-1976. *593*
—. Puritans. Sermons. Taylor, Edward ("Upon the Types of the Old Testament"). Theology. Typology. 1693-1706. *3639*
—. Union College. 1890-1900. *621*
Nebraska (Omaha). Charities. Judaism (Orthodox, Reform). Political Leadership. Refugees. Settlement. 1820-1937. *4102*
—. Episcopal Church, Protestant. Missions and Missionaries (associate). 1891-1902. *1562*
—. Franklin, Leo M. Judaism. Rabbis. Temple Israel. 1892-99. *4094*
—. Judaism (Reform). Temple Israel. 1867-1908. *4207*
Nebraska (Weyerts). Clergy. Helmreich, Christian. Letters. Lutheran Church. 1887-88. *3308*
Necrology. Kuhnle, Howard A. Lutheran Church. 1950-73. *222*
Needlework. Catholic Church. Quebec (Quebec). Ursulines. ca 1655-1890's. *1850*
Neely, Phillip Phillips. Alabama. Clergy. Methodist Episcopal Church (South). Secession. 1861. *1213*
Neff, Christian. Mennonite World Conference. 1910-78. *446*
Negroes *See also* Black Muslims; Black Nationalism; Black Power; Civil War; Confederate States of America; Discrimination; Race Relations; Racism; Reconstruction; Slavery.
—. 1970's. *155*
—. 19c-20c. *21*
—. Abel, Elijah. Clergy. Mormons. ca 1830-79. *3944*
—. Abolition Movement. Baptists. Education. First African Baptist Church. Meachum, John Berry. Missouri (St. Louis). 1815-54. *2482*
—. Abolition Movement. Christology. Clergy. Congregationalism. New York. Ward, Samuel Ringgold. 1839-51. *2462*
—. Abolition Movement. Clergy. Protestant churches. 1830-60. *2472*
—. Abolition movement. Constitutional Amendments (15th). Douglass, Frederick. Theology. 1825-86. *2495*
—. Abolition Movement. Cornish, Samuel E. *Freedom's Journal* (newspaper). Journalism. Presbyterian Church. 1820's-59. *2498*
—. Adolescents. Church attendance. Religiosity. South. Whites. 1964-74. *99*
—. Adventists. First Harlem Church. Humphrey, James K. New York City. Schisms. Utopia Park. 1920's-30's. *2143*
—. Africa. Economic Conditions. Slave trade. Social Customs. ca 1500-1940's. *24*
—. Africans' School. Benezet, Anthony. Education. Friends, Society of. Pennsylvania (Philadelphia). 1770's-80's. *527*
—. Alabama (Aliceville). Baptists, Primitive. Civil rights. Corder, James. Personal narratives. 1965-75. *2555*
—. American Baptist Home Mission Society. Baptists. Leadership. Missions and Missionaries. Paternalism. Virginia Union University. 1865-1905. *644*
—. American Colonization Society. Crummell, Alexander. Education. Episcopal Church, Protestant. Liberia. Missions and Missionaries. 1853-73. *1671*
—. American Missionary Association. Civil War. Education. Missouri. 1862-65. *547*
—. American Missionary Association. Congregationalism. Missions and Missionaries. South. 1846-80. *1617*
—. Archival catalogs and inventories. Emmett, Daniel. Hymns. Minstrel Shows. Ohio Historical Society. Sermons. 1838-96. 1976. *2064*
—. Armies. Butler, Benjamin F. Chaplains. Civil War. Diaries. Fort Fisher (battle). North Carolina. Turner, Henry M. 1864-65. *2685*
—. Attitudes. Brooklyn College. Catholic Church. Immigration. Judaism. New York City. Protestant Ethic. West Indian Americans. 1939-78. *350*
—. Baker, Ray Stannard. Civil rights. DuBois, W. E. B. Episcopal Church, Protestant. Liberalism. Personal narratives. Whites. Wilmer, Cary Breckenridge. 1900-10. *2151*
—. Baptists. Bethel African Methodist Episcopal Church. California (San Francisco). Civil rights. Methodist Episcopal Zion Church, African. Pressure groups. Third Baptist Church. 1860's. *1289*
—. Baptists. California. Political activity. St. Andrew's African Methodist Episcopal Church. 1850-73. *981*
—. Baptists. Chaplains. Courts Martial and Courts of Inquiry. Fort Robinson. Nebraska. Plummer, Henry V. 1884-94. *2695*
—. Baptists. City Government. Maryland (Baltimore). Political protest. Public schools. 1865-1900. *583*
—. Baptists. Civil rights. King, Martin Luther, Jr. Nonviolence. 1950's-68. *2533*
—. Baptists. Civil Rights. King, Martin Luther, Jr. ("Letter from Birmingham Jail"). 1963. *2534*
—. Baptists. Clergy. Davis, Noah. Maryland (Baltimore). Meachum, John Berry. Missouri (St. Louis). Slavery. 1818-66. *3094*
—. Baptists. Clergy. Jay Street Church. Massachusetts (Boston). Paul, Thomas (and family). 1773-1973. *3048*
—. Baptists. First African Baptist Church. Jasper, John. Sermons. Virginia (Richmond). 1812-1901. *2990*
—. Baptists. Georgia. 1750's-1830's. *3077*
—. Baptists. Georgia (Richmond County). Kiokee Church. Marshall, Daniel. Settlement. 1784-1819. *3020*
—. Baptists. Jack (man). Rhode Island (Newport). 1630's-52. *3017*
—. Baptists. Kentucky (Stoney Point). Social Conditions. 1848-1969. *2999*
—. Baptists. Massachusetts (Boston). Social Reform. 1800-73. *3040*
—. Baptists. Methodism. New York. Segregation. 1865-68. *2139*
—. Baptists. New York (Buffalo). Shiloh Baptist Church. 1920's-30's. *3097*
—. Baptists. Protestantism. Socialism. Woodbey, George Washington. 1902-15. *2563*
—. Baptists, American. Education. Missions. South. 1862-81. *739*
—. Baptists, Southern. Education. Paternalism. 1880's-90's. *553*
—. Baptists, Southern. Education. Racism. Reconstruction. 1865-76. *2149*
—. Black theology. Christianity. Feminism. Reform. Theology. 1960's-70's. *2426*
—. Blue laws. Church and state. Legislators. Louisiana. Reconstruction. Sabbath. 1867-75. *2285*
—. Bossism. City Politics. Clergy. Crump, Edward Hull. Tennessee (Memphis). 1927-48. *1318*

—. Bottoms, Lawrence W. Personal narratives. Presbyterian Church, Southern. South. 1930-75. *2529*
—. Bratton, Theodore DuBose. Conference for Education in the South. Episcopal Church, Protestant. Mississippi. Racism. 1908. *2148*
—. Cain, Richard Harvey. Methodist Episcopal Church, African. Politics. Reconstruction. Social conditions. South Carolina. 1850's-87. *2407*
—. California. Cantwell, John J. Catholic Church. 1920's. *3896*
—. Catholic Church. Cities. Civil rights movement. Protestant churches. Social Classes. 1960's-70's. *2539*
—. Catholic Church. Cities. North or Northern States. Occupations. Social Status. 1968. *2613*
—. Catholic Church. Education. Georgia (Skidaway Island). Orphanages. Poor Clares. Women. 1885-87. *3806*
—. Catholic University of America. Colleges and Universities. Discrimination. District of Columbia. Wesley, Charles H. 1914-48. *3729*
—. Centennial United Methodist Church. Indiana (Gary). Methodist Church, United. Methodist Church, United. Personal narratives. Robinson, Roosevelt. White flight. 1976. *3467*
—. Chambers, Samuel D. (testimonies). Converts. Mormons. Slavery. Utah (Salt Lake City). 1844-76. *4059*
—. Chaplains. Garvey, Marcus. Universal Negro Improvement Association. 1920's. *2366*
—. Cheshire, Joseph Blount, Jr. Episcopal Church, Protestant. North Carolina. Paternalism. Race Relations. 1870-1932. *2140*
—. Christianity. -1973. *25*
—. Christianity. Civil rights. Equality. 19c-20c. *2536*
—. Christianity. Civil Rights. Fernando (slave). Key, Elizabeth. Law. Virginia. 1607-90. *2153*
—. Christianity. Civil rights. Militance. 1960's-70's. *2538*
—. Christianity. Discrimination. Folklore. Jews. Stereotypes. 18c-1974. *2091*
—. Christianity. Family. Social change. Values. War. 1960's-70's. *875*
—. Christianity. King, Martin Luther, Jr. 1900-70. *2773*
—. Christianity. Race relations. 1939-79. *2544*
—. Christianity. Whites. 1975. *2802*
—. Christianity (review article). Nelsen, Ann Kusener. Nelsen, Hart M. 1960's. 1975. *2736*
—. Christianity (unaffiliated). Social Indicators. 1977. *2629*
—. Church and Social Problems. Protestant Churches. 1970's. *2452*
—. Church of England. Laity. Neau, Elias. New York City. Society for the Propagation of the Gospel. 1704-22. *3193*
—. Church of God in Christ. Holiness movement. Music. New York (Binghamton). 1971-74. *3289*
—. City life. Folklore. Indiana (East Chicago, Gary, Hammond). Voodoo. 1976. *2182*
—. Civil rights programs. Clergy. Education. New York (Buffalo). 1969-70. *2554*
—. Clergy. 1960's-70's. *2739*
—. Clergy. Equality. Mormons (Reorganized). Schisms. Women. 1860-1979. *4032*
—. Clergy. Integration. Kimball, Spencer W. Mormons. Revelation. 1950-78. *4051*
—. Clergy. Lutheran Church (North Carolina Synod). 1865-89. *3328*
—. Clergy. Political Leadership. Texas (Beaumont). 1972. *1315*
—. Clergy. Presbyterian Church. 1885-1975. *3594*
—. Clergy. Presbyterian Church, United. 1855-1973. *3595*
—. Clergy. Protestant churches. Race Relations. South. ca 1800-65. *2816*
—. Collectors and Collecting. Folklore. Hyatt, Harry Midddleton. Illinois (Adams County). Small, Minnie Hyatt. South. Witchcraft. 1920-78. *2190*
—. Colonization. Liberia. Methodist Episcopal Church. Missions and Missionaries. Sierra Leone. 1833-48. *1702*
—. Congregationalism. Georgia (Atlanta). Social Work. 1886-1970. *2432*
—. Connecticut (New Haven). Pentecostal movement. Prayer meetings. Psychology. Social conditions. 1978. *3521*
—. Converts. Letters. Lynch, James. Methodist Episcopal Church. Methodist Episcopal Church, African. 1867. *3462*
—. Country Life. Murder. South. Whites. 1916-20. *156*
—. Cults. Father Divine. Jones, Jim. Peace Mission (movement). People's Temple. 1920-79. *4254*
—. Democratic Party. Liberty Party. New York. Referendum. Suffrage. Whig Party. 1840-47. *1264*
—. Ecumenism. Protestantism. Reform. World Conference of Christian Youth, 1st. Youth. 1939-79. *2884*
—. Emigration. Ethiopia (Addis Ababa). Ford, Arnold. Judaism. 1930-35. *4143*
—. Episcopal Church, Protestant. Music. 1790-1975. *1934*
—. Episcopal Church, Protestant. Racism. Society for the Propagation of the Gospel. ca 1700-1974. *3169*
—. Evangelicalism. Faith Healing. Indiana (Gary). Music (gospel). Theology. 1976. *2868*
—. Evangelicalism. Farmers. South. 1800-60. *2845*
—. Father Divine. Father Jehovia (pseud. of Samuel Morris). Georgia (Valdosta). St. John the Vine Hickerson. 1899-1914. *4259*
—. Father Divine. Peace Mission (movement). Sermons. 1915-65. *4249*
—. Federal Aid to Education. Methodist Episcopal Church, African. Ohio. Wilberforce University (Combined Normal and Industrial Department). 1887-91. *518*
—. Florida (Tallahassee). Protestant Churches. Race Relations. Social control. 1865-85. *2864*
—. Friends, Society of. Maryland (Baltimore). Methodist Episcopal Church, African. Presbyterian Church. Private Schools. Sunday Schools. 1794-1860. *633*
—. Georgia (Atlanta). Haven, Gilbert. Protestant Churches. Segregation. 1865-1906. *2145*
—. Greek Americans. Ohio (Cincinnati). Racism. 1970's. *2146*
—. Jackson, Jesse. People United to Save Humanity. Social Status. Southern Christian Leadership Conference. 1966-78. *2423*
—. Knights of Columbus. Military. Salvation Army. World War I. Young Men's Christian Association. 1917-18. *2720*
—. Leadership. South Carolina. 1919. *2617*
—. Leftism. Methodist Episcopal Zion Church, African. Music. Robeson, Paul. 1898-1976. *3470*
—. Letters. Lynch, James. Methodist Episcopal Church. Mississippi. Reconstruction. 1868-69. *3461*
—. Louisiana (New Orleans). Music (jazz). Voodoo. Women. ca 19c. *2181*
—. Lutheran Church. Methodist Episcopal Church, African. Payne, Daniel Alexander. Wilberforce University. 1830-93. *2905*
—. Lutheran Church (Alpha Synod). North Carolina. 1889-91. *3327*
—. Methodist Church. 1769-1968. *444*
—. Militancy. Orthodoxy. South. 1964-75. *1292*
—. Missouri (Caldwell, Jackson counties). Mormons. Social Problems. 1830-39. *4030*
—. Mormons. Priesthood. 1978-79. *3946*
—. Mormons. Priesthood. Utah. 1844-52. *2137*
—. Mormons. Priesthood. Young, Brigham. 1843-52. *3962*
—. Mormons. Race Relations. Theology. 1831-1973. *4058*
—. Mormons. Social Theory. Strang, James Jesse. Thompson, Charles B. 1844-73. *2138*
—. Moving Star Hall. Protestantism. South Carolina (Johns Island). 18c-1970. *2830*
—. Music. New York City. Pennsylvania (Philadelphia). Protestant churches. ca 1800-44. *1948*
—. Music. Racism. 17c-20c. *1943*
—. Pentecostal movement. 1906-72. *3525*
—. Presbyterian Church, United. 20c. *3593*
—. Protestantism. Segregation. South. 1885-90's. *2135*
—. Sectarianism. Whites. Working Class. 1969. *94*
Neighborhoods. Business. California (San Francisco; San Bruno Avenue). Esther Hellman Settlement House. Jews. 1901-68. *4130*
—. California (Los Angeles). Catholic Church. Christmas. Mexican Americans. Posadas (celebrations). Rites and Ceremonies. 1975-80. *3794*
—. Catholic Church. City Life. Illinois (Chicago). 1900-30. *3771*
Neisser, George. American Revolution. Georgia. Historians. Hymns. Moravian Church. New York. Pennsylvania, eastern. ca 1735-84. *197*
Nelsen, Ann Kusener. Christianity (review article). Negroes. Nelsen, Hart M. 1960's. 1975. *2736*
Nelsen, Hart M. Christianity (review article). Negroes. Nelsen, Ann Kusener. 1960's. 1975. *2736*
Nelson, E. Clifford. Ecumenism. Lutheran Church, American. Schiotz, Fredrik A. 1945-69. *485*
Nelson, Edward O. Personal narratives. Salvation Army (Scandinavian Corps). Scandinavian Americans. 1877-1977. *3293*
Nelson, William E. (review article). Industrialization. Law and society. Massachusetts. Secularization. Social change. 1760-1830. *53*
Neoorthodoxy. Agriculture. Landlords and Tenants. Mississippi. Protestant Churches. Theologians. 1936-40. *2566*
—. Catholic Church. Liberalism. Pluralism. Secularism. Theology. 1936-74. *3899*
Netherlands. American Revolution. Calvinism. Kuyper, Abraham. Political systems. 1775-83. 19c-1920. *1332*
—. Annulments. Birth Control. Canon law. Catholic Church. Divorce. 1945-77. *914*
—. Cantors. Congregation Shearith Israel. Judaism (Orthodox). New York. Pinto, Joseph Jesurun. Travel. 1759-82. *4196*
—. Congregationalism. Exiles. Great Britain. Hooker, Thomas. New England. Theology. 1631-33. *3650*
—. Great Britain. Iroquois Indians. Jesuits. Missions and Missionaries. New York. 1642-1719. *1654*
—. Immigrants. Reformed Christian Church. Reformed Dutch Church. Schisms. 1834-80. *3163*
—. Massachusetts (Plymouth). Pilgrims. 1607-20. *3139*
Neumann, Saint John Nepomucene. Antislavery Sentiments. Catholic Church. Emigration. Germans, Sudeten. Journalism. Missions and Missionaries. Republican Party. 19c-20c. *3826*
—. Bohemia. Catholic Church. Pennsylvania (Philadelphia). 1811-1977. *3904*
—. Bohemia (Prague). Religious Education. 1833-35. *3763*
—. Canonization processes. Heroic virtue. Vatican Council II. 19c. 1962-65. *3835*
—. Catholic Church. Pennsylvania (Philadelphia). 1830's-1963. *3774*
Neurology. Handsome Lake (Seneca). Indian Shaker Church. Revitalization movements. Slocum, John. Trances. 18c-20c. *2756*
Neutrality. American Revolution. Dunkards. Friends, Society of. Mennonites. Moravian Church. Pacifism. Schwenkfelders. Taxation. 1765-83. *2670*
—. *Christliche Apologete* (periodical). German Americans. Methodists. World War I. 1914-18. *3458*
Nevada *See also* Far Western States.
—. Agriculture. Indians. Mormons. Utah. 1847-60. *4037*
—. Annexation. Church and state. Idaho, southern. Legislation. Mormons. Stewart, William. Suffrage. 1887-88. *1089*
—. Elections. Liberal Party. Mormons. Utah. 1860-70. *1252*
—. Mormons. Smith, Joseph. Utah. Voting and Voting Behavior. Young, Brigham. 1835-50's. *1251*
Nevada (Austin). Hebrew Benevolent Association. Jews. Letters. Silver mining. 1864-82. *4164*
Nevada (Eureka). *American Israelite* (newspaper). Jews. Letters. 1875. *4163*
Nevada (Muddy River Valley). Mormons. Settlement. 1865-75. *3953*
Nevada (Panaca). Driggs, Nevada W. Personal narratives. Polygamy. Utah. 1890-93. *832*
—. Mining camps. Mormons. Social Customs. ca 1860-80. *3929*
Nevada (Reno). Episcopal Church, Protestant. Girls. Schools. Whitaker, Ozi William. 1876-94. *769*
Nevada (Smith Valley). California (Bodie). Clay, Eugene O. Funerals. Methodist Church. Personal narratives. Sermons. 1915. *3456*
Nevada (Virginia City). Atheism. Ingersoll, Robert. Lectures. Public Opinion. 1877. *4304*

Nevin, John W. Adger, John B. Dabney, Robert L. Hodge, Charles. Mercersburg theology. Presbyterian Church. Sacramental controversy. 1845-75. *3551*
—. Divinity (issue). Hodge, Charles *(Systematic Theology)*. Jesus Christ. Presbyterian Church. Theology. 1872. *3581*
New Brunswick *See also* Atlantic Provinces.
—. Acadians. Catholic Church. Discrimination. Irish Canadians. 1860-1900. *3855*
—. Anglin, Timothy Warren. Catholic Church. Irish Canadians. Newspapers. St. John *Freeman* (newspaper). 1849-83. *3680*
—. Anti-Catholicism. Pitts, Herman H. Religion in the Public Schools. 1871-90. *574*
—. Autobiography. Baptists. Clergy. Crandall, Joseph. 1795-1810. *2993*
—. Christianity. Indian-White Relations. Micmac Indians. Missions and Missionaries. Nova Scotia. 1803-60. *1649*
—. Education. Socialism. Stuart, Henry Harvey. 1873-1952. *2369*
New Brunswick (Fredericton). Bishops. Church of England. Letters. Medley, John. Oxford Movement. Pusey, Edward Bouverie. ca 1840-44. *3190*
New Brunswick (Saint John). Aged. Catholic Church. Charities. Education. Immigration. Orphans. Sisters of Charity of the Immaculate Conception. 1854-64. *2509*
New Catholic Encyclopedia. Catholic Church. Clergy. Editors and Editing. Historiography. Polish Americans. Swastek, Joseph Vincent (obituary). 1913-77. *227*
New Deal. Agricultural Reform. Catholic Church. Roosevelt, Franklin D. (administration). Social Theory. 1933-39. *2572*
—. Catholic Church. Farm programs. Rural life movement. 1930's. *2573*
New Divinity (doctrines). Congregationalism. Edwards, Jonathan. Hopkins, Samuel. New England. Social reform. Theology. 1730-1803. *2373*
New Divinity movement. Congregationalism. Evangelism. New England, western. 1740-1800. *3117*
New England *See also* individual states; Northeastern or North Atlantic States.
—. Abolition Movement. Attitudes. Puritans. Slavery. 1641-1776. *2164*
—. Abolition Movement. Civil War (antecedents). Clergy. Parker, Theodore. Transcendentalism. Violence. 1850-60. *2467*
—. Acculturation. Catholic Church. French Canadians. Nationalism. ca 1610-1975. *309*
—. Adams, John. American Revolution. Paine, Thomas. Political theory. Puritans. Rhetoric. 17c-1770's. *1424*
—. Allen, Thomas. American Revolution. Chaplains. 1774-77. *2680*
—. Almanacs. Astronomy. Infinity (concept). Puritanism. 1650-85. *2325*
—. American Revolution. Baptists. Pennsylvania. Religious liberty. Virginia. 1775-91. *1100*
—. American Revolution. Canada. Church of England. Cossitt, Ranna. Loyalists. Missions and Missionaries. 1773-1815. *1317*
—. American Revolution. Chauncy, Charles. Clergy. Congregationalism. 1770's. *1269*
—. American Revolution (antecedents). Benefices. Church of England. Religious Liberty. Society for the Propagation of the Gospel. 1689-1775. *1054*
—. Americanization. Attitudes. Pilgrims. 17c. *323*
—. Antinomianism. Cotton, John. Eliot, John. Government. Millenarianism. Missions and Missionaries. Puritans. Rhode Island (Portsmouth). 1630-90. *3635*
—. Antislavery sentiments. Puritans. 1652-1795. *2485*
—. Architecture. Churches. Episcopal Church, Protestant. Vaughan, Henry. 1845-1917. *1800*
—. Architecture. Meetinghouses. Stairwells. 18c. *1761*
—. Arminiamism. Church of England. Congregationalism. Converts. Johnson, Samuel (1696-1772). Sacramentalism. 1715-22. *3183*
—. Assurance, doctrine of. Hooker, Thomas. Puritans. Theology. 1630-60. *3644*
—. Attitudes. Congregationalism. Dwight, Timothy. New York. Travel (accounts). Wilderness. 1790's. *2066*
—. Attitudes. Court records. Law Enforcement. Sodomy. 1630-80. *2428*
—. Attitudes. Exercise. Health. Recreation. Transcendentalists. 1830-60. *1453*
—. Attitudes. Hymnals. Puritans. Regular Singing movement. 1720's. *1933*
—. Attitudes. Mather, Cotton. Puritans. Sermons. Women. 1650-1800. *880*
—. Augustine, Saint. Calvinism. Edwards, Jonathan. Heart concept. Psychology. 17c. *2311*
—. Axtell, James (review article). Education. Puritans. Social Organization. 17c-18c. 1974. *526*
—. Baptism. Baptists. Great Britain (London). Jessey, Henry. Letters. Puritans. Toleration. Tombes, John. 1645. *997*
—. Baptists. Church and state. McLoughlin, William G. (review article). 1630-1833. *1077*
—. Baptists, Separate. Evangelism. General Association of Separate Baptists in Christ. Kentucky. 1755-1977. *3064*
—. Beauty, perception of. Congregationalism. Edwards, Jonathan. Knowledge. Mental activity theory. 1730-69. *2323*
—. Beecher, Lyman. Congregationalism. Dwight, Timothy. Presbyterian Church. Republicanism. Taylor, Nathaniel William. 1790-1840. *1356*
—. Bible. Music. Puritans. Pythagoreanism. 1640-1726. *1912*
—. Bibliographies. Puritans. Sermons. 1652-1700. 1903. *1964*
—. Bosom serpentry (concept). Folklore. Mormons. Puritans. Snakes. Utah. 17c-19c. *2765*
—. Botany. Friends, Society of. Logan, James. Mather, Cotton. Natural History. Puritans. 17c-18c. *2300*
—. Bradstreet, Anne. Clap, Roger. Devotions. Puritans. Sewall, Samuel. Shepard, Thomas. Worship. 17c. *3627*
—. Burg, B. R. Clergy (review article). Congregationalism. Mather, Richard. Youngs, J. William T., Jr. ca 1700-50. 1976. *3124*
—. Calvinism. Cotton, John. Elegies. Fiske, John. Poetry. Puritans. 17c. *1985*
—. Calvinism. Diphtheria. Enlightenment. Great Awakening. Sermons. 1735-40. *2260*
—. Calvinism. Emerson, Mary Moody. Emerson, Ralph Waldo. 19c. *2721*
—. Capital Punishment. Clergy. Protestantism. Sermons. 1674-1750. *2822*
—. Captivity narratives. Catholic Church. Congregationalism. French Canadians. Indians. Williams, John *(The Redeemed Captive)*. 1704-06. *3133*
—. Cartoons and Caricatures. Great Britain. Puritans. Satire. 1770-76. *2005*
—. Catholic Church. French Canadians. LaPatrie (colony). Quebec. Repatriation Act (Canada, 1875). ca 1875-80. *3792*
—. Catholic Church. Theology. Transcendentalists. 19c. *2777*
—. Children. Death and Dying. Puritans. 17c-1750. *929*
—. Christianity. Indians. Missions and Missionaries. New France. 17c. *1621*
—. Church and State. Clergy. Income. 1700-75. *1011*
—. Church discipline. Friends, Society of. Ireland. New York. 1690-1789. *3283*
—. Church Membership. Puritans. 1620-1700. *3655*
—. Church of England. Clergy. Congregationalism. Vestries. 1630-1775. *312*
—. Church of England. Congregationalism. Cutler, Timothy. Edwards, Jonathan. Gibson, Edmund. Great Awakening. Letters. Stoddard, Solomon. 1739. *2263*
—. Church of England. Great Awakening. Whitefield, George. 1735-70. *2239*
—. Cities (review article). New York. Pennsylvania (Philadelphia; Germantown). Protestantism. 1660's-18c. *2828*
—. Clergy. Congregationalism. 1700-60. *3141*
—. Clergy. Congregationalism. Great Awakening. New Lights. Old Lights. Social Classes. 1734-85. *2627*
—. Clergy. Congregationalism. Presbyterian Church. Professionalism. Scott, Donald M. (review article). 1750-1850. 1979. *2865*
—. Clergy. Emigration. Intellectuals. 1640-60. *3653*
—. Clergy. Great Awakening. Professionalism. Theology. 1740-49. *2257*
—. Clergy. Great Britain. Immigration. Puritans. 1629-65. *3661*
—. Clergy. Historiography. Puritans. Women. 1668-1735. *936*
—. Clergy. Puritans. 17c. *3599*
—. Clothing. Legislation. Puritans. Social Status. 1630-90. *2427*
—. Cobbett, Thomas *(Practical Discourse of Prayer)*. Prayer. Puritans. 1630-85. *3607*
—. Colonization. Pragmatism. Puritans. Social Change. 1620-90. *3608*
—. Communion. Puritanism. Stoddard, Solomon. 1679. *3614*
—. Composers. Hymnals. Music. Publishers and publishing. Thomas, Isaiah. 1784-19c. *1936*
—. Congregationalism. Cooper, Samuel. Funerals. Music. Sermons. Social Customs. 18c. *3113*
—. Congregationalism. Dark Day. Stiles, Ezra. Weather. 1780. *2326*
—. Congregationalism. Dwight, Timothy. Political attitudes. 1775-1817. *1369*
—. Congregationalism. Edwards, Jonathan. Hopkins, Samuel. New Divinity (doctrines). Social reform. Theology. 1730-1803. *2373*
—. Congregationalism. Exiles. Great Britain. Hooker, Thomas. Netherlands. Theology. 1631-33. *3650*
—. Congregationalism. Family. Methodism. Mormons. New York, western. Young, Brigham. 18c-1830's. *2840*
—. Congregationalism. Great Awakening. Ordination. Parkman, Ebenezer. 1630-1740. *3157*
—. Conversion. Puritans. Semiology. Theology. 1600's. *3612*
—. Correspondence, theory of. Transcendentalists. 1836-44. *1962*
—. Covenant theology. Poetry. Puritans. Wigglesworth, Michael *(Day of Doom)*. 1662. *3597*
—. Dartmouth College. Lane Theological Seminary. Presbyterian Church. Stowe, Calvin Ellis. Stowe, Harriet Beecher. 1824-86. *3555*
—. Death and dying. Folklore. 1630-1790. *2903*
—. Death and Dying. Infants. Parents. Puritans. Theology. 1620-1720. *925*
—. Death and Dying. Puritans. 17c-18c. *3651*
—. Drunkenness. Puritans. 17c. *2590*
—. Earthquakes. Literature. Puritans. 1727. *2289*
—. Eddy, Mary Baker. Hypnotism. Psychiatry. Quimby, Phineas Parkhurst. 1820's-66. *1442*
—. Education. Great Britain. Greaves, Richard L. Mather (family). Middlekauff, Robert. Puritans. 1596-1728. *607*
—. Edwards, Jonathan. Millenarianism. Mission, concept of. Puritans. 18c. *1154*
—. Elliott, Emory. Puritans (review article). Sabbath. Sermons. Solberg, Winton U. 17c-18c. 1975-77. *3623*
—. Equality. Sex roles. Shakers. Women. 1810-60. *821*
—. Folk art. New York (Long Island). Tombstones. 1660-18c. *1900*
—. Folklore. Puritans. Sermons. 1625-60. *1981*
—. Friends, Society of. Great Britain. Missions and Missionaries. 1656-1775. *1662*
—. Friends, Society of. Howgill, Francis. Persecution. Puritans. ca 1650-60. *1027*
—. Friends, Society of. King Philip's War. Politics. Toleration. Williams, Roger *(George Fox)*. 1672-77. *993*
—. Great Awakening. Puritans. Religious Education. 1690-1750. *655*
—. Great Britain. Jeremiads. Pamphlets. Puritans. Ward, Nathaniel. 1645-50. *1975*
—. Great Britain. Local government. Massachusetts. Political theory. Puritans. Social change. 1600-50. *3604*
—. Great Britain. Puritans. Rhetoric. Sermons. 1620's-50's. *1980*
—. Great Britain. Williams, Roger. 1629-82. *2876*
—. Historiography. Indian-White Relations. Missions and Missionaries. Puritans. Theology. 17c-20c. *1641*
—. Historiography. Intuition. Parker, Theodore. Reason. Theology. Transcendentalism. Unitarianism. 18c-1860. 1920-79. *4074*
—. Historiography. Miller, Perry. Puritanism. 1620-1775. 1939-74. *258*
—. Historiography, neoconservative. Puritans. Social Organization. 17c. 1930's-60's. *3619*
—. Holifield, E. Brooks. Lowrie, Ernest Benson. Puritans (review article). Sacraments. Theology. Willard, Samuel. 16c-17c. 1974. *3637*
—. Holmes, Oliver Wendell *(Elsie Venner)*. Literature. Original Sin. 1861. *2024*
—. Iconography. Poetry. Puritans. Sermons. Tombstones. 17c. *1977*
—. Indian-White Relations. Puritans. Race. 1620-90. *2150*

—. Intellectuals. Poetry. Radicals and Radicalism. Socialism. Wheelwright, John (1897-1940). 18c-1940. *1419*
—. Irving, Washington. Witchlore. 1809-24. *2008*
—. Jeremiads. Puritans. Sermons. Sports. 17c-18c. *3659*
—. Jews. Old Testament. Pilgrims. Puritans. 1620-1700. *2936*
—. Kibbutzim. Palestine. Puritans. Social Organization. Towns. 17c. 20c. *3633*
—. Mather, Cotton *(Magnalia Christi Americana)*. Morality. Puritans. Suffering (meaning). 1690's-1702. *3626*
—. Miller, Perry *(The New England Mind: The Seventeenth Century)*. Puritans. 17c. 1939. *257*
—. Myths and Symbols. Puritans. Regionalism. Theology. 17c. *3611*
—. Novels. Presbyterian Church. Salvation. Stowe, Harriet Beecher. Theology. Women. 1845-85. *2038*
—. Pilgrims. Puritans. 1606-1790. *2886*
—. Price controls. Puritans. 1629-76. *2570*
—. Psychology, faculty. Puritans. Stoddard, Solomon *(Safety of Appearing)*. 1630-1746. *2299*
—. Puritans. Recreation. 17c. *3660*
—. Puritans. Satire. Ward, Nathaniel *(The Simple Cobler of Aggawam in America)*. 1647. *3647*
—. Puritans. Scientific thought. Winthrop, John. Winthrop, John, Jr. Winthrop, John (1714-79). 1620-1779. *2295*
—. Puritans. Sermons. Sex roles. Theology. Women. 1690-1730. *883*
—. Puritans. Stoddard, Solomon. Theology. 1672-1729. *3634*
—. Puritans. Witchcraft. Women. ca 1630-1978. *2185*
—. Revivals. Textile industry. Women. ca 1790-1840. *2228*
New England Company. Christianity. Indians. Missions and Missionaries. Royal Society. 1660's-70's. *1554*
New England Conscience (term). Appleton, Thomas Gold. Calvinism. James, Henry. Unitarianism. 1875-95. *4075*
New England Courant (newspaper). Clergy. Congregationalism. Franklin, Benjamin. Massachusetts (Boston). Smallpox. *Spectator* (newspaper). 1720-23. *2023*
New England Meeting for Sufferings. Backus, Isaac *(History of New England)*. Baptists. Friends, Society of. Sectarianism. Theology. 17c-1784. *2953*
New England Quarterly (periodical). Historians. Morison, Samuel Eliot (obituary). Puritans. 1928-76. *276*
New England (review article). Lucas, Paul R. Puritans. Social Organization. VanDeventer, David E. 1623-1741. 1976. *3621*
New England, western. Congregationalism. Evangelism. New Divinity movement. 1740-1800. *3117*
New France *See also* Louisiana; Nova Scotia; Quebec.
—. Architecture. Catholic Church. 1600-1760. *1807*
—. Attitudes. France. Indians. Jesuits. Missions and Missionaries. 1611-72. *1495*
—. Brébeuf, Jean de. Catholic Church. Indian-White Relations. Ledesme, R. P. *(Doctrine Chrestienne)*. Translating and Interpreting. Wyandot Indians. 16c-17c. *1639*
—. Catholic Church. 17c-18c. *3732*
—. Catholic Church. Church and State. Protestantism. ca 1625-1760's. *2818*
—. Catholic church. Clergy. Trade. 1627-1760. *337*
—. Catholic Church. Nobility. Sulpicians. 17c-18c. *2611*
—. Christianity. Indians. Missions and Missionaries. New England. 17c. *1621*
—. France. Huguenots. 1541-1760. *3252*
—. France. Trials. Witchcraft. 17c. *2203*
—. Historiography. Lescarbot, Marc *(Histoire de la Nouvelle-France)*. 1606-30's. *2032*
—. Land. Law. Sulpicians. 1667. *3782*
New France (Sovereign Council). Catholic Church. Church and state. Governors, provincial. Laval, François de. Trade. 1659-84. *1020*
New Hampshire *See also* New England; Northeastern or North Atlantic States.
—. Abolition Movement. Friends, Society of. Haverford College Library (Quaker Collection). Portsmouth Anti-Slavery Society. Rogers, Nathaniel Peabody. 1830-46. *2465*
—. Calvinism. Founding fathers. Giles, Benjamin. Libraries. 1760's-87. *2908*
—. Clergy (dismissal). Congregationalism. Presbyterian Church. Social change. 1633-1790. *2885*
—. Maine. Revivals. Whitefield, George. 1727-48. *2249*
New Hampshire (Acworth). Baptists. Church and state. Congregationalism. Meetinghouses. Taxation. Toleration Act (New Hampshire, 1819). Universalists. 1783-1822. *1113*
New Hampshire (Chesterfield). Embury, Philip. Methodist Church. Sermons. 1754-1805. *3488*
New Hampshire (Claremont). Assimilation. Orthodox Eastern Church, Russian. Russian Americans. ca 1907-75. *2809*
New Hampshire (Cornish, Enfield). Historical Sites and Parks. Meetinghouses. Shakers. 1793-1902. *1777*
New Hampshire Covenant. Baptists, Southern. Brown, J. Newton. Covenants. 1833-1972. *3006*
New Hampshire (Enfield). Cumings, John. Shakers. Utopias. 1829-1923. *394*
New Hampshire (Londonderry). Tombstones. Wight, John. 1718-75. *1841*
New Hampshire (Manchester). Catholic Church. Church Schools. Girls. McDonough, Madrienne C. Mount St. Mary Convent. Personal narratives. 1902-09. *692*
New Hampshire (Portsmouth). Architecture. Episcopal Church, Protestant. St. John's Episcopal Church. 1807-09. *1780*
New Hampshire (Washington). Adventists. Oakes, Rachel. Preble, T. M. Sabbath. Wheeler, Frederick. 1841-44. *2287*
New Israel concept. Bellah, Robert N. Church and state. Civil religion. Judeo-Christian thought. National self-image. 19c-20c. *1199*
New Jersey *See also* Northeastern or North Atlantic States.
—. Alexander Hall (building). Presbyterian Church. Princeton Theological Seminary. 1815. *595*
—. American Revolution. Dutch Americans. New York. Reformed Dutch Church. 1775-83. *1208*
—. American Revolution. Green, Jacob. Politics. 1770-90. *1398*
—. American Revolution. Historiography. New York. Pennsylvania. Social conditions. 1680-1790's. 1960's-70's. *59*
—. Buchman, Frank. Evangelicalism. Moral Re-Armament movement. Princeton University. 1938. *2858*
—. Charities. Law. Morristown Female Charitable Society. Presbyterian Church. Women. 1813-1978. *2510*
—. Church and State. Church of England. Colleges and Universities (administration). Friends, Society of. Presbyterians. Princeton University. 1745-60. *661*
—. Constitutions, State. North Carolina. Pennsylvania. Presbyterian Church. 1775-87. *1285*
—. Davies, Samuel. Diaries. Fund raising. Great Britain. Presbyterian Church. Princeton University. 1753-54. *636*
—. Presbyterian Church. Princeton University (library). 18c. *622*
New Jersey (East Rutherford, Trenton). Concordia Collegiate Institute. Lutheran Church. New York City (Brooklyn). Steege, Martin. 1921-73. *3343*
New Jersey (Hackensack). American Revolution. New York City. Reformed Dutch Church (coetus, conferentie). 1750-83. *1311*
New Jersey Historical Society. Manuscripts. McDowell, William A. Presbyterian Church. South Carolina (Charleston). Third Presbyterian Church. 1820's-30's. *259*
New Jersey (Jersey City). Catholic Church. Progressivism. Protestantism. Social reform. Whittier House. 1890-1917. *2449*
New Jersey (Morristown). Barnes, Albert *(Way of Salvation)*. Presbyterian Church. Schisms. Sermons. Theology. Trials. 1829-37. *3576*
New Jersey (Newark). Catholic Church. Church and Social Problems. German Americans. Irish Americans. 1840-70. *3830*
—. Presbyterian Church. See, Isaac M. Sermons. Women. 1876. *805*
New Jersey (Oldman's Creek). Moravian Church. 1743-1800. *3513*
New Jersey (Perth Amboy, Red Bank). Communes. North American Phalanx. Raritan Bay Union. Spring, Marcus. 1843-59. *413*
New Jersey (Pitman Grove). Revivals. Settlement. Urbanization. 1860-1975. *2262*
New Jersey (Princeton). Hodge, Charles. Princeton University. Women. 1825-55. *857*
New Jersey (Tenafly). Camp Lejeune. Lamb Studios. Marines. North Carolina. Protestantism. Stained glass windows. 1775-1943. *1867*
New Jersey (Woodcliff). "Angel Dancers". Communalism. Folklore. Howell, Jane. Huntsman, Manson T. Rumors. Sects, Religious. 1890-1920. *389*
"New Jerusalem" (manuscript). Massachusetts. Mather, Increase. Millenarianism. Puritans. 1669-1710. *3632*
New Left *See also* Communism; Leftism; Radicals and Radicalism; Socialism.
—. Calvinism. Great Awakening. New Lights. Youth. 1740's. 1960's. *2265*
New Lights. American Revolution. American Revolution. Cleaveland, John. Congregationalism. Daily life. Great Awakening. Ideology. Jedrey, Christopher M. (review article). Massachusetts (Chebacco). 1740-79. *2241*
—. Calvinism. Great Awakening. New Left. Youth. 1740's. 1960's. *2265*
—. Clergy. Congregationalism. Great Awakening. New England. Old Lights. Social Classes. 1734-85. *2627*
—. Congregationalism. Connecticut (New London). Great Awakening. Schisms. Shepherd's Tent (college). 1720-50. *2250*
—. Congregationalism. Connecticut (New London). Great Awakening. Shepherd's Tent (college). 1742-46. *774*
New Madrid Earthquake. Christianity. Converts. Earthquakes. Mississippi River. Missouri. 1811-12. *2789*
New Mexico *See also* Western States.
—. Arizona. Bandelier, Adolph Francis. Manuscripts. Mexico (Chihuahua, Sonora). Missions and Missionaries. Vatican Library. 16c-17c. 1886-1964. 1975-79. *1618*
—. Arizona. Catholic Church. Colonial Government. Jurisdictions, ecclesiastical. Spain. 1548-1969. *3739*
—. California (Monterey). Discovery and Exploration. Dominguez, Francisco Atanasio. Escalante, Silvestre Velez de. Overland Journeys to the Pacific. 1765-1805. *1480*
—. Calvin, Ross Randall. Episcopal Church, Protestant. Literature. Nature. 1889-1970. *2332*
—. Catholic Church. Cofradías (brotherhoods). Mexican Americans. Penitentes. Rio Grande Valley. ca 1770-1970. *3675*
—. Catholic Church. Colorado. Folk art. Penitentes. 19c-20c. *3898*
—. Catholic Church. Colorado. Passion plays. Spain. 1830's-1978. *1890*
—. Catholic Church. Design. Folk art. Iconography. Manuscripts. 16c-17c. *1858*
—. Catholic Church. Feast days. Mexican Americans. 20c. *3903*
—. Catholic Church. Fiestas. Rites and Ceremonies. Saints, patron. Villages. 1970's. *3892*
—. Catholic Church. Flagellants. Penitentes. 13c-20c. *3779*
—. Catholic Church. Folk art. Santos (statues). 1780-1900. *1903*
—. Catholic Church. Folklore. Hispanic Americans. Penitentes. Rites and Ceremonies. Social customs. 16c-20c. *3829*
—. Catholic Church. Frontier and Pioneer Life. Settlement. 17c-1810. *3852*
—. Catholic Church. Penitentes. Sangre de Cristo Mountains. 19c-1979. *3893*
—. Church and state. Libraries. 1598-1912. *1111*
—. Colonial Government. Documents. Franciscans. Missions and Missionaries. Spain. Vélez Cachupín, Thomas. ca 1754. *1586*
—. Franciscans. Indian-White Relations. Inquisition. Marriage. Missions and Missionaries. Plains Apache Indians. Romero, Diego. 1660-78. *3773*
New Mexico (Albuquerque). Catholic Church. Penitentes. Roybal, Max. Santos, statues. Wood Carving. 20c. *1901*
—. Congregationalism. Education. Prohibition. Social gospel. 1900-17. *2448*
—. Jacobs, Pizer. Judaism (Reform). Temple Albert (dedication). 1900. *4232*
New Mexico (Bernalillo). Catholic Church. Feast days. Lawrence, Saint. Social Customs. 1974. *3853*

New Mexico (Bernalillo, Manzana). Indians. Mexican Americans. Witchcraft. 1970-74. *2193*
New Mexico (Cordova). Catholic Church. Folk art. Lopez, George. Lopez, José Dolores. Santos, statues. 20c. *1844*
New Mexico, northern. Catholic Church. Colorado, southern. Death Carts. Hispanic Americans. Penitentes. 1860-90's. *3856*
New Mexico (Peralta). Faith healing. Mysticism. Schlatter, Francis. 1895-96. *1429*
New Mexico (Sandoval). Adventists. Education. Missions and Missionaries. Spanish-American Seminary. 1928-53. *751*
New Mexico (Santa Fe). Bishops. Catholic Church. Indian-white relations. Lamy, Jean Baptiste. Social customs. 1849-88. *3761*
—. Catholic Church. Chapels. 1850's-70's. *1821*
—. Catholic Church. Chapels. Third Order of Saint Francis. ca 1805-32. *1776*
—. Catholic Church. Colorado. Diaries. Hospitals. Mallon, Catherine. Sisters of Charity. 1865-1901. *1454*
—. Catholic Church. St. Vincent's Hospital. Sisters of Charity. 1865-1948. *1449*
—. Christian Schools, Brothers of. St. Michael's High School. Secondary Education. 1859-1959. *742*
New Mexico (Shiprock). Assimilation. Indians. Navajo Indians. Sherman Institute for Indians. Women. 1900-20. *589*
New Mexico (Taos). Cather, Willa *(Death Comes for the Archbishop)*. Fiction. Martinez, Antonio Jose. 1830's. 1927. *2077*
New Mexico (Torrance County). Mexican Americans. Superstitions. Witchcraft. 1970's. *2184*
New Netherland *See also* New York.
—. Brazil. Clergy. Polhemius, Johannes Theodorus. Reformed Dutch Church. 1598-1676. *3165*
—. Clergy. Michaelius, Jonas. Reformed Dutch Church. 1590's-1633. *3164*
—. Dutch Americans. Religious liberty. Smith, George L. (review article). Trade. 17c. *1109*
New Netherland (New Amsterdam). Dutch Americans. Mennonites. Shecut, John L. E. W. *(The Eagle of the Mohawks)*. Universalists. 17c. 1800-36. *2012*
New Theology. Protestantism. Roe, Edward Payson *(Barriers Burned Away)*. Sheldon, Charles M. *(In His Steps)*. Social Gospel. 1860's-90's. *2058*
New Thought movement. Correspondence courses. Idaho (Moscow). Psychiana (religion). Robinson, Frank Bruce. 1929-48. *4260*
—. Evans, Warren Felt. Idealism. Mental healing. Mysticism. Romanticism. 1864-89. *1460*
—. Philosophy. Quimby, Phineas Parkhurst. 1850's-1917. *62*
New York *See also* Northeastern or North Atlantic States.
—. Abolition Movement. Christology. Clergy. Congregationalism. Negroes. Ward, Samuel Ringgold. 1839-51. *2462*
—. Accademia (association). Catholic Church. Clergy. 1865-1907. *296*
—. Adventists. Albany Conference. Millerites. 1844-45. *2961*
—. Adventists. Fuller, Nathan. Pennsylvania. 1858-71. *2975*
—. Albany Diocese. Bishops. Episcopal Church, Protestant. Oldham, George Ashton. 1922-47. *3176*
—. American Revolution. Dutch Americans. New Jersey. Reformed Dutch Church. 1775-83. *1208*
—. American Revolution. Episcopal Church, Protestant. Nonconformists. Political Factions. Provincial government. 1768-71. *1294*
—. American Revolution. Georgia. Historians. Hymns. Moravian Church. Neisser, George. Pennsylvania, eastern. ca 1735-84. *197*
—. American Revolution. Historiography. New Jersey. Pennsylvania. Social conditions. 1680-1790's. 1960's-70's. *59*
—. Ararat (colony). Judaism (Orthodox). Noah, Mordecai Manuel. Rhode Island (Newport). 1813-21. *4178*
—. Architecture. Banner, Peter. Congregationalism. First Congregational Society Church. Vermont (Burlington). 1794-1815. *1829*
—. Assimilation. Church and state. Politics. Reformed Dutch Church. 1664-91. *1121*
—. Attitudes. Congregationalism. Dwight, Timothy. New England. Travel (accounts). Wilderness. 1790's. *2066*
—. Baptists. Bingham, Abel. Diaries. Indian-White Relations. Iroquois Indians (Seneca). Missions and Missionaries. Red Jacket (leader). Tonawanda Indian Reservation. 1822-28. *1513*
—. Baptists. Galusha, Elon. Millerites. 1825-56. *2921*
—. Baptists. Methodism. Negroes. Segregation. 1865-68. *2139*
—. Bishops. Episcopal Church, Protestant. Huntington, Frederick (and family). Social reform. Theology. Women. 1869-1904. *3213*
—. Burned-over district (theory). Cross, Whitney R. Dissent. Millerites. 1830's-40's. 20c. *2974*
—. Cantors. Congregation Shearith Israel. Judaism (Orthodox). Netherlands. Pinto, Joseph Jesurun. Travel. 1759-82. *4196*
—. Catholic Church. Conservatism. Corrigan, Michael. Economic Theory. George, Henry. McGlynn, Edward. 1886-94. *2562*
—. Catholic Church. Dolan, Jay P. (review article). German Americans. Irish Americans. Social Conditions. 1815-65. 1975. *3793*
—. Chautauqua School of Theology. Methodist Church. Seminaries, correspondence. Vincent, John Heyl. 1881-98. *763*
—. Church and state. Civil Rights. Colleges and Universities. Federal Aid to Education. Political attitudes. Students. 1972. *1119*
—. Church discipline. Friends, Society of. Ireland. New England. 1690-1789. *3283*
—. Church of England. Connecticut. Letters. Missions and Missionaries. Muirson, George. ca 1697-1708. *1535*
—. Cities (review article). New England. Pennsylvania (Philadelphia; Germantown). Protestantism. 1660's-18c. *2828*
—. Congregationalism. Edwards, Jonathan. Presbyterian Church. Sermons. 1722-23. *2883*
—. Courtship. Field, Eliza. Great Britain (London). Indians. Jones, Peter. Methodism. 1820's-33. *1637*
—. Democratic Party. Liberty Party. Negroes. Referendum. Suffrage. Whig Party. 1840-47. *1264*
—. Education. France. Hymns. Neau, Elias. Protestant Churches. Slaves. ca 1689-1722. *1913*
—. *Engel* v. *Vitale* (US, 1962). Nonsectarianism. Prayer. Public opinion. Public schools. 1962. *581*
—. Family. Illinois (Nauvoo). Mormons. Young, Brigham. 1824-45. *861*
—. Family. Noyes, John Humphrey. Oneida Community. Sex. 1848-80. *431*
—. Finney, Charles G. Revivals. 1820-40. *2243*
—. Friends, Society of. Political Factions. Seneca Indians. Tribal government. 1848. *1202*
—. Frontier and Pioneer Life. Immigration. Irish Americans. Pennsylvania. Presbyterian Church. Virginia (Shenandoah Valley). 17c-1776. *3558*
—. Genetics. Noyes, John Humphrey. Oneida Community. Stirpicultural experiment. Utopias. 1848-86. *946*
—. Great Britain. Iroquois Indians. Jesuits. Missions and Missionaries. Netherlands. 1642-1719. *1654*
—. Judaism (Orthodox). Schools. Social relations. 18c. *4175*
—. Lee, Ann. Shakers. Theology. 1774-20c. *4065*
—. Letters. Mormons. Reformed Dutch Church. Willers, Diedrich. 1830. *2766*
—. Literature. Presbyterian Church. Satire. Social criticism. Whitcher, Frances Miriam Berry *(Widow Bedott Papers)*. 1847-55. *2056*
—. Noyes, John Humphrey. Oneida Community. Sex. Social Status. Women. 1848-79. *863*
New York (Auburn). Attitudes. Friends, Society of. Pennsylvania. Prisons. Reform. 1787-1845. *2393*
New York (Binghamton). Church of God in Christ. Holiness movement. Music. Negroes. 1971-74. *3289*
New York (Bucks Bridge). Adventists. Byington, John. Methodist Church, Wesleyan. Methodist Episcopal Church. 1840's-52. *3509*
New York (Buffalo). Baptists. Negroes. Shiloh Baptist Church. 1920's-30's. *3097*
—. Civil rights programs. Clergy. Education. Negroes. 1969-70. *2554*
—. Council of Churches of Buffalo and Erie County. Sanderson, Ross W. 1937-42. *447*
—. Evangelism. Sunday, Billy. 1917. *2218*
New York (Buffalo area; Cheektowaga). Alsace-Lorraine. Batt, Joseph. Catholic Church. Chapel of Our Lady of Help of Christians. Immigration. 1789-1872. *1760*
New York City. Adler, Samuel. Judaism (Reform). Morality. Theology. ca 1829-91. *4208*
—. Adventists. First Harlem Church. Humphrey, James K. Negroes. Schisms. Utopia Park. 1920's-30's. *2143*
—. Agnosticism. Ethnicity. Hillquit, Morris. Jews. Socialism. 1890's-1933. *1331*
—. American Revolution. Clergy. Loyalists. Lydekker, Gerrit. Reformed Dutch Church. 1765-94. *977*
—. American Revolution. New Jersey (Hackensack). Reformed Dutch Church (coetus, conferentie). 1750-83. *1311*
—. Americanization. Catholics. Church attendance. Ethnicity. -1974. *3810*
—. Anti-Catholicism. Breslin, Jimmy. Brooklyn Diocese. Flaherty, Joe. Hamill, Pete. Irish Americans. Novels. 1960's-70's. *2098*
—. Architecture. Cathedral Church of St. John the Divine. Episcopal Church, Protestant. Manning, William Thomas. Sabbatarianism. Sports. 19c-1920's. *3243*
—. Architecture. Catholic Church. Church of St. Paul the Apostle. Decorative Arts. LaFarge, John. 1876-99. *1833*
—. Assimilation. Ethnicity. Greek Americans. Orthodox Eastern Church. St. Demetrios Church. St. Markela Church. 1970's. *318*
—. Attitudes. Brooklyn College. Catholic Church. Immigration. Judaism. Negroes. Protestant Ethic. West Indian Americans. 1939-78. *350*
—. Baptists. Clergy. First Presbyterian Church. Fosdick, Harry Emerson. Presbyterian Church. Theology. 1918-24. *466*
—. Baptists, Seventh-Day. Conversion. Daland, William C. Friedlaender, Herman. Jews. *Peculiar People* (newspaper). 1880's-90's. *1633*
—. Beecher, Henry Ward. Feminism. Radicals and Radicalism. Sex. Social Reform. Spiritualism. Vanderbilt, Cornelius. Woodhull, Victoria Claflin. 1868-90's. *2386*
—. Bergner, Peter. Bethel Ships. Evangelism. Merchant Marine. Methodist Church. Swedish Americans. 1832-66. *1661*
—. Bergner, Peter. Immigrants. *John Wesley* (vessel). Methodist Episcopal Church. Seamen. 1830-77. *3478*
—. Bible. Embury, Philip. Ireland. Methodism. 1760-1834. *3489*
—. Bishops. Catholic Church. Colombia (Bogotá). Hughes, John. Letters. Mosquera, Manuel José. 1853. *3762*
—. Blum, Abraham. California (Los Angeles). Judaism (Reform). Rabbis. Texas (Galveston). 1866-1921. *4217*
—. Boycotts. Consumers. Jews. Meat, kosher. Prices. Riots. Women. 1902. *4112*
—. Brown, Robert McAfee. Personal Narratives. Presbyterian Church. Union Theological Seminary. VanDusen, Henry Pitney. 1945-75. *767*
—. California (San Francisco). Goldie, Albert. Judaism (Orthodox, Reform). Poor. Synagogues. Weinstock, Harris. 1906. *4166*
—. Catholic Church. Civil War. Copperheads. Editors and Editing. *Metropolitan Record* (newspaper). Mullaly, John. 1861-64. *1234*
—. Catholic Church. Clergy. Human rights. Social progress. Varela, Félix. 1823-53. *2357*
—. Catholic Church. Democratic Party. Immigrants. Prohibition. Protestantism. Tammany Hall. 1840-60. *2594*
—. Charities. Episcopal Church, Protestant. Iowa (Iowa City). Orphans' Home of Industry. Townsend, Charles Collins. 1854-68. *2507*
—. Charities. Federation for the Support of Jewish Philanthropic Societies. Judaism. 1917-33. *2516*
—. Christianity. Episcopal Church, Protestant. Fiction. Grace Church. Melville, Herman ("The Two Temples"). Trinity Church. 1845-50. *2061*
—. Church of England. Laity. Neau, Elias. Negroes. Society for the Propagation of the Gospel. 1704-22. *3193*
—. Churches. Dutch Americans. Reformed Dutch Church. 1686-88. *3166*
—. Churches. Episcopal Church, Protestant. Roofs. Trinity Church. Upjohn, Richard. 1839-42. *1774*
—. Churches. Idealism. LaFarge, John. Painting. 1877-88. *1898*

—. City Life. Cromwell, James W. Friends, Society of. Personal narratives. 1842-60. *3271*
—. Congregation Kahal Kadosh Shearith Israel. Ethnicity. Falkenau, Jacob J. M. Hebrew. Jews. Lyons, Jacques Judah. Pique, Dob. Poetry. 1786-1841. *2062*
—. Congregation Shearith Israel. Judaism (Orthodox). Rhode Island (Newport). Touro Synagogue. 1893-1902. *4183*
—. Domesticity. Methodism. Palmer, Phoebe. Women. ca 1825-60. *877*
—. Episcopal Church, Protestant. Newspapers. Racism. Riots. St. Philip's Church. Williams, Peter, Jr. 1830-50. *2142*
—. Fund raising. Jewish Theological Seminary. Judaism (Orthodox). Mergers. Seminaries. Yeshiva College. 1925-28. *736*
—. Jesus Christ. Judaism (Orthodox, Reform). Sermons. Theology. Wise, Stephen Samuel. 1925-26. *4153*
—. Librarians. Presbyterian Church. Smith, Henry B. Union Theological Seminary. 1851-77. *758*
—. Libraries. Pettee, Julia. Presbyterian Church. Rockwell, William Walker. Union Theological Seminary Library. 1908-58. *759*
—. Matthews, Robert ("Matthias the Prophet"). Retrenchment Society. Sects, Religious. 1828-35. *70*
—. Music. Negroes. Pennsylvania (Philadelphia). Protestant churches. ca 1800-44. *1948*
—. Protestant churches. Social problems. 1970's. *2421*
New York City (Brooklyn). American Revolution. Daily life. Great Britain. Johnson, Jeremiah. Military Occupation. Personal narratives. 1775-83. *63*
—. Architecture, Gothic Revival. Bolton, William J. Church of the Holy Trinity. Episcopal Church, Protestant. Stained glass windows. 1845-47. *1847*
—. Catholic Church. Dialects. French Language. Haitian Americans. 1970's. *3699*
—. Catholic Church. Holy Family Slovak Parish. Slovak Americans. 1905-80. *3869*
—. Concordia Collegiate Institute. Lutheran Church. New Jersey (East Rutherford, Trenton). Steege, Martin. 1921-73. *3343*
New York City (Brooklyn; Boro Park). Children. Judaism (Orthodox). Parents. Social Status. 1973. *4187*
New York City (Greenwich Village). Immigration. Italian Americans. Presbyterian Church. University Place Church. 1900-30. *3564*
New York City (Lower East Side). Ghettos. Jews. 1890-1920. *4108*
New York City (Queens). Clergy. Emanuel Lutheran Church. Lutheran Church. Personal narratives. Wyneken, Frederick G. 1887-1907. *3348*
New York Conference. Canada. Methodism. Missions and Missionaries. 1766-1862. *1607*
New York (Cornwall-on-the-Hudson). Abbott, Lyman. Clergy. Congregationalism. Parsons, Edward Smith. Personal narratives. 1885. *3136*
New York (Dansville). Adventists. Hydrotherapy. Jackson, James Caleb. Medical reform. White, Ellen G. 1864-65. *1451*
New York (East Hampton). Beecher, Lyman. Clergy. Presbyterian Church. Temperance Movements. 1799-1810. *2585*
New York (Finger Lakes area). Finch, John. Letters. Skaneateles Community. Utopias. 1843-45. *4302*
New York (Graymoor). Catholic Church. Chapel-of-St. John's-in-the-Wilderness. Ecumenism. Episcopal Church, Protestant. Society of the Atonement. Wattson, Paul James. White, Lurana Mary. 1909-18. *461*
New York Herald (newspaper). Bennett, James Gordon. Catholic Church. Immigration. 1835-70. *3850*
New York (Kingston). Jews. Laity. Leadership. Political Leadership. Protestant Churches. Social Status. 1825-60. *2600*
New York (Long Island). Dutch Americans. Reformed Dutch Church. 1636-1700. *3162*
—. Folk art. New England. Tombstones. 1660-18c. *1900*
New York (Low Hampton). Baptists. Letters. Miller, William. 1828. *2831*
New York (New Lebanon, Watervliet). Cohoon, Hannah Harrison. Massachusetts (Hancock). Painting. Shakers. 1817-64. *1902*
New York (Oneida County). Congregationalism. Finney, Charles G. Presbyterian Church. Revivals. 1825-27. *2245*
New York (review article). Bonomi, Patricia U. Ethnic Groups. Klein, Milton M. Pluralism. Provincial Government. 1690's-1770's. 1971-74. *1204*
New York (Rochester). Boyer, Paul. City Life. Johnson, Paul E. Middle Classes. Missions and Missionaries. Morality. Revivals. 1815-1920. 1978. *2800*
—. Congregationalism. Plymouth Church. 1853-1904. *3115*
—. Crapsey, Algernon Sidney. Episcopal Church, Protestant. Heresy. Humanitarian Reform. St. Andrew's Church. Trials. 1879-1927. *3234*
—. Dogberry, Obediah. Free thinkers. Freedom of thought. *Liberal Advocate* (newspaper). Religious liberty. 1832-34. *1003*
—. Friends, Society of. Larson, Lars. Larson, Martha. Norwegian Americans. Religious Liberty. Women. 1807-44. *3263*
—. Radicals and Radicalism. Revivalism. Social Reform. 1830-56. *2416*
New York (Rockland County; Clarkstown, Clarksville). Kanniff, Jane. Witchcraft. 1816. *2213*
New York State Lunatic Asylum. Assassination. Gray, John P. Moral insanity. Psychiatry. Trials. 1854-86. *2346*
New York Thruway. Folklore. Jesus Christ. Vanishing hitchhiker (theme). 1971. *2737*
New York *Tribune* (newspaper). Adventists. Dowling, John. Greeley, Horace. Miller, William. 1842. *2963*
New York (Utica). Evangelicalism. Revivals. Women. 1800-40. *922*
—. Evil eye. Folklore. Italian Americans. 20c. *2192*
New York, western. Anti-Masonic movement. Baptists. Freemasonry. Morgan, William. 1826-30. *2362*
—. Congregationalism. Family. Methodism. Mormons. New England. Young, Brigham. 18c-1830's. *2840*
—. France. Indians. Jesuits. Missions and Missionaries. Rings. ca 1630-87. *1664*
—. Friends, Society of. Frontier and Pioneer Life. Hutchinson, Mathias. Ontario. Pennsylvania, central. Travel (accounts). 1819-20. *3280*
—. Great Plains. Indian-White Relations. Mormons. Utah. Young, Brigham. 1835-51. *3948*
New York Yearly Meeting. Friends, Society of. Massachusetts. Schisms. Vermont. 1845-1949. *3259*
New York (Yonkers). Catholic Church. Independence Movements. Kubašek, John J. Slovak Americans. 1902-50. *3870*
Newcomb, Horace. Baptists, Southern. Personal narratives. 1940's-70's. *3052*
Newcomer, Christian. Boehm, Martin. Mennonites. Pennsylvania Germans. Revivalism. 1740-1850. *2266*
Newell, Samuel. Baptists. Judson, Adoniram. Missions and Missionaries. 1810-21. *1731*
Newfoundland *See also* Labrador.
—. Bishops. Catholic Church. Church of England. Evangelicalism. Feild, Edward. Liturgy. Methodism. Presbyterian Church. 1765-1852. *3197*
—. Bishops. Catholic Church. Church of England. Liberal Party. Provincial government. 1860-62. *1253*
—. Bishops. Church of England. Education. Feild, Edward. Great Britain. 1826-44. *3198*
—. Catholic Church. Feild, Edward. Irish Canadians. Mullock, John Thomas. Politics. Protestant Churches. 19c. *1254*
—. Coughlin, Lawrence. Methodism. 1765-1815. *3477*
Newfoundland (Avalon Peninsula). Calvert, George (1st Lord Baltimore). Catholic Church. Colonization. Protestant churches. Religious Liberty. 1620's. *2755*
Newman Clubs. *America* (periodical). Catholic Church. Colleges and Universities. LaFarge, John. 1904-50's. *515*
Newman, John Henry. Brownson, Orestes A. Catholic University of Ireland. Great Britain. Ireland. 1853-54. *3837*
Newman, John Henry *(Apologia pro Vita Sua).* Attitudes. Autobiography. Brownson, Orestes A. *(The Convert).* Catholic Church. Converts. Great Britain. Protestantism. 1857-64. *3681*
Newmark, Joseph. California (Los Angeles). Judaism (Reform). Letters. Rabbis. Wilshire Boulevard Temple. 1881. *4236*
Newspapers *See also* Editors and Editing; Freedom of the Press; Journalism; Periodicals; Press.
—. Adventists. Massachusetts, western. Miller, William. Public opinion. 1840's. *2079*
—. Anglin, Timothy Warren. Catholic Church. Irish Canadians. New Brunswick. St. John *Freeman* (newspaper). 1849-83. *3680*
—. Anti-Semitism. California (San Francisco). D'Ancona, David Arnold. Letters. Pixley, Frank M. 1883. *2128*
—. Antislavery Sentiments. Editors and Editing. Kansas. Providence. Rhetoric. 1855-58. *2034*
—. Attitudes. Clergy. Lyche, Hans Tambs. Norway. Travel (accounts). Unitarianism. 1880-92. *4081*
—. Baptists. Methodist Episcopal Church, South. Presbyterian Church (Cumberland, Old School). Texas. 1829-61. *2907*
—. Baptists, Southern. Graves, James Robinson. Seminaries. *Tennessee Baptist* (newspaper). 1820-93. *3076*
—. Baptists, Southern. History. Research. 1977. *209*
—. Beiliss, Mendel. California (Oakland, San Francisco). Christianity. Jews. Russia. Trials. 1911-13. *4105*
—. Bibliographies. Mormons. 1977. *4042*
—. *Boston Evening Post* (newspaper). Fleet, Thomas. Freedom of the press. Great Awakening. Massachusetts (Boston). 1740's. *1423*
—. California. Catholic Church. Mission San Gabriel Arcangel. 1867. *1658*
—. Catholic Church. Conservatism. Nativism. Political Commentary. Protestantism. *Providence Visitor* (newspaper). Rhode Island. 1916-24. *2118*
—. Catholic Church. Education. Ontario. 1851-1948. *543*
—. Catholic Church. German Americans. Immigrants. Kansas (Atchison). Pluralism. 1854-59. *3877*
—. Catholic Church. Journalism. 1822-1975. *3831*
—. Chinese Americans. Christianity. Judaism. Nativism. Pacific Coast. Slavery. 1848-65. *75*
—. Episcopal Church, Protestant. New York City. Racism. Riots. St. Philip's Church. Williams, Peter, Jr. 1830-50. *2142*
—. Fugitive Slave Act (US, 1850). Methodist Church. Slavery. 1850. *3476*
—. Fundamentalism. Ham, Mordecai F. North Carolina (Elizabeth City). Revivals. Saunders, William O. 1924. *2217*
—. Jews. Letters-to-the-editor. Mexico (Tamaulipas; Matamoros). Texas (Brownsville). 1876-82. *4165*
—. Methodist Episcopal Church, South. South. 1861-65. *3487*
—. Methodist Episcopal Church (South). South. Spanish-American War. 1898. *2691*
—. Mormons. Periodicals. Public Opinion. 1970's. *2071*
Newton, Thomas. Boudinot, Elias. Millenarianism. Presbyterian Church. Theology. 1787-1821. *3569*
Newton, William. Alberta (Edmonton). Church of England. Indians. Métis. 1875-1900. *3196*
Nez Percé Indians. Idaho. McBeth, Sue L. Missions and Missionaries. Presbyterian Church. 1874. *1591*
—. Indians. McBeth, Sue L. Missions and Missionaries. Presbyterian Church. 1873-93. *1509*
Nicholet, Charles. Clergy (tenure). Higginson, John. Massachusetts (Salem). Puritans. Social change. 1672-76. *3620*
Nichols, Clarina I. H. Feminism. Kansas. Letters. Sex roles. Theology. 1857-69. *843*
Nicholson, David Bascom, III. Baptist Student Center. Education. Georgia (Athens). 1925-52. *631*
Nicoll, John R. A. Catholic Church. Great Britain. Isolationism. Roosevelt, Franklin D. (administration). World War II. 1943. *1241*
Niebuhr, H. Richard. Bergson, Henri. Historiography. Morality. Troeltsch, Ernst. 1925-37. *255*
—. Bibliographies. Dissertations. Edwards, Jonathan. Niebuhr, Reinhold. Presbyterian Church. Reformed Churches. Tillich, Paul. 18c-20c. 1965-72. *2815*
—. Social sciences. Theology. ca 1930-70. *125*

Niebuhr, Reinhold. American experience. Theology, public. 1974. *2896*
—. Barth, Karl. Ethics. Liberalism. 1920's-60. *2359*
—. Beard, Charles A. Foreign policy. 20c. *1364*
—. Bibliographies. Dissertations. Edwards, Jonathan. Niebuhr, H. Richard. Presbyterian Church. Reformed Churches. Tillich, Paul. 18c-20c. 1965-72. *2815*
—. Capitalism. Marxism. *Radical Religion* (periodical). Roosevelt, Franklin D. (administration). 1930-43. *1343*
—. Carter, Jimmy. South. 1976. *1233*
—. Christian Realism. Eschatology. Radicalism. 20c. *2927*
—. Christian realism. Freedom. 1915-63. 1960's-70's. *2360*
—. Christian realism. Liberalism. Philosophy. 1920's. *1359*
—. Christian realism. Politics. Theodicy. ca 1940-73. *1403*
—. Christianity. Judaism. 1930-60. *137*
—. Christianity. Muste, A. J. Pacifism. Political Theory. Thomas, Norman. 1914-38. *2687*
—. Christianity. Philosophy of history. 20c. *2859*
—. Conservatism. 20c. *1394*
—. Democracy. Liberals. 1930-45. *1367*
—. German Evangelical Synod of North America. Pacifism. Patriotism. Theology. World War I. 1915-18. *2639*
—. History. Theology. 1974. *2856*
—. Liberalism. Marxism. Philosophy. 1927-69. *1422*
—. Liberalism. Political Theory. ca 1920-72. *1355*
—. Pacifism. 1932-34. *2638*
—. Philosophy. Secularism. Theology. 1974. *2855*
—. Philosophy. Theology. 1974. *2940*
—. Political thought. Theology. 1927-59. *1417*
—. Politics. Theology. 20c. *2895*
—. Theology. 1892-1971. *2825*
Niebuhr, Reinhold *(Moral Man and Immoral Society)*. Sin (doctrine). Theology. 1930's. *2909*
—. 1932-59. *2933*
Niebuhr, Reinhold (review article). Freudianism. Marxism. Original sin. Protestantism. Theology. 1939-70. *2838*
Nieto, Jacob. California. Charities. Disaster relief. Economic aid. Jews. Rabbis. San Francisco Earthquake and Fire. 1906. *2520*
—. California (San Francisco). Jews. Rabbis. Rubin, Max. Temple Sherith Israel. 1893. *4148*
Nihilism. James, William. Psychology. 1870-1910. 1975. *50*
Nilsson, Frederik Olaus. Baptists. Circuit riders. Diaries. Immigrants. Minnesota. Swedish Americans. 1855-65. *3046*
Ninth Street Baptist Church. Baptists. Methodist Church. Ohio (Cincinnati). Political protest. Temperance Movements. Wesley Chapel. Women's Christian Temperance Union. 1874. *2582*
Nissenbaum, Stephen. Boyer, Paul. Massachusetts (Salem). Puritans. Witchcraft (review article). 1550-1690. 1974-76. *2200*
Nixon, Richard M. Civil religion. Elections (presidential). Voting and Voting Behavior. 1972. *1197*
—. Hoover, Herbert C. Johnson, Lyndon B. Protestant ethic. Public welfare. Rhetoric. Roosevelt, Franklin D. Weber, Max. 1905-79. *348*
—. McGovern, George S. Political Campaigns (presidential). Rhetoric. Voting and Voting Behavior. 1972. *1228*
Noah, Mordecai Manuel. Ararat (colony). Judaism (Orthodox). New York. Rhode Island (Newport). 1813-21. *4178*
Nobili, John. California. Jesuits. Santa Clara, University of. 1850-55. *695*
Nobility *See also* Aristocracy.
—. Catholic Church. New France. Sulpicians. 17c-18c. *2611*
Nolan, Edward J. Church and state. France. Gibbons, James. Letters. Sabatier, Paul. 1906. *1016*
Nome Hebrew Benevolent Society. Alaska. Fur trade. Gold rushes. Jews. 1867-1916. *4103*
Nominations for office. Bishops. Canada, western. Catholic Church. French Canadians. Irish Canadians. 1900-75. *3765*
Nonconformists. American Revolution. Episcopal Church, Protestant. New York. Political Factions. Provincial government. 1768-71. *1294*
—. American Revolution. Great Britain. 1765-83. *1401*
—. Great Britain. Methodism. Revivals. 1828-43. *2223*
Non-Sectarian Church of St. Louis. Cave, Robert Catlett. Disciples of Christ. Liberalism. Missouri (St. Louis). Theology. 1867-1923. *2913*
Nonsectarianism. *Engel* v. *Vitale* (US, 1962). New York. Prayer. Public opinion. Public schools. 1962. *581*
Nonviolence. Baptists. Civil rights. King, Martin Luther, Jr. Negroes. 1950's-68. *2533*
—. Baptists. King, Martin Luther, Jr. Muelder, W. G. Personalism. Theology. Tillich, Paul. Wieman, Henry Nelson. 1955-68. *2552*
—. Catholic Church. Cities. Merton, Thomas. Reform. Social criticism. 1960's. *2417*
—. Friends, Society of. Indian Wars. Paxton Boys. Pennsylvania (Philadelphia). 1764-67. *2693*
Normal School. *See* Teachers Colleges.
Norman, Jeremiah. Diaries. Evangelism. Georgia (Augusta Circuit). Methodist Episcopal Church. 1798-1801. *1642*
Norris, J. Frank. Anti-Catholicism. Baptists. Fundamentalism. Morality. Texas. 1920's. *2889*
—. Baptists, Southern. Bureaucracies. Democracy. 1920-40. *3084*
North America. Agriculture. Hutterites. Lifestyles. Social Customs. Technological innovation. 18c-20c. *3349*
—. Amish. Doukhobors. Hutterites. Mennonites. Molokans. ca 1650-1977. *2769*
—. Anti-Catholicism. Colonization. Great Britain. Ideology. Ireland. Protestantism. ca 1550-1600. *2086*
—. Antislavery Sentiments. Friends, Society of. 1671-1771. *2480*
—. Archival Catalogs and Inventories. Congregatio de Propaganda Fide. France. Vatican. 1622-1799. 1979. *182*
—. Bibliographies. Europe. Folk religion. 1900-74. 16c-20c. *42*
—. Brethren, Swiss. Immigration. Mennonites. Surnames. 1680-1880. *3417*
—. Catholic Church. Church and State. Europe, Western. Politics. 1870-1974. *1326*
—. Christianity. Latin America. Socialism. 20c. *953*
—. Colleges and Universities. Consortium of Peace Research, Education and Development. Mennonites. Peace Studies. 1965-80. *2650*
—. Diaries. Great Britain. Physicians. Theologians. Ward, John. 17c. *2312*
—. Emigration. Epp, Johann. Letters. Mennonites. Russia. 1875. *3373*
—. Mennonites. Morality. Officeholding. Voting and Voting Behavior. 1860-1940. *955*
North American Phalanx. Communes. New Jersey (Perth Amboy, Red Bank). Raritan Bay Union. Spring, Marcus. 1843-59. *413*
North Carolina *See also* South; Southeastern States.
—. American Revolution. Church of England. Conspiracies. Llewelyn, John. Loyalists. 1776-77. *1224*
—. Americanization. Church of England. Great Britain. Parishes. 1701-12. *298*
—. Anti-Catholicism. Anti-Semitism. Education. Minorities. Prejudice. Religious beliefs. 1957-73. *2093*
—. Armies. Butler, Benjamin F. Chaplains. Civil War. Diaries. Fort Fisher (battle). Negroes. Turner, Henry M. 1864-65. *2685*
—. Arts and Crafts. Girls. Moravian Church. Pennsylvania. Students. 19c. *1862*
—. Baptists. Bode, Frederick A. (review article). Capitalism. Methodist Church. Populism. 1894-1903. 1975. *1287*
—. Baptists. Church and State. Church of England. Presbyterians. Provincial Government. Tryon, William. 1765-76. *1036*
—. Baptists. Social control. 1772-1908. *2445*
—. Baptists, Southern. Southeastern Baptist Theological Seminary. Wake Forest College. 1945-51. *748*
—. Bibliographies. 1975-76. *20*
—. Bibliographies. Dissertations. Prehistory-1970's. *28*
—. Brickell, John. Clayton, John. Letters. Natural History. Plagiarism. 1693-1737. *2341*
—. Camp Lejeune. Lamb Studios. Marines. New Jersey (Tenafly). Protestantism. Stained glass windows. 1775-1943. *1867*
—. Cheshire, Joseph Blount, Jr. Episcopal Church, Protestant. Negroes. Paternalism. Race Relations. 1870-1932. *2140*
—. Church of God. Personal narratives. Reed, Granny. 20c. *3520*
—. Clergy. Methodist Church. Personal narratives. Young, John. 1747-1837. *3507*
—. Confederate States of America. Conscientious objectors. Friends, Society of. 1861-65. *2708*
—. Constitutions, State. New Jersey. Pennsylvania. Presbyterian Church. 1775-87. *1285*
—. Doub, Peter. Education. Methodist Episcopal Church. Slavery. Women. 1796-1869. *3469*
—. Episcopal Church, Protestant. Religious commitment. Salience. 1975. *3222*
—. Localism. Social classes. Temperance Movements. 1969-70. *2599*
—. Lutheran Church (Alpha Synod). Negroes. 1889-91. *3327*
North Carolina (Durham). Academic freedom. Bassett, John Spencer. Duke University. Methodist Church. Racism. *South Atlantic Quarterly* (periodical). 1902-03. *3497*
North Carolina, east. Church of England. Public Administration. St. John's Church. St. Paul's Church. 1729-75. *3240*
North Carolina (Elizabeth City). Fundamentalism. Ham, Mordecai F. Newspapers. Revivals. Saunders, William O. 1924. *2217*
North Carolina (Halifax County). Civil War. Letters. Methodist Church. Slavery. Wills, Washington. 1861-65. *2171*
North Carolina (Piedmont region). Pluralism. Protestantism. 1890-1952. *2813*
North Carolina (Salem). Dissent. Economic conditions. Military Service. Moravian Church. Slavery. Social change. Women. 1772-1860. *3516*
North Central States *See also* individual states; Old Northwest; Midwest.
—. Adventists. Automobile Industry and Trade. Worth, William O. 1890-1913. *361*
—. Brethren in Christ. Canada. Holiness movement. 1910-50. *3435*
—. Bygdelag movement. Ethnicity. Nationalism. Norwegian Americans. 1901-30. *3319*
—. Catholic Church. French Canadians. Settlement. Social Customs. 19c. *3804*
—. Catholic Church. Louisiana. Rosati, Joseph (review article). 1818-43. *3734*
—. Clergy. Disciples of Christ. Frontier. Personal narratives. Snethen, Abraham. 1794-1830. 1977. *3112*
—. Cultural Pluralism. Jensen, Richard. Kleppner, Paul. Political behavior. 1850-1900. *1214*
—. Fundamentalism. Long, Huey P. Populism. Progressivism. Smith, Gerald L. K. 1934-48. *975*
—. Methodist Church, Primitive. 1842-1976. *3508*
North Dakota *See also* Western States.
—. Architecture. Churches (Gothic Revival, Victorian Gothic). Episcopal Church, Protestant. Upjohn, Richard. 1874-1903. *1815*
—. Bishops. Catholic Church. Irish Americans. Jamestown Diocese. Minnesota (St. Paul). Shanley, John. 1852-1909. *3731*
—. Catholic Church. Education. Indians. Missions and Missionaries. Pioneers. Presentation of the Blessed Virgin Mary, Sisters of the. South Dakota. Women. 1880-96. *727*
—. Christianity. Frontier and Pioneer Life. Red River of the North. ca 1870-97. *2733*
—. Clergy. Lutheran Church, Norwegian. Norwegian Americans. Red River of the North. 1871-99. *3318*
—. Dutch Americans. Immigration. Reformed Dutch Church. South Dakota. 1880's-1951. *3161*
—. Methodist Church. Missions and Missionaries. Settlement. 1871-1914. *1523*
North Dakota (Grand Forks). Jews. Papermaster, Benjamin. 1890-1934. *4135*
North Dakota (Hannaford). Church suppers. Ladies Aid Society. Lutheran Church (Norwegian). Norwegian Americans. 1941. *3310*
North Dakota (Ross). Depressions. Juma, Charlie. Personal narratives. Syrian Americans. 1900's-30's. *35*

North, Frank M. Federal Council of the Churches of Christ in America. Methodist Federation for Social Service. Social Creed of Methodism. Ward, Harry F. 1907-12. *2388*

North or Northern States *See also* individual states.

—. Catholic Church. Cities. Negroes. Occupations. Social Status. 1968. *2613*

—. Civil War. Puritan tradition. South. 1840's-60's. *2842*

—. Death and Dying. Literature. Protestantism. Women. 1830-80. *2846*

—. Friends, Society of. Lawrence, Daniel. Printing. 1788-1812. *3258*

—. Slavery. South. Unitarianism. 1831-60. *2174*

Northeastern or North Atlantic States *See also* individual states; New England.

—. Adventists. Camp meetings. 1840's. *2231*

—. Attitudes. Ethnicity. Israel. Jews. Students. Zionism. 1973-76. *4155*

—. Baptists. Folger, Peter. Indians. Jones, David. Missionaries. Williams, Roger. 1638-1814. *1619*

—. Baptists, Southern. Language. Missions. Southern Baptist Convention Home Missions Board. 1950-75. *1620*

—. Children. Evangelicalism. Protestant Churches. Sunday Schools. Theology. 1820's. *604*

—. Church of England. Clergy. Delaware. Vestries. 1690-1775. *311*

—. Congregationalism. Dwight, Timothy *(Travels in New England and New York).* 1796-1815. *2022*

—. Dunkards. Evangelism. German Americans. Great Awakening. Immigration. Lutheran Church. Moravian Church. Reformed churches. 1720-60. *2237*

—. Fund raising. Hyde, Orson. Illinois (Nauvoo). Mormons. Tabernacle project. 1845-46. *4048*

Northwest Rebellion. Canada. Letters. Millenarianism. Riel, Louis. 1876-78. 1885. *965*

—. Messianic Movements. Prairie Provinces. Riel, Louis. 1869-85. *964*

Northwest Territories *See also* Yukon Territory.

—. Catholic Church. Discrimination. Teachers colleges. 1884-1900. *77*

—. Church of England. Indians. McDonald, Robert. Missions and Missionaries. Yukon Territory. 1850's-1913. *1604*

Northwest Territories (Baffin Island). Church Missionary Society. Church of England. Eskimos. Hudson's Bay Company. Missionaries. Peck, E. J. Trade. 1894-1913. *1660*

Northwestern College (Zwemer Hall). Architecture. Iowa (Orange City). Reformed Dutch Church. 1890-1924. *1806*

Norway. Americanization. Methodist Episcopal Church. Missions and Missionaries. Petersen, Ole Peter. 1830-53. *1706*

—. Attitudes. Clergy. Lyche, Hans Tambs. Newspapers. Travel (accounts). Unitarianism. 1880-92. *4081*

—. Clergy. Ecumenism. Lutheran Church (Missouri Synod, Norwegian). Munch, Johan Storm. Wisconsin (Wiota). 1827-1908. *3324*

Norwegian Americans. Altarpieces. Christenson, Lars. Folk art. Lutheran Church. Minnesota (Benson). Wood Carving. 1887-1904. *1874*

—. Bygdelag movement. Ethnicity. Nationalism. North Central States. 1901-30. *3319*

—. Church and State. Diaries. Lutheran Church. Preus, Herman A. Wisconsin (Columbia, Dane counties). 1851-60. *1104*

—. Church suppers. Ladies Aid Society. Lutheran Church (Norwegian). North Dakota (Hannaford). 1941. *3310*

—. Clergy. Country stores. Duus, O. F. Knoph, Thomas. Ledgers. Lutheran Church. Wisconsin (Waupaca township; Scandinavia). 1853-56. *3334*

—. Clergy. Janson, Kristofer. Minnesota (Minneapolis). Unitarianism. 1881-82. *4078*

—. Clergy. Lutheran Church, Norwegian. North Dakota. Red River of the North. 1871-99. *3318*

—. Friends, Society of. Larson, Lars. Larson, Martha. New York (Rochester). Religious Liberty. Women. 1807-44. *3263*

—. Hymnals. Lutheran Church (Hauge's Synod, Norwegian Synod). Lutheran Church in America, Norwegian. Youth. 1878-1916. *1915*

—. Immigrants. Letters. Pennsylvania (Harmony, New Harmony). Rapp, George. 1816-26. *378*

—. Lutheran Free Church. Religious Liberty. Sermons. Sverdrup, Georg. Thanksgiving. 1896-1907. *3304*

Nova Scotia *See also* Atlantic Provinces.

—. Acadians. Acculturation. Catholic Church. Exiles. France. Great Britain. 18c. *3750*

—. Alline, Henry. Charisma. Integration. Revivals. 1776-83. *2264*

—. American Revolution. Bailey, Jacob. Church of England. Exiles. Letters. 1784. *3226*

—. Antigonish Movement. Catholic Church. Rural Development. Social change. ca 1928-73. *2409*

—. Baptists. McKim, Andrew. Politics. Provincial Legislatures. 1784-1840. *1309*

—. Christianity. Indian-White Relations. Micmac Indians. Missions and Missionaries. New Brunswick. 1803-60. *1649*

—. Church of England. Dalhousie University. King's College, University of. Mergers. Presbyterian Church. 1821-37. *684*

—. Church of England. Loyalists. Society for the Propagation of the Gospel. 1787-1864. *1644*

—. Coke, Thomas. Garrettson, Freeborn. Letters. Methodist Church. Missions and Missionaries. Wesley, John. 1786. *1490*

—. Colleges and Universities. Common Sense school. Curricula. Dalhousie University. King's College. Lyall, William. Philosophy. Pine Hill Divinity Hall. Presbyterian Church. 1850-90. *719*

—. Colleges and universities. Dalhousie University. McCulloch, Thomas. Missions and Missionaries. Pictou Academy. Presbyterian Church. ca 1803-42. *591*

—. Communalism. Holy Ghost and Us Society. *Kingdom Come, Ark of the Holy Ghost and US Society* (vessel). Sanford, Frank. Sects, Religious. Shipwrecks. 1910-48. *4261*

—. Cromwell, James. Garrettson, Freeborn. Methodist Episcopal Church. Missionaries. USA. 1785-1800. *1581*

—. German Canadians. Immigrants. Protestants. 1749-52. *2852*

—. Literature. McCulloch, Thomas *(Letters of Mephibosheth Stepsure).* Presbyterian Church. Satire. 1821-22. *2067*

—. Missionaries. Raymond, Eliza Ruggles. Sierra Leone (Sherbro Island). Slaves. Women. 1839-50. *1692*

Nova Scotia (Annapolis Valley). Baptists. Creeds. 1760-1980. *3060*

Nova Scotia (Barney's River). Blair, Duncan Black. Gaelic language. Poets. Presbyterianism. Scholarship. 1848-93. *2069*

Nova Scotia (Cornwallis Township). Disciples of Christ. 1812-1910. *3103*

Nova Scotia (Dartmouth). Friends, Society of. Marriage. 1786-89. *864*

Nova Scotia (Halifax). Anti-Catholicism. Civil Rights. Irish Canadians. Law. 1749-1829. *1105*

—. Barnes, James. Editorials. Murray, Robert. *Presbyterian Witness and Evangelical Advocate* (newspaper). 1848-1910. *3584*

—. *Challenger* (vessel). Honeyman, David. Oceanography. 1872-76. *2329*

—. Church of England. Missions and Missionaries. St. Paul's Church. Society for the Propagation of the Gospel. Tutty, William. 1749-52. *1646*

—. Churches. 1784-1825. *1763*

—. Editors and Editing. "Letter to My Country Friends" (series). Murray, Robert. *Presbyterian Witness* (newspaper). 1863. *987*

Nova Scotia (Lochaber). Catholic Church. Daily Life. Presbyterians. Rural Settlements. 1830-1972. *2747*

Nova Scotia (Pictou). MacGregor, James. Missions and Missionaries. Presbyterian Church of Scotland. 1786-1830. *1634*

Nova Scotia (Pictou County). Blair, Duncan Black. Gaelic language. Poetry. Presbyterianism. Scholars. Scotland. 1846-93. *2070*

—. Factionalism. Presbyterian Church. Scottish Canadians. Social Conditions. 1898-1966. *3533*

Nova Scotia (Springhill). Clergy. Presbyterian Church. 1874-1925. *3532*

—. Ecumenism. Methodist Church. Presbyterian Church. St. Andrew's Wesley United Church of Canada. United Church of Canada. 1800-1976. *2829*

Nova Scotia (Yarmouth). Economic Conditions. Great Awakening. Social Conditions. 1760's-70's. *2626*

Novels. Anti-Catholicism. Breslin, Jimmy. Brooklyn Diocese. Flaherty, Joe. Hamill, Pete. Irish Americans. New York City. 1960's-70's. *2098*

—. Baptists. Dayton, Amos Cooper. Landmark Movement. South. 1850-65. *1995*

—. Brúnum, Eiríkur á. Iceland. Laxness, Halldór *(Paradise Reclaimed).* Mormons. 1870-1900. 1960. *2075*

—. Caldwell, Erskine. Caldwell, Ira Sylvester. Presbyterian Church, Associate Reformed. South. 1900-78. *2017*

—. Catholic Church. Popular Culture. 1970's. *2054*

—. Christianity. 1870-1900. *2074*

—. Christianity. Lewis, Sinclair. Science. Secular humanism. 1900-50. *2003*

—. Church of England. Clergy. Episcopal Church, Protestant. Ingraham, Joseph Holt. Prisons. Public Schools. Reform. Tennessee (Nashville). 1847-51. *3241*

—. Folklore. Steinbeck, John *(Winter of Our Discontent).* Witchcraft. 1961. *2046*

—. Hawthorne, Nathaniel. History. Puritan tradition. Social reform. Symbolism in Literature. 1825-63. *2019*

—. Humor. Illustration. Mormons. Periodicals. 1850-60. *2004*

—. Literary movement, regional. Mormons. Utah. 1940's. *2025*

—. Massachusetts (Boston). Unitarianism. Ware, William. 1837-52. *2010*

—. New England. Presbyterian Church. Salvation. Stowe, Harriet Beecher. Theology. Women. 1845-85. *2038*

Novels (western). Emmett, James Simpson. Friendship. Grey, Zane. Mormons. Utah. 1907. *2072*

Novitiate of St. Stanislaus. Anti-Catholicism. Conscription, Military. Jesuits. Ontario (Guelph). Protestantism. World War I. 1918-19. *2657*

Noyes, John Humphrey. Authority. Charisma. Oneida Community. 1875-81. *418*

—. Family. New York. Oneida Community. Sex. 1848-80. *431*

—. Genetics. New York. Oneida Community. Stirpicultural experiment. Utopias. 1848-86. *946*

—. New York. Oneida Community. Sex. Social Status. Women. 1848-79. *863*

—. Oneida Community. Thomas, Robert David (review article). Utopias. 1811-86. 1977. *406*

Nullification crisis. Butler, Elizur. Cherokee Indians. Indian-White Relations. Marshall, John. Missions and Missionaries. Worcester, Samuel A. *Worcester* v. *Georgia* (US, 1832). 1828-33. *1583*

Numbers, Ronald L. (review article). Adventists. Health. Reform. White, Ellen G. ca 1840's-1915. 1976. *1457*

Nursery Schools. *See* Day Nurseries.

Nurses and Nursing *See also* Children; Hospitals.

—. Adventists. Battle Creek Sanitarium. California. Loma Linda University. Medical Education. Michigan. 1884-1979. *1425*

—. Canada. Charities. Slovak Americans. Slovak Canadians. USA. Vincentian Sisters of Charity. Women. 1902-78. *2525*

Nutting, John Danforth. Congregationalism. Evangelism. Far Western States. Mormons. Photographs. Utah Gospel Mission. 1900-50. *1560*

O

Oakes, Rachel. Adventists. New Hampshire (Washington). Preble, T. M. Sabbath. Wheeler, Frederick. 1841-44. *2287*

Oakes, Urian *(Elegie).* Poetry. Puritans. 1650-81. *1976*

Oaks, Dallin H. Assassination. Hill, Marvin S. Illinois (Carthage). Mormons. Smith, Joseph. Trials (review article). 1844. 1977. *2126*

O'Beirne, Eugene Francis. Anti-Catholicism. Manitoba (Red River country). Travel. 1860's. *2120*

Oberlin College. Adrian College. Baptists, Free Will. Hillsdale College. Methodist Church, Wesleyan. Michigan. Ohio. Olivet College. Social Reform. 1833-70. *741*

—. American Board of Commissioners for Foreign Missions. Ayer, Frederick. Chippewa Indians. Minnesota. Missions and Missionaries. Red Lake Mission. 1842-59. *1496*

Objectivist apologetics. Bible. Evangelicals. Inerrancy (doctrine). Montgomery, John W. (review article). 1972. *2882*
Oblates of Mary Immaculate. Canada, western. Catholic Church. Indians. Missions and Missionaries. 1818-70. *1502*
O'Brien, Alice. Catholic Church. Minnesota (St. Paul). Philanthropy. Women. 1914-62. *2419*
Occult Sciences *See also* Astrology; Magic; Witchcraft.
—. Ballard, Edna. Ballard, Guy. I AM sect. 1930's-75. *4273*
—. British North America. Christianity. Deviant Behavior. Government. Historiography. 1600-1760. *2180*
—. Charismatic movement. Europe. Folk Religion (review article). Health. Science. 16c-19c. 1975-76. *7*
—. Church of Satan. LaVey, Anton Szandor. Satanism. 1966-75. *4240*
—. Church of the Sun. Middle Classes. 1960's. *4257*
—. Cults. Deviant Behavior. Transcendental Meditation. 1948-79. *4239*
—. *The Exorcist*, film (review article). Social Psychology. 1975. *2211*
—. German Americans. Pennsylvania. 17c-20c. *2183*
—. Jacobs, David M. (review article). UFO controversy. 1975. *2188*
Occupational mobility. Church membership. Cities. Education. Midwest. 1955-75. *2616*
Occupational status. Catholic Church. Children. Public schools. Socialization. -1974. *3784*
Occupations. Canada. Immigrants. Lifestyles. Lutheran Church. Settlement. Social Organizations. Swedish Americans. USA. 1893-1979. *3325*
—. Catholic Church. Cities. Negroes. North or Northern States. Social Status. 1968. *2613*
—. Catholic Church. Educational attainment. Immaculate Conception Primary School. Lithuanian Americans. Missouri (St. Louis). 1948-68. *2607*
—. Labor. Quebec (Montreal). Sex roles. Women. 1911-41. *1471*
Oceania. Missions and Missionaries. Pease, Benjamin. Pirates. 1867-70. *1685*
Oceanography. *Challenger* (vessel). Honeyman, David. Nova Scotia (Halifax). 1872-76. *2329*
O'Connell, William Henry. Catholic Church. Clergy. Massachusetts (Boston). 1915-44. *3741*
O'Connor, Michael. Bishops. Catholic Church. Church Finance. Frenaye, Mark Anthony. Letters. Pennsylvania (Pittsburgh). 1843-49. *368*
O'Conor, Charles. Anti-Catholicism. Constitutional Law. Ireland. Irish Americans. O'Conor, Charles Owen. Political reform. Reconstruction. 1865-85. *1031*
O'Conor, Charles Owen. Anti-Catholicism. Constitutional Law. Ireland. Irish Americans. O'Conor, Charles. Political reform. Reconstruction. 1865-85. *1031*
O'Dea, Thomas F. Mormons. Scholarship. 1957-74. *4012*
Oetgen, Jerome (review article). Benedictines. Catholic Church. Frontier and Pioneer Life. Wimmer, Boniface. 1809-87. *3685*
O'Farrell, Patrick (review article). Australia. Catholic Church. 17c-1977. *3733*
Officeholding. Church and State. Church of England. Congregationalism. Connecticut. Factionalism. Great Awakening. 1730-76. *1310*
—. Mennonites. Morality. North America. Voting and Voting Behavior. 1860-1940. *955*
Ogden, John C. Elections (presidential). Episcopal Church, Protestant. Illuminati controversy. Philadelphia *Aurora* (newspaper). Religious liberty. 1798-1800. *957*
O'Hare, Kate Richards. Christianity. Socialist Party. Women. 1901-17. *2559*
Ohio *See also* North Central States.
—. Adrian College. Baptists, Free Will. Hillsdale College. Methodist Church, Wesleyan. Michigan. Oberlin College. Olivet College. Social Reform. 1833-70. *741*
—. American Revolution. Delaware Indians. Indians. Missions and Missionaries. Moravian Church. Pennsylvania, western. 1775-83. *1532*
—. Antislavery Sentiments. Political attitudes. Revivals. Voting and Voting Behavior. 1825-70. *2866*
—. Assimilation. Authority. Bishops. Catholic Church. Cleveland Diocese. German Americans. Irish Americans. Rappe, Louis Amadeus. 1847-70. *3788*
—. Brethren in Christ (Wengerites). Indiana. Pentecostals. 1836-1924. *3432*
—. California. Circuit riders. Civil War. Frontier and Pioneer Life. Manuscripts. Methodism. Phillips, George. 1840-64. *3494*
—. Cedar Creek Monthly Meeting. Emancipation. Farms. Friends, Society of. Moorman, Clark Terrell. Virginia (Caroline County). 1766-1814. *2487*
—. Constitutional Amendments, State. Prohibition. Women's Christian Temperance Union. 1874-85. *2597*
—. Episcopal Church, Protestant. Evangelism. Frontier and Pioneer Life. McIlvaine, Charles Petit. Oxford Movement. 1800-75. *3187*
—. Evangelical Association. United Brethren in Christ. 1806-39. *3663*
—. Federal Aid to Education. Methodist Episcopal Church, African. Negroes. Wilberforce University (Combined Normal and Industrial Department). 1887-91. *518*
—. Indiana. Mennonites. Mumaw, George Shaum. Personal narratives. Singing Schools. 1900-57. *1941*
—. Indians. Kansas. Methodism. Removal policy. Wyandot Indians. 1816-60. *1598*
Ohio Antislavery Society. Finney, Charles G. Higher law (doctrine). Political Participation. Revivalism. 1835-60. *2253*
Ohio (Bedford). Catholic Church. Mary, Virgin. Our Lady of Levoča (statue). Slovakia (Spiš; Levoča). ca 13c-1975. *1884*
Ohio (Bluffton). Christmas. Emmanuel Church. Immigration. Reformed Tradition. Swiss Americans. 1840's-1900. *2857*
Ohio (Canton). Bible. Darwinism. Episcopal Church, Protestant. Europe. Excommunication. Hermeneutics. MacQueary, Howard. St. Paul's Church. Universalism. 1890-91. *3178*
—. Churches. Tilden, Guy. 1880's-1920's. *1790*
Ohio (Cincinnati). Academic Freedom. Hebrew Union College. Judaism, Reform. Kohler, Kaufmann. Zionism. 1903-07. *724*
—. Anti-Catholicism. City Politics. Ethnic groups. Immigrants. Temperance Movements. 1845-60. *2584*
—. Antislavery sentiments. Integration. Presbyterian Church, Reformed. Reformed Presbyterian Theological Seminary. 1845-49. *610*
—. Baptists. Methodist Church. Ninth Street Baptist Church. Political protest. Temperance Movements. Wesley Chapel. Women's Christian Temperance Union. 1874. *2582*
—. Cary, Samuel Fenton. Temperance movements. 1845-1900. *2583*
—. Catholic Church. Judaism. Lutheran Church. Public Schools. Religious Education. 19c. *545*
—. Catholic Church. Xavier University. 1831-61. *708*
—. Colleges and Universities. Hebrew Union College. Judaism (Reform). Judaism, Reform. Wise, Isaac Mayer. 1870's-1900. *613*
—. Education. Sisters of Charity of St. Joseph. Social Work. Women. 1809-1979. *2514*
—. Greek Americans. Negroes. Racism. 1970's. *2146*
—. Hebrew Union College. Judaism (Reform). 1942-45. *750*
—. Hebrew Union College. Judaism (Reform). Rabbis. Seminaries. Wise, Isaac Mayer. 1817-90's. *701*
—. Hexter, Maurice B. Jews. Personal narratives. Social Work. United Jewish Charities. 1910's. *2508*
Ohio (Cleveland). Anti-Catholicism. Elections (presidential). Ethnic Groups. Nativism. Republican Party. 1860. *1265*
—. Benedictine High School. Boys. Catholic Church. Secondary Education. 1928-78. *787*
—. Catholic Church. Church membership. 1860. *65*
Ohio (Columbus). Baptists, Southern. Clergy. Evangelism. 1969-76. *2988*
—. Charities. Federation movement. Judaism. 1904-48. *2522*
—. Cities. Congregationalism. Gladden, Washington. Reform. Social gospel. 1850's-1914. *2425*
Ohio Historical Society. Archival catalogs and inventories. Emmett, Daniel. Hymns. Minstrel Shows. Negroes. Sermons. 1838-96. 1976. *2064*
Ohio (Kirtland). Banking. Dissent. Mormons. 1837-90. *3980*
—. Coe, Truman. Letters. Mormons. Presbyterians. 1836. *2718*
—. Economic Conditions. Mormons. Smith, Joseph. 1830's. *351*
Ohio (Median County). Colleges and Universities. Immigration. Mennonites. Wadsworth Institute. 1825-80. *674*
Ohio (Mount Pleasant). Attitudes. Daily Life. Friends, Society of. 1795-1918. *3260*
Ohio (Western Reserve). Congregationalism. Connecticut. Free Thinkers. Frontier and Pioneer Life. Ingersoll, Robert. Wright, Elizur (and family). Yale University. 1762-1870. *56*
Ohio (Worthington). Congregationalism. Converts. Episcopal Church, Protestant. Kilbourne, James. Letters. Pioneers. 1844-49. *2823*
—. Episcopal Church, Protestant. Kilbourne, James. Settlement. 1744-1816. *3170*
Ohio Yearly Meeting. Emigration. Evangelism. Friends, Society of (Hicksite). 1828-1919. *3270*
Ohio (Youngstown). Anti-Catholicism. Anti-Semitism. Attitudes. Ku Klux Klan. Morality. Reform. 1920's. *2402*
Oil Industry and Trade. Clergy. Labor. Lynd, Robert S. Presbyterian Church. Wyoming (Elk Basin). 1921. *3562*
Oklahoma. Catholic Church. Church finance. Education. Indian-White Relations. Quapaw Indians. 1876-1927. *3727*
—. Catholic Church. Morality. Politics. Protestant Churches. Referendum. Sabbatarianism. Voting and Voting Behavior. 1959-76. *1290*
—. Catholic Church. National Prohibition League. Prohibition. Religious Liberty. State Government. 1907-18. *2580*
—. Cherokee Indians. Foreman, Stephen. Georgia. Indians. Presbyterian Church. 1820's-81. *3538*
—. Circuit riders. Frontier and Pioneer Life. German Americans. Lutheran Church (Missouri Synod). Texas. Wacker, Hermann Dietrich. 1847-1938. *3342*
—. Indians. Methodism. Missions and Missionaries. 1820-45. *1650*
Oklahoma (Oklahoma City). Ethnicity. Evangelical and Reformed Church. German Americans. Kamp, Henry. 1906-57. *3123*
Oklahoma (Penola County). Bloomfield Academy. Chickasaw Indians. Downs, Ellen J. Girls. Indians. Methodist Church. Personal Narratives. Schools. 1853-66. *772*
Oklahoma (Tulsa). Fasman, Oscar Z. Hebrew Theological College. Judaism (Orthodox). Ontario (Ottawa). Personal narratives. Rabbis. 1929-79. *4177*
Oklahoma, western. Church and State. Education. Episcopal Church, Protestant. Indians (agencies). Stouch, George W. H. Whirlwind Day School. ca 1904-14. *1086*
Oklahoma (Wichita Mountains). Baptists, American. Crawford, Isabel. Indians. Kiowa Indians. Missions and Missionaries. Women's American Baptist Home Missionary Society. 1893-1961. *1590*
Old Lights. Clergy. Congregationalism. Great Awakening. New England. New Lights. Social Classes. 1734-85. *2627*
Old Northwest *See also* North Central States.
—. Agriculture. Catholic Church. Federal Programs. Friends, Society of. Indian-White Relations. Missions and Missionaries. Moravian Church. 1789-1820. *1529*
—. Catholic Church. Church and state. Democracy. Dominicans. Mazzuchelli, Samuel Charles *(Memoirs)*. 1806-63. *1384*
Old South Church. Congregationalism. Historians. Massachusetts (Boston). Prince, Thomas. 1718-58. *275*
Old Southwest. Blackburn, Gideon. Cherokee Indians. Indians. Missions and Missionaries. Presbyterian Church. Schools. Whiskey. 1809-10. *700*
Old Swedes' Church. Gloria Dei Congregation. Lutheran Church. Pennsylvania (Philadelphia). Swedish Americans. 1638-98. *3302*
Old Zion Reformed Church. Pennsylvania (Brickerville). Reformed churches. 1732. *2935*

Oldham, George Ashton. Albany Diocese. Bishops. Episcopal Church, Protestant. New York. 1922-47. *3176*
O'Leary, Henry Joseph. Alberta, University of. Catholic Church. Colleges and Universities. Legal, Emile. St. Joseph's University College. 1906-26. *619*
Olier, Jean Jacques. Catholic Church. Quebec (Montreal). Sulpicians. 1630's-50's. *3798*
Olivet College. Adrian College. Baptists, Free Will. Hillsdale College. Methodist Church, Wesleyan. Michigan. Oberlin College. Ohio. Social Reform. 1833-70. *741*
Olivetan Benedictine Sisters, American. Arkansas (Jonesboro). Catholic Church. Missions and missionaries. Renggli, Rose (Mother Mary Beatrice). 1847-1942. *1652*
Olney, Thomas, Jr. Baptists. Fox, George. Friends, Society of. Politics. Rhode Island. 1672-73. *967*
Omaha Indians. Davies, David Jones. Davies, Gwen. Indians. Methodist Church, Calvinistic. Missions and Missionaries. Nebraska, eastern. 1853-60. *1514*
Oneida Community. Authority. Charisma. Noyes, John Humphrey. 1875-81. *418*
—. California (Orange County). Communalism. Middle Classes. Social Organization. Townerites. 1848-1910. *417*
—. Family. New York. Noyes, John Humphrey. Sex. 1848-80. *431*
—. Genetics. New York. Noyes, John Humphrey. Stirpicultural experiment. Utopias. 1848-86. *946*
—. Mormons. Sex roles. Shakers. Utopias. Women. ca 1825-90. *842*
—. New York. Noyes, John Humphrey. Sex. Social Status. Women. 1848-79. *863*
—. Noyes, John Humphrey. Thomas, Robert David (review article). Utopias. 1811-86. 1977. *406*
—. Utopias. 1837-86. *398*
Ontario. Algoma Diocese. Episcopal Church, Protestant. Missions and Missionaries. Society for the Propagation of the Gospel. 1873-1973. *1653*
—. Anti-Catholicism. Great Britain. Irish Canadians. Orange Order. Patriotism. 1830-1900. *2111*
—. Archives. Bishops. Catholic Church. Church History. Kingston, Archdiocese of. 1800-1966. *247*
—. Art. Fraktur. German Canadians. 1976. *1843*
—. Bishops. Catholic Church. Lynch, John Joseph. Poor. Toronto Savings Bank. 1870's. *369*
—. Boundaries. Catholic Church. Missions and Missionaries. Settlement. 1840-1910. *3709*
—. Brubacher, Henry. Brubacher, Jacob. Daily life. Letters. Mennonites. Pennsylvania. 1817-46. *3374*
—. Catholic Church. Church of England. Colonial Government. Macdonnell, Alexander. Ontario (Kingston, Toronto). Strachan, John. 1820's-30's. *1108*
—. Catholic Church. Clergy. Harris, William Richard. Toronto Archdiocese. 1846-1923. 1974. *3846*
—. Catholic Church. Education. Newspapers. 1851-1948. *543*
—. Catholic Church. French Canadians. Guigues, Joseph-Eugène. Ottawa Diocese. 1848-74. *3713*
—. Catholics. Great Britain. Immigration. Macdonnell, Alexander. Scottish Canadians. 1770's-1814. *3862*
—. Cultural history. Protestantism. 1840's-1900. *2844*
—. Education. Friends, Society of. Girls. 1790-1820. *749*
—. Friends, Society of. Frontier and Pioneer Life. Hutchinson, Mathias. New York, western. Pennsylvania, central. Travel (accounts). 1819-20. *3280*
—. Higher education. Methodist Church. Women. 19c. *3504*
—. Mennonites, Old Order. 1786-1980. *3367*
Ontario (Algoma, Huron). Church of England. Education. Indians. Methodist Church. Missions and Missionaries. Wilson, Edward F. 1868-93. *1596*
Ontario (Bruce County; Waterloo). Catholic Church. Cemeteries. German Alsatians. Gravemarkers. Iron work. 1850-1910. *1880*
Ontario (Cobourg). Church of England. Clergy. Diocesan Theological Institute. Frontier and Pioneer Life. Strachan, John. 1840-55. *732*
Ontario (Guelph). Anti-Catholicism. Conscription, Military. Jesuits. Novitiate of St. Stanislaus. Protestantism. World War I. 1918-19. *2657*
Ontario (Hamilton). Fuga, Francis J. Shrine of Our Lady of Klocočov. Slovak Canadians. Uniates. 1952-77. *3911*
Ontario (Kingston). All Saints Church. Church of England. Theology. Working class. 1867-1906. *3173*
—. Catholic Church. Congregation of Notre Dame (Sisters). Religious education. Women. 1841-48. *596*
—. Catholic Church. St. Mary's Cathedral of the Immaculate Conception. 1843-1973. *3738*
—. Church of England. Morris, William. Presbyterians. Queen's College. 1836-42. *711*
Ontario (Kingston, Smith Falls). Canada. Great Britain. Queen's College. Romanes, George. Romanes, George John. Science. Scientific Experiments and Research. Theology. 1830-90. *2918*
Ontario (Kingston, Toronto). Catholic Church. Church of England. Colonial Government. Macdonnell, Alexander. Ontario. Strachan, John. 1820's-30's. *1108*
Ontario (Lake Superior). Evans, James. Methodism. Missions and Missionaries. Voyages. 1837-38. *1564*
Ontario (London). Catholic Church. Charities. Education. Moore, Julia. Personal narratives. Sisters of St. Joseph. Women. 1868-85. *2517*
Ontario (Moosonee). Church Missionary Society. Church of England. Hudson's Bay Company. Missions and Missionaries. Vincent, Thomas. 1835-1910. *1638*
Ontario (Ottawa). Cameron, John. Church of England. Letters. Politics. Thompson, Annie Affleck. Thompson, John S. D. 1867-94. *1127*
—. Fasman, Oscar Z. Hebrew Theological College. Judaism (Orthodox). Oklahoma (Tulsa). Personal narratives. Rabbis. 1929-79. *4177*
Ontario (Oxford, Waterloo counties). Blenheim Mennonite Church. Mennonites. 1839-1974. *3352*
Ontario, southern. Friends, Society of. 19c. *3277*
Ontario (Toronto). Assimilation. Evangelism. Jews. Presbyterian Church. 1912-18. *1540*
—. Baptists. Factionalism. Fundamentalism. Jarvis Street Baptist Church. Modernism. Social Classes. 1895-1934. *2605*
—. Baptists. Fundamentalism. Jarvis Street Baptist Church. Shields, Thomas Todhunter. 1891-1955. *3067*
—. Baptists. McMaster Hall. McMaster, Susan Moulton Fraser. Michigan (Bay City). Women. 1819-1916. *3000*
—. Bengough, John Wilson. City government. *Grip* (periodical). Political Reform. Protestantism. 1873-1910. *1266*
—. Bishops. Church of England. Liturgy. Strachan, John. Theology. 1802-67. *3214*
—. Canadian Catholic Historical Association. Catholic Church. 1933-73. *241*
—. Catholic Church. St. Basil's Seminary. Seminaries. Vatican Council II. 1962-67. *3775*
—. Catholic Church. Saints Cyril and Methodius Parish. Slovak Canadians. 1934-77. *3905*
—. Charities. Church of England. Evangelicals. Temperance Movements. Theology. 1870-1900. *3205*
—. Church and State. Church of England. King's College (charter). Scotland. Strachan, John. 1815-43. *506*
Ontario (Upper Canada). Catholic Church. Church of England. Government. Indian-White Relations. Manitoulin project. Methodist Church. Missions and Missionaries. 1820-40. *1537*
—. Church and state. Church of England. Endowments. Land. Rolph, John. Strachan, John. University of Toronto. 1820-70. *1026*
—. Exiles. Loyalists. McDowall, Robert James. Missions and Missionaries. Reformed Dutch Church. 1790-1819. *1588*
—. Methodist Episcopal Church. Missions and Missionaries. Quebec (Lower Canada). 1788-1812. *1580*
—. Social control. Sunday schools. 19c. *643*
Ontario (Waterloo County). Conservatism. Liberalism. Mennonites. 1977. *3368*
Ontario (York Factory). Anglican Communion. Autobiography. Cree Indians. Faries, Richard. Missions and Missionaries. 1896-1961. *1528*
Opechancanough (chief). Colonization. Indians. Jesuits. Menéndez de Avilés, Pedro. Missions and Missionaries. Powhatan Indians. Spain. Virginia. 1570-72. *1622*
Opera. California (Stockton). Davidson, Herman. Judaism (Reform). Rabbis. Russia. 1846-1911. *4204*
Oral History *See also* Personal Narratives.
—. Baptist studies. Church History. 1940-75. *178*
—. Baptist studies. Methodology. 1973. *231*
—. Baptists, Southern. Illinois State Baptist Association. 1976. *210*
—. Bethel College. Conscientious Objectors. Mennonites. World War I. 1917-18. 1974. *262*
—. British Columbia (Vancouver Island; Nootka Sound). Catholic Church. Indians. Missions and Missionaries. Spain. 1789-95. 19c. *1563*
—. Conscientious objectors. Mennonites. World War I. 1917-20. *2660*
—. Illinois (Nauvoo). Lyon, T. Edgar. Mormons. Smith, Hyrum. Smith, Joseph. 1840's-1978. *4005*
Oral history program. Baptists. 1970-75. *177*
—. Baptists. 1975. *268*
Oral tradition. Baptists (Two-Seed-in-the-Spirit). Evangelism. Indiana (Putnam County). Music. Otter Creek Predestinarian Church. Sermons. 1820-1975. *1940*
—. Folklore. Mormons. 19c-20c. *4054*
Orange Order. Anti-Catholicism. Great Britain. Irish Canadians. Ontario. Patriotism. 1830-1900. *2111*
Oration. Emerson, Ralph Waldo. Theology. Transcendentalism. ca 1836-60. *4072*
Orchard, Harry. Christianity. Converts. Idaho. Murder. 1899-1906. *2760*
Order of Friars Minor. *See* Franciscans.
Order of the Holy Cross. Episcopal Church, Protestant. Huntington, James Otis Sargent. Monasticism. Single tax. Social reform. 1878-90. *2430*
Ordination. Baptists, Southern. 1677-1980. *3079*
—. Bishop of London. Clergy. Methodists. Petitions. Pilmoor, Joseph. Virginia (Norfolk County). 1774. *3465*
—. Canada. McClung, Nellie. Methodist Church. United Church of Canada. Women. 1915-46. *852*
—. Canon Law. Episcopal Church, Protestant. Women. 1966-74. *937*
—. Church of England. Congregationalism. Connecticut. Great Britain. Johnson, Samuel (1696-1772). Yale University. 1722-23. *2843*
—. Clergy. Methodist Church. Social Change. 1771-1975. *3473*
—. Clergy. United Brethren in Christ. Women. 1889. *847*
—. Congregationalism. Great Awakening. New England. Parkman, Ebenezer. 1630-1740. *3157*
—. Presbyterian Church (Committee of Four). Women. 1926-30. *809*
—. Protestantism. Social change. Women. World Council of Churches. 1945-75. *879*
Oregon *See also* Far Western States.
—. American Protective Association. Anti-Catholicism. Chinese Americans. Guardians of Liberty. Ku Klux Klan. Nativism. Racism. ca 1840-1945. *2100*
—. Aurora Colony. Communes. Music. Pioneer Band. Society of Bethel. 1855-1920's. *1942*
—. Bailey, Margaret Jewett *(Ruth Rover).* Business. Methodist Church. Missionaries. 1854. *1522*
—. Beeson, John. Blaine, David E. Indian-White Relations. Methodists. Washington. 1850-59. *3495*
—. Catholic Church. Hudson's Bay Company. Indians. Methodist Church. Missions and Missionaries. Presbyterian Church. 1830's - 1840's. *1482*
—. Communes. German Americans. Keil, William. Letters. Missouri. Society of Bethel. Weitling, Wilhelm. 1844-83. *405*
—. Drury, Clifford M. Historians. Missions and Missionaries. Presbyterian Church. Washington. 1928-74. *190*
—. Drury, Clifford M. Indians. Lee, Jason. Methodism. Missions and Missionaries. Settlement. 1834-43. 1970's. *3480*
—. French Canadians. Government, provisional. Gray, William. Lee, Jason. Methodist Church. Missions and Missionaries. 1843. *1271*
—. Historiography. Indians. Lee, Jason. Methodism. Missions and Missionaries. 1838-43. *1569*

—. Historiography. Marshall, William I. Missions and Missionaries. Whitman, Marcus. Winters, Herbert D. ca 1842-43. 1930. *1553*
Oregon (Pendleton). Episcopal Church, Protestant. 1864-1971. *3225*
Oregon (Portland). Charities. Judaism, Reform. Organizations. Temple Beth Israel. 1885. *4235*
—. Commerce. Judaism (Orthodox, Reform). Organizations. 1888. *4162*
—. Daily Life. Elections. Judaism. Temple Beth Israel. 1878. *4237*
—. Lutheran Church (Missouri Synod). Rimbach, John Adam. Trinity Church. Washington. 1906-41. *3333*
Oregon (Salem). Architecture, academy. Catholic Church. Piper, William W. Sacred Heart Academy. 1834-83. *1828*
—. Catholic Church. Daily life. Documents. Girls. Holy Names of Jesus and Mary, Sisters of the. Sacred Heart Academy. 1863-73. *699*
Oregon (Siletz). Indian Shaker Church. Johnson, Jakie. Missions and Missionaries. Siletz Indians. ca 1881-1970. *2776*
Oregon (Willamette Valley). Baptists. Clergy. Missouri. Powell, Joab. Westward movement. 1852-73. *3093*
Oregon (Willamette Valley, The Dalles). Business. Indians. Lee, Daniel. Letters. Methodist Church. Missions and Missionaries. 1834-43. *1570*
Organizational change. Catholic Church. Clergy. National Federation of Priests' Councils. Values. -1973. *3859*
Organizational stress. Ecumenism. National Council of Churches. 1908-69. *478*
Organizational structure. Baptists, Southern. Theology. 16c-20c. *3049*
—. Catholic Church. Centralization. Influence, distribution of. 1970's. *3866*
—. Children of God. 1968-76. *2732*
—. Jehovah's Witnesses. Rescue missions. Skid Rows. Watch Tower movement. 1970's. *2722*
Organizational Theory *See also* Public Administration.
—. Divine Light Mission. Maharaj Ji. 1930's-70's. *4285*
Organizations *See also* Social Organizations; Voluntary Associations.
—. Alberta (Coaldale). Germans, Russian. Mennonites. Social Change. 1920-76. *3411*
—. Beth Olam Cemetery. California (San Jose). Congregation Bickur Cholim. Judaism (Orthodox, Reform). 1850-1900. *4123*
—. Canada. Deprogramming. Sects, religious. USA. 1960's-70's. *4267*
—. Charities. Judaism, Reform. Oregon (Portland). Temple Beth Israel. 1885. *4235*
—. Commerce. Judaism (Orthodox, Reform). Oregon (Portland). 1888. *4162*
—. Culture. Mormons. Pioneers. Utah. 1850's-70's. *523*
—. Missions and Missionaries. Protestant Churches. Women. 1870's-90's. *894*
Orientalism. Johnson, Samuel (1822-82). Massachusetts. Theology. Transcendentalism. 1840's-82. *4071*
Original sin. Catholic Church. Europe. Theology. 1966-71. *3751*
—. Freudianism. Marxism. Niebuhr, Reinhold (review article). Protestantism. Theology. 1939-70. *2838*
—. Holmes, Oliver Wendell *(Elsie Venner)*. Literature. New England. 1861. *2024*
Orlov, Vasilii. Alaska. Diaries. Indian-White Relations. Library of Congress (Alaska Church Collection). Missions and Missionaries. Orthodox Eastern Church, Russian. 1886. *1632*
Orphanages. Catholic Church. Education. Georgia (Skidaway Island). Negroes. Poor Clares. Women. 1885-87. *3806*
—. Francke, Gottfried. Georgia (Ebenezer). Germany. Immigrants. Kiefer, Theobald, II. Letters. Lutheran Church. Pietism. Whitefield, George. 1738. 1750. *2878*
Orphans. Aged. Catholic Church. Charities. Education. Immigration. New Brunswick (Saint John). Sisters of Charity of the Immaculate Conception. 1854-64. *2509*
—. Charities. Edgewood Children's Center. Missouri (Webster Groves). Protestantism. St. Louis Protestant Orphan Asylum. 1834-1979. *2518*
—. Education. Georgia (Savannah). Great Awakening. Whitefield, George. 1738-71. *731*
Orphans' Home of Industry. Charities. Episcopal Church, Protestant. Iowa (Iowa City). New York City. Townsend, Charles Collins. 1854-68. *2507*
Orthodox Eastern Church. Assimilation. Ethnicity. Greek Americans. New York City. St. Demetrios Church. St. Markela Church. 1970's. *318*
—. Church and state. Democracy. Symphonia theory. 17c-20c. *1048*
—. Lutheran Church. Methodist Church. Pennsylvania Historical and Museum Commission. Pennsylvania Historical Association. Reformed Dutch Church. Research conference. Uniates. 1977. *2791*
Orthodox Eastern Church, Greek. *Alaska Herald* (newspaper). Clergy. Far Western States. Honcharenko, Agapius. Ukrainian Americans. 1832-1916. *2805*
—. Alberta (Rabbit Hill). Ukrainian Canadians. 1900. *2808*
—. Assimilation. 1918-73. *2812*
—. Fundamentalism. Immigrants. Ruthenians. Uniates. Vermont (Proctor). 1914-73. *2757*
Orthodox Eastern Church, Russian. Alaska. Church finance. Documents. Education. Russian-American Company. Veniaminov, Metropolitan Innokentii. 1858. *2806*
—. Alaska. Diaries. Indian-White Relations. Library of Congress (Alaska Church Collection). Missions and Missionaries. Orlov, Vasilii. 1886. *1632*
—. Arguello, Maria de la Concepcion. California. Catholic Church. Rezanov, Nikolai. 1806. *2797*
—. Assimilation. New Hampshire (Claremont). Russian Americans. ca 1907-75. *2809*
Orthodox Eastern Church, Russian (Old Believers). Alaska (Kenai Peninsula). Freedom of religion. Russian Americans. 1920's-76. *2810*
—. Russian Americans. 1890's-1970's. *2804*
Orthodox Eastern Church (Syrian). Assimilation. Catholic Church. Maronite Catholics. Melkite Catholics. Syrian Americans. Uniates. 1900-73. *3908*
Orthodox Jewish Sabbath Alliance. Central Conference of American Rabbis. Drachman, Bernard. Judaism. Judaism (Orthodox). Sabbath. Saturday. 1903-30. *2277*
Orthodoxy. Christianity. Church and State. Religious liberty. 17c-20c. *1085*
—. Furniture and Furnishings. Shakers. Social Change. Theology. 1815-1969. *4067*
—. Militancy. Negroes. South. 1964-75. *1292*
Ortynsky, Soter. Ruthenians. Uniates. 1907-16. *3910*
Osborn, Sarah. Congregationalism. Fish, Josiah. Revivals. Rhode Island (Newport). Women. 1766-67. *904*
Osborn, William H. Augustana College and Theological Seminary. Illinois (Paxton). Lutheran Church (Augustana Synod). Railroads. Swedish Americans. 1853-73. *3321*
Osgood, Thaddeus. Canada. Evangelism. Religious Education. 1807-52. *2900*
Oshinsky, David. Anti-Communist Movements. Catholic Church. Crosby, Donald F. Labor Unions and Organizations. McCarthy, Joseph R. (review article). 1950-54. 1976-78. *1212*
Ostracism. Converts. Letters. Missouri. Mormons. Partridge, Edward. 1837. *3989*
Otey, James Hervey. Diaries. Episcopal Church, Protestant. Harris, N. Sayre. Indian Territory. Missions and Missionaries. 1844. *1533*
—. Episcopal Church, Protestant. St. Paul's Church. Tennessee (Franklin). 1827-34. *1802*
Ottawa Diocese. Catholic Church. French Canadians. Guigues, Joseph-Eugène. Ontario. 1848-74. *3713*
Otter Creek Predestinarian Church. Baptists (Two-Seed-in-the-Spirit). Evangelism. Indiana. Parker, Daniel. 1820-1974. *3047*
—. Baptists (Two-Seed-in-the-Spirit). Evangelism. Indiana (Putnam County). Music. Oral tradition. Sermons. 1820-1975. *1940*
Otterbein, Philip Wilhelm. Clergy. Germany. Herborn, University of. Maryland. Pennsylvania. Theology. United Brethren in Christ. 1726-1813. *3666*
Ottoman Empire *See also* constituent parts, e.g. Palestine, Armenia, etc.; Turkey.
—. Diplomacy. Great Britain. Missionaries. Protestantism. 1824-42. *1697*
—. Jesuits. Missions and Missionaries. Protestant Churches. Syria. 1840's. *1698*
Our Hope (periodical). Attitudes. Fundamentalism. Gaebelein, Arno C. Stroeter, Ernst F. Zionism. 1894-97. *80*
—. Fundamentalism. Gaebelein, Arno C. Genocide. Germany. Jews. 1937-45. *136*
Our Lady of Levoča (statue). Catholic Church. Mary, Virgin. Ohio (Bedford). Slovakia (Spiš; Levoča). ca 13c-1975. *1884*
Overland Journeys to the Pacific. California. Methodist Episcopal Church. Missions and missionaries. Owen, Isaac. 1849. *1611*
—. California (Monterey). Discovery and Exploration. Dominguez, Francisco Atanasio. Escalante, Silvestre Velez de. New Mexico. 1765-1805. *1480*
Owen, Isaac. California. Methodist Episcopal Church. Missions and missionaries. Overland Journeys to the Pacific. 1849. *1611*
Owen, Robert. Fraud. Pennsylvania (New Harmony). Rapp, Frederick. Real Estate. 1825. *327*
Owen, Robert Dale. Social Organization. Utopias. Wright, Frances. 1826-32. *411*
Oxford Conference (1937). Anti-Communist Movements. Dulles, John Foster. Ecumenism. Morality. Presbyterian Church. Protestantism. World order movement. 1937-48. *1375*
Oxford Movement. Bishops. Church of England. Letters. Medley, John. New Brunswick (Fredericton). Pusey, Edward Bouverie. ca 1840-44. *3190*
—. Christianity. Longshoremen. Strikes. Washington (Seattle). 1921-34. *1477*
—. Episcopal Church, Protestant. Evangelism. Frontier and Pioneer Life. McIlvaine, Charles Petit. Ohio. 1800-75. *3187*

P

Paca, William. Boucher, Jonathan. Chase, Samuel. Church and State. Maryland. Taxation. 1770-73. *1141*
Pacific Coast. Chinese Americans. Christianity. Judaism. Nativism. Newspapers. Slavery. 1848-65. *75*
Pacific Northwest. Agriculture. Communalism. Education. German Americans. Hutterites. Pacifism. 20c. *392*
—. Bible. British Columbia. California. Christianity. Indians. Missions and Missionaries. Myths and Symbols. 1830-50. *1612*
—. District of Columbia. Missions and Missionaries. National Statuary Hall. Pariseau, Mother Mary Joseph. Sisters of Charity of Providence. Women. 1856-1902. 1977. *1629*
—. Episcopal Church, Protestant. Hudson's Bay Company. Indians. Missions and Missionaries. 1825-75. *1555*
Pacific Press Publishing Company. Adventists. California (Mountain View, Oakland). Jones, Charles Harriman. Publishers and Publishing. 1879-1923. *362*
Pacific, South. Missions and Missionaries. Modernization. Mormons. 1955-80. *1682*
Pacifism *See also* Conscientious Objectors; Peace Movements.
—. Agriculture. Communalism. Education. German Americans. Hutterites. Pacific Northwest. 20c. *392*
—. American Revolution. Brown, Joshua. Friends, Society of. Pennsylvania (Little Britain Township). Prisoners. South Carolina (Ninety Six). 1778. *2633*
—. American Revolution. Diaries. Drinker family. Friends, Society of. Pennsylvania (Philadelphia). Prisoners. Virginia (Winchester). 1777-81. *2683*
—. American Revolution. Dunkards. Friends, Society of. Mennonites. Moravian Church. Neutrality. Schwenkfelders. Taxation. 1765-83. *2670*
—. American Revolution. Dunkards. Loyalists. Mennonites. 1776-84. *2635*
—. Angers, François-Albert. Canada. Catholic Church. French Canadians. Values. 1940-79. *2654*
—. Asia, central. Immigration. Kansas. Mennonites. Nebraska. 1884-93. *3350*
—. Belk, Fred R. Immigration. Mennonites. Russia. 1880-84. *3351*
—. Buttrick, George Arthur. Presbyterian Church. 1915-74. *2642*
—. Canada. Fairbairn, R. Edis. United Church of Canada. World War II. 1939. *2688*

—. Christianity. Muste, A. J. Niebuhr, Reinhold. Political Theory. Thomas, Norman. 1914-38. *2687*
—. Clark, Bertha W. Hutterites. Social change. South Dakota. 1921. *3385*
—. Dunkards. Friends, Society of. Historic Peace Churches (meeting). Kansas (Newton). Krehbiel, H. P. Mennonites. 1935-36. *2663*
—. Dunkards. Friends, Society of. Mennonites. Militarism. 1900-78. *2646*
—. Friends, Society of. King George's War. Penn, Thomas. Pennsylvania. Politics. Provincial Government. 1726-42. *1314*
—. German Americans. Mennonites. Military conscription. Public opinion. World War I. 1914-18. *2696*
—. German Evangelical Synod of North America. Niebuhr, Reinhold. Patriotism. Theology. World War I. 1915-18. *2639*
—. Jewish Peace Fellowship. World War II. 1943. *2706*
—. Kansas. Liberty bonds. Mennonites. Vigilantism. World War I. 1918. *2659*
—. Kansas. Patriotism. Sects, Religious. World War I. 1917-18. *2677*
—. Literature. Mennonites. 20c. *2073*
—. Massacres. Mennonites. Paxton Boys. Pennsylvania. Politics. Presbyterian Church. 1763-68. *2702*
—. Mormons. Spanish-American War. Young, Brigham, Jr. ca 1840-98. *2682*
—. Niebuhr, Reinhold. 1932-34. *2638*
Paddock, Algernon Sidney. Mormons. Polygamy. Utah Commission. 1882-86. *1117*
Padilla Gold Plates. Archaeology. Engraving. Fraud. Mexico (Guerrero). Mormons. 1952-78. *4007*
Paine, Thomas. Adams, John. American Revolution. New England. Political theory. Puritans. Rhetoric. 17c-1770's. *1424*
Paine, Thomas *(Age of Reason)*. Clergy. Deism. Virginia. 1794-97. *86*
Paine, Thomas *(Common Sense)*. American Revolution. Calvinism. Eschatology. 1776. *1393*
Painting *See also* Landscape Painting.
—. Allegory. Art. Folwell, Samuel *(Sacred to the Illustrious Washington)*. Mourning (theme). Protestantism. ca 1800. *1885*
—. Bock, Anna. Indiana (Elkhart County). Mennonites, Old Order. 1830's-1970's. *1845*
—. Catholic Church. Indians. Juan Antonio (neophyte). Mission San Gabriel Arcangel. 1800-1976. *1883*
—. Childhood. Dreams. Italy (Rome). Symbolism in Art. Vedder, Elihu. 1856-1923. *1888*
—. Christianity. Cole, Thomas. Iconography. Romanticism. 1830's-40's. *1865*
—. Churches. Idealism. LaFarge, John. New York City. 1877-88. *1898*
—. Cohoon, Hannah Harrison. Massachusetts (Hancock). New York (New Lebanon, Watervliet). Shakers. 1817-64. *1902*
—. Folk art. Friends, Society of. Hicks, Edward *(Peaceable Kingdom)*. Pennsylvania (Bucks County). 1780-1849. *1857*
—. Poetry. Puritans. Smith, Thomas. ca 1690. *1839*
Painting (realist tradition). Catholic Church. Indians. Juan Antonio (neophyte). Mission San Gabriel Arcangel. 1800. 1976. *1882*
Palestine *See also* Israel.
—. American Christian Palestine Committee. Great Britain. Lobbying. Zionism. 1940's. *1316*
—. Bible. Diaries. Fiction. Melville, Herman. Travel. 1857. *2039*
—. Biblical studies. Ecumenism. Missions and Missionaries. Protestantism. 1812-1975. *1748*
—. Judaism (Reform). Kerman, Julius C. Personal narratives. Rabbis. World War I. 1913-71. *4214*
—. Kibbutzim. New England. Puritans. Social Organization. Towns. 17c. 20c. *3633*
Palestine Liberation Organization. American Friends Service Committee. Arab-Israeli conflict. Foreign Policy. Friends, Society of. 1970's. *1250*
Palestinians. Friends, Society of. Israel. 1977. *1278*
Palm Sunday. Lutheran Church. Personal narratives. Schreiber, Clara Seuel. Wisconsin (Freistadt). 1898. *3338*
Palmer, Edwin R. Adventists. Australia. Missions and Missionaries. Publishers and Publishing. 1894-1915. *2968*
Palmer, Elihu. Allen, Ethan. Deism. Franklin, Benjamin. Historiography. Jefferson, Thomas. 1750-1820. *4277*
Palmer, Phoebe. Domesticity. Methodism. New York City. Women. ca 1825-60. *877*
—. Feminism. Holiness Movement. Wesley, Susanna. 1732-1973. *829*
Pamphlets. Clergy (dismissal). Episcopal Church, Protestant. Illinois (Chicago). Rites and Ceremonies. Swope, Cornelius E. Trinity Church. Unonius, Gustaf. 1850-51. *3179*
—. Great Britain. Jeremiads. New England. Puritans. Ward, Nathaniel. 1645-50. *1975*
Papagiannis, Michael D. Assimilation. Greek Americans. Personal narratives. USA (impressions). 20c. *2811*
Papago Indians. Architecture. Arizona, southern. Catholic Church. Chapels. Folk religion. 20c. *1783*
—. Arizona (Pisinimo). Catholic Church. Clergy. Frembling, Lambert. Refugees. 1939-77. *3825*
Papal Infallibility. Catholic Church. 1870. *3848*
Papal legates. Canada. Catholic Church. Conroy, George. 1873-77. *3883*
Papermaster, Benjamin. Jews. North Dakota (Grand Forks). 1890-1934. *4135*
Paquette, Albiny. Barbeau, Victor. Catholic Church. Cooperatives. Medical Reform. Politics. Quebec. 1900-45. *3874*
Parachurch groups. Baptists, Southern. 1970's. *2981*
Parades. California (San Diego). Christmas. Drama. Social Customs. 1769-1980. *2714*
Paraguay. Catholic Church. Culture. Spain. 1513-20c. *3737*
Parents. Children. Judaism (Orthodox). New York City (Brooklyn; Boro Park). Social Status. 1973. *4187*
—. Children. Minnesota, southern. Religiosity. Socialization. 1975. *128*
—. Church and State. Compulsory education. Constitutional Amendments (1st). *Pierce* v. *Society of Sisters* (US, 1925). 1925. 1976. *587*
—. Death and Dying. Infants. New England. Puritans. Theology. 1620-1720. *925*
—. Ethnicity. Jews. Maryland, University of. Students. 1949-71. *4128*
Pariseau, Mother Mary Joseph. District of Columbia. Missions and Missionaries. National Statuary Hall. Pacific Northwest. Sisters of Charity of Providence. Women. 1856-1902. 1977. *1629*
Parish registers. Catholic Church. Government. Quebec. 1539-1973. *3694*
Parishes. Americanization. Church of England. Great Britain. North Carolina. 1701-12. *298*
—. Assimilation. Catholic Church. Pennsylvania (Philadelphia). 1759-1975. *3745*
—. Calvinism. Massachusetts (Boston). Puritans. Switzerland (Geneva). 16c-17c. *3631*
—. Catholic Church. French Canadians. Migration, Internal. Quebec (Compton County). Rural-Urban Studies. 1851-91. *3791*
—. Ethnicity. Language. Nationalism. Polish National Catholic Church. 1880's-1930's. *313*
Parker, Daniel. Baptists (Two-Seed-in-the-Spirit). Evangelism. Indiana. Otter Creek Predestinarian Church. 1820-1974. *3047*
Parker, Lois Stiles. Dickey, Sarah. Heck, Barbara. Leadership. Methodist Church. Shaw, Anna Howard. Stereotypes. Willard, Frances E. Women. 19c. *812*
Parker, Theodore. Abolition Movement. Civil War (antecedents). Clergy. New England. Transcendentalism. Violence. 1850-60. *2467*
—. Historiography. Intuition. New England. Reason. Theology. Transcendentalism. Unitarianism. 18c-1860. 1920-79. *4074*
Parkman, Ebenezer. Childbirth. Congregationalism. Death and Dying. Diaries. Diseases. Massachusetts (Westborough). Social Organization. 1724-82. *1447*
—. Congregationalism. Great Awakening. New England. Ordination. 1630-1740. *3157*
Parochial Schools. *See* Church Schools; Religious Education.
Parody. Humor. Popular Culture. 1976. *2052*
Parsonages. Family. Lutheran Church. 1974. *802*
Parsons case. Massachusetts (Springfield). Puritans. Witchcraft. 1650-55. *2210*
Parsons' Cause. Anglican Communion. Anticlericalism. Church and State. Virginia. 1730-60. *1058*
—. Church and state. Church of England. Clergy. Tobacco. Virginia. Wages. 1750-70. *1052*
—. Church and state. Clergy. Henry, Patrick. Maury, James. Personal narratives. Speeches, Addresses, etc. Virginia. 1758-65. *1080*
Parsons, Edward Smith. Abbott, Lyman. Clergy. Congregationalism. New York (Cornwall-on-the-Hudson). Personal narratives. 1885. *3136*
Parsons, Wilfrid. Bibliographies. Catholic Church. Catholic University of America. Hogan Schism. Pennsylvania (Philadelphia). Schisms. 1785-1825. 1975. *3845*
Parties, Political. *See* Political Parties.
Partisanship. Church and state. County Government. Judicial Administration. Mormons. Probate courts. Utah. 1855-72. *1039*
Partridge, Edward. Converts. Letters. Missouri. Mormons. Ostracism. 1837. *3989*
Passenger lists. Immigration. Mennonites. Quebec. Russia. 1874-80. *3364*
Passion plays. Catholic Church. Colorado. New Mexico. Spain. 1830's-1978. *1890*
Patent medicines. Advertising. Men. Mormons. Stereotypes. Virility. 1884-1931. *819*
Paternalism. American Baptist Home Mission Society. Baptists. Leadership. Missions and Missionaries. Negroes. Virginia Union University. 1865-1905. *644*
—. Baptists, Southern. Education. Negroes. 1880's-90's. *553*
—. Brent, Charles Henry. Episcopal Church, Protestant. Missions and Missionaries. Philippines. 1901-18. *1738*
—. Cheshire, Joseph Blount, Jr. Episcopal Church, Protestant. Negroes. North Carolina. Race Relations. 1870-1932. *2140*
Patriarchal attitudes. Feminism. Prehistory-1970's. *859*
Patrick, William. Canada. Ecumenism. Methodist Church. Presbyterian Church. 1900-11. *443*
Patriote de l'Ouest (newspaper). Catholic Church. French language. Saskatchewan. 1910-41. *3764*
Patriotism. American Revolution. Church of England. Clergy. 1770-85. 1895-98. *982*
—. American Revolution. Georgia (Savannah). Presbyterian Church. Zubly, John Joachim. 1766-81. *985*
—. American Revolution. Historiography. Millenarianism. Nationalism. Politics. 1740-89. *1347*
—. Anti-Catholicism. Great Britain. Irish Canadians. Ontario. Orange Order. 1830-1900. *2111*
—. Antislavery Sentiments. Eliot, Samuel A. Fugitive Slave Act (US, 1850). Massachusetts (Boston). Unitarianism. 1850-60. *4085*
—. Church of England. Hunt, Edward. Jacobitism. Keith, William. Pennsylvania. 1720. *1130*
—. Church of England. Poetry. Rising glory of America (theme). Smith, William. 1752. *1337*
—. French Canadians. Literature. Quebec. Sociology. 19c. *2085*
—. German Evangelical Synod of North America. Niebuhr, Reinhold. Pacifism. Theology. World War I. 1915-18. *2639*
—. Kansas. Pacifism. Sects, Religious. World War I. 1917-18. *2677*
—. Revivals. Sunday, Billy. World War I. 1917-18. *2676*
Patronage. Allen, Bennet. Church of England. Colonial Government. Ecclesiastical pluralism. Jordan, John Morton. Maryland. Sharpe, Horatio. 1759-70. *1051*
Paul, Saint. Bible (New Testament; Epistles). Primitivism. Theology. Williams, Roger. 1630-83. *2939*
—. Christianity. Grimké, Sarah. Nature. Social organization. Women. 1c. 1830's. *921*
Paul, Thomas (and family). Baptists. Clergy. Jay Street Church. Massachusetts (Boston). Negroes. 1773-1973. *3048*
Paxton Boys. Friends, Society of. Indian Wars. Nonviolence. Pennsylvania (Philadelphia). 1764-67. *2693*
—. Friends, Society of. Indians. Pennsylvania. Politics. Presbyterian Church. Riots. 1763-64. *3530*
—. Massacres. Mennonites. Pacifism. Pennsylvania. Politics. Presbyterian Church. 1763-68. *2702*
Payne, Daniel Alexander. Lutheran Church. Methodist Episcopal Church, African. Negroes. Wilberforce University. 1830-93. *2905*

Peabody, Endicott. Arizona (Tombstone). Clergy. Episcopal Church, Protestant. 1882. *3237*
—. Episcopal Church, Protestant. Groton School. Massachusetts. Religious education. 1884-1940. *671*
Peace *See also* Pacifism.
—. Art. Attitudes. Centennial Exposition of 1876. Friends, Society of. Pennsylvania (Philadelphia). Sabbatarianism. Temperance Movements. 1876. *3256*
Peace Mission (movement). Cults. Father Divine. Jones, Jim. Negroes. People's Temple. 1920-79. *4254*
—. Father Divine. Negroes. Sermons. 1915-65. *4249*
Peace Movements *See also* Antiwar Sentiment.
—. Antiwar Sentiment. Catholic Association for International Peace. 1917-68. *2673*
—. Catholic Church. National Catholic Welfare Conference. National Council of Catholic Women. Women. World War II. 1919-46. *2669*
—. Cobden, Richard. Great Britain. Millenarianism. Protestant churches. 1840-60. *2701*
Peace Studies. Colleges and Universities. Consortium of Peace Research, Education and Development. Mennonites. North America. 1965-80. *2650*
Peale, Norman Vincent. Graham, Billy. Popular culture. Protestantism. 1950's. *2901*
Peasants *See also* Agricultural Labor; Farmers; Land Tenure; Working Class.
—. Land. Massachusetts (Barnstable County). Pilgrims. Values. 1620's-1720's. *3151*
Pease, Benjamin. Missions and Missionaries. Oceania. Pirates. 1867-70. *1685*
Peck, E. J. Church Missionary Society. Church of England. Eskimos. Hudson's Bay Company. Missionaries. Northwest Territories (Baffin Island). Trade. 1894-1913. *1660*
Peck, Jesse T. Bishops. Methodist Episcopal Church. Social gospel. 1850-83. *2396*
Peckham, Robert. Congregationalism. Folk Art. Massachusetts. Portraits. ca 1838-44. *1861*
Peculiar People (newspaper). Baptists, Seventh-Day. Conversion. Daland, William C. Friedlaender, Herman. Jews. New York City. 1880's-90's. *1633*
Pedagogy. *See* Teaching.
Pendell, Thomas Roy. International cooperation. Methodism. Personal narratives. USSR. World Conference of Christian Youth, 1st. 1939-79. *1402*
Pendleton, James Madison. Abolition Movement. Baptists. Landmark Movement. 1835-91. *2998*
Penitentes. Catholic Church. Cofradías (brotherhoods). Mexican Americans. New Mexico. Rio Grande Valley. ca 1770-1970. *3675*
—. Catholic Church. Colorado. Folk art. New Mexico. 19c-20c. *3898*
—. Catholic Church. Colorado, southern. Death Carts. Hispanic Americans. New Mexico, northern. 1860-90's. *3856*
—. Catholic Church. Flagellants. New Mexico. 13c-20c. *3779*
—. Catholic Church. Folklore. Hispanic Americans. New Mexico. Rites and Ceremonies. Social customs. 16c-20c. *3829*
—. Catholic Church. New Mexico. Sangre de Cristo Mountains. 19c-1979. *3893*
—. Catholic Church. New Mexico (Albuquerque). Roybal, Max. Santos, statues. Wood Carving. 20c. *1901*
Penn, Thomas. Friends, Society of. King George's War. Pacifism. Pennsylvania. Politics. Provincial Government. 1726-42. *1314*
Penn, William. Friends, Society of. Humanism. Intellectuals. Radicals and Radicalism. Social reform. 1650-1700. *2353*
Pennsylvania *See also* Northeastern or North Atlantic States.
—. Abolition Movement. Fox, George. Friends, Society of. Slave trade. 1656-1754. *2479*
—. Abolition Movement. Friends, Society of (Longwood Meeting). Reform. 1850's-1940. *2450*
—. Adventists. Fuller, Nathan. New York. 1858-71. *2975*
—. American Revolution. Baptists. New England. Religious liberty. Virginia. 1775-91. *1100*
—. American Revolution. Biddle, Owen. Friends, Society of. Lacey, John, Jr. Military Service. 1775-83. *2684*
—. American Revolution. Civilian Service. Moravian Church. 1775-1783. *2703*
—. American Revolution. Historiography. New Jersey. New York. Social conditions. 1680-1790's. 1960's-70's. *59*
—. American Revolution (antecedents). Conscientious Objectors. Dunkards. Mennonites. Petitions. 1775. *2710*
—. Amish. Education. Military. Trials. Wisconsin. 1755-1974. *3401*
—. Amish. Folk Art. Mennonites. Persecution. Quiltmaking. 16c-1935. *1893*
—. Amish. Folk medicine. Magic. Mennonites. Powwowing. ca 1650-1979. *2206*
—. Amish. France (Alsace). Germany (Palatinate). Immigrants. 1693-1803. *3406*
—. Amish. Genealogy. Zug family. 1718-1886. *3441*
—. Archival catalogs and inventories. Letters. Mennonites. Mensch, Jacob B. 1835-1912. *251*
—. Art. Bartram, John. Bartram, William. Botany. Friends, Society of. Travel (accounts). 1699-1823. *2304*
—. Arts and Crafts. Girls. Moravian Church. North Carolina. Students. 19c. *1862*
—. Assimilation. Lutheran Church. Muhlenberg, Henry Melchior. Politics. Swedish Americans. Wrangel, Carl Magnus. 1749-69. *1283*
—. Attitudes. Friends, Society of. New York (Auburn). Prisons. Reform. 1787-1845. *2393*
—. Attitudes. Lancaster Mennonite High School. Mennonites. Rites and Ceremonies. Students. 1974-78. *3354*
—. Baptists. Bucknell University. Franklin and Marshall College. Friends, Society of (Hicksite). Reformed German Church. Swarthmore College. Urbanization. 1865-1915. *685*
—. Bishops. Durr, John N. Mennonite Conference, Allegheny. 1872-1934. *3440*
—. Blue Laws. Church and state. Church of England. Friends, Society of. Law and Society. Presbyterian Church. 1682-1740. *2278*
—. Brethren, Old Order River. Love feast. ca 1773-1973. *3383*
—. Brubacher, Henry. Brubacher, Jacob. Daily life. Letters. Mennonites. Ontario. 1817-46. *3374*
—. Canada. Eby, Ezra E. Immigration. Loyalists. Mennonites. 18c-1835. *1237*
—. Catholic Church. First Catholic Slovak Union (Jednota). Sabol, John. Slovak Americans. 1920's-60's. *3821*
—. Catholic Church. Lawyers. Progressivism. Smith, Walter George. 1900-22. *2365*
—. Charities. Friends, Society of. Philadelphia Society for Organizing Charitable Relief and Repressing Mendicancy. 1800-1900. *2523*
—. Christianity. Huidekoper, Frederick. Judaism. Meadville Theological School. Seminaries. Unitarianism. 1834-92. *4086*
—. Church of England. Colonial Government. Ethnic Groups. Friends, society of. Reformed churches. 1755-80. *1215*
—. Church of England. Ethnic Groups. Friends, Society of. Presbyterian Church. Provincial Politics. 1775-80. *1248*
—. Church of England. Hunt, Edward. Jacobitism. Keith, William. Patriotism. 1720. *1130*
—. Clergy. Diaries. Lutheran Church. Muhlenberg, Henry Melchior. Women. 1742-87. *828*
—. Clergy. Friends, Society of. Keith, George. Schisms. Schisms. 1660-1720. *3261*
—. Clergy. Germany. Herborn, University of. Maryland. Otterbein, Philip Wilhelm. Theology. United Brethren in Christ. 1726-1813. *3666*
—. Clergy. Lutheran Church. Muhlenberg, Henry Melchior. Pietism. 18c. *3337*
—. Communalism. German Americans. Harmony Society. Indiana. Protestantism. Rapp, George. 1804-47. *425*
—. Conewago Colony. Reformed Dutch Church. 1760's-70's. *3159*
—. Constitutions, State. New Jersey. North Carolina. Presbyterian Church. 1775-87. *1285*
—. Country Life. Farms. Haswell, David R. Letters. Protestants. Revivals. 1808-31. *2234*
—. Education. Family. Friends, Society of. Social Customs. Socialization. ca 1740-76. *3279*
—. Education. Mennonites, old order. Social change. 1653-1975. *664*
—. Evolution. Friends, Society of. Provincial Government. Revivals. 1735-75. *2222*
—. Fishbourn, William. Friends, Society of. Settlement. 1680-1739. *3272*
—. Fort Duquesne. Frontier and Pioneer Life. Indian-White Relations. Moravian Church. Post, Christian Frederick. 1758-59. *1505*
—. Friends, Society of. Indians. Paxton Boys. Politics. Presbyterian Church. Riots. 1763-64. *3530*
—. Friends, Society of. Irish Americans. Settlement. 1682-1750. *3276*
—. Friends, Society of. Keith, George. Pusey, Caleb. Schisms. Theology. 17c. *3273*
—. Friends, Society of. Keith, George. Schisms. 1693-1703. *3262*
—. Friends, Society of. King George's War. Pacifism. Penn, Thomas. Politics. Provincial Government. 1726-42. *1314*
—. Frontier and Pioneer Life. Immigration. Irish Americans. New York. Presbyterian Church. Virginia (Shenandoah Valley). 17c-1776. *3558*
—. Gerhart, Emanuel Vogel. Mercersburg Theological Seminary. Reformed German Church. Theology. 1831-1904. *3287*
—. German Americans. Good, Merle. Literature. Mennonites. Personal narratives. 1975. *2057*
—. German Americans. Lutheran Church. Reformed Churches. Slavery. Social change. 1779-88. *2162*
—. German Americans. Occult Sciences. 17c-20c. *2183*
—. German language. Protestant Churches. Sermons. 18c. *1989*
—. Harmony Society. Rapp, George. State Legislatures. Utopias. 1805-07. *380*
—. Hess, Katie Charles. Mennonites. Personal narratives. Women. 1883-1978. *3356*
—. Massacres. Mennonites. Pacifism. Paxton Boys. Politics. Presbyterian Church. 1763-68. *2702*
—. Mennonites. Raikes, Robert. Sunday schools. 1780-1980. *641*
—. Philadelphia Archeparchy. Senyshyn, Ambrose (obituary). Ukrainian Americans. Uniates. 1903-76. *3906*
—. Reform. Revivals. 1794-1860. *2399*
Pennsylvania (Allentown). Blumer, Abraham. Reformed German Church. Swiss Americans. Zion Reformed Church. 1771-1822. *3285*
Pennsylvania (Bethlehem). American Revolution. Civilian Service. Moravian Church. 1775-83. *2652*
—. Art. Daily life. Moravian Church. Social Organization. 1741-1865. *3515*
—. Materialism. *Moravian* (newspaper). Nationalism. Slavery. 1850-76. *3518*
—. Moravian Archives. Music. 1740-1978. *180*
Pennsylvania (Bethlehem, Nazareth). Architecture. Moravian Church. 1740-68. *1791*
Pennsylvania (Brickerville). Old Zion Reformed Church. Reformed churches. 1732. *2935*
Pennsylvania (Bucks County). Folk art. Friends, Society of. Hicks, Edward *(Peaceable Kingdom)*. Painting. 1780-1849. *1857*
Pennsylvania, central. Anabaptists. Methodism. 1815-1942. *2880*
—. Friends, Society of. Frontier and Pioneer Life. Hutchinson, Mathias. New York, western. Ontario. Travel (accounts). 1819-20. *3280*
Pennsylvania (Chester, Delaware counties). Churches. Friends, Society of. Meetinghouses. ca 1700-1903. *1814*
Pennsylvania (Coatesville). Chapman, John Jay. Christianity. Lynching. Poetry. Race Relations. Rhetoric. Speeches, Addresses, etc. 1912. *1971*
Pennsylvania (Conestoga Valley). Beissel, Johann Conrad. Communalism. Eckerlin, Emmanuel. Ephrata Cloister. 1732-68. *390*
Pennsylvania (Danville). Catholic Church. St. Cyril Academy. Sisters of SS. Cyril and Methodius. Slovak Americans. Social customs. 1909-73. *3885*
Pennsylvania (Delaware Valley). Children. Family. Friends, Society of. Theology. 1681-1735. *874*
Pennsylvania (East Penn Valley). Communes. Economic conditions. Education. Mennonites, Old Order. 1949-75. *410*
Pennsylvania, eastern. American Revolution. Georgia. Historians. Hymns. Moravian Church. Neisser, George. New York. ca 1735-84. *197*
Pennsylvania (Easton). American Revolution. Burgoyne, John. Friends, Society of. Indians. ca 1776. *3282*
Pennsylvania (Economy). Harmony Society. Rapp, George. Utopias. 1785-1847. *381*

—. Harmony Society. Wrede, Friedrich Wilhelm von. 1842. *401*
Pennsylvania (Economy, Harmony). Architecture. Harmony Society. Indiana (New Harmony). Preservation. Rapp, George. Restorations. Utopias. 1804-25. 20c. *420*
—. City Planning. Communes. Harmony Society. Indiana (New Harmony). Social customs. 1820's-1905. *391*
Pennsylvania (Elkins Park). Historians. Jews. Kenesseth Israel Synagogue. Korn, Bertram Wallace (obituary). 1918-79. *248*
Pennsylvania (Ephrata). Baptists (Seventh-Day). Communalism. Letters. Müller, Johan Peter. Social Conditions. 1743. *428*
Pennsylvania Germans. American Revolution. Folk religion. National Characteristics. 1775-83. *2948*
—. Astrology. Astronomy. Comets. 18c-19c. *2209*
—. Astronomy. *Horologium Achaz* (scientific device). Pietism. Witt, Christopher. 1578-1895. *2349*
—. Baptismal certificates. Birth certificates. Folk art. 1750-1850. *1899*
—. Boehm, Martin. Mennonites. Newcomer, Christian. Revivalism. 1740-1850. *2266*
—. Fraktur. Mennonites. 1740's-1860's. *1904*
Pennsylvania (Groffdale). Mennonites. Metzler congregation. 1728-1978. *3415*
Pennsylvania (Harmony, New Harmony). Immigrants. Letters. Norwegian Americans. Rapp, George. 1816-26. *378*
Pennsylvania (Havertown). Catholic Church. Irish Americans. Kelly, Dennis. St. Denis Parish. 1825-1975. *3683*
Pennsylvania (Hereford). Diaries. Gehman, John B. Mennonites. Speak Schools. 1853. *566*
Pennsylvania Historical and Museum Commission. Lutheran Church. Methodist Church. Orthodox Eastern Church. Pennsylvania Historical Association. Reformed Dutch Church. Research conference. Uniates. 1977. *2791*
Pennsylvania Historical Association. Lutheran Church. Methodist Church. Orthodox Eastern Church. Pennsylvania Historical and Museum Commission. Reformed Dutch Church. Research conference. Uniates. 1977. *2791*
Pennsylvania Hospital for the Sick Poor. Charities. Friends, Society of. Pennsylvania (Philadelphia). Poor. 18c. *2519*
Pennsylvania (Indian Field). American Revolution. Excommunication. Funk, Christian. Mennonites (Funkite). 1760-1809. *3376*
Pennsylvania (Intercourse). Amish. Land use. Mennonites. Mormons. Theology. Utah (Escalante). 1973. *2767*
Pennsylvania (Lampeter). Cemeteries. Mennonites. 18c-20c. *3366*
Pennsylvania (Lancaster). Attitudes. Ethnicity. Mennonites. Private Schools. Socialization. 1974-76. *673*
—. Clergy. Franklin and Marshall College. Gerhart, Emanuel Vogel. Reformed German Church. Theology. 1840-1904. *3286*
—. Clergy. Mennonites. Weaver, Benjamin W. 1853-1928. *3433*
—. Holy Trinity Parish. Lutheran Church (Evangelical). 1730-1980. *3306*
Pennsylvania (Lancaster County). Amish. Schisms. Stoltzfus, John. Theology. 1850-77. *3439*
—. Amish, Old Order. Church schools. 1937-73. *626*
—. Amish (Old Order). Daily Life. Diaries. Farms. King family. Loomis, Charles P. 1940. *3403*
—. Brethren in Christ. Canada. Engel, Jacob. Sects, Religious. 1775-1964. *3437*
—. Friends, society of. Local politics. Provincial politics. 1700-76. *1008*
—. Little Britain Presbyterian Church. Presbyterian Church. 1740-1860. *3587*
Pennsylvania (Lancaster County; Rapho Township). Bishops. Immigration. Lehman, Hans (and family). Mennonites. Swiss Americans. ca 1727-1909. *3400*
Pennsylvania (Lancaster, Mifflin counties). Amish. Baptism. Stoltzfus, John. Tennessee. 1820-74. *3438*
Pennsylvania (Little Britain Township). American Revolution. Brown, Joshua. Friends, Society of. Pacifism. Prisoners. South Carolina (Ninety Six). 1778. *2633*
Pennsylvania (Meadville). Christian Connection (church). Huidekoper, Harm Jan. Meadville Theological School. Unitarianism. 1844-56. *762*
Pennsylvania (Middle Octorara). American Revolution. Presbyterian Church. 1740-83. *969*
—. Presbyterian Church. 1727-1977. *3590*
Pennsylvania (Morgantown). Amish. Church History. Documents. Plank, D. Heber. 1668-1790's. 20c. *3388*
Pennsylvania (Nazareth). Land. Moravian Church. Settlement. Whitefield House. 1740-1978. *3517*
Pennsylvania (New Geneva; Pleasant Hill School District). Books. Protestantism. Sunday schools. 1823-57. *592*
Pennsylvania (New Harmony). Fraud. Owen, Robert. Rapp, Frederick. Real Estate. 1825. *327*
Pennsylvania, northwest. Architecture. Churches (Gothic Revival). Country Life. Furniture and Furnishings. Presbyterian Church. 1850-1905. 1979. *1797*
Pennsylvania (Philadelphia). Abolition Movement. Assassination. Brooks, Phillips. Episcopal Church, Protestant. Lincoln, Abraham. Sermons. 1865. 1893. *2463*
—. Adventists. Centennial Exposition of 1876. Kellogg, John Harvey. 1876. *2969*
—. Africans' School. Benezet, Anthony. Education. Friends, Society of. Negroes. 1770's-80's. *527*
—. Aitken, Robert. Bible. Continental Congress. English language. Publishers and Publishing. 1782. *1979*
—. American Revolution. Charities. Friends, Society of. Great Britain. Ireland. 1778-97. *2503*
—. American Revolution. Diaries. Drinker family. Friends, Society of. Pacifism. Prisoners. Virginia (Winchester). 1777-81. *2683*
—. American Revolution. Friends, Society of. Loyalists. 1770's. *1282*
—. American Revolution. Friends, Society of. Reform. 1741-90. *2674*
—. American Revolution. German Americans. Lutherans. 1776-81. *1304*
—. American Revolution. Germany. *Heinrich Mullers Pennsylvanischer Staatsbote* (newspaper). Moravian Church. Muller, Johann Heinrich. Printing. 1722-82. *3514*
—. American Revolution (antecedents). Business. Friends, Society of. Leadership. Radicals and radicalism. 1769-74. *1293*
—. Americanization. Episcopal Church, Protestant. White, William. ca 1789-1836. *324*
—. Antislavery Sentiments. Friends, Society of. Lay, Benjamin. 1690's-1759. *2460*
—. Archaeology. Kensington Methodist Episcopal Church. Methodist Episcopal Church. Preservation. 18c. 1950's-75. *1769*
—. Archives. Ecumenism. Historical Societies. Presbyterian Historical Society. 1852-1977. *260*
—. Art. Attitudes. Centennial Exposition of 1876. Friends, Society of. Peace. Sabbatarianism. Temperance Movements. 1876. *3256*
—. Artisans. Identity. Methodism. Morality. Social customs. Work ethic. Working Class. 1820-50. *3479*
—. Assimilation. Catholic Church. Parishes. 1759-1975. *3745*
—. Atkinson, James H. Friends Historical Association. 1873-1923. *234*
—. Baltzell, E. Digby (review article). Friends, Society of. Massachusetts (Boston). Puritans. Social Classes. 17c-1979. *2920*
—. Bibliographies. Catholic Church. Catholic University of America. Hogan Schism. Parsons, Wilfrid. Schisms. 1785-1825. 1975. *3845*
—. Bicentennial Conference of Religious Liberty. Religious liberty. 1976. *1040*
—. Bohemia. Catholic Church. Neumann, Saint John Nepomucene. 1811-1977. *3904*
—. Catholic Church. Centennial Exposition of 1876. Periodicals. 1876. *3864*
—. Catholic Church. Charismatic Movement. Italian Americans. Jesu, Father. Working Class. 1920's-30's. *1576*
—. Catholic Church. Church records. Immigrants. Italian Americans. Methodology. 1789-1900. *3770*
—. Catholic church. City Politics. Construction. Contractors. Irish Americans. 1846-1960's. *338*
—. Catholic Church. Ethnic Groups. Judaism. Social classes. Voting and Voting Behavior. 1924-40. *1308*
—. Catholic Church. Jankola, Matthew. Sisters of SS. Cyril and Methodius. Slovak Americans. 1903-70's. *3822*
—. Catholic Church. Literature. Walter, William Joseph *(Thomas More)*. 1839-46. *2063*
—. Catholic Church. Neumann, Saint John Nepomucene. 1830's-1963. *3774*
—. Catholic Church. Religious education. Sisters of Charity of the Blessed Virgin Mary. 1833-43. *609*
—. Centennial Exposition of 1876. Methodist Episcopal Church. Prayer. Simpson, Matthew. 1876. *3502*
—. Chain of interest (concept). Loyalists. Presbyterian Church. 1770's. *984*
—. Charities. Friends, Society of. Pennsylvania Hospital for the Sick Poor. Poor. 18c. *2519*
—. Children's Aid Society. Family. Foster care. Home Missionary Society. Protestantism. 1880-1905. *2504*
—. Christ Church Hospital. Episcopal Church, Protestant. Hospitals. Kearsley, John. Women. 1778-1976. *1455*
—. Church of England. Duche, Jacob, Jr. Great Britain. Pietism. Swedenborgianism. 1750-1800. *2738*
—. Clergy. Diaries. Hodge, Charles. Presbyterian Church. Theology. 1819-20. *3534*
—. Ecumenism. Presbyterian Church, Cumberland. World Alliance of Reformed Churches. 1870-80. *455*
—. Education. Women. Young Ladies Academy. 1780's-90's. *520*
—. Fell, Margaret. Feminism. Friends, Society of. Great Britain (Lancashire). Women. 1670's. *928*
—. Folklore. Gomez, Dolorez Amelia. Witchcraft. 1974. *2179*
—. Friends Asylum. Hinchman, Morgan. Mental Illness. Moral insanity. Trials. 1847. *1432*
—. Friends, Society of. Great Britain. Law. *Mary and Charlotte* (vessel). War relief. 1778-84. *3266*
—. Friends, Society of. Indian Wars. Nonviolence. Paxton Boys. 1764-67. *2693*
—. Gloria Dei Congregation. Lutheran Church. Old Swedes' Church. Swedish Americans. 1638-98. *3302*
—. Independence Hall. Philanthropy. Seybert, Henry. Spiritualism. 1793-1882. *4292*
—. Music. Negroes. New York City. Protestant churches. ca 1800-44. *1948*
—. Pius IX, Pope. Public Opinion. 1848. *2781*
Pennsylvania (Philadelphia; Germantown). Cities (review article). New England. New York. Protestantism. 1660's-18c. *2828*
Pennsylvania (Philadelphia, Pittsburgh). Bishops. Canevin, Regis. Catholic Church. Flick, Lawrence. 1870's-1927. *3843*
Pennsylvania (Philadelphia; review article). Benjamin, Philip S. Feldberg, Michael. Friends, Society of. Miller, Richard G. Sinclair, Bruce. 1790-1920. 1974-76. *3269*
Pennsylvania (Pittsburgh). Acculturation. Catholic Church. Irish Americans. St. Andrew Parish. 1863-90. *3748*
—. Bishops. Catholic Church. Church Finance. Frenaye, Mark Anthony. Letters. O'Connor, Michael. 1843-49. *368*
—. Immigrants. Jews. Religious Education. 1862-1932. *754*
Pennsylvania (Reading). Bethel African Methodist Episcopal Church. Methodist Episcopal Church, African. Restorations. 1834-1979. *1784*
Pennsylvania (Rockdale). Evangelicalism. Social change. Wallace, Allen F. C. (review article). 1820-65. *2861*
Pennsylvania (St. Marys). Catholic Church. St. Joseph's Convent. Walburga, Saint. 1852-1974. *3778*
Pennsylvania (Schuylkill County). Anti-Catholicism. Antislavery Sentiments. Bannan, Benjamin. Nativism. Temperance Movements. Whig Party. 1852-54. *1238*
Pennsylvania (Shenandoah). Clergy. Uniates. 1884-1907. *3909*
Pennsylvania (Snyder County). Clergy. Mennonites. 1780's-1970's. *3371*
Pennsylvania, southeastern. Brethren churches. Quiltmaking. 1700-1974. *1891*
—. Brethren in Christ. Kansas (Dickinson). Westward Movement. 1879. *3381*
Pennsylvania (Uniontown). Higher Education. Madison College. Methodist Protestant Church. 1851-58. *617*
Pennsylvania, University of. Andrews, John. Clergy. Education. Episcopal Academy. 1765-1810. *507*

Pennsylvania, western. American Revolution. Delaware Indians. Indians. Missions and Missionaries. Moravian Church. Ohio. 1775-83. *1532*
—. American Tract Society. Evangelicalism. Missions and Missionaries. Wright, Elizur, Jr. 1828-29. *1536*
—. Evangelical Association. 1800-33. *3662*
Pentecostal Assemblies of Canada. Canada. Pentecostal Bible School. Purdie, James Eustace. Religious education. Theology. 1925-50. *747*
Pentecostal Bible School. Canada. Pentecostal Assemblies of Canada. Purdie, James Eustace. Religious education. Theology. 1925-50. *747*
Pentecostal Holiness Church. Appalachia, southern. Hensley, George Went. Snakehandlers. 1909-73. *3522*
Pentecostal Movement *See also* Charismatic Movement.
—. Americanization. Evangelical Covenant Church. Evangelical Free Church of America. Methodism. Salvation Army. Swedish Baptist Church. 1870-1973. *321*
—. Appalachia. Folk Religion. Snakehandlers. 1974. *3519*
—. Catholic Church. 1967-75. *3799*
—. Catholic Church. Clergy. Middle Classes. Students. 1970's. *3753*
—. Catholic Church. Dissent. Episcopal Church, Protestant. 1950's-70's. *2742*
—. Catholic Church. Revivals. 1969. *3752*
—. Catholicism. Underground church. 1969-73. *3802*
—. Christianity. 1972-73. *3524*
—. Connecticut (New Haven). Negroes. Prayer meetings. Psychology. Social conditions. 1978. *3521*
—. Negroes. 1906-72. *3525*
Pentecostalism. Charismatic Movement. Jesus People. Revivals. Transcendental Meditation. 1960's-78. *127*
Pentecostals. Appalachia, southern. Rites and ceremonies. Snakehandlers. Trances. 1909-74. *3523*
—. Arkansas, northeast. Baptists. Folk religion. Theology. Worship. 1972-78. *2836*
—. Arkansas, northeast. Faith healing. Sects, Religious. 1937-73. *1433*
—. Arkansas, northeastern. Clergy. Radio. Rhetoric. 1972-73. *1959*
—. Brethren in Christ (Wengerites). Indiana. Ohio. 1836-1924. *3432*
—. Revivals. 1970's. *2269*
People United to Save Humanity. Jackson, Jesse. Negroes. Social Status. Southern Christian Leadership Conference. 1966-78. *2423*
People's Institute of Applied Religion. Labor Unions and Organizations. South. Williams, Claude. Williams, Joyce. 1940-75. *1478*
People's Party. Anti-Catholicism. California (San Francisco). City Politics. Know-Nothing Party. Vigilance Committee. 1854-56. *1307*
People's Temple. Apocalypse (concept). Guyana (Jonestown). Jones, Jim. 1953-78. *4252*
—. California. Guyana (Jonestown; review article). Jones, Jim. 1931-78. *4251*
—. California (San Francisco). Guyana (Jonestown). Jones, Jim. Leftism. 1960's-78. *4247*
—. Charisma. Guyana (Jonestown). Jones, Jim. Leadership. Models. Suicide, mass. 1978. *4253*
—. Cults. Father Divine. Jones, Jim. Negroes. Peace Mission (movement). 1920-79. *4254*
—. Guyana (Jonestown). Jones, Jim. Personality. Suicide, mass. 1965-78. *4238*
—. Guyana (Jonestown). Jones, Jim. Sects, Religious. ca 1950-79. *4262*
Percy, Walker (*Love in the Ruins*). Christianity. Technology. Western civilization. 1971. *2028*
Perfectionism. Abolition Movement. Hersey, John. Methodist Church. Millenarianism. 1786-1862. *3446*
—. Civil Religion. Finney, Charles G. Mahan, Asa. Millenarianism. National Self-image. 19c. *1189*
—. Evangelism. Faith healing. Theology. 1870-90. *1434*
Perfectionists. Free love. Rhode Island (Cumberland). Theology. 1748-68. *2898*
Performance licensing. Lawsuits. Licenses. Music, gospel. 1950's. *1919*
Periodicals *See also* Editors and Editing; Freedom of the Press; Newspapers; Press.
—. Acculturation. Americanism. Catholic Church. Leo XIII, Pope (*Testem Benevolentiae*). Protestantism. 1899. *319*
—. Assemblies of God. Church of God. Civil rights movement. Presbyterian Church, Southern. South. 1950's-60's. *2528*
—. Baptists. Bible. Theology. 1925-75. *3014*
—. Baptists. Bibliographies. 1979. *3099*
—. Baptists. Historical societies. South. 1950's-70's. *186*
—. Bible. Catholic Church. Hermeneutics. 1893-1908. *3812*
—. Bibliographies. 17c-1970's. *44*
—. Bibliographies. 1977. *43*
—. Bibliographies. Presbyterian Church. Reformed churches. 1973. *2957*
—. Bibliographies. Psychology of religion. Research. 1950-74. *168*
—. Bibliographies. South. 18c-20c. 1977-78. *45*
—. Books. Children's literature. Death and Dying. Protestantism. 1800-60. *2914*
—. Catholic Church. Centennial Exposition of 1876. Pennsylvania (Philadelphia). 1876. *3864*
—. *Christian History* (periodical). Evangelicalism. Great Britain. Methodist Church, Calvinistic. Whitefield, George. 1740's. *2233*
—. Humor. Illustration. Mormons. Novels. 1850-60. *2004*
—. Mormons. Newspapers. Public Opinion. 1970's. *2071*
Persecution *See also* Anti-Semitism; Civil Rights; Religious Liberty.
—. Amish. Folk Art. Mennonites. Pennsylvania. Quiltmaking. 16c-1935. *1893*
—. Canada. Doukhobors. Immigration. Russia. Sects, Religious. 1654-1902. *3917*
—. Catholic Church. Immigration. Prince Edward Island. Scotland. 1769-74. *3702*
—. Charles I. Friends, Society of. Massachusetts. 1661. *1018*
—. Church and State. Government, Resistance to. Jehovah's Witnesses. Theology. 1870's-1960's. *1097*
—. Civil religion. Counter Culture. Public Opinion. Sects, Religious. 19c-20c. *4263*
—. Friends, Society of. Howgill, Francis. New England. Puritans. ca 1650-60. *1027*
—. Friends, Society of. Massachusetts. Southwick (family). 1639-61. *1066*
Personal Narratives *See also* Autobiography; Oral History; Travel Accounts.
—. Abbott, Lyman. Clergy. Congregationalism. New York (Cornwall-on-the-Hudson). Parsons, Edward Smith. 1885. *3136*
—. Abolition Movement. James, Thomas. Methodist Episcopal Church, African. 1804-80. *2476*
—. Adventist Medical Cadet Corps. Armies. Dick, Everett N. Korean War. World War II. 1934-53. *2644*
—. Adventists. California (Arlington). Loma Linda University. Robison, James I. 1922. *745*
—. Adventists. Evangelism. Hill, W. B. Iowa. Minnesota. 1877. 1881. *1547*
—. Agriculture. Factionalism. Germans, Russian. Mennonites. Saskatchewan (Rosthern). Settlement. 1891-1900. *3442*
—. Alabama (Aliceville). Baptists, Primitive. Civil rights. Corder, James. Negroes. 1965-75. *2555*
—. Alberta (Edmonton, Mellowdale). Concordia College. Lutheran Church (Missouri Synod). Schwermann, Albert H. USA. 1891-1976. *753*
—. American Revolution. Daily life. Great Britain. Johnson, Jeremiah. Military Occupation. New York City (Brooklyn). 1775-83. *63*
—. Anti-Semitism. Fiction. Fiedler, Leslie. Judaism. 1970's. *2043*
—. Arkansas, University of. Baptists. Hays, Brooks. Students. Values. ca 1915-20. *3025*
—. Arrington, Leonard J. Historiography. Mormons. Western states. 20c. *171*
—. Assimilation. Greek Americans. Papagiannis, Michael D. USA (impressions). 20c. *2811*
—. Baker, Ray Stannard. Civil rights. DuBois, W. E. B. Episcopal Church, Protestant. Liberalism. Negroes. Whites. Wilmer, Cary Breckenridge. 1900-10. *2151*
—. Baptists. Civil rights movement. Ebenezer Baptist Church. Georgia (Atlanta). Roberts, Joseph L., Jr. 1960-75. *2556*
—. Baptists. Clergy. Dahlberg, Edwin. Rauschenbusch, Walter. Social reform. 1914-18. *2440*
—. Baptists. Clergy. Frontier and Pioneer Life. Montana. Spencer, James Hovey. 1888-97. *3095*
—. Baptists. Country Life. Farms. Illinois (southern). Lentz, Lula Gillespie. 1883-1929. *3037*
—. Baptists, Southern. Campbell, Will. Clergy. Garner, Thad. South. 20c. *2994*
—. Baptists, Southern. Newcomb, Horace. 1940's-70's. *3052*
—. Baur, John C. Concordia Seminary. Fund raising. Lutheran Church (Missouri Synod). Missouri (Clayton, St. Louis). 1923-26. *594*
—. Berger, Elmer. Judaism (Reform). Rabbis. Zionism. ca 1945-75. *4202*
—. Bloomfield Academy. Chickasaw Indians. Downs, Ellen J. Girls. Indians. Methodist Church. Oklahoma (Penola County). Schools. 1853-66. *772*
—. Boarding Schools. Chatham Hall. Episcopal Church, Protestant. Ferguson, Anne Williams. Virginia. Women. 1940's. *628*
—. Bottoms, Lawrence W. Negroes. Presbyterian Church, Southern. South. 1930-75. *2529*
—. Braude, William G. Judaism. Wolfson, Harry. 1932-54. *4090*
—. British Columbia. Daily life. Doukhobors. Immigration. Russia. 1880's-1976. *3918*
—. Brown, Robert McAfee. New York City. Presbyterian Church. Union Theological Seminary. VanDusen, Henry Pitney. 1945-75. *767*
—. Buettner, George L. Concordia Publishing House. Lutheran Church (Missouri Synod). Missouri (St. Louis). Publishers and publishing. 1888-1955. *336*
—. California. Franklin, Harvey B. Jews. Rabbis. 1916-57. *4099*
—. California (Bodie). Clay, Eugene O. Funerals. Methodist Church. Nevada (Smith Valley). Sermons. 1915. *3456*
—. Canada. China. Church of England. Missionary Society of the Canadian Church. Scovil, G. C. Coster. 1946-47. *1744*
—. Canada. China. Hurford, Grace Gibberd. Missions and Missionaries. Teaching. World War II. 1928-45. *1711*
—. Canadian Pacific Railway. Clergy. Construction crews. Manitoba (Virden). McLeod, Finlay J. C. Presbyterian Church. 1881-82. *3567*
—. Catholic Church. Charities. Education. Moore, Julia. Ontario (London). Sisters of St. Joseph. Women. 1868-85. *2517*
—. Catholic Church. Chicoutimi, Séminaire de. Church and State. Personal narratives. Simard, Ovide-D. 1873-1973. *757*
—. Catholic Church. Chicoutimi, Séminaire de. Church and State. Personal narratives. Simard, Ovide-D. 1873-1973. *757*
—. Catholic Church. Church Schools. Girls. McDonough, Madrienne C. Mount St. Mary Convent. New Hampshire (Manchester). 1902-09. *692*
—. Catholic Church. Clergy. Czechoslovakia. Refugees. Social Change. Zubek, Theodoric. 1950-78. *3902*
—. Catholicism. French Canadians. Lévesque, Georges-Henri. Nationalism. Quebec. Youth movements. 1930's. *3790*
—. Centennial United Methodist Church. Indiana (Gary). Methodist Church, United. Methodist Church, United. Negroes. Robinson, Roosevelt. White flight. 1976. *3467*
—. Church and state. Clergy. Henry, Patrick. Maury, James. Parsons' Cause. Speeches, Addresses, etc. Virginia. 1758-65. *1080*
—. Church history. Presbyterian Church. Thompson, Ernest Trice. Union Theological Seminary. Virginia (Richmond). 1920-75. *689*
—. Church of God. North Carolina. Reed, Granny. 20c. *3520*
—. City Life. Cromwell, James W. Friends, Society of. New York City. 1842-60. *3271*
—. Civil Rights movement. Discrimination. Florida (Miami). Louisiana (New Orleans). Murray, Hugh T., Jr. Tulane Interfaith Council. 1959-60. *2548*
—. Civil War. Country Life. Mississippi (Pontotoc County). Shady Grove Baptist Church. Smith, Andrew Jackson. 1864-69. *3035*
—. Clark, Joseph. Education, Finance. Fund raising. Princeton University (Nassau Hall). Travel. 1802-04. *612*

—. Clergy. Concordia Seminary. Illinois (Hahlen, Nashville). Lutheran Church (Missouri Synod). St. Peter's Lutheran Church. Scharlemann, Ernst K. Seminaries. 1905-18. *3335*
—. Clergy. Consultation on Church Union. Henderlite, Rachel. Presbyterian Church, Southern. South. Women. 1945-77. *804*
—. Clergy. Disciples of Christ. Frontier. North Central States. Snethen, Abraham. 1794-1830. 1977. *3112*
—. Clergy. Emanuel Lutheran Church. Lutheran Church. New York City (Queens). Wyneken, Frederick G. 1887-1907. *3348*
—. Clergy. German language. Hansel, William H. Lutheran Church (Missouri Synod). 1907-62. *3305*
—. Clergy. Methodist Church. North Carolina. Young, John. 1747-1837. *3507*
—. Congregationalism. Conversion. Great Awakening. Massachusetts (Freetown). 1749-70. *2221*
—. Coray, Howard. Leadership. Mormons. Smith, Joseph. 1840's. *3990*
—. Country Life. Iowa. Langland, Joseph. Lutheran Church. Poetry. Youth. 1917-30's. 1977. *2027*
—. Depressions. Juma, Charlie. North Dakota (Ross). Syrian Americans. 1900's-30's. *35*
—. Driggs, Nevada W. Nevada (Panaca). Polygamy. Utah. 1890-93. *832*
—. Dwellings. Jacobsen, Florence S. Mormons. Restorations. Utah (St. George). Young, Brigham. 19c. 1970's. *1789*
—. Ecumenism. Education. Mackay, John A. Presbyterian Church of the United States of America. Princeton Theological Seminary. Theology. 1910-75. *3543*
—. Elementary Education. Johnson, Emeroy. Lutheran Church. Minnesota. Religious education. Swedish Americans. ca 1854-ca 1920. *666*
—. Evangelism. Horstman, Otto K. Indiana (Shelbyville). Lutheran Church, Evangelical. Missions and Missionaries. 1934. *1551*
—. Fasman, Oscar Z. Hebrew Theological College. Judaism (Orthodox). Oklahoma (Tulsa). Ontario (Ottawa). Rabbis. 1929-79. *4177*
—. Gates, Susa Young. Marriage. Mormons. Utah. Women. Young, Brigham. Young, Lucy Bigelow. 1830-1905. *3972*
—. German Americans. Good, Merle. Literature. Mennonites. Pennsylvania. 1975. *2057*
—. Gordon, Helen Skinner. King, Gordon J. Manitoba (Winnipeg). Presbyterian Church. Woman's Missionary Society of the Presbyterian and United Churches. 1890's-1961. *3548*
—. Hawaii. Judaism. Zwerin, Kenneth C. 1935. *4158*
—. Hertzberg, Arthur. Judaism (Conservative). Rabbis. 1940's-79. *4168*
—. Hess, Katie Charles. Mennonites. Pennsylvania. Women. 1883-1978. *3356*
—. Hexter, Maurice B. Jews. Ohio (Cincinnati). Social Work. United Jewish Charities. 1910's. *2508*
—. Holt, Benjamin M. Lutheran Church. Minnesota. 1882-1974. *3309*
—. Immanuel Lutheran School. Lutheran Church (Missouri Synod). Religious education. Wulff, O. H. 1908-75. *781*
—. Indiana. Mennonites. Mumaw, George Shaum. Ohio. Singing Schools. 1900-57. *1941*
—. International cooperation. Methodism. Pendell, Thomas Roy. USSR. World Conference of Christian Youth, 1st. 1939-79. *1402*
—. Judaism (Reform). Kerman, Julius C. Palestine. Rabbis. World War I. 1913-71. *4214*
—. Keisker, Walter. Lutheran Church. Missouri (Concordia). Religious Education. St. Paul's College. Students. 1913-19. 1980. *669*
—. Kimball, Edward L. Kimball, Spencer W. Mormons. 1943-78. *3994*
—. Kramer, William A. Lutheran Church. Missouri (Perry County). ca 1890-1910. *3314*
—. Lutheran Church. Mission Festival Sunday. Missions and Missionaries. Schreiber, Clara Seuel. Wisconsin (Freistadt). 1900. *1630*
—. Lutheran Church. Palm Sunday. Schreiber, Clara Seuel. Wisconsin (Freistadt). 1898. *3338*
—. Nelson, Edward O. Salvation Army (Scandinavian Corps). Scandinavian Americans. 1877-1977. *3293*
Personalism. Baptists. King, Martin Luther, Jr. Muelder, W. G. Nonviolence. Theology. Tillich, Paul. Wieman, Henry Nelson. 1955-68. *2552*
Personality. Child-rearing. Protestantism. 1640-1800. *814*
—. Christian Science. Eddy, Mary Baker. Lee, Ann. Shakers. Theology. Women. 1736-1910. *2753*
—. Converts. Psychology. Puritans. 1630-1740. *3640*
—. Guyana (Jonestown). Jones, Jim. People's Temple. Suicide, mass. 1965-78. *4238*
Personality (review article). Child-rearing. Death and Dying. Fischer, David H. Greven, Philip. Lynn, Kenneth S. Politics. Protestantism. Stannard, David E. 18c. 1977. *2943*
Pessimism. Fiction. Hawthorne, Nathaniel. Melville, Herman *(Moby Dick).* 1850-51. *2042*
Petersen, Ole Peter. Americanization. Methodist Episcopal Church. Missions and Missionaries. Norway. 1830-53. *1706*
Petitions. Agricultural Labor. Canary Islanders. Fernandez de Santa Ana, Benito. Indians. Missions and Missionaries. Provincial Government. Texas (Villa San Fernando). 1741. *1542*
—. American Revolution (antecedents). Conscientious Objectors. Dunkards. Mennonites. Pennsylvania. 1775. *2710*
—. Bishop of London. Clergy. Methodists. Ordination. Pilmoor, Joseph. Virginia (Norfolk County). 1774. *3465*
—. Church Government. Church of England. House of Burgesses. Public policy. Virginia. 1700-75. *999*
Pettee, Julia. Libraries. New York City. Presbyterian Church. Rockwell, William Walker. Union Theological Seminary Library. 1908-58. *759*
Pfeffer, Leo. Christianity. Judaism. Politics. Secular Humanism. Social Change. 1958-76. *132*
Philadelphia Archeparchy. Pennsylvania. Senyshyn, Ambrose (obituary). Ukrainian Americans. Uniates. 1903-76. *3906*
Philadelphia *Aurora* (newspaper). Elections (presidential). Episcopal Church, Protestant. Illuminati controversy. Ogden, John C. Religious liberty. 1798-1800. *957*
Philadelphia Society for Organizing Charitable Relief and Repressing Mendicancy. Charities. Friends, Society of. Pennsylvania. 1800-1900. *2523*
Philanthropy *See also* Charities.
—. Business. 19c. *342*
—. Catholic Church. Minnesota (St. Paul). O'Brien, Alice. Women. 1914-62. *2419*
—. Claflin, Lee. Methodist Episcopal Church. 19c. *2513*
—. Independence Hall. Pennsylvania (Philadelphia). Seybert, Henry. Spiritualism. 1793-1882. *4292*
—. Mormons. Settlement. Smart, William Henry. Utah (Uinta Basin). 1862-1937. *4031*
Philippines. Annexation. Catholic Church. Converts. Imperialism. Methodist Episcopal Church. Missions and Missionaries. 1899-1913. *1689*
—. Brent, Charles Henry. Episcopal Church, Protestant. Missions and Missionaries. Paternalism. 1901-18. *1738*
—. Catholic Church. Methodists. Missions and Missionaries. 1899-1916. *1688*
Phillips Academy. Calvinism. Education. Massachusetts (Andover). 1778-1978. *584*
Phillips, George. California. Circuit riders. Civil War. Frontier and Pioneer Life. Manuscripts. Methodism. Ohio. 1840-64. *3494*
Phillips, Jeremiah. Baptists (freewill). India. Missions and Missionaries. Santals (tribe). 19c. *1733*
Phillips, Wendell. Abolition Movement. Christianity. Enlightenment. Morality. Nationalism. 1830-84. *1399*
Philosophy *See also* Ethics; Mysticism; Pragmatism; Rationalism; Transcendentalism.
—. Aesthetics. Emerson, Ralph Waldo. Plotinus. Science. Transcendentalism. 1836-60. *2302*
—. American Philosophical Association. Catholic Church. Colleges and Universities. Religious Education. 1933-79. *775*
—. Attitudes. Hasidism. Judaism. 1970's. *4189*
—. Bledsoe, Albert Taylor. Liberty. Theology. 19c. *1360*
—. Canada. Grant, George. Politics. Schmidt, Larry (review article). Theology. 1945-78. *509*
—. Catholic Church. Christian Renaissance. Converts. Literature. Science. Stern, Karl. 1920's-60's. *2758*
—. Catholic Church. Church Schools. Theology. 1920-60. *3747*
—. Christian realism. Liberalism. Niebuhr, Reinhold. 1920's. *1359*
—. Christianity. Conservatism. South. Weaver, Richard M. ca 1930-63. *1363*
—. Christianity. Marti, Fritz. Scholarship. Swiss Americans. Theology. 1894-1979. *2803*
—. Colleges and Universities. Common Sense school. Curricula. Dalhousie University. King's College. Lyall, William. Nova Scotia. Pine Hill Divinity Hall. Presbyterian Church. 1850-90. *719*
—. Common Sense school. Comte, Auguste. Positivism. Reformed churches. Social Gospel. Theology. ca 1850's-80's. *2833*
—. Congregationalism. Edwards, Jonathan. Theological empiricism. 1740-46. *3145*
—. Diplomacy. Hocking, William Ernest. Idealism. Political attitudes. 1918-66. *1368*
—. Fowler, Lorenzo Niles. Fowler, Orson Squire. Millenarianism. Phrenology. ca 1820-60's. *2350*
—. Fuller, Margaret. Spiritualism. Transcendentalism. Women. 1840's. *4068*
—. Laurens, Henry. Republicanism. Social Reform. South Carolina. 1764-77. *2385*
—. Liberalism. Marxism. Niebuhr, Reinhold. 1927-69. *1422*
—. McCosh, James. Protestantism. World Alliance of Reformed Churches. 1850-75. *453*
—. Nature. Poetry. Whitman, Walt ("Song of Myself"). 1855. *64*
—. New Thought movement. Quimby, Phineas Parkhurst. 1850's-1917. *62*
—. Niebuhr, Reinhold. Secularism. Theology. 1974. *2855*
—. Niebuhr, Reinhold. Theology. 1974. *2940*
—. Science. 1974. *2294*
Philosophy of History *See also* Historiography.
—. Albright, William Foxwell. Archaeology. Biblical studies. Science. 1918-70. *2328*
—. Apocalypticism. Counter culture. 1950-73. *148*
—. Christianity. Islam. Judaism. Medieval culture. Wolfson, Harry Austryn. 6c-16c. 1910-74. *278*
—. Christianity. Methodism. Wesley, John. ca 1740's-80's. *3453*
—. Christianity. Niebuhr, Reinhold. 20c. *2859*
—. Conversion. Edwards, Jonathan *(History of the Work of Redemption).* Theology. 1739. *3140*
—. Elliott, Stephen. Episcopal Church, Protestant. Providence. South. 1840-66. *3212*
—. Fiction. Hawthorne, Nathaniel. Massachusetts. Puritans. 1820's-60's. *2081*
Philosophy of Science. LeConte, Joseph. Sociology. South. ca 1840-60. *2301*
Philtres. Aphrodisiacs. Charms. Folk Medicine. Witchcraft. -1973. *2199*
Phips, William. Massachusetts. Mather, Cotton *(Life of Phips).* Politics. Puritans. 1690-1705. *3622*
Photographs. Adventists. California. Loma Linda Sanitarium. 1905-19. *1458*
—. Alabama. Lutheran Church. South. 1971-74. *3347*
—. California (Los Angeles; Chavez Ravine). Cemeteries. Hebrew Benevolent Society of Los Angeles. Home of Peace Jewish Cemetery. Judaism. 1855-1910. *4161*
—. Cheyenne Indians. Institutions. Mennonites. Missions and Missionaries. Social customs. 1880-1940. *3398*
—. Churches. Georgia. 1751-1900's. *1830*
—. Congregationalism. Evangelism. Far Western States. Mormons. Nutting, John Danforth. Utah Gospel Mission. 1900-50. *1560*
Photography *See also* Films.
—. Anderson, George Edward. Mormons. Utah, southern. 1877-1928. *3970*
—. Bossard, Gisbert. Florence, Max. Mormon Temple. Smith, Joseph Fielding. Utah (Salt Lake City). 1911. *1762*
Phrenology. Fowler, Lorenzo Niles. Fowler, Orson Squire. Millenarianism. Philosophy. ca 1820-60's. *2350*
—. Mormons. 1842-1940. *2298*
Physicians. Diaries. Great Britain. North America. Theologians. Ward, John. 17c. *2312*
—. Herbs. Medicine (practice of). Mormons. 1820-1979. *1459*
Physiology. Bartholow, Roberts. Medical reports. Mormons. Polygamy. Utah. Vollum, E. P. 1850-75. *1430*

Pictou Academy. Colleges and universities. Dalhousie University. McCulloch, Thomas. Missions and Missionaries. Nova Scotia. Presbyterian Church. ca 1803-42. *591*
Pierce, George Foster. Clergy. Georgia. Methodist Episcopal Church, South. Pierce, Lovick. 1785-1884. *3454*
Pierce, Lovick. Clergy. Georgia. Methodist Episcopal Church, South. Pierce, George Foster. 1785-1884. *3454*
Pierce v. *Society of Sisters* (US, 1925). Church and State. Compulsory education. Constitutional Amendments (1st). Parents. 1925. 1976. *587*
Piercy, Frederick *(Illustrated Route)*. Great Britain. Immigrants. Landscape Painting. Mormons. Portraits. Travel guides. Western states. 1848-57. *1869*
Pierpont, Benjamin. Bible. Clergy. Congregationalism. Edwards, Jonathan. Marginalia. Massachusetts (Deerfield). Theology. 1726-30. *3146*
Pietism. American Revolution (antecedents). Great Awakening. Individualism. Republicanism. 1735-75. *1385*
—. Astronomy. *Horologium Achaz* (scientific device). Pennsylvania Germans. Witt, Christopher. 1578-1895. *2349*
—. Baptists. Canada. Disciples of Christ. Great Plains. Lutheran Church. Methodism. Prairie Radicals. Radicals and Radicalism. 1890-1975. *954*
—. Church of England. Duche, Jacob, Jr. Great Britain. Pennsylvania (Philadelphia). Swedenborgianism. 1750-1800. *2738*
—. Clergy. Lutheran Church. Muhlenberg, Henry Melchior. Pennsylvania. 18c. *3337*
—. Conversion. Germany. Great Britain. Lutheran Church. Puritanism. 17c-18c. *2942*
—. Enlightenment. National self-image. Puritanism. 17c-20c. *1184*
—. Europe, Western. Evangelicalism. Methodism. Reformed Dutch Church. Revivals. Social Conditions. 1674-19c. *2959*
—. Francke, Gottfried. Georgia (Ebenezer). Germany. Immigrants. Kiefer, Theobald, II. Letters. Lutheran Church. Orphanages. Whitefield, George. 1738. 1750. *2878*
—. Georgia. Germany (Halle). Methodism. 1736-70. *3510*
—. Puritans. Radical catholicity principle. Theology. 17c-18c. *2950*
Piety. Diaries. Massachusetts (Cambridge). Puritans. Shepard, Thomas. 1640-44. *3656*
Pigeon Creek Baptist Church. Baptists. Indiana. Lincoln, Abraham. 1822-30. *3098*
Pilgrims. Americanization. Attitudes. New England. 17c. *323*
—. Bradford, William *(Of Plymouth Plantation)*. Historiography. Plymouth Colony. Social Organization. 1630-50. *3153*
—. Bradford, William *(Of Plymouth Plantation)*. Historiography. Plymouth Colony. Theology. 1630. *3126*
—. Historiography. Massachusetts. Merry Mount incident. Morton, Thomas. 1625-1970's. *2050*
—. Hobomok (shaman). Indian-White Relations. Plymouth Colony. Polytheism. Squanto (Wampanoag Indian). Theology. ca 1620-30. *3144*
—. Indians. Massachusetts. Morton, Thomas. Puritans. Values. 1625-45. *2956*
—. Jews. New England. Old Testament. Puritans. 1620-1700. *2936*
—. Land. Massachusetts (Barnstable County). Peasants. Values. 1620's-1720's. *3151*
—. Massachusetts (Plymouth). Netherlands. 1607-20. *3139*
—. New England. Puritans. 1606-1790. *2886*
Pilmoor, Joseph. Bishop of London. Clergy. Methodists. Ordination. Petitions. Virginia (Norfolk County). 1774. *3465*
Pine Hill Divinity Hall. Colleges and Universities. Common Sense school. Curricula. Dalhousie University. King's College. Lyall, William. Nova Scotia. Philosophy. Presbyterian Church. 1850-90. *719*
Piner Baptist Church. Baptists. Indiana. 1833-1906. *3026*
Pinto, Joseph Jesurun. Cantors. Congregation Shearith Israel. Judaism (Orthodox). Netherlands. New York. Travel. 1759-82. *4196*
Pioneer Band. Aurora Colony. Communes. Music. Oregon. Society of Bethel. 1855-1920's. *1942*
Pioneer life. Family. Land. Mormons. Utah (Kanab). 1874-80. *4009*
—. Great Plains. Mennonites. Wheat. 1870-1974. *3443*
—. Mormons. Travel. Utah. Young, Brigham. 1850-77. *3987*
Pioneers *See also* Frontier and Pioneer Life; Mountain Men; Voyages.
—. Agriculture. Grasshoppers. Utah. 1854-79. *3941*
—. Badgley, David. Baptists. Illinois (New Design). 1769-1824. *3096*
—. California (Stockton). Clergy. Presbyterian Church. Woods, James. 1850-54. *3526*
—. Canada. Ecumenism. Mennonites (Canadian Conference). 1873-1978. *475*
—. Catholic Church. Education. Indians. Missions and Missionaries. North Dakota. Presentation of the Blessed Virgin Mary, Sisters of the. South Dakota. Women. 1880-96. *727*
—. Clergy. Dulík, Joseph J. Slovak Americans. Vaniščák, Gregory. 1909-38. *3823*
—. Congregationalism. Converts. Episcopal Church, Protestant. Kilbourne, James. Letters. Ohio (Worthington). 1844-49. *2823*
—. Crockett, Davy. Nature. Popular Culture. 1830's. *2712*
—. Culture. Mormons. Organizations. Utah. 1850's-70's. *523*
—. Manitoba. Mennonites. 1875. *3353*
Piper, William W. Architecture, academy. Catholic Church. Oregon (Salem). Sacred Heart Academy. 1834-83. *1828*
Pique, Dob. Congregation Kahal Kadosh Shearith Israel. Ethnicity. Falkenau, Jacob J. M. Hebrew. Jews. Lyons, Jacques Judah. New York City. Poetry. 1786-1841. *2062*
Pirates. Missions and Missionaries. Oceania. Pease, Benjamin. 1867-70. *1685*
Pitcairn (vessel). Adventists. Missions and Missionaries. Visions. White, Ellen G. 1848-90. *1704*
Pitts, Herman H. Anti-Catholicism. New Brunswick. Religion in the Public Schools. 1871-90. *574*
Pittsburgh Platform (1885). Judaism (Reform). Science. Theology. Voorsanger, Jacob. 1872-1908. *2337*
Pius IX, Pope. Catholic Church. Elections. Leo XIII, Pope. Press. Protestantism. 1878. *2786*
—. Pennsylvania (Philadelphia). Public Opinion. 1848. *2781*
Pius IX, Pope *(Syllabus of Errors)*. Canada. Catholic Church. Church and state. Encyclicals. Press. Public opinion. 1864-65. *1019*
Pius XII, Pope. Diplomacy. Taylor, Myron C. Vatican. World War II. 1940-50. *1025*
Pixley, Frank M. Anti-Semitism. California (San Francisco). D'Ancona, David Arnold. Letters. Newspapers. 1883. *2128*
Place Names. *See* Toponymy.
Plagiarism. American Revolution. Great Britain. Methodism. Politics. Wesley, John *(A Calm Address to our American Colonies)*. 1775-79. *1377*
—. Brickell, John. Clayton, John. Letters. Natural History. North Carolina. 1693-1737. *2341*
Plains Apache Indians. Franciscans. Indian-White Relations. Inquisition. Marriage. Missions and Missionaries. New Mexico. Romero, Diego. 1660-78. *3773*
Plank, D. Heber. Amish. Church History. Documents. Pennsylvania (Morgantown). 1668-1790's. 20c. *3388*
Plantations. Jesuits. Maryland (St. Marys County). St. Inigoes Church. Slavery. 1806-1950. *326*
—. Marriage. Protestantism. Slaves. South. ca 1750's-1860. *2928*
Plants. Hallucinations. Southwest. Trances. Witchcraft. 17c-20c. *2207*
Pleasant Hill (community). Kentucky. Restorations. Shakers. Utopias. 1805-1970's. *385*
Pleasants, Robert. Friends, Society of. Virginia. 17c-18c. *3267*
Plessis, Joseph-Octave. Atlantic Provinces. Bishops. Catholic Church. Diaries. Quebec Archdiocese. 1812-15. *3704*
—. Catholic Church. Maritime Provinces. Travel (accounts). 1812-15. *3703*
Plotinus. Aesthetics. Emerson, Ralph Waldo. Philosophy. Science. Transcendentalism. 1836-60. *2302*
Plummer, Henry V. Baptists. Chaplains. Courts Martial and Courts of Inquiry. Fort Robinson. Nebraska. Negroes. 1884-94. *2695*
Plural establishment, theory of. Arnold, Matthew. Ethnicity. 19c-20c. *15*
Pluralism. Ahlstrom, Sydney E. (review article). Religious history. 1974. *17*
—. American Revolution. Education. Great Awakening. Theology. 1776. *1386*
—. Americanization. Catholic Church. Ecumenism. Europe. Theology. 1775-1820. *295*
—. Assimilation. German Americans. Michigan (Ann Arbor). Protestantism. 1830-1955. *284*
—. Bonomi, Patricia U. Ethnic Groups. Klein, Milton M. New York (review article). Provincial Government. 1690's-1770's. 1971-74. *1204*
—. Catholic Church. German Americans. Immigrants. Kansas (Atchison). Newspapers. 1854-59. *3877*
—. Catholic Church. Liberalism. Neoorthodoxy. Secularism. Theology. 1936-74. *3899*
—. Christianity. Economic growth. Ethnic Groups. Michigan (Detroit). 1880-1940. *2748*
—. Church and State. Public policy. 1970's. *1064*
—. Civil religion. Law and Society. 1953-72. *1161*
—. Democracy. National characteristics. 1640's-1840's. *71*
—. Demography. Religiosity. 1970's. *150*
—. Ecumenism. Social reform. Tolerance. 1975. *105*
—. Ethics. Literature. Styron, William *(Confessions of Nat Turner)*. 1970's. *2053*
—. Idealism. National characteristics. Puritan tradition. 1620's-1940's. *1*
—. Ideology. Middle Classes. Secularization. Social Change. 17c-20c. *12*
—. North Carolina (Piedmont region). Protestantism. 1890-1952. *2813*
Plymouth Church. Congregationalism. New York (Rochester). 1853-1904. *3115*
Plymouth Colony. Bradford, William *(Of Plymouth Plantation)*. Historiography. Pilgrims. Social Organization. 1630-50. *3153*
—. Bradford, William *(Of Plymouth Plantation)*. Historiography. Pilgrims. Theology. 1630. *3126*
—. Hobomok (shaman). Indian-White Relations. Pilgrims. Polytheism. Squanto (Wampanoag Indian). Theology. ca 1620-30. *3144*
—. Property. Puritans. 1621-75. *2569*
Poe, Edgar Allan *(The Pit and the Pendulum)*. Revivals. Symbolism in Literature. ca 1800-50. *2084*
Poetry. *Advent Review and Sabbath Herald* (newspaper). Adventists. Prophecy. Smith, Uriah. 1853. *1997*
—. Adventists. Hymns. Smith, Annie Rebekah. 1850's. *1926*
—. American Revolution. Church of England. Freneau, Philip ("A Political Litany"). Intellectuals. 1775. *1998*
—. American Revolution. Great Britain. Loyalists. Methodism. Political Commentary. Wesley, Charles. 1775-83. *1339*
—. Antislavery Sentiments. Congregationalism. Connecticut. Dwight, Theodore. 1788-1829. *2468*
—. Attitudes. Puritans. 16c-17c. *1973*
—. Baptists. Hermeneutics. Strong, Augustus Hopkins. Theology. 1897-1916. 1978. *1974*
—. Baptists. Massachusetts (Ashfield). Political Protest. Religious Liberty. Smith, Ebenezer. 1772. *2048*
—. Billings, William. Hymnals. Music. Read, Daniel. Watts, Isaac. 1761-85. *1920*
—. Blair, Duncan Black. Gaelic language. Nova Scotia (Pictou County). Presbyterianism. Scholars. Scotland. 1846-93. *2070*
—. Bogan, Louise. Catholic Church. Women. 1920's-70. *2059*
—. *Book of Common Worship*. Humor. Lampton, William J. Presbyterian Church, Southern. Rites and Ceremonies. VanDyke, Henry. 1906. *3557*
—. Bradstreet, Anne. Elegies. Massachusetts. Puritans. Women. 1665. *2044*
—. Brophy, Robert J. Jeffers, Robinson. Morris, Adelaide Kirby. Stevens, Wallace. Theology (review article). 20c. *2065*
—. Bucke, Richard Maurice. Whitman, Walt. 1877-1902. *68*
—. Buddhism (Zen). Snyder, Gary. 1960-74. *2055*
—. Calvinism. Cotton, John. Elegies. Fiske, John. New England. Puritans. 17c. *1985*

—. Chain of being. Church of England. Cradock, Thomas. Maryland (Baltimore County). Sermons. Social theory. 1700-80. *3227*
—. Chapman, John Jay. Christianity. Lynching. Pennsylvania (Coatesville). Race Relations. Rhetoric. Speeches, Addresses, etc. 1912. *1971*
—. Church of England. Clergy. Cradock, Thomas. Maryland (Baltimore County). Sermons. 1700-70. *3229*
—. Church of England. Patriotism. Rising glory of America (theme). Smith, William. 1752. *1337*
—. Congregation Kahal Kadosh Shearith Israel. Ethnicity. Falkenau, Jacob J. M. Hebrew. Jews. Lyons, Jacques Judah. New York City. Pique, Dob. 1786-1841. *2062*
—. Country Life. Iowa. Langland, Joseph. Lutheran Church. Personal narratives. Youth. 1917-30's. 1977. *2027*
—. Covenant theology. New England. Puritans. Wigglesworth, Michael *(Day of Doom)*. 1662. *3597*
—. Creative innocence, concept of. Maritain, Jacques. Maritain, Raissa. Merton, Thomas. Theology. 1940's-75. *3863*
—. Dickinson, Emily. Identity. Intellectual history. Myths and Symbols. Puritanism. Transcendentalism. Women. 1860's. *51*
—. Ecology. Hopkins, Gerard Manley. Humanities. Jesuits. Science. ca 1840-70's. *3701*
—. Fiske, John. Puritans. Taylor, Edward. Tree of Life metaphor. 1650-1721. *1969*
—. Folklore. Samplers. Social Customs. 19c. *2021*
—. Iconography. New England. Puritans. Sermons. Tombstones. 17c. *1977*
—. Intellectuals. New England. Radicals and Radicalism. Socialism. Wheelwright, John (1897-1940). 18c-1940. *1419*
—. Leadership. Mormons. Prophecy. Snow, Eliza Roxey. Utah. Women. 1804-87. *3936*
—. Nature. Philosophy. Whitman, Walt ("Song of Myself"). 1855. *64*
—. Oakes, Urian *(Elegie)*. Puritans. 1650-81. *1976*
—. Painting. Puritans. Smith, Thomas. ca 1690. *1839*
—. Proverbs. Puritans. Taylor, Edward ("Gods Determinations"). 1685. 1973. *1963*
—. Puritans. Science. Taylor, Edward. 1706. *2342*
—. Wheatley, Phillis. Women. 1773. *2031*
Poets. Blair, Duncan Black. Gaelic language. Nova Scotia (Barney's River). Presbyterianism. Scholarship. 1848-93. *2069*
—. Transcendentalism. Unitarianism. Very, Jones. 1833-70. *2774*
Polemics. Morality. Mormons. Polygamy. ca 1860-1900. *823*
Polhemius, Johannes Theodorus. Brazil. Clergy. New Netherland. Reformed Dutch Church. 1598-1676. *3165*
Police protection. Boys. Illinois (Nauvoo). Mormons. Whistling and Whittling Brigade. 1845. *4014*
Polish Americans. Actors and Actresses. California (Los Angeles area). Catholic Church. Modjeska, Helena. 1876-1909. *3786*
—. Addams, Jane. Dudzik, Mary Theresa. Franciscan Sisters of Chicago. Illinois. Social Work. Women. 1860-1918. *2511*
—. Americanization. Catholic Church. Clergy. Irish Americans. 1920-40's. *290*
—. Americanization. Catholic Church. Connecticut (New Britain). 1890-1955. *3692*
—. Assimilation. Catholic Church. Connecticut (New Britain). Holy Cross Church. 1928-76. *3693*
—. Assimilation. Catholic Church. Immigrants. 1860's-1930's. *3700*
—. Bójnowski, Lucyan. Buczek, Daniel Stephen (review article). Catholic Church. Clergy. Connecticut (New Britain). 1895-1960. *3865*
—. California (Los Angeles). Catholic Church. Ethnology. Methodology. Sandberg, Neil C. (review article). 1968-74. *3813*
—. Catholic Church. Church Schools. 1874-1960's. *675*
—. Catholic Church. Church Schools. Felicians. Social Work. Women. 1855-1975. *3828*
—. Catholic Church. Clergy. Editors and Editing. Historiography. *New Catholic Encyclopedia*. Swastek, Joseph Vincent (obituary). 1913-77. *227*
—. Catholic Church. Clergy. Lemke, John A. Michigan (Detroit). 1866-90. *3875*
—. Catholic Church. Colorado (Denver; Globeville). St. Joseph Parish. 1902-78. *3724*
—. Catholic Church. Family. Immigrants. Social control. Values. 20c. *913*
—. Catholic Church. Immigration. Letters. Moczygemba, Leopold. Texas (Panna Marya). 1855. *3679*
—. Catholic Church. Labor Unions and Organizations. Political Leadership. Progressivism. Socialism. Wisconsin (Milwaukee). 1900-30. *1299*
—. Catholic Church. Wisconsin (Milwaukee). 1846-1940. *3690*
—. Michigan (Detroit). St. Albertus Church. St. Casimir Church. 1870-1970. *3827*
Polish Canadians. British Canadians. Country life. Ethnic groups. French Canadians. Manitoba. Mennonites. Migration. Ukrainian Canadians. 1921-61. *3389*
—. Catholic Church. Discrimination. Economic Conditions. Prairie Provinces. 1880's-1970's. *3796*
Polish National Catholic Church. Assimilation. Immigrants. Kubiak, Hieronim (review article). 1897-1965. *306*
—. Ethnicity. Language. Nationalism. Parishes. 1880's-1930's. *313*
—. Hodur, Francis. 1896-1907. *310*
Polish Roman Catholic Union. Barzynski, Wincenty. Catholic Church. Illinois (Chicago). St. Stanislaus Kortka Church. Texas. 1838-99. *3678*
Political activism. California. Chavez, Cesar. Christianity. Mexican Americans. Rhetoric. Texas. Tijerina, Reies. 1960's-70's. *2391*
—. Church and Social Problems. Clergy. Protestant Churches. 1960's-70's. *2431*
Political activity. Baptists. California. Negroes. St. Andrew's African Methodist Episcopal Church. 1850-73. *981*
—. Church and Social Problems. 1974. *1328*
—. Church and state. Colorado (Denver). Tax exemption. *United States* v. *Christian Echoes National Ministry, Inc.* 1950's-1970's. *1063*
Political attitudes. American Revolution. Christian humanism. Puritans. Values. 18c. *1395*
—. American Revolution. Freedom. Liberation movements. Theology. 1765-20c. *1342*
—. American Revolution. Great Britain. Methodism. Wesley, John. Whigs, Radical. 1775-78. *1391*
—. American Revolution. Mormon, Book of. Mormons. Smith, Joseph. 1820's. *1353*
—. American Revolution. Presbyterians. Princeton University. 1765-76. *960*
—. Anti-Catholicism. Canada. Italy. Protestants. Risorgimento. 1846-60. *2114*
—. Antislavery Sentiments. Ohio. Revivals. Voting and Voting Behavior. 1825-70. *2866*
—. Assimilation. Jews. South Carolina (Charleston). 1970's. *4136*
—. Bellah, Robert N. Civil religion. National self-image. Values. 1775-20c. *1200*
—. California, University of (Regents). Catholic Church. Clergy. Irish Americans. Yorke, Peter C. 1900-12. *560*
—. Church and Social Problems. Ethics. Evangelicals. Graham, Billy. War. 1970's. *2932*
—. Church and state. Civil Rights. Colleges and Universities. Federal Aid to Education. New York. Students. 1972. *1119*
—. Church of England. Clergy. Government. Loyalists. Theology. 1770-83. *1387*
—. Civil Rights. Higher education. 1968. *1390*
—. Congregationalism. Dwight, Timothy. New England. 1775-1817. *1369*
—. Diplomacy. Hocking, William Ernest. Idealism. Philosophy. 1918-66. *1368*
—. Elites. Social Classes. Tennessee (Davidson County). 1835-61. *1232*
—. Idaho. Mormons. Voting and Voting Behavior. 1880's. *1273*
—. Reform. Settlement Movement. 1880's-90's. *2405*
Political behavior. Cultural Pluralism. Jensen, Richard. Kleppner, Paul. North Central States. 1850-1900. *1214*
Political Campaigns *See also* Elections; Political Speeches.
—. Drinan, Robert F. Jesuits. Massachusetts. 1970. *1267*
Political Campaigns (gubernatorial). Anti-Catholicism. Bryan, Nathan P. Catts, Sidney J. Democratic Party. Florida. Primaries (senatorial). Trammell, Park M. 1915-16. *1258*
Political Campaigns (mayoral). California (Los Angeles). Judaism. Social Classes. Voting and Voting Behavior. 1969. *1276*
Political Campaigns (presidential). Anti-Catholicism. Fillmore, Millard. Know-Nothing Party. Nativism. Whig Party. 1850-56. *1305*
—. Attitudes. Carter, Jimmy. Civil religion. Evangelicalism. Political Speeches. Rhetoric. 1976. *1229*
—. Baptists. Carter, Jimmy. 1976. *1272*
—. Candler, Warren A. Methodist Episcopal Church, South. Prohibition. Smith, Al. 1928. *1210*
—. Catholic Church. Church and state. Kennedy, John F. Presbyterian Church. 1959-60. *992*
—. Hoover, Herbert C. Smith, Al. Tennessee, west. 1928. *1279*
—. McGovern, George S. Nixon, Richard M. Rhetoric. Voting and Voting Behavior. 1972. *1228*
Political Commentary. American Revolution. Great Britain. Loyalists. Methodism. Poetry. Wesley, Charles. 1775-83. *1339*
—. Anti-Catholicism. Anti-Semitism. Conspiracy theories. Fundamentalism. Kansas. Winrod, Gerald Burton. 1933-57. *2090*
—. Arts. Propaganda. 1975. *1873*
—. Catholic Church. Conservatism. Nativism. Newspapers. Protestantism. *Providence Visitor* (newspaper). Rhode Island. 1916-24. *2118*
Political Corruption *See also* Elections; Lobbying; Political Reform.
—. Cannon, James, Jr. Glass, Carter. Methodist Church. Virginia. 1909-34. *1295*
Political Factions *See also* Lobbying.
—. American Revolution. Episcopal Church, Protestant. New York. Nonconformists. Provincial government. 1768-71. *1294*
—. Friends, Society of. New York. Seneca Indians. Tribal government. 1848. *1202*
Political institutions. Civil religion. Democracy. Ideology. Puritan tradition. 17c-20c. *1150*
Political knowledge. Canada. Colleges and Universities. Public opinion. Students. 1974. *978*
Political Leadership. Anti-Catholicism. Know-Nothing Party. Thompson, Richard W. 1850's. *1291*
—. Baptists. Georgia. State Politics. 1772-1823. *1260*
—. Benson, Ezra Taft. Morality. Mormons. Presbyterian Church. Wallace, Henry A. 1933-60. *1303*
—. Burr, Aaron. Presbyterian Church. 1772-1805. *3542*
—. Carroll, Charles (of Carrollton). Catholic Church. Declaration of Independence. Maryland. 1737-1832. *3705*
—. Carter, Jimmy. Cromwell, Oliver. Great Britain. Rickover, Hyman. Roosevelt, Theodore. 20c. *974*
—. Catholic Church. Labor Unions and Organizations. Polish Americans. Progressivism. Socialism. Wisconsin (Milwaukee). 1900-30. *1299*
—. Charities. Judaism (Orthodox, Reform). Nebraska (Omaha). Refugees. Settlement. 1820-1937. *4102*
—. Clergy. Negroes. Texas (Beaumont). 1972. *1315*
—. Diaries. Mormons. Musser, Elise Furer. Social Reform. Utah. Women. 1897-1967. *811*
—. Jews. Laity. Leadership. New York (Kingston). Protestant Churches. Social Status. 1825-60. *2600*
Political participation. Documents. Friends, Society of. Methodism. National Characteristics. Shakers. Tocqueville, Alexis de. 1831-40. *2780*
—. Equal Rights Amendment. Texas. Women. 1977. *933*
—. Finney, Charles G. Higher law (doctrine). Ohio Antislavery Society. Revivalism. 1835-60. *2253*
—. Protestants. Racism. Sexism. Whites. Women. 1974-75. *907*
Political Parties *See also* names of political parties, e.g. Democratic Party, Republican Party, etc.; Elections; Political Campaigns.
—. Anti-Catholicism. Chicago *Tribune* (newspaper). Editors and Editing. Illinois. 1853-61. *2112*
—. Bryan, William Jennings. Reagan, Ronald. Revivals. Social Change. 1730-1980. *1329*
—. Catholic Church. Ethnicity. Protestantism. 1968-72. *1220*

—. Church and State. Prince Edward Island. Prince of Wales College Act (1860). School Boards. 1860-63. *744*
—. Education. 1960's-74. *1261*
—. Evangelism. Michigan. State Legislatures. 1837-61. *1300*
—. Johnson, Benton. Protestant ethic. 1960's-70's. *1302*
—. Kleppner, Paul (review article). 1853-92. 1979. *1205*
Political philosophy. Alison, Francis. American Revolution. Presbyterian Church. Witherspoon, John. 1750-87. *1382*
—. American Revolution. Church of England. Clergy. Maryland. 1770-80. *1388*
Political power. Attitudes. Ethnic groups. Working class. 1974. *2612*
—. Baptists, Southern. Corporate wealth. Methodism. Presbyterian Church. South. 1930's-75. *2926*
—. Christian Science. Eddy, Mary Baker. Political Protest. Women. 1879-99. *840*
Political Protest *See also* Civil Disobedience; Revolution; Riots; Youth Movements.
—. Baptists. City Government. Maryland (Baltimore). Negroes. Public schools. 1865-1900. *583*
—. Baptists. Massachusetts (Ashfield). Poetry. Religious Liberty. Smith, Ebenezer. 1772. *2048*
—. Baptists. Methodist Church. Ninth Street Baptist Church. Ohio (Cincinnati). Temperance Movements. Wesley Chapel. Women's Christian Temperance Union. 1874. *2582*
—. Canada. Church and State. Jesuits' Estates Act. Protestants. 1880-90. *1088*
—. Christian Science. Eddy, Mary Baker. Political power. Women. 1879-99. *840*
—. Jews. Vietnam War. Youth. 1960's. *2694*
Political rallies. Camp meetings. Crowd control. Rhetoric. Tennessee. 1828-60. *1259*
Political Reform *See also* names of reform movements, e.g. Progressivism, etc.; Lobbying; Political Corruption.
—. Anti-Catholicism. Constitutional Law. Ireland. Irish Americans. O'Conor, Charles. O'Conor, Charles Owen. Reconstruction. 1865-85. *1031*
—. Attitudes. Great Awakening. Social Change. 18c. 1975. *2216*
—. Bengough, John Wilson. City government. *Grip* (periodical). Ontario (Toronto). Protestantism. 1873-1910. *1266*
Political repression. Canada. Catholic Church. Clergy. Craig, James Henry. French Canadians. Nationalism. Quebec (Lower Canada). 1810. *1319*
Political Science *See also* Constitutional Law; Democracy; Government; Imperialism; Law; Legislation; Nationalism; Politics; Public Administration; Revolution; Utopias.
—. Capitalism. Ideology. Management. Protestantism. Theology. Weber, Max. 16c-1974. *376*
Political socialization. Canada. Voting and Voting Behavior. 1965. *1249*
Political Speeches *See also* Debates; Speeches.
—. Attitudes. Carter, Jimmy. Civil religion. Evangelicalism. Political Campaigns (presidential). Rhetoric. 1976. *1229*
—. Christianity. Civil religion. South. 1960's-70's. *1193*
Political systems. American Revolution. Calvinism. Kuyper, Abraham. Netherlands. 1775-83. 19c-1920. *1332*
—. Economics. Public Policy. ca 1920-72. *1247*
—. Historiography. Massachusetts. Puritans. Suffrage. 1620-99. 1954-74. *1350*
Political Theory *See also* kinds of political theory, e.g. Democracy; Political Science.
—. Adams, John. American Revolution. New England. Paine, Thomas. Puritans. Rhetoric. 17c-1770's. *1424*
—. American Revolution. Baptists. Clergy. Georgia. Marshall, Daniel. 1747-1823. *1372*
—. American Revolution (antecedents). Church of England. Colonial Government. Great Britain. Shipley, Jonathan. 1773-75. *1376*
—. American Revolution (antecedents). Clergy. Sermons. 1750's-75. *1415*
—. Baptists. Religious liberty. 1619-1776. 1973. *1122*
—. Bascom, John. Commons, John R. Ely, Richard T. Evolution. Social gospel. Wisconsin, University of. 1870-1910. *2394*
—. Calvinism. Congregationalism. Government, Resistance to. Massachusetts (Boston). Mayhew, Jonathan. Sermons. 1750. *1381*
—. Catholic Worker Movement. Maurin, Peter ("Easy Essays"). Social Reform. 1920's-33. *2571*
—. Christianity. Muste, A. J. Niebuhr, Reinhold. Pacifism. Thomas, Norman. 1914-38. *2687*
—. Church and State. Civil religion. ca 1940's-74. *1188*
—. Civil religion. Mazzuchelli, Samuel Charles. Tocqueville, Alexis de. 1831-63. *1164*
—. Constitutions. Founding fathers. Historiography. Theology. 18c. *1405*
—. Great Britain. Local government. Massachusetts. New England. Puritans. Social change. 1600-50. *3604*
—. Liberalism. Niebuhr, Reinhold. ca 1920-72. *1355*
Political thought. Congregationalism. Democracy. Massachusetts. Wise, John. 17c-18c. *1354*
—. Niebuhr, Reinhold. Theology. 1927-59. *1417*
Political Violence. *See* Violence.
Politicians. Anti-Catholicism. France. Maryland. Protestants. 1750's. *2095*
Politics *See also* headings beginning with the word political; City Politics; Elections; Geopolitics; Government; Lobbying; Local Politics; Presidents; State Politics.
—. Aberhart, William. Alberta. Economic reform. Prime ministers. Radio. 1934-37. *1216*
—. Agriculture. Missions and Missionaries. Settlement. South Dakota. 1850-1900. *66*
—. American Revolution. Baptists. Georgia. Mercer, Silas. Theology. 1770-96. *3030*
—. American Revolution. Church of England. Clergy. Maryland. Social Status. 1775. *2618*
—. American Revolution. Constitutionalism. Historiography. Law. 1775-83. 1790-1950. *961*
—. American Revolution. Great Britain. Methodism. Plagiarism. Wesley, John *(A Calm Address to our American Colonies).* 1775-79. *1377*
—. American Revolution. Green, Jacob. New Jersey. 1770-90. *1398*
—. American Revolution. Historiography. Millenarianism. Nationalism. Patriotism. 1740-89. *1347*
—. American Revolution (antecedents). Church and state. Connecticut. Devotion, Ebenezer. Theology. 1714-71. *1397*
—. Antislavery sentiments. Campbell, Alexander. Civil religion. Disciples of Christ. Indians. War. Women. 1823-55. *3108*
—. Apostolic Delegates. Catholic Church. Conroy, George. Nationalism. Quebec. Vatican. 1877-78. *1098*
—. Assimilation. Church and state. New York. Reformed Dutch Church. 1664-91. *1121*
—. Assimilation. Lutheran Church. Muhlenberg, Henry Melchior. Pennsylvania. Swedish Americans. Wrangel, Carl Magnus. 1749-69. *1283*
—. Attitudes. California (Berkeley). Converts. Davis, Rennie. Divine Light Mission. Maharaj Ji. 1973. *4286*
—. Augustana College and Theological Seminary. Bethany College. Immigration. Lutheran Church. Midwest. Railroads. Religious education. Swedish Americans. Swensson, Carl Aaron. 1873-1904. *726*
—. Authority. Bellah, Robert N. Civil religion. Myths and Symbols. Secularization. 1977. *1165*
—. Bacon, Thomas. Church of England. Clergy. Education. Maryland. Slavery. Theology. ca 1745-68. *3175*
—. Baptists. Clergy. Emigration. Great Britain. Harris, Theophilus. Social conditions. 1793-1810. *3050*
—. Baptists. Fox, George. Friends, Society of. Olney, Thomas, Jr. Rhode Island. 1672-73. *967*
—. Baptists. Laity. 1715-1975. *1243*
—. Baptists. McKim, Andrew. Nova Scotia. Provincial Legislatures. 1784-1840. *1309*
—. Baptists. Social Reform. 1976. *1244*
—. Baptists, Southern. Individualism. Social problems. 18c-1976. *968*
—. Barbeau, Victor. Catholic Church. Cooperatives. Medical Reform. Paquette, Albiny. Quebec. 1900-45. *3874*
—. Bartlett, Robert. Election sermons. Religious liberty. Universalist Church of America. Vermont. 1817-30. *1045*
—. Bible reading. Catholic Church. Prince Edward Island. Protestants. Religion in the Public Schools. 1856-60. *580*
—. Bourassa, Henri. Catholic Church. Provincial Government. Quebec. 1902-71. *976*
—. *Brown* v. *Les Curé et Marguilliers de l'Oeuvre et de la Fabrique de la Paroisse de Montréal* (1874). Catholic Church. Church and state. Guibord, Joseph. Liberalism. Quebec. Ultramontanism. 1870-74. *1067*
—. Cain, Richard Harvey. Methodist Episcopal Church, African. Negroes. Reconstruction. Social conditions. South Carolina. 1850's-87. *2407*
—. California (San Francisco). Judaism. 1935-65. *1226*
—. Calvinism. Social Change. 16c-20c. *980*
—. Cameron, John. Church of England. Letters. Ontario (Ottawa). Thompson, Annie Affleck. Thompson, John S. D. 1867-94. *1127*
—. Canada. Grant, George. Philosophy. Schmidt, Larry (review article). Theology. 1945-78. *509*
—. Canada. Ideology. King, William Lyon Mackenzie. Liberal Party. Protestantism. Social Classes. 1900-50. *1421*
—. Catholic Church. Church and State. Europe, Western. North America. 1870-1974. *1326*
—. Catholic Church. Church and State. French language. Langevin, Adélard. Manitoba. Private schools. 1890-1916. *608*
—. Catholic Church. Conservatism. 1970's. *970*
—. Catholic Church. Elites. Ethnicity. Immigrants. Protestants. Reform. 1890's-1970's. *1225*
—. Catholic Church. Feild, Edward. Irish Canadians. Mullock, John Thomas. Newfoundland. Protestant Churches. 19c. *1254*
—. Catholic Church. German Americans. Language. Religious education. St. Peter's Colony. Saskatchewan. 1903-16. *779*
—. Catholic Church. Morality. Oklahoma. Protestant Churches. Referendum. Sabbatarianism. Voting and Voting Behavior. 1959-76. *1290*
—. Charities. Cities. Evangelism. Muhlenberg, Augustus. Protestantism (review article). Social Problems. 1812-1900. *2930*
—. Child-rearing. Death and Dying. Fischer, David H. Greven, Philip. Lynn, Kenneth S. Personality (review article). Protestantism. Stannard, David E. 18c. 1977. *2943*
—. Christian realism. Niebuhr, Reinhold. Theodicy. ca 1940-73. *1403*
—. Christianity. Judaism. Pfeffer, Leo. Secular Humanism. Social Change. 1958-76. *132*
—. Church and state. Colleges and universities. 1740's-60's. *651*
—. Church and state. Federal government. 1776-1976. *1057*
—. Cities. Revivals. Social conditions. 1857-77. *2261*
—. Civil religion. Croly, Herbert. Millenarianism. Wilson, Woodrow. 1909-19. *1159*
—. Colleges and Universities (administration). Desha, Joseph. Holley, Horace. Kentucky. Presbyterians. State government. Transylvania College. Unitarianism. 1818-27. *537*
—. Connecticut. Ethics. Fitch, James. Land. Puritans. 1679-1727. *3646*
—. Democratic Party. Letters. Mennonites. Risser, Johannes. Slavery. 1856-57. *994*
—. Ecumenism. Federal Council of the Churches of Christ in America. Hopkins, Charles Howard. Protestant Churches. Social gospel. 1880-1908. *487*
—. Elites. Government. Protestants. 1960's-70's. *1207*
—. Friends, Society of. Indians. Paxton Boys. Pennsylvania. Presbyterian Church. Riots. 1763-64. *3530*
—. Friends, Society of. King George's War. Pacifism. Penn, Thomas. Pennsylvania. Provincial Government. 1726-42. *1314*
—. Friends, Society of. King Philip's War. New England. Toleration. Williams, Roger *(George Fox).* 1672-77. *993*
—. Indiana. Lutherans. Theology. 1835-70. *3344*
—. Massachusetts. Mather, Cotton *(Life of Phips).* Phips, William. Puritans. 1690-1705. *3622*
—. Massacres. Mennonites. Pacifism. Paxton Boys. Pennsylvania. Presbyterian Church. 1763-68. *2702*
—. Mennonites. Separatism. Social Reform. 1840's-1930's. *3418*
—. Millenarianism. Social Conditions. 1920's-50's. *1420*
—. Mormons. Utah (Weber County; Ogden). 1850-1924. *1324*
—. Niebuhr, Reinhold. Theology. 20c. *2895*

—. Religiosity. 1968-78. *162*
—. Revivals. 19c. *1242*
Politics (review article). Formisano, Ronald P. Hackney, F. Sheldon. Kleppner, Paul. Methodology. 1827-1900. 1969-71. *1263*
Polk, Leonidas. Bishops. Episcopal Church, Protestant. Louisiana (Shreveport). 1830-1916. *3184*
—. Education. Episcopal Church, Protestant. Louisiana (New Orleans). Slavery. 1805-65. *3219*
Polls. *See* Public Opinion.
Polygamy. Arizona. Edmunds Act (US, 1882). Federal government. Mormons. 1880's. *1000*
—. Arizona (Short Creek). Church and state. Mormons. Utah. 1953. *1076*
—. Atheism. Freedom of Speech. *Lucifer's Lantern* (periodical). Mormons. Schroeder, Theodore. Utah. 1889-1900. *2125*
—. Baldwin, Nathaniel. Fundamentalism. Inventions. Mormons. Radio. Utah. 1900's-61. *4036*
—. Bartholow, Roberts. Medical reports. Mormons. Physiology. Utah. Vollum, E. P. 1850-75. *1430*
—. Cannon, Martha Hughes. Great Britain. Letters. Mormons. Utah (Salt Lake City). Women. 1885-96. *4002*
—. Church and state. Cowley, Matthias F. Mormons. Smoot, Reed. Taylor, John W. Theology. Woodruff Manifesto. 1890-1911. *1060*
—. Church and state. Feminism. House of Representatives. Roberts, Brigham Henry. Utah. 1898-1900. *1133*
—. Civil disobedience. Clawson, Rudger. Federal government. Mormons. Sharp, John. Utah. 1862-91. *996*
—. Congress. Hayes, Rutherford B. Mormons. Suffrage. Women. 1877-81. *797*
—. Constitutional Law. Morality. Mormons. Religious Liberty. *Reynolds* v. *United States* (US, 1878). Supreme Court. 1862-78. *1024*
—. Dalton, Edward Meeks. Edmunds Act (US, 1882). Mormons. Utah. 1852-86. *1028*
—. Divorce. Mormons. Utah. 1844-90. *822*
—. Driggs, Nevada W. Nevada (Panaca). Personal narratives. Utah. 1890-93. *832*
—. Economic Conditions. Mormons. Railroads. Salt Lake and Fort Douglas Railroad. Statehood. Utah. Young, John W. 1883-1924. *3993*
—. Edmunds Act (US, 1882). Mormons. Prisons. Utah. 1880's. *1004*
—. Equality. Lincoln, Abraham. Mormons. Slavery. Smith, Joseph. 1840-64. *986*
—. Exiles. Letters. Mormons. Utah. Woodruff, Emma Smith. Woodruff, Wilford. 1885. *1050*
—. Fertility. Mormons. 19c. *926*
—. Folklore. Mormons. Scandinavian Americans. Temples. Utah (Sanpete-Sevier area). 1849-1979. *4053*
—. Law. Leadership. Mormons. Utah. 1890-1905. *824*
—. Morality. Mormons. Polemics. ca 1860-1900. *823*
—. Mormons. 1842. *839*
—. Mormons. Paddock, Algernon Sidney. Utah Commission. 1882-86. *1117*
Polytheism. Hobomok (shaman). Indian-White Relations. Pilgrims. Plymouth Colony. Squanto (Wampanoag Indian). Theology. ca 1620-30. *3144*
Pontifical Commission for the Revision of the Code of Canon Law. Canon Law Society of America. Catholicism. 1917-73. *3686*
Pool, Reuben B. Great Britain (London). Libraries. Young Men's Christian Association. 1844-1974. *2887*
Poor *See also* Poverty.
—. Advocate role. Charities. Children. Indians. St. Vincent de Paul Society. 1900-10. *2515*
—. Aged. Folklore. West Virginia. Witchcraft. Women. 1975. *2201*
—. Bishops. Catholic Church. Lynch, John Joseph. Ontario. Toronto Savings Bank. 1870's. *369*
—. Blackthink. Church and Social Problems. Human Relations. 1963-75. *2537*
—. California (San Francisco). Goldie, Albert. Judaism (Orthodox, Reform). New York City. Synagogues. Weinstock, Harris. 1906. *4166*
—. Catholic Church. Charities. Irish Canadians. McMahon, Patrick. Quebec (Quebec). St. Bridget's Home. 1847-1972. *2521*
—. Charities. Friends, Society of. Pennsylvania Hospital for the Sick Poor. Pennsylvania (Philadelphia). 18c. *2519*
—. Charities. Mormons. Utah. 1850-1930's. *2501*
Poor Clares. Catholic Church. Education. Georgia (Skidaway Island). Negroes. Orphanages. Women. 1885-87. *3806*
Popular Culture *See also* Daily Life; Folk Art; Social Conditions.
—. A. A. Allen Revival, Incorporated. Arizona (Miracle Valley). Fundamentalism. Language. Revivals. 1970's. *2270*
—. Authors. Marshall, Catherine. Presbyterian Church. Theology. Women. 1949-78. *3546*
—. British Americans. California (Los Angeles). Protestant Churches. Social Classes. 1920's. 1977. *2624*
—. Catholic Church. Novels. 1970's. *2054*
—. Crockett, Davy. Nature. Pioneers. 1830's. *2712*
—. Graham, Billy. Peale, Norman Vincent. Protestantism. 1950's. *2901*
—. Humor. Parody. 1976. *2052*
Population *See also* names of ethnic or racial groups, e.g. Jews, Negroes, etc.; Aged; Birth Control; Birth Rate; Census; Demography; Fertility; Migration, Internal.
—. -1973. *989*
—. California (San Diego). Judaism (Reform). Temple Beth Israel. 1889-1978. *4224*
—. Catholic Church. Cotton mills. French Canadians. Immigration. Massachusetts (Springfield). Working Class. 1870. *3710*
—. Catholic Church. Family size preference. Women. Women. 1964-74. *915*
—. Communalism. Equal opportunity. Hutterites. Leadership. Prairie Provinces. Social Organization. Succession. 1940's-70's. *387*
—. Family size preference. Teenagers. 1971-74. *808*
—. Mormons. 19c. 1978. *794*
Populism. Baptists. Bode, Frederick A. (review article). Capitalism. Methodist Church. North Carolina. 1894-1903. 1975. *1287*
—. Clergy. Congregationalism. Herron, George David. Iowa College. National Christian Citizen League. Progressivism. Socialism. 1880's-1900. *2561*
—. Fundamentalism. Long, Huey P. North Central States. Progressivism. Smith, Gerald L. K. 1934-48. *975*
—. Historiography. South. 1865-1900. *1281*
Portraits *See also* Cartoons and Caricatures; Photography.
—. Congregationalism. Folk Art. Massachusetts. Peckham, Robert. ca 1838-44. *1861*
—. Great Britain. Immigrants. Landscape Painting. Mormons. Piercy, Frederick *(Illustrated Route)*. Travel guides. Western states. 1848-57. *1869*
Ports. American Seamen's Friend Society. Evangelicalism. Merchant Marine. 1828-38. *2376*
Portsmouth Anti-Slavery Society. Abolition Movement. Friends, Society of. Haverford College Library (Quaker Collection). New Hampshire. Rogers, Nathaniel Peabody. 1830-46. *2465*
Portugal. American Board of Commissioners for Foreign Missions. Angola. Church and State. Missions and Missionaries. Protestant Churches. Umbundu (tribe). 1880-1922. *1746*
Portuguese Americans. Congregation Beth Elohim. Congregation Beth Elohim Unveh Shallom. Judaism (Orthodox). South Carolina (Charleston). 1784-91. *4173*
Posadas (celebrations). California (Los Angeles). Catholic Church. Christmas. Mexican Americans. Neighborhoods. Rites and Ceremonies. 1975-80. *3794*
Positivism. Common Sense school. Comte, Auguste. Philosophy. Reformed churches. Social Gospel. Theology. ca 1850's-80's. *2833*
—. France. Great Britain. Unitarianism. 1816-90. *4077*
Post, Christian Frederick. Fort Duquesne. Frontier and Pioneer Life. Indian-White Relations. Moravian Church. Pennsylvania. 1758-59. *1505*
Postage stamps. Adventists. 1847-1978. *2972*
Postal Service. Evangelism. Sects, Religious. 1970's. *1118*
Post-American (periodical). Christianity. Values. 1974. *2792*
Postcards. Adventists. Sanatoriums. 1900's-10's. *1427*
Potawatomi Indians. Baptists. Education. Indians. Kansas. Lykins, Johnston. Pottawatomie Baptist Manual Labor Training School. 1846-67. *508*
Pott, Francis L. H. China (Shanghai). Colleges and Universities. Episcopal Church, Protestant. Missions and Missionaries. St. John's University. 1888-1941. *1707*
Pottawatomie Baptist Manual Labor Training School. Baptists. Education. Indians. Kansas. Lykins, Johnston. Potawatomi Indians. 1846-67. *508*
Potter, Francis. Anti-Catholicism. Antichrist. Edwards, Jonathan. Mather, Cotton. Puritans. ca 1700-58. *2937*
Poverty *See also* Charities; Economic Conditions; Poor; Public Welfare.
—. Abolition Movement. Attitudes. Competition. Economic conditions. Evangelicalism. ca 1830-60. *2473*
—. Canada. Church of England National Task Force on the Economy (report). Income. Social Classes. Theology. 1977. *2564*
—. Church and Social Problems. Education. Racism. 1970's. *2435*
Powell, Joab. Baptists. Clergy. Missouri. Oregon (Willamette Valley). Westward movement. 1852-73. *3093*
Powhatan Indians. Colonization. Indians. Jesuits. Menéndez de Avilés, Pedro. Missions and Missionaries. Opechancanough (chief). Spain. Virginia. 1570-72. *1622*
Powwowing. Amish. Folk medicine. Magic. Mennonites. Pennsylvania. ca 1650-1979. *2206*
Prager, Abraham J. Hebrew Union College. Judaism, Reform. Letters. Rabbis. Wise, Isaac Mayer. 1854-1900. *4227*
Pragmatism. Colonization. New England. Puritans. Social Change. 1620-90. *3608*
—. Episcopal Church, Protestant. National Characteristics. 1650-1975. *3239*
Prairie Provinces *See also* Alberta; Manitoba; Saskatchewan.
—. Anglophones. Catholics. Church Discipline. Church History. Francophones. Morality. 1900-30. *3715*
—. Bryan, William Jennings. Fund raising. Lectures. Presbyterian Church. Young Men's Christian Association. 1909. *2446*
—. Catholic Church. Church schools. French language. Langevin, Adélard. Laurier, Wilfrid. Liberal Party. Religion in the Public Schools. 1890-1915. *569*
—. Catholic Church. Discrimination. Economic Conditions. Polish Canadians. 1880's-1970's. *3796*
—. Communalism. Equal opportunity. Hutterites. Leadership. Population. Social Organization. Succession. 1940's-70's. *387*
—. Discrimination. Ethnicity. Hutterites. Legislation. Provincial government. 1960's-79. *1099*
—. Indians. McDougall, John. Methodist Church, Wesleyan. Missions and Missionaries. 1860-1917. *1534*
—. Letters. Métis. Religious beliefs. Riel, Louis. Taché, Alexandre Antonin. 1880's. *966*
—. Messianic Movements. Northwest Rebellion. Riel, Louis. 1869-85. *964*
Prairie Radicals. Baptists. Canada. Disciples of Christ. Great Plains. Lutheran Church. Methodism. Pietism. Radicals and Radicalism. 1890-1975. *954*
Prairie States. *See* Great Plains.
Pratt, Orson. Heresy. Mormons. Revelation. Young, Brigham. 1853-68. *3938*
—. Mathematics. Mormons. Utah. ca 1836-70. *2318*
Pratt, Orson (confession). Mormons. Theology. 1860. *4024*
Pratt, Parley P. McLean, Eleanor. McLean, Hector. Mormons. Murder. Women. 1841-57. *4025*
Pratt, Rey I. Mexico (Mexico City). Missions. Mormons. 1906-24. *1677*
Prayer. Attitudes. Catholic Church. Students. 1961-71. *3808*
—. Centennial Exposition of 1876. Methodist Episcopal Church. Pennsylvania (Philadelphia). Simpson, Matthew. 1876. *3502*
—. Church and State. Church schools. Conscientious objection. Holidays. Public finance. Public Schools. Religious Liberty. Supreme Court. 1950-70's. *1112*
—. Church schools. Education, Finance. Government. Public opinion. Religion in the Public Schools. 1962-68. *504*

—. Cobbett, Thomas *(Practical Discourse of Prayer)*. New England. Puritans. 1630-85. *3607*
—. *Engel* v. *Vitale* (US, 1962). New York. Nonsectarianism. Public opinion. Public schools. 1962. *581*
Prayer circles. Mormons. 1829-1978. *4026*
Prayer meetings. Connecticut (New Haven). Negroes. Pentecostal movement. Psychology. Social conditions. 1978. *3521*
Prayer petitions. Congregationalism. Edwards, Jonathan. Massachusetts (Northampton). 1730-49. *3147*
Praying towns. Assimilation. Eliot, John. Indians. Massachusetts. Puritans. 1646-74. *1592*
Preble, T. M. Adventists. New Hampshire (Washington). Oakes, Rachel. Sabbath. Wheeler, Frederick. 1841-44. *2287*
Pregnancy. Behavior. Puritanism. Sex. Social control. 1640-1971. *949*
Prejudice. Anti-Catholicism. Anti-Semitism. Education. Minorities. North Carolina. Religious beliefs. 1957-73. *2093*
Preparationism. Conversion. Hooker, Thomas. Puritans. Ramus, Petrus. Shepard, Thomas. Theology. 1608-49. *3643*
—. Conversion. Puritans. Stoddard, Solomon. Taylor, Edward. Theology. 1690-94. *3642*
Presburg, Joseph. Church of England. Letters. Maryland. 1713-32. *3199*
Presbyterian Board of Foreign Missions. Indians. Missionaries. Slavery. 1837-61. *3568*
Presbyterian Church. Abolition Movement. Anderson, Isaac. Southern and Western Theological Seminary. Tennessee (Maryville). 1819-50's. *723*
—. Abolition Movement. Berea College. Fee, John Gregg. Kentucky. Religious education. 1855-1904. *777*
—. Abolition Movement. Civil War (antecedents). South. Stanton, Robert. 1840-55. *2484*
—. Abolition Movement. Cornish, Samuel E. *Freedom's Journal* (newspaper). Journalism. Negroes. 1820's-59. *2498*
—. Abolition movement. Douglass, Frederick. Ireland (Belfast). Smyth, Thomas. 1846. *2165*
—. Acculturation. Blackburn, Gideon. Cherokee Indians. Missions and missionaries. Schools. Tennessee. 1804-10. *1491*
—. Adger, John B. Dabney, Robert L. Hodge, Charles. Mercersburg theology. Nevin, John W. Sacramental controversy. 1845-75. *3551*
—. Africa. American Colonization Society. Colonization. McDonough, David. Medical Education. Slavery. 1840-50. *2483*
—. Africa. Congregationalism. Missions and Missionaries. Reformed Dutch Church. Reformed German Church. 19c-20c. *1709*
—. Africa, West. Missions and Missionaries. Social change. Women. 1850-1915. *1686*
—. Alabama. Church schools. Livingston Female Academy. Women. 1835-1910. *686*
—. Alabama (Mobile). China. Missions and Missionaries. Stuart, Mary Horton. Women. 1840's-1947. *1705*
—. Alaska. Brady, John Green (and family). Business. Governors. Morality. 1878-1906. *3549*
—. Albanese, Catherine L. Beecher family. Caskey, Marie. Congregationalism. Connecticut. Massachusetts. Transcendentalism (review article). Unitarianism. 1800-60. *2763*
—. Alexander, Archibald. Princeton Theological Seminary. Scripture, doctrine of. 1772-1929. *3566*
—. Alexander, Archibald *(Thoughts on Religious Experience)*. Theology. 1841. *3556*
—. Alexander Hall (building). New Jersey. Princeton Theological Seminary. 1815. *595*
—. Alison, Francis. American Revolution. Political philosophy. Witherspoon, John. 1750-87. *1382*
—. American Revolution. Antislavery sentiments. Slavery. 1750-1818. *2493*
—. American Revolution. Baptists. Church of England. Congregationalism. Friends, Society of. Georgia. Judaism. Lutheran Church. 1733-90. *88*
—. American Revolution. Calvinism. Church and state. Clergy. Jefferson, Thomas. Linn, William. 1775-1808. *1335*
—. American Revolution. Clergy. Congregationalism. Social status. 1774-1800. *2849*
—. American Revolution. Cummings, Charles. Indians. Virginia, southwest. 1760's-80's. *2634*
—. American Revolution. Georgia (Savannah). Patriotism. Zubly, John Joachim. 1766-81. *985*
—. American Revolution. Immigrants. Scotch-Irish. Scottish Americans. 1700-75. *1268*
—. American Revolution. Pennsylvania (Middle Octorara). 1740-83. *969*
—. Americanization. Christianity. Janes, Leroy Lansing. Japan (Kumamoto). Missions and Missionaries. 1838-76. *1732*
—. Anti-Catholicism. Church and State. Clergy. Education, Finance. MacKinnon, Murdoch. Saskatchewan. School Act (Saskatchewan, 1930; amended). Scott, Walter. 1913-26. *528*
—. Anti-Communist Movements. Dulles, John Foster. Ecumenism. Morality. Oxford Conference (1937). Protestantism. World order movement. 1937-48. *1375*
—. Antislavery sentiments. Christianity. Civil War. Stowe, Harriet Beecher. Women. ca 1850-80. *2474*
—. Antislavery Sentiments. Davies, Samuel. Great Awakening. Virginia. 1740-59. *2238*
—. Appalachia. Baptists. Lifestyles. Methodism. 1788-1974. *2873*
—. Architecture. Churches (Gothic Revival). Country Life. Furniture and Furnishings. Pennsylvania, northwest. 1850-1905. 1979. *1797*
—. Archives. Canada. Methodist Church. United Church of Canada. 18c-1973. *269*
—. Arizona. Baptists. Catholic Church. Episcopal Church, Protestant. Methodism. Missions and Missionaries. Mormons. 1859-99. *1501*
—. Arkansas (Texarkana). Congregationalism. Maddox, Finis Ewing. Schisms. Theology. 1908. *2869*
—. Art. Illinois (Chicago). Second Presbyterian Church. Stained glass windows. 1872-74. *1855*
—. Assimilation. Evangelism. Jews. Ontario (Toronto). 1912-18. *1540*
—. Assimilation. Indians (agencies). Lowrie, John C. Missions and Missionaries. 1870-82. *1655*
—. Attitudes. China. Missions and Missionaries. 1837-1900. *1691*
—. Attitudes. Indians. Missions and Missionaries. 1837-93. *1510*
—. Austin College. Baker, Daniel. Legal education. Texas (Huntsville). 1849-57. *529*
—. Authors. Marshall, Catherine. Popular Culture. Theology. Women. 1949-78. *3546*
—. Baptists. Clergy. First Presbyterian Church. Fosdick, Harry Emerson. New York City. Theology. 1918-24. *466*
—. Baptists. Creek Indians. Indian Territory. Methodist Church. Missions and Missionaries. 1835-60's. *1517*
—. Baptists. Methodist Church. Slavery. South. 1740-1860. *2168*
—. Baptists, Southern. Corporate wealth. Methodism. Political power. South. 1930's-75. *2926*
—. Baptists, Southern. Disciples of Christ. Evolution. Kentucky. Methodist Church. Schisms. 1920's. *2310*
—. Barnes, Albert *(Way of Salvation)*. New Jersey (Morristown). Schisms. Sermons. Theology. Trials. 1829-37. *3576*
—. Beecher, Lyman. Clergy. New York (East Hampton). Temperance Movements. 1799-1810. *2585*
—. Beecher, Lyman. Congregationalism. Dwight, Timothy. New England. Republicanism. Taylor, Nathaniel William. 1790-1840. *1356*
—. Beecher, Lyman. Evangelical Alliance. Great Britain. Temperance Movements. World Temperance Convention. 1846. *3563*
—. Belgian Congo (Kasai). Missions and Missionaries. 1871-1964. *1729*
—. Benson, Ezra Taft. Morality. Mormons. Political Leadership. Wallace, Henry A. 1933-60. *1303*
—. Bible (New Testament). Exegesis. Germany. Hodge, Charles. Liberalism. Princeton Theological Seminary. 1820-78. *3573*
—. Biblical Theology Movement. Smith, William Robertson. Theology. 1870-83. *590*
—. Bibliographies. Canada. Congregationalism. Historiography. Lutheran Church. Methodist Church. United Church of Canada. 1825-1973. *2892*
—. Bibliographies. Dissertations. Edwards, Jonathan. Niebuhr, H. Richard. Niebuhr, Reinhold. Reformed Churches. Tillich, Paul. 18c-20c. 1965-72. *2815*
—. Bibliographies. Periodicals. Reformed churches. 1973. *2957*
—. Bishops. Catholic Church. Church of England. Evangelicalism. Feild, Edward. Liturgy. Methodism. Newfoundland. 1765-1852. *3197*
—. Blackburn, Gideon. Cherokee Indians. Indians. Missions and Missionaries. Old Southwest. Schools. Whiskey. 1809-10. *700*
—. Blue Laws. Church and state. Church of England. Friends, Society of. Law and Society. Pennsylvania. 1682-1740. *2278*
—. Boudinot, Elias. Millenarianism. Newton, Thomas. Theology. 1787-1821. *3569*
—. Boycotts. Church Schools. Mexican Americans. Mexican Presbyterian Mission School. Public schools. Segregation. Texas (San Angelo). 1910-15. *618*
—. Bradley, Lucas. Churches. Missouri (St. Louis). Wisconsin (Racine). 1840-90. *1810*
—. Breckinridge, Robert Jefferson. Clergy. Danville Theological Seminary. Education. Emancipation. Kentucky. 1800-71. *3544*
—. Breckinridge, Robert Jefferson. Danville Theological Seminary. Emancipation. Kentucky. Theology. 1832-71. *3545*
—. British Columbia (Bennett). Construction. St. Andrew's Church. 1898. *1820*
—. Brown, Robert McAfee. New York City. Personal Narratives. Union Theological Seminary. VanDusen, Henry Pitney. 1945-75. *767*
—. Bryan, William Jennings. Christianity. Evolution. 1921-25. *2297*
—. Bryan, William Jennings. Evolution. Fundamentalism. 1875-1920's. *2344*
—. Bryan, William Jennings. Fund raising. Lectures. Prairie Provinces. Young Men's Christian Association. 1909. *2446*
—. Bryan, William Jennings. Fundamentalism. 1860-1925. *1407*
—. Buck, Pearl S. Fiction. Missions and Missionaries. 1931-69. *2068*
—. Budgets. Missions and Missionaries. 1763-1978. *1488*
—. Bureau of Indian Affairs. Catholic Church. Indian-White Relations. Iowa. Schools. Winnebago Indians. 1834-48. *737*
—. Burr, Aaron. Political Leadership. 1772-1805. *3542*
—. Buttrick, George Arthur. Pacifism. 1915-74. *2642*
—. California (Placerville). Ecumenism. El Dorado County Federated Church. Methodist Church. 1850-1950. *492*
—. California (Stockton). Clergy. Pioneers. Woods, James. 1850-54. *3526*
—. Calvinism. Evangelicalism. 17c-19c. *3570*
—. Calvinism. Faulkner, William. Literature. 1920's-75. *2035*
—. Calvinism. Millenarianism. Proslavery Sentiments. South. 1800-65. *2166*
—. Canada. Church Schools. East Indians. Missions and Missionaries. Trinidad and Tobago. 1868-1912. *1726*
—. Canada. Ecumenism. Methodist Church. Patrick, William. 1900-11. *443*
—. Canada. United Church of Canada. 1925. *2902*
—. Canadian Pacific Railway. Clergy. Construction crews. Manitoba (Virden). McLeod, Finlay J. C. Personal narratives. 1881-82. *3567*
—. Catholic Church. Church and state. Kennedy, John F. Political Campaigns (presidential). 1959-60. *992*
—. Catholic Church. Hudson's Bay Company. Indians. Methodist Church. Missions and Missionaries. Oregon. 1830's - 1840's. *1482*
—. Censorship. *Christian Observer* (newspaper). Civil War. Converse, Amasa. 1861-65. *1115*
—. Centennial Celebrations. Georgia (Jonesboro). 1879-1979. *3531*
—. Chain of interest (concept). Loyalists. Pennsylvania (Philadelphia). 1770's. *984*
—. Charities. Equality. Missions and Missionaries. Women. 1800-1975. *908*
—. Charities. Law. Morristown Female Charitable Society. New Jersey. Women. 1813-1978. *2510*
—. Cherokee Indians. Foreman, Stephen. Georgia. Indians. Oklahoma. 1820's-81. *3538*
—. Cherokee Indians. Indians. Martin, John. Missions and Missionaries. Richardson, William. Tennessee. Virginia. 1755-63. *1511*
—. Chile. Journalism. Missions and Missionaries. Religious liberty. Trumbull, David. 1845-89. *1703*

—. China. Diplomacy. Japan. Missions and Missionaries. Stuart, John Leighton. 1937-41. *1745*
—. Chinese Americans. Immigrants. Race Relations. 1851-1977. *3561*
—. Christianity. Constitutional Amendments. Strong, William. Supreme Court. 1864-80. *3588*
—. Church and State. Church of England. Livingston, William. ca 1750-90. *1091*
—. Church and State. Slavery. South. 1850-80. *1074*
—. Church and State. Virginia. 1770-85. *1015*
—. Church history. Personal narratives. Thompson, Ernest Trice. Union Theological Seminary. Virginia (Richmond). 1920-75. *689*
—. Church of England. Dalhousie University. King's College, University of. Mergers. Nova Scotia. 1821-37. *684*
—. Church of England. Ethnic Groups. Friends, Society of. Pennsylvania. Provincial Politics. 1775-80. *1248*
—. Church of Scotland. Communion. Maine (Boothbay). 1750-75. *3578*
—. Church Property. Constitutional Amendments (1st). Courts. Kentucky (Louisville). Walnut Street Presbyterian Church. *Watson* v. *Jones* (US, 1860). 1860-1970. *1129*
—. Clergy. Congregationalism. New England. Professionalism. Scott, Donald M. (review article). 1750-1850. 1979. *2865*
—. Clergy. Davies, Samuel. Eulogies. National Self-image. Washington, George. 1789-1815. *1157*
—. Clergy. Democratic Party. Eaton, Margaret (Peggy) O'Neale. Ely, Ezra Stiles. Jackson, Andrew. 1829-30. *3536*
—. Clergy. Diaries. Hodge, Charles. Pennsylvania (Philadelphia). Theology. 1819-20. *3534*
—. Clergy. Dickinson, Jonathan. Subscription controversy. Westminster Standards. 1700-50. *3560*
—. Clergy. Ellis, Edwin M. Montana. Sunday schools. Travel. 1870's-1927. *3537*
—. Clergy. Fundamentalism. Macartney, Clarence E. 1901-53. *3579*
—. Clergy. Georgia (Savannah). Swiss Americans. Zubly, John Joachim. 1724-58. *3565*
—. Clergy. Kentucky. Templin, Terah. 1780-1818. *3592*
—. Clergy. Labor. Lynd, Robert S. Oil Industry and Trade. Wyoming (Elk Basin). 1921. *3562*
—. Clergy. Miller, Samuel. Princeton Theological Seminary. Religious Education. 1813-50. *764*
—. Clergy. Negroes. 1885-1975. *3594*
—. Clergy. Nova Scotia (Springhill). 1874-1925. *3532*
—. Clergy. Reese, Thomas. South Carolina. 1773-96. *3585*
—. Clergy (dismissal). Congregationalism. New Hampshire. Social change. 1633-1790. *2885*
—. Colleges and Universities. Colorado. Jackson, Sheldon. Westminster University. 1874-1917. *597*
—. Colleges and Universities. Common Sense school. Curricula. Dalhousie University. King's College. Lyall, William. Nova Scotia. Philosophy. Pine Hill Divinity Hall. 1850-90. *719*
—. Colleges and universities. Dalhousie University. McCulloch, Thomas. Missions and Missionaries. Nova Scotia. Pictou Academy. ca 1803-42. *591*
—. Colleges and Universities. Mormons. Utah (Salt Lake City). Westminster College. 1875-1913. *559*
—. Colonialism. India, north. Missions and Missionaries. ca 1800-1950. *1673*
—. Conflict and Conflict Resolution. Theology. 1960's-70's. *3550*
—. Congregationalism. Edwards, Jonathan. New York. Sermons. 1722-23. *2883*
—. Congregationalism. Finney, Charles G. New York (Oneida County). Revivals. 1825-27. *2245*
—. Connecticut Valley. Great Awakening. Massachusetts (Hatfield). Williams, William. 1686-1741. *2240*
—. Conservatism. Smyth, Thomas. Social theory. South Carolina. Theology. 1831-70. *3552*
—. Constitutions, State. New Jersey. North Carolina. Pennsylvania. 1775-87. *1285*
—. Converts. Immigration. Kansas. Mennonites. Milling. Warkentin, Bernhard. 1847-1908. *3380*
—. Crittenden, Lyman B. Higher Education. Jackson, Sheldon. McMillan, Duncan M. Montana. 1869-1918. *598*
—. Dartmouth College. Lane Theological Seminary. New England. Stowe, Calvin Ellis. Stowe, Harriet Beecher. 1824-86. *3555*
—. Davies, Samuel. Diaries. Fund raising. Great Britain. New Jersey. Princeton University. 1753-54. *636*
—. *Directory of Worship*. Worship. 1788-1979. *3583*
—. Divinity (issue). Hodge, Charles *(Systematic Theology)*. Jesus Christ. Nevin, John W. Theology. 1872. *3581*
—. Douglas, William O. Humanism. Religious liberty. Supreme Court. 1915-80. *1128*
—. Doukhobors. Galicians. Hospitals. Lake Geneva Mission. Missions and Missionaries. Saskatchewan (Wakaw). 1903-42. *1492*
—. Drury, Clifford M. Historians. Missions and Missionaries. Oregon. Washington. 1928-74. *190*
—. Dulles, John Foster. Federal Council of the Churches of Christ in America. UN. 1941-45. *1312*
—. Economic conditions. Frontier and Pioneer life. Indians. Missions and Missionaries. South Dakota. 1840-1900. *3540*
—. Ecumenism. 1549-1979. *451*
—. Ecumenism. Evangelical Alliance. Evangelicalism. 1867-73. *456*
—. Ecumenism. Evangelical and Reformed Church. Richards, George Warren. World Alliance of Reformed Churches. 1900-55. *481*
—. Ecumenism. Great Awakening. Moravian Church. Tennent, Gilbert. Theology. Zinzendorf, Nikolaus. 1740-41. *2226*
—. Ecumenism. Methodist Church. Nova Scotia (Springhill). St. Andrew's Wesley United Church of Canada. United Church of Canada. 1800-1976. *2829*
—. Education. Missions and Missionaries. Puerto Rico. Social Customs. 1898-1917. *1727*
—. Educational Policy. Princeton University (trustees). 1806-07. *541*
—. Elders. Laity. Miller, Samuel. Republicanism. 1813-50. *3559*
—. Factionalism. Nova Scotia (Pictou County). Scottish Canadians. Social Conditions. 1898-1966. *3533*
—. First Presbyterian Church. Tennessee (Nashville). 1814-1976. *3553*
—. Friends, Society of. Indians. Paxton Boys. Pennsylvania. Politics. Riots. 1763-64. *3530*
—. Friends, Society of. Maryland (Baltimore). Methodist Episcopal Church, African. Negroes. Private Schools. Sunday Schools. 1794-1860. *633*
—. Frontier and Pioneer Life. Immigration. Irish Americans. New York. Pennsylvania. Virginia (Shenandoah Valley). 17c-1776. *3558*
—. Fundamentalism. Machen, J. Gresham. South. 1920's-35. *3580*
—. Fundamentalism. Matthews, Mark Allison. Social reform. Washington (Seattle). 1900-40. *2434*
—. Gold Rushes. Yukon Territory. 1897-1910. *3571*
—. Gordon, Helen Skinner. King, Gordon J. Manitoba (Winnipeg). Personal narratives. Woman's Missionary Society of the Presbyterian and United Churches. 1890's-1961. *3548*
—. Green, Jacob. Seminaries. 1775. *714*
—. Higher Education. Miller, Howard (review article). 1707-1837. 1976. *760*
—. Idaho. McBeth, Sue L. Missions and Missionaries. Nez Percé Indians. 1874. *1591*
—. Immigration. Italian Americans. New York City (Greenwich Village). University Place Church. 1900-30. *3564*
—. Indians. McBeth, Sue L. Missions and Missionaries. Nez Percé Indians. 1873-93. *1509*
—. Jones, Charles Colcock. Missions and Missionaries. Slavery. South. 1825-63. *2177*
—. Librarians. New York City. Smith, Henry B. Union Theological Seminary. 1851-77. *758*
—. Libraries. New York City. Pettee, Julia. Rockwell, William Walker. Union Theological Seminary Library. 1908-58. *759*
—. Literature. Marriage. Marshall, Catherine. Sex roles. Women. 1950's. *806*
—. Literature. McCulloch, Thomas *(Letters of Mephibosheth Stepsure)*. Nova Scotia. Satire. 1821-22. *2067*
—. Literature. New York. Satire. Social criticism. Whitcher, Frances Miriam Berry *(Widow Bedott Papers)*. 1847-55. *2056*
—. Little Britain Presbyterian Church. Pennsylvania (Lancaster County). 1740-1860. *3587*
—. Loyalists. Zubly, John Joachim. 1770-81. *1400*
—. Manuscripts. McDowell, William A. New Jersey Historical Society. South Carolina (Charleston). Third Presbyterian Church. 1820's-30's. *259*
—. Massacres. Mennonites. Pacifism. Paxton Boys. Pennsylvania. Politics. 1763-68. *2702*
—. Metropolitan Areas. Missions and Missionaries. 1869-1977. *1608*
—. Mexican Americans. Southwest. 1830-1977. *3528*
—. Missions and Missionaries. 1706-1977. *1739*
—. Missions and Missionaries. Puerto Rico. 1899-1914. *1728*
—. Missions and Missionaries. Race Relations. 1562-1977. *3535*
—. Morality. Republicanism. Revivals. South. 1825-60. *2244*
—. New England. Novels. Salvation. Stowe, Harriet Beecher. Theology. Women. 1845-85. *2038*
—. New Jersey. Princeton University (library). 18c. *622*
—. New Jersey (Newark). See, Isaac M. Sermons. Women. 1876. *805*
—. Pennsylvania (Middle Octorara). 1727-1977. *3590*
—. *Princeton Review* (periodical). Providence. Science. Social problems. 1789-1860. *3527*
—. Religious Education. Sherrill, Lewis. ca 1900-57. *778*
—. Segregation. Slavery. South Carolina (Charleston). 1845-60. *2154*
—. Sermons. Sunday, Billy. Virtue. Women. Working class. 1915. *890*
—. Slavery. Stowe, Harriet Beecher. 1830's-1870's. *3554*
—. Social justice. 1770-1977. *2398*
—. Stained glass windows. Willet family. 19c-20c. *1887*
—. Women. 1764-1974. *3582*
—. Women. 1920's. *849*
Presbyterian Church, Associate Reformed. Caldwell, Erskine. Caldwell, Ira Sylvester. Novels. South. 1900-78. *2017*
Presbyterian Church (Committee of Four). Ordination. Women. 1926-30. *809*
Presbyterian Church (Cumberland). Archko collection. Forgeries. Jesus Christ. Mahan, William D. Mormons. Wallace, Lew *(Ben-Hur)*. 1880's. *3928*
—. Clergy. McGown, A. J. Publishers and Publishing. *Texas Presbyterian* (newspaper). 1846-73. *3586*
—. Ecumenism. Pennsylvania (Philadelphia). World Alliance of Reformed Churches. 1870-80. *455*
—. Ecumenism. Presbyterian Church of the United States of America. 1906. *437*
—. Ecumenism. Theology. World Alliance of Reformed Churches. 1880-84. *470*
Presbyterian Church (Cumberland, Old School). Baptists. Methodist Episcopal Church, South. Newspapers. Texas. 1829-61. *2907*
Presbyterian Church (General Assembly). Princeton Theological Seminary (trustees). Theology. 1920-29. *647*
Presbyterian Church (New Church Synod). Kentucky. Schisms. 1837-58. *3574*
Presbyterian Church (New School). Abolition Movement. Beecher, Lyman. Colonization. 1820-50. *2492*
—. Anti-Catholicism. Congregationalism. Cox, Samuel Hanson. Ecumenism. Episcopal Church, Protestant. Evangelicalism. Slavery. 1840's. *471*
—. Kentucky (Woodford County). Seminaries. 1837-51. *722*
Presbyterian Church of Scotland. MacGregor, James. Missions and Missionaries. Nova Scotia (Pictou). 1786-1830. *1634*
Presbyterian Church of the United States of America. Auburn Affirmation (document). Church government. Theology. 1920-25. *3577*
—. Ecumenism. Education. Mackay, John A. Personal narratives. Princeton Theological Seminary. Theology. 1910-75. *3543*
—. Ecumenism. Presbyterian Church, Cumberland. 1906. *437*

Presbyterian Church, Reformed. Antislavery sentiments. Integration. Ohio (Cincinnati). Reformed Presbyterian Theological Seminary. 1845-49. *610*
Presbyterian Church, Southern. Assemblies of God. Church of God. Civil rights movement. Periodicals. South. 1950's-60's. *2528*
—. *Book of Common Worship*. Humor. Lampton, William J. Poetry. Rites and Ceremonies. VanDyke, Henry. 1906. *3557*
—. Bottoms, Lawrence W. Negroes. Personal narratives. South. 1930-75. *2529*
—. Cable, George Washington. Fiction. Louisiana (New Orleans). Reform. ca 1870-1925. *3539*
—. Clergy. Consultation on Church Union. Henderlite, Rachel. Personal narratives. South. Women. 1945-77. *804*
—. Colleges and Universities. Foreman, Kenneth J., Sr. *Presbyterian Outlook* (newspaper). Theology. 1922-67. *3547*
—. Ecumenism. South. 1861-74. *477*
—. South. Wilson, Joseph Ruggles. 1844-1903. *3572*
Presbyterian Church, Southern (administration). Bureaucracies. Conservatism. Roberts, William Henry. Theology. 1884-1920. *3541*
Presbyterian Church (Synod of the West). German Americans. 1912-59. *3529*
Presbyterian Church, United. 1640-1978. *3575*
—. America (views of). Anti-Communist Movements. Internationalism. 1973. *1373*
—. Clergy. Negroes. 1855-1973. *3595*
—. Negroes. 20c. *3593*
Presbyterian Historical Society. Archives. China. Japan. Korea. Missions and Missionaries. 1852-1911. *189*
—. Archives. Ecumenism. Historical Societies. Pennsylvania (Philadelphia). 1852-1977. *260*
Presbyterian Outlook (newspaper). Colleges and Universities. Foreman, Kenneth J., Sr. Presbyterian Church (southern). Theology. 1922-67. *3547*
Presbyterian Witness and Evangelical Advocate (newspaper). Barnes, James. Editorials. Murray, Robert. Nova Scotia (Halifax). 1848-1910. *3584*
Presbyterian Witness (newspaper). Editors and Editing. "Letter to My Country Friends" (series). Murray, Robert. Nova Scotia (Halifax). 1863. *987*
Presbyterianism. Baldwin, Theron. Congregationalism. Higher education. Society for the Promotion of Collegiate and Theological Education at the West. 1843-73. *629*
—. Blair, Duncan Black. Gaelic language. Nova Scotia (Barney's River). Poets. Scholarship. 1848-93. *2069*
—. Blair, Duncan Black. Gaelic language. Nova Scotia (Pictou County). Poetry. Scholars. Scotland. 1846-93. *2070*
—. Immigrants. McDonald, Donald. Millenarianism. Prince Edward Island. Scottish Canadians. ca 1828-67. *3591*
Presbyterians. Abolition Movement. Breckinridge, Robert Jefferson. Breckinridge, William Lewis. Constitutions, State. Emancipation Party. Kentucky. 1849. *2475*
—. Alma College. Colleges and Universities. Michigan. 1883-86. *694*
—. American Revolution. Documents. National character. 1729-87. *3596*
—. American Revolution. Political attitudes. Princeton University. 1765-76. *960*
—. Baptists. Church and State. Church of England. North Carolina. Provincial Government. Tryon, William. 1765-76. *1036*
—. Catholic Church. Daily Life. Nova Scotia (Lochaber). Rural Settlements. 1830-1972. *2747*
—. Church and State. Church of England. Colleges and Universities (administration). Friends, Society of. New Jersey. Princeton University. 1745-60. *661*
—. Church of England. Morris, William. Ontario (Kingston). Queen's College. 1836-42. *711*
—. Coe, Truman. Letters. Mormons. Ohio (Kirtland). 1836. *2718*
—. Colleges and Universities (administration). Desha, Joseph. Holley, Horace. Kentucky. Politics. State government. Transylvania College. Unitarianism. 1818-27. *537*
—. Education. Evangelism. Freedmen. 1872-1900. *3589*
—. Slavery. South. 1787-1817. *2156*
Preservation *See also* Restorations.
—. Archaeology. Kensington Methodist Episcopal Church. Methodist Episcopal Church. Pennsylvania (Philadelphia). 18c. 1950's-75. *1769*
—. Architecture. Harmony Society. Indiana (New Harmony). Pennsylvania (Economy, Harmony). Rapp, George. Restorations. Utopias. 1804-25. 20c. *420*
—. Catholic Church. Church records. Louisiana, north. 1716-1840's. 1930's-74. *185*
—. Catholic Church. Georgia (Augusta). Local history. Sacred Heart Church. 1976-78. *1823*
—. Concordia Historical Institute. Farms. Lutheran Church (Missouri Synod). Missouri (Perry County). Saxon Lutheran Memorial. 1958-64. *220*
—. Kentucky (Pleasant Hill; Shakertown). Shakers. Utopias. 1805-1976. *436*
Presidency (mystique). Clergy. Eulogies. Sermons. Washington, George. 1799. *1190*
Presidents *See also* names of individual presidents.
—. Christianity. 1788-1979. *2726*
—. Inaugural addresses. 1789-1941. *1176*
—. Inaugural addresses. Myths and Symbols. National Characteristics. Protestantism. 17c-20c. *1174*
Presley, Elvis. Music (rock and roll, white gospel). 1956-77. *1954*
Press *See also* Books; Editors and Editing; Journalism; Newspapers; Periodicals.
—. Adventists. Fiction. Miller, William. 1830's-40's. *2014*
—. Canada. Catholic Church. Church and state. Encyclicals. Pius IX, Pope *(Syllabus of Errors)*. Public opinion. 1864-65. *1019*
—. Catholic Church. Elections. Leo XIII, Pope. Pius IX, Pope. Protestantism. 1878. *2786*
Pressure groups. Baptist Joint Committee on Public Affairs. Church and State. 1973. *1298*
—. Baptists. Bethel African Methodist Episcopal Church. California (San Francisco). Civil rights. Methodist Episcopal Zion Church, African. Negroes. Third Baptist Church. 1860's. *1289*
Preus, Herman A. Church and State. Diaries. Lutheran Church. Norwegian Americans. Wisconsin (Columbia, Dane counties). 1851-60. *1104*
Price controls. New England. Puritans. 1629-76. *2570*
Price, Richard. American Revolution. Chauncy, Charles. Church and State. Congregationalism. Great Britain. Letters. Slavery. 1727-87. *3129*
Prices *See also* Wages.
—. Boycotts. Consumers. Jews. Meat, kosher. New York City. Riots. Women. 1902. *4112*
Priesthood. Mormons. Negroes. 1978-79. *3946*
—. Mormons. Negroes. Utah. 1844-52. *2137*
—. Mormons. Negroes. Young, Brigham. 1843-52. *3962*
Priesthood (Aaronic). Mormons. 1851-83. *3978*
Priesthood-Auxiliary Movement. Mormons. 1928-38. *3955*
Primaries (senatorial). Anti-Catholicism. Bryan, Nathan P. Catts, Sidney J. Democratic Party. Florida. Political Campaigns (gubernatorial). Trammell, Park M. 1915-16. *1258*
Primary Education. *See* Elementary Education.
Prime ministers. Aberhart, William. Alberta. Economic reform. Politics. Radio. 1934-37. *1216*
Primitivism. Bible (New Testament; Epistles). Paul, Saint. Theology. Williams, Roger. 1630-83. *2939*
Prince Edward Island. Bible reading. Catholic Church. Politics. Protestants. Religion in the Public Schools. 1856-60. *580*
—. Catholic Church. Immigration. Persecution. Scotland. 1769-74. *3702*
—. Church and State. Political Parties. Prince of Wales College Act (1860). School Boards. 1860-63. *744*
—. Immigrants. McDonald, Donald. Millenarianism. Presbyterianism. Scottish Canadians. ca 1828-67. *3591*
Prince of Wales College Act (1860). Church and State. Political Parties. Prince Edward Island. School Boards. 1860-63. *744*
Prince, Thomas. Congregationalism. Historians. Massachusetts (Boston). Old South Church. 1718-58. *275*
Princeton Review (periodical). Presbyterian Church. Providence. Science. Social problems. 1789-1860. *3527*
Princeton Theological Seminary. Alexander, Archibald. Presbyterian Church. Scripture, doctrine of. 1772-1929. *3566*
—. Alexander Hall (building). New Jersey. Presbyterian Church. 1815. *595*
—. Alexander, Joseph A. Biblical criticism. Seminaries. Theater. 1830-61. *705*
—. Bible (New Testament). Exegesis. Germany. Hodge, Charles. Liberalism. Presbyterian Church. 1820-78. *3573*
—. Clergy. Miller, Samuel. Presbyterian Church. Religious Education. 1813-50. *764*
—. Ecumenism. Education. Mackay, John A. Personal narratives. Presbyterian Church of the United States of America. Theology. 1910-75. *3543*
Princeton Theological Seminary (trustees). Presbyterian Church (General Assembly). Theology. 1920-29. *647*
Princeton University. American Revolution. Political attitudes. Presbyterians. 1765-76. *960*
—. Brown University. Colleges and Universities. Harvard University. Libraries. Yale University. 18c. *672*
—. Buchman, Frank. Evangelicalism. Moral Re-Armament movement. New Jersey. 1938. *2858*
—. Church and State. Church of England. Colleges and Universities (administration). Friends, Society of. New Jersey. Presbyterians. 1745-60. *661*
—. Davies, Samuel. Diaries. Fund raising. Great Britain. New Jersey. Presbyterian Church. 1753-54. *636*
—. Hodge, Charles. New Jersey (Princeton). Women. 1825-55. *857*
Princeton University Library. Mormons. Smith, Joseph *(Book of Commandments)*. 1820-1975. *3956*
—. New Jersey. Presbyterian Church. 18c. *622*
Princeton University (Nassau Hall). Clark, Joseph. Education, Finance. Fund raising. Personal narratives. Travel. 1802-04. *612*
Princeton University (trustees). Educational Policy. Presbyterian Church. 1806-07. *541*
Printing *See also* Books.
—. 1638-1776. *85*
—. American Revolution. Germany. *Heinrich Mullers Pennsylvanischer Staatsbote* (newspaper). Moravian Church. Muller, Johann Heinrich. Pennsylvania (Philadelphia). 1722-82. *3514*
—. Book of Common Prayer. Episcopal Church, Protestant. Merrymount Press. Typeface. 1922-30. *1986*
—. Education. Engelhardt, Zephyrin. Franciscans. Holy Childhood Indian School Printery. Indians. Michigan (Harbor Springs). 1894-1913. *1584*
—. Friends, Society of. Lawrence, Daniel. North or Northern States. 1788-1812. *3258*
Prisoners. American Revolution. Brown, Joshua. Friends, Society of. Pacifism. Pennsylvania (Little Britain Township). South Carolina (Ninety Six). 1778. *2633*
—. American Revolution. Diaries. Drinker family. Friends, Society of. Pacifism. Pennsylvania (Philadelphia). Virginia (Winchester). 1777-81. *2683*
Prisoners of War. Catholic Church. Confederate Army. Duke, Basil W. Fort Delaware. Wood, James F. 1864. *3844*
Prisons *See also* Crime and Criminals; Criminal Law.
—. Attitudes. Friends, Society of. New York (Auburn). Pennsylvania. Reform. 1787-1845. *2393*
—. Church of England. Clergy. Episcopal Church, Protestant. Ingraham, Joseph Holt. Novels. Public Schools. Reform. Tennessee (Nashville). 1847-51. *3241*
—. Edmunds Act (US, 1882). Mormons. Polygamy. Utah. 1880's. *1004*
Private Schools *See also* Boarding Schools; Church Schools.
—. Attitudes. Ethnicity. Mennonites. Pennsylvania (Lancaster). Socialization. 1974-76. *673*
—. Catholic Church. Church and State. French language. Langevin, Adélard. Manitoba. Politics. 1890-1916. *608*
—. Catholic Church. Compulsory education. Edwards Law (Illinois, 1889). Ethnic Groups. Illinois. Public schools. State Politics. 1889-93. *551*
—. Catholic Church. Family. Judaism. 1960's-70's. *654*

—. Clergy. Diaries. Episcopal Church, Protestant. Salt industry. Trade. Ward, Henry Dana. West Virginia (Kanawha Valley, Charleston). 1845-47. *3172*
—. Friends, Society of. Maryland (Baltimore). Methodist Episcopal Church, African. Negroes. Presbyterian Church. Sunday Schools. 1794-1860. *633*
Probasco, Harriet. Carroll, Anna Ella. Nativism. Women. 1840's-61. *851*
Probate courts. Church and state. County Government. Judicial Administration. Mormons. Partisanship. Utah. 1855-72. *1039*
Professionalism. Clergy. Congregationalism. New England. Presbyterian Church. Scott, Donald M. (review article). 1750-1850. 1979. *2865*
—. Clergy. Great Awakening. New England. Theology. 1740-49. *2257*
—. Hadassah. Jews. National Council of Jewish Women. Voluntary Associations. Women. 1890-1980. *4146*
—. Social mobility. Spiritualists. Women. 19c. *4294*
Professions. Catholic Church. Quebec. Religious orders. Secondary education. Women. 1908-54. *871*
Program failure. Employment. Public Policy. Rescue missions. Skid rows. Social Reform. 1960's-70's. *2524*
Progress, concept of. Congregationalism. Edwards, Jonathan. Judaism. Luria, Isaac. Millenarianism. 16c-18c. *84*
Progressivism. Barkley, Alben. Gambling, pari-mutuel. Kentucky. Louisville Churchmen's Federation. 1917-27. *2437*
—. California (San Francisco). Catholic Church. City Politics. Clergy. Irish Americans. Yorke, Peter C. 1900's. *3889*
—. Catholic Church. Labor Unions and Organizations. Polish Americans. Political Leadership. Socialism. Wisconsin (Milwaukee). 1900-30. *1299*
—. Catholic Church. Lawyers. Pennsylvania. Smith, Walter George. 1900-22. *2365*
—. Catholic Church. New Jersey (Jersey City). Protestantism. Social reform. Whittier House. 1890-1917. *2449*
—. Christianity. Country Life. Ecumenism. Protestant Churches. Reform. Wisconsin. 1904-20. *2723*
—. Clergy. Congregationalism. Herron, George David. Iowa College. National Christian Citizen League. Populism. Socialism. 1880's-1900. *2561*
—. Colorado (Denver). Congregation Beth Ha Medrosh Hagodol. Judaism (Orthodox). Kauvar, Charles E. H. 1902-71. *4194*
—. Community centers. Country life movement. Rural Settlements. 1900's-20's. *2447*
—. Forssell, G. D. Iowa. Lectures. Minnesota. Social Conditions. 1890-95. *1967*
—. Fundamentalism. Long, Huey P. North Central States. Populism. Smith, Gerald L. K. 1934-48. *975*
Prohibition. Alaska. Women's Christian Temperance Union. 1842-1917. *2596*
—. Arkansas. Baptists. Brough, Charles Hillman. Elections (presidential). Evolution. 1928-29. *1270*
—. Candler, Warren A. Methodist Episcopal Church, South. Political Campaigns (presidential). Smith, Al. 1928. *1210*
—. Catholic Church. Democratic Party. Immigrants. New York City. Protestantism. Tammany Hall. 1840-60. *2594*
—. Catholic Church. National Prohibition League. Oklahoma. Religious Liberty. State Government. 1907-18. *2580*
—. Catholic Church. Social reform. Zurcher, George. 1884-1920's. *2579*
—. Congregationalism. Education. New Mexico (Albuquerque). Social gospel. 1900-17. *2448*
—. Constitutional Amendments, State. Ohio. Women's Christian Temperance Union. 1874-85. *2597*
—. League of Nations. Mormons. Republican Party. Roberts, Brigham Henry. Smith, Joseph Fielding. Suffrage. Utah. Women. ca 1900. *1284*
—. Local option campaign. Louisiana. Shreveport Ministerial Association. 1950-52. *2591*
—. Mormons. Utah. 1900's-1910's. *2592*
—. Nation, Carry Amelia. Temperance Movements. Women. 1890's-1911. *2576*
—. Willard, Frances E. Women's Christian Temperance Union. 1878-98. *2595*
Prohibition (repeal). Adventists. Constitutional Amendments (21st). 1932-34. *2598*
—. Constitutional Amendments (21st). Mormons. Utah. 1932-33. *2587*
Prohibition (review article). Blocker, Jack S., Jr. Clark, Norman H. 1890-1913. 1976. *2577*
Prohibitionists. Ethnic groups. Saloons. Values. Working Class. 1890-1920. *2588*
Project North. Canada. Christianity. Civil rights. Eskimos. Indians. Métis. 1975-79. *2545*
Proletariat. *See* Working class.
Propaganda *See also* Advertising; Public Opinion.
—. Arts. Political commentary. 1975. *1873*
—. Catholic Church. École Sociale Populaire. Quebec (Montreal). Syndicalism. Working Class. 1911-49. *1473*
—. Catholic Church. Great Britain. World War I. 1918. *1240*
—. Church of England. Inglis, Charles. Loyalists. Sermons. 1770-80. *1370*
Property *See also* Income; Property Tax; Real Estate.
—. Amnesty. Loyalists. Massachusetts. Public Opinion. 1783-84. *1357*
—. Bidamon, Emma Smith. Illinois (Nauvoo). Mormons. Schisms. Smith, Joseph. Women. Women. Young, Brigham. 1832-79. *3932*
—. Plymouth Colony. Puritans. 1621-75. *2569*
Property tax. Church and State. Sects, Religious. 1847-1979. *1005*
Prophecy. *Advent Review and Sabbath Herald* (newspaper). Adventists. Poetry. Smith, Uriah. 1853. *1997*
—. Adventists. Bible. World War I (antecedents). 1912-18. *2664*
—. Adventists. Charisma. White, Ellen G. Women. 1848-1901. *2976*
—. Arkansas (Pine Bluff). Burnett, Ellen. Storms. Women. 1903. *74*
—. Leadership. Mormons. Poetry. Snow, Eliza Roxey. Utah. Women. 1804-87. *3936*
Proposition 6 (1978). California. Catholic Church. Homosexuality. Public schools. Referendum. Teachers. 1978. *1320*
Proslavery Sentiments *See also* Antislavery Sentiments.
—. Calvinism. Millenarianism. Presbyterian Church. South. 1800-65. *2166*
—. Christianity. Colleges and Universities. Curricula. Graham, William. Liberty Hall Academy. Virginia. ca 1786-96. *2173*
—. Christianity. South. 1844-1977. *2167*
—. Clergy. National Characteristics. Social Status. 1699-1865. *2628*
—. Whitefield, George. 1740-48. *2175*
Protestant Churches *See also* names of churches, e.g. Methodist Church, etc.; Protestantism.
—. Abolition Movement. Clergy. Negroes. 1830-60. *2472*
—. Abortion. Right To Life organizations. South. 1970's. *945*
—. Agriculture. Landlords and Tenants. Mississippi. Neoorthodoxy. Theologians. 1936-40. *2566*
—. Alabama. Reconstruction. 1865-67. *457*
—. American Board of Commissioners for Foreign Missions. Angola. Church and State. Missions and Missionaries. Portugal. Umbundu (tribe). 1880-1922. *1746*
—. American Board of Commissioners for Foreign Missions. Boutwell, William Thurston. Chippewa Indians. Indian-White Relations. Minnesota. Missions and Missionaries. 1831-47. *1572*
—. American Board of Commissioners for Foreign Missions. Missions and Missionaries. Social customs. South Africa. Zulus. 1835-60's. *1695*
—. American Revolution. Historiography. 1775-82. *1396*
—. Americanization. Missions and Missionaries. Puerto Rico. 1898-1917. *1734*
—. Anti-Catholicism. Attitudes. Independence Movements. Latin America. 1810-25. *2107*
—. Antiwar Sentiments. Clergy. Vietnam War. ca 1966-73. *2700*
—. Asia. Canada. Colleges and Universities (review article). Missions and Missionaries. 1850-1971. *1675*
—. Attitudes. Censorship. Films. Television. 1921-80. *2820*
—. Attitudes. Mexico. Missions and Missionaries. Social Darwinism. Travel accounts. 1867-1911. *1690*
—. Boer War. Canada. Clergy. English Canadians. 1899-1902. *2675*
—. British Americans. California (Los Angeles). Popular culture. Social Classes. 1920's. 1977. *2624*
—. Calvert, George (1st Lord Baltimore). Catholic Church. Colonization. Newfoundland (Avalon Peninsula). Religious Liberty. 1620's. *2755*
—. Canada. Catholic Church. Industrialization. Judaism. Religiosity. 1921-71. *93*
—. Canada. Ecumenism. Immigration. Nationalism. United Church of Canada. 1902-25. *491*
—. Catholic Church. China. Communists. Missionaries. 1948-50. *1752*
—. Catholic Church. Church attendance. Religiosity. 1974. *2713*
—. Catholic Church. Cities. Civil rights movement. Negroes. Social Classes. 1960's-70's. *2539*
—. Catholic Church. Clergy. Sex discrimination. Women. 1970's. *939*
—. Catholic Church. Democratic Party. Elections (presidential). Louisiana. Smith, Al. Temperance Movements. 1928. *1330*
—. Catholic Church. Dissent. Michigan (Detroit). Religious Education. 1958-71. *3777*
—. Catholic Church. District of Columbia. Jews. Judaism. Psychological well-being. Religiosity. Worship. 1970's. *130*
—. Catholic Church. Education. Missions and Missionaries. Prucha, Francis Paul (review article). 1888-1912. *1538*
—. Catholic Church. Feild, Edward. Irish Canadians. Mullock, John Thomas. Newfoundland. Politics. 19c. *1254*
—. Catholic Church. Hawaii. Independence Movements. Missions and Missionaries. Simpson, George. 1842-43. *1723*
—. Catholic Church. Human Relations. Judaism (Orthodox). Rhode Island. 18c. *2087*
—. Catholic Church. Mexican Americans. Music. 1963-75. *1911*
—. Catholic Church. Morality. Oklahoma. Politics. Referendum. Sabbatarianism. Voting and Voting Behavior. 1959-76. *1290*
—. Catholic Church. Social Classes. 1970's. *2623*
—. Charters. Institutionalization. Mennonites (Franconia Conference). 1840-1940. *3382*
—. Child-rearing. Converts. Psychology. Religious Education. Sunday schools. 19c. *603*
—. Children. Evangelicalism. Northeastern or North Atlantic States. Sunday Schools. Theology. 1820's. *604*
—. Chinese Americans. Hawaii. Missions and Missionaries. 1872-98. *1717*
—. Christianity. Country Life. Ecumenism. Progressivism. Reform. Wisconsin. 1904-20. *2723*
—. Church and Social Problems. Clergy. Political Activism. 1960's-70's. *2431*
—. Church and Social Problems. Negroes. 1970's. *2452*
—. Clergy. Frontier. Missouri. Schools. ca 1800-30. *639*
—. Clergy. Johnson, Andrew. Public Opinion. 1865-68. *1219*
—. Clergy. Negroes. Race Relations. South. ca 1800-65. *2816*
—. Clergy. Religious beliefs. 1965. *2890*
—. Clergy. Textbooks. Theology. 1850-1900. *2925*
—. Clergy, dissident. Ideology. Leadership. -1973. *2439*
—. Cobden, Richard. Great Britain. Millenarianism. Peace movements. 1840-60. *2701*
—. Congregationalism. Connecticut. Hawaii. Kanui, William Tennooe. Missions and Missionaries. 1796-1864. *1493*
—. Ecumenism. Europe. World War II. 1900-45. *465*
—. Ecumenism. Federal Council of the Churches of Christ in America. Hopkins, Charles Howard. Politics. Social gospel. 1880-1908. *487*
—. Ecumenism. Jews. National Council of Churches (General Assembly). 1969-74. *502*
—. Education. France. Hymns. Neau, Elias. New York. Slaves. ca 1689-1722. *1913*
—. Ethnic Groups. Michigan (Detroit). Social organization. 1880-1940. *2877*
—. Europe. History, comparative. Liberalism. Social Gospel. 1885-1975. *2395*
—. Feminism. Radicals and Radicalism. Social reform. South. Women. 1920's. *789*
—. Feminism. Women. -1973. *891*

—. Florida (Tallahassee). Negroes. Race Relations. Social control. 1865-85. *2864*
—. Georgia (Atlanta). Haven, Gilbert. Negroes. Segregation. 1865-1906. *2145*
—. German language. Pennsylvania. Sermons. 18c. *1989*
—. Higher education. India. Missionaries. Social Gospel. 1883. *1680*
—. Homosexuality. Theology. 1970's. *815*
—. Indian-White Relations. Missions and Missionaries. Spokan Indians. Walker, Elkanah. Washington (Tshimakain). 1838-48. *1520*
—. Jesuits. Land Tenure. Legislation. Mercier, Honoré. Quebec. 1886. *1087*
—. Jesuits. Missions and Missionaries. Ottoman Empire. Syria. 1840's. *1698*
—. Jesus People. Mormons. Restitutionism. Revivals. 19c-20c. *2744*
—. Jews. Laity. Leadership. New York (Kingston). Political Leadership. Social Status. 1825-60. *2600*
—. Missions and Missionaries. 1792-1970. *1722*
—. Missions and Missionaries. Organizations. Women. 1870's-90's. *894*
—. Missions and Missionaries. Women. 19c. *943*
—. Music. Negroes. New York City. Pennsylvania (Philadelphia). ca 1800-44. *1948*
—. New York City. Social problems. 1970's. *2421*
Protestant Ethic. Attitudes. Brooklyn College. Catholic Church. Immigration. Judaism. Negroes. New York City. West Indian Americans. 1939-78. *350*
—. Calling (concept). Equality. Great Chain of Being (theme). Puritans. 17c-18c. *340*
—. Canada. Elites. Ethnicity. Senators. Values. 1971. *958*
—. Capitalism. Values. Weber, Max. 1770-1920. *355*
—. Economic development. Reformation. -1973. *339*
—. Family misfortune, theme of. Folklore. 20c. *335*
—. Franklin, Benjamin. Weber, Max *(The Protestant Ethic and the Spirit of Capitalism)*. 18c-1978. *330*
—. Hoover, Herbert C. Johnson, Lyndon B. Nixon, Richard M. Public welfare. Rhetoric. Roosevelt, Franklin D. Weber, Max. 1905-79. *348*
—. Industrialization. Labor. Leisure. Values. 19c-20c. *334*
—. Johnson, Benton. Political parties. 1960's-70's. *1302*
—. Massachusetts (Webster). Methodism. Textile industry. Working class. 1820's-50's. *372*
Protestantism *See also* Evangelism; Fundamentalism.
—. Abolition Movement. Education. Freedmen. McPherson, James M. (review article). Missions and Missionaries. 1865-1910. 1975. *563*
—. Abolition Movement. Great Britain. Historiography. 18c-19c. *2499*
—. Abortion. Birth Control. 19c. *869*
—. Acculturation. Americanism. Catholic Church. Leo XIII, Pope (*Testem Benevolentiae*). Periodicals. 1899. *319*
—. Acculturation. Catholic Church. Indian-White Relations. Missionaries. Wisconsin. 1830-48. *1640*
—. Adolescence. Boys. Canada. USA. Young Men's Christian Association. 1870-1920. *2414*
—. Adventists. Bible. Republicanism. 1850's-60's. *2962*
—. Allegory. Art. Folwell, Samuel *(Sacred to the Illustrious Washington)*. Mourning (theme). Painting. ca 1800. *1885*
—. American Board of Commissioners for Foreign Missions. Arabic. Bible. Missions and Missionaries. Moslems. Translating and Interpreting. 1843-60. *1740*
—. American Institute for Education. Country life. Educational Reform. Elites. Massachusetts. Nationalism. 1830-37. *573*
—. American Revolution. Connecticut (Norfield). Sermons. Sherwood, Samuel. 1776. *1414*
—. American Revolution. Evangelism. Great Awakening. 1770-1800. *2267*
—. Anglican Communion. Canada. Education. Great Britain. Missionaries. Sudan Interior Mission. 1937-55. *1741*
—. Anglo-Saxonism. Interventionism. Reform. Strong, Josiah. 1885-1915. *2418*
—. Anti-Catholicism. Anti-Semitism. Colorado (Denver). Ku Klux Klan. Social Classes. 1921-25. *2609*
—. Anti-Catholicism. Cheverus, Jean Louis Lefebvre de. Daley, Dominic. Halligan, James. Irish Americans. Massachusetts (Northampton). Trials. 1805-06. *2097*
—. Anti-Catholicism. Cheverus, Jean Louis Lefebvre de. Irish Americans. Lyon, Marcus. Massachusetts (Northampton). Murder. Trials. 1805-06. *2099*
—. Anti-Catholicism. Chicopee Manufacturing Company. Immigration. Irish Americans. Massachusetts (Chicopee). Mills. Nativism. 1830-75. *2103*
—. Anti-Catholicism. Church and state. Ethnic groups. Evangelism. Quebec (Lower Canada). Rebellion of 1837. 1766-1865. *2110*
—. Anti-Catholicism. Clergy. Ku Klux Klan. Republican Party. Rhode Island. 1915-32. *2116*
—. Anti-Catholicism. Colonization. Great Britain. Ideology. Ireland. North America. ca 1550-1600. *2086*
—. Anti-Catholicism. Conscription, Military. Jesuits. Novitiate of St. Stanislaus. Ontario (Guelph). World War I. 1918-19. *2657*
—. Anticlericalism. Enlightenment. Europe. Revivals. 1640's-1830's. *2912*
—. Anti-Communist Movements. Dulles, John Foster. Ecumenism. Morality. Oxford Conference (1937). Presbyterian Church. World order movement. 1937-48. *1375*
—. Appalachia. Bibliographies. 1905-75. *2879*
—. Art. Bunyan, John *(Pilgrim's Progress)*. Huntington, Daniel. *Mercy's Dream* (painting). National characteristics. 1678. 1841-70. *1856*
—. Assimilation. Brethren in Christ. 1770-1973. *3422*
—. Assimilation. German Americans. Michigan (Ann Arbor). Pluralism. 1830-1955. *284*
—. Attitudes. Autobiography. Brownson, Orestes A. *(The Convert)*. Catholic Church. Converts. Great Britain. Newman, John Henry *(Apologia pro Vita Sua)*. 1857-64. *3681*
—. Attitudes. Canada. Catholic Church. Ethnic Groups. Jews. Social Status. 1968. *2088*
—. Attitudes. Church and state. Civil Religion. Hoover, Herbert C. 1928-32. *1167*
—. Baconianism. Bozeman, Theodore Dwight (review article). Science. 1800's-60's. 1977. *2324*
—. Baptists. Negroes. Socialism. Woodbey, George Washington. 1902-15. *2563*
—. Barth, Karl. Germany. Theology. 1919-39. *2946*
—. Benevolence (doctrine). Finney, Charles G. Social reform. 1815-65. *2422*
—. Bengough, John Wilson. City government. *Grip* (periodical). Ontario (Toronto). Political Reform. 1873-1910. *1266*
—. Bible. Creation theory. Dana, James Dwight. Guyot, Arnold. Science. 1850's. *2333*
—. Bible. Folklore. South. Visions. 20c. *2178*
—. Bible. Music (Gospel). 18c-1980. *1949*
—. Bible (King James version). Catholic Church. Church Schools. City Politics. Education, Finance. Michigan (Detroit). Religion in the Public Schools. 1842-53. *2716*
—. Bible reading. Catholic Church. Desmond, Humphrey. Religion in the Public Schools. *Wisconsin ex rel. Frederick Weiss et al.* v. *District School Board of School District 8* (1890). 1888-90. *571*
—. Biblical studies. Ecumenism. Missions and Missionaries. Palestine. 1812-1975. *1748*
—. Books. Children's literature. Death and Dying. Periodicals. 1800-60. *2914*
—. Books. Pennsylvania (New Geneva; Pleasant Hill School District). Sunday schools. 1823-57. *592*
—. California. Catholic Church. Mountain Men. Rogers, Harrison. Smith, Jedediah Strong. 1826-27. *2798*
—. Calvin, John. Luther, Martin. National Characteristics. 16c-18c. *2870*
—. Camp Lejeune. Lamb Studios. Marines. New Jersey (Tenafly). North Carolina. Stained glass windows. 1775-1943. *1867*
—. Canada. Capitalism. Fur trade. Hudson's Bay Company. Scottish Canadians. 18c-1970's. *377*
—. Canada. Communion. United Church of Canada. 1952-72. *3670*
—. Canada. Ideology. King, William Lyon Mackenzie. Liberal Party. Politics. Social Classes. 1900-50. *1421*
—. Canada. Sweet, H. C. 1866-1960. *2888*
—. Capital Punishment. Clergy. New England. Sermons. 1674-1750. *2822*
—. Capitalism. Ideology. Management. Political Science. Theology. Weber, Max. 16c-1974. *376*
—. Capitalism. Individualism. Social ethic. 20c. *345*
—. Catholic Church. Church and state. Great Britain. Military government. Quebec. 18c. *1125*
—. Catholic Church. Church and State. New France. ca 1625-1760's. *2818*
—. Catholic Church. Connecticut (New Haven). Ethnic Groups. Jews. Marriage. 1900-50. *906*
—. Catholic Church. Conservatism. Nativism. Newspapers. Political Commentary. *Providence Visitor* (newspaper). Rhode Island. 1916-24. *2118*
—. Catholic Church. Converts. Marriage. 1960's-70's. *848*
—. Catholic Church. Democratic Party. Immigrants. New York City. Prohibition. Tammany Hall. 1840-60. *2594*
—. Catholic Church. Ecumenism. Weigel, Gustave. 1950-64. *497*
—. Catholic Church. Elections. Leo XIII, Pope. Pius IX, Pope. Press. 1878. *2786*
—. Catholic church. Elections (presidential). Smith, Al. West Virginia. 1928. *1217*
—. Catholic Church. Ethnicity. Political Parties. 1968-72. *1220*
—. Catholic Church. Evangelism. Massachusetts (Boston). Settlement houses. South End House. Woods, Robert A. 1891-1910. *2438*
—. Catholic Church. Freedmen. Law. Texas. 1836-60. *2799*
—. Catholic Church. Kansas. Religion in the Public Schools. 1861-1900. *568*
—. Catholic Church. Mexican Americans. Music. 1962-75. *1910*
—. Catholic Church. New Jersey (Jersey City). Progressivism. Social reform. Whittier House. 1890-1917. *2449*
—. Charities. Edgewood Children's Center. Missouri (Webster Groves). Orphans. St. Louis Protestant Orphan Asylum. 1834-1979. *2518*
—. Charities. Fosdick, Harry Emerson. Friendship. Liberalism. Rockefeller, John D., Jr. Social control. Wealth. 1920-36. *364*
—. Child-rearing. Death and Dying. Fischer, David H. Greven, Philip. Lynn, Kenneth S. Personality (review article). Politics. Stannard, David E. 18c. 1977. *2943*
—. Child-rearing. Greven, Philip (review article). 17c-19c. 1977. *886*
—. Child-rearing. Greven, Philip (review article). Self-perception. 1620-18c. *836*
—. Child-rearing. Personality. 1640-1800. *814*
—. Children's Aid Society. Family. Foster care. Home Missionary Society. Pennsylvania (Philadelphia). 1880-1905. *2504*
—. Church location. Congregationalism. Economic conditions. Maryland (Baltimore). 1840-70. *2853*
—. Cities (review article). New England. New York. Pennsylvania (Philadelphia; Germantown). 1660's-18c. *2828*
—. Civil religion. Golden Age concept. Rationalism. Reformation. 16c-19c. *1173*
—. Civil Religion. Nationalism. Social Organization. Technology. ca 1630-1974. *1171*
—. Civil religion. Secularization. Socialism. 16c-20c. *2910*
—. Civil War. South. 1861-65. *2841*
—. Clergy. Conflict and Conflict Resolution. Laity. 19c-20c. *2954*
—. Clergy. Folklore. Georgia, west-central. Humor. 19c-20c. *2839*
—. Clergy. Sore throats. 1830-60. *1431*
—. Colleges and Universities. 19c. *698*
—. Colleges and Universities. Emerson, Joseph. Lyon, Mary. Mount Holyoke College. Women. 1760's-1850's. *552*
—. Communalism. German Americans. Harmony Society. Indiana. Pennsylvania. Rapp, George. 1804-47. *425*
—. Connecticut. Great Awakening (antecedents). 1700's-40's. *2256*
—. Connecticut (Hartford). Democratic Party. Ethnic groups. Middle Classes. Voting and Voting Behavior. 1896-1940. *1203*
—. Cultural history. Ontario. 1840's-1900. *2844*
—. Darwinism. Great Britain. Moore, James R. (review article). 1870-1900. *2319*
—. Death and Dying. Literature. North or Northern States. Women. 1830-80. *2846*
—. Denominationalism. Ecumenism. 16c-1979. *480*

—. Diaries. Maine. Missions and Missionaries. Sewall, Jotham. 1778-1848. *1645*
—. Dickinson, Emily. Women. 1840-54. *73*
—. Diplomacy. Great Britain. Missionaries. Ottoman Empire. 1824-42. *1697*
—. Discrimination, Educational. Women. 1818-91. *2899*
—. Douglas, Ann. Feminization. Reform. Sex roles. Stereotypes. ca 1820-75. 1977-80. *918*
—. Ecumenism. Evangelism. Social change. Social justice. Student Christian Movement. 19c-20c. *440*
—. Ecumenism. Negroes. Reform. World Conference of Christian Youth, 1st. Youth. 1939-79. *2884*
—. Education (review article). Germany. Greven, Philip. Strauss, Gerald. Youth. 16c-19c. *850*
—. Emigration. Sweden. Unonius, Gustaf. 1858-63. *2922*
—. Enlightenment. Theology. 1920's-75. *2881*
—. Episcopal Church, Protestant. Great Britain. Maurice, Frederick Denison. Revelation. Social reform. Theology. 1860-1900. *3171*
—. Evangelism. Slavery. South. 18-19c. *2169*
—. Family. France. Quebec. Trade. 1740-60. *333*
—. Foreign Policy. Israel. Zionism (review article). 1945-48. *2944*
—. Freudianism. Marxism. Niebuhr, Reinhold (review article). Original sin. Theology. 1939-70. *2838*
—. Friends, Society of. Sex roles. Women. 17c-18c. *835*
—. Genovese, Eugene D. (review article). Millenarianism. Slavery. South. 17c-1865. *2163*
—. Graham, Billy. Peale, Norman Vincent. Popular culture. 1950's. *2901*
—. Great Britain. Law. Secularization. 1800-1970. *10*
—. History. Theology. 1900-70. *2850*
—. Hutchison, William R. (review article). Modernism. 19c-1976. *2872*
—. Immigrants. Scandinavian Americans. 1849-1900. *303*
—. Immigration. Public Schools. 1890-1970. *546*
—. Inaugural addresses. Myths and Symbols. National Characteristics. Presidents. 17c-20c. *1174*
—. Indiana (Gary, Valparaiso). Ku Klux Klan. Nativism. 1920's. *2358*
—. Lectures. Public Opinion. 1840's-50's. *2923*
—. Liberalism. Theology. 1880's-1930's. *2945*
—. Marriage. Plantations. Slaves. South. ca 1750's-1860. *2928*
—. McCosh, James. Philosophy. World Alliance of Reformed Churches. 1850-75. *453*
—. Middle classes. Myths and Symbols. 1975. *2606*
—. Millenarianism. Millerites. 1830's-40's. *2977*
—. Millenarianism. Nationalism. 1740-1800. *1151*
—. Morality. Sex. Women. 1790-1850. *827*
—. Moving Star Hall. Negroes. South Carolina (Johns Island). 18c-1970. *2830*
—. Music. South. Walker, William. 1830-50. *1914*
—. Nationalism. Social organization. Voluntary associations. 19c. *2931*
—. Negroes. Segregation. South. 1885-90's. *2135*
—. New Theology. Roe, Edward Payson *(Barriers Burned Away)*. Sheldon, Charles M. *(In His Steps)*. Social Gospel. 1860's-90's. *2058*
—. North Carolina (Piedmont region). Pluralism. 1890-1952. *2813*
—. Ordination. Social change. Women. World Council of Churches. 1945-75. *879*
—. Radical catholicity principle. Theology. Transcendence. 1975. *2949*
—. Rhetoric. Sermons. 1952-74. *1972*
—. Statistics. Texas, north. Whites. 1965-73. *2874*
Protestantism (review article). Caskey, Marie. Mathews, Donald G. Moorhead, James H. Reform. Walters, Ronald. 1830-80. 1976-78. *2368*
—. Charities. Cities. Evangelism. Muhlenberg, Augustus. Politics. Social Problems. 1812-1900. *2930*
Protestants. Abortion. Attitudes. Catholics. Whites. 1962-75. *888*
—. Anti-Catholicism. Canada. Italy. Political Attitudes. Risorgimento. 1846-60. *2114*
—. Anti-Catholicism. France. Maryland. Politicians. 1750's. *2095*
—. Anti-Catholicism. Ku Klux Klan. Saskatchewan. 1927-30. *2096*
—. Bible reading. Catholic Church. Politics. Prince Edward Island. Religion in the Public Schools. 1856-60. *580*
—. Burchard, Jedediah. Revivals. Social Conditions. Vermont. 1835-36. *2246*
—. Canada. Church and State. Jesuits' Estates Act. Political Protest. 1880-90. *1088*
—. Carroll, John. Catholic Church. Ecumenism. Immigrants. Nativism. 1790-1820. *496*
—. Catholic Church. Conversion. France (Alsace). Immigration policy. Louisiana. 1753-59. *3719*
—. Catholic Church. Elites. Ethnicity. Immigrants. Politics. Reform. 1890's-1970's. *1225*
—. Catholics. Church membership. Migration, Internal. Rhode Island. 1926-71. *152*
—. Catholics. Colleges and Universities. 1960's-70's. *565*
—. Church membership. Ethnicity. Illinois (Chicago). Jews. 1960's-70's. *121*
—. Conservatism. Quebec (Montreal). Social Reform. Women's Protective Immigration Society. 1882-1917. *919*
—. Country Life. Farms. Haswell, David R. Letters. Pennsylvania. Revivals. 1808-31. *2234*
—. Elites. Government. Politics. 1960's-70's. *1207*
—. German Canadians. Immigrants. Nova Scotia. 1749-52. *2852*
—. Political Participation. Racism. Sexism. Whites. Women. 1974-75. *907*
Proulx, Nicholas. Catholic Church. French Canadians. Immigration. Massachusetts (Holyoke). Working Class. 1850-1900. *3691*
Proverbs. Poetry. Puritans. Taylor, Edward ("Gods Determinations"). 1685. 1973. *1963*
Providence. Antislavery Sentiments. Editors and Editing. Kansas. Newspapers. Rhetoric. 1855-58. *2034*
—. Apocalypse. Bible (Revelation). Edwards, Jonathan. Theology. 1720-24. *3148*
—. Christianity. Ethics. Theology. 19c. *2728*
—. Civil religion. Nationalism. 1789-1812. *1158*
—. Civil War. Diaries. Episcopal Church, Protestant. Robertson, Martha Wayles. South Carolina (Chesterfield County). Women. 1860-66. *3191*
—. Colonies. Stamp Act crisis. 1765-66. *1156*
—. Elliott, Stephen. Episcopal Church, Protestant. Philosophy of History. South. 1840-66. *3212*
—. Great Awakening. 18c. *1155*
—. National Characteristics. 17c-20c. *1172*
—. Presbyterian Church. *Princeton Review* (periodical). Science. Social problems. 1789-1860. *3527*
—. Theology. ca 1830's-60. *2779*
Providence Visitor (newspaper). Catholic Church. Conservatism. Nativism. Newspapers. Political Commentary. Protestantism. Rhode Island. 1916-24. *2118*
Provincial Council of Baltimore (4th). Bishops. Catholic Church. Intellectuals. Letters. Walter, William Joseph. 1840-43. *3842*
Provincial Government. Aberhart, William. Alberta. Ideology. Social Credit Party. Theology. 1935-43. *1365*
—. Agricultural Labor. Canary Islanders. Fernandez de Santa Ana, Benito. Indians. Missions and Missionaries. Petitions. Texas (Villa San Fernando). 1741. *1542*
—. American Revolution. Episcopal Church, Protestant. New York. Nonconformists. Political Factions. 1768-71. *1294*
—. Baptists. Church and State. Church of England. North Carolina. Presbyterians. Tryon, William. 1765-76. *1036*
—. Bishops. Catholic Church. Church of England. Liberal Party. Newfoundland. 1860-62. *1253*
—. Black, Conrad. Catholic Church. Church and state. Duplessis, Maurice (review article). Quebec. Rumilly, Robert. 1930's-77. *1124*
—. Bonomi, Patricia U. Ethnic Groups. Klein, Milton M. New York (review article). Pluralism. 1690's-1770's. 1971-74. *1204*
—. Bourassa, Henri. Catholic Church. Politics. Quebec. 1902-71. *976*
—. Calvert, Cecilius (2d Lord Baltimore). Catholic Church. Great Britain. Maryland. Religious Liberty. 1634-49. *1068*
—. Discrimination. Ethnicity. Hutterites. Legislation. Prairie Provinces. 1960's-79. *1099*
—. Evolution. Friends, Society of. Pennsylvania. Revivals. 1735-75. *2222*
—. Friends, Society of. King George's War. Pacifism. Penn, Thomas. Pennsylvania. Politics. 1726-42. *1314*
Provincial legislation. Catholic Church. Church Schools. Manitoba. McCarthy, D'Alton. 1870-90. *72*
Provincial Legislatures. Baptists. McKim, Andrew. Nova Scotia. Politics. 1784-1840. *1309*
—. City Government. Congregationalism. Massachusetts (Tiverton). Religious liberty. Taxation. 1692-1724. *1084*
Provincial Politics. Church of England. Ethnic Groups. Friends, Society of. Pennsylvania. Presbyterian Church. 1775-80. *1248*
—. Friends, society of. Local politics. Pennsylvania (Lancaster County). 1700-76. *1008*
Provo Outrage. Civil-Military Relations. Fort Rawlins. Mormons. Utah. 1870-71. *4000*
Provost, T. S. Catholic Church. Colonization. Economic development. French Canadians. Geopolitics. Quebec (Mattawinie district). 17c-1890. *3809*
Prucha, Francis Paul (review article). Catholic Church. Education. Missions and Missionaries. Protestant Churches. 1888-1912. *1538*
Psalmody. Massachusetts (Boston). Mather, Cotton. Puritans. Sermons. Singing. 1721. *1938*
Psychiana (religion). Correspondence courses. Idaho (Moscow). New Thought movement. Robinson, Frank Bruce. 1929-48. *4260*
Psychiatry *See also* Mental Illness; Psychology.
—. Assassination. Gray, John P. Moral insanity. New York State Lunatic Asylum. Trials. 1854-86. *2346*
—. Depression. 1973. *2348*
—. Eddy, Mary Baker. Hypnotism. New England. Quimby, Phineas Parkhurst. 1820's-66. *1442*
Psychoanalysis *See also* Psychology.
—. Dependence. Religiosity. 1974. *142*
—. Emmanuel movement. Freud, Sigmund. Myers, Frederic W. H. 1906-10. *2334*
Psychocultural therapy. City life. Family. Witchcraft. 1968. *2197*
—. Witchcraft. 1968-73. *2196*
Psychohistory. Catholic Church. Georgia. Judaism. State Politics. Watson, Thomas E. 1856-1922. *55*
Psychological well-being. Catholic Church. District of Columbia. Jews. Judaism. Protestant churches. Religiosity. Worship. 1970's. *130*
Psychology *See also* Behaviorism; Psychiatry; Psychoanalysis; Social Psychology.
—. Anthropology. Historiography. Massachusetts (Salem). Puritans. Witchcraft. 1691-92. *2187*
—. Augustine, Saint. Calvinism. Edwards, Jonathan. Heart concept. New England. 17c. *2311*
—. Behaviorism. Calvinism. Watson, John Broadus. 1890-1919. *2308*
—. Child-rearing. Converts. Protestant Churches. Religious Education. Sunday schools. 19c. *603*
—. Connecticut (New Haven). Negroes. Pentecostal movement. Prayer meetings. Social conditions. 1978. *3521*
—. Converts. Personality. Puritans. 1630-1740. *3640*
—. Edwards, Jonathan. Grace. Locke, John. Theology. 1740's. *3158*
—. Edwards, Jonathan. Hasidism (Habad). Theology (comparative). 18c. *2338*
—. Great Britain. Religious experience. 1975-77. *114*
—. James, William. Nihilism. 1870-1910. 1975. *50*
—. Myths and Symbols. Science fiction. Sensitivity movement. 1960's-70's. *2060*
Psychology, faculty. Emotions. Intellect. Puritanism. 17c. *2313*
—. New England. Puritans. Stoddard, Solomon *(Safety of Appearing)*. 1630-1746. *2299*
Psychology of Religion. 1880-1930. *3*
—. Bibliographies. Periodicals. Research. 1950-74. *168*
Psychotherapy. Conversion. Eastern Religions. Mysticism. 1970's. *2290*
—. Cult practices. Puerto Rico. Social organization. Spiritualism. 1975. *1445*
Public Administration *See also* Bureaucracies; Civil-Military Relations; Government.
—. Calvinism. Centralization. Executive branch. Reform. Revivals. ca 1880-1930's. *959*

—. Church of England. North Carolina, east. St. John's Church. St. Paul's Church. 1729-75. *3240*
Public affairs. Baptists. 1936-71. *3022*
Public Finance *See also* Budgets.
—. Church and State. Church schools. Conscientious objection. Holidays. Prayer. Public Schools. Religious Liberty. Supreme Court. 1950-70's. *1112*
—. Church schools. Education, Finance. Supreme Court. 1971-73. *663*
Public Opinion *See also* Propaganda.
—. Adventists. Massachusetts, western. Miller, William. Newspapers. 1840's. *2079*
—. Alberta (Edmonton). Hutterites. Social customs. 1966-75. *3404*
—. Amnesty. Loyalists. Massachusetts. Property. 1783-84. *1357*
—. Atheism. Ingersoll, Robert. Lectures. Nevada (Virginia City). 1877. *4304*
—. Canada. Catholic Church. Church and state. Encyclicals. Pius IX, Pope *(Syllabus of Errors)*. Press. 1864-65. *1019*
—. Canada. Colleges and Universities. Political knowledge. Students. 1974. *978*
—. Chinese Americans. Discrimination. Frontier and Pioneer Life. Montana. Supreme courts (state). 1864-1902. *2152*
—. Church schools. Education, Finance. Government. Prayer. Religion in the Public Schools. 1962-68. *504*
—. Civil religion. Counter Culture. Persecution. Sects, Religious. 19c-20c. *4263*
—. Clergy. Johnson, Andrew. Protestant Churches. 1865-68. *1219*
—. *Engel* v. *Vitale* (US, 1962). New York. Nonsectarianism. Prayer. Public schools. 1962. *581*
—. German Americans. Mennonites. Military conscription. Pacifism. World War I. 1914-18. *2696*
—. Lafayette, Marquis de. Social Problems. Travel. 1824-25. *61*
—. Lectures. Protestantism. 1840's-50's. *2923*
—. Mormons. Newspapers. Periodicals. 1970's. *2071*
—. Mormons. Railroads. Train, George Francis. Utah. Young, Brigham. 1860's-70's. *3939*
—. Pennsylvania (Philadelphia). Pius IX, Pope. 1848. *2781*
—. Social Psychology. 1970's. *124*
Public policy. Catholic Worker Movement. Equality. Human Rights. 1933-78. *2436*
—. Church and State. Church schools. Education, Finance. Jews. Religion in the Public Schools. 1961-71. *512*
—. Church and State. Pluralism. 1970's. *1064*
—. Church Government. Church of England. House of Burgesses. Petitions. Virginia. 1700-75. *999*
—. Economics. Political systems. ca 1920-72. *1247*
—. Employment. Program failure. Rescue missions. Skid rows. Social Reform. 1960's-70's. *2524*
Public Schools *See also* High Schools; Schools.
—. Acculturation. Church Schools. Mexican Americans. Texas (San Antonio). 1973. *677*
—. Acculturation. Educational reform. Immigration. 19c-1910's. *532*
—. Anderson, James T. M. Anti-Catholicism. Saskatchewan. School Act (Saskatchewan, 1930; amended). Secularization. 1929-34. *575*
—. Baptists. City Government. Maryland (Baltimore). Negroes. Political protest. 1865-1900. *583*
—. Bible reading. Letters. Massachusetts (Amesbury). Whittier, John Greenleaf. 1853. *577*
—. Boycotts. Church Schools. Mexican Americans. Mexican Presbyterian Mission School. Presbyterian Church. Segregation. Texas (San Angelo). 1910-15. *618*
—. Bryan, William Jennings. Church and state. Darwinism. Evolution. Fundamentalism. 1920-73. *2317*
—. California. Catholic Church. Homosexuality. Proposition 6 (1978). Referendum. Teachers. 1978. *1320*
—. Catholic Church. Children. Occupational status. Socialization. -1974. *3784*
—. Catholic Church. Compulsory education. Edwards Law (Illinois, 1889). Ethnic Groups. Illinois. Private schools. State Politics. 1889-93. *551*
—. Catholic Church. Judaism. Lutheran Church. Ohio (Cincinnati). Religious Education. 19c. *545*
—. Church and state. 1940-60. *582*
—. Church and State. Church schools. Conscientious objection. Holidays. Prayer. Public finance. Religious Liberty. Supreme Court. 1950-70's. *1112*
—. Church of England. Clergy. Episcopal Church, Protestant. Ingraham, Joseph Holt. Novels. Prisons. Reform. Tennessee (Nashville). 1847-51. *3241*
—. Doukhobors. Saskatchewan. 1905-50. *533*
—. Educational Policy. Fundamentalism. Textbooks. West Virginia (Kanawha County). 1975. *576*
—. *Engel* v. *Vitale* (US, 1962). New York. Nonsectarianism. Prayer. Public opinion. 1962. *581*
—. Immigration. Protestantism. 1890-1970. *546*
—. Mormons. National Education Association. Sinclair, Upton. Teachers. Utah. 1920-24. *567*
—. Religious studies. Social sciences. 1979. *558*
Public Welfare *See also* Charities; Children; Day Nurseries; Hospitals; Social Work.
—. Adoption policies. Children. 1954-71. *845*
—. Hoover, Herbert C. Johnson, Lyndon B. Nixon, Richard M. Protestant ethic. Rhetoric. Roosevelt, Franklin D. Weber, Max. 1905-79. *348*
Publications. Communes. Labor Department. Library of Congress. Western states. 1830's-1930's. *430*
Publications programs. Baptists, Southern. Foreign Mission Board. Missions and Missionaries. 1899-1976. *1708*
Publishers and Publishing *See also* Books; Copyright; Editors and Editing; Press; Printing.
—. Adventists. Australia. Missions and Missionaries. Palmer, Edwin R. 1894-1915. *2968*
—. Adventists. California (Mountain View, Oakland). Jones, Charles Harriman. Pacific Press Publishing Company. 1879-1923. *362*
—. Aitken, Robert. Bible. Continental Congress. 1777-82. *1983*
—. Aitken, Robert. Bible. Continental Congress. English language. Pennsylvania (Philadelphia). 1782. *1979*
—. Buettner, George L. Concordia Publishing House. Lutheran Church (Missouri Synod). Missouri (St. Louis). Personal Narratives. 1888-1955. *336*
—. China (Shanghai). Methodist Episcopal Church, South. Missions and Missionaries. 1898-1920. *1737*
—. Clergy. McGown, A. J. Presbyterian Church, Cumberland. *Texas Presbyterian* (newspaper). 1846-73. *3586*
—. Clergy. Puritanism. 1630-1763. *1991*
—. Composers. Hymnals. Music. New England. Thomas, Isaiah. 1784-19c. *1936*
—. Franklin, Benjamin. Friendship. Morality. Religious liberty. Whitefield, George. 1739-70. *58*
Puck (periodical). Cartoons and Caricatures. Mormons. Stereotypes. 1904-07. *2001*
Pueblo Indians. Indians. Mexican Americans. Navajo Indians. Southwest. Witchcraft. 19c-1930's. *2214*
Pueblo Revolt (1680). Catholic Church. Indians. Missions and Missionaries. Southwest. 1590-1680. *1499*
Puerto Rico. Adolescents. Hispanic Americans. Identity. Mexico. Religiosity. Whites. 1970's. *108*
—. Americanization. Missions and Missionaries. Protestant Churches. 1898-1917. *1734*
—. Bishops. Byrne, Edwin V. Caruana, George J. Catholic Church. Jones, William A. San Juan Diocese. 1866-1963. *3814*
—. Catholic Church. Church and State. Law. ca 1863-1908. *1041*
—. Catholic University of Puerto Rico. Colleges and Universities. 1900's-74. *652*
—. Cult practices. Psychotherapy. Social organization. Spiritualism. 1975. *1445*
—. Documents. Episcopal Church, Protestant. Missions and Missionaries. 1870-1952. *1679*
—. Education. Missions and Missionaries. Presbyterian Church. Social Customs. 1898-1917. *1727*
—. Folk art. Lithography. Mexico. Southwest. 1300-1974. *1868*
—. Missions and Missionaries. Presbyterian Church. 1899-1914. *1728*
Pulp mills. Capitalism. Catholic Church. Clergy. Elites. Quebec (Chicoutimi). Working class. 1896-1930. *2601*
Purdie, James Eustace. Canada. Pentecostal Assemblies of Canada. Pentecostal Bible School. Religious education. Theology. 1925-50. *747*
Puritan Tradition. American Revolution. Hawthorne, Nathaniel. Literature. National character. 1775-83. 1830-40. *2082*
—. Civil religion. Democracy. Ideology. Political institutions. 17c-20c. *1150*
—. Civil War. North or Northern States. South. 1840's-60's. *2842*
—. Hawthorne, Nathaniel. History. Novels. Social reform. Symbolism in Literature. 1825-63. *2019*
—. Idealism. National characteristics. Pluralism. 1620's-1940's. *1*
Puritanism. Almanacs. Astronomy. Infinity (concept). New England. 1650-85. *2325*
—. American Revolution. 1630-1776. *956*
—. Antinomianism. Emerson, Ralph Waldo. Sermons. Social reform. Transcendentalism. 1820's-30's. *4070*
—. Behavior. Pregnancy. Sex. Social control. 1640-1971. *949*
—. Citizenship. Democracy. Jefferson, Thomas. Locke, John. 17c-18c. *1408*
—. Clergy. Publishers and Publishing. 1630-1763. *1991*
—. Communion. New England. Stoddard, Solomon. 1679. *3614*
—. Conservatism. Ideology. 17c. *1361*
—. Conversion. Germany. Great Britain. Lutheran Church. Pietism. 17c-18c. *2942*
—. Covenant Theology. Divine Sovereignty. Ethics. 17c-18c. *3618*
—. Dickinson, Emily. Identity. Intellectual history. Myths and Symbols. Poetry. Transcendentalism. Women. 1860's. *51*
—. Emotions. Intellect. Psychology, faculty. 17c. *2313*
—. Enlightenment. National self-image. Pietism. 17c-20c. *1184*
—. Gorton, Samuel. Great Britain. Massachusetts. Radicals and Radicalism. Rhode Island. Rhode Island. Theology. 1636-77. *2862*
—. Great Britain. 1560-1660. *3617*
—. Historiography. Miller, Perry. New England. 1620-1775. 1939-74. *258*
—. Literature. Romanticism. 1620-1946. *2016*
—. Milton, John. Transcendentalism. 1820's-30's. *2731*
—. Science. Winthrop, John (1714-79). 1738-79. *2315*
—. Skinner, B. F. ca 1730-1974. *2339*
Puritans *See also* Calvinism; Church of England; Congregationalism; Pilgrims.
—. Abolition Movement. Attitudes. New England. Slavery. 1641-1776. *2164*
—. Adams, John. American Revolution. New England. Paine, Thomas. Political theory. Rhetoric. 17c-1770's. *1424*
—. Agnosticism. Ingersoll, Robert. Winthrop, John. ca 1630-1890's. *54*
—. American Revolution. Christian humanism. Political attitudes. Values. 18c. *1395*
—. American Revolution. Ideology. Literature. 1775-83. 19c. *1344*
—. Anthropology. Historiography. Massachusetts (Salem). Psychology. Witchcraft. 1691-92. *2187*
—. Anti-Catholicism. Antichrist. Edwards, Jonathan. Mather, Cotton. Potter, Francis. ca 1700-58. *2937*
—. Antinomian Controversy. Church and state. Hutchinson, Anne. Massachusetts. Social Organization. Trials. Women. 1637. *1135*
—. Antinomian Controversy. Cotton, John. Hutchinson, Anne. Massachusetts (Boston). 1636. *3652*
—. Antinomian controversy. Hutchinson, Anne. Massachusetts (Boston). Trials. Winthrop, John. 1634-38. *3641*
—. Antinomianism. Cotton, John. Eliot, John. Government. Millenarianism. Missions and Missionaries. New England. Rhode Island (Portsmouth). 1630-90. *3635*
—. Antinomianism. Hutchinson, Anne. Language. Massachusetts. Trials. 1636-38. *3609*
—. Antislavery sentiments. New England. 1652-1795. *2485*
—. Assimilation. Eliot, John. Indians. Massachusetts. Praying towns. 1646-74. *1592*
—. Assurance, doctrine of. Hooker, Thomas. New England. Theology. 1630-60. *3644*
—. Attitudes. 1630's-80's. *3602*

—. Attitudes. Hymnals. New England. Regular Singing movement. 1720's. *1933*
—. Attitudes. Jeremiads. Sports. 1620-1720. *3658*
—. Attitudes. Mather, Cotton. New England. Sermons. Women. 1650-1800. *880*
—. Attitudes. Poetry. 16c-17c. *1973*
—. Axtell, James (review article). Education. New England. Social Organization. 17c-18c. 1974. *526*
—. Baltzell, E. Digby (review article). Friends, Society of. Massachusetts (Boston). Pennsylvania (Philadelphia). Social Classes. 17c-1979. *2920*
—. Baptism. Baptists. Great Britain (London). Jessey, Henry. Letters. New England. Toleration. Tombes, John. 1645. *997*
—. Bercovitch, Sacvan (review article). Massachusetts. Mather, Cotton. National Characteristics. 17c-18c. 1975. *3630*
—. Bible. Music. New England. Pythagoreanism. 1640-1726. *1912*
—. Bibliographies. Discovery and Exploration. Historians. Morison, Samuel Eliot (obituary). 1887-1976. *233*
—. Bibliographies. New England. Sermons. 1652-1700. 1903. *1964*
—. Bosom serpentry (concept). Folklore. Mormons. New England. Snakes. Utah. 17c-19c. *2765*
—. Botany. Friends, Society of. Logan, James. Mather, Cotton. Natural History. New England. 17c-18c. *2300*
—. Boyer, Paul. Massachusetts (Salem). Nissenbaum, Stephen. Witchcraft (review article). 1550-1690. 1974-76. *2200*
—. Bradstreet, Anne. Clap, Roger. Devotions. New England. Sewall, Samuel. Shepard, Thomas. Worship. 17c. *3627*
—. Bradstreet, Anne. Elegies. Massachusetts. Poetry. Women. 1665. *2044*
—. Bradstreet, Anne. Hutchinson, Anne. Literature. Massachusetts. Social change. Theology. Women. 1630's-70's. *865*
—. Brattle Street Church. Coleman, Benjamin. Elites. Gentility (concept). Massachusetts (Boston). 1715-45. *2622*
—. Bulkeley, Peter (and family). Covenant theology. Massachusetts (Concord). 1635-1731. *3645*
—. Bulkeley, Peter *(Gospel-Covenant).* Covenant theology. Massachusetts. 1640's-50's. *3636*
—. Calling (concept). Equality. Great Chain of Being (theme). Protestant Ethic. 17c-18c. *340*
—. Calvinism. Cotton, John. Elegies. Fiske, John. New England. Poetry. 17c. *1985*
—. Calvinism. Massachusetts (Boston). Parishes. Switzerland (Geneva). 16c-17c. *3631*
—. Cambridge Platform. Church and state. Massachusetts. 1630-79. *1017*
—. Cartoons and Caricatures. Great Britain. New England. Satire. 1770-76. *2005*
—. Charles I. Cotton, John. Great Britain. Massachusetts (Boston). Regicide. Sermons. 1650. *1349*
—. Children. Death and Dying. New England. 17c-1750. *929*
—. Christmas carols. Great Britain. Music. Virginia. 1662-70. *2787*
—. Church and Social Problems. Church membership. Half-Way Covenant. Massachusetts (Dorchester). Religious scrupulosity. 1660-1730. *3601*
—. Church and State. College of William and Mary. Harvard University. Yale University. 1636-1700. *650*
—. Church History. Court records. Excommunication. Massachusetts (Salem). 1629-80. *3600*
—. Church membership. Half-Way Covenant. Massachusetts. 1662. *3624*
—. Church Membership. New England. 1620-1700. *3655*
—. Church of England. James, Henry *(The American).* National Characteristics. 1700-1880. *2036*
—. City Planning. Connecticut (New Haven). 1628-39. *3598*
—. Civil religion. Europe. Rousseau, Jean-Jacques. 18c-20c. *1177*
—. Civil War. Disasters. Lincoln, Abraham. Rhetoric. Sermons. 1650-1870. *1968*
—. Clergy. Great Britain. Immigration. New England. 1629-65. *3661*
—. Clergy. Historiography. New England. Women. 1668-1735. *936*
—. Clergy. New England. 17c. *3599*
—. Clergy (tenure). Higginson, John. Massachusetts (Salem). Nicholet, Charles. Social change. 1672-76. *3620*
—. Clothing. Legislation. New England. Social Status. 1630-90. *2427*
—. Cobbett, Thomas *(Practical Discourse of Prayer).* New England. Prayer. 1630-85. *3607*
—. Coffman, Ralph J. (review article). Stoddard, Solomon. 1660's-1729. 1978. *3615*
—. Colonization. New England. Pragmatism. Social Change. 1620-90. *3608*
—. Commerce. 17c. *373*
—. Communion. Mather, Increase. Sermons. ca 1680-1710. *3629*
—. Connecticut. Constitutional Law. Government. Hooker, Thomas. 1635-39. *3603*
—. Connecticut. Ethics. Fitch, James. Land. Politics. 1679-1727. *3646*
—. Connecticut (Milford). Family. 1639-90's. *897*
—. Consensus. Ideology. National Characteristics. 1630-1865. *1345*
—. Conversion. Hooker, Thomas. Preparationism. Ramus, Petrus. Shepard, Thomas. Theology. 1608-49. *3643*
—. Conversion. New England. Semiology. Theology. 1600's. *3612*
—. Conversion. Preparationism. Stoddard, Solomon. Taylor, Edward. Theology. 1690-94. *3642*
—. Converts. Indians. Massachusetts (Martha's Vineyard). Mayhew, Thomas, Jr. Missions and Missionaries. 1645-57. *1635*
—. Converts. Personality. Psychology. 1630-1740. *3640*
—. Covenant theology. Edwards, Jonathan. Great Awakening. 18c. *2219*
—. Covenant theology. New England. Poetry. Wigglesworth, Michael *(Day of Doom).* 1662. *3597*
—. Crime and Criminals. Massachusetts (Middlesex County). Social classes. 17c. *3616*
—. Death and Dying. Infants. New England. Parents. Theology. 1620-1720. *925*
—. Death and Dying. New England. 17c-18c. *3651*
—. Diaries. Massachusetts (Cambridge). Piety. Shepard, Thomas. 1640-44. *3656*
—. Divorce. Law. Massachusetts. Social conditions. Women. 1639-92. *941*
—. Drunkenness. New England. 17c. *2590*
—. Earthquakes. Literature. New England. 1727. *2289*
—. Education. Great Britain. Greaves, Richard L. Mather (family). Middlekauff, Robert. New England. 1596-1728. *607*
—. Edwards, Jonathan. Millenarianism. Mission, concept of. New England. 18c. *1154*
—. Eliot, John. Indians. Massachusetts. Missions and Missionaries. 1620-80. *1624*
—. Eliot, John. Indians. Massachusetts (Natick). Missions and Missionaries. 1646-74. *1602*
—. Elites. Immigrants. Local government. Massachusetts (Charlestown). 1630-40. *3613*
—. Enlightenment. Mather, Cotton. Theology. 1680-1728. *3657*
—. Erikson, Erik H. Excommunication. First Church. Hibbens, Ann. Massachusetts (Boston). Rites and Ceremonies. 1640-41. 1960's-70's. *3610*
—. Family. Government. Ideology. Massachusetts. Social cohesion. 1630-85. *3606*
—. Fiction. Hawthorne, Nathaniel. Massachusetts. Philosophy of History. 1820's-60's. *2081*
—. Fiske, John. Poetry. Taylor, Edward. Tree of Life metaphor. 1650-1721. *1969*
—. Folklore. New England. Sermons. 1625-60. *1981*
—. Friends, Society of. Howgill, Francis. New England. Persecution. ca 1650-60. *1027*
—. Godfrey, John. Massachusetts. Social Conditions. Trials. Witchcraft. 1634-75. *2186*
—. Great Awakening. New England. Religious Education. 1690-1750. *655*
—. Great Britain. Jeremiads. New England. Pamphlets. Ward, Nathaniel. 1645-50. *1975*
—. Great Britain. Local government. Massachusetts. New England. Political theory. Social change. 1600-50. *3604*
—. Great Britain. New England. Rhetoric. Sermons. 1620's-50's. *1980*
—. Historians. Morison, Samuel Eliot (obituary). *New England Quarterly* (periodical). 1928-76. *276*
—. Historiography. Indian-White Relations. Missions and Missionaries. New England. Theology. 17c-20c. *1641*
—. Historiography. Massachusetts. Political Systems. Suffrage. 1620-99. 1954-74. *1350*
—. Historiography. Mather, Cotton *(Magnalia Christi Americana).* Winthrop, John. 1702. *1966*
—. Historiography. Morison, Samuel Eliot (obituary). 1887-1976. *172*
—. Historiography, neoconservative. New England. Social Organization. 17c. 1930's-60's. *3619*
—. Hooker, Thomas. Mather, Cotton. Rhetoric. Winthrop, John. 17c. *1965*
—. Humanism. Mather, Cotton *(Magnalia Christi Americana).* Renaissance. Rhetoric. 1702. *1996*
—. Iconography. New England. Poetry. Sermons. Tombstones. 17c. *1977*
—. Immigrants. Massachusetts. 1590-1660. *3605*
—. Indians. Irish. Massachusetts. Stereotypes. 17c. *2144*
—. Indians. Massachusetts. Morton, Thomas. Pilgrims. Values. 1625-45. *2956*
—. Indian-White Relations. New England. Race. 1620-90. *2150*
—. Indian-White Relations. Racism. 17c. *2136*
—. Jeremiads. New England. Sermons. Sports. 17c-18c. *3659*
—. Jews. New England. Old Testament. Pilgrims. 1620-1700. *2936*
—. Kibbutzim. New England. Palestine. Social Organization. Towns. 17c. 20c. *3633*
—. Levin, David (review article). Mather, Cotton. 1663-1703. 1978. *3625*
—. Literature. Murdock, Kenneth Ballard (obituary). 20c. *225*
—. Lucas, Paul R. New England (review article). Social Organization. VanDeventer, David E. 1623-1741. 1976. *3621*
—. Manuscripts. Massachusetts. Mather, Increase. Theology. 1670's. *3628*
—. Massachusetts. Mather, Cotton *(Life of Phips).* Phips, William. Politics. 1690-1705. *3622*
—. Massachusetts. Mather, Increase. Millenarianism. "New Jerusalem" (manuscript). 1669-1710. *3632*
—. Massachusetts. Sports. 1630-1730. *3654*
—. Massachusetts. Taylor, Edward. Taylor, Thomas *(Christ Revealed).* Typology. 1635-98. *3649*
—. Massachusetts (Boston). Mather, Cotton. Psalmody. Sermons. Singing. 1721. *1938*
—. Massachusetts (Springfield). Parsons case. Witchcraft. 1650-55. *2210*
—. Massachusetts (Westfield). Sermons. Taylor, Edward ("Upon the Types of the Old Testament"). Theology. Typology. 1693. *3638*
—. Mather, Cotton *(Essays to Do Good).* Morality. Social Organization. 1700-25. *331*
—. Mather, Cotton *(Magnalia Christi Americana).* Morality. New England. Suffering (meaning). 1690's-1702. *3626*
—. Miller, Perry *(The New England Mind: The Seventeenth Century).* New England. 17c. 1939. *257*
—. Myths and Symbols. New England. Regionalism. Theology. 17c. *3611*
—. Nebraska (Lincoln). Sermons. Taylor, Edward ("Upon the Types of the Old Testament"). Theology. Typology. 1693-1706. *3639*
—. New England. Pilgrims. 1606-1790. *2886*
—. New England. Price controls. 1629-76. *2570*
—. New England. Psychology, faculty. Stoddard, Solomon *(Safety of Appearing).* 1630-1746. *2299*
—. New England. Recreation. 17c. *3660*
—. New England. Satire. Ward, Nathaniel *(The Simple Cobler of Aggawam in America).* 1647. *3647*
—. New England. Scientific thought. Winthrop, John. Winthrop, John, Jr. Winthrop, John (1714-79). 1620-1779. *2295*
—. New England. Sermons. Sex roles. Theology. Women. 1690-1730. *883*
—. New England. Stoddard, Solomon. Theology. 1672-1729. *3634*
—. New England. Witchcraft. Women. ca 1630-1978. *2185*
—. Oakes, Urian *(Elegie).* Poetry. 1650-81. *1976*
—. Painting. Poetry. Smith, Thomas. ca 1690. *1839*
—. Pietists. Radical catholicity principle. Theology. 17c-18c. *2950*
—. Plymouth Colony. Property. 1621-75. *2569*

—. Poetry. Proverbs. Taylor, Edward ("Gods Determinations"). 1685. 1973. *1963*
—. Poetry. Science. Taylor, Edward. 1706. *2342*
Puritans (review article). Elliott, Emory. New England. Sabbath. Sermons. Solberg, Winton U. 17c-18c. 1975-77. *3623*
—. Holifield, E. Brooks. Lowrie, Ernest Benson. New England. Sacraments. Theology. Willard, Samuel. 16c-17c. 1974. *3637*
Pusey, Caleb. Friends, Society of. Keith, George. Pennsylvania. Schisms. Theology. 17c. *3273*
Pusey, Edward Bouverie. Bishops. Church of England. Letters. Medley, John. New Brunswick (Fredericton). Oxford Movement. ca 1840-44. *3190*
Pythagoreanism. Bible. Music. New England. Puritans. 1640-1726. *1912*

Q

Quakers. *See* Friends, Society of.
Quapaw Indians. Catholic Church. Church finance. Education. Indian-White Relations. Oklahoma. 1876-1927. *3727*
Quebec. Agnosticism. Catholic Church. Colleges and Universities. Students. 1970-78. *505*
—. Apostolic Delegates. Catholic Church. Conroy, George. Nationalism. Politics. Vatican. 1877-78. *1098*
—. Art. Catholic Church. Folk religion. French Canadians. Musée Historique de Vaudreuil. 17c-20c. *174*
—. Association Catholique de la Jeunesse Canadienne-Française. Catholic Church. French Canadians. Morality. 1903-14. *2355*
—. Attitudes. Catholic Church. Death and Dying. Wills. 1663-1760. *3718*
—. Barbeau, Victor. Catholic Church. Cooperatives. Medical Reform. Paquette, Albiny. Politics. 1900-45. *3874*
—. Bishops. Catholic Church. Sherbrooke Diocese. 1868-72. *3882*
—. Black, Conrad. Catholic Church. Church and state. Duplessis, Maurice (review article). Provincial Government. Rumilly, Robert. 1930's-77. *1124*
—. Bourassa, Henri. Catholic Church. Politics. Provincial Government. 1902-71. *976*
—. British Empire. Catholic Church. Ideology. Imperialism. 19c-20c. *1411*
—. *Brown* v. *Les Curé et Marguilliers de l'Oeuvre et de la Fabrique de la Paroisse de Montréal* (1874). Catholic Church. Church and state. Guibord, Joseph. Liberalism. Politics. Ultramontanism. 1870-74. *1067*
—. Canada. Catholic Church. Education. French Canadians. Rinfret, Fernand. Siegfried, André *(Le Canada, les deux races: Problèmes politiques contemporains)*. Social Sciences. 1906-07. *3873*
—. Canada, western. Catholic Church. French Canadians. Historiography. Migration, Internal. 1870-1915. *3819*
—. Catholic Church. Church and State. 18c-20c. *1070*
—. Catholic Church. Church and state. Great Britain. Military government. Protestantism. 18c. *1125*
—. Catholic Church. Church Finance. Economic Development. LaRocque, Paul. Sherbrooke Diocese. 1893-1926. *3783*
—. Catholic Church. Church names. Toponymy. 1600-1925. *3841*
—. Catholic Church. Cistercians. Mistassini, monastery of. Trappists. 1900-03. *3721*
—. Catholic Church. Clergy. Working conditions. 1968-77. *3861*
—. Catholic Church. Colonial Government. Intendants. 1633-1760. *1030*
—. Catholic Church. Debt. LaRocque, Charles. St. Hyacinthe Diocese. 1866-73. *3695*
—. Catholic Church. École Sociale Populaire. Labor Unions and Organizations. Social Change. 1911-75. *1469*
—. Catholic Church. Economic development. Social Conditions. 1850-1950. *3743*
—. Catholic Church. Economic Theory. French Canadians. Minville, Esdras. 20c. *2558*
—. Catholic Church. Fédération Nationale Saint-Jean-Baptiste. Feminism. Gérin-Lajoie, Marie. 1907-33. *870*
—. Catholic Church. Feminism. Religious Orders. Women. 1640-1975. *833*
—. Catholic Church. French Canadians. Groulx, Lionel. Secularism. Separatist Movements. 1897-1928. *1409*
—. Catholic Church. French Canadians. LaPatrie (colony). New England. Repatriation Act (Canada, 1875). ca 1875-80. *3792*
—. Catholic Church. French Canadians. Minville, Esdras (eulogy). 1975. *3674*
—. Catholic Church. French Canadians. Self-perception. Social Customs. Values. 17c-1978. *3789*
—. Catholic Church. French Canadians. Social Organization. Women. 1960's-70's. *2013*
—. Catholic Church. Government. Parish registers. 1539-1973. *3694*
—. Catholic Church. Groulx, Lionel. 1895-1905. *3688*
—. Catholic Church. Hospitals. Hôtel-Dieu. Indian-White Relations. 1635-98. *1446*
—. Catholic Church. International Union of Catholic Women's Leagues (congress). Italy (Rome). Suffrage. Women. 1922. *935*
—. Catholic Church. Laval, François de. 17c. *3766*
—. Catholic Church. Nationalism. 1608-1978. *1012*
—. Catholic Church. Professions. Religious orders. Secondary education. Women. 1908-54. *871*
—. Catholic Church. Social Change. 17c. 20c. *3876*
—. Catholicism. French Canadians. Lévesque, Georges-Henri. Nationalism. Personal narratives. Youth movements. 1930's. *3790*
—. Christianity. Cooperatives. 1940-78. *2574*
—. Diseases (classification). Etiology. Folk Medicine. 1976-77. *1428*
—. Earthquakes. Jesuits. *Relation de 1663* (report). 1663. *2296*
—. Family. France. Protestantism. Trade. 1740-60. *333*
—. French Canadians. Literature. Patriotism. Sociology. 19c. *2085*
—. Immigration. Mennonites. Passenger lists. Russia. 1874-80. *3364*
—. Jesuits. Lacouture, Onésime. Spiritual movement. 1931-50. *3730*
—. Jesuits. Land Tenure. Legislation. Mercier, Honoré. Protestant Churches. 1886. *1087*
Quebec Archdiocese. Atlantic Provinces. Bishops. Catholic Church. Diaries. Plessis, Joseph-Octave. 1812-15. *3704*
Quebec (Beauce County). Catholic Church. Devotions, popular. Shrines, roadside. Social customs. 1970's. *1788*
Quebec (Brome County). Benedictines. St. Benoît-du-Lac (abbey). 1955-79. *1770*
Quebec (Chicoutimi). Capitalism. Catholic Church. Clergy. Elites. Pulp mills. Working class. 1896-1930. *2601*
Quebec (Chicoutimi Basin). Catholic Church. Eudists. Industrialization. Working class. 1903-30. *1466*
Quebec (Compton County). Catholic Church. French Canadians. Migration, Internal. Parishes. Rural-Urban Studies. 1851-91. *3791*
Quebec (Drummond County). Catholic Church. Drummond County Mechanics Institute. Farmers. Labor Unions and Organizations. 1856-90. *1472*
Quebec (Eastern Townships). Catholic Church. Missions and Missionaries. Social Conditions. 1825-53. *1568*
—. Catholicism. Colonization. French Canadians. Settlement. 1800-60. *3780*
Quebec (Gaspé). Bishops. Catholic Church. Education. Medicine. Ross, François Xavier. Social Conditions. 1923-45. *3787*
Quebec (Hébertville, Lake St. John). Catholic Church. Settlement. ca 1840-1900. *3847*
Quebec (Hull). Labor. Match industry. Syndicat Catholique des Allumettières. Women. 1919-24. *1470*
Quebec (Lake St. John, Portneuf counties). Catholic Church. Cults. Devotions, popular. 1970's. *3851*
Quebec (Lower Canada). Anti-Catholicism. Church and state. Ethnic groups. Evangelism. Protestantism. Rebellion of 1837. 1766-1865. *2110*
—. Canada. Catholic Church. Clergy. Craig, James Henry. French Canadians. Nationalism. Political repression. 1810. *1319*
—. Economic Development. Government. Social classes. Ultramontanism. 19c. *962*
—. Methodist Episcopal Church. Missions and Missionaries. Ontario (Upper Canada). 1788-1812. *1580*
Quebec (Mattawinie district). Catholic Church. Colonization. Economic development. French Canadians. Geopolitics. Provost, T. S. 17c-1890. *3809*
Quebec (Montreal). Bishops. Church of England. Councils and Synods. Fulford, Francis. 1850-68. *3209*
—. Bourget, Ignace. Catholic Church. Church History. Faillon, Etienne-Michel. Letters. 1850. *3824*
—. Brotherhood of the Holy Family. Catholic Church. Chaumonot, Joseph-Marie-Pierre. Elites. Laval, François de. 1663-1760. *3717*
—. Catholic Church. École Sociale Populaire. Propaganda. Syndicalism. Working Class. 1911-49. *1473*
—. Catholic Church. Olier, Jean Jacques. Sulpicians. 1630's-50's. *3798*
—. Child care. Day Nurseries. Dominicans. Women. 1858-1920. *2505*
—. Church Schools. Education. Hasidism (Lubavitch). Judaism. 1969-71. *550*
—. Conservatism. Protestants. Social Reform. Women's Protective Immigration Society. 1882-1917. *919*
—. Hasidism. Judaism. 1942-71. *4179*
—. Immigration. Jews. Morocco. 1960's-70's. *4121*
—. Labor. Occupations. Sex roles. Women. 1911-41. *1471*
Quebec (Oka). Algonkin Indians. Architecture. Calvary (chapels). Iroquois Indians. Missionaries. Sulpicians. 1700's-1800's. *1811*
—. Catholic Church. Language. Métis. Missions and Missionaries. Religious Education. Rocheblave, Charlotte de. 19c. *1507*
Quebec (Quebec). Bourget, Ignace. Catholic Church. Colleges and Universities. Laval University. 1840's-50's. *676*
—. Catholic Church. Charities. Irish Canadians. McMahon, Patrick. Poor. St. Bridget's Home. 1847-1972. *2521*
—. Catholic Church. Needlework. Ursulines. ca 1655-1890's. *1850*
Quebec (review article). Catholic Church. Clergy. 19c. 1979. *3840*
Quebec (Rimouski). Action Catholique. Catholic Church. Courchesne, Georges. 1940-67. *2356*
Quebec (Saguenay). Bishops. Catholic Church. Chicoutimi, Séminaire de. 1873-1973. *721*
—. Catholic Church. Chicoutimi, Petit-Séminaire de. Religious Education. Students. 1873-1930. *756*
Quebec (Sherbrooke). Emigration. Foreign Relations. France. Trappists. 1903-14. *3785*
Quebec (Three Rivers). Church of England. Clergy. Education. Missions and Missionaries. Wood, Samuel. 1822-68. *3202*
Queen's College. Canada. Great Britain. Ontario (Kingston, Smith Falls). Romanes, George. Romanes, George John. Science. Scientific Experiments and Research. Theology. 1830-90. *2918*
—. Church of England. Morris, William. Ontario (Kingston). Presbyterians. 1836-42. *711*
Quiltmaking. Amish. Folk Art. Mennonites. Pennsylvania. Persecution. 16c-1935. *1893*
—. Brethren churches. Pennsylvania, southeastern. 1700-1974. *1891*
Quimby, Phineas Parkhurst. Eddy, Mary Baker. Hypnotism. New England. Psychiatry. 1820's-66. *1442*
—. New Thought movement. Philosophy. 1850's-1917. *62*
Quinte Mission. Canada. Fort Frontenac. Indian-White Relations. Iroquois Indians. Missions and Missionaries. Sulpician order. 1665-80. *1610*

R

Rabbinical Council of America. Judaism (Orthodox). Jung, Leo. 1926-42. *4171*
Rabbis. Adelman, Samuel. Colorado (Denver). Congregation Beth Ha Medrosh Hagodol. Judaism (Conservative, Orthodox). Kauvar, Charles E. H. 1949-58. *4193*
—. Alpert, Abraham. Immigration. Judaism. Massachusetts (Boston). 20c. *4087*
—. Americanization. Judaism. Law. Rabbis (responsa). Social customs. 1862-1937. *300*
—. Assimilation. Jews. Reading. 1970's. *4132*
—. Berger, Elmer. Judaism (Reform). Personal Narratives. Zionism. ca 1945-75. *4202*
—. Blum, Abraham. California (Los Angeles). Judaism (Reform). New York City. Texas (Galveston). 1866-1921. *4217*

—. California. Charities. Disaster relief. Economic aid. Jews. Nieto, Jacob. San Francisco Earthquake and Fire. 1906. 2520
—. California. Franklin, Harvey B. Jews. Personal narratives. 1916-57. 4099
—. California (Los Angeles). Church finance. Judaism (Reform). Wilshire Boulevard Temple. 1897. 4231
—. California (Los Angeles). Judaism (Reform). Letters. Newmark, Joseph. Wilshire Boulevard Temple. 1881. 4236
—. California (Sacramento). Judaism (Reform). Letters. Levy, J. Leonard. 1892. 4219
—. California (Sacramento, San Francisco). Henry, Henry Abraham. Issacs, Samuel Meyer. Jews. Letters. Travel (accounts). 1858. 4106
—. California (San Francisco). *Emanu-El* (newspaper). Immigration. Jews, East European. Letters-to-the-editor. Rosenthal, Marcus. Voorsanger, Jacob. 1905. 4141
—. California (San Francisco). Franklin, Lewis Abraham. Judaism. Sermons. Yom Kippur. 1850. 4100
—. California (San Francisco). Henry, Henry Abraham. Judaism. 1857-69. 4107
—. California (San Francisco). Jews. Nieto, Jacob. Rubin, Max. Temple Sherith Israel. 1893. 4148
—. California (Stockton). Davidson, Herman. Judaism (Reform). Opera. Russia. 1846-1911. 4204
—. Canon law. Circumcision. Europe. Illowy, Bernard. Judaism (Orthodox). Louisiana (New Orleans). 1853-65. 4176
—. Charities. Ecumenism. Hungarian Americans. Judaism (Reform). Wise, Stephen Samuel. World War II. Zionism. 1890's-1949. 4229
—. Congregation Kahal Kadosh Beth Israel. Georgia (Macon). Judaism. Leeser, Isaac. Letters. Loewenthal, Henry. 1854-70. 4124
—. Congregation Sons of Zion. Finesilver, Moses Ziskind. Judaism. Rhode Island (Providence). 1880-83. 4122
—. Fasman, Oscar Z. Hebrew Theological College. Judaism (Orthodox). Oklahoma (Tulsa). Ontario (Ottawa). Personal narratives. 1929-79. 4177
—. Franklin, Leo M. Judaism. Nebraska (Omaha). Temple Israel. 1892-99. 4094
—. Hebrew Union College. Judaism, Reform. Letters. Prager, Abraham J. Wise, Isaac Mayer. 1854-1900. 4227
—. Hebrew Union College. Judaism (Reform). Letters. Stolz, Joseph. Wise, Isaac Mayer. 1882-1900. 4220
—. Hebrew Union College. Judaism (Reform). Ohio (Cincinnati). Seminaries. Wise, Isaac Mayer. 1817-90's. 701
—. Hertzberg, Arthur. Historians. Judaism (Conservative). 1980. 4167
—. Hertzberg, Arthur. Judaism (Conservative). Personal narratives. 1940's-79. 4168
—. Judaism (Reform). Kerman, Julius C. Palestine. Personal narratives. World War I. 1913-71. 4214
Rabbis (responsa). Americanization. Judaism. Law. Rabbis. Social customs. 1862-1937. 300
Race. Debates. Ecumenism. Methodist Episcopal Church. Methodist Episcopal Church (South). Virginia. 1924-25. 467
—. Indian-White Relations. New England. Puritans. 1620-90. 2150
Race (issue). Ahlstrom, Sydney E. Christianity (review article). Handy, Robert T. Historiography. Marty, Martin E. 16c-1978. 2743
Race Relations *See also* Acculturation; Discrimination; Emigration; Ethnology; Human Relations; Immigration; Indian-White Relations; Negroes.
—. Baptists. Social change. Violence. 1960-69. 2420
—. Baptists, Southern. Civil Rights. Leadership. Texas. 1954-68. 2553
—. Baptists, Southern. First Baptist Church. Merry, Nelson. Tennessee (Nashville). 1810-65. 3078
—. Chapman, John Jay. Christianity. Lynching. Pennsylvania (Coatesville). Poetry. Rhetoric. Speeches, Addresses, etc. 1912. 1971
—. Cheshire, Joseph Blount, Jr. Episcopal Church, Protestant. Negroes. North Carolina. Paternalism. 1870-1932. 2140
—. Chinese Americans. Immigrants. Presbyterian Church. 1851-1977. 3561
—. Christianity. Negroes. 1939-79. 2544
—. *Christianity Today*, periodical. Civil rights. Evangelicalism. Malone College. 1956-59. 2549
—. Church of Christ. Evangelism. Keeble, Marshall. 1878-1968. 2550
—. Civil rights movement. Episcopal Church, Protestant. Theology. 1800-1965. 2540
—. Clergy. Negroes. Protestant churches. South. ca 1800-65. 2816
—. Evangelicalism. Jones, Charles Colcock. South. Utopias. 1804-63. 2543
—. Florida (Tallahassee). Negroes. Protestant Churches. Social control. 1865-85. 2864
—. Missions and Missionaries. Presbyterian Church. 1562-1977. 3535
—. Mormons. Negroes. Theology. 1831-1973. 4058
—. Reform. Social gospel. 1877-98. 2412
Racial attitudes. Baptists. Carey, William. Rauschenbusch, Walter. Williams, Roger. 1776-1976. 3100
Racism. Academic freedom. Bassett, John Spencer. Duke University. Methodist Church. North Carolina (Durham). *South Atlantic Quarterly* (periodical). 1902-03. 3497
—. American Colonization Society. Finley, Robert. 1816-40. 2470
—. American Protective Association. Anti-Catholicism. Chinese Americans. Guardians of Liberty. Ku Klux Klan. Nativism. Oregon. ca 1840-1945. 2100
—. Ames, Jessie Daniel. Association of Southern Women for the Prevention of Lynching. Lynching. Methodist Woman's Missionary Council. South. Women. Young Women's Christian Association. 1930's. 2535
—. Antislavery Sentiments. Clergy. Kentucky. 1791-1824. 2455
—. Baptists. Imperialism. National Characteristics. Virginia. Women. 1865-1900. 3001
—. Baptists, Southern. Education. Negroes. Reconstruction. 1865-76. 2149
—. Boles, John B. (review article). Evangelicalism. Revivals. Smith, H. Shelton (review article). South. 1972. 2867
—. Bratton, Theodore DuBose. Conference for Education in the South. Episcopal Church, Protestant. Mississippi. Negroes. 1908. 2148
—. Catholic Church. Democracy. Intellectuals. Liberalism. 1924-59. 2532
—. Christianity. Methodology. 1960's-70's. 2141
—. Church and Social Problems. Education. Poverty. 1970's. 2435
—. Elections (presidential). Hoover, Herbert C. Smith, Al. Tennessee, west. 1928. 1280
—. Episcopal Church, Protestant. Negroes. Society for the Propagation of the Gospel. ca 1700-1974. 3169
—. Episcopal Church, Protestant. New York City. Newspapers. Riots. St. Philip's Church. Williams, Peter, Jr. 1830-50. 2142
—. Greek Americans. Negroes. Ohio (Cincinnati). 1970's. 2146
—. Historians. Massachusetts (Salem). Tituba (Indian). Witchcraft. 1648-1953. 2191
—. Indian-White Relations. Puritans. 17c. 2136
—. Music. Negroes. 17c-20c. 1943
—. Political Participation. Protestants. Sexism. Whites. Women. 1974-75. 907
—. Religion, traditional. 1965-73. 2147
Radical catholicity principle. Christianity. National Characteristics. 18c-20c. 41
—. Pietists. Puritans. Theology. 17c-18c. 2950
—. Protestantism. Theology. Transcendence. 1975. 2949
Radical Religion (periodical). Capitalism. Marxism. Niebuhr, Reinhold. Roosevelt, Franklin D. (administration). 1930-43. 1343
Radicals and Radicalism *See also* Leftism; Political Reform; Revolution; Social Reform.
—. American Revolution (antecedents). Business. Friends, Society of. Leadership. Pennsylvania (Philadelphia). 1769-74. 1293
—. Antimasons. 1820's. 1236
—. Antislavery Sentiments. Friends, Society of. Great Britain. Libertarianism. 18c-1865. 2497
—. Baptists. Canada. Disciples of Christ. Great Plains. Lutheran Church. Methodism. Pietism. Prairie Radicals. 1890-1975. 954
—. Beecher, Henry Ward. Feminism. New York City. Sex. Social Reform. Spiritualism. Vanderbilt, Cornelius. Woodhull, Victoria Claflin. 1868-90's. 2386
—. Christian Realism. Eschatology. Niebuhr, Reinhold. 20c. 2927
—. Christianity. Clergy. Social status. 1960-74. 2764
—. Declaration of Independence. Ideology. Utopias. 1730's-1890's. 426
—. Feminism. Protestant Churches. Social reform. South. Women. 1920's. 789
—. Friends, Society of. Humanism. Intellectuals. Penn, William. Social reform. 1650-1700. 2353
—. Gorton, Samuel. Great Britain. Massachusetts. Puritanism. Rhode Island. Rhode Island. Theology. 1636-77. 2862
—. Intellectuals. New England. Poetry. Socialism. Wheelwright, John (1897-1940). 18c-1940. 1419
—. Jewish Student Movement. Massachusetts (Boston). Social Change. Youth Movements. 1960-75. 2433
—. New York (Rochester). Revivalism. Social Reform. 1830-56. 2416
Radio *See also* Audiovisual Materials.
—. Aberhart, William. Alberta. Economic reform. Politics. Prime ministers. 1934-37. 1216
—. Arkansas, northeastern. Clergy. Pentecostals. Rhetoric. 1972-73. 1959
—. Baldwin, Nathaniel. Fundamentalism. Inventions. Mormons. Polygamy. Utah. 1900's-61. 4036
—. California (Los Angeles). Evangelism. International Church of the Foursquare Gospel. McPherson, Aimee Semple. 1920-44. 1958
—. Federal Communications Commission. Lansman, Jeremy. Milam, Lorenzo. Religious references. Television. 1972-75. 1116
—. Mormons. Television. 1922-77. 347
Raikes, Robert. Mennonites. Pennsylvania. Sunday schools. 1780-1980. 641
Railroads. Augustana College and Theological Seminary. Bethany College. Immigration. Lutheran Church. Midwest. Politics. Religious education. Swedish Americans. Swensson, Carl Aaron. 1873-1904. 726
—. Augustana College and Theological Seminary. Illinois (Paxton). Lutheran Church (Augustana Synod). Osborn, William H. Swedish Americans. 1853-73. 3321
—. Economic Conditions. Mormons. Polygamy. Salt Lake and Fort Douglas Railroad. Statehood. Utah. Young, John W. 1883-1924. 3993
—. Elections. Labor. Law. Mormons. Utah (Ogden). 1869-70. 1262
—. Finance. Mormons. Tourism. Utah. Young, John W. 1867-91. 332
—. Mormons. Public Opinion. Train, George Francis. Utah. Young, Brigham. 1860's-70's. 3939
Rainbows. Congregationalism. Edwards, Jonathan. Science. Theology. 1740-45. 2343
Ramm, Charles A. California. Catholic Church. Charities. Ethnic groups. 1863-1951. 3888
Ramus, Petrus. Conversion. Hooker, Thomas. Preparationism. Puritans. Shepard, Thomas. Theology. 1608-49. 3643
Randall, Edwin M. Clergy. Gold Mines and Mining. Klondike Stampede. Lippy, Thomas S. Methodist Church. Transportation. Yukon Territory. 1896-99. 3492
Randall, Gurdon Paine. Architecture (Gothic Revival). Churches. Congregationalism. Iowa (Iowa City). 1868-69. 1822
Raphael, Mark Lee. Cities. Gartner, Lloyd P. Gurock, Jeffrey S. Hertzberg, Steven. Jews (review article). 1840-1979. 4150
Rapp, Frederick. Fraud. Owen, Robert. Pennsylvania (New Harmony). Real Estate. 1825. 327
Rapp, George. Architecture. Harmony Society. Indiana (New Harmony). Pennsylvania (Economy, Harmony). Preservation. Restorations. Utopias. 1804-25. 20c. 420
—. Communalism. German Americans. Harmony Society. Indiana. Pennsylvania. Protestantism. 1804-47. 425
—. Harmony Society. Indiana (New Harmony). Utopias. 1814-47. 421
—. Harmony Society. Indiana (New Harmony). Utopias. 1822-30. 379
—. Harmony Society. Pennsylvania. State Legislatures. Utopias. 1805-07. 380
—. Harmony Society. Pennsylvania (Economy). Utopias. 1785-1847. 381
—. Immigrants. Letters. Norwegian Americans. Pennsylvania (Harmony, New Harmony). 1816-26. 378
Rappe, Louis Amadeus. Assimilation. Authority. Bishops. Catholic Church. Cleveland Diocese. German Americans. Irish Americans. Ohio. 1847-70. 3788

Rare Books. Lambdin, William. Mormons. Smith, Joseph *(Book of Commandments)*. West Virginia (Wheeling). 1830-33. *2124*
Raritan Bay Union. Communes. New Jersey (Perth Amboy, Red Bank). North American Phalanx. Spring, Marcus. 1843-59. *413*
Rationalism *See also* Atheism; Deism; Enlightenment.
—. Cabala. Counter Culture. Jews. Mysticism. Traditionalism. 1940's-70's. *4140*
—. Christianity. Ethics. Science. White, Andrew Dickson. 1888-90's. *2288*
—. Civil religion. Golden Age concept. Protestantism. Reformation. 16c-19c. *1173*
—. James, William *(Varieties of Religious Experience, Will to Believe)*. 1897-1902. *52*
Rauschenbusch, Walter. Baptists. Carey, William. Racial attitudes. Williams, Roger. 1776-1976. *3100*
—. Baptists. Catholic Church. Clergy. Social reform. Theology. Vatican Council II. 1912-65. *2380*
—. Baptists. Christian Socialism. Clergy. Social consciousness. Theology. 1891-1918. *2400*
—. Baptists. Clergy. Dahlberg, Edwin. Personal narratives. Social reform. 1914-18. *2440*
—. Baptists. Clergy. Hudson, Winthrop. Liberalism. Social theory. Theology. 1880-1978. *2351*
—. Baptists. Darwin, Charles. Evolution. Hofstadter, Richard *(Social Darwinism in American Thought)*. Social Gospel. Spencer, Herbert. 1879-1918. *3002*
—. Baptists, North American. German Americans. Theology. 1814-1949. *3062*
Rawlins, Joseph L. Church and state. Statehood. Utah. 1850-1926. *1049*
Raymond, Eliza Ruggles. Missionaries. Nova Scotia. Sierra Leone (Sherbro Island). Slaves. Women. 1839-50. *1692*
Read, Daniel. Billings, William. Hymnals. Music. Poetry. Watts, Isaac. 1761-85. *1920*
Reader's Digest (periodical). Middle Classes. Values. 1976. *2015*
Reading. Assimilation. Jews. Rabbis. 1970's. *4132*
—. Documents. Free Thinkers. German Americans. Immigrants. Missouri. Religious liberty. St. Louis Free Congregation Library. 1850-99. *1123*
Reading, Philip. American Revolution. Church of England. Delaware (Appoquiniminck). Loyalists. Society for the Propagation of the Gospel. 1775-78. *1221*
Reagan, Ronald. Bryan, William Jennings. Political parties. Revivals. Social Change. 1730-1980. *1329*
Real Estate *See also* Land Tenure.
—. Fraud. Owen, Robert. Pennsylvania (New Harmony). Rapp, Frederick. 1825. *327*
Rearticulation. Genealogy. Methodology. Religious studies. Translating and Interpreting. 1975. *232*
Reason. Historiography. Intuition. New England. Parker, Theodore. Theology. Transcendentalism. Unitarianism. 18c-1860. 1920-79. *4074*
Rebellion of 1837. Anti-Catholicism. Church and state. Ethnic groups. Evangelism. Protestantism. Quebec (Lower Canada). 1766-1865. *2110*
Rebellions *See also* particular mutinies, insurrections, and rebellions by name, e.g. Kronstadt Mutiny, Warsaw ghetto uprising; Political Protest; Revolution.
—. Church and State. Civil religion. Constitutional conventions, state. Massachusetts. 1780. *1071*
Reconstruction *See also* Confederate States of America; Emancipation; Freedmen; Ku Klux Klan; Negroes.
—. Alabama. Protestant Churches. 1865-67. *457*
—. American Missionary Association. Federal agencies. Freedmen. Georgia (Atlanta). Methodist Episcopal Church. 1865-69. *556*
—. Anti-Catholicism. Constitutional Law. Ireland. Irish Americans. O'Conor, Charles. O'Conor, Charles Owen. Political reform. 1865-85. *1031*
—. Baptists, Southern. Education. Negroes. Racism. 1865-76. *2149*
—. Blue laws. Church and state. Legislators. Louisiana. Negroes. Sabbath. 1867-75. *2285*
—. Cain, Richard Harvey. Methodist Episcopal Church, African. Negroes. Politics. Social conditions. South Carolina. 1850's-87. *2407*
—. Letters. Lynch, James. Methodist Episcopal Church. Mississippi. Negroes. 1868-69. *3461*
Recreation *See also* Community Centers; Games; Leisure; Resorts; Sports.
—. Attitudes. Exercise. Health. New England. Transcendentalists. 1830-60. *1453*
—. Grant, Heber J. Letters. Mormons. Smith, Joseph Fielding. 1930's. *3954*
—. New England. Puritans. 17c. *3660*
Red Horse (periodical). *Defender* (periodical). Evolution. Kansas (Wichita). Science. Winrod, Gerald Burton. 1925-57. *2305*
Red Jacket (leader). Baptists. Bingham, Abel. Diaries. Indian-White Relations. Iroquois Indians (Seneca). Missions and Missionaries. New York. Tonawanda Indian Reservation. 1822-28. *1513*
Red Lake Mission. American Board of Commissioners for Foreign Missions. Ayer, Frederick. Chippewa Indians. Minnesota. Missions and Missionaries. Oberlin College. 1842-59. *1496*
Red River of the North. Christianity. Frontier and Pioneer Life. North Dakota. ca 1870-97. *2733*
—. Clergy. Lutheran Church, Norwegian. North Dakota. Norwegian Americans. 1871-99. *3318*
—. Indians. Mennonites. Métis. Red River of the North. Removals, forced. Saskatchewan River Valley. Settlement. 1869-95. *3360*
—. Indians. Mennonites. Métis. Red River of the North. Removals, forced. Saskatchewan River Valley. Settlement. 1869-95. *3360*
Red River Rebellion. Church of England. Clergy. Corbett, Griffiths Owen. Manitoba. Métis. 1863-70. *3215*
Reed, Granny. Church of God. North Carolina. Personal narratives. 20c. *3520*
Reese, Thomas. Clergy. Presbyterian Church. South Carolina. 1773-96. *3585*
Referendum. California. Catholic Church. Homosexuality. Proposition 6 (1978). Public schools. Teachers. 1978. *1320*
—. Catholic Church. Morality. Oklahoma. Politics. Protestant Churches. Sabbatarianism. Voting and Voting Behavior. 1959-76. *1290*
—. Democratic Party. Liberty Party. Negroes. New York. Suffrage. Whig Party. 1840-47. *1264*
Reform *See also* types of reform, e.g. Economic Reform, Political Reform, etc.; reform movements, e.g. Abolition Movements, Temperance Movements, etc.; Social Conditions; Social Problems; Utopias.
—. Abolition Movement. Dugdale, Joseph A. Friends, Society of. 1810-96. *2361*
—. Abolition Movement. Friends, Society of (Longwood Meeting). Pennsylvania. 1850's-1940. *2450*
—. Adventists. Health. Numbers, Ronald L. (review article). White, Ellen G. ca 1840's-1915. 1976. *1457*
—. Alabama. Baptists, Southern. Social issues. 1877-90. *2372*
—. Alabama (Birmingham). Anti-Catholicism. Anti-Semitism. City Politics. Social Gospel. 1900-30. *11*
—. Albanese, Catherine L. Beecher, Henry Ward. Civil Religion. Clark, Clifford E., Jr. Douglas, Ann. Handy, Robert T. McLoughlin, William G. Revivals (review article). Women. 1607-1978. *6*
—. American Revolution. Friends, Society of. Pennsylvania (Philadelphia). 1741-90. *2674*
—. American Union for the Relief and Improvement of the Colored Race. Congregationalism. Emancipation. Massachusetts (Boston). 1835-37. *2490*
—. Anglo-Saxonism. Interventionism. Protestantism. Strong, Josiah. 1885-1915. *2418*
—. Anti-Catholicism. Anti-Semitism. Attitudes. Ku Klux Klan. Morality. Ohio (Youngstown). 1920's. *2402*
—. Antislavery Sentiments. Great Britain. 18c-19c. *2457*
—. Apes, William. Indian-white relations. Massachusetts (Mashpee). Methodist Church. Wampanoag Indians. 1830-40. *2546*
—. Arizona. Christianity. Frontier and Pioneer Life. Suffrage. Temperance Movements. Women. 1850's-1912. *837*
—. Attitudes. Friends, Society of. New York (Auburn). Pennsylvania. Prisons. 1787-1845. *2393*
—. Baptists. Bishop, Harriet E. Minnesota (St. Paul). Social reform. Women. 1847-83. *801*
—. Baptists (Ketocton Association). Evangelicalism. Slavery. Stringfellow, Thornton. Virginia. 1800-70. *2158*
—. Berkeley, George. Church of England. Education. Rhode Island (Newport). Sectarianism. 1704-34. *3230*
—. Bishops. Laity. Methodist Protestant Church. 1779-1832. *320*
—. Black theology. Christianity. Feminism. Negroes. Theology. 1960's-70's. *2426*
—. Book of Common Prayer. Episcopal Church, Protestant. 1785. *291*
—. Cable, George Washington. Fiction. Louisiana (New Orleans). Presbyterian Church, Southern. ca 1870-1925. *3539*
—. Calvinism. Centralization. Executive branch. Public Administration. Revivals. ca 1880-1930's. *959*
—. Caskey, Marie. Mathews, Donald G. Moorhead, James H. Protestantism (review article). Walters, Ronald. 1830-80. 1976-78. *2368*
—. Catholic Church. Cities. Merton, Thomas. Nonviolence. Social criticism. 1960's. *2417*
—. Catholic Church. Elites. Ethnicity. Immigrants. Politics. Protestants. 1890's-1970's. *1225*
—. Christianity. Country Life. Ecumenism. Progressivism. Protestant Churches. Wisconsin. 1904-20. *2723*
—. Church of England. Clergy. Episcopal Church, Protestant. Ingraham, Joseph Holt. Novels. Prisons. Public Schools. Tennessee (Nashville). 1847-51. *3241*
—. Cities. Congregationalism. Gladden, Washington. Ohio (Columbus). Social gospel. 1850's-1914. *2425*
—. Douglas, Ann. Feminization. Protestantism. Sex roles. Stereotypes. ca 1820-75. 1977-80. *918*
—. Ecumenism. Negroes. Protestantism. World Conference of Christian Youth, 1st. Youth. 1939-79. *2884*
—. Evangelism. Wright, Henry Clarke. 1820-60. *2444*
—. Finland. Finnish Americans. Lutheranism. Marxism. 1900-76. *990*
—. Grundtvig, Nikolai Frederik Severin. Lutheran Church. 19c-1972. *3313*
—. Pennsylvania. Revivals. 1794-1860. *2399*
—. Political attitudes. Settlement Movement. 1880's-90's. *2405*
—. Race Relations. Social gospel. 1877-98. *2412*
—. Romanticism. Utopias. 1820's-60. *2364*
Reform (review article). Beecher, Catharine. Church of England. Congregationalism. Johnson, Samuel (1696-1772). Washington, Booker T. Women. 1696-1901. *2847*
—. Cities. Social control. 1812-1900. 1970's. *2411*
Reformation. Anabaptists. Theology. 16c. 1945-77. *3408*
—. Civil religion. Golden Age concept. Protestantism. Rationalism. 16c-19c. *1173*
—. Economic development. Protestant Ethic. -1973. *339*
Reformed Christian Church. Calvinism. Church Membership. 1964-79. *3160*
—. Immigrants. Netherlands. Reformed Dutch Church. Schisms. 1834-80. *3163*
Reformed churches. Bibliographies. Dissertations. Edwards, Jonathan. Niebuhr, H. Richard. Niebuhr, Reinhold. Presbyterian Church. Tillich, Paul. 18c-20c. 1965-72. *2815*
—. Bibliographies. Periodicals. Presbyterian Church. 1973. *2957*
—. Church of England. Colonial Government. Ethnic Groups. Friends, society of. Pennsylvania. 1755-80. *1215*
—. Common Sense school. Comte, Auguste. Philosophy. Positivism. Social Gospel. Theology. ca 1850's-80's. *2833*
—. Dunkards. Evangelism. German Americans. Great Awakening. Immigration. Lutheran Church. Moravian Church. Northeastern or North Atlantic States. 1720-60. *2237*
—. Ecumenism. World Alliance of Reformed Churches. 1957-62. *472*
—. German Americans. Lutheran Church. Pennsylvania. Slavery. Social change. 1779-88. *2162*
—. Old Zion Reformed Church. Pennsylvania (Brickerville). 1732. *2935*
Reformed Dutch Church. Africa. Congregationalism. Missions and Missionaries. Presbyterian Church. Reformed German Church. 19c-20c. *1709*

—. American Revolution. Artifacts. Dutch Americans. 17c-18c. *1866*
—. American Revolution. Clergy. Loyalists. Lydekker, Gerrit. New York City. 1765-94. *977*
—. American Revolution. Dutch Americans. 1740-90. *1227*
—. American Revolution. Dutch Americans. New Jersey. New York. 1775-83. *1208*
—. American Revolution. Factionalism. 1650-1840. *1211*
—. Architecture. Iowa (Orange City). Northwestern College (Zwemer Hall). 1890-1924. *1806*
—. Assimilation. Church and state. New York. Politics. 1664-91. *1121*
—. Brazil. Clergy. New Netherland. Polhemius, Johannes Theodorus. 1598-1676. *3165*
—. Catholic Church. Country Life. Ethnic Groups. Lutheran Church. Voting and Voting Behavior. 1890-98. *1257*
—. Church of England. Columbia University. Johnson, Samuel (1696-1772). Livingston, William. 1751-63. *635*
—. Churches. Dutch Americans. New York City. 1686-88. *3166*
—. Clergy. Michaelius, Jonas. New Netherland. 1590's-1633. *3164*
—. Conewago Colony. Pennsylvania. 1760's-70's. *3159*
—. Dutch Americans. Immigration. North Dakota. South Dakota. 1880's-1951. *3161*
—. Dutch Americans. New York (Long Island). 1636-1700. *3162*
—. Europe, Western. Evangelicalism. Methodism. Pietism. Revivals. Social Conditions. 1674-19c. *2959*
—. Exiles. Loyalists. McDowall, Robert James. Missions and Missionaries. Ontario (Upper Canada). 1790-1819. *1588*
—. Immigrants. Netherlands. Reformed Christian Church. Schisms. 1834-80. *3163*
—. Letters. Mormons. New York. Willers, Diedrich. 1830. *2766*
—. Lutheran Church. Methodist Church. Orthodox Eastern Church. Pennsylvania Historical and Museum Commission. Pennsylvania Historical Association. Research conference. Uniates. 1977. *2791*
Reformed Dutch Church (coetus, conferentie). American Revolution. New Jersey (Hackensack). New York City. 1750-83. *1311*
Reformed German Church. Africa. Congregationalism. Missions and Missionaries. Presbyterian Church. Reformed Dutch Church. 19c-20c. *1709*
—. Baptists. Bucknell University. Franklin and Marshall College. Friends, Society of (Hicksite). Pennsylvania. Swarthmore College. Urbanization. 1865-1915. *685*
—. Blumer, Abraham. Pennsylvania (Allentown). Swiss Americans. Zion Reformed Church. 1771-1822. *3285*
—. Clergy. Franklin and Marshall College. Gerhart, Emanuel Vogel. Pennsylvania (Lancaster). Theology. 1840-1904. *3286*
—. Gerhart, Emanuel Vogel. Mercersburg Theological Seminary. Pennsylvania. Theology. 1831-1904. *3287*
—. German Americans. Immigration. Spotswood, Alexander. Virginia (Germanna). 1714-21. *3284*
Reformed Presbyterian Theological Seminary. Antislavery sentiments. Integration. Ohio (Cincinnati). Presbyterian Church, Reformed. 1845-49. *610*
Reformed Swiss Church. Grueningen, Johann Jakob von. Swiss Americans. Wisconsin (Sauk City). 1876-1911. *2860*
Reformed Tradition. Christmas. Emmanuel Church. Immigration. Ohio (Bluffton). Swiss Americans. 1840's-1900. *2857*
Refugees *See also* Exiles.
—. Arizona (Pisinimo). Catholic Church. Clergy. Frembling, Lambert. Papago Indians. 1939-77. *3825*
—. California (Oakland). Disaster relief. Jews. San Francisco Earthquake and Fire. Temple Sinai. 1906. *2527*
—. Canada. Czechoslovakia. Jesuits. Refugees. 1950. *3776*
—. Canada. Czechoslovakia. Jesuits. Refugees. 1950. *3776*
—. Catholic Church. Clergy. Czechoslovakia. Personal narratives. Social Change. Zubek, Theodoric. 1950-78. *3902*
—. Charities. Judaism (Orthodox, Reform). Nebraska (Omaha). Political Leadership. Settlement. 1820-1937. *4102*
Regenerate Membership (doctrine). Baptists, Southern. Theology. 16c-20c. *3059*
Regicide. Charles I. Congregationalism. Folklore. Rhode Island. Stiles, Ezra. Whale, Theophilus. 17c. 1755-85. *3131*
—. Charles I. Cotton, John. Great Britain. Massachusetts (Boston). Puritans. Sermons. 1650. *1349*
Regina Diocese. Anglophiles. Catholic Church. Francophiles. Mathieu, Olivier-Elzéar. Saskatchewan. 1905-30. *3714*
—. Catholic Church. Immigration. Manitoba. Mathieu, Olivier-Elzéar. Saskatchewan. 1911-31. *3781*
Regionalism. 1974. *149*
—. Canada. Catholic Church. Geographic Space. Missions and Missionaries. 1615-1851. *1486*
—. Fiction. Mormons. 1930-50. *2026*
—. Myths and Symbols. New England. Puritans. Theology. 17c. *3611*
Regular Singing movement. Attitudes. Hymnals. New England. Puritans. 1720's. *1933*
Rehine, Zalma. Baltimore Hebrew Congregation. Judaism (Orthodox). Maryland (Baltimore). 1830-31. *4191*
Relation de 1663 (report). Earthquakes. Jesuits. Quebec. 1663. *2296*
Religion (definitions). Church and State. Federal Regulation. Law. 1950's-70's. *1131*
Religion in the Public Schools. Anti-Catholicism. New Brunswick. Pitts, Herman H. 1871-90. *574*
—. Bible (King James version). Catholic Church. Church Schools. City Politics. Education, Finance. Michigan (Detroit). Protestantism. 1842-53. *2716*
—. Bible reading. Catholic Church. Desmond, Humphrey. Protestantism. *Wisconsin ex rel. Frederick Weiss et al.* v. *District School Board of School District 8* (1890). 1888-90. *571*
—. Bible reading. Catholic Church. Politics. Prince Edward Island. Protestants. 1856-60. *580*
—. Catholic Church. Church schools. French language. Langevin, Adélard. Laurier, Wilfrid. Liberal Party. Prairie Provinces. 1890-1915. *569*
—. Catholic Church. Kansas. Protestantism. 1861-1900. *568*
—. Church and State. Church schools. Education, Finance. Jews. Public Policy. 1961-71. *512*
—. Church Schools. Constitutional Amendments (1st). Education, Finance. Government. 1950's-70's. *564*
—. Church schools. Education, Finance. Government. Prayer. Public opinion. 1962-68. *504*
—. Civil religion. Courts. Teaching. 1947-76. *572*
Religion, traditional. Racism. 1965-73. *2147*
Religiosity *See also* Church Attendance.
—. Academic disciplines. College teachers. 1965-73. *531*
—. Adolescents. Church attendance. Negroes. South. Whites. 1964-74. *99*
—. Adolescents. Hispanic Americans. Identity. Mexico. Puerto Rico. Whites. 1970's. *108*
—. Age. Church membership. Lutheran church. 1974. *3311*
—. Attitudes. Catholic Church. Students. 1961-71. *3807*
—. Attitudes. Colleges and Universities. Sex roles. Stereotypes. Students. Women. 1970's. *793*
—. Attitudes. Colleges and Universities. Students. Vietnam War. 1968-72. *2636*
—. Baptists, Southern. Cities. Men. Women. 1968. *3008*
—. Canada. Catholic Church. Industrialization. Judaism. Protestant Churches. 1921-71. *93*
—. Catholic Church. Church attendance. Protestant Churches. 1974. *2713*
—. Catholic Church. District of Columbia. Jews. Judaism. Protestant churches. Psychological well-being. Worship. 1970's. *130*
—. Children. Minnesota, southern. Parents. Socialization. 1975. *128*
—. Church and state. 17c-20c. *26*
—. Church attendance. Students. Williams College. 1948-74. *113*
—. Colleges and Universities. Teachers. 1973. *555*
—. Conversion. 1970's. *138*
—. Death and Dying. 1970's. *116*
—. Demography. Pluralism. 1970's. *150*
—. Dependence. Psychoanalysis. 1974. *142*
—. Education. Middle classes. Troeltsch, Ernst. 1960's-70's. *2602*
—. Education. Social Conditions. Technology. 1945-75. *561*
—. Ethnicity. Students. 1972. *110*
—. Family. Generations. 1940-75. *160*
—. Germany. Students. 1960-77. *96*
—. Herberg, Will. Historiography. Sociology of Religion. 1790's-1970's. *39*
—. Higher education. 1968-73. *562*
—. Higher Education. Students. 1970. *106*
—. Illinois (Nauvoo). Mormons. Social stability. 1833-46. *3981*
—. Jesus movement. Self-conceptions. 1960's-70's. *2783*
—. Metropolitan areas. South. 1970's. *123*
—. Politics. 1968-78. *162*
—. Students. 1973. *117*
Religious beliefs. Anti-Catholicism. Anti-Semitism. Education. Minorities. North Carolina. Prejudice. 1957-73. *2093*
—. Attitudes. Conservatism. Social Surveys. 1970-74. *1380*
—. Christians. Citizenship. 100-1974. *1126*
—. Church attendance. 1957-68. *115*
—. Clergy. Protestant Churches. 1965. *2890*
—. Kentucky. Language. Wills. 1808-53. *48*
—. Letters. Métis. Prairie Provinces. Riel, Louis. Taché, Alexandre Antonin. 1880's. *966*
—. Mennonites. Values. 20c. *3434*
Religious commitment. Episcopal Church, Protestant. North Carolina. Salience. 1975. *3222*
Religious consciousness. Future. Leisure. 1973-. *103*
Religious Education *See also* Church Schools; Religion in the Public Schools; Seminaries; Theology.
—. Abolition Movement. Berea College. Fee, John Gregg. Kentucky. Presbyterian Church. 1855-1904. *777*
—. Adventists. Bible Research Fellowship. 1943-52. *611*
—. American Philosophical Association. Catholic Church. Colleges and Universities. Philosophy. 1933-79. *775*
—. Augustana College and Theological Seminary. Bethany College. Immigration. Lutheran Church. Midwest. Politics. Railroads. Swedish Americans. Swensson, Carl Aaron. 1873-1904. *726*
—. Baptists. Bristol Baptist College. Great Britain (Bristol). Missions and Missionaries. Terrill, Edward. 1634-1979. *3024*
—. Baptists. Clergy. Great Britain. 1600's-1980. *725*
—. Baptists. Elementary education. Secondary education. State Aid to Education. 1850-1910. *718*
—. Baptists. *Keystone Graded Lessons.* Literature. Sunday schools. 1824-1909. *637*
—. Bergel, Siegmund. California (San Bernardino). Jews. 1868-1912. *765*
—. Bohemia (Prague). Neumann, Saint John Nepomucene. 1833-35. *3763*
—. California (Oroville, San Francisco, Woodland). Congregation Beth Israel. Judaism (Orthodox). Messing, Aron J. Sabbath Schools. Travel. 1879. *4201*
—. California (San Bernardino). Confirmation. Henrietta Hebrew Benevolent Society. Judaism (Reform). 1891. *788*
—. Canada. Evangelism. Osgood, Thaddeus. 1807-52. *2900*
—. Canada. Pentecostal Assemblies of Canada. Pentecostal Bible School. Purdie, James Eustace. Theology. 1925-50. *747*
—. Canadians. Theology. USA. 1760-1980. *646*
—. Catholic Church. 1960's-70's. *642*
—. Catholic Church. Chicoutimi, Petit-Séminaire de. Quebec (Saguenay). Students. 1873-1930. *756*
—. Catholic Church. Congregation of Notre Dame (Sisters). Ontario (Kingston). Women. 1841-48. *596*
—. Catholic Church. Diaries. Healy, James A. Holy Cross College. Massachusetts (Worcester). 1849. *640*
—. Catholic Church. Dissent. Michigan (Detroit). Protestant Churches. 1958-71. *3777*
—. Catholic Church. German Americans. Language. Politics. St. Peter's Colony. Saskatchewan. 1903-16. *779*
—. Catholic Church. Germans, Russian. St. Angela's Convent. Saskatchewan (Prelate). Ursulines. Women. 1919-34. *680*

—. Catholic Church. Judaism. Lutheran Church. Ohio (Cincinnati). Public Schools. 19c. *545*
—. Catholic Church. Language. Métis. Missions and Missionaries. Quebec (Oka). Rocheblave, Charlotte de. 19c. *1507*
—. Catholic Church. Pennsylvania (Philadelphia). Sisters of Charity of the Blessed Virgin Mary. 1833-43. *609*
—. Catholic Church. Saskatchewan. Youth. 1870-1978. *715*
—. Centenary College. Methodist Church. Mississippi (Brandon Springs). Mississippi Conference. 1838-44. *656*
—. Child-rearing. Converts. Protestant Churches. Psychology. Sunday schools. 19c. *603*
—. Clergy. Miller, Samuel. Presbyterian Church. Princeton Theological Seminary. 1813-50. *764*
—. Coca-Cola Company. Emory University. Methodist Church. South. Vanderbilt University. 1840's-1970's. *3466*
—. Colleges and Universities. 1939-79. *733*
—. Congregationalism. Connecticut. Girls. Indian-White Relations. Wheelock, Eleazar. 1761-69. *766*
—. Education. Mormons. Utah. 1890-1929. *735*
—. Elementary Education. Johnson, Emeroy. Lutheran Church. Minnesota. Personal narratives. Swedish Americans. ca 1854-ca 1920. *666*
—. Episcopal Church, Protestant. Groton School. Massachusetts. Peabody, Endicott. 1884-1940. *671*
—. Great Awakening. New England. Puritans. 1690-1750. *655*
—. Hebrew Day Schools. Judaism (Orthodox). 1960's-70's. *662*
—. Immanuel Lutheran School. Lutheran Church (Missouri Synod). Personal narratives. Wulff, O. H. 1908-75. *781*
—. Immigrants. Jews. Pennsylvania (Pittsburgh). 1862-1932. *754*
—. Judaism. Michigan (Detroit). Sholom Aleichem Institute. 1926-71. *746*
—. Judaism (Orthodox). Yeshivot (schools). 1896-1979. *648*
—. Keisker, Walter. Lutheran Church. Missouri (Concordia). Personal narratives. St. Paul's College. Students. 1913-19. 1980. *669*
—. Presbyterian Church. Sherrill, Lewis. ca 1900-57. *778*
—. Seminaries. 1808-50. *709*
Religious experience. Great Britain. Psychology. 1975-77. *114*
—. National Aeronautics and Space Administration. Science fiction. Space exploration. 1960-76. *146*
Religious history. Ahlstrom, Sydney E. (review article). 1972. *31*
—. Ahlstrom, Sydney E. (review article). Pluralism. 1974. *17*
—. Christianity. God is Dead Theology. Islam. Methodology. Secularism. Smith, Wilfred Cantwell. Theology. 1940-73. *134*
—. Mead, Sidney E. National Characteristics. 20c. *235*
Religious institutions. Ethnic groups. Family. Government. Morality. 1960's-70's. *899*
Religious Liberty *See also* Church and State; Persecution.
—. Acculturation. American Indian Defense Association. Collier, John. Indians. 1920-26. *1101*
—. Adventists. Illinois. Jones, Alonzo Trevier. Sabbath. World's Columbian Exposition (Chicago, 1893). 1893. *2280*
—. American Revolution. Baptists. 1775-1800. *1001*
—. American Revolution. Baptists. New England. Pennsylvania. Virginia. 1775-91. *1100*
—. American Revolution (antecedents). Benefices. Church of England. New England. Society for the Propagation of the Gospel. 1689-1775. *1054*
—. Americanization. Catholic Church. Church and state. Europe. Maryland. ca 1634-1786. *304*
—. Anti-Catholicism. Know-Nothing Party. 1770's-1850's. *2934*
—. Antifederalists. Constitutions. Federalists. 1776-92. *1010*
—. Aristocracy. Clergy. French Americans. Huguenots. Richebourg, Claude Phillipe de. 1680-1719. *3250*
—. Authority. Constitutional Amendments (1st). Health. Supreme Court. 1963-79. *1439*
—. Baptists. 1612-1974. *1137*
—. Baptists. Bennett, Robert. Clarke, John. Great Britain (London). Letters. Rhode Island. 1655-58. *1132*
—. Baptists. Massachusetts (Ashfield). Poetry. Political Protest. Smith, Ebenezer. 1772. *2048*
—. Baptists. Political theory. 1619-1776. 1973. *1122*
—. Baptists. Virginia. 1600-1800. *1090*
—. Bartlett, Robert. Election sermons. Politics. Universalist Church of America. Vermont. 1817-30. *1045*
—. Bicentennial Conference of Religious Liberty. Pennsylvania (Philadelphia). 1976. *1040*
—. Boucher, Jonathan. Catholic Church. Church of England. Maryland. 1774-97. *2729*
—. California (Eight Mile, Blue Creek). Forest Service. Indians. Supreme Court. 1975. *1102*
—. Calvert, Cecilius (2d Lord Baltimore). Catholic Church. Colonization. Maryland. 1634-92. *1061*
—. Calvert, Cecilius (2d Lord Baltimore). Catholic Church. Great Britain. Maryland. Provincial Government. 1634-49. *1068*
—. Calvert, George (1st Lord Baltimore). Catholic Church. Colonization. Newfoundland (Avalon Peninsula). Protestant churches. 1620's. *2755*
—. Catholic Church. National Prohibition League. Oklahoma. Prohibition. State Government. 1907-18. *2580*
—. Chile. Journalism. Missions and Missionaries. Presbyterian Church. Trumbull, David. 1845-89. *1703*
—. Christianity. Church and State. Orthodoxy. 17c-20c. *1085*
—. Christianity. History. Rhode Island. Williams, Roger. 17c. *1047*
—. Church and State. -1973. *1138*
—. Church and State. Church schools. Conscientious objection. Holidays. Prayer. Public finance. Public Schools. Supreme Court. 1950-70's. *1112*
—. Church and State. Colonial Government. Defoe, Daniel. South Carolina. 1704-06. *1014*
—. City Government. Congregationalism. Massachusetts (Tiverton). Provincial Legislatures. Taxation. 1692-1724. *1084*
—. Civil Rights. Deprogramming. Sects, religious. 1970's. *1062*
—. Constitutional Amendments (1st). 1960's-75. *1092*
—. Constitutional Amendments (1st). Courts. 1878-1972. *1038*
—. Constitutional Law. Morality. Mormons. Polygamy. *Reynolds* v. *United States* (US, 1878). Supreme Court. 1862-78. *1024*
—. Debates. Maryland. State Government. 1776-85. *1107*
—. Declaration of Independence. Jefferson, Thomas. Virginia. 1743-1826. *1022*
—. Documents. Free Thinkers. German Americans. Immigrants. Missouri. Reading. St. Louis Free Congregation Library. 1850-99. *1123*
—. Documents. Friends, Society of. Missions and Missionaries. Virginia. Wilson, George. 1650-62. *1007*
—. Dogberry, Obediah. Free thinkers. Freedom of thought. *Liberal Advocate* (newspaper). New York (Rochester). 1832-34. *1003*
—. Douglas, William O. Humanism. Presbyterian Church. Supreme Court. 1915-80. *1128*
—. Dutch Americans. New Netherland. Smith, George L. (review article). Trade. 17c. *1109*
—. Elections (presidential). Episcopal Church, Protestant. Illuminati controversy. Ogden, John C. Philadelphia *Aurora* (newspaper). 1798-1800. *957*
—. Franklin, Benjamin. Friendship. Morality. Publishers and Publishing. Whitefield, George. 1739-70. *58*
—. Freedmen. Methodist Episcopal Church, Colored. Methodist Episcopal Church, South. Segregation. South. 1865-70. *3464*
—. Friends, Society of. Larson, Lars. Larson, Martha. New York (Rochester). Norwegian Americans. Women. 1807-44. *3263*
—. Georgia. Judaism (Orthodox). 1733-90. *4188*
—. Indians. 1609-1976. *1134*
—. Judaism (Orthodox). Letters. Rhode Island (Newport). Seixas, Moses. Washington, George. 1790. 1974. *1081*
—. Legislation. Lobbying. 1950's-70's. *1136*
—. Lutheran Free Church. Norwegian Americans. Sermons. Sverdrup, Georg. Thanksgiving. 1896-1907. *3304*
Religious movements. Hegel, Georg. Troeltsch, Ernst. Weber, Max. 19c-20c. *33*
Religious Orders *See also* religious orders by name, e.g. Franciscans, Jesuits; Convents; Monasteries.
—. Anglican communion. Catholic Church. Ecumenism. Hughes, John Jay. -1973. *493*
—. Catholic Church. Clergy. Men. Social classes. Women. 1650-1762. *2614*
—. Catholic Church. Feminism. Quebec. Women. 1640-1975. *833*
—. Catholic Church. History. Literature. Women. 19c-1978. *868*
—. Catholic Church. Massachusetts (Boston). Teaching. Voluntarism. Women. 1870-1940. *717*
—. Catholic Church. Professions. Quebec. Secondary education. Women. 1908-54. *871*
Religious Persecution. *See* Persecution.
Religious references. Federal Communications Commission. Lansman, Jeremy. Milam, Lorenzo. Radio. Television. 1972-75. *1116*
Religious Revivals. *See* Revivals.
Religious scrupulosity. Church and Social Problems. Church membership. Half-Way Covenant. Massachusetts (Dorchester). Puritans. 1660-1730. *3601*
Religious studies. Church and State. Colleges and Universities. Constitutions. Supreme Court. 1970's. *578*
—. Genealogy. Methodology. Rearticulation. Translating and Interpreting. 1975. *232*
—. Judaism. Tradition. 20c. *4133*
—. Public schools. Social sciences. 1979. *558*
Religious studies departments. Higher Education. Jewish studies. 1972-74. *539*
Religious thought (review article). Clebsch, William A. Dissent. Gaustad, Edwin Scott. 17c-20c. *18*
Removal policy. Indians. Kansas. Methodism. Ohio. Wyandot Indians. 1816-60. *1598*
Removals, forced. American Board of Commissioners for Foreign Missions. Cherokee Indians. Georgia. Indian-White Relations. Law Enforcement. Missions and Missionaries. Worcester, Samuel A. 1831. *1667*
—. Indians. Mennonites. Métis. Red River of the North. Red River of the North. Saskatchewan River Valley. Settlement. 1869-95. *3360*
Renaissance. Humanism. Mather, Cotton *(Magnalia Christi Americana).* Puritans. Rhetoric. 1702. *1996*
Renggli, Rose (Mother Mary Beatrice). Arkansas (Jonesboro). Catholic Church. Missions and missionaries. Olivetan Benedictine Sisters, American. 1847-1942. *1652*
—. Benedictine sisters. Immigration. Missouri (Conception). Switzerland. Women. 1874. *3832*
Repatriation Act (Canada, 1875). Catholic Church. French Canadians. LaPatrie (colony). New England. Quebec. ca 1875-80. *3792*
Republican Party. Ames Church. Education. Freedmen. Hartzell, Joseph C. Methodist Episcopal Church. Missionaries. South. 1870-73. *3481*
—. Anti-Catholicism. Antislavery Sentiments. Know-Nothing Party. Massachusetts. Voting and Voting Behavior. 1850's. *1201*
—. Anti-Catholicism. Clergy. Ku Klux Klan. Protestantism. Rhode Island. 1915-32. *2116*
—. Anti-Catholicism. Elections (presidential). Ethnic Groups. Nativism. Ohio (Cleveland). 1860. *1265*
—. Anti-Catholicism. Know-Nothing Party. Massachusetts. Voting and Voting Behavior. 1850's. *1209*
—. Antislavery Sentiments. Catholic Church. Emigration. Germans, Sudeten. Journalism. Missions and Missionaries. Neumann, Saint John Nepomucene. 19c-20c. *3826*
—. League of Nations. Mormons. Prohibition. Roberts, Brigham Henry. Smith, Joseph Fielding. Suffrage. Utah. Women. ca 1900. *1284*
Republicanism. Adventists. Bible. Protestantism. 1850's-60's. *2962*
—. American Revolution (antecedents). Great Awakening. Individualism. Pietism. 1735-75. *1385*
—. American Revolution (antecedents). Revivals. Rhetoric. 1730-75. *1993*
—. Beecher, Lyman. Congregationalism. Dwight, Timothy. New England. Presbyterian Church. Taylor, Nathaniel William. 1790-1840. *1356*
—. Elders. Laity. Miller, Samuel. Presbyterian Church. 1813-50. *3559*
—. Laurens, Henry. Philosophy. Social Reform. South Carolina. 1764-77. *2385*

—. Morality. Presbyterian Church. Revivals. South. 1825-60. *2244*
Rescue missions. Employment. Program failure. Public Policy. Skid rows. Social Reform. 1960's-70's. *2524*
—. Jehovah's Witnesses. Organizational structure. Skid Rows. Watch Tower movement. 1970's. *2722*
—. Skid rows. Washington (Seattle). 1973. *2502*
Research *See also* Methodology.
—. Amish, Old Order. Hutterites. Minorities. 1977. *3363*
—. Baptists, Southern. History. Newspapers. 1977. *209*
—. Bibliographies. Periodicals. Psychology of religion. 1950-74. *168*
—. Carroll, John. Catholic Church. Clergy. Documents. Hanley, Thomas O'Brien *(The John Carroll Papers).* 18c-19c. 1976-78. *3872*
—. Church membership. Elites. 19c. 1975. *2615*
—. Genealogical Society of Utah. Mormons. Utah. 1894-1976. *246*
—. Historiography. Manuscripts. Mormons. Young, Brigham. 19c-1978. *192*
Research conference. Lutheran Church. Methodist Church. Orthodox Eastern Church. Pennsylvania Historical and Museum Commission. Pennsylvania Historical Association. Reformed Dutch Church. Uniates. 1977. *2791*
Resettlement. Baptists. Discrimination. Japanese Americans. World War II. 1890-1970. *2547*
Residence. Atheism. Morality. Theology. Tolerance. Traditionalism. 1958. *159*
—. Catholic Church. Church attendance. 1953-69. *3696*
Resorts. California (Santa Monica). Jews. 1875-1939. *4160*
—. Camp meetings. Methodism. Revivals. 19c. *2252*
Restitutionism. Jesus People. Mormons. Protestant Churches. Revivals. 19c-20c. *2744*
Restoration movement. Disciples of Christ. Dunkards. Hostetler, Joseph. Indiana. Revivals. 1800-27. *3104*
Restorations *See also* Historical Sites and Parks; Preservation.
—. Architecture. Harmony Society. Indiana (New Harmony). Pennsylvania (Economy, Harmony). Preservation. Rapp, George. Utopias. 1804-25. 20c. *420*
—. Architecture, Gothic Revival. Churches. Episcopal Church, Protestant. Holy Trinity Episcopal Church. Tennessee (Nashville). 1840's-1970's. *1801*
—. Artists. Carmelites. Louisiana (DeSoto Parish). St. Anne's Chapel. 1891-1975. *1796*
—. Bethel African Methodist Episcopal Church. Methodist Episcopal Church, African. Pennsylvania (Reading). 1834-1979. *1784*
—. California. Catholic Church. Mission San Juan Capistrano. 1797-1979. *1803*
—. Dwellings. Jacobsen, Florence S. Mormons. Personal narratives. Utah (St. George). Young, Brigham. 19c. 1970's. *1789*
—. Kentucky. Pleasant Hill (community). Shakers. Utopias. 1805-1970's. *385*
Retrenchment Society. Matthews, Robert ("Matthias the Prophet"). New York City. Sects, Religious. 1828-35. *70*
Revel, Bernard. Adler, Cyrus. American Academy for Jewish Research. Intellectuals. Judaism (Orthodox, Reform). Society of Jewish Academicians. 1916-22. *4139*
Revelation. Clergy. Integration. Kimball, Spencer W. Mormons. Negroes. 1950-78. *4051*
—. Episcopal Church, Protestant. Great Britain. Maurice, Frederick Denison. Protestantism. Social reform. Theology. 1860-1900. *3171*
—. Heresy. Mormons. Pratt, Orson. Young, Brigham. 1853-68. *3938*
Revista Catolica (periodical). Catholic Church. Jesuits. Southwest. 1875-1962. *3884*
Revitalization movements. Handsome Lake (Seneca). Indian Shaker Church. Neurology. Slocum, John. Trances. 18c-20c. *2756*
—. Indian Shaker Church. Indians. Rites and Ceremonies. Salishan Indians. 1840's-1978. *2715*
Revival meetings. Methodist Era. 1825-1914. *3474*
Revivalism. Audiences. Graham, Billy. Social classes. -1974. *2604*
—. Boehm, Martin. Mennonites. Newcomer, Christian. Pennsylvania Germans. 1740-1850. *2266*
—. Canada. Gospel Temperance Movement. Rine, D. I. K. Temperance Movements. 1877-82. *2575*
—. Darby, John Nelson. Evangelical Free Church of America. Franson, Fredrik. Millenarianism. Moody, Dwight L. Scandinavian Americans. 1875-95. *2863*
—. Democracy. Finney, Charles G. Human nature. Social Theory. 1820-30. *2268*
—. Finney, Charles G. Higher law (doctrine). Ohio Antislavery Society. Political Participation. 1835-60. *2253*
—. New York (Rochester). Radicals and Radicalism. Social Reform. 1830-56. *2416*
Revivals *See also* Great Awakening.
—. Abolition Movement. Finney, Charles G. Social reform. South. 1833-69. *2466*
—. Adolescence. Baptists. Congregationalism. Finney, Charles G. Massachusetts (Boston). Methodism. 1822-42. *2258*
—. Adventists. Great Disappointment. Millenarianism. 18c-1973. *2970*
—. A. A. Allen Revival, Incorporated. Arizona (Miracle Valley). Fundamentalism. Language. Popular culture. 1970's. *2270*
—. Alline, Henry. Charisma. Integration. Nova Scotia. 1776-83. *2264*
—. American Revolution (antecedents). Republicanism. Rhetoric. 1730-75. *1993*
—. Amish. Mennonites. 1860-90. *2255*
—. Amusements. Georgia. Jones, Sam. Methodist Episcopal Church, South. Morality. Self-reliance. 1872-1906. *3498*
—. Anticlericalism. Enlightenment. Europe. Protestantism. 1640's-1830's. *2912*
—. Antislavery Sentiments. Ohio. Political attitudes. Voting and Voting Behavior. 1825-70. *2866*
—. Behavior. Conversion. Graham, Billy. 1968-75. *2275*
—. Boles, John B. (review article). Evangelicalism. Racism. Smith, H. Shelton (review article). South. 1972. *2867*
—. Boyer, Paul. City Life. Johnson, Paul E. Middle Classes. Missions and Missionaries. Morality. New York (Rochester). 1815-1920. 1978. *2800*
—. British Columbia (Metlakatla). Church Missionary Society. Church of England. Hall, A. J. Indian-White Relations. Missions and Missionaries. Tsimshian Indians. 1877. *1616*
—. Bryan, William Jennings. Political parties. Reagan, Ronald. Social Change. 1730-1980. *1329*
—. Burchard, Jedediah. Protestants. Social Conditions. Vermont. 1835-36. *2246*
—. Calvinism. Centralization. Executive branch. Public Administration. Reform. ca 1880-1930's. *959*
—. Calvinism. Mather, Moses. Theology. 1719-1850. *2248*
—. Camp meetings. Methodism. Resorts. 19c. *2252*
—. Catholic Church. Pentecostal movement. 1969. *3752*
—. Charismatic movement. Faith healing. Harrell, David Edwin, Jr. (review article). 1947-75. *2782*
—. Charismatic Movement. Jesus People. Pentecostalism. Transcendental Meditation. 1960's-78. *127*
—. Cities. Politics. Social conditions. 1857-77. *2261*
—. Congregationalism. Connecticut. Evangelism. Vermont. 1781-1803. *1609*
—. Congregationalism. Edwards, Jonathan. Goen, C. C. (review essay). Great Awakening. 1734-1751. *2224*
—. Congregationalism. Finney, Charles G. New York (Oneida County). Presbyterian Church. 1825-27. *2245*
—. Congregationalism. Fish, Josiah. Osborn, Sarah. Rhode Island (Newport). Women. 1766-67. *904*
—. Country Life. Farms. Haswell, David R. Letters. Pennsylvania. Protestants. 1808-31. *2234*
—. Disciples of Christ. Dunkards. Hostetler, Joseph. Indiana. Restoration movement. 1800-27. *3104*
—. Domesticity. Industrialization. Womanhood, sentimental. 1830-70. *817*
—. Europe. Social reform. 1400-1900. *2429*
—. Europe, Western. Evangelicalism. Methodism. Pietism. Reformed Dutch Church. Social Conditions. 1674-19c. *2959*
—. Evangelicalism. New York (Utica). Women. 1800-40. *922*
—. Evolution. Friends, Society of. Pennsylvania. Provincial Government. 1735-75. *2222*
—. Finney, Charles G. Law and Society. 1800-50. *2271*
—. Finney, Charles G. New York. 1820-40. *2243*
—. Finney, Charles G. Theology. 1821-75. *2251*
—. Fundamentalism. Ham, Mordecai F. Newspapers. North Carolina (Elizabeth City). Saunders, William O. 1924. *2217*
—. Great Britain. Methodism. Nonconformists. 1828-43. *2223*
—. Holiness Movement. Inskip, John S. Inskip, Martha Jane. Methodist Church. Women. 1836-90. *3448*
—. Holiness Movement. Methodist Church. 1835-1920. *3291*
—. Jesus People. Mormons. Protestant Churches. Restitutionism. 19c-20c. *2744*
—. Laity. 1858. *2259*
—. Maine. New Hampshire. Whitefield, George. 1727-48. *2249*
—. McLoughlin, William G. (review article). Social Change. 1607-1978. *2220*
—. Mennonites. Modernization. 1683-1850. *2254*
—. Morality. Presbyterian Church. Republicanism. South. 1825-60. *2244*
—. Mountaineers. Music. South. 1798-1970. *1935*
—. New England. Textile industry. Women. ca 1790-1840. *2228*
—. New Jersey (Pitman Grove). Settlement. Urbanization. 1860-1975. *2262*
—. Patriotism. Sunday, Billy. World War I. 1917-18. *2676*
—. Pennsylvania. Reform. 1794-1860. *2399*
—. Pentecostals. 1970's. *2269*
—. Poe, Edgar Allan *(The Pit and the Pendulum).* Symbolism in Literature. ca 1800-50. *2084*
—. Politics. 19c. *1242*
Revivals (review article). Albanese, Catherine L. Beecher, Henry Ward. Civil Religion. Clark, Clifford E., Jr. Douglas, Ann. Handy, Robert T. McLoughlin, William G. Reform. Women. 1607-1978. *6*
Revolution *See also* American Revolution; Government, Resistance to; Radicals and Radicalism; Rebellions; Riots.
—. *America* (weekly). Carranza, Venustiano. Catholic Church. Mexico. Tierney, Richard Henry. 1914-17. *3722*
—. Butler, John Wesley. Letters. Methodist Church. Mexico. Missions and Missionaries. 1910-11. *1725*
—. China. Diplomatic recognition. Missions and Missionaries. Sun Yat-sen. 1911-13. *1724*
—. Dye, Alexander V. Mexico (Sonora). Mormons. Settlement. 1912. *4016*
—. Europe. Nationalism. Romanticism. Social criticism. 1630-1876. *950*
Reynolds v. *United States* (US, 1878). Constitutional Law. Morality. Mormons. Polygamy. Religious Liberty. Supreme Court. 1862-78. *1024*
Rezanov, Nikolai. Arguello, Maria de la Concepcion. California. Catholic Church. Orthodox Eastern Church, Russian. 1806. *2797*
Rhetoric *See also* Lectures; Political Speeches.
—. Adams, John. American Revolution. New England. Paine, Thomas. Political theory. Puritans. 17c-1770's. *1424*
—. American Revolution. Congregationalism. Cooper, Samuel. Massachusetts (Boston). Sermons. 1768-80. *1352*
—. American Revolution (antecedents). Republicanism. Revivals. 1730-75. *1993*
—. Antislavery Sentiments. Editors and Editing. Kansas. Newspapers. Providence. 1855-58. *2034*
—. Arkansas, northeastern. Clergy. Pentecostals. Radio. 1972-73. *1959*
—. Attitudes. Carter, Jimmy. Civil religion. Evangelicalism. Political Campaigns (presidential). Political Speeches. 1976. *1229*
—. Bible. Disciples of Christ. 19c. *1978*
—. Bible. Georgia Trustees. Sermons. Slavery. 1731-50. *2161*
—. California. Chavez, Cesar. Christianity. Mexican Americans. Political activism. Texas. Tijerina, Reies. 1960's-70's. *2391*
—. Camp meetings. Crowd control. Political rallies. Tennessee. 1828-60. *1259*
—. Chapman, John Jay. Christianity. Lynching. Pennsylvania (Coatesville). Poetry. Race Relations. Speeches, Addresses, etc. 1912. *1971*

—. Civil War. Disasters. Lincoln, Abraham. Puritans. Sermons. 1650-1870. *1968*
—. Congregationalism. Harvard University (Hollis Professorship of Divinity). Latin language. Wigglesworth, Edward. 1722. *667*
—. Great Britain. New England. Puritans. Sermons. 1620's-50's. *1980*
—. Hooker, Thomas. Mather, Cotton. Puritans. Winthrop, John. 17c. *1965*
—. Hoover, Herbert C. Johnson, Lyndon B. Nixon, Richard M. Protestant ethic. Public welfare. Roosevelt, Franklin D. Weber, Max. 1905-79. *348*
—. Humanism. Mather, Cotton *(Magnalia Christi Americana)*. Puritans. Renaissance. 1702. *1996*
—. McGovern, George S. Nixon, Richard M. Political Campaigns (presidential). Voting and Voting Behavior. 1972. *1228*
—. Protestantism. Sermons. 1952-74. *1972*
Rhode Island *See also* New England; Northeastern or North Atlantic States.
—. American Jewish Historical Society. Archival catalogs and inventories. Judaism. 1692-1975. *273*
—. American Revolution. Great Britain. Judaism (Orthodox). Touro, Isaac. 1782. *4184*
—. Anti-Catholicism. Clergy. Ku Klux Klan. Protestantism. Republican Party. 1915-32. *2116*
—. Baptists. Bennett, Robert. Clarke, John. Great Britain (London). Letters. Religious Liberty. 1655-58. *1132*
—. Baptists. Fox, George. Friends, Society of. Olney, Thomas, Jr. Politics. 1672-73. *967*
—. Bibliographies. Historiography. Williams, Roger. 17c-1972. *2911*
—. Birth Control. Fertility. 1968-69. *803*
—. Catholic Church. Conservatism. Nativism. Newspapers. Political Commentary. Protestantism. *Providence Visitor* (newspaper). 1916-24. *2118*
—. Catholic Church. Human Relations. Judaism (Orthodox). Protestant Churches. 18c. *2087*
—. Catholics. Church membership. Migration, Internal. Protestants. 1926-71. *152*
—. Charles I. Congregationalism. Folklore. Regicide. Stiles, Ezra. Whale, Theophilus. 17c. 1755-85. *3131*
—. Christianity. History. Religious liberty. Williams, Roger. 17c. *1047*
—. Church and state. Colonial Government. Great Britain. Williams, Roger. 1629-83. *1042*
—. Gorton, Samuel. Great Britain. Massachusetts. Puritanism. Radicals and Radicalism. Rhode Island. Theology. 1636-77. *2862*
—. Gorton, Samuel. Great Britain. Massachusetts. Puritanism. Radicals and Radicalism. Rhode Island. Theology. 1636-77. *2862*
—. Human relations. Social Theory. Williams, Roger. 1643-76. *2826*
—. Toleration. Williams, Roger. ca 1603-83. *1120*
Rhode Island (Barrington). Baptists. Church and state. Congregationalism. Massachusetts (Swansea). 1711-46. *1082*
Rhode Island (Cumberland). Free love. Perfectionists. Theology. 1748-68. *2898*
Rhode Island (Narragansett). Humanism. Indians. More, Thomas *(Utopia)*. Utopias. Williams, Roger *(A Key into the Language of America)*. 1640's. *2938*
Rhode Island (Newport). American Revolution. Antislavery Sentiments. Congregationalism. Hopkins, Samuel. ca 1770-1803. *2464*
—. Ararat (colony). Judaism (Orthodox). New York. Noah, Mordecai Manuel. 1813-21. *4178*
—. Artifacts. Moravian Church. 1767-1835. *3511*
—. Baptists. Jack (man). Negroes. 1630's-52. *3017*
—. Baptists, Seventh-Day. Churches. 1664-1929. *1775*
—. Berkeley, George. Church of England. Education. Reform. Sectarianism. 1704-34. *3230*
—. Carigal, Hakham Raphael Haim Isaac. Jews. 1771-77. *4190*
—. Catholic Church. Church of St. John the Evangelist. Construction. 1883-1934. *1772*
—. Churches. Harrison, Peter. Touro Synagogue. Wren, Christoper. 1670-1775. *1819*
—. Clockmakers. Friends, Society of. 1780's-1850's. *3268*
—. Congregation Shearith Israel. Judaism (Orthodox). New York City. Touro Synagogue. 1893-1902. *4183*
—. Congregationalism. Decorative Arts. Interior decoration. United Congregational Church. 1879-80. *1897*
—. Congregationalism. Fish, Josiah. Osborn, Sarah. Revivals. Women. 1766-67. *904*
—. Construction. Friends, Society of. Historic Preservation. Meetinghouses. 1657-1974. *1838*
—. Judaism (Orthodox). Letters. Religious Liberty. Seixas, Moses. Washington, George. 1790. 1974. *1081*
—. Judaism (Orthodox). Touro Synagogue. 1654-1977. *4200*
—. Judaism (Orthodox). Touro Synagogue. 1658-1963. *4185*
—. Judaism (Orthodox). Touro Synagogue. 1902. *4174*
Rhode Island (Portsmouth). Antinomianism. Cotton, John. Eliot, John. Government. Millenarianism. Missions and Missionaries. New England. Puritans. 1630-90. *3635*
Rhode Island (Providence). African Society. Colonization. Congregationalism. Freedmen. Hopkins, Samuel. Sierra Leone. 1789-95. *2459*
—. Belkin, Samuel. Brown University. Judaism (Orthodox). 1932-35. *4172*
—. Catholic Church. Conflict and Conflict Resolution. Italian Americans. 1890-1930. *3682*
—. Congregation Sons of Zion. Finesilver, Moses Ziskind. Judaism. Rabbis. 1880-83. *4122*
Rhode Island (West Warwick). Congregation Ahavath Shalom. Judaism. 1912-38. *4152*
Rhode Island (Woonsocket). Assimilation. Catholic Church. French Canadians. Nationalism. 1924-29. *3854*
Rhodes families. Mennonites. Virginia. 1770's-1900. *3426*
Rice, Luther. Baptist Triennial Convention. Church Finance. Education. Missions and missionaries. Wayland, Francis. 1823-26. *3018*
Richards, George Warren. Ecumenism. Evangelical and Reformed Church. Presbyterian Church. World Alliance of Reformed Churches. 1900-55. *481*
Richards, Willard. Great Britain. Letters. Mormons. Young, Brigham. 1840. *1754*
Richardson, Henry Hobson. Churches (Gothic Revival). Decorative Arts. LaFarge, John. Massachusetts (Boston). Trinity Church. 1876. *1832*
Richardson, William. Cherokee Indians. Indians. Martin, John. Missions and Missionaries. Presbyterian Church. Tennessee. Virginia. 1755-63. *1511*
Richebourg, Claude Phillipe de. Aristocracy. Clergy. French Americans. Huguenots. Religious liberty. 1680-1719. *3250*
Richey, James Arthur Morrow. Catholic Church. Clergy. Converts. Episcopal Church, Protestant. ca 1900-33. *2754*
Richmond College. Baptists. Colleges and Universities. Virginia (Richmond). 1843-60. *616*
Richter, Peyton. Kateb, George. Utopias (review article). 19c. 1971. *400*
Rickover, Hyman. Carter, Jimmy. Cromwell, Oliver. Great Britain. Political Leadership. Roosevelt, Theodore. 20c. *974*
Riel, Louis. Canada. Letters. Millenarianism. Northwest Rebellion. 1876-78. 1885. *965*
—. Letters. Métis. Prairie Provinces. Religious beliefs. Taché, Alexandre Antonin. 1880's. *966*
—. Messianic Movements. Northwest Rebellion. Prairie Provinces. 1869-85. *964*
Right To Life organizations. Abortion. Protestant churches. South. 1970's. *945*
Riis, Jacob. Anti-Semitism. Europe, Eastern. Immigration. 1890-1914. *2132*
—. Christianity. Civil Rights. Jews. Social Organization. 1870-1914. *2129*
Riley, William Bell. Baptists. Fundamentalism. Graham, Billy. Minnesota (Minneapolis). World Christian Fundamental Association. ca 1900-65. *3068*
Rimbach, John Adam. Lutheran Church (Missouri Synod). Oregon (Portland). Trinity Church. Washington. 1906-41. *3333*
Rine, D. I. K. Canada. Gospel Temperance Movement. Revivalism. Temperance Movements. 1877-82. *2575*
Rinfret, Fernand. Canada. Catholic Church. Education. French Canadians. Quebec. Siegfried, André *(Le Canada, les deux races, Problèmes politiques contemporains)*. Social Sciences. 1906-07. *3873*
Ringgold, Samuel. Christ Church. Civil War. Episcopal Church, Protestant. Kentucky (Bowling Green). Tennessee (Knoxville). 1860-1911. *3168*
—. Civil-Military Relations. Episcopal Church, Protestant. Kentucky (Bowling Green). Tennessee (Clarksville). 1861-65. *998*
Rings. France. Indians. Jesuits. Missions and Missionaries. New York, western. ca 1630-87. *1664*
Rio Grande Annual Conference. Methodist Church. Mexican Americans. Southwest. 1874-1978. *3491*
Rio Grande Valley. Catholic Church. Cofradías (brotherhoods). Mexican Americans. New Mexico. Penitentes. ca 1770-1970. *3675*
Riobó, Juan Antonio García. Alaska. Catholic Church. Missionaries. Spain. Voyages. 1779. *1643*
Riots *See also* Strikes.
—. Anti-Catholicism. Antislavery sentiments. Ideology. Massachusetts (Boston). Social Classes. Ursulines. 1834-35. *2109*
—. Boycotts. Consumers. Jews. Meat, kosher. New York City. Prices. Women. 1902. *4112*
—. Episcopal Church, Protestant. New York City. Newspapers. Racism. St. Philip's Church. Williams, Peter, Jr. 1830-50. *2142*
—. Friends, Society of. Indians. Paxton Boys. Pennsylvania. Politics. Presbyterian Church. 1763-64. *3530*
Rising glory of America (theme). Church of England. Patriotism. Poetry. Smith, William. 1752. *1337*
Risorgimento. Anti-Catholicism. Canada. Italy. Political Attitudes. Protestants. 1846-60. *2114*
Risser, Johannes. Democratic Party. Letters. Mennonites. Politics. Slavery. 1856-57. *994*
Rister, Carl Coke. Baptists. Historiography. Western States. 1920's-55. *223*
Rites and Ceremonies *See also* Liturgy.
—. Appalachia, southern. Pentecostals. Snakehandlers. Trances. 1909-74. *3523*
—. Attitudes. Lancaster Mennonite High School. Mennonites. Pennsylvania. Students. 1974-78. *3354*
—. *Book of Common Worship*. Humor. Lampton, William J. Poetry. Presbyterian Church, Southern. VanDyke, Henry. 1906. *3557*
—. British North America. Jews. Myers, Myer. Silversmithing. 1723-95. *1905*
—. California (Los Angeles). Catholic Church. Christmas. Mexican Americans. Neighborhoods. Posadas (celebrations). 1975-80. *3794*
—. Catholic Church. Fiestas. New Mexico. Saints, patron. Villages. 1970's. *3892*
—. Catholic Church. Folklore. Hispanic Americans. New Mexico. Penitentes. Social customs. 16c-20c. *3829*
—. Christianity. Judaism. Metalwork. ca 1650-1888. *1854*
—. Clergy (dismissal). Episcopal Church, Protestant. Illinois (Chicago). Pamphlets. Swope, Cornelius E. Trinity Church. Unonius, Gustaf. 1850-51. *3179*
—. Coke, Thomas. Great Britain. Methodism. Wesley, John *(Sunday Service)*. 1780's. *3460*
—. Episcopal Church, Protestant. Theology. 1607-1978. *3216*
—. Erikson, Erik H. Excommunication. First Church. Hibbens, Ann. Massachusetts (Boston). Puritans. 1640-41. 1960's-70's. *3610*
—. Ethnic Groups. 1797-1960. *37*
—. Illinois (Nauvoo). Mormons. Smith, Joseph. Temples. 1841-45. *1766*
—. Indian Shaker Church. Indians. Revitalization movements. Salishan Indians. 1840's-1978. *2715*
Ritter, Joseph E. Catholic Church. Church Schools. Glennon, John J. Missouri (St. Louis). School Integration. 1935-47. *2542*
Ritualization. Mormon history. Utah. 1830-1975. *3942*
Roberts, Brigham Henry. Church and state. Feminism. House of Representatives. Polygamy. Utah. 1898-1900. *1133*
—. Historiography. Hunter, Howard W. Jenson, Andrew. Lund, A. William. Lyon, T. Edgar. Mormons. 1913-70. *226*

—. League of Nations. Mormons. Prohibition. Republican Party. Smith, Joseph Fielding. Suffrage. Utah. Women. ca 1900. *1284*
Roberts, Joseph L., Jr. Baptists. Civil rights movement. Ebenezer Baptist Church. Georgia (Atlanta). Personal narratives. 1960-75. *2556*
Roberts, William Henry. Bureaucracies. Conservatism. Presbyterian Church, Southern (administration). Theology. 1884-1920. *3541*
Robertson, Martha Wayles. Civil War. Diaries. Episcopal Church, Protestant. Providence. South Carolina (Chesterfield County). Women. 1860-66. *3191*
Robeson, Paul. Leftism. Methodist Episcopal Zion Church, African. Music. Negroes. 1898-1976. *3470*
Robinson, Frank Bruce. Correspondence courses. Idaho (Moscow). New Thought movement. Psychiana (religion). 1929-48. *4260*
Robinson, Roosevelt. Centennial United Methodist Church. Indiana (Gary). Methodist Church, United. Methodist Church, United. Negroes. Personal narratives. White flight. 1976. *3467*
Robison, James I. Adventists. California (Arlington). Loma Linda University. Personal narratives. 1922. *745*
Rocheblave, Charlotte de. Catholic Church. Language. Métis. Missions and Missionaries. Quebec (Oka). Religious Education. 19c. *1507*
Rockefeller, John D., Jr. Charities. Fosdick, Harry Emerson. Friendship. Liberalism. Protestantism. Social control. Wealth. 1920-36. *364*
Rockwell, William Walker. Libraries. New York City. Pettee, Julia. Presbyterian Church. Union Theological Seminary Library. 1908-58. *759*
Rocky Mountains. Colorado. Haven, Gilbert. Methodist Church. Utah (Salt Lake City). 1875. *3463*
Roe, Edward Payson *(Barriers Burned Away)*. New Theology. Protestantism. Sheldon, Charles M. *(In His Steps)*. Social Gospel. 1860's-90's. *2058*
Rogers, Harrison. California. Catholic Church. Mountain Men. Protestantism. Smith, Jedediah Strong. 1826-27. *2798*
Rogers, Nathaniel Peabody. Abolition Movement. Friends, Society of. Haverford College Library (Quaker Collection). New Hampshire. Portsmouth Anti-Slavery Society. 1830-46. *2465*
Rollins College. Colleges and Universities. Congregationalism. Florida (Winter Park). Hooker, Edward P. 1885-1900. *678*
Rolph, John. Church and state. Church of England. Endowments. Land. Ontario (Upper Canada). Strachan, John. University of Toronto. 1820-70. *1026*
Rolvaag, O. E. *(Giants in the Earth)*. Acculturation. Frontier and Pioneer Life. Immigrants. Lutheran Church. South Dakota. 1870. 1927. *3307*
Roman Catholic Church. *See* Catholic Church.
Roman Law. Crime and criminals. Ecclesiastical law. Great Britain. Massachusetts. 17c. *972*
Romanes, George. Canada. Great Britain. Ontario (Kingston, Smith Falls). Queen's College. Romanes, George John. Science. Scientific Experiments and Research. Theology. 1830-90. *2918*
Romanes, George John. Canada. Great Britain. Ontario (Kingston, Smith Falls). Queen's College. Romanes, George. Science. Scientific Experiments and Research. Theology. 1830-90. *2918*
Romanticism. Calvinism. Literature. Muir, John. 1838-1914. *2929*
—. Christianity. Cole, Thomas. Iconography. Painting. 1830's-40's. *1865*
—. Church History. 1760-1840. *47*
—. Europe. Nationalism. Revolution. Social criticism. 1630-1876. *950*
—. Evans, Warren Felt. Idealism. Mental healing. Mysticism. New Thought Movement. 1864-89. *1460*
—. Literature. Puritanism. 1620-1946. *2016*
—. Reform. Utopias. 1820's-60. *2364*
Romero, Diego. Franciscans. Indian-White Relations. Inquisition. Marriage. Missions and Missionaries. New Mexico. Plains Apache Indians. 1660-78. *3773*
Roofs. Churches. Episcopal Church, Protestant. New York City. Trinity Church. Upjohn, Richard. 1839-42. *1774*
Roosevelt, Franklin D. Hoover, Herbert C. Johnson, Lyndon B. Nixon, Richard M. Protestant ethic. Public welfare. Rhetoric. Weber, Max. 1905-79. *348*
Roosevelt, Franklin D. (administration). Agricultural Reform. Catholic Church. New Deal. Social Theory. 1933-39. *2572*
—. Capitalism. Marxism. Niebuhr, Reinhold. *Radical Religion* (periodical). 1930-43. *1343*
—. Catholic Church. Great Britain. Isolationism. Nicoll, John R. A. World War II. 1943. *1241*
Roosevelt, Theodore. Anti-Catholicism. Georgia. Letters. Watson, Thomas E. 1915. *2104*
—. Carter, Jimmy. Cromwell, Oliver. Great Britain. Political Leadership. Rickover, Hyman. 20c. *974*
Roots, Eliza McCook. China. Episcopal Church, Protestant. Missions and Missionaries. Roots, Logan H. 1900-34. *1743*
Roots, Logan H. China. Episcopal Church, Protestant. Missions and Missionaries. Roots, Eliza McCook. 1900-34. *1743*
Rosati, Joseph (review article). Catholic Church. Louisiana. North Central States. 1818-43. *3734*
Rosenblatt, Josef "Yosele". California (Los Angeles). Cantors. Concerts. Judaism. Loew's State Theatre. Music, liturgical. Vaudeville. 1925. *1917*
Rosenbloom, Charles J. Collectors and Collecting. Yale University. 1918-75. *280*
Rosenthal, Marcus. California (San Francisco). *Emanu-El* (newspaper). Immigration. Jews, East European. Letters-to-the-editor. Rabbis. Voorsanger, Jacob. 1905. *4141*
Ross, François Xavier. Bishops. Catholic Church. Education. Medicine. Quebec (Gaspé). Social Conditions. 1923-45. *3787*
Ross, James. Converts. Immigration. Mormons. Scotland. 1842-1900. *4011*
Round Valley Indian Reservation. California, northern. Converts. Ghost Dance. Indians. Methodist Church. 1870. *3484*
Rousseau, Jean-Jacques. Civil religion. Europe. Puritans. 18c-20c. *1177*
Rowen, Margaret W. Adventists. Fullmer, Bert E. Visions. Women. 1916-29. *2979*
Royal Canadian Mounted Police. Doukhobors. Ethnic groups. Federal government. Saskatchewan. Settlement. 1899-1909. *1006*
Royal Society. Christianity. Indians. Missions and Missionaries. New England Company. 1660's-70's. *1554*
Roybal, Max. Catholic Church. New Mexico (Albuquerque). Penitentes. Santos, statues. Wood Carving. 20c. *1901*
Rubin, Max. California (San Francisco). Jews. Nieto, Jacob. Rabbis. Temple Sherith Israel. 1893. *4148*
Rubio, José Gonzalez. California. Catholic Church. Mexico. Tithing. 1848. *3894*
Rumilly, Robert. Black, Conrad. Catholic Church. Church and state. Duplessis, Maurice (review article). Provincial Government. Quebec. 1930's-77. *1124*
Rumors. "Angel Dancers". Communalism. Folklore. Howell, Jane. Huntsman, Manson T. New Jersey (Woodcliff). Sects, Religious. 1890-1920. *389*
Rural Cemetery Movement. Cemeteries. Family. Social change. Tombstones. 1830's-40's. *87*
Rural Development. Antigonish Movement. Catholic Church. Nova Scotia. Social change. ca 1928-73. *2409*
—. Clergy. Council of Southern Mountain Workers. South. Standard of Living. 1913-72. *2451*
Rural Life. *See* Country Life.
Rural life movement. Catholic Church. Farm programs. New Deal. 1930's. *2573*
Rural Settlements *See also* Settlement; Villages.
—. Architecture. Catholic Church. Fundamentalists. German Americans. Social customs. Southerners. Texas (Cooke, Denton counties). 1860-1976. *2750*
—. Catholic Church. Daily Life. Nova Scotia (Lochaber). Presbyterians. 1830-1972. *2747*
—. Community centers. Country life movement. Progressives. 1900's-20's. *2447*
—. Cooperatives. Idaho (Paris). Mormons. 1869-96. *360*
Rural-Urban Studies. Adolescents. Children. Christianity. Social classes. 1920's-70's. *2762*
—. Catholic Church. French Canadians. Migration, Internal. Parishes. Quebec (Compton County). 1851-91. *3791*
Rush, Benjamin. Social Reform. 1770's-1813. *2375*
Russell, Charles Taze. Adventists. Friends of Man. Interior Lay Missionary Movement. Jehovah's Witnesses. 1852-1916. *3921*
—. Jehovah's Witnesses. Millenarianism. 1879-1916. *3919*
Russia *See also* Finland; USSR.
—. Asia, central. Immigration. Mennonites. 1870's-1920's. *3386*
—. Beiliss, Mendel. California (Oakland, San Francisco). Christianity. Jews. Newspapers. Trials. 1911-13. *4105*
—. Belk, Fred R. Immigration. Mennonites. Pacifism. 1880-84. *3351*
—. British Columbia. Daily life. Doukhobors. Immigration. Personal narratives. 1880's-1976. *3918*
—. California (Stockton). Davidson, Herman. Judaism (Reform). Opera. Rabbis. 1846-1911. *4204*
—. Canada. Doukhobors. Immigration. 1652-1908. *3915*
—. Canada. Doukhobors. Immigration. Persecution. Sects, Religious. 1654-1902. *3917*
—. Christianity. Deism. Jefferson, Thomas *(Life and Morals of Jesus of Nazareth)*. Jesus Christ. Morality. Theology. Tolstoy, Leo *(Christ's Christianity)*. 1800-85. *4278*
—. Clergy. Funk, John F. Manitoba. Mennonites. Settlement. Travel. 1873. *3393*
—. Clergy. Immigration. Manitoba. Mennonite Brethren Church. Warkentin, Johann. 1879-1948. *3409*
—. Emigration. Epp, Johann. Letters. Mennonites. North America. 1875. *3373*
—. Great Plains. Immigration. Manitoba. Mennonites. 1871-74. *3395*
—. Immigration. Manitoba. Mennonites. Shantz, Jacob Y. Travel accounts. 1873. *3425*
—. Immigration. Mennonites. Passenger lists. Quebec. 1874-80. *3364*
—. Immigration. Mennonites. South Dakota. Unruh, Daniel. 1820-82. *3430*
—. Immigration. Ukrainian Americans. 1850's-1945. *2785*
—. Mormons. 1857-72. *3965*
Russia (St. Petersburg). *Khristianski Pobornik* (periodical). Methodist Episcopal Church. Missions and Missionaries. Simons, George Albert. 1881-1917. *1696*
Russian Americans. Alaska (Kenai Peninsula). Freedom of religion. Orthodox Eastern Church, Russian (Old Believers). 1920's-76. *2810*
—. Assimilation. New Hampshire (Claremont). Orthodox Eastern Church, Russian. ca 1907-75. *2809*
—. Kansas (McPherson County). Mennonites. Social Change. 1874-1974. *3372*
—. Orthodox Eastern Church, Russian (Old Believers). 1890's-1970's. *2804*
Russian Canadians. British Columbia. Doukhobors. Saskatchewan. 1652-1976. *3916*
—. Immigration. Manitoba. Mennonites. Travel accounts. 1873. *3391*
—. Immigration. Mennonites. Saskatchewan (Rosthern). Social conditions. 1923. *3399*
Russian Revolution. Baerg, Anna. Canada. Diaries. Immigration. Mennonites. Women. 1917-23. *3362*
Russian-American Company. Alaska. Church finance. Documents. Education. Orthodox Eastern Church, Russian. Veniaminov, Metropolitan Innokentii. 1858. *2806*
Ruthenians. Fundamentalism. Immigrants. Orthodox Eastern Church, Greek. Uniates. Vermont (Proctor). 1914-73. *2757*
—. Ortynsky, Soter. Uniates. 1907-16. *3910*
Rutledge, Arthur B. Baptists, Southern. Garrott, William Maxfield. Graham, Agnes Nora. Missions and Missionaries. 20c. *1694*
Ryan, John A. Catholic Church. George, Henry. Single tax doctrine. Taxation. 1935. *2557*
Rytas (newspaper). Assimilation. Catholic Church. Connecticut (Waterbury). Lithuanian Americans. Zebris, Joseph. 1896-98. *3901*

S

Sabatier, Paul. Church and state. France. Gibbons, James. Letters. Nolan, Edward J. 1906. *1016*
Sabbatarianism. Architecture. Cathedral Church of St. John the Divine. Episcopal Church, Protestant. Manning, William Thomas. New York City. Sports. 19c-1920's. *3243*

—. Art. Attitudes. Centennial Exposition of 1876. Friends, Society of. Peace. Pennsylvania (Philadelphia). Temperance Movements. 1876. *3256*
—. California. Church and state. Supreme Courts, state. 1855-83. *2283*
—. Canada. Church and state. Cities. Streetcars. Values. 1890-1914. *2281*
—. Canada. Church and state. Lord's Day Act (Canada, 1906). Sports. 1906-77. *2284*
—. Catholic Church. Morality. Oklahoma. Politics. Protestant Churches. Referendum. Voting and Voting Behavior. 1959-76. *1290*
Sabbath. Adventists. Illinois. Jones, Alonzo Trevier. Religious liberty. World's Columbian Exposition (Chicago, 1893). 1893. *2280*
—. Adventists. New Hampshire (Washington). Oakes, Rachel. Preble, T. M. Wheeler, Frederick. 1841-44. *2287*
—. Baseball. Blue laws. Church and state. West Virginia. Wheeling Nailers (team). 1889. *2279*
—. Baseball. Social change. Values. 1892-1934. *2282*
—. Blue laws. Church and state. Legislators. Louisiana. Negroes. Reconstruction. 1867-75. *2285*
—. Central Conference of American Rabbis. Drachman, Bernard. Judaism. Judaism (Orthodox). Orthodox Jewish Sabbath Alliance. Saturday. 1903-30. *2277*
—. Congregationalism. Drummer, Jeremiah. Letters. Massachusetts. Sewall, Samuel. Taylor, Edward. 1704. *2276*
—. Elliott, Emory. New England. Puritans (review article). Sermons. Solberg, Winton U. 17c-18c. 1975-77. *3623*
—. Law enforcement. Licenses. Taverns. Virginia. ca 1630-1850. *2286*
Sabbath Schools. California (Oroville, San Francisco, Woodland). Congregation Beth Israel. Judaism (Orthodox). Messing, Aron J. Religious education. Travel. 1879. *4201*
Sabol, John. Catholic Church. First Catholic Slovak Union (Jednota). Pennsylvania. Slovak Americans. 1920's-60's. *3821*
Sacramental controversy. Adger, John B. Dabney, Robert L. Hodge, Charles. Mercersburg theology. Nevin, John W. Presbyterian Church. 1845-75. *3551*
Sacramental love tradition. Christianity. Hawthorne, Nathaniel. Literature. 1838-60. *2080*
Sacramentalism. Arminiamism. Church of England. Congregationalism. Converts. Johnson, Samuel (1696-1772). New England. 1715-22. *3183*
Sacraments. Holifield, E. Brooks. Lowrie, Ernest Benson. New England. Puritans (review article). Theology. Willard, Samuel. 16c-17c. 1974. *3637*
Sacred fire. Christianity. Gerhardt, Paul. Hymns. Symbolism in Literature. Translating and Interpreting. Wesley, John. 1760's-1930's. *1952*
Sacred Heart Academy. Architecture, academy. Catholic Church. Oregon (Salem). Piper, William W. 1834-83. *1828*
—. Catholic Church. Daily life. Documents. Girls. Holy Names of Jesus and Mary, Sisters of the. Oregon (Salem). 1863-73. *699*
Sacred Heart Church. Catholic Church. Georgia (Augusta). Local history. Preservation. 1976-78. *1823*
St. Albertus Church. Michigan (Detroit). Polish Americans. St. Casimir Church. 1870-1970. *3827*
St. Andrew Parish. Acculturation. Catholic Church. Irish Americans. Pennsylvania (Pittsburgh). 1863-90. *3748*
St. Andrew's African Methodist Episcopal Church. Baptists. California. Negroes. Political activity. 1850-73. *981*
St. Andrew's Church. Architecture. Catholic Church. Churches. Virginia (Roanoke). 1882-1975. *1834*
—. British Columbia (Bennett). Construction. Presbyterian Church. 1898. *1820*
—. Crapsey, Algernon Sidney. Episcopal Church, Protestant. Heresy. Humanitarian Reform. New York (Rochester). Trials. 1879-1927. *3234*
St. Andrew's Wesley United Church of Canada. Ecumenism. Methodist Church. Nova Scotia (Springhill). Presbyterian Church. United Church of Canada. 1800-1976. *2829*
St. Angela's Convent. Catholic Church. Germans, Russian. Religious Education. Saskatchewan (Prelate). Ursulines. Women. 1919-34. *680*
St. Anne's Chapel. Artists. Carmelites. Louisiana (DeSoto Parish). Restorations. 1891-1975. *1796*
St. Anne's Church. Church of England. Malcolm, Alexander. Maryland (Annapolis). Music. Society for the Propagation of the Gospel. Teaching. 1721-63. *1931*
St. Anne's Parish. Edson, Theodore. Episcopal Church, Protestant. Massachusetts (Lowell). Textile industry. 1800-65. *366*
St. Basil's Seminary. Catholic Church. Ontario (Toronto). Seminaries. Vatican Council II. 1962-67. *3775*
St. Benoît-du-Lac (abbey). Benedictines. Quebec (Brome County). 1955-79. *1770*
St. Bridget's Home. Catholic Church. Charities. Irish Canadians. McMahon, Patrick. Poor. Quebec (Quebec). 1847-1972. *2521*
St. Casimir Church. Michigan (Detroit). Polish Americans. St. Albertus Church. 1870-1970. *3827*
St. Cyril Academy. Catholic Church. Pennsylvania (Danville). Sisters of SS. Cyril and Methodius. Slovak Americans. Social customs. 1909-73. *3885*
St. Demetrios Church. Assimilation. Ethnicity. Greek Americans. New York City. Orthodox Eastern Church. St. Markela Church. 1970's. *318*
St. Denis Parish. Catholic Church. Irish Americans. Kelly, Dennis. Pennsylvania (Havertown). 1825-1975. *3683*
St. Hyacinthe Diocese. Catholic Church. Debt. LaRocque, Charles. Quebec. 1866-73. *3695*
St. Inigoes Church. Jesuits. Maryland (St. Marys County). Plantations. Slavery. 1806-1950. *326*
St. James Church. Episcopal Church, Protestant. Unonius, Gustaf. Wisconsin (Manitowoc). 1848-49. *3181*
St. James Episcopal Church. Architecture. Churches. Episcopal Church, Protestant. Virginia (Accomac). 1838. *1825*
St. John *Freeman* (newspaper). Anglin, Timothy Warren. Catholic Church. Irish Canadians. New Brunswick. Newspapers. 1849-83. *3680*
St. John the Vine Hickerson. Father Divine. Father Jehovia (pseud. of Samuel Morris). Georgia (Valdosta). Negroes. 1899-1914. *4259*
St. John's Church. Church of England. North Carolina, east. Public Administration. St. Paul's Church. 1729-75. *3240*
—. Clergy. Episcopal Church, Protestant. Kentucky (Versailles). 1829-1976. *3220*
St. John's College. Freemasonry. Maryland (Annapolis). State Legislatures. 1784. *517*
St. John's Episcopal Church. Architecture. Episcopal Church, Protestant. New Hampshire (Portsmouth). 1807-09. *1780*
—. Churches (Gothic Revival). Delaware (Wilmington). Episcopal Church, Protestant. Grace Methodist Church. Methodist Church. 1850-90. *1786*
St. John's Evangelical Lutheran Church (Old Dutch Church). Indiana (Elletsville). Lutheran Church (Evangelical). 1830-1956. *3330*
St. John's University. China (Shanghai). Colleges and Universities. Episcopal Church, Protestant. Missions and Missionaries. Pott, Francis L. H. 1888-1941. *1707*
St. Joseph Parish. Catholic Church. Colorado (Denver; Globeville). Polish Americans. 1902-78. *3724*
St. Joseph's College (Alberta). Alberta (Edmonton). Catholic Church. Colleges and Universities. MacDonald, John Roderick. 1922-23. *710*
St. Joseph's Convent. Catholic Church. Pennsylvania (St. Marys). Walburga, Saint. 1852-1974. *3778*
St. Joseph's Indian Normal School. American Protective Association. Anti-Catholicism. Church Schools. Indiana. Indians. 1888-96. *57*
St. Joseph's University College. Alberta, University of. Catholic Church. Colleges and Universities. Legal, Emile. O'Leary, Henry Joseph. 1906-26. *619*
St. Louis Free Congregation Library. Documents. Free Thinkers. German Americans. Immigrants. Missouri. Reading. Religious liberty. 1850-99. *1123*
St. Louis Protestant Orphan Asylum. Charities. Edgewood Children's Center. Missouri (Webster Groves). Orphans. Protestantism. 1834-1979. *2518*
St. Markela Church. Assimilation. Ethnicity. Greek Americans. New York City. Orthodox Eastern Church. St. Demetrios Church. 1970's. *318*
St. Mary's Cathedral of the Immaculate Conception. Catholic Church. Ontario (Kingston). 1843-1973. *3738*
St. Mary's Episcopal School for Indian Girls. Education. Episcopal Church, Protestant. Girls. Indians. South Dakota (Springfield). 1873-1973. *687*
St. Mary's of the Barrens. Catholic Church. Kenrick, Peter Richard. Missouri (Carondelet, St. Louis). Seminaries. 1840-48. *752*
St. Michael's High School. Christian Schools, Brothers of. New Mexico (Santa Fe). Secondary Education. 1859-1959. *742*
St. Paul's Church. Bible. Darwinism. Episcopal Church, Protestant. Europe. Excommunication. Hermeneutics. MacQueary, Howard. Ohio (Canton). Universalism. 1890-91. *3178*
—. Church of England. Missions and Missionaries. Nova Scotia (Halifax). Society for the Propagation of the Gospel. Tutty, William. 1749-52. *1646*
—. Church of England. North Carolina, east. Public Administration. St. John's Church. 1729-75. *3240*
—. Episcopal Church, Protestant. Otey, James Hervey. Tennessee (Franklin). 1827-34. *1802*
St. Paul's College. Keisker, Walter. Lutheran Church. Missouri (Concordia). Personal narratives. Religious Education. Students. 1913-19. 1980. *669*
St. Paul's Lutheran Church. Lutheran Church. Tennessee (Wartburg). 1844-1975. *3300*
St. Paul's Parish. American Revolution. Church of England. Georgia (Augusta). Loyalists. Seymour, James. 1775-83. *1301*
St. Peter's Colony. Catholic Church. German Americans. Language. Politics. Religious education. Saskatchewan. 1903-16. *779*
St. Peter's Lutheran Church. Clergy. Concordia Seminary. Illinois (Hahlen, Nashville). Lutheran Church (Missouri Synod). Personal narratives. Scharlemann, Ernst K. Seminaries. 1905-18. *3335*
St. Philip's Church. Episcopal Church, Protestant. New York City. Newspapers. Racism. Riots. Williams, Peter, Jr. 1830-50. *2142*
St. Stanislaus Kortka Church. Barzynski, Wincenty. Catholic Church. Illinois (Chicago). Polish Roman Catholic Union. Texas. 1838-99. *3678*
St. Thomas More College. Catholics. Colleges and Universities. Saskatchewan (Regina, Saskatoon). 1918-21. *620*
St. Vincent Academy. Catholic Church. Louisiana (Shreveport). -1973. *1799*
St. Vincent de Paul Society. Advocate role. Charities. Children. Indians. Poor. 1900-10. *2515*
St. Vincent's Hospital. Catholic Church. New Mexico (Santa Fe). Sisters of Charity. 1865-1948. *1449*
Saints Cyril and Methodius Parish. Catholic Church. Ontario (Toronto). Slovak Canadians. 1934-77. *3905*
Saints, patron. Catholic Church. Fiestas. New Mexico. Rites and Ceremonies. Villages. 1970's. *3892*
Salaries. *See* Wages.
Salience. Episcopal Church, Protestant. North Carolina. Religious commitment. 1975. *3222*
Salinan Indians. Acculturation. California (Monterey, San Luis Obispo counties). Catholic Church. Indians. Missions and Missionaries. 1770's-1830's. *1550*
Salishan Indians. Indian Shaker Church. Indians. Revitalization movements. Rites and Ceremonies. 1840's-1978. *2715*
Saloons. Ethnic groups. Prohibitionists. Values. Working Class. 1890-1920. *2588*
Salt industry. Clergy. Diaries. Episcopal Church, Protestant. Private Schools. Trade. Ward, Henry Dana. West Virginia (Kanawha Valley, Charleston). 1845-47. *3172*
Salt Lake and Fort Douglas Railroad. Economic Conditions. Mormons. Polygamy. Railroads. Statehood. Utah. Young, John W. 1883-1924. *3993*
Salubria (religious community). Communalism. Free thinkers. Iowa. Kneeland, Abner. 1827-44. *383*
Salvation. Cults. Social Customs. 1960-76. *4270*
—. New England. Novels. Presbyterian Church. Stowe, Harriet Beecher. Theology. Women. 1845-85. *2038*

Salvation Army. Americanization. Evangelical Covenant Church. Evangelical Free Church of America. Methodism. Pentecostal movement. Swedish Baptist Church. 1870-1973. *321*
—. Knights of Columbus. Military. Negroes. World War I. Young Men's Christian Association. 1917-18. *2720*
Salvation Army (Scandinavian Corps). Nelson, Edward O. Personal narratives. Scandinavian Americans. 1877-1977. *3293*
Samoa. Dean, Joseph Harry. Gibson, Walter Murray. Hawaii. Missions and Missionaries. Mormons. 1860's-90. *1683*
Samplers. Folklore. Poetry. Social Customs. 19c. *2021*
Samuel Colgate Baptist Historical Library. American Baptist Historical Society. *Baptist Bibliography*. Starr, Edward Caryl. 1935-76. *263*
—. American Baptist Historical Society. Baptists. Librarians. Starr, Edward Caryl. 1930's-76. *208*
San Francisco Earthquake and Fire. California. Charities. Disaster relief. Economic aid. Jews. Nieto, Jacob. Rabbis. 1906. *2520*
—. California (Oakland). Disaster relief. Jews. Refugees. Temple Sinai. 1906. *2527*
San Juan Diocese. Bishops. Byrne, Edwin V. Caruana, George J. Catholic Church. Jones, William A. Puerto Rico. 1866-1963. *3814*
Sanatoriums. Adventists. Postcards. 1900's-10's. *1427*
Sandberg, Neil C. (review article). California (Los Angeles). Catholic Church. Ethnology. Methodology. Polish Americans. 1968-74. *3813*
Sanders, James W. (review article). Catholic Church. Church Schools. Ethnic Groups. Illinois (Chicago). 1833-1965. 1977. *614*
Sanderson, Ross W. Council of Churches of Buffalo and Erie County. New York (Buffalo). 1937-42. *447*
Sanford, Frank. Communalism. Holy Ghost and Us Society. *Kingdom Come, Ark of the Holy Ghost and US Society* (vessel). Nova Scotia. Sects, Religious. Shipwrecks. 1910-48. *4261*
Sangre de Cristo Mountains. Catholic Church. New Mexico. Penitentes. 19c-1979. *3893*
Santa Clara, University of. California. Jesuits. 1849-51. *696*
—. California. Jesuits. Nobili, John. 1850-55. *695*
—. California (Santa Clara). Catholic Church. 1851-80. *697*
Santals (tribe). Baptists (freewill). India. Missions and Missionaries. Phillips, Jeremiah. 19c. *1733*
Santos, statues. Catholic Church. Folk art. Lopez, George. Lopez, José Dolores. New Mexico (Cordova). 20c. *1844*
—. Catholic Church. Folk art. New Mexico. 1780-1900. *1903*
—. Catholic Church. New Mexico (Albuquerque). Penitentes. Roybal, Max. Wood Carving. 20c. *1901*
Sartre, Jean-Paul. Buber, Martin. God is Dead Theology. Heidegger, Robert. Theology. 1961-64. *153*
Saskatchewan *See also* Prairie Provinces.
—. Anderson, James T. M. Anti-Catholicism. Public schools. School Act (Saskatchewan, 1930; amended). Secularization. 1929-34. *575*
—. Anglophiles. Catholic Church. Francophiles. Mathieu, Olivier-Elzéar. Regina Diocese. 1905-30. *3714*
—. Anti-Catholicism. Church and State. Clergy. Education, Finance. MacKinnon, Murdoch. Presbyterian Church. School Act (Saskatchewan, 1930; amended). Scott, Walter. 1913-26. *528*
—. Anti-Catholicism. Ku Klux Klan. Protestants. 1927-30. *2096*
—. Archives. Women. 1880's-1970's. *170*
—. *Bote* (newspaper). Germans, Russian. Mennonites. Nazism. USSR. Völkisch thought. 1917-39. *3431*
—. British Columbia. Doukhobors. Russian Canadians. 1652-1976. *3916*
—. Catholic Church. Co-operative Commonwealth Federation. Social reform. Socialism. 1930-50. *2567*
—. Catholic Church. French language. *Patriote de l'Ouest* (newspaper). 1910-41. *3764*
—. Catholic Church. German Americans. Language. Politics. Religious education. St. Peter's Colony. 1903-16. *779*
—. Catholic Church. Immigration. Manitoba. Mathieu, Olivier-Elzéar. Regina Archdiocese. 1911-31. *3781*
—. Catholic Church. Religious Education. Youth. 1870-1978. *715*
—. Communalism. Doukhobors. 1904. *415*
—. Doukhobors. Ethnic groups. Federal government. Royal Canadian Mounted Police. Settlement. 1899-1909. *1006*
—. Doukhobors. Public schools. 1905-50. *533*
Saskatchewan (Grenfell). Bee, William. Methodist Church, Primitive. Settlement. 1882. *3449*
Saskatchewan (Hague-Osler area). Mennonites. Social Change. 1895-1977. *3359*
Saskatchewan (Ile-à-la-Crosse). Catholic Church. Chipewyan Indians. Indian-White Relations. Letters. Mission St. Jean-Baptiste. Taché, Alexandre Antonin. 1823-54. *1503*
Saskatchewan (Prelate). Catholic Church. Germans, Russian. Religious Education. St. Angela's Convent. Ursulines. Women. 1919-34. *680*
Saskatchewan (Regina, Saskatoon). Catholics. Colleges and Universities. St. Thomas More College. 1918-21. *620*
Saskatchewan River Valley. Indians. Mennonites. Métis. Red River of the North. Red River of the North. Removals, forced. Settlement. 1869-95. *3360*
Saskatchewan (Rosthern). Agriculture. Factionalism. Germans, Russian. Mennonites. Personal narratives. Settlement. 1891-1900. *3442*
—. Immigration. Mennonites. Russian Canadians. Social conditions. 1923. *3399*
Saskatchewan (Wakaw). Doukhobors. Galicians. Hospitals. Lake Geneva Mission. Missions and Missionaries. Presbyterian Church. 1903-42. *1492*
Satanism. Church of Satan. LaVey, Anton Szandor. Occult Sciences. 1966-75. *4240*
—. Counter culture. Millenarianism. Mysticism. Social reform. 1960's-70's. *4243*
Satire. Cartoons and Caricatures. Great Britain. New England. Puritans. 1770-76. *2005*
—. Literature. McCulloch, Thomas (*Letters of Mephibosheth Stepsure*). Nova Scotia. Presbyterian Church. 1821-22. *2067*
—. Literature. New York. Presbyterian Church. Social criticism. Whitcher, Frances Miriam Berry (*Widow Bedott Papers*). 1847-55. *2056*
—. New England. Puritans. Ward, Nathaniel (*The Simple Cobler of Aggawam in America*). 1647. *3647*
Saturday. Central Conference of American Rabbis. Drachman, Bernard. Judaism. Judaism (Orthodox). Orthodox Jewish Sabbath Alliance. Sabbath. 1903-30. *2277*
Saunders, William O. Fundamentalism. Ham, Mordecai F. Newspapers. North Carolina (Elizabeth City). Revivals. 1924. *2217*
Saxon Lutheran Memorial. Concordia Historical Institute. Farms. Lutheran Church (Missouri Synod). Missouri (Perry County). Preservation. 1958-64. *220*
Scandinavian Americans. Converts. Mormons. Young, Kimball. 1893-1972. *3979*
—. Darby, John Nelson. Evangelical Free Church of America. Franson, Fredrik. Millenarianism. Moody, Dwight L. Revivalism. 1875-95. *2863*
—. Folklore. Mormons. Polygamy. Temples. Utah (Sanpete-Sevier area). 1849-1979. *4053*
—. Immigrants. Protestantism. 1849-1900. *303*
—. Mormons. Utah. ca 1873-1900. *3943*
—. Nelson, Edward O. Personal narratives. Salvation Army (Scandinavian Corps). 1877-1977. *3293*
Scanlan, Laurence. Catholicism. Clergy. Utah. 1875-79. *3897*
Scharlemann, Ernst K. Clergy. Concordia Seminary. Illinois (Hahlen, Nashville). Lutheran Church (Missouri Synod). Personal narratives. St. Peter's Lutheran Church. Seminaries. 1905-18. *3335*
Schiotz, Fredrik A. Ecumenism. Lutheran Church, American. Nelson, E. Clifford. 1945-69. *485*
Schisms. Abolition Movement. American Free Baptist Mission Society. Baptists. Missions and Missionaries. 1830-69. *2481*
—. Adventists. First Harlem Church. Humphrey, James K. Negroes. New York City. Utopia Park. 1920's-30's. *2143*
—. Amish. Pennsylvania (Lancaster County). Stoltzfus, John. Theology. 1850-77. *3439*
—. Arkansas (Texarkana). Congregationalism. Maddox, Finis Ewing. Presbyterian Church. Theology. 1908. *2869*
—. Baptists, Southern. Disciples of Christ. Evolution. Kentucky. Methodist Church. Presbyterian Church. 1920's. *2310*
—. Barnes, Albert (*Way of Salvation*). New Jersey (Morristown). Presbyterian Church. Sermons. Theology. Trials. 1829-37. *3576*
—. Besant, Annie. California (San Diego). Theosophy. Tingley, Katharine Augusta Westcott. 1897. *4298*
—. Bibliographies. Catholic Church. Catholic University of America. Hogan Schism. Parsons, Wilfrid. Pennsylvania (Philadelphia). 1785-1825. 1975. *3845*
—. Bidamon, Emma Smith. Illinois (Nauvoo). Mormons. Property. Smith, Joseph. Women. Women. Young, Brigham. 1832-79. *3932*
—. Clergy. Equality. Mormons (Reorganized). Negroes. Women. 1860-1979. *4032*
—. Clergy. Friends, Society of. Keith, George. Pennsylvania. Schisms. 1660-1720. *3261*
—. Clergy. Friends, Society of. Keith, George. Pennsylvania. Schisms. 1660-1720. *3261*
—. Congregationalism. Connecticut (Canterbury). Family. Great Awakening. Local politics. 1742-50. *2242*
—. Congregationalism. Connecticut (New London). Great Awakening. New Lights. Shepherd's Tent (college). 1720-50. *2250*
—. Ethnic groups. Evangelical Association. 1887-94. *3664*
—. Excommunication. Godbe, William Samuel. Mormonism. 1840's-80's. *4047*
—. Friends, Society of. Keith, George. Pennsylvania. 1693-1703. *3262*
—. Friends, Society of. Keith, George. Pennsylvania. Pusey, Caleb. Theology. 17c. *3273*
—. Friends, Society of. Massachusetts. New York Yearly Meeting. Vermont. 1845-1949. *3259*
—. Historians. Letters. Mormons. Wight, Lyman. Woodruff, Wilford. 1857-58. *4049*
—. Immigrants. Netherlands. Reformed Christian Church. Reformed Dutch Church. 1834-80. *3163*
—. Kentucky. Presbyterian Church (New Church Synod). 1837-58. *3574*
—. Methodist Episcopal Church. Methodist Protestant Church. 1775-1820. *294*
—. Mormons. 1840-1978. *3922*
—. Mormons. Morris, Joseph. Utah (Weber River). War. Young, Brigham. 1861-62. *3926*
Schlatter, Francis. Faith healing. Mysticism. New Mexico (Peralta). 1895-96. *1429*
Schlutius, Emma. California (Santa Cruz). Converts. Judaism. 1877. *4098*
Schmidt, Larry (review article). Canada. Grant, George. Philosophy. Politics. Theology. 1945-78. *509*
Schmucker, Samuel Simon. Ecumenism. Lutheran Church. 1838. *474*
—. Evangelical Alliance. Lutheran Church (General Synod). 1843-51. *3294*
Scholars. Blair, Duncan Black. Gaelic language. Nova Scotia (Pictou County). Poetry. Presbyterianism. Scotland. 1846-93. *2070*
Scholarship. Baptists. Church and Social Problems. Clergy. Dawson, Joseph Martin. 1879-1973. *3015*
—. Blair, Duncan Black. Gaelic language. Nova Scotia (Barney's River). Poets. Presbyterianism. 1848-93. *2069*
—. Christianity. Marti, Fritz. Philosophy. Swiss Americans. Theology. 1894-1979. *2803*
—. Historiography. Jews. 1948-76. *207*
—. Mormons. O'Dea, Thomas F. 1957-74. *4012*
Scholasticism. Arts. California. Catholic Church. Historiography (Anglo-American). Missions and Missionaries. 1740's-1976. *1878*
School Act (Saskatchewan, 1930; amended). Anderson, James T. M. Anti-Catholicism. Public schools. Saskatchewan. Secularization. 1929-34. *575*
—. Anti-Catholicism. Church and State. Clergy. Education, Finance. MacKinnon, Murdoch. Presbyterian Church. Saskatchewan. Scott, Walter. 1913-26. *528*
School boards. Anti-Catholicism. Georgia (Atlanta). Ku Klux Klan. 1916-27. *2115*
—. Church and State. Political Parties. Prince Edward Island. Prince of Wales College Act (1860). 1860-63. *744*
School Integration. Catholic Church. Church Schools. Glennon, John J. Missouri (St. Louis). Ritter, Joseph E. 1935-47. *2542*

Schools *See also* Church Schools; Colleges and Universities; Education; High Schools; Private Schools; Public Schools; Students; Teaching.
—. Acculturation. Blackburn, Gideon. Cherokee Indians. Missions and missionaries. Presbyterian Church. Tennessee. 1804-10. *1491*
—. Arizona (Coconino County). Frontier. Immigrants. Mormons. 1875-1900. *510*
—. Asylums. Catholic Church. Hospitals. Illinois (Chicago). Wisconsin (Milwaukee). 19c. *3886*
—. Blackburn, Gideon. Cherokee Indians. Indians. Missions and Missionaries. Old Southwest. Presbyterian Church. Whiskey. 1809-10. *700*
—. Bloomfield Academy. Chickasaw Indians. Downs, Ellen J. Girls. Indians. Methodist Church. Oklahoma (Penola County). Personal Narratives. 1853-66. *772*
—. Bureau of Indian Affairs. Catholic Church. Indian-White Relations. Iowa. Presbyterian Church. Winnebago Indians. 1834-48. *737*
—. Clergy. Frontier. Missouri. Protestant Churches. ca 1800-30. *639*
—. Episcopal Church, Protestant. Girls. Nevada (Reno). Whitaker, Ozi William. 1876-94. *769*
—. Hymns. Music. Singing. 1775-1820. *1951*
—. Judaism (Orthodox). New York. Social relations. 18c. *4175*
Schreiber, Clara Seuel. Lutheran Church. Mission Festival Sunday. Missions and Missionaries. Personal narratives. Wisconsin (Freistadt). 1900. *1630*
—. Lutheran Church. Palm Sunday. Personal narratives. Wisconsin (Freistadt). 1898. *3338*
Schreiber, Emanuel. California (Los Angeles). Judaism (Reform). Wilshire Boulevard Temple. 1881-1932. *4216*
Schroeder, Theodore. Atheism. Freedom of Speech. *Lucifer's Lantern* (periodical). Mormons. Polygamy. Utah. 1889-1900. *2125*
Schulze, Ernst Carl Ludwig. Clergy. Lutheran Church. Steup, Henry Christian. 1852-1931. *3339*
Schurz, Carl. District of Columbia. Johnson, Andrew. Lincoln, Abraham. Seance. Spiritualism. 1865. *4293*
Schwan, Henry C. Exegesis. Luther, Martin *(Small Catechism)*. 1893-1912. *3332*
Schwartz, Auguste von. Immigration. Iowa. Lutheran Church. Wartburg College. Women. 1861-77. *3320*
Schwenkfelders. American Revolution. Dunkards. Friends, Society of. Mennonites. Moravian Church. Neutrality. Pacifism. Taxation. 1765-83. *2670*
Schwermann, Albert H. Alberta (Edmonton, Mellowdale). Concordia College. Lutheran Church (Missouri Synod). Personal narratives. USA. 1891-1976. *753*
Science *See also* headings beginning with the word scientific; Astronomy; Botany; Ethnology; Mathematics; Natural History.
—. 1960-74. *2340*
—. Aesthetics. Emerson, Ralph Waldo. Philosophy. Plotinus. Transcendentalism. 1836-60. *2302*
—. Albright, William Foxwell. Archaeology. Biblical studies. Philosophy of History. 1918-70. *2328*
—. Attitudes. Chiropractic. Cultism. Medicine (practice of). 1850's-1970's. *2314*
—. Baconianism. Bozeman, Theodore Dwight (review article). Protestantism. 1800's-60's. 1977. *2324*
—. Baptists. Educational Policy. Evolution. Kentucky. 1922-28. *2347*
—. Bible. Creation theory. Dana, James Dwight. Guyot, Arnold. Protestantism. 1850's. *2333*
—. California. Church and state. Creationism. Curricula. Educational Policy. Evolution. 1963-74. *2331*
—. Canada. Great Britain. Ontario (Kingston, Smith Falls). Queen's College. Romanes, George. Romanes, George John. Scientific Experiments and Research. Theology. 1830-90. *2918*
—. Catholic Church. Christian Renaissance. Converts. Literature. Philosophy. Stern, Karl. 1920's-60's. *2758*
—. Charismatic movement. Europe. Folk Religion (review article). Health. Occult sciences. 16c-19c. 1975-76. *7*
—. Christianity. Ethics. Rationalism. White, Andrew Dickson. 1888-90's. *2288*
—. Christianity. Lewis, Sinclair. Novels. Secular humanism. 1900-50. *2003*
—. Colleges and Universities. Curricula. Massachusetts (South Hadley). Mount Holyoke College. Women. 1839-88. *2320*
—. Congregationalism. Edwards, Jonathan. Epistemology. 1703-58. *2327*
—. Congregationalism. Edwards, Jonathan. Rainbows. Theology. 1740-45. *2343*
—. Counter culture. Technology. Values. 1960's-70's. *2292*
—. *Defender* (periodical). Evolution. Kansas (Wichita). *Red Horse* (periodical). Winrod, Gerald Burton. 1925-57. *2305*
—. Ecology. Hopkins, Gerard Manley. Humanities. Jesuits. Poetry. ca 1840-70's. *3701*
—. Education. Friends, Society of. Hallowell, Benjamin. Virginia (Alexandria). 1824-60. *3281*
—. God is Dead theology. Theology. 1600-1970. *2306*
—. Judaism (Reform). Pittsburgh Platform (1885). Theology. Voorsanger, Jacob. 1872-1908. *2337*
—. Mathews, Shailer. Modernism. Social gospel movement. Theology. 1864-1930. *2443*
—. Moore, R. Laurence (review article). Spiritualism. 1850-1977. *4290*
—. Morality. Social studies. Teaching. 1977. *2321*
—. Philosophy. 1974. *2294*
—. Poetry. Puritans. Taylor, Edward. 1706. *2342*
—. Presbyterian Church. *Princeton Review* (periodical). Providence. Social problems. 1789-1860. *3527*
—. Puritanism. Winthrop, John (1714-79). 1738-79. *2315*
Science fiction. Myths and Symbols. Psychology. Sensitivity movement. 1960's-70's. *2060*
—. National Aeronautics and Space Administration. Religious experience. Space exploration. 1960-76. *146*
Science League of America. Adventists. California (San Francisco). Debates. Educational Policy. Evolution. 1925. *2291*
Scientific Experiments and Research. Canada. Great Britain. Ontario (Kingston, Smith Falls). Queen's College. Romanes, George. Romanes, George John. Science. Theology. 1830-90. *2918*
Scientific thought. New England. Puritans. Winthrop, John. Winthrop, John, Jr. Winthrop, John (1714-79). 1620-1779. *2295*
Scopes, John Thomas. Candler, Warren A. Conservatism. Evolution. Leopold, Nathan. Loeb, Richard. Methodist Episcopal Church, South. Trials. 1921-41. *2293*
Scopes Trial. Bryan, William Jennings. Darrow, Clarence. Evolution. Tennessee (Dayton). Trials. 1925. *2336*
Scotch-Irish. American Revolution. Immigrants. Presbyterian Church. Scottish Americans. 1700-75. *1268*
Scotland. Blair, Duncan Black. Gaelic language. Nova Scotia (Pictou County). Poetry. Presbyterianism. Scholars. 1846-93. *2070*
—. Catholic Church. Immigration. Persecution. Prince Edward Island. 1769-74. *3702*
—. Church and State. Church of England. King's College (charter). Ontario (Toronto). Strachan, John. 1815-43. *506*
—. Converts. Immigration. Mormons. Ross, James. 1842-1900. *4011*
Scott, Donald M. (review article). Clergy. Congregationalism. New England. Presbyterian Church. Professionalism. 1750-1850. 1979. *2865*
Scott, Walter. Anti-Catholicism. Church and State. Clergy. Education, Finance. MacKinnon, Murdoch. Presbyterian Church. Saskatchewan. School Act (Saskatchewan, 1930; amended). 1913-26. *528*
Scottish Americans. American Revolution. Immigrants. Presbyterian Church. Scotch-Irish. 1700-75. *1268*
Scottish Canadians. Canada. Capitalism. Fur trade. Hudson's Bay Company. Protestantism. 18c-1970's. *377*
—. Catholics. Great Britain. Immigration. Macdonnell, Alexander. Ontario. 1770's-1814. *3862*
—. Factionalism. Nova Scotia (Pictou County). Presbyterian Church. Social Conditions. 1898-1966. *3533*
—. Immigrants. McDonald, Donald. Millenarianism. Presbyterianism. Prince Edward Island. ca 1828-67. *3591*
Scovil, G. C. Coster. Canada. China. Church of England. Missionary Society of the Canadian Church. Personal narratives. 1946-47. *1744*
Scripture, doctrine of. Alexander, Archibald. Presbyterian Church. Princeton Theological Seminary. 1772-1929. *3566*
Scudder, Vida Dutton. Christianity. Industrial Relations. Massachusetts (Lawrence). Social reform. Socialism. Women. 1912. *2374*
Seabury, Samuel (pseud. A. W. Farmer). American Revolution. Church of England. Continental Congress. Loyalists. 1774-84. *1378*
Seamen. Bergner, Peter. Immigrants. *John Wesley* (vessel). Methodist Episcopal Church. New York City. 1830-77. *3478*
Seamen's Bethel. Massachusetts (Boston). Methodist Church. Taylor, Edward Thompson. 1793-1871. *3452*
—. Massachusetts (Boston, New Bedford). Methodist Church. Mudge, Enoch. Taylor, Edward Thompson. 1776-1850. *3457*
Seance. District of Columbia. Johnson, Andrew. Lincoln, Abraham. Schurz, Carl. Spiritualism. 1865. *4293*
Secession *See also* States' Rights.
—. Alabama. Clergy. Methodist Episcopal Church (South). Neely, Phillip Phillips. 1861. *1213*
Second Presbyterian Church. Art. Illinois (Chicago). Presbyterian Church. Stained glass windows. 1872-74. *1855*
Secondary Education *See also* High Schools; Private Schools; Public Schools.
—. Baptists. Elementary education. Religious Education. State Aid to Education. 1850-1910. *718*
—. Baptists. Georgia (Cartersville). Moon, Lottie. Women. 1870-1903. *2985*
—. Benedictine High School. Boys. Catholic Church. Ohio (Cleveland). 1928-78. *787*
—. Catholic Church. Professions. Quebec. Religious orders. Women. 1908-54. *871*
—. Christian Schools, Brothers of. New Mexico (Santa Fe). St. Michael's High School. 1859-1959. *742*
—. Immanuel Lutheran School. Lutheran Church. Wisconsin (Milwaukee). 1903-78. *785*
Secret societies. Methodist Connection, Wesleyan. 1843-60. *2363*
Sectarianism. Backus, Isaac *(History of New England)*. Baptists. Friends, Society of. New England Meeting for Sufferings. Theology. 17c-1784. *2953*
—. Baptists, Southern. Sectionalism. 1970's. *2987*
—. Berkeley, George. Church of England. Education. Reform. Rhode Island (Newport). 1704-34. *3230*
—. Christianity. Deism. Jefferson, Thomas. Letters. 1784-1800. *4280*
—. Negroes. Whites. Working Class. 1969. *94*
Sectionalism. Baptists, Southern. Sectarianism. 1970's. *2987*
—. Friends, Society of. Social status. West Virginia. 18c-19c. *3257*
Sects, Religious. "Angel Dancers". Communalism. Folklore. Howell, Jane. Huntsman, Manson T. New Jersey (Woodcliff). Rumors. 1890-1920. *389*
—. Arkansas, northeast. Faith healing. Pentecostals. 1937-73. *1433*
—. Baptists. Landmark movement. Theology. 1850-1950. *3089*
—. Baptists, Primitive. Georgia, northwest. 1830-41. *3036*
—. Brethren in Christ. Canada. Engel, Jacob. Pennsylvania (Lancaster County). 1775-1964. *3437*
—. California (San Francisco; Potrero Hill). Ethnicity. Molokans. 1906-76. *2807*
—. Canada. Deprogramming. Organizations. USA. 1960's-70's. *4267*
—. Canada. Doukhobors. Immigration. Persecution. Russia. 1654-1902. *3917*
—. Church and State. Property tax. 1847-1979. *1005*
—. Civil religion. Counter Culture. Persecution. Public Opinion. 19c-20c. *4263*
—. Civil Rights. Deprogramming. Religious liberty. 1970's. *1062*
—. Communalism. Holy Ghost and Us Society. *Kingdom Come, Ark of the Holy Ghost and US Society* (vessel). Nova Scotia. Sanford, Frank. Shipwrecks. 1910-48. *4261*
—. Converts. Deprogramming. 1970's. *4265*

—. Cults. Sociologists. Youth. 1960's-70's. *4256*
—. Emigration. Illinois. Janssonists. Social Classes. Sweden. 1845-47. *2620*
—. Evangelism. Postal Service. 1970's. *1118*
—. Fund raising. 1945-79. *4245*
—. Guyana (Jonestown). Jones, Jim. People's Temple. ca 1950-79. *4262*
—. Jesus movement. 1960's-70's. *2771*
—. Kansas. Pacifism. Patriotism. World War I. 1917-18. *2677*
—. Matthews, Robert ("Matthias the Prophet"). New York City. Retrenchment Society. 1828-35. *70*
—. Mennonites. Mormons. ca 19c-20c. *32*
Secular Humanism. Christianity. Judaism. Pfeffer, Leo. Politics. Social Change. 1958-76. *132*
—. Christianity. Lewis, Sinclair. Novels. Science. 1900-50. *2003*
Secularism. Bible. Business. 1900-29. *344*
—. Calvinism. 18c-20c. *1186*
—. Catholic Church. French Canadians. Groulx, Lionel. Quebec. Separatist Movements. 1897-1928. *1409*
—. Catholic Church. Liberalism. Neoorthodoxy. Pluralism. Theology. 1936-74. *3899*
—. Childhood. Leadership. Sex roles. Women. 1636-1930. *881*
—. Christianity. God is Dead Theology. Islam. Methodology. Religions, history of. Smith, Wilfred Cantwell. Theology. 1940-73. *134*
—. Niebuhr, Reinhold. Philosophy. Theology. 1974. *2855*
Secularization. 1964-73. *205*
—. Anderson, James T. M. Anti-Catholicism. Public schools. Saskatchewan. School Act (Saskatchewan, 1930; amended). 1929-34. *575*
—. Authority. Bellah, Robert N. Civil religion. Myths and Symbols. Politics. 1977. *1165*
—. California. Durán, Narciso. Franciscans. Indians. Missions. 1826-46. *1093*
—. Church and State. Education. Great Britain. India. 19c. *522*
—. Civil religion. Protestantism. Socialism. 16c-20c. *2910*
—. Great Britain. Law. Protestantism. 1800-1970. *10*
—. Ideology. Middle Classes. Pluralism. Social Change. 17c-20c. *12*
—. Industrialization. Law and society. Massachusetts. Nelson, William E. (review article). Social change. 1760-1830. *53*
—. Jews. Self-perception. 1957-77. *4127*
—. Millenarianism. 1850-1914. *78*
See, Isaac M. New Jersey (Newark). Presbyterian Church. Sermons. Women. 1876. *805*
Segregation *See also* Desegregation; Discrimination; Minorities; Negroes.
—. American Anti-Slavery Society. Female Anti-Slavery Society. Foster, Abigail Kelley. Fox, George. Friends, Society of. Mott, Lucretia Coffin. 17c. 1837-66. *791*
—. Baptists. Methodism. Negroes. New York. 1865-68. *2139*
—. Boycotts. Church Schools. Mexican Americans. Mexican Presbyterian Mission School. Presbyterian Church. Public schools. Texas (San Angelo). 1910-15. *618*
—. Catholic Church. Church Schools. 1972. *704*
—. Freedmen. Methodist Episcopal Church, Colored. Methodist Episcopal Church, South. Religious liberty. South. 1865-70. *3464*
—. Georgia (Atlanta). Haven, Gilbert. Negroes. Protestant Churches. 1865-1906. *2145*
—. Negroes. Protestantism. South. 1885-90's. *2135*
—. Presbyterian Church. Slavery. South Carolina (Charleston). 1845-60. *2154*
Seixas, Moses. Judaism (Orthodox). Letters. Religious Liberty. Rhode Island (Newport). Washington, George. 1790. 1974. *1081*
Self-conceptions. Jesus movement. Religiosity. 1960's-70's. *2783*
Self-determination. Black power. Church and Social Problems. Economic Aid. Episcopal Church, Protestant. General Convention Special Program. 1963-75. *2541*
—. Christianity. Ecumenism. 1960's-70's. *473*
Self-made man doctrine. Success. Swedish Americans. 1870's-1910's. *370*
Self-perception *See also* Identity.
—. Catholic Church. French Canadians. Quebec. Social Customs. Values. 17c-1978. *3789*
—. Child-rearing. Greven, Philip (review article). Protestantism. 1620-18c. *836*
—. Jews. Secularization. 1957-77. *4127*
Self-reliance. Amusements. Georgia. Jones, Sam. Methodist Episcopal Church, South. Morality. Revivals. 1872-1906. *3498*
Seminaries. Abolition Movement. Andover Seminary. Congregationalism. Massachusetts. Theology. 1825-35. *2491*
—. Alexander, Joseph A. Biblical criticism. Princeton Theological Seminary. Theater. 1830-61. *705*
—. Autobiography. Buenger, Theodore Arthur. Clergy. Concordia Seminary. German Americans. Lutheran Church (Missouri Synod). 1886-1909. *3297*
—. Baptists, Southern. Graves, James Robinson. Newspapers. *Tennessee Baptist* (newspaper). 1820-93. *3076*
—. Baptists, Southern. Kentucky (Louisville). 1877-1977. *690*
—. Catholic Church. Kenrick, Peter Richard. Missouri (Carondelet, St. Louis). St. Mary's of the Barrens. 1840-48. *752*
—. Catholic Church. Ontario (Toronto). St. Basil's Seminary. Vatican Council II. 1962-67. *3775*
—. Christianity. Huidekoper, Frederick. Judaism. Meadville Theological School. Pennsylvania. Unitarianism. 1834-92. *4086*
—. Clergy. Concordia Seminary. Illinois (Hahlen, Nashville). Lutheran Church (Missouri Synod). Personal narratives. St. Peter's Lutheran Church. Scharlemann, Ernst K. 1905-18. *3335*
—. Concordia Seminary. Daily Life. Kansas (Clay Center). Lutheran Church (Missouri Synod). Mueller, Peter. Students. 1883-89. *707*
—. Episcopal Church, Protestant. Letters. Nashotah House. Unonius, Gustaf. Wisconsin (Nashotah). 1884. *585*
—. Fund raising. Jewish Theological Seminary. Judaism (Orthodox). Mergers. New York City. Yeshiva College. 1925-28. *736*
—. Green, Jacob. Presbyterian Church. 1775. *714*
—. Hebrew Union College. Jewish Institute of Religion. 1875-1974. *786*
—. Hebrew Union College. Judaism (Reform). Ohio (Cincinnati). Rabbis. Wise, Isaac Mayer. 1817-90's. *701*
—. Kentucky (Woodford County). Presbyterian Church (New School). 1837-51. *722*
—. Lifestyles. Lutheran Church. Missouri (St. Louis). Students. 1922-28. *703*
—. Religious Education. 1808-50. *709*
Seminaries, correspondence. Chautauqua School of Theology. Methodist Church. New York. Vincent, John Heyl. 1881-98. *763*
Seminole Indians. Episcopal Church, Protestant. Florida. Gray, William Crane. Indian-White Relations. Missions and missionaries. 1893-1914. *1558*
Semiology. Conversion. New England. Puritans. Theology. 1600's. *3612*
Senate *See also* House of Representatives; Legislation.
—. Christianity. Civil religion. Nationalism. Webster, Daniel. 1813-52. *1191*
Senators. Canada. Elites. Ethnicity. Protestant ethic. Values. 1971. *958*
Seneca Indians. Friends, Society of. New York. Political Factions. Tribal government. 1848. *1202*
Sensitivity movement. Myths and Symbols. Psychology. Science fiction. 1960's-70's. *2060*
Senyshyn, Ambrose (obituary). Pennsylvania. Philadelphia Archeparchy. Ukrainian Americans. Uniates. 1903-76. *3906*
Separatism. Mennonites. Politics. Social Reform. 1840's-1930's. *3418*
Separatist Movements. Catholic Church. French Canadians. Groulx, Lionel. Quebec. Secularism. 1897-1928. *1409*
Sephardic Hebrew Center. California (Los Angeles). Immigration. Jews (Rhodesli). Judaism (Orthodox). 1900-74. *4180*
Seri Indians. Arizona (Nogales). Buena, Mariano. Catholic Church. Gil, Juan. Indians. 1768-72. *1559*
Serials. *See* Periodicals.
Sermons. Abolition Movement. Assassination. Brooks, Phillips. Episcopal Church, Protestant. Lincoln, Abraham. Pennsylvania (Philadelphia). 1865. 1893. *2463*
—. Adolescence. 1700-30. *856*
—. American Revolution. Church of England. Government, Resistance to. Griffith, David. Virginia Convention. 1775. *1351*
—. American Revolution. Congregationalism. Cooper, Samuel. Massachusetts (Boston). Rhetoric. 1768-80. *1352*
—. American Revolution. Connecticut (Norfield). Protestantism. Sherwood, Samuel. 1776. *1414*
—. American Revolution. Cooke, Samuel. History Teaching. Langdon, Samuel. Mayhew, Jonathan. West, Samuel. Witherspoon, John. 1750-76. 1975. *1406*
—. American Revolution. Cooper, Samuel. Massachusetts (Boston). 1776. *1146*
—. American Revolution (antecedents). Clergy. Political theory. 1750's-75. *1415*
—. Antinomianism. Cotton, John. Hutchinson, Anne. Massachusetts. Shepard, Thomas. Theology. 1630's. *3648*
—. Antinomianism. Emerson, Ralph Waldo. Puritanism. Social reform. Transcendentalism. 1820's-30's. *4070*
—. Archival catalogs and inventories. Emmett, Daniel. Hymns. Minstrel Shows. Negroes. Ohio Historical Society. 1838-96. 1976. *2064*
—. Associates of Dr. Bray. Church of England. Georgia Trustees. 1733-50. *3231*
—. Attitudes. Mather, Cotton. New England. Puritans. Women. 1650-1800. *880*
—. Baptists. Cameron, William Andrew. Canada. Clergy. Shields, Thomas Todhunter. 1910-41. *3021*
—. Baptists. First African Baptist Church. Jasper, John. Negroes. Virginia (Richmond). 1812-1901. *2990*
—. Baptists, Southern. 1707-1980. *1984*
—. Baptists (Two-Seed-in-the-Spirit). Evangelism. Indiana (Putnam County). Music. Oral tradition. Otter Creek Predestinarian Church. 1820-1975. *1940*
—. Barnes, Albert *(Way of Salvation)*. New Jersey (Morristown). Presbyterian Church. Schisms. Theology. Trials. 1829-37. *3576*
—. Bible. Cave, Robert Catlett. Disciples of Christ. Missouri (St. Louis). Theology. 1840's-90's. *3111*
—. Bible. Georgia Trustees. Rhetoric. Slavery. 1731-50. *2161*
—. Bibliographies. Clergy. Friends, Society of. 1653-1700. *204*
—. Bibliographies. New England. Puritans. 1652-1700. 1903. *1964*
—. Bibliographies. Vermont. Women. 1800-1915. *909*
—. California (Bodie). Clay, Eugene O. Funerals. Methodist Church. Nevada (Smith Valley). Personal narratives. 1915. *3456*
—. California (San Francisco). Franklin, Lewis Abraham. Judaism. Rabbis. Yom Kippur. 1850. *4100*
—. Calvinism. Congregationalism. Government, Resistance to. Massachusetts (Boston). Mayhew, Jonathan. Political Theory. 1750. *1381*
—. Calvinism. Diphtheria. Enlightenment. Great Awakening. New England. 1735-40. *2260*
—. Capital Punishment. Clergy. New England. Protestantism. 1674-1750. *2822*
—. Catholic Church. Democracy. Manuscripts. Tocqueville, Alexis de. Yale University. 1831-40. *1990*
—. Chain of being. Church of England. Cradock, Thomas. Maryland (Baltimore County). Poetry. Social theory. 1700-80. *3227*
—. Charles I. Cotton, John. Great Britain. Massachusetts (Boston). Puritans. Regicide. 1650. *1349*
—. Christians. Massachusetts. War. 1640-1740. *2630*
—. Church of England. Clergy. Cradock, Thomas. Maryland (Baltimore County). Poetry. 1700-70. *3229*
—. Church of England. Inglis, Charles. Loyalists. Propaganda. 1770-80. *1370*
—. Civil War. Disasters. Lincoln, Abraham. Puritans. Rhetoric. 1650-1870. *1968*
—. Civil War. Elliott, John H. Episcopal Church, Protestant. South Carolina (Camden). 1862. *1982*
—. Clergy. Congregations. Morality. 1970's. *2904*
—. Clergy. Eulogies. Presidency (mystique). Washington, George. 1799. *1190*
—. Communion. Mather, Increase. Puritans. ca 1680-1710. *3629*
—. Congregationalism. Cooper, Samuel. Funerals. Music. New England. Social Customs. 18c. *3113*
—. Congregationalism. Edwards, Jonathan. New York. Presbyterian Church. 1722-23. *2883*

—. Connecticut (Enfield). Edwards, Jonathan ("Sinners in the Hands of an Angry God"). Theology. 1741. *1994*
—. Deity. Illinois (Nauvoo). Mormons. Smith, Joseph (King Follett Discourse). Theology. 1844. *3976*
—. Elliott, Emory. New England. Puritans (review article). Sabbath. Solberg, Winton U. 17c-18c. 1975-77. *3623*
—. Embury, Philip. Methodist Church. New Hampshire (Chesterfield). 1754-1805. *3488*
—. Father Divine. Negroes. Peace Mission (movement). 1915-65. *4249*
—. Folklore. New England. Puritans. 1625-60. *1981*
—. German language. Pennsylvania. Protestant Churches. 18c. *1989*
—. Great Britain. New England. Puritans. Rhetoric. 1620's-50's. *1980*
—. Iconography. New England. Poetry. Puritans. Tombstones. 17c. *1977*
—. Illinois (Nauvoo). Mormons. Smith, Joseph (King Follett Discourse). Theology. 1844-1978. *3947*
—. Jeremiads. New England. Puritans. Sports. 17c-18c. *3659*
—. Jesus Christ. Judaism (Orthodox, Reform). New York City. Theology. Wise, Stephen Samuel. 1925-26. *4153*
—. Lutheran Free Church. Norwegian Americans. Religious Liberty. Sverdrup, Georg. Thanksgiving. 1896-1907. *3304*
—. Massachusetts (Boston). Mather, Cotton. Psalmody. Puritans. Singing. 1721. *1938*
—. Massachusetts (Westfield). Puritans. Taylor, Edward ("Upon the Types of the Old Testament"). Theology. Typology. 1693. *3638*
—. Nebraska (Lincoln). Puritans. Taylor, Edward ("Upon the Types of the Old Testament"). Theology. Typology. 1693-1706. *3639*
—. New England. Puritans. Sex roles. Theology. Women. 1690-1730. *883*
—. New Jersey (Newark). Presbyterian Church. See, Isaac M. Women. 1876. *805*
—. Presbyterian Church. Sunday, Billy. Virtue. Women. Working class. 1915. *890*
—. Protestantism. Rhetoric. 1952-74. *1972*
—. Theology. 18c-20c. *1988*
Serra, Junípero. California. Catholic Church. Mission San Juan Capistrano. 1775-76. *1601*
—. California. Dominicans. Franciscans. Jesuits. Missions and Missionaries. 1768-76. *1575*
Serra Museum. California (San Diego). Catholic Church. Excavations. Military Camps and Forts. Missions and Missionaries. 1769-75. 1964-70's. *1526*
Servants. Anti-Catholicism. Maryland. Slave Revolts. 1745-58. *2117*
Seton, Elizabeth Ann. Catholic Church. Church Schools. White House (school). 1774-1821. *625*
Settlement *See also* Colonization; Frontier and Pioneer Life; Pioneers; Resettlement; Rural Settlements.
—. Agriculture. Factionalism. Germans, Russian. Mennonites. Personal narratives. Saskatchewan (Rosthern). 1891-1900. *3442*
—. Agriculture. Idaho. Mormons. Snake River. 1880-1914. *3940*
—. Agriculture. Missions and Missionaries. Politics. South Dakota. 1850-1900. *66*
—. Alberta. Hutterites. Nativism. 1918-72. *2089*
—. American Revolution. Canada. France. Huguenots. USA. Whaling industry and Trade. 17c-20c. *3251*
—. Amish (Old Order). 1717-1977. *3355*
—. Atlantic Provinces. Mennonites. 1950-70. *3410*
—. Baptists. Georgia (Richmond County). Kiokee Church. Marshall, Daniel. Negroes. 1784-1819. *3020*
—. Bee, William. Methodist Church, Primitive. Saskatchewan (Grenfell). 1882. *3449*
—. Bibliographies. Historiography. Mormons. Utah. 1840-1976. *4046*
—. Boundaries. Catholic Church. Missions and Missionaries. Ontario. 1840-1910. *3709*
—. British Columbia (Queen Charlotte Islands). Church of England. Haida Indians. Methodist Church. Missions and Missionaries. Social Change. 1876-1920. *1545*
—. Canada. Immigrants. Lifestyles. Lutheran Church. Occupations. Social Organizations. Swedish Americans. USA. 1893-1979. *3325*
—. Catholic Church. French Canadians. Minnesota (Gentilly). Theillon, Elie. 1870's-1974. *3687*
—. Catholic Church. French Canadians. North Central States. Social Customs. 19c. *3804*
—. Catholic Church. Frontier and Pioneer Life. New Mexico. 17c-1810. *3852*
—. Catholic Church. Quebec (Hébertville, Lake St. John). ca 1840-1900. *3847*
—. Catholicism. Colonization. French Canadians. Quebec (Eastern Townships). 1800-60. *3780*
—. Charities. Judaism (Orthodox, Reform). Nebraska (Omaha). Political Leadership. Refugees. 1820-1937. *4102*
—. City Planning. Mormons. Smith, Joseph. Western states. 19c. *3988*
—. Clergy. Funk, John F. Manitoba. Mennonites. Russia. Travel. 1873. *3393*
—. Doukhobors. Ethnic groups. Federal government. Royal Canadian Mounted Police. Saskatchewan. 1899-1909. *1006*
—. Drury, Clifford M. Indians. Lee, Jason. Methodism. Missions and Missionaries. Oregon. 1834-43. 1970's. *3480*
—. Dutch Americans. Genealogy. Iowa. Mennonites. Swiss Americans. 1839-1974. *3370*
—. Dye, Alexander V. Mexico (Sonora). Mormons. Revolution. 1912. *4016*
—. Episcopal Church, Protestant. Kilbourne, James. Ohio (Worthington). 1744-1816. *3170*
—. Fishbourn, William. Friends, Society of. Pennsylvania. 1680-1739. *3272*
—. Folklore. Mormons. Utah (Great Salt Lake valley). Young, Brigham. 1842-1970's. *4023*
—. Friends, Society of. Irish Americans. Pennsylvania. 1682-1750. *3276*
—. Idaho (Cassia County). Mormons. 1873-1921. *3930*
—. Indians. Mennonites. Métis. Red River of the North. Red River of the North. Removals, forced. Saskatchewan River Valley. 1869-95. *3360*
—. Iowa (Lee County). Mormons. Young, Brigham. 1838-46. *3998*
—. Land. Moravian Church. Pennsylvania (Nazareth). Whitefield House. 1740-1978. *3517*
—. Methodist Church. Missions and Missionaries. North Dakota. 1871-1914. *1523*
—. Mormons. Nevada (Muddy River Valley). 1865-75. *3953*
—. Mormons. Philanthropy. Smart, William Henry. Utah (Uinta Basin). 1862-1937. *4031*
—. New Jersey (Pitman Grove). Revivals. Urbanization. 1860-1975. *2262*
Settlement houses. Catholic Church. Evangelism. Massachusetts (Boston). Protestantism. South End House. Woods, Robert A. 1891-1910. *2438*
Settlement Movement. Political attitudes. Reform. 1880's-90's. *2405*
Seventh-day Adventists. *See* Adventists.
Sewall, Jotham. Diaries. Maine. Missions and Missionaries. Protestantism. 1778-1848. *1645*
Sewall, Samuel. Bradstreet, Anne. Clap, Roger. Devotions. New England. Puritans. Shepard, Thomas. Worship. 17c. *3627*
—. Congregationalism. Drummer, Jeremiah. Letters. Massachusetts. Sabbath. Taylor, Edward. 1704. *2276*
Sex *See also* Homosexuality; Men; Women.
—. Beecher, Henry Ward. Feminism. New York City. Radicals and Radicalism. Social Reform. Spiritualism. Vanderbilt, Cornelius. Woodhull, Victoria Claflin. 1868-90's. *2386*
—. Behavior. Pregnancy. Puritanism. Social control. 1640-1971. *949*
—. California, northern. Morality. Mormons. Utah (Salt Lake City). Youth. 1967-69. *885*
—. Children of God. Christianity. Converts. 1970's. *2793*
—. Communalism (review article). Fellman, Michael. Marriage. Muncy, Raymond Lee. Social Organization. 19c. 1973. *384*
—. Family. New York. Noyes, John Humphrey. Oneida Community. 1848-80. *431*
—. Morality. Mormons. Social Change. 1820's-90's. *853*
—. Morality. Mormons. Students. 1930's-68. *825*
—. Morality. Mormons. Students. Western States. 1950-72. *927*
—. Morality. Protestantism. Women. 1790-1850. *827*
—. New York. Noyes, John Humphrey. Oneida Community. Social Status. Women. 1848-79. *863*
Sex discrimination. Catholic Church. Clergy. Protestant Churches. Women. 1970's. *939*
—. Clergy. Episcopal Church, Protestant. Women. 1973. *841*
Sex roles. Attitudes. Colleges and Universities. Religiosity. Stereotypes. Students. Women. 1970's. *793*
—. Canada. Christianity. Missions and Missionaries. Women. 1815-99. *854*
—. Childhood. Leadership. Secularism. Women. 1636-1930. *881*
—. Christianity. Social Change. Women. World Conference of Christian Youth, 1st. 1939-79. *844*
—. Douglas, Ann. Feminization. Protestantism. Reform. Stereotypes. ca 1820-75. 1977-80. *918*
—. Equality. New England. Shakers. Women. 1810-60. *821*
—. Evangelicalism. Sunday School Movement. Women. 1790-1880. *807*
—. Family. Farms. Literature. Social Status. South. Women. 1800-60. *816*
—. Feminism. Kansas. Letters. Nichols, Clarina I. H. Theology. 1857-69. *843*
—. Friends, Society of. Protestantism. Women. 17c-18c. *835*
—. Labor. Occupations. Quebec (Montreal). Women. 1911-41. *1471*
—. Literature. Marriage. Marshall, Catherine. Presbyterian Church. Women. 1950's. *806*
—. Mormons. Oneida Community. Shakers. Utopias. Women. ca 1825-90. *842*
—. New England. Puritans. Sermons. Theology. Women. 1690-1730. *883*
Sexism. Political Participation. Protestants. Racism. Whites. Women. 1974-75. *907*
Sexual behavior. Christianity. Human nature. Kinsey, Alfred C. 1948-54. *2749*
Sexuality. Christianity. Theology. 1970's. *2740*
Seybert, Henry. Independence Hall. Pennsylvania (Philadelphia). Philanthropy. Spiritualism. 1793-1882. *4292*
Seymour, James. American Revolution. Church of England. Georgia (Augusta). Loyalists. St. Paul's Parish. 1775-83. *1301*
Shady Grove Baptist Church. Civil War. Country Life. Mississippi (Pontotoc County). Personal narratives. Smith, Andrew Jackson. 1864-69. *3035*
Shakers. Architecture. Kentucky. 1805-60. *1824*
—. Archives. Cathcart, Wallace H. Western Reserve Historical Society. 1911-12. *202*
—. Cathcart, Wallace H. Manuscripts. Western Reserve Historical Society. 1774-1920. *245*
—. Children's Order of the United Society of Believers. Education. Utopias. Utopias. 1780-1900. *4064*
—. Christian Science. Eddy, Mary Baker. Lee, Ann. Personality. Theology. Women. 1736-1910. *2753*
—. Christian Science. Leadership. Spiritualism. Theosophy. Women. 19c. *795*
—. Civil War. Kentucky. Utopias. 1861-65. *419*
—. Cohoon, Hannah Harrison. Massachusetts (Hancock). New York (New Lebanon, Watervliet). Painting. 1817-64. *1902*
—. Communalism. Kentucky (Pleasant Hill). 1805-1922. *432*
—. Communalism. Maine (Sabbathday Lake). 1974. *395*
—. Connecticut (Canterbury). Maine (Sabbathday Lake). Theology. Utopias. 1774-1974. *434*
—. Cumings, John. New Hampshire (Enfield). Utopias. 1829-1923. *394*
—. Diaries. Maine. Wilson, Delmer. 1887. *4066*
—. Documents. Friends, Society of. Methodism. National Characteristics. Political participation. Tocqueville, Alexis de. 1831-40. *2780*
—. Equality. New England. Sex roles. Women. 1810-60. *821*
—. Fiction. ca 1780-1900. *2006*
—. Furniture and Furnishings. Orthodoxy. Social Change. Theology. 1815-1969. *4067*
—. Historical Sites and Parks. Meetinghouses. New Hampshire (Cornish, Enfield). 1793-1902. *1777*
—. Kentucky. Pleasant Hill (community). Restorations. Utopias. 1805-1970's. *385*
—. Kentucky (Pleasant Hill; Shakertown). Preservation. Utopias. 1805-1976. *436*
—. Lee, Ann. New York. Theology. 1774-20c. *4065*
—. Mormons. Oneida Community. Sex roles. Utopias. Women. ca 1825-90. *842*

Shambaugh, Bertha Horak. Amana Society. Communalism. Iowa. Wick, Barthinius L. ca 1900-34. *404*
Shanley, John. Bishops. Catholic Church. Irish Americans. Jamestown Diocese. Minnesota (St. Paul). North Dakota. 1852-1909. *3731*
Shannon, James. Colleges and Universities. Culver-Stockton University. Democratic Party. Disciples of Christ. Missouri. Slavery. 1821-59. *3107*
Shantz, Jacob Y. Immigration. Manitoba. Mennonites. Russia. Travel accounts. 1873. *3425*
Sharp, John. Civil disobedience. Clawson, Rudger. Federal government. Mormons. Polygamy. Utah. 1862-91. *996*
Sharp, Solomon Zook. Education. Mennonites. 1860-1931. *755*
Sharpe, Horatio. Allen, Bennet. Church of England. Colonial Government. Ecclesiastical pluralism. Jordan, John Morton. Maryland. Patronage. 1759-70. *1051*
Shaw, Anna Howard. Clergy. Methodist Protestant Church. Social Gospel Movement. Suffrage. Women. 1880-1919. *3506*
—. Dickey, Sarah. Heck, Barbara. Leadership. Methodist Church. Parker, Lois Stiles. Stereotypes. Willard, Frances E. Women. 19c. *812*
Shaw, Joseph Coolidge. Catholic Church. Clergy. Diaries. Vermont (Brattleboro). 1848. *3849*
Shecut, John L. E. W. *(The Eagle of the Mohawks)*. Dutch Americans. Mennonites. New Netherland (New Amsterdam). Universalists. 17c. 1800-36. *2012*
Sheed, Frank. Catholicism. Intellectuals. 20c. *3706*
Sheldon, Charles M. *(In His Steps)*. New Theology. Protestantism. Roe, Edward Payson *(Barriers Burned Away)*. Social Gospel. 1860's-90's. *2058*
Shepard, Thomas. Antinomianism. Cotton, John. Hutchinson, Anne. Massachusetts. Sermons. Theology. 1630's. *3648*
—. Bradstreet, Anne. Clap, Roger. Devotions. New England. Puritans. Sewall, Samuel. Worship. 17c. *3627*
—. Conversion. Hooker, Thomas. Preparationism. Puritans. Ramus, Petrus. Theology. 1608-49. *3643*
—. Diaries. Massachusetts (Cambridge). Piety. Puritans. 1640-44. *3656*
Shepherd's Tent (college). Congregationalism. Connecticut (New London). Great Awakening. New Lights. 1742-46. *774*
—. Congregationalism. Connecticut (New London). Great Awakening. New Lights. Schisms. 1720-50. *2250*
Sherbrooke Diocese. Bishops. Catholic Church. Quebec. 1868-72. *3882*
—. Catholic Church. Church Finance. Economic Development. LaRocque, Paul. Quebec. 1893-1926. *3783*
Sherman Institute for Indians. Assimilation. Indians. Navajo Indians. New Mexico (Shiprock). Women. 1900-20. *589*
Sherrill, Lewis. Presbyterian Church. Religious Education. ca 1900-57. *778*
Sherwood, Samuel. American Revolution. Connecticut (Norfield). Protestantism. Sermons. 1776. *1414*
Shields, Thomas Todhunter. Baptists. Cameron, William Andrew. Canada. Clergy. Sermons. 1910-41. *3021*
—. Baptists. Fundamentalism. Jarvis Street Baptist Church. Ontario (Toronto). 1891-1955. *3067*
Shiloh Baptist Church. Baptists. Negroes. New York (Buffalo). 1920's-30's. *3097*
Shimeta, Neesima. Congregationalism. Converts. Japan. Massachusetts. Voyages. 1860's-90. *1701*
Shipley, Jonathan. American Revolution (antecedents). Church of England. Colonial Government. Great Britain. Political theory. 1773-75. *1376*
Shipwrecks. Communalism. Holy Ghost and Us Society. *Kingdom Come, Ark of the Holy Ghost and US Society* (vessel). Nova Scotia. Sanford, Frank. Sects, Religious. 1910-48. *4261*
Sholom Aleichem Institute. Judaism. Michigan (Detroit). Religious Education. 1926-71. *746*
Shreveport Ministerial Association. Local option campaign. Louisiana. Prohibition. 1950-52. *2591*
Shrine of Our Lady of Klocočov. Fuga, Francis J. Ontario (Hamilton). Slovak Canadians. Uniates. 1952-77. *3911*
Shrines, roadside. Catholic Church. Devotions, popular. Quebec (Beauce County). Social customs. 1970's. *1788*
Shuck, Eliza G. Sexton. Baptists. China. Missions and Missionaries. 1844-51. *1713*
Siegfried, André *(Le Canada, les deux races: Problèmes politiques contemporains)*. Canada. Catholic Church. Education. French Canadians. Quebec. Rinfret, Fernand. Social Sciences. 1906-07. *3873*
Sierra Leone *See also* Africa, West.
—. African Society. Colonization. Congregationalism. Freedmen. Hopkins, Samuel. Rhode Island (Providence). 1789-95. *2459*
—. Black nationalism. Colonization. Cuffe, Paul. Friends, Society of. 1810's. *2478*
—. Colonization. Liberia. Methodist Episcopal Church. Missions and Missionaries. Negroes. 1833-48. *1702*
Sierra Leone (Sherbro Island). Missionaries. Nova Scotia. Raymond, Eliza Ruggles. Slaves. Women. 1839-50. *1692*
Sigourney, Lydia Huntley. Connecticut (Hartford). Episcopal Church, Protestant. Evangelicalism. Literature. Women. 1800-65. *3194*
Siletz Indians. Indian Shaker Church. Johnson, Jakie. Missions and Missionaries. Oregon (Siletz). ca 1881-1970. *2776*
Silk industry. Mormons. Utah. Women. 1855-1905. *328*
Silva Mind Control. Charismatic Movement. Durkheim, Emile. Social organization. 1970's. *158*
Silver mining. Hebrew Benevolent Association. Jews. Letters. Nevada (Austin). 1864-82. *4164*
Silversmithing. British North America. Jews. Myers, Myer. Rites and Ceremonies. 1723-95. *1905*
Simard, Ovide-D. Catholic Church. Chicoutimi, Séminaire de. Church and State. Personal narratives. Personal narratives. 1873-1973. *757*
Simmons, Joseph M. Appleby, William. Calligraphy. Mormons. Young, Brigham. 1851-53. *1895*
Simons, George Albert. *Khristianski Pobornik* (periodical). Methodist Episcopal Church. Missions and Missionaries. Russia (St. Petersburg). 1881-1917. *1696*
Simpson, George. Catholic Church. Hawaii. Independence Movements. Missions and Missionaries. Protestant Churches. 1842-43. *1723*
Simpson, Matthew. Centennial Exposition of 1876. Methodist Episcopal Church. Pennsylvania (Philadelphia). Prayer. 1876. *3502*
Sin (doctrine). Niebuhr, Reinhold *(Moral Man and Immoral Society)*. Theology. 1930's. *2909*
Sin, sense of. Attitudes. Social reform. 1830's-60's. *2389*
Sinclair, Bruce. Benjamin, Philip S. Feldberg, Michael. Friends, Society of. Miller, Richard G. Pennsylvania (Philadelphia; review article). 1790-1920. 1974-76. *3269*
Sinclair, Upton. Mormons. National Education Association. Public schools. Teachers. Utah. 1920-24. *567*
Singer, Milton. Culture. Social activities. 1964-74. *165*
Singing. Baptists. Hymnals. 1650-1850. *1945*
—. Hymns. Music. Schools. 1775-1820. *1951*
—. Massachusetts (Boston). Mather, Cotton. Psalmody. Puritans. Sermons. 1721. *1938*
Singing Schools. Indiana. Mennonites. Mumaw, George Shaum. Ohio. Personal narratives. 1900-57. *1941*
Single tax. Episcopal Church, Protestant. Huntington, James Otis Sargent. Monasticism. Order of the Holy Cross. Social reform. 1878-90. *2430*
—. George, Henry. ca 1870's-90's. *2568*
Single tax doctrine. Catholic Church. George, Henry. Ryan, John A. Taxation. 1935. *2557*
Sioux Indians. Black Hills. Episcopal Church, Protestant. Hinman, Samuel D. Indians. Missions and Missionaries. 1860-76. *1484*
—. Catholic Church. Eisenmann, Sylvester. South Dakota. Yankton Reservation (Marty Mission). 1918-49. *3900*
Sisters of Charity. Catholic Church. Colorado. Diaries. Hospitals. Mallon, Catherine. New Mexico (Santa Fe). 1865-1901. *1454*
—. Catholic Church. New Mexico (Santa Fe). St. Vincent's Hospital. 1865-1948. *1449*
Sisters of Charity of Providence. District of Columbia. Missions and Missionaries. National Statuary Hall. Pacific Northwest. Pariseau, Mother Mary Joseph. Women. 1856-1902. 1977. *1629*
Sisters of Charity of St. Joseph. Education. Ohio (Cincinnati). Social Work. Women. 1809-1979. *2514*
Sisters of Charity of the Blessed Virgin Mary. Catholic Church. Pennsylvania (Philadelphia). Religious education. 1833-43. *609*
Sisters of Charity of the Immaculate Conception. Aged. Catholic Church. Charities. Education. Immigration. New Brunswick (Saint John). Orphans. 1854-64. *2509*
Sisters of St. Ann. Alaska. Catholic Church. Holy Cross Mission. Indians. Jesuits. Missions and Missionaries. Yukon River, lower. 1887-1956. *1615*
—. Alaska (Juneau). Catholic Church. Hospitals. 1886-1968. *3757*
Sisters of St. Joseph. Catholic Church. Charities. Education. Moore, Julia. Ontario (London). Personal narratives. Women. 1868-85. *2517*
Sisters of Service. Canada, Western. Catholic Church. Immigration. Missions and Missionaries. 1920-30. *1665*
Sisters of SS. Cyril and Methodius. Catholic Church. Jankola, Matthew. Pennsylvania (Philadelphia). Slovak Americans. 1903-70's. *3822*
—. Catholic Church. Pennsylvania (Danville). St. Cyril Academy. Slovak Americans. Social customs. 1909-73. *3885*
Sisters of the Congregation of Notre Dame. Catholic Church. Ontario (Kingston). Religious education. Women. 1841-48. *596*
Sisters of the Holy Names of Jesus and Mary. Catholic Church. Daily Life. Documents. Girls. Oregon (Salem). Sacred Heart Academy. 1863-73. *699*
Sisters of the Presentation of the Blessed Virgin Mary. Catholic Church. Education. Indians. Missions and Missionaries. North Dakota. Pioneers. South Dakota. Women. 1880-96. *727*
Sisters of the Visitation. Cardome (home). Catholic Church. Education. Kentucky (Scott County; Georgetown). Mount Admirabilis (academy). 1875-1975. *600*
Siu Pheong Aheong. Congregationalism. Hawaiian Evangelical Association. Missions and Missionaries. ca 1838-76. *1687*
Sjöborg, Sofia Charlotta. Diaries. Emigration. Florida. Lutheran Church. Sweden. 1871. *3340*
Skaneateles Community. Finch, John. Letters. New York (Finger Lakes area). Utopias. 1843-45. *4302*
Skid rows. Employment. Program failure. Public Policy. Rescue missions. Social Reform. 1960's-70's. *2524*
—. Jehovah's Witnesses. Organizational structure. Rescue missions. Watch Tower movement. 1970's. *2722*
—. Rescue missions. Washington (Seattle). 1973. *2502*
Skinner, B. F. Behaviorism. Social Psychology. 1948-74. *154*
—. Puritanism. ca 1730-1974. *2339*
Skousen, W. Cleon. City Politics. Lee, J. Bracken. Morality. Mormons. Utah (Salt Lake City). 1956-60. *4006*
Slave Revolts. Anti-Catholicism. Maryland. Servants. 1745-58. *2117*
—. Christianity. Styron, William *(Confessions of Nat Turner)*. Turner, Nat. 1820-31. 1968. *2047*
—. Gruber, Jacob. Maryland (Washington County). Methodism. Trials. 1818-20. *2456*
Slave trade. Abolition Movement. Fox, George. Friends, Society of. Pennsylvania. 1656-1754. *2479*
—. Africa. Economic Conditions. Negroes. Social Customs. ca 1500-1940's. *24*
—. Suicide. 1690-1852. *76*
Slavery *See also* Abolition Movement; Antislavery Sentiments; Emancipation; Freedmen; Negroes; Proslavery Sentiments; Slave Trade.
—. Abolition Movement. Attitudes. New England. Puritans. 1641-1776. *2164*
—. Africa. American Colonization Society. Colonization. McDonough, David. Medical Education. Presbyterian Church. 1840-50. *2483*

—. American Revolution. Antislavery sentiments. Presbyterian Church. 1750-1818. *2493*
—. American Revolution. Chauncy, Charles. Church and State. Congregationalism. Great Britain. Letters. Price, Richard. 1727-87. *3129*
—. Anti-Catholicism. Congregationalism. Cox, Samuel Hanson. Ecumenism. Episcopal Church, Protestant. Evangelicalism. Presbyterian Church, New School. 1840's. *471*
—. Arkansas. Baptists. ca 1830-60. *2176*
—. Asbury, Francis. Coke, Thomas. Methodist Episcopal Church. 1780-1816. *2155*
—. Attitudes. Baptists. Virginia. 1785-97. *2157*
—. Attitudes. Episcopal Church, Protestant. Fletcher, C. B. Letters. Vermont. 1777-1864. *2159*
—. Bacon, Thomas. Church of England. Clergy. Education. Maryland. Politics. Theology. ca 1745-68. *3175*
—. Baptists. Clergy. Davis, Noah. Maryland (Baltimore). Meachum, John Berry. Missouri (St. Louis). Negroes. 1818-66. *3094*
—. Baptists. Converts. Evangelism. Louisiana (New Orleans). Methodism. 1800-61. *2916*
—. Baptists. Methodist Church. Presbyterian Church. South. 1740-1860. *2168*
—. Baptists. Virginia (Richmond). 1820-65. *3055*
—. Baptists. Wayland, Francis. 1830-45. *2160*
—. Baptists (Ketocton Association). Evangelicalism. Reform. Stringfellow, Thornton. Virginia. 1800-70. *2158*
—. Bible. Georgia Trustees. Rhetoric. Sermons. 1731-50. *2161*
—. Capers, William. *Christian Advocate* (newspaper). Ecumenism. Letters. Methodist Episcopal Church. Methodist Episcopal Church (South). 1854. 1875. *479*
—. Catholic Church. South. 1619-1860. *2170*
—. Chambers, Samuel D. (testimonies). Converts. Mormons. Negroes. Utah (Salt Lake City). 1844-76. *4059*
—. Chinese Americans. Christianity. Judaism. Nativism. Newspapers. Pacific Coast. 1848-65. *75*
—. Choctaw Indians. Congregationalism. Harkins, Richard. Missions and Missionaries. Murder. 1858-59. *3132*
—. Church and State. Presbyterian Church. South. 1850-80. *1074*
—. Civil War. Letters. Methodist Church. North Carolina (Halifax County). Wills, Washington. 1861-65. *2171*
—. Clapp, Theodore. Louisiana (New Orleans). Theology. Unitarianism. 1822-56. *4084*
—. Colleges and Universities. Culver-Stockton University. Democratic Party. Disciples of Christ. Missouri. Shannon, James. 1821-59. *3107*
—. Democratic Party. Letters. Mennonites. Politics. Risser, Johannes. 1856-57. *994*
—. Dissent. Economic conditions. Military Service. Moravian Church. North Carolina (Salem). Social change. Women. 1772-1860. *3516*
—. Doub, Peter. Education. Methodist Episcopal Church. North Carolina. Women. 1796-1869. *3469*
—. Education. Episcopal Church, Protestant. Louisiana (New Orleans). Polk, Leonidas. 1805-65. *3219*
—. Equality. Lincoln, Abraham. Mormons. Polygamy. Smith, Joseph. 1840-64. *986*
—. Evangelism. Methodism. Wesley, John. 1725-1974. *3505*
—. Evangelism. Protestantism. South. 18-19c. *2169*
—. Fugitive Slave Act (US, 1850). Methodist Church. Newspapers. 1850. *3476*
—. Genovese, Eugene D. (review article). Millenarianism. Protestantism. South. 17c-1865. *2163*
—. German Americans. Lutheran Church. Pennsylvania. Reformed Churches. Social change. 1779-88. *2162*
—. Indians. Missionaries. Presbyterian Board of Foreign Missions. 1837-61. *3568*
—. Jesuits. Maryland (St. Marys County). Plantations. St. Inigoes Church. 1806-1950. *326*
—. Jones, Charles Colcock. Missions and Missionaries. Presbyterian Church. South. 1825-63. *2177*
—. Lutheran Church. South. 1790-1865. *2172*
—. Materialism. *Moravian* (newspaper). Nationalism. Pennsylvania (Bethlehem). 1850-76. *3518*
—. North or Northern States. South. Unitarianism. 1831-60. *2174*
—. Presbyterian Church. Segregation. South Carolina (Charleston). 1845-60. *2154*
—. Presbyterian Church. Stowe, Harriet Beecher. 1830's-1870's. *3554*
—. Presbyterians. South. 1787-1817. *2156*
—. Social Organization. 1740-76. *2824*
Slaves. Education. France. Hymns. Neau, Elias. New York. Protestant Churches. ca 1689-1722. *1913*
—. Marriage. Plantations. Protestantism. South. ca 1750's-1860. *2928*
—. Missionaries. Nova Scotia. Raymond, Eliza Ruggles. Sierra Leone (Sherbro Island). Women. 1839-50. *1692*
Slocum, John. Handsome Lake (Seneca). Indian Shaker Church. Neurology. Revitalization movements. Trances. 18c-20c. *2756*
Slovak Americans. Acculturation. Catholics. Immigration. 1860's-1970's. *3879*
—. Canada. Charities. Nurses and Nursing. Slovak Canadians. USA. Vincentian Sisters of Charity. Women. 1902-78. *2525*
—. Catholic Church. First Catholic Slovak Union (Jednota). Pennsylvania. Sabol, John. 1920's-60's. *3821*
—. Catholic Church. Holy Family Slovak Parish. New York City (Brooklyn). 1905-80. *3869*
—. Catholic Church. Independence Movements. Kubašek, John J. New York (Yonkers). 1902-50. *3870*
—. Catholic Church. Jankola, Matthew. Pennsylvania (Philadelphia). Sisters of SS. Cyril and Methodius. 1903-70's. *3822*
—. Catholic Church. Pennsylvania (Danville). St. Cyril Academy. Sisters of SS. Cyril and Methodius. Social customs. 1909-73. *3885*
—. Clergy. Dulík, Joseph J. Pioneers. Vaniščák, Gregory. 1909-38. *3823*
Slovak Canadians. Canada. Charities. Nurses and Nursing. Slovak Americans. USA. Vincentian Sisters of Charity. Women. 1902-78. *2525*
—. Catholic Church. Ontario (Toronto). Saints Cyril and Methodius Parish. 1934-77. *3905*
—. Fuga, Francis J. Ontario (Hamilton). Shrine of Our Lady of Klocočov. Uniates. 1952-77. *3911*
Slovak Catholic Federation of America. Catholic Church. 1911-79. *3671*
Slovakia (Spiš; Levoča). Catholic Church. Mary, Virgin. Ohio (Bedford). Our Lady of Levoča (statue). ca 13c-1975. *1884*
Slums. *See* Cities.
Small, Minnie Hyatt. Collectors and Collecting. Folklore. Hyatt, Harry Midddleton. Illinois (Adams County). Negroes. South. Witchcraft. 1920-78. *2190*
Smallpox. Clergy. Congregationalism. Franklin, Benjamin. Massachusetts (Boston). *New England Courant* (newspaper). *Spectator* (newspaper). 1720-23. *2023*
—. Epidemics. Inoculation. Massachusetts (Boston). Mather, Cotton. 1721-22. *1464*
Smart, William Henry. Mormons. Philanthropy. Settlement. Utah (Uinta Basin). 1862-1937. *4031*
Smith, Al. Candler, Warren A. Methodist Episcopal Church, South. Political Campaigns (presidential). Prohibition. 1928. *1210*
—. Catholic Church. Democratic Party. Elections (presidential). Louisiana. Protestant Churches. Temperance Movements. 1928. *1330*
—. Catholic church. Elections (presidential). Protestantism. West Virginia. 1928. *1217*
—. Elections (presidential). Hoover, Herbert C. Racism. Tennessee, west. 1928. *1280*
—. Hoover, Herbert C. Political Campaigns (presidential). Tennessee, west. 1928. *1279*
Smith, Albert Edward. Canada. Communist Party. Labour Party. Methodism. Social Gospel. 1893-1924. *983*
Smith, Andrew Jackson. Civil War. Country Life. Mississippi (Pontotoc County). Personal narratives. Shady Grove Baptist Church. 1864-69. *3035*
Smith, Annie Rebekah. Adventists. Hymns. Poetry. 1850's. *1926*
Smith, Ebenezer. Baptists. Massachusetts (Ashfield). Poetry. Political Protest. Religious Liberty. 1772. *2048*
Smith, Emma. Hymns. Mormons. 1835. *1953*
Smith, George L. (review article). Dutch Americans. New Netherland. Religious liberty. Trade. 17c. *1109*
Smith, Gerald L. K. Fundamentalism. Long, Huey P. North Central States. Populism. Progressivism. 1934-48. *975*
Smith, Gerrit. Abolition Movement. Birney, James. Clergy. Evangelism. Stanton, H. B. Weld, Theodore. 1820-50. *2488*
Smith, H. Shelton (review article). Boles, John B. (review article). Evangelicalism. Racism. Revivals. South. 1972. *2867*
Smith, Henry B. Librarians. New York City. Presbyterian Church. Union Theological Seminary. 1851-77. *758*
Smith, Hyrum. Illinois (Nauvoo). Lyon, T. Edgar. Mormons. Oral history. Smith, Joseph. 1840's-1978. *4005*
Smith, Jedediah Strong. California. Catholic Church. Mountain Men. Protestantism. Rogers, Harrison. 1826-27. *2798*
Smith, Joseph. American Revolution. Mormon, Book of. Mormons. Political attitudes. 1820's. *1353*
—. Anthropology. Archaeology. Indians. Lost Tribes of Israel. Mormons. 1830. *2335*
—. Architecture. City Planning. Mormons. Western states. 1833-90. *1767*
—. Assassination. Hill, Marvin S. Illinois (Carthage). Mormons. Oaks, Dallin H. Trials (review article). 1844. 1977. *2126*
—. Bidamon, Emma Smith. Illinois (Nauvoo). Mormons. Property. Schisms. Women. Women. Young, Brigham. 1832-79. *3932*
—. Brodie, Fawn *(No Man Knows My History).* Historiography. Mormons. 19c. 1945-73. *3983*
—. City Planning. Mormons. Settlement. Western states. 19c. *3988*
—. Constitutions. Mormons. Speeches, Addresses, etc. 1840. *1374*
—. Coray, Howard. Leadership. Mormons. Personal narratives. 1840's. *3990*
—. Diaries. Illinois (Nauvoo). Laub, George. Mormons. Young, Brigham. 1845-46. *3961*
—. Economic Conditions. Mormons. Ohio (Kirtland). 1830's. *351*
—. Equality. Lincoln, Abraham. Mormons. Polygamy. Slavery. 1840-64. *986*
—. Folklore. Mormons. Murder. 1659-1900. *4022*
—. Galland, Isaac. Iowa (Lee County). Land. Mormons. Speculation. 1830's-58. *3950*
—. Illinois (Nauvoo). Jones, Dan. *Maid of Iowa* (vessel). Mormons. Steamboats. 1843-45. *346*
—. Illinois (Nauvoo). Kimball, Vilate. Letters. Mormons. Murder. Women. 1844. *3963*
—. Illinois (Nauvoo). Lyon, T. Edgar. Mormons. Oral history. Smith, Hyrum. 1840's-1978. *4005*
—. Illinois (Nauvoo). Mormons. Rites and Ceremonies. Temples. 1841-45. *1766*
—. Knight, Joseph, Sr. Manuscripts. Mormons. 1772-1847. *3991*
—. Letters. Miller, George. Mormons. 1842. *3952*
—. Mormons. Nevada. Utah. Voting and Voting Behavior. Young, Brigham. 1835-50's. *1251*
—. Mormons. Succession. Young, Brigham. 1834-44. *4027*
—. Mormons. Theology. ca 1800-44. *3982*
Smith, Joseph *(Book of Commandments).* Lambdin, William. Mormons. Rare Books. West Virginia (Wheeling). 1830-33. *2124*
—. Princeton University Library. 1820-1975. *3956*
Smith, Joseph (King Follett Discourse). Deity. Illinois (Nauvoo). Mormons. Sermons. Theology. 1844. *3976*
—. Illinois (Nauvoo). Mormons. Sermons. Theology. 1844-1978. *3947*
Smith, Joseph Fielding. Bible. History. Israel. Mormons. Snell, Heber C. Theology. 1937-52. *4035*
—. Bossard, Gisbert. Florence, Max. Mormon Temple. Photography. Utah (Salt Lake City). 1911. *1762*
—. Grant, Heber J. Letters. Mormons. Recreation. 1930's. *3954*
—. League of Nations. Mormons. Prohibition. Republican Party. Roberts, Brigham Henry. Suffrage. Utah. Women. ca 1900. *1284*
Smith, Julia Evelina. Bible. Translating. Women. 1840-76. *1992*
Smith, Luther Wesley. Baptist Board of Education and Publication. Church Schools. 1941-56. *630*
Smith, Samuel Stanhope. Educators. Hampden-Sydney College. Virginia (Farmville area). 1776-1815. *513*

Smith, Thomas. Painting. Poetry. Puritans. ca 1690. *1839*
Smith, Uriah. *Advent Review and Sabbath Herald* (newspaper). Adventists. Poetry. Prophecy. 1853. *1997*
—. Adventists. Engraving. Michigan (Battle Creek). Wood. 1852-70's. *1889*
Smith, Walter George. Catholic Church. Lawyers. Pennsylvania. Progressivism. 1900-22. *2365*
Smith, Wilfred Cantwell. Christianity. God is Dead Theology. Islam. Methodology. Religions, history of. Secularism. Theology. 1940-73. *134*
Smith, William. Church of England. Patriotism. Poetry. Rising glory of America (theme). 1752. *1337*
Smith, William Robertson. Biblical Theology Movement. Presbyterian Church. Theology. 1870-83. *590*
Smoot, Reed. Church and state. Cowley, Matthias F. Mormons. Polygamy. Taylor, John W. Theology. Woodruff Manifesto. 1890-1911. *1060*
Smyth, Frederick Hastings *(Manhood into God)*. Anglican Communion. Massachusetts (Cambridge). Society of the Catholic Commonwealth. Theology. Utopias. 1940. *3200*
Smyth, Thomas. Abolition movement. Douglass, Frederick. Ireland (Belfast). Presbyterian Church. 1846. *2165*
—. Conservatism. Presbyterian Church. Social theory. South Carolina. Theology. 1831-70. *3552*
Snake River. Agriculture. Idaho. Mormons. Settlement. 1880-1914. *3940*
Snakehandlers. Appalachia. Folk Religion. Pentecostal Movement. 1974. *3519*
—. Appalachia, southern. Hensley, George Went. Pentecostal Holiness Church. 1909-73. *3522*
—. Appalachia, southern. Pentecostals. Rites and ceremonies. Trances. 1909-74. *3523*
Snakes. Bosom serpentry (concept). Folklore. Mormons. New England. Puritans. Utah. 17c-19c. *2765*
Snell, Heber C. Bible. History. Israel. Mormons. Smith, Joseph Fielding. Theology. 1937-52. *4035*
Snethen, Abraham. Clergy. Disciples of Christ. Frontier. North Central States. Personal narratives. 1794-1830. 1977. *3112*
Snethen, Nicholas. Bond, Thomas Emerson. Church government. Laity. Methodist Episcopal Church. Stockton, William S. 1820-56. *288*
—. Clergy. Methodist Protestant Church. 1769-1845. *315*
Snow, Eliza Roxey. Diaries. Illinois (Nauvoo). Mormons. Women. 1842-44. *4044*
—. Frontier and Pioneer Life. Heywood, Martha Spence. Intellectuals. King, Hannah Tapfield. Mormons. Utah. Women. 1850-70. *4045*
—. Leadership. Mormons. Poetry. Prophecy. Utah. Women. 1804-87. *3936*
—. Mormons. Women. 1830-90. *900*
Snyder, Gary. Buddhism (Zen). Poetry. 1960-74. *2055*
Social activities. Culture. Singer, Milton. 1964-74. *165*
Social Change *See also* Economic Growth; Industrialization; Modernization.
—. Africa, West. Missions and Missionaries. Presbyterian Church. Women. 1850-1915. *1686*
—. Alberta (Coaldale). Germans, Russian. Mennonites. Organizations. 1920-76. *3411*
—. Algonkian Indians, northeastern. Indians. Maine. Maritime Provinces. Missionaries. 1610-1750. *1512*
—. American Revolution (antecedents). Great Awakening. Liberalism. Social theory. ca 1725-75. *1338*
—. Americanization. Asbury, Francis. Methodism. 1766-1816. *286*
—. Amish, Old Order. Hutterites. Mennonites. ca 1930-77. *3357*
—. Amish, Old Order. Tradition. ca 1650-1976. *3384*
—. Antigonish Movement. Catholic Church. Nova Scotia. Rural Development. ca 1928-73. *2409*
—. Attitudes. Great Awakening. Political reform. 18c. 1975. *2216*
—. Baptists. Church of England. Elites. Values. Virginia (Lunenburg County). 1746-74. *2819*
—. Baptists. Race relations. Violence. 1960-69. *2420*
—. Baseball. Sabbath. Values. 1892-1934. *2282*
—. Bradstreet, Anne. Hutchinson, Anne. Literature. Massachusetts. Puritans. Theology. Women. 1630's-70's. *865*
—. British Columbia (Queen Charlotte Islands). Church of England. Haida Indians. Methodist Church. Missions and Missionaries. Settlement. 1876-1920. *1545*
—. Bryan, William Jennings. Political parties. Reagan, Ronald. Revivals. 1730-1980. *1329*
—. Calvinism. Politics. 16c-20c. *980*
—. Catholic Church. Clergy. Czechoslovakia. Personal narratives. Refugees. Zubek, Theodoric. 1950-78. *3902*
—. Catholic Church. École Sociale Populaire. Labor Unions and Organizations. Quebec. 1911-75. *1469*
—. Catholic Church. Quebec. 17c. 20c. *3876*
—. Cemeteries. Family. Rural Cemetery Movement. Tombstones. 1830's-40's. *87*
—. Christianity. Education. Games, board. Mansion of Happiness (game). Values. 1832-1904. *2711*
—. Christianity. Family. Negroes. Values. War. 1960's-70's. *875*
—. Christianity. Judaism. Pfeffer, Leo. Politics. Secular Humanism. 1958-76. *132*
—. Christianity. Sex roles. Women. World Conference of Christian Youth, 1st. 1939-79. *844*
—. Cities. Historiography. Mormons. Utah. 1849-1970's. *4008*
—. Clark, Bertha W. Hutterites. Pacifism. South Dakota. 1921. *3385*
—. Clergy. Methodist Church. Ordination. 1771-1975. *3473*
—. Clergy (dismissal). Congregationalism. New Hampshire. Presbyterian Church. 1633-1790. *2885*
—. Clergy (tenure). Higginson, John. Massachusetts (Salem). Nicholet, Charles. Puritans. 1672-76. *3620*
—. Colonization. New England. Pragmatism. Puritans. 1620-90. *3608*
—. Congregationalism. Connecticut (Windham). Conversion. Great Awakening. 1723-43. *2274*
—. Congregationalism. Connecticut (Windham). Converts. Great Awakening. 1721-43. *2273*
—. Converts. 1975-76. *129*
—. Converts. Glock, Charles Y. Models. Stark, Rodney. 1960's-70's. *144*
—. Democracy. Education. Fundamentalism. Local Politics. Morality. Vigilantism. 1920's. *2387*
—. Dissent. Economic conditions. Military Service. Moravian Church. North Carolina (Salem). Slavery. Women. 1772-1860. *3516*
—. Ecumenism. Evangelism. Protestantism. Social justice. Student Christian Movement. 19c-20c. *440*
—. Education. Mennonites, old order. Pennsylvania. 1653-1975. *664*
—. Evangelicalism. Pennsylvania (Rockdale). Wallace, Allen F. C. (review article). 1820-65. *2861*
—. Furniture and Furnishings. Orthodoxy. Shakers. Theology. 1815-1969. *4067*
—. German Americans. Lutheran Church. Pennsylvania. Reformed Churches. Slavery. 1779-88. *2162*
—. Great Britain. Local government. Massachusetts. New England. Political theory. Puritans. 1600-50. *3604*
—. Ideology. Middle Classes. Pluralism. Secularization. 17c-20c. *12*
—. Industrialization. Law and society. Massachusetts. Nelson, William E. (review article). Secularization. 1760-1830. *53*
—. Irrigation. Mormons. Utah. 1840-1900. *329*
—. Jewish Student Movement. Massachusetts (Boston). Radicals and Radicalism. Youth Movements. 1960-75. *2433*
—. Kansas (McPherson County). Mennonites. Russian Americans. 1874-1974. *3372*
—. McLoughlin, William G. (review article). Revivals. 1607-1978. *2220*
—. Mennonites. Saskatchewan (Hague-Osler area). 1895-1977. *3359*
—. Morality. Mormons. Sex. 1820's-90's. *853*
—. Mormons. Utah. 1830-1974. *4018*
—. Ordination. Protestantism. Women. World Council of Churches. 1945-75. *879*
—. Social Organization. 1960-78. *119*
Social Classes *See also* Aristocracy; Elites; Middle Classes; Social Mobility; Social Status; Upper Classes; Working Class.
—. Adolescents. Children. Christianity. Rural-Urban Studies. 1920's-70's. *2762*
—. American Revolution. Great Awakening. Social theory. Urbanization. 1740's-70's. *2230*
—. Anti-Catholicism. Anti-Semitism. Colorado (Denver). Ku Klux Klan. Protestantism. 1921-25. *2609*
—. Anti-Catholicism. Antislavery sentiments. Ideology. Massachusetts (Boston). Riots. Ursulines. 1834-35. *2109*
—. Audiences. Graham, Billy. Revivalism. -1974. *2604*
—. Baltzell, E. Digby (review article). Friends, Society of. Massachusetts (Boston). Pennsylvania (Philadelphia). Puritans. 17c-1979. *2920*
—. Baptists. Factionalism. Fundamentalism. Jarvis Street Baptist Church. Modernism. Ontario (Toronto). 1895-1934. *2605*
—. British Americans. California (Los Angeles). Popular culture. Protestant Churches. 1920's. 1977. *2624*
—. California (Los Angeles). Judaism. Political Campaigns (mayoral). Voting and Voting Behavior. 1969. *1276*
—. Canada. Church of England National Task Force on the Economy (report). Income. Poverty. Theology. 1977. *2564*
—. Canada. Ideology. King, William Lyon Mackenzie. Liberal Party. Politics. Protestantism. 1900-50. *1421*
—. Catholic Church. Cities. Civil rights movement. Negroes. Protestant churches. 1960's-70's. *2539*
—. Catholic Church. Clergy. Men. Religious Orders. Women. 1650-1762. *2614*
—. Catholic Church. Ethnic Groups. Judaism. Pennsylvania (Philadelphia). Voting and Voting Behavior. 1924-40. *1308*
—. Catholic Church. Protestant Churches. 1970's. *2623*
—. Catholics. Church Schools. 1961-73. *3735*
—. Christianity. Judaism. Minority groups. 1974. *2610*
—. Clergy. Congregationalism. Great Awakening. New England. New Lights. Old Lights. 1734-85. *2627*
—. Country life. Ethnic groups. Evangelical United Brethren Church. Theology. 1800-1968. *3668*
—. Crime and Criminals. Massachusetts (Middlesex County). Puritans. 17c. *3616*
—. Economic Development. Government. Quebec (Lower Canada). Ultramontanism. 19c. *962*
—. Elites. Political attitudes. Tennessee (Davidson County). 1835-61. *1232*
—. Emigration. Illinois. Janssonists. Sects, Religious. Sweden. 1845-47. *2620*
—. Localism. North Carolina. Temperance Movements. 1969-70. *2599*
Social cohesion. Family. Government. Ideology. Massachusetts. Puritans. 1630-85. *3606*
Social compassion. Church attendance. Values. 1973. *2370*
Social Conditions *See also* Cities; Counter Culture; Country Life; Daily Life; Economic Conditions; Family; Labor; Marriage; Migration, Internal; Popular Culture; Social Classes; Social Mobility; Social Problems; Social Reform; Social Surveys; Standard of Living.
—. Acadians. Catholic Church. English Canadians. Maritime Provinces. 1763-1977. *3871*
—. American Revolution. Historiography. New Jersey. New York. Pennsylvania. 1680-1790's. 1960's-70's. *59*
—. Baptists. Clergy. Emigration. Great Britain. Harris, Theophilus. Politics. 1793-1810. *3050*
—. Baptists. Kentucky (Stoney Point). Negroes. 1848-1969. *2999*
—. Baptists (Seventh-Day). Communalism. Letters. Müller, Johan Peter. Pennsylvania (Ephrata). 1743. *428*
—. Bishops. Catholic Church. Education. Medicine. Quebec (Gaspé). Ross, François Xavier. 1923-45. *3787*
—. Burchard, Jedediah. Protestants. Revivals. Vermont. 1835-36. *2246*
—. Cain, Richard Harvey. Methodist Episcopal Church, African. Negroes. Politics. Reconstruction. South Carolina. 1850's-87. *2407*
—. Catholic Church. Dolan, Jay P. (review article). German Americans. Irish Americans. New York. 1815-65. 1975. *3793*
—. Catholic Church. Economic development. Quebec. 1850-1950. *3743*

—. Catholic Church. Illinois (Chicago). Immigration. Mexican Americans. 1910's-20's. *3833*
—. Catholic Church. Missions and Missionaries. Quebec (Eastern Townships). 1825-53. *1568*
—. Cities. Politics. Revivals. 1857-77. *2261*
—. Civil religion. 1973. *1170*
—. Civil religion. Freedom. 1776-1900. *1179*
—. Connecticut (New Haven). Negroes. Pentecostal movement. Prayer meetings. Psychology. 1978. *3521*
—. Divorce. Law. Massachusetts. Puritans. Women. 1639-92. *941*
—. Economic Conditions. Ethnic groups. Folklore. Mail-Order Business. Voodoo. 1970-79. *2205*
—. Economic Conditions. Great Awakening. Nova Scotia (Yarmouth). 1760's-70's. *2626*
—. Education. Religiosity. Technology. 1945-75. *561*
—. Europe, Western. Evangelicalism. Methodism. Pietism. Reformed Dutch Church. Revivals. 1674-19c. *2959*
—. Factionalism. Nova Scotia (Pictou County). Presbyterian Church. Scottish Canadians. 1898-1966. *3533*
—. Forssell, G. D. Iowa. Lectures. Minnesota. Progressivism. 1890-95. *1967*
—. Godfrey, John. Massachusetts. Puritans. Trials. Witchcraft. 1634-75. *2186*
—. Immigration. Mennonites. Russian Canadians. Saskatchewan (Rosthern). 1923. *3399*
—. Literature. Morality. 17c-1976. *2037*
—. Millenarianism. Politics. 1920's-50's. *1420*
—. Social Gospel. Sociology. 1890-1972. *2390*
—. Transcendentalism. 1830's-50's. *2367*
Social consciousness. Baptists. Christian Socialism. Clergy. Rauschenbusch, Walter. Theology. 1891-1918. *2400*
—. Mennonites. 1890-1905. *3369*
Social control. Baptists. North Carolina. 1772-1908. *2445*
—. Behavior. Pregnancy. Puritanism. Sex. 1640-1971. *949*
—. Catholic Church. Family. Immigrants. Polish Americans. Values. 20c. *913*
—. Charities. Fosdick, Harry Emerson. Friendship. Liberalism. Protestantism. Rockefeller, John D., Jr. Wealth. 1920-36. *364*
—. Cities. Reform movements (review article). 1812-1900. 1970's. *2411*
—. Florida (Tallahassee). Negroes. Protestant Churches. Race Relations. 1865-85. *2864*
—. Ontario (Upper Canada). Sunday schools. 19c. *643*
Social Credit Party. Aberhart, William. Alberta. Ideology. Provincial Government. Theology. 1935-43. *1365*
Social Creed of Methodism. Federal Council of the Churches of Christ in America. Methodist Federation for Social Service. North, Frank M. Ward, Harry F. 1907-12. *2388*
Social criticism. American League for Peace and Democracy. Methodist Federation for Social Service. Ward, Harry F. 1900-40. *2408*
—. Catholic Church. Cities. Merton, Thomas. Nonviolence. Reform. 1960's. *2417*
—. Europe. Nationalism. Revolution. Romanticism. 1630-1876. *950*
—. Literature. New York. Presbyterian Church. Satire. Whitcher, Frances Miriam Berry *(Widow Bedott Papers).* 1847-55. *2056*
Social Customs. Africa. Economic Conditions. Negroes. Slave trade. ca 1500-1940's. *24*
—. Agriculture. Hutterites. Lifestyles. North America. Technological innovation. 18c-20c. *3349*
—. Agriculture. Immigration. Lutheran Church. Minnesota (Isantic County). Sweden (Dalarna). 1840-1910. *3329*
—. Alberta (Edmonton). Hutterites. Public Opinion. 1966-75. *3404*
—. American Board of Commissioners for Foreign Missions. Missions and Missionaries. Protestant Churches. South Africa. Zulus. 1835-60's. *1695*
—. Americanization. Judaism. Law. Rabbis. Rabbis (responsa). 1862-1937. *300*
—. Anthropology. Death and dying. Memorial Day. 1945-74. *90*
—. Appalachia, southern. Ballads. Calendar, Gregorian. "Christmas, Old". 1753-1977. *2955*
—. Architecture. Catholic Church. Fundamentalists. German Americans. Rural Settlements. Southerners. Texas (Cooke, Denton counties). 1860-1976. *2750*
—. Artisans. Identity. Methodism. Morality. Pennsylvania (Philadelphia). Work ethic. Working Class. 1820-50. *3479*
—. Attitudes. Death and Dying. 17c-1977. *19*
—. Bishops. Catholic Church. Indian-white relations. Lamy, Jean Baptiste. New Mexico (Santa Fe). 1849-88. *3761*
—. British North America. Death and Dying. Funerals. 17c-18c. *2772*
—. California (San Diego). Christmas. Drama. Parades. 1769-1980. *2714*
—. Canada. Mennonites. Urbanization. USA. 1961-71. *3358*
—. Catholic Church. Devotions, popular. Quebec (Beauce County). Shrines, roadside. 1970's. *1788*
—. Catholic Church. Feast days. Lawrence, Saint. New Mexico (Bernalillo). 1974. *3853*
—. Catholic Church. Folklore. Hispanic Americans. New Mexico. Penitentes. Rites and Ceremonies. 16c-20c. *3829*
—. Catholic Church. French Canadians. North Central States. Settlement. 19c. *3804*
—. Catholic Church. French Canadians. Quebec. Self-perception. Values. 17c-1978. *3789*
—. Catholic Church. Pennsylvania (Danville). St. Cyril Academy. Sisters of SS. Cyril and Methodius. Slovak Americans. 1909-73. *3885*
—. Cemeteries. Christianity. Folklore. Texas. 1830-1950. *2751*
—. Cheyenne Indians. Institutions. Mennonites. Missions and Missionaries. Photographs. 1880-1940. *3398*
—. Christianity. Farmers. South. Travel accounts. 1850-70. *2795*
—. City Planning. Communes. Harmony Society. Indiana (New Harmony). Pennsylvania (Harmony, Economy). 1820's-1905. *391*
—. Congregationalism. Cooper, Samuel. Funerals. Music. New England. Sermons. 18c. *3113*
—. Cults. Salvation. 1960-76. *4270*
—. Education. Family. Friends, Society of. Pennsylvania. Socialization. ca 1740-76. *3279*
—. Education. Missions and Missionaries. Presbyterian Church. Puerto Rico. 1898-1917. *1727*
—. Folklore. Poetry. Samplers. 19c. *2021*
—. Jewish Jubilee Year. ca 3000 BC-1975. *4149*
—. Mining camps. Mormons. Nevada (Panaca). ca 1860-80. *3929*
Social Darwinism. Attitudes. Mexico. Missions and Missionaries. Protestant churches. Travel accounts. 1867-1911. *1690*
—. Christianity. Corporations. Education, Finance. Higher education. 1860-1930. *540*
Social ethic. Capitalism. Individualism. Protestantism. 20c. *345*
Social factors. Baptists, Southern. Evangelism. 1940-75. *2989*
Social Gospel. Alabama (Birmingham). Anti-Catholicism. Anti-Semitism. City Politics. Reform. 1900-30. *11*
—. Antireligious Movements. Communism. USSR. 1921-26. *104*
—. Asians. Conservatism. Immigration. Methodist Episcopal Church. 1865-1908. *2404*
—. Baptists. Darwin, Charles. Evolution. Hofstadter, Richard *(Social Darwinism in American Thought).* Rauschenbusch, Walter. Spencer, Herbert. 1879-1918. *3002*
—. Bascom, John. Commons, John R. Ely, Richard T. Evolution. Political theory. Wisconsin, University of. 1870-1910. *2394*
—. Bashford, James W. China. Methodist Episcopal Church. Missions and Missionaries. 1889-1919. *1712*
—. Bishops. Methodist Episcopal Church. Peck, Jesse T. 1850-83. *2396*
—. Bland, Salem. Canada. Methodism. Theology. 1880-86. *3444*
—. Bliss, William D. P. Christianity. Leftism. 1876-1926. *2377*
—. Canada. Communist Party. Labour Party. Methodism. Smith, Albert Edward. 1893-1924. *983*
—. Canada. Fiction. Labor. 1890's. *2078*
—. Canada. Labor. Socialism. 20c. *2441*
—. Canada. Methodism. 1890-1914. *2381*
—. Christian Commonwealth Colony. Communes. Georgia (Columbus). 1896-1900. *397*
—. Cities. Congregationalism. Gladden, Washington. Ohio (Columbus). Reform. 1850's-1914. *2425*
—. Clergy. Methodist Protestant Church. Shaw, Anna Howard. Suffrage. Women. 1880-1919. *3506*
—. Common Sense school. Comte, Auguste. Philosophy. Positivism. Reformed churches. Theology. ca 1850's-80's. *2833*
—. Congregationalism. Education. New Mexico (Albuquerque). Prohibition. 1900-17. *2448*
—. Congregationalism. Minnesota (Minneapolis). 1850-90. *2410*
—. Congregationalism. Missions and Missionaries. Nationalism. Strong, Josiah. Wyoming (Cheyenne). 1871-1916. *3134*
—. Ecumenism. Federal Council of the Churches of Christ in America. Hopkins, Charles Howard. Politics. Protestant Churches. 1880-1908. *487*
—. Ecumenism. Liberalism. Manitoba. United Church of Canada. 1870's-1925. *449*
—. Europe. History, comparative. Liberalism. Protestant Churches. 1885-1975. *2395*
—. God is Dead theology. Theology, avant-garde. 1960's. *2768*
—. Higher education. India. Missionaries. Protestant Churches. 1883. *1680*
—. Mathews, Shailer. Modernism. Science. Theology. 1864-1930. *2443*
—. New Theology. Protestantism. Roe, Edward Payson *(Barriers Burned Away).* Sheldon, Charles M. *(In His Steps).* 1860's-90's. *2058*
—. Race Relations. Reform. 1877-98. *2412*
—. Social conditions. Sociology. 1890-1972. *2390*
Social History. Alger, Horatio. Capitalism. Evangelicalism. Literature. Success (concept of). 1820-1910. *2958*
Social indicators. Alienation. Christianity. Converts. Cults. Human potential movement. 1960's-70's. *143*
—. Christianity (unaffiliated). Negroes. 1977. *2629*
Social issues. Alabama. Baptists, Southern. Reform. 1877-90. *2372*
—. Attitudes. Clergy. Theology. 1974. *2378*
—. Canada. Church and State. Leadership. Mennonite Conference of 1970. Students. 1917-74. *1029*
—. Clergy. Denominationalism. Theology. Values. 1960's-70's. *2401*
Social justice. *Catholic Worker* (newspaper). Day, Dorothy. Maurin, Peter. 20c. *1468*
—. Dreiser, Theodore. Fiction. 1900-45. *2020*
—. Ecumenism. Evangelism. Protestantism. Social change. Student Christian Movement. 19c-20c. *440*
—. Evangelicalism. Henry, Carl F. (review essay). 1971. *2415*
—. Presbyterian Church. 1770-1977. *2398*
Social mobility. Professionalism. Spiritualists. Women. 19c. *4294*
Social Organization. 1960's-77. *91*
—. Acculturation. Catholic Church. Italian Americans (review article). 1880-20c. *3820*
—. Agriculture. Amish. Economic conditions. Illinois. 1960-72. *3428*
—. Amish. Deviant Behavior. 1977. *3429*
—. Amish. Indiana (Allen County). Mennonites. 1850-1950. *3412*
—. Antinomian Controversy. Church and state. Hutchinson, Anne. Massachusetts. Puritans. Trials. Women. 1637. *1135*
—. Art. Daily life. Moravian Church. Pennsylvania (Bethlehem). 1741-1865. *3515*
—. Attitudes. Mormons. Utah. Women. Young, Brigham. 1840's-77. *830*
—. Axtell, James (review article). Education. New England. Puritans. 17c-18c. 1974. *526*
—. Bradford, William *(Of Plymouth Plantation).* Historiography. Pilgrims. Plymouth Colony. 1630-50. *3153*
—. California. Chumash Indians. Indians. Marriage. Mission Santa Barbara. Yanunali, Pedro (chief). 1787-1806. *940*
—. California (Orange County). Communalism. Middle Classes. Oneida Community. Townerites. 1848-1910. *417*
—. Capitalism. Church and State. 1960's-70's. *1075*
—. Catholic Church. French Canadians. Quebec. Women. 1960's-70's. *2013*
—. Catholic Church. Italian Americans. 1880-1940. *3834*
—. Charismatic Movement. Durkheim, Emile. Silva Mind Control. 1970's. *158*
—. Childbirth. Congregationalism. Death and Dying. Diaries. Diseases. Massachusetts (Westborough). Parkman, Ebenezer. 1724-82. *1447*
—. Christianity. Civil Rights. Jews. Riis, Jacob. 1870-1914. *2129*

—. Christianity. Grimké, Sarah. Nature. Paul, Saint. Women. 1c. 1830's. *921*
—. Civil Religion. Nationalism. Protestantism. Technology. ca 1630-1974. *1171*
—. Communalism. Equal opportunity. Hutterites. Leadership. Population. Prairie Provinces. Succession. 1940's-70's. *387*
—. Communalism (review article). Fellman, Michael. Marriage. Muncy, Raymond Lee. Sex. 19c. 1973. *384*
—. Communes. 19c-1976. *422*
—. Cult practices. Psychotherapy. Puerto Rico. Spiritualism. 1975. *1445*
—. Ethics. Liturgy. 1970's. *2735*
—. Ethnic Groups. Michigan (Detroit). Protestant Churches. 1880-1940. *2877*
—. Historiography, neoconservative. New England. Puritans. 17c. 1930's-60's. *3619*
—. Kibbutzim. New England. Palestine. Puritans. Towns. 17c. 20c. *3633*
—. Leadership. Manson Family. Millerites. Nazism. Women's Liberation Movement. 19c-20c. *2964*
—. Lucas, Paul R. New England (review article). Puritans. VanDeventer, David E. 1623-1741. 1976. *3621*
—. Mather, Cotton *(Essays to Do Good).* Morality. Puritans. 1700-25. *331*
—. Nationalism. Protestantism. Voluntary associations. 19c. *2931*
—. Owen, Robert Dale. Utopias. Wright, Frances. 1826-32. *411*
—. Slavery. 1740-76. *2824*
—. Social change. 1960-78. *119*
Social organizations. Archives. Emigrant Institute. Lutheran Church. Sweden (Växjö). 1800-1970. *282*
—. Canada. Immigrants. Lifestyles. Lutheran Church. Occupations. Settlement. Swedish Americans. USA. 1893-1979. *3325*
—. Christianity. Eastern religions. Youth Movements. 1968-74. *141*
—. Civil Religion. 1975. *1183*
—. Commission on the Status and Role of Women in the United Methodist Church. Feminism. Methodism. 1869-1974. *893*
—. Goal submergence concept. Methodist Church. Temperance movements. 1919-72. *2586*
—. Lutheran Church. Methodist Church. Swedish Americans. 1850-1951. *2951*
Social Philosophy. Brownson, Orestes A. Catholic Church. Intellectuals. 1803-76. *3677*
Social Policy. Baptists, Southern. Church organization. 19c-1970's. *3090*
Social Problems *See also* Charities; Crime and Criminals; Divorce; Emigration; Immigration; Public Welfare; Race Relations; Skid Rows.
—. Antislavery Sentiments. British North America. Friends, Society of. Woolman, John. 1720-72. *2371*
—. Baptists, Southern. Individualism. Politics. 18c-1976. *968*
—. Charities. Cities. Evangelism. Muhlenberg, Augustus. Politics. Protestantism (review article). 1812-1900. *2930*
—. Lafayette, Marquis de. Public Opinion. Travel. 1824-25. *61*
—. Missouri (Caldwell, Jackson counties). Mormons. Negroes. 1830-39. *4030*
—. New York City. Protestant churches. 1970's. *2421*
—. Presbyterian Church. *Princeton Review* (periodical). Providence. Science. 1789-1860. *3527*
Social progress. Catholic Church. Clergy. Human rights. New York City. Varela, Félix. 1823-53. *2357*
Social Psychology *See also* Human Relations; Violence.
—. Behaviorism. Skinner, B. F. 1948-74. *154*
—. *The Exorcist*, film (review article). Occult sciences. 1975. *2211*
—. History. 17c-20c. *228*
—. Public opinion. 1970's. *124*
Social Reform *See also* names of reform movements, e.g. Temperance Movements; Social Problems.
—. 1790-1815. *2352*
—. Abolition Movement. Finney, Charles G. Revivals. South. 1833-69. *2466*
—. Adrian College. Baptists, Free Will. Hillsdale College. Methodist Church, Wesleyan. Michigan. Oberlin College. Ohio. Olivet College. 1833-70. *741*
—. Agriculture. Judaism (Reform). Krauskopf, Joseph. 1880's-1923. *4228*
—. Antinomianism. Emerson, Ralph Waldo. Puritanism. Sermons. Transcendentalism. 1820's-30's. *4070*
—. Attitudes. Sin, sense of. 1830's-60's. *2389*
—. Baptists. Bishop, Harriet E. Minnesota (St. Paul). Reform. Women. 1847-83. *801*
—. Baptists. Catholic Church. Clergy. Rauschenbusch, Walter. Theology. Vatican Council II. 1912-65. *2380*
—. Baptists. Clergy. Dahlberg, Edwin. Personal narratives. Rauschenbusch, Walter. 1914-18. *2440*
—. Baptists. Massachusetts (Boston). Negroes. 1800-73. *3040*
—. Baptists. Politics. 1976. *1244*
—. Beecher, Henry Ward. Feminism. New York City. Radicals and Radicalism. Sex. Spiritualism. Vanderbilt, Cornelius. Woodhull, Victoria Claflin. 1868-90's. *2386*
—. Benevolence (doctrine). Finney, Charles G. Protestantism. 1815-65. *2422*
—. Bishops. Episcopal Church, Protestant. Huntington, Frederick (and family). New York. Theology. Women. 1869-1904. *3213*
—. Canada. Women. Young Women's Christian Association. 1870-1900. *895*
—. Catholic Church. Co-operative Commonwealth Federation. Saskatchewan. Socialism. 1930-50. *2567*
—. Catholic Church. New Jersey (Jersey City). Progressivism. Protestantism. Whittier House. 1890-1917. *2449*
—. Catholic Church. Prohibition. Zurcher, George. 1884-1920's. *2579*
—. Catholic Worker Movement. Maurin, Peter ("Easy Essays"). Political Theory. 1920's-33. *2571*
—. Christianity. Industrial Relations. Massachusetts (Lawrence). Scudder, Vida Dutton. Socialism. Women. 1912. *2374*
—. Church and Social Problems. Episcopal Church, Protestant. Missions and Missionaries. ca 1960-73. *2384*
—. Colorado (Boulder). Feminism. Temperance Movements. Women's Christian Temperance Union. 1881-1967. *2741*
—. Commission on Training Camp Activities. Jewish Welfare Board. Knights of Columbus. Leisure. Morality. War Department. World War I. Young Men's Christian Association. Young Women's Christian Association. 1917-18. *2379*
—. Congregationalism. Edwards, Jonathan. Hopkins, Samuel. New Divinity (doctrines). New England. Theology. 1730-1803. *2373*
—. Conservatism. Protestants. Quebec (Montreal). Women's Protective Immigration Society. 1882-1917. *919*
—. Counter culture. Millenarianism. Mysticism. Satanism. 1960's-70's. *4243*
—. Diaries. Mormons. Musser, Elise Furer. Political Leadership. Utah. Women. 1897-1967. *811*
—. Ecumenism. Pluralism. Tolerance. 1975. *105*
—. Education. Indian-White Relations. Missionaries. ca 1609-1900. *1498*
—. Employment. Program failure. Public Policy. Rescue missions. Skid rows. 1960's-70's. *2524*
—. Episcopal Church, Protestant. Great Britain. Maurice, Frederick Denison. Protestantism. Revelation. Theology. 1860-1900. *3171*
—. Episcopal Church, Protestant. Huntington, James Otis Sargent. Monasticism. Order of the Holy Cross. Single tax. 1878-90. *2430*
—. Episcopal Church, Protestant. Missouri (St. Louis). 1880-1920. *2403*
—. Europe. Revivals. 1400-1900. *2429*
—. Feminism. Identity. 1820's-60. *884*
—. Feminism. Protestant Churches. Radicals and Radicalism. South. Women. 1920's. *789*
—. Friends, Society of. Humanism. Intellectuals. Penn, William. Radicals and Radicalism. 1650-1700. *2353*
—. Fundamentalism. Matthews, Mark Allison. Presbyterian Church. Washington (Seattle). 1900-40. *2434*
—. Hawthorne, Nathaniel. History. Novels. Puritan tradition. Symbolism in Literature. 1825-63. *2019*
—. Intellectuals. McConnell, Francis John. Methodist Church. Theology. 1894-1937. *2382*
—. Laurens, Henry. Philosophy. Republicanism. South Carolina. 1764-77. *2385*
—. Liberal Institute. Mormons. Spiritualism. Utah (Salt Lake City). 1869-84. *4296*
—. Mennonites. Politics. Separatism. 1840's-1930's. *3418*
—. Mexican Americans. 1974. *2413*
—. New York (Rochester). Radicals and Radicalism. Revivalism. 1830-56. *2416*
—. Rush, Benjamin. 1770's-1813. *2375*
Social relations. Judaism (Orthodox). New York. Schools. 18c. *4175*
Social Sciences *See also* Economics; Political Science; Social Change; Sociology.
—. Canada. Catholic Church. Education. French Canadians. Quebec. Rinfret, Fernand. Siegfried, André *(Le Canada, les deux races: Problèmes politiques contemporains).* 1906-07. *3873*
—. Niebuhr, H. Richard. Theology. ca 1930-70. *125*
—. Public schools. Religious studies. 1979. *558*
Social stability. Illinois (Nauvoo). Mormons. Religiosity. 1833-46. *3981*
Social Status. American Revolution. Church of England. Clergy. Maryland. Politics. 1775. *2618*
—. American Revolution. Clergy. Congregationalism. Presbyterian Church. 1774-1800. *2849*
—. Attitudes. Canada. Catholic Church. Ethnic Groups. Jews. Protestantism. 1968. *2088*
—. Baptists. Clergy. Education. Income. 1651-1980. *2603*
—. Catholic Church. Cities. Negroes. North or Northern States. Occupations. 1968. *2613*
—. Catholic Church. Clergy. Ethnicity. 1947-80. *3867*
—. Children. Judaism (Orthodox). New York City (Brooklyn; Boro Park). Parents. 1973. *4187*
—. Christianity. Clergy. Radicals and radicalism. 1960-74. *2764*
—. Church attendance. 1970. *2619*
—. Clergy. National Characteristics. Proslavery Sentiments. 1699-1865. *2628*
—. Clothing. Legislation. New England. Puritans. 1630-90. *2427*
—. Economic Conditions. Judaism. 1970-71. *4129*
—. Family. Farms. Literature. Sex roles. South. Women. 1800-60. *816*
—. Friends, Society of. Sectionalism. West Virginia. 18c-19c. *3257*
—. Jackson, Jesse. Negroes. People United to Save Humanity. Southern Christian Leadership Conference. 1966-78. *2423*
—. Jews. Laity. Leadership. New York (Kingston). Political Leadership. Protestant Churches. 1825-60. *2600*
—. New York. Noyes, John Humphrey. Oneida Community. Sex. Women. 1848-79. *863*
Social Structure. *See* Social Organization; Social Status.
Social studies. Morality. Science. Teaching. 1977. *2321*
Social Surveys *See also* Sociology.
—. Attitudes. Conservatism. Religious beliefs. 1970-74. *1380*
Social Theory. Agricultural Reform. Catholic Church. New Deal. Roosevelt, Franklin D. (administration). 1933-39. *2572*
—. American Revolution. Great Awakening. Social Classes. Urbanization. 1740's-70's. *2230*
—. American Revolution (antecedents). Great Awakening. Liberalism. Social Change. ca 1725-75. *1338*
—. Baptists. Clergy. Hudson, Winthrop. Liberalism. Rauschenbusch, Walter. Theology. 1880-1978. *2351*
—. Behavior. Communalism. Hutterites. ca 1650-1977. *382*
—. Chain of being. Church of England. Cradock, Thomas. Maryland (Baltimore County). Poetry. Sermons. 1700-80. *3227*
—. Conservatism. Presbyterian Church. Smyth, Thomas. South Carolina. Theology. 1831-70. *3552*
—. Democracy. Finney, Charles G. Human nature. Revivalism. 1820-30. *2268*
—. Edwards, Jonathan. Massachusetts (Northampton). Millenarianism. 1720's-50's. *3154*
—. Human relations. Rhode Island. Williams, Roger. 1643-76. *2826*
—. Mormons. Negroes. Strang, James Jesse. Thompson, Charles B. 1844-73. *2138*
Social thought. Canada. Catholic Church. Journalism. Somerville, Henry. 1915-53. *2354*
—. Catholic Church. Gibbons, James. Knights of Labor. Taschereau, Elzéar Alexandre. 1880's. *1476*
Social Welfare. *See* Public Welfare.

Social Work *See also* Charities; Counseling; Public Welfare.
—. Addams, Jane. Dudzik, Mary Theresa. Franciscan Sisters of Chicago. Illinois. Polish Americans. Women. 1860-1918. *2511*
—. California (Huntington Park, Los Angeles). Frey, Sigmund. Jewish Orphan's Home. Judaism (Reform). 1870's-1930. *2500*
—. Catholic Church. Church Schools. Felicians. Polish Americans. Women. 1855-1975. *3828*
—. Congregationalism. Georgia (Atlanta). Negroes. 1886-1970. *2432*
—. Education. Ohio (Cincinnati). Sisters of Charity of St. Joseph. Women. 1809-1979. *2514*
—. Hexter, Maurice B. Jews. Ohio (Cincinnati). Personal narratives. United Jewish Charities. 1910's. *2508*
Socialism *See also* Capitalism; Communism; Labor; Labor Unions and Organizations; Leftism; Marxism; Utopias.
—. Agnosticism. Ethnicity. Hillquit, Morris. Jews. New York City. 1890's-1933. *1331*
—. Anti-Catholicism. Capitalism. DeLeon, Daniel. 1891-1914. *2113*
—. Baptists. Negroes. Protestantism. Woodbey, George Washington. 1902-15. *2563*
—. Canada. Labor. Social Gospel. 20c. *2441*
—. Catholic Church. Co-operative Commonwealth Federation. Saskatchewan. Social reform. 1930-50. *2567*
—. Catholic Church. Labor Unions and Organizations. Polish Americans. Political Leadership. Progressivism. Wisconsin (Milwaukee). 1900-30. *1299*
—. Christianity. Church and Social Problems. Labor Unions and Organizations. 1880-1913. *1465*
—. Christianity. Industrial Relations. Massachusetts (Lawrence). Scudder, Vida Dutton. Social reform. Women. 1912. *2374*
—. Christianity. Latin America. North America. 20c. *953*
—. Civil religion. Protestantism. Secularization. 16c-20c. *2910*
—. Clergy. Congregationalism. Herron, George David. Iowa College. National Christian Citizen League. Populism. Progressivism. 1880's-1900. *2561*
—. Education. New Brunswick. Stuart, Henry Harvey. 1873-1952. *2369*
—. Intellectuals. New England. Poetry. Radicals and Radicalism. Wheelwright, John (1897-1940). 18c-1940. *1419*
Socialist Party. Christianity. O'Hare, Kate Richards. Women. 1901-17. *2559*
Socialization *See also* Political Socialization.
—. Attitudes. Ethnicity. Mennonites. Pennsylvania (Lancaster). Private Schools. 1974-76. *673*
—. Catholic Church. Children. Occupational status. Public schools. -1974. *3784*
—. Children. Minnesota, southern. Parents. Religiosity. 1975. *128*
—. Communes. Convents. Cults. Tnevnoc Cult. 19c. 1970-79. *386*
—. Education. Family. Friends, Society of. Pennsylvania. Social Customs. ca 1740-76. *3279*
—. Illinois (Chicago). Judaism. 1974. *4110*
Society for the Promotion of Collegiate and Theological Education at the West. Baldwin, Theron. Congregationalism. Higher education. Presbyterianism. 1843-73. *629*
Society for the Propagation of the Gospel. Algoma Diocese. Episcopal Church, Protestant. Missions and Missionaries. Ontario. 1873-1973. *1653*
—. American Revolution. Church of England. Delaware (Appoquiniminck). Loyalists. Reading, Philip. 1775-78. *1221*
—. American Revolution (antecedents). Benefices. Church of England. New England. Religious Liberty. 1689-1775. *1054*
—. Archives. Church of England. Missions and Missionaries. 1700-80. *215*
—. Church of England. Laity. Neau, Elias. Negroes. New York City. 1704-22. *3193*
—. Church of England. Loyalists. Nova Scotia. 1787-1864. *1644*
—. Church of England. Malcolm, Alexander. Maryland (Annapolis). Music. St. Anne's Church. Teaching. 1721-63. *1931*
—. Church of England. Missions and Missionaries. Nova Scotia (Halifax). St. Paul's Church. Tutty, William. 1749-52. *1646*
—. Episcopal Church, Protestant. Negroes. Racism. ca 1700-1974. *3169*
Society of Bethel. Aurora Colony. Communes. Music. Oregon. Pioneer Band. 1855-1920's. *1942*
—. Communes. German Americans. Keil, William. Letters. Missouri. Oregon. Weitling, Wilhelm. 1844-83. *405*
Society of Free Brethren and Sisters. Anti-Christian sentiments. Christianity. Cochran, Jacob. Free love. Maine (York County). 1817-19. *89*
Society of Jesus. *See* Jesuits.
Society of Jewish Academicians. Adler, Cyrus. American Academy for Jewish Research. Intellectuals. Judaism (Orthodox, Reform). Revel, Bernard. 1916-22. *4139*
Society of the Atonement. Catholic Church. Chapel-of-St. John's-in-the-Wilderness. Ecumenism. Episcopal Church, Protestant. New York (Graymoor). Wattson, Paul James. White, Lurana Mary. 1909-18. *461*
—. Catholic Church. Ecumenism. Episcopal Church, Protestant. Wattson, Paul James. White, Lurana. Women. 1870-1928. *459*
Society of the Catholic Commonwealth. Anglican Communion. Massachusetts (Cambridge). Smyth, Frederick Hastings *(Manhood into God)*. Theology. Utopias. 1940. *3200*
Society of the New Jerusalem. Andrews, Joseph. Art. Massachusetts (Boston). Swedenborgianism. 1830-73. *4062*
Sociologists. Cults. Sects, religious. Youth. 1960's-70's. *4256*
Sociology *See also* Cities; Emigration; Family; Immigration; Labor; Marriage; Population; Race Relations; Slavery; Social Classes; Social Conditions; Social Organization; Social Problems; Social Surveys.
—. Bibliographies. History. 1960-70. *120*
—. French Canadians. Literature. Patriotism. Quebec. 19c. *2085*
—. History. -1973. *188*
—. LeConte, Joseph. Philosophy of Science. South. ca 1840-60. *2301*
—. Mysticism. Troeltsch, Ernst. Weber, Max. 20c. *111*
—. Social conditions. Social Gospel. 1890-1972. *2390*
—. Women. 1950's-70's. *902*
Sociology of religion. Attitudes. Daily life. Yinger, J. Milton. 1946-77. *166*
—. Bellah, Robert N. (review article). Civil religion. 1959-75. *112*
—. Bibliographies. Civil religion. 17c-20c. 1960's-70's. *1168*
—. Doherty, Robert W. Historiography. Methodology. 1974. *264*
—. Herberg, Will. Historiography. Religiosity. 1790's-1970's. *39*
—. Magic. 1940-73. *147*
Sociology of religion concept. Greeley, Andrew M. (review essays). Theology. 1960's-70's. *167*
Sodomy. Attitudes. Court records. Law Enforcement. New England. 1630-80. *2428*
Soelle, Georg. Maine (Waldoboro). Missions and Missionaries. Moravian Church. 1762-70. *3512*
Solberg, Winton U. Elliott, Emory. New England. Puritans (review article). Sabbath. Sermons. 17c-18c. 1975-77. *3623*
Solomon, Hannah G. American, Sadie. Congress of Jewish Women. Jews. Women. World Parliament of Religions. World's Columbian Exposition (Chicago, 1893). 1893. *846*
Somerville, Henry. Canada. Catholic Church. Journalism. Social thought. 1915-53. *2354*
Sore throats. Clergy. Protestantism. 1830-60. *1431*
South *See also* individual states; South Central and Gulf States; Southeastern States.
—. Abolition Movement. Civil War (antecedents). Presbyterian Church. Stanton, Robert. 1840-55. *2484*
—. Abolition Movement. Finney, Charles G. Revivals. Social reform. 1833-69. *2466*
—. Abortion. Protestant churches. Right To Life organizations. 1970's. *945*
—. Adolescents. Church attendance. Negroes. Religiosity. Whites. 1964-74. *99*
—. Alabama. Bakke, Niles J. Lutheran Church. Young, Rosa J. 1839-1965. *3299*
—. Alabama. Lutheran Church. Photographs. 1971-74. *3347*
—. American Missionary Association. Congregationalism. Missions and Missionaries. Negroes. 1846-80. *1617*
—. Ames Church. Education. Freedmen. Hartzell, Joseph C. Methodist Episcopal Church. Missionaries. Republican Party. 1870-73. *3481*
—. Ames, Jessie Daniel. Association of Southern Women for the Prevention of Lynching. Lynching. Methodist Woman's Missionary Council. Racism. Women. Young Women's Christian Association. 1930's. *2535*
—. Antislavery sentiments. Evangelicalism. 1820-30. *2489*
—. Architecture, Gothic Revival. Episcopal Church, Protestant. Upjohn, Richard. Wills, Frank. 1835-60. *1809*
—. Assemblies of God. Church of God. Civil rights movement. Periodicals. Presbyterian Church, Southern. 1950's-60's. *2528*
—. Attitudes. Calvinism. Faulkner, William *(The Sound and the Fury)*. 1929. *2018*
—. Baptists. Dayton, Amos Cooper. Landmark Movement. Novels. 1850-65. *1995*
—. Baptists. Graves, James Robinson. Landmark movement. Missions and Missionaries. Whitsitt Controversy. 1850-1950. *3057*
—. Baptists. Historical societies. Periodicals. 1950's-70's. *186*
—. Baptists. Methodist Church. Presbyterian Church. Slavery. 1740-1860. *2168*
—. Baptists, American. Education. Missions. Negroes. 1862-81. *739*
—. Baptists, Primitive. Music (Sacred Harp). 1840's-1977. *1918*
—. Baptists, Southern. Campbell, Will. Clergy. Garner, Thad. Personal narratives. 20c. *2994*
—. Baptists, Southern. Church membership. Country life. Evangelicalism. Urbanization. 1920's. *3085*
—. Baptists, Southern. Corporate wealth. Methodism. Political power. Presbyterian Church. 1930's-75. *2926*
—. Barr, D. Eglinton. Chaplains. Civil War. Episcopal Church, Protestant. 1851-72. *2648*
—. Bible. Folklore. Protestantism. Visions. 20c. *2178*
—. Bibliographies. Periodicals. 18c-20c. 1977-78. *45*
—. Boles, John B. (review article). Evangelicalism. Racism. Revivals. Smith, H. Shelton (review article). 1972. *2867*
—. Bottoms, Lawrence W. Negroes. Personal narratives. Presbyterian Church, Southern. 1930-75. *2529*
—. Caldwell, Erskine. Caldwell, Ira Sylvester. Novels. Presbyterian Church, Associate Reformed. 1900-78. *2017*
—. Calvinism. Millenarianism. Presbyterian Church. Proslavery Sentiments. 1800-65. *2166*
—. Carter, Jimmy. Niebuhr, Reinhold. 1976. *1233*
—. Catholic Church. Slavery. 1619-1860. *2170*
—. Christianity. Civil religion. Political Speeches. 1960's-70's. *1193*
—. Christianity. Conservatism. Philosophy. Weaver, Richard M. ca 1930-63. *1363*
—. Christianity. Farmers. Social Customs. Travel accounts. 1850-70. *2795*
—. Christianity. Proslavery Sentiments. 1844-1977. *2167*
—. Church and State. Presbyterian Church. Slavery. 1850-80. *1074*
—. Civil religion. Lost Cause (theme). 1865-1920. *1196*
—. Civil War. North or Northern States. Puritan tradition. 1840's-60's. *2842*
—. Civil War. Protestantism. 1861-65. *2841*
—. Clergy. Consultation on Church Union. Henderlite, Rachel. Personal narratives. Presbyterian Church, Southern. Women. 1945-77. *804*
—. Clergy. Council of Southern Mountain Workers. Rural Development. Standard of Living. 1913-72. *2451*
—. Clergy. Negroes. Protestant churches. Race Relations. ca 1800-65. *2816*
—. Coca-Cola Company. Emory University. Methodist Church. Religious education. Vanderbilt University. 1840's-1970's. *3466*
—. Collectors and Collecting. Folklore. Hyatt, Harry Midddleton. Illinois (Adams County). Negroes. Small, Minnie Hyatt. Witchcraft. 1920-78. *2190*
—. Country Life. Murder. Negroes. Whites. 1916-20. *156*
—. Death and Dying. Evangelism. Literature. 1800-65. *1970*
—. Ecumenism. Presbyterian Church, Southern. 1861-74. *477*

—. Elliott, Stephen. Episcopal Church, Protestant. Philosophy of History. Providence. 1840-66. *3212*
—. Evangelicalism. Farmers. Negroes. 1800-60. *2845*
—. Evangelicalism. Jones, Charles Colcock. Race Relations. Utopias. 1804-63. *2543*
—. Evangelicalism. Mathews, Donald G. (review article). 18c-19c. 1977. *2835*
—. Evangelicals. Twain, Mark. 1870-1910. *2875*
—. Evangelism. Protestantism. Slavery. 18-19c. *2169*
—. Family. Farms. Literature. Sex roles. Social Status. Women. 1800-60. *816*
—. Feminism. Protestant Churches. Radicals and Radicalism. Social reform. Women. 1920's. *789*
—. Freedmen. Methodist Episcopal Church, Colored. Methodist Episcopal Church, South. Religious liberty. Segregation. 1865-70. *3464*
—. Fundamentalism. Machen, J. Gresham. Presbyterian Church. 1920's-35. *3580*
—. Genovese, Eugene D. (review article). Millenarianism. Protestantism. Slavery. 17c-1865. *2163*
—. Historiography. Populism. 1865-1900. *1281*
—. Jones, Charles Colcock. Missions and Missionaries. Presbyterian Church. Slavery. 1825-63. *2177*
—. Labor Unions and Organizations. People's Institute of Applied Religion. Williams, Claude. Williams, Joyce. 1940-75. *1478*
—. LeConte, Joseph. Philosophy of Science. Sociology. ca 1840-60. *2301*
—. Lutheran Church. Slavery. 1790-1865. *2172*
—. Marriage. Plantations. Protestantism. Slaves. ca 1750's-1860. *2928*
—. Methodist Episcopal Church, South. Newspapers. 1861-65. *3487*
—. Methodist Episcopal Church (South). Newspapers. Spanish-American War. 1898. *2691*
—. Metropolitan areas. Religiosity. 1970's. *123*
—. Militancy. Negroes. Orthodoxy. 1964-75. *1292*
—. Morality. Presbyterian Church. Republicanism. Revivals. 1825-60. *2244*
—. Mormons. Violence. 1884-1905. *2127*
—. Mountaineers. Music. Revivals. 1798-1970. *1935*
—. Music. Protestantism. Walker, William. 1830-50. *1914*
—. Negroes. Protestantism. Segregation. 1885-90's. *2135*
—. North or Northern States. Slavery. Unitarianism. 1831-60. *2174*
—. Presbyterian Church, Southern. Wilson, Joseph Ruggles. 1844-1903. *3572*
—. Presbyterians. Slavery. 1787-1817. *2156*
South Africa. American Board of Commissioners for Foreign Missions. Missions and Missionaries. Protestant Churches. Social customs. Zulus. 1835-60's. *1695*
South Africa (Ginani). Boers. Champion, George. Missions and Missionaries. Zulus. 1836-41. *1719*
South Atlantic Quarterly (periodical). Academic freedom. Bassett, John Spencer. Duke University. Methodist Church. North Carolina (Durham). Racism. 1902-03. *3497*
South Carolina *See also* South; Southeastern States.
—. Bishop of London. Church of England. Commissaries. Great Britain. 1715-32. *3242*
—. Cain, Richard Harvey. Methodist Episcopal Church, African. Negroes. Politics. Reconstruction. Social conditions. 1850's-87. *2407*
—. Church and State. Colonial Government. Defoe, Daniel. Religious liberty. 1704-06. *1014*
—. Clergy. Presbyterian Church. Reese, Thomas. 1773-96. *3585*
—. Conservatism. Presbyterian Church. Smyth, Thomas. Social theory. Theology. 1831-70. *3552*
—. Laurens, Henry. Philosophy. Republicanism. Social Reform. 1764-77. *2385*
—. Leadership. Negroes. 1919. *2617*
—. Libraries. Lutheran Church. Theological Seminary Library of Lexington, South Carolina. 1832-59. *645*
South Carolina (Anderson County). Baptists. Ebenezer Methodist Church. Inscriptions. Methodist Church. Mount Bethel Baptist Church. Tombstones. 1856-1978. *2848*
South Carolina (Camden). Civil War. Elliott, John H. Episcopal Church, Protestant. Sermons. 1862. *1982*
—. Friends, Society of. Irish Americans. Milhouse, Robert. Wyly, Samuel. 1751-93. *3265*
South Carolina (Charleston). Assimilation. Jews. Political Attitudes. 1970's. *4136*
—. Congregation Beth Elohim. Congregation Beth Elohim Unveh Shallom. Judaism (Orthodox). Portuguese Americans. 1784-91. *4173*
—. Judaism (Reform). Kahal Kadosh Beth Elohim (synagogue). 1695-1978. *1764*
—. Manuscripts. McDowell, William A. New Jersey Historical Society. Presbyterian Church. Third Presbyterian Church. 1820's-30's. *259*
—. Methodism. Wesley, John. 1737. *1487*
—. Presbyterian Church. Segregation. Slavery. 1845-60. *2154*
South Carolina (Chesterfield County). Civil War. Diaries. Episcopal Church, Protestant. Providence. Robertson, Martha Wayles. Women. 1860-66. *3191*
South Carolina (Johns Island). Moving Star Hall. Negroes. Protestantism. 18c-1970. *2830*
South Carolina (Ninety Six). American Revolution. Brown, Joshua. Friends, Society of. Pacifism. Pennsylvania (Little Britain Township). Prisoners. 1778. *2633*
South Dakota *See also* Western States.
—. Acculturation. Frontier and Pioneer Life. Immigrants. Lutheran Church. Rolvaag, O. E. *(Giants in the Earth)*. 1870. 1927. *3307*
—. Agriculture. Missions and Missionaries. Politics. Settlement. 1850-1900. *66*
—. Canada. Communalism. Hutterites. Lifestyles. 1874-1975. *403*
—. Catholic Church. Education. Indians. Missions and Missionaries. North Dakota. Pioneers. Presentation of the Blessed Virgin Mary, Sisters of the. Women. 1880-96. *727*
—. Catholic Church. Eisenmann, Sylvester. Sioux Indians. Yankton Reservation (Marty Mission). 1918-49. *3900*
—. Clark, Bertha W. Hutterites. Pacifism. Social change. 1921. *3385*
—. Compulsory Education. Hutterites. Legislation. Values. 1700-1970's. *659*
—. Dutch Americans. Immigration. North Dakota. Reformed Dutch Church. 1880's-1951. *3161*
—. Economic conditions. Frontier and Pioneer life. Indians. Missions and Missionaries. Presbyterian Church. 1840-1900. *3540*
—. Immigration. Mennonites. Russia. Unruh, Daniel. 1820-82. *3430*
South Dakota Historical Resource Center. Christianity. Frontier and Pioneer Life. Manuscripts. 1976. *217*
South Dakota (Springfield). Education. Episcopal Church, Protestant. Girls. Indians. St. Mary's Episcopal School for Indian Girls. 1873-1973. *687*
South End House. Catholic Church. Evangelism. Massachusetts (Boston). Protestantism. Settlement houses. Woods, Robert A. 1891-1910. *2438*
Southeastern Baptist Theological Seminary. Baptists, Southern. North Carolina. Wake Forest College. 1945-51. *748*
Southeastern States *See also* South; individual states.
—. American Board of Commissioners for Foreign Missions. Brainerd Mission. Cherokee Indians. Education. Indian-White Relations. Letters. 1817-38. *1605*
—. Baptists, Southern. Clergy. Manly, Basil. Teachers. 1798-1868. *3041*
—. Folklore. Music, bluegrass gospel. 1770-1970. *1937*
Southern and Western Theological Seminary. Abolition Movement. Anderson, Isaac. Presbyterian Church. Tennessee (Maryville). 1819-50's. *723*
Southern Baptist Convention Home Missions Board. Baptists, Southern. Evangelism. 1845-1973. *1544*
—. Baptists, Southern. Language. Missions. Northeastern or North Atlantic States. 1950-75. *1620*
Southern Baptist Theological Seminary. Carver, William Owen. Missions and Missionaries. 1859-1954. *1518*
—. Clergy. Denominationalism. Theology. 18c-1980. *3075*
Southern Christian Leadership Conference. Jackson, Jesse. Negroes. People United to Save Humanity. Social Status. 1966-78. *2423*
Southern Methodist University. Educational innovation. Methodist Church, United. Student activists. Texas (Dallas). 1972-74. *720*
Southerners. Architecture. Catholic Church. Fundamentalists. German Americans. Rural Settlements. Social customs. Texas (Cooke, Denton counties). 1860-1976. *2750*
Southwest *See also* individual states; Far Western States.
—. Bolton, Herbert Eugene. Catholic Church. Colonization. Historiography. Missions and Missionaries. Spain. 1917-79. *1489*
—. Catholic Church. Frontier and Pioneer Life. Missions and Missionaries. Spain. 16c-18c. *1497*
—. Catholic Church. Indians. Missions and Missionaries. Pueblo Revolt (1680). 1590-1680. *1499*
—. Catholic Church. Jesuits. *Revista Catolica* (periodical). 1875-1962. *3884*
—. Esteyneffer, Juan de *(Florilegio Medicinal)*. Herbs. Indians. Jesuits. Medicine (practice of). Missions and Missionaries. 1711. *1444*
—. Folk art. Lithography. Mexico. Puerto Rico. 1300-1974. *1868*
—. Hallucinations. Plants. Trances. Witchcraft. 17c-20c. *2207*
—. Indians. Mexican Americans. Navajo Indians. Pueblo Indians. Witchcraft. 19c-1930's. *2214*
—. Methodist Church. Mexican Americans. Rio Grande Annual Conference. 1874-1978. *3491*
—. Mexican Americans. Presbyterian Church. 1830-1977. *3528*
Southwestern College. Evolution. Goldsmith, William. Hawkins, Robert W. Kansas (Winfield). Methodist Episcopal Church. 1920-25. *2316*
Southwestern history. California. Catholic Church. Engelhardt, Zephyrin. Mission Santa Barbara. Missions and Missionaries. 1851-1934. *176*
Southwick (family). Friends, Society of. Massachusetts. Persecution. 1639-61. *1066*
Space exploration. National Aeronautics and Space Administration. Religious experience. Science fiction. 1960-76. *146*
Spain. Alaska. Catholic Church. Missionaries. Riobó, Juan Antonio García. Voyages. 1779. *1643*
—. American Revolution. California. Indians. Missions. 1776-83. *1321*
—. Arizona. Catholic Church. Colonial Government. Jurisdictions, ecclesiastical. New Mexico. 1548-1969. *3739*
—. Arizona. Indians. Jesuits. Kino, Eusebio Francisco. Missions and Missionaries. 1680's-1711. *1565*
—. Bolton, Herbert Eugene. Catholic Church. Colonization. Historiography. Missions and Missionaries. Southwest. 1917-79. *1489*
—. British Columbia (Vancouver Island; Nootka Sound). Catholic Church. Indians. Missions and Missionaries. Oral History. 1789-95. 19c. *1563*
—. California. Church and state. Colonial Government. Indians. Laws of the Indies. Missions and Missionaries. 18c. *1143*
—. California (San Diego). Colonization. Indians. Missions and Missionaries. 1769-1834. *1668*
—. Catholic Church. Colorado. New Mexico. Passion plays. 1830's-1978. *1890*
—. Catholic Church. Culture. Paraguay. 1513-20c. *3737*
—. Catholic Church. Frontier and Pioneer Life. Missions and Missionaries. Southwest. 16c-18c. *1497*
—. Church and state. Colonization. West Florida. 1780's. *1055*
—. Colonial Government. Documents. Franciscans. Missions and Missionaries. New Mexico. Vélez Cachupín, Thomas. ca 1754. *1586*
—. Colonization. Indians. Jesuits. Menéndez de Avilés, Pedro. Missions and Missionaries. Opechancanough (chief). Powhatan Indians. Virginia. 1570-72. *1622*
Spalding, Solomon. Congregationalism. Mormon, Book of. 1761-1816. *2796*
Spanish-American Seminary. Adventists. Education. Missions and Missionaries. New Mexico (Sandoval). 1928-53. *751*
Spanish-American War. Anti-imperialism. Baptists, American. Horr, George. Vietnam War. *Watchman*. 1876-1974. *2698*
—. Methodist Episcopal Church (South). Newspapers. South. 1898. *2691*
—. Mormons. Pacifism. Young, Brigham, Jr. ca 1840-98. *2682*
Sparks, Jared. Clergy. Documents. Editors and Editing. Historians. Unitarianism. Washington, George. 1815-30. *4076*

Speak Schools. Diaries. Gehman, John B. Mennonites. Pennsylvania (Hereford). 1853. *566*
Special Interest Groups. *See* Pressure Groups; Lobbying; Political Factions.
Spectator (newspaper). Clergy. Congregationalism. Franklin, Benjamin. Massachusetts (Boston). *New England Courant* (newspaper). Smallpox. 1720-23. *2023*
Speculation. Galland, Isaac. Iowa (Lee County). Land. Mormons. Smith, Joseph. 1830's-58. *3950*
Speeches, Addresses, etc. *See also* Lectures; Political Speeches.
—. Chapman, John Jay. Christianity. Lynching. Pennsylvania (Coatesville). Poetry. Race Relations. Rhetoric. 1912. *1971*
—. Church and state. Clergy. Henry, Patrick. Maury, James. Parsons' Cause. Personal narratives. Virginia. 1758-65. *1080*
—. Congregationalism. Harvard University. Latin language. Leverett, John. Massachusetts (Cambridge). 1722. *668*
—. Constitutions. Mormons. Smith, Joseph. 1840. *1374*
—. Mormons. Utah. 1776-1976. *1103*
—. Women. Wright, Frances. 1828-30. *4303*
Spencer, Herbert. Baptists. Darwin, Charles. Evolution. Hofstadter, Richard *(Social Darwinism in American Thought).* Rauschenbusch, Walter. Social Gospel. 1879-1918. *3002*
Spencer, James Hovey. Baptists. Clergy. Frontier and Pioneer Life. Montana. Personal narratives. 1888-97. *3095*
Spiritual growth. Christianity. 1973. *102*
Spiritual movement. Jesuits. Lacouture, Onésime. Quebec. 1931-50. *3730*
Spiritualism. Baptists, Free Will. Cheney Family Singers. Cheney, Moses. Music. Vermont. 1839-91. *1932*
—. Beecher, Henry Ward. Feminism. New York City. Radicals and Radicalism. Sex. Social Reform. Vanderbilt, Cornelius. Woodhull, Victoria Claflin. 1868-90's. *2386*
—. Christian Science. Leadership. Shakers. Theosophy. Women. 19c. *795*
—. Cult practices. Psychotherapy. Puerto Rico. Social organization. 1975. *1445*
—. District of Columbia. Johnson, Andrew. Lincoln, Abraham. Schurz, Carl. Seance. 1865. *4293*
—. Fuller, Margaret. Philosophy. Transcendentalism. Women. 1840's. *4068*
—. Independence Hall. Pennsylvania (Philadelphia). Philanthropy. Seybert, Henry. 1793-1882. *4292*
—. Liberal Institute. Mormons. Social Reform. Utah (Salt Lake City). 1869-84. *4296*
—. Lincoln, Abraham. Lincoln, Mary Todd. 1848-64. *4295*
—. Moore, R. Laurence (review article). Science. 1850-1977. *4290*
—. Professionalism. Social mobility. Women. 19c. *4294*
—. Wisconsin. 1840-90. *4291*
Spirituality. Channing, William Ellery. Clergy. Unitarianism. 1830-80. *4083*
Spokan Indians. Diaries. Indians. Missions and Missionaries. Walker, Elkanah. Walker, Mary. Washington, eastern. 1839-48. *1521*
—. Indian-White Relations. Missions and Missionaries. Protestant Churches. Walker, Elkanah. Washington (Tshimakain). 1838-48. *1520*
Sports *See also* Games.
—. Architecture. Cathedral Church of St. John the Divine. Episcopal Church, Protestant. Manning, William Thomas. New York City. Sabbatarianism. 19c-1920's. *3243*
—. Attitudes. Jeremiads. Puritans. 1620-1720. *3658*
—. Canada. Church and state. Lord's Day Act (Canada, 1906). Sabbatarianism. 1906-77. *2284*
—. Jeremiads. New England. Puritans. Sermons. 17c-18c. *3659*
—. Massachusetts. Puritans. 1630-1730. *3654*
—. National character. 20c. *98*
Spotswood, Alexander. German Americans. Immigration. Reformed German Church. Virginia (Germanna). 1714-21. *3284*
Spring, Marcus. Communes. New Jersey (Perth Amboy, Red Bank). North American Phalanx. Raritan Bay Union. 1843-59. *413*
Sprunger, David. Courtship. Diaries. Indiana. Marriage. Mennonites. 1893-95. *3427*
Squanto (Wampanoag Indian). Hobomok (shaman). Indian-White Relations. Pilgrims. Plymouth Colony. Polytheism. Theology. ca 1620-30. *3144*
St. John, J. Hector. *See* Crevecoeur, Michel Guillaume Jean de.
Stained glass windows. Architecture, Gothic Revival. Bolton, William J. Church of the Holy Trinity. Episcopal Church, Protestant. New York City (Brooklyn). 1845-47. *1847*
—. Art. Illinois (Chicago). Presbyterian Church. Second Presbyterian Church. 1872-74. *1855*
—. British Columbia (Vancouver). Canadian Memorial Chapel (Manitoba memorial window). 1928. *1848*
—. Camp Lejeune. Lamb Studios. Marines. New Jersey (Tenafly). North Carolina. Protestantism. 1775-1943. *1867*
—. Presbyterian Church. Willet family. 19c-20c. *1887*
Staines, William C. Mormons. Utah. 1818-81. *3964*
Stairwells. Architecture. Meetinghouses. New England. 18c. *1761*
Stamp Act crisis. Colonies. Providence. 1765-66. *1156*
Standard of Living. Clergy. Council of Southern Mountain Workers. Rural Development. South. 1913-72. *2451*
Stannard, David E. Child-rearing. Death and Dying. Fischer, David H. Greven, Philip. Lynn, Kenneth S. Personality (review article). Politics. Protestantism. 18c. 1977. *2943*
Stannard, David E. (review article). Christianity. Death and Dying. 17c-20c. *2746*
Stanton, H. B. Abolition Movement. Birney, James. Clergy. Evangelism. Smith, Gerrit. Weld, Theodore. 1820-50. *2488*
Stanton, Robert. Abolition Movement. Civil War (antecedents). Presbyterian Church. South. 1840-55. *2484*
Stark, Rodney. Converts. Glock, Charles Y. Models. Social Change. 1960's-70's. *144*
Starr, Edward Caryl. American Baptist Historical Society. *Baptist Bibliography.* Samuel Colgate Baptist Historical Library. 1935-76. *263*
—. American Baptist Historical Society. Baptists. Librarians. Samuel Colgate Baptist Historical Library. 1930's-76. *208*
State Aid to Education. Baptists. Elementary education. Religious Education. Secondary education. 1850-1910. *718*
—. Church Schools. Colleges and Universities. Supreme Court. 1971-76. *682*
—. Church Schools. Constitutional Amendments (1st). Supreme Court. 1970's. *728*
State Department. Catholic Church. China (Kanchow). Foreign policy. Missions and Missionaries. 1929-32. *1710*
State Government *See also* Constitutions, State; Governors; State Legislatures; State Politics; States' Rights; Territorial Government.
—. California. Church and state. Church Finance. Worldwide Church of God. 1970's. *1139*
—. Catholic Church. National Prohibition League. Oklahoma. Prohibition. Religious Liberty. 1907-18. *2580*
—. Church and state. Constitutional Law. Fund raising. Local Government. 1970's. *1059*
—. Colleges and Universities (administration). Desha, Joseph. Holley, Horace. Kentucky. Politics. Presbyterians. Transylvania College. Unitarianism. 1818-27. *537*
—. Debates. Maryland. Religious liberty. 1776-85. *1107*
—. Elections. Lee, J. Bracken. Mormons. Utah. 1944-56. *1274*
State Legislatures. Disfranchisement. Federal government. Mormons. Suffrage. 1882-92. *1046*
—. Evangelism. Michigan. Political parties. 1837-61. *1300*
—. Freemasonry. Maryland (Annapolis). St. John's College. 1784. *517*
—. Harmony Society. Pennsylvania. Rapp, George. Utopias. 1805-07. *380*
State Politics *See also* Elections; Governors; Political Campaigns; Political Parties; State Government.
—. Adventists. Nebraska. Williams, George A. 1925-31. *1325*
—. Anti-Catholicism. District of Columbia. Marquette, Jacques. Statuary Hall. Wisconsin. 1887-1904. *2101*
—. Baptists. Georgia. Political Leadership. 1772-1823. *1260*
—. Catholic Church. Compulsory education. Edwards Law (Illinois, 1889). Ethnic Groups. Illinois. Private schools. Public schools. 1889-93. *551*
—. Catholic Church. Georgia. Judaism. Psychohistory. Watson, Thomas E. 1856-1922. *55*
Statehood. Church and state. Lobbying. Mormons. Trumbo, Isaac. Utah. 1887-96. *1072*
—. Church and state. Rawlins, Joseph L. Utah. 1850-1926. *1049*
—. Economic Conditions. Mormons. Polygamy. Railroads. Salt Lake and Fort Douglas Railroad. Utah. Young, John W. 1883-1924. *3993*
—. Mormons. Suffrage. Utah. Women. 1867-96. *798*
States' Rights *See also* Secession.
—. Conscientious objection. Constitutional Amendments (2nd). Federal government. Friends, Society of. Madison, James. Military service. 1787-92. *2686*
Statistics *See also* Social Surveys.
—. Baptists. 1978. *3086*
—. Protestantism. Texas, north. Whites. 1965-73. *2874*
Statuary Hall. Anti-Catholicism. District of Columbia. Marquette, Jacques. State Politics. Wisconsin. 1887-1904. *2101*
Statues. *See* Monuments.
Statute. *See* Law; Legislation.
St.Cloud Diocese. Catholic Church. Culture region. Minnesota. 1860-1973. *3881*
Steamboats. Economic growth. Illinois (Nauvoo). Mississippi River. Mormons. 1839-46. *367*
—. Illinois (Nauvoo). Jones, Dan. *Maid of Iowa* (vessel). Mormons. Smith, Joseph. 1843-45. *346*
Steege, Martin. Concordia Collegiate Institute. Lutheran Church. New Jersey (East Rutherford, Trenton). New York City (Brooklyn). 1921-73. *3343*
Steinbeck, John *(Winter of Our Discontent).* Folklore. Novels. Witchcraft. 1961. *2046*
Stereotypes. Advertising. Men. Mormons. Patent medicines. Virility. 1884-1931. *819*
—. Anti-Semitism. Drama. Literature. 1830's-1920's. *2011*
—. Attitudes. Colleges and Universities. Religiosity. Sex roles. Students. Women. 1970's. *793*
—. Cartoons and Caricatures. Mormons. *Puck* (periodical). 1904-07. *2001*
—. Cartoons and Caricatures. Mormons. Women. 1830-1914. *800*
—. Christianity. Discrimination. Folklore. Jews. Negroes. 18c-1974. *2091*
—. Dickey, Sarah. Heck, Barbara. Leadership. Methodist Church. Parker, Lois Stiles. Shaw, Anna Howard. Willard, Frances E. Women. 19c. *812*
—. Douglas, Ann. Feminization. Protestantism. Reform. Sex roles. ca 1820-75. 1977-80. *918*
—. Historiography. Mormons. Women. 19c. 1976. *796*
—. Indians. Irish. Massachusetts. Puritans. 17c. *2144*
Stern, Karl. Catholic Church. Christian Renaissance. Converts. Literature. Philosophy. Science. 1920's-60's. *2758*
Steup, Henry Christian. Clergy. Lutheran Church. Schulze, Ernst Carl Ludwig. 1852-1931. *3339*
Stevens, Wallace. Brophy, Robert J. Jeffers, Robinson. Morris, Adelaide Kirby. Poetry. Theology (review article). 20c. *2065*
Stewart, Levi. Mormons. United Order. Utah (Kanab). Young, Brigham. Young, John R. 1874-84. *4029*
Stewart, William. Annexation. Church and state. Idaho, southern. Legislation. Mormons. Nevada. Suffrage. 1887-88. *1089*
Stiles, Ezra. Archives. Congregationalism. Manuscripts. Yale University. 1748-1975. *3142*
—. Charles I. Congregationalism. Folklore. Regicide. Rhode Island. Whale, Theophilus. 17c. 1755-85. *3131*
—. Colleges and Universities. Congregationalism. Dwight, Timothy. Human Relations. Yale University. 1778-95. *706*
—. Congregationalism. Connecticut. Theology. Thomism. 1792-94. *3130*
—. Congregationalism. Dark Day. New England. Weather. 1780. *2326*
Stirpicultural experiment. Genetics. New York. Noyes, John Humphrey. Oneida Community. Utopias. 1848-86. *946*

Stocken, H. W. G. Alberta. Bible. Blackfoot Indians. Indians. Missions and Missionaries. Translating and Interpreting. Wolf Collar (shaman). 1870-1928. *1500*
Stockton, William S. Bond, Thomas Emerson. Church government. Laity. Methodist Episcopal Church. Snethen, Nicholas. 1820-56. *288*
Stoddard, Solomon. Church of England. Congregationalism. Cutler, Timothy. Edwards, Jonathan. Gibson, Edmund. Great Awakening. Letters. New England. 1739. *2263*
—. Coffman, Ralph J. (review article). Puritans. 1660's-1729. 1978. *3615*
—. Communion. New England. Puritanism. 1679. *3614*
—. Conversion. Preparationism. Puritans. Taylor, Edward. Theology. 1690-94. *3642*
—. New England. Puritans. Theology. 1672-1729. *3634*
Stoddard, Solomon *(Safety of Appearing).* New England. Psychology, faculty. Puritans. 1630-1746. *2299*
Stoesz, David. Bergthal Colony. Bishops. Immigration. Manitoba. Mennonites. Ukraine. 1872-76. *3390*
Stoltzfus, John. Amish. Baptism. Pennsylvania (Lancaster, Mifflin counties). Tennessee. 1820-74. *3438*
—. Amish. Pennsylvania (Lancaster County). Schisms. Theology. 1850-77. *3439*
Stolz, Joseph. Hebrew Union College. Judaism (Reform). Letters. Rabbis. Wise, Isaac Mayer. 1882-1900. *4220*
Stone buildings. Architecture, folk. Mormons. Utah (Beaver City). 1855-1975. *1812*
Storms *See also* Tornadoes.
—. Arkansas (Pine Bluff). Burnett, Ellen. Prophecy. Women. 1903. *74*
Stouch, George W. H. Church and State. Education. Episcopal Church, Protestant. Indians (agencies). Oklahoma, western. Whirlwind Day School. ca 1904-14. *1086*
Stowe, Calvin Ellis. Dartmouth College. Lane Theological Seminary. New England. Presbyterian Church. Stowe, Harriet Beecher. 1824-86. *3555*
Stowe, Harriet Beecher. Antislavery sentiments. Christianity. Civil War. Presbyterian Church. Women. ca 1850-80. *2474*
—. Dartmouth College. Lane Theological Seminary. New England. Presbyterian Church. Stowe, Calvin Ellis. 1824-86. *3555*
—. New England. Novels. Presbyterian Church. Salvation. Theology. Women. 1845-85. *2038*
—. Presbyterian Church. Slavery. 1830's-1870's. *3554*
Strachan, John. Bishops. Church of England. Liturgy. Ontario (Toronto). Theology. 1802-67. *3214*
—. Catholic Church. Church of England. Colonial Government. Macdonnell, Alexander. Ontario. Ontario (Kingston, Toronto). 1820's-30's. *1108*
—. Church and state. Church of England. Endowments. Land. Ontario (Upper Canada). Rolph, John. University of Toronto. 1820-70. *1026*
—. Church and State. Church of England. King's College (charter). Ontario (Toronto). Scotland. 1815-43. *506*
—. Church of England. Clergy. Diocesan Theological Institute. Frontier and Pioneer Life. Ontario (Cobourg). 1840-55. *732*
Strang, James Jesse. Lake Michigan. Michigan (Beaver Island). Mormons. Utopias. Wisconsin (Voree). 1820-56. *433*
—. Mormons. Negroes. Social Theory. Thompson, Charles B. 1844-73. *2138*
Strauss, Gerald. Education (review article). Germany. Greven, Philip. Protestantism. Youth. 16c-19c. *850*
Streetcars. Canada. Church and state. Cities. Sabbatarianism. Values. 1890-1914. *2281*
Streiker, Lowell D. (review essay). Evangelicalism. Graham, Billy. Middle America. Strober, Gerald S. (review essay). -1972. *2621*
Strikes *See also* Labor Unions and Organizations.
—. Christianity. Longshoremen. Oxford Movement. Washington (Seattle). 1921-34. *1477*
Stringfellow, Thornton. Baptists (Ketocton Association). Evangelicalism. Reform. Slavery. Virginia. 1800-70. *2158*
Stritch, Samuel A. Bishops. Catholic Church. Farrelly, John P. Irish Americans. Morris, John. Tennessee. 19c-1958. *3860*
Strober, Gerald S. (review essay). Evangelicalism. Graham, Billy. Middle America. Streiker, Lowell D. (review essay). -1972. *2621*
Stroeter, Ernst F. Attitudes. Fundamentalism. Gaebelein, Arno C. *Our Hope* (periodical). Zionism. 1894-97. *80*
Strong, Augustus Hopkins. Baptists. Hermeneutics. Poetry. Theology. 1897-1916. 1978. *1974*
Strong, Josiah. Anglo-Saxonism. Interventionism. Protestantism. Reform. 1885-1915. *2418*
—. Congregationalism. Missions and Missionaries. Nationalism. Social Gospel. Wyoming (Cheyenne). 1871-1916. *3134*
Strong, William. Christianity. Constitutional Amendments. Presbyterian Church. Supreme Court. 1864-80. *3588*
Stuart, Henry Harvey. Education. New Brunswick. Socialism. 1873-1952. *2369*
Stuart, John Leighton. China. Diplomacy. Japan. Missions and Missionaries. Presbyterian Church. 1937-41. *1745*
Stuart, Mary Horton. Alabama (Mobile). China. Missions and Missionaries. Presbyterian Church. Women. 1840's-1947. *1705*
Stuck, Hudson. Alaska. Discovery and Exploration. Educators. Episcopal Church, Protestant. Missions and Missionaries. 1904-20. *1647*
Student activists. Educational innovation. Methodist Church, United. Southern Methodist University. Texas (Dallas). 1972-74. *720*
Student Christian Movement. Ecumenism. Evangelism. Protestantism. Social change. Social justice. 19c-20c. *440*
Students *See also* Colleges and Universities; Schools.
—. Abortion. Attitudes. Catholic Church. Colleges and Universities. 1970's. *855*
—. Agnosticism. Catholic Church. Colleges and Universities. Quebec. 1970-78. *505*
—. American Board of Commissioners for Foreign Missions. Assimilation. Connecticut (Cornwall). Foreign Mission School. Indian-White Relations. 1816-27. *586*
—. Arkansas, University of. Baptists. Hays, Brooks. Personal narratives. Values. ca 1915-20. *3025*
—. Arts and Crafts. Girls. Moravian Church. North Carolina. Pennsylvania. 19c. *1862*
—. Attitudes. Catholic Church. Prayer. 1961-71. *3808*
—. Attitudes. Catholic Church. Religiosity. 1961-71. *3807*
—. Attitudes. Colleges and Universities. Religiosity. Sex roles. Stereotypes. Women. 1970's. *793*
—. Attitudes. Colleges and Universities. Religiosity. Vietnam War. 1968-72. *2636*
—. Attitudes. Ethnicity. Israel. Jews. Northeastern or North Atlantic States. Zionism. 1973-76. *4155*
—. Attitudes. Lancaster Mennonite High School. Mennonites. Pennsylvania. Rites and Ceremonies. 1974-78. *3354*
—. Brigham Young University. Fundamentalism. Mormons. Utah (Provo). 1935-73. *606*
—. Canada. Church and State. Leadership. Mennonite Conference of 1970. Social issues. 1917-74. *1029*
—. Canada. Colleges and Universities. Political knowledge. Public opinion. 1974. *978*
—. Canada. Ethnicity. 1971. *100*
—. Catholic Church. Chicoutimi, Petit-Séminaire de. Quebec (Saguenay). Religious Education. 1873-1930. *756*
—. Catholic Church. Clergy. Middle Classes. Pentecostal movement. 1970's. *3753*
—. Church and state. Civil Rights. Colleges and Universities. Federal Aid to Education. New York. Political attitudes. 1972. *1119*
—. Church attendance. Religiosity. Williams College. 1948-74. *113*
—. Concordia Seminary. Daily Life. Kansas (Clay Center). Lutheran Church (Missouri Synod). Mueller, Peter. Seminaries. 1883-89. *707*
—. Ethnicity. Jews. Maryland, University of. Parents. 1949-71. *4128*
—. Ethnicity. Religiosity. 1972. *110*
—. Germany. Religiosity. 1960-77. *96*
—. Higher Education. Religiosity. 1970. *106*
—. Keisker, Walter. Lutheran Church. Missouri (Concordia). Personal narratives. Religious Education. St. Paul's College. 1913-19. 1980. *669*
—. Lifestyles. Lutheran Church. Missouri (St. Louis). Seminaries. 1922-28. *703*
—. Morality. Mormons. Sex. 1930's-68. *825*
—. Morality. Mormons. Sex. Western States. 1950-72. *927*
—. Religiosity. 1973. *117*
Stuermer, Herbert. Canada, Western. Ecumenism. Lutheran Church. 1922. *489*
Sturkie Resolution. Anti-Catholicism. Catts, Sidney J. Elections (gubernatorial). Florida. Guardians of Liberty. Knott, William V. 1916. *1231*
Styron, William *(Confessions of Nat Turner).* Christianity. Slave Revolts. Turner, Nat. 1820-31. 1968. *2047*
—. Literature. Pluralism. 1970's. *2053*
Subscription controversy. Clergy. Dickinson, Jonathan. Presbyterian Church. Westminster Standards. 1700-50. *3560*
Success. Self-made man doctrine. Swedish Americans. 1870's-1910's. *370*
Success (concept of). Alger, Horatio. Capitalism. Evangelicalism. Literature. Social History. 1820-1910. *2958*
Succession. Bishops. Catholic Church. Chicago Diocese. Clergy. Duggan, James. Illinois. McMullen, John. 1865-81. *3742*
—. Communalism. Equal opportunity. Hutterites. Leadership. Population. Prairie Provinces. Social Organization. 1940's-70's. *387*
—. Mormons. Smith, Joseph. Young, Brigham. 1834-44. *4027*
Sudan Interior Mission. Anglican Communion. Canada. Education. Great Britain. Missionaries. Protestantism. 1937-55. *1741*
Suffering (meaning). Mather, Cotton *(Magnalia Christi Americana).* Morality. New England. Puritans. 1690's-1702. *3626*
Suffrage *See also* Voting and Voting Behavior.
—. Annexation. Church and state. Idaho, southern. Legislation. Mormons. Nevada. Stewart, William. 1887-88. *1089*
—. Arizona. Christianity. Frontier and Pioneer Life. Reform. Temperance Movements. Women. 1850's-1912. *837*
—. Baptists, Southern. Women. 1910-20. *3082*
—. Catholic Church. International Union of Catholic Women's Leagues (congress). Italy (Rome). Quebec. Women. 1922. *935*
—. Clergy. Methodist Protestant Church. Shaw, Anna Howard. Social Gospel Movement. Women. 1880-1919. *3506*
—. Congress. Hayes, Rutherford B. Mormons. Polygamy. Women. 1877-81. *797*
—. Democratic Party. Liberty Party. Negroes. New York. Referendum. Whig Party. 1840-47. *1264*
—. Disfranchisement. Federal government. Mormons. State Legislatures. 1882-92. *1046*
—. Historiography. Massachusetts. Political Systems. Puritans. 1620-99. 1954-74. *1350*
—. Kimball, Sarah Melissa Granger. Mormons. Utah. Women. 15th Ward Relief Society. 1818-98. *901*
—. League of Nations. Mormons. Prohibition. Republican Party. Roberts, Brigham Henry. Smith, Joseph Fielding. Utah. Women. ca 1900. *1284*
—. Mormons. Statehood. Utah. Women. 1867-96. *798*
—. Mormons. Utah. Women. 1895. *944*
Suicide. Slave trade. 1690-1852. *76*
Suicide, mass. Charisma. Guyana (Jonestown). Jones, Jim. Leadership. Models. People's Temple. 1978. *4253*
—. Guyana (Jonestown). Jones, Jim. People's Temple. Personality. 1965-78. *4238*
Sulpicians. Algonkin Indians. Architecture. Calvary (chapels). Iroquois Indians. Missionaries. Quebec (Oka). 1700's-1800's. *1811*
—. Catholic Church. Fort Frontenac. Indian-White Relations. Iroquois Indians. Missions and Missionaries. New France. Quinte Mission. 1665-80. *1610*
—. Catholic Church. New France. Nobility. 17c-18c. *2611*
—. Catholic Church. Olier, Jean Jacques. Quebec (Montreal). 1630's-50's. *3798*
—. Land. Law. New France. 1667. *3782*
Sun faces (motif). Connecticut Valley. Folk art. Tombstones. Vermont (Rockingham). 1786-1812. *1842*
Sun Yat-sen. China. Diplomatic recognition. Missions and Missionaries. Revolution. 1911-13. *1724*
Sunday, Billy. Evangelism. New York (Buffalo). 1917. *2218*
—. Patriotism. Revivals. World War I. 1917-18. *2676*
—. Presbyterian Church. Sermons. Virtue. Women. Working class. 1915. *890*
Sunday School Movement. Evangelicalism. Sex roles. Women. 1790-1880. *807*

Sunday Schools. Asbury, Francis. Letters. Methodist Episcopal Church. 1791. *782*
—. Baptists. *Keystone Graded Lessons.* Literature. Religious Education. 1824-1909. *637*
—. Books. Pennsylvania (New Geneva; Pleasant Hill School District). Protestantism. 1823-57. *592*
—. Child-rearing. Converts. Protestant Churches. Psychology. Religious Education. 19c. *603*
—. Children. Evangelicalism. Northeastern or North Atlantic States. Protestant Churches. Theology. 1820's. *604*
—. Clergy. Ellis, Edwin M. Montana. Presbyterian Church. Travel. 1870's-1927. *3537*
—. Friends, Society of. Maryland (Baltimore). Methodist Episcopal Church, African. Negroes. Presbyterian Church. Private Schools. 1794-1860. *633*
—. Mennonites. Pennsylvania. Raikes, Robert. 1780-1980. *641*
—. Ontario (Upper Canada). Social control. 19c. *643*
Supernatural. Ballads, British. Death and Dying. Folk Songs. 1830-1930. *1923*
Superstitions. Chain letters. Law. 1930's-70's. *133*
—. Mexican Americans. New Mexico (Torrance County). Witchcraft. 1970's. *2184*
Supreme Court. Americanization. Church Schools. German language. Lutheran Church (Missouri Synod). Nebraska Council of Defense. 1917-23. *305*
—. Authority. Constitutional Amendments (1st). Health. Religious liberty. 1963-79. *1439*
—. Baptists. *Brown* v. *Board of Education* (US, 1954). Desegregation. Georgia. 1954-61. *511*
—. Berns, Walter (review article). Church and state. Constitutional Amendments (1st). 18c-20c. *1114*
—. Burger, Warren E. Church and state. Church schools. Constitutional Amendments (1st). 1950-75. *602*
—. California (Eight Mile, Blue Creek). Forest Service. Indians. Religious liberty. 1975. *1102*
—. Christianity. Constitutional Amendments. Presbyterian Church. Strong, William. 1864-80. *3588*
—. Church and State. 1960's. *1035*
—. Church and State. Church schools. Conscientious objection. Holidays. Prayer. Public finance. Public Schools. Religious Liberty. 1950-70's. *1112*
—. Church and State. Colleges and Universities. Constitutions. Religious studies. 1970's. *578*
—. Church Schools. Colleges and Universities. State Aid to Education. 1971-76. *682*
—. Church Schools. Constitutional Amendments (1st). State Aid to Education. 1970's. *728*
—. Church schools. Education, Finance. Public finance. 1971-73. *663*
—. Constitutional Law. Morality. Mormons. Polygamy. Religious Liberty. *Reynolds* v. *United States* (US, 1878). 1862-78. *1024*
—. Douglas, William O. Humanism. Presbyterian Church. Religious liberty. 1915-80. *1128*
—. Morgan, Richard E. (review article). 1972-74. *1023*
Supreme Court decisions. 1963-74. *1021*
—. Church and State. 1963-75. *1034*
Supreme Courts, state. California. Church and state. Sabbatarianism. 1855-83. *2283*
—. Chinese Americans. Discrimination. Frontier and Pioneer Life. Montana. Public opinion. 1864-1902. *2152*
Surgery. Friends, Society of. Maryland (Baltimore). Medicine (practice of). Taylor, Sarah. Women. 1823. *3264*
Surnames. Brethren, Swiss. Immigration. Mennonites. North America. 1680-1880. *3417*
Surveillance. Catholic Church. Church and state. Inquisition. Louisiana. 1762-1800. *1044*
—. Diaries. Federal government. Malone, R. J. Mennonites. Military Intelligence. World War I. 1914-19. *2697*
Sutherland, Edward A. Adventists. Battle Creek College. Madison College. Michigan. Tennessee. 1897-1904. *743*
—. Adventists. Colleges and Universities. Educational Reform. 1904-50. *693*
Suzuki, Diasetz Teitaro. Buddhism (Zen). Catholic Church. Merton, Thomas. 1935-70. *498*
Sverdrup, Georg. Lutheran Free Church. Norwegian Americans. Religious Liberty. Sermons. Thanksgiving. 1896-1907. *3304*
Swarthmore College. Baptists. Bucknell University. Franklin and Marshall College. Friends, Society of (Hicksite). Pennsylvania. Reformed German Church. Urbanization. 1865-1915. *685*
Swastek, Joseph Vincent (obituary). Catholic Church. Clergy. Editors and Editing. Historiography. *New Catholic Encyclopedia.* Polish Americans. 1913-77. *227*
Sweden. Adventists. Germany. Great Britain. Millenarianism. Miller, William. 19c. *2967*
—. American Baptist Publishing Society. Baptists. Converts. Immigration. Lutheran Church. Travel (accounts). Wiberg, Anders. 1852-53. *3054*
—. Bäck, Olof. Clergy. Esbjörn, Lars Paul. Janssonists. Letters. Lutheran Church. Methodism. 1846-49. *2906*
—. Clergy. Converts. Episcopal Church, Protestant. Lutheran Church. Unonius, Gustaf. Wisconsin (Pine Lake). 1841-58. *2854*
—. Diaries. Emigration. Florida. Lutheran Church. Sjöborg, Sofia Charlotta. 1871. *3340*
—. Emigration. Illinois. Janssonists. Sects, Religious. Social Classes. 1845-47. *2620*
—. Emigration. Protestantism. Unonius, Gustaf. 1858-63. *2922*
Sweden (Dalarna). Agriculture. Immigration. Lutheran Church. Minnesota (Isantic County). Social customs. 1840-1910. *3329*
Sweden (Växjö). Archives. Emigrant Institute. Lutheran Church. Social organizations. 1800-1970. *282*
Swedenborg, Emanuel. Arthur, Timothy Shay *(Ten Nights in a Bar-Room).* Temperance Movements. 18c. 1854. *2041*
—. Correspondence, theory of. Thoreau, Henry David. Transcendentalism. ca 1850-62. *4069*
—. James, Henry (1811-82). Letters. Theology. Wilkinson, James John Garth. 1844-55. *4060*
Swedenborgianism. Andrews, Joseph. Art. Massachusetts (Boston). Society of the New Jerusalem. 1830-73. *4062*
—. Church of England. Duche, Jacob, Jr. Great Britain. Pennsylvania (Philadelphia). Pietism. 1750-1800. *2738*
—. James, Henry (1811-82). Literature. Swedenborgians. Theology. 1840's-81. *4061*
—. Lundeberg, Axel Johan Sigurd Mauritz. Minnesota. Swedish Americans. 1852-1940. *4063*
Swedish Americans. American Revolution. Clergy. Delaware River Valley. Episcopal Church, Protestant. Lutheran Church. 1655-1831. *285*
—. Americanization. Ecumenism. Episcopal Church, Protestant. Lutheran Church, Swedish. 1630-1850. *322*
—. Andersson, Joris Per. Letters. Lutheran Church. Minnesota (Chisago Lake). 1851-53. *3312*
—. Arvedson, Peter. Episcopal Church, Protestant. Illinois. 1822-80. *1600*
—. Assimilation. Lutheran Church. Muhlenberg, Henry Melchior. Pennsylvania. Politics. Wrangel, Carl Magnus. 1749-69. *1283*
—. Augustana College and Theological Seminary. Bethany College. Immigration. Lutheran Church. Midwest. Politics. Railroads. Religious education. Swensson, Carl Aaron. 1873-1904. *726*
—. Augustana College and Theological Seminary. Illinois (Paxton). Lutheran Church (Augustana Synod). Osborn, William H. Railroads. 1853-73. *3321*
—. Augustana College and Theological Seminary. Illinois (Rock Island). Immigrants. Lutheran Church. 1855-1956. *599*
—. Baptists. Circuit riders. Diaries. Immigrants. Minnesota. Nilsson, Frederik Olaus. 1855-65. *3046*
—. Bergner, Peter. Bethel Ships. Evangelism. Merchant Marine. Methodist Church. New York City. 1832-66. *1661*
—. Bishop Hill Colony. Illinois. Immigrants. Janssonists. Utopias. 1846-60. *393*
—. Bishop Hill Colony. Illinois. Janssonists. Letters. 1847. *416*
—. Canada. Immigrants. Lifestyles. Lutheran Church. Occupations. Settlement. Social Organizations. USA. 1893-1979. *3325*
—. Clergy. Immigrants. Lutheran Church (Augustana Synod). Wives. 1860-1962. *3296*
—. Clergy. Lutheran Church (Missouri Synod). Minnesota. Missouri. Wihlborg, Niels Albert. 1893-1918. *3331*
—. Elementary Education. Johnson, Emeroy. Lutheran Church. Minnesota. Personal narratives. Religious education. ca 1854-ca 1920. *666*
—. Gloria Dei Congregation. Lutheran Church. Old Swedes' Church. Pennsylvania (Philadelphia). 1638-98. *3302*
—. Lundeberg, Axel Johan Sigurd Mauritz. Minnesota. Swedenborgianism. 1852-1940. *4063*
—. Lutheran Church. Methodist Church. Social Organizations. 1850-1951. *2951*
—. Lutheran Church (Augustana Synod). 1860-1973. *287*
—. Self-made man doctrine. Success. 1870's-1910's. *370*
Swedish Baptist Church. Americanization. Evangelical Covenant Church. Evangelical Free Church of America. Methodism. Pentecostal movement. Salvation Army. 1870-1973. *321*
Sweet, H. C. Canada. Protestantism. 1866-1960. *2888*
Sweet, William Warren. Church History. Historiography. Latourette, Kenneth Scott. ca 1910-65. *175*
Swensson, Carl Aaron. Augustana College and Theological Seminary. Bethany College. Immigration. Lutheran Church. Midwest. Politics. Railroads. Religious education. Swedish Americans. 1873-1904. *726*
Swiss Americans. Bishops. Immigration. Lehman, Hans (and family). Mennonites. Pennsylvania (Lancaster County; Rapho Township). ca 1727-1909. *3400*
—. Blumer, Abraham. Pennsylvania (Allentown). Reformed German Church. Zion Reformed Church. 1771-1822. *3285*
—. Christianity. Marti, Fritz. Philosophy. Scholarship. Theology. 1894-1979. *2803*
—. Christmas. Emmanuel Church. Immigration. Ohio (Bluffton). Reformed Tradition. 1840's-1900. *2857*
—. Clergy. Georgia (Savannah). Presbyterian Church. Zubly, John Joachim. 1724-58. *3565*
—. Dutch Americans. Genealogy. Iowa. Mennonites. Settlement. 1839-1974. *3370*
—. Grueningen, Johann Jakob von. Reformed Swiss Church. Wisconsin (Sauk City). 1876-1911. *2860*
Switzerland. Americanization. Benedictines. Germany. Monasticism. 1846-1900. *314*
—. Anabaptists. Germany. Mennonites. Taxation. War. 16c-1973. *2662*
—. Benedictine sisters. Immigration. Missouri (Conception). Renggli, Rose (Mother Mary Beatrice). Women. 1874. *3832*
Switzerland (Geneva). Calvinism. Massachusetts (Boston). Parishes. Puritans. 16c-17c. *3631*
Swope, Cornelius E. Clergy (dismissal). Episcopal Church, Protestant. Illinois (Chicago). Pamphlets. Rites and Ceremonies. Trinity Church. Unonius, Gustaf. 1850-51. *3179*
Symbolism in Art. Childhood. Dreams. Italy (Rome). Painting. Vedder, Elihu. 1856-1923. *1888*
—. Folk art. Friends, Society of. Hicks, Edward *(Peaceable Kingdom).* 1825-49. *1851*
Symbolism in Literature. American Revolution. Environment. Literature. Millenarianism. 1770's-1800. *1192*
—. Christianity. Gerhardt, Paul. Hymns. Sacred fire. Translating and Interpreting. Wesley, John. 1760's-1930's. *1952*
—. Hawthorne, Nathaniel. History. Novels. Puritan tradition. Social reform. 1825-63. *2019*
—. Poe, Edgar Allan *(The Pit and the Pendulum).* Revivals. ca 1800-50. *2084*
Symonds, Herbert. Canada. Church of England. Ecumenism. 1897-1921. *483*
Symphonia theory. Church and state. Democracy. Orthodox Eastern Church. 17c-20c. *1048*
Synagogues. California (San Francisco). Goldie, Albert. Judaism (Orthodox, Reform). New York City. Poor. Weinstock, Harris. 1906. *4166*
—. California (San Francisco). Jews (German, Polish). Temple Emanu-El. Temple Sherith Israel. 1848-1900. *4126*
—. Kahal Kadosh Elohim. Judaism (Reform). South Carolina (Charleston). 1695-1978. *1764*
Syncretism. Assimilation. Christianity. Indians. Missions and Missionaries. 19c-20c. *2794*
Syndicalism *See also* Anarchism and Anarchists; Communism; Labor Unions and Organizations; Socialism.

—. Catholic Church. École Sociale Populaire. Propaganda. Quebec (Montreal). Working Class. 1911-49. *1473*
Syndicat Catholique des Allumettières. Labor. Match industry. Quebec (Hull). Women. 1919-24. *1470*
Synods. *See* Councils and Synods.
Syria. Arabs. Missions and Missionaries. Nationalism. 1842-1918. *1670*
—. Jesuits. Missions and Missionaries. Ottoman Empire. Protestant Churches. 1840's. *1698*
Syrian Americans. Assimilation. Catholic Church. Eastern Orthodox Church, Syrian. Maronite Catholics. Melkite Catholics. Uniates. 1900-73. *3908*
—. Depressions. Juma, Charlie. North Dakota (Ross). Personal narratives. 1900's-30's. *35*

T

Tabernacle project. Fund raising. Hyde, Orson. Illinois (Nauvoo). Mormons. Northeastern or North Atlantic States. 1845-46. *4048*
Taché, Alexandre Antonin. Catholic Church. Chipewyan Indians. Indian-White Relations. Letters. Mission St. Jean-Baptiste. Saskatchewan (Île-à-la-Crosse). 1823-54. *1503*
—. Letters. Métis. Prairie Provinces. Religious beliefs. Riel, Louis. 1880's. *966*
Tahitians. Congregationalism. Diaries. Hawaii. Missions and Missionaries. Toketa (teacher). 1820's-30's. *1676*
Tammany Hall. Catholic Church. Democratic Party. Immigrants. New York City. Prohibition. Protestantism. 1840-60. *2594*
Tanzania. Mennonites (Lancaster Conference). Missions and Missionaries. 1934-71. *1674*
Tappan, Lewis. Abolition Movement. Evangelicalism. Friendship. 1830-61. *2469*
Taschereau, Elzéar Alexandre. Catholic Church. Gibbons, James. Knights of Labor. Social thought. 1880's. *1476*
Taverns. Law enforcement. Licenses. Sabbath. Virginia. ca 1630-1850. *2286*
Tax exemption. Church and state. Church property. Freedom of religion. 1960's-70's. *1094*
—. Church and state. Colorado (Denver). Political activity. *United States* v. *Christian Echoes National Ministry, Inc.* 1950's-1970's. *1063*
Taxation *See also* Property Tax; Single Tax.
—. American Revolution. Dunkards. Friends, Society of. Mennonites. Moravian Church. Neutrality. Pacifism. Schwenkfelders. 1765-83. *2670*
—. Anabaptists. Germany. Mennonites. Switzerland. War. 16c-1973. *2662*
—. Anti-Catholicism. Church and state. Cox Library. Discrimination. *Koester* v. *Pardeeville* (1929). Libraries. Wisconsin (Pardeeville). 1927-29. *1033*
—. Baptists. Church and state. Congregationalism. Meetinghouses. New Hampshire (Acworth). Toleration Act (New Hampshire, 1819). Universalists. 1783-1822. *1113*
—. Boucher, Jonathan. Chase, Samuel. Church and State. Maryland. Paca, William. 1770-73. *1141*
—. Catholic Church. George, Henry. Ryan, John A. Single tax doctrine. 1935. *2557*
—. City Government. Congregationalism. Massachusetts (Tiverton). Provincial Legislatures. Religious liberty. 1692-1724. *1084*
Taylor, Edward. Congregationalism. Drummer, Jeremiah. Letters. Massachusetts. Sabbath. Sewall, Samuel. 1704. *2276*
—. Conversion. Preparationism. Puritans. Stoddard, Solomon. Theology. 1690-94. *3642*
—. Fiske, John. Poetry. Puritans. Tree of Life metaphor. 1650-1721. *1969*
—. Massachusetts. Puritans. Taylor, Thomas *(Christ Revealed).* Typology. 1635-98. *3649*
—. Poetry. Puritans. Science. 1706. *2342*
Taylor, Edward ("Gods Determinations"). Poetry. Proverbs. Puritans. 1685. 1973. *1963*
Taylor, Edward ("Upon the Types of the Old Testament"). Massachusetts (Westfield). Puritans. Sermons. Theology. Typology. 1693. *3638*
—. Nebraska (Lincoln). Puritans. Sermons. Theology. Typology. 1693-1706. *3639*
Taylor, Edward Thompson. Massachusetts (Boston). Methodist Church. Seamen's Bethel. 1793-1871. *3452*
—. Massachusetts (Boston, New Bedford). Methodist Church. Mudge, Enoch. Seamen's Bethel. 1776-1850. *3457*
Taylor, John W. Church and state. Cowley, Matthias F. Mormons. Polygamy. Smoot, Reed. Theology. Woodruff Manifesto. 1890-1911. *1060*
Taylor, Myron C. Diplomacy. Pius XII, Pope. Vatican. World War II. 1940-50. *1025*
Taylor, Nathaniel William. Beecher, Lyman. Congregationalism. Dwight, Timothy. New England. Presbyterian Church. Republicanism. 1790-1840. *1356*
Taylor, Sarah. Friends, Society of. Maryland (Baltimore). Medicine (practice of). Surgery. Women. 1823. *3264*
Taylor, Thomas *(Christ Revealed).* Massachusetts. Puritans. Taylor, Edward. Typology. 1635-98. *3649*
Teachers *See also* Educators; Teaching.
—. Academic freedom. Concordia Seminary. Lutheran Church (Missouri Synod). Missouri (St. Louis). Tenure. 1968-74. *771*
—. Baptists, Southern. Clergy. Manly, Basil. Southeastern States. 1798-1868. *3041*
—. California. Catholic Church. Homosexuality. Proposition 6 (1978). Public schools. Referendum. 1978. *1320*
—. Colleges and Universities. Religiosity. 1973. *555*
—. Mormons. National Education Association. Public schools. Sinclair, Upton. Utah. 1920-24. *567*
Teachers colleges. Catholic Church. Discrimination. Northwest Territories. 1884-1900. *77*
Teaching *See also* Education; History Teaching; Schools; Teachers.
—. Adventists. Anesthesia. California. Dentistry. Jorgensen, Niels Bjorn. Loma Linda University. 1923-74. *1441*
—. Buddhism. Hinduism. Western Nations. 1969-75. *4287*
—. Canada. China. Hurford, Grace Gibberd. Missions and Missionaries. Personal narratives. World War II. 1928-45. *1711*
—. Catholic Church. Massachusetts (Boston). Religious Orders. Voluntarism. Women. 1870-1940. *717*
—. Christianity. Letters. Willard, Frances Langdon. 1835-51. *542*
—. Church of England. Malcolm, Alexander. Maryland (Annapolis). Music. St. Anne's Church. Society for the Propagation of the Gospel. 1721-63. *1931*
—. Civil religion. Courts. Religion in the Public Schools. 1947-76. *572*
—. Morality. Science. Social studies. 1977. *2321*
Technological innovation. Agriculture. Hutterites. Lifestyles. North America. Social Customs. 18c-20c. *3349*
Technology *See also* Inventions; Science.
—. Christianity. Lifestyles. Values. 20c. *2725*
—. Christianity. Percy, Walker *(Love in the Ruins).* Western civilization. 1971. *2028*
—. Civil Religion. Nationalism. Protestantism. Social Organization. ca 1630-1974. *1171*
—. Counter culture. Science. Values. 1960's-70's. *2292*
—. Education. Religiosity. Social Conditions. 1945-75. *561*
Teed, Cyrus Read. Florida (Estero). Illinois (Chicago). Koreshan Unity. Millenarianism. Utopias. 1886-1903. *396*
Television *See also* Audiovisual Materials.
—. Attitudes. Censorship. Films. Protestant Churches. 1921-80. *2820*
—. Baptists. Films. History Teaching. Videotape. 1977. *267*
—. Evangelicalism. 1978. *1961*
—. Federal Communications Commission. Lansman, Jeremy. Milam, Lorenzo. Radio. Religious references. 1972-75. *1116*
—. Mormons. Radio. 1922-77. *347*
Temperance Movements. Adventists. Music. 1850's-90's. *2965*
—. *American Mercury* (periodical). Editors and Editing. Ku Klux Klan. Mencken, H. L. Methodist Episcopal Church (South). 1910-33. *2033*
—. Anti-Catholicism. Antislavery Sentiments. Bannan, Benjamin. Nativism. Pennsylvania (Schuylkill County). Whig Party. 1852-54. *1238*
—. Anti-Catholicism. City Politics. Ethnic groups. Immigrants. Ohio (Cincinnati). 1845-60. *2584*
—. Arizona. Christianity. Frontier and Pioneer Life. Reform. Suffrage. Women. 1850's-1912. *837*
—. Art. Attitudes. Centennial Exposition of 1876. Friends, Society of. Peace. Pennsylvania (Philadelphia). Sabbatarianism. 1876. *3256*
—. Arthur, Timothy Shay *(Ten Nights in a Bar-Room).* Swedenborg, Emanuel. 18c. 1854. *2041*
—. Baptists. Methodist Church. Ninth Street Baptist Church. Ohio (Cincinnati). Political protest. Wesley Chapel. Women's Christian Temperance Union. 1874. *2582*
—. Beecher, Lyman. Clergy. New York (East Hampton). Presbyterian Church. 1799-1810. *2585*
—. Beecher, Lyman. Evangelical Alliance. Great Britain. Presbyterian Church. World Temperance Convention. 1846. *3563*
—. Canada. Gospel Temperance Movement. Revivalism. Rine, D. I. K. 1877-82. *2575*
—. Cary, Samuel Fenton. Ohio (Cincinnati). 1845-1900. *2583*
—. Catholic Church. Democratic Party. Elections (presidential). Louisiana. Protestant Churches. Smith, Al. 1928. *1330*
—. Charities. Church of England. Evangelicals. Ontario (Toronto). Theology. 1870-1900. *3205*
—. Colorado (Boulder). Feminism. Social reform. Women's Christian Temperance Union. 1881-1967. *2741*
—. Goal submergence concept. Methodist Church. Social Organizations. 1919-72. *2586*
—. Gough, John B. 1828-86. *2593*
—. Localism. North Carolina. Social classes. 1969-70. *2599*
—. Methodism. Wesley, John. 1725-91. *2581*
—. Michigan (Adrian). Women's Christian Temperance Union. 1873-74. *2578*
—. Nation, Carry Amelia. Prohibition. Women. 1890's-1911. *2576*
—. Willard, Frances E. Women's Christian Temperance Union. 19c-1920. *2589*
Temple Albert (dedication). Jacobs, Pizer. Judaism (Reform). New Mexico (Albuquerque). 1900. *4232*
Temple Beth Israel. California (San Diego). Judaism (Reform). Population. 1889-1978. *4224*
—. Charities. Judaism, Reform. Oregon (Portland). Organizations. 1885. *4235*
—. Daily Life. Elections. Judaism. Oregon (Portland). 1878. *4237*
Temple B'nai Israel. Judaism (Reform). Leadership. Levi, Abraham. Texas (Victoria). 1850-1902. *4225*
Temple Emanu-El. Architecture. California (Los Angeles, San Francisco). Judaism (Reform). Wilshire Boulevard Temple. 1937. *4205*
—. California (San Francisco). Jews (German, Polish). Synagogues. Temple Sherith Israel. 1848-1900. *4126*
Temple Israel. Franklin, Leo M. Judaism. Nebraska (Omaha). Rabbis. 1892-99. *4094*
—. Judaism (Reform). Nebraska (Omaha). 1867-1908. *4207*
Temple Sherith Israel. California (San Francisco). Jews. Nieto, Jacob. Rabbis. Rubin, Max. 1893. *4148*
—. California (San Francisco). Jews (German, Polish). Synagogues. Temple Emanu-El. 1848-1900. *4126*
Temple Sinai. California (Oakland). Disaster relief. Jews. Refugees. San Francisco Earthquake and Fire. 1906. *2527*
Temples. Architecture. Illinois (Nauvoo). Mormons. Utah. Weeks, William. 1840's-1900. *1758*
—. Folklore. Mormons. Polygamy. Scandinavian Americans. Utah (Sanpete-Sevier area). 1849-1979. *4053*
—. Illinois (Nauvoo). Mormons. Rites and Ceremonies. Smith, Joseph. 1841-45. *1766*
—. Mormons. Utah (Logan). 1850-1900. *1759*
Templin, Terah. Clergy. Kentucky. Presbyterian Church. 1780-1818. *3592*
Tennent, Gilbert. Ecumenism. Great Awakening. Moravian Church. Presbyterian Church. Theology. Zinzendorf, Nikolaus. 1740-41. *2226*
Tennessee. Acculturation. Blackburn, Gideon. Cherokee Indians. Missions and missionaries. Presbyterian Church. Schools. 1804-10. *1491*
—. Adventists. Battle Creek College. Madison College. Michigan. Sutherland, Edward A. 1897-1904. *743*

—. Amish. Baptism. Pennsylvania (Lancaster, Mifflin counties). Stoltzfus, John. 1820-74. *3438*
—. Bishops. Catholic Church. Farrelly, John P. Irish Americans. Morris, John. Stritch, Samuel A. 19c-1958. *3860*
—. Camp meetings. Crowd control. Political rallies. Rhetoric. 1828-60. *1259*
—. Cherokee Indians. Indians. Martin, John. Missions and Missionaries. Presbyterian Church. Richardson, William. Virginia. 1755-63. *1511*
—. Education. Frontier and Pioneer Life. 1758-96. *544*
Tennessee Baptist (newspaper). Baptists, Southern. Graves, James Robinson. Newspapers. Seminaries. 1820-93. *3076*
Tennessee (Brownsville). Baptists. Higher education. West Tennessee Baptist Female College. Women. 1850-1910. *658*
Tennessee (Clarksville). Civil-Military Relations. Episcopal Church, Protestant. Kentucky (Bowling Green). Ringgold, Samuel. 1861-65. *998*
Tennessee (Clinton). Baptists. Desegregation. Turner, Paul. Violence. 1956. *2531*
Tennessee (Davidson County). Elites. Political attitudes. Social Classes. 1835-61. *1232*
Tennessee (Dayton). Bryan, William Jennings. Darrow, Clarence. Evolution. Scopes Trial. Trials. 1925. *2336*
Tennessee (Franklin). Episcopal Church, Protestant. Otey, James Hervey. St. Paul's Church. 1827-34. *1802*
Tennessee (Haywood, Lauderdale, Tipton counties). Baptists, Big Hatchie. Baptists, Southern. Ecumenism. 1903-78. *3010*
Tennessee (Jackson). Baptists. Colleges and Universities. Union University. 1825-1975. *776*
Tennessee (Knoxville). Christ Church. Civil War. Episcopal Church, Protestant. Kentucky (Bowling Green). Ringgold, Samuel. 1860-1911. *3168*
Tennessee (Maryville). Abolition Movement. Anderson, Isaac. Presbyterian Church. Southern and Western Theological Seminary. 1819-50's. *723*
Tennessee (Memphis). Architecture. Churches. 19c. *1813*
—. Bossism. City Politics. Clergy. Crump, Edward Hull. Negroes. 1927-48. *1318*
Tennessee (Nashville). Architecture. Baptists. First Baptist Church. Heiman, Adolphus. 1837-62. *1808*
—. Architecture, Gothic Revival. Churches. Episcopal Church, Protestant. Holy Trinity Episcopal Church. Restorations. 1840's-1970's. *1801*
—. Baptists, Southern. First Baptist Church. Merry, Nelson. Race Relations. 1810-65. *3078*
—. Business. 1960's-70's. *349*
—. Christ Church. Churches. Episcopal Church, Protestant. 1829-1979. *3174*
—. Church of England. Clergy. Episcopal Church, Protestant. Ingraham, Joseph Holt. Novels. Prisons. Public Schools. Reform. 1847-51. *3241*
—. First Presbyterian Church. Presbyterian Church. 1814-1976. *3553*
Tennessee (Wartburg). Lutheran Church. St. Paul's Lutheran Church. 1844-1975. *3300*
Tennessee, west. Elections (presidential). Hoover, Herbert C. Racism. Smith, Al. 1928. *1280*
—. Hoover, Herbert C. Political Campaigns (presidential). Smith, Al. 1928. *1279*
Tenure. Academic freedom. Concordia Seminary. Lutheran Church (Missouri Synod). Missouri (St. Louis). Teachers. 1968-74. *771*
Terrill, Edward. Baptists. Bristol Baptist College. Great Britain (Bristol). Missions and Missionaries. Religious Education. 1634-1979. *3024*
Territorial Government *See also* State Government.
—. Fillmore, Millard. Mormons. Utah. 1850-53. *1053*
Terry, Milton S. Creeds. Evangelical Association. Methodism. Theology. United Evangelical Church. 1894-1921. *3667*
Tewksbury, Donald G. (review article). Colleges and Universities. 1776-1860. 1932. *538*
Texas. Anti-Catholicism. Baptists. Fundamentalism. Morality. Norris, J. Frank. 1920's. *2889*
—. Art. Baptist Heritage Picture Set. History. 17c-20c. 1977. *211*
—. Baptists. Methodist Episcopal Church, South. Newspapers. Presbyterian Church (Cumberland, Old School). 1829-61. *2907*
—. Baptists, Southern. Civil Rights. Leadership. Race Relations. 1954-68. *2553*
—. Barzynski, Wincenty. Catholic Church. Illinois (Chicago). Polish Roman Catholic Union. St. Stanislaus Kortka Church. 1838-99. *3678*
—. California. Chavez, Cesar. Christianity. Mexican Americans. Political activism. Rhetoric. Tijerina, Reies. 1960's-70's. *2391*
—. Castañeda, Carlos Eduardo. Catholic church. Historians. Mexican Americans. 1896-1927. *169*
—. Castañeda, Carlos Eduardo *(Our Catholic Heritage).* Catholic Church. Colonization. 1693-1731. 1933-43. *3673*
—. Catholic Church. Freedmen. Law. Protestantism. 1836-60. *2799*
—. Cemeteries. Christianity. Folklore. Social Customs. 1830-1950. *2751*
—. Church of Christ. Disciples of Christ. Fundamentalism. 1972. *3105*
—. Circuit riders. Frontier and Pioneer Life. German Americans. Lutheran Church (Missouri Synod). Oklahoma. Wacker, Hermann Dietrich. 1847-1938. *3342*
—. Councils and Synods. Delegates. Episcopal Church, Protestant (Annual Council). Kinsolving, George Herbert. Veto. Women. 1921-70. *813*
—. Equal Rights Amendment. Political Participation. Women. 1977. *933*
Texas (Beaumont). Clergy. Negroes. Political Leadership. 1972. *1315*
Texas (Brownsville). Jews. Letters-to-the-editor. Mexico (Tamaulipas; Matamoros). Newspapers. 1876-82. *4165*
Texas (Cooke, Denton counties). Architecture. Catholic Church. Fundamentalists. German Americans. Rural Settlements. Social customs. Southerners. 1860-1976. *2750*
Texas (Dallas). Educational innovation. Methodist Church, United. Southern Methodist University. Student activists. 1972-74. *720*
Texas (Galveston). Blum, Abraham. California (Los Angeles). Judaism (Reform). New York City. Rabbis. 1866-1921. *4217*
Texas (Huntsville). Austin College. Baker, Daniel. Legal education. Presbyterian Church. 1849-57. *529*
Texas, north. Protestantism. Statistics. Whites. 1965-73. *2874*
Texas (Panna Marya). Catholic Church. Immigration. Letters. Moczygemba, Leopold. Polish Americans. 1855. *3679*
Texas Presbyterian (newspaper). Clergy. McGown, A. J. Presbyterian Church, Cumberland. Publishers and Publishing. 1846-73. *3586*
Texas (San Angelo). Boycotts. Church Schools. Mexican Americans. Mexican Presbyterian Mission School. Presbyterian Church. Public schools. Segregation. 1910-15. *618*
Texas (San Antonio). Acculturation. Church Schools. Mexican Americans. Public Schools. 1973. *677*
—. Catholic Church. Coahuiltecan Indians. Missions and Missionaries. 1792. *1566*
Texas, southern. Catholic Church. Mexican Americans. 1836-1911. *3769*
Texas (Victoria). Judaism (Reform). Leadership. Levi, Abraham. Temple B'nai Israel. 1850-1902. *4225*
Texas (Villa San Fernando). Agricultural Labor. Canary Islanders. Fernandez de Santa Ana, Benito. Indians. Missions and Missionaries. Petitions. Provincial Government. 1741. *1542*
Textbooks. Censorship. Educators. Fundamentalists. Virginia. 1974. *570*
—. Clergy. Protestant churches. Theology. 1850-1900. *2925*
—. Educational Policy. Fundamentalism. Public schools. West Virginia (Kanawha County). 1975. *576*
Textile industry. Edson, Theodore. Episcopal Church, Protestant. Massachusetts (Lowell). St. Anne's Parish. 1800-65. *366*
—. Massachusetts (Webster). Methodism. Protestant Ethic. Working class. 1820's-50's. *372*
—. New England. Revivals. Women. ca 1790-1840. *2228*
Thanksgiving. 1578-1863. *81*
—. 1620-1979. *1166*
—. Lutheran Free Church. Norwegian Americans. Religious Liberty. Sermons. Sverdrup, Georg. 1896-1907. *3304*
Theater *See also* Actors and Actresses; Drama; Films; Opera.
—. Alexander, Joseph A. Biblical criticism. Princeton Theological Seminary. Seminaries. 1830-61. *705*
—. Baptists. Catholic Church. Hispanic Americans. Indiana (East Chicago, Gary). 1920-76. *1864*
—. Christianity. France. Great Britain. Judaism. ca 1957-78. *1853*
Theillon, Elie. Catholic Church. French Canadians. Minnesota (Gentilly). Settlement. 1870's-1974. *3687*
Theocratic principles. Brownson, Orestes A. Catholic Church. Democracy. 19c. *1379*
Theodicy. Christian realism. Niebuhr, Reinhold. Politics. ca 1940-73. *1403*
Theologians. Agriculture. Landlords and Tenants. Mississippi. Neoorthodoxy. Protestant Churches. 1936-40. *2566*
—. Diaries. Great Britain. North America. Physicians. Ward, John. 17c. *2312*
—. Evjen, John O. Lutheran Church. Minnesota. 1874-1942. *3303*
Theological empiricism. Congregationalism. Edwards, Jonathan. Philosophy. 1740-46. *3145*
Theological Seminary Library of Lexington, South Carolina. Libraries. Lutheran Church. South Carolina. 1832-59. *645*
Theology *See also* Atheism; Christianity; Creeds; Deism; Ethics; Mysticism; Religious Beliefs.
—. 1974. *40*
—. Aberhart, William. Alberta. Ideology. Provincial Government. Social Credit Party. 1935-43. *1365*
—. Abolition Movement. Andover Seminary. Congregationalism. Massachusetts. Seminaries. 1825-35. *2491*
—. Abolition movement. Constitutional Amendments (15th). Douglass, Frederick. Negroes. 1825-86. *2495*
—. Academic Freedom. Baptists. Foster, George Burman. Illinois. University of Chicago Divinity School. 1895-1918. *557*
—. Academic freedom. Lutheran Church (Missouri Synod). 1973. *649*
—. Adler, Samuel. Judaism (Reform). Morality. New York City. ca 1829-91. *4208*
—. Adventists. Evangelicals. 1948-60. *503*
—. Alexander, Archibald *(Thoughts on Religious Experience).* Presbyterian Church. 1841. *3556*
—. All Saints Church. Church of England. Ontario (Kingston). Working class. 1867-1906. *3173*
—. American dream. Christianity. Civil religion. Evil. Myths and Symbols. 1973. *2724*
—. American Revolution. Baptists. Georgia. Mercer, Silas. Politics. 1770-96. *3030*
—. American Revolution. Civil Religion. 1760-75. *1148*
—. American Revolution. Education. Great Awakening. Pluralism. 1776. *1386*
—. American Revolution. Freedom. Liberation movements. Political Attitudes. 1765-20c. *1342*
—. American Revolution (antecedents). Church and state. Connecticut. Devotion, Ebenezer. Politics. 1714-71. *1397*
—. Americanization. Catholic Church. Ecumenism. Europe. Pluralism. 1775-1820. *295*
—. Amish. Land use. Mennonites. Mormons. Pennsylvania (Intercourse). Utah (Escalante). 1973. *2767*
—. Amish. Pennsylvania (Lancaster County). Schisms. Stoltzfus, John. 1850-77. *3439*
—. Anabaptists. Reformation. 16c. 1945-77. *3408*
—. Anglican Communion. Massachusetts (Cambridge). Smyth, Frederick Hastings *(Manhood into God).* Society of the Catholic Commonwealth. Utopias. 1940. *3200*
—. Antimodernism. Christianity. Ecumenism. 1975. *2734*
—. Antinomianism. Cotton, John. Hutchinson, Anne. Massachusetts. Sermons. Shepard, Thomas. 1630's. *3648*
—. Apocalypse. Bible (Revelation). Edwards, Jonathan. Providence. 1720-24. *3148*
—. Appalachia. Baptists, Primitive. Folklore. 1800's-1977. *3083*
—. Arkansas, northeast. Baptists. Folk religion. Pentecostals. Worship. 1972-78. *2836*
—. Arkansas (Texarkana). Congregationalism. Maddox, Finis Ewing. Presbyterian Church. Schisms. 1908. *2869*

—. Assurance, doctrine of. Hooker, Thomas. New England. Puritans. 1630-60. *3644*
—. Atheism. Morality. Residence. Tolerance. Traditionalism. 1958. *159*
—. Attitudes. Clergy. Social issues. 1974. *2378*
—. Auburn Affirmation (document). Church government. Presbyterian Church of the United States of America. 1920-25. *3577*
—. Authority. Baptists, Southern. 1600-1978. *3016*
—. Authors. Marshall, Catherine. Popular Culture. Presbyterian Church. Women. 1949-78. *3546*
—. Autobiography. Congregationalism. Edwards, Jonathan. Identity. 1729-58. *3152*
—. Autonomy. Church Finance. Episcopal Church, Protestant. Isolationism. Missions and Missionaries. 1953-77. *1720*
—. Backus, Isaac *(History of New England).* Baptists. Friends, Society of. New England Meeting for Sufferings. Sectarianism. 17c-1784. *2953*
—. Bacon, Thomas. Church of England. Clergy. Education. Maryland. Politics. Slavery. ca 1745-68. *3175*
—. Baptism. Illinois (Nauvoo). Mormons. 1830-43. *4028*
—. Baptist Faith and Message (confession). Baptists, Southern. 1920-75. *3028*
—. Baptists. Bible. Church Government. 1707-1814. *3071*
—. Baptists. Bible. Periodicals. 1925-75. *3014*
—. Baptists. Bibliographies. Clarke, William Newton. Evolution. Immanentism. 1894-1912. *3065*
—. Baptists. Catholic Church. Clergy. Rauschenbusch, Walter. Social reform. Vatican Council II. 1912-65. *2380*
—. Baptists. Christian Socialism. Clergy. Rauschenbusch, Walter. Social consciousness. 1891-1918. *2400*
—. Baptists. Civil Rights. King, Martin Luther, Jr. Transcendentalism. 1840's-50's. 1950's-60's. *2530*
—. Baptists. Clergy. First Presbyterian Church. Fosdick, Harry Emerson. New York City. Presbyterian Church. 1918-24. *466*
—. Baptists. Clergy. Hudson, Winthrop. Liberalism. Rauschenbusch, Walter. Social theory. 1880-1978. *2351*
—. Baptists. Hermeneutics. Poetry. Strong, Augustus Hopkins. 1897-1916. 1978. *1974*
—. Baptists. King, Martin Luther, Jr. Muelder, W. G. Nonviolence. Personalism. Tillich, Paul. Wieman, Henry Nelson. 1955-68. *2552*
—. Baptists. Landmark movement. Sects, Religious. 1850-1950. *3089*
—. Baptists (American). Missions and Missionaries. 1810-26. *1735*
—. Baptists, North American. German Americans. Rauschenbusch, Walter. 1814-1949. *3062*
—. Baptists, Southern. Barton, A. J. Denominationalism. Gambrell, James Bruton. Lawrence, J. B. 1910-80. *3039*
—. Baptists, Southern. Fraternal Address. Mullins, Edgar Young. 1919-20. *2995*
—. Baptists, Southern. Fundamentalism. Graves, James Robinson. Landmark Movement. Modernism. Mullins, Edgar Young. 1840-1928. *3058*
—. Baptists, Southern. Mullins, Edgar Young. 1860-1928. *3009*
—. Baptists, Southern. Organizational structure. 16c-20c. *3049*
—. Baptists, Southern. Regenerate Membership (doctrine). 16c-20c. *3059*
—. Baptists, Southern. Values. 1700-1977. *3044*
—. Barnes, Albert *(Way of Salvation).* New Jersey (Morristown). Presbyterian Church. Schisms. Sermons. Trials. 1829-37. *3576*
—. Barth, Karl. Germany. Protestantism. 1919-39. *2946*
—. Bennett, Anne M. Bennett, John C. Minorities. Women's liberation. 1974. *799*
—. Bible. Campbell, Alexander. Disciples of Christ. ca 1830-60. *3110*
—. Bible. Cave, Robert Catlett. Disciples of Christ. Missouri (St. Louis). Sermons. 1840's-90's. *3111*
—. Bible. Clergy. Congregationalism. Edwards, Jonathan. Marginalia. Massachusetts (Deerfield). Pierpont, Benjamin. 1726-30. *3146*
—. Bible. History. Israel. Mormons. Smith, Joseph Fielding. Snell, Heber C. 1937-52. *4035*
—. Bible. Mormons. 1830-1900. *4013*
—. Bible (New Testament; Epistles). Paul, Saint. Primitivism. Williams, Roger. 1630-83. *2939*
—. Biblical Theology Movement. Presbyterian Church. Smith, William Robertson. 1870-83. *590*
—. Bishops. Church of England. Liturgy. Ontario (Toronto). Strachan, John. 1802-67. *3214*
—. Bishops. Episcopal Church, Protestant. Huntington, Frederick (and family). New York. Social reform. Women. 1869-1904. *3213*
—. Black theology. Christianity. Feminism. Negroes. Reform. 1960's-70's. *2426*
—. Bland, Salem. Canada. Methodism. Social Gospel. 1880-86. *3444*
—. Bledsoe, Albert Taylor. Liberty. Philosophy. 19c. *1360*
—. Blewett, George John. Canada. Methodist Church. 1873-1912. *3496*
—. Boudinot, Elias. Millenarianism. Newton, Thomas. Presbyterian Church. 1787-1821. *3569*
—. Bradford, William *(Of Plymouth Plantation).* Historiography. Pilgrims. Plymouth Colony. 1630. *3126*
—. Bradstreet, Anne. Hutchinson, Anne. Literature. Massachusetts. Puritans. Social change. Women. 1630's-70's. *865*
—. Breckinridge, Robert Jefferson. Danville Theological Seminary. Emancipation. Kentucky. Presbyterian Church. 1832-71. *3545*
—. Buber, Martin. God is Dead Theology. Heidegger, Robert. Sartre, Jean-Paul. 1961-64. *153*
—. Bureaucracies. Conservatism. Presbyterian Church, Southern (administration). Roberts, William Henry. 1884-1920. *3541*
—. Bushnell, Horace. Clergy. Congregationalism. Elites. 19c. *3114*
—. Business. Ethics. Mormons. Watergate scandal. 1974. *995*
—. Calvinism. Mather, Moses. Revivals. 1719-1850. *2248*
—. Canada. Church of England National Task Force on the Economy (report). Income. Poverty. Social Classes. 1977. *2564*
—. Canada. Grant, George. Philosophy. Politics. Schmidt, Larry (review article). 1945-78. *509*
—. Canada. Great Britain. Ontario (Kingston, Smith Falls). Queen's College. Romanes, George. Romanes, George John. Science. Scientific Experiments and Research. 1830-90. *2918*
—. Canada. Pentecostal Assemblies of Canada. Pentecostal Bible School. Purdie, James Eustace. Religious education. 1925-50. *747*
—. Canadians. Religious Education. USA. 1760-1980. *646*
—. Capital punishment. Mormons. Utah. 1843-1978. *3971*
—. Capitalism. Ideology. Management. Political Science. Protestantism. Weber, Max. 16c-1974. *376*
—. Catholic Church. Church Schools. Philosophy. 1920-60. *3747*
—. Catholic Church. Europe. Original sin. 1966-71. *3751*
—. Catholic Church. Liberalism. Neoorthodoxy. Pluralism. Secularism. 1936-74. *3899*
—. Catholic Church. New England. Transcendentalists. 19c. *2777*
—. Cave, Robert Catlett. Disciples of Christ. Liberalism. Missouri (St. Louis). Non-Sectarian Church of St. Louis. 1867-1923. *2913*
—. Channing, William Ellery. Great Britain. Humanitarianism. Irresistible compassion. ca 1660-19c. *2851*
—. Charities. Church of England. Evangelicals. Ontario (Toronto). Temperance Movements. 1870-1900. *3205*
—. Children. Evangelicalism. Northeastern or North Atlantic States. Protestant Churches. Sunday Schools. 1820's. *604*
—. Children. Family. Friends, Society of. Pennsylvania (Delaware Valley). 1681-1735. *874*
—. Christian Science. Eddy, Mary Baker. Lee, Ann. Personality. Shakers. Women. 1736-1910. *2753*
—. Christianity. Church and Social Problems. Civil religion. Ecumenism. 1967-70's. *1181*
—. Christianity. Conservatism. Meyer, Frank Straus. 1909-72. *1362*
—. Christianity. Deism. Jefferson, Thomas *(Life and Morals of Jesus of Nazareth).* Jesus Christ. Morality. Russia. Tolstoy, Leo *(Christ's Christianity).* 1800-85. *4278*
—. Christianity. Ethics. Providence. 19c. *2728*
—. Christianity. Europe. Frontier and Pioneer Life. 18c-1979. *301*
—. Christianity. God is Dead Theology. Islam. Methodology. Religions, history of. Secularism. Smith, Wilfred Cantwell. 1940-73. *134*
—. Christianity. Marti, Fritz. Philosophy. Scholarship. Swiss Americans. 1894-1979. *2803*
—. Christianity. Sexuality. 1970's. *2740*
—. Christianity. University of Chicago Divinity School. Wieman, Henry Nelson. 1890's-1920's. *2717*
—. Christians. Genocide. Jews. World War II. 1945-74. *101*
—. Church and state. Cowley, Matthias F. Mormons. Polygamy. Smoot, Reed. Taylor, John W. Woodruff Manifesto. 1890-1911. *1060*
—. Church and state. Founding fathers. 1695-1830. *1096*
—. Church and State. Government, Resistance to. Jehovah's Witnesses. Persecution. 1870's-1960's. *1097*
—. Church of England. Clergy. Government. Loyalists. Political Attitudes. 1770-83. *1387*
—. Church of England. Clergy. Loyalists. 1774-83. *1346*
—. Church of England. Congregationalism. Connecticut (New Haven). Conversion. Johnson, Samuel (1696-1772). Yale University. 1710-22. *3177*
—. Civil rights movement. Episcopal Church, Protestant. Race Relations. 1800-1965. *2540*
—. Clapp, Theodore. Louisiana (New Orleans). Slavery. Unitarianism. 1822-56. *4084*
—. Clergy. Denominationalism. Social issues. Values. 1960's-70's. *2401*
—. Clergy. Denominationalism. Southern Baptist Theological Seminary. 18c-1980. *3075*
—. Clergy. Diaries. Hodge, Charles. Pennsylvania (Philadelphia). Presbyterian Church. 1819-20. *3534*
—. Clergy. Franklin and Marshall College. Gerhart, Emanuel Vogel. Pennsylvania (Lancaster). Reformed German Church. 1840-1904. *3286*
—. Clergy. Germany. Herborn, University of. Maryland. Otterbein, Philip Wilhelm. Pennsylvania. United Brethren in Christ. 1726-1813. *3666*
—. Clergy. Great Awakening. New England. Professionalism. 1740-49. *2257*
—. Clergy. Protestant churches. Textbooks. 1850-1900. *2925*
—. Colleges and Universities. Foreman, Kenneth J., Sr. Presbyterian Church (southern). *Presbyterian Outlook* (newspaper). 1922-67. *3547*
—. Common Sense school. Comte, Auguste. Philosophy. Positivism. Reformed churches. Social Gospel. ca 1850's-80's. *2833*
—. Conflict and Conflict Resolution. Presbyterian Church. 1960's-70's. *3550*
—. Congregationalism. Connecticut. Stiles, Ezra. Thomism. 1792-94. *3130*
—. Congregationalism. Covenant theology. Iconography. Tombstones. Vermont (Grafton, Rockingham). 1770-1803. *1896*
—. Congregationalism. Edwards, Jonathan. Great Awakening. Intellectuals. Massachusetts (Northampton, Stockbridge). Youth. ca 1730-1880. *3150*
—. Congregationalism. Edwards, Jonathan. Hopkins, Samuel. New Divinity (doctrines). New England. Social reform. 1730-1803. *2373*
—. Congregationalism. Edwards, Jonathan. Rainbows. Science. 1740-45. *2343*
—. Congregationalism. Exiles. Great Britain. Hooker, Thomas. Netherlands. New England. 1631-33. *3650*
—. Connecticut (Canterbury). Maine (Sabbathday Lake). Shakers. Utopias. 1774-1974. *434*
—. Connecticut (Enfield). Edwards, Jonathan ("Sinners in the Hands of an Angry God"). Sermons. 1741. *1994*
—. Conservatism. Presbyterian Church. Smyth, Thomas. Social theory. South Carolina. 1831-70. *3552*
—. Constitutions. Founding fathers. Historiography. Political Theory. 18c. *1405*
—. Conversion. Edwards, Jonathan *(History of the Work of Redemption).* Philosophy of History. 1739. *3140*
—. Conversion. Hooker, Thomas. Preparationism. Puritans. Ramus, Petrus. Shepard, Thomas. 1608-49. *3643*

—. Conversion. New England. Puritans. Semiology. 1600's. *3612*
—. Conversion. Preparationism. Puritans. Stoddard, Solomon. Taylor, Edward. 1690-94. *3642*
—. Country life. Ethnic groups. Evangelical United Brethren Church. Social classes. 1800-1968. *3668*
—. Creative innocence, concept of. Maritain, Jacques. Maritain, Raissa. Merton, Thomas. Poetry. 1940's-75. *3863*
—. Creeds. Evangelical Association. Methodism. Terry, Milton S. United Evangelical Church. 1894-1921. *3667*
—. Death and Dying. Infants. New England. Parents. Puritans. 1620-1720. *925*
—. Deism. Jefferson, Thomas. 1800-25. *4276*
—. Deity. Illinois (Nauvoo). Mormons. Sermons. Smith, Joseph (King Follett Discourse). 1844. *3976*
—. Divinity (issue). Hodge, Charles *(Systematic Theology)*. Jesus Christ. Nevin, John W. Presbyterian Church. 1872. *3581*
—. Dualism. Thoreau, Henry David. Transcendentalism. 1853-1906. *4073*
—. Economic theory. 1974. *374*
—. Ecumenism. Education. Mackay, John A. Personal narratives. Presbyterian Church of the United States of America. Princeton Theological Seminary. 1910-75. *3543*
—. Ecumenism. Great Awakening. Moravian Church. Presbyterian Church. Tennent, Gilbert. Zinzendorf, Nikolaus. 1740-41. *2226*
—. Ecumenism. Presbyterian Church, Cumberland. World Alliance of Reformed Churches. 1880-84. *470*
—. Education. Mormons. Universe. 1830-75. *3977*
—. Edwards, Jonathan. Grace. Locke, John. Psychology. 1740's. *3158*
—. Emerson, Ralph Waldo. Oration. Transcendentalism. ca 1836-60. *4072*
—. Enlightenment. Mather, Cotton. Puritans. 1680-1728. *3657*
—. Enlightenment. Presbyterian Evangelical Calvinists. 17c-19c. *3570*
—. Enlightenment. Protestantism. 1920's-75. *2881*
—. Episcopal Church, Protestant. 1973. *716*
—. Episcopal Church, Protestant. Great Britain. Maurice, Frederick Denison. Protestantism. Revelation. Social reform. 1860-1900. *3171*
—. Episcopal Church, Protestant. Missions. 1972-73. *3249*
—. Episcopal Church, Protestant. Rites and Ceremonies. 1607-1978. *3216*
—. Eschatology. Future. Millenarianism. 18c. *1180*
—. Ethics. Methodist Church. Wesley, John. 1744-91. 1879-1974. *2397*
—. Ethics. Women's Liberation Movement. 1973. *838*
—. Ethnicity. Immigrants. Lutheran Church (Missouri Synod). Migration. 1847-1970. *3323*
—. Evangelicalism. 1517-20c. *2817*
—. Evangelicalism. Faith Healing. Indiana (Gary). Music (gospel). Negroes. 1976. *2868*
—. Evangelism. Faith healing. Perfectionism. 1870-90. *1434*
—. Feminism. Kansas. Letters. Nichols, Clarina I. H. Sex roles. 1857-69. *843*
—. Finney, Charles G. Revivals. 1821-75. *2251*
—. Finnish Americans. Lutheran Church. 1688-1970's. *3316*
—. Franklin, Benjamin. Great Awakening. Great Britain. Whitefield, George. 1739-64. *2272*
—. Free love. Perfectionists. Rhode Island (Cumberland). 1748-68. *2898*
—. Freudianism. Marxism. Niebuhr, Reinhold (review article). Original sin. Protestantism. 1939-70. *2838*
—. Friends, Society of. Keith, George. Pennsylvania. Pusey, Caleb. Schisms. 17c. *3273*
—. Furniture and Furnishings. Orthodoxy. Shakers. Social Change. 1815-1969. *4067*
—. Geiger, Abraham. Holdheim, Samuel. Judaism, Reform. 19c. *4221*
—. Gerhart, Emanuel Vogel. Mercersburg Theological Seminary. Pennsylvania. Reformed German Church. 1831-1904. *3287*
—. German Evangelical Synod of North America. Niebuhr, Reinhold. Pacifism. Patriotism. World War I. 1915-18. *2639*
—. God is Dead theology. Science. 1600-1970. *2306*
—. Gorton, Samuel. Great Britain. Massachusetts. Puritanism. Radicals and Radicalism. Rhode Island. Rhode Island. 1636-77. *2862*
—. Great Awakening. Massachusetts (Hampshire County). 1730's-40's. *2235*
—. Greeley, Andrew M. (review essays). Sociology of religion concept. 1960's-70's. *167*
—. Hirsch, Samuel. History. Judaism, Reform. 1815-89. *4209*
—. Historiography. Indian-White Relations. Missions and Missionaries. New England. Puritans. 17c-20c. *1641*
—. Historiography. Intuition. New England. Parker, Theodore. Reason. Transcendentalism. Unitarianism. 18c-1860. 1920-79. *4074*
—. History. Niebuhr, Reinhold. 1974. *2856*
—. History. Protestantism. 1900-70. *2850*
—. Hobomok (shaman). Indian-White Relations. Pilgrims. Plymouth Colony. Polytheism. Squanto (Wampanoag Indian). ca 1620-30. *3144*
—. Holifield, E. Brooks. Lowrie, Ernest Benson. New England. Puritans (review article). Sacraments. Willard, Samuel. 16c-17c. 1974. *3637*
—. Homosexuality. Protestant Churches. 1970's. *815*
—. Identity. Lutheran Church. 18c-20c. *3326*
—. Illinois (Nauvoo). Mormons. 1839-46. *4004*
—. Illinois (Nauvoo). Mormons. Sermons. Smith, Joseph (King Follett Discourse). 1844-1978. *3947*
—. Indiana. Lutherans. Politics. 1835-70. *3344*
—. Intellectuals. McConnell, Francis John. Methodist Church. Social Reform. 1894-1937. *2382*
—. James, Henry (1811-82). Letters. Swedenborg, Emanuel. Wilkinson, James John Garth. 1844-55. *4060*
—. James, Henry (1811-82). Literature. Swedenborgianism. Swedenborgians. 1840's-81. *4061*
—. Jesus Christ. Judaism (Orthodox, Reform). New York City. Sermons. Wise, Stephen Samuel. 1925-26. *4153*
—. Johnson, Samuel (1822-82). Massachusetts. Orientalism. Transcendentalism. 1840's-82. *4071*
—. Judaism, Conservative. 1945-70's. *4169*
—. Judaism (Reform). Pittsburgh Platform (1885). Science. Voorsanger, Jacob. 1872-1908. *2337*
—. Judaism, Reform. Wise, Isaac Mayer. 19c. *4223*
—. Koehler, J. P. Lutheran Church. *Wisconsin Lutheran Quarterly* (periodical). 1880's-1915. *3317*
—. Lectures of Faith. Mormons. 1834-1921. *3973*
—. Lee, Ann. New York. Shakers. 1774-20c. *4065*
—. Liberalism. Protestantism. 1880's-1930's. *2945*
—. Literature. Trumbull, John. 1769-73. *2029*
—. Manuscripts. Massachusetts. Mather, Increase. Puritans. 1670's. *3628*
—. Massachusetts (Westfield). Puritans. Sermons. Taylor, Edward ("Upon the Types of the Old Testament"). Typology. 1693. *3638*
—. Mathews, Shailer. Modernism. Science. Social gospel movement. 1864-1930. *2443*
—. Methodist Episcopal Church. 1919-39. *3483*
—. Millenarianism. Missions and Missionaries. Weber, Timothy P. (review article). 1875-1925. *2897*
—. Mormons. 19c-1973. *4039*
—. Mormons. Negroes. Race Relations. 1831-1973. *4058*
—. Mormons. Pratt, Orson (confession). 1860. *4024*
—. Mormons. Smith, Joseph. ca 1800-44. *3982*
—. Myths and Symbols. New England. Puritans. Regionalism. 17c. *3611*
—. Nebraska (Lincoln). Puritans. Sermons. Taylor, Edward ("Upon the Types of the Old Testament"). Typology. 1693-1706. *3639*
—. New England. Novels. Presbyterian Church. Salvation. Stowe, Harriet Beecher. Women. 1845-85. *2038*
—. New England. Puritans. Sermons. Sex roles. Women. 1690-1730. *883*
—. New England. Puritans. Stoddard, Solomon. 1672-1729. *3634*
—. Niebuhr, H. Richard. Social sciences. ca 1930-70. *125*
—. Niebuhr, Reinhold. 1892-1971. *2825*
—. Niebuhr, Reinhold. Philosophy. 1974. *2940*
—. Niebuhr, Reinhold. Philosophy. Secularism. 1974. *2855*
—. Niebuhr, Reinhold. Political thought. 1927-59. *1417*
—. Niebuhr, Reinhold. Politics. 20c. *2895*
—. Niebuhr, Reinhold *(Moral Man and Immoral Society)*. 1932-59. *2933*
—. Niebuhr, Reinhold *(Moral Man and Immoral Society)*. Sin (doctrine). 1930's. *2909*
—. Pietists. Puritans. Radical catholicity principle. 17c-18c. *2950*
—. Preaching. 18c-20c. *1988*
—. Presbyterian Church (General Assembly). Princeton Theological Seminary (trustees). 1920-29. *647*
—. Protestantism. Radical catholicity principle. Transcendence. 1975. *2949*
—. Providence. ca 1830's-60. *2779*
Theology, avant-garde. God is Dead theology. Social Gospel. 1960's. *2768*
Theology (comparative). Edwards, Jonathan. Hasidism (Habad). Psychology. 18c. *2338*
Theology, conservative (review essay). Fundamentalism. 1920-74. *2814*
Theology of the Republic (concept). Democracy. Enlightenment. Equality. Mead, Sidney E. 17c-20c. *1366*
Theology, public. American experience. Niebuhr, Reinhold. 1974. *2896*
Theology (review article). Brophy, Robert J. Jeffers, Robinson. Morris, Adelaide Kirby. Poetry. Stevens, Wallace. 20c. *2065*
Theosophical Institute. California (San Diego; Point Loma). Church Schools. Tingley, Katherine Augusta Westcott. 1897-1940. *4297*
Theosophy. Art, Symbolist. California (San Diego; Point Loma). ca 1875-1910. *1863*
—. Australia. Canada. Finland. Kurikka, Matti. Utopias. 1883-1915. *435*
—. Besant, Annie. Blavatsky, Helena Petrovna. Hindu renaissance. India. Vedanta. 1875-1900. *4283*
—. Besant, Annie. California (San Diego). Schisms. Tingley, Katharine Augusta Westcott. 1897. *4298*
—. California (Point Loma). Communes. Tingley, Katherine Augusta Westcott. Universal Brotherhood and Theosophical Society. 1897-1942. *4299*
—. Christian Science. Leadership. Shakers. Spiritualism. Women. 19c. *795*
Theses. American Studies. Colleges and Universities. Great Britain. 1975-76. *46*
—. Bibliographies. Dissertations. Mormons. 19c-1977. *4041*
Theses, Doctoral. *See* Dissertations.
Third Baptist Church. Baptists. Bethel African Methodist Episcopal Church. California (San Francisco). Civil rights. Methodist Episcopal Zion Church, African. Negroes. Pressure groups. 1860's. *1289*
Third Order of Saint Francis. Catholic Church. Chapels. New Mexico (Santa Fe). ca 1805-32. *1776*
Third Presbyterian Church. Manuscripts. McDowell, William A. New Jersey Historical Society. Presbyterian Church. South Carolina (Charleston). 1820's-30's. *259*
Third World. *See* Developing Nations.
Thomas, Isaiah. Composers. Hymnals. Music. New England. Publishers and publishing. 1784-19c. *1936*
Thomas, Norman. Christianity. Muste, A. J. Niebuhr, Reinhold. Pacifism. Political Theory. 1914-38. *2687*
Thomas, Robert D. *(Hanes Cymry America)*. Congregationalism. Guidebooks. Illinois. Immigration. Welsh Americans. 19c. *3119*
—. Guidebooks. Immigration. Iowa. Welsh Americans. 1790-1890. *3155*
—. Guidebooks. Immigration. Kansas. Welsh Americans. 1838-84. *3121*
—. Guidebooks. Immigration. Missouri. Welsh Americans. 1872. *3120*
Thomas, Robert David (review article). Noyes, John Humphrey. Oneida Community. Utopias. 1811-86. 1977. *406*
Thomism. Congregationalism. Connecticut. Stiles, Ezra. Theology. 1792-94. *3130*
Thompson, Annie Affleck. Cameron, John. Church of England. Letters. Ontario (Ottawa). Politics. Thompson, John S. D. 1867-94. *1127*
Thompson, Charles B. Mormons. Negroes. Social Theory. Strang, James Jesse. 1844-73. *2138*
Thompson, Ernest Trice. Church history. Personal narratives. Presbyterian Church. Union Theological Seminary. Virginia (Richmond). 1920-75. *689*

Thompson, John S. D. Cameron, John. Church of England. Letters. Ontario (Ottawa). Politics. Thompson, Annie Affleck. 1867-94. *1127*
Thompson, Richard W. Anti-Catholicism. Know-Nothing Party. Political Leadership. 1850's. *1291*
Thomson, Samuel. Calomel. Medicine (practice of). Mormons. 1793-1865. *1438*
Thoreau, Henry David. Correspondence, theory of. Swedenborg, Emanuel. Transcendentalism. ca 1850-62. *4069*
—. Dualism. Theology. Transcendentalism. 1853-1906. *4073*
Thoreau, Henry David *(Walden)*. Capitalism. Defoe, Daniel *(Robinson Crusoe)*. Great Britain. Materialism. Transcendentalism. 18c-19c. *354*
Thorpe, Christian Scriver. Clergy. Frontier. Letters. Lutheran Church in America, Norwegian. Montana, eastern. 1906-08. *3295*
Tierney, Richard Henry. *America* (weekly). Carranza, Venustiano. Catholic Church. Mexico. Revolution. 1914-17. *3722*
Tijerina, Reies. California. Chavez, Cesar. Christianity. Mexican Americans. Political activism. Rhetoric. Texas. 1960's-70's. *2391*
Tilden, Guy. Churches. Ohio (Canton). 1880's-1920's. *1790*
Tillich, Paul. Baptists. King, Martin Luther, Jr. Muelder, W. G. Nonviolence. Personalism. Theology. Wieman, Henry Nelson. 1955-68. *2552*
—. Bibliographies. Dissertations. Edwards, Jonathan. Niebuhr, H. Richard. Niebuhr, Reinhold. Presbyterian Church. Reformed Churches. 18c-20c. 1965-72. *2815*
Tilly, Dorothy. Civil rights. Georgia. Methodist Church. 1900's-70. *2551*
Tingley, Katharine Augusta Westcott. Besant, Annie. California (San Diego). Schisms. Theosophy. 1897. *4298*
—. California (Point Loma). Communes. Theosophy. Universal Brotherhood and Theosophical Society. 1897-1942. *4299*
—. California (San Diego; Point Loma). Church Schools. Theosophical Institute. 1897-1940. *4297*
Tithes. Church of England. Clergy. Cotton, William. Lawsuits. Virginia (Accomack County). 1633-39. *1013*
Tithing. California. Catholic Church. Mexico. Rubio, José Gonzalez. 1848. *3894*
Tituba (Indian). Historians. Massachusetts (Salem). Racism. Witchcraft. 1648-1953. *2191*
Tlingit Indians. Alaska. Assimilation. Brady, John Green. Economic Conditions. Indian-White Relations. Missions and Missionaries. 1878-1906. *1548*
Tnevnoc Cult. Communes. Convents. Cults. Socialization. 19c. 1970-79. *386*
Tobacco. Church and state. Church of England. Clergy. Parson's Cause. Virginia. Wages. 1750-70. *1052*
—. Law. Mormons. Utah. 1896-1923. *2442*
Tocqueville, Alexis de. Authority. Church and state. France. Liberalism. 1830's. *1144*
—. Catholic Church. Democracy. Manuscripts. Sermons. Yale University. 1831-40. *1990*
—. Christianity. Civil religion. Democracy. France. 1820-50. *1175*
—. Civil religion. Mazzuchelli, Samuel Charles. Political theory. 1831-63. *1164*
—. Documents. Friends, Society of. Methodism. National Characteristics. Political participation. Shakers. 1831-40. *2780*
Toketa (teacher). Congregationalism. Diaries. Hawaii. Missions and Missionaries. Tahitians. 1820's-30's. *1676*
Toleration. Atheism. Morality. Residence. Theology. Traditionalism. 1958. *159*
—. Attitudes. 1958-71. *151*
—. Baptism. Baptists. Great Britain (London). Jessey, Henry. Letters. New England. Puritans. Tombes, John. 1645. *997*
—. Baptists. Church of England. Lifestyles. Virginia. 1765-75. *3032*
—. Catholic Church. Economic Growth. Immigration. Irish Americans. Michigan (Detroit). 1850. *2790*
—. Ecumenism. Pluralism. Social reform. 1975. *105*
—. Friends, Society of. King Philip's War. New England. Politics. Williams, Roger *(George Fox)*. 1672-77. *993*
—. Rhode Island. Williams, Roger. ca 1603-83. *1120*
Toleration Act (New Hampshire, 1819). Baptists. Church and state. Congregationalism. Meetinghouses. New Hampshire (Acworth). Taxation. Universalists. 1783-1822. *1113*
Tolles, Frederick Barnes (obituary). Friends, Society of. Historiography. 1915-75. *213*
Tollig, Paulus. Alexian Brothers. Bernard, Alexius. Catholic Church. German Americans. Hospitals. Missouri (St. Louis). 1869-1980. *1456*
Tolstoy, Leo *(Christ's Christianity)*. Christianity. Deism. Jefferson, Thomas *(Life and Morals of Jesus of Nazareth)*. Jesus Christ. Morality. Russia. Theology. 1800-85. *4278*
Tombes, John. Baptism. Baptists. Great Britain (London). Jessey, Henry. Letters. New England. Puritans. Toleration. 1645. *997*
Tombstones. Baptists. Ebenezer Methodist Church. Inscriptions. Methodist Church. Mount Bethel Baptist Church. South Carolina (Anderson County). 1856-1978. *2848*
—. Baptists. Louisiana (Union Parish). Methodist Church, Wesleyan. 1839-1970's. *2834*
—. Cemeteries. Family. Rural Cemetery Movement. Social change. 1830's-40's. *87*
—. Congregationalism. Covenant theology. Iconography. Theology. Vermont (Grafton, Rockingham). 1770-1803. *1896*
—. Connecticut, eastern. Wheeler, Obadiah. 1702-49. *1886*
—. Connecticut Valley. Folk art. Sun faces (motif). Vermont (Rockingham). 1786-1812. *1842*
—. Folk art. German Americans. Harmony Methodist Church Cemetery. Methodist Church. West Virginia (Jane Lew). 1827-55. *1892*
—. Folk art. New England. New York (Long Island). 1660-18c. *1900*
—. Iconography. New England. Poetry. Puritans. Sermons. 17c. *1977*
—. New Hampshire (Londonderry). Wight, John. 1718-75. *1841*
Tonawanda Indian Reservation. Baptists. Bingham, Abel. Diaries. Indian-White Relations. Iroquois Indians (Seneca). Missions and Missionaries. New York. Red Jacket (leader). 1822-28. *1513*
Toponymy. Bible. 17c-1940. *23*
—. Catholic Church. Church names. Quebec. 1600-1925. *3841*
Tornadoes *See also* Storms.
—. Arkansas (Jonesboro). Attitudes. Folk Religion. Folklore. 1973. *95*
Toronto Archdiocese. Catholic Church. Clergy. Harris, William Richard. Ontario. 1846-1923. 1974. *3846*
Toronto Savings Bank. Bishops. Catholic Church. Lynch, John Joseph. Ontario. Poor. 1870's. *369*
Toronto, University of. Church and State. Church of England. Endowments. Land. Ontario (Upper Canada). Rolph, John. Strachan, John. 1820-70. *1026*
Tourism *See also* Resorts; Voyages.
—. Finance. Mormons. Railroads. Utah. Young, John W. 1867-91. *332*
Touro, Isaac. American Revolution. Great Britain. Judaism (Orthodox). Rhode Island. 1782. *4184*
Touro Synagogue. Churches. Harrison, Peter. Rhode Island (Newport). Wren, Christoper. 1670-1775. *1819*
—. Congregation Shearith Israel. Judaism (Orthodox). New York City. Rhode Island (Newport). 1893-1902. *4183*
—. Judaism (Orthodox). Rhode Island (Newport). 1654-1977. *4200*
—. Judaism (Orthodox). Rhode Island (Newport). 1658-1963. *4185*
—. Judaism (Orthodox). Rhode Island (Newport). 1902. *4174*
Townerites. California (Orange County). Communalism. Middle Classes. Oneida Community. Social Organization. 1848-1910. *417*
Towns. Kibbutzim. New England. Palestine. Puritans. Social Organization. 17c. 20c. *3633*
Townsend, Charles Collins. Charities. Episcopal Church, Protestant. Iowa (Iowa City). New York City. Orphans' Home of Industry. 1854-68. *2507*
Toynbee, Arnold. Anti-Semitism. Christians. World War II. ca 1940-1975. *2130*
Tractarians. Canada. Church of England. Liturgy. 1840-68. *3189*
Trade. Canada, eastern. Christianity. Europe. Micmac Indians. 15c-18c. *1574*
—. Catholic Church. Church and state. Governors, provincial. Laval, François de. New France (Sovereign Council). 1659-84. *1020*
—. Catholic church. Clergy. New France. 1627-1760. *337*
—. Church Missionary Society. Church of England. Eskimos. Hudson's Bay Company. Missionaries. Northwest Territories (Baffin Island). Peck, E. J. 1894-1913. *1660*
—. Clergy. Diaries. Episcopal Church, Protestant. Private Schools. Salt industry. Ward, Henry Dana. West Virginia (Kanawha Valley, Charleston). 1845-47. *3172*
—. Dutch Americans. New Netherland. Religious liberty. Smith, George L. (review article). 17c. *1109*
—. Family. France. Protestantism. Quebec. 1740-60. *333*
Trade Unions. *See* Labor Unions and Organizations.
Tradition. Amish, Old Order. Social Change. ca 1650-1976. *3384*
—. Judaism. Religious studies. 20c. *4133*
Tradition (periodical). *Jewish Observer* (periodical). Judaism, Orthodox. 1880-1974. *4197*
Traditionalism. Atheism. Morality. Residence. Theology. Tolerance. 1958. *159*
—. Cabala. Counter Culture. Jews. Mysticism. Rationalism. 1940's-70's. *4140*
Train, George Francis. Mormons. Public Opinion. Railroads. Utah. Young, Brigham. 1860's-70's. *3939*
Trall, Russell Thacher. Adventists. Diaries. Kellogg, Merritt. Medicine, practice of. 1844-77. *1452*
Trammell, Park M. Anti-Catholicism. Bryan, Nathan P. Catts, Sidney J. Democratic Party. Florida. Political Campaigns (gubernatorial). Primaries (senatorial). 1915-16. *1258*
Trances. Appalachia, southern. Pentecostals. Rites and ceremonies. Snakehandlers. 1909-74. *3523*
—. Hallucinations. Plants. Southwest. Witchcraft. 17c-20c. *2207*
—. Handsome Lake (Seneca). Indian Shaker Church. Neurology. Revitalization movements. Slocum, John. 18c-20c. *2756*
Transcendence. Communes. Counter culture. 1960's-70's. *4246*
—. Protestantism. Radical catholicity principle. Theology. 1975. *2949*
Transcendental Meditation. Charismatic Movement. Jesus People. Pentecostalism. Revivals. 1960's-78. *127*
—. Civil religion. Values. 20c. *1182*
—. Cults. Deviant Behavior. Occult Sciences. 1948-79. *4239*
Transcendentalism. Abolition Movement. Civil War (antecedents). Clergy. New England. Parker, Theodore. Violence. 1850-60. *2467*
—. Aesthetics. Emerson, Ralph Waldo. Philosophy. Plotinus. Science. 1836-60. *2302*
—. Antinomianism. Emerson, Ralph Waldo. Puritanism. Sermons. Social reform. 1820's-30's. *4070*
—. Baptists. Civil Rights. King, Martin Luther, Jr. Theology. 1840's-50's. 1950's-60's. *2530*
—. Brisbane, Albert. Brook Farm. Channing, William Henry. Fourierism. 1840-46. *399*
—. Capitalism. Defoe, Daniel *(Robinson Crusoe)*. Great Britain. Materialism. Thoreau, Henry David *(Walden)*. 18c-19c. *354*
—. Congregationalism. Edwards, Jonathan. ca 1725-58. *3135*
—. Correspondence, theory of. Swedenborg, Emanuel. Thoreau, Henry David. ca 1850-62. *4069*
—. Dickinson, Emily. Identity. Intellectual history. Myths and Symbols. Poetry. Puritanism. Women. 1860's. *51*
—. Dualism. Theology. Thoreau, Henry David. 1853-1906. *4073*
—. Emerson, Ralph Waldo. Hedge, Frederic Henry. Maine (Bangor). Unitarianism. 1833. *2761*
—. Emerson, Ralph Waldo. Oration. Theology. ca 1836-60. *4072*
—. Fuller, Margaret. Philosophy. Spiritualism. Women. 1840's. *4068*
—. Historiography. Intuition. New England. Parker, Theodore. Reason. Theology. Unitarianism. 18c-1860. 1920-79. *4074*
—. Johnson, Samuel (1822-82). Massachusetts. Orientalism. Theology. 1840's-82. *4071*

—. Milton, John. Puritanism. 1820's-30's. *2731*
—. Poets. Unitarianism. Very, Jones. 1833-70. *2774*
—. Social Conditions. 1830's-50's. *2367*
Transcendentalism (review article). Albanese, Catherine L. Beecher family. Caskey, Marie. Congregationalism. Connecticut. Massachusetts. Presbyterian Church. Unitarianism. 1800-60. *2763*
Transcendentalists. Attitudes. Exercise. Health. New England. Recreation. 1830-60. *1453*
—. Catholic Church. New England. Theology. 19c. *2777*
—. Correspondence, theory of. New England. 1836-44. *1962*
Translating and Interpreting. Alberta. Bible. Blackfoot Indians. Indians. Missions and Missionaries. Stocken, H. W. G. Wolf Collar (shaman). 1870-1928. *1500*
—. American Board of Commissioners for Foreign Missions. Arabic. Bible. Missions and Missionaries. Moslems. Protestantism. 1843-60. *1740*
—. Anticlericalism. Bible. Deism. Jefferson, Thomas. Jesus Christ. 1813-20. *4279*
—. Bible. Smith, Julia Evelina. Women. 1840-76. *1992*
—. Brébeuf, Jean de. Catholic Church. Indian-White Relations. Ledesme, R. P. *(Doctrine Chrestienne).* New France. Wyandot Indians. 16c-17c. *1639*
—. Christianity. Gerhardt, Paul. Hymns. Sacred fire. Symbolism in Literature. Wesley, John. 1760's-1930's. *1952*
—. Genealogy. Methodology. Rearticulation. Religious studies. 1975. *232*
Transportation *See also* names of transportation vehicles, e.g. Automobiles, Ships, Buses, Trucks, Railroads, etc.; Commerce; Merchant Marine; Postal Service.
—. Clergy. Gold Mines and Mining. Klondike Stampede. Lippy, Thomas S. Methodist Church. Randall, Edwin M. Yukon Territory. 1896-99. *3492*
Transylvania College. Colleges and Universities (administration). Desha, Joseph. Holley, Horace. Kentucky. Politics. Presbyterians. State government. Unitarianism. 1818-27. *537*
Trappists. Asia. Catholic Church. Merton, Thomas. Monasteries. 1940's-68. *3707*
—. Catholic Church. Cistercians. Mistassini, monastery of. Quebec. 1900-03. *3721*
—. Emigration. Foreign Relations. France. Quebec (Sherbrooke). 1903-14. *3785*
—. Holy Cross Abbey. Virginia (Shenandoah Valley). Wormeley Manor. 1744-1980. *3890*
Travel *See also* Voyages.
—. Anti-Catholicism. Manitoba (Red River country). O'Beirne, Eugene Francis. 1860's. *2120*
—. Baptists. Broaddus, Andrew, I. Clergy. Diaries. Kentucky. 1817. *2986*
—. Bible. Diaries. Fiction. Melville, Herman. Palestine. 1857. *2039*
—. Bishops. Catholic Church. Kenrick, Peter Richard. Letters. Missouri. 1847. *3839*
—. California (Oroville, San Francisco, Woodland). Congregation Beth Israel. Judaism (Orthodox). Messing, Aron J. Religious education. Sabbath Schools. 1879. *4201*
—. Cantors. Congregation Shearith Israel. Judaism (Orthodox). Netherlands. New York. Pinto, Joseph Jesurun. 1759-82. *4196*
—. Clark, Joseph. Education, Finance. Fund raising. Personal narratives. Princeton University (Nassau Hall). 1802-04. *612*
—. Clergy. Ellis, Edwin M. Montana. Presbyterian Church. Sunday schools. 1870's-1927. *3537*
—. Clergy. Funk, John F. Manitoba. Mennonites. Russia. Settlement. 1873. *3393*
—. Lafayette, Marquis de. Public Opinion. Social Problems. 1824-25. *61*
—. Mormons. Pioneer life. Utah. Young, Brigham. 1850-77. *3987*
Travel accounts *See also* Personal Narratives.
—. American Baptist Publishing Society. Baptists. Converts. Immigration. Lutheran Church. Sweden. Wiberg, Anders. 1852-53. *3054*
—. Art. Bartram, John. Bartram, William. Botany. Friends, Society of. Pennsylvania. 1699-1823. *2304*
—. Attitudes. Californios. Europeans. 1780's-1840's. *2122*
—. Attitudes. Clergy. Lyche, Hans Tambs. Newspapers. Norway. Unitarianism. 1880-92. *4081*
—. Attitudes. Congregationalism. Dwight, Timothy. New England. New York. Wilderness. 1790's. *2066*
—. Attitudes. Mexico. Missions and Missionaries. Protestant churches. Social Darwinism. 1867-1911. *1690*
—. Burton, Richard *(City of the Saints).* Mormons. Utah. 1860-61. *4052*
—. California (Sacramento, San Francisco). Henry, Henry Abraham. Issacs, Samuel Meyer. Jews. Letters. Rabbis. 1858. *4106*
—. California, southern. Choynski, Isidor Nathan. Cities. Jews. Journalism. 1881. *4144*
—. Catholic Church. Maritime Provinces. Plessis, Joseph-Octave. 1812-15. *3703*
—. Christianity. Farmers. Social Customs. South. 1850-70. *2795*
—. Friends, Society of. Frontier and Pioneer Life. Hutchinson, Mathias. New York, western. Ontario. Pennsylvania, central. 1819-20. *3280*
—. Great Britain. 1800-30's. *2730*
—. Immigration. Manitoba. Mennonites. Russia. Shantz, Jacob Y. 1873. *3425*
—. Immigration. Manitoba. Mennonites. Russian Canadians. 1873. *3391*
Travel guides. Great Britain. Immigrants. Landscape Painting. Mormons. Piercy, Frederick *(Illustrated Route).* Portraits. Western states. 1848-57. *1869*
Travis, John. Circuit riders. Clark, John. Evangelism. Methodism. Missouri. 1796-1851. *1561*
Tree of Life metaphor. Fiske, John. Poetry. Puritans. Taylor, Edward. 1650-1721. *1969*
Trials *See also* Courts Martial and Courts of Inquiry; Crime and Criminals.
—. Amish. Education. Military. Pennsylvania. Wisconsin. 1755-1974. *3401*
—. Anti-Catholicism. Cheverus, Jean Louis Lefebvre de. Daley, Dominic. Halligan, James. Irish Americans. Massachusetts (Northampton). Protestantism. 1805-06. *2097*
—. Anti-Catholicism. Cheverus, Jean Louis Lefebvre de. Irish Americans. Lyon, Marcus. Massachusetts (Northampton). Murder. Protestantism. 1805-06. *2099*
—. Antinomian Controversy. Church and state. Hutchinson, Anne. Massachusetts. Puritans. Social Organization. Women. 1637. *1135*
—. Antinomian controversy. Hutchinson, Anne. Massachusetts (Boston). Puritans. Winthrop, John. 1634-38. *3641*
—. Antinomianism. Hutchinson, Anne. Language. Massachusetts. Puritans. 1636-38. *3609*
—. Anti-Semitism. California (Fresno). Foote, William D. Johnson, Grove L. 1893. *2134*
—. Assassination. Gray, John P. Moral insanity. New York State Lunatic Asylum. Psychiatry. 1854-86. *2346*
—. Barnes, Albert *(Way of Salvation).* New Jersey (Morristown). Presbyterian Church. Schisms. Sermons. Theology. 1829-37. *3576*
—. Beiliss, Mendel. California (Oakland, San Francisco). Christianity. Jews. Newspapers. Russia. 1911-13. *4105*
—. Bryan, William Jennings. Darrow, Clarence. Evolution. Scopes Trial. Tennessee (Dayton). 1925. *2336*
—. Candler, Warren A. Conservatism. Evolution. Leopold, Nathan. Loeb, Richard. Methodist Episcopal Church, South. Scopes, John Thomas. 1921-41. *2293*
—. Crapsey, Algernon Sidney. Episcopal Church, Protestant. Heresy. Humanitarian Reform. New York (Rochester). St. Andrew's Church. 1879-1927. *3234*
—. Editors and Editing. Germany. Mennonites. Miller, Samuel H. World War I. 1917-18. *2658*
—. France. New France. Witchcraft. 17c. *2203*
—. Friends Asylum. Hinchman, Morgan. Mental Illness. Moral insanity. Pennsylvania (Philadelphia). 1847. *1432*
—. Godfrey, John. Massachusetts. Puritans Social Conditions. Witchcraft. 1634-75. *2186*
—. Gruber, Jacob. Maryland (Washington County). Methodism. Slave Revolts. 1818-20. *2456*
Trials (review article). Assassination. Hill, Marvin S. Illinois (Carthage). Mormons. Oaks, Dallin H. Smith, Joseph. 1844. 1977. *2126*
Tribal government. Friends, Society of. New York. Political Factions. Seneca Indians. 1848. *1202*
Trinidad and Tobago. Canada. Church Schools. East Indians. Missions and Missionaries. Presbyterian Church. 1868-1912. *1726*
Trinity Church. Batchelder, John. Episcopal Church, Protestant. Frontier and Pioneer Life. Illinois (Jacksonville). 1830-40. *3192*
—. Christianity. Episcopal Church, Protestant. Fiction. Grace Church. Melville, Herman ("The Two Temples"). New York City. 1845-50. *2061*
—. Churches. Episcopal Church, Protestant. New York City. Roofs. Upjohn, Richard. 1839-42. *1774*
—. Churches (Gothic Revival). Decorative Arts. LaFarge, John. Massachusetts (Boston). Richardson, Henry Hobson. 1876. *1832*
—. Clergy (dismissal). Episcopal Church, Protestant. Illinois (Chicago). Pamphlets. Rites and Ceremonies. Swope, Cornelius E. Unonius, Gustaf. 1850-51. *3179*
—. Lutheran Church (Missouri Synod). Oregon (Portland). Rimbach, John Adam. Washington. 1906-41. *3333*
Trinity Episcopal Church. Architecture (Gothic Revival). Churches. Episcopal Church, Protestant. Iowa (Iowa City). Upjohn, Richard. 1871-72. *1787*
Troeltsch, Ernst. Bergson, Henri. Historiography. Morality. Niebuhr, H. Richard. 1925-37. *255*
—. Education. Middle classes. Religiosity. 1960's-70's. *2602*
—. Hegel, Georg. Religious movements. Weber, Max. 19c-20c. *33*
—. Mysticism. Sociology. Weber, Max. 20c. *111*
Troeltsch, Ernst (review). DuBois, W. E. B. James, William *(Varieties of Religious Experience).* 1912. *67*
Trumbo, Isaac. Church and state. Lobbying. Mormons. Statehood. Utah. 1887-96. *1072*
Trumbull, David. Chile. Journalism. Missions and Missionaries. Presbyterian Church. Religious liberty. 1845-89. *1703*
Trumbull, John. Literature. Theology. 1769-73. *2029*
Truss design. Architecture. Benjamin, Asher. Massachusetts (Boston). West Church. 1805-23. *1827*
Trusteeism. Bishops. Catholic Church. 1785-1860. *293*
—. Catholic Church. Democracy. Laity. 1785-1855. *292*
Tryon, William. Baptists. Church and State. Church of England. North Carolina. Presbyterians. Provincial Government. 1765-76. *1036*
Tsimshian Indians. Alaska (Metlakahtla). British Columbia. Capitalism. Duncan, William. Missions and Missionaries. 1857-1974. *1519*
—. British Columbia (Metlakatla). Church Missionary Society. Church of England. Hall, A. J. Indian-White Relations. Missions and Missionaries. Revivals. 1877. *1616*
Tulane Interfaith Council. Civil Rights movement. Discrimination. Florida (Miami). Louisiana (New Orleans). Murray, Hugh T., Jr. Personal narratives. 1959-60. *2548*
Turkey *See also* Ottoman Empire.
—. Armenia. Lambert, Rose. Letters. Mennonites. Missions and Missionaries. 1898-1911. 1969. *1756*
Turner, Henry M. Armies. Butler, Benjamin F. Chaplains. Civil War. Diaries. Fort Fisher (battle). Negroes. North Carolina. 1864-65. *2685*
Turner, Nat. Christianity. Slave Revolts. Styron, William *(Confessions of Nat Turner).* 1820-31. 1968. *2047*
Turner, Paul. Baptists. Desegregation. Tennessee (Clinton). Violence. 1956. *2531*
Tutty, William. Church of England. Missions and Missionaries. Nova Scotia (Halifax). St. Paul's Church. Society for the Propagation of the Gospel. 1749-52. *1646*
Twain, Mark. Aga Khan III. Agnosticism. India (Bombay). 1885. *4301*
—. Evangelicals. South. 1870-1910. *2875*
Typeface. Book of Common Prayer. Episcopal Church, Protestant. Merrymount Press. Printing. 1922-30. *1986*
Typography. *See* Printing.
Typology. Massachusetts. Puritans. Taylor, Edward. Taylor, Thomas *(Christ Revealed).* 1635-98. *3649*
—. Massachusetts (Westfield). Puritans. Sermons. Taylor, Edward ("Upon the Types of the Old Testament"). Theology. 1693. *3638*
—. Nebraska (Lincoln). Puritans. Sermons. Taylor, Edward ("Upon the Types of the Old Testament"). Theology. 1693-1706. *3639*

U

UFO controversy. Jacobs, David M. (review article). Occult sciences. 1975. *2188*
UFO cults. Conversion. Cultic milieu. 1970's. *4241*
Ukraine. Agriculture. Immigration. Kansas. Mennonites. Warkentin, Bernhard. 1872-1908. *3379*
—. Bergthal Colony. Bishops. Immigration. Manitoba. Mennonites. Stoesz, David. 1872-76. *3390*
—. Canada. Immigration. Mennonites. 1922-23. *3365*
Ukrainian Americans. *Alaska Herald* (newspaper). Clergy. Far Western States. Honcharenko, Agapius. Orthodox Eastern Church, Greek. 1832-1916. *2805*
—. Immigration. Russia. 1850's-1945. *2785*
—. Pennsylvania. Philadelphia Archeparchy. Senyshyn, Ambrose (obituary). Uniates. 1903-76. *3906*
Ukrainian Canadians. Alberta (Rabbit Hill). Orthodox Eastern Church, Greek. 1900. *2808*
—. British Canadians. Country life. Ethnic groups. French Canadians. Manitoba. Mennonites. Migration. Polish Canadians. 1921-61. *3389*
Ultramontanism. *Brown* v. *Les Curé et Marguilliers de l'Oeuvre et de la Fabrique de la Paroisse de Montréal* (1874). Catholic Church. Church and state. Guibord, Joseph. Liberalism. Politics. Quebec. 1870-74. *1067*
—. Economic Development. Government. Quebec (Lower Canada). Social classes. 19c. *962*
Umbundu (tribe). American Board of Commissioners for Foreign Missions. Angola. Church and State. Missions and Missionaries. Portugal. Protestant Churches. 1880-1922. *1746*
UN. Dulles, John Foster. Federal Council of the Churches of Christ in America. Presbyterian Church. 1941-45. *1312*
Underdeveloped Nations. *See* Developing Nations.
Underground church. Catholicism. Pentecostal movement. 1969-73. *3802*
Uniates. Assimilation. Catholic Church. Eastern Orthodox Church, Syrian. Maronite Catholics. Melkite Catholics. Syrian Americans. 1900-73. *3908*
—. Bishops. Catholic Church. Clergy. Marriage. 1890-1907. *3907*
—. Chaldean Church. Immigrants. Iraqi Americans. Michigan (Detroit). Middle East. Nationalism. ca 1940's-74. *1306*
—. Clergy. Pennsylvania (Shenandoah). 1884-1907. *3909*
—. Fuga, Francis J. Ontario (Hamilton). Shrine of Our Lady of Klokočov. Slovak Canadians. 1952-77. *3911*
—. Fundamentalism. Immigrants. Orthodox Eastern Church, Greek. Ruthenians. Vermont (Proctor). 1914-73. *2757*
—. Lutheran Church. Methodist Church. Orthodox Eastern Church. Pennsylvania Historical and Museum Commission. Pennsylvania Historical Association. Reformed Dutch Church. Research conference. 1977. *2791*
—. Ortynsky, Soter. Ruthenians. 1907-16. *3910*
—. Pennsylvania. Philadelphia Archeparchy. Senyshyn, Ambrose (obituary). Ukrainian Americans. 1903-76. *3906*
Unification Church. Alaska (Kodiak). Canneries. Fishing. 1978-79. *325*
—. Anti-Semitism. Deprogramming. Moon, Sun Myung. 1946-76. *4269*
—. Authoritarianism. Civil religion. Moon, Sun Myung. 1970-76. *4264*
—. Conflict and Conflict Resolution. 1970's. *4266*
—. Deprogrammers. 1970's. *4244*
—. Evangelism. Models. 1965-75. *4255*
—. Moon, Sun Myung. 1970's. *4258*
Union College. Adventists. Nebraska (Lincoln). 1891-1976. *593*
—. Nebraska (Lincoln). 1890-1900. *621*
Union of American Hebrew Congregations. Fund raising. Hebrew Union College. Judaism (Reform). Western States. Wise, Isaac Mayer. 1873-75. *784*
—. Judaism, Reform. 1873-1973. *495*
—. Judaism (Reform). 1873-1973. *4206*
—. Judaism (Reform). 1873-1973. *4233*
Union Theological Seminary. Brown, Robert McAfee. New York City. Personal Narratives. Presbyterian Church. VanDusen, Henry Pitney. 1945-75. *767*
—. Church history. Personal narratives. Presbyterian Church. Thompson, Ernest Trice. Virginia (Richmond). 1920-75. *689*
—. Librarians. New York City. Presbyterian Church. Smith, Henry B. 1851-77. *758*
Union Theological Seminary Library. Libraries. New York City. Pettee, Julia. Presbyterian Church. Rockwell, William Walker. 1908-58. *759*
Union University. Baptists. Colleges and Universities. Tennessee (Jackson). 1825-1975. *776*
Union (USA 1861-65). *See* Civil War; also names of US Government agencies, bureaus, and departments, e.g., Bureau of Indian Affairs, War Department.
Unions. *See* Labor Unions and Organizations.
Unitarianism. Abolition movement. Clergy. Conservatism. Constitutions. Massachusetts (Boston). Missouri (St. Louis). 1828-57. *1413*
—. Agriculture. Clergy. Colman, Henry. Massachusetts. 1820-49. *4082*
—. Albanese, Catherine L. Beecher family. Caskey, Marie. Congregationalism. Connecticut. Massachusetts. Presbyterian Church. Transcendentalism (review article). 1800-60. *2763*
—. Andover-Harvard Theological Library. Manuscripts. Massachusetts. Universalism. 1800-1925. *256*
—. Antislavery Sentiments. Eliot, Samuel A. Fugitive Slave Act (US, 1850). Massachusetts (Boston). Patriotism. 1850-60. *4085*
—. Appleton, Thomas Gold. Calvinism. James, Henry. New England Conscience (term). 1875-95. *4075*
—. Attitudes. Clergy. Lyche, Hans Tambs. Newspapers. Norway. Travel (accounts). 1880-92. *4081*
—. Attitudes. Diaries. Hitchcock, Ethan Allen. Military Service. 1836-54. *2656*
—. Biographical dictionary. Clergy. Universalism. Women. 1860-1976. *4079*
—. Buckminster, Joseph Stevens. Congregationalism. Massachusetts (Boston). 1804-12. *3116*
—. Channing, William Ellery. Clergy. Spirituality. 1830-80. *4083*
—. Christian Connection (church). Huidekoper, Harm Jan. Meadville Theological School. Pennsylvania (Meadville). 1844-56. *762*
—. Christianity. Huidekoper, Frederick. Judaism. Meadville Theological School. Pennsylvania. Seminaries. 1834-92. *4086*
—. Clapp, Theodore. Louisiana (New Orleans). Slavery. Theology. 1822-56. *4084*
—. Clergy. Documents. Editors and Editing. Historians. Sparks, Jared. Washington, George. 1815-30. *4076*
—. Clergy. Janson, Kristofer. Minnesota (Minneapolis). Norwegian Americans. 1881-82. *4078*
—. Colleges and Universities (administration). Desha, Joseph. Holley, Horace. Kentucky. Politics. Presbyterians. State government. Transylvania College. 1818-27. *537*
—. Emerson, Ralph Waldo. Hedge, Frederic Henry. Maine (Bangor). Transcendentalism. 1833. *2761*
—. France. Great Britain. Positivism. 1816-90. *4077*
—. Historiography. Intuition. New England. Parker, Theodore. Reason. Theology. Transcendentalism. 18c-1860. 1920-79. *4074*
—. Massachusetts (Boston). Novels. Ware, William. 1837-52. *2010*
—. North or Northern States. Slavery. South. 1831-60. *2174*
—. Poets. Transcendentalism. Very, Jones. 1833-70. *2774*
United Brethren in Christ *See also* Evangelical United Brethren Church.
—. Clergy. Germany. Herborn, University of. Maryland. Otterbein, Philip Wilhelm. Pennsylvania. Theology. 1726-1813. *3666*
—. Clergy. Ordination. Women. 1889. *847*
—. Clergy. Wright, Milton. 1828-1917. *3665*
—. Evangelical Association. Ohio. 1806-39. *3663*
United Church of Canada. Archives. Canada. Methodist Church. Presbyterian Church. 18c-1973. *269*
—. Authority. Canada. 1925-73. *3669*
—. Bibliographies. Canada. Congregationalism. Historiography. Lutheran Church. Methodist Church. Presbyterian Church. 1825-1973. *2892*
—. Canada. Church History. Ecumenism. 1920-76. *442*
—. Canada. Communion. Protestantism. 1952-72. *3670*
—. Canada. Ecumenism. Immigration. Nationalism. Protestant churches. 1902-25. *491*
—. Canada. Fairbairn, R. Edis. Pacifism. World War II. 1939. *2688*
—. Canada. McClung, Nellie. Methodist Church. Ordination. Women. 1915-46. *852*
—. Canada. Methodism. 18c-20c. *3468*
—. Canada. Presbyterian Church. 1925. *2902*
—. Ecumenism. Liberalism. Manitoba. Social gospel. 1870's-1925. *449*
—. Ecumenism. Methodist Church. Nova Scotia (Springhill). Presbyterian Church. St. Andrew's Wesley United Church of Canada. 1800-1976. *2829*
United Church of Christ. Ecumenism. 19c-20c. *494*
United Congregational Church. Congregationalism. Decorative Arts. Interior decoration. Rhode Island (Newport). 1879-80. *1897*
United Evangelical Church. Creeds. Evangelical Association. Methodism. Terry, Milton S. Theology. 1894-1921. *3667*
United Jewish Charities. Hexter, Maurice B. Jews. Ohio (Cincinnati). Personal narratives. Social Work. 1910's. *2508*
United Order. Economic Conditions. Mormons. ca 1870's-90's. *2565*
—. Mormons. Stewart, Levi. Utah (Kanab). Young, Brigham. Young, John R. 1874-84. *4029*
United States. *See* entries beginning with the word American; US; states; regions, e.g. New England, Western States, etc.; British North America; also names of government agencies and departments, e.g., Bureau of Indian Affairs, State Department, etc..
United States v. *Christian Echoes National Ministry, Inc.* Church and state. Colorado (Denver). Political activity. Tax exemption. 1950's-1970's. *1063*
United Synagogue of America. Judaism (Conservative). 1910-13. *4170*
Universal Brotherhood and Theosophical Society. California (Point Loma). Communes. Theosophy. Tingley, Katherine Augusta Westcott. 1897-1942. *4299*
Universal Negro Improvement Association. Chaplains. Garvey, Marcus. Negroes. 1920's. *2366*
Universalism. Andover-Harvard Theological Library. Manuscripts. Massachusetts. Unitarianism. 1800-1925. *256*
—. Bible. Darwinism. Episcopal Church, Protestant. Europe. Excommunication. Hermeneutics. MacQueary, Howard. Ohio (Canton). St. Paul's Church. 1890-91. *3178*
—. Biographical dictionary. Clergy. Unitarianism. Women. 1860-1976. *4079*
—. Great Britain. Murray, John. Vidler, William. Winchester, Elhanan. 1770-1825. *4080*
Universalist Church of America. Bartlett, Robert. Election sermons. Politics. Religious liberty. Vermont. 1817-30. *1045*
Universalists. Baptists. Church and state. Congregationalism. Meetinghouses. New Hampshire (Acworth). Taxation. Toleration Act (New Hampshire, 1819). 1783-1822. *1113*
—. Dutch Americans. Mennonites. New Netherland (New Amsterdam). Shecut, John L. E. W. *(The Eagle of the Mohawks).* 17c. 1800-36. *2012*
Universe *See also* Astronomy.
—. Education. Mormons. Theology. 1830-75. *3977*
Universe: The Catholic Herald and Visitor (newspaper). Catholic Church. Civil War. Irish Americans. 1860-70. *3746*
University Place Church. Immigration. Italian Americans. New York City (Greenwich Village). Presbyterian Church. 1900-30. *3564*
Unonius, Gustaf. Clergy. Converts. Episcopal Church, Protestant. Lutheran Church. Sweden. Wisconsin (Pine Lake). 1841-58. *2854*
—. Clergy (dismissal). Episcopal Church, Protestant. Illinois (Chicago). Pamphlets. Rites and Ceremonies. Swope, Cornelius E. Trinity Church. 1850-51. *3179*
—. Emigration. Protestantism. Sweden. 1858-63. *2922*
—. Episcopal Church, Protestant. Letters. Nashotah House. Seminaries. Wisconsin (Nashotah). 1884. *585*

—. Episcopal Church, Protestant. St. James Church. Wisconsin (Manitowoc). 1848-49. *3181*
Unruh, Daniel. Immigration. Mennonites. Russia. South Dakota. 1820-82. *3430*
Updike, John. Fiction. Kierkegaard, Sören. 1932-77. *2009*
Upjohn, Richard. Architecture. Churches (Gothic Revival, Victorian Gothic). Episcopal Church, Protestant. North Dakota. 1874-1903. *1815*
—. Architecture (Gothic Revival). Churches. Episcopal Church, Protestant. Iowa (Iowa City). Trinity Episcopal Church. 1871-72. *1787*
—. Architecture, Gothic Revival. Episcopal Church, Protestant. South. Wills, Frank. 1835-60. *1809*
—. Churches. Episcopal Church, Protestant. New York City. Roofs. Trinity Church. 1839-42. *1774*
Upper Classes. Attitudes. Billings, William. Music (choral). 1750-1800. *1907*
—. Attitudes. Domestic servants. 1800-65. *1475*
Urbanization *See also* City Planning; Modernization; Rural-Urban Studies.
—. American Revolution. Great Awakening. Social Classes. Social theory. 1740's-70's. *2230*
—. Anti-Catholicism. Irish Americans. 1920's. *2102*
—. Baptists. Bucknell University. Franklin and Marshall College. Friends, Society of (Hicksite). Pennsylvania. Reformed German Church. Swarthmore College. 1865-1915. *685*
—. Baptists, Southern. Church membership. Country life. Evangelicalism. South. 1920's. *3085*
—. Canada. Mennonites. Social Customs. USA. 1961-71. *3358*
—. New Jersey (Pitman Grove). Revivals. Settlement. 1860-1975. *2262*
Ursulines. Anti-Catholicism. Antislavery sentiments. Ideology. Massachusetts (Boston). Riots. Social Classes. 1834-35. *2109*
—. Catholic Church. Germans, Russian. Religious Education. St. Angela's Convent. Saskatchewan (Prelate). Women. 1919-34. *680*
—. Catholic Church. Needlework. Quebec (Quebec). ca 1655-1890's. *1850*
USSR *See also* Russia.
—. Antireligious Movements. Communism. Social gospel. 1921-26. *104*
—. *Bote* (newspaper). Germans, Russian. Mennonites. Nazism. Saskatchewan. Völkisch thought. 1917-39. *3431*
—. International cooperation. Methodism. Pendell, Thomas Roy. Personal narratives. World Conference of Christian Youth, 1st. 1939-79. *1402*
Usury. Letters. Lutheran Church. Mennicke, Christopher A. Walther, Carl F. W. 1866. *353*
Utah *See also* Far Western States.
—. Aaronic Order. Glendenning, Maurice L. Middle classes. Millenarianism. Mormons. 1930-79. *3933*
—. Agriculture. Grasshoppers. Pioneers. 1854-79. *3941*
—. Agriculture. Indians. Mormons. Nevada. 1847-60. *4037*
—. Architecture. Churches. Mormons. 1847-1929. *1817*
—. Architecture. City Planning. Mormons. 1847-1975. *1781*
—. Architecture. Illinois (Nauvoo). Mormons. Temples. Weeks, William. 1840's-1900. *1758*
—. Arizona (Short Creek). Church and state. Mormons. Polygamy. 1953. *1076*
—. Atheism. Freedom of Speech. *Lucifer's Lantern* (periodical). Mormons. Polygamy. Schroeder, Theodore. 1889-1900. *2125*
—. Attitudes. Mormons. Social Organization. Women. Young, Brigham. 1840's-77. *830*
—. Baldwin, Nathaniel. Fundamentalism. Inventions. Mormons. Polygamy. Radio. 1900's-61. *4036*
—. Bartholow, Roberts. Medical reports. Mormons. Physiology. Polygamy. Vollum, E. P. 1850-75. *1430*
—. Bibliographies. Historiography. Mormons. Settlement. 1840-1976. *4046*
—. Bosom serpentry (concept). Folklore. Mormons. New England. Puritans. Snakes. 17c-19c. *2765*
—. Brigham Young University. Centennial Celebrations. Colleges and Universities. Mormons. 1876-1976. *783*
—. Buchanan, James. Church and state. Federal Policy. Historiography. Military. Mormons. 1857-58. *1073*
—. Burton, Richard *(City of the Saints)*. Mormons. Travel Accounts. 1860-61. *4052*
—. Business. Depressions. Grant, Heber J. Mormons. 1893. *375*
—. Capital punishment. Mormons. Theology. 1843-1978. *3971*
—. Catholic Church. Colleges and Universities. High Schools. 1875-1975. *624*
—. Catholicism. Clergy. Scanlan, Laurence. 1875-79. *3897*
—. Charities. Mormons. Poor. 1850-1930's. *2501*
—. Church and state. County Government. Judicial Administration. Mormons. Partisanship. Probate courts. 1855-72. *1039*
—. Church and state. Feminism. House of Representatives. Polygamy. Roberts, Brigham Henry. 1898-1900. *1133*
—. Church and state. Lobbying. Mormons. Statehood. Trumbo, Isaac. 1887-96. *1072*
—. Church and state. Rawlins, Joseph L. Statehood. 1850-1926. *1049*
—. Cities. Historiography. Mormons. Social change. 1849-1970's. *4008*
—. Civil disobedience. Clawson, Rudger. Federal government. Mormons. Polygamy. Sharp, John. 1862-91. *996*
—. Civil-Military Relations. Fort Rawlins. Mormons. Provo Outrage. 1870-71. *4000*
—. Clergy. Mormons. Negroes. 1844-52. *2137*
—. Constitutional Amendments (21st). Mormons. Prohibition (repeal). 1932-33. *2587*
—. Culture. Mormons. Organizations. Pioneers. 1850's-70's. *523*
—. *Daily Union Vedette* (newspaper). Fort Douglas. Mormons. 1863-67. *4020*
—. Dalton, Edward Meeks. Edmunds Act (US, 1882). Mormons. Polygamy. 1852-86. *1028*
—. Dance. Mormons. 1830-80. *3984*
—. Diaries. Mormons. Musser, Elise Furer. Political Leadership. Social Reform. Women. 1897-1967. *811*
—. Divorce. Mormons. Polygamy. 1844-90. *822*
—. Driggs, Nevada W. Nevada (Panaca). Personal narratives. Polygamy. 1890-93. *832*
—. Economic Conditions. Mormons. Polygamy. Railroads. Salt Lake and Fort Douglas Railroad. Statehood. Young, John W. 1883-1924. *3993*
—. Editors and Editing. Mormons. *Woman's Exponent* (periodical). Women. 1872-1914. *3937*
—. Edmunds Act (US, 1882). Mormons. Polygamy. Prisons. 1880's. *1004*
—. Education. Mormons. Religious education. 1890-1929. *735*
—. Elections. Lee, J. Bracken. Mormons. State Government. 1944-56. *1274*
—. Elections. Liberal Party. Mormons. Nevada. 1860-70. *1252*
—. Emmett, James Simpson. Friendship. Grey, Zane. Mormons. Novels (western). 1907. *2072*
—. Exiles. Letters. Mormons. Polygamy. Woodruff, Emma Smith. Woodruff, Wilford. 1885. *1050*
—. Federal government. Mormons. Westward Movement. 1846-50's. *4034*
—. Fillmore, Millard. Mormons. Territorial government. 1850-53. *1053*
—. Finance. Mormons. Railroads. Tourism. Young, John W. 1867-91. *332*
—. Fort Bridger. Mormons. Mountain men. 1847-57. *3975*
—. Friendship. Kimball, Heber C. Mormons. Young, Brigham. 1829-68. *3996*
—. Frontier and Pioneer Life. Heywood, Martha Spence. Intellectuals. King, Hannah Tapfield. Mormons. Snow, Eliza Roxey. Women. 1850-70. *4045*
—. Gates, Susa Young. Marriage. Mormons. Personal narratives. Women. Young, Brigham. Young, Lucy Bigelow. 1830-1905. *3972*
—. Genealogical Society of Utah. Mormons. Research. 1894-1976. *246*
—. Genealogy. Missions and Missionaries. Mormons. 1885-1900. *1525*
—. Great Plains. Indian-White Relations. Mormons. New York, western. Young, Brigham. 1835-51. *3948*
—. Identity. Mormons. Westward Movement. 1846-69. *3999*
—. Income. Mormons. Wealth. 1857. *2625*
—. Irrigation. Mormons. Social Change. 1840-1900. *329*
—. Kimball, Sarah Melissa Granger. Mormons. Suffrage. Women. 15th Ward Relief Society. 1818-98. *901*
—. Labor Unions and Organizations. Mormons. 1850-96. *1467*
—. Landownership. Mormons. 1847-69. *4003*
—. Law. Leadership. Mormons. Polygamy. 1890-1905. *824*
—. Law. Mormons. Tobacco. 1896-1923. *2442*
—. Leadership. Mormons. Poetry. Prophecy. Snow, Eliza Roxey. Women. 1804-87. *3936*
—. Leadership. Mormons. Young, Brigham. 1801-77. *1206*
—. Leadership. Mormons. Young, Brigham. 1840's-77. *3960*
—. League of Nations. Mormons. Prohibition. Republican Party. Roberts, Brigham Henry. Smith, Joseph Fielding. Suffrage. Women. ca 1900. *1284*
—. Lee, John Doyle. Mormons. Mountain Meadows Massacre. 1857-77. *4043*
—. Literary movement, regional. Mormons. Novels. 1940's. *2025*
—. Mathematics. Mormons. Pratt, Orson. ca 1836-70. *2318*
—. Mormon history. Ritualization. 1830-1975. *3942*
—. Mormons. Morrisite War. 1862. *3986*
—. Mormons. National Education Association. Public schools. Sinclair, Upton. Teachers. 1920-24. *567*
—. Mormons. Nevada. Smith, Joseph. Voting and Voting Behavior. Young, Brigham. 1835-50's. *1251*
—. Mormons. Pioneer life. Travel. Young, Brigham. 1850-77. *3987*
—. Mormons. Prohibition. 1900's-1910's. *2592*
—. Mormons. Public Opinion. Railroads. Train, George Francis. Young, Brigham. 1860's-70's. *3939*
—. Mormons. Scandinavian Americans. ca 1873-1900. *3943*
—. Mormons. Silk industry. Women. 1855-1905. *328*
—. Mormons. Social change. 1830-1974. *4018*
—. Mormons. Speeches, Addresses, etc. 1776-1976. *1103*
—. Mormons. Staines, William C. 1818-81. *3964*
—. Mormons. Statehood. Suffrage. Women. 1867-96. *798*
—. Mormons. Suffrage. Women. 1895. *944*
—. Mormons. Watt, George D. 1840's-81. *4050*
Utah (Beaver City). Architecture, folk. Mormons. Stone buildings. 1855-1975. *1812*
Utah (Centerville). Chase, Josephine Streeper. Daily life. Diaries. Mormons. Women. 1881-94. *3957*
Utah Commission. Mormons. Paddock, Algernon Sidney. Polygamy. 1882-86. *1117*
Utah (Davis County). Leonard, Truman. Mormons. 1820-97. *4001*
Utah (Escalante). Amish. Land use. Mennonites. Mormons. Pennsylvania (Intercourse). Theology. 1973. *2767*
Utah Gospel Mission. Congregationalism. Evangelism. Far Western States. Mormons. Nutting, John Danforth. Photographs. 1900-50. *1560*
Utah (Great Salt Lake valley). Folklore. Mormons. Settlement. Young, Brigham. 1842-1970's. *4023*
Utah (Kanab). Family. Land. Mormons. Pioneer life. 1874-80. *4009*
—. Mormons. Stewart, Levi. United Order. Young, Brigham. Young, John R. 1874-84. *4029*
Utah (Logan). Mormons. Temples. 1850-1900. *1759*
Utah (Ogden). Elections. Labor. Law. Mormons. Railroads. 1869-70. *1262*
Utah (Parowan). Decker, Mahonri M. Hymns. Mormons. 1919. *1921*
Utah (Provo). Brigham Young University. Education. Mormons. 1831-1970's. *588*
—. Brigham Young University. Fundamentalism. Mormons. Students. 1935-73. *606*
—. Brigham Young University Library. Genealogy. Immigration studies. Mormons. 1830-1978. *236*
Utah (Provo, Salt Lake City). Architects. Churches. Folsom, William Harrison. Mormons. ca 1850's-1901. *1757*
Utah (St. George). Dwellings. Jacobsen, Florence S. Mormons. Personal narratives. Restorations. Young, Brigham. 19c. 1970's. *1789*

Utah (Salt Lake City). Alienation. Ecumenism. Judaism (Conservative, Reform). Liberalism. 1971. *499*
—. Archives. Libraries. Mormons. 1830-1970's. *194*
—. Bossard, Gisbert. Florence, Max. Mormon Temple. Photography. Smith, Joseph Fielding. 1911. *1762*
—. California, northern. Morality. Mormons. Sex. Youth. 1967-69. *885*
—. Cannon, Martha Hughes. Great Britain. Letters. Mormons. Polygamy. Women. 1885-96. *4002*
—. Chambers, Samuel D. (testimonies). Converts. Mormons. Negroes. Slavery. 1844-76. *4059*
—. Church Schools. Colleges and Universities. Mormons. Young University. 1876-94. *734*
—. City Politics. Lee, J. Bracken. Morality. Mormons. Skousen, W. Cleon. 1956-60. *4006*
—. Colleges and Universities. Mormons. Presbyterian Church. Westminster College. 1875-1913. *559*
—. Colorado. Haven, Gilbert. Methodist Church. Rocky Mountains. 1875. *3463*
—. Congregation Kol Ami. Ecumenism. Judaism. 1964-76. *482*
—. Congregation Sharey Tzedick. Judaism (Orthodox). 1916-48. *4195*
—. Dwellings. Mormons. Young, Amelia Folsom. Young, Brigham. 1863-1926. *1785*
—. Liberal Institute. Mormons. Social Reform. Spiritualism. 1869-84. *4296*
—. Mines. Mormons. 1863-1979. *4033*
Utah (Sanpete-Sevier area). Folklore. Mormons. Polygamy. Scandinavian Americans. Temples. 1849-1979. *4053*
Utah, southern. Anderson, George Edward. Mormons. Photography. 1877-1928. *3970*
—. Competition. Economic Growth. Mormons. 500-1979. *4038*
Utah (Spring City). Architecture (Scandinavian). City Planning. Country Life. Mormons. 1851-1975. *1816*
Utah (Uinta Basin). Mormons. Philanthropy. Settlement. Smart, William Henry. 1862-1937. *4031*
Utah (Weber County; Ogden). Mormons. Politics. 1850-1924. *1324*
Utah (Weber River). Mormons. Morris, Joseph. Schisms. War. Young, Brigham. 1861-62. *3926*
Utah Women's Conference. Feminism. Mormons. National Women's Conference, 1st. Women. 1977. *858*
Utopia Park. Adventists. First Harlem Church. Humphrey, James K. Negroes. New York City. Schisms. 1920's-30's. *2143*
Utopias *See also* Communes.
—. Anglican Communion. Massachusetts (Cambridge). Smyth, Frederick Hastings *(Manhood into God)*. Society of the Catholic Commonwealth. Theology. 1940. *3200*
—. Architecture. Harmony Society. Indiana (New Harmony). Pennsylvania (Economy, Harmony). Preservation. Rapp, George. Restorations. 1804-25. 20c. *420*
—. Attitudes. Ballou, Adin Augustus. Hopedale Community. Massachusetts (Milford). 1830-42. *427*
—. Australia. Canada. Finland. Kurikka, Matti. Theosophy. 1883-1915. *435*
—. Ballou, Adin Augustus. Draper, E. D. Hopedale Community. Massachusetts (Milford). 1824-56. *388*
—. Bishop Hill Colony. Illinois. Immigrants. Janssonists. Swedish Americans. 1846-60. *393*
—. Children's Order of the United Society of Believers. Education. Shakers. Utopias. 1780-1900. *4064*
—. Children's Order of the United Society of Believers. Education. Shakers. Utopias. 1780-1900. *4064*
—. Christian Catholic Church. Dowie, John Alexander. Evangelism. Illinois (Zion). 1888-1907. *409*
—. Christianity. 1790-1970. *423*
—. Civil War. Kentucky. Shakers. 1861-65. *419*
—. Connecticut (Canterbury). Maine (Sabbathday Lake). Shakers. Theology. 1774-1974. *434*
—. Cumings, John. New Hampshire (Enfield). Shakers. 1829-1923. *394*
—. Declaration of Independence. Ideology. Radicals and Radicalism. 1730's-1890's. *426*
—. Evangelicalism. Jones, Charles Colcock. Race Relations. South. 1804-63. *2543*
—. Finch, John. Letters. New York (Finger Lakes area). Skaneateles Community. 1843-45. *4302*
—. Florida (Estero). Illinois (Chicago). Koreshan Unity. Millenarianism. Teed, Cyrus Read. 1886-1903. *396*
—. Genetics. New York. Noyes, John Humphrey. Oneida Community. Stirpicultural experiment. 1848-86. *946*
—. Harmony Society. Indiana (New Harmony). Rapp, George. 1814-47. *421*
—. Harmony Society. Indiana (New Harmony). Rapp, George. 1822-30. *379*
—. Harmony Society. Pennsylvania. Rapp, George. State Legislatures. 1805-07. *380*
—. Harmony Society. Pennsylvania (Economy). Rapp, George. 1785-1847. *381*
—. Humanism. Indians. More, Thomas *(Utopia)*. Rhode Island (Narragansett). Williams, Roger *(A Key into the Language of America)*. 1640's. *2938*
—. Kentucky. Pleasant Hill (community). Restorations. Shakers. 1805-1970's. *385*
—. Kentucky (Pleasant Hill; Shakertown). Preservation. Shakers. 1805-1976. *436*
—. Lake Michigan. Michigan (Beaver Island). Mormons. Strang, James Jesse. Wisconsin (Voree). 1820-56. *433*
—. Mormons. Oneida Community. Sex roles. Shakers. Women. ca 1825-90. *842*
—. Noyes, John Humphrey. Oneida Community. Thomas, Robert David (review article). 1811-86. 1977. *406*
—. Oneida Community. 1837-86. *398*
—. Owen, Robert Dale. Social Organization. Wright, Frances. 1826-32. *411*
—. Reform. Romanticism. 1820's-60. *2364*
Utopias (review article). Kateb, George. Richter, Peyton. 19c. 1971. *400*

V

Valparaiso University. Colleges and Universities. Lutheran Church. 1636-1973. *683*
Values *See also* Attitudes; Public Opinion.
—. American Revolution. Christian humanism. Political attitudes. Puritans. 18c. *1395*
—. Angers, François-Albert. Canada. Catholic Church. French Canadians. Pacifism. 1940-79. *2654*
—. Architecture. Churches. Decorative Arts. 1970's. *1837*
—. Arkansas, University of. Baptists. Hays, Brooks. Personal narratives. Students. ca 1915-20. *3025*
—. Baptists. Church of England. Elites. Social Change. Virginia (Lunenburg County). 1746-74. *2819*
—. Baptists, Southern. Theology. 1700-1977. *3044*
—. Baseball. Sabbath. Social change. 1892-1934. *2282*
—. Bellah, Robert N. Civil religion. National self-image. Political attitudes. 1775-20c. *1200*
—. Birth control. Mormons. 19c-20c. *818*
—. Canada. Church and state. Cities. Sabbatarianism. Streetcars. 1890-1914. *2281*
—. Canada. Elites. Ethnicity. Protestant ethic. Senators. 1971. *958*
—. Capitalism. Protestant ethic. Weber, Max. 1770-1920. *355*
—. Catholic Church. Clergy. 1970's. *3744*
—. Catholic Church. Clergy. National Federation of Priests' Councils. Organizational change. -1973. *3859*
—. Catholic Church. Family. Immigrants. Polish Americans. Social control. 20c. *913*
—. Catholic Church. French Canadians. Quebec. Self-perception. Social Customs. 17c-1978. *3789*
—. Christianity. Education. Games, board. Mansion of Happiness (game). Social Change. 1832-1904. *2711*
—. Christianity. Family. Negroes. Social change. War. 1960's-70's. *875*
—. Christianity. Lifestyles. Technology. 20c. *2725*
—. Christianity. *Post-American* (periodical). 1974. *2792*
—. Church attendance. Social compassion. 1973. *2370*
—. Civil religion. Transcendental Meditation. 20c. *1182*
—. Clergy. Denominationalism. Social issues. Theology. 1960's-70's. *2401*
—. Compulsory Education. Hutterites. Legislation. South Dakota. 1700-1970's. *659*
—. Counter culture. Science. Technology. 1960's-70's. *2292*
—. Episcopal Church, Protestant. 1974. *3247*
—. Ethnic groups. Prohibitionists. Saloons. Working Class. 1890-1920. *2588*
—. Evangelicalism. Methodism. 1784-1924. *2406*
—. Indians. Massachusetts. Morton, Thomas. Pilgrims. Puritans. 1625-45. *2956*
—. Industrialization. Labor. Leisure. Protestant Ethic. 19c-20c. *334*
—. Land. Massachusetts (Barnstable County). Peasants. Pilgrims. 1620's-1720's. *3151*
—. Mennonites. Religious beliefs. 20c. *3434*
—. Middle Classes. *Reader's Digest* (periodical). 1976. *2015*
—. Mississippi. Music, gospel. 1890-1978. *1922*
Vanderbilt, Cornelius. Beecher, Henry Ward. Feminism. New York City. Radicals and Radicalism. Sex. Social Reform. Spiritualism. Woodhull, Victoria Claflin. 1868-90's. *2386*
Vanderbilt University. Coca-Cola Company. Emory University. Methodist Church. Religious education. South. 1840's-1970's. *3466*
VanDeventer, David E. Lucas, Paul R. New England (review article). Puritans. Social Organization. 1623-1741. 1976. *3621*
VanDusen, Henry Pitney. Brown, Robert McAfee. New York City. Personal Narratives. Presbyterian Church. Union Theological Seminary. 1945-75. *767*
VanDyke, Henry. *Book of Common Worship.* Humor. Lampton, William J. Poetry. Presbyterian Church, Southern. Rites and Ceremonies. 1906. *3557*
Vaniščák, Gregory. Clergy. Dulík, Joseph J. Pioneers. Slovak Americans. 1909-38. *3823*
Vanishing hitchhiker (theme). Folklore. Jesus Christ. New York Thruway. 1971. *2737*
—. Folklore. Mormons. 1933-74. *4056*
Varela, Félix. Catholic Church. Clergy. Human rights. New York City. Social progress. 1823-53. *2357*
Vatican. Apostolic Delegates. Catholic Church. Conroy, George. Nationalism. Politics. Quebec. 1877-78. *1098*
—. Archival Catalogs and Inventories. Congregatio de Propaganda Fide. France. North America. 1622-1799. 1979. *182*
—. Catholic Church. Documents. Identity. National Catholic Welfare Council. 1922. *3803*
—. Diaries. Jesuits. McCormick, Vincent A. World War II. 1942-45. *3755*
—. Diplomacy. Pius XII, Pope. Taylor, Myron C. World War II. 1940-50. *1025*
—. Ecumenism. France. Jews. 1975. *501*
Vatican Council I. Benedictines. Catholic Church. Missions and Missionaries. Wimmer, Boniface. 1866-87. *3815*
Vatican Council II. Architecture. Benedictines. Churches. Monasteries. 1962-75. *1805*
—. Baptists. Catholic Church. Clergy. Rauschenbusch, Walter. Social reform. Theology. 1912-65. *2380*
—. Canonization processes. Heroic virtue. Neumann, Saint John Nepomucene. 19c. 1962-65. *3835*
—. Catholic Church. Ontario (Toronto). St. Basil's Seminary. Seminaries. 1962-67. *3775*
Vatican Library. Arizona. Bandelier, Adolph Francis. Manuscripts. Mexico (Chihuahua, Sonora). Missions and Missionaries. New Mexico. 16c-17c. 1886-1964. 1975-79. *1618*
Vaudeville. California (Los Angeles). Cantors. Concerts. Judaism. Loew's State Theatre. Music, liturgical. Rosenblatt, Josef "Yosele". 1925. *1917*
Vaughan, Henry. Architecture. Churches. Episcopal Church, Protestant. New England. 1845-1917. *1800*
Vedanta. Besant, Annie. Blavatsky, Helena Petrovna. Hindu renaissance. India. Theosophy. 1875-1900. *4283*
Vedder, Elihu. Childhood. Dreams. Italy (Rome). Painting. Symbolism in Art. 1856-1923. *1888*
Vélez Cachupín, Thomas. Colonial Government. Documents. Franciscans. Missions and Missionaries. New Mexico. Spain. ca 1754. *1586*
Veniaminov, Metropolitan Innokentii. Alaska. Church finance. Documents. Education. Orthodox Eastern Church, Russian. Russian-American Company. 1858. *2806*
Verin, Philip (sons). Massachusetts (Salem). 1635-90. *2941*
Vermont *See also* New England; Northeastern or North Atlantic States.

—. Americanization. Catholic Church. French language. 1917-75. *308*
—. Attitudes. Episcopal Church, Protestant. Fletcher, C. B. Letters. Slavery. 1777-1864. *2159*
—. Baptists, Free Will. Cheney Family Singers. Cheney, Moses. Music. Spiritualism. 1839-91. *1932*
—. Bartlett, Robert. Election sermons. Politics. Religious liberty. Universalist Church of America. 1817-30. *1045*
—. Bibliographies. Sermons. Women. 1800-1915. *909*
—. Bingham, Hiram. Congregationalism. Converts. Family. Missions and Missionaries. 1789-1819. *1585*
—. Burchard, Jedediah. Protestants. Revivals. Social Conditions. 1835-36. *2246*
—. Congregationalism. Connecticut. Evangelism. Revivals. 1781-1803. *1609*
—. Divorce. Law. 1777-1815. *792*
—. Friends, Society of. Massachusetts. New York Yearly Meeting. Schisms. 1845-1949. *3259*
Vermont (Brattleboro). Catholic Church. Clergy. Diaries. Shaw, Joseph Coolidge. 1848. *3849*
—. Catholic Church. Cunningham, Patrick. Documents. Irish Americans. 1847-98. *3725*
Vermont (Burlington). Architecture. Banner, Peter. Congregationalism. First Congregational Society Church. New York. 1794-1815. *1829*
Vermont (Grafton, Rockingham). Congregationalism. Covenant theology. Iconography. Theology. Tombstones. 1770-1803. *1896*
Vermont Pilgrims ("Mummyjums"). Bullard, Isaac. Christianity. 1817-24. *408*
Vermont (Proctor). Fundamentalism. Immigrants. Orthodox Eastern Church, Greek. Ruthenians. Uniates. 1914-73. *2757*
Vermont (Rockingham). Connecticut Valley. Folk art. Sun faces (motif). Tombstones. 1786-1812. *1842*
Very, Jones. Poets. Transcendentalism. Unitarianism. 1833-70. *2774*
Vestments. Architecture. Church of England. Liturgy. 18c. *3188*
Vestries. Blair, James. Church of England. Clergy. Virginia. 1700-75. *3186*
—. Church of England. Clergy. Congregationalism. New England. 1630-1775. *312*
—. Church of England. Clergy. Delaware. Northeastern or North Atlantic States. 1690-1775. *311*
Veto. Councils and Synods. Delegates. Episcopal Church, Protestant (Annual Council). Kinsolving, George Herbert. Texas. Women. 1921-70. *813*
Videotape. Baptists. Films. History Teaching. Television. 1977. *267*
Vidler, William. Great Britain. Murray, John. Universalism. Winchester, Elhanan. 1770-1825. *4080*
Vietnam War. Amnesty. Ethics. 1974. *2704*
—. Anti-imperialism. Baptists, American. Horr, George. Spanish-American War. *Watchman.* 1876-1974. *2698*
—. Antiwar Sentiments. Clergy. Protestant churches. ca 1966-73. *2700*
—. Attitudes. Colleges and Universities. Religiosity. Students. 1968-72. *2636*
—. Christianity. Conscientious Objectors. 1960's-70's. *2653*
—. Jews. Political Protest. Youth. 1960's. *2694*
Vietnamese. Filipinos. Indians. War crimes. 1636-1970's. *2640*
Vigilance Committee. Anti-Catholicism. California (San Francisco). City Politics. Know-Nothing Party. People's Party. 1854-56. *1307*
Vigilantism. Democracy. Education. Fundamentalism. Local Politics. Morality. Social Change. 1920's. *2387*
—. Kansas. Liberty bonds. Mennonites. Pacifism. World War I. 1918. *2659*
Villages *See also* Rural Settlements.
—. Catholic Church. Fiestas. New Mexico. Rites and Ceremonies. Saints, patron. 1970's. *3892*
Vincent, John Heyl. Chautauqua School of Theology. Methodist Church. New York. Seminaries, correspondence. 1881-98. *763*
Vincent, Thomas. Church Missionary Society. Church of England. Hudson's Bay Company. Missions and Missionaries. Ontario (Moosonee). 1835-1910. *1638*
Vincentian Sisters of Charity. Canada. Charities. Nurses and Nursing. Slovak Americans. Slovak Canadians. USA. Women. 1902-78. *2525*
Violence. Abolition Movement. Civil War (antecedents). Clergy. New England. Parker, Theodore. Transcendentalism. 1850-60. *2467*
—. Baptists. Desegregation. Tennessee (Clinton). Turner, Paul. 1956. *2531*
—. Baptists. Race relations. Social change. 1960-69. *2420*
—. Mormons. South. 1884-1905. *2127*
Virginia *See also* South; Southeastern States.
—. American Revolution. Baptists. New England. Pennsylvania. Religious liberty. 1775-91. *1100*
—. American Revolution. Church and State. 1776-86. *1106*
—. Anglican Communion. Anticlericalism. Church and State. Parsons' Cause. 1730-60. *1058*
—. Anti-Catholicism. Church of England. Gavin, Anthony *(A Master-Key to Popery).* Great Britain. Literature. 1724-73. *2108*
—. Anticlericalism. Church of England. Great Britain. ca 1635-1783. *3238*
—. Antislavery Sentiments. Davies, Samuel. Great Awakening. Presbyterian Church. 1740-59. *2238*
—. Architecture. Churches. Episcopal Church, Protestant. 1800-1920. *1798*
—. Attitudes. Baptists. Slavery. 1785-97. *2157*
—. Attitudes. Bradford family. Letters. Missouri. Mormons. 1838-39. *4057*
—. Baptists. Church and state. 1775-1810. *1043*
—. Baptists. Church government. Women. 1765-1800. *878*
—. Baptists. Church of England. Lifestyles. Toleration. 1765-75. *3032*
—. Baptists. Imperialism. National Characteristics. Racism. Women. 1865-1900. *3001*
—. Baptists. Religious Liberty. 1600-1800. *1090*
—. Baptists (Ketocton Association). Evangelicalism. Reform. Slavery. Stringfellow, Thornton. 1800-70. *2158*
—. Behavior. Boucher, Jonathan. Church of England. Loyalists. Maryland. 1738-89. *1348*
—. Blair, James. Church of England. Church of Scotland. College of William and Mary. Converts. 1679-1720. *2924*
—. Blair, James. Church of England. Clergy. Vestries. 1700-75. *3186*
—. Blair, James. Church of England. College of William and Mary. Governors. Missions and Missionaries. ca 1685-1743. *3223*
—. Boarding Schools. Chatham Hall. Episcopal Church, Protestant. Ferguson, Anne Williams. Personal narratives. Women. 1940's. *628*
—. Cannon, James, Jr. Glass, Carter. Methodist Church. Political Corruption. 1909-34. *1295*
—. Censorship. Educators. Fundamentalists. Textbooks. 1974. *570*
—. Cherokee Indians. Indians. Martin, John. Missions and Missionaries. Presbyterian Church. Richardson, William. Tennessee. 1755-63. *1511*
—. Christianity. Civil Rights. Fernando (slave). Key, Elizabeth. Law. Negroes. 1607-90. *2153*
—. Christianity. Colleges and Universities. Curricula. Graham, William. Liberty Hall Academy. Proslavery Sentiments. ca 1786-96. *2173*
—. Christmas carols. Great Britain. Music. Puritans. 1662-70. *2787*
—. Church and state. Church of England. Clergy. Parson's Cause. Tobacco. Wages. 1750-70. *1052*
—. Church and state. Clergy. Henry, Patrick. Maury, James. Parsons' Cause. Personal narratives. Speeches, Addresses, etc. 1758-65. *1080*
—. Church and State. Presbyterian Church. 1770-85. *1015*
—. Church Government. Church of England. House of Burgesses. Petitions. Public policy. 1700-75. *999*
—. Church of England. Clergy (recruitment). 1726-76. *3185*
—. Clergy. Deism. Paine, Thomas *(Age of Reason).* 1794-97. *86*
—. Clergy. Episcopal Church, Protestant. Jarratt, Devereux. Letters. 1770-1800. *3195*
—. Colonization. Indians. Jesuits. Menéndez de Avilés, Pedro. Missions and Missionaries. Opechancanough (chief). Powhatan Indians. Spain. 1570-72. *1622*
—. Debates. Ecumenism. Methodist Episcopal Church. Methodist Episcopal Church (South). Race. 1924-25. *467*
—. Declaration of Independence. Jefferson, Thomas. Religious liberty. 1743-1826. *1022*
—. Documents. Friends, Society of. Missions and Missionaries. Religious Liberty. Wilson, George. 1650-62. *1007*
—. Friends, Society of. Pleasants, Robert. 17c-18c. *3267*
—. Law enforcement. Licenses. Sabbath. Taverns. ca 1630-1850. *2286*
—. Mennonites. Rhodes families. 1770's-1900. *3426*
Virginia (Accomac). Architecture. Churches. Episcopal Church, Protestant. St. James Episcopal Church. 1838. *1825*
Virginia (Accomack County). Church of England. Clergy. Cotton, William. Lawsuits. Tithes. 1633-39. *1013*
Virginia (Alexandria). Education. Friends, Society of. Hallowell, Benjamin. Science. 1824-60. *3281*
Virginia (Caroline County). Cedar Creek Monthly Meeting. Emancipation. Farms. Friends, Society of. Moorman, Clark Terrell. Ohio. 1766-1814. *2487*
Virginia (Charlottesville). Clergy. Letters. Lipscomb, Bernard F. Methodist Church. 1889-92. *3471*
Virginia Convention. American Revolution. Church of England. Government, Resistance to. Griffith, David. Sermons. 1775. *1351*
Virginia (Dunmore County). Church of England. Clergy. Muhlenberg, John Peter Gabriel. 1772-76. *3221*
Virginia (Farmville area). Educators. Hampden-Sydney College. Smith, Samuel Stanhope. 1776-1815. *513*
Virginia (Germanna). German Americans. Immigration. Reformed German Church. Spotswood, Alexander. 1714-21. *3284*
Virginia (Lancaster County). Carter, Robert. Christ Church. Church of England. Churches. 18c. *1849*
Virginia (Lunenburg County). Baptists. Church of England. Elites. Social Change. Values. 1746-74. *2819*
Virginia (Norfolk County). Bishop of London. Clergy. Methodists. Ordination. Petitions. Pilmoor, Joseph. 1774. *3465*
Virginia Regiment, 3rd. American Revolution. Bishops. Chaplains. Church of England. Griffith, David. 1774-89. *3235*
Virginia (Richmond). Baptists. Colleges and Universities. Richmond College. 1843-60. *616*
—. Baptists. First African Baptist Church. Jasper, John. Negroes. Sermons. 1812-1901. *2990*
—. Baptists. Slavery. 1820-65. *3055*
—. Calish, Edward Nathan. Judaism, Reform. Zionism. Zionism. 1891-1945. *4203*
—. Church history. Personal narratives. Presbyterian Church. Thompson, Ernest Trice. Union Theological Seminary. 1920-75. *689*
—. Earlham College. Evolution. Friends, Society of. Moore, Joseph. 1861. *2307*
Virginia (Roanoke). Architecture. Catholic Church. Churches. St. Andrew's Church. 1882-1975. *1834*
Virginia (Shenandoah Valley). Frontier and Pioneer Life. Immigration. Irish Americans. New York. Pennsylvania. Presbyterian Church. 17c-1776. *3558*
—. Holy Cross Abbey. Trappists. Wormeley Manor. 1744-1980. *3890*
Virginia, southwest. American Revolution. Cummings, Charles. Indians. Presbyterian Church. 1760's-80's. *2634*
Virginia Union University. American Baptist Home Mission Society. Baptists. Leadership. Missions and Missionaries. Negroes. Paternalism. 1865-1905. *644*
Virginia (Winchester). American Revolution. Diaries. Drinker family. Friends, Society of. Pacifism. Pennsylvania (Philadelphia). Prisoners. 1777-81. *2683*
Virility. Advertising. Men. Mormons. Patent medicines. Stereotypes. 1884-1931. *819*
Virtue. Presbyterian Church. Sermons. Sunday, Billy. Women. Working class. 1915. *890*
Visions. Adventists. Fullmer, Bert E. Rowen, Margaret W. Women. 1916-29. *2979*
—. Adventists. Missions and Missionaries. *Pitcairn* (vessel). White, Ellen G. 1848-90. *1704*
—. Bible. Folklore. Protestantism. South. 20c. *2178*
Viticulture. California. Franciscans. Missions. 18c-19c. *371*
—. California. Catholic Church. Missions and Missionaries. 1697-1858. *1659*
Vocabulary. *See* Language.

Völkisch thought. *Bote* (newspaper). Germans, Russian. Mennonites. Nazism. Saskatchewan. USSR. 1917-39. *3431*
Vollum, E. P. Bartholow, Roberts. Medical reports. Mormons. Physiology. Polygamy. Utah. 1850-75. *1430*
Voluntarism. Baptists, Southern. Evangelism. 1940's-78. *2997*
—. Catholic Church. England, John. Ireland. 1808-50. *3708*
—. Catholic Church. Massachusetts (Boston). Religious Orders. Teaching. Women. 1870-1940. *717*
Voluntary Associations. California (San Francisco). 1850's. *69*
—. Christianity. Ethnic Groups. Voting turnout. 1967-75. *1313*
—. Feminization. Missions and Missionaries. Women. 1800-60. *942*
—. Hadassah. Jews. National Council of Jewish Women. Professionalism. Women. 1890-1980. *4146*
—. Nationalism. Protestantism. Social organization. 19c. *2931*
Voodoo. City life. Folklore. Indiana (East Chicago, Gary, Hammond). Negroes. 1976. *2182*
—. Economic Conditions. Ethnic groups. Folklore. Mail-Order Business. Social Conditions. 1970-79. *2205*
—. Louisiana (New Orleans). Music (jazz). Negroes. Women. ca 19c. *2181*
Voorsanger, Jacob. California (San Francisco). *Emanu-El* (newspaper). Immigration. Jews, East European. Letters-to-the-editor. Rabbis. Rosenthal, Marcus. 1905. *4141*
—. Judaism (Reform). Pittsburgh Platform (1885). Science. Theology. 1872-1908. *2337*
Voting and Voting Behavior *See also* Elections; Suffrage.
—. Abramson, Harold J. Catholics. Ethnicity (review article). Hays, Samuel. 1973. *3740*
—. Anti-Catholicism. Antislavery Sentiments. Know-Nothing Party. Massachusetts. Republican Party. 1850's. *1201*
—. Anti-Catholicism. Know-Nothing Party. Massachusetts. Republican Party. 1850's. *1209*
—. Antislavery Sentiments. Ohio. Political attitudes. Revivals. 1825-70. *2866*
—. Archives. Church membership. Historical societies. Methodology. 1776-1860. 1977. *1235*
—. California (Los Angeles). Judaism. Political Campaigns (mayoral). Social Classes. 1969. *1276*
—. Canada. Catholic Church. Macdonald, John. 1850's-91. *1286*
—. Canada. Political socialization. 1965. *1249*
—. Catholic Church. Country Life. Ethnic Groups. Lutheran Church. Reformed Dutch Church. 1890-98. *1257*
—. Catholic Church. Ethnic Groups. Judaism. Pennsylvania (Philadelphia). Social classes. 1924-40. *1308*
—. Catholic Church. Morality. Oklahoma. Politics. Protestant Churches. Referendum. Sabbatarianism. 1959-76. *1290*
—. Civil religion. Elections (presidential). Nixon, Richard M. 1972. *1197*
—. Connecticut (Hartford). Democratic Party. Ethnic groups. Middle Classes. Protestantism. 1896-1940. *1203*
—. Idaho. Mormons. Political Attitudes. 1880's. *1273*
—. McGovern, George S. Nixon, Richard M. Political Campaigns (presidential). Rhetoric. 1972. *1228*
—. Mennonites. Morality. North America. Officeholding. 1860-1940. *955*
—. Mormons. Nevada. Smith, Joseph. Utah. Young, Brigham. 1835-50's. *1251*
Voting behavior. Abortion. Legislators. Western States. 1975. *139*
Voting turnout. Christianity. Ethnic Groups. Voluntary associations. 1967-75. *1313*
Voyages *See also* Travel; Whaling Industry and Trade.
—. Alaska. Catholic Church. Missionaries. Riobó, Juan Antonio García. Spain. 1779. *1643*
—. Congregationalism. Converts. Japan. Massachusetts. Shimeta, Neesima. 1860's-90. *1701*
—. Evans, James. Methodism. Missions and Missionaries. Ontario (Lake Superior). 1837-38. *1564*

W

Wacker, Hermann Dietrich. Circuit riders. Frontier and Pioneer Life. German Americans. Lutheran Church (Missouri Synod). Oklahoma. Texas. 1847-1938. *3342*
Wadsworth Institute. Colleges and Universities. Immigration. Mennonites. Ohio (Median County). 1825-80. *674*
Wages *See also* Prices.
—. Church and state. Church of England. Clergy. Parson's Cause. Tobacco. Virginia. 1750-70. *1052*
Wagner, William. Lutheran Church, Missouri Synod. Manitoba (Township Berlin). ca 1870. *3345*
Wake Forest College. Baptists, Southern. North Carolina. Southeastern Baptist Theological Seminary. 1945-51. *748*
Walburga, Saint. Catholic Church. Pennsylvania (St. Marys). St. Joseph's Convent. 1852-1974. *3778*
Waldner, Jakob. Camp Funston. Conscientious objectors. Diaries. Hutterites. Kansas. World War I. 1917-18. *2690*
Walker, Elkanah. Diaries. Indians. Missions and Missionaries. Spokan Indians. Walker, Mary. Washington, eastern. 1839-48. *1521*
—. Indian-White Relations. Missions and Missionaries. Protestant Churches. Spokan Indians. Washington (Tshimakain). 1838-48. *1520*
Walker, Mary. Diaries. Indians. Missions and Missionaries. Spokan Indians. Walker, Elkanah. Washington, eastern. 1839-48. *1521*
Walker, William. Music. Protestantism. South. 1830-50. *1914*
Wallace, Allen F. C. (review article). Evangelicalism. Pennsylvania (Rockdale). Social change. 1820-65. *2861*
Wallace, Henry A. Benson, Ezra Taft. Morality. Mormons. Political Leadership. Presbyterian Church. 1933-60. *1303*
Wallace, Lew. *Ben-Hur* (play, novel). Christianity. Drama. 1880-1900. *1872*
Wallace, Lew *(Ben-Hur)*. Archko collection. Forgeries. Jesus Christ. Mahan, William D. Mormons. Presbyterian Church (Cumberland). 1880's. *3928*
Walnut Street Presbyterian Church. Church Property. Constitutional Amendments (1st). Courts. Kentucky (Louisville). Presbyterian Church. *Watson* v. *Jones* (US, 1860). 1860-1970. *1129*
Walter, William Joseph. Authors. Catholic Church. More, Thomas. 1820's-46. *2049*
—. Bishops. Catholic Church. Intellectuals. Letters. Provincial Council of Baltimore (4th). 1840-43. *3842*
Walter, William Joseph *(Thomas More)*. Catholic Church. Literature. Pennsylvania (Philadelphia). 1839-46. *2063*
Walters, Ronald. Caskey, Marie. Mathews, Donald G. Moorhead, James H. Protestantism (review article). Reform. 1830-80. 1976-78. *2368*
Walther, Carl F. W. Letters. Lutheran Church. Mennicke, Christopher A. Usury. 1866. *353*
Wampanoag Indians. Apes, William. Indian-white relations. Massachusetts (Mashpee). Methodist Church. Reform. 1o30-40. *2546*
War *See also* names of wars, battles, etc., e.g. American Revolution, Gettysburg (battle), etc.; Antiwar Sentiment; Civil War; Military; Peace; Prisoners of War; Refugees.
—. Anabaptists. Germany. Mennonites. Switzerland. Taxation. 16c-1973. *2662*
—. Antislavery sentiments. Campbell, Alexander. Civil religion. Disciples of Christ. Indians. Politics. Women. 1823-55. *3108*
—. Attitudes. Baptists. Brown University. Wayland, Francis. 1826-65. *2649*
—. Attitudes. Youth. 1975. *2666*
—. Christianity. Family. Negroes. Social change. Values. 1960's-70's. *875*
—. Christianity. Lobbying. 1939-79. *1327*
—. Christians. Massachusetts. Sermons. 1640-1740. *2630*
—. Church and Social Problems. Ethics. Evangelicals. Graham, Billy. Political attitudes. 1970's. *2932*
—. Mormons. Morris, Joseph. Schisms. Utah (Weber River). Young, Brigham. 1861-62. *3926*
War bond drives. Kansas. Mennonites. World War I. 1917-18. *2647*
War crimes. Filipinos. Indians. Vietnamese. 1636-1970's. *2640*
War Department. Commission on Training Camp Activities. Jewish Welfare Board. Knights of Columbus. Leisure. Morality. Social Reform. World War I. Young Men's Christian Association. Young Women's Christian Association. 1917-18. *2379*
War relief. Friends, Society of. Great Britain. Law. *Mary and Charlotte* (vessel). Pennsylvania (Philadelphia). 1778-84. *3266*
Ward, Harry F. American League for Peace and Democracy. Methodist Federation for Social Service. Social criticism. 1900-40. *2408*
—. Federal Council of the Churches of Christ in America. Methodist Federation for Social Service. North, Frank M. Social Creed of Methodism. 1907-12. *2388*
Ward, Henry Dana. Clergy. Diaries. Episcopal Church, Protestant. Private Schools. Salt industry. Trade. West Virginia (Kanawha Valley, Charleston). 1845-47. *3172*
Ward, John. Diaries. Great Britain. North America. Physicians. Theologians. 17c. *2312*
Ward, Nathaniel. Great Britain. Jeremiads. New England. Pamphlets. Puritans. 1645-50. *1975*
Ward, Nathaniel *(The Simple Cobler of Aggawam in America)*. New England. Puritans. Satire. 1647. *3647*
Ward Relief Society (15th). Kimball, Sarah Melissa Granger. Mormons. Suffrage. Utah. Women. 1818-98. *901*
Ward, Samuel Ringgold. Abolition Movement. Christology. Clergy. Congregationalism. Negroes. New York. 1839-51. *2462*
Ware, William. Massachusetts (Boston). Novels. Unitarianism. 1837-52. *2010*
Warkentin, Bernhard. Agriculture. Immigration. Kansas. Mennonites. Ukraine. 1872-1908. *3379*
—. Converts. Immigration. Kansas. Mennonites. Milling. Presbyterian Church. 1847-1908. *3380*
Warkentin, Johann. Clergy. Immigration. Manitoba. Mennonite Brethren Church. Russia. 1879-1948. *3409*
Wartburg College. Immigration. Iowa. Lutheran Church. Schwartz, Auguste von. Women. 1861-77. *3320*
Washington *See also* Far Western States.
—. Beeson, John. Blaine, David E. Indian-White Relations. Methodists. Oregon. 1850-59. *3495*
—. Clergy. Columbia River. Congregationalism. Fort Vancouver. Hawaiians. Hudson's Bay Company. Kaulehelehe, William R. 1845-69. *3128*
—. Drury, Clifford M. Historians. Missions and Missionaries. Oregon. Presbyterian Church. 1928-74. *190*
—. Lutheran Church (Missouri Synod). Oregon (Portland). Rimbach, John Adam. Trinity Church. 1906-41. *3333*
Washington, Booker T. Beecher, Catharine. Church of England. Congregationalism. Johnson, Samuel (1696-1772). Reform (review article). Women. 1696-1901. *2847*
Washington, eastern. Diaries. Indians. Missions and Missionaries. Spokan Indians. Walker, Elkanah. Walker, Mary. 1839-48. *1521*
Washington, George. American Revolution. 1761-99. *1147*
—. American Revolution. Baptists. Chaplains. Gano, John. 1727-1804. *2631*
—. American Revolution. Chaplains. Church of England. 1775-83. *2643*
—. Clergy. Davies, Samuel. Eulogies. National Self-image. Presbyterian Church. 1789-1815. *1157*
—. Clergy. Documents. Editors and Editing. Historians. Sparks, Jared. Unitarianism. 1815-30. *4076*
—. Clergy. Eulogies. Presidency (mystique). Sermons. 1799. *1190*
—. Judaism (Orthodox). Letters. Religious Liberty. Rhode Island (Newport). Seixas, Moses. 1790. 1974. *1081*
Washington (Seattle). Christianity. Longshoremen. Oxford Movement. Strikes. 1921-34. *1477*
—. Fundamentalism. Matthews, Mark Allison. Presbyterian Church. Social reform. 1900-40. *2434*
—. Rescue missions. Skid rows. 1973. *2502*

Washington (Tshimakain). Indian-White Relations. Missions and Missionaries. Protestant Churches. Spokan Indians. Walker, Elkanah. 1838-48. *1520*
Watch Tower movement. Jehovah's Witnesses. Organizational structure. Rescue missions. Skid Rows. 1970's. *2722*
Watchman. Anti-imperialism. Baptists, American. Horr, George. Spanish-American War. Vietnam War. 1876-1974. *2698*
Watergate scandal. Business. Ethics. Mormons. Theology. 1974. *995*
Watson, John Broadus. Behaviorism. Calvinism. Psychology. 1890-1919. *2308*
Watson, Thomas E. Anti-Catholicism. Georgia. Letters. Roosevelt, Theodore. 1915. *2104*
—. Catholic Church. Georgia. Judaism. Psychohistory. State Politics. 1856-1922. *55*
Watson v. *Jones* (US, 1860). Church Property. Constitutional Amendments (1st). Courts. Kentucky (Louisville). Presbyterian Church. Walnut Street Presbyterian Church. 1860-1970. *1129*
Watt, George D. Mormons. Utah. 1840's-81. *4050*
Watts, Alan. Buddhism (Zen). Christianity. Merton, Thomas. 1930-73. *4288*
Watts, Isaac. Billings, William. Hymnals. Music. Poetry. Read, Daniel. 1761-85. *1920*
Wattson, Paul James. Anglo-Catholics. Catholic Church. Clergy. Ecumenism. Episcopal Church, Protestant. *Lamp* (periodical). 1903-09. *460*
—. Catholic Church. Chapel-of-St. John's-in-the-Wilderness. Ecumenism. Episcopal Church, Protestant. New York (Graymoor). Society of the Atonement. White, Lurana Mary. 1909-18. *461*
—. Catholic Church. Ecumenism. Episcopal Church, Protestant. Society of the Atonement. White, Lurana. Women. 1870-1928. *459*
—. Catholic Near East Welfare Association. Charities. 1904-26. *2512*
Wayland, Francis. Attitudes. Baptists. Brown University. War. 1826-65. *2649*
—. Baptist Triennial Convention. Church Finance. Education. Missions and missionaries. Rice, Luther. 1823-26. *3018*
—. Baptists. Child-rearing. Evangelicalism. 1831. 1975. *948*
—. Baptists. Slavery. 1830-45. *2160*
Wealth. Anti-Bigamy Act (US, 1862). Mormons. Young, Brigham. 1847-77. *341*
—. Attitudes. Benezet, Anthony. Friends, Society of. Woolman, John. 1740-83. *358*
—. Charities. Fosdick, Harry Emerson. Friendship. Liberalism. Protestantism. Rockefeller, John D., Jr. Social control. 1920-36. *364*
—. Income. Mormons. Utah. 1857. *2625*
Weather *See also* Storms.
—. Congregationalism. Dark Day. New England. Stiles, Ezra. 1780. *2326*
Weaver, Benjamin W. Clergy. Mennonites. Pennsylvania (Lancaster). 1853-1928. *3433*
Weaver, Richard M. Christianity. Conservatism. Philosophy. South. ca 1930-63. *1363*
Webb, Thomas. Clergy. Letters. Methodist Church. Montgomery, Daniel. 1771. *3490*
Weber, Max. Capitalism. Ideology. Management. Political Science. Protestantism. Theology. 16c-1974. *376*
—. Capitalism. Protestant ethic. Values. 1770-1920. *355*
—. Hegel, Georg. Religious movements. Troeltsch, Ernst. 19c-20c. *33*
—. Hoover, Herbert C. Johnson, Lyndon B. Nixon, Richard M. Protestant ethic. Public welfare. Rhetoric. Roosevelt, Franklin D. 1905-79. *348*
—. Mysticism. Sociology. Troeltsch, Ernst. 20c. *111*
Weber, Max *(The Protestant Ethic and the Spirit of Capitalism).* Franklin, Benjamin. Protestant Ethic. 18c-1978. *330*
Weber, Timothy P. (review article). Millenarianism. Missions and Missionaries. Theology. 1875-1925. *2897*
Webster, Daniel. Christianity. Civil religion. Nationalism. Senate. 1813-52. *1191*
Week of Prayer for Foreign Missions. Baptists. Missions and Missionaries. Moon, Lottie. Woman's Missionary Union. 1888-1979. *1747*
Weeks, William. Architecture. Illinois (Nauvoo). Mormons. Temples. Utah. 1840's-1900. *1758*
Weigel, Gustave. Catholic Church. Ecumenism. Protestantism. 1950-64. *497*
Weinstock, Harris. California (San Francisco). Goldie, Albert. Judaism (Orthodox, Reform). New York City. Poor. Synagogues. 1906. *4166*
Weitling, Wilhelm. Communes. German Americans. Keil, William. Letters. Missouri. Oregon. Society of Bethel. 1844-83. *405*
Weld, Theodore. Abolition Movement. Birney, James. Clergy. Evangelism. Smith, Gerrit. Stanton, H. B. 1820-50. *2488*
Welfare. *See* Public Welfare.
Weller, George. Adams, John. American Revolution (antecedents). Church of England. Letters. 1770's. 1824-25. *971*
Welsh Americans. Congregationalism. Guidebooks. Illinois. Immigration. Thomas, Robert D. *(Hanes Cymry America).* 19c. *3119*
—. Congregationalism. Guidebooks. Immigration. Iowa. Thomas, Robert D. *(Hanes Cymry America).* 1790-1890. *3155*
—. Congregationalism. Guidebooks. Immigration. Kansas. Thomas, Robert D. *(Hanes Cymry America).* 1838-84. *3121*
—. Congregationalism. Guidebooks. Immigration. Missouri. Thomas, Robert D. *(Hanes Cymry America).* 1872. *3120*
Welter, Barbara. Feminization. Historiography. Women. 1820's-30's. 1970's. *920*
Wesley Chapel. Baptists. Methodist Church. Ninth Street Baptist Church. Ohio (Cincinnati). Political protest. Temperance Movements. Women's Christian Temperance Union. 1874. *2582*
Wesley, Charles. American Revolution. Great Britain. Loyalists. Methodism. Poetry. Political Commentary. 1775-83. *1339*
Wesley, Charles H. Catholic University of America. Colleges and Universities. Discrimination. District of Columbia. Negroes. 1914-48. *3729*
Wesley, John. American Revolution. Asbury, Francis. Great Britain. Methodism. 1770-90. *1334*
—. American Revolution. Great Britain. 1775. *1336*
—. American Revolution. Great Britain. Methodism. 1760-89. *1404*
—. American Revolution. Great Britain. Methodism. Political Attitudes. Whigs, Radical. 1775-78. *1391*
—. Christianity. Gerhardt, Paul. Hymns. Sacred fire. Symbolism in Literature. Translating and Interpreting. 1760's-1930's. *1952*
—. Christianity. Methodism. Philosophy of history. ca 1740's-80's. *3453*
—. Coke, Thomas. Garrettson, Freeborn. Letters. Methodist Church. Missions and Missionaries. Nova Scotia. 1786. *1490*
—. Creeds. Methodism. 19c-20c. *3493*
—. Ethics. Methodist Church. Theology. 1744-91. 1879-1974. *2397*
—. Evangelism. Methodism. Slavery. 1725-1974. *3505*
—. Folk Medicine. Georgia. Great Britain. Indians. Medicine (practice of). Methodism. 1740's. *1426*
—. Methodism. South Carolina (Charleston). 1737. *1487*
—. Methodism. Temperance Movements. 1725-91. *2581*
Wesley, John *(A Calm Address to our American Colonies).* American Revolution. Great Britain. 1770-76. *1340*
—. Great Britain. Methodism. Plagiarism. Politics. 1775-79. *1377*
Wesley, John *(Sunday Service).* Coke, Thomas. Great Britain. Methodism. Rites and Ceremonies. 1780's. *3460*
Wesley, Susanna. Feminism. Holiness Movement. Palmer, Phoebe. 1732-1973. *829*
West Church. Architecture. Benjamin, Asher. Massachusetts (Boston). Truss design. 1805-23. *1827*
West Florida. Church and state. Colonization. Spain. 1780's. *1055*
—. Colonization. Florida (Campbell Town). Great Britain. Huguenots. 1763-70. *3254*
West Indian Americans. Attitudes. Brooklyn College. Catholic Church. Immigration. Judaism. Negroes. New York City. Protestant Ethic. 1939-78. *350*
West, John. Books (editions). Canada, western. Church of England. Diaries. Missions and Missionaries. 1820-27. *1530*
West, Samuel. American Revolution. Cooke, Samuel. History Teaching. Langdon, Samuel. Mayhew, Jonathan. Sermons. Witherspoon, John. 1750-76. 1975. *1406*
West Tennessee Baptist Female College. Baptists. Higher education. Tennessee (Brownsville). Women. 1850-1910. *658*
West Virginia *See also* Southeastern States.
—. Aged. Folklore. Poor. Witchcraft. Women. 1975. *2201*
—. Baseball. Blue laws. Church and state. Sabbath. Wheeling Nailers (team). 1889. *2279*
—. Catholic church. Elections (presidential). Protestantism. Smith, Al. 1928. *1217*
—. Devil. Folklore. Witchcraft. 1950-67. *2202*
—. Friends, Society of. Sectionalism. Social status. 18c-19c. *3257*
West Virginia (Jane Lew). Folk art. German Americans. Harmony Methodist Church Cemetery. Methodist Church. Tombstones. 1827-55. *1892*
West Virginia (Kanawha County). Educational Policy. Fundamentalism. Public schools. Textbooks. 1975. *576*
West Virginia (Kanawha Valley; Charleston). Clergy. Diaries. Episcopal Church, Protestant. Private Schools. Salt industry. Trade. Ward, Henry Dana. 1845-47. *3172*
West Virginia (Webster County). Church records. Clergy. Grimes, Addison McLaughlin. Methodist Episcopal Church. 1880's-1963. *3455*
West Virginia (Wheeling). Lambdin, William. Mormons. Rare Books. Smith, Joseph *(Book of Commandments).* 1830-33. *2124*
Western civilization. Christianity. Percy, Walker *(Love in the Ruins).* Technology. 1971. *2028*
Western Examiner (periodical). Atheism. Bobb, John. Missouri (St. Louis). 1834-35. *4300*
Western Nations. Buddhism. Hinduism. Teaching. 1969-75. *4287*
Western Reserve Historical Society. Archives. Cathcart, Wallace H. Shakers. 1911-12. *202*
—. Cathcart, Wallace H. Manuscripts. Shakers. 1774-1920. *245*
Western States *See also* individual states; Far Western States; Southwest.
—. Abortion. Legislators. Voting behavior. 1975. *139*
—. Architecture. City Planning. Mormons. Smith, Joseph. 1833-90. *1767*
—. Arrington, Leonard J. Historiography. Mormons. Personal Narratives. 20c. *171*
—. Baptists. Historiography. Rister, Carl Coke. 1920's-55. *223*
—. Bibliographies. Indian-White relations. *Journal of the West* (periodical). 1970-74. *1593*
—. City Planning. Mormons. Settlement. Smith, Joseph. 19c. *3988*
—. Communalism. Frontier and Pioneer Life. Hutterites. 1874-1977. *429*
—. Communes. Labor Department. Library of Congress. Publications. 1830's-1930's. *430*
—. Documents. Indian-White Relations. Missions and Missionaries. 1812-1923. *1483*
—. Fund raising. Hebrew Union College. Judaism (Reform). Union of American Hebrew Congregations. Wise, Isaac Mayer. 1873-75. *784*
—. Great Britain. Immigrants. Landscape Painting. Mormons. Piercy, Frederick *(Illustrated Route).* Portraits. Travel guides. 1848-57. *1869*
—. Literature. 19c-20c. *2007*
—. Morality. Mormons. Sex. Students. 1950-72. *927*
Westminster College. Colleges and Universities. Mormons. Presbyterian Church. Utah (Salt Lake City). 1875-1913. *559*
Westminster Standards. Clergy. Dickinson, Jonathan. Presbyterian Church. Subscription controversy. 1700-50. *3560*
Westminster University. Colleges and Universities. Colorado. Jackson, Sheldon. Presbyterian Church. 1874-1917. *597*
Westward Movement *See also* Frontier and Pioneer Life; Overland Journeys to the Pacific; Pioneers.
—. Baptists. Clergy. Missouri. Oregon (Willamette Valley). Powell, Joab. 1852-73. *3093*
—. Brethren in Christ. Kansas (Dickinson). Pennsylvania, southeastern. 1879. *3381*
—. Federal government. Mormons. Utah. 1846-50's. *4034*
—. Identity. Mormons. Utah. 1846-69. *3999*

Whale, Theophilus. Charles I. Congregationalism. Folklore. Regicide. Rhode Island. Stiles, Ezra. 17c. 1755-85. *3131*
Whaling industry and Trade. American Revolution. Canada. France. Huguenots. Settlement. USA. 17c-20c. *3251*
Wheat. Great Plains. Mennonites. Pioneer life. 1870-1974. *3443*
Wheat industry. Baptists. Catholic Church. Germans, Russian. Immigration. Kansas. Lutheran Church. Mennonites. 1874-77. *2778*
Wheatley, Phillis. Abolition Movement. American Revolution. Letters. Massachusetts (Boston). Whigs. 1767-80. *2454*
—. Poetry. Women. 1773. *2031*
Wheeler, Frederick. Adventists. New Hampshire (Washington). Oakes, Rachel. Preble, T. M. Sabbath. 1841-44. *2287*
Wheeler, Obadiah. Connecticut, eastern. Tombstones. 1702-49. *1886*
Wheeling Nailers (team). Baseball. Blue laws. Church and state. Sabbath. West Virginia. 1889. *2279*
Wheelock, Eleazar. Congregationalism. Connecticut. Girls. Indian-White Relations. Religious Education. 1761-69. *766*
Wheelwright, John (1897-1940). Intellectuals. New England. Poetry. Radicals and Radicalism. Socialism. 18c-1940. *1419*
Whig Party. Anti-Catholicism. Antislavery Sentiments. Bannan, Benjamin. Nativism. Pennsylvania (Schuylkill County). Temperance Movements. 1852-54. *1238*
—. Anti-Catholicism. Fillmore, Millard. Know-Nothing Party. Nativism. Political Campaigns (presidential). 1850-56. *1305*
—. Democratic Party. Liberty Party. Negroes. New York. Referendum. Suffrage. 1840-47. *1264*
Whigs. Abolition Movement. American Revolution. Letters. Massachusetts (Boston). Wheatley, Phillis. 1767-80. *2454*
Whigs, Radical. American Revolution. Great Britain. Methodism. Political Attitudes. Wesley, John. 1775-78. *1391*
Whirlwind Day School. Church and State. Education. Episcopal Church, Protestant. Indians (agencies). Oklahoma, western. Stouch, George W. H. ca 1904-14. *1086*
Whiskey. Blackburn, Gideon. Cherokee Indians. Indians. Missions and Missionaries. Old Southwest. Presbyterian Church. Schools. 1809-10. *700*
Whistling and Whittling Brigade. Boys. Illinois (Nauvoo). Mormons. Police protection. 1845. *4014*
Whitaker, Ozi William. Episcopal Church, Protestant. Girls. Nevada (Reno). Schools. 1876-94. *769*
Whitcher, Frances Miriam Berry *(Widow Bedott Papers)*. Literature. New York. Presbyterian Church. Satire. Social criticism. 1847-55. *2056*
White, Andrew Dickson. Christianity. Ethics. Rationalism. Science. 1888-90's. *2288*
White, Ellen G. Adventists. California. Letters. Loma Linda Sanitarium. 1905. *1461*
—. Adventists. Charisma. Prophecy. Women. 1848-1901. *2976*
—. Adventists. Health. Numbers, Ronald L. (review article). Reform. ca 1840's-1915. 1976. *1457*
—. Adventists. Hydrotherapy. Jackson, James Caleb. Medical reform. New York (Dansville). 1864-65. *1451*
—. Adventists. Missions and Missionaries. *Pitcairn* (vessel). Visions. 1848-90. *1704*
White flight. Centennial United Methodist Church. Indiana (Gary). Methodist Church, United. Methodist Church, United. Negroes. Personal narratives. Robinson, Roosevelt. 1976. *3467*
White House (school). Catholic Church. Church Schools. Seton, Elizabeth Ann. 1774-1821. *625*
White, Lurana Mary. Catholic Church. Ecumenism. Episcopal Church, Protestant. Society of the Atonement. Wattson, Paul James. Women. 1870-1928. *459*
—. Catholic Church. Chapel-of-St. John's-in-the-Wilderness. Ecumenism. Episcopal Church, Protestant. New York (Graymoor). Society of the Atonement. Wattson, Paul James. 1909-18. *461*
White, Lynn, Jr. Christianity. Environmental crisis. 1c-20c. *2309*
White Path's Rebellion. Acculturation. Cherokee Indians. Georgia. Missions and Missionaries. 1824-28. *1578*
White, Thomas. American Revolution. Asbury, Francis. Delaware. Loyalists. Maryland. Methodists. 1777-80. *3482*
White, William. Americanization. Episcopal Church, Protestant. Pennsylvania (Philadelphia). ca 1789-1836. *324*
Whitefield, George. Bordley, Stephen. Church of England. Great Awakening. Letters. Maryland. 1730-40. *2229*
—. *Christian History* (periodical). Evangelicalism. Great Britain. Methodist Church, Calvinistic. Periodicals. 1740's. *2233*
—. Church of England. Great Awakening. New England. 1735-70. *2239*
—. Cole, Nathan ("Spiritual Travels"). Congregationalism. Great Awakening. 1740-65. *2227*
—. Education. Georgia (Savannah). Great Awakening. Orphans. 1738-71. *731*
—. Evangelism. Great Awakening. Great Britain. 1714-70. *2232*
—. Francke, Gottfried. Georgia (Ebenezer). Germany. Immigrants. Kiefer, Theobald, II. Letters. Lutheran Church. Orphanages. Pietism. 1738. 1750. *2878*
—. Franklin, Benjamin. Friendship. Morality. Publishers and Publishing. Religious liberty. 1739-70. *58*
—. Franklin, Benjamin. Great Awakening. Great Britain. Theology. 1739-64. *2272*
—. Maine. New Hampshire. Revivals. 1727-48. *2249*
—. Proslavery Sentiments. 1740-48. *2175*
Whitefield, Henry. Daily life. Evangelism. Illinois (Chicago). Methodist Church. 1833-71. *1508*
Whitefield House. Land. Moravian Church. Pennsylvania (Nazareth). Settlement. 1740-1978. *3517*
Whites. Abortion. Attitudes. Catholics. Protestants. 1962-75. *888*
—. Adolescents. Church attendance. Negroes. Religiosity. South. 1964-74. *99*
—. Adolescents. Hispanic Americans. Identity. Mexico. Puerto Rico. Religiosity. 1970's. *108*
—. Baker, Ray Stannard. Civil rights. DuBois, W. E. B. Episcopal Church, Protestant. Liberalism. Negroes. Personal narratives. Wilmer, Cary Breckenridge. 1900-10. *2151*
—. Christianity. Negroes. 1975. *2802*
—. Country Life. Murder. Negroes. South. 1916-20. *156*
—. Marriage, interfaith. 1973-75. *790*
—. Negroes. Sectarianism. Working Class. 1969. *94*
—. Political Participation. Protestants. Racism. Sexism. Women. 1974-75. *907*
—. Protestantism. Statistics. Texas, north. 1965-73. *2874*
Whitman, Marcus. Historiography. Marshall, William I. Missions and Missionaries. Oregon. Winters, Herbert D. ca 1842-43. 1930. *1553*
Whitman, Walt. Bucke, Richard Maurice. Poetry. 1877-1902. *68*
Whitman, Walt ("Song of Myself"). Nature. Philosophy. Poetry. 1855. *64*
Whitsitt Controversy. Baptists. Graves, James Robinson. Landmark movement. Missions and Missionaries. South. 1850-1950. *3057*
Whittier House. Catholic Church. New Jersey (Jersey City). Progressivism. Protestantism. Social reform. 1890-1917. *2449*
Whittier, John Greenleaf. Bible reading. Letters. Massachusetts (Amesbury). Public schools. 1853. *577*
Wiberg, Anders. American Baptist Publishing Society. Baptists. Converts. Immigration. Lutheran Church. Sweden. Travel (accounts). 1852-53. *3054*
Wick, Barthinius L. Amana Society. Communalism. Iowa. Shambaugh, Bertha Horak. ca 1900-34. *404*
Wieman, Henry Nelson. Baptists. King, Martin Luther, Jr. Muelder, W. G. Nonviolence. Personalism. Theology. Tillich, Paul. 1955-68. *2552*
—. Christianity. Theology. University of Chicago Divinity School. 1890's-1920's. *2717*
Wigglesworth, Edward. Congregationalism. Harvard University (Hollis Professorship of Divinity). Latin language. Rhetoric. 1722. *667*
Wigglesworth, Michael *(Day of Doom)*. Covenant theology. New England. Poetry. Puritans. 1662. *3597*
Wigglesworth, Samuel. Clergy. Congregationalism. Massachusetts (Ipswich). 1714-68. *3138*
Wight, John. New Hampshire (Londonderry). Tombstones. 1718-75. *1841*
Wight, Lyman. Historians. Letters. Mormons. Schisms. Woodruff, Wilford. 1857-58. *4049*
Wihlborg, Niels Albert. Clergy. Lutheran Church (Missouri Synod). Minnesota. Missouri. Swedish Americans. 1893-1918. *3331*
Wilberforce, Robert. Anglophiles. Catholic Church. World War II (antecedents). 1940. *1239*
Wilberforce University. Lutheran Church. Methodist Episcopal Church, African. Negroes. Payne, Daniel Alexander. 1830-93. *2905*
Wilberforce University (Combined Normal and Industrial Department). Federal Aid to Education. Methodist Episcopal Church, African. Negroes. Ohio. 1887-91. *518*
Wilderness *See also* Nature.
—. Attitudes. Congregationalism. Dwight, Timothy. New England. New York. Travel (accounts). 1790's. *2066*
—. Bible. Environment. History. 18c-20c. *36*
Wilkinson, James John Garth. James, Henry (1811-82). Letters. Swedenborg, Emanuel. Theology. 1844-55. *4060*
Willard, Frances E. Dickey, Sarah. Heck, Barbara. Leadership. Methodist Church. Parker, Lois Stiles. Shaw, Anna Howard. Stereotypes. Women. 19c. *812*
—. Prohibition. Women's Christian Temperance Union. 1878-98. *2595*
—. Temperance movements. Women's Christian Temperance Union. 19c-1920. *2589*
Willard, Frances Langdon. Christianity. Letters. Teaching. 1835-51. *542*
Willard, Samuel. Holifield, E. Brooks. Lowrie, Ernest Benson. New England. Puritans (review article). Sacraments. Theology. 16c-17c. 1974. *3637*
Willers, Diedrich. Letters. Mormons. New York. Reformed Dutch Church. 1830. *2766*
Willet family. Presbyterian Church. Stained glass windows. 19c-20c. *1887*
Williams, Claude. Labor Unions and Organizations. People's Institute of Applied Religion. South. Williams, Joyce. 1940-75. *1478*
Williams College. Church attendance. Religiosity. Students. 1948-74. *113*
Williams, George A. Adventists. Nebraska. State Politics. 1925-31. *1325*
Williams, John *(The Redeemed Captive)*. Captivity narratives. Catholic Church. Congregationalism. French Canadians. Indians. New England. 1704-06. *3133*
Williams, Joyce. Labor Unions and Organizations. People's Institute of Applied Religion. South. Williams, Claude. 1940-75. *1478*
Williams, Michael. Catholic Church. *Commonweal* (periodical). Editors and Editing. 1922-38. *3716*
Williams, Peter, Jr. Episcopal Church, Protestant. New York City. Newspapers. Racism. Riots. St. Philip's Church. 1830-50. *2142*
Williams, Roger. Baptists. Carey, William. Racial attitudes. Rauschenbusch, Walter. 1776-1976. *3100*
—. Baptists. Folger, Peter. Indians. Jones, David. Missionaries. Northeastern or North Atlantic States. 1638-1814. *1619*
—. Bible (New Testament; Epistles). Paul, Saint. Primitivism. Theology. 1630-83. *2939*
—. Bibliographies. Historiography. Rhode Island. 17c-1972. *2911*
—. Christianity. History. Religious liberty. Rhode Island. 17c. *1047*
—. Church and state. Colonial Government. Great Britain. Rhode Island. 1629-83. *1042*
—. Great Britain. New England. 1629-82. *2876*
—. Human relations. Rhode Island. Social Theory. 1643-76. *2826*
—. Rhode Island. Toleration. ca 1603-83. *1120*
Williams, Roger *(A Key into the Language of America)*. Humanism. Indians. More, Thomas *(Utopia)*. Rhode Island (Narragansett). Utopias. 1640's. *2938*
Williams, Roger *(George Fox)*. Friends, Society of. King Philip's War. New England. Politics. Toleration. 1672-77. *993*
Williams, William. Connecticut Valley. Great Awakening. Massachusetts (Hatfield). Presbyterian Church. 1686-1741. *2240*
Wills. Attitudes. Catholic Church. Death and Dying. Quebec. 1663-1760. *3718*
—. Kentucky. Language. Religious Beliefs. 1808-53. *48*

Wills, Frank. Architecture, Gothic Revival. Episcopal Church, Protestant. South. Upjohn, Richard. 1835-60. *1809*
Wills, Washington. Civil War. Letters. Methodist Church. North Carolina (Halifax County). Slavery. 1861-65. *2171*
Wilmer, Cary Breckenridge. Baker, Ray Stannard. Civil rights. DuBois, W. E. B. Episcopal Church, Protestant. Liberalism. Negroes. Personal narratives. Whites. 1900-10. *2151*
Wilshire Boulevard Temple. Architecture. California (Los Angeles, San Francisco). Judaism (Reform). Temple Emanu-El. 1937. *4205*
—. California (Los Angeles). Church finance. Judaism (Reform). Rabbis. 1897. *4231*
—. California (Los Angeles). Judaism (Reform). Letters. Newmark, Joseph. Rabbis. 1881. *4236*
—. California (Los Angeles). Judaism (Reform). Schreiber, Emanuel. 1881-1932. *4216*
—. Cemeteries. Judaism (Reform). *4234*
Wilson, Delmer. Diaries. Maine. Shakers. 1887. *4066*
Wilson, Edward F. Church of England. Education. Indians. Methodist Church. Missions and Missionaries. Ontario (Algoma, Huron). 1868-93. *1596*
Wilson, George. Documents. Friends, Society of. Missions and Missionaries. Religious Liberty. Virginia. 1650-62. *1007*
Wilson, Joseph Ruggles. Presbyterian Church, Southern. South. 1844-1903. *3572*
Wilson, Woodrow. Civil religion. Croly, Herbert. Millenarianism. Politics. 1909-19. *1159*
Wimmer, Boniface. Benedictines. Catholic Church. Frontier and Pioneer Life. Oetgen, Jerome (review article). 1809-87. *3685*
—. Benedictines. Catholic Church. Missions and Missionaries. Vatican Council I. 1866-87. *3815*
—. Benedictines. Monasteries. 19c. 1960's-70's. *3754*
—. Letters. Missionaries. 1847-55. *1626*
Winans, William. Louisiana (New Orleans). Methodist Church. 1813-14. *3472*
Winchester, Elhanan. Great Britain. Murray, John. Universalism. Vidler, William. 1770-1825. *4080*
Winnebago Indians. Bureau of Indian Affairs. Catholic Church. Indian-White Relations. Iowa. Presbyterian Church. Schools. 1834-48. *737*
Winnipeg Archdiocese. Anglophones. Catholics. French Canadians. Langevin, Adélard. Manitoba. 1905. *3711*
Winrod, Gerald Burton. Anti-Catholicism. Anti-Semitism. Conspiracy theories. Fundamentalism. Kansas. Political Commentary. 1933-57. *2090*
—. *Defender* (periodical). Evolution. Kansas (Wichita). *Red Horse* (periodical). Science. 1925-57. *2305*
Winters, Herbert D. Historiography. Marshall, William I. Missions and Missionaries. Oregon. Whitman, Marcus. ca 1842-43. 1930. *1553*
Winthrop, John. Agnosticism. Ingersoll, Robert. Puritans. ca 1630-1890's. *54*
—. Antinomian controversy. Hutchinson, Anne. Massachusetts (Boston). Puritans. Trials. 1634-38. *3641*
—. Historiography. Mather, Cotton *(Magnalia Christi Americana).* Puritans. 1702. *1966*
—. Hooker, Thomas. Mather, Cotton. Puritans. Rhetoric. 17c. *1965*
—. New England. Puritans. Scientific thought. Winthrop, John, Jr. Winthrop, John (1714-79). 1620-1779. *2295*
Winthrop, John, Jr. New England. Puritans. Scientific thought. Winthrop, John. Winthrop, John (1714-79). 1620-1779. *2295*
Winthrop, John (1714-79). New England. Puritans. Scientific thought. Winthrop, John. Winthrop, John, Jr. 1620-1779. *2295*
—. Puritanism. Science. 1738-79. *2315*
Wisconsin *See also* North Central States.
—. Acculturation. Catholic Church. Indian-White Relations. Missionaries. Protestantism. 1830-48. *1640*
—. Amish. Education. Military. Pennsylvania. Trials. 1755-1974. *3401*
—. Anti-Catholicism. District of Columbia. Marquette, Jacques. State Politics. Statuary Hall. 1887-1904. *2101*
—. Chippewa Indians. Documents. Fullerton, Thomas. Indians. Methodist Episcopal Church. Minnesota. Missions and Missionaries. 1841-44. *1531*
—. Christianity. Country Life. Ecumenism. Progressivism. Protestant Churches. Reform. 1904-20. *2723*
—. Spiritualism. 1840-90. *4291*
Wisconsin (Columbia, Dane counties). Church and State. Diaries. Lutheran Church. Norwegian Americans. Preus, Herman A. 1851-60. *1104*
Wisconsin ex rel. Frederick Weiss et al. v. *District School Board of School District 8* (1890). Bible reading. Catholic Church. Desmond, Humphrey. Protestantism. Religion in the Public Schools. 1888-90. *571*
Wisconsin (Freistadt). Lutheran Church. Mission Festival Sunday. Missions and Missionaries. Personal narratives. Schreiber, Clara Seuel. 1900. *1630*
—. Lutheran Church. Palm Sunday. Personal narratives. Schreiber, Clara Seuel. 1898. *3338*
Wisconsin Lutheran Quarterly (periodical). Koehler, J. P. Lutheran Church. Theology. 1880's-1915. *3317*
Wisconsin (Manitowoc). Episcopal Church, Protestant. St. James Church. Unonius, Gustaf. 1848-49. *3181*
Wisconsin (Milwaukee). Asylums. Catholic Church. Hospitals. Illinois (Chicago). Schools. 19c. *3886*
—. Catholic Church. Labor Unions and Organizations. Polish Americans. Political Leadership. Progressivism. Socialism. 1900-30. *1299*
—. Catholic Church. Polish Americans. 1846-1940. *3690*
—. Immanuel Lutheran School. Lutheran Church. Secondary education. 1903-78. *785*
Wisconsin (Nashotah). Episcopal Church, Protestant. Letters. Nashotah House. Seminaries. Unonius, Gustaf. 1884. *585*
Wisconsin (Pardeeville). Anti-Catholicism. Church and state. Cox Library. Discrimination. *Koester* v. *Pardeeville* (1929). Libraries. Taxation. 1927-29. *1033*
Wisconsin (Pine Lake). Clergy. Converts. Episcopal Church, Protestant. Lutheran Church. Sweden. Unonius, Gustaf. 1841-58. *2854*
Wisconsin (Racine). Bradley, Lucas. Churches. Missouri (St. Louis). Presbyterian Church. 1840-90. *1810*
Wisconsin (Sauk City). Grueningen, Johann Jakob von. Reformed Swiss Church. Swiss Americans. 1876-1911. *2860*
Wisconsin, University of. Bascom, John. Commons, John R. Ely, Richard T. Evolution. Political theory. Social gospel. 1870-1910. *2394*
Wisconsin (Voree). Lake Michigan. Michigan (Beaver Island). Mormons. Strang, James Jesse. Utopias. 1820-56. *433*
Wisconsin (Waupaca township; Scandinavia). Clergy. Country stores. Duus, O. F. Knoph, Thomas. Ledgers. Lutheran Church. Norwegian Americans. 1853-56. *3334*
Wisconsin (Wiota). Clergy. Ecumenism. Lutheran Church (Missouri Synod, Norwegian). Munch, Johan Storm. Norway. 1827-1908. *3324*
Wise, Isaac Mayer. Colleges and Universities. Hebrew Union College. Judaism (Reform). Judaism, Reform. Ohio (Cincinnati). 1870's-1900. *613*
—. Fund raising. Hebrew Union College. Judaism (Reform). Union of American Hebrew Congregations. Western States. 1873-75. *784*
—. Hebrew Union College. Judaism, Reform. Letters. Prager, Abraham J. Rabbis. 1854-1900. *4227*
—. Hebrew Union College. Judaism (Reform). Letters. Rabbis. Stolz, Joseph. 1882-1900. *4220*
—. Hebrew Union College. Judaism (Reform). Ohio (Cincinnati). Rabbis. Seminaries. 1817-90's. *701*
—. Judaism, Reform. Theology. 19c. *4223*
Wise, John. Congregationalism. Democracy. Massachusetts. Political thought. 17c-18c. *1354*
Wise, Stephen Samuel. Charities. Ecumenism. Hungarian Americans. Judaism (Reform). Rabbis. World War II. Zionism. 1890's-1949. *4229*
—. Jesus Christ. Judaism (Orthodox, Reform). New York City. Sermons. Theology. 1925-26. *4153*
Wit and Humor. *See* Humor.
Witchcraft *See also* Folklore; Occult Sciences.
—. Aged. Folklore. Poor. West Virginia. Women. 1975. *2201*
—. Anthropology. Historiography. Massachusetts (Salem). Psychology. Puritans. 1691-92. *2187*
—. Aphrodisiacs. Charms. Folk Medicine. Philtres. -1973. *2199*
—. Bibliographies. Connecticut. Massachusetts. 17c. 1976. *2194*
—. City life. Family. Psychocultural therapy. 1968. *2197*
—. Collectors and Collecting. Folklore. Hyatt, Harry Midddleton. Illinois (Adams County). Negroes. Small, Minnie Hyatt. South. 1920-78. *2190*
—. Devil. Folklore. West Virginia. 1950-67. *2202*
—. Folk medicine. Folklore. Jones, Louis C. 1945-49. *2189*
—. Folklore. Gomez, Dolorez Amelia. Pennsylvania (Philadelphia). 1974. *2179*
—. Folklore. Kentucky, eastern. 1977. *2198*
—. Folklore. Novels. Steinbeck, John *(Winter of Our Discontent).* 1961. *2046*
—. France. New France. Trials. 17c. *2203*
—. Godfrey, John. Massachusetts. Puritans. Social Conditions. Trials. 1634-75. *2186*
—. Hallucinations. Plants. Southwest. Trances. 17c-20c. *2207*
—. Historians. Massachusetts (Salem). Racism. Tituba (Indian). 1648-1953. *2191*
—. Indians. Mexican Americans. 16c-20c. *2204*
—. Indians. Mexican Americans. Navajo Indians. Pueblo Indians. Southwest. 19c-1930's. *2214*
—. Indians. Mexican Americans. New Mexico (Bernalillo, Manzana). 1970-74. *2193*
—. Kanniff, Jane. New York (Rockland County; Clarkstown, Clarksville). 1816. *2213*
—. Massachusetts (Springfield). Parsons case. Puritans. 1650-55. *2210*
—. Mexican Americans. New Mexico (Torrance County). Superstitions. 1970's. *2184*
—. New England. Puritans. Women. ca 1630-1978. *2185*
—. Psychocultural therapy. 1968-73. *2196*
Witchcraft (review article). Boyer, Paul. Massachusetts (Salem). Nissenbaum, Stephen. Puritans. 1550-1690. 1974-76. *2200*
Witchlore. Irving, Washington. New England. 1809-24. *2008*
Withers, Frederick C. Architecture. 1840's-1901. *1793*
Witherspoon, John. Alison, Francis. American Revolution. Political philosophy. Presbyterian Church. 1750-87. *1382*
—. American Revolution. Cooke, Samuel. History Teaching. Langdon, Samuel. Mayhew, Jonathan. Sermons. West, Samuel. 1750-76. 1975. *1406*
Witt, Christopher. Astronomy. *Horologium Achaz* (scientific device). Pennsylvania Germans. Pietism. 1578-1895. *2349*
Wives. Clergy. Immigrants. Lutheran Church (Augustana Synod). Swedish Americans. 1860-1962. *3296*
Wolf Collar (shaman). Alberta. Bible. Blackfoot Indians. Indians. Missions and Missionaries. Stocken, H. W. G. Translating and Interpreting. 1870-1928. *1500*
Wolfson, Harry. Braude, William G. Judaism. Personal narratives. 1932-54. *4090*
Wolfson, Harry Austryn. Christianity. Islam. Judaism. Medieval culture. Philosophy of history. 6c-16c. 1910-74. *278*
Womanhood, sentimental. Domesticity. Industrialization. Revivals. 1830-70. *817*
Woman's Exponent (periodical). Editors and Editing. Mormons. Utah. Women. 1872-1914. *3937*
Woman's Missionary Society of the Presbyterian and United Churches. Gordon, Helen Skinner. King, Gordon J. Manitoba (Winnipeg). Personal narratives. Presbyterian Church. 1890's-1961. *3548*
Woman's Missionary Union. Baptists. Missions and Missionaries. Moon, Lottie. Week of Prayer for Foreign Missions. 1888-1979. *1747*
—. Baptists, Southern. Missions and Missionaries. 19c. *1527*
Women *See also* Divorce; Family; Feminism; Girls; Marriage; Sex Discrimination; Wives.
—. Abortion. Catholic Church. Hawaii. Methodology. 1965-74. *872*
—. Addams, Jane. Dudzik, Mary Theresa. Franciscan Sisters of Chicago. Illinois. Polish Americans. Social Work. 1860-1918. *2511*

—. Addams, Jane. Education. Friends, Society of. Hull House. Ideology. Illinois (Chicago). 1875-1930. *911*

—. Adventists. Charisma. Prophecy. White, Ellen G. 1848-1901. *2976*

—. Adventists. Clement, Lora E. Editors and Editing. *Youth's Instructor* (newspaper). 1927-52. *1987*

—. Adventists. Fullmer, Bert E. Rowen, Margaret W. Visions. 1916-29. *2979*

—. Africa, West. Missions and Missionaries. Presbyterian Church. Social change. 1850-1915. *1686*

—. Age. Birth rate. Marriage. Mormons. 1800-69. *892*

—. Aged. Folklore. Poor. West Virginia. Witchcraft. 1975. *2201*

—. Alabama. Church schools. Livingston Female Academy. Presbyterian Church. 1835-1910. *686*

—. Alabama (Mobile). China. Missions and Missionaries. Presbyterian Church. Stuart, Mary Horton. 1840's-1947. *1705*

—. Albanese, Catherine L. Beecher, Henry Ward. Civil Religion. Clark, Clifford E., Jr. Douglas, Ann. Handy, Robert T. McLoughlin, William G. Reform. Revivals (review article). 1607-1978. *6*

—. American, Sadie. Congress of Jewish Women. Jews. Solomon, Hannah G. World Parliament of Religions. World's Columbian Exposition (Chicago, 1893). 1893. *846*

—. Ames, Jessie Daniel. Association of Southern Women for the Prevention of Lynching. Lynching. Methodist Woman's Missionary Council. Racism. South. Young Women's Christian Association. 1930's. *2535*

—. Amish. Fertility. Income. Indiana. 20c. *882*

—. Anglican Communion. Manitoba (Red River). Missions and Missionaries. 1820-37. *1750*

—. Antinomian Controversy. Church and state. Hutchinson, Anne. Massachusetts. Puritans. Social Organization. Trials. 1637. *1135*

—. Antislavery sentiments. Campbell, Alexander. Civil religion. Disciples of Christ. Indians. Politics. War. 1823-55. *3108*

—. Antislavery sentiments. Christianity. Civil War. Presbyterian Church. Stowe, Harriet Beecher. ca 1850-80. *2474*

—. Archives. Saskatchewan. 1880's-1970's. *170*

—. Arizona. Christianity. Frontier and Pioneer Life. Reform. Suffrage. Temperance Movements. 1850's-1912. *837*

—. Arkansas (Pine Bluff). Burnett, Ellen. Prophecy. Storms. 1903. *74*

—. Assimilation. Indians. Navajo Indians. New Mexico (Shiprock). Sherman Institute for Indians. 1900-20. *589*

—. Attitudes. Colleges and Universities. Religiosity. Sex roles. Stereotypes. Students. 1970's. *793*

—. Attitudes. Mather, Cotton. New England. Puritans. Sermons. 1650-1800. *880*

—. Attitudes. Mormons. Social Organization. Utah. Young, Brigham. 1840's-77. *830*

—. Authors. Marshall, Catherine. Popular Culture. Presbyterian Church. Theology. 1949-78. *3546*

—. Baerg, Anna. Canada. Diaries. Immigration. Mennonites. Russian Revolution. 1917-23. *3362*

—. Baptists. Bishop, Harriet E. Minnesota (St. Paul). Reform. Social reform. 1847-83. *801*

—. Baptists. Church government. Virginia. 1765-1800. *878*

—. Baptists. Georgia (Cartersville). Moon, Lottie. Secondary Education. 1870-1903. *2985*

—. Baptists. Higher education. Tennessee (Brownsville). West Tennessee Baptist Female College. 1850-1910. *658*

—. Baptists. Imperialism. National Characteristics. Racism. Virginia. 1865-1900. *3001*

—. Baptists. McMaster Hall. McMaster, Susan Moulton Fraser. Michigan (Bay City). Ontario (Toronto). 1819-1916. *3000*

—. Baptists, Southern. 1700-1974. *887*

—. Baptists, Southern. 1860-1975. *873*

—. Baptists, Southern. Cities. Men. Religiosity. 1968. *3008*

—. Baptists, Southern. Deaconesses. 1600-1976. *831*

—. Baptists, Southern. Suffrage. 1910-20. *3082*

—. Beecher, Catharine. Church of England. Congregationalism. Johnson, Samuel (1696-1772). Reform (review article). Washington, Booker T. 1696-1901. *2847*

—. Benedictine sisters. Immigration. Missouri (Conception). Renggli, Rose (Mother Mary Beatrice). Switzerland. 1874. *3832*

—. Bible. Smith, Julia Evelina. Translating. 1840-76. *1992*

—. Bibliographies. *Minnesota History* (periodical). 1915-76. *905*

—. Bibliographies. Sermons. Vermont. 1800-1915. *909*

—. Bidamon, Emma Smith. Bidamon, Lewis C. Illinois (Nauvoo). Marriage. Mormons. 1842-80. *3931*

—. Bidamon, Emma Smith. Illinois (Nauvoo). Mormons. Property. Schisms. Smith, Joseph. Women. Young, Brigham. 1832-79. *3932*

—. Bidamon, Emma Smith. Illinois (Nauvoo). Mormons. Property. Schisms. Smith, Joseph. Women. Young, Brigham. 1832-79. *3932*

—. Biographical dictionary. Clergy. Unitarianism. Universalism. 1860-1976. *4079*

—. Bishops. Episcopal Church, Protestant. Huntington, Frederick (and family). New York. Social reform. Theology. 1869-1904. *3213*

—. Boarding Schools. Chatham Hall. Episcopal Church, Protestant. Ferguson, Anne Williams. Personal narratives. Virginia. 1940's. *628*

—. Boardinghouses. Labor. Minnesota (Minneapolis). Women's Christian Association. 1880's-1979. *2526*

—. Bogan, Louise. Catholic Church. Poetry. 1920's-70. *2059*

—. Boycotts. Consumers. Jews. Meat, kosher. New York City. Prices. Riots. 1902. *4112*

—. Bradstreet, Anne. Elegies. Massachusetts. Poetry. Puritans. 1665. *2044*

—. Bradstreet, Anne. Hutchinson, Anne. Literature. Massachusetts. Puritans. Social change. Theology. 1630's-70's. *865*

—. California-Nevada Conference. Clergy. Methodist Church. 1873-78. *3503*

—. Canada. Charities. Nurses and Nursing. Slovak Americans. Slovak Canadians. USA. Vincentian Sisters of Charity. 1902-78. *2525*

—. Canada. Christianity. Missions and Missionaries. Sex roles. 1815-99. *854*

—. Canada. McClung, Nellie. Methodist Church. Ordination. United Church of Canada. 1915-46. *852*

—. Canada. Social Reform. Young Women's Christian Association. 1870-1900. *895*

—. Cannon, Martha Hughes. Great Britain. Letters. Mormons. Polygamy. Utah (Salt Lake City). 1885-96. *4002*

—. Canon Law. Episcopal Church, Protestant. Ordination. 1966-74. *937*

—. Carroll, Anna Ella. Nativism. Probasco, Harriet. 1840's-61. *851*

—. Cartoons and Caricatures. Mormons. Stereotypes. 1830-1914. *800*

—. Catholic Church. Charities. Education. Moore, Julia. Ontario (London). Personal narratives. Sisters of St. Joseph. 1868-85. *2517*

—. Catholic Church. Church Schools. Felicians. Polish Americans. Social Work. 1855-1975. *3828*

—. Catholic Church. Clergy. Men. Religious Orders. Social classes. 1650-1762. *2614*

—. Catholic Church. Clergy. Protestant Churches. Sex discrimination. 1970's. *939*

—. Catholic Church. College of St. Teresa. Franciscan Sisters. Minnesota (Winona). Molloy, Mary Aloysius. 1903-54. *670*

—. Catholic Church. Congregation of Notre Dame (Sisters). Ontario (Kingston). Religious education. 1841-48. *596*

—. Catholic Church. Ecumenism. Episcopal Church, Protestant. Society of the Atonement. Wattson, Paul James. White, Lurana. 1870-1928. *459*

—. Catholic Church. Education. Georgia (Skidaway Island). Negroes. Orphanages. Poor Clares. 1885-87. *3806*

—. Catholic Church. Education. Indians. Missions and Missionaries. North Dakota. Pioneers. Presentation of the Blessed Virgin Mary, Sisters of the. South Dakota. 1880-96. *727*

—. Catholic Church. Family size preference. Population. Women. 1964-74. *915*

—. Catholic Church. Family size preference. Population. Women. 1964-74. *915*

—. Catholic Church. Feminism. Quebec. Religious Orders. 1640-1975. *833*

—. Catholic Church. French Canadians. Quebec. Social Organization. 1960's-70's. *2013*

—. Catholic Church. Germans, Russian. Religious Education. St. Angela's Convent. Saskatchewan (Prelate). Ursulines. 1919-34. *680*

—. Catholic Church. History. Literature. Religious Orders. 19c-1978. *868*

—. Catholic Church. International Union of Catholic Women's Leagues (congress). Italy (Rome). Quebec. Suffrage. 1922. *935*

—. Catholic Church. Massachusetts (Boston). Religious Orders. Teaching. Voluntarism. 1870-1940. *717*

—. Catholic Church. Minnesota (St. Paul). O'Brien, Alice. Philanthropy. 1914-62. *2419*

—. Catholic Church. National Catholic Welfare Conference. National Council of Catholic Women. Peace Movements. World War II. 1919-46. *2669*

—. Catholic Church. Professions. Quebec. Religious orders. Secondary education. 1908-54. *871*

—. Charities. Equality. Missions and Missionaries. Presbyterian Church. 1800-1975. *908*

—. Charities. Law. Morristown Female Charitable Society. New Jersey. Presbyterian Church. 1813-1978. *2510*

—. Chase, Josephine Streeper. Daily life. Diaries. Mormons. Utah (Centerville). 1881-94. *3957*

—. Child care. Day Nurseries. Dominicans. Quebec (Montreal). 1858-1920. *2505*

—. Childhood. Leadership. Secularism. Sex roles. 1636-1930. *881*

—. Christ Church Hospital. Episcopal Church, Protestant. Hospitals. Kearsley, John. Pennsylvania (Philadelphia). 1778-1976. *1455*

—. Christian Science. Eddy, Mary Baker. 1840's-1926. *3914*

—. Christian Science. Eddy, Mary Baker. Gottschalk, Stephen (review article). 1885-1910. *3913*

—. Christian Science. Eddy, Mary Baker. Lee, Ann. Personality. Shakers. Theology. 1736-1910. *2753*

—. Christian Science. Eddy, Mary Baker. Political power. Political Protest. 1879-99. *840*

—. Christian Science. Leadership. Shakers. Spiritualism. Theosophy. 19c. *795*

—. Christianity. Church history. 1975. *889*

—. Christianity. Divorce. National Fertility Study. 1970's. *934*

—. Christianity. Ecumenism. World Conference of Christian Youth, 1st. Young Women's Christian Association. 1939-79. *488*

—. Christianity. Grimké, Sarah. Nature. Paul, Saint. Social organization. 1c. 1830's. *921*

—. Christianity. Industrial Relations. Massachusetts (Lawrence). Scudder, Vida Dutton. Social reform. Socialism. 1912. *2374*

—. Christianity. Judaism. 17c-1978. *860*

—. Christianity. O'Hare, Kate Richards. Socialist Party. 1901-17. *2559*

—. Christianity. Sex roles. Social Change. World Conference of Christian Youth, 1st. 1939-79. *844*

—. Civil War. Diaries. Episcopal Church, Protestant. Providence. Robertson, Martha Wayles. South Carolina (Chesterfield County). 1860-66. *3191*

—. Clergy. Consultation on Church Union. Henderlite, Rachel. Personal narratives. Presbyterian Church, Southern. South. 1945-77. *804*

—. Clergy. Diaries. Lutheran Church. Muhlenberg, Henry Melchior. Pennsylvania. 1742-87. *828*

—. Clergy. Episcopal Church, Protestant. Sex Discrimination. 1973. *841*

—. Clergy. Equality. Mormons (Reorganized). Negroes. Schisms. 1860-1979. *4032*

—. Clergy. Friends, Society of. 19c. *820*

—. Clergy. Historiography. New England. Puritans. 1668-1735. *936*

—. Clergy. Methodist Protestant Church. Shaw, Anna Howard. Social Gospel Movement. Suffrage. 1880-1919. *3506*

—. Clergy. Ordination. United Brethren in Christ. 1889. *847*

—. Colleges and Universities. Curricula. Massachusetts (South Hadley). Mount Holyoke College. Science. 1839-88. *2320*

—. Colleges and Universities. Emerson, Joseph. Lyon, Mary. Mount Holyoke College. Protestantism. 1760's-1850's. *552*

—. Congregationalism. Fish, Josiah. Osborn, Sarah. Revivals. Rhode Island (Newport). 1766-67. *904*

—. Congregationalism. Friends, Society of. ca 1620-1765. *834*

—. Congress. Hayes, Rutherford B. Mormons. Polygamy. Suffrage. 1877-81. *797*
—. Connecticut (Hartford). Episcopal Church, Protestant. Evangelicalism. Literature. Sigourney, Lydia Huntley. 1800-65. *3194*
—. Councils and Synods. Delegates. Episcopal Church, Protestant (Annual Council). Kinsolving, George Herbert. Texas. Veto. 1921-70. *813*
—. Daily life. Diaries. Illinois (Nauvoo). Jacobs, Zina Diantha Huntington. Mormons. 1844-45. *3935*
—. Death and Dying. Literature. North or Northern States. Protestantism. 1830-80. *2846*
—. Diaries. Illinois (Nauvoo). Mormons. Snow, Eliza Roxey. 1842-44. *4044*
—. Diaries. Mormons. Musser, Elise Furer. Political Leadership. Social Reform. Utah. 1897-1967. *811*
—. Dickey, Sarah. Heck, Barbara. Leadership. Methodist Church. Parker, Lois Stiles. Shaw, Anna Howard. Stereotypes. Willard, Frances E. 19c. *812*
—. Dickinson, Emily. Identity. Intellectual history. Myths and Symbols. Poetry. Puritanism. Transcendentalism. 1860's. *51*
—. Dickinson, Emily. Protestantism. 1840-54. *73*
—. Discrimination, Educational. Protestantism. 1818-91. *2899*
—. Dissent. Economic conditions. Military Service. Moravian Church. North Carolina (Salem). Slavery. Social change. 1772-1860. *3516*
—. District of Columbia. Missions and Missionaries. National Statuary Hall. Pacific Northwest. Pariseau, Mother Mary Joseph. Sisters of Charity of Providence. 1856-1902. 1977. *1629*
—. Divorce. Law. Massachusetts. Puritans. Social conditions. 1639-92. *941*
—. Domesticity. Methodism. New York City. Palmer, Phoebe. ca 1825-60. *877*
—. Doub, Peter. Education. Methodist Episcopal Church. North Carolina. Slavery. 1796-1869. *3469*
—. Editors and Editing. Mormons. Utah. *Woman's Exponent* (periodical). 1872-1914. *3937*
—. Education. Ohio (Cincinnati). Sisters of Charity of St. Joseph. Social Work. 1809-1979. *2514*
—. Education. Pennsylvania (Philadelphia). Young Ladies Academy. 1780's-90's. *520*
—. Equal Rights Amendment. Ideology. 1933-75. *810*
—. Equal Rights Amendment. Political Participation. Texas. 1977. *933*
—. Equality. New England. Sex roles. Shakers. 1810-60. *821*
—. Evangelicalism. New York (Utica). Revivals. 1800-40. *922*
—. Evangelicalism. Sex roles. Sunday School Movement. 1790-1880. *807*
—. Family. Farms. Literature. Sex roles. Social Status. South. 1800-60. *816*
—. Fell, Margaret. Feminism. Friends, Society of. Great Britain (Lancashire). Pennsylvania (Philadelphia). 1670's. *928*
—. Feminism. Mormons. National Women's Conference, 1st. Utah Women's Conference. 1977. *858*
—. Feminism. Protestant churches. -1973. *891*
—. Feminism. Protestant Churches. Radicals and Radicalism. Social reform. South. 1920's. *789*
—. Feminization. Historiography. Welter, Barbara. 1820's-30's. 1970's. *920*
—. Feminization. Missions and Missionaries. Voluntary Associations. 1800-60. *942*
—. Friends, Society of. Larson, Lars. Larson, Martha. New York (Rochester). Norwegian Americans. Religious Liberty. 1807-44. *3263*
—. Friends, Society of. Maryland (Baltimore). Medicine (practice of). Surgery. Taylor, Sarah. 1823. *3264*
—. Friends, Society of. Protestantism. Sex roles. 17c-18c. *835*
—. Frontier and Pioneer Life. Heywood, Martha Spence. Intellectuals. King, Hannah Tapfield. Mormons. Snow, Eliza Roxey. Utah. 1850-70. *4045*
—. Fuller, Margaret. Philosophy. Spiritualism. Transcendentalism. 1840's. *4068*
—. Gates, Susa Young. Marriage. Mormons. Personal narratives. Utah. Young, Brigham. Young, Lucy Bigelow. 1830-1905. *3972*
—. Hadassah. Jews. National Council of Jewish Women. Professionalism. Voluntary Associations. 1890-1980. *4146*
—. Hess, Katie Charles. Mennonites. Pennsylvania. Personal narratives. 1883-1978. *3356*
—. Higher education. Methodist Church. Ontario. 19c. *3504*
—. Historiography. Mormons. Stereotypes. 19c. 1976. *796*
—. Hodge, Charles. New Jersey (Princeton). Princeton University. 1825-55. *857*
—. Holiness Movement. Inskip, John S. Inskip, Martha Jane. Methodist Church. Revivals. 1836-90. *3448*
—. Illinois (Nauvoo). Kimball, Vilate. Letters. Mormons. Murder. Smith, Joseph. 1844. *3963*
—. Immigration. Iowa. Lutheran Church. Schwartz, Auguste von. Wartburg College. 1861-77. *3320*
—. Judaism. 1920's-30's. *916*
—. Kimball, Sarah Melissa Granger. Mormons. Suffrage. Utah. 15th Ward Relief Society. 1818-98. *901*
—. Labor. Match industry. Quebec (Hull). Syndicat Catholique des Allumettières. 1919-24. *1470*
—. Labor. Occupations. Quebec (Montreal). Sex roles. 1911-41. *1471*
—. Leadership. Mormons. Poetry. Prophecy. Snow, Eliza Roxey. Utah. 1804-87. *3936*
—. League of Nations. Mormons. Prohibition. Republican Party. Roberts, Brigham Henry. Smith, Joseph Fielding. Suffrage. Utah. ca 1900. *1284*
—. Literature. Marriage. Marshall, Catherine. Presbyterian Church. Sex roles. 1950's. *806*
—. Louisiana (New Orleans). Music (jazz). Negroes. Voodoo. ca 19c. *2181*
—. McLean, Eleanor. McLean, Hector. Mormons. Murder. Pratt, Parley P. 1841-57. *4025*
—. Methodist Church (Women's Division of Christian Service). 1880's-1975. *930*
—. Methodist Protestant Church. 19c. *903*
—. Missionaries. Nova Scotia. Raymond, Eliza Ruggles. Sierra Leone (Sherbro Island). Slaves. 1839-50. *1692*
—. Missions and Missionaries. 19c. *1721*
—. Missions and Missionaries. Organizations. Protestant Churches. 1870's-90's. *894*
—. Missions and Missionaries. Protestant Churches. 19c. *943*
—. Morality. Protestantism. Sex. 1790-1850. *827*
—. Mormons. Oneida Community. Sex roles. Shakers. Utopias. ca 1825-90. *842*
—. Mormons. Silk industry. Utah. 1855-1905. *328*
—. Mormons. Snow, Eliza Roxey. 1830-90. *900*
—. Mormons. Statehood. Suffrage. Utah. 1867-96. *798*
—. Mormons. Suffrage. Utah. 1895. *944*
—. Nation, Carry Amelia. Prohibition. Temperance Movements. 1890's-1911. *2576*
—. New England. Novels. Presbyterian Church. Salvation. Stowe, Harriet Beecher. Theology. 1845-85. *2038*
—. New England. Puritans. Sermons. Sex roles. Theology. 1690-1730. *883*
—. New England. Puritans. Witchcraft. ca 1630-1978. *2185*
—. New England. Revivals. Textile industry. ca 1790-1840. *2228*
—. New Jersey (Newark). Presbyterian Church. See, Isaac M. Sermons. 1876. *805*
—. New York. Noyes, John Humphrey. Oneida Community. Sex. Social Status. 1848-79. *863*
—. Ordination. Presbyterian Church (Committee of Four). 1926-30. *809*
—. Ordination. Protestantism. Social change. World Council of Churches. 1945-75. *879*
—. Poetry. Wheatley, Phillis. 1773. *2031*
—. Political Participation. Protestants. Racism. Sexism. Whites. 1974-75. *907*
—. Presbyterian Church. 1764-1974. *3582*
—. Presbyterian Church. 1920's. *849*
—. Presbyterian Church. Sermons. Sunday, Billy. Virtue. Working class. 1915. *890*
—. Professionalism. Social mobility. Spiritualists. 19c. *4294*
—. Sociology. 1950's-70's. *902*
—. Speeches, Addresses, etc. Wright, Frances. 1828-30. *4303*
Women's American Baptist Home Missionary Society. Baptists, American. Crawford, Isabel. Indians. Kiowa Indians. Missions and Missionaries. Oklahoma (Wichita Mountains). 1893-1961. *1590*
Women's Christian Association. Boardinghouses. Labor. Minnesota (Minneapolis). Women. 1880's-1979. *2526*
Women's Christian Temperance Union. Alaska. Prohibition. 1842-1917. *2596*
—. Baptists. Methodist Church. Ninth Street Baptist Church. Ohio (Cincinnati). Political protest. Temperance Movements. Wesley Chapel. 1874. *2582*
—. Colorado (Boulder). Feminism. Social reform. Temperance Movements. 1881-1967. *2741*
—. Constitutional Amendments, State. Ohio. Prohibition. 1874-85. *2597*
—. Michigan (Adrian). Temperance Movements. 1873-74. *2578*
—. Prohibition. Willard, Frances E. 1878-98. *2595*
—. Temperance movements. Willard, Frances E. 19c-1920. *2589*
Women's Foreign Missionary Society. Methodist Episcopal Church. Missions and Missionaries. 1869-1900. *862*
Women's liberation. Bennett, Anne M. Bennett, John C. Minorities. Theology. 1974. *799*
Women's Liberation Movement. -1973. *931*
—. Abortion. Catholic Church. -1973. *898*
—. Ethics. Theology. 1973. *838*
—. Leadership. Manson Family. Millerites. Nazism. Social Organization. 19c-20c. *2964*
Women's Missionary Society. Mennonites. Missions and Missionaries. 1900-30. *866*
Women's Protective Immigration Society. Conservatism. Protestants. Quebec (Montreal). Social Reform. 1882-1917. *919*
Wood *See also* Wood Carving.
—. Adventists. Engraving. Michigan (Battle Creek). Smith, Uriah. 1852-70's. *1889*
Wood Carving. Altarpieces. Christenson, Lars. Folk art. Lutheran Church. Minnesota (Benson). Norwegian Americans. 1887-1904. *1874*
—. Catholic Church. New Mexico (Albuquerque). Penitentes. Roybal, Max. Santos, statues. 20c. *1901*
Wood, James F. Catholic Church. Confederate Army. Duke, Basil W. Fort Delaware. Prisoners of War. 1864. *3844*
Wood, Samuel. Church of England. Clergy. Education. Missions and Missionaries. Quebec (Three Rivers). 1822-68. *3202*
Woodbey, George Washington. Baptists. Negroes. Protestantism. Socialism. 1902-15. *2563*
Woodhull, Victoria Claflin. Beecher, Henry Ward. Feminism. New York City. Radicals and Radicalism. Sex. Social Reform. Spiritualism. Vanderbilt, Cornelius. 1868-90's. *2386*
Woodland Female College. Baptists. Colleges and Universities. Georgia (Cedartown). 1851-87. *634*
Woodruff, Emma Smith. Exiles. Letters. Mormons. Polygamy. Utah. Woodruff, Wilford. 1885. *1050*
Woodruff Manifesto. Church and state. Cowley, Matthias F. Mormons. Polygamy. Smoot, Reed. Taylor, John W. Theology. 1890-1911. *1060*
Woodruff, Wilford. Diaries. Mormons. 1830-1906. *3923*
—. Exiles. Letters. Mormons. Polygamy. Utah. Woodruff, Emma Smith. 1885. *1050*
—. Historians. Letters. Mormons. Schisms. Wight, Lyman. 1857-58. *4049*
Woods, James. California (Stockton). Clergy. Pioneers. Presbyterian Church. 1850-54. *3526*
Woods, Robert A. Catholic Church. Evangelism. Massachusetts (Boston). Protestantism. Settlement houses. South End House. 1891-1910. *2438*
Woolman, John. Antislavery Sentiments. British North America. Friends, Society of. Social problems. 1720-72. *2371*
—. Attitudes. Benezet, Anthony. Friends, Society of. Wealth. 1740-83. *358*
Worcester, Samuel A. American Board of Commissioners for Foreign Missions. Cherokee Indians. Georgia. Indian-White Relations. Law Enforcement. Missions and Missionaries. Removals, forced. 1831. *1667*
—. Butler, Elizur. Cherokee Indians. Indian-White Relations. Marshall, John. Missions and Missionaries. Nullification crisis. *Worcester* v. *Georgia* (US, 1832). 1828-33. *1583*

Worcester v. *Georgia* (US, 1832). Butler, Elizur. Cherokee Indians. Indian-White Relations. Marshall, John. Missions and Missionaries. Nullification crisis. Worcester, Samuel A. 1828-33. *1583*
Words. *See* Language; Lexicology.
Work ethic. Artisans. Identity. Methodism. Morality. Pennsylvania (Philadelphia). Social customs. Working Class. 1820-50. *3479*
Workers. *See* Labor; Working Class.
Working Class *See also* Labor; Peasants; Social Classes.
—. All Saints Church. Church of England. Ontario (Kingston). Theology. 1867-1906. *3173*
—. Artisans. Identity. Methodism. Morality. Pennsylvania (Philadelphia). Social customs. Work ethic. 1820-50. *3479*
—. Attitudes. Ethnic groups. Political power. 1974. *2612*
—. Betten, Neil. Catholic Church (review article). Dolan, Jay P. 1830-1978. *3698*
—. Capitalism. Catholic Church. Clergy. Elites. Pulp mills. Quebec (Chicoutimi). 1896-1930. *2601*
—. Catholic Church. Charismatic Movement. Italian Americans. Jesu, Father. Pennsylvania (Philadelphia). 1920's-30's. *1576*
—. Catholic Church. Cotton mills. French Canadians. Immigration. Massachusetts (Springfield). Population. 1870. *3710*
—. Catholic Church. École Sociale Populaire. Propaganda. Quebec (Montreal). Syndicalism. 1911-49. *1473*
—. Catholic Church. Eudists. Industrialization. Quebec (Chicoutimi Basin). 1903-30. *1466*
—. Catholic Church. French Canadians. Immigration. Massachusetts (Holyoke). Proulx, Nicholas. 1850-1900. *3691*
—. Ethnic groups. Prohibitionists. Saloons. Values. 1890-1920. *2588*
—. Great Britain. Missions and Missionaries. Mormons. 1840-41. *1672*
—. Massachusetts (Webster). Methodism. Protestant Ethic. Textile industry. 1820's-50's. *372*
—. Negroes. Sectarianism. Whites. 1969. *94*
—. Presbyterian Church. Sermons. Sunday, Billy. Virtue. Women. 1915. *890*
Working conditions. Catholic Church. Clergy. Quebec. 1968-77. *3861*
World Alliance of Reformed Churches. Ecumenism. Evangelical and Reformed Church. Presbyterian Church. Richards, George Warren. 1900-55. *481*
—. Ecumenism. Pennsylvania (Philadelphia). Presbyterian Church, Cumberland. 1870-80. *455*
—. Ecumenism. Presbyterian Church, Cumberland. Theology. 1880-84. *470*
—. Ecumenism. Reformed churches. 1957-62. *472*
—. McCosh, James. Philosophy. Protestantism. 1850-75. *453*
World Christian Fundamental Association. Baptists. Fundamentalism. Graham, Billy. Minnesota (Minneapolis). Riley, William Bell. ca 1900-65. *3068*
World Conference of Christian Youth, 1st. Africa. Christianity. Independence movements. Missions and Missionaries. 1939-74. *1751*
—. Canadian Council of Churches. Ecumenism. Youth. 1939-79. *464*
—. Christianity. Ecumenism. Women. Young Women's Christian Association. 1939-79. *488*
—. Christianity. Sex roles. Social Change. Women. 1939-79. *844*
—. Ecumenism. Negroes. Protestantism. Reform. Youth. 1939-79. *2884*
—. International cooperation. Methodism. Pendell, Thomas Roy. Personal narratives. USSR. 1939-79. *1402*
World Council of Churches. Baptists. Canadian Council of Churches. Ecumenism. 1907-79. *462*
—. Cavert, Samuel McCrea. Christianity. Ecumenism. Germany, West. 1945-46. *486*
—. Ordination. Protestantism. Social change. Women. 1945-75. *879*
World Order Movement. Anti-Communist Movements. Dulles, John Foster. Ecumenism. Morality. Oxford Conference (1937). Presbyterian Church. Protestantism. 1937-48. *1375*
World Parliament of Religions. American, Sadie. Congress of Jewish Women. Jews. Solomon, Hannah G. Women. World's Columbian Exposition (Chicago, 1893). 1893. *846*
World Temperance Convention. Beecher, Lyman. Evangelical Alliance. Great Britain. Presbyterian Church. Temperance Movements. 1846. *3563*
World War I *See also* battles and campaigns by name.
—. Anti-Catholicism. Conscription, Military. Jesuits. Novitiate of St. Stanislaus. Ontario (Guelph). Protestantism. 1918-19. *2657*
—. Attitudes. Baptists, Southern. 1918-20. *2699*
—. Bethel College. Conscientious Objectors. Mennonites. Oral history. 1917-18. 1974. *262*
—. Camp Funston. Conscientious objectors. Diaries. Hutterites. Kansas. Waldner, Jakob. 1917-18. *2690*
—. Catholic Church. Great Britain. Propaganda. 1918. *1240*
—. *Christliche Apologete* (periodical). German Americans. Methodists. Neutrality. 1914-18. *3458*
—. Commission on Training Camp Activities. Jewish Welfare Board. Knights of Columbus. Leisure. Morality. Social Reform. War Department. Young Men's Christian Association. Young Women's Christian Association. 1917-18. *2379*
—. Conscientious objectors. Mennonites. Oral History. 1917-20. *2660*
—. Diaries. Federal government. Malone, R. J. Mennonites. Military Intelligence. Surveillance. 1914-19. *2697*
—. Editors and Editing. Germany. Mennonites. Miller, Samuel H. Trials. 1917-18. *2658*
—. German Americans. Mennonites. Military conscription. Pacifism. Public opinion. 1914-18. *2696*
—. German Evangelical Synod of North America. Niebuhr, Reinhold. Pacifism. Patriotism. Theology. 1915-18. *2639*
—. Judaism (Reform). Kerman, Julius C. Palestine. Personal narratives. Rabbis. 1913-71. *4214*
—. Kansas. Liberty bonds. Mennonites. Pacifism. Vigilantism. 1918. *2659*
—. Kansas. Mennonites. War bond drives. 1917-18. *2647*
—. Kansas. Pacifism. Patriotism. Sects, Religious. 1917-18. *2677*
—. Knights of Columbus. Military. Negroes. Salvation Army. Young Men's Christian Association. 1917-18. *2720*
—. Patriotism. Revivals. Sunday, Billy. 1917-18. *2676*
World War I (antecedents). Adventists. Bible. Prophecy. 1912-18. *2664*
World War II *See also* battles and campaigns by name.
—. Adventist Medical Cadet Corps. Armies. Dick, Everett N. Korean War. Personal narratives. 1934-53. *2644*
—. Anti-Semitism. Christians. Toynbee, Arnold. ca 1940-1975. *2130*
—. Attitudes. Baptists, Southern. Kelsey, George (review article). Kentucky. 1941-45. 1973. *2681*
—. Baptists. Discrimination. Japanese Americans. Resettlement. 1890-1970. *2547*
—. Canada. China. Hurford, Grace Gibberd. Missions and Missionaries. Personal narratives. Teaching. 1928-45. *1711*
—. Canada. Conference of Historic Peace Churches. Conscientious objectors. Mennonites. ca 1914-45. *2671*
—. Canada. Fairbairn, R. Edis. Pacifism. United Church of Canada. 1939. *2688*
—. Catholic Church. Great Britain. Isolationism. Nicoll, John R. A. Roosevelt, Franklin D. (administration). 1943. *1241*
—. Catholic Church. National Catholic Welfare Conference. National Council of Catholic Women. Peace Movements. Women. 1919-46. *2669*
—. Catholics. Conscientious Objectors. 1941-45. *2672*
—. Charities. Ecumenism. Hungarian Americans. Judaism (Reform). Rabbis. Wise, Stephen Samuel. Zionism. 1890's-1949. *4229*
—. Christians. Genocide. Jews. Theology. 1945-74. *101*
—. Civilian service. Conscription, military. Mennonites. 1930's-45. *2661*
—. Conscientious Objectors. Courts. Flag salute. Jehovah's Witnesses. 1930's-40's. *2655*
—. Diaries. Jesuits. McCormick, Vincent A. Vatican. 1942-45. *3755*
—. Diplomacy. Pius XII, Pope. Taylor, Myron C. Vatican. 1940-50. *1025*
—. Ecumenism. Europe. Protestant Churches. 1900-45. *465*
—. Jewish Peace Fellowship. Pacifism. 1943. *2706*
World War II (antecedents). Anglophiles. Catholic Church. Wilberforce, Robert. 1940. *1239*
World's Columbian Exposition (Chicago, 1893). Adventists. Illinois. Jones, Alonzo Trevier. Religious liberty. Sabbath. 1893. *2280*
—. American, Sadie. Congress of Jewish Women. Jews. Solomon, Hannah G. Women. World Parliament of Religions. 1893. *846*
Worldwide Church of God. California. Church and state. Church Finance. State Government. 1970's. *1139*
Wormeley Manor. Holy Cross Abbey. Trappists. Virginia (Shenandoah Valley). 1744-1980. *3890*
Worship. Arkansas, northeast. Baptists. Folk religion. Pentecostals. Theology. 1972-78. *2836*
—. Artifacts. Ceramics. Glass. Moravian Church. 18c-19c. *1879*
—. Bradstreet, Anne. Clap, Roger. Devotions. New England. Puritans. Sewall, Samuel. Shepard, Thomas. 17c. *3627*
—. Catholic Church. District of Columbia. Jews. Judaism. Protestant churches. Psychological well-being. Religiosity. 1970's. *130*
—. *Directory of Worship*. Presbyterian Church. 1788-1979. *3583*
Worth, William O. Adventists. Automobile Industry and Trade. North Central States. 1890-1913. *361*
Wrangel, Carl Magnus. Assimilation. Lutheran Church. Muhlenberg, Henry Melchior. Pennsylvania. Politics. Swedish Americans. 1749-69. *1283*
Wrede, Friedrich Wilhelm von. Harmony Society. Pennsylvania (Economy). 1842. *401*
Wren, Christoper. Churches. Harrison, Peter. Rhode Island (Newport). Touro Synagogue. 1670-1775. *1819*
Wright, Elizur (and family). Congregationalism. Connecticut. Free Thinkers. Frontier and Pioneer Life. Ingersoll, Robert. Ohio (Western Reserve). Yale University. 1762-1870. *56*
Wright, Elizur, Jr. American Tract Society. Evangelicalism. Missions and Missionaries. Pennsylvania, western. 1828-29. *1536*
Wright, Frances. Owen, Robert Dale. Social Organization. Utopias. 1826-32. *411*
—. Speeches, Addresses, etc. Women. 1828-30. *4303*
Wright, Henry Clarke. Evangelism. Reform. 1820-60. *2444*
Wright, Milton. Clergy. United Brethren in Christ. 1828-1917. *3665*
Wulff, O. H. Immanuel Lutheran School. Lutheran Church (Missouri Synod). Personal narratives. Religious education. 1908-75. *781*
Wyandot Indians. Brébeuf, Jean de. Catholic Church. Indian-White Relations. Ledesme, R. P. *(Doctrine Chrestienne)*. New France. Translating and Interpreting. 16c-17c. *1639*
—. Indians. Kansas. Methodism. Ohio. Removal policy. 1816-60. *1598*
Wyly, Samuel. Friends, Society of. Irish Americans. Milhouse, Robert. South Carolina (Camden). 1751-93. *3265*
Wyneken, Frederick G. Clergy. Emanuel Lutheran Church. Lutheran Church. New York City (Queens). Personal narratives. 1887-1907. *3348*
Wyoming *See also* Western States.
—. Crow Indians. Diaries. Doederlein, Paul Ferdinand. Indians. Lutheran Church. Missions and Missionaries. 1859-60. *1589*
Wyoming (Cheyenne). Congregationalism. Missions and Missionaries. Nationalism. Social Gospel. Strong, Josiah. 1871-1916. *3134*
Wyoming (Elk Basin). Clergy. Labor. Lynd, Robert S. Oil Industry and Trade. Presbyterian Church. 1921. *3562*

X

Xavier University. Catholic Church. Ohio (Cincinnati). 1831-61. *708*

Y

Yale University. Archives. Congregationalism. Manuscripts. Stiles, Ezra. 1748-1975. *3142*
—. Brown University. Colleges and Universities. Harvard University. Libraries. Princeton University. 18c. *672*
—. Catholic Church. Democracy. Manuscripts. Sermons. Tocqueville, Alexis de. 1831-40. *1990*
—. Church and State. College of William and Mary. Harvard University. Puritans. 1636-1700. *650*
—. Church and State. Colleges and Universities (review article). Columbia University. Dartmouth College. Harvard University. Johnson, Samuel (1696-1772). 1696-1970. 1972-74. *524*
—. Church of England. Congregationalism. Connecticut. Great Britain. Johnson, Samuel (1696-1772). Ordination. 1722-23. *2843*
—. Church of England. Congregationalism. Connecticut (New Haven). Conversion. Johnson, Samuel (1696-1772). Theology. 1710-22. *3177*
—. Church of England. Congregationalism. Harvard University. ca 1722-90. *660*
—. Collectors and Collecting. Rosenbloom, Charles J. 1918-75. *280*
—. Colleges and Universities. Congregationalism. Dwight, Timothy. Human Relations. Stiles, Ezra. 1778-95. *706*
—. Congregationalism. Connecticut. Free Thinkers. Frontier and Pioneer Life. Ingersoll, Robert. Ohio (Western Reserve). Wright, Elizur (and family). 1762-1870. *56*
Yale University Library (Bingham Family Papers). Bingham Family. Congregationalism. Hawaii. Micronesia. Missions and Missionaries. 1815-1967. *1714*
Yale University Library (Kohut Collection). Book Collecting. Judaism. Kohut, George Alexander. 1901-33. *179*
Yankton Reservation (Marty Mission). Catholic Church. Eisenmann, Sylvester. Sioux Indians. South Dakota. 1918-49. *3900*
Yanunali, Pedro (chief). California. Chumash Indians. Indians. Marriage. Mission Santa Barbara. Social Organization. 1787-1806. *940*
Yeshiva College. Fund raising. Jewish Theological Seminary. Judaism (Orthodox). Mergers. New York City. Seminaries. 1925-28. *736*
Yeshivot (schools). Judaism (Orthodox). Religious Education. 1896-1979. *648*
Yinger, J. Milton. Attitudes. Daily life. Sociology of religion. 1946-77. *166*
Yom Kippur. California (San Francisco). Franklin, Lewis Abraham. Judaism. Rabbis. Sermons. 1850. *4100*
Yorke, Peter C. California (San Francisco). Catholic Church. City Politics. Clergy. Irish Americans. Progressivism. 1900's. *3889*
—. California (San Francisco). Catholic Church. Clergy. Editors and Editing. Ethnicity. Irish Americans. ca 1885-1925. *3887*
—. California, University of (Regents). Catholic Church. Clergy. Irish Americans. Political attitudes. 1900-12. *560*
Young, Amelia Folsom. Dwellings. Mormons. Utah (Salt Lake City). Young, Brigham. 1863-1926. *1785*
Young, Brigham. Anti-Bigamy Act (US, 1862). Mormons. Wealth. 1847-77. *341*
—. Appleby, William. Calligraphy. Mormons. Simmons, Joseph M. 1851-53. *1895*
—. Attitudes. Mormons. Social Organization. Utah. Women. 1840's-77. *830*
—. Bidamon, Emma Smith. Illinois (Nauvoo). Mormons. Property. Schisms. Smith, Joseph. Women. Women. 1832-79. *3932*
—. Clergy. Mormons. Negroes. 1843-52. *3962*
—. Congregationalism. Family. Methodism. Mormons. New England. New York, western. 18c-1830's. *2840*
—. Diaries. Illinois (Nauvoo). Laub, George. Mormons. Smith, Joseph. 1845-46. *3961*
—. Dwellings. Jacobsen, Florence S. Mormons. Personal narratives. Restorations. Utah (St. George). 19c. 1970's. *1789*
—. Dwellings. Mormons. Utah (Salt Lake City). Young, Amelia Folsom. 1863-1926. *1785*
—. Family. Illinois (Nauvoo). Mormons. New York. 1824-45. *861*
—. Folklore. Mormons. Settlement. Utah (Great Salt Lake valley). 1842-1970's. *4023*
—. Friendship. Kimball, Heber C. Mormons. Utah. 1829-68. *3996*
—. Gates, Susa Young. Marriage. Mormons. Personal narratives. Utah. Women. Young, Lucy Bigelow. 1830-1905. *3972*
—. Great Britain. Letters. Mormons. Richards, Willard. 1840. *1754*
—. Great Plains. Indian-White Relations. Mormons. New York, western. Utah. 1835-51. *3948*
—. Heresy. Mormons. Pratt, Orson. Revelation. 1853-68. *3938*
—. Historiography. Manuscripts. Mormons. Research. 19c-1978. *192*
—. Historiography. Mormons. 1801-77. 1977. *4015*
—. Iowa (Lee County). Mormons. Settlement. 1838-46. *3998*
—. Leadership. Mormons. Utah. 1801-77. *1206*
—. Leadership. Mormons. Utah. 1840's-77. *3960*
—. Medicine, practice of. Mormons. ca 1840-75. *1463*
—. Mormons. 1832-75. *3992*
—. Mormons. Morris, Joseph. Schisms. Utah (Weber River). War. 1861-62. *3926*
—. Mormons. Nevada. Smith, Joseph. Utah. Voting and Voting Behavior. 1835-50's. *1251*
—. Mormons. Pioneer life. Travel. Utah. 1850-77. *3987*
—. Mormons. Public Opinion. Railroads. Train, George Francis. Utah. 1860's-70's. *3939*
—. Mormons. Smith, Joseph. Succession. 1834-44. *4027*
—. Mormons. Stewart, Levi. United Order. Utah (Kanab). Young, John R. 1874-84. *4029*
Young, Brigham, Jr. Mormons. Pacifism. Spanish-American War. ca 1840-98. *2682*
Young, John. Clergy. Methodist Church. North Carolina. Personal narratives. 1747-1837. *3507*
Young, John R. Mormons. Stewart, Levi. United Order. Utah (Kanab). Young, Brigham. 1874-84. *4029*
Young, John W. Economic Conditions. Mormons. Polygamy. Railroads. Salt Lake and Fort Douglas Railroad. Statehood. Utah. 1883-1924. *3993*
—. Finance. Mormons. Railroads. Tourism. Utah. 1867-91. *332*
Young, Kimball. Converts. Mormons. Scandinavian Americans. 1893-1972. *3979*
Young Ladies Academy. Education. Pennsylvania (Philadelphia). Women. 1780's-90's. *520*
Young, Lucy Bigelow. Gates, Susa Young. Marriage. Mormons. Personal narratives. Utah. Women. Young, Brigham. 1830-1905. *3972*
Young Men's Christian Association. Adolescence. Boys. Canada. Protestantism. USA. 1870-1920. *2414*
—. Bryan, William Jennings. Fund raising. Lectures. Prairie Provinces. Presbyterian Church. 1909. *2446*
—. Commission on Training Camp Activities. Jewish Welfare Board. Knights of Columbus. Leisure. Morality. Social Reform. War Department. World War I. Young Women's Christian Association. 1917-18. *2379*
—. Great Britain (London). Libraries. Pool, Reuben B. 1844-1974. *2887*
—. Knights of Columbus. Military. Negroes. Salvation Army. World War I. 1917-18. *2720*
Young, Rosa J. Alabama. Bakke, Niles J. Lutheran Church. South. 1839-1965. *3299*
Young University. Church Schools. Colleges and Universities. Mormons. Utah (Salt Lake City). 1876-94. *734*
Young Women's Christian Association. Ames, Jessie Daniel. Association of Southern Women for the Prevention of Lynching. Lynching. Methodist Woman's Missionary Council. Racism. South. Women. 1930's. *2535*
—. Canada. Social Reform. Women. 1870-1900. *895*
—. Christianity. Ecumenism. Women. World Conference of Christian Youth, 1st. 1939-79. *488*
—. Commission on Training Camp Activities. Jewish Welfare Board. Knights of Columbus. Leisure. Morality. Social Reform. War Department. World War I. Young Men's Christian Association. 1917-18. *2379*
Youngs, J. William T., Jr. Burg, B. R. Clergy (review article). Congregationalism. Mather, Richard. New England. ca 1700-50. 1976. *3124*
Youth *See also* Adolescence; Children; Youth Movements.
—. Attitudes. War. 1975. *2666*
—. California, northern. Morality. Mormons. Sex. Utah (Salt Lake City). 1967-69. *885*
—. Calvinism. Great Awakening. New Left. New Lights. 1740's. 1960's. *2265*
—. Canadian Council of Churches. Ecumenism. World Conference of Christian Youth, 1st. 1939-79. *464*
—. Catholic Church. Fiction, juvenile. Finn, Francis J. 1889-1928. *2051*
—. Catholic Church. Religious Education. Saskatchewan. 1870-1978. *715*
—. Congregationalism. Edwards, Jonathan. Great Awakening. Intellectuals. Massachusetts (Northampton, Stockbridge). Theology. ca 1730-1880. *3150*
—. Converts. Divine Light Mission. Hare Krsna Movement. 1960's-70's. *4284*
—. Counter Culture. 1960's. *4242*
—. Country Life. Iowa. Langland, Joseph. Lutheran Church. Personal narratives. Poetry. 1917-30's. 1977. *2027*
—. Cults. 1960's-70's. *4248*
—. Cults. Sects, religious. Sociologists. 1960's-70's. *4256*
—. Ecumenism. Negroes. Protestantism. Reform. World Conference of Christian Youth, 1st. 1939-79. *2884*
—. Education (review article). Germany. Greven, Philip. Protestantism. Strauss, Gerald. 16c-19c. *850*
—. Hymnals. Lutheran Church (Hauge's Synod, Norwegian Synod). Lutheran Church in America, Norwegian. Norwegian Americans. 1878-1916. *1915*
—. Japan. Mysticism. 1976. *4282*
—. Jews. Political Protest. Vietnam War. 1960's. *2694*
Youth movements. Catholicism. French Canadians. Lévesque, Georges-Henri. Nationalism. Personal narratives. Quebec. 1930's. *3790*
—. Christianity. Eastern religions. Social Organizations. 1968-74. *141*
—. Counter culture. Fundamentalism. Jesus People. 1960's. *2719*
—. Divine Light Mission. Maharaj Ji. 1970's. *4281*
—. Jewish Student Movement. Massachusetts (Boston). Radicals and Radicalism. Social Change. 1960-75. *2433*
Youth's Instructor (newspaper). Adventists. Clement, Lora E. Editors and Editing. Women. 1927-52. *1987*
Yukon River, lower. Alaska. Catholic Church. Holy Cross Mission. Indians. Jesuits. Missions and Missionaries. Sisters of St. Ann. 1887-1956. *1615*
Yukon Territory *See also* Northwest Territories.
—. Church of England. Indians. McDonald, Robert. Missions and Missionaries. Northwest Territories. 1850's-1913. *1604*
—. Clergy. Gold Mines and Mining. Klondike Stampede. Lippy, Thomas S. Methodist Church. Randall, Edwin M. Transportation. 1896-99. *3492*
—. Gold Rushes. Presbyterian Church. 1897-1910. *3571*
Yuman Indians. California (San Diego). Franciscans. Jayme, Luís (death). Mission San Diego de Alcalá. 1775. *1657*

Z

Zebris, Joseph. Assimilation. Catholic Church. Connecticut (Waterbury). Lithuanian Americans. *Rytas* (newspaper). 1896-98. *3901*
Ziegler, Eustace Paul. Alaska. Art. Episcopal Church, Protestant. Missions and Missionaries. 1900-69. *1515*
Zimmer, Anne Y. (review article). Boucher, Jonathan. Church of England. Great Britain. Loyalists. Maryland. 1770's-90's. *1358*
Zinzendorf, Nikolaus. Ecumenism. Great Awakening. Moravian Church. Presbyterian Church. Tennent, Gilbert. Theology. 1740-41. *2226*
Zion Reformed Church. Blumer, Abraham. Pennsylvania (Allentown). Reformed German Church. Swiss Americans. 1771-1822. *3285*
Zionism *See also* Jews.

—. Academic Freedom. Hebrew Union College. Judaism, Reform. Kohler, Kaufmann. Ohio (Cincinnati). 1903-07. *724*
—. American Christian Palestine Committee. Great Britain. Lobbying. Palestine. 1940's. *1316*
—. Attitudes. Catholic Church. Israel. 1945-48. *963*
—. Attitudes. Ethnicity. Israel. Jews. Northeastern or North Atlantic States. Students. 1973-76. *4155*
—. Attitudes. Fundamentalism. Gaebelein, Arno C. *Our Hope* (periodical). Stroeter, Ernst F. 1894-97. *80*
—. Berger, Elmer. Judaism (Reform). Personal Narratives. Rabbis. ca 1945-75. *4202*
—. Calish, Edward Nathan. Judaism, Reform. Virginia (Richmond). Zionism. 1891-1945. *4203*
—. Charities. Ecumenism. Hungarian Americans. Judaism (Reform). Rabbis. Wise, Stephen Samuel. World War II. 1890's-1949. *4229*
—. Fundamentalism. Gaebelein, Arno C. Methodist Episcopal Church. Missions and Missionaries. 1893-1945. *1613*
—. Judaism, Reform. Nazism. 1917-41. *4215*
Zionism (review article). Foreign Policy. Israel. Protestantism. 1945-48. *2944*
Zubek, Theodoric. Catholic Church. Clergy. Czechoslovakia. Personal narratives. Refugees. Social Change. 1950-78. *3902*
Zubly, John Joachim. American Revolution. Georgia (Savannah). Patriotism. Presbyterian Church. 1766-81. *985*
—. Clergy. Georgia (Savannah). Presbyterian Church. Swiss Americans. 1724-58. *3565*
—. Loyalists. Presbyterian Church. 1770-81. *1400*
Zug family. Amish. Genealogy. Pennsylvania. 1718-1886. *3441*
Zulus. American Board of Commissioners for Foreign Missions. Missions and Missionaries. Protestant Churches. Social customs. South Africa. 1835-60's. *1695*
—. Boers. Champion, George. Missions and Missionaries. South Africa (Ginani). 1836-41. *1719*
Zurcher, George. Catholic Church. Prohibition. Social reform. 1884-1920's. *2579*
Zwerin, Kenneth C. Hawaii. Judaism. Personal narratives. 1935. *4158*

AUTHOR INDEX

A

Abbey, Sue Wilson 2094
Abbott, Kenneth A. 3561
Abernathy, Mollie C. 789
Abler, Thomas S. 1202
Abrahams, Edward 3919
Abu-Ghazaleh, Adnan 1670
Achenbaum, W. Andrew 284
Adamec, Joseph V. 3671
Adams, David Wallace 2711
Adams, Eleanor B. 1480
Adams, William C. 504
Adasiak, Allan 325
Adler, Douglas D. 3922
Admiraal, C. A. 1332
Agonito, Joseph 326 496 3672
Aguirre, B. E. 3920
Ahlstrom, Sydney E. 1 47 950 1145
Ahluwalia, Harsharan Singh 3597
Ainsley, W. Frank 2813
Akers, Charles W. 951 1146 1333 2454
Akpan, M. B. 1671
Albanese, Catherine L. 90 1147 1148 1962 2712
Albritton, Sherodd 1906
Alderfer, Owen H. 1334
Aleshire, Daniel 2141
Alexander, Jon A. T. 2630
Alexander, Thomas G. 3923
Allaire, Georges 505
Allard, Joseph 1839
Allen, H. David 3810
Allen, James B. 996 1672 3924 3925
Allen, Jeffrey Brooke 2455
Allen, Richard 3444
Allis, Frederick S., Jr. 584
Allison, C. FitzSimons 3167
Almaráz, Félix D., Jr. 169 3673
Almeida, Deidre 1481
Alpert, David B. 4087
Alston, Jon P. 790 888 1315 2713 3920
Alter, James P. 1673
Altschuler, Glenn C. 2288 2351
Alvarez, David J. 1203
Amero, Richard W. 2714
Ames, John T. 437
Ames, Michael 1482
Amoss, Pamela 2715
Anchak, G. Ronald 1674
Andelson, Robert V. 2557
Anderson, Ann Leger 170
Anderson, Avis R. 3295
Anderson, C. LeRoy 3926 3927
Anderson, Gary Clayton 1483
Anderson, Gillian B. 1907 3113
Anderson, Godfrey T. 2960
Anderson, Grant K. 1484
Anderson, Harry H. 585
Anderson, Paul L. 1757
Anderson, Philip J. 997 1335
Anderson, Richard Lloyd 3928
Anderson, Walter 1840
Anderson-Green, Paula Hathaway 2178
Andresen, Grant W. 285
Andrew, John 586
Andrews, Edward Deming 4064
Andrews, Faith 4064
Andrews, Stuart 1336
Andrews, William D. 1337 1998 2289
Angers, François-Albert 2558 3674
Angrave, James 506
Angus, David L. 2716
Anstey, Roger 2499
Anthony, Dick 140 141 2290 4263 4264 4265
Appleby, Joyce 1338
Aragón, Janie Louise 3675
Archdeacon, Thomas J. 952 1204
Archer, John 3598
Archibald, Robert R. 1485
Arès, Richard 1486
Argersinger, Peter H. 1205
Armentrout, Don S. 438
Armour, Rollin S. 2980
Arndt, Karl J. R. 327 378 379 380 381 439
Arner, Robert D. 1963
Arnold, Bob 2215
Arnold, Harvey 2814
Arnon, Ruth Soulé 1675
Arons, Stephen 587
Arrington, Chris Rigby 328
Arrington, J. Earl 1758
Arrington, Leonard J. 171 329 588 1206 1759 1999 3929 3930
Arthur, David T. 2961
Ascher, Carol 4088
Ashbrook, James B. 3100
Ashby, Rickie Zayne 48
Ashdown, Paul G. 998 3168
Ashley, Yvonne 589
Ashmore, Harry S. 2216
Askol'dova, S. M. 1465
Aspinwall, Bernard 3676 3677
Atteberry, Maxine 1425
Avery, Valeen Tippetts 3931 3932
Axe, Ruth Frey 2500
Axel, Larry E. 2717
Axelrad, Allan M. 330
Aycock, Martha B. 2815
Ayers, Edward 4290

B

Babcock, C. Merton 3599
Backman, Milton V., Jr. 2718
Bacon, Margaret H. 791 3256
Baechler, Jean 4238
Baer, Hans A. 3349 3933
Bailey, Kenneth K. 2135 2816
Bailey, Raymond C. 999
Bailey, Warner M. 590
Bailyn, Bernard 172
Bainbridge, William Sims 2 4239 4271
Bair, Jo Ann W. 1000
Baird, Anne 3526
Baird, Frank, Jr. 591
Bak, Felix 4240
Baker, Alonzo L. 2291
Baker, Donald S. 1339
Baker, Frank 286 1340 1487 3445
Baker, Gordon C. 592
Baker, James T. 2217
Baker, Nathan Larry 2981
Baker, Robert A. 1001 2982 2983 2984
Baker, T. Lindsay 3678 3679
Baker, Van R. 507
Baker, Wesley C. 1488
Baker, William M. 1341 3680
Balch, Robert W. 4241
Baldwin, Leland D. 1149
Balitzer, Alfred 1150
Ballard, Paul H. 2817
Balswick, Jack 2719
Baltzell, E. Digby 1207
Bandel, Betty 792
Banner, Lois W. 942 2352
Bannon, John Francis 1489
Barbeau, Art 2720
Barbour, Hugh 2353
Barbour, Ian G. 2292
Barcus, James E. 3681
Barcus, Nancy 2721
Bardaglio, Peter W. 3682
Bardell, Eunice Bonow 1426
Barnes, Howard A. 1002 3114
Barnes, Joseph W. 1003
Barnett, Steven G. 3934
Barns, William D. 3257
Barone, Constance 1208
Barr, Thomas P. 508
Barr, William R. 1342
Barrere, Dorothy 1676
Barrett, Joseph 3683
Barrett, William 49 50
Barrish, Gerald 793
Barry, Colman J. 3684 3685
Bartel, Deena 593
Barton, Betty L. 2501
Barton, H. Arnold 2922
Barton, J. Hamby 1490
Basen, Neil K. 2559
Bashore, Melvin L. 1004
Bass, Dorothy C. 1491
Bassett, Paul M. 3288
Bassett, William W. 3686
Bathory, Peter Dennis 1144
Batt, Ronald E. 1760
Baughman, Ernest W. 3600
Baum, Dale 1209
Baum, Gregory 953
Bauman, Mark K. 1210 2293
Baur, John C. 594
Beach, Frank L. 173
Beal, William C., Jr. 3662
Beales, Ross W., Jr. 3601
Beam, Christopher M. 1151
Beaman, Robert S. 595
Bean, Lee L. 794 892
Beardslee, John W., III 1211
Beck, Jane C. 2179
Beck, Jeanne M. 2354
Becker, A. 1492
Becker, Sandra Hartwell 4089
Becker, William H. 1343
Beckford, James A. 91 2722
Bédard, Marc-André 2818
Bedau, Hugo Adam 2294
Bednarowski, Mary Farrell 795 4291
Beebe, Robert L. 1005
Beecher, Dale F. 1677
Beecher, Maureen Ursenbach 796 3935 3936
Beeman, Richard R. 2819
Beeton, Beverly 797 798
Begnal, Calista 596
Behiels, Michael 2355
Beit-Hallahmi, Benjamin 3
Beitz, U. 4242
Bélanger, Noël 2356
Beliajeff, Anton S. 2804
Belk, Fred R. 3350 3351
Belknap, Michal R. 1212
Bell, James B. 2000
Bell, Stephen Hugh 1213
Bell, Susan N. 1493
Bellah, Robert N. 1152 1199 1200
Beltman, Brian W. 2723
Bender, Elizabeth 1908 2690 3373 3438
Bender, Norman J. 597 598
Benedí, Claudio F. 2357
Benes, Peter 1761 1841 1842
Benne, Robert 2724
Bennett, Anne M. 799
Bennett, James D. 1909
Bennett, John C. 799
Bennett, John W. 382
Bennett, Lawrence 1951
Bennett, Robert A. 3169
Bennett, W. Lance 1153
Bennion, Sherilyn Cox 3937
Benoit, Virgil 3687
Bensch, Donald E. 3260
Bensusan, Guy 1910 1911
Benton, Robert M. 1964 2295
Berckman, Edward M. 2820
Bercovitch, Sacvan 1154 1344 1345 1965 1966
Berenbaum, May 2218
Berens, John F. 1155 1156 1157 1158 1346 1347
Berg, Philip L. 2136
Berge, Dennis E. 4297
Bergendoff, Conrad 287 599 3296
Berger, Elmer 4202
Bergera, Gary James 1762 3938
Bergeron, Réjean 3688
Bergey, Lorna L. 3352
Berk, Daniel W. 1427
Berkin, Carol Ruth 520 552 835 1348 2535
Berman, Myron 4203
Bernardin, Joseph L. 3689
Berner, Robert L. 2219
Bernhard, Virginia 331
Bernstein, Louis 4171
Berquist, Goodwin F., Jr. 2823 3170
Betke, Carl 1006
Betten, Neil 2358
Bettis, Joseph 2359
Betts, E. Arthur 1763
Beveridge, Lowell P. 1912
Bevil, Gladys Davis Topping 2631
Bevins, Ann B. 600
Bewley, Fred W. 1494
Bibby, Reginald W. 92 93 2502
Bicha, Karel D. 954
Bideaux, Michel 1495 2296
Bielewicz, Bohdan 3690
Bigglestone, William E. 1496
Billings, Warren M. 1007 2153
Bilodeau, Therese 3691
Bingham, Afred M. 1678
Birchard, Roy 2821
Birchler, Allen 2297
Bird, Michael 1843
Birdwhistell, Jack 2632
Birrell, A. J. 2575
Bischoff, Volker 4075
Bishirjian, Richard J. 1159
Bishop, Grace H. 2576
Bishop, M. Guy 332
Bitton, Davis 800 2001 2004 2298 2303 3939 3940 3941 3942
Bixler, Julius Seelye 601
Bjork, Kenneth O. 3943
Black, Margie 2985
Blackwelder, Julia Kirk 2528
Blair, John L. 2986
Blandre, Bernard 3921
Blejwas, Stanislaus A. 3692 3693
Blight, James G. 2299
Blocker, Jack S., Jr. 1214
Blodgett, Geoffrey 2577
Blosser, Janet K. 955
Bloy, Myron B., Jr. 2725
Bluestein, Gene 2002
Blumin, Stuart M. 2600
Bockelman, Wayne L. 1008 1215
Bodemann, Y. Michal 4243
Bodemer, Charles W. 2300
Bogardus, Ralph F. 1967
Bogert, Frederick W. 3159
Boggs, Beverly 3289
Boileau-DeSerres, Andrée 174
Boles, Donald E. 602
Boles, John B. 2456 3446
Bolhouse, G. E. 3511
Bolin, Winifred D. Wandersee 801
Boling, T. Edwin 94 2987 2988 2989
Boller, Paul F., Jr. 2360 2726
Bollinger, Heil D. 440
Bolt, Christine 947 2168 2457
Bolton, Herbert Eugene 1497
Bomberger, Herbert L. 802
Bonenfant, Jean-Charles 2085
Bonney, Margaret Atherton 383
Booth, Karen Marshall 1679
Borden, Morton 1009 1010 1498
Bordin, Ruth 2578
Bormann, Ernest G. 1968
Bormann, Pauline C. 3602
Borrego, John E. 2003
Bosco, Ronald A. 2822
Bose, Anima 1680
Bosher, J. F. 333
Bosman, Sarah Williams 3603
Bosworth, Timothy W. 2095
Botein, Stephen 1011
Bouchard, Gérard 1466 2601 3694
Boucher, Réal 3695
Boudreau, Joseph A. 1216
Bouma, Gary D. 166 3160 3533
Bourg, Carroll J. 334 1200
Bourgeault, Guy 1012
Bouvier, Leon F. 803 3696
Bouvy, Jane Faulkner 3697
Bouyer, Louis 2727
Bowden, Henry Warner 4 175 1160 1499
Bower, Robert K. 2361
Bowers, Paul C., Jr. 2823 3170
Bowler, Clara Ann 1013
Boyd, Lois A. 804 805
Boyer, Paul 384 806
Boylan, Anne M. 603 604 807
Bozeman, Theodore Dwight 2220 2301 3527
Braby, Junia 3985
Brackbill, Yvonne 808
Brackenridge, R. Douglas 804 809 2529 3528
Brackney, William H. 2362 2363
Bradford, Richard H. 1217
Bradley, A. Day 2633 3258 3259
Bradley, Michael R. 2824
Bradley, Patricia Hayes 3447
Bradley, Preston 2560
Brado, Edward B. 3353
Brady, David W. 810
Brady, James E. 2579
Brandes, Stanley H. 335
Brannan, Emora T. 288
Branson, Branley Allan 385
Brass, Maynard F. 3529
Brasser, Ted J. 1500
Bratt, James D. 5
Bratton, Mary J. 2990
Braude, William G. 4090 4172
Brauer, Jerald 956
Bray, James 1969
Breen, Timothy H. 3604 3605 3606
Breeze, Lawrence E. 3448
Breibart, Solomon 1764 4173
Brekke, Milo L. 3311
Bremer, Barbara A. 3607
Bremer, Francis J. 1349 3607
Brewer, Paul D. 2991
Briceland, Alan V. 957
Bridenbaugh, Carl 3608
Briggs, Charles L. 1844
Briggs, Richard 570
Brill, Earl H. 3247
Bringhurst, Newell G. 2137 2138 3944
Brinks, Herbert J. 5
Brinsfield, John W. 1014
Britsch, R. Lanier 1681 1682 1683 1684 3945
Broach, Claude U. 2992
Broadbent, Charles D. 3115
Broderick, Francis L. 3698
Brodwin, Stanley 2302
Bromley, David G. 386 4244 4245 4266
Bronner, Edwin B. 2458
Bronner, Simon J. 1845
Brooks, George E., Jr. 2459
Brooks, Juanita 811
Brooks, William H. 3449 3450
Brosseau, Mathilde 1765
Brown, Bruce T. 1218
Brown, C. G. 3171
Brown, Douglas Summers 2634
Brown, Earl Kent 812
Brown, Katherine B. 1350
Brown, Lawrence L. 289 813
Brown, Lisle G. 1766 2124
Brown, Richard D. 814
Brown, Robert McAfee 2825
Brown, Sharon 907
Brown, Thomas Elton 2580
Brown, Wallace 2364
Browning, Don S. 815
Browning, J. D. 3732
Browning, Mary 1685
Brownlow, Paul C. 1219
Bruce, Dickson D., Jr. 1970
Brudnoy, David 2125
Brugge, David M. 1656
Brunel, Gilles 1428
Brunkow, Robert deV 2826

Bruns, Roger A. 2460 2461
Brunvand, Jan Harold 1767
Bryant, Keith L., Jr. 816
Brydon, G. MacLaren 1351
Bryson, Thomas A. 2365
Buchanan, Frederick S. 567
Buchanan, John G. 1352
Buchanan, Susan Huelsebusch 3699
Buchdahl, David 165
Buckley, Cathryn 605
Buckley, Thomas E. 1015
Buczek, Daniel S. 290 3700
Budick, E. Miller 51
Buell, James 1846
Buell, Lawrence 3116
Buenger, Richard E. 3297
Buenger, Theodore Arthur 3297
Buettner, George L. 336
Bullock, Alice 1429
Bump, Jerome 3701
Bumsted, J. M. 6 2221 2993 3702
Bunker, Gary L. 800 2001 2004 2298 2303
Bunkle, Phillida 817
Burbick, Joan 2827
Burch, Francis F. 1016
Burdick, Norman R. 1971
Burg, B. R. 1017
Burke, James L. 3260
Burke, John C. 4174
Burke, Ronald K. 2462
Burkett, Randall K. 2366
Burnbaugh, Donald F. 2635
Burnett, Ivan, Jr. 2581
Burns, S. A. M. 509
Burrus, Ernest J. 176
Buryk, Michael 2805
Bush, Lester E., Jr. 818 819 1430 3946 4058
Bushman, Richard L. 1353 2005
Butchart, Ronald E. 510
Butler, Janet G. 811
Butler, Jon 7 1913 2180 2828 2962 3261 3262
Butzin, Peter A. 3530
Byars, Patti W. 3531
Byrkit, James W. 1501
Byrne, Cyril 3703 3704

C

Cadbury, Henry J. 1018
Cadwalader, Mary H. 3705
Calcote, A. Dean 291
Calderwood, William 2096
Caldwell, Patricia 3609
Calkin, Homer L. 3451
Callahan, Nancy 2304
Callam, Daniel 1019
Calvo, Janis 820
Cameron, J. M. 3706
Campbell, Bertha J. 2829 3532
Campbell, Bruce L. 822
Campbell, Colin 958 2602
Campbell, D'Ann 821
Campbell, Douglas F. 3533
Campbell, Eugene E. 822
Campbell, George Duncan 3452
Campbell, Keith E. 2636
Campbell, Penelope 1686
Campbell, Roy 2305
Campbell, Will D. 2994 3519
Campeau, Lucien 337 1020
Camposeo, James M. 2097
Canavan, Francis 1021
Cannon, Charles A. 823
Cannon, Donald Q. 3947
Cannon, Kenneth L., II 606 824
Cannon, William R. 3453 3454
Canny, Nicholas P. 2086
Canuteson, Richard L. 3263
Cappon, Lester J. 4076
Capps, Donald 168 3610
Capps, Walter H. 3707
Carawan, Candy 2830
Carawan, Guy 2830
Card, Edith B. 1914
Cardwell, Jerry D. 117
Carey, Patrick 292 293 3708
Carey, Ralph A. 2958
Carlet, Yves 2367
Carmody, John T. 441
Carner, Vern 2831 2963
Carpenter, Charles 3172
Carpenter, Joel A. 2832
Carper, James Carothers 568
Carr, Stephen M. 2637
Carrière, Gaston 1502 1503
Carriker, Robert C. 1504
Carroll, Jackson W. 4246
Carroll, Kenneth L. 2222 2503 3264 3265 3266 3267
Carter, George E. 2530
Carter, James E. 2603 2995 2996
Carter, Paul A. 2306
Cartford, Gerhard M. 1915
Cartwright, D. G. 3709
Carvalho, Joseph, III 3710
Carwardine, Richard 2223 2368
Casey, Daniel J. 2098
Cashdollar, Charles D. 2728 2833 3534 4077
Cassedy, James H. 1431
Cate, Herma R. 2006
Caulfield, Ernest 1886
Cavalli, Ennio 1916
Cavin, Susan 2181
Cawelti, John G. 2007
Cawthon, John Ardis 2834
Champion, Walter T., Jr. 1505
Champlin, Brad 1506
Champlin, Richard L. 3268
Chandler, Douglas R. 294
Chapman, Berlin B. 3455
Chapman, James K. 2369
Chapman, Phillip C. 1354
Chaput, Donald 1507
Char, Tin-Yuke 1687
Charles, Daniel E. 3354
Charlton, Thomas L. 177 178
Chase, J. Smeaton 1627
Chaudhuri, Joyotpaul 1354 1408
Chernov, S. A. 1355
Cherry, Charles L. 1432
Cherry, Conrad 1356 2224 3611
Chesnick, Eugene 52
Chianese, Mary Lou 1022
Chiel, Arthur A. 179
Childress, James F. 2638
Chinnici, Joseph P. 295
Choquette, Robert 569 3711 3712 3713 3714 3715
Christensen, Harold T. 606 825
Christenson, James A. 991 2370
Christian, William A., Sr. 2371
Christopher, Louise 1508
Chrystal, William G. 2639
Church, F. Forrester 1357
Clapson, Clive 3173
Clar, Bayard S. 2463
Clar, Reva 1917 4182 4204 4216 4217 4218
Clark, Andrienne G. 2099
Clark, David L. 1958
Clark, Dennis 338 3269
Clark, James W., Jr. 2008
Clark, M. Will 1942
Clark, Malcolm, Jr. 2100
Clark, Michael 3612
Clark, Michael D. 1358 2729
Clark, Peter 387
Clark, Roger W. 2582
Clark, Thomas D. 1972 4298
Clark, Tom C. 1023
Clark, Willene B. 1847
Clarke, Erskine 2154
Clay, Eugene O. 3456
Claypool, Richard D. 180
Clayton, James L. 1024
Clebsch, William A. 181 2835
Clelland, Donald A. 2275 2604
Clement, Priscilla Ferguson 2504
Clements, Robert B. 3716
Clements, William M. 95 1433 1959 2225 2730 2836
Clemmons, William 2997
Cleveland, Len G. 511
Cleveland, Mary L. 2531
Cleven, Harry T. 1733
Cliche, Marie-Aimée 3717 3718
Clifford, N. K. 442 443
Cloyd, Daniel Lee 2372
Clymer, Kenton J. 1688 1689
Coalter, Milton J., Jr. 2226
Coates, Lawrence G. 3948
Cobb, Buell E., Jr. 1918
Cochran, David R. 3249
Codignola, Luca 182
Cody, Mary Alice Bull 3298
Coe, Michael 3949
Coffey, David M. 388
Coffey, John W. 1359
Coffman, Ralph J. 3613
Cohen, David Steven 389
Cohen, Michael 959
Cohen, Naomi W. 512
Cohen, Ronald D. 607
Cohen, Sheldon S. 960
Cohen, Steven Martin 826 1220
Coke, Fletch 3174
Colburn, Dorothy 1221
Cole, Garold L. 1690
Cole, Nathan 2227
Cole, Phyllis 2731
Cole, William A. 1161
Coleman, Michael C. 1509 1510 1691
Coleman, Richard J. 2837
Coles, Robert 2838
Coleson, Edward 339
Collins, Patrick W. 497
Colmant, Berta 2839
Comeault, Gilbert-L. 608
Compton, Bob 2998
Conard, A. Mark 1511
Conforti, Joseph A. 2373 2464 3117
Conkling, Robert 1512
Conrad, Glenn R. 3719
Constantin, Charles 340
Conway, John S. 1025
Coogan, M. Jane 609 3720
Cook, Blanche Wiesen 2640
Cook, Lyndon W. 3950 3951 3952
Cooke, J. W. 1360 2999
Cooley, Gilbert E. 2182
Cooper, Patricia Irvin 1768
Cooper, William 2307
Copeland, Robert M. 610
Corbett, Beatrice 3000
Corbett, Pearson Starr 3953
Corcoran, Theresa 2374
Cornwall, Rebecca 2840
Cosette, Joseph 183
Costello, John R. 2183
Côté, André 3721
Cott, Nancy F. 827 2228
Cotter, John L. 1769
Cottrell, Raymond F. 611
Cousins, Leone B. 1692
Cowan, Richard O. 3954 3955
Cox, Dwayne 3722
Cox, Richard J. 8 2229
Cox, Steven 2465
Crahan, Margaret E. 1693
Craig, G. M. 1026
Crandall, Ralph J. 3613
Crane, Elaine F. 2087
Crauder, Bruce 3270
Craven, W. Frank 612
Crawford, David 1919
Crawford, Michael J. 2227 3118
Crawford, Richard 1920
Crawley, Peter 3956
Creelan, Paul G. 2308
Crews, Clyde F. 3723
Croft, David James 341
Cromwell, Jarvis 3271
Cronbach, Abraham 613
Cronon, E. David 2101
Crosby, Donald F. 1222 1223
Croskey, Robert 2806
Crossin, Alan L. 1848
Crouch, Archie 3535
Crow, Jeffrey J. 1224
Crowell, John C. 184
Crowley, Sue Mitchell 2009
Crowley, Weldon S. 2375
Crowley, William K. 3355
Crowson, E. T. 513
Crunden, Robert M. 2561
Cuba, Stanley L. 3724
Cuddy, Edward 2102
Culpepper, Hugo H. 1694
Cumming, John 1513
Cummings, Scott 570 1225
Cunningham, Barbara 828
Cunningham, Patrick 3725
Cunningham, Raymond J. 1434
Curcione, Nicholas R. 3726
Curran, Robert Emmett 296 2562
Currey, Cecil B. 4275
Currick, Max C. 4205
Curry, Thomas J. 614
Curtis, James E. 2088
Curtis, Peter H. 2641
Curtis, Ralph E., Jr. 3727
Curtis, Thomas E. 141 2290 4264
Czuchlewski, Paul E. 2532

D

DaCosta, Emilia Viotti 2499
Dahl, Curtis 2010 3457 3536
Dalin, David G. 1226
Dallmann, Roger Howard 615
Daly, Lydia 1435
Daly, Robert 1973
Damsteegt, P. Gerard 1436
D'Ancona, David Arnold 2128
Daniel, W. Harrison 9 616 617 2155 2156 2841 3001
Daniels, Bruce E. 2230
Daniels, Doris Groshen 4175
Dann, Norman K. 3290
Dannenbaum, Jed 2583 2584
D'Antoni, Blaise C. 185
Dargo, George 53
Darragh, Ian 1770
Davidson, Charles N., Jr. 2642
Davies, J. Kenneth 1467
Davies, Phillips G. 1514 3119 3120 3121 3155
Davis, David Brion 2499
Davis, Dennis R. 3002
Davis, Edwin S. 2643
Davis, Hugh H. 2376
Davis, Jacaleen 2184
Davis, Rex 2732
Davis, Thomas M. 2276 3614 3615
Dawe, Louise Belote 1849
Dawson, Jan C. 2842
Dawson, Joyce Taylor 1850
Dayton, Donald W. 829
Dayton, Lucille Sider 829
DeArmond, R. N. 1515
Deck, Raymond H., Jr. 4060
Decker, Raymond G. 10
Decter, Midge 4247
Deibert, William E. 3175
DeJong, Gerald F. 3161 3162
DeJong, Gordon F. 96
Delaney, E. Theo 1516
DeLeon, Arnoldo 618
Deloria, Vine, Jr. 97
DelPino, Julius E. 444
DeMille, George E. 635 2843 3176 3177
Demos, John 2185 2186
Denlinger, A. Martha 3356
Dennis, William Cullen 1361
Dennison, Mary S. 3178
DeProspo, R. C. 3158
Derfner, Phyllis 1851
DeRose, Christine A. 3728
Derr, Jill Mulvay 830
Derr, Thomas Sieger 2309
Derrick, W. Edwin 1517
Detweiler, Robert 2187
Detwiller, Frederic C. 1771
deValk, Alphonse 619 620
DeVane, F. Arthur 514
DeVilliers-Westfall, William E. 2844
DeVries, George, Jr. 1227
Deweese, Charles W. 186 831 3003 3004 3005 3006
Dewing, Rolland 98
Dexter, Lorraine Le H. 1772
Dick, Ernest J. 187
Dick, Everett N. 621 2231 2644 2645
Dickinson, George E. 99
Dickson, D. Bruce, Jr. 2845
Diekemper, B. 1542
Dietrich, Bobbie Morrow 3250
Dinnerstein, Myra 1695
Ditsky, John 1027
Divett, Robert T. 1437 1438
Dix, Fae Decker 1028 1921 3957
Dix, William S. 622
Dixon, Blase 3729
Dobbins, Gaines S. 1518
Dobkowski, Michael N. 2011
Dodd, Damon C. 3007
Doepke, Dale K. 4300
Doerries, Reingard R. 297
Doherty, Robert W. 188
Doherty, William T., Jr. 342 343 344
Doig, Ivan 1519
Donahue, Bernard F. 1228
Donald, James M. 445
Doress, Irvin 4248
Dorfman, Mark H. 390
Dosker, Nina Ellis 3537
Doucas, Madeline 2290 4264
Douglas, Ann 2846 2847
Douglas, Crerar 1974
Douglas, Paul H. 391
Douglas, Walter B. T. 2232
Dove, Kay L. 189
Dovre, Paul J. 2733
Dow, James R. 1852
Downey, Fairfax 2585
Downey, James 1922
Downs, Arthur Channing, Jr. 1773 1774
Doyle, Daniel P. 4271
Doyle, James 2012
Doyle, John E. 2103
Draxten, Nina 4078
Drescher, Seymour 947 2168 2457
Dressner, Richard B. 2377
Driedger, Leo 100 1029 2378 3357 3358 3359 3360 3361 4091
Driggs, Nevada W. 832
Drolet, Jean Claude 3730
Drolet, Yves 3688
Drury, Clifford M. 190 623 1520 1521
Dubé, Jean-Claude 1030
Duchschere, Kevin A. 3731
Duffy, John J. 2246
Dulles, Avery 2734
Dumais, Monique 2013
Dumas, David W. 3122
Dumont-Johnson, Micheline 833 2505
Duncan, Janice K. 1522
Dunlap, E. Dale 3291
Dunleavy, Gareth W. 1031
Dunleavy, Janet E. 1031
Dunn, Ethel 2807
Dunn, Mary Maples 834 835
Dunn, Stephen P. 2807
Dunstan, John 1696
DuPasquier, Thierry 3251
Durden, Susan 2233
Durham, Weldon B. 2379
Durnbaugh, Donald 2646
Dushnyck, Walter 3906
Dwyer, James A. 3458 3510
Dwyer, Robert J. 624
Dybdahl, Tom 2143
Dyck, Cornelius J. 446
Dyck, Peter J. 3362
Dyer, Thomas G. 2104

E

East, John P. 1362 1363
Easton, Carol 392
Eaton, E. L. 3103
Eccles, W. J. 3732
Eckardt, Alice L. 101
Ede, Alfred J. 2380
Ederer, Rupert J. 345
Edgar, Irving I. 4092 4093 4094
Edgley, Charles K. 2270
Ediger, Marlow 3363
Edmonds, Victor 2711

Edmund, T. 2533
Edward, C. 625
Edwards, Herbert O. 3100
Edwards, Katharine Bush 2848
Edwards, O. C., Jr. 3248
Edwards, Paul M. 191 3922
Edwards, Tilden H., Jr. 102
Egan, James 1975
Ehat, Andrew F. 3958
Ehrlich, James 2014
Eichler, Margit 2964
Eidem, R. J. 1523
Eisen, George 1524
Eisenach, Eldon J. 961
Eisendrath, Maurice N. 4206
Ekirch, Arthur A., Jr. 1364
Elder, Harris J. 3123
Elias, Mohamed 4301
Elifson, Kirk W. 3008
Ellenson, David 4176
Eller, David B. 3104
Elliott, David R. 1365
Elliott, Emory 2849
Elliott, Jean Leonard 126
Elliott, Josephine M. 421
Elliott, R. Sherman 1775
Elliott, Willis 103
Ellis, Bill 1923
Ellis, Bruce T. 1776
Ellis, John Tracy 3733
Ellis, Joseph 836
Ellis, William E. 2310 2605 3009
Ellwanger, Walter H. 3299
Elmen, Paul 393 3179
Elzey, Wayne 2015 2606
Embry, Jessie L. 1525
Emery, George N. 2381
Emlen, Robert P. 394 1777
Endelman, Judith E. 4095 4096 4113
Enders, Donald L. 346 3959
Endy, Melvin B. 1162
Engel, J. Ronald 1366
Engel, Rose-Anne 680
England, Eugene 995 3960 3961 4058
Engle, Irvin A. 3459
English, Thelouizs 3521
Ens, Adolph 3364
Ensley, F. Gerald 2382
Entz, Margaret 2647
Epley, Rita J. 116
Epp, Frank H. 3365
Erdt, Terrence 2311
Erickson, Gary Lee 1163
Erickson, Keith V. 1229 4249
Erisman, Fred 2016
Esh, Levi A. 626
Eshleman, Wilmer J. 3366
Espenshade, Kevin R. 3354
Esplin, Fred C. 347
Esplin, Ronald K. 192 193 1206 3962 3963
Esselmont, Harriet A. E. 3180
Essig, James David 2157 2466
Ethridge, F. Maurice 3105
Evans, E. Raymond 3538
Evans, John Whitney 515
Evans, Mary Ellen 1164
Evans, Max J. 193 194 3964
Evans, Simon 2089
Evans, Teddy H. 3010 3011
Everett, Robert 3710
Everett, William 1032
Everett, William W. 2735
Everman, H. E. 627
Ezell, Paul 1526

F

Faber, Eli 3616
Fader, Larry A. 498
Faherty, William Barnaby 3734
Fahmy-Eid, Nadia 962
Fain, Elaine 1033
Fair, Daryl R. 1034
Fairbanks, David 2383
Falk, Gerhard 348
Falls, Helen Emery 1527
Farah, Caesar E. 1697 1698
Faramelli, Norman J. 2384
Faries, Richard 1528
Farley, Benjamin W. 2017 3539
Farley, Ena L. 2139
Farmerie, Janice C. 2234
Farmerie, Samuel A. 2234
Farrell, Richard 1529
Fasman, Oscar Z. 4177
Fast, Vera 1530
Fattic, Grosvenor 2965
Faue, Jeffrey L. 3550
Faulkner, Joseph E. 96 106
Faust, Drew Gilpin 2158
Fay, Leo F. 3735
Feagin, Joe R. 2736 3105
Fear, Jacqueline 516
Fedder, Norman J. 1853
Fee, Joan L. 1230
Feigenbaum, Rita 1905
Feldblum, Esther 963 3736
Fellman, Michael 2467 2472 2473 2488
Fenn, Richard K. 1165 1199
Fennero, Matthew John 104
Fennimore, Donald L. 1854
Ferguson, Anne Williams 628
Ferguson, Richard G., Jr. 4065
Ferm, Deane William 2850
Ferm, Robert L. 54
Fernández-Shaw, Carlos M. 3737
Ferranti, Frank T. 395
Ferron, Jean-Olivier 3880
Fetzer, Leland 3965
Feucht, Oscar E. 3300
Fichter, Joseph H. 105
Field, Phyllis F. 1264
Fiering, Norman S. 2851
Filsinger, Erik E. 106
Findlay, James 195 629
Fine, Howard D. 396
Fingard, Judith 2852
Finlayson, Michael G. 3617
Fireman, Bert M. 4097
Fischer, Christiane 837
Fischer, Emil C. 1778
Fish, John O. 397
Fish, Lydia M. 2737
Fishbourn, William 3272
Fisher, Albert L. 2506
Fisher, Brad 1779
Fisher, Jeanne Y. 4303
Fisher, Marcelia C. 2507
Flake, Chad J. 3966 3967 3968 3969
Flanagan, Thomas E. 964 965 966
Flanders, Robert 196
Fleming, Sandford 630
Fletcher, Charlotte 517
Fletcher, James E. 499
Fletcher, Jesse C. 1699 1700
Fletcher, Mary Dell 2018
Florin, John W. 2813
Flowers, Ronald B. 1035 1439
Flynn, Louis J. 3738
Flynt, Wayne 11 1231
Fogarty, Gerald P. 3907
Fogarty, Robert S. 398
Fogelson, George J. 4098
Fogle, Richard Harter 2019
Foley, Marya 4068
Foley, Ruth Howard 1701
Foley, Timothy 3887
Folsom, Burton W., II 1232
Foner, Philip S. 2563
Forbes, Bruce David 1531 3540 3541
Forell, George Wolfgang 1532
Forrer, Richard 3618
Forrey, Robert 2020
Foss, Daniel A. 4281
Foster, A. Durwood 838
Foster, Gaines M. 2140
Foster, Lawrence 839
Foster, Mary C. 2235 2236
Foster, John B. 2235 2236
Foster, Stephen 3124 3605 3606
Fowler, Arlen L. 2648
Fowler, Franklin T. 1440
Fox, Francis J. 3739
Fox, Margery 840
Fox, Richard W. 1367 3740
Fox, Sandie Wightman 139
Fracchia, Charles A. 107
Franch, Michael S. 2853
Francis, Rell G. 3970
Francis, Richard 399
Frank, Albert H. 197
Frank, Douglas 1368
Frank, Robert G., Jr. 2312
Frank, Thomas E. 2649
Franklin, Benjamin, V. 2468
Franklin, D. Bruce 1702
Franklin, Harvey B. 4099
Franklin, Lewis A. 4100
Franklin, Robert L. 631
Franks, Henry A. 1533
Frantz, John B. 2237
Franzoni, Janet Brenner 55
Frary, Joseph P. 841
Fratto, Toni Flores 2021
Frazier, Arthur H. 4292
Frech, Laura P. 2385
Freeman, Mark 1320
Freeze, Gary 1036
Freimarck, Vincent 2022
French, David 56
Fretz, J. Winfield 3361 3367 3368
Fried, Lewis 2129
Friedland, Edward I. 400
Friedman, Lawrence J. 2469 2470
Friedmann, F. G. 1233 1468
Friesen, Duane K. 2650
Friesen, Gerhard K. 401
Friesen, John W. 219 1534
Friesen, Steve 198 3369
Frigon, F. J. 1469
Friman, Axel 2854 3181
Frizzell, Robert W. 3301
Frost, Harlan M. 447
Frost, J. William 967 2471 3273
Frueh, Erne R. 1855
Frueh, Florence 1855
Fryer, Judith 842 2386
Fulcher, J. Rodney 2313
Fulkerson, Richard P. 2534
Furman, D. E. 12
Furtwangler, Albert 2023

G

Gabbert, Mark 2564
Gaddy, C. Welton 968
Gadzhiev, K. S. 3619
Gaffey, James P. 3741 3742
Gaffney, Thomas L. 89
Gage, Patricia Anthony 3292
Gagnon, Alain 3743
Gallup, Donald 280
Galvin, John T. 632
Gambone, Joseph G. 843
Gamwell, Franklin I. 2855
Gannon, Thomas M. 3744
Garcia-Treto, Francisco O. 3528
Gardner, Bettye 633
Gardner, Martin R. 3971
Gardner, Robert G. 199 634 3012 3013
Garland, John M. 298
Garner, Stanton 2024
Garr, Daniel J. 1037
Garrett, Clarke 2738
Garrett, James Leo, Jr. 1038 3014 3015 3016
Garrett, Samuel M. 1535 3182
Garson, Robert A. 2387
Garvin, James L. 1780
Gaskin, J. M. 177
Gates, Susa Young 3972
Gaustad, Edwin S. 200 3017
Gavelis, Vytautus 2607
Gaventa, John 349
Gavigan, Kathleen 3745
Geary, Edward A. 2025 2026
Gecas, Viktor 108
Gee, Elizabeth D. 1039
Geffen, M. David 4101
Gehman, John B. 566
Geiger, John O. 571
Geiger, Maynard 1924
Geissler, Suzanne B. 3542
Geldbach, Erich 1040
Gelpi Barrios, Juan 1041
Gendler, Carol 4102 4207
Genné, Elizabeth 844
Gentry, Leland H. 3973
George, A. Raymond 3460
George, Carol V. R. 2472
George, Joseph, Jr. 1234 2105 3746
Gephart, Jerry C. 499
Gerardi, Donald F. M. 3183
Gerber, David A. 518
Gerdts, William H. 1856
Gerlach, Dominic B. 57
Gerlach, Don R. 635 2843 3177
Gerlach, Larry R. 201 960
Gerrard, Ginny 3184
Gervin, J. Barry 969
Ghent, Joyce Maynard 2608
Gianakos, Perry E. 4250
Gibbons, Russell W. 2314
Gibson, Harry W. 2651
Gilbert, Dan Paul 1925
Gilbert, Daniel R. 2652
Gilborn, Craig 636
Gildner, Judith 2027
Gildrie, Richard P. 3620
Gilkey, Langdon 2856
Gillespie, Paul 3520
Gillette, Gerald W. 3543
Gilliam, Will D., Jr. 3544 3545
Gilpin, W. Clark 448
Gilreath, James W. 202
Gilson, Estelle 4167
Gina, Terry 637
Gingerich, Melvin 3370
Gingrich, J. Lloyd 3371
Gizycki, Horst von 402 403
Gladden, Richard K. 638
Glantz, Oscar 350
Glanz, Rudolf 4103
Glauert, Ralph E. 639
Gleason, Philip 299 572 640 3747
Glenn, Norval D. 2739
Glickstein, Jonathan A. 2473
Glock, Charles Y. 2133
Glogower, Rod 300
Godfrey, Kenneth W. 3974
Godin, Gerald 519
Godshalk, W. L. 2028
Goen, C. C. 203 301
Goering, Jacob D. 3372
Goetsch, Bertha Louise 2857
Goin, Mary Elisabeth 3546
Goldberg, Robert A. 2609
Goldowsky, Seebert J. 4178
Goldstick, D. 109
Gollub, Sylvia L. 845
Golomb, Deborah Grand 846
Good, L. Douglas 1369
Good, Noah G. 641
Good, Patricia K. 3748
Goodheart, Lawrence B. 1536
Goodloe, James C., IV 3547
Goodman, Paul 1235
Goodpasture, H. McKennie 1703
Goodwin, Grethe 3512
Gordon, Ann D. 520
Gordon, Ernest 2858
Gordon, J. King 3548
Gordon, Mary MacDougall 573
Goresky, Isidore 2808
Gorrell, Donald K. 847 2388 3663
Gorsuch, Richard L. 2141
Goss, Peter L. 1781
Goss, Robert C. 1782
Gotard, Erin 2739
Gottlieb, David 110
Goulding, Stuart D. 1042
Gowans, Fred R. 3975
Goyder, John C. 2610
Graffagnino, J. Kevin 2159
Gragg, Larry 58 2966
Graham, Louis 2315
Granberg, Donald 2636
Granger, Bruce 2029
Grant, H. Roger 404 405 4302
Grant, John Webster 1537
Grattan-Guinness, I. 2188
Gravely, William B. 3461 3462 3463 3464
Graves, Michael P. 204
Gray, Ina Turner 2316
Graybill, Ron 1926
Greeley, Andrew M. 205 521 565 642 848 970 2106 3749
Green, Dee 206
Green, Jesse C., Jr. 1043
Green, Michael D. 1538
Greenberg, Douglas 59 3621
Greenberg, Gershon 4208 4209 4210 4211
Greenberg, Michael 2238
Greenlaw, William A. 2859
Greenleaf, Richard E. 1044
Greenwood, N. H. 60
Greer, Allan 643
Gregory, Annadora F. 3125
Greninger, Edwin T. 1166
Gribbin, William 61 971 1045 1236 2107 2389
Griessman, B. Eugene 13
Griffin, Clifford S. 406
Griffiss, James E. 2740
Griffith, Ezra E. H. 3521
Griffith, James S. 1783
Griffiths, Naomi 3750
Griggs, Walter S., Jr. 2653
Gripe, Elizabeth Howell 849
Groberg, Joseph H. 1046
Groos, Seymour 2030
Gross, Leonard 1237 2709 2710 3373 3374 3375 3376
Groulx, Lionel 2611
Grover, Kathryn 2809
Grube, John 2654
Grueningen, John Paul von 2860
Grulich, Rudolf 1539
Grumet, Elinor 4144
Grundman, Adolph H. 644
Gruneir, Robert 1540
Gudelunas, William, Jr. 1238
Guelzo, Allen C. 2239 2861 3302
Guest, Francis F. 1143 1541
Guggisberg, Hans R. 850 1047
Gundersen, Joan Rezner 2108 3185 3186 3465
Gunn, Giles 4061
Gunn-Walberg, Kenneth W. 449
Gunter, Mary F. 1370
Gura, Philip F. 2240 2862 3622
Gustafson, Merlin D. 1167
Gustafson, Paul M. 111
Guttenberg, John P., Jr. 1857
Gutwirth, Jacques 4179 4251

H

Haag, Herbert 3751
Habegger, David 3377
Habibuddin, S. M. 522
Habig, Marion A. 1542 1566
Hachey, Thomas E. 1239 1240 1241
Hadaway, Christopher Kirk 144 145
Hadden, Jeffrey K. 112 166 167 2390 2890 4256
Haebler, Peter 302
Hahn, Stephen S. 645
Hahn, T. G. 1976
Haims, Lynn 1977
Hair, P. E. H. 949
Halan, Y. C. 1927
Halberstam, Joshua 4104
Halbrooks, G. Thomas 2160 3018
Hale, Frederick 303 2863
Hale, Van 3976
Hales, Jean Gould 851
Halford, Larry J. 3926
Hall, Bob 3466
Hall, David D. 3623
Hall, E. Boyd 1858
Hall, Jacquelyn Dowd 2535
Hall, John R. 4252
Hall, Mark Heathcote 3187
Hall, Michael G. 3624 3625 3628
Hall, Robert L. 2864
Hallett, Mary E. 852
Halliburton, R., Jr. 2317
Halliday, E. M. 407
Hallowell, Benjamin 3274
Halttunen, Karen 3626
Halvorson, Peter L. 4134
Ham, F. Gerald 408
Hambrick-Stowe, Charles E. 3627
Hamilton, William B. 2865
Hammerback, John C. 2391

Hammett, Theodore M. 1371 2109
Hammond, John L. 1242 2866
Hammond, Phillip E. 1161 1168
Hamre, James S. 3303 3304
Hand, Wayland D. 2189 2190
Handlin, Oscar 207
Handy, Robert T. 646 3019 3101
Hanrahan, James 14
Hansel, William H. 3305
Hansen, Chadwick 2191
Hansen, Klaus J. 853
Hanson, Grant W. 638
Harakas, Stanley S. 1048
Harder, Fred M. 1704
Harder, Mary W. 2783
Harding, Brian R. 4069
Harding, Vincent 2536
Hardy, B. Carmon 1060 3977
Hardy, René 2110
Hardy, Robert T. 208
Hargroves, V. Carney 450
Harmon, Nolan B. 1928
Harms, Marianne 3378
Harnik, Peter 2392
Harrington, Michael L. 2867
Harris, Katherine 2741
Harris, Waldo P., III 1372 3020
Harrison, Barbara Grizzuti 2655
Harrison, Michael I. 2742 3752 3753 4129
Harrop, G. Gerald 3021
Harrow, Joan Ray 1049
Hart, Columba 1929
Hart, John W. 647
Hartdagen, Gerald E. 3228
Hartley, William G. 1050 3978
Hartman, Mary 942
Hartman, Peter 2192
Hartman, Susan B. 1784
Hartwell, Mrs. Charles K. 1705
Haskins, George L. 972
Hasse, John 2868 3467
Hasselmo, Nils 2951 3046
Hassing, Arne 1706
Hasson, Aron 4180
Hastey, Stan L. 1243 3022
Hastings, C. B. 3023
Hastings, Philip K. 113
Hastings, Robert J. 209 210
Hatch, Nathan O. 1169 2241
Hatch, Roger D. 2743
Hatchett, Marion J. 3188
Hatfield, Michael 574
Hatton, Russ 2545
Haupt, Jon 1999
Haury, David A. 3379 3380
Haury, Samuel S. 1543
Havlik, John F. 1544
Haw, James 1051
Hawes, Joseph M. 2393
Hawkins, John N. 1707
Hawley, Richard A. 1930
Hay, David 114
Hay, Marguerite 2275
Hayden, Jess, Jr. 1441
Hayden, Roger 3024
Hayes, Alan L. 3468
Hays, Brooks 1244 3025
Hayward, Larry R. 2869
Head, Keith 3520
Headon, Christopher F. 854 3189 3190
Hearne, Erwin M., Jr. 211
Heath, Alden R. 409
Hefner, Philip 2724
Heiges, George L. 3306
Heilman, Samuel C. 4181
Heim, S. Mark 500
Heimer, David D. 855
Heinerman, Joseph 523 1785
Heinrich, Thelma C. 2870
Heintze, James R. 1931
Heisey, Terry M. 3664
Heizer, Robert 1668
Helgeland, John 3307
Helmreich, Ernst C. 3308
Helmreich, Jonathan E. 3191
Helmreich, William B. 648 4155
Hemmen, Alcuin 3754
Hench, John B. 212 213
Henderlite, Rachel 451
Henderson, John R. 1545
Hendricks, Sylvia C. 3026
Hendrickson, Walter B. 3192
Hendrix, Scott H. 649
Henig, Gerald S. 4105
Hennesey, James 304 3755 3756
Henry, Henry Abraham 4106
Henry, Marcus H. 4107
Hensley, Carl Wayne 1978
Herberg, Will 1170
Herbst, Jurgen 524 525 650 651
Hernández Borch, Carmen 652
Herscher, Uri D. 4108
Hershberger, Guy F. 214
Hertel, Bradley R. 115
Hertsberg, Steven 4109
Hertzberg, Arthur 4168
Hertzler, James R. 2161
Hertzler, John R. 3381
Hesslink, George K. 3979
Hesten, Richard L. 653
Hewitt, John H. 2142 3193
Hexter, Maurice B. 2508
Hickey, James C. 1129
Hickman, James T. 2871
Higginbotham, Mary Alves 1546
Higham, John 1171
Highes, Charles W. 1932
Hill, A. Shrady 1052
Hill, Beth 3757
Hill, Marvin S. 351 3980 3981 3982 3983
Hill, Samuel S., Jr. 2744
Hill, Thomas W. 1708
Hill, W. B. 1547
Himmelfarb, Harold S. 654 4110 4111
Himmelfarb, Milton 15
Hinckley, Ted C. 1548 3549
Hindus, Michael S. 949 2126
Hiner, N. Ray 655 856
Hinson, E. Glenn 452 3027
Hinton, Wayne K. 1053
Hinz, Evelyn J. 2938 2939
Hirsch, Lester M. 1442
Hitchcock, Ethan Allen 2656
Hitchcock, James 1245 3758 3759
Hitchings, Catherine F. 4079
Hites, Margaret Ann 3469
Hobbs, Herschel H. 3028
Hobbs, R. Gerald 3669
Hochbaum, H. Albert 1549
Hoehn, Richard A. 2537
Hoelter, Jon W. 116
Hoeveler, J. David, Jr. 453 2394
Hoffecker, Carol E. 1786 3275
Hoffmann, John 526
Hogan, Brian F. 16 2657 2745 3760
Hogan, Edward R. 2318
Hoge, Dean R. 113 1373 3550
Hogeland, Ronald W. 857
Hoggard, J. Clinton 3470
Hogue, William M. 1054 3194
Hohner, Robert A. 3471
Holbrook, Leona 3984
Holder, Ray 656 3472
Holifield, E. Brooks 2872 3551 3552
Holland, Dorothy Garesche 657
Hollenbach, Raymond E. 566
Hollinger, David A. 2319 2746
Hollingsworth, Gerelyn 3276
Hollow, Elizabeth Patton 658
Hollstein, Milton 1960
Holmes, David L. 973 3195
Holmes, Jack D. L. 1055
Holmes, Urban T. 3249
Holmgren, Eric J. 3196
Holmgren, Laton E. 1979
Holt, Benjamin M. 3309
Holt, Michael F. 1246
Hoobler, James A. 3553
Hood, Fred J. 1709
Hood, Thomas C. 2275 2604
Hoover, Robert Linville 1550
Hope, Clifford R., Jr. 2090
Horgan, Paul 3761
Horgan, Terence B. 3762
Hornick, Nancy Slocum 527
Horowitz, Irving Louis 2612
Horstman, Otto K. 1551
Horton, Loren N. 1787
Hostetler, Beulah S. 3382 3383
Hostetler, John A. 2769 3384
Hotter, Don W. 3473
Hough, Brenda 215
Hougland, James G., Jr. 2586
Houston, Cecil 2111
Houston, Jourdan 2320
Hovet, Theodore R. 2474 3554
Hovey, Kenneth Alan 3126
Hovinen, Elizabeth 3277
Howard, Barbara 3985
Howard, G. M. 3986
Howard, Victor B. 2475
Howe, Charles A. 4080
Howe, Claude L. 3029
Howell, Embry M. 808
Hoyt, Frederick B. 1710
Hruneni, George A., Jr. 216
Huber, August Kurt 3763
Huber, Donald L. 1056
Huddlestun, J. R. 3030
Hudson, Winthrop S. 1057 1172 3031 3474
Huefner, Dixie Snow 858
Huel, Raymond 528 575 3764 3765
Huenemann, Mark W. 659
Hughes, Arthur J. 974
Hughes, Richard T. 1173 3106
Humpherys, A. Glen 1552
Humphrey, David C. 660 661
Humphrey, Edna H. 3555
Humphrey, Richard A. 2873
Humphreys, Claire 565
Humphreys, James 576
Humphries, Jack W. 529
Hunnicutt, Benjamin Kline 2277
Hunsberger, Bruce 168
Hunt, Janet G. 2538 2539 2613
Hunt, Larry L. 2538 2539 2613
Hunt, Richard A. 2874
Hunter, Lloyd A. 2875
Huntley, William B. 4276
Hurford, Grace Gibberd 1711
Hurt, Wesley R., Jr. 2193
Hurtubise, Pierre 2614 3766
Hurvitz, Nathan 2091
Husband, Michael B. 1553
Hutcheson, John D. 1247
Hutchinson, Gerald M. 3475
Hutchison, William R. 17 18 2395
Hyman, Paula E. 4112
Hynson, Leon O. 2396 2397

I

Iglitzin, Lynne B. 859
Inbar, Efraim 662
Inglis, R. E. 2747
Ingram, Henry Black 1894
Ireland, Owen S. 1215 1248 2162
Irvin, Dale T. 2398
Irvine, William P. 1249
Irving, Gordon 3987
Irwin, Joyce 1933
Isaac, Rael Jean 1250
Isaac, Rhys 1058 3032
Isani, Mukhtar Ali 2031
Isetti, Ronald E. 1174
Israel, Jerry 1712
Israelsen, L. Dwight 2565

J

Jable, J. Thomas 2278 2399
Jack, Ronald C. 1251 1252
Jacklin, Thomas M. 2566
Jackson, Carl T. 62
Jackson, Charles O. 19
Jackson, Claire 3310
Jackson, Gordon E. 3556
Jackson, Hermione Dannelly 1713
Jackson, Irene V. 1934
Jackson, Richard H. 3988
Jacob, J. R. 1554
Jacob, Paul 1788
Jacobs, Phoebe Lloyd 1859
Jacobsen, Florence S. 1789
Jacobson, Robert L. 663
Jaehn, Klaus Juergen 2400
Jaenen, Cornelius J. 2032 3252 3767
Jaffe, Irma B. 1860
Jaher, Frederic Cople 2608
James, Janet Wilson 860
James, Sydney V. 2876
James, Thomas 2476
Janis, Ralph 2748 2877
Jarvenpa, Robert 377
Javersak, David T. 2279
Jeansonne, Glen 975
Jeffries, John W. 2242
Jeffries, Vincent 2401
Jenkins, William D. 2402
Jennings, Warren A. 3989
Jensen, Richard J. 2391
Jensen, Richard L. 1000 3929
Jentsch, Theodore W. 410 664
Jentz, John 2163
Jervey, Edward D. 2033
Jeske, Jeff 3614
Jessee, Dean C. 861 1374 3990 3991 3992
Jessett, Thomas E. 1555
Jeter, Joseph R., Jr. 454
Jimerson, Randall C. 1714
Johannesen, Eric 1790
Johansen, Robin B. 1059
Johnsen, Leigh 665
Johnsen, Thomas C. 3912
Johnson, Arthur L. 3311
Johnson, Benton 1200
Johnson, C. Lincoln 3768
Johnson, Dale T. 1861
Johnson, David W. 2034
Johnson, Doyle Paul 4253
Johnson, Emeroy 666 3312
Johnson, Greg 1443
Johnson, James E. 2243
Johnson, Jeremiah 63
Johnson, Kathleen Eagen 1862
Johnson, Niel M. 305
Johnson, Richard G. 1784
Johnson, Robert C. 2749
Johnson, Robert L. 2035
Johnson, Theodore E. 4066
Johnson, Weldon T. 2619
Johnston, Edwin D. 3033
Johnston, Patricia Condon 1556
Jones, Arnita Ament 411
Jones, Charles Edwin 3127
Jones, Clifton H. 217 3385
Jones, Frederick 1253 1254 3197 3198
Jones, Garth N. 1715
Jones, George Fenwick 2878
Jones, H. G. 20
Jones, Lawrence N. 21
Jones, Loyal 2879 3034
Jones, Phyllis M. 1980 1981
Jones, Ronald W. 2403
Jones, Walter L. 3035
Jordan, Albert F. 1791
Jordan, David W. 3199
Jordan, Philip D. 455 456 2404
Jordan, Terry G. 2750 2751
Jorgensen, Victor W. 1060
Joseph, Ted 2658
Joyce, William 3624
Joyce, William L. 3628 3629
Juárez, José Roberto 3769
Juhnke, James C. 262 1543 1557 1716 2659 2660 3386 3387
Juliani, Richard J. 3770
Jurden, D. A. 4277

K

Kadelbach, Ada 1908
Kagan, Paul 4299
Kaganoff, Nathan M. 4113 4114 4115 4116 4117 4118 4119 4120
Kaiser, Leo M. 667 668
Kalberg, Stephen 2405
Kambeitz, Teresita 2567
Kamerling, Bruce 1863
Kane, Steven M. 3522 3523
Kanellos, Nicolás 1864
Kantowich, Edward 3771
Kantrow, Alan M. 2036
Kaplan, Lawrence J. 4169
Kapsis, Robert E. 1220
Kardonne, Rick 4121
Karlin, Athanasius 3772
Karp, Abraham J. 4212
Karsten, Peter 2656
Kasson, Joy S. 1865
Kastens, Dennis A. 1717
Kater, John L., Jr. 2540 2541 3200
Katz, Irving I. 4213
Katz-Hyman, Martha B. 4114 4116 4117 4118 4119 4120 4122
Kauffman, Earl H. 2880
Kauffman, S. Duane 3388
Kavanagh, Jack 704
Kawashima, Yasuhide 3630
Kay, Margarita Artschwager 1444
Kayal, Philip M. 3908
Kazin, Alfred 2037
Kearnes, John 1255 2587
Keddie, Phillip D. 3389
Keefe, Thomas M. 1256 2112
Keeney, Steven H. 2194
Keim, Albert N. 1375 2661
Keisker, Walter 669
Keller, Allan 1061
Keller, Charles L. 3993
Keller, Ralph A. 3476
Keller, Rosemary Skinner 862
Kelley, Bruce Gunn 1257
Kelley, Dean M. 1062 1063
Kelley, Mary 2881
Kelly, Richard Edward 577
Kemper, Donald J. 2542
Kendall, Kathleen Edgerton 4303
Kennedy, E. William 2882
Kennedy, Estella 2509
Kennelly, Karen 670
Kenney, Alice P. 1866
Kepner, Diane 64
Kerber, Stephen 1258
Kerman, Julius C. 4214
Kern, Louis J. 863
Kerr, Hugh T. 3557
Kerr, Joseph R. 1867
Kerrine, Theodore M. 1064
Kersey, Harry A. 1558
Kershaw, Gordon E. 352
Kerstan, Reinhold J. 412
Kessell, John L. 1065 1559 3773
Kessler, Sanford 1175
Kewley, Arthur E. 3477
Keyes, Jane 864
Keys, Thomas Bland 4293
Kihlstrom, Mary F. 2510
Killea, Lucy L. 1668
Kimball, Edward L. 3994
Kimball, Gayle 2038
Kimball, James L., Jr. 3995
Kimball, Stanley B. 1560 3996 3997 3998
Kimnach, Wilson H. 2883
Kincheloe, Joe L., Jr. 1259 2959
Kindermann, A. 3774
King, Anne 865
King, Irving H. 1376
King, Morton B. 2874
King, Robert R. 3999
King, Spencer B., Jr. 1260
Kingdon, Robert M. 3631
Kingsdale, Jon M. 2588
Kingsley, J. Gordon, Jr. 218
Kinney, John M. 3201
Kinsey, Stephen D. 4123
Kintrea, Frank 671
Kirby, Rich 1935
Kirchmann, George 413
Kirk, Russell 530
Kirkendoll, Chester A. 2884
Kirker, Harold 1792
Kirkham, Donald Henry 1377
Kirkpatrick, Gabriel W. 1066
Kirley, Kevin 3775
Kirsch, George B. 2885
Kirschbaum, J. M. 3776
Kirwan, Kent A. 2113

Kit-Ching, Chau Lau 1718
Klaassen, Walter 2662
Klan, Yvonne Mearns 3128
Klassen, Henry C. 414
Kleber, John E. 4304
Kleber, Louis C. 2752
Klein, Janice 2753
Klein, Maury 3558
Klemmack, David L. 117
Klemp, Alberta H. 1561
Kline, Lawrence O. 2406
Klingelsmith, Sharon 866 3387
Klippenstein, Lawrence 219 475 3387 3390 3391 3392 3393
Kluegel, James R. 118
Knaplund, Paul 4081
Knawa, Anne Marie 2511
Knee, Stuart E. 4215
Knight, James A. 3394
Knight, Virginia C. 2589
Knoke, David 1261 1313
Knopff, Rainer 1067
Knudsen, Johannes 3313
Kocher, Helen J. 2886
Koedel, R. Craig 3578
Koehler, Lyle 867
Kolb, Robert 353
Kolbenschlag, Madonna Claire 354 355
Koller, Douglas B. 3777
Kolmer, Elizabeth 868
Konvitz, Milton R. 2039
Korn, Bertram W. 4124
Kortz, Edwin W. 3513
Koss, Joan D. 1445
Kotter, Richard E. 1262
Kousser, J. Morgan 1263
Kowsky, Francis R. 1793
Krahn, Cornelius 3395 3396 3397
Kramer, Gerhardt 220
Kramer, William A. 221 1589 3314 3315
Kramer, William M. 765 4125 4126 4147 4182 4198 4216 4217 4218 4227
Kraus, Joe W. 672 2887
Krausz, Ernest 4127
Kraut, Alan M. 1264
Kraybill, Donald B. 673 3354
Krebs, Sylvia 457
Kreider, Rachel 674
Kreider, Robert 446 2663 3398 3399
Kremm, Thomas W. 65 1265
Kreuter, Gretchen 670 801 2419
Kring, Hilda Adam 3778
Kroeger, Karl 1936
Kronick, Jane C. 928
Krugler, John D. 1068
Krummel, John W. 458
Kuhnle, Howard A. 222
Kukkonen, Walter J. 3316
Kunz, P. R. 912 926
Kurihara, Akira 4282
Kusinitz, Bernard 4183
Kutcher, Stan 1266
Kutolowski, Kathleen Smith 2615
Kutz, Jack 3779
Kuznicki, Ellen Marie 675
Kuzniewski, Anthony 306
Kverndal, Roald 3478
Kydd, Ronald 2888

L

LaBrèque, Marie-Paule 3780
LaFontaine, Charles V. 459 460 461 1176 1562 2512 2754
Lahey, R. J. 2755
Lalonde, André N. 3781
Lamar, Howard R. 66
Lambert, James H. 676 3202
Lambert, Neal 2040
Lambert, Ronald D. 2088
Lamirande, Émilien 1563
Lamontagne, Leopold 2085
Lampe, Philip E. 677 2321
Lancaster, Paul 1719
Land, Gary 1794 2664
Landon, Fred 1564
Lane, Belden C. 3559
Lane, Jack C. 678
Lange, Yvonne 1868
Langlais, Antonio 3782
Langum, David J. 2122
Lankford, John 22 119 120
Lannie, Vincent P. 679
LaPalm, Loretta 1446
Laperrière, Guy 3783
Lapointe, Michelle 1470
Lapomarda, Vincent A. 1267
Larkin, Melvin A. 1759
Larkin, Ralph W. 4281
LaRose, André 3694
LaSorte, Michael A. 869
Lathrop, Alan K. 1795
Lauer, Bernarda 680
Lauer, Robert H. 2616 3784
Launitz-Shurer, Leopold, Jr. 1378
Lauricella, Francis, Jr. 2041
Laurie, Bruce 3479
Lavallée, Jean-Guy 3785
Lavender, Abraham D. 4128
Lavender, David 1565
Lavigne, Marie 870 1471
Lawson-Peebles, Bob 2568
Layton, Monique 2195
Layton, Stanford J. 4000
Lazerson, Marvin 681
Lazerwitz, Bernard 121 4129
Leat, Diana 122
Leavy, Edward N. 682
LeBeau, Bryan F. 3560
Lebhar, Neil 1720
LeCheminant, Wilford Hill 1869
Leckie, William H. 223
Ledbetter, Cal, Jr. 2322
Ledbetter, Patsy 2889
Lee, Che-Fu 915
Lee, Danielle Juteau 871
Lee, Elizabeth 3561
Lee, Ellen K. 3786
Lee, George R. 3107
Lee, Jerry J. 3036
Lee, Knute 683
Lee, Sang Hyun 2323
Leefe, John 684
Legebokoff, Peter P. 3915
Lehman, Daniel R. 3400
Lehman, Edward C., Jr. 531
Lehman, James O. 2665
Lehman, Thomas L. 3401
Leibo, Steven A. 4130
Leighly, John 23
Leininger, Madeleine 2196 2197
Leisy, Bruce R. 356
Leliaert, Richard M. 1379
Lemieux, Donald 1069
Leming, Michael R. 1380
Lemke, Lloyd H. 3317
LeMoignan, Michel 3787
Lender, Mark 2590
Leneman, Leah 4283
Lentz, Lula Gillespie 3037
León, Argeliers 24
Leon, Joseph J. 872
Leonard, Bill J. 3038 3039
Leonard, Glen M. 4001
Leonard, Henry B. 3788
Leslie, W. Bruce 685
Letsinger, Norman H. 873
Leubking, Sandra 3417
Leutenegger, Benedict 1542 1566
LeVan, Sandra W. 3278
Lévesque, Delmas 1070 3789
Levesque, George A. 3040
Lévesque, Georges-Henri 3790
Levey, Samson H. 4100
Levinson, H. S. 2324
Levitsky, Ihor 4278
Levitt, Joseph 976
Levy, Barry 874
Levy, I. Judson 462
Levy, J. Leonard 4219
Lewis, Reid H. 1567
Lewis, Robert A. 2666
Lewis, Ronald L. 2407
Lewis, Theodore 4184 4185
Lewis, Wilber H. 1796
Lex, Barbara W. 2756
Leyburn, James G. 1268
Libert, Herman W. 280
Lieber, Constance L. 4002
Liebman, Charles S. 4186
Liechty, Joseph C. 3402
Liggin, Edna 463
Liggio, Leonard P. 532
Light, E. S. 3224
Lightfoot, William E. 2198
Lincoln, C. Eric 875 4254
Lindberg, D. R. 3318
Lindén, Ingemar 2967
Lindner, Robert D. 1177
Lindsey, David 1721
Lindsey, Jonathan A. 3041
Lineback, Donald J. 3514
Linford, Lawrence L. 4003
Link, Eugene P. 2408
Lippy, Charles H. 1071 1269 3129
Lipsey, C. M. 2275 2604
Lipsitt, Lewis P. 948
Lisenby, William Foy 224 1270
Littell, Franklin H. 2130
Little, John I. 1568 3791 3792
Locke, William R. 2477
Lockett, Darby Richardson 876
Lockhart, Wilfred C. 464
Lockwood, Rose A. 1447 2325
Loewenberg, Robert 4131
Loewenberg, Robert J. 1271 1569 1570 3480
Lofland, John 4255
Long, Charles H. 25 67
Long, Eleanor R. 2199
Long, Theodore E. 4256
Longino, Charles F., Jr. 2390 2890
Loomis, Charles P. 3403
Loomis, Sally 2478
Lord, Clyde W. 2891
Lotz, Denton 1571
Lotz, Jim 2409
Loveland, Anne C. 877 2244 3481
Loving, Jerome M. 2042
Løvoll, Odd Sverre 3319 3324
Lowance, Mason I., Jr. 225 3632
Lowry, Charles B. 3633
Lozynsky, Artem 68
Lucas, Glenn 2892
Lucas, Paul R. 2410 3634
Luce, W. Ray 2667
Lucet, Charles 1272
Luckingham, Bradford 69
Ludlow, Peter W. 465
Luebke, Frederick C. 3793
Luke, Miriam L. 2668
Luker, Ralph E. 2411 2412
Lumpkin, William L. 878
Lutz, Cora E. 2326 3130 3131
Lydecker, William J. F. 977
Lyman, Edward Leo 1072 1273
Lynch, Claire 1572
Lynch, Frederick R. 4257
Lynch, John E. 879
Lynd, Staughton 3562
Lyon, Joseph L. 1448
Lyon, Ralph M. 686
Lyon, T. Edgar 226 4004 4005
Lyons, John 533
Lythgoe, Dennis L. 1274 2071 4006

M

Mabee, Charles 4279
MacCarthy, Esther 2669
MacDonald, Robert James 534
MacGregor-Villarreal, Mary 3794
Machalek, Richard 123
Macias, Ysidro Ramón 2413
Mackie, Marlene 3404
Mackinley, Peter W. 2164
Mackinnon, William P. 1073
Maclean, Hugh D. 3203
Maclear, J. F. 2165 2893 3563 3635
MacLeod, David 2414
MacMaster, Richard K. 2670
Macnab, John B. 466 3564
MacPeek, Gertrude A. 687
MacPhail, Elizabeth C. 535
MacPhee, Donald A. 2415 2958
Madaj, M. J. 227
Maddex, Jack P., Jr. 1074 2166 2167
Maddox, William S. 1275
Madron, Thomas W. 1292
Maghami, Farhat Ghaem 978
Magnusson, Gustav A. 357
Magocsi, Paul R. 2757
Maguire, Mary Ann 2904
Mahone, Rene C. 3795
Main, Elaine 3320
Małajny, Ryszard M. 1075
Mallard, William 124
Maller, Allen S. 1276 4132
Malmsheimer, Lonna M. 880
Maloney, Stephen R. 2758
Maloney, Wiley S. 1076
Maltby, Charles 1573
Mamiya, Lawrence H. 4254
Maniha, Barbara B. 881
Maniha, John K. 881 2742
Manis, Andrew M. 3042
Mansfield, John H. 1077
Manton, Kenneth 2599
Mappen, Marc 3204
Marable, W. Manning 2479
Marcus, Jacob Rader 1277
Marietta, Jack D. 358 3279
Mariner, Kirk 467
Markle, G. E. 882
Marks, John D. 4258
Maros dell'Oro, Angiolo 359
Marsden, George 2894 2958
Marsh, John L. 1797
Marshall, Howard Wight 1937
Marshall, Paul 2759
Marszalek, John F. 1982 2617
Martens, Hildegard M. 2671
Marti, Donald B. 2513 4082
Marti, Fritz 2803
Martin, Calvin 1574
Martin, Jean-Pierre 1381 2327
Martin, Michael 123
Martin, Roger A. 3565
Martinez, Reyes 3829
Marty, Martin E. 26 167 228 1078 1722 2895 2896 3913
Marx, Leo 1178
Maser, Frederick E. 229 1983
Masilamoni, E. H. Leelavathi 2043
Masson, Margaret W. 883
Masters, D. C. 3205
Matejko, Alexander 3796
Matejko, Joanna 3796
Matheny, Ray T. 4007
Mather, Eleanore Price 1870
Mathes, W. Michael 1575
Mathews, Donald G. 2168 2169 2543
Mathias, Elizabeth 1576
Mathis, Ray 536
Mathisen, Robert R. 2897
Matter, Robert Allen 1079
Matthews, Jean V. 884
Matthies, Katherine 3797
Maurault, Olivier 3798
Maurer, Marvin 1278
Mauss, Armand L. 885 910 2502
Mawer, Randall R. 2044
Maxwell, John Francis 2480
May, Dean L. 329 360 794 2625 4008 4009
May, George S. 361
May, Henry F. 886
May, James W. 3482
May, Lynn E., Jr. 230 468
Maydell, Bodo von 27
Mayer, Egon 4187
Mayfield, Violet 3521
Mayo, Janet 688
Mayo, Louise Abbie 2045
Mays, Benjamin E. 2544
Mayse, Edgar C. 689
McAdams, Donald R. 362 2968
McAllister, James L., Jr. 1382 1798
McArthur, Ben 2280
McBeth, Harry Leon 231 887 3043
McCall, Duke K. 690
McCants, David A. 1080
McCants, Sister Dorothea Olga 1799
McCarthy, G. Michael 1279 1280
McCarthy, Kevin M. 2046
McCarthy, Rockne 1179
McClellan, Albert 3044
McCluskey, Neil G. 691
McCook, James 1723
McCormick, John S. 4010
McCormick, P. L. 415
McCue, Robert J. 1669
McCullum, Hugh 2545
McCutcheon, William J. 3483
McDade, Thomas M. 70
McDonnell, Kilian 3799
McDonough, Madrienne C. 692
McElrath, James L. 469
McElroy, James L. 2416
McEnery, Jean N. 3807 3808
McFarland, J. Wayne 693
McFarland, T. A. 693
McGiffert, Michael 3636
McGill, William J. 694 2047
McGinty, Brian 3800
McGinty, Garnie W. 3045
McGinty, Park 232
McGloin, John Bernard 3801
McGlothlin, William J. 537
McGoldrick, James E. 1383
McGreal, Mary Nona 1384
McGuckin, Michael 1577
McGuire, Meredith B. 3802
McInerny, Dennis Q. 2417
McIntosh, Hugh E. 3321
McIntosh, Karyl 2192
McIntosh, William Alex 790 888 2713
McKay, David P. 1938 1939
McKeown, Elizabeth 3803
McKevitt, Gerald 695 696 697
McKibbens, Thomas R., Jr. 1984
McKillop, Lucille 1081
McKim, Donald K. 3566
McKinney, William J., Jr. 125
McKivigan, John R. 2481
McKnight, Roger 3046
McLachlan, James 698
McLaughlin, Eleanor 889
McLear, Patrick E. 1281
McLellan, Sara J. 699
McLeod, Dean L. 4011
McLeod, Finlay J. C. 3567
McLoughlin, William G. 700 890 948 979 1082 1083 1084 1385 1578 1579 2048 2898 3132 3568
McNairn, Norman A. 1580 1581
McNamara, Patrick H. 167
McNamara, Robert F. 2049
McNeal, Patricia 2672 2673
McQuaid, Kim 2546
McQuillan, D. Aidan 3804
McWilliams, John P., Jr. 2050
Mead, Sidney E. 71 1085 2881
Mealing, F. M. 3916
Means, Richard L. 166
Meen, Sharon P. 2281
Meier, Kenneth J. 1290
Mekeel, Arthur J. 1282
Melder, Keith 2899
Melville, Annabelle M. 3805
Menard, Johanne 1472
Mensing, Raymond C., Jr. 3806
Mercy, James 570
Meredith, Howard 1086
Mesar, Joe 2143
Metallo, Michael V. 1724
Metcalf, Keyes 233
Metcalf, Michael F. 1283
Metz, Judith 2514
Meyer, Carl S. 3322
Meyer, D. H. 4083
Meyer, Judith W. 3323
Meyer, Michael A. 701 4220
Meyer, Paul R. 2418
Michaelsen, Robert S. 578 4012
Michel, Jack 2674
Michels, Eileen Manning 2419
Micks, Marianne H. 891
Middlekauff, Robert 702 3637

Middleton, Robert G. 2420
Middleton, Russell 2133
Midelfort, H. C. Erik 2200
Miessler, Ernst Gustav Herman 1582
Miessler, H. C. 1582
Mignon, Charles W. 3638 3639
Mikkelsen, D. Craig 1284
Miles, Edwin A. 1583
Miles, John A., Jr. 2328
Miles, William 1584
Millar, W. P. J. 2900
Miller, Carman 2675
Miller, Char 1585
Miller, Darline 200
Miller, David L. 3405
Miller, Douglas T. 2901
Miller, Glenn T. 363 1180 1386 1387 3569 3570
Miller, H. Earl 703
Miller, Howard 1285
Miller, J. Virgil 3406
Miller, James R. 72 1087 1088 1286
Miller, Randall M. 2170 2171
Miller, Robert Moats 364 1287
Miller, Robert Ryal 1586
Miller, Rodney K. 1388 2618
Miller, Steven I. 704
Miller, Terry E. 1940 3047
Miller, Virginia P. 3484
Millett, David 126
Millett, Richard 1725
Millman, Thomas R. 1587 3206 3207 3208 3209
Mills, Eric L. 2329
Mills, Frederick V., Sr. 3210 3211 3485
Mills, Thora McIlroy 3571
Milspaw, Yvonne J. 2201
Mineau, G. P. 892
Minns, Martyn 1720
Miscamble, Wilson D. 1288
Mitchell, J. Marcus 3048
Mitchell, Joseph 3486 3487
Mitchell, Norma Taylor 893
Mitchinson, Wendy 894 895
Moberg, David O. 3807 3808
Moench, Melodie 4013
Moffatt, Frederick C. 1871
Moffitt, Robert Emmet 1389
Mohler, Dorothy A. 2515
Mohs, Mayo 2421
Moir, John S. 1588
Moldenhauer, Roger 1589
Molson, Francis J. 73 2051
Monahan, Thomas P. 896
Mondello, Salvatore 1590 2547
Monteiro, George 2052
Montero, Darrel 1390
Montesano, Philip M. 1289
Montgomery, James W. 2760
Moody, Dale 3049
Moody, Eric N. 1089
Moody, Robert 74
Moody, Thurman Dean 4014
Moore, Deborah Dash 2516
Moore, Donald S. 2902
Moore, James R. 2330
Moore, John A. 2331
Moore, John Hammond 3050
Moore, John M. 234
Moore, John S. 1090
Moore, Julia 2517
Moore, Leroy 235 3051
Moore, Marie D. 28
Moore, N. Webster 2482
Moore, R. Laurence 4294
Moorhead, James H. 705 2422
Moorman, Donald R. 4015
Moran, Gerald F. 897
Morgan, David R. 1290
Morgan, David T. 1391 2676 4188
Morgan, Edmund S. 706
Morgan, William 1800
Moriarty, Claire 898
Morissette, Luc 1428
Morissonneau, Christian 3809
Morisy, Ann 114
Morrill, Allen C. 1591
Morrill, Eleanor D. 1591
Morris, Ann N. 2518
Morrison, Howard Alexander 2245
Morrison, John L. 579 3108 3109 3110
Morrison, Kenneth M. 1592 3133
Morrison, Lorrin L. 1593
Morrow, Hubert W. 470
Morrow, Lance 2423
Morrow, Sara Sprott 1801 1802
Morsberger, Katharine M. 1872
Morsberger, Robert E. 1872
Morton, R. E. 3732
Moseley, James G. 2053
Moses, H. Vincent 1392
Moses, L. G. 2332
Moses, Wilson J. 2424
Moss, Arthur Bruce 3488 3489 3490
Moss, Robert F. 2054
Mott, Wesley T. 4070
Motto, Sytha 1449
Mounger, Dwyn Mecklin 471 3212
Mount, Graeme S. 1726 1727 1728
Moynihan, Daniel Patrick 899
Mudge, Lewis S. 472
Muelder, Walter George 127
Mueller, Charles W. 2619
Mueller, Peter Dietrich 707
Mueller, Roger C. 4071
Mueller, Samuel A. 167 2586
Mufuka, N. Nyamayaro 1729
Mühlenfels, Astrid Schmitt-v 1985
Mulder, John M. 980 1091 2425 3572
Mulder, William 236
Muldoon, James 2144
Muller, Dorothea R. 3134
Muller, H. N., III 2246
Mulligan, Robert W. 708
Mulvay, Jill C. 900 901
Mumaw, George Shaum 1941
Munch, Peter A. 307 3324
Munn, Daniel M. 3248
Murphey, Murray G. 3640
Murphy, Larry George 981
Murphy, Rosalie 2030
Murray, Andrew E. 2483
Murray, Hugh T., Jr. 2548
Murray, Pauli 2426
Musick, Ruth Ann 2202
Musselman, Thomas H. 2591
Myers, Raymond E. 3284
Myerson, Joel 2761
Myhrman, Anders 3325

N

Naglack, James 2903
Nall, T. Otto 473
Nanez, Alfredo 3491
Nash, Gary B. 2519
Nash, Ray 1986
Naylor, Natalie A. 538 709
Naylor, Thomas H. 4016
Neal, Marie Augusta 902
Nearing, Peter 710
Neatby, Hilda 711
Neatby, Leslie H. 1594
Neely, Mark E. 1291
Neely, Sharlotte 712
Neff, LaVonne 1987
Neier, Aryeh 1092
Nelsen, Hart M. 115 128 159 1292 2762 2904 3810
Nelson, Arnold 3492
Nelson, Charles H. 2620
Nelson, David 1873
Nelson, E. Clifford 3326
Nelson, Edward O. 3293
Nelson, Helen 3492
Nelson, Larry E. 2592
Nelson, Marion John 1874
Nelson, Richard Alan 1875
Nelson, Rudolph L. 2055
Nelson, Steven 1448
Nelson, Vernon H. 3515
Neri, Michael C. 1093 3811
Ness, John H., Jr. 3665
Nettles, Tom J. 1595
Neuchterlein, James A. 365
Neuerburg, Norman 1803 1876
Neufer, P. Dale 3493
Neuhaus, Richard John 1064
Neusner, Jacob 539 4133
Newberry, Daniel Clever 1730
Newcomb, Horace 3052
Newcomb, Wellington 3641
Newell, Linda King 3931 3932
Newell, Robert C. 1731
Newman, Harvey K. 2145
Newman, Stephen 1393
Newman, William M. 4134
Newport, Frank 129
Newport, John 1877
Newsome, Jerry 3053
Nibley, Hugh 4058
Nicholls, Michael L. 201
Niebling, Howard V. 1804 1805
Niemeyer, Gerhart 713
Nieto, Jacob 2520
Nieuwenhuis, Nelson 1806
Nix, James R. 2969
Noble, David W. 1394
Nobles, Gregory H. 2247
Nock, David 1596
Nolan, James L. 1878
Noll, Mark A. 237 540 541 714 1395 1396 1397 1398 2248
Noll, William T. 903
Noon, Rozanne E. 3213
Noon, Thomas R. 2172 2905 3327 3328
Noonan, Brian 715
Noone, Bernard 3812
Noppen, Luc 1807
Nordbeck, Elizabeth C. 2249
Norlin, Dennis A. 474
Norris, Richard A., Jr. 716
North, Gary 2427 2569 2570
Norton, John E. 416 2906 3054
Norton, Mary Beth 520 552 835 904 2535
Norton, Wesley 75 2907
Nortrup, Jack 542
Norwood, Frederick A. 1597 1598 3494 3495
Norwood, W. Frederick 1450
Notehelfer, F. G. 1732
Novitsky, Anthony 2571
Noyes, Richard 2908
Numbers, Ronald L. 1451 1452 2333
Nunis, Doyce B., Jr. 238 239 240
Nye, Russel B. 2909
Nyhagen, Johan 1733

O

Oaks, Bert F. 2428
Oaks, Robert F. 1293
Oates, Mary J. 717
Obidinski, Eugene 3813
O'Brien, John T. 3055
O'Brien, Miriam 3814
O'Donnell, Thomas F. 2056
O'Driscoll, Dennis 543
Oetgen, Jerome 3815 3816
O'Farrell, John K. A. 241
O'Gallagher, Marianna 2521
Ogasapian, John 366
Ognibene, Richard 718
Ohlmann, Erich H. 1599
Olbricht, Thomas H. 3573
Olds, Mason 3914
Olfert, Sharon 3407
Olin, Spencer C., Jr. 417 418
Oliver, John W., Jr. 2549
Olsen, Deborah M. 1942
Olson, James S. 1294
Olsson, Nils William 1600
O'Malley, J. Steven 3666
O'Neill, Ynez Violé 1601
Onuf, Peter S. 2250
Oostenbaam, J. A. 3408
Opie, John 2251
Orban, Edmond 308 309
Orfalea, Greg 2810
Orr, David 1769
Orr, J. Edwin 2429
Orzell, Laurence 310
Osborn, Ronald E. 1181 1988
Osmond, Oliver R. 3214
Osofsky, Gilbert 1399
O'Steen, Neal 544
Ostergren, Robert 3329
Ostrander, Gilman M. 2763
Otis, Virginia Ladd 1602
O'Toole, James M. 242
Ottensoser, Milton D. 1119
Ousley, Stanley 3817
Owen, John E. 29
Oyer, John S. 243

P

Packard, Hyland B. 3818
Paetkau, Peter 475
Page, F. Hilton 719
Painchaud, Robert 3819
Painter, Borden W., Jr. 311 476
Painter, Bordon W., Jr. 312
Palmer, Arlene M. 1879
Palmer, Richard F. 2840
Palmer, Steven C. 720
Palmquist, Bonnie Beatson 905
Pankratz, Herbert L. 2677
Pannekoek, Frits 3215
Panting, Gerald E. 30
Pantojas García, Emilio 1734
Papagiannis, Michael D. 2811
Papermaster, Isadore 4135
Paré, Marius 721
Pargament, Kenneth I. 130
Park, Roberta J. 1453
Parker, Charles A. 2252
Parker, David L. 3642 3643
Parker, Harold M., Jr. 477 722 723 3574
Parker, Russell D. 2253
Parker, William H. 3135
Parsons, Edward Smith 3136
Parsons, Talcott 2910
Parsons, William T. 3285
Parzen, Herbert 724
Pasco, Sharon 882
Passi, Michael M. 3820
Paterson, Morton 3496
Paterwick, Stephen 419
Patrick, James 1808 1809
Patrick, John W. 131
Patt, Jack Michael 2970
Patterson, James A. 1735
Patterson, Michael S. 1295
Patterson, Nancy Lou 1880
Patterson, W. Morgan 231 725 3056 3057 3058
Patton, Frank, Jr. 1094
Patton, Helen 1810
Patton, Richard D. 244 3059
Paučo, Joseph 3821 3822 3823
Paul, Rodman W. 4017 4018
Pauley, William E., Jr. 1400
Payne, Ernest A. 1296 1401
Paz, D. G. 2430
Peabody, Velton 4019
Peace, Nancy E. 2911
Peach, Ceri 906
Peachey, Paul 2764
Peake, Frank A. 1603 1604
Pearl, Jonathan L. 2203
Pearson, Alden B., Jr. 2678
Pearson, Daniel M. 726
Pearson, Fred Lamar, Jr. 4259
Pearson, Ralph L. 4089
Pearson, Samuel C., Jr. 31 1095 1096 2912 2913 3111
Peavy, Charles D. 1881
Peden, Joseph R. 532
Pedersen, Lyman C., Jr. 4020
Peek, Charles W. 907
Pelzel, Thomas O. 1882
Pemberton, Prentiss 3100
Pendell, Thomas Roy 1402
Penfield, Janet Harbison 908
Penner, Peter 3409 3410
Penner, Rita 3364
Penton, M. James 1097
Pepe, Faith L. 909
Perdue, Theda 1605
Perin, Roberto 1098
Perkin, James R. C. 3060
Perkins, Richard B. 3222
Perko, F. Michael 545
Perlmutter, Philip 2092
Perry, Everett L. 3575
Perry, Lewis 2472 2473 2488
Perry, Margaret T. 3575
Perry, William Stevens 982
Peter, Karl A. 1099
Petersen, Larry R. 910
Petersen, William H. 3216
Peterson, E. T. 912
Peterson, Keith 4260
Peterson, Robert W. 3867
Peterson, Susan 727 4021
Peterson, Walfred H. 728 1297 1298
Petropoulos, Nicholas P. 2146
Petrusak, Frank 4136
Petryshyn, J. 983
Pettit, Norman 3644
Petuchowski, Jakob J. 4221
Pfaller, Louis L. 2679
Pfeffer, Leo 132 729
Pfisterer, K. Dieterich 1100
Phelan, Michael 1182
Philip, Kenneth 1101
Phillips, Dennis H. 1736
Phillips, George Harwood 1606 1883
Phillips, J. O. C. 911
Phillips, Loretta 2593
Phillips, Paul D. 2550
Phillips, Prentice 2593
Phillips, Romeo Eldridge 1943
Phinney, William R. 1607
Pichaske, David R. 730
Pickering, Samuel, Jr. 2914
Pienkos, Donald E. 1299
Pierard, Richard V. 2621 2915
Piersen, William D. 76
Pike, Kermit J. 245
Pilarzyk, Thomas 4284
Pilkington, Luann Foster 1737
Pilling, Arnold R. 1102
Pineo, Peter C. 2610
Pinkele, Carl 1315
Pinsker, Sanford 2057 4189
Pitcher, B. L. 912
Pitcher, W. Alvin 2147
Pitterman, Marvin 4190
Pitzer, Donald E. 420 421
Plato, W. R. 3670
Platt, Warren C. 313
Plesur, Milton 348 1368
Poelzer, Irene A. 77
Poethig, Richard P. 1608
Poll, Richard D. 1103
Polzin, Theresita 913
Poole, David R., Jr. 731
Pope, Earl A. 3576
Porter, Earl W. 3497
Porter, Jack Nusan 4248
Porter, John D. 1811
Potash, Paul Jeffrey 1609
Poteet, James M. 3645 3646
Pototschnig, Franz 914
Potter, Gail M. 2680 3137
Potvin, Raymond H. 915 2762
Pouliot, Léon 3824
Poulsen, Richard C. 1812 2765 4022 4023
Pousett, Gordon H. 3061
Powell, Jonathan 984
Powell, Robert Charles 2334
Powell, Ted F. 246
Powers, Robert M. 3825
Pratt, Henry J. 478
Pratt, Norma Fain 916
Pratt, Orson 4024
Pratt, Steven 4025
Preston, Michael J. 133
Preus, J. C. K. 1104
Price, Brian J. 247
Price, John A. 2335
Price, Joseph L. 2681
Price, Maeve 4285
Prichard, Bob 3217
Priddy, Benjamin, Jr. 1813
Priestley, David T. 3062
Prieur, Vincent 422
Principe, Angelo 2114
Prinz, Friedrich 3826
Pritchard, James S. 1610
Procko, Bohdan P. 3909 3910
Proctor, Emerson 3063
Pruett, Gordon E. 134
Puig, Francis J. 1814
Pullease, Donald E. 1558

Pulsifer, Janice Goldsmith 3138
Punch, Terrence M. 1105
Purdy, J. D. 732
Purdy, John R., Jr. 1611

Q

Quandt, Jean B. 78
Quillian, William F., Jr. 733
Quimby, Rollin W. 79
Quinley, Harold E. 2431
Quinlivan, Mary E. 1106
Quinn, D. Michael 734 735 2682 2766 4026 4027 4028
Quirk, Charles E. 3577

R

Racine, Philip N. 2115
Radbill, Kenneth A. 2683 2684
Radzialowski, Thaddeus C. 3827 3828
Rael, Juan B. 3829
Ragsdale, W. B. 2336
Rainbolt, John Corbin 1107
Raines, John C. 1403
Raitz, Karl B. 2767
Rakeffet-Rothkoff, Aaron 736
Ralph, John H. 546
Ralph, Raymond M. 3830
Rambo, Lewis 168
Ramírez, David Piñera 1143
Ramsey, David A. 3578
Ramsey, Jarold 1612
Ramsey, Ron 1815
Rankin, Jane 3139
Ransohoff, Paul 168
Raphael, Marc Lee 248 2337 2522 4137 4138
Raps, Eric Alan 682
Raskoff, Roger W. 3524
Rathbun, John W. 2768
Rauch, Julia B. 2523
Rausch, David A. 80 135 136 1613
Rawls, Andrew B. 249
Ray, Mary Lyn 4067
Ray, Roberta K. 4072
Rayman, Ronald 737
Raymond, Allan 1404
Rea, J. E. 1108
Real, Michael R. 3831
Reck, W. Emerson 81
Reddig, Ken 250
Redekop, Calvin 32 423 2769
Rediger, Beatrice 1543
Redkey, Edwin S. 2685
Reed, Myer S., Jr. 2390
Regeher, Ted D. 3411
Regis, Mary 1884
Rehkopf, Charles F. 3218
Rehmer, R. F. 1614
Rehmer, Rudolph F. 3330
Reilly, Michael C. 1738
Reilly, P. T. 4029
Reilly, Timothy F. 2484 2916 3219 4084
Reily, Duncan A. 479
Reinford, Wilmer 251
Reist, Ilse 2690
Reith, Ferdinand 3331
Renault, James Owen 3064
Renggli, M. Beatrice 3832
Renner, Louis L. 1615
Renner, Richard Wilson 2686
Rensi, Ray C. 3498
Renzi, Mario 917
Repp, Arthur C. 3332
Ressler, Martin E. 1944
Rettig, Andrew 1616
Reynierse, Peter J. 3220
Reynolds, Arthur 252
Reynolds, David Spencer 918 2058
Reynolds, John F. 1300
Reynolds, Keld J. 738 2971
Reynolds, Noel B. 1405
Reynolds, William J. 1945
Rice, Cindy 1816
Rice, Dan 137
Richardson, Evelyn M. 4261
Richardson, Fredrick 739
Richardson, James T. 138 139 140 2732 2770 2771 2783 2917 4262
Richardson, Joe M. 547 548 1617
Richey, Russell E. 480 3499
Richey, Susan 2687
Richling, Barnett 424
Richter, Thomas 1454
Ridgeway, Jacqueline 2059
Riess, Steven 2282
Riest, Irwin W. 3065
Rightmyer, Thomas Nelson 3221
Riley, Jobie E. 1989
Rimbach, Raymond W. 3333
Ringenberg, William C. 740 741 3412
Ringereide, Mabel 2918
Rippinger, Joel 314
Riser, Ellen Lucille 742
Ritchie, Robert C. 1109
Rittenhouse, Floyd O. 743
Ritter, Christine C. 425
Riverin, Bérard 756
Rives, Ralph Hardee 315
Roach, Robert A. 2972
Robbins, Caroline 2919
Robbins, Peggy 2772 4295
Robbins, Thomas 140 141 166 2290 4263 4264 4265
Roberts, Allen D. 1817
Roberts, Barbara 919
Roberts, George B. 1455
Roberts, Wesley A. 2773
Robertson, Darrel M. 920
Robertson, Heard 1301
Robertson, Ian Ross 580 744
Robertson, R. J., Jr. 4030
Robertson, Roland 33 166
Robinson, David 2774
Robinson, Ira 4139
Robinson, William J. 1818
Robison, James I. 745
Robison, Joseph B. 1110
Robson, David W. 2173
Rock, Kenneth W. 2775
Rock, Rosalind Z. 1111
Rockaway, Robert A. 4222
Rodack, Madeline 1618
Rodgers, Daniel T. 2920
Rodgers, James 426
Roditi, Edouard 4140
Rodrigues, Lêda Boechat 1112
Roeber, Anthony Gregg 2622
Roemig, Madeline 1852
Rogers, Charles A. 4073
Rogers, George A. 549
Rogers, George Truett 1619
Rogers, Kristen Smart 4031
Rogers, William R. 142
Rojek, Dean G. 1302
Rollins, Richard M. 427
Romig, Michael C. 481
Romo, Oscar I. 1620
Ronda, James P. 1621
Roof, Wade Clark 143 144 145 2093 2623 3222
Rooker, C. Keith 351
Rooney, James F. 2524
Rorabaugh, William J. 2594
Rosales, Francisco Arturo 3833
Roselle, Daniel 1406
Rosen, Sanford Jay 1059
Rosenblum, Herbert 4170
Rosenshine, Jay 746
Rosenthal, Bernard 2485
Rosenthal, Marcus 4141
Rosenwaike, Ira 4142 4191
Rosholt, Malcolm 3334
Rosoli, Gianfausto 3834
Ross, Aileen 3253
Ross, Brian R. 747 3500 3501
Ross, Don S. 1183
Ross, Edyth L. 2432
Ross, Ruth 859
Rossman, Michael 4286
Roth, Arnold 2283
Roth, Gary G. 748
Rothchild, Sylvia 2433
Rothfork, John 146 2060
Rothwell, David R. 2688
Rouse, Parke, Jr. 1622 3223
Routh, Porter 3066
Rowe, David L. 2921 2973 2974
Rowe, Kenneth E. 316 782 1410 3494 3502
Rowland, Beryl 2061
Rowlett, Martha 3503
Rowley, Dennis 367
Roy, Andrew T. 1739
Royce, Marion V. 749 3504
Rubenstein, Richard L. 750
Rubinoff, Michael W. 4192 4193 4194
Rubinson, Richard 546
Rubinstein, Aryeh 4223
Rudd, Hynda 482 4195
Rudolph, L. C. 253
Ruether, Rosemary Radford 921
Ruggle, Richard 483
Runeby, Nils 2922
Rushby, William F. 3413
Rushforth, Brent N. 995
Rushing, Stan 254
Rusk, Alfred C. 3835
Russell, C. Allyn 1407 2434 3067 3068 3579 3580
Russell, Francis H. 3069
Russell, William D. 4032
Ruth, John 3414
Rutledge, Arthur B. 1623
Rutter, Suzanna 280
Ruybalid, M. Keith 751
Ryan, H. R. S. 3224
Ryan, Mary P. 922
Ryan, Pat M. 3280
Ryan, Thomas R. 3836 3837 3838
Ryan, Walter A. 1113
Rybolt, John E. 752 3839

S

Sabine, David B. 2689
Sackett, Lee 2776
Sadler, Richard W. 4033
Sahlins, Marshall 1676
St. Amant, Jean-Claudeet 1473
Saliba, Issa A. 1740
Salisbury, Neal 1624
Salomon, H. P. 4196
Saloutos, Theodore 2812
Sancton, Thomas A. 82
Sandeen, Ernest R. 484
Sanderson, Lilian 1741
Sandon, Leo, Jr. 255
Sanfilippo, M. Helena 2777
Santos Hernández, Angel 1625
Sarna, Jonathan D. 2062
Sauder, David L. 3415
Sauer, Walter 1626
Saul, Norman E. 2778
Saum, Lewis O. 2779
Saunders, Charles Frances 1627
Saunders, Davis L. 1742
Saunders, R. Frank, Jr. 549
Savard, Pierre 3840 3841
Sawatzky, H. L. 3416
Sayad, Elizabeth Gentry 1456
Scaff, Lawrence A. 1408
Scanlon, Harold P. 3667
Schappes, Morris U. 83
Schapsmeier, Edward L. 1303
Schapsmeier, Frederick H. 1303
Scharlemann, E. K. 3335
Scharlemann, M. H. 3335
Schatz, Klaus 2486
Scheick, William J. 3140 3647
Scheidt, David L. 1304
Schelbert, Leo 428 985 1184 2803 3417
Schelin, Robert C. 1305
Schiavo, Bartholomew 4190
Schiotz, Fredrik A. 485
Schlabach, Theron F. 1628 2254 2255 2690 3418
Schlegel, Ronald J. 3336
Schleifer, James T. 1990 2780
Schlesinger, Arthur M., Jr. 1185 1186
Schless, Nancy Halverson 1819
Schlicke, Carl P. 1629
Schloss, Ruth 1743
Schmandt, Raymond H. 368 2063 2781 3842 3843 3844
Schmidt, Dennis 3419
Schmidt, John F. 3420
Schmidt, Thomas V. 3845
Schmidt, William J. 486
Schmitt, Dale J. 2256
Schmotter, James W. 2257 3141
Schneider, Gilbert D. 2064
Schneider, Louis 147
Schneider, Mary L. 2782
Schoenherr, Richard A. 3867
Scholz, Robert F. 3337
Schomakers, G. 4034
Schorsch, Anita 1885
Schrag, Martin H. 3421 3422
Schreiber, Clara Seuel 1630 3338
Schreiber, William I. 1946
Schrock, Nancy Carlson 4062
Schrodt, Barbara 2284
Schultz, Joseph P. 84 2338
Schulze, Eldor P. 3339
Schupe, Anson D., Jr. 4266
Schwantes, Carlos A. 1474
Schwartz, Henry 4224
Schwartz, Hillel 2258
Schwartz, Jack 1135
Schwarz, Philip J. 2487
Schweikart, Larry 986
Schwermann, Albert H. 753
Schwieder, Dorothy A. 429 3423
Schwieder, Elmer 3423
Scollard, Robert J. 3846
Scott, Donald M. 2488 2923
Scott, James A. 2435
Scott, Kenneth 3166
Scott, Nathan A., Jr. 148
Scott, P. G. 2924
Scott, Robert Ian 2065
Scott, Stephen E. 3424
Scott, William R. 4143
Scovil, G. C. Coster 1744
Seaburg, Alan 256
Searcey, Mildred 3225
Searl, Stanford J., Jr. 257
Sears, Donald A. 1947
Sears, John F. 2066
Segal, Sheila F. 923
Segers, Mary C. 2436
Séguin, Norman 3847
Selavan, Ida Cohen 754
Selement, George 258 1991 3648
Selesky, Harold E. 3142
Senese, P. M. 1409
Sengstock, Mary C. 1306
Senkewicz, Robert M. 1307
Sernett, Milton C. 2925
Sessions, Gene A. 1631 2127
Sessions, Jim 2926
Sewrey, Charles L. 3848
Sexton, Robert F. 2437
Shafer, Elizabeth 2595
Shaffer, Thomas I. 1114
Shaffir, William 550
Shalkop, Antoinette 1632
Shanabruch, Charles 551
Shanklin, Thomas L. 1410
Shankman, Arnold M. 1115 1633 2551 2691
Shantz, Jacob Y. 3425
Shapiro, Deanne Ruth 3101
Shapiro, Edward S. 2438 2572 2573
Shapiro, Henry D. 1457
Shapiro, Walter 1116
Sharman, V. 2067
Sharp, John E. 755
Sharpe, Eric J. 4287
Sharrow, Walter G. 2692
Shaw, Joseph Coolidge 3849
Shaw, Richard 3850
Shea, Daniel B., Jr. 2339 3143
Shepherd, Allen L. 1117
Sherlock, Richard 4035
Sherwood, Roland Harold 1634
Shils, Edward 2340
Shinn, Roger L. 2927
Shipps, Howard Fenimore 2259
Shockley, Grant S. 3505
Shook, Robert W. 4225
Short, Ron 3070
Shortridge, James R. 149 150
Shover, John L. 1308
Showalter, Grace I. 3426
Shriver, George H. 3581
Shryock, Harold 1458
Shuffelton, Frank 3144
Shupe, Anson D., Jr. 386 1118 2439 4244 4245 4267 4268
Shurden, Walter B. 3071 3072 3073 3074 3075
Shute, Michael N. 2260
Sibbison, Virginia 110
Sides, Sudie Duncan 2928
Siegel, Martin A. 499
Siegenthaler, David 3226
Siegman, Henry 501
Sigall, Michael W. 1119
Sihelvik, LaVerne 2525
Silver, A. I. 1411
Silver, Charles 2068
Silverberg, David 4269
Silvia, Philip T., Jr. 317
Simard, Jean Paul 756 3851
Simard, Ovide-D. 757
Simmonds, R. B. 2783
Simmonds, Robert B. 2784 2917
Simmons, Marc 2204 3852
Simmons, William S. 1635
Simms, Adam 2131
Simms, L. Moody, Jr. 2148
Simon, Andrea J. 318
Simonson, Harold P. 2929
Simpson, George Eaton 3525
Simpson, Marcus B., Jr. 2341
Simpson, Sallie W. 2341
Sinclair, D. M. 2069 2070
Sinclair, James M. 1820
Sinclair, John L. 1821 3853
Singer, David 4197
Singer, Merrill 4036
Singer, Milton 165
Singerman, Robert 4144
Singleton, Gregory H. 2624 2930 2931
Sisk, John P. 4270
Sizelove, Linda 1636
Sizer, Sandra 2261
Sjöborg, Sofia Charlotta 3340
Skaggs, David Curtis 3227 3228 3229
Skarsten, Trygve R. 3341
Skemer, Don C. 259
Skemp, Sheila 3230
Skjelver, Mabel C. 1822
Sklar, Kathryn Kish 552
Sklare, Marshall 4145
Skoglund, John E. 2440
Skolnick, Mark 794 892 924
Slater, James A. 1886
Slater, Peter G. 925
Slavens, Thomas P. 758 759
Slethaug, Gordon E. 3649
Sloan, David 2693
Sluder, Lawrence Lan 2342
Smaby, Beverly P. 4037
Smelser, Marshall 1120
Smidt, Corwin 1187
Smillie, Benjamin G. 2441
Smith, Becky 2596
Smith, Bruce R. 3281
Smith, Daniel Scott 949
Smith, Dean 85
Smith, Donald B. 1637
Smith, Harold S. 3076
Smith, J. E. 926
Smith, James 1309
Smith, John Abernathy 487 3294
Smith, John E. 3145
Smith, John S. H. 2442
Smith, Julia Floyd 3077
Smith, Kalmin D. 1188
Smith, Kenneth 2443
Smith, Melvin T. 4038
Smith, N. Lee 1459
Smith, Norman W. 2116
Smith, Timothy Lawrence 5 34 1189
Smith, Wilford E. 927
Smith, Wilson 760
Smucker, Donovan E. 3361
Smylie, James H. 86 260 1190 1887 2932 2933 3582 3583
Smylie, Robert F. 1745
Smyth, William J. 2111

Snow, Loudell F. 2205
Snyder, Marsha 1638
Snyder, Walter W. 3342
Sobel, Mechal 3078
Sochen, June 4146
Sokolow, Jayme A. 2444
Soland, Martha Jordan 2934
Soltow, Lee 2625
Soper, Marley 761
Soremekun, Fola 1746
Sorenson, John 4039
Soria, Regina 1888
Sorrell, Richard S. 3854
Sorrill, Bobbie 1747
Southern, Eileen 1948
Spalding, James C. 1412
Spalding, Phinizy 1823 3231
Speck, William A. 261
Speizman, Milton D. 928
Spencer, Ralph W. 3506
Spielmann, Roger 4267 4268
Spigelman, Martin S. 3855
Spotts, Charles D. 2935
Sprunger, Keith L. 262 3650
Sprunger, Milton F. 3427
Sprunk, Larry J. 35
Stachiw, Matthew 2785
Stange, Douglas C. 1413 2174 4085
Stannard, David E. 87 929 3651
Stansfield, Charles 2262
Stark, Rodney 2 2133 4239 4271
Starr, Edward C. 263
Starr, J. Barton 3254
Starr, Jerold M. 2694
Stathis, Stephen W. 2071 2796 4040 4041
Stauffer, J. Paul 1889
Stearns, Monroe 2936
Steckley, John 1639
Steege, Martin 3343
Steele, David L. 3507
Steele, Robert E. 130
Steele, Thomas J. 1890 3856
Steelman, Robert F. 180
Steely, John E. 3079
Stegmaier, Mark J. 2117
Steiber, Steven R. 151
Stein, K. James 3668
Stein, Stephen J. 1414 2175 2343 2937 3146 3147 3148 3149
Steiner, Bruce E. 1310
Steinert, Steven 4136
Steinhoff, Patricia G. 872
Steinkraus, Warren E. 2552
Stekelenburg, H. A. V. M. van 3857
Stenerson, Douglas C. 2263
Stephens, Bruce M. 762 763 764 4086
Stern, Madeleine B. 1992
Stern, Malcolm H. 4226
Stern, Marc D. 1110
Stern, Norton B. 765 4126 4147 4148 4198 4199 4227
Stern, Steve J. 1121
Stevens, Clifford 3858
Stevens, Meribah L. 1415
Stevens, Michael E. 1640
Stevens, Thelma 930
Stevenson, E. M. 987 3584
Stevenson, W. Taylor 36
Stewart, Gordon 2264 2626
Stewart, James Brewer 2489
Stewart, James H. 3859
Stewart, Mary White 2770 2917
Stewart, Susan 1891
Stewart, Thomas H. 1949
Steyer, Beatrice 1110
Stigall, Sam 4267 4268
Stineback, David C. 1641
Stipe, Claude E. 37
Stirn, James R. 2490
Stoddart, Jennifer 1471
Stoever, William R. B. 3652
Stokes, Durward T. 1642 3585
Stokes, G. Allison 200
Stoloff, Carolyn 931
Stoltzfus, Victor 3428 3429
Stone, Donald 4272
Stone, Michael 1950
Stone, William J., Jr. 3586
Stoneburner, Tony 3247
Stookey, Robert W. 1748
Storey, John W. 553 2149 2553
Stortz, Gerald J. 369
Stott, Graham St. John M 2072
Stout, Harry S. 264 1993 2627 3653
Stover, Earl F. 2695
Stover, Margaret Harris 3255
Stowe, Walter Herbert 988
Strayer, Brian 2975
Stritch, Thomas J. 3860
Strober, Gerald S. 502
Strombeck, Rita 370
Strommen, Merton P. 3311
Stroupe, Henry S. 2445
Strout, Cushing 1144 2265
Strum, Harvey 2446
Struna, Nancy 3654
Stryckman, Paul 3861
Stryker-Rodda, Kenn 3166
Stuart, Reginald C. 1416
Stuart, Robert Lee 1994
Stubbs, Charles H. 3587
Studer, Gerald C. 2206
Stuhler, Barbara 670 801 2419
Stupple, David 4273
Suderman, Elmer F. 2073 2074
Suelflow, August R. 265 266
Sugeno, Frank E. 3232 3233
Sullivan, James L. 3080 3081
Sullivan, John L. 989
Sumners, Bill 3082
Sunter, Ronald 3862
Surratt, Jerry L. 3516
Suther, Judith D. 3863
Sutherland, Daniel E. 1475
Sutherland, John F. 4228
Sutter, Sem C. 2266
Sutton, Brett 3083
Svengalis, Kendall F. 3344
Swan, George Steven 554
Swanson, Merwin 2447
Swanton, Carolyn 3234
Swearer, Donald K. 4288
Sweeney, Odile 488
Sweet, Douglas H. 2267
Sweet, Leonard 2443
Sweet, Leonard I. 2268
Sweetland, James H. 430
Swidler, Arlene 3864
Swierenga, Robert 3163
Swisher, Bob 1892
Swope, Wilmer D. 2709
Sydnor, William 3235
Sylvain, Philippe 1476
Symmons-Symonolewicz, Konstantin 3865
Szafran, Robert F. 3866 3867
Szasz, Ferenc M. 1191 1967 2344
Szasz, Margaret Connell 766 2448

T

Tally, Frances M. 2190
Tanenhaus, Ruth Amdur 1893
Tanis, James 1311
Tanzone, Daniel F. 3868 3869 3870
Tarr, Dennis L. 1312
Tate, George A. 2075
Tatum, W. Barnes 1894
Taulman, James E. 1995
Taylor, David 4241
Taylor, George A. 1247
Taylor, James S. 1370
Taylor, Orville W. 1122 2176
Taylor, Robert 264
Taylor, Sandra C. 932
Teaford, Jon C. 3588
Teaham, John F. 1460
Tedin, Kent L. 810 933
Tegborg, Lennart 581 582
Teichroew, Allan 2696 2697
Tenenbaum, Marc H. 4149
Tero, Richard D. 1643
Terry, Thomas D. 371
Teunissen, John J. 2938 2939
Thalheimer, Fred 555
Tharpe, Jac 38
Thatcher, Linda 4042
Theobald, Robin 2976
Theriault, Leon 3871
Thode, Frieda Oehlschlaeger 1749
Thomas, Bettye C. 583
Thomas, C. E. 1644
Thomas, Charles P. 1645
Thomas, Darwin L. 108
Thomas, Donna 2118
Thomas, E. E. 1646
Thomas, G. E. 2150
Thomas, Ivor B. 2698
Thomas, James C. 1824
Thomas, N. Gordon 2977
Thomas, Robert David 431
Thomas, Samuel J. 319 2786
Thomas, Samuel W. 432
Thomasson, Gordon C. 4058
Thompson, Arthur N. 1750
Thompson, Dean J. 767
Thompson, Dennis L. 1417
Thompson, Ernest T. 3589
Thompson, J. Earl, Jr. 2491 2492 2493
Thompson, James J., Jr. 2119 2345 2699 3084 3085
Thompson, Kenneth W. 2940
Thompson, Paul E. 1647
Thomson, Randall 1313
Thornbery, Jerry 556
Thornton, Arland 934
Thornton, Bob 267
Thorp, Malcolm R. 1672
Threinen, Norman J. 489 3345
Threlfall, John B. 2941
Tichi, Cecelia 1192
Tierney, Gail D. 2207
Tierney, John J. 3872
Tiller, Carl W. 490 3086
Tipson, Baird 2942 3655 3656
Tise, Larry Edward 2628
Titon, Jeff Todd 2269
Tobin, Eugene M. 2449
Tobler, Douglas F. 768
Toll, William 4150
Tolzmann, Don Heinrich 1123 4063
Tomberlin, Joseph Aaron 4259
Tomlinson, Juliette 3236
Toney, Michael B. 152
Tonks, A. Ronald 177 268 1648 3087 3088
Topping, Gary 2076
Toury, Jacob 4151
Towne, Edgar A. 557
Townley, Carrie M. 769
Toy, Eckard V., Jr. 1477
Tracy, Patricia 3150
Trendel, Robert 2494
Trépanier, Pierre 1124 3873 3874
Trépannier, Lise 3873
Treppa, Allan R. 3875
Trifiro, Luigi 935
Trivers, Howard 1418
Troop, Hiram G. 3590
Trotter, F. Thomas 153
Troubetzkoy, Ulrich 2787
Troy, Bill 1478
Trudel, Marcel 1125 3876
True, Edmond J. 1203
Truzzi, Marcello 2208
Tucker, Barbara M. 372
Tucker, Bruce 2943
Tucker, Glenn 2788
Tucker, Janey 3677
Tucker, Kathryn 1751
Tucker, Nancy Bernkopf 1752
Tucker, Theodore L. 1751
Tuerk, Richard 2132
Tull, James E. 3089
Tullis, LaMond 1753
Tully, Alan 1314
Turk, Eleanor L. 3877
Turman, Nora Miller 1825
Turner, Ronny E. 2270 2554
Turney, Catherine 4043
Tusseau, Jean-Pierre 3878
Tuttle, William M., Jr. 2151
Tweed, Tommy 2120
Tweedie, Stephen W. 1961
Twersky, Rebecca 4152
Tybor, M. Martina 3879
Tygart, Clarence E. 2401 2700
Tyler, Forrest B. 130
Tyner, Wayne C. 2177
Tyrrell, Alexander 2701
Tyrrell, Charles W. 3508

U

Ulle, Robert F. 2702 2710
Ulrich, Laurel Thatcher 936
Umetsu, Jun-ichi 373
Underwager, Ralph C. 3311
Unruh, John D. 3430
Unruh, John D., Jr. 3430
Unruh, T. E. 503
Unsicker, Joan I. 770
Upton, L. F. S. 1649
Urkowitz, Steven 1951
Urofsky, Melvin I. 2944 4153 4229
Ursenbach, Maureen 4044 4045

V

Vaillancourt, François 3880
Valentine, Foy 1126 3090
Vanausdall, Jeanette 558
VanBeeck, Frans Josef 937
VanCromphout, Gustaaf 1996
VanDeburg, William L. 2495 2496
VanDusen, Henry P. 2945
vanMelle, J. J. Ferdinand 3164
VanMeter, Mary 1826
Vann, Richard T. 938
VanWyck, Philip 3165
Varenne, Hervé 165
Varesano, Angelamaria 1576
Vartanian, Pershing 3657
Vedlitz, Arnold 1315
Ventimiglia, J. C. 4244
Vernon, Walter N. 772 1650
Vigil, Ralph H. 2077
Viitanen, Wayne 2789
Vinatieri, Joseph A. 559
Vincent, Charles 2285
Vinyard, Jo Ellen 2790
Vipond, Mary 491 2078
Vittands, Alexander T. 1651
Vogeler, Ingolf 3881
Voisine, Nive 3882 3883
Vollmar, Edward R. 3884
Voskuil, Dennis N. 2946
Voss, Carl Hermann 1316
Voth, M. Agnes 1652 3832
Voye, Nancy S. 1827

W

Waddell, Louis M. 2791
Wade, Mason 1317
Wadley, W. 1653
Wagenaar, John 154
Wagner, Jonathan F. 3431
Wagner, Peter 3658 3659 3660
Wagner, William 3885
Wagoner, Gerald C. 3432
Wahl, Albert F. 2450
Wahlquist, Wayne L. 4046
Waite, P. B. 1127
Wakely, Francis E. 1654
Walaskay, Paul William 3091
Walch, Timothy 773 3886
Wald, Alan M. 1419
Waldinger, Robert J. 2346
Walker, Arthur L., Jr. 3092
Walker, Charles O. 88 270 271
Walker, Henry Pickering 3237
Walker, Jerald C. 374
Walker, Randolph Meade 1318
Walker, Ronald W. 375 1754 4047 4296
Wallace, Ruth A. 939
Waller, John O. 1997 3509
Wallfisch, M. Charles 1128
Wallis, Jim 2792
Wallis, Roy 2793 4274
Wallot, Jean Pierre 1319
Walsh, James P. 560 3238 3887 3888 3889
Walters, Jonathan 3890
Walters, Stanley D. 1952
Waltmann, Henry G. 1655 3346
Walton, Elisabeth 1828
Walton, John 3239
Wangler, Thomas E. 3891
Warburton, Rennie 1669
Warch, Richard 774
Ward, Albert E. 1656
Ward, Leo R. 775
Ward, Michael 1320
Ward, Richard Hiram 776
Ward, W. R. 39
Warford, Malcolm L. 777
Wargelin, Raymond W. 990
Warland, Rex H. 96 106
Warman, John B. 320 2947
Warner, Madeleine 2079
Warren, Claude N. 940
Warren, Matthew M. 561
Warren, Nancy 3892
Warren, William Lamson 1829
Warsen, Allen A. 4154
Wartluft, David J. 272
Washington, Joseph R., Jr. 155
Wasserman, Ira M. 156
Waterhouse, Richard 3661
Waters, John J. 3151
Watkins, T. H. 3893
Watner, Carl 2497
Watson, Alan D. 3240
Watson, Elden J. 4048
Watt, Ronald G. 194 1895 4049 4050
Watters, David 1896 3632
Watters, William R., Jr. 157
Watts, John D. W. 1755
Watts, Kit 2978
Wax, Bernard 273 4200
Wax, Murray L. 2794
Wax, Rosalie H. 2794
Waxman, Chaim I. 4155
Weale, David 3591
Weathersby, Robert W., II 3241
Weaver, Bill L. 2347
Webb, Bernard L. 1830
Weber, David J. 1497 1903 2122 3852
Weber, Francis J. 274 1321 1573 1657 1658 1659 1831 3894 3895 3896 3897
Weber, Paul J. 2113
Weddle, David L. 2271 3152
Weeks, Louis 1129 3592
Weeks, Louis B., III 778
Weeks, Robert P. 433
Weems, Lovett Hayes, Jr. 1322
Weigert, Andrew J. 108 3768
Weight, Newell B. 1953
Weigle, Martha 3898
Weinberg, Helene Barbara 1832 1833 1897 1898
Weinberg, Julius 4230
Weiner, Lynn 2526
Weinfeld, Morton 4156
Weinlick, John R. 2703 3517
Weisberg, D. Kelly 941
Weiser, Frederick S. 1899
Weisheit, Eldon J. 3347
Weitz, Martin M. 2348
Welch, Michael R. 793 2629
Welch, Richard F. 1900
Wellborn, Charles 1193
Weller, Robert H. 3696
Welter, Barbara 942 943
Welton, Mike 2759
Wendel, Thomas 1130
Wenger, Edna K. 3433
Wennersten, John R. 1323
Wenska, Walter P. 3153
Wentz, Richard E. 40 562 2948 2949 2950
Werly, John M. 1420
Werner, Alfred 1905
Wertz, Richard E. 41
Wesson, Kenneth R. 2795
West, Elliot 275
Westbrook, Robert B. 3154
Westerberg, Wesley M. 321 2951 3340
Westly, Frances 158
Wettan, Richard G. 3243
Wettstein, A. Arnold 4280
Wheeler, Otis B. 2080

Whelan, Charles M. 1131
Whisnant, David E. 2451
Whitaker, F. M. 2597
Whitaker, James W. 3155
Whitaker, Reginald 1421
White, B. R. 1132
White, Clinton O. 779
White, Daryl 4051
White, Ellen G. 1461
White, Gavin 1660
White, Jean Bickmore 944 1324
White, Joyce L. 322
White, Larry 2598 2979
White, O. Kendall, Jr. 4051
White, Paula K. 2081
White, Peter 4074
White, William G. 1325
White, William Griffin, Jr. 1133
Whitehill, Walter Muir 276
Whitmore, Allan R. 2121
Whitney, John R. 1194
Whitson, Mont 1195
Whitt, Hugh P. 159
Whittaker, David J. 277
Whittier, Charles H. 2796
Whitwell, W. L. 1834
Whorton, James C. 1462
Whyman, Henry C. 1661
Whyte, John H. 1326
Wiebe, Menno 3434
Wieseltier, Leon 278
Wieting, Stephen G. 160
Wilbanks, Dana W. 2704
Wilcox, Linda P. 1463 3941
Wilks, Flo 1901
Will, Herman 1327
Willauer, G. J., Jr. 1662
Williams, Catherine 3093
Williams, Claude 1478
Williams, Dorothy M. 3282
Williams, George W. 3242
Williams, James H. 2452
Williams, John P., Jr. 2082
Williams, John R. 2272
Williams, Michael Patrick 3094
Williams, Preston N. 161
Williams, Priscilla Parish 945
Williams, Richard L. 434
Williams, Robert 3372
Williams, William Carlos 323
Williams, William H. 1663
Williamson, Norman J. 780
Williamson, Rene De Visme 1328
Willingham, William F. 2273 2274
Willis, Joe D. 3243
Wilson, Charles Reagan 1196
Wilson, Frank T. 3593 3594 3595
Wilson, J. Donald 435
Wilson, James Q. 1329
Wilson, John 2599
Wilson, John F. 3156
Wilson, John R. M. 2705
Wilson, Laura Foster 4052
Wilson, Major L. 2952
Wilson, Samuel, Jr. 1835
Wilson, Spencer 3095
Wilson, W. Emerson 3244 3245
Wilson, William A. 4053 4054 4055 4056
Wimberley, Ronald C. 162 991 1197 1198 2275 2604
Wimmer, Larry T. 351
Winchester, Alice 436
Wingo, Barbara C. 1330
Winkler, Louis 2209 2349
Winquist, Charles E. 163
Winter, J. Alan 376
Winter, Robert 1836
Winzenz, David J. 163
Witheridge, David E. 1134
Withington, Anne Fairfax 1135
Wittlinger, Carlton O. 3435 3436 3437
Woehrmann, Paul 3112
Wogaman, J. Philip 1136
Wolf, William J. 3899
Wolfe, Charles 1954
Wolfe, Edward C. 1955 1956
Wolfe, James S. 992
Wolfe, Ruth 1902
Wolff, Gerald W. 3900
Wolkinson, Benjamin W. 1479
Wolkovich-Valkavičius, William 3901
Wolniewicz, Richard 1837
Wolseley, Roland E. 2498
Wolters, Raymond 563
Wood, Alice S. 1664
Wood, James E., Jr. 564 1137 1138
Wood, James R. 2439 2586
Wood, Jerome H., Jr. 2953
Wood, Raymund F. 2797 2798
Woodcock, George 3917
Woodrum, Eric 2954
Woolfolk, George Ruble 2799
Woolverton, John F. 324 1957 3246
Worrall, Arthur J. 993 3283
Worthing, Sharon L. 1139
Wright, C. M. 1838
Wright, Louise M. 790
Wright, Malcolm E. 492
Wright, Robert J. 493
Wright, Rochelle 2083
Wrobel, Arthur 2350
Wrona, Christine 2210
Wroth, William 1903
Wrzeszcz, Maciej 2211
Wu, Nai-te 1422
Wukasch, Peter 2453
Wulff, O. H. 781
Wunder, John R. 2152
Wuthnow, Robert 2212
Wyatt, Philip R. 946
Wyatt-Brown, Bertram 947 2800
Wyneken, Chet A. 3348
Wyneken, Frederick G. 3348
Wynne, Edward J., Jr. 782

Y

Yackel, Peter G. 1140
Yates, W. Ross 3518
Yeager, Lyn Allison 2801 3096
Yearwood, Lennox 3097
Yellowitz, Irwin 1331
Yinger, J. Milton 166
Yodelis, M. A. 1423
Yoder, Don 42 164 1904
Yoder, Paton 2286 3438 3439
Yokley, Raytha L. 1292
Young, Chester Raymond 2955
Young, David M. 2287
Young, Mary Lawrence 432
Young, Michael 2706
Youngs, J. William T., Jr. 3157
Yrigoyen, Charles, Jr. 3286 3287
Yurtinus, John F. 2707

Z

Zanger, Jules 2084
Zaslow, Morris 279
Zehr, Dan 1029
Zehrer, Karl 3510
Zelt, Roger P. 1464
Zenner, Walter P. 377
Ziebarth, Marilyn 4299
Ziff, Larzer 1424
Zikmund, Barbara Brown 494
Zimmer, Anne Y. 1141
Zimmerman, Noah L. 3371
Zink, Ella 1665
Zinsmeister, Robert, Jr. 3098
Zipperstein, Steve 4157
Zook, Lois Ann 3440 3441
Zubek, Theodoric 3902
Zuber, Richard L. 2708
Zuckerman, Michael 2956
Zwerin, Kenneth C. 4158

LIST OF PERIODICALS

A

AAUP Bulletin (see Academe: Bulletin of the AAUP)
Academe: Bulletin of the AAUP
Acadiensis: Journal of the History of the Atlantic Region [Canada]
Action Nationale [Canada]
Administration and Society
Adventist Heritage
Afro-Americans in New York Life and History
Agricultural History
Air University Review
Alabama Historical Quarterly
Alabama Review
Alaska Journal (ceased pub 1980)
Alberta Historical Review (see Alberta History) [Canada]
Alberta History [Canada]
American Archivist
American Art and Antiques (see Art and Antiques)
American Art Journal
American Behavioral Scientist
American Benedictine Review
American Book Collector (ceased pub 1976)
American Heritage
American Historical Review
American History Illustrated
American Jewish Archives
American Jewish Historical Quarterly (see American Jewish History)
American Jewish History
American Journal of Economics and Sociology
American Journal of International Law
American Journal of Legal History
American Journal of Political Science
American Journal of Sociology
American Literature
American Neptune
American Quarterly
American Review of Canadian Studies
American Scholar
American Sociological Review
American Studies (Lawrence, KS)
American West
Americas: A Quarterly Review of Inter-American Cultural History (Academy of American Franciscan History)
Américas (Organization of American States)
Amerikastudien/American Studies [German Federal Republic]
Anglican Theological Review
Annals of Iowa
Annals of Science [Great Britain]
Annals of the American Academy of Political and Social Science
Annals of the Association of American Geographers
Anthropologica [Canada]
Antioch Review
Antonianum [Italy]
Appalachian Journal
APT Bulletin [Canada]
Archives de Sciences Sociales des Religions [France]
Arizona and the West
Arkansas Historical Quarterly
Art & Antiques
Art in America
Arte y Arqueología (IHE) [Bolivia]
Arts in Society (ceased pub 1976)
Atlantis: A Women's Studies Journal [Canada]
Aztlán

B

Baptist History and Heritage
Baptist Quarterly [Great Britain]
BC Studies [Canada]
Beaver [Canada]
Biography
Bohemia [German Federal Republic]
Boletín de Historia y Antigüedades [Colombia]
Brigham Young University Studies
Bulletin de la Société de l'Histoire du Protestantisme Français [France]
Bulletin d'Histoire de la Culture Matérielle (see Material History Bulletin = Bulletin d'Histoire de la Culture Matérielle) [Canada]
Bulletin of Bibliography
Bulletin of Bibliography and Magazine Notes (see Bulletin of Bibliography)
Bulletin of Research in the Humanities
Bulletin of the Atomic Scientists (briefly known as Science
Bulletin of the Committee on Archives of the United Church of Canada [Canada]
Bulletin of the History of Medicine
Bulletin of the New York Public Library (superseded by Bulletin of Research in the Humanities)
Bulletin of the United Church of Canada (see Bulletin of the Committee on Archives of the United Church of Canada) [Canada]
Business History Review

C

Cahiers de Géographie de Québec [Canada]
Cahiers d'Études Africaines [France]
California Historian
California Historical Quarterly (see California History)
California History
Canada: An Historical Magazine (ceased pub 1976) [Canada]
Canadian Dimension [Canada]
Canadian Ethnic Studies = Études Ethniques au Canada
Canadian Geographic [Canada]
Canadian Geographical Journal (see Canadian Geographic) [Canada]
Canadian Historic Sites [Canada]
Canadian Historical Association Historical Papers (see Historical Papers) [Canada]
Canadian Historical Review [Canada]
Canadian Journal of History = Annales Canadiennes d'Histoire [Canada]
Canadian Journal of History of Sport and Physical Education (see Canadian Journal of History of Sport) [Canada]
Canadian Journal of History of Sport = Revue Canadienne de l'Histoire des Sports [Canada]
Canadian Journal of Political Science = Revue Canadienne de Science Politique [Canada]
Canadian Review of American Studies [Canada]
Canadian Review of Sociology and Anthropology = Revue Canadienne de Sociologie et d'Anthropologie [Canada]
Canadian Review of Studies in Nationalism = Revue Canadienne des Études sur le Nationalisme [Canada]
Canadian Slavic Studies (see Canadian-American Slavic Studies)
Canadian Slavonic Papers = Revue Canadienne des Slavistes [Canada]
Catholic Historical Review
Centennial Review
Center Magazine
Change
Chicago History
Ch'ing-shih Wen-t'i
Christian Scholar's Review
Chronicle
Chronicles of Oklahoma
Church History
Cincinnati Historical Society Bulletin
Cithara
Civil Liberties Review (ceased pub 1979)
Civil War History
Civil War Times Illustrated
Clio
Clio Medica [Netherlands]
Colorado Magazine
Colorado Quarterly
Commentary
Communication Monographs
Compact
Comparative Studies in Society and History [Great Britain]
Concordia Historical Institute Quarterly
Connecticut Antiquarian
Connecticut History
Contemporary Review [Great Britain]
Crisis
Cuadernos Hispanoamericanos [Spain]
Current History

D

Daedalus
Dalhousie Review [Canada]
Daughters of the American Revolution Magazine
Delaware History
Dialogue: A Journal of Mormon Thought
Diplomatic History
Dissent
Dix-Septième Siècle [France]
Durham University Journal [Great Britain]

E

Early American Life
Early American Literature
Economia e Storia [Italy]
Education and Urban Society
Eighteenth-Century Studies
Éire-Ireland
Encounter [Great Britain]
Essex Institute Historical Collections
Ethnic and Racial Studies [Great Britain]
Ethnic Groups
Ethnicity
Ethnohistory
Études Françaises [Canada]
European Journal of Sociology [Great Britain]
Explorations in Economic History
Explorations in Ethnic Studies

F

Family Heritage (ceased pub 1979)
Feminist Studies
Fides et Historia
Filson Club History Quarterly
Florida Historical Quarterly
Foundations: A Baptist Journal of History and Theology
Frankfurter Hefte [German Federal Republic]
Freeman
Frontiers

G

Gandhi Marg [India]
Gateway Heritage
Geographical Review
Georgia Historical Quarterly
Georgia Life (ceased pub 1980)
Georgia Review
Government Publications Review Part A: Research Articles
Great Plains Journal
Greek Orthodox Theological Review
Guam Recorder (ceased pub 1979)

H

Halve Maen
Harvard Educational Review
Harvard Library Bulletin
Harvard Theological Review
Hawaiian Journal of History
Hayes Historical Journal
Hebrew Union College Annual
Historian
Historic Preservation
Historical Archaeology
Historical Journal [Great Britain]
Historical Journal of Massachusetts
Historical Journal of Western Massachusetts (see Historical Journal of Massachusetts)
Historical Magazine of the Protestant Episcopal Church
Historical Methods
Historical Methods Newsletter (see Historical Methods)
Historical New Hampshire
Historical Papers = Communications Historiques [Canada]
Historical Reflections = Réflexions Historiques [Canada]
Historische Zeitschrift [German Federal Republic]
History of Childhood Quarterly: The Journal of Psychohistory (see Journal of Psychohistory)
History of Education Quarterly
History of Religions
History Teacher
History Today [Great Britain]
Horizon
Horizontes [Puerto Rico]
Human Organization
Huntington Library Quarterly

I

Idaho Yesterdays
Immigration History Newsletter
Indian Historian (see Wasseje Indian Historian)
Indian Journal of American Studies [India]
Indian Journal of Politics [India]
Indiana Folklore
Indiana Magazine of History
Indiana Social Studies Quarterly
Indica [India]
Industrial Relations = Relations Industrielles [Canada]
Inland Seas
Innes Review [Great Britain]
International Journal of African Historical Studies
International Journal of Middle East Studies [Great Britain]
International Journal of Women's Studies [Canada]
International Migration Review
International Social Science Bulletin (see International Social Science Journal) [France]
International Social Science Journal [France]
International Socialist Review
Islamic Quarterly [Great Britain]
Italian Americana

J

Japan Interpreter [Japan]
Jednota Annual Furdek
Jewish Social Studies
Journal for the Scientific Study of Religion
Journal of American Folklore
Journal of American History
Journal of American Studies [Great Britain]
Journal of Arizona History
Journal of Bible and Religion (see Journal of the American Academy of Religion)
Journal of Black Studies
Journal of California and Great Basin Anthropology
Journal of California Anthropology (see Journal of California and Great Basin Anthropology)
Journal of Canadian Studies = Revue d'Études Canadiennes [Canada]
Journal of Cherokee Studies
Journal of Church and State
Journal of Communication
Journal of Contemporary History [Great Britain]
Journal of Current Social Issues
Journal of Ecclesiastical History [Great Britain]
Journal of Ecumenical Studies
Journal of Ethnic Studies
Journal of Family History: Studies in Family, Kinship, and Demography
Journal of Historical Geography
Journal of Interdisciplinary History
Journal of Intergroup Relations
Journal of Jazz Studies
Journal of Libertarian Studies
Journal of Library History, Philosophy, and Comparative Librarianship
Journal of Long Island History
Journal of Mexican American History
Journal of Mississippi History
Journal of NAL Associates
Journal of Negro Education
Journal of Negro History
Journal of Oriental Studies [Hong Kong]
Journal of Palestine Studies [Lebanon]
Journal of Politics
Journal of Popular Culture
Journal of Popular Film (see Journal of Popular Film and Television)
Journal of Presbyterian History
Journal of Psychohistory
Journal of Religion
Journal of Religion in Africa = Religion en Afrique [Netherlands]
Journal of Religious History [Australia]
Journal of San Diego History
Journal of Social History
Journal of Social Issues
Journal of Southern History
Journal of Sport History
Journal of the American Academy of Religion
Journal of the American Historical Society of Germans from Russia
Journal of the Canadian Church Historical Society [Canada]
Journal of the Folklore Institute
Journal of the History of Ideas
Journal of the History of Medicine and Allied Sciences
Journal of the History of Philosophy
Journal of the History of Sociology
Journal of the History of the Behavioral Sciences
Journal of the Illinois State Historical Society
Journal of the Lancaster County Historical Society
Journal of the Society of Architectural Historians
Journal of the United Reformed Church History Society [Great Britain]
Journal of the Universalist Historical Society
Journal of the West
Journal of the West Virginia Historical Association
Journal of Urban History
Journalism Quarterly
Judaica [Switzerland]

K

Kansas Historical Quarterly (superseded by Kansas History)
Kansas History
Kansas Quarterly
Kentucky Folklore Record: A Regional Journal of Folklore and Folklife
Kiva
Kyrkohistorisk Årsskrift [Sweden]

L

Labor History
Labour = Travailleur [Canada]
Latin American Research Review
Leo Baeck Institute. Year Book [Great Britain]
Library [Great Britain]
Library History Review [India]
Library Quarterly
Lincoln Herald
Lituanus
Louisiana History
Louisiana Studies (see Southern Studies: An Interdisciplinary Journal of the South)
Lutheran Quarterly (ceased pub 1977)
Lychnos [Sweden]

M

Maine Historical Society Quarterly
Malaysian Journal of Education (ceased pub 1976) [Malaysia]
Manitoba History [Canada]
Manitoba Pageant (superseded by Manitoba History) [Canada]
Mankind
Manuscripta
Manuscripts
Marin County Historical Society Bulletin *
Marine Corps Gazette
Marxist Perspectives
Maryland Historian
Maryland Historical Magazine
Massachusetts Historical Society Proceedings
Massachusetts Review
Masterkey
Material History Bulletin = Bulletin d'Histoire de la Culture Matérielle [Canada]
Mémoires de la Société Royale du Canada (see Transactions of the Royal Society of Canada = Mémoires de la Société Royale du Canada) [Canada]
Mennonite Historical Bulletin
Mennonite Life
Mennonite Quarterly Review
Methodist History
Michael: On the History of the Jews in the Diaspora [Israel]
Michigan Academician
Michigan Jewish History
Mid-America
Middle East Journal
Midstream
Midwest Quarterly
Military Affairs
Minnesota History
Missionalia Hispanica [Spain]
Mississippi Quarterly
Missouri Historical Review
Missouri Historical Society. Bulletin (superseded by Gateway Heritage)
Modern Age
Montana Magazine of History (see Montana: Magazine of Western History)
Montana: Magazine of Western History
Moreana [France]
Mormonia (ceased pub 1973)
Mouvement Social [France]
Muslim World

N

Names
Nebraska History
Negro History Bulletin
Nevada Historical Society Quarterly
New England Historical and Genealogical Register
New England Quarterly
New England Social Studies Bulletin
New Jersey History
New Mexico Historical Review
New Scholar
New York Affairs
New York Folklore
New York Folklore Quarterly (superseded by New York Folklore)
New York History
New-England Galaxy
Newport History
New-York Historical Society Quarterly
Niagara Frontier
Nineteenth-Century Fiction
North Carolina Historical Review
North Dakota History
North Dakota Quarterly
North Louisiana Historical Association Journal
Norwegian-American Studies
Nouvelle Revue des Deux Mondes [France]
Nova Scotia Historical Quarterly [Canada]
Nova Scotia Historical Society Collections [Canada]
Novaia i Noveishaia Istoriia [Union of Soviet Socialist Republic]

O

Ohio History
Old Northwest
Old-Time New England
Ontario History [Canada]
Oregon Historical Quarterly
Österreichisches Archiv für Kirchenrecht [Austria]

P

Pacific Historian
Pacific Historical Review
Pacific Northwest Quarterly
Pacific Northwesterner
Pacific Sociological Review
Pacific Viewpoint [New Zealand]
Paedagogica Historica [Belgium]
Palacio
Palimpsest
Pan-African Journal [Kenya]
Patterns of Prejudice [Great Britain]
Peace and Change
Pennsylvania Folklife
Pennsylvania Heritage
Pennsylvania History
Pennsylvania Magazine of History and Biography
Pennsylvania Mennonite Heritage
Perspectives in American History
Pharmacy in History
Philippine Studies [Philippines]
Phylon
Pioneer America
Plains Anthropologist
Plantation Society in the Americas
Plateau
Policy Studies Journal
Polish American Studies
Political Science Quarterly
Political Theory: an International Journal of Political Philosophy
Polity
Population Studies [Great Britain]
Prairie Forum [Canada]
Present Tense
Presidential Studies Quarterly
Princeton History
Princeton University Library Chronicle
Problemi di Ulisse [Italy]
Proceedings of the American Antiquarian Society
Proceedings of the American Philosophical Society
Proceedings of the Annual Meeting of the Western Society for French History
Prologue: the Journal of the National Archives
Protée [Canada]
Przegląd Zachodni [Poland]
Psychiatry: Journal for the Study of Interpersonal Processes
Psychohistory Review
Public Welfare

Q

Quaker History
Quarterly Journal of Speech
Quarterly Journal of Studies on Alcohol (see Journal of Studies on Alcohol)
Quarterly Journal of the Library of Congress
Queen's Quarterly [Canada]

R

Radical America
Radical History Review
RA-nytt [Sweden]
Rassegna Storica del Risorgimento [Italy]
Recherches Sociographiques [Canada]
Records of the American Catholic Historical Society of Philadelphia
Red River Valley Historian
Red River Valley Historical Review
Register of the Kentucky Historical Society
Relations Industrielles (see Industrial Relations = Relations Industrielles) [Canada]
Religion in Life (ceased pub 1980)
Rendezvous
Research Studies
Resources for Feminist Research/Documentation sur la Recherche Féministe [Canada]
Review of Politics
Reviews in American History
Revista Brasileira de Estudos Políticos [Brazil]
Revista de Ciencias Sociales [Puerto Rico]
Revista Española de Derecho Canónico [Spain]
Revista Interamericana de Bibliografía (see Inter-American Review of Bibligraphy = Revista Interamericana de Bibliografía)
Revue de l'Histoire des Religions [France]
Revue de l'Université d'Ottawa (see University of Ottawa Quarterly = Revue de l'Université d'Ottawa) [Canada]
Revue d'Études Canadiennes (see Journal of Canadian Studies = Revue d'Études Canadiennes) [Canada]
Revue d'Histoire de l'Amérique Française [Canada]
Revue d'Histoire Urbaine (see Urban History = Revue d'Histoire Urbaine) [Canada]
Revue Française d'Études Américaines [France]
Revue Internationale d'Histoire de la Banque [Italy]
Rhode Island History
Rhode Island Jewish Historical Notes
Richmond County History
Rochester History
Rural Sociology
Russian Review

S

Saeculum [German Federal Republic]
Santiago [Cuba]
Saskatchewan History [Canada]
Search: Journal for Arab and Islamic Studies
Sessions d'Étude: Société Canadienne d'Histoire de l'Église Catholique (published simultaneously in one volume with Study Sessions: Canadian Catholic Historical Association) [Canada]
Shakaikeizaishigaku (Socio-Economic History) [Japan]
Signs: Journal of Women in Culture and Society
Slovakia
Smithsonian
Social Education
Social Forces
Social History = Histoire Sociale [Canada]
Social Policy
Social Research
Social Science
Social Science Journal
Social Service Review
Social Studies
Social Studies of Science [Great Britain]
Societas
Society
Sociological Analysis
Sociological Inquiry
Sociological Quarterly
Sociological Review [Great Britain]
Sociology and Social Research
Sociology of Education
Sound Heritage [Canada]
Soundings (Nashville, TN)
South Asian Review (ceased pub 1975) [Great Britain]
South Atlantic Quarterly
South Carolina Historical Magazine
South Dakota History
Southern California Quarterly
Southern Exposure
Southern Folklore Quarterly
Southern Humanities Review
Southern Quarterly
Southern Review
Southern Speech Communication Journal
Southern Studies: An Interdisciplinary Journal of the South
Southern Voices (ceased pub 1974)
Southwest Review
Southwestern Art (ceased pub 1978)
Southwestern Historical Quarterly
Speech Monographs (see Communication Monographs)
Spiegel Historiael [Netherlands]
Ssu yü Yen (Thought and Word) [Taiwan]
Stadion [German Federal Republic]
Stimmen der Zeit [German Federal Republic]
Studia Hibernica [Republic of Ireland]
Studia Nauk Politycznych [Poland]
Studia Rosenthaliana [Netherlands]
Studies: An Irish Quarterly Review of Letters, Philosophy and
Studies in History and Society (suspended pub 1977)
Studies in Romanticism
Studies in the American Renaissance
Studium [Italy]
Study Sessions: Canadian Catholic Historical Association (published simultaneously in one volume with Sessions d'Étude: Société Canadienne d'Histoire de l'Église Catholique) [Canada]
Sudetenland [German Federal Republic]
Swedish Pioneer Historical Quarterly
Swiss American Historical Society Newsletter
Synthesis

T

Tampa Bay History
Teachers College Record
Tennessee Folklore Society Bulletin
Tennessee Historical Quarterly
Texana (ceased pub 1974)
Thought
Thought and Word (see Ssu yü Yen) [Taiwan]
Towson State Journal of International Affairs
Transactions of the Historical and Scientific Society of Manitoba (superseded by Manitoba History) [Canada]
Transactions of the Moravian Historical Society
Transactions of the Royal Society of Canada = Mémoires de la Société Royale du Canada [Canada]
Transactions of the Unitarian Historical Society [Great Britain]
Travailleur (see Labour = Travailleur) [Canada]
Turun Historiallinen Arkisto [Finland]

U

Ukrainian Quarterly
Upper Ohio Valley Historical Review
Urban and Social Change Review
Urban History Review = Revue d'Histoire Urbaine [Canada]
Utah Historical Quarterly

V

Vermont History
Vestnik Moskovskogo Universiteta, Seriia 9: Istoriia (superseded by Vestnik Moskovskogo Universiteta, Seriia 8: Istoriia) [Union of Soviet Socialist Republic]
Viewpoints: Georgia Baptist History
Virginia Cavalcade
Virginia Magazine of History and Biography
Virginia Quarterly Review
Voprosy Filosofii [Union of Soviet Socialist Republic]
Voprosy Istorii [Union of Soviet Socialist Republic]

W

Washington Monthly
Wasseje Indian Historian
West Georgia College Studies in the Social Sciences
West Tennessee Historical Society Papers
West Virginia History
Western American Literature
Western Folklore
Western Historical Quarterly
Western Humanities Review
Western Illinois Regional Studies
Western Journal of Speech Communication
Western Pennsylvania Historical Magazine
Western Political Quarterly
Western Speech Communication (see Western Journal of Speech Communication)
Western States Jewish Historical Quarterly
Westways
William and Mary Quarterly
Winterthur Portfolio
Wisconsin Magazine of History
Wissenschaftliche Zeitschrift der Karl-Marx Universität Leipzig. Gesellschafts- und Sprachwissenschaftliche Reihe [German Democratic Republic]
Women's Studies
Working Papers from the Regional Economic History Center
World Affairs
Worldview

Y

Yale University Library Gazette
Yivo Annual of Jewish Social Science
York State Tradition (ceased pub 1974)
Youth and Society

Z

Zeitschrift für Kirchengeschichte [German Federal Republic]
Zeitschrift für Religions- und Geistesgeschichte [German Federal Republic]
Życie i Myśl [Poland]
Zygon

LIST OF ABSTRACTERS

A

Aimone, A. C.
Aldrich, R.
Alexander, G. M.
Alvis, R.
Andrew, J. A., III
Athey, L. L.
Atkins, L. R.
Atkinson, J. L. B.
Auffenberg, T. L.

B

Baatz, S.
Bailey, E. C.
Barkan, E.
Bassett, T. D. S.
Bates, C.
Bauer, K. J.
Bauhs, T. H.
Baylen, J. O.
Beaber, P. A.
Belles, A. G.
Benson, J. A.
Billigmeier, J. C.
Blaser, L. K.
Bobango, G. J.
Bowers, D. E.
Bradford, J. C.
Broussard, J. H.
Brown, C. B.
Brown, L.
Burckel, N. C.
Burnett, B.
Burnett, R.
Burns, H. M.
Burns, R. I.
Buschen, J. J.
Bushnell, D.
Butchart, R. E.

C

Calkin, H. L.
Cameron, D. D.
Campbell, E. R.
Carp, E. W.
Casada, J. A.
Chan, L. B.
Chandler, B. J.
Chaput, D.
Chard, D. F.
Chard, E. A.
Churchill, E. A.
Cleyet, G. P.
Coleman, P. J.
Collon, C.
Conner, S. P.
Correia-Afonso, J.
Crandall, R. J.
Crowther, K. N. T.
Curtis, G. H.

D

D'Aniello, C. A.
Davis, G. H.
Davison, S. R.
Dean, D. M.
Dewees, A. C.
Dibert, M. D.
Dickinson, J. N.
Dodd, D.
Driggs, O. T.
Dubay, R. W.

E

Ehrlich, J. K.
Eid, L. V.
Elison, W. W.
Eminhizer, E. E.
Engler, D. J.
English, J. C.
Erlebacher, A.
Evans, A. J.
Evans, H. M.

F

Falk, J. D.
Farmerie, S. A.
Feingold, M.
Fenske, B. L.
Findling, J. E.
Frame, R. M., III
Frank, S. H.
Frenkley, N.
Frey, M. L.
Friedel, J. N.
Fulton, R. T.

G

Gagnon, G. O.
Gammage, J.
Garfinkle, R. A.
Garland, A. N.
Geist, C. D.
Genung, M.
Geyer, M.
Gillam, M. R.
Gilmont, K. E.
Glasrud, B. A.
Grant, C. L.
Gunter, C. R.

H

Hardacre, P. H.
Harling, F. F.
Hartford, D. A.
Hartig, T. H.
Hazelton, J. L.
Held, C. H.
Henry, B. W.
Herstein, S. R.
Hewlett, G. A.
Hillje, J. W.
Hively, W. R.
Hobson, W. K.
Hoffman, A.
Holzinger, J.
Homan, G. D.
Hoobs, M. A.
Hough, C. M.
Howell, A. W.
Howell, R.
Huff, A. V., Jr.
Human, V. L.
Hunley, J. D.

I

Iklé, F. W.

J

Jirran, R. J.
Johnson, B. D.
Johnson, D. W.
Johnson, E. S.
Jordan, D. P.

K

Kaufman, M.
Kearns, W. A.
Kennedy, P. W.
Kerens, S.
Kicklighter, J. A.
Krenkel, J. H.
Krzyzaniak, M.
Kubicek, R. V.
Kuntz, N. A.
Kurland, G.

L

LaBue, B. J.
Lambert, D. K.
Larson, A. J.
LeBlanc, A. E.
Ledbetter, B. D.
Lederer, N.
Lee, J. M.
Leedom, J. W.
Legan, M. S.
Leonard, I. M.
Lester, E. R.
Lewis, J.
Lewis, J. A.
Lifka, M. L.
Linkfield, T. P.
Lokken, R. N.
Lovin, H. T.
Lowitt, R.
Lucas, M. B.

M

Maloney, L. M.
Marks, H. S.
Marr, W. L.
Marshall, P. C.
Marti, D. B.
Mattar, P. J.
McCarthy, E.
McCarthy, J. M.
McCarthy, M. M.
McDonald, D. R.
McDorman, K. S.
McGinnis, D.
McGinty, G. W.
McKinney, G. B.
McKinney, G. M.
McKinstry, E. R.
McLaughlin, P. L.
McNeill, C. A.
Mendel, R. B.
Meyers, R. C.
Miller, Randall M.
Moen, N. W.
Moore, J.
Moriarty, T. F.
Morrison, S. C.
Mulligan, W. H.
Murdoch, D. H.
Murdock, E. C.
Mycue, D. J.
Myers, R. C.
Myres, S. L.

N

Neal, D. C.
Neville, J. D.
Newton, C. A.
Nielson, D. G.
Nirmal, C. J.
Novitsky, A. W.

O

Oaks, R. F.
O'Brien, E. J.
Ohrvall, C. W.
Olbrich, W. L.
Olson, C. W.
Olson, G. L.
Orr, R. B.
Osur, A. M.
Overbeck, J. A.

P

Panting, G. E.
Papalas, A. J.
Parker, H. M.
Patterson, S. L.
Patzwald, G.-A.
Paul, B. J.
Paul, J. F.
Pavia, J. R.
Pearson, S. C.
Pergl, G. E.
Petersen, P. L.
Pickens, D. K.
Piersen, W. D.
Pliska, S. R.
Pollaczek, F.
Porter, B. S.
Powers, T. L.
Pragman, J. H.
Puffer, K. J.
Pusateri, C. J.

R

Rahmes, R. D.
Raife, L. R.
Reith, L. J.
Richardson, D. C.
Rilee, V. P.
Ritter, R. V.
Rodríguez, R. D.
Rollins, R. M.
Roosen, W. J.
Rosenthal, F.
Rossi, G. J.
Rowe, D. L.
Rowe, E. L.
Russell, L.

S

Sapper, N. G.
Sarna, J. D.
Sassoon, T.
Savitt, T. L.
Sbacchi, A.
Schermerhorn, D. L.
Schoenberg, P. E.
Schoonover, T. D.
Schroeder, G. R.
Schulz, C. B.
Selleck, R. G.
Sevilla, S.
Shapiro, E. S.
Sherer, R. G.
Simmerman, T.
Sliwoski, R. S.
Smith, D. L.
Smith, G. L.
Smith, L. C.
Smith, L. D.
Smith, S. R.
Smith, T. W.
Soff, H. G.
Sokolow, J.
Souby, A. R.
Spira, T.
Sprague, S. S.
Stack, R. E.
Standley, A. E.
Stickney, E. P.
Stoesen, A. R.
Storey, B. A.
Street, J. B.
Street, N. J.
Stromberg, R.
Summers, N.
Svengalis, K. F.
Swiecicka, M. A. J.
Swift, D. C.

T

Talley, K.
Tate, M. L.
Taylorson, P. J.
Tennyson, B. D.
Thacker, J. W.
Tharaud, B. C.
Tomlinson, R. H.
Trauth, M. P.
Tutorow, N. E.

V

Vance, M. M.
Velicer, L. F.
Vivian, J. F.

W

Wagnleitner, R.
Walker, W. T., III
Ward, G. W. R.
Ward, H. M.
Watson, C. A.
Wechman, R. J.
Weltsch, R. E.
Wendel, T. H.
Wentworth, M. J.
West, K. B.
Wharton, D. P.
Whitham, W. B.
Wiederrecht, A. E.
Wiegand, W. A.
Willson, J. R.
Woehrmann, P. J.
Woodward, R. L.
Wyk, L. W. Van

Y

Yanchisin, D. A.
Yerburgh, M. R.

Z

Zabel, O. H.
Ziewacz, L. E.
Zolota, M.
Zornow, W. F.

LIST OF ABBREVIATIONS

A. .... Author-prepared Abstract
Acad. .... Academy, Academie, Academia
Agric. .... Agriculture, Agricultural
AIA .... Abstracts in Anthropology
Akad. .... Akademie
Am. .... America, American
Ann. .... Annals, Annales, Annual, Annali
Anthrop. .... Anthropology, Anthropological
Arch. .... Archives
Archaeol. .... Archaeology, Archaeological
Art. .... Article
Assoc. .... Association, Associate
Biblio. .... Bibliography, Bibliographical
Biog. .... Biography, Biographical
Bol. .... Boletim, Boletin
Bull. .... Bulletin
c. .... century (in index)
ca. .... circa
Can. .... Canada, Canadian, Canadien
Cent. .... Century
Coll. .... College
Com. .... Committee
Comm. .... Commission
Comp. .... Compiler
DAI .... Dissertation Abstracts International
Dept. .... Department
Dir. .... Director, Direktor
Econ. .... Economy, Econom-.
Ed. .... Editor, Edition
Educ. .... Education, Educational
Geneal. .... Genealogy, Genealogical, Genealogique
Grad. .... Graduate
Hist. .... History, Hist-.
IHE .... Indice Historico Espanol
Illus. .... Illustrated, Illustration
Inst. .... Institute, Institut-.
Int. .... International, Internacional, Internationaal, Internationaux, Internazionale
J. .... Journal, Journal-prepared Abstract
Lib. .... Library, Libraries
Mag. .... Magazine
Mus. .... Museum, Musee, Museo
Nac. .... Nacional
Natl. .... National, Nationale
Naz. .... Nazionale
Phil. .... Philosophy, Philosophical
Photo. .... Photograph
Pol. .... Politics, Political, Politique, Politico
Pr. .... Press
Pres. .... President
Pro. .... Proceedings
Publ. .... Publishing, Publication
Q. .... Quarterly
Rev. .... Review, Revue, Revista, Revised
Riv. .... Rivista
Res. .... Research
RSA .... Romanian Scientific Abstracts
S. .... Staff-prepared Abstract
Sci. .... Science, Scientific
Secy. .... Secretary
Soc. .... Society, Societe, Sociedad, Societa
Sociol. .... Sociology, Sociological
Tr. .... Transactions
Transl. .... Translator, Translation
U. .... University, Universi-.
US .... United States
Vol. .... Volume
Y. .... Yearbook

Abbreviations also apply to feminine and plural forms.
Abbreviations not noted above are based on *Webster's Third New International Dictionary* and the *United States Government Printing Office Style Manual.*